MW01670743

**RELIGION AND THE STATE IN AMERICAN LAW**

*Religion and the State in American Law* provides a comprehensive and up-to-date overview of religion and government in the United States, from historical origins to modern laws and rulings. In addition to extensive coverage of the religion clauses of the First Amendment, it addresses many statutory, regulatory, and common-law developments at both the federal and state levels. Topics include the history of church-state relations and religious liberty, religion in the classroom, and expressions of religion in government. This book also covers the role of religion in specific areas of law such as contracts, taxation, employment, land-use regulation, torts, criminal law, and domestic relations, as well as in specialized contexts such as prisons and the military. Accessible to the general as well as the professional reader, it will be of use to scholars, judges, practicing lawyers, and the media.

Boris I. Bittker (1916–2005) was a professor at the Yale Law School for over five decades. He was named Southmayd Professor in 1958, then Sterling Professor of Law in 1970, and he retired as Sterling Professor Emeritus. The leading tax scholar of his era, he helped pioneer the study of federal tax law as a serious academic discipline. Updated versions of his casebooks, including the groundbreaking *Estate and Gift Taxation* (1951), are still in use today. He continued his amazing scholarly productivity until his death in 2005.

Scott C. Idleman is Professor of Law at the Marquette University Law School. He has written articles on constitutional law, law and religion, and the federal courts in the nation's top journals, including the *Cornell Law Review*, the *Virginia Law Review*, and the *University of Pennsylvania Law Review*.

Frank S. Ravitch is Professor of Law and Walter H. Stowers Chair in Law and Religion at Michigan State University College of Law. He is the author of several books and numerous articles on law and religion, civil rights, and constitutional law and frequently serves as an expert in the media on the same topics. His most recent book is *Marketing Creation: The Law and Intelligent Design* (2011).

*Chapter Contributors*

The authors of this book were privileged to have leading experts contribute major chapters to the book:

Angela C. Carmella, Professor of Law, Seton Hall University School of Law: Chapter 12, Land Use

Jennifer A. Drobac, Professor of Law, Indiana University Robert H. McKinney School of Law, and Jill L. Wesley, Indiana University Robert H. McKinney School of Law: Chapter 11, Employment

Cynthia Lee Starnes, Professor of Law and John F. Schaefer Chair in Matrimonial Law, Michigan State University College of Law: Chapter 15, Family Law

# Religion and the State in American Law

**Boris I. Bittker**
Late Sterling Professor of Law, Yale Law School

**Scott C. Idleman**
Marquette University Law School

**Frank S. Ravitch**
Michigan State University College of Law

CAMBRIDGE
UNIVERSITY PRESS

CAMBRIDGE
UNIVERSITY PRESS

32 Avenue of the Americas, New York, NY 10013-2473, USA

Cambridge University Press is part of the University of Cambridge.

It furthers the University's mission by disseminating knowledge in the pursuit of education, learning, and research at the highest international levels of excellence.

www.cambridge.org
Information on this title: www.cambridge.org/9781107419285



First published 2015

Printed in the United States of America

*A catalog record for this publication is available from the British Library.*

*Library of Congress Cataloging in Publication Data*
Bittker, Boris I., author.
Religion and the state in American law / Boris I. Bittker, Yale Law School (deceased); Scott C. Idleman, Marquette University Law School; Frank S. Ravitch, Michigan State University College of Law.
pages cm
Includes bibliographical references and index.
ISBN 978-1-107-07182-7 (hardback) – ISBN 978-1-107-41928-5 (paperback)
1. Religion and state – United States. 2. Freedom of religion – United States. 3. Church and state – United States. I. Idleman, Scott C., 1966– author. II. Ravitch, Frank S., 1966– author. III. Title.
KF4865.B55 2015
342.7308′52–dc23 2015003340

ISBN 978-1-107-07182-7 Hardback
ISBN 978-1-107-41928-5 Paperback

In memory of Boris I. Bittker, whose towering intellect, remarkable industry, generous spirit, and inimitable sense of humor continue to inspire those of us who try, however imperfectly, to follow in his extraordinary footsteps.

— S.C.I. and F.S.R.

To Elizabeth, my wife and dearest friend; to Sue, my mother and lifelong inspiration; and to Katherine and Peter, my wonderful children, without whom my life would be unfulfilled.

— S.C.I.

To Chika, my remarkably smart and caring wife and companion; to Elysha and Ariana, my daughters, whose intelligence and creativity add perspective to all my work; and to my parents, Arline and Carl, whose love and support are inspiring.

— F.S.R.

# Contents

# Preface

*Religion and the State in American Law* provides a comprehensive view of law and religion in the United States. It addresses the traditional First Amendment questions but goes well beyond to cover every area where questions of law and religion intersect. It is designed to be a comprehensive treatise that will enable readers to explore any topic in law and religion from school prayer to tax issues. The book was written over several years with the generous support of the Lilly Endowment.

Law and religion intersect in every area of law in the United States. Sometimes this simply results in the application of a given legal doctrine to religious entities or individuals. In many cases, however, the religious nature of a party affects what courts will consider and enforce. This can be seen in cases involving, for example, property disputes, employment, family law, and criminal law. Moreover, some fields, such as tax law, have complex systems in place to address claims involving religious entities. Exploring these cases from within a given field of law, whether criminal law, torts, or taxation, allows readers to use this book as a research tool for any area of law to see if, and how, the law is applied to cases involving religious entities and individuals.

*Religion and the State in American Law* was conceived by Boris Bittker, who wrote several chapters but unfortunately passed away before the project was completed. Boris' idea was to have a comprehensive treatise covering every topic in law and religion. There has never been anyone better qualified to undertake such a task than Boris, and the co-authors Boris brought onto the project, Scott Idleman and Frank S. Ravitch, were humbled to be part of the project and hope that the end result is one with which Boris would have been pleased.


## Acknowledgments

First and foremost, we want to thank Boris Bittker for his vision in conceiving this project and his kindness in bringing us in to help write this book.

Scott Idleman wishes to thank his wife, Elizabeth, for her guidance and understanding throughout the duration of this project. I am grateful for the encouragement of my children, Katherine and Peter, as well as that of my mother and father, the latter of whom unfortunately was able to see only the earliest phase of this work. For financial and institutional support, I would like to express my gratitude to the Lilly Endowment, Marquette University Law School, and Yale Law School, particularly Yale's John Simon, who was instrumental in securing funding for the project, and the many Yale administrators involved in its management. For his cooperative spirit and seemingly endless patience, I am indebted to my superb co-author, Frank Ravitch. I also wish to thank the numerous research assistants whose efforts contributed to this book. Finally, I am deeply appreciative of the opportunity to publish with Cambridge University Press and to work with its excellent editorial staff.

Frank S. Ravitch would like to thank many people for their support and advice during the writing and production of this book. I thank my wife, Chika, and my daughters, Elysha and Ariana, whose smiles and love make life brighter and add balance to everything I do. I also thank my parents, Carl and Arline Ravitch, who are a source of constant support and love and who are an inspiration for all three of their children. Thanks go to my late Bubby and Pop Pop, who are always close to my heart and who embodied all that is best in religion and in law without being lawyers or overtly religious. I thank my sisters, Sharon and Elizabeth, and their families, my Uncle Gary and Aunt Mindy, and my Aunt Jackie and Uncle Ken, who have been exceptionally supportive of all my work and who each in their own way have an interest in law and/or religion.

I am grateful to the Lilly Endowment, which supported this project; John Simon, who was instrumental in obtaining the grant through Yale Law School; the Yale Law School Grants Department for serving as an excellent resource on the grant; and the Michigan State University College of Law, which provides an excellent environment for research productivity. My deepest gratitude also goes to my wonderful research assistants who worked on this project under the grant over the years (listed from earliest to most recent): Colin Boes, Adrianne Whitehead, Holly Shannon, Andrew Davis, Michael Epstein, Zachary Risk, Heather Snider, Jim Zeimer, Philip Berens, Caitlin Keene, Cheyna Roczkowski, Erin Dombros, Calvin Boyd, and David Louden. Thank you for your excellent research. I also thank Jacklyn Beard for her wonderful secretarial support. This project would have never come to print without the support of Cambridge University Press, John Berger, Jim Madru, and Ramesh Karunakaran. I am also grateful to my co-author, Scott Idleman, who is a wonderful co-author with whom to work.

# 1 History and Introduction

## A. Church-State Relations in the Colonies from Their Founding to the Declaration of Independence

### 1. *Introduction*

During the century and a half that passed between the first permanent English settlements in Virginia (1607) and Massachusetts (1620) and the signing of the Declaration of Independence, there were seismic changes in the political and religious characteristics of the colonies that became the thirteen original states of the Union.[1] Although liberty proved to be the ultimate destination in both these arenas, the journeys were taken in fits and starts rather than smoothly, and the process of change took longer in the church-state relationships than in the political links between the colonies and England.[2] Political

[1] 1620 and 1630, for the Pilgrims and Puritans, respectively, *see generally* JAMES TRUSLOW ADAMS, THE FOUNDING OF NEW ENGLAND (1933). For the early documents, *see* THE FOUNDING OF MASSACHUSETTS, HISTORIANS AND THE SOURCES (Bobbs-Merrill, Edmund S. Morgan ed., 1964). For statistics of religious affiliations, *see* WILLIAM M. NEWMAN & PETER L. HALVORSON, ATLAS OF AMERICAN RELIGIONS: THE DENOMINATIONAL ERA, 1776–1990 (Rowman & Littlefield, 2000).

[2] *See generally* SANFORD H. COBB, THE RISE OF RELIGIOUS LIBERTY IN AMERICA (Macmillan 1902); 1 ANSON PHELPS STOKES, CHURCH AND STATE IN THE UNITED STATES (Harper 1950) (notable for its comprehensive compendium of documents – not merely famous items but obscure letters, newspaper accounts, etc.); ANSON PHELPS STOKES & LEO PFEFFER, CHURCH AND STATE IN THE UNITED STATES (1964) (summary of Stokes' magisterial three-volume work). There are also numerous studies of the changes in church-state relations in particular states, some of which are cited later, as well as histories of changes in particular religions and denominations, a notable example of which is WILLIAM G. MCLOUGHLIN, NEW ENGLAND DISSENT: THE BAPTISTS AND THE SEPARATION OF CHURCH AND STATE (Harvard Univ. Press 1971) (two volumes). For an exhaustive annotated bibliography, *see* CHURCH AND STATE IN AMERICA, THE COLONIAL AND EARLY NATIONAL PERIODS (Greenwood, John F. Wilson ed., 1986). For detailed examination of particular churches, *see* EDWARD F. HUMPHREY, NATIONALISM AND RELIGION IN AMERICA, 1774–1789 (1924) (out-of-date but still useful). *See also* JOHN T. NOONAN, THE BELIEVER AND THE POWERS THAT ARE: CASES, HISTORY, AND OTHER DATA BEARING ON THE RELATION OF RELIGION AND GOVERNMENT (Macmillan 1987); AMERICAN CIVIL RELIGION (Edwin Mellen Press Donald G. Jones & Russell E. Richey eds., 1990); RONALD B. FLOWERS, THAT GODLESS COURT? SUPREME COURT DECISIONS ON CHURCH STATE RELATIONSHIPS (2d ed., 2005); EVARTS B. GREENE, RELIGION AND THE STATE: THE MAKING AND TESTING OF AN AMERICAN TRADITION (N.Y. Univ. Press 1941); WILL HERBERG, PROTESTANT, CATHOLIC, JEW: AN ESSAY IN AMERICAN RELIGIOUS SOCIOLOGY (Univ. Chicago Press 1983) (1960); Michael Ariens, *On the Road of Good Intentions: Justice Brennan and the Religion Clauses*, 27 CAL. W. L. REV. 311, 313 (1991) ("good intentions … have led to suspicion, misunderstanding, and confusion, not enlightenment, tolerance, and respect"); H. Frank Way, *The Death of the*

liberty for the United States was presaged in 1776 by the Declaration of Independence and was recognized by Great Britain in 1783 in the Treaty of Paris and a second time in 1814 in the Treaty of Ghent, which ended the War of 1812 (sometimes called our "second war of independence").[3] Neither treaty dealt with religious issues. The Treaty of Paris, however, was dipped in religiosity: it was promulgated "[i]n the name of the Most Holy and Undivided Trinity," credited "Divine Providence" with having disposed the two parties to "forget all past misunderstandings," and is dated "in the year of our Lord" 1783.

The achievement of religious liberty in America, by contrast, was not declared or recognized by so crisp an event or document, and attainment of that goal proceeded separately in each of the colonies, unlike the achievement of political independence, which occurred for all the colonies at the national level.[4] Moreover, disestablishment of the state church in Massachusetts did not occur until 1833, and as late as 1892, a unanimous Supreme Court quoted, seemingly with approval, the proposition that Christianity was part of the common law of Pennsylvania and, by implication, of the other states as well.[5] As recently as 1961, Maryland urged (though without success) that the Supreme Court should uphold the validity of its antiquated constitutional provision requiring candidates for the post of notary public to declare their belief in the existence of God,[6] and every year this provision spawns a sizable body of church-state lawsuits, as this work will demonstrate.

By contrast, the nation's political independence is so routinely acknowledged that a leading compendium of constitutional documents does not include, summarize, or even cite the 1783 Treaty of Paris, though, of course, it reprints the Declaration of Independence.[7] In our era, there are, to be sure, occasional fervid laments that the nation

*Christian Nation: The Judiciary and Church-State Relations*, 29 J. CHURCH & ST. 509, 510 (1987) (noting that between 1800 and 1920, there were 254 decisions from appellate courts related to church-state questions) ("The issues presented were often persistent and fairly widespread and, in the aggregate, the decisions indicate that courts began to assume a role in redefining church-state relations."); Kurt T. Lash, *The Second Adoption of the Establishment Clause: The Rise of the Nonestablishment Principle*, 27 ARIZ. ST. L.J. 1085, 1095 (1996) ("In a variety of controversies that arose in the early nineteenth century, both Congress and the Supreme Court interpreted the Establishment Clause as a limitation on the power of Congress, and a preservation of power in the states."); Joan DelFattore, *What Is Past Is Prelude: Newdow and the Evolution of Thought on Religious Affirmations in Public Schools*, 8 U. PA. J. CONST. L. 641 (2006) (summarizing post–Civil War lawsuits over bible reading and prayer in school, including Board of Education v. Minor, 23 Ohio St. 211 (1872)); Andrew Koppelman, *Corruption of Religion and the Establishment Clause*, 50 WM. & MARY L. REV. 1831, 1848–93 (2009) (summarizing various formulations of the Founders' belief that religion must be protected from the corruption of government).

3 For the Treaty of Paris, *see* WILLIAM M. MALLOY, TREATIES, CONVENTIONS, INTERNATIONAL ACTS, PROTOCOLS, AND AGREEMENTS BETWEEN THE UNITED STATES OF AMERICA AND OTHER POWERS, S. DOC. NO. 61–357, at 586 (2d Sess. 1910); for the provisional agreement preceding the definitive treaty, *see id.* at 580; for the Treaty of Ghent, *see id.* at 612.

4 The piecemeal allocation of religious freedom in each of the American colonies contrasts with the more expansive move toward religious freedom in England, as noted by Parliament's enactment of the Toleration Act in 1689, which granted freedom of worship to Protestant Nonconformists by allowing, among other privileges, independent places of worship. *See* ALBERT VENN DICEY, LECTURES ON THE RELATION BETWEEN LAW AND PUBLIC OPINION IN ENGLAND 54 (Macmillan, 2d ed. 1914); John Spurr, *The Church of England, Comprehension, and the Toleration Act of 1689*, ENG. HIST. REV. 927 (Oct. 1989).

5 *See* Church of Holy Trinity v. United States, 143 U.S. 457, 466 (1892) (federal statute forbidding importation of aliens under employment contracts held inapplicable to clergyman).

6 *See* Torcaso v. Watkins, 367 U.S. 488 (1961). For disestablishment in Massachusetts, *see infra* Section A.2.a and authorities therein cited.

7 *See* 1 THE FOUNDERS' CONSTITUTION (Univ. Chicago Press, Philip B Kurland & Ralph Lerner eds., 1987). The 1776 Declaration was followed by the Massachusetts Constitution of 1780, which announced the

has surrendered its long-vaunted independence to such international bodies as the United Nations and the World Trade Organization, but these claims are often routinely dismissed by the citizenry as a whole as farfetched alarms, though they may well be hints of world unity to come.[8] These tinges of political globalism, moreover, are often accepted with equanimity by those who routinely warn that the nation's doctrine of religious liberty and its "wall of separation" between church and state are threatened by state and federal laws and other official actions.[9]

With this in mind, the debates that occurred in the eighteenth century regarding religious liberty and disestablishment may be of use in centering contemporary concerns regarding separation of church and state. Review of the literature from the period illustrates that the founding generation was as divided as to church-state relations as are citizens of today.[10] Present attempts to bind discourse on church-state relations to the established attitudes of the founding generation are inadequate because consensus itself did not exist.[11] The strict divide between federalist opposition to disestablishment and reformist promotion of religious liberty was, in actuality, illusory because there existed vast disagreement among early Americans as to what exactly disestablishment entailed. Underlying the issue of the unintelligibility of the various positions surrounding the meaning of disestablishment and the applicability of the Establishment Clause was the fact that the First Amendment to the federal Constitution was interpreted by some as having no applicability whatsoever to states already possessing an established religion, whereas in other instances the Establishment Clause was used to protect state-sanctioned religions.[12]

Those colonial states with established religions emphasized the Protestant Christian tradition.[13] Indeed, Christianity was deemed so universal that the religious freedoms guaranteed by state constitutions and legislative enactments mainly pertained to Protestant Christian denominations and completely ignored the experiences of Jews, Muslims, Catholics, agnostics, and atheists.[14] This emphasis on Christianity was furthered by a

formation of "a free, sovereign, and independent body-politic or state, by the name of the Commonwealth of Massachusetts." *Id.* at 11. Similar manifestos existed in the other colonies, and there were the Articles of Confederation, the Northwest Ordinance, and the Constitution itself.

8 Although from the current vantage such world unity is only likely in the distant future.

9 For the "wall" between church and state, *see infra* at Chapter 4.

10 Carol Weisbrod, *On Evidences and Intentions: The More Proof, The More Doubt*, 18 CONN. L. REV. 803, 810–20 (1985), using, as an example, the debates in Connecticut that occurred up until the mid-nineteenth century regarding witness qualification or the proposition that one be a religious, namely, Christian, observer in order to take a legal oath. This was one area where the role of religion continued to be debated well after formation of the idea of separation of church and state. Of particular issue was not only whether a witness could be disqualified altogether for lacking established religious views but whether the credibility of a witness could be impeached by his or her lack of religious beliefs. *Id.* at 813, 818–19.

11 Colin Kidd, *Civil Theology and Church Establishments in Revolutionary America*, 42 HIST. J. 1007, 1008 & 1017 (1999); Weisbrod, *supra* note 10, at 825.

12 Discrepancies between federal provisions regarding separation of church and state and state provisions often were exacerbated by the fact that some states continued to follow laws enacted under colonial rule. An example of this is Connecticut, which until the enactment of its first constitution in 1818 was still operating under its original royal charter, dating from the seventeenth century. Weisbrod, *supra* note 10, at 804, 807.

13 *E.g.*, Weisbrod, *supra* note 10, at 808–9; Kidd, *supra* note 11, at 1017.

14 B. H. Hartogensis, *Denial of Equal Rights to Religious Minorities and Non-Believers in the United States*, 39 YALE L.J. 650, 659 (1930) ("by providing equal rights and religious freedom for all, [the Establishment Clause] ... succeeded merely in giving all Christian sects equal rights before the law. Rights have consistently been denied other religious minorities."). Recognition of religious expression outside of Christianity was not

revival in religious sentiment during the prerevolutionary period, reaching a "crescendo" of fervor in 1740, known as the "Great Awakening."[15] Long characterized by scholars of history as furthering the political sentiment of the colonists toward revolution,[16] the Great Awakening also has been credited with "crystalliz[ing]" differences within colonial American churches, causing the splintering of established churches into dissenting denominations.[17]

The profusion of new denominations, whose interests were at odds with those of established churches, makes it difficult for modern scholars to accurately identify early American consensus toward church-state relations. Most obviously, denominations that benefited from establishment, such as the Anglican Church in Virginia and the Congregationalists in Massachusetts and Connecticut, were reluctant to relinquish privileges guaranteed by the state.[18] Such privileges included the collection of taxes to support clergy, the requirement to attend services at the established church subject to fines and other legal penalties, and the exclusive right to perform baptisms and consecrate marriages.[19] In addition to commonly explicated liberal rationales for the separation of

within the purview of the Framers generally, and in the instance of Connecticut, it was not until 1965 that reference to Christianity was removed from the state's constitution. *See* CONN. CONST. art. VII, § I (1965). For further examples of the preference given to Christianity in the grant of religious freedom, *see* text accompanying notes 5 & 6, *supra* at 1–3, regarding Massachusetts, Pennsylvania, and Maryland. While the history of colonial America traditionally has been devoid of the experiences of non-Christians and non-Protestant Christians, contemporary scholars recognize the importance of the contribution of other religious and non-religious experiences to the social and cultural formation of the nascent nation. For a history of the Jewish experience, *see, e.g.*, JACOB R. MARCUS, THE COLONIAL AMERICAN JEW: 1492–1776 (Wayne State Univ. Press 1970) (multivolume). For a history of the Muslim experience, *see, e.g.*, Michael A. Gomez, *Muslims in Early America*, 60 J. S. HIST. 671 (1994), and for a history of Catholicism in colonial America, *see* JAY P. DOLAN, THE AMERICAN CATHOLIC EXPERIENCE: A HISTORY FROM COLONIAL TIMES TO THE PRESENT (Doubleday 1985).

15 ALAN HEIMERT, RELIGION AND THE AMERICAN MIND: FROM THE GREAT AWAKENING TO THE REVOLUTION 2 (Harvard Univ. Press 1966).

16 Jon Butler, *Enthusiasm Described and Decried: The Great Awakening as Interpretative Fiction*, 69 J. AM. HIST. 305–6 (1982), referencing works such as William G. McLoughlin, *Enthusiasm for Liberty: The Great Awakening as the Key to the Revolution, in* PREACHERS AND POLITICIANS: TWO ESSAYS ON THE ORIGINS OF THE AMERICAN REVOLUTION 47–73 (Jack P. Greene & William G. McLoughlin eds., 1977); Harry S. Stout, *Religion, Communications, and the Ideological Origins of the American Revolution*, 34 WM. & MARY Q. 519 (1977); Rhys Isaac, *Preachers and Patriots: Popular Culture and the Revolution in Virginia, in* THE AMERICAN REVOLUTION: EXPLORATIONS IN THE HISTORY OF AMERICAN RADICALISM 125 (Alfred F. Young ed., 1976). Butler questions the significance that historians give to the impact of the "Great Awakening" on the revolutionary sentiments of the colonists, arguing both that "contemporaries never homogenized the eighteenth-century colonial religious revivals by labeling them the 'Great Awakening'" and that by ignoring the particularities of individual revivals, the label itself "distorts the extent, nature, and cohesion of the revivals that did exist in the eighteenth-century colonies," *supra*, at 307–8.

17 HEIMERT, *supra* note 15, at 2, *but see* Butler, *supra* note 16, at 313 n. 19 ("Although many American historians infer that denominational growth stemmed from revivalism and a commitment to evangelicalism, the evidence does not allow them to say that the organization of each new congregation stemmed from a local revival.").

18 Edward L. Bond & Joan R. Gondersen, *The Episcopal Church in Virginia, 1607–2007*, 115 VA. MAG. HIST. & BIO. 163, 190 (2007); Kelly Olds, *Privatizing the Church: Disestablishment in Connecticut and Massachusetts*, 102 J. POL. ECON. 277–8 (1994); *see also* Kidd, *supra* note 11, at 1020 (remarking that even after the Revolution, "[r]epublicanism was not considered incompatible with state support of religion.").

19 John A. Ragosta, *Fighting for Freedom: Virginia Dissenters' Struggle for Religious Liberty during the American Revolution*, 116 VA. MAG. HIST. & BIO. 227 (2008); Michael W. McConnell, *Establishment and Disestablishment at the Founding, Part I: Establishment of Religion*, 44 WM. & MARY L. REV. 2105, 2146–58 (2003); *see also* Olds, *supra* note 18, at 278–81 (discussing tax benefits afforded to established churches).

church and state, religious arguments also were used in support of disestablishment, especially among dissenting denominations such as Baptists and other evangelicals, who condemned the secular influences of politics as contaminating Christianity.[20]

Except for Rhode Island, all thirteen colonies had, at least in their earliest days, either an established church or some other entanglement with religion on a scale that would be unthinkable today[21] given the Establishment Clause of the First Amendment and its application to the states by virtue of the Fourteenth Amendment.[22] The prototype for these local establishments was the Church of England, described by a leading authority on colonial church history as follows:

> [T]he Church of England was an establishment because by law it made the King the head of the church, it imposed an episcopal form of polity, it defined the thirty-nine Articles to which all inhabitants must swear their belief, and it set up ecclesiastical courts to govern all the churches.... By the [British] Act of Conformity and the Toleration Act dissent was tolerated only at the cost of grave civil disabilities, and no one, of any sect,

[20] Kidd, *supra* note 11, at 1008–9, 1025 (reviewing modern developments in the history of political thought that have "displac[ed] the [idea of] the Lockean liberal tradition which had hitherto underpinned America's myth of origins"); Donald S. Lutz, *The Relative Influence of European Writers on Late Eighteenth Century American Political Thought*, 78 AM. POL. SCI. REV. 189, 190–3 (1984) (surveying American political writings from 1760 to 1805 and finding that Montesquieu and Blackstone were the two most cited European thinkers during this era). *See also* JOHN EUSTACE GILES, SEPARATION OF CHURCH AND STATE: TWO LECTURES, EXPLANATORY OF THE OBJECTS OF THE ANTI-STATE-CHURCH CONFERENCE DELIVERED IN SOUTH-PARADE CHAPEL, LEEDS 17–18 (London, Simpkin, Marshall & Co. 1844), for contemporary opinion regarding the ills of secular state influence on religion. Speaking before the Leeds Sunday School Union, Giles, a Baptist minister, invoked biblical exegesis in support for his anti–church-state position:

> Instead of the affairs of the Church being managed by spiritual men, they are managed, it is well known, by men of the world ... if you look at the Church and State system, you will find, that instead of calling upon its officers to come out from the world, and to be separate; it invests them with all the pomp, power, wealth, and splendor of the world.... Jesus Christ has declared that his kingdom is not of this world. He has said that his servants shall not fight in his cause. He has declared that they who draw the sword shall perish by the sword. He has told us, if he needed any agents to fight in support of his kingdom, that he has legions of angels at his disposal for that that purpose; but that neither men nor angels shall draw the sword for him, because his kingdom is not of this world.... But the union of Church and State declares that his kingdom is of this world; that it is altogether a political and worldly Establishment; that the sword ought to be drawn in its defense, and that if legions of angels cannot be got for the purpose, solid and substantial regiments and infantry shall.

[21] Arguably, Pennsylvania and its split-off, Delaware, belong with Rhode Island in the church-free category, but they both restricted religious liberty enough (*see infra* Section A.4.d and e, respectively) so that Cobb, a stern separationist, discerns "a marked difference" between them and Rhode Island:

> In fact, every American colony, from its foundation down to the revolution, with the exception of Rhode Island (if, indeed, that state be an exception) did openly, by the whole course of its laws and institutions, support and sustain, in some form, the Christian religion.

*See* COBB, *supra* note 2, at 422–53; *see also* JOSEPH STORY, 3 COMMENTARIES ON THE CONSTITUTION OF THE UNITED STATES, § 1867, at 724 (1833). For a brief, readable account of the early days of each colony (with an extensive bibliography), *see* ALAN TAYLOR, AMERICAN COLONIES: THE SETTLING OF NORTH AMERICA (Eric Foner ed., Penguin History of United States, 2001). For accounts of the social and political context of each colony's church-state relations, *see* HISTORY OF THE AMERICAN COLONIES IN THIRTEEN VOLUMES (Milton M. Klein & Jacob E. Cooke eds., 1986). *See also* WILLIAM WARREN SWEET, RELIGION IN COLONIAL AMERICA (Charles Scribner's Sons 1942); McConnell, *supra* note 19.

[22] For the "incorporation" of the First Amendment's religious clauses into the Fourteenth Amendment, *see* discussion *infra* Section I.2.

was exempt from supporting the state church by paying tithes. In addition, the bishops and archbishops of the Church of England were allowed to sit in the House of Lords where they shared in the lawmaking for all inhabitants of the realm.[23]

The Church of England was established in the colonies mainly by royal charters from which the colonies obtained their land; however, the nascent states introduced many changes in their religious institutions in the century and a half between their inception and the Revolution. These changes, by and large, loosened the tight link between the states and their churches. In one respect, though, some colonies introduced a new element of church-state union through the imposition of a tax specifically earmarked for the support of the local church's clergy and for the construction and repair of its buildings.[24] The imposition of these levies on dissenters and nonbelievers was deemed consistent with claims of religious tolerance, the justifying rationale being that supporting religion and religious institutions was comparable to supporting other institutions constituted for the welfare of the populace as a whole, such as courts, schools, roads, and the armed forces.[25] Thus an early judicial panegyric attempted to reconcile the incongruity between recognizing individual freedom of conscience and upholding the mandatory taxation of the claimant, a religious nonbeliever, for the financial maintenance of local clergy by stating

> He need not believe as the teacher or the [local] majority believe.... His conscience is free, his civil rights unimpaired. It is his misfortune that, in electing a teacher of religion and morality, he happens to be in the minority.... Society has the right to judge what will promote the good of society and to provide for it at the expense of the whole.[26]

Even so, taxes for the support of religion, as will be seen, evoked in their turn grievances and complaints that dominated the colonial church-state landscape in the period between the Revolution and the framing of the First Amendment. By then, only six states still maintained what the First Amendment calls "an establishment of religion."[27]

## 2. *The New England Puritans*

By the eve of the Revolution, New England colonists had transitioned from being stewards of their Puritan forebears' covenant to pioneer a godly kingdom in the New World,

[23] 1 McLoughlin, New England Dissent, *supra* note 2, at 615. It was not until 1988 that a Jewish leader was granted the same privilege. Immanuel Jakobovits, chief rabbi of the United Hebrew Congregations of the British Commonwealth of Nations, was the first rabbi to sit in the House of Lords, under the title Lord Jakobovits, Baron of Regent's Park. *See The House of Lords Seats Its First Rabbi*, N.Y. Times, Feb. 10, 1988, at A1. For further details of Lord Jakobovits' religious and political experiences, *see* Immanuel Jakobovits & Michael Shashar, Lord Jakobovits in Conversation (Edward Levin, trans., 2000).

[24] *See* 1 McLoughlin, New England Dissent, *supra* note 2, at 201; *see also* sources cited *supra* note 19.

[25] *See* 1 McLoughlin, New England Dissent, *supra* note 2, at 610; Olds, *supra* note 18, at 280.

[26] Muzzy v. Wilkins, 1 Smith's (N.H.) 1 (1803), *reprinted in* Decisions of the Superior and Supreme Courts of New Hampshire, from 1802 to 1809, and from 1813 to 1816, Selected from the Manuscript Reports of the Late Jeremiah Smith, Chief Justice of Those Courts 13–14 (Boston, Little, Brown 1879).

[27] The states upholding established religions at the time of the framing of the First Amendment were Massachusetts, Connecticut, New Hampshire, Georgia, South Carolina, and Maryland, with the disestablishment of the Congregational Church occurring in Massachusetts (1833), Connecticut (1813), and New Hampshire (1790) and the Church of England in Georgia (1789), South Carolina (1790), and Maryland (1776); *see* McConnell, *supra* note 19, at 2017.

as first set down in the Mayflower Compact – "We whose names are underwritten … having undertaken, for the glory of God, and advancement of the Christian faith, … a voyage to plant the first colony"[28] – and later affirmed by John Winthrop's ideal of a "city on a hill"[29] to advancing arguments for the separation of religious and civic polities.

### a. Massachusetts

Although the Puritans, on embarking from England for Massachusetts, professed their esteem for the Church of England ("our dear mother"),[30] they lost no time in pursuing their aim of purifying their parent of the rituals and forms of internal government that they despised.[31] The result in New England was a "Bible Commonwealth" whose union of church and state was, if anything, even more hostile to dissenters than the royal church they sought to reform. A harsh instance of Puritan intolerance was the hanging in 1658–1661 of four Quakers who returned to Massachusetts after being banished for

28 Mayflower Compact, *in* THE AMERICAN REPUBLIC: PRIMARY SOURCES 11 (Bruce Frohnen ed., 2002) (hereinafter PRIMARY SOURCES). For useful brief accounts of each colony, *see* MICHAEL S. ARIENS & ROBERT A. DESTRO, RELIGIOUS LIBERTY IN A PLURALISTIC SOCIETY 45 *passim* (Carolina Academic Press 1996).

29 Written aboard the *Arbella* in transit to the New World, Winthrop preached of the divine mission of the New England settlers:

> We are a company professing ourselves fellow members of Christ.… It is by a mutual consent, through a special over-valuing providence and a more than an ordinary approbation of the churches of Christ, to seek out a place of cohabitation and consortship under a due form of government both civil and ecclesiastical.… [W]hen God gives a special commission He looks to have it strictly observed in every article.… Thus stands the cause between God and us. We are entered into covenant with Him for this work.… For this end, we must be knit together, in this work, as one man. We must entertain each other in brotherly affection. We must be willing to abridge ourselves of our superfluities, for the supply of others' necessities. We must uphold a familiar commerce together in all meekness, gentleness, patience and liberality. We must delight in each other; make others' conditions our own; rejoice together, mourn together, labor and suffer together, always having before our eyes our commission and community in the work, as members of the same body. So shall we keep the unity of spirit in the bond of peace.… For we must consider that we shall be as a city upon a hill. The eyes of all people are upon us. So that if we shall deal falsely with our God in this work we have undertaken, and so cause Him to withdraw His present help from us, we shall be made a story and a by-word through the world.

John Winthrop, Sermon, A Modell of Christian Charity (1630), *in* COLLECTIONS OF THE MASSACHUSETTS HISTORICAL SOCIETY, ser. 3, pt. 7, at 44–7 (1838). A modernized version of the text, reproduced *supra*, is available in MATTHEW S. HOLLAND, BONDS OF AFFECTION: CIVIC CHARITY AND THE MAKING OF AMERICA 261–76 (Georgetown Univ. Press 2007). For additional authorities discussing the mission of the Puritan settlers and their covenant with God, *see* PERRY MILLER, ERRAND INTO THE WILDERNESS 11, 88–90 (Belknap Press 1956). *But see* Theodore Dwight Bozeman, *The Puritans' "Errand into the Wilderness" Reconsidered*, 59 NEW ENG. Q. 231 (1986) (questioning historians' reliance on Miller's "errand" thesis of an exemplary Puritan mission in settling New England).

30 EDMUND S. MORGAN, THE PURITAN DILEMMA: THE STORY OF JOHN WINTHROP 53 (Little, Brown & Co. 1958) ("[Y]ou would be pleased to take notice of the principals, and body of our company, as those who esteeme it our honour, to call the Church of England, from whence wee rise, our deare Mother, and cannot part from our native Country, where she specially resideth, without much sadnes of heart.").

31 *See* A HISTORY OF NEW ENGLAND 29–30 (R. H. Howard & Henry E. Crocker eds., Boston, Crocker & Co. 1879) ("To the ordinary reader it can never cease … to be a matter of profound wonder that these original Puritan colonists, ministers and laymen, born and bread in the bosom of Episcopacy, should have suddenly and so completely … severed the associations of a life-time; and, on coming to New England, become metamorphosed into uncompromising Episcopal-hating, Dissenting Congregationalists."); MORGAN, PURITAN DILEMMA, *supra* note 30, at 103 (remarking on the change in Thomas Dudley,

their religious beliefs.[32] The Pilgrims, whose settlement at Plymouth antedated the Puritan settlement on Massachusetts Bay by a decade, originally rejected the Church of England wholeheartedly, whereas the Puritans called for its reform from within. With the passage of time, though, their differences diminished, and the Pilgrims, many fewer in number, soon merged with the Puritan theocracy.[33]

In keeping with Puritan opposition to the centralized control of the Church of England and to the authority vested in its bishops – elements of church government that to the Puritans smacked of Roman Catholicism – they organized their Massachusetts churches in independent congregations connected only by synods. Congregationalism was recognized locally as the established church of Massachusetts,[34] but before the Revolution, the Puritans avoided open challenges to the Church of England's status.[35] Congregationalism's close link between religious faith and civil government was

deputy governor of the colony, who having once recognized the authority of the Anglican Church by 1633 believed that doing so would "pollute" him).

32 For an account of the persecution of the Quakers in Massachusetts during the seventeenth century, *see* Rufus M. Jones, The Quakers in the American Colonies 63–89 (Macmillan & Co. 1911).

33 For a description of the differing beliefs of the Pilgrims, who settled Plymouth Colony, and the Puritans, who established Massachusetts Bay Colony, and the subsequent establishment of the Congregational Church as the ecclesiastical authority of the region due to the unification of both colonies in 1691, *see* Jacob Conrad Meyer, Church and State in Massachusetts: From 1740 to 1833, at 1–31 (W. Reserve Univ. Press 1930). *See also* Adams, *supra* note 1; William Bradford, Of Plymouth Plantation, 1620–1647 (Samuel Eliot Morison ed., Knopf 1952); Cobb, *supra* note 2, at 133–48.

By an irony of fate, the tiny band of Pilgrims who landed at Plymouth Rock are memorialized by Plymouth Church (in Brooklyn, New York), nineteenth-century Protestant Christianity's most-famous locale. *See* Lyman Abbott, Henry Ward Beecher: A Sketch of His Career, with Analyses of His Power as Preacher, Lecturer, Orator and Journalist and Incidents and Reminiscences of His Life (Honolulu, U. P. Pacific 2002) (1882). An unlikely descendant of the Puritan ethos, who epitomized the burgeoning nation's evolution in religious sentiment and thought, was Henry Ward Beecher, son of Calvinist minister Lyman Beecher, himself a charismatic preacher described as "a combination of St. Augustine, Barnum, and John Barrymore." Sinclair Lewis, *Foreword in* Paxton Hibben, Henry Ward Beecher: An American Portrait, vii (Readers Club Press 1942) (1927).

An anecdote regarding the presidential election of 1884 sheds light on Beecher's own personal behavior and mind-set. In response to claims that Cleveland fathered an illegitimate child during his time practicing law in Buffalo, Beecher declared that "[i]f every man in New York State tonight, who has broken the seventh commandment, voted for Cleveland, he would be elected by 200,000 majority." Hibben, *supra*, at 307. Referencing long-standing rumors of Beecher's affinity for women other than his wife and his trial in 1875 charging alienation of affection, Benjamin F. Butler, running on an opposing party ticket, cleverly retorted: "As an expert in such matters Mr. Beecher must know better than I." *Id.*

In summarizing the significance of his subject, Hibben notes that "Beecher stood forth a prodigious figure, not by blazing a path in any wilderness, but by the fact that his inner experience was identical with that of millions of his fellow countrymen.... He began in the flint-like faith of the Puritans.... He ended his days an apostle of evolution, an advocate of women's suffrage and the higher education of women, a clergyman who attended the theater and who drank his wine or beer when he felt like it." *Id.* at xiv.

34 Commentators almost universally refer to Congregationalism as "the" established church of Massachusetts, although the singular term applies awkwardly to Congregationalism's ecclesiastical organization – a multiplicity of self-governing local organisms – as noted by Mark DeWolfe Howe, The Garden and the Wilderness: Religion and Government in American Constitutional History 34 (Univ. Chicago Press 1965); *see also* Baker v. Fales, 16 Mass. (1 Tyng) 488, 498–501 (1820) (detailing the transition from *de facto* to *de jure* establishment of Congregationalism in Massachusetts); Weld v. May, 63 Mass (1 Cush.) 181, 184–6 (1852) (detailing the development of congregational churches in Massachusetts). For disestablishment in Massachusetts, *see supra* notes 18–20 and accompanying text.

35 *See* Leonard W. Levy, The Establishment Clause: Religion and the First Amendment 16 (Macmillan 1986) (taxes for religion divided in Swansea, Massachusetts, equally between Baptists and Congregationalists); *see also* Susan Reed Stifler, Church and State in Massachusetts: 1691–1740, at 148–89 (Univ. Ill. Press 1914); Meyer, *supra* note 33, at 2.

evidenced by the enactment of taxes for the support of the Congregational churches, which required the inhabitants of each town to support "an able, learned and orthodox minister ... to dispense the word of God" regardless of the taxpayer's own faith, subject from time to time to grudgingly awarded exceptions.[36]

John Cotton, who regarded even toleration as "anti-Christian," responded to an English nobleman sympathetic to the Puritan cause and interested in emigrating to Massachusetts, yet who expressed concern regarding the colony's requirement of church membership in order to hold political office, by stating that theocracy is "the best forme of government in the commonwealth, as well as in the church."[37] In describing Congregational polity and the relationship between ministerial leadership and church membership, Samuel Stone remarked that the Massachusetts church was "a speaking aristocracy in the face of a silent democracy."[38] The pioneer Baptist leader John Clarke wrote of Massachusetts during this period: "[T]hey have Laws thus to proceed to force all to their worship, and to restrain those that differ from them."[39] Perry Miller, an eminent authority on the New England Puritans described, as follows, the concept of the state held by the Puritans: "New England political theory made the state almost a kind of second incarnation, a Messiah fathered by God and born of the people.... [W]hen they covenant among themselves, when they combine their several regenerate wills into one all-inclusive will, the state becomes another savior, the child of God and man, leading men to righteousness and preparing them for final reckoning."[40] Thus the Puritan government of Massachusetts, and later Connecticut, was best characterized as a dictatorship – "not of a single tyrant, or of an economic class, or of a political faction, but of the holy and regenerate" – and those not adhering to the truth, as established by Puritan leaders, were free to stay away.[41]

### b. Connecticut

Connecticut, like Massachusetts, maintained Congregationalism as its established church until after ratification of the First Amendment, although it split away from Massachusetts in 1634 to blaze a less rigorous route, one that did not restrict citizenship and the suffrage to church members.[42] On moving to Connecticut, these Bay Staters

36 LEVY, *supra* note 35, at 15. For a concise explanation of the methods used by the Puritans to determine an inhabitant's church membership, *see* EDMUND S. MORGAN, VISIBLE SAINTS: THE HISTORY OF A PURITAN IDEA 64 *passim* (Cornell Univ. Press 1965).

37 Letter from John Cotton to Lord Say and Seal (1636), *in* PRIMARY SOURCES, *supra* note 28, at 68–71. Cotton further expounded on his religious and political ideology by stating: "It is better that the commonwealth be fashioned to the setting forth of Gods house, which is his church: than to accommodate the church frame to the civill state. Democracy, I do not conceive that ever God did ordeyne as a fitt government eyther for church or commonwealth. If the people be governors, who shall be governed?" Needless to say, the nobleman did not immigrate to New England. *Id.*

38 1 COTTON MATHER, MAGNALIA CHRISTI AMERICANA 437 (Hartford, S. Andrus & Sons 1853).

39 JOHN CLARKE, ILL NEWES FROM NEW-ENGLAND (London, Henry Hills Printing 1652), *reprinted in* COLONIAL BAPTISTS: MASSACHUSETTS AND RHODE ISLAND 65 (Edwin S. Gaustad ed., 1980).

40 PERRY MILLER, THE NEW ENGLAND MIND: THE SEVENTEENTH CENTURY 419 (Harvard Univ. Press 1939).

41 MILLER, *supra* note 29, at 143–4.

42 *See* M. LOUISE GREENE, THE DEVELOPMENT OF RELIGIOUS LIBERTY IN CONNECTICUT 61–2 (Houghton, Mifflin & Co. 1905). By 1634, settlers from Massachusetts, disgruntled by the colony's requirement of church membership for franchise, a right so strictly guarded that only one man out of six possessed it, settled in the Connecticut River Valley. *See, e.g.*, GEORGE L. CLARK, A HISTORY OF CONNECTICUT 7–11

brought Congregationalism with them, and arguably, Connecticut had two establishments for a few decades: Congregationalism and the Church of England.[43] An admiring historian of religious liberty in America asserts that the citizens of Connecticut "were fully ready to concede the truth that the Christian religion could vitalize other forms of polity and worship than their own"[44] and that Connecticut's

> [w]orst sins against religious liberty were in the exercise of authority over the Church and the assessment upon the entire community for the support of the establishment. In these respects only did her Church laws differ from the full liberty conferred by Williams on Rhode Island, and by Baltimore on Maryland. And even these provisions of law Connecticut, so soon as occasion arose, learned to relax for the relief of dissenting Churches.[45]

Ultimately, though, Connecticut's "exercise of authority over the Church" was detailed and comprehensive:

> This care was intimate, concerning itself with many minor items; the erection of meetinghouses, the calling and support of ministers, the location and boundary of parishes, the composition of any troubles arising in the affairs of any parish. The care was shown also, not only by the enactment of general laws, but by the action of the general court in an endless number of individual cases. Everything touching Church management, any change in Church or in meeting-house, from one end of the commonwealth to the other, was brought to the legislature for indirection or permission. Any wrong suffered by any individual by way of discipline found its echo in the general court. Any

(G.P. Putnum & Sons 1914); MORGAN, *supra* note 36, at 106–8. In March of 1638, a settlement started in New Haven, under the religious leadership of John Davenport, who, as described by Cotton Mather,

> did now at New-Haven make *church purity* to be one of his greatest concerns and endeavors.... [H]e used a more than ordinary exactness in trying those that were admitted unto the communion of the church: indeed, so very thoroughly, and I had almost said, severely strict, were the terms of his communion, and so much, I had well nigh said over-much, were the golden snuffers of the sanctuary employed by him in his exercise of discipline towards those that were admitted, that he did all that was possible to render the renowned church of New-Haven like the New-Jerusalem.

MATHER, *supra* note 38, at 327–8, *quoted in* MORGAN, *supra* note 36, at 108. At the height of Davenport's pure church polity, more than half of New Haven's settlers were disenfranchised, giving the colony a strong likeness to the political and ecclesiastical structure of Massachusetts. CLARK, *supra* at 20. In fact, when New Haven was eventually annexed to Connecticut colony in 1662, Davenport returned to Massachusetts. Citing this example, one learned scholar posits: "Do we have here, in their differing views of church membership and the attendant question of freemanship, one explanation for the coolness that always existed between Connecticut and the New Haven colony?" MORGAN, *supra* note 36, at 108–9. *See also* COBB, *supra* note 2, at 238–90, for a history of Connecticut and New Haven colonies.

43 *See* LEVY, *supra* note 35, at 21–2.

44 Cobb acknowledges an outbreak of hostility to the Quakers when they arrived in Connecticut but refuses to describe the antipathy as "very severe." COBB, *supra* note 2, at 260. For a description of the enmity and harsh treatment with which Quakers were treated in New Haven, *see* CLARK, *supra* note 42, at 128–9. For the difference in treatment of Quakers in Connecticut Colony versus New Haven Colony, *see* GREENE, *supra* note 42, at 165–6. For the reaction against the short-lived New Haven theocracy, *see infra* notes 49 & 50 and accompanying text.

45 COBB, *supra* note 2, at 244; *see also* Herbert J. Santos, *Birth of a Liberal State: Connecticut's Fundamental Orders*, 1 CONN. L. REV. 386, 399 (1968) (noting that Connecticut's "Fundamental Orders" of 1639 deemed "America's first constitution" had no requirement for religious affiliation for voting rights).

disturbance in a Church soon brought the paternal bidding of the court to consider the things which make for peace.[46]

Thus tolerance in Connecticut was limited only to those "varying shades of opinions within a common faith and fold."[47] The arrival of "new elements," however, gave rise to the adoption in 1743 of legislation denying tolerance to Roman Catholics and ordering the arrest "of foreigners and suspected persons who sow and spread false and dangerous doctrines of religion amongst us," a measure that was evidently aimed primarily at Moravian missionaries engaged in preaching to the Indians.[48] The intolerant sentiment of mid-eighteenth-century Connecticut finds its precursor not in the liberal tradition of Connecticut colony but in the theocracy of New Haven, which on its founding in 1638 attempted to establish a religious government more stringent than Massachusetts, "in which every public utterance and action was to be guided by, and an expression of, the divine law."[49]

Ultimately, Connecticut emulated the aspiration of its founder, Thomas Hooker, by promoting the ideals of liberty of conscience.[50] Its 1776 constitution provided the following:

> The People of this State, being by the Providence of God, free and independent, have the sole and exclusive Right of governing themselves as a free, sovereign, and independent State; and having from their Ancestors derived a free and excellent Constitution of the Government whereby the Legislature depends on the free and annual Election of the People, they have the best Security for the Preservation of their civil and religious Rights and liberties. And forasmuch as the free Fruition of such Liberties and Privileges as Humanity, Civility and Christianity call for, as is due to every Man in his Place and Proportion, without Impeachment or Infringement, hath ever been, and will be the Tranquility and Stability of Churches and Commonwealths; and the Denial thereof, the Disturbance, if not the Ruin of both.[51]

46 COBB, *supra* note 2, at 246.

47 GREENE, *supra* note 42, at 117.

48 *See* COBB, *supra* note 2, at 277–8.

49 *Id.* at 280. Ultimately, the end of this independent theocracy was reflected by, among other things, the fact that three of the regicides responsible for condemning Charles I to death found refuge in New Haven (which still honors their actions by the names of three of its avenues (Dixwell, Goffe, and Whalley). *See* FEDERAL WRITERS' PROJECT, WORKS PROJECT ADMINISTRATION, CONNECTICUT: A GUIDE TO ITS ROADS, LORE, AND PEOPLE 229–33, 251–2 (1938). For an example of the esteem to which the regicides were held in New Haven, *see* President Stiles of Yale College's dedication in his account of the regicides:

> To all the patrons of real, perfect, and unpolluted liberty, civil and religious, throughout the world; this history of three of its most illustrious and heroic, but unfortunate defenders, is humbly submitted, and dedicated, by a hitherto uncorrupted friend to universal liberty.

EZRA STILES, A HISTORY OF THREE OF THE JUDGES OF KING CHARLES I (Hartford, Elisha Babcock Printing 1794) (signed Yale College, November 1793); *see also* CLARK, *supra* note 42, at 164–6 (describing the plight of the regicide judges).

50 *See* GREENE, *supra* note 42, at 62–3 ("[I]t was [Hooker's] political foresight which made him urge upon the colonists a more representative government than would be obtainable from a franchise based upon church-membership where, as in the colonial churches, admission to such membership was conditioned upon exacting tests."); Santos, *supra* note 45, at 397 ("In Connecticut, as in the Bay Colony, Hooker called for the election of all branches of government, but he proposed no religious or property qualifications for the franchise.").

51 1 BEN[JAMIN] PERLEY POORE, THE FEDERAL AND STATE CONSTITUTIONS, COLONIAL CHARTERS, AND OTHER ORGANIC LAWS OF THE UNITED STATES 257–8 (Washington, Gov't Prtg. Off. 1877).

In a 1784 act, its last major religious legislation before ratifying the First Amendment, Connecticut granted Christians who did not belong to its established church an exception from the state's church-support taxes provided that they "attend public worship, and support the gospel ministry in a way agreeable to their consciences" and filed a certificate to that effect issued by their own minister.[52]

### c. New Hampshire

As with Rhode Island and Connecticut, New Hampshire owed its establishment in 1679 by royal charter to the religious intolerance of the Massachusetts Puritans.[53] While asserting that the groundwork of the colony was based on a religious, specifically Christian, foundation, New Hampshire relaxed Massachusetts' union of church and state by allowing all qualified Protestants, not merely members of the established Congregationalist church, to vote.[54] An example of the tenacity of the New Hampshire colonists' support for liberty of conscience is the failure, in 1682, of the royal governor's vigorous effort to force the Church of England on the colony's residents.[55] An analysis not matched in the other colonies was the examination in 1725 by New Hampshire's legislature of a religious treatise, which it found so full of doctrinal error that it impounded the work so that "no one shall have a copy."[56] This curious event, evidently unique in our history, demonstrates that whatever its views on liberty of conscience, the New Hampshire colonial legislature was hardly committed to a separation of church and state.

### d. Rhode Island

Besides spawning the established churches of Connecticut and New Hampshire, the fissiparous Puritans of Massachusetts launched a totally novel species of the church-state relationship by expelling Roger Williams, a Salem minister, for advocating the separation of church and state and for compounding his offense by questioning the legal validity of the colony's charter on the ground that it violated the rights of the local Indians.[57]

[52] *See An act for securing the rights of conscience in matters of religion to Christians of every denomination in this state*, ACTS AND LAWS OF THE STATE OF CONNECTICUT IN AMERICA 22 (New London: T. Green [prtg.] 1784); *see also* 2 MCLOUGHLIN, *supra* note 2, at 922–3. For disestablishment in Connecticut, usually credited to its 1818 Constitution, *see* Weisbrod, *supra* note 10, at 803. *See also* 2 MCLOUGHLIN, *supra* note 2, at 962–1062. For text of the Connecticut 1818 Constitution pertaining to disestablishment, *see* 1 POORE, *supra* note 51, at 264.

[53] *See* COBB, *supra* note 2, at 290.

[54] *See id.* at 291. For a more detailed account of church-state relations in New Hampshire, *see* CHARLES B. KINNEY, JR., CHURCH AND STATE: THE STRUGGLE FOR SEPARATION IN NEW HAMPSHIRE (Columbia Univ. Press 1955).

[55] *See* COBB, *supra* note 2, at 295–6.

[56] *Id.* at 300.

[57] *Id.* at 423 *passim*. For background on the evolution of the doctrine of separation of church and state, in contradiction to medieval doctrines upholding civil government's authority over religious and spiritual affairs, *see* Stephen Phillips, *Roger Williams and the Two Tables of the Law*, 38 J. CHURCH & ST. 547–56 (1996), and Jimmy D Neff, *Pious Puritan and Strict Separationist*, 38 J. CHURCH & ST. 529–31 (1996). For the impact of separatists' writings on Williams' theology, *see* Phillips, *supra*, at 556–68, and Neff, *supra*, at 536–46. For a full analysis of Williams' theological beliefs, *see* EDMUND S. MORGAN, ROGER WILLIAMS: THE CHURCH AND THE STATE (Harcourt, Brace & World 1967), and *see also* OLA ELIZABETH WINSLOW, MASTER ROGER WILLIAMS: A BIBLIOGRAPHY (Macmillan 1957), and PERRY MILLER, ROGER WILLIAMS: HIS CONTRIBUTION TO THE AMERICAN TRADITION (Bobbs-Merrill Co. 1953).

Williams, banished from Massachusetts in 1636, set out to establish a society governed only in civil matters, whereby conscience – "a persuasion fixed in the mind and heart of man" – could be freely expressed.[58] Rhode Island and Providence Plantations, established to "hold forth a livelie [*sic*] experiment," was granted a royal charter in 1663, which provided that "[n]o person within the said colony, at any time hereafter, shall be any wise molested, punished, disqualified, or called in question for any difference of opinion in matters of religion ... every person may at all times freely and fully enjoy his own judgment and Conscience in matters of religious concernments."[59]

Williams was revolutionary in his commitment to freedom of conscience and his requisite belief in the separation of church and state, as related by an admiring chronicler of religious liberty in America:

> Himself [i.e., Roger Williams] the first among philosophers and statesmen, since the day of Constantine, to proclaim the complete freedom of mind and conscience from all civil bonds, he became the founder of the first state in whose fundamental law that freedom was incorporated, not only as a charter of liberty, but as the actual reason and purpose of the state's existence. In this latter particular, indeed, the colony of Rhode Island stands alone, owing its origin, not only to that desire for liberty which brought the Pilgrim and Puritan to New England, but to the act and acknowledged purpose, a purpose confessed by its founders and assented to by the king, "to hold forth a lively experiment, that a most flourishing civil state may stand and best be maintained, with a full liberty of religious concernments."[60]

Williams is a source of the metaphor "a wall of separation" between church and state, which is perhaps the most misunderstood figure of speech in constitutional law, if not in the entire *corpus juris*.[61] He is often credited with inspiring the First Amendment. Perhaps his views percolated in American intellectual life from his day until 1789, but whether they did or did not, the church-state practices of Rhode Island were surely well known to the Founders and Framers of the Constitution even if Williams himself, as an expounder of theory, has not been considered politically influential by historians.[62]

58 *See* James Ernst, Roger Williams: New England Firebrand 435 (Macmillan 1932) (quoting Williams). For a description of Williams' banishment, *see* Cobb, *supra* note 2, at 423–34.

59 2 Poore, *supra* note 51, at 1596–7.

60 Cobb, *supra* note 2, at 423. Cobb's mention of Constantine refers to Emperor Constantine's "Edict of Milan," which in A.D. 313 proclaimed freedom of worship and universal religious tolerance in the Roman Empire. *See generally* A. H. M. Jones, Constantine and the Conversion of Europe 76–8 (Collier 1962) (describing Constantine's influence on the spread of Christianity).Cobb's equation of Williams' belief in complete separation of church and state to Constantine is seemingly ironic, however, because Williams wrote that Constantine did more harm to Christianity by cloaking it in the support of the state than did Nero, who burned Christians alive for entertainment. *See* Roger Williams, The Bloody Tenent Yet More Bloody (London, Giles Calvert 1652), *reprinted in* 4 Publications of the Narragansett Club 72 (Samuel L. Caldwell ed., Providence Press 1870) ("It is apparent that then the *Christian Religion* gloriously flourished ... when the *Roman Emperours* took not power to themselves to reform the *abuses* in the *Christian Church*, but persecuted it; and then the *church* was ruined and overwhelmed with *Apostacy* [*sic*] and *Antichristianism* [*sic*], when the *Emperours* took that power unto themselves; And then it was ... that *Christianitie* [*sic*] lost more, even in *Constantines* [*sic*] time, than under bloody *Nero*.").

61 *See infra* Chapter 4. As noted there, the metaphor is often attributed to Jefferson. It is impossible to ascertain whether the metaphor was borrowed by him from Roger Williams, was derived by both of them from still earlier theoreticians, or was kindled in both minds independently.

62 *See* Ariens & Destro, *supra* note 28, at 55. For a summary of how various scholars have interpreted Williams' historical impact, *see* LeRoy Moore, Jr., *Roger Williams and the Historians*, 32 Church Hist. 432–51 (1963).

In these respects, Rhode Island was unique among the thirteen colonies, though even its record of tolerance and liberty is not entirely free of blemishes. For example, Roman Catholics were at one time denied citizenship, and a bill was proposed in 1665 to outlaw the practice of Quakerism because of its prohibition on bearing arms.[63] However, on the arrival of Roman Catholic faithful, in the form of French naval officers and sailors aiding the Colonies during the Revolutionary period, the opprobrious law denying citizenship to Catholics was expunged, whereas there is no record of the bill proposing the prohibition of Quakerism ever passing.[64]

### 3. *The Anglican Southern Colonies*

#### a. Introduction

As much as Massachusetts was the epitome of church-state relations in Puritan New England, except, of course, for Rhode Island, so Virginia set the standard in the southern colonies for church-state relations with the Church of England.[65] There was a pronounced difference between the two regions in their passion for their established churches and in the rigor of their application of their religious convictions. The Puritans were far stronger in both. Religion impelled their immigration to America and took the form of a homegrown product, whereas the Virginians' established church – the Church of England – was headed by the King, their allegiance to whom was undermined as they gravitated toward political independence.

The two geographic groups also differed in their paths to disestablishment. This disparity reflected a difference in loyalty to their established churches, as explained by a distinguished historian:

> Many reasons have been offered for the different paths [Virginia and Massachusetts] followed. First, while the Virginians were disestablishing the Anglican Church, which was closely allied with the King in both its institutional form and in its behavior, those in Massachusetts who favored disestablishment had to attack a church which was staunchly patriotic and locally controlled. Second, the Anglican Church, lacking a colonial episcopate, had never been a strong force in the colonial life of Virginia nor was it an

For a recent discussion on the impact of Williams' theology on the political discourse in America, *see* John M. Barry, Roger Williams and the Creation of the American Soul (Viking Adult 2012). *Compare* Miller, *supra* note 57, at 254–7 (arguing that Williams' thought and impact were primarily religious and not political), *with* Edmund S. Morgan, *Miller's Williams*, 38 New Eng. Q. 513, 522–3 (1965) [reviewing The Complete Writings of Roger Williams (James Hammond Trumbull et al. eds., 1963)] ("On further consideration one senses the connection between Miller's two observations that Williams contributed nothing to the American tradition and that he is a threat to every establishment.... [I]n its history ever since, the [United States] ... has retained some sense of the divine mission that Winthrop had originally assigned to New England and that Williams had rejected. In spite of the fact that the United States has separated church and state, Americans continue to think of their government as embodying some sort of righteousness. By Williams' view, all governments were useful.... They all gained their authority simply from the agreement of the people who established them.... The seditious character of such a belief lay less in its substance than in the relentless rationality with which Williams applied it.... Reason applied to government, or for that matter to any institution, is not only the most constructive but also the most subversive instrument at man's command.").

63 Cobb, *supra* note 2, at 437–8.

64 *Id.* at 437.

65 *See generally* S. Charles Bolton, Southern Anglicanism: The Church of England in Colonial South Carolina 1–36 (Praeger 1982).

> integral part of the social and intellectual fabric of the people; but in Massachusetts, the Congregational churches were the warp and woof of life. Third, the Anglican Church had taken a very hostile attitude toward dissenters in Virginia and although it had never practiced the extreme intolerance of seventeenth century Puritanism neither had it been willing to grant the broad tolerance to dissenters (by exempting them from taxes and granting them full freedom of worship) which the Puritans had extended in the eighteenth century.... Finally, the leaders of the fight for disestablishment in Virginia included some of the most distinguished and influential members of the ruling elite (Jefferson, Mason, Madison), but in Massachusetts the ruling elite were almost solidly united in favor of maintaining the establishment.[66]

Still another disparity between the church-state history of Massachusetts and its counterpart in Virginia deserves attention because it has had a powerful – but unwarranted – influence on the contemporary jurisprudence of the First Amendment's Establishment Clause. This disparity is that in ascribing a meaning to the Establishment Clause, judicial historians have relied almost solely on the writings of Virginia's Jefferson and Madison to the disregard of the countervailing influence of church-state commentators in Massachusetts during the very same years.

### b. Virginia

Virginia's first royal charter, granted shortly before the 1606 departure of the first Virginia settlers from England, admonished them to follow the rites and doctrines of the Church of England, both for themselves and in discharging their missionary function of converting the native population, deemed "people [who] as yet live in darkness and miserable ignorance of the true knowledge and worship of God."[67] The establishment of Anglicanism as the colony's religion was repeated in the charter of 1609, which permitted the inhabitants to accept more settlers provided that they took an oath of supremacy to the Church of England.[68] In practice, however, Virginia's Anglican facsimile was only a "faulty imitation" of the mother church, lacking, among other things, a resident bishop for nearly a century and a half.[69]

As it happened, less than a month before the nation's Declaration of Independence was promulgated, Virginia adopted a Declaration of Rights, Article 16 of which is devoted to religion:

66 1 McLoughlin, *supra* note 2, at 592. The author also cites other factors for the regions' differing paths to disestablishment, including the democratic control of the numerous Congregational churches in New England, which weakened allegations that establishment in New England threatened parishioners' liberty. *Id.* at 593.

67 *See* 2 Poore, *supra* note 51, at 1888–93, *reprinted in* 1 Documents of American History 8–10 (Henry Steele Commager ed., 1958) (hereinafter Documents).

68 *See* 2 Poore, *supra* note 51, at 1893–1902, *reprinted in* 1 Documents, *supra* note 66, at 10–12 [expressing particular concern about the presence of "any person ... suspected to affect the Superstitions of the Church of *Rome*" (emphasis in original)].

For a brief account of Virginia's religious practices from its founding to the disestablishment of the Church of England, *see* Stokes, *supra* note 2, at 366–97. For more detailed accounts of Virginia's religious practices, *see* Cobb, *supra* note 2, at 74–115. *See also* Rhys Isaac, Transformation of Virginia, 1740–1790 (Univ. of N. Carolina Press 1982); Thomas E. Buckley, Church and State in Revolutionary Virginia (Univ. Press of Va. 1977). For the social, political, and religious nature Virginia on the eve of independence, *see* Buckley, *supra*, at 9–37; *see also* Charles F. James, Documentary History of the Struggle for Religious Liberty in Virginia (Da Capo Press 1971) (1899).

69 *See* Buckley, *supra* note 68, at 9; *see also* Wesley Frank Craven, The Southern Colonies in the Seventeenth Century 178–82 (La. State Univ. Press 1949) (comparing the Anglican Church in England

> That religion, or the duty which we owe to our Creator, and the manner of discharging it, can be directed only by reason and conviction, not by force or violence; and therefore all men are equally entitled to the free exercise of religion, according to the dictates of conscience; and that it is the mutual duty of all to practice Christian forbearance, love, and charity towards each other.[70]

The first version of the Declaration of Rights, as originally drafted by George Mason, adhered to the contemporary view that valued religious toleration, but not religious freedom, by providing that "all men should enjoy the fullest toleration of the exercise of religion."[71] Under Mason's view, the state could support and maintain specific Christian denominations so long as individuals espousing other religious views were tolerated.[72] James Madison, however, believed that "the right to every man is to liberty – not to toleration"[73] and subscribed to Thomas Paine's aphorism that "[t]oleration is not the opposite of intolerance but is the counterfeit of it."[74]

Madison argued that merely tolerating religion casts the practice of personal religious beliefs as a revocable privilege rather than an inalienable right.[75] As noted by historians, "[i]n Madison's mind, the right of religious exercise was too important to be cast in the form of a mere privilege allowed by the ruling civil polity and enjoyed as a grant of

and Virginia). For a discussion of the protracted controversy surrounding the issue of bishops for the American branches of the Church of England, *see* 1 STOKES, *supra* note 2, at 231–40; COBB, *supra* note 2, at 478–81. For a more detailed analysis, *see* CARL BRIDENBAUGH, MITRE AND SCEPTRE: TRANSATLANTIC FAITHS, IDEAS, PERSONALITIES, AND POLITICS, 1689–1775 (Oxford Univ. Press 1962).

70 2 POORE, *supra* note 51, at 1908–9, *reprinted in* 1 DOCUMENTS, *supra* note 66, at 103–4; *see also* SYDNEY E. AHLSTROM, A RELIGIOUS HISTORY OF THE AMERICAN PEOPLE 380 (Yale Univ. Press 1972) (describing this manifesto as the "most sensational" grant of religious liberty in the revolutionary era).

A companion buttress for religious liberty proposed by Madison – the prohibition of financial support for the established Church of England – was, however, rejected. Other features of the priority given to the Anglican establishment, such as the church's exclusive right to perform marriage ceremonies, also were left untouched by the proclamation, which was so groundbreaking in other respects. *See* BUCKLEY, *supra* note 68, at 36. A commentator observed in 1961 that by the end of the American Revolution, "every state either had fashioned a separate bill of rights or had passed statutes with similar provisions. In a good many cases the work was done with scissors, paste pot, and a copy of the Virginia Declaration." Daniel L. Dreisbach, *Church-State Debate in the Virginia Legislature: From the Declaration of Rights to the Statute for Establishing Religious Freedom, in* RELIGION AND POLITICAL CULTURE IN JEFFERSON'S VIRGINIA 135, 137 (Garrett Ward Sheldon & Daniel L. Dreisbach eds., 2000).

For a detailed examination of Virginia's 1776 Declaration of Rights and the gradual disestablishment of its Anglican Church, *see* BUCKLEY, *supra* note 68, at 8–71; Dreisbach, *supra*, at 135–55. *See also* H. J. ECKENRODE, SEPARATION OF CHURCH AND STATE IN VIRGINIA: A STUDY IN THE DEVELOPMENT OF THE REVOLUTION (Va. State Library, Archives Div. 1910). For briefer accounts of this subject, *see* THOMAS J. CURRY, THE FIRST FREEDOMS: CHURCH AND STATE IN AMERICA TO THE PASSAGE OF THE FIRST AMENDMENT 135–6 (Oxford Univ. Press 1986); WILLIAM LEE MILLER, THE FIRST LIBERTY: RELIGION AND THE AMERICAN REPUBLIC 5–7 (Knopf 1985); 1 STOKES, *supra* note 2, at 303–5, 380; ARIENS & DESTRO, *supra* note 28, at 45–63. For a more broadly ranging cultural survey of this area, *see* ISAAC, *supra* note 67. For discussion of the enactment in 1786 of Jefferson's Statute for Religious Freedom, the important sequel to the widely influential 1776 Declaration of Rights, *see infra* F in this chapter.

71 *See* RODNEY K. SMITH, PUBLIC PRAYER AND THE CONSTITUTION: A CASE STUDY IN CONSTITUTIONAL INTERPRETATION 37–9 (1987); BUCKLEY, *supra* note 68, at 18; *see also* CUSHING STROUT, THE NEW HEAVENS AND NEW EARTH: POLITICAL RELIGION IN AMERICA 84 (Harper & Row 1973).

72 *See* SMITH, *supra* note 71, at 40.

73 *See id.*

74 Dreisbach, *supra* note 70, at 138 [quoting THOMAS PAINE, THE RIGHTS OF MAN: BEING AN ANSWER TO MR. BURKE'S ATTACK ON THE FRENCH REVOLUTION (1791)]; *see also* STROUT, *supra* note 71, at 84.

75 *See* Dreisbach, *supra* note 70, at 138; BUCKLEY, *supra* note 68, at 18.

governmental benevolence. Rather, he viewed religious liberty as a natural and unalienable right, possessed equally by all citizens."[76] The pledge of "equal entitle[ment] to the free exercise of religion" was therefore substituted and ultimately adopted by the legislature.[77] However, as one scholar notes, "[t]he convention was willing to make the alteration in wording, but failed to grasp its implications,"[78] for, in discarding the term "toleration," used up to that point as designating "in some degree ... a symbol of liberty," Madison exposed the term's "intrinsic fallacious[ness]" and "erected a new and loftier platform for the fabric of religious freedom."[79]

Because Virginia's Declaration of Rights did not explicitly alter the Church of England's legal status in Virginia, it left open the question of who would be the proper recipient of the colony's subsidies – either George III, whose status as Defender of the Faith (unlike his political role as King of Great Britain) was not disputed by the colonists' push toward independence, or an undetermined successor to the Church of England. The liturgy of the established church was eventually altered to eliminate its references to George III and the royal family, and prayers for Virginia's own magistrates were instead substituted.[80] This action presupposed that Virginia's legislature had the authority to prescribe rules for the conduct of religious observance, and it demonstrates that the Declaration of Rights distinguished between the right of free exercise of religion and the establishment of a state church. Virginians who wanted the former but not the latter, however, argued that the levy of taxes for the benefit of a state church was tantamount to imposing a burden on dissenting denominations' free exercise of religion, a sentiment that was expressed in verse at the time:

> Tax all things, water, air and light,
> If need there is, yea tax the night
> But let our brave heroic minds
> Move freely, like celestial winds.
> Make vice and folly feel your rod,
> But leave our consciences to God.[81]

76 Dreisbach, *supra* note 70, at 138.

77 *Id.* Historians commentating on Article 16 of the Declaration are surprisingly reticent, however, about what in today's America would be considered a puzzling contradiction between its last clause – prescribing the practice of Christian virtues as the "mutual duty of all" – and its guarantee of religious freedom. For example, one historian flatly states that "Anglicans, Roman Catholics, Evangelists, Jews and unbelievers were placed on the same civil footing." ECKENRODE, *supra* note 70, at 45. Although another historian is more guarded, observing that "in the longer history [the "equally entitled" language of the Declaration] ... would mean that heathens, pagans, and nonbelievers had rights equal to those of believers, although liberty that broad would not have been publicized in Williamsburg, Virginia, in June of 1776." MILLER, *supra* note 70, at 6.

The language in the Declaration linking "Creator," "religion," and "conscience," and significantly, the call to practice "Christian forbearance, love, and charity," rests, notes scholars, on two assumptions: "first, that the rights of conscience envisioned by the Virginia Convention were to be exercised in a theistic context, and second, that it involves not only a relationship between one man and his God, but also the relationship of each man to his neighbor." Dreisbach, *supra* note 69, at 140.

78 BUCKLEY, *supra* note 68, at 18.

79 COBB, *supra* note 2, at 492 [quoting 1 WILLIAM C. RIVES, HISTORY OF THE LIFE AND TIMES OF JAMES MADISON 146 (Boston, Little Brown 1859)].

80 *See* BUCKLEY, *supra* note 68, at 21.

81 BUCKLEY, *supra* note 68, at 22 [citing Otto Lohrenz, *The Virginia Clergy and the American Revolution* 263–4 (1970) (unpublished Ph.D. dissertation, Univ. of Kansas) (on file with Van Pelt Library, Univ. of Pennsylvania)]. The forces favoring disestablishment and freedom from religious assessments aligned in

This sentiment was widely shared, and taxes for the support of the Anglican Church were not levied after 1776, although enough financial support for the church was generated during the next decade to cause some historians to date Virginia's disestablishment later in time to the legislative defeat of a religious tax assessment proposed in 1785.[82]

### c. South Carolina

The Church of England became the established church of the Carolinas as the result of a 1663 royal charter covering the area that includes present-day North and South Carolina. The grantees of the charter promptly bestowed freedom and liberty of conscience to non-Anglicans, provided that they "behav[e] themselves peaceably, and not us[e] this liberty to licentiousness, nor to the civil injury, or outward disturbance of others."[83] These two themes – an established church and freedom of religion for outsiders – became recurrent elements of the Fundamental Constitutions of Carolina, drafted in 1669.[84] The promise of religious liberty fitted neatly into the effort of the

their distrust of the effect of institutionalized church-state relations on the general populace, although they differed in their reasons. Rationalists, such as Jefferson and Madison, found religion to be a "private affair," whereby personal beliefs about divinity and conscience are the purview of religion only, not government. For Jefferson, "[t]ruth can stand by itself," and government support is not needed. *See* STROUT, *supra* note 71, at 79–89. Evangelicals, on the other hand, denounced religious assessments as corrupting the purity of the church. *See* BUCKLEY, *supra* note 68, at 140, 149–50. A petition from Washington County seeking to overturn the assessment is indicative of this broader sentiment: "civil policy ... can never make us Christians, neither can Christianity be benefited by the laws of the commonwealth, but only by the constitutions of Christ." *Id.* at 150.

82 *See, e.g.*, 1 STOKES, *supra* note 2, at 383; BUCKLEY, *supra* note 68, at 113–44.

83 2 POORE, *supra* note 51, at 1397 (Charter of Carolina, dated 1665). Both the Charter of 1663 and the Charter of 1665 acknowledged the existence of religious sentiment in the Carolinas of persons who "cannot, in their private opinions, conform to the public exercise of religion according to the liturgy, forms and ceremonies of the Church of England" (*id.*), yet only the Charter of 1665 safeguarded non-Anglicans from acts of molestation or punishment. *See also* 2 POORE, *supra*, at 1382–9 (Charter of Carolina, dated 1663). *See generally* COBB, *supra* note 2, at 116–17 (discussing Carolina Charters of 1663 and 1665).

84 For text of the Fundamental Constitutions of Carolina (1669), *see* 5 FRANCIS NEWTON THORPE, THE FEDERAL AND STATE CONSTITUTIONS COLONIAL CHARTERS, AND OTHER ORGANIC LAWS OF THE STATES, TERRITORIES, AND COLONIES NOW OR HERETOFORE FORMING THE UNITED STATES OF AMERICA 2772, 2783–5 (Washington, Gov't Prtg. Office 1909). For discussion of the significance of the Fundamental Constitutions, *see* COBB, *supra* note 2, at 119–23. *See also* JOHN WESLEY BRINSFIELD, RELIGION AND POLITICS IN COLONIAL SOUTH CAROLINA (1983); CHARLES S. BOLTON, SOUTHERN ANGLICISM: THE CHURCH OF ENGLAND IN COLONIAL SOUTH CAROLINA (1982); ROBERT M. WEIR, COLONIAL SOUTH CAROLINA (1983). The Fundamental Constitutions are attributed to John Locke and are credited with establishing the Church of England in the Carolinas. *See, e.g.*, BRINSFIELD, *supra* at 7–9; COBB, *supra* note 2, at 119. One historian describes the document as "the most singular and fantastic instrument of government ever devised by the human mind." COBB, *supra* note 2, at 119. Positing that "the deepest philosophic mind may be at fault, when called to deal with practical affairs [of church-state relations]," Cobb describes the Fundamental Constitutions as "essay[ing] to combine relics of a dead feudalism with institutions of the new popular power in a mixture both absurd and unserviceable.... These articles are eleven in number, entering into matters of detail with a notable particularity, and while extending a large liberty to certain sorts of dissent, put other sorts under a sharp ban." *Id.* at 119–20. For instance, atheists and nonpracticing persons of European descent were not only barred from political life in the colony but also were actively criminalized, whereas native populations, deemed "strangers to Christianity," were afforded civil protections for their differing beliefs. *See* THORPE, *supra* at 2783–5; COBB, *supra* note 2, at 120–2. As scholars note, the aim of the Fundamental Constitutions was not to espouse freedom of conscience but to provide for freedom of religion. *See, e.g.*, COBB, *supra* note 2, at 122 (under the Fundamental Constitutions, "while a broad dissent is allowed to the very limit of theism, every

colony's leaders to attract a broad array of settlers – a successful strategy, bringing sizable groups of Quakers, Huguenots, Presbyterians, Baptists, Dutch Reformed, and Jews to the colony.[85]

South Carolina's constitution, ratified in 1778, prescribed the "Christian Protestant religion" as the established religion of the state and provided that "all denominations of Christian Protestants … demeaning themselves peaceably and faithfully, shall enjoy equal religious and civil privileges."[86] The newly enacted constitution then went on to provide that any group of fifteen or more males over twenty-one years of age, who professed belief in Protestant Christianity, could organize themselves into an established church, subject, however, to the maintenance of a record book in which members subscribed to the following beliefs:

> 1st. That there is one eternal God, and a future state of rewards and punishments.
> 2nd. That God is publicly to be worshiped.
> 3rd. That the Christian religion is the true religion.
> 4th. That the holy scriptures of the Old and New Testaments are of divine inspiration, and are the rule of faith and practice.
> 5th. That it is lawful and the duty of every man being therunto called by those that govern, to bear witness to the truth.[87]

Not content with the requirement of attestation to the foregoing statement of beliefs, South Carolina's constitution also required every minister to be elected by a majority of his religious society and to declare

> That he is determined by God's grace out of the holy scriptures, to instruct the people committed to his charge, and to teach nothing as required of necessity to eternal salvation but that which he shall be persuaded may be concluded and proved from the scripture … that he will be diligent in prayers, and in reading of the holy scriptures, and in such studies as help to the knowledge of the same; that he will be diligent to frame and fashion his own self and his family according to the doctrine of Christ, and to make both himself and them, as much as in him lieth, wholesome examples and patterns to the flock of Christ; that he will maintain and set forwards, as much as he can, quietness, peace, and love among all people, and especially among those that are or shall be committed to his charge.[88]

In keeping with the installation of Protestant Christianity as the state's established religion, South Carolina's constitution also provided the legislature with the right to

citizen must have some religion and be a communicant in some Church, or be an outlaw."); BRINSFIELD, *supra* at 8 [noting that the Fundamental Constitutions "affirmed in general deist terms … that 1) There is a God, and 2) He ought to be publically worshipped"].

85 *See, e.g.*, COBB, *supra* note 2, at 118 (describing immigration of dissenting Christian denominations to Carolinas); *see also* LEON HÜHNER, JEWS OF SOUTH CAROLINA FROM EARLIEST SETTLEMENT TO THE END OF THE AMERICAN REVOLUTION (1904).

86 2 POORE, *supra* note 51, at 1626.

87 *Id.*

88 *Id.* at 1627.1 STOKES, *supra* note 2, at 432, describes South Carolina's effort to ensure a Protestant state as "probably without parallel in our national history," a mild comment in light of Cobb's description of the Constitution of 1778 as "a most curious mingling of political and religious ideas, having in part the ordinary expressions of civil law, and in other part assuming the attitude and motive of a superior spiritual court or confession of faith." COBB, *supra* note 2, at 505. *But see supra* note 56 and accompanying text regarding the New Hampshire legislature's condemnation and impoundment, in 1725, of a religious treatise found to be objectionable.

intervene in such religious matters as the salaries of clergymen, the duties of the rector of a specific chapel, and the repairs of designated church buildings.[89]

Contemporaries viewed the Revolution as a watershed for South Carolina's political, social, and ecclesiastical history.[90] By 1790, South Carolina's new constitution provided for the complete separation of church and state, enfranchised Roman Catholics, and provided for religious freedom "without distinction or preference."[91]

d. North Carolina

North Carolina was part of a much larger territory governed by a royal grant of 1663, subject in religious matters to the Church of England, which was always nominally the official religion of the colony.[92] However, in 1715, the North Carolina colonists, led by their governing assembly, endorsed the establishment of the Church of England as the official religion of the colony while also providing for the grant of indulgences to Protestant dissenters.[93] Despite its exalted status on paper, North Carolina's Anglican Church was rather weak in real life because its members were not vigorous in their observances, and many of the colony's inhabitants were followers of dissenting denominations.[94] Moreover, there was a protracted dispute in North Carolina over the distribution of power within the established church, the royalists favoring a centralized ecclesiastical system and the dissenters seeking substantial local control.[95]

The establishment's grip on the populace grew steadily weaker, and a 1775 declaration of independence, known as the "Mecklenburg Resolutions," announced that "the Crown of Great Britain never can be considered as holding rights, privileges, or authorities" in the colony.[96] This was followed in November of 1776 by a constitution that explicitly terminated the establishment and recognized a wide freedom of religion:

> [T]here shall be no establishment of any one religious church or denomination in this State, in preference to any other; neither shall any person, on any pretence whatsoever,

89 *See* 2 Poore, *supra* note 51, at 1626–7; *see also* Cobb, *supra* note 2, at 505–7.

90 *See* Brinsfield, *supra* note 84, at 136 [citing Alexander Hewatt, Historical Account of the Rise and Progress of the Colonies of South Carolina and Georgia 16 (London, A. Donaldson 1779)].

91 *See* 2 Poore, *supra* note 51, at 1628–34 (text of South Carolina's Constitution of 1790); *see also* Cobb, *supra* note 2, at 517; Brinsfield, *supra* note 84, at 133. For more lengthy discussion of disestablishment in South Carolina, *see* Mark Douglas McGarvie, One Nation Under Law: America's Early National Struggles to Separate Church and State 131–51 (2004).

92 *See* Paul Conkin, *The Church Establishment in North Carolina, 1765–1778*, *in* 32 N.C. Hist. Rev. 1, 2 (1955). *Also see* discussion, *supra* Section I.B.3, regarding the establishment of the colony of Carolina. It was not until 1710 that North and South Carolina became officially separated. *See, e.g.*, N.C. Hist. Comm'n, Work Projects Admin., How North Carolina Grew 15 (1941) [hereinafter How North Carolina Grew].

93 *See* How North Carolina Grew, *supra* note 92, at 16. *See generally* Conkin, *supra* note 92, *passim*; Stephen Beauregard Weeks, Religious Development in the Province of North Carolina (John Hopkins Press 1892); Stephen Beauregard Weeks, Church and State in North Carolina (Baltimore, Johns Hopkins Press 1896). Later legislative acts – the Vestry Act of 1764 and the Orthodox Clergy Act of 1765 – which together provided for monetary support and acreage for clergy, cemented the establishment of the Church of England in North Carolina. *See* Conkin, *supra* note 92, at 4–5.

94 *See* Bolton, *supra* note 65, at 159; *see also* Conkin, *supra* note 92, at 5–10 (noting the decentralized ecclesiastical system of the Church of England in North Carolina prior to 1765 and the rise of dissenting denominations in the colony).

95 *See generally* Conkin, *supra* note 92, at 10–11.

96 *See* 2 Poore, *supra* note 51, at 1408–9.

be compelled to attend any place of worship contrary to his own faith or judgment, nor be obliged to pay, for the purchase of any glebe, or the building of any house of worship. Or for the maintenance of any minister or ministry, contrary to what he believes right, or has voluntarily and personally engaged to perform; but all persons shall be at liberty to exercise their own mode of worship.[97]

### e. Georgia

The last of the thirteen colonies to be chartered, Georgia received its grant from George II in 1732, who accorded "liberty of conscience … in the worship of God" to all persons and the right to the "free exercise of religion" to all (except "papists") if they did not give "offense" or "scandal" to the government.[98] At least on its face, this grant encompassed both Jews and Muslims.[99] The acrimony afforded to Catholics, however, can be explained by not only the strong tinges of nativism that characterize American history but also by the Protestant belief that Roman Catholicism and "popery" were anti-Christian and "the very embodiment of evil."[100]

In 1758, Georgia established the Church of England, but its privileged status was evidently exercised only rarely.[101] Despite an established church, Georgia maintained elements of freedom of conscience, first expounded in its royal charter, by providing in its Constitution of 1777 that "all persons whatever shall have the free exercise of their religion; provided it be not repugnant to the peace and safety of the State; and shall not, unless by consent, support any teacher or teachers except those of their own profession."[102] The commitment to the free exercise of religion, established by the 1777 Constitution,

97 *See id.* at 1413.

98 *See* 1 Poore, *supra* note 51, at 375.

99 *See, e.g.*, Oscar Handlin, From American Jews: Their Story 12 (1958) ("Already in the seventeenth century, some Americans had wished to 'maintain full and free toleration of religion to all men,' including the Jews. In the eighteenth century that attitude became universal as the country filled up with sects of every sort who showed in practice the ability to live together."); John Franklin Jameson, *Autobiography of Omar ibn Said, Slave in North Carolina, 1831*, 30 Am. Hist. Rev. 787–95 (1925), *reprinted in* African Muslims in Antebellum America 450 (Allan D. Austin ed., 1984) (while converting to Christianity, Omar ibn Said maintained aspects of his Muslim faith). *But see* Michael A. Gomez, *Muslims in Early America*, 60 J. S. Hist. 671, 672 (1994) ("The study of Muslims in the American colonial and antebellum periods has yet to be undertaken seriously because materials on the subject are scarce."); 1 The Jewish Encyclopedia 495–505 (New York, Funk & Wagnalls Co. 1901) (condensed history of Jewish settlement in early America including depiction of instances of antipathetic sentiment toward Jews).

100 Charles H. Metzger, Catholics and the American Revolution: A Study in Religious Climate 5, 20 *passim* (Loyola Univ. Press 1962); *see* Marjule Anne Drury, *Anti-Catholicism in Germany, Britain, and the United States: A Review and Critique of Recent Scholarship*, 70 Church Hist. 98, 101–10 (2001) (summarizing arguments that the development of anti-Catholicism in Britain, and later in America, stemmed from a state of near-constant war with France and the use of Protestantism as a type of "cultural glue"); *see also* John D. Basil, *South Carolina Catholics before Roman Discipline: 1670–1820*, 45 J. Church & St. 787–8 (2003) ("A long record of hostility had actually begun in the mother country in 1534 when King Henry VIII defied the authority of Rome and had himself placed at the head of an independent Anglican Church."). For the continued plea of Roman Catholics for freedom of conscience, *see* James A. M'Faul, *Catholics and American Citizenship*, 171 N. Am. Rev. 320, 331 (1900) ("We ask no favors, we beg no privileges; but we demand that our religion shall not be made a bar to the attainment of our rights under the Constitution. It is not to bring our religion into politics that an appeal is made to the Catholic laity of America; on the contrary, it is to keep religion out of politics.").

101 *See* Cobb, *supra* note 2, at 421. *See generally* Kenneth Coleman, Colonial Georgia: A History 144–73 (Kraus Int'l Publ. 1976).

102 *See* 1 Poore, *supra* note 51, at 377–83. Only Protestants, however, were allowed to serve in the state legislature. *Id.* at 379.

was carried forward and expanded by a later constitution, enacted in 1789, that eliminated the religious test for legislators.[103] Both the 1777 and 1789 Constitutions seemingly authorized the legislature to require all citizens to support their own religions, but this feature was explicitly eliminated by a Constitution enacted in 1798 that provided that

> [n]o person within this State shall, upon any pretence, be deprived of the inestimable privilege of worshiping God in a manner agreeable to his own conscience, nor be compelled to attend any place of worship contrary to his own faith and judgment; nor shall he ever be obliged to pay tithes, taxes, or any other rate, for the building or repairing any place of worship, or for the maintenance of any minister or ministry, contrary to what he believes to be right, or hath voluntarily engaged to do. No one religious society shall ever be established in this State, in preference to another; nor shall any person be denied the enjoyment of any civil right merely on account of his religious principles.[104]

### 4. *The Middle Colonies*

#### a. Introduction

Unlike the other eleven colonies, which were launched under the authority of the English Crown, New York and New Jersey were formed in 1626 as a commercial venture of the Dutch West Indies Company, and this difference accounts for two important features of New Netherlands' church-state relations – the ethnic and religious diversity of its settlers and the absence of any claim by the Church of England to a religious monopoly in the colony's earliest years. The Dutch Reformed Church, a Calvinist denomination, was the established church of the territory, but a broad-based tolerance prevailed, though a perceived need for discipline in an era of hardship may have led the newly established colonies to be less tolerant of dissenters than the mother country.[105]

#### b. New York

In 1664, an English fleet, acting under a grant given by Charles II to his brother, the Duke of York, threatened to invade New Netherland. Bowing to its superior force, Peter Stuyvesant, the area's governor, surrendered before a shot had been fired.[106] New York, as the area was renamed, adopted a conciliatory policy calculated to encourage trade and commerce, with the objective of reaping custom duties and taxes.[107] Thus the Dutch

103 *See id.* at 384.

104 *See id.* at 395.

105 *See, e.g.*, John Webb Pratt, Religion, Politics, and Diversity, The Church-State Theme in New York History 1–80 (Cornell Univ. Press 1967); George Bancroft, 2 History of the United States 278–82 (Boston, Little, Brown 1866) (recounting the organization of the Dutch West India Company and the settlement of New Netherland); *see also* Randall Balmer, A Perfect Babel of Confusion: Dutch Religion and English Culture in the Middle Colonies 29–50 (Oxford Univ. Press 1989) (recounting fear and persecution of Catholics stemming from events of Glorious Revolution in England); Cobb, *supra* note 2, at 314–20 (recounting the persecution of Lutherans and Quakers in New Netherlands and Stuyvesant's edict prohibiting Jews from entering the territory). It was Peter Minuit, the first governor of New Netherlands, who made the famous 1626 purchase of Manhattan from the Canarsee Indians for approximately twenty-four dollars, or sixty Dutch guilders. *See* Bancroft, *supra*, at 179.

106 *See* Cobb, *supra* note 2, at 322.

107 *See* Pratt, *supra* note 105, at 27.

inhabitants were granted freedom of worship and officeholders were not required to belong to any religious denomination.[108] Each town, however, was required to build a church, financed by taxes levied on all, whether members of the majority denomination or not, and the power to regulate public morals (including bans on Sabbath breaking and blasphemy) also was vested in each town.[109] This localized arrangement represented an advancement in religious liberties over the former Dutch provisions because it was "[f]rom these local situations that the germ of the idea of church-state separation would later arise."[110]

Political events across the Atlantic eventually whittled away the religious freedoms afforded to New Yorkers. With the ascension of William and Mary to the throne, increasing attempts to establish the Church of England in New York were made, most notably by the enactment of the Ministry Act in 1693, which prescribed the establishment of six Protestant ministers in four New York counties.[111] The act was deemed "remarkable for both its requirements and its omissions" because it failed to "refer to the Church of England, or to the book of common prayer."[112] In addition,

> there [was] no requirement of services 'according to the rites' of the English Church, nor any acknowledgment of the supremacy of the crown, nor any allowance of patronage to the governor.... Thus, while the act did create a Church establishment in the places noted, it yet established neither any Church for the province at large, nor any particular Church for the localities specified.[113]

Reflecting on this arrangement, it can be argued that the Dutch Reformed Church had as good a right to claim its establishment in New York as did the Church of England.[114]

As New York grew restive under English colonial rule and joined the movement for independence, the Church of England's appeal diminished. In 1777, New York's constitution provided for its disestablishment: "All such parts of the ... common law, and all such ... statutes, and acts ... or parts thereof, as may be construed to establish or maintain any particular denomination to Christians, or their Ministers, ... hereby are, abrogated and rejected."[115]

108 *See id.* at 28–9.

109 *See id.* at 29–32.

110 *Id.* at 30.

111 *See* An Act for Settling a Ministry and Raising a Maintenance for Them in the City of New York, County of Richmond, Westchester, and Queens County, *reprinted in* 1 THE COLONIAL LAWS OF NEW YORK FROM THE YEAR 1664 TO THE REVOLUTION 328–31 (Albany, James B. Lyon 1896) (hereinafter The Ministry Act) (enacted Sept. 22, 1693).Subsequent to the passage of the Ministry Act, increased restrictions on religious practice and tolerance became common as the Church of England attempted to consolidate its authority. For the first time in the colony, under English rule, a religious test was prescribed for public office, Catholicism was outlawed, and religious affiliation increasingly became a measure of social standing. *See* PRATT, *supra* note 105, at 37.

112 *See* COBB, *supra* note 2, at 339.

113 *Id.*.

114 *See id.*; *cf.* PRATT, *supra* note 105, at 39 ("The crown and its representatives were as equally determined to see the Church of England established in New York. This was achieved, but in a form never entirely satisfactory to the Anglican church.").

115 *See* 2 POORE, *supra* note 51, at 1328–40. The omission of an explicit mention of the Church of England may reflect a conciliatory attitude vis-à-vis the state's Anglican members; *see also* PRATT, *supra* note 105, at 90–7 (describing the enactment of the constitution).

### c. New Jersey

When the English sailed into New York Bay and appropriated the area of New Netherland from the Dutch, their acquisition included not only the area that became New York but also that which became New Jersey.[116] The latter included some scattered settlements inhabited by Swedes, whose control had been wrested from them by the Dutch in 1655, thus ending Sweden's incipient empire in the New World.[117] In 1664, a charter was adopted for New Jersey that granted religious freedom in broad terms and did not provide for an established church:

> No person … shall be any ways molested, punished, disquieted or called in question for any difference in opinion or practice. In matter of religious concernments, who do not actually disturb the civil peace of the said Province; but that all and every such person and persons may from time to time, and at all times, freely and fully have and enjoy his and their judgments and consciences in matters of religion throughout the said Province they behaving themselves peaceably and quietly, and not using this liberty to licentiousness, nor to the civil injury or outward disturbance of others.[118]

Two years later, the colony's first assembly, influenced by the settlement of Puritans from New Haven colony along the Passaic, "transferred the chief features of the New England codes to the statute book of New Jersey."[119] The diverse populace, however, was too enamored of religious freedom to accept the Puritan model for public life.[120] The area was divided for a short period between East New Jersey, focused primarily on commercial ventures, and West New Jersey, manifesting a Quaker-dominated vision that was much influenced by William Penn.[121]

116 *See supra* text accompanying note 106.

117 *See* 2 BANCROFT, *supra* note 105, at 296–8. For a background on the settlement of New Jersey, *see, e.g.*, COBB, *supra* note 2, at 399–418; *see also* RICHARD P. MCCORMICK, NEW JERSEY FROM COLONY TO STATE, 1609–1789 at 1–13 (Rutgers Univ. Press 1964).

118 *See* 2 POORE, *supra* note 51, at 783–5.

119 *See* 2 BANCROFT, *supra* note 105, at 318; *see also* COBB, *supra* note 2, at 399.

120 *See* COBB, *supra* note 2, at 399–400.

121 *See* 5 THORPE, *supra* note 84, at 2546–8, 2560–5 (Duke of York's grant to lords proprietors, establishing East and West New Jersey; Duke of York's second grant to William Penn establishing West New Jersey). The difference between East and West New Jersey's estimation of freedom of conscience was exemplified by their discrepant provisions for religious liberty in each of their fundamental constitutions. For example, West New Jersey's Charter of Fundamental Laws, enacted in 1676, provided that "no men … hath power or authority to rule over men's consciences in religious matters, therefore it is consented, agreed and ordained, that no person or persons whatsoever within the said Province … shall be any ways upon any pretense whatsoever, called in question, or in the least punished or hurt, either in person, estate, or privilege, for the sake of his opinion, judgment, faith or worship towards God in matters of religion." 5 THORPE, *supra* note 84, at 2549. This sentiment was later upheld by a proviso enacted in 1681 that prohibited discrimination against officeholders with respect to their religious beliefs. *Id.* at 2567. The Fundamental Constitution of East New Jersey, enacted in 1683, however, took a much more strict and limited view of individual belief and practice. While allowing those "who confess and acknowledge the one Almighty and Eternal God," freedom from compulsion to attend services or maintain specific denominational affiliations, the East New Jersey constitution prohibited those who did not profess faith in Jesus Christ from holding office and specifically delineated prohibited beliefs and behaviors, including "atheism, irreligiousness … cursing, swearing, drunkenness, prophaness [*sic*], whoring, adultery, murdering or any kind of violence, or indulging … in stage plays, masks, revels or such like abuses." *Id.* at 2579–80. For an exhaustive account of the territorial division of New Jersey into East and West in 1674 to its reunification in 1702, *see* JOHN E. POMFRET, THE PROVINCE OF WEST NEW JERSEY

In 1702, the two New Jerseys were reunited as a royal province, which included a renunciation by the proprietors of their "pretences" to the powers of government.[122] Despite the colony's royal oversight, the Church of England was never officially established in New Jersey, although it was favored among Protestant denominations.[123] With the adoption of its 1776 Constitution – two days before the Declaration of Independence – New Jersey both prohibited the adoption of an established church and granted freedom of religion, restricting the latter, along with the right to hold office, to Protestant Christians only:

> [T]here shall be no establishment or any one religious sect in this Province, in preference to another; and ... no Protestant inhabitant of this Colony shall be denied the enjoyment of any civil right, merely on account of his religious principles; but ... all persons, professing a belief in the faith of any Protestant sect, who shall demean themselves peaceably under the government, as hereby established, shall be capable of being elected into any office of profit or trust, or being a member of either branch of the Legislature, and shall fully and freely enjoy every privilege and immunity, enjoyed by others their fellow subjects.[124]

To buttress this part of the 1776 Constitution, the state's legislators were required to swear on taking office that "I will not assent to any law ... that shall annul, repeal, or alter" any part of the religious provisions just quoted.[125]

d. Pennsylvania

As a colony, Pennsylvania began life as a "holy experiment" by William Penn, a dedicated Quaker, who received a grant of land from Charles II in 1681.[126] The royal charter made no mention of religion or of an established church, except for an evidently unexercised provision authorizing any twenty inhabitants to request the Bishop of London of the Church of England to appoint a resident preacher.[127] Penn's vision embraced a colony with very broad religious freedom, but within a Christian context, making his "holy experiment" more qualified than Rhode Island's "lively experiment."[128] The phrase "holy experiment" was used by Penn in a letter sent to James Harrison in 1681 contemplating that "virtuous men, laboring

1609–1702: A History of the Origins of an American Colony (Princeton Univ. Press 1956), and John E. Pomfret, The Province of East New Jersey 1609–1702: The Rebellious Proprietary (Princeton Univ. Press 1962). *See generally* Wallace N. Jamison, Religion in New Jersey: A Brief History 1–29 (Van Nostrand 1964) (recounting the early history of New Jersey, the formation of East and West New Jersey and their reunification); McCormick, *supra* note 117, at 14–79 (same).

122 *See* 5 Thorpe, *supra* note 84, at 2585–90; 3 Bancroft, *supra* note 105, at 47–8; Cobb, *supra* note 2, at 405.

123 *See* Cobb, *supra* note 2, at 406–8; Jamison, *supra* note 121, at 43–7; Bancroft, *supra* note 105, at 48–9. Historians speculate that the Church of England's establishment was either "taken for granted" once New Jersey became a royal province or that the lack of Anglican congregations in the region dissuaded the legislation or royal decree necessary to establish the Church. *See* Cobb, *supra* note 2, at 406–8.

124 *See* 2 Poore, *supra* note 51, at 1313.

125 *Id.* at 1313–14.

126 *See generally* Sally Schwartz, A Mixed Multitude: The Struggle for Toleration in Colonial Pennsylvania (N.Y. Univ. Press 1988) (detailing the establishment of Pennsylvania).

127 *See* 2 Poore, *supra* note 51, at 1515.

128 For discussion of Rhode Island as a "lively experiment," *see supra* notes 58 & 59 and accompanying text. *See also* Schwartz, *supra* note 126 (detailing William Penn's "holy experiment" in the settling of Pennsylvania).

under divine guidance, might establish a virtuous government and society as an example to all mankind."[129] Thus Pennsylvania's First Frame of Government, drafted by Penn himself in 1682, provided that the fledgling colony's officeholders and legislators must "possess faith in Christ Jesus."[130] Other inhabitants, however, were granted religious freedom, provided they qualified as monotheists:

> [A]ll persons living in this province, who confess and acknowledge the one almighty and eternal God to be the Creator, Upholder, and Ruler of the world; and that hold themselves obliged in conscience to live peaceably and justly in civil society, shall, in no ways be molested or prejudiced for their religious persuasion, or practice, in matters of faith and worship, nor shall they be compelled, at any time, to frequent or maintain any religious worship, place or ministry whatever.[131]

Advocates of an "impregnable" wall of separation between church and state sometimes claim William Penn and his "holy experiment" as precursors.[132] But Penn himself held beliefs in this respect that separationists ought to find unpalatable. Thus he averred that "government seems to me a part of religion itself, a thing sacred in its institution and end" and that "the divine right of government" is to "terrify ill evil-doers" and to "cherish those that do well."[133] A Pennsylvania Sabbath-keeping law, enacted in 1682, exemplified Penn's belief in the divine right of government to repel "evil-doers":

> [T]o the end that Looseness, irreligion [*sic*], and Atheism may not Creep in under any pretense of Conscience in this Province, *Be it ... enacted* ... [t]hat, according to the example of the primitive Christians, and for the ease of the Creation, Every first day of the week, called the Lord's day, People shall abstain from their usual and common toil and labor, That whether Masters, Parents, Children, or Servants, they may the better dispose themselves to read the Scriptures of truth at home, or frequent such meetings of religious worship abroad, as may best suit their respective persuasions."[134]

Moreover, in conformity with the wishes of the monarchy, persons applying for naturalization were required to renounce Roman Catholic beliefs and to have taken the

129 *See* Letter from William Penn to James Harrison (August 25, 1681), *in* 2 THE PAPERS OF WILLIAM PENN 108–9 (Richard S. Dunn & Mary Maples Dunn eds., 1982); *see also* EDWIN B. BRONNER, WILLIAM PENN'S "HOLY EXPERIMENT": THE FOUNDING OF PENNSYLVANIA, 1681–1701 at 1 (Columbia Univ. Press 1962).

130 *See* 2 POORE, *supra* note 51, at 1518–27.

131 *Id.* at 1526.

132 Penn's call for a society where "God may have his due, Caesar his due, and the people their due," in the preamble to a set of laws drafted in 1682, is often used as support for this assertion. *See* The Body of Laws of the Province of Pennsilvania [*sic*] and Territories thereunto Belonging (1682), *in* CHARTER TO WILLIAM PENN, AND LAWS OF THE PROVINCE OF PENNSYLVANIA, PASSED BETWEEN THE YEARS 1682 AND 1700, at 107 (George Staughton et al. eds., Harrisburg, Lane S. Hart Prtg. 1879) (hereinafter CHARTER TO WILLIAM PENN). However, Williams invoked the metaphor of "a hedge or wall of separation between the Garden of the Church and the Wilderness of the world," long before Penn's preamble or Jefferson's Statute for Religious Freedom. *See* ROGER WILLIAMS, MR. COTTON'S LETTER EXAMINED AND ANSWERED (1644), *reprinted in* 1 THE COMPLETE WRITINGS OF ROGER WILLIAMS 392 (Perry Miller ed., 2005); *see also* discussion *infra* Section G.4, regarding Jefferson's Statute for Religious Freedom and the "wall of separation" between church and state, respectively.

133 *See* 2 POORE, *supra* note 51, at 1518–19 [preface to PENN'S FRAME OF GOVERNMENT (1682)]; *see also* BRONNER, *supra* note 129, at 11. *Compare* with notes 57–62 and accompanying text regarding Williams' view of church-state relations.

134 *See* The Body of Laws of the Province of Pennsilvania [*sic*] and Territories thereunto Belonging (1682), *in* CHARTER TO WILLIAM PENN, *supra* note 132, at 108; *see also* COBB, *supra* note 2, at 443–4.

sacrament of the Lord's Supper within the previous month.[135] This oath and other religious restrictions led a leading historian of religious freedom to note a paradox in Pennsylvania's practices:

> So far, then, as terms are concerned, Pennsylvania was much less liberal than most of the colonies, and is not to be classed with Rhode Island on her broad platform of full religious liberty. The one point of close resemblance is in the absence of a religious establishment. Pennsylvania never made any attempts toward establishing a Church. This fact makes the rigid insistence on religious tests one of the strangest things in colonial history, for in all other cases of such insistence the oath has been in the interest of some State-Church. With the Quakers of Pennsylvania its demand was in the interests simply of Protestantism. Protestantism was established, in a sense.[136]

Pennsylvania's 1776 Constitution, adopted about a month after the nation's Declaration of Independence, carries forward William Penn's vision of freedom of religion:

> [A]ll men have a natural and unalienable right to worship Almighty God according to the dictates of their own consciences and under-standing: And ... no man ought or of right can be compelled to attend any religious worship, or erect or support any place of worship, or maintain any ministry, contrary to, or against, his own free will and consent: Nor can any man, who acknowledges the being of a God, be justly deprived or abridged of any civil right as a citizen, on account of his religious sentiments or peculiar mode of religious worship: And that no authority can or ought to be vested in, or assumed by any power whatever, that shall in any case interfere with, or in any manner control, the right of conscience in the free exercise of religious worship.[137]

e. Delaware

In 1683, two years after Charles II gave William Penn the territory that became Pennsylvania, the King's brother, the Duke of York, augmented Penn's proprietorship by granting him the land that became Delaware, which was settled at that time mainly by the Dutch and Swedes.[138] The validity of this transfer was disputed in the English courts by Lord Baltimore, the proprietor of Maryland, and the dispute was not settled until 1750, when the Lord Chancellor decided in favor of Penn.[139] By that time, Delaware had been carved out of Pennsylvania as a separate colony, though for a time the two shared a common governor.

Delaware's first charter, promulgated by William Penn in 1701, provided for a breadth of religious liberty that carried forward the spirit of its parent, Pennsylvania:

> Because no people can be truly happy, though under the greatest enjoyment of civil liberties, if abridged of the freedom of their consciences as to their religious profession and worship: and Almighty God being the only Lord of Conscience, father of Lights and

135 *See* Cobb, *supra* note 2, at 449.
136 *Id.*
137 2 Poore, *supra* note 51, at 1541.
138 *See supra* note 126 and accompanying text; *see also* 2 Poore, *supra* note 51, at 1541; 2 Bancroft, *supra* note 105, at 281–7; *see generally* Federal Writers' Project, Works Progress Admin., Delaware: A Guide to the First State 19–33 (1938); John A. Munroe, A History of Delaware *passim* (Univ. of Del. Press, 4th ed. 2001).
139 *See* Munroe, *supra* note 138, at 40.

> Spirits; and the Author as well as Object of all divine Knowledge, Faith and Worship, who only doth enlighten the minds, and persuade and confine the understandings of People. I [William Penn] do hereby grant and declare, that no person or persons, inhabiting in this province or territories, who shall confess and acknowledge *One* almighty God, the Creator, Upholder and Ruler of the World; and professes him or themselves obliged to live quietly under the civil government, shall be in any case molested or prejudiced, in his or their person or estate, because of his or their conscientious persuasion or practice, nor be compelled to frequent or maintain any religious worship, place or ministry, contrary to his or their mind, or to do or suffer any other act or thing, contrary to their religious persuasion.
>
> And that all persons who also profess to believe in Jesus Christ, the Savior of the World, shall be capable (notwithstanding their other persuasions and practices in point of conscience and religion) to serve this government in any capacity, both legislatively and executively.[140]

To reinforce the strength of these commitments, the charter goes on to provide that its "liberty of conscience" provisions shall continue in force "without any alteration, inviolably, for ever."[141]

In 1776, Delaware adopted its first constitution, which prohibited any "establishment of any one religious sect in this state in preference to another."[142] It also provided, like some other state constitutions of the day, that

> [n]o clergyman or preacher of the gospel, of any denomination, shall be capable of holding any civil office in this State, or of being a member of either of the branches of the legislature, while they continue in the exercise of the pastoral function.[143]

140 1 POORE, *supra* note 51, at 270–1.

141 *Id.* at 272.

142 *Id.* at 277. The prohibition against religious preference was carried forward by Delaware's constitutions of 1792 and 1831. *See id.* at 278 & 289.

143 *Id.* at 277–8; *see, e.g.*, 2 POORE, *supra*, at 1413 (Amendment to North Carolina Constitution of 1776); *id.* at 1911 (Virginia Constitution of 1776); *id.* at 1338–9 (New York Constitution of 1777); *id.* at 1624 (South Carolina Constitution of 1778). The popular belief is that such prohibitions were based on the purpose of securing the separation of church and state; however, such prohibitions were the product of both historical tradition and evangelical sentiment. *See* William M. Hogue, *The Civil Disability of Ministers of Religion in State Constitutions*, 36 J. CHURCH & ST. 329, 348–9 (1994) (arguing against the presupposition that the prohibition on clergy holding a public office stemmed from concern for separation of church and state). The medieval doctrine that established the separateness of the priesthood from the secular laity conferred on clergy state-sponsored "privileges and disabilities not accorded [to] laymen," one privilege being their exemption from the House of Commons. *Id.* at 330–1 & 349. Thus exclusion, on the one hand, can be seen simply as a continuation of English custom and colonial institutions. *Id.* at 336. Similarly, the prohibition against clergy and ministers from holding public office stemmed from the social value placed on the ministry, which was enforced by radical evangelical belief that religion and civil government were incompatible. *Id.* at 341. For example, South Carolina's prohibition originated from the concern that "ministers of the gospel [who] are by their profession dedicated to the service of God and the cure of souls ... ought not to be diverted from the great duties of their function." 2 POORE, *supra*, at 1624; *see also id.* at 1338–9 (language from New York Constitution indicating same).Ultimately, the abolishment of the exclusion of clergy from holding public office was based on claims of unconstitutionality, in that persons fulfilling a religious vocation were denied freedom of religion and freedom of speech by the continued adherence to these laws. *See* McDaniel v. Paty, 435 U.S. 618 (1978) (Tennessee statute that excluded clergy from participation in constitutional convention as well as from holding legislative seat deemed unconstitutional as violating free exercise of religion); Kirkley v. Maryland, 381 F. Supp. 327 (D. Md. 1974) (Maryland statute prohibiting clergy from being state legislators deemed unconstitutional under the free exercise of religion clause of the First Amendment); *see also* Hogue, *supra*, at 345–6.

The Constitution also prescribed an oath, to be taken by the state's legislators and office-holders, emphasizing a Trinitarian belief in Christian scriptures:

> I ... do profess faith in God the Father, and in Jesus Christ His only Son, and in the Holy Ghost, one God, blessed for evermore; and I do acknowledge the holy scriptures of the Old and New Testament to be given by divine inspiration.[144]

As read literally, this oath did not exclude Roman Catholics from public office, but it did bar non-Trinitarian Christians, such as Unitarians, and non-Christians generally from holding office.[145]

#### f. Maryland

George Calvert, the first Lord Baltimore, a convert to Roman Catholicism and a friend of James I, appealed to his son, King Charles I, for a grant of land in the New World.[146] After failing because of the severe winters to create a settlement in Newfoundland, he renewed his request, choosing the Chesapeake area as his target. In 1632, after Baltimore's death, this grant was issued to his son, the second Lord Baltimore.[147] Maryland was the only American colony launched by Roman Catholics, but its first settlers included more Protestants than Catholics, and unlike the Puritan settlements in New England, Maryland opened its doors to members of all Christian churches. This breadth of religious freedom evoked from a famous American historian the ironic observation that in Maryland, "Protestants were sheltered from Protestants."[148]

The 1632 charter did not compel the colony to grant religious liberty to its settlers, and it provided that "nothing shall be done contrary to God's Holy religion"[149]; religious liberty, however, emerged in the colony's earliest days. Its first legislative act provided that the "Holy Church within this province shall have and enjoy all her Rights, liberties and franchises wholly and without blemish," a sufficiently ambiguous announcement to permit any Christian church to claim that it was sheltered by this

144 1 Poore, *supra* note 51, at 276.

145 *Compare* Ga. Const. of 1777, art. VI, § 5, *reprinted in* 1 The Federal and State Constitutions, *supra* note 51, at 377, 379 ("The representatives ... shall be of the Protestant religion."); N.H. Const. of 1784, pt. 2, *reprinted in* 2 The Federal and State Constitutions, *supra* note 51, at 1280, 1286–7 (requiring all senators, representatives, and the state president be "of the protestant religion"); N.J. Const. of 1776, art. XIX, *reprinted in* 2 The Federal and State Constitutions, *supra* note 51, at 1310, 1313 ("[A]ll persons, professing a belief in the faith of any Protestant sect ... shall be capable of being elected into any office of profit or trust, or being a member of either branch of the Legislature."); S.C. Const. of 1778, arts. III, XII, XIII, *reprinted in* 2 The Federal and State Constitutions, *supra* note 51, at 1620, 1621–3 (requiring all senators, representatives, and the governor be "of the Protestant religion"); *see also* Gerard V. Bradley, *The No Religious Test Clause and the Constitution of Religious Liberty: A Machine that Has Gone of Itself*, 37 Case W. Res. L. Rev. 674, 682 (1987).

146 *See* Matthew Page Andrews, The Founding of Maryland 47 (Williams & Wilkins 1933).

147 *See generally* Andrews, *supra* note 146; Albert Warwick Werline, Problems of Church and State in Maryland (College Press 1948). Extracts from the 1632 charter are reprinted in Commager, Documents, *supra* note 67 at 21–2; for the full text, *see* III Thorpe, *supra* note 84, at 1677ff.

148 Cobb, *supra* note 2, at 373, *citing* George Bancroft, 1 History of the United States 248 (23d ed. 1964).

149 N.D. Mereness, Maryland as a Proprietary Province 507–20 (New York 1901).

holy umbrella.[150] Another early enactment prescribed this oath for all the colony's officeholders:

> I will not, by myself or any other, directly or indirectly, trouble, molest, or discountenance any person, professing to believe in Jesus Christ, for, or in respect of, religion; but merely as they shall be found faithful and well-deserving; my aim shall be public unity, and if any person or officer shall molest any person, professing to believe in Jesus Christ, on account of his religion, I will protect the person molested and punish the offender.[151]

As for an official establishment of religion, there was a division of opinion, with some claiming that the foregoing and other Maryland provisions implied that the Church of England was established. This dispute was not settled until 1702, when, after Lord Baltimore's 1632 charter was annulled, the Church of England gained official recognition as Maryland's established church.[152]

Maryland's 1776 Constitution, adopted about a month after the nation's Declaration of Independence, provided that

> it is the duty of every man to worship God in such manner as he thinks most acceptable to him; all persons, professing the Christian religion, are equally entitled to protection in their religious liberty; wherefore no person ought by any law to be molested in his person or estate on account of his religious persuasion or profession, or for his religious practice; unless, under colour of religion, any man shall disturb the good order, peace or safety of the State, or shall infringe the laws of morality, or injure others, in their natural, civil, or religious rights; nor ought any person to be compelled to frequent or maintain, or contribute, unless on contract, to maintain any particular place of worship, or any particular ministry; yet the Legislature may, in their discretion, lay a general and equal tax for the support of the Christian religion.[153]

Attempts to exercise the legislative power to levy taxes for the support of Christianity were defeated in 1776 and 1784, and the power was revoked in 1810.[154]

A 1776 document labeled, "Form of Government," prescribing the details of the state's government, required every officeholder to sign a "declaration of his belief in the Christian religion," a provision that two centuries later was held by the Supreme Court to be unconstitutional when applied to an aspiring notary public.[155]

## B. Religion and the Declaration of Independence

In Bernard Bailyn's widely praised work, *The Ideological Origins of the American Revolution*, the major engine of revolutionary thought was not the passion for religious liberty, either in its moderate tolerance[156] or free exercise forms or in its more confrontational modality in demanding disestablishment of the state churches; the author instead

150 The language, after all, did not specify the "Holy Church."

151 COBB, *supra* note 2, at 372, citing FRANCIS LISTER HAWKS, 2 CONTRIBUTIONS TO THE ECCLESIASTICAL HISTORY OF THE UNITED STATES 27 (Harper & Bros. 1836).

152 COBB, *supra* note 2, at 385–6.

153 3 THORPE, *supra* note 84, at 1689.

154 *Stated in* ARIENS & DESTRO, *supra* note 28, at 59.

155 THORPE *supra* note 84; *id.* at 1700; Torcaso v. Watkins, 367 U.S. 488 (1961); for discussion of this decision, *see* Chapter 6.A.3.

156 BERNARD BAILYN, THE IDEOLOGICAL ORIGINS OF THE AMERICAN REVOLUTION (Belknap 1967).

portrays religious liberty more as a torch that was ignited by other revolutionary forces and ideas. Disestablishment, Bailyn wrote, "was neither an original goal nor completely a product of the Revolution"; instead, the random and jumbled roots of disestablishment "were touched by the magic of Pre-revolutionary thought, and were transformed."[157] Bailyn observes: "[t]hat establishments of such irregularity and weakness should have come under fire at all is a measure of the contagiousness of Revolutionary thought."[158] Bailyn's view, however, has not gone unchallenged by authors who argue that a main force in creating public opinion was the preacher.[159] Others have gone so far as to claim that the American Revolution was in itself a religious experience.

The Declaration of Independence begins by focusing on dissolution of "the political bonds" connecting the colonies with the mother country and ends by announcing that "all political connection between [the colonies] and the State of Great Britain is and ought to be totally dissolved."[160] But its bill of particulars of George III's misdeeds – certainly not terse – does not complain about his behavior as Defender of the Faith, nor does it purport to sever the religious links between the colonies and the established Church of England. Even so, the Declaration invokes the Deity more frequently than does the Constitution, it contains four references to the Almighty ("Nature's God," the "Creator," the "Supreme Judge of the World," and "Divine Providence"), and it ends with a pledge by the signers of their "sacred Honor."[161] But the American *independentists* who objected to the colonial church establishments could hardly have blamed George III for the restrictions on religious liberty on this side of the Atlantic; it was their fellow colonists who launched the demanding features of New England's religious structure. The Church of England, as established in the southern colonies, was a model of relaxation,[162] even somnolence, compared with New England's homegrown religious establishments.

Although Anson Phelps Stokes, author of the most compendious study of American church-state relations, asserted that the Declaration of Independence's "ideal is of course a definitely Christian one," evidencing "the huge degree to which Christian theism and

157 *Id.* at 271; *see also id.* at 246ff. "At that time the preacher was the leading politician"; for a detailed analysis, church by church, of the role played by religion in the creation of American nationalism, *see* Edward Frank Humphrey, Nationalism and Religion in America, 1774–1789, at 10, 19–166 (Chipman Law Publ. Co. 1924); *see also* Donald Weber, Rhetoric and History in Revolutionary New England (Oxford Univ. Press 1988). For a hefty compendium of eighteenth-century sermons, *see* Political Sermons of the American Founding Era, 1730–1805 (Ellis Sandoz ed., Liberty Fund, 2d ed. 1991) (two volumes). For a brief account of the support given to the revolutionary cause by colonial preachers, *see* Patricia U. Bonomi, Under the Cope of Heaven 209ff (Oxford Univ. Press 1986). For a comparison of the American Revolution with other eighteenth-century revolutions, *see* R.R. Palmer, The Age of the Democratic Revolution (Princeton Univ. Press 1959).

158 Bailyn, *supra* note 156.

159 For a view of colonial pamphlets and newspapers as rivals for the pulpit in forming public opinion and development of the idea that "the American Revolution was *in itself* a religious experience, a hierophany collectively manifested and received, which provided the fundamental basis for American civil religion as we know it" (emphasis in original), *see* Catherine L. Albanese, Sons of the Fathers 6, 11, & *passim* (Temple Univ. Press 1976).

160 Declaration of Independence (1776).

161 Of these references to the Deity, two did not appear in Jefferson's draft of the Declaration but were added by the Continental Congress, *viz.*, the appeal "to the Supreme Judge of the world for the rectitude of our intentions" and the assertion of "a firm reliance on the protection of Divine Providence." *See* Pauline Maier, American Scripture 148–9 (Knopf 1997).

162 *See supra* Section A.3.

Christian social ideals had been accepted by the founders of the republic," he cites precious little concrete evidence to support this claim.[163] A recent commentator on the Declaration cites its "conventional references" to the Deity but argues that the document does not "reflect any distinctive Christian gospel," noting that its signatories included only one clergyman and that none of "the famous names of the Revolution" were noted for their active work in any religious denomination.[164] Their ideas, he notes, were derived from the "secular political philosophy" of authors such as John Locke, not from such religion-drenched notables as Luther, Calvin, Cotton Mather, or Jonathan Edwards. To be sure, Jefferson used the terms "reverence," "sacred," and "holy" to describe the facsimile of the document presented to him by Congress in 1824, but these lofty words characterized the place the Declaration had attained in the nation's self-saga, not the intellectual or spiritual sources that led to its adoption.[165]

The most recent analyst of the Declaration applies the terms "American Scripture" and "sacred text" to the document, but these reverential words are seemingly employed with their twentieth-century secular connotations, and the analyst contrasts the Declaration with such contemporary counterparts as Virginia's Declaration of Rights (issued June 12, 1776), which vigorously proclaim religious tolerance and liberty, doing so not merely as ideals but in some cases as legally enforceable commitments.[166]

The foregoing comments use "religion" in its conventional sense,[167] but sociologists and theologians of the second half of the twentieth century have popularized the idea of an "American civil religion," with symbols and rituals taking the form of flags, parades, anthems, fireworks, holidays, orations, and proclamations, and this enlarged and pervasive "religion" makes it possible to describe the American Revolution as a religious experience "in itself"[168] and even to argue that "the American Revolution and the American civil religion" are the same thing.[169]

163 1 Stokes, *supra* note 2, at 462. Carl Becker's highly regarded book-length essay, The Declaration of Independence: A Study in the History of Political Ideas (Knopf 1922), published in 1922 and republished with a new introduction in 1942, mentions the subject of religion only in passing and contains nothing to support Stokes' claim that the Declaration embodies any distinctively Christian themes.

164 Cushing Strout, The New Heavens and New Earth: Political Religion in America (Harper & Row 1974). For a work whose breadth is denoted by its title, which makes only two brief references to the Declaration of Independence, *see* John Witte, Jr., Religion and the American Constitutional Experiment: Essential Rights and Liberties 35 & 60 (Westview 2000). For exhaustive analyses of the Declaration, *see* Maier, *supra* note 161. The religious affiliations of the fifty-six signers of the Declaration of Independence were thirty-four Episcopalian, thirteen Congregationalist, six Presbyterian, one Baptist, one Quaker, and one Roman Catholic. [1 Stokes, at 464; this classification is described by Stokes as "exact," but he cites (*id.* at 910) "some authorities," not named, as crediting the Quakers with one of the signers listed as Presbyterian.]

165 For the 1824 episode, *see* Maier, *supra* note 161, at 185; *see also id.* at 235–41, showing how Jefferson's draft was amended before it was promulgated.

166 Maier, *supra* note 161; for the contrast between the Declaration of Independence and Virginia's Declaration of Rights, *see id.* For the Virginia document, *see* Commager, *supra* note 67, at 103; 2 Thorpe, *supra* note 84, Vol. II at 1008.

167 *See infra* Sections D and E.

168 Albanese, *supra* note 159.

169 Robert N. Bellah *in* Religion and the American Revolution 55 (Jerald C. Brauer ed., Fortress Press 1976); *see also* Sidney E. Mead, The Nation with the Soul of a Church (Mercer Univ. Press 1985); The Lively Experiment Continued (Mercer Univ. Press, Jerald C. Brauer ed., 1987).

## C. Religion and the Constitution

Unlike the Declaration of Independence, the Constitution, as proposed and ratified, contains no appeal to the Deity, although the contrary might have been expected, given the conventional view that the delegates to the Philadelphia Convention were more conservative than the signatories of the Declaration.[170] However, there is no commitment to religious liberty in the Declaration, whereas the Constitution makes three contributions to religious liberty – not overwhelming in their weight but at least worthy of note – the prohibition on religious tests for federal officers, the option permitting the president to affirm rather than swear to the oath of office, and the similar option granted to senators, representatives, and other national and state officials.[171] A proposal to include this provision in the embryonic Constitution was evidently not discussed and died without action:

> The legislature of the United States shall pass no law on the subject of religion.[172]

The Constitution's lack of explicit religious invocations contrasts sharply with the religious orientation of the Continental Congress (1774–1789), the political mechanism that the Constitution displaced. Its proclamations and other state papers "are so filled with Biblical phrases as to resemble Old Testament ecclesiastical documents."[173] They unabashedly extol Protestant Christianity, calling themselves "Free Protestant Colonies"; in this vein, the Continental Congress invoked, as a sanction for its acts, "God," "Almighty God," "Nature's God," "God of Armies," "Lord of Hosts," "His Goodness," "God's Superintending Providence," "Providence of God," "Providence," "Supreme and Universal Providence," "Overruling Providence of God," "Creator of All," "Indulgent Creator," "Great Governor of the World," "the Divinity," "Supreme Judge of the Universe," "Supreme Disposer of All Events," and "Holy Ghost."[174]

Another religion-imbued event in the life of the Continental Congress is this episode showing concern for the availability of bibles:

> To meet an impending bible shortage, a group of Presbyterian clergy offered a petition to the Continental Congress in the summer of 1777 requesting that bibles be procured because of their high price coupled with the "Scarcity and Difficulty in importing them from Europe." Congress replied by calling for bids from various printers for the work ... After considering the bids, the Congress decided that it would be much cheaper and

170 For a detailed account of the Philadelphia Convention, *see* COLLIER & COLLIER, DECISION IN PHILADELPHIA (Random House 1986); for earlier accounts, *see* CLINTON ROSSITER, 1787: THE GRAND CONVENTION (Macmillan 1966); PAGE SMITH, THE CONSTITUTION: A DOCUMENTARY AND NARRATIVE HISTORY (Morrow 1978), NEIL H. COGAN, CONTEXTS OF THE CONSTITUTION (Foundation Press 1999) (compendium of background documents), ch. VII; *see also* FRED RODELL, 55 MEN: THE STORY OF THE CONSTITUTION (Telegraph 1936). For a "rational choice" and game-theory analysis of the federalized governmental structure created by the Constitution, *see* Norman Schofield, *Evolution of the Constitution*, 32 BRIT. J. POL. SCI. 1 (2002) (cost of war against Britain and of European hostility outweighed by benefits to colonies of thwarting Napoleonic and Spanish domination of American west, as achieved by Louisiana Purchase of 1803–1804; author acknowledges element of happenstance in chaotic circumstances).

171 U.S. CONST. art. VI; art. II, § 1; art. VI.

172 *See* MAX FARRAND (ED.) RECORDS OF THE FEDERAL CONVENTION OF 1787 (rev. ed., New Haven, Yale Univ. Press 1937).

173 EDWARD F. HUMPHREY, NATIONALISM AND RELIGION IN AMERICA, 1774–1789 at 407 (Chipman 1924); *see also* DEREK H. DAVIS, RELIGION AND THE CONTINENTAL CONGRESS, 1774–1789 (Oxford Univ. Press 2000).

174 HUMPHREY, *supra* note 173, at 402–3.

> more reliable simply to import bibles, and so they decided to attempt to procure 20,000 bibles from Holland. No action was ever taken on this decision, for soon after it was made, the Congress had to flee Philadelphia. This petition for bibles, and the idea of importation of bibles from Holland, faded into the background forever as the Congress found itself with the more pressing concerns of war.[175]

In sharp contrast, a familiar episode in the 1787 Philadelphia convention's deliberations was the explicit rejection of a proposal by Benjamin Franklin, one of the assembly's most respected elder statesmen, to offer prayers at the opening of each daily session. His proposal came about a month after the assembly began its deliberations, at a time of troubled disagreement about the proper representation in Congress to be accorded to the small states. As reported by Madison, Franklin soberly entreated his audience:

> In this situation of this Assembly, groping as it were in the dark to find political truth, and scarce able to distinguish it when presented to us, how has it happened, Sir, that we have not hitherto once thought of humbly applying to the Father of lights to illuminate our understandings? In the beginning of the Contest with G. Britain, when we were sensible of danger we had daily prayer in this room for the divine protection. – Our prayers, Sir, were heard, and they were graciously answered.... I have lived, Sir, a long time, and the longer I live, the more convincing proofs I see of this truth – *That God governs in the affairs of men*. And if a sparrow cannot fall to the ground without his notice, is it probable that an empire can rise without his aid? We have been assured, Sir, in the sacred writings, that "except the Lord build the House they labour in vain that build it." I firmly believe this; and I also believe that without his concurring aid we shall succeed in this political building no better than the Builders of Babel. ...
>
> I therefore beg leave to move – that henceforth prayers imploring the assistance of Heaven, and its blessings on our deliberations, be held in this Assembly every morning before we proceed to business, and that one or more of the Clergy of this City be requested to officiate in that service.[176]

Franklin's proposal was rejected after Hamilton and others expressed fear that however proper the resolution might have been at the beginning of the convention, its belated adoption might bring on some "disagreeable animadversions" and lead the public to believe (accurately!) that embarrassments and dissensions within the convention had suggested the measure.[177] Another delegate, however, commented that "the true cause of the omission" was that the convention had no funds, and a vote on Franklin's proposal was dodged by adjournment.[178] In a letter written in 1834, Madison suggested that "the discord of religious opinions within the Convention" might have been another reason for rejecting Franklin's proposal.[179]

[175] PAUL C. GUTJAHN, AN AMERICAN BIBLE: A HISTORY OF THE GOOD BOOK IN THE UNITED STATES 1777–1880, at 1–147 n. 150 (Stanford Univ. Press 1999).

[176] 1 FARRAND, RECORDS OF THE FEDERAL CONVENTION OF 1787 at 451–2 (Yale Univ. Press 1911, 1937) (emphasis in original). For Franklin's belief in the value of a "public religion," *see* JOHN F. WILSON, PUBLIC RELIGION IN AMERICAN CULTURE 7 (Temple Univ. Press 1979). In his youth, Franklin had often mocked organized religion, but he became a deist in his mature years. *See* WALTER ISAACSON, BENJAMIN FRANKLIN, AN AMERICAN LIFE 44–6 and 86ff (Simon & Schuster 2003).

[177] *Id.* 1 FARRAND, *supra* note 176, at 452.

[178] *Id.*

[179] Letter to Thomas S. Grimke, dated January 6, 1834, *reprinted in* 5 DOCUMENTARY HISTORY OF THE CONSTITUTION OF THE UNITED STATES 395 (Department of State 1905).

Like the American Revolution, however, the Constitution has come to be enshrouded in reverence. Thus a 2002 commentator observed that "the American civic religion [the Constitution] accords Biblical or Koranic status, even to the point of seeing it as divinely inspired."[180]

## D. Religion and Ratification of the Constitution

The Articles of Confederation, agreed on by the Continental Congress in 1777 and ratified by the states in 1781, provided for amendment only if the Congress approved and the alteration was thereafter confirmed by the legislatures of every state, and when the Continental Congress called in 1787 for a convention of delegates to be held in Philadelphia, the resolution similarly provided that the convention's recommendations should be reported to the Congress and, if agreed to, should then be submitted for confirmation to the state legislatures.[181] On completing their work in 1787, however, the Philadelphia delegates departed from their mandate and from the Confederation's principles of unanimity and state legislative supremacy by submitting the draft Constitution to the Congress and to popular conventions of the states and by providing that ratification by nine of the thirteen states "should be sufficient for the establishment of this Constitution between the states so ratifying the same."[182] This arguably unconstitutional procedure touched off a bitter ratification battle when the nascent Constitution was submitted to the state conventions.[183]

As the labels for the two antagonistic groups in the ratification struggle – Federalists and Anti-Federalists – imply, the main bone of contention was the proposed shift from a loose coalition – the Confederacy – to a stronger central government. ("Antifederalist" was already the sobriquet for the disorganized and unpopular opponents of a national tax to support the Revolution.) The core of the conflict is described by the author of two detailed studies of this crucial period in the nation's early history as follows:

180 Hendrik Hertzberg, *reviewing* Robert A. Dahl's, *How Democratic Is the American Constitution?* (Yale 2002), *in* The New Yorker (July 29, 2002) at 85.

181 1 Documentary History of the Ratification of the Constitution 185 (Merrill Jensen ed., State Hist. Soc'y of Wis. 1978).

182 U.S. Const. art. VII.

183 Robert Allen Rutland, The Ordeal of the Constitution: The Antifederalists and the Ratification Struggle of 1787–1788 at 5–6 (Univ. of Okla. Press 1966). For relevant documents, *see* The Anti-Federalist Papers and the Constitutional Convention Debates (Ralph Ketcham ed., New Am. Library 1986). For a multivolume compendium of relevant documents, *see* Documentary History of the Ratification, *supra* note 181. For a state-by-state account of ratification, linked to political trends in the particular state, with detailed bibliographic notes, *see* Patrick T. Conley & John P. Kaminski, The Constitution and the States: The Role of the Original Thirteen in the Framing and Adoption of the Federal Constitution (Madison House 1988). Some of the opponents called for a second convention to supplant the product of the 1787 Philadelphia convention. Rutland gives this abortive gambit a full chapter (XV) in his *Ordeal of the Constitution*, *supra*. *See also* Bernard Schwartz, The Bill of Rights: A Documentary History 1229 (index) (Chelsea House 1971); Humphrey, *supra* note 2, at chs. XV & XVII. In the first Federal Congress, referring to the possibility of amending the new Constitution, Congressman Bland (an anti-federalist from Virginia) reported that Virginia had requested Congress to call a convention for this purpose and that his proposal had been sent to the other states, "but that few of them seemed to have coincided with Virginia in opinion." Daily Advertiser, May 6, 1789, *reprinted in* Creating the Bill of Rights: The Documentary Record From the First Federal Congress 571 (Helen E. Veit, Kenneth R. Bowling & Charlene Bangs Bickford eds., Johns Hopkins Univ. Press 1991).

> The common ground for opposition to ratification in 1787–88, as in most political struggles, was the distribution of political power. The Revolution had transferred the seat of power from Britain to her former colonies, and then distributed it among thirteen sovereign states, occupying a thousand miles of coast line. Jealousy and fear of a strong, centralized government prompted the thirteen states to surrender so few powers to the national government that the Articles of Confederation barely kept the loose alliance intact during the war years.... [W]ith the return of peace came renewed rivalries and scrambles for power. Since widespread confusion was the result, desperate measures seemed necessary. The Constitution was conceived by its framers, as Madison was to state with such clarity, as a means of throttling all the power struggles by placing the higher authority in a national government under "the supreme law of the land." For some citizens this quick transition of power from local or regional levels to a national or federal level was simply a matter of moving too fast and going too far.[184]

When our "Godless Constitution" – the provocative but approving title of a recent book of constitutional commentary[185] – was submitted to the states for ratification, it was welcomed by religion-minded people with dismay; its only references to the Almighty were its date (September 17, 1787, "in the year of our Lord") and the exclusion of Sundays in counting the time allowed to the president to approve legislation. Moreover, in the first of the *Federalist Papers*, written to bolster the ratification process, Publius (Madison) focused on the political character of the ratification controversy, omitting any reference to religion:

> I propose, in a series of papers, to discuss the following interesting particulars [of the draft constitution]: – *The utility of the Union to your political prosperity – The insufficiency of the present Confederation to preserve that Union – The necessity of a government at least equally energetic with the one proposed, to the attainment of this object – The conformity of the proposed Constitution to the true principles of republican government – Its analogy to your own State constitution* – and lastly, *The additional security which its adoption will afford to the preservation of that species of government, to liberty, and to property.*[186]

Despite this unswerving focus on the political character of the ratification campaign, the Federalists gained some support from antiestablishment churchmen (especially Baptists and Presbyterians), but this choice of sides did not dilute the political flavor of the debates. The opposing sides were known as "Federalists" and "AntiFederalists," never as "Establishment" and "Disestablishment" factions. Moreover, the *Federalist* makes no claim of divine inspiration or sanction for the Constitution, nor does it invoke the Almighty's blessings on the ratifiers. To the contrary, its principal reference to religion is an assurance that the new republic will be protected against religious oppression:

> Whilst all authority in it will be derived from and dependent on the society, the society itself will be broken into so many parts, interests and classes of citizens, that the rights

[184] Robert A. Rutland, The Birth of the Bill of Rights, 1776-1791 at 4-5 (rev. ed., Northeastern Univ. Press 1991).

[185] Isaac Kramnick & R. Laurence Moore, The Godless Constitution: The Case against Religious Correctness (W.W. Norton & Co. 1996).

[186] The Federalist (George W. Carey & James McClellan eds., Liberty Fund 2001) No. 1. *The Federalist*, by Alexander Hamilton, John Jay, and James Madison, was written primarily to influence the ratification struggle in New York and Virginia; although frequently cited as evidence of the intent of the ratifiers, it was issued over a period of time; some numbers were published well after ratification had already been approved by the earlier states to act.

> of individuals or of the minority, will be in little danger from interested combinations of the majority. In a free government, the security for civil rights must be the same as for religious rights. It consists in the one case in the multiplicity of interests, and in the other, in the multiplicity of sects. The degree of security in both cases will depend on the number of interests and sects; and this may be presumed to depend on the extent of country and number of people comprehended under the same government.... In the extended republic of the United States, and among the great variety of interests, parties and sects which it embraces, a coalition of a majority of the whole society could seldom take place on any other principles than those of justice and the general good.[187]

*Federalist* No. 10 similarly asserts that religious convictions have "inflamed [mankind] with mutual animosity" and rendered them "much more disposed to vex and oppress each other, than to co-operate for their common good." Another reference to religion in the *Federalist* is its well-known rejection of any analogy of the president as contemplated by the Constitution to the British King because, among other differences, "[t]he one has no particle of spiritual jurisdiction; the other is the supreme head and governor of the national church."[188]

Attempts by critics of the "Godless Constitution" to defeat its ratification got nowhere, but the ratifiers in five states accompanied their favorable votes with declarations extolling religious liberty and recommendations for amending the Constitution to correct what they viewed as its deficiencies in dealing with religious matters.[189] These proposals led to the postratification Bill of Rights, including the Anti-Establishment and Free Exercise Clauses of the First Amendment.[190] Thus New Hampshire's delegates to its ratifying convention acknowledged "with grateful hearts the goodness of the Supreme ruler of the Universe in affording the people of the United States in the course of his Providence an opportunity, deliberately & peaceably without fraud or surprise of entering into an explicit and solemn compact with each other by assenting to & ratifying a new Constitution, in order to form a more perfect union, establish justice, insure domestic tranquility, provide for the common defence, promote the general welfare and secure the Blessings of Liberty to themselves & their posterity," and they recommended an amendment to provide that "Congress shall make no law touching religion, or to infringe the rights of conscience."[191]

Virginia accompanied its ratification with (1) a declaration proclaiming that "no right of any denomination can be cancelled, abridged or modified by the Congress by the Senate or House of Representatives acting in any capacity by the President or any department or office of the United States except in those instances in which power is given by

187 THE FEDERALIST NO. 51. *See generally* MORTON WHITE, PHILOSOPHY, THE FEDERALIST, AND THE CONSTITUTION esp. 241–2 (Oxford Univ. Press 1987).

188 THE FEDERALIST NO. 69, *id.* at 422. *See also* MILLER, *supra* note 70, at 111 ["[T]he silence of *Federalist* (re religious matters) is almost as striking as the silence of the Constitution."].

189 An out-of-step proposal by South Carolina was a recommendation that the provision stating that "no religious test shall ever be required as a qualification to any office or public trust under the United States" be amended to read "no *other* religious test" (emphasis added), a change that would evidently (but presumably inadvertently) have permitted the "oath or affirmation" provision to be employed to require a religious test.

190 *See infra* Section F. For the ticklish possibility that some states might indulge in "conditional" ratifications, *see* KURLAND AND LERNER, 46 THE FOUNDERS' CONSTITUTION 648–71; *see also* RUTLAND, ORDEAL OF THE CONSTITUTION *supra* note 183, at 218.

191 II DOCUMENTARY HISTORY OF THE CONSTITUTION 141–4 (Department of State 1894).

the Constitution for those purposes and that among other essential rights the liberty of conscience and of the press cannot be abridged, restrained or modified by any authority of the United States" and (2) a recommendation that the Constitution should include a Declaration or Bill of Rights "asserting and securing from encroachment the essential and unalienable rights of the people" in such manner as the following:

> That any person religiously scrupulous of bearing arms ought to be exempted upon payment of an equivalent to employ another to bear arms in his stead [and] That religion, or the duty which we owe to our Creator, and the manner of discharging it, can be directed only by reason and conviction, not by force or violence, and therefore all men have an equal, natural and unalienable right to the free exercise of religion according to the dictates of conscience, and that no particular religious sect or society ought to be favoured or established by law in preference to others.[192]

North Carolina's ratification included a proposal to amend "the most ambiguous and exceptional parts of the Constitution" with provisions identical to Virginia's proposals relating to conscientious objectors to bearing arms, to the free exercise of religion, and to the granting of religious preferences.[193]

New York's ratification included this declaration:

> That the People have an equal, natural and unalienable right, freely and peaceably to exercise their Religion according to the dictates of Conscience, and that no Religious Sect or Society ought to be favoured or established by Law in preference of others.[194]

Although New York also recommended amendments to the Constitution relating to a large number of issues, the list does not include an explicit proposal to protect religious liberty.

Finally, Rhode Island ratified the Constitution on May 29, 1790, with a declaration identical to Virginia's proposals relating to conscientious objectors to bearing arms, to the free exercise of religion, and to the granting of religious preferences.[195] This action by Rhode Island, however, did not occur until almost a year after Congress drafted the Bill of Rights and sent it to the states for ratification.

A few intransigent foes of the "Godless Constitution" urged their followers to boycott the federal elections until the Constitution was amended to restore the Deity to a proper place of supremacy, and there were several unsuccessful national campaigns to achieve this result.[196] During his presidency, George Washington deployed a different justification for the Constitution's alleged deficiency in failing to invoke the Deity – a defense that presages the currently popular principle of the separate roles of government and religion – by writing to a group of clergymen:

> [T]he path of true piety is so plain as to require but little political direction. To this consideration we ought to ascribe the absence of any regulation, respecting religion, from the Magna-Charta of our country.

192 *Id.* at 1027–30.
193 *Id.* at 1044–7.
194 *Id.* at 1090.
195 *Id.* at 310.
196 *See* Daniel L. Dreisbach, *In Search of a Christian Commonwealth: An Examination of Selected Nineteenth-Century Commentaries on References to God and the Christian Religion in the United States Constitution*, 48 Baylor L. Rev. 927, 931-6 (1996).

> To the guidance of the ministers of the gospel this important object is, perhaps, more properly committed – It will be your care to instruct the ignorant and to reclaim the devious – and in the progress of morality and science, to which our government will give every furtherance, we may confidently expect the advancement of true religion, and the completion of our happiness.[197]

## E. The Drafting of the Religion Clauses of the First Amendment

### 1. *Introduction*

Less than a year after the new Constitution was ratified by the requisite nine states,[198] the First Federal Congress submitted twelve amendments to the states, ten of which were ratified and became known as the "Bill of Rights." The process of adopting these changes was begun by Madison[199] – in a speech in the new Congress on June 8, 1789.[200]

When interpreting the First Amendment, the Supreme Court has searched for clues to its meaning in "the background and environment of the period in which that constitutional language was fashioned and adopted."[201] This allegedly wide-angle vision, as will be noted later in this work, has in actuality focused narrowly on the pre-1789 history of Virginia (examined in detail later), and even this limited data bank has been restricted by the Supreme Court almost exclusively to three documents: (1) an unenacted Virginia "General Assessment to Support Teachers of Christianity," (2) Madison's "Memorial and Remonstrance against Religious Assessments," denouncing the proposed general assessment, and (3) a successful alternate to the taxing statute, the Virginia Statute for Religious Freedom, written by Thomas Jefferson.[202] The Supreme Court's stress on these documents disregards the principle expressed by Madison in interpreting the Constitution itself, *viz.*, that the intentions of the delegates to the Philadelphia convention were not controlling because they produced a mere proposal, which came into force only when ratified.[203]

In sharp contrast to the judicial preoccupation with these documents and with the roles of Madison and Jefferson in their native state, some commentators and constitutional theorists have given their primary attention to the legislative history of the First Federal Congress, which was the venue in which the First Amendment was drafted. We turn first to the raw materials used by these scholars in their vigorous battles over the meaning of the religion clauses of the First Amendment.[204]

197 *Id.* at 956.

198 U.S. Const. art. VII.

199 *See infra* Section E.2.a.

200 *See infra* text accompanying notes 218 and 220.

201 Everson v. Bd. of Educ., 330 U.S. 1, 8 (1947); *see also id.* at 28–9, 31–43 (Rutledge, J., dissenting).

202 *See id.* at 11–14. For detailed analysis of this case, *see* Chapter 16.D.

203 If the Bill of Rights had not been ratified, of course, it would not have come into force through constitutional amendment, although Hamilton and others argued that the rights might exist anyway, even without a Bill of Rights.

204 Two excellent compilations of documents relating to the drafting of the First Amendment are The Complete Bill of Rights: The Drafts, Debates, Sources and Origins (Neil H. Cogan ed., Oxford Univ. Press 1997) (for religion clauses, *see* 1–82) and Creating the Bill of Rights, *supra* note 183. The latter is derived from an exhaustive compendium; *see* Documentary History of the First Federal Congress of the United States of America, March 4, 1789–March 3, 1791

## 2. *The Documentary Record*

The First Federal Congress, sitting in New York City and Philadelphia in 1789–1791, drafted and sent to the states for ratification the religion clauses of what became the First Amendment. Commentators, influenced and often dominated by the originalist standard of constitutional interpretation,[205] frequently cite, quote, and rely on the *Annals of Congress* and the *Congressional Register* for the language of the 1789–1791 congressional debates, sometimes seemingly believing that these publications are as official as their titles imply.[206] Alas, the legislative debates were not officially recorded; as a result, any account of the House debates must be pieced together from fragmentary and sometimes conflicting private and newspaper accounts of the proceedings in the House, and the Senate's deliberations are even more elusive because its sessions were closed to outsiders.[207] A recent meticulous and exhaustive description of these deplorably incomplete sources states

> At the beginning of its first session the House of Representatives began admitting the public to its debates. Three newspaper publishers and shorthand writer Thomas Lloyd, an individual entrepreneur who came to the seat of government with the declared

(Linda Grant De Pauw ed., Johns Hopkins Univ. Press 1972–2012) (numerous volumes), sponsored by the National Historical Publications Commission. For the editorial policies of the DePauw work, *see* this from Vol. X, p. xiii:

> All newspapers printed at the seat of government were read and compared, and it was determined that with rare exceptions only three papers printed original accounts of the first and second session debates: *The Gazette of the United States, the Daily Advertiser*, and the *New York Daily Gazette*. Other New York papers took their accounts from these sources.... On rare occasions, newspapers printed outside the seat of government contained an original version of a speech that the editor received from a congressman or an intermediary.

*See also* BERNARD SCHWARTZ, THE BILL OF RIGHTS: A DOCUMENTARY HISTORY (Chelsea House Publ. 1971) (includes useful editorial commentary by editor); EDWARD DUMBAULD, THE BILL OF RIGHTS AND WHAT IT MEANS TODAY (Univ. of Okla. Press 1957); Gaspare J. Saladino, *The Bill of Rights, A Bibliographic Essay*, *in* CONLEY & KAMINSKI, *supra* note 183, at 461–510 (comprehensive, with helpful commentary).

For analysis of the relevant documents, *see inter alia* AKHIL AMAR, THE BILL OF RIGHTS: CREATION AND RECONSTRUCTION (Yale Univ. Press 1998); LEVY, *supra* note 35; THOMAS J. CURRY, THE FIRST FREEDOMS 193–222 (Oxford Univ. Press 1986); GERARD V. BRADLEY, CHURCH-STATE RELATIONSHIPS IN AMERICA 85–110 (Greenwood Press 1987); ROBERT L. CORD, SEPARATION OF CHURCH AND STATE: HISTORICAL FACT AND CURRENT FICTION (Lambeth Press 1982); WITTE, *supra* note 164, at 57–86; Douglas Laycock, *"Nonpreferential" Aid to Religion: A False Claim about Original Intent*, 27 WM. & MARY L.J. 875 (1986); RUTLAND, THE BIRTH OF THE BILL OF RIGHTS, *supra* note 184, at 218; MILLER, *supra* note 70.

For a concise, readable account of the political history leading to the convening of the First Federal Congress and its submission of the Bill of Rights to the states for ratification, see RUTLAND, THE BIRTH OF THE BILL OF RIGHTS, *supra* note 184, ch. IX (*The Campaign Pledge Fulfilled*).

205 For this and other standards of constitutional interpretation, *see infra* Section J. Regarding original understanding of the definition of religion, *see* Chapter 7.C.1

206 For the House and Senate legislative journals, which endured damage during transfers from one place to another and also were damaged by fire when the British attacked the Capitol, *see infra* Section E.2.d–f.

207 The diary of Senator William Maclay contains rough notes on the Senate debates, but it did not come to public attention until 1880 and then only in an abbreviated and expurgated form, and it has seemed to have escaped the attention of jurists and scholars. *See* IX DOCUMENTARY HISTORY OF THE FIRST FEDERAL CONGRESS, *supra* note 204, at xi–xviii, which painstakingly reconstructs the diary; its index contains no reference to "religion" or to "church."

> intention of publishing the debates, made serious attempts at recreating portions of the debates for the news-hungry public. Lloyd supported his efforts to produce the most complete account of the happenings on the floor through subscriptions to his *Congressional Register*, which contained only the debates. John Fenno began publishing the *Gazette of the United States* specifically for the purpose of reporting on and supporting the new government. Francis Childs (joined in July 1789 by John Swaine) and Archibald McLean had already established *The* [New York] *Daily Advertiser* and *The New-York Daily Gazette* respectively. These papers reported the debates only sporadically at first but eventually, probably in part because of Lloyd's long delays in publication, their accounts became more complete.
>
> These reports should be regarded as the results of an effort to record the debates while facing some very difficult odds. Reporters attended the sessions alone, trying to keep up with the debate while coping with dim lighting, quill pens, and poor acoustics. Without any of the modern day aids such as guides picturing the members, an excellent sound system, a board that shows recorded votes, and videotapes of the sessions to review, the reporters struggled to put together a coherent picture of the proceedings – which may not have been coherent at all! Thus, the debates they published represent their best efforts, but are not a verbatim or complete transcript.[208]

Because Lloyd's reports as published in his *Congressional Register* became the base of the much-quoted *Annals of Congress*,[209] it should be noted that he was given to the use of ardent spirits and that Madison condemned the results:

> The face of the debates shows that they are defective, and desultory, where not revised, or written out by the Speakers. In some instances, [Lloyd] ... makes them inconsistent with themselves, by erroneous reports of their speeches at different times on the same subject. He was indolent and sometimes filled up blanks in his notes from memory or imagination. I recollect that he put into my mouth, a speech, drawn much from the latter and in its style suited rather to a youthful declaimer than to me in my situation. He finally, became a votary of the bottle and perhaps made too free use of it sometimes at the period of his printed debates.[210]

An enterprising 1940 study sponsored by the Library of Congress[211] disclosed that contemporary historians and commentators who seek to reconstruct "the original intent" of the constitutional Framers from the "legislative history" of the religion clauses of the First Amendment have their work cut out for them. According to one account:

> In 1940, the Library of Congress acquired the manuscript of [Lloyd's] shorthand notes of the debates from April 8 to May 15, 1789, and from January 19 to June 3, 1790. These

208 *See* Creating the Bill of Rights, *supra* note 183; for a more detailed account, *see* X Documentary History of the First Federal Congress, *supra* note 204, at x–xl.

209 *Annals of Congress* was not published until 1834 and is incomplete, relying for its reports exclusively on Lloyd's *Congressional Register* and then (after Lloyd ceased publication) on the *Gazette of the United States*; indeed, it is possible that its publishers were unaware of the fact that the debates were more or less contemporaneously reported by several other newspapers, and "they introduced some new errors into the text through mistranscriptions from the original source." X Documentary History of the First Federal Congress, *supra* note 204, at xxvii.

210 Letter from James Madison to Edward Everett (January 7, 1832), *in* Edward Everett Papers, *quoted in* Marion Tinling, *Thomas Lloyd's Reports of the First Federal Congress*, 18 Wm. & Mary Q. 519, 537-8 (1961).

211 *See* Tinling, *supra* note 210.

> notes were transcribed, insofar as they could be, by a shorthand expert, and the transcription was compared to the debates printed by Lloyd in the *Congressional Register*. It was discovered that what Lloyd published "bears only slight resemblance to the literal transcript of his own notes. Sometimes a speech is printed for which no notes or only very brief notes exist; sometimes a long speech reported in the manuscript is printed very briefly or not at all." Another investigator has reported that Lloyd's reports were frequently "garbled" and that he neglected to report speeches whose texts are known to exist elsewhere. Lloyd's manuscript also demonstrates a wandering mind, for it is periodically interrupted by doodling, sketches of members, horses, and landscapes, and by poetry.... It is thus little wonder that on May 9, 1789, Madison condemned the *Congressional Register* as exhibiting "the strongest evidence of mutilation and perversion," and that Eldridge Gerry, after accusing Lloyd of persisting in his Federalist partisanship, complained that "[s]ometimes members were introduced as uttering arguments directly the reverse of what they had advanced."[212]

The author of this account reaches these conclusions:

> If we conclude that this array of defects has corrupted the historical documentation of the Constitution, it would appear to be impossible to rely upon the documentary record to discover the intentions of the Framers. A jurisprudence of original intention is not precluded by these findings, but it would be obliged to seek the intention of the Framers in the words of the Constitution, as the Framers themselves intended.[213]

A striking instance of the contrast between the documentary record and today's debates among commentators is a spate of arguments turning on whether an eighteenth-century legislator used the definite article "the" or the indefinite article "a" in a discussion.[214]

Scholars who search today for the original intent of the Framers of the Bill of Rights are aided – and simultaneously burdened – by a *Documentary History of the First Federal Congress (1789–1791)* that compiles the variant accounts of the debates of the House of Representatives in five bulky volumes, refers the reader to an additional five volumes of relevant material, and then offers the following bleak advice: "It is the task of the user to sift through these accounts with their inconsistencies and potential bias and come to an understanding of what actually transpired on the floor of the House."[215]

### a. Legislative History of the Religion Clauses

Early in 1789, Jefferson commented, in a letter to John Paul Jones, on the need for a "bill of rights" to mollify critics of the newly ratified Constitution:

> Our new constitution was acceded to in the course of the last summer by all the states except N. Carolina and Rhode Island. Massachusetts, Virginia and New York, tho they accepted unconditionally, yet gave it as a perpetual instruction to their future delegates never to cease urging certain amendments. N. Carolina insisted that the amendments

212 James H. Hutson, *The Creation of the Constitution: The Integrity of the Documentary Record*, 65 Tex. L. Rev. 1, 36–8 (1986).

213 *Id.* at 39.

214 *See* Smith, *supra* note 71, at 81 & 92. For an echo of this agonizing over a one-syllable word, *see* Somini Sengupta, *Report of United Nations Negotiations over the Convention on the Rights of the Child*, N.Y. Times, May 12, 2002.

215 *Supra* note 204, vol. X, at xliii.

> should be made before she would accede. The Most important of these amendments will be effected by adding a bill of rights; and even the friends of the Constitution are become sensible of the expediency of such an addition were it only to conciliate the opposition. In fact this security for liberty seems to be demanded by the general voice of America, and we may conclude it will unquestionably be added.[216]

On June 8, 1789, as though responding to Jefferson's prediction, Madison introduced, in the first session of the Federal Congress, a series of amendments to the month-old Constitution, which as revised and ratified became known as the "Bill of Rights." Madison prefaced his proposals by explaining that he desired to soothe the unease of Federalists and Anti-Federalists alike:

> He had no design to propose any alterations which in the view of the most sanguine friends to the constitution could affect its main structure or principles, or do it any possible injury – His object was to quiet the mind of the people by giving them some early assurance of a disposition in the house to provide expressly against all encroachments on their liberties, and against the abuses to which the principles of the constitution were liable.[217]

### b. Madison's Proposals of June 8, 1789

Madison's proposed amendments to the Constitution, introduced by him on June 8, 1789, read (as reported) in part as follows:

> That in article 1st, section 9, between clauses 3 and 4 [of the Constitution, relating respectively to bills of attainder and direct taxes] be inserted these clauses, to wit, The civil rights of none shall be abridged on account of religious belief or worship, nor shall any national religion be established, nor shall the full and equal rights of conscience be in any manner, or on any pretext infringed.[218]

216 *See* 2 SCHWARTZ, *supra* note 183, at 1003; *reprinting* Letter from Thomas Jefferson to John Paul Jones, March 23, 1789, *in* 14 THE PAPERS OF THOMAS JEFFERSON 686–9 (Julian P. Boyd ed., Princeton Univ. Press 1958). Jefferson's summary of North Carolina's posture overstates its opposition; its ratification was not conditional but less intransigent: the amendments "ought to be laid before Congress and the convention of the states … for their consideration." *Id.*

217 CREATING THE BILL OF RIGHTS, *supra* note 183, at 63; *Annals of Congress*. For the drafting of the First Amendment, *see* RUTLAND, *supra* note 183, ch. IX, at 190–218 (*Birth of Bill of Rights, The Campaign Pledge Fulfilled*). For comments on Madison's speech and a copy of his rough outline, *see* SCHWARTZ, *supra* note 183, at 1006–9 & 1042–3 ("rightly considered one of the great addresses in our history," *id.* at p. 1007). By focusing the First Federal Congress' attention to amending the Constitution to modify its critics, Madison put an end to the troublesome proposal to call a second convention. For the impact of the amendments recommended by the states on the provisions proposed by Madison for inclusion in what became the Bill of Rights, *see* Donald S. Lutz, *The States and the U.S. Bill of Rights*, 16 S. ILL. U. L.J. 251, 259 (1992).

218 CREATING THE BILL OF RIGHTS, *supra* note 183, at 12; *see also id.* at 31. Although Madison's amendment as written would have been inserted into the body of the Constitution itself, Madison referred to his proposals as "A Bill of Rights" (*see id.* at 67), and as related below, they were redrafted to stand as separate amendments. For a version of an integrated Constitution, "revised" to carry out Madison's original plan, *see* Edward Hartnett, *A "Uniform and Entire" Constitution; or, What If Madison Had Won?*, 15 CONST. COMM. 251 (1998). For detailed reviews of the legislative debates, *see* SMITH, *supra* note 71, at 73ff; DANIEL L. DREISBACH, REAL THREAT AND MERE SHADOW: RELIGIOUS LIBERTY AND THE FIRST AMENDMENT 57ff (Crossway 1987).

As proposed, the employment of the passive verbs in this draft might have evoked claims that it would bind the states as well as the national government.[219] Such an inference would not have upset Madison because his proposed amendments also included the following explicit limit on the states:

> No state shall violate the equal rights of conscience, or the freedom of the press, or the trial by jury in criminal cases.[220]

This restriction on the states, described by Madison as "the most valuable amendment in the whole list,[221] would have anticipated by about 150 years the "incorporation" of the First Amendment into the Fourteenth,[222] and it was actually passed by the House; but it then faded away, leading it to be dubbed the "lost amendment."[223] In the same vein, a potential restriction on the states arising by inference from Madison's language ("the civil rights of none shall be abridged") disappeared when the draft was amended to restrict explicitly only Congress.[224]

A meticulous compilation identifies twenty-two versions of Madison's religion proposal as it moved through the House, the Senate, and a conference committee, en route to the document submitted by the new Congress to the states for ratification.[225] The four most important versions, which culminated in the First Amendment's now-familiar religion clauses, are set out in the next subsection. Many of the other changes were typographical or cosmetic.

### c. Redraft by Committee of Eleven: Report of July 28, 1789

Madison's proposals, including the religious clauses, were referred by the House of Representatives to a select committee of eleven members (one from each state, except North Carolina and Rhode Island, which had not yet ratified the Constitution), and this so-called committee of eleven revised the provisions to read as follows:

219 *See* Congressman Huntington, as reported by the CONGRESSIONAL REGISTER; THE COMPLETE BILL OF RIGHTS *supra* note 204, at 60; *see also* I WILLIAM W. CROSSKEY, POLITICS AND THE CONSTITUTION IN THE HISTORY OF THE UNITED STATES 1066 & 1073 (Univ. of Chicago Press 1953 and 1980).
*See* Barron v. Baltimore, 7 Pet. (32 U.S.) 243 (1833), holding that despite the passive voice in the "takings" clause of the Fifth Amendment, the provision bound only the federal government, not the states. For criticism of Barron v. Baltimore, *see* II WILLIAM W. CROSSKEY, POLITICS AND THE CONSTITUTION IN THE HISTORY OF THE UNITED STATES 1076ff (Univ. of Chicago Press 1953 and 1980); *see also* IV G. EDWARD WHITE, HISTORY OF SUPREME COURT OF THE UNITED STATES xxx.

220 CREATING THE BILL OF RIGHTS, *supra* note 183, at 13; for discussion, *see* CURRY, *supra* note 70, at 204ff; MILLER, *supra* note 70, at 123.

221 THE COMPLETE BILL OF RIGHTS, *supra* note 204.

222 As noted by Akhil Amar, *in* THE BILL OF RIGHTS, *supra* note 204, at 22, this language (prophetically) appeared as number fourteen on Madison's list. For the "incorporation," almost two centuries later, of the First Amendment through the Fourteenth, *see infra* section I.2.

223 *See, e.g.*, Gary C. Leedes, *Rediscovering the Link between the Establishment Clause and the Fourteenth Amendment: The Citizenship Declaration*, 26 IND. L. REV. 469, 498-9 (1993).

224 CREATING THE BILL OF RIGHTS, *supra* note 183, at 48. *See also* Barron v. Baltimore, 32 U.S. (7 Pet.) 243 (1833), *infra* section I.1, ruling that the passive verb in the First Amendment, providing that property shall not "be taken" without just compensation, binds only Congress, not the states.

225 THE COMPLETE BILL OF RIGHTS, *supra* note 204, at 1–11; there were twenty versions according to WITTE, *supra* note 164, at 72.

> No religion shall be established by law, nor shall the equal rights of conscience be infringed.[226]

Because the committee of eleven left no record of its deliberations, its deletion of the adjective "national" from Madison's draft is not officially explained. The change may have been intended to reinforce Madison's theory that the new federal government, vested with only its enumerated powers, had no authority over religious matters[227] or, assuming that members of the committee thought that this theory was fallacious or at least debatable, they may have concluded that it would be wise to deny explicitly that Congress could establish a religion for either the nation or for any state or region. The committee of eleven's other substantive change – dropping Madison's proposed protection of "religious belief or worship" – may have reflected verbal parsimony rather than a policy judgment because the deleted phrase could be viewed as virtually synonymous with "the rights of conscience."

A reasonable inference from the committee's language – "No religion shall be established by law" – is that the prohibition did not apply to the states[228] because surely there would have been an outcry from the New England Puritans if Congregationalism was to be deprived of its status as the established church in Massachusetts, New Hampshire, and Vermont.

The committee of eleven also carried forward (as part of a provision to protect free speech, a free press, and the right to trial by jury in criminal cases) Madison's ban on state infringements of "the equal rights of conscience," and the committee's draft echoed the recommendations of three states (made when they ratified the Constitution) by providing that "no person religiously scrupulous shall be compelled to bear arms."[229] Both of these provisions, however, were eventually dropped from the First Amendment, as later recommended by a conference committee.[230]

#### d. House Debate on August 15 and 20, 1789

On August 15, 1789, when the House took up the committee of eleven's redraft of Madison's proposal of June 8, the first speaker, Peter Sylvester of New York, expressed his "doubts of the propriety of the mode of expression used" because it "was liable to a construction different from what had been made by the Committee." He "feared it might be thought to have a tendency to abolish religion altogether."[231] Commentators have found this comment puzzling, but perhaps Sylvester thought that the proposed language could be stretched by foes of religion to mean that neither the states nor the new national government could do anything to aid religion. At any rate, after three other members also

[226] The Complete Bill of Rights, *supra* note 164, §§ 1.1, 1.3, at 2. The committee also proposed (without explanation) to relocate the religion provisions to follow art. I, § 9's second clause (relating to the writ of habeas corpus).

[227] *See* Vincent Phillip Muñoz, *The Original Meaning of the Establishment Clause and the Impossibility of Its Incorporation*, 8 U. Pa. J. Const. L. 585, 625 (2006).

[228] For a verbal analogy, *see* Barron v. Baltimore, *supra* note 219.

[229] *See supra* section D.

[230] For the exemption, two centuries later, of conscientious objectors from the Selective Service Act, *see* Chapter 18.H.1.

[231] Congressional Register, Aug. 15, 1789, *reprinted in* IX Documentary History of the First Federal Congress, *supra* note 204, at 1260; Creating the Bill of Rights, *supra* note 183, at 157.

expressed unease, Madison took the floor and offered his understanding of "the meaning of the words," saying that

> he apprehended the meaning of the words to be, that Congress should not establish a religion, and enforce the legal observation of it by law, nor compel men to worship God in any manner contrary to their conscience. Whether the words are necessary or not he did not mean to say, but they had been required by some of the State Conventions, who seemed to entertain an opinion that under [Article I, Section 8] ... of the constitution, which gave power to Congress to make all laws necessary and proper to carry into execution the constitution, and the laws made under it, enabled them to make laws of such a nature as might infringe the rights of conscience, or establish a national religion; to prevent these effects he presumed the amendment was intended, and he thought it as well expressed as the nature of the language would admit.[232]

Madison also proposed, but almost immediately withdrew, a motion to modify the committee of eleven's phrase "No religion shall be established by law" by restoring "national" before the word "religion."[233] Explaining this short-lived suggestion, he observed

> [I]f the word national was inserted before religion, it would satisfy the minds of honorable gentlemen. He believed that the people feared one sect might obtain a pre-eminence, or two combine together and establish a religion to which they would compel others to conform; he thought if the word national was introduced, it would point the amendment directly to the object it was intended to prevent.[234]

When withdrawing his motion, Madison alluded to the allegations of the Anti-Federalists that the new federal government was a "national" entity with independently broad powers (not candidly acknowledged, according to them) rather than a creature of the states. Madison asserted that the words "No national religion shall be established by law" did

232 IX Documentary History, *supra* note 204, at 1261. A recent commentator has asserted that in this speech, Madison made an error; in two places Madison misquoted his own proposal, adding a word to it by saying that Congress should not establish *a* religion. The additional word is significant. If it had been in the original, Sylvester would never have objected. If the added word had been in Madison's clause, it could not have been read as a prohibition of indirect, nondiscriminatory assistance to religion.

Malbin, Religion and Politics: The Intentions of the Authors of the First Amendment 8 (Am. Enterprise Inst. 1978) (emphasis in original). This Madisonian "misquotation" is also noted by several other authors; thus Dreisbach, *in* Real Threat and Mere Shadow *supra* note 218, at 60, accepts the claim of a Madisonian misquotation, describing it as "significant," as does Berns, The First Amendment and the Future of American Democracy 9 (Basic Books 1976); *see also* John E. Dunsford, *Prayer in the Well: Some Heretical Reflections on the Establishment Syndrome*, 1984 Utah L. Rev. 1, 24.

Madison's "misquotation" of "his own proposal" (which referred neither to "a religion" nor to "the religion"), however, lies wholly in the eye of the beholder. The reference to "a religion" occurred during the House's discussion of the committee of eleven's version of the First Amendment; it was that draft (not Madison's own proposal) whose language, rightly or wrongly, elicited Congressman Sylvester's "fears," as well as Madison's effort to reassure Sylvester and his fellow critics; it also elicited comments by Representative Vining ("suggested the propriety of transposing the two members of the [committee's] sentence") and Representative Gerry ("it would read better if it was, that no religious doctrine shall be established by law"). Creating the Bill of Rights, *supra* note 183, at 157. This episode suggests that given the unsatisfactory state of the reports of the legislative debates, attempts to attach weight to Madison's use of the indefinite article "a" are a tempest in a murky legislative teapot, as noted by Levy, *supra* note 35, at 94.

233 *See* Creating the Bill of Rights, *supra* note 183, at 30; *see also id.* at 158–9.

234 *Id.* at 158.

not imply that the government was a national one.[235] This disclaimer seems designed to calm Anti-Federalist fears.

A motion to alter the language to read "The Congress shall make no laws touching religion or the rights of conscience" was then introduced. The phrase "touching religion," possibly taken from New Hampshire's proposal when ratifying the Constitution,[236] seemingly would have broadened the committee of eleven's prohibition on Congress very substantially, and it attracted a favorable vote. However, it was then abandoned. The House settled on August 24 on the following language, which was thereupon referred to the Senate:

> Congress shall make no law establishing religion or prohibiting the free exercise thereof, nor shall the rights of conscience be infringed.[237]

The House may have confined its prohibition to Congress not in order to leave room for actions affecting religion by the other two branches of the new federal government but rather to protect state establishments of religion from federal interference. This "jurisdictional" construction of the Establishment Clause is embraced by Akhil Amar in his magisterial *The Bill of Rights*, quoting the identical point as expressed by Joseph Story in his early nineteenth-century *Commentaries of the Constitution*: "[T]he whole power over the subject of religion is left exclusively to the state governments."[238] Story, however, overstates somewhat because Congress was almost certainly left with some control over religious matters (e.g., in the District of Columbia, on Indian reservations, and in other federal enclaves).[239]

#### e. Senate Revision of September 9, 1789

We know from the Senate's journal that it defeated three proposals that would have altered the House's Establishment Clause to read as follows:

1. "Congress shall make no law establishing one religious sect or society in preference to others";
2. "Congress shall not make any law, infringing the rights of conscience, or establishing any religious sect or society"; and
3. "Congress shall make no law establishing any particular denomination of religion in preference to another or prohibiting the free exercise thereof, nor shall the rights of conscience be infringed."

The defeat of each of these proposals is the foundation of a claim by a few commentators that the Senate favored a broad prohibition on all possible establishments over a narrower one that would have forbidden an establishment only if it preferred one sect over another.[240] However, the precisely contrary inference emerges when we see

235 The Complete Bill of Rights, *supra* note 204, at 77.

236 *Id.* at 12.

237 *Id.* at 3. On leaving the reports of the House debates, it is worth noting again the characterizations of their tone, owing in some unknown measure to defects in the journalists' reports.

238 Amar, *supra* note 204; Story, *supra* note 21, at § 1873.

239 *See* Robert G. Natelson, *The Original Meaning of the Establishment Clause*, 14 Wm. & Mary Bill Rts. J. 73, 94, 137 (2005).

240 Levy, *supra* note 35, seeks (at 82) to buttress this claim by asserting that after defeating the three proposals quoted earlier, "[t]he Senate then adopted the language of the House." Levy's account is wrong.

what the Senate, after rejecting these three versions, actually voted for and sent to the House:

> Congress shall make no law establishing articles of faith, or a mode of worship.

This version of the Establishment Clause obviously would have prohibited only a particular species of religious preference and hence was a very narrow limit. Moreover, if a law prescribed articles of faith or a mode of worship, it *necessarily* created a preference in favor of the religion whose articles of faith or mode of worship was endorsed. Thus the version of the Establishment Clause that was proposed by the Senate prohibited – just as did the three versions it rejected – religious preferences. The difference between the three rejected versions and the chosen instrument was that the latter was much weaker, a mere shadow.[241] If adopted, a religion could have been established for all practical purposes without violating its prohibition. (In actuality, the six states with established churches in 1789 did not prescribe articles of faith or modes of worship; those matters were left to be fixed by the established churches on their own.) The Senate's watered-down version of the prohibition, however, did not survive. It was rejected by the House on September 21, whereupon it, together with the version that had been approved by the House on August 24, was sent to a joint committee of the two houses of Congress.

### f. Conference Committee Report of September 24, 1789

Without leaving any record of its discussion, the conference committee reported this version of Madison's amendment, which on approval by both houses of Congress and ratification by the states became the first portion of the First Amendment:

> Congress shall make no law respecting an establishment of religion, or prohibiting the free exercise thereof.[242]

The *Senate Journal* reports that the second proposal quoted earlier was defeated on September 3 and that "[t]he question was then taken on the adoption of the third article, as it came from the House of Representatives, when it was decided in the negative." *See* Schwartz, *supra* note 183, at 1147–8. Contrary to Levy's assertion, the Senate never adopted "the language of the House." If it had, the House version would have been submitted to the states for ratification; there would have been no need for a conference committee to iron out differences between the two branches of Congress.

241 The Senate's language and its rejection of the three earlier versions do not fit it into Curry's theory that the "Senate debate can be seen as a discussion about style, not substance" or that it concerned merely "how to state the common agreement that the new government had no authority whatsoever in religious matters." *See* CURRY, *supra* note 70, at 213–15.

242 For an comprehensive and objective analysis of the range of interpretations that emerge from a detailed examination of this constitutional language, studied in its context, *see* WITTE, *supra* note 164, at 72–86. Because the meaning of "establishment of religion" is frequently brought into question, it is worth noting that the number of states with establishments when the Establishment Clause was drafted, adopted, and ratified is open to debate:

> Cobb's 1902 study found two states with establishments or religion during the founding period. Pfeffer concludes that four had a "substantial establishment," Van Alstyne identifies five; Levy says there were seven. The truth is that by the standards of modern doctrine, almost every state in post-Revolutionary America had laws establishing religion.

Jed Rubenfeld, *Antidisestablishmentarianism: Why RFRA Really Was Unconstitutional*, 95 MICH. L. REV. 2347, 2351 (1997).

Although an admirer of Madison asserts that "[w]ithout a doubt, this final version of the first guarantee of the First Amendment was written by Madison,"[243] no recorded evidence supports this claim, and a more plausible account is that

> [h]istorians do not know which of the six conference members drafted the final language regarding religious liberty, how the passive phrase "respecting an establishment of" replaced the more active verb "establishing," whether that change was significant to some (or all) of the members of Congress, whether the phrase "nor shall the rights of conscience be infringed," was deleted because it was deemed surplusage, or because the rights of conscience might be infringed, nor finally, whether the language was intended to create two separate clauses, two interdependent clauses, or one clause.[244]

Still another commentator asks this self-answering question:

> How, in any case, can authorship determine the meaning of a collective compromise in Congress, whose operative significance resides in the actions of thirteen differentiated state legislatures?[245]

## F. Ratification of the Bill of Rights

On September 25, 1789, the First Federal Congress completed its work on twelve amendments to the Constitution – ten of which were to become the Bill of Rights – and these proposals were sent a few days later by President Washington to the thirteen states, including North Carolina and Rhode Island, even though they had not yet ratified the Constitution. Prompt action by nine states would have been sufficient to ratify the amendments, but before this occurred, North Carolina and Rhode Island joined the Union, increasing the number of states required for ratification of the amendments to ten. This number rose to eleven on February 3, 1791, when Vermont became the fourteenth state. The requisite number of state ratifications was reached on December 15, 1791, when Virginia ratified. The three laggards – Massachusetts, Georgia, and Connecticut – did not ratify the Bill of Rights until 1939 – their belated action being a *coup de théâtre* commemorating the bill's sesquicentennial anniversary.[246]

Our knowledge of the ratification process is deplorable, according to the editor of a compendium of the available scraps of information:

> It is amazing, considering the crucial significance of the Bill of Rights, that we know practically nothing about what went on in the state legislatures during the ratification process. At the time, there was nothing in the states comparable even to the *Annals of Congress*, which reported, however sketchily, proceedings and debates in the federal legislature. Even the contemporary newspapers are virtually silent on the ratification

243 2 Schwartz, *supra* note 183, at 1159. For a typical example of the assumption that Madison was virtually the sole framer and founder of the religion clauses of First Amendment so that a departure from his views is impliedly tantamount to unconstitutionality, *see* Marci A. Hamilton, *Free? Exercise*, 42 Wm. & Mary L. Rev. 823 (2001).

244 Ariens & Destro, *supra* note 28, at 88. *See also* Donald L. Drakeman, *Religion and the Republic: James Madison and the First Amendment*, 25 J. Church & St., 427 (1983).

245 Bradley, *supra* note 204, at 87.

246 *See generally* 2 Schwartz, *supra* note 183, at 1171–1203. The relevant volumes of Documentary History of the Ratification of the Constitution (Merrill Jensen ed., Madison State Hist. Soc. of Wis.) have not yet been published.

> debates in the states. Nor is this to be explained by the fact that ratification was a mere perfunctory matter, since there was virtually no opposition in the state legislatures. The first two of the amendments proposed by Congress were never ratified, being rejected or postponed by five of the states which ratified the Bill of Rights (Delaware, New Hampshire, New Jersey, New York, and Pennsylvania). Certainly, there must have been some sharp debates in those states on the matter.
>
> Even in the states which ratified all twelve proposed amendments, there must have been sharp division and debate. We know this from the fragmentary knowledge we have of the Virginia ratification.[247] The Virginia legislature began its consideration of the amendments in October, 1789, but it was not until December, 1791, that Virginia could announce its ratification. As [a] letter from [a Virginian legislator] puts it, "The antifederal gentlemen in our assembly do not relish the amendments," and they were able, as other letters ... show, to secure the temporary rejection of the amendments. It is unfortunate that we do not have any report of the debates which led to this result, other than the fragmentary glimpses in the newspaper excerpts and letters which follow this commentary.[248]

The raw materials adduced by the editor do not shed any light on the intent of the ratifiers when approving the religion clauses of the First Amendment. To be sure, eight Virginia legislators opposed ratification, claiming that the First Amendment "does not prohibit the rights of conscience from being violated or infringed; and although it goes to restrain Congress from passing laws establishing any national religion, they might notwithstanding, levy taxes to any amount, for the support of religion or its preachers; and any particular denomination of Christians might be so favored and supported by the General Government, as to give it a decided advantage over others, and in process of time render it as powerful and dangerous as if it was established as the national religion of the country.... This amendment then, when considered as it relates to any of the rights it pretended to secure, will be found totally inadequate."[249] There is no way to ascertain whether the Virginia legislators who successfully favored ratification agreed with this interpretation of the Establishment Clause or thought it was specious, and *a fortiori*, the same is true of the legislators in the ten other states who voted for ratification before Virginia. Nor is there any evidence that the interpretation put forward by the Virginia dissenters came to the attention of the ratifiers in any other state or that it arose independently outside Virginia.

## G. The Postindependence Struggle for Religious Freedom in Virginia: Key to the Meaning of the Religion Clauses of the First Amendment?

### 1. *Introduction*

In two major nineteenth- and twentieth-century encounters with the religion clauses of the First Amendment, the Supreme Court announced that their meaning was largely dictated by the Virginia struggle over the roles of church and state in the years between the Declaration of Independence and the state's adoption of Jefferson's "Virginia Bill

[247] *See generally supra* note 204, at ch. 5.

[248] SCHWARTZ, *supra* note 183, at 1171. For the *Annals of Congress*, *see supra* Section E.2.

[249] *Quoted by* Leonard W. LEVY, SEASONED JUDGMENTS: THE AMERICAN CONSTITUTION, RIGHTS, AND HISTORY 188 (Transaction 1995).

for Religious Liberty," which was drafted in 1777 and enacted in 1784.[250] The triggering events of this Virginia struggle was a proposed tax for the support of teachers of Christianity, which elicited the vigorous opposition of Madison, expressed in his "Memorial and Remonstrance against Religious Assessments," and of Jefferson, who drafted the 1784 Virginia bill enacted on the defeat of the tax bill.[251]

Thus, in *Reynolds v. United States* (1878) (ruling that religious conviction was not a valid defense to the prosecution of a Mormon for bigamy), decided almost a century after these Virginia events, the Supreme Court announced that "the true distinction between what properly belongs to the Church and what to the State" is to be found in two sentences of Jefferson's bill, and in *Everson v. Board of Education* (1947) (upholding the constitutionality of a municipality's reimbursement of the cost of bus transportation to attend a parochial school), the Court linked the First Amendment to Jefferson's 1784 Virginia bill.[252] Although the *Everson* Court was split on application of the Establishment Clause to the facts before it, the entire bench (both the prevailing justices and the four dissenters) agreed that the eighteenth-century dispute in Virginia was the context determining the meaning of the Establishment Clause. Thus, speaking for the majority, Justice Black observed that "the provisions of the First Amendment, in the drafting and adoption of which Madison and Jefferson played such leading roles, had the same objective and were intended to provide the same protection against governmental intrusion on religious liberty as the [1784] Virginia statute,"[253] and Justice Rutledge, dissenting in *Everson*, asserted that "[a]ll the great instruments of the Virginia struggle for religious liberty ... became warp and woof of our constitutional tradition, not simply by the course of history, but by the common unifying forces of Madison's life, thought and sponsorship."[254]

So emphatic and unqualified are these invocations of Virginia's history that a novice, on reading *Reynolds* and *Everson*, might be excused for thinking that the Court was elucidating the meaning of *Virginia's* constitution rather than our national charter. On

250 In neither of these applications of the originalism mode of interpreting the Constitution did the Supreme Court refer to the 1789 debates in the First Federal Congress, where the First Amendment was framed and discussed. By contrast, the academic commentators on the meaning of the Establishment Clause have focused mainly on the 1789 legislative debates.

251 As noted earlier, the general assessment bill was scheduled in 1784 for a final vote in 1785, but the bill then evaporated. Rather than say that it died without even a whimper, however, one can say that there was a bang – the enactment of a substitute, Jefferson's 1784 statute. Unlike Madison's "Memorial," however, this bill was not written for the express purpose of defeating the general assessment. It stemmed, instead, from Jefferson's comprehensive revision of the laws of Virginia following its declaration of independence in 1776.

252 Reynolds v. United States, 98 U.S. (8 Otto) 145 (1879); Everson v. Bd. of Educ., 330 U.S. 1 (1947).

253 Everson, 330 U.S. at 13. Given this flat assertion by the Supreme Court in *Everson*, it is not surprising that the lower federal courts have cited Jefferson's statute in scores of First Amendment cases; *see* DREISBACH, *supra* note 218, at 174 n. 77.

254 *Id.* 330 U.S. at 38; for Madison's "Memorial and Remonstrance," *see infra* Section G.3. For Jefferson's statute, *see generally* THE VIRGINIA STATUTE FOR RELIGIOUS FREEDOM (Merrill D. Peterson & Robert C. Vaughan eds., Cambridge Univ. Press 1988) (survey of statute and its influence, published on bicentennial anniversary of its enactment in 1788 by Virginia's General Assembly); CHARLES FENTON JAMES, DOCUMENTARY HISTORY OF THE STRUGGLE FOR RELIGIOUS LIBERTY IN VIRGINIA 1900 (reprint ed., Da Capo Press 1970) (reprints many petitions from church groups, etc.). A frequently acclaimed biography of Madison similarly presupposes that his intent determines the meaning of the First Amendment. *See* IRVING BRANT, JAMES MADISON: FATHER OF THE CONSTITUTION 264–75 (Bobbs-Merrill 1950).

realizing this error, the reader might ask: when the religion clauses of the First Amendment were drafted, where were the voices of the philosopher-statesmen of Massachusetts and Connecticut, who did not worship so devoutly at the altar of the French Enlightenment as Madison and Jefferson? Is it plausible that they would have stood mute when the First Federal Congress, allegedly, constitutionalized the rationalist convictions of Jefferson and Madison, who had little use for the spirit of Puritan New England?

In assessing the validity of the Supreme Court's claims that the religion clauses of the First Amendment, particularly the Establishment Clause, can be traced to a few polemical writings by Madison and Jefferson, the documents must be examined with great care, especially if originalism is to be the guiding interpretative principle. As will be seen, any link between the Madison and Jefferson documents and the First Amendment is more tenuous than the Court has acknowledged.[255] It is surely worthy of note that Kurland, editor of *The Founders' Constitution*, probably the most lasting scholarly legacy of the bicentennial of the ratification of the Constitution, has announced "that I have been unable to discover any recorded connection between the Virginia [Act for Establishing Religious Freedom] and the first amendment religion clauses other than the similarity in language."[256] It may be a bit too strong to classify the judicial linkage as the offspring of *post hoc ergo propter hoc* reasoning, but it comes close to this fallacy.

### 2. *Virginia's Proposed General Assessment to Support Teachers of Christianity*

Between 1776 and 1787, when the First Amendment was drafted, Virginia debated, adopted, rejected, or deferred action on a variety of bills relating to religion, of which the most noteworthy for present purposes was a proposed "general assessment" for the support of teachers of Christianity.[257] The most relevant version of this bill required the tax to be collected by the sheriff or other official of each county, to be paid (less a 5 percent collection fee) to the "society of Christians" designated by the taxpayer, to be used to provide "a Minister or Teacher of the Gospel" of the taxpayer's denomination, or to provide "places of divine worship."[258] Amounts collected from taxpayers who did not designate a recipient were to be paid by the sheriff into the state's treasury, to be expended as directed by the General Assembly "for the encouragement of seminaries of learning" in the locality wherein the undesignated funds were collected.[259] Recognizing that Quakers and "menonists" (presumably Mennonites) were governed by organizational rules differing from those of other denominations, the proposal authorized those groups to receive amounts collected from their members "to be disposed of in a manner which they shall

255 *See supra* Section A.3.a and b.

256 Philip B. Kurland, *The Origins of the Religion Clauses of the Constitution*, 27 WM. & MARY L. REV. 839, 855 (1986).

257 For background, *see* THOMAS E. BUCKLEY, CHURCH AND STATE IN REVOLUTIONARY VIRGINIA, 1776–1787 (Univ. of Virginia Press 1939) and H. J. ECKENRODE, SEPARATION OF CHURCH AND STATE IN VIRGINIA (Va. Dept. of Archives & Hist. 1910). Jefferson's verdict on this bill, letter to Madison, 7 THE PAPERS OF THOMAS JEFFERSON 595 (Julian P. Boyd ed., Princeton Univ. Press 1953): "Should the bill ever pass into a law in its present form it may and will be easily eluded. It is chiefly obnoxious on account of its dishonourable principle and dangerous tendency."

258 For the 1784 version, *see* BUCKLEY, *supra* note 257, app. 2, at 188.

259 For a discussion of the General Assembly's authority, *see* BUCKLEY, cited by Laycock, *supra* note 204, at 897.

think best calculated to promote their particular mode of worship." No such provision was made for Roman Catholics in the 1784 version, though earlier amendments to the proposal were evidently intended to qualify them for participation in the program.[260] Still other denominations protested that the bill would interfere with their forms of ecclesiastical government; the Presbyterians, for example, objected to the bill because it overrode their view of the proper allocation of power between the ministry and the laity.[261] The most glaring denominational preference was that assessments paid by Jews and other non-Christians had to be allocated by them to Christian groups or left unallocated, in which event the General Assembly could evidently assign the funds to Christian groups of its selection if it so desired.[262]

A few commentators have argued that the assessment did not prefer Christians because amounts that were not designated for payment to a Christian society were to be paid into the public treasury and could be used by the General Assembly to support "seminaries of learning," a term that arguably might include non-Christian or non-Protestant schools. But the possibility that any of the funds would actually flow to any secular (or even to any non-Christian) society was very remote because it would have depended on a series of intertwined contingencies: (1) that some of the assessed funds would not be "appropriated" by the person assessed to a Christian society of his choice, (2) that any such funds would have their source in a county with a "seminary of learning," (3) that the seminary (if any) would be a secular or non-Christian organization, and finally, (4) that such a "non-Christian" seminary (if any) would be selected by the General Assembly as a beneficiary of the hypothesized unappropriated funds. A Christian preference, therefore, was virtually inherent in the proposed tax, as its title implied.[263] The bill also played other favorites, as noted earlier, by allowing Quakers and Mennonites greater freedom in the allocation of funds to their denominations than was accorded to others, as the Presbyterians complained.

### 3. *Madison's "Memorial and Remonstrance against Religious Assessments"*

In *Everson*, Justice Rutledge credited Madison's "Memorial and Remonstrance against Religious Assessments" with having "killed" Virginia's proposed general assessment – a verdict that is also embraced by several of Madison's biographers.[264] As explained

260 *See* Laycock, *supra* note 204, at 896–7.

261 Miller, *supra* note 70, at 40.

262 Although the General Assembly could have directed unassigned funds to secular educational institutions, it was not required to do so. *See* the exchange on this point between Justices Thomas and Souter, Rosenberger v. Rector & Visitors of Univ. of Va., 515 U.S. 819, 853 n.1 (1995) (Thomas, J., concurring); *id.* at 872 n.2 (Souter, J., dissenting).

263 For an explicit recognition of this preference, *see* the Memorial of the Virginia Presbyterian Church protesting that the bill evidenced "an impolitic partiality which we are sorry to have observed so long," *quoted in* Edward Frank Humphrey, Nationalism and Religion in America, 1774–1789 at 400 (Chipmen 1924). In a very long footnote to his dissenting opinion in *Rosenberger v. Univ. of Virginia*, Justice Souter asserts that the proposed assessment, if enacted, "*would* have funded secular as well as religious instruction" (emphasis added). Rosenberger, 515 U.S. at 869 n. 1 (Souter, J., dissenting). True, unallocated funds *could* have been used by Virginia's legislature to support secular seminaries (assuming that there were any in the county where the unallocated funds were collected), but that outcome was not mandatory.

264 Everson, 330 U.S. at 38; Rives, *supra* note 79, at 663 ("the crowning victory in the momentous [general assessment] contest"); 1 Stokes, *supra* note 2, at 391 ("Madison's remarkable paper was largely responsible" for defeat of the general assessment). For an exhaustive account of the "Memorial and

in this section, however, this claim exaggerates the impact of the "Memorial and Remonstrance."[265] Issued anonymously and not publicly acknowledged by Madison as his work until 1826, the "Memorial and Remonstrance" was elicited by the near success of the general assessment bill in December of 1785, when it was favored by Virginia's General Assembly by votes of forty-seven to thirty-two and forty-four to forty-two on its first and second readings. Fearing enactment, Madison managed to persuade the legislature to postpone the third and final reading until the next session, scheduled for 1785; in doing so, Madison, it is reported, hoped for the death during this interim of Patrick Henry, the bill's passionate and most eloquent supporter. If so, he sublimated this ignoble hope by aiding in elevating Henry to the post of governor, which prevented his participation in the later legislative debates.[266] This political emasculation of his rival achieved, Madison drafted his "Memorial and Remonstrance" in the summer of 1785, evidently cloaking his authorship because he and his coterie of eighteenth-century Enlightenment deists were not overly popular in the Virginia of their own day, however irresistible their views came to be for such twentieth-century jurists as Black, Rutledge, Frankfurter, and Jackson when they decided the *Everson* case.[267]

Quoting from Virginia's 1776 Bill of Rights,[268] the "Memorial" charges

> [T]he [general assessment proposal] violates that equality which ought to be the basis of every law.... If "all men are by nature equally free and independent," all men are to be considered as entering into Society on equal conditions; as relinquishing no more, and therefore retaining no less, one than another, of their natural rights. Above all are they to be considered as retaining an "equal title to the free exercise of Religion according to the dictates of conscience." Whilst we assert for ourselves a freedom to embrace, to profess and to observe the Religion which we believe to be of divine origin, we cannot deny an equal freedom to those whose minds have not yet yielded to the evidence which has convinced us. If this freedom be abused, it is an offence against God, not against man: To God, therefore, not to men, must an account of it be rendered. As the [assessment] Bill violates equality by subjecting some to peculiar burdens; so it violates the same principle, by granting to others peculiar exemptions.[269]

In the same spirit, the "Memorial and Remonstrance" warns of worse to come:

> Who does not see that the same authority which can establish Christianity, in exclusion of all other Religions, may establish with the same ease any particular sect of Christians, in exclusion of all other Sects? That the same authority which can force a citizen to

Remonstrance," *see* 8 THE PAPERS OF JAMES MADISON 295–8 & 304–6) (Robert A. Rutland & William M.E. Rachal eds., Univ. of Chicago Press 1973). For a detailed account of the development of Madison's religious convictions and their relationship to his political philosophy, *see* GARRETT WARD SHELDON, THE POLITICAL PHILOSOPHY OF JAMES MADISON (Johns Hopkins Univ. Press 2000).

265 *See infra* text at notes 274–80.

266 *See* ECKENRODE, *supra* note 70, at 94; for the votes by the delegates, with thumbnail sketches of their church-state views, *see* BUCKLEY, *supra* note 68, app. II, at 194.

267 For the text of the "Memorial and Remonstrance," *see* the appendix of the *Everson* case (330 U.S. at 63). The "Memorial and Remonstrance" adheres closely to an outline that Madison prepared for his participation in the General Assembly's debates on the general assessment bill, captioned by him "Debate on Bill for Relig. Establishment proposed by Mr. [Patrick] Henry." 8 PAPERS OF JAMES MADISON, *supra* note 264, at 197.

268 *See supra* Section A.3.b.

269 330 U.S. at 66. The quotations are from arts. 1 and 16 of Virginia's 1776 Bill of Rights.

contribute three pence only of his property for the support of any one establishment, may force him to conform to any other establishment in all cases whatsoever?[270]

The much-quoted "three pence" caveat of the "Memorial and Remonstrance" is, of course, an echo of the three-penny Boston tax that triggered the Boston Tea Party.[271] As though this history lesson were not sufficient, the "Memorial and Remonstrance" asserts that the proposed Virginia assessment would differ only in degree from the Spanish Inquisition: "The one is the first step, the other the last in the career of intolerance."[272] Summing up almost fifteen centuries of history, the "Memorial and Remonstrance" – a faithful document of the Enlightenment – asserts that the fruits of legally established Christianity have been "[m]ore or less in all places, pride and indolence in the Clergy, ignorance and servility in the laity; in both, superstition, bigotry and persecution."[273]

Madison did not himself sign the "Memorial and Remonstrance," but many of his fellow citizens did, and it merged with scores of other antiassessment petitions that bombarded Virginia's legislators in 1785. Justice Rutledge was almost certainly creating history, however, rather than unearthing it when he singled out the "Memorial and Remonstrance" from this welter of antiassessment protests and credited it with having "killed" the assessment bill.[274] Of the approximately eleven thousand Virginians who signed eighty antiassessment petitions, less than a fifth subscribed to the "Memorial and Remonstrance."[275]

The influence of the "Memorial and Remonstrance" also was rivaled, if not exceeded, by other antiassessment forces that were prominent in the legislative battle. These included a large vocal, and probably decisive, group of evangelical Christians who objected to the assessment bill but not because they agreed with Madison that religion should be privatized. By contrast with him, they wanted not a secular state but a Christian America, and their religious convictions did not stem from rationalism but from their interpretation of scripture and of God's will.[276] It is not surprising, however, that Madison's "Memorial and Remonstrance" was more compelling in Justice Rutledge's reading of history; he (and the justices who joined him in *Everson*) would hardly have wanted to erect the "impregnable" wall of separation on a religious foundation.[277]

Moreover, the assessment advocates made a political blunder in simultaneously agitating (successfully) for a bill incorporating the Protestant Episcopal Church, which confirmed its title to the established Angelican Church's property – a measure that smacked

[270] 330 U.S. at 65.

[271] David A. Copeland, Debating the Issues in Colonial Newspapers 288–92 (Greenwood 2000).

[272] Madison's comparison may itself be compared with the hyperbole that Cardozo dubbed a "sanguinary simile" in *Jones v. SEC*, 297 U.S. 1, 33 (1936), likening the Securities and Exchange Commission (SEC) to the Court of Star Chamber. Would Madison have accepted an accusation, in the same vein, that the use of public funds to provide bus transportation to a parochial school, ruled constitutional in *Everson*, will lead inevitably to the establishment of Roman Catholicism as the state religion of New Jersey?

[273] 330 U.S. at 67 (appendix).

[274] *Supra* note 264 and accompanying text. Madison himself asserted that the "Memorial and Remonstrance" "crushed" the assessment bill, but he made this claim more than thirty years after the controversy; *see* Buckley, *supra* note 68, at 175 n. 2.

[275] *Id.* at 175.

[276] *See generally id.* at chs. 4 & 5; Eckenrode, *supra* note 70, at 106–15; James, *supra* note 68, at 122–49, 251–5.

[277] The constitutional wall of separation between church and state was described as "high and impregnable" by Justice Black in *Everson*. 330 U.S. at 18.

of sectarian favoritism.[278] Still another source of trouble for the assessment proposal, similarly independent of Madison's "Memorial and Remonstrance," was no doubt the hostility that always greets a new tax – a force that might have been quiescent in 1784 but that came to life as the proposal elicited greater attention in 1785.

In a recent broad-based cultural history, a penetrating author summarized the influence of Madison and his deist colleagues:

> In the torrent of signatures that ultimately swept away the [general assessment] bill, a significant group of supporters of Enlightenment secularism stood side by side with a much greater number of evangelical separationists. For the moment the two groups were united against the traditional conception of community as a hierarchy of head and members whose corporateness was symbolically expressed in an obligation to provide for public worship.[279]

In the same vein, another careful commentator concluded

> [T]he role of Madison and Jefferson and the liberal elements who gathered under their banner can be overplayed, just as the significance of the "Memorial and Remonstrance" as representative of the sentiments of Virginians can be overemphasized.... Despite the best efforts of Madison's allies to circulate the memorial, less than one fifth of those who signed petitions against the assessment in 1785 put their names beneath his composition. The key to understanding the nature of the religious settlement in Virginia rests with the dissenters, the members of the evangelical churches, for they wrote and signed the overwhelming majority of the memorials which engulfed the legislature that year; and their representatives provided the votes in the Assembly which determined the outcome.[280]

It also should be noted that Madison's "Memorial and Remonstrance" is suffused with a devout spirit that ill befits a document that has become a classic of separationism. It begins by asserting that everyone "must be considered as a subject of the Governor of the Universe" and that this status is prior "in order of time and degree of obligation, to the claims of Civil Society," with the consequence that membership in "any particular Civil Society" must be assumed "with a saving of [one's] allegiance to the Universal Sovereign." In keeping with this subordination of the secular to the divine, the "Memorial and Remonstrance" – as though fearful that its rational arguments against the assessment bill might fall on deaf, or worse, hostile, ears – concludes on a religious note: "earnestly praying, as we are in duty bound, that the Supreme lawgiver of the Universe, by illuminating those to whom [the "Memorial and Remonstrance"] is addressed, may on the one hand, turn their councils from every act which would affront his holy prerogative, or violate the trust committed to them: and on the other, guide them into every measure which may be worthy of his ... [blessing]."[281]

278 James, *supra* note 68, at 128; Eckenrode, *supra* note 70, at 100–1; Buckley, *supra* note 68, at 27.

279 Isaac, *supra* note 68, at 292–3; *see also* Sidney E. Mead, The Lively Experiment: The Shaping of Christianity in America 55–71 (Harper & Row 1963).

280 Buckley, *supra* note 68, at 175. Buckley buttresses his conclusion with a member-by-member compilation of the votes of the members of Virginia's legislature (his app. II, at 192). A metaphor floated by one of Madison's admiring biographers was picturesque but grossly excessive: the "table of [Virginia's] House of Delegates almost sunk under the weight of the memorial sent forward from the different counties." *Quoted by* Smith, *supra* note 71, at 59.

281 "Memorial and Remonstrance," final sentence; the bracketed word "blessing" has faded from the original manuscript but appears in the published version. *See* 8 Papers of James Madison, *supra* note 264, at 306 n. 15.

The "Memorial and Remonstrance" also relies heavily on claims that enactment of the proposed assessment would undermine Christianity; for example, that it would "weaken in those who profess [Christianity] a pious confidence in its innate excellence [and would] foster in those who still reject it, a suspicion that its friends are too conscious of its fallacies, to trust it to its own merits" and that the assessment bill "is adverse to the diffusion of the light of Christianity" because it would discourage religious persons from migrating to Virginia. An astute recent commentator on the "Memorial and Remonstrance" notes that Madison's objection to the proposed Virginia tax "was not that it aided or accommodated religion generally but that it aided Christianity to the exclusion of other religions."[282]

Moreover, in any attempt to link the "Memorial and Remonstrance" to the litigated issues that arise in the twenty-first century, it should be noted that it was drafted and issued for the primary – if not the sole – purpose of defeating the eighteenth-century Virginia general assessment bill and that when it is deployed to blast other targets, it may fire far afield. Thus, when aimed in the twenty-first century at a governmental program that treats all religious groups alike and that does not distinguish between religious and secular recipients of the benefits, the antifavoritism rhetoric of the "Memorial and Remonstrance" simply falls flat. The plethora of antiassessment reasons proffered by the "Memorial and Remonstrance" may have been an astute argumentative device for building a coalition, but they engender a troublesome by-product for anyone hoping to count its signatories as stalwart advocates of a wall of separation between church and state, let alone a "high and impregnable" wall. This is so because many Virginians might well have subscribed to the "Memorial and Remonstrance" even though they were strongly tempted to favor the proposed assessment but were won over by Madison's claim that the assessment would diminish the appeal of Christianity to the unconverted. Such faint-hearted signers of the "Memorial and Remonstrance" might well have accepted, or even favored, governmental actions that an uncompromising advocate of the wall of separation would oppose, such as a Christmas crèche on the village green or public financing for the transport of children to and from parochial schools. Indeed, one could sign the "Memorial and Remonstrance" even though one's only objection to the proposed assessment was that it did not provide financial support for non-Christian religious groups. In short, the "Memorial and Remonstrance" was a broad umbrella, not a dogmatic manifesto, appealing only to hard-core separationists.

There are two other shortcomings in the attempt to employ Madison's "Memorial and Remonstrance" as an authoritative guide to the meaning of the religion clauses of the First Amendment:

1. In framing the First Amendment, the "Memorial and Remonstrance" had no official status: it was not a committee report, a legislative resolution, or an early draft of the amendment, and there is no evidence that it played a significant role in the thinking of either the draftsmen or the ratifiers of the First Amendment.
2. It is far from clear that the "Memorial and Remonstrance," written with Virginians as its intended audience, would have evoked the concurrence of the contemporary political theorists and statesmen in the New England states or that a proposed to enact a general assessment in those states could have been similarly defeated.

[282] Smith, *supra* note 71, at 53.

Thus the very first objection of the "Memorial and Remonstrance" to the Virginia assessment – "that it is the duty of every man to render to the Creator such homage, *and only such*, as he believes to be acceptable to him" (emphasis added) – presupposes a personal character to religion that would have been anathema to the numerous New Englanders for whom religion gained its force not from the convictions of the individual but from tradition and the overwhelming power of the bible as interpreted by an educated clergy. Indeed, in 1780, the people of Massachusetts adopted a constitution avowing principles that were virtually identical with those fueling the Virginia general assessment that Madison's "Memorial and Remonstrance" was written to defeat:

> As the happiness of a people, and the good order and preservation of civil government, essentially depend upon piety, religion and morality, and as these cannot be generally diffused through a community but by the institution of the public worship of GOD; and of public instructions in piety, religion, and morality: Therefore, to promote their happiness and to secure the good order and preservation of their government, the people of this Commonwealth have a right to invest their legislature with power to authorize and require, and the legislature shall, from time to time, authorize and require, the several towns, parishes, precincts, and other bodies politic or religious societies, to make suitable provision, at their own expense, for the institution of the public worship of GOD and for the support and maintenance of public protestant teachers of piety, religion and morality, in all cases where such provision shall not be made voluntarily.[283]

### 4. *Jefferson's Virginia Statute for Religious Freedom*

#### a. Background

In 1786, Virginia's path-breaking "Declaration of Rights," discussed earlier in this work,[284] was augmented by the Virginia's General Assembly's enactment of what is commonly called Jefferson's "Virginia Statute for Religious Freedom," which is often paired (as in the *Everson* case) with Madison's "Memorial and Remonstrance," as though they were fraternal twins, in narrating the postrevolutionary struggle for religious freedom in Virginia, in accounting for the defeat of Virginia's proposed general assessment for the support of teachers of Christianity and in interpreting the religion clauses of the First Amendment. But the two documents differ in fundamental features. Madison's "Memorial and Remonstrance" was designed explicitly as a weapon to defeat the general assessment bill; Jefferson's statute, however, was drafted as part of a comprehensive revision of Virginia's laws, launched in 1776, and it became a rival to the assessment proposal more by an accident of chronology than by design.[285] The "Memorial and Remonstrance" was signed by a respectable (but far from decisive) fraction of Virginia's residents, but there is no way to ascertain how many of its melange of antiassessment arguments gained the agreement of Virginia's lawmakers; by contrast, Jefferson's statute

283 *See* Ronald M. Peters, Jr., The Massachusetts Constitution of 1780: A Social Compact 52 (Univ. of Mass. Press 1978); *see also* Adams v. Howe, 14 Mass. 149 (1817).

284 *See supra* Section A.3.b.

285 For Jefferson's statute, *see* The Virginia Statute for Religious Freedom, *supra* note 254; Strout, *supra* note 71, at 88.

can claim the imprimatur of enactment by the state's General Assembly. What the two documents share is an impressive unintended achievement: persuading the jurists and academicians of the second half of twentieth-century America that these Virginia laws are a key to the intended meaning of the religion clauses of the First Amendment despite the absence of any objective evidence that any member of the First Federal Congress, which drafted the First Amendment, mentioned either document in the legislative discussions.

### b. Jefferson's Statute in Its Church-State Context

Both Justice Black's opinion for the Court in *Everson* and Justice Rutledge's dissenting opinion treat the 1786 Virginia statute as drafted by Jefferson as though it was a singular event, flowing perhaps from Jefferson's solitary musings in Monticello about the rights of conscience. In point of fact, however, it was only a small portion of a dauntingly ambitious project: nothing less than a comprehensive revision of the laws of Virginia, a natural result of its declaration of independence in 1776, which originated in a bill, sponsored by Jefferson in Virginia's General Assembly, to "revise, alter, amend, repeal, or introduce any or all" of the Commonwealth's laws.[286] Jefferson was named chairman of a five-man committee for this task. Two of the nominees bowed out, excusing themselves because they were not lawyers, and Jefferson took over the lion's share of the labor. He prepared 126 bills for the legislature, ranging in subject matter from a division of the state's counties into senatorial districts to the repeal of certain laws of Parliament. The bills, with bibliographic details, can be found in the pages of Jefferson's papers; of the 126 bills, bill number 82 is the Statute for Religious Freedom, and bills number 83 through 86 cover the closely related subjects of preserving the property of the established Anglican church, punishing disturbers of religious worship and Sabbath breakers, designating days of public fasting and thanksgiving, and regulating the mode of solemnizing marriages.[287] These adjacent statutory revisions were obviously intended to be consistent with bill number 82, and it with them.

Of these companion bills, bill number 84 (punishing disturbers of religious worship and Sabbath breakers) merits special interest because its provisions are glaringly disregarded by both Justice Black and Justice Rutledge in their *Everson* opinions.[288] Thus bill number 84's ten-shilling fine on any person who "shall be found laboring in his own or any other trade"[289] on Sunday could not have been reconciled by Justice Black with his claim in *Everson* that the Establishment Clause prohibits "laws which aid

286 For a detailed account of this project, including an analysis of each bill, *see* 2 THE PAPERS OF THOMAS JEFFERSON 305–665 (Julian P. Boyd ed., Princeton Univ. Press 1950).

287 *Id.* 545–53 (no. 82), 553–8 (nos. 83–86). Jefferson evidently was responsible for drafting all five of these bills; *see* DREISBACH, *supra* note 218, at 184 n. 134.

288 *See* Daniel L. Dreisbach, *Thomas Jefferson and Bills Number 82–86 of the Revision of the Laws of Virginia, 1776–1786: New Light on the Jeffersonian Model of Church-State Relations*, 69 N.C. L. REV. 159 (1988). For the political context of the Statute for Religious Freedom, the enactment of which reflected a joinder of evangelical Christians with the supporters of the proposed general assessment for the support of teachers of Christianity, *see* BUCKLEY, *supra* note 68, at 179–82; *see also* RICHARD BEALE DAVIS, INTELLECTUAL LIFE IN JEFFERSON'S VIRGINIA, 1790–1830 (Univ. of North Carolina Press 1964). Bills number 82 and 84 were introduced in the General Assembly by Madison on the same day; *see* Robert L. Cord, *Church-State Separation: Restoring the "No Preference" Doctrine of the First Amendment*, 9 HARV. J. L. & PUB. POL'Y 129, 135 (1986).

289 II PAPERS OF THOMAS JEFFERSON, *supra* note 286, at 555.

one religion, aid all religions, or prefer one religion over another," and bill number 84 would have created a similar hurdle for Justice Rutledge, who asserted in *Everson* that the Establishment Clause was intended "to create a complete and permanent separation of the spheres of religious activity and civil authority by comprehensively forbidding every form of public aid or support for religion."[290] In short, if Jefferson could propose enacting *both* the Statute for Religious Freedom *and* a fine for working on Sunday (treated by bill number 84 as the "Sabbath"), how could Justices Black and Rutledge claim that he proposed to separate church from state by a "high and impregnable wall"?[291] Still another breach in the hypothetical wall is a portion of bill number 86 that annuls marriages "prohibited by the Levitical law."[292] Finally, what sort of a wall can be discerned between church and the state of Virginia's General Assembly, which denounced departures from "the plan of the Holy author of our religion" when enacting the Statute for Religious Freedom?

Jefferson's bill number 82 ended with a bid for immortality: acknowledging that the General Assembly could not bind its successors and that a declaration of irrevocability would have no legal effect, the bill nevertheless launches an anticipatory anathema against future changes by asserting that "we are free to declare, and do declare, that the rights hereby asserted are of the natural rights of mankind, and that if any act shall be hereafter passed to repeal the present or to narrow its operation, such act will be an infringement of natural right."[293] The bill gained another link with posterity: in keeping with Jefferson's wishes, his tombstone records that the bill was one of his three most esteemed achievements, along with authoring the Declaration of Independence and founding the University of Virginia.[294]

## H. Government-Sponsored Private Behavior: "State Action"

Although the First Amendment's injunction – "Congress shall make no law …" – has been construed to forbid almost all types of governmental action, whether by Congress or not and even if not embodied in a formal "law,"[295] it does not prohibit action by private individuals and organizations, except in a small category of situations involving governmental sponsorship or participation. This fundamental distinction between governmental and private action (along with its narrow exceptions) has long played a crucial role in the civil rights area, reaching at least as far back as the beginning with the Supreme

290 330 U.S. at 15; *id.* at 31–2 (Rutledge, J., dissenting).

291 *Id.* at 18.

292 *See* LEVITICUS, xvii, 16; xx, 91 (glossed in Christian theology to forbid marriage to a brother's widow), *but see* DEUTERONOMY, xxv 5 (understood by ancient Hebrews to favor or require such a marriage, especially if the brother died childless – a duty claimed by some theologians to have been abrogated by the coming of Christ). This biblical conflict was not an obscure enigma to educated eighteenth-century statesmen because Henry VIII had relied on Leviticus to annul his marriage to Catherine of Aragon and thus to clear his way to marrying Anne Boleyn. *See* J. J. SCARISBRICK, HENRY VIII 163–97 (Univ. of California Press 1968).

293 *Id.* at 546–7.

294 For Jefferson's sketch of this memorial, *see* RHYS ISAAC, *supra* note 274; for its wording, *see* PAULINE MEIER, AMERICAN SCRIPTURE 186 (Knopf 1997); for Jefferson and religion at the University of Virginia., *see* STROUT, *supra* note 71, at 89.

295 *See, e.g.*, Holloman *ex rel.* Holloman v. Harland, 370 F.3d 1252, 1284 (11th Cir. 2004); Canell v. Lighter, 143 F.3d 1210, 1214 (9th Cir. 1998).

Court's 1888 decision in a group of decisions known as the *Civil Rights Cases*.[296] In those cases, the Court struck down as unconstitutional a central part of the Civil Rights Act of 1875, which outlawed racial segregation by inns, public conveyances, and places of public amusement, ruling that the power of Congress to enforce the Fourteenth Amendment was limited to actions by the states:

> [The Fourteenth Amendment] declares that "no state shall make or enforce any law which shall abridge the privileges or immunities of citizens of the United States; nor shall any state deprive any person of life, liberty, or property without due process of law; nor deny to any person within its jurisdiction the equal protection of the laws." It is state action of a particular character that is prohibited. *Individual invasion of individual rights is not the subject-matter of the amendment*.... [T]he last section of the amendment invests congress with power to enforce it by appropriate legislation. To enforce what? To enforce the prohibition. To adopt appropriate legislation for correcting the effects of such prohibited state law and state acts, and thus to render them effectually null, void, and innocuous. This is the legislative power conferred upon congress, and this is the whole of it.
>
> An inspection of [Civil Rights Act] shows that it makes no reference whatever to any supposed or apprehended violation of the fourteenth amendment on the part of the states.... It does not profess to be corrective of any constitutional wrong committed by the states.[297]

In a similar vein, it can be persuasively asserted that the religion clauses of the First Amendment prohibit action by the federal government (and, since adoption of the Fourteenth Amendment in 1868, by the states) but not the behavior of private individuals and organizations. Justice Harlan, sole dissenter in the 1888 *Civil Rights Cases*, argued that the targets of the disputed legislation – inns, public conveyances, and public places of amusement – were cloaked with a public interest and engaged in quasi-public activities and that this feature distinguished them from purely private activities:

[296] Civil Rights Cases, 109 U.S. 3 (1888) (divided court). For the five cases decided under this label, with a detailed analysis of contemporary editorial commentary, *see* Charles Fairman, Reconstruction and Reunion, 1864–88 [vol. VII of the Holmes Devise History of the Supreme Court of the United States 550–88 (Macmillan 1987)]. *See also* Kevin Christopher Newsom, *Setting Incorporationism Straight: A Reinterpretation of the Slaughter-House Cases*, 109 Yale L.J. 643 (2000), which includes this historical correction:

> Although today we generally view the *Civil Rights Cases* as the fountainhead of the so-called "state action" doctrine – the principle that "[n]early all of the Constitution's self-executing, and therefore judicially enforceable, guarantees of individual rights shield individuals only from government action," not private action – that distinction actually belongs to *Cruikshank* [25 F. Cas. 707 (C.C.D. La.) 1874 (No. 14,897)]. In fact, when the Court in the *Civil Rights Cases* held that "[i]t is State action of a particular character that is prohibited" by the Fourteenth Amendment and observed that "[i]ndividual invasion of individual rights is not the subject-matter of the amendment," it noted that "[a] quite full discussion of this aspect of the amendment may be found in *United States v. Cruikshank*."

Newsom, *supra*, at 717 (footnote omitted). For an extensive analysis of *Cruikshank*, including its sequel in the Supreme Court, *see* Fairman, *supra* note 296, at 263–89.

[297] 109 U.S. at 30 (emphasis added). The Court also ruled that the legislation was not authorized by the Thirteenth Amendment, abolishing slavery and involuntary servitude. No effort was made to ground the contested law on the federal power over interstate commerce, nor did the Court pass on the impact of the legislation in the District of Columbia or other federal enclaves or territories. *See id.* at 26.

> In every material sense applicable to the practical enforcement of the Fourteenth Amendment, railroad corporations, keepers of inns, and managers of places of public amusement are agents of the state, because amenable, in respect of their public duties and functions, to public regulation.[298]

Although Justice Harlan failed to win over any of his colleagues, his line of argument foreshadowed the emergence, many years later, of the "state action" concept, under which the First and Fourteenth Amendments have been applied to enterprises that, though privately owned and operated, perform "public" functions, are sponsored by the government, or are otherwise entangled with state or federal governmental agencies. In *Marsh v. Alabama* (1946), for example, the Court reversed the criminal trespass conviction of a Jehovah's Witness for distributing religious literature on the premises of a "company town," described by the Court as follows:

> The town, a suburb of Mobile, Alabama, known as Chickasaw, is owned by the Gulf Shipbuilding Corporation. Except for that it has all the characteristics of any other American town. The property consists of residential buildings, streets, a system of sewers, a sewage disposal plant and a "business block" on which business places are situated. A deputy of the Mobile county Sheriff, paid by the company, serves as the town's policeman. Merchants and service establishments have rented the stores and business places on the business block and the United States uses one of the places as a post office from which six carriers deliver mail to the people of Chickasaw and the adjacent area.... [The residents] make use of a company-owned, paved street and sidewalk located alongside the store fronts in order to enter and leave the stores and the post office.... In short the town and its shopping district are accessible to and freely used by the public in general and there is nothing to distinguish them from any other town and shopping center except the fact that the title to the property belongs to a private corporation.[299]

Given these facts, the Court reached its conclusion with relatively little discussion:

> When we balance the Constitutional rights of owners of property against those of the people to enjoy freedom of press and religion, as we must here, we remain mindful of the fact that the latter occupy a preferred position.... In our view the circumstance that the property rights to the premises where the deprivation of liberty, here involved, took place, were held by others than the public, is not sufficient to justify the State's permitting a corporation to govern a community of citizens so as to restrict their fundamental liberties and the enforcement of such restraint by the application of a State statute. Insofar as the State has attempted to impose criminal punishment on appellant for undertaking to distribute religious literature in a company town, its action cannot stand.[300]

This "state action" concept also was employed by *Burton v. Wilmington Parking Authority* (1961), holding that the Equal Protection Clause of the Fourteenth Amendment was violated when a privately owned restaurant in a publicly financed and state-owned parking facility refused to serve an African-American because

> The State has so far insinuated itself into a position of interdependence with [the restaurant] ... that it must be recognized as a joint participant in the challenged activity

298 *Id.* at 58-9.

299 Marsh v. Alabama, 326 U.S. 501, 502–3 (1946) (divided court).

300 109 U.S. at 503; *see also* Evans v. Newton, 382 U.S. 296 (1966) (city park); Reitman v. Mulkey, 387 U.S. 369 (1967) (real property transactions).

which, on that account, cannot be considered to have been so "purely private" as to fall without the scope of the Fourteenth Amendment.[301]

However, the Court has refused to apply the "state action" concept to an electric utility company, privately owned but heavily regulated, despite its partial monopoly of the business of supplying service to an area including the city of York, Pennsylvania, or to the membership rules of a national fraternal order.[302]

At the height of the civil rights movement, efforts were made to impose the "state action" label on virtually all private action that was tolerated (or that *could be* regulated) by the state, as though "state action is a sea in which everything else floats."[303] The religion clauses of the First Amendment have played only a minor role in the development of the "state action" concept, even though a Jehovah's Witness was present at its creation.

## I. Application of the Religion Clauses of the First Amendment to the States: "Incorporation" of the Bill of Rights into the Fourteenth Amendment

### 1. *Introduction*

The Establishment and Free Exercise Clauses of the First Amendment are applied so frequently in testing the constitutionality of action by the states that it is easy to forget that the First Amendment itself explicitly prohibits only the federal Congress from enacting laws respecting the establishment of religion or prohibiting its free exercise.[304] The later expansion of religious liberty by the Fourteenth Amendment to restrict action by the states is now routinely encapsulated by the Supreme Court in the briefest of phrases; in *Murdock v. Pennsylvania* (1943), for example, the Court merely referred to "[t]he First Amendment, which the Fourteenth makes applicable to the states,"[305] deeming it unnecessary to offer any explanation of the constitutional nexus between the two amendments or to cite any of the Court's earlier decisions. Three years earlier, in *Cantwell v. Connecticut* (1940), "in a slightly more expansive mood, the Court had explained its

301 Burton v. Wilmington Parking Auth., 365 U.S. 715, 725 (1961) (divided court); *see also* Am. Mfrs. Mut. Ins. Co. v. Sullivan, 526 U.S. 40 (1999) (divided court) (*Wilmington* "refined" by later cases to exclude from "joint participation" category privately owned enterprises providing services that the state would not provide, even if extensively regulated).

302 *See* Jackson v. Metropolitan Edison Co., 419 U.S. 345 (1974); Moose Lodge v. Irvis, 407 U.S. 163 (1972) ("nothing approaching the symbolic relationship between lessor and lessee that was present in *Burton*). For a shopping center, *see* Hudgens v. NLRB, 424 U.S. 507 (1976) [overruling Amalgamated Food Employees Union v. Logan Valley Plaza, 391 U.S. 308 (1968)].

303 C. Edwin Baker, *Private Power, the Press, and the Constitution*, 10 CONST. COMM. 421, 422 (1993). The concept, however, is somewhat quiescent now in the civil rights area because of the breadth of Civil Rights Act of 1964 (and some parallel state laws); and breadth of federal enforcement power under the Thirteenth Amendment as construed in Jones v. Meyer, 392 U.S. 409 (1968). Charles L. Black, Jr., *The Supreme Court, 1966 Term—Foreword: "State Action," Equal Protection, and California's Proposition 14*, 81 HARV. L. REV. 69, 95 (1967) (describing the field of state action as a "conceptual disaster area").

304 *See* U.S. CONST. amend. I ("Congress shall make no law respecting an establishment of religion, or prohibiting the free exercise thereof.").

305 Murdock v. Pennsylvania, 319 U.S. 105, 108 (1943) (divided court) (city licensing ordinance held unconstitutional as applied to Jehovah's Witnesses engaged in door-to-door distribution and sale of evangelical pamphlets).

invalidation of a state law that convicted several Jehovah's Witnesses for violating a state statute prohibiting the public solicitation of funds unless the appeal was certified as legitimate by a state official" by stating

> We hold that the statute, as construed and applied to the applicants, deprives them of their liberty without due process of law in contravention of the Fourteenth Amendment. The fundamental concept of liberty embodied in that Amendment embraces the liberties guaranteed by the First Amendment. The First Amendment declares that Congress shall make no law respecting an establishment of religion or prohibiting the free exercise thereof. The Fourteenth Amendment has rendered the legislatures of the states as incompetent as Congress to enact such laws.[306]

As will be seen, this process of "incorporating" the religion clauses of the First Amendment (and most of the other provisions of the Bill of Rights) into the Fourteenth Amendment and thereby subjecting the states as well as the federal government to these constitutional guarantees was protracted and sporadic, and it has not yet come to its conclusion.

The introductory words of the First Amendment – "Congress shall make no law" – plainly do not limit action by the state legislatures, and this conclusion is buttressed as to the amendment's religion provisions by the fact that, as related earlier in this work, Madison's so-called lost amendment, which would have imposed parallel restrictions on the states, died in the First Federal Congress when it was drafting what became the First Amendment.[307] In explicitly designating Congress as its target, the First Amendment differed from most of its companions in the Bill of Rights, which were not so clearly focused; the Second Amendment, for example, states vaguely that "the right of the people to keep and bear arms shall not be infringed, and the Fifth Amendment provides that "property shall [not] be taken for public use without just compensation." These provisions, neither of which specifies whom it restricts, open the door to claims that they limit the states as well as the federal government, unlike the First Amendment's explicit specification of Congress as the target of its prohibitions.

An important early commentator deduced from this difference in constitutional language that the less explicit provisions of the Bill of Rights "are to be more generally construed, and considered as applying to the state legislatures as well as that of the Union."[308] This expansive interpretation was rejected, however, in 1833, when the Supreme Court ruled in *Barron v. Baltimore*, per Chief Justice Marshall, that the Fifth Amendment's Takings Clause (and, by implication, the rest of the vaguely aimed provisions of the Bill of Rights) restricted only the federal government:

> The Constitution was ordained and established by the people of the United States for themselves, for their own government, and not for the government of the individual States. Each State established a constitution for itself, and in that constitution provided such limitations and restrictions on the powers of its particular government as its judgment dictated. The people of the United States framed such a government for the United States as they supposed best adapted to their situation, and best calculated to promote their interests. The powers they conferred on this government were to be

306 Cantwell v. Connecticut, 310 U.S. 296, 303 (1940).

307 For the "lost amendment," *see supra* note 223 and accompanying text.

308 William Rawle, A View of the Constitution of the United States of America (2d ed., H. C. Carey 1829).

exercised by itself; and the limitations on power, if expressed in general terms, are naturally, and, we think, necessarily applicable to the government created by the instrument. They are limitations of power granted in the instrument itself; not of distinct governments, framed by different persons and for different purposes.

If these propositions be correct, the fifth amendment must be understood as restraining the power of the general government, not as applicable to the States.[309]

So the matter rested until the Fourteenth Amendment was drafted and ratified. Unlike the Bill of Rights, this amendment explicitly and deliberately imposed its limitations on the states, using language that might have been construed to adopt or absorb – "incorporate," in today's legal parlance – some or all of the limitations that were imposed on the federal government by the Bill of Rights:

> No State shall make or enforce any law which shall abridge the privileges or immunities of citizens of the United States; nor shall any State deprive any person of life, liberty, or property, without due process of law; nor deny to any person within its jurisdiction the equal protection of the laws.

Despite the breadth of this language, however, it took some time to eliminate the Supreme Court's pre-1868 double standard, under which the federal government was subject to restrictions that did not restrict the states unless their own constitutions imposed analogous limits. Thus the leading commentator on church-state relations asserted in 1902 that

> [I]f one of the states, even today, should change its own constitution and set up a State-Church, with the peculiar perquisites and power of an establishment, and should put such Church upon the public treasury for support, the general government has no power to prevent it.[310]

In the *Slaughter-House Cases* (1873), the first case to allude to what has come to be called the "Incorporation Doctrine," the Supreme Court ruled that the Privileges or Immunities Clause of the Fourteenth Amendment protected only the rights of national citizenship and not those of state citizenship.[311] Although this was a plausible reading of an ambiguous provision, it reduced the Privileges or Immunities Clause to "a vain and idle enactment," to quote Justice Field's dissent in the 1873 *Slaughter-House Cases*, because in the majority's view, the privileges and immunities of *state* citizenship – not protected by the Fourteenth Amendment – are those "which are fundamental, which belong of right to the citizens of all free governments, and which have at all times been enjoyed by citizens of the several states which compose this Union, from the time of their becoming free, independent and sovereign ... [including] the right to acquire and possess property of every kind, and to pursue and obtain happiness and safety, subject,

309 Barron v. Baltimore, 32 U.S. (7 Pet.) 243, 243–50 (1833). This case took on a special force given that its states-rights rationale emanated from the pen of the "Great Federalist" himself. For reasons why Chief Justice Marshall might have rejected a rationale that would have made *Barron v. Baltimore* "the capstone of [the Marshall Court's] assault on state sovereignty," *see* Edward R. White, The Marshall Court and Cultural Change, 1815–35 at 589–93 (Macmillan 1988). *See also* United States v. Cruikshank, 92 U.S. (2 Otto) 542, 591 (1876) ("[I]t is now too late to question the correctness" of the *Barton* case and others of like import).

310 Cobb, *supra* note 2, at 510.

311 Slaughter House Cases, 83 U.S. (16 Wall.) 36 (1873); for an exhaustive narrative account of this litigation, *see* Fairman, *supra* note 296, at 1320–63 ; *see also* Crosskey, II Politics and the Constitution 1119–30 (Univ. of Chicago Press 1953).

nevertheless to such restraints as the government may prescribe for the general good of the whole."[312] On this theory, state rather than national citizenship is the source of virtually all of a citizen's rights to participate in public affairs; thus the *Slaughter-House* plaintiff's right to pursue the business of slaughtering livestock was a privilege of state rather than national citizenship, and therefore, it was not protected by the Fourteenth Amendment against a Louisiana-granted monopoly to a rival group of wholesale butchers.

Having asserted in the majority opinion in the *Slaughter-House Cases* that the rights of *state* citizenship "embrace nearly every civil right for the establishment and protection of which organized government is established,"[313] Justice Miller was accused of leaving little that can be attributed to national citizenship, qualifying for protection by the Fourteenth Amendment against invasion by the states. Responding to this allegation, Justice Miller observed that a definition of the rights of national citizenship could be deferred until the Court was required by a specific case to provide one, but he went on to offer examples, such as the citizen's right of free access to the District of Columbia and the country's seaports; the right to federal protection for life, liberty, and property when on the high seas or in a foreign country; and the rights to travel on the country's navigable waters, to assemble and petition the government for a redress of grievances, to the protection afforded by the writ of habeas corpus, to become a citizen of any state on establishing residence therein, and to exercise the rights granted by the Thirteenth and Fifteenth Amendments.[314] More generally, Justice Miller pointed out that the Privileges or Immunities Clause forbids a state's impairment of rights that "owe their existence to the Federal Government, its National character, its Constitution, or its laws."[315] Except for the rights created by the Thirteenth and Fifteenth Amendments, however, the rights mentioned by Justice Miller were seemingly already protected against state invasion by the Supremacy Clause of the Constitution and hence needed no buttress from the Fourteenth Amendment.

### 2. *Incorporation via the Due Process Clause of the Fourteenth Amendment*

In 1925, the Incorporation Doctrine received a powerful boost – but not its current name – when the Supreme Court, in *Gitlow v. New York*, upheld the constitutionality of a New York law punishing "criminal anarchy," stating that "[f]or present purposes we may and do assume that freedom of speech and of the press – which are protected by the First Amendment from abridgement by Congress – are among the fundamental personal rights and 'liberties' protected by the due process clause of the Fourteenth Amendment from impairment by the States."[316] Although in form this was only an acceptance

312 83 U.S. at 96, quoting and adopting the language of Corfield v. Coryell, 6 F. Cas. 546 (C.C.E.D. Pa. 1823) (No. 3,230). For a penetrating autopsy of the *Slaughter-House Cases*, arguing for resuscitation of the Privileges or Immunities Clause; *see* Kevin Christopher Newsom, *Setting Incorporationism Straight: A Reinterpretation of the Slaughter-House Cases*, 109 YALE L.J., 643 (2000); for another trenchant analysis of *Slaughter-House*, *see* DAVID P. CURRIE, THE CONSTITUTION IN THE SUPREME COURT: THE FIRST HUNDRED YEARS, 1789–1888 at 342–50 (Univ. of Chicago Press 1985).

313 Slaughter-House Cases, 83 U.S. (16 Wall.) 36 (1873); for analysis of these "uniquely federal" rights of state citizenship, *see* Newsom, *supra* note 312, at 675–83.

314 For a later list of the protected privileges and immunities of national citizenship, *see* Twining v. New Jersey, 211 U.S. 78, 97 (1908), *overruled on other grounds by* Malloy v. Hogan, 378 U.S. 1 (1964).

315 83 U.S. at 79.

316 Gitlow v. New York, 268 U.S. 652, 666 (1925) (divided court).

*arguendo* that the Fourteenth Amendment incorporated the Free Speech and Free Press Clauses of the First Amendment, its tentative and diffident tone was belied by the fact that the Court went on in *Gitlow* to brush aside "the incidental statement" in an opinion – announced only three years earlier – that "the Fourteenth Amendment imposes no restrictions on the States concerning freedom of speech,"[317] and the Court observed flatly that the question presented by *Gitlow* is "whether the [New York] statute, as construed and applied in this case by the State courts, deprived the defendant of his liberty of expression in violation of the due process clause of the Fourteenth Amendment."[318] Although the Court did not say so in *Gitlow*, it could have cited a string of cases in which it had employed the Due Process Clause of the Fourteenth Amendment to invalidate legislation by the states on the ground that the disputed law impaired freedom of contract. In general, the "rights" giving rise to these "substantive" due process cases (so-called because they went beyond the guarantee of "procedural fairness" in the application of state laws and regulations) were not explicitly attributed to the Bill of Rights but rather to some vaguely defined rights of citizens and their corporations to practice their occupations, engage in business, and hold property free of "unreasonable" or "arbitrary" rules and regulations by either the federal or state government.[319]

Even if the *Gitlow* Court truly desired to hold in abeyance the question whether the Free Speech and Free Press Clauses of the First Amendment were imposed on the states by the Fourteenth Amendment, Justice Holmes, who was joined by Justice Brandeis, announced in a brief dissent that

> [t]he general principle of free speech, it seems to me, must be taken to be included in the Fourteenth Amendment, in view of the scope that has been given to the word "liberty" as there used, although perhaps it may be accepted with a somewhat larger latitude of interpretation than is allowed to Congress by the sweeping language that governs or ought to govern the laws of the United States.[320]

Later decisions routinely cited *Gitlow* as though it incorporated the Free Speech and Free Press Clauses of the First Amendment into the Due Process Clause of the Fourteenth Amendment, not as merely an *arguendo* assumption to that effect, but the Court did not follow up the suggestion floated by Justice Holmes in his *Gitlow* dissent that the states might be accorded by the Fourteenth Amendment "a somewhat greater latitude" than is allowed by the First Amendment to Congress.

### 3. *The Incorporation Doctrine's Loose Ends*

The still unsettled issues of the Incorporation Doctrine – the portion of the Fourteenth Amendment on which incorporation rests and whether incorporation was "selective" or total – arise primarily in the area of criminal law, where the battles have been both contentious and confused. By contrast, incorporation of the First Amendment's religion clauses into the Fourteenth Amendment has been seemingly complete and free of controversy. Indeed, the process began in what might be termed the "preincorporation era,"

[317] Prudential Ins. Co. v. Check, 259 U.S. 520, 543 (1922).
[318] 268 U.S. at 664.
[319] *See, e.g.*, Prudential Ins. Co., 259 U.S. 530–43.
[320] 268 U.S. at 672.

when the Supreme Court held in *Meyer v. Nebraska* (1923) that the "liberty" protected by the Due Process Clause of the Fourteenth Amendment against state impairment "denotes not merely freedom from bodily restraint but also the right of the individual ... to worship God according to the dictates of his own conscience and generally to enjoy those privileges long recognized at common law as essential to the orderly pursuit of happiness by free men."[321] The Court evidently regarded this guarantee – announced "[w]ithout doubt" – as so well-settled that no historical or textual analysis or other argument was adduced – only a string of federal and state decisions, none of them explicitly passing on the validity of an alleged state denial of the freedom of religious worship.[322]

The court's opinion in the *Meyer* case did not mention the religion clauses of the First Amendment, and it might be distinguished from the Court's later "incorporation" cases because its reliance on the Fourteenth Amendment's Due Process Clause, unaided by the specific guarantees of the First Amendment, might be read to imply that the latter's explicit Free Exercise Clause was superfluous. Moreover, *Meyer* also left open the possibility (never actually explored by the case law) that the boundaries of the religious "liberty" protected against impairment by the states by the Fourteenth Amendment's Due Process Clause are either narrower or broader than the religious liberty guaranteed against federal interference by the Free Exercise Clause of the First Amendment.

This possibility that freedom of religious worship might rest on two constitutional foundations – as an essential element of "liberty" protected by the Due Process Clause of the Fourteenth Amendment and, separately, as a feature of the Free Exercise Clause, made applicable to the states by the same Due Process Clause (or possibly by a resuscitated Privileges or Immunities Clause)[323] – each with its own boundaries – has never emerged from the realm of speculation. Instead, the Incorporation Doctrine has monopolized the field, and alleged state interferences with religious worship have been analyzed by the Supreme Court as Free Exercise Clause issues. The implicit rejection of a bifurcated constitutional foundation for religious liberty can be dated from *Cantwell v. Connecticut* (1940), which invalidated the conviction of three Jehovah's Witnesses (a father and his two sons) for distributing religious literature in the streets of New Haven and soliciting contributions, in violation of a state law requiring solicitors of such funds to obtain a certificate of "approval" from a state official.[324] Although the Court (which was unanimous in *Cantrell*) did not use the term "incorporation," it embodied the substance of that doctrine in its opinion:

> We hold that the [Connecticut] statute, as construed and applied to the appellants, deprives them of their liberty without due process of law in contravention of the Fourteenth Amendment. The fundamental concept of liberty embodied in that amendment embraces the liberties guaranteed by the First Amendment. The First Amendment declares that Congress shall make no law respecting an establishment of religion or prohibiting the free exercise thereof. The Fourteenth Amendment has rendered the legislatures of the states as incompetent as Congress to enact such laws.[325]

321 Meyer v. Nebraska, 262 U.S. 390, 399 (1923) (Justices Holmes and Sutherland dissenting, without opinion) (invalidating Nebraska law prohibiting the teaching of any subject in elementary schools, whether public or private, in any language other than English).

322 *See id.*

323 *See supra* Section I.1 (discussing the Privileges or Immunities Clause).

324 Cantwell v. Connecticut, 310 U.S. 296 (1940).

325 *Id.* at 303.

Not surprisingly, *Cantwell* was later described as having "completed in 1940 the process of absorption of the Free Exercise Clause."[326]

Lest this reference to the Free Exercise Clause be thought to imply doubt about whether the Establishment Clause also was "absorbed" by the Fourteenth Amendment, two slightly later cases (*Murdock* and *Everson*) explicitly brought both religion clauses within the ambit of the Fourteenth Amendment. Thus, in *Murdock v. Pennsylvania* (1943), invalidating a Pennsylvania law requiring a license for the sale of merchandise of any kind in the public streets, as applied to Jehovah's Witnesses who were offering religious books for sale, the Court stated flatly that "[t]he First Amendment, which the Fourteenth makes applicable to the states, declares that 'Congress shall make no law respecting an establishment of religion, or prohibiting the free exercise thereof; or abridging the freedom of speech, or of the press.'"[327]

Because *Cantwell* and *Murdock* could have been grounded on the First Amendment's Freedom of Speech Clause rather than on its Free Exercise Clause, some commentators award primacy in time in adopting the Incorporation Doctrine to *Everson v. Board of Education* (1947), which upheld a New Jersey ordinance under which the parents of pupils attending religious schools were reimbursed for the cost of bus transportation incurred to transport their children to school.[328] Like *Murdock*, *Everson* does not argue the issue of incorporation; it simply cites *Murdock* as the source of the Court's authority to pass on the constitutionality of the disputed law:

> The New Jersey statute is challenged as a "law respecting an establishment of religion." The First Amendment, as made applicable to the states by the Fourteenth, *Murdock v. Commonwealth of Pennsylvania* ... commands that a state "shall make no law respecting an establishment of religion, or prohibiting the free exercise thereof."[329]

## J. Meaning of Terms Used in the First Amendment

### 1. *"Establishment" of Religion*

The most notable example of the term "establishment" when the First Amendment was drafted and ratified and the meaning that almost certainly first came to mind when the term was used by the Framers of the amendment was the Church of England. It was the established church in the principal southern states and the target of reform in the New England states. Other churches could be, and in fact were, established by most of the states, but the criteria that "established" these churches in colonial and early statehood days derived from the features of the Church of England.[330] Thus a "local" church came

326 Sch. Dist. of Abington Twp. v. Schempp, 374 U.S. 203, 253–4 (1963).

327 Murdock v. Pennsylvania, 319 U.S. 105, 108 (1943). Although Justices Reed, Frankfurter, and Jackson filed vigorous dissents in *Murdock*, they did not contest the Court's tacit acceptance of incorporation – nor did Frankfurter argue that the "selective" version of the incorporation doctrine espoused by him in earlier cases would omit the religion clauses. *See id.* at 166–82 (Jackson, J., dissenting, joined by Frankfurter, J.); *id.* at 117–34 (Reed, J., joined by Roberts, Frankfurter, and Jackson, JJ.); *id.* at 134–40 (Frankfurter, J., dissenting, joined by Jackson, J.).

328 Everson v. Bd. of Educ., 330 U.S. 1 (1947) (divided court).

329 *Id.* at 8.

330 For a compendium of the characteristics of "established" churches in colonial days, *see* Chester J. Antieau, Arthur T. Downey & Edward C. Roberts, Freedom from Federal Establishment: Formation and Early History of the First Amendment Religion Clauses (Bruce 1964):

to be described as "established" – whether that term was used in a neutral, benign, or pejorative sense – if it was vested by the state with characteristics that marked the Church of England – not necessarily all these characteristics but a critical mass of them.

The inherent and dominating features of the Church of England were its official recognition by English law, the King's right to nominate its bishops, Parliament's power to prescribe its doctrines and rites (illustrated by the *Thirty-Nine Articles of Religion* and the *Book of Common Prayer*), and its financial support by tithes paid by English landowners.[331] As noted earlier in this work, in 1789, the Church of England was still established in several southern states, and it was a rival to the Congregational churches of New England.

Although the locally established churches of the various states differed from the Church of England in many details, all shared with it one fundamental characteristic: a state-granted preference over other churches and religions.[332] No colony or state granted a preference to any non-Christian religion, and some were even more exclusionary, denying to Roman Catholicism and a variety of marginal Christian denominations, such as the Quakers and Mennonites, the preferences accorded to other Christian denominations. As noted by Leonard Levy, author of an influential (but controversial) work on establishmentarianism, "In no state or colony ... was there ever an establishment of religion that included every religion without exception. In three of the seven multiple establishments existing in 1791, the establishment included only Protestant churches, and in the other four, all Christian churches."[333]

1. A state church officially recognized and protected by the sovereign;
2. A state church whose members along were eligible to vote, to hold public office, and to practice a profession;
3. A state church which compelled religious orthodoxy under penalty of fine and imprisonment;
4. A state church willing to expel dissenters from the commonwealth;
5. A state church financed by taxes upon all members of the community;
6. A state church which alone could freely hold public worship and evangelize;
7. A state church which alone could perform valid marriages, burials, etc.

*Id.* at 1. It is not clear whether the authors believe that all these features are essential or, if not, which or how many are needed to brand a church as "established." Presumably the term "state church" is used in a geographic sense; if it is a term connoting state creation or sponsorship, it is circular in import: of course, a "state" church is "established."

331 *Church of England*, *in* OXFORD COMPANION TO LAW 217 (David M. Walker ed., Oxford Univ. Press 1980).

332 In McGowan v. Maryland, 366 U.S. 420 (1961), Justice Frankfurter, writing separately, observed that "[i]n view of the competition among religious creeds, whatever 'establishes' one sect disadvantages another, and vice versa." *Id.* at 463. It is worth noting that even when the term "establishment" is used in today's social or political commentary, outside the church-state context, for example, a preference or exclusion is inherent in the term, as in such phrases as "the foreign policy establishment" or the "Protestant Establishment." *See, e.g.*, E. DIGBY BALTZELL, THE PROTESTANT ESTABLISHMENT: ARISTOCRACY AND CASTE IN AMERICA (Vintage Books 1964).

333 LEONARD W. LEVY, ORIGINS OF THE BILL OF RIGHTS 101 (Yale Univ. Press 1999). Given these facts of life, it is surprising to find that Levy earlier asserted in 1986 that after the American Revolution, "[N]ot one state maintained a single or preferential establishment of religion." LEVY, *supra* note 35, at xvi. It is possible that the 1999 extract from Levy quoted in the text is a corrective revision of his 1986 assertion, but more likely it reflects his idiosyncratic theory that establishments confined to Protestant Christianity can be properly described as "nonpreferential." For this claim, *see infra* Section J.2. This survey shows that none of the Framers (of the First Amendment) had a working model of nonpreferential establishment on which to draw. Every time a nonpreferential establishment had been proposed, it had been

If a litmus test is sought to identify "establishment" status, a governmental grant of preferences to a particular religion or church (or a group of religions or churches) that was withheld from other religions or churches is always a sufficient, and almost always a necessary, condition. In his magisterial three-volume work, *Church and State in the United States*, Anson Phelps Stokes endorses the definition of "establishment" employed by the classic ninth edition of the *Encyclopedia Britannica*, observing that the term first appears in 1731:

> [Establishment] implies the existence of some definite and distinctive relation between the state and a religious society (or conceivably more than one) other than that which is shared in by other societies of the same general character.[334]

The only substitute for such a preference is the legislative endorsement of the doctrine of the established religion or church, illustrated in the case of the Church of England by Parliament's ratification of its *Book of Common Prayer*.[335] There may have been instances of this practice in colonial establishments,[336] but it was not a characteristic of the religious establishments of the states when the Bill of Rights was being drafted by the First Federal Congress. During the evolution of the Establishment Clause, however, the Senate voted to provide that "Congress shall make no law establishing articles of faith, or a mode of worship," but this language was rejected by the House as well as by the conference committee appointed to resolve the differences between the two houses.[337]

The virtually universal use of the term "establishment" to mean a religion or church favored by the government with preferences that are not accorded to other religions or churches has continued to the present day. Thus the *Encyclopedia Britannica* defines "established church" as follows:

> [A] church recognized by law as the official church of a state or nation and supported by civil authority. Though not strictly created by a legal contract, the legal establishment is more like a contractual entity than like anything else and, therefore, ordinarily cannot be varied or repudiated by only one party to it. The church is not free to make changes in such things as doctrine, order, or worship without the consent of the state. In accepting such obligations, the church usually, though not always, receives financial support and other special privileges.
>
> Among numerous examples of established churches or state religions are the following: Anglicanism in England, Lutheranism in the Scandinavian countries, Roman Catholicism in Italy and Spain, Judaism in Israel, Islam in Saudi Arabia and Egypt, Buddhism in Thailand and Sikkim, and Shinto in Japan before World War II. In pluralistic societies and under modern forms of government, religious establishment has tended, on the whole, to diminish in importance.[338]

rejected. The allegedly nonpreferential systems in New England did not work well and demonstrably caused bitter religious strife. *See also* Laycock, *supra* note 204, at 902; Laycock also argues that "[a]t the very least, the framing of a federal rule [to govern church-state relations] required a choice among the diverse practices in the states." *Id.* at 895.

334 1 Stokes, *supra* note 2, at 29.

335 *See* McConnell, *supra* note 19, at 2112-13.

336 For a proposal in the Continental Congress to publish a "National Bible," *see* Derek H. Davis, Religion and the Continental Congress 1774-1789: Contributions to Original Intent 145–8 (Oxford Univ. Press 2000).

337 *See supra* Section E.2.e.

338 *Encyclopædia Britannica Online*, *at* http://www.britannica.com/EBchecked/topic/193250/established-church.

The principal denominational encyclopedias are in agreement with this secular reference work. Thus the *Catholic Encyclopedia* states

> The union of Church and State setting up a definite and distinctive relation between the two is frequently expressed in English by use of the word "establishment," applied to such union in both Catholic and Protestant States, in spite of the fundamental differences of principle which characterize them. "The Establishment" or "the Established Church" is often used as a distinctive name for the ecclesiastical system established by law in Scotland, in Ireland (until 1869), but especially in England.[339]

Innumerable standard reference works agree with the foregoing definitions.[340]

## 2. *"Nonpreferential," "Multiple," and "Universal" Establishments*

This overwhelming body of authority defining the term "establishment" to mean an official status or a governmental grant of preferences or privileges to one or more religions or churches that are not enjoyed by their religious rivals is rejected by a recent constitutional theorist. In recent claims that the Establishment Clause bars not only "denominational preferences" – legal measures that favor one religious denomination or sect over another – but also laws that aid all religions impartially, a few commentators have argued that the generation that enacted the Establishment Clause was familiar with what might be called "universal establishments" (impartial [or "nonpreferential"] legislative sponsorship of all religions) and that this practice was forbidden for the future by the Establishment Clause.[341] A fundamental, even fatal, flaw in this concept of "universal

339 V The Catholic Encyclopedia: An International Work of Reference on the Constitution, Doctrine, Discipline, and History of the Catholic Church 548 (Charles G. Herbermann et al. eds., Robert Appleton Co. 1909).

340 *See* III Oxford English Dictionary (2d ed. 1989) ("the church as by law established in any country, as the public or state-recognized form of religion"); Collins English Dictionary 528 (5th ed. 2000) (a "church that is officially recognized as a national institution"); American Heritage Dictionary of the English Language (4th ed. 2000) (a "church that a government officially recognizes as a national institution and to which it accords support"); Random House Dictionary of the English Language 663 (2d ed. 1987) (a "church that is recognized by law, and sometimes financially supported, as the official church of a nation"); Abington Dictionary of Living Religions 240 (Keith Crim ed., 1981) ("any church recognized by civil law as the official religion of a country or religion"); Oxford Dictionary of World Religions 319 (1997) ("any church recognized by state law as the official religion of a country"); Webster's Third New International Dictionary 778 (3d ed. 1986) ("a church that is recognized by law as the official church of a nation, that is supported by civil authority, and that receives in most instances financial support from the government through some system of taxation"); Concise Dictionary of American History 344 (1983) ("churches supported by tax funds or by direct grants of aid"); Dictionary of Christianity in America 401 (2d ed. 1989) ("churches enjoying privileged status").

341 For the early history of "multiple establishments," *viz.*, establishments embracing all Protestant denominations (but excluding Roman Catholicism), *see* Robert B.C. Howell, The Early Baptists of Virginia 165–6 (Am. Baptist Hist. Soc'y Press 1857): "Meantime a new theory of a *State Religious Establishment* was devised, and began, in private circles, to be warmly discussed. This theory had its origin with the Presbyterians, and was in their subsequent memorials tenaciously and elaborately advocated. It proposed, not the abrogation of the State Religious Establishment, the measure demanded by the Baptists, but that the State, instead of selecting one denomination, as the Episcopal, and establishing that as the religion of the State, and giving to that alone its support, should establish all the denominations, Presbyterians, Methodists, and Baptists, as well as the Episcopalians, and make them all equally and alike *the religion of the State*, and to be *supported by the State*.... Of this plan of reconciling and harmonizing all parties,

establishments" is that when the First Amendment was drafted and ratified, no existing establishment – and, so far as the authors can ascertain, no proposed establishment – included Judaism. The result of this exclusion is that all establishments known to the First Amendment's draftsmen and ratifiers embodied a basic preference by favoring some or all Christian denominations but not non-Christian faiths.[342] Twentieth-century scholars sometimes refer to a state preference for some or all Christian denominations as a "multiple establishment," distinguishing this phenomenon from the New England Puritan establishments, which favored only the Congregational church, and from the Southern preferences for the Anglican church, but such a "multiple establishment" should not be confused with an arrangement that grants nonexclusive aid to religions of every species (a "universal establishment"). Despite a tendency in some discussions to treat multiple establishments – which actually existed – as though they were what might be termed "universal establishments" – which existed nowhere except in twentieth-century tendentious arguments – the two notions should be sharply distinguished.[343]

To obliterate this inconvenient fact of life, advocates of "universal establishmentarism" argue that the eighteenth-century American establishments embraced what was, for practical purposes, the entire population. Thus Leonard Levy asserts

> In each of the six states where multiple establishments existed [in 1789] the establishment included the churches of every denomination and sect with a sufficient number of adherents to form a church. There were a few isolated towns or counties in each of the states where the letter of the law was not followed, particularly where a congregation of a sect such as the Quakers conscientiously opposed compulsory tax support of even their own church, but such cases were comparatively rare. In general, where Protestantism was established, it was synonymous with religion; there were either no Jews and Catholics or too few of them to make a difference; and where Christianity was established, as in Maryland which had many Catholics, Jews were scarcely known.... The uniqueness of the American experience justifies defining an establishment of religion as any support of religion by government, whether the support be to religion in general, to all churches, some churches, or one church.[344]

This attempt to explain the denial to Roman Catholics of the privileges accorded by five of the six states to Protestants because there were so few local Romanists probably has reversed cause and effect. It is more likely that few Catholics chose to reside in colonies

Patrick Henry was the ablest and most eloquent advocate. It had the merit of British precedent, since Episcopalianism in England, and Presbyterianism in Scotland, were alike the Established Religion of the Empire."

342 For a recognition of this fact by Levy, the protagonist of "nonpreferential establishments," *see* LEVY, *supra* note 333, at 101.

343 *See, e.g.*, this observation in CURRY, *supra* note 70, at 210: The New England States (Rhode Island excepted) continued to provide public support for religion, and scholars commonly refer to this practice as a "multiple establishment," i.e., a system by which all denominations received state support. To avoid confusion, this statement needs to be revised to read "all Christian denominations." Curry, in fact, goes on to state accurately

> The dominant image of establishment Americans carried with them from the colonial period on was that of an exclusive government preference for one religion.

344 *See also* Levy's assertion that "[i]ndeed, at the time of the framing of the Bill of Rights all state establishments which still existed in America were *multiple* establishments of *all* churches, something unknown in European experience" (emphasis in original). LEONARD W. LEVY, JUDGMENTS: ESSAYS ON AMERICAN CONSTITUTIONAL HISTORY 191 (Quadrangle Books 1972).

excluding their church from the privileges of the local establishment than that the privileges were denied because the local Catholics were few in number. Moreover, today's advocates of Levy's dubious causal claim may have been seduced by the religious tolerance of contemporary national life into projecting backward the notion that differences between Roman Catholicism and Protestantism are so trivial that no one favoring an established church would have insisted on a distinction among Christian denominations.

The notion that the state establishments known to the Framers of the First Amendment were universal because non-Christians were not thought numerous enough to constitute a distinct religious grouping implicitly assumes that given more Jewish residents, their religion would have been granted the privileges of establishment.[345] This claim is absurd because it presupposes that Judaism's denial of the divinity of Jesus and the authority of the New Testament would not have been a barrier in the eighteenth century to the legislative establishment of Judaism. Indeed, if there ever was a "high and impregnable" wall of separation[346] in American church-state relations, it was the boundary between Christianity and Judaism in the era when the First Amendment was adopted.[347] The widespread tolerance of Judaism was one thing; leaping beyond that laudable step to vesting Judaism with the preferences accorded Christianity would have been something fundamentally different. If the religious insiders of colonial days had wanted to take the breathtaking leap (which had not merely been avoided but more likely not even contemplated in Western Europe) of bringing Judaism into the religious establishment, they would almost certainly have done it explicitly rather than hiding it with language that was not interpreted to equate Judaism and Christianity in one big established church for more than two centuries, to be discovered at long last not by theologians or historians of religion but by a legal commentator who disclosed his findings in legal publications after it could have had any practical consequences in the religious world.

Moreover, if they had openly declared that they were prepared to admit Judaism (and Islam?) to the inner circle of established religions, they undoubtedly would have been attacked in sermons and the popular press as enemies of the revealed truth.[348] The theological debates of the eighteenth century were tumultuous, but Levy cites no evidence that anyone thought that the Christian establishments of the day would have been willing to open its doors to non-Christians.

### 3. *Judaism as a "Nonpreferred" or "Excluded" Religion*

The assertion that the Jews were too small a flock in the America of 1789 to figure as a distinct religious group disregards the incontrovertible fact that they were far more

[345] The usual count is 2,500 to 3,000, but it is often unclear whether the estimate relates to the number of families or of individuals. For estimates, *see* the compilation of "population data" – more accurately described as, at best, a compodium of educated guesses – in JACOB RADER MARCUS, TO COUNT A PEOPLE: AMERICAN JEWISH POPULATION DATA, 1585–1984 (Univ. Press of Am. 1990); *see also* ATLAS OF EARLY AMERICAN HISTORY: THE REVOLUTIONARY ERA 1760–1790 (Lester J. Cappon ed., Princeton Univ. Press 1976).

[346] Everson v. Bd. of Educ., 330 U.S. 1, 18 (1947).

[347] This is not to say that a Christian reference might not sometimes be properly construed to include non-Christians. *See, e.g.*, Internal Revenue Code, § 170, for reference to "ministers of the gospel," construed to include rabbis and probably similarly extended to other religions. *See* Chapter 10.C.2.c.

[348] *See* text accompanying note 66 (discussing relative tolerance of dissent between Virginia and Massachusetts establishments).

visible than their numbers would suggest.[349] First and foremost, the notion that Jews did not appear on the public radar screen is refuted by the many statutes, ordinances, and rules that identified them as a distinct group either to impose burdens or to bestow benefits[350]; these rules were promulgated for practical purposes, not to embrace an unknown demographic group. Second, though some Jews were unobtrusive itinerant peddlers, most were city dwellers in such communities as Newport, New York, Philadelphia,[351] Richmond, Charleston, and Savannah, where their activities in finance, commerce, and international trade routinely brought them to the center of the economic stage. Indeed, in Revolutionary America, Jews may well have been the most cosmopolitan of any American demographic group regardless of size.

The importance of eighteenth-century American Jews in finance is documented by none other than James Madison, who recorded in 1783 that "I have for some time been a pensioner on the favor of Haym Salomon,"[352] and a later government report asserted that Salomon "supported from his private means many of the principal men of the Revolution, who otherwise, as stated by themselves, could not have attended to their public duties, among whom are mentioned Jefferson, Madison, Lee, von Steuben, Mifflin, St. Clair, Mercer, Blond, Jones, Monroe, Wilson and others."[353] Salomon also aided Robert Morris, often recognized as the principal financier of the American Revolution, in his official activities.[354] The prominence of American Jewish merchants

349 *See generally* the admirably comprehensive three-volume work JACOB R. MARCUS, 3 THE COLONIAL AMERICAN JEW 1345ff (Wayne State Univ. Press 1970) (without bibliography); *see also* the same author's two-volume work EARLY AMERICAN JEWRY (Jewish Publ. Soc'y 1951–53) (organized colony by colony); ELI FABER, A TIME FOR PLANTING: THE FIRST MIGRATION, 1654–1820 (Johns Hopkins Univ. Press 1992); LEON HUHNER, JEWS IN AMERICA IN COLONIAL AND REVOLUTIONARY TIMES (Gertz Bros. 1959); LEON HUHNER, JEWS IN THE LEGAL AND MEDICAL PROFESSIONS IN AMERICA PRIOR TO 1800 at 147–65 (Am. Jewish Hist. Soc'y 1914); SAMUEL BROCHES, JEWS IN NEW ENGLAND (Bloch Publishing 1942); CHARLES P. DALY, THE SETTLEMENT OF THE JEWS IN NORTH AMERICA (Philip Cowen 1893); Leo Hershkowitz, *Original Inventories of Early New York Jews*, 90 AM. JEWISH HIST. 237 (first installment of massive work in progress). Some of the articles cited in this section are reprinted in facsimile by AMERICAN JEWISH HISTORY (Jeffrey S. Gurock ed., Rutledge 1998), vol. I of an eight-volume series.

350 *See* STANLEY F. CHAYET, THE POLITICAL RIGHTS OF THE JEWS IN THE UNITED STATES, 1776–1840 (Am. Jewish Archives April 1958).

351 Philadelphia's 1780 list for a wartime tax on real and personal estates shows that more than a third of the amount assessed was imposed on seventeen Jewish merchants, at a time when the city's population was estimated to be about 28,000 (based on U.S. Dept. of Interior Geological Survey). LAURENS R. SCHWARTZ, JEWS AND THE AMERICAN REVOLUTION: HAYM SALOMON AND OTHERS 35 (McFarland 1987); for the identity of the persons on the list, *see* HENRY S. MORAIS, THE JEWS OF PHILADELPHIA *passim* (Levytype 1894).

352 *Quoted in* Sen. Document No. 178, 69th Cong., 2d Sess., 1926, 3 (including a brief summary of Salomon's life). *See also* SCHWARTZ, *supra* note 351; CHARLES EDWARD RUSSELL, HAYM SALOMON AND THE REVOLUTION (Cosmopolitan 1930); LEON HUHNER, THE JEWS OF VIRGINIA FROM THE EARLIEST TIMES TO THE CLOSE OF THE EIGHTEENTH CENTURY 93 (Am. Jewish Hist. Soc'y 1911) (quoting Madison: when the "pecuniary resources of the members of Congress both public and private were cut off, recourse was had to Mr. [Haym] Salamon for means to answer their current expenses and he was always found extending his friendly hand" and "he obstinately rejects all recompense.").

353 Senate Doc. 178 (1926), *supra* note 352.

354 Salomon's financial support for and cooperation with Morris have occasionally led writers to decorate Salomon with the "financier of the American Revolution" label, normally conferred on Morris himself. *See* MADISON CLINTON PETERS, HAYM SALOMON, THE FINANCIER OF THE REVOLUTION (Trow Press 1911) (with a foreword by President William Howard Taft); ROBERT A. EAST, BUSINESS ENTERPRISE IN THE AMERICAN REVOLUTIONARY ERA 158 (Columbia Univ. Press 1938) (Salomon "a foremost financial figure of Philadelphia"); 2 STOKES, *supra* note 2, fig. 2 (following 410) (reproduction of Washington-Morris-Salomon Monument, Chicago). Robert Morris' papers contain 114 references

in the international trade of the mid-eighteenth century was fostered by their relatives and coreligionists in such major seaports as London, Amsterdam, Jamaica, Barbados, Curaçao, and Surinam.

Rivaling Haym Salomon in prominence but active in other segments of the colonial economy, Aaron Lopez was a major businessman during Newport's golden age of commerce and industry and its largest taxpayer.[355] Lopez owned a large fleet of ships, which in 1772 transported both his own goods and those of others to Jamaica, Haiti, Barbados, Dominica, St. Eustatius, Surinam, Honduras, Newfoundland, Quebec, England, Ireland, the Netherlands, Sweden, Spain, Portugal, the Azores and Canaries, Africa, and the North American coast.[356] The scope of his ventures is illustrated by this account:

> [H]e and [his partner] Rivera sent aboard the *Sally* to Surinam in November 1768; flour, fish, beef, pork, bread, salt, tobacco, candles, whale oil, bricks, staves, headings, dismantled hogsheads, hoops, chairs, tables, tallow, horses, hay, oats, saddles, bridles – and twenty-nine bottles of superfine mustard. On his own account, Aaron added silverware and mahogany platters to the cargo. A few days later on the schooner *Eleanore* he and two partners dispatched to Hispaniola: lumber, shingles, disassembled barrels, staves, hoops, oars, naval stores, bread, oil, corn, peas, fish, beef, pork, lard, candles, and teakettles.... [Except for tobacco and land speculation] everything from distilling to the production of shoes to the exporting of kosher foods to the construction and overhauling of ships to the raising of mules – played some part in the unfolding of the Lopez regime. His shop on Thames Street in Newport supplied its customers with everything from Bibles and bottled beer to looking glasses and violins.[357]

Lest it be thought that somehow this member of an allegedly "scarcely known" religious group[358] managed to escape public attention, it should be noted that his tombstone, composed by Ezra Stiles (a Newport Congregational minister then serving as president of Yale University), bears this tribute:

> He was a merchant of eminence.... An ornament and valuable pillar to the Jewish society, of which he was a member. His knowledge in commerce was unbounded and his integrity irreproachable; thus he lived and died, much regretted, esteemed and loved by all.[359]

Finally, the public-minded Framers and Founders would almost certainly have known about the Jews in their midst from such extraordinarily diverse political, military, financial, and social events as Oliver Cromwell's readmittance of Jews to England[360]; the theory

to Haym Salomon and 48 to other Jewish financiers. A DOCUMENTARY HISTORY OF THE JEWS IN THE UNITED STATES, 1654–1875 at 579 n. 3 (3d ed., Morris U. Schappes ed., Schocken Books 1971).

355 *See* STANLEY F. CHAYET, LOPEZ OF NEWPORT, COLONIAL AMERICAN MERCHANT PRINCE 127 (Wayne State Univ. Press 1970).

356 *Id.* at 118.

357 *Id.* at 119, 128; in his Diary, Ezra Stiles observed that "for Honor & Extent of commerce [Lopez was] probably surpassed by no Merch[ant] in America.... He was my intimate Friend & Acquaintance! Oh! How often have I wished that sincere pious & candid mind could have perceived the Evidences of [Christiani]ty." III THE LITERARY DIARY OF EZRA STILES 24 (Franklin Bowditch Dextes ed., Charles Scribner's Sons 1901) (June 8, 1782).

358 *See supra* text at note 344.

359 CHAYET, *supra* note 350, at 195.

360 ROBERT S. PAUL, THE LORD PROTECTOR: RELIGION AND POLITICS IN THE LIFE OF OLIVER CROMWELL 331–2 (Lutterworth Press 1955).

that the American Indians were descended from the lost tribes of Israel[361]; the "paroxysm of excitement" provoked in mid-eighteenth-century England by the enactment and hasty repeal of the so-called Jew Bill authorizing Parliament to naturalize professing Jews[362]; the 1711 contributions by New York City Jews, including their rabbi, to help pay for a steeple for Trinity Church[363]; the 1740 enactment by Parliament of a law permitting Jews to become naturalized citizens of the American colonies without taking the normally prescribed oath "upon the true faith of a Christian"[364]; Peter Stuyvesant's efforts to exclude Jews from New Amsterdam, rebuked by the directors of the Dutch East India Company[365]; the life-long hopes of Cotton Mather for the conversion of the Jews to Christianity[366]; the election of Moses Levy to the office of constable in New York City and his declining to serve[367]; the highly publicized 1722 conversion of Judah Monis to Christianity in Harvard's College Hall and his subsequent employment by Harvard to teach Hebrew and his receipt of an honorary Harvard degree[368]; the controversial subscription of wealthy Jewish merchants in London to encourage the emigration of indigent Jews to Georgia, ultimately approved by Governor Oglethorpe[369]; notable mixed marriages, such as the elopement of Phila Franks, daughter of a prominent New York Jewish merchant, with Oliver DeLancy, son of a wealthy Huguenot family[370]; the scalping during the Revolution of Francis Salvador, an elected member of South Carolina's first colonial assembly[371]; the court martial acquittal of Maj. David S. Franks, aide-de-camp to General Benedict Arnold, and his subsequent services in France and Spain[372]; the 1778 capture by the British of Mordecai Sheftall, commissary general of Georgia's troops[373]; the fact that Georgia's Jews were such vigorous backers of American independence that its colonial governor proposed in 1781 that no Jews be permitted to return or to settle in Georgia, "these People" ... having been "found to a Man to have been violent Rebels & Persecutors of the King's Loyal Subjects"[374]; the

361 *See* Richard Popkin, *The Rise and Fall of the Jewish Indian Theory*, *in* MENASSEH BEN ISRAEL AND HIS WORLD 63–82 (Yosef Kaplan et al. eds., E. J. Brill 1989).

362 *See* THOMAS W. PERRY, PUBLIC OPINION, PROPAGANDA, AND POLITICS IN EIGHTEENTH-CENTURY ENGLAND: A STUDY OF THE JEW BILL OF 1753 at 1, 2 n. 2 (Harvard Univ. Press 1962) [quoting W.E.H. LECKY, I THE HISTORY OF ENGLAND IN THE EIGHTEENTH CENTURY 285 (New York 1878)].

363 NOTES RELATING TO THE CELEBRATION OF THE 250TH ANNIVERSARY OF THE SETTLEMENT OF THE JEWS IN THE UNITED STATES 17 (New York 1905).

364 *Id.* at 15.

365 *See* ABRAM VOSSEN GOODMAN, AMERICAN OVERTURE: JEWISH RIGHTS IN COLONIAL TIMES 74–86 (Jewish Publishing Soc'y of Am. 1947); HENRY S. KESSLER & EUGENE RACHLIS, PETER STUYVESANT, AND HIS NEW YORK 176–86 (Random House 1959).

366 III DIARY OF COTTON MATHER (Boston, Mass. Hist. Soc'y Collection 1911). [Extracts in THE JEW IN A GENTILE WORLD 227–31 (Arnold A. Rogow ed., Macmillan 1961).]

367 DOCUMENTARY HISTORY OF THE JEWS OF THE UNITED STATES, *supra* note 354, at 19–20.

368 II MARCUS, *supra* note 349, at 1096–1103; *see also* LEE M. FRIEDMAN, EARLY AMERICAN JEWS 24–38 (Harvard Univ. Press 1934).

369 For a more detailed account of the early Jewish community in Savannah, preceding the 1800 election of David Emanuel as governor of Georgia, *see* GOODMAN, *supra* note 365, at 168–200; MARCUS, *supra* note 349, at 349–53.

370 Jon Butler, *The New York World of Myer Myers*, *in* DAVID L. BARQUIST, MYER MYERS: JEWISH SILVERSMITH IN COLONIAL NEW YORK 2 (Yale Univ. Press 2001); *see also* MORAIS, *supra* note 351, at 34–5.

371 *See* 3 MARCUS, *supra* note 349, at 1306–9.

372 *See* SIMON WOLF, THE AMERICAN JEW AS PATRIOT, SOLDIER AND CITIZEN 27–32 (Gregg Press 1972).

373 MARCUS, *supra* note 349, at 1275–6.

374 III COLLECTIONS OF THE GEORGIA HISTORICAL SOCIETY 341 (Savannah 1873) (letter of Governor James Wright to Lord George Germain, Mar. 9, 1781).

1787 letter from Jonas Phillips to the Philadelphia Constitutional Convention urging the delegates not to incorporate an oath requiring officials to swear that the New Testament was the product of divine inspiration[375]; Benjamin Franklin's contribution to a campaign to help finance a synagogue in Philadelphia[376]; the tortuous role played by Moses Lindo in the founding of Rhode Island College (later to become Brown University) and its 1770 exemption of Jewish students from the Christian worship requirements imposed on other students[377]; the claim by Henry James Pye, England's anti-Semitic poet laureate, that the democratic spirit of the American Revolution reflected in part the influence of Jews[378]; the perception of colonial theologians that there were democratic strands in the Hebrew Old Testament[379]; the 1778 British arrest and imprisonment of Hyam Salomon, charging (probably with justification) that he attempted to sabotage British military facilities on orders from General Washington[380]; the prominence of Jews in the Masonic order at a time when many leading revolutionary figures were Masons, including George Washington, Benjamin Franklin, Lafayette, Madison, and Pulaski[381]; the presence of seven Jewish lieutenant colonels and majors and at least six captains in the Continental forces (a number that was probably much in excess of their proportion in the population), one of whom, Major Benjamin Nones, served on Washington's staff and was known as "the Jewish Lafayette"[382]; the appointment of Rabbi Gershom Seixas to be a regent of Columbia University (then King's College) in 1784[383]; the fact that Jewish merchants often closed their business premises on Saturday, a religious practice that evidently led Aaron Lopez to avoid having his ships leave Newport on Saturdays[384]; and the facts that Rhode Island's General Assembly and Supreme Court held sessions in Newport's Touro Synagogue during the period 1780–1784 and that the building (designated a National Historical Site in 1946) was the locale of a town meeting during George Washington's visit in 1781.[385]

375 3 FARRAND, *supra* note 172, at 78–9. Article VI's prohibition of any religious test for federal officials was adopted by the delegates shortly before this letter was received.

376 MORAIS, *supra* note 351, at 20 (subscription list for Congregation Mikveh Israel April 30, 1788). The original is held by Congregation Mikveh Israel in Philadelphia; *see* Subscription List for Congregation Mikveh Israel, Philadelphia, April 30, 1788, Document 5605, The Papers of Benjamin Franklin, Yale University.

377 GOODMAN, *supra* note 365, at 61–8.

378 DOCUMENTARY HISTORY OF THE JEWS IN THE UNITED STATES, *supra* note 354, at 84–8 & 588–9.

379 *Id*. at 70–1; *see generally* HUMPHREY, *supra* note 2.

380 Senate Doc. No. 178, *supra* note 352, at 7.

381 *See* SCHWARTZ, *supra* note 351, at 103–9; III MARCUS, *supra* note 349, 1168–72. It was even said that one had to be a Mason to become a member of George Washington's staff; Washington took his presidential oath of office on a Masonic Bible, and his funeral followed the Masonic tradition.

382 Speech by President Coolidge, May 8, 1925, Senate Doc. No. 178, *supra* note 352, at 15. Although the known facts are fragmentary, Jewish participation in the armed forces during the revolution may have been disproportionate to their population. THE TOLL OF INDEPENDENCE: ENGAGEMENTS & BATTLE CASUALTIES OF THE AMERICAN REVOLUTION 132–3 (Howard H. Peckham ed., Univ. of Chicago Press 1974), reports that about 7 percent of the estimated American population served (200,000 of 2,781,000), most of them not known by name. 3 MARCUS, *supra* note 349, at 1304, states that thirty-four South Carolina Jews served, a number that is more than 10 percent of that colony's estimated Jewish population (34 of 300).

383 *See* ROBERT A. MCCAUGHEY, STAND, COLUMBIA: A HISTORY OF COLUMBIA UNIVERSITY IN THE CITY OF NEW YORK, 1754–2004 at 53 (Columbia Univ. Press 2003).

384 Butler, *supra* note 370, at 18.

385 *See* ANTOINETTE F. DOWNING & VINCENT J. SCULLY, JR., THE ARCHITECTURAL HERITAGE OF NEWPORT, RHODE ISLAND, 1640–1915 at 87 (2d ed., Clarkson N. Potter 1967).

# 2 Church and State in the Nineteenth Century

## A. Introduction

During the century and a half between the ratification of the First Amendment in 1791 and the Supreme Court's 1947 decision in the *Everson* case upholding the constitutionality of using public funds to finance the bus transportation of children attending church-sponsored schools, the Court rarely addressed the meaning of the Establishment and Free Exercise Clauses.[1] Moreover, these early applications of the religion clauses affected no more than a small fraction of the nation's populace. For example, *Terrett v. Taylor*, decided in 1815, ruled that a Virginia law confiscating certain real estate owned by the Protestant Episcopal Church (in the course of its disestablishment) was unconstitutional,[2] and *Reynolds v. United States* (1878) held that a Mormon's religious belief that polygamy was divinely inspired was not a valid defense to a federal prosecution for committing bigamy.[3]

The paucity of Supreme Court litigation should not lead readers to infer that the nineteenth century was devoid of episodes requiring the religion clauses of the First Amendment to be interpreted. In fact, numerous church-state clashes were resolved by the executive and legislative branches of government at both the federal and state levels, as well by the state courts, and these collisions sometimes elicited implicit or explicit interpretations of the religion clauses that were no less important than formal judicial resolutions of the disputes would have been. This chapter concerns itself with these nineteenth-century actions – or, sometimes, failures to act – by the nation's executive and legislative bodies, as well as other public events involving the church-state relationship.

In his three-volume ground-breaking historical survey, *Church and State in the United States*, Anson Phelps Stokes provides a useful list of the links between religion in early America, especially New England transcendentalism, and social reform in the nineteenth century:

> The beginnings in America of effective urban social-welfare work by the Churches through the appointment in 1826 by the American Unitarian Association of the

1 For discussion of Everson v. Board of Education, 330 U.S. 1 (1947), *see* Chapter 16.D.

2 Terrett v. Taylor, 13 U.S. (Cranch) 43 (1815) (citing "the spirit and the letter of the constitution of the United States" without naming its pertinent letter).

3 Reynolds v. United States, 98 U.S. (8 Otto) 145 (1879); *See also* Davis v. Beason, 133 U.S. 333 (1890) (rejecting First Amendment Free Exercise Clause defense to criminal prosecution for refusing to swear oath that defendant was not a polygamist or part of an organization that supported polygamy).

> Reverend Joseph Tuckerman (1778–1840) as minister-at-large in Boston – an appointment that led the way to making the city foremost in America in the administration of charity.
>
> The reforming pastorate of Lyman Beecher (1775–1863) in the Hanover Street Church from 1826 to 1832, with the remarkable stimulus it gave to the temperance movement, the education of the West, and various reforms.
>
> The development of Americanization agencies to meet the needs of the new immigrants (which the Roman Catholic Church was striving to serve through its new parochial schools), and to overcome through the preaching of tolerance the extreme anti-Catholic feeling coming to the surface in most parts of the country. [Church-affiliates] … played a large part in the discussion of temperance, history, philosophy, science, social problems (including slavery), ethics, books, and the need of public libraries. It was the first large-scale adult-education movement started in this country. Emerson was the most distinguished of its lecturers, going about the country spreading the views of Boston's literary elite, especially those of culture, progress, idealism, the overcoming of social abuses, and tolerance. As to the last, his interest and that of some other Transcendentalists in the fundamental unity of all true religions was destined to help break down the intellectual barriers of creed.
>
> The improvements in the opportunities for women's education as shown by the founding of the first American coeducational high school, in Massachusetts in 1826, and the first well-established college for women, Mount Holyoke, in 1836.[4]

Another scholar wrote

> The wave of popular religious movements that broke upon the United States in the half-century after independence did more to Christianize American society than anything before or since. Nothing makes that point clearer than the growth of Methodists and Baptists as mass movements among white and black Americans. Starting from scratch just prior to the Revolution, the Methodists in America grew at a rate that terrified other denominations, reaching a quarter of a million members by 1820 and doubling again by 1830. Baptist membership multiplied tenfold in the three decades after the Revolution, the number of churches increasing from 500 to over 2,500. The black church in America was born amidst the crusading vigor of these movements and quickly assumed its own distinct character and broad appeal among people of color. By the middle of the nineteenth century, Methodist and Baptist churches had splintered into more different denominational forms than one cares to remember.[5]

Stokes summed up, saying

> In at least three respects the popular religious movements of the early republic articulated a profoundly democratic spirit. First, they rejected the age-old distinction that set the clergy apart as a separate order of men and refused to defer to learned theologians and received orthodoxies. All were democratic or populist in the way they instinctively associated virtue with ordinary people rather than with elites, exalted the vernacular in word and song as the hallowed channel for communicating with and about god, and freely turned over the reigns of power. These groups also shared with the Jeffersonian Republicans an overt rejection of the past as a repository of wisdom.

4 Anson Phelps Stokes, 1 Church and State in the United States 715–16 (Harper & Bros. 1950).

5 Nathan O. Hatch, *The Democratization of Christianity and the Character of American Politics*, *in* Religion and American Politics 92, 96–8 (Mark A. Noll ed., Oxford Univ. Press 1990).

> Second, these movements empowered ordinary people by taking their deepest spiritual impulses at face value rather than subjecting them to the scrutiny of orthodox doctrine and the frowns of respectable clergymen. In the last two decades of the [eighteenth] century, preachers from a wide range of new religious movements openly fanned the flames of religious ecstasy. ... Such a shift in emphasis, accompanied by rousing gospel singing rather than formal church music, reflected the success of common people in defining for themselves the nature of faith.
>
> The early republic was also a democratic moment in a third sense. Religious outsiders were flushed with confidence about their prospects and had little sense of their own limitations. They dreamed that a new age of religious and social harmony would spring up naturally out of their own efforts to overthrow coercive and authoritarian structures.[6]

## B. Early Religious Ceremonies, Symbols, and Proclamations

Although the Constitution prescribes the oath of office to be taken by the president-elect, George Washington set the stage for augmenting the constitutional formula by adding, with his hand on a bible, "so help me God," establishing a precedent that has been uniformly followed, except for Franklin Pierce.[7] Moreover, Washington acknowledged the hand of God in his first inaugural address:

> No People can be bound to acknowledge and adore the invisible hand, which conducts the Affairs of men more than the People of the United States. Every step, by which they have advanced to the character of an independent nation, seems to have been distinguished by some token of providential agency.[8]

In this devotional tone, the members of the First Federal Congress solemnized President Washington's inauguration by accompanying him to St. Paul's Chapel, an Episcopalian church, "to hear divine service, to be performed by the Chaplain of Congress," who was bishop of the Episcopal Diocese of New York.[9] While this ceremony preceded ratification of the First Amendment, the Establishment Clause of which prohibited religious favoritism, it set the custom for presidential inaugurations thereafter.

Washington's presidential tenure not only began with but also ended in a religious posture, as witness this extract from his 1796 "Farewell Address":

> Of all the dispositions and habits which lead to political prosperity, Religion and morality are indispensable supports. ... Let it simply be asked where is the security for property, for reputation, for life, if the sense of religious obligation desert the oaths, which are the instruments of investigation in Courts of Justice? And let us with caution indulge the supposition, that morality can be maintained without religion. Whatever may be conceded to the influence of refined education on minds of peculiar structure, reason

6 1 STOKES *supra* note 4, at 715–17. For the social and intellectual history of religion in America from the seventeenth to the middle of the nineteenth centuries, *see generally* MARK A. NOLL. AMERICA'S GOD: FROM JONATHAN EDWARDS TO ABRAHAM LINCOLN (Oxford Univ. Press 2002).

7 *See* Jams Pfander, *So Help Me God: Religion and the Presidential Oath Taking, in* 16 CONSTITUTIONAL COMMENTARY 549 (1999); *see also* JOSEPH NATHAN KANE, FACTS ABOUT THE PRESIDENTS 85 (H.W. Wilson, 6th ed. 1993). Pierce's decision was based on his understanding of Matthew 5:34–7.

8 GEORGE WASHINGTON: A COLLECTION 461 (W.B. Allen ed., Liberty Classics 1988).

9 1 STOKES *supra* note 4, at 484–6. For the constitutional status of legislative chaplains, *see* Marsh v. Chambers, 463 U.S. 783 (1983), discussed at Chapter 3.E.

and experience both forbid us to expect that National morality can prevail in exclusion of religious principle.[10]

Our nation's seal, currency, flag, and anthems are sprinkled with religious emblems and associations, some of them reaching back to its earliest days, and some of these insignia of religion are watered down from earlier, more explicit religious indicia. Thus Benjamin Franklin suggested that the national seal should show Moses lifting up his wand to divide the Red Sea, with the inscription, "Rebellion to tyrants is obedience to God," whereas Jefferson favored an image of the children of Israel wandering in the desert guided by a cloud by day and a pillar of fire by night. The winning version portrays a radiant Eye of Providence above a pyramid, with the motto, "E Pluribus Unum," alluding to "the many interpositions of Providence in favor of the American cause."[11] These symbols are also found on the standard dollar bill.[12] Stretching the facts a bit, the colors of the flag are said to have a religious origin reaching back to the Hebrew Arc of the Covenant.[13]

The most prominent national ceremony that is dominated by a religious spirit is Thanksgiving Day. Carrying forward a tradition that was already entrenched in colonial days, the First Federal Congress adopted a resolution requesting President Washington to recommend to the American people "a day of public Thanksgiving and Prayer, to be observed by acknowledging, with grateful hearts the many signal favors of Almighty God, especially by affording them an opportunity peacefully to establish a Constitution of government for their safety and happiness."[14] This resolution was adopted on September 25, 1789, the same day the Congress had submitted the First Amendment to the states for ratification and two years before its adoption. President Washington responded to the congressional request on October 3, 1789, by issuing a proclamation in a similarly devout tone,[15] and without waiting to be prompted by Congress, President Adams proclaimed Thanksgiving Day in 1798.[16] Although he was a son of New England, schooled in a different religious tradition than Virginia's George Washington, John Adams' appeals to "Almighty God," the "Redeemer of the World," and "His Holy Spirit" were not markedly different in spirit from Washington's proclamation. In 1799, Adams recommended that his fellow citizens "call to mind our numerous offenses against the Most High God, confess them before Him with the sincerest penitence, implore His pardoning mercy, through the Great Mediator and Redeemer, for our past transgressions, and [pray] that

[10] *Farewell Address, in* 35 WRITINGS OF WASHINGTON 214, 229 (Sept. 19, 1796) (John C. Fitzpatrick ed., Govt. Prnt'g Office 1940); 1 STOKES, *supra* note 4, at 494.

[11] 1 STOKES, *supra* note 4, at 467–8.

[12] *Id.* at 468 (citing GAILLARD HUNT, HISTORY OF SEAL OF UNITED STATES 8). The national seal and dollar bills also bear the motto "*Annuit Coeptis*" (Latin for "the Eye of Providence, has favored our undertakings"). This motto originated with Vergil and invoked Jupiter; despite the pagan source, the Framers surely intended a reference to the Christian God.

[13] 1917 (erroneously printed as 1817) NAT'L GEO. MAG. 303.

[14] *Annals of Congress*, September 25, 1789; *see generally* H. S. J. SICKEL, THANKSGIVING: ITS SOURCE, PHILOSOPHY AND HISTORY 24 (Philadelphia, Nat'l Publ. Co. 1940). President Bush's Thanksgiving Proclamation for 2003 refers back to George Washington's 1789 proclamation and recited that "we … thank God for the many blessings he has given us, and ask God to continue to guide and watch over our country." N.Y. TIMES, Nov. 22, 2003, at 136.

[15] COMPILATION OF THE MESSAGES AND PAPERS OF THE PRESIDENTS 56 (James D. Richardson) (multivolume) (1902 and 1904).

[16] H. S. J. SICKEL, THANKSGIVING: ITS SOURCES, PHILOSOPHY, AND HISTORY 156–7 (Int'l Prnt'g Co. 1940).

through the grace of His Holy Spirit we may be disposed and enabled to yield a more suitable obedience to His righteous requisitions in time to come."[17]

Another instance of church-state intermingling – striking even though it did not advance beyond a blueprint – was Pierre Charles L'Enfant's 1791 proposal for the construction of a "grand church" as an integral part of his plan for "a national city," presented to President Washington and accepted by him: "This Church is intended for national purposes, such as public prayer, thanksgivings, funeral Orations, &c., and assigned to the special use of no particular Sect or denomination, but equally open to all."[18] Although this part of L'Enfant's plan was not built, Congress did grant a charter for construction of the Washington Cathedral in 1893. Under the L'Enfant plan, plots of land were to be allocated to different religious denominations on which to build churches in the capital. There appears to be nothing to indicate that this was thought by Washington or anyone else in a position of authority to create any constitutional objection, and the proposal was consistent with the actual conduct of religious services on many occasions in the hall of the House of Representatives.[19]

A diligent researcher has published a compendium of these and other instances of early and contemporary "ceremonial deism,"[20] including the national motto ("In God We Trust"), the invocation routinely used by the Supreme Court ("God save the United States and this Honorable Court"), and the 1954 statutory addition of "under God" to the nation's Pledge of Allegiance.[21] (Another example, rarely cited, is the formula, "May God have mercy on your soul," used in the death chamber.) The author, a relentless foe of ceremonial deism, distinguishes between "core" and "fringe" instances of ceremonial deism and condemns as unconstitutional all "core" examples – those that "have been noncontroversial, have resulted in very little litigation, and have never been held unconstitutional by any court."[22] His forensic strategy is that if, as he asserts, these examples of ceremonial deism are unconstitutional, the bypassed "fringe" examples are unconstitutional *a fortiori*. The "core" category includes all practices involving

1. [A]ctual, symbolic, or ritualistic [symbols or recitals];
2. [P]rayer, invocation, benediction, supplication, appeal, reverent reference to, or embrace of, a general or particular deity;
3. [C]reated, delivered, sponsored, or encouraged by government officials;
4. [D]ring governmental functions or ceremonies, in the form of patriotic expressions, or associated with holiday observances;
5. [W]hich, in and of themselves, are unlikely to indoctrinate or proselytize their audience;

[17] *Id.* at 158–9; *see also* Charles Ellis Dickson, *Jeremiads in the New American Republic: The Case of National Fasts in the John Adams Administration*, 60 N. ENGL. Q. 187–207 (June 1987).

[18] 1 STOKES, *supra* note 4, at 493.

[19] *Id.* at 493–4, 499–507.

[20] Dean Eugene V. Rostow, of the Yale Law School, is credited by Arthur E. Sutherland, in a book review, 40 IND. L.J. 83, 86 n. 7 (1965), with coining this term. Owing to a lapse of memory or a typographical error, however, Epstein credits the term to Walter Rostow, allegedly dean of the Yale Law School, a mythical brother of Eugene V. Rostow and Walt Whitman Rostow. *See* Steven B. Epstein, *Rethinking the Constitutionality of Ceremonial Deism*, 96 COLUM. L. REV. 2083, 2091 (1996).

[21] *See* Elk Grove Unified Sch. Dist. v. Newdow, 542 U.S. 1, 7 (2004); Epstein *supra* note 20, at 2083.

[22] Epstein, *supra* note 20, at 2095 (emphasis added).

6. [W]hich are not specifically designed to accommodate the free religious exercise of a particular group of citizens; and
7. [W]hich, as of this date, are deeply rooted in the nation's history and traditions.[23]

Some of these "core" practices of ceremonial deism have been explicitly endorsed as constitutional by the Supreme Court, but most are cited by the Court or legal practitioners as the major premise of a syllogism (the "no more than" syllogism) that takes this form: (1) *major premise:* the cited historic practices must pass constitutional muster or they would not have been tolerated so long; (2) *minor premise:* the practice before the court does not advance religion any more than the items in the major premise; (3) *conclusion:* therefore, the litigated practice must also pass constitutional muster.[24] Consistently with this theory, in commenting on some examples of ceremonial deism, justices of the Supreme Court have minimized their constitutional import. In 1962, for example, Justice Black observed in a decision holding that a state-drafted school prayer was unconstitutional

> There is of course nothing in the decision reached here that is inconsistent with the fact that school children and others are officially encouraged to express love for our country by reciting historical documents such as the Declaration of Independence which contain references to the Deity or by signing officially espoused anthems which include the composer's professions of faith in a Supreme Being, or with the fact that there are many manifestations in our public life of belief in God. Such patriotic or ceremonial occasions bear no true resemblance to the unquestioned religious exercise that the State of New York has sponsored in this instance.[25]

In 1963, Justice Brennan similarly commented

> [T]he "Establishment" Clause does not ban federal or state regulation of conduct whose reason or effect merely happens to coincide or harmonize with the tenets of some or all religions. This rationale suggests that the use of the motto "In God We Trust" on currency, on documents and public buildings and the like may not offend the clause. It is not that the use of those four words can be dismissed as "de minimis" – for I suspect there would be intense opposition to the abandonment of that motto. The truth is that we have simply interwoven the motto so deeply into the fabric of our civil polity that its

[23] *Id.* Although Chief Justice Burger included religious paintings in the "ceremonial deism" category, Epstein disagrees with this classification:

> Religious paintings in art museums, however, do not fit within the rubric of ceremonial deism because they do not involve a governmental embrace of religion. Rather, they involve a governmental embrace of art, which only incidentally embodies a religious theme.

*Id.* at 2174 n. 52. One wonders if Epstein would also palliate "The Battle Hymn of the Republic" if sung in public schools as an exercise in history, given its religion-drenched words:

> Mine eyes have seen the glory of the coming of the Lord
> He is trampling out the vintage where the grapes of wrath are stored,
> He has loosed the fateful lightening of His terrible swift sword
> His truth is marching on.
> Glory! Glory! Hallelujah!

[24] *Id.* at 2087.

[25] Engel v. Vitale 370 U.S. 421, 436 n. 21 (1962). For discussion of this decision, *see* Chapter 16.F.2.

present use may well not present that type of involvement which the First Amendment prohibits.

This general principle might also serve to insulate the various patriotic exercises and activities used in the public schools and elsewhere which, whatever may have been their origins, no longer have a religious purpose or meaning. The reference to divinity in the revised pledge of allegiance, for example, may merely recognize the historical fact that our Nation was believed to have been founded "under God." Thus reciting the pledge may be no more of a religious exercise than the reading aloud of Lincoln's Gettysburg Address, which contains an allusion to the same historical fact.[26]

Speaking for the Court in a 1984 decision upholding a nativity crèche in a municipal Christmas display, Chief Justice Burger recited at length an "unbroken" and "replete" history of official references to the value of divine guidance in the conduct of our national affairs.[27] A similar recital of symbols and invocations was set out even earlier by Justice Douglas, who added this caustic verdict: "A fastidious atheist or agnostic could even object to the supplication with which the Court opens each session: 'God save the United States and this Honorable Court.'"[28] Other justices who have likewise rejected attacks on examples of ceremonial deism (sometimes using, implicitly, the "no more than" syllogism) are Justices Scalia, Kennedy, Burger, and Rehnquist.

Attacking this formidable chorus of yea-sayers, a lonely opponent of every instance of ceremonial deism asserts that all of them violate the "no endorsement of religion maxim," the shorthand code for *Lemon* and related Supreme Court decisions.[29] Despite his earnest and detailed argument, however, these arguments against ceremonial deism is unlikely to win over a majority of the justices in the foreseeable future, except for possible instances in which the litigated instance of ceremonial deism is only the tip of an iceberg that, taken as a whole, qualifies as "a law respecting an establishment of religion" as that constitutional phrase is currently interpreted and applied.

## C. Disestablishment of State-Established Churches, 1791–1833

Ratification of the Bill of Rights in 1791 imposed the Establishment Clause of the First Amendment on the federal government but left the state-established churches (in Massachusetts and Virginia, for example) free from federal intervention. Indeed, some commentators view this insulation of state-established churches from federal interference as the primary objective of the Establishment Clause,[30] but whether this was its principal goal or only a by-product, the right of the states to accord an establishment preference to a chosen religious denomination was retained in 1791 but withered away within the first few decades of the nineteenth century.[31] Disestablishment in Massachusetts occurred in

[26] Sch. Dist. of Abington Twp. v. Schempp, 374 U.S. 203, 303–4 (1963) (Brennan, J., concurring) (internal citation omitted).

[27] Lynch v. Donnelly, 465 U.S. 668, 674ff (1984).

[28] Zorach v. Clauson, 343 U.S. 306, 313 (1952).

[29] Epstein, *supra* note 20, at 2904.

[30] *See* Chapter 1.E.2.d.

[31] For a brief account of each state's path to disestablishment, with mention of the residual traces, as of 1902, of the old dispensation, *see* Sanford H. Cobb, The Rise of Religious Liberty in America 510–28 (Macmillan 1902). Almost every state's steps to disestablishment are chronicled by at least one massive volume. *See* M. Louise Greene, The Development of Religious Liberty in Connecticut

1833 – almost a century and a half after Massachusetts began life by requiring every town to hire "an able, learned orthodox minister" and to support public worship by taxation.[32] The dates ordinarily given for disestablishment in the states that still had established churches after 1791 are Vermont (1807), Connecticut (1818), New Hampshire (1819) and Massachusetts (1833). Even before the establishment rules were wiped from the new republic's statute books, however, a mounting variety of exemptions, coupled with haphazard enforcement, turned the formal establishment status of some churches into dead letters.[33] The direction in which the wind of change was blowing also was reflected in the fact that after 1791, no state took advantage of its freedom from the constraints of the Establishment Clause to create a *new* religious establishment, except for the widely condemned Mormon establishment (more comprehensive and transigent than any of the febrile post-1791 state establishments), which was abandoned when Utah become a state in 1896.[34]

Disestablishment after 1791 had a variety of causes, which varied and overlapped from state to state: The immigration of dissenters and unchurched inhabitants into states with established churches brought with it objections to the privileged status of the chosen religions; religious convictions to state aid to any religious faith, especially among the rapidly growing Baptists; the belief that all religions should stand or fall on the voluntary choice of their adherents; the clash between faiths that sought to monopolize state aid for themselves; mass evangelism among Methodists, Baptists, and some Presbyterians, inevitably threatening the hierarchical claims of established churches; the flowering of lay preachers, especially among Methodists, who repudiated any allegiance to central church governing bodies; the corrosive impact of political independence on the Church of England; and doctrinal splits within the established churches themselves (such as the defection of Unitarianism from Congregationalism in Massachusetts). Finally, disestablishment was undoubtedly spurred on by the nagging sense that the established churches were inconsistent – no matter how many specific exceptions were allowed and despite the growth of tolerance – with every individual's right to the free exercise of religion.

## D. Jefferson's 1800 Presidential Campaign: The Electorate's Use of Religious Test

Although the ban on any "religious test" as a qualification for holding public office, as set out in Article VI of the Constitution, does not explicitly say so, it prohibits only legally prescribed religious tests, not religious tests employed by the citizenry in choosing

445ff (Books for Libraries Press 1905, reprinted 1970); Jerry B. Smith, Disestablishment in Virginia and Massachusetts, 1733–1833 (1970) (unpublished Wheaton College dissertation).

32 *See* Chapter 1.A.1 and 2.

33 *See* John D. Cushing, *Notes on Disestablishment in Massachusetts, 1780–1833*, 26 WM. & MARY Q. (1969); *see also* John Witte, Jr., *"A Most Mild and Equitable Establishment of Religion": John Adams and the Massachusetts Experiment*, 41 J. CHURCH & ST. 213 (1999). For the Cambridge Platform of 1648, in which the Puritan leaders of Massachusetts and Connecticut proclaimed "the Duty of the Magistrate to take care of matters of Religion" (2 STOKES, *supra* note 4, at 46, 280); for a briefer account, *see* ROBERT T. HANDY, A CHRISTIAN AMERICA, PROTESTANT HOPES AND HISTORICAL REALITIES 12ff (Oxford Univ. Press 1971).

34 *See infra* Section L.

among candidates for public office. Throughout our history, a candidate's religion has often – openly or covertly – been an important, even a dominant feature of national and local electoral campaigns. In 1876, for example, the Democrats were denounced as the party of "Rum, Romanism, and Rebellion"[35]; in 1928, Al Smith's presidential candidacy evoked allegations that he would consult the Pope on national issues[36]; and late in the twentieth century, John F. Kennedy believed that his Catholicism made it necessarily wise for him to avow in major addresses that he did not speak for his church or it for him both in seeking the Democratic Party's nomination for the presidency and later when campaigning for that office.[37] Indeed, a common feature of today's elections is a "balanced ticket," which uses a religious test, drained of animus by allocating to each major religion its "place" on the electoral roster.

In short, when voting, our countrymen have not followed the principle of separating church from state. This lamentable (or, as some might argue, laudable) practice began with a vengeance with the 1800 candidacy of Jefferson for president, when his religious beliefs became a matter for ardent debate. (The Electoral College was then, to some extent, a filter through which popular views had to pass, but a visitor from afar, observing the focus on Jefferson himself, might have thought that the electorate voted directly for the president in person.) Lest the voters fail to probe deeply enough into Jefferson's religious beliefs, Federalist ministers used their pulpits to surmount the wall between church and state in order to launch attacks on Jefferson in a practice that, as summarized by a recent scholar, was utterly inconsistent with the Jeffersonian principle of separating church from state:

> Beginning in the 1790s, and now [in the 1800 election], with renewed effort Federalist ministers inveighed against Jefferson, often from their pulpits, excoriating his infidelity and deism. For some politicians, such as Alexander Hamilton, this onslaught was part of a deliberate plan of "opposing the honest enthusiasm of Religious Opinion to the phrenzy of Political fanaticism." Most clergymen, however, were hardly so calculating. Understanding their religion as a fully integrated part of the life of the nation, and oblivious to the risks to themselves and the country of employing their pulpits for partisan ends, Federalist ministers felt obliged to bring their faith to bear upon party politics, especially against the man who, more than any other American, seemed to regard religion with indifference – who was notorious for apparently suggesting that religion and morality and thus also religion and politics were specialized, less than fully integrated, features of human life.[38]

This two-track denunciation of Jefferson – as a nondenominational deist[39] and as an enemy of the routine use of the pulpit to preach politics – produced a campaign, at the very dawn of the new republic, that was as bitter as any in our history.[40] (It should be noted that in the course of defending Jefferson, the Republicans came close to denying

[35] *See infra* Section K.1.

[36] *See* Christopher M. Finan & Alfred E. Smith: The Happy Warrior 209–20 (Hill & Wang 2002).

[37] Robert Dallek, An Unfinished Life, John F. Kennedy, 1917–1963 at 282–3 (Little, Brown 2003).

[38] Philip Hamburger, Separation of Church and State 111–12 (Harvard Univ. Press 2002) (internal citation omitted).

[39] *See* G. Adolph Koch, Religion of the American Enlightenment (Thomas Y. Crowell 1968).

[40] For a massive compendium of the Anti-Federalist newspapers of the era, *see* Donald H. Stewart, The Opposition Press of the Federalist Period (State Univ. of New York 1969) (based on a survey of 550 papers), *Preface* at x, 395–418.

the free-speech rights of the Federalist ministers.[41]) In the 1800 presidential campaign, Jefferson's Federalist enemies hurled many charges against him; the most common was that he was an atheist. This claim was false; he was a deist, but the claim was difficult to answer because Jefferson's conviction that religion was a man's private affair led him to remain largely silent.[42] According to Jefferson's best-known biographer, the atheist allegation was made not only in the public press but often in the pulpit as well, where the French Revolution (viewed by Jefferson as tolerable or even laudable) was held up as a "terrible warning of things to come" – including, according to some, a time when bibles would have to be hidden from view.[43] In a private letter commenting on these attacks, Jefferson wrote his famous manifesto: "for I have sworn upon the altar of God eternal hostility against every form of tyranny over the mind of man."[44]

In 1815, Jefferson enunciated a curiously legalistic theory of a minister's right to offer political advice from the pulpit. Starting with the presupposition that ministers are selected by their parishioners so that the scope of the minister's role is governed by contract law, Jefferson also presupposed that "[i]n choosing our pastors we look to his religious qualifications, without enquiring into his physical or political dogmas." This leads to the conclusion that in the pulpit, the clergyman should stick to religious matters. Otherwise, "the association being voluntary, the majority has no right to apply the contributions of the minority to purposes unspecified in the agreement of congregation." However, Jefferson wrote, "I do not deny that a congregation may if they please, agree with their preacher that he shall instruct them in Medicine also, or Law, or Politics." In these instances (presumably rare), lectures on the agreed-upon subjects from the pulpit "become not only a matter of right, but of duty also." Finally, Jefferson acknowledged that in his leisure time, "the preacher has the right equally with every other citizen, to express his sentiments, in speaking or writing on the subjects of Medicine, Law, Politics, etc., his leisure time being his own."[45]

## E. Nativism, No-Popery, Know-Nothingism, and the "Protestant Crusade" of 1800–1860

Belying our nation's justifiable pride in its religious tolerance, and simultaneously undermining the hope of keeping religion out of politics, there was a plethora of anti-Catholic episodes, many of them violent, during the first half of America's nineteenth century. These "nativist" events, aimed especially at immigrants in the cities of the Atlantic seaboard and in the nascent centers of population in the Midwest, have collectively been aptly dubbed the "Protestant Crusade" of 1800–1860, which, like some of its ancestors of the distant past, generated collateral damage far out of proportion to the spiritual good

[41] *See* citations in HAMBURGER, *supra* note 38, at 112 n. 2.

[42] The campaign centered on the selection of presidential electors; the Electoral College had not yet been reduced to a formality. *See generally* DUMAS MALONE, 3 JEFFERSON AND HIS TIME: JEFFERSON AND THE ORDEAL OF LIBERTY ch. 29 (Little, Brown 1962).

[43] *Id.* at 481–3.

[44] *Id.* at 483. This proclamation is memorialized on the Jefferson Memorial in Washington, DC.

[45] Letter to P. H. Wendover, 1815, *in* BASIC WRITINGS OF THOMAS JEFFERSON 738–9 (Philip S. Foner ed., Halcyon House 1944).

that was its announced goal.[46] This avalanche of bigotry, however, did not spring full grown from the new republic's native soil; it built, instead, on a broad anti-Catholic foundation, going back in England to the days of Henry VIII, two centuries preceding the American Revolution. In the mother country, this religious hatred was celebrated every year by Guy Fawkes Day, with its symbolic search of Parliament's basement for residual evidence of the Jesuits' 1605 "Gunpowder Plot" to blow up the buildings and kill James I and members of Parliament.[47] This festival could not be persuasively carried forward intact by the Puritans of New England, to be sure, because their ancestors had joyfully beheaded James I's son Charles, but it was perpetuated by "Pope Day," the most national of our early holidays, after Thanksgiving and the Fourth of July.[48]

Other remembered historical sources for America's anti-Catholicism in the nineteenth century were England's wars with Catholic France; the reign of "Bloody Mary," the attempt to restore Mary Queen of Scots to the English throne; the Spanish Armada; and the Jacobite Rebellion of 1745–1746, when Bonnie Prince Charles (the "Young Pretender") valiantly tried but failed to make good his claim to the English crown. These events evoked a series of English restrictions on Catholics, briefly summarized as follows:

> Catholics were excluded from the legal profession, from teaching and from the universities, priests were banished under penalty of death, poorer Catholics were afforded the same treatment, and even the well-to-do were ordered to stay within five miles of their estates and attend the services of the Church of England. With the Gunpowder Plot, popular indignation was reflected in even more rigorous penal laws. The fines against those Catholics who failed to attend the established ... [Church of England] were increased, all were required to take a new oath of allegiance to the king, and the professions which they could enter were still further narrowed.[49]

The American colonists had their differences with the home country in religious matters, but most brought with them a shared hatred of "popery," no less vitriolic even though the colonies harbored only a relative handful of Catholics.[50] Intolerance gradually diminished here, but by 1700, despite America's vaunted freedom of religion, Catholics enjoyed unfettered civil and religious rights only in Rhode Island (if there). Their status improved gradually during the eighteenth century, however, fed by France's support of the colonies during the American Revolution, and the Constitution's ban on religious tests for federal officeholders did not encounter much opposition.[51] Within a few decades, though, there was a pretext for a revival of the no-popery clamor, *viz.*, a flood of immigrants, especially Irish Catholics, reflecting the reduction in Europe of its wartime employment rolls, the parallel decline of wages during the industrial revolution, and the harsh treatment (including deportation) of paupers from England and Germany.

46 *See generally* Ray Allen Billington, The Protestant Crusade, 1800–1860 (Rinehard & Co. 1938) (admirably detailed and copiously illustrated); *see also* Sydney E. Ahlstrom, A Religious History of the American People 555–69 (Yale Univ. Press 1972).

47 For a lively and well-illustrated account of the Gunpowder Plot and Guy Fawkes Day, *see* Alan Haynes, The Gunpowder Plot (Sutton 1994).

48 For Pope Day, *see* Mary Augustina Ray, American Opinion of Roman Catholicism in the Eighteenth Century 256–61 (Columbia Univ. Press 1936).

49 Billington, *supra* note 46, at 3–4.

50 *See* John G. Shea, The Catholic Church in Colonial Days (New York 1886).

51 For this provision of the Constitution, *see* Chapter 6.A.

Deists like Jefferson and his followers did not join the nativist ranks, but their independent hostility to Roman Catholicism and papal "superstition" meant that they did not actively seek to discourage the nativists.

The Papal Jubilee of 1827 inspired Catholic priests in the United States to seek converts, a step that evoked anxiety among American Protestants, especially when the Catholic Diocese of Baltimore, headed by a vigorous and ambitious bishop, warned Catholic parents against "corrupt translations of the Bible" (i.e., the King James and other Protestant versions, then being circulated by the American Bible Society) and promoted the construction of parochial schools to protect Catholic children from the "perversion" they encountered in the public schools.[52] Moreover, an internal dispute pitted Catholic priests against their parishioners over the legal ownership of church buildings: was the rightful owner the bishop of the diocese (as prescribed by Catholic doctrine) or trustees representing the lay members? Protestant observers thought that the bishops' claim was inconsistent with American traditions and reflected centralized papal authority that violated the nation's democratic spirit.[53] This was one of the few nineteenth-century church-state controversies to find its way into litigation, which was resolved in favor of the bishopric claim,[54] and though diehard Protestants carried the battle into the state legislative bodies, they lost there also.

Anti-Catholic outcries gained force from a surprising source: popular suspicions about the secretive Masons, even though they were historically enemies of Roman Catholicism, which led citizens to sniff out conspiracies everywhere and to accept lurid tales about the inner workings of the Catholic Church. Another unexpected source of anti-Catholicism was the enactment in England of the 1829 Catholic Emancipation Act, which inspired American Protestants to circulate memories of the Gunpowder Plot and other alleged Catholic atrocities in order launch a preemptive campaign to forestall such a measure in the United States. Gathering force, the anti-Catholic clamor attracted "[r]eligious and political adventurers, profit seekers, publicity hounds, fanatics, opportunists, 'joiners' of all kinds, and some men who in retrospect seem almost mad," along with a sprinkling of respectable church leaders.[55]

These nativist suspicions of Catholicism were fueled by a barrage of fantastic revelations, often with a salacious tinge, about the Church's confessional, life in the convents, and other inner-church matters. This propaganda was published in more than a score of anti-Catholic newspapers, augmented by numerous books and pamphlets. A best-seller was the tale of Maria Monk, whose "Awful Disclosures of the Hotel Dieu Nunnery of

[52] For a graphic account of the beating given a ten-year-old Catholic boy who refused to recite passages from a Protestant edition of the bible in a Boston public school, *see The Eliot School Rebellion, Boston, 1857, in* John T. McGreevy, Catholicism and American Freedom (W.W. Norton 2003). Fuller account: Robert H. Lord, John E. Sexton & Edward T. Harrington, 2 History of the Archidioceses of Boston 535ff (Wood, Shield & Ward 1944). *See also* Diane Ravitch, The Great School Wars, New York City, 1805–1913, A History of the Public Schools as Battlefield of Social Change (Basic Books 1974).

[53] For a brief account of this dispute, *see* The Catholic Encyclopedia (Broderick ed., 1987); for details, *see* Joseph L.J. Kirlin, Catholicity in Philadelphia (1909).

[54] For a detailed account of the early problems of property ownership and control of individual churches, confused because the Catholic Church was not recognized as a corporation or legal entity, *see* Carl Zollmann, American Church Law 103–24 (West Publ. Co. 1933); for contemporary law, *see* Chapter 8.A.

[55] Ahlstrom, *supra* note 46, at 559.

Montreal" disclosed "the practice of criminal intercourse" between nuns and priests, followed by the baptism and strangulation of their babies, who were thus "sent out of the world before they had time to do anything wrong."[56] Equally alarmist, though on a different level of appeal, was the nativist theory that the Pope, in company with Europe's despotic rulers, was plotting to gain control of the Mississippi area and to flood it with Catholic settlers in order to dispel American freedom and liberty and substitute papal authority. Not surprisingly, the Jesuits were seen as the advance agents of this papal crusade. Samuel F. B. Morse, inventor of the telegraph, was an early leader in publicizing the plot in his widely circulated, "A Foreign Conspiracy against the Liberties of the United States." In an 1835 book-length expansion of this work, he warned his nativist followers against the Jesuits and their alleged puppets, Catholic immigrants:

> Americans, you are marked for their prey, not by foreign bayonets, but by weapons surer of effecting the conquest of liberty than all the munitions of physical combat in the military or naval storehouses of Europe. Will you not awake to the apprehension of the reality and extent of your danger? ... Up! Up! I beseech you. Awake! To your posts! Let the tocsin sound from Maine to Louisiana. Fly to protect the vulnerable places of your Constitution and Laws. Place your guards; you will need them, and quickly ... shut your [immigration] gates.[57]

Despite Morse's fervor, neither his warning nor the nativist movement as a whole succeeded in barring entry to immigrants; they were accepted, if not welcomed, throughout the nineteenth century. Their number surged from approximately 150,000 in the 1820s to almost 600,000 in the 1830s and to an astonishing 2,300,000 in the 1850s[58] amid charges that immigration was causing a growth in pauperism, labor-class rowdyism, and crime. Despite these alarms, immigration was not subjected to ethnic, religious, or country-of-origin limits until enactment of the Chinese Exclusion Act of 1882.[59]

In the 1850s, the nativist movement was propelled to its crest by a patriotic society, the Order of the Star-Spangled Banner, whose avowed secrecy won its members a memorably provocative name, the "Know-Nothings,"[60] and this group branched out into national politics. Electing 75 members of a 234-member Congress in 1854, the Know-Nothings seemed poised for a presidential victory in 1856, but unsuccessful in attempting to straddle the slavery issue, they actually declined in number and then fell into obscurity when the new Republican Party, soon to be the party of Lincoln, came to the fore.

[56] *See* Billington, *supra* note 46, at 99–108.

[57] *Id.* at 122–5; *see also id.* at 322–44; Edward L. Morse & Samuel F.B. Morse, Samuel F.B. Morse: His Letters and Journals (Houghton Mifflin 1914). One of Morse's prominent supporters was Lyman Beecher, an influential and respected Protestant preacher (and father of Harriet Beecher Stowe), whose 1834 *Plea for the West* warned of an alleged papal-monarchial conspiracy to win control of the Mississippi Valley.

[58] Maldwyn Allen Jones, American Immigration 93 (Univ. of Chicago Press 1960).

[59] *See* Erika Lee, At America's Gates: Chinese Immigration during the Exclusion Era, 1882–1943 at 4 (Univ. of N. Carolina Press 2003).

[60] For a brief account of the rise, decline, and fall of Know-Nothingism, *see* Billington, *supra* note 46, at 380–436; for details, *see* Brian Nelson Fry, Alien Nations: Varieties of Nativism and Perceptions of Threat (1998) (Michigan State Univ. Ph.D. thesis); John Higham, Strangers in the Land: Patterns of American Nativitism, 1860–1925 (2d ed., Rutgers Univ. Press 1998); Tyler Gregory Anbinder, Nativism and Slavery: The Northern Know Nothings and the Politics of the 1850s (Oxford Univ. Press 1992); Mark Voss-Hubbard, Beyond Party: Cultures of Antipartisanship in Northern Politics Before the Civil War (Johns Hopkins Univ. Press 2002).

With this summary of American nativism, note should be taken of one of its manifestations that was relatively free of imagined Catholic horror stories and conspiracies: controversies over the use of the King James translation of the bible and its concomitant, Protestant indoctrination in the growing public school system, most dramatically in New York City.[61] Its nonprofit Public School Society, partly financed with public funds, had been formed in 1805 to conduct schools for children whose parents could not afford to send them to religious or private schools. By 1840, it operated nearly a hundred schools, many with practices that were objectionable to Catholic parents, such as bible reading, daily prayers, Protestant hymns, and instruction in history that denigrated the role of Catholics.[62] In 1840, New York's governor, sympathetic to these Catholic complaints, proposed the state financing of schools in which Catholic children could be taught by Catholic teachers. This intervention led Catholics, under the leadership of an energetic and passionate spokesman, Bishop John Hughes, to demand that their parochial schools be allowed to share in the allocation of public funds. The outcome of this dispute and its impact in later years on the role of religion in the public school system are discussed later in this work.[63]

## F. Religion and the Abolition of Slavery

In 1987, Justice Scalia observed that "yesterday's religious activism resulted in the abolition of slavery."[64] If Justice Scalia was right, religious activism can be credited with ramming a massive breach in the wall between church and state, one with a unique characteristic, *viz.*, a breach that the American Civil Liberties Union should applaud. Early American misgivings about the institution of slavery are evidenced by the prohibition of slavery in the territory covered by the Northwest Ordinance of 1787, the inclusion in the early constitutions of the northern states of bans and sunset rules on slavery, and the federal Constitution's provision permitting Congress to prohibit the slave trade after 1807.[65] The American Colonization Society, founded in 1817 to raise funds to purchase slaves from their owners for shipment back to Africa, was dominated by clergymen and their churches; Quakers were especially prominent in the abolitionist movement; and the Methodists and Presbyterians were gradually but steadily calling for abolition of the evil. The most famous manifesto in the history of abolitionism was written by William Lloyd Garrison, the Baptist founder of the antislavery journal *The Liberator*, for its first issue:

61 *See* Billington, *supra* note 46, at 142–65; *see also* Carl F. Kaestle, Pillars of the Republic: Common Schools and American Society (Hill & Wang 1983); *Who Defines What Is Common? Roman Catholics and the Common School Movement, 1801–1892*, *in* James W. Fraser, Between Church and State: Religion and Public Education in Multicultural America ch. 3 (St. Martin's Press 1999).

62 For an influential 1854 state decision holding that a Catholic student could be expelled from the state's public schools for refusing to read from the Protestant bible, *see* Donahoe v. Richards, 38 Me. 379 (1854).

63 *See* Chapter 16.

64 Edwards v. Aguillard, 482 U.S. 578, 615 (1987) (invalidating on First Amendment grounds a state statute that forbid public schools from teaching evolution without also teaching creation science).

65 For the pre–Civil War law of slavery, *see* Thomas R. Cobb, An Inquiry into the Law of Negro Slavery in the United States (Univ. of Georgia Press 1999). For slavery in the North, *see, e.g.*, Leslie M. Harris, In the Shadow of Slavery: African Americans in New York City, 1626–1863 (Univ. of Chicago Press 2003); Shane White, Stories of Freedom in Black New York (Harvard Univ. Press 2002).

> I *will* be as harsh as truth, and as uncompromising as justice. On this subject [of slavery] I do not wish to think, or speak, or write, with moderation. ... I am in earnest – I will not equivocate – I will not excuse – I will not retreat a single inch – AND I *WILL* BE HEARD.[66]

Garrison's uncompromising stance led him to demand that the North secede from the union because the Constitution, by tolerating slavery, was a "covenant with death and an agreement with hell."[67] The antislavery movement split again and again as its members – little given to compromise – embraced a bewilderingly wide range of opinions and tactics, and no niche was without its ardent clergymen and devout laymen.

Although Harriet Beecher Stowe, author of *Uncle Tom's Cabin*, was not herself a militant abolitionist, she was the daughter, sister, and wife of leading religious foes of slavery (Lyman Beecher, Henry Ward Beecher, and Calvin Stowe, respectively), and Lincoln famously credited her with bringing on the Civil War.[68] The association of religion with the abolition of slavery is also attested by the ubiquitous involvement of religious leaders in the antislavery cause. Henry Ward Beecher, for example, used his pulpit to solicit funds to fight slavery in "Bleeding Kansas" so that the term "Beecher's Bibles" meant rifles, and the bible-reading Puritan John Brown led a famous attack on Harper's Ferry.[69] In time, the men in blue marched into war singing the religion-drenched "Battle Hyman of the Republic." ("Mine eyes have seen the glory of the coming of the Lord"). However, the defense of slavery, voiced mostly by southerners, also could claim support from religious leaders, although these southern religious defenders of slavery were numerous and less fervent than their antislavery northern counterparts.[70] The southern defense of slavery often was grounded on its economic importance to the South and on regional loyalty, the South's most eloquent and respected spokesman being John C. Calhoun.[71]

Slavery was not only the cause of incessant religious intervention into politics, but it also brought political influences to bear on the churches, resulting most dramatically in schisms within some denominations as their pro- and antislavery wings chose to go their separate ways. Thus the Methodists found that neither neutrality nor silence on the subject of slavery was feasible, and in a series of steps, the antislavery Methodists seceded. Before long, there were two bitterly separated Methodist Episcopal Churches. The Baptists also divided into northern and southern wings, though their fission was less marked by vitriol because, unlike the Methodists, they were organized into local congregations and lacked a binding national hierarchy.[72] The Presbyterians also split, though more slowly; theirs was the third of the religions to which Calhoun alluded in an 1850 speech in the Senate in which he lamented that "already three great evangelical churches have been torn asunder" by the slavery issue.[73] The principal churches that

[66] William Lloyd Garrison 23 (George M. Fredrickson ed., Prentice-Hall 1968).

[67] *Id.* at 63. Garrison's characterization was based on Isaiah 28:15.

[68] Frank Donovan, Mr. Lincoln's Proclamation 47 (Dodd, Mead & Co. 1964) (quoting President Lincoln, based on reports by Stowe's relatives, as asking, "Is this the little lady who made the great war?").

[69] *See generally* Louis Filler, Crusade Against Slavery 1830–1860 (Harper's 1960); James Brewer Stewart, Holy Warriors: The Abolitionists and American Slavery (Hill & Wang 1976).

[70] For the pre–Civil War law of slavery, *see* Cobb, *supra* note 31.

[71] *See The Bible in Defense of Slavery*, *in* Noll, *supra* note 6, at 388–9.

[72] For analysis of the legal issues created by intradenominational schisms, *see* Chapter 8.

[73] Ahlstrom, *supra* note 46, at 660. For a brief account of these and other divisions, *see id.* at 657–68; for more detailed histories, *see* 2 Stokes, *supra* note 4, at 156–203.

managed to avoid an internal division until the Civil War compelled them to split were the Lutheran, Protestant Episcopal, and Roman Catholic churches.

The schisms were so bitter that even after the defeat of the Confederacy, some northern clergymen opposed a reunion of their southern wings, whose failure to condemn slavery, one church newspaper wrote, buried "[t]he apostate church … beneath a flood of divine wrath."[74] The three churches accounting for most of the southern church membership – Methodist, Baptist, and Presbyterian – maintained their independence after the Civil War, thus "providing the Lost Cause with its own altars."[75]

## G. Religion and Women's Rights

One of the features of the eighteenth- and nineteenth-century "democratization of Christianity" and its incorporation into popular culture was the entry of women into the arena of religious instruction, both in the home (through their role in supervising their children) and in public, as they began to preach and expound theological doctrines to both female and male audiences.[76] Women were able to enter the pulpit long before they could enter the electoral booth because suffrage required the approval of all-male legislative bodies, whereas there was no gender barrier to becoming a preacher.[77] To buttress claims that women's rights (including suffrage) were consistent with Christian teachings, Elizabeth Cady Stanton, a leading advocate, published "The Woman's Bible" in 1895, but this link was not a new concept.[78] Even at the trail-blazing 1848 Seneca Falls (New York) Women's Rights Convention, the resolution supporting woman suffrage barely mustered a majority vote.[79] The doubts expressed at this meeting were reflected by actions in the outside world:

> Public opinion and politicians were more sympathetic to feminists' economic demands than to their political ones. In the mid-1850's, state legislatures began to respond

74 *The Independent*, as quoted by AHLSTROM, *supra* note 46, at 695–6.

75 AHLSTROM, *supra* note 46, at 715–29; EUGENE D. GENOVESE, A CONSUMING FIRE: THE FALL OF THE CONFEDERACY IN THE MIND OF THE WHITE CHRISTIAN SOUTH (Univ. of Georgia Press 1998).

76 *See generally* PATRICIA U. BONOMI, UNDER THE COPE OF HEAVEN: RELIGION, SOCIETY, AND POLITICS IN COLONIAL AMERICA 105–15, 123–4 (Oxford Univ. Press 1986); AHLSTROM, *supra* note 46, at 642ff; 3 STOKES, *supra* note 4, at 35–9 (*Women's Rights in Church and State*); *see also* Richard H. Chused, *Married Women's Property Law: 1800–1850*, 71 GEO. L.J. 1359, 1421 (1983); WOMEN'S RIGHTS IN THE UNITED STATES: A DOCUMENTARY HISTORY (Winston E. Langley & Vivian Fox eds., Greenwood Press 1994) (prominent women writing or speaking about moral, religious, or ethical issues in early nineteenth century).

77 *See generally* KEITH E. MELDER, BEGINNINGS OF SISTERHOOD: THE AMERICAN WOMAN'S RIGHTS MOVEMENT, 1800–1850; L. P. BROCKETT, WOMAN: HER RIGHTS, WRONGS, PRIVILEGES, AND RESPONSIBILITIES (Shacker Books 1977); ELLEN CAROL DUBOIS, FEMINISM AND SUFFRAGE: THE EMERGENCE OF AN INDEPENDENT WOMEN'S MOVEMENT IN AMERICA, 1848–1869 (Cornell Univ. Press 1978).

78 For this work, *see* COALITION TASK FORCE ON WOMEN AND RELIGION, THE WOMAN'S BIBLE (1891) (reprint with commentary of Elizabeth Cady Stanton). *See also* Ariela R. Dubler, *In the Shadow of Marriage: Single Women and the Legal Construction of the Family and the State*, 112 YALE L.J. 1641 (2003). Discrimination in the right to vote on account of sex was not prohibited by the Constitution until the ratification in 1920 of the Nineteenth Amendment.

79 Some recent scholars have argued against the "centrality of suffrage" to the women's rights movement (notwithstanding the sobriquet "suffragette"), calling attention to "a deeply religious sensibility which stressed the interconnections between rights and responsibilities, between civil and domestic relations, and

> favorably to women's lobbying and petition efforts for reforms in property law. By 1860, fourteen states had passed some form of women's property rights legislation. Encouraged by these victories, the movement escalated its demands and shifted its emphasis from property rights to the suffrage. This was clearest in the case of New York. Initially, to gain maximum support for the less controversial demand, activists there circulated separate petitions for property rights and for the vote. As the movement gained strength, however, they included both economic and political demands on a single petition, and, in 1857, presented a unified program to the legislature. Three years later, the New York legislature passed the most comprehensive piece of women's rights legislation in the United States, the Married Women's Property Act. This law granted New York women all the economic rights they demanded, but still refused women the right to vote.[80]

The "economic rights" demanded and often granted included such matters as the right of women to receive their own earnings, to enter into contracts, and to bequeath their property. The nineteenth-century reforms of women's rights also dealt with such noneconomic matters as divorce and the custody of children.[81]

The link between religion and women's rights was manifested from the birth of the Seneca Falls Convention to its conclusion: held in a Wesleyan chapel, it was convened "to discuss the social, civil, and religious rights of women," and it ended with a resolution "to enlist the pulpit and press on our behalf."[82] After cataloging the "history of repeated injuries and usurpations on the part of man toward women," phrased in a style echoing the nation's 1776 Declaration of Independence, the Seneca Falls Convention presented a call to vigorous action. Among the resolutions, which were "carried with but two or three dissenting voices," were these:

> Resolved, That we deplore the apathy and indifference of woman in regard to her rights, thus restricting her to an inferior position in social, religious, and political life, and we urge her to claim an equal right to act on all subjects that interest the human family.
>
> Resolved, That the assumption of law to settle estates of men who die without wills, having widows, is an insult to woman, and ought to be regarded as such by every lover of right and equality.
>
> Whereas, The husband has the legal right to hire out his wife to service, collect her wages and appropriate it to his own exclusive and independent benefit; and, whereas, this has contributed to establish that hideous custom, the promise of obedience in the

between the workings of the state and of the home." Elizabeth B. Clark, *Religion, Rights, and Difference in the Early Women's Rights Movement*, 3 Wis. Women's L.J. 29, 30 (1987). Another revisionist feature of recent studies of the early history of the women's rights movement is a reexamination of the conventional theory that it was a natural offshoot of the prominence of women in the agitation for the abolition of slavery. *See* Peggy A. Rabkin, Fathers to Daughters, The Legal Foundations of Female Emancipation 3ff (Greenwood Press 1980).

80 DuBois, *supra* note 77, at 41–2. For a path-breaking historical account of the nineteenth-century reforms of the property rights of married women, *see* Chused, *supra* note 76.

81 For the early legal history of the principles governing the allocation of custody between parents, *see* Jamil S. Zainaldin, *The Emergence of a Modern American Family Law: Child Custody, Adoption, and the Courts, 1796–1851*, 73 Nw. U. L. Rev. 1038 (1979); Norma Basch, *Relief in the Premises: Divorce as a Woman's Remedy in New York and Indiana, 1815–1870*, 8 L. & Hist. Rev. 1 (1990); Elizabeth B. Clark, *Matrimonial Bonds: Slavery and Divorce in Nineteenth-Century America*, 8 L. & Hist. Rev. 25 (1990).

82 Proceedings of the Women's Rights Convention, held at Seneca Falls & Rochester, N.Y., July & August, 1848, at 1 & 9 (Robert J. Johnston, 1870; reprint Anno New York Times 1969); after adjournment on July 20, 1848, the Seneca Falls Convention reassembled at the Unitarian Church in Rochester, New York, on August 2, 1848.

> marriage contract, effectually, though insidiously, reducing her almost to the condition of a slave, whatever freedom she may have in these respects, being granted as a privilege, not as a right, therefore,
>
> Resolved, That we will seek the overthrow of this barbarous and unrighteous law, and conjure women no longer to promise obedience in the marriage covenant.
>
> Resolved, That those who believe the laboring classes of women are oppressed ought to do all in their power to raise their wages, beginning with their own household servants.
>
> Resolved, That it is the duty of woman, whatever her complexion, to assume, as soon as possible, her true position of equality in the social circle, the church, and the state.[83]

The results of the nineteenth-century movement for reform of the property rights of married women have been summarized recently as follows:

> As the nineteenth century began, real property owned by a married woman in a legal estate was subject to the management and control of her husband. Personal property of a wife became the property of her husband as soon as he reduced it to possession. Where equity courts existed, separate equitable estates could be created for married women's property, but the protections to be provided a wife by the equitable forum had to be specifically delineated in the document creating the estate. ... Several reforms including the liberalization of inheritance rules and divorce laws and the enlargement of benefits for widows and abandoned women, appeared in the early decades of the nineteenth century. Meanwhile, developments in the culture at large created a milieu sympathetic to changes in coverture law. Romantic notions of family formation and maintenance, introduction of industrial production, and increases in literacy and educational goals for children gave women significant family roles. When distressed economic times appeared after 1839, the moment was right for legislatures to codify a portion of the equitable separate estate tradition by insulating wives' property from their spouses' creditors. The acts, usually adopted with little lobbying from women, created a special set of assets available for family use when husbands found themselves in trouble with creditors. Only after this initial wave of debtor protection measures appeared did the women's movement get deeply and successfully involved in substantial reform of coverture law.[84]

## H. Religion and Temperance

In the nineteenth century's arena of social reform, drunkenness rivaled slavery, the treatment of Native Americans, and women's rights in the attention it received from religious leaders and in the extent to which they advocated legal changes that belied any claim that church could be separated from the state by a wall of separation, let alone one that was "high and impregnable."[85] The temperance movement – described by a historian of religion as "that most intemperate of reform impulses"[86] in America – had its beginnings in the seventeenth century, like the abolition of slavery and correction of the maltreatment of Native Americans, but the excessive consumption of distilled spirits differed

83 *Id.* at 15. These resolutions were adopted at the Rochester meeting.

84 Chused, *supra* note 76, at 1361.

85 Everson v. Bd. of Educ. of Ewing Twp., 330 U.S. 1, 18 (1947). *See generally* John Allen Krout, The Origins of Prohibition (Knopf 1925) (history to 1851); Ernest H. Cherrington, The Evolution of Prohibition in the United States (Patterson Smith 1969) (chronological list of significant events, with commentary, 1609–1920); Ahlstrom, *supra* note 46, *passim*.

86 Ahlstrom, *supra* note 46, at 867.

from these two other evils in that its remedies were widely diverse because the legislators of the various states greatly differed in prescribing remedies. Slavery and the treatment of Native Americans, by contrast, were both primarily within the jurisdiction of the national government. Not until 1919, when the Eighteenth Amendment was ratified, was liquor subjected to a unified national prohibition, and this federal hegemony lasted only until 1933, when the Eighteenth Amendment was repealed by the Twenty-First Amendment, reviving the cacophony of state-by-state regulation of the liquor industry.[87]

A notable illustration of the seventeenth- and eighteenth-century religious roots of the temperance movement is a 1673 pamphlet entitled, "Woe to Drunkards," by Increase Mather, an illustrious Congregational minister who was equally distinguished in the political arena.[88] Despite these and other admonitions by the clergy, the excessive use of distilled spirits multiplied as the manufacture and export of rum became a major eighteenth-century industry, Native Americans became addicted to drinking "firewater," revolutionary troops demanded a daily ration of liquor, and civilian wages were sometimes paid partly in rum. When local governments taxed liquor and saloons, however, they ironically acquired an economic interest in the continued use of whisky and rum.[89]

In the early nineteenth century, the temperance movement grew rapidly as its tactics shifted from sermons by individual preachers to organized opposition. Lyman Beecher – who, it has been said, "like most of the New England divines of his day, was as much politician as preacher"[90] – was a leader of this change, and in 1812, his church issued a proposal for reform in which it would work hand in glove with the state:

> It ... suggested the following measures: that [religious groups] abstain from the use of ardent spirits at ecclesiastical meetings, that members of churches abstain from unlawful vending or purchase of liquor, that farmers, mechanics and manufacturers substitute monetary compensation for the ration of spirits, that voluntary associations aid the civil magistrates to enforce the laws, and that the pamphlet of Dr. Rush be printed and circulated.[91]

This 1812 report was but the first of an avalanche of nineteenth-century publications and organizations, all of them advocating one or another mode of suppressing the consumption of "ardent" spirits and, somewhat less frequently, wine, beer, and cider as well. Religious leaders and church members were prominent in these groups, and many temperance organizations were explicitly subject to control by Protestant denominations, particularly Methodists, Baptists, Congregationalists, Presbyterians, and Quakers. Moreover, women were especially prominent in the temperance movement; liquor was seen as threatening the sanctity and even the existence of the home in the days when the home was viewed as the domain more of women than of men.[92] Before long, advocacy

[87] *See generally* John R. Vile, A Companion to the United States Constitution and Its Amendments (3d ed., Praeger 2001).

[88] Krout, *supra* note 85, at 52–4.

[89] *See generally id.* at 58–63.

[90] *Id.* at 85.

[91] *Id.* Dr. Rush, a signer of the Declaration of Independence, was the author of several widely admired publications on the deleterious physiological effects of distilled spirits, including a 1784 pamphlet entitled, "An Inquiry into the Effects of Spirituous Liquors on the Human Body and Mind." *See id.* at 72–82.

[92] *See* Elizabeth B. Clark, *Religion, Rights, and Difference in the Early Woman's Rights Movement*, 3 Wis. Women's L.J. 29, 40 (1987); *see also* Ruth Bordin, *A Maternal Struggle*, in Woman and Temperance 3–14 (Temple Univ. Press 1981).

of temperance took on the trappings of a religious observance, similar in passion to the revival meetings of the so-called Second Awakening:

> Temperance workers were evangelists preaching a new gospel, and they stated its dogmas in the pulpit phraseology of the day. ... Appropriate verses, set to familiar gospel tunes, were sung with all the fervour of religious exaltation. The emotional appeals of the speakers and the "testimony" of the pledge-signers strongly suggested the revivals of the evangelical sects. Indeed, the most effective propagandist for temperances was usually the Protestant clergyman who devoted a large proportion of his sermons to denunciation of the liquor traffic, indicting intemperance as the great barrier in the way of the church militant as it marched forward to become the church triumphant.[93]

The religion-dominated temperance movement (and its indispensable link between church and state, illustrated by a myriad of legislative debates and regulations) expanded rapidly during the first half of the nineteenth century. A scholar has painstakingly documented this conclusion: "Both the opponents and supporters of the campaign against the use of intoxicants felt that the single greatest force in the movement was the power of evangelical Protestantism," and "the battle was to be waged not by precept and example, but by political action. ... Temperance advocates were well aware of the value of an alliance with organized religion. In season and out they stressed the divine origin of their reform and the religious character of their propaganda."[94] This "greatest and most unified of all [nineteenth-century] Protestant crusades" reached a crescendo in 1873, when countless "pray-ins" were staged by groups of women at entrances to the nation's saloons, challenging the customers with this battle hymn:

> And where are the hands red with slaughter?
> Behold them each day as you pass
> The places where death and destruction
> Are retailed at ten cents a glass.[95]

A year later, delegates of women from eighteen states, mostly with religious backgrounds, organized the Women's Christian Temperance Union (WTCU), described as "the greatest women's organization of the century."[96] The rapid growth of this organization was facilitated by a network of women's groups promoting temperance:

> The missionary societies of the several Protestant denominations, as well as the churches themselves, provided already functioning female networks that could be converted into WCTU chapters. The temperance movement, the WCTU in particular, was ecumenical from the beginning, and in this it differed from church groups such as missionary societies; but the WCTU was certainly church-oriented, and almost all of its members were church-going Protestants.[97]

[93] Krout, Foreword & 113–15, 300. For the Second Awakening and its religious predecessor, the Great Awakening of the eighteenth century, *see* Ahlstrom, *supra* note 46, at 422–8 & 280–94; *see also* The Great Awakening: Event and Exegesis (Darrett Bruce Rutman ed., Wiley 1970).

[94] For a tabular list of the major events in the temperance movement, *see* Cherrington, *supra* note 85.

[95] Ahlstrom, *supra* note 46, at 867. For a detailed account of the Woman's Crusade of 1873–1874, *see A Western Prairie Fire, in* Ruth Bordin, Woman and Temperance: The Quest for Power and Liberty 15–33 (Temple Univ. Press 1981).

[96] Ahlstrom, *supra* 46, at 868.

[97] Bordin, *supra* note 95, at 9. For the religious composition of the WCTU in its early years, *see id.* at 168–70.

Early in the twentieth century, the WCTU, imbued with the evangelical spirit, exploited every political tactic known to humankind in demanding legislation to prohibit the manufacture and sale of alcoholic beverages. The WCTU succeeded in achieving its objective, first in many states and finally, in 1919, at the national level, with enactment of the Eighteenth Amendment to the national Constitution.[98] If any prohibitionists were distressed because the WCTU constantly breached the wall between church and state, their voices were drowned out by their beats of victory.

## I. Religion, the Churches, and the Civil War

During the Civil War, northern churches marched arm in arm with the northern states in going to war, and the southern churches similarly embraced the states of the Confederacy.[99] An illustration: the Protestant Episcopal Bishop of Rhode Island prayed for his state's Civil War militia, assuring the troops that "it is a holy and righteous cause in which you enlist." In the same vein, the Episcopal Bishop of Louisiana left the pulpit to become a major general in the Confederacy, writing that "it is for our constitutional liberty, which seems to have fled to use for refuge, for our hearth-stones and altars that we strike."[100] After quoting these and similar appeals, the leading historian of religion in the United States concluded that "for violence of statement and ultimacy of appeal, the clergy and the religious press seem to have led the multitude" in welcoming the Civil War.[101] This should be no surprise:

> Churchmen played leading roles in the moral revolutions that swept the North and the South in opposite directions between 1830 and 1860. Between 1846 and 1860, churchmen gradually converted the antislavery movement into a massive juggernaut, and dedicated the South to preserving a biblically supported social order. To these opposing causes, moreover, they transmitted the overcharged intensity of revivalism, carrying it even to the troops when war finally came.
>
> A Northern church leader, responding to allegations that the church brought about the Civil War, exulted "I believe it is true that we did bring it about, and I glory in it, for it is a wreath of glory around our brow."[102]

Conversely, "the most violent and radical pro-slavery men in [the South] were ministers," and "the church in the South constituted the major resource of the Confederacy in the building and maintenance of civilian morale."[103] Both religious groups supplied

98 For the Eighteenth Amendment, *see* IRVING FISHER, THE "NOBLE EXPERIMENT" (Alcohol Information Committee 1930). For repeal of the Eighteenth Amendment by the Twenty-First Amendment, *see supra* note 87 and accompanying text.

99 For the schisms in Protestant churches into northern and southern wings because of differences over the slavery issue, *see supra* Section F.

100 AHLSTROM, *supra* note 46, at 670.

101 *Id.* at 672. At the end of the war, Henry Ward Beecher pronounced this verdict on the pro-slavery political leaders of the South:

> [T]hese guiltiest and most remorseless traitors, these high and cultured men with might and wisdom … shall be whirled aloft and plunged downward forever and ever in an endless retribution.

*Id.* at 684.

102 *Id.* at 673.

103 *Id.* at 672 & 673.

chaplains to their respective sides, and there were numerous battlefield conversions.[104] A Christian Commission was founded by northern civilians, which provided the Union's armed forces with "vast numbers" of bibles, tracts, medical facilities, and "luxuries" not furnished by the armed forces.[105] There were similar programs by religious southerners:

> [T]his outpouring raised the charitable and missionary plans of the churches to a new order of magnitude. It extended the American reformer's conception of the possible, and because its effects were enduring, it opened a new philanthropic era in American history. On this same theme one must add that the churches, not only on account of their role in stimulating this philanthropy, but because of their entire involvement in sectional controversy and war work, were permanently altered in their public stance and in their attitudes toward social affairs.[106]

One might add that this historical trend left little room for a wall between church and state.

The nation's memories of the Civil War are enshrined in songs and literary works, among the best known of which are the "Battle Hymn of the Republic," Lincoln's Second Inaugural and Gettysburg addresses, and Walt Whitman's paean to Lincoln following his assassination ("When Lilacs Last in the Dooryard Bloom'd") – all echoing the vocabulary, phrases, rhythms, and themes of the bible.[107]

## J. Religion and Reconstruction

With the end of the Civil War, the nation entered the troubled era of Reconstruction, which began with high hopes for the revived union but ended in failure. The Protestant churches of the North supported the Radical Republicans, who sought to suppress the rise of southern political forces in order to ensure a safe place for the emancipated slaves. Working through the American Missionary Association (and little troubled by the "wall of separation" between church and state), the northern churches marshaled millions of dollars and supported thousands of teachers and school administrators for work among the southern blacks: "One of the noblest and least recognized chapters in Reconstruction history was written by these poorly paid educators, most of them women, as they struggled amid penury, ridicule, hostility, and sometimes outright violence to demonstrate their faith in the nation's ideals and in the Negro's natural capacity to enter fully into American life."[108]

Led by Thaddeus Stevens and Charles Sumner, the Radical Republicans won widespread electoral victories in 1866, which enabled them to override President Johnson's political compromises and to treat the southern states as "conquered provinces."[109] Their

104 *Id.* at 671 (internal citations omitted).
105 *Id.* at 678–9.
106 *Id.* at 681.
107 For a brief account of these and similar works, including Southern tributes to the "Lost Cause," *see id.* at 681–9; *see also* Garry Wills, Lincoln at Gettysburg: The Words that Remade America (Simon & Schuster 1992).
108 Ahlstrom, *supra* 46, at 694–5.
109 *See generally* Kenneth M. Stampp, The Era of Reconstruction, 1865–1877 (Knopf 1970); Jane G. Randall & David Donald, Civil War and Reconstruction (Little, Brown 1969) (discussion of religious aspects of abolition movement at 25–6).

principal instruments were the Thirteenth, Fourteenth, and Fifteenth Amendments to the Constitution, the Civil Rights Acts of 1866 and later years, the federal Freedman's Bureau, and the statutory conditions imposed by Congress on the Confederate states when they applied for readmission to the Union.[110] These engines of change, however, were subject to constricted judicial interpretation,[111] political delays, weak leadership, and racist opposition, and crucial though they were, they encountered and were often defeated by southern intransigence. Reconstruction dwindled away to an ignominious end with the Compromise of 1877, which settled the disputed presidential election of 1876 by awarding victory to Rutherford B. Hayes (Republican), although he received fewer popular votes than his Democratic rival, Samuel J. Tilden. Hayes pledged federal subsidies to improve the South's war-damaged and obsolete economic infrastructure but did little to back up his promises. Moreover, the Compromise of 1877 included the removal of the last federal troops that remained in the South. The states of the old Confederacy thereafter became the Democratic Party's "Solid South" for almost a century.[112] The losers were the ex-slaves, who were left without political champions to face segregation and the Ku Klux Klan; their life was punctuated by sporadic lynchings if they violated the harsh southern social code or otherwise stepped out of their assigned "place" or were suspected of, or charged with, such an offense

## K. The Blaine Amendment and Its State Constitutional Offshoots

### 1. *Introduction*

In his 1875 State of the Union message to Congress, President Grant proposed an amendment to the constitution: "I suggest for your earnest consideration ... a constitutional amendment ... making it the duty of each of the several States to establish and forever maintain free public schools adequate to the education of all children ... [and] forbidding the teaching in aid schools of religious, atheistic, or pagan tenets; and prohibiting the granting of any school funds or school taxes, or any past thereof ... for the benefit of or in aid, directly or indirectly, of any religious sect or denomination.[113] Within a week, James G. Blaine, Republican Speaker of the House of Representatives, soon to become an aspirant for his party's nomination for the presidency, introduced this resolution:

> No state shall make any law respecting an establishment of religion, or prohibiting the free exercise thereof; and no money raised by taxation in any State, for the support of

110 *See* Michael Perman, Reunion Without Compromise: The South and Reconstruction, 1865–1868 (Cambridge Univ. Press, 1973). *See also* Ludwell H. Johnson, Division and Reunion: America 1848–1877 (Wiley 1978).

111 The Civil Rights Act, as interpreted, applied only to governmental misconduct, not to private acts, even if widespread and organized, and the Fourteenth Amendment's equal protection clause was ruled to tolerate legally enforced segregation. *See* Chapter 1.H.

112 *See generally* Keith I. Polakoff, The Politics of Inertia: the Election of 1876 and the End of Reconstruction (Louisiana St. Univ. Press 1973); Eric Foner, Reconstruction: America's Unfinished Revolution (Harper & Row 1988); Charles Fairman, Five Justices and the Electoral Commission of 1877 (Macmillan 1988).

113 Grant's papers: *Seventh Annual Message to Congress, December 7, 1875, in* Ulysses S. Grant 1822–1885 at 92 (Philip R. Moran ed., Oceana Publ. 1968). Grant made a similar proposal in an earlier speech to a reunion of Civil War veterans ("resolve that not one dollar, appropriated for [the support of free public schools] shall be appropriated to the support of any sectarian schools").

> the public schools or derived from any public fund therefore, shall ever be under the control of any religious sect, nor shall any money so raised ever be divided between religious sects or denominations.[114]

Divorced from its political and cultural context, this version of the Blaine proposal seems rather bland, proposing rules elaborating on the rules emerging when the Establishment Clause of the First Amendment was ultimately held by the Supreme Court to be binding on the states because it was "incorporated" into the Fourteenth Amendment.[115] Moreover, several states already had similar prohibitions in their state constitutions. Even so, the Blaine Amendment both revived and stimulated the nativist, anti-immigrant, and anti-Catholic views of the 1830s. Senator Blaine himself seems to have lost interest in the amendment after he gained whatever transitory political benefits it furnished; at any rate, he did not mention it in his autobiography.[116] Glorified in his day as the "Plumed Knight" of the Republican Party, Blaine has been dubbed the "prince of opportunists." In the same vein, Blaine was credited with denouncing the Democratic Party as the party of "Rum, Romanism, and Rebellion," although this alliterated R's phrase emanated from one of his obscure followers, whose defamatory words he renounced, albeit not convincingly.[117]

## 2. *The Proposed Amendment's Context*

Although Blaine displayed only tepid enthusiasm for "his" amendment, it gained many ardent advocates who were infuriated by actual and proposed contributions of public funds to support Catholic parochial schools and by Catholic demands that the public schools (attended by most Catholic pupils) cease their Protestant evangelism. The *Catholic World* responded to the Blaine proposal by reproaching the "politicians who hope to ride into power by awakening the spirit of fanaticism and religious bigotry among us" and announcing that the proposed amendment "will disturb the foundations of our government, will create religious strife, and blast the hopes of freedom not only in this country, but all the world over."[118]

In the course of this struggle, the Blaine Amendment was revised to read as follows:

> No State shall make any law respecting an establishment or religion, or prohibiting the free exercise thereof; and no religious test shall ever be required as a qualification to any

114 4 Cong. Rec. 5191 (1876). *See generally* F. William O'Brien, *The Blaine Amendment 1875–1876*, 41 U. Det. L.J. 137 (1963); Steven K. Green, *The Blaine Amendment Reconsidered*, 36 Am. J. Leg. Hist. 38 (1992); Joseph P. Viteritti, *Blaine's Wake: School Choice, the First Amendment, and State Constitutional Law*, 21 Harv. J.L. & Pub. Pol'y 657 (1998).

115 For the "incorporation" issue, *see infra* Section K.4.

116 *See generally* Richard E. Morgan, The Politics of Religious Conflict (Pegasus 1968). For evidence supporting the charge of the *Nation* in May 1876 that "all that Mr. Blaine means to do or can do with his amendment is, not to pass it but to use it in the [political] campaign to catch anti-Catholic votes"; *see* Green, *supra* note 114, at 54.

117 For this episode, *see* H. Wayne Morgan, From Hayes to McKinley, National Party Politics, 1877–1896 at 226–9 (Syracuse Univ. Press 1969). It was not a period known for political civility; e.g., the Republican Party's national platform accused the Democratic Party of having "sympathized with treason." *See* Kirk H. Porter & Donald Bruce Johnson, National Party Platforms, 1840–1964 at 55 (Univ. of Illinois Press. 1966).

118 Porter & Johnson, *supra* note 117, at 53–4.

> office or public trust under any State. No public property and no public revenue, nor any loan of credit by or under the authority of the United States, or any State, Territory, District, or municipal corporation, shall be appropriated to or made or used for the support of any school, educational or other institution under the control of any religious or anti-religious sect, organization, or denomination, or wherein the particular creeds or tenets shall be taught. And no such particular creeds or tenets … shall be read or taught in any school or institution supported in whole or in part by such revenue or loan of credit; and no such appropriation or loan of credit shall be made to any religious or anti-religious sect, organization, or denomination, or to promote its interests or tenets. This article shall not be construed to prohibit the reading of the Bible in any school or institution, and it shall not have the effect to impair rights of property already vested.[119]

In addition to applying its limitations to the federal government, this revision closed a "loophole" in Blaine's original language: the possibility that it applied only to funds that had somehow been dedicated when appropriated for the public schools (and were then diverted to sectarian schools), not to funds accumulated in the state's general treasury or raised explicitly to aid sectarian schools, but the proposal continued in common parlance to be known as the "Blaine Amendment."[120]

Despite the changes, because of them, or perhaps as a result of the changes taken in combination, the revised version failed to get the necessary two-thirds vote in the Senate,[121] but it did not die quietly. Thus its central theme was carried forward in the Republican Party's 1880 national platform:

> The Constitution wisely forbids Congress to make any law respecting the establishment of religion, but it is idle to hope that the Nation can be protected against the influence of secret sectarianism while each State is exposed to its domination. We, therefore, recommend that the Constitution be so amended as to lay the same prohibition upon the Legislature of each State, and to forbid the appropriation of public funds to the support of sectarian schools.[122]

### 3. *State "Blaine Amendments"*

In 1888, Senator Henry Blair, a New Hampshire Republican, endeavored to resuscitate the Blaine Amendment, but against a different enemy.[123] Blaine feared not the Catholics but the newly prominent Mormons. He pointed out that the First Amendment's Establishment Clause bound only Congress, leaving the states free to create established churches[124] – an institution that would be easy for the territory of Utah (which was about to become a state), which could revise its constitution and establish Mormonism as the state religion.

119 4 Cong. Rec. 5184, 5453 (1876).

120 For a detailed analysis of the changes in Blaine's verbiage, *see* O'Brien, *supra* note 114, at 155–90.

121 *Id.* at 186–7. For an analysis of the vote, *see id.* at 192 [citing 4 Cong. Rec. 5589, 5590 (1876)].

122 *See* Porter & Johnson, *supra* note 117, at 61.

123 For Blair's amendment, *see* F. William O'Brien, *The States and "No Establishment": Proposed Amendments to the Constitution since 1798*, 4 Washburn L.J. 183, 196–202 (1965). For a list of the proposed amendments, *see id.* at 210.

124 This was before the Supreme Court held that the Bill of Rights was "incorporated" into the Fourteenth Amendment so as to bind the states.

In the states, matters developed quite differently. The case of New York was an instance of developments at this level of government. In an 1894 state constitutional convention, meeting to draft a new charter, the delegates adopted the following language as part of the new state constitution, urged on by the illustrious Elihu Root, who argued that an amendment explicitly prohibiting aid to religious schools was essential for "maintaining the great American principle of eternal separation between Church and State." The language inserted in the New York constitution is similar to that adopted by the thirty-three states between 1877 and 1913. It read as follows:

> Neither the state nor any subdivision thereof shall use its property, or credits or any public money, or authorize or permit either to be used directly or indirectly, in aid or maintenance, other than for examination or inspection, of any school or institution of learning wholly or in part under the control or direction of any religious denomination, or in which any denominational tenet or doctrine is taught.

Although there is no direct connection between these state enactments and the efforts of Senator Blaine, who in fact died (in 1893) before some states acted, they do indicate the deep reservoir of opposition to any form of state aid to Catholic schools in late nineteenth- and early twentieth-century America, into which Blaine and other Republicans hoped to tap. That they are today called "Blaine Amendments" (or "baby-Blaine Amendments") appears to be due to the label affixed to such measures by the editors of the Jesuit-edited *America* magazine, who possibly hoped to settle a score with the man who had once described the Jesuits as a "'Black Legion' and an 'enemy of this country' whose goal was 'destroying the public school system.'"[125]

### 4. *The Blaine Amendment and "Incorporation" of the Bill of Rights by the Fourteenth Amendment*

After decades of somnolescence, the Blaine Amendment suddenly attracted an abundance of scholarly attention in the middle of the twentieth century not because of its substantive content but rather because of what was *not* said when it was being debated in the 1870s. The context of this curious revival of interest in the Blaine Amendment was the Supreme Court's twentieth-century cases ruling that the Bill of Rights was binding on the states as well as on the federal government – the so-called incorporation doctrine.[126] Historians who thought that the "incorporation" claim distorted history pointed to the Blaine Amendment as evidence, arguing that it would have been an idle gesture – an unnecessary precaution – if the incorporation theory was correct because in that event it would have already been unconstitutional for the states to finance religious education. Yet both the advocates and the enemies of the Blaine Amendment assumed in their debates that state financing of church-affiliated schools was permissible under existing law:

> [T]he near passage of the Blaine Amendment – with its provision applying the first amendment religion clauses to the states – reveals that the members of the 44th Congress [which debated the Blaine proposal] did not believe the fourteenth amendment already

125 Jon Lauck, *"You Can't Mix Wheat and Potatoes in the Same Bin": Anti-Catholicism in Early Dakota*, 38 S.D. Hist. 1, 32 (2008).

126 *See* Chapter 1.I.

> applied the first amendment ... to state actions. Under this view, the fact that Congress considered the Blaine Amendment within seven years of the passage of the fourteenth amendment, and that several lawmakers voted for both amendments, indicates that none of the lawmakers understood the protections of the first amendment to be included within the concept of liberty under the fourteenth amendment's due process clause.[127]

To bolster this anti-incorporation claim, a painstaking scholar points out

> For ... eight months, Blaine's proposal was discussed in the leading journals and newspapers across the nation while several Congressmen wrote pro and con addresses. It is highly significant that there appears to have been no speaker or writer who contested the assumption upon which [Congressman Blaine] ... grounded his argument that a constitutional amendment was needed. Yet it is incredible to say that the full import of the fourteenth amendment [i.e., its application of the Establishment Clause of the First Amendment to the states] could have so quickly been forgotten by every public figure and every responsible journal.
>
> The House Committee on the Judiciary [of the 44th Congress], which had Blaine's Amendment under advisement for eight months consisted of eleven members, all lawyers, several of whom might be called distinguished in the legal profession. One had been in the House in the 39th Congress when the fourteenth amendment was debated and approved. Another was in the state legislature of Maine when that body voted to ratify the [Fourteenth] amendment.
>
> The House in which the [Blaine] amendment was suggested [included] ... ten members of the 39th Congress, amongst whom was Blaine himself. Thirty seven others had been in the legislatures of twenty-four different states when these bodies debated and voted upon the fourteenth amendment. Three had been Governors in their respective states and had presented the amendment to their legislatures with messages of explanation. At least eleven other members of the 44th Congress had been candidates for public office, federal or state, at the very time that the then recently proposed amendment was a burning election issue. They must perforce have acquainted themselves with its provisions. In addition, many others held significant positions as attorney generals or judges on state or federal courts, offices almost demanding that their incumbents investigate a constitutional question which was provoking so much current public debate.[128]

Dismissing the importance of these failures to mention the Fourteenth Amendment in debating the Blaine proposal, however, a recent scholar argued

> The Blaine Amendment was the direct result of Republican attempts to gain political mileage from a growing public concern over Catholic and immigrant inroads into American culture. The Democrats were no less culpable through their [opposition to] ... the amendment to garner Catholic support. The debate surrounding the Blaine Amendment centered on resolving the School Question – and on how each party could benefit from the controversy – and not on the meaning and scope of the fourteenth amendment. Thus the modern-day emphasis placed on the Blaine Amendment is misplaced. The Amendment may say less about nineteenth century conceptions of liberty protected under the fourteenth amendment and more about our nation's continual willingness to use religious issues for political ends.[129]

127 Green, *supra* note 114, at 38–9.
128 O'Brien, *supra* note 114, at 200–1.
129 Green, *supra* note 114, at 69.

Without rejecting this assessment of the rival efforts to use the Blaine proposal as a political weapon, however, one can say that it does not rebut the claim that given the propensity of journalists, politicians, and legislators to use every conceivable argument in a war of words, a sizable number of them would have asserted that Blaine's fears were phantoms of his imagination, given the recent ratification of the Fourteenth Amendment, if it "incorporated" the First Amendment. Thus it remains baffling that the Blaine proposal was not dismissed as an idle gesture if its mandate had already been achieved by the Fourteenth Amendment's incorporation of the Bill of Rights. A more recent scholarly attempt to explain "this remarkable transformation" was that a then-recent Supreme Court decision had affirmed the Court's much earlier rulings that the Bill of Rights limited only the federal government, not the states. The result was that "[t]he true and intended meaning of the Fourteenth Amendment was, by this time [i.e., when the Blaine Amendment was debated] of only academic interest."[130] This explanation could be persuasive, perhaps even convincing, if the Blaine debaters were all precedent-dominated graduates of the Harvard Law School, fearful of proffering weak legal arguments, but it does not explain why an undisciplined mob of politicians, ready to use any stick to beat a dog, would have been so austere in their concept of legal relevance.

## L. Mormonism

Mormonism, the doctrine of the Church of Jesus Christ of Latter-Day Saints, originated in western New York in the 1820s, but its members, ridiculed and persecuted by their neighbors, moved in 1833 to Ohio and Missouri.[131] In 1844, their founder, Joseph Smith, was murdered in Nauvoo, Illinois,[132] and they began an arduous trek under the leadership of Brigham Young that took them in 1847 to what is now Utah. Their State of Deseret, shielded from the rest of the nation by the Rocky Mountains, combined church and state, with "plural marriage" as a social practice that shocked and infuriated the non-Mormons ("Gentiles").

In 1857, the Mormons engaged in the "Utah War" with the United States Army. The army succeeded in ousting Brigham Young from his post as governor, but the Mormons themselves managed to preserve their tight-knit community and the practice of "plural marriage" for several decades, though polygamy was forbidden by a series of federal laws.[133] The federal prohibition was held constitutional, despite the Free Exercise Clause of the First Amendment, in *Reynolds v. United States* (1878), a test case that was followed by criminal prosecutions of many Mormons.[134] By 1890, however, with the coveted

[130] MICHAEL KENT CURTIS, NO STATE SHALL ABRIDGE: THE FOURTEENTH AMENDMENT AND THE BILL OF RIGHTS (Duke Univ. Press 1986). Curtis does in fact cite one reference to the narrow judicial construction of the Fourteenth Amendment, *id.* at 170; it remains inexplicable that this sentiment was not repeated again and again in the Blaine debates.

[131] *See generally* SARAH BARRINGER GORDON, THE MORMON QUESTION: POLYGAMY AND CONSTITUTIONAL CONFLICT IN NINETEENTH CENTURY AMERICA (Univ. of North Carolina Press 2002); ROBERT MULLEN, THE LATTER-DAY SAINTS: THE MORMONS YESTERDAY AND TODAY (Doubleday 1966) (with annotated bibliography at 289); for a briefer account, *see* AHLSTROM, *supra* note 46, at 501–9).

[132] *See* Dallin H. Oakes, *The Suppression of the Nauvoo Expositor*, 9 UTAH L.REV. 862 (1965).

[133] *See* Orma Linford, *The Mormons and the Law: The Polygamy Cases*, 9 UTAH L.REV. 308 & 543 (1964–5).

[134] Reynolds v. United States, 98 U.S. (8 Otto) 145 (1879).

status of statehood on the horizon, the church renounced plural marriage as a religious principle and reorganized its political arrangements to accept the separation of church and state.[135]

## M. Rise of the "Social Gospel" Theme in Religious Theory

As related earlier in this chapter, the record of church-state relations in the nineteenth century displayed many instances that disregarded the principle of separation between church and state. This feature of the American religious culture was illustrated again, and with a vengeance, by the "social gospel" theme in Protestant theology in the 1870s and 1880s, which became even more pronounced in the early years of the twentieth century. Acknowledging that the system of religious beliefs known as the Social Gospel "does not permit of precise definition," a standard reference work essays this description:

> The Social Gospel criticized the Protestantism of its day for being too individualistic and too little concerned with practical social service. ... [The Social Gospel] did not reject the notion of individual salvation, but stressed that the fruits of that salvation must be seen in the social sphere.
>
> Its chief theological focus was "the kingdom of God," which it understood as being the heart of the ethical system of Jesus, a collective notion and the only alternative to "the greedy ethics of capitalism and militarism." Against the kingdom of God are ranged the manifestations of "the kingdom of evil." Purely individual notions of sin are inadequate to explain the universal yoke of evil and suffering in human experience. The Social Gospel therefore sought to identify social, collective evil, and to foster a spirit of solidarity among Christians over against those manifestations. This involved the possibility of collective repentance and collective conversion for nations, organizations, companies and other social units.[136]

To apply these principles to contemporary American life – the central aim of the Social Gospel – these abstractions had to be brought down to earth. The movement's best-known

[135] *See* Leonard J. Arrington, 1 History of Idaho 319–448 (Univ. of Idaho Press 1994).

[136] Alan Richardson and John Bowden, The Westminster Dictionary of Christian Theology 540–1 (Westminster Press 1983). For detailed accounts of the Social Gospel movement, see Ahlstrom, *supra* note 46, at 785–804; *id.* at 639 [tracing the concept back to Joseph Tuckerman (1778–1840), a Unitarian minister, for his "conviction that Christianity was a social principle and not merely a private pact with God," The Social Gospel in America, 1870–1920 (Robert T. Handy ed., Oxford Univ. Press 1966); Charles H. Hopkins, The Rise of the Social Gospel in American Protestantism 1865–1915 (Yale Univ. Press 1940); Paul T. Phillips, A Kingdom on Earth, Anglo-American Social Christianity, 1880–1940 (Penn State Univ. Press 1996)]. Criticizing in his The Kingdom of God in America (Willett, Clark & Co. 1937), H. Richard Neibuhr suggests (at 193) that the Social Gospel theologians were "naively optimistic" for implying that

> A God without wrath brought men without sin into a kingdom without judgment through the ministrations of a Christ without a cross.

Commenting on the 2004 motion picture *The Passion of the Christ*, a critic observed that "[d]espite its muscular excess, this film is a welcome repudiation of all that." *See* Kenneth L. Woodward, *Do You Recognize This Jesus?*, N.Y. Times, Feb. 25, 2004, at A23.

theologian, Walter Rauschenbusch (1861–1918), did this in a program setting out his proposals for the reconstruction (and purification) of the nation's economic system:

1. [A]ppropriation of economic rent by the taxation of ground values apart from improvements [the so-called single tax advocated by Henry George][137];
2. [A]ppropriation of some of the chief sources of profit by municipal ownership of natural monopolies, e.g., water, gas, electric light and power, and surface roads;
3. [E]xtension of the industrial machinery and capacity of the organized people by control of the express and telegraph business through the machinery of the post office;
4. [B]y the income derived from these sources, extension of … museums, parks, playgrounds, baths, etc., to promote the welfare of the people;
5. [B]reaking up the accumulations of great capital by a steeply graduated inheritance tax;
6. [O]rganization of trades, partly to maintain wages and improve the condition of labor, and partly to create a social organization of the people, on which the social management of industry can devolve when it becomes necessary; and
7. [L]abor legislation to shorten the working time, improve the sanitary conditions of labor, prevent child labor, restrict female labor, etc.[138]

Not one of these reforms, let alone the full nine yards, could be achieved by Rauschenbusch and his Social Gospel followers without employing to the hilt all the political tactics that are customary in achieving economic and social reform, and this means that the Social Gospel is utterly inconsistent with the theory that church and state should be separated by a "high and impregnable wall," to quote Justice Black.[139]

By presenting the platform as an illustration of what the Social Gospel taught him, Rauschenbusch impliedly acknowledged that however persuasive the program's "secular" foundation may be for nonbelievers, the Social Gospel was what impelled him to present it as an example of the ethical system of Jesus. Rauschenbusch was sometimes called a "Christian socialist," a term implying that the materialistic features of political socialism were repellent to him.[140] Surely he did not offer a "secular" program as a route to the "Kingdom of God." Moreover, the religious character of Rauschenbusch's economic program is attested to by the fact that it is the only detailed set of reforms presented in a leading work on the Social Gospel. It would be an unsettling anticlimax to announce that Rauschenbusch's list of reforms could just as well have been published to exhibit his "secular" conclusions about what should be done to improve the nation's economic and political health.

## N. Christianity as Part of the Law of the Land

The nineteenth-century record of church-state relations is sprinkled with assertions – sometimes characterized as a "maxim" – that Christianity is part of the law of the land.

137 For Henry George's proposed "single tax," *see* HENRY GEORGE, PROGRESS AND POVERTY: AN INQUIRY INTO THE CAUSE OF INDUSTRIAL DEPRESSIONS AND OF INCREASE OF WANT WITH INCREASE OF WEALTH, THE REMEDY (Garden City, NY, Doubleday, Page, & Co. 1912), *available at* http://oll.libertyfund.org/titles/328.

138 Walter Rauschenbusch, *Dogmatic and Practical Socialism, in* THE SOCIAL GOSPEL IN AMERICA (list slightly reorganized), *supra* note 136, at 321; *see also* Rauschenbusch, *The Social Principles of Jesus, id.* at 371.

139 For the "wall of separation," *see* Chapter 1.

140 *See* THE SOCIAL GOSPEL IN AMERICA, *supra* note 136, observing (at 308) that Rauschenbusch's socialism was "mild, revisionist, evolutionary, and non-doctrinaire."

This proposition is sometimes enunciated in a triumphal model, as by Daniel Webster in his argument in the *Girard Will* case:

> All proclaim that Christianity, general, tolerant Christianity, Christianity independent of sects and parties, that Christianity to which the sword and fagot are unknown, general tolerant Christianity, is the law of the land."[141]

More often, however, the announcement is qualified, as though it conflicted with the nation's vaunted spirit of religious freedom, as in Thomas Cooley's widely praised work on constitutional law:

> It is frequently said that Christianity is a part of the law of the land. In a certain sense and for certain purposes this is true. The best features of the common law, and especially those which regard the family and social relations; which compel the parent to support the child, the husband to support the wife; which make the marriage-tie permanent and forbid polygamy, – if not derived from, have at least been improved and strengthened by the prevailing religion and the teachings of its sacred Book. But the law does not attempt to enforce the precepts of Christianity on the ground of their sacred character or divine origin. Some of those precepts, though we may admit their continual and universal obligation, we must nevertheless recognize as being incapable of enforcement by human laws. That standard of morality which requires one to love his neighbor as himself we must admit is too elevated to be accepted by human tribunals as the proper test by which to judge the conduct of the citizen; and one could hardly be held responsible to the criminal laws if in goodness of heart and spontaneous charity he fell something short of the Good Samaritan. The precepts of Christianity, moreover, affect the heart, and address themselves to the conscience; while the laws of the State can regard the outward conduct only; and for these several reasons Christianity is not a part of the law of the land in any sense which entitles the courts to take notice of and base their judgments upon it, except so far as they can find that its precepts and principles have been incorporated in and made a component part of the positive law of the State.[142]

Except for its power to annoy or inflame deists and strict church-state separationists – Jefferson denounced it as a "judicial forgery"[143] – the concept has been of minor practical importance. It has been employed, however, in a few cases to support a prosecution for blasphemy when the criminal law of the jurisdiction lacked a formal codification of the crime.[144]

A leading case in which an influential nineteenth-century court rejected Cooley's caution and applied the maxim with vigor is *People v. Ruggles*, decided by James Kent, the distinguished chief justice of the New York Supreme Court of Judicature in 1811, later to become famous as "America's Blackstone" for his authoritative *Commentaries on American Law*.[145] For proclaiming that "Jesus Christ was a bastard, and his mother must be a whore," Ruggles was convicted of blasphemy and sentenced to imprisonment

141 ZOLLMANN, *supra* note 54, at 27 [discussing Vidal v. Girard's Executors, 43 U.S. (2 How.) 127 (1844)].

142 THOMAS M. COOLEY, 2 CONSTITUTIONAL LIMITATIONS 976 (8th ed., Little Brown 1927).

143 *See* ZOLLMANN, *supra* note 54, at 27 n. 12.

144 *See, e.g.*, People v. Ruggles, 8 Johns. 290 (N.Y. 1811) (upholding common-law blasphemy conviction).

145 People v. Ruggles, 8 Johns. 290 (N.Y. 1811); for Kent, *see* THEODORE HORTON, A STUDY IN CONSERVATISM, 1763–1847 (Lawbook Exchange 1939); *id.* at 265 ("[T]he names of Blackstone and Kent are never to be disjoined.").

for three months and a fine of $500.[146] His defense was that blasphemy was not a crime because it was not punishable by law in New York, unlike its status in Great Britain, where the establishment of the Church of England made Christianity (including the offense of blasphemy) part of the law of the land. Rejecting this defense, Chancellor Kent asserted

> We stand equally in need, now as formerly, of all that moral discipline, and of those principles of virtue, which help to bind society together. The people of this state, in common with the people of this country, profess the general doctrines of Christianity, as the rule of their faith and practice; and to scandalize the author of these doctrines is not only, in a religious point of view, extremely impious, but, even in respect to the obligations due to society, is a gross violation of decency and good order. Nothing could be more offensive to the virtuous part of the community, or more injurious to the tender morals of the young, than to declare such profanity lawful.[147]
>
> This declaration (noble and magnanimous as it is, when duly understood) never meant to withdraw religion in general, and with it the best sanctions of moral and social obligation from all consideration and notice of the law. It will be fully satisfied by a free and universal toleration, without any of the tests, disabilities, or discriminations, incident to a religious establishment. To construe it as breaking down the common law barriers against licentious, wanton, and impious attacks upon Christianity itself, would be an enormous perversion of its meaning.[148]

Although Kent was willing in 1811 to convict Ruggles without the foundation of a pertinent criminal statute, he seemed in later years to be uncomfortable with this action because when the validity of *Ruggles* was debated in an 1821 New York constitutional convention, Kent asserted that his court had not ruled that Christianity was the law of the land and that blasphemy was a crime only if an attack on Christianity offended public morals. His murky revision of the issue was that "[i]n a sense, we may consider the duties and injunction of the Christian religion as interwoven with the law of the land, and as part and parcel of the common law."[149]

[146] For a detailed historical analysis of the law of blasphemy, *see* Leonard W. Levy, Blasphemy (Knopf 1993) [*see* especially ch. 10 ("Christianity Becomes the Law of the Land") and ch. 18 ("Early American State Cases")].

[147] Ruggles, 8 Johns. at 294.

[148] *Id* at 296.

[149] Levy, *supra* note 146, at 405.

# 3 Religious Influences and Expressions in Law and Government

## A. Introduction

Religion appears to be a pervasive, perhaps indelible dimension of human existence.[1] Approximately 87 percent of the world's population has been characterized as religiously adherent,[2] and in the United States, the percentage of self-identified religious individuals is roughly 89 percent, over 93 percent of whom are affiliated with specific religious traditions.[3] Nearly two-thirds of Americans consider religion to be an important part of their daily lives.[4] From a social science standpoint, it can be said that human beings appear consistently to contemplate questions and to form answers and belief systems regarding matters that have historically been deemed religious in nature.[5] There is evidence as well that underlying or influencing this pattern of human activity are distinct biological factors.[6] Even when traditional religion is removed from the picture, human beings nevertheless seem driven to embrace alternative frameworks of belief that exhibit characteristics of transcendence or that seek to answer the so-called ultimate questions of human existence.[7] This might explain why totalitarian political regimes, in an effort to shape the moral and conceptual frameworks of their citizens, attempt not simply to suppress conventional religious belief systems but also to supplant those systems with ideological frameworks that purport to supply their citizens with statist worldviews.[8]

1 *See* John C. Super & Briane K. Turley, Religion in World History 2 (2006) ("The evidence proves that since the remote past religion has been a part of our mental and emotional make-up. Even non-believers usually agree that the term *homo religiosus* aptly describes the human experience. Men and women by their nature are religious, and efforts to eliminate religion, as many social and political movements have done since the eighteenth century, come up short.").

2 *See* 1 Religions of the World: A Comprehensive Encyclopedia of Beliefs and Practices (J. Gordon Melton & Martin Baumann eds., 2002).

3 The Pew Forum on Religion & Public Life, U.S. Religious Landscape Survey 5 (Feb. 2008), *available at*: http://religions.pewforum.org/pdf/report-religious-landscape-study-full.pdf.

4 *See* Gallup, *State of the States: Importance of Religion* (Jan. 28, 2009); *available at*: http://www.gallup.com/poll/114022/state-states-importance-religion.aspx.

5 *See* Roger Trigg, Equality, Freedom, and Religion 18–25 (2012).

6 Super & Turley, *supra* note 1, at 2 ("[O]ne explanation is that the psychology of the brain has been so ordered that we are born with spiritual inclinations that lead us beyond ourselves … In a literal sense the wiring of our brains, the chemistry of our organs, and the functioning of our senses lead us – no, compel us – to follow a spiritual journey.").

7 *See, e.g.*, Amit Goswami, God Is Not Dead: What Quantum Physics Tells Us about Our Origins and How We Should Live (repr. 2012).

8 *See* Fascism, Totalitarianism and Political Religion (Roger Griffin ed., 2006); William L. Shirer, The Rise and Fall of the Third Reich: A History of Nazi Germany 212–13

In the United States, religion has been part of the nation's narrative since its beginnings.[9] To be sure, "[t]he idea that God has directed the history of the United States has become a commonplace in American life, a way of imagining America's purpose and history that seems so thoroughly familiar that one can easily overlook its essential oddness."[10] When the rebellious American colonies prevailed over the British, given the dim prospect of victory at the Revolution's outset, the notion that Providence looked favorably on the new nation predictably served as an explanatory framework.[11] When the country was divided during the Civil War, many in both the Confederacy and the Union – President Lincoln prominently among them[12] – viewed the conflict as well as the outcome in religious, even apocalyptic terms.[13] Imbued with religious significance, to be sure, have been many, if not most, of the nation's major events or developments: westward expansion across the continent,[14] World War I,[15]

("[T]he Nazi regime intended eventually to destroy Christianity in Germany, if it could, and substitute the old paganism of the early tribal Germanic gods and the new paganism of the Nazi extremists."); Michael Burleigh, *National Socialism as a Political Religion*, *in* 1 TOTALITARIAN MOVEMENTS AND POLITICAL RELIGIONS 1 (Michael Burleigh, Robert Mallett & Emilio Gentile eds., 2000); Emilio Gentile, *Fascism as Political Religion*, 25 J. CONTEMP. HIST. 229 (1990).

9 *See* Sch. Dist. of Abington Twp. v. Schempp, 374 U.S. 203, 212 (1963) (noting "that religion has been closely identified with our history and government"); MARK A. NOLL, AMERICA'S GOD: FROM JONATHAN EDWARDS TO ABRAHAM LINCOLN (2002). Regarding eighteenth-century religious influences, *see* the two volumes of ELLIS SANDOZ, POLITICAL SERMONS OF THE AMERICAN FOUNDING ERA: 1730–1805 (2d ed. 1998).

10 NICHOLAS GUYATT, PROVIDENCE AND THE INVENTION OF THE UNITED STATES, 1607–1876 at 1–2 (2007).

11 *See* JAMES P. BYRD, SACRED SCRIPTURE, SACRED WAR: THE BIBLE AND THE AMERICAN REVOLUTION (2013); JAMES H. HUTSON, CHUCH AND STATE IN AMERICA: THE FIRST TWO CENTURIES 97–101 (2008); THOMAS S. KIDD, GOD OF LIBERTY: A RELIGIOUS HISTORY OF THE AMERICAN REVOLUTION (2010). On the particular religious views of members of the founding-era generation, *see* GREGG L. FRAZER, THE RELIGIOUS BELIEFS OF AMERICA'S FOUNDERS: REASON, REVELATION, REVOLUTION (2012); DAVID L. HOLMES, THE FAITHS OF THE FOUNDING FATHERS (2006); THE FOUNDERS ON GOD AND GOVERNMENT (Daniel L. Dreisbach et al. eds., 2004).

12 *See, e.g.*, JAMES TACKACH, LINCOLN'S MORAL VISION: THE SECOND INAUGURAL ADDRESS (2002); Mark A. Noll, *"Both ... Pray to the Same God": The Singularity of Lincoln's Faith in the Era of the Civil War*, 18 J. ABRAHAM LINCOLN ASS'N 1 (Winter 1997); Ronald C. White, Jr., *Lincoln's Sermon on the Mount: The Second Inaugural*, *in* RELIGION AND THE AMERICAN CIVIL WAR 208 (Randall M. Miller et al. eds., 1998). Most recently, *see* FERENC MORTON SZASZ & MARGARET CONNELL SZASZ, LINCOLN AND RELIGION (2014).

13 *See* MARK A. NOLL, THE CIVIL WAR AS A THEOLOGICAL CRISIS (2006); TERRIE DOPP AAMODT, RIGHTEOUS ARMIES, HOLY CAUSES: APOCALYPTIC IMAGERY IN THE CIVIL WAR (2002); GEORGE C. RABLE, GOD'S ALMOST CHOSEN PEOPLES: A RELIGIOUS HISTORY OF THE AMERICAN CIVIL WAR (2010); MITCHELL SNAY, GOSPEL OF DISUNION: RELIGION AND SEPARATISM IN THE ANTEBELLUM SOUTH (1997); HARRY S. STOUT, UPON THE ALTAR OF THE NATION: A MORAL HISTORY OF THE CIVIL WAR (2006); STEVEN E. WOODWORTH, WHILE GOD IS MARCHING ON: THE RELIGIOUS WORLD OF CIVIL WAR SOLDIERS (2001). To take just one notable example, Julia Ward Howe's poem, which when set to an extant Union marching tune became the "Battle Hymn of the Republic," is a fierce statement of postmillennialist apocalypticism. On its legacy in American culture, *see* JOHN STAUFFER & BENJAMIN SOSKIS, THE BATTLE HYMN OF THE REPUBLIC: A BIOGRAPHY OF THE SONG THAT MARCHES ON (2013).

14 *See* NICHOLAS GUYATT, PROVIDENCE AND THE INVENTION OF THE UNITED STATES 1607–1876, at 218–21 (2007).

15 PHILIP JENKINS, THE GREAT AND HOLY WAR: HOW WORLD WAR I BECAME A RELIGIOUS CRUSADE 10–11, 92–5 (2014); Charles H. Lippy, *Politics*, *in* RELIGION IN AMERICAN HISTORY 249, 251–2 (Amanda Porterfield & John Corrigan eds., 2010) ("Led by a president, Woodrow Wilson, a devout Presbyterian, the American people unconsciously imposed religious images onto the war effort. Wilson's rhetoric, especially in wartime, drew from the emphasis on preaching from the Bible, a form of sermonic proclamation

World War II,[16] the cold war,[17] and the civil rights movement of the 1950s and 1960s,[18] to mention just a few prominent examples.[19]

In turn, it is hardly surprising that the religiosity of Americans and the religious dimensions of the nation's culture and history have been and continue to be acknowledged by law and government in a variety of ways. Some of these acknowledgments are declaratory, such as when the Supreme Court observed in 1952 that Americans "are a religious people whose institutions presuppose a Supreme Being."[20] Canvassing the state and federal constitutions, as well as other documents, the Court similarly observed, sixty years earlier, that "[t]here is a universal language pervading them all, having one meaning. They affirm and reaffirm that this is a religious nation. These are not individual sayings, declarations of private persons. They are organic utterances. They speak the voice of the entire people."[21] Also canvassing the documentary terrain of early America, Professor John Witte richly summarizes the governmental acknowledgments of religion during that period:

> Government officials … regularly acknowledged and endorsed religious beliefs and practices. "In God We Trust" and similar confessions appeared on currency and stamps. Various homages to God and religion appeared on state seals and state documents. The Ten Commandments and favorite Bible verses were inscribed on the walls of court houses, schools, and other public buildings. Crucifixes and other Christian symbols were erected in state parks and on state house grounds. Flags flew at half mast on Good Friday and other high holy days. Christmas, Easter, and other holy days were official holidays. Sundays remained official days of rest. Government-sponsored chaplains were appointed to Congress, the military, and various governmental asylums, prisons, and hospitals. Prayers were offered at the commencement of each session of Congress and of many state legislatures. Thanksgiving Day prayers were offered by presidents, governors, and other state officials.[22]

from his Calvinist heritage that Wilson absorbed almost by osmosis as the son of an ordained Presbyterian seminary professor. The war to make the world safe for democracy was in Wilson's mind a sacred crusade, with the American nation anointed to bring regeneration to a lost world. In other words, the political task of the American state in the war was essentially a religious task, a Protestant Christian one.").

16 *See, e.g.*, ANDREW PRESTON, SWORD OF THE SPIRIT, SHIELD OF FAITH: RELIGION IN AMERICAN WAR AND DIPLOMACY 347–8 (2012).

17 *See, e.g.*, WILLIAM INBODEN III, RELIGION AND AMERICAN FOREIGN POLICY, 1945–1960: THE SOUL OF CONTAINMENT (2010); JASON W. STEVENS, GOD-FEARING AND FREE: A SPIRITUAL HISTORY OF AMERICA'S COLD WAR (2010); Lippy, *supra* note 15, at 252.

18 *See, e.g.*, DAVIS W. HOUCK & DAVID E. DIXON, RHETORIC, RELIGION AND THE CIVIL RIGHTS MOVEMENT 1954–1965 (2006).

19 *See* 1 W. COLE DURHAM, ROBERT SMITH & WILLIAM BASSETT, RELIGIOUS ORGANIZATIONS AND THE LAW § 1:2 (2012) (discussing the role of religion in the abolitionist, women's suffrage, and civil rights movements).

20 Zorach v. Clauson, 343 U.S. 306, 313 (1952); *see also* Van Orden v. Perry, 545 U.S. 677, 683 (2005) (plurality opinion) ("Our institutions presuppose a Supreme Being, yet these institutions must not press religious observances upon their citizens. One face looks to the past in acknowledgment of our Nation's heritage, while the other looks to the present in demanding a separation between church and state.").

21 Holy Trinity Church v. United States, 143 U.S. 457, 470 (1892). In the same case, the Court also observed, more specifically, that these documents as well as a host of public practices illustrate that "this is a Christian nation." *Id.* at 471.

22 John Witte, Jr., *The Essential Rights and Liberties of Religion in the American Constitutional Experiment*, 71 NOTRE DAME L. REV. 371, 406 (1996). Witte continues: "Government officials afforded various forms of aid to religious groups. States underwrote the costs of Bibles and liturgical books for rural churches

A number of these practices, which the Supreme Court has occasionally noted as well,[23] continue to the present and, in the view of many, effectively constitute a national tradition of "ceremonial deism" or an American civil religion.[24] Most recently, the Supreme Court, in upholding a town board's practice of opening its meetings with prayers by local clergy and community members, remarked that "[c]eremonial prayer is but a recognition that, since this Nation was founded and until the present day, many Americans deem that their own existence must be understood by precepts far beyond the authority of government to alter or define and that willing participation in civic affairs can be consistent with a brief acknowledgment of their belief in a higher power."[25]

With these observations as a backdrop, this chapter focuses on the extent to which the laws and legal institutions of American society, past and present, reflect in various ways the religious principles, values, and beliefs associated with the nation's religious traditions. Following an overview of the nation's changing religious demography, this

and occasionally donated land and services to them. Federal and state subsidies were given to Christian missionaries who proselytized among the native American Indians. Property grants and tax subsidies were furnished to Christian schools and charities. Special criminal laws protected the property and clergy of the churches. Tax exemptions were accorded to the real and personal properties of many churches, clerics, and charities." *Id.* at 406–7.

23 *See, e.g.*, Town of Greece, N.Y. v. Galloway, 134 S. Ct. 1811, 1825 (2014) ("As a practice that has long endured, legislative prayer has become part of our heritage and tradition, part of our expressive idiom, similar to the Pledge of Allegiance, inaugural prayer, or the recitation of 'God save the United States and this honorable Court' at the opening of this Court's sessions."); Engel v. Vitale, 370 U.S. 421, 435 n. 21 (1962) (noting that "that school children and others are officially encouraged to express love for our country by reciting historical documents such as the Declaration of Independence which contain references to the Deity or by singing officially espoused anthems which include the composer's professions of faith in a Supreme Being" and that "there are many manifestations in our public life of belief in God"); Zorach, 343 U.S. at 312–13 (noting the practice of "[p]rayers in our legislative halls; the appeals to the Almighty in the messages of the Chief Executive; the proclamations making Thanksgiving Day a holiday; 'so help me God' in our courtroom oaths" and "the supplication with which the Court opens each session: 'God save the United States and this Honorable Court'"); *cf. also* Elk Grove Unified Sch. Dist. v. Newdow, 542 U.S. 1, 26–30 (2004) (Rehnquist, J., concurring in the judgment) (noting several "patriotic invocations of God and official acknowledgments of religion's role in our Nation's history"); Loudon Cnty. Pub. Schs., 418 F.3d 395, 403–4 (4th Cir. 2005) (opinion of Williams, J.) (noting legislative prayer, the explicit religious references in the Declaration of Independence and the implicit ones in the Constitution, and various legislative and executive pronouncements of a religious nature, and further observing that these "patriotic references to the Deity … are not limited to the time surrounding the founding of our nation" and then noting various practices, such as the Supreme Court's opening of its sessions with 'God save the United States and this honorable court,' the reference to 'under God' in Lincoln's "Gettysburg Address," and the use of what is now the national motto, 'In God We Trust,' on coinage and then currency).

24 *See, e.g.*, Cnty. of Allegheny v. ACLU Greater Pittsburgh Chapter, 492 U.S. 573, 630 (1989) (O'Connor, J., concurring in part and concurring in the judgment); ACLU of Ohio v. Capitol Square Rev. & Advis. Bd., 243 F.3d 289, 300 (6th Cir. 2001) (noting the "country's long and deeply entrenched tradition of civic piety, or 'ceremonial deism'"); N.C. Civil Liberties Union v. Constangy, 947 F.2d 1145, 1151 (4th Cir. 1991), *cert. denied*, 505 U.S. 1219 (1992); Jones v. Clear Creek Indep. Sch. Dist., 930 F.2d 416, 420 (5th Cir. 1991); Stein v. Plainwell Cmty. Schs., 822 F.2d 1406, 1408–10 (6th Cir. 1987) (embracing a "civil religion" standard for ceremonial invocations and benedictions, and invalidating two high school commencement ceremonies because of the specificity of their religious content); Caroline Mala Corbin, *Ceremonial Deism and the Reasonable Religious Outsider*, 57 UCLA L. Rev. 1545 (2010); Steven B. Epstein, *Rethinking the Constitutionality of Ceremonial Deism*, 96 Colum. L. Rev. 2083 (1996); James J. Knicely & John W. Whitehead, *In God We Trust: The Judicial Establishment of American Civil Religion*, 43 J. Marshall L. Rev. 869 (2010); Michael M. Maddigan, *Comment, The Establishment Clause, Civil Religion, and the Public Church*, 81 Cal. L. Rev. 293 (1993).

25 Town of Greece, 134 S. Ct. at 1827–8.

chapter will examine the religious origins of selected legal provisions, principles, and doctrines, whereas the section that follows will explore various invocations of religion in specific legal or government documents – from state constitutions to presidential proclamations – some of which exemplify the ceremonial deism discussed in the preceding paragraph. The final section of this chapter then will look at the specific institution of legislative chaplaincies and the attendant practice of legislative prayer. The premise underlying this survey is not that the efficacious functioning of the law necessarily requires a robust or manifest connection to religion, although that position was held by various constitutional Framers and still can be argued with some force today. Rather, it is that American law and legal institutions simply and quite naturally embody or reflect the religious dimensions of the nation's culture.

## B. Religious Demography: From Protestantism to Pluralism

At the time of the founding and for at least the following century, these religious dimensions consisted largely of the influences of Protestant Christianity, which in manifold forms held sway over most of the cultural landscape.[26] Although from a modern vantage point the early nation may be perceived as having been religiously homogeneous, those of the revolutionary generation likely viewed their new country as remarkably diverse, especially when compared with most regions of Europe.[27] Episcopalians, Congregationalists, Presbyterians, and other denominations that are today seen as collectively constituting mainline Protestantism were at that time separated by intense questions of doctrine and practice.[28]

If there was homogeneity, it was largely to be found in regions and communities. New England, for example, was dominated by Calvinism and its derivative denominations,[29] whereas the South was heavily Anglican,[30] and the mid-Atlantic region was

26 *See, e.g.*, United States v. Macintosh, 283 U.S. 605, 625 (1931) (declaring that Americans "are a Christian people"); Holy Trinity Church v. United States, 143 U.S. 457, 471 (1892) ("[V]iew[ing] ... American life, as expressed by its laws, its business, its customs, and its society, we find every where a clear recognition of the same truth. Among other matters note the following: The form of oath universally prevailing, concluding with an appeal to the Almighty; the custom of opening sessions of all deliberative bodies and most conventions with prayer; the prefatory words of all wills, 'In the name of God, amen'; the laws respecting the observance of the Sabbath, with the general cessation of all secular business, and the closing of courts, legislatures, and other similar public assemblies on that day; the churches and church organizations which abound in every city, town, and hamlet; the multitude of charitable organizations existing every where under Christian auspices; the gigantic missionary associations, with general support, and aiming to establish Christian missions in every quarter of the globe. These, and many other matters which might be noticed, add a volume of unofficial declarations to the mass of organic utterances that this is a Christian nation."); Daniel O. Conkle, *The Path of American Religious Liberty: From the Original Theology to Formal Neutrality and an Uncertain Future*, 75 IND. L.J. 1, 4 (2000) (observing that "throughout most of our country's history, there has been an overt Christian, and primarily Protestant, dominance in American law and public life"). *But cf.* Treaty of Peace and Friendship art. XI (signed at Tripoli, Nov. 4, 1796) (ratified by the U.S. Senate, Jun. 10, 1797) (declaring that "the government of the United States of America is not in any sense founded on the Christian Religion," though presumably doing so as much for diplomatic as for other reasons); *available at*: http://avalon.law.yale.edu/18th_century/bar1796t.asp.

27 *See* SYDNEY E. AHLSTROM, A RELIGIOUS HISTORY OF THE AMERICAN PEOPLE 123 (2d ed. 1972).

28 *See* EDWIN GAUSTAD & LEIGH SCHMIDT, THE RELIGIOUS HISTORY OF AMERICA: THE HEART OF THE AMERICAN STORY FROM COLONIAL TIMES TO TODAY 74 (rev'd ed. 2004).

29 *See* AHLSTROM, *supra* note 27, at 517; GAUSTAD & SCHMIDT, *supra* note 28, at 49.

30 *See* AHLSTROM, *supra* note 27, at 188–99, 517; GAUSTAD & SCHMIDT, *supra* note 28, at 36.

characterized by a diverse religious milieu consisting not only of the leading Protestant denominations but also of Baptists, Methodists, Quakers, German Lutherans, French Huguenots, and Dutch Reformed, among others.[31] Small Jewish communities could be found in some Atlantic seaports, most notably Newport, Rhode Island. Catholic adherents were generally located in the mid-Atlantic region, especially in Maryland, where a diocese in Baltimore had been established in 1789,[32] and to some extent on the frontiers with scattered populations of French traders as well as Métis and Native American converts.[33] Among mostly enslaved African Americans as well as Native American tribes, various levels of syncretism between traditional beliefs and Christianity also could be found.[34] Further compounding the religious diversity of early America were radical, Enlightenment-inspired cosmologies such as Unitarianism and various strains of Deism. Often far exceeding the boundaries of Protestant orthodoxy, these belief systems claimed adherents even among the nation's Founders and constitutional Framers.[35]

Given the country's religious pluralism in the late eighteenth century, it is improbable that any single denomination could have secured a national establishment of its religion – unlike, for example, Anglicanism in England or Catholicism in Spain – though religious establishments existed in several states until 1833, when Massachusetts ended its effective establishment of Congregational churches.[36] In short, there was, as James Madison described it, a "multiplicity of sects" across the nation.[37] At the same time, some commonality and intensity of religious belief were sufficiently present in the young republic that an entirely secular state, based on one or more strands of Enlightenment rationalism, would for most have been far too radical, especially prior to or even after – for some, especially after – the revolution in France. To be sure, the original Constitution's failure to acknowledge God, coupled with its ban on religious tests for federal office, generated more than a little controversy when the document was sent to the states for ratification.[38]

Although historical changes in the American religious landscape can be explained in many ways, during the nineteenth and early twentieth centuries this landscape was clearly transformed by immigration.[39] Most significant in this regard is the large influx of Irish in

31 *See* AHLSTROM, *supra* note 27, at 517; GAUSTAD & SCHMIDT, *supra* note 28, at 74–94.

32 *See* Michael S. Carter, *"Under the Benign Sun of Toleration": Mathew Carey, The Douai Bible, and the Catholic Print Culture, 1789–1791*, 27 J. EARLY REPUBLIC 437, 447 (2007).

33 *See, e.g.*, Keith R. Widder, *The Convergence of Native Religion, Roman Catholicism, and Evangelical Protestantism at Mackinaw Mission, 1823–1837*, 77(3) J. PRESBYTERIAN HIST. 167–8 (1999).

34 *See* AHLSTROM, *supra* note 27, at 700–4.

35 Thomas Jefferson, John Adams, and Thomas Paine were just a few of the leading Revolutionaries and Framers adhering to the Enlightenment's rational approach to religious belief. *See id.* at 366–8.

36 *See* John D. Cushing, *Notes on Disestablishment in Massachusetts, 1780–1833*, 26(2) WM. & MARY Q. 169 (Apr. 1969).

37 THE FEDERALIST No. 51, at 283 (J.R. Pole ed., 2005) (James Madison) ("In a free government, the security for civil rights must be the same as that for religious rights. It consists in the one case in the multiplicity of interests, and in the other, in the multiplicity of sects. The degree of security in both cases will depend on the number of interests and sects."); *see also* THE FEDERALIST No. 10, *supra*, at 54 (James Madison) ("The influence of factious leaders may kindle a flame within their particular states, but will be unable to spread a general conflagration through the other states: A religious sect, may degenerate into a political faction in a part of the confederacy; but the variety of sects dispersed over the entire face of it, must secure the national councils against any danger from that source."); Witte, *supra* note 22, at 396 n. 126.

38 *See* Daniel L. Dreisbach, *The Constitution's Forgotten Religion Clause: Reflections on the Article IV Religious Test Ban*, 38 J. CHURCH & ST. 261, 273–84 (1996); Steven D. Smith, *Our Agnostic Constitution*, 83 N.Y.U. L. REV. 120, 127 (2008).

39 *See* GAUSTAD & SCHMIDT, *supra* note 28, at 209.

the middle to late nineteenth century, which resulted mainly from the infamous potato famine beginning in 1845 and which brought nearly 4.5 million immigrants to U.S. soil by century's end.[40] With them, of course, also came their Roman Catholic faith, and by 1850, Roman Catholicism constituted the largest single denomination in the United States, a status that persists to this day.[41] In many instances, however, these Irish Catholic immigrants were not warmly received. In fact, their mass arrival engendered the most violent period of the nation's religious history because deep-seated anti-Catholicism as well as socioeconomic dynamics spawned a potent nativist movement.[42] Whether rooted in concerns that the Vatican would control and thus destroy American self-government[43] or that an overwhelming foreign labor force would undermine the country's prosperity, nativism and anti-Catholicism were frequently one and the same.[44] Political parties such as the Know-Nothings, formed solely on nativist and anti-Catholic platforms, became increasingly popular among American Protestants and revealed a darker side to the nation's culture that would endure well into the subsequent century.[45]

Whereas Catholicism's rapid growth chiefly occurred prior the Civil War, immigration of European Jews took place at differing points throughout the nineteenth and early twentieth centuries and involved a variety of ethnic groups with different views regarding the future of Judaism in the New World.[46] In the mid-nineteenth century, a large number of German Jews, influenced by European political philosophy, arrived in America with liberal, relatively modern perspectives and were open to altering or even jettisoning long-standing Jewish traditions.[47] Perhaps fearing that they might face in America the same "ghettoization" that they had faced in Germany, they viewed their new home as a place to effect reform and to escape from ethnic and traditional Jewish roots, eventually culminating in a major presence of Reformed Judaism in America.[48] Jews emigrating from Eastern Europe, by contrast, generally lacked such reformist aspirations. Effectively forced out by Russian persecution and first arriving in America in the late nineteenth century, these Orthodox Jews came with the hope of practicing their traditional faith unchanged and uninhibited.[49] All told, the influx of Jewish immigrants from Germany, Russia, and other European countries transformed the United States, by the twentieth century, into one of the world's major population centers for Jews.[50]

40 *See* Ahlstrom, *supra* note 27, at 541. Of the 5 million American immigrants between 1815 to the Civil War, 40 percent were Irish. *See* Gaustad & Schmidt, *supra* note 28, at 170.

41 *See* Gaustad & Schmidt, *supra* note 28, at 170.

42 *See* Ahlstrom, *supra* note 27, at 555.

43 *See* John Butler, Grant Wacker, & Randall Balmer, Religion in American Life: A Short History 256 (2d ed. 2011) ("Protestants believed that the long history of the Catholic Church in Europe proved that the church would tyrannize the state if it got the chance. ... These Protestant suspicions were grounded upon some fact. For centuries the papacy had insisted that the church ultimately should control the state. When democratic revolutions swept Europe in the late 1840s, the pope condemned them. In 1864 the pope issued a letter ... attacking modern errors, including the notion of church-state separation.").

44 *See* Ahlstrom, *supra* note 27, at 556–7.

45 *See id.* at 564–8; Tyler G. Anbinder, Nativism and Slavery: The Northern Know Nothings and the Politics of the 1850s (1992); Pierre Schrag, Not Fit for Our Society: Immigration and Nativism in America 29–34 (2010).

46 *See* Gaustad & Schmidt, *supra* note 28, at 214.

47 *See* Ahlstrom, *supra* note 27, at 575–8.

48 *See id.* at 580–2.

49 *See* Gaustad & Schmidt, *supra* note 28, at 214.

50 *See id.* at 212.

Although immigration accounted for much of the non-Protestant religious growth in nineteenth-century America, it resulted in the arrival or expansion of certain Protestant groups as well. After the Civil War, for instance, substantial numbers of Lutherans, primarily from Scandinavia, settled in what are now the Midwest and upper Great Plains regions of the United States.[51] Cultural and linguistic affinities largely shaped Lutheran geographic patterns because many Scandinavians refused to worship outside their own ethnicity or nationality, especially with the German Lutherans who had settled earlier in the century.[52] Similar to German Jewish immigrants of the mid-nineteenth century, Scandinavian Lutherans often viewed emigration to America as an opportunity to rid their faith of lingering European influences, particularly the liturgical and even dogmatic remnants of Catholicism.[53] Many German Lutherans already present in America, by comparison, held strongly to European traditions despite their Catholic semblance.[54] By the twentieth century, however, the prevalence of ethnic distinctions and divisions between the reformers and traditionalists ultimately gave way to a more generalized American Lutheranism, though conservative and progressive factions within Lutheranism (as they do within most Protestant denominations) continue to the present.[55]

Although the principal religious traditions in nineteenth-century America were Christian and to a growing extent Jewish, that period also witnessed the emergence of non-Western religions, such as Confucianism and Buddhism, as a result of Asian immigration to the American West.[56] Even more than perhaps the Irish, and also the result of a confluence of religious and economic as well as racial reasons, Chinese immigrants were largely subjected to an atmosphere of intolerance despite their critical contributions to the nation's infrastructural and agricultural development. In 1882, Congress notoriously adopted its first Chinese exclusion act,[57] which stopped all immigration from China for ten years.[58] The statute and its subsequent extensions were not officially repealed until 1943,[59] and in 2011 and 2012, the U.S. Senate and House of Representatives, respectively, passed resolutions formally apologizing for the Chinese exclusion laws.[60]

The exogenous force of immigration was only one influence on the nation's religious demography in the nineteenth and early twentieth centuries. Legal and cultural dynamics also allowed for the endogenous development of modified or entirely new religious belief systems, often related to the Second Great Awakening,[61] some of which have long since

51 *See id.* at 216.
52 *See id.*
53 *Id.*
54 *See* AHLSTROM, *supra* note 27, at 524–5.
55 *See* GAUSTAD & SCHMIDT, *supra* note 28, at 217.
56 *See id.* at 219.
57 Act of May 6, 1882, ch. 126, 22 Stat. 58.
58 *See* GAUSTAD & SCHMIDT, *supra* note 28, at 219.; ANDREW GYORY, CLOSING THE GATE: RACE, POLITICS, AND THE CHINESE EXCLUSION ACT (1998); ERIKA LEE, AT AMERICA'S GATES: CHINESE IMMIGRATION DURING THE EXCLUSION ERA, 1882–1943 (2003).
59 *See* Chinese Exclusion Repeal Act, Pub. L. No. 78–199, ch. 344, § 1, 57 Stat. 600 (Dec. 17, 1943).
60 *See* Moni Basu, *In Rare Apology, House Regrets Exclusionary Laws Targeting Chinese*, Jun. 19, 2012; *available at:* http://inamerica.blogs.cnn.com/2012/06/19/in-rare-apology-house-regrets-exclusionary-laws-targeting-chinese/.
61 *See* BUTLER ET AL., *supra* note 43, at 171–83.

disappeared and others of which flourished in the ensuing decades.[62] Historians Roger Finke and Rodney Stark theorize that American religious history and demography should be seen through an economic lens and that, ultimately, there are "winners and losers in a free market religious environment that exposed religious organizations to relentless competition."[63] An example of an eventual winner, in this view, would be the Church of Jesus Christ of Latter-Day Saints, or Mormonism, which was founded by Joseph Smith in the late 1820s and which claimed, among other things, that Christ had first come to North America prior to his birth as depicted in the *New Testament*[64] – an otherwise heterodox view that nevertheless resonated with a number of citizens who adhered to notions such as American Exceptionalism and Manifest Destiny.[65] Among the long-term losers, by comparison, are the various utopian movements that formed or crystallized in the nineteenth century, such as the Shakers, who practiced celibacy but nevertheless persisted into the late twentieth century, and the Oneida Community, whose members believed that a form of communitarianism should replace traditional patriarchal and matriarchal roles for the raising of children and that sexual freedom should replace monogamy in order to "lift up humankind to the level where a truly spiritual revolution could occur."[66]

For others, a more tangible type of freedom contributed to the birth of new religious denominations. Former slaves in the American South created "Black churches," such as the Colored Methodist Episcopal Church[67] and various Baptist sects.[68] African-Americans in the late nineteenth century felt largely unwelcome in white-dominated denominations and desired churches that better reflected their musical and sermonic practices, often based on modes of worship conducted by slaves during the antebellum era.[69] These pioneering churches also allowed the newly freed African-Americans to assume greater roles than they would have had in the established white churches of the Reconstruction South.[70] Finally, the black churches "served as a center for many aspects of life. Excluded from white-run schools, businesses, and churches, blacks created a separate world of their own inside the limits of their churches."[71]

In the twentieth century, the religious topography of America underwent further modifications, some again resulting from external influences such as immigration and world

62 *See* Gaustad & Schmidt, *supra* note 28, at 140. Regarding a few of the more prominent yet ultimately unsuccessful religious experiments, *see, e.g.*, Spencer Klaw, Without Sin: The Life and Death of the Oneida Community (1993); David L. Rowe, God's Strange Work: William Miller and the End of the World (2008); William E. Wilson, The Angel and the Serpent: The Story of New Harmony (1983).

63 Roger Finke & Rodney Stark, The Churching of America 1776–2005: Winners and Losers in Our Religious Economy 2 (2d ed. 2005).

64 *See* 1 Scott A. Merriman, Religion and the Law in America: An Encyclopedia of Personal Belief and Public Policy 253–54 (2007).

65 *See id.* at 254.

66 *See* Gaustad & Schmidt, *supra* note 28, at 151. Whereas the Shakers and the Oneida Community were met with public skepticism and varying levels of disapproval, the Mormons, who effectively advocated a theocratic succession to the nation's traditional Christianity, were often met with disdain, if not violence. Laws outlawing polygamy, which was widely practiced by church leaders, forced the Mormons West, ultimately into the federal territories. *See* 1 Merriman, *supra* note 64, at 254.

67 It was later renamed the Christian Methodist Episcopal Church. *See id.* 1 Merriman, *supra* note 6, at 218.

68 *See id.*

69 *See* Butler et al., *supra* note 43, at 229; 1 Merriman, *supra* note 64, at 218.

70 *See* 1 Merriman, *supra* note 64, at 218–19.

71 Butler et al., *supra* note 43, at 229.

events and others resulting from domestic developments such as the civil rights movement and the sexual revolution. Though the twentieth century, unlike the eighteenth and nineteenth centuries, did not experience a Great Awakening as such, it did see the rise of Christian fundamentalism,[72] a continued and at times politically prominent role for evangelical Protestantism[73] and, in the 1960s and 1970s, a new culture of religious or spiritual experimentation not unlike the utopian movements of the 1800s.[74] It also saw the persistence of religiosity among Americans, 96 percent of whom in 1957 associated themselves with an identifiable religious tradition.[75]

In addition, the United States in the twentieth century witnessed evolving relationships between religion and government owing to such factors as the First Amendment's application to the states and demands for increased neutrality or secularity in government.[76] One new area of legal wrangling involved the impact of the so-called Blaine Amendments, which a number of states adopted (and the U.S. Congress had attempted to adopt in the 1870s) in order to prevent tax dollars from going to religious, primarily Catholic, schools.[77] Among other things, these amendments reflected lingering nativist and anti-Catholic sentiments so prominent in the mid-1800s, with many state legislatures and school boards in late nineteenth- and early twentieth-century America still heavily under Protestant control or influence.[78] Although Blaine-type amendments remain in some state constitutions, they are generally justified today by more modern notions of church-state separation.[79] Eventually, much of the religious nativism and anti-Catholicism would itself subside, and in 1960, the nation would elect John F. Kennedy as its first Catholic President.[80]

Issues of moral controversy in the United States also influenced the relationship among law, religion, and politics. Following the 1973 court decision of *Roe v. Wade*,[81] for example, the abortion question became a call-to-arms for religious conservatives, who increasingly attempted in the century's closing decades to infuse the legal and political processes with traditional moral values.[82] To be sure, religious conservatives and the

[72] *See* MALISE RUTHVEN, FUNDAMENTALISM: A VERY SHORT INTRODUCTION 6–7 (2007).

[73] *See* PAUL A. DJUPE & LAURA R. OLSON, ENCYCLOPEDIA OF AMERICAN RELIGION AND POLITICS 157 (2003) (noting three waves of evangelical influence in the legal or political developments of the twentieth century).

[74] *See* BUTLER ET AL., *supra* note 43, at 382–91.

[75] *See* 1 MERRIMAN, *supra* note 64, at 341.

[76] *See id.* at 350.

[77] *See id.* at 147; Mark Edward DeForrest, *An Overview and Evaluation of State Blaine Amendments: Origins, Scope, and First Amendment Concerns*, 26 HARV. J.L. & PUB. POL'Y 551 (2003); Meir Katz, *The State of Blaine: A Closer Look at the Blaine Amendments and Their Modern Application*, 12 ENGAGE: J. FEDERALIST SOC'Y PRAC. GROUPS 111 (2011).

[78] *See* 1 MERRIMAN, *supra* note 64, at 147.

[79] *See id.*

[80] *See id.* at 343. As of 2014, moreover, the nine-member Supreme Court consisted of six Catholic and three Jewish Justices – a far cry from the Protestant hegemony that had characterized the Court well into the twentieth century.

[81] 410 U.S. 113 (1973).

[82] *See* GAUSTAD & SCHMIDT, *supra* note 28, at 366; *see also* STEPHEN L. CARTER, THE CULTURE OF DISBELIEF: HOW AMERICAN LAW AND POLITICS TRIVIALIZE RELIGIOUS DEVOTION 58 (1993) ("For many religious conservatives, *Roe* was like a cold shower. All at once, the nascent pro-life movement … exploded into the national prominence. The very same Christian fundamentalists who had preached for decades that their followers should ignore the secular world, and perhaps not even vote, looked around and decided that the secular world was on the verge of destroying the tight religious cocoons in which they had bound their communities."); GARRY WILLS, UNDER GOD: RELIGION AND AMERICAN POLITICS 320–4

pro-life movement played a prominent role in the ascendancy of Ronald Reagan in the 1980 presidential election, prompting him as president to attend national prayer broadcasts and even to propose a constitutional amendment to allow prayer in public schools and institutions.[83]

At the same time, changes in the demographics of denominations resulted from twentieth-century America's growing diversity, especially with a resurgence of Hispanic or Latino immigration in the century's closing decades.[84] Though traditionally of the Roman Catholic faith – today they make up 33 percent of the country's Catholic population[85] – for many years these groups struggled for recognition by Church leaders in the United States. By the 1980s and 1990s, however, the nation's Catholic bishops were preaching greater inclusion of Hispanics or Latinos within the structure and life of the Church.[86] Asian immigration also has exerted influences on the diversity and demography of American religion. Beginning in the 1990s, Asian immigrants have been the fastest-growing demographic in the country, bringing with them a panoply of religions – Buddhism, Taoism, Islam, Hinduism, Jainism, and Sikhism, among others – and in some instances offering alternatives to extant religious traditions, such as Vietnamese-influenced Catholicism or Korean Presbyterianism.[87] The freedom to practice these religions not only has allowed Asian immigrants to continue their traditional faiths but also, much like the Mormon and utopian movements in the nineteenth century, has provided Americans who are perhaps alienated from the Western religions of their forebears to find new spiritual domiciles, most notably within the varieties of Buddhism.[88]

In at least two chief respects, the foregoing survey of religious demography from the founding to the present has relevance to this chapter's focus on religious influences and expressions in law and government. First, because legal or governmental embodiments of religion in the United States have resulted from the force of culture rather than the force of law, as in a state with an established church, these embodiments have always been broader than a single denomination and, arguably, have expanded in rough proportion to the diversification of religion in the nation. Thus, to the extent that there is an American civil religion, premised on a common ground of transcendent notions and values, it has necessarily been shaped by and cognizant of many religious traditions as well as constitutional principles, such as equality, neutrality, and tolerance. Second, and related to these principles, the contemporary governmental expressions of religion, and especially the prudential and legal limits on those expressions, reflect the entirety – good and bad – of the nation's religious experience. Though religious diversity in the United States is admired in retrospect and often celebrated today, as this historical survey indicates, it has occasionally also served as fertile ground for persecution and even violence, especially in conjunction with nativist reactions to immigration or during periods of national stress such as wars or economic downturns. Different periods in the nation's history have witnessed surges of animus – in some instances localized, in others widespread – directed toward

(1990) (tracing the intellectual roots of the modern evangelical-fundamentalist pro-life movement, and in turn the Religious Right itself, to the work of Francis Schaeffer in response to the *Roe* decision).

83 *See* Gaustad & Schmidt, *supra* note 28, at 406.

84 *See* Ahlstrom, *supra* note 27, at 1108.

85 *See* Pew Research Center, *The Shifting Religious Identity of Latinos in the United States* 10 (May 7, 2014); *available at:* http://www.pewforum.org/files/2014/05/Latinos-Religion-07-22-full-report.pdf.

86 *See* Gaustad & Schmidt, *supra* note 28, at 379–81.

87 *See id.* at 415.

88 *See id.*

Catholics,[89] Jews,[90] Mormons,[91] and Jehovah's Witnesses,[92] as well as concerted efforts to suppress the beliefs and practices of various Native American religions.[93] More recently, the events of September 11, 2001, engendered heightened and indiscriminate suspicion or antipathy toward Muslims, at times accompanied by criminal acts against people and their property.[94] Nor is it always citizens, acting apart from government, who have orchestrated the intolerance, as the nineteenth-century federal policies toward Mormons and American Indians illustrate. In short, it is important to recognize that these events, too, are part of the nation's history of law and religion, and – no less than the First Amendment, Lincoln's "Gettysburg Address," or Franklin D. Roosevelt's "Four Freedoms" – they also can influence as well as illuminate how law and religion in America are understood today.

## C. Religious Origins of Legal Principles and Doctrines

America's religious demography is important, for present purposes, because the law is fundamentally a cultural institution, one that both reflects and shapes, serving and governing, the society to which it is attached. Given the religious dimensions of American culture and heritage, it is unremarkable that the nation's laws might be rooted in or might otherwise embody the religious beliefs, premises, moral strictures, and even cosmologies of past and current generations of Americans. This section will briefly examine some of these relationships, beginning with the Establishment and Free Exercise Clauses of the First Amendment.

### 1. *The First Amendment Religion Clauses*

Although the Constitution is, on its face, "a secular document,"[95] this does not mean that the nation's charter rested on or incorporated exclusively secular assumptions about the

89 *See id.* at 170–2; Edward McGlynn Gaffney, Jr., *Hostility to Religion, American Style*, 42 DePaul L. Rev. 263, 279–92 (1992); Douglas Laycock, *A Survey of Religious Liberty in the United States*, 47 Ohio St. L.J. 409, 417–18 (1986). Regarding anti-Catholicism's larger effect on American law and politics, including the conception of religious freedom, *see* Elizabeth Fenton, Religious Liberties: Anti-Catholicism and Liberal Democracy in Nineteenth-Century U.S. Literature and Culture (2011).

90 *See* Leonard Dinnerstein, Antisemitism in America (1994).

91 *See* Edwin Brown Firmage & R. Collin Mangrum, Zion in the Courts: A Legal History of the Church of Jesus Christ of Latter-Day Saints, 1830–1900 (2001); Sarah Barringer Gordon, The Mormon Question: Polygamy and Constitutional Conflict in Nineteenth-Century America (2001); Christine Talbot, *Turkey Is in Our Midst: Orientalism and Contagion in Nineteenth Century Anti-Mormonism*, 8 J.L. & Fam. Stud. 363 (2006).

92 *See* Shawn Francis Peters, Judging Jehovah's Witnesses: Religious Persecution and the Dawn of the Rights Revolution (2001).

93 *See* George Dargo, *Religious Toleration and Its Limits in Early America*, 16 N. Ill. U. L. Rev. 341, 358–60 (1996); Allison M. Dussias, *Ghost Dance and Holy Ghost: The Echoes of Nineteenth-Century Christianization Policy in Twentieth-Century Native American Free Exercise Cases*, 49 Stan. L. Rev. 773, 787–805 (1997); Lee Irwin, *Freedom, Law, and Prophecy: A Brief History of Native American Religious Resistance*, 21 Am. Indian Q. 35 (1997).

94 *See* American-Arab Anti-Discrimination Committee, Report on Hate Crimes and Discrimination Against Arab Americans: The Post-September 11 Backlash (2003); U.S. Department of Justice Civil Rights Division, *Enforcement and Outreach Following the September 11 Terrorist Attacks; available at:* http://www.usdoj.gov/crt/legalinfo/discrimupdate.php.

95 Hutson, *supra* note 11, at 141. The Constitution "contains no conspicuous acknowledgment of God nor does it attempt to incorporate religion into the structure or operations of government." *Id. See also* Daniel

nature of human beings, society, and governance either in general or with respect to specific constitutional principles and guarantees. To the contrary, early America was permeated by the influences of Christianity, especially Protestant conceptions of law, politics, and morality,[96] and "Christian values and insights were intrinsically connected to the political culture of the new nation."[97] These influences undergirded and shaped various aspects of the Constitution,[98] including notably the Establishment Clause and Free Exercise Clause – the so-called the religion clauses – of the First Amendment.[99] These provisions, as Professor John Witte observes, "express both theological and political sentiments."[100] Prominent among such sentiments were those of congregational Puritans and free-church evangelicals: the former envisioned separation yet interdependence of church and state and had a tolerant but limited view of religious liberty,[101] whereas the latter envisioned a rigid separation of church and state and a robust, voluntarism-based conception of religious freedom.[102]

It has even been argued that "for the Founders, *the* central justification for religious liberty was distinctly religious" and was "based on the combination of two theological principles: first, that religious duties are more important than secular duties, and second, that individuals must undertake their religious duties voluntarily, not under legal compulsion."[103] More generally, many of those who framed or ratified the First Amendment based their understanding of religious liberty on "the theological premise that God exists and is sovereign over both government and the individual citizen"[104] and on "the perception that th[e] higher call of God makes the exercise of religious faith a uniquely transcendent and intimate human activity, distinct from other human interests or pursuits."[105]

L. Dreisbach, *In Search of a Christian Commonwealth: An Examination of Selected Nineteenth-Century Commentaries on References to God and the Christian Religion in the United States Constitution*, 48 Baylor L. Rev. 927, 930 (1996) (noting that the Constitution, "unlike the Declaration of Independence and most public documents of the era," has "no clear affirmation of the existence of a superintendent, transcendent being and no acknowledgment that society and civil government are dependent on and governed by God").

96 *See* Conkle, *supra* note 26, at 4–5.

97 *Id.* at 4.

98 *See* Sch. Dist. of Abington Twp. v. Schempp, 374 U.S. 203, 213 (1963) ("The fact that the Founding Fathers believed devotedly that there was a God and that the unalienable rights of man were rooted in Him is clearly evidenced in their writings, from the Mayflower Compact to the Constitution itself."); Donald S. Lutz, *Religious Dimensions in the Development of American Constitutionalism*, 39 Emory L.J. 21 (1990); Fernando Rey Martinez, *The Religious Character of the American Constitution: Puritanism and Constitutionalism in the United States*, 12 Kan. J.L. & Pub. Pol'y 459 (2003); David L. Wardle, *Reason to Ratify: The Influence of John Locke's Religious Beliefs on the Creation and Adoption of the United States Constitution*, 26 Seattle U. L. Rev. 291 (2002); John Witte, Jr., *How to Govern a City on a Hill: The Early Puritan Contribution to American Constitutionalism*, 39 Emory L.J. 41 (1990). For a contemporary assessment, *see* Bradley P. Jacob, *The Bible and the Constitution*, 17 Trinity L. Rev. 1 (2011).

99 *See* Conkle, *supra* note 26, at 3–4; Mark S. Scarberry, *John Leland and James Madison: Religious Influence on the Ratification of the Constitution and on the Proposal of the Bill of Rights*, 113 Penn St. L. Rev. 733 (2009); Steven D. Smith, *The Rise and Fall of Religious Freedom in Constitutional Discourse*, 140 U. Pa. L. Rev. 149, 154–66 (1991); E. Gregory Wallace, *Justifying Religious Freedom: The Western Tradition*, 114 Penn St. L. Rev. 485, 488–91 (2009).

100 Witte, *supra* note 22, at 476.

101 *See id.* at 378–80.

102 *See* Witte, *supra* note 22, at 381–3.

103 Conkle, *supra* note 26, at 3 (emphasis added).

104 Wallace, *supra* note 99, at 489–90.

105 *Id.* at 490.

As illustrated in Chapters 4 and 5, the principles and doctrines that today frame the interpretation and application of the religion clauses do not, at least on their surface, reflect the kind of overtly religious phrasing that characterized the arguments for religious liberty and against religious establishments of, say, James Madison.[106] Nevertheless, many of the contemporary principles and doctrines correspond to at least some of these original religiously informed views. The prohibition on religious coercion, for example, which is a modern doctrinal component of both religion clauses, correlates with the theologically important and original principle of voluntarism in the matter of responding to one's religious obligations,[107] even if today's version may be cast mostly in terms of personal autonomy no different from the autonomy associated with other constitutional rights.[108] It also has been forcefully argued that the belief-conduct distinction so prominent in the Supreme Court's interpretation of the Free Exercise Clause "is a manifestation of a world view which is decidedly Protestant in structure."[109] Occasionally, one even encounters theological phrasing in the pages of the modern *United States Reports*, such as when Justice Souter asserted that scope of the Free Exercise Clause "defines nothing less than the respective relationships ... of the individual to government and to God."[110]

## 2. *Other Elements of Constitutional, Statutory, or Common Law*

Many areas of contemporary domestic law embody religious principles or rest on religious foundations, even though their modern tenor is nearly always secular in nature.[111] Among these subjects are torts,[112] criminal law and punishment,[113] family

106 *See, e.g.*, James Madison, *Memorial and Remonstrance against Religious Assessments* ¶ 1 (1785); *available at:* http://religiousfreedom.lib.virginia.edu/sacred/madison_m&r_1785.html.

107 *See* Chapter 5.B.1.

108 *See, e.g.*, Planned Parenthood of Southeastern Pa. v. Casey, 505 U.S. 833, 851 (1992) ("Our law affords constitutional protection to personal decisions relating to marriage, procreation, contraception, family relationships, child rearing, and education. ... These matters, involving the most intimate and personal choices a person may make in a lifetime, choices central to personal dignity and autonomy, are central to the liberty protected by the Fourteenth Amendment. At the heart of liberty is the right to define one's own concept of existence, of meaning, of the universe, and of the mystery of human life. Beliefs about these matters could not define the attributes of personhood were they formed under compulsion of the State.").

109 Marci A. Hamilton, *The Belief/Conduct Paradigm in the Supreme Court's Free Exercise Jurisprudence: A Theological Account of the Failure to Protect Religious Conduct*, 54 OHIO ST. L.J. 713, 716 (1993).

110 Church of the Lukumi Babalu Aye, Inc. v. City of Hialeah, 508 U.S. 520, 577 (1993) (Souter, J., concurring in part and concurring in the judgment).

111 *See generally* HAROLD J. BERMAN: LAW AND REVOLUTION: THE FORMATION OF THE WESTERN LEGAL TRADITION (1983); Harold J. Berman, *The Religious Foundations of Western Law*, 24 CATH. U.L. REV. 490 (1975).

112 *See, e.g.*, ABA Special Committee on the Tort Liability System, *Towards a Jurisprudence of Injury: The Continuing Creation of a System of Substantive Justice in American Tort Law*, COMMITTEE'S PREFACE at 1-1 (1984) ("So far as we know, there is no word in the Bible for 'torts.' Yet the 'norms' which the Creator told Moses to set before the Israelites, in the chapter of Exodus following the Ten Commandments, are filled with what we think of as 'tort' rules. ... We have indicated the depth of the roots of tort law in the Judeo-Christian tradition."), *quoted in* Douglas H. Cook, *Negligence or Strict Liability? A Study in Biblical Tort Law*, 13 WHITTIER L. REV. 1, 2 (1992).

113 *See, e.g.*, TERANCE D. MIETHE & HONG LU, PUNISHMENT: A COMPARATIVE HISTORICAL PERSPECTIVE 17, 22–4 (2005) (noting the religious origins or consonance of various objectives or philosophies of criminal punishment such as retribution, rehabilitation, and restoration); JOEL SAMAHA, CRIMINAL LAW

law,[114] contracts,[115] property,[116] and various rules of evidence and procedure that may cut across multiple subjects.[117] What today may be referred to as "morals legislation," such as a prohibition against gambling or adultery, is often traceable to religious premises or values and, indeed, in many states descends directly from religiously based legislation of early statehood.[118] As one commentator has noted with regard to early American legal systems:

> Government officials predicated some of their laws and policies directly on the moral and religious teachings of the Bible and the church. The first public schools and state universities had mandatory courses in religion and theology and compulsory attendance in daily chapel and Sunday worship services. Employees in state prisons, reformatories, orphanages, and asylums were required to know and to teach basic Christian beliefs and values. Polygamy, prostitution, pornography, and other sexual offenses against Christian morals and mores were prohibited. Blasphemy, sacrilege, and false swearing were still prosecuted. Gambling houses, lotteries, fortune-telling, and other activities that depended on fate or magic were forbidden. In many jurisdictions, these and other laws and policies were predicated on explicitly religious, and usually Christian, grounds. It was a commonplace of nineteenth century legal thought that "Christianity is a part of the common law."[119]

As this commentator further notes, however, the promulgation and enforcement of these legal norms at times engendered significant legislative and judicial disagreement based on converging and diverging religious and political perspectives. "Those inclined to Puritan and civic republican views saw these laws and policies as appropriate forms of nonpreferential state aid to, and accommodation of, the civic and sectarian religions of the nation. Those inclined to enlightenment and evangelical perspectives saw them as vestiges of traditional religious establishments and compromises of the ideals of separationism and voluntarism."[120]

Even as late as 1892, however, the Supreme Court reaffirmed the notion that Christianity was part of the common law, considering its "truth" to be a matter of

22–3 (10th ed. 2011) (same regarding retribution); Jonathan Burnside, *Retribution and Restoration in Biblical Texts*, *in* Handbook of Restorative Justice 132 (Gerry Johnstone & Daniel W. Van Ness eds., 2007) (noting that "the Judaeo-Christian tradition has been highly influential in the development of Western understandings of criminal justice"); John E. Witte & Thomas C. Arthur, *The Three Uses of the Law: A Protestant Source of the Purposes of Criminal Punishment?* 10 J.L. & Religion 433 (linking Reformation theology to punishment in criminal law).

114 *See, e.g.*, Vivian E. Hamilton, *Principles of U.S. Family Law*, 75 Fordham L. Rev. 31, 46–56 (2006).

115 *See, e.g.*, Harold J. Berman, *The Religious Sources of General Contract Law: An Historical Perspective*, 4 J.L. & Religion 103 (1986).

116 *See, e.g.*, William W. Fisher III, *Ideology, Religion, and the Constitutional Protection of Private Property: 1760–1860*, 39 Emory L.J. 65 (1990).

117 *See, e.g.*, James Q. Whitman, The Origins of Reasonable Doubt: Theological Roots of the Criminal Trial (2008); Daniel G. Ashburn, *Appealing to a Higher Authority? Jewish Law in American Judicial Opinions*, 71 U. Det. Mercy L. Rev. 295, 303–14 (1994) (documenting Jewish law's influences on procedural and evidentiary rulings).

118 *See generally* William G. Miller, Faith, Reason, and Consent: Legislating Morality in Early American States (2008).

119 Witte, *supra* note 22, at 407. *See, e.g.*, State v. Chandler, 2 Del. (2 Harr.) 553 (Del. Ct. Gen. Sess. 1837); People v. Ruggles, 8 Johns. 290, 294–8 (N.Y. 1811); Updegraph v. Commonwealth, 11 Serg. & Rawle 394, 400–3 (Pa. 1824).

120 Witte, *supra* note 22, at 407.

"general recognition."[121] Though it is likely correct that "[t]his notion would have few adherents today,"[122] it is likely also correct that important strands of religious thinking remain embedded in contemporary law, and, of course, the religiosity of citizens and government officials still can influence currents of legal thought, especially given the religious demographics of the nation's citizenry and the vibrancy of visibly religious participation in the processes of law and governance.[123]

## D. Religious References in Legal or Governmental Documents

Consistent with the notion that religion has traditionally influenced American law and government, one can find many key documents from the early years of the United States containing explicit religious references. For example, the opening paragraphs of the nation's first public legal document, the protostates' Declaration of Independence, refer to "Nature's God" and famously proclaim that "all men are created equal" and "endowed by their Creator with certain unalienable Rights," and the Declaration's closing paragraph appeals to "the Supreme Judge of the world" and "the protection of divine Providence."[124] Such references, even accounting for Jefferson's Enlightenment Deism, are plainly religious or theological in nature.[125] So, too, is the passage in the Articles of Confederation, adopted in 1781, that speaks of "pleas[ing] the Great Governor of the World."[126] Likewise, the Northwest Ordinance of 1787 asserts matter-of-factly that "[r]eligion, morality, and knowledge" are "necessary to good government and the happiness of mankind."[127]

As noted, the Constitution itself, by comparison, is largely secular in tone, with no comparable references to a creator or to nature's (or any other) god. The religious references that it does have – the exception of Sundays from the president's ten-day veto period[128] and the convention's completion date being designated "in the Year of our Lord,"[129] the latter of which is addressed later in this section – are certainly not as direct as, say, a supplication for "the protection of divine Providence." This omissive aspect of the Constitution is as significant as it is anomalous. From the founding to the present, the federal and state governments have issued numerous laws, declarations, proclamations, and other documents with explicit religious components; they have engaged in religious practices, such as prayer at the outset of legislative sessions and other government functions; and they have incorporated religious artwork and symbols in the architecture of government buildings and on publicly owned lands.[130] These many invocations and uses

121 Holy Trinity Church v. United States, 143 U.S. 457, 470–1 (1892).

122 Stuart Banner, *When Christianity Was Part of the Common Law*, 16 L. & Hist. Rev. 27, 27 (1998).

123 *See* Ted G. Jelen, *The Constitutional Basis of Religious Pluralism in the United States: Causes and Consequences*, 612 Ann. Am. Acad. Pol. & Soc. Sci. 26, 33–4 (2007) (describing current and past influences of religion on public policy).

124 Declaration of Independence (Jul. 4, 1776).

125 For an argument that Jefferson's phrasing is based, at least partly, on theological but not Christian principles, *see* Rick Fairbanks, *The Laws of Nature and of Nature's God: The Role of Theological Claims in the Argument of the Declaration of Independence*, 11 J.L. & Religion 551 (1995).

126 Articles of Confederation art. XIII (Mar. 1, 1781).

127 Northwest Ordinance art. III (Jul. 13, 1787).

128 U.S. Const. art. I, § 7, ¶ 2.

129 *Id.* art. VII, cl. 2.

130 Regarding the artwork and architecture of the U.S. Capitol, *see* William C. Allen, History of the United States Capitol: A Chronicle of Design, Construction, and Politics (2001); *available*

of religion can be significant insofar as they evince cultural understandings about the acceptable if not proper relationship between religion and the government and its laws.

Examined in this section are five categories of legal or governmental documents or practices that in some manner or another implicate religion: the various state constitutions, the Attestation Clause of the U.S. Constitution, the national motto, the Pledge of Allegiance, and several presidential or congressional proclamations. By no means, of course, do these categories exhaust the expressions of religion in American public life. One could also note, for example, that at the outset of each sitting of the U.S. Supreme Court and some lower federal courts, the Marshal proclaims, "God save the United States and this Honorable Court."[131] Or one could observe that traditional renditions of governmental oaths, beginning with President Washington's first inauguration, tend to conclude with "So help me God."[132] The five categories addressed do, however, paint a fairly representative portrait of the types of roles and appearances that religion, at both the state and federal levels, has assumed in law and governance.

### 1. *The State Constitutions*

The heavily Protestant Christian complexion of early America is reflected not only in available historical data but also in the states' constitutions, which embodied (and many of which continue to embody) monotheistic if not explicitly Christian beliefs

*at:* http://www.aoc.gov/capitol-hill/art. Religious art abounds in the Capitol building. For example, the National Statuary Hall Collection, in which each state selects two figures to memorialize, contains statues of several religious leaders. Catholic missionaries St. Damien of Molokai, Fr. Jacques Marquette, S.J., Franciscan Fr. Junípero Serra, and Fr. Eusebio Francisco Kino, S.J., represent the states of Hawaii, Wisconsin, California, and New Mexico, respectively. New Mexico is also represented by a statute of Po'pay, the Pueblo religious leader who spearheaded a 1680 revolt against the Spanish. Puritan John Winthrop, several-time governor of the Massachusetts Bay Colony, represents Massachusetts, whereas Brigham Young, the Utah Territory's first governor and the Mormon Church's second president, is memorialized on behalf of Utah. In addition to statues depicting significant figures, the Capitol also houses many religiously themed paintings. Most notable, perhaps, is the fresco in the Capitol Dome, *The Apotheosis of Washington*, by Italian painter Constantino Brumidi. *Apotheosis* is a Greek theological term similar to the Latin *deificati* ("deification"). In the 1865 artwork, Washington is depicted as a divine figure in heaven joined by Roman gods, including Mercury, Vulcan, and Neptune. Though that particular work is obviously allegorical, other paintings depict overtly Christian scenes. These include John Gadsby Chapman's *Baptism of Pocahontas*, depicting her kneeling before an Anglican Priest and preparing to be christened; Robert W. Weir's *Embarkation of the Pilgrims*, showing the religious separatist founders of the Plymouth Colony kneeling in prayer on the deck of their ship; and William H. Powell's *Discovery of the Mississippi by De Soto*, a scene that at one time also would find its way onto the $500 bill, in which Spanish conquistadors are raising a large crucifix as clergymen reverence it with incense.

131 The full chant is "The Honorable, the Chief Justice and the Associate Justices of the Supreme Court of the United States. Oyez! Oyez! Oyez! All persons having business before the Honorable, the Supreme Court of the United States, are admonished to draw near and give their attention, for the Court is now sitting. God save the United States and this Honorable Court!" *See* Supreme Court of the U.S., *The Court and Its Procedures*; *available at:* http://www.supremecourt.gov/about/procedures.aspx; *see also* Myers v. Loudon Cnty. Pub. Schs., 418 F.3d 395, 404 (4th Cir. 2005) (opinion of Williams, J.) ["The Supreme Court has opened its sessions since the time of Chief Justice John Marshall in the early nineteenth century with 'God save the United States and this honorable court.' Our own court, since its infancy in 1891, has opened sessions with the same refrain" (citation omitted)].

132 On Washington's inauguration, in which he himself added those words after finishing the prescribed oath of U.S. Const. art. II, § 1, ¶ 8; *see* Elk Grove Unified Sch. Dist. v. Newdow, 542 U.S. 1, 26–7 (Rehnquist, C.J., concurring in the judgment).

or principles.[133] Some of the early constitutions are the most explicit. The Delaware Constitution of 1776, for example, required an expressly Christian oath from all officers – "[I] profess faith in God the Father, and in Jesus Christ His only Son, and in the Holy Ghost, one God, blessed forever more; and I do acknowledge the Holy Scriptures of the Old and New Testament to be given by divine inspiration"[134] – and the Massachusetts Constitution of 1780 spoke of the "right" and "duty" of all citizens to "worship the SUPREME BEING, the great Creator and Preserver of the universe."[135]

Many early state constitutions, much like that of Massachusetts, portray a God with particular characteristics. As Professor William Miller has observed, virtually all these documents described "(1) the holiness of God and (2) the relational nature of God."[136] Miller explains that "[t]erms including omnipotence (what the states refer to as 'almighty'), omniscience, and immutability describe attributes that fall into the category of holiness" in that they "describe characteristics of God that set the divine being apart from any other being."[137] Concurrently, God is often described as one "who engages with human beings and expects to be engaged by humans. Creatures are created with a design to engage in a certain kind of relationship with the Creator."[138] In particular, "[r]eferences to the incarnate god-man Jesus Christ portray the divine as having a communicative nature. This explicitly Christian view of God, along with references to God as Creator and the 'Author of Existence,' differs from pantheism, for example, in that the divine is a separate entity from everything in the created universe."[139]

Today's state constitutions continue to have many explicit religious and theological references, including those of both states that formed the original nation and states that joined many decades later. The constitutions of all fifty states, in fact, contain some kind

133 Examples from current state constitutions include ARK. CONST. art. II, § 24 ("Almighty God"); CONN. CONST. art. VII ("Supreme Being"); DEL. CONST. art. I, § 1 ("Almighty God"); GA. CONST. art. I, § 1, ¶ III ("God"); IND. CONST. art. I, § 2 ("ALMIGHTY GOD"); KAN. CONST. BILL OF RTS. § 7 ("God"); KY. CONST. BILL OF RTS. § 1 ("Almighty God"); ME. CONST. art. I, § 3 ("Almighty God"); MD. CONST. DECL. OF RTS. art. 36 ("God"); MASS. CONST. pt. I, art. II ("SUPREME BEING, the great Creator and Preserver of the universe"); *id.* pt. I, art. III ("GOD"); MINN. CONST. art. I, § 16 ("God"); MO. CONST. art. I, § 5 ("Almighty God"); NEB. CONST. art. I, § 4 ("Almighty God"); N.H. CONST. pt. I, art. 5 ("God"); N.J. CONST. art. I, ¶ 3 ("Almighty God"); N.M. CONST. art. II, § 11 ("God"); N.C. CONST. art. I, § 13 ("Almighty God"); OHIO CONST. art. I, § 7 ("Almighty God"); OR. CONST. art. I, § 2 ("Almighty God"); PA. CONST. art. I, § 3 ("Almighty God"); R.I. CONST. art. I, § 3 ("Almighty God" and "God"); S.D. CONST. art. VI, § 3 ("God"); TENN. CONST. art. I, § 3 ("Almighty God"); TEX. CONST. art. I, § 6 ("Almighty God"); VA. CONST. art. I, § 16 ("Creator" and "Christian forbearance, love, and charity"); VT. CONST. ch. I, art. 3 ("Almighty God" and "every sect or denomination of christians ought to observe the sabbath or Lord's day, and keep up some sort of religious worship, which to them shall seem most agreeable to the revealed will of God"); WIS. CONST. art. I, § 18 ("Almighty God").

134 DEL. CONST. art. XXII (1776), *quoted in* Holy Trinity Church v. United States, 143 U.S. 457, 469 (1892); *available at:* http://avalon.law.yale.edu/18th_century/de02.asp. This language appears, however, not to have been carried over to subsequent versions of Delaware's constitution, beginning as early as 1792.

135 MASS. CONST. pt. I, art. II (1780), *quoted in* Holy Trinity Church, 143 U.S. at 469; *available at:* http://press-pubs.uchicago.edu/founders/print_documents/v1ch1s6.html. As noted in the next paragraph, this language is retained by Massachusetts' current constitution, though it was subsequently accompanied by provisions protecting free exercise and prohibiting certain public funding for religious institutions. *See* MASS. CONST. art. 18.

136 MILLER, *supra* note 118, at 29.

137 *Id.* at 30.

138 *Id.*

139 *Id.*

of religious or theological reference, and "nearly every state constitution expresses deference to a being denominated 'God,' 'Almighty God,' 'the Supreme Ruler of the Universe,' or 'the Sovereign Ruler of the Universe.'"[140] Broadly viewed, the contemporary state constitutions invoke religious or theological terms or ideas in three ways: to express (in their preambles) gratitude, deference, or appeals to God; to explain the basis or scope of their religious freedom or nonestablishment guarantees; and to express an understanding about the relationship between religion and government or society more generally.[141]

With regard to the first function, of the forty-eight state constitutions with preambles,[142] forty-five, unlike the U.S. Constitution's preamble, contain supplications or expressions of thankfulness or devotion to God.[143] A few declare that the people are "grateful to God" or "Almighty God" in a general sense,[144] whereas many explain that they are grateful to God specifically for God's guidance or protection[145] or for their liberties,[146] for their right of self-government,[147] or for both.[148] Unique among these are Montana's proclamation that the state's people are "grateful to God for the quiet beauty of our state, the grandeur of our mountains, [and] the vastness of our rolling plains,"[149] as well as North Carolina's declaration of gratitude to God "for the preservation of the American Union."[150] Still others "invok[e] the favor and guidance of Almighty God,"[151] express their "profound

140 Smith, *supra* note 83, at 126.

141 For additional discussion, *see* Christopher Hammons, *State Constitutions, Religious Protection, and Federalism*, 7 U. St. Thomas J.L. & Pub. Pol'y 226 (2013).

142 The New Hampshire and Vermont Constitutions lack preambles.

143 The preambles to the Oregon and Virginia Constitutions contain no religious references, while the Tennessee Constitution's preamble contains several uses of "year of our Lord" in reference to dates. All three constitutions elsewhere refer to "Almighty God" or "our Creator."

144 *See, e.g.*, Alaska Const. preamble; Iowa Const. preamble; Miss. Const. preamble; Mo. Const. preamble.

145 *See* Haw. Const. preamble; *see also* Me. Const. preamble ("acknowledging with grateful hearts the goodness of the Sovereign Ruler of the Universe in affording us an opportunity, so favorable to the design; and, imploring God's aid and direction in its accomplishment").

146 *See, e.g.*, Ariz. Const. preamble; Cal. Const. preamble; Fla. Const. preamble; Idaho Const. preamble; Ill. Const. preamble; Kan. Const. preamble; Ky. Const. preamble; La. Const. preamble; Md. Const. preamble; Mich. Const. ch. 1 preamble; Minn. Const. preamble; Neb. Const. preamble; Nev. Const. preamble; N.J. Const. preamble; N.M. Const. preamble; N.Y. Const. preamble; N.C. Const. preamble; N.D. Const. preamble; Ohio Const. preamble; Pa. Const. preamble; R.I. Const. preamble; S.C. Const. preamble; S.D. Const. preamble; Utah Const. preamble; Wash. Const. preamble; W. Va. Const. preamble; Wis. Const. preamble; Wyo. Const. preamble.

147 *See, e.g.*, Conn. Const. preamble; Ind. Const. preamble; Me. Const. preamble; Mass. Const. preamble.

148 *See, e.g.*, Ark. Const. preamble.

149 Mont. Const. preamble.

150 N.C. Const. preamble.

151 Ala. Const. preamble; *see also* Ga. Const. preamble ("relying upon the … guidance of Almighty God"); Ill. Const. preamble ("seeking His blessing upon our endeavors"); Ky. Const. preamble ("invoking the continuance of these blessings"); Me. Const. preamble ("imploring God's aid and direction"); Mass. Const. preamble ("devoutly imploring His direction"); Miss. Const. preamble ("invoking his blessing on our work"); N.J. Const. preamble ("looking to Him for a blessing upon our endeavors to secure and transmit the same unimpaired to succeeding generations"); Pa. Const. preamble ("humbly invoking His guidance"); R.I. Const. preamble ("looking to Him for a blessing upon our endeavors to secure and to transmit [the civil and religious liberty which He hath so long permitted us to enjoy], unimpaired, to succeeding generations"); Tex. Const. preamble ("Humbly invoking the blessings of Almighty God").

reverence for the Supreme Ruler of the Universe,"[152] or acknowledge their reliance or dependence on God.[153]

The second function of religious or theological notions in state constitutions is to provide a basis for protecting religious liberty or, if different, for prohibiting the harms of religious establishments. Though a number of state constitutional preambles express gratitude to God for their citizens' religious liberty,[154] constitutions fulfilling this function specifically in their religious freedom provisions are all, interestingly, from original states: Connecticut, Delaware, Maryland, Massachusetts, Rhode Island, and Virginia. The Massachusetts Constitution, for example, still speaks of "the right as well as the duty of all men in society, publicly, and at stated seasons to worship the SUPREME BEING, the great Creator and Preserver of the universe,"[155] and Connecticut's Constitution employs comparable language and directly connects it to a prohibition on compulsion.[156] The Delaware Constitution proclaims that "it is the duty of all men frequently to assemble together for the public worship of Almighty God,"[157] and Maryland's Constitution similarly declares that "it is the duty of every man to worship God in such manner as he thinks most acceptable to Him" and links this to a guarantee of equality of religious liberty.[158] Virginia's Constitution recognizes as well "the duty which we owe to our Creator" and links not only with equality of religious liberty but also with "the mutual duty of all to practice Christian forbearance, love, and charity towards each other."[159] Lastly is Rhode Island, which of these states has the most elaborate religious freedom provision, not only referencing God (twice) but also guaranteeing both voluntarism and equality:

> Whereas Almighty God hath created the mind free; and all attempts to influence it by temporal punishments or burdens, or by civil incapacitations, tend to beget habits of hypocrisy and meanness; and whereas a principal object of our venerable ancestors, in their migration to this country and their settlement of this state, was, as they expressed it, to hold forth a lively experiment that a flourishing civil state may stand and be best maintained with full liberty in religious concernments; we, therefore, declare that no person shall be compelled to frequent or to support any religious worship, place, or ministry whatever, except

152 COLO. CONST. preamble; *see also* MO. CONST. preamble (same).

153 *See, e.g.*, GA. CONST. preamble ("relying upon the protection ... of Almighty God"); IOWA CONST. preamble ("feeling our dependence on Him for a continuation of those blessings [hitherto enjoyed]"); N.C. CONST. preamble ("acknowledging our dependence upon Him for the continuance of those blessings to us and our posterity"); W. VA. CONST. preamble ("reaffirm[ing] our faith in and constant reliance upon God").

154 *See, e.g.*, ARK. CONST. preamble; DEL. CONST. preamble; KAN. CONST. preamble; LA. CONST. preamble; MD. CONST. preamble; MINN. CONST. preamble; N.J. CONST. preamble; N.C. CONST. preamble; PA. CONST. preamble; R.I. CONST. preamble; S.D. CONST. preamble; W. VA. CONST. preamble; WYO. CONST. preamble.

155 MASS. CONST. pt. I, art. II.

156 *See* CONN. CONST. art. VII ("It being the right of all men to worship the Supreme Being, the Great Creator and Preserver of the Universe, and to render that worship in a mode consistent with the dictates of their consciences, no person shall by law be compelled to join or support, nor be classed or associated with, any congregation, church or religious association.").

157 DEL. CONST. art. I, § 1.

158 MD. CONST. DECL. OF RTS. art. 36 ("That as it is the duty of every man to worship God in such manner as he thinks most acceptable to Him, all persons are equally entitled to protection in their religious liberty.").

159 VA. CONST. art. I, § 16.

> in fulfillment of such person's voluntary contract; nor enforced, restrained, molested, or burdened in body or goods; nor disqualified from holding any office; nor otherwise suffer on account of such person's religious belief; and that every person shall be free to worship God according to the dictates of such person's conscience, and to profess and by argument to maintain such person's opinion in matters of religion; and that the same shall in no wise diminish, enlarge, or affect the civil capacity of any person.[160]

Many state constitutions are also rather explicit about the nature of the right and the types of conduct that are protected by their religion-related provisions, which again contrasts with the U.S. Constitution's rather generic reference to the "free exercise" of religion. Several of them, for example, specifically protect the act of "worship"[161] or "public worship"[162] and, further, often describe the right as natural and either "inalienable,"[163] "unalienable,"[164] or "indefeasible."[165]

The third and final function of religious or theological phrasing in state constitutions is to identify religion as an important, if not necessary, force in the maintenance of a prosperous society or of good government.[166] Several employ phrasing, much like the Northwest Ordinance of 1787, to the effect that religion, morality, and knowledge are "essential to good government" or "the happiness of mankind" and then provide for the protection of public worship or the provision of public schools or libraries.[167] Some, especially of the original states, are even more particular about the role of religion in public life. The Delaware Constitution, for instance, declares that "it is the duty of all men

160 R.I. CONST. art. I, § 3

161 *See, e.g.*, ARK. CONST. art. II, § 24; CONN. CONST. art. VII; GA. CONST. art. I, § 1, ¶ III; IND. CONST. art. I, § 2; KAN. CONST. BILL OF RTS. § 7; KY. CONST. BILL OF RTS. § 1; ME. CONST. art. I, § 3; MD. CONST. DECL. OF RTS. art. 36; MINN. CONST. art. I, § 16; MO. CONST. art. I, § 5; NEB. CONST. art. I, § 4; N.H. CONST. pt. I, art. 5; N.J. CONST. art. I, ¶ 3; N.M. CONST. art. II, § 11; N.C. CONST. art. I, § 13; OHIO CONST. art. I, § 7; OR. CONST. art. I, § 2; PA. CONST. art. I, § 3; R.I. CONST. art. I, § 3; S.D. CONST. art. VI, § 3; TENN. CONST. art. I, § 3; TEX. CONST. art. I, § 6; VT. CONST. ch. I, art. 3; WIS. CONST. art. I, § 18.

162 *See, e.g.*, ARK. CONST. art. II, § 25; DEL. CONST. art. I, § 1; MASS. CONST. pt. I, arts. II, III; NEB. CONST. art. I, § 4; OHIO CONST. art. I, § 7.

163 *See, e.g.*, GA. CONST. art. I, § 1, ¶ III; KY. CONST. BILL OF RTS. § 1; N.C. CONST. art. I, § 13.

164 *See, e.g.*, ME. CONST. art. I, § 3; N.H. CONST. pt. I, art. 5; VT. CONST. ch. I, art. 3.

165 *See, e.g.*, ARK. CONST. art. II, § 24; MO. CONST. art. I, § 5; NEB. CONST. art. I, § 4; OHIO CONST. art. I, § 7; PA. CONST. art. I, § 3; TENN. CONST. art. I, § 3; TEX. CONST. art. I, § 6.

166 *Cf.* Holy Trinity Church v. United States, 143 U.S. 457, 468 (1892) (remarking that all of the state constitutions at that time "contain[ed] language which, either directly or by clear implication, recognizes a profound reverence for religion, and an assumption that its influence in all human affairs is essential to the well-being of the community").

167 *See, e.g.*, ARK. CONST. art. II, § 25 ("Religion, morality and knowledge being essential to good government, the General Assembly shall enact suitable laws to protect every religious denomination in the peaceable enjoyment of its own mode of public worship."); MICH. CONST. art. VIII, § 1 ("Religion, morality and knowledge being necessary to good government and the happiness of mankind, schools and the means of education shall forever be encouraged."); NEB. CONST. art. I, § 4: "Religion, morality, and knowledge, however, being essential to good government, it shall be the duty of the Legislature to pass suitable laws to protect every religious denomination in the peaceable enjoyment of its own mode of public worship, and to encourage schools and the means of instruction."); N.C. CONST. art. IX, § 1 ("Religion, morality, and knowledge being necessary to good government and the happiness of mankind, schools, libraries, and the means of education shall forever be encouraged."); OHIO CONST. art. I, § 7 ("Religion, morality, and knowledge, however, being essential to good government, it shall be the duty of the General Assembly to pass suitable laws, to protect every religious denomination in the peaceable enjoyment of its own mode of public worship, and to encourage schools and the means of instruction.").

frequently to assemble together for the public worship of Almighty God" and that "the prosperity of communities depends" on "piety and morality,"[168] and the New Hampshire Constitution proclaims that "morality and piety, rightly grounded on high principles, will give the best and greatest security to government, and will lay, in the hearts of men, the strongest obligations to due subjection."[169] The Massachusetts Constitution is equally specific and unequivocal, stating that "[t]he public worship of GOD and instructions in piety, religion and morality, promote the happiness and prosperity of a people and the security of a republican government."[170]

## 2. *The U.S. Constitution: The Attestation Clause*

Article VII of the U.S. Constitution provides that the document would be "Establish[ed]" and effective upon its ratification by nine of the thirteen states. The delegates then dated the Convention's proceedings as concluding on "the Seventeenth Day of September in the Year of our Lord one thousand seven hundred and Eighty seven and of the Independence of the United States of America the Twelfth."[171] As noted earlier, the Constitution as a whole, unlike the Declaration of Independence or the state constitutions, is largely devoid of manifestly religious references, but the most apparent exception to this is the use of "the Year of our Lord" in the so-called Attestation Clause following Article VII.[172] Assuming that the "Lord" referenced in the clause is, as most assume, the Jesus of Christianity, then it is necessary to assess how the reference should be understood. Should it be viewed, for example, as simply a routine dating convention, with no particular religious implications, or should it instead be seen as a constitutional affirmation of Christianity or of God's authority over human affairs?[173] This section examines the possible significance of the Attestation Clause, beginning with the origins and development of the phrase "in the year of our Lord" and ending with a discussion of cases that have assessed the constitutionality of its use.

The phrase "year of our Lord" is an English translation of the Latin phrase "*Anno Domini*," commonly abbreviated as A.D., with its counterpart being "Before Christ," or B.C. The system of marking time in terms of years before and since Christ's nativity was developed by Dionysius Exiguus, a sixth-century Catholic monk.[174] Various systems of tracking years had been used in the Roman Empire, including dating events in relation to the legendary founding of Rome by Romulus and Remus and tracking dates based on the names of the two consuls who assumed office (an event that took place on the first day of each year).[175] Various Christian calendars also were in existence with start dates based

168 Del. Const. art. I, § 1.

169 N.H. Const. pt. I, art. 6.

170 Mass. Const. pt. I, art. III.

171 U.S. Const. art. VII.

172 An additional but more subtle religion-recognizing aspect of the Constitution is the exemption of Sundays from the president's ten-day window within which to exercise the veto power. *See* U.S. Const. art. I, § 7.

173 *See* Dreisbach, *supra* note 95, at 965–7.

174 *See* Michael Ostling, *BC/AD Dating: In the Year of Whose Lord?* 59 Hist. Today (Oct. 2009); *available at:* http://www.historytoday.com/michael-ostling/bcad-dating-year-whose-lord.

175 *See* Christopher S. Mackey, *Consuls of the Roman Republic*, 1998; *available at:* http://www.ualberta.ca/~csmackay/Consuls.List.html; *The Roman Calendar*; *available at:* http://penelope.uchicago.edu/~grout/encyclopaedia_romana/calendar/romancalendar.html (accessed Jul. 30, 2014). On the

on the creation of the world, the Resurrection, and the commencement of Christian persecutions under Emperor Diocletian.[176] Dionysius Exiguus devised his calendar based on the birth of Christ as the point on which all of history pivoted, though many scholars today place Jesus' birth at roughly 4 B.C.[177] The primary importance of calendar systems for Dionysius was their use in tabulating the date of holy days, especially Easter.[178] The dominance of the A.D. usage in calendars in the Anglo-Saxon world was a result of the system being used by the eighth-century monk and scholar known as Venerable Bede in his sweeping *Historica ecclesiastica gentis Anglorum* (*Ecclesiastical History of the English People*), completed *circa* A.D. 731.[179] Eventually, Dionysius Exiguus' system became the predominate method of tracking years in much of the world. Pope Gregory XIII reformed the calendar in 1582 to account for advances in understanding in astronomy.[180] However, the Protestant British Empire, including its North American colonies, stubbornly held out with the less-accurate Julian calendar until 1752, when reform was finally implemented, with Wednesday, September 2, of that year being followed by Thursday, September 14.[181]

In short, the calendar system employed by the Constitution's Framers, and still largely employed today, was at once commonplace yet rich with religious, political, and ideological significance.[182] To be sure, this significance was not lost on the highly secularist French revolutionaries, who in 1793 introduced a new "Republican Calendar," which redesignated 1792, when the first French Republic was established, as Year I.[183] Under this calendar, months and days were all renamed, and months were divided into three groups of ten days (the tenth being a festival day), with the hope of extirpating the Christian Sabbath from the culture.[184] Though France returned in 1806 to the traditional Christian calendar,[185] recent years have witnessed a new and not unrelated development: the disuse of A.D. and B.C. in historical dating, based largely on a concern for inclusiveness in light of

Iberian Peninsula, a system of denoting years from Spain's incorporation into the Roman Empire was used until the fifteenth century, whereas religious minorities such as Jews maintained their own calendars. *See* MEDIEVAL IBERIA: AN ENCYCLOPEDIA 190 (Michael E. Gerli ed., 2003).

176 *See* Ostling, *supra* note 174.

177 *See id.*

178 *See* Charles A. Sullivan, *Dionysius Exiguus and the AD Calendar System*, Apr. 12, 2012; *available at:* http://charlesasullivan.com/1842/dionysius-exiguus-and-the-ad-calendar-system/.

179 In its English translation, *see* http://www.gutenberg.org/files/38326/38326-h/38326-h.html. In Latin, *see* http://www.thelatinlibrary.com/bede.html.

180 *See* Mark M. Smith, *Culture, Commerce, and Calendar Reform in Colonial America*, 55 WM. & MARY Q. 557–9 (1998).

181 *See id.*

182 By the date of the U.S. Constitution's drafting and ratification, then, the extant system of time keeping was largely the product of the work of Roman Catholic clerics and reflected a Christian concept of time, even though the days and months retained names based on pagan gods, *e.g.*, Saturday based on Saturn and March based on Mars. Indeed, pious Quakers in the early American republic used a system of tracking time that relied only on numbers so as to avoid using the names of the ancient gods. *See* Henry J. Cadbury, *Heathen Names of Days of the Week and Months*, 17(2) BULL. FRIENDS HIST. ASS'N 54–7 (1928).

183 Prior to the Republic Calendar being promulgated, some French citizens had viewed 1789 as the first year of a new era, the "Era of Liberty." *See* George G. Andrews, *Making the Revolutionary Calendar*, 36 AM. HIST. REV. 515, 517 (1931); Eviatar Zerubavel, *The French Republican Calendar: A Case Study of the Sociology of Time* 42 AM. SOCIOL. REV. 868–70 (1977).

184 *See* Dreisbach, *supra* note 95, at 966.

185 *See* Zerubavel, *supra* note 183, at 874.

modern religious diversity. Under this new approach, A.D. is replaced with C.E. ("Common Era"), and B.C. with B.C.E. ("Before the Common Era").

As the generally secular nature of the Constitution and the near-contemporaneous experience of the French Revolution would indicate, the Constitution's authors could have avoided altogether a reference to the Christian calendar.[186] The notion of removing Christian influences in tracking time was well within the realm of Enlightenment ideas and certainly in vogue in some quarters even in pre-Revolutionary France, where several of the most influential Founders – Jefferson, Franklin, and, less happily, Adams – had all spent time.[187] For deists and atheists, the notion that the historical event on which the epochs of time pivoted would be the supposed birth of God incarnate in ancient Palestine was presumably not well regarded. If there were ever a time for America to break off from not only the political but also the religious traditions of the Old World and to fashion a new society steeped in Enlightenment rationalism, the Constitutional Convention provided such an opportunity.

The Framers' use of "the Year of our Lord" to date the closing of the Constitutional Convention may have involved multiple intentions or motivations. For some, perhaps for many, it may have had no meaningful religious significance at all. In the view of Professor Steven Smith, "[t]he reference to 'the Year of our Lord' simply employed the conventional dating method of the era; it seems no more a purposive invocation of God than does attaching the letters 'A.D.' or 'B.C.' to a historical date. If the Framers meant to pay their devotions, they surely chose an oblique and even impious way to do so – as if, rather than welcoming deity in through the front door, they instead limited themselves to an almost imperceptible wave through the back window."[188] Alternatively, "the delegates might have used the conventional phrase 'the Year of our Lord' merely as a way of differentiating that date from the second, more significant" date of the twelfth year of the nation's independence.[189]

For others, by comparison, using "the Year of our Lord" may have been perceived as a counterpoint to emergent currents of radical enlightenment thinking (which just a few years hence would culminate in the French Revolution and its aftermath),[190] much like

186 *See* Dreisbach, *supra* note 95, at 967 ("[I]f the Constitution was deliberately secular or hostile to traditional religion, the reference to Jesus Christ could have been avoided. The framers broke with tradition by omitting from the body of the text all references to the Deity, and they could have just as easily omitted the reference to Christ in the dating clause.").

187 *See* Paul M. Spurlin, *The World of the Founding Fathers and France*, 49 FRENCH REV. 909, 916–18 (1976).

188 Smith, *supra* note 38, at 125 n. 19.

189 Suzanna Sherry, *Enlightening the Religion Clauses*, 7 J. CONTEMP. LEGAL ISSUES 473, 483 n. 52 (1996).

190 *See* Dreisbach, *supra* note 95, at 965; Carl H. Esbeck, *Uses and Abuses of Textualism and Originalism in Establishment Clause Interpretation*, 2011 UTAH L. REV. 489, 498 ["One may regard the Western use of a calendar that begins with the birth of Jesus Christ as but a trifle mention of religion. However, as historian William Lee Miller points out, such trifles in the aggregate do contrast the American Revolution with, for example, the anti-Christianity of the French Revolution. The American founders were not repudiating their Christian past or being hostile to it, hence, they absentmindedly used the Christian calendar and unconsciously assumed Sunday would be the president's Sabbath. Similarly, the Convention delegates worked six-day weeks from late May to mid-September, with Sunday excepted. While the American founders were intentional about breaking with their European past of a confessional state, it is also well documented that they viewed the Protestant religion as a friend to republicanism and as an aid to the expansion of liberty" (footnotes omitted) referencing WILLIAM LEE MILLER, THE BUSINESS OF MAY NEXT: JAMES MADISON & THE FOUNDING 114–15 (1992)].

adding "under God" to the Pledge of Allegiance in the 1950s was understood, in part, as a counterpoint to the godless and unlimited government of Soviet communism.[191] From this perspective, the reference may be less an affirmation of a personal Christian faith and more a recognition of the new nation's place in relation to God or its heritage within the context of European Christendom. To be sure, some nineteenth-century observers "ascribed great significance" to the language following Article VII: "At the very least, the framers paid tribute – whether inadvertently or not is unclear – to Christianity and its calendar. At the very most, the phrase declared the lordship of Jesus Christ and recognized that all civil government is under God."[192]

Certainly the lawsuits challenging the use of "year of our Lord" (or its Latin equivalent) suggest, by their institution, that the phrase can be perceived by some as an affirmation or invocation of religion in general or Christianity in particular.[193] This is not to imply that such challenges have legal merit, but they do indicate that the use of "year of our Lord" or "*Anno Domini*" or "A.D." can be seen as more than just a chronological convention. On the merits, in fact, these claims have not been successful. A government employee's challenge to the use of A.D. on a federal document, for example, failed under the Free Exercise Clause, and the court implied that an Establishment Clause claim would fail as well.[194] In particular, the court found "the use of the abbreviation in question … to be a constitutionally permissible chronological referent. The abbreviation, 'A.D.,' as used on [the form] has a purely secular usage" and "the extended use of 'A.D.' through recent centuries as an annual or chronological reference point and its incorporation into the Constitution have worked to evolve the term into an entirely secular designation" especially "in the context of its appearance" on a government form.[195] Similarly, a state's inclusion of "in the year of our Lord" on law licenses and notarial commissions was held not to violate the Establishment Clause.[196] The court concluded that the phrase, in addition to surviving the three-part *Lemon* test,[197] "is an example of 'ceremonial deism,' a practice which should not be understood as conveying governmental approval of a particular religious belief."[198]

191 *See* Grace Y. Kao, *"One Nation under God" or Taking the Lord's Name in Vain? Christian Reflections on the Pledge of Allegiance*, 27 J. SOC'Y CHRISTIAN ETHICS 183, 195 (2007).

192 Dreisbach, *supra* note 95, at 966.

193 *See, e.g.*, Barnes v. Clinton, No. 02-6057, 57 Fed. App'x 240 (6th Cir. Jan. 31, 2003) (unpublished) (alleging that the phrase "is based on the establishment of the Christian religion"), *cert. denied*, 540 U.S. 905 (2003); benMeriam v. Office of Personnel Mgt., 647 F. Supp. 84 (M.D.N.C. 1986) (challenge by a government employee to use of "A.D." on government form).

194 *See* benMeriam, 647 F. Supp. at 85–6.

195 *Id.* at 85.

196 *See* Doe v. La. Supr. Ct., No. Civ. A. No. 91–1635, 1992 WL 373566, at *5-*7 (E.D. La. Dec. 8, 1992) (unpublished).

197 *See id.* at *7. For an overview of the *Lemon* test, *see* Chapter 4.C.1.

198 *See* Doe, 1992 WL 373566, at *6 [citing Marsh v. Chambers, 463 U.S. 783 (1983); Sch. Dist of Abington Twp. v. Schempp, 374 U.S. 203, 212–14 (1963); Zorach v. Clauson, 343 U.S. 306, 313 (1952)]; *see also* Commonwealth v. Callahan, 519 N.E.2d 245, 252 (Mass. 1988) (holding that "[t]he words 'in the year of our Lord' in [an] indictment form and 'so help me God' in the oaths [administered to the jurors and witnesses] do not constitute an establishment of religion" but rather "are simply two examples of many permissible, secular 'references to the Almighty that run through our laws, our public rituals, [and] our ceremonies'" quoting Colo. v. Treasurer & Receiver Gen., 392 N.E.2d 1195, 1201 (Mass. 1979)].

### 3. *The National Motto*

The nation's first unofficial motto was "*E pluribus unum*" ("Out of many, one"), which was proposed in 1776, adopted in 1782, and to this day is part of the Great Seal of the United States.[199] *E pluribus unum* first appeared on coinage in 1795 and in 1873 was required on all U.S. coinage, followed in 1935 by its appearance on the back of the one-dollar note.[200] Beginning in the 1860s, however, a new vernacular phrase, "In God we trust," also began to emerge on the nation's coins. Nearly a century later, in 1956, Congress adopted "In God we trust" as the official motto of the United States.[201] This section explores the history, significance, and constitutionality of this national motto.

The initial request for the addition of some kind of divine recognition on U.S. coinage appears to have come from a Pennsylvania minister writing in 1861 to Secretary of the Treasury Salmon P. Chase.[202] In November of that year, Chase instructed the director of the mint at Philadelphia to prepare "a motto expressing in the fewest and tersest words possible" the "trust of our people in God," and from this emerged the terse phrase "In God we trust," which first appeared on two-cent coins in 1864.[203] The next year, Congress authorized the use of "In God we trust" on "such coins hereafter to be issued as shall admit of such legend thereon,"[204] and it has been inscribed on all U.S. coinage since 1938.[205] In 1955, Congress further mandated that the phrase be imprinted on U.S. paper currency.[206] It first appeared on paper money two years later, and by the 1960s, it was present on all major denominations.[207]

Today, most Americans – 90 percent according to a 2003 poll – endorse the use of "In God we trust" on U.S. coins, and presumably a similar percentage support that phrase as the official national motto.[208] Indeed, when a new series of dollar coins bearing the images of presidents in chronological order was introduced in 2007,[209] concern was

199 *See Original Design of the Great Seal of the United States; available at:* http://www.ourdocuments.gov/doc.php?flash=true&doc=5.

200 *See* http://www.treasury.gov/about/budget-performance/strategic-plan/Pages/dlinks.aspx ["The Latin phrase *E Pluribus Unum* is found in the *Journals of the Continental Congress*, June 20, 1782, where it was used to describe the Great Seal adopted that day. From the Great Seal's earliest depiction, *E Pluribus Unum* has appeared on coins since 1795 and has graced the back of $1 notes since 1935. The phrase has been required on all U.S. coinage by law since February 12, 1873" (internal references omitted)].

201 Pub. L. No. 84–851 (Joint Resolution), ch. 795, 70 Stat. 732 (Jul. 30, 1956) (presently codified at 36 U.S.C. § 302) (formerly codified at 36 U.S.C. § 186).

202 *See* U.S. Dep't of the Treasury, *History of "In God We Trust,"* Mar. 8, 2011; *available at:* http://www.treasury.gov/about/education/Pages/in-god-we-trust.aspx.

203 *See* Anson Phelps Stokes & Leo Pfeffer, Church and State in the United States 568 (rev'd ed. 1964); *History of "In God We Trust," supra* note 202.

204 Act of Mar. 3, 1865, ch. 100, § 5, 13 Stat. 517, 518. Congress did so again eight years later. *See* Act of Feb. 12, 1873, ch. 131, § 18, 17 Stat. 424, 427 (authorizing the Secretary of the Treasury to "cause the motto 'In God we trust' to be inscribed upon such coins as shall admit of such motto").

205 *See History of "In God We Trust," supra* note 202.

206 Pub. L. No. 84–140, ch. 303, 69 Stat. 290 (Jul. 11, 1955) [presently codified at 31 U.S.C. § 5112(d)(1) (coinage), § 5114(b) (printed currency); formerly codified at 31 U.S.C. §§ 320, 324a].

207 *See History of "In God We Trust," supra* note 202.

208 *See* Frank Newport, *Americans Approve of Public Displays of Religious Symbols*, Gallup News Service, Oct. 3, 2003; *available at:* http://www.gallup.com/poll/9391/americans-approve-public-displays-religious-symbols.aspx.

209 *See* Presidential $1 Coin Act of 2005, Pub. L. No. 109–45, 119 Stat. 2664 (Dec. 22, 2005); U.S. Mint, *The Presidential $1 Coin Act of 2005; available at:* http://www.usmint.gov/mint_programs/$1coin/?action=coinAct2005.

raised by some citizens that the new coins lacked the motto.[210] As it turns out, the words were there, but printed on the outer edge of the coins. Congress in 2008 then mandated that the words return to a place of prominence on the obverse (either face) of the coins.[211]

The roots of the national motto may extend back to Maryland lawyer Francis Scott Key and his 1814 lyrics, "Defence of Fort M'Henry," which were likely arranged for an existing tune but would later be set to different music and eventually become "The Star Spangled Banner," the American national anthem.[212] Key was an Episcopalian and in 1817 became the vice president of the American Bible Society, a post he held until his death in 1843.[213] In the seldom-sung fourth stanza, Key writes

> Oh, thus be it ever when free men shall stand,
> Between their loved homes and the war's desolation;
> Blest with vict'ry and peace, may the heav'n-rescued land
> Praise the Power that has made and preserved us as a nation.
> Then conquer we must, when our cause is just,
> And this be our motto: "In God is our trust";
> And the star-spangled banner in triumph shall wave
> O'er the land of the free and the home of the brave.[214]

It is unknown whether Key's lyrics actually influenced the Treasury Department's selection of "In God we trust" and thus provide the original source of the national motto, though regardless they give some insight into religious understandings of national events in the nineteenth century. In all events, Key's lyrics were clearly noted by Congress when it officially adopted the motto in 1956.[215]

From the late 1960s to the present, several lawsuits have argued that the use of "In God we trust" on U.S. coinage and paper currency is unconstitutional under the Establishment Clause.[216] More recently, claims alleging a violation of the Free Exercise

210 *See "Godless Dollars,"* May 27, 2009; *available at:* http://www.factcheck.org/2009/05/godless-dollars/. Some coins did, in fact, omit "In God we trust" from the edge, but those were minting errors and not part of the design. *See id.*

211 *See Presidential $1 Coins: 'In God We Trust' Motto Moves in 2009: Are Coin Edge-Letterings Gone Forever?* Dec. 30, 2007; *available at:* http://www.coinnews.net/2007/12/30/presidential-1-coins-in-god-we-trust-motto-moves-in-2009-are-coin-edge-letterings-gone-forever-3914/.

212 *See* Epstein, *supra* note 24, at 2122. The song based on Key's lyrics was not formally adopted as the national anthem until 1931, when President Herbert Hoover signed it into law. *See* Pub. L. No. 71–823, ch. 436, 46 Stat. 1508 (Mar. 3, 1931) [presently codified at 36 U.S.C. § 301(a)] ("The composition consisting of the words and music known as the Star-Spangled Banner is the national anthem.") (formerly codified at 36 U.S.C. § 170). Prior to 1931, "The Star Spangled Banner" competed with other patriotic songs such as "My Country, 'Tis of Thee" and "Hail, Columbia," both of which also contain overt religious references, for preeminence at official government functions [*see United States (to 1931); available at:* http://www.nationalanthems.info/us-31.htm], although the 1931 act had been preceded by a 1916 executive order by President Woodrow Wilson to the same effect.

213 *See Francis Scott Key; available at:* http://www.nps.gov/fomc/historyculture/francis-scott-key.htm; *History of American Bible Society; available at:* http://www.americanbible.org/about/history.

214 *See The Lyrics,* Nat'l Museam of Am. Hist.; *available at:* http://amhistory.si.edu/starspangledbanner/the-lyrics.aspx.

215 Epstein, *supra* note 24, at 2122 n. 232 [citing H.R. Rep. No. 84–1959 (1956)].

216 *See* Newdow v. Peterson, 753 F.3d 105 (2d Cir. 2014) (*per curiam*); Kidd v. Obama, No. 10–5006, 387 Fed. App'x 2 (D.C. Cir. Jul. 21, 2010) (*per curiam*) (unpublished); Newdow v. Lefevre, 598 F.3d 638 (9th Cir. 2010), *cert. denied,* 131 S. Ct. 1612 (2011); Gaylor v. United States, 74 F.3d 214 (10th Cir. 1996), *cert. denied,* 517 U.S. 1211 (1996); O'Hair v. Murray, 588 F.2d 1144 (5th Cir. 1979) (*per curiam*), *cert. denied,* 442 U.S. 930 (1979); Aronow v. United States, 432 F.2d 242 (9th Cir. 1970).

Clause or the Religious Freedom Restoration Act[217] also have been asserted.[218] As with the 2008 Detroit Lions, however, these suits have produced only losses.[219] Challenges to the use of the motto in other contexts, such as on government buildings, also have been rejected by the courts,[220] as has a challenge to Ohio's similar state motto.[221] Most courts, in addition to heeding each other's rulings, take their lead from numerous comments by Supreme Court justices, in majority or separate opinions, indicating that they consider the national motto to be valid under the Establishment Clause.[222] Finally, the Supreme Court itself also has suggested in dictum that the motto's inclusion on currency, as opposed to a license plate, poses no problem of forced expression under the Free Speech Clause.[223] Were it included on a license plate or similar medium, in fact, an individual presumably would be entitled to cover it up, much like the plaintiffs in *Wooley v. Maynard* had a right to conceal New Hampshire's motto, "Live Free or Die," on their license plates.[224]

### 4. *The Pledge of Allegiance*

The Pledge of Allegiance was originally authored by Francis Bellamy, a nineteenth-century Baptist minister and self-styled Christian socialist. Bellamy's pledge first appeared in a children's magazine and was quickly disseminated in school districts as part of honoring the 400th anniversary of Christopher Columbus' landfall in the Americas.[225] The wording of the pledge has been modified a number of times since Bellamy's version, with the 1954 addition of the phrase "under God" being the most recent and, for present purposes, the most notable.[226]

The idea for this particular change came from Louis A. Bowman, chaplain to the Illinois chapter of the Sons of the American Revolution, who began using his amended version of the pledge in 1948.[227] Bowman claimed that he took inspiration for use of the

217 Pub. L. No. 103–41, 107 Stat. 1488 (Nov. 16, 1993) (codified as amended at 42 U.S.C. §§ 2000bb to 2000bb-4).

218 *See Newdow*, 753 F.3d at 106; *Newdow*, 598 F.3d at 640.

219 *See Lions First NFL Team to Finish 0–16*; *available at*: http://scores.espn.go.com/nfl/recap?gameId=281228009. Indeed, few applications of the Establishment Clause and few NFL teams have exhibited such consistent results.

220 *See* Lambeth v. Bd. of Comm'rs of Davidson Cnty., N.C., 407 F.3d 266 (4th Cir. 2005) (motto inscribed on the facade of a county government center), *cert. denied*, 546 U.S. 1015 (2005); Schmidt v. Cline, 127 F. Supp. 2d 1169, 1177–80 (D. Kan. 2000) (motto displayed on a poster inside county offices).

221 *See* ACLU of Ohio v. Capitol Square Review & Advisory Bd., 243 F.3d 289 (6th Cir. 2001) (*en banc*) (upholding Ohio's official state motto, "With God, All Things Are Possible").

222 *See, e.g.*, Newdow, 753 F.3d at 108; Kidd, 387 Fed. App'x. at 2; Newdow, 598 F.3d at 644–5; Gaylor, 74 F.3d at 216, 217.

223 *See* Wooley v. Maynard, 430 U.S. 705, 717 n. 15 (1977) ("It has been suggested that today's holding will be read as sanctioning obliteration of the National Motto, 'In God We Trust,' from United States coins and currency. … [W]e note that currency, which is passed from hand to hand, differs in significant respects from an automobile, which is readily associated with its operator. Currency is generally carried in a purse or pocket and need not be displayed by the public. The bearer of currency is thus not required to publicly advertise the National Motto.").

224 *See id.* at 713–17.

225 *See* Elk Grove Unified Sch. Dist. v. Newdow, 542 U.S. 1, 6 (2004); John W. Baer, The Pledge of Allegiance: A Revised History and Analysis (2007); *available in part at:* http://www.oldtimeislands.org/pledge/pdgech0.htm.

226 *See* Kao, *supra* note 191, at 183.

227 *See* Scott A. Merriman, Religion and the Law in America: An Encyclopedia of Personal Belief and Public Policy 111 (2007).

phrase from Lincoln's "Gettysburg Address."[228] The Daughters of the American Revolution quickly supported Bowman's idea,[229] and by the early 1950s, the Knights of Columbus started using "under God" when reciting the pledge at their meetings. It also began lobbying Congress to make the change official.[230]

In February 1954, in honor of Abraham Lincoln's birthday, President Dwight Eisenhower went to services at the New York Avenue Presbyterian Church, where Lincoln had been known occasionally to attend.[231] Eisenhower himself was raised in a Jehovah's Witness household but had recently been baptized a Presbyterian.[232] The pastor at the church, George MacPherson Docherty, gave a sermon that drew on the "Gettysburg Address" and also discussed the pledge, declaring that "there was something missing in the pledge, and that which was missing was the characteristic and definitive factor in the American way of life."[233] That missing factor, one that would set the United States apart from the atheism of the Soviet Bloc, was an acknowledgment of God as sitting above government and as endowing the people with their liberties.[234]

Following the service, Eisenhower and Docherty discussed the topic, and the president voiced his support for inserting "under God" into the pledge.[235] Just four months later, on June 14, 1954, the phrase was officially incorporated into the pledge after Eisenhower signed a congressional joint resolution amending the 1942 Flag Code.[236] A House committee report captured some of the thinking about the change:

> Since our flag is symbolic of our Nation, its constitutional government and the morality of our people, the committee believes it most appropriate that the concept of God be included in the recitations of the pledge. … It should be pointed out that the … legislation in no way runs contrary to the provisions of the first amendment to the Constitution. This is not an act establishing a religion or one interfering with the "free exercise" of religion. A distinction must be made between the existence of a religion as an institution and a belief in the sovereignty of God. The phrase "under God" recognizes only the guidance of God in our national affairs.[237]

228 Lincoln's address ends with the following: "It is rather for us to be here dedicated to the great task remaining before us – that from these honored dead we take increased devotion to that cause for which they gave the last full measure of devotion – that we here highly resolve that these dead shall not have died in vain, that this nation under God shall have a new birth of freedom, and that government of the people, by the people, for the people shall not perish from the earth." *See* http://avalon.law.yale.edu/19th_century/gettyb.asp.

229 *See* Merriman, *supra* note 227, at 111–12.

230 *See id.*

231 *See* Tom Gibb, *How the Pledge Got God*, Pittsburgh Post-Gazette, Jun. 28, 2002, *available at*: http://old.post-gazette.com/nation/20020628undergod0628p3.asp; Stephen Wylder, *The Sermon That Put "Under God" in the Pledge*, Spectator, Aug. 24, 2009; *available at*: http://www.examiner.com/article/the-sermon-that-put-under-god-the-pledge.

232 *See* Mark Tooley, *Eisenhower's Religion*, Am. Spectator, Feb. 14, 2011; *available at*: http://spectator.org/articles/38107/eisenhowers-religion.

233 Tom Gibb, *Minister Reprises "under God" Sermon*, Pittsburgh Post-Gazette, Aug. 19, 2002; *available at*: http://old.post-gazette.com/nation/20020819pledge0819p1.asp. The full sermon can be found at www.christianheritagemins.org/articles/UNDER%20GOD.pdf.

234 *See* Newdow v. Rio Linda Union Sch. Dist., 597 F.3d 1007, 1032 (9th Cir. 2010); Merriman, *supra* note 227, at 111.

235 *See* Gibb, *How the Pledge Got God*, *supra* note 233.

236 Pub. L. No. No. 83–396, ch. 297, 68 Stat. 249 (Jun. 14, 1954) (formerly codified at 36 U.S.C. § 172). The pledge and the proper manner of its recitation are today codified at 4 U.S.C. § 4.

237 H.R. Rep. No. 1693, 83d Cong., 2d Sess. 3 (1954), *quoted in Comment, The Supreme Court, the First Amendment, and Religion in the Public Schools*, 63 Colum. L. Rev. 73, 85 (1963).

Challenges involving the pledge, or state-directed recitation of it, arose before the addition of "under God," and they have certainly arisen since. In 1943, at the height of World War II, the Supreme Court in *West Virginia State Board of Education v. Barnette*[238] upheld the First Amendment right of public school students (in that case, Jehovah's Witnesses) not to salute the American flag and recite the pledge at the mandate of the state.[239] Shortly after the pledge was changed in 1954, the New York courts addressed a challenge to a state education regulation recommending use of the amended version in public schools.[240] The courts rejected the challenge, however, holding that the option not to recite the pledge (as recognized in *Barnette*) eliminated any possible constitutional problem.[241] In recent decades, legal opposition to the pledge has surfaced again. In 1992, the Seventh Circuit upheld an Illinois state law requiring recitation of the pledge in public schools because, as in the New York case, students could opt out[242] and, further, because the collective weight of tradition and the considered dicta of various Supreme Court justices suggested that the pledge was not unconstitutional.[243] Likewise, and on similar grounds, the Fourth Circuit in 2005 upheld a Virginia statute providing for daily, voluntary recitation of the pledge in its public schools.[244]

Among modern challenges to the pledge, the most visible and controversial case arose out of a 2000 lawsuit filed against the state of California, two of its school districts, and the president as well as the Congress of the United States. The complaint alleged that both the pledge itself (as codified in federal law) and its recitation in public schools (pursuant to state law and school district policy) violated the Establishment Clause of the First Amendment. Though the suit was dismissed by the federal district court, a three-judge panel of the Ninth Circuit reversed and held that both a school district policy and the pledge violated the Establishment Clause.[245] The panel's ruling, which made national headlines for days during the summer of 2002 and smoldered for months thereafter in the Ninth Circuit, was eventually accepted for review by the Supreme Court, thus promising a potential end to the controversy.[246] The end that came, however, was not with a

238 319 U.S. 624 (1943).

239 *See id.* at 637–42. Nor, apparently, can students who opt not to recite the pledge be forced to leave the classroom during the recitation [*see* Goetz v. Ansell, 477 F.2d 636, 638 (2d Cir. 1973); Frain v. Baron, 307 F. Supp. 27 (E.D.N.Y. 1969)] or to stand while the pledge is being recited. *See* Lipp v. Morris, 579 F.2d 834, 836 (3d Cir. 1978); Goetz, 477 F.2d at 637–8; Banks v. Bd. of Pub. Instr. of Dade Cnty., 450 F.2d 1103 (5th Cir. 1971) (*per curiam*) (affirming order holding that requirement to stand was unconstitutional).

240 Lewis v. Allen, 159 N.Y.S.2d 807 (N.Y. Supr. Ct. Albany Cnty. 1957), *aff'd*, 207 N.Y.S.2d 862 (N.Y. App. Div. 1960), *aff'd*, 200 N.E.2d 767 (N.Y. 1964), *cert. denied*, 379 U.S. 923 (1964).

241 *See id.* at 813 ("Petitioners' right to disbelieve is guaranteed by the First Amendment, and neither they nor their children can be compelled to recite the words 'under God' in the pledge of allegiance. But the First Amendment affords them no preference over those who do believe in God and who, in pledging their allegiance, choose to express that belief."). The Appellate Division, affirming, ruled likewise. *See* 207 N.Y.S.2d at 865–6. It also rejected the "contention that the teaching and recitation of the pledge 'involve' improper use of the schools for the dissemination of 'religious dogma.'" *Id.* [relying on Zorach v. Clauson, 343 U.S. 306, 312–14 (1952)].

242 *See* Sherman v. Cmty. Consol. Sch. Dist. 21 of Wheeling Twp., 980 F.2d 437, 442–5 (7th Cir. 1992), *cert. denied*, 508 U.S. 950 (1993).

243 *See id.* at 445–8.

244 *See* Myers v. Loudoun Cnty. Pub. Schs., 418 F.3d 395 (4th Cir. 2005).

245 *See* Newdow v. U.S. Congress, 292 F.3d 597, 605–12 (9th Cir. 2002).

246 *See* Newdow v. U.S. Congress, 321 F.3d 772 (9th Cir. 2003), *republished at* 328 F.3d 466 (9th Cir. 2003), *cert. denied*, 540 U.S. 962 (2003), *and cert. granted in part*, 540 U.S. 945 (2003).

bang but a whimper. Instead of ruling on the merits, the Court held that the plaintiff lacked standing – and had from the outset of the suit – such that every ruling to that point would need to be vacated and the suit dismissed.[247] Some years later, the same plaintiff orchestrated a similar lawsuit against various California officials and school districts as well as several federal defendants, but this time the Ninth Circuit rejected the claims on the merits, holding that the pledge did not violate any possibly applicable test of the Establishment Clause.[248] "In the context of the Pledge," said the court, "the phrase 'one Nation under God' constitutes a powerful admission by the government of its own limitations. Although the phrase also has religious connotations, 'one Nation under God' in the Pledge is a reference to the historical and political underpinnings of our nation."[249] Eight months later, in a wholly different action, the First Circuit likewise upheld New Hampshire's voluntary recitation program.[250]

### 5. *Governmental Proclamations and Addresses*

The practice of governmental leaders expressing gratitude and urging prayers for divine blessings is a deep and prominent tradition in Western culture. In Shakespeare's *Henry V*, on triumphing in the Battle of Agincourt, a grateful King proclaims, "Do we all holy rites; Let there be sung 'Non nobis' and 'Te Deum.'"[251] On American soil, this tradition took root in the colonies, most notably with the practice of Thanksgiving celebrations. The popular understanding of the origins of Thanksgiving involves a harvest feast held by devout New England Puritans and local Native Americans in 1621.[252] Although most contemporary Thanksgiving celebrations are at best mild quasi-reenactments of the 1621 affair, in colonial America and in the nation's early years, they were literal expressions of gratitude to God for present bounties and blessings.[253] A late seventeenth-century Thanksgiving proclamation by the town council of Charlestown, Massachusetts, conveys a sense of thanks to a Christian God who is deeply involved in the affairs of mankind:

> The COUNCIL has thought meet to appoint and set apart the 29th day of this instant June, as a day of Solemn Thanksgiving and praise to God for such his Goodness and Favour, many Particulars of which mercy might be Instanced, but we doubt not those who are sensible of God's Afflictions, have been as diligent to espy him returning to us; and that the Lord may behold us as a People offering Praise and thereby glorifying Him; the Council doth commend it to the Respective Ministers, Elders and people of this

247 *See* Elk Grove Unified Sch. Dist. v. Newdow, 542 U.S. 1, 11–18 (2004).

248 *See* Newdow v. Rio Linda Union Sch. Dist., 597 F.3d 1007, 1017–40 (9th Cir. 2010).

249 *Id.* at 1037 (footnote omitted). "The phrase 'under God' is a recognition of our Founder's [*sic*] political philosophy that a power greater than the government gives the people their inalienable rights. Thus, the Pledge is an endorsement of our form of government, not of religion or any particular sect." *Id.*

250 *See* Freedom from Religion Found. v. Hanover Sch. Dist., 626 F.3d 1 (2010), *cert. denied*, 131 S. Ct. 2992 (2011). Also in 2010, the Fifth Circuit upheld the addition of "one state under God" to the Texas pledge of allegiance, required by state law to be recited by public school students. *See* Croft v. Perry, 624 F.3d 157 (5th Cir. 2010). It is not clear, in all events, that a state can impose a pledge recitation requirement on *private* schools within the state. *See* The Circle Sch. v. Pappert, 381 F.3d 172, 181–3 (3d Cir. 2004) (holding that such a requirement violated the private schools' First Amendment right to freedom of expressive association).

251 *See The Life of King Henry the Fifth*; *available at*: http://shakespeare.mit.edu/henryv/henryv.4.8.html.

252 *See* Edwin T. Greninger, *Thanksgiving: An American Holiday*, 54(1) Soc. Sci. 3 (Winter 1979).

253 *See id.*

> Jurisdiction; Solemnly and seriously to keep the same Beseeching that being perswaded by the mercies of God we may all, even this whole people offer up our bodies and soulds as a living and acceptable Service unto God by Jesus Christ.[254]

Just over a century later, in the waning days of the Revolution, the Confederation Congress continued this tradition when issuing its Thanksgiving proclamation of 1782.[255] Like the Charlestown proclamation, it speaks of a God who is active in the lives of individuals (as opposed to the uninvolved God of deism) and to whom thanks and praise should be rendered, though it is broader in its appeal, omitting explicit references to Christ or to doctrines that might be readily associated with any particular denomination or sect:

> It being the indispensable duty of all nations, not only to offer up their supplications to Almighty God, the giver of all good, for his gracious assistance in a time of distress, but also in a solemn and public manner to give him praise for his goodness in general, and especially for great and signal interpositions of his Providence in their behalf; therefore the United States in Congress assembled, taking into their consideration the many instances of divine goodness to these States, in the course of the important conflict in which they have been so long engaged; the present happy and promising state of public affairs; and the events of the war, in the course of the year now drawing to a close … the success of the armies of the United States and those of their allies, and the acknowledgment of their independence by another European power, whose friendship and commerce must be of great and lasting advantage to these States; do hereby recommend to the inhabitants of these States in general, to observe … Thursday, the twenty-eighth day of November next, as a day of solemn thanksgiving to God for all his mercies; and they do further recommend to all ranks and testify to their gratitude of God for his goodness, by a cheerful obedience to his laws, and by protecting, each in his station, and by his influence, the practice of true and undefiled religion, which is the great foundation of public prosperity and national happiness.[256]

As president, George Washington maintained the tradition of Thanksgiving proclamations.[257] In October of 1789, at the request of Congress, Washington issued his first such proclamation, in which he declared that "it is the duty of all Nations to acknowledge the providence of Almighty God, to obey his will, to be grateful for his benefits, and humbly to implore his protection and favor" and then urged Americans to observe "a day of

254 The Portable Patriot: Documents, Speeches, and Sermons That Compose the American Soul 13 (Joel L. Miller & Kristen Parrish eds., 2012).

255 *See* Epstein, *supra* note 24, at 2113.

256 Quoted in 1 Anson Phelps Stokes, Church and State in the United States 453–4 (1950).

257 *See* Epstein, *supra* note 24, at 2113. Washington also instituted both the use of a bible during and the declaration of "So help me God" at the end of presidential inaugurations. The Constitution itself prescribes an oath but does not use that phrase. *See* U.S. Const. art. II, § 1, cl. 8. At his first inauguration, Washington took the oath with his hand on a bible and then, after concluding the prescribed oath, declared "So help me God" and kissed the bible. *See President George Washington's First Inaugural Speech* (Apr. 30, 1789); *available at:* http://www.ourdocuments.gov/doc.php?flash=true&doc=11; Michael Riccards, A Republic, If You Can Keep It: The Foundation of the American Presidency, 1700–1800, at 73–4 (1987). Robert R. Livingston, who administered the oath, then turned to the crowd of spectators and proclaimed, "Long live George Washington, President of the United States!" – which they heartily echoed in reply. *See President George Washington's First Inaugural Speech*, *supra*. Livingston's jubilant exclamation, similar to the cry of "*Vivat Rex*" ("Long Live the King"), intoned in the coronation of a British monarch. *See Guide to the Coronation Service*; *available at:* http://www.westminster-abbey.org/our-history/royals/coronations/guide-to-the-coronation-service.

public thanksgiving and prayer ... by acknowledging with grateful hearts the many signal favors of Almighty God especially by affording them an opportunity peaceably to establish a form of government for their safety and happiness."[258]

Religiously imbued declarations marking Thanksgiving or other events of significance, by presidents and other public officials, certainly did not end with Washington and the First Congress.[259] As the Supreme Court observed in 1962, "[e]ach of our Presidents, from George Washington to John F. Kennedy, has upon assuming his Office asked the protection and help of God."[260] The nineteenth century, for example, "offers countless instances in which political leaders, acting in their official capacities, thanked God for the blessings bestowed on the Republic and prayed that the nation might continue to enjoy His favor. Most presidents have followed the example of President Washington in proclaiming a public day of thanksgiving to God."[261] Some of the best-known examples of that century come, of course, from the pen of President Lincoln, particularly in the later years of the Civil War. In the final Emancipation Proclamation of 1863, for instance, Lincoln invokes "the gracious favor of Almighty God,"[262] and toward the close of that year, at Gettysburg, he famously implored that the war dead "shall not have died in vain – that this nation, under God, shall have a new birth of freedom – and that government of the people, by the people, for the people, shall not perish from the earth."[263] The following year, Lincoln (at Congress' request) appointed "a day of national humiliation

258 George Washington, *Thanksgiving Proclamation* (Oct. 3, 1789); *available at:* http://lcweb2.loc.gov/ammem/GW/gw004.html. Washington continued: "Now therefore I do recommend and assign Thursday the 26th day of November next to be devoted by the People of these States to the service of that great and glorious Being, who is the beneficent Author of all the good that was, that is, or that will be – That we may then all unite in rendering unto him our sincere and humble thanks – for his kind care and protection of the People of this Country previous to their becoming a Nation – for the signal and manifold mercies, and the favorable interpositions of his Providence which we experienced in the course and conclusion of the late war – for the great degree of tranquility, union, and plenty, which we have since enjoyed – for the peaceable and rational manner, in which we have been enabled to establish constitutions of government for our safety and happiness, and particularly the national One now lately instituted – for the civil and religious liberty with which we are blessed; and the means we have of acquiring and diffusing useful knowledge; and in general for all the great and various favors which he hath been pleased to confer upon us."

259 *See* Elk Grove Unified Sch. Dist. v. Newdow, 542 U.S. 1, 27 (2004) (Rehnquist, C.J., concurring in the judgment) (observing that "[a]lmost all succeeding Presidents have issued similar Thanksgiving proclamations" and that "[l]ater Presidents, at critical times in the Nation's history, have likewise invoked the name of God").

260 Engel v. Vitale, 370 U.S. 421, 448 (1962); *see id.* at 448 n. 3 (quoting the remarks of Presidents George Washington, John Adams, Thomas Jefferson, James Madison, Abraham Lincoln, Grover Cleveland, Woodrow Wilson, Franklin Roosevelt, Dwight Eisenhower, and John Kennedy).

261 ACLU of Ohio v. Capitol Square Rev. & Advis. Bd., 243 F.3d 289, 299 (6th Cir. 2001) (citations omitted) [citing CATHERINE L. ALBANESE, SONS OF THE FATHERS: THE CIVIL RELIGION OF THE AMERICAN REVOLUTION 183–99 (1976); RICHARD J. CARWARDINE, EVANGELICALS AND POLITICS IN ANTEBELLUM AMERICA 19–22, 40–2 (1993); JOHN WITTE, JR., RELIGION AND THE AMERICAN CONSTITUTIONAL EXPERIMENT 96–8 (2000) and quoting Abraham Lincoln, *Address at Gettysburg* (Nov. 16, 1863), *in* 7 THE WORKS OF ABRAHAM LINCOLN 20 (1906)].

262 Abraham Lincoln, *Emancipation Proclamation* (Jan. 1, 1863); *available at:* http://www.archives.gov/exhibits/featured_documents/emancipation_proclamation/transcript.html. On the proclamation's appeal to God, *see* ALLEN C. GUELZO, LINCOLN'S EMANCIPATION PROCLAMATION: THE END OF SLAVERY IN AMERICA 179–80 (2006).

263 Abraham Lincoln, *Gettysburg Address* (Nov. 19, 1863) (Bliss copy); *available at:* http://www.abrahamlincolnonline.org/lincoln/speeches/gettysburg.htm.

and prayer," urging all officials and "all the other loyal and law-abiding people of the United States, to assemble in their preferred places of public worship on that day, and there and then to render to the almighty and merciful Ruler of the Universe such homages and such confessions and to offer to Him … supplications."[264] And in his second inaugural address, just over a month before his assassination, Lincoln situated the entire war and the nation's destiny within a divine framework:

> If we shall suppose that American slavery is one of those offenses which, in the providence of God, must needs come, but which, having continued through His appointed time, He now wills to remove, and that He gives to both North and South this terrible war as the woe due to those by whom the offense came, shall we discern therein any departure from those divine attributes which the believers in a living God always ascribe to Him? Fondly do we hope, fervently do we pray, that this mighty scourge of war may speedily pass away. Yet, if God wills that it continue until all the wealth piled by the bondsman's two hundred and fifty years of unrequited toil shall be sunk, and until every drop of blood drawn with the lash shall be paid by another drawn with the sword, as was said three thousand years ago, so still it must be said "the judgments of the Lord are true and righteous altogether."[265]

The practice of religious references in official declarations continued unabated through the twentieth century, from Theodore Roosevelt's Thanksgiving Proclamation in 1901[266] to Bill Clinton's in 2000.[267] In 1952, a congressional joint resolution requested the president to declare a "National Day of Prayer,"[268] and in 1988 it codified the practice,[269] with annual proclamations and observances to the present day.[270] Just as the Confederation Congress' 1782 Thanksgiving Proclamation differed from Charlestown's 1676 Proclamation, however, today's religious declarations, particularly at the national level, tend to be even more inclusive or ecumenical than their counterparts from earlier centuries, no doubt reflecting an awareness of the nation's comparative religious diversity. President Barack Obama's Thanksgiving Proclamation of 2012, for example, urged Americans to "spend th[e] day by lifting up those we love, mindful of the grace bestowed upon us by God and by all who have made our lives richer with their presence" and "to join together – whether in our homes, places of worship, community centers, or any

264 Abraham Lincoln, *Proclamation 114* (Jul. 7, 1864); *available at:* http://www.presidency.ucsb.edu/ws/?pid=69994.

265 Abraham Lincoln, *Second Inaugural Address* (Mar. 4, 1865); *available at:* http://www.ourdocuments.gov/doc.php?doc=38&page=transcript.

266 *See* Theodore Roosevelt, *Proclamation 466 – Thanksgiving Day, 1901* (Nov. 2, 1901); *available at:* http://www.presidency.ucsb.edu/ws/index.php?pid=69381.

267 *See* William J. Clinton, *Proclamation 7381 – Thanksgiving Day, 2000* (Nov. 17, 2000); *available at:* http://www.presidency.ucsb.edu/ws/index.php?pid=62407.

268 *See* Pub. L. No. 82–324 (joint resolution), 66 Stat. 64 (Apr. 17, 1952).

269 *See* Pub. L. No. 100–307, 102 Stat. 456 (May 5, 1988). This was followed by a new law a decade later. *See* Pub. L. No. 105–225, § 1, 112 Stat. 1258 (Aug. 12, 1998) (codified at 36 U.S.C. § 119) ("The President shall issue each year a proclamation designating the first Thursday in May as a National Day of Prayer on which the people of the United States may turn to God in prayer and meditation at churches, in groups, and as individuals.").

270 *See, e.g.*, Barack Obama, *Presidential Proclamation – National Day of Prayer, 2014* (May 1, 2014); *available at:* http://www.whitehouse.gov/the-press-office/2014/05/01/presidential-proclamation-national-day-prayer-2014. A challenge to the statute and the presidential practice was dismissed for lack of standing. *See* Freedom from Religion Found., Inc. v. Obama, 641 F.3d 803 (7th Cir. 2011).

place of fellowship for friends and neighbors – and give thanks for all we have received in the past year, express appreciation to those whose lives enrich our own, and share our bounty with others."[271] This is clearly a recognition of the role that religion, particularly monotheistic religion, plays in the lives of many citizens. At the same time, however, it invokes a God that is not specific to Christianity, Judaism, Islam, or any other monotheistic tradition while still allowing most readers or listeners to identify, in the president's message, the God of their specific faith.

## E. Legislative Chaplaincies and Prayer

Governmentally appointed and paid chaplaincies can be found in a variety of contexts, including in the armed forces, in prisons and other institutionalized settings, and in the service of legislative or quasi-legislative bodies.[272] The last of these, the legislative chaplaincy, dates to the earliest years of the nation, first in the Continental and Confederation Congresses and then in the U.S. Congress.[273] This congressional tradition of opening House and Senate sessions with chaplain-delivered prayer, while it may seem to conflict with modern notions of church-state separation, is in fact far different from the practices of European nations with established churches. The upper house of the British Parliament is, after all, the House of Lords Spiritual and Temporal, and to this day Anglican Bishops comprise a necessary segment of its membership.[274] Likewise, the French Estates General, meeting on the eve of the French Revolution in 1789, consisted of three estates, the first being the clergy.[275]

Legislative prayer, led by appointed chaplains, was a practice common to several colonial legislatures and was duly instituted by the First Continental Congress in 1774. At the Constitutional Convention in 1787, a chaplaincy proposal was introduced by Benjamin Franklin in the following words:

> All of us who were engaged in the struggle must have observed frequent instances of a Superintending providence in our favor. To that kind providence we owe this happy opportunity of consulting in peace on the means of establishing our future national

271 Barack Obama, *Presidential Proclamation – Thanksgiving Day, 2012* (Nov. 20, 2012); *available at:* http://www.whitehouse.gov/the-press-office/2012/11/20/presidential-proclamation-thanksgiving-day-2012.

272 Regarding military chaplaincies, *see* Chapter 18.I. Regarding prison chaplaincies, *see* Chapter 18.B.3 and D.3.

273 Regarding the Continental and Confederation Congresses, *see* Derek H. Davis, Religion and the Continental Congress, 1774–1789: Contributions to Original Intent (2000). Regarding the U.S. Congress, *see* 2 Robert C. Byrd, The Senate, 1789–1989, at 297–310 (1982); *available at:* http://www.senate.gov/artandhistory/history/resources/pdf/Chaplain.pdf; U.S. House of Representatives Office of the Chaplain, *History of the Chaplaincy*; *available at:* http://chaplain.house.gov/chaplaincy/history.html [hereinafter *History of the Chaplaincy*]; U.S. Senate, *Senate Chaplain*; *available at:* http://www.senate.gov/artandhistory/history/common/briefing/Senate_Chaplain.htm [hereinafter *Senate Chaplain*].

274 As of 2014, twenty-six Anglican archbishops and bishops sit in the House of Lords. *See* http://www.parliament.uk/business/lords/whos-in-the-house-of-lords/members-and-their-roles/diverse-experience/. Traditionally, they have been seen as providing a necessary voice in a Parliament that legislates for England's established Anglican Church. For additional reading, including proposed reforms to expand clerical membership in Parliament to represent England's religious diversity, *see* Janet Lewis-Jones, *Reforming the Lords: The Role of the Bishops* 3 (Jun. 1999); *available at:* https://www.ucl.ac.uk/spp/publications/unit-publications/41.pdf.

275 *See* Debora B. Schwartz, *The Three Estates*; *available at:* http://cla.calpoly.edu/~dschwart/engl430/estates.html.

> felicity. And have we now forgotten that powerful friend? or do we imagine that we no longer need his assistance? I have lived, Sir, a long time, and the longer I live, the more convincing proofs I see of this truth – *that God governs in the affairs of men*. And if a sparrow cannot fall to the ground without his notice, is it probable that an empire can rise without his aid? We have been assured, Sir, in the sacred writings, that "except the Lord build the House they labour in vain that build it." I firmly believe this; and I also believe that without his concurring aid we shall succeed in this political building no better than the Builders of Babel: We shall be divided by our little partial local interests; our projects will be confounded, and we ourselves shall become a reproach and bye word down to future ages.
>
> I therefore beg leave to move – that henceforth prayers imploring the assistance of Heaven, and its blessings on our deliberations, be held in this Assembly every morning before we proceed to business, and that one or more of the Clergy of this City be requested to officiate in that service.[276]

Objecting to Franklin's motion, Alexander Hamilton feared that securing a chaplain "might at this late day … bring on it some disagreeable animadversions" and "lead the public to believe that the embarrassments and dissentions within the convention, had suggested this measure."[277] Ultimately, the Convention's delegates declined to act on the proposal, and "[y]ears later, Madison … mentioned three considerations that may have contributed to the failure of Franklin's motion: its deviation from the Quaker method of worship, the differing religious convictions of the delegates, and the differing convictions of the members of the Philadelphia clergy."[278]

The U.S. Congress, by contrast, from the outset provided for chaplains, with the initial Senate and House chaplains being appointed just days apart in the spring of 1789.[279] The Senate's first eight chaplains were Episcopalian,[280] whereas the House chaplaincy was dominated originally by Presbyterians, with Methodists becoming more common over the course of the nineteenth century.[281] The first and only Catholic appointed as Senate Chaplain was Father Charles Constantine Pise, who, while serving at St. Matthew's Parish in Washington, DC, "attracted the attention of Henry Clay at whose instance he was unanimously elected Chaplain to the United States Senate."[282] The House did not appoint its first Catholic chaplain until 2000.[283]

Despite the prominence of Congress' chaplaincy program, the most significant case involving legislative chaplaincies arose not in Washington, DC, but in Lincoln, Nebraska, culminating in the Supreme Court's 1983 ruling in *Marsh v. Chambers*.[284]

276 1 The Records of the Federal Convention of 1787 at 451–2 (Max Farrand ed., 1911) (footnote omitted; emphasis in original).

277 *Id.* at 452; *see also* Louis J. Sirico, Jr., *Benjamin Franklin, Prayer, and the Constitutional Convention: History as Narrative*, 10 Legal Commun. & Rhetoric: JALWD 89, 93 (2013); *available at*: http://www.alwd.org/wp-content/uploads/2013/09/9Sirico-TEXT.pdf (2013).

278 Sirico, *supra* note 277, at 94.

279 *See* 2 Byrd, *supra* note 273, at 298; *History of the Chaplaincy*, *supra* note 273.

280 *See Senate Chaplain*, *supra* note 273.

281 *See History of the Chaplaincy*, *supra* note 273.

282 3 The Catholic Church in the United States of America: Undertaken to Celebrate the Golden Jubilee of His Holiness Pope Pius X 549 (1914).

283 *See History of the Chaplaincy*, *supra* note 273.

284 463 U.S. 783 (1983). There had been earlier challenges, in other states, to opening prayers at local government meetings. *See* Bogen v. Doty, 598 F.2d 1110 (8th Cir. 1979) (upholding a Minnesota county's practice of having local clergy deliver prayers at county board meetings); Lincoln v. Page, 241 A.2d 799

From statehood in 1855 onward, Nebraska's unicameral legislature, much like the U.S. Congress, has opened its sessions with prayer. In 1965, it hired a Presbyterian minister as its chaplain, paying him with public funds and reappointing him for several years thereafter. State Senator Ernest Chambers challenged the legislative chaplaincy as a violation of the Establishment Clause and prevailed in both the federal district court and then the Eighth Circuit Court of Appeals. The appeals court, in particular, held that the legislature's selection and payment of the same minister for sixteen years, "representing one denomination, to open each legislative session with prayer" followed by the publication of "his prayers for distribution to members and nonmembers of the legislature" violated all three parts of the so-called *Lemon* test of the Establishment Clause.[285]

A year later, the Supreme Court reversed, essentially refusing to apply the *Lemon* test and instead adverting to original understanding and the weight of tradition. It noted, in particular, that the same Congress that had sent the First Amendment to the states for ratification more or less simultaneously authorized the hiring of congressional chaplains. As a matter of original understanding, the Court surmised, "[i]t can hardly be thought that in the same week Members of the First Congress voted to appoint and to pay a Chaplain for each House and also voted to approve the draft of the First Amendment for submission to the States" and that "they intended the Establishment Clause of the Amendment to forbid what they had just declared acceptable."[286] But the Court was moved by more than just this original understanding. It further noted that the federal congressional chaplaincy had "continued without interruption ever since" and similar practices had "also been followed consistently in most of the states"[287] such that "the practice of opening legislative sessions with prayer has become part of the fabric of our society."[288] Ultimately, the Court found that the chaplaincy posed no actual danger of a present or future religious establishment. "From colonial times through the founding of the Republic and ever since," it said, "the practice of legislative prayer has coexisted with the principles of disestablishment and religious freedom."[289] "The unbroken practice for two centuries in the National Congress, for more than a century in Nebraska and in many other states, gives abundant assurance that there is no real threat."[290]

Following *Marsh*, courts have upheld many, though not all, practices related to legislative or quasi-legislative prayer,[291] and the Second Circuit, relying on *Marsh* as well as the unique religious interests at stake, has ruled that the U.S. Army's chaplaincy program is not inconsistent with the Establishment Clause.[292] But *Marsh* should not be understood as sanctioning any kind of prayer or invocation at any kind of governmental event. *Marsh* itself indicated that an Establishment Clause problem might arise if a

(N.H. 1968) (upholding a New Hampshire town's practice of inviting local clergy to give invocations at various town meetings).

285 *See* Chambers v. Marsh, 675 F.2d 228, 234 (8th Cir. 1982), *rev'd*, 463 U.S. 783 (1983). The *Lemon* test is described at length in Chapter 4.C.1, and *Marsh* is further addressed in Chapter 4.D.1.

286 Marsh, 463 U.S. at 790. "Clearly the men who wrote the First Amendment Religion Clause did not view paid legislative chaplains and opening prayers as a violation of that Amendment." *Id.* at 788.

287 *Id.* at 788–9.

288 *Id.* at 792. "The opening of sessions of legislative and other deliberative public bodies with prayer is deeply embedded in the history and tradition of this country." *Id.* at 786.

289 *Id.* at 786.

290 *Id.* at 795.

291 These are addressed in Chapter 4.D.1.

292 *See* Katcoff v. Marsh, 755 F.2d 223 (2d Cir. 1985). *Katcoff* is addressed at length in Chapter 18.I.2.

practice, such as the selection of clergy, "stem[s] from an impermissible motive" such as religious discrimination[293] or if "the prayer opportunity [is] exploited to proselytize or advance any one, or to disparage any other, faith or belief."[294] And in subsequent cases, the Court refused to extend *Marsh* to the public education context if only because "free public education was virtually nonexistent at the time the Constitution was adopted."[295] In 2014, the Court revisited and reaffirmed *Marsh*, this time upholding a town board's practice of inviting local clergy and community members to deliver prayers at the outset of its meetings.[296] That most of the clergy were Christian was not problematic in light of the town's religious demography and the town's open invitation to the public,[297] nor was it problematic that some of the prayers were explicitly Christian.[298] Only if it shown that "a pattern of prayers … over time denigrate, proselytize, or betray an impermissible government purpose" will a practice be called into question under Establishment Clause.[299]

293 *Marsh*, 463 U.S. at 793.
294 *Id.* at 794–5.
295 Edwards v. Aguillard, 482 U.S. 578, 583 n.4 (1987); *see also* Lee v. Weisman, 505 U.S. 577, 596–7 (1992).
296 *See* Town of Greece, N.Y. v. Galloway, 134 S. Ct. 1811 (2014).
297 *See id.* at 1824.
298 *See id.* at 1820–2.
299 *Id.* at 1824.

# 4 The Establishment Clause

## A. Introduction

The Establishment Clause of the First Amendment textually provides that "Congress shall make no law respecting an establishment of religion."[1] In the period since its framing and ratification, now extending well over two centuries, the meaning and reach of the clause have moved beyond a strict understanding of its text.[2] Three developments in particular warrant mention at the outset. The first is that the clause has been held to apply to all *branches* of government – legislative, executive, and judicial – not simply to the first of these, as the term "Congress" might suggest. The second is that by virtue of a doctrine called "Fourteenth Amendment incorporation,"[3] the clause also has been held to apply to all *levels* of government – federal, state, and local[4] – such that today it essentially applies to virtually every form of legal or governmental action.[5] From the Congress

1 U.S. CONST. amend. I. Its companion provision, the Free Exercise Clause, addressed in Chapter 5, provides that "Congress shall make no law ... prohibiting the free exercise thereof," referring back to the word "religion" as found in the Establishment Clause. Some have suggested that these two provisions, at least grammatically, constitute a single clause. *See, e.g.*, Akhil Reed Amar, *The Supreme Court, 1999 Term – Foreword: The Document and the Doctrine*, 114 HARV. L. REV. 26, 119–20 (2000); Carl H. Esbeck, *The Establishment Clause as a Structural Restraint on Governmental Power*, 84 IOWA L. REV. 1, 103 n. 441 (1998).

2 Regarding the much-debated origins and historical evolution of the clause, *see* Chapter 1.

3 "Incorporation" is the judicial interpretive process of recognizing various Bill of Rights guarantees, such as the First Amendment prohibition on "law[s] respecting an establishment of religion" as part of the guarantee of due process in Section 1 the Fourteenth Amendment, thereby rendering them applicable to state and local governmental actions. The Establishment Clause's incorporation was recognized in Everson v. Bd. of Educ., 330 U.S. 1, 14–15 (1947). Absent such incorporation, the clause would apply only against the federal government.

4 *See* Elk Grove Unified Sch. Dist. v. Newdow, 542 U.S. 1, 8 n. 4 (2004) (reaffirming that "[t]he Religion Clauses apply to the States by incorporation into the Fourteenth Amendment"); Holloman *ex rel.* Holloman v. Harland, 370 F.3d 1252, 1284 (11th Cir. 2004) (noting that the Establishment Clause "has been made applicable to states, as well as state-created entities and their employees, through the Due Process Clause of the Fourteenth Amendment"). Regarding the debate over the Establishment Clause's incorporation, *see* Frederick Mark Gedicks, *Incorporation of the Establishment Clause Against the States: A Logical, Textual, and Historical Account*, 88 IND. L.J. 669 (2013); William K. Lietzau, *Rediscovering the Establishment Clause: Federalism and the Rollback of Incorporation*, 39 DEPAUL L. REV. 1191 (1990); Vincent Phillip Muñoz, *The Original Meaning of the Establishment Clause and the Impossibility of Its Incorporation*, 8 U. PA. J. CONST. L. 585 (2006); *Note, Rethinking the Incorporation of the Establishment Clause: A Federalist View*, 105 HARV. L. REV. 1700 (1992).

5 Thus the term "law" includes "not only ... statutes, but acts and decisions of individual governmental actors." Holloman *ex rel.* Holloman v. Harland, 370 F.3d 1252, 1284 (11th Cir. 2004); *accord* Canell

and the president of the United States, to the agencies, universities, and court systems of the fifty states, to the school districts and police departments of every municipality, all are bound by the limits and prohibitions of the Establishment Clause.[6] State and local governments are further constrained, moreover, by the analogous provisions of their own state constitutions.[7] These provisions, though largely not addressed in this chapter, can differ markedly from the Establishment Clause, and several state constitutions, either by these or other provisions, specifically restrict the relationship between religion and public education or the use of public revenue for religious institutions or purposes.[8]

The third development, which is as much cultural as legal, is that the contemporary reach and impact of the clause are also a product of developing notions of what counts as "law respecting an establishment of religion,"[9] which itself reflects changing understandings of the American political community. Concerns that animated the clause's inclusion – "the church exercising the coercive power of government," "direct financial support of the church ... through general tax revenue," and "control by the state over

v. Lighter, 143 F.3d 1210, 1214 (9th Cir. 1998) ("For the purpose of an Establishment Clause violation, a state policy need not be formal, written, or approved by an official body to qualify as state sponsorship of religion."). For the government itself to be liable, however, the plaintiff must show that the individual actor "was acting pursuant to an official policy or custom of the [government]" or "had the authority to make policy" or "that the government ratified or endorsed his actions." Canell, 143 F.3d at 1214.

6 The one domestic exception is that the Establishment Clause, like most of the Constitution, does not directly bind Native American tribal governments. *See* Native Am. Church of N. Am. v. Navajo Tribal Council, 272 F.2d 131, 134–5 (10th Cir. 1959). Even Congress' application to tribes of statutory versions of various Bill of Rights guarantees (*see* Indian Civil Rights Act, 25 U.S.C. §§ 1301–4) specifically omits a prohibition on laws respecting religious establishments. *See* Santa Clara Pueblo v. Martinez, 436 U.S. 49, 62–3 (1978).

7 *See* Ala. Const. art. I, § 3; Alaska Const. art. I, § 4; Ariz. Const. art. II, § 12; *id.* art. XI, § 7; Ark. Const. art. II, § 24; Cal. Const. art. I, § 4; Colo. Const. art. II, § 4; Conn. Const. art. VII; Del. Const. art. I, § 1; Fla. Const. art. I, § 3; Haw. Const. art. I, § 4; Idaho Const. art. I, § 4; Ill. Const. art. I, § 3; Ind. Const. art. I, § 4; Iowa Const. art. I, § 3; Kan. Const. Bill of Rts. § 7; Ky. Const. Bill of Rts. § 5; La. Const. art. I, § 8; Me. Const. art. I, § 3; Md. Const. Decl. of Rts. art. 36; Mass. Const. pt. I, art. III; Mich. Const. art. I, § 4; Minn. Const. art. I, § 16; Miss. Const. art. III, § 18; Mo. Const. art. I, §§ 6, 7; Mont. Const. art. II, § 5; Neb. Const. art. I, § 4; Nev. Const. art. I, § 4; N.H. Const. pt. I, art. 6; N.J. Const. art. I, ¶¶ 3, 4; N.M. Const. art. II, § 11; Ohio Const. art. I, § 7; Pa. Const. art. I, § 3; R.I. Const. art. I, § 3; S.C. Const. art. I, § 2; S.D. Const. art. VI, § 3; Tenn. Const. art. I, § 3; Tex. Const. art. I, § 6; Utah Const. art. I, § 4; Vt. Const. ch. I, art. 3; Va. Const. art. I, § 16; Wash. Const. art. I, § 11; W. Va. Const. art. III, § 15; Wis. Const. art. I, § 18; Wyo. Const. art. I, § 18.

8 *See* Ala. Const. art. I, § 3; Alaska Const. art. VII, § 1; Ariz. Const. art. II, § 12; *id.* art. XI, § 7; Ark. Const. art. II, § 24; Cal. Const. art. IX, §§ 8, 9(f); *id.* art. XVI, § 5; Colo. Const. art. IX, § 8; Del. Const. art. I, § 1; *id.* art. X, § 3; Fla. Const. art. I, § 3; Ga. Const. art. I, § 2, ¶ VII; Haw. Const. art. X, § 1; Idaho Const. art. IX, §§ 5, 6; Ill. Const. art. X, § 3; Ind. Const. art. I, § 6; Iowa Const. art. I, § 3; Kan. Const. art. VI, § 6(c); Ky. Const. § 189; Md. Const. Decl. of Rts. art. 36; Mass. Const. amend. art. 18, § 2; *id.* amend. art. 48, pt. 2, § 2; Mich. Const. art. I, § 4; Minn. Const. art. I, § 16; *id.* art. XIII, § 2; Miss. Const. art. VIII, § 208; Mo. Const. art. I, §§ 6, 7; *id.* art. IX, § 8; Mont. Const. art. X, §§ 6, 7; Neb. Const. art. I, § 4; *id.* art. VII, § 11; Nev. Const. art. XI, §§ 9, 10; *id.* art. XII, § 9; N.H. Const. pt. I, art. 6; N.J. Const. art. I, ¶ 3; N.M. Const. art. II, § 11; N.Y. Const. art. XI, § 3; N.D. Const. art. VIII, §§ 1, 5; Ohio Const. art. I, § 7; *id.* art. VI, § 2; Okla. Const. art. II, § 5; Or. Const. art. I, § 5; Pa. Const. art. I, § 3; R.I. Const. art. I, § 3; S.C. Const. art. XI, § 4; S.D. Const. art. VI, § 3; Tenn. Const. art. I, § 3; Tex. Const. art. I, §§ 6, 7; Utah Const. art. I, § 4; Vt. Const. ch. I, art. 3; Va. Const. art. I, § 16; *id.* art. IV, § 16; *id.* art. VIII, § 11; Wash. Const. art. I, § 11; *id.* art. IX, § 4; W. Va. Const. art. III, § 15; Wis. Const. art. I, § 18; *id.* art. X, § 3; Wyo. Const. art. I, §§ 18, 19; *id.* art. VII, §§ 8, 12; *id.* art. XXI, § 28.

9 As the Second Circuit has noted, "the Clause [most obviously] prohibits the establishment of a national or state church, but the [Supreme] Court has never construed its mandate to apply only to this most obvious proscription." Skoros v. City of N.Y., 437 F.3d 1, 16 (2d Cir. 2006), *cert. denied*, 549 U.S. 1205 (2007).

the church"[10] – still persist but for many may not seem like looming threats.[11] Conversely, institutions and practices that may today immediately arouse establishment concerns – breaches in the metaphorical wall of separation between church and state – were or would have been mostly unproblematic within the world of Protestant Christianity and limited government that largely defined early America. That world, though pluralistic for its time in comparison with most European societies, had yet to experience the full-blown religious diversity that the nation exhibits today, and it certainly lacked the vast system of public education, social welfare, and administrative regulation to which many Americans have grown accustomed.[12]

The present-day legal result of these developments, manifest as various tests and doctrines and borne out in volumes of case law, will provide the focus of much of this chapter. Before examining the modern analytical framework, however, it is first necessary to examine several historical and contemporary principles of nonestablishment that both shape and reflect this framework.

## B. Historical and Contemporary Nonestablishment Principles

Nowhere is the importance of doctrine more evident than in the analytical context of the Establishment Clause. Though the tasks of constitutional interpretation and analysis often begin with the text or phrasing of the constitutional provision at issue, "[t]he First Amendment contains no textual definition of 'establishment,' and the term is certainly not self-defining."[13] Today, in fact, the understanding of whether a "law respect[s] an establishment of religion" is sufficiently removed from these words that it is customary in Establishment Clause cases to start not with the text but instead with authoritative judicial interpretations.[14] As it happens, the Supreme Court has distilled from the history and theory of the clause several guiding principles and from these principles several doctrinal requirements that all legal enactments must satisfy.[15]

10 Brett G. Scharffs, *The Autonomy of Church and State*, 2004 B.Y.U. L. Rev. 1217, 1232 (footnotes omitted).

11 *But see* Hosanna-Tabor Evangelical Lutheran Church & Sch. v. EEOC, 132 S. Ct. 694, 706 (2012) (holding that the religion clauses prohibit the application of antidiscrimination laws to the employment of ministers and like personnel, in part because such application would "[a]ccord the state the power to determine which individuals will minister to the faithful" in violation of the Establishment Clause).

12 "Diversity" is a relative term. "The actual extent of religious difference in the United States is controversial; indeed, it might be argued that the apparent diversity of American religion is confined to a very narrow range of theological beliefs or religious practices." Ted G. Jelen, *The Constitutional Basis of Religious Pluralism in the United States: Causes and Consequences*, 612 Ann. Am. Acad. Pol. & Soc. Sci. 26, 30 (2007) (citations omitted).

13 McCreary Cnty., Ky. v. ACLU of Ky., 545 U.S. 844, 874–5 (2005); *see also* Lemon v. Kurtzman, 403 U.S. 602, 612 (1971) (describing the text of the Establishment Clause as "opaque").

14 *See* Witters v. Wash. Dep't of Servs. for Blind, 474 U.S. 481, 485 (1986) {noting that "the Court's opinions in this area have at least clarified 'the broad contours of our inquiry'" [quoting Cmte. for Pub. Educ. & Religious Liberty v. Nyquist, 413 U.S. 756, 761 (1973)]}; Wolman v. Walter, 433 U.S. 229, 236 (1977) {"[T]he wall of separation that must be maintained between church and state 'is a blurred, indistinct, and variable barrier depending on all the circumstances of a particular relationship.' Nonetheless, the Court's numerous precedents 'have become firmly rooted' and now provide substantial guidance" [quoting Lemon v. Kurtzman, 403 U.S. 602, 614 (1971), and Nyquist, 413 U.S. at 761, respectively]}.

15 The Supreme Court has "repeatedly emphasized [its] unwillingness to be confined to any single test or criterion in this sensitive area." Lynch v. Donnelly, 465 U.S. 668, 679 (1984). For each individual case, "[t]he decision to apply a particular Establishment Clause test rests upon the nature of the Establishment Clause

As suggested, there is, between the general text of the Establishment Clause and the specific doctrinal tests invoked in actual cases, an intermediate realm of principle and theory in which the central underlying themes and core objectives of the clause are identified, labeled, and to some extent prioritized. The chief purpose of doctrinal formulation, in turn, is essentially to translate these broad principles into more manageable forms, ones with which judges, attorneys, and scholars can meaningfully work. Insofar as these translations are many times imperfect, incomplete, or contested, however, the resulting doctrines are rarely entirely freestanding, making resort to underlying principles a useful, if not necessary, ongoing exercise.[16]

One can derive from Supreme Court decisions, as well as other judicial, academic, and historical sources, at least five core principles, themes, or objectives of nonestablishment: neutrality, separation, equality, liberty, and civil peace. Importantly, these are neither exclusive nor entirely exhaustive in scope. Some of them (neutrality and equality, for example) can share significant common ground, whereas other principles not listed here, such as tolerance and inclusiveness, might provide additional insight into the Establishment Clause's interpretation independent of those that are addressed.[17] Nevertheless, these five themes or principles – in various forms, conceptions, and combinations – can confirm or explain many of the cases decided under the Establishment Clause, if not also the Free Exercise Clause.[18]

## 1. *Neutrality*

A central and recurring theme of contemporary Establishment Clause jurisprudence has been government *neutrality* in relation to religion.[19] The Court's 1947 decision in

violation asserted." Freiler v. Tangipahoa Parish Bd. of Educ., 185 F.3d 337, 344 (5th Cir, 1999), *cert. denied*, 530 U.S. 1251 (2000). Not directly addressed are comparable nonestablishment limitations found in various state constitutions, a number of which are broader or more specific than those of the First Amendment. *See* Neil McCabe, *The State and Federal Religion Clauses: Differences in Degree and Kind*, 5 St. Thomas L. Rev. 49 (1992); G. Alan Tarr, *Church and State in the States*, 64 Wash. L. Rev. 73 (1989); Robert F. Williams, *State Constitutional Religion Clauses: Lessons from the New Judicial Federalism*, 7 U. St. Thomas J.L. & Pub. Pol'y 192 (2013); Linda S. Wendtland, *Note, Beyond the Establishment Clause: Enforcing Separation of Church and State Through State Constitutional Provisions*, 71 Va. L. Rev. 625 (1985).

16 *Cf.* Douglas Laycock, *Notes on the Role of Judicial Review, the Expansion of Federal Power, and the Structure of Constitutional Rights*, 99 Yale L.J. 1711, 1741 (1990) (book review) ("[T]he Supreme Court's [analytical, doctrinal] formulas ... are often constructed from snippets of old opinions, with each snippet erected into an independent test.... Such snippets did not originate as a coordinated test and are unlikely to be either cumulatively complete or mutually exclusive. They were not designed as a formula, and their character is wholly changed when they are converted into one. In the establishment clause example, creation of the formula changed the substantive meaning of the snippets. Phrases that originated as explanations of neutrality were converted into separate elements of a test that seemed to forbid any significant benefit to religion, even where the effect of withholding a benefit was to inflict disproportionate harms.").

17 *See, e.g.*, Lisa Shaw Roy, *The Establishment Clause and the Concept of Inclusion*, 83 Or. L. Rev. 1 (2004).

18 *See* Chapter 5.B (identifying several free exercise principles). These themes or principles can be as controversial as they are illuminating, however. Perhaps more than any other area of constitutional law, in fact, their identification, and in particular their expression through specific words or metaphors, has itself been highly contested. That they should then essentially demarcate the universe of acceptable doctrine would partly explain why the various tests and standards of the Establishment Clause, apart from any internal shortcomings that they may exhibit, have for decades been the object of fairly harsh and relatively widespread criticism.

19 In Sch. Dist. of Abington Twp. v. Schempp, 374 U.S. 203 (1963), the Court justified the principle of neutrality on two bases: (1) "a recognition of the teachings of history that powerful sects or groups might bring

*Everson v. Board of Education*,[20] which ushered in the modern era of nonestablishment,[21] emphasized this principle's importance through its declaration that the Establishment Clause "requires the state to be a neutral in its relations with groups of religious believers and non-believers; it does not require the state to be their adversary. State power is no more to be used so as to handicap religions, than it is to favor them."[22] With regard to favoritism, in particular, the Court explained that "[n]either a state nor the Federal Government ... can pass laws which aid one religion, aid all religions, or prefer one religion over another."[23] Five years later, in *Zorach v. Clausen*,[24] the Court reiterated that "[t]he government must be neutral when it comes to competition between sects,"[25] an admonition that it has repeated several times since.[26]

To a large extent, neutrality is a relative concept depending not only on the particular facts of the case or outlook of the legal decision maker[27] but also – and perhaps more critically – on the reference point or baseline against which the interplay between government and religion should be gauged. It is relative or contingent, not in any postmodern sense, but simply because it presupposes an ideal relational framework within which particular circumstances can be labeled acceptable (i.e., neutral) or unacceptable (i.e., nonneutral).[28] As Professor Douglas Laycock has noted, neutrality may, among other things, be formal or substantive. "Formal neutrality or formal equality teaches that

about a fusion of governmental and religious functions or a concert or dependency of one upon the other to the end that official support of the State or Federal Government would be placed behind the tenets of one or of all orthodoxies" and (2) the "Free Exercise Clause['s] ... recogni[tion] [of] the value of religious training, teaching and observance and, more particularly, the right of every person to freely choose his own course with reference thereto, free of any compulsion from the state." *Id.* at 222.

20 330 U.S. 1 (1947).

21 On the significance of *Everson*, *see* Daniel L. Dreisbach, *A Lively and Fair Experiment: Religion and the American Constitutional Tradition*, 49 Emory L.J. 223, 224 & n. 4 (2000) (noting commentary) [reviewing John Witte, Jr., Religion and the American Constitutional Experiment: Essential Rights and Liberties (2000)].

22 Everson. 330 U.S. at 18

23 *Id.* at 15.

24 343 U.S. 306 (1952).

25 *Id.* at 314.

26 *See, e.g.*, McCreary Cnty., Ky. v. ACLU of Ky., 545 U.S. 844, 860 (2005) ("The touchstone for our analysis is the principle that the 'First Amendment mandates governmental neutrality between religion and religion, and between religion and nonreligion'" [quoting Epperson v. Arkansas, 393 U.S. 97, 104 (1968)]); Schempp, 374 U.S. at 225, 226 (noting "the command of the First Amendment that the Government maintain strict neutrality, neither aiding nor opposing religion" and declaring that "[i]n the relationship between man and religion, the State is firmly committed to a position of neutrality"); *see also* Engel v. Vitale, 370 U.S. 421, 443 (1962) (Douglas, J., concurring) {"By reason of the First Amendment government is commanded 'to have no interest in theology or ritual', for on those matters 'government must be neutral.' The First Amendment leaves the Government in a position not of hostility to religion but of neutrality. The philosophy is that the atheist or agnostic – the nonbeliever – is entitled to go his own way. The philosophy is that if government interferes in matters spiritual, it will be a divisive force. The First Amendment teaches that a government neutral in the field of religion better serves all religious interests" [quoting McGowan v. Maryland, 366 U.S. 420, 564 (1961) (Douglas, J., dissenting)]).

27 *See* Selman v. Cobb Cnty. Sch. Dist., 449 F.3d 1320, 1322–3 (11th Cir. 2006) ("[N]eutrality cannot be clearly defined for all times in absolute terms.... Knowledge of the particular facts and specific circumstances is essential to a determination of whether the governmental acts in question are religiously neutral.").

28 *See* Van Orden v. Perry, 351 F.3d 173, 178 (5th Cir. 2003) (observing that "neutrality is not self-defining"), *aff'd*, 545 U.S. 677 (2005); Ronald F. Thiemann, Religion in Public Life: A Dilemma for Democracy 60 (1996) (calling it a "protean concept").

religious liberty consists of no discrimination against religion – that religion should be treated just like every other activity and institution in the society," whereas "[s]ubstantive neutrality, or liberty, includes the right of religion to be let alone, whether or not other activities and institutions are let alone, save only when government has a compelling reason to interfere."[29]

Today, the Court's understanding of neutrality appears to depend on the type of government action involved. With regard to funding, the Court largely conceives of neutrality in terms of equal treatment. Thus an educational voucher or grant program will be deemed neutral if it is extended more or less equally to religious and nonreligious schools (or, at least initially, to the parents of schoolchildren) alike,[30] although the Court, somewhat counterintuitively, also has indicated that the exclusion of religious schools from such programs is not itself constitutionally problematic.[31] With regard to issues of endorsement or symbolism, by comparison, neutrality apparently means that the government may not outwardly favor or disfavor religion, even though it may outwardly favor or disfavor nonreligious ideas, images, or ideologies.[32] Thus a municipality may include

29 Douglas Laycock, *Summary and Synthesis: The Crisis in Religious Liberty*, 60 GEO. WASH. L. REV. 841, 848 (1992); *see generally* Douglas Laycock, *Formal, Substantive, and Disaggregated Neutrality Toward Religion*, 39 DEPAUL L. REV. 993 (1990).

30 *See, e.g.*, Zelman v. Simmons-Harris, 536 U.S. 639, 652 (2002) (upholding such a program, explaining that "where a government aid program is neutral with respect to religion, and provides assistance directly to a broad class of citizens who, in turn, direct government aid to religious schools wholly as a result of their own genuine and independent private choice, the program is not readily subject to challenge under the Establishment Clause"); Mitchell v. Helms, 530 U.S. 793 (2000) (plurality opinion) (holding that chapter 2 of the 1981 Education Consolidation and Improvement Act, which channels federal funds to local education agencies to acquire, for use in public and private schools, instructional and educational materials, including library, media, and computer, does not violate the Establishment Clause because it offers aid on a religiously neutral basis to a broad range of groups, goes to religious institutions only as the result of private individual choices, and does not have an impermissible religious content); Agostini v. Felton, 521 U.S. 203 (1997) (holding that a federally funded program providing supplemental, remedial instruction to disadvantaged children on a religiously neutral basis does not violate the Establishment Clause when such instruction is given on the premises of religious schools by government employees under a program containing safeguards such as those in New York City's Title I program). *See also* Kotterman v. Killian, 972 P.2d 606 (Ariz. 1999) (holding that state statute allowing a tax credit for donations to organizations that in turn provided tuition assistance to private schools, including religious schools, does not violate the Establishment Clause), *cert. denied*, 528 U.S. 810, 921 (1999); Simmons-Harris v. Goff, 711 N.E.2d 203 (Ohio 1999) (holding that Ohio's program largely satisfied the Establishment Clause, though invalidating it under the state constitution); Campbell v. Manchester Bd. of Sch. Dirs., 641 A.2d 352 (Vt. 1994) (holding that governmental reimbursement of tuition at a religious school pursuant to a general reimbursement statute did not violate the Establishment Clause); Jackson v. Benson, 578 N.W.2d 602 (Wis. 1998) (upholding voucher program allowing participation by religious schools), *cert. denied*, 525 U.S. 997 (1998).

31 *See* Locke v. Davey, 540 U.S. 712 (2004) (upholding, under the Free Exercise Clause, a post–secondary educational aid program that specifically excluded students pursuing theology degrees); *see also* Eulitt *ex rel.* Eulitt v. Me. Dep't of Educ., 386 F.3d 344 (1st Cir. 2004) (holding that the Equal Protection Clause does not require a state "to extend tuition payments to private sectarian secondary schools on behalf of students who reside in a school district that makes such payments available on a limited basis to private nonsectarian secondary schools"); Strout v. Albanese, 178 F.3d 57 (1st Cir. 1999) (holding that the exclusion of religious schools from an educational assistance program is not unconstitutional under the Establishment, Free Exercise, Free Speech, Due Process, or Equal Protection Clauses), *cert. denied*, 528 U.S. 931 (1999); Bagley v. Raymond Sch. Dep't, 728 A.2d 127 (Me. 1999) (similar), *cert. denied*, 528 U.S. 947 (1999).

32 *See, e.g.*, Warnock v. Archer, 380 F.3d 1076, 1080 (8th Cir. 2004) ("The government, of course, may speak on a large number of different issues. The Constitution, however, forbids it from conveying the message that it decisively endorses a particular religious position.").

within its official seal or emblem a symbol that endorses capitalism or environmentalism, for instance, but it may not include an icon that similarly endorses Christianity.[33] The same conception of neutrality more or less governs issues of excessive entanglement as well. Accordingly, the government can greatly involve itself in all aspects and institutions of, say, medicine or agriculture, but its involvement in the realm of religion is distinctly circumscribed by the First Amendment despite the obvious disparity in treatment.[34]

## 2. *Separation*

What may actually guide judicial analysis of apparent endorsement or entanglement is not so much the notion of neutrality, conventionally understood, but rather the principle of *separation*, which in these contexts essentially entails institutional noninvolvement,[35] be it avoiding governmental financial support for religion[36] or not delegating or usurping each other's official functions.[37] To quote again the Court in *Everson*, which very much expresses a separationist view, the Establishment Clause means that "[n]either a state nor the Federal Government can, openly or secretly, participate in the affairs of any religious organizations or groups and vice versa."[38] Referring to a letter written by Thomas Jefferson, the Court then declares that "the clause against establishment of religion by law was intended to erect 'a wall of separation between Church and State.'"[39]

Despite the strict separationist tone of some of its opinions, however, the Court has never entirely subscribed to a rigid understanding of separationism and, in fact, has several times expressly countenanced some level of religion-government interaction.[40]

33 *See, e.g.*, Robinson v. City of Edmond, 68 F.3d 1226 (10th Cir. 1995) (invalidating a four-quadrant, circular municipal seal depicting in one quadrant a steam engine and oil derrick, in a second a tower, in a third a covered wagon with the number 1889, and in the fourth a Christian cross – because of the religious content of the fourth quadrant), *cert. denied*, 517 U.S. 1201 (1996).

34 *See infra* Section C.1.c.

35 *See* Sherbert v. Verner, 374 U.S. 398, 409 (1963) (stating that "it is the object of the Establishment Clause to forestall [involvement of religious with secular institutions]"). According to Professor Douglas Laycock, "[t]he central meaning of separation is to separate the authority of the church from the authority of the state, so that 'no religion can invoke government's coercive power and no government can coerce any religious act or belief.'" Douglas Laycock, *The Underlying Unity of Separation and Neutrality*, 46 Emory L.J. 43, 46 (1997) (footnote omitted) [quoting Douglas Laycock, *Religious Liberty as Liberty*, 7 J. Contemp. Legal Issues 313, 319 (1996)].

36 Everson v. Bd. of Educ., 330 U.S. 1, 15–16 (1947) (explaining that "[n]o tax in any amount, large or small, can be levied to support any religious activities or institutions").

37 *See, e.g.*, Lemon v. Kurtzman, 403 U.S. 602, 614 (1971) ("The objective is to prevent, as far as possible, the intrusion of either into the precincts of the other."); McCollum v. Bd. of Educ., 333 U.S. 203, 227 (1948) (Frankfurter, J., writing separately) ("Separation is a requirement to abstain from fusing functions of Government and of religious sects, not merely to treat them all equally."). More generally, *see* John Witte, Jr., *The Essential Rights and Liberties of Religion in the American Constitutional Experiment*, 71 Notre Dame L. Rev. 371, 399–401 (1996).

38 Everson, 330 U.S. at 15–16.

39 *Id.* at 16 [quoting Reynolds v. United States, 98 U.S. (8 Otto) 145, 164 (1879)]. President Jefferson's *Letter to the Danbury Baptist Association*, dated January 1, 1802, can be found at http://www.loc.gov/loc/lcib/9806/danpre.html. The Court's unqualified endorsement of this principle continues today. *See* Cutter v. Wilkinson, 544 U.S. 709, 719 (2005) (explaining that "the Establishment Clause ... commands a separation of church and state"). For a critical examination of separationism's genealogy, especially its nativist and anti-Catholic roots, *see* Philip Hamburger, Separation of Church and State (2002).

40 *See* Lemon, 403 U.S. at 614 ("Our prior holdings do not call for total separation between church and state; total separation is not possible in an absolute sense.").

Already noted, for example, is the effective distribution of funding to religious schools or institutions pursuant to a formally neutral program, even though such distribution and the attendant administrative conditions clearly amount to religion-government interaction. In addition, the Court has indicated that such interaction will not necessarily violate the Establishment Clause if it is unavoidable,[41] is insubstantial,[42] or is so rooted in original understanding and tradition that many of the Court's doctrinal tests simply should not be applied.[43]

This tension between the logical demands of separation and the reality of modern society is clearly expressed just five years after *Everson* in *Zorach v. Clausen*[44]:

> There cannot be the slightest doubt that the First Amendment reflects the philosophy that Church and State should be separated. And so far as interference with the "free exercise" of religion and an "establishment" of religion are concerned, the separation must be complete and unequivocal. The First Amendment within the scope of its coverage permits no exception; the prohibition is absolute. The First Amendment, however, does not say that in every and all respects there shall be a separation of Church and State.... Otherwise the state and religion would be aliens to each other – hostile, suspicious, and even unfriendly. Churches could not be required to pay even property taxes. Municipalities would not be permitted to render police or fire protection to religious groups. Policemen who helped parishioners into their places of worship would violate the Constitution. Prayers in our legislative halls; the appeals to the Almighty in the messages of the Chief Executive; the proclamations making Thanksgiving Day a holiday; "so help me God" in our courtroom oaths – these and all other references to the Almighty that run through our laws, our public rituals, our ceremonies would be flouting the First Amendment. A fastidious atheist or agnostic could even object to the supplication with which the Court opens each session: "God save the United States and this Honorable Court."[45]

Recognizing the difficulties that would attend a purist understanding of separationism, the Court in *Lemon v. Kurtzman*, less than two decades after *Zorach*, conceded that "the line of separation, far from being a 'wall,' is a blurred, indistinct, and variable barrier depending on all the circumstances of a particular relationship."[46]

Today, perhaps due to societal changes, the principle of separation has become less prominent both in relation to other principles, such as neutrality, and in comparison with its prior significance.[47] To be sure, the separationism of most of the current justices could fairly be described as moderate and accommodationist rather than strict or rigid. This is not to suggest, of course, that the Court is truly of one mind. To the contrary,

[41] *See id.* at 614 (explaining that "[s]ome relationship between government and religious organizations is inevitable").

[42] *See id.* at 613 (requiring only that entanglement not be "excessive").

[43] *See, e.g.*, Town of Greece, N.Y. v. Galloway, 134 S. Ct. 1811, 1828 (2014) (upholding a practice of citizen-delivered prayer before town board meetings insofar as it "comports with our tradition and does not coerce participation by nonadherents"); Marsh v. Chambers, 463 U.S. 783 (1983) (upholding state legislative prayer, offered by a state-sponsored chaplain, because of its pedigree and relative neutrality).

[44] 343 U.S. 306 (1952).

[45] *Id.* at 312–13.

[46] Lemon, 403 U.S. at 614 (1971).

[47] *See* Thomas C. Berg, *Religious Liberty in America at the End of the Century*, 16 J.L. & RELIGION 187 (2001); Ira C. Lupu, *The Lingering Death of Separationism*, 62 GEO. WASH. L. REV. 230 (1993). *But cf.* Douglas Laycock, *The Underlying Unity of Separation and Neutrality*, 46 EMORY L.J. 43 (1997).

its members are quite divided over the propriety of providing public funding to religious institutions[48] and the place of religious practices and symbols in the domain of government.[49] Moreover, the persistence of the endorsement test, which prohibits the government from creating the objective appearance that it endorses or disfavors religion or a particular religious practice, indicates that separationism, while diminished in some quarters, nevertheless continues to be a meaningful force in others.

### 3. *Equality*

A third objective or theme associated with the Establishment Clause, especially in the modern era, is *equality*, which at points can overlap with the principle of neutrality. There are, in fact, two forms of equality or nondiscrimination that the clause, as interpreted today, addresses. The first is equality between or among religious beliefs or conduct, sometimes called "denominational nonpreferentialism," whereas the second is equality between religious and nonreligious beliefs or conduct. In the Supreme Court's words, it is "a principle at the heart of the Establishment Clause, that government should not prefer one religion to another, or religion to irreligion."[50]

The bar on denominational preferentialism is largely considered to be one of the original and central aims of the First Amendment, and as a core principle, it is therefore unremarkable.[51] To be sure, the Court has called it "[t]he clearest command of the Establishment Clause."[52] The very notion of establishment, after all, contemplates the governmental elevation of one religious tradition or denomination over most or all others, rendering that denomination the state's preferred, and ordinarily tax-supported, religion. At the same time, however, the "Court has rejected unequivocally the contention that the Establishment Clause forbids only governmental preference of one religion over another."[53] In fact, it is the other equality principle – requiring evenhandedness between religion and nonreligion – that has uniquely emerged within the last half-century and that has arguably contributed both to the vast expansion of the Establishment Clause's substantive reach and, most recently, to the modern judicial understanding of neutrality in the context of public funding.

According to the *Everson* Court, the Establishment Clause dictates that "[n]either a state nor the Federal Government ... can pass laws which aid one religion, aid all

48 *See, e.g.*, Zelman v. Simmons-Harris, 536 U.S. 639 (2002) (upholding, by a five-to-four vote, a state school choice program involving mostly religious schools); Mitchell v. Helms, 530 U.S. 793 (2000) (upholding, by a six-to-three vote but in an opinion only by four members, government funding as applied to religious schools); Agostini v. Felton, 521 U.S. 203 (1997) (upholding, by a five-to-four vote, availability of government funding to religious schools).

49 *See, e.g.*, Town of Greece, N.Y. v. Galloway, 134 S. Ct. 1811 (2014) (upholding, by a five-to-four vote, a practice of citizen-delivered prayer before town board meetings); McCreary Cnty., Ky. v. ACLU of Ky., 545 U.S. 844 (2005) (invalidating, by a five-to-four vote, Ten Commandments displays at courthouses); Van Orden v. Perry, 545 U.S. 677 (2005) (upholding, by a five-to-four vote with no majority opinion, a Ten Commandments monument on the grounds of a state capitol).

50 Bd. of Educ. of Kiryas Joel Vill. Sch. Dist. v. Grumet, 512 U.S. 687, 703 (1994) [citing Wallace v. Jaffree, 472 U.S. 38, 52–4 (1985); Epperson v. Arkansas, 393 U.S. 97, 104 (1968); Sch. Dist. of Abington Twp. v. Schempp, 374 U.S. 203, 216–17 (1963)].

51 *See* Witte, *supra* note 37, at 398–9.

52 Larson v. Valente, 456 U.S. 228, 244 (1982) ("The clearest command of the Establishment Clause is that one religious denomination cannot be officially preferred over another.").

53 Sch. Dist. of Abington Twp. v. Schempp, 374 U.S. 203, 216 (1963).

religions, or prefer one religion over another."[54] By the 1960s, the prohibition on "aid[ing] all religions" had become a prohibition on discriminating, detrimentally or beneficially, between religion and nonreligion. "The First Amendment," said the Court in *Epperson v. Arkansas*,[55] "mandates governmental neutrality between religion and religion, and between religion and nonreligion"[56] or, as it was phrased roughly a quarter-century later, "government should not prefer one religion to another, or religion to irreligion."[57] By the 1980s and 1990s, the emphasis on equality had transformed neutrality, at least in some contexts, into an authorization for the government to treat religious and nonreligious entities equally, even if it would mean that "a vast majority of program benefits [go] to religious ... [entities]."[58]

### 4. *Liberty*

Another nonestablishment principle, perhaps the most fundamental, is *liberty*. Although this particular term is not always employed at the doctrinal level, there is plainly a constellation of Establishment Clause doctrines or tenets that together reflect a concern for individual freedom or institutional autonomy, which is not surprising insofar as "the common purpose of the Religion Clauses 'is to secure religious liberty.'"[59] Indeed, to the extent that liberty, as a principle, is prior to – or is the ultimate goal of – neutrality, separation, and equality, then these latter principles arguably should be defined and applied in a manner that furthers rather than frustrates liberty. As Professor Thomas Berg has written,

> equality between religion and nonreligion, or separation between church and state, can sometimes come in conflict with the direct advancement of religious liberty in a particular case. Strict versions of separation, disqualifying religious entities or individuals from government benefits available to others or barring their expression in public institutions, can prevent individuals from practicing their faith. Equality, strictly applied, may mean that religious exercise, far from being "free," can be highly regulated because other institutions in society are highly regulated.[60]

54 330 U.S. at 15.

55 393 U.S. 97 (1968).

56 *Id.* at 103–4 ("Government in our democracy, state and national, must be neutral in matters of religious theory, doctrine, and practice. It may not be hostile to any religion or to the advocacy of nonreligion; and it may not aid, foster, or promote one religion or religious theory against another or even against the militant opposite. The First Amendment mandates governmental neutrality between religion and religion, and between religion and nonreligion."); *see also* Schempp, 374 U.S. at 305 (Goldberg, J., concurring) ("The fullest realization of true religious liberty requires that government neither engage in nor compel religious practices, that it effect no favoritism among sects or between religion and nonreligion.").

57 Bd. of Educ. of Kiryas Joel Vill. Sch. Dist. v. Grumet, 512 U.S. 687, 703 (1994).

58 Zelman v. Simmons-Harris, 536 U.S. 639, 658 (2002).

59 Santa Fe Indep. Sch. Dist. v. Doe, 530 U.S. 290, 313 (2000) [citing Engel v. Vitale, 370 U.S. 421, 430 (1962), and quoting Wallace v. Jaffree, 472 U.S. 38, 68 (1985) (O'Connor, J., concurring in the judgment)]; *see also* Noah Feldman, *From Liberty to Equality: The Transformation of the Establishment Clause*, 90 CAL. L. REV. 673 (2002); Robert A. Holland, *Comment, A Theory of Establishment Clause Adjudication: Individualism, Social Contract, and the Significance of Coercion in Identifying Threats to Religious Liberty*, 80 CAL. L. REV. 1595, 1641 n. 303 (1992) (noting other sources reaching this conclusion).

60 Thomas C. Berg, *Religious Liberty in America at the End of the Century*, 16 J.L. & RELIGION 187, 191 (2001); *see also* Van Orden v. Perry, 351 F.3d 173, 178 (5th Cir. 2003) ("Religion and government cannot be ruthlessly separated without encountering other First Amendment constraints, including its guaranty of the free exercise of religion."), *aff'd*, 545 U.S. 677 (2005).

The doctrinal manifestations of liberty, as indicated, are several. First and foremost, there is a clear prohibition on the coercion of religious activity or the coerced profession of religious belief.[61] In recent years, the concept of coercion has been expanded to include not only pressure resulting from palpable adverse legal consequences but also – at least for minors in the public-school setting – pressure from social circumstances that the government in part facilitates or magnifies.[62] Second and correspondingly, there is a prohibition against imposing legal disabilities on someone for professing a particular religious or irreligious belief.[63] As the Court explained in *Wallace v. Jaffree*,

> the individual freedom of conscience protected by the First Amendment embraces the right to select any religious faith or none at all. This conclusion derives support not only from the interest in respecting the individual's freedom of conscience, but also from the conviction that religious beliefs worthy of respect are the product of free and voluntary choice by the faithful, and from recognition of the fact that the political interest in forestalling intolerance extends beyond intolerance among Christian sects – or even intolerance among "religions" – to encompass intolerance of the disbeliever and the uncertain.[64]

At a more institutional level, the principle of liberty is reflected in the so-called church autonomy doctrine, which shields core religious institutional decision making from the application of certain regulatory laws,[65] as well as the prohibition on excessive entanglement, which restricts the government from unduly monitoring, usurping the functions of, or delegating its authority to religious officials or organizations.[66] The First Amendment, the Court has explained, "rests upon the premise that both religion and government can best work to achieve their lofty aims if each is left free from the other within its respective sphere."[67] Even the prohibition against preferentialism may be described as a doctrine of liberty or autonomy, for "[w]hen the government favors a particular religion or sect, [it] ... may fear being 'taint[ed] ... with a corrosive secularism.' The favored religion may

61 *See* Lee v. Weisman, 505 U.S. 577, 587 (1992) ("It is beyond dispute that, at a minimum, the Constitution guarantees that government may not coerce anyone to support or participate in religion or its exercise, or otherwise act in a way which 'establishes a [state] religion or religious faith, or tends to do so.'" [quoting Lynch v. Donnelly, 465 U.S. 668, 678 (1984)]); Torcaso v. Watkins, 367 U.S. 488, 495 (1961) ["[N]either a State nor the Federal Government can constitutionally force a person 'to profess a belief or disbelief in any religion.' Neither can constitutionally pass laws or impose requirements which aid all religions as against non-believers, and neither can aid those religions based on a belief in the existence of God as against those religions founded on different beliefs." (footnote omitted)]; Zorach v. Clauson, 343 U.S. 306, 314 (1952) ("The government ... may not thrust any sect on any person. It may not make a religious observance compulsory. It may not coerce anyone to attend church, to observe a religious holiday, or to take religious instruction.").

62 *See* Santa Fe Indep. Sch. Dist. v. Doe, 530 U.S. 290, 310–12 (2000); Lee, 505 U.S. at 592.

63 *See* Everson v. Bd. of Educ. of Ewing Twp., 330 U.S. 1, 15–16 (1947) ("No person can be punished for entertaining or professing religious beliefs or disbeliefs, for church attendance or non-attendance."); *cf.* Employment Div. v. Smith, 494 U.S. 872, 877 (1990) [explaining, albeit in the free exercise context, that "[t]he government may not ... punish the expression of religious doctrines it believes to be false" or "impose special disabilities on the basis of religious views or religious status" (citation omitted)].

64 472 U.S. 38, 53–4 (1985) (footnotes omitted).

65 *See* Chapters 5.H and 8. For example, the "ministerial exemption" bars "an employment discrimination suit brought on behalf of a minister, challenging [a] church's decision to fire [the minister]." Hosanna-Tabor Evangelical Lutheran Church & Sch. v. EEOC, 132 S. Ct. 694, 710 (2012).

66 *See infra* Section C.1.c.

67 McCollum v. Bd. of Educ., 333 U.S. 203, 212 (1948).

be compromised as political figures reshape the religion's beliefs for their own purposes; it may be reformed as government largesse brings government regulation."[68]

## 5. *Civil Peace*

A fifth and final principle, *civil peace* or *civil harmony*, is directed at limiting political division along religious lines.[69] The Court in *Lemon v. Kurtzman*,[70] while recognizing that political debate and division are a natural and healthy part of democracy, specifically characterized political fragmentation along religious lines as "one of the principal evils against which the First Amendment was intended to protect."[71] On the modern Court, the chief proponent of this principle has been Justice Stephen Breyer.[72] In his view, a key purpose of the religion clauses is to

> assure the fullest possible scope of religious liberty and tolerance for all. They seek to avoid that divisiveness based upon religion that promotes social conflict, sapping the strength of government and religion alike. They seek to maintain that "separation of church and state" that has long been critical to the "peaceful dominion that religion exercises in [this] country," where the "spirit of religion" and the "spirit of freedom" are productively "united," "reign[ing] together" but in separate spheres "on the same soil."[73]

The principle of civil harmony can effectively augment the principle of liberty by limiting government involvement with religion and by removing issues of religious orthodoxy and praxis from political debate. At the same time, it can complement the principle of neutrality insofar as the presence of political division along religious lines may be a consequence of the government's failure to maintain neutrality in relation to the religious realm.[74]

68 Lee v. Weisman, 505 U.S. 577, 608 (1992) (Blackmun, J., concurring) [quoting Sch. Dist. of Grand Rapids v. Ball, 473 U.S. 373, 385 (1985)].

69 *See* Feldman, *supra* note 59, at 691 (explaining that, in *Lemon*, "the Court developed the argument that the Clause aimed to avoid the divisive effects of religion in the public sphere"). The principle was most recently invoked in Town of Greece, N.Y. v. Galloway, 134 S. Ct. 1811 (2014), though as a reason to uphold rather than invalidate an interaction of religion and government. *See id.* at 1819.

70 403 U.S. 602 (1971).

71 *Id.* at 622.

72 *See* Van Orden v. Perry, 545 U.S. 677, 698–9 (2005) (Breyer, J., concurring); Zelman v. Simmons-Harris, 536 U.S. 639, 718–26 (2002) (Breyer, J., dissenting). Justice Breyer was also a member of the majority both in McCreary Cnty., Ky. v. ACLU of Ky., 545 U.S. 844 (2005), which mentioned the concern over divisiveness multiple times (*see id.* at 861, 863, 876, 881) and in Santa Fe Indep. Sch. Dist. v. Doe, 530 U.S. 290 (2000), which found that a school district policy effectively "encourage[d] divisiveness along religious lines in a public school setting, a result at odds with the Establishment Clause." *Id.* at 311.

73 Van Orden v. Perry, 545 U.S. 677, 698 (2005) (Breyer, J., concurring) (citations omitted) [quoting Alexis de Tocqueville, Democracy in America 282–3 (1835) (H. Mansfield & D. Winthrop trans. and eds., 2000)]. For a critical analysis of civil harmony or civil peace as a rationale for religious liberty, from an historical or originalist perspective, *see* Steven D. Smith, *The Rise and Fall of Religious Freedom in Constitutional Discourse*, 140 U. Pa. L. Rev. 149, 163–5 (1991). "[W]hile the civil peace rationale probably influenced the founding generation, the contention that it was the historical rationale, or even the primary rationale, seems anachronistic; it likely reflects what in the view of some modern interpreters should have been the Framers' primary rationale, but not what Americans of that period actually regarded as their principal ground for religious freedom." *Id.* at 163.

74 *See* McCreary Cnty., 545 U.S. at 875–6 ["Given the variety of interpretative problems, the principle of neutrality has provided a good sense of direction: the government may not favor one religion over another, or religion over irreligion, religious choice being the prerogative of individuals under the Free Exercise Clause.

## C. Current Doctrines, Tests, and Standards

Having described the major themes or principles of the contemporary Establishment Clause, the focus now turns to the various doctrines, tests, and standards into which these principles have been translated. Today there are essentially three doctrinal frameworks within which courts can assess the constitutionality of government actions under the Establishment Clause. These are *first*, the *Lemon* test, which, in turn, consists of multiple prongs and variations, including the endorsement test; *second*, a prohibition on religious coercion; and *third*, certain limitations on discrimination with regard to religion.

### 1. *The Lemon Test as Modified by the Endorsement Test*

The most prominent and most criticized doctrinal analysis stems from the Supreme Court's 1971 opinion in *Lemon v. Kurtzman*.[75] Known as the "*Lemon* test," it is comprised of three parts or prongs: (1) a purpose prong, (2) an effect prong, and (3) an entanglement prong.[76] To be constitutional, a law must satisfy all three parts.[77] "Notwithstanding oft-aired criticism and debate about the *Lemon* test," moreover, "*Lemon* remains the law, providing the framework in Establishment Clause cases ... until such time as it is explicitly overruled or abandoned by the Supreme Court."[78]

#### a. The Purpose Prong

*Lemon*'s first prong examines a law's purposes or objectives. There are two formulations, which may or may not be coextensive. A law will be deemed an impermissible establishment of religion if the law lacks a legitimate or "clearly" secular purpose[79] or if its actual, primary, or predominant purpose is to advance or inhibit religion.[80] Inasmuch as they do in fact differ, these two formulations will be examined separately.

The principle has been helpful simply because it responds to one of the major concerns that prompted adoption of the Religion Clauses. The Framers and the citizens of their time intended not only to protect the integrity of individual conscience in religious matters, but to guard against the civic divisiveness that follows when the government weighs in on one side of religious debate; nothing does a better job of roiling society, a point that needed no explanation to the descendants of English Puritans and Cavaliers (or Massachusetts Puritans and Baptists). A sense of the past thus points to governmental neutrality as an objective of the Establishment Clause, and a sensible standard for applying it." (citations omitted)].

75 403 U.S. 602 (1971).

76 *See id.* at 612–13 {"First, the statute must have a secular legislative purpose; second, its principal or primary effect must be one that neither advances nor inhibits religion; finally, the statute must not foster 'an excessive government entanglement with religion.'" (citation omitted) [quoting Walz v. Tax Comm'n of N.Y. City, 397 U.S. 664, 674 (1970)]}.

77 *See* Edwards v. Aguillard, 482 U.S. 578, 583 (1987) ("State action violates the Establishment Clause if it fails to satisfy any of these prongs."); Stone v. Graham, 449 U.S. 39, 40–1 (1980) (*per curiam*) (explaining that "a statute violates any of these three principles, it must be struck down under the Establishment Clause").

78 ACLU of Ohio Found., Inc. v. Ashbrook, 375 F.3d 484, 490 n.5 (6th Cir. 2004), *cert. denied*, 545 U.S. 1152 (2005).

79 *See* Lee v. Weisman, 505 U.S. 577, 585 (1992); Cnty. of Allegheny v. ACLU, Greater Pittsburgh Chapter, 492 U.S. 573, 592 (1989); Bowen v. Kendrick, 487 U.S. 589, 602–03 (1988); Edwards, 482 U.S. at 589–4; Wallace v. Jaffree, 472 U.S. 38, 56 (1985); Stone, 449 U.S. at 41–2; Lemon, 403 U.S. at 612.

80 *See* Agostini v. Felton, 521 U.S. 203, 222–3 (1997); Edwards, 482 U.S. at 585; Wallace, 472 U.S. at 56; Sch. Dist. of Abington Twp. v. Schempp, 374 U.S. 203, 222 (1963).

i. *The Secular Purpose Requirement.* Under the first formulation, a law must have at least one plausible and nonmarginal secular purpose.[81] This requirement has been described as "a fairly low hurdle"[82] that "is often easily satisfied,"[83] and the Supreme Court itself has recognized that the secular purpose requirement has been a "seldom dispositive" element in its cases.[84] To be sure, "invalidation of statutes or ordinances under *Lemon*'s purpose prong is relatively rare."[85] Religious purposes in conjunction with a secular purpose can be valid and will not defeat that secular purpose as long as they are neither "predominant,"[86] "pre-eminent,"[87] primary,[88] nor exclusive.[89] Thus "[t]he [Supreme] Court has invalidated legislation or governmental action on the ground that a secular purpose was lacking, but only when it has concluded there was no question that the statute or activity was motivated *wholly* by religious considerations."[90] Indeed, "[w]ere the test that the government must have 'exclusively secular' objectives, much of the conduct and legislation th[e] Court has approved in the past would have been invalidated."[91]

Courts begin with the presumption that any given law or governmental action possesses a secular purpose and "generally accept the government's stated rationale for its action"[92]

[81] *See* Lynch v. Donnelly, 465 U.S. 668, 681 n. 6 (1984) (explaining that "all that *Lemon* requires" is that a law "ha[ve] a secular purpose" and not that its purposes be "exclusively secular").

[82] Barghout v. Bureau of Kosher Meat & Food Control, 66 F.3d 1337, 1345 (4th Cir. 1995); *accord* Freethought Soc'y of Greater Phila. v. Chester Cnty., 334 F.3d 247, 267 (3d Cir. 2003) (noting "the relatively low threshold required by the purpose prong of *Lemon*"); Osediacz v. City of Cranston *ex rel.* Rossi, 344 F. Supp. 2d 799, 804 (D.R.I. 2004) ("A government program may be found unconstitutional because it has a religious purpose. The bar, however, is a high one.").

[83] Commack Self-Serv. Kosher Meats, Inc. v. Weiss, 294 F.3d 415, 431 (2d Cir. 2002), *cert. denied*, 537 U.S. 1187 (2003).

[84] McCreary Cnty., Ky. v. ACLU of Ky., 545 U.S. 844, 859 (2005). For criticism of *McCreary*'s rendition of the purpose prong as *ever* dispositive by itself, and for an analysis of the Court's apparent "shift from a search for actual government purpose toward a search for the objective observer's perception of government intent," *see* Note, *The Supreme Court, 2004 Term – Leading Cases*, 119 HARV. L. REV. 258, 262–8 (2005).

[85] Utah Gospel Mission v. Salt Lake City Corp., 316 F. Supp. 2d 1201 (D. Utah 2004), *aff'd*, 425 F.3d 1249 (10th Cir. 2005).

[86] McCreary Cnty., 545 U.S. at 865; *see also* Newdow v. Rio Linda Union Sch. Dist., 597 F.3d 1007 (9th Cir. 2010) {"That certain enactments can have both secular and religious purposes and still be constitutional has been recognized by the Supreme Court. 'A religious purpose alone is not enough to invalidate an act of a state legislature. The religious purpose must predominate.'" [quoting *Edwards*, 482 U.S. at 598 (Powell, J., concurring)]}.

[87] Stone, 449 U.S. at 41.

[88] *See* McCreary Cnty., Ky. v. ACLU of Ky., 545 U.S. 844, 864 (2005) (explaining that "the secular purpose required has to be … not merely secondary to a religious objective").

[89] *See* Bowen v. Kendrick, 487 U.S. 589, 602 (1988) (explaining that "a court may invalidate a statute only if it is motivated wholly by an impermissible purpose"); Newdow, 597 F.3d at 1036 ["The *Lemon* test … asks whether a challenged statute or governmental action is *predominantly* religious or secular, not exclusively secular. This formulation makes sense because oftentimes what one person considers secular, another considers religious." (citation omitted)]; United States v. Corum, 362 F.3d 489, 496 (8th Cir. 2004) ("The fact [a statute] may have been motivated in part by a religious purpose is not fatal. *Lemon* only requires there be a secular purpose for the legislation, not that there be a solely secular purpose."); Jewish War Veterans of U.S. v. United States, 695 F. Supp. 3, 12 (D.D.C. 1988) ("The Supreme Court has never required an *exclusively* secular purpose.").

[90] Lynch, 465 U.S. at 680 (emphasis added); *see also* Wallace v. Jaffree, 472 U.S. 38, 56 (1985) (explaining that "the First Amendment requires that a statute must be invalidated if it is entirely motivated by a purpose to advance religion" and "a statute that is motivated in part by a religious purpose may satisfy the first criterion [of *Lemon*]").

[91] Lynch, 465 U.S. at 681 n. 6.

[92] Satawa v. Macomb Cnty. Rd. Comm'n, 689 F.3d 506, 526 (6th Cir. 2012).

if only to be consistent with the presumption of constitutionality that attends all legislative enactments,[93] as well as a general judicial reluctance to inquire too deeply into the workings of the legislative process.[94] Accordingly, "[t]o warrant a finding that a statute is unconstitutional for lack of secular purpose, a challenger must demonstrate conclusively that the statute 'was motivated wholly by religious considerations.'"[95] This is not to suggest that the government can immunize an action merely by appending to it a single secular purpose of only secondary significance.[96] As the Sixth Circuit has explained, "Although a 'totally secular purpose is not required,' it is clear that the secular purpose 'requirement is not satisfied … by the mere existence of some secular purpose, however dominated by religious purposes.'"[97] Nor is it to suggest that the government simply may remain silent; as a practical adjudicative matter, it should and typically does defend its laws by affirmatively expounding their nonreligious objectives.[98] But courts should "normally [be]

93 *See* Cohen v. City of Des Plaines, 8 F.3d 484, 489–90 (7th Cir. 1993), *cert. denied*, 512 U.S. 1236 (1994); Utah Gospel Mission v. Salt Lake City Corp., 316 F. Supp. 2d 1201, 1237 n. 42 (D. Utah, 2004) ("Such judicial deference under the Establishment Clause comports with the traditional deference to the stated purposes of any legislative action challenged as unconstitutional.").

94 *See* Kosydar v. Wolman, 353 F. Supp. 744, 752 n.4 (S.D. Ohio 1972) [The infrequent significance of the secular purpose requirement "does not reflect anything unusual about First Amendment cases. Courts are, in general, highly reluctant to scrutinize a legislature's motivation or predominant purpose for enacting a given law. The reason for this deferential attitude on the part of the judiciary is in part generated by courts' respect for a coequal branch of government, and in part is necessitated by the futility of attempting to supervise this aspect of the legislative process. Even assuming that a dominant or sole legislative motivation is always ascertainable, there is a certain disutility for a court invalidating a law merely on the ground of improper motivation. This approach leaves unadjudicated the substantive merits of the law itself and allows the legislature to redraft an identical law in a less forthright fashion. In addition, in those states where legislatures keep journals of their proceedings … such an approach might well inhibit free and open debate or discourage the accurate keeping of records." (citations omitted)], *stay denied*, 410 U.S. 903 (1973), *aff'd sub nom.* Grit v. Wolman, 413 U.S. 901 (1973).

95 People v. Carter, 592 N.E.2d 491, 497 (Ill. Ct. App.) (emphasis in original omitted), *appeal denied*, 602 N.E.2d 461 (Ill. 1992); *accord* Cholla Ready Mix, Inc. v. Civish, 382 F.3d 969, 975 (9th Cir. 2004) (finding no violation of the purpose prong where the challenger "has alleged no facts that would support a conclusion that the state defendants were not motivated at least in part by this secular purpose"), *cert. denied*, 544 U.S. 974 (2005); ACLU of Ohio Found., Inc. v. Ashbrook, 375 F.3d 484, 491 (6th Cir. 2004) ("[A] plaintiff must show that the predominate purpose for a challenged display is religious, although a totally secular purpose is not required."), *cert. denied*, 545 U.S. 1152 (2005); Bauchman v. W. High Sch., 132 F.3d 542, 554 (10th Cir. 1997), *cert. denied*, 524 U.S. 953 (1998); Associated Contract Loggers, Inc. v. U.S. Forest Serv., 84 F. Supp. 2d 1029, 1037 (D. Minn. 2000), *aff'd*, No. 00-1730, 10 Fed. App'x. 397, 2001 WL 605010 (8th Cir. Jun. 5, 2001) (*per curiam*) (unpublished).

96 *See* McCreary Cnty., 545 U.S. at 864–85 (cautioning that its remarks to the effect that a government action will be invalid only if entirely motivated by religious purposes or considerations should not be read "in isolation," thereby suggesting "a fairly complaisant attitude" or "a timid standard"). The *McCreary* majority specifically rejected the position that "the purpose test is satisfied so long as any secular purpose for the government action is apparent" because "this position is inconsistent with the language of the [Court's] cases," "would leave the purpose test with no real bite, given the ease of finding some secular purpose for almost any government action," and "has not been the way the Court has approached government action that implicates establishment." *Id.* at 865 n. 13.

97 Adland v. Russ, 307 F.3d 471, 480 (6th Cir. 2002) (citation omitted) [quoting ACLU v. City of Birmingham, 791 F.2d 1561, 1565 (6th Cir. 1986), *cert. denied*, 479 U.S. 939 (1986), and Lynch v. Donnelly, 465 U.S. 668, 690–1 (1984) (O'Connor, J., concurring)], *cert. denied*, 538 U.S. 999 (2003).

98 Failure to do so, moreover, may be critical, particularly in the absence of an otherwise obvious secular purpose. *See* Wallace, 472 U.S. at 57 (emphatically and perhaps dispositively noting that "[t]he State did not present evidence of *any* secular purpose"); Epperson v. Arkansas, 393 U.S. 97, 107 (1968) (observing that "[n]o suggestion has been made that … [the challenged state] law may be justified by considerations of state policy other than the religious views of some of its citizens").

deferential to a State's articulation of a secular purpose"[99] and "reluctan[t] to attribute unconstitutional motives to the state, particularly when a plausible secular purpose … may be discerned from the face of the statute."[100] In this regard, it is important to note that a government's efforts "to avoid potential Establishment Clause violations" can themselves constitute "a valid secular purpose under *Lemon*."[101] "Establishment Clause jurisprudence would be unworkable if it were any other way: 'For [a] court … to hold that the removal of … objects to cure an Establishment Clause violation would itself violate the Establishment Clause would … result in an inability to cure an Establishment Clause violation and thus totally eviscerate the [E]stablishment [C]lause.' "[102]

Even "[w]hen a governmental entity professes a secular purpose for an arguably religious policy, the government's characterization is … entitled to *some* deference. But it is nonetheless the duty of the courts to 'distinguis[h] a sham secular purpose from a sincere one.' "[103] To be sure, the government will begin to run afoul of the secular purpose requirement where the real purpose or purposes of its law or action, often evidenced by the nature of the law or action itself, appear not truly to be secular. Thus, if the challenger can meaningfully call into question the law's purposes, and if the government cannot then either point to an enumerated secular purpose or articulate a persuasive secular purpose in litigation,[104] then the presumption of constitutionality will be removed, if not reversed.[105] This, once again, is an uncommon occurrence and typically results when the government's articulation is not "plausible" or is a "sham,"[106] when the secular purpose is "merely secondary

99 Edwards v. Aguillard, 482 U.S. 578, 586 (1987); *accord* McCreary Cnty., Ky. v. ACLU of Ky., 545 U.S. 844, 864 (2005) (explaining that "a legislature's stated reasons will generally get deference"); Lemon v. Kurtzman, 403 U.S. 602, 613 (1971); Brown v. Gilmore, 258 F.3d 265, 276 (4th Cir. 2001), *application for injunction denied*, 533 U.S. 1301 (2001) (per Rehnquist, C.J.), *cert. denied*, 534 U.S. 996 (2001); Gonzales v. N. Twp. of Lake Cnty., Ind., 4 F.3d 1412, 1419 (7th Cir. 1993).

100 Mueller v. Allen, 463 U.S. 388, 394–5 (1983); *accord* Adland v. Russ, 307 F.3d 471, 483 (6th Cir. 2002) ("Given the uncertainty with which state and local governments must often act, we believe that it is particularly appropriate to accord a measure of deference to a state or local government's avowed secular purpose and to refrain from hastily imputing unconstitutional motives to state legislators."), *cert. denied*, 538 U.S. 999 (2003).

101 Vasquez v. L.A. Cnty., 487 F.3d 1246, 1255–6 (9th Cir. 2007).

102 *Id.* at 1256 n. 8 [quoting McGinley v. Houston, 282 F. Supp. 2d 1304, 1307 (M.D. Ala. 2003), *aff'd*, 361 F.3d 1328 (11th Cir. 2004)].

103 Santa Fe, 530 U.S. at 308 (emphasis added) [quoting Wallace, 472 U.S. at 75 (O'Connor, J., concurring in the judgment)].

104 The credibility of this articulation may itself be assessed by the court. *See, e.g.*, Adland v. Russ, 307 F.3d 471, 482 (6th Cir. 2002) (rejecting an attempt to recast statutory purpose when "it is notably absent from the preamble" and the government "wait[ed] until its reply brief to put forth a secular explanation for statements with an agreed religious meaning … [thereby] suggest[ing] that its asserted secular justification is intended merely to avoid Establishment Clause liability rather than to actually further a legitimate secular purpose"), *cert. denied*, 538 U.S. 999 (2003).

105 *See* Koenick v. Felton, 190 F.3d 259, 265 (4th Cir. 1999) ["[The state's purpose] need not … be entirely secular, but if there is no evidence of a legitimate, secular purpose, then the statute must fail." (citation omitted)], *cert. denied*, 528 U.S. 1118 (2000); Metzl v. Leininger, 57 F.3d 618, 622 (7th Cir. 1995) ("When there is no evidence concerning a critical fact, here the feasibility of keeping the public schools of Illinois open on Good Friday, the allocation of the burden of production of evidence becomes critical. We think it properly belongs on the state in this case.… On its face, and even without regard to the governor's proclamation, the challenged statute, given the unambiguously sectarian character of Good Friday, promotes one religion over others.").

106 The stated purpose must be "sincere and not a sham." Edwards, 482 U.S. at 587; *accord* Bowen v. Kendrick, 487 U.S. 589, 604 (1988); Freiler v. Tangipahoa Parish Bd. of Educ., 185 F.3d 337, 344 (5th Cir. 1999); Chaudhuri v. Tennessee, 130 F.3d 232, 236 (6th Cir. 1997), *cert. denied*, 523 U.S. 1024 (1998).

to a religious objective,"[107] or when the very subject matter of the law is "intrinsically religious."[108] Examples of the last category, in particular, include a state mandate that the Ten Commandments (a religious compendium) be posted in public-school classrooms,[109] a program that aims to teach the bible (obviously a religious text) as metaphysical truth,[110] the specific addition of prayer ("perhaps the quintessential religious practice"[111]) to an existing moment-of-silence statute,[112] a statutory scheme that effectively encourages the teaching of creationism (ordinarily a religious concept) in public schools,[113] and the display of a crucifix (a religious symbol) in a public park.[114]

Importantly, a statute's original purposes are probably but not necessarily dispositive of an assessment of its present-day constitutionality. This is particularly true where there is reason to believe that the original and potentially unconstitutional purposes have been abandoned or augmented[115] or, conversely, where the original and likely constitutional

107 McCreary Cnty., Ky. v. ACLU of Ky., 545 U.S. 844, 864 (2005).

108 Jager v. Douglas Cnty. Sch. Dist., 862 F.2d 824, 830 (11th Cir. 1989), *cert. denied*, 490 U.S. 1090 (1989); *see also* Edwards, 482 U.S. at 585.

109 *See, e.g.*, Stone v. Graham, 449 U.S. 39, 41–2 (1980) (*per curiam*); Books v. City of Elkhart, Ind., 235 F.3d 292, 302–4 (7th Cir. 2000), *cert. denied*, 532 U.S. 1058 (2001). More recently, compare McCreary Cnty., Ky. v. ACLU of Ky., 545 U.S. 844 (2005) (invalidating a practice of posting the Ten Commandments in county courthouses) with Van Orden v. Perry, 545 U.S. 677 (2005) (upholding a Ten Commandments monument on the grounds of a state capitol).

110 *See* Doe v. Porter, 370 F.3d 558, 562–3 (6th Cir. 2004) ["Several lesson plans from the 2000–2001 academic year are singularly religious. For example, the objective of one lesson plan for second graders is to 'Teach the children God's commandments and that we should obey all of them.' A subsequent lesson plan expressed a teacher's intention to 'Teach them how God gives us the best and leads us where He wants us to go.' The lessons also seek to 'teach the kids that God provides for us, even in the worst situations.' Moreover, in explaining 'How I Plan to Help Students See the Truth,' one BEM teacher wrote, 'Teach – 'Read your Bible, pray every day.' 'Jesus loves you.' – (if acceptable)?" Such statements cannot be described as having a secular purpose."]; *see also* Staley v. Harris Cnty., Tex., 332 F. Supp. 2d 1030, 1036–7 (S.D. Tex. 2004) (explaining that "[t]he Bible can have a secular purpose ... when read as literature in a classroom or in studying the development of the English language" but concluding that the purpose of "prominently displaying an open Bible in an illuminated case tilted toward passersby in a heavily frequented plaza in front of the main entrance to the Courthouse" is clearly – and unconstitutionally – "to encourage people to read the Bible"), *appeal dismissed*, 485 F.3d 305 (5th Cir. 2007) (*en banc*).

111 Karen B. v. Treen, 653 F.2d 897, 901 (5th Cir. Unit A Aug. 1981), *aff'd*, 455 U.S. 913 (1982).

112 *See, e.g.*, Wallace v. Jaffree, 472 U.S. 38, 58 (1985); *see also* Holloman *ex rel.* Holloman v. Harland, 370 F.3d 1252, 1285 (11th Cir. 2004) {"Because prayer is 'a primary religious activity in itself,' a teacher or administrator's intent to facilitate or encourage prayer in a public school is *per se* an unconstitutional intent to further a religious goal." [quoting Karen B. v. Treen, 653 F.2d 879, 901 (5th Cir. Unit A Aug. 1981), *aff'd*, 455 U.S. 913 (1982)]}; Hall v. Bradshaw, 630 F.2d 1018, 1021 (4th Cir. 1980) (invalidating the inclusion of a "Motorist's Prayer" on a state-published and state-distributed map, noting that "[a] prayer, because it is religious, does advance religion, and the limited nature of the encroachment does not free the state from the limitations of the Establishment Clause"), *cert. denied*, 450 U.S. 965 (1981).

113 *See, e.g.*, Edwards, 482 U.S. at 593; *cf. also* Epperson v. Arkansas, 393 U.S. 97, 106 (1968).

114 *See, e.g.*, Gonzales v. N. Twp. of Lake Cnty., Ind., 4 F.3d 1412, 1419–21 (7th Cir. 1993); ACLU of Ga. v. Rabun Cnty. Chamber of Commerce, Inc., 698 F.2d 1098, 1110–11 (11th Cir. 1983).

115 *See* Gallagher v. Crown Kosher Super Mkt. of Mass., Inc., 366 U.S. 617, 626 (1961); McGowan v. Maryland, 366 U.S. 420, 444–5 (1961); Newdow v. Rio Linda Union Sch. Dist., 597 F.3d 1007, 1032–4 (9th Cir. 2010); Metzl v. Leininger, 57 F.3d 618, 621 (7th Cir. 1995); Cammack v. Waihee, 932 F.2d 765, 776 (9th Cir. 1991), *cert. denied*, 505 U.S. 1219 (1992); Hatheway v. Sec'y of Army, 641 F.2d 1376, 1383–4 (9th Cir. 1981), *cert. denied*, 454 U.S. 864 (1981); ACLU of Ky. v. Rowan Cnty., Ky., 513 F. Supp. 2d 889, 904–5 (E.D. Ky. 2007); Jewish War Veterans of U.S. v. United States, 695 F. Supp. 3, 12 (D.D.C. 1988). *But see* Turner v. Habersham Cnty., Ga., 290 F. Supp. 2d 1362 (N.D. Ga. 2003) (finding that a Ten Commandments display, supplemented by historical, functionally nonreligious documents

purposes have been supplanted by constitutionally dubious ones or where the doctrinal context has changed.[116] However, although an objectively discernible change in purpose is entirely possible, the Supreme Court has cautioned that "the world is not made brand new every morning.... [R]easonable observers have reasonable memories, and [the Court's] precedents sensibly forbid an observer 'to turn a blind eye to the context in which [the] policy arose.'"[117] Correspondingly, "[w]hen determining whether a statute *retains* a secular purpose, [courts] look not to the purpose of the statute when enacted, but at its contemporary purpose."[118] Such an inquiry may be appropriate when an originally valid law appears over time to have lost its secular purpose or to have acquired a predominant religious purpose, in which case it may today be deemed invalid.[119]

In addition, while it is true that "*Lemon* requires ... that the law at issue serve a 'secular legislative purpose' ... [t]his does not mean that the law's purpose must be unrelated to religion."[120] It is "a lawful secular purpose," for example, to "[a]ccommodat[e] ... a religious minority to let them practice their religion without penalty."[121] Likewise, the Court has repeatedly explained that a statute will not be deemed to have "an impermissible religious

after litigation was instituted, still lacked a secular purpose insofar as the government did not repudiate its original religious purpose).

116 *Cf., e.g.*, Staley v. Harris Cnty., Tex., 461 F.3d 504, 505 (5th Cir. 2006) (assessing a monument on courthouse grounds and finding "that although the monument at one time may have passed constitutional scrutiny, its recent history would force an objective observer to conclude that it is a religious symbol of a particular faith, located on public grounds – public grounds that may not reflect preference in matters of religion under the Establishment Clause of the First Amendment of the United States Constitution as interpreted and applied by modern day jurisprudence"), *vacated and dismissed on juris. grounds*, 485 F.3d 305 (5th Cir. 2007) (*en banc*), *cert. denied*, 552 U.S. 1038 (2007).

117 McCreary, Ky. v. ACLU of Ky., 545 U.S. 844, 866 (2005) [quoting Santa Fe Indep. Sch. Dist. v. Doe, 530 U.S. 290, 315 (2000)]; *cf. also* Friedman v. Bd. of Cnty. Comm'rs of Bernalillo Cnty., 781 F.2d 777, 780 n.3 (10th Cir. 1985), *cert. denied*, 476 U.S. 1169 (1986).

118 Koenick v. Felton, 190 F.3d 259, 266 (4th Cir. 1999) (emphasis added) (citing McGowan, 366 U.S. at 431), *cert. denied*, 528 U.S. 1118 (2000). This rule does not conflict with the Supreme Court's position that it "has previously found the post-enactment elucidation of the meaning of a statute to be of little relevance in determining the intent of the legislature contemporaneous to the passage of the statute." Edwards, 482 U.S. at 596 n. 19. Contemporary purposes that differ from original purposes and contemporary interpretations of original purposes are different objects of inquiry.

119 *See* Rojas v. Fitch, 928 F. Supp. 155, 163 n.4 (D.R.I. 1996), *aff'd*, 127 F.3d 184 (1st Cir. 1997), *cert. denied*, 524 U.S. 937 (1998); DiLoreto v. Bd. of Educ., 87 Cal. Rptr. 2d 791, 797 (Cal. Ct. App. 1999); *cf.* McCreary Cnty., 545 U.S. at 866 n.14 ("One consequence of taking account of the purpose underlying past actions is that the same government action may be constitutional if taken in the first instance and unconstitutional if it has a sectarian heritage.").

120 Corp. of Presiding Bishop of Church of Jesus Christ of Latter-Day Saints v. Amos, 483 U.S. 327, 335 (1987) [quoting Lemon v. Kurtzman, 403 U.S. 602, 612 (1971)]; *accord* Bauchman for Bauchman v. W. High Sch., 132 F.3d 542, 553 (10th Cir. 1997), *cert. denied*, 524 U.S. 953 (1998). Nor "does ... [it] follow ... that government policies with secular objectives may not incidentally benefit religion" or "that legislative categories make no explicit reference to religion." Tex. Monthly, Inc. v. Bullock, 489 U.S. 1, 10 (1989). "Even where the benefits to religion were substantial ... [the Court has seen] a secular purpose and no conflict with the Establishment Clause." Lynch v. Donnelly, 465 U.S. 668, 680 (1984) (citations omitted).

121 Kong v. Scully, 341 F.3d 1132, 1140 (9th Cir. 2003), *amended on denial of reh'g*, 357 F.3d 895 (9th Cir. 2004). The Supreme Court most recently addressed the constitutionality of religious freedom accommodations in Cutter v. Wilkinson, 544 U.S. 709 (2005), which upheld a facial Establishment Clause challenge to 42 U.S.C. § 2000cc-1, the institutionalized persons section of the Religious Land Use and Institutionalized Persons Act, Pub. L. No. 106–274, 114 Stat. 803 (Sept. 22, 2000) (codified at 42 U.S.C. §§ 2000cc to 2000cc-5).

purpose simply because some of the goals of the statute coincide with the beliefs of certain religious organizations."[122] As the Ninth Circuit has observed,

> [c]ourts have long recognized that certain secular beliefs, views, and positions coincide with religious beliefs, views, and positions. In such cases, government speech or action with respect to a secular issue is not considered endorsement of religion simply because the government's views are consistent with religious tenets. That is, the same belief can have both religious and secular dimensions; the government is not stripped of its secular purpose simply because the same concept can be construed as religious.[123]

Nor will a law be invalidated merely because it serves dual or mixed purposes (religious and secular) as long as it is animated in part by a "substantial, objectively verifiable secular purpose."[124]

There has been significant debate about whether examination of a law's purposes – as stated in the law or in litigation or as evidenced by the law's design[125] – allows a court also to examine individual legislators' motivations or the premises on which they based their votes. The Supreme Court, despite previous remarks about the role of motivations, most recently indicated that purpose alone ought to be examined.[126] "[A]n understanding of official objective," said the Court, should "emerge from readily discoverable fact, without any judicial psychoanalysis of a drafter's heart of hearts. The eyes that look to purpose belong to an objective observer, one who takes account of the traditional external signs

122 Bowen v. Kendrick, 487 U.S. 589, 604 n. 8 (1988); *accord* Van Orden v. Perry, 545 U.S. 677, 690 (2005) (plurality opinion) ("Simply having religious content or promoting a message consistent with a religious doctrine does not run afoul of the Establishment Clause."); Marsh v. Chambers, 463 U.S. 783, 792 (1983); Harris v. McRae, 448 U.S. 297, 319–20 (1980); Bob Jones Univ. v. United States, 461 U.S. 574, 604 n. 30 (1983); McGowan v. Maryland, 366 U.S. 420, 442 (1961); Clayton by Clayton v. Place, 884 F.2d 376, 380–1 (8th Cir. 1989), *cert. denied*, 494 U.S. 1081 (1990); People v. Baldwin, 112 Cal. Rptr. 290, 291–2 (Cal. Ct. App. 1974); Hogan v. State, 139 P.3d 907, 934 (Okla. Ct. Crim. App. 2006), *cert. denied*, 549 U.S. 1139 (2007); DePriest v. Commonwealth, 537 S.E.2d 1, 6 (Va. Ct. App. 2000).

123 Catholic League for Religious & Civil Rights v. City & Cnty. of S.F., 567 F.3d 595, 603 (9th Cir. 2009), *on reh'g en banc*, 624 F.3d 1043 (9th Cir. 2010), *cert. denied*, 131 S. Ct. 2875 (2011); *see also* Connor v. State, 490 S.W.2d 114, 115 (Ark. 1973) ("Of the allegation that [certain conduct] should not be regulated because such acts are regarded as sinful by some religious groups, little need be said. If that theory were adopted then many of our criminal statutes would be emasculated."), *appeal dismissed*, 414 U.S. 991 (1973); Eckl v. Davis, 124 Cal. Rptr. 685, 695 (Cal. Ct. App. 1975) ("[T]he fact that [a] regulation is consonant with moral principles espoused by religious bodies – a situation not uncommon in the development of the common law and in the present-day judicial and legislative expressions of law – does not bring into operation the constitutional concept of separation of church and state."); Sumpter v. State, 306 N.E.2d 95, 101 (Ind. 1974) ("Appellant argues that the prostitution statute violates the federal and state constitutional prohibitions against establishment of religion and constitutional guarantees of religious liberty, by giving Judaeo-Christian ethics the force of criminal law. We find this contention to be utterly frivolous. Virtually all criminal laws are in one way or another the progeny of Judaeo-Christian ethics. We have no intention to overrule the The Commandments."), *appeal dismissed*, 419 U.S. 811 (1974).

124 Utah Gospel Mission v. Salt Lake City Corp., 316 F. Supp. 2d 1201, 1238 (D. Utah May 3, 2004), *aff'd*, 425 F.3d 1249 (10th Cir. 2005). "[M]ixed-purpose situations – where the purpose of the government's action is to advance both secular and religious goals – still pass muster under the secular purpose inquiry." *Id.* at 1236.

125 *See* United States v. Allen, 760 F.2d 447, 451–2 (2d Cir. 1985) (assessing satisfaction of secular purpose requirement in light of "the statute's broad scope"). "The eyes that look to purpose belong to an 'objective observer,' one who takes account of the traditional external signs that show up in the 'text, legislative history, and implementation of the statute,' or comparable official act." McCreary Cnty., Ky. v. ACLU of Ky., 545 U.S. 844, 862 (2005).

126 *See* McCreary Cnty., 545 U.S. at 861–2.

that show up in the text, legislative history, and implementation of the statute, or comparable official act."[127] Or, as stated by a plurality of justices in an earlier case, "what is relevant is the legislative *purpose* of the statute, not the possibly religious *motives* of the legislators who enacted the law."[128] Motives or premises may in some cases confirm an initial judicial determination of purpose, thus inviting an examination of legislative history.[129] Ordinarily, however, courts do not determine purpose solely by such an examination,[130] and of course, "the legislative history cannot be construed to override the express statutory language articulating a clear secular purpose and also disclaiming a religious purpose."[131] In all events, it is understood that the secular purpose requirement (as well as the alternatively formulated limit on religious purposes) is at least in part a subjective inquiry, focusing on what the governmental actor actually intended.[132]

ii. *The Limit on Religious Purposes.* The alternative formulation of *Lemon*'s purpose prong forbids laws that have the purpose of advancing or inhibiting religion.[133] This formulation simply may be another way of expressing the rule that religious purposes, while

127 *Id.* at 862 (citation omitted) (internal quotation marks omitted).

128 Bd. of Educ. v. Mergens, 496 U.S. 226, 249 (1990) (plurality opinion); *accord Utah Gospel Mission*, 316 F. Supp. 2d at 1237 ("[T]he secular purpose inquiry does not probe the personal motives of those involved in passing a statute or ordinance."); McLean v. Ark. Bd. of Educ., 529 F. Supp. 1255, 1263 (E.D. Ark. 1982); Todd v. State, 643 So. 2d 625, 629 (Fla. Ct. App. 1994), *review denied*, 651 So. 2d 1197 (Fla. 1995), *cert. denied*, 515 U.S. 1143 (1995). "Legislative purpose should not be confused with legislative motive. A judicial inquiry may not go into the motive of each legislator supporting a legislative bill. A motive analysis would have implications not only for the denial of religious freedom, but also for violating separation of powers." Carl H. Esbeck, *A Restatement of the Supreme Court's Law of Religious Freedom: Coherence, Conflict, or Chaos?*, 70 Notre Dame L. Rev. 581, 599 n. 67 (1995) (citations omitted).

129 *See, e.g.*, Wallace v. Jaffree, 472 U.S. 38, 56–61 (1985) (examining legislative history to confirm the absence of an evident secular purpose); Bown v. Gwinnett Cnty. Sch. Dist., 112 F.3d 1464, 1471 (11th Cir. 1997) (examining legislative history and concluding that it is "not inconsistent with the express statutory language articulating a clear secular purpose and disclaiming a religious purpose").

130 *See, e.g.*, Roach v. Quarterman, No. 05-70051, 220 Fed. App'x 270, 277–8, 2007 WL 625067, at *5 (5th Cir. Feb. 26, 2007) (unpublished) (rejecting the claim that Texas' capital murder and death penalty statutes had only religious purposes based on legislative history indicating that "the sponsor used a religious argument to refute an opponent's religious argument" because those arguments constituted only "a small part of the legislative process" and did not "state the purpose of the statute" and also because "the primary sponsor invited prosecutors to testify about the effect of the death penalty on deterrence and incapacitation" and "[t]hat testimony stated secular purposes for the death penalty"); Discount Records, Inc. v. City of N. Little Rock, 671 F.2d 1200, 1221–2 (8th Cir. 1982) (*per curiam*) (rejecting a "post hoc attempt to reconstruct legislative intent contrary to the stated [legislative] purpose"). There also remains the problem of multiple motivations or premises. *See* Holberg v. State, 38 S.W.3d 137, 140 (Tex. Crim. App. 2000) ("[I]n assessing the legislative purpose, a court cannot assume that the selected statements of a few legislators, even the sponsors of the legislation, reflected the motivation of the entire Legislature."), *cert. denied*, 534 U.S. 972 (2001).

131 Bown, 112 F.3d at 1472. For critiques of motivation analysis, *see* Edwards v. Aguillard, 482 U.S. 578, 636–9 (1987) (Scalia, J., dissenting); Hal Culbertson, *Note, Religion in the Political Process: A Critique of Lemon's Purpose Test*, 1990 U. Ill. L. Rev. 915; Jeffrey S. Theuer, *Comment, The Lemon Test and Subjective Intent in Establishment Clause Analysis: The Case for Abandoning the Purpose Prong*, 76 Ky. L.J. 1061 (1987–8).

132 *See, e.g.*, ACLU of Ohio Found., Inc. v. Bd. of Comm'rs of Lucas Cnty., Ohio, 444 F. Supp. 2d 805, 811 (N.D. Ohio 2006) {"The first, or 'purpose,' prong [of *Lemon*] involves a subjective inquiry into the governmental actor's intent: i.e., did such actor intend to send a message endorsing a particular religion." [citing Lynch v. Donnelly, 465 U.S. 668, 691 (1984) (O'Connor, J., concurring)]}.

133 *See* Agostini v. Felton, 521 U.S. 203, 222–3 (1997); Wallace, 472 U.S. at 56.

generally valid, cannot be preeminent, much less exclusive (and correspondingly that the secular purpose cannot be marginal). However, several cases indicate that this alternative formulation prohibits not merely laws that have *the* purpose of religious advancement (which suggests preeminence or exclusivity) but also laws that have the *predominant* or *primary* purpose of religious advancement,[134] and these qualifiers are potentially broader than the term "preeminent." Taken literally, in fact, this prohibition could invalidate a law with multiple nonmarginal secular purposes if it also had as its predominant or primary (but not preeminent) purpose the advancement or inhibition of religion.

As with the secular purpose formulation, some courts have explicitly distinguished between religious purposes and religious motivations.[135] Thus, for example, even if one votes for civil rights or antipoverty laws out of religious conviction, as many legislators do, the statutory objectives still should be seen as the eradication of inequality and poverty. It is only when the very objective of the statute is religious in nature – when, for example, the government attempts to save souls – that the objective clearly will be deemed religious.[136] Alternatively, at least one federal appeals court has suggested that "explicit statutory incorporation of a particular religion's belief may violate the Establishment Clause."[137] Thus, although "Judaeo-Christian religio[us] oppos[ition] [to] stealing does not mean that a State or the Federal Government may not ... enact laws prohibiting larceny,"[138] if "a religion only opposed stealing from a particular group and the state outlawed stealing only from that group, it might be a closer case ... and would require inquiry into the legitimacy of government interests."[139]

In summary, like the requirement of a secular purpose, the limitation on religious purposes – specifically that the predominant or primary purpose not be to advance or inhibit religion – is not often of real consequence for most Establishment Clause defendants. In fact, "a finding of impermissible purpose should be rare. Only 'where an understanding of official objective emerges from readily discoverable fact' is judicial scrutiny warranted."[140]

134 *See* McCreary Cnty., 545 U.S. at 865; Edwards, 482 U.S. at 593; Levitt v. Comm. for Pub. Educ. & Religious Liberty, 413 U.S. 472, 481 (1973); Newdow v. Rio Linda Unified Sch. Dist., 597 U.S. 1007, 1035–6 (9th Cir. 2010); ACLU of Ohio v. Capitol Square Review & Advisory Bd., 243 F.3d 289, 308 (6th Cir. 2001); Books v. City of Elkhart, 235 F.3d 292, 302 (7th Cir. 2000), *cert. denied*, 532 U.S. 1058 (2001); Droz v. Comm'r, 48 F.3d 1120, 1124 (9th Cir. 1995), *cert. denied*, 516 U.S. 1042 (1996); Hall v. Bd. of Sch. Comm'rs, 656 F.2d 999, 1002 (5th Cir. Unit B Sept. 1981); Hatcher v. Comm'r, 688 F.2d 82, 84 (10th Cir. 1978).

135 *See, e.g.*, Dean v. Dist. of Columbia, Civ. A. No. 90-13892, 1992 WL 685364, at *5 (D.C. Super. Ct. June 2, 1992) (unpublished) ("[T]here is a difference between a purpose to 'advance or endorse' religion, on the one hand, and merely being motivated by religious convictions, on the other. Only the former is forbidden under *Lemon*."), *aff'd*, 653 A.2d 307 (D.C. 1995) (*per curiam*).

136 *See, e.g.*, State v. West, 263 A.2d 602, 605 (Md. Ct. Spec. App. 1970) (invalidating a state antiblasphemy law in part because it was "[p]atently ... intended to protect and preserve and perpetuate the Christian religion in this State" and "to serve as a mantle of protection by the State to believers in Christian orthodoxy").

137 Jane L. v. Bangerter, 61 F.3d 1505, 1516 (10th Cir. 1995).

138 Harris v. McRae, 448 U.S. 297, 319 (1980).

139 Jane L., 61 F.3d at 1516 n. 10. *Compare, e.g.*, Epstein v. Maddox, 277 F. Supp. 613, 618 (N.D. Ga. 1967) (holding that an alcohol sale prohibition on all Sundays does not violate the Establishment Clause's purpose limitations), *aff'd*, 401 F.2d 777 (5th Cir. 1968) (*per curiam*), *with* Griswold Inn, Inc. v. State, 441 A.2d 16, 20–21 (Conn. 1981) (holding that an alcohol prohibition only on Good Friday, but no other holiday, violates these purpose limitations).

140 ACLU of Ky. v. Mercer Cnty., Ky., 432 F.3d 624, 630 (6th Cir. 2005) [quoting McCreary Cnty., Ky. v. ACLU of Ky., 545 U.S. 844, 862 (2005)].

As one district court has explained, "[s]ince the primary purpose of a statute can rarely be successfully challenged in court, the tripartite *Lemon* test will, almost invariably, be deemed satisfied or violated by examining the relationship of the primary effect of the given statute to its potential for entanglement."[141]

### b. The Effect Prong

Often of greater concern to defendants, as suggested earlier, is the second prong of *Lemon*, which prohibits laws that have the principal or primary effect of advancing or inhibiting religion.[142] Subsequent to *Lemon*, the Supreme Court modified this prong, as well as the alternative formulation of the purpose prong, to account specifically for the *outward appearance* of governmental actions that in some way relate to religion. In particular, the Court has held that the Establishment Clause not only forbids laws that have the purpose or primary effect of advancing or inhibiting religion but also forbids laws that would appear to a reasonable observer to be endorsing or disapproving of religion.[143] Thus the effect prong now has two formulations: advancement/inhibition and endorsement/disapproval.

i. *Advancement or Inhibition of Religion.* The issue of whether a law's primary effect is the advancement or inhibition of religion commonly arises in the context of government funding or other material aid, and it is often the critical analysis in such cases.[144] In fact, it is largely the effect prong in this context that the Supreme Court reworked in recent years, thereby increasing the constitutional feasibility of broadly available funding programs such as school or charitable choice.[145] Importantly, the Court has never fully

141 Kosydar v. Wolman, 353 F. Supp. 744, 752 (S.D. Ohio 1972), *stay denied*, 410 U.S. 903 (1973), *judgment aff'd sub nom.* Grit v. Wolman, 413 U.S. 901 (1973).

142 *See* Agostini, 521 U.S. at 223; Edwards, 482 U.S. at 583; Lemon, 403 U.S. at 612.

143 *See* Capitol Square Review & Advisory Bd. v. Pinette, 515 U.S. 753, 763–9 (1995); Cnty. of Allegheny v. ACLU, Greater Pittsburgh Chapter, 492 U.S. 573, 593–4 (1989); Robinson v. City of Edmond, 68 F.3d 1226, 1229 (10th Cir. 1995) ("The first and second parts of the test have been modified, or at least recast, to ask whether the challenged government action was intended to endorse, or has the effect of endorsing, religion."), *cert. denied*, 517 U.S. 1201 (1996).

144 It does not exclusively arise in this context, however. "Symbolic benefit to religion is enough; it 'need not be material and tangible advancement.'" Utah Gospel Mission v. Salt Lake City Corp., 425 F.3d 1249, 1260 (10th Cir. 2005) [quoting Friedman v. Bd. of Cnty. Comm'rs of Bernalillo Cnty., 781 F.2d 777, 781 (10th Cir. 1985)].

145 Charitable choice is the catchphrase describing the contractual disbursement of government funding to private organizations, nonreligious and religious alike, for the provision of social services. The federal statute ordinarily associated with charitable choice is 42 U.S.C. § 604, enacted as part of the Personal Responsibility and Work Opportunity Reconciliation Act of 1996 (also known as the Welfare Reform Act) and complemented by executive directives. *See, e.g.*, Exec. Order No. 13,498, *Amendments to Executive Order 13199 and Establishment of the President's Advisory Council for Faith-Based and Neighborhood Partnerships*, 74 FED. REG. 6533 (Feb. 5, 2009) (issued by President Barack Obama); Exec. Order No. 13,199, *Establishment of White House Office of Faith-Based and Community Initiatives*, 66 FED. REG. 8499 (Jan. 29, 2001) (issued by President George W. Bush). For various analyses of charitable choice programs, *see* Stanley W. Carlson-Thies, *"Don't Look to Us": The Negative Responses of the Churches to Welfare Reform*, 11 NOTRE DAME J.L. ETHICS & PUB. POL'Y 667 (1997); Carl H. Esbeck, *Charitable Choice and the Critics*, 57 N.Y.U. ANN. SURV. AM. L. 17 (2000); Michele Estrin Gilman, *Fighting Poverty with Faith: Reflections on Ten Years of Charitable Choice*, 10 J. GENDER RACE & JUST. 395 (2007); Steven K. Green, *Charitable Choice and Neutrality Theory*, 57 N.Y.U. ANN. SURV. AM. L. 33 (2000); Jonathan Friedman, *Comment, Charitable Choice and the Establishment Clause*, 5 GEO. J. ON FIGHTING POVERTY 103 (1997); Eric L. Gomez, *Note, Charitable Choice under the Lemon*

adopted the view that "no aid" may go to religious institutions, nor, of course, has it held that aid may permissibly be given only to such institutions. Rather, it has often struggled to maintain an intermediate position, sometimes leading to seemingly ad hoc and inconsistent rulings, allowing some forms of financial or in-kind assistance while disallowing others that appear indistinguishable. Among the more important factors on which the Court has traditionally focused are, *first*, whether the aid is *neutrally* distributed and broadly available without regard to the religious or nonreligious identity of beneficiaries,[146] *second*, whether the aid is *directly* provided to religious institutions, as opposed to indirectly provided through the intervening and voluntary decisions of private individuals or entities,[147] and *third*, whether the religious institutions ultimately receiving the aid, particularly direct aid, are *pervasively sectarian*,[148] although the viability of this last factor is questionable.[149]

In *Agostini v. Felton*,[150] a 1997 ruling, the Court stated that "three primary criteria [are] currently use[d] to evaluate whether government aid has the effect of advancing religion: ... [whether it] result[s] in governmental indoctrination; define[s] its recipients by reference to religion; or create[s] an excessive entanglement."[151] The first two appear to reaffirm the factors of private choice and neutrality, whereas the last (as will be noted in the subsequent treatment of entanglement) is an incorporation of *Lemon*'s third prong into the second. *Agostini* did not simply reaffirm but also modified these criteria. Regarding governmental indoctrination, for example, the issue is not one of religious indoctrination per se but rather of whether such indoctrination can be attributed to the government.[152] The Court, in turn, has diminished the likelihood of attribution in at least three ways: by giving greater weight to the element of intervening private decision making,[153] by "abandon[ing]

*Test: Historical and Empirical Support for a Constitutional Defense*, 44 COLUM. J.L. & SOC. PROBS. 353 (2011); Andrea Pallios, *Note, Should We Have Faith in the Faith-Based Initiative?: A Constitutional Analysis of President Bush's Charitable Choice Plan*, 30 HASTINGS CONST. L.Q. 131 (2002).

146 *See* Witters v. Wash. Dep't of Servs. for Blind, 474 U.S. 481, 487 (1986); Mueller v. Allen, 463 U.S. 388, 398–9 (1983); Cmte. for Pub. Educ. & Religious Liberty v. Nyquist, 413 U.S. 756, 782 n. 38 (1973).

147 *See* Zobrest v. Catalina Foothills Sch. Dist., 509 U.S. 1, 10 (1993); Mueller, 463 U.S. at 399–400; Nyquist, 413 U.S. at 771.

148 *See* Bowen v. Kendrick, 487 U.S. 589, 610–12 (1988). "A pervasively sectarian institution is one in which religion so pervades its functions that any government aid it receives, even if designated for secular activities, impermissibly assists religion because the institution is unable to separate the funded secular activities from its religious mission. Conversely, an institution is not pervasively sectarian if its primary function is secular and if this function can be effectively separated from its religious activity." Children's Healthcare Is a Legal Duty, Inc. v. Min De Parle, 212 F.3d 1084, 1095–8 (8th Cir. 2000) (citations omitted), *cert. denied*, 532 U.S. 957 (2001).

149 *See infra* note 159 and accompanying text [discussing the repudiation of this criterion by the plurality opinion of Mitchell v. Helms, 530 U.S. 793 (2000) but further noting its continued use by lower courts].

150 521 U.S. 203 (1997) (upholding the state use of federal funds under Title I of the Elementary and Secondary Education Act to send public school teachers into parochial schools to provide remedial education to disadvantaged children).

151 *Id.* at 234.

152 *See* Corp. of Presiding Bishop of Church of Jesus Christ of Latter-Day Saints v. Amos, 483 U.S. 327, 337 (1987) ("For a law to have forbidden 'effects' under *Lemon*, it must be fair to say that the *government itself* has advanced religion through its own activities and influence."); *cf.* Mitchell v. Helms, 530 U.S. 793, 809 (2000) (plurality opinion) (asking "whether any religious indoctrination that occurs in [religious] schools could reasonably be attributed to governmental action").

153 *See* Zelman v. Simmons-Harris 536 U.S. 639, 652–53 (2002); Agostini, 521 U.S. at 225–6.

the presumption ... that the placement of public employees on parochial school grounds inevitably results in the impermissible effect of state-sponsored indoctrination,"[154] and by holding, with regard to the concern about "creating a financial incentive to undertake religious indoctrination," that "[t]his incentive is not present" where the aid is neutrally allocated and generally available.[155] As will also be noted later in this chapter, the Court has similarly modified the excessive entanglement inquiry, making such entanglement unlikely absent an unusually intrusive government arrangement.

In 2000, a four-justice plurality in *Mitchell v. Helms*[156] went even further, focusing exclusively on the criteria of neutrality and private decision making and rejecting consideration of whether the aid is direct or indirect,[157] whether the aid is divertible to religious use,[158] and whether the institution is pervasively sectarian (a criterion "born of [anti-Catholic] bigotry").[159] In so doing, however, the plurality forwent the vote of Justice O'Connor (the author of *Agostini*), who wrote an opinion concurring only in the judgment (joined, curiously, by Justice Breyer, an *Agostini* dissenter). In particular, O'Connor was troubled by the singular emphasis on neutrality, the rejection of the distinction between direct and indirect aid, and the deemphasis on whether otherwise secular aid is actually diverted to advance an institution's religious mission. As summarized by the Fourth Circuit, "[t]he O'Connor concurring opinion ... replaced the pervasively sectarian test with a principle of 'neutrality plus.' Neutrality is a necessary and important consideration in judging Establishment Clause cases, but it may not be sufficient in and of itself. Instead, courts must examine whether actual diversion of aid occurs and whether the 'particular facts of each case' reveal that the Establishment Clause has been violated."[160]

154 Agostini, 521 U.S. at 223.

155 *Id.* at 231.

156 530 U.S. 793 (2000) (upholding federal funding under Title I of the Elementary and Secondary Education Act of 1965 for state and local governmental agencies to lend educational materials and equipment to public and private schools, including religious schools). *See generally* Steven K. Green, *The Constitutionality of Vouchers after Mitchell v. Helms*, 57 N.Y.U. ANN. SURV. AM. L. 57 (2000).

157 *See* Mitchell, 530 U.S. at 816 ("Although the presence of private choice is easier to see when aid literally passes through the hands of individuals ... there is no reason why the Establishment Clause requires such a form.").

158 *See id.* at 820–5.

159 *Id.* at 829. It also overruled Meek v. Pittenger, 421 U.S. 349 (1975), and Wolman v. Walter, 433 U.S. 229 (1977). *See* Mitchell, 530 U.S. at 808. The overrulings' plurality status makes them somewhat uncertain, but Justice O'Connor also agreed that they should be overruled "[t]o the extent ... [they] are inconsistent with the Court's judgment[.]" *Id.* at 837 (O'Connor, J., concurring in the judgment). Notwithstanding *Mitchell*, some lower courts continue to apply the "pervasively sectarian" standard. *See, e.g.*, Wirtz v. City of S. Bend, 813 F. Supp. 2d 1051, 1065 (N.D. Ind. 2011), *appeal dismissed*, 669 F.3d 860 (7th Cir. 2012); ACLU of Minn. v. Tarek ibn Ziyad Acad., 788 F. Supp. 2d 950, 965 (D. Minn. 2011); Murray v. Geithner, 763 F. Supp. 2d 860, 869 (E.D. Mich. 2011), *aff'd*, 681 F.3d 744 (6th Cir. 2012), *cert. denied*, 133 S. Ct. 792 (2012); Conley v. Jackson Twp. Trs., 376 F. Supp. 2d 776, 783 & n. 4 (N.D. Ohio 2005).

160 Columbia Union Coll. v. Oliver, 254 F.3d 496, 504 (4th Cir. 2001) [quoting *Mitchell*, 530 U.S. at 844 (O'Connor, J., concurring in the judgment) (alterations in original)]. Thus, while Justice O'Connor (and apparently Justice Breyer) would have upheld the federal aid program (Title I of the Elementary and Secondary Education Act of 1965), she would have done so under the authority of *Agostini*, so construed. *Cf.* Barnes-Wallace v. Boy Scouts of Am., 275 F. Supp. 2d 1259, 1266 (S.D. Cal. 2003) (surmising that "[t]he differences between the plurality opinion and Justice O'Connor's concurrence suggest *Agostini's*

The Court clarified its approach two years later in *Zelman v. Simmons-Harris*.[161] Writing for a majority that now included O'Connor, Chief Justice Rehnquist held that a school voucher program in Cleveland, Ohio, did not violate the Establishment Clause because the program employed neutral criteria and because any benefits that it provided to religious institutions, which overwhelmingly made up the institutions participating in the program, were the result of genuine private choices.[162] First, "the Ohio program is neutral in all respects toward religion.... It confers educational assistance directly to a broad class of individuals defined without reference to religion, i.e., any parent of a school-age child who resides in the Cleveland City School District. The program permits the participation of all schools within the district, religious or nonreligious.... Program benefits are available to participating families on neutral terms, with no reference to religion."[163] Moreover, the fact that the program's funding ends up disproportionately in the hands of religious institutions does not render the program itself nonneutral. "That 46 of the 56 private schools now participating in the program are religious schools does not condemn it as a violation of the Establishment Clause."[164] "Cleveland's preponderance of religiously affiliated private schools certainly did not arise as a result of the program; it is a phenomenon common to many American cities.... It is true that 82% of Cleveland's participating private schools are religious schools, but it is also true that 81% of private schools in Ohio are religious schools."[165]

According to the Court, the critical "Establishment Clause question is whether Ohio is coercing parents into sending their children to religious schools" and thus itself causing the seemingly disproportional receipt of program funds by religious schools.[166] Far from finding such coercion, the Court determined that the Ohio program "permits ... individuals [defined only by financial need and residence in a particular school district] to exercise genuine choice among options public and private, secular and religious."[167] "Cleveland schoolchildren enjoy a range of educational choices: They may remain in public school as before, remain in public school with publicly funded tutoring aid, obtain a scholarship and choose a religious school, obtain a scholarship and choose

limits"), *aff'd in part and rev'd in part*, 530 F.3d 776 (9th Cir. 2008), *cert. denied*, 559 U.S. 1106 (2010). Standing alone, of course, her views would not have been of particular significance, but consensus among lower courts, at least initially, was that "[t]he O'Connor concurring opinion ... is the controlling opinion from *Mitchell*." Columbia Union Coll., 254 F.3d at 504; *accord* DeStefano v. Emergency Hous. Group, Inc., 247 F.3d 397, 418 (2d Cir. 2001); Johnson v. Econ. Dev. Corp. of Oakland Cnty., 241 F.3d 501, 510 n. 2 (6th Cir. 2001); Am. Jewish Cong. v. Corp. for Nat'l & Cmty. Serv., 323 F. Supp. 2d 44, 59 (D.D.C. 2004). As the Supreme Court itself has explained, "[w]hen a fragmented Court decides a case and no single rationale explaining the result enjoys the assent of five Justices, 'the holding of the Court may be viewed as that position taken by those Members who concurred in the judgments on the narrowest grounds.'" Marks v. United States, 430 U.S. 188, 193 (1977) [quoting Gregg v. Georgia, 428 U.S. 153, 169 n. 15 (1976) (opinion of Stewart, Powell, and Stevens, JJ)]. Precisely "[b]ecause the plurality opinion for the Court [in *Mitchell*] did not garner a majority" [Columbia Union Coll., 254 F.3d at 504 & n.1 (4th Cir. 2001)], Justice O'Connor's concurrence in the judgment, taking a more restricted view of *Agostini*, thus represented the narrowest ground of decision.

161 536 U.S. 639 (2002).

162 *See id.* at 662.

163 *Id.* at 653.

164 *Id.* at 655–6.

165 *Id.* at 656–7.

166 *Id.* at 655–6.

167 *Id.* at 662.

a nonreligious private school, enroll in a community school, or enroll in a magnet school."[168] "The program is therefore a program of true private choice."[169]

*Zelman* clarifies that the two principal factors in assessing a funding program under the Establishment Clause are indeed neutrality and private choice. It also makes clear that disproportionate distribution of funding to religious institutions, when effected by means of private choices pursuant to a neutral program, is normally irrelevant. However, *Zelman* does not wholly or definitively resolve the status of certain other factors that the *Mitchell* plurality attempted to discard (but that Justice O'Connor in *Mitchell* wished to retain), such as the divertibility of funding to advance the religious missions of participating institutions[170] and the extent to which the recipient institutions are pervasively sectarian.[171] The majority opinion in *Zelman* basically leaves these considerations unaddressed, though they do not escape the attention of the dissenters.[172] The Court also leaves somewhat uncertain the possible significance of whether a program creates incentives for use specifically at religious institutions, discussing the issue but finding it nondispositive with regard to Ohio's program.[173]

ii. *Endorsement or Disapproval of Religion.* Under the endorsement test, a modification or enhancement of *Lemon*, a plaintiff "must allege facts indicating [that] the [law] ha[s] a *principal* or *primary* effect of ... endorsing religion"[174] or that "the objective effect of [the law's] passage is to suggest government preference for a particular religious view or for religion in general."[175] Despite criticism by many,[176] the test remains part of the Court's jurisprudence and, where relevant, continues to be invoked and developed by lower courts.[177] According to the Court, "the prohibition against governmental

168 *Id.* at 655.

169 *Id.* at 662.

170 *See* Mitchell, 530 U.S. at 839–42 (O'Connor, J., concurring in the judgment); Zobrest, 509 U.S. at 12.

171 *See* Mitchell, 530 U.S. at 841, 850 (O'Connor, J., concurring in the judgment).

172 Regarding the divertibility of funding, *see* Zelman, 536 U.S. at 688, 692–4 (Souter, J., dissenting); *id.* at 727 (Breyer, J., dissenting). Regarding the pervasively sectarian nature of recipient institutions, *see id.* at 692, 709 n. 19 (Souter, J., dissenting).

173 *See id.* at 653–4.

174 Bauchman v. W. High Sch., 132 F.3d 542, 555 (10th Cir. 1997) (as corrected), *cert. denied*, 524 U.S. 953 (1998).

175 Barghout v. Bureau of Kosher Meat & Food Control, 66 F.3d 1337, 1345 (4th Cir. 1995). Because the test is one of objective effect, courts "do not examine the [government's] motivations ... but consider the [religious display's] effect on the reasonable observer, determining whether the reasonable observer would perceive it as an endorsement of religion." Modrovich v. Allegheny Cnty., Pa., 385 F.3d 397, 401 (3d Cir. 2004).

176 *See, e.g.*, Jesse H. Choper, *The Endorsement Test: Its Status and Desirability*, 18 J.L. & Pol. 499, 499 (2002) (concluding that "despite its advantages, it provides neither a workable nor a wise judicial standard"); Steven D. Smith, *Symbols, Perceptions, and Doctrinal Illusions: Establishment Neutrality and the "No Endorsement" Test*, 86 Mich. L. Rev. 266 (1987); Kirsten K. Wendela, *Context is in the Eye of the Beholder: Establishment Clause Violations and the More-Than-Reasonable Person*, 80 Chi.-Kent L. Rev. 981 (2005). In support of the test, as is or as modified, *see* Eliott M. Berman, *Endorsing the Supreme Court's Decision to Endorse Endorsement*, 24 Colum. J.L. & Soc. Probs. 1 (1990); Shari Seidman Diamond & Andrew Koppelman, *Measured Endorsement*, 60 Md. L. Rev. 713 (2001).

177 *See, e.g.*, Ind. Civil Liberties Union v. O'Bannon, 259 F.3d 766, 772–3 (7th Cir. 2001); Elewski v. City of Syracuse, 123 F.3d 51, 53–4 (2d Cir. 1997), *cert. denied*, 523 U.S. 1004 (1998); Kunselman v. W. Reserve Local Sch. Dist., 70 F.3d 931, 932–3 (6th Cir. 1995); King v. Village of Waunakee, 517 N.W.2d 671, 676–82 (Wis. 1994). With the departure of Justices Stevens, O'Connor, and Souter, and the added membership of only Justices Sotomayor and Kagan, it is not clear that the test could probably still garner the necessary five votes on the Supreme Court.

endorsement of religion 'preclude[s] government from conveying or attempting to convey a message that religion or a particular religious belief is *favored* or *preferred*.' "[178] The "essential principle" of the prohibition is that government may not "appear to take a position on questions of religious belief or ... 'mak[e] adherence to a religion relevant in any way to a person's standing in the political community."[179] Because it is perception based, "the endorsement test is particularly concerned with whether governmental practices create a 'symbolic union' of church and state."[180]

Not all such symbolic unions are or could be forbidden, and the endorsement test, as a consequence, has two primary refining characteristics. First, its analytical focus is both highly fact specific and purposefully holistic.[181] Challenged laws or practices must be "viewed in context and in their entirety."[182] This contextual analysis allows a court to assess the extent to which the conduct can truly be attributed to the government,[183] as well as to extent to which certain extrinsic factors might "neutralize the message of governmental endorsement"[184] that otherwise could be perceived using a more reductionist perspective.[185] Second, the test is objective, not subjective: a government action is

178 Cnty. of Allegheny, 492 U.S. at 593–4 [quoting Wallace v. Jaffree, 472 U.S. 38, 70 (1985) (O'Connor, J., concurring in the judgment)]. "While the Establishment Clause is often invoked to protect against the state's endorsement of religion over non-religion, it is equally applicable to claims that the state action is 'hostile' to religion." Demmon v. Loudoun Cnty. Pub. Schs., 279 F. Supp. 2d 689, 697 (E.D. Va. 2003).

179 *Id.* [quoting Lynch v. Donnelly, 465 U.S. 668, 687 (1984) (O'Connor, J., concurring)].

180 Brooks v. City of Oak Ridge, 222 F.3d 259, 264 (6th Cir. 2000) [quoting Agostini v. Felton, 521 U.S. 203, 220–3, 227 (1997)], *cert. denied*, 531 U.S. 1152 (2001).

181 *See, e.g.*, Freedom from Religion Found., Inc. v. City of Marshfield, Wis., 203 F.3d 487, 495 (7th Cir. 2000) ("look[ing] to the unique facts and circumstances ... to determine whether a reasonable person would perceive the ... [government action as] promot[ing] or disfavor[ing] religion or a particular religious belief"); *accord* Elewski, 123 F.3d at 53; ACLU of N.J. v. Black Horse Pike Reg'l Bd. of Educ., 84 F.3d 1471, 1486 (3d Cir. 1996); Bonham v. D.C. Library Admin., 989 F.2d 1242, 1245 (D.C. Cir. 1993).

182 Bauchman v. W. High Sch., 132 F.3d 542, 555 (10th Cir. 1997), *cert. denied*, 524 U.S. 953 (1998); *accord* Trunk v. City of San Diego, 629 F.3d 1099, 1110 (9th Cir. 2011) (in a challenge to a Latin cross erected as a war memorial, "consider[ing] fine-grained, factually specific features of the Memorial, including the meaning or meanings of the Latin cross at the Memorial's center, the Memorial's history, its secularizing elements, its physical setting, and the way the Memorial is used"), *cert. denied*, 132 S. Ct. 2535 (2012); Adland v. Russ, 107 F. Supp. 2d 782, 786 (E.D. Ky. 2000) (examining "the entirety" of a Ten Commandments display, including its "historical context, location, and size"), *aff'd*, 307 F.3d 471 (6th Cir. 2002), *cert. denied*, 538 U.S. 999 (2003).

183 *See, e.g.*, Ams. United for Separation of Church & State v. City of Grand Rapids, 980 F.2d 1538, 1544–6 (6th Cir. 1992) (holding that a private religious symbol on public property, labeled by a sign as private and displayed pursuant to a government policy allowing all parties to have expressive access to the property, did not engender an endorsement test violation); Staley v. Harris Cnty., Tex., 332 F. Supp. 2d 1030, 1035 (S.D. Tex. 2004) (distinguishing between private expression in a public forum, which normally cannot be attributed to – and therefore can be seen as being endorsed by – the government, and private expression in a nonpublic forum, which, especially when subject to approval by the government, normally can be attributed to the government), *appeal dismissed*, 485 F.3d 305 (5th Cir. 2007) (*en banc*), *cert. denied*, 552 U.S. 1038 (2007).

184 Elewski, 123 F.3d at 54.

185 *See* Lynch v. Donnelly, 465 U.S. 668, 692 (1984) (O'Connor, J., concurring) (explaining that the particular setting may "negate any message of endorsement of [religious] content"); *accord* Gonzales v. N. Twp. of Lake Cnty., Ind., 4 F.3d 1412, 1421–2 (7th Cir. 1993); Bonham, 989 F.2d at 1245. This includes disclaimers to the effect that the display is not an endorsement of religion. *See* Brooks v. City of Oak Ridge, 222 F.3d 259, 266 (6th Cir. 2000), *cert. denied*, 531 U.S. 1152 (2001); ACLU v. Wilkinson, 895 F.2d 1098, 1104–6 (6th Cir. 1990). Courts also may facilitate the mitigation of endorsement by requiring such disclaimers. *See* Doe v. Small, 964 F.2d 611, 621 (7th Cir. 1992) ("If the district court found the conduct of the City violative of the Establishment Clause, it should have ordered a remedy that would have directly addressed the violation.").

problematic only if it would be seen as an endorsement or disapproval of religion from the vantage point of a "reasonable observer,"[186] a construct similar to the hypothetical reasonable person of tort law.[187]

What makes this observer "reasonable" appears, in turn, to be a function of at least three characteristics. First, the observer is neither "omniscient"[188] nor "absent-minded"[189] but instead possesses reasonable familiarity with the relevant community's history, traditions, and contemporary practices in general[190] and with the background of the government's challenged action in particular.[191] The observer also may possess reasonable familiarity with the governing constitutional principles,[192] although lower courts remain uncertain "as to the proper level of understanding to impute onto [this] mythical reasonable observer."[193] Second, the observer is an individual of reasonable sensitivity and "does not look upon religion with a jaundiced eye."[194] A court "do[es] not ask whether there is *any* person who could find an endorsement of religion, whether *some* people may be offended by the ... [government's action], or whether some reasonable person *might* think ... [the government] endorses religion. Instead, [the court] ask[s] whether *the* reasonable observer *would* conclude that ... [the government] endorses religion by ...

186 *See* Chaudhuri v. Tennessee, 130 F.3d 232, 237 (6th Cir. 1997), *cert. denied*, 523 U.S. 1024 (1998); Elewski, 123 F.3d at 53; Barghout v. Bureau of Kosher Meat & Food Control, 66 F.3d 1337, 1345 (4th Cir. 1995). As a consequence, the number of persons actually viewing or encountering the alleged endorsement is apparently immaterial to the analysis. *See* Buono v. Norton, 371 F.3d 543, 549 (9th Cir. 2004). Indeed, "[g]iven the dizzying religious heterogeneity of our Nation, adopting a subjective approach would reduce the test to an absurdity. Nearly any government action could be overturned as a violation of the Establishment Clause if a 'heckler's veto' sufficed to show that its message was one of endorsement." Hansen v. Wis. Dep't of Revenue, No. 06-C-290-C, 2006 WL 1589648, at *5 (W.D. Wis. Jun. 5, 2006) (unpublished).

187 *See* Capitol Square Review & Advisory Bd. v. Pinette, 515 U.S. 753, 779–80 (1995) (O'Connor, J., concurring in part and concurring in the judgment); ACLU of Ohio v. Capitol Square Review & Advisory Bd., 243 F.3d 289, 302 (6th Cir. 2001).

188 Green v. Haskell Cnty. Bd. of Comm'rs, 568 F.3d 784, 800 (10th Cir. 2009), *cert. denied*, 559 U.S. 970 (2010); *Capital Square Review & Advisory Bd.*, 243 F.3d at 302.

189 McCreary Cnty., Ky. v. ACLU of Ky., 545 U.S. 844, 866 (2005); *see also* Capital Square Review & Advisory Bd., 243 F.3d at 303 (explaining that the reasonable observer should not be "as ill-informed as he or she almost certainly would be in real life"); Ams. United for Separation of Church & State v. City of Grand Rapids, 980 F.2d 1538, 1553 (6th Cir. 1992) ("The plaintiffs posit a "reasonable observer" who knows nothing about the nature of the exhibit – he simply sees the religious object in a prominent public place and ignorantly assumes that the government is endorsing it. We refuse to rest important constitutional doctrines on such unrealistic legal fictions.").

190 *See* Bauchman, 132 F.3d at 555; Elewski, 123 F.3d at 54; Chabad-Lubavitch of Ga. v. Miller, 5 F.3d 1383, 1390 n.11 (11th Cir. 1993); Kreisner v. City of San Diego, 1 F.3d 775, 784 (9th Cir. 1993), *cert. denied*, 510 U.S. 1044 (1994).

191 *See* McCreary Cnty., 545 U.S. at 866 (explaining that the "objective observer" should be "presumed to be familiar with the history of the government's actions and competent to learn what history has to show"); Green, 568 F.3d at 800 (explaining in relation to a Ten Commandments monument on a courthouse lawn that "the reasonable observer ... would be aware of the nature and history of the Haskell County community, the circumstances surrounding the Monument's placement on the courthouse lawn, its precise location on the lawn and its spatial relationship to the other courthouse monuments, and also the Haskell County community's response to the Monument").

192 *See* Chabad-Lubavitch, 5 F.3d at 1390 n. 11; Kreisner, 1 F.3d at 784.

193 Freedom from Religion Found., Inc. v. City of Marshfield, Wis., 203 F.3d 487, 495 n. 2 (7th Cir. 2000) (citing cases).

194 Ams. United, 980 F.2d at 1553.

[its action]."[195] Third and finally, the observer can reasonably situate and comprehend a government action in proper context, neither overemphasizing nor underemphasizing its religious dimensions.[196]

By design, the endorsement test is most suited to cases involving public religious symbolism, such as nativity scenes, as well as to cases involving primary and secondary public schools.[197] This is so because the inherently expressive nature of symbols and the relative impressionability of school children, respectively, create heightened probabilities of perceived governmental communication of religious approval.[198] Additionally, some courts have employed the endorsement test when examining public holidays that neatly correspond to religious observances, such as Good Friday, although various factors – including the legitimating element of religious accommodation and the settled validity of Sunday closing laws[199] – have confounded judicial analysis and produced divergent holdings in the holiday context.[200] Apart from these areas, the endorsement test's applicability remains uncertain,[201] and the Supreme Court, for its part, has only marginally invoked it in other contexts, such as government funding.[202]

Although claims under the endorsement test almost always allege just that – endorsement – the test, as formulated, also prohibits government actions that a reasonable observer would perceive as *disapproving* of religion in general or of one or more religions

195 *Id.* at 1544 (6th Cir. 1992), *cited in part with approval by* Capitol Square Review & Advisory Bd. v. Pinette, 515 U.S. 753, 780 (1995) (O'Connor, J., concurring in part and concurring in the judgment); *accord* Van Orden v. Perry, 351 F.3d 173, 177–8 (5th Cir. 2003) ("This is the observation of a reasonable observer, not of the uninformed, the casual passerby, the heckler, or the reaction of a single individual."), *aff'd*, 545 U.S. 677 (2005); Bauchman, 132 F.3d at 555.

196 *See* Elewski, 123 F.3d at 54.

197 *See* Santa Fe Indep. Sch. Dist. v. Doe, 530 U.S. 290, 305, 307, 316 (2000) (briefly but repeatedly noting the existence of "perceived and actual endorsement").

198 *But see* Rusk v. Crestview Local Sch. Dist, 379 F.3d 418, 421 (6th Cir. 2004) {"The Supreme Court has ... expressed general 'heightened concerns' about the impressionability of elementary school students. But despite such concerns, the Court has never ruled that a school's practice might amount to an impermissible endorsement of religion because of the impressionability of the school's young students. The Court's opinion in *Good News Club v. Milford Cent. Sch.*, 533 U.S. 98 (2001), suggests just the opposite – that elementary school students' possible misperceptions of endorsement are an insufficient basis for finding an Establishment Clause violation." (citations omitted) [citing Edwards v. Aguillard, 482 U.S. 578, 583–4 (1987); Widmar v. Vincent, 454 U.S. 263, 274 n. 14 (1981)]}.

199 *See* McGowan v. Maryland, 366 U.S. 420, 448–53 (1961).

200 *Compare* Koenick v. Felton, 190 F.3d 259 (4th Cir. 1999) (upholding Friday–Monday Easter holiday for public schools), *cert. denied*, 528 U.S. 1118 (2000), Bridenbaugh v. O'Bannon, 185 F.3d 796 (7th Cir. 1999) (upholding Good Friday holiday for state employees), *cert. denied*, 529 U.S. 1003 (2000), Granzeier v. Middleton, 173 F.3d 568 (6th Cir. 1999) (upholding Good Friday closing of governmental offices), Cammack v. Waihee, 932 F.2d 765 (9th Cir. 1991) (upholding state Good Friday holiday), *cert. denied*, 505 U.S. 1219 (1992), *with* Metzl v. Leininger, 57 F.3d 618 (7th Cir. 1995) (invalidating state law requiring public school closure on Good Friday), and Freedom from Religion Found., Inc. v. Thompson, 920 F. Supp. 969 (W.D. Wis. 1996) (invalidating state Good Friday holiday).

201 *See* DeStefano v. Emergency Hous. Group, Inc., 247 F.3d 397, 411 (2d Cir. 2001) (interpreting certain Supreme Court rulings "as casting doubt on the vitality of the endorsement test as a stand-alone measure of unconstitutionality in most Establishment Clause cases" but noting that it "remains a viable test of constitutionality in certain unique and discrete circumstances – for example, where the government embraces a religious symbol or allows the prominent display of religious imagery on public property").

202 *See* Agostini v. Felton, 521 U.S. 203, 235 (1997) (noting, largely as an analytical postscript, that a government aid program did not result in endorsement).

in particular.[203] It is well settled in this regard that the Establishment Clause is not violated simply because a secularly oriented government action is offensive to the religious sensibilities of citizens and, as a consequence, may have the secondary effect of disparaging their beliefs or advancing a contrary moral position.[204] Legislatures, by nature, must render judgments on the morality and regulability of conduct, and the judiciary has taken the pragmatic position that the incidental, nonsystematic disfavoritism of particular religious norms or beliefs is not itself sufficient to render such judgments doctrinally invalid under the Establishment Clause. This view roughly corresponds to the understanding, also well settled, that the incidental favoritism of particular religious norms or beliefs inherent in certain legislative judgments, which may have the secondary effect of endorsing or otherwise advancing those norms or beliefs, likewise does not create an Establishment Clause violation,[205] particularly given the inevitable environmental influence of religion in American law and politics.[206] It is only when the favoritism of those norms is more than incidental – when the endorsement of religion becomes, in actuality, the direct or primary effect – that the second prong of *Lemon* presumably would render the law invalid.

### c. The Entanglement Prong

The third and final prong of *Lemon* provides that a law will violate the Establishment Clause if the challenger can demonstrate that the law fosters an "excessive entanglement" of government and religion.[207] As this wording suggests, "[n]ot all interaction between the

203 For a thorough exploration of this side of the test, *see* Jay Wexler, *Government Disapproval of Religion*, 2013 B.Y.U. L. Rev. 119 (2013).

204 *See, e.g.*, Altman v. Bedford Cent. Sch. Dist., 245 F.3d 49, 76 (2d Cir. 2001) ("[T]he Establishment Clause does not prohibit teaching about a doctrine, such as evolution, merely because it conflicts with the beliefs of a religious group."), *cert. denied*, 534 U.S. 827 (2001); Fleischfresser v. Dirs. of Sch. Dist. 200, 15 F.3d 680, 689 (7th Cir. 1994) (similar); Crowley v. Smithsonian Inst., 636 F.2d 738, 742–3 (D.C. Cir. 1980) (similar); Florey v. Sioux Falls Sch. Dist. 49-5, 619 F.2d 1311, 1318 (8th Cir. 1980) (similar), *cert. denied*, 449 U.S. 987 (1980).

205 By the same token, it is unlikely that a reasonable observer – who is familiar with the political process and not beholden to a radically materialistic vision of law – would conclude that the primary effect of such legislative judgments is the endorsement of religion. *Cf.* Vernon v. City of L.A., 27 F.3d 1385, 1398–9 (9th Cir. 1994) (explaining that inferable incidental disapproval of certain religious beliefs does not violate the endorsement test where it "cannot objectively be construed as the primary focus or effect" of the governmental action), *cert. denied*, 513 U.S. 1000 (1994).

206 *See* Daniel O. Conkle, *Religious Purpose, Inerrancy, and the Establishment Clause*, 67 Ind. L.J. 1, 7 (1991) ("In addressing social problems, lawmakers inevitably make value judgments. These judgments require a resolution of competing claims concerning what is good and what is evil. In a society as religious as ours, it is hardly surprising that citizens and their representatives frequently rely on religious beliefs in resolving these questions."); *cf.* Bauchman v. W. High Sch., 132 F.3d 542, 554 (10th Cir. 1997) {"Courts have long recognized the historical, social and cultural significance of religion in our lives and in the world, generally. Courts also have recognized that 'a variety of motives and purposes are implicated' by government activity in a pluralistic society." [quoting Lynch v. Donnelly, 465 U.S. 668, 680 (1984)]}, *cert. denied*, 524 U.S. 953 (1998).

207 *See* Agostini v. Felton, 521 U.S. 203, 222–3 (1997); Larkin v. Grendel's Den, Inc., 459 U.S. 116, 126–7 (1982); Lemon v. Kurtzman, 403 U.S. 602, 613 (1971); Walz v. Tax Comm'n, 397 U.S. 664, 674 (1970). As with the other prongs, the burden is on the challenger to demonstrate entanglement. *See, e.g.*, Cholla Ready Mix, Inc. v. Civish, 382 F.3d 969, 976 (9th Cir. 2004) (finding no violation of the entanglement prong where the challenger "has not alleged facts that would support an inference that the defendants' actions foster excessive government entanglement with religion"), *cert. denied*, 544 U.S. 974 (2005).

government and religious authority … runs afoul of the Establishment Clause."[208] Rather, "[i]nteraction between church and state is inevitable, and [the Supreme Court] … ha[s] always tolerated some level of involvement between the two. Entanglement must be 'excessive' before it runs afoul of the Establishment Clause."[209] In turn, the Court has characterized entanglement as "a question of kind and degree"[210] and has indicated that the clause, "in a complex modern society," must allow for "[s]ome limited and incidental entanglement between church and state authority."[211] Whether there is excessive entanglement in any given interaction between these authorities, therefore, necessarily "depend[s] on all the circumstances of a particular relationship."[212]

Although entanglement can be categorized in many ways,[213] the three broad categories are administrative entanglement, doctrinal entanglement, and political entanglement.

i. *Administrative Entanglement.* Administrative entanglement is ordinarily a function of the government's presence in or oversight of a religious institution that receives government funding (e.g., through an educational assistance program) or that is subject to general regulatory laws (e.g., labor or civil rights statutes). Typically, it "involves comprehensive, discriminating, and continuing state surveillance of religion."[214] Thus, for example, "[a]n excessive entanglement may occur where there is a sufficiently intrusive investigation by a government entity into a church's employment of its clergy."[215] In *Lemon* itself, the Court invalidated an educational assistance law that created "comprehensive, discriminating, and continuing state surveillance" of religious schools receiving funding and "state inspection and evaluation of the religious content of a religious organization."[216] By contrast, "[t]he Establishment Clause does not exempt religious organizations from such secular governmental activity as fire inspections and building and zoning regulations,"[217] nor does it exempt them from record-keeping requirements, such as those of the Fair Labor Standards Act,[218] as long as such requirements, even if "more

208 Coles v. Cleveland Bd. of Educ., 171 F.2d 369, 385 (6th Cir. 1999).

209 Agostini, 521 U.S. at 233 (citation omitted); *accord* Cholla Ready Mix, 382 F.3d at 977; Koenick, 190 F.3d at 268.

210 Lynch v. Donnelly, 465 U.S. 668, 684 (1984).

211 Larkin v. Grendel's Den, Inc., 459 U.S. 116, 123 (1982); *accord* Carter v. Broadlawns Med. Ctr., 857 F.2d 448, 456 (8th Cir. 1988) (upholding a county hospital's paid chaplaincy even though "[i]t is obvious that employing a chaplain causes some entanglement"), *cert. denied*, 489 U.S. 1096 (1989).

212 Lemon, 403 U.S. at 614.

213 *See* Laurence H. Tribe, American Constitutional Law § 14-11, at 1226–32 (2d ed. 1988) (dividing entanglement into administrative, vesting, political, regulatory, and doctrinal); Robert A. Destro, *Developments in Liability Theories and Defenses*, 37 Cath. Law. 83, 96–7 (1997) ("There are three basic types of entanglement … 1) administrative entanglement, such as oversight of church or church-school use of state moneys … 2) doctrinal entanglement, such as utilizing courts to decide matters of doctrine … and 3) political entanglement, such as excessive church involvement in political affairs."); *Note, Government Noninvolvement with Religious Institutions*, 59 Tex. L. Rev. 921, 935–9 (1981) (explaining the distinction between doctrinal and administrative entanglement, elaborating on the former).

214 Vernon v. City of L.A., 27 F.3d 1385, 1399 (9th Cir. 1994), *cert. denied*, 513 U.S. 1000 (1994). According to the Second Circuit, "[e]ntanglement concerns can also arise where extensive monitoring is required to ensure that a public entity is not promoting religion." Am. Atheists, Inc. v. Port Auth. of N.Y. & N.J., 760 F.3d 227, 245 (2d Cir. 2014).

215 EEOC v. Catholic Univ. of Am., 83 F.3d 455, 467 (D.C. Cir. 1996).

216 Lemon v. Kurtzman, 403 U.S. 602, 619–20 (1971).

217 Tony & Susan Alamo Found. v. Sec'y of Labor, 471 U.S. 290, 305 (1985).

218 *See id.* at 305–6.

burdensome in terms of paperwork, are not significantly more intrusive into religious affairs."[219]

In the context of government funding, the Supreme Court has modified the inquiry into administrative entanglement, indicating that it should be analyzed as a component of *Lemon*'s "effect" prong. According to the Court,

> [w]hether a government aid program results in such an entanglement has consistently been an aspect of our Establishment Clause analysis. We have considered entanglement both in the course of assessing whether an aid program has an impermissible effect of advancing religion, and as a factor separate and apart from "effect." Regardless of how we have characterized the issue, however, the factors we use to assess whether an entanglement is "excessive" are similar to the factors we use to examine "effect." That is, to assess entanglement, we have looked to "the character and purposes of the institutions that are benefited, the nature of the aid that the State provides, and the resulting relationship between the government and religious authority." Similarly, we have assessed a law's "effect" by examining the character of the institutions benefited (e.g., whether the religious institutions were "predominantly religious"), and the nature of the aid that the State provided (e.g., whether it was neutral and nonideological).[220]

This collapse of the entanglement criterion into the effect inquiry corresponds more generally to the Court's apparent relaxation of the entanglement notion within the administrative funding context. Overruling prior decisions, the Court has repudiated, among other things, the presumption that public employees at religious schools will inculcate religion or that the monitoring of such employees, or of the religious institutions themselves, will unduly entangle the government with religion.[221] In addition, the Court only infrequently considers the entanglement-related potential for political divisiveness resulting from a government action to have constitutional import,[222] and it may have no independence significance,[223] although it has played a role in cases involving

[219] *Id.* at 306; *see also* Vernon v. City of L.A., 27 F.3d 1385, 1399–1400 (9th Cir. 1994) (finding no excessively administrative entanglement where a city's investigation of whether a police official's religious views adversely affected his duties did not involve "continuing or systematic investigation of religious beliefs" and "several specific precautions were taken by the [city] to limit the scope and duration of the investigation"), *cert. denied*, 513 U.S. 1000 (1994); NLRB v. Hanna Boys Ctr., 940 F.2d 1295, 1304–5 (9th Cir. 1991) (finding no excessive administrative entanglement with a church-affiliated organization where the National Labor Relation Board's "jurisdiction … require[d] governmental involvement only with respect to specific charges which may be filed" and did "not involve the Board in continuing or systematic monitoring of the Church's activities" or "monitoring [of] the religious aspects of [the organization's] activities at all" such that "Board involvement [would] not create the reality or the appearance of the government's supervising or collaborating with the Church"), *cert. denied*, 504 U.S. 985 (1992).

[220] Agostini, 521 U.S. at 232 (citations omitted) (quoting Lemon, 403 U.S. at 615).

[221] *See id.* at 233–4 [overruling Aguilar v. Felton, 473 U.S. 402 (1985) and overruling in part Sch. Dist. of Grand Rapids v. Ball, 473 U.S. 373 (1985)].

[222] *See id.* at 233–4; Lynch v. Donnelly, 465 U.S. 668, 684 (1984).

[223] *See* Am. Fam. Ass'n, Inc. v. City & Cnty. of S.F., 277 F.3d 1114, 1123 (9th Cir. 2002) {"Political divisiveness … 'has never been relied upon as an independent ground for holding a government practice unconstitutional.'" [quoting Brown v. Woodland Jt. Unified Sch. Dist., 27 F.3d 1373, 1383 (9th Cir. 1994)]}, *cert. denied*, 537 U.S. 886 (2002); Brooks v. City of Oak Ridge, 222 F.3d 259, 266 (6th Cir. 2000) (observing that "divisiveness alone, in the absence of administrative entanglement, is not enough to render a practice unconstitutional"), *cert. denied*, 531 U.S. 1152 (2001).

governmental endorsement of religious expression[224] and (of less precedential certainty today) governmental funding of religious schools.[225]

ii. *Doctrinal Entanglement.* A second species of entanglement, *doctrinal*, arises when the government endeavors to interpret or decide issues of religious doctrine or ecclesiastical law.[226] It is unclear, and the lower courts cannot agree, whether the Court's recent merger of entanglement and effect is limited to funding-related administrative entanglement or also extends to doctrinal and political entanglement.[227] For present purposes, and not without some basis, these latter forms will be treated as separate analyses.[228]

Problems with doctrinal entanglement can arise in a variety of contexts. The classic scenario is the attempted adjudication of property or other assets between intradenominational institutions or factions, each of which claims that it is the proper church body (often as a matter of dogma or church law) and thus the rightful possessor of the property.[229] In recent decades, doctrinal entanglement problems also have arisen when religious institutions or clergy are alleged to have committed tortious conduct and the plaintiff essentially seeks a declaration that the clergymember or his or her superior has acted unreasonably.[230] Lastly, one may encounter doctrinal entanglement problems when, as can occur with kosher labeling statutes, the law employs religious terminology or concepts.[231]

224 *See* McCreary Cnty., Ky. v. ACLU of Ky., 545 U.S. 844, 876 (2005); Santa Fe Indep. Sch. Dist. v. Doe, 530 U.S. 290, 310–11 (2000).

225 *See* Bowen v. Kendrick, 487 U.S. 589, 617 n. 14 (1988); *see also* Vernon, 27 F.3d at 1401 (noting this role).

226 *See* Hernandez v. Comm'r, 490 U.S. 680, 696 (1989) (noting that impermissible entanglement may occur when the government makes "inquiries into religious doctrine").

227 *Compare* Koenick v. Felton, 190 F.3d 259, 265 n. 6 (4th Cir. 1999) (explaining that even after *Agostini*, in some contexts "the two inquiries are best considered separately"), *cert. denied*, 528 U.S. 1118 (2000), *with* Holloman *ex rel.* Holloman v. Harland, 370 F.3d 1252, 1284–5 (11th Cir. 2004) (in light of *Agostini*, analytically placing entanglement within the inquiry into effect), *and* ACLU of N.J. *ex rel.* Lander v. Schundler, 168 F.3d 92, 97 (3d Cir. 1999) ("[T]he statement [in *Agostini*] appears to mean that entanglement, standing alone, will not render an action unconstitutional if the action does not have the overall effect of advancing, endorsing, or disapproving of religion.").

228 The *Mitchell* plurality stated that the *Agostini* Court "modified *Lemon* for purposes of evaluating aid to schools" [Mitchell v. Helms, 530 U.S. 793, 807 (2000) (plurality opinion)], suggesting that it did not necessarily modify *Lemon* for other types of cases.

229 *See, e.g.*, Jones v. Wolf, 443 U.S. 595 (1979); Serbian E. Orthodox Diocese for the U.S. of Am. & Can. v. Milivojevich, 426 U.S. 696 (1976); Presbyterian Church in the U.S. v. Mary Elizabeth Blue Hull Mem'l Presbyterian Church, 393 U.S. 440 (1969); Kedroff v. St. Nicholas Cathedral of Russian Orthodox Church in N. Am., 344 U.S. 94 (1952); Watson v. Jones, 80 U.S. (13 Wall.) 679 (1872); Wis. Conf. Bd. of Trs. of the United Methodist Church, Inc. v. Culver, 627 N.W.2d 469 (Wis. 2001); Kerler v. Evangelical Emanuel's Church, 292 N.W. 887 (Wis. 1940). This line of cases is addressed in Chapter 8.

230 *See* L.L.N. v. Clauder, 563 N.W.2d 434, 440–5 (Wis. 1997) (holding that the First Amendment precluded adjudication of a negligent supervision claim against a diocese regarding a priest's alleged misconduct); Pritzlaff v. Archdiocese of Milw., 533 N.W.2d 780 (Wis. 1995) (holding that the First Amendment precluded adjudication of various negligence claims against an archdiocese regarding a priest's alleged misconduct), *cert. denied*, 516 U.S. 1116 (1996); Scott C. Idleman, *Tort Liability, Religious Entities, and the Decline of Constitutional Protection*, 75 Ind. L.J. 219, 229–38 (2000) (examining the risk of doctrinal entanglement in the context of tort adjudication).

231 *See, e.g.*, Commack Self-Serv. Kosher Meats, Inc. v. Rubin, 294 F.3d, 415, 425–30 (2d Cir. 2002), *cert. denied*, 537 U.S. 1187 (2003); Barghout v. Bureau of Kosher Meat & Food Control, 66 F.3d 1337, 1344 n. 13 (4th Cir. 1995); Ran-Dav's Cnty. Kosher, Inc. v. State, 608 A.2d 1353, 1362 (N.J. 1992), *cert. denied*, 507 U.S. 952 (1993); Mark Popovsky, *Note, The Constitutional Complexity of Kosher Food Laws*, 44 Colum. J.L. & Soc. Probs. 75 (2010).

In these situations and others, the courts have emphatically explained that "[i]t is not the province of government officials or courts to determine religious orthodoxy"[232]; that judges, and presumably other officers of government, must "abst[ain] from evaluating the merits of a scriptural interpretation"[233]; and that "[t]he entanglement test ... forbids government adoption and enforcement of religious law."[234] In the words of the Supreme Court, "to inquire into the significance of words and practices to different religious faiths, and in varying circumstances by the same faith ... would tend inevitably to entangle the State with religion in a manner forbidden by our cases."[235]

When faced with a potential for doctrinal entanglement, the government (usually the judiciary) has essentially two options. First, courts may proceed to adjudicate if their decision making rests on "neutral principles of law," that is, legal rules or standards that have been developed and are regularly applied in a given field of law, such as property or torts, without particular regard to religious institutions or doctrines.[236] The U.S. Supreme Court has not sanctioned the neutral principles approach outside the relatively limited context of intrachurch property disputes,[237] although several lower courts not only have adopted it in the property context[238] but also have extended its application to actions in tort,[239] contract,[240] and employment discrimination.[241] Even within the property context, moreover, the Court has explained that the neutral principles approach is permissible but not necessary, and that courts have a second option. Assuming that the facts and circumstances allow it, this is to defer to the decision of an intrachurch decisional tribunal if such a decision has already been issued.[242] Overwhelmingly, this will be the highest or

232 Teterud v. Burns, 522 F.2d 357, 360 (8th Cir. 1975); *accord* Saunders-El v. Tsoulos, 1 F. Supp. 2d 845, 848 (N.D. Ill. 1998); Havurah v. Zoning Bd. of Appeals, 418 A.2d 82, 87 (Conn. 1979).

233 Callahan v. Woods, 658 F.2d 679, 686 (9th Cir. 1981); *accord* Thomas v. Review Bd. of Ind. Employment Sec. Div., 450 U.S. 707, 716 (1981); Glass v. First United Pentecostal Church of DeRidder, 676 So. 2d 724, 731 (La. Ct. App. 1996).

234 Ran-Dav's Cnty. Kosher, 608 A.2d at 1362. "That test also forbids government resolution of religious disputes. The government may not 'lend its power to one or the other side in controversies over religious authority or dogma.'" *Id.* [quoting Employment Div. v. Smith, 494 U.S. 872, 877 (1990)].

235 Widmar v. Vincent, 454 U.S. 263, 269 n. 6 (1981).

236 Jones v. Wolf, 443 U.S. 595, 602–4 (1979); Presbyterian Church in the U.S. v. Mary Elizabeth Blue Hull Mem'l Presbyterian Church, 393 U.S. 440, 449 (1969); Maktab Tarighe Oveyssi Shah Maghsoudi, Inc. v. Kianfar, 179 F.3d 1244, 1249 (9th Cir. 1999). "'Neutral principles' are wholly secular legal rules whose application to religious parties does not entail theological or doctrinal evaluations." S. Jersey Catholic Sch. Teachers Org. v. St. Teresa of the Infant Jesus Church Elem. Sch., 696 A.2d 709, 723 (N.J. 1997).

237 *See* Hutchison v. Thomas, 789 F.2d 392, 396 (6th Cir. 1986) (noting this point).

238 *See, e.g.*, Wis. Conf. Bd. of Trustees of the United Methodist Church, Inc. v. Culver, 627 N.W.2d 469, 475–6 (Wis. 2001).

239 *See, e.g.*, Smith v. O'Connell, 986 F. Supp. 73, 77–80 (D.R.I. 1997); Isely v. Capuchin Province, 880 F. Supp. 1138, 1151 (E.D. Mich. 1995); Moses v. Diocese of Colo., 863 P.2d 310, 320–1 (Colo. 1993) (*en banc*), *cert. denied*, 511 U.S. 1137 (1994); Odenthal v. Minn. Conf. of Seventh-Day Adventists, 649 N.W.2d 426, 435–6 (Minn. 2002); L.L.N. v. Clauder, 563 N.W.2d 434, 440 (Wis. 1997). *But see* El-Farra v. Sayyed, 226 S.W.3d 792, 795 (Ark. 2006) (refusing to extend the neutral principles approach to contract disputes).

240 *See, e.g.*, Kleppinger v. Anglican Catholic Church, Inc., 715 A.2d 1033, 1038 (N.J. Super. Ct. Ch. Div. 1998).

241 *See, e.g.*, Doe v. Lutheran High Sch. of Greater Minneapolis, 702 N.W.2d 322, 327 (Minn. Ct. App. 2005) (holding that adjudication of a minister's claim of sexual orientation discrimination by his church-employer could not be resolved using neutral principles and would therefore create excessive entanglement).

242 *See* Jones, 443 U.S. at 604. This is basically the approach adopted by, for example, the State of Washington. *See* Elvig v. Ackles, 98 P.3d 524, 526 (Wash. Ct. App. 2004) {"In Washington, civil courts may adjudicate church-related disputes only if the dispute does not involve ecclesiastical or doctrinal issues. 'The First

final tribunal of the religious entity, given the ordinary jurisdictional demands of exhaustion and ripeness. Whether or not to use the deference approach appears ultimately to be a matter of state discretion, presumably (although not necessarily) exercised by each state's judicial branch. The decision to defer also obviously can arise from the lack of available neutral principles. A more thorough exposition and analysis of these two options, set within the church property dispute context, can be found in Chapter 8.

iii. *Political Entanglement.* A third kind of entanglement, *political,* arises when the government delegates civil authority to religious institutions or officials because of their religious status.[243] The category of political entanglement sometimes can encompass the concern over political divisiveness along religious lines, which was addressed in the treatment of administrative entanglement. In addition, the analysis of political entanglement is related to that of doctrinal entanglement – but with a different focus. Under this analysis, the concern is not that the government will be interpreting and expounding religious doctrine but that the government may, perhaps in an effort to prevent doctrinal entanglement, hand over its interpretive or enforcement authority to religious institutions or officials. The case law makes clear, however, that this is impermissible.

Although the government cannot preclude clergy in their general capacity as citizens from holding political office and thereby exercising governmental power,[244] its relationship to clergy in their specific capacity as clergy is more restricted. In particular, although it may select them because of their status as clergy to serve in a nonbinding advisory role,[245] it may not vest them because of that status with actual civil authority.[246] In the words of the Supreme Court, "[t]he Framers did not set up a system of government in which important, discretionary governmental powers would be delegated to or shared with religious institutions."[247]

Amendment does not provide churches with absolute immunity to engage in tortious conduct. So long as liability is predicated on secular conduct and does not involve the interpretation of church doctrine or religious beliefs, it does not offend constitutional principles.' But if the church accused of wrongdoing is a member of a hierarchically-organized church that has ecclesiastical judicial tribunals, civil courts must defer to the highest church tribunal's resolution of the matter, despite the fact that the dispute could be resolved by a civil court." (footnotes omitted) [quoting C.J.C. v. Corp. of Catholic Bishop of Yakima, 985 P.2d 262, 277 (Wash. 1999)]}.

243 *See* Larkin v. Grendel's Den, Inc., 459 U.S. 116, 125–7 (1982); Barghout v. Bureau of Kosher Meat & Food Control, 66 F.3d 1337, 1342–3 (4th Cir. 1995); State v. Celmer, 404 A.2d 1, 6 (N.J. 1979) (explaining that "there can be no question but that … [the First Amendment] precludes a state from ceding governmental powers to a religious organization"), *cert. denied sub nom.* Ocean Grove Camp Mtg. Ass'n of United Methodist Church v. Celmer, 444 U.S. 951 (1979).

244 *See* McDaniel v. Paty, 435 U.S. 618, 626–9 (1978) (plurality opinion) (holding that Free Exercise Clause prohibits the exclusion of clergy from political office).

245 *See* N.Y. State Sch. Bds. Ass'n v. Sobol, 591 N.E.2d 1146, 1148–52 (N.Y. 1992), *cert. denied,* 506 U.S. 909 (1992).

246 *See* Larkin, 459 U.S. at 126–7 (invalidating a state law vesting in churches and schools the power to veto liquor license applications within 500 feet of them); Barghout, 66 F.3d at 1342–3 (4th Cir. 1995) (invalidating a state kosher labeling law because "it fosters excessive entanglement of religious and secular authority by vesting significant investigative, interpretive, and enforcement power in a group of individuals based on their membership in a specific religious sect"); Voswinkel v. City of Charlotte, 495 F. Supp. 588, 598 (W.D.N.C. 1980) (invalidating a police chaplaincy as excessive entanglement in part because "[t]he chaplain is either a church employee who must answer in his employment to the police chief; or he is a police employee in some respect answerable to the Church; or he is in some way responsible to both in the performance of what purports to be a public function").

247 Larkin, 459 U.S. at 127.

## 2. *The Prohibition on Coercion*

The *Lemon* test's limitations on purpose, effect, and entanglement do not exhaust the Establishment Clause's doctrinal expanse.[248] Also prohibited are laws that are actually or effectively coercive in some religiously significant manner. In recent years, in fact, "[w]hile the *Lemon* test dominates Establishment Clause jurisprudence, coercion has emerged as a prevailing consideration in the school prayer context."[249]

### a. Actual Coercion

Under the prohibition against actual coercion, the government may not require or restrict conduct that either is intrinsically religious or is regulated by the government because of its potential religious meaning.[250] More specifically, the government may not compel participation in or support of religious programs,[251] much less compel religious profession or observance outright,[252] and it may not impose legal penalties on persons because they claim adherence to a particular religion or to no religion at all.[253] The Supreme Court has in turn declared that the government, at least in the financing context, "may not place its ... coercive authority ... behind a single religious faith or behind religious belief in general, compelling nonadherents to support the practices or proselytizing of favored religious organizations."[254]

Normally, "[t]o satisfy the coercion test, a plaintiff must show that she was forced to participate in a religious activity,"[255] such as prayer or theistic profession, "regardless of whether those practices are in some ways consistent with [her] beliefs."[256] "The essence of the Establishment Clause is its prohibition of coercion by governmental

[248] *See* Hunt v. McNair, 413 U.S. 734, 741 (1973) (calling them "no more than helpful signposts").

[249] Mellen v. Bunting, 327 F.3d 355, 370 (4th Cir. 2003), *cert. denied*, 541 U.S. 1019 (2004).

[250] *See* Lee v. Weisman, 505 U.S. 577, 587 (1992); Everson v. Bd. of Educ., 330 U.S. 1, 15–16 (1947). This prohibition is duplicated and to some extent complemented by the requirements of the Free Exercise Clause. *See* Employment Div. v. Smith, 494 U.S. 872, 877 (1990); Venters v. City of Delphi, 123 F.3d 956, 970 (7th Cir. 1997).

[251] *See, e.g.*, Town of Greece, N.Y. v. Galloway, 134 S. Ct. 1811, 1825 (2014); Warner v. Orange Cnty. Dep't of Prob., 115 F.3d 1068, 1075 (2d Cir. 1996); Kerr v. Farrey, 95 F.3d 472, 476–80 (7th Cir. 1996); Griffen v. Coughlin, 673 N.E.2d 98 (N.Y. 1996), *cert. denied*, 519 U.S. 1054 (1997).

[252] *See* Torcaso v. Watkins, 367 U.S. 488, 492–6 (1961) (invalidating state constitutional requirement of theistic profession to hold office); Anderson v. Laird, 466 F.2d 283, 283–4 (D.C. Cir. 1972) (*per curiam*) (holding that the federal military academies' chapel attendance requirement violated the First Amendment), *cert. denied*, 409 U.S. 1076 (1972); O'Hair v. White, No. Civ. A-78-CA-220, 1984 WL 251621, at *1 (W.D. Tex. July 27, 1984) (recognizing invalidity of similar requirement); *see generally* Santa Fe Indep. Sch. Dist. v. Doe, 530 U.S. 290, 311–12 (2000); Lee, 505 U.S. at 591–8; Sch. Dist. v. Schempp, 374 U.S. 203, 223 (1963); Zorach v. Clauson, 343 U.S. 306, 314 (1952).

[253] *See* Venters, 123 F.3d at 970; Doe v. Harlan Cnty. Sch. Dist., 96 F. Supp. 2d 667, 679 (E.D. Ky. 2000); Moore v. Gaston Cnty. Bd. of Educ., 357 F. Supp. 1037, 1043 (W.D.N.C. 1973); *see also* Warsoldier v. Woodford, 418 F.3d 989, 996 (9th Cir. 2005) ("[P]unishments to coerce a religious adherent to forgo her or his religious beliefs is an infringement on religious exercise.").

[254] Tex. Monthly, Inc. v. Bullock, 489 U.S. 1, 9 (1989).

[255] Chaudhuri v. Tennessee, 886 F. Supp. 1374, 1383 (M.D. Tenn. 1995), *aff'd*, 130 F.3d 232 (6th Cir. 1997), *cert. denied*, 523 U.S. 1024 (1998). An exception is apparently made in the taxation context, where the coerced activity (payment of taxes) is not itself religious, but the government then spends the revenue generated by the coerced activity in the direct pursuit of religious ends. *See* DeStefano v. Emergency Hous. Group, Inc., 247 F.3d 397, 407 (2d Cir. 2001).

[256] Turner v. Hickman, 342 F. Supp. 2d 887, 895 (E.D. Cal. 2004).

power applied for the benefit of religion. Such coercion may consist in compulsion to participate in religious activities or ceremonies, or in compulsion to pay taxes for the support of religious activities or programs."[257] Actual religious coercion is uncommon today, although there has emerged in recent years a line of cases challenging requirements on inmates or probationers (as a condition of sentencing or probation) that they attend rehabilitation or substance abuse counseling, such as a twelve-step program, that has religious or arguably religious components.[258] As summarized by one federal district court, "[f]orced attendance or coercion is shown if a prison official, a parole board, or another state actor requires an inmate to attend a program that emphasizes religion or faith as a condition of his [or her] probation or sentencing. In contrast, merely suggesting or recommending a religious program, without force or coercion or when secular options are equally available, is not a First Amendment violation."[259] In other words, coercion presumably will not be found if participation in a religiously based program is truly voluntary (i.e., nonparticipation will not adversely affect any legally cognizable interest)[260] and a person independently chooses to participate in such a program, fully understanding that it has religious dimensions,[261] or if an adequate nonreligious alternative program is also made available.[262] These principles also will apply to other

257 Donovan v. Tony & Susan Alamo Found., 722 F.2d 397, 403 (8th Cir. 1983), *aff'd*, 471 U.S. 290 (1985).

258 *See, e.g.*, Jackson v. Nixon, 747 F.3d 537, 541–3 (8th Cir. 2014) (finding potential coercion where progress toward early parole appeared to be conditioned on participation in a rehabilitative program with religious components); Ams. United for Separation of Church & State v. Prison Fellowship Ministries, Inc. 509 F.3d 406, 421–3 (8th Cir. 2007) (finding a religious prison rehabilitative program unconstitutional because amenities were made available to members that were not available to members of similar secular programs); Warner v. Orange Cnty. Dep't of Probation, 115 F.3d 1068, 1075 (2d Cir. 1997) (holding that requiring a probationer to attend AA meetings, which had a central religious component, violated the Establishment Clause); Kerr v. Farrey, 95 F.3d 472, 479–80 (7th Cir. 1996) (holding that requiring an inmate's attendance at NA meetings, where failure to attend would result in "significant penalties" such as "classification to a higher security risk category and adverse notations in his prison record that could affect his chances for parole," violated the Establishment Clause); Edmundson v. Curry, No. Civ. 05-CV-445-JD, 2006 WL 1134913, at *5–*6 (D.N.H. Apr. 3, 2006) (unpublished); Raines v. James, No. 2:98CV290-MHT, 2006 WL 691236, at *3–*5 (M.D. Ala. Mar. 17, 2006) (unpublished); Catala v. Comm'r, No. Civ. 05-CV-106-JD, 2005 WL 3133036 (D.N.H. Nov. 22, 2005) (unpublished); Bobko v. Lavan, No. Civ. 1:CV-04-0158, 2005 WL 1309072, at *3 (M.D. Pa. May 31, 2005) (unpublished), *aff'd*, No. 05-3184, 157 Fed. App'x 516 (3d Cir. 2005) (unpublished); Turner v. Hickman, 342 F. Supp. 2d 887, 895–7 (E.D. Cal. 2004); Nusbaum v. Terrangi, 210 F. Supp. 2d 784, 787–9 (E.D. Va. 2002); Baucsch v. Sumiec, 139 F. Supp. 2d 1029, 1033–7 (E.D. Wis. 2001); Ross v. Keelings, 2 F. Supp. 2d 810, 816–18 (E.D. Va. 1998). *See generally* Stanton Peele & Charles Bufe, Resisting 12-Step Coercion: How to Fight Forced Participation in AA, NA, or 12-Step Treatment ch. 4 (2000); Rachel F. Calabro, *Comment, Correction Through Coercion: Do State Mandated Alcohol and Drug Treatment Programs in Prisons Violate the Establishment Clause?* 47 DePaul L. Rev. 565 (1998).

259 Catala, 2005 WL 3133036, at *1 (citation omitted).

260 *See, e.g.*, Henderson v. Frank, No. 05-2684, 190 Fed. App'x 507, 509 (7th Cir. Aug. 3, 2006) (unpublished) (rejecting an inmate's challenge to a religiously based behavior modification program where the inmate "never provided any evidence that he was denied parole, advancement through the level system, or a transfer for refusing to complete a behavior modification program").

261 *See* Freedom from Religion Found., Inc. v. McCallum, 324 F.3d 880, 881–2 (7th Cir. 2003).

262 *See, e.g.*, Bobko v. Levan, No. 05-3184, 157 Fed. App'x 516, 517 (3d Cir. 2005) (unpublished) (holding that required participation in a therapeutic program as a condition of parole was not religiously coercive where "defendants submitted evidence establishing that … a secular approach to recovery … [was also] available in the … program"); Arnold v. Tenn. Bd. of Paroles, 956 S.W.2d 478, 484 (Tenn. 1997) (noting that "to require a prisoner to attend or participate in … a treatment program would constitute a violation

nonrehabilitative social services, such as government-operated or -affiliated vocational programs[263] and homeless shelters.[264]

### b. Effective Coercion

In 1992, in *Lee v. Weisman*,[265] the Supreme Court expanded the prohibition on coercion to include, at least in the precollegiate public-school context, government actions that may fairly be perceived as being obligatory, even if they do not, in fact, impose actual requirements or penalties. At issue in *Lee* were a Rabbi's invocation and benediction at a middle-school graduation. Even though attendance was not mandatory and those attending were not required to participate, the Court invalidated the exercise because, from the vantage point of graduates, "their attendance and participation in the state-sponsored religious activity [we]re in a fair and real sense obligatory."[266] According to the Court, "the school district's supervision and control of a … graduation ceremony places public pressure, as well as peer pressure, on attending students to stand as a group or, at least, maintain respectful silence during the invocation and benediction. This pressure, though subtle and indirect, can be as real as any overt compulsion."[267]

In 2000, in *Santa Fe Independent School District v. Doe*,[268] the Court again applied this principle and invalidated a high school policy allowing student-initiated and student-led prayer at football games. The Court rejected the notion that "high school students do not feel immense social pressure, or have a truly genuine desire, to be involved in the extracurricular event that is American high school football."[269] For many students, observed the Court, "the choice between whether to attend these games or to risk facing a personally offensive religious ritual is in no practical sense an easy one," and "[e]ven if [one] regard[s] every high school student's decision to attend a home football game as purely voluntary … the delivery of a pregame prayer has the improper effect of coercing those present to participate in an act of religious worship."[270]

of the Establishment Clause" if the program is religious and "there are no alternative secular treatment programs offered"); Griffin, 673 N.E.2d at 108 (finding an Establishment Clause violation where participation in Alcoholics Anonymous was "mandated" and it was the "exclusive drug addiction and alcoholism rehabilitation program").

263 *See* Moeller v. Bradford Cnty., No. 3:05CV334, 2006 WL 319288, at *6 (M.D. Pa. Feb. 10, 2006) (unpublished) (holding that plaintiffs stated a claim that an outside vocational program for inmates that included religious instruction and discussion, where no other program was offered, violated the Establishment Clause, observing that "the choice between foregoing educational and vocational training in prison or enduring the [program's] efforts to proselytize may be no choice at all").

264 *See* Cmty. House, Inc. v. City of Boise, No. CV-05-283-S-BLW, 2005 WL 2847390, at *6 (D. Idaho Oct. 28, 2005) (unpublished) (enjoining a city-coordinated program to shelter the homeless, where the contracted organization required participants affirmatively to opt out of attendance at religious services, explaining that "requir[ing] the homeless person to explain why he or she would be offended by the religious meeting … can easily amount to a subtle, and even not-so-subtle, form of coercion … [and] brings the [organization] perilously close to advocating attendance rather than allowing an unhindered free choice."), *aff'd in part and rev'd in part on other grounds*, 490 F.3d 1041 (9th Cir. 2007).

265 505 U.S. 577 (1992).

266 *Id.* at 586.

267 *Id.* at 593.

268 530 U.S. 290 (2000).

269 *Id.* at 311.

270 *Id.* at 312.

Even more recently, the Seventh Circuit, sitting en banc,[271] held that a public school district's decision to hold a high school graduation in a church building likewise generated impermissible coercion, even though no intrinsically religious activities, such as prayer, transpired at the behest of the government.[272] Among other things, the majority concluded that "*Lee* and *Santa Fe* cannot be meaningfully distinguished ... on the ground that the school district did not coerce overt religious activity."[273] "Once the school district creates a captive audience, the coercive potential of endorsement can operate. When a student who holds minority (or no) religious beliefs observes classmates at a graduation event taking advantage of [the church's] offerings or meditating on its symbols (or posing for pictures in front of them) or speaking with its staff members, '[t]he law of imitation operates,' and may create subtle pressure to honor the day in a similar manner. The only way for graduation attendees to avoid the dynamic is to leave the ceremony. That is a choice, *Lee v. Weisman* teaches, the Establishment Clause does not force students to make."[274]

Importantly, not all coercion that is in some way related to religion will violate the Establishment Clause. According to the Fourth Circuit, "school administrators can 'coerce' student action of all kinds without engaging in unconstitutional coercion.... [T]he critical question ... is not just whether the [school] would be 'coercing' students to ... [undertake certain conduct], but whether that translates into *unconstitutional* government coercion in violation of the Establishment Clause."[275] In particular, the court distinguished (perhaps now in tension with the Seventh Circuit's graduation case) between impermissibly coercing children to "participat[e] in an inherently religious activity," such as scripture reading or prayer,[276] and lawfully coercing children to engage in a categorically nonreligious activity, even one that is has some relationship to religion.[277]

In addition, whether there is effective coercion depends not only of the activity in question but also on the nature of the educational environment and the characteristics, particularly the maturity, of the allegedly coerced individuals. A number of courts have held, for example, that the effective coercion prohibition does not apply (or at least does

[271] *See* Doe *ex rel.* Doe v. Elmbrook Sch. Dist., 687 F.3d 840 (7th Cir. 2012) (*en banc*), *cert. denied*, 134 S. Ct. 2283 (2014). The *en banc* vote was seven to three. The denial of *certiorari* by the Supreme Court took place only after several conferences, spanning two terms, and over the dissent of two Justices. *See* Elmbrook Sch. Dist. v. Doe, 134 S. Ct. 2283 (2014) (Scalia, J., dissenting, joined by Thomas, J.).

[272] *See* Elmbrook Sch. Dist., 687 F.3d at 854–6.

[273] *Id.* at 855.

[274] *Id.* at 855–6 (citation omitted) [quoting Wallace v. Jaffree, 472 U.S. 38, 60 n. 51 (1985)].

[275] Child Evangelism Fellowship of Md., Inc. v. Montgomery Cnty. Pub. Schs., 373 F.3d 589, 597 (4th Cir. 2004).

[276] *Id.* at 599 ["They would not be forced to engage in any formal religious exercise; they would not be made to read the Bible or to pray, nor would they be bound to sit by while other students or faculty pray. They would not be required, or even encouraged, to accept a religious tract, or asked to read or listen to a religious message." (citations omitted)].

[277] In that case, the students were given flyers by a religious organization, advertising a religious event, which the students were then supposed to take home to their parents. According to the court, "A student who receives a Good News Club flyer and delivers it to his parents is no more engaging in a religious activity than a child who receives the same flyer from a street-corner evangelist and turns to give it to his mother. In both of these cases, the children are merely delivering an invitation to participate in a religious activity, not engaging in that activity." *Id.* at 600. *See also* Myers v. Loudoun Cnty. Pub. Schs., 418 F.3d 395, 406–7 (4th Cir. 2005) (noting that "all of the cases holding that indirect coercion of religious activity violates the Establishment Clause presuppose that the challenged activity is a *religious* exercise").

not apply with equal force) to the university setting, given both the critical nature of higher education and the comparative age of students.[278] The Supreme Court, with one exception, has not addressed the reach of the effective coercion test beyond high school, although a 2004 denial of *certiorari* (accompanied by multiple opinions) indicates some degree of disagreement over the test's scope of application or at least disagreement over the interpretation of the test by lower courts.[279]

The one exception, addressed more thoroughly later in this chapter, involves prayers at the outset of legislative or quasi-legislative meetings. In 1983, the Court upheld state legislative prayer delivered by a paid chaplain,[280] although with regard to the question of coercion it noted only that "the individual claiming injury by the practice is an adult, presumably not readily susceptible to 'religious indoctrination,' or peer pressure."[281] In 2014, the Court upheld a town's practice of having citizens deliver prayers before town board meetings, but this time, having decided both *Lee* and *Santa Fe* since 1983, it addressed the coercion question at greater length.[282] Distinguishing both the environment and the audience in *Lee*, the Court found no evidence that "members of the public are dissuaded from leaving the meeting room during the prayer, arriving late, or even, as happened here, making a later protest."[283] The Court continued: "Should nonbelievers choose to exit the room during a prayer they find distasteful, their absence will not stand out as disrespectful or even noteworthy. And should they remain, their quiet acquiescence will not, in light of our traditions, be interpreted as an agreement with the words or ideas expressed. Neither choice represents an unconstitutional imposition as to mature adults."[284]

### 3. *The Limitations on Religious Discrimination*

In addition to the strictures of *Lemon* and the prohibition on coercion, contemporary Establishment Clause doctrine also includes limitations on discrimination, one covering discrimination between or among religions[285] and the other between religion

278 *See, e.g.*, Chaudhuri v. Tennessee, 130 F.3d 232, 238–9 (6th Cir. 1997), *cert. denied*, 523 U.S. 1024 (1998); Tanford v. Brand, 104 F.3d 982, 985–6 (7th Cir. 1997), *cert. denied*, 522 U.S. 814 (1997). To the extent that the effective coercion analysis applies outside the educational context, a similar distinction between adults and children has been made. *See, e.g.*, Newdow v. Bush, 391 F. Supp. 2d 95, 101 n. 3 (D.D.C. 2005) ("Consideration of the coercive effect of a prayer pertains only to the special case of school children, not to mature, sophisticated adults.").

279 *Compare* Bunting v. Mellen, 541 U.S. 1019, 1021 (2004) (Stevens, J., respecting denial of *certiorari*) (remarking "the absence of a direct conflict among the Circuits"), *with id.* at 1022 (Scalia, J., dissenting from denial of *certiorari*) ("The weighty questions raised by petitioners – about the proper application of *Lee* where adults rather than children are the subjects, and about the constitutionality of traditional religious observance in military institutions – deserve this Court's attention, particularly since the decisions of two other Circuits are in apparent contradiction as to whether *Lee* can extend so far."). Justice Scalia's dissent from the denial of *certiorari* in *Elmbrook School District* (*see supra* note 271) raises similar arguments but does not cite his *Bunting* opinion.

280 *See* Marsh v. Chambers, 463 U.S. 783 (1983).

281 *Id.* at 792 [quoting Tilton v. Richardson, 403 U.S. 672, 686 (1971)].

282 *See* Town of Greece, N.Y. v. Galloway, 134 S. Ct. 1811, 1824–8 (2014).

283 *Id.* at 1827.

284 *Id.*

285 *See* Bd. of Educ. v. Grumet, 512 U.S. 687, 703 (1994); Larson v. Valente, 456 U.S. 228, 244–6 (1982); Epperson v. Arkansas, 393 U.S. 97, 103–4 (1968); Everson v. Bd. of Educ., 330 U.S. 1, 15 (1947);

and nonreligion.[286] Notably, these are described as limitations rather than prohibitions insofar as they operate differently from the other doctrines thus far addressed: discrimination among religions is not prohibited altogether but rather is subject to strict judicial scrutiny, whereas discrimination between religion and nonreligion is more of an idea than an absolute, principally because the First Amendment itself provides for the unique treatment of religion in relation to the government.

### a. Between Religions or Denominations

Discrimination between or among religions or the government's use of a "denominational preference"[287] has been a long-standing concern under the Establishment Clause,[288] and some have considered its prohibition to be one of the clause's few historically legitimate objectives.[289] According to the Tenth Circuit, "statutes involving discrimination on the basis of religion, including interdenominational discrimination, are subject to heightened scrutiny whether they arise under the Free Exercise Clause, the Establishment Clause, or the Equal Protection Clause,"[290] though, of these options, they are typically pursued or decided under the Establishment Clause.[291]

Perhaps the most distinctive contemporary feature of the law of denominational discrimination is that unlike the other doctrines, which function within their reach as total prohibitions, this doctrine renders facial religious discrimination presumptively, but not conclusively, unconstitutional. Converging with the balancing methodology of equal protection, it subjects such discrimination to judicial "strict scrutiny" and assesses the legal and logical necessity of the government's action.[292] More precisely, it requires the government to demonstrate that the discrimination "is justified by a compelling governmental interest ... and ... is closely fitted to further that interest."[293] The alleged compelling interest must be invoked to solve an actual, concrete problem rather than merely

Sasnett v. Litscher, 197 F.3d 290, 292–3 (7th Cir. 1999); Olsen v. DEA, 878 F.2d 1458, 1461 (D.C. Cir. 1989), *cert. denied*, 495 U.S. 906 (1990).

286 *See* Grumet, 512 U.S. at 703; Epperson, 393 U.S. at 103–4.

287 Larson, 456 U.S. at 245.

288 *See id.* at 244–5.

289 *See, e.g.*, Wallace v. Jaffree, 472 U.S. 38, 113 (1985) (Rehnquist, J., dissenting); Robert L. Cord, *Church-State Separation: Restoring the "No Preference" Doctrine of the First Amendment*, 9 Harv. J.L. & Pub. Pol'y 129 (1986).

290 Colo. Christian Univ. v. Weaver, 534 F.3d 1245, 1266 (10th Cir. 2008) (citations omitted); *see also* Olsen, 878 F.2d at 1463 n. 5 (observing that in cases involving an alleged denominational preference, "establishment clause and equal protection analyses converge"), *cert. denied*, 495 U.S. 906 (1990).

291 *See, e.g.*, Bd. of Educ. v. Grumet, 512 U.S. 687, 703 (1994); Larson, 456 U.S. at 244–6; Epperson v. Arkansas, 393 U.S. 97, 103–4 (1968); Everson v. Bd. of Educ., 330 U.S. 1, 15 (1947); Awad v. Ziriax, 670 F.3d 1111, 1126–31 (10th Cir. 2012); Children's Healthcare Is a Legal Duty, Inc. v. Min De Parle, 212 F.3d 1084, 1090 (8th Cir. 2000), *cert. denied*, 532 U.S. 957 (2001); Sasnett v. Litscher, 197 F.3d 290, 292–3 (7th Cir. 1999); Am. Jewish Cong. v. City of Beverly Hills, 90 F.3d 379, 383–6 (9th Cir. 1996) (*en banc*).

292 *See* Hernandez v. Comm'r, 490 U.S. 680, 695 (1989); Larson, 456 U.S. at 246–7; Koenick v. Felton, 190 F.3d 259, 264 (4th Cir. 1999), *cert. denied*, 528 U.S. 1118 (2000); Wilson v. NLRB, 920 F.2d 1282, 1286–7 (6th Cir. 1990), *cert. denied*, 505 U.S. 1218 (1992). *But cf.* Am. Jewish Cong., 90 F.3d at 386 (holding that a standardless access policy for erecting displays on municipal land, used to grant access for one religious group's display but not other group's displays, violated the Establishment Clause without further scrutiny of the city policy or actions).

293 Larson, 456 U.S. at 247 (citation omitted).

speculative harms.[294] Strict scrutiny will apply, however, only if the denominational preference is facial – that is, if it is evident from the statute's text, design, or manifest purpose, apart from its application to any specific set of facts. "If no such facial preference exists, [the court] … proceed[s] to apply the customary three-pronged Establishment Clause inquiry derived from … [*Lemon*]."[295]

Interestingly, there are cases – principally, if not exclusively, from the Seventh Circuit – suggesting that denominationally discriminatory laws should be subjected to a different, less rigorous standard. According to that court, "[t]he Establishment Clause … prohibits the government from favoring one religion over another without a *legitimate* secular reason."[296] In particular, "the First Amendment does not allow a state to make it easier for adherents of one faith to practice their religion than for adherents of another faith to practice their religion, unless there is a secular justification for the difference in treatment."[297] Though this language roughly describes the standard used in certain cases arising under Title VII of the 1964 Civil Rights Act, it seems to be an anomalous and possibly incorrect rendition of Establishment Clause doctrine.

It appears, in all events, that courts often prefer to address the issue of denominational preferentialism under one or more of *Lemon*'s three prongs rather than as a free-standing analysis.[298] To a large extent, this is not surprising. It may frequently be much easier, on a variety of levels, to hold that a law's predominant purpose or primary effect is or is not religious in a generic sense than to hold that a law's text or design discriminates in favor of or against a particular religion or denomination. Moreover, a law that transgresses one of these standards under *Lemon* would be conclusively invalid, whereas under the anti-discrimination approach, the law, though presumptively invalid, would further have to be subjected to strict scrutiny.

### b. Between Religion and Nonreligion

In addition to presumptively prohibiting denominational discrimination, the Establishment Clause restricts discrimination between religion, on the one hand, and nonreligion or irreligion, on the other hand, although the scope and meaning of these categories are, as one might expect, uncertain and disputed.[299] Normally, the bar on

294 *See* Awad, 670 F.3d at 1129–30.

295 Hernandez, 490 U.S. at 695.

296 Kaufman v. McCaughtry, 419 F.3d 678, 683 (7th Cir. 2005) (emphasis added) [citing Linnemeir v. Bd. of Trs. of Purdue Univ., 260 F.3d 757, 759 (7th Cir. 2001); Metzl v. Leininger, 57 F.3d 618, 621 (7th Cir. 1995); Berger v. Rensselaer Cent. Sch. Corp., 982 F.2d 1160, 1168–9 (7th Cir. 1993), *cert. denied*, 508 U.S. 911 (1993)].

297 Metzl, 57 F.3d at 621.

298 *See, e.g.*, Yabr v. Rapides Parish Sch. Bd. *ex rel.* Metoyer, 171 F. Supp. 2d 653, 660–1 (W.D. La. 2001) (using the endorsement formulation of *Lemon*'s second prong to assess, and hold invalid, the distribution of the New Testament in public schools); *cf.* Awad, 670 F.3d at 1127 (noting "*Larson*'s rare use").

299 The Court has varied in its terms when delineating the components of this form of discrimination. *See, e.g.*, McCreary Cnty., Ky. v. ACLU of Ky., 545 U.S. 844, 875 (2005) ("religion over irreligion"); Bd. of Educ. of Kiryas Joel Vill. Sch. Dist. v. Grumet, 512 U.S. 687, 703 (1994) ("religion to irreligion"); Cnty. of Allegheny v. ACLU Greater Pittsburgh Chapter, 492 U.S. 573, 605 (1989) ("religion over nonreligion"); Epperson v. Arkansas, 393 U.S. 97, 104 (1968) ("religion and nonreligion"). The plurality opinion in *Mitchell v. Helms*, 530 U.S. 793 (2000), spoke of "the religious, irreligious, and areligious" (*id.* at 809), where "areligious" presumably means nonreligious and "irreligious" presumably means either

such discrimination is invoked when a government action allegedly benefits religious practices or beliefs but not their nonreligious analogues. At least in theory, however, the restriction should operate both ways. As stated by one federal district court, revealing the intersection between this restriction and the endorsement test, "[a]lthough the Establishment Clause is most generally invoked to protect against government endorsement of religion, it is equally applicable to claims that the government is hostile to religion. The government cannot establish a religion of secularism in the sense of affirmatively showing hostility to religion, opposing religion, or showing preference to those who believe in no religion over those who do believe in a religion."[300] That being said, it is certainly true that the government must distinguish between religion and nonreligion – potentially discriminating against the former – when complying with the Establishment Clause, and conversely, it may and sometimes must discriminate in favor of religion, or its exercise, when accommodating religious practices under the Free Exercise Clause.[301]

In terms of doctrine, the restriction on discrimination between religion and nonreligion is somewhat elusive, particularly when compared with the presumptive prohibition on denominational discrimination. Even more than the latter, in fact, this restriction seems to be addressed by courts at best indirectly through the *Lemon* analysis by holding either that a law lacks a secular purpose or that its primary effect is to advance religion.[302] Indeed, given these components of *Lemon*, it is unclear whether this prohibition has any independent analytical significance. It is also unclear whether, if triggered, it would apply categorically (like the prongs of *Lemon*) or through balancing (like the presumptive bar on denominational discrimination).

At a thematic level, by comparison, the norm of equal treatment between religion and nonreligion has been a key feature of the conceptual transformation of neutrality over the last two decades. What has emerged, in particular, is a rule of relative governmental discretion: the government may, but need not always, include religious entities within a general funding scheme. On the one hand, as long as "the link between government funds and religious training is broken by the independent and private choice of recipients," a funding program permissibly may include religious participants.[303] On the other hand, the First Amendment is also not violated if the program excludes religious entities

nonreligious or antireligious. *See* WEBSTER'S NEW UNIVERSAL UNABRIDGED DICTIONARY 971 (2d ed. 1983) [defining irreligious as (1) "not religious" or "indifferent or hostile to religion" and (2) "not in accord with religious principles"; "impious"; "profane"; or "wicked"].

300 Seidman v. Paradise Valley Unified Sch. Dist. No. 69, 327 F. Supp. 2d 1098, 1119 (D. Ariz. 2004) [citing Sch. Dist. of Abington Twp. v. Schempp, 374 U.S. 203, 225 (1963)].

301 These issues, and the limits on distinguishing between religion and nonreligion, are explored elsewhere in the treatise at greater length. *See* Chapter 5.E.1.a (examining when nonestablishment concerns provide a compelling interest sufficient to defeat a free exercise claim); Chapter 6.B.2 (examining the overlap between the nondiscrimination mandates of the Equal Protection Clause and the First Amendment); Chapter 6.C.2 (examining situations where religious and nonreligious speech may be treated differently).

302 *See, e.g.*, Tex. Monthly, Inc. v. Bullock, 489 U.S. 1, 15–17 (1989) (finding no secular objective because a sales tax exemption applied only to religious organizations).

303 Locke v. Davey, 540 U.S. 712, 719 (2004) [citing Zelman v. Simmons–Harris, 536 U.S. 639, 652 (2002); Zobrest v. Catalina Foothills Sch. Dist., 509 U.S. 1, 13–14 (1993); Witters v. Wash. Dep't of Servs. for Blind, 474 U.S. 481, 487 (1986); Mueller v. Allen, 463 U.S. 388, 399–400 (1983)].

from participation,[304] even though the program therefore may be fairly characterized as nonneutral with regard to religion.[305]

## D. Special Applications of the Establishment Clause

The possibility that one of the doctrines examined in previous sections might by its normal application preclude certain governmental actions does not end the Establishment Clause analysis. In fact, the Supreme Court has effectively recognized certain types of government action that call for either the nonapplication or at least the modified application of these doctrines. Two such circumstances will be addressed here – one involving traditional government practices and the other the discretionary accommodation of religious practices – although the latter, given the nation's history of accommodation, arguably may be just a subset or variation of the former.

### 1. *To Traditional Government Practices*

In its 1983 ruling in *Marsh v. Chambers*,[306] the Supreme Court recognized that there are some government practices so rooted in the nation's history and traditions, especially those condoned by the First Amendment's Framers,[307] that they should not be analyzed using the ordinary array of Establishment Clause doctrines, such as the three-part *Lemon* test.[308] The *Marsh* Court indicated that a practice, to qualify for this modified application of the Establishment Clause, should exhibit certain characteristics, such as *antiquity*, the existence of the practice in some form at the nation's founding[309]; *continuity*, its continuation to the present[310]; and *ubiquity*, its widespread use or observance.[311] In two subsequent cases, accordingly, the Court refused to extend the methodology of *Marsh*

304 Regarding the Establishment Clause, *see* Strout v. Albanese, 178 F.3d 57 (1st Cir. 1999) (holding that the exclusion of religious schools from an educational assistance program is not unconstitutional), *cert. denied*, 528 U.S. 931 (1999); Bagley v. Raymond Sch. Dep't, 728 A.2d 127 (Me. 1999) (similar), *cert. denied*, 528 U.S. 947 (1999); *cf. also* Bush v. Holmes, 886 So. 2d 340 (Fla. 2004) (upholding state restriction on voucher funding to religious schools, premised on a state constitutional provision, FLA. CONST. art. I, § 3, which provides that "[n]o revenue of the state ... shall ever be taken from the public treasury directly or indirectly in aid ... of any sectarian institution"), *aff'd in part on other grounds*, 919 So. 2d 392 (Fla. 2006). Regarding the Free Exercise Clause, *see* Locke, 540 U.S. at 720–5 (upholding a post–secondary educational aid program that specifically excluded students pursuing devotional theology degrees).

305 *See* Locke, 540 U.S. at 720 (not denying the characterization of such a program as nonneutral but instead "reject[ing] [the challenger's attendant] claim of presumptive unconstitutionality").

306 463 U.S. 783 (1983).

307 *See id.* at 790–1.

308 *See* Van Orden v. Perry, 545 U.S. 677, 699 (2005) (Breyer, J., concurring in the judgment) [observing that the Court's doctrinal tests cannot "readily explain the Establishment Clause's tolerance, for example, of the prayers that open legislative meetings; certain references to, and invocations of, the Deity in the public words of public officials; the public references to God on coins, decrees, and buildings; or the attention paid to the religious objectives of certain holidays, including Thanksgiving" (citation omitted) (citing *Marsh*)]; Allen v. Consol. City of Jacksonville, Fla., 719 F. Supp. 1532, 1538 (M.D. Fla. 1989) (similar), *aff'd*, 880 F.2d 420 (11th Cir. 1989) (*per curiam*).

309 *See* Marsh, 463 U.S. at 786–9, 795 (200 years nationally; 100 years for state); *cf.* Tanford v. Brand, 104 F.3d 982, 986 (7th Cir. 1997) (155 years old), *cert. denied*, 522 U.S. 814 (1997).

310 *See* Marsh, 463 U.S. at 786, 788, 792, 795.

311 *See id.* at 788–9, 795; *accord* Tanford, 104 F.3d at 986.

to the public-education context precisely because "free public education was virtually nonexistent at the time the Constitution was adopted."[312]

In *Marsh* itself, the Court addressed and upheld the practice of state legislative prayer by a government-paid chaplain because that practice "is deeply embedded in the history and tradition of this country,"[313] "has continued without interruption ever since [an] early session of Congress ... [and] been followed consistently in most of the states,"[314] and, through an "unambiguous and unbroken history of more than 200 years ... has become part of the fabric of our society."[315] In particular, the Court noted that "the Continental Congress, beginning in 1774, adopted the traditional procedure of opening its sessions with a prayer offered by a paid chaplain" and that "the First Congress, as one of its early items of business, adopted the policy of selecting a chaplain to open each session with prayer" and – just three days before reaching agreement on the language of the Bill of Rights – enacted a "statute providing for the payment of these chaplains."[316] Given this historical footing, which "sheds light not only on what the draftsmen intended the Establishment Clause to mean, but also on how they thought that Clause applied to the practice authorized by the First Congress,"[317] the Court concluded that "the practice of opening legislative sessions with prayer" and more generally the "invo[cation] [of] Divine guidance on a public body entrusted with making the laws is not, in these circumstances, an 'establishment' of religion or a state towards establishment; it is simply a tolerable acknowledgment of beliefs widely held among the people of this country."[318]

Nor, in light of the historical background, was it problematic that the state legislature employed, at public expense, the same chaplain (a Presbyterian minister) for many years and that the chaplain's prayers were in the Judeo-Christian tradition.[319] When upholding the paid chaplaincy and the prayers, the Court did, however, note two possible limitations to the use of its original understanding/tradition-based approach. First, the employment of a minister of the same denomination for several years was acceptable in part because there was no "proof that the chaplain's reappointment stemmed from an impermissible motive,"[320] thus suggesting that it may have been problematic had the chaplain been reappointed only or principally because of his denominational affiliation or beliefs and not "because his performance and personal qualities were acceptable to the body appointing him."[321] Second, the Court found that "there [was] ... no indication" that the chaplaincy "ha[d] been exploited to proselytize or advance any one, or to disparage any other, faith or belief," and for that reason, the "content of the prayer [was] not of concern," and the Court would not "embark on a sensitive evaluation or to parse the content of a particular prayer."[322] The implication is that had there been such

312 Edwards v. Aguillard, 482 U.S. 578, 583 n. 4 (1987); *see also* Lee v. Weisman, 505 U.S. 577, 596–7 (1992) (refusing to apply *Marsh* to a middle school graduation); *cf.* Engel v. Vitale, 370 U.S. 421 (1962).

313 Marsh, 463 U.S. at 786.

314 *Id.* at 788–9.

315 *Id.* at 792.

316 *Id.* at 787–8.

317 *Id.* at 790.

318 *Id.* at 792.

319 *See id.* at 793–5.

320 *Id.* at 793.

321 *Id.* In addition, the state-employed chaplain "was not the only clergyman heard by the Legislature; guest chaplains have officiated at the request of various legislators and as substitutes during [his] absences." *Id.* And Congress, too, had employed chaplains for extended terms. *See id.* at 794 n. 17.

322 *Id.* at 794–5.

evidence of exploitation, the chaplaincy would have faced a different or more searching Establishment Clause analysis.[323]

Just over two decades later, in *Town of Greece v. Galloway*,[324] the Court revisited and once again applied the methodology of *Marsh*, this time upholding, by a five-to-four vote, a town board's practice of opening its meeting with prayers led by community members, usually clergy. At each meeting, before the start of business, the town supervisor "would invite a local clergyman to the front of the room to deliver an invocation ... intended to place town board members in a solemn and deliberative frame of mind" and "invoke divine guidance in town affairs," after which the supervisor "would thank the minister for serving as the board's 'chaplain for the month' and present him with a commemorative plaque."[325] A list of prayer givers, all unpaid, was drawn up by a town employee after contacting congregations listed in a local directory, though the town "at no point excluded or denied an opportunity to a would-be prayer giver. Its leaders maintained that a minister or layperson of any persuasion, including an atheist, could give the invocation. But nearly all of the congregations in town were Christian; and from 1999 to 2007, all of the participating ministers were too."[326] The town did not direct the content of the prayers, which often contained "both civic and religious themes" and some of which were explicitly Christian and "invoked religious holidays, scripture, or doctrine."[327] After complaints (by the eventual litigants) "that Christian themes pervaded the prayers, to the exclusion of citizens who did not share those beliefs, the town invited a Jewish layman and the chairman of the local Baha'i temple to deliver prayers. A Wiccan priestess who had read press reports about the prayer controversy requested, and was granted, an opportunity to give the invocation."[328]

The Court in *Town of Greece* both clarified and applied its approach in *Marsh*. At the outset, the Court both rejected the characterization of *Marsh* as creating an exception to Establishment Clause tests – *Marsh*, it said, "found those tests unnecessary because history supported the conclusion that legislative invocations are compatible with the Establishment Clause"[329] – and repudiated the notion that *Marsh* "permit[s] a practice that would amount to a constitutional violation if not for its historical foundation."[330] Rather, "*Marsh* stands for the proposition that it is not necessary to define the precise boundary of the Establishment Clause where history shows that the specific practice is permitted. Any test the Court adopts must acknowledge a practice that was accepted by the Framers and has withstood the critical scrutiny of time and political change."[331] Having clarified *Marsh*, the Court then inquired "whether the prayer practice in the town of Greece fits within the tradition long followed in Congress and the state legislatures," especially given the Christian content of several of the prayers and

323 *See* Snyder v. Murray City Corp., 159 F.3d 1227, 1233–4 & nn. 10 & 11 (10th Cir. 1998) (exploring this limitation), *cert. denied*, 526 U.S. 1039 (1999); Stein v. Plainwell Cmty. Schs., 822 F.2d 1406, 1410 (6th Cir. 1987) (similar, albeit in the context of a high school graduation).

324 134 S. Ct. 1811 (2014).

325 *Id.* at 1816.

326 *Id.*

327 *Id.*

328 *Id.* at 1817.

329 *Id.* at 1818.

330 *Id.* at 1819.

331 *Id.*

the alleged pressure on attendees either to participate or to leave the room during the invocation.[332]

As for the content of the prayers, the Court explained that "[t]he tradition reflected in *Marsh* permits chaplains to ask their own God for blessings of peace, justice, and freedom that find appreciation among people of all faiths. That a prayer is given in the name of Jesus, Allah, or Jehovah, or that it makes passing reference to religious doctrines, does not remove it from that tradition."[333] To allow only "nonsectarian or ecumenical prayer as a single, fixed standard is not consistent with th[is] tradition," and indeed, "[t]he Congress that drafted the First Amendment would have been accustomed to invocations containing explicitly religious themes."[334] After noting several such congressional prayers from the late eighteenth through mid-nineteenth centuries, the Court emphasized that

> [t]he decidedly Christian nature of these prayers must not be dismissed as the relic of a time when our Nation was less pluralistic than it is today. Congress continues to permit its appointed and visiting chaplains to express themselves in a religious idiom. It acknowledges our growing diversity not by proscribing sectarian content but by welcoming ministers of many creeds.[335]

The Court further remarked that a rule requiring invocations to "be nonsectarian would force the legislatures that sponsor prayers and the courts that are asked to decide these cases to act as supervisors and censors of religious speech" and thus "would involve government in religious matters to a far greater degree than is the case under the town's current practice of neither editing or approving prayers in advance nor criticizing their content after the fact."[336]

The Court denied, however, that "no restraints remain" on the content of such prayers. It would, the majority said, be a "different case" where a "course and practice over time shows that the invocations denigrate nonbelievers or religious minorities, threaten damnation, or preach conversion,"[337] though it cautioned that a few prayers reflecting these characteristics, as arguably happened in the town of Greece, "do not despoil a practice that on the whole reflects and embraces our tradition." In short, there must be "a pattern of prayers that over time denigrate, proselytize, or betray an impermissible government purpose" before an Establishment Clause problem is found.[338] The Court also did not find it problematic that the town invited predominantly Christian clergy to deliver prayers because the town "made reasonable efforts to identify all of the congregations located within its borders and represented that it would welcome a prayer by any minister or layman who wished to give one. That nearly all of the congregations in town turned out to be Christian does not reflect an aversion or bias on the part of town leaders against minority faiths."[339] Indeed, "requir[ing] it to search beyond its borders for non-Christian

[332] *Id.* at 1819–20.
[333] *Id.* at 1823.
[334] *Id.* at 1820.
[335] *Id.* at 1820–1.
[336] *Id.* at 1822. "It would be but a few steps removed from that prohibition for legislatures to require chaplains to redact the religious content from their message in order to make it acceptable for the public sphere. Government may not mandate a civic religion that stifles any but the most generic reference to the sacred any more than it may prescribe a religious orthodoxy." *Id.*
[337] *Id.* at 1823.
[338] *Id.* at 1824.
[339] *Id.*

prayer givers in an effort to achieve religious balancing" would entail "a form of government entanglement with religion that is far more troublesome than the [town's] current approach."[340]

As for the alleged coercion of attendees at the town meetings, a plurality of three justices, employing "a fact-sensitive … [inquiry] that considers both the setting in which the prayer arises and the audience to whom it is directed" determined that there was no actionable compulsion.[341] Turning to the reasonable observer of the endorsement test, the plurality explained that this observer would be familiar with the tradition of legislative prayer, would understand "that its purposes are to lend gravity to public proceedings and to acknowledge the place religion holds in the lives of many private citizens, not to afford government an opportunity to proselytize or force truant constituents into the pews," and thus would appreciate that the "principal audience for these invocations is not, indeed, the public but lawmakers themselves."[342] The justices stated that their "analysis would be different if town board members directed the public to participate in the prayers, singled out dissidents for opprobrium, or indicated that their decisions might be influenced by a person's acquiescence in the prayer opportunity."[343] However, noting that the attendees at issues are adults,[344] and distinguishing the precedents involving prayer at public school events,[345] the plurality emphasized that the invocations occur "during the ceremonial portion of the town's meeting" when the board is "not engaged in policymaking"; that "members of the public are [not] dissuaded from leaving the meeting room during the prayer, arriving late, or even, as happened here, making a later protest"; that "[s]hould nonbelievers choose to exit the room during a prayer they find distasteful, their absence will not stand out as disrespectful or even noteworthy"; and that "should they remain, their quiet acquiescence will not, in light of our traditions, be interpreted as an agreement with the words or ideas expressed."[346]

Following *Town of Greece*, then, a government's use of "[c]eremonial prayer"[347] may be upheld under the methodology of *Marsh*, based on original and traditional understanding, as long as the practice neither evinces "a pattern of prayers that over time denigrate,

340 *Id.*

341 *Id.* at 1825 (opinion of Kennedy, J., joined by Roberts, C.J., and Alito, J.). Justices Scalia and Thomas did not join this portion of Kennedy's opinion. *See id.* at 1835 (Thomas, J., concurring in part and concurring in the judgment, joined in part by Scalia, J.).

342 *Id.*

343 *Id.* at 1826.

344 *See id.* ("[R]respondents stated that the prayers gave them offense and made them feel excluded and disrespected. Offense, however, does not equate to coercion. Adults often encounter speech they find disagreeable; and an Establishment Clause violation is not made out any time a person experiences a sense of affront from the expression of contrary religious views in a legislative forum, especially where, as here, any member of the public is welcome in turn to offer an invocation reflecting his or her own convictions."); *id.* at 1827 [noting that the litigants and other attendees "mature adults, who 'presumably' are 'not readily susceptible to religious indoctrination or peer pressure.' (quoting Marsh, 463 U.S., at 792)].

345 *See id.* at 1827 [distinguishing Lee v. Weisman, 505 U.S. 577 (1992), and Santa Fe Indep. Sch. Dist. v. Doe, 530 U.S. 290 (2000)].

346 *Id.*

347 *Id.* at 1827. "Ceremonial prayer is but a recognition that, since this Nation was founded and until the present day, many Americans deem that their own existence must be understood by precepts far beyond the authority of government to alter or define and that willing participation in civic affairs can be consistent with a brief acknowledgment of their belief in a higher power, always with due respect for those who adhere to other beliefs.… It is not an unconstitutional establishment of religion." *Id.* at 1827–8.

proselytize, or betray an impermissible government purpose"[348] nor "direct[s] the public to participate in the prayers, single[s] out dissidents for opprobrium, or indicate[s] that [the government's] decisions might be influenced by a person's acquiescence in the prayer opportunity."[349] Nevertheless, questions still remain following *Town of Greece*. In particular, to what practices of government may *Marsh*'s (and now *Town of Greece*'s) methodology apply, especially apart from prayer, and what specifically might trigger the limitations articulated in *Marsh* and clarified in *Town of Greece*?

As for the applicability of a *Marsh*-type analysis, the available data points from the Court's own rulings are small in number and modest in illumination. Obviously, *Marsh*'s methodology can apply to federal, state, and local legislative or quasi-legislative prayer. Conversely, as noted, the Court has explicitly refused to extend it to the public-school context, even when the government practice might be characterized as ceremonial prayer. Apart from governmental prayer, reliance on historical and traditional understanding as a primary methodological consideration has surfaced in at least three other Establishment Clause cases from the Court. Two of these were decided after *Marsh*: a 1984 Court decision upholding a municipality's display of a nativity scene[350] and a 2005 plurality opinion (though majority judgment) upholding a Ten Commandments monument on the grounds of a state capitol.[351] The third case was decided in 1970, well before *Marsh*, but similarly relied on historical and traditional understanding to upheld a state-authorized property tax exemption for religious organizations.[352]

Lower courts, for their part, have differed with regard to the applicability of *Marsh*'s approach. Some lower courts, after *Marsh* but before *Town of Greece*, expressed reluctance to extend *Marsh*'s reasoning beyond the particular domain of legislative prayer,[353] and the Fourth Circuit held that a supper prayer at a state military institute did not fall within the ambit of *Marsh* because "the supper prayer does not share *Marsh*'s 'unique history.' In fact, public universities and military colleges ... did not exist when the Bill of Rights was adopted."[354] More recently, following *Town of Greece*, the Seventh Circuit refused to extend the methodology of *Marsh* and *Town of Greece* to analyze a state law allowing only religious officials to solemnize marriages. A critical aspect of those cases, the court reasoned, is that "they concern what a chosen agent of the government says as part of the government's own operations. They do not concern how a state regulates private conduct." The challenged state marriage law, "by contrast, is regulatory. It specifies which private actors are entitled to engage in a particular act in private venues. So although *Marsh* and *Greece* show that a government may, consistent with the First Amendment, open legislative sessions with Christian prayers while not inviting leaders of

348 *Id.* at 1824.
349 *Id.* at 1826.
350 *See* Lynch v. Donnelly, 465 U.S. 668, 673–7 (1984).
351 *See* Van Orden v. Perry, 545 U.S. 677, 686–90 (2005) (plurality opinion). Justice Breyer did not join the plurality opinion but concurred in, and provided a fifth vote for, the judgment. While he cited *Marsh*, his overall analysis was not rooted primarily in the history and tradition of the practice. *See id.* at 698–705 (Breyer, J., concurring in the judgment).
352 *See* Walz v. Tax Comm'n, 397 U.S. 664, 676–8 (1970).
353 *See, e.g.*, Cammack v. Waihee, 932 F.2d 765, 772 (9th Cir. 1991) (finding it inapplicable to an assessment of a state Good Friday holiday), *cert. denied*, 505 U.S. 1219 (1992); Graham v. Cent. Cmty. Sch. Dist., 608 F. Supp. 531, 535 (S.D. Iowa 1985) (limiting it to "the legislative setting").
354 Mellen v. Bunting, 327 F.3d 355, 370 (4th Cir. 2003), *cert. denied*, 541 U.S. 1019 (2004).

other religions, they do not begin to suggest that a state could limit the solemnization of weddings to Christians, while excluding Judaism, Islam, Buddhism, and – humanism."[355]

By comparison, a number of other lower courts before *Town of Greece* extended *Marsh*'s approach to assess and uphold a variety of practices, including the creation of a legislative prayer room in a state capitol building,[356] the provision and financing of a military chaplaincy program,[357] the use of an invocation and benediction at a state university graduation,[358] the commencement of school board meetings with prayer delivered by board members[359] or by members of the public,[360] the practice of privately led prayer at the start of county commission meetings[361] and city council meetings (now ratified by *Town of Greece*),[362] and the *selection* of opening prayers at a city council meeting (a slight variation on *Town of Greece*).[363]

As for the interpretation and application of *Marsh*'s limitations, lower courts prior to *Town of Greece* exhibited similar division, though typically over the issue of denominational specificity. For example, in a ruling now presumably abrogated by *Town of Greece*, the Fourth Circuit struck down a town council's practice of opening its meetings with prayers that specifically referred to Jesus Christ.[364] In contrast, the Eleventh Circuit (correctly anticipating *Town of Greece*'s reasoning) upheld a county's practice of opening commission meetings with prayers by volunteer clergy or lay community members, even though the majority of speakers were Christian and some of the prayers invoked religion-specific doctrines and terms.[365] However, and also presumably consistent with *Town of Greece*, the Eleventh Circuit further held that the county's prior selection policy, which had categorically excluded certain faiths, was not constitutional because it

355 Ctr. for Inquiry, Inc. v. Marion Circuit Ct. Clerk, 758 F.3d 869, 874 (7th Cir. 2014) (citation omitted). "*Marsh* and *Greece* observe that the meaning of the Constitution's religion clauses depends in part on historical practices. One cannot understand centuries-old language apart from the culture in which the language was written and originally operated. The history of marriage is that the state came late to the party. For hundreds of years, in the legal tradition that we inherited from England, the persons who could solemnize marriages included clergy, public officials, sea captains, notaries public, and the celebrants themselves. When Indiana codified the list in 1857 ... it left off captains, notaries, and the marrying couple, though it included Quakers and German Baptists. It also left off Islam, Baha'i, and Mormons, which now have their own accommodations." *Id.* at 875.

356 *See* Van Zandt v. Thompson, 839 F.2d 1215, 1218–20 (7th Cir. 1988).

357 *See* Katcoff v. Marsh, 755 F.2d 223, 232–3 (2d Cir. 1985).

358 *See* Tanford v. Brand, 104 F.3d 982, 986 (7th Cir. 1997) (upholding an invocation and benediction at a state university commencement because the practice "has prevailed for 155 years and is widespread throughout the nation"), *cert. denied*, 522 U.S. 814 (1997).

359 *See* Dobrich v. Walls, 380 F. Supp. 2d 366, 377 (D. Del. 2005); *but cf.* Coles v. Cleveland Bd. of Educ., 171 F.3d 369, 376–7 (6th Cir. 1999) (holding that the *Marsh* analysis does not apply to school board meetings).

360 *See* Bacus v. Palo Verde Unified Sch. Dist. Bd. of Educ., 11 F. Supp. 2d 1192, 1196–8 (C.D. Cal. 1998).

361 *See* Pelphrey v. Cobb Cnty., Ga., 547 F.3d 1263, 1275–7 (11th Cir. 2008).

362 *See* Rubin v. City of Lancaster, 710 F.3d 1087, 1091 (9th Cir. 2013).

363 *See* Snyder v. Murray City Corp., 159 F.3d 1227, 1233–6 (10th Cir. 1998) (*en banc*), *cert. denied*, 526 U.S. 1039 (1999).

364 *See* Wynne v. Town of Great Falls, S.C., 376 F.3d 292, 298 (4th Cir. 2004), *cert. denied*, 545 U.S. 1152 (2005). The Fourth Circuit reached a similar result in Joyner v. Forsyth Cnty., N.C., 653 F.3d 341 (4th Cir. 2011), *cert. denied*, 132 S. Ct. 1097 (2012), although in that case "almost every ... invocation ... closed with the phrase, 'For we do make this prayer in Your Son Jesus' name, Amen.'" *Id.* at 342.

365 *See, e.g.*, Pelphrey, 547 F.3d at 1277–8; *see also* Rubin, 710 F.3d at 1091–1101 (upholding a city council meeting practice that yielded similar prayers).

demonstrated the "impermissible motive" – purposeful religious discrimination – disallowed under *Marsh*.[366] Likewise, a federal district court enjoined a practice by a county council pursuant to which the council president, at the start of every meeting, would himself face the audience and recite the Lord's Prayer – specifically a Protestant version of that prayer.[367]

## 2. *To Permissible Accommodations of Religious Exercise*

A second circumstance in which the Establishment Clause is applied distinctively or flexibly is when the government is providing a permissible or discretionary accommodation to religious practices; that is, when it is attempting to protect religious liberty above and beyond what the Free Exercise Clause requires.[368] At the legislative level, such efforts can take the form of customized exceptions to particular statutes (described by some as "retail" accommodations), or they can take the form of widely applicable religious freedom statutes, such as the Religious Freedom Restoration Act (RFRA) or its many state analogues (so-called wholesale accommodations).[369] At the administrative level, permissible accommodations similarly may be spelled out in particular regulations, much like the first legislative approach, or they may be available on request pursuant to a standing published policy governing an agency as a whole or governing one or more of an agency's functions. Whatever their form, they are addressed here because their subject matter being religion, they must abide by the Establishment Clause, but the application of the clause to permissible accommodations may differ from its ordinary application as described Section C.

Accommodations of religion date from the nation's founding, with two of the most well known being relief from militia duty for religious pacifists[370] and relief from taxation for church property.[371] Yet these exemptions from otherwise generally applicable obligations were not necessarily required by the religious freedom guarantees of the federal or state

366 *See* Pelphrey, 547 F.3d at 1281–2.

367 *See* Mullin v. Sussex Cnty., Del., 861 F. Supp. 2d 411, 424 (D. Del. 2012).

368 Permissible accommodations and their constitutionality are also addressed by the treatise at Chapters 5.G.2 and 18.D.1 and I.2.

369 *See, e.g.*, Richard C. Schragger, *The Role of the Local in the Doctrine and Discourse of Religious Liberty*, 117 Harv. L. Rev. 1810, 1844 (2004) (distinguishing "between wholesale, blanket religion-benefiting trumps, and retail, localized religion-benefiting accommodations").

370 *See* Michael W. McConnell, *The Origins and Historical Understanding of the Free Exercise of Religion*, 103 Harv. L. Rev. 1409, 1468–9 (1990) (quoting a resolution from the Continental Congress as well as earlier colonial exemptions). Proposed exemptions under what would become the Second Amendment were considered but rejected. *See id.* at 1500–3; Robert R. Russell, *Development of Conscientious Objector Recognition in the United States*, 20 Geo. Wash. L. Rev. 409, 414–17 (1952).

371 *See* Walz v. Tax Comm'n of City of N.Y., 397 U.S. 664, 676–7 (1970) (recounting the early history of state and federal tax exemptions for churches and religious societies). Another example, also with deep historical roots, is the provision of chaplains to persons who are incarcerated; *see* Hartmann v. Cal. Dep't of Corr. & Rehab., 707 F.3d 1114, 1126 (9th Cir. 2013) ("Prison employment of full-time chaplains to assist inmates in their religious exercise is a permissible accommodation within the established parameters of the First Amendment."); Chapter 18.D.3, or to members of the armed forces. *See* McCreary Cnty., Ky. v. ACLU of Ky., 545 U.S. 844, 845 (2005) ("[S]pending government money on the clergy looks like establishing religion, but if the government cannot pay for military chaplains a good many soldiers and sailors would be kept from the opportunity to exercise their chosen religions."); Katcoff v. Marsh, 755 F.2d 223 (2d Cir. 1985) (upholding the U.S. Army's chaplaincy program); Chapter 18.I.2.

constitutions. Rather, they appear to have been, in today's terms, permissible or discretionary accommodations as opposed to accommodations that are constitutionally compelled and judicially mandated. In modern times, the Supreme Court has sanctioned the basic concept of permissible accommodations[372] and has recognized "that 'there is room for play in the joints between' the Free Exercise and Establishment Clauses, allowing the government to accommodate religion beyond free exercise requirements, without offense to the Establishment Clause."[373] Thus, though it may "seem strange to say that accommodating religion can constitute a 'secular' or non-religious purpose; nevertheless ... the government may 'accommodate the free exercise of religion by relieving people from generally applicable rules that interfere with their religious callings' without violating the establishment clause."[374]

The Court also has indicated, however, that governments may not provide such accommodations without limit and that the Establishment Clause will, beyond certain bounds, convert the permissible into the impermissible. For example, when the Court in *Cutter v. Wilkinson*[375] upheld a discretionary accommodation scheme (essentially for prisoners) as part of the Religious Land Use and Institutionalized Persons Act (RLUIPA),[376] it noted three factors that rendered the scheme, as written, valid under the Establishment Clause.[377] First, the scheme "alleviates exceptional government-created

[372] *See* Bd. of Educ. of Kiryas Joel Vill. Sch. Dist. v. Grumet, 512 U.S. 687, 705–6 (1994); Employment Div. v. Smith, 494 U.S. 872, 890 (1990); Corp. of Presiding Bishop of Church of Jesus Christ of Latter-Day Saints v. Amos, 483 U.S. 327, 334–5 (1987).

[373] Cutter v. Wilkinson, 544 U.S. 709, 713 (2005) [quoting Locke v. Davey, 540 U.S. 712, 718 (2004)]; *see also id.* at 719 ["Our decisions recognize that 'there is room for play in the joints' between the Clauses, some space for legislative action neither compelled by the Free Exercise Clause nor prohibited by the Establishment Clause." (citation omitted) (quoting Walz, 397 U.S. at 669)]; Kaufman v. McCaughtry, 419 F.3d 678, 684 (7th Cir. 2005) ("[I]n certain circumstances the government may make special accommodations for religious practices that are not extended to nonreligious practices without violating the Establishment Clause."); Ehlers-Renzi v. Connelly Sch. of the Holy Child, Inc., 224 F.3d 283, 287 (4th Cir. 2000) (explaining that "the government is entitled to accommodate religion without violating the Establishment Clause, and at times the government must do so" and that "[t]his authorized ... accommodation of religion is a necessary aspect of the Establishment Clause jurisprudence because, without it, government would find itself effectively and unconstitutionally promoting the absence of religion over its practice"), *cert. denied*, 531 U.S. 1192 (2001).

[374] Kaufman v. McCaughtry, 422 F. Supp. 2d 1016, 1020 (W.D. Wis. 2006) [quoting Lee v. Weisman, 505 U.S. 577, 627 (1992)]. "Consequently, courts have said that the establishment clause does not bar all governmental preference for religion over irreligion." *Id.* [citing Van Orden v. Perry, 545 U.S. 677, 684 n. 3 (2005)].

[375] 544 U.S. 709 (2005).

[376] Pub. L. No. 106–274, 114 Stat. 803 (Sept. 22, 2000) (codified at 42 U.S.C. §§ 2000cc to 2000cc-5).

[377] *See* Cutter, 544 U.S. at 720 (concluding that the scheme "fits within the corridor between the Religion Clauses: On its face, the Act qualifies as a permissible legislative accommodation of religion that is not barred by the Establishment Clause"). Several lower courts have upheld under the Establishment Clause the other major federal accommodation law, the Religious Freedom Restoration Act, Pub. L. No. 103–141, 107 Stat. 1488 (codified as amended at 42 U.S.C. §§ 2000bb to 2000bb-4). *See* Hankins v. Lyght, 441 F.3d 96, 108–9 (2d Cir. 2006); Christians v. Crystal Evangelical Free Church, 141 F.3d 854, 861–3 (8th Cir. 1998); EEOC v. Catholic Univ. of Am., 83 F.3d 455, 470 (D.C. Cir. 1996). They have also upheld the religious antidiscrimination protections of Title VII of the Civil Rights Act of 1964, 42 U.S.C. §§ 2000e(j) and 2000e-2, even though the burdens (apart from public employment) are not government created. *See* EEOC v. Ithaca Indus., Inc., 849 F.2d 116, 119 (4th Cir. 1988), *cert. denied*, 488 U.S. 924 (1988); Int'l Ass'n of Machinists & Aerospace Workers, Lodge 751 v. Boeing Co., 833 F.3d 165, 170–1 (9th Cir. 1987), *cert. denied*, 485 U.S. 1014 (1988); Protos v. Volkswagen of Am., Inc., 797 F.2d 129, 135–7 (3d Cir. 1986), *cert. denied*, 479 U.S. 972 (1986);

burdens on private religious exercise" and, in particular, removes burdens on "persons who are unable freely to attend to their religious needs and are therefore dependent on the government's permission and accommodation for exercise of their religion."[378] Second, it allows, if not requires, courts to "take adequate account of the burdens a requested accommodation may impose on nonbeneficiaries,"[379] including a correctional institution's "need to maintain order and safety."[380] Third, and lastly, its prescriptions can (and must) "be administered neutrally among different faiths."[381]

The Court's analysis in *Cutter* sheds significant light on the relationship between discretionary accommodations and the Establishment Clause.[382] For one thing, the Court did not apply the *Lemon* test at all, even though various components of *Lemon* are routinely applied in Establishment Clause cases and even though the Sixth Circuit had

McDaniel v. Essex Int'l, Inc., 696 F.2d 34, 36–7 (6th Cir. 1982); Anderson v. Gen. Dynamics Convair Aerospace Div., 648 F.2d 1247 (9th Cir. 1981), *cert. denied*, 454 U.S. 1145 (1982); Nottelson v. Smith Steel Workers D.A.L.U. 19806, AFL-CIO, 643 F.2d 445, 454–5 (7th Cir. 1981), *cert. denied*, 454 U.S. 1046 (1981); Hardison v. Trans World Airlines, Inc., 527 F.2d 33 (8th Cir. 1975), *rev'd on other grounds*, 432 U.S. 63 (1977).

378 Cutter, 544 U.S. at 721 [citing Kiryas Joel, 512 U.S. at 705; Amos, 483 U.S. at 349 (O'Connor, J., concurring in the judgment)]; *see also* Tex. Monthly, Inc. v. Bullock, 489 U.S. 1, 15, 18 (1989); Midrash Sephardi, Inc. v. Town of Surfside, 366 F.3d 1214, 1241 (11th Cir. 2004); Children's Healthcare Is a Legal Duty, Inc. v. Min De Parle, 212 F.3d 1084, 1094 (8th Cir. 2000) (examining the substantiality of the burden alleviated, though not requiring the degree of burden necessitating a mandatory accommodation under the Free Exercise Clause), *cert. denied*, 532 U.S. 957 (2001); Kent Greenawalt, *Establishment Clause Limits on Free Exercise Accommodations*, 110 W. Va. L. Rev. 343, 348–50 (2007) (addressing this requirement, noting its possible variations); *cf.* Forest Hills Early Learning Ctr., Inc. v. Lukhard, 728 F.2d 230, 239–40 (4th Cir. 1984) ("It does not seem possible – without wholly abdicating the judicial review function – to hold the accommodation a valid secular legislative purpose for the exemption except on the basis of an independent judicial determination that free exercise rights justifying the accommodation did in fact exist.")

379 Cutter, 544 U.S. at 720 (citing Estate of Thornton v. Caldor, Inc., 472 U.S. 703 (1985)); *see also* Tex. Monthly, 489 U.S. at 15; Children's Healthcare, 212 F.3d at 1093–5; Greenawalt, *supra* note 378, at 353–6. *Estate of Thornton* struck down a state law providing an unqualified right of employees not to work on the Sabbath, taking no account of whether the statute's application "would cause [an] employer substantial economic burdens or ... require the imposition of significant burdens on other employees required to work in place of the Sabbath observers." Estate of Thornton, 472 U.S. at 710. For a critical assessment of *Estate of Thornton*, *see* Greenawalt, *supra* note 378, at 345–7.

380 Cutter, 544 U.S. at 722.

381 *Id.* at 720 (citing *Kiryas Joel*); *see also* Walz, 397 U.S. at 673 (upholding a tax exemption scheme that had "not singled out one particular church or religious group or even churches as such" but rather extended "to all houses of religious worship"); Ctr. for Inquiry, Inc. v. Marion Circuit Ct. Clerk, 758 F.3d 869, 872 (7th Cir. 2014) ["Neutrality is essential to the validity of an accommodation. A state could not, for example, permit Catholic priests to solemnize weddings while forbidding Baptist ministers to do so." (citations omitted)]; Children's Healthcare Is a Legal Duty, Inc. v. Vladeck, 938 F. Supp. 1466, 1479–81, 1483–5 (D. Minn. 1996) (invalidating the exemption only of Christian Science sanatoria from federal Medicaid statutes). *Kiryas Joel* invalidated an accommodation in part because it was granted not pursuant to a standardized scheme but rather on an ad hoc, seemingly sect-specific basis, which both increased the prospect of religious favoritism or disfavoritism and decreased the ability of courts to discern whether such favoritism or disfavoritism has taken place. *See* Kiryas Joel, 512 U.S. at 702–5.

382 Prior to *Cutter*, the permissible accommodations landscape was less clear. Although it was understood that "the range of permissible state accommodation to free exercise rights runs ... out to limits ultimately imposed by the establishment clause ... [w]here those limits of permissible accommodation lie in a particular case involve[d] a 'value judgment' guided only by historical inquiry and prior authoritative judicial decisions." Forest Hills Early Learning Ctr., Inc. v. Lukhard, 728 F.2d 230, 241 (4th Cir. 1984) (citation omitted) (quoting Walz, 397 U.S. at 669).

relied on the test.[383] This could be indicative of *Lemon*'s own uncertain status in the realm of Establishment Clause analysis.[384] More likely, however, it reveals the Court's view that governmental efforts to accommodate religious practices should be assessed differently than, say, county executives' decisions to post the Ten Commandments in their courthouses[385] or public school district policies that encourage student-led prayers before high school football games.[386] For another thing, the Court's assessment of RLUIPA was based on a *facial* challenge to the statute; that is, it upheld the statute as written and did not assess its application to any particular litigant or set of facts. Accordingly, RLUIPA could engender accommodations that *do* violate the Establishment Clause if one or more of the three considerations identified by the Court are not honored – if, for example, the statute is applied in a way that alleviates burdens on religious exercise that are not "exceptional" or not "government-created" or is applied without taking "adequate account of the burdens a requested accommodation may impose on nonbeneficiaries," such as prisons officials or other inmates, or is not in fact "administered neutrally among different faiths."[387]

Besides the three limitations identified in *Cutter*, the Court's earlier decisions as well as various lower court rulings suggest that the Establishment Clause may impose at least two other constraints on discretionary accommodations, although the status of these other possible constraints is not entirely clear.[388] First, and consistent with the Establishment Clause's limit on discrimination between religion and nonreligion, some of the Court's cases suggest that an accommodation may be less problematic under the Establishment Clause if it is offered to nonreligious persons or institutions as well as religious ones, as opposed to the latter alone.[389] However, the fact that RLUIPA, which accommodates only religious practices, was upheld by a unanimous Court that did not

383 *See* Cutter, 544 U.S. at 717 & n. 6 (noting the lower court's use of the *Lemon* test and then simply remarking that it would "resolve this case on other grounds").

384 *See, e.g.*, Van Orden v. Perry, 545 U.S. 677, 686 (2005) (plurality opinion) (not applying *Lemon* to evaluate a Ten Commandments monument on the grounds of a state capitol, expressing uncertainty regarding "the fate of the *Lemon* test in the larger scheme of Establishment Clause jurisprudence"); Zelman v. Simmons-Harris, 536 U.S. 639 (2002) (not applying *Lemon* to assess a school voucher program).

385 *See* McCreary Cnty., Ky. v. ACLU of Ky., 545 U.S. 844 (2005) (using *Lemon*).

386 *See* Santa Fe Indep. Sch. Dist. v. Doe, 530 U.S. 290, 314–16 (2000) (using *Lemon*).

387 *See* Cutter, 544 U.S. at 725 ["In upholding RLUIPA's institutionalized-persons provision, we emphasize that [the prison officials] 'have raised a facial challenge to [the Act's] constitutionality, and have not contended that under the facts of any of [prisoners'] specific cases ... [that] applying RLUIPA would produce unconstitutional results.'" (quoting district court opinion)].

388 In addition to the three *Cutter* limits and the two possible other limits identified here, an accommodation will not be valid if it "impermissibly assign[s] political authority to a religious group on the basis of religion." Greenawalt, *supra* note 378, at 350 [citing Kiryas Joel, 512 U.S. at 699; *id.* at 722 (Kennedy, J., concurring in the judgment)].

389 *See* Kiryas Joel, 512 U.S. at 704–5; Tex. Monthly, 489 U.S. at 15–17; *cf. also* Ctr. for Inquiry, Inc. v. Marion Circuit Ct. Clerk, 758 F.3d 869, 873 (7th Cir. 2014) ("A state may accommodate religious views that impose extra burdens ... but this does not imply an ability to favor religions over non-theistic groups that have moral stances that are equivalent to theistic ones except for non-belief in God or unwillingness to call themselves religions."); Hernandez v. Comm'r, 819 F.2d 1212, 1225 (1st Cir. 1987) ("[I]f the government were lured into granting special tax deductions because of particular religious beliefs but for no other reasons, it would run up against the Establishment clause prohibition of religious endorsement."), *aff'd*, 490 U.S. 680 (1989); Greenawalt, *supra* note 378, at 353. *But see* Amos, 483 U.S. at 338 ("Where ... government acts with the proper purpose of lifting a regulation that burdens the exercise of religion, we see no reason to require that the exemption comes packaged with benefits to secular entities.").

mention this consideration suggests that, at least within government-controlled settings such as prisons, it is no longer as meaningful as it may once have been,[390] though it may have application to exemptions in other settings such as regulatory or tax laws.[391] Second, some lower courts have indicated that the Establishment Clause may be triggered by an accommodation scheme that induces, rather than simply facilitates, religious belief or practice.[392] Other lower courts essentially disagree.[393] The *Cutter* Court, for its part, addressed this consideration only tangentially, commenting that "[w]hile some accommodations of religious observance ... might attract joiners seeking a break in their closely guarded day, we doubt that all accommodations would be perceived as 'benefits.' "[394] The Court also may have addressed it implicitly by its declaration that prison officials "would be free to resist the imposition" of RLUIPA's prescriptions if "inmate requests for religious accommodations become excessive."[395] In all events, it is fair to say that the present status of this second additional possible consideration is as uncertain as, if not more uncertain than, the first.

## E. Standing and the Establishment Clause

Article III of the Constitution empowers the federal courts to hear only certain categories of suits and, within those categories, only suits that can be deemed "Cases"

390 *See, e.g.*, Madison v. Riter, 355 F.3d 310, 318 (4th Cir. 2003) (in a pre-*Cutter* challenge to RLUIPA's prison accommodation scheme, rejecting "the theory ... that Congress impermissibly advances religion when it acts to lift burdens on religious exercise yet fails to consider whether other rights are similarly threatened"), *cert. denied*, 545 U.S. 1103 (2005)

391 *See, e.g.*, Freedom from Religion Found., Inc. v. Lew, 983 F. Supp. 2d 1051, 1062–3 (W.D. Wis. 2013) (invalidating a tax exemption exclusively for "ministers of the gospel" because it "results in preferential treatment for religious messages over secular ones" and distinguishing "the cases in which the Supreme Court has upheld religious accommodations" as arising "in contexts that otherwise would result in severe restrictions on free exercise"); Gospel Missions of Am. v. Bennett, 951 F. Supp. 1429, 1448 n. 18 (C.D. Cal. 1997) [addressing exemptions in a municipal solicitation ordinance, asserting that "[s]tatutes that confer benefits upon religious organizations have generally withstood constitutional attack only where 'the benefits derived by religious organizations flowed to a large number of nonreligious groups as well' " (quoting Tex. Monthly, 489 U.S. at 11)].

392 *See* Kong v. Scully, 341 F.3d 1132, 1139 (9th Cir. 2003) (noting that "[n]o one would become a Christian Scientist in order to obtain admission to [a religious nonmedical health care institution, which under federal law is now subject to Medicaid and Medicare reimbursement] ... when the cost of such a conversion would be renunciation of all medical treatment"), *opinion amended on denial of reh'g*, 357 F.3d 895 (9th Cir. 2004); Children's Healthcare, 212 F.3d at 1098 (finding that the challenged law "does not create any more of an incentive for persons to engage in religion than other religious accommodations that have been upheld by the Supreme Court"); Greenawalt, *supra* note 378, at 350–1 (discussing this aspect of accommodations); Michael W. McConnell, *Accommodation of Religion: An Update and a Response to Critics*, 60 GEO. WASH. L. REV. 685, 700–2 (1992) (same).

393 *See, e.g.*, Madison, 355 F.3d at 319 (finding it "not a concern under the Establishment Clause" that RLUIPA "may create incentives for secular prisoners to cloak secular requests in religious garb and thus may increase the burden on state and local officials in processing RLUIPA claims").

394 Cutter, 544 U.S. at 721 n. 10. "For example, congressional hearings on RLUIPA revealed that one state corrections system served as its kosher diet 'a fruit, a vegetable, a granola bar, and a liquid nutritional supplement – each and every meal.' " *Id.* [quoting Hearing on Protecting Religious Freedom after *Boerne v. Flores* before the Subcommittee on the Constitution of the House Committee on the Judiciary, 105th Cong., 2d Sess., pt. 3, at 39 (1998) (statement of Isaac M. Jaroslawicz, Director of Legal Affairs for the Aleph Institute)].

395 *Id.* at 726.

or "Controversies."[396] The Supreme Court, in turn, has explained that "Cases" and "Controversies" are disputes exhibiting specific characteristics, chief among them that the party invoking a federal court's jurisdiction – at the trial level, usually the plaintiff – have *standing*, which itself requires proof of three elements: *first*, that the party is suffering a so-called injury-in-fact, or factual injury; *second*, that this injury is fairly traceable to the defendant's conduct; and *third*, that a favorable ruling would likely redress the injury.[397] In addition to these three elements of standing, which the Court describes as constitutionally required,[398] the Court has further placed on the jurisdiction of federal courts certain "prudential" limits, which are not constitutionally required but which rest on constitutional principles such as the separation of powers.[399]

This final section of the chapter will address two aspects of standing that are potentially unique to suits alleging violations of the Establishment Clause. The first is an exception that the Court recognized in the case of *Flast v. Cohen*.[400] This so-called *Flast* exception, though increasingly narrowed since its inception, continues to be retained by the Court despite calls by some justices to eliminate it altogether. The second aspect of standing that will be explored is the extent to which the domain of sufficient factual injuries in Establishment Clause suits, particularly those alleging harm by governmental religious expression, might be broader or at least different from the domain of factual injuries ordinarily necessary to demonstrate constitutional standing.

### 1. *The Availability of Taxpayer Standing*

In 1968, at a time when the substantive scope of the Establishment Clause was itself arguably expanding,[401] the Court recognized in the Establishment Clause case of *Flast v. Cohen* an exception within its standing jurisprudence. The plaintiffs in *Flast*, who were challenging congressional education expenditures, alleged that they had suffered injuries as federal taxpayers. At that time and today, however, one's status as a federal taxpayer (no matter how much one pays in taxes) is normally not adequate to create an injury for the purpose of standing: either the harm is not sufficiently individualized or personal to satisfy the *constitutional* requirement of factual injury,[402] or the harm is

396 U.S. Const. art. III, § 2. Prominent among the categories are suits that present questions "arising under this Constitution" or "the Laws of the United States" (*id.*), which is why federal courts can hear claims under the First Amendment, for example, or under RFRA or RLUIPA.

397 *See* Lujan v. Defenders of Wildlife, 504 U.S. 555, 560–1 (1990); Allen v. Wright, 468 U.S. 737, 751 (1984).

398 *See* Allen, 468 U.S. at 751 ("The requirement of standing ... has a core component derived directly from the Constitution. A plaintiff must allege personal injury fairly traceable to the defendant's allegedly unlawful conduct and likely to be redressed by the requested relief.").

399 *See* Elk Grove Unified Sch. Dist. v. Newdow, 542 U.S. 1, 12 (2004) ["Although we have not exhaustively defined the prudential dimensions of the standing doctrine, we have explained that prudential standing encompasses 'the general prohibition on a litigant's raising another person's legal rights, the rule barring adjudication of generalized grievances more appropriately addressed in the representative branches, and the requirement that a plaintiff's complaint fall within the zone of interests protected by the law invoked.'" (quoting Allen, 468 U.S. at 751)]; Valley Forge Christian Coll. v. Ams. United for Separation of Church & State, 454 U.S. 464, 474–5 (1982).

400 392 U.S. 83 (1968).

401 *See, e.g.*, Epperson v. Arkansas, 393 U.S. 97 (1968); Sch. Dist. of Abington Twp., Pa. v. Schempp, 374 U.S. 203 (1963); Engel v. Vitale, 370 U.S. 421 (1962).

402 *See* Lujan, 504 U.S. at 560 n. 1 (explaining that an injury, in order to trigger Article III jurisdiction, must "must affect the plaintiff in a personal and individual way").

so broadly distributed among all taxpayers that it is classified as a "generalized grievance," which the *prudential* limits on standing preclude courts from adjudicating.[403] Nevertheless, the *Flast* Court found that the taxpayers had standing and that the federal judiciary could hear their suit because their pleadings demonstrated two things. First, there was "a logical link between th[eir] status [as federal taxpayers] and the type of legislative enactment attacked" because they "allege[d] the unconstitutionality ... of [an] exercise of congressional power under the taxing and spending clause of Art. I, § 8, of the Constitution."[404] Second, there was "a nexus between that status and the precise nature of the constitutional infringement alleged."[405] In particular, they claimed that "the challenged enactment exceeds [a] specific constitutional limitation imposed upon the exercise of the congressional taxing and spending power and not simply that the enactment is generally beyond the powers delegated to Congress by Art. I, § 8."[406] Given evidence of original intent and the historical relationship between taxation or spending and religious establishments, the Court found that the Establishment Clause was such a "specific constitutional limitation" on the taxing and spending power of Congress.[407]

In the ensuing decades, the *Flast* exception has survived but has exhibited some notable features and undergone significant transformation.[408] For example, the Court has yet to identify any other "specific constitutional limitation" on the taxing and spending power of Congress besides the Establishment Clause that is sufficient to satisfy the exception, thus effectively confining the exception to suits under that clause.[409] Since *Flast*, moreover, the Court itself has rarely found the exception to have been met.[410] A key reason for this is that the Court has interpreted with increasing narrowness the type of spending action that will trigger the exception. In a 1982 ruling, for instance, the Court deemed the exception inapplicable to challenges to administrative agency spending, even though the funds ultimately derive from congressional appropriations. *Flast*, it said, "limited taxpayer standing to challenges directed 'only [at] exercises of

403 *See* Allen, 468 U.S. at 751 (setting forth as a prudential limitation "the rule barring adjudication of generalized grievances more appropriately addressed in the representative branches"); Valley Forge, 454 U.S. at 474–5 ("[E]ven when [a] plaintiff has alleged redressable injury sufficient to meet the requirements of Art. III, the Court has refrained from adjudicating 'abstract questions of wide public significance' which amount to 'generalized grievances,' pervasively shared and most appropriately addressed in the representative branches."); Frothingham v. Mellon, 262 U.S. 447 (1923) (disallowing federal taxpayer standing because the plaintiff's interest as a single taxpayer was too minor, uncertain, and indirect).

404 Flast, 392 U.S. at 102. By comparison, federal taxpayer standing has not been found when the challenged enactment stems from a power other than taxing and spending. *See, e.g.*, Valley Forge, 454 U.S. at 480 (Property Clause, U.S. Const. art. IV, § 3).

405 Flast, 392 U.S. at 102.

406 *Id.* at 102–3.

407 *See id.* at 103–4.

408 *See* 13A Charles Alan Wright et al., Federal Practice & Procedure § 3531.1 (3d ed. updated Apr. 2014) ("Fate has not been kind to the *Flast* decision. In the field of taxpayer standing, it has been limited to very narrow confines.").

409 *See, e.g.*, DaimlerChrisler Corp. v. Cuno, 547 U.S. 332, 347–9 (2006) (refusing to extend the *Flast* exception to an alleged violation of the Commerce Clause, U.S. Const. art. I, § 8, cl. 3); Schlesinger v. Reservists Comm. to Stop the War, 418 U.S. 208 (1974) (same regarding the Ineligibility Clause, U.S. Const. art. I, § 6); United States v. Richardson, 418 U.S. 166 (1974) (same regarding the Accounts Clause, U.S. Const. art. I, § 9, cl. 7); *cf.* Frothingham v. Mellon, 262 U.S. 447 (1923) (finding no standing in suit alleging violations of U.S. Const. amend. X as well as the Due Process Clause, U.S. Const. amend. V, as distinguished in Flast, 392 U.S. at 105).

410 *See, e.g.*, Bowen v. Kendrick, 487 U.S. 589, 618–20 (1988).

congressional power.' "[411] A similar result was reached in 2007 by a plurality of justices, who first cautioned that *Flast* should be interpreted narrowly[412] and then reaffirmed that it applies, if at all, only to a "specific congressional action or appropriation" and not to "general appropriations to the Executive Branch" that lead to "expenditures result[ing] from executive discretion."[413] (Importantly, there could have been a majority opinion, but two justices declined to join because they wanted to overrule *Flast* outright.[414]) Finally, in 2011, the Court refused to equate legislatively created tax credits with legislative expenditures, thus further confining the reach and availability of the *Flast* exception.[415]

At the same time that it has narrowed the domain of relevant spending actions, the Court has arguably moved the basis or location of the *Flast* exception away from prudential standing to constitutional standing, thus further reducing any potential flexibility in its application. A widely shared interpretation of *Flast*'s exception, even in recent years, has been that it effected, at least in part, a judicial carve-out to the judicially imposed prudential limit on the adjudication of generalized grievances.[416] Precisely because the constitutional components of standing are an "irreducible ... minimum"[417] and thus cannot technically have exceptions, the Court's recognition of an "exception" suggested that it was operating within the prudential dimension of standing or at the interface of the prudential and constitutional dimensions (*Flast* does, after all, refer to Article III) and not within the constitutional dimension alone. If nothing else, the Court's language in *Flast* and certain post-*Flast* cases generated significant uncertainty in this regard.[418]

Its more recent rulings, however, have indicated that the *Flast* exception and the limitations on taxpayer standing, and more broadly, the prohibition on generalized grievances, arise strictly from the dictates of Article III, not from the discretionary prudential realm. A 1982 ruling suggested such an understanding, at least as to *Flast*,[419] but a 2006 ruling clearly characterized taxpayer standing (and perhaps all generalized grievances) as a problem under Article III's injury-in-fact requirement,[420] and a 2007 plurality opinion

411 Valley Forge, 454 U.S. at 479 (quoting Flast, 392 U.S. at 102).

412 *See* Hein v. Freedom from Religion Found., Inc., 551 U.S. 587, 602 (2007) (plurality opinion).

413 *Id.* at 605.

414 *See id.* at 618 (Scalia, J., concurring in the judgment, joined by Thomas, J.).

415 *See* Ariz. Christian Sch. Tuition Org. v. Winn, 131 S. Ct. 1436, 1447 (2011).

416 *See, e.g.*, Winkler v. Gates, 481 F.3d 977, 980 (7th Cir. 2007) (surmising that the exception may rest on prudential and constitutional grounds); Bell v. City of Kellogg, 922 F.2d 1418, 1423 (9th Cir. 1991) (noting "the prudential rule of *Flast*"); ACLU of Mass. v. Sebelius, 697 F. Supp. 2d 200, 204 (D. Mass. 2010) ("[T]he *Flast* Court concluded that its holding was likely motivated by prudential concerns."); Mark C. Rahdert, *Forks Taken and Roads Not Taken: Standing to Challenge Faith-Based Spending*, 32 CARDOZO L. REV. 1009, 1034 (2011) ("*Flast* ... authoriz[es] a prudential suspension of the usual prudential rule against taxpayer standing."); Craig A. Stern, *Another Sign from Hein: Does the Generalized Grievance Fail a Constitutional or a Prudential Test of Federal Standing to Sue?* 12 LEWIS & CLARK L. REV. 1169, 1208 (2008) ["[T]he *Flast* opinion for the Court itself casts the rule against hearing generalized grievances as prudential and not demanded by Article III. Two other opinions in *Flast* agree, and other authorities have so understood the *Flast* Court." (footnotes omitted)].

417 Lujan, 504 U.S. at 560.

418 *See* Duke Power Co. v. Carolina Envt'l Study Group, Inc., 438 U.S. 59, 79 n. 25 (1978) ["Both at the time of its formulation, and more recently, there have been questions as to whether the nexus requirement [of *Flast*], even in the context of taxpayers' suits, is constitutionally mandated or is instead simply a prudential limitation." (citations omitted)].

419 *See* Valley Forge, 454 U.S. at 476–9.

420 *See* DaimlerChrysler Corp., 547 U.S. at 344.

stated unequivocally that "*Flast* ... carved out a narrow exception to the general *constitutional* prohibition against taxpayer standing."[421] In 2014, a unanimous Court surmised that its larger "reluctance to entertain generalized grievances" may be a "concept that [it has] previously classified as an aspect of 'prudential standing' but for which, upon closer inspection, [it has] found that label inapt" to the extent that it has since "held that such suits do not present constitutional 'cases' or 'controversies.'"[422] Although this most recent speculation was dictum, and though the case implicated neither the Establishment Clause nor the *Flast* exception, nevertheless it currently appears that the exception, in addition to being "largely ... confined to its facts"[423] and seldom available, is very likely situated not in the discretionary realm of prudential standing but instead in the strict realm of constitutional standing.

## 2. *The Approach to Cognizable Factual Injuries*

Somewhat related to the *Flast* exception, particularly now that it seems squarely to be an aspect of constitutional standing, is another potentially unique feature of Establishment Clause standing, namely, the range or type of alleged harms that may serve as factual injuries sufficient to trigger federal court jurisdiction. According to the Supreme Court, the factual injury element of constitutional standing requires the "invasion of a legally protected interest"[424] that is "distinct and palpable,"[425] "actual or imminent,"[426] and "concrete and particularized,"[427] where "particularized ... mean[s] that the injury must affect the plaintiff in a personal and individual way."[428] Conversely, the injury (as discussed with regard to taxpayer standing) cannot be generalized or too broadly distributed, nor can it be "abstract or conjectural or hypothetical."[429]

When one's religious practices are being restricted by a criminal or regulatory law, or when one has been penalized for practicing religion, the necessary injury-in-fact is normally quite apparent, and one might then be able to invoke a federal court's jurisdiction to adjudicate a claim under the Free Exercise Clause. Such distinct and individualized harms associated with alleged Establishment Clause violations, however, are not always so apparent, and "there is uncertainty concerning how to apply the injury-in-fact requirement in the Establishment Clause context."[430] If a Ten Commandments monument is sitting on the grounds outside of a state capitol building, for example, or if a municipality sets up a static Christmas display in the corner a public park, it may be difficult to demonstrate that one has been or is being distinctly, palpably, concretely, personally, individually, and actually or imminently injured by

421 Hein, 551 U.S. at 602 (plurality opinion).
422 Lexmark Int'l, Inc. v. Static Control Components, Inc., 134 S. Ct. 1377, 1387 n. 3 (2014).
423 Hein, 551 U.S. at 609 (plurality opinion).
424 Lujan, 504 U.S. at 560.
425 Allen, 468 U.S. at 751 (internal quotations omitted).
426 Lujan, 504 U.S. at 560 (internal quotations omitted).
427 *Id.*
428 *Id.* at 560 n. 1.
429 Allen, 468 U.S. at 751 (citations and internal quotations omitted).
430 Cooper v. U.S. Postal Serv., 577 F.3d 479, 490 (2d Cir. 2009), *cert denied*, 559 U.S. 971 (2010). Moreover, "[s]everal times, the Supreme Court has considered the problem of standing in the Establishment Clause context, but so far the Court has announced no reliable and handy principles of analysis." *Id.* at 489.

simply viewing or knowing about the monument or display.[431] One might try to sue as a taxpayer, where the injury then would be economic and even quantifiable, but taxpayer suits are, as noted, vulnerable to characterization as generalized grievances and thus outside the federal courts' jurisdiction.

The often intangible nature of the alleged injuries in such cases and the prospect of no person or organization being able to challenge what may very well be an Establishment Clause violation are two factors that have led to a somewhat different or more flexible approach to the concept of factual injury in Establishment Clause cases when compared with the concept as developed and applied apart from that clause. To be sure, the normal understanding of federal court jurisdiction is that having to observe the government violate the law is not by itself a cognizable factual injury,[432] and further, the possibility that "no one would have standing … is not a reason to find standing."[433] Yet, as one district court has observed, "various Circuits [in Establishment Clause cases] have found sufficient injury-in-fact based upon the observation of offensive religious materials where plaintiffs have alleged a 'personal connection' with the challenged conduct. Such cases … [look to] the proximity of the plaintiffs to the conduct they challenged, examining circumstances such as the frequent contact between the plaintiff and the offensive conduct or display."[434]

Illustrative of this modified approach to the injury-in-fact requirement is the Fourth Circuit's decision in *Suhre v. Haywood County*,[435] in which the plaintiff claimed that a marble display of the Ten Commandments on the wall a county courtroom (a room used for a variety of county functions) "cause[d] him distress" and "filled him with revulsion" but did not actually "cause him to alter his conduct in any way."[436] Reversing the district court, the Fourth Circuit concluded that the plaintiff had standing in light of three considerations: his "*unwelcome direct contact* with a religious display that appear[ed] to be endorsed by the state,"[437] his "*personal connection* between the plaintiff and the challenged display *in his … home community*,"[438] and the fact that "the display that cause[d]

431 *See* Cooper, 577 F.3d at 489 ["Standing is often a tough question in the Establishment Clause context, where the injuries alleged are to the feelings alone. This is often the case in religious display cases where the fact of exposure becomes the basis for injury and jurisdiction." (footnote omitted)].

432 *See* Allen, 468 U.S. at 755 (noting that plaintiffs "have no standing to complain simply that their Government is violating the law").

433 Schlesinger v. Reservists Cmte. to Stop the War, 418 U.S. 208, 227 (1974); *accord* Clapper v. Amnesty Int'l USA, 133 S. Ct. 1138, 1154 (2013); Valley Forge, 454 U.S. at 489.

434 Newdow v. Cong. of U.S. of Am., 435 F. Supp. 2d 1066, 1073 (E.D. Cal. 2006) (citations omitted) [quoting Newdow v. Bush, 355 F. Supp. 2d 265, 278 (D.D.C. 2005), and citing Suhre v. Haywood Cnty., 131 F.3d 1083, 1086 (4th Cir. 1997); Washegesic v. Bloomingdale Pub. Sch., 33 F.3d 679, 682 (6th Cir. 1994); Saladin v. City of Milledgeville, 812 F.2d 687, 691 (11th Cir. 1987); Newdow, 355 F. Supp. 2d at 277–8], *aff'd sub nom.* Newdow v. Lefevre, 598 F.3d 638 (9th Cir. 2010), *cert. denied*, 131 S. Ct. 1612 (2011).

435 131 F.3d 1083 (4th Cir. 1997).

436 *Id.* at 1085.

437 *Id.* at 1086 (emphasis added). In that case, the plaintiff "has had two kinds of direct contacts with the Ten Commandments display.… First, [he] comes into contact with the Ten Commandments display as a customer of the courthouse" (*id.* at 1090). "Second, [he] comes into contact with the Ten Commandments display as a participant in local government. He attends public meetings in the courtroom on matters of local concern" (*Id*).

438 *Id.* at 1087 (emphases added). "The circuits have … recognized that '[t]he practices of our own community may create a larger psychological wound than someplace we are just passing through.' Plaintiffs who 'are part of the [community where challenged religious symbolism is located] and are directly affronted

[his] distress [was] located *within a public facility*" to the extent that "[r]eligious displays in public buildings may seem more in the nature of endorsements and may potentially impair the use of the affected facilities by individuals who harbor strong objections to a religious message."[439] The Fourth Circuit specifically held, however, that a plaintiff does not actually have to alter his conduct because of the display (e.g., by avoiding the courtroom), though it noted some division among courts on this point.[440]

As such division suggests, not all approaches to Establishment Clause standing are or can be as accommodating as the Fourth Circuit's approach in *Suhre*, though much depends on the context and circumstances in each case. Consider as a possible counterpoint the D.C. Circuit's *In re Navy Chaplaincy* opinion from 2008, in which it found that the plaintiffs had not demonstrated a sufficient factual injury, and thus lacked standing, based on their exposure to governmental policies or decisions that in their view contravened the Establishment Clause.[441] Specifically, a group of nonliturgical Protestant Navy chaplains challenged the Navy's retirement system, claiming that it favored Catholic chaplains in violation of the Establishment Clause's general prohibition on denominational discrimination.[442] In addition to asserting taxpayer standing pursuant to the *Flast* exception, which the court rejected because the plaintiffs were not challenging specific congressional expenditures,[443] the plaintiffs "also claim[ed] injury-in-fact from their being subjected to the 'message' of religious preference conveyed by the Navy's allegedly preferential retirement program for Catholic chaplains" insofar as the program made "them feel like second-class citizens within the Navy Chaplaincy even if they themselves have not suffered discrimination on account of their religion."[444] The D.C. Circuit, however, deemed their alleged injury inadequate. After noting the ordinary rule that "mere personal offense to government action does not give rise to standing to sue,"[445] it then refused to analogize the plaintiffs' situation to that of the religious display and prayer cases because in the latter "the Government was actively and directly communicating a religious message through religious words or religious symbols," whereas in the chaplaincy situation "the Navy [was] not communicating a religious message through religious words or religious symbols."[446] "Under plaintiffs' theory," the court reasoned, "every government *action* that allegedly violates the Establishment Clause could be re-characterized as a governmental *message* promoting religion. And therefore everyone who becomes aware of the 'message' would have standing to sue."[447]

by the presence of [this symbolism]' certainly 'have more than an abstract interest in seeing that [the government] observes the Constitution.'" *Id.* (citations omitted) (quoting Washegesic, 33 F.3d at 683, and Saladin, 812 F.2d at 693, respectively).

439 *Id.* (emphasis added).

440 *See id.* at 1087–9. "Such an extraordinary showing of injury, while sufficient, is not necessary to support standing to bring an Establishment Clause claim." *Id.* at 1088.

441 534 F.3d 756 (D.C. Cir. 2008), *cert. denied sub nom.* Chaplaincy of Full Gospel Churches v. Dep't of Navy, 556 U.S. 1167 (2009).

442 *See id.* at 758–9.

443 *See id.* at 762.

444 *Id.* at 763.

445 *Id.*

446 *Id.* at 764.

447 *Id.*

# 5 The Free Exercise Clause

## A. Introduction and Note on *Smith* and Its Aftermath

Central to the liberty of Americans is, and has long been, freedom of religion. This is true historically, given the country's tradition of religious dissent and tolerance since at least the eighteenth century. It is true demographically, given the diversity of faiths that have emerged and today coexist across the national landscape. It is true aspirationally, as manifest in the "Four Freedoms" of both the 1939 New York World's Fair[1] and President Franklin D. Roosevelt's 1941 address to Congress.[2] And it is true constitutionally, as embodied in the First Amendment, which protects religious freedom both directly, by barring the prohibition of its free exercise, and indirectly, by barring laws respecting an establishment of religion.[3]

The first of these constitutional protections, the Free Exercise Clause, is the focus of this chapter; the latter, the Establishment Clause, is addressed in Chapter 4.[4] The Free Exercise Clause, which provides that "Congress shall make no law … prohibiting the free exercise [of religion],"[5] protects both freedom of religious belief or profession and, as the text indicates, freedom of religious exercise or conduct. However, though it has often been said that religious belief is absolutely protected,[6] case law and common sense dictate that religious exercise – defined by one court as "the robust putting into practice of a person's religious beliefs"[7] – is protected only to a point.[8] That point is effectively determined by a balancing of

1 *See The Four Freedoms* at http://www.1939nyworldsfair.com/worlds_fair/wf_tour/statues/4-freedoms.htm (*Religion* being one of Leo Friedlander's *The Four Freedoms* sculptures).

2 *See* Franklin D. Roosevelt, Annual Message to Congress on the State of the Union (Jan. 6 1941) (listing as the second of four freedoms the "freedom of every person to worship God in his own way – everywhere in the world"); *available at:* http://www.fdrlibrary.marist.edu/pdfs/fftext.pdf.

3 *See* U.S. Const. amend. I ("Congress shall make no law respecting an establishment of religion, or prohibiting the free exercise thereof.").

4 Some have suggested that these two provisions, at least grammatically, actually constitute a single clause. *See, e.g.*, Akhil Reed Amar, *The Supreme Court, 1999 Term – Foreword: The Document and the Doctrine*, 114 Harv. L. Rev. 26, 119–20 (2000); Carl H. Esbeck, *The Establishment Clause as a Structural Restraint on Governmental Power*, 84 Iowa L. Rev. 1, 103 n.441 (1998).

5 U.S. Const. amend. I.

6 *See* Employment Div. v. Smith, 494 U.S. 872, 877 (1990). "The Free Exercise Clause categorically prohibits government from regulating, prohibiting, or rewarding religious beliefs as such" [McDaniel v. Paty, 435 U.S. 618, 626 (1978)], and "neither a State nor the Federal Government can constitutionally force a person 'to profess a belief or disbelief in any religion.'" Torcaso v. Watkins, 367 U.S. 488, 495 (1961) [quoting Everson v. Bd. of Educ., 330 U.S. 1, 15 (1947)].

7 Peterson v. Minidoka Cnty. Sch. Dist. No. 331, 118 F.3d 1351, 1356 (9th Cir. 1997), *amended by* 132 F.3d 1258 (9th Cir. 1997).

8 *See* Forest Hills Early Learning Ctr., Inc. v. Lukhard, 728 F.2d 230, 240 (4th Cir. 1984) (noting "the fundamental proposition that the freedom to act upon religious beliefs – to engage in religious

the respective interests of the free exercise claimant and of the government or of the public that it represents, where the precise balance or level of judicial scrutiny will vary based on the claimant's evidentiary showings.[9]

This chapter presents an overview of this balancing methodology from the required components of a free exercise claim, to the ways in which the government may or must respond to such a claim, to the different levels of judicial scrutiny that have been recognized, as well as to the factors that can determine which level of scrutiny may apply. In addition, the chapter briefly addresses the forms of religious accommodation available under the Free Exercise Clause as well as the doctrines of religious institutional autonomy that are grounded, at least partly, in that provision. As a prelude to these topics, this chapter also examines several principles that guide the protection of religious liberty in the first instance. These principles remain relevant to litigation because they continue to shape the overarching doctrinal framework and to capture intuitive or cultural sensibilities that inform legislative, judicial, and public opinion.

At the outset, major shifts and features of the religious freedom landscape must be noted. From the 1960s to 1990, the general framework of free exercise analysis as defined by the U.S. Supreme Court was understood to be this: if a claimant demonstrated that the government meaningfully burdened a practice stemming from the claimant's sincerely held religious beliefs, then the government had to show that imposing the burden was necessary to achieve a compelling interest (so-called judicial strict scrutiny).[10] In 1990, in *Employment Division v. Smith*,[11] the Court announced that this was not, or would no longer be, the general framework; rather, such strict scrutiny of a challenged law or government action would occur only if the law or action were shown to be not neutral toward religion or not generally applicable or, perhaps, if one or two other circumstances pertain.[12]

The consequences of *Smith* have been numerous and significant. The role of the federal Free Exercise Clause has been heavily diminished, and its residual doctrine

activity – is not absolute, as is the right to hold those beliefs; activity may be curtailed in some circumstances for the protection of sufficiently compelling societal interests"); *In re* Palmer, 386 A.2d 1112, 1114 (R.I. 1978) ("Despite the exalted status so rightly afforded to religious beliefs and activities that are motivated by and embody those beliefs, the freedom of an individual to practice his [or her] religion does not enjoy absolute immunity from infringement by the state."). "While the distinction between religious beliefs and religious action is more semantic than conceptual, it is still employed in First Amendment analysis. Only the former is accorded absolute protection." Int'l Soc'y for Krishna Consciousness, Inc. v. Barber, 650 F.2d 430, 444 n. 20 (2d Cir. 1981) (citation omitted). More generally, "purported ornamentations of First Amendment freedoms warrant no constitutional protection when such activities are not essential to the enjoyment of a particular right, or may otherwise be harmful to public health, safety, order, or general welfare." NYC C.L.A.S.H., Inc. v. City of N.Y., 315 F. Supp. 2d 461, 474 (S.D.N.Y. 2004).

9 *See* Wisconsin v. Yoder, 406 U.S. 205, 221 (1972) ("Where fundamental claims of religious freedom are at stake ... we must searchingly examine the interests that the State seeks to promote ... and the impediment to those objectives that would flow from recognizing the claimed [religious] exemption.").

10 *See* Hobbie v. Unemployment Appeals Comm'n, 480 U.S. 136, 141–2 (1987); Thomas v. Review Bd. of Ind. Employment Sec. Div., 450 U.S. 707, 718 (1981); Yoder, 406 U.S. at 215; Sherbert v. Verner, 374 U.S. 398, 406 (1963).

11 494 U.S. 872 (1990).

12 Not all agree that *Smith* worked a major doctrinal change or that *Smith*'s framework has yielded markedly different consequences for free exercise claimants. *See* John P. Forren, *Revisiting Four Popular Myths about the Peyote Case*, 8 U. Pa. J. Const. L. 209 (2006).

continues to be marked by uncertain content and unclear boundaries.[13] Meanwhile, the role of federal statutory law in protecting religious freedom has taken on unprecedented prominence. And state law – for much of the twentieth century largely quiet, if not dormant, in the realm of religious freedom – likewise has assumed an important place in litigation. Correspondingly, state legislatures and courts have become principal forums for debate over the protection of religious freedom, particularly when that protection might conflict with other claims of civil rights.

At the federal level, Congress in 1993 responded by enacting the Religious Freedom Restoration Act (RFRA), which reinstated the strict scrutiny standard even against neutral and generally applicable laws.[14] In 1997, however, the Supreme Court invalidated RFRA's application to state and local governments,[15] though it has apparently accepted as valid RFRA's continued application to federal law.[16] In 2000, after examining a number of possible responses to RFRA's partial demise, Congress then enacted the Religious Land Use and Institutionalized Persons Act (RLUIPA), which reimposes the strict scrutiny test on state and local governments in two distinct realms: actions relating to institutionalized persons (for the most part, prisoners) and decisions relating to land use.[17]

At the state level, over this same period and also largely in response to *Smith* or to RFRA's invalidation, several states have modified or interpreted their own laws to protect religious freedom above the federal constitutional standard, usually at the pre-*Smith* standard of strict scrutiny. In many instances (at last count, eighteen), these state law modifications have taken the form of statutory enactments, so-called state RFRAs.[18] Typically, these statutes use portions of the language of RFRA, modifying the text to exclude certain types of claims[19] or to account for subsequent developments

13 The U.S. Supreme Court has not issued a fully analyzed Free Exercise Clause case and thus has offered no further development of *Smith* for over two decades. *See* Church of the Lukumi Babalu Aye, Inc. v. City of Hialeah, 508 U.S. 520 (1993). Two intervening cases, Locke v. Davey, 540 U.S. 712 (2004) and Hosanna-Tabor Evangelical Lutheran Church & Sch. v. EEOC, 132 S. Ct. 694, 705 (2012) did involve the Free Exercise Clause but shed little light on the operation of either *Smith*'s main rule or its exceptions.

14 Pub. L. No. 103–141, 107 Stat. 1488 (Nov. 16, 1993) (codified as amended at 42 U.S.C. §§ 2000bb to 2000bb-4).

15 *See* City of Boerne v. Flores, 521 U.S. 507 (1997).

16 *See, e.g.*, Gonzales v. O Centro Espirita Beneficente Uniao do Vegetal, 546 U.S. 418 (2006) (upholding RFRA's application to federal governmental action, though not facing a direct challenge to the constitutionality of such application).

17 Religious Land Use and Institutionalized Persons Act (RLUIPA), Pub. L. No. 106–274, 114 Stat. 803–7 (Sept. 22, 2000) (codified at 42 U.S.C. §§ 2000cc to 2000cc-5). RLUIPA was upheld against a facial Establishment Clause challenge in Cutter v. Wilkinson, 544 U.S. 709, 720–6 (2005).

18 In alphabetical order by state, *see* Ariz. Rev. Stat. Ann. §§ 41–1493 to 41–1493.02; Conn. Gen. Stat. Ann. § 52–571b; Fla. Stat. Ann. §§ 761.01–761.05; Idaho Code §§ 73–401 to 73–404; 75 Ill. Comp. Stat. Ann. 35/1 to 35/99; Kan. Stat. Ann. §§ 60–5301 to 60-5305; Ky. Rev. Stat. Ann. § 446.350; La. Rev. Stat. §§ 5231–5242; Miss. Religious Freedom Restoration Act, 2014 Miss. Laws WL No. 196 (S.B. 2681) (Apr. 3, 2014) (enacted but not yet codified); Vernon's Ann. Mo. Stat. §§ 1.302 & 1.307; N.M. Stat. Ann. §§ 28-22-1 to 28-22-5; Okla. Stat. Ann. §§ 51-251 to 51-258; 71 Pa. Stat. Ann. §§ 2401–2407; R.I. Gen. Laws. §§ 42-80.1-1 to 42.80.1-4; S.C. Code Ann. §§ 1-32-10 to 1-32-60; Tenn. Code Ann. § 4-1-407; Tex. Civ. Prac. & Rem. Code §§ 110.001 to 110.012; Va. Code Ann. § 57-2.02.

19 *See* Thomas C. Berg, *Religious Liberty in America at the End of the Century*, 16 J.L. & Religion 187, 203 (2001) (noting that "[s]ome states exclude religious freedom claims by state prisoners" and that "Texas excludes claims against land use regulations and against civil rights laws"); Douglas Laycock, *The Religious Exemption Debate*, 11 Rutgers J.L. & Religion 139, 156 (2009) (noting several exceptions or modifications to state religious freedom laws).

or state-specific considerations.[20] In other instances (at last count, roughly a dozen), the state law modifications have entailed the judicial interpretation or reinterpretation of existing state constitutional guarantees,[21] often making reference to the pre-*Smith* cases and standards but then explicitly adopting them as part of the religious freedom provisions found in the states' own constitutions.[22] In at least one instance, the change occurred by means of state constitutional amendment.[23] The remaining states either have opted against embracing a standard more demanding than *Smith* or have simply not yet addressed the matter definitively.[24]

These changes in the topography and sources of religious freedom have enormous significance for litigants, practitioners, and judges. They also have significance for this chapter, which attempts to focus mainly on the Free Exercise Clause but invariably draws on cases decided under RFRA, RLUIPA, and various state laws. Where appropriate, this chapter will attempt to indicate reliance on or reference to religious freedom laws other than the Free Exercise Clause and occasionally also will highlight, particularly with respect to RFRA and RLUIPA, points of doctrinal or operational difference.

20 *See generally* Thomas C. Berg, *State Religious Freedom Statutes in Private and Public Education*, 32 U.C. Davis L. Rev. 531 (1999); W. Cole Durham, Jr., *State RFRAs and the Scope of Free Exercise Protection*, 32 U.C. Davis L. Rev. 665 (1999); Christopher C. Lund, *Religious Liberty After Gonzales: A Look at State RFRAs*, 55 S.D. L. Rev. 466 (2010).

21 In alphabetical order by state, *see* Swanner v. Anchorage Equal Rights Comm'n, 874 P.2d 274, 280–4 (Alaska 1994) (interpreting Alaska Const. art. I, § 4), *cert. denied*, 513 U.S. 979 (1994); City Chapel Evangelical Free, Inc. v. City of S. Bend, Ind., 744 N.E.2d 443, 445–51 (Ind. 2001) (interpreting Ind. Const. art. I, §§ 2–4); Fortin v. Roman Catholic Bishop of Portland, 871 A.2d 1208, 1227–8 (Me. 2005) (interpreting Me. Const. art. I, § 3, eliminating doubt from prior cases); Att'y Gen. v. Desilets, 636 N.E.2d 233, 235–6 (Mass. 1994) (interpreting Mass. Const. amend. art. 46, § 1); McCready v. Hoffius, 586 N.W.2d 723, 729 (Mich. 1998) (interpreting Mich. Const. art. I, § 4), *vacated in part on other grounds*, 593 N.W.2d 545 (Mich. 1999); State v. Hershberger, 462 N.W.2d 393, 397–9 (Minn. 1990) (interpreting Minn. Const. art. I, § 16); St. John's Lutheran Church v. State Comp. Ins. Fund, 830 P.2d 1271, 1276–7 (Mont. 1992) (interpreting Mont. Const. art. II, § 5); Humphrey v Lane, 728 N.E.2d 1039, 1043–5 (Ohio 2000) (interpreting Ohio Const. art. I, § 7), *cert. denied sub nom.* Fink v. Ohio, 531 U.S. 912 (2000); Hunt v. Hunt, 648 A.2d 843, 852–3 (Vt. 1994) (interpreting Vt. Const. ch. I, art. 3); Munns v. Martin, 930 P.2d 318, 321 (Wash. 1997) (interpreting Wash. Const. art. I, § 11); State v. Miller, 549 N.W.2d 235, 239–41 (Wis. 1996) (interpreting Wis. Const. art. I, § 18); *cf. In re* Williams, 152 S.E.2d 317, 326 (N.C. 1967) (interpreting what is now N.C. Const. art. I, § 13 but was then N.C. Const. art. I, § 26, though doing so well prior to *Smith*). *See also* Catholic Charities of Diocese of Albany v. Serio, 859 N.E.2d 459, 466 (N.Y. 2006) (interpreting N.Y. Const. art. I, § 3, as requiring an intermediate rather than strict level of scrutiny), *cert. denied*, 552 U.S. 816 (2007).

22 *See generally* Angela C. Carmella, *State Constitutional Protection of Religious Exercise: An Emerging Post-*Smith *Jurisprudence*, 1993 BYU L. Rev. 275; Daniel A. Crane, *Beyond RFRA: Free Exercise of Religion Comes of Age in the State Courts*, 10 St. Thomas L. Rev. 235 (1998); Christine M. Durham, *What Goes Around Comes Around: The New Relevancy of State Constitution Religion Clauses*, 38 Val. U.L. Rev. 353 (2004); Tracey Levy, *Rediscovering Rights: State Courts Reconsider the Free Exercise Clauses of Their Own Constitutions in the Wake of Employment Division v. Smith*, 67 Temp. L. Rev. 1017 (1994); Paul Benjamin Linton, *Religious Freedom Claims and Defenses under State Constitutions*, 7 U. St. Thomas J.L. & Pub. Pol'y 103 (2013); Robert F. Williams, *State Constitutional Religion Clauses: Lessons from the New Judicial Federalism*, 7 U. St. Thomas J.L. & Pub. Pol'y 192 (2013); Stuart G. Parsell, *Note, Revitalization of the Free Exercise of Religion under State Constitutions: A Response to Employment Division v. Smith*, 68 Notre Dame L. Rev. 747 (1993).

23 *See* Ala. Const. amend. No. 622.

24 For a listing of those states, current to 2010, *see* Eugene Volokh, *Religious Exemption Law Map of the United States; available at:* http://volokh.com/2010/07/09/religious-exemption-law-map-of-the-united-states/.

## B. Historical and Contemporary Free Exercise Principles

Broadly speaking, religious liberty may warrant protection both from the government and by the government for any number or combination of reasons: political pragmatism,[25] economic theory,[26] liberal political theory,[27] republican political theory,[28] theological doctrine,[29] social contract,[30] or a generalized sense of basic morality or

[25] *See, e.g.*, David Little, *The Reformed Tradition and the First Amendment*, *in* THE FIRST FREEDOM: RELIGION AND THE BILL OF RIGHTS 17 (James E. Wood, Jr. ed., 1990) (asserting that "present-day commitments owe very little to a principled belief in religious liberty" evidenced by our predecessors and that, historically, "[m]uch more is owed to the effects of pragmatic compromise and mutual convenience").

[26] *See, e.g.*, Michael W. McConnell & Richard A. Posner, *An Economic Approach to Issues of Religious Freedom*, 56 U. CHI. L. REV. 1, 1 (1989) (proposing the use of "an economic definition of 'neutrality' to determine when government action impinges impermissibly on religious choice").

[27] *See, e.g.*, JAY NEWMAN, ON RELIGIOUS FREEDOM 135 (1991) (stating that "most instances of political interference in the religious affairs of individuals and groups trouble my conscience and strike me, on the basis of my own utilitarian calculations, as being contributory in the 'long run' to a diminution of 'general happiness'"); Gail Merel, *The Protection of Individual Choice: A Consistent Understanding of Religion under the First Amendment*, 45 U. CHI. L. REV. 805, 811 (1978) (noting that the Free Exercise and Establishment Clauses of the Constitution demonstrate that an "individual is freed from both the weight of government opinion and the oppressive effects of government regulation in order to believe or disbelieve as he [or she] chooses"); William L. Miller, *The Principle of Religious Liberty*, 6 J. CHURCH & ST. 85, 87 (1964) (arguing that the risk of anarchy is the necessary price of religious liberty, and the risk of anarchy in that sense is preferable to the risk of tyranny inherent in restrictions on liberty); Steven D. Smith, *The Rise and Fall of Religious Freedom in Constitutional Discourse*, 140 U. PA. L. REV. 149, 202–4 (1991) (describing the personal autonomy rationale for religious freedom, which states that religious liberty is important to a person's sense of self or of who [he or] she is and what [he or] she wants to be); Aldir Guedes Soriano, *Liberal Democracy and the Right to Religious Freedom*, 2013 BYU L. REV. 581.

[28] *See, e.g.*, Timothy L. Hall, *Religion and Civic Virtue: A Justification of Free Exercise*, 67 TUL. L. REV. 87, 90 (1992) (attempting to "construct a theory of free exercise from the insights of civic republicanism"); William L. Miller, *The Moral Project of the American Founders*, *in* ARTICLES OF FAITH, ARTICLES OF PEACE 18 (James D. Hunter & Os Guinness eds., 1990) (asserting that "Americans resisted monofounderism … as they did monarchy, on republican principle"); Mark Tushnet, *The Constitution of Religion*, 18 CONN. L. REV. 701, 735–8 (1986) (discussing the possibility of using the tradition of civic republicanism as a basis for interpreting the religion clauses).

[29] *See, e.g.*, RELIGIOUS LIBERTY: AN END AND A BEGINNING (John C. Murray ed., 1966) (focusing on a Catholic understanding of religious liberty and the 1965 Declaration on Religious Freedom); John Coventry, *The Theology of Religious Freedom*, 80–81 LAW & JUST. 100, 104 (1984) (stating that the doctrine of religious freedom is ultimately a doctrine about the irresistible freedom of God); Robert Gordis, *Judaism and Religious Liberty*, *in* RELIGIOUS LIBERTY IN THE CROSSFIRE OF CREEDS 25, 26 (Franklin H. Littell ed., 1978) (asserting three aspects of religious liberty: the right to practice a faith without interference from others, the extension of freedom of conscience by one group to another that differs in belief and practice, and the granting of freedom of thought and action by a group to dissidents in its own ranks); Winthrop S. Hudson, *The Theological Basis for Religious Freedom*, 3 J. CHURCH & ST. 130, 136 (1961) (arguing that there are theological justifications for the religious freedom enjoyed by U.S. citizens); Franklin H. Littell, *The Basis of Religious Liberty in Christian Belief*, 6 J. CHURCH & ST. 132, 145 (1964) (noting that religious liberty rests on an understanding of obedience to the will of God, which is voluntary service to fellow man); Mohamed Talbi, *Religious Liberty: A Muslim Perspective*, *in* RELIGIOUS LIBERTY AND HUMAN RIGHTS IN NATIONS AND IN RELIGIONS 175–87 (Leonard Swidler ed., 1986) (demonstrating that Muslim theology supports the maintenance of religious freedom); Pope Paul VI, *Declaration on Religious Freedom*, DIGNITATIS HUMANAE (Dec. 7, 1965); *available at:* http://www.vatican.va/archive/hist_councils/ii_vatican_council/documents/vat-ii_decl_19651207_dignitatis-humanae_en.html.

[30] *See, e.g.*, Abner S. Greene, *The Political Balance of the Religion Clauses*, 102 YALE L.J. 1611, 1634 (1993) (arguing that free exercise of religion should be interpreted pursuant to a reading of the religion clauses as embodying a contractual theory of law and politics); *cf.* THE WILLIAMSBURG CHARTER (1988), *reprinted in* ARTICLES OF FAITH, *supra* note 28, app. at 123 (drafted by representatives of the leading faiths in

fairness.[31] Corresponding to several of these reasons, the following subsections elaborate on what are arguably the major principles underlying or animating the Free Exercise Clause and its contemporary interpretation, at least from the perspectives of sitting judges and practicing attorneys. On the scholarly front, some commentators have basically deemed futile any effort to interpret and apply the First Amendment's religion clauses through the medium of one or two principles or theories of religious freedom.[32] Likewise, in the related context of the Establishment Clause, Justice O'Connor expressed comparable skepticism, remarking that "[w]hen bedrock principles collide, they test the limits of categorical obstinacy and expose the flaws and dangers of a Grand Unified Theory that may turn out to be neither grand nor unified."[33]

Though taking note of these concerns, it is important to keep in mind the basic purpose and significance of identifying the principles that follow and, in particular, to draw certain key distinctions. At the outset, it should be acknowledged that the text of the First Amendment provides only one interpretive point, albeit a critical and unassailably relevant one, in defining the substance and scope of religious freedom under the U.S. Constitution. Preceding the text were historical experiences and matters of political and theological principle that motivated the drafting and ratification of the First Amendment – both what it included and what it omitted and how it was thought to relate to other guarantees.[34] These historical and original influences are also important, but even they are not always able to provide sufficient illumination of the text so as to determine the resolution of actual free exercise disputes. Courts thus strive to identify a core set of functional principles that incorporate, are generally consistent with, but are not circumscribed by the motives or purposes of the Framers or Ratifiers. They then distill these principles into much more workable standards, rule, or tests – collectively called "doctrine" – that judges and litigants can invoke in particular disputes or circumstances with relative consistency, coherence, and predictability. The purpose of this section is to identify the core functional principles, whereas the remaining sections essentially explicate the doctrine that courts and litigants apply to actual controversies.

America to address the dilemmas, challenges, and opportunities posed by religious liberty in American public life).

31 *See, e.g.*, Newman, *supra* note 27, at 135–7 (examining the position that religious liberty is justifiable either as an application of the "golden rule" – that one's moral treatment of others should stem from one's desired treatment by others – or as an application of the principle that one should not engage in conduct that might seem negligible if isolated but would undermine the social order if its practice were to become universal); J. Morris Clark, *Guidelines for the Free Exercise Clause*, 83 Harv. L. Rev. 327, 337 (1969) (stating that "[a] far more important interest protected by the free exercise clause relates to fairness to the individual").

32 *See, e.g.*, Frederick Mark Gedicks, The Rhetoric of Church and State: A Critical Analysis of Religion Clause Jurisprudence (1995); Steven D. Smith, Foreordained Failure: The Quest for a Constitutional Principle of Religious Freedom (1995); Frederick Mark Gedicks, *The Improbability of Religion Clause Theory*, 27 Seton Hall L. Rev. 1233 (1997); Steven D. Smith, *Unprincipled Religious Freedom*, 7 J. Contemp. Legal Issues 497, 499 (1996) (arguing that "there is no satisfactory principle of religious freedom" and further that "the principled approach is undesirable on prudential grounds").

33 Rosenberger v. Rector & Visitors of Univ. of Va., 515 U.S. 819, 852 (1995) (O'Connor, J., concurring); *see also* Bd. of Educ. of Kiryas Joel Vill. Sch. Dist. v. Grumet, 512 U.S. 687, 718 (1994) (O'Connor, J., concurring in part and concurring in the judgment).

34 *See, e.g.*, Vincent Phillip Muñoz, *The Original Meaning of the Free Exercise Clause: The Evidence from the First Congress*, 31 Harv. J.L. & Pub. Pol'y 1083 (2008).

### 1. *Voluntarism and Noncoercion*

One of the most entrenched rationales for protecting religious freedom is a respect for the voluntary and autonomous decisions of individuals within the sphere of faith and conscience.[35] Conversely, the coercion or compulsion of religious professions or practices is viewed as anathema to this tradition, and coercion of religious faith itself is often considered futile or meaningless as well as immoral.[36] The writings of key Framers or Framing-era statesmen, as well as several state constitutions, emphatically express this position. James Madison's "Memorial and Remonstrance against Religious Assessments," penned in 1785 in opposition to a Virginia proposal to tax the citizenry in order to fund religious Christian teachers, declared that "[t]he Religion ... of every man must be left to the conviction and conscience of every man" and "cannot follow the dictates of other men,"[37] and Thomas Jefferson's "Act for Establishing Religious Freedom," originally drafted in 1779 and enacted by Virginia in 1786, asserted that "Almighty God hath created the mind free" and "that all attempts to influence it by temporal punishments or burdens, or by civil incapacitations ... are a departure from the plan of the Holy Author of our religion, who being Lord both of body and mind, yet chose not to propagate it by coercions on either."[38] Similarly, Delaware's 1792 Constitution (like its present constitution) proclaimed that "no man shall or ought to be compelled to attend any religious worship, to contribute to the erection or support of any place of worship, or to the maintenance of any ministry, against his own free will and consent,"[39] whereas New Hampshire's 1784 Constitution provided (and still provides today) that "[e]very individual has a natural and unalienable right to worship God according to the dictates of his own conscience, and reason; and no subject shall be hurt, molested, or restrained, in his peers on, liberty, or estate, for worshipping God in the manner and season most agreeable to the dictates of his own conscience."[40] Virginia's 1776 Constitution, perhaps

35 *See* Int'l Soc'y for Krishna Consciousness, Inc. v. Barber, 650 F.2d 430, 439 (1981) ("The free exercise of religion promotes the inviolability of individual conscience and voluntarism, recognizing that private choice, not official coercion, should form the basis for religious conduct and belief."); John Witte, Jr., *The Essential Rights and Liberties of Religion in the American Constitutional Experiment*, 71 NOTRE DAME L. REV. 371, 390–1 (1996).

36 *See* Clark, *supra* note 31, at 337 ("The violation of a man's religion or conscience often works an exceptional harm to him which, unless justified by the most stringent social needs, constitutes a moral wrong in and of itself, far more than would the impairment of his freedoms of speech, press or assembly. ... The moral condemnation implicit in the threat of criminal sanctions is likely to be very painful to one motivated by belief.").

37 James Madison, *Memorial and Remonstrance Against Religious Assessments* ¶ 1 (1785); *available at:* http://religiousfreedom.lib.virginia.edu/sacred/madison_m&r_1785.html.

38 Thomas Jefferson, Virginia Act for Establishing Religious Freedom (1786); *available at:* http://religiousfreedom.lib.virginia.edu/sacred/vaact.html.

39 DEL. CONST. art. I, § 1.

40 N.H. CONST. pt. I, art. 5; *see also* CONN. CONST. art. VII ("It being the right of all men to worship the Supreme Being, the Great Creator and Preserver of the Universe, and to render that worship in a mode consistent with the dictates of their consciences, no person shall by law be compelled to join or support, nor be classed or associated with, any congregation, church or religious association."); MASS. CONST. pt. I, art. II ("It is the right as well as the duty of all men in society, publicly, and at stated seasons to worship the SUPREME BEING, the great Creator and Preserver of the universe. And no subject shall be hurt, molested, or restrained, in his person, liberty, or estate, for worshipping GOD in the manner and season most agreeable to the dictates of his own conscience."); N.J. CONST. art. XVIII (1776) ("That no person shall ever, within this Colony, be deprived of the inestimable privilege of worshipping Almighty God in a manner, agreeable to the dictates of his own conscience; nor, under any presence whatever, be compelled

not surprisingly, was quite direct about voluntarism and coercion: "religion, or the duty which we owe to our Creator, and the manner of discharging it, can be directed only by reason and conviction, not by force or violence; and therefore all men are equally entitled to the free exercise of religion, according to the dictates of conscience."[41]

"Today," as Professor Daniel Conkle observes, "the value of religious voluntarism promotes the right to choose any religion or none at all, and it guards not only against governmental compulsion or coercion, but also against more subtle forms of governmental influence."[42] Supreme Court opinions reflect this understanding. In 1963, the Court stated that the Free Exercise Clause "recognizes … the right of every person to freely choose his [or her] own course with reference thereto, free of any compulsion from the state."[43] The importance of voluntarism and noncoercion necessarily overlaps with the Establishment Clause, leading the Court to comment in 1962 that "[w]hen the power, prestige and financial support of government is [*sic*] placed behind a particular religious belief, the indirect coercive pressure upon religious minorities to conform to the prevailing officially approved religion is plain."[44] Even in *Employment Division v. Smith*, which curtailed the availability of rigorous free exercise protection, the Court nevertheless

to attend any place of worship, contrary to his own faith and judgment; nor shall any person, within this Colony, ever be obliged to pay tithes, taxes, or any other rates, for the purpose of building or repairing any other church or churches, place or places of worship, or for the maintenance of any minister or ministry, contrary to what he believes to be right, or has deliberately or voluntarily engaged himself to perform."), *superseded by* N.J. CONST. art. I, ¶ 3 (1844 & 1947); N.C. CONST. DECL. RTS. art. XIX (1776) ("[A]ll men have a natural and unalienable right to worship Almighty God according to the dictates of their own consciences."), *superseded by* N.C. CONST. art. I, § 26 (1868), *superseded by* N.C. CONST. art. I, § 13 (1971); PA. CONST. DECL. RTS. art. II (1776) ("[A]ll men have a natural and unalienable right to worship Almighty God according to the dictates of their own consciences and understanding: And that no man ought or of right can be compelled to attend any religious worship, or erect or support any place of worship, or maintain any ministry, contrary to, or against, his own free will and consent: Nor can any man, who acknowledges the being of a God, be justly deprived or abridged of any civil right as a citizen, on account of his religious sentiments or peculiar mode of religious worship: And that no authority can or ought to be vested in, or assumed by any power whatever, that shall in any case interfere with, or in any manner controul, the right of conscience in the free exercise of religious worship."), *superseded by* PA. CONST. art. IX, § 3 (1790 & 1838), *superseded by* PA. CONST. art. I, § 3 (1874 & 1968); VT. CONST. ch. I, art. 3 ("[A]ll persons have a natural and unalienable right, to worship Almighty God, according to the dictates of their own consciences and understandings, as in their opinion shall be regulated by the word of God; and that no person ought to, or of right can be compelled to attend any religious worship, or erect or support any place of worship, or maintain any minister, contrary to the dictates of conscience, nor can any person be justly deprived or abridged of any civil right as a citizen, on account of religious sentiments, or peculia[r] mode of religious worship; and that no authority can, or ought to be vested in, or assumed by, any power whatever, that shall in any case interfere with, or in any manner control the rights of conscience, in the free exercise of religious worship.").

41 VA. CONST. BILL OF RTS. § 16 (1776). This provision eventually became art. I, § 16, of the current (1971) Virginia Constitution.

42 DANIEL O. CONKLE, CONSTITUTIONAL LAW: THE RELIGION CLAUSES 38 (2003).

43 Sch. Dist. of Abington Twp., Pa. v. Schempp, 374 U.S. 203, 222 (1963); *accord* En Gao v. Holder, 721 F.3d 893, 895 (7th Cir. 2013) ("The right to choose one's religion is part of the religious freedom that is recognized in the United States.").

44 Engel v. Vitale, 370 U.S. 421, 431 (1962). More generally, it also overlapped with the Court's free speech jurisprudence, emphasizing – at a time when the world witnessed the rise of totalitarian government – the need for freedom of thought and expression. *See, e.g.*, W. Va. State Bd. of Educ. v. Barnette, 319 U.S. 624, 642 (1943) ("If there is any fixed star in our constitutional constellation, it is that no official, high or petty, can prescribe what shall be orthodox in politics, nationalism, religion, or other matters of opinion or force citizens to confess by word or act their faith therein.").

reiterated the principle of voluntarism, emphasizing that "[t]he free exercise of religion means, first and foremost, the right to believe and profess whatever religious doctrine one desires" and that "[t]he government may not compel affirmation of religious belief, punish the expression of religious doctrines it believes to be false, [or] impose special disabilities on the basis of religious views or religious status."[45]

## 2. *Limited Civil and Religious Jurisdiction*

Closely related to the voluntarist conception of religious liberty is the notion that the government and religion should occupy separate though intersecting spheres – civil and ecclesiastical, temporal and spiritual, profane and sacred – and that each one's jurisdiction is circumscribed by its respective authority, roles, and competence. Superficially, this idea more naturally befits the federal government, which is explicitly limited in its powers and thus its functions, but as a matter of principle, it has no less applicability to state governments, even though they, unlike the national government, possess general authority as embodied in the "police power," that is, the inherent sovereign power to regulate on behalf of health, welfare, safety, and morals.[46] Once again, certain Founding-era writers and early state constitutions attest to the original resonance of this notion. Madison, in his "Memorial and Remonstrance," denies that "the Civil Magistrate is a competent Judge of Religious Truth; or that he may employ Religion as an engine of Civil policy"[47] and that religion is "not within the cognizance of Civil Government."[48] Likewise, early state constitutions (in language often still found today) declare that "no power shall or ought to be vested in or assumed by any magistrate that shall in any case interfere with, or in any manner control the rights of conscience, in the free exercise of religious worship"[49] and that "no authority can or ought to be vested in, or assumed by any power whatever, that shall in any case interfere with, or in any manner control, the right of conscience in the free exercise of religious worship."[50] The civil magistrate's authority, instead, extends only to "acts of licentiousness"[51] or to conduct that "disturb[ed] the public peace, or obstruct[ed] others in their religious worship."[52]

Although this separate-spheres jurisdictional conception of the state and religion may have less distinct resonance today than it had in the late eighteenth century, when religious establishments both abroad and at home were still intact, nevertheless, it survives both thematically and doctrinally in the jurisprudence of the Free Exercise Clause as well as the Establishment Clause. Thematically, it has been expressly embraced by the

45 494 U.S. 872, 877 (1990) (citations omitted).

46 *See* Nat'l Fed'n of Indep. Bus. v. Sebelius, 132 S. Ct. 2566, 2578 (2012); Berman v. Parker, 348 U.S. 26, 32 (1954); Manigault v. Springs, 199 U.S. 473, 480 (1905); Johnson v. Collins Entm't Co., 199 F.3d 710, 720 (4th Cir. 1999); State v. Brenan, 772 So. 2d 64, 73 (La. 2000); Christensen v. State, 468 S.E.2d 188, 190 (Ga. 1996); Rothman v. Rothman, 320 A.2d 496, 499 (N.J. 1974); Smith v. State Hwy. Comm'n, 346 P.2d 259, 267 (Kan. 1959).

47 Madison, *Memorial and Remonstrance*, *supra* note 37, at ¶ 5.

48 *Id.* at ¶ 8.

49 Del. Const. art. I, § 1.

50 Pa. Const. Decl. Rts. art. II (1776), *superseded by* Pa. Const. art. IX, § 3 (1790 & 1838), *superseded by* Pa. Const. art. I, § 3 (1874 & 1968); *see also* Vt. Const. ch. I, art. 3 (similar).

51 N.Y. Const. art. XXXVIII (1777). This provision eventually became art. I, § 3 of the current New York Constitution.

52 Mass. Const. pt. I, art. II; *see also* N.H. Const. pt. I, art. 5 (similar);

U.S. Supreme Court, which in 1948 explained that "the First Amendment rests upon the premise that both religion and government can best work to achieve their lofty aims if each is left free from the other within its respective sphere."[53] Doctrinally, it persists under both religion clauses through a constellation of cases and doctrines centered on church autonomy, which can be viewed, in part, as a form of corporate or institutional free exercise. Recently, the Court adopted one prominent component of this constellation, namely, the so-called ministerial exception, which, at the very least, "precludes application of [employment discrimination laws] … to claims concerning the employment relationship between a religious institution and its ministers."[54] According to the Court,

> [r]equiring a church to accept or retain an unwanted minister, or punishing a church for failing to do so … interferes with the internal governance of the church, depriving the church of control over the selection of those who will personify its beliefs. By imposing an unwanted minister, the state infringes the Free Exercise Clause, which protects a religious group's right to shape its own faith and mission through its appointments. According the state the power to determine which individuals will minister to the faithful also violates the Establishment Clause, which prohibits government involvement in such ecclesiastical decisions.[55]

But, of course, the jurisdictional limitations run both ways, and the Court also has held, under the Establishment Clause's prohibition on excessive entanglement, that the government may not delegate civil authority to religious institutions or officials because of their religious status,[56] nor may it "lend its power to one or the other side in controversies over religious authority or dogma."[57]

### 3. *Equality or Neutrality*

Another key principle or dimension of religious freedom law in the United States is equality or – as it is sometimes translated in the First Amendment religion context – neutrality.[58] That equality is a core free exercise principle is hardly surprising given the strong jurisprudential commitment to equal treatment more generally both in constitutional

53 People of State of Ill. *ex rel.* McCollum v. Bd. of Educ. of Sch. Dist. No. 71, 333 U.S. 203, 212 (1948).

54 Hosanna-Tabor Evangelical Lutheran Church & Sch. v. EEOC, 132 S. Ct. 694, 705 (2012).

55 *Id.* at 706.

56 *See* Larkin v. Grendel's Den, Inc., 459 U.S. 116, 125–7 (1982); Commack Self-Service Kosher Meats, Inc. v. Weiss, 294 F.3d 415, 425, 428–9 (2d Cir. 2002), *cert. denied*, 537 U.S. 1187 (2003); Barghout v. Bureau of Kosher Meat & Food Control, 66 F.3d 1337, 1342–3 (4th Cir. 1995); Espresso, Inc. v. Dist. of Columbia, 884 F. Supp. 7, 11 (D.D.C. 1995); Voswinkel v. City of Charlotte, 495 F. Supp. 588, 598 (W.D.N.C. 1980); State v. Celmer, 80 N.J. 405, 416, 404 A.2d 1, 6 (N.J. 1979), *cert. denied*, 444 U.S. 951 (1979).

57 Employment Div. v. Smith, 494 U.S. 872, 877 (1990) [citing Presbyterian Church in U.S. v. Mary Elizabeth Blue Hull Mem. Presbyterian Church, 393 U.S. 440, 445–52 (1969); Kedroff v. St. Nicholas Cathedral, 344 U.S. 94, 95–119 (1952); Serbian Eastern Orthodox Diocese v. Milivojevich, 426 U.S. 696, 708–25 (1976)].

58 *See* Conkle, *supra* note 42, at 40–1; Michael J. Perry, *What Do the Free Exercise and Nonestablishment Norms Forbid? Reflections on the Constitutional Law of Religious Freedom*, 1 U. St. Thomas L.J. 549, 553 (2003) ("The free exercise norm … is an antidiscrimination norm… [T]he only sound conception of religious liberty is founded upon protecting religious exercise against persecution, discrimination, insensitivity, or hostility."); Witte, *supra* note 35, at 398–9.

law[59] and in background legal traditions.[60] As with many areas of American law and culture, however, the conception and breadth of equality or neutrality have changed significantly and sometimes abruptly since the nation's founding. At first, the aspiration was equal tolerance between Protestant and related Christian denominations and perhaps between Catholics and Jews, though the existence of an established church, at least at the state level, plainly did not seem inconsistent with the prevailing concept of equality. With time, however, the nation's religious diversity, both from within and from without, expanded greatly, eventually exerting pressure on previously adequate baselines of equality or neutrality.

By the middle of the twentieth century, after the tumult of two world wars and after witnessing anew the state-sanctioned suppression of minority faiths and peoples in Europe, judicial enforcement through the religion clauses of a revised equality or neutrality norm grew more aggressive. As with race under an evolving norm of equal protection,[61] the Supreme Court announced new First Amendment doctrines that did not blindly accept the traditions and baselines that had guided decision making in prior decades. Under the Establishment Clause, this approach led to the gradual displacement of mainstream Protestant Christian influence, particularly in public schools, notwithstanding the fact that this influence had previously been upheld, indeed embraced, and was hardly inconsistent with the views held by many of the Founding generation.[62] Under the Free Exercise Clause, correspondingly, the Court's new approach led to greater scrutiny of laws that imposed burdens on nonmainstream religious adherents,[63] notwithstanding the fact that the burdens often were the incidental effect of applying laws that were not enacted out of religious animus.

59 *See, e.g.*, U.S. CONST. amend. XIV, § 1 (prohibiting each state from "deny[ing] to any person within its jurisdiction the equal protection of the laws"); Bolling v. Sharpe, 347 U.S. 497, 499–500 (1954) (reading a comparable guarantee into the Fifth Amendment Due Process Clause, which binds the federal government); Romer v. Evans, 517 U.S. 620, 633 (1996) ("Central both to the idea of the rule of law and to our own Constitution's guarantee of equal protection is the principle that government and each of its parts remain open on impartial terms to all who seek its assistance."); Daniel O. Conkle, *The Path of American Religious Liberty: From the Original Theology to Formal Neutrality and an Uncertain Future*, 75 IND. L.J. 1, 5–24 (2000).

60 *See, e.g.*, Evan H. Caminker, *Precedent and Prediction: The Forward-Looking Aspects of Inferior Court Decisionmaking*, 73 TEX. L. REV. 1, 39 (1994) (noting that the principle "that similarly situated litigants are treated equally … is considered a hallmark of fairness in a regime committed to the rule of law").

61 *See, e.g.*, Brown v. Bd. of Educ., 347 U.S. 483 (1954); McLaurin v. Okla. State Regents, 339 U.S. 637 (1950); Sweatt v. Painter, 339 U.S. 629 (1950); Mo. *ex rel.* Gaines v. Canada, 305 U.S. 337 (1938)

62 *See, e.g.*, Wallace v. Jaffree, 472 U.S. 38 (1985) (invalidating state statute authorizing a daily period of silence in public schools for meditation or voluntary prayer); Stone v. Graham, 449 U.S. 39 (1980) (*per curiam*) (invalidating state statute requiring that Ten Commandments be posted in all public school classrooms); Cmte. for Pub. Educ. & Religious Liberty v. Nyquist, 413 U.S. 756 (1973) (invaliding various components of state program providing financial assistance to nonpublic, including religious, schools); Sch. Dist. of Abington Twp., Pa. v. Schempp, 374 U.S. 203 (1963) (invalidating state laws providing for bible readings and recitation of the Lord's Prayer as part of opening exercises in public schools); Engel v. Vitale, 370 U.S. 421 (1962) (invalidating state program providing for prayer as part of opening exercises at public schools).

63 *See, e.g.*, Wisconsin v. Yoder, 406 U.S. 205 (1972) (invalidating application of state educational requirements to Old Order Amish); Sherbert v. Verner, 374 U.S. 398 (1963) (invaliding application of state unemployment compensation qualification requirement to Seventh Day Adventist). This framework resulted in what Professor Douglas Laycock has called substantive neutrality as opposed to mere formal neutrality *See* Douglas Laycock, *Formal, Substantive, and Disaggregated Neutrality Toward Religion*, 39 DEPAUL L. REV. 993 (1990).

As has happened to some extent with race and equal protection, however, the Court, beginning as early as the mid-1980s, started to recalibrate its understanding of equality or neutrality, returning the doctrinal framework to a less demanding, more formalistic baseline and effectively ratcheting down the judicial scrutiny under both religion clauses.[64] For the Establishment Clause, this has led, at least in funding and access cases, to more focus on the formal attributes of a government action and less, if any, on it effects.[65] For the Free Exercise Clause, the pattern has been the same, as evidenced by the main rule of the 1990 case, *Employment Division v. Smith*[66]: when a law is generally applicable and enacted without regard to religion (i.e., is neutral), ordinarily it will not be strictly scrutinized by the judiciary regardless of how substantial a burden it imposes on religious adherents. Thus, in terms of formal equality, it is fair to say that "[i]n recent decades, religious equality has grown to become a dominant value under the Religion Clauses. Indeed, it may now be the most important value of all, at least in the eyes of the contemporary Supreme Court."[67]

### 4. *Social Utility: Religion as Ally, Religion as Antagonist*

Religious freedom is sometimes valued because the effects of religion, as an institution that shapes society and its members, are themselves valued. In many instances, the value is of a superficially agreeable sort: religion can complement government objectives such as obedience to law, loyalty to country, preservation of social norms, integrity and industry in one's vocation, commitment to family, service to community, and charity toward the less fortunate.[68] The religious freedom guarantees of several state

64 *See* generally Berg, *supra* note 19; Conkle, supra note 59.

65 *See, e.g.*, Zelman v. Simmons-Harris, 536 U.S. 639 (2002); Good News Club v. Milford Central Sch., 533 U.S. 98, 112–19 (2001); Mitchell v. Helms, 530 U.S. 793 (2000) (plurality); Agostini v. Felton, 521 U.S. 203 (1997); Rosenberger v. Rector & Visitors of Univ. of Va., 515 U.S. 819, 837–46 (1995); Lamb's Chapel v. Ctr. Moriches Union Free Sch. Dist., 508 U.S. 384, 394–7 (1993). Outside these contexts, however, the Court has generally maintained a more aggressive, realism-based approach. *See, e.g.*, Santa Fe Indep. Sch. Dist. v. Doe, 530 U.S. 290 (2000); Lee v. Weisman, 505 U.S. 577 (1992). *But cf.* Town of Greece, N.Y. v. Galloway, 134 S. Ct. 1811 (2014).

66 494 U.S. 872 (1990).

67 CONKLE, *supra* note 42, at 40.

68 *See, e.g.*, Walz v. Tax Comm'n of City of N.Y., 397 U.S. 664, 689 (1970) (Brennan, J., concurring) (noting that "religious organizations … uniquely contribute to the pluralism of American society by their religious activities"); 1 W. COLE DURHAM, ROBERT SMITH & WILLIAM BASSETT, RELIGIOUS ORGANIZATIONS AND THE LAW § 1:3 (2012) (discussing the relationship between religious adherence and philanthropy); JAMES H. HUTSON, CHURCH AND STATE IN AMERICA: THE FIRST TWO CENTURIES 107–13 (2008) (noting the early American view "that religion served the 'public utility'"); RELIGION IN AMERICAN HISTORY 3 (Amanda Porterfield & John Corrigan, eds., 2010) (observing that religion in America has "operated as an agent of national unity and cultural homogenization" and "contributed to overarching conceptions of nationhood and to patriotic devotion to the ideals of liberty, equality, and justice that people have often believed America to represent"); Michael E. Smith, *The Special Place of Religion in the Constitution*, 1983 SUP. CT. REV. 83, 102–3 (describing instances where the Court has observed that freedom of religion produces social benefits because of the community ties established and strengthened through religious participation and by bearing burdens that would otherwise have to be met by general taxation); Steven D. Smith, *The Rise and Fall of Religious Freedom in Constitutional Discourse*, 140 U. PA. L. REV. 149, 199–202 (1991) (arguing that "religion is essential to our republic because it helps to inculcate in citizens the moral character necessary for a democratic society"). As stated by the N.Y. Court of Appeals in 1956 (in what was perhaps a more innocent era), "church and school and accessory uses are, in themselves, clearly in furtherance of the public morals and general welfare. The church is the teacher and guardian

constitutions, in fact, are explicitly premised on the importance, if not necessity, of religion to the community and to good government.[69] In other instances, the social and political value of religion may initially be less obvious but no less significant: religion can serve as an antagonist to the state by encouraging civil disobedience, conscientious objection to military or other civic obligations, disruption of social norms, overt resistance to government policies or actions, prevention of assimilation, and competition for the ultimate loyalty of the populace.[70] Indeed, "religion may provide a buffer against some of the worst tendencies of democratic political cultures" by "allow[ing] stable, transcendent, or 'prophetic' values to enter the democratic dialogue and to

of morals, and 'an educational institution, whose curriculum complies with the state law, is considered an aid to the general welfare.'" Diocese of Rochester v. Planning Bd. of Town of Brighton, 136 N.E.2d 827, 836–7 (N.Y. 1956) (citation omitted) [quoting Roman Catholic Archbishop of Diocese of Or. v. Baker, 140 Or. 600, 613, 15 P.2d 391, 395 (Or. 1932)].

69 *See, e.g.*, Ark. Const. art. II, § 25 ("Religion, morality and knowledge being essential to good government, the General Assembly shall enact suitable laws to protect every religious denomination in the peaceable enjoyment of its own mode of public worship."); Del. Const. art. I, § 1 ("Although it is the duty of all men frequently to assemble together for the public worship of Almighty God; and piety and morality, on which the prosperity of communities depends, are hereby promoted; yet no man shall or ought to be compelled to attend any religious worship, to contribute to the erection or support of any place of worship, or to the maintenance of any ministry, against his own free will and consent."); Mass. Const. pt. I, art. III ("[T]he public worship of GOD and instructions in piety, religion and morality, promote the happiness and prosperity of a people and the security of a republican government."); Neb. Const. art. I, § 4 ("Religion, morality, and knowledge, however, being essential to good government, it shall be the duty of the Legislature to pass suitable laws to protect every religious denomination in the peaceable enjoyment of its own mode of public worship, and to encourage schools and the means of instruction."); Ohio Const. art. I, § 7 ("Religion, morality, and knowledge … being essential to good government, it shall be the duty of the General Assembly to pass suitable laws, to protect every religious denomination in the peaceable enjoyment of its own mode of public worship, and to encourage schools and the means of instruction.").

70 *See, e.g.*, Stephen L. Carter, The Culture of Disbelief: How American Law and Politics Trivialize Religious Devotion 132 (1993) ("[I]f … religions are at their most useful when they serve as democratic intermediaries and preach resistance, then it is at precisely that moment, the moment when the religious tradition most diverges from the mainstream, that protection is both most needed and most deserved."); *id.* at 134 ("[T]he reason for accommodation [i.e., granting a religious exemption from a generally applicable law] becomes not the protection of individual conscience, but the preservation of the religions as independent power bases that exist in large part in order to resist the state."); Religion in American History, *supra* note 68, at 3 (observing that religion in the United States "has contributed both to centrifugal forces of diversity, fragmentation, and factionalism" by "preserv[ing] ethnic traditions, inspir[ing] countless forms of charity, education, and social activism, and br[inging] an esthetic complexity to American life that stimulated the arts and enriched many lives" but also that "[r]eligious diversity also contributed to the fragmentation and factionalism of American life, promoting boundaries between groups, and stimulating misunderstanding and hatred"); Clark, *supra* note 31, at 337 ("[R]eligious or conscientious values frequently represent an idealism which serves a valuable function in society even though the idealist's conclusions may be rejected. Exemption of conscientious objectors to war, for example, may be tolerated as a valuable reminder to the nation that war is undesirable and that evil should be returned with good."); Michael W. McConnell, *Free Exercise Revisionism and the Smith Decision*, 57 U. Chi. L. Rev. 1109, 1139 (1990) ("The ideal of free exercise is counter-assimilationist; it strives to allow individuals of different religious faiths to maintain their differences in the face of powerful pressures to conform."); *see generally* Eric William Cernyar, *The Checking Value of Free Exercise: Religious Clashes with the State*, 3 Tex. Rev. L. & Pol. 191 (1999); Jane Rutherford, *Religion, Rationality, and Special Treatment*, 9 Wm. & Mary Bill Rts. J. 303 (2001); Marci A. Hamilton, *The First Amendment's Challenge Function and the Confusion in the Supreme Court's Contemporary Free Exercise Jurisprudence*, 29 Ga. L. Rev. 81 (1994).

empower the expression of minority viewpoints."[71] Religious organizations, in particular, can be especially effective at creating or mobilizing this spirit of dissent and resistance among adherents.[72]

From this perspective, protecting free exercise thus protects these many and often bipolar roles of religion in society and the life of the state. In turn, a meaningful jurisprudence of free exercise, frequently in conjunction with the freedoms of speech, association, and assembly, provide the necessary space within which religious institutions and adherents can develop their faith and then apply that faith to the temporal sphere, whether supporting or opposing the laws and decisions of the government. A survey of U.S. history reveals that both these roles have been and remain important. For example, religious support – or, more broadly, a spiritual basis – for fighting the Third Reich in World War II, especially as a reason to sacrifice one's life for what otherwise might be an abstract cause, was likely critical to the nation's determination in that conflict.[73] By the same token, religious opposition to the legally protected institution of slavery prior to and during the Civil War was equally critical to the consummation of that conflict, in which abolitionists and eventually Union soldiers alike often risked their lives for others' freedom. This is not to suggest that these events saw uniform alignment of religious adherents on what retrospectively is the morally correct side; to the contrary, religious institutions and individuals have been and are divided on most, if not all, major legal, political, economic, environmental, and social issues.[74] But a meaningful free exercise guarantee, while not dictating morally correct outcomes, ensures the deliberation and division that are often necessary to arrive at such outcomes by religious communities and individuals, and such outcomes, if and when reached, can inhere very much to the nation's benefit.

### 5. *Other Principles*

Whether one looks to Madison's writings, to particular court decisions, or to scholarly publications, one can certainly find other rationales for protecting religious freedom, minimally if not robustly, some of which were noted briefly at the outset. In this last portion of the section, two additional rationales will be explored in slightly greater depth owing largely to their logical or historical value to the question of why religious freedom, particularly in the United States, warrants and has warranted special protection.

71 Ted G. Jelen, *The Constitutional Basis of Religious Pluralism in the United States: Causes and Consequences*, 612 ANN. AM. ACAD. POL. & SOC. SCI. 26, 35 (2007). "The fact that religious principles are grounded in beliefs that are not based on the social and political exigencies of the moment allows for such beliefs to serve as independent sources of criticism of the prevailing political mood." *Id.*

72 *See* CARTER, *supra* note 70, at 126 (contending that religions can "stand as intermediaries between sovereign and citizen, thus limiting the prospect of majoritarian tyranny" and that this role is particularly important today, when the state is "characterized by a regulatory regime far more intrusive than the Founders could possibly have contemplated").

73 For a more nuanced institutional view, *see* GERALD L. SITTSER, A CAUTIOUS PATRIOTISM: THE AMERICAN CHURCHES AND THE SECOND WORLD WAR (1997).

74 Regarding the Civil War, for example, *see* C.C. GOEN, BROKEN CHURCHES, BROKEN NATION: DENOMINATIONAL SCHISMS AND THE COMING OF THE CIVIL WAR (1997); ROBERT J. MILLER & JAMES M. MCPHERSON, BOTH PRAYED TO THE SAME GOD: RELIGION AND FAITH IN THE AMERICAN CIVIL WAR (2007). Regarding abolitionism in the antebellum period, *see* CLAUDINE L. FERRELL, THE ABOLITION MOVEMENT 52–3 (2006).

The first is that the harms perceived by adherents, resulting from the disobedience of religious tenets in order to conform to temporal laws, may be of a nature or magnitude that can differ in kind from the harms perceived by nonreligious dissidents. The threat of defying one's creator and of losing one's salvation or facing eternal punishment, or of jeopardizing the souls of one's relatives, is presumably a source of immeasurable angst, possibly having no counterpart in the realm of secular conscience.[75] This focus on "extratemporal consequences" has been most consistently and forcefully developed by Jesse Choper,[76] and while, strictly construed, it could leave a great number of religious practices unprotected,[77] it can nonetheless form one of a cluster of rationales that collectively have a broader sweep.[78]

The other rationale worthy of mention is the original Enlightenment-era belief – still resonant today with many Americans – that religious liberty is a natural, inalienable right that is prior to the state in terms of both chronology and importance.[79] As noted by Professor Philip Hamburger, commenting on the decline of this conception, "Americans once considered the free exercise of religion to be the most inalienable of rights. ... In contrast to the English, who had subjected religious liberty to conditions that preserved the interests of government, numerous eighteenth-century Americans ... viewed the free exercise of religion as a right so personal and inalienable that it could not be conditioned or otherwise determined or measured by the concerns of society or government."[80] The classic formulation is this view is found, once again, in Madison's "Memorial and Remonstrance," in which he asserts that the right to religious exercise

> is in its nature an unalienable right. It is unalienable, because the opinions of men, depending only on the evidence contemplated by their own minds cannot follow the dictates of other men: It is unalienable also, because what is here a right towards men, is a duty towards the Creator. It is the duty of every man to render to the Creator such homage and such only as he believes to be acceptable to him. This duty is precedent, both in order of time and in degree of obligation, to the claims of Civil Society. Before

75 *See* Clark, *supra* note 31, at 337 ("[T]he cost to a principled individual of failing to do his [or her] moral duty is generally severe, in terms of supernatural sanction or the loss of moral self-respect. In the face of these costs, the individual's refusal to obey the law may be inevitable, and therefore in some perhaps unusual sense of the word, involuntary.").

76 *See* Jesse H. Choper, *Defining "Religion" in the First Amendment*, 1982 U. Ill. L. Rev. 579, 597–601.

77 *See* John H. Garvey, *Is There a Principle of Religious Liberty?* 84 Mich. L. Rev. 1379, 1384 (1996) (book review) ("[T]he theory of extratemporal consequences, though it is a useful shibboleth, leaves out some pretty clearly religious actors and actions. Strict Calvinists believe that our actions don't affect our chances of salvation. They get no exemptions."); Kent Greenawalt, *Religion as a Concept in Constitutional Law*, 72 Cal. L. Rev. 753, 802–6 (1984); Gary J. Simson, *Endangering Religious Liberty*, 84 Cal. L. Rev. 441, 446–51 (1996).

78 In addition, courts might be unwilling or unable to assess whether a given practice implicates possible extratemporal consequences, much like the judicial hesitancy to assess the importance or "centrality" of given religious beliefs; *see* Smith, 494 U.S. at 886–7 & n. 4, in which case the prospect of undercoverage may be reduced.

79 *See* Arlin M. Adams & Charles J. Emmerich, A Nation Dedicated to Religious Liberty: The Constitutional Heritage of the Religion Clauses 37–40 (1990) (discussing historical precedent for "liberty of conscience" along with the Madisonian assertion that "[c]onscience is the most sacred of all property"); W. Cole Durham, Jr., *Religious Liberty and the Call of Conscience*, 42 DePaul L. Rev. 71, 80–4 (1992) (discussing historical precedent for religious liberty and focusing particularly on the Madisonian view of religious liberty); Philip Hamburger, *More Is Less*, 90 Va. L. Rev. 835, 839–57 (2004).

80 Hamburger, *supra* note 79, at 839.

> any man can be consider[e]d as a member of Civil Society, he must be considered as a subject of the Governour of the Universe: And if a member of Civil Society, do it with a saving of his allegiance to the Universal Sovereign.[81]

Thomas Jefferson, likewise, grounded much of his thinking on religious freedom in terms of its status as a natural right,[82] at one point describing religious liberty as "the most inalienable and sacred of all human rights."[83] Attesting to its general influence throughout the late eighteenth and nineteenth centuries, the natural or inalienable character of religious liberty is declared, essentially as self-evident, by numerous state constitutions.[84]

Nor is this understanding of the right merely an historical artifact, though Professor Hamburger correctly observes that it at least appears to be conceptually inconsistent with the modern balancing methodology in free exercise cases.[85] A more modern constitutional formulation, for example, is provided by the late Professor Paul Kauper:

> The Constitution ... does not create religious liberty. ... [R]eligious freedom is deemed to be not a concession or grant by the state but an indefeasible right of the person, which the government must recognize, respect and protect. Religious liberty is not to be confused with religious tolerance. Tolerance as a legal concept is premised on the assumption that the state has ultimate control over religion and the churches, and that whether

[81] Madison, *Memorial and Remonstrance*, *supra* note 37, at ¶ 1.

[82] *See* Chester James Antieau, *Natural Rights and the Founding Fathers – The Virginians*, 17 WASH. & LEE L. REV. 43, 44–7 (1960).

[83] Thomas Jefferson, *Freedom of Religion at the University of Virginia* (Oct. 7, 1822), *in* THE COMPLETE JEFFERSON 957, 958 (Saul K. Padover ed., 1943).

[84] *See, e.g.*, ARK. CONST. art. II, § 24 ("All men have a natural and indefeasible right to worship Almighty God according to the dictates of their own consciences; no man can, of right, be compelled to attend, erect, or support any place of worship; or to maintain any ministry against his consent."); GA. CONST. art. I, § 1, ¶ III ("Each person has the natural and inalienable right to worship God, each according to the dictates of that person's own conscience."); IND. CONST. art. I, § 2 ("All people shall be secured in the natural right to worship ALMIGHTY GOD, according to the dictates of their own consciences."); KY. CONST. BILL OF RTS. § 1 ("All men are, by nature, free and equal, and have certain inherent and inalienable rights, among which may be reckoned ... Second: The right of worshipping Almighty God according to the dictates of their consciences."); ME. CONST. art. I, § 3 ("All individuals have a natural and unalienable right to worship Almighty God according to the dictates of their own consciences, and no person shall be hurt, molested or restrained in that person's liberty or estate for worshipping God in the manner and season most agreeable to the dictates of that person's own conscience, nor for that person's religious professions or sentiments."); MO. CONST. art. I, § 5 ("That all men have a natural and indefeasible right to worship Almighty God according to the dictates of their own consciences."); NEB. CONST. art. I, § 4 ("All persons have a natural and indefeasible right to worship Almighty God according to the dictates of their own consciences."); N.H. CONST. pt. I, art. 5 ("Every individual has a natural and unalienable right to worship God according to the dictates of his own conscience, and reason."); N.C. CONST. art. I, § 13 ("All persons have a natural and inalienable right to worship Almighty God according to the dictates of their own consciences."); OHIO CONST. art. I, § 7 ("All men have a natural and indefeasible right to worship Almighty God according to the dictates of their own conscience."); OR. CONST. art. I, § 2 ("All men shall be secure in the Natural right, to worship Almighty God according to the dictates of their own consciences."); PA. CONST. art. I, § 3 ("All men have a natural and indefeasible right to worship Almighty God according to the dictates of their own consciences."); TENN. CONST. art. I, § 3 ("That all men have a natural and indefeasible right to worship Almighty God according to the dictates of their own conscience."); TEX. CONST. art. I, § 6 ("All men have a natural and indefeasible right to worship Almighty God according to the dictates of their own consciences."); VT. CONST. ch. I, art. 3 ("[A]ll persons have a natural and unalienable right, to worship Almighty God, according to the dictates of their own consciences and understandings, as in their opinion shall be regulated by the word of God.").

[85] *See* Hamburger, *supra* note 79, at 858–61.

> and to what extent religious freedom will be granted and protected is a matter of state policy. Tolerance of minority religious groups and of nonconformists was an important half-way step in the struggle for religious liberty as evidenced in American colonial history. But our constitutional system embodies the full-blown concept of religious freedom as a natural right which limits the government, rather than a privilege dispensed by governmental authority in pursuing a policy of benevolent toleration.[86]

Admittedly, this final conception of the basis of religious liberty may seem more like a tenet of faith than a principle of deduction, and it does not necessarily yield an obvious doctrinal formulation, although these features arguably are also exhibited by the aforementioned principles of limited jurisdiction, equality or neutrality, and social utility. In all events, the view of religious liberty as an inalienable natural right is sufficiently deep rooted and resonant that it cannot rightly or easily be excluded from an inventory of significant free exercise principles.

## C. Elements of Prima Facie Free Exercise Claim

A free exercise claim necessarily consists of several elements, and ordinarily a free exercise claimant must prove each one to a legally sufficient extent, with variations based on the stage of pleadings or litigation. There is, it should be noted, more than one acceptable way to delineate the doctrinal components and limitations of a free exercise claim and that the approach employed here, though certainly within conventional bounds, does not purport to be exclusive or exhaustive. Indeed, as the ensuing analysis reveals, the demarcation and even the content of these elements, particularly the concepts of "religion" and "substantial burden," are not always matters of settled doctrine.

Broadly speaking, there are at least four elements to a free exercise claim. The claimant, whether an individual or an institution,[87] must demonstrate every element, though the order of their demonstration can vary. First, the claimant must show that the alleged infringer is a government agency or official or the equivalent of the government (as opposed to a purely private actor) and that the allegedly infringing action involves an exercise of the government's sovereign authority. Second, the claimant must show that the practice or behavior that the government's action is somehow restricting is religious in origin or nature.[88] Third, the claimant must show that this restriction imposes

86 Paul G. Kauper, *Legal Aspects of Religious Liberty*, *in* Religious Liberty 25 (Cedric W. Tilberg ed., 1968); *cf. also* Girouard v. United States, 328 U.S. 61, 68 (1946) ("The struggle for religious liberty has through the centuries been an effort to accommodate the demands of the State to the conscience of the individual. The victory for freedom of thought recorded in Our Bill of Rights recognizes that in the domain of conscience there is a moral power higher than the State. Throughout the ages men have suffered death rather than subordinate their allegiance to God to the authority of the State. Freedom of religion guaranteed by the First Amendment is the product of that struggle.").

87 Religious organizations, even those that are incorporated, can invoke the Free Exercise Clause. *See* Primera Iglesia Bautista Hispana of Boca Raton, Inc. v. Broward Cnty., 450 F.3d 1295, 1305 (11th Cir. 2006) ("Although the rights of corporate persons and natural persons are not entirely coextensive … corporations plainly possess the right [of the] free exercise of religion.").

88 *See* Levitan v. Ashcroft, 281 F.3d 1313, 1320 (D.C. Cir. 2002) (explaining that "the practices at issue must be of a religious nature"); United States v. Meyers, 95 F.3d 1475, 1482 (10th Cir. 1996) (RFRA: "The government need only accommodate the exercise of actual religious convictions."), *cert. denied*, 522 U.S. 1006 (1997); New Creation Fellowship of Buffalo v. Town of Cheektowaga, N.Y., No. 99-CV-460A(F), 2004 WL 1498190, at *30 (W.D.N.Y. July 2, 2004) (Magis. J. Rpt. & Recomm.) ("[A] § 1983 claim for abridgement of the Free Exercise Clause requires a plaintiff demonstrate, at the outset, that the alleged

a substantial burden on the allegedly religious practice[89] and may have to demonstrate, either separately or as part of this showing, that the practice is a significant, central, or even required part of his or her faith.[90] Finally, the claimant must demonstrate that he or she sincerely holds the religious beliefs that underlie this practice.[91]

These showings are described as ordinarily rather than always required because there appear to be exceptions, some of which are formal and others of which are functional in nature. A handful of courts, for example, have held that "if a law is not neutral and of general applicability, a plaintiff is not required to prove that his or her free exercise of religion has been 'substantially burdened.'"[92] Likewise, the sincerity of a claimant's beliefs and the status of those beliefs as religious, though formally required, are not regularly challenged to any significant extent, especially when they are conventional in nature and especially, it seems, outside of high-litigation contexts such as prisons. As a practical matter, then, claimants are often allowed to assert these elements with little or no affirmative evidentiary effort. Of course, parties cannot assume that they will be the beneficiaries of these exceptional doctrines or tendencies, and therefore, it is important to examine all four in greater detail. Indeed, as the phrasing of the elements suggests, not all beliefs are religious in origin and nature, not all burdens are constitutionally substantial, not all practices are sufficiently related to a claimant's beliefs, and not all religious beliefs are sincerely held.

### 1. *Action by the Government*

A free exercise claimant normally must show that the alleged infringer is an officer, branch, or instrumentality of the federal, state, or local government[93] and that the

religion and related exercises sought to be protected from official impairment constitute a 'religion' within the purview of the First Amendment's protection."), *aff'd*, No. 05-0159-CV, 164 Fed. App'x 5 (2d Cir. Dec. 6, 2005) (unpublished).

89 The government's action need not be accompanied by any particular state of mind. However, courts have ruled that at least under 42 U.S.C. § 1983, claims of *negligent* free exercise violations are not actionable. *See* Gallagher v. Shelton, 587 F.3d 1063, 1070 (10th Cir. 2009); Lovelace v. Lee, 472 F.3d 174, 201 (4th Cir. 2006). A "[p]laintiff must assert more than negligence to state a valid § 1983 claim for the violation of his Free Exercise rights" but "[i]nstead … must allege conscious or intentional acts that burden his free exercise of religion." Lewis v. Mitchell, 416 F. Supp. 2d 935, 944 (S.D. Cal. 2005).

90 *See* Hernandez v. Comm'r, 490 U.S. 680, 699 (1989) ("The free exercise inquiry asks whether government has placed a substantial burden on the observation of a central religious belief or practice."); Weir v. Nix, 114 F.3d 817, 820 (8th Cir. 1997) ("As an initial matter, a person claiming that a governmental policy or action violates his right to exercise his religion freely must establish that the action substantially burdens his sincerely held religious belief."); Vernon v. City of L.A., 27 F.3d 1385, 1393 (9th Cir. 1994) (noting that "the plaintiff must first establish that the government has placed a substantial burden on his or her free exercise of religion"), *cert. denied*, 513 U.S. 1000 (1994); State v. DeLaBruere, 154 Vt. 237, 249, 577 A.2d 254, 261 (Vt. 1990) ("In a First Amendment case, the party asserting the violation has the initial burden of proving that the state requirement or restriction imposes a burden on religious belief or practice.").

91 *See* Levitan v. Ashcroft, 281 F.3d 1313, 1320 (D.C. Cir. 2002) (explaining that "[t]he litigant's beliefs must be sincere").

92 Rader v. Johnston, 924 F. Supp. 1540, 1543 n. 2, 1555 (D. Neb. 1996) [citing Hartmann v. Stone, 68 F.3d 973, 979 n.4 (6th Cir. 1995); Brown v. Borough of Mahaffey, Pa., 35 F.3d 846, 849 (3d Cir. 1994)]; *accord* Larsen v. U.S. Navy, 346 F. Supp. 2d 122, 138 (D.D.C. 2004) (explaining that "because the plaintiffs do not challenge a neutral or generally applicable law, the plaintiffs need not plead a substantial burden").

93 *See* Shymatta v. Microsoft Corp., No. 04-55206, 150 Fed. App'x 637, 2005 WL 2358375, at *1 (9th Cir. Sept. 27, 2005) (unpublished) (holding that plaintiff's free exercise claim "lack[ed] merit because [the defendant] is not a state actor"), *cert. denied*, 546 U.S. 1225 (2006); Lown v. Salvation Army, Inc., 393

allegedly infringing action involves an exercise of that government's sovereign authority.[94] By the text of the Free Exercise Clause, the government action must be a "law," but that term has been broadly interpreted and can take the form of a statute, regulation, rule, directive, order, ruling, policy, practice, or even an official's individual decision, though liability in that instance might extend only to the individual actor.[95] This does not mean that every action by government is a "law" under the First Amendment or otherwise. In particular, the term may not include entirely declaratory actions, such as many legislative resolutions and executive proclamations, that do "not exact any particular behavior from any individual" or "impose no penalties or sanctions of any kind."[96]

The range of governments to which the Free Exercise Clause applies is also broad. As written, of course, the Free Exercise Clause binds only Congress, the legislative branch of the federal government.[97] Subsequent interpretations and developments make clear, however, that the clause also binds the national government's judicial and executive branches.[98]

F. Supp. 2d 223, 244 (S.D.N.Y. 2005) ("Because the allegedly discriminatory acts of the Salvation Army cannot properly be considered state action, plaintiffs' claims against the Salvation Army for violation of the Equal Protection Clause and the Free Exercise Clause are dismissed."); Hack v. President & Fellows of Yale Coll., 16 F. Supp. 2d 183, 188–92 (D. Conn. 1998) (dismissing a free exercise challenge under 42 U.S.C. § 1983 for want of state action), *aff'd*, 237 F.3d 81 (2d Cir. 2000), *cert. denied*, 534 U.S. 888 (2001).

94 *See* United States v. Int'l Bhd. of Teamsters, Chauffeurs, Warehousemen & Helpers of Am., 941 F.2d 1292, 1295–6 (2d Cir. 1991) {"Because the United States Constitution regulates only the Government, not private parties, a litigant claiming that his constitutional rights have been violated must first establish that the challenged conduct constitutes 'state action.' To qualify as state action, the conduct in question 'must be caused by the exercise of some right or privilege created by the State or by a rule of conduct imposed by the State or by a person for whom the State is responsible,' and 'the party charged with the [conduct] must be a person who may fairly be said to be a state actor.'" (citation omitted) [quoting Lugar v. Edmondson Oil Co., 457 U.S. 922, 937 (1982)]}, *cert. denied*, 502 U.S. 1091 (1992). One who asserts a federal constitutional claim against a municipal or state defendant must normally do so under 42 U.S.C. § 1983 rather than directly under the Constitution itself. *See* Baxter v. Vigo Cnty. Sch. Corp., 26 F.3d 728, 732 n. 3 (7th Cir. 1994); Ward v. Caulk, 650 F.2d 1144, 1148 (9th Cir. 1981). Accordingly, the state action requirement is, in the first instance, really a statutory element, usually subsumed under section 1983's requirement that the defendant have acted "under color of" of state law. *See* Reed v. City of Chicago, 77 F.3d 1049, 1051 (7th Cir. 1996) ["To state a claim under 42 U.S.C. § 1983, a plaintiff must allege that: (1) the defendant deprived the plaintiff of a right secured by the Constitution and laws of the United States, and (2) the defendant acted under color of state law."]. Thus a government employee's conduct may not give rise to a free exercise violation when it exceeds the scope of his employment or is not authorized. *See, e.g.*, Canell v. Lightner, 143 F.3d 1210, 1214 (9th Cir. 1998) (finding no free exercise violation where a prisoner did not allege that correctional officer, who in effect religiously harassed the prisoner, "acted pursuant to any state or prison policy authorizing prison staff to interfere with the religious freedoms of inmates").

95 *See* Holloman *ex rel.* Holloman v. Harland, 370 F.3d 1252, 1284 (11th Cir. 2004) (explaining in an Establishment Clause case that the term "law" includes "not only … statutes, but acts and decisions of individual governmental actors.").

96 Zwerling v. Reagan, 576 F. Supp. 1373, 1378 (C.D. Cal. 1983) (holding that neither a joint congressional resolution nor a presidential proclamation, each concerning the designation of 1983 as the "Year of the Bible," was a "law" under the First Amendment). "The joint resolution of Congress … does not exact any particular behavior from any individual. Nor does it authorize the President to exact any particular behavior from any individual. It certainly imposes no penalties or sanctions of any kind. It is not a 'law.'" *Id.* [citing Am. Banana Co. v. United Fruit Co., 213 U.S. 347 (1909); U.S. Fidelity & Guaranty Co. v. Guenther, 281 U.S. 34 (1929)].

97 *See* U.S. Const. amend. I; Peterson v. Minidoka Cnty. Sch. Dist. No. 331, 118 F.3d 1351, 1356 (9th Cir. 1997) (noting that "[t]he free exercise of religion … is guaranteed against congressional impairment by the Bill of Rights"), *amended by* 132 F.3d 1258 (9th Cir. 1997); Nicholas Quinn Rosenkranz, *The Subjects of the Constitution*, 62 Stan. L. Rev. 1209, 1252–3 (2010).

98 *See* Shrum v. City of Coweta, Okla., 449 F.3d 1132, 1140–3 (10th Cir. 2006); Rosenkranz, *supra* note 97, at 1253 n. 6 (noting cases). Though it applies to all branches of government, nevertheless "[u]nder

By means of judicially recognized incorporation through the Due Process Clause of the Fourteenth Amendment, moreover, the clause today equally applies to all branches and officers of state and local governments as well.[99]

It does not, however, directly constrain the actions of foreign governments[100] or domestic tribal governments,[101] nor does it constrain the conduct of private, nongovernmental parties that are not acting in a meaningful relationship with a government,[102] although civil rights statutes or ordinances may impose on these parties comparable duties and limitations.[103] "In certain circumstances," however, "the government may become so entangled in private conduct that 'the deed of an ostensibly private organization or individual is to be treated … as if a State had caused it to be performed.'"[104] Normally, "to hold that private parties … are State actors, [a] court must conclude that … (1) the State has coerced or at least significantly encouraged the action alleged to violate the Constitution ('State compulsion test'); (2) the private parties performed a public function that was traditionally the exclusive prerogative of the State ('public function test'); or (3) 'the State had so far insinuated itself into a position of interdependence with the [private parties] … that it was a joint participant in the enterprise' ('nexus/joint action test')."[105]

Even when a named defendant is governmental, one must further show that the defendant, when allegedly infringing on the claimant's religious freedom, was exercising

our constitutional system, courts have a long tradition of resolving questions of religious freedom." Suhre v. Haywood Cnty., 131 F.3d 1083, 1091 (4th Cir. 1997).

99 *See* Church of the Lukumi Babalu Aye, Inc. v. City of Hialeah, 508 U.S. 520, 531 (1993); Shrum, 449 F.3d at 1140–3; Peterson, 118 F.3d at 1356 (noting that "[t]he free exercise of religion … is … insured against intrusion by state or municipal authority through the incorporation of the First Amendment's guarantees into the Fourteenth Amendment"). "Incorporation" is the judicial interpretive process of recognizing various Bill of Rights liberties, such as the First Amendment guarantee of free exercise, as part of the guarantee of due process in Section I the Fourteenth Amendment, thereby rendering them applicable to state and local governmental actions. The Free Exercise Clause's incorporation was recognized in Cantwell v. Connecticut, 310 U.S. 296, 303 (1940). Absent such incorporation, the clause would apply only against the federal government. *See* Permoli v. Mun. No. 1 of City of New Orleans, 44 U.S. (3 How.) 589 (1845).

100 *See* Naoko Ohno v. Yuko Yasuma, 723 F.3d 984, 993 (9th Cir. 2013).

101 *See* Native Am. Church of N. Am. v. Navajo Tribal Council, 272 F.2d 131, 134–5 (10th Cir. 1959) (holding that tribes are not bound by the First Amendment); Toledo v. Pueblo De Jemez, 119 F. Supp. 429, 431–2 (D.N.M. 1954) (alleged tribal violation of religious liberty not an action under color of state law). Tribal governments, instead, are subject to a federal statutory analog, part of the Indian Civil Rights Act, that forbids them from "mak[ing] or enforc[ing] any law prohibiting the free exercise of religion." 25 U.S.C. § 1302(a)(1).

102 *See* 2 Harold S. Lewis, Jr., Police Misconduct and Civil Rights § 10–12 (2d ed. 2002). When confronted with a constitutional suit against a seemingly private actor, courts generally will ask "first whether the claimed constitutional deprivation resulted from the exercise of a right or privilege having its source in state authority, and second, whether the private party charged with the deprivation could be described in all fairness as a state actor." Edmonson v. Leesville Concrete Co., 500 U.S. 614, 620 (1991) (citations omitted).

103 *See, e.g.*, 42 U.S.C. § 2000e-2 (prohibiting private employers, employment agencies, and labor unions from engaging in employment-related religious discrimination); *id.* § 3604 (prohibiting religious discrimination in the private sale or rental of housing).

104 Wickersham v. City of Columbia, 481 F.3d 591, 597 (8th Cir. 2007) [quoting Brentwood Acad. v. Tenn. Secondary Sch. Athletic Ass'n, 531 U.S. 288, 295 (2001)], *cert. denied*, 552 U.S. 950 (2007).

105 Rayburn *ex rel.* Rayburn v. Hogue, 241 F.3d 1341, 1347 (11th Cir. 2001) [quoting NBC, Inc. v. Commun. Workers of Am., 860 F.2d 1022, 1026–7 (11th Cir. 1988)]; *accord* Wittner v. Banner Health, 720 F.3d 770, 775–81 (10th Cir. 2013); Santiago v. Puerto Rico, 655 F.3d 61, 68 (1st Cir. 2011).

sovereign governmental authority or, to use the phrasing of 42 U.S.C. § 1983, was acting "under color of law."[106] This showing is simple when what is being challenged is an actual law or policy or its proper implementation by a government actor; in those instances, the sovereign action is inherent. It can be more complicated, however, if the government official or agent is not clearly acting within the scope of his or her employment or authority or, as indicated earlier, if the government action being challenged has no legal effect, in which case it may not be considered a "law" at all.

Finally, it should be noted that the types of defendants and conduct that may be challenged under RFRA and RLUIPA can, because of the specific language of those statutes, differ from those that may be challenged under the Free Exercise Clause. For one thing, the Free Exercise Clause applies to both federal and state governments, the former by its text and the latter by Fourteenth Amendment incorporation. However, RFRA applies only to the federal government[107] and apparently only to federal law,[108] whereas RLUIPA applies only to state and local governments and to state law (and, of course, only to conduct relating to institutionalized persons and land use).[109] For another thing, the Free Exercise Clause often arises without controversy in suits between private parties, where the court's application of statutory or common law, such as tort law, implicates the free exercise interests of one of the parties.[110] Some courts, however, have held or suggested that RFRA, as a matter of statutory language and congressional intent, does not apply to suits between private parties.[111] Finally, suits for alleged Free Exercise Clause violations

[106] *See, e.g.*, Montano v. Hedgepeth, 120 F.3d 844, 851 (8th Cir. 1997) (holding that state-employed prison chaplain, sued under 42 U.S.C. § 1983 for allegedly violating an inmate's free exercise of religion, did not act "under color of law" and was "not a state actor when he engage[d] in inherently ecclesiastical functions").

[107] *See* 42 U.S.C. § 2000bb-2(1) ["[T]he term 'government' includes a branch, department, agency, instrumentality, and official (or other person acting under color of law) of the United States, or of a covered entity."]; *id.* § 2000bb-2(2) ("[T]he term 'covered entity' means the District of Columbia, the Commonwealth of Puerto Rico, and each territory and possession of the United States.").

[108] *See id.* § 2000bb-3(a) ("This chapter applies to all Federal law, and the implementation of that law, whether statutory or otherwise, and whether adopted before or after November 16, 1993.").

[109] *See id.* § 2000cc-5(4) (defining "government" as "a State, county, municipality, or other governmental entity created under the authority of a State;" "any branch, department, agency, instrumentality, or official of [the aforementioned entities]"; and "any other person acting under color of State law").

[110] *See, e.g.*, Naoko Ohno v. Yuko Yasuma, 723 F.3d 984, 1010 (9th Cir. 2013) (explaining that a church could "invoke the protection of the Religion Clauses against a judgment in tort" by "demonstrat[ing] that imposing liability in damages substantially burdened its sincerely held religious beliefs or practices and that the state's justifications for that burden did not outweigh any infringement on the Church's religious freedom"); Paul v. Watchtower Bible & Tract Soc'y of N.Y., Inc., 819 F.2d 875, 880 (9th Cir. 1997) ("State laws whether statutory or common law, including tort rules, constitute state action ... Clearly, the application of tort law to activities of a church or its adherents in their furtherance of their religious belief is an exercise of state power. When the imposition of liability would result in the abridgement of the right to free exercise of religious beliefs, recovery in tort is barred."), *cert. denied*, 484 U.S. 926 (1987); Sands v. Living Word Fellowship, 34 P.3d 955, 958 (Alaska 2001) ("If conduct is protected by the free exercise clause of the First Amendment to the U.S. Constitution ... a tort action based on that conduct is barred.").

[111] *Compare* Gen. Conf. Corp. of Seventh-Day Adventists v. McGill, 617 F.3d 402, 410–12 (6th Cir. 2010) (holding RFRA inapplicable), *cert. denied*, 131 S. Ct. 2097 (2011), *and* Rweyemamu v. Cote, 520 F.3d 198, 203 n.2 (2d Cir. 2008) (questioning its applicability), *and* Tomic v. Catholic Diocese of Peoria, 442 F.3d 1036, 1042 (7th Cir. 2006) (holding RFRA inapplicable), *and* Worldwide Church of God v. Phila. Church of God, Inc., 227 F.3d 1110, 1121 (9th Cir. 2000) (questioning RFRA's applicability), *cert. denied*, 532 U.S. 958 (2001), *with* Hankins v. Lyght, 441 F.3d 96, 103 (2d Cir. 2006) (holding RFRA applicable, though not unqualifiedly). *See generally* Shruti Chaganti, *Note, Why the Religious Freedom*

normally can be brought against federal and state governments or their officials, and relief for proven violations potentially can include monetary damages depending on a number of circumstances.[112] Under RLUIPA, however, the Supreme Court has held that the statute's spending power–based provision does not waive state sovereign immunity such that monetary damages cannot be recovered by prisoners in suits against states or state agents named in their official capacities.[113] Likewise, some lower courts have held that RFRA does not waive the federal government's sovereign immunity and thus disallows monetary relief against the federal government or its agents in official-capacity suits.[114] At the same time, several lower courts also have held that RLUIPA does not permit suits against state prison officials in their individual capacities, thereby foreclosing a potential alternative avenue of monetary relief.[115]

## 2. *Religious Basis for the Practice*

A free exercise claimant also must demonstrate that his or her practice stems from religion, or a religious belief system, or is otherwise religious in nature.[116] By its text, the

*Restoration Act Provides a Defense in Suits by Private Plaintiffs*, 99 VA. L. REV. 343 (2013). Regarding the issue of who can and cannot sue under RFRA, the Supreme Court has held that statute may be invoked by closely held for-profit corporations [*see* Burwell v. Hobby Lobby Stores, Inc., 134 S. Ct. 2751, 2768–75 (2014)], whereas lower courts have held that the statute does not provide for claims by nonresident aliens [*see* Rasul v. Myers, 563 F.3d 527, 532–33 (D.C. Cir. 2009), *cert. denied*, 558 U.S. 1091 (2009); Bukhari v. Piedmont Reg'l Jail. Auth., Civ. Action No. 01:09-cv-1270, 2010 WL 3385179, at *4–*5 (E.D. Va. Aug. 20, 2010) (unpublished)], and at least one lower court has also strongly suggested that RFRA may not be used by enemy combatants in military detention. *See* Lebron v. Rumsfeld, 670 F.3d 540, 557–60 (4th Cir. 2012), *cert. denied*, 132 S. Ct. 2751 (2012).

112 *See* Al-Jundi v. Estate of Rockefeller, 885 F.2d 1060, 1065–7 (2d Cir. 1989) (explaining the availability of damages against state or local officials under 42 U.S.C. § 1983); *cf.* Ashcroft v. Iqbal, 556 U.S. 662, 675 ("assum[ing], without deciding," that a damages claim against federal governmental defendants for alleged religious discrimination in violation of the First Amendment "is actionable"); Jihaad v. O'Brien, 645 F.2d 556 (6th Cir. 1981) (entertaining claim against federal defendants for alleged free exercise violation); Turkmen v. Ashcroft, 915 F. Supp. 2d 314, 352–4 (E.D.N.Y. 2013) (expressly recognizing a damages claim against federal defendants for allegedly violating the Free Exercise Clause).

113 *See* Sossamon v. Texas, 131 S. Ct. 1651, 1658–61 (2011).

114 *See, e.g.*, Webman v. Fed. Bureau of Prisons, 441 F.3d 1022 (D.C. Cir. 2006); *see id.* at 1026 n. 2 (listing several federal district court cases so concluding).

115 *See, e.g.*, Washington v. Gonyea, 731 F.3d 143, 145–6 (2d Cir. 2013) (holding that RLUIPA does not create a cause of action to sue prison officials in their individual capacity; citing other circuit courts so holding); Sharp v. Johnson, 669 F.3d 144, 154–5 (3d Cir. 2012) ("RLUIPA does not permit an action against … [state prison officials] in their individual capacities. [The state] … not [the officials], was the direct recipient of any federal funds. Thus, RLUIPA cannot impose direct liability on [the officials], who were not parties to the contract created between [the state] and the federal government."), *cert. denied*, 133 S. Ct. 41 (2012).

116 *See* Levitan v. Ashcroft, 281 F.3d 1313, 1320 (D.C. Cir. 2002) ("The litigant's … practices at issue must be of a religious nature."); DeHart v. Horn, 227 F.3d 47, 51 (3d Cir. 2000) ("The mere assertion of a religious belief does not automatically trigger First Amendment protections … To the contrary, only those beliefs which are … religious in nature are entitled to constitutional protection."); United States v. Ward, 989 F.2d 1015, 1017 (9th Cir. 1992) ("[A court] must determine as a threshold matter whether [a person]'s beliefs are within the ambit of the First Amendment. In order for [a person] to invoke 'the protection of the Religion Clauses, [the person's] claims must be rooted in religious belief.'" [quoting Wisconsin v. Yoder, 406 U.S. 205, 215 (1972)]; Otero v. State Election Bd. of Okla., 975 F.2d 738, 740 (10th Cir. 1992) ("[T]he burden is upon the plaintiff to establish that his belief or practice is truly rooted in a religious belief."), *cert. denied*, 507 U.S. 977 (1993); Grosz v. City of Miami Beach, Fla., 721 F.2d 729, 736 (11th Cir. 1983) ("Only conduct flowing from religious belief merits free exercise

Free Exercise Clause protects only exercise rooted in "religion,"[117] and "[t]he government need only accommodate the exercise of actual religious convictions."[118] The Supreme Court, in turn, has clearly indicated that secular or philosophical beliefs, even if strongly held, cannot themselves trigger the Free Exercise Clause.[119] As noted by the Third Circuit, "the free exercise clause does not protect all deeply held beliefs, however 'ultimate' their ends or all-consuming their means. An individual or group may adhere to and profess certain political, economic, or social doctrines, perhaps quite passionately. The first amendment, though, has not been construed, at least as yet, to shelter strongly held ideologies of such a nature, however all-encompassing their scope."[120] What *does* qualify as a religion or religious practice under the First Amendment has been the subject of extensive judicial and academic analysis. Even so, or perhaps as a result, it largely remains an unclarified legal question, and "[t]he determination of what is a 'religious' belief or practice is more often than not a difficult and delicate task."[121] Ultimately, however, it appears to be a question of law, albeit one with factual dimensions, and is thus an issue that a court, rather than jury or the parties, must decide.[122]

protection; no weight measures on the side of religion unless the government action ultimately affects a religious practice."), *cert. denied*, 469 U.S. 827 (1984); New Creation Fellowship of Buffalo v. Town of Cheektowaga, N.Y., No. 99-CV-460A(F), 2004 WL 1498190, at *32 (W.D.N.Y. July 2, 2004) (Magis. J. Rpt. & Recomm.) (unpublished) ("To avoid summary judgment on a § 1983 claim based on the Free Exercise Clause, the essential characteristics qualifying the asserted religion as one entitled to the Clause's protection must appear in the record."), *aff'd*, No. 05-0159-CV, 164 Fed. App'x 5 (2d Cir. Dec. 6, 2005) (unpublished).

117 *See* U.S. Const. amend. I; Thomas v. Review Bd., 450 U.S. 707, 713 (1981) ("Only beliefs rooted in religion are protected by the Free Exercise Clause, which, by its terms, gives special protection to the exercise of religion."). That said, courts have held that it also protects the nonreligious from religious coercion. *See* Johnson v. Bd. of Cnty. Comm'rs, 528 F. Supp. 919, 921 (D.N.M. 1981), *rev'd on other grounds*, 781 F.2d 777 (10th Cir. 1985), *cert. denied*, 476 U.S. 1169 (1986); Seegers v. Parker, 241 So. 2d 213, 216 n. 4 (La. 1970), *cert. denied*, 403 U.S. 955 (1971). This principle does not necessarily mean that the Free Exercise Clause protects atheism or agnosticism in and of itself, though it might. *See, e.g.*, Kaufman v. McCaughtry, 419 F.3d 678, 681–2 (7th Cir. 2005) (accepting atheism as functionally religious under the Free Exercise Clause); Soc'y of Separationists, Inc. v. Herman, 939 F.2d 1207, 1215–17 (5th Cir. 1991) (sustaining atheist's challenge to a court affirmation requirement, countenancing her argument "that a God-free affirmation is nonetheless a 'religious statement,' hence objectionable"). Rather, it reflects the quite logical notion that coerced religious exercise, no matter the beliefs of the person coerced, simply cannot be *free* exercise within the meaning of the clause. For further analysis of the status of atheism under the First Amendment, *see* Caroline Corbin, *Nonbelievers and Government Religious Speech*, 97 Iowa L. Rev. 347 (2011); Nelson Tebbe, *Nonbelievers*, 97 Va. L. Rev. 1111 (2011).

118 United States v. Meyers, 95 F.3d 1475, 1482 (10th Cir. 1996) (RFRA case), *cert. denied*, 522 U.S. 1006 (1997).

119 *See* Frazee v. Ill. Dep't of Employment Sec., 489 U.S. 829, 833 (1989) ("Purely secular views do not suffice."); Wisconsin v. Yoder, 406 U.S. 205, 216 (1972) (distinguishing between "religious" and "philosophical and personal" beliefs); Sanders v. Casa View Baptist Church, 134 F.3d 331, 336 (4th Cir. 1998) ("[T]he constitutional guarantee of *religious* freedom cannot be construed to protect *secular* beliefs and behavior, even when they comprise part of an otherwise religious relationship between a minister and a member of his or her congregation."), *cert. denied*, 525 U.S. 868 (1998); McGlothin v. Jackson Mun. Separate Sch. Dist., 829 F. Supp. 853, 865–6 & n.19 (S.D. Miss. 1992).

120 Africa v. Commonwealth of Pa., 662 F.2d 1025, 1034 (3d Cir. 1981), *cert. denied*, 456 U.S. 908 (1982).

121 Thomas v. Review Bd. of Ind. Employment Sec. Div., 450 U.S. 707, 714 (1981).

122 *See* New Creation Fellowship of Buffalo, 2004 WL 1498190, at *32 {"The determination of whether the purported religion qualifies for First Amendment protection is a question for the court." [citing Africa v. Pennsylvania, 662 F.2d 1025, 1037 (3d Cir. 1981), *cert. denied*, 456 U.S. 908 (1982); Malnak v. Yogi, 592 F.2d 197, 199 (3d Cir. 1979) (*per curiam*)]}; *cf.* United States v. Quaintance, 471 F. Supp. 2d 1153, 1156 (D.N.M. 2006) ("Whether a particular set of beliefs are 'religious' within the meaning of RFRA

Though the definition of religion is a matter taken up at greater length elsewhere in this book,[123] a few observations at this juncture are warranted. First, the belief systems animating most free exercise claims are not contested as being nonreligious in large measure because free exercise claims ordinarily involve belief systems, even if nonconventional, that are widely or at least sufficiently recognized as religious. The disputes in litigation, instead, often focus on the nature of the challenged law, the extent to which the law is actually burdening the claimant's religious practice, and if the claim proceeds far enough, whether the government can justify its imposition. Second, when a court is faced with a contention that the claimant's belief system is not religious, and especially where precedent regarding that belief system is sparse or nonexistent, it will likely avoid definitively deciding the matter unless it absolutely must do so, given a general norm against avoiding unnecessary constitutional questions,[124] given the delicacy of the task (enhanced by ambient nonestablishment, equal protection, and institutional concerns), and not least important, given the lack of authoritative guidance from the U.S. Supreme Court. To the extent, in fact, that the court anticipates ruling against the claimant on some alternative basis, the court simply may assume, for purpose of the analysis, that the belief system is a religion, thereby minimizing any precedential effect. Lastly, having noted these considerations, it also should be emphasized that a court is fully empowered to determine whether or not a belief system comprises a religion, or a practice is religious, under the First Amendment [125]; that the evidentiary burden in this regard is on the claimant (although "the threshold for establishing the religious nature of [a claimant's] beliefs is low"[126]); and that a court will find against the claimant on this point if insufficient proof is adduced before or during trial.[127]

is a legal question reviewed *de novo*."), *aff'd*, 608 F.3d 717 (10th Cir. 2010), *cert. denied*, 131 S. Ct. 544 (2010); State v. White, 271 P.3d 1217, 1221 (Idaho Ct. App 2011) (interpreting Idaho's Free Exercise of Religion Protected Act, stating that "the issue of whether a belief motivating a particular practice is 'religious' is a question of law").

123 *See* Chapter 7.

124 *See* Clinton v. Jones, 520 U.S. 681, 690 & n. 11 (1997); Lyng v. Northwest Indian Cemetery Protective Ass'n, 485 U.S. 439, 445 (1988); Rescue Army v. Mun. Ct. of City of L.A., 331 U.S. 549, 570 n. 34 (1947); Spector Motor Serv., Inc. v. McLaughlin, 323 U.S. 101, 105 (1944); Lisa A. Kloppenberg, *Avoiding Constitutional Questions*, 35 B.C. L. Rev. 1003 (1994); Brian C. Murchison, *Interpretation and Independence: How Judges Use the Avoidance Canon in Separation of Powers Cases*, 30 Ga. L. Rev. 85 (1995);

125 *See* Jones v. Bradley, 590 F.2d 294, 295 (9th Cir. 1979) ["It is clearly impermissible to inquire into the 'truth' of religious doctrines or beliefs. There is no prohibition, however, against ruling whether or not a set of beliefs constitutes a religion when deciding if First Amendment protections apply." (citation omitted)]; *see also* Ben-Yahudah v. Bolden, No. 94–2438, 98 F.3d 1341, 1996 WL 571145, at *4 n. 1 (6th Cir. 1996) (*per curiam*) (unpublished). *But see* United States v. Daly, 756 F.2d 1076, 1081 (5th Cir. 1985) ("[C]ourts may not determine whether a given belief is or is not a religion." [citing United States v. Ballard, 322 U.S. 78, 86–8 (1944)], *cert. denied*, 474 U.S. 1022 (1985).

126 United States v. Meyers, 95 F.3d 1475, 1482–3 (10th Cir. 1996), *cert. denied*, 522 U.S. 1006 (1997). "[I]f there is any doubt about whether a particular set of beliefs constitutes a religion, the court will err on the side of freedom and find that the beliefs are a religion." State v. Pedersen, 679 N.W.2d 368, 374 (Minn. Ct. App. 2004).

127 *See, e.g.*, United States v. Meyers, 95 F.3d 1475, 1482–4 (10th Cir. 1996) (preamendment RFRA case) (finding the "Church of Marijuana" to be not religious), *cert. denied*, 522 U.S. 1006 (1997); Ephraim v. Angelone, 313 F. Supp. 2d 569, 578 (E.D. Va. 2003) ["Plaintiff has provided no evidence that his dietary request is rooted in a religious belief. Plaintiff claims that as a Charismatic Christian, he is required to eat only fresh fruit, raw vegetables, whole grains, milk, and cheese. Yet Plaintiff has provided no objective evidence of the dietary requirements of Charismatic Christianity. Absent such evidence, Plaintiff has not established that his claims are rooted in a religious belief so as to invoke the protection of the First

### 3. *Substantial Burden on the Practice*

It is not enough under the Free Exercise Clause that a claimant's practice be religious. The text also dictates that a claimant's "free exercise" be "prohibit[ed]" by the government. According to the courts, this does not mean that the claimant must demonstrate that the governmental action by its own terms or operation completely forbids the claimant's desired practice, as the word "prohibit" might suggest. To the contrary, a free exercise violation potentially may arise when the government simply makes the practice of one's religion more difficult. Nor does the law have to be prohibitory if that is understood to mean that the law must be criminal in nature.[128] Instead, as indicated by many of the cases addressed in this chapter, the clause may be triggered by any type of governmental action, be it regulation,[129] taxation,[130] or even adjudication.[131]

The Supreme Court has emphasized, nevertheless, that the term "prohibit" denotes that the Free Exercise Clause is a negative guarantee against, and not an affirmative guarantee of, government action. That is, "[t]he Free Exercise Clause affords an individual protection from certain forms of governmental compulsion; it does not afford an individual a right to dictate the conduct of the Government's internal procedures."[132] According to the Court, "[t]he crucial word in the constitutional text is 'prohibit' … '[f]or the Free Exercise Clause is written in terms of what the government cannot do to the individual, not in terms of what the individual can exact from the government.'"[133]

Amendment." (citation omitted)], *aff'd*, No. 03-6411, 68 Fed. App'x 460, 2003 WL 21380621 (4th Cir. Jun. 27, 2003) (unpublished), *cert. denied*, 124 S. Ct. 1084 (2004); Theriault v. Silber, 453 F. Supp. 254, 260–1 (W.D. Tex. 1978) (finding the "Church of the New Song" to be not religious), *appeal dismissed*, 579 F.2d 302 (5th Cir. 1978), *cert. denied*, 440 U.S. 917 (1979); State v. Pederson, 679 N.W.2d 368, 376 (Minn. Ct. App. 2004) (holding that the defendant did not sufficiently demonstrate that beliefs were religious); State v. Brashear, 593 P.2d 63, 68 (N.M. Ct. App. 1979) (same).

128 Interestingly, the possibility that the Free Exercise Clause may be *less* protective against criminal laws was raised by the Court's decision in Employment Division v. Smith, 494 U.S. 872 (1990). *See, e.g.*, Miller v. Reed, 176 F.3d 1202, 1207 (9th Cir. 1999) {noting that it had "indicated in dicta in prior cases that *Smith* only applies when the challenged law 'punishes conduct which constitutes a criminal act,'" although now rejecting that view [quoting NLRB v. Hanna Boys Ctr., 940 F.2d 1295, 1305 (9th Cir. 1991)]}; Salvation Army v. Dep't of Cmty. Affairs, 919 F.2d 183, 194 (3d Cir. 1990) (noting that "[t]here are a number of phrases in the Court's opinion that might support such a limited reading," although ultimately rejecting such an interpretation). It is settled, however, that even though "*Smith* involved a criminal law … its rule also applies in the context of non-criminal laws and regulations." Tenafly Eruv Ass'n, Inc. v. Borough of Tenafly, 309 F.3d 144, 165 n. 25 (3d Cir. 2002), *cert. denied*, 539 U.S. 942 (2003).

129 *See, e.g.*, Tenafly Eruv Ass'n, 309 F.3d at 178 (addressing a challenge to an ordinance regulating signage, finding that the claimants were likely to prevail)

130 *See, e.g.*, Follett v. Town of McCormick, S.C., 321 U.S. 573, 576–8 (1944) (invalidating the application of a business license tax to a preacher). It should be noted, however, that free exercise challenges to taxation are rarely, if ever, successful. *See* FEDERAL TAX COORDINATOR ¶ V-2769 (2d ed. 1997 & Supp. June 2014) (cataloging several adverse cases); Michelle O'Connor, *The Religious Freedom Restoration Act: Exactly What Rights Does It "Restore" in the Federal Tax Context?* 36 ARIZ. ST. L.J. 321 (2004). For more on taxation, *see* Chapter 10.

131 *See, e.g.*, *In re* Palmer, 386 A.2d 1112, 1114–16 (R.I. 1978) (holding that a trial judge violated the free exercise rights of a person appearing before the court).

132 Bowen v. Roy, 476 U.S. 693, 700 (1986).

133 Lyng v. Northwest Indian Cemetery Protective Ass'n, 485 U.S. 439, 451 (1988) [quoting *Sherbert*, 374 U.S. at 412 (Douglas, J., concurring)]; *see also* Taylor v. City of Gary, Ind., No. 06-3550, 2007 WL 1317130, at *1 (7th Cir. May 7, 2007) (*per curiam*) (unpublished); Prater v. City of Burnside, Ky., 289 F.3d 417, 427–8 (6th Cir. 2002), *cert. denied*, 537 U.S. 1018 (2002).

Even with this limitation, however, courts have consistently struggled with the task of coherently separating cognizable from uncognizable prohibitions on religious free exercise.

What the Supreme Court has often employed in this regard is a requirement that one's religious practices be *burdened* or *substantially burdened* by some action of the government. In developing this notion, "[t]he Court's articulation of what constitutes a 'substantial burden' has varied over time,"[134] and these formulations, including the diverse factors they bring to bear, are the main focus of this subsection. It should be noted, before assessing the various formulations, that the true objective or effect of the burden inquiry is a matter of some dispute, in part turning on differing conceptions of the judicial process. The courts themselves are likely to explain that the inquiry is simply an attempt to interpret the term "prohibit" or perhaps the meaning of "free" exercise and that concerns about line drawing are inherently part of that process but are far from paramount or determinative. Others, however, have maintained that the burden concept is fundamentally about demarcation, akin, perhaps, to the determination of proximate cause in the law of torts. It has been argued by Professor Ira Lupu, for example, that the courts employ the burden requirement as a "gatekeeper doctrine … function[ing] to increase the likelihood of failure at the prima facie stage,"[135] thereby "obviat[ing] the need for judicial determination of other, perhaps more troubling questions."[136]

Whatever the actual objective of the burden analysis, at least three aspects of it are known with relative certainty. First, as part of the prima facie case, a claimant must "allege facts … showing that [government's] actions substantially burdened his ability to practice his religion,"[137] and failure to make this threshold evidentiary showing will doom the claimant's case,[138] even if the government has in fact greatly burdened the claimant's religion and no matter how sincere and devout the claimant's faith might be.[139] Although a few courts in recent years have questioned whether the substantial-burden requirement remains valid,[140]

134 Midrash Sephardi, Inc. v. Town of Surfside, 366 F.3d 1214, 1226–7 (11th Cir. 2004), *cert. denied*, 543 U.S. 1146 (2005); *accord* Westchester Day Sch. v. Vill. of Mamaroneck, 379 F. Supp. 2d 550, 557 (S.D.N.Y. 2005) (noting that "[t]he Supreme Court … has articulated the substantial burden test differently over the years"); Guru Nanak Sikh Soc'y of Yuba City v. Cnty. of Sutter, 326 F. Supp. 2d 1140, 1151 (E.D. Cal. 2003) (same), *aff'd*, 456 F.3d 978 (9th Cir. 2006). Likewise, "[c]ircuit courts have articulated different definitions of substantial burden as applied to Section 2(a)(1) RLUIPA cases." Westchester Day Sch. v. Vill. of Mamaroneck, 417 F. Supp. 2d 477, 546 (S.D.N.Y. 2006), *aff'd*, 504 F.3d 338 (2d Cir. 2007). *See also* Karla L. Chaffee & Dwight H. Merriam, *Six Fact Patterns of Substantial Burden in RLUIPA: Lessons for Potential Litigants*, 2 ALB. GOV'T L. REV. 437 (2009).

135 Ira C. Lupu, *Where Rights Begin: The Problem of Burdens on the Free Exercise of Religion*, 102 HARV. L. REV. 933, 935 (1989).

136 *Id.* at 936; *see also id.* at 953–60 (examining the types of troubling questions that can be avoided, including the claimant's sincerity and the religiosity of the claimant's beliefs or practices). This pattern or practice apparently continued under RFRA. *See* Ira C. Lupu, *The Failure of RFRA*, 20 U. ARK. LITTLE ROCK L.J. 575, 593–6 (1998).

137 Shakur v. Schriro, 514 F.3d 878, 885 (9th Cir. 2008).

138 *See* Levitan v. Ashcroft, 281 F.3d 1313, 1320 (D.C. Cir. 2002) ("[T]his threshold showing must be made before the First Amendment is implicated.").

139 *See, e.g.*, United States v. Mitchell, 502 F.3d 931, 949 (9th Cir. 2007) (holding that executing an individual whose religion opposes capital punishment does not impose a cognizable burden on that individual's religious beliefs), *cert. denied*, 553 U.S. 1094 (2008).

140 *See, e.g.*, McEachin v. McGuinnis, 357 F.3d 197, 202–3 (2d Cir. 2004); Tenafly Eruv Ass'n v. Borough of Tenafly, 309 F.3d 144, 170–1 (3d Cir. 2002), *cert. denied*, 539 U.S. 942 (2003).

especially in light of some language in *Smith*,[141] the vast majority of courts retain the inquiry, and under RFRA, RLUIPA, and many state religious freedom laws, courts are textually required to determine whether or not a substantial burden has been demonstrated.

Second, the fundamental focus of the substantial-burden inquiry is essentially the following: is there something about the government's imposition on a given claimant's religious practice that warrants careful judicial scrutiny and potential invalidation of the law or policy causing the imposition? This inquiry may entail assessment of the government's action, the claim itself, or both, but the bottom-line question is whether "an impediment to a religious practice is significant enough to warrant judicial intervention."[142] Third and last, the burden analysis, for many litigants, judges, and scholars, poses perhaps the most frustratingly elusive issue of modern free exercise doctrine, which as noted extends today to RFRA, RLUIPA, and a host of state laws. To be sure, whereas RFRA and RLUIPA provide relatively elaborate statutory definitions of "religious exercise,"[143] their explication of the meaning of "substantial burden" is more wanting.[144] Indeed, neither statute has an outright definition for the term despite the fact that it is employed five times in RFRA and over twenty times in RLUIPA, though it is true that their definition of religious exercise refers to factors that have often been part of a Free Exercise Clause burden analysis.[145]

In any event, the conventional formulation of the burden standard under the Free Exercise Clause is that as an initial matter, a claimant must show that the government has placed a *substantial* burden on his or her religious practice and potentially that this practice is itself an important, central, or even required aspect of his or her faith. Several courts have attempted to define "substantiality" by means of synonyms and antonyms: it is "undu[e]"[146] or "significantly great"[147] and not simply "de minimis,"[148]

141 *See* Employment Div. v. Smith, 494 U.S. 872, 887 & n. 4 (1990) (suggesting that it is inappropriate "for judges to determine the 'centrality' of religious beliefs" and then observing that "'[c]onstitutionally significant burden' would seem to be 'centrality' under another name").

142 *See* McEachin, 357 F.3d at 202–3 (describing the inquiry as such, though expressing concern about the validity of such an inquiry, but then recasting it as a question of whether the government "significantly interfered" with a claimant's religious practice).

143 *See* 42 U.S.C. § 2000cc-5(7)(A) (RLUIPA); *id.* § 2000bb-2(4) (RFRA) (as amended, employing RLUIPA's definition).

144 *See* Mack v. O'Leary, 80 F.3d 1175, 1178 (7th Cir. 1996) (noting at least three different approaches among the federal appeals courts to defining "substantial burden" under the original version of RFRA), *judgment vacated on other grounds*, 522 U.S. 801 (1997).

145 This is the clarification in RLUIPA that one's "exercise" of religion need not be "compelled by" or "central to" one's religious belief system. *See* 42 U.S.C. § 2000cc-5(7)(A); *infra* text accompanying notes 176–211 (discussing these potential factors in the substantial burden analysis). RFRA was amended to incorporate this standard from RLUIPA. *See id.* § 2000bb-2(4).

146 Wisconsin v. Yoder, 406 U.S. 205, 220 (1972).

147 *See* Roman Catholic Bishop of Springfield v. City of Springfield, 724 F.3d 78, 96 (1st Cir. 2013) (RLUIPA case) ("A 'burden' is '[s]omething that hinders or oppresses,' or 'something oppressive or worrisome.' … Next, something is 'substantial' when it is 'important' or 'significantly great.'" (citations omitted) [quoting Black's Law Dictionary 223 (9th ed. 2009), Merriam-Webster's Collegiate Dictionary 152 (10th ed. 1993), and *id.* at 1174, respectively)]; San Jose Christian College v. City of Morgan Hill, 360 F.3d 1024, 1034 (9th Cir. 2004) (RLUIPA case) {"A 'burden' is 'something that is oppressive.' 'Substantial,' in turn, is defined as 'considerable in quantity' or 'significantly great.' Thus, for a land use regulation to impose a 'substantial burden,' it must be 'oppressive' to a 'significantly great' extent. That is, a 'substantial burden' on 'religious exercise' must impose a significantly great restriction or onus upon such exercise." (citations omitted) [quoting Black's Law Dictionary 190 (7th ed. 1999), and Merriam-Webster's Collegiate Dictionary 1170 (10th ed. 2002), respectively]}.

148 *See, e.g.*, Rapier v. Harris, 172 F.3d 999, 1006 n. 4 (7th Cir. 1999) {"De minimis burdens on the free exercise of religion are not of constitutional dimension." [citing Walsh v. La. High Sch. Athletic Ass'n,

"inconsequential,"[149] or "an inconvenience."[150] The Supreme Court, for its part, has said that the government imposes a substantial burden when it "put[s] substantial pressure on an adherent to modify his [or her] behavior and to violate his [or her] beliefs … [even though] the compulsion may be indirect"[151]; forces a person to "choose between following the precepts of [his or] her religion and forfeiting [governmental] benefits, on the one hand, and abandoning one of the precepts of [his or] her religion … on the other hand"[152]; or, phrased more stringently, "affirmatively compel[s] [claimants], by threat of sanctions, to refrain from religiously motivated conduct or to engage in conduct that they find objectionable for religious reasons."[153] In the view of the Tenth Circuit, speaking in a prisoner case under the original version of RFRA, "[t]o exceed the 'substantial burden' threshold, government regulation must significantly inhibit or constrain conduct or expression that manifests some central tenet of [an individual's] beliefs; must meaningfully curtail [an individual's] ability to express adherence to his or her faith; or must deny [an individual] reasonable opportunities to engage in those activities that are fundamental to … [the individual's] religion."[154] Alternatively, as described in more demanding terms by a Seventh Circuit RLUIPA land-use decision, a government action "that imposes a substantial burden on religious exercise is one that necessarily bears direct, primary, and fundamental responsibility for rendering religious exercise … effectively impracticable."[155]

616 F.2d 152, 158 (5th Cir. 1980), *cert. denied*, 449 U.S. 1124 (1981); Windsor Park Baptist Church, Inc. v. Ark. Activities Ass'n, 658 F.2d 618, 622–4 (8th Cir. 1981)]}. Indeed, "[t]he substantial burden test … presupposes that there will be cases in which it comfortably could be said that a belief or practice is so peripheral to the plaintiff's religion that any burden can be aptly characterized as constitutionally de minimis." Ford v. McGinnis, 352 F.3d 582, 593 (2d Cir. 2003).

149 Levitan v. Ashcroft, 281 F.3d 1313, 1320 (D.C. Cir. 2002) (explaining that a challenged law must "impose a substantial, as opposed to inconsequential, burden on the litigant's religious practice").

150 Midrash Sephardi, Inc. v. Town of Surfside, 366 F.3d 1214, 1227 (11th Cir. 2004) (stating that "a 'substantial burden' must place more than an inconvenience on religious exercise"), *cert. denied*, 543 U.S. 1146 (2005); Graham v. Comm'r, 822 F.2d 844, 851 (9th Cir. 1987) (explaining that "[t]his interference must be more than an inconvenience"), *aff'd*, 490 U.S. 680 (1989).

151 Thomas v. Review Bd. of Ind. Employment Sec. Div., 450 U.S. 707, 718 (1981).

152 Sherbert v. Verner, 374 U.S. 398, 404 (1963); *see also* C.L.U.B. v. City of Chicago, 157 F. Supp. 2d 903, 914 (N.D. Ill. 2001) ["A substantial burden exists when the government pressures a plaintiff to modify [his or] her behavior and violate [his or] her beliefs, by, for example, discriminating against [him or] her because of [his or] her religious belief, inhibiting [his or] her dissemination of particular religious views or pressuring [his or] her to forgo a religious practice." (citation omitted)], *aff'd*, 342 F.3d 752 (7th Cir. 2003), *cert. denied*, 541 U.S. 1096 (2004).

153 Bowen v. Roy, 476 U.S. 693, 703 (1986) (plurality opinion) (footnote omitted).

154 Werner v. McCotter, 49 F.3d 1476, 1480 (10th Cir. 1995) (citations omitted), *cert. denied*, 515 U.S. 1166 (1995); *see also* Horen v. Commonwealth, 23 Va. App. 735, 745, 479 S.E.2d 553, 558 (Va. Ct. App. 1997) {"A substantial burden is imposed on the free exercise of religion where governmental action compels a party to affirm a belief they do not hold, discriminates on the basis of religious beliefs, inhibits the dissemination of particular religious beliefs, or compels a party to forgo their religious practices." [citing Battles v. Anne Arundel Cnty. Bd. of Educ., 904 F. Supp. 471, 476–7 (D. Md. 1995)]}. The Eighth Circuit has subsequently carried this definition into the RLUIPA context. *See* Murphy v. Mo. Dep't of Corrections, 372 F.3d 979, 988 (8th Cir. 2004), *cert. denied*, 543 U.S. 991 (2004).

155 Civil Liberties for Urban Believers v. City of Chicago, 342 F.3d 752, 761 (7th Cir. 2003), *cert. denied*, 541 U.S. 1096 (2004). Unlike some interpretations of the Free Exercise Clause, however, RLUIPA protects "any exercise of religion, *whether or not compelled by, or central to*, a system of religious belief." 42 U.S.C. § 2000cc-5(7)(A) (emphasis added). Accordingly, RLUIPA cases may not always be an appropriate, much less authoritative, source for defining substantial burden under the First Amendment [*see* Meyer v. Teslik, 411 F. Supp. 2d 983, 990 (W.D. Wis. 2006) (recognizing this point)], nor may First

Ultimately, the substantial-burden component of the free exercise analysis may encompass as many as four inquiries: (1) the severity of the legal consequences to the claimant should the claimant defy the law, (2) the degree to which the claimant's religious practice is actually restricted or obstructed by the government's action, (3) the extent to which the religious practice is significant within the claimant's religious belief system, and (4) whether the practice is mandated by or simply motivated by this belief system. The first two inquiries, which are potentially related to each other, focus on the government's action, whereas the latter two, which are also potentially interrelated, focus on the claimant's practice and belief system. The following subsections will explore and evaluate each inquiry in greater detail.

### a. Severity of the Legal Consequences

One way that courts discern a substantial burden is by examining the formal legal consequences that have resulted, or could result, from a claimant's exercise of religion. "As a general rule, the greater the cost of practicing one's religion, the more probable that the statute creates an unconstitutional infringement."[156] Will the claimant, for example, be charged with a felony or misdemeanor, or be exacted an administrative fine, or face a loss of access to public resources or a denial of government benefits? The Tenth Circuit, in a RFRA case, has described the inquiry as assessing "*the intensity of the coercion* applied by the government."[157] Criminal penalties are generally quite sufficient in this respect, as are many civil penalties, as long as the claimant can be viewed as being worse off as a result of the governmental action.[158] By comparison, where a claimant is not disadvantaged per se but merely not advantaged in relation to other citizens who do not observe similar religious practices, courts are generally less willing to find a substantial burden.[159]

Amendment cases always be an appropriate or authoritative source for defining substantial burden under RLUIPA.

156 Lakewood, Ohio Congregation of Jehovah's Witnesses, Inc. v. City of Lakewood, Ohio, 699 F.2d 303, 305 (6th Cir. 1983), *cert. denied*, 464 U.S. 815 (1983).

157 Hobby Lobby Stores, Inc. v. Sebelius, 723 F.3d 1114, 1137 (10th Cir. 2013), *aff'd*, 134 S. Ct. 2751 (2014); *see also* Korte v. Sebelius, 735 F.3d 654, 683 (7th Cir. 2013) (agreeing with the Tenth Circuit that "the substantial-burden inquiry evaluates the coercive effect of the governmental pressure on the adherent's religious practice"), *cert. denied*, 134 S. Ct. 2903 (2014).

158 *See* Burwell v. Hobby Lobby Stores, Inc., 134 S. Ct. 2751, 2775–6 (2014) (RFRA case) (finding a substantial burden where the claimants' adherence to religious beliefs in derogation of legal requirements would generate taxes or penalties that "are surely substantial"); Grosz v. City of Miami, Fla., 721 F.2d 729, 739 (11th Cir. 1983) (explaining that the burden on the claimants did not trigger the Free Exercise Clause because it did "not rise to the level of criminal liability, loss of livelihood, or denial of a basic income sustaining public welfare benefit"), *cert. denied*, 469 U.S. 827 (1984); Episcopal Student Found. v. City of Ann Arbor, 341 F. Supp. 2d 691, 701 (E.D. Mich. 2004) ("[C]ourts routinely find substantial burdens where compliance with the statute itself violates the individual's religious beliefs and noncompliance may subject him to criminal sanctions or the loss of a significant government privilege or benefit.").

159 *See, e.g.*, *Bowen*, 476 U.S. at 703, 704 (plurality) (finding no burden where claimants simply "seek benefits from the Government and … assert that, because of certain religious beliefs, they should be excused from compliance with a condition that is binding on all other persons who seek the same benefits," explaining "that denial of such benefits by a uniformly applicable statute neutral on its face is of a wholly different, less intrusive nature than affirmative compulsion or prohibition, by threat of penal sanctions, for conduct that has religious implications"); Adkins v. Kaspar, 393 F.3d 559, 569–70 (5th Cir. 2004) (RLUIPA prison case) ("[A] government action or regulation does not rise to the level of a substantial burden on religious exercise if it merely prevents the adherent from either enjoying some benefit that is not otherwise generally available or acting in a way that is not otherwise generally allowed."),

The difficult cases, to be sure, often involve governmental benefits, such as educational or social welfare programs, precisely because the extent to which one is actually disadvantaged by the denial of these benefits is a matter of perspective and legitimate disagreement. On the one hand, being benefits, it is difficult to say that a citizen is "worse off" without them. On the other hand, economic reality and modern social contract theory may be such that the loss of such benefits often can lead to unreasonable and significant hardship. The Supreme Court has indicated that a benefit must be "important" if its denial is to trigger a constitutionally cognizable burden. Accordingly, "[w]here the state conditions receipt of an important benefit upon conduct proscribed by a religious faith, or where it denies such a benefit because of conduct mandated by religious belief, thereby putting substantial pressure on an adherent to modify his [or her] behavior and to violate his beliefs, a burden upon religion exists."[160] The Seventh Circuit, for its part, has endorsed a more flexible approach, explaining that "[t]he more valuable the benefit to the claimant and hence the greater the burden on him [or her] of forgoing it in order to continue to observe his [or her] religion, the greater must be the burden on the government of relaxing the conditions it places on that benefit for a refusal to make an exception for the claimant to survive a challenge based on the First Amendment."[161] Other lower courts have arguably set a lower bar, indicating that the benefit must simply be "nontrivial."[162] Of course, whether a benefit is "important" or "nontrivial," or whether its loss is "unreasonably costly,"[163] can be a highly contextual and relative determination grounded in baseline understandings of what is required or "commonly expected in our society."[164]

Not surprisingly, the burden issue thus has played a pivotal role in several cases involving educational funding or programs, where such societal expectations may be shifting and uncertain.[165] Consider, for example, the case of *Locke v. Davey*,[166] in which the

*cert. denied*, 545 U.S. 1104 (2005); Gary S. v. Manchester Sch. Dist., 374 F.3d 15, 20 (1st Cir. 2004) ("[D]enying … benefits … to which [the claimants] have no cognizable entitlement … do[es] not burden their free exercise rights."), *cert. denied*, 543 U.S. 988 (2004); Swanson *ex rel.* Swanson v. Guthrie Indep. Sch. Dist. No. I-L, 135 F.3d 694, 702 (10th Cir. 1998) (finding that the Free Exercise Clause, or specifically the individualized assessment exception of *Sherbert*, is not triggered where what plaintiffs sought was "special treatment not accorded other home-schooled or private-schooled students," i.e., "an added exception to the part-time attendance policy, that would accommodate people who home-school for religious reasons").

160 Thomas v. Review Bd. of Ind. Employment Sec. Div., 450 U.S. 707, 717–18 (1981); *see also Grosz*, 721 F.2d at 739 (stating that a burden can result from "denial of a basic income sustaining public welfare benefit").

161 Menora v. Ill. High Sch. Ass'n, 683 F.2d 1030, 1033 (7th Cir. 1982), *cert. denied*, 459 U.S. 1156 (1983).

162 *See, e.g.*, Adkins v. Kaspar, 393 F.3d 559, 569–70 (5th Cir. 2004) (RLUIPA prison case) ("[T]he effect of a government action or regulation is significant when it … forces the adherent to choose between, on the one hand, enjoying some generally available, non-trivial benefit, and, on the other hand, following his religious beliefs."), *cert. denied*, 545 U.S. 1104 (2005).

163 Menora, 683 F.2d at 1033 ("Free exercise of religion does not mean costless exercise of religion, but the state may not make the exercise of religion unreasonably costly.").

164 Gary S., 374 F.3d at 20 n. 2.

165 *See, e.g.*, D.L. *ex rel.* K.L. v. Baltimore Bd. of Sch. Comm'rs, 706 F.3d 256, 262–4 (4th Cir. 2013); Gary S., 374 F.3d at 19–20; Eulitt *ex. rel.* Eulitt v. Me. Dep't of Educ., 386 F.3d 344, 353–6 (1st Cir. 2004); Swanson, 135 F.3d at 697–702; Goodall by Goodall v. Stafford Cnty. Sch. Bd., 60 F.3d 168, 172–3 (4th Cir. 1995) (RFRA case); Valencia v. Blue Hen Conf., 476 F. Supp. 809, 822 (D. Del. 1979), *aff'd*, 615 F.2d 1355 (3d Cir. 1980).

166 540 U.S. 712 (2004).

Supreme Court upheld a state's refusal to have public scholarship dollars be used in pursuit of devotional theology (ministry) degrees. The Court found no cognizable burden in part because a scholarship recipient still could attend a religious school and could pursue, at that or any other school, any other degree. "[T]he State's disfavor of religion (if it can be called that) … imposes neither criminal nor civil sanctions on any type of religious service or rite. It does not deny to ministers the right to participate in the political affairs of the community. And it does not require students to choose between their religious beliefs and receiving a government benefit. The State has merely chosen not to fund a distinct category of instruction."[167] The reasoning of *Locke* has been extended recently beyond educational benefits to the context of other government resources.[168]

### b. Extent of the Governmental Restriction

As a corollary to examining the legal consequences faced by a claimant who elevates religious practice above a government directive, a second approach to discerning the presence of a substantial burden is to examine the extent to which the government directive actually restricts the religious practice in the first instance. Is the religious practice totally or effectively prohibited, or is it instead made more costly or inconvenient, and if the latter, to what degree is it made more costly or inconvenient? Though it is clear that a substantial burden may be found even where a claimant's practice is not entirely prohibited, some courts, as part of the burden inquiry, do examine the extent to which a governmental action actually does limit or inhibit the practice.

Obviously, and consistent with the prior consideration, an effective total prohibition of a practice by the imposition of criminal or meaningful civil penalties for its occurrence represents a degree of restriction that could easily be deemed substantial in a court's burden analysis.[169] After canvassing several cases under the Free Exercise Clause, RFRA, and RLUIPA, for example, the Fifth Circuit declared that "[t]he upshot of these opinions is that, at a minimum, the government's *ban* of conduct sincerely motivated by religious belief substantially burdens an adherent's free exercise of that religion. … If a government's restriction of religious conduct may be a substantial burden, then a complete ban presents a much stronger case."[170] Likewise, the Ninth Circuit in a RLUIPA prisoner case stated that it had "little difficulty in concluding that an outright ban on a particular religious exercise is a substantial burden on that religious exercise."[171]

Not all government actions, however, are so restrictive. At the other end of the spectrum are laws that impose nothing more than a chilling or stigmatic effect on religious

[167] *Id.* at 720–1 (footnote and citations omitted).

[168] *See* Bronx Household of Faith v. Bd. of Educ. of City of N.Y., 750 F.3d 184, 190 (2d Cir. 2014).

[169] *See* Grosz, 721 F.2d at 736 {"[I]t is clear that when the government totally precludes religious conduct by imposing criminal sanctions, the burden weighs at its heaviest." [citing Yoder, 406 U.S. at 215; Cantwell v. Connecticut, 310 U.S. 296, 307–8 (1940)]}.

[170] Merced v. Kasson, 577 F.3d 578, 590 (5th Cir. 2009) (Texas RFRA case) (emphasis in original).

[171] Greene v. Solano Cnty. Jail, 513 F.3d 982, 988 (9th Cir. 2008) [citing Murphy v. Mo. Dep't of Corrections, 372 F.3d 979, 988 (8th Cir. 2004); Meyer v. Teslik, 411 F. Supp. 2d 983, 989 (W.D. Wis. 2006)]; *accord* Yellowbear v. Lampert, 741 F.3d 48, 56 (10th Cir. 2014) (RLUIPA prisoner case) (finding a substantial burden where the Native American inmate's religion "requires at least *some* access to a sweat lodge" and "[t]he prison refuses *any* access" and distinguishing these facts from "a situation where the claimant is left with some degree of choice in the matter and we have to inquire into the degree of the government's coercive influence on that choice").

practitioners, having no actual legal or tangible impact on the ability to practice the religion, in which case courts appear unwilling to find a substantial burden no matter how subjectively afflicted these practitioners may feel.[172] It is between these extremes of prohibition, on the one end, and of mere discouragement, on the other, where courts must render heavily factual and contextual judgments about the degree to which a specific law or government action is actually interfering with a religious practice. In reaching such judgments, some courts appear to adopt an approach that assesses whether and to what extent a claimant has alternative means or opportunities to practice his or her religion.[173] As part of this inquiry, or separately, courts may define with relative specificity the religious practice at issue and then assess to what degree the government action burdens this specific religious practice or, instead, burdens conduct apart from that practice.[174] Still other courts look at the duration or frequency of the government's action in relation to the claimant's religious practice, holding that the action may not impose a substantial burden if it persists for only a "brief period" or is "relatively short term and sporadic."[175]

### c. Significance of the Religious Practice

Courts also have defined and discerned a burden's substantiality by examining the extent to which a particular practice is significant within the claimant's religious framework or belief system. Courts have phrased the criterion of significance in a number of ways,

172 *See, e.g.*, Am. Family Ass'n, Inc. v. City & Cnty. of S.F., 277 F.3d 1114, 1124 (9th Cir. 2002) ("[W]hen the challenged government action is neither regulatory, proscriptive or compulsory, alleging a subjective chilling effect on free exercise rights is not sufficient to constitute a substantial burden."), *cert. denied*, 537 U.S. 886 (2002).

173 *See, e.g.*, Episcopal Student Found. v. City of Ann Arbor, 341 F. Supp. 2d 691, 705 (E.D. Mich. 2004) ("Although it may be 'incredibly beneficial' if [the claimant's practices] were … [accommodated], there is no indication that [the claimant] cannot continue to [engage in these practices] at such alternate locations, and thus fulfill its religious mission."); Valencia v. Blue Hen Conf., 476 F. Supp. 809, 822 (D. Del. 1979) (finding no "constitutionally significant" burden in part because "of the minimal degree of the burden imposed on the plaintiffs" and because "there are means available to … the plaintiffs to alleviate the burdens complained of here that do not create any conflicts with the precepts of [their] religion"), *aff'd*, 615 F.2d 1355 (3d Cir. 1980).

174 *See, e.g.*, Reed v. Town of Gilbert, Ariz., 707 F.3d 1057, 1076 (9th Cir. 2013) ("[W]hile [the claimants] may be obligated to spread their message and advertise their events, there is no suggestion that [their] tenets require that they do so in any particular way. Accordingly … [the government's restrictions] … do not constitute a substantial burden on [their] free exercise rights."), *cert. granted*, 134 S. Ct. 1900 (2014); Guam v. Guerrero, 290 F.3d 1210, 1222–3 (9th Cir. 2002) (RFRA case) (distinguishing, for the purpose of discerning a substantial burden, the criminalization of possessing a controlled substance, which could be a burden, from the criminalization of importing or intending to distribute the controlled substance, which would not be a burden); Loop v. United States, Civ. No. 05-575 (JRT/FLN), 2006 WL 1851140, at *3 (D. Minn. June 30, 2006) (unpublished) (similarly distinguishing between, on the one hand, the possession and use of marijuana as part of the claimant's religious practice and, on the other hand, the possession of paraphernalia while visiting a courthouse and finding no substantial burden in restricting the latter), *aff'd*, No. 06-3402, 225 Fed. App'x 420 (8th Cir. May 30, 2007) (unpublished); *Valencia*, 476 F. Supp. at 822 (finding no constitutionally significant burden in part because of "the remoteness of [any burden imposed by the government] … to the exercise of [the claimants'] religion").

175 Canell v. Lightner, 143 F.3d 1210, 1215 (9th Cir. 1998) ["[The claimant's] only allegation is that on some occasions [the defendant] interfered with his prayer activities … While [the defendant's conduct] may have constituted an intrusion upon [the claimant's] prayers on some occasions during the brief period involved … these intrusions were relatively short-term and sporadic and did not constitute a substantial interference." (internal quotations omitted)].

asking, for example, whether a religious practice at issue is "*integrally related* to the underlying beliefs"[176] or "*central*" to the claimant's religion[177]; whether the law "constitutes 'grave interference with *important* … religious tenets' or … affirmatively compels [a claimant] to 'perform acts undeniably at odds with *fundamental* tenets of [his or her] religious beliefs'"[178]; or whether "[t]he challenged rule … burden[s] a *central* tenet or *important* practice of the litigant's religion."[179] Conversely, "[t]he substantial burden test … presupposes that there will be cases in which it comfortably could be said that a belief or practice is so peripheral to the plaintiff's religion that any burden can be aptly characterized as constitutionally de minimis."[180]

According to one federal appeals court, a claimant who wishes to demonstrate the religious importance of a particular object or undertaking cannot simply make that assertion and present no additional supporting evidence.[181] In particular, where an incarcerated

176 Lakewood, 699 F.2d at 306 (emphasis added)

177 *See, e.g.*, Hernandez v. Comm'r, 490 U.S. 680, 699 (1989) (emphasis added) (explaining that "[t]he free exercise inquiry asks whether government has placed a substantial burden on the observation of a central religious belief or practice" though noting the judiciary's inability "to question the centrality of particular beliefs or practices to a faith"); Ford v. McGinnis, 352 F.3d 582, 593–4 (2d Cir. 2003) ("The relevant question in determining whether [a claimant's] religious beliefs were substantially burdened is whether … [a specific activity], in particular, is considered central or important to [the claimant's] practice of … [his or her religion]."); Levitan v. Ashcroft, 281 F.3d 1313, 1321 (D.C. Cir. 2002) (explaining that a burden is not "constitutionally cognizable" where claimant "can make no credible showing that the affected practice is either central or important in their religious scheme" but also that a rule "ban[ning] a practice that is not 'central' to an adherent's religious practice might nonetheless impose a substantial burden, if the practice is important and based on a sincere religious belief"); *Lakewood*, 699 F.2d at 306 ("The centrality of the burdened religious observance to the believer's faith influences the determination of an infringement."); Int'l Soc'y for Krishna Consciousness, Inc. v. Barber, 650 F.2d 430, 441–2 (2d Cir. 1981) ["In determining centrality … we look to the role that the rite or belief plays in the ritual and theology of the religion in question. Sacramental practices are given great weight. Affirmative duty-creating commands are also considered 'central' to a religion's doctrines." (citations omitted)]; Sequoyah v. Tenn. Valley Auth., 620 F.2d 1159, 1164 (1980) (using centrality), *cert. denied*, 449 U.S. 953 (1980).

178 Griffin High Sch. v. Ill. High Sch. Ass'n, 822 F.2d 671, 674 (7th Cir. 1987) (citations omitted) (emphases added) [quoting Wisconsin v. Yoder, 406 U.S. 205, 218 (1972)]; *see also* Messiah Baptist Church v. Cnty. of Jefferson, Colo., 859 F.2d 820, 826 (10th Cir. 1988) (finding no burden where enforcement of zoning law did "not involve the compromise of the Church's fundamental tenets"), *cert. denied*, 490 U.S. 1005 (1989).

179 Levitan, 281 F.3d at 1320 (emphases added); *accord* Werner v. McCotter, 49 F.3d 1476, 1480 (10th Cir. 1995) (RFRA case) ("To exceed the 'substantial burden' threshold, government regulation must significantly inhibit or constrain conduct or expression that manifests some central tenet of a prisoner's individual beliefs … ."), *cert. denied*, 515 U.S. 1166 (1995); Graham v. Comm'r, 822 F.2d 844, 851 (9th Cir. 1987) (explaining that "the burden must be … an interference with a tenet or belief that is central to religious doctrine"), *aff'd sub nom.* Hernandez v. Comm'r, 490 U.S. 680 (1989); Forest Hills Early Learning Ctr., Inc. v. Lukhard, 728 F.2d 230, 240 (4th Cir. 1984) ("Whether … the holding or active expression of particular beliefs involves the observance of 'religion' depends upon the sincerity of the beliefs held and the centrality of those beliefs to an identifiable religious faith or commitment; only those laws that impede the holding or active expression of sufficiently sincere and central religious beliefs impinge upon free exercise rights."); Charles v. Verhagen, 220 F. Supp. 2d 937, 948 (W.D. Wis. 2002) {"In determining whether a prisoner's religious freedom is substantially burdened … the question is … whether 'the practices in question are important to the votaries of the religion.'" [quoting Mack v. O'Leary, 80 F.3d 1175, 1180 (7th Cir. 1996), *judgment vacated on other grounds*, 522 U.S. 801 (1997)]}, *aff'd*, 348 F.3d 601 (7th Cir. 2003).

180 Ford v. McGinnis, 352 F.3d 582, 593 (2d Cir. 2003).

181 *See* Borzych v. Frank, 439 F.3d 388, 390 (7th Cir. 2006). An exception, perhaps, is where the object or undertaking is so widely understood to be religiously significant that the court can take judicial notice of that fact.

claimant's "only evidence on this point is his [or her] unreasoned say-so, plus equivalent declarations by other inmates," that "is insufficient to create a material dispute that would require a trial."[182] Instead, a claimant must put forth "objective evidence support[ing] his [or her] assertion that the [object or undertaking is] important to [his or her religion]"[183] or "that he [or she] would be unable to practice [his or her religion] effectively without the benefit of a weekly study group."[184]

It is vital to note two important caveats about the inquiry into whether a claimant's belief or practice is a significant aspect or tenet of his or her religion. First, both RLUIPA and RFRA (the latter by referring to the former) expressly define "religious exercise" as "any exercise of religion, whether or not compelled by, *or central to*, a system of religious belief."[185] That is, they both explicitly reject centrality as a means of including or excluding certain practices from protection under the statutes. (Their simultaneous declaration that an exercise need not be "compelled" will be discussed shortly.) This rejection of centrality arguably ought to be construed as a rejection of the many synonyms for central – for example, important, core, and fundamental – that courts employ to capture essentially the same notion of significance. However, that is a normative legal contention, and courts could plausibly inquire into significance by these or other means, as long as they avoid using the specific criteria that the statutes disavow.[186]

Second, and more critically, an inquiry into whether or not a belief or practice is "central" arguably poses Establishment Clause concerns and, perhaps for that reason, was specifically denounced in the *Smith* decision (as, indeed, was the larger inquiry of whether or not a burden is "constitutionally significant"). As for the Establishment Clause concern, the Supreme Court for many decades has held that government actions, including judicial rulings, may not foster an excessively entanglement with religion,[187] and this includes so-called doctrinal entanglement.[188] In one of the church property cases, for example, the Court explained that "First Amendment values are plainly jeopardized when ... litigation is made to turn on the resolution by civil courts of controversies over religious doctrine and practice"[189] and, in particular, that civil courts may not "determine matters at the very core of a religion – the interpretation of particular church

[182] *Id.* [citing Kaufmann v. McCaughtry, 419 F.3d 678, 682–83 (7th Cir. 2005); Stefanow v. McFadden, 103 F.3d 1466, 1471 (9th Cir. 1996)].

[183] *Id.*

[184] Kaufmann, 419 F.3d at 683.

[185] *See* 42 U.S.C. § 2000cc-5(7)(A) (RLUIPA); *id.* § 2000bb-2(4) (RFRA).

[186] *See, e.g.*, Charles v. Verhagen, 220 F. Supp. 2d 937, 948 (W.D. Wis. 2002) (RLUIPA prisoner case) {"In determining whether a prisoner's religious freedom is substantially burdened ... the question is ... whether 'the practices in question are important to the votaries of the religion.'" [quoting Mack v. O'Leary, 80 F.3d 1175, 1180 (7th Cir. 1996) (RFRA case), *judgment vacated on other grounds*, 522 U.S. 801 (1997)]}, *aff'd*, 348 F.3d 601 (7th Cir. 2003).

[187] *See* Lemon v. Kurtzman, 403 U.S. 602, 613 (1971) {explaining that a statute, among other things, "statute must not foster 'an excessive government entanglement with religion.'" (quoting Walz v. Tax Comm'n of N.Y. City, 397 U.S. 664, 674 (1970))}; *see also* Agostini v. Felton, 521 U.S. 203, 222–3 (1997); Larkin v. Grendel's Den, Inc., 459 U.S. 116, 126–7 (1982).

[188] *See* Hernandez v. Comm'r, 490 U.S. 680, 696 (1989) (noting that impermissible entanglement may occur when the government makes "inquiries into religious doctrine"); Barghout v. Bureau of Kosher Meat & Food Control, 66 F.3d 1337, 1344 n. 13 (4th Cir. 1995); Commack Self-Serv. Kosher Meats, Inc. v. Weiss, 294 F.3d 415, 425–8 (2d Cir. 2002), *cert. denied*, 537 U.S. 1187 (2003).

[189] Presbyterian Church in U.S. v. Mary Elizabeth Blue Hull Mem. Presbyterian Church, 393 U.S. 440, 449 (1969).

doctrines and the importance of those doctrines to the religion."[190] Likewise, in a more conventional Establishment Clause case, the Court has stated that "inquir[ing] into the significance of words and practices to different religious faiths, and in varying circumstances by the same faith ... would tend inevitably to entangle the State with religion in a manner forbidden by our cases."[191] Yet, asking and assessing whether a particular belief or practice is central or fundamental or important to a particular religion, and then definitively ruling that it is or is not, would seem no less effectively to entangle the government with religious doctrine.

As for *Smith*, the Court in that case rather bluntly declared that "[i]t is no more appropriate for judges to determine the 'centrality' of religious beliefs before applying a 'compelling interest' test in the free exercise field, than it would be for them to determine the 'importance' of ideas before applying the 'compelling interest' test in the free speech field. What principle of law or logic can be brought to bear to contradict a believer's assertion that a particular act is 'central' to his [or her] personal faith?"[192] Had the *Smith* Court stopped there, the problem of inquiring into centrality would have appeared to be a matter of the limits of judicial reasoning and competence, a point that the Court had expressed before.[193] As the Second Circuit has observed, "distinguish[ing] important from unimportant religious beliefs [is] a task for which ... courts are particularly ill-suited. Always present is the danger that courts will make conclusory judgments about the unimportance of the religious practice to the adherent rather than confront the often more difficult inquiries into sincerity, religiosity and the sufficiency of the [government's] interest asserted to justify the burden."[194]

The *Smith* Court did not stop with the issue of judicial competence, however. Instead, it continued, "Judging the centrality of different religious practices is akin to the unacceptable 'business of evaluating the relative merits of differing religious claims.' ... Repeatedly and in many different contexts, we have warned that courts must not presume to determine the place of a particular belief in a religion or the plausibility of a religious claim."[195] Then, in a footnote, the Court essentially called into question the larger inquiry into whether or not a practice has been substantially burdened, commenting that "'[c]onstitutionally significant burden' would seem to be 'centrality' under another name,"[196] as well as the alternative approach of assessing the impact on the claimant, stating that "inquiry into 'severe impact' is no different from inquiry into centrality. [One is] ... merely substitut[ing] for the question 'How important is X to the religious adherent?' the question 'How great will be the harm to the religious adherent if X is taken away?'"[197]

190 *Id*. at 450.

191 Widmar v. Vincent, 454 U.S. 263, 269 n. 6 (1981).

192 Employment Div. v. Smith, 494 U.S. 872, 886–7 (1990).

193 *See, e.g. Hernandez*, 490 U.S. at 699 (recognizing centrality as part of the inquiry but then admonishing that "[i]t is not within the judicial ken to question the centrality of particular beliefs or practices to a faith, or the validity of particular litigants' interpretations of those creeds"); *cf*. Thomas v. Review Bd. of Ind. Employment Sec. Div., 450 U.S. 707, 716 (1981) ("[I]t is not within the judicial function and judicial competence to inquire whether [a claimant] or his fellow [adherent] more correctly perceived the commands of their common faith. Courts are not arbiters of scriptural interpretation.").

194 Ford v. McGinnis, 352 F.3d 582, 593 (2d Cir. 2003).

195 Smith, 494 U.S. at 887 [quoting United States v. Lee, 455 U.S. 252, 263 n. 2 (1982) (Stevens, J., concurring)].

196 *Id*. at 887 n. 4.

197 *Id*.

These passages from *Smith* suggest that inquiring into centrality, or virtually any variation on it, not only pushes or exceeds the limits of judicial competence but, more seriously, risks violating the religion clauses themselves. Not surprisingly, lower courts, on the basis of one or both of these prospects, are divided or uncertain regarding the continued validity of using centrality or a related inquiry as part of a free exercise analysis[198] or, for that matter, of using a comparable inquiry as part of a RFRA or RLUIPA analysis.[199] In turn, several courts "have rightly shied away from attempting to gauge how central a sincerely held belief is to the believer's religion,"[200] with some rejecting centrality as a free exercise standard altogether,[201] going so far as to suggest that sincerity (along with religiousness) remains the only threshold factor to be considered.[202] Other courts, by contrast, have either retained the centrality inquiry outright or have adopted a substantively similar criterion to fill its analytical role.[203]

198 *See* Salahuddin v. Goord, 467 F.3d 263, 275 n. 5 (2d Cir. 2006) (noting but not "resolv[ing] the parties' disagreement about whether the substantial-burden test includes an inquiry into the centrality or importance of a burdened practice to the plaintiff's system of religious belief"); Levitan, 281 F.3d at 1320 {sanctioning the use of centrality or importance, though noting that the court was "mindful of the Supreme Court's warning that judging the centrality of different religious practices is akin to 'the unacceptable business of evaluating the relative merits of differing religious claims'" (quoting Smith, 494 U.S. at 887) (internal quotations omitted)]}.

199 *Compare* Korte v. Sebelius, 735 F.3d 654, 682 (7th Cir. 2013) (RFRA case) ["[A] substantial burden exists when the government compels a religious person to 'perform acts undeniably at odds with fundamental tenets of [his] religious beliefs.'" (quoting Yoder, 406 U.S. at 218)], *cert. denied*, 134 S. Ct. 2903 (2014), *and* Sossamon v. Lone Star State of Tex., 560 F.3d 316, 332 (5th Cir. 2009) (RLUIPA prisoner case) (rejecting centrality, per the statute's text, but requiring importance: "The practice burdened need not be central to the adherent's belief system, but the adherent must have an honest belief that the practice is important to his free exercise of religion."), *aff'd*, 131 S. Ct. 1651 (2011), *and* Odom v. Dixion, No. 04-CV-889F, 2008 WL 466255, at *7 (W.D.N.Y. Feb. 15, 2008) (unpublished) (RLUIPA prisoner case) (not using centrality but asking whether the government is "interfering with or violating a key tenet" of the claimant's religion), *with* Grace United Methodist Church v. City of Cheyenne, 451 F.3d 643, 663 (10th Cir. 2006) (RLUIPA land use case) (rejecting, as part of the substantial burden analysis, an inquiry into whether the claimant's religious conduct was "fundamental" because of the statute's rejection of centrality as a requirement).

200 Watts v. Fla. Int'l Univ., 495 F.3d 1289, 1295 (11th Cir. 2007).

201 *See, e.g.*, Shakur v. Schriro, 514 F.3d 878, 885 (9th Cir. 2008); Watts, 495 F.3d at 1295 ("While the Free Exercise Clause may be aimed primarily at protecting 'central' religious practices, it is beyond the competence of the courts to determine the centrality of a particular religious belief or practice."); McEachin v. McGuinnis, 357 F.3d 197, 202 (2d Cir. 2004) ("[A] court must determine when an impediment to a religious practice is significant enough to warrant judicial intervention. But it must do this without passing judgment on 'the centrality of different religious practices,' which is a misguided enterprise that the Supreme Court has called 'akin to the unacceptable business of evaluating the relative merits of differing religious claims.'" [quoting Smith, 494 U.S. at 887)]; Tenafly Eruv Ass'n, Inc. v. Borough of Tenafly, 309 F.3d 144, 170–1 (3d Cir. 2002) (construing *Smith* as barring inquiry into centrality and viewing this construction as harmonious with *Smith*'s limitation of the clause's applicability to claims of discrimination insofar as such claims obviate the need to demonstrate a substantial burden), *cert. denied*, 539 U.S. 942 (2003).

202 *See* Shakur, 514 F.3d at 885 ("Given the Supreme Court's disapproval of the centrality test, we are satisfied that the sincerity test … determines whether the Free Exercise Clause applies."); Watts, 495 F.3d at 1295 ("The test is sincerity, not centrality.").

203 *See, e.g.*, Rogers v. Hellenbrand, No. 04-1918, 118 Fed. App'x 80, 82–3 (7th Cir. Nov. 24, 2004) (unpublished) ("The Free Exercise Clause is violated when the government substantially burdens the 'exercise' of religion, i.e., an act or practice mandated by or central to a particular religion."); Skoros v. City of N.Y., 437 F.3d 1, 39 (2d Cir. 2006) (retaining centrality), *cert. denied*, 549 U.S. 1205 (2007); Altman v. Minn. Dep't of Corrections, 251 F.3d 1199, 1204 (8th Cir. 2001) (retaining centrality and fundamentality: "Government significantly burdens the exercise of religion if it significantly constrains conduct or

### d. Necessity of the Religious Practice

A fourth and final potential factor in the burden analysis is whether the practice allegedly restricted by the government is compelled or mandated by, rather than simply motivated or animated by, the claimant's religious belief system.[204] At the outset, it should be noted that consideration of this factor, like centrality, is inappropriate under RLUIPA and RFRA, which in relevant part define "religious exercise" to include "any exercise of religion, *whether or not compelled by* … a system of religious belief."[205] Its status under the Free Exercise Clause, by contrast, is a matter of judicial disagreement.

Several courts have held or indicated that while compulsion may be relevant to the substantial burden analysis, it is not critical to that analysis and that motivation or animation can be sufficient to find a substantial burden.[206] Adopting such an approach, the Second Circuit has reasoned that "confin[ing] the protection of the First Amendment

expression that manifests a central tenet of a person's religious beliefs, meaningfully curtails the ability to express adherence to a particular faith, or denies reasonable opportunities to engage in fundamental religious activities."); Werner v. McCotter, 49 F.3d 1476, 1480 (10th Cir. 1995) (preamendment RFRA case) ("To exceed the 'substantial burden' threshold, government regulation must significantly inhibit or constrain conduct or expression that manifests some central tenet of a prisoner's individual beliefs."), *cert. denied*, 515 U.S. 1166 (1995).

204 *See, e.g.*, Thomas v. Review Bd. of Ind. Employment Sec. Div., 450 U.S. 707, 717–18 (1982) (explaining that "a burden upon religion exists" if the government denies an important benefit "because of conduct mandated by religious belief"); Graham v. Comm'r, 822 F.2d 844, 850–1 (9th Cir. 1987) {"[T]he religious adherent … has the obligation to prove that a governmental regulatory mechanism burdens the adherent's practice of his or her religion … by preventing him or her from engaging in conduct or having a religious experience which the faith mandates." [citing Hobbie v. Unemployment Appeals Comm'n of Fla., 480 U.S. 136, 141 (1987); Sherbert v. Verner, 374 U.S. 398, 404 (1963)]}, *aff'd sub nom.* Hernandez v. Comm'r, 490 U.S. 680 (1989); Sequoyah v. Tenn. Valley Auth., 620 F.2d 1159, 1164 (1980) (discussing "indispensability"), *cert. denied*, 449 U.S. 953 (1980); State v. Brave Heart, 326 N.W.2d 220, 222–3 (S.D. 1982) (finding no free exercise violation where the specific practice prohibited by law was not shown to be "required" by the claimants' faith), *appeal dismissed*, 460 U.S. 1064 (1983).

205 42 U.S.C. § 2000cc-5(7)(A) (RLUIPA) (emphasis added); *id.* § 2000bb-2(4) (RFRA) (as amended, incorporating RLUIPA's definition). *See* Kikumura v. Hurley, 242 F.3d 950, 960 (10th Cir. 2001) (explaining, in light of the amendment, that "a religious exercise need not be mandatory for it to be protected under RFRA"). It still may be appropriate if one completely separates this definition of "religious exercise" from the question of substantial burden. *See, e.g.*, Navajo Nation v. U.S. Forest Serv., 535 F.3d 1058, 1076–7 (9th Cir. 2008) [rejecting the "conflat[ion] [of] two distinct questions under RFRA: (1) what constitutes an 'exercise of religion' and (2) what amounts to a 'substantial burden' on the exercise of that religion" and explaining that "RFRA's amended definition of 'exercise of religion' merely expands the scope of what may not be substantially burdened" and "does not change what level or kind of interference constitutes a 'substantial burden' upon such religious exercise"], *cert. denied*, 556 U.S. 1281 (2009). Such a strict separation may be textually valid, even correct, though it does not reflect judicial practice under the Free Exercise Clause before, and to some extent after, *Smith*.

206 *See, e.g.*, Ford v. McGinnis, 352 F.3d 582, 593 (2d Cir. 2003) ["Whether a particular practice is religiously mandated is surely relevant to resolving whether a particular burden is substantial. Neither the Supreme Court nor we, however, have ever held that a burdened practice must be mandated in order to sustain a prisoner's free exercise claim. Nor do we believe that substantial burden can or should be so narrowly defined." (citation omitted)]; Levitan v. Ashcroft, 281 F.3d 1313, 1319–20 (D.C. Cir. 2002) (observing that "[a] requirement that a religious practice be mandatory to warrant First Amendment protection finds no support in the cases of the Supreme Court or of this court" but noting that "[t]he fact that a regulation affects a mandatory religious practice is, obviously, relevant evidence of an infringement on the free exercise of religion"); Chalifoux v. New Caney Indep. Sch. Dist., 976 F. Supp. 659, 670 (S.D. Tex. 1997) (applying a motivation-type standard under the Free Exercise Clause); Meggett v. Pa. Dep't of Corrections, 892 A.2d 872, 882 (Pa. Commw. Ct. 2006) (refusing "[t]o extend protection only to practices mandated by a religion").

to only those religious practices that are mandatory would necessarily lead us down the unnavigable road of attempting to resolve intra-faith disputes over religious law and doctrine. It would furthermore except from constitutional protection many religions or sects that do not oblige adherents to engage in certain practices or maintain certain beliefs by commandments, edicts or threat of condemnation or godly retribution."[207] As Professor Christopher Lund has commented, the compulsion standard embraces "the old troublesome view that equates religious exercise with the following of commands – the idea being that if the law's requirements do not contradict any of God's commands, then there is no significant burden on religious exercise. But this is not right. Religion is more than just obeying commands. God might not demand that you sing in the church choir or go to church on Sunday rather than Tuesday. But those things are surely religious exercise. And were the government to start forbidding church choirs or Sunday worship, it would just as surely burden the free exercise of religion."[208]

Other courts, however, have retained a compulsion standard, insisting that a practice be a requirement or obligation of the claimant's religion.[209] Still others have suggested that a practice may need to be required within the claimant's understanding of his or her religious beliefs but that if the claimant adheres to an organized religion, the practice need not be mandatory within that religion either based on organizational teachings or based on the understandings of fellow adherents.[210] As the Ninth Circuit has remarked, "[t]here is nothing in the First Amendment's guarantee of the free exercise of religion that restricts the guarantee to the requirements of a church. ... That an act was 'mandated' by religious belief has been a judicial category used in upholding a free exercise claim. What is mandated by religion, however, is not to be equated with what is minimally required of adherents of a religion. What is mandated is what the individual human being perceives to be the requirement of the transhuman Spirit to whom he or she gives allegiance."[211]

207 Ford, 352 F.3d at 593 (citations omitted); *accord* Levitan, 281 F.3d at 1320 (noting that, under a compulsion standard, "religions that lack the concepts of commandments necessary for the salvation of the soul would find themselves outside the scope of First Amendment protection altogether" and that "[n]othing in the free exercise clause suggests that it only protects religions that incorporate mandatory tenets"); Meggett, 892 A.2d at 882 ("[E]xcluding protection to those religious practices that are optional ... would require courts to engage in the study of religious dogma and to make doctrinal rulings.").

208 Christopher C. Lund, *In Defense of the Ministerial Exception*, 90 N.C. L. Rev. 1, 36–7 (2011).

209 *See, e.g.*, Rogers v. Hellenbrand, No. 04-1918, 118 Fed. App'x 80, 82–3 (7th Cir. Nov. 24, 2004) (unpublished) ("The Free Exercise Clause is violated when the government substantially burdens the 'exercise' of religion, i.e., an act or practice mandated by or central to a particular religion."); Nieuwenhuis by Nieuwenhuis v. Delavan-Drien Sch. Dist. Bd. of Educ., 996 F. Supp. 855, 863 (E.D. Wis. 1998) (finding no cognizable burden, at least to trigger the hybrid claim exception, where "the government is neither compelling an act that violates a religious belief nor forbidding an act required by religious belief"); Cape v. Crossroads Correctional Ctr., 99 P.3d 171, 175 (Mont. 2004) {"[I]n order to be protected as a constitutional right, a dietary request must be essential to the practice of a particular religion." [citing Spies v. Voinovich, 173 F.3d 398, 406–7 (6th Cir. 1999)]}; *see also* Henderson v. Kennedy, 253 F.3d 12, 16–17 (D.C. Cir. 2001) (preamendment RFRA case) (rejecting a motivation standard), *cert. denied*, 535 U.S. 986 (2002).

210 *See, e.g.*, Daley v. Lappin, No. 12–3393, 555 Fed. App'x 161, 164–5 (3d Cir. Jan. 29, 2014) (unpublished) ("[A] religious practice is protected even if it is not deemed to be mandatory or practiced by every member of the religion.").

211 Peterson v. Minidoka Cnty. Sch. Dist. No. 331, 118 F.3d 1351, 1357 (9th Cir. 1997) (citation and line break omitted), *amended by* 132 F.3d 1258 (9th Cir. 1997).

### 4. *Sincerity of the Religious Belief*

Under the Free Exercise Clause, a claimant also must demonstrate that his or her religious beliefs, especially those relating to the practice in question, are sincerely held.[212] The sincerity inquiry, as characterized by the Second Circuit, "seeks to determine an adherent's good faith in the expression of his [or her] religious belief" and as such "provides a rational means of differentiating between those beliefs that are held as a matter of conscience and those that are animated by motives of deception and fraud."[213] Indeed, "[w]ithout some sort of required showing of sincerity on the part of the individual or organization seeking judicial protection of its beliefs, the first amendment would become 'a limitless excuse for avoiding all unwanted legal obligations.'"[214] Thus, although "the question of 'sincerity in the religious exercise context is understood to be 'exceedingly amorphous,' and although it may understandably appear to overlap with the test for what is 'religious' inasmuch as that test examines the private and subjective ... sincerity remains a discrete element in ... Free Exercise analyses."[215]

Being a sensible threshold element, a sincerity requirement also has been read into both RFRA and RLUIPA,[216] even though neither statute specifically requires that one's practice stem from *sincerely held* beliefs, as they do require, for example, that the burden on one's practice be "substantial." As an inquiry into credibility, sincerity is treated as a question of fact,[217] and "the trier of fact may determine whether a belief is truly held

[212] *See* Levitan v. Ashcroft, 281 F.3d 1313, 1320 (D.C. Cir. 2002) (explaining that a "litigant's beliefs must be sincere"); Mosier v. Maynard, 937 F.2d 1521, 1526 (10th Cir. 1991) ("A religious belief which is not sincerely held ... does not require the ... [government] to consider accommodation."); Sourbeer v. Robinson, 791 F.2d 1094, 1102 (3d Cir. 1986) ("A sincere religious belief is a prerequisite to any free exercise claim."), *cert. denied*, 483 U.S. 1032 (1987).

[213] Patrick v. LeFevre, 745 F.2d 153, 157 (2d Cir. 1984); *accord* Yellowbear v. Lampert, 741 F.3d 48, 54 (10th Cir. 2014) (RLUIPA prisoner case) ("When inquiring into a claimant's sincerity ... our task is ... limited to asking whether the claimant is (in essence) seeking to perpetrate a fraud on the court – whether he [or she] actually holds the beliefs he [or she] claims to hold – a comparatively familiar task for secular courts that are regularly called on to make credibility assessments – and an important task, too, for ensuring the integrity of any judicial proceeding."); Int'l Soc'y for Krishna Consciousness, Inc. v. Barber, 650 F.2d 430, 441 (2d Cir. 1981) ["Sincerity analysis seeks to determine the subjective good faith of an adherent in performing certain rituals. The goal, of course, is to protect only those beliefs which are held as a matter of conscience." (citation omitted)].

[214] Africa v. Commonwealth of Pa., 662 F.2d 1025, 1030 (3d Cir. 1981) [quoting LAURENCE H. TRIBE, AMERICAN CONSTITUTIONAL LAW 859 (1978)], *cert. denied*, 456 U.S. 908 (1982).

[215] United States v. Manneh, 645 F. Supp. 2d 98, 111 (E.D.N.Y. 2008) (quoting Patrick, 745 F.2d at 157).

[216] *See, e.g.*, Cutter v. Wilkinson, 544 U.S. 709, 725 n. 13 (2005) ("[P]rison officials may appropriately question whether a prisoner's religiosity, asserted as the basis for a requested accommodation, is authentic ... [RLUIPA] does not preclude inquiry into the sincerity of a prisoner's professed religiosity."); Moussazadeh v. Tex. Dep't of Crim. Justice, 703 F.3d 781, 791 (5th Cir. 2012) ("Sincerity of a belief is an essential initial matter in a RLUIPA claim."); United States v. Zimmerman, 514 F.3d 851, 853 (9th Cir. 2007) (*per curiam*) (stating that a claimant "may only invoke RFRA if his [or her] beliefs are ... 'sincerely held'" [quoting Callahan v. Woods, 658 F.2d 679, 683 (9th Cir. 1981)]; United States v. Israel, 317 F.3d 768, 771 (7th Cir. 2003) [approving of the district court's formulation "that under RFRA, a plaintiff establishes a prima facie violation if he [or she] can demonstrate that the government's action was a (1) substantial burden on a (2) sincere (3) exercise of religion"].

[217] *See* Murphy v. Mo. Dep't of Corrections, 372 F.3d 979, 983 (8th Cir. 2004), *cert. denied*, 543 U.S. 991 (2004); Mosier, 937 F.2d at 1526; *see also* United States v. Seeger, 380 U.S. 163, 185 (1965) (noting in the statutory conscientious objection context that "the threshold question of sincerity which must be resolved in every case ... is, of course, a question of fact"); United States v. Zimmerman, 514 F.3d 851, 854 (9th Cir. 2007) (RFRA case).

without violating the First Amendment,"[218] with its finding subject to appellate review, like most questions of fact, for clear error.[219] A claimant's failure to demonstrate sincerity, no less than a failure to demonstrate government action, a substantial burden, or the religiousness of one's beliefs, will lead to the demise of his or her claim.

As with the other elements of the prima facie case, however, the sincerity component has certain areas of logical, institutional, and doctrinal uncertainty that can complicate its analysis in any given case. First, there may be several ways to phrase or focus the inquiry into sincerity. Broadly approached, for example, one could ask whether or not the claimant sincerely believes in or adheres to a religious belief system as a whole, of which the particular practice at issue is simply a constituent. Alternatively, and more narrowly, one could ask whether or not the claimant sincerely believes that the particular practice is part of the claimant's faith and – overlapping with the burden inquiry – whether the claimant sincerely believes it is an important, central, or even mandatory part of that faith. One also could ask (perhaps again overlapping with the burden inquiry) whether the claimant sincerely believes that his or her not engaging in the practice will have particular consequences, such as the commission of sin or the loss of salvation.

Second, and partly due to the nature of some of these formulations, courts frequently express hesitation about pursuing a sincerity inquiry too aggressively.[220] As the next section will discuss, courts are not permitted to assess the truth or reasonableness of a claimant's alleged religious beliefs, and it can be a fine line between questioning sincerity and engaging in these prohibited assessments. Given that sincerity is a factual question that may go to a jury, moreover, judicial concerns about inadvertently crossing this line or effecting an end-run around the bar on evaluating reasonableness are justifiably heightened. Perhaps based on these and related concerns, some courts have indicated that an inquiry into sincerity is itself forbidden,[221] but "[t]he case authority since *Seeger* makes it clear that in evaluating a free exercise claim, courts can examine this factual question of whether an individual sincerely holds a religious belief."[222] Government agencies can and often must do so as well.[223] Nevertheless, many times the government in litigation

[218] United States v. Daly, 756 F.2d 1076, 1081 (5th Cir. 1985), *cert. denied*, 474 U.S. 1022 (1985); *see also* Patrick, 745 F.2d at 159 ("In determining whether [a claimant's] beliefs are to be accorded first amendment protection, the factfinder must delve into the internal workings of [his or her] mind and assess the credibility of his [or her] claims. In so doing, subjective issues of sincerity of belief and the perceived nature of that belief must be confronted squarely.").

[219] *See* Thiry v. Carlson, 78 F.3d 1491, 1495 (10th Cir. 1996), *cert. denied*, 519 U.S. 821 (1996); Iron Eyes v. Henry, 907 F.2d 810, 813 (8th Cir. 1990); Sourbeer, 791 F.2d at 1102.

[220] *See* Frazee v. Ill. Dep't of Employment Sec., 489 U.S. 829, 833 (1989) (noting "the difficulty ... in determining whether a professed belief is sincerely held"); Murphy, 372 F.3d at 988 (noting that under both the Free Exercise Clause and RLUIPA "we hesitate to make judgments about whether a religious belief is sincere or not"); Mosier, 937 F.2d at 1526 (noting that, with few exceptions, "courts carefully avoid inquiring into the merits of particular religious beliefs in an effort to gauge sincerity").

[221] *See, e.g.*, Peeler v. The Way Int'l, Inc., No. E2005-01692-COA-R3-CV, 2006 WL 1864662, at *6 (Tenn. Ct. App. July 5, 2006) (unpublished) ("[W]e may not pass judgment upon the legitimacy of [claimants'] religious beliefs or the sincerity with which they profess them.").

[222] Thacker v. Dixon, 784 F. Supp. 286, 292 (E.D.N.C. 1991) [referencing United States v. Seeger, 380 U.S. 163 (1965), and citing Martinelli v. Dugger, 817 F.2d 1499, 1503 (11th Cir. 1987), *cert. denied*, 484 U.S. 1012 (1988); Sourbeer v. Robinson, 791 F.2d 1094, 1102 (3d Cir. 1986), *cert. denied sub nom.* Patton v. Sourbeer, 483 U.S. 1032 (1987); United States v. Daly, 756 F.2d 1076, 1081 (5th Cir. 1985), *cert. denied*, 474 U.S. 1022 (1985)].

[223] *See* Gartrell v. Ashcroft, 191 F. Supp. 2d 23, 39 (D.D.C. 2002) ("The Supreme Court has made clear that governmental agencies not only can assess bona fides when deciding whether to accommodate religious

will concede the sincerity of a claimant's beliefs[224] or courts will assume, *arguendo*, this element's satisfaction, particularly if doing so does not determine the outcome of the case.[225]

Third, when a sincerity analysis is undertaken, there can be related hesitancy and legal uncertainty about what forms of evidence may permissibly be used to demonstrate the presence or absence of sincerity.[226] Among the types of evidence that have been entertained to confirm or question sincerity are the claimant's own consistency or inconsistency of observance of practice,[227] the claimant's knowledge of his or her religion or religious practice,[228] whether or not the claimant's beliefs grossly deviate from a belief system to which he or she explicitly claims adherence,[229] whether or not there

beliefs, but often must do so in order to properly assess religious accommodation claims."), *appeal dismissed*, No. 02-5179, 2003 WL 1873847 (D.C. Cir. Apr. 11, 2003) (unpublished).

224 *See* Moussazadeh v. Tex. Dep't of Crim. Justice, 703 F.3d 781, 791 (5th Cir. 2012) {observing that "'[t]he sincerity of a religious belief is not often challenged' but instead "is generally presumed or easily established" [quoting McAlister v. Livingston, 348 Fed. App'x 923, 935 (5th Cir. 2009) (unpublished)]}, *reh'g en banc denied*, 709 F.3d 487 (5th Cir. 2013).

225 *See, e.g.*, Dierks v. Does, No. 4:12-CV-00382-KGB, 2013 WL 5820267, at *9 (E.D. Ark. Oct. 29, 2013) (unpublished) ("assum[ing], without deciding, that [claimant's] religious beliefs are sincerely held" but then finding no free exercise violation); Haight v. Thompson, No. 5:11-CV-00118, 2013 WL 1092969, at *6 (W.D. Ky. Mar. 15, 2013) (unpublished) ("assum[ing] that the Plaintiffs' beliefs were sincerely held and that … [there] was a substantial burden on the exercise of that belief" but then finding no free exercise violation); Dawson v. Cal. Dep't of Correction & Rehabilitation, No. C 10–4066 CW, 2011 WL 3957015, at *2 (N.D. Cal. Sep. 7, 2011) (unpublished) ("assum[ing] without deciding that Plaintiff's beliefs are sincerely held" and then finding no free exercise violation); Tabbaa v. Chertoff, No. 05-CV-582S, 2005 WL 3531828, at *16 n. 14 (W.D.N.Y. Dec. 22, 2005) (unpublished) ("assum[ing] that Plaintiffs' religious beliefs are sincerely held and that the government's actions constitute a burden sufficient to trigger the First Amendment and RFRA" but then finding no violations), *aff'd*, 509 F.3d 89 (2d Cir. 2007).

226 *See* Moussazadeh, 703 F.3d at 791 {"Though the sincerity inquiry is important, it must be handled with a light touch, or 'judicial shyness.' We limit ourselves to 'almost exclusively a credibility assessment' when determining sincerity. To examine religious convictions any more deeply would stray into the realm of religious inquiry, an area into which we are forbidden to tread." (citations omitted) [quoting A.A. *ex rel.* Betenbaugh v. Needville Indep. Sch. Dist., 611 F.3d 248, 262 (5th Cir. 2010), and Kay v. Bemis, 500 F.3d 1214, 1219 (10th Cir. 2007), respectively]}; Colvin v. Caruso, 852 F. Supp. 2d 862, 869 (W.D. Mich. 2012) ("The 'sincerity' test is one of those broad legal pronouncements that looks good on paper, but is difficult to apply. How does one determine another person's sincerity?").

227 *See, e.g.*, Laurensau v. Romarowics, No. 13–1283, 528 Fed. App'x 136, 139 (3d Cir. Jun. 13, 2013) (inmate who requested Kosher meals occasionally still chose non-Kosher meals); Reed v. Faulkner, 842 F.2d 960, 963 (7th Cir. 1988) (noting that "[e]vidence of nonobservance is relevant on the question of sincerity"); Int'l Soc'y for Krishna Consciousness, Inc. v. Barber, 650 F.2d 430, 441 (2d Cir. 1981) (observing that "an adherent's belief would not be 'sincere' if he [or she] acts in a manner inconsistent with that belief"). "Evidence of nonobservance … is especially important in the prison setting, for an inmate may adopt a religion merely to harass the prison staff with demands to accommodate his new faith." Reed, 842 F.2d at 963. "If [an inmate's] request [for different treatment] is not a constituent part of a larger pattern of religious observance on the part of the inmate … the asserted religious basis for the request may be rejected as pretext." DeHart v. Horn, 227 F.3d 47, 52 n. 3 (3d Cir. 2000).

228 *See, e.g.*, Colvin, 852 F. Supp. 2d at 869 ("[A] person's knowledge of the tenets of his/her claimed religion, as well as his [or her] knowledge … [of the practice in question] has some bearing upon sincerity.").

229 *See, e.g.*, Levitan v. Ashcroft, 281 F.3d 1313, 1321 (D.C. Cir. 2002) ("[A] litigant's assertion of a view so totally foreign to the creed with which he [or she] claimed to affiliate might well lead the court to question his [or her] sincerity."); Lewis v. Califano, 616 F.2d 73, 80 n. 12 (3d Cir. 1980) (explaining that an examination of the tenets of a sect to which the claimant belongs "is proper in helping to establish sincerity").

are evident nonreligious factors, such as possible material gain or a desire to harass government officials, that could be motivating the claimant,[230] whether and to what extent the claimant has submitted documentary evidence (such as others' statements, his or her own statement, and a record of past requests or accommodations),[231] and during trial, of course, whether or not the claimant expresses his or her beliefs with sufficient credibility.[232] But all these factors are usually seen as matters of degree such that occasional inconsistency or incomplete adherence or idiosyncratic interpretations, for example, might be insufficient to show insincerity,[233] especially if they form no overall pattern of apparent insincerity.[234]

Furthermore, all these factors, if deployed indelicately, may easily lead a court or jury to transgress the prohibitions, discussed in the next section, against assessing the verity or reasonableness of a claimant's beliefs and holding a claimant to the beliefs of others. As the Second Circuit has observed, "[s]incerity analysis is exceedingly amorphous, requiring the factfinder to delve into the claimant's most veiled motivations and vigilantly separate the issue of sincerity from the factfinder's perception of the religious nature of the claimant's beliefs. This need to dissever is most acute where unorthodox beliefs are implicated. There, the factfinder's temptation to merge sincerity and verity is as great as the need to guard against this conjugation."[235]

230 *See, e.g.*, Int'l Soc'y for Krishna Consciousness, 650 F.2d at 441 (surmising that "an adherent's belief would not be 'sincere' … if there is evidence that the adherent materially gains by fraudulently hiding secular interests behind a veil of religious doctrine"); Thacker v. Dixon, 784 F. Supp. 286, 295–7 (E.D.N.C. 1991) (Magis. J. Rpt. & Recomm.) (finding that a claimant's lawsuit was "instituted, not out of any sincere desire to obtain first amendment protection for a religious practice, but for the purpose of harassing prison officials and essentially making [them] jump through hoops for [his] amusement"), *aff'd*, 953 F.2d 639 (4th Cir. 1992).

231 *See, e.g.*, Mosier, 937 F.2d at 1527; United States v. Adeyemo, 624 F. Supp. 2d 1081, 1086 (N.D. Cal. 2008) (accepting as evidence of sincerity the claimant's own sworn declarations as well as the "declarations from experts demonstrating how … [the claimant's practice] arises from [his] religion"); Boone v. Boozman, 217 F. Supp. 2d 938, 941–5 (E.D. Ark. 2002) (finding sincerity based in on claimant's affidavit and hearing testimony), *appeal dismissed sub nom.* McCarthy v. Ozark Sch. Dist., 359 F.3d 1029 (8th Cir. 2004).

232 *See, e.g.*, Patrick v. LeFevre, 745 F.2d 153, 157 (2d Cir. 1984) ("[A]ssessing a claimant's sincerity of belief demands a full exposition of facts and the opportunity for the factfinder to observe the claimant's demeanor during direct and cross-examination."); Thacker, 784 F. Supp. at 296 (basing insincerity finding partly on the basis of "observ[ing] plaintiff's demeanor and hear[ing] his answers to questions").

233 *See, e.g.*, Moussazadeh v. Tex. Dep't of Crim. Justice, 703 F.3d 781, 791 (5th Cir. 2012) ["A showing of sincerity does not necessarily require strict doctrinal adherence to standards created by organized religious hierarchies. … A finding of sincerity does not require perfect adherence to beliefs expressed by the … [claimant], and even the most sincere practitioner may stray from time to time." (line break omitted)]; Reed, 842 F.2d at 963 (cautioning that "the fact that a person does not adhere steadfastly to every tenet of his [or her] faith does not mark him [or her] as insincere"); Lewis, 616 F.2d at 80 n. 12 (noting that "the mere absence of a sect supporting an individual's belief need not require a presumption that the belief is insincere"); *see also* Wall v. Wade, 741 F.3d 492, 500 (4th Cir. 2014) (RLUIPA prison case) ("[P]rison administrators may not assume that a 'lack of sincerity (or religiosity) with respect to one practice [of a given religion] means lack of sincerity with respect to others.'" [quoting Lovelace v. Lee, 472 F.3d 174, 188 (2006)]).

234 Even a history of excessive litigation, allegedly done for pecuniary gain or to harass officials, may not by itself "be definitive; [the claimant] … could certainly be both litigious and observant." Shaheed-Muhammed v. Dipaolo, 393 F. Supp. 2d 80, 91 (D. Mass. 2005).

235 Patrick, 745 F.2d at 157.

## D. Limitations on the Government's Rebuttal

To the extent that a claimant makes the evidentiary showings outlined in the preceding section, the government then may attempt to challenge their factual or legal sufficiency. In so doing, however, the government will find that some of its efforts are restricted by other doctrines of the First Amendment. In particular, courts are uncomfortable with the notion that either they or any other governmental entity should be able to easily second-guess a claimant's allegation that his or her beliefs constitute a "religion" or that the burdened practice is "religious,"[236] much less that the claimant's religious belief or practice is adequate. As summarized by the Second Circuit, "free exercise claims often test the boundaries of the judiciary's competence, as courts are 'singularly ill-equipped to sit in judgment on the verity of an adherent's religious beliefs.'"[237] This discomfort is reflected in several attendant restrictions.

First, while the government is not categorically disabled from deeming a claimant's beliefs or practices altogether nonreligious – it is "clearly entitled to assure [itself] that there is an ample predicate for invoking the Free Exercise Clause"[238] – it cannot do so merely because the beliefs are "not … acceptable, logical, consistent, or comprehensible to others"[239]; are inconsistent with the beliefs of fellow adherents to the same religion[240];

236 *See* Frazee v. Ill. Dep't of Employment Sec., 489 U.S. 829, 833 (1989) (explaining that the Court does not "underestimate the difficulty of distinguishing between religious and secular convictions"); Alvarado v. City of San Jose, 94 F.3d 1223, 1227 (9th Cir. 1996) ("Attempting to define religion … is a notoriously difficult, if not impossible, task."); Remmers v. Brewer, 361 F. Supp. 537, 540 (S.D. Iowa 1973) (commenting that "a succinct and comprehensive definition of … [religion] would appear to be a judicial impossibility"), *aff'd*, 494 F.2d 1277 (8th Cir. 1974), *cert. denied*, 419 U.S. 1012 (1974). For overview and analysis of the definition of religion, *see* Chapter 7.

237 Ford v. McGinnis, 352 F.3d 582, 588 (2d Cir. 2003) [quoting Patrick v. LeFevre, 745 F.2d 153, 157 (2d Cir. 1984)].

238 Frazee v. Ill. Dep't of Employment Sec., 489 U.S. 829, 833 (1989).

239 Thomas v. Review Bd., 450 U.S. 707, 714 (1981); *accord* Fowler v. Rhode Island, 345 U.S. 67, 70 (1953); Dekoven v. Bell, 140 F. Supp. 2d 748, 762 (E.D. Mich. 2001). *But see* State v. Phelps, 266 Kan. 185, 195, 967 P.2d 304, 311 (Kan. 1998) ["The First Amendment to the United States Constitution does offer a defense to protected speech and religious freedom. It does not, however, allow one to commit a crime and then seek protection based on a personal interpretation of the Bible *not shared by a recognized religious group* or clearly exercised as a religious act." (emphasis added)]; State v. Pedersen, 679 N.W.2d 368, 376 (Minn. Ct. App. 2004) [explaining that "it is necessary that … [a claimant's religious practice] be somehow tied to [his or] her religion and the *established* practices and beliefs within [his or] her religion" (emphasis added)]. Even *Thomas* itself, however, acknowledges that a claim might be "so bizarre, so clearly nonreligious in motivation, as not to be entitled to protection under the Free Exercise Clause." Thomas, 450 U.S. at 714.

240 *See, e.g.*, Hernandez v. Comm'r, 490 U.S. 680, 699 (1989); Lyng v. Northwest Indian Cemetery Protective Ass'n, 485 U.S. 439, 457–8 (1988); Thomas, 450 U.S. at 715–16; EEOC v. Abercrombie & Fitch Stores, Inc., 731 F.3d 1106, 1117 (10th Cir. 2013) [noting that in First Amendment cases "courts consistently focus on the individual's belief system rather than the beliefs of a religious group with which the individual may (or may not) be associated"]. "The issue in free exercise cases … is not whether an adherent has correctly divined the religious commands of his faith, but whether his [or her] understanding of what his [or her] religion requires, however unorthodox, is based on a sincerely held religious belief." Hudson v. Maloney, 326 F. Supp. 2d 206, 211 n. 3 (D. Mass. 2004). In short, "[t]he relevant inquiry for the Court is what plaintiff sincerely believes, not what others consider an important religious practice." Smith v. Sears, Nos. 1-03-CV-189 & 1:03-CV-422, 2005 WL 1652166, at *6 (S.D. Ohio Jun. 11, 2005) (unpublished). *But cf.* Levitan v. Ashcroft, 281 F.3d 1313, 1321 (D.C. Cir. 2002) ("A court may … consider whether the litigants' beliefs find any support in the religion to which they subscribe or whether the litigants are merely relying on a self-serving view of religious practice. This inquiry is not a matter of deciding whether appellants' beliefs accord in every particular with the religious orthodoxy of their

or have only been recently acquired or perceived by the claimant.[241] These considerations may affect a determination of whether the claimant's beliefs are sincerely held,[242] but generally they cannot be used to assess whether the beliefs in the first instance are religious.

Second, "[w]hen considering assertions that these provisions exempt a person from regulatory mandates when compliance would contravene his [or her] religious beliefs, courts avoid questioning the rationality of those beliefs."[243] The government may permissibly conclude as a factual matter that a certain religious belief is not sincerely held by a claimant,[244] but it may not assess the ultimate or objective validity – that is, the "plausibility,"[245] "truth or falsity,"[246] "reasonableness,"[247] "verity,"[248] "correctness,"[249] or "worthiness"[250] – of the religious belief itself.[251] As one court has written, "[t]he freedom to exercise religious beliefs cannot be made contingent on the objective truth of such beliefs"[252] in part because such assessment creates a form of establishment and in part because "the judiciary is singularly ill-equipped to sit in judgment on the verity of an adherent's religious beliefs."[253] Typically, in fact, the judiciary in difficult cases has erred toward an inclusive conception of religion, often bypassing the issue entirely and simply assuming or concluding that a particular claim is, in fact, religious.[254]

church. Nor is it a matter of adjudicating intrafaith differences in practice or belief. Instead, a court may determine whether the litigants' views have any basis whatsoever in the creed or community on which they purport to rest their claim." (citations omitted)).

241 *See, e.g.*, Hobbie v. Unemployment Appeals Comm'n, 480 U.S. 136, 144 (1987).

242 *See supra* notes 212–35 and accompanying text.

243 Toca v. State, 834 So. 2d 204, 207 (Fla. Dist. Ct. App. 2002), *review denied*, 846 So. 2d 1150 (Fla. 2003).

244 *See, e.g.*, Lipton v. Peters, No. SA-99-CA-O235-EP, 1999 WL 33289705, at *4–*5 (W.D. Tex. Oct. 12, 1999) (unpublished) (finding insincerity), *aff'd*, 240 F.3d 1074 (5th Cir. 2000).

245 Employment Div. v. Smith, 494 U.S. 872, 887 (1990).

246 Sherbert v. Verner, 374 U.S. 398, 407 (1963) (noting "the prohibition against judicial inquiry into the truth or falsity of religious beliefs"); Williams v. Bright, 658 N.Y.S.2d 910, 914 (N.Y. App. Div. 1997) ("American courts have no business endorsing or condemning the truth or falsity of anyone's religious beliefs."), *appeal dismissed*, 686 N.E.2d 1368 (N.Y. 1997).

247 Callahan v. Woods, 658 F.2d 679, 685 (9th Cir. 1981) ("In applying the free exercise clause of the First Amendment, courts may not inquire into the truth, validity, or reasonableness of a claimant's religious beliefs."); Estate of Supple v. Roman Catholic Archbishop, 55 Cal. Rptr. 542, 545 (Cal. Ct. App. 1966) (equating a challenge to "the reasonableness of [one's religious] beliefs" with a challenge to "the truth or scientific validity of such beliefs").

248 United States v. Ballard, 322 U.S. 78, 86 (1944) (holding that "the truth or verity" of a party's religious claims, even if disputed by another party, may not be submitted to the jury); Philbrook v. Ansonia Bd. of Educ., 757 F.2d 476, 481 (2d Cir. 1985) (contrasting "sincerity," which is a permissible object of inquiry, with "verity," which is not), *aff'd*, 479 U.S. 60 (1986).

249 Smith by Smith v. Bd. of Educ., 844 F.2d 90, 93 (2d Cir. 1988) ("Generally it is not proper for courts to evaluate the truth or correctness of an individual's sincerely held religious beliefs.").

250 Kaplan v. Hess, 694 F.2d 847, 851 (D.C. Cir. 1982) (citing *Ballard* and holding that "the court may not inquire into the worthiness of appellants' religious beliefs to ascertain whether they merit First Amendment protection").

251 *See* Ford v. McGinnis, 352 F.3d 582, 593–4 (2d Cir. 2003) (expressly rejecting an objective test in favor of a subjective test); United States v. Lemon, 723 F.2d 922, 938 n.49 (D.C. Cir. 1983); Cohen v. United States, 297 F.2d 760, 765 (9th Cir. 1962), *cert. denied*, 369 U.S. 865 (1962).

252 Patrick v. LeFevre, 745 F.2d 153, 157 (2d Cir. 1984).

253 *Id.* at 157.

254 *See, e.g.*, United States v. Meyers, 95 F.3d 1475, 1482–3 (10th Cir. 1996) (RFRA case) (explaining "that the threshold for establishing the religious nature of his beliefs is low"), *cert. denied*, 522 U.S. 1006 (1997); State v. Pedersen, 679 N.W.2d 368, 374 (Minn. Ct. App. 2004) ("[I]f there is any doubt about

## E. Levels and Components of Judicial Scrutiny

As indicated in the introductory section, the appropriate standard of judicial review in the religious freedom context has for many years generated both interpretive discord within the Supreme Court and institutional wrangling between the Court and Congress. From the 1960s to the 1980s, several of the Court's opinions indicated that in *any* instance where a claimant could demonstrate a substantial governmental burden on a religious practice rooted in sincerely held religious beliefs, the government had to prove that its law was necessary to achieve a compelling interest (strict scrutiny), even if the law was neutral and generally applicable and the free exercise burden was merely incidental or inadvertent. In 1990, however, the Court definitively rejected this reading of the First Amendment,[255] holding instead that strict scrutiny is triggered only in limited circumstances, most prominently, a lack of neutrality or general applicability.[256]

In 1993, the Congress responded by enacting the Religious Freedom Restoration Act (RFRA),[257] which purported to reimpose by statute the strict scrutiny standard on all federal, state, and local laws, including neutral and generally applicable laws, that placed a substantial burden, even incidentally, on a claimant's religious practices. In 1997, the Court then held that RFRA's application to state and local governments exceeded Congress' enforcement power under the Fourteenth Amendment,[258] once again leaving neutral and generally applicable state and local laws largely subject only to rational basis review as a matter of federal law.[259] Finally, in 2000, Congress enacted yet another religious

whether a particular set of beliefs constitutes a religion, the court will err on the side of freedom and find that the beliefs are a religion.").

255 *See* Smith, 494 U.S. at 878–80; *see also* City of Hialeah, 508 U.S. at 531.

256 *See* Smith, 494 U.S. at 878–84; Carol M. Kaplan, *Note, The Devil Is in the Details: Neutral, Generally Applicable Laws and Exceptions from Smith*, 75 N.Y.U. L. Rev. 1045, 1051–60 (2000) (discussing the underlying purposes, doctrinal modifications, and wider implications of *Smith*). For general reading on *Smith*, *see* Carolyn N. Long, Religious Freedom and Indian Rights: The Case of Oregon v. Smith (Univ. Press of Kan. 2000).

257 42 U.S.C. § 2000bb to 2000bb-4. For the text of the statute, *see* Appendix C.

258 *See* City of Boerne v. Flores, 521 U.S. 507 (1997). Congress subsequently amended RFRA to conform to the Court's holding. *See* Pub. L. No. 106–274, § 7, 114 Stat. 803, 806 (Sept. 22, 2000). Whether RFRA remains valid as applied to the federal government has not been decided by the Supreme Court. Lower courts, for their part, have generally upheld the statute. *See, e.g.*, Blackhawk v. Pennsylvania, 381 F.3d 202, 212 (3d Cir. 2004) (stating that RFRA "remained applicable to the federal government despite *City of Boerne*"); O'Bryan v. Bureau of Prisons, 349 F.3d 399, 401 (7th Cir. 2003) (upholding RFRA's application to the federal government); Henderson v. Kennedy, 265 F.3d 1072, 1073 (D.C. Cir. 2001) (same), *cert. denied*, 535 U.S. 986 (2002); Guam v. Guerrero, 290 F.3d 1210, 1219–21 (9th Cir. 2002) (same); Kikumura v. Hurley, 242 F.3d 950, 958–9 (10th Cir. 2001) (same); Christians v. Crystal Evangelical Free Church, 141 F.3d 854, 859–61 (8th Cir. 1998) (same), *cert. denied*, 525 U.S. 811 (1998); *but cf.* United States v. Indianapolis Baptist Temple, 224 F.3d 627, 629 n. 1 (7th Cir. 2000); La Voz Radio de la Communidad v. FCC, 223 F.3d 313, 319 (6th Cir. 2000). Scholars, by contrast, are divided. *Compare* Thomas C. Berg, *The Constitutional Future of Religious Freedom Legislation*, 20 U. Ark. Little Rock L.J. 715, 727–47 (1998) (arguing that the act is constitutional), *with* Marci Hamilton, *The Religious Freedom Restoration Act Is Unconstitutional, Period*, 1 U. Pa. J. Const. L. 1 (1998) (arguing that it is not).

259 Some have argued that RFRA, even if otherwise valid as applied to the federal government (*see supra* note 258) is nevertheless invalid under the Establishment Clause. *See, e.g.*, Boerne, 521 U.S. at 536–7 (Stevens, J., concurring); Christopher L. Eisgruber & Lawrence G. Sager, *Why the Religious Freedom Restoration Act Is Unconstitutional*, 69 N.Y.U. L. Rev. 437, 452–60 (1994). Most courts have not accepted this argument, however. *See, e.g.*, Hankins v. Lyght, 441 F.3d 96, 107–9 (2d Cir. 2006) (finding no establishment); Christians, 141 F.3d at 861–3 (same); EEOC v. Catholic Univ. of Am., 83 F.3d 455,

freedom statute, the Religious Land Use and Institutionalized Persons Act (RLUIPA).[260] However, although this statute, like RFRA, reapplies the strict scrutiny standard to the decisions of state and local government,[261] as its title implies, it does so only to decisions relating to land use and institutionalized persons, such as prisoners. Thus, after several years of judicial and congressional sparring, state and local governmental decision making that burdens the religious practices of claimants will now, as a matter of federal law, largely be subject to rational basis review, absent one of the exceptions in *Smith* or one of the conditions of RLUIPA.[262]

470 (D.C. Cir. 1996) (same). And the Supreme Court's rejection of a facial Establishment Clause challenge to RFRA's sibling statute, RLUIPA [Cutter v. Wilkinson, 544 U.S. 709, 719–24 (2005)], arguably supports these holdings.

260 42 U.S.C. §§ 2000cc to 2000cc-5.

261 *See id.* §§ 2000cc(a)(1), 2000cc-1(a). For a spirited overview and history, *see* Marci A. Hamilton, *Federalism and the Public Good: The True Story Behind the Religious Land Use and Institutionalized Persons Act*, 78 IND. L.J. 311 (2003). The statute has been upheld against an array of constitutional challenges. *See* Cutter, 544 U.S. at 719–24 (upholding prisoner portion of RLUIPA under the Establishment Clause); Guru Nanak Sikh Soc'y of Yuba City v. Cnty. of Sutter, 456 F.3d 978, 992–5 (9th Cir. 2006) (upholding RLUIPA under Section 5 of the 14th Amendment Enforcement Power); Benning v. Georgia, 391 F.3d 1299 (11th Cir. 2004) (upholding the prisoner portion of RLUIPA under Spending Power, 10th Amendment, and Establishment Clause); Midrash Sephardi, Inc. v. Town of Surfside, 366 F.3d 1214, 1236–43 (11th Cir. 2004) (upholding land use portion of RLUIPA under Section 5, the Establishment Clause, and the 10th Amendment), *cert. denied*, 543 U.S. 1146 (2005); Madison v. Riter, 355 F.3d 310, 316–22 (4th Cir. 2003) (holding that RLUIPA does not violate the Establishment Clause), *cert. denied*, 545 U.S. 1103 (2005); Charles v. Verhagen, 348 F.3d 601 (7th Cir. 2003) (upholding statute); Mayweathers v. Newland, 314 F.3d 1062 (9th Cir. 2002) (same), *cert. denied*, 540 U.S. 815 (2003); Williams v. Bitner, 285 F. Supp. 2d 593 (M.D. Pa. 2003) (same); Westchester Day Sch. v. Vill. of Mamaroneck, 280 F. Supp. 2d 230 (S.D.N.Y. 2003) (same), *vacated on other grounds*, 386 F.3d 183 (2d Cir. 2004); Johnson v. Martin, 223 F. Supp. 2d 820 (W.D. Mich. 2002) (same); Freedom Baptist Church of Delaware Cnty. v. Twp. of Middletown, 204 F. Supp. 2d 857 (E.D. Pa. 2002) (same). For various assessments of the statute's constitutionality, *see* Shawn P. Bailey, *The Establishment Clause and the Religious Land Use and Institutionalized Persons Act of 2000*, 16 REGENT U. L. REV. 53 (2003); Roman P. Storzer & Anthony R. Picarello, Jr., *The Religious Land Use and Institutionalized Persons Act of 2000: A Constitutional Response to Unconstitutional Zoning Practices*, 9 GEO. MASON L. REV. 929 (2001); Gregory S. Walston, *Federalism and Federal Spending: Why the Religious Land Use and Institutionalized Persons Act of 2000 Is Unconstitutional*, 23 U. HAW. L. REV. 479 (2001); Caroline R. Adams, *Note, The Constitutional Validity of the Religious Land Use and Institutionalized Persons Act of 2000: Will RLUIPA's Strict Scrutiny Survive the Supreme Court's Strict Scrutiny?* 70 FORDHAM L. REV. 2361 (2002); Joshua R. Geller, *Note, The Religious Land Use and Institutionalized Persons Act of 2000: An Unconstitutional Exercise of Congress's Power Under Section Five of the Fourteenth Amendment*, 6 N.Y.U. J. LEGIS. & PUB. POL'Y 561 (2002); Evan M. Shapiro, *Comment, The Religious Land Use and Institutionalized Persons Act: An Analysis under the Commerce Clause*, 76 WASH. L. REV. 1255 (2001); Ada-Marie Walsh, *Note, Religious Land Use and Institutionalized Persons Act of 2000: Unconstitutional and Unnecessary*, 10 WM. & MARY BILL RTS. J. 189 (2001). For analysis of the statute as applied to land use and preservation laws, *see* James L. Noles, Jr., *Can Historic Preservation Coexist with Protections for Religious Land Uses?* 17 NAT. RES. & ENV'T 89 (Fall 2002); Storzer & Picarello, *supra*; Robert W. Tuttle, *How Firm a Foundation? Protecting Religious Land Uses after Boerne*, 68 GEO. WASH. L. REV. 861 (2000).

262 *See* Tenafly Eruv Ass'n, Inc. v. Borough of Tenafly, 309 F.3d 144, 165 (3d Cir. 2002) ("Depending on the nature of the challenged law or government action, a free exercise claim can prompt either strict scrutiny or rational basis review."), *cert. denied*, 539 U.S. 942 (2003); *accord* Fifth Ave. Presbyterian Church v. City of N.Y., 293 F.3d 570, 574 (2d Cir. 2002). As indicated earlier, however, several states have amended or interpreted their own constitutions or passed their own religious freedom restoration acts to provide a level of protection comparable to that of the *Sherbert* and *Yoder* cases. *See supra* notes 18–23 and accompanying text.

### 1. *Strict Scrutiny*

Strict scrutiny is marked by two key features. First, the governmental action loses its presumption of constitutionality – indeed, the law is now presumed unconstitutional – such that the evidentiary burden shifts to the government, and the judiciary will no longer provide the kind of salvaging assistance characteristic of rational basis review.[263] Second, the government is required to meet a test that by design is much more rigorous than the rational basis test. Specifically, "[t]o survive strict scrutiny, a challenged government action must be narrowly tailored to advance a compelling government interest, whereas rational basis review requires merely that the action be rationally related to a legitimate government objective."[264] Satisfaction of strict scrutiny has been aptly described by one court as a "daunting task."[265] As a practical matter, many laws are premised on legitimate but not compelling interests, and laws are seldom written or designed so precisely as to make them "narrowly tailored" (or "necessary" or the "least restrictive means") to achieve the government's interest, especially under the retrospective lens of judicial scrutiny.[266]

#### a. Compelling Government Interest

To justify the imposition of a substantial burden on a claimant's religious practice, the government must first show that imposing the burden furthers a compelling interest, which is a question of law to be decided by a court, subject to *de novo* appellate review.[267] Although "[t]here is … little guidance from the Supreme Court in determining what qualifies as a compelling interest,"[268] by definition, compelling interests should comprise a comparatively small set of government objectives, having also been described by the Court as "interests of the highest order."[269] At their broadest, compelling interests forestall

263 *See* Qutb v. Strauss, 11 F.3d 488, 492 (5th Cir. 1993), *cert. denied*, 511 U.S. 1127 (1994).

264 Tenafly Eruv Ass'n, Inc. v. Borough of Tenafly, 309 F.3d 144, 165 n. 24 (3d Cir. 2002), *cert. denied*, 539 U.S. 942 (2003).

265 Axson-Flynn v. Johnson, 356 F.3d 1277, 1294 (10th Cir. 2004) ("Unless Defendants succeed in showing that the … [law] was a neutral rule of general applicability, they will face the daunting task of establishing that the requirement was narrowly tailored to advance a compelling governmental interest."); *see also* City of Boerne v. Flores, 521 U.S. 507, 534 (1997) ("Requiring a State to demonstrate a compelling interest and show that it has adopted the least restrictive means of achieving that interest is the most demanding test known to constitutional law.").

266 *See* Skinner v. Ry. Labor Executives' Ass'n, 489 U.S. 602, 629 n. 9 (1989) [remarking in the search-and-seizure context that "judges engaged in *post hoc* evaluations of government conduct can almost always imagine some alternative means by which the objectives of the … [government] might have been accomplished" (brackets in original) (internal quotations omitted)].

267 *See* United States v. Hardman, 297 F.3d 1116, 1127 (10th Cir. 2002) ("Whether something qualifies as a compelling interest is a question of law."). Apparently, so also is the question of whether a compelling interest outweighs a free exercise interest. *See* Peterson v. Minidoka Cnty. Sch. Dist. No. 331, 118 F.3d 1351, 1357 (9th Cir. 1997) ("When the facts are undisputed, it is a question of law, not a question of fact, whether [the government's] concerns outweigh [a claimant's] exercise of his [or her] constitutional right."), *amended by* 132 F.3d 1258 (9th Cir. 1997).

268 Hardman, 297 F.3d at 1127; *accord* Grosz v. City of Miami Beach, Fla., 721 F.2d 729, 737 (11th Cir. 1983) (noting that "the standards are vague as to what government interests will counterbalance free exercise interests"), *cert. denied*, 469 U.S. 827 (1984); *see* Stephen E. Gottlieb, *Compelling Governmental Interests: An Essential but Unanalyzed Term in Constitutional Adjudication*, 68 B.U. L. Rev. 917 (1988).

269 Wisconsin v. Yoder, 406 U.S. 205, 215 (1972).

"some substantial threat to public health, safety, peace, or order."[270] Thus highway safety concerns have been repeatedly recognized as comprising a compelling interest,[271] as has the interest in protecting the health and welfare of children.[272] By comparison, compelling interests seldom include otherwise valid governmental concerns about aesthetics,[273] administrative convenience,[274] cost reduction,[275] or certain other internal fiscal interests,[276] though the interest in maintaining the integrity of a major government program, such as the federal Social Security or tax systems, has been held to be compelling.[277]

Complicating the compelling interest analysis post-*Smith* are four factors. First, government interests often do not gravitate neatly toward one pole (manifestly compelling) or the other (manifestly not compelling); rather, they are spread out across the range of government objectives and functions. Second, whether or not an interest is compelling can be contextual – with some exceptions, compelling interests do not approximate universals or Platonic ideals – and courts therefore must assess any given interest in its own legal framework and in relation to the facts of the case. Third, and related, the Supreme Court in a RFRA case has made clear that the government, at least in an as-applied challenge, may not assert its allegedly compelling interest in a blanket fashion but instead must show that it has a compelling interest in applying its law or policy specifically to (and in not exempting) the litigant's conduct, taking into account any comparable exemptions that exist or in the past have been recognized.[278] Whether there is a compelling interest, in other words, must be assessed in a particularized rather than a generalized manner. Noting the differential significance of these two approaches, the

270 Forest Hills Early Learning Ctr., Inc. v. Lukhard, 728 F.2d 230, 241 (4th Cir. 1984) [citing Wisconsin v. Yoder, 406 U.S. 205, 221–9 (1972)]; *see also* Westchester Day Sch. v. Vill. of Mamaroneck, 417 F. Supp. 2d 477, 550 (S.D.N.Y. 2006) (RLUIPA land use case) ("Compelling governmental interests are those that protect public health, safety or welfare."), *aff'd*, 504 F.3d 338 (2d Cir. 2007).

271 *See, e.g.*, Satawa v. Bd. of Cnty. Rd. Comm'rs, 687 F. Supp. 2d 682, 699–700 (E.D. Mich. 2009) (interest sufficient to override claim of religious speech); *cf.* State v. Miller, 549 N.W.2d 235, 241 (Wis. 1996) (finding "a compelling interest in public safety on the highways" under analogous test of WIS. CONST. art. I, § 18).

272 *See, e.g.*, Prince v. Massachusetts, 321 U.S. 158, 166–7 (1944).

273 *See* Cottonwood Christian Ctr. v. Cypress Redevelopment Agency, 218 F. Supp. 2d 1203, 1228 (C.D. Cal. 2002) (explaining that aesthetics can give rise to substantial, but not compelling, interests); Keeler v. Mayor & City Council of Cumberland, 940 F. Supp. 879, 886 (D. Md. 1996) (so concluding and citing authorities).

274 Courts *may* be persuaded, however, by administrative arguments that coincide with their own institutional interest in keeping the scope of the free exercise guarantee within manageable bounds. Thus, for example, a credible assertion that allowing a claimant to prevail would effectively open the free exercise floodgates – either because of the number of similarly situated claimants or because of an inability to distinguish insincere claims – may be influential in the judicial scrutiny process.

275 One exception is apparently in the prison context. *See* Phipps v. Morgan, No. CV-04-5108-MWL, 2006 WL 543896, at *2, *9 (E.D. Wash. Mar. 6, 2006) (unpublished) (approving a magistrate judge's finding "that Defendants established a compelling justification for the denial of Halal meals to Plaintiff under RLUIPA, i.e., reducing costs, streamlining food production, limiting the number of required staff, maintaining consolidation of vendors, and limiting security risks").

276 *See, e.g.*, Blackhawk v. Pennsylvania, 381 F.3d 202, 214 (3d Cir. 2004) (finding it "doubtful" that "maintaining the fiscal integrity of its permit fee system" would "qualify as [a] compelling interest"); Church on the Rock v. City of Albuquerque, 84 F.3d 1273, 1280 (10th Cir. 1996) ("A city or state's desire for federal funds is not a compelling government interest.").

277 *See* Hernandez v. Comm'r, 490 U.S. 680, 699 (1989) (taxation); United States v. Lee, 455 U.S. 252, 258–9 (1982) (Social Security).

278 *See* Gonzales v. O Centro Espirita Beneficente Uniao do Vegetal, 546 U.S. 418 (2006).

Tenth Circuit recently remarked (before adopting the particularized approach for prisoner cases under RLUIPA)

> [t]he more abstract the level of inquiry, often the better the governmental interest will look. At some great height, after all, almost any state action might be said to touch on "one or another of the fundamental concerns of government: public health and safety, public peace and order, defense, revenue," and measuring a highly particularized and individual interest "directly against one of these rarified values inevitably makes the individual interest appear the less significant."[279]

Fourth and finally, given the post-*Smith* reliance on pre-*Smith* jurisprudence (such as what counts as a compelling interest), it is important to note that the pre-*Smith* cases seemed to accept as compelling a range of interests that in other contexts employing strict scrutiny arguably would not so easily have been deemed compelling.[280] On the one hand, there are ample situations in which a compelling interest identified in a free exercise case also could be found, or likely would be found, in these other contexts, such as eradicating racial discrimination in education,[281] raising and regulating the armed forces,[282] ensuring national security,[283] maintaining prison safety,[284] providing public school education,[285] prohibiting plural marriage,[286] enforcing drug laws,[287] and protecting the public from future crime,[288] among others.[289] On the other hand, there do seem to be a number of free exercise cases in which a compelling interest was found even

279 Yellowbear v. Lampert, 741 F.3d 48, 57 (10th Cir. 2014) (quoting Clark, *supra* note 31, at 330–1).

280 *See* Mark E. Chopko & Marissa Parker, *Still a Threshold Question: Refining the Ministerial Exception Post-Hosanna-Tabor*, 10 First Amend. L. Rev. 233, 254 (2012) ["By the end of the 1980's ... the robust compelling interest doctrine was in retreat. Judges and commentators noted that courts more routinely accepted as "compelling" any government assertion of an important interest." (footnotes omitted)].

281 *See* Bob Jones Univ. v. United States, 461 U.S. 574, 604 (1983).

282 *See* Gillette v. United States, 401 U.S. 437, 462 (1971); United States v. Schmucker, 815 F.2d 413, 417 (6th Cir. 1987) ("institut[ing] conscription quickly").

283 *Cf.* Office of Foreign Assets Control v. Voices in Wilderness, 329 F. Supp. 2d 71, 81 (D.D.C. 2004) (RFRA case).

284 *See* Ochs v. Thalacker, 90 F.3d 293, 296 (8th Cir. 1996).

285 *See* Fleischfresser v. Dirs. of Sch. Dist. 200, 15 F.3d 680, 690 (7th Cir. 1994).

286 *See* Potter v. Murray City, 760 F.2d 1065, 1070 (10th Cir. 1985), *cert. denied*, 474 U.S. 849 (1985).

287 *See* Olsen v. DEA, 878 F.2d 1458, 1462 (D.C. Cir. 1989), *cert. denied*, 495 U.S. 906 (1990); United States v. Middleton, 690 F.2d 820, 825–6 (11th Cir. 1982) ("regulating the possession and distribution of drugs"), *cert. denied*, 460 U.S. 1051 (1983); Leary v. United States, 383 F.2d 851, 860 (5th Cir. 1967), *rev'd on other grounds*, 395 U.S. 6 (1969); Peyote Way Church of God, Inc. v. Meese, 698 F. Supp. 1342, 1349 (N.D. Tex. 1988), *aff'd*, 922 F.2d 1210 (5th Cir. 1991); *cf.* United States v. Lafley, 656 F.3d 936, 940 (9th Cir. 2011) (RFRA case).

288 *See* Boone v. State, 147 S.W.3d 801, 806 (Mo. Ct. App. 2004); *cf. also In re* Grand Jury Empaneling of Special Grand Jury, 171 F.3d 826, 832 (3d Cir. 1999) (RFRA case) ("securing the evidence needed to punish the criminal activity").

289 *See, e.g.*, Trubin v. Mazzuca, No. 04 Civ. 6156(LAP)(GWG), 2006 WL 1876669, at *9 (S.D.N.Y. July 6, 2006) (Magis. Rpt. & Rec.) (unpublished) {"'maintaining the integrity of the jury's deliberations'" [quoting Morgan v. Walsh, 2002 U.S. Dist. Lexis 26734, at *27 n. 9 (S.D.N.Y. Nov. 27, 2002), *adopted by* 2003 U.S. Dist. LEXIS 14813 (S.D.N.Y. Aug. 27, 2003)]}; S. Jersey Catholic Sch. Teachers Ass'n v. St. Teresa of Infant Jesus Church Elem. Sch., 675 A.2d 1155, 1170–1 (N.J. Super. Ct. App. Div. 1996) (applying labor laws), *aff'd as modified*, 696 A.2d 709 (N.J. 1997); Niemann v. Vaughn Cmty. Church, 77 P.3d 1208, 1211 n.2 (Wash. Ct. App. 2003) ("eradicating [religiously] discriminatory property ownership"). Some cases, in fact, involved both religion and another constitutional right protected by strict scrutiny, such as speech. *See, e.g.*, Lumpkin v. Brown, 109 F.3d 1498, 1501 (9th Cir. 1997) (removing a city human rights commissioner for making antihomosexual remarks), *cert. denied*, 522 U.S. 995 (1997).

though it is questionable whether the same interest could comparably justify another circumstance where strict scrutiny is triggered, such as content censorship of speech or intentional racial discrimination. Examples of such purportedly compelling interests ranged from the protection of endangered or threatened species[290] and the management of natural resources,[291] including "protecting and preserving our national forests for this and future generations,"[292] to the application of zoning laws[293] and the elimination of marital discrimination in housing.[294] The government no doubt has legitimate interests in these matters, perhaps even important interests, but it is hard to say that it has *compelling* interests – could forest preservation, for example, really justify racial segregation? – though admittedly free exercise claims arise in such an array of contexts and present such diverse fact patterns that direct comparisons to strict scrutiny under the Free Speech and Equal Protection Clauses may not be entirely appropriate.

One government interest that is periodically asserted against a religious freedom claim is that of preventing violations of the Establishment Clause, although in recent decades such assertions have been less successful in part due to changes in Establishment Clause doctrine. The Supreme Court has clearly stated in several religious speech cases that the prevention of an actual Establishment Clause violation can be a compelling interest sufficient to justify content discrimination,[295] although perhaps not viewpoint discrimination.[296] A more difficult question is whether the prevention of a *possible* but not definite Establishment Clause violation also can qualify as a compelling interest sufficient to justify a free exercise or free speech infringement. The Court, for its part, has issued

290 *See, e.g.*, United States v. Hugs, 109 F.3d 1375, 1378 (9th Cir. 1997) (*per curiam*); *cf. also* United States v. Adeyemo, 624 F. Supp. 2d 1081, 1089 (N.D. Cal. 2008) (RFRA case) ("the conservation and protection of endangered leopard species"); United States v. Winddancer, 435 F. Supp. 2d 687, 695 (M.D. Tenn. 2006) (RFRA case) ("the preservation of bald and golden eagles").

291 *See, e.g.*, Crow v. Gullet, 706 F.2d 856, 858 (8th Cir. 1983) (per curiam), *cert. denied*, 464 U.S. 977 (1983); Badoni v. Higginson, 638 F.2d 172, 177 (10th Cir. 1980), *cert. denied*, 452 U.S. 954 (1981); *cf. also* Navajo Nation v. U.S. Forest Serv., 408 F. Supp. 2d 866, 906 (D. Ariz. 2006) (RFRA case) ("managing the public land for recreational uses such as skiing"), *aff'd*, 535 F.3d 1058 (9th Cir. 2008) (*en banc*).

292 United States v. Little, 638 F. Supp. 337, 339 (D. Mont. 1986).

293 *See, e.g.*, Grosz v. City of Miami Beach, Fla., 721 F.2d 729, 738 (11th Cir. 1983) ("enforcing ... zoning laws so as to preserve the residential quality of ... [certain] zones"), *cert. denied*, 469 U.S. 827 (1984); Daytona Rescue Mission v. City of Daytona Beach, Fla., 885 F. Supp. 1554, 1560 (M.D. Fla. 1995) (RFRA case) ("regulating homeless shelters and food banks").

294 *Cf., e.g.*, Swanner v. Anchorage Equal Rights Comm'n, 974 P.2d 274, 282–3 (Alaska 1994) (using the comparable test of ALASKA CONST. art. I, § 4), *cert. denied*, 513 U.S. 979 (1994).

295 *See, e.g.*, Good News Club v. Milford Central Sch., 533 U.S. 98, 112 (2001); Capitol Square Review & Advisory Bd. v. Pinette, 515 U.S. 753, 761–2 (1995). Lower courts, moreover, have held that the interest in preventing an Establishment Clause violation generally will have a secular purpose such that its furtherance would not itself violate the Establishment Clause. *See, e.g.*, Vasquez v. L.A. Cnty., 487 F.3d 1246, 1255–6 (9th Cir. 2007); Utah Gospel Mission v. Salt Lake City Corp., 425 F.3d 1249, 1258–60 (10th Cir. 2005); Bishop v. Aronov, 926 F.2d 1066, 1077–8 (11th Cir. 1991), *cert. denied*, 505 U.S. 1218 (1992).

296 *See* Good News Club, 533 U.S. at 133 (noting that "it is not clear whether a State's interest in avoiding an Establishment Clause violation would justify viewpoint discrimination"); Peck *ex rel.* Peck v. Baldwinsville Cent. Sch. Dist., 426 F.3d 617, 633 (2d Cir. 2005) (noting this uncertainty). According to one lower court, "cases that find that Establishment Clause concerns justify viewpoint regulation ... rely, in part, on the coercive environment and proselytizing nature of the speech involved." Seidman v. Paradise Valley Unified Sch. Dist. No. 69, 327 F. Supp. 2d 1098, 1113 (D. Ariz. 2004) [citing Lee v. Weisman, 505 U.S. 577, 578–9 (1992); Cole v. Oroville Union High Sch., 228 F.3d 1092 (9th Cir. 2000), *cert. denied*, 532 U.S. 905 (2001)].

mixed signals, particularly with its ruling in *Locke v. Davey*,[297] which held that a state's nonestablishment concerns, heightened by the language of its own constitution, justified a ban on using state scholarship funding to pursue a degree in devotional theology, even though "there is no doubt that the State could, consistent with the Federal Constitution, permit [a scholarship recipient] … to pursue [such] a degree."[298] Lower courts, at least in free speech cases, have generally required that in order for a state effort to be compelling, it must prevent an actual rather than a conjectural or perceived Establishment Clause violation, particularly when the state effort entails the differential treatment of religion and nonreligion.[299] As the Sixth Circuit has stated, "a program that violates the Free Exercise Clause cannot be saved by relying on implausible Establishment Clause concerns."[300]

Indeed, with the apparent exception of certain Establishment Clause–based government actions, as in *Locke*, the differential treatment of religion and nonreligion (or of one religion versus another) is basically a death knell for government action under the compelling interest prong of the strict scrutiny test. In particular, such differential treatment poses two problems for the government. First, the law's unyielding application to religious conduct, when it is not unwaveringly applied to all comparable nonreligious activities, undermines the notion that the law's objective is actually compelling. If an interest is truly compelling, its achievement should be sought generally, not selectively.[301] Second, because the law is not religiously neutral, the government's asserted

297 540 U.S. 712 (2004).

298 *Id.* at 719. Specifically, the state constitution, in comparison with federal Establishment Clause doctrine, has stricter limits on indirect government funding of religion. The Court emphasized that such limits could find parallel historical concerns about the relationship been government funding and religious establishments. "Even though the differently worded Washington Constitution draws a more stringent line than that drawn by the United States Constitution, the interest it seeks to further is scarcely novel. In fact, we can think of few areas in which a State's antiestablishment interests come more into play. Since the founding of our country, there have been popular uprisings against procuring taxpayer funds to support church leaders, which was one of the hallmarks of an 'established' religion." *Id.* at 722 (footnote omitted). Presumably, a government's heightened nonestablishment concerns that lack this historical parallel may not be so readily invoked to justify differential treatment with regard to religion.

299 *See, e.g.*, Child Evangelism Fellowship of Minn. v. Minneapolis Sch. Dist. No. 1, 690 F.3d 996, 1002–4 (8th Cir. 2012); Satawa v. Macomb Cnty. Rd. Comm'n, 689 F.3d 506, 524–5 (6th Cir. 2012); Badger Catholic, Inc. v. Walsh, 620 F.3d 775 (7th Cir. 2010), *cert. denied*, 131 S. Ct. 1604 (2011); Wigg v. Sioux Falls Sch. Dist. 49-5, 382 F.3d 807, 814–15 (8th Cir. 2004); Donovan *ex rel.* Donovan v. Punxsutawney Area Sch. Bd., 336 F.3d 211, 226–7 (3d Cir. 2003); Columbia Union College v. Oliver, 254 F.3d 496, 510 (4th Cir. 2001); Orin v. Barclay, 272 F.3d 1207, 1215–16 (9th Cir. 2001), *cert. denied*, 536 U.S. 958 (2002); Church on the Rock v. City of Albuquerque, 84 F.3d 1273, 1280 (10th Cir. 1996), *cert. denied*, 519 U.S. 949 (1996); Hartmann v. Stone, 68 F.3d 973, 979 (6th Cir. 1995); Good News/Good Sports Club v. Sch. Dist. of City of Ladue, 28 F.3d 1501, 1507–10 (8th Cir. 1994), *cert. denied*, 515 U.S. 1173 (1995); Ams. United for Separation of Church & State v. City of Grand Rapids, 980 F.2d 1538, 1541–53 (6th Cir. 1992).

300 Hartmann, 68 F.3d at 979.

301 *See* Church of the Lukumi Babalu Aye, Inc. v. City of Hialeah, 508 U.S. 520, 546–7 (1993); Tenafly Eruv Ass'n, Inc. v. Borough of Tenafly, 309 F.3d 144, 172 (3d Cir. 2002), *cert. denied*, 539 U.S. 942 (2003); Peyote Way Church of God, Inc. v. Smith, 742 F.2d 193, 201 (5th Cir. 1984); Rader v. Johnston, 924 F. Supp. 1540, 1557 (D. Neb. 1996); *cf. also* Gonzales v. O Centro Espirita Beneficente Uniao do Vegetal, 546 U.S. 418, 432–7 (2006) (concluding that a statutory exemption for one controlled substance, peyote, undermined the government's contention that allowing an exemption for another controlled substance, hoasca, would undermine the efficacy of the Controlled Substances Act).

interest must not simply necessitate the law as such but must specifically necessitate the religious discrimination.[302]

### b. Least Restrictive Means

The "means" or "fit" portion of strict scrutiny asks whether the statute is narrowly tailored, necessary, essential, or the least restrictive means to achievement of the government's interest.[303] In particular, it asks whether there is an equally efficacious alternative that would be less restrictive of the claimant's religious practices.[304] If so, then the court's task is essentially to hold the government to the less restrictive alternative.[305] Unlike the compelling interest analysis, which can be relatively legal and categorical, this inquiry is normally rather factual or empirical, turning on the specific data, expert testimony, and other evidence that the parties present to the court.[306]

As part of its inquiry into narrow tailoring, moreover, a court may specifically examine the extent to which a law (1) is underinclusive or underbroad (i.e., not encompassing conduct, whether by exemption or otherwise, that, like the religious practice, also might thwart its alleged objectives),[307] (2) is overinclusive or overbroad (i.e., encompassing conduct, especially religious conduct, the restriction of which bears no relation to achieving its objectives),[308] and (3) as written, actually would or would not achieve its purported objectives.[309] Further, unlike in rational basis scrutiny, courts employing strict scrutiny are not under any particular obligation to save the law from its own potential unconstitutionality by, for example, conceiving of possible compelling interests that might support the law or discerning an internal logic to the law that might render it the least restrictive means of achieving its objectives.

302 *See, e.g.*, Fraternal Order of Police Newark Lodge No. 12 v. City of Newark, 170 F.3d 359, 365 (3d Cir. 1999) (rejecting governmental efforts to distinguish between medical exemptions, which were provided, and religious exemptions, which were not), *cert. denied*, 528 U.S. 817 (1999).

303 All these formulations are found in Free Exercise Clause cases. *See* City of Hialeah, 508 U.S. at 546 ("narrowly tailored"); Employment Div. v. Smith, 494 U.S. 872, 883 (1990) ("necessary"); Peyote Way Church of God, Inc. v. Smith, 742 F.2d 193, 201 (5th Cir. 1984) (same); United States v. Lee, 455 U.S. 252, 257 (1982) ("essential"); Callahan v. Woods, 736 F.2d 1269, 1272–3 (9th Cir. 1984) ("least restrictive means"). RFRA and RLUIPA, by comparison, specifically require that a government use "the least restrictive means" to further its compelling interest. *See* 42 U.S.C. § 2000bb-1(b)(2) (RFRA); *id.* § 2000cc(a)(1)(B) (RLUIPA land use provision); *id.* § 2000cc-1(a)(2) (RLUIPA institutionalized persons provision).

304 *See* Sherbert v. Verner, 374 U.S. 398, 407 (1963) (requiring that there be "no alternative forms of regulation [that] would combat [the] abuses [that threaten the government's interests] without infringing First Amendment rights").

305 *See, e.g.*, Fraternal Order of Police, 170 F.3d at 366–7; Rader, 924 F. Supp. at 1558; *cf.* State v. Miller, 549 N.W.2d 235, 241–2 (Wis. 1996) (applying strict scrutiny under Wis. Const. art. I, § 18).

306 *See, e.g.*, Walsh, 616 F.2d at 159.

307 *See* City of Hialeah, 508 U.S. at 546 (deeming it problematic that the challenged ordinances were "underinclusive in substantial respects" and "not pursued with respect to analogous non-religious conduct"); Tenafly Eruv Ass'n, 309 F.3d at 172; *cf.* Colo. Christian Univ. v. Weaver, 534 F.3d 1245, 1268 (10th Cir. 2008) (finding underinclusiveness using strict scrutiny under the Establishment Clause).

308 *See* City of Hialeah, 508 U.S. at 546 (deeming it problematic that the challenged ordinances were "overbroad … in substantial respects" and "achiev[able] by narrower ordinances that burdened religion to a far lesser degree").

309 *See, e.g.*, Tenafly Eruv Ass'n, 309 F.3d at 172 (explaining that "it is hard to see how the [claimant's religious practice] somehow undermines [the government's] objective"); Stormans, Inc. v. Selecky, 854 F. Supp. 2d 925, 989–90 (W.D. Wash. 2012).

### 2. Rational Basis Scrutiny

If there is no cause for heightened review – either strict or, perhaps in some cases, intermediate scrutiny – then a court will apply rational basis scrutiny, also called "rationality review" or the "rational basis test."[310] This is true even if the government's action imposes an undeniably severe burden on an indisputably sincere religious practice and is based on nothing more than routine administrative interests.[311] Some courts have suggested that a claimant who fails to trigger heightened scrutiny may no longer have a free exercise claim at all,[312] although this perspective, even if correct, could be inconsequential insofar as a claimant, through appropriate pleading, can always obtain rational basis scrutiny of a law under the baseline guarantees of due process and equal protection.[313]

Rational basis scrutiny exhibits several key features, all of which, relatively speaking, are favorable to the government. At the outset, for example, laws and other government actions are ordinarily presumed constitutional,[314] and under rationality review, this presumption persists. Accordingly, the claimant must continue to shoulder the evidentiary burden throughout. What the claimant must demonstrate, in turn, is that the law or government action is *not* rationally or reasonably related to a legitimate government interest,

310 *See* United States v. Hardman, 297 F.3d 1116, 1126 (10th Cir. 2002) (*en banc*) ("[I]f the law is 'a valid and neutral law of general applicability,' then it must simply be rationally related to a legitimate government end."); Hyman v. City of Louisville, 132 F. Supp. 2d 528, 538 (E.D. Ky. 2001); Gingerich v. Commonwealth, 382 S.W.3d 835, 841 (Ky. 2012); State *ex rel.* Comm'r of Transp. v. Medicine Bird Black Bear White Eagle, 63 S.W.3d 734, 763 (Tenn. Ct. App. 2001).

311 Goshtasby v. Bd. of Trs. of Univ. of Ill., 141 F.3d 761, 769 (7th Cir. 1998) (explaining that, after *Smith*, "the Free Exercise Clause does not require states to make exceptions to neutral and generally applicable laws even when those laws significantly burden religious practices" (citing *Smith*, 494 U.S. at 887), *abrogated on other grounds by* Kimel v. Fla. Bd. of Regents, 528 U.S. 62 (2000); Berg, *supra* note 19, at 192 (observing that the *Smith* rule applies "no matter how seriously the law burdens religious conscience or how minimal the government's interest is in applying it"). This does not mean, of course, that the claimant's conduct is of no constitutional value or significance but simply that the Free Exercise Clause – one of many possible constitutional guarantees – does not provide an independent and meaningful degree of protection.

312 *See, e.g.*, Jacobs v. Clark Cnty. Sch. Dist., 526 F.3d 419, 439–40 (9th Cir. 2008) (after finding that a law is neutral and generally applicable and that no other possible exception under *Smith* applied, simply ending its analysis, with no subsequent use of rational basis scrutiny); Youngblood v. Fla. Dep't of Health, No. 06-11523, 225 Fed. App'x 909, 913, 2007 WL 914239, at *2 (11th Cir. Mar. 28, 2007) (unpublished) ("An attempt by state and local officials to enforce a neutral and generally applicable law or regulatory structure is no violation of the Free Exercise Clause."); Axson-Flynn v. Johnson, 356 F.3d 1277, 1294 (10th Cir. 2004) {"Neutral rules of general applicability ordinarily do not raise free exercise concerns even if they incidentally burden a particular religious practice or belief. When it comes to the enforcement of such rules, 'the Free Exercise Clause offers no protection.'" (footnote omitted) (citations omitted) [quoting Tenafly Eruv Ass'n, Inc. v. Borough of Tenafly, 309 F.3d 144, 165 (3d Cir. 2002), *cert. denied*, 539 U.S. 942 (2003)]}; Am. Life League, Inc. v. Reno, 47 F.3d 642, 654 (4th Cir. 1995) (citing Smith and declaring that "a neutral, generally applicable law does not offend the Free Exercise Clause, even if the law has an incidental effect on religious practice"), *cert. denied*, 516 U.S. 809 (1995).

313 *Cf.* Bowen v. Roy, 476 U.S. 693, 727 (1986) (O'Connor, J., concurring in part and dissenting in part) (explaining that a free exercise analysis that "would uphold any facially neutral and uniformly applicable governmental requirement if the Government shows its rule to be a reasonable means of promoting a legitimate public interest' … relegates a serious First Amendment value to the barest level of minimal scrutiny that the Equal Protection Clause already provides" [quoting *id.* at 708 (majority opinion)].

314 *See* Branson v. O.F. Mossberg & Sons, Inc., 221 F.3d 1064, 1065 n. 4 (8th Cir. 2000) ("[S]tate statutes are presumed constitutional, and the plaintiff has the burden to show otherwise.").

and this can be a rather onerous task.[315] This is true not simply because of placement of the evidentiary burden but also, and more critically, because of the ease with which a government action can satisfy the test. Legitimate interests are, or ought to be, readily available. For the federal government, they include anything within the government's constitutionally enumerated powers as well as the mundane needs of governmental administration, such as cost minimization and resource allocation. Even more broadly, for state governments they include these administrative needs, too, plus anything within a state's traditional police power, which encompasses "the health, welfare, safety, and morals of its citizens."[316]

Moreover, a reasonable or rational relationship between a law's design and one of these legitimate interests should be virtually impossible not to articulate. To be sure, courts at this level of review have been willing to accept after-the-fact characterizations of a law's objectives or internal logic and in some instances, consistent with the presumption of the law's constitutionality, have even been willing to divine them on their own.[317] Courts using the rational basis test also will tolerate both underinclusiveness[318] and overinclusiveness,[319] either of which could be fatal under heightened scrutiny.

### 3. Other Levels of Scrutiny

In addition to strict and rational basis scrutiny, some lower courts have indicated that there may be particular free exercise circumstances or contexts in which an intermediate level of scrutiny could be applied, although it is important to highlight that the Supreme Court has not spoken clearly with regard to the appropriate level of scrutiny in these situations. The idea of an intermediate level of scrutiny is just that: a standard more demanding that rationality review but less demanding than strict scrutiny. For instance, under the equal protection guarantee's version of intermediate scrutiny for gender discrimination, the evidentiary burden (as under strict scrutiny) shifts to the government and then specifically requires the government to demonstrate that its challenged law is substantially related to an important government interest.[320] As a general conceptual matter, important interests are less readily available than legitimate interests but not as scarce as compelling interests, and a substantial relationship is more carefully

315 *See* Fitz v. Dolyak, 712 F.2d 330, 333 (8th Cir. 1983) ("[A] party seeking to challenge a statute under [the rationality] standard bears a heavy burden.").

316 Johnson v. Collins Entm't Co., 199 F.3d 710, 720 (4th Cir. 1999); *see* Manigault v. Springs, 199 U.S. 473, 480 (1905); State v. Brenan, 772 So. 2d 64, 73 (La. 2000); Christensen v. State, 468 S.E.2d 188, 190 (Ga. 1996); Rothman v. Rothman, 320 A.2d 496, 499 (N.J. 1974); Smith v. State Hwy. Comm'n, 346 P.2d 259, 267 (Kan. 1959). *But cf.* Lawrence v. Texas, 539 U.S. 558, 578 (2003) (holding that the police power does not extend to consensual adult conduct, in private, that does not cause harm to other persons or institutions, thus precluding the recognition of a legitimate state interest in such circumstances).

317 *See, e.g.*, United States v. Castillo, 140 F.3d 874, 883 (10th Cir. 1998) {using rationality review under the equal protection guarantee: "We need not find that the legislature ever articulated this reason, nor that it actually underlay the legislative decision, nor even that it was wise." (citations omitted) [citing Flemming v. Nestor, 363 U.S. 603, 612 (1960); City of Dallas v. Stanglin, 490 U.S. 19, 27 (1989)]}.

318 *See, e.g.*, Ry. Express Agency v. People of State of N.Y., 336 U.S. 106, 110 (1949) (using rationality review under the Equal Protection Clause).

319 *See, e.g.*, N.Y. City Transit Auth. v. Beazer, 440 U.S. 568, 593 (1979) (using rationality review under the Equal Protection Clause).

320 *See* United States v. Virginia, 518 U.S. 515, 533 (1996) (involving gender discrimination); Craig v. Boren, 429 U.S. 190, 197 (1976) (same).

constructed than a mere rational relationship but not as precise as a relationship characterized by narrow tailoring, necessity, or least restrictive means.[321]

Based on case law, there are possibly four free exercise scenarios in which some kind of intermediate scrutiny might apply: (1) public employment, (2) hybrid rights situations under *Smith*, (3) the military, and (4) prisons. These possibilities will be discussed only briefly here because each of these subjects is addressed elsewhere in this book.[322] First, a number of courts have reasoned, based on the Supreme Court's public-employee free speech cases, that a public-employee claim triggering heightened review under *Smith* should be evaluated using intermediate rather than strict scrutiny, where the parameters of that intermediate scrutiny are either custom fashioned for the Free Exercise Clause[323] or simply imported from the Free Speech Clause.[324] Second, a few courts recognizing a hybrid rights exception under *Smith* – where the combination of free exercise and another constitutional claim may generate heightened scrutiny – have suggested or held that the heightened scrutiny, if obtained, should be intermediate rather than strict.[325] Third, the *Smith* Court left intact its decision in *Goldman*

321 Other forms of intermediate scrutiny are formulated differently. A content-neutral restriction in speech in a public forum, for example, must be "narrowly tailored to serve a significant governmental interest" and must "leave open ample alternative channels for communication of the information" [Clark v. Cmty. for Creative Non-Violence, 468 U.S. 288, 293 (1984)], whereas a restriction on commercial speech must be "narrowly tailored" to serve a "substantial" government interest. *See* Bd. of Trs. of State Univ. of N.Y. v. Fox, 492 U.S. 469, 480–1 (1989).

322 Regarding public employment, *see* Chapter 11; regarding hybrid rights, *see Infra* Section F.4 of this chapter; and regarding the military and prisons, *see* Chapter 18.

323 *See, e.g.*, Tenafly Eruv Ass'n, Inc. v. Borough of Tenafly, 309 F.3d 144, 165 n. 24 (3d Cir. 2002) (noting that "an intermediate level of scrutiny may apply in the public employment context"), *cert. denied*, 539 U.S. 942 (2003); Fraternal Order of Police Newark Lodge No. 12 v. City of Newark, 170 F.3d 359, 366 n. 7 (3d Cir. 1999) (applying by assumption "an intermediate level of scrutiny" similar to the gender discrimination standard "since this case arose in the public employment context and since the Department's actions cannot survive even that level of scrutiny"), *cert. denied*, 528 U.S. 817 (1999).

324 *See* Draper v. Logan Cnty. Pub. Library, 403 F. Supp. 2d 608, 622 (W.D. Ky. 2005) {so doing and noting that some courts "have applied the … balancing test [of Pickering v. Bd. of Educ. of Twp. High Sch. Dist. 205, 391 U.S. 563 (1968)] used in public employment free speech jurisprudence" [citing Brown v. Polk Cnty., Iowa, 61 F.3d 650 (8th Cir. 1995) (*en banc*); Baz v. Walters, 782 F.2d 701, 708 (7th Cir. 1986); Shahar v. Bowers, 836 F. Supp. 859, 866 (N.D. Ga. 1993), *aff'd*, 114 F.3d 1097 (11th Cir.1997) (*en banc*)]}; *see also* Finnie v. Lee Cnty., Miss., 907 F. Supp. 2d 750, 767–9 (N.D. Miss. 2012); Shatkin v. Univ. of Tex. at Arlington, No. 4:06-CV-882-Y, 2009 WL 614788, at *7 (N.D. Tex. 2009) (unpublished). In addition, "[s]ome courts have applied *Pickering*'s test to situations involving religious speech without specifying whether they were evaluating a free speech or free exercise claim." Draper, 403 F. Supp. 2d at 622 [citing Lumpkin v. Brown, 109 F.3d 1498, 1500–1 (9th Cir. 1997)].

325 *See, e.g.*, Leebaert v. Harrington, 332 F.3d 134, 144 (2d Cir. 2003) (declining to recognize strict scrutiny – and perhaps any kind of heightened scrutiny – for hybrid claims); Chalifoux v. New Caney Indep. Sch. Dist., 976 F. Supp. 659, 671 (S.D. Tex. 1997) (so holding); Church at 925 S. 18th St. v. Employment Dep't, 28 P.3d 1185, 1192 (Or. Ct. App. 2001) (noting uncertainty, observing that, "[s]trictly speaking, the [*Smith*] Court did not say that, in any particular class of cases, a neutral, generally applicable law will be subject to strict scrutiny" but instead "simply noted – without reference to any particular standard – that, in the past, the Court had struck down neutral, generally applicable laws when a case 'involved' both the Free Exercise Clause and some other constitutional protection"), *review denied*, 36 P.3d 974 (Or. 2001). *Compare* Brown v. Hot, Sexy & Safer Prods., Inc., 68 F.3d 525, 539 (1st Cir. 1995) (indicating that strict scrutiny would apply, but not finding an adequate hybrid claim), *cert. denied*, 516 U.S. 1159 (1996), Miller v. Reed, 176 F.3d 1202, 1207–8 (9th Cir. 1999) (same); Swanson *ex rel.* Swanson v. Guthrie Indep. Sch. Dist. No. I-L, 135 F.3d 694, 699–700 (10th Cir. 1998) (same); Hicks *ex rel.* Hicks v. Halifax Cnty. Bd. of Educ., 93 F. Supp. 2d 649, 662–3 (E.D.N.C. 1999) (using strict scrutiny).

*v. Weinberger*,[326] which applied to a military officer's free exercise claim a standard that was lower than strict scrutiny but, at the same time, only partially resembled rational basis scrutiny, suggesting that in the military context – a specialized public-employment context – a modest intermediate level of scrutiny might be applicable.[327] Finally, *Smith* also left intact its decision in *O'Lone v. Estate of Shabazz*,[328] which extended to prisoner free exercise claims a multipart test that the Court had developed for other constitutional claims by prisoners.[329] This test, drawn from *Turner v. Safley*,[330] is somewhat more demanding than a rational basis analysis[331] and thus may properly also be classified as a type of low-level intermediate scrutiny.[332]

## F. Causes of Heightened Scrutiny under *Smith*

*Smith* and *City of Hialeah* clearly indicate, and all lower courts agree, that strict scrutiny obtains if a law or other government action is either not religiously neutral[333] or not generally applicable.[334] *Smith* also indicates that there may be two other circumstances in which strict scrutiny, or some type of heightened scrutiny, also applies: (1) if the government refuses to consider a religious exemption even though the regulation "len[ds] itself to individualized governmental assessment of the reasons for the relevant conduct"[335] and (2) if the free exercise claim is asserted "in conjunction with other constitutional protections."[336] Lower courts disagree, however, on whether these two additional circumstances are or ought to be treated as independent bases for heightened review and, if so, how exactly they should operate.[337] Acknowledging this disagreement where appropriate,

326 475 U.S. 503 (1986).

327 The Court simply stated that "when evaluating whether military needs justify a particular restriction on religiously motivated conduct, courts must give great deference to the professional judgment of military authorities concerning the relative importance of a particular military interest" (*id.* at 507) and that in the case held that the challenged regulations "reasonably and evenhandedly" furthered the military's interest. *Id.* at 510.

328 482 U.S. 342 (1987).

329 *See id.* at 349–53.

330 482 U.S. 78 (1987).

331 According to *Turner*: (1) "there must be a 'valid, rational connection' between the prison regulation and the legitimate governmental interest put forward to justify it" {*id.* at 89 [quoting Block v. Rutherford, 468 U.S. 576, 586 (1984)]}; (2) there should be "alternative means of exercising the rights that remain open to prison inmates" (*id.* at 90); (3) a court should consider "the impact accommodation of the asserted constitutional right will have on guards and other inmates, and on the allocation of prison resources generally" (*id.*); and (4) a court should consider whether there exists "an alternative that fully accommodates the prisoner's rights at *de minimis* cost to valid penological interests" (*id.* at 91). The focus on alternatives in the second and fourth factors, a result presumably of the confined nature of incarceration, is not something found in an ordinary rational basis test.

332 "Lower courts adopted a similarly deferential test for probation conditions that incidentally interfered with religious practices." Eugene Volokh, *A Common-Law Model for Religious Exemptions*, 46 UCLA L. Rev. 1465, 1495 (1999) [citing United States v. Juvenile No. 1 (LWQ), 38 F.3d 470, 473 (9th Cir. 1994); United States v. Tolla, 781 F.2d 29, 36 n. 3 (2d Cir. 1986); State v. Emery, 593 A.2d 77, 79–80 (Vt. 1991)].

333 *See* Church of the Lukumi Babalu Aye, Inc. v. City of Hialeah, 508 U.S. 520, 531, 546 (1993); Employment Div. v. Smith, 494 U.S. 872, 877–8 (1990).

334 *See* City of Hialeah, 508 U.S. at 531, 542, 546; *Smith*, 494 U.S. at 877–8.

335 *See* Smith, 494 U.S. at 884.

336 *Id.* at 881.

337 *See* Kaplan, *supra* note 256, at 1060–73 (cataloging the confusion).

the following subsections will address each of the four heightened scrutiny–triggering circumstances.[338]

### 1. *Lack of Neutrality*

A governmental action will be subjected to strict scrutiny if it is not religiously "neutral," that is, if its "object … is to infringe upon or restrict practices because of their religious motivation"[339] or if the law itself "is discriminatorily motivated and applied."[340] By comparison, "[a] law is neutral so long as its object is something other than the infringement or restriction of religious practices."[341] This neutrality must exist not only among religions but also "*between* religion and nonreligion."[342] Accordingly, "[a] rule that uniformly bans all religious practice is not neutral."[343]

Most obviously, nonneutrality can inhere in a law or policy as it is enacted, in which case the law would be said to lack facial neutrality.[344] Thus a court will look first and foremost at an enactment's wording.[345] "Even if a law passes the test of facial neutrality," moreover, "it is still necessary to ask whether it embodies a more subtle or masked hostility to religion."[346] As part of this inquiry, a court may examine a law's breadth and structure, its apparent objectives, the history and context of its enactment, and its intended

338 In addition to potentially providing heightened scrutiny under these circumstances, the Free Exercise Clause, in conjunction with the Establishment Clause, contains a protective doctrine of church autonomy that operates in a categorical fashion – i.e., if triggered, it can be absolutely protective without inquiring into the objectives or mode of the government's action. *See infra* § 5.08.

339 City of Hialeah, 508 U.S. at 533; *see also id.* at 532 (explaining that "the protections of the Free Exercise Clause pertain if the law at issue discriminates against some or all religious beliefs or regulates or prohibits conduct because it is undertaken for religious reasons"). Conversely, "[a] law is neutral with respect to religion if it does not use religion as a basis of classification – that is, if the religious character of the beliefs and practices of those to whom a law applies is irrelevant to the goals of its classification scheme." Frederick Mark Gedicks, *The Normalized Free Exercise Clause: Three Abnormalities*, 75 IND. L.J. 77, 96–7 (2000).

340 Blackhawk v. Pennsylvania, 381 F.3d 202, 209 (3d Cir. 2004) ("A law is 'neutral' if it does not target religiously motivated conduct either on its face or as applied in practice."); Axson-Flynn v. Johnson, 356 F.3d 1277, 1294 (10th Cir. 2004) ("A rule that is discriminatorily motivated and applied is not a neutral rule of general applicability."); Grosz v. City of Miami Beach, Fla., 721 F.2d 729, 733 (11th Cir. 1983) ("[G]overnmental action violates the Constitution if it is based upon disagreement with religious tenets or practices, or if it is aimed at impeding religion." [citing Braunfeld v. Brown, 366 U.S. 599, 607 (1961)], *cert. denied*, 469 U.S. 827 (1984).

341 Grace United Methodist Church v. City of Cheyenne, 451 F.3d 643, 649–50 (10th Cir. 2006).

342 Hartmann v. Stone, 68 F.3d 973, 978 (6th Cir. 1995) (emphasis in original).

343 *Id.*

344 An example of a nonneutral law is Ky. Rev. Stat. § 437.060, which provides that "[a]ny person who displays, handles or uses any kind of reptile in connection with any religious service or gathering shall be fined not less than fifty dollars ($50) nor more than one hundred dollars ($100)." The law textually targets only conduct at religious services or gatherings and does not purport to be based on a neutral rationale, such as human safety or animal welfare. An example of a neutral and generally applicable statute that also covers religious snake handling is Tenn. Code § 39-17-101, which makes it "an offense for a person to display, exhibit, handle, or use a poisonous or dangerous snake or reptile in a manner that endangers the life or health of any person." *Id.* § 39-17-101(a).

345 *See* City of Hialeah, 508 U.S. at 533–4.

346 St. John's United Church of Christ v. City of Chicago, 502 F.3d 616, 633 (7th Cir. 2007), *cert. denied*, 553 U.S. 1032 (2008).

and actual mode of operation.[347] Other than instances in which the government is attempting to avoid an Establishment Clause violation, however, few laws or policies are enacted today that expressly provide for or otherwise have the object of the adverse treatment of religious practices.[348] This is not to suggest that such bias does not exist or does not manifest through the law – the facts of *City of Hialeah* plainly show that it does – but simply that it is not extremely common and, in all events, can be quite difficult to detect, much less demonstrate in a court of law.[349]

The more likely risk is that an otherwise neutral law or policy may be discriminatorily applied, that is, that it is not "operationally neutral,"[350] particularly among religions and especially against unpopular or unorthodox religious practices. For example, a neutral law may be applied in a targeted or selective manner,[351] a possibility that the case law suggests may be particularly problematic in the absence of clear standards of implementation that lend themselves to judicial review.[352] "Discrimination may not be inferred,

347 *See* City of Hialeah, 508 U.S. at 534–5; St. John's United Church of Christ, 502 F.3d at 633; Stormans, Inc. v. Selecky, 854 F. Supp. 2d 925, 984–7 (W.D. Wash. 2012); Hyman v. City of Louisville, 132 F. Supp. 2d 528, 537–8 (W.D. Ky. 2001); Yeshiva Chofetz Chaim Radin, Inc. v. Vill. of New Hempstead, 98 F. Supp. 2d 347, 352–4 (S.D.N.Y. 2000); Storm v. Town of Woodstock, N.Y., 32 F. Supp. 2d 520, 527 (N.D.N.Y.), *aff'd*, 165 F.3d 15 (2d Cir. 1998); *see, e.g.*, Horen v. Commonwealth, 479 S.E.2d 553, 557 (Va. Ct. App. 1997) (holding that a state criminal law was not neutral where its prohibition applied "except as specifically permitted by law" and where there was no religion exception); *cf.* Children's Healthcare Is a Legal Duty, Inc. v. Min De Parle, 212 F.3d 1084, 1090 (8th Cir. 2000) (explaining primarily as part of an Establishment Clause analysis that religious discrimination "can be evidenced by objective factors such as the law's legislative history and its practical effect while in operation"), *cert. denied*, 532 U.S. 957 (2001).

348 "In fact, there are almost no cases in which an arm of the government has prohibited a religious practice because it was a religious practice. The majority of cases deal with at least ostensibly neutral laws." Hartmann, 68 F.3d at 979. Periodically, governmental entities, particularly in the educational setting, enact or implement policies concerning expression or access to resources (such as funding or building access) that explicitly discriminate on the basis of religion, purportedly in an effort to comply with the Establishment Clause. However, such regulations in recent years have generally been invalidated, often on free speech grounds. *See, e.g.*, Good News Club v. Milford Cent. Sch., 533 U.S. 98, 107–12 (2001) (after-hours access to school facilities); Rosenberger v. Rectors & Visitors, 515 U.S. 819, 828–37 (1995) (funding for student organizations); Lamb's Chapel v. Ctr. Moriches Union Free Sch. Dist., 508 U.S. 384, 393–4 (1993) (after-hours access to school facilities).

349 As the *City of Hialeah* Court itself noted, "[t]he principle that government may not enact laws that suppress religious belief or practice is so well understood that few violations are recorded in our opinions." City of Hialeah, 508 U.S. at 523.

350 Mitchell Cnty. v. Zimmerman, 810 N.W.2d 1, 10 (Iowa 2012).

351 *See, e.g.*, Rader v. Johnston, 924 F. Supp. 1540, 1554–5 (D. Neb. 1996) (concluding that a university housing policy, though "neutral on its face and in its purpose," was not "enforced in a neutral manner" when it exempted over one-third of students for a variety of reasons but not religious reasons and "when administrators base decisions upon their own religious experiences and their own perceptions of the religious beliefs of others"); *see also* Booth v. State of Md., 327 F.3d 377, 380–1 (4th Cir. 2003) (confirming that otherwise neutral policies can be challenged if applied nonneutrally); *cf.* Jocham v. Tuscola Cnty., 289 F. Supp. 2d 887 (E.D. Mich. 2003) (finding, interestingly, an Equal Protection Clause violation where county board members discriminatorily applied an otherwise neutral five-minute public comment rule against atheist speakers because of the county board's disapproval of their religious viewpoint).

352 *See* Bd. of Educ. of Kiryas Joel Vill. Sch. Dist. v. Grumet, 512 U.S. 687, 703 (1994) (explaining that where a "legislature's exercise of state authority" is "anomalously case-specific," the judiciary is left "without any direct way to review such state action for the purpose of safeguarding a principle at the heart of the Establishment Clause, that government should not prefer one religion to another, or religion to irreligion").

however, simply because a public program is incompatible with a religious organization's spiritual priorities. The Free Exercise Clause 'does not ... offer to reconcile the various competing demands on government, many of them rooted in sincere religious belief, that inevitably arise in so diverse a society as ours.'"[353] A free exercise claimant, in other words, "must show more than disparate impact in order to prove discriminatory animus on the part of the ... [government]."[354]

As for noncodified official actions or decisions, which as-applied challenges could easily involve, these obviously have to be assessed entirely by their motivations, purposes, and operation, as informed by the real-life context of their formulation and implementation.[355] Moreover, to the extent that the nonneutral application is more than simply an aberration and becomes a repetitive practice of which responsible government officials become aware, then the government itself may be liable for damages as if it had enacted and applied a nonneutral law in the first instance.[356]

Finally, the case law since *Smith* indicates that the command of neutrality obtains whether the governmental conduct at issue is conceptualized as the withholding of benefits or the imposition of burdens. For example, in a Seventh Circuit decision affirming a law enforcement agency's decision not to accommodate an employee who objected on religious grounds to working at casinos, the court noted that the claimant did "not contend that he was treated more severely than he would have been had he refused the same position for secular reasons. As a result, neither the posting [of the claimant at the casino] nor the decision not to accommodate ... [the claimant's] desire for different duties violated the free exercise clause of the first amendment, as *Smith* understands that clause."[357] In other words, the question for the court is not necessarily whether it is unjust to deny an exemption or accommodation of the claimant; instead, it is whether *all* potential claimants, religious or nonreligious, face such a denial.

### 2. *Lack of General Applicability*

A law also may be subject to strict scrutiny if it is selectively applicable rather than generally applicable. Applicability describes a law's breadth of coverage in relation to comparably situated persons or activities. A generally applicable law, accordingly, is one that basically applies to all such persons or activities, except where noncoverage is congruent with the law's particular objectives.[358] "A law fails the general applicability requirement

353 Prater v. City of Burnside, Ky., 289 F.3d 417, 428 (6th Cir. 2002) [quoting Lyng v. Northwest Indian Cemetery Protective Ass'n, 485 U.S. 439, 452 (1988)], *cert. denied*, 537 U.S. 1018 (2002).

354 *Id.* at 429; *see also* City of Hialeah, 508 U.S. at 535; *St. John's United Church of Christ*, 502 F.3d at 634.

355 *See, e.g.*, Heartland Academy Cmty. Church v. Waddle, 317 F. Supp. 2d 984, 1103 (E.D. Mo. 2004) ("To determine if the object of an official's act which interferes with the Free Exercise Clause is neutral or discriminatory, the Court may consider both direct and circumstantial evidence."), *aff'd*, 427 F.3d 525 (8th Cir. 2005).

356 *See* New Creation Fellowship of Buffalo v. Town of Cheektowaga, N.Y., No. 99-CV-460A(F), 2004 WL 1498190, at *30 (W.D.N.Y. July 2, 2004) (Magis. J. Rpt. & Recomm.) (unpublished), *aff'd*, No. 05-0159-CV, 164 Fed. App'x 5 (2d Cir. Dec. 6, 2005) (unpublished).

357 Endres v. Ind. State Police, 349 F.3d 922, 924 (7th Cir. 2003).

358 *Cf., e.g.*, Fraternal Order of Police Newark Lodge No. 12 v. City of Newark, 170 F.3d 359, 366 (3d Cir. 1999) (explaining the heightened scrutiny will not be triggered by statutory exceptions which "do not undermine the [government's] interest" or that allow "activities that [the government] does not have an interest in preventing"), *cert. denied*, 528 U.S. 817 (1999). *See* Jeffrey M. Shaman, *Rules of General Applicability*, 10 First Amend. L. Rev. 419 (2012).

if it burdens a category of religiously motivated conduct but exempts or does not reach a substantial category of conduct that is not religiously motivated and that undermines the purposes of the law to at least the same degree as the covered conduct that is religiously motivated."[359] A highway speed limit, for example, is considered generally applicable, even though ambulances may be allowed to exceed it to preserve life or health (the principal purpose of the limit) and even though police officers may be allowed to exceed it in the process of apprehending speeders (a necessary means by which this purpose is achieved).[360]

For free exercise purposes, the issue of selective applicability is relevant when a law (or perhaps its application) appears to exempt from its coverage one or more nonreligious activities, persons, or institutions but does not comparably exempt those of a religious nature.[361] More specifically, a reviewing court will examine whether the nonexemption of religion is so unwarranted or so aberrational that it may fairly be said that the "government ... [has] in a selective manner impose[d] burdens only on conduct motivated by religious belief."[362] Because "[a]ll laws are selective to some extent,"[363] the test is necessarily one of *substantial underinclusiveness*,[364] wherein a court will carefully examine the effective scope of the law (the "categories of selection"[365]) and the precise justifications for that scope and determine whether or not the nonexemption of religion is "inconsequential."[366] In assessing a law's effective scope, moreover, courts will take into account

359 Blackhawk v. Pennsylvania, 381 F.3d 202, 209 (3d Cir. 2004).

360 For criticism of the general applicability criterion, insofar as "it depends on random, arbitrary factors, and the protection it provides is sporadic, idiosyncratic, unprincipled, and unpredictable," *see* Christopher C. Lund, *A Matter of Constitutional Luck: The General Applicability Requirement in Free Exercise Jurisprudence*, 26 Harv. J.L. & Pub. Pol'y 627 (2003).

361 *See, e.g.*, Stormans Inc. v. Selecky, 844 F. Supp. 2d 1172, 1190 (W.D. Wash. 2012) (finding that a state pharmacy board's stocking and delivery rules, challenged by a pharmacy and pharmacists on religious grounds, "are riddled with exemptions for secular conduct, but contain no such exemptions for identical religiously-motivated conduct," that the rules' objectives are "undermined by secular exceptions," and that the state pharmacy board "failed to explain why a refuse and refer policy creates greater difficulties when a pharmacy declines to stock a drug for religious reasons, rather than for secular reasons").

362 Church of the Lukumi Babalu Aye, Inc. v. City of Hialeah, 508 U.S. 520, 543 (1993). Needless to say, "[n]eutrality and general applicability are interrelated, and ... failure to satisfy one requirement is a likely indication that the other has not been satisfied." *Id.* at 531. *See also id.* at 557–8 (Scalia, J., concurring in part and concurring in the judgment) ("[C]ertainly a law that is not of general applicability ... can be considered 'nonneutral'; and certainly no law that is nonneutral (in the relevant sense) can be thought to be of general applicability.").

363 City of Hialeah, 508 U.S. at 542.

364 *See id.* at 543, 546, 547.

365 *See id.* at 542.

366 *Id.* at 543. *See, e.g., id.* at 543–5 (finding that municipal ordinances prohibiting ritualistic or sacrificial animal slaughter were not generally applicable when, by their text and context, it remained lawful to, among other things, exterminate mice and rats, euthanize animals, hunt and fish, and kill animals for agricultural or food purposes); Rader v. Johnston, 924 F. Supp. 1540, 1553 (D. Neb. 1996) (finding that a state university rule requiring freshman to live in university housing was not generally applicable where "exceptions are granted ... for a variety of non-religious reasons ... [but] are not granted for religious reasons" and, because of the exceptions, "[o]ver one third of the freshman students ... are not required to comply with the parietal rule"); Mitchell Cnty. v. Zimmerman, 810 N.W.2d 1, 15–16 (Iowa 2012) (finding that a facially neutral county road protection ordinance, which did not allow for Mennonite Church member to operate a tractor with steel-cleated wheels on a hard surfaced roadway, "lack[ed] sufficient general applicability" because it underinclusively allowed uses that disserved the ordinance's two alleged objectives and "chose to prohibit only a particular source of harm to the roads that had a religious origin").

not only the exemptions expressly provided for in the law but also those comparable persons or activities that the law, by its apparent silence, simply does not cover.[367]

### 3. *Exclusion from an Extant System of Individualized Assessment*

A third condition that may trigger strict scrutiny is "where the [government] … has in place a system of individual exemptions" but "refuse[s] to extend that system to cases of … 'religious hardship.'"[368] More specifically, strict scrutiny may apply if the law, by its terms or actual implementation, "len[ds] itself to individualized governmental assessment of the reasons for the … conduct [for which the claimant seeks an exemption],"[369] but the government categorically refuses to consider religious beliefs or practices as a potential basis of exemption. Although the Court has spoken of this condition almost entirely in relation to unemployment compensation cases,[370] the Court has not explicitly limited its relevance to that context.[371] In short, as stated by the Tenth Circuit, "[b]ased on *Smith* and *City of Hialeah*, the individualized exemption exception inquiry can be summarized as follows: as long as a law remains exemptionless, it is considered generally applicable and religious groups cannot claim a right to exemption; however, when a law has secular exemptions, a challenge by a religious group becomes possible."[372]

For example, the zoning context, though largely covered by RLUIPA, typically involves, through variances and the like, some degree of individualized assessment,[373] such that a municipality's denial of a religious organization's permit application could subject the denial to a strict scrutiny analysis.[374] However, simply because a law has exemptions does

367 *See City* of Hialeah, 508 U.S. at 543–4 (assessing the applicability of ordinances by citing the activities that the ordinances' narrow drafting leaves unprohibited).

368 Employment Div. v. Smith, 494 U.S. 872, 884 (1990) [quoting Bowen v. Roy, 476 U.S. 693, 708 (1986)]; *see, e.g.*, Fraternal Order of Police Newark Lodge No. 12 v. City of Newark, 170 F.3d 359, 365–7 (3d Cir. 1999) (holding that a police department's no-beard rule, to which an exception had been made for medical conditions, could not be applied without like consideration of religious objections and ultimately that an exemption was required), *cert. denied*, 528 U.S. 817 (1999).

369 Smith, 494 U.S. at 884; *see also* Swanson *ex rel.* Swanson v. Guthrie Indep. Sch. Dist. No. I-L, 135 F.3d 694, 701–2 (10th Cir. 1998); Rader, 924 F. Supp. at 1552–3. According to a more recent Tenth Circuit opinion, "[b]ased on *Smith* and *City of Hialeah*, the individualized exemption exception inquiry can be summarized as follows: as long as a law remains exemptionless, it is considered generally applicable and religious groups cannot claim a right to exemption; however, when a law has secular exemptions, a challenge by a religious group becomes possible." Grace United Methodist Church v. City of Cheyenne, 451 F.3d 643, 650 (10th Cir. 2006).

370 *See* Smith, 494 U.S. at 882–4; Swanson, 135 F.3d at 701 (noting "some doubt concerning the continued validity of the … analysis outside the unemployment context").

371 *See* City of Hialeah, 508 U.S. at 537 (invoking it in a case involving municipal animal slaughter ordinances); Rader, 924 F. Supp. at 1552 n. 23 ("Whether individualized exemptions constitute an exception to the *Smith* rule or merely preclude a finding of general applicability … I see no justifiable basis for limiting consideration of them to only those cases involving unemployment compensation.").

372 Grace United Methodist Church, 451 F.3d at 650.

373 *See* Castle Hills First Baptist Church v. City of Castle Hills, 2004 WL 546792, at *15 (W.D. Tex. Mar. 17, 2004) (unpublished) {"Zoning, and the special use permit application process specifically, inherently depend upon a system of individualized assessment. Moreover, courts have already recognized that land use regulations that require individualized assessment fall within the scope of the remaining strict scrutiny treatment left in the wake of *Smith* and *Hialeah*." [citing Keeler v. Mayor & City Council of Cumberland, 940 F. Supp. 879, 886 (D. Md. 1996); Alpine Christian Fellowship v. Cnty. Comm'rs of Pitkin Cnty., 870 F. Supp. 991, 994–5 (D. Colo. 1994)]}.

374 *See* Church of Hills of Twp. of Bedminster v. Twp. of Bedminster, No. Civ. 05-3332(SRC), 2006 WL 462674, at *4 (D.N.J. Feb. 24, 2006) (unpublished) ("Under the First Amendment's Free Exercise

not mean that it erects a system of individualized assessment, where the regulatory scheme "contains broad, objective exceptions" that are not readily susceptible to subjective, discretionary application.[375] Importantly, even in cases in which strict scrutiny is triggered, it is not necessarily because of the refusal of the religious exemption per se but rather because of the government's blanket refusal to consider religion as a possible reason for an exemption.[376]

The individualized assessment situation would seem to overlap with the condition of selective applicability and thus seem to be a subset of the inquiry into general applicability, and some courts have indeed analyzed them together.[377] The difference appears to concern the mode and perhaps the degree of nonapplicability. The inquiry into general applicability examines the enumerated exceptions, if any, in the law, whereas the inquiry into individual assessment examines the existence of some discretionary device, such as a "good cause" or "necessity" or "exceptional circumstances" standard,[378] that the government uses on a case-by-case basis to determine whether an individual should be excused from the law's otherwise general application.[379] Alternatively, the government simply may have a history or demonstrable practice of granting exemptions on a case-by-case basis, even though it is neither formally adopted nor written.[380] The premise at work under either scenario is the following: if the government has in place an open-ended mechanism for assessing individual hardship and employs it to assess secular reasons but

protections, religious justifications for such an exemption cannot be denied unless the [government] can demonstrate a compelling state interest for the denial and that the denial represents the least restrictive means available to further that interest."); Castle Hills, 2004 WL 546792, at *15 (explaining that the "outright denial of [a church's] permit application [would be] subject to strict scrutiny"). Several circuit courts, however, have "have rejected a per se approach and instead apply a fact-specific inquiry to determine whether the regulation at issue was motivated by discriminatory animus, or whether the facts support an argument that the challenged rule is applied in a discriminatory fashion that disadvantages religious groups or organizations." Grace United Methodist Church, 451 F.3d at 651 [citing Civil Liberties for Urban Believers v. City of Chicago, 342 F.3d 752, 764–5 (7th Cir. 2003); First Assembly of God of Naples v. Collier Cnty., 20 F.3d 419, 423–4 (11th Cir. 1994); Cornerstone Bible Church v. City of Hastings, 948 F.2d 464, 472 (8th Cir. 1991)].

375 *See* Grace United Methodist Church, 451 F.3d at 654. "Consistent with the majority of our sister circuits ... we ... [do not] interpret *Smith* as standing for the proposition that a secular exemption automatically creates a claim for a religious exemption." *Id.* at 651.

376 *See* Brian A. Freeman, *Expiating the Sins of Yoder and Smith: Toward a Unified Theory of First Amendment Exemptions from Neutral Laws of General Applicability*, 66 Mo. L. Rev. 9, 50–1 (2001).

377 *See* Kaplan, *supra* note 256, at 1062.

378 Respectively, *see* Smith, 494 U.S. at 884 (discussing the "good cause" standard in the unemployment compensation context); City of Hialeah, 508 U.S. at 537 (analyzing a municipal ordinance prohibiting one from "unnecessarily" killing animals); and Rader, 924 F. Supp. at 1546–7 (addressing a university policy requiring that freshman live on campus that provided for discretionary exemptions, such as medical or family-related matters, based on a showing of "significant and truly exceptional circumstances which would make living on-campus impossible"). *See also* Stinemetz v. Kan. Health Pol'y Auth., 252 P.3d 141, 155 (Kan. Ct. App. 2011) (invoking the exception where state law provided a medical exception that allowed for coverage, beyond its terms, "at the choice" of a government official).

379 *Cf.* Fraternal Order of Police, 170 F.3d at 365 (distinguishing between "a mechanism for individualized exemptions" and "a categorical exemption for individuals with a secular objection but not for individuals with a religious objection").

380 *See* Axson-Flynn v. Johnson, 356 F.3d 1277, 1299 (10th Cir. 2004) ("The 'system of individualized exemptions' need not be a written policy, but rather the plaintiff may show a pattern of ad hoc discretionary decisions amounting to a 'system.' If we were to require the plaintiff to show that the 'system of individualized exemptions' was contained in a written policy, we would contradict the general principle that greater discretion in the hands of governmental actors makes the action taken pursuant thereto more, not less, constitutionally suspect.").

refuses to employ it to assess religious reasons – "when the government makes a value judgment in favor of secular motivations, but not religious motivations"[381] – then a court may reasonably infer that religious disfavoritism explains the differential treatment.[382]

## 4. *Assertion of a Hybrid Claim*

A final possible condition for triggering heightened scrutiny is a claimant's assertion of free exercise in conjunction with another constitutional claim,[383] although, as noted in the preceding section, what level of scrutiny is actually prompted by such a "hybrid situation,"[384] as the Court describes it in *Smith*, remains uncertain.[385] At present, the judiciary is divided over the meaning and even the existence of this particular concept.[386] Though

381 Fraternal Order of Police, 170 F.3d at 366.

382 *See* Bowen v. Roy, 476 U.S. 693, 708 (1986) (plurality opinion).

383 *See* Smith, 494 U.S. at 881–2. For commentary and analysis, *see* Steven H. Aden & Lee J. Strang, *When a "Rule" Doesn't Rule: The Failure of the Oregon Employment Division v. Smith "Hybrid Rights Exception,"* 108 PENN. ST. L. REV. 573 (2003); Ming Hsu Chen, *Note, Two Wrongs Make a Right: Hybrid Claims of Discrimination*, 79 N.Y.U. L. REV. 685 (2004); William L. Esser IV, *Note, Religious Hybrids in the Lower Courts: Free Exercise Plus or Constitutional Smoke Screen?* 74 NOTRE DAME L. REV. 211 (1998); William J. Haun, *Comment, A Standard for Salvation: Evaluating "Hybrid-Rights" Free-Exercise Claims*, 61 CATH. U.L. REV. 265 (2011); Jonathan B. Hensley, *Comment, Approaches to the Hybrid-Rights Doctrine in Free Exercise Cases*, 68 TENN. L. REV. 119 (2000); Michael E. Lechliter, *Note, The Free Exercise of Religion and the Public Schools: The Implications of Hybrid Rights on the Religious Upbringing of Children*, 103 MICH. L. REV. 2209 (2005); Hope Lu, *Comment, Addressing the Hybrid-Rights Exception: How the Colorable-Plus Approach Can Revive the Free Exercise Clause*, 63 CASE W. RES. L. REV. 257 (2012); Timothy J. Santoli, *Note, A Decade after Employment Division v. Smith: Examining How Courts Are Still Grappling with the Hybrid-Rights Exception to the Free Exercise Clause of the First Amendment*, 34 SUFFOLK U. L. REV. 649 (2001); Kyle Still, *Comment, Smith's Hybrid Rights Doctrine and the Pierce Right: An Unintelligent Design*, 85 N.C. L. REV. 385 (2006); *Note, The Best of a Bad Lot: Compromise and Hybrid Religious Exemptions*, 123 HARV. L. REV. 1494 (2010).

384 Smith, 494 U.S. at 882.

385 *Cf.* Tenafly Eruv Ass'n, Inc. v. Borough of Tenafly, 309 F.3d 144, 165 n. 26 (3d Cir. 2002) (stating that "[s]trict scrutiny may also apply" in hybrid situations), *cert. denied*, 539 U.S. 942 (2003), *with* Watchtower Bible & Tract Soc'y of N.Y., Inc. v. Vill. of Stratton, Ohio, 240 F.3d 553, 561–2 (6th Cir. 2001) ("reject[ing] … [the] assertion that the Supreme Court established in … *Smith* that laws challenged by hybrid rights claims are subject to strict scrutiny"), *rev'd on other grounds*, 536 U.S. 150 (2002), *and* Church at 925 S. 18th St. v. Employment Dep't, 28 P.3d 1185, 1192 (Or. Ct. App. 2001) (noting the conflict among courts and, for its part, observing that, "[s]trictly speaking, the Court did not say that, in any particular class of cases, a neutral, generally applicable law will be subject to strict scrutiny" but rather that "[i]t simply noted – without reference to any particular standard – that, in the past, the Court had struck down neutral, generally applicable laws when a case 'involved' both the Free Exercise Clause and some other constitutional protection"), *review denied*, 333 Or. 73, 36 P.3d 974 (Or. 2001). One consequence of this ongoing uncertainty may be the availability of qualified immunity for defendants. *See, e.g.*, Axson-Flynn, 356 F.3d at 1301 ["[T]he law regarding this controversial 'hybrid-rights' exception is not clearly established, and even this Court has recognized that '[i]t is difficult to delineate the exact contours of the hybrid-rights theory discussed in *Smith*.' Because the law was not clearly established on hybrid-rights at the time of Defendants' actions, Defendants are entitled to qualified immunity." (quoting Swanson, 135 F.3d at 699)].

386 *See* Axson-Flynn, 356 F.3d at 1297 (noting with regard to both the individualized assessment and the hybrid rights exceptions that "courts and commentators are divided"); Thomas v. Anchorage Equal Rights Comm'n, 165 F.3d 692, 704–7 (9th Cir. 1999) (canvassing the problem), *withdrawn by* 192 F.3d 1208 (9th Cir. 1999); Swanson *ex rel.* Swanson v. Guthrie Indep. Sch. Dist. No. I-L, 135 F.3d 694, 699 (10th Cir. 1998) ("It is difficult to delineate the exact contours of the hybrid-rights theory discussed in *Smith*."); Castle Hills First Baptist Church v. City of Castle Hills, No. SA-01-CA-1149-RF, 2004 WL 546792, at *16 (W.D. Tex. Mar. 17, 2004) (noting "the theory's inherent difficulties"); Green v. City of

a few courts have basically repudiated it,[387] and though "the hybrid rights theory has been roundly criticized from every quarter,"[388] most courts have at least nominally accepted it[389] and have wrestled instead with such issues as what types of accompanying or conjunctive claims will qualify, how viable these claims must be, and perhaps, what level of scrutiny should apply if a hybrid rights situation is adequately pleaded.[390] Assuming, in all events, that the hybrid rights approach exists as an independent means to obtaining heightened review, both the free exercise claim and the conjunctive claim presumably must be leveled against the same law or governmental conduct, and their mere presence together in the same lawsuit would not be sufficient.

As for what types of conjunctive claims might be asserted along with free exercise, the Supreme Court itself has explicitly identified "freedom of speech and of the press ... the right of parents ... to direct the education of their children"[391] and possibly "freedom of association."[392] It has not clearly indicated, however, whether this enumeration is exclusive or merely illustrative,[393] and some lower courts have expressed reluctance to extend the hybrid rights concept beyond these enumerated claims.[394] Other courts, by contrast,

Philadelphia, No. Civ. A. 03-1476, 2004 WL 1170531, at *5–*7 (E.D. Pa. May 26, 2004) (unpublished) (observing, with case citations, that "[f]or several years since the *Smith* decision, a debate regarding the existence and application of a hybrid rights exception has been brewing in the circuit courts"); Roman Catholic Archbishop of L.A. v. Superior Court, 32 Cal. Rptr. 3d 209, 223 (Cal. Ct. App. 2005) ("As a doctrinal matter, the nature and scope of the so-called hybrid rights exception to *Smith* is rather nebulous."), *cert. denied*, 547 U.S. 1071 (2006); Thomas v. Anchorage Equal Rights Comm'n, 102 P.3d 937, 944 (Alaska 2004) ("[C]onsiderable uncertainty continues to surround the doctrine's meaning, scope, and correct application – and, indeed, its very existence."), *cert. denied*, 544 U.S. 1060 (2005); City Chapel Evangelical Free, Inc. v. City of S. Bend, Ind., 744 N.E.2d 443, 452–3 & nn. 11 & 12 (Ind. 2001) (noting different federal and state court interpretations of the hybrid claim concept).

387 *See, e.g.*, Leebaert v. Harrington, 332 F.3d 134, 144 (2d Cir. 2003) ("We ... can think of no good reason for the standard of review to vary simply with the number of constitutional rights that the plaintiff asserts have been violated."); Kissinger v. Bd. of Trs. of Ohio State Univ., 5 F.3d 177, 180 & n. 1 (6th Cir. 1993); *cf.* Warner v. City of Boca Raton, 64 F. Supp. 2d 1272, 1288 n. 2 (S.D. Fla. 1999).

388 Axson-Flynn, 356 F.3d at 1296; *see also* Jacobs v. Clark Cnty. Sch. Dist., 526 F.3d 419, 440 n. 45 (9th Cir. 2008) (observing that "[t]he 'hybrid rights' doctrine has been widely criticized").

389 *See, e.g.*, Civil Liberties for Urban Believers v. Chicago, 342 F.3d 752, 765 (7th Cir. 2003); Tenafly Eruv Ass'n, Inc. v. Borough of Tenafly, 309 F.3d 144, 165 n. 26 (3d Cir. 2002); Miller v. Reed, 176 F.3d 1202, 1207–8 (9th Cir. 1999); Swanson, 135 F.3d at 699–700; EEOC v. Catholic Univ. of Am., 83 F.3d 455 (D.C. Cir. 1996); Brown v. Hot, Sexy & Safer Productions, Inc., 68 F.3d 525, 539 (1st Cir. 1995), *cert. denied*, 516 U.S. 1159 (1996); Cornerstone Bible Church v. City of Hastings, 948 F.2d 464, 473 (8th Cir. 1991).

390 This chapter will use the term "conjunctive claim" to describe the claim asserted along with free exercise to constitute the hybridized claim. Others employ varying terms. *See, e.g.*, Miller v. Reed, 176 F.3d 1202, 1207 (9th Cir. 1999) ("companion right"); Kaplan, *supra* note 256, at 1069 n. 107 ("conjoined constitutional claim").

391 Employment Div. v. Smith, 494 U.S. 872, 881 (1990) (citations omitted); *and see* Hicks ex rel. Hicks v. Halifax Cnty. Bd. of Educ., 93 F. Supp. 2d 649, 657–63 (E.D.N.C. 1999) (finding a hybrid free exercise–parental rights situation and applying strict scrutiny as a result); Chalifoux v. New Caney Indep. Sch. Dist., 976 F. Supp. 659, 671 (S.D. Tex. 1997) (finding a hybrid free exercise–free speech situation and employing heightened, though not strict, scrutiny as a result).

392 *Id.* at 882; *and see* City Chapel, 744 N.E.2d at 454 (entertaining the possibility of a hybrid free association–free exercise claim).

393 *See* Smith, 494 U.S. at 882.

394 *See, e.g.*, United States v. Carlson, No. 90-10465, 959 F.2d 242, 1992 WL 64772, at *2 (9th Cir. Apr. 2, 1992) (unpublished) (questioning the hybridization of equal protection), *cert. denied*, 505 U.S. 1227 (1992); Jane L. v. Bangerter, 794 F. Supp. 1537, 1547 n. 11 (D. Utah 1992) (limiting hybridization to claims involving communicative activity or parental rights).

have been willing to entertain the hybridization of free exercise with constitutional guarantees relating to the nonestablishment of religion,[395] the right to keep and bear arms,[396] the rights of property,[397] the guarantee of equal protection,[398] the concept of substantive due process,[399] and the right to life,[400] though even they have drawn the line at the infamous "right to employ" of *Lochner v. New York*.[401] At least one court has specifically rejected the proposition that a federal free exercise claim can be hybridized with a free exercise claim under a state constitution, but it left open the question of whether a federal free exercise claim can be hybridized with other state constitutional rights.[402]

This issue of defining the domain of potential conjunctive claims goes to the very coherence and administrability of the hybrid rights concept itself. Certainly it cannot be the case that litigants simply may add to their free exercise claims one or more "garden variety" constitutional claims, each of which would ordinarily prompt only rational basis review, and expect that strict scrutiny will alchemically result from the blend.[403] If nothing else, the omnipresence of potential due process and equal protection claims, normally prompting only rationality review, reveals the unmanageability of such an approach. But the alternative – to recognize only conjunctive claims that independently trigger heightened scrutiny – would seem to empty the hybrid rights concept of any significance.[404] If the

395 *See* EEOC v. Catholic Univ. of Am., 83 F.3d 455, 467 (D.C. Cir. 1996); Brown v. Buhman, 947 F. Supp. 2d 1170, 1222 (D. Utah 2013).

396 *See* Green v. City of Philadelphia, No. Civ. A. 03-1476, 2004 WL 1170531, at *7 (E.D. Pa. May 26, 2004) (unpublished).

397 *Cf.* Thomas v. Anchorage Equal Rights Comm'n, 165 F.3d 692, 707–9 (9th Cir. 1999), *withdrawn by* 192 F.3d 1208 (9th Cir. 1999).

398 *See* Brown, 947 F. Supp. 2d at 1222; Vineyard Christian Fellowship of Evanston, Inc. v. City of Evanston, 250 F. Supp. 2d 961, 989 (N.D. Ill. 2003); *cf.* Lighthouse Inst. for Evangelism, Inc. v. City of Long Branch, 406 F. Supp. 2d 507, 520 (D.N.J. 2005), *aff'd in part and vacated in part on other grounds*, 510 F.3d 253 (3d Cir. 2007), *cert. denied*, 553 U.S. 1065 (2008).

399 *See* Brown, 947 F. Supp. 2d at 1222.

400 *Cf.* Matter of Baby K, 832 F. Supp. 1022, 1030–1 (E.D. Va. 1993), *aff'd*, 16 F.3d 590 (4th Cir. 1994), *cert. denied*, 513 U.S. 825 (1994).

401 *See* Am. Friends Serv. Cmte. Corp. v. Thornburgh, 951 F.2d 957, 960 (9th Cir. 1991), *amended by* 961 F.2d 1405 (9th Cir. 1991). Apparently unavailing as well, at least in terms of outcome, are attempts to hybridize free exercise with the parental right to direct a child's upbringing and education. *See* Combs v. Homer Ctr. Sch. Dist., 468 F. Supp. 2d 738, 775 (W.D. Pa. 2006) [citing Crowley v. McKinney, 400 F.3d 965 (7th Cir. 2005); Littlefield v. Forney Indep. Sch. Dist., 268 F.3d 275 (5th Cir. 2001); Hooks v. Clark Cnty. Sch. Dist., 228 F.3d 1036 (9th Cir. 2000); Swanson *ex rel.* Swanson v. Guthrie Indep. Sch. Dist. No. 1-L, 135 F.3d 694 (10th Cir. 1998); Herndon v. Chapel Hill-Carrboro City Bd. of Educ., 89 F.3d 174 (4th Cir. 1996); Leebaert v. Harrington, 332 F.3d 134 (2d Cir. 2003); Brown v. Hot. Sexy & Safer Prods., Inc., 68 F.3d 525 (1st Cir. 1995)], *aff'd in part and vacated in part on other grounds*, 540 F.3d 231 (3d Cir. 2008), *cert. denied*, 555 U.S. 1138 (2009).

402 Hill v. N.J. Motor Veh. Comm'n, No. A-1676-04T2, 2005 WL 2924832, at *2–*3 (N.J. Super. App. Div. Nov. 7, 2005) (*per curiam*) (unpublished).

403 *See* Castle Hills First Baptist Church v. City of Castle Hills, 2004 WL 546792, at *15 (W.D. Tex. Mar. 17, 2004) (unpublished) ("A plaintiff cannot establish a hybrid rights claim merely by combining a substantial free exercise claim with tenuous claims and mere allegations of violations of other rights.").

404 *See* Church at 925 S. 18th St. v. Employment Dep't, 28 P.3d 1185, 1192–3 (Or. Ct. App. 2001) ("Why the addition of another constitutional claim would affect the standard of review of a free exercise claim is not immediately obvious. Indeed, if the mere allegation of an additional constitutional claim has the effect of altering the standard articulated in Smith, then the 'hybrid' exception likely would swallow the *Smith* rule; free exercise claims will frequently also pose at least a colorable free speech claim. On the other hand, if the Court meant that strict scrutiny pertains only when an additional constitutional claim

conjunctive claim on its own would lead to heightened or strict scrutiny, then the presence of the free exercise claim adds nothing, and there really is no hybridization after all.[405] One potential application for the concept, therefore, is for conjunctive claims that by themselves trigger some form of intermediate scrutiny (more than rational basis but less than strict), whereby hybridization plausibly could increase the level of review to strict scrutiny.[406] But the intermediate scrutiny standard is not extremely common,[407] and opportunities to invoke the hybrid rights concept would, as a consequence, be proportionately infrequent, although perhaps this is precisely what the Supreme Court intended.[408]

Another uncertainty is the extent to which the conjunctive claim must be legally viable. Obviously, the conjunctive claim cannot be frivolous,[409] nor would it probably be workable if the claim were merely nonfrivolous.[410] As the D.C. Circuit remarked of an attempt to assert a hybridized free exercise–free speech claim, where neither claim had merit, "in law as in mathematics zero plus zero equals zero."[411] Just as plainly, however, courts cannot require that the conjunctive claim be demonstrated to be definitively successful, for then the free exercise claim and the resulting strict scrutiny become an unnecessary postscript.[412] Accordingly, several courts have adopted what is perceived to be an intermediate position: the conjunctive claim must be shown to be "colorable,"[413]

is successfully asserted, then the rule of *Smith* becomes mere surplusage, as the church already would win under the alternate constitutional theory."), *review denied*, 36 P.3d 974 (Or. 2001).

405 *See* Church of the Lukumi Babalu Aye, Inc. v. City of Hialeah, 508 U.S. 520, 567 (1993) (Souter, J., concurring in part and concurring in the judgment).

406 *See supra* note 325 and accompanying text.

407 *See, e.g.*, United States v. Virginia, 518 U.S. 515, 533 (1996) (gender discrimination); Fla. Bar v. Went For It, Inc., 515 U.S. 618, 623–4 (1995) (commercial speech); Supr. Ct. of Va. v. Friedman, 487 U.S. 59, 65 (1988) (residency discrimination under the Privileges and Immunities Clause, U.S. CONST. art. IV, § 2); Mills v. Habluetzel, 456 U.S. 91, 99 (1982) (illegitimacy); United States v. O'Brien, 391 U.S. 367, 377 (1968) (content-neutral regulations of expression).

408 *See* Axson-Flynn v. Johnson, 356 F.3d 1277, 1296 (10th Cir. 2004) (surmising that "the *Smith* Court itself did not have an expansive standard in mind for a separate hybrid-rights cause of action or it would have found a hybrid-rights claim on the facts before it" [citing Michael W. McConnell, *Free Exercise Revisionism and the* Smith *Decision*, 57 U. CHI. L. REV. 1109, 1122)].

409 *See* Miller v. Reed, 176 F.3d 1202, 1208 (9th Cir. 1999) ("[A] plaintiff does not allege a hybrid-rights claim entitled to strict scrutiny analysis merely by combining a free exercise claim with an utterly meritless claim of the violation of another alleged fundamental right or a claim of an alleged violation of a non-fundamental or non-existent right."); Castle Hills First Baptist Church v. City of Castle Hills, No. SA-01-CA-1149-RF, 2004 WL 546792, at *15 (W.D. Tex. Mar. 17, 2004) (unpublished) ("A plaintiff cannot establish a hybrid rights claim merely by combining a substantial free exercise claim with tenuous claims and mere allegations of violations of other rights."); Roman Catholic Archdiocese of L.A. v. Superior Court, 32 Cal. Rptr. 3d 209, 224 (Cal. Ct. App. 2005) (refusing to hybridize "a free exercise claim with a meritless establishment clause claim"), *cert. denied*, 547 U.S. 1071 (2006).

410 *See, e.g.*, Axson-Flynn, 356 F.3d at 1295–6 ("The adoption of a 'non-frivolous' standard would open the floodgates for hybrid-rights claims, as nearly every plaintiff with a free exercise claim would be able to assert an additional non-frivolous constitutional claim.").

411 Henderson v. Kennedy, 253 F.3d 12, 19 (D.C. Cir. 2001), *cert. denied*, 535 U.S. 986 (2002); *accord* Civil Liberties for Urban Believers v. City of Chicago, 342 F.3d 752, 765 (7th Cir. 2003); Miller, 176 F.3d at 1207–8.

412 *See* Axson-Flynn, 356 F.3d at 1296–7 ("[I]t makes no sense to adopt a strict standard that essentially requires a *successful* companion claim because such a test would make the free exercise claim unnecessary. If the plaintiff's additional constitutional claim is successful, he or she would typically not need the free exercise claim and the hybrid-rights exception would add nothing to the case.").

413 *See, e.g.*, Miller, 176 F.3d at 1207–8; Swanson *ex rel.* Swanson v. Guthrie Indep. Sch. Dist. No. I-L, 135 F.3d 694, 700 (10th Cir. 1998).

that is, having "'a fair probability or a likelihood, but not a certitude, of success on the merits.'"[414] According to the Tenth Circuit, "[t]his inquiry is very fact-driven and must be used to examine hybrid rights on a case-by-case basis."[415] In addition to or as part of this colorability showing, courts also generally have required that the conjunctive claim fall within the specific, precedentially defined parameters of an existing constitutional right.[416] Regarding the parental right to direct a child's education, for example, the Tenth Circuit requires "a colorable showing of infringement of recognized and specific constitutional rights, rather than the mere invocation of a general right such as the right to control the education of one's child."[417]

## G. Forms and Limits of Accommodation

### 1. *Mandatory Accommodation*

If a law or regulation fails judicial scrutiny, the court will require by injunction that the defendant accommodate the claimant's religious practice. This is sometimes described as "mandatory" or "constitutionally compelled accommodation."[418] Ordinarily, the regulation as a whole will remain constitutionally valid, but as applied to the claimant's religious practice, under the facts presented to the court, it will be declared violative of the Free Exercise Clause. In such a case, the result is one of judicially ordered accommodation, subsequent denial of which by the government can result in a declaration of contempt of court, subject to fine or other penalty.

### 2. *Discretionary Accommodation*

If so inclined, legislatures and administrative agencies may proactively accommodate religious practices, even when it is clear that they are not constitutionally required to do so. Likewise, a government official or entity presented with an accommodation request, if properly empowered, may choose to accommodate the claimant's religious practice, even though, once again, it does not appear that the law requires such an accommodation. Called "discretionary" or "permissible accommodation," this method has been explicitly sanctioned by the Supreme Court[419] and can be employed prospectively by governments to "avoid conflicts between [the] secular and religious activities" of their citizens or employees, or it can be instituted responsively to eliminate or lessen a conflict

[414] Miller, 176 F.3d at 1207 (internal quotation marks omitted).

[415] Axson-Flynn, 356 F.3d at 1297.

[416] *See, e.g.*, Miller, 176 F.3d at 1208; *Swanson*, 135 F.3d at 699–700; Vandiver v. Hardin Cnty. Bd. of Educ., 925 F.2d 927, 933 (6th Cir. 1991).

[417] Swanson, 135 F.3d at 700; *see also* Brown v. Hot, Sexy & Safer Prods., Inc., 68 F.3d 525, 539 (1st Cir. 1995), *cert. denied*, 516 U.S. 1159 (1996).

[418] *See* Arlin M. Adams & Sarah Barringer Gordon, *The Doctrine of Accommodation in the Jurisprudence of the Religion Clauses*, 37 DePaul L. Rev. 317, 318–19 (1988) (distinguishing among permissible, mandatory, and impermissible accommodation).

[419] *See* Cutter v. Wilkinson, 544 U.S. 709, 719–24 (2005); Bd. of Educ. of Kiryas Joel Vill. Sch. Dist. v. Grumet, 512 U.S. 687, 705–6 (1994); Employment Div. v. Smith, 494 U.S. 872, 890 (1990); Corp. of Presiding Bishop of Church of Jesus Christ of Latter-Day Saints v. Amos, 483 U.S. 327, 334–5 (1987).

that is presently occurring.[420] In addition to evincing respect for the claimant's practice and recognition of the gravity of the conflict, discretionary accommodations also may be advantageous to the extent that they avoid the potential cost and publicity associated with a suit seeking court-compelled accommodation because the quantitative and qualitative burdens of such a suit still may exist even if the claim eventually fails in court.

The only specific qualification to the method of permissible accommodation is that it must abide by certain limits of the Establishment Clause.[421] However, as the Eleventh Circuit has noted, "[i]n requiring neutrality toward religion, the government need not be 'oblivious to impositions that legitimate exercises of state power may place on religious belief and practice,' nor must the 'government show a callous indifference to religious groups.' Where … a law's purpose is to alleviate significant government interference with the exercise of religion, that purpose does not violate the Establishment Clause."[422] Indeed, these limits appear to be somewhat relaxed where the government is genuinely attempting to accommodate religious practices,[423] especially in governmentally controlled contexts.[424] In particular, although a discretionary accommodation may be either informal (a one-time nonapplication of the rule) or formal (the inclusion and application of an express exception to the rule for religious practices), the Court has suggested that the latter method is constitutionally preferable because it reduces the likelihood of nonneutrality or discrimination among religious practices.[425]

Accommodations may even take the form of wide-ranging exemptions to otherwise applicable statutes. RFRA, RLUIPA, and the many RFRA-like state religious freedom statutes are all examples of such broad-based exemption schemes. The Supreme Court, moreover, has upheld RLUIPA's institutionalized persons provision against a facial challenge under the Establishment Clause, finding that "it alleviates exceptional

420 Student Members of Playcrafters v. Bd. of Educ. of Teaneck Twp., 424 A.2d 1192, 1198 (N.J. Super. Ct. App. Div.), *aff'd*, 438 A.2d 543 (N.J. 1981). "When the state … cooperates with religious authorities by adjusting the schedule of public events to sectarian needs, it … respects the religious nature of our people and accommodates the public service to their spiritual needs. To hold that it may not would be to find in the Constitution a requirement that the government show a callous indifference to religious groups." Zorach v. Clauson, 343 U.S. 306, 313–14 (1952).

421 *See* Kiryas Joel, 512 U.S. at 696–705; Estate of Thornton v. Caldor, Inc., 472 U.S. 703, 708–11 (1985). For additional discussion, *see* Chapter 4.D.2.

422 Midrash Sephardi, Inc. v. Town of Surfside, 366 F.3d 1214, 1241 (11th Cir. 2004) (quoting Kiryas Joel, 512 U.S. at 705, and Zorach, 343 U.S. at 314, respectively); *accord* Cholla Ready Mix, Inc. v. Civish, 382 F.3d 969, 975 (9th Cir. 2004) (citing additional cases).

423 *See, e.g.*, Ehlers-Renzi v. Connelly Sch. of the Holy Child, Inc., 224 F.3d 283, 287 (4th Cir. 2000) (explaining that "the government is entitled to accommodate religion without violating the Establishment Clause, and at times the government must do so" and that "[t]his authorized … accommodation of religion is a necessary aspect of the Establishment Clause jurisprudence because, without it, government would find itself effectively and unconstitutionally promoting the absence of religion over its practice"), *cert. denied*, 531 U.S. 1192 (2001).

424 *See, e.g.*, Montano v. Hedgepeth, 120 F.3d 844, 850 n. 10 (8th Cir. 1997) ("[S]tates might commit a technical violation of the Establishment Clause by even hiring prison chaplains. Nonetheless, this is condoned as a permissible accommodation for persons whose free exercise rights would otherwise suffer."); Persad v. Savage, No. 02-CV-336S(F), 2004 WL 1570286, at *5 (W.D.N.Y. May 25, 2004) (Magis. J. Rpt. & Recomm.) (unpublished) ("[I]n the prison setting, th[e] [*Lemon*] test is tempered by an inmate's free exercise rights and legitimate penological interests."), *adopted by* No. 02-CV-336S, 2004 WL 1858140 (W.D.N.Y. Aug. 19, 2004) (unpublished).

425 *See* Kiryas Joel, 512 U.S. at 702–5.

government-created burdens on private religious exercise," allows courts to "take adequate account of the burdens a requested accommodation may impose on nonbeneficiaries," and can "be administered neutrally among different faiths."[426] Lower courts generally have yielded the same assessment of RFRA,[427] with the Second Circuit finding that RFRA has "a secular legislative purpose ... namely, to protect individual First Amendment rights as interpreted by the Congress," yields a "principal effect [that] neither advances nor inhibits religion," and "decreases rather than fosters government entanglement with religion."[428] Courts likewise have upheld civil rights statutes prohibiting religious discrimination (including disparate impact discrimination) in employment, such as Title VII of the Civil Rights Act of 1964[429] and its state law counterparts.[430]

## H. Religious Institutional Autonomy: The Ministerial Exception

In addition to the doctrines and limitations discussed in prior sections, the Free Exercise Clause, in conjunction with the Establishment Clause, contains a protective array of doctrines traditionally placed under the heading of "church autonomy" or, as this section is titled, "religious institutional autonomy."[431] Included within this array are, *first*, a limitation on adjudicating disputes between or within religious organizations; *second*, a "right of religious organizations to formulate their own beliefs and doctrines ... and develop their own organizational structures"[432]; and *third*, a prohibition on interfering with an organization's or congregation's selection of its clergy and other ministerial personnel. The focus in this section largely will be on the last of these doctrines, known as the "ministerial exception," whereas Chapter 8 addresses the adjudicating of property disputes and Chapter 4 addresses the right to formulate beliefs and doctrines insofar as it

426 Cutter v. Wilkinson, 544 U.S. 709, 720 (2005) (citation omitted).

427 *See, e.g.*, Hankins v. Lyght, 441 F.3d 96, 108–9 (2d Cir. 2006); Christians v. Crystal Evangelical Free Church, 141 F.3d 854, 861–3 (8th Cir. 1998); EEOC v. Catholic Univ. of Am., 83 F.3d 455, 470 (D.C. Cir. 1996).

428 Hankins, 441 F.3d at 108. The court also noted "that the Supreme Court approved of and invited legislative enactments of religious exceptions to neutral laws in *Smith* itself." *Id.* at 109.

429 *See, e.g.*, EEOC v. Ithaca Indus., Inc., 849 F.2d 116, 119 (4th Cir. 1988), *cert. denied*, 488 U.S. 924 (1988); Int'l Ass'n of Machinists & Aerospace Workers, Lodge 751 v. Boeing Co., 833 F.3d 165, 170–1 (9th Cir. 1987), *cert. denied*, 485 U.S. 1014 (1988); Protos v. Volkswagen of Am., Inc., 797 F.2d 129, 135–7 (3d Cir. 1986), *cert. denied*, 479 U.S. 972 (1986); McDaniel v. Essex Int'l, Inc., 696 F.2d 34, 36–7 (6th Cir. 1982); Anderson v. Gen. Dynamics Convair Aerospace Div., 648 F.2d 1247 (9th Cir. 1981), *cert. denied*, 454 U.S. 1145 (1982); Nottelson v. Smith Steel Workers D.A.L.U. 19806, AFL-CIO, 643 F.2d 445, 454–5 (7th Cir. 1981), *cert. denied*, 454 U.S. 1046 (1981); Hardison v. Trans World Airlines, Inc., 527 F.2d 33 (8th Cir. 1975), *rev'd on other grounds*, 432 U.S. 63 (1977).

430 *See, e.g.*, Montgomery v. Bd. of Educ., 71 P.3d 94, 102 n. 17 (Or. Ct. App. 2003) (upholding Or. Rev. Stat. § 659.850).

431 "Church autonomy is also commonly known as the 'religious autonomy principle' and the 'ecclesiastical abstention doctrine,' and it is the oldest strand of religion-related jurisprudence in the Supreme Court, predating the cases articulating the Religion Clauses." W. Cole Durham, Robert Smith & William Bassett, 1 Religious Organizations and the Law § 1:14 (2012).

432 *See id.* "The Free Exercise Clause protects not only the individual's right to believe and profess whatever religious doctrine one desires, but also a religious institution's right to decide matters of faith, doctrine, and church governance." Petruska v. Gannon Univ., 462 F.3d 294, 306 (3d Cir. 2006) (internal quotation marks and citation omitted), *cert. denied*, 550 U.S. 903 (2007); *accord* Bryce v. Episcopal Church in Diocese of Colo., 289 F.3d 648, 655 (10th Cir. 2002).

effectively gives rise to a bar on the governmental assessment and resolution of religious questions.

Beginning in the latter part of the nineteenth century and extending through the twentieth century, the U.S. Supreme Court issued several rulings involving church governance that collectively articulated a doctrine of church autonomy. In effect, the doctrine circumscribed the government's power to interfere in matters of internal church governance, particularly when a matter had already been resolved by an authoritative church tribunal.[433] At first, this church autonomy doctrine was characterized as a matter more of common law than constitutional law, but by the mid-twentieth century it was expressly grounded in the First Amendment.[434] One footing of the doctrine seemed to be the Free Exercise Clause in that it shielded institutional religious practices from infringing government action. Yet another seemed to be the Establishment Clause in that it maintained a literal, jurisdictional separation of church and state authority and, in more modern doctrinal terms, prevented excessive entanglement of courts in fundamentally religious disputes.

With the passage of the Civil Rights Act of 1964, and in particular the employment discrimination prohibitions of Title VII of that act,[435] new and serious questions of church autonomy emerged. Although Title VII exempted religious entities and their educational institutions from the bar on religious discrimination,[436] it left intact the prohibitions on race, gender, and national original discrimination,[437] and the issue naturally arose whether these prohibitions could or should be applied to a religious entity's hiring and firing of personnel, particularly clergy or those with clergy-like functions. On the one hand, religious organizations, like nonreligious organizations, enjoy the benefits of a progressive regulatory state and should presumptively be subject to a generally applicable law of that state, especially when their discrimination thwarts the law's objectives no

433 *See* Serbian E. Orthodox Diocese for U.S. & Can. v. Milivojevich, 426 U.S. 696, 720–5 (1976); Kedroff v. St. Nicholas Cathedral, 344 U.S. 94, 95–119 (1952); Gonzalez v. Roman Catholic Archbishop of Manila, 280 U.S. 1, 16 (1929), *overruled in part by Milivojevich*, 426 U.S. at 713; Watson v. Jones, 80 U.S. (13 Wall.) 679 (1871); Lund, *supra* note 208, at 12–20 (surveying the cases).

434 *See* Kedroff, 344 U.S. at 116; Nat'l Spiritual Assembly of Baha'is of U.S. Under Hereditary Guardianship, Inc. v. Nat'l Spiritual Assembly of Baha'is of U.S., Inc., 628 F.3d 837, 845 (7th Cir. 2010) (noting that "*Kedroff* constitutionalized the general common-law principle announced in *Watson* ... that civil authorities may not make judgments about religious controversies when deciding church property disputes").

435 42 U.S.C. §§ 2000e to 2000e-4, Pub. L. No. 88–352, Title VII, § 703, 78 Stat. 255 (July 2, 1964) (as amended).

436 *See* 42 U.S.C. § 2000e-1(a) (exempting "a religious corporation, association, educational institution, or society with respect to the employment of individuals of a particular religion to perform work connected with the carrying on by such corporation, association, educational institution, or society of its activities"); *id.* § 2000e-2(e)(2) (exempting "a school, college, university, or other educational institution or institution of learning [with regard] to hir[ing] and employ[ing] employees of a particular religion if such school, college, university, or other educational institution or institution of learning is, in whole or in substantial part, owned, supported, controlled, or managed by a particular religion or by a particular religious corporation, association, or society, or if the curriculum of such school, college, university, or other educational institution or institution of learning is directed toward the propagation of a particular religion"). The constitutionality of § 2000e-1(a) was upheld in Corp. of Presiding Bishop of Church of Jesus Christ of Latter-day Saints v. Amos, 483 U.S. 327, 335–9 (1987).

437 *See id.* § 2000e-2(a); Rayburn v. Gen. Conf. of Seventh-Day Adventists, 772 F.2d 1164, 1166–7 (4th Cir. 1985) (noting that while Title VII "makes clear that religious institutions may base relevant hiring decisions upon religious preferences, [it] does not confer upon religious organizations a license to make those same decisions on the basis of race, sex, or national origin"), *cert. denied*, 478 U.S. 1020 (1986).

less than discrimination by nonreligious entities. On the other hand, religious organizations often make theologically informed employment decisions based generally on more than economics or bigotry, and governmental interference with those decisions may be seen as much more intrusive or imperious than interference with the decisions of nonreligious entities, especially ordinary commercial operations.

In the 1970s and 1980s, lower federal courts, relying on the Supreme Court's church autonomy cases, began ruling that the application of Title VII to a religious organization's clergy employment decisions violated the First Amendment.[438] Dubbed the "ministerial exception,"[439] the doctrine exhibited five key characteristics. First, it used a functional assessment of the employee's position at issue: the critical element was not the title of a position or the ordained status of an employee but rather whether the position had functions and duties similar to those of a clergy member[440] and "whether a position is important to the spiritual and pastoral mission of the church."[441] Thus courts applied the exception to employment decisions concerning, among others, church music and choir directors,[442] the faculty at a seminary,[443] an archdiocesan communications manager,[444] a lay theology teacher at a religious high school,[445] and a kosher food supervisor at a Jewish residence for the aged.[446] Second, many courts grounded the exception under both religion clauses, and even those that grounded the exception mostly under one clause typically invoked the precedents, principles, and doctrines of both clauses when recognizing

438 *See* Rayburn, 772 F.2d at 1167–72 (doing so under both clauses); McClure v. Salvation Army, 460 F.2d 553, 558–61 (5th Cir. 1972) (doing so under the Free Exercise Clause, though also invoking Establishment Clause cases and language), *cert. denied*, 409 U.S. 896 (1972).

439 Rayburn, 772 F.2d at 1168. For selected commentary on the exception, *see* Bruce N. Bagni, *Discrimination in the Name of the Lord: A Critical Evaluation of Discrimination by Religious Organizations*, 79 Colum. L. Rev. 1514 (1979); Janet S. Belcove-Shalin, *Ministerial Exception and Title VII Claims: Case Law Grid Analysis*, 2 Nev. L.J. 86 (2002); Chopko & Parker, *supra* note 280; Caroline Mala Corbin, *Above the Law? The Constitutionality of the Ministerial Exception from Antidiscrimination Law*, 75 Fordham L. Rev. 1965 (2007); Douglas Laycock, *Hosanna-Tabor and the Ministerial Exception*, 35 Harv. J.L. & Pub. Pol'y 839 (2012); Lund, *supra* note 208; Ira C. Lupu, *Free Exercise and Religious Institutions: The Case of Employment Discrimination*, 67 B.U. L. Rev. 391 (1987); Gregory A. Kalscheur, *Civil Procedure and the Establishment Clause: Exploring the Ministerial Exception, Subject-Matter Jurisdiction, and the Freedom of the Church*, 17 Wm. & Mary Bill Rts. J. 43 (2008); Jane Rutherford, *Equality as the Primary Constitutional Value: The Case for Applying Employment Discrimination Laws to Religion*, 81 Cornell L. Rev. 1049 (1996).

440 *See, e.g.*, Shaliehsabou v. Hebrew Home of Greater Wash., Inc., 363 F.3d 299, 306 (D.C. Cir. 2004) [noting that the court has "applied a 'primary duties' test to determine whether an individual falls within the ministerial exception … focus[ing] on 'the function of the position,' and not whether the individual holding that position is formally ordained" (quoting Rayburn, 772 F.2d at 1168, 1169)]; Starkman v. Evans, 198 F.3d 173, 175–6 (5th Cir. 1999) ("examin[ing] the employment duties and requirements of the [employee] as well as her actual role at the church"), *cert. denied*, 531 U.S. 814 (2000).

441 Rayburn, 772 F.2d at 1169 (citation omitted).

442 *See* EEOC v. Roman Catholic Diocese of Raleigh, 213 F.3d 795, 800–5 (4th Cir. 2000); Starkman, 198 F.3d at 175–7.

443 *See* EEOC v. Southwestern Baptist Theological Seminary, 651 F.2d 277, 283–4 (5th Cir. 1981), *cert. denied*, 456 U.S. 905 (1982); *see also* EEOC v. Catholic Univ. of Am., 83 F.3d 455, 461, 463–5 (D.C. Cir. 1996) (nun who was a member of canon law faculty). More recently, *see* Kirby v. Lexington Theological Seminary, 426 S.W.3d 597, 611–13 (Ky. 2014).

444 *See* Alicea-Hernandez v. Catholic Bishop of Chicago, 320 F.3d 698, 704 (7th Cir. 2003)

445 *See* Powell v. Stafford, 859 F. Supp. 1343, 1346–7 (D. Colo. 1994).

446 *See* Shaliehsabou, 363 F.3d at 307.

and applying the exception.[447] Third, these courts overwhelmingly agreed that although the Free Exercise Clause is a key foundation of the ministerial exception, the exception exists apart from the main rule of *Employment Division v. Smith*,[448] which holds that the Free Exercise Clause will ordinarily not shield conduct from neutral and generally applicable laws.[449] Fourth, perhaps partly due to accumulated holdings and partly due to its implication of the Establishment Clause, which tends to operating categorically rather than by balancing (as does the Free Exercise Clause), the exception effectively became an unqualified bar to applying employment laws to clergy hiring and firing by religious organizations. Accordingly, by the first decade of the new century, at which time all relevant federal appeals courts had adopted the exception,[450] it was understood that once a position was deemed ministerial, Title VII's application to that position was not a matter of case-by-case balancing but instead was simply prohibited. Finally, being constitutional in origin, its application was not limited to Title VII, and gradually it was applied to other federal employment discrimination laws,[451] as well as comparable state and local laws.[452]

In 2012, four decades after its initial articulation by the Fifth Circuit, the Supreme Court unanimously recognized the ministerial exception, largely embracing the exception's primary characteristics as developed by the lower courts.[453] Regarding its functional

447 *See, e.g.*, Bollard v. Cal. Province of the Soc'y of Jesus, 196 F.3d 940, 944 (9th Cir. 1999) (referring to both religion clauses).

448 494 U.S. 872 (1990).

449 *See, e.g.*, Roman Catholic Diocese of Raleigh, 213 F.3d at 800 n. *; Gellington v. Christian Methodist Episcopal Church, Inc., 203 F.3d 1299, 1302–4 (11th Cir. 2000); Combs v. Central Tex. Annual Conf. of the United Methodist Church, 173 F.3d 343, 349 (5th Cir. 1999); EEOC v. Catholic Univ. of Am., 83 F.3d 455, 461–3 (D.C. Cir. 1996); Miller v. Bay View United Methodist Church, Inc., 141 F. Supp. 2d 1174, 1180–3 (E.D. Wis. 2001).

450 *See* Rweyemamu v. Cote, 520 F.3d 198, 207–9 (2d Cir. 2008); Hollins v. Methodist Healthcare, Inc., 474 F.3d 223 (6th Cir. 2007), *cert. denied*, 552 U.S. 857 (2007); Petruska v. Gannon Univ., 462 F.3d 294 (3d Cir. 2006), *cert. denied*, 550 U.S. 903 (2007); Elvig v. Calvin Presbyterian Church, 375 F.3d 951 (9th Cir. 2004); Bryce v. Episcopal Church in the Diocese, 289 F.3d 648 (10th Cir. 2002); EEOC v. Roman Catholic Diocese of Raleigh, N.C., 213 F.3d 795 (4th Cir. 2000); Gellington v. Christian Methodist Episcopal Church, Inc., 203 F.3d 1299 (11th Cir. 2000); Starkman v. Evans, 198 F.3d 173 (5th Cir. 1999); Combs v. Cent. Tex. Annual Conf. of the United Methodist Church, 173 F.3d 343 (5th Cir. 1999); EEOC v. Catholic Univ. of Am., 83 F.3d 455 (D.C. Cir. 1996); Young v. N. Ill. Conf. of United Methodist Church, 21 F.3d 184 (7th Cir. 1994), *cert. denied*, 513 U.S. 929 (1994); Scharon v. St. Luke's Episcopal Presbyterian Hosps., 929 F.2d 360 (8th Cir. 1991); Natal v. Christian & Missionary Alliance, 878 F.2d 1575 (1st Cir. 1989). The other appeals court, the Federal Circuit, essentially does not have subject matter jurisdiction of the sort that would implicate Title VII's application against a religious organization.

451 *See, e.g.*, Shaliehsabou v. Hebrew Home of Greater Wash., Inc., 363 F.3d 299 (4th Cir. 2004) (Fair Labor Standards Act); Starkman v. Evans, 198 F.3d 173, 175–7 (5th Cir. 1999) (Americans with Disabilities Act), *cert. denied*, 531 U.S. 814 (2000); Minker v. Baltimore Annual Conf. of United Methodist Church, 894 F.2d 1354, 1356–8 (D.C. Cir. 1990) (Age Discrimination in Employment Act); Fassl v. Our Lady of Perpetual Help Roman Catholic Church, No. Civ. A. 05-CV-0404, 2005 WL 2455253, at *2 (E.D. Pa. Oct. 5, 2005) (unpublished) (Family and Medical Leave Act); *see also* Corbin, *supra* note 439, at 1975–6 (citing these and other federal laws to which the exception has been applied).

452 *See* Corbin, *supra* note 439, at 1976 n. 58 (citing examples); Lund, *supra* note 208, at 22 n. 97 (same). As the Ninth Circuit has commented, "[j]ust as there is a ministerial exception to Title VII, there must also be a ministerial exception to any state law cause of action that would otherwise impinge on the church's prerogative to choose its ministers or to exercise its religious beliefs in the context of employing its ministers." Bollard, 196 F.3d at 950.

453 *See* Hosanna-Tabor Evangelical Lutheran Church & Sch. v. EEOC, 132 S. Ct. 694 (2012).

focus, for example, the Court "agree[d]" with the lower court rulings "that the ministerial exception is not limited to the head of a religious congregation," though it was "reluctant … to adopt a rigid formula for deciding when an employee qualifies as a minister."[454] In addition, as had many lower courts, the Supreme Court expressly grounded the exception in both religion clauses, explaining that "[t]he Establishment Clause prevents the Government from appointing ministers, and the Free Exercise Clause prevents it from interfering with the freedom of religious groups to select their own."[455] With regard to the Free Exercise Clause, in particular, the Court maintained that "[r]equiring a church to accept or retain an unwanted minister, or punishing a church for failing to do so … interferes with the internal governance of the church, depriving the church of control over the selection of those who will personify its beliefs. By imposing an unwanted minister, the state infringes the Free Exercise Clause, which protects a religious group's right to shape its own faith and mission through its appointments."[456]

As for the main rule of *Smith*, the Supreme Court, like most lower courts, deemed it inapplicable: "*Smith* involved government regulation of only outward physical acts. The present case, in contrast, concerns government interference with an internal church decision that affects the faith and mission of the church itself."[457] Also like the lower courts, the Court applied the ministerial exception without a case-specific balancing of competing interests, indicating that the exception, once triggered, is categorical in operation. Having determined that the employee "was a minister within the meaning of the exception, the First Amendment require[d] dismissal of th[e] employment discrimination suit against her religious employer."[458] In turn, run-of-the-mill employment discrimination issues, such as remedies and employer motivation analysis, thus were simply irrelevant.[459]

Finally, the case implied, though it did not hold, that the ministerial exception would similarly prohibit the application of other laws that interfered with clergy employment. *Hosanna-Tabor* itself involved the Americans with Disabilities Act, and it is easy to foresee that the Court also would adopt the exception under Title VII (where it initially

454 *Id.* at 707.

455 *Id.* at 703; *see also id.* at 702, 706.

456 *Id.* at 706. Regarding the Establishment Clause, the Court explained that "[a]ccording the state the power to determine which individuals will minister to the faithful also violates the Establishment Clause, which prohibits government involvement in such ecclesiastical decisions." *Id.*

457 *Id.* at 707. For other reasons that the ministerial exception might escape *Smith*'s main rule, *see* Laycock, *supra* note 439, at 855–8; Lund, *supra* note 208, at 57–60.

458 Hosanna-Tabor, 132 S. Ct. at 709. The Court, noting a circuit court split, clarified that "the [ministerial] exception operates as an affirmative defense to an otherwise cognizable claim, not a jurisdictional bar." *Id.* at n.4. This has judicial procedural implications (*see* Chopko & Parker, *supra* note 280, at 289–90 & n. 338), and it also suggests that the exception, like most constitutional claims, may be waived or abandoned.

459 "An award of … [monetary damages] would operate as a penalty on the Church for terminating an unwanted minister, and would be no less prohibited by the First Amendment than an order overturning the termination. Such relief would depend on a determination that [the church] was wrong to have relieved [the employee] of her position, and it is precisely such a ruling that is barred by the ministerial exception." *Id.* And the assertion that the church's "asserted religious reason for firing [the employee] … was pretextual … misses the point of the ministerial exception. The purpose of the exception is not to safeguard a church's decision to fire a minister only when it is made for a religious reason. The exception instead ensures that the authority to select and control who will minister to the faithful – a matter 'strictly ecclesiastical' – is the church's alone." *Id.* (citation omitted) (quoting Kedroff, 344 U.S. at 119).

and widely arose in the lower courts), the Age Discrimination in Employment Act, and similar laws governing the hiring, firing, and promotion of employees. Moreover, the Court itself noted matter-of-factly that the employee in *Hosanna-Tabor* did "not dispute that if the ministerial exception bar[red] her retaliation claim under the ADA, it [would] also bar her retaliation claim under [state] law."[460] Though the Court explicitly disavowed a broad holding – "express[ing] no view on whether the exception bars other types of suits, including actions by employees alleging breach of contract or tortious conduct by their religious employers"[461] – the Court's reasoning would seem to prohibit the application of any law that interferes with or penalizes a religious organization's ministerial employment decision. Accordingly, as Professor Douglas Laycock has observed with regard to contract suits, a minister's claim "for unpaid salary or retirement benefits surely can proceed to the merits," but "[a] minister discharged for cause, suing in contract on the theory that the church lacked adequate cause to discharge him [or her], should be squarely within the rationale of *Hosanna-Tabor*."[462] "Similarly, in tort, a minister's workers' compensation claim for physical injury surely can proceed to the merits. A defamation claim alleging that church officials made false statements in the proceedings leading to his [or her] discharge, or when they explained the discharge to the congregation, should be barred."[463] As for tort suits over clergy sexual exploitation of congregants, the exception's applicability likewise will depend on the tort theory asserted and the alleged conduct to which liability might attach, but there is nothing inherent in these types of tort actions, notwithstanding their grave and high-profile nature, that renders them immune from the constitutional bar on adjudicating ministerial employment decisions.[464]

## I. Religious Freedom, Native Americans, and Public Lands

Among the most challenging religious freedom claims confronting civil courts can be those asserted by practitioners of Native American religions.[465] Their potentially difficult

460 *Id.* at 709 n. 3

461 *Id.* at 710. "The case before us is an employment discrimination suit brought on behalf of a minister, challenging her church's decision to fire her. Today we hold only that the ministerial exception bars such a suit." *Id.*

462 Laycock, *supra* note 439, at 861.

463 *Id.* at 861–2. *Compare* Cha v. Korean Presbyterian Church of Wash., 553 S.E.2d 511, 516–17 (Va. 2001) (not permitting such a claim to proceed), *cert. denied*, 535 U.S. 1035 (2002), *with* Tubra v. Cooke, 225 P.3d 862, 868–73 (Or. Ct. App. 2010) (allowing such a claim to proceed), *review denied*, 237 P.3d 221 (Or. 2010), *cert. denied*, 131 S. Ct. 1569 (2011).

464 *Cf., e.g.*, Doe No. 2 v. Norwich Roman Catholic Diocesan Corp., No. HHDX07CV125036425S, 56 Conn. L. Rptr. 460, 2013 WL 3871430, at *2 (Conn. Super. Ct. Jul. 8, 2013) (unpublished) (noting, in such a case brought against a diocese and several church officials, that "*Hosanna-Tabor* may indeed bar some of the allegations found in the complaint, such as the defendants' allegedly wrongful failure to remove Father Shea from the priesthood"), *with* Doe v. Corp. of Catholic Bishop of Yakima, 957 F. Supp. 2d 1225, 1232 (E.D. Wash. 2013) (in such a case, confining *Hosanna-Tabor* to "claims by former ministers who are terminated pursuant to church policies" and not applying it so as to bar a negligent hiring claim).

465 The discussion here focuses on challenges to federal, state, and local governments brought pursuant to the federal Constitution. Challenges to *tribal* governments must be asserted in tribal court either under tribal law or under the Indian Civil Rights Act, 25 U.S.C. § 1302(a), or, if a custodial situation is involved, in federal court under that act's *habeas corpus* provision. *Id.* § 1303. The federal Constitution's First Amendment, like all of the Bill of Rights, does not by its own force apply to tribal governments. *See supra* note 101.

nature stems from a number of factors. For one thing, certain characteristics of many Native American religious traditions can easily make their legal claims incongruent with the premises and design of conventional free exercise analysis.[466] Often problematic, for example, is the importance of location or place. Whereas "[t]he majority Judeo-Christian religions are commemorative, tracing their origins to a specific person or event (Jesus, Buddha, the Exodus)," tribal religions emphasize location and "observe new revelations at each ceremony. Relocations of the sites of tribal rituals are impossible and even sacrilegious."[467] Likewise problematic is the extent to which religion cannot always be differentiated, much less distilled, from culture.[468] Although "[m]ost religions divide the world into the sacred and the profane … Indians see the sacred as embedded in all phenomena."[469] In turn, "[a]ccessing this [sacredness] is a major ritual goal, and access points or portals, either well established or revealed in visions, are essential, as are a sense of place and time, along with an exacting ceremonialism."[470]

For another thing, it is likely difficult for some judges, lawyers, legislators, and scholars to analyze Native American religious freedom claims without appreciating, even subconsciously, the often unpleasant history of Native American and European American relations.[471] Religious practices were, in fact, frequently the specific target of governmental efforts to dismantle Native American tribalism and culture,[472] the most notorious

466 According to one scholar, "courts do not understand the nature of Indian religious beliefs because most judges are confined intellectually by Judeo-Christian notions of what constitutes a religion," and "[t]his bias is reflected in the judicially constructed legal doctrines for determining the constitutional validity of religious claims." John Rhodes, *An American Tradition: The Religious Persecution of Native Americans*, 52 Mont. L. Rev. 13, 17 (1991). In turn, "because these doctrines are framed in Western concepts of religiosity, they are prejudicial to the non-Western religions of Native Americans." *Id.* at 16–17. *See generally* Brian E. Brown, Religion, Law, and the Land: Native Americans and the Judicial Interpretation of Sacred Land (1999); Jace Weaver, Other Words: American Indian Literature, Law, and Culture 179–88 (2001); Lori G. Beaman, *Aboriginal Spirituality and the Legal Construction of Freedom of Religion*, 44 J. Church & St. 135 (2002); Allison M. Dussias, *Ghost Dance and Holy Ghost: The Echoes of Nineteenth-Century Christianization Policy in Twentieth-Century Native American Free Exercise Cases*, 49 Stan. L. Rev. 773, 805–19 (1997); Bryan J. Rose, *Comment, A Judicial Dilemma: Indian Religion, Indian Land, and the Religion Clauses*, 7 Va. J. Soc. Pol'y & L. 103 (1999).

467 Rita Sabina Mandosa, *Another Broken Promise: Reexamining the National Policy of the American Indian Religious Freedom Act*, 40 Fed. B. News & J. 109, 110 (1993); *see also* Michelle Kay Albert, *Note, Obligations and Opportunities to Protect Native American Sacred Sites Located on Public Lands*, 40 Colum. Hum. Rts. L. Rev. 479, 481–3 (2009).

468 Accordingly, though Congress has imposed on Native American tribes most of the limitations set forth in the Bill of Rights [*see* 25 U.S.C. § 1302(a)], one of the few that it omitted is the First Amendment's prohibition on making laws "respecting an establishment of religion." *See* Santa Clara Pueblo v. Martinez, 436 U.S. 49, 62–3 (1978).

469 Mandosa, *supra* note 467, at 110; Dean B. Suagee, *American Indian Religious Freedom and Cultural Resources Management: Protecting Mother Earth's Caretakers*, 10 Am. Indian L. Rev. 1, 3 (1982) ("Tribal religions tend to see all life in religious terms, rather than divided into domains clearly religious or nonreligous.").

470 Mandosa, *supra* note 467, at 110.

471 *See, e.g.*, State *ex rel.* Comm'r of Transp. v. Medicine Bird Black Bear White Eagle, 63 S.W.3d 734, 759 (Tenn. Ct. App. 2001) ["At the outset, we must acknowledge the long history of the mistreatment of Native Americans at the hands of European settlers and their governments. We are not unmindful of the removal of the eastern tribes that was pursued so vigorously and cruelly in the early nineteenth century. These federal and state policies undermined the Native Americans' religion and way of life by removing them from their ancestral homelands that were their source of strength." (footnote omitted)].

472 *See* George Dargo, *Religious Toleration and Its Limits in Early America*, 16 N. Ill. U. L. Rev. 341, 358–60 (1996); Lee Irwin, *Freedom, Law, and Prophecy: A Brief History of Native American Religious Resistance*, 21 Am. Indian Q. 35 (1997); Rhodes, *supra* note 466.

instance being the criminalization of the "Ghost Dance."[473] Given this context, modern claims by Native American are likely imbued with a moral character that most other claims generally lack,[474] although whether this character alters the outcomes of cases, and not simply their justification, is debatable. To be sure, claims of Native American religious freedom are, as a formal matter, subject to the same analytical framework by which other religious freedom claims are addressed. That is, they will ordinarily not trigger heightened scrutiny, much less warrant accommodation, as long as the law or governmental action in question is neutral and generally applicable. Indeed, the modern case most closely associated with that framework, *Employment Division v. Smith*,[475] itself involved Native American claimants who were denied unemployment compensation after losing their jobs due to the sacramental use of peyote, a controlled substance under federal law.[476]

One of the special topical areas into which cases involving Native American claimants often fall is the use of governmentally owned and managed lands. Because of the emphasis by certain Native American religions on location and natural surroundings, and owing to the government's ownership of many former tribal areas,[477] the interests of Native Americans and the government sometimes can clash. One such conflict culminated in *Sequoyah v. Tennessee Valley Authority*,[478] handed down in 1980 by the Ninth Circuit, a decade before the *Smith* decision. The case involved a challenge to the government's efforts to construct a hydroelectric dam on the Little Tennessee River, which would have caused the flooding of an area that, according to the Cherokee plaintiffs, included "sacred sites, medicine gathering sites, holy places and cemeteries."[479] In particular, they asserted that the flooding would "disturb the sacred balance of the land" and cause "irreversible loss to the culture and history" of the Cherokees.[480] Ultimately, the Ninth Circuit affirmed the judgment in favor of the government, finding that "damage to tribal and family folklore and traditions, more than particular religious observances … appear[ed] to be at stake"[481] and determining that the plaintiffs had not demonstrated a cognizable burden on their religious practices.[482]

Perhaps the most famous pre-*Smith* case involving a conflict between government land and Native American religious practices was the Supreme Court's decision in *Lyng*

473 Dussias, *supra* note 466, at 787–805 (recounting the nineteenth-century federal governmental suppression of Native American ceremonial dancing, notably the Ghost Dance).

474 *Cf.* United States v. Rush, 738 F.2d 497, 513 (1st Cir. 1984) (noting, in the context of assessing a non–Native American religious freedom claim, the unique legal status of Native Americans and congressional findings and policies regarding the special need to preserve Native American religion and culture), *cert. denied*, 470 U.S. 1004 (1985).

475 494 U.S. 872 (1990).

476 Subsequent to *Smith*, an exemption for Native American religious practitioners was added to federal law. *See* American Indian Religious Freedom Act Amendments of 1994, Pub. L. No. 103–344, § 2, 108 Stat. 3125 (Oct. 6, 1994) (codified at 42 U.S.C. § 1996a).

477 *See* Albert, *supra* note 467, at 483–5.

478 620 F.2d 1159 (9th Cir. 1980), *cert. denied*, 449 U.S. 953 (1980); *see also* Badoni v. Higginson, 638 F.2d 172 (10th Cir. 1980) (another pre-*Smith* flooding case in which the court reached the balancing test but found that the government's interest in supplying citizens with water outweighed the tribe's interest in maintaining a site unchanged for worship), *cert. denied*, 452 U.S. 954 (1981).

479 Sequoyah, 620 F.2d at 1160.

480 *Id.*

481 *Id.* at 1164.

482 *See id.* at 1164–5.

*v Northwest Indian Cemetery Protective Association*.[483] In *Lyng*, the Court addressed a challenge to the federal government's plan to pave a timbering road through an area of Six Rivers National Forest in California, a portion of which was considered sacred by Native American tribes from the region. In particular, the tribes claimed that their religious practices depended on the "privacy, silence, and an undisturbed natural setting" of the area.[484] Like the Ninth Circuit in *Sequoyah*, however, the Supreme Court essentially found no cognizable burden on the Native Americans' religious practices. "Even if we assume that … [the] road will virtually destroy the … Indians' ability to practice their religion, the Constitution simply does not provide a principle that could justify upholding [their] legal claims."[485] The Court continued: "Whatever rights the Indians may have to the use of the area … those rights do not divest the Government of its right to use what is, after all, *its* land."[486]

As *Sequoyah* and *Lyng* suggest, "[c]ourts consistently have refused to disturb governmental land management decisions that have been challenged by Native Americans on free exercise grounds."[487] Given that this conclusion obtained pre-*Smith*, when free exercise protection was most robust, the impact of *Smith* and then of RFRA (and similar legal developments) has effectively been negligible. Instructive in this regard is a more recent case out of the Ninth Circuit, this one involving a RFRA-based challenge by several Native American tribes, among others, to the federal government's decision to use treated sewage effluent to generate artificial snow at a commercial ski area. In the initial panel decision, the court held that the application of sewage-derived snow on an area that the tribes considered sacred placed a substantial burden on their religious practice, thus triggering strict scrutiny under RFRA.[488] It then found that the government's interest in creating snow for the area was not compelling.[489] When the Ninth Circuit chose to hear the case *en banc*, however, the outcome was very different. The *en banc* court agreed that RFRA, and thus the pre-*Smith* analysis, applied to the case. Under that analysis, however, the court now held that the plaintiffs failed to show a substantial burden on their exercise of religion and, as a result, "failed to establish a prima facie RFRA claim."[490]

The other branches of the federal government also have weighed in on the matter of Native American religious land use, although the effectiveness of their efforts has varied. In 1978, for example, Congress passed the American Indian Religious Freedom Act (AIRFA),[491] a primary concern of which was the denial of access to religious sites.[492] AIRFA declares that

483 485 U.S. 439 (1988).

484 *Id.* at 442.

485 *Id* at 451–2 (quotations and citation omitted).

486 *Id.* at 453 (emphasis in original).

487 United States v. Means, 858 F.2d 404, 407 (8th Cir. 1988) (*en banc*) (holding that Native Americans did not adequately show that a requested use of federal lands was essential to their religion and thus failed to demonstrate a cognizable burden on their religious practice), *cert. denied*, 492 U.S. 910 (1989).

488 *See* Navajo Nation v. U.S. Forest Serv., 479 F.3d 1024, 1042–3 (9th Cir. 2007).

489 *See id.* at 1043–6.

490 *See* Navajo Nation v. U.S. Forest Serv., 535 F.3d 1058, 1078 (9th Cir. 2008) (*en banc*), *cert. denied*, 556 U.S. 1281 (2009).

491 American Indian Religious Freedom Act of 1978, Pub. L. No. 95–341, § 1, 92 Stat. 469 (Aug. 11, 1978) (codified at 42 U.S.C. § 1996).

492 *See* Wilson v. Block, 708 F.2d 735, 746 (D.C. Cir. 1983) (citing legislative history), *cert. denied*, 464 U.S. 956 (1983).

> it shall be the policy of the United States to protect and preserve for American Indians their inherent right of freedom to believe, express, and exercise the traditional religions of the American Indian, Eskimo, Aleut, and Native Hawaiians, including but not limited to access to sites, use and possession of sacred objects, and the freedom to worship through ceremonials and traditional rites.[493]

As the Court in *Lyng* pointed out, however, "nowhere in the law is there so much as a hint of any intent to create a cause of action or any judicially enforceable individual rights."[494] Several lower court decisions, both before and after *Lyng*, echo this observation,[495] and even those suggesting that AIRFA may be independently actionable have been hesitant to read it as demanding anything more than what the Free Exercise Clause already requires.[496] At most, they conclude, AIRFA is a procedural enactment requiring consultation and consideration[497] but "not prohibit[ing] agencies from adopting all land uses that conflict with traditional Indian religious beliefs or practices."[498]

Almost two decades after AIRFA, President Clinton issued Executive Order 13007, entitled "Indian Sacred Sites."[499] The order directs federal agencies "to the extent practicable, permitted by law, and not clearly inconsistent with essential agency functions," to "accommodate access to and ceremonial use of Indian sacred sites by Indian religious practitioners" and to "avoid adversely affecting the physical integrity of such sites."[500] Despite the seemingly robust coverage of this directive, however, courts have tempered this coverage in light of the order's prefatory qualifying language. For example, the Ninth Circuit has indicated that agencies, though bound by the order, fulfill their obligations

493 42 U.S.C. § 1996.

494 Lyng, 485 U.S. *at* 455.

495 *See, e.g.*, Henderson v. Terhune, 379 F.3d 709, 715 (9th Cir. 2004) ["AIRFA is simply a policy statement that is judicially unenforceable." (citing Lyng, 485 U.S. at 455)]; Lockhart v. Kenops, 927 F.2d 1028, 1036 (8th Cir. 1991) ["AIRFA is merely a statement of federal policy to protect Indians' exercise of their religion; it confers no cause of action." (citing Lyng)], *cert. denied*, 502 U.S. 863 (1991); Saunders v. Patsavouras, No. 86–7271, 808 F.2d 835 (4th Cir. 1986) (*per curiam*) (unpublished) ("42 U.S.C. § 1996 was merely a joint resolution by Congress stating a policy, and created no substantive rights."); Crow v. Gullet, 541 F. Supp. 785, 793 (D.S.D. 1982) ("[T]he Act does not create a cause of action in federal courts for violation of rights of religious freedom. The Act is merely a statement of the policy of the federal government with respect to traditional Indian religious practices."), *aff'd*, 706 F.2d 856 (8th Cir. 1983) (*per curiam*), *cert. denied*, 464 U.S. 977 (1983).

496 *See, e.g.*, Attakai v. United States, 746 F. Supp. 1395, 1405 (D. Ariz. 1990) ("The legislative history provides that the Act was meant to insure that American Indians were given the protection guaranteed under the First Amendment to all persons, not to grant them rights in excess of those guarantees."); Crow, 541 F. Supp. at 794 ("[T]he conduct of defendants complied with the dictates of the first amendment. The American Indian Religious Freedom Act requires no more.").

497 *See* Wilson, 708 F.2d at 747 ("AIRFA requires federal agencies to consider, but not necessarily to defer to, Indian religious values … [A]n agency undertaking a land use project will be in compliance with AIRFA if, in the decision-making process, it obtains and considers the views of Indian leaders, and if, in project implementation, it avoids unnecessary interference with Indian religious practices."); *see also* Conservation Law Found. v. FERC, 216 F.3d 41, 50 (D.C. Cir. 2000); New Mex. Navajo Ranchers Ass'n v. ICC, 850 F.2d 729, 732–3 (D.C. Cir. 1988) (restating these procedural agency obligations, though noting that whether the statute actually imposes such obligations, in light of the Supreme Court's intervening decision in *Lyng*, "is debatable").

498 Wilson, 708 F.2d at 747; *accord* Havasupai Tribe v. United States, 752 F. Supp. 1471, 1488 (D. Ariz. 1990), *aff'd*, 943 F.2d 32 (1991), *cert. denied*, 503 U.S. 959 (1992).

499 61 Fed. Reg. 26771 (May 24, 1996).

500 *Id.* § 1(a).

under it simply by not acting arbitrarily and capriciously in their consideration of Native American sacred sites while implementing their larger statutory mandates.[501] In a more recent decision, the Ninth Circuit has flatly stated that the executive order "has no force and effect on its own."[502]

Generally speaking, the most successful protections for Native American religious practitioners have come from administrative agencies that have affirmatively acted in accordance with both the letter and spirit of AIRFA, Executive Order 13007, and other statutory or internal agency directives.[503] Indeed, attesting perhaps to their efficacy, some agency efforts on this front have been challenged under the Establishment Clause on the ground that the agency has preferentially favored Native American religions, excessively entangled itself with Native American religious beliefs, or coerced non-Native Americans into observing Native American religious practices.[504] Where agency initiatives provide for no more than public educational programs and voluntary public participation, however, such Establishment Clause challenges have not been successful.[505]

501 *See* S. Fork Band Council of W. Shoshone of Nev. v. U.S. Dep't of Interior, 588 F.3d 718, 724 (9th Cir. 2009) (holding that a tribe failed to meet standards for a preliminary injunction under the Federal Land Policy and Management Act and Executive Order 13007 but did meet that burden as to certain environmental claims); *accord* Te-Moak Tribe of W. Shoshone Indians of Nev. v. U.S. Dep't of the Interior, No. 12-15412, 2014 WL 1244275, at *2 (9th Cir. Mar. 27, 2014) (unpublished).

502 Te-Moak Tribe, 2014 WL 1244275, at *1.

503 *See* Marcia Yalbon, *Note, Property Rights and Sacred Sites: Federal Regulatory Responses to American Indian Religious Claims on Public Land*, 113 YALE L.J. 1623 (2004); *see also* Erik B. Bluemel, *Accommodating Native American Cultural Activities on Federal Public Lands*, 41 IDAHO L. REV. 475, 531–41 (2005) (examining particular federal agency mandates and directives).

504 *See, e.g.*, Wyo. Sawmills Inc. v. U.S. Forest Serv., 383 F.3d 1241 (10th Cir. 2004) (entertaining such a challenge, though finding that the plaintiff lacked standing), *cert. denied*, 546 U.S. 811 (2005); *cf. also* Rayellen Resources, Inc. v. N.M. Cultural Props. Review Cmte., 319 P.3d 639, 656 (N.M. 2014) (challenge to state listing of public land as a registered cultural property).

505 *See, e.g.*, Natural Arch & Bridge Soc'y v. Alston, 209 F. Supp. 2d 1207, 1223–6 (D. Utah 2002) (holding that an agency plan that educated visitors and encouraged but did not require them to avoid a sacred site, in order to accommodate, Native American religious practices did not violate Establishment Clause), *aff'd*, No. 02-4099, 98 Fed. App'x 711 (10th Cir. 2004) (unpublished), *cert. denied*, 543 U.S. 1145 (2005); Bear Lodge Multiple Use Ass'n v. Babbitt, 2 F. Supp. 2d 1448, 1454–6 (D. Wyo. 1998) (holding, in relevant part, that a National Park Service "voluntary" ban on climbing Devil's Tower National Monument during the month of June, out of deference to the local Native American tribe's belief that that monument and that month were sacred, did not violate the Establishment Clause), *aff'd*, 175 F.3d 814 (10th Cir. 1999), *cert. denied*, 529 U.S. 1037 (2000).

# 6 The Religious Test, Equal Protection, and Free Speech Clauses

The First Amendment's Free Exercise and Establishment Clauses are undoubtedly the most prominent constitutional provisions governing the relationship among religion, the citizenry, and the state. They are, to be sure, frequently described as "*the* Religion Clauses."[1] But they are not the only constitutional provisions that govern this relationship. There is, for example, another and often overlooked clause that expressly deals with religion – the only provision of the unamended Constitution that does so – namely, the Religious Test Clause of Article VI. In addition, the equal protection guarantees of the Fifth and Fourteenth Amendments have been held to protect against discrimination on the basis of one's religious affiliation or conduct. Finally, there is an extensive interrelationship between the First Amendment's religion clauses, especially the Free Exercise Clause, and the best-known provision of that amendment, the Free Speech Clause. This chapter surveys these additional constitutional provisions and specifically how they govern or relate to matters of religion.

## A. The Religious Test Clause

In the last section of the original Constitution's last substantive article, one finds the following provisions:

> The Senators and Representatives ... and the Members of the several State Legislatures, and all executive and judicial Officers, both of the United States and of the several States, shall be bound by Oath or Affirmation, to support this Constitution; but no religious Test shall ever be required as a Qualification to any Office or public Trust under the United States.[2]

The latter clause, which clearly modifies the former,[3] is commonly referred to as the "Religious Test Clause" or, among some scholars, the "No Religious Test Clause."[4]

1 *E.g.*, Hosanna-Tabor Evangelical Lutheran Church & Sch. v. EEOC, 132 S. Ct. 694, 703 (2012); McCreary Cnty., Ky. v. ACLU of Ky., 545 U.S. 844, 876, 880 (2005); Bd. of Educ. of Kiryas Joel Village Sch. Dist. v. Grumet, 512 U.S. 687, 705 (1994); Lemon v. Kurtzman, 411 U.S. 192, 201–2 (1973).

2 U.S. Const. art. VI, § 3.

3 *See* John H. Garvey & Amy V. Coney, *Catholic Judges in Capital Cases*, 81 Marq. L. Rev. 303, 349 (1998) ("The evident meaning of the religious test clause is that those whom the first part of the sentence requires to take an oath shall not have to swear to any religious propositions.").

4 *See, e.g.*, Francis J. Beckwith, *The Court of Disbelief: The Constitution's Article VI Religious Test Prohibition and the Judiciary's Religious Motive Analysis*, 33 Hastings Const. L.Q. 337, 337–8, 359 (2006); Gerard V. Bradley, *The No Religious Test Clause and the Constitution of Religious Liberty: A Machine That Has Gone*

The Religious Test Clause is perceived by many as an unfamiliar or even irrelevant provision – at best, a distant and curious relative of the First Amendment religion clauses.[5] Perhaps befitting its contemporary obscurity, the Religious Test Clause seems largely to have been uncontroversial when proposed during the drafting of the Constitution.[6] Charles Pinckney of South Carolina submitted an initial draft on August 20, 1787, providing that "[n]o religious test or qualification shall ever be annexed to any oath of office under the authority of the U.S."[7] After slight modification of the wording, a revised version was then approved on August 30 without significant dissent.[8] At the state-level ratification phase, by comparison, the proposed Religious Test Clause was markedly more contentious,[9] due in part to perceptions that it further reinforced the relatively nonreligious nature of the proposed Constitution[10] or posed a risk of eventual Catholic infiltration and domination of public offices.[11]

## 1. *Historical and Contemporary Understanding*

As a matter of principle or conventional retrospective understanding, the Religious Test Clause was ostensibly designed to "prevent the bitter English experience of flushing out dissenters or those not loyal enough to the English Crown, mainly Roman Catholics, atheists, or separatists, a practice which also continued in the colonies and early states."[12] The animating English practice was most prominently codified in a series of seventeenth-century Restoration-era statutes, most notably the Corporation Act of 1661,[13] which limited office

*of Itself*, 37 CASE W. RES. L. REV. 674 (1987); Steven K. Green, *A "Spacious Conception": Separationism as an Idea*, 85 OR. L. REV. 443, 471–3 (2006); Paul Horwitz, *Religious Tests in the Mirror: The Constitutional Law and Constitutional Etiquette of Religion in Judicial Nominations*, 15 WM. & MARY BILL RTS. J. 75 (2006); *Note*, An *Originalist Analysis of the No Religious Test Clause*, 120 HARV. L. REV. 1649 (2007).

5 *See* Daniel L. Dreisbach, *The Constitution's Forgotten Religion Clause: Reflections on the Article IV Religious Test Ban*, 38 J. CHURCH & ST. 261–2 (1996) (commenting on its obscurity in relation to the First Amendment religion clauses); Horwitz, *supra* note 4, at 76 (noting this view).

6 *See* Vincent Philip Muñoz, *The Original Meaning of the Establishment Clause and the Impossibility of Its Incorporation*, 8 U. PA. J. CONST. L. 585, 614 n. 158 (2006) (discussing the minimal debate accompanying the Religious Test Clause).

7 Pinckney had submitted a more general proposal as early as May 1787. but the delegates did not act on it. *See* Dreisbach, *supra* note 5, at 270.

8 *See* Bradley, *supra* note 4, at 692–3; Dreisbach, *supra* note 5, at 271. Regarding the issue of consensus, "the records of the Philadelphia Convention reveal only that article VI, Section 3 (in the words of Luther Martin, a Maryland delegate) 'was adopted by a great majority of the convention, and without much debate.' In fact there is *no* recorded 'debate'; all that survives is Roger Sherman's critical observation that article VI was 'unnecessary, the prevailing liberality being a sufficient security [against] such tests.'" Bradley, *supra* note 4, at 688–9 (footnote omitted).

9 *See* Dreisbach, *supra* note 5, at 273–84 (summarizing several arguments for and against the federal religious test ban). *But see* James E. Wood, Jr., *"No Religious Test Shall Ever Be Required": Reflections on the Bicentennial of the U.S. Constitution*, 29 J. CHURCH & ST. 199, 200 (1987) ("Although the ban on religious tests met with some opposition, primarily from certain religionists, it was widely applauded throughout the states.").

10 *See* Bradley, *supra* note 4, at 694–6.

11 *See id.* at 699–701.

12 Edward J. Eberle, *Religion in the Classroom in Germany and the United States*, 81 TUL. L. REV. 67, 81 (2006) (footnote omitted).

13 An Act for the well Governing and Regulating of Corporations, 13 Car. II, stat. 2 ch. 1. The Corporation Act did not stand alone. The so-called Cavalier Parliament "passed a series of severe statutes known as the Clarendon Code (Corporation Act, 1661; Act of Uniformity, 1662; Conventicle Act, 1664; Five Mile

holding to persons in communion with the Church of England, and the Test Acts of 1673[14] and 1678,[15] which required professions against belief in distinctly Catholic doctrines such as transubstantiation.

But that conventional understanding is only partially explanatory, especially when one considers that "[t]he U.S. Constitution's prohibition on religious tests for federal officeholders was historically unprecedented ... not only mark[ing] a break with Old World establishment practices but also ... depart[ing] from the prevailing policies in the original American colonies and, following independence, in the nascent states."[16] Indeed, given the accepted desirability and continuation of such tests at the state level, it has been argued that the Religious Test Clause was inserted and adopted by the Framers not so much out of high-minded principle but out of then-perceived common sense. Under this view, the Constitution's advocates argued that religious tests "were useless, counterproductive, and unnecessary. 'Useless' because unprincipled men with no firm beliefs could pass them by faking the required piety. 'Counterproductive' because therefore only principled, good men scrupulous of the test – Baptists for instance, and perhaps even Papists, Jews, and those possessing only 'natural religion' – would be excluded. 'Unnecessary' because in a pious, more or less democratic society, only 'good' characters stood a chance of winning election anyway."[17]

Today, the Religious Test Clause is infrequently litigated, though a number of the cases in which it has been implicated have involved the potential recusal or disqualification of sitting judges. In such suits, a litigant alleges that a judge's religious beliefs or involvement with a religious organization, the views of which in some way conflict with the litigants' claims, effectively renders the judge biased or not disinterested, thereby disqualifying the judge or warranting the judge's recusal.[18] Generally speaking, these efforts

Act, 1665). Their object was to exclude nonconformists from any share in central or local government." Christopher Hill, The Century of Revolution, 1603–1714, at 194 (2d ed., Routledge 2001).

14 An Act for preventing Dangers which may happen from Popish Recusants, 25 Car. II, ch. 2. This act is sometimes dated at 1672.

15 An Act for the more effectuall preserving the Kings Person and Government by disableing Papists from sitting in either House of Parlyament, 30 Car. II, stat. 2 ch. 1.

16 Dreisbach, *supra* note 5, at 263 (footnote omitted).

17 Bradley, *supra* note 4, at 698 (footnotes omitted); *see also* Dreisbach, *supra* note 5, at 294 ("[T]he federal test ban was not driven by a condemnation of religious tests as a matter of principle. The fact that religious tests accorded with popular wishes is confirmed by their presence in most state constitutions of the revolutionary era.... [S]ome delegates at the Philadelphia Convention who endorsed the federal ban had previously participated in framing religious tests for their respective state constitutions. Even among the most ardent proponents of Article VI, few denied the advantage of placing devout Christians in public office. The issue debated was the efficacy of religious tests for attaining this objective.").

18 Examples of such cases, not all invoking the Religious Test Clause, include *In re* McCarthey, 368 F.3d 1266, 1270 (10th Cir. 2004); Bryce v. Episcopal Church in the Diocese of Colo., 289 F.3d 648, 660 (10th Cir. 2002); Feminist Women's Health Ctr. v. Codispoti, 69 F.3d 399, 400–1 (9th Cir. 1995); Singer v. Wadman, 745 F.2d 606, 608 (10th Cir. 1984); Petruska v. Gannon Univ., No. 1:04-cv-80-SJM, 2007 WL 3072237, at *2 (W.D. Pa. Oct. 19, 2007) (unpublished); Hoatson v. N.Y. Archdiocese, No. 05 Civ. 10467, 2006 WL 3500633, at *5 (S.D.N.Y. Dec. 1, 2006) (unpublished); Menora v. Ill. High Sch. Ass'n, 527 F. Supp. 632, 634 (N.D. Ill. 1981); Idaho v. Freeman, 507 F. Supp. 706, 729 (D. Idaho 1981). *See also* Jake Garn & Lincoln C. Oliphant, *Disqualification of Federal Judges Under 28 U.S.C. § 455(a): Some Observations on and Objections to an Attempt by the United States Department of Justice To Disqualify a Judge on the Basis of His Religion and Church Position*, 4 Harv. J.L. & Pub. Pol'y 1, 49–59 (1981) (discussing *Freeman*); Garvey & Coney, *supra* note 3, at 348–50; Raymond J. McKoski, *Disqualifying Judges When Their Impartiality Might Reasonably Be Questioned: Moving Beyond a Failed Standard*, 56 Ariz.

have not succeeded, and "courts have consistently held that membership in a church does not create sufficient appearance of bias to require recusal."[19] One reason for this categorical position is the difficulty of assessing any particular judge's adherence to a given religious tenet or, more broadly, the judge's religious devoutness. As noted by Judge Noonan of the Ninth Circuit, when asked to recuse himself from a case involving abortion (to which his church, the Catholic Church, is opposed), "the plaintiffs qualify my beliefs as 'fervently-held' as if to distinguish my beliefs from those that might be lukewarmly maintained.... [T]he distinction is not workable. The question is whether incapacitating prejudice flows from religious belief.... As long as a person holds the creed of one of the religious bodies condemning abortion as sinful he [or she] must be accounted unfit to judge a case involving abortion; the application of an objective, reasonable-person standard leads inexorably to this conclusion if the plaintiffs' contention is supportable. No thermometer exists for measuring the heatedness of a religious belief objectively. Either religious belief disqualifies or it does not. Under Article VI it does not."[20]

## 2. *Inapplicability to State Offices*

By its terms, the Religious Test Clause applies only to *federal* offices, consistent with the view "that the banning of the religious test oath in the Constitution was to keep the Federal Government from creating an established religion"[21] or from interfering with state religious arrangements.[22] Thus, although the Religious Test Clause "prohibited [and still prohibits] States from imposing [religious] qualifications on federal legislators,"[23] it did not, and textually does not, prohibit by its own force the imposition of religious qualifications on *state* offices or officeholders.

To be sure, early state constitutions often required public officers to take religious oaths demonstrating fidelity to denominational establishments or certain Protestant Christian beliefs[24] or otherwise denying allegiance to the Catholic Church,[25] and "religious test oaths remained operative in many state constitutions well into the twentieth century."[26] A number of states also prohibited clergy from holding certain state offices,

L. Rev. 411, 455–7 (2014); Winston E. Calvert, *Note, Judicial Selection and the Religious Test Clause*, 82 Wash. U. L.Q. 1129 (2004).

19 Bryce, 289 F.3d at 660.

20 Feminist Women's Health Ctr. v. Codispoti, 69 F.3d 399, 400 (9th Cir. 1995) (Noonan, J.).

21 Anderson v. Laird, 316 F. Supp. 1081, 1093 (D.C.C. 1970), *rev'd on other grounds*, 466 F.2d 283 (D.C. Cir. 1972), *cert denied*, 409 U.S. 1076 (1972).

22 *See* Dreisbach, *supra* note 5, at 286 (discussing the possible role of federalism and observing that "many framers did not believe religious tests, at least not at the state level, were the equivalent of an establishment").

23 U.S. Term Limits, Inc. v. Thornton, 514 U.S. 779, 825 n. 35 (1995).

24 *See id.* (noting that "[s]everal State Constitutions ... imposed religious qualifications on state representatives" and specifically noting the denominational tests of New Hampshire, North Carolina, Georgia, and South Carolina); Dreisbach, *supra* note 5, at 265–8, 287–9; Eberle, *supra* note 12, at 81 n. 94; John K. Wilson, *Religion under the State Constitutions, 1776–1800*, 32 J. Church & St. 753 (1990). "Even Delaware, New Jersey, and Pennsylvania, which had no histories of an established church during the colonial period, nonetheless maintained religious tests for office in their state constitutions." Wood, *supra* note 9, at 202.

25 *See* Bradley, *supra* note 4, at 681–3.

26 Dreisbach, *supra* note 5, at 272; *see also* Eberle, *supra* note 12, at 81 (commenting that the state-level "practice of requiring religious tests through mandated oaths stubbornly persisted until 1961, when the Supreme Court declared it unconstitutional") [referencing Torcaso v. Watkins, 367 U.S. 488, 489 (1961)].

usually legislative seats, a practice that was potentially animated by different concerns but that essentially functioned, at least from the clergy member's standpoint, as a religious test for office.[27] These practices suggest an understanding, congruent with Religious Test Clause's language, that the clause did not originally apply to state offices, and though courts have issued mixed signals,[28] no subsequent developments strongly suggest that it does today. Unlike the religion clauses of the First Amendment, moreover, the guarantee against religious tests for office has not been judicially recognized as an incorporated liberty apart from the rights of the First Amendment or as an independent substantive guarantee within the Due Process Clause of the Fourteenth Amendment, either of which would then render it applicable to the states.

Merely because the Religious Test Clause might not apply directly to states, however, does not mean that states or their political subdivisions may freely subject appointees or applicants for public office to religious tests. As will be discussed shortly, the First Amendment religion clauses, which *are* applicable to the states through the Fourteenth Amendment, have themselves been held to prohibit such tests. Several states through their own constitutions, moreover, expressly prohibit religious tests for public office in a manner analogous to Article VI of the federal Constitution.[29] Additionally or

27 *E.g.*, Tenn. Const. art. IX, § 1 ("Whereas ministers of the gospel are, by their profession, dedicated to God and the care of Souls, and ought not to be diverted from the great duties of their functions; therefore, no minister of the gospel, or priest of any denomination whatever, shall be eligible to a seat in either House of the legislature."), *invalidated by* McDaniel v. Paty, 435 U.S. 618 (1978); Tex. Const. art. III, § 27 (1845) (removed in 1869) ("Ministers of the gospel being, by their profession, dedicated to God, and the care of souls, ought not to be diverted from the great duties of their functions; therefore, no minister of the gospel, or priest of any denomination whatever, shall be eligible to the legislature."); Wood, *supra* note 9, at 205–6. As Justice Brennan noted, "a unique disability upon those who exhibit a defined level of intensity of involvement in protected religious activity … as much imposes a test for office based on religious conviction as one based on denominational preference. A law which limits political participation to those who eschew prayer, public worship, or the ministry as much establishes a religious test as one which disqualifies Catholics, or Jews, or Protestants." McDaniel v. Paty, 435 U.S. 618, 632 (1978) (Brennan, J., concurring in the judgment).

28 *See, e.g.*, Torcaso, 367 U.S. at 489 n. 1 ("find[ing] it unnecessary to consider appellant's contention that this provision applies to state as well as federal offices"); Martinez v. Clark Cnty., Nev., 846 F. Supp. 2d 1131, 1144–5 (D. Nev. 2012) (ostensibly applying the Religious Test Clause directly to state law); Silverman v. Campbell, 486 S.E.2d 1, 2 (S.C. 1997) (same).

29 *See, e.g.*, Ala. Const. art. I, § 3 ("[N]o religious test shall be required as a qualification to any office or public trust under this state."); Ariz. Const. art. II, § 12 ("No religious qualification shall be required for any public office or employment."); Ark. Const. art. II, § 26 ("No religious test shall ever be required of any person as a qualification to vote or hold office."); Del. Const. art. I, § 2 ("No religious test shall be required as a qualification to any office, or public trust, under this State."); Ga. Const. art. I, § 1, ¶ IV ("No inhabitant of this state shall be molested in person or property or be prohibited from holding any public office or trust on account of religious opinions."); Ind. Const. art. I, § 5 ("No religious test shall be required, as a qualification for any office of trust or profit."); Iowa Const. art. I, § 4 ("No religious test shall be required as a qualification for any office, or public trust."); Kan. Const. Bill of Rts. § 7 ("No religious test … shall be required for any office of public trust."); Me. Const. art. I, § 3 ("[N]or shall any religious test be required as a qualification for any office or trust, under this State."); Md. Const. Decl. of Rts. art. 37 ("That no religious test ought ever to be required as a qualification for any office of profit or trust in this State."), *as modified by* Torcaso v. Watkins, 367 U.S. 488 (1961); Minn. Const. art. I, § 17 ("No religious test … shall be required as a qualification for any office of public trust in the state."); Miss. Const. art. III, § 18 ("No religious test as a qualification for office shall be required."); Mo. Const. art. I, § 5 ("[N]o person shall, on account of his religious persuasion or belief, be rendered ineligible to any public office or trust or profit in this state."); Neb. Const. art. I, § 4 ("No religious test shall be required as a qualification for office."); Nev. Const. art. XI, § 3 ("The right of any citizen of the state to … hold office

alternatively, a number of states generally prohibit any kind of civil disability on the basis of religious belief, which could be construed to accompany rights relating to eligibility for public office.[30] Finally, with regard to the religious tests that states included in their early constitutions, these provisions have been subsequently removed or modified,[31] have been held unconstitutional,[32] or, if still intact but as yet unchallenged, are presumably invalid.[33]

... shall never be restricted, abridged or impaired on account of religion."); N.J. CONST. art. I, ¶ 4 ("[N]o religious ... test shall be required as a qualification for any office or public trust."); OHIO CONST. art. I, § 7 ("No religious test shall be required, as a qualification for office."); OR. CONST. art. I, § 4 ("No religious test shall be required as a qualification for any office of trust or profit."); PA. CONST. art. I, § 4 ("No religious test shall be required as a qualification for any office of trust or profit."); R.I. CONST. art. I, § 3 ("[N] o person shall be ... disqualified from holding any office ... on account of such person's religious belief."); TENN. CONST. art. I, § 4 ("[N]o political or religious test, other than an oath to support the Constitution of the United States and of this State, shall ever be required as a qualification to any office or public trust under this State."); TEX. CONST. art. I, § 4 ("No religious test shall ever be required as a qualification to any office, or public trust, in this State; nor shall any one be excluded from holding office on account of his religious sentiments."), *as modified by* O'Hair v. White, Civ. No. A-78-CA-220, 1984 WL 251621 (W.D. Tex. July 27, 1984) (unpublished); UTAH CONST. art. I, § 4 "[N]o religious test shall be required as a qualification for any office of public trust."); WASH. CONST. art. I, § 11 ("No religious qualification shall be required for any public office or employment."); WIS. CONST. art. I, § 19 ("No religious tests shall ever be required as a qualification for any office of public trust under the state."); WYO. CONST. art. I, § 18 ("[N]o person shall be rendered incompetent to hold any office of trust or profit ... because of his opinion on any matter of religious belief whatever.").

30 *See, e.g.*, ALA. CONST. art. I, § 3 ("[T]he civil rights, privileges, and capacities of any citizen shall not be in any manner affected by his religious principles."); COLO. CONST. art. II, § 4 ("[N]o person shall be denied any civil or political right, privilege or capacity, on account of his opinions concerning religion."); IDAHO CONST. art. I, § 4 ("[N]o person shall be denied any civil or political right, privilege, or capacity on account of his religious opinions."); ILL. CONST. art. I, § 3 ("[N]o person shall be denied any civil or political right, privilege or capacity, on account of his religious opinions."); IOWA CONST. art. I, § 4 ("[N]o person shall be deprived of any of his rights, privileges, or capacities, or disqualified from the performance of any of his public or private duties ... in consequence of his opinions on the subject of religion."); KY. CONST. BILL OF RTS. § 5 ("[T]he civil rights, privileges or capacities of no person shall be taken away, or in anywise diminished or enlarged, on account of his belief or disbelief of any religious tenet, dogma or teaching."); MICH. CONST. art. I, § 4 ("The civil and political rights, privileges and capacities of no person shall be diminished or enlarged on account of his religious belief."); N.M. CONST. art. II, § 11 ("[N]o person shall ever be ... denied any civil or political right or privilege on account of his religious opinion or mode of religious worship."); OKLA. CONST. art. I, § 2 ("[N]o religious test shall be required for the exercise of civil or political rights."); VT. CONST. ch. I, art. 3 ("[N]or can any person be justly deprived or abridged of any civil right as a citizen, on account of religious sentiments, or peculia[r] mode of religious worship."); VA. CONST. art. I, § 16 ("[A]ll men shall be free to profess and by argument to maintain their opinions in matters of religion, and the same shall in nowise diminish, enlarge, or affect their civil capacities."); W. VA. CONST. art. III, § 11 ("No religious or political test oath shall be required as a prerequisite or qualification to vote, serve as a juror, sue, plead, appeal, or pursue any profession or employment."); *id.* art. III, § 15 ("[A]ll men shall be free to profess and by argument, to maintain their opinions in matters of religion; and the same shall, in nowise, affect, diminish or enlarge their civil capacities.").

31 *See* U.S. Term Limits, Inc. v. Thornton, 514 U.S. 779, 825 n. 35 (1995); Dreisbach, *supra* note 5, at 272–3.

32 *See* Torcaso v. Watkins, 367 U.S. 488 (1961) (Maryland); O'Hair v. White, Civ. No. A-78-CA-220, 1984 WL 251621 (W.D. Tex. July 27, 1984) (unpublished) (Texas); Silverman v. Campbell, 486 S.E.2d 1, 1–2 (S.C. 1997) (South Carolina).

33 The following provisions appear not to have been modified, repealed, or judicially reviewed: ARK. CONST. art. XIX, § 1 ("No person who denies the being of a God shall hold any office in the civil departments of this State, nor be competent to testify as a witness in any Court."); MISS. CONST. art. XIV, § 265 ("No person who denies the existence of a Supreme Being shall hold any office in this state."); N.C. CONST. art. VI, § 8 ("The following persons shall be disqualified for office: First, any person who shall deny the being of Almighty God."); PA. CONST. art. I, § 4 ("No person who acknowledges the being of a God and a future state of rewards and punishments shall, on account of his religious sentiments, be disqualified to hold any office or place of trust or profit under this Commonwealth."); and TENN. CONST. art. 9, § 2 ("No person

### 3. *Overlap with the First Amendment*

As indicated earlier, the primary basis for the present-day unconstitutionality of religious tests for state office is not the Religious Test Clause per se but instead the U.S. Supreme Court's recognition in *Torcaso v. Watkins*[34] that the First Amendment religion clauses effectively embody a comparable prohibition on such tests.[35] *Torcaso*, a 1961 ruling, involved an appointee to the office of notary public in Maryland who sued after being barred from office based on his unwillingness to declare his belief in God. The obligation that he make such an avowal stemmed from an article in the Maryland Constitution providing (and still providing today) that "no religious test ought ever to be required as a qualification for any office of profit or trust in this State, other than a declaration of belief in the existence of God."[36] The Supreme Court ultimately held that Maryland's religious test was unconstitutional under the First Amendment because it "invade[d] [Torcaso's] freedom of belief and religion" under the First and Fourteenth Amendments.[37]

Several observations about *Torcaso* are warranted. First, its holding should not be, and should not have been, especially surprising. Although the Court in *Torcaso* did mention the purpose and history of the Religious Test Clause,[38] its decision to rely instead on the First Amendment can be justified both by the practical reality that a religious test does in fact civilly disable persons because of their religious beliefs, which the Court had already deemed absolutely protected,[39] and by the historical reality that religious tests often were characteristic features of religious establishments.[40] Second, although *Torcaso* creates

who denies the being of God, or a future state of rewards and punishments, shall hold any office in the civil department of this State."). A challenge to the Arkansas provision was dismissed for lack of standing [*see* Flora v. White, 692 F.2d 53 (8th Cir. 1982) (*per curiam*)], with the court commenting in dictum on its apparent unconstitutionality. *See id.* at 54 n. 2 In all likelihood, these provisions are not actively enforced today. Not included in this list are prescribed oaths of office that end with "So help me God" and do not provide a generally available alternative, such as an affirmation under penalty of perjury. *See, e.g.*, ALA. CONST. art. XVI, § 279; DEL. CONST. art. 14, § 1; FLA. CONST. art. 2 § 5(b); KY. CONST. § 228; LA. CONST. art. 10, § 30; MASS. CONST. pt. II, ch. VI, art. I & amend. art. VI (specifically exempting Quakers); MISS. CONST. art. 4, § 40; N.H. CONST. pt. II, art. 84 (specifically exempting Quakers); N.C. CONST. art. VI, § 7; S.C. CONST. art. III, § 26 & art. VI, § 5; TEX. CONST. art. 16, § 1.

34 367 U.S. 488 (1961).

35 *See* Torcaso, 367 U.S. at 495; *accord* O'Hair v. White, Civ. No. A-78-CA-220, 1984 WL 251621 (W.D. Tex. July 27, 1984) (unpublished) (recognizing that a Texas state constitutional provision requiring officeholders to "acknowledge the existence of a Supreme Being" violates the Establishment Clause). *Torcaso* was presaged by Girouard v. United States, 328 U.S. 61 (1946), which construed the naturalization law as not barring religious objectors to combat service in part because "[t]he test oath is abhorrent to our tradition. Over the years Congress has meticulously respected that tradition and even in time of war has sought to accommodate the military requirements to the religious scruples of the individual. We do not believe that Congress intended to reverse that policy when it came to draft the naturalization oath." *Id.* at 69.

36 MD. CONST. DECL. OF RTS. art. 37.

37 Torcaso, 367 U.S. at 496.

38 *See, e.g., id.* at 491, 495 n. 10.

39 *See* Cantwell v. Connecticut, 310 U.S. 296, 303 (1940); *cf.* Reynolds v. United States, 98 U.S. (8 Otto) 145, 166 (1878).

40 *See* Torcaso, 367 U.S. at 490 (noting that "it was largely to escape religious test oaths and declarations that a great many of the early colonists left Europe and came here hoping to worship in their own way" but that "many of those who had fled to escape religious test oaths turned out to be perfectly willing, when they had the power to do so, to force dissenters from their faith to take test oaths in conformity with that faith"). Thus, in Virginia's Act for Establishing Religious Freedom, Jefferson bemoans "the proscribing any citizen as unworthy the public confidence by laying upon him an incapacity of being called to the offices of trust and emolument, unless he profess or renounce this or that religious opinion." The Virginia Act for Establishing Religious Freedom (1786); *available at:* http://religiousfreedom.lib.virginia.edu/sacred/vaact.html.

redundancy with respect to federal offices – arguably it renders the Religious Test Clause unnecessary – such redundancy may be seen as less problematic as a matter of constitutional interpretation than either the countertextual step of applying the Religious Test Clause directly to state offices or the extratextual step of recognizing a ban on religious tests as an incorporated liberty, or a free-standing substantive right, under the Fourteenth Amendment. Third, *Torcaso*'s reliance on the First Amendment effectively obviates any further need, or eliminates any temptation, to determine whether the Religious Test Clause does directly prohibit religious tests for state office.[41] Finally, and instead, *Torcaso* directs litigants, whether challenging restrictions on state or federal offices, to employ the doctrinal frameworks of the First Amendment religion clauses, which were even in 1961 – and certainly are today – much more familiar and developed than the doctrine of the Religious Test Clause.[42] In turn, the Religious Test Clause "has received little, if any, attention from the courts," which "have usually resolved questions which could arise under article VI under the first amendment."[43] The Establishment Clause, in particular, also may provide a more accessible avenue for litigants, especially those asserting so-called taxpayer standing. This is so because there persists a thus-far unique opportunity for taxpayer standing under the Establishment Clause,[44] and at least one court has indicated that this opportunity may not be available under the Religious Test Clause despite its close connection to the idea of nonestablishment.[45]

Following *Torcaso*, state and lower federal courts have necessarily invalidated other state religious tests for public office. In 1997, for instance, the South Carolina Supreme Court confronted a challenge to a state constitutional provision declaring that "[n]o person who denies the existence of the Supreme Being shall hold any office under this Constitution."[46] The Court, partly following *Torcaso*, ruled that this prohibition "violate[d] the First Amendment ... of the United States Constitution."[47] Likewise, a federal district court in 1984 recognized that a Texas state constitutional provision requiring officeholders to "acknowledge the existence of a Supreme Being" violates the Establishment Clause.[48]

41 The Court, for its part, left the matter undecided. *See* Torcaso, 367 U.S. at 489 n. 1.

42 *See* State of Idaho v. Freeman, 507 F. Supp. 706, 729 (D. Idaho 1981) ("From the Supreme Court's approach to article VI, clause 3, it is far from clear what its true scope is.").

43 *Id.*

44 *See* Flast v. Cohen, 392 U.S. 83, 102–6 (1968). The so-called *Flast* exception has been narrowed and never again favorably invoked by the Supreme Court, yet the Court has refused to overrule it. *See* Ariz. Christian Sch. Tuition Org. v. Winn, 131 S. Ct. 1436, 1445–9 (2011); Hein v. Freedom from Religion Found., Inc., 551 U.S. 587, 602–15 (2007) (plurality); Valley Forge Christian College v. Ams. United for Separation of Church & State, 454 U.S. 464, 478–82 (1982).

45 *See* Newdow v. Eagen, 309 F. Supp. 2d 29 (D.D.C. 2004). *Newdow* involved allegations that Congress' practices regarding legislative prayer and chaplains violated, among other constitutional provisions, the Religious Test Clause, but the district court held that the plaintiff lacked taxpayer standing with regard to a Religious Test Clause claim. *See id.* at 37. In particular, the court noted that the Religious Test Clause, unlike the Establishment Clause, had never been recognized as a specific constitutional limitation on Congress' taxing and spending power. *See id.* at 38 n. 5.

46 S.C. Const. art. VI, § 2.

47 Silverman v. Campbell, 486 S.E.2d 1, 2 (S.C. 1997). The Court also held that it violated the Article VI Religious Test Clause, but, as noted, the applicability of the Religious Test Clause itself to state offices is questionable and arguably unwarranted by precedent.

48 O'Hair v. White, Civ. No. A-78-CA-220, 1984 WL 251621, at *1 (W.D. Tex. Jul. 27, 1984) (unpublished).

As noted earlier, a number of states, in addition to having religious tests for public office, also had prohibitions on office holding specifically by clergy, which could be viewed as a cousin, if not a species, of religious tests. "By the time of the adoption of the Constitution," in fact, "a majority of the original states had constitutional provisions prohibiting members of the clergy from serving in state legislatures (Maryland, Virginia, North Carolina, and Georgia) and, in some cases, from holding any political or public office (New York, Delaware, and South Carolina)."[49] Six subsequently admitted states "similarly excluded clergymen from some political offices."[50] Most of these prohibitions were eliminated by the states themselves in the nineteenth century,[51] but at least two – those of Maryland and Tennessee – persisted well into the twentieth century.

In 1974, a federal district court invalidated under the Free Exercise Clause the prohibition in the Maryland Constitution that had provided that "[n]o Minister or Preacher of the Gospel, or of any religious creed, or denomination, and no person holding any civil office of profit, or trust, under this State, except Justices of the Peace, shall be eligible as Senator or Delegate."[52] Then, just four years later, the U.S. Supreme Court in *McDaniel v. Paty*[53] struck down the prohibition in the Tennessee Constitution, which provided (and, unrepealed, still provides) "[w]hereas ministers of the gospel are, by their profession, dedicated to God and the care of Souls, and ought not to be diverted from the great duties of their functions; therefore, no minister of the gospel, or priest of any denomination whatever, shall be eligible to a seat in either House of the legislature."[54] Though all eight participating justices agreed that this provision was unconstitutional, the lead opinion, authored by Chief Justice Burger, garnered only a four-member plurality. Two aspects of *McDaniel* are of particular relevance. First, the plurality expressly stated that "*Torcaso* [did] not govern" the case.[55] According to the opinion, "the Tennessee disqualification operate[d] against McDaniel because of his status as a 'minister' or 'priest'" and state law "indicate[d] that ministerial status is defined in terms of conduct and activity rather than in terms of belief."[56] In turn, "[b]ecause the Tennessee disqualification [was] directed primarily at status, acts, and conduct it [was] unlike the requirement in *Torcaso*, which focused on belief."[57] Second, the plurality nevertheless, like *Torcaso*, based its holding on the Free Exercise Clause, under which it strictly scrutinized the Tennessee provision as a burden on McDaniel's clerical status and found that Tennessee could not demonstrate that its prohibition served an interest "of the highest order."[58]

[49] Wood, *supra* note 9, at 205.
[50] McDaniel v. Paty, 435 U.S. 618, 622 (1978) (plurality).
[51] *See* Wood, *supra* note 9, at 206.
[52] Md. Const. art. III, § 11. *See* Kirkley v. State of Md. by Mandel, 381 F. Supp. 327, 329–31 (D. Md. 1974).
[53] 435 U.S. 618 (1978).
[54] Tenn. Const. art. 9, § 1, *quoted in* McDaniel, 435 U.S. at 621 n.1.
[55] McDaniel, 435 U.S. at 626.
[56] *Id.* at 627.
[57] *Id.*
[58] *Id.* at 628. As for the other four justices, two would have held it unconstitutional under the Free Exercise and Establishment Clauses [*see id.* at 630 (Brennan, J., concurring in the judgment, joined by Marshall, J.)]; one would have held it unconstitutional under the Free Exercise Clause pursuant to *Torcaso* [*see id.* at 642–3 (Stewart, J., concurring in the judgment)]; and one would have held it unconstitutional under the Fourteenth Amendment Equal Protection Clause [*see id.* at 643 (White, J., concurring in the judgment)].

## B. The Equal Protection Guarantees

### 1. *Equal Protection Doctrine in General*

Section 1 of the Fourteenth Amendment provides that no state shall, among other things, "deny to any person within its jurisdiction the equal protection of the laws."[59] Included within "state," and thus bound by this equal protection mandate, are the agencies and instrumentalities of states, such as public universities,[60] as well as the branches, agencies, and instrumentalities of the political subdivisions of states, such as counties and municipalities.[61] An equal protection guarantee also binds the federal government, according to the Supreme Court, through the Due Process Clause of the Fifth Amendment.[62]

The primary conceptualization of equal protection under modern case law – indeed, the guarantee's governing motif – is that "all persons similarly situated should be treated alike."[63] Of course, governments necessarily treat persons differently with great regularity: people pay different tax rates based on income, receive different benefits based on economic need, and attend different school districts based on geographic and other distinctions. Accordingly, courts start with the premise that governmental "classifications ... are ... constitutional, and the burden of showing a statute to be unconstitutional is on the challenging party, not on the party defending the statute."[64] At the outset, in other words, courts will presume that there has not been a denial of equal protection, and the challenger, in order to overcome this presumption, must show that the government's discrimination exhibits certain undesirable characteristics. Specifically, the challenger must show that the government has textually or purposefully discriminated on the basis of a so-called suspect classification (such as race, alienage, or national origin) or quasi-suspect classification (such as gender or illegitimacy) or in relation to fundamental right (such as the right to vote or to travel interstate).[65] In such instances, the

[59] U.S. Const. amend. XIV, § 1.

[60] *See* Moose Lodge No. 107 v. Irvis, 407 U.S. 163, 179 (1972) ("State action, for purposes of the Equal Protection Clause, may emanate from rulings of administrative and regulatory agencies as well as from legislative or judicial action.").

[61] *See* Edelman v. Jordan, 415 U.S. 651, 667 n. 12 (noting "the long-established rule that while county action is generally state action for purposes of the Fourteenth Amendment"); Adickes v. S.H. Kress & Co., 398 U.S. 144, 173 (1970) (noting that town ordinances and customs are subject to the Equal Protection Clause); Cooper v. Aaron, 358 U.S. 1, 16 (1958) (noting that a public school board and superintendent were, "from the point of view of the Fourteenth Amendment ... agents of the State").

[62] *See* Adarand Constructors, Inc. v. Pena, 515 U.S. 200, 215 (1995); Bolling v. Sharpe, 347 U.S. 497, 500 (1954).

[63] City of Cleburne, Tex, v. Cleburne Living Ctr., Inc. 473 U.S. 432, 439 (1985). "Different types of equal protection claims call for different forms of review.... But in each instance, 'to assert a viable equal protection claim, plaintiffs must first make a threshold showing that they were treated differently from others who were similarly situated to them.'" Brown v. Montoya, 662 F.3d 1152, 1172–3 (10th Cir. 2011) [quoting Barney v. Pulsipher, 143 F.3d 1299, 1312 (10th Cir. 1998)].

[64] N.Y. State Club Ass'n, Inc. v. City of N.Y., 487 U.S. 1, 17 (1988).

[65] *See* City of Cleburne, 473 U.S. at 440–1; Mass. Bd. of Retirement v. Murgia, 427 U.S. 307, 312–13 & nn. 3 & 4 (1976). As the Fourth Circuit has explained, "[t]o succeed on an equal protection claim, a plaintiff must first demonstrate that he has been treated differently from others with whom he is similarly situated and that the unequal treatment was the result of intentional or purposeful discrimination. Once this showing is made, the court proceeds to determine whether the disparity in treatment can be justified under the requisite level of scrutiny." Morrison v. Garraghty, 239 F.3d 648, 654 (4th Cir. 2001); *accord* Knight v. Conn. Dep't of Pub. Health, 275 F.3d 156, 166 (2d Cir. 2001); Foy v. Holston, 94 F.3d 1528, 1533 (11th Cir. 1996); Muhammad v. Lynaugh, 966 F.2d 901, 903 (5th Cir. 1992); Cornerstone Bible Church v. City

government's action, be it a statute or policy or agency rule, will not simply lose its presumption of constitutionality but will be presumed unconstitutional and then be subjected to some kind of heightened judicial review.[66]

When the discrimination involves suspect classifications and fundamental rights, this heightened review ordinarily will take the form of strict scrutiny.[67] The evidentiary burden shifts to the government, which must then prove that its discriminatory law or action is necessary or narrowly tailored to achieve – or is the least discriminatory or restrictive means of achieving – a compelling interest.[68] When the discrimination involves a quasi-suspect classification, the heightened review will, by comparison, take the form of intermediate scrutiny. The evidentiary burden likewise shifts to the government, but the standard is somewhat less demanding: the government must show that its discriminatory law or action is substantially related to an important interest.[69]

Absent a reason for heightened review, the judiciary will assess the government action only for reasonableness or rationality, or what it calls a "rational basis." The presumption of constitutionality persists, leaving the evidentiary burden on the challenger, who must show "that there exists no fairly conceivable set of facts that could ground a rational relationship between the challenged classification and the government's legitimate goals" and, further, "must rule out every plausible rationale that might support the law at issue."[70] As this language suggests, rationality review is normally quite deferential – "[u]nder the best of circumstances, [it] is a steep uphill climb for a plaintiff"[71] – and government actions subject to it ordinarily will be upheld.[72]

### 2. *Overlap with the First Amendment*

Broadly speaking, religion-related equal protection claims can be approached in two ways: by alleging discrimination on the basis of religious belief, affiliation, or perhaps

of Hastings, 948 F.2d 464, 472 n. 13 (8th Cir. 1991); Andrews v. Philadelphia, 895 F.2d 1469, 1478 (3d Cir. 1990).

66 *See* Int'l Paper Co. v. Town of Jay, 928 F.2d 480, 485 n. 2 (1st Cir. 1991) (explaining that the "general rule [of deferring to legislation, requiring only that it be rational] does not apply when the statute involves suspect classifications such as race, alienage, or national origin, or 'quasi-suspect' classifications such as gender and illegitimacy, or if the statute affects personal and fundamental rights").

67 *See* Bowman v. United States, 564 F.3d 765, 772 (6th Cir. 2008) ("Strict scrutiny applies where the classification affecting eligibility for benefits is based on religion or burdens the exercise of religion."), *cert. denied*, 558 U.S. 815 (2009).

68 *See* Fisher v. Univ. of Tex. at Austin, 133 S. Ct. 2411, 2419 (2013); Johnson v. California, 543 U.S. 499, 505 (2005); Gratz v. Bollinger, 539 U.S. 244, 270 (2003); City of Cleburne, 473 U.S. at 440.

69 *See* United States v. Virginia, 518 U.S. 515, 533 (1996); Miss. Univ. for Women v. Hogan, 458 U.S. 718, 724 (1982).

70 Eulitt *ex rel.* Eulitt v. Me. Dep't of Educ., 386 F.3d 344, 356 (1st Cir. 2004).

71 *Id.*

72 *See* City of Cleburne, 473 U.S. at 440 ["The general rule is that legislation is presumed to be valid and will be sustained if the classification drawn by the statute is rationally related to a legitimate state interest. When social or economic legislation is at issue, the Equal Protection Clause allows the States wide latitude, and the Constitution presumes that even improvident decisions will eventually be rectified by the democratic processes." (citations omitted)]; *accord* Knapp v. Hanson, 183 F.3d 786, 789 (8th Cir. 1999); Bowman, 564 F.3d at 776 (noting that the test is "extremely deferential" and "quite liberal"); Sutton v. Stewart, 22 F. Supp. 2d 1097, 1106 n. 14 (D. Ariz. 1998) (commenting "that rationality review is typically so deferential that virtually any conceivable justification will suffice"), *aff'd*, 185 F.3d 869 (9th Cir. 1999) (*per curiam*).

conduct (where religion is characterized as a suspect classification) or by alleging discrimination that interferes with one's religious free exercise (where religion is characterized as a fundamental right). Before addressing each approach, however, two qualifications or caveats must be noted. The first is that both approaches – perhaps, for that matter, *all* assertions of religious interests in the equal protection context – overlap significantly with the First Amendment religion clauses and, in cases of religious expression, with the First Amendment Free Speech Clause as well. Not only do they overlap; in practice, they are effectively and regularly eclipsed by these other provisions. The second caveat, which is related to the first, is that the differential treatment of religion, unlike race, is often entirely permissible. The First Amendment religion clauses themselves single out religion for differential treatment; in turn, courts have held that the government can take cognizance of religion and treat it differently, either to accommodate its exercise or to prevent its establishment, in ways that the government could not possibly do in relation to other suspect classifications.

With respect to claims alleging discrimination on the basis of religious belief, affiliation, or conduct, as a result, equal protection is not frequently or prominently invoked by claimants (especially outside of the prison setting), and it is even less often employed by courts as a basis for resolving cases[73] and, when employed, may be invoked in an after-the-fact manner.[74] As the Second Circuit has observed, "[u]nlike the race and gender contexts, religious discrimination challenges are rarely brought under the equal protection clause, thanks to the existence of the First Amendment."[75] Given the predominant role of the religion clauses, in fact, a claimant's effort to bring a religion-related equal protection challenge could be seen as an indicator that the claimant is unable or unlikely to prevail, or to obtain heightened scrutiny, under these other provisions.[76] At least

73 *See* James A. Kushner, Government Discrimination: Equal Protection Law and Litigation § 5:21 (updated Nov. 2013) ("Religion-based discrimination is rarely challenged under the equal protection clause."). Some have argued for a greater role of equal protection in religion-related claims. *See, e.g.*, Susan Gellman & Susan Looper-Friedman, *Thou Shalt Use the Equal Protection Clause for Religion Cases (Not Just the Establishment Clause)*, 10 U. Pa. J. Const. L. 665 (2008) (advocating such a role with regard to challenges to governmental religious expression); Michael A. Paulsen, *Religion, Equality, and the Constitution: An Equal Protection Approach to Establishment Clause Adjudication*, 61 Notre Dame L. Rev. 311, 315 (1986) (arguing that Establishment Clause doctrine should be refocused toward "[t]he equal protection of the free exercise of religion"). For an historical assessment, as least with regard to free exercise, *see* Bernadette Meyler, *The Equal Protection of Free Exercise: Two Approaches and Their History*, 47 B.C. L. Rev. 275 (2006).

74 *See, e.g.*, Ctr. for Inquiry, Inc. v. Marion Circuit Ct. Clerk, 758 F.3d 869, 874–5 (7th Cir. 2014) (after a moderately extensive Establishment Clause analysis, declaring that the state law in question "violates the Equal Protection Clause of the Fourteenth Amendment as well as the First Amendment" because it "is irrational").

75 United States v. Brown, 352 F.3d 654, 669 n. 18 (2d Cir. 2003); *see also* Sherbert v. Verner, 374 U.S. 398, 410 (1963) ("In view of the result we have reached under the First and Fourteenth Amendments' guarantee of free exercise of religion, we have no occasion to consider appellant's claim that the denial of benefits also deprived her of the equal protection of the laws in violation of the Fourteenth Amendment."); State v. Hodge, 248 Conn. 207, 244 n. 43, 726 A.2d 531, 552 n. 43 (Conn. 1999) {"Because religion-based constitutional challenges generally are raised under the free exercise or establishment clauses of the first amendment to the United States constitution, '[r]eligious discrimination rarely is challenged under the [federal] equal protection clause.'" [quoting J. Suzanne Bell Chambers, *Note, Applying the Break: Religion and the Peremptory Challenge*, 70 Ind. L.J. 569, 591 (1995)]}, *cert. denied*, 528 U.S. 969 (1999).

76 *See, e.g.*, Locke v. Davey, 540 U.S. 712, 720 n. 3 (2004) [explaining that in light of its antecedent finding of no free exercise violation, it would "apply rational-basis scrutiny to [the challenger's] equal protection

a few courts have even held that "[i]n the context of an equal protection claim based on religion, the Fourteenth Amendment is supplanted by the Free Exercise Clause of the First Amendment except as to a claim of arbitrariness unrelated to the character of the activity allegedly discriminated against."[77] In part this is "because the Fourteenth Amendment's general protections should not be invoked when a more specific textual source of the constitutional protection exists in another amendment"[78] and "because the Fourteenth Amendment simply applies the First Amendment to state actions."[79] To quote the Seventh Circuit, which has strongly developed this position, "[d]iscrimination by an official body can always be attacked as a violation of the equal protection clause – but that would usually add nothing, when the discrimination was alleged to be based on religion, to a claim under the religion clauses of the First Amendment."[80]

With respect to a claim alleging discrimination that interferes with one's fundamental right to exercise religion, this approach likewise appears to be – or is often treated as being – simply an alternative means of pleading the Free Exercise Clause or, if the exercise is expressive, the Free Speech Clause. There is case law, to be sure, suggesting that the equal protection guarantee does not exceed the Free Exercise Clause.[81] In the 1974 case of *Johnson v. Robison*,[82] for example, the Supreme Court specifically proclaimed within

claims" (citation omitted)]; Teen Ranch v. Udow, 389 F. Supp. 2d 827, 841 (W.D. Mich. 2005) (similar), *aff'd*, 479 F.3d 403 (6th Cir. 2007).

77 Hicks v. Meyers, No. 01C50099, 2003 WL 22383577, at *2 (N.D. Ill. Oct. 17, 2003) (unpublished) [citing Reed v. Faulkner, 842 F.2d 960, 962 (7th Cir. 1988)]; *see also* United States v. Kuch, 288 F. Supp. 439, 451 (D.D.C. 1968) ("[I]t would appear that this argument is not, in fact, an equal protection argument but, rather, a novel attempt to take a second bite at the free exercise apple."). According to the Seventh Circuit, the First Amendment itself requires that the efforts of prison administrators, in fulfilling their duty to "afford all inmates a reasonable opportunity to practice their religion ... when assessed in their totality, must be evenhanded. Prisons cannot discriminate against a particular religion. The rights of inmates belonging to minority or non-traditional religions must be respected to the same degree as the rights of those belonging to larger and more traditional denominations. Of course, economic and, at times, security constraints may require that the needs of inmates adhering to one faith be accommodated differently from those adhering to another. Nevertheless, the treatment of all inmates must be qualitatively comparable." Al-Alamin v. Gramley, 926 F.2d 680, 686 (7th Cir. 1991) (citations omitted).

78 Filinovich v. Claar, No. 04C7189, 2006 WL 1994580, at *3 (N.D. Ill. July 14, 2006) (unpublished) [citing Graham v. Connor, 490 U.S. 386, 395 (1989); Conyers v. Abitz, 416 F.3d 580, 586 (7th Cir. 2005)].

79 *Id.* [citing Malloy v. Hogan, 378 U.S. 1, 10 (1964)].

80 World Outreach Conference Ctr. v. City of Chicago, 591 F.3d 531, 534 (7th Cir. 2009); *see also* Conyers v. Abitz, 416 F.3d 580, 586 (7th Cir. 2005) (forgoing analysis under equal protection, remarking that "the free-exercise claim arises under the First Amendment and gains nothing by attracting additional constitutional labels").

81 *See, e.g.*, Wirzburger v. Galvin, 412 F.3d 271, 282 (1st Cir. 2005) {explaining that "[w]here a plaintiff's First Amendment Free Exercise claim has failed, the Supreme Court has applied only rational basis scrutiny in its subsequent review of an equal protection fundamental right to religious free exercise claim based on the same facts" [citing Locke v. Davey, 540 U.S. 712, 721 n. 3 (2004)]}; St. John's United Church of Christ v. City of Chicago, 502 F.2d 616, 638 (7th Cir. 2007) (relying on *Wirzburger*), *cert. denied*, 553 U.S. 1032 (2008); Bowers v. Raney, No. 97–6400, 172 F.3d 47, 1998 WL 939835, at *1 (6th Cir. Dec. 21, 1998) (unpublished) (holding that because a defendant "was not deprived of the fundamental right of religious liberty [as asserted in his first claim], his equal protection rights were not violated as asserted in the second claim"); *cf.* Fields v. City of Tulsa, 753 F.3d 1000, 1012 (10th Cir. 2014) (ruling against an equal protection claim after finding no free exercise violation, though possibly due to poor pleading "[b]ecause we hold that [government] did not violate [the claimant's] free-exercise rights and his equal-protection claim is nothing more than a 'rephrasing' of his free-exercise claim, '[i]t falls with [his argument] based on denial of religious freedom'" [quoting Prince v. Massachusetts, 321 U.S. 158, 170 (1944)].

82 415 U.S. 361 (1974).

the equal protection context that the free exercise of religion "[u]nquestionably ... is a fundamental constitutional right."[83] It then went on to state, however, that, having found no violation of a plaintiff's First Amendment free exercise of religion, it had "no occasion to apply to the challenged classification a standard of scrutiny stricter than the traditional rational-basis test."[84] In 2004, the Court renewed this position in *Locke v. Davey*.[85] After holding that a state scholarship program, which expressly barred the use of funds for a degree in devotional theology, did not violate a recipient's free exercise under the First Amendment, the Court, citing *Robison*, explained that it would only "apply rational-basis scrutiny to his equal protection claims,"[86] particularly in the absence of proof that exclusion from the program was motivated by "animus toward religion."[87] According to one appellate court's interpretation of *Locke*, "[w]here a plaintiff's First Amendment Free Exercise claim has failed, the Supreme Court has applied only rational basis scrutiny in its subsequent review of an equal protection fundamental right to religious free exercise claim based on the same facts."[88]

To summarize, religion-related equal protection claims are potentially qualified by two major caveats: *first*, they may overlap substantially with the First Amendment religion and speech clauses and, indeed, often may be subsumed under these other protections, and *second*, largely because of the First Amendment religion clauses, religion (or nonreligion) may be treated constitutionally quite unequally, even though the equal protection guarantee would normally forbid such differential treatment respecting a suspect classification or fundamental right. With these caveats in mind, the next two subsections will examine in greater detail the treatment of religion-related claims under the guarantee of equal protection based on the relatively limited number of cases that address such claims directly under that guarantee.

83 *Id.* at 375 n. 14.

84 *Id.*

85 540 U.S. 712 (2004). For an argument that the equal protection guarantee should not be coextensive with the Free Exercise Clause, *see* Alan Trammell, *Note, The Cabining of Rosenberger: Locke v. Davey and the Broad Nondiscrimination Principle That Never Was*, 92 VA. L. REV. 1957, 1983–5 (2006). In particular, this author contends that a party "might be able to argue that facially disparate treatment of religion cannot satisfy even rational basis scrutiny absent an actual Establishment Clause violation." *Id.* at 1985.

86 Locke, 540 U.S. at 720 n. 3.

87 *Id.* at 725. The Court found that the state's interest in preventing religious establishment, though not required by the First Amendment Establishment Clause, was both "historic and substantial." *Id.*

88 Wirzburger v. Galvin, 412 F.3d 271, 282 (1st Cir. 2005) (citing Locke, 540 U.S. at 721 n. 3). At issue in *Wirzburger* was a provision of the Massachusetts Constitution providing that "[n]o measure that relates to religion, religious practices or religious institutions ... shall be proposed by an initiative petition." MASS. CONST. amend. art. 48, pt. 2, § 2. Upholding the provision, the court remarked that it "kn[e]w of no constitutional principle that prevents a state from determining that sensitive measures that relate to religion, religious practices, or religious institutions should not be made or initiated by the public initiative process but rather only via the legislature." Wirzburger, 412 F.3d at 284. A year prior, the First Circuit had stated that "[i]n *Davey*, the Supreme Court clearly rejected th[e] ... effort to erect a separate and distinct framework for analyzing claims of religious discrimination under the Equal Protection Clause.... [T]he Court held that if a challenged program comports with the Free Exercise Clause, that conclusion wraps up the religious discrimination analysis. Thus, rational basis scrutiny applies to any further equal protection inquiry." Eulitt *ex rel.* Eulitt v. Me. Dep't of Educ., 386 F.3d 344, 354 (1st Cir. 2004) (citation omitted); *see also* Gary S. v. Manchester Sch. Dist., 374 F.3d 15 (1st Cir. 2004) (upholding denial of funding for special education services provided by religious schools even though funding was available when such services were provided by public schools), *cert. denied*, 543 U.S. 988 (2004).

### 3. *Religion as a Suspect Classification*

Within the scheme of suspect and quasi-suspect classifications, it is generally accepted that religion, like race, is a suspect classification and that textual or purposeful religious discrimination by the government thus will be subject to heightened or strict scrutiny using the analytical framework of equal protection.[89] Indeed, in the Supreme Court's famous footnote 4 of *Carolene Products*, when discussing the possibility of heightened scrutiny for politically defective legislation adversely affecting minorities, the Court leads off the list with religious minorities, followed by national and racial minorities.[90] It is, of course, an interesting question whether or not religion *ought* to be designated a suspect or quasi-suspect classification,[91] either as a matter of original meaning[92] or using the various criteria that the Supreme Court has deemed relevant when considering that designation for particular groups or traits.[93] These include whether the groups in question – here religious groups in general or specific religious groups in particular[94] – have been subjected to "a history of purposeful unequal treatment,"[95] have "been subjected to unique disabilities on the basis of stereotyped characteristics not truly indicative

[89] *See* Miller v. Johnson, 515 U.S. 900, 911 (1995); Burlington N. R.R. Co. v. Ford, 504 U.S. 648, 651 (1992); City of New Orleans v. Dukes, 427 U.S. 297, 303 (1976); Abcarian v. McDonald, 617 F.3d 931, 938 (7th Cir. 2010), *cert. denied*, 131 S. Ct. 1685 (2011); Abdulhaseeb v. Calbone, 600 F.3d 1301, 1322 n. 10 (10th Cir. 2010), *cert. denied*, 131 S. Ct. 469 (2010); Bowman v. United States, 564 F.3d 765, 772 (6th Cir. 2008); Patel v. U.S. Bur. of Prisons, 515 F.3d 807, 816 (8th Cir. 2008); Knight v. Conn. Dep't of Pub. Health, 275 F.3d 156, 166 (2d Cir. 2001); Tolchin v. Supr. Ct. of the State of N.J., 111 F.3d 1099, 1113–14 (3d Cir. 1997); Christian Sci. Reading Rm. Jointly Maintained v. City & Cnty. of S.F., 784 F.2d 1010, 1012 (9th Cir. 1986), *amended*, 792 F.2d 124 (9th Cir. 1986), *cert. denied*, 479 U.S. 1066 (1987); Seoane v. Ortho Pharmaceuticals, Inc., 660 F.2d 146, 149 (5th Cir. 1981); King's Garden, Inc. v. FCC, 498 F.2d 51, 57 (D.C. Cir. 1974), *cert. denied*, 419 U.S. 996 (1974); *cf.* Olsen v. Comm'r, 709 F.2d 278, 283 (4th Cir. 1983) (principally citing a First Amendment case for the proposition that "[h]eightened scrutiny is applied to an equal protection challenge to a regulation which applies selectively to religious activity only if the plaintiff can show the basis for the distinction was religious and not secular in nature"); *see also* Bd. of Educ. of Kiryas Joel Vill. Sch. Dist. v. Grumet, 512 U.S. 687, 715 (1994) (O'Connor, J., concurring in part and concurring in the judgment) (discussing the theme of equal treatment and stating that "the Religion Clauses – the Free Exercise Clause, the Establishment Clause, the Religious Test Clause, Art. VI, cl. 3, and the Equal Protection Clause as applied to religion – all speak with one voice on this point: Absent the most unusual circumstances, one's religion ought not affect one's legal rights or duties or benefits").

[90] *See* United States v. Carolene Products Co., 304 U.S. 144, 152 n. 4 (1938).

[91] *See, e.g.*, Wirzburger, 412 F.3d at 283 & n. 6 (questioning whether religion is actually a suspect classification).

[92] *See* Steven G. Calabresi & Abe Salander, *Religion and the Equal Protection Clause: Why the Constitution Requires School Vouchers*, 65 Fla. L. Rev. 909, 913 (2013) (arguing "that, as a matter of original meaning, the Fourteenth Amendment, standing alone, forbids all discrimination on the basis of religion just as it forbids all discrimination on the basis of race and gender").

[93] *See* Windsor v. United States, 699 F.3d 169, 181 (2d Cir. 2012) (summarizing the criteria), *aff'd*, 133 S. Ct. 2675 (2013).

[94] Though claims in regard to groups – demographic or other classes of individuals – are the classic form that equal protection challenges take, a claim by an individual or organization as a so-called class of one is possible under equal protection doctrine. *See* Village of Willowbrook v. Olech, 528 U.S. 562, 564 (2000) (*per curiam*).

[95] San Antonio Indep. Sch. Dist. v. Rodriguez, 411 U.S. 1, 28 (1973); *see also* Lyng v. Castillo, 477 U.S. 635, 638 (1986) (asking whether "[a]s a historical matter, they have not been subjected to discrimination"); Mass. Bd. of Ret. v. Murgia, 427 U.S. 307, 313 (1976) (*per curiam*).

of their abilities,"[96] "exhibit obvious, immutable, or distinguishing characteristics that define them as a discrete group,"[97] and "are … a minority or politically powerless."[98] Certainly different religious groups vary in the degree to which of these criteria describe them. Some can be described by two or three, whereas others by none, and arguably there are at least a few nonreligious demographic groups, such as those with significant physical or developmental disabilities, that can claim equal or greater satisfaction of the criteria but that the Supreme Court has refused, at least formally, to recognize as a suspect or quasi-suspect class.[99]

In all events, based on the precedent-supported assumption that religion can be a suspect classification, and applying to the religion context the principle that those similarly situated be treated similarly, several forms of religious discrimination may be actionable. One is an allegation that religious and nonreligious (or secular) individuals or groups, otherwise comparably situated, have been treated differently. This contention can emerge from either side of the equation: religious claimants may allege less favorable treatment than that given to their nonreligious counterparts,[100] or nonreligious claimants may allege less favorable treatment than comparable individuals or groups that are religious.[101] Claims such as this, perhaps especially when brought by religious claimants, are the most likely to implicate the caveat, raised in the preceding section, that government

96 Murgia, 427 U.S. at 313; *see also* City of Cleburne, 473 U.S. at 440–1.

97 Lyng, 477 U.S. at 638; *see also* Bowen v. Gilliard, 483 U.S. 587, 602 (1987).

98 Lyng, 477 U.S. at 638; *see also* Bowen, 483 U.S. at 602.

99 *See, e.g.*, City of Cleburne, 473 U.S. at 442–6 (explaining the refusal). For critique and analysis, *see* Anita Silvers & Michael Ashley Stein, *Disability, Equal Protection, and the Supreme Court: Standing at the Crossroads of Progressive and Retrogressive Logic in Constitutional Classification*, 35 U. Mich. J.L. Ref. 81 (2001); Aaron J. Walker, *Note, "No Distinction Would Be Tolerated": Thaddeus Stevens, Disability, and the Original Intent of the Equal Protection Clause*, 19 Yale L. & Pol'y Rev. 265 (2000). Essentially consistent with the view that religion is a protected status under equal protection, some courts have held that "[m]embers of a particular religion or the holders of a particular religious belief are generally considered to be members of a protected class" under 42 U.S.C. § 1985(3). 1 Civil Actions Against State and Local Government: Its Divisions, Agencies and Officers § 8:56 (2d ed. rev'd 2014) (hereinafter 1 Civil Actions). *Compare* Taylor v. Gilmartin, 686 F.2d 1346, 1355–8 (10th Cir. 1982) (so holding), *cert. denied*, 459 U.S. 1147 (1983), *and cert. denied*, 463 U.S. 1229 (1983), *and* Ward v. Connor, 657 F.2d 45, 48 (4th Cir. 1981) (so holding), *cert. denied*, 455 U.S. 907 (1982), *with* Word of Faith World Outreach Ctr. Church, Inc. v. Sawyer, 90 F.3d 118, 124 (5th Cir. 1996) (limiting statute to conspiracies based on racial animus), *cert. denied*, 520 U.S. 1117 (1997). Section 1985(3), among other things, authorizes damage actions against private conspiracies to "depriv[e], either directly or indirectly, any person or class of persons of the equal protection of the laws." The theory behind recognizing this protection is akin to the criteria for identifying suspect classifications: "[r]eligion is considered to be a protected class because, although belief in a particular religion is not an immutable characteristic such as race, membership in a minority religious group has often excited irrational fear and hatred in the majority, similar to feelings excited in the majority by members of a racial minority." 1 Civil Actions, *supra*, § 8:56.

100 *See, e.g.*, Trinity Lutheran Church of Columbia, Inc. v. Pauley, 976 F. Supp. 2d 1137 (W.D. Mo. 2013) (challenging, partly under equal protection, the denial to a church of government funding, to be used for playground resurfacing, based on a policy of not providing grants to religious organizations); *cf. also* Teen Ranch v. Udow, 389 F. Supp. 2d 827, 841 (W.D. Mich. 2005) (challenging, partly under equal protection, a government funding moratorium on an organization's faith-based services, though there was not a total exclusion of religious organizations), *aff'd*, 479 F.3d 403 (6th Cir. 2007), *cert. denied*, 552 U.S. 1039 (2007).

101 *See, e.g.*, Am. Atheists, Inc. v. Shulman, 21 F. Supp. 3d 856 (E.D. Ky. 2014) (challenging, partly under equal protection, various federal income tax exemptions or benefits for churches and religious organizations); Freedom from Religion Found., Inc. v. Lew, 983 F. Supp. 2d 1051 (W.D. Wis. 2013) (challenging, partly under equal protection, a federal income tax exemption for "ministers of the gospel").

may permissibly treat religion differently in ways that would not be acceptable with regard to other suspect classifications. In some circumstances, specifically, the government can accommodate or protect only religious conduct if its purpose and effect are to eliminate a burden on free exercise or to limit government entanglement with religion.

For example, in *Corporation of Presiding Bishop v. Amos*,[102] which upheld the religious accommodation provision of Title VII of the 1964 Civil Rights Act, the Supreme Court explained that as long as the statute is legitimately accommodating religion and otherwise complies with the Establishment Clause, any differential treatment of religion and nonreligion should be assessed under equal protection only for rationality and need not satisfy heightened scrutiny. According to the Court, "where a statute is neutral on its face [among religions] and motivated by a permissible purpose of limiting governmental interference with the exercise of religion, we see no justification for applying strict scrutiny.... The proper inquiry is whether ... [the government] has chosen a rational classification to further a legitimate end."[103] Likewise, as noted in the earlier discussion of *Locke v. Davey*, a governmental effort to prevent a religious establishment potentially can justify less favorable treatment of religion and will only be subject to rationality review under equal protection, at least as long as there is no free exercise violation and no evidence of religious animus.[104]

A second type of claim, generally not subject to the foregoing caveat, is an allegation that the government has created a so-called denominational preference[105] by discriminating among religions or religious groups, treating some more favorably than others. According to the Tenth Circuit, "statutes involving discrimination on the basis of religion, including interdenominational discrimination, are subject to heightened scrutiny whether they arise under the Free Exercise Clause, the Establishment Clause, or the Equal Protection Clause,"[106] though, of these options, they are typically pursued or decided under the Establishment Clause.[107] It appears that allegations of interdenominational discrimination often and predictably arise within government-operated environments, such as prisons[108] or the military,[109] or in the context of government taxing or funding,[110] perhaps because high competition for scarce resources impels

[102] 483 U.S. 327 (1987).

[103] *Id.* at 339; *accord* Dayton Area Visually Impaired Persons, Inc. v. Fisher, 70 F.3d 1474, 1482–3 (6th Cir. 1995), *cert. denied*, 517 U.S. 1135 (1996).

[104] *See supra* notes 85–8 and accompanying text.

[105] Larson v. Valente, 456 U.S. 228, 245–6 (1982).

[106] Colo. Christian Univ. v. Weaver, 534 F.3d 1245, 1266 (10th Cir. 2008) (citations omitted); *see also* Olsen v. DEA, 878 F.2d 1458, 1463 n. 5 (D.C. Cir. 1989) (observing that, in cases involving an alleged denominational preference, "establishment clause and equal protection analyses converge"), *cert. denied*, 495 U.S. 906 (1990).

[107] *See, e.g.*, Bd. of Educ. v. Grumet, 512 U.S. 687, 703 (1994); Larson, 456 U.S. at 244–6; Epperson v. Arkansas, 393 U.S. 97, 103–4 (1968); Everson v. Bd. of Educ., 330 U.S. 1, 15 (1947); Awad v. Ziriax, 670 F.3d 1111, 1126–31 (10th Cir. 2012); Children's Healthcare Is a Legal Duty, Inc. v. Min De Parle, 212 F.3d 1084, 1090 (8th Cir. 2000), *cert. denied*, 532 U.S. 957 (2001); Sasnett v. Litscher, 197 F.3d 290, 292–3 (7th Cir. 1999).

[108] *See, e.g.*, Rouser v. White, 630 F. Supp. 2d 1165, 1199–1200 (E.D. Cal. 2009) (accepting claim against a summary judgment motion).

[109] *See, e.g.*, *In re* Navy Chaplaincy, 738 F.3d 425, 428–30 (D.C. Cir. 2013) (rejecting claim), *cert. denied*, 135 S. Ct. 86 (2014).

[110] *See, e.g.*, Warnke v. United States, 641 F. Supp. 1083, 1089–92 (E.D. Ky. 1986) (rejecting challenge to availability of parson's allowance exclusion under federal tax law).

governments to make distinctions that are often seen as unnecessary in run-of-the-mill regulatory schemes.[111]

A third type of discrimination claim, principally a function of the public-employment context, is that of religious harassment.[112] As the First Circuit has explained, "[h]arassment of an employee because of [his or] her faith, whatever guise it assumes, may constitute religious discrimination under the Equal Protection Clause of the Fourteenth Amendment."[113] As with other types of religious discrimination claims, however, it is probable that harassment and related claims are typically brought or decided under the First Amendment religion clauses, especially the Establishment Clause, insofar as public employer actions that religiously harass employees also likely could constitute religious endorsement or disfavoritism, advancement or inhibition, coercion, or even entanglement in violation of the Establishment Clause.[114]

Finally, some (though not all) courts have held that "the equal protection clause of the fourteenth amendment ... prohibits the exercise of a peremptory challenge to excuse a venireperson because of his or her religious affiliation."[115] As this phrasing indicates, what is most significant about this recognition is that following the analysis of *Batson v. Kentucky*[116] and *J.E.B. v. Alabama ex rel. T.B.*,[117] it may not provide for any judicial scrutiny other than allowing the alleged perpetrator to offer a neutral basis for the peremptory challenge.[118] In other words, it may entail a categorical prohibition, which obviously differs from the strict scrutiny that religious discrimination would normally trigger under either the guarantee of equal protection or the religion clauses.

To the extent that an equal protection claim is pursued, whatever its variety, it can essentially take two forms. It can be a so-called facial challenge, alleging that the very text or manifest purpose of the contested law or government policy is discriminatory with regard to religion in general or one or more religions in particular.[119] The standard for a facial

111 Specialized contexts, such as prisons and the military, are addressed separately in Chapter 18.

112 Harassment, or a hostile work environment, is an employment discrimination theory under Title VII of the Civil Rights Act of 1964 and analogous state laws, which generally cover both public and private employment. *See, e.g.*, Feingold v. New York, 366 F.3d 138, 149–51 (2d Cir. 2004) (Title VII); Abrahamson v. William Paterson College of N.J., 260 F.3d 265, 276–80 (3d Cir. 2001) (Title VII and the New Jersey Law Against Discrimination).

113 Rivera v. P.R. Aqueduct & Sewers Auth., 331 F.3d 183, 192 n. 7 (1st Cir. 2003).

114 *See, e.g.*, Milwaukee Deputy Sheriffs' Ass'n v. Clarke, 588 F.3d 523, 529 (7th Cir. 2009) (ruling unconstitutional a sheriff's providing for "a [group's] heavily Christian-focused presentation at a mandatory conference for government employees"; his "subsequently invit[ing] them to present at mandatory roll calls during work hours, granting them unfiltered access to a captive audience of subordinates"; his command staff's "personal introduc[tion] [of them]" at the roll calls; his permitting them "to distribute additional Christian-focused literature"; and his "refusal to cease the presentations after some of the deputies complained of the [group's] proselytizing").

115 State v. Hodge, 726 A.2d 531, 553 (Conn. 1999). For further discussion of peremptory challenges involving religion, *see* Chapter 14.D.2.a.

116 476 U.S. 79 (1986) (holding that peremptory challenges cannot be premised on a prospective juror's race).

117 511 U.S. 127 (1994) (holding that peremptory challenges cannot be premised on a prospective juror's gender).

118 *See* Hodge, 726 A.2d at 553–5.

119 *Cf.* Washington v. Davis, 426 U.S. 229, 239–41 (1976) (setting forth the standards, in particular the element of purpose, for facial challenges alleging racial discrimination); *see, e.g.*, Congregation Rabbinical College of Tartikov, Inc. v. Village of Pomona, 915 F. Supp. 2d 574, 616–17 (S.D.N.Y. 2013) (finding sufficient pleading of discriminatory intent to survive motion to dismiss facial challenge).

challenge is high[120] but, if successful, will result in the law's partial or total invalidation.[121] Alternatively, it can be an as-applied challenge, alleging that the law or policy, though not itself textually or intentionally discriminatory, nevertheless is or was applied in a selective manner with a discriminatory motive or purpose.[122] As summarized by the Second Circuit, "an equal protection violation based upon selective application of a facially lawful state regulation is properly found when: '(1) the person, compared with others similarly situated, was selectively treated, and (2) the selective treatment was motivated by an intention to discriminate on the basis of impermissible considerations, such as … religion, to punish or inhibit the exercise of constitutional rights, or by a malicious or bad faith intent to injure the person.'"[123] As-applied challenges also include allegations of selective enforcement[124] or selective prosecution, though the task of demonstrating selection prosecution can be quite demanding. "'In order to dispel the presumption that a prosecutor has not violated equal protection, a criminal defendant must present clear evidence to the contrary,' demonstrating that the government was motivated by a discriminatory purpose to adopt a prosecutorial policy with a discriminatory effect. To make this showing, a defendant must 'establish both (1) that similarly situated individuals of a different … [religion] were not prosecuted, and (2) that the decision to prosecute was invidious or in bad faith.'"[125]

[120] In United States v. Salerno, 481 U.S. 739 (1987), the Court stated that "the challenger must establish that no set of circumstances exists under which the Act would be valid." *Id.* at 745. The scope and applicability of the *Salerno* standard, however, has been a matter of debate. *See* Doe v. City of Albuquerque, 667 F.3d 1111, 1124 (10th Cir. 2012) (contending that "[t]he idea that the Supreme Court applies the 'no set of circumstances' test to every facial challenge is simply a fiction" and citing cases); United States v. Comstock, 627 F.3d 513, 518–19 (4th Cir. 2010) (noting this debate), *cert. denied*, 131 S. Ct. 3026 (2011). To be sure, there are specific contexts in which courts have expressly or impliedly held the *Salerno* standard to be inapplicable. The most notable and well established are so-called overbreadth challenges under the Free Speech Clause. In addition, facial challenges to abortion regulations are often not subjected to the *Salerno* standard. And there is some indication that facial Fourth Amendment challenges may not, or may not always, have to meet *Salerno*'s rigorous test. *Cf.* Chandler v. Miller, 520 U.S. 305 (1997).

[121] A clear example of a facially unconstitutional law – one that had an impact on religion, among other activities – was a 1983 policy adopted by the City of Los Angeles Board of Airport Commissioners declaring that "the Central Terminal Area at Los Angeles International Airport is not open for First Amendment activities by any individual and/or entity," which the Supreme Court unanimously invalidated in Bd. of Airport Comm'rs of City of L.A. v. Jews for Jesus, Inc., 482 U.S. 569 (1987).

[122] *See* Barren v. Harrington, 152 F.3d 1193, 1194 (9th Cir. 1998) ("To state a claim under 42 U.S.C. § 1983 for a violation of the Equal Protection Clause of the Fourteenth Amendment a plaintiff must show that the defendants acted with an intent or purpose to discriminate against the plaintiff based upon membership in a protected class."), *cert. denied*, 525 U.S. 1154 (1999); *see, e.g.*, Open Homes Fellowship, Inc. v. Orange Cnty., Fla., 325 F. Supp. 2d 1349, 1364–5 (M.D. Fla. 2004) (holding that county zoning ordinance, as applied to a church, violated the Equal Protection Clause).

[123] Terminate Control Corp. v. Horowitz, 28 F.3d 1335, 1352 (2d Cir. 1994) (line break removed) [quoting FSK Drug Corp. v. Perales, 960 F.2d 6, 10 (2d Cir. 1992)]; *see also* Diesel v. Town of Lewisboro, 232 F.3d 92, 103 (2d Cir. 2000).

[124] *See, e.g.*, Jocham v. Tuscola Cnty., 289 F. Supp. 2d 887, 895–7 (E.D. Mich. 2003) (finding sufficient evidence to survive a summary judgment motion that county board members selectively treated atheist speakers opposed to a nativity scene differently, and adversely in their application of an otherwise neutral time-limit rule for speaking at board meetings).

[125] United States v. Venable, 666 F.3d 893, 900 (4th Cir. 2012) [quoting United States v. Armstrong, 517 U.S. 456, 463 (1996), and United States v. Olvis, 97 F.3d 739, 743 (4th Cir. 1996), respectively]; *accord* United States v. Lewis, 517 F.3d 20, 25 (1st Cir. 2008); Branch Ministries v. Rossotti, 211 F.3d 137, 144 (D.C. Cir. 2000).

### 4. *Religion as a Fundamental Right*

The other means of potentially triggering some type of heightened scrutiny using the equal protection guarantee is to demonstrate governmental discrimination that infringes on a fundamental right.[126] The Supreme Court has indicated that the free exercise of religion is indeed a fundamental right,[127] and several lower federal and state courts have followed suit.[128] The critical question in this regard is actually not whether free exercise should be recognized a fundamental right, but rather, consistent with the second caveat noted earlier, the question is whether such recognition does or should make a meaningful difference within any given case. After all, under both the Free Exercise and Establishment Clauses, the nonneutral treatment of religion (or of a particular religious practice or denomination) ordinarily yields a presumption of unconstitutionality and strict scrutiny of the law in question,[129] which is the most that the equal protection guarantee itself can provide. Correspondingly, a failure to demonstrate a free exercise violation yields at best a rationality analysis under the First Amendment and, according to the cases, the same standard under the equal protection guarantee in turn.[130]

This effective marginalization of equal protection is likely problematic for most would-be claimants and certainly could explain the relatively infrequent use of equal protection in religion cases, either as an independent basis for meaningfully scrutinizing government actions or as the ultimate ground on which lawsuits are resolved.

126 *See, e.g.*, Eisenstadt v. Baird, 405 U.S. 438 (1972) (contraception); Loving v. Virginia, 388 U.S. 1 (1967) (marriage); Skinner v. Oklahoma, 316 U.S. 535 (1942) (procreation).

127 *See* Johnson v. Robison, 415 U.S. 361, 375 n. 14 (1974) (stating, in the context of equal protection, that "[u]nquestionably, the free exercise of religion is a fundamental constitutional right"); *cf.* Williams v. Rhodes, 393 U.S. 23, 30–1 (1968) (recognizing another First Amendment right, the freedom of association, as fundamental for equal protection purposes).

128 *See, e.g.*, Village Church v. Village of Long Grove, 468 F.3d 975, 1000 (7th Cir. 2006) ("Heightened scrutiny [under the Equal Protection Clause] is appropriate when government action interferes with a person's fundamental rights, such as freedom of … religion."), *cert. denied,* 552 U.S. 940 (2007); Equality Found. of Greater Cincinnati, Inc. v. City of Cincinnati, 128 F.3d 289, 292 n. 1 (6th Cir. 1997) (explaining that "[w]here a statute or ordinance … invades a 'fundamental right' such as speech or religious freedom, the rigorous 'strict scrutiny' standard governs"); Thompson v. Kentucky, 712 F.2d 1078, 1082 (6th Cir. 1983) (describing "the right to exercise one's religion" as "a fundamental right"); Reaching Hearts Int'l, Inc. v. Prince George's Cnty., 584 F. Supp. 2d 766, 781 n. 9 (D. Md. 2008) (same), *aff'd*, No. 08-2281, 368 Fed. Appx. 370 (4th Cir. Mar. 3, 2010) (unpublished); Feinerman v. Jones, 356 F. Supp. 252, 258 (M.D. Pa. 1973); Shepherd Montessori Ctr. Milan v. Ann Arbor Charter Twp., 675 N.W.2d 271, 283 (Mich. Ct. App. 2003) ("[C]ourts apply a strict scrutiny test in evaluating equal protection issues where a statute encroaches on a fundamental right, such as the right to free exercise of religion."); State v. Purcell, 18 P.3d 113, 120 (Ariz. Ct. App. 2001) ["A classification receives strict scrutiny under the Equal Protection Clause when it discriminates against a person on the basis of that person's exercise of a fundamental right, of which the free exercise of religion is one." (citation omitted)]; Casarez v. State, 913 S.W.2d 468, 478–9 (Tex. Crim. Ct. App. 1994) ["The right to the free exercise of religion is unquestionably a fundamental right and any impairment of that right is subject to strict scrutiny review. Consequently, we hold the Equal Protection Clause of the Fourteenth Amendment prohibits the use of a peremptory challenge on the basis of religion absent a compelling governmental interest." (footnote omitted)].

129 *See* State v. Hodge, 726 A.2d 531, 552 n. 43 (Conn. 1999) ("Government action that discriminates on the basis of religion under either the free exercise clause or the establishment clause is … subject to strict scrutiny.").

130 *See supra* notes 77–88 and accompanying text.

However, the foregoing is only a general description of the legal terrain, and there may be specific instances in which the use of equal protection to advance one's free exercise of religion is a worthwhile approach. One such opportunity, which seems to arise disproportionately in the prison context, is an allegation that the government has treated different religious faiths or practices unequally and that this differential treatment is irrational.[131] Assuming that the claimant cannot obtain a standard above rationality (because of a lack of textual or intentional discrimination) and that a straightforward free exercise claim likely will fail (because, viewed in isolation, the government's treatment of the claimant does not seem irrational), the perspective of readily discernible, similarly situated individuals being treated differently apparently can create a basis for concluding that the differential treatment, particularly an accommodation scheme's limited scope, is irrational.[132] The prison context is likely a fruitful venue for such claims for two reasons: *first*, the closed and monitored nature of the prison environment readily allows for the direct comparison of the treatment of different religious practices, and *second*, prison administrators by constitutional necessity must accommodate some religious practices yet by practical necessity cannot accommodate them all.[133] In particular, although prison officials need not provide "every religious sect or group within a prison – however few in number – ... identical facilities or personnel,"[134] they must provide each inmate "a reasonable opportunity of pursuing his [or her] faith comparable to the opportunity afforded fellow prisoners who adhere to conventional religious precepts."[135]

131 *See, e.g.*, Brown v. Borough of Mahaffey, Pa., 35 F.3d 846, 850 (3d Cir. 1994) (explaining that where "the plaintiffs argue that the violation of their fundamental right to free exercise of religion constitutes an equal protection violation ... in order to maintain an equal protection claim with any significance independent of the free exercise [clause] ... the plaintiffs must ... allege and prove that they received different treatment from other similarly situated individuals or groups); *see also* Allen v. Toombs, 827 F.2d 563, 568–9 (9th Cir. 1987) (entertaining, though rejecting, such a claim); Sutton v. Stewart, 22 F. Supp. 2d 1097, 1107 (D. Ariz. 1998) (explaining, in the prison context, that "the relevant inquiry in the equal protection context is not simply whether legitimate penological interests justify limitations on Plaintiff's free exercise, but also whether those limitations are reasonable *when measured against the limitations placed on other inmates*"), *aff'd*, 185 F.3d 869 (9th Cir. 1999); Lucero v. Hensley, 920 F. Supp. 1067, 1075 (C.D. Cal. 1996) (similar).

132 *Cf.* Sasnett v. Litscher, 197 F.3d 290, 292–3 (7th Cir. 1999) (invaliding, under the Free Exercise Clause, that a prison regulation allowing prisoners to possess crosses attached to rosaries, but not allowing prisoners to possess crosses by themselves, finding that the different treatment lacked any reasonable justification).

133 Equal protection claims in the incarceration context have been held to be judicially reviewable under the relatively deferential four-factor analysis of Turner v. Safley, 482 U.S. 78, 89–90 (1987). *See, e.g.*, DeHart v. Horn, 227 F.3d 47, 61 (3d Cir. 2000).

134 Cruz v. Beto, 405 U.S. 319, 322 n. 2 (1972). "A special chapel or place of worship need not be provided for every faith regardless of size; nor must a chaplain, priest, or minister be provided without regard to the extent of the demand." *Id.*

135 *Id.* at 322. In addition, though not relevant to the type of claim discussed here, inmates cannot be "treated differently than others similarly situated as a result of intentional or purposeful discrimination" by prison officials. Phillips v. Girdich, 408 F.3d 124, 129 (2d Cir. 2005); *accord* Davis v. Flores, No. 11–15296, 484 Fed. App'x. 108, 110, 2012 WL 1898657, at *1 (9th Cir. May 25, 2012) (*per curiam*) (unpublished) (explaining that equal protection plaintiff must "allege facts showing he was intentionally treated differently from similarly situated inmates"); Sweet v. Sec'y, Dep't of Corr., 467 F.3d 1311, 1318–19 (11th Cir. 2006) (similar), *cert. denied*, 550 U.S. 922 (2007); Taylor v. Johnson, 257 F.3d 470, 473 (5th Cir. 2001) (similar).

## C. The Free Speech Clause

In addition to the Free Exercise and Establishment Clauses, the First Amendment famously prohibits the government from "abridging the freedom of speech."[136] The relationship between the Free Exercise and Free Speech Clauses, in particular, is extensive and in recent years has been doctrinally dynamic. Many religious practices, from prayer to proselytization, are expressive or communicative in nature,[137] and "[r]eligious expression holds a place at the core of the type of speech that the First Amendment was designed to protect."[138] As a consequence, claims involving expressive religious activity often can be analyzed under either clause and in some instances also can be protected and analyzed under the Establishment Clause,[139] the right of association (an implied right of the First Amendment),[140] or, as noted in the preceding section, the guarantee of equal protection. The focus here, particularly in light of its contemporary importance, is the Free Speech Clause.

### 1. *Free Speech Doctrine in General*

Free speech analysis employs a variety of criteria or inquiries, but there are two that tend to predominate when analyzing the government's regulation of expressive activity by private individuals or organizations: *first*, whether the governmental action in question is content neutral or content based (and if content based, whether or not it is viewpoint neutral) and, *second*, whether the location or medium of the speech is a traditional public, designated public, or nonpublic forum. As a preface to these two inquiries, of course, one also must determine whether the speech or expressive conduct at issue falls within the protective scope of the Free Speech Clause[141] and, if so, the extent to which it does

136 U.S. Const. amend. I. Originally applicable only to the federal government, the Free Speech Clause has been recognized as applicable to state and local governments by means of incorporation through the Due Process Clause of Section 1 of the Fourteenth Amendment. *See* Fiske v. Kansas, 274 U.S. 380, 386–7 (1927); Gitlow v. New York, 268 U.S. 652, 666 (1925).

137 The Free Speech Clause protects "a message … delivered by conduct that is intended to be communicative and that, in context, would reasonably be understood by the viewer to be communicative." Clark v. Cmty. for Creative Non-Violence, 468 U.S. 288, 294 (1984).

138 DeBoer v. Village of Oak Park, 267 F.3d 558, 570 (7th Cir. 2001) [citing Capitol Square Rev. & Advisory Bd. v. Pinette, 515 U.S. 753, 760 (1995)].

139 *See, e.g.*, Larson v. Valente, 456 U.S. 228 (1982) (invalidating under the Establishment Clause certain requirements of a state charitable solicitation statute that granted denominational preferences); Kalman v. Cortes, 723 F. Supp. 2d 766 (E.D. Pa. 2010) (holding that a state blasphemy statute violated both the Establishment and Free Speech Clauses). "While the Establishment Clause is often invoked to protect against the state's endorsement of religion over non-religion, it is equally applicable to claims that the state action is 'hostile' to religion." Demmon v. Loudon Cnty. Pub. Schs., 342 F. Supp. 2d 474, 490 (E.D. Va. 2004).

140 *See* Bd. of Directors of Rotary Int'l v. Rotary Club of Duarte, 481 U.S. 537, 544 (1987) (noting "the freedom of individuals to associate for the purpose of engaging in protected speech or religious activities"); Roberts v. U.S. Jaycees, 468 U.S. 609 (1984) (noting that it "has recognized a right to associate for the purpose of engaging in those activities protected by the First Amendment – speech, assembly, petition for the redress of grievances, and the exercise of religion"); *accord* Sanitation & Recycling Indus., Inc. v. City of N.Y., 107 F.3d 985, 996 (2d Cir. 1997); Hobbs v. Hawkins, 968 F.2d 471, 482 (5th Cir. 1992).

141 In addition to "the spoken or written word," Texas v. Johnson, 491 U.S. 397, 404 (1989), First Amendment speech includes symbolic conduct accompanied by "[a]n intent to convey a particularized message … and in the surrounding circumstances the likelihood [i]s great that the message would be understood by those who view it." Spence v. State of Washington, 418 U.S. 405, 410–11 (1974) (per curiam); *see also*

because not all types of expression receive the same level of protection,[142] with some receiving virtually no protection at all.[143]

Content-neutral or so-called time, place, and manner regulations restrict expression incidentally without regard to its message.[144] Examples might include a library prohibition on all loud speech (even though a person may be engaged in, say, political speech) or an open-burning ordinance (even though it may be applied to a person who happens to be symbolically burning the American Flag). Content-based regulations, in contrast, either by their text or by their application, target the content or message of the expression itself. Examples might include an ordinance that textually prohibits profane or offensive language[145] or a law that specifically prohibits "desecrat[ing] ... a state or national flag."[146] The government in these examples is not principally attempting to target nonexpressive conduct, or even the possible secondary harms of expression, but instead is targeting the very content or message of the speech or expressive conduct precisely because listeners or viewers might find it disagreeable or disturbing. It is this quite different focus that has constitutional importance, for "[t]he First Amendment generally prevents government from proscribing speech ... or even expressive conduct ... because of disapproval of the ideas expressed."[147]

Clark v. Cmty. for Creative Non-Violence, 468 U.S. 288, 294 (1984) ("[A] message may be delivered by conduct that is intended to be communicative and that, in context, would reasonably be understood by the viewer to be communicative."). Subsequently, the Court has announced that "a narrow, succinctly articulable message is not a condition of constitutional protection, which if confined to expressions conveying a 'particularized message' would never reach the unquestionably shielded painting of Jackson Pollock, music of Arnold Schöenberg, or Jabberwocky verse of Lewis Carroll." Hurley v. Irish-Am. Gay, Lesbian & Bisexual Group of Boston, 515 U.S. 557, 569 (1995). However, the Court's "cases reject the 'view that an apparently limitless variety of conduct can be labeled 'speech' whenever the person engaging in the conduct intends thereby to express an idea.'" Wisconsin v. Mitchell, 508 U.S. 476, 484 (1993).

142 The Court has employed a different, less demanding standard for many restrictions on so-called commercial speech. *See* Bd. of Trs. of State Univ. of N.Y. v. Fox, 492 U.S. 469, 475–80 (1989); Central Hudson Gas & Elec. Corp. v. Pub. Serv. Comm'n of N.Y., 447 U.S. 557, 561–6 (1980).

143 These include defamation, fighting words, obscenity, child pornography, incitement to imminent unlawful activity, true threats, and speech that is used as evidence of a crime. *See* Virginia v. Black, 538 U.S. 343, 359–60 (2003); Mitchell, 508 U.S. at 489; R.A.V. v. City of St. Paul, Minn., 505 U.S. 377, 383 (1992); Osborne v. Ohio, 495 U.S. 103, 108–11 (1990); Hess v. Indiana, 414 U.S. 105, 107–8 (1973). They are generally, but not absolutely, unprotected by the Free Speech Clause. *See* R.A.V., 505 U.S. at 383–6.

144 *See* Ward v. Rock Against Racism, 491 U.S. 781, 791 (1989) ["The principal inquiry in determining content neutrality, in speech cases generally and in time, place, or manner cases in particular, is whether the government has adopted a regulation of speech because of disagreement with the message it conveys. The government's purpose is the controlling consideration. A regulation that serves purposes unrelated to the content of expression is deemed neutral, even if it has an incidental effect on some speakers or messages but not others. Government regulation of expressive activity is content neutral so long as it is '*justified* without reference to the content of the regulated speech.'" (citations omitted) (quoting *Clark*, 468 U.S. at 293)].

145 *See* Plummer v. City of Columbus, Ohio, 414 U.S. 2 (1973) (*per curiam*) (invalidating an ordinance making it unlawful to "abuse another by using menacing, insulting, slanderous, or profane language"); Gooding v. Wilson, 405 U.S. 518 (1972) (invalidating a state law prohibiting the use of "opprobrious words or abusive language" toward another).

146 *See* Texas v. Johnson, 491 U.S. 397 (1989) (invaliding a state law criminalizing such conduct); *see also* United States v. Eichman, 496 U.S. 310 (1990) (invalidating a federal law that made it a crime to "knowingly mutilate, deface, physically defile ... maintain on the floor or ground, or trample upon any flag of the United States").

147 R.A.V., 505 U.S. at 382 (citations omitted).

These limitations on government discrimination against content or viewpoint have been especially important in recent years, including for religious speakers, principally for two reasons. First, they have been actively employed in the context of government funding, taking into account the expressive character of the applicant's identity or conduct. "Even where the government subsidizes, rather than penalizes, private speech it usually cannot 'favor some viewpoints or ideas at the expense of others.'"[148] Second, and relatedly, they have been applied to the question of access to government facilities, such as community centers or public schools (after hours), which the government makes available for use by civic groups.[149] In addition, some courts, based on the particular facts presented, also have extended these limitations to certain government-created or -facilitated informational conduits, such as municipal bulletin boards or public school take-home packets.[150]

The nature of the law, however, is not the only consideration. Also critical to many free speech analyses is the character of the *forum* – the space or medium – in which the expression takes place.[151] On purely private property (at least one's own), one's speech is, not surprisingly, highly protected.[152] On public or governmental property, by comparison, the metes and bounds of free speech can vary greatly insofar as "the government need not permit all forms of speech on property that it owns and controls."[153] The Supreme Court has identified several types of governmental forums, which in this chapter will be classified as the traditional public forum, the designated (including limited-purpose) public forum, and the nonpublic forum. It should be noted, however, that courts and commentators sometimes differ in the labels and parameters they associate with speech-related

148 Columbia Union College v. Clarke, 159 F.3d 151, 156 (4th Cir. 1998) [quoting Lamb's Chapel v. Ctr. Moriches Union Free Sch. Dist., 508 U.S. 384, 394 (1993)], *cert. denied*, 527 U.S. 1013 (1999). However, "the government, provided it does not violate the Establishment Clause, may selectively aid certain kinds of private speech and thereby 'regulate the content of what is or is not expressed' in two clearly defined instances. First, the government may provide assistance to certain viewpoints when 'it enlists private entities to convey its [the government's] own message.' Second, the government may appropriate public funds 'to promote a particular policy of its own.'" *Id.* (citations omitted) [quoting Rosenberger v. Rector & Visitors of the Univ. of Va., 515 U.S. 819, 833 (1995)].

149 *See, e.g.*, Good News Club v. Milford Central Sch., 533 U.S. 98 (2001); Lamb's Chapel v. Ctr. Moriches Union Free Sch. Dist., 508 U.S. 384 (1993); DeBoer v. Village of Oak Park, 267 F.3d 558 (7th Cir. 2001); Culbertson v. Oakridge Sch. Dist. No. 76, 258 F.3d 1061 (9th Cir. 2001).

150 *See, e.g.*, Hills v. Scottsdale Unified Sch. Dist. No. 48, 329 F.3d 1044 (9th Cir. 2003), *cert. denied*, 540 U.S. 1149 (2004).

151 *See* Downs v. L.A. Unified Sch. Dist., 228 F.3d 1003, 1009 (9th Cir. 2000) ("When an individual speaks, the government's ability to regulate that speech depends in some situations on the designation of the forum in which the individual chooses to speak."), *cert. denied*, 532 U.S. 994 (2001).

152 *See* Jones v. Parmley, 465 F.3d 46, 56 (2d Cir. 2006) ("First Amendment protections ... are especially strong where an individual engages in speech activity from his or her own private property."); Metro Display Advertising, Inc. v. City of Victorville, 143 F.3d 1191, 1195 (9th Cir. 1998) ("Private property affords the strongest protection to free speech."). As the Supreme Court has remarked, "[a] special respect for individual liberty in the home has long been part of our culture and our law; that principle has special resonance when the government seeks to constrain a person's ability to speak there.... Whereas the government's need to mediate among various competing uses, including expressive ones, for public streets and facilities is constant and unavoidable, its need to regulate temperate speech from the home is surely much less pressing." City of Ladue v. Gilleo, 512 U.S. 43, 58 (1994) (citations omitted).

153 Int'l Soc'y for Krishna Consciousness, Inc. v. Lee, 505 U.S. 672, 678 (1992). "State ownership or control of property does not automatically open that property to the public wholesale." Wis. Interscholastic Athletic Ass'n v. Gannett Co., Inc., 658 F.3d 614, 622 (7th Cir. 2011) [citing U.S. Postal Serv. v. Council of Greenburgh Civic Ass'ns, 453 U.S. 114, 129 (1981)].

governmental forums.[154] Regardless of these differences, however, it is essentially true that "[o]nce the government has set the boundaries of its forum, it may not renege" but "must respect its own self-imposed boundaries"[155] and that "[t]he level of scrutiny applicable to the government's actions in this type of free speech case differs depending on the nature of forum from which the speaker has been excluded."[156]

The first type of venue, the traditional public forum, includes spaces such as sidewalks, "streets and parks which 'have immemorially been held in trust for the use of the public, and, time out of mind, have been used for purposes of assembly, communicating thoughts between citizens, and discussing public questions.'"[157] In a traditional public forum, a content- or viewpoint-based law or governmental action will be subjected to strict scrutiny, requiring the government to "show that its regulation is necessary to serve a compelling state interest and that it is narrowly drawn to achieve that end."[158] It may even be the case that viewpoint discrimination, rather than being subjected to strict scrutiny, is altogether prohibited.[159] By comparison, a law or government action that restricts speech or expressive conduct neutrally and incidentally rather than on the basis of content or viewpoint ordinarily will be upheld as long as it is "narrowly tailored to serve a significant governmental interest" and "leave[s] open ample alternative channels for communication of the information."[160]

The second type of venue is the designated public forum, including the limited-purpose public forum. Informing or shaping this second category are two potentially overlapping concepts – designation and limitation – and it is their relationship, in fact, that is the source of much, though not all, of the previously noted taxonomical debate.[161]

154 For example, in Christian Legal Soc'y v. Walker, 453 F.3d 853 (7th Cir. 2006), the Seventh Circuit observed that "[t]he forum nomenclature is not without confusion. Court decisions also speak of 'limited public' fora; most recently this phrase has been used interchangeably with 'nonpublic' fora, which means both are subject to a lower level of scrutiny. But 'limited public forum' has also been used to describe a subcategory of 'designated public forum,' meaning that it would be subject to the strict scrutiny test." *Id.* at 865 n. 2 (citations omitted). And in Byrne v. Rutledge, 623 F.3d 46 (2d Cir. 2010), the Second Circuit recognized "the traditional public forum, the designated public forum, and the nonpublic forum" (*id.* at 53), but then in a footnote further observed that "the law of this Court and the Supreme Court also occasionally speaks of a 'limited public forum'" (*Id.* at 53 n. 6).

155 Christian Legal Soc'y, 453 F.3d at 866.

156 *Id.* at 865.

157 Perry Educ. Ass'n v. Perry Local Educators' Ass'n, 460 U.S. 37, 45 (1983) [quoting Hague v. CIO, 307 U.S. 496, 515 (1939)]. The Ninth Circuit "consider[s] three factors in determining whether government property is a traditional public forum: (1) 'the actual use and purposes of the property, particularly status as a public thoroughfare and availability of free public access to the area,' (2) 'the area's physical characteristics, including its location and the existence of clear boundaries delimiting the area,' and (3) 'traditional or historic use of both the property in question and other similar properties.'" Wright v. Incline Village Gen. Improvement Dist., 665 F.3d 1128, 1135 (9th Cir. 2011) [quoting ACLU of Nev. v. City of Las Vegas, 333 F.3d 1092, 1100–01 (9th Cir. 2003) (citations omitted)].

158 Perry Educ. Ass'n, 460 U.S. at 45; *accord* Capitol Square Review & Advisory Bd. v. Pinette, 515 U.S. 753, 761 (1995) (explaining that, on "property [that] has by law or tradition been given the status of a public forum" a government "may regulate expressive *content* only if such a restriction is necessary, and narrowly drawn, to serve a compelling state interest").

159 *See* Pleasant Grove City, Utah v. Summum, 555 U.S. 460, 469 (2009) (stating unqualifiedly that "restrictions based on viewpoint are prohibited").

160 Clark, 468 U.S. at 293; Perry Educ. Ass'n, 460 U.S. at 45. "[T]he four-factor standard of *United States v. O'Brien*, 391 U.S. 367 (1968), for validating a regulation of expressive conduct ... in the last analysis is little, if any, different from the standard applied to time, place, or manner restrictions." Clark, 468 U.S. at 298.

161 *See* Chiu v. Plano Indep. Sch. Dist., 260 F.3d 330, 345–6 & nn. 10–12 (5th Cir. 2001). "Two terms – 'designated public forum' and 'limited public forum' – have been utilized ... yet there has not been

When a space or medium is a "designated" public forum, the idea is that the space is not a traditional or quintessential venue for public expression but instead is "public property which the state has opened for use by the public as a place for expressive activity."[162] When a space or medium is a "limited purpose" public forum, the idea is that the government has "created [it] for a limited purpose such as use by certain groups or for the discussion of certain subjects."[163] Examples might include a government-run website for public input on pending legislation and a comment session during a school board meeting.[164] The general view among federal appeals courts is that although all limited-purpose public forums are in some sense designated, not all designated forums are limited purpose because a nontraditional space may be opened up for all expression by all speakers.[165]

Differentiating between these types forums can be critical with regard to the resulting restrictions on government and thus the scope of one's free speech protection.[166] In a designated but nonlimited public forum, for example, the restrictions appear to be

agreement on their meaning. Specifically, it has not been clear whether the terms could be used interchangeably to describe the middle tier of forum, or in fact described different types of forums subject to different levels of First Amendment scrutiny." *Id.* at 345–6 (footnotes omitted); *see also* United Food & Commercial Workers Local 1099 v. City of Sidney, 364 F.3d 738, 750 (6th Cir. 2004) (observing that it and other circuit courts "have noted the confusion surrounding the use of the terms 'designated public forum' and 'limited public forum'").

162 Perry Educ. Ass'n, 460 U.S. at 45; *accord* Child Evangelism Fellowship of Md., Inc. v. Mongtomery Cnty. Pub. Schs., 457 F.3d 376, 382 (4th Cir. 2006) {"In a designated public forum ... the government makes public property (that would not otherwise qualify as a traditional public forum) generally accessible to all speakers. In such a forum, regulations on speech are 'subject to the same limitations as that governing a traditional public forum' – namely, strict scrutiny." [quoting Int'l Soc'y for Krishna Consciousness, Inc. v. Lee, 505 U.S. 672, 678–79 (1992)]}. "In considering whether a designated public forum has been created, [courts] look to 'the policy and practice of the government, the nature of the property and its compatibility with expressive activity and whether the forum was designed and dedicated to expressive activities.'" Hills v. Scottsdale Unified Sch. Dist. No. 48, 329 F.3d 1044, 1049 (9th Cir. 2003) [quoting Children of the Rosary v. City of Phoenix, 154 F.3d 972, 976 (9th Cir. 1998), *cert. denied*, 526 U.S. 1131 (1999)], *cert. denied*, 540 U.S. 1149 (2004). "In addition to these factors, courts examine the selectivity with which the forum was open to particular forms of expression. In general, the more restrictive the criteria for admission and the more administrative control over access, the less likely a forum will be deemed public." Hopper v. City of Pasco, 241 F.3d 1067, 1078 (9th Cir. 2001) [citing Ark. Educ. Television Comm'n v. Forbes, 523 U.S. 666, 679 (1998); Cinevision Corp. v. City of Burbank, 745 F.2d 560, 570 (9th Cir. 1984), *cert. denied*, 471 U.S. 1054 (1985)], *cert. denied*, 534 U.S. 951 (2001).

163 Perry Educ. Ass'n, 460 U.S. at 46 n. 7 (citations omitted). "A limited public forum exists when the government intentionally opens a nonpublic forum to expressive activity by a certain class of speakers to address a particular class of topics." Ariz. Life Coalition, Inc. v. Stanton, 515 F.3d 956, 969 (9th Cir. 2008), *cert. denied*, 555 U.S. 815 (2008).

164 *See, e.g.*, City of Madison Joint Sch. Dist. No. 8 v. Wis. Employment Relations Comm'n, 429 U.S. 167, 175–6 (1976); Fairchild v. Liberty Indep. Sch. Dist., 597 F.3d 747, 759 (5th Cir. 2010)

165 *See* Child Evangelism Fellowship of Md., 457 F.3d at 382 n. 3 {noting that many courts "have held that a limited public forum, a forum opened only to certain speakers or for discussion of certain subjects, is in fact a subset of the larger category of designated public forums specifically opened by the government for use by all speakers." [citing Bowman v. White, 444 F.3d 967, 976 (8th Cir. 2006); Make the Road by Walking, Inc. v. Turner, 378 F.3d 133, 143 (2d Cir. 2004); Donovan v. Punxsutawney Area Sch. Bd., 336 F.3d 211, 225 (3d Cir. 2003); Chiu v. Plano Indep. Sch. Dist., 260 F.3d 330, 346 n. 12 (5th Cir. 2001); Hopper v. City of Pasco, 241 F.3d 1067, 1074 (9th Cir. 2001); Chabad-Lubavitch of Ga. v. Miller, 5 F.3d 1383, 1391 n. 13 (11th Cir. 1993)]}.

166 *See* Alpha Delta Chi-Delta Chapter v. Reed, 648 F.3d 790, 797 (9th Cir. 2011) (observing that "[s]peech in a designated public forum has significantly greater protection than speech in a limited public forum"), *cert. denied*, 132 S. Ct. 1743 (2012).

identical to those of a traditional public forum: content- and viewpoint-based regulations must be necessary to achieve a compelling interest, and neutral time, place, or manner regulations must be narrowly tailored to achieve a significant interest.[167] In a limited public forum, however, "the State is not required to and does not allow persons to engage in every type of speech"[168] and, by definition, engages in some kinds of discrimination at the outset. In particular, the government may impose content-based limits that are "reasonable in light of the purpose served by the forum"[169] – a municipal budget meeting may be limited to discussing the municipal budget – but the government may "not discriminate against speech on the basis of viewpoint"[170] and must "provide adequate safeguards to protect against the improper exclusion of viewpoints."[171]

Finally, as a third category, a governmentally established or controlled location or medium may be a nonpublic forum. This category potentially consists of "[a]ll remaining public property" not falling under one of the foregoing categories[172] or at least the remaining government property that may be deemed a forum.[173] Although, here too, there is some confusion over the meaning of this category – "most recently th[e] phrase ['limited public' fora] has been used interchangeably with 'nonpublic' fora"[174] – it will be used here in a fairly narrow sense so as to attempt to distinguish it as much as possible from other categories. Accordingly, a nonpublic forum is a space or medium that while owned by the government and financed by public monies has not been opened up for general or, more definitively, even limited public expression.[175] Starkly illustrative examples could include the interior of the White House (especially when not hosting public functions),[176] the NORAD Command Center,[177] or the Supreme Court justices' conference room[178]; more mundane ones include a public school or school room that has not been opened up for public expression,[179] a government committee meeting to which the public is not invited,[180] a state's

167 *See* DiLoreto v. Downey Unified Sch. Dist. Bd. of Educ., 196 F.3d 958, 964–5 (9th Cir. 1999) ("Restrictions on expressive activity in designated public fora are subject to the same limitations that govern a traditional public forum.").

168 Good News Club v. Milford Central Sch., 533 U.S. 98, 106 (2001).

169 Cornelius v. NAACP Legal Def. & Educ. Fund, Inc., 473 U.S. 788, 806 (1985).

170 Good News Club, 533 U.S. at 106–7.

171 Child Evangelism Fellowship of Md., 457 F.3d at 384 [citing Bd. of Regents v. Southworth, 529 U.S. 217, 235 (2000); Santa Fe Indep. Sch. Dist., 530 U.S. at 304–5)].

172 Hotel Employees & Restaurant Employees Union, Local 100 v. City of N.Y. Dep't of Parks & Recreation, 311 F.3d 534, 546 (2d Cir. 2002); DiLoreto, 196 F.3d at 965.

173 *See* Ark. Educ. Television Comm'n v. Forbes, 523 U.S. 666, 677 (1998) (explaining that properties other than traditional and designated or limited public forums "are either nonpublic fora or not fora at all").

174 Christian Legal Soc'y v. Walker, 453 F.3d 853, 865 n. 2 (7th Cir. 2006) (noting further the concern that this interchange, if correct, would mean that both categories "are subject to a lower level of scrutiny").

175 Accordingly, "[t]o maintain a nonpublic forum, the government must employ 'selective access' policies, whereby forum participation is governed by 'individual, non-ministerial judgments.'" Child Evangelism Fellowship of Md., 457 F.3d at 381 (quoting *Forbes*, 523 U.S. at 680).

176 By contrast, "the street in front of the White House is a public forum." Mahoney v. Doe, 642 F.3d 1112, 1117 (D.C. Cir. 2011).

177 *Cf.* Greer v. Spock, 424 U.S. 828, 836–8 (1976) (federal military reservation).

178 *See* Byrne, 623 F.3d at 53 ("Property falling into this third category includes airport terminals, military bases, prisons, and similar properties.").

179 *See, e.g.*, Nurre v. Whitehead, 580 F.3d 1087, 1093 (9th Cir. 2009) (noting that "schools are typically non-public fora"), *cert. denied*, 559 U.S. 1025 (2010); Peck *ex rel.* Peck v. Baldwinsville Central Sch. Dist., 426 F.3d 617, 626–7 (2d Cir. 2005), *cert. denied*, 547 U.S. 1097 (2006).

180 *See, e.g.*, Perez v. Hoblock, 368 F.3d 166, 172–3 (2d Cir. 2004).

specialty license plate program,[181] or the area inside the Jefferson Memorial.[182] The central premise with respect to nonpublic forums is that "the State, no less than a private owner of property, has power to preserve the property under its control for the use to which it is lawfully dedicated"[183] and has 'maximum control over communicative behavior.'"[184]

Of course, the government is not truly an ordinary private owner, and as a result, the First Amendment places some limitations on its capacity to restrict expression even in nonpublic forums.[185] "In addition to [imposing] time, place, and manner regulations, the state may reserve the forum for its intended purposes, communicative or otherwise, as long as the regulation on speech is reasonable and not an effort to suppress expression merely because public officials oppose the speaker's view."[186] This mandate of viewpoint neutrality means that while "the government may permissibly restrict content by prohibiting *any* speech on a given topic or subject matter, once the government has permitted *some* comment on a particular subject matter or topic, it may not then 'regulate speech in ways that favor some viewpoints or ideas at the expense of others.'"[187] Such viewpoint discrimination, should it occur, apparently will be subject to judicial strict scrutiny, whereby the government must show that the discrimination is necessary to achieve a compelling interest.[188]

Over and above the foregoing content-focused and forum-based analyses, free speech jurisprudence also incorporates a constellation of doctrines reflecting unique concerns about the historic and contemporary place of free expression in American society. One of these is a general prohibition on compelled private expression of a "religious, political, and ideological" nature,[189] including as a condition to receiving a government benefit,[190]

181 *See, e.g.*, Choose Life Ill., Inc. v. White, 547 F.3d 853, 864–5 (7th Cir. 2008); Perry v. McDonald, 280 F.3d 159, 167–9 (2d Cir. 2001). *Compare* Ariz. Life Coalition, Inc. v. Stanton, 515 F.3d 956, 969–71 (9th Cir. 2008) (deeming such a program a limited public forum where the program's "purpose was to open up its license plate forum to a certain class of organizations for expressive activity"), *cert. denied*, 555 U.S. 815 (2008).

182 *See* Oberwetter v. Hilliard, 639 F.3d 545, 552–3 (D.C. Cir. 2011).

183 U.S. Postal Serv. v. Council of Greenburgh Civic Ass'ns, 453 U.S. 114, 129 (1981). "Where the government is acting as a proprietor, managing its internal operations, rather than acting as lawmaker with the power to regulate or license, its action will not be subjected to the heightened review to which its actions as a lawmaker may be subject." Int'l Soc'y for Krishna Consciousness, 505 U.S. at 678; *accord* Wis. Interscholastic Athletic Ass'n v. Gannett Co., Inc., 658 F.3d 614, 622 (7th Cir. 2011).

184 Byrne, 623 F.3d at 53 [quoting Paulsen v. Cnty. of Nassau, 925 F.2d 65, 69 (2d Cir. 1991)].

185 *See* Chiu v. Plano Indep. Sch. Dist., 260 F.3d 330, 347 (5th Cir. 2001) ("A nonpublic forum ... is not a private forum, and because it is a government-sponsored medium of communication, it is still subject to First Amendment constraints.").

186 Perry Educ. Ass'n, 460 U.S. at 46; *accord* Int'l Soc'y for Krishna Consciousness, 505 U.S. at 678–9; Cornelius, 473 U.S. 788 at 806 (1985); Milwaukee Deputy Sheriffs' Ass'n v. Clarke, 588 F.3d 523, 530 (7th Cir. 2009) ("Exclusion from nonpublic fora is permitted subject to two conditions: the government cannot engage in viewpoint discrimination against speech otherwise within the forum's limitations, and the restriction must be reasonable in light of the purpose served by the forum."); Child Evangelism Fellowship of Md., 457 F.3d at 383 (same).

187 Byrne, 623 F.3d at 54–5 [quoting Lamb's Chapel v. Ctr. Moriches Union Free Sch. Dist., 508 U.S. 384, 394 (1993)].

188 *See* Gen. Media Communications, Inc. v. Cohen, 131 F.3d 273, 281 n. 9 (2d Cir. 1997) (noting cases suggesting that strict scrutiny is the appropriate standard for viewpoint discrimination in a nonpublic forum), *cert. denied*, 524 U.S. 951 (1998).

189 Wooley v. Maynard, 430 U.S. 705, 714 (1977); *see* Agency for Int'l Dev. v. Alliance for Open Soc'y Int'l, Inc., 133 S. Ct. 2321, 2327 (2013); W. Va. Bd. of Educ. v. Barnette, 319 U.S. 624 (1943).

190 *See* Agency for Int'l Dev., 133 S. Ct. at 2327–32.

absent proof by the government that such compulsion is necessary or narrowly tailored to achieve a compelling government interest.[191] "[T]he right of freedom of thought protected by the First Amendment against state action includes both the right to speak freely and the right to refrain from speaking at all. A system which secures the right to proselytize religious, political, and ideological causes must also guarantee the concomitant right to decline to foster such concepts."[192]

A second distinct concern of the First Amendment, and a counterpart of sorts to the first, is a general aversion to so-called prior restraints, which entail censoring speech preemptively or "deny[ing] use of a forum in advance of actual expression" in the absence of "precise and clear standards" to constrain government officials.[193] Though a prior restraint is "not unconstitutional per se," it " 'comes to [the judiciary] bearing a heavy presumption against its constitutional validity' "[194] and, in order to be upheld, must possess a variety of procedural safeguards.[195] Yet a third special concern of free speech doctrine not unrelated to the aversion to prior restraints is that persons' expressive inclinations might be "chilled" by vague or overreaching laws and the attendant fear of liability for their violation. When there is a genuine concern about the chilling of free speech, therefore, courts may be unwilling to countenance in a law an ordinarily tolerable

191 *See* Wooley, 430 U.S. at 715–16; Evergreen Ass'n, Inc. v. City of N.Y. 740 F.3d 233, 244–5, 246–51 (2d Cir. 2014) (employing strict scrutiny, though noting exceptions warranting lower scrutiny); Planned Parenthood, Minn., N.D. & S.D. v. Rounds, 530 F.3d 724, 733 (8th Cir. 2008) (explaining that if "a claim that a state action violates the right not to speak . . . implicates First Amendment protections . . . the court must determine whether the action is narrowly tailored to serve a compelling state interest."). The limitation on compelled speech can also include compelled monetary contributions that are used specifically to subsidize others' speech, especially political or ideological speech. *See* Harris v. Quinn, 134 S. Ct. 2618, 2623 (2014) (fees imposed on "personal care providers," effectively private-sector employees, "to subsidize speech on matters of public concern" – i.e., the collective bargaining process – "by a union that they do not wish to join or support"); Keller v. State Bar of Cal., 496 U.S. 1 (1990) (portion of attorneys' state bar association dues used for political or ideological activities unrelated to regulating the legal profession and improving the quality of legal services); Abood v. Detroit Bd. of Educ., 431 U.S. 209 (1977) (portion of public teachers' union dues used for political or ideological activities unrelated to collective bargaining). *Compare* Bd. of Regents of Univ. of Wis. Sys. v. Southworth, 529 U.S. 217 (2000) (upholding mandatory student fee used to subsidize political, ideological, and other organizations where distribution of revenue was viewpoint-neutral). " 'Compelled support of government' – even those programs of government one does not approve – is of course perfectly constitutional, as every taxpayer must attest. And some government programs involve, or entirely consist of, advocating a position. . . . [The Court has] generally assumed, though not yet squarely held, that compelled funding of government speech does not alone raise First Amendment concerns." Johanns v. Livestock Mtkg. Ass'n, 544 U.S. 550, 559 (2005).

192 Wooley, 430 U.S. at 714. When the speech is not of a religious, political, or ideological nature, it may more readily be compelled. *See, e.g.*, United States v. Arnold, 740 F.3d 1032, 1033–4 (5th Cir. 2014) (mandatory sex offender registration); United States v. Sindel, 53 F.3d 874, 877–8 (8th Cir. 1995) (mandatory disclosure of information on IRS form). But not always. *See* Riley v. Nat'l Fed'n of the Blind of N.C., Inc., 487 U.S. 781, 795–801 (1988) (strictly scrutinizing and invalidating a government mandate on professional fund raisers to disclose certain factual information to potential donors). For an extended analysis, *see* Howard M. Wasserman, *Compelled Expression and the Public Forum Doctrine*, 77 Tul. L. Rev. 163 (2002).

193 Southeastern Promotions, Ltd. v. Conrad, 420 U.S. 546, 553 (1975).

194 *Id.* at 558 [quoting Bantam Books, Inc. v. Sullivan, 372 U.S. 58, 70 (1963)].

195 In particular, "the burden of instituting judicial proceedings, and of proving that the material is unprotected, must rest on the censor"; "any restraint prior to judicial review can be imposed only for a specified brief period and only for the purpose of preserving the status quo," and "a prompt final judicial determination must be assured." *Id.* at 560.

degree of vagueness[196] or overbreadth.[197] Additionally, in order to expose and eliminate speech-chilling laws, courts have recognized unique opportunities for speech-based facial challenges on the basis of overbreadth, even by speakers whose own expression is constitutionally unprotected.[198]

Having highlighted some points of special solicitude under the First Amendment, it also must be noted that there are certain forms or contexts of expression that, for a variety of reasons, garner less First Amendment protection than others. Mentioned already, for example, are categories of less protected or basically unprotected speech.[199] In addition, there are several institutional contexts in which free speech is potentially subject to greater regulation, including public employment,[200] public education,[201] incarceration,[202] and the military.[203] Insofar as these contexts can involve controversies over religious expression, in particular, they are appropriately addressed more fully in other chapters of this book.[204]

196 "Where a statute's literal scope, unaided by a narrowing state court interpretation, is capable of reaching expression sheltered by the First Amendment, the [vagueness] doctrine demands a greater degree of specificity than in other contexts." Smith v. Goguen, 415 U.S. 566, 573 (1974). "The prohibition against vague regulations of speech is based in part on the need to eliminate the impermissible risk of discriminatory enforcement, for history shows that speech is suppressed when either the speaker or the message is critical of those who enforce the law." Gentile v. State Bar of Nev., 501 U.S. 1030, 1050 (1991) (citations omitted). Also, "[w]here a vague statute 'abut(s) upon sensitive areas of basic First Amendment freedoms,' it 'operates to inhibit the exercise of (those) freedoms.'" Grayned v. City of Rockford, 408 U.S. 104, 109 (1972).

197 "Overbreadth is a judicially created doctrine designed to prevent the chilling of protected expression." Massachusetts v. Oakes, 491 U.S. 576, 584 (1989). It "prohibits the Government from banning unprotected speech if a substantial amount of protected speech is prohibited or chilled in the process." Ashcroft v. Free Speech Coalition, 535 U.S. 234, 255 (2002).

198 *See* Forsyth Cnty., Ga. v. Nationalist Movement, 505 U.S. 123, 129–30 (1992). {"[T]he Court has altered its traditional rules of standing to permit – in the First Amendment area – 'attacks on overly broad statutes with no requirement that the person making the attack demonstrate that his own conduct could not be regulated by a statute drawn with the requisite narrow specificity.' Litigants, therefore, are permitted to challenge a statute not because their own rights of free expression are violated, but because of a judicial prediction or assumption that the statute's very existence may cause others not before the court to refrain from constitutionally protected speech or expression." Broadrick v. Oklahoma, 413 U.S. 601, 612 (1973) [quoting Dombrowski v. Pfister, 380 U.S. 479, 486 (1965)]}.

199 *See supra* notes 142–3 and accompanying text.

200 *See* Johnson v. Poway Unified Sch. Dist., 658 F.3d 954, 961 (9th Cir. 2011) {"[T]he Supreme Court has held that where the government acts as both sovereign and employer, this general forum-based analysis does not apply.... Instead, the Court applies a distinct *Pickering*-based analysis that 'reconcile[s] the employee's right to engage in speech and the government employer's right to protect its own legitimate interests in performing its mission.'" [quoting City of San Diego, Cal. v. Roe, 543 U.S. 77, 80 (2004), and citing Garcetti v. Ceballos, 547 U.S. 410, 417–19 (2006); Roe, 543 U.S. at 80; Pickering v. Bd. of Educ. of Twp. High Sch. Dist. 205, 391 U.S. 563, 568 (1968)]}, *cert. denied*, 132 S. Ct. 1807 (2012).

201 *See, e.g.*, Morse v. Frederick, 551 U.S. 393 (2007); Bethel Sch. Dist. No. 403 v. Fraser, 478 U.S. 675, 685 (1986); Tinker v. Des Moines Indep. Cmty. Sch. Dist., 393 U.S. 503, 511 (1969).

202 *See, e.g.*, Turner v. Safley, 482 U.S. 78, 89–91 (1987).

203 *See, e.g.*, Parker v. Levy, 417 U.S. 733, 758–61 (1974); United States v. Wilcox, 66 M.J. 442 (Ct. App. Armed Forces 2008); Michael C. Friess, *A Specialized Society: Speech Offenses in the Military*, ARMY LAWYER, Sep. 2009, at 18.

204 Regarding public employment, *see* Chapter 11; public education, *see* Chapter 16; and incarceration and the military, *see* Chapter 18.

## 2. *Religious Expression by Private Parties*

The clear judicial trend in recent decades has been to require the government to accord religious expression the same content and forum protections enjoyed by nonreligious expression. Thus, if the government has opened up a nontraditional public forum, it cannot exclude religious speech absent a compelling interest, nor can it easily (or ever) exclude religious viewpoints while allowing nonreligious viewpoints, even in the context of a nonpublic forum, much less in a limited-purpose public forum. At the same time, it appears that the judiciary has become increasingly unwilling, under strict scrutiny, to accept as a basis for suppressing religious speech a government's alleged effort to avoid perceived establishment problems partly because the Supreme Court in recent years has relaxed or modified certain Establishment Clause doctrines.

Even before these modern developments, however, constitutional protection for religious speech was a prominent part of the First Amendment landscape. In a 1940 decision, *Cantwell v. Connecticut*,[205] the Court reversed the convictions of two Jehovah's Witnesses for unauthorized solicitation and incitement to breach of the peace resulting from their door-to-door religious proselytizing and requesting of donations for literature.[206] Regarding the first basis for conviction, the Court reasoned that "to condition the solicitation of aid for the perpetuation of religious views or systems upon a license, the grant of which rests in the exercise of a determination by state authority as to what is a religious cause, is to lay a forbidden burden upon the exercise of liberty protected by the Constitution."[207] Regarding the second, the Court found "no assault or threatening of bodily harm, no truculent bearing, no intentional discourtesy, no personal abuse. On the contrary, [it found] only an effort to persuade a willing listener to buy a book or to contribute money in the interest of what Cantwell, however misguided others may think him, conceived to be true religion."[208]

Just three years later, in *Murdock v. Pennsylvania*,[209] the Court again reversed the convictions of Jehovah's Witnesses for unauthorized solicitation. The Court noted:

> The hand distribution of religious tracts is an age-old form of missionary evangelism – as old as the history of printing presses. It has been a potent force in various religious movements down through the years.... It is more than preaching; it is more than distribution of religious literature. It is a combination of both. Its purpose is as evangelical as the revival meeting. This form of religious activity occupies the same high estate under the First Amendment as do worship in the churches and preaching from the pulpits. It has the same claim to protection as the more orthodox and conventional exercises of religion. It also has the same claim as the others to the guarantees of freedom of speech and freedom of the press.[210]

205 Cantwell v. Connecticut, 310 U.S. 296 (1940).

206 One year prior, the Court reversed several convictions involving a variety of municipal ordinances on hand-billing and the like, stating that "[a]lthough a municipality may enact regulations in the interest of the public safety, health, welfare or convenience, these may not abridge the individual liberties secured by the Constitution to those who wish to speak, write, print or circulate information or opinion." Schneider v. State (Town of Irvington), 308 U.S. 147, 160 (1939).

207 Cantwell, 310 U.S. at 307.

208 *Id.* at 310.

209 319 U.S. 105 (1943).

210 *Id.* at 108–9. Three years later, the Court reversed the conviction of a Jehovah's Witness for engaging in similar activities, without municipal authorization, in a company-owned town. *See* Marsh v. Alabama, 326 U.S. 501 (1946).

Nearly six decades later, the Court, once more in a suit involving Jehovah's Witnesses, invalidated a government attempt to require a permit for door-to-door advocacy.[211] Before the justices was a village ordinance that, as summarized by the Court, "prohibit[ed] 'canvassers' from going on private property for the purpose of explaining or promoting any 'cause,' unless they receive[d] a permit and the residents visited ha[d] not opted for a 'no solicitation' sign."[212] The Court deemed the ordinance dangerously broad in its coverage and, more critically, not sufficiently tailored to serve the municipality's stated interests.[213]

Today, the protection of private religious expression is defined by a variety of principles that often complement or intersect with the doctrines set forth in the preceding section (i.e., the focus on the nature of the regulation and the forum of the expression as well as the aversion to prior restraints and vague or overbroad laws that preemptively chill speech). This protection is sufficiently robust, in fact, that religious speakers often find the Free Speech Clause more attractive than the Free Exercise Clause, especially given the latter's constriction in *Employment Division v. Smith*.[214] First, the judiciary has emphasized that not only is religious expression clearly safeguarded by the Free Speech Clause,[215] but it is normally protected at least as much as any genre of nonreligious speech.[216] In this regard, the Supreme Court has stated that "private religious speech, far from being a First Amendment orphan, is as fully protected under the Free Speech Clause as secular private expression."[217] Second, and as a result, the category of "religious speech" necessarily includes nonverbal and nonwritten forms of

211 Watchtower Bible & Tract Soc'y of N.Y., Inc. v. Village of Stratton, 536 U.S. 150 (2002).

212 *Id.* at 165.

213 *See id.* at 165–9.

214 494 U.S. 872 (1990). This phenomenon has not been without critics. *See, e.g.*, Patrick M. Garry, *Inequality Among Equals: Disparities in the Judicial Treatment of Free Speech and Religious Exercise Claims*, 39 Wake Forest L. Rev. 361 (2004). "The disparity in judicial treatment between speech and religious liberty cases has produced more than just a constitutional imbalance. It has also created a constitutional distortion, in which plaintiffs seeking religious protection frequently abandon the Free Exercise Clause and resort instead to the Free Speech Clause. Thus, what should otherwise be characterized as religious exercise is labeled as free speech." *Id.* at 363. Moreover, "[a] focus on free speech may blind the courts to certain accommodations that free exercise might demand. The Free Exercise Clause carries an affirmative aspect (a requirement of accommodation) that the Free Speech Clause does not. The latter encompasses a negative freedom, a simple prohibition of government infringement; whereas with free exercise, the government may have to affirmatively require certain things so as not to constrain religious liberty." *Id.* at 392.

215 *See* Widmar v. Vincent, 454 U.S. 263, 269 (1981) ("[R]eligious worship and discussion ... are forms of speech and association protected by the First Amendment.").

216 It has been suggested that "[r]eligious speech is ... entitled to *exactly* the same protection from government restriction as any other kind of speech – *no more and no less*." Kreisner v. City of San Diego, 1 F.3d 775, 790 (9th Cir. 1993) (Kozinski, J., concurring) (emphases added). As a generalization, this may be true, and as a matter of principle, it may be a good idea, but as a matter of practice, it is not necessarily accurate. As explained *infra* notes 223–40 and accompanying text, the First Amendment religion clauses may in some instances effectively provide a benefit or protection to religion or religious expression that is denied to nonreligion or nonreligious expression, whereas in other instances they may effectively deny to religion or religious expression a benefit or protection that is provided to nonreligion or nonreligious expression.

217 Capitol Square Review & Advisory Bd. v. Pinette, 515 U.S. 753, 760 (1995). However, "[t]he Supreme Court has never held that religious speech is entitled to more protection than non-religious speech." Axson-Flynn v. Johnson, 356 F.3d 1277, 1292 n. 13 (10th Cir. 2004).

symbolic, communicative conduct.[218] Third, this category does not admit of subcategories of greater- and lesser-protected expression; all forms are equally protected.[219] In short, religious expression receives significant and generally equal protection under the Free Speech Clause, and absent the government's satisfaction of strict scrutiny, it cannot be subject to content or viewpoint discrimination in a traditional or unlimited designated public forum,[220] nor can it be subject to viewpoint discrimination in a limited public[221] or nonpublic forum.[222]

This equality of protection for religious and nonreligious speech is a general norm, however, and not a steadfast rule admitting of no exceptions or variations. In fact, the First Amendment religion clauses may effectively provide to religious speech, when compared with nonreligious speech, both greater protection in some instances and lesser protection in others. The greater protection may arise either from a Free Exercise Clause–based accommodation of religious expression (when not available or accorded to nonreligious expression) or from an inability of courts, under one or both religion clauses, to provide a remedy against speech that is religious and tortious or otherwise unlawful (and that, if equally injurious but nonreligious, would normally result in liability). An example of the former scenario, even after *Employment Division v. Smith*,[223] would be a judicially mandated exemption to a rule against potentially expressive conduct, such as having facial hair or wearing jewelry, where the court finds that the rule is not generally applicable or neutral toward religion.[224] In such a case, the religious claimant could very well get an exemption under the Free Exercise Clause, but nonreligious claimants (unless already exempted by the rule or unless the rule is struck down *in toto*) would not. An example of the latter scenario would be an otherwise defamatory statement that the court cannot adjudicate either because addressing an underlying religious question (e.g., the truth or falsity of the statement) would create excessive entanglement

218 *See* Chabad-Lubavitch of Ga. v. Miller, 5 F.3d 1383, 1387 (11th Cir. 1993) (so holding and citing cases); Ams. United for Separation of Church & State v. City of Grand Rapid, 980 F.2d 1538, 1542 (6th Cir. 1992) (so holding).

219 Church on the Rock v. City of Albuquerque, 84 F.3d 1273, 1278 (10th Cir. 1996) (noting that "[t]he Supreme Court … has rejected the notion that speech about religion, religious speech designed to win converts, and religious worship by persons already converted should be treated differently under the First Amendment"), *cert. denied*, 519 U.S. 949 (1996).

220 *See* Orin v. Barclay, 272 F.3d 1207, 1215–16 (9th Cir. 2001) (community college official's instruction to demonstrators to refrain from religious worship or instruction in a designated public forum was subject to, and failed, strict scrutiny), *cert. denied*, 536 U.S. 958 (2002).

221 *See* Good News Club v. Milford Central Sch., 533 U.S. 98, 112 (2001) ("[S]peech discussing otherwise permissible subjects cannot be excluded from a limited public forum on the ground that the subject is discussed from a religious viewpoint.").

222 *See* Summum v. Callaghan, 130 F.3d 906, 918 (10th Cir. 1997) ("If, for example, the government permits secular displays on a nonpublic forum, it cannot ban displays discussing otherwise permissible topics from a religious perspective.").

223 494 U.S. 872 (1990).

224 *See, e.g.*, Fraternal Order of Police Newark Lodge No. 12 v. City of Newark, 170 F.3d 359, 364–7 (3d Cir. 1999) (finding a free exercise violation where a police department policy allowed beards for medical but not religious reasons), *cert. denied*, 528 U.S. 817 (1999); Nichol v. ARIN Intermediate Unit 28, 268 F. Supp. 2d 536, 548–55 (W.D. Pa. 2003) (finding a free exercise violation where public school policy specifically prohibited wearing "religious emblems, dress, or insignia"); *cf. also* Erin J. Cox, *Comment, Freeing Exercise at Expression's Expense: When RFRA Privileges the Religiously Motivated Speaker*, 56 UCLA L. Rev. 169 (2008) (recognizing though criticizing this prospect under RFRA).

under the Establishment Clause or because adjudication would interfere with internal church governance (e.g., the selection of clergy) under one or both of the First Amendment religion clauses.[225]

Conversely, religious speech, when compared with nonreligious speech, sometimes may effectively receive less protection. At least two types of scenarios could yield this result. First, this could happen where, once again, a court is disabled by the First Amendment religion clauses from adjudicating a claim resting on the speech (whereas a comparable claim resting on nonreligious speech would not face that obstacle). Second, it could happen where the speech, otherwise private, is sufficiently comingled with or attributable to the government – for example, student-led prayer at a high school football game[226] – that the government, in order to achieve the compelling interest in preventing an Establishment Clause violation, can forbid the speech (whereas private nonreligious expression, no matter how entangled with or attributed to the government, would not be subject to that fate).[227]

This last basis warrants further analysis, particularly given the prefatory comment at the outset of this section that courts seem increasingly less willing to accept nonestablishment concerns as compelling reasons that can justify government suppression of or discrimination against private speech. The Supreme Court itself has explained that "a state interest in avoiding an Establishment Clause violation 'may be characterized as compelling,' and therefore may justify content-based discrimination"[228] though it has expressly

225 *See, e.g.*, Hutchison v. Thomas, 789 F.2d 392, 393–6 (6th Cir. 1986), *cert. denied*, 479 U.S. 885 (1986); Hartwig v. Albertus Magnus College, 93 F. Supp. 2d 200, 218–19 (D. Conn. 2000); Klagsbrun v. Va'ad Harabonim of Greater Monsey, 53 F. Supp. 2d 732, 739–42 (D.N.J. 1999), *aff'd*, 263 F.3d 158 (3d Cir. 2001); Sands v. Living Word Fellowship, 34 P.3d 955, 960 (Alaska 2001); El-Farra v. Sayyed, 226 S.W.3d 792, 796–7 (Ark. 2006); Thibodeau v. Am. Baptist Churches of Conn., 994 A.2d 212, 221–4 (Conn. Ct. App. 2010), *certification denied*, 3 A.3d 74 (Conn. 2010); O'Connor v. Diocese of Honolulu, 885 P.2d 361, 367–8 (Hawai'i 1994); Brazauskas v. Fort Wayne-South Bend Diocese, Inc., 714 N.E.2d 253, 260–3 (Ind. Ct. App. 1999), *transfer denied*, 726 N.E.2d 313 (Ind. 1999); Bourne v. Ctr. on Children, Inc., 838 A.2d 371, 380 (Md. Ct. Spec. App. 2003), *cert. denied*, 846 A.2d 401 (Md. 2003); Hiles v. Episcopal Diocese of Mass., 773 N.E.2d 929, 935–9 (Mass. 2002); Trice v. Burress, 137 P.3d 1253, 1258–60 (Okla. Civ. Ct. App. 2006); *In re* Godwin, 293 S.W.3d 742, 748–9 (Tex. Ct. App. 2009); Cha v. Korean Presbyterian Church of Wash., 553 S.E.2d 511, 516–17 (Va. 2001), *cert. denied*, 535 U.S. 1035 (2002); David Blaikie & Diana Ginn, The Legal Guide for Religious Institutions: Churches, Synagogues, Mosques, Temples, and Other Religious Communities 148–9 (2010).

226 *See, e.g.*, Santa Fe Indep. Sch. Dist. v. Doe, 530 U.S. 290 (2000) (holding that a student prayer delivered before public high school football games violated the Establishment Clause because it was delivered over the school's public address system, was "authorized by a government policy and [took] place on government property at government-sponsored school-related events" because the school district "failed to divorce itself from the religious content in the invocations" and because some students were required to attend while "many" others likely felt pressured to do so); Cole v. Oroville Union High Sch. Dist., 228 F.3d 1092, 1102 (9th Cir. 2000) (following *Santa Fe* and prohibiting student delivery of a sectarian invocation at graduation where "the District authorized an invocation as part of the graduation ceremony held on District property, allowed only a student selected by a vote of his classmates to give an invocation and no doubt would have used a microphone or public address system to amplify the invocation to the audience at the graduation ceremony"), *cert. denied*, 532 U.S. 905 (2001).

227 *See* Draper v. Logan Cnty. Pub. Library, 403 F. Supp. 2d 608, 620 (W.D. Ky. 2005) ("At times, the state's interest in avoiding an Establishment Clause violation may provide justification for infringing upon free speech or free exercise rights otherwise protected by the First Amendment.").

228 Good News Club v. Milford Central Sch., 533 U.S. 98, 112 (2001) (quoting Widmar v. Vincent, 454 U.S. 263, 271 (1981)); *accord* Capitol Square Review & Advisory Bd. v. Pinette, 515 U.S. 753, 761–2 (1995) ("There is no doubt that compliance with the Establishment Clause is a state interest sufficiently compelling to justify content-based restrictions on speech.").

not decided "whether a State's interest in avoiding an Establishment Clause violation would justify viewpoint discrimination."[229] As one state supreme court has observed, however, although it is true that the government "undeniably has an interest in avoiding Establishment Clause violations ... the interest must be grounded in reality; the ... mere fear of an Establishment Clause violation will not justify burdening First Amendment protections. If the ... [government is] acting to avoid an Establishment Clause violation, there actually need[s] to be an Establishment Clause violation to avoid."[230] It is on this basis, then, that the Supreme Court in recent years has "[m]ore than once ... rejected the position that the Establishment Clause even justifies, much less requires, a refusal to extend free speech rights to religious speakers who participate in broad-reaching government programs neutral in design."[231] Lower courts, for their part, not only have remarked on this trend in Supreme Court jurisprudence[232] but also have themselves regularly refused to uphold content- or viewpoint-based discrimination against religious speech where no actual Establishment Clause violation would occur in the absence of such discrimination.[233] At bottom, these cases reflect the principle that "the Establishment

[229] Good News Club, 533 U.S. at 113 (citing *Lamb's Chapel*, 508 U.S. at 394–5).

[230] Freshwater v. Mt. Vernon City Sch. Dist. Bd. of Educ., 1 N.E.3d 335, 352–3 (Ohio 2013) (citation omitted), *cert. denied*, 135 S. Ct. 60 (2014); *accord* Satawa v. Macomb Cnty. Rd. Comm'n, 689 F.3d 506, 524–5 (6th Cir. 2012) {"For the Establishment Clause to serve as a compelling state interest, the speech suppressed must actually violate the Constitution. If the government's 'posited fears of an Establishment Clause violation are unfounded,' an Establishment Clause defense will not do." [quoting Lamb's Chapel v. Ctr. Moriches Union Free Sch. Dist., 508 U.S. 384, 395 (1993)]}.

[231] Rosenberger v. Rector & Visitors of Univ. of Va., 515 U.S. 819, 839 (1995) [citing Lamb's Chapel, 508 U.S. at 393–4; Bd. of Educ. of Westside Cmty. Schs. v. Mergens, 496 U.S. 226, 248, 252 (1990); Widmar, 454 U.S. at 274–5].

[232] *See, e.g.*, Donovan *ex rel.* Donovan v. Punxsutawney Area Sch. Bd., 336 F.3d 211, 226–7 (3d Cir. 2003) ["The Supreme Court has repeatedly rejected Establishment Clause defenses in free speech cases." (citing Good News Club, Lamb's Chapel, and Widmar)]; Peck v. Upshur Cnty. Bd. of Educ., 155 F.3d 274, 279 (4th Cir. 1998) {"The Supreme Court has, over the past decade, consistently sustained against Establishment Clause challenge neutral government policies that permit private religious speech on and within state educational and other properties on the same terms as private secular speech is permitted." [citing Rosenberger, Lamb's Chapel, Mergens, and Widmar as well as Capitol Square Review & Advisory Bd. v. Pinette, 515 U.S. 753 (1995) (plurality)]}.

[233] *See* Child Evangelism Fellowship of Minn. v. Minneapolis Sch. Dist. No. 1, 690 F.3d 996, 1002–4 (8th Cir. 2012) (viewpoint discrimination against religious speech unjustified because no actual Establishment Clause violation); Satawa, 689 F.3d at 524–5 (with an actual Establishment Clause violation, denial of permit to religious speaker in order to "prevent an Establishment Clause violation ... was not compelling"); Badger Catholic, Inc. v. Walsh, 620 F.3d 775 (7th Cir. 2010) (holding that university's refusal to denying funding to student organizations that engaged in prayer, proselytizing, or religious instruction amounted to viewpoint discrimination, and there was no Establishment Clause violation to provide a compelling interest), *cert. denied*, 131 S. Ct. 1604 (2011); Donovan, 336 F.3d at 226–7 (viewpoint discrimination against religious speech was unjustified because no actual Establishment Clause violation); Columbia Union College v. Oliver, 254 F.3d 496, 510 (4th Cir. 2001) (viewpoint discrimination against religious funding applicant invalid because no actual Establishment Clause violation); Orin v. Barclay, 272 F.3d 1207, 1215–16 (9th Cir. 2001) (content discrimination against religious speech unjustified because no actual Establishment Clause violation), *cert. denied*, 536 U.S. 958 (2002); Church on the Rock v. City of Albuquerque, 84 F.3d 1273, 1280 (10th Cir. 1996) (nonestablishment interest may be compelling, but restriction on speech not necessary), *cert. denied*, 519 U.S. 949 (1996); Good News/Good Sports Club v. Sch. Dist. of City of Ladue, 28 F.3d 1501, 1507–10 (8th Cir. 1994) (viewpoint discrimination against religious expression invalid because no actual Establishment Clause violation), *cert. denied*, 515 U.S. 1173 (1995); Ams. United for Separation of Church & State v. City of Grand Rapids, 980 F.2d 1538, 1541–53 (6th Cir. 1992) (content discrimination against religious speech unjustified because no actual Establishment Clause violation).

Clause requires neutrality, as opposed to hostility, towards religion. And as the Supreme Court has stated and restated, 'neutrality is respected, not offended, when the government, following neutral criteria and evenhanded policies, extends benefits to recipients whose ideologies and viewpoints, including religious ones, are broad and diverse.'"[234]

As it turns out, however, this is also a general principle that, in application, can exhibit exceptions or variations. For example, governments may have some flexibility to engage in narrowly crafted forms of differential treatment with respect to some religious activities, particularly in the area of funding. As discussed in the section on equal protection, the Supreme Court's 2004 decision in *Locke v. Davey*[235] upheld a state scholarship program's explicit prohibition on using scholarship funds to pursue a degree in devotional theology, accepting as a rationale a state constitutional norm of nonestablishment that plainly exceeded (i.e., was not required by) the doctrine of the federal Establishment Clause. Although the case involved free exercise and equal protection claims, it could plausibly have been recast as a free speech claim insofar as the pursuit of a degree in a particular subject can be seen as expressive of one's faith and views. Critical to the Court's ruling, however, was the perceived lack of animus toward religion – one could otherwise use the funds at religious schools or to pursue (nonministerial) religious studies – and the fact that the government did not need to create the program at all.

In addition, governments also may have some flexibility to exclude religious activities specifically when creating a limited-purpose public forum, as long as the exclusion is based solely on content rather than viewpoint and is otherwise reasonable. This is the teaching of a 2011 ruling from the Second Circuit that upheld a board of education policy expressly prohibiting the use of school facilities by outside groups, during nonschool hours, for "religious worship services."[236] Finding that "the challenged rule does not constitute viewpoint discrimination because it does not seek to exclude expressions of religious points of view or of religious devotion, but rather excludes for valid non-discriminatory reasons only a type of activity – the conduct of worship services," and further finding that the school board "reasonably seek[s] by the rule to avoid violating the Establishment Clause," the Second Circuit held that "the exclusion ... is a reasonable content-based restriction, which does not violate the Free Speech Clause."[237] However, "religious worship" was very precisely and narrowly defined under the policy[238] such that the court could rely on the distinction "between excluding the *conduct of an event or activity* that includes expression of a point of view, and excluding the *expression* of that point of view."[239] In addition, and perhaps more critically, the court stated that it did not need to decide "whether use of the school for worship services would in fact

234 Child Evangelism Fellowship of Minn. v. Minneapolis Sch. Dist. No. 1, 690 F.3d 996, 1003 (8th Cir. 2012) (citation omitted) (quoting Rosenberger, 515 U.S. at 839).

235 540 U.S. 712 (2004).

236 *See* Bronx Household of Faith v. Bd. of Educ. of City of N.Y., 650 F.3d 30 (2d Cir. 2011), *cert. denied*, 132 S. Ct. 816 (2011).

237 *Id.* at 33.

238 *See id.* at 36–7 ("Prayer, religious instruction, expression of devotion to God, and the singing of hymns, whether done by a person or a group, do not constitute the conduct of worship services.... What is prohibited ... is solely the conduct of a particular type of event: a collective activity characteristically done according to an order prescribed by and under the auspices of an organized religion, typically but not necessarily conducted by an ordained official of the religion.").

239 *Id.* at 37.

violate the Establishment Clause"; instead, it was enough to find that "the Board ha[d] a strong basis to believe that allowing the conduct of religious worship services in schools would give rise to a sufficient appearance of endorsement to constitute a violation of the Establishment Clause."[240] It is not clear that this approach to evaluating a nonestablishment justification is sound in light of other circuit court rulings, although it is perhaps meaningful that the Establishment Clause concern was part of a low-level rather than strict scrutiny. Nonetheless, it does provide some flexibility to governmental access policies and their treatment of private religious expression that otherwise would not be evident from the majority of cases.

### 3. *Religious Expression by the Government*

Governments, of course, express a variety of ideas and views, whether by the symbols or mottos they adopt, the laws or policies they enact, the public campaigns they undertake, or the educational curricula they develop and implement. Although it is generally thought that governments do not have free speech rights of their own,[241] they are correspondingly not constrained in their own speech by the First Amendment doctrines that normally protect private speech against their control.[242] Thus, for example, "when the State is the speaker, it may make content-based choices"[243] and may "select the views that it wants to express."[244] That is, "even ordinarily impermissible viewpoint-based distinctions drawn by the government may be sustained where the government itself speaks or where it uses private speakers to transmit its message."[245] One chief reason for this rule is the government's "accountability inherent in the political process: ... where the government itself is responsible, and therefore accountable, for the message that its speech sends, the danger ordinarily involved in governmental viewpoint-based choices is not present."[246]

240 *Id.* at 40.

241 *See* EEOC v. Mitsubishi Motor Mfg. of Am., Inc., 960 F. Supp. 164, 167 n. 2 (C.D. Ill. 1997); Julian N. Eule & Jonathan D. Varat, *Transporting First Amendment Norms to the Private Sector: With Every Wish There Comes a Curse*, 45 UCLA L. Rev. 1537, 1602 & n. 281 (1998) (noting this understanding, though observing that "[t]he public educational institution may be an exception to this rule").

242 *See* Pleasant Grove City, Utah v. Summum, 555 U.S. 460, 467 (2009) ("The Free Speech Clause restricts government regulation of private speech; it does not regulate government speech."); Johanns v. Livestock Mktg. Ass'n, 544 U.S. 550, 553 (2005) (noting that "the Government's own speech ... is exempt from ... scrutiny" under the Free Speech Clause). This includes the ordinary restrictions on compelled speech, which do not apply "to situations where the government imposes an excise tax on private citizens and then uses the money to speak in the name of the government itself." R.J. Reynolds Tobacco Co. v. Shewry, 423 F.3d 906, 917 (9th Cir. 2005), *cert. denied*, 546 U.S. 1176 (2006).

243 Rosenberger, 515 U.S. at 833; *accord* Downs v. L.A. Unified Sch. Dist., 228 F.3d 1003, 1013 (9th Cir. 2000) ("[W]hen a public high school is the speaker, its control of its own speech is not subject to the constraints of constitutional safeguards and forum analysis, but instead is measured by practical considerations applicable to any individual's choice of how to convey oneself: among other things, content, timing, and purpose."), *cert. denied*, 532 U.S. 994 (2001).

244 Summum, 555 U.S. at 468. In particular, the government may "refus[e] to fund activities, including speech, which are specifically excluded from the scope of the project funded." Rust v. Sullivan, 500 U.S. 173, 194–5 (1991).

245 Sons of Confederate Veterans, Inc. *ex rel.* Griffin v. Comm'n of Va. Dep't of Motor Vehicles, 288 F.3d 610, 618 (4th Cir. 2002), *reh'g en banc denied*, 305 F.3d 241 (4th Cir. 2002).

246 *Id.*

When it comes to religious expression, however, what most certainly can constrain government speech, as opposed to private speech, is the Establishment Clause.[247] It is this very consideration, in fact, that can make the private-government speech distinction so consequential when it comes to religious expression. If the religious speech is deemed private, then the government is bound by the Free Speech Clause but is largely unconstrained by the Establishment Clause.[248] However, if the speech is deemed governmental, then the government is bound by the Establishment Clause but is essentially liberated from the Free Speech Clause.[249]

It is a critical threshold task, therefore, to determine whether any given expression alleged to be religious in nature is government speech or private speech. The task is not always a simple one – "the 'government speech' doctrine is still relatively new, and its precise contours are uncertain"[250] – and even the Supreme Court has acknowledged that "[t]here may be situations in which it is difficult to tell whether a government entity is speaking on its own behalf or is providing a forum for private speech."[251] The task is made only more difficult by the reality that there may coexist government and private speech in the same space,[252] that there may be a category of hybrid private-governmental speech,[253] and finally, that the government may be deemed to speak in a variety of ways. The government can, of course, speak for itself, as it does when it enacts a law or policy or directly operates a program. But it also can enlist otherwise private speakers to convey its message,[254] such as when it places the state motto on license plates[255] or when it disburses funding and specifically wishes to subsidize, by the funding, the transmission of its message.[256] Lastly, and sometimes the most difficult to assess, it can encourage or facilitate what is otherwise (and perhaps still seemingly) private speech and do so to such

247 *See* Summum, 555 U.S. at 468 ("[G]overnment speech must comport with the Establishment Clause."); Rosenberger, 515 U.S. at 841 [noting the "critical difference 'between *government* speech endorsing religion, which the Establishment Clause forbids, and *private* speech endorsing religion, which the Free Speech and Free Exercise Clauses protect'" (quoting *Mergens*, 496 U.S. at 250 (plurality opinion))].

248 "The Free Speech Clause restricts government regulation of private speech" [Pleasant Grove City, Utah v. Summum, 555 U.S. 460, 467 (2009)], and "*private* speech endorsing religion ... [is protected by] the Free Speech and Free Exercise Clauses" [Bd. of Educ. of Westside Cmty. Schs. v. Mergens, 496 U.S. 226, 250 (1990) (plurality opinion)].

249 *See* Summum, 555 U.S. at 467, 468 (noting that "[t]he Free Speech Clause ... does not regulate government speech" but that "government speech must comport with the Establishment Clause").

250 Tex Div., Sons of Confederate Veterans, Inc. v. Vandergriff, No. A-11-CA-1049, 2013 WL 1562758, at *13 (W.D. Tex. Apr. 12, 2013) (unpublished), *rev'd on other grounds*, 759 F.3d 588 (5th Cir. 2014), *cert. granted*, 135 S. Ct. 752 (2014).

251 Summum, 555 U.S. at 470.

252 *See* Freedom from Religion Found., Inc. v. City of Warren, Mich., 707 F.3d 686, 697 (6th Cir. 2013) (noting that "the lawn of a statehouse may serve as a forum for the announcement of an official government proclamation *and* a political rally" and recognizing that "the mere existence of private speakers in a particular space does not transform all speech in all parts of the space into private speech").

253 *See* ACLU of N.C. v. Tata, 742 F.3d 563, 568 (4th Cir. 2014) ("recogniz[ing] that speech may be not purely government or private but instead implicate both"); W.V. Ass'n of Club Owners Fraternal Servs., Inc. v. Musgrave, 553 F.3d 292, 298–300 (4th Cir. 2009) (finding hybrid speech).

254 *See* Summum, 555 U.S. at 468.

255 *See* Wooley v. Maynard, 430 U.S. 705 (1977). In a unfunded situation, such as the license plate motto at issue in *Wooley*, the private party clearly retains a free speech interest independent of the government speech. *See id.* at 715.

256 *See* Rosenberger, 515 U.S. at 833; Harvey v. Veneman, 396 F.3d 28, 42–3 (1st Cir. 2005).

an extent that the speech may be ultimately attributed to the government, even though its apparent relationship to the speech is attenuated.

With regard to religious expression in particular, the private-government speech distinction takes on unparalleled significance because it directly intersects with the endorsement test and, in certain contexts, the coercion prohibitions of the Establishment Clause. Under the endorsement test, the government may not speak or act in ways that a reasonable observer would perceive as having the principal or primary purpose or effect of endorsing or disfavoring religion[257] or, more generally, as "appearing to take a position on questions of religious belief or ... 'making adherence to a religion relevant in any way to a person's standing in the political community.'"[258] Under the prohibition on coercion, the government may not directly compel participation in religious programs[259] or compel religious profession or observance,[260] may not impose legal penalties on persons because they claim adherence to a particular religion or to no religion,[261] and, at least in the public-school setting, may not have a meaningful hand in the effective compulsion of persons to participate in religious activities.[262] If speech is truly private, then neither endorsement nor coercion is a constitutional concern. If speech is deemed governmental, though, whether it emanates from an official or a private individual at the behest of government, then these limitations can apply. Of course, under the endorsement test, part of what makes the observer "reasonable" is an appreciation of the history, context, and dynamic behind the challenged expression, and this may very well include a reasonable ability to distinguish between private and government speech in the first instance.

Instructive, regarding both the analysis of the speech and the consequences of the resulting determination, are the cases of *Santa Fe Independent School District v. Doe*[263] and *Pleasant Grove City, Utah v. Summum*.[264] In *Santa Fe*, the Supreme Court examined the practice of having a prayer delivered by a student, selected by the student body, prior to a public high school's football games. Although the student ordinarily would have been a private speaker or a speaker whose expression would not have been attributable to the government, the Court found that the circumstances under which the

257 *See* Cnty. of Allegheny v. ACLU Greater Pittsburgh Chapter, 492 U.S. 573, 592–3 (1989); Green v. Haskell Cnty. Bd. of Comm'rs, 568 F.3d 784, 799–800 (10th Cir. 2009).

258 Cnty. of Allegheny, 492 U.S. at 594 [quoting Lynch v. Donnelly, 465 U.S. 668, 687 (1984) (O'Connor, J., concurring)].

259 *See, e.g.*, Warner v. Orange Cnty. Dep't of Prob., 115 F.3d 1068, 1075 (2d Cir. 1996); Kerr v. Farrey, 95 F.3d 472, 476–80 (7th Cir. 1996); Griffen v. Coughlin, 673 N.E.2d 98 (N.Y. 1996), *cert. denied*, 519 U.S. 1054 (1997).

260 *See* Torcaso v. Watkins, 367 U.S. 488, 492–6 (1961) (invalidating state constitutional requirement of theistic profession to hold office); Anderson v. Laird, 466 F.2d 283, 283–4 (D.C. Cir. 1972) (*per curiam*) (holding that the federal military academies' chapel attendance requirement violated the First Amendment), *cert. denied*, 409 U.S. 1076 (1972); *see generally* Sch. Dist. of Abington Twp., Pa. v. Schempp, 374 U.S. 203, 223 (1963); Zorach v. Clauson, 343 U.S. 306, 314 (1952).

261 *See* Venters, 123 F.3d at 970; Doe v. Harlan Cnty. Sch. Dist., 96 F. Supp. 2d 667, 679 (E.D. Ky. 2000); Moore v. Gaston Cnty. Bd. of Educ., 357 F. Supp. 1037, 1043 (W.D.N.C. 1973); *see also* Warsoldier v. Woodford, 418 F.3d 989, 996 (9th Cir. 2005) ("[P]unishments to coerce a religious adherent to forgo her or his religious beliefs is an infringement on religious exercise.").

262 *See* Santa Fe Indep. Sch. Dist. v. Doe, 530 U.S. 290 (2000); Lee v. Weisman, 505 U.S. 577 (1992). For further analysis of the prohibition on coercion, *see* Chapter 4.C.2.

263 530 U.S. 290 (2000).

264 555 U.S. 460 (2009), and, on remand, Summum v. Pleasant Grove City, No. 2:05CV638 DAK, 2010 WL 2330336 (D. Utah Jun. 3, 2010) (unpublished).

student delivered the prayer resulted in government, rather than private, speech. In particular, the student's selection and authorization to deliver a prayer took place pursuant to a school policy that provided a forum only for the one student, and the prayer was delivered at a school-sponsored event on school property using the school's public address system.[265] In turn, as expression for which the government was responsible, a reasonable observer would perceive that the school encouraged and approved of the student's prayer, thus running afoul of the endorsement test.[266] At the same time, the school's action involved impermissible coercion insofar as some students had to attend the event, and others doubtless felt pressure to attend,[267] and those in attendance likely experienced pressure "to participate in an act of public worship."[268]

A very different outcome resulted in the *Summum* case, which involved a municipality's refusal to allow a private group to place a permanent monument in a city park populated by other privately donated monuments. The private group's monument contained religious content, as did at least one of the monuments (which included the Ten Commandments) already in the park. Accordingly, the group alleged that not allowing its monument in the park constituted governmental discrimination against private speech and, after losing on that claim before the Supreme Court, argued on remand that the government's continued exclusion of the group's monument, coupled with its retention of the Ten Commandments monument, violated the Establishment Clause. On the free speech question, the Supreme Court determined that the monuments in the park were government and not private speech. Conceding that "[t]here may be situations in which it is difficult to tell whether a government entity is speaking on its own behalf or is providing a forum for private speech … [p]ermanent monuments displayed on public property typically represent government speech."[269] Correspondingly, the monument donation and selection process was not some kind of designated or other public forum in which private expression generally could not be subject to discrimination; thus the group's free speech rights were not implicated much less infringed.[270] On remand, the private group lodged an Establishment Clause challenge, essentially arguing that either the Ten Commandments monument must be removed or its monument must be accepted. The district court, however, found that the inclusion of the Ten Commandments was acceptable under the Supreme Court's ruling in *Van Orden v. Perry*,[271] in which five justices – four as a plurality and a fifth concurring in the judgment – agreed that the Establishment Clause was not violated by a Ten Commandments monument on public grounds in light of the independent historical, nonreligious significance of

265 *See* Santa Fe, 530 U.S. at 302–8.

266 *See id.* at 308.

267 *See id.* at 311–12.

268 *Id.* at 312.

269 Summum, 555 U.S. at 470. "Just as government-commissioned and government-financed monuments speak for the government, so do privately financed and donated monuments that the government accepts and displays to the public on government land." *Id.* at 470–1.

270 *See id.* at 478–80. "[I]t is hard to imagine how a public park could be opened up for the installation of permanent monuments by every person or group wishing to engage in that form of expression." *Id.* at 479. "[I]f public parks were considered to be traditional public forums for the purpose of erecting privately donated monuments, most parks would have little choice but to refuse all such donations. And where the application of forum analysis would lead almost inexorably to closing of the forum, it is obvious that forum analysis is out of place." *Id.* at 480.

271 545 U.S. 677 (2005).

the monument.[272] As for the exclusion of the private group's monument, the district court found that there was "no evidence that anyone in [the municipal] government had any idea what [the group]'s religious beliefs were, and thus it cannot be said that the … government demonstrated a preference for one religion over another."[273]

Lower courts, for their part, have attempted to clarify the inquiry into whether speech is private or governmental by identifying several factors or considerations. For example, the Tenth Circuit, borrowing from the Eighth Circuit, has developed a four-factor analysis to determine whether speech is ultimately attributable to a private party or to the government: "(1) whether the 'central purpose' of the project is to promote the views of the government or of the private speaker; (2) whether the government exercised 'editorial control' over the content of the speech; (3) whether the government was the 'literal speaker'; and (4) whether 'ultimate responsibility' for the project rested with the government."[274] Using these or similar factors, courts have fairly consistently found that, for example, winter holiday displays, including nativity scenes and menorahs, are typically government speech where they are owned, maintained, or controlled by the government and are erected by it on government property, with the consequence being that private speech can be excluded but that the displays must comply with the Establishment Clause.[275] Courts also have held, with somewhat less obvious consistency, that a state's decision to allow a private highway patrol association to erect memorial crosses on public roadsides gave rise to government speech that violated the Establishment Clause[276] but that a government board's decision not to allow a private organization to erect a cross on a traditional public forum involved only private speech, which the board had infringed and which could not violate the Establishment Clause.[277] Other examples of government speech have included the determination of curricula and likely the selection of textbooks for public schools,[278] the creation of a town website,[279] the inclusion and removal of the books in a public-school library,[280] and the operation of a specialty license

272 *See* Summum, 2010 WL 2330336, at *3 [citing Van Orden, 545 U.S. at 690 (plurality), and *id.* at 701–3 (Breyer, J., concurring in the judgment)].

273 *Id.*

274 Fleming v. Jefferson Cnty. Sch. Dist. R-1, 298 F.3d 918, 923 (10th Cir. 2002) [quoting Wells v. City & Cnty. of Denver, 257 F.3d 1132, 1141 (10th Cir. 2001), *cert. denied*, 534 U.S. 997 (2001)], *cert. denied*, 537 U.S. 1110 (2003). The antecedent Eighth Circuit decision is Knights of the Ku Klux Klan v. Curators of Univ. of Mo., 203 F.3d 1085 (8th Cir. 2000), *cert. denied*, 531 U.S. 814 (2000). The Fourth Circuit subsequently found the Tenth Circuit's factors "instructive" though without "conclud[ing] that the[y] … constitute an exhaustive or always-applicable list." Sons of Confederate Veterans, 288 F.3d at 619.

275 *See, e.g.*, Freedom from Religion Found., Inc. v. City of Warren, Mich., 707 F.3d 686, 692–5, 696–7 (6th Cir. 2013); Wells v. City & Cnty. of Denver, 257 F.3d 1132, 1140–52 (10th Cir. 2001), *cert. denied*, 534 U.S. 997 (2001).

276 *See* Am. Atheists, Inc. v. Davenport, 616 F.3d 1145 (10th Cir. 2010), *amended on denial of reh'g*, 637 F.3d 1095 (10th Cir. 2010), *cert. denied*, 132 S. Ct. 12 (2011). *See also* Green v. Haskell Cnty. Bd. of Comm'rs, 568 F.3d 784 (10th Cir) (holding that a county board's decision to place a Ten Commandments monument on the county courthouse lawn yielded government speech that violated the Establishment Clause where several commissioners endorsed the religious motivation underlying the decision).

277 *See* Capitol Square Review & Advisory Bd. v. Pinette, 515 U.S. 753, 760–70 (1995) (plurality opinion).

278 *See* Chiras v. Miller, 432 F.3d 606, 611–18 (5th Cir. 2005).

279 *See* Sutliffe v. Epping Sch. Dist., 584 F.3d 314, 331 (1st Cir. 2009).

280 *See* ACLU of Fla., Inc. v. Miami-Dade Cnty. Sch. Bd., 557 F.3d 1177, 1202–3 (11th Cir. 2009), *cert. denied*, 558 U.S. 1023 (2009). However, "[t]he question of what standard applies to school library book removal decisions is unresolved." *Id.* at 1202.

plate program,[281] though courts have yielded different outcomes regarding specialty plate programs based partly on factual differences among the programs.[282] By comparison, it has been held that a school teacher on school property – easily a source or conduit of government speech – engaged in private speech when participating in a religious group's meetings after school hours[283] and that a school board member (and parent of a graduate) likewise engaged in private speech when spontaneously delivering a prayer during a commencement address[284] such that the expression in both instances did not and could not violate the Establishment Clause.[285]

281 *See* ACLU of Tenn. v. Bredesen, 441 F.3d 370, 375–7 (6th Cir. 2006), *cert. denied*, 548 U.S. 906 (2006).

282 *Compare* Bredesen, 441 F.3d at 375–7 (government speech), *with* Sons of Confederate Veterans, Inc. *ex rel.* Griffin v. Comm'r of Va. Dep't of Motor Vehicles, 288 F.3d 610 (4th Cir. 2002) (mixed government-private speech), *with* Roach v. Stouffer, 560 F.3d 860, 868 (8th Cir. 2009), *and* Choose Life of Ill., Inc. v. White, 547 F.3d 853, 863–4 (7th Cir. 2008) (private speech), *cert. denied*, 558 U.S. 816 (2009), *and* Ariz. Life Coalition v. Stanton, 515 F.3d 956, 965–7 (9th Cir. 2008) (private speech), *cert. denied*, 555 U.S. 815 (2008). By comparison, courts have normally held that vanity plate programs create a forum for private speech. *See, e.g.*, Byrne v. Rutledge, 623 F.3d 46 (2d Cir. 2010); Lewis v. Wilson, 253 F.3d 1077, 1079 (8th Cir. 2001), *cert. denied*, 535 U.S. 986 (2002).

283 *See* Wigg v. Sioux Falls Sch. Dist. 49-5, 382 F.3d 807, 815 (8th Cir. 2004).

284 *See* Doe *ex rel.* Doe v. Sch. Dist. of City of Norfolk, 340 F.3d 605, 612–13 (8th Cir. 2003).

285 *Cf.* Borden v. Sch. Dist. of Twp. of E. Brunswick, 523 F.3d 153, 165–71, 175–9 (3d Cir. 2008) (finding that public high school teacher-coach's participation in pregame football team prayers, being government employee speech, violated the Establishment Clause and was not shielded by the Free Speech Clause), *cert. denied*, 555 U.S. 1212 (2009).

# 7 The Definition of Religion

## A. The Current Lack of an Authoritative Definition

At most points in this book, it is essentially assumed that the belief system of a given claimant is in fact a "religion" within the meaning of the Free Exercise Clause or that the object of an alleged government establishment involves "religion" under the Establishment Clause. Much of the time, both for this book and for litigation, this turns out to be a fair and workable assumption because the belief systems at issue are often widely recognized as being religious. Occasionally, however, government officials are confronted with so novel or unconventional a belief system – typically as part of a religious freedom claim and disproportionately, it seems, in the prison context – that they must inquire whether or not the beliefs amount to a legally cognizable religion as a threshold matter. In the coming decades, as the diversity and idiosyncrasy of religious beliefs and practices in the United States continue to grow, such inquiries are likely only to increase.[1]

As it turns out, "religion" appears to be one of the few key terms of the First Amendment, if not the only key term of that provision, that the contemporary Supreme Court has not authoritatively defined in a comprehensive or systematic manner.[2] The most that the Court has said, in relatively dated cases of unknown or dubious precedential authority, is that

1 *See* Rebecca French, *Shopping for Religion: The Change in Everyday Religious Practice and Its Importance to the Law*, 51 Buff. L. Rev. 127, 127–8 (2003) (noting that "[t]he last thirty-five years have seen an exponential increase in American pluralism, and in the number and diversity of religions" including "an explosion of New Religions, break-away churches from traditional denominations and immigrant religions from Asia"; that "individual practitioners now emphasize spiritual identity and personal choice … routinely shop[ping] for a new religion when relocating to a different part of the country or creat[ing] their own personal practice, picking and choosing from a wide variety of possibilities"; and that "many of the basic functions of religion such as a connection to the divine, counseling, and ritual ceremonies are being comfortably displaced by other activities").

2 *See* United States v. Meyers, 906 F. Supp. 1494, 1500 (D. Wyo. 1995) (commenting that "the Supreme Court has done little to identify positively what 'religion' is for First Amendment purposes"), *aff'd*, 95 F.3d 1475 (10th Cir. 1996), *cert. denied*, 522 U.S. 1006 (1997); Daniel O. Conkle, The Religion Clauses 60 (2003) ("Remarkably, … the Supreme Court has never adopted a constitutional definition [of religion] as such and, indeed, it has offered no more than partial and sometimes conflicting suggestions."); Michael W. McConnell, John H. Garvey & Thomas C. Berg, Religion and the Constitution 762 (3d ed. 2011) (observing that the Court "has never provided an authoritative definition of the constitutional term"); Jonathan C. Lipson, *On Balance: Religious Liberty and Third-Party Harms*, 84 Minn. L. Rev. 589, 597 (2000) (remarking that "the Supreme Court has been reluctant to define religion" and "has circled around the issue for over one hundred years").

religion involves a person's relationship to God[3] or to "the ultimate mystery of the universe."[4] Conversely, the Court has explained that religion under the First Amendment does *not* encompass "purely secular considerations" or "philosophical and personal" beliefs such as those held by Henry David Thoreau,[5] but this category of exclusion remains elusive as well.[6]

Even among the multitude of other Article III judges past and present, only a modest number have ventured into this definitional abyss and yielded substantial (and sometimes quite different) definitions.[7] To be sure, it is not uncommon for lower courts, when faced with an allegedly religious belief system that is unknown or extremely unusual, simply to assume that the beliefs are religious for sake of the litigation, particularly when the case is then resolved against the claimant on some other basis.[8] Legal scholars, by comparison, have produced an abundance of literature on defining religion,[9] though,

3 *See* Davis v. Beason, 133 U.S. 333, 342 (1890) ("The term 'religion' has reference to one's views of his relations to his Creator, and to the obligations they impose of reverence for his being and character, and of obedience to his will."), *overruled on other grounds by* Romer v. Evans, 517 U.S. 620, 634 (1996); Reynolds v. United States, 98 U.S. (8 Otto) 145, 163–4 (1879) (similar, invoking the writings of James Madison and Thomas Jefferson).

4 Minersville Sch. Dist. v. Gobitis, 310 U.S. 586, 593 (1940) ("the affirmative pursuit of one's convictions about the ultimate mystery of the universe and man's relation to it"), *overruled on other grounds by* W. Va. State Bd. of Educ. v. Barnette, 319 U.S. 624 (1943).

5 *See* Wisconsin v. Yoder, 406 U.S. 205, 216 (1972).

6 *See* Moore-King v. Cnty. of Chesterfield, Va., 708 F.3d 560, 571 (4th Cir. 2013) [noting that "*Yoder* provides guidance on the distinction between a religion and a way of life" and that "defining the borders between the personal and philosophical on one side, and the religious on the other 'present[s] a most delicate question'" (quoting Yoder, 406 U.S. at 215)].

7 *See, e.g.*, Africa v. Pennsylvania, 662 F.2d 1025, 1031–6 (3d Cir. 1982), *cert. denied*, 456 U.S. 908 (1982); Malnak v. Yogi, 592 F.2d 197, 200–10 (3d Cir. 1979) (Adams, J., concurring in the result); Founding Church of Scientology of Wash., D.C. v. United States, 409 F.2d 1146, 1160 (D.C. Cir. 1969), *cert. denied*, 396 U.S. 963 (1969); United States v. Meyers, 906 F. Supp. 1494, 1502–3 (D. Wyo. 1995), *aff'd*, 95 F.3d 1475, 1482–4 (10th Cir. 1996), *cert. denied*, 522 U.S. 1006 (1997).

8 *See, e.g.*, Wells v. City & County of Denver, 257 F.3d 1132, 1152 (10th Cir. 2001) (atheism), *cert. denied*, 534 U.S. 997 (2001); Kalka v. Hawk, 215 F.3d 90, 98 (D.C. Cir. 2000) (humanism); *In re* Long Term Admin. Segregation of Inmates Designated as Five Percenters, 174 F.3d 464, 468 (4th Cir. 1999) ("Five Percenters"), *cert. denied sub nom.* Mickle v. Moore, 528 U.S. 874 (1999); Kunselman v. W. Reserve Local Sch. Dist., 70 F.3d 931, 931 (6th Cir. 1995) (Satanism); Brown v. Woodland Joint Unified Sch. Dist., 27 F.3d 1373, 1378 (9th Cir. 1994) (Wicca); McCabe v. Arave, 827 F.2d 634, 637 n. 2 (9th Cir. 1987) ("Church Jesus Christ Christian"); United States v. Middleton, 690 F.2d 820, 824 (11th Cir. 1982) ("Ethiopian Zion Coptic Church"), *cert. denied*, 460 U.S. 1051 (1983); Ciempa v. Jones, 745 F. Supp. 2d 1171, 1187 (N.D. Okla. 2010) ("Five Percent Nation" or "Nation of Gods and Earths"), *aff'd*, Nos. 12–5087 & 12–5088, 511 Fed. App'x 781 (10th Cir. Feb. 20, 2013) (unpublished); Winford v. Frank, No. 06-C-1000, 2008 WL 359728, at *5 n. 2 (E.D. Wis. Feb. 8, 2008) (unpublished) (Satanism); Lepp v. Gonzales, No. C-05-0566, 2005 WL 1867723, at *9 (N.D. Cal. Aug. 2, 2005) (unpublished) ("Universal Life Church"), *aff'd sub nom.* Harris v. Mukasey, No. 05-16695, 265 Fed. App'x. 461 (9th Cir. Jan. 22, 2008) (unpublished); Kaufman v. Frank, No. 03-C-27-C, 2003 WL 23277423, at *7 (W.D. Wis. Mar. 27, 2003) (atheism); Haff v. Cooke, 923 F. Supp. 1104, 1108 (E.D. Wis. 1996) (Identity Christianity); Faheem-El v. Lane, No. 82 C 4404, 1984 WL 717, at *2 n. 1 (N.D. Ill. June 29, 1984) ("El Rukn Science Temple") (unpublished); *see also* MICHAEL WOLF ET AL., RELIGION IN THE WORKPLACE: A COMPREHENSIVE GUIDE TO RELIGIOUS DISCRIMINATION AND ACCOMMODATION 31 (1993) (noting in the administrative context that, "[i]n practice, when an employee attaches the appellation 'religious' to a set of beliefs, the courts are reluctant to dig beneath the surface").

9 *See, e.g.*, Andrew W. Austin, *Faith and the Constitutional Definition of Religion*, 22 CUMB. L. REV. 1 (1991); Donald L. Beschle, *Does a Broad Free Exercise Right Require a Narrow Definition of "Religion,"* 39 HAST. CONST. L.Q. 357 (2012); Anita Bowser, *Delimiting Religion in the Constitution: A Classification Problem*, 11 VAL. U. L. REV. 163 (1977); A. Stephen Boyan, Jr., *Defining Religion in Operational and Institutional Terms*, 116 U. PA. L. REV. 479 (1968); Jesse H. Choper, *Defining "Religion" in the First Amendment*, 1982 U. ILL. L. REV. 579 (1982); James M. Donovan, *God Is as God Does: Law, Anthropology,*

of course, their proposals carry no formal weight in a court of law, which may explain their willingness to devise definitional schemes and, in turn, the relative volume of their work. As one commentator has observed, "[s]cholars may debate definitions of religions at leisure, but when judges do so, their definitions are authoritative acts of state power."[10]

It should be noted that unlike some other components of a free exercise claim,[11] the meaning of "religion" under the Free Exercise Clause appears to correspond or be equivalent to the terms "religion" under the Religious Freedom Restoration Act (RFRA)[12] and "religious" under the Religious Land Use and Institutionalized Persons Act (RLUIPA),[13] which is significant because a large portion of federal religious freedom claims today are based on RFRA or RLUIPA either in addition to or in place of the Free Exercise Clause.[14] Perhaps based on a concern that a different definition could create independent First Amendment problems, in fact, a number of federal and state laws and their enforcement rely heavily and broadly on the apparent meaning and scope of "religion" under the Free Exercise Clause as found in various judicial decisions.[15]

*and the Definition of "Religion,"* 6 SETON HALL CONST. L.J. 23 (1995); Dmitry N. Feofanov, *Defining Religion: An Immodest Proposal*, 23 HOFSTRA L. REV. 309 (1994); George C. Freeman III, *The Misguided Search for the Constitutional Definition of "Religion,"* 71 GEO. L.J. 1519 (1983); Kent Greenawalt, *Religion as a Concept in Constitutional Law*, 72 CAL. L. REV. 753 (1984); Stanley Ingber, *Religion or Ideology: A Needed Clarification of the Religion Clauses*, 41 STAN. L. REV. 233 (1989); John C. Knechtle, *If We Don't Know What It Is, How Do We Know if It's Established?* 41 BRANDEIS L.J. 521 (2003); Val D. Ricks, *To God God's, to Caesar Caesar's, and to Both the Defining of Religion*, 26 CREIGHTON L. REV. 1053 (1993); Jane M. Ritter, *The Legal Definition of Religion: From Eating Cat Food to White Supremacy*, 20 TOURO L. REV. 751 (2004); Karen Sandrik, *Towards a Modern Definition of Religion*, 85 U. DET. MERCY L. REV. 561 (2008); L. Scott Smith, *Constitutional Meanings of 'Religion' Past and Present: Explorations in Definition and Theory*, 14 TEMP. POL. & CIV. RTS. L. REV. 89 (2004); C. John Sommerville, *Defining Religion and the Present Supreme Court*, 6 U. FLA. J.L. & PUB. POL'Y (1994); Jeffrey Omar Usman, *Defining Religion: The Struggle to Define Religion under the First Amendment and the Contributions and Insights of Other Disciplines of Study Including Theology, Psychology, Sociology, the Arts, and Anthropology*, 83 N.D. L. REV. 123 (2007); Jeffrey L. Oldham, *Note, Constitutional "Religion": A Survey of First Amendment Definitions of Religion*, 6 TEX. FORUM ON CIV. LIB. & CIV. RTS. 117 (2001); *Note, Toward a Constitutional Definition of Religion*, 91 HARV. L. REV. 1056 (1978).

10 BETTE NOVIT EVANS, INTERPRETING THE FREE EXERCISE OF RELIGION: THE CONSTITUTION AND AMERICAN PLURALISM 48 (1997).

11 *See* Chapter 5.C.3 (discussing the substantial burden requirement).

12 Pub. L. No. 103–141, 107 Stat. 1488 (Nov. 16, 1993) (codified as amended at 42 U.S.C. §§ 2000bb to 2000bb-4). *See* United States v. Meyers, 906 F. Supp. 1494, 1502–3 (D. Wyo. 1995) (holding that "religion" under preamendment RFRA is identical to "religion" under the First Amendment), *aff'd*, 95 F.3d 1475, 1482–4 (10th Cir. 1996), *cert. denied*, 522 U.S. 1006 (1997).

13 Pub. L. No. 106–274, 114 Stat. 803–07 (Sept. 22, 2000) (codified at 42 U.S.C. §§ 2000cc to 2000cc-5). *See* Marria v. Broaddus, No. 97 Civ. 8297 NRB, 2003 WL 21782633, at *11–*12 (S.D.N.Y. Jul. 31, 2003) (conducting simultaneous and identical inquiry into whether claimant's beliefs were "religious" under RLUIPA and the Free Exercise Clause).

14 RLRA and RLUIPA do define "religious exercise" in a way that is broader than many free exercise interpretations. *See* 42 U.S.C. 42 U.S.C. § 2000cc-5(7)(A) (RLUIPA); *id.* § 2000bb-2(4) (RFRA) (incorporating RLUIPA's definition). But there is no textual indication that the meaning of "religion" under RFRA and "religious" under both statutes should differ from their constitutional meaning, acknowledging, of course, that the First Amendment uses the noun "religion" rather than the adjective "religious."

15 *See, e.g.*, 29 C.F.R. § 1605.1 (providing the U.S. Equal Employment Opportunity Commission's broad definition of religion for enforcement of Title VII the Civil Rights Act of 1964); MASS. GEN. LAWS ANN. ch. 151B, § 4, ¶ 1A (providing, for the state's employment discrimination law, that "the words 'creed or religion' mean any sincerely held religious beliefs, without regard to whether such beliefs are approved, espoused, prescribed or required by an established church or other religious institution or organization"). Conversely, many courts interpreting the federal Free Exercise Clause or comparable state constitutional

## B. Some Difficulties of Legally Defining Religion

The lack of an authoritative and meaningful definition of "religion" – a key constitutional term that has been part of extensive litigation for decades – is, as suggested earlier, rather anomalous. Most other operative terms in the First Amendment, such as "establishment,"[16] "free exercise,"[17] "speech,"[18] "peaceable assembly,"[19] and "petition,"[20] have been defined or delineated at least by individual justices if not by the Court itself.[21] Even the speech subterm "obscenity," the famous object of Justice Stewart's statement that "I know it when I see it,"[22] has its own three-part definition.[23]

provisions have taken their lead from the Supreme Court's broad interpretation of the Selective Service Act's conscientious objector provision in cases such as United States v. Seeger, 380 U.S. 163 (1965), and Welsh v. United States, 398 U.S. 333 (1970).

16 *See* Lee v. Weisman, 505 U.S. 577, 587–98 (1992) (nonpunitive coercion); Cnty. of Allegheny v. ACLU Greater Pittsburgh Chapter, 492 U.S. 573, 592–4 (1989) (endorsement); Larson v. Valente, 456 U.S. 228 (1982) (discrimination); Lemon v. Kurtzman, 403 U.S. 602, 612–13 (1971) (purpose, effect, and entanglement); Everson v. Bd. of Educ., 330 U.S. 1, 15–16 (1947) (listing a multitude of prohibitions).

17 *See* Locke v. Davey, 540 U.S. 712, 720 (2004) (indicating that free exercise encompasses the ability to engage in a "religious service or rite" without "criminal or civil sanctions" as well as the right of "ministers ... to participate in the political affairs of the community"); Hernandez v. Comm'r of Internal Revenue, 490 U.S. 680, 699 (1989) (stating that free exercise includes "the observation of a central religious belief or practice"); Employment Div. v. Smith, 494 U.S. 872, 877–82 (1990) [explaining that free exercise includes "the right to believe and profess whatever religious doctrine one desires," religious conduct that does not conflict with neutral laws of generally applicability, and religious conduct "in conjunction with other constitutional[ly] protect[ed] [liberties], such as freedom of speech and of the press or the right of parents to direct the education of their children" (citations omitted)]; Thomas v. Review Bd. of Ind. Employment Sec. Div., 450 U.S. 707, 717–18 (1981) (free exercise includes the ability to engage in "conduct mandated by religious belief" or not to engage in "conduct proscribed by a religious faith" without the resulting denial of an important government benefit); Wisconsin v. Yoder, 406 U.S. 205, 215–19 (1972) (finding, with regard to Old Order Amish, that free exercise can encompass an entire way of life).

18 In addition to "the spoken or written word," Texas v. Johnson, 491 U.S. 397, 404 (1989), First Amendment "speech" includes symbolic conduct accompanied by "[a]n intent to convey a particularized message ... and in the surrounding circumstances the likelihood [i]s great that the message would be understood by those who view it." Spence v. State of Washington, 418 U.S. 405, 410–11 (1974) (*per curiam*); *see also* Clark v. Cmty. for Creative Non-Violence, 468 U.S. 288, 294 (1984) ("[A] message may be delivered by conduct that is intended to be communicative and that, in context, would reasonably be understood by the viewer to be communicative.").

19 *See* United States v. Cruikshank, 92 U.S. (2 Otto) 542, 551–3 (1876).

20 *See* McDonald v. Smith, 42 U.S. 479, 486–90 (1985) (Brennan, J., concurring).

21 At least one commentator has written that the Court has also not defined the term "press." *See* Troy L. Booher, *Finding Religion for the First Amendment*, 38 John Marshall L. Rev. 469, 483 (2004). The Court has stated, however, that "[f]reedom of the press ... 'is not confined to newspapers and periodicals. It necessarily embraces pamphlets and leaflets.... The press in its historic connotation comprehends every sort of publication which affords a vehicle of information and opinion." Branzburg v. Hayes, 408 U.S. 665, 704 (1972) [quoting Lovell v. City of Griffin, 303 U.S. 444, 450 (1938)]; *see also* First Nat'l Bank of Boston v. Bellotti, 435 U.S. 765, 798–802 (1978) (Burger, C.J., concurring). This does appear to be a fairly developed definition, though concededly the notion of "definition" can itself be a contested, or at least relative, concept.

22 Jacobellis v. Ohio, 378 U.S. 184, 197 (1964) (Stewart, J., concurring).

23 *See* Miller v. California, 413 U.S. 15, 24 (1973) {explaining that a work can be deemed obscene if "'the average person, applying contemporary community standards' would find that the work, taken as a whole, appeals to the prurient interest; ... [if] the work depicts or describes, in a patently offensive way, sexual conduct specifically defined by the applicable state law; and ... [if] the work, taken as a whole, lacks serious literary, artistic, political, or scientific value" (citations omitted) [quoting Kois v. Wisconsin, 408 U.S. 229, 230 (1972)]}.

When it comes to defining "religion," however, the Court essentially "has demonstrated an aversion to the task."[24]

This void and its anomalous nature imply that the Court has sensed one or more serious difficulties attending this task.[25] If this is the case, then the Court is almost certainly right, and it is definitely not alone. At the extreme, some judges and scholars contend that "a succinct and comprehensive definition of … [religion] would appear to be a judicial impossibility."[26] According to one commentator, "there simply is no essence of religion, no single feature or set of features that all religions have in common and that distinguishes religion from everything else."[27] Others argue that the process of defining "religion" for legal purposes, across the board or even in a given case, not only is impossible but also can itself be a source of injustice and intolerance, necessarily excluding persons of faith who do not fit neatly within the framework of legal classification.[28] Still others argue that any judicial definition of "religion" would itself violate the First Amendment by fostering excessive entanglement with religion in violation of the Establishment Clause[29] or by encompassing some belief systems but not others,[30]

[24] Smith, *supra* note 9, at 91. Apparently, this was equally true over four decades ago. *See* United States v. Kuch, 288 F. Supp. 439, 443 (D.D.C. 1968) ("The dividing line between what is, and what is not, a religion is difficult to draw. The Supreme Court has given little guidance. Indeed, the Court appears to have avoided the problem with studied frequency in recent years.").

[25] It could be argued that this avoidance by the Supreme Court, in particular, stems from a lack of opportunity. The Court's own rule on granting review by writ of certiorari, for example, emphasizes the need for a split between or among federal or state appellate courts over an important federal legal issue (S. Ct. R. 10) or at least a lower court decision that decides "an important federal question in a way that conflicts with relevant decisions of th[e] [Supreme] Court" [*id.* 10(c)]. But some of this lack of opportunity reflects, rather than constrains, the Court's actions. Though it may be true that there is no definitive split (partly because not many courts have taken up the matter), the inability to conclude that a lower court decision has clearly contradicted the Supreme Court's precedents stems from the fact that these precedents themselves provide little guidance.

[26] Remmers v. Brewer, 361 F. Supp. 537, 540 (S.D. Iowa 1973), *aff'd*, 494 F.2d 1277 (8th Cir. 1974), *cert. denied*, 419 U.S. 1012 (1974), *see also* Alvarado v. City of San Jose, 94 F.3d 1223, 1227 (9th Cir. 1996) ("Attempting to define religion, in general and for the purposes of the Establishment Clause, is a notoriously difficult, if not impossible, task."); Booher, *supra* note 21 (arguing that "religion" should be contextually defined and that finding a single definition is neither possible nor productive); Freeman, *supra* note 9.

[27] Freeman, *supra* note 9, at 1565.

[28] *See, e.g.*, Winnifred Fallers Sullivan, The Impossibility of Religious Freedom (2005).

[29] *See, e.g.*, Andrews v. Va. Union Univ., No. 3:07CV447, 2008 WL 2096964, at *6 (E.D. Va. May 16, 2008) (unpublished) (noting, in relation to Title VII of the 1964 Civil Rights Act and its implementing regulations, that "[o]ne purpose of defining 'religion' so broadly is to minimize the need for judicial decisions on which particular beliefs and practices qualify as a 'religion' in order to avoid the excessive entanglement of church and state prohibited by the First Amendment"); William P. Marshall, *The Case Against the Constitutionally Compelled Free Exercise Exemption*, 40 Case W. Res. L. Rev. 357, 386–8 (1990).

[30] *See, e.g.*, Derek Davis, *The Courts and the Constitutional Meaning of "Religion": A History and Critique, in* The Role of Government in Monitoring and Regulating Religion in Public Life 89, 91 (James E. Wood, Jr. & Derek Davis, eds., 1993); Lipson, *supra* note 2, at 601; Ira C. Lupu, *Where Rights Begin: The Problem of Burdens on the Free Exercise of Religion*, 102 Harv. L. Rev. 933, 957–8 (1989); Jonathan Weiss, *Privilege, Posture and Protection: "Religion" in the Law*, 73 Yale L.J. 593, 604 (1964); Sharon L. Worthing, *"Religion" and "Religious Institutions" Under the First Amendment*, 7 Pepp. L. Rev. 313, 345–6 (1980); *cf.* Bd. of Educ. v. Barnette, 319 U.S. 624, 658 (1943) (Frankfurter, J., dissenting) ("Certainly this Court cannot be called upon to determine what claims of conscience should be recognized and what should be rejected as satisfying the 'religion' which the Constitution protects. That would indeed resurrect the very discriminatory treatment of religion which the Constitution sought forever to forbid.").

thereby according selective protection under the Free Exercise Clause in violation of the Establishment Clause's general bar on interreligious discrimination.[31]

It is unlikely, of course, that any of these categorical objections corresponds to or fully explains the reluctance of the Supreme Court, specifically, to define "religion." The impossibility argument, for example, is weakened by the Court's willingness to expound on other constitutional terms or concepts – such as "person,"[32] "cruel and unusual,"[33] and religion's companion term "establishment"[34] – that are by no means easy to define.[35] Moreover, the Court itself has acknowledged that "[a]lthough a determination of what is a 'religious' belief or practice entitled to constitutional protection may present a most delicate question, the very concept of ordered liberty precludes allowing every person to make his [or her] own standards on matters of conduct in which society as a whole has important interests."[36] Even less explanatory, it would seem, is the Establishment

31 *See* Bd. of Educ. v. Grumet, 512 U.S. 687, 703 (1994); Larson v. Valente, 456 U.S. 228, 244–6 (1982); Gillette v. United States, 401 U.S. 437, 449 (1971); Epperson v. Arkansas, 393 U.S. 97, 103–4 (1968); Everson v. Bd. of Educ., 330 U.S. 1, 15 (1947). More recently, the Court has stated that the government violates the constitutional mandate of neutrality when it "[m]anifest[s] a purpose to favor one faith over another." McCreary Cnty., Ky. v. ACLU of Ky., 545 U.S. 844, 860 (2005).

32 *See, e.g.*, Plyler v. Doe, 457 U.S. 202, 210 (1982) (includes illegal aliens); Roe v. Wade, 410 U.S. 113, 157–8 (1973) (excludes the unborn); Levy v. Louisiana, 391 U.S. 68, 70 (1968) (includes illegitimate children); South Carolina v. Katzenbach, 383 U.S. 301, 323–4 (1966) (excludes states); Michael D. Rivard, *Comment, Toward a General Theory of Constitutional Personhood: A Theory of Constitutional Personhood for Transgenic Humanoid Species*, 39 UCLA L. Rev. 1425, 1452 n. 103 (1992) (compiling Supreme Court cases holding that corporations are Fourteenth Amendment persons as to property rights).

33 *See, e.g.*, Gregg v. Georgia, 428 U.S. 153, 173 (1976) {"[P]ublic perceptions of standards of decency with respect to criminal sanctions are not conclusive. A penalty also must accord with the dignity of man,' which is the 'basic concept underlying the Eighth Amendment.' This means, at least, that the punishment not be 'excessive.' When a form of punishment in the abstract ... rather than in the particular ... is under consideration, the inquiry into 'excessiveness' has two aspects. First, the punishment must not involve the unnecessary and wanton infliction of pain. Second, the punishment must not be grossly out of proportion to the severity of the crime." (citations omitted) [quoting Trop v. Dulles, 356 U.S. 86, 100–1 (1958) (plurality opinion)]}.

34 *See, e.g.*, Cnty. of Allegheny v. ACLU Greater Pittsburgh Chapter, 492 U.S. 573, 593–4 (1989) [announcing that an establishment occurs when the "government ... convey[s] or attempt[s] to convey a message that religion or a particular religious belief is *favored* or *preferred*" (original quotation marks omitted)]; Tex. Monthly, Inc. v. Bullock, 489 U.S. 1, 9 (1989) (stating that an establishment exists when the government "place[s] its ... coercive authority ... behind a single religious faith or behind religious belief in general, compelling nonadherents to support the practices or proselytizing of favored religious organizations"); Lemon v. Kurtzman, 403 U.S. 602, 612–13 (1971) {explaining that an establishment arises when a law lacks "a secular legislative purpose," when "its principal or primary effect" is to advance or inhibit religion, or when it "foster[s] 'an excessive government entanglement with religion'" [quoting Walz v. Tax Comm'n, 397 U.S. 664, 674 (1970)]}; Everson v. Bd. of Educ., 330 U.S. 1, 15–16 (1947) (enumerating a list of criteria for discerning an establishment). The Court has fashioned this composite definition, moreover, even while recognizing that the First Amendment, just as it includes no definition of religion, "contains no textual definition of 'establishment,' and the term is certainly not self-defining." *McCreary Cnty.*, 545 U.S. at 874–5.

35 It is true, of course, that there are other constitutional terms that the Court has avoided defining, but often these avoidances are characterized as constitutional obligations pursuant to the separation of powers or federalism. *See, e.g.*, Taylor v. Beckham, 178 U.S. 548, 578 (1900) (referring to the guaranty of a "republican form of government" in U.S. Const. art. IV, § 4, and explaining that "[i]t was long ago settled that the enforcement of this guaranty belonged to the political department").

36 Wisconsin v. Yoder, 406 U.S. 205, 215–16 (1972) (footnote omitted); *see also* Founding Church of Scientology of Wash., D.C. v. United States, 409 F.2d 1146, 1160 (D.C. Cir. 1969) ["Though litigation of the question whether a given group or set of beliefs is or is not religious is a delicate business, our legal system sometimes requires it." (footnote omitted)]; Dmitry N. Feofanov, *Defining Religion: An Immodest*

Clause objection. The very inclusion of the word in the Constitution's text is a strong warrant for its meaningful interpretation,[37] with the Court's job being not to deem it untouchable but to reconcile it with the remainder of the text.[38] Additionally, assuming that religion has the same scope under both religion clauses, if a given belief system were not considered a "religion" under the Free Exercise Clause, then this exclusion presumably would not be cognizable as discrimination among "religion[s]" under the Establishment Clause.

However, although these categorical objections likely would not be embraced by the Court, they do point to larger issues of potential concern, ones, in fact, that are hardly confined to the First Amendment or the judiciary. Even in disciplines or fields outside of law, which are not directly constrained by the consequentialist considerations that must be part of the legal definitional process, efforts to define "religion" have necessarily "struggled to avoid, on the one hand, the Scylla of hard, sharp, particularistic definition and, on the other hand, the Charybdis of meaningless generalities."[39] In turn, the definitional assertions among philosophers, social scientists, and others are quite varied.

Some scholars do offer definitions, although they are rarely fully congruent with one another and often may be of limited utility outside their disciplines of origin. One philosopher, for example, proposes that "a religion is a conceptual system that provides an interpretation of the world and the place of human beings in it, bases an account of how life should be lived given that interpretation, and expresses this interpretation and lifestyle in a set of rituals, institutions, and practices."[40] A pair of historians, by comparison, define religion as "a system of beliefs, rituals, and practices, usually institutionalized in one manner or another, which connects this world with the beyond" and "provides the bridge that allows humans to approach the divine, the universal life force that both encompasses and transcends the world,"[41] whereas a cultural anthropologist posits that religion can be defined "an institution consisting of culturally patterned interaction with culturally postulated superhuman beings."[42]

Other scholars are less enthusiastic about the definitional enterprise at the outset. Thus one professor of religious studies has concluded "that 'religion,' 'religious,' and 'religions' are Western folk concepts, that their meaning is unstable and contested, and that they cannot be defined so as to specify anything uniquely,"[43] and another philosopher has

*Proposal*, 34 Hofstra L. Rev. 309, 313–16 (1994) (providing several reasons why the Court should define the term).

37 *Cf.* Widmar v. Vincent, 454 U.S. 263, 271 n. 9 (1981) (noting, in a religious speech case, that "the Establishment Clause requires the State to distinguish between 'religious' speech ... and 'nonreligious' speech" and that "[t]his distinction is required by the plain text of the Constitution").

38 From this perspective, the Court no more violates the Establishment Clause by defining religion than it violates the separation of powers by defining the respective authority of the Congress or the president. *See, e.g.*, United States v. Lopez, 514 U.S. 549, 551 (1995) (holding that Congress exceeded its authority under U.S. Const. art. I, § 8, cl. 3); Youngstown Sheet & Tube Co. v. Sawyer, 343 U.S. 579, 589 (1952) (holding that the president exceeded his authority under U.S. Const. art. II).

39 11 Gale Encyclopedia of Religion 7693 (2d ed., Lindsay Jones ed., 2005).

40 Keith E. Yandell, Philosophy of Religion: A Contemporary Introduction 16 (1999) (emphases omitted).

41 John C. Super & Briane K. Turley, Religion in World History 2 (2006).

42 Melford E. Spiro, Culture and Human Nature 197 (1987).

43 Ann Taves, Religious Experience Reconsidered: A Building-Block Approach to the Study of Religion and Other Special Things 25 (2009).

declared that "'[r]eligion,' in the singular, as just one thing, is nowhere to be found; it is too maddeningly polyvalent and too uncontainably diverse for us to fit it all under one roof. There are Western religions, Eastern religions, ancient religions, modern religions, monotheistic, polytheistic, and even slightly atheistic religions; too many to count, too many to master, in too many languages to learn."[44] In short, based on this scholarly dissensus, it would be fair to say that the judiciary's, and in particular the Supreme Court's, overall disinclination toward systematically defining "religion" or its inability to settle on one definition is hardly unique.

The judiciary does, of course, have its own norms and obligations, which, in turn, give rise to particular concerns of the sort that could explain with greater precision the general reluctance to provide a comprehensive or systematic definition of "religion." Among the many potential difficulties posed by the task of legally defining "religion" are, *first*, a concern that a chosen definition, particularly under the Free Exercise Clause, will be too narrow or exclusionary and, as such, will be discredited and discarded in time; *second*, a concern that a more expansive definition under the Free Exercise Clause could prove problematic under the Establishment Clause, assuming the need for a single definition for both clauses; and *third*, a concern that a broad definition under the Free Exercise Clause, in addition, could invite an unmanageable number of claims given the nation's increasing religious diversity and expanded government presence.

### 1. *Narrowness*

One concern no doubt animating the common judicial reluctance to define "religion" is that any readily workable definition might not be sufficiently inclusive and will, in time, be rejected as anachronistic, if not intolerant. The modern judiciary is well aware of this prospect, cognizant of past constitutional rationales or conceptualizations now deemed misguided, from the Court's exclusionary understanding of citizenship in *Dred Scott*,[45] to Justice Bradley's patronizing conceptualization of women in *Bradwell v. State*,[46] to the pseudoscientific view of mental disability, genetics, and criminality in *Buck v. Bell*.[47] The task of defining "religion" poses a comparable risk of adverse retrospective judgment, especially as the American religious landscape increases in diversity and the collective sense of what constitutes inclusive or equal treatment continue to change.

44 John D. Caputo, On Religion 1 (2001).

45 Dred Scott v. Sandford, 60 U.S. (19 How.) 393, 404–5 (1857) (concluding that African-Americans, "considered ... a subordinate and inferior class of beings" at the time of the framing, "are not ... and were not intended to be included, under the word 'citizens' in the Constitution, and can therefore claim none of the rights and privileges which that instrument provides for and secures to citizens of the United States"), *superseded by* U.S. Const. Amend. XIV.

46 83 U.S. (16 Wall.) 130, 141 (1873) (Bradley, J., concurring) ("The paramount destiny and mission of woman are to fulfil the noble and benign offices of wife and mother. This is the law of the Creator."). "Fortunately, we emerged long ago from Justice Bradley's legal dark ages." Mueller v. Auker, 576 F.3d 979, 999 (9th Cir. 2009) [citing Reed v. Reed, 404 U.S. 71 (1971); Frontiero v. Richardson, 411 U.S. 677 (1973)].

47 Buck v. Bell, 274 U.S. 200, 207 (1927) ("It is better for all the world, if instead of waiting to execute degenerate offspring for crime, or to let them starve for their imbecility, society can prevent those who are manifestly unfit from continuing their kind."). *See* Paul A. Lombardo, *Three Generations, No Imbeciles: New Light on Buck v. Bell*, 60 NYU L. Rev. 30 (1985). The contemporary perspective is that *Buck v. Bell*'s view of mental disability has been largely repudiated. *See* Fieger v. Thomas, 74 F.3d 740, 750 (6th Cir. 1996); State v. Trujillo, 206 P.3d 125, 134 (N.M. 2009).

To take just one example, the Western theological or ontological tendency to differentiate between the religious and the secular – to dichotomize the sacred and the profane – can easily fail to capture the nature of religions outside (and even inside) the Western tradition. "Many practical and conceptual difficulties arise when one attempts to apply such a dichotomous pattern across the board to all cultures. In primitive societies, for instance, what the West calls religious is such an integral part of the total ongoing way of life that it is never experienced or thought of as something separable or narrowly distinguishable from the rest of the pattern. Or if the dichotomy is applied to that multifaceted entity called Hinduism, it seems that almost everything can be and is given a religious significance by some sect."[48] More generally, any use of qualifying characteristics in a definition is likely to exclude a number of recognized religious or faith traditions at the outset. A definition premised on monotheism, for instance, will leave out polytheistic and nontheistic religions,[49] whereas a definition that anticipates scripture-based tenets will leave out nonscriptural, orally based religions,[50] and a definition that expects systematic expositions of beliefs will exclude certain noncreedal religions or spiritual belief systems.[51]

## 2. *Interoperability*

A second potential problem impeding the definitional task stems from the fact that the term "religion" is an essential element of and must function under two related but differently interpreted provisions: the Free Exercise Clause and the Establishment Clause. Precisely because the same term is used in both clauses, presumptively it should be defined the same way under each clause.[52] Such a unitary interpretation, in turn, means

48 11 Gale Encyclopedia of Religion, *supra* note 39, at 7692; *and see* Patrick v. LeFevre, 745 F.2d 153, 155 (2d Cir. 1984) ("[W]ith the advent of the theological revolution, the already acute tension between spiritual liberty and secular intervention has been exacerbated. Religious impulses, once ensconced in a theocentric, transcendental mode, now extend to the imminence of meaning in the natural order. This implosion of conscience tests the resiliency of first amendment doctrine, and places demands of inordinate difficulty on the judiciary as it strives to resolve conflicts with dispatch and fairness.").

49 For example, some liberal Quakers are nontheistic [*see* Pink Dandelion, Quakerism: A Very Short Introduction 67–8 (2008); Godless for God's Sake: Nontheism in Contemporary Quakerism (David Boulton ed., 2006)], as are adherents to Humanistic Judaism (*see Society for Humanistic Judaism, available at:* http://www.shj.org/). Certain forms of Buddhism and Taoism can be functionally nontheistic [*see* Wing-Tsit Chan et al., The Great Asian Religions: An Anthology 71, 150 (1969)], whereas others, like a number of native South American religions, can be polytheistic [*see* 1 Religions of the World: A Comprehensive Encyclopedia of Beliefs and Practices 152, 234–5 (J. Gordon Melton & Martin Baumann eds., 2002)].

50 Native African religions and most Native American religions generally involve no scriptures or holy books, relying instead largely on oral tradition. *See* John S. Mbiti, Introduction to African Religion 15 (1975); Richard C. Bush et al., The Religious World: Communities of Faith 13 (Robert F. Weir ed., 1982).

51 Unitarian Universalism, for example, is essentially noncreedal, though the denomination or association does affirm general principles. *See* Unitarian Universalist Association, *Our Unitarian Universalist Principles and Sources, available at:* http://www.uua.org/beliefs/principles/index.shtml.

52 *See, e.g.*, Everson v. Bd. of Educ., 330 U.S. 1, 32 (1947) (Rutledge, J., dissenting); Malnak v. Yogi, 440 F. Supp. 1284, 1316 n. 20 (D.N.J. 1977), *aff'd*, 592 F.2d 197, 211 (3d Cir. 1979); *see also Malnak*, 592 F.2d at 211 (Adams, J., concurring); Greenawalt, *supra* note 9, at 758 (explaining that a unitary definition is "strongly" indicated by text and overall preferable, though not ruling out dual definitions); Leo Pfeffer, *Freedom and/or Separation: The Constitutional Dilemma of the First Amendment*, 64 Minn. L. Rev. 561, 567 n. 30 (1980). *But see* United States v. Allen, 760 F.2d 447, 450 (2d Cir. 1985) (adopting a dual approach "acknowledg[ing] that 'religion' can have a different meaning depending on which religion clause of the First Amendment is at issue").

that any definition must exhibit interoperability between the religion clauses, functioning reasonably well in both environments. As it turns out, the idea of using a single definition for both clauses gives rise to a particular concern about breadth or reach, specifically under the Establishment Clause.[53]

On the one hand, the Court is likely concerned from a practical and normative standpoint (as partly discussed earlier) that the Free Exercise Clause should encompass many religions and religious practices, including highly nonconventional or emergent ones.[54] It has even admonished, within the free exercise context, that "[t]he determination of what is a 'religious' belief or practice … is not to turn upon a judicial perception of the particular belief or practice in question; religious beliefs need not be acceptable, logical, consistent, or comprehensible to others to merit First Amendment protection."[55] On the other hand, the Court is likely also concerned from a practical and normative standpoint that the scope of the Establishment Clause not be so broad that the operations of government become unduly hindered by increased allegations of endorsement, material advancement, entanglement, or unequal treatment. Yet a generous definition of "religion," developed under and then imported from the Free Exercise Clause, could create precisely this risk,[56] yielding Establishment Clause challenges to celebrating Earth Day,

[53] *See* Fausto v. Diamond, 589 F. Supp. 451, 469 n. 23 (D.R.I. 1984) [noting the allure of adopting dual meanings, "defin[ing] 'religion' less expansively for Establishment Clause purposes (lest all activities of a spread-eagled government be deemed constitutionally suspect) and more expansively for Free Exercise Clause purposes (lest new variations and permutations of religious expression be placed beyond the pale of constitutional protection)"].

[54] *See* Daniel O. Conkle, *The Path of American Religious Liberty: From the Original Theology to Formal Neutrality and an Uncertain Future*, 75 IND. L.J. 1, 30 (2000) (explaining that "the Court appears to agree that a definition like *Seeger*'s might be well-suited for the end of the twentieth century and that, if anything, America has outgrown even the capacious approach of *Seeger*").

[55] Thomas v. Review Bd., 450 U.S. 707, 714 (1981).

[56] *See* Grove v. Mead Sch. Dist. No. 354, 753 F.2d 1528, 1537 (9th Cir. 1985) ("To borrow the ultimate concern test from the free exercise context and use it with present establishment clause doctrines would be to invite attack on all programs that further the ultimate concerns of individuals or entangle the government with such concerns."); Int'l Soc'y for Krishna Consciousness, Inc. v. Barber, 650 F.2d 430, 439 n. 12 (2d Cir. 1981) (noting that a "narrow definition is necessary in an age of pervasive governmental activity" insofar as "a broad reading of religion would bar the government on establishment clause grounds from providing even the most essential public services to religious organizations"); Booher, *supra* note 21, at 470 ("A more expansive definition of the term 'religion' … creates problems in interpreting the Establishment Clause. For example, if a deeply-held, but non-theistic, moral objection to war could qualify for protection under the Free Exercise Clause, then arguably, the moral theory that generates the objection cannot be taught in public schools without violating the Establishment Clause. Yet such a result is legally unacceptable."); Conkle, *supra* note 54, at 30 (contending that a broad conception of religion under the Free Exercise Clause could yield unmanageable effects under both clauses). An analogous concern arises for scholars and others when considering the acceptable role or influence of religious input in public discourse, largely apart from what the First Amendment might dictate. Seeking to ensure that this discourse is rational and universally accessible or that the political processes are not unduly divisive, commentators have proposed various self-observed limitations on that input, particularly in relation to the motivations or justifications for legal or political decision making. *See, e.g.*, ROBERT AUDI, RELIGIOUS COMMITMENT AND SECULAR REASON (2000); BRUCE A. ACKERMAN, SOCIAL JUSTICE IN THE LIBERAL STATE 10 (1980); KENT GREENAWALT, PRIVATE CONSCIENCES AND PUBLIC REASONS (1995); KENT GREENAWALT, RELIGIOUS CONVICTIONS AND POLITICAL CHOICE (1988); William P. Marshall, *The Other Side of Religion*, 44 HASTINGS L.J. 843 (1993); Suzanna Sherry, *The Sleep of Reason*, 84 GEO. L.J. 453 (1996). Much turns, however, on one's definition or conceptualization of religion insofar as "the broader one's definition of religion or religious values, the greater the consequences of either allowing or disallowing … [legal or political decision makers] to invoke religious values in their decision making."

for example, or having Halloween symbols in public schools,[57] or the claim that a public school reading program unconstitutionally "focuses on supernatural beings including 'wizards, sorcerers, giants and unspecified creatures with supernatural powers.'"[58]

Conversely, a more limited definition designed for the Establishment Clause could create problems under both clauses. A narrow definition crafted with the Establishment Clause in mind and then imported to the Free Exercise Clause would pose the concern, noted in the preceding paragraph, that an inadequate diversity of religious beliefs and practices would be protected from governmental infringement, including the intentional suppression of or discrimination against nonmainstream belief systems.[59] Even under the Establishment Clause, too narrow a definition might mean that the clause would have no application to, say, the teaching of transcendental meditation in public schools[60] or the domination of local government by a nonmainstream spiritual group.[61] Finally, to the extent that the operative content and reach of the clauses become more divergent and complex – as in the 1970s, when they were matter-of-factly said to be in "tension"[62] – these various risks, their effects, or at least the uncertainty of them likely will only increase.

### 3. *Breadth*

Finally, even if the Court were able to craft a broad definition of "religion" without serious Establishment Clause repercussions, such a definition, when combined with the country's increasing religious diversity and the growth in government functions or presence over the past several decades, potentially could yield an unmanageable number and variety of claims, especially in unique contexts such as prisons and public schools.[63] In recent decades, for example, courts have been asked to determine, under either the Free Exercise Clause, the Establishment Clause, RFRA, or RLUIPA, the religiousness

Scott C. Idleman, *The Limits of Religious Values in Judicial Decision Making*, 81 MARQ. L. REV. 537, 539 (1998). Conceiving of religion narrowly, thereby keeping the consequences of these extralegal limitations more manageable, would not be consistent with many contemporary understandings of religion. Conceiving of it broadly and then applying these limitations, however, "might cause the [legal and political] process[es] either to be stripped of all meaningful moral influence or (more likely) to degenerate into a medium in which religious values are simply invoked in an ad hoc and selective manner." *Id.* at 540.

57 *See, e.g.*, Altman v. Bedford Central Sch. Dist., 245 F.3d 49 (2d Cir. 2001) (Earth Day), *cert. denied*, 534 U.S. 827 (2001); Guyer v. Sch. Bd. of Alachua Cnty., 634 So. 2d 806 (Fla. Dist Ct. App. 1994) (Halloween), *review denied*, 641 So. 2d 1345 (Fla. 1994), *cert. denied*, 513 U.S. 1044 (1994).

58 *See* Fleischfresser v. Dirs. of Sch. Dist. 200, 15 F.3d 680, 683 (7th Cir. 1994) (quoting plaintiffs' amended complaint); *see also* Brown v. Woodland Jt. Unified Sch. Dist., 27 F.3d 1373 (9th Cir. 1994).

59 *See, e.g.*, Late Corp. of Church of Jesus Christ of Latter-Day Saints v. United States, 136 U.S. 1, 49 (1890) (allowing federal criminalization of polygamy, notwithstanding the Free Exercise Clause, because polygamy could not be considered a legitimate religious practice).

60 *See, e.g.*, Malnak v. Yogi, 592 F.2d 197 (3d Cir. 1979) (*per curiam*).

61 *See, e.g.*, State of Or. v. City of Rajneeshpuram, 598 F. Supp. 1208 (D. Or. 1984).

62 Tilton v. Richardson, 403 U.S. 672, 677 (1971).

63 *See* CONKLE, *supra* note 2, at 63 (noting that under a very broad *constitutional* conception of religion, similar to that employed by the Supreme Court in statutory case of *United States v. Seeger*, 380 U.S. 163 (1965), "the Free Exercise Clause could be read to protect a wide range of morally-based objections to legal burdens, and the Establishment Clause might broadly preclude the government from conferring legal benefits or favor on various moral perspectives" and that, "[e]specially in an era of pervasive government, religious liberty could potentially become unmanageable").

of the Church of Marijuana,[64] the Church of the New Song,[65] the Church of Saint Dennis,[66] the Nation of Gods and Earth,[67] the Creativity Movement,[68] the El Rukn Science Temple,[69] atheism,[70] Identity Christianity,[71] Odinism or Wotanism,[72] Satanism,[73] and Wicca.[74] The continued emergence of new and alternative religious movements, the reappearance of ancient religious traditions, and the constant influx of religious diversity through immigration would suggest that courts and other government officials will, in coming decades, face an even greater variety of claims.[75]

Moreover, if, under the Free Exercise Clause or another religious freedom guarantee, some sort of heightened judicial scrutiny were to result from every adequately pleaded prima facie case (of which religion is one component), then it would not merely be the number or variety of claims that could prove unmanageable but also their potential impact on the operations of government. Of course, the Court could try to diminish these claims doctrinally, as it attempted to do in *Employment Division v. Smith*,[76] by essentially limiting the types and thus the number of cognizable violations that can trigger heightened scrutiny. But the aftereffects of *Smith* – that is, the contravening federal statutes, the broad state statutory and constitutional revisions, and certain expansive lower court interpretations of *Smith*'s exceptions[77] – suggest that doctrinal attempts to cabin the consequences of a broad definition might be of limited effect. Legislatures writing prospective statutes and lower courts deciding individual cases are likely to be less sensitive than the Supreme Court to the cumulative transjurisdictional effects of

64 *See* United States v. Meyers, 95 F.3d 1475, 1482–4 (10th Cir. 1996) (deeming it not a religion under RFRA), *cert. denied*, 522 U.S. 1006 (1997).

65 *Cf.* Theriault v. Silber, 453 F. Supp. 254, 260–1 (W.D. Tex. 1978) (deeming it not a religion under the Free Exercise Clause), *appeal dismissed*, 579 F.2d 302 (5th Cir. 1978), *cert. denied*, 440 U.S. 917 (1979), *with* Remmers v. Brewer, 494 F.2d 1277, 1278 (8th Cir. 1974) (*per curiam*) (treating it as a religion under the Free Exercise Clause), *cert. denied*, 419 U.S. 1012 (1974).

66 *See* Jacques v. Hilton, 569 F. Supp. 730, 736 (D.N.J. 1983) (deeming it not a religion under the Free Exercise Clause), *aff'd*, 738 F.2d 422 (3d Cir. 1984).

67 *See* Panayoty v. Annucci, 898 F. Supp. 2d 469, 482–3 (N.D.N.Y. 2012) (Magis. J. Rpt. & Recomm.) (deeming it a religion under the Free Exercise Clause), *adopted by* No. 9:11-CV-159, 2012 WL 4378127 (N.D.N.Y. Sep. 25, 2012) (unpublished).

68 *See* Conner v. Tilton, No. C 07-4965 MMC-PR, 2009 WL 4642392, at *7–*13, *15 (N.D. Cal. Dec. 2, 2009) (unpublished) (deeming it not a religion under the Free Exercise Clause and RLUIPA).

69 *See* Faheem-El v. Lane, No. 82 C 4404, 1984 WL 717, at *2 n. 1 (N.D. Ill. June 29, 1984) (unpublished) (assuming that it is a religion under the Free Exercise Clause).

70 *See* Wells v. City & Cnty. of Denver, 257 F.3d 1132, 1152 (10th Cir. 2001) (assuming that it is a religion under the Free Exercise Clause).

71 *See* Haff v. Cooke, 923 F. Supp. 1104, 1108 (E.D. Wis. 1996) (assuming that it is a religion under RFRA).

72 *See* Lindell v. McCallum, 352 F.3d 1107, 1110 (7th Cir. 2003) (treating it as a religion under RLUIPA); Borzych v. Frank, 340 F. Supp. 2d 955 (W.D. Wis. 2004) (treating it as a religion under the Free Exercise Clause and RLUIPA).

73 *See* Kunselman v. W. Reserve Local Sch. Dist., 70 F.3d 931, 931 (6th Cir. 1995) (assuming that it is a religion under the Establishment Clause).

74 *See* Brown v. Woodland Joint Unified Sch. Dist., 27 F.3d 1373, 1378 (9th Cir. 1994) (assuming that it is a religion under the Establishment Clause); Dettmer v. Landon, 799 F.2d 929, 932 (4th Cir. 1986) (deeming it a religion under the Free Exercise Clause), *cert. denied*, 483 U.S. 1007 (1987).

75 *See* Encyclopedia of New Religious Movements (Peter B. Clarke ed., 2006); 1–5 Introduction to New and Alternative Religions in America (Eugene V. Gallagher & W. Michael Ashcraft eds., 2006).

76 494 U.S. 872 (1990).

77 *See* Chapter 5.A & F.

broad definitional changes, and the Court's awareness of this dynamic presumably gives its members pause when confronted with the task of defining "religion."

## C. Potential Definitional Criteria

Notwithstanding the foregoing difficulties, the nature of law, indeed the rule of law, requires that there exist some kind of authoritative, working definition of "religion." "Whatever else 'religion' may be – a concept used and studied in philosophy, in sociology, in psychology, and of course in theology – it is also a legal term, used to define individual rights and governmental limits under the First Amendment. It is thus inescapable that the courts (and the other branches of government) must sometimes say what counts as 'religion' in our legal system and what does not."[78] It is famously, after all, the "province and duty of the judicial department to say what the law is."[79] In addition, the Constitution itself, through the guarantee of due process, requires that operative legal terms be "set out in terms that the ordinary person exercising ordinary common sense can sufficiently understand and comply with,"[80] and it would be ironic, if not intolerable, were the Court's own interpretations, or silence, not able to satisfy this basic norm of fairness and limited government.

Accordingly, government officials, whether prison administrators or trial judges, are necessarily empowered to determine whether or not a given belief or practice, set of beliefs or practices, or worldview is "religious" within the meaning of the First Amendment,[81] notwithstanding an occasional judicial declaration to the contrary.[82] As the Ninth Circuit has stated, while it is "clearly impermissible to inquire into the 'truth' of religious doctrines or beliefs ... [t]here is no prohibition ... against ruling whether or not a set of beliefs constitutes a religion when deciding if First Amendment protections apply."[83] In turn, when faced, for example, with free exercise claimants asserting unconventional beliefs, governments "are clearly entitled to assure themselves that there is an

78 Michael W. McConnell, John H. Garvey & Thomas C. Berg, Religion and the Constitution 761 (3d ed., 2011); *see also* United States v. Kuch, 288 F. Supp. 439, 443–4 (D.D.C. 1968) ("Subtle and difficult though the inquiry may be, it should not be avoided for reasons of convenience. There is need to develop a sharper line of demarkation between religious activities and personal codes of conduct that lack spiritual import. Those who seek the constitutional protections for their participation in an establishment of religion and freedom to practice its beliefs must not be permitted the special freedoms this sanctuary may provide merely by adopting religious nomenclature ... In a complex society where the requirements of public safety, health and order must be recognized, those who seek immunity from these requirements on religious grounds must at the very least demonstrate adherence to ethical standards and a spiritual discipline.").

79 Marbury v. Madison, 5 U.S. (1 Cranch) 137, 177 (1803) (emphasis added); *see also* Legal Servs. Corp. v. Velazquez, 531 U.S. 533, 545 (2001) ("Interpretation of the law and the Constitution is the primary mission of the judiciary when it acts within the sphere of its authority to resolve a case or controversy."); United States v. Dickson, 40 U.S. (15 Pet.) 141, 162 (1841).

80 U.S. Civil Serv. Comm'n v. Nat'l Ass'n of Letter Carriers, 413 U.S. 548, 579 (1973); *see generally* Joseph E. Murphy, *The Duty of the Government to Make the Law Known*, 51 Fordham L. Rev. 255 (1982).

81 *See, e.g.*, Ben-Yahudah v. Bolden, No. 94-2438, 98 F.3d 1341, 1996 WL 571145, at *4 n. 1 (6th Cir. 1996) (*per curiam*) (unpublished); Jones v. Bradley, 590 F.2d 294, 295 (9th Cir. 1979).

82 *See, e.g.*, United States v. Daly, 756 F.2d 1076, 1081 (5th Cir. 1985) {"[C]ourts may not determine whether a given belief is or is not a religion." [citing United States v. Ballard, 322 U.S. 78, 86–8 (1944)]}, *cert. denied*, 474 U.S. 1022 (1985).

83 Jones, 590 F.2d at 295.

ample predicate for invoking the Free Exercise Clause" and may "distinguish between religious and secular convictions" as well as "determin[e] whether a professed belief is sincerely held."[84]

Given, then, both the authority and the necessity of governments to define "religion," this section will explore various potential approaches to this task. Drawn from judicial decisions and academic commentary, four approaches, each with a different primary focus or criterion, will be examined: original intent or meaning, comparative similarity, functional equivalence, and subjective characterization. Also considered will be the prospect of an integrated or hybrid approach that incorporates two or more of the foregoing criteria, which seems increasingly to be the method favored by lower courts. Taxonomically, the first two approaches can be considered "substantive," whereas the third (and possibly fourth) can be called "functional" based on the notion that "substantive definitions focus on what religion *is*, whereas functional definitions try to say what religion *does*."[85] The last approach, which is a blend of the others, thus likely would be classified as both substantive and functional.

### 1. *Original Intent or Meaning*

Given the prominence and evident rise of originalism in constitutional jurisprudence since the 1980s,[86] and given the prior role of originalism in First Amendment interpretations,[87] it is worthwhile to consider first an approach to defining religion that looks to original intent, meaning, or understanding. Though the generation that drafted and ratified the First Amendment was not entirely of one mind when it came to notions of religion, including the meaning of religious tolerance and the mandates of religious liberty, nevertheless the predominant understanding, heavily informed by Protestant Christianity, was that genuine religion involved the discernment of one's obligations in relation to the God that created the world and humankind and then the fulfillment of those obligations, be they the worship of God or the love of neighbor.[88] As Professor Daniel Conkle has observed, "for the Founders and for generations that followed, the

84 Frazee v. Ill. Dep't of Employment Sec., 489 U.S. 829, 833 (1989); *see also* Africa v. Commonwealth of Pa., 662 F.2d 1025, 1031 (3d Cir. 1981) ("Few tasks that confront a court require more circumspection than that of determining whether a particular set of ideas constitutes a religion.... Nonetheless, when an individual invokes the first amendment to shield himself or herself from otherwise legitimate state regulation, we are required to make such uneasy differentiations."), *cert. denied*, 456 U.S. 908 (1982).

85 Peter Beyer, *Contemporary Social Theory as it Applies to the Understanding of Religion in Cross-cultural Perspective*, *in* The Blackwell Companion to Sociology of Religion 422 (Richard K. Fenn ed., 2003).

86 *See* Frank B. Cross, The Failed Promise of Originalism 106 (2013) (noting that "[t]he recent history of originalism demonstrates its significance to the Court" though questioning its actual usefulness as a methodology).

87 *See, e.g.*, Reynolds v. United States, 98 U.S. (8 Otto) 145, 162 (1879) ("The word 'religion' is not defined in the Constitution. We must go elsewhere, therefore, to ascertain its meaning, and nowhere more appropriately, we think, than to the history of the times in the midst of which the provision was adopted.").

88 Thus Webster's 1828 edition, for example, defined religion as (1) "a belief in the being and perfections of God, in the revelation of his will to man, in man's obligation to obey his commands, in a state reward and punishment, and in man's accountableness to God;" and (2) "godliness or real piety in practice, consisting in the performance of all known duties to God and our fellow men, in obedience to divine command, or from love to God and his law." 2 Noah Webster, An American Dictionary of the English Language (1828) (unpaginated).

defining characteristic of religion was easily stated and utterly uncontroversial: it was the performance of duties owed to God. This understanding encompassed not only the various strands of Protestant Christianity, but also other traditional religions, including Catholic Christianity and Judaism."[89]

Such an understanding would have been agreeable to the main religious viewpoints of the time, including not only the more influential Protestant denominations (Episcopal, Congregational, and Presbyterian) but also emerging or traditionally separatist denominations (Baptist, Methodist, and Quaker) as well as some varieties of Enlightenment deism.[90] This conception of religion would, in turn, have encompassed most, if not all, of these denominations or religious communities, even though they variously conceptualized God. For many, such a conception, as Professor Conkle notes, also would have encompassed non-Protestant faiths such as Judaism and Catholicism and likely even Islam, however much these latter faith traditions may otherwise have enjoyed only minimal tolerance.[91]

Something akin to an originalist definition of religion arguably persisted in both law and common understanding through the nineteenth century, if not also into the first decades of the twentieth century.[92] In the 1879 decision of *Reynolds v. United States*,[93] for example, the Court defined religion and the scope of free exercise chiefly by relying on the writings of James Madison, principal author of the First Amendment, and Thomas Jefferson, who, along with Madison, was instrumental in defining religious freedom for the Commonwealth of Virginia. Of Madison the Court quoted the assertion in his "Memorial and Remonstrance against Religious Assessments" that religion refers to "'the duty we owe the Creator,'"[94] while of Jefferson the Court quoted his letter to the Danbury Baptist Association, in which he states that "'religion is a matter which lies solely between man and his God.'"[95] Just over a decade later, in *Davis v. Beason*,[96] the Court employed a definition of religion that was theistic (presumably monotheistic),

89 Conkle, *supra* note 2, at 60–1; *see also* Micah Schwartzman, *What If Religion Is Not Special?* 79 U. Chi. L. Rev. 1351, 1405–6 (2012) (noting the monotheistic conception of religion at the time of the framing).

90 Regarding the religious beliefs of the Framers, or those prevalent at the time of the framing, *see* Gregg L. Frazer, The Religious Beliefs of America's Founders: Reason, Revelation, and Revolution (2012); David L. Holmes, The Faiths of the Founding Fathers (2006); Frank Lambert, The Founding Fathers and the Place of Religion in America (2003).

91 Thomas Jefferson, though not technically a First Amendment Framer or Ratifier, anticipated the future citizenship and rights of Muslims, even though at that time Islam remained a largely unknown religion among Americans. *See* Denise A. Spellberg, Thomas Jefferson's Qur'an: Islam and the Founders 106–10 (2013).

92 *See, e.g.*, Daniel Lyons, The American Dictionary of the English Language 360 (1899) (defining religion as "the performance of our duties of love and obedience towards God: piety: any system of faith and worship"); Noah Webster, A Dictionary of the English Language 358 (acad. ed., William G. Webster & William A. Wheeler eds., 1868) [defining religion as (1) "[r]ecognition of God as an object of worship, love, and obedience" and (2) "[a]ny system of faith and worship"]. For a broad overview of the legal and religious culture of the nineteenth century, *see* Daniel F. Piar, *Majority Rights, Minority Freedoms: Protestant Culture, Personal Autonomy, and Civil Liberties in Nineteenth-Century America*, 14 Wm. & Mary Bill Rts. J. 987 (2006).

93 98 U.S. (8 Otto) 145 (1879).

94 *Id.* at 163 [quoting Robert B. Semple, A History of the Rise and Progress of the Baptists in Virginia (unknown year)]. Madison's "Memorial and Remonstrance" is available at: http://founders.archives.gov/documents/Madison/01-08-02-0163.

95 *Id.* at 164 [quoting 8 Paul Leicester Ford, The Works of Thomas Jefferson 113 (unknown year)]. Jefferson's letter is available at: http://www.loc.gov/loc/lcib/9806/danpre.html.

96 133 U.S. 333 (1890), *overruled on other grounds by* Romer v. Evans, 517 U.S. 620, 634 (1996).

that contemplated a relationship between the adherent and the deity, and that entailed obligations on the adherent arising from this relationship. According to the *Davis* Court,

> [t]he term "religion" has reference to one's views of his relations to his Creator, and to the obligations they impose of reverence for his being and character, and of obedience to his will. It is often confounded with the cultus or form of worship of a particular sect, but is distinguishable from the latter. The first amendment to the constitution, in declaring that congress shall make no law respecting the establishment of religion or forbidding the free exercise thereof, was intended to allow every one under the jurisdiction of the United States to entertain such notions respecting his relations to his Maker and the duties they impose as may be approved by his judgment and conscience, and to exhibit his sentiments in such form of worship as he may think proper, not injurious to the equal rights of others, and to prohibit legislation for the support of any religious tenets, or the modes of worship of any sect.[97]

Later that same year, the Court reiterated this conceptualization and further suggested that a true religion, or at least the kind protected by the First Amendment, would not countenance beliefs or conduct too far afield from the moral norms of the Christian tradition. Specifically, in *Church of Jesus Christ of LatterDay Saints v. United States*,[98] the Court characterized polygamy as a "return to barbarism"[99] that did not qualify as a cognizable religious belief or practice because it was "contrary to the spirit of Christianity and of the civilization which Christianity has produced in the Western world."[100]

By the middle of the twentieth century, however, the Court had discarded not simply the monotheism but also even the theism of these late nineteenth-century cases as the means by which to understand "religion" in the First Amendment.[101] In its 1940 decision in *Minersville School District v. Gobitis*,[102] a case it famously overruled just three years later,[103] the Court suggested that religion involves "the affirmative pursuit of one's convictions about the ultimate mystery of the universe and man's relation to it,"[104] thereby implying that the concept included a great deal more than theistic traditions, let alone the monotheism of Christianity.[105] Then, in a footnote from the 1961 case of *Torcaso v. Watkins*,[106] the Court commented that "[a]mong religions in this country which do not teach what would generally be considered a belief in the existence of God are Buddhism, Taoism, Ethical Culture, Secular Humanism and others."[107] Though

97 *Id.* at 342.
98 136 U.S. 1 (1890).
99 *Id.* at 49.
100 *Id.*
101 *But cf.* Church of the Lukumi Babalu Aye, Inc. v. City of Hialeah, 508 U.S. 520, 577 (1993) (Souter, J., concurring in part and concurring in the judgment) ("The extent to which the Free Exercise Clause requires government to refrain from impeding religious exercise defines nothing less than the respective relationships in our constitutional democracy of the individual to government and to God.").
102 Minersville Sch. Dist. v. Gobitis, 310 U.S. 586 (1940).
103 *See* W. Va. State Bd. of Educ. v. Barnette, 319 U.S. 624 (1943).
104 Gobitis, 310 U.S. at 593.
105 *See also id.* ("Government may not interfere with organized or individual expression of belief or disbelief. Propagation of belief – or even of disbelief in the supernatural – is protected, whether in church or chapel, mosque or synagogue, tabernacle or meetinghouse.").
106 367 U.S. 488 (1961).
107 *Id.* at 495 n. 11.

the passage "might be characterized as dictum,"[108] unnecessary for resolving the case at hand, the Court presumably intended its comment not to be taken as a sociological or anthropological observation but rather as a statement relevant to the scope and meaning of the First Amendment. The context indicates that the latter view is correct. For one thing, *Torcaso* was itself a case about the First Amendment religion clauses, ultimately holding that Maryland's theistic test for public office violated an appointee's freedom of religion.[109] For another thing, the text corresponding to the footnote was a declaration on the meaning of the religion clauses – "neither a State nor the Federal Government ... can aid those religions based on a belief in the existence of God as against those religions founded on different beliefs"[110] – and one of the two cases cited as references in the footnote directly addressed the demands of the First Amendment when defining religion.[111] Moreover, in the preceding footnote, which corresponds to the same sentence, the Court quotes James Iredell's suggestion that the principle of religious freedom would allow the citizenry to "'choose representatives who have no religion at all, and that pagans and Mahometans may be admitted into offices.'"[112]

This shift from a Christian-centered monotheistic view of religion to theism more generally and eventually to nontheism or even atheism suggests that an originalist approach to defining religion, if viewed as a take-all-or-none proposition, is no longer in accord with the contemporary constitutional conception of religion, however underdefined that conception may be. But well-regarded interpretive sources or authorities are often not embraced wholesale, and in that light, originalism need not be deemed irrelevant to present-day efforts to define or conceptualize religion. Insofar as a core focus of the Framers or Ratifiers, for example, was on transcendent or higher duties and the conscientious citizen's efforts to fulfill those duties, that focus certainly can have application to contemporary cases, even if the element of transcendence or the source of higher duties is not the God worshipped or contemplated by the Framers or Ratifiers themselves. Likewise, the original emphasis on voluntarism as an essential component of religious liberty can inform the assessment of what kinds of beliefs or attendant practices may be deemed religious. In addition, the notion of separate civil and religious spheres, discussed along with voluntarism in Chapter 5.B.1, may shed light on what sorts of matters lie within the domain of conscience and beyond the jurisdiction and control of the state, even though they may not be readily recognizable using certain characteristics of religion as understood by those who drafted or approved of the First Amendment.[113]

108 Ctr. for Inquiry, Inc. v. Marion Circuit Ct. Clerk, 758 F.3d 869, 873 (7th Cir. 2014). Even so, some courts recognize that they typically have an "obligation to accord great deference to Supreme Court *dicta*." United States v. Colasuonno, 697 F.3d 164, 179 (2d Cir. 2012).

109 *See* Torcaso, 367 U.S. at 496.

110 *Id.* at 495.

111 *See id.* at 495 n. 11 [citing Fellowship of Humanity v. Cnty. of Alameda, 315 P.2d 394 (Cal. Ct. App. 1957)].

112 *Id.* at 495 n. 10 [quoting 4 Jonathan Elliott, Debates in the Several State Conventions on the Adoption of the Federal Constitution 194 (unknown year)].

113 *Cf.* Conkle, *supra* note 2, at 65 [arguing that certain language from the Supreme Court's abortion decision in Planned Parenthood v. Casey, 505 U.S. 833 (1992), "strongly suggests that the contemporary Court finds constitutional value in decisions of conscience, that is, decisions of moral self-definition and self-determination that might or might not be religious in a conventional sense"].

### 2. *Comparative Similarity*

A second, largely substantive approach to defining "religion" is to delineate certain features that indicate what one would expect to find in a "religion" – some archetype or ideal, typically drawn from belief systems that are widely recognized as religious – and then to assess whether a given belief system exhibits or lacks these features. This method focuses, in other words, on indicia of comparative similarity; hence it is sometimes also called an "analogical approach."[114] The points of similarity can concern both the interior content of a belief system (e.g., teachings, ethics, or principles) and its outward manifestations (e.g., rituals, practices, or institutions). It should be noted that few analogical approaches are wholly substantive as opposed to functional because some of the anticipated features – say, a comprehensive set of strict moral obligations – likely are closely linked to how the belief system actually operates in the lives of faithful adherents.

The most comprehensive analogical or similarity-based definition in the religious freedom context comes from *United States v. Meyers*,[115] a federal district court decision authored by Judge Clarence Brimmer and affirmed by the Tenth Circuit, involving an adherent (the founder, in fact) of the Church of Marijuana, who challenged under RFRA his federal prosecution for marijuana possession and distribution. Even though the district court was construing RFRA, it "decided that 'religion' under RFRA is the same as 'religion' under the First Amendment,"[116] drawing heavily on First Amendment case law[117] and nowhere suggesting that its proposed broad definition would not also apply with equal force under the Free Exercise Clause.[118] Based on its survey of prior definitional efforts, Judge Brimmer drew up a list of several factors – five main ones, with the fifth having several components – in order to determine whether or not a given belief constitutes a religion:

1. **Ultimate Ideas.** Religious beliefs often address fundamental questions about life, purpose, and death.... These matters may include existential matters, such as man's perception of life; ontological matters, such as man's sense of being; teleological matters, such as man's purpose in life; and cosmological matters, such as man's place in the universe.
2. **Metaphysical Beliefs.** Religious beliefs often are "metaphysical," that is, they address a reality which transcends the physical and immediately apparent world. Adherents to many religions believe that there is another dimension, place, mode, or temporality, and they often believe that these places are inhabited by spirits, souls, forces, deities, and other sorts of inchoate or intangible entities.
3. **Moral or Ethical System.** Religious beliefs often prescribe a particular manner of acting, or way of life, that is "moral" or "ethical." In other words, these beliefs often describe certain acts in normative terms, such as "right and wrong," "good and evil," or "just and unjust." The beliefs then proscribe those acts that are "wrong," "evil,"

114 *See, e.g*, Greenawalt, *supra* note 9, at 762.

115 906 F. Supp. 1494 (D. Wyo. 1995), *aff'd*, 95 F.3d 1475 (10th Cir. 1996), *cert. denied*, 522 U.S. 1006 (1997).

116 *Id.* at 1499.

117 *See id.* at 1499–1501.

118 *See, e.g.*, Huffman v. State, 204 P.3d 339, 345 n. 28 (Alaska 2009) (referring in a case involving the Free Exercise Clause to the *Meyers* factors as adopted by the Tenth Circuit's affirmance of the district court); *cf.* State v. Pedersen, 679 N.W.2d 368, 375–6 (Minn. Ct. App. 2004) (applying the *Meyers* factors to assess whether beliefs were religious under Minn. Const. art. I, § 16).

or "unjust." A moral or ethical belief structure also may create duties – duties often imposed by some higher power, force, or spirit – that require the believer to abnegate elemental self-interest.

4. **Comprehensiveness of Beliefs.** Another hallmark of "religious" ideas is that they are comprehensive. More often than not, such beliefs provide a *telos*, an overarching array of beliefs that coalesce to provide the believer with answers to many, if not most, of the problems and concerns that confront humans. In other words, religious beliefs generally are not confined to one question or a single teaching.
5. **Accoutrements of Religion.** By analogy to many of the established or recognized religions, the presence of the following external signs may indicate that a particular set of beliefs is "religious":
   a. **Founder, Prophet, or Teacher.** Many religions have been wholly founded or significantly influenced by a deity, teacher, seer, or prophet who is considered to be divine, enlightened, gifted, or blessed.
   b. **Important Writings.** Most religions embrace seminal, elemental, fundamental, or sacred writings. These writings often include creeds, tenets, precepts, parables, commandments, prayers, scriptures, catechisms, chants, rites, or mantras.
   c. **Gathering Places.** Many religions designate particular structures or places as sacred, holy, or significant. These sites often serve as gathering places for believers. They include physical structures, such as churches, mosques, temples, pyramids, synagogues, or shrines; and natural places, such as springs, rivers, forests, plains, or mountains.
   d. **Keepers of Knowledge.** Most religions have clergy, ministers, priests, reverends, monks, shamans, teachers, or sages. By virtue of their enlightenment, experience, education, or training, these people are keepers and purveyors of religious knowledge.
   e. **Ceremonies and Rituals.** Most religions include some form of ceremony, ritual, liturgy, sacrament, or protocol. These acts, statements, and movements are prescribed by the religion and are imbued with transcendent significance.
   f. **Structure or Organization.** Many religions have a congregation or group of believers who are led, supervised, or counseled by a hierarchy of teachers, clergy, sages, priests, etc.
   g. **Holidays.** As is etymologically evident, many religions celebrate, observe, or mark "holy," sacred, or important days, weeks, or months.
   h. **Diet or Fasting.** Religions often prescribe or prohibit the eating of certain foods and the drinking of certain liquids on particular days or during particular times.
   i. **Appearance and Clothing.** Some religions prescribe the manner in which believers should maintain their physical appearance, and other religions prescribe the type of clothing that believers should wear.
   j. **Propagation.** Most religious groups, thinking that they have something worthwhile or essential to offer non-believers, attempt to propagate their views and persuade others of their correctness. This is sometimes called "mission work," "witnessing," "converting," or proselytizing.[119]

Several things about these factors are noteworthy. First, and again, to the extent that they are assessed descriptively, without regard to how they actually unfold in the adherent's life apart from the particular belief or practice giving rise to the legal conflict, they render the *Meyers* approach substantive in nature because they look fundamentally to

[119] Meyers, 906 F. Supp. at 1502–3 (footnotes omitted).

the content and features, not the function, of a belief system. This is especially apparent with regard to the last factor, covering the so-called accoutrements of religion, though it can readily apply to the others as well. Second, the court itself "emphasize[d] that no one of these factors is dispositive" and "recognize[d] that it ... [could not] rely solely on established or recognized religions to guide it in determining whether a new and unique set of beliefs warrants inclusion."[120] Third and relatedly, the court cautioned that "[t]he threshold for inclusion ... is low" and that this "ensures that the Court errs ... on the side of religious freedom"[121] and also that the factors do not dictate an outcome but rather, "if minimally satisfied, counsel the inclusion of beliefs within the term 'religion.'"[122] Fourth, after noting several beliefs that presumably would or likely qualify as "religious" pursuant to the factors,[123] the court noted that "[p]urely personal, political, ideological, or secular beliefs probably would not satisfy enough criteria for inclusion" and provided several examples of such beliefs: "nihilism, anarchism, pacifism, utopianism, socialism, libertarianism, Marxism, vegetism, and humanism."[124] Fifth, from a legal authority standpoint, it bears emphasis that not only did the Tenth Circuit Court of Appeals affirm the district court, it expressly "adopt[ed]" the "district court's thorough analysis of the indicia of religion,"[125] albeit with one of the three panel judges dissenting specifically over the basic propriety of systematically defining religion.[126]

Finally, it should be noted that Judge Brimmer did not design his analysis from scratch and that the prior work of judges and scholars was expressly invoked and assimilated into his analysis. In particular, *Meyers* drew especially on the opinions of Third Circuit Judge Arlin Adams, whose proposed definitional approach was highly influential before *Meyers* and remains so afterward. Judge Adams' initial efforts to provide a constitutional definition to religion came in a concurring opinion in 1979,[127] in which he observed as a starting point that the originalist and nineteenth-century theistic understanding of religion was "no longer sustainable" and that "'religion' is not confined to the relationship of man with his Creator, either as a matter of law or as a matter of theology."[128]

120 *Id.* at 1503.

121 *Id.* at 1501.

122 *Id.* at 1503.

123 *See id.* at 1503–4 ("[T]he Court presumes that the following sets of beliefs are 'religious': Judaism, Christianity, Islam, Hinduism, Buddhism, Shintoism, Confucianism, and Taoism. Undoubtedly, the test also would lead to the conclusion that the beliefs of the following groups are 'religious': Hare Krishnas, Bantus, Mormons, Seventh Day Adventists, Christian Scientists, Scientologists, Branch Davidians, Unification Church Members, and Native American Church Members (whether Shamanists or Ghost Dancers). More likely than not, the test also includes obscure beliefs such as Paganism, Zoroastrianism, Pantheism, Animism, Wicca, Druidism, Satanism, and Santeria. And, casting a backward glance over history, the test assuredly would have included what we now call 'mythology': Greek religion, Norse religion, and Roman religion.").

124 *Id.* at 1504.

125 Meyers, 95 F.3d at 1484.

126 *See id.* at 1489–92 (Brorby, J., dissenting).

127 *See* Malnak v. Yogi, 592 F.2d 197, 207–10 (3d Cir. 1979) (Adams, J., concurring). Nor was Judge Adams the first to develop a multipart analogical analysis for defining religion. *See, e.g.*, Founding Church of Scientology of Wash., D.C. v. United States, 409 F.2d 1146, 1160 (D.C. Cir. 1969) (considering criteria such as whether an alleged religion "[i]t is incorporated as ... [a religion within its jurisdiction"; "[i]t has ministers, who are licensed as such, with legal authority to marry and to bury"; "[i]ts fundamental writings contain a general account of man and his nature comparable in scope, if not in content, to those of some recognized religions"), *cert. denied*, 396 U.S. 963 (1969).

128 *Id.* at 207.

Rather, the Supreme Court's mid-twentieth-century cases indicated movement toward "a definition by analogy" that "looks to the familiar religions as models in order to ascertain, by comparison, whether the new set of ideas or beliefs is confronting the same concerns, or serving the same purposes, as unquestioned and accepted 'religions.'"[129]

Judge Adams then proceeded to identify "three useful indicia that are basic to our traditional religions and that are themselves related to the values that undergird the first amendment."[130] "The first and most important of these indicia is the nature of the ideas in question": does a belief system address "the deeper and more imponderable questions the meaning of life and death, man's role in the Universe, the proper moral code of right and wrong"?[131] The second of the indicia, according to Judge Adams, is "comprehensiveness": does a belief system "lay claim to an ultimate and comprehensive 'truth'" and "proffer a systematic series of answers to … [ultimate concerns] that might begin to resemble a religion"?[132] Third, and last, does the belief system display "any formal, external, or surface signs that may be analogized to accepted religions," such as "formal services, ceremonial functions, the existence of clergy, structure and organization, efforts at propagation, observation of holidays and other similar manifestations associated with the traditional religions"?[133] Like the court in *Meyers*, Judge Adams cautioned that "[a]lthough these indicia will be helpful, they should not be thought of as a final 'test' for religion. Defining religion is a sensitive and important legal duty. Flexibility and careful consideration of each belief system are needed."[134] Two years later, Judge Adams, now writing for a unanimous Third Circuit panel, had the opportunity to apply the three indicia, concluding that an organization called MOVE was not a religion such that one of its incarcerated members could not invoke the Free Exercise Clause to request a special diet allegedly based on MOVE's principles.[135]

In addition to the opinions of Judges Brimmer and Adams, the writings of Professor Kent Greenawalt also have done much on the academic front to advance an analogical approach to defining religion.[136] Greenawalt's proposal is "that in both free exercise and establishment cases, courts should decide whether something is religious by comparison with the indisputably religious, in light of the particular legal problem involved," but that "[n]o single characteristic should be regarded as essential to religiousness."[137] In succinct form, his proposal is as follows:

> To use the analogical approach to determine the boundaries of religion, one begins with instances of the indisputably religious…. For example, no one doubts that Roman Catholicism, Greek Orthodoxy, Lutheranism, Methodism, and Orthodox Judaism are religions. Our society identifies what is indubitably religious largely by reference to their beliefs, practices, and organizations. These include: a belief in God; a comprehensive

129 *Id.*

130 *Id.* at 207–8.

131 *Id.* at 208.

132 *Id.* at 209.

133 *Id.*

134 *Id.* at 210 (footnote omitted).

135 *See* Africa v. Commonwealth of Pa., 662 F.2d 1025, 1032–6 (3d Cir. 1981), *cert. denied*, 456 U.S. 908 (1982).

136 *See* 1 Kent Greenawalt, Religion and the Constitution: Free Exercise and Fairness 139–41 (2006); Greenawalt, *supra* note 9.

137 Greenawalt, *supra* note 9, at 753.

> view of the world and human purposes; a belief in some form of afterlife; communication with God through ritual acts of worship and through corporate and individual prayer; a particular perspective on moral obligations derived from a moral code or from a conception of God's nature; practices involving repentence and forgiveness of sins; "religious" feelings of awe, guilt, and adoration; the use of sacred texts; and organization to facilitate the corporate aspects of religious practice and to promote and perpetuate beliefs and practices. This list could be expanded or organized differently. The main point is that among religions typical in this society a number of different elements are joined together.[138]

Much like Judges Brimmer and Adams, Greenawalt qualifies his proposal by noting that the absence of any given feature should not be dispositive – "[a] set of beliefs and practices would still be religious, for example, if it were based on polytheism or non-theism rather than monotheism, if it failed to assert any claim between transcendental reality and proper moral practices, or if it did not involve any corporate organization"[139] – and, further, that the presence of some characteristics, such as the rituals and ethical codes of professional or fraternal organizations or the comprehensiveness and depth of Marxism, should not lead to the conclusion that an organization or belief system is thus religious.[140] Rather, "[i]n seeking to categorize an organization or a broad set of practices, one must examine the combination of characteristics that constitute it. A final decision to consider something religious depends on how closely the combination of characteristics resembles those of the paradigm instances, judged in light of the particular reason for the inquiry."[141]

### 3. *Functional Equivalence*

A third approach to defining "religion," already hinted at when discussing the analogical or similarity-based approaches, focuses not on the content or external characteristics of a belief or belief system but instead on its actual role or function in the life of an adherent and specifically whether it functions with a depth, intensity, or totality often associated with genuine religious devotion. Appropriately, this method has been labeled a "functional approach," though it obviously shares some aspects of the analogical or substantive approaches, including an effective comparison between the belief system in question and some archetypal or illustrative notion of what true religion is or should be. Nevertheless, the fundamental focus is sufficiently distinct – how meaningfully the beliefs shape and direct the adherent's life as opposed to what they proclaim or how they are externally manifested – that it is useful to examine this approach on its own terms.

138 *Id.* at 767–8 (footnotes omitted).

139 *Id.* at 768.

140 *See id.* One assumes, for example, that Greenawalt would not be inclined to deem "religious" the contrived holiday of Festivus, which reached public awareness through the television show *Seinfeld*, even though it has its own symbol (the Festivus Pole), stories, music, and rituals. *See Happy Festivus, available at:* http://festivusweb.com/; *Festivus, available at:* http://en.wikipedia.org/wiki/Festivus. Nor, presumably, would atheist churches be considered religious, despite having organized corporate forms quite similar to many Christian congregations. *See* Josh Sanburn, *Nonbelief System: Atheist "Churches" Take Hold, Even in the Bible Belt*, Time, Aug. 4, 2014, at 52.

141 Greenawalt, *supra* note 9, at 768.

During the era of America's military involvement in Vietnam, the Supreme Court adopted a heavily functional approach to defining "religion" in its construction of the conscientious objector exception to the Selective Service Act of 1948,[142] as amended by the Universal Military Training and Service Act of 1951.[143] In the early and mid-1960s, when the cases before the Court first arose, the exemption in the federal conscription statute required that a conscientious objector's opposition to war had to stem from "religious training and belief," which it defined as "an individual's belief in relation to a Supreme Being involving duties superior to those arising from any human relation, but ... not includ[ing] essentially political, sociological, or philosophical views or a merely personal moral code."[144]

In *United States v. Seeger*,[145] the first of its two primary cases, the Court was asked to decide whether the statutory requirement encompassed only conventionally theistic belief systems and, if so, whether this limitation ran afoul of the First Amendment.[146] The Court concluded that the statutory exemption should be construed to include any sincere belief that is "based upon a power or being, or upon a faith, to which all else is subordinate or upon which all else is ultimately dependent" and that "occupies in the life of its possessor a place parallel to that filled by the God of those admittedly qualifying for the exemption."[147] The Court's approach can be described as essentially functional because it asked not so much what the registrant professed or what his belief system taught (other than opposition to all war) and certainly did not look for conventional indicia of organized religions; instead, it asked how the belief or belief system functioned in the life of the claimant – whether the beliefs were, "in his own scheme of things, religious"[148]

142 Pub. L. No. 80-759, 62 Stat. 604 (Jun. 24, 1948) (codified as amended at 50 U.S.C. app. §§ 451–73). The Supreme Court was not the first tribunal to read a federal conscription law in such a manner. *See, e.g.*, United States v. Kauten, 133 F.2d 703, 708 (2d Cir. 1943) (construing the 1940 Selective Training and Service Act's requirement that one's conscientious objection be "by reason of religious training and belief" to include "a compelling voice of conscience" or "a response of the individual to an inward mentor, call it conscience or God, that is for many persons at the present time the equivalent of what has always been thought a religious impulse").

143 Pub. L. No. 82-51, § 1, 65 Stat. 75 (Jun. 19, 1951).

144 50 U.S.C. app. § 456(j) (1958 ed.), *quoted in* United States v. Seeger, 380 U.S. 163, 165 (1965). The statute has since been amended. *See* 50 U.S.C. app. § 456(j) (2006) ("Nothing contained in this title shall be construed to require any person to be subject to combatant training and service in the armed forces of the United States who, by reason of religious training and belief, is conscientiously opposed to participation in war in any form. As used in this subsection, the term 'religious training and belief' does not include essentially political, sociological, or philosophical views, or a merely personal moral code."). There are also regulations implementing the statute, formerly published at 32 C.F.R. pt. 75, but in 2007, the Department of Defense withdrew them from publication, explaining that "[t]he document on which this part was based has been revised and is limited only to DoD personnel management matters, affects only DoD military personnel, and has no impact on the public." 72 Fed. Reg. 33,677 (Jun. 19, 2007). The general standards and procedures are set forth, however, in Department of Defense Instruction 1300.06 (May 5, 2007).

145 380 U.S. 163 (1965).

146 *See id.* at 165. According to the Court, "[t]he question is not ... one between theistic and atheistic beliefs.... Our question ... is the narrow one: Does the term 'Supreme Being' as used in § 6(j) mean the orthodox God or the broader concept of a power or being, or a faith, 'to which all else is subordinate or upon which all else is ultimately dependent'?" *Id.* at 173–4 [quoting Webster's New International Dictionary (2d ed., year unknown)].

147 *Id.* at 176; *see also id.* at 184 ("While the applicant's words may differ, the test is simple of application. It is essentially an objective one, namely, does the claimed belief occupy the same place in the life of the objector as an orthodox belief in God holds in the life of one clearly qualified for exemption?").

148 *Id.* at 185.

and whether its role was parallel or comparable to that ascribed to recognized religions in the lives of their adherents.[149] Five years later, in *Welsh v. United States*,[150] a plurality of the Court employed again the approach it had developed in *Seeger*, holding that a Selective Service registrant who had specifically crossed out the term "religious" on his form[151] still could qualify for conscientious objector status if his "opposition to war stem[med] from … moral, ethical, or religious beliefs about what is right and wrong" and if "these beliefs … [were] held with the strength of traditional religious convictions" and "impose[d] upon him a duty of conscience to refrain from participating in any war at any time," thus "occupy[ing] in the life of that individual 'a place parallel to that filled by … God' in traditionally religious persons."[152]

Importantly, the *Seeger* and *Welsh* Courts were not directly interpreting the First Amendment and did not purport to do so but were instead construing the federal conscription statute. In turn, the definition they adopted is technically applicable only to that statute (and its predecessors) and is not authoritative or binding when it comes to the religion clauses.[153] Nevertheless, it is thought that constitutional considerations likely informed the Court's statutory construction,[154] and Mr. Seeger in his case specifically alleged that the exemption, as written and if strictly applied, "violat[ed] the Establishment Clause of the First Amendment, the Due Process Clause of the Fifth Amendment, and

149 Comparably broad constructions of the statute have also come from the lower federal courts. *See, e.g.*, United States v. Levy, 419 F.2d 360, 365 (8th Cir. 1969); United States v. Haughton, 413 F.2d 736, 739–42 (9th Cir. 1969); *cf.* United States v. Kauten, 133 F.2d 703, 708 (2d Cir. 1943). In 1967, following *Seeger*, Congress amended the federal conscription law, removing the "Supreme Being" language. *See* Pub. L. No. 90-40, § 1(7), 81 Stat. 100, 104 (Jun. 30, 1967).

150 398 U.S. 333 (1970) (plurality opinion).

151 *See id.* at 337, 341.

152 *Id.* at 340 (quoting Seeger, 380 U.S. at 176). The following year, the Court decided a third conscription case, Gillette v. United States, 401 U.S. 437 (1971), but the Court had no occasion to alter or expand on its definition of religion as set forth in *Seeger* and *Welsh*. *See id.* at 447. The issue, instead, was whether one could qualify for the exemption if one had an objection only to particular wars rather that all war. The Court held that one could not (*see id.* at 443) and that this limitation did not violate the First Amendment (*see id.* at 448–62).

153 *See* United States v. Meyers, 906 F. Supp. 1494, 1500 (D. Wyo. 1995) (concluding that the functional approach invoked in the Selective Service Act cases does not carry over into the constitutional realm), *aff'd*, 95 F.3d 1475 (10th Cir. 1996), *cert. denied*, 522 U.S. 1006 (1997); *cf.* Wisconsin v. Yoder, 406 U.S. 205, 248–9 (1972) (Douglas, J., dissenting) (arguing that the majority's description of what does not qualify as a religion under the First Amendment is "contrary to what [the Court] held in … *Seeger*" and *Welsh* under the Selective Service Act). *But see* Loney v. Scurr, 474 F. Supp. 1186, 1193 n. 5 (S.D. Iowa 1979) ("The Supreme Court has appeared to give 'religion' and 'religious' an expansive meaning in both the statutory and First Amendment free exercise contexts, and this Court does not believe *Welsh*, *Seeger* and like cases can be distinguished on the ground that they involved the interpretation of a statute." [citing Torcaso v. Watkins, 367 U.S. 488, 495 n. 11 (1961)].

154 *See* Ctr. for Inquiry, Inc. v. Marion Circuit Ct. Clerk, 758 F.3d 869, 873 (7th Cir. 2014) (observing that "the Court interpreted the conscription statutes to avoid a declaration of unconstitutionality"); Jesse H. Choper, *Congressional Power To Expand Judicial Definitions of the Substantive Terms of the Civil War Amendments*, 67 MINN. L. REV. 299, 336–7 (1982). For example, after recounting the diversity of religious beliefs in the nation, the Court noted the importance of Congress' "fashioning of an exemption which would be in keeping with its long-established policy of not picking and choosing among religious beliefs." Seeger, 380 U.S. at 175. This could be viewed as simply an application of statutory construction principles, but it certainly brings to mind the Court's admonition, under the Establishment Clause, that "[n]either a state nor the Federal Government can … prefer one religion over another." Everson v. Bd. of Educ. of Ewing Twp., 330 U.S. 1, 15 (1947).

the religious test clause of Article VI."[155] More important, the impact of the Court's approach in *Seeger* and *Welsh*, whether directly or indirectly as part of the tests employed in *Meyers* and the Third Circuit, has been substantial in lower court interpretations of both the Free Exercise Clause[156] and the Establishment Clause[157] as well as constructions of RLUIPA,[158] other federal statutes,[159] and various state laws concerning religious freedom[160] or nondiscrimination.[161]

### 4. *Subjective Characterization*

In recent years, heeding the Supreme Court's admonitions that judges should not assess the "centrality" of religious beliefs[162] and that the "determination of what is a 'religious' belief or practice ... is not to turn upon a judicial perception of the particular belief or practice in question"[163] – indeed, that "religious beliefs need not be acceptable, logical, consistent, or comprehensible to others in order to merit First Amendment protection"[164] – a number of courts have, it seems, effectively retreated from the business of assessing religiousness by relying chiefly, if not entirely, on a litigant's own declarations that certain beliefs are, or are not, religious. Borrowing in part from *Seeger*, these courts consider the First Amendment satisfied as long as a litigant's beliefs are sincerely held and are, in the litigant's "'own scheme of things, religious.'"[165] In turn, the requirement of sincerity can become the pivotal, if not exclusive, inquiry in the analysis, with

155 United States v. Seeger, 216 F. Supp. 516, 520 (S.D.N.Y. 1963), *rev'd*, 326 F.2d 846 (2d Cir. 1964), *aff'd*, 380 U.S. 163 (1965).

156 *See, e.g.*, Kaufman v. McCaughtry, 419 F.3d 678, 681–2 (7th Cir. 2005); Fleischfresser v. Directors of Sch. Dist. 200, 15 F.3d 680, 688 n. 5 (7th Cir. 1994); United States v. Ward, 973 F.2d 730, 732 (9th Cir. 1992); Dettmer v. Landon, 799 F.2d 929, 931–2 (4th Cir. 1986), *cert. denied*, 483 U.S. 1007 (1987); Int'l Soc'y for Krishna Consciousness, Inc. v. Barber, 650 F.2d 430, 440 (2d Cir. 1981).

157 *See, e.g.*, Kaufman, 419 F.3d at 681–2, 683–4 (using analysis initially under the Free Exercise Clause and then applying its determination under the Establishment Clause).

158 *See, e.g.*, Moore-King v. Cnty. of Chesterfield, Va., 708 F.3d 560, 570–2 (4th Cir. 2013).

159 *See, e.g.*, Adeyeye v. Heartland Sweeteners, LLC, 721 F.3d 444, 448 (7th Cir. 2013) (unpublished) (Title VII of the 1964 Civil Rights Act); Peterson v. Wilmur Communications, Inc., 205 F. Supp. 2d 1014, 1022–3 (E.D. Wis. 2002) (same); 29 C.F.R. § 1605.1 (regulation implementing Title VII).

160 *See, e.g.*, State v. Bontrager, 683 N.E.2d 126, 128 (Ohio Ct. App. 1996) (Ohio Const. art. I, § 7), *appeal dismissed*, 675 N.E.2d 1249 (Ohio 1997).

161 *See, e.g.*, Friedman v. S. Cal. Permanente Med. Group, 125 Cal. Rptr. 2d 663 (Cal. Ct. App. 2002) (state antidiscrimination law), *cert. denied*, 538 U.S. 1033 (2003).

162 *See* Employment Div. v. Smith, 494 U.S. 872, 886–7 & n. 4 (1990); Hernandez v. Comm'r, 490 U.S. 680, 699 (1989) ("It is not within the judicial ken to question the centrality of particular beliefs or practices to a faith, or the validity of particular litigants' interpretations of those creeds.").

163 Thomas v. Review Bd. of Ind. Employment Sec. Div., 450 U.S. 707, 714 (1981).

164 *Id.*

165 *See, e.g.*, Moore-King v. Cnty. of Chesterfield, Va., 708 F.3d 560, 570–2 (4th Cir. 2013) (Free Exercise Clause and RLUIPA) [quoting United States v. Seeger, 380 U.S. 163, 185 (1965)]; Watts v. Fla. Int'l Univ., 495 F.3d 1289, 1298 (11th Cir. 2007) (Free Exercise Clause) (quoting Seeger, 380 U.S. at 185); Ford v. McGinnis, 352 F.3d 582, 588 (2d Cir. 2003) (Free Exercise Clause) [quoting Fifth Ave. Presbyterian Church v. City of N.Y., 293 F.3d 570, 574 (2d Cir. 2002)]; Bryant v. Johnson, Civ. Action No. 7:11-cv-00075, 2012 WL 4458214, at *13 (W.D. Va. Aug. 21, 2012) (unpublished) (RLUIPA) (quoting *Seeger*, 380 U.S. at 185); Isbell v. Ryan, No. CV 11-0391-PHX-JAT-JFM, 2011 WL 6050337, at *5 (D. Ariz. Dec. 6, 2011) (unpublished) (Free Exercise Clause and RLUIPA) (quoting Seeger, 380 U.S. at 185); Omar v. Casterline, 414 F. Supp. 2d 582, 592 (W.D. La. 2006) (RFRA) (quoting Ford, 352 F.3d at 588).

the element of religiousness turning essentially on the litigant's characterization of his or her own beliefs.[166]

Were this not an approach potentially embraced by a growing number of courts, it might not deserve mention in a chapter on defining religion if only because, in a sense, it is not an effort to define religion. However, given its apparent expanding use, a few critical observations are warranted. First of all, it is not clear that a subjectivist approach is faithful to the judiciary's interpretive obligations under the First Amendment for reasons noted at the outset of this section.[167] It is true that such an approach may relieve the judiciary of much of the difficulty of defining and discerning religion, including concerns about doctrinal entanglement and judicial competence, but "because the religion clauses protect 'religion,' it seems implausible that the clauses could be meaningful without a definition of 'religion,' or a definition that includes anything one asserts is a religion."[168]

Nor is it clear that a subjectivist approach is truly consistent with the Supreme Court's own commentary on the scope of religion under the First Amendment. In *Wisconsin v. Yoder*[169] – an expansive free exercise case, to be sure – the Court could not have been more unambiguous: "Although a determination of what is a 'religious' belief or practice entitled to constitutional protection may present a most delicate question, the very concept of ordered liberty precludes allowing every person to make his [or her] own standards on matters of conduct in which society as a whole has important interests."[170] Likewise, while the Court in a subsequent decision certainly did say that "religious beliefs need not be acceptable, logical, consistent, or comprehensible,"[171] it also recognized that "[o]ne can … imagine an asserted claim so bizarre, so clearly nonreligious in motivation, as not to be entitled to protection under the Free Exercise Clause"[172] – a recognition that can have meaning only if courts remain able to assess religiousness in some structured way above and beyond a litigant's subjective perceptions. Even the *Welsh* plurality, at the same time that it was capaciously construing the federal conscription law, refused to allow a registrant's own characterization of his views dictate the ultimate legal analysis.[173]

Finally, it is hardly evident that a sincerity requirement alone can adequately shoulder the burden of distinguishing meritorious from nonmeritorious claims. Although such

166 *See, e.g.*, Watts v. Fla. Int'l Univ., 495 F.3d 1289, 1299 (11th Cir. 2007) (rejecting centrality in favor of sincerity, but arguably also repudiating any independent inquiry into religiousness, seemingly accepting a litigant's assertion of religiousness at face value).

167 *See supra* notes 78–80 and accompanying text.

168 Ivan E. Bodensteiner, *The Demise of the First Amendment as a Guarantor of Religious Freedom*, 27 Whittier L. Rev. 415, 426 (2005).

169 406 U.S. 205 (1972).

170 *Id.* at 215–16 (footnote omitted); *see also* Malnak v. Yogi, 592 F.2d 197, 210 n.45 (3d Cir. 1979) (Adams, J., concurring) ("[T]he question of the definition of religion for first amendment purposes is one for the courts, and is not controlled by the subjective perceptions of believers. Supporters of new belief systems may not 'choose' to be non-religious.").

171 Thomas, 450 U.S. at 714.

172 *Id.* at 715.

173 *See* Welsh, 398 U.S. at 341 ("When a registrant states that his objections to war are 'religious,' that information is highly relevant to the question of the function his beliefs have in his life. But very few registrants are fully aware of the broad scope of the word 'religious' as used in … [the conscientious objector exemption], and accordingly a registrant's statement that his beliefs are nonreligious is a highly unreliable guide for those charged with administering the exemption.").

a requirement can separate many genuine from sham claims, even palpably contrived beliefs or belief systems, as long as they are accompanied by credible claims of adherence, still potentially could exploit a definition of religion that turned mostly or exclusively on subjective perceptions and characterizations.[174] More generally, a reluctance to assess religiousness, at least in any meaningful way, could permit and encourage such exploitation under both religion clauses – the free exercise claimant seeking some benefit, the Establishment Clause litigant trying to elude the strictures of nonestablishment[175] – precisely because the judicial oversight that normally prevents such legal gamesmanship would not be present.

### 5. *An Integrated Approach*

As indicated earlier, it is not common to find courts using a purely substantive or purely functional definition or using just one of the foregoing approaches, and this reality suggests that the best overall approach might very well be one that entails an integration of substantive and functional, as well as objective and subjective, considerations. This final subsection will not make the case for such an integrated approach other than to note that it allows courts to fulfill their role in interpreting the First Amendment (a role seemingly inhibited by a subjectivist approach) and, at the same time, potentially accords them a balance of structure and flexibility that at once can legitimize their decision making yet permit them to operate across a range of factual scenarios. The focus here, rather, will be on the qualities that should attend an integrated definition so as to maximize its validity and utility while minimizing its possible downsides. Insofar as the *Meyers* factors arguably provide a solid foundation for developing an integrated approach – as solid a foundation as any available analysis – the remaining comments thus will build on them.

First, the *Meyers* framework presumably should be enhanced, in a balanced way, with more of the functionalism of *Seeger* and *Welsh*. Second, whatever approach is developed, it should be interoperable between the Free Exercise and Establishment Clauses. Third, it should be assessed using a variety of real and hypothetical test cases, such as the lists of included and excluded beliefs found in *Meyers*. One possible criticism of the *Meyers* opinion, in fact, is that the lists it provides seem not to have been constructed through a rigorous use of the factors, and it was not always obvious why certain items were on one list rather than the other. Fourth, an integrated approach should be accompanied by the caveat (articulated in one form or another by Judges Brimmer and Adams and Professor Greenawalt) that no single factor should be deemed dispositive. But, and last, the factors probably should not remain unranked or ungrouped in terms of importance, however difficult it may be to rank or group them, and there should be some indication as to how many factors ordinarily will be sufficient to qualify under the definition. Whether as a matter of legitimacy for courts or as a matter of due process for litigants, it is problematic

174 *See* Carole M. Cusack, Invented Religions: Imagination, Fiction and Faith (2010); *cf.* Bobby Henderson, The Gospel of the Flying Spaghetti Monster (2006).

175 *See, e.g.*, Malnak v. Yogi, 592 F.2d 197, 210 n. 45 (3d Cir. 1979) (Adams, J., concurring) (in an Establishment Clause challenge to the teaching of transcendental meditation in schools, noting that there was "some indication that SCI/TM has attempted a transformation from a religion to a secular science in order to gain access to the public schools").

simply to offer up a pool of considerations with no guidance regarding which ones are more and less critical and regarding how many normally must be demonstrated by litigants. Although such guidance may render the definition less flexible and seemingly less inclusive, in reality, the absence of such guidance invites the selective or discriminatory application of the factors and, more generally, the arbitrary and unpredictable use of the definition as a whole.[176]

[176] *See* Aaron Xavier Fellmeth, *Civil and Criminal Sanctions in the Constitution and Courts*, 94 GEO. L.J. 1, 36–7 (2005) ("Multifactor tests give guidance in extreme circumstances (i.e., when most factors clearly weigh in favor of one side), but in all other cases, a subjective judgment is merely clothed with the legitimacy of an ostensibly reasoned decision. The concept of 'rule of law' comports poorly with highly subjective judgments of legality, particularly when the rule is designed to guarantee fundamental civil liberties.").

# 8 Church Property Disputes and Church Schisms

The issues underlying church property disputes and church schisms are directly connected to the role of courts vis-à-vis religion.[1] Central to this role is the notion that state and federal courts do not involve themselves in ecclesiastical disputes, but courts may address issues concerning civil or property rights as long as they need not resolve ecclesiastical issues in order to do so.[2] This rule raises numerous questions, and several settled principles of law have arisen as a result, but different jurisdictions have sometimes interpreted these rules in different ways. For the most part, as will be seen herein, each question that arises seems to garner a majority approach and several minority approaches that are generally closely related to the majority approach. One of the first questions most jurisdictions ask in church property dispute and church schism cases is what kind of

1 The terms "church property disputes" and "church schisms" are used throughout this chapter simply because most courts use this terminology and for ease of reference. Obviously, the terms cover other religious institutions, such as synagogues, mosques, Buddhist temples, Hindu temples, Sikh temples, Quaker meeting houses, Baha'i congregations, and so on. Use of these terms is not intended to be Christocentric but rather is simply a pragmatic use because the vast majority of the cases involve churches. Where a religious institution other than a church is referenced, the proper term for that religious institution will be used.

2 *See, e.g.*, Jones v. Wolf, 443 U.S. 595 (1979) (saying that, as a general proposition, courts may decide such disputes using neutral principles, but the First Amendment severely limits the role of the courts); Presbyterian Church in U.S. v. Mary Elizabeth Blue Hall Memorial Presbyterian Church, 393 U.S. 440 (1969) (holding that courts may decide property church property disputes as long as they do not need to deal with ecclesiastical matters); Watson v. Jones, 80 U.S. 679 (1871) (discussing the questions and rules to apply when considering whether the court would need to resolve ecclesiastical issues in the case); Murphy v. Green, 794 So.2d 325 (Ala. 2000) (holding that courts may address nonecclesiastical matters, based on neutral principles, without running afoul of the First Amendment); New York Annual Conference of United Methodist Church v. Fisher, 438 A.2d 62 (Conn. 1980) (holding that courts may resolve church property disputes as long as they may do so without deciding ecclesiastical matters); Fluker Community Church v. Hitchens, 419 So.2d 445 (La. 1982) (saying that courts may resolve church property disputes through neutral principles of law); Cavalry Baptist Church of Port Huron v. Shay, 290 N.W. 890 (Mich. 1940) (holding that where church property is at issue, subject to civil law, the courts may decide these rights but may not determine ecclesiastical matters); Berthiaume v. McCormack, 891 A.2d 539 (N.H. 2006) (reaffirming the proposition that courts may determine church property disputes as long as they do not involve doctrinal matters); Presbytery of Cimarron v. Westminster Presbyterian Church, 515 P.2d 211 (Okla. 1973) (saying that courts may determine property rights but not ecclesiastical matters); In re Church of St. James the Less, 888 A.2d 795 (Pa. 2005) (holding that courts may resolve church property disputes but not doctrinal matters); First Baptist Church of Paris v. Ford, 54 S.W. 892 (Tex. 1900) (determining that church property disputes may be resolved by the courts by applying ordinary principles of law without inquiry into the religious matters).

religious institution is involved? Is it hierarchical or congregational?[3] If the former, what is its structure?[4] If the latter, how does it govern itself?[5] The next question that is often

3 *See, e.g.*, Bouldin v. Alexander, 82 U.S. 131 (1872) (congregational religious institution); Jones, 443 U.S. 595 (dealing with a hierarchical religious institution but contrasting hierarchical institutions with congregational institutions); Kedroff v. St. Nicholas Cathedral of Russian Orthodox Church in North America, 344 U.S. 94 (1952) (hierarchical religious institution); Presbyterian Church in U.S., 393 U.S. 440 (hierarchical religious institution); Watson, 80 U.S. 679 (discussing general rules for both congregational and hierarchical churches but focusing on hierarchical determinations because the church in question was such); Mount Olive Primitive Baptist Church v. Patrick, 42 So.2d 617 (Ala. 1949) (congregational religious institution); Britton v. Jackson, 250 P. 763 (Ariz. 1926) (hierarchical religious institution); Protestant Episcopal Church v. Barker, 171 Cal. Rprt. 541 (Cal. Ct. App. 2d Dist 1981) (hierarchical religious institution); Trustees of Pencader Presbyterian Church in Pencader Hundred v. Gibson, 22 A.2d 782 (Del. 1941) (overturning a referee's conclusion that the religious institution was congregational and finding it to be hierarchical); Carnes v. Smith, 222 S.E.2d 322 (Ga. 1976) (hierarchical religious institution); Little Grove Church v. Todd, 26 N.E.2d 485 (Ill. 1940) (congregational religious institution); Fonken v. Community Church of Kamrar, 339 N.W.2d 810 (Iowa 1983) (hierarchical religious institution); Graffam v. Wray, 437 A.2d 627 (Me. 1981) (congregational religious institution); Shay, 290 N.W. at 890 (congregational religious institution); Protestant Episcopal Church in Diocese of New Jersey v. Graves, 417 A.2d 19 (N.J. 1980) (hierarchical religious institution); Cape v. Moore, 253 P. 506 (Okla. 1927) (congregational religious institution); Niemann v. Vaughn Community Church, 113 P.3d 463 (Wash. 2005) (congregational religious institution).

4 *See, e.g.*, Jones, 443 U.S. at 595 ("The government of the church is exercised by and through an ascending series of 'judicatories,' known as Church Sessions, Presbyteries, Synods, and a General Assembly."); Kedroff, 344 U.S. at 107–8 (holding that the legislature of New York could not break the hierarchical connection with "the central governing hierarchy of the Russian Orthodox Church, the Patriarch of Moscow and the Holy Synod" and that the creation of an autonomous North American branch of the church by the legislature violated the Fourteenth Amendment); Presbyterian Church in U.S., 393 U.S. 441–2 ["Presbyterian Church in the United States is an association of local Presbyterian churches governed by a hierarchical structure of tribunals which consists of, in ascending order, (1) the Church Session, composed of the elders of the local church; (2) the Presbytery, composed of several churches in a geographical area; (3) the Synod, generally composed of all Presbyteries within a State; and (4) the General Assembly, the highest governing body."]; Britton, 250 P. at 101 ("The local Church of God in Christ affiliated itself with the national organization having headquarters in Memphis, Tenn., and … the local church accepted and followed the doctrines and discipline of the Memphis organization."); Gibson, 22 A.2d at 786 (holding that the Pencader Church, as a member church, could not break free of the parent church, Presbyterian Church, in the hierarchical structure and take the church property with them); Fonken, 339 N.W.2d at 814 ("Like *Jones v. Wolf*, the present case involves a hierarchical church and a dispute between factions of the local congregation. The national organization in *Jones*, however, was the Presbyterian Church of the United States (PCUS) rather than UPCUSA. The constitution of UPCUSA contains provisions dealing with church government that were not shown in *Jones* to be in the PCUS constitution. Therefore the neutral principles approach would not necessarily produce the same result in this case.").

5 *See, e.g.*, Bouldin, 82 U.S. at 133 ("A congregation had by this time been organized with sufficient regularity and in full conformity with the constitution of the general Baptist Church of the United States, in which, as is known, the congregational form of government prevails; and there was at this time no serious dissensions in the particular Third Church of which we are speaking. 'The Rules of Church Order,' making part of the Baptist Manual, an authoritative book in the Baptist church generally, required that 'seven trustees' should be elected in January of each year, but provided that in case of any omission to hold an election then, the election should be held 'at the next regular meeting for business.' "); Patrick, 42 So.2d at 619 ("In the instant case the church, through its congregation, was the final arbiter, no action by a higher body having been taken. The lower court therefore correctly held that the matters complained of were not of that character which allowed court intervention."); Todd, 26 N.E.2d at 487 (finding that the church property, which was governed by an elected board of trustees, remains with the faction who "adheres to the tenets and doctrines originally taught by the congregation to whose use the property was originally dedicated" and that in this case the plaintiffs failed to show that the defendants departed from such tenets); Graffam, 437 A.2d at 629 (finding the church to be run through a series of "parliamentary rules" and meetings and by elected officials from within the body).

asked is whether the issue involved in the case requires the determination of ecclesiastical matters.[6] If so, the courts generally find that they have no jurisdiction.[7] If not, the analysis generally continues.[8]

Church property disputes often involve church schisms, but property cases are frequently held to be addressable by the courts using either neutral principles of law or another acceptable method.[9] Church schism cases that do not involve property can involve a variety of issues such as employment disputes,[10] disputes over membership status,[11]

[6] *See, e.g.*, Jones, 443 U.S. at 604 ("If in such a case the interpretation of the instruments of ownership would require the civil court to resolve a religious controversy, then the court must defer to the resolution of the doctrinal issue by the authoritative ecclesiastical body."); Watson, 80 U.S. 679 (finding that there was a question of an ecclesiastical nature).

[7] *See, e.g.*, Kreshik v. Saint Nicolas Cathedral, 363 U.S. 190 (1960) (finding that the question of who had the right to the position of archbishop of the North American Archdiocese of the Russian Orthodox Greek Catholic Church was an ecclesiastical matter and should be left up to the ecclesiastical authorities); Watson, 80 U.S. 726–7 (finding that this case involved a hierarchical church and that the courts should defer the matter, due to its ecclesiastical nature, to the church authority).

[8] *See, e.g.*, Jones, 443 U.S. at 607 (remanding the case to determine whether the facts of the case would require delving into ecclesiastical matters; if not, the analysis may continue without impugning the First Amendment); Maryland and Virginia Eldership of Churches of God v. Church of God at Sharpsburg, Inc., 396 U.S. 367 (1970) (holding that because the Maryland Court of Appeals had not impermissibly delved into ecclesiastical matters, its judgment would be upheld).

[9] Jones, 443 U.S. at 60 (holding that courts may employ neutral principles of law in church property disputes but are not required to and may adopt other constitutionally permissible methods).

[10] *See, e.g.*, Gonzalez v. Roman Catholic Archbishop of Manila, 280 U.S. 1 (1929) (holding that Gonzalez was not entitled to the position of chaplain); Serbian Eastern Orthodox Diocese for U.S. of America and Canada v. Milivojevich, 426 U.S. 696, 709 (1976) (finding that the lower courts detailed inquiry into the defrockment of a bishop was improper); Foster v. St. John's Baptist Church, 406 So.2d 389 (Ala. 1981) (holding that a pastor's removal through a congregational election was an ecclesiastical matter that the court could not resolve); Kedrovsky v. Burdikoff, 146 A. 613 (upholding a lower court's determination that there was no evidence to show that Kedrovsky was the archbishop and that even if he were found to be the archbishop, there was nothing that said he had a right to summarily dismiss the priest); Sanders v. Edwards, 34 S.E.2d 167 (Ga. 1945) (holding that where a pastor has been legally removed through church procedures, the courts may enter an order to support that action when needed); Pierce v. Iowa-Missouri Conference of Seventh-Day Adventists, 534 N.W.2d 425, 427 (Iowa 1995) (finding that the First Amendment prohibits the court's inquiry into a minister's relationship with the church because it related to an employment dispute); LeBlanc v. Davis, 432 So.2d 239, 242–3 (La. 1983) (finding that the court did have subject-matter jurisdiction and would not be improperly delving into ecclesiastical matters with regard to entertaining the question of whether a pastor had been dismissed by a majority of church members and refused to leave); Blauert v. Schupmann, 63 N.W.2d 578, 583 (Minn. 1954) (holding that where nothing under the church's constitution or the pastor's contract specified a definite term, the employment was at will, and as such, the majority of the congregation could terminate his employment at any time); Daniels v. Union Baptist Church, Inc., 55 P.3d 1012, 1014 (Okla. 2001) (holding that the question of the pastor's employment involved ecclesiastical matters that the court could not delve into); Williams v. Wilson, 563 S.E.2d 320, 325 (S.C. 2002) [holding that the congregation (in a congregational church), not the board of trustees, had the power to remove the pastor, so his removal by the board was "a nullity" and also holding that the congregation's vote to replace the trustees was not valid because the congregation failed to provide notice to the trustees in accordance with church bylaws]; Cha v. Korean Presbyterian Church of Washington, 553 S.E.2d 511, 515 (Va. 2001) (holding that the court lacked jurisdiction to determine the pastor's claim for wrongful termination due to the ecclesiastical nature of the inquiry); Gillespie v. Elkins Southern Baptist Church, 350 S.E.2d 715, 719 (W. Va. 1986) (holding that where a congregational church has authority to terminate a pastor and they exercise that authority to remove a pastor and provide adequate notice of the meeting, the court may go no further in their inquiry).

[11] *See, e.g.*, Taylor v. Jackson, 273. F. 345, 347 (C.A.D.C. 1921) (finding that the court's "inquiry must be confined to an examination of the rules of the church organization, for the purpose of determining whether

disputes over control of the church,[12] and disputes over financial matters.[13] This chapter will address the law applicable to church property disputes and that applicable to church schisms in separate sections. The law addressing church property disputes is

there has been a substantial compliance with those rules" and holding that only one of the members was not accorded notice in compliance with the rules and would be reinstated; the other members reinstatements were reversed); U.S v. First Colored Baptist Church, 3 F.2d 296, 297 (C.A.D.C 1926) (holding that the courts could not review the determination of a church to remove a member due to the ecclesiastical nature of the inquiry); Abyssinnia Missionary Baptist Church v. Nixon, 340 So.2d 746, 748 (Ala. 1977) (reversing the lower court's finding that the court lacked jurisdiction to inquire into the removal of several former Baptist church members and on remand allowing the former members to present evidence as to whether the proper procedures, in accordance with church policy, were followed); First Free Will Baptist Church of Blountstown v. Franklin, 4 So.2d 390, 393 (Fla. 1941) (finding that the court could not interfere with a church's decision to expel certain members as long as they followed their own procedures and there was no evidence of "a showing of fraud, collusion or arbitrariness."); Kompier v. Thegza, 13 N.E.2d 229, 232 (Ind. 1938) ("It is not the province of the court to decide who is a member of a church or whether the excommunicated have been denied membership justly or unjustly, regularly or irregularly. The decision of the church authorities upon that subject is final."); Bowen v. Green, 272 S.E.2d 433, 435 (S.C. 1980) (The court said, "Generally, a civil court has no authority to intervene in cases involving expulsion from church membership where there is no question of an invasion of a civil, property or contract right." Notwithstanding this general rule, the court determined that where the congregation normally had the power of excommunication and the expelled members were excommunicated by the board of trustees and deacons with no explanation as to the source of their authority to do so, the court would restore the "status quo.").

12 *See, e.g.*, Bouldin, 103 U.S. at 331 (involving a dispute between two different boards of trustees for control of the Third Colored Baptist Church); Yates v. El Bethel Primitive Baptist Church, 847 So.2d 331 (Ala. 2002) (concerning a dispute between a reverend and a board of deacons and trustees as to the election of a new board); Epperson v. Myers, 58 So.2d 150, 152 (Fla. 1952) ("When a 'faction' of the church arrogates authority to itself, disrupts the organization and sets at naught well-defined rules of church order, there is no course left for those who desire their rights settled through orderly processes but resort to the courts."); Moustakis v. Hellenic Orthodox of Peabody and Salem, 159 N.E. 453, 455 (Mass. 1928) (determining that a dispute as to who should be recognized as an archbishop was a purely ecclesiastical matter that could not be determined by the courts); Second Baptist Church of Reno v. Mount Zion Baptist Church, 466 P.2d 212, 215 (Nev. 1970) (holding that a court has the power to oversee a church election to determine control of the church); First Presbyterian v. United Presbyterian, 464 N.E.2d 454, 458 (N.Y. 1984) (holding that during a dispute over control of the church, the courts may not delve into whether the local church had a right to withdraw from the regional church; it was an ecclesiastical matter that civil courts may not entertain); Chrapko v. Kobasa, 114 A. 254, 255 (Pa. 1921) ("The law is clear that even a majority faction cannot divert a church from the purpose for which it was established, and those adhering to that purpose, though a minority, are the true congregation.").

13 *See, e.g.*, Bouldin, 103 U.S. 330, 331 (determining that no further payments were due to Bouldin for use of the Church unless he came forward with the records requested by the court); Gonzalez, 280 U.S. at 18 (determining that since Gonzalez was not entitled to the chaplaincy, he was not entitled to the funds from the position); Smith v. Swormstedt, 57 U.S. 288, 303 (1853) (determining that a church fund known as the "Book of Concern" should be split between the northern and southern branches of the Methodist Episcopal Church); Edwards v. Thomas, 51 S.E.2d 855 (Ga. 1949) (finding that the court could not rule on matters of speculation that the pastor might take the funds in the church treasury when the real issue was the internal workings of the church); Graffam, 437 A.2d at 635 (holding that the lower court erred in dismissing a suit that involved questions involving the handling of church funds because this was not a purely ecclesiastical matter); Second International Baha'i Council v. Chase, 106 P.3d 1168, 1174 (Mont. 2005) (holding that the court could determine questions of corporate control and funds without delving into ecclesiastical matters); Second Baptist Church of Reno, 466 P.2d at 217 (holding that one side in the church dispute over money was bound by their stipulation that they would accept the court's determination of the outcome); Pearson v. Church of God, 478 S.E.2d 849, 853 (S.C. 1996) (finding that a case involving the discontinuation of a retired minister's pension was a contract matter that could be decided without inquiry into ecclesiastical matters).

frequently used in church schism cases,[14] so we will first address church property disputes and then church schisms.

## A. Church Property Disputes

The most recognized rule applicable to church property disputes comes from *Watson v. Jones*,[15] decided by the U.S. Supreme Court in 1871. The *Watson* case involved a dispute over church property at the Walnut Street Presbyterian Church, located in Kentucky.[16] The ultimate question was which of two factions claiming to have authority to control church property was entitled to exercise that authority.[17] The dispute arose over the Civil War and the issue of slavery. The General Assembly of the Presbyterian Church denounced slavery and required those who aided the Confederacy or who supported slavery to repent, and both the Louisville Presbytery and the Synod of Kentucky split over this issue.[18] In the case of the Walnut Street Church those who wanted to leave the national church sought and obtained admission to a newly formed entity, the Presbyterian Church of the Confederacy.[19] The schism in the Walnut Street Church arose as a result of these events.[20]

The U.S. Supreme Court ultimately had to determine which of these two factions was entitled to control the church property constituted the Walnut Street Church. As the Court explained in its decision, it had to do so without determining purely ecclesiastical matters; that is, the Court could address civil and property rights in a church dispute, but only to the extent that it did not have to determine ecclesiastical issues in the process.[21] In an oft-quoted passage that has stood as a fundamental tenet of the law applicable to church property disputes, the Court laid out the following rule:

> The questions which have come before civil courts concerning the rights to property held by ecclesiastical bodies, may … be profitably classified under three general heads.
>
> 1. The first of these is when the property which is the subject of the controversy has been, by the deed or will of the donor, or other instrument by which the property

[14] *See, e.g.*, Milivojevich, 426 U.S. at 709 (1976) (applying the principles applied to church property disputes to an employment question and holding that the lower court's detailed inquiry into ecclesiastical matters was improper); Williams v. Jones, 61 So.2d 101 (Ala. 1952) (applying the general principle that courts may not determine ecclesiastical matters, only matters such as civil rights and property, to a case involving questions of church membership and control of the church); Partin v. Tucker, 172 So. 89 (Fla. 1937) (applying the general principles laid out in *Watson* to a case involving a dispute over control of a church and expelled members); Kompier, 13 N.E.2d 229 (holding that the courts may not review ecclesiastical matters in church membership matters); Brown v. Mt. Olive Baptist Church, 124 N.W.2d 445, 446 (holding that, as a general rule, courts may not exercise jurisdiction over ecclesiastical matters, in this case as applied to church membership and expulsion); Chase, 106 P.3d 1173–4 (applying the laws used to decide church property disputes to a schism case involving questions of board membership and the continuing effect of a resolution); Pearson, 478 S.E.2d at 852 (recognizing that, consistent with the law of church property disputes, courts have no authority to resolve ecclesiastical matters but must try civil matters); Gillespie, 350 S.E.2d at 718 (saying that in matters involving hierarchical churches, the court must wait for final appeal through the church structure, but in congregational matters, final action by the local church can be reviewed).

[15] 80 U.S. 679 (1871).

[16] *Id.*

[17] *Id.* at 717.

[18] *Id.* at 690–2.

[19] *Id.* at 691–2.

[20] *Id.* at 690–9.

[21] *Id.* at 713–14, 727–9.

is held, by the express terms of the instrument devoted to the teaching, support, or spread of some specific form of religious doctrine or belief.

2. The second is when the property is held by a religious congregation which, by the nature of its organization, is strictly independent of other ecclesiastical associations, and so far as church government is concerned, owes no fealty or obligation to any higher authority.
3. The third is where the religious congregation or ecclesiastical body holding the property is but a subordinate member of some general church organization in which there are superior ecclesiastical tribunals with a general and ultimate power of control more or less complete, in some supreme judicatory over the whole membership of that general organization.[22]

The Court held that the Presbyterian Church was in the third category (i.e., it is a hierarchical church) and held that in this category civil courts should defer to the decision of the highest church judicatory "to which the matter has been carried."[23] Moreover, the Court held that the second category (i.e., congregational churches) should be governed "by the ordinary principles that govern voluntary associations,"[24] which frequently are governed by majority rule or which vest control in congregational officers.[25] It is important to note at this point that another approach based on "neutral principles of law" has been added to the fray.[26] This latter approach, and its interaction with the former approach at the state court level, will be discussed in subsection A.4. In *Watson*, the Court deferred to the decision of the original church hierarchy, which vested control in the faction that did not seek to leave the church.[27] The other faction, the Court held, had in effect abandoned its right to control church property by splitting off into a new church against the will of the original church's hierarchy.[28]

### 1. *Express and Implied Trusts*

The first category of situations involved in church property disputes set forth by the *Watson* Court is express trusts and similar devices reflecting the express will of the donor to give the property for a specified use or to devote it to the propagation of a specific faith or set of doctrines.[29] Many jurisdictions still require an express trust or similar legally valid document reflecting the will of the donor.[30] A few jurisdictions also recognize

[22] *Id.* at 722–3.
[23] *Id.* at 726–7.
[24] *Id.* at 725.
[25] *Cf. Id.*
[26] Jones v. Wolf, 443 U.S. 595 (1979); *Cf.* Presbyterian Church in U.S. v. Mary Elizabeth Blue Hull Memorial Presbyterian Church, 393 U.S. 440 (1969).
[27] Watson, 80 U.S. at 728–9, 735.
[28] *Id.* at 735.
[29] *Id.* at 722.
[30] *See, e.g.*, Britton, 250 P. at 765–6 (finding that whoever the beneficiary of the express trust was would prevail); Korean United Presbyterian Church v. Presbytery of the Pacific, 281 Cal. Rptr. 396, 413 (Cal. Ct. App. 2d Dist. 1991) (requiring an express trust); Mt. Olive African Methodist Episcopal Church of Fruitland, Inc. v. Board of Incorporators of African Methodist Episcopal Church Inc., 703 A.2d 194, 202 (Md. Ct. App.) ("[The] three ways in which hierarchical denominations may insure that they maintain control over local church property: 1. requiring the local churches to place reverter clauses in the deeds to its property; 2. providing in their constitutions or other authoritative sources for the reversion of local church property upon the withdrawal by a local congregation, with an implied consent by the local church

implied trusts as valid evidence that church property was intended for a specific use or to support a particular faith or set of religious commitments.[31] Several jurisdictions generally fit within the first group of jurisdictions but have recognized a limited number of circumstances where an implied trust will be recognized.[32] California is an unusually strict express trust jurisdiction. In California, absent an express trust or other document (e.g., church bylaws, etc.) expressly stating that a church property is meant to be controlled by a regional or national church, local churches own such property and have a right to control it even when they are part of a much larger hierarchical church as set forth in subsection A.3.[33]

to the reversion provision; 3. obtaining from the General Assembly an Act providing for that result."); Bennison v. Sharp, 329 N.W.2d 466. 470 (Mich. Ct. App. 1982) (requiring a showing of an express trust for a faction, even if a majority, who no longer adheres to the beliefs of the parent church in hierarchical structure to retain the property); Boyles v. Roberts, 121 S.W. 805, 807–8 (Miss. 1909) (saying that the property of a congregational church, absent an express trust, is generally controlled by the majority).

31 *See, e.g.*, Holiman v. Dovers, 366 S.W.2d 197 (Ark. 1963) (finding, essentially, an implied trust that recognized a right to the property for those who continued to follow the original beliefs of the church even if they be in the minority); Bishop and Diocese of Colorado v. Mote, 716 P.2d 85, 100 (Colo. 1986) ("Colorado recognizes that the intent to create a trust can be inferred from the nature of property transactions, the circumstances surrounding the holding of and transfer of property, the particular documents or language employed, and the conduct of the parties."); Fisher, 438 A.2d at 68–9 ("Where the property is not subject to an express trust, we must decide, without becoming entangled in religious controversy, what is the nature of the relationship between the Methodist Church and the local church, and the nature of the affiliation of Round Hill to the Methodist Church."); St. John's Presbytery v. Central Presbyterian Church of St. Petersburg, 102 So.2d 714, 719 (Fla. 1958) (recognizing an implied trust where the property was given to the local church at no cost from the parent church, there was an implied trust in favor of the faction that adhered to the beliefs of the parent church); Fonken, 339 N.W.2d at 818 (recognizing an implied trust in the parent church based on the church constitution); Presbytery of Bismarck v. Allen, 22 N.W.2d 625, 632 (N.D. 1946) ("Where real property is conveyed to a local religious association or corporation, which local society is a subordinate member of a general church organization, with superior ecclesiastical tribunals with ultimate power in some supreme judicatory, and the conveyance contains no special trust, then the property is not owned by the local congregation or the individuals thereof, but is held in trust for the general church body and it cannot be used in contravention of the decisions of the superior church judicatory."); Foss v. Dykstra, 342 N.W.2d 220, 223 (S.D. 1983) (finding that a local church's connection with a national church was not such as to create a trust and requiring an express trust for the national church to have a claim).

32 *See, e.g.*, Carnes, 222 S.E.2d at 328–9 (Ga. 1976) (While an implied trust may not be recognized under certain circumstances, i.e., when the general church provided none of the funding, it may be recognized when a conveyance is made to the local church from the parent church in certain circumstances, such as where church documents provide for it.); Fortin v. Roman Catholic Bishop of Worcester, 625 N.E.2d 1352, 1357–8 (Mass. 1994) ("Likewise the plaintiffs' claims of equitable ownership based on a theory of constructive trust were properly dismissed. Under Massachusetts law, a court will declare a party a constructive trustee of property for the benefit of another if he [or she] acquired the property through fraud, mistake, breach of duty, or in other circumstances indicating that he [or she] would be unjustly enriched.").

33 *See* California-Nevada Annual Conference of United Methodist Church v. St. Luke;s United Methodist Church, 17 Cal. Rptr. 3d 442, 452–3 (Cal. Ct. App. 5th Dist. 2004) (holding that while there was an express trust in the national church, this trust was revocable by the local church who created it absent express terms in the trust to the contrary); Guardian Angel Polish Nat. Catholic Church of Los Angeles, Inc. v. Grotnik, 13 Cal. Rptr. 3d 552, 561 (Cal. Ct. App. 2d Dist. 2004) (holding that while California laws do require an express trust or other document for the national church to have an interest in the local church property, in this case the church bylaws and constitution provided such a trust); Korean United Presbyterian Church, 281 Cal. Rptr. at 413 (determining that an express trust, as required, in the national church did exist); Barker, 171 Cal. Rptr. at 552–3 (requiring a national church to show an express trust to lay claim to local church property).

One of the most common questions that arise in trust cases is how to approach a situation where the donor sets forth an intent that a property should be used for the propagation of a specific sect and the document of conveyance mentions specific doctrines of that sect, but in subsequent years the sect changes some of the relevant doctrines.[34] Most courts to address this issue have held that the donor understood that the sect might alter some doctrines in the future and as long as the church is still a member of the specified sect, the grant of the property to that sect remains valid.[35] Another variation on this theme is where the sect itself merges with another sect or sects. In such situations, many courts look to whether the new entity reflects the faith specified in the trust, but do so without determining ecclesiastical questions.[36] That is, the court must determine if the new entity is consistent with the old but must often rely on the actions of the new entity to make such determinations.[37] Some jurisdictions use the concept of implied trust to deal with changes to church doctrine or polity which may not have been foreseen by the conveyor of an express trust.[38] A few eschew the distinction between implied and express trusts and focus solely on the intent of the conveyance as set forth in the language of relevant documents along with other evidence of the intent of the donor.[39]

[34] *See, e.g.*, Watson, 80 U.S. at 722 (holding that when the trust designates the property for the "teaching, support, or spread of some specific form of religious doctrine or belief," the court will recognize the right to the property in those who still follow the doctrine in the trust); Swormstedt, 57 U.S. 288, 294 (1853) (dealing with a question of whether the local church could retain the property that was in trust for the parent church if the parent church organization had been destroyed and reorganized).

[35] *See, e.g.*, Gibson, 22 A.2d at 789 (recognizing the principle that in a case where a church has deviated from the express trust, the court must inquire whether the deviation was "so far variant as to defeat the declared objects of the trust"); Partin, 172 So. at 93 (holding that for a church to lose its property, which was dedicated to the Christian religion, it must have abandoned the fundamental principles of Christianity); Little Grove Church v. Todd, 26 N.E.2d 485, 487 (Ill. 1940) (holding that for a court to intervene, the changes "must be a real substantial departure from the purpose of the trust"); Davis v. Scher, 97 N.W.2d 137, 141 (Mich. 1959) ("The Michigan Supreme Court has held on numerous occasions that the membership of a congregation, which is one of several congregations belonging to a particular religious faith to which the local church property and practice is [*sic*] dedicated, does not have the right to effect, by vote of a momentary majority, a change in religious practice, not conformable with the origin and historic character of the faith of the church of which the local congregation is one member, as against those who faithfully adhere to the characteristic doctrine of the church, and thereby deprive the minority of the use of the church property."); Kensaw Free Baptist Church v. Lattimer, 174 N.W. 296, 297 (Neb. 1919) ("When … property is given to a church which is a strictly congregational or independent organization … with no specific trust attached, other than that it is given for church purposes … the ordinary contributor to a particular church regards it as a living organism, subject to change and growth. He [or she] would not attach conditions to the contrary, if he [or she] could. So long as it continues by regular succession, retaining its identity as the church to which the donation was made, he [or she] will not complain, even though there are changes of doctrine or method which do not amount to an abandonment of the original purpose.").

[36] *See* Boyles, 121 S.W. at 849–50 (dealing with a merger). *But see* Berkaw v. Mayflower Congregational Church, 170 N.W.2d 905, 907–8 (Mich. Ct. App. 1969) ("Where there is no agreement that a departure [from church doctrine] has occurred, the ecclesiastical conflict destroys civil court jurisdiction to resolve the property dispute.").

[37] *See* Boyles, 121 S.W. 805, 849 (Miss. 1909) (finding the differences in the merging sects to be minimal).

[38] *See* St. John's Presbytery, 102 So.2d at 719 (recognizing an implied trust in the members of a church who were loyal to the parent church for which the original trust was created).

[39] *See, e.g.*, Harris v. Apostolic Overcoming Holy Church of God, Inc., 457 So.2d 385, 388 (Ala. 1984) (focusing solely on the intent of the trust); Mote, 716 P.2d at 87 (focusing on the intent as set forth in church documents); First Rebecca Baptist Church Inc. v. Atlantic Cotton Mills, 440 S.E.2d 159, 160 (Ga. 1993) (interpreting the express trust narrowly and only looking at the intent of the donor); Fluker Community Church, 419 So.2d at 448 (determining the rights based on the intent of the donor);

## 2. *Congregational Churches*

The general rule for determining who governs and controls property in congregational churches is roughly that set forth in *Watson*.[40] Most courts recognize the will of the majority in congregations,[41] unless the congregation has adopted an alternative governance structure through a constitution, bylaws, or other governing document.[42] Courts frequently apply neutral principles of law, as discussed later, to church property disputes,[43] but one of the neutral principles many courts have applied is the governance structure and governing documents of the congregation.[44] Thus in some cases the doctrine from *Watson* is implicitly woven together with the neutral principles of law concept,[45] whereas in other cases this connection is explicit.[46] Without addressing ecclesiastical matters, courts will look to the secular indicia of property ownership and

Lindstrom v. Tell, 154 N.W. 969, 969 (Minn. 1915) ("Where a church corporation is formed for the purpose of promoting certain defined doctrines of religious faith which are set forth in its corporate articles, the church property which it acquires is impressed with a trust to carry out that purpose, and a majority of the congregation cannot divert the property to other inconsistent uses against the protest of a minority, however small."); Mt. Helm Baptist Church v. Jones, 30 So. 714, 717 (Miss. 1901) ("The property is held in trust by the church for the purpose for which it was dedicated by the donor, and for that purpose alone."); Niemann, 113 P.3d at 467 (looking only at the intent of the express trust, but looking to extrinsic evidence to determine the true intent).

40 *See, e.g.*, Maryland and Virginia Eldership of the Churches of God v. Church of God at Sharpsburg, Inc., 396 U.S. 367, 368–9 (1970) (explicitly recognizing the *Watson* rules for congregational churches); Crumbley v. Solomon, 254 S.E.2d 330, 333 (Ga. 1979) (following the *Watson* rules); Graffam, 437 A.2d at 632 (same); Boyles, 121 S.W. at 842–3 (same); Cape, 253 P. at 509 (same); First Baptist Church of Paris v. Fort, 54 S.W. 892, 896 (Tex. 1900) (same).

41 *See, e.g.*, Bouldin, 82 U.S. at 140 ("In a congregational church, the majority, if they adhere to the organization and to the doctrines, represent the church."); Crumbley, 254 S.E.2d at 333 (recognizing that in a congregational church, the will of the majority rules); Graffam, 437 A.2d at 632 (same); Shay, 290 N.W. at 892 (same); Smith v. St. John Baptist Church of Bozeman, 211 P.2d 975, 977 (Mont. 1949) (same); Cape v. Moore, 253 P. 506, 509 (Okla. 1927) (same); Fort, 54 S.W. at 897–8 (same).

42 Holiman, 366 S.W.2d at 200 ("It is firmly settled that the controlling faction will not be permitted to divert the church property to another denomination or to the support of doctrines, usages, and practices basically opposed to those characteristic of the particular church."); Boyles, 121 S.W. at 842–3 (recognizing the right of the minority against a majority when they remain faithful to the trust); Cape, 253 P. at 509 (saying that the outcome, which recognized the will of the majority, may have been different had there been conditions attached to the deed).

43 *See, e.g.*, Jones, 443 U.S. at 602–3 (finding that the use of neutral principles of law to decide church property disputes is constitutional); Presbyterian Church in U.S., 393 U.S. at 449 (dealing with a hierarchal church but broadly recognizing that neutral principles of law may be used to decide church property disputes); Clough v. Wilson, 368 A.2d 231, 234 (Conn. 1976) (applying the neutral principles of law approach); Carnes, 222 S.E.2d at 323 (using neutral principles analysis); Graffam, 437 A.2d at 634 (applying neutral principles approach); Berthiaume, 891 A.2d at 545 (using a neutral principles of law approach); Atkins v. Walker, 200 S.E.2d 641, 650 (N.C. 1973) (applying neutral principles approach).

44 *See, e.g.*, Clough, 368 A.2d at 234 (recognizing that the lower court could have looked to the church's articles of incorporation to help make a decision based on neutral principles of law); Graffam, 437 A.2d at 633 (looking to the church constitution); Atkins, 200 S.E.2d at 650 (looking to the governing structure of the Baptist church and the church constitution); Piletich v. Deretich, 328 N.W.2d 696, 700–1 (looking to governing documents and structure of the church under a neutral principles of law approach).

45 *See, e.g.*, Mote, 716 P.2d at 95 (recognizing the neutral principals of law approach and implicitly weaving some of the *Watson* doctrine into it); Graffam, 437 A.2d at 633–4 (same); Atkins, 200 S.E.2d at 650 (N.C. 1973) (same); Piletich, 328 N.W.2d at 701 (same).

46 *See, e.g.*, Mote, 716 P.2d at 95 (recognizing the neutral principals of law approach and implicitly weaving some of the *Watson* doctrine into it); Graffam, 437 A.2d at 633–4 (same); Atkins, 200 S.E.2d at 650 (N.C. 1973) (same); Piletich, 328 N.W.2d at 701 (same).

control, such as deeds, church governance documents, state property law, and wills and trusts granting the property.[47] These and other means for determining church property disputes under neutral principles will be discussed further in Section A.4.

Most courts will go to great lengths to avoid hearing ecclesiastical questions because it has long been held that civil courts have no jurisdiction over such matters.[48] As a practical matter, however, it is sometimes hard to determine where the secular ends and the ecclesiastical begins, so the majority of courts defer to congregational decisions and/or secular documents and will only get involved in questioning congregational decisions when the procedure used to reach such decisions is contrary to church governance documents[49] or, in some cases, state law governing charitable and/or religious corporations.[50] When the dispute is over who constitutes the congregation courts will generally defer to the body or faction that constitutes the majority of a congregational church.[51] This enables courts to answer the civil law questions without making religious determinations. A small minority of jurisdictions, however, focus on which parties continue to follow the religious principles held by the congregational church prior to the schism or other events giving rise to the property dispute.[52] They do so without determining the validity or nature

47 *See, e.g.*, Mote, 716 P.2d at 95 (recognizing the neutral principals of law approach and implicitly weaving some of the *Watson* doctrine into it); Graffam, 437 A.2d at 633–4 (same); Atkins, 200 S.E.2d at 650 (N.C. 1973) (same); Piletich, 328 N.W.2d at 701 (same).

48 *See, e.g.*, Jones, 443 U.S. at 604 (1979) (holding that civil courts have no jurisdiction of ecclesiastical matters); Presbyterian Church in U.S., 393 U.S. at 449 (1969) (same); Watson, 80 U.S. at 710 (same).

49 *See, e.g.*, Bouldin, 82 U.S. at 140 (1872) ("In a congregational church, the majority, if they adhere to the organization and to the doctrines, represent the church."); Patrick, 42 So.2d at 618 (recognizing the principle that courts will only intervene in congregational decisions when they are a "radical departure of doctrine to justify court action"); Elston v. Wilborn, 186 S.W.2d 662, 664 (Ark. 1945) (deferring to the decisions of the congregation and their governing structure regarding the election of trustees); Partin, 172 So. at 93 (deferring to congregational decisions unless they are a significant departure from church doctrine or principals); Christian Church of Tama v. Carpenter, 79 N.W. 375, 376 (Iowa 1899) (finding the decisions of the church leaders to be contrary to the primary governing document, the New Testament); Enix v. Owns, 271 S.W. 1091, 1093 (Ky. Ct. App. 1925) (interpreting a trust narrowly to allow the majority of the church to join a different assembly); Shay, 290 N.W. at 892 (Mich. 1940) (deferring to the congregation's decisions so long as they conformed with Baptist principles); Anderson v. Byers, 69 N.W.2d 227, 232 (Wis. 1955) ("The evidence in this case supports the trial court's finding that there has been no 'real and substantial' departure from the Baptist faith and doctrine by defendants, and under the law the property must remain in the majority.").

50 *See, e.g.*, Samoan Congregational etc. Church in U.S. v. Samoan Congregational etc. Church of Oceanside, 135 Cal.Rptr. 793, 798 (Cal.App. 1977) (recognizing that state law could be used to help determine a property dispute in a congregational church); First Rebecca Baptist Church, Inc. v. Atlantic Cotton Mills, 440 S.E.2d 159, 161 (Ga. 1993) (holding that a reverter clause under state law was enforceable against a congregational church); Enix, 271 S.W. at 1093 (saying that the minority's remedy was a specific state law protecting the minority of a church in the case of a schism); St. John Baptist Church of Bozeman, 211 P.2d 975 (Mont. 1949) (using state law regarding whether or not a trustee of a congregation could sell the church property); Reid v. Johnston, 85 S.E.2d 114, 118 (N.C.1954) (The court cites state law as support for the proposition that the majority of a congregation "is supreme and is entitled to control its church property only so long as the majority remains true to the fundamental faith, usages, customs, and practices of this particular church, as accepted by both factions before the dispute arose.").

51 *See, e.g.*, Bouldin, 82 U.S. at 140 ("In a congregational church, the majority, if they adhere to the organization and to the doctrines, represent the church."); Crumbley, 254 S.E.2d at 333 (recognizing that in a congregational church, the will of the majority rules); Graffam, 437 A.2d at 632 (same); Shay, 290 N.W. at 892 (same); St. John Baptist Church of Bozeman, 211 P.2d at 977 (same); Cape, 253 P. at 509 (same); Fort, 54 S.W. 892, 896, 897–8 (Tex. 1900) (same).

52 Holiman, 366 S.W.2d at 200 ("It is firmly settled that the controlling faction will not be permitted to divert the church property to another denomination or to the support of doctrines, usages, and practices basically

of such principles, but still in these jurisdictions the principles in place prior to the property dispute remain an important focus.[53]

In such jurisdictions, the courts do not claim to have jurisdiction over ecclesiastical matters but rather argue that religious doctrine may be explored to validate civil and property rights.[54] The courts do not analyze the doctrines for their religious significance but rather for what they say about the civil or property rights involved.[55] Thus these courts leave the ecclesiastical doctrines as they found them, only using these doctrines as understood before the dispute began in order to determine civil or property rights.[56] It should seem obvious that such jurisdictions come much closer to the secular-ecclesiastical dispute line than most jurisdictions and therefore increase the risk of affecting religious decisions and/or doctrines, albeit unintentionally.[57] Every jurisdiction has rejected on Establishment and Free Exercise Clause grounds the old English rule allowing civil courts to make ecclesiastical decisions.[58] Given First Amendment concerns, jurisdictions in the United States are uniform in their refusal to adjudicate ecclesiastical disputes.[59]

opposed to those characteristic of the particular church."); Davis, 97 N.W.2d at 141 (Mich. 1959) (recognizing the right of a minority when they remain faithful to the original religious practices); Boyles, 121 S.W. at 842–3 (recognizing the right of the minority against a majority when they remain faithful to the trust); Cape, 253 P. at 509 (saying that the outcome, which recognized the will of the majority, may have been different had there been conditions attached to the deed); Hughes v. Grossman, 201 P.2d 670, 674 (Kan. 1949) (recognizing the right of the minority if they remain faithful to the beliefs of the religious society as it existed prior to the schism).

53 Holiman, 366 S.W.2d at 200 (Ark. 1963) (discussing how the principles in place prior to the dispute come into play); Davis, 97 N.W.2d 137, 141 (Mich. 1959) (discussing the principles of Jewish Orthodox Law).

54 *See, e.g.*, Holiman, 366 S.W.2d at 199 (arguing that an inquiry into doctrine, protecting the minority is necessary in the case of congregational churches because "there is no recourse within the denomination"); Davis, 97 N.W.2d at 140–1 (admitting that while the courts do not have jurisdiction over ecclesiastical matters, they may intervene to protect property rights and the freedom of religion of the minority).

55 *See, e.g.*, Holiman, 366 S.W.2d at 200 (avoiding comment on ecclesiastical matters and focusing on how the congregation's doctrine applies to the property involved); Davis, 97 N.W.2d at 140–1 (Mich. 1959) (determining that because the congregation was an Orthodox Jewish congregation and that Orthodox Jews may not participate in services with mixed seating, this prevented members from participating in the services and placed in conflict a property right as it relates to the Orthodox doctrine).

56 *See, e.g.*, Holiman, 366 S.W.2d at 200–1 (using the church doctrine, as understood before the schism, to determine if the departures were significant enough for the court to intervene); Davis, 97 N.W.2d at 141 (applying the fundamental precepts of Jewish Orthodox doctrine to determine if a property right was involved and who remained faithful to the original doctrine).

57 *See, e.g.*, Holiman, 366 S.W.2d at 201 (The court looked to the church doctrines and determined that there had been a substantial departure from doctrine by the majority. While the court insisted that it did not delve into ecclesiastical matters, the inquiry, by its very nature, involved matters of religious doctrine.); Davis, 97 N.W.2d at 144 (In this case there was an explicit question of whether the court had gone too far and was in fact determining ecclesiastical questions, but the court dismissed this argument in this particular case "because of defendants' calculated risk of not offering proofs, no dispute exists as to the teaching of Orthodox Judaism as to mixed seating.").

58 *See, e.g.*, Jones, 443 U.S. 595, 618 (rejecting the English rule on First Amendment grounds); Presbyterian Church in U.S., 393 U.S. at 446–9 (same); Watson, 80 U.S. at 724 (rejecting the English rule); Decker v. Berean Baptist Church, 624 P.2d 1094, 1097–8 (Or. App. 1981) (recognizing that the First Amendment severely limits the courts' inquires into church property disputes and may not determine matters which are wholly ecclesiastical); Original Glorious Church of God in Christ, Inc. of Apostolic Faith v. Myers, 367 S.E.2d 30, 31 (W. Va. 1988).

59 *See, e.g.*, Jones, 443 U.S. at 618 (recognizing that courts do not have authority over purely ecclesiastical matters); Watson, 80 U.S. 679, 724 (same); Odoms v. Woodall, 20 So.2d 849, 851 (Ala. 1945) (same); Carnes, 222 S.E. at 325 (same); Hackney v. Vawter, 18 P. 699, 703 (Kan. 1888) (same); Western Conference of Original Free Will Baptists of N.C. v. Miles, 129 S.E.2d 600, 606 (same); Decker v. Berean Baptist

### 3. *Hierarchical Churches*

Hierarchical churches are, as the term suggests, churches with formal hierarchies.[60] The most obvious examples include the Roman Catholic Church, Eastern Orthodox Churches, the Episcopalian Church, and the Presbyterian Church.[61] There are a number of others.[62] These churches share several traits that place them in this category. As will be seen, however, there are some churches that do not fit neatly into this category but that have nonetheless been considered hierarchical by courts.[63]

The factors most often used by courts to determine that a given church is hierarchical include whether there are ecclesiastical courts that can bind churches and church members[64]; whether there is a general set of rules and procedures that purports to bind individual churches within the broader church[65]; whether a church has bound itself in some way to a national, regional, or international body[66]; whether religious precepts are

Church, 624 P.2d 1094, 1097–8 (Or. App. 1981) (same); Landrith v. Hudgins, 120 S.W. 783, 807 (Tenn. 1907) (same); Fort, 54 S.W. at 896 (same).

60 Watson, 80 U.S. at 722–3.

61 *See, e.g.*, Jones, 443 U.S. at 597 (dealing with the hierarchy of the Presbyterian Church in the United States); Serbian Eastern Orthodox Diocese for the United States and Canada, v. Milivojevich, 426 U.S. 696, 696 (1976) (dealing with the hierarchy of the Serbian Orthodox Church); Presbyterian Church in the U.S., 393 U.S. at 441–2 (dealing with the hierarchy of the Presbyterian Church); Kedroff, 344 U.S. at 100–1 (dealing with the hierarchy of the Russian Orthodox Church); Protestant Episcopal Church v. Barker, 171 Cal. Rptr. 541, 543 (Cal. Ct. App. 2d Dist. 1981) (dealing with the hierarchy of Protestant Episcopal Church); Mote, 716 P.2d at 87 (dealing with the hierarchy of the Protestant Episcopal Church in the United States); Fonken, 339 N.W.2d at 811 (dealing with the hierarchy of the United Presbyterian Church); Fluker Community Church v. Hitchens, 419 So.2d 445, 447 (La. 1844) (dealing with the hierarchy of the African Methodist Episcopal Church); Fortin, 625 N.E.2d at 1353–4 (dealing with the hierarchy of the Roman Catholic Church); Berthiaume, 891 A.2d at 545–6 (dealing with the hierarchy of the Roman Catholic Church).

62 *See, e.g.*, Britton, 250 P. at 764 (dealing with the Church of God in Christ, a hierarchical church); East Lake Methodist Episcopal Church, Inc. v. Trustees of Peninsula-Delaware Annual Conference of the United Methodist, 731 A.2d 798, 810 (Del. 1999) (dealing with the United Methodist Church, a hierarchical church); Carnes, 222 S.E.2d 322, 325 (Ga. 1976) (dealing with the United Methodist Church); Church of God Pentecostal, Inc. v. Freewill Pentecostal Church of God, Inc., 716 So.2d 200 (Miss. 1998) (dealing with the Church of God Pentecostal, a hierarchical church); Harlem Church of Seventh Day Adventists v. Greater New York Corporation of Seventh Day Adventists, 198 N.E. 615, 616 (N.Y. Ct. App. 1935) (dealing with the Seventh Day Adventists organization, which is structured hierarchically); Myers, 367 S.E.2d at 31 (W. Va. 1988) (dealing with the Original Glorious Church of God in Christ, a hierarchical church).

63 *See* Emberry Community Church v. Bloomington District Missionary and Church Extension Society, Inc., 482 N.E.2d 288 (Ind. 1985) (paying money to Conference, elections in accordance with cannons, rules and regulations of Conference, and Conference's maintenance of records sufficient to create hierarchical relationship).

64 *See* Kendysh v. Holy Spirit B.A.O.C., 683 F. Supp. 1501 (E.D. Mich 1987) (holding that B.A.O.C. intended to be hierarchal because "the congregation which holds the property is subordinate to 'superior ecclesiastical tribunals with a general and ultimate power of control.'"); *affd.* 850 F.2d 692 (6th Cir. 1988) (unpublished).

65 *See, e.g.*, Serbian-Eastern Orthodox Diocese v. Milivojevich, 426 U.S. 696, 708–9 (1976); Kendysh, 683 F. Supp. at 1506–7.

66 *See, e.g.*, Shirley v. Christian Episcopal Methodist Church, 748 So.2d 672 (Miss. 1999) (facts show clear intent by the church that it be considered a part of the CME national organization.); Harris v. Apostolic Overcoming Holy Church of God, Inc., 457 So.2d 385 (Ala. 1984) (local church held hierarchical because local congregation required to affirm ownership by hierarchal religious organization before purchasing property); Fonken v. Community Church of Kamrar, 339 N.W.2d 810, 817 (Iowa 1983) (local

dictated by some centralized body[67]; and whether a centralized body has the authority to appoint or remove clergy.[68] Some churches share all these traits and thus are easily categorized as hierarchical,[69] whereas others may share only one or a few of these traits, thus requiring courts to make the decision whether a church is hierarchical for civil law purposes based on all the relevant facts.[70]

If a church is hierarchical, courts generally defer to the decisions of the highest authority within the church hierarchy.[71] This ostensibly prevents civil courts from having to make ecclesiastical determinations in such cases.[72] As noted earlier, courts cannot determine ecclesiastical questions without running afoul of the Establishment and Free Exercise Clauses of the First Amendment to the United States Constitution.[73] Some have suggested that this deference may itself interfere with First Amendment rights,[74] and some courts avoid using categories such as hierarchical or congregational, instead relying on neutral principles of law to determine church property disputes.[75] Even then, some of the factors relevant to determining whether or not a given church is hierarchical can be used as neutral principles of law.[76] Not surprisingly, a number of jurisdictions use both approaches in determining church property disputes.[77] These jurisdictions

church voluntarily submitted to system of church government); Fluker Community Church v. Hitchens, 419 So.2d 445 (La. 1982) (acts of local church fully affiliated it with A.M.E.).

67 *See* Milivojevich, 426 U.S. at 722.

68 *See* Kedroff v. St. Nicholas Cathedral of Russian Orthodox Church in North America, 344 U.S. 94, 116 (1954); Southern Ohio State Exec. Offices of Church of God v. Fairborn Church of God, 573 N.E.2d 172 (Ohio Ct. App. 1989).

69 *See, e.g.*, Mt. Olive African Methodist Episcopal Church of Fruitland, Inc. v. Board of Incorporators of African Methodist Episcopal Church, Inc., 703 A.2d 194 (Md. Ct. App. 1997) (holding that AME is hierarchical); Southern Ohio State Executive Officers of Church of God v. Fairborn Church of God, 573 N.E.2d 172 (Ohio Ct. App. 1989) (holding that Church of God is hierarchical); Bennison v. Sharp, 329 N.W.2d 466 (Mich. Ct. App. 1982) (holding that Protestant Episcopal Church is hierarchical); Carnes v. Smith, 222 S.E.2d 322 (Ga. 1976) (holding that United Methodist Church is hierarchical).

70 *See* Trustees of Pencader Presbyterian Church in Pencander Hundred v. Gibson, 22 A.2d 782 (Del. 1941) (holding that the Presbyterianism occupies "an intermediate position between episcopacy and congregationalism").

71 Milivojevich, 426 U.S. at 709; Paradise Hills Church, Inc. v. Int'l Church of the Foursquare Gospel, 467 F. Supp. 357 (D. Ariz. 1979); Fonken, 339 N.W.2d at 816.

72 Milivojevich, 426 U.S. 696 (1976); Jones, 80 U.S. at 604; Harris, 457 So.2d 385 (Ala. 1984).

73 Presbyterian Church in U.S. v. Mary Elizabeth Blue Hull Memorial Presbyterian Church, 393 U.S. 440, 447, 449 (1969); Milivojevich, 426 U.S. at 709.

74 Arlin M. Adams & William R. Hanlon, *Jones v. Wolf: Church Autonomy and the Religion Clauses of the First Amendment*, 128 U. Pa. L. Rev. 1291, 1294–5 (1980).

75 *Id.*

76 *See, e.g.*, Presbytery of Hudson River, 821 N.Y.S.2d at 836 (application of neutral principles includes review of terms of local church charter and provisions in the constitution of the general church related to control and ownership of church property); Wisconsin Conference Bd. of Trustees of United Methodist Church, Inc. v. Culver, 614 N.W.2d 523, 527 (Wis. Ct. App. 2000) ("'[N]eutral principles of law' method permits a civil court to examine certain religious documents, such as a church constitution, deed or corporate charter, which inform on the question."); Mote, 716 P.2d at 98 (court examined, among other things, the articles of incorporation of the church, the corporate bylaws, and the canons and constitutions of the national church and the local diocese).

77 *See, e.g.*, Culver, 614 N.W.2d 523 (using both neutral principals and an examination of the hierarchical relationship); Fairborn, 573 N.E.2d at 179–80 (discussing requirements of using both neutral principles and establishing whether or not a church is hierarchical); Aglikin, 516 N.E.2d at 707 (noting that doctrinal issues require deference to church's highest ecclesiastical authority, but if the controversy is not doctrinal, deference is not required, and neutral principles analysis may be used); Fonken, 339 N.W.2d at 816 (using

frequently apply neutral principles to determine property disputes, but whether or not a church is congregational or hierarchical influences the principles applied and their application.[78]

In jurisdictions that do not apply neutral principles to property disputes within hierarchical churches complete deference is often given to the highest judicial authority within the general church.[79] Courts still must determine whether a church is hierarchical in the first place and who the highest authority is, but usually these things are reasonably clear from the documents, traditions, and/or practices within the broader church.[80] Where this is not clear, courts generally avoid determining any ecclesiastical questions and use secular criteria based on the evidence to decide who is the highest authority within a church.[81] Courts use similar mechanisms when there are internal struggles within the church as to who represents the hierarchy, such as cases where two bishops claim to control a given locale.[82] In such cases, courts will look to the history of the dispute, church governance documents, statements of high-ranking church officials as to who is the proper authority, and the overall governance system of the church.[83] In doing so, courts avoid purely ecclesiastical questions and take the preceding evidence at face value.[84] Courts do sometimes determine whether church hierarchies have followed their own procedural rules in determining property disputes, but such courts do not pass judgment on the substantive correctness of those decisions.[85]

both approaches); Bennison, 329 N.W.2d at 475 (indicating that in other situations like express trusts, application of neutral principles would be appropriate); Protestant Episcopal Church in Diocese of New Jersey v. Graves, 417 A.2d 19 (N.J. 1980) (declaring use of neutral principles only in the absence of hierarchical control).

78 *See, e.g.*, Culver, 614 N.W.2d at 355 (indicating that relevant issue is severance of hierarchical relationship); Fairborn, 573 N.E.2d at 179–80 (discussing application of both neutral principles and establishing whether or not a church is hierarchical).

79 Fonken, 339 N.W.2d at 816 (compulsory deference approach requires that a decision of the highest authority in a hierarchical church be conclusive on the civil courts in church property disputes); Bennison, 329 N.W.2d at 470 (courts are required to defer to the resolution of issues of religious doctrine or polity by the highest court of a hierarchical church organization); Graves, 417 A.2d at 22 (when "ecclesiastical tribunals have been created to decide disputes over governmental direction of subordinate bodies, the Constitution requires that civil courts accept their decisions as binding upon them.").

80 *See, e.g.*, Milivojevich, 426 U.S. 696 (1976); Kedroff, 344 U.S. 94 (1954); Shirley, 748 So.2d 672 (Miss. 1999); Fairborn, 573 N.E.2d 172 (Ohio Ct. App. 1989); Kendysh, 683 F. Supp. 1501 (E.D. Mich 1987); Harris, 457 So.2d 385 (Ala. 1984).

81 *See* Emberry, 482 N.E.2d 288 (Ind. 1985) (determining church to be hierarchical because it paid money to the conference; held elections pursuant to the cannons, rules, and regulations of the conference; and allowed the conference to maintain records on the church's pastors and membership); Fonken, 339 N.W.2d at 817 (holding that church was hierarchical because it "indisputably subordinated itself to UPCUSA through expression and action" because the contention that the "church actually functioned as an ecumenical church, would require an impermissible inquiry into doctrine to determine whether this function was consistent with Presbyterian teachings"); Fluker, 419 So.2d 445 (La. 1982) (holding that church's actions show that it chose to affiliate itself with A.M.E., a hierarchical denomination).

82 Kedroff, 344 U.S. 94 (1954).

83 *Id.* at 105–6, 109–10, 115.

84 *Id.* at 120 ("Even in those cases when the property rights follow as an incident from decisions of the church custom or law on ecclesiastical issues, the church rule controls.").

85 *Id.* at 96–7, 120 (determination of the issue depends on which procedure validly selects the ruling hierarch for the American churches; evidence shows no abdication of power by Russian Orthodox Church; church rule controls).

### 4. *"Neutral Principles of Law"*

For nearly 100 years, courts generally followed the approach set forth in *Watson v. Jones* in church property dispute cases. In 1969, however, in *Presbyterian Church in U.S. v. Mary Elizabeth Blue Hull Memorial Presbyterian Church*,[86] the Supreme Court referred to "neutral principles of law" that could be applied to church property disputes.[87] The language was basically dicta, but the Georgia Supreme Court, whose decision was at issue in that case,[88] as well as some other state courts, began to apply neutral principles to church property disputes.[89] The next year, in *Maryland and Virginia Eldership of the Churches of God v. Church of God at Sharpsburg, Inc.*, the Court again approvingly referred to "neutral principles of law."[90] In 1979, in *Jones v. Wolf*,[91] a case from Georgia, a state which had begun applying neutral principles after the Court's decision in *Mary Elizabeth Hull*, the Court formally acknowledged that a neutral principles approach was both constitutional and beneficial in deciding church property disputes.[92]

Neutral principles are a mechanism courts can use to avoid getting involved in ecclesiastical questions, including those related to the governance of churches.[93] Thus the Court held that such principles are consistent with the long-standing principles that civil courts cannot determine ecclesiastical issues without running afoul of the Free Exercise and Establishment Clauses,[94] and in fact, a neutral principles approach will better avoid crossing the boundary between secular and ecclesiastical matters than the traditional approach.[95] Moreover, a neutral principles approach that relies on deeds, state corporations law, trust documents, church bylaws, and so on (the principles themselves will be set forth later) would allow hierarchical as well as congregational churches to spell out the ownership of church property before disputes arise, thus essentially predetermining the outcomes in such cases.[96]

Since *Jones v. Wolf* was decided, more and more courts have adopted a neutral principles approach either by itself[97] or in conjunction with the categories set forth in *Watson*

86 393 U.S. 440 (1969).

87 *Id.* at 449.

88 Presbyterian Church in U.S. v. Eastern Heights Presbyterian Church, 159 S.E.2d 690 (Ga. 1968).

89 *See* Presbytery of the Covenant v. First Presbyterian Church of Paris, Inc., 552 S.W.2d 865, (Tex. App. 1977); Clough v. Wilson, 368 A.2d 231 (Conn. 1976); Carnes, 222 S.E.2d 322 (Ga. 1976); Board of Church Extension v. Eads, 230 S.E.2d 911, (W.Va. 1976); Bangor Spiritualist Church, Inc. v. Littlefield, 330 A.2d 793, (Me. 1975); Fairmount Presbyterian Church, Inc. v. Presbytery of Holston of Presbyterian Church of U. S., 531 S.W.2d 301 (Tenn. App. 1975); Adickes v. Adkins, 215 S.E.2d 442 (S.C. 1975); Norfolk Presbytery v. Bollinger, 201 S.E.2d 752 (Va. 1974); St. Michael & Archangel Russian Orthodox Greek Catholic Church v. Uhniat, 301 A.2d 655 (Pa. 1973); Polen v. Cox, 267 A.2d 201 (Md. 1970).

90 396 U.S. 367 (1970).

91 443 U.S. 595 (1979).

92 *Id.* at 602–3.

93 *Id.* at 605.

94 *Id.* at 605–6.

95 *Id.* at 604–7.

96 *Id.* at 604.

97 *See* Church of God Pentecostal, Inc. v. Freewill Pentecostal Church of God, Inc., 716 So.2d 200 (Miss. 1998); Mote, 716 P.2d 85 (Colo. 1986); Beaver-Butler, 489 A.2d 1317 (Pa. 1985); Harris, 457 So.2d 385 (Ala. 1984); Graffam v. Wray, 437 A.2d 627 (Me. 1981).

*v. Jones*.[98] Today, most jurisdictions rely on a neutral principles of law approach to some degree or another. Still, some jurisdictions have rejected the neutral principles approach because it was not mandated by the Court.[99] As noted earlier, a large number of jurisdictions have combined the traditional approach from *Watson v. Jones* with the neutral principles of law approach.[100] There is language from *Jones v. Wolf* that directly supports deference to an "authoritative ecclesiastical body" in cases where church documents or other "instruments of ownership" incorporate religious concepts.[101] The reason for this is that, as noted earlier, civil courts cannot determine ecclesiastical matters without running afoul of the First Amendment.[102]

So what are neutral principles of law? Neutral principles are those used in many trust and property disputes.[103] Thus courts using neutral principles will look at deeds,[104] trust documents,[105] other documents of conveyance such as wills,[106] church constitutions,[107] church bylaws,[108] and/or state corporation laws relevant to church incorporation (assuming that the church is incorporated).[109] This list is not exhaustive given the many varying factual scenarios in such cases, but it does represent factors that have been considered in the vast majority of cases applying neutral principles of law. The idea, as noted earlier, is that civil courts can use these neutral principles to determine church property disputes in the same manner as most other property disputes without delving into ecclesiastical concerns.[110]

98 *See, e.g.*, Culver, 614 N.W.2d 523 (Wis. Ct. App. 2000); Fairborn, 573 N.E.2d 172 (Ohio Ct. App. 1989); Aglikin, 516 N.E.2d 704, 707 (Ill. App. Ct. 1987); Fonken, 339 N.W.2d 810 (Iowa 1983); Bennison, 329 N.W.2d 466 (Mich. Ct. App. 1982); Graves, 417 A.2d 19 (N.J. 1980).

99 *See* Southside Tabernacle v. Pentecostal Church of God, 650 P.2d 231 (Wash. 1982) (noting that although there is confusion regarding whether to apply neutral principles, it need not be addressed because "Washington has adopted the Watson compulsory deference rule."); Schismatic and Purported Casa Linda Presbyterian Church in America v. Grace Union Presbytery, Inc., 710 S.W.2d 700 (Tex. App. Dallas 1986) (noting that the "intermediate appellate courts have consistently followed the deference rule in deciding hierarchical church property disputes"); New York Annual Conference of United Methodist Church v. Fisher, 438 A.2d 62, 68 (Conn. 1980) ("The first amendment thus requires that civil courts defer to the highest court of the hierarchical church organization to resolve issues of religious doctrine or practice.).

100 *See, e.g.*, Culver, 614 N.W.2d 523 (Wis. Ct. App. 2000); Fairborn, 573 N.E.2d 172 (Ohio Ct. App. 1989); Aglikin, 516 N.E.2d 704, 707 (Ill. App. Ct. 1987); Fonken, 339 N.W.2d 810 (Iowa 1983); Bennison, 329 N.W.2d 466 (Mich. Ct. App. 1982); Graves, 417 A.2d 19 (N.J. 1980).

101 Jones, 443 U.S. at 604.

102 *Id.* at 603–4.

103 *Id.* at 603.

104 *See, e.g.*, Church of God Pentecostal, 716 So.2d 200 (Miss. 1998) (reviewing deeds and by-laws); Berthiaume v. McCormack, 891 A.2d 539 (N.H. 2006) (examining statutes creating corporation and deeds); Presbytery of Hudson River, 821 N.Y.S.2d 834 (2006) (reviewing deeds and church constitution); Foss, 342 N.W.2d 220 (S.D. 1983) (reviewing deeds, mortgage, and church constitution).

105 *See* California-Nevada Annual Conference of United Methodist Church v. St. Luke's United Methodist Church, 17 Cal. Rptr. 3d 442 (Cal. Ct. App. 5th Dist. 2004) (discussing creation and revocation of trust); *Cf.* Foss, 342 N.W.2d 220 (S.D. 1983) (reviewing mortgage, deed, and church constitution).

106 Foss, 342 N.W.2d 220 (S.D. 1983) (reviewing mortgage, deed, and church constitution).

107 *See* Presbytery of Hudson River, 821 N.Y.S.2d 834 (N.Y. 2006) [reviewing church constitution (Book of Order) and deeds]; Foss, 342 N.W.2d 220 (S.D. 1983) (reviewing church constitution, mortgage, and deed).

108 *See* Church of God Pentecostal, 716 So.2d 200 (Miss. 1998) (reviewing bylaws and deeds).

109 *See* Berthiaume, 891 A.2d 539 (N.H. 2006) (examining statutes creating corporation and deeds); St. Luke's, 17 Cal. Rptr. 3d 442 (Cal. Ct. App. 5th Dist. 2004) (examining provisions of California Corporations Code).

110 Jones, 443 U.S. at 603.

There are also a small number of cases that rely exclusively on state incorporation laws without addressing neutral principles or any other constitutionally driven test.[111] These cases are arguably de facto neutral principle cases even if they never raise the issue.[112] Most cases looking at state incorporation laws do so in the context of neutral principles analysis, where the state laws are used to determine who controls church property and other assets.[113] As with other neutral principles, the state laws serve as a mechanism for helping to determine church property disputes without delving into ecclesiastical questions.[114] In the end, this is the primary goal of a neutral principles approach regardless of which specific principle or principles courts rely on.

## B. Church Schisms

The law governing church schisms is intertwined with that applicable to church property disputes. This makes sense because most church property disputes themselves arise as the result of a schism within a church.[115] Thus neutral principles and the hierarchical-congregational approach can be sensibly applied in the church schism context.[116] Moreover, the constitutional duty civil courts have to avoid becoming

111 *See In re* Roman Catholic Archbishop of Portland in Oregon, 335 B.R. 842 (Bankr. D. Or. 2005) (relying on bankruptcy and state incorporation statutes to determine ownership); St. Luke's, 17 Cal. Rptr. 3d 442 (Cal. Ct. App. 5th Dist. 2004) (relying on California Corporations Code provisions regarding trusts); *see also* Protestant Episcopal Church v. Barker, 171 Cal. Rptr. 541 (Cal Ct. App. 2d Dist. 1981) (relying on church articles of incorporation but also discussing neutral principles).

112 Under *Jones*, articles of incorporation of the church, deeds to the disputed property, and relevant state statutes are all neutral principles on which a state court can rely. *See* St. Luke's, 17 Cal. Rptr. 3d at 449–50 [citing Protestant Episcopal Church v. Barker, 171 Cal. Rptr. 541, 553 (Cal Ct. App. 2d Dist. 1981)].

113 *See* Culver, 614 N.W.2d 523 (Wis. Ct. App. 2000) (using statutory definitions of "dissolved" or "defunct" in conjunction with other neutral principles).

114 *See* Culver, 614 N.W.2d at 527 (noting that the "neutral principles of law" doctrine requires the court to not address which group was more "doctrinally pure" to the religion but rather to "look from a secular perspective to the authorities and documents that inform us on the issue," including Wisconsin statutes); Barker, 171 Cal. Rptr. at 543 ("neutral principles promise to free a court from the necessity of inquiry into church doctrine … and allow[s] it to rely on objective, well-established concepts of trust and property law"); Harris, 457 So.2d. at 387 (Neutral principles such as deeds and state statutes governing the holding of church property keep courts from deciding property disputes on the basis of religious doctrine and practice.).

115 *See, e.g.*, Watson v. Jones, 80 U.S. 679 (1871). (A Presbyterian Church became divided on the issue of slavery. Both groups claim that they are the group mostly closely aligned with the Church's original doctrine. Jones filed a bill to restrain by injunction Watson and thirty others from using church property.); Brundage v. Deardorf, 55 F. 839 (N.D. Ohio 1893); Norfolk Presbytery v. Bollinger, 201 S.E. 752 (Va. 1974); Church of God Pentecostal, Inc. v. Freewill Pentecostal Church of God, Inc., 716 So.2d 200 (Miss 1998).

116 *See, e.g.*, Presbyterian Church in U.S. v. Mary Elizabeth Blue Hull Memorial Presbyterian Church, 393 U.S. 440, 449 (1969). (Neutral principles of law may be applied in all property disputes without establishing churches.); Jones v. Wolf, 443 U.S. 595, 602–5 (1979)[holding that "(1) a state is constitutionally entitled to adopt neutral principles of law as a means of adjudicating church property disputes; (2) if state has adopted a presumptive rule of majority representation, defeasible upon showing that identity of local church is to be determined by some other means, this would be consistent with both neutral principles analysis and the First Amendment, but (3) if state law provides that identity of local church is to be determined according to the 'laws and regulations' of the general church, then the First Amendment requires that state courts give deference to determination of that church's identity by the authoritative ecclesiastical body."]; Watson v. Jones, 80 U.S. 679 (1871)[stating three general heads to classify property issues

involved in determining ecclesiastical issues is equally applicable – if not more so – in the church schism context.[117] It should be obvious that church property disputes are often a type of church schism case, but given the significant attention paid to property disputes by civil courts, property disputes have essentially become a category in and of themselves. Non-property-oriented schism cases most often involve disputes between church factions over issues such as retention or termination of clergy or other church employees,[118] dismissal of church members from membership,[119] calls for financial accounting within the church,[120] questions over who controls church governance,[121]

regarding ecclesiastical bodies: (1) property deeded or donated through a will in order to further the teachings of the religious doctrinal beliefs, (2) property owned by a religious congregation without any other higher authority obligations, and (3) property held by a religious congregation that is subordinate to a higher ecclesiastical body].

117 *See, e.g.*, Watson v. Jones, 80 U.S. (13 Wall.) 679, 727, 20 L.Ed. 666 (1871) (holding that church decisions regarding "questions of discipline, or of faith, or ecclesiastical rule, custom, or law" are final); Kreshik v. St. Nicholas Cathedral, 363 U.S. 190, 191, 80 S.Ct. 1037, 4 L.Ed.2d 1140 (1960) (*per curiam*) (holding that constitutional principles prevent the judiciary from intruding on freedom of religion); Serbian E. Orthodox Diocese v. Milivojevich, 426 U.S. 696, 713, 717, 96 S.Ct. 2372, 49 L.Ed.2d 151 (1976) (holding that "religious controversies are not the proper subject of civil court inquiry, and that a civil court must accept the ecclesiastical decisions of church tribunals as it finds them"); Bollard v. California Province of Society of Jesus, 211 F.3d 1331, 1332 (9th Cir. 2000) (stating that the issue in this case requires that the judiciary "delve into religious matters," which is forbidden under the Constitution.).

118 *See, e.g.*, Serbian Eastern Orthodox Diocese for U. S. of America and Canada v. Milivojevich, 426 U.S. 696, 718 (1976) (holding that under the First and Fourteenth Amendments, it is impermissible for a state court to rule on an issue regarding the "defrockment of a bishop of a hierarchical church in whose sole discretion the authority to make such ecclesiastical decisions was vested."); Kedroff v. St. Nicholas Cathedral of Russian Orthodox Church in North America, 344 U.S. 94, 116 (holding that the freedom to chose clergy has constitutional protection under the Free Exercise Clause); Rayburn v. General Conference of Seventh-Day Adventists, 772 F.2d 1164, 1169 (4th Cir. 1985) (holding that to subject church employment decisions to Title VII scrutiny would cause government entanglement with a religious institution, which is prohibited under the Establishment Clause); Schmidt v. Bishop, 779 F.Supp 321 (S.D.N.Y. 1991)(holding that is would be inappropriate and unconstitutional for the court to rule whether or not the church authorities negligently supervised a pastor who allegedly sexually assaulted the plaintiff).

119 *See, e.g.*, Tubiolo v. Abundant Life Church, Inc., 605 S.E.2d 161, 162 (N.C. App. 2004) (After two years of disagreement, the church terminated memberships of founding members. Founding members brought suit claiming that the termination of their memberships was a due process violation.); Burgess v. Rock Creek Baptist Church, 734 F. Supp. 30, 33 (D.D.C. 1990) (Former church member sued the church for emotional distress after she was terminated as a member and treated as a nonmember.); Owen v. Board of Directors of Rosicrucian Fellowship, 342 P.2d 424, 425 (Cal. App. 1959) (Expelled members of the church sought a writ of mandamus to compel the church to reinstate them as members and allow them to examine the members' mailing list.); Mount Olive Primitive Baptist, 42 So. 2d 617, 618 (Ala. 1949) (Appellates filed a petition to be reinstated as members of the church after they were ousted without notice.).

120 *See, e.g.*, Levitt v. Calvary Temple of Denver, 33 P.3d 1227 (Colo. App. 2001) (Church member requested church financial records and brought suit against the church when he was denied.).

121 *See, e.g.*, Kedroff v. St. Nicholas Cathedral of Russian Orthodox Church of North America, 344 U.S. 73, 104 (U.S. 1952) (After a history of political instability tied to the Russian Orthodox Church, the Mother Church attempted to control its American offshoot denomination.); The Serbian Eastern Orthodox Diocese for the United States of America and Canada v. Milivojevich, 426 U.S. 696, 721 (1976) (The Court noted that reorganization of the diocese is an internal church governance issue, which relates to an ecclesiastical question as well as a governance one.); Wooten v. Cryton, 845 N.E.2d 1213, 1221 (Mass. App. Ct. 2006)(A faction within the church was vying for control over both the congregation and the church's property.).

and cases where churches or factions within churches seek to affiliate with another denomination or where churches or factions within them seek to disaffiliate from a denomination.[122]

The central tenet of church schism cases is that civil courts will not get involved in deciding ecclesiastical matters, but courts can determine civil and property rights as long as they can do so without determining ecclesiastical matters.[123] This rule has significant implications for cases involving disputes over clergy employment and cases involving church membership. Any substantive decisions on such matters are beyond the jurisdiction of civil courts.[124] Courts may, however, look at the processes applied to clergy employment and membership expulsion issues to make sure that the church followed its own procedural rules.[125] Even if a court finds that a church failed to follow its own procedures, the court will simply undo the procedurally flawed decision and leave it to the church to follow its procedures, potentially arriving at the same decision.[126] Most courts avoid delving even into church procedure when in order to do so the court would need to

122 *See, e.g.*, Permanent Committee of Missions of the Pacific Synod of the Cumberland Presbyterian Church in the United States v. Pacific Synod of the Presbyterian Church, U.S.A., 106 P. 395, 397 (Cal. 1909)(Local church created a constitutionally planned union with the Presbyterian Church of the United States.); Trustees of Pencander Presbyterian Church in Pencader Hundred v. Gibson, 22 A.2d 782, 786 (Del. 1941)(Local church broke away from parent church arguing that the parent church was disloyal to the church's "constitution and doctrinal standards."); Sanders v. Stone, 255 Ga. 704, 705 (Ga. 1986)(Church faction voted to stay affiliated with the United Methodist Church despite a different church faction's attempt to break away.).

123 *See, e.g.*, Watson v. Jones, 80 U.S. 679 (1871)(holding that the rule for civil court "whenever the questions of discipline, or of faith, or ecclesiastical rule, custom, or law have been decided by the highest of church judiciaries," the court must accept these decisions as final); Presbyterian Church in U.S. v. Mary Elizabeth Blue Hull Memorial Presbyterian Church, 393 U.S. 440, 449 (1969)(The First Amendment is in danger of being violated when civil courts adjudicate church property disputes by attempting to resolve ecclesiastical differences and issues.), Serbian Eastern Orthodox Diocese for the United States & Canada v. Milivojevich, 426 U.S. 696, 714–15 (1976)(holding that "it is the essence of religious faith that ecclesiastical decisions are reached and are to be accepted as matters of faith whether or not rational or measurable by objective criteria.").

124 *See, e.g.*, Watson v. Jones, 80 U.S. 679, 727 (1872)(deciding that when an issue of discipline, faith, ecclesiastical custom, or law has been decided by the highest church adjudicators, civil courts are bound by that decision.); Bell v. Presbyterian Church (U.S.A.), 126 F.3d 328, 331 (4th Cir. 1997) {stating that "[i]t has thus become established that the decisions of religious entities about the appointment and removal of ministers and persons in other positions of similar theological significance are beyond the ken of civil courts" [citing Serbian Eastern Orthodox Diocese for the United States & Canada v. Milivojevich, 426 U.S. 696, 713 (1976)]}; Burgess v. Rock Creek Baptist Church, 734 F.Supp.30, 33 (D.D.C. 1990)(The Court cannot make a ruling regarding membership of the church without violating the First Amendment because the church's constitution expressly determines who maybe a member.); Hutchinson v. Thomas, 789 F.2d 392, 396 (6th Cir. 1986)(stating that neutral principles have never been applied in religious causes of action regarding "church government, order, and discipline" and should not be).

125 Kennedy v. Gray, 248 Kan. 486, 807 P.2d 670 (Ka. 1991); *Cf.* Burgess v. Rock Creek Baptist Church, 734 F.Supp. 30, 33 (D.D.C. 1990)(The court looks to the Church's constitution to ensure that it followed its own definition membership.).

126 *See, e.g.*, Serbian Eastern Orthodox Diocese for the United States & Canada v. Milivojevich, 426 U.S. 696, 713 (1976)(holding that under the "narrow rubrics" of fraud or collision, "when church tribunals act in bad faith for secular purposes, no 'arbitrariness' exception in the sense of an inquiry whether the decisions of the highest ecclesiastical tribunal of a hierarchical church complied with church laws and regulations is consistent with the constitutional mandate that civil courts are bound to accept the decisions of the highest judicatories of a religious organization of hierarchical polity on matters of discipline, faith, internal organization, or ecclesiastical rule, custom, or law").

address ecclesiastical issues.[127] Some courts will go further than others by more narrowly defining "ecclesiastical" in these cases.[128] The following subsections will address some of the more common types of church schism cases. It is not a coincidence that the same principles arise again and again in these cases because the over-arching rules are generally the same for all schism cases.

### 1. *Clergy Employment Cases*

Civil courts have repeatedly held that it is inappropriate to question church decisions regarding the employment of clergy barring a procedural issue.[129] The reason for this is quite simple: the hiring and firing of clergy is central to the religious aspects of a church because the role of clergy is central to the religious functioning of most religious institutions.[130] It

[127] *See, e.g.*, Serbian Eastern Orthodox Diocese for the United States & Canada v. Milivojevich, 426 U.S. 696, 713 (1976)(stating that for "civil courts to analyze whether the ecclesiastical actions of a church" requires the court to inquire into the canon or ecclesiastical law that the church follows; this inquiry is prohibited by the First Amendment and requires a civil court to accept the ecclesiastical determinations of the church); Knuth v. Lutheran Church Missouri Synod, 643 F. Supp. 444, 447 (D.Kan. 1986)(A motion to dismiss based on lack of personal jurisdiction was granted because the facts of this case went beyond the narrow exception of fraud or collusion in church schism cases.); Kaufmann v. Sheehan, 707 F.2d 355, 358 (8th Cir.1983).

[128] *See, e.g.*, Simpson v. Wells Lamont Corp., 484 F.2d 490, 493 (C.A. Miss. 1974)(stating that only on rare occasions where there is a compelling government interest in regulating public health, safety, and general welfare will courts delve into this protected area of law); Nunn v. Black, 506 F.Supp.444, 447 (D.C.Va. 1981)(using the narrow definition when court may intrude into ecclesiastical matters laid out in *Simpson*, the court determined that the facts of this case did not fall within that narrow definition, and plaintiff must accept the church's decision); Burgess v. Rock Creek Baptist Church, 734 F.Supp. 30, 32 (D. D.C. 1990)(While every case in which a church is a party will to some degree involve an ecclesiastical matter, there are certain narrow circumstances in which it may be appropriate for a court to adjudicate. Those narrow circumstances include disputes where a court can decide the issue without becoming unduly entangled in the ecclesiastical matter and possibly where a decision of a church tribunal is the product of fraud of collusion.).

[129] Hosanna-Tabor Evangelical Lutheran Church and School v. EEOC, 565 U.S., 132 S.Ct. 694 (2012). *See also In re* Galilee Baptist Church, 186 So.2d 102, 106 (Ala. 1966) (stating that "[s]piritualities are beyond the reach of temporal courts, and a pastor may be deposed by a majority of the members at a congregational meeting at any time, so far as the civil courts are concerned, subject only to inquiry by the courts as to whether the church, or its appointed tribunal has proceeded according to the law of the church"); Young v. Northern Illinois Conference of United Methodist Church, 21 F.3d 184, 187 (7th Cir. 1994) (holding that religious bodies may make decisions affecting the employment status of their clergy members free from civil court review.); Bell v. Presbyterian Church (U.S.A.), 126 F.3d 328 (4th Cir. 1997); Hutchison v. Thomas, 789 F.2d 392 (6th Cir. 1986); Farley v. Wisconsin Evangelical Lutheran Synod, 821 F.Supp. 1286 (D. Minn. 1993); United Methodist Church, Baltimore Annual Conference v. White, 571 A.2d 790 (D.C. 1990); Goodman v. Temple Shir Ami, Inc., 712 So. 2d 775 (Fla. Dist. Ct. App. 3d Dist. 1998), *review granted*, 727 So.2d 905 (Fla. 1998) *and appeal dismissed as improvidently granted*, 737 So.2d 1077 (Fla. 1999), *cert. denied*, 528 U.S. 1075, 120 S. Ct. 789, 145 L. Ed. 2d 666 (2000); Bledsoe v. Morningside Baptist Church of Atlanta, 232 Ga. App. 122, 501 S.E.2d 292 (1998); Marsh v. Johnson, 259 Ky. 305, 82 S.W.2d 345 (1935); Roppolo v. Moore, 644 So.2d 206 (La. Ct. App. 4th Cir. 1994), *writ denied*, 650 So.2d 253 (La. 1995); Graham v. Lockhart, 42 N.C. App. 377, 256 S.E.2d 518 (1979); Knotts v. Williams, 319 S.C. 473, 462 S.E.2d 288 (1995); Schumacher v. Giedt, 79 S.D. 421, 112 N.W.2d 898 (1962); Dean v. Alford, 994 S.W.2d 392 (Tex. App. Fort Worth 1999).

[130] *See, e.g.*, Serbian Eastern Orthodox Diocese for U. S. of America and Canada v. Milivojevich, 426 U.S. 696, 718 (1979)(stating that "the State court's 'detailed review' of evidence in challenge to proceedings resulting in removal and defrockment of bishop of hierarchical church by religious bodies in

is therefore nearly impossible to separate out ecclesiastical concerns when deciding such cases.[131] When, however, there are established church procedures regarding employment decisions[132] or, in a few cases, where the clergy member has contractual rights to pay or enjoys procedural safeguards,[133] courts will sometimes hear such issues without addressing

whose sole discretion the authority to make such ecclesiastical decisions was vested was impermissible under First and Fourteenth Amendments"); Scharon v. St. Luke's Episcopal Presbyterian Hospitals, 929 F.2d 360, 363 (8th Cir. 1991)(stating that "[p]ersonnel decisions by church-affiliated institutions affecting clergy are *per se* religious matters and cannot be reviewed by civil courts, for to review such decisions would require the courts to determine the meaning of religious doctrine and canonical law and to impose a secular court's view of whether in the context of the particular case religious doctrine and canonical law support the decision the church authorities have made"); Kaufmann v. Sheehan, 707 F.2d 355 (8th Cir.1983)(Priest filed suit against archdiocese claiming defamation and conspiracy, dismissed); Natal v. Christian and Missionary Alliance, 878 F.2d 1575 (1st Cir.1989)(Clergyman filed wrongful termination suit against incorporated religious nonprofit, dismissed); Minker v. Baltimore Annual Conference of United Methodist Church, 894 F.2d 1354, 1356 (D.C.Cir. 1990)(Pastor's suit for violation of federal age discrimination statute dismissed); United Methodist Church, Baltimore Annual Conference v. White, 571 A.2d 790, 794 (D.C. 1990)(Former minister filed suit for breach of employment contract, dismissed.); Rayburn v. General Conf. of Seventh-Day Adventists, supra, 772 F.2d 1164 (minister's claims of race and sex discrimination dismissed); Simpson v. Wells Lamont Corporation, 494 F.2d 490 (United Methodist minister's suit for wrongful discharge, dismissed); Hutchinson v. Thomas, *cert. denied*, 479 U.S. 885 (1986) (Methodist minister's common-law claims challenging forced retirement by the church, dismissed); Knuth v. Lutheran Church Missouri Synod, 643 F.Supp. 444 (D.Kan. 1986) (Pastor's claim of breach of contract and implied duty of good faith and fair dealing, seeking damages for removal and attempt to regain pastoral status, dismissed); Hafner v. Lutheran Church-Missouri Synod, 616 F.Supp. 735 (N.D.Ind.1985) (Pastor's suit for alleged denial of benefits based on interpretation of church synod constitution, dismissed); *See also* Hosanna-Tabor, 565 U.S., 132 S.Ct. 694 (finding this even in a case where the "clergy member" was a "called" teacher who disputed her role as a "minister").

131 *Id.*; Hosanna-Tabor, 565 U.S., 132 S.Ct. 694.

132 *See, e.g.*, Barton v. Fitzpatrick, 65 So. 390, 393 (Ala. 1914)(analyzing whether the church followed its laws regarding the dismissal of its pastor; because the church was organized on the congregational plan, the court was limited to determining whether the church acted as a congregation); *In re* Galilee Baptist Church,186 So.2d 102, 106 (Ala. 1966)(stating that "a pastor may be deposed by a majority of the members at a congregational meeting at any time, so far as the civil courts are concerned, subject only to inquiry by the courts as to whether the church, or its appointed tribunal has proceeded according to the law of the church"); Epperson v. Myers, 58 So.2d 150 (Fla. 1952); Stubbs v. Vetry of St. John's Church, 53 A. 917 (Md. 1903); Briscoe v. Williams, 192 S.W. 643 (Mo. App. 1946); Chavis v. Rowe, 459 A.2d 674 (N.J. 1983); Graham v. Lockhart, 256 S.E.2d 518 (N.C. App. 1979); Morris Street Baptist Church v. Dart, 45 S.E. 753 (S.C. 1903); Ervin v. Lilydale Progressive Missionary Baptist Church, 813 N.E.2d 1073, 1078 (Ill. App. 1 Dist. 2004)(deciding that "the congregation did not authorize its boards to terminate its pastor's service without following the bylaw procedures for terminating a pastor. The court can decide the issue by applying neutral legal principles to interpret the church's bylaws, handbook and covenant.").

133 *See, e.g.*, Stony Island Church of Christ v. Stephens, 369 N.E.2d 1313, 1317 (Ill. App. 1 Dist. 1997) (stating that the record presents a secular, contractual issue between the church and the pastor regarding his termination and his right to possess the parsonage); Jewish Center of Sussex County v. Whale, 397 A.2d 712, 714 (N.J. Sup. Ct. 1978)(noting that it has long been recognized that contractual arrangements between a pastor and his congregation are subject to civil court enforcement); Waters v. Hargest, 593 S.W.2d 363 (Tex. Civ. App. 1979)(stating that the issue regarding the pastor's contract may be determined by application of neutral principles of law); Minker v. Baltimore Annual Conference of United Methodist Church, 894 F.2d 1354, 1359 (D.C. Cir. 1990)(stating that a church is always free to burden its activities voluntarily through contracts and that such contracts are fully enforceable in civil court).

the substantive merits of the employment decision.[134] If a court needs to address the latter to determine the former, most jurisdictions refuse to hear the case.[135]

In a few cases, the procedure for calling meetings is set forth in deeds or articles of incorporation under state incorporation laws, and those laws become relevant to whether the church followed appropriate procedures regarding any action taken in relation to clergy employment.[136] Most courts look to neutral principles such as church documents, legal documents, and/or corporation laws to determine procedural or other rights relevant to the case.[137] Many combine the neutral principles approach with discussion of the nature of the religious institution; that is, is it hierarchical or congregational.[138] With the exception of cases where the clergy member has a written contract for a term of years entitling him or her to specific pay regardless of the basis for termination,[139] the most

134 *See, e.g.*, Morris Street Baptist Church v. Dart, 45 S.E. 753, 754 (S.C. 1903)(stating that the court would only consider whether the church had ordered the pastor's exclusion but not whether it was right in doing so; the court also would only determine whether the resolution to exclude the pastor was passed according to the canon law of the church and whether it was the church in fact that made the determination); Le Blanc v. Davis, 432 So.2d 239 (La. 1983)(stating that ecclesiastical matters were not at issue because the pastor had been dismissed but refused to leave; the church members sough an injunctive relief from the court); Graham v. Lockhart, 256 S.E.2d 518, 519 (N.C. App. 1979)(noting that matters of church doctrine were not in dispute in this case; the only issue was whether the pastor had been properly dismissed by the church, which is in congregational form); Barton v. Fitzpatrick, 65 So. 390, 393 (Ala. 1914); In re Galilee Baptist Church,186 So.2d 102, 106 (Ala. 1966); Epperson v. Myers, 58 So.2d 150 (Fla. 1952); Stubbs v. Vetry of St. John's Church, 53 A. 917 (Md. 1903); Briscoe v. Williams, 192 S.W. 643 (Mo. App. 1946); Chavis v. Rowe, 459 A.2d 674 (N.J. 1983); Stony Island Church of Christ v. Stephens, 369 N.E.2d 1313, 1317 (Ill. App. 1 Dist. 1997); Jewish Center of Sussex County v. Whale, 397 A.2d 712, 714 (N.J. Sup. Ct. 1978).

135 *See, e.g.*, Dobrota v. Free Serbian Orthodox Church St. Nicholas, 952 P.2d 1190, 1194 (Ariz. App. Div. 1 1998)(stating that reviewing the discharged priest's breach of contract claim would have cause the trial court to delve into matters of internal church discipline, faith, and organization, which is prohibited by the First Amendment); Leavy v. Congregation Beth Shalom, 490 F.Supp. 2d 1011, 1028 (N.D. Iowa 2007)(stating that the claims leave the court with a significant risk of entangling itself in the process a congregation uses to choose its leader); United Methodist Church, Baltimore Annual Conference v. White, 571 A.2d 790, 796 (D.C. 1990)(holding that the minister's claim was not clearly separate from his ecclesiastical claims, which, therefore, does not permit the court to adjudicate his claim).

136 *See, e.g.*, Stubbs v. Vestry of St. John's Church, 53 A. 917, 917 (Md. 1903)(Looking to the ninth clause of the deed of incorporation, the court found that the vestry shall have the power to appoint the rector and fill vacancies of the church offices.).

137 *See, e.g.*, Stubbs v. Vestry of St. John's Church, 53 A. 917, 917 (Md. 1903); Williams v. Wilson, 563 S.E.2d 320, 324 (S.C. 2002)(stating that "[t]he church bylaws clearly reserve to the congregation the right to dismiss the preacher which is consistent with the convention of Christian Churches as congregational"); Chavis v. Rowe, 459 A.2d 674, 678 (N.J. 1983)(reaffirming that depending on the church structure, courts are to use neutral principles in adjudicating disputes within a congregational church.); In re Galilee Baptist Church, 186 So.2d 102, 107 (Ala. 1966)(In determining whether the vote to dismiss the pastor was proper, the court stated that "so far as we can determine from the church manual, all members of a Baptist church are entitled to vote at a meeting, regardless of age."); United Methodist Church, Baltimore Annual Conference v. White, 571 A.2d 790, 794 (D.C. 1990)(In determining whether the pastor's claim was ecclesiastically based, the court noted that the Discipline of the United Methodist Church is a religious document that the court was not permitted to hear claims on.); Briscoe v Williams, 129 S.W.2d 643 (Mo. App. 1946); Walker Memorial Baptist Church v. Saunders, 35 N.E.2d 42 (N.Y. 1941).

138 *See, e.g.*, Serbian Eastern Orthodox Diocese for the United States of American and Canada v. Milivojevich, 426 U.S. 696 (1976); Presbyterian Church in U.S. v. Mary Elizabeth Blue Hull Memorial, 393 U.S. 440 (1969); Jones v. Wolf, 443 U.S. 595 (1979).

139 *See, e.g.*, Goodman v. Temple Shir Ami, Inc., 712 So.2d 775, 777 (Fla. App. 3 Dist. 1998)(stating that the claim by the rabbi that the temple failed to pay all compensation due under the employment contract did

that a clergy member can expect from a civil court is an order finding that the church failed to follow its own procedures and thus the action taken is void, and the clergy member is entitled to any lost compensation or clergy status that occurred as the result of the procedurally flawed decision.[140] Of course, there is then nothing to stop a church or church faction from using proper procedures to achieve the same ends.[141] The clergy member may continue with the church if the faction seeking his or her ouster cannot prevail under proper procedures (which is sometimes the reason those procedures were not followed), but courts will not question substantive decisions made by a church using proper church procedures.[142]

In congregational churches, unless the church constitution or bylaws provide otherwise, the procedure is generally a majority vote of the congregation at a properly called meeting that provides adequate notice to congregants and clergy.[143] Courts defer completely to such decisions when made according to church procedures.[144] In hierarchical churches, the procedures generally are laid out in church documents, and courts give total deference to substantive decisions made by proper church authorities in conformity with church procedures.[145] Some courts have an almost per se rule of never hearing

not preclude civil court intervention because there was no excessive entanglement); Minker v. Baltimore Annual Conference of United Methodist Church, 894 F.2d 1354 (D.C. Cir. 1990).

140 *See, e.g.*, Barton v. Fitzpatrick, 65 So. 390, 393 (Ala. 1914); Holt v. Trone, 67 N.W.2d 125 (Mich. 1954); Vincent v. Raglin, 318 N.W.2d 629 (Mich. App. 1982); Harrison v. Floyd, 97 A.2d 761 (N.J. Sup. Ct. 1953).

141 *See e.g.*, In re Galilee Baptist Church, 186 So.2d 102 (Ala. 1966)(stating that "there is nothing tending to show that such meeting was not held in such a manner but that the business of the congregation could be transacted. We hold therefore that the congregational meeting of 19 September 1964, was not void and therefore as a result of such meeting Thomas Thornes was dismissed as pastor of the Galilee Baptist Church."); Williams v. Cupp, 597 S.W.2d 855 (Ark. App. 1980)(holding that there was sufficient evidence that the pastor's removal was valid); Foster v. St. John's Baptist Church, Inc., 406 So.2d 389 (Ala. 1981); Le Blanc v. Davis, 432 So.2d 239 (La. 1983); Stony Island Church of Christ v. Stephens, 369 N.E.2d 1313 (Ill. App. 1977); Quinn v. First Evangelist Baptist Church, 135 So. 753 (La. App. 1931); Sance v. Monroe, 39 So.2d 174 (La. App. 1949); Stubbs v. Vestry of St. John's Church, 53 A. 917 (Md. 1903); Blauert v. Schupmann, 63 N.W.2d 578 (Minn. 1954).

142 *See, e.g.*, Serbian Eastern Orthodox Diocese v. Milivojevich, 426 U.S. 696 (1976)(stating that courts must defer to the decisions of religious organizations on matters of discipline, faith, internal organization, or ecclesiastical rule, custom or law); Bell v. Presbyterian Church (U.S.A.), 126 F.3d 328 (Va.1997); Epperson v. Myers, 58 So.2d 150 (Fla. 1952); Barton v. Fitzpatrick, 65 So. 390 (Ala. 1914).

143 *See, e.g.*, In re Galilee Baptist Church, 186 So.2d 102 (Ala. 1966); Williams v. Cupp, 597 S.W.2d 855 (Ark. App. 1980); Stony Island Church of Christ v. Stephens, 369 N.E.2d 1313 (Ill. App. 1977)(noting that a conclusive adjudication of a Church of Christ pastor's termination by written notice signed by the church elders).

144 *See, e.g.*, Barton v. Fitzpatrick, 65 S.O. 390, 393 (Ala. 1914)(holding that congregations are only subject to inquiries regarding whether the church proceeded according to the law of the church); In re Galilee Baptist Church, 186 So.2d 102 (Ala. 1966); Briscoe v. Williams, 192 S.W.2d 643, 646 (Mo. App. 1946) (holding that civil courts have no ecclesiastical jurisdiction and ordinarily cannot question acts of church disciple or the removal of a pastor); Graham v. Lockhart, 256 S.E. 518 (N.C. App. 1979); Schumacker v. Giedt, 112 N.W.2d 898, 902 (S.D. 1962)(reasoning that because the congregation had the power to discharge the pastor, the civil court was bound by the church's decision).

145 *See, e.g.*, Hutchison v. Thomas, 789 F.2d 392, 395 (Ohio 1986)(concluding that "civil courts are bound to accept the decisions of the highest judicatories of a religious organization of hierarchical polity on matters of discipline, faith, internal organization, or ecclesiastical rule, custom, or law"); Concord Christian Center v. Open Bible Standard Churches, 34 Cal. Rptr.3d 412 (Cal. App. 1 Dist. 2005)(In an action against a hierarchical national church, the court held that the trial court appropriately applied the ecclesiastical rule to abstain from making a determination as to the propriety of the national church's revocation of the pastor as a member of the church.); Jay v. Christian Methodist Episcopal Church, 531 S.E.2d

clergy employment disputes even when procedural irregularities exist so long as written and binding contract rights are not involved.[146] Even when contract rights are involved, most courts will not determine whether a termination or discipline of a clergy member violated the contract because it is up to church officials to determine the substantive questions regarding just cause and similar employment concepts.[147] Courts will enforce clear contract rights but will not question church decisions arrived at after properly following church procedures.[148]

## 2. *Other Employee Cases*

Some nonclergy employees, such as choir directors, are governed by the same doctrine as clergy in most jurisdictions.[149] Their function is seen as being inseparable from the

369, 370 (Ga. App. 2000)(stating that the structure of the church was hierarchical, and hierarchical religious organization are permitted to establish rules to govern by. The trial court lack subject-matter jurisdiction in this case where the underlying issue was whether the bishop failed to comply with church's internal rules when transferring him to another location.)

146 *See, e.g.*, Lewis v. Seventh Day Adventists Lake Region Conference, 978 F.2d 940, 943 (Mich. 1992) (concluding that the First Amendment bars civil courts from reviewing decisions of religious judicatory bodies relating to employment of clergy even where there are allegations that the religious tribunal decisions was based on misapplication of its own procedure and laws).

147 *See, e.g.*, Sance v. Monroe, 39 So.2d 174, 176 (La. App. 1949)(stating that the pastor's contract of employment and his right to occupy the parsonage could be terminated at will by a majority of the congregation); Stubbs v. Vestry of St. John's Church, 53 A. 917, 919 (Md. 1903)(noting that the "relation of the appellant to the vestry was a contractual one, that his employment was at the will of the vestry, and that he had no vested right to the office or its incidents, and was consequently not entitled to notice that the question as to the severing of that relation would be considered by the vestry"); Jewish Center of Sussex County v. Whale, 411 A.2d 475, (N.J. 1978)(holding that the congregation had no obligation to continue the synagogue's rabbi as spiritual leader under the employment contract, which was procured as a result of the rabbi's fraudulent conduct); Music v. United Methodist Church, 864 S.W.2d 286, 288 (Ky. 1993) (Minister claims that there was a breach of his employment contract when the church and bishop failed to follow the procedures set for the in the church's book of disciple. The court held that the minister's claim could not be separated from an interpretation of church law and would cause excessive entanglement with religion and thus prohibited the court's jurisdiction.).

148 *See, e.g.*, Callahan v. First Congregational Church of Haverhill, 808 N.E.2d 301, 311 (Mass. 2004) (stating that the Free Exercise Clause prevented the court from having subject-matter jurisdiction over the pastor's breach of contract claim. The court could not inquired into reasons for church's decisions regarding pastor's ministry without intruding into matters of internal management of church.); Barton v. Fitzpatrick, 65 So. 390, 393 (Ala. 1914)(analyzing whether the church followed its laws regarding the dismissal of its pastor. Because the church was organized on the congregational plan, the court was limited to determining whether the church acted as a congregation.); *In re* Galilee Baptist Church,186 So.2d 102, 106 (Ala. 1966)(stating that "a pastor may be deposed by a majority of the members at a congregational meeting at any time, so far as the civil courts are concerned, subject only to inquiry by the courts as to whether the church, or its appointed tribunal has proceeded according to the law of the church"); Morris Street Church v. Dart, 45 S.E. 753 (S.C. 1903); State v. Bibb Street Church, 4 So. 40 (Ala. 1888).

149 *See, e.g.*, Hollins v. Methodist Healthcare, Inc., 474 F.3d 223, 225 (Tenn. 2007)(stating that the ministerial exception is a doctrine rooted in the First Amendment's guarantees of religious freedom); Starkman v. Evans, 198 F.3d 173, 175 (La. 1999)(holding that the choir director qualified as a "minister" for purposes of the First Amendment's ministerial exception. The "minister exception" of the First Amendment prohibiting undue interference with the personnel decisions of church and religious leaders encompasses all employees of a religious institution, whether ordained or not, whose primary function is to serve its spiritual and pastoral mission.); McClure v. Salvation Army, 460 F.2d 553, 559 (5th Cir. 1972) (stating that the ministerial exception does not depend on ordination but on the function of the position);

religious aspects of the church.[150] Moreover, battles over these employees can result in schisms for reasons similar to clergy disputes.[151] Yet religious institutions often have other employees such as secretarial and custodial staff. These employees are not necessarily central to the religious aspects of the church.[152] Most courts that address employment cases involving this type of employee will use contract language and general employment law concepts (to the extent that churches are not immune from those laws) to determine outcomes.[153] These cases rarely involve church schisms and thus will be discussed in Chapter 11.

### 3. *Membership Cases*

There have been a number of cases brought by former church members who have been expelled from their church.[154] These disputes are frequently the result of a schism within the church.[155] Sometimes the expelled members claim to be the true representatives of

EEOC v. Catholic University of America, 83 F.3d 455, 463 (D.C. Cir. 1996)(stating that the ministerial exception encompasses all employees of a religious institution, whether ordained or not, whose primary function is to serve its spiritual and pastoral mission); Rayburn v. General Conference of Seventh-Day Adventists, 772 F.2d 1164, 1169 (4th Cir. 1985)[citing EEOC v. Southwestern Baptist Seminary, 651 F.2d 277, 283 (5th Cir. 1981)(stating that as a general rule, if the employee's primary duties consist of teaching, spreading the faith, church governance, supervision of a religious order, or supervision or participation in religious ritual and worship, he or she should be considered 'clergy')]. These cases are especially relevant since the Supreme Court decided, Hosanna-Tabor Evangelical Lutheran Church and School v. EEOC, 565 U.S. ___, 132 S. Ct. 694 (2012) (this is a new and important case that was not yet decided when the original chapter was drafted).

150 *Id.*

151 *Cf.* Patton v. Jones, 212 S.W. 3d 541, 545 (Tex. App. 2006)(Employee was the leader of youth activities and outings, which involved bringing youth together in fellowship and religious worship. His work was important to the spiritual and pastoral mission of the church. Some members of the congregation, however, were upset by the youth minister's interactions with girls at the church.).

152 *See, e.g.*, E.E.O.C. v. Roman Catholic Diocese of Raleigh, N.C., 213 F.3d 795, 801(N.C. 2000)(stating that the ministerial exception does not apply to employment decisions concerning purely custodial or administrative personnel); E.E.O.C. v. Mississippi College, 626 F.2d 477 (5th Cir. 1980)(involving the promotion of a secular school teacher in a religious educational institution); E.E.O.C. v. Southwestern Baptist Theological Seminary, 651 F.2d 277 (5th Cir. 1981)(involving administrative and support staff at a seminary); Whitney v. Greater New York Corporation of Seventh-Day Adventists, 401 F.Supp. 1363 (S.D.N.Y. 1975)(involving a typist-receptionist).

153 *Id.*

154 *See, e.g.*, Serbian Eastern Orthodox Diocese v. Milivojevich, 426 U.S. 696, 725 (1976)(accepting as the fundamental position that a church's decision as to the status of a person's church membership must be considered as binding and beyond the reviewing power of courts); Hadnot v. Shaw, 826 P.2d 978, 986 (Okl. 1992); First Presbyterian Church of Perry v. Myers, 50 P. 70, 74 (1897); Bouldin v. Alexander, 82 U.S. 131, 140 (1872)(stating that the court must take the fact of excommunication as conclusive proof that the persons exscinded are not members); Bowen v. Green, 275 S.C. 431, 272 S.E.2d 433 (1980) (Excommunicated members brought suit seeking to have the minister restrained from interfering with their rights as members.); Watson v. Jones, 80 U.S. 679, 681 (1872); Ramsey v. Hicks, 91 N.E. 344, 351 (1910); Hatfield v. Cummins, 85 N.E. 359, 361 (1908); Hendryx v. People's United Church of Spokane, 84 P. 1123, 1125 (1906); Pounder v. Ashe, 63 N.W. 48, 51 (1895); Nance v. Busby, 18 S.W. 874, 881 (1892); Deloisted v. Hilson, 235 N.W. 340 (1931); Caples v. Nazareth Church of Hopewell Ass'n., 18 So.2d 383, 386 (1944).

155 Watson v. Jones, 80 U.S. 679 (1872); Bouldin v. Alexander, 82 U.S. 131 (1872); Jones v. Wolf, 443 U.S. 595 (1979); Serbian Eastern Orthodox Diocese for U.S. of America and Canada, 426 U.S. 696 (1976).

the church.[156] As with clergy disputes, courts will not get involved in the ecclesiastical debates over expulsion – that is, the substantive bases for expulsion of church members.[157] Courts sometimes will, however, determine whether the procedures used in the expulsion follow established church procedures.[158] In this regard, courts will sometimes look at whether the expelling authorities within the church actually represented the church.[159] This can be done through neutral principles such as church bylaws or constitutions,[160] deference to church hierarchies,[161] deference to the majority in a congregational church,[162] or some combination of neutral principles and the latter two rules.[163]

156 *See, e.g.*, Gewin v. Mt. Pilgrim Baptist Church, 51 So. 947, 949 (Ala. 1909)(holding that the expulsion was invalid because the court found that the expelling body was not the real church); Caples v. Nazareth Church, 18 So.2d 383, 384 (Ala. 1944)(a suit brought by expelled members who claim to be the church).

157 *See, e.g.*, Nance v. Busby, 18 S.W. 874, 879 (Tenn. 1892)(stating that civil courts deal only with civil and property rights and that they have, in this country, no ecclesiastical jurisdiction); Brown v. Mt. Olive Baptist Church, 124 N.W.2d 445 (Iowa 1963)(stating that ordinarily the courts have no jurisdiction over, and no concern with, purely ecclesiastical questions and controversies, including membership in a church organization); Gipson v. Brown, 749 S.W.2d 297, 298 (Ark. 1988)(stating that the underlying dispute between the elders and members of the church is essentially religious in nature, and its resolution is more properly reserved to the church).

158 *See, e.g.*, Kennedy v. Gray, 807 P.2d 670, 672 (Kan. 1991)(holding that a church member had the right under common-law principle to have the church follow its expulsion procedure if the congregational church provides a procedure for expulsion of a member); Bouldin v. Alexander, 82 U.S. 131, 140 (1872); David v. Carter, 222 S.W.2d 900, 906 (Tex. Civ. App. 1949)(stating that although the courts will not disturb any action by the church as long as it is in accordance with the rules by which it is governed, they will grant relief from disciplinary action when the facts show a radical departure from the accepted customs and rules of the organization); Baugh v. Thomas, 265 A.2d 675, 678 (N.J. 1970)(stating that judicial review may exist in claims where the outers' actions show a departure from the rules and regulations of the church); Taylor v. Jackson, 273 F. 345 (C.A.D.C. 1921); Walker Memorial Baptist Church v. Saunders, 35 N.E.2d 42 (1941); Randolf v. First Baptist Church, 20 N.E.2d 485 (Ohio Ct. C.P. 1954); Linke v. Church of Jesus Christ of Latter Day Saints, 163 P.2d 44 (1945).

159 *See, e.g.*, Jones v. Wolf, 443 U.S. 595 (1979); Jarrel v. Sproles, 49 S.W. 904 (Tex. Civ. App. 1899)(In the case, there was evidence that the pastor of the majority and some members in fact believed in some of its doctrines. The minority was recognized then by the convention, council, and the Baptist association as the true church.); Brown v Mt. Olive Baptist Church, 124 N.W.2d 445 (Iowa 1963); Mt. Zion Baptist Church v. Whitmore, 49 N.W. 81, 86 (1891)(holding that the true church was the only one adhering to the church's adopted articles of faith); Christian Church of Tama v. Carpenter, 79 N.W. 375, 376 (Iowa 1899)(holding that the expelled members were the true church because the opposite faction was engaging in new practices contrary to the practices of the church); Gewin v. Mt. Pilgrim Baptist Church, 51 So. 947, 948 (Ala. 1909)(in order to determine whether the expulsion was actually that act of the church, the court will look to the church's ecclesiastical law and custom).

160 *Id.*

161 *See, e.g.*, Serbian Eastern Orthodox Diocese v. Milivojevich, 426 U.S. 696, 709 (1976)(declaring that where resolution of the disputes cannot be made without extensive inquiry into religious law and polity, courts must accept the applicable decision of the highest church body in a hierarchical church as binding); Elmora Hebrew Center, Inc. v. Fishman, 593 A.2d 725, 730 (N.J. 1991)(Regarding disputes involving a church governed by a hierarchical structure, courts should defer to the result reached by the highest church authority to have considered the religious question at issue.); Watson v. Jones, 80 U.S. 679, 727 (1871); Chavis v. Rowe, 459 A.2d 674, 677 (N.J. 1983); Dixon v. Edwards, 290 F.3d 699 (4th Cir. 2002); Elvig v. Ackles, 98 P.3d 524 (Wash. Ct. App. Div. 1 2004).

162 *See, e.g.*, Bouldin v. Alexander, 82 U.S. 131, 140 (1872)(stating that in a congregational church, the majority, if they adhere to the organization and to the doctrines, represent the church; an expulsion of the majority by a minority is a void act); Elmora Hebrew Center, Inc., v. Fishman, 592 A.2d 725, 730 (N.J. 1991)(stating that in disputes involving a church with a congregational structure, courts should defer to resolutions by a majority of the church's governing body); Chavis v. Rowe, 459 A.2d 674, 677 (N.J. 1983).

163 *See, e.g.*, Jones v. Wolf, 443 U.S. 595, 603 (1979)(stating that the primary advantages of the neutral principles approach are that it is completely secular in operation and yet flexible enough to accommodate

The general possibilities in membership cases are that the court holds it cannot decide the matter without engaging ecclesiastical issues and thus will not hear the case[164]; that the court will hear the case, but only examine procedural flaws,[165] sometimes resulting in reinstatement due to flawed procedures[166] and sometimes upholding the action[167]; that the court may hold it must defer to the appropriate church authorities in the matter, thus either reinstating the ousted members when the church determines they represent the church[168] or keeping them out when the opposite is true[169]; and that the court

all forms of religious organization and polity); Elmora Hebrew Center, Inc. v. Fishman, 593 A.2d 725, 730 (N.J. 1991)(stating that neutral principles sometimes may be invoked to resolve disputes concerning a religious entity's membership); Hardwick v. First Baptist Church, 524 A.2d 1298, 1301 (N.J. Super. 1987)(stating that courts can examine the bylaws and church policies to resolve membership disputes).

164 *See, e.g.*, Tubiolo v. Abundant Life Church, Inc., 605 S.E.2d 161, 164 (N.C.Ct. App. 2004)(stating that membership in a church is a core ecclesiastical matter because power to control church membership is ultimately the power to control the church, and it is an area where the courts should not become involved); Brown v. Mt. Olive Baptist Church, 124 N.W.2d 445, 446 (Iowa 1963)(stating that it is a general rule that courts do not have jurisdiction regarding purely ecclesiastical questions and controversies, including membership in a church organization; jurisdiction may exist, however, if there is an issue regarding a civil, contract, and/or property rights).

165 *See, e.g.*, Bouldin v. Alexander, 82 U.S. 131, 140 (1872); David v. Carter, 222 S.W.2d 900, 906 (Tex. Civ. App. 1949)(stating that although the courts will not disturb any action by the church as long as it is in accordance with the rules by which it is governed, they will grant relief from disciplinary action when the facts show a radical departure from the accepted customs and rules of the organization); Baugh v. Thomas, 265 A.2d 675, 678 (N.J. 1970)(stating that judicial review may exist in claims where the outers' actions show a departure from the rules and regulations of the church); Taylor v. Jackson, 273 F. 345 (C.A.D.C. 1921); Walker Memorial Baptist Church v. Saunders, 35 N.E.2d 42 (1941); Randolf v. First Baptist Church, 20 N.E.2d 485 (Ohio Ct. C.P. 1954); Linke v. Church of Jesus Christ of Latter Day Saints, 163 P.2d 44 (1945).

166 *See, e.g.*, Bowen v. Green, 272 S.E.2d 433, 435 (S.C. 1980)(Because the minister of a congregational church failed to demonstrate the source of authority whereby boards of trustees and deacons, rather than church members, exercised the power of excommunication, the court would restore the status quo, entitling the excommunicated members to reinstatement and to congregational meeting to review the pastoral office.); Randolph v. First Baptist Church of Lockland, 120 N.E.2d 485, 496 (Ohio Com. Pl. 1954) (holding that the attempted expulsion was void and had no effect because the member was not given a fair and impartial investigation).

167 *See, e.g.*, Brown v. Mt. Olive Baptist Church, 124 N.W.2d 445, 477 (Iowa 1963)(holding that the trial court was in error in going behind the authority of the majority of the church); Fowler v. Bailey, 844 P.2d 141, 145 (Okl. 1992)(stating that a church's decision as to the status of a person's church membership must be considered as binding and beyond the reviewing power of courts such as ours); Serbian Eastern Orthodox Diocese v. Milivojevich, 426 U.S. 696 (1976); Hadnot v. Shaw, 826 P.2d 978, 986 (Okl. 1992); First Presbyterian Church of Perry v. Myers, 50 P. 70, 74 (1897).

168 Bowen v. Green, 272 S.E.2d 433, 435 (S.C. 1980)(stating that "it is the function of this court, however, in these circumstances, to assure that the church itself has spoken. If it has, this court inquires no further. If it has not, this court may restore the status quo to enable the church to act."); Smith v. Pedigo, 44 N.E. 363, 365 (Ind. 1893)(stating that the expulsion that was done by the members who ceased to act in harmony with the original church doctrine, law, customs, principles, and practices held by the real church was an invalid expulsion).

169 *See, e.g.*, Nunn v. Black, 506 F.Supp. 444, 448 (D.C. Va. 1981)(holding that while the local church may have departed arbitrarily from its established expulsion procedures in removing the members, it is of no constitutional consequence); Mount Olive Primitive Baptist Church v. Patrick, 42 So.2d 617, 618 (Ala. 1949)(holding that it is established in this jurisdiction that courts will not intervene to settle a dispute regarding the right of membership); Fowler v. Bailey, 844 P.2d 141, 145 (Okl. 1992)(noting that church membership, by itself, is not a civil or property right subject to civil judicial regulation, and "we will not compel a church to reinstate a member.").

may hold by joining the congregation the former congregants subjected themselves to its rules and decisions.[170]

### 4. *Governance and Accounting Cases*

Two issues that come up repeatedly in the church schism cases are battles over who controls the workings of the church and cases involving concern over financial improprieties. The former cases frequently involve battles over who the proper church board or deacons are.[171] These types of cases seem to be more common in congregational churches but also appear in hierarchical churches.[172] The minister is sometimes the central focus of the factions that arise in the church,[173] but sometimes the schism arises out of religious disagreements.[174] The central question in most of these cases is who has

170 *See, e.g.*, Linke v. Church of Jesus Christ of Latter Day Saints, 163 P.2d 44, 45 (Cal. App. 1 Dist. 1945) (stating that a religious organization such as Church of Jesus Christ of Latter Day Saints is purely voluntary, and one joining it submits himself or herself to the disciplinary power of the body, and his or her rights as a member are governed by the constitution and bylaws thereof, and courts will not interfere unless the church authorities have proceeded contrary to the rules of the association in subjecting him or her to disciplinary penalties); State *ex rel.* Morrow v. Hill, 364 N.E.2d 1156, 1160 (Ohio 1977)(noting that one who becomes a member of a church is presumed to have voluntarily submitted to all the known tenets of congregational discipline, with an implied consent to its government, and is bound by its laws, usages, customs, and principles); Guinn v. Church of Christ of Collinsville, 775 P.2d 766 (Okla. 1989) (noting that there is a presumption that while you are member of a church, you voluntarily submit to all known tenets of congregational discipline).

171 *See, e.g.*, Barton v. Fitzpatrick, 65 So. 390, 391 (Ala. 1914) (involving a dispute over whether to retain a pastor and also involving some questions of legitimacy as to some of the deacons); State v. Getty, 37 A. 687, 688 (Conn. 1897) (involving a dispute as to who constituted the duly elected church committee); Trustees of Delaware Annual Conference of Union American Methodist Episcopal Church v. Ennis, 29 A.2d 374, 375 (Del. 1942) (involving a dispute over who was the proper pastor and against the church trustees); Epperson v. Myers, 58 So.2d 150, 151 (Fla. 1952) (involving a dispute as to who constituted the proper board of trustees); Borgman v. Bultema, 182 N.W. 91, 91 (Mich. 1921) (involving a dispute over who the proper minister, deacons, and elders of the church were); Williams v. Wilson, 563 S.E.2d 320, 321 (S.C. 2002) (involving a dispute over who constituted the church trustees).

172 *See, e.g.*, Barton, 65 So. at 392 (involving a question of control of a congregational church); Getty, 37 A. at 688 (involving a question of control of the church in the Roman Catholic Church, a hierarchical religious society); Ennis, 29 A.2d at 375 (involving a question of control of the church in the Union American Methodist Episcopal Church, a hierarchical religious society); Epperson, 58 So.2d at 151 (involving a dispute over the proper board of trustees in a Baptist church, a congregational religious society); Borgman, 182 N.W. at 91 (involving a dispute over who constituted the proper deacons and elders of a hierarchical church); Williams, 563 S.E.2d at 321 (involving a dispute over who constituted the church trustees in a congregational church).

173 *See, e.g.*, Barton, 65 So. at 391 (involving a dispute over whether to retain a pastor); Ennis, 29 A.2d at 375 (involving a question of whether the dismissal of a pastor was proper as the focus of the dispute); Epperson, 58 So.2d 150, 151 (Fla. 1952) (involving a question as to who was the proper board of trustees, with the firing of the pastor as the focal point of the dispute); Vaughan, 170 S.W.2d at 897–8 (involving a factional dispute over the pastor and control of the church); LeBlanc v. Davis, 432 So.2d 239, 241 (La. 1983) (involving a dispute over whether the pastor could retain his office in light of a majority vote against him by the body of the church); Furmanski v. Iwanowski, 108 A. 27, 29 (Pa. 1919) (involving a dispute over whether the bishop had the right to remove a priest from his position); Williams, 563 S.E.2d at 321 (involving a dispute where the church trustees sought to dismiss a minister and the congregation reacted by voting to elect new trustees).

174 *See, e.g.*, Partin v. Tucker, 172 So. 89, 93 (Fla. 1937) (finding that in a schism for the trustees to lose control of the property they must act in a way fundamentally opposed to the purpose and faith for which the property was originally acquired); Vaughan, 170 S.W.2d at 897–8 (involving a factional dispute over the pastor and claims that the majority of the congregation had departed from the tenants of the United

the right to control the local church.[175] Courts tend to evaluate these cases through the rules set forth in church documents and practices.[176] Thus, in most congregational churches, a majority must elect the church leaders at a properly noticed and held meeting.[177] Courts will not get involved in doctrinal disputes and will only look at which faction or leaders have the right to act on behalf of the church under church procedures.[178] Therefore, when the

Baptist faith); Saltman v. Nesson, 88 N.E. 3, 4 (Mass. 1909) (dealing with a controversy over which form of a religious ceremony to use); Schumacher v. Giedt, 112 N.W.2d 898, 900 (S.D. 1962) (arising out of a disagreement as to whether or not to leave the Wisconsin Synod).

175 *See, e.g.*, Barton, 65 So. at 391 (involving a question of who would control church property); Partin, 172 So. at 89 (determining that the only question the court need determine was who would control the church property); Ramsey v. Hicks, 91 N.E. 344 (Ind. 1910) (determining, in this case, who had the right to control of church property and whether they could merge with another church); Vaughan, 170 S.W.2d at 899 (determining who had the right to control the church property and finding in favor of the majority); Borgman, 182 N.W. at 91–2 (dealing with a question as to who had the right to control the local church); Williams, 563 S.E.2d at 324 (involving a dispute between the body of a congregational church and trustees as to who would have control of the church).

176 *See, e.g.*, Barton, 65 So. at 392 (The court held that they may only evaluate the dispute in "decision[s] by the congregation acting as an organized body in conformity with the law and practice of the church."); Getty, 37 A. at 688 (using church governance practices and documents to determine whether the election by the congregation was valid); Ennis, 29 A.2d at 376–7 (determining that the bishop's termination of a pastor was not proper under the procedures of the church); Epperson, 58 So.2d at 152 (using the common practices of the Baptist Church to evaluate the claims brought before the court and finding that the faction had not acted in accordance with the practices of the Baptist Church); Vaughan, 170 S.W.2d at 898 (evaluating the case based on church governance documents and the practices of the Baptist Church); Borgman, 182 N.W. 91, 92 (Mich. 1921) (using the church's articles, which were akin to a church constitution, to help determine the outcome of the case); Furmanski, 108 A. at 29 ("In matters relating to a church or other voluntary organization, its members are bound by and required to conform to its laws, and on a proper occasion will be enjoined from acting otherwise. Where it has appropriate tribunals to decide what are the scope and effect of its laws, their decisions duly made are binding on the members unless in violation of the law of the land."); Williams, 563 S.E.2d at 323–4 (S.C. 2002) (looking to church bylaws and practices to determine who had the ultimate authority and finding that the trustees had not overcome the presumptive burden in favor of the congregation in a congregational church).

177 *See, e.g.*, Barton, 65 So. 390, 392 (determining that in a congregational church, a majority, through proper notice, at meetings control the election of church officials); LeBlanc, 432 So.2d at 242 (inquiring into whether the body of a congregational church had held a proper meeting wherein they voted to remove the church's pastor); Williams, 563 S.E.2d at 325 (involving a dispute over the election of trustees, and the court found that the election was improper because there was not a properly noticed and held meeting).

178 *See, e.g.*, Barton, 65 So. at 392 ("It is familiar law that where factional differences occur in an ecclesiastical body, the rule of the civil courts in dealing with the property rights disputed between the factions is to give effect to the will of that part of the organization acting in harmony with the ecclesiastical laws, usages, customs, and principles which were accepted among them before the dispute arose."); Getty, 37 A. at 688 (focusing on church procedures to determine who had the right to act); Ennis, 29 A.2d at 377 (finding that the bishop did not act in accordance with church procedures and that his actions were thus invalid); Epperson, 58 So.2d at 152 (determining the outcome of the case by looking to which faction acted in accordance with church procedures); Ramsey, 91 N.E. at 354 (recognizing the right of the church's general assembly to act under church doctrine and procedure); Brown v. Mt. Olive Baptist Church, 124 N.W.2d 445, 446–7 (Iowa 1963) (determining only that the majority faction acted in accordance with church procedures pursuant to the church constitution and were thus justified in acting to expel certain members from the church); Vaughan, 170 S.W.2d at 898 (looking to church documents and procedures to determine who had the right to act under church law); LeBlanc, 432 So.2d at 241 (finding that the court had jurisdiction to determine the dispute because it was not ecclesiastical in nature and only would inquire as to whether the majority's dismissal of the pastor was valid under existing church procedures); Williams v. Wilson, 563 S.E.2d 320, 324–5 (S.C. 2002) (involving a dispute over who constituted the church trustees and an action to remove the pastor, and the court looked only at who had the right to act on behalf of the church and whether proper procedures were followed).

debate is over church doctrines or a church decision to split from a denomination or stay within one, courts generally will only determine who, based on church procedures, has a right to make the substantive decision.[179] The ecclesiastical decision is itself beyond a court's competence (and jurisdiction) to reach.[180]

One important note in this regard – a point relevant to all church schism cases – is that many courts distinguish between the church itself and it's corporate board.[181] Thus a number of courts have held corporate boards of incorporated churches cannot make nontemporal decisions (e.g., decisions involving membership, clergy, doctrine, or church leadership).[182] At the same time, the corporation and corporate board cannot be held liable for religiously based activities or decisions of the church.[183]

179 *See, e.g.*, Ramsey, 91 N.E. at 354 (involving a question over whether the Cumberland Presbyterian Church should merge with the Presbyterian Church in the United States of America and finding that the faction supporting merger had the right to make the determination); Saltman, 88 N.E. at 4 (determining that in the debate over church doctrine, the court may only determine whether the proper church procedures were followed); Lindstrom v. Tell, 154 N.W. 969, 971 (Minn. 1915) (deciding that the church could not be used for purposes other than those it was founded on based on the church constitution); Schumacher, 112 N.W.2d at 901–2 (reviewing the church documents and procedures and determining that the decision to remain with the Wisconsin Synod was valid under church procedures).

180 *See, e.g.*, Barton, 65 So. at 392–3 (finding that ecclesiastical matters are beyond the authority of the courts to rule on); Partin, 172 So. at 91 (recognizing that courts cannot determine ecclesiastical matters); Epperson, 58 So.2d at 152 (The court recognized that most decisions by a church are ecclesiastical and generally beyond the competence of the court but finding exceptions to this rule when there is a "showing of fraud, collusion or arbitrary conduct on the part of the church authorities."); Kompier v. Thegza, 13 N.E.2d 229, 231 (Ind. 1938) (recognizing that the courts may not deal with purely ecclesiastical matters); Brown, 124 N.W.2d at 446 (same); LeBlanc, 432 So.2d at 241 (same); Berry v. Bruce, 27 N.W.2d 67, 71 (Mich. 1947) (same); Morris Street Baptist Church v. Dart, 45 S.E. 753, 754 (S.C. 1903) (same).

181 *See, e.g.*, Blount v. Sixteenth Baptist Church, 90 So. 602, 603 (Ala. 1921) (recognizing that the corporate board is separate and distinct from the church itself); German Evangelical Congregation v. Pressler, 1865 WL 2445, *3 (La.) (distinguishing the church board from the church itself); Hardin v. Baptist Church, 16 N.W. 311, 311–12 (Mich. 1883) ("[T]he corporation has nothing to do with the church except as it provides for the church wants."); Lindstrom, 154 N.W. at 971 (recognizing a distinction between the church's corporate body and the church itself); St. Michael's Ukrainian Greek Catholic Church of Woonsocket v. Bohachewsky, 196 A. 796, 808 (R.I. 1938) (recognizing that the corporate board dealt with the temporal matters, as distinguished from other church business); Reinke v. German Evangelical Lutheran Trinity Church, 96 N.W. 90, 90 (S.D. 1903) (recognizing a distinction between the corporate board and the church).

182 *See, e.g.*, Blount, 90 So. at 603 (recognizing that the corporate board cannot make decisions involving church membership, church faith, or other nontemporal decisions); Pressler, 1865 WL 2445 at *3 ("There is one principle common to the trustees of all incorporated churches. They have the possession and the custody of the temporalities of the church. They are considered *virtute officii* entitled to the possession, and are lawfully seized of the grounds, buildings and other property belonging to the church."); Hardin, 16 N.W. at 312 (The corporate board of a church "cannot alter the church faith or covenant, it cannot receive members, it cannot expel members, it cannot prevent the church receiving or expelling whomsoever that body shall see fit to receive or expel."); Lindstrom, 154 N.W. at 971 (saying that even a majority, through the corporate body of the church, may not divert the church property from the original faith, even if those who remain faithful are only a minority); Bohachewsky, 196 A. at 809 (determining that the corporate board could not divert the church property to another faith, doctrine of leadership and thus had acted illegally); Reinke, 96 N.W. at 90 (determining that the corporation could have no part in making nontemporal decisions within the church).

183 *See, e.g.*, Blount, 90 So. at 603 (recognizing that the corporate board is separate and distinct from the church itself, and therefore, the corporation cannot be held liable for the religiously based activities of the church); Hardin, 16 N.W. at 312 (The church and corporation are separate and distinct, and the corporation may not be held liable for the religious acts of the church.); Reinke, 96 N.W. 90, 90 (S.D. 1903) (determining that the corporation, which had no part in making nontemporal decisions within the church, could not be held liable for the religious acts, such as in this case excommunicating a member).

The second type of case, which is often intertwined with the first, involves the desire of some in the congregation for a financial accounting because of concern over financial improprieties by the minister, church leadership, or both.[184] Sometimes church rules allow congregants to seek such an accounting[185] or at least congregants who hold a certain status within the church based on donations, voting right, or similar criterion.[186] Other times it is unclear if this is the case.[187] In both situations, courts will generally defer to church procedures and rules to determine whether the congregants requesting an accounting are so entitled.[188] Sometimes the congregants seeking the accounting are

184 *See, e.g.*, Abyssinia Missionary Church v. Nixon, 340 So.2d 746, 747 (Ala. 1977) (involving a suit brought by members who were expelled from the church claiming mismanagement of funds by the minister and church secretary and demanding an accounting); Hemphill v. Zion Hope Primitive Church of Pensacola, Inc, 447 So.2d 976, 977 (Fla. Dist. Ct. App. 1984) (involving a suit brought by members of the church against the pastor for an accounting); Graffam v. Wray, 437 A.2d 627, 635 (Me. 1981) (overturning a lower court decision that the matter of a financial accounting against the officers of the church was outside the court's subject-matter jurisdiction and allowing, if the plaintiffs so wished, them to present their evidence as to the accounting); Evans v. Shiloh Baptist Church, 77 A.2d 160, 161 (Md. 1950) (involving an action by members of a church and a fired assistant pastor who were concerned about the actions and potential financial improprieties of the pastor, so they brought suit against the church as a corporate entity for an accounting); Berry v. Bruce, 27 N.W.2d 67, 67–8 (Mich. 1947) (Several members of the church brought suit against the pastor and officials of the church); Fowler v. Bailey, 844 P.2d 141, 143 (Okla. 1992) (Several members of the church requested an accounting of the financial activities of the pastor and church deacons and trustees; after making this request, they were immediately kicked out of the church.).

185 *See, e.g.*, Abyssinia Missionary Church, 340 So.2d at 748 (Ala. 1977) (determining that a majority rules in a Baptist Church and therefore implicit in this statement is a right of a majority to demand an accounting); Greer v. Davis, 534 S.E.2d 853, 855 (Ga. Ct. App. 2000) ("Church bylaws provided that any member or his attorney may inspect the books and records of the Church for any proper purpose and at any reasonable time upon written demand and under oath stating the purpose.").

186 *See, e.g.*, Levitt v. Calvary Temple of Denver, 33 P.3d 1227, 1228–9 (Colo. Ct. App. 2001) (holding that state law entitled members of a nonprofit corporation, like the church in question, to an accounting, but since the plaintiff had been expelled, he could not avail himself of this provision); Russian Orthodox All Saints Church v. Darin, 192 N.W. 697, 705 (Mich. 1923) (withholding an accounting until the members of the church who could vote elected a new church committee or board of directors); Dragelevich v. Rajsich, 263 N.E.2d 778, 784 (Ohio Ct. App. 1970) (determining that the church officeholders were entitled to an accounting).

187 *See, e.g.*, Kennedy v. Gray, 807 P.2d 670, 673 (Kan. 1991) (In this case it was unclear if there was a right to an accounting; the court focused on determining the plaintiffs' right to a fair proceeding from expulsion from the church, and if they were to be reinstated, the court did not determine whether they were entitled to an accounting, although it seemed implicit.); Graffam, 437 A.2d at 635 (The court overturned a lower court decision that the matter of a financial accounting against the officers of the church was outside the court's subject-matter jurisdiction and allowed the plaintiffs, if so wished, to present their evidence as to the accounting, but it was unclear if such an accounting was right.); Evans, 77 A.2d at 162 (involving a question of whether a particular state law that required a showing of the church's activities in a public meeting allowed for five members or more to force both a meeting and the accounting; the court held that the provision did not grant them the authority to call the meeting.); Fowler, 844 P.2d at 150 (Several members of the church requested an accounting of the financial activities of the pastor and church deacons and trustees; after making this request, they were immediately kicked out of the church. It was unclear in this case whether or not the church had any procedures to request an accounting, and the court upheld the church's decision to kick the members in question out and not require an accounting, going so far as to say that even church members in good standing may not have been able to force an accounting.).

188 Abyssinia Missionary Church, 340 So.2d at 747 (allowing expelled church members to present evidence as to the proper procedures of the church regarding expulsion and accounting); Levitt, 33 P.3d at 1228–9 (holding that while state law entitled members of a nonprofit corporation, like the church in question, to an accounting, the court would defer to the church's decision to expel the plaintiff as a member); Evans,

also expelled, and the rules set forth earlier come into play.[189] Courts have on rare occasions ordered an accounting,[190] but more often than not the court simply determines that the party seeking an accounting is entitled to one.[191]

### 5. *Denominational Schism Cases*

Denominational schism cases can take any number of forms. One common type of case is where a congregational church votes to affiliate with another denomination or disaffiliate with a denomination. In such cases, courts look to make sure that church procedures were followed,[192] and if so, the courts defer to the appropriate church authorities

77 A.2d at 162 (deferring to church procedures as to when a meeting could be called, at which meeting it might have been possible for the plaintiffs to get an accounting under state law); Dragelevich, 263 N.E.2d at 784 (following church procedures to determine who constituted the proper church officers and finding that they were entitled to an accounting).

189 *See, e.g.*, Abyssinia Missionary Church, 340 So.2d at 748 (involving a suit brought by members who were expelled from the church and demanded an accounting, and the Court held that they were entitled to present evidence as to whether the proper procedures were followed in their expulsion); Levitt, 33 P.3d at 1228–9 (holding that the court would defer to the church's decision to expel the plaintiff as a member and therefore prevent him from obtaining an accounting); Kennedy, 807 P.2d at 673 (involving a suit for an accounting brought by church members who were expelled after bringing suit); Fowler, 844 P.2d at 150 (Okla. 1992) (Several members of the church requested an accounting of the financial activities of the pastor and church deacons and trustees; after making this request, they were immediately kicked out of the church.).

190 *See, e.g.*, Bhatti v. Singh, 773 N.E.2d 605, 608 (Ohio Ct. App. 2002) (affirming a lower court ruling which, in part, ordered an accounting).

191 *See, e.g.*, Greer, 534 S.E.2d at 855 (finding that the plaintiffs, under church bylaws, were entitled to an accounting); Saltman, 88 N.E. at 5 (determining that the corporation was entitled to an accounting); Graffam, 437 A.2d at 635 (The Court overturned a lower court decision that the matter of a financial accounting against the officers of the church was outside the court's subject-matter jurisdiction and allowed the plaintiffs, if so wished, to present their evidence as to the accounting, but it was unclear if such an accounting was right. While it was unclear if the accounting was a right, the Court did determine that the plaintiffs were, at the very least, entitled to present their evidence on the matter.); Dragelevich, 263 N.E.2d 778, 784 (Ohio Ct. App. 1970) (finding that church officers were entitled to an accounting against the plaintiffs). *But see* Levitt, 33 P.3d at 1228–9 (Colo. Ct. App. 2001) (holding that while state law entitled members of a nonprofit corporation, like the church in question, to an accounting, the court would defer to the church's decision to expel the plaintiff as a member, and he was therefore not entitled to an accounting); Fowler, 844 P.2d at 150 (Several members of the church requested an accounting of the financial activities of the pastor and church deacons and trustees; after making this request, they were immediately kicked out of the church. It was unclear in this case whether or not the church had any procedures to request an accounting, and the court upheld the church's decision to kick the members in question out and not require an accounting, going so far as to say that even church members in good standing may not have been able to force an accounting.).

192 Scotts African Union Methodist Protestant Church v. Conference of African Union First Colored Methodist Protestant Church, 98 F.3d 78, 82 (3rd Circuit 1996)(The Scott's Church certificate of incorporation states that "its trustee, except as such act be authorized by a two-thirds vote of the Church body members." But neither the church body nor the trustee ever approved the transfer of the church property, and as a result, the church voted to disaffiliate with the Conference.); Calvary Presbyterian Church v. Presbytery of Lake Huron of the United Presbyterian Church, 384 N.W. 2d 92, 93 (Mich. App. 1986) (The court ruled that there is a possibility that a Church that disaffiliates with a hierarchical denominational church might have a right to the property if the title is free simple to the church. This is different from the earlier rule, which stated that civil law did not interfere with a hierarchical church's affairs. This new rule calls for the court to examine church deeds, constitutions, and similar documents in order to apply them to secular law without considering any theological issues.).

(usually a majority of the congregation in congregational churches).[193] Sometimes, however, it becomes clear that church procedures were not followed.[194] For example, where proper notice of relevant meetings was not given.[195] In such cases, courts will invalidate affiliation or disaffiliation decisions on procedural grounds, leaving it up to the congregation to decide according to church procedures.[196] This is similar to situations where church property disputes involve affiliation with a new denomination or disaffiliation from a former denomination,[197] but in property cases the added factor of trust documents or other documents of conveyance may affect the result in a given case.[198]

Another common scenario is where affiliation or disaffiliation with a hierarchical church is involved. In these cases, courts often defer to the highest authority within the church hierarchy,[199] or they rely on neutral principles of law, which often involve church governance rules within the hierarchical church.[200] Courts are less likely to recognize disaffiliation in these cases unless the rules of the hierarchical church clearly allow for disaffiliation in the manner used by the relevant local church.[201]

193 Watson v. Jones, 80 U.S. 679, 727 (1871)(The rule that should govern civil courts is "whenever the questions of discipline, or of faith, or ecclesiastical rule, custom, or law have been decided by the highest of these church judicatories to which the matter has been carried to the legal tribunals must accept such decisions as final" and binding.); Kaufman v. Sheehan, 707 F.2d 355, 359 (8th Cir. 1983)(Due process arguments within a church deal solely with church procedures established by church authorities and, therefore, is "not a claim cognizable to civil courts."); Solid Rock Baptist Church v. Carlton, 789 A. 2d 149, 156 (N.J. Super. 2002)("While it is true that in a congregational church setting the majority may rule, it does not follow that if a congregational church is involved, the majority must rule.").

194 Evans v. Criss, 240 N.Y.S.2d 517, 522 (N.Y. Sup. 1963)(The Baptist faith demands a "fair, democratic, and impartial hearing on due and timely notice before the entire church congregation," which then will vote. The Court held that the church did not follow its own policy.); Yates v. El Bethel Primitive Baptist Church, 847 So.2d 331, (Ala. 2002)(The board of deacons and trustees of the church wanted an injunction to prevent their reverend and a newly elected board from interfering with church issues. Proper notice was not given to either the executive board or association according to the church's bylaws.).

195 *Id.*

196 *Id.*

197 *See, e.g.*, Watson v. Jones, 80 U.S. 679 (1871); Presbyterian Church in U.S. v. Mary Elizabeth Blue Hull Memorial Presbyterian Church, 393 U.S. 440, 449 (1969); Jones v. Wolf, 443 U.S. 595, 602–5 (1979).

198 *See, e.g.*, Presbyterian Church in U.S. v. Mary Elizabeth Blue Hull Memorial Presbyterian Church, 393 U.S. 440, 449 (1969)(The underlying law in both cases supported applying the implied trust doctrine to church property disputes.); Scotts African Union Methodist Protestant Church v. Conference of African Union First Colored Methodist Protestant Church, 98 F.3d 78, 96 (3rd Cir. 1996)(The Court held that in the absence of trust provision, the hierarchical rule under *Watson* should apply; that is, the hierarchical has title to the church property if the local congregation decides to disaffiliate with the larger denomination.); Fonken v. Community Church of Kamrar, 339 N.W.2d 810, 814 (Iowa 1983)(The local church property was held in trust for the national United Presbyterian Church in the United States of America (UPCUSA). The UPCUSA petitioned for injunctive relief that the trust be honored after a theological divide.).

199 *See, e.g.*, Serbian Eastern Orthodox Diocese v. Milivojevich, 426 U.S. 696, 724–5 (1976) (The issue in this case is doctrinal in nature because an ecclesiastical decision will determine the ownership of the local church property. Therefore, the civil courts must defer to the church authorities on the issue and accept their decision.); Scotts African Union Methodist Protestant Church v. Conference of African Union First Colored Methodist Protestant Church, 98 F.3d 78 (3rd Cir. 1996).

200 *See, e.g.*, Jones v. Wolf, 443 U.S. 595, 604 (1979)(The Court held that courts must defer to the church hierarchy and neutral principles of law when an interpretation of a deed or other church document would require the court to resolve a religious controversy.); Serbian Eastern Orthodox Diocese v. Milivojevich, 426 U.S. 696, 724–5 (1976)(The courts cannot resolve church property disputes based on religious doctrine, but they may apply neutral principles of law.)

201 *See, e.g.*, Serbian Eastern Orthodox Diocese v. Milivojevich, 426 U.S. 696, 709 (1976)(The Court ruled that when the dispute cannot be resolved without courts delving into ecclesiastical law, the courts

Perhaps the most common type of denominational dispute involves basic questions of who controls the church and church doctrines, as discussed in subsection B.4. When the dispute is over purely ecclesiastical concerns civil courts will not get involved, barring procedural problems or secular rights that may be determined by a civil court.[202] Otherwise, civil courts leave such ecclesiastical disputes to be worked out within the church.[203]

## C. A Note about Subject-Matter Jurisdiction in Church Property Dispute and Schism Cases

Most courts hold that they have no subject-matter jurisdiction to hear claims involving ecclesiastical matters,[204] and therefore can only hear claims involving failure to follow church procedures and cases involving civil or property rights.[205] A few courts come to the same conclusion without mentioning subject-matter jurisdiction.[206] It seems odd to

must accept the decision of the highest church body the hierarchy.); Scotts African Union Methodist Protestant Church v. Conference of African Union First Colored Methodist Protestant Church, 98 F.3d 78, 90 (3rd Cir. 1996)(In the absence of an expressed trust, when there is no hierarchical church control over the local church property, neutral principles of law apply.); Presbytery of Elijah Parish Lovejoy v. Jaeggi, 682 S.W.2d 465 (MO 1984)(The national church's constitution allowed local churches to voluntarily associate with the national church.).

202 *See, e.g.*, Jones v. Wolf, 443 U.S. 595, 604 (1979)(The Court held that courts must defer to the church hierarchy and neutral principles of law when an interpretation of a deed or other church document would require the court to resolve a religious controversy.); Serbian Eastern Orthodox Diocese v. Milivojevich, 426 U.S. 696, 709 (1976); Bell v. Presbyterian Church (U.S.A.), 126 F.3d. 328, 331 (4th Cir. 1997) (Claims involving religious organizations appointing or removing ministers or other employees involve a "theological significance [that is] beyond the ken of civil courts."); Kaufman v. Sheehan, 707 F.2d 355, 359 (8th Cir. 1983)(Due process arguments within a church deal solely with church procedures established by church authorities and, therefore, are "not a claim cognizable to civil courts."); Klagsbrun v. Va'ad Harabonim of Greater Monsey, 53 F.Supp.2d 732, 738 (D.N.J. 1999)(Secular courts may decide civil disputes involving religious entities, but courts may not become entangled with matters of faith, discipline, or doctrine.).

203 *See, e.g.*, Serbian Eastern Orthodox Diocese v. Milivojevich, 426 U.S. 696 (1976); Natal v. Christian and Missionary Alliance, 878 F.2d 1575 (1st Cir. 1989)(The Court would not intrude into ecclesiastical law.); Kaufman v. Sheehan, 707 F.2d 355, 359 (8th Cir. 1983); First Presbyterian Church of Schnectady v. United Presbyterian Church of the United States, 430 F.Supp. 450, 456 (D.C.N.Y. 1977)(Disputes whose resolutions are under ecclesiastical law "are not ones for judicial inquiry and decision.").

204 *See, e.g.*, Serbian Eastern Orthodox Diocese v. Milivojevich, 426 U.S. 696 (1976); Natal v. Christian and Missionary Alliance, 878 F.2d 1575 (1st Cir. 1989); Simpson v. Wells Lamont Corp., 494 F.2d 490, 493 (5th Cir. 1974)(The Court stated that issues regarding church government, especially those of faith and doctrine, do not fall under the Court's review, and, therefore, the case was properly dismissed for lack of subject-matter jurisdiction.); Bell v. Presbyterian Church (U.S.A.), 126 F.3d. 328, 331 (4th Cir. 1997); Kaufman v. Sheehan, 707 F.2d 355, 359 (8th Cir. 1983).

205 *See, e.g.*, Presbyterian Church v. Mary Elizabeth Blue Hull Memorial Presbyterian Church, 393 U.S. 440 (1969); Jones v. Wolf, 443 U.S. 595 (1979); William v. Jones, 61 So.2d 101, 104 (Ala. 1952) (Civil courts have jurisdiction in disputes of religious organizations when the issue involves either property rights or civil rights.); Stalling v. Finney, 122 N.E. 369, 370 (Ill. 1919)(Civil courts are not to interfere with the exercise of ecclesiastical authority unless it involves property rights or civil rights.).

206 *Cf.* Serbian Eastern Orthodox Diocese v. Milivojevich, 426 U.S. 696 (1976); Natal v. Christian and Missionary Alliance, 878 F.2d 1575 (1st Cir. 1989); Kaufman v. Sheehan, 707 F.2d 355, 359 (8th Cir. 1983); Blue v. Jones, 230 So.2d 569, 570 (Miss. 1970)(Even though there is no doctrinal schism, the dispute is over who is the proper pastor, trustees, and deacons, which is an ecclesiastical question that cannot be answered by this court.).

deny subject-matter jurisdiction in these cases because courts certainly have jurisdiction over tort, contract, property, employment, and some kinds of membership claims.[207] The Establishment and Free Exercise Clauses in essence preclude civil courts from hearing ecclesiastical claims,[208] but at least theoretically, courts have jurisdiction over these matters and are simply prohibited by substantive law from deciding the claim.[209] Significantly, whether this is characterized as a lack of subject-matter jurisdiction or a constitutionally mandated defense, the result is the same.

207 *Id.*

208 Presbyterian Church v. Mary Elizabeth Blue Hull Memorial Presbyterian Church, 393 U.S. 440, 449 (1969)(A civil court presiding over church disputes must avoid violating the Free Exercise and Establishment Clauses by not deciding a controversy involving religious doctrine.); Dixon v. Edwards, 290 F.3d 699, 714 (4th Cir. 2002)(Civil courts have a limited role in deciding church disputes. "This limited role is premised on First Amendment principles that preclude a court from deciding issues of religious doctrine and practice, or from interfering with internal church government."); Simpson v. Wells Lamont Corp., 494 F.2d 490, 493 (5th Cir. 1974).

209 *See, e.g.*, Watson v. Jones, 80 U.S. 679, 727 (1871)(If the claim involves "questions of discipline, or of faith, or ecclesiastical rule, custom, or law that have been decided by the highest church" authorities, then the civil courts must accept the decision as final and binding.); Presbyterian Church v. Mary Elizabeth Blue Hull Memorial Presbyterian Church, 393 U.S. 440 (1969); Serbian Eastern Orthodox Diocese for the United States & Canada v. Milivojevich, 426 U.S. 696 (1976); Bell v. Presbyterian Church (U.S.A.), 126 F.3d. 328, 331 (4th Cir. 1997)(Claims involving religious organizations appointing or removing ministers or other employees involve a "theological significance [that is] beyond the ken of civil courts.").

# 9 Contracts

Perhaps the most remarkable thing about application of the general law of contracts to religious entities and religious individuals is how unremarkable that application is in most situations. In most situations, religious entities and individuals are bound to contracts they make in the same fashion as other entities and individuals. Thus, for example, if a religious entity contracts for the services of a general contractor to build a church or for the purchase of goods or a religious individual contracts to purchase goods, the same law applies as would apply in other contract cases.[1] The fact that the entity or individual is religious would not affect the legal analysis of the contract in most of these general contract cases.[2]

Courts also have been willing to enforce basic employment contracts between religious entities and individuals.[3] As long as the court need not interpret a religious issue,

1 Jones v. Wolf, 443 U.S. 595, 606 (1979) (stating that courts are always allowed to resolve contracts governing "the manner in which churches own property, hire employees, or purchase goods"); *see also* St. Paul Church, Inc. v. Bd. of Trs. of the Ak. Missionary Conference of the United Methodist Church Inc., 145 P.3d 541 (Ak. 2007); Hope Presbyterian Church v. Presbyterian Church (U.S.A.), 242 Ore. App. 485 (2011); In re Multi-Circuit Episcopal Church Prop. Litig., 76 Va. Cir. 894 (2008); Episcopal Church Cases, 45 Cal. 4th 467 (2009); Heartland Presbytery v. Gashland Presbyterian Church, 364 S.W.3d 575 (Mo. Ct. App. 2012); Moses v. Diocese of Colo., 863 P.2d 310 (Colo. 1993); Bishop & Diocese of Colo. v. Mote, 716 P.2d 85 (Colo. 1986); Huber v. Jackson, 175 Cal. App. 4th 663 (2009); Minker v. Balt. Annual Conference of United Methodist Church, 894 F.2d 1354, 1359 (D.C. Cir. 1990) (the court held that a breach of an oral contract claim can be held by the court because "[a] church is always free to burden its activities voluntarily through contracts, and such contracts are fully enforceable in civil court"); Medcom Contracting Servs., Inc., v. Shepherdsville Christian Church Disciples of Christ, et al, 290 S.W.3d 681 (Ky. Ct. App. 2009) (contract with general contractor enforcing arbitration provisions); New Hope Missionary Baptist Church v. Paragon Builders, 667 S.E.2d 1 (Va. 2008) (enforcing contract and arbitration agreement contained therein).

2 77 C.J.S. Religious Societies, § 85, at 108–9 (2006) (stating that "[civil courts] do have jurisdiction as to civil contract and property rights even though such rights are involved in, or arise from, a church controversy"); McKelvey v. Pierce, 800 A.2d 840, 851 (N.J. 2002) (stating that if "the dispute can be resolved by application of purely neutral principles of law and without impermissible government intrusion (e.g., where the church offers no religious-based justification for its actions and points to no internal governance rights that would actually be affected), there is no First Amendment shield to litigation"); Barr v. United Methodist Church, 153 Cal. Rptr. 322 (1979) (stating that just because one of the defendants is a religious body does not preclude a suit based on breach of contract); Encore Prods., Inc. v. Promise Keepers, 53 F.Supp.2d 1101 (D. Colo. 1999) (holding that "[d]istrict courts have the power to enforce secular contract rights, despite the fact that one of the contracting parties may base their rights on religious affiliations").

3 DeMarco v. Holy Cross High School, 4 F.3d 166 (2d Cir. 1993) (enforcing employment contract between catholic school and teacher); Guinan v. Roman Catholic Archdiocese of Indianapolis, 42 F.Supp.2d

the court may apply neutral principles of law, in these situations contract principles, to enforce the contract.[4] Of course, as is the case with the law of employment contracts, specific performance is unlikely to be ordered.[5] This is even more true in cases involving religious entities and clergy or teachers because of the general unwillingness of courts to interfere in core religious questions, such as who should serve as the clergy member of a church or teach religious school there.[6] Thus, even if a contract violation is found, damages are more likely to be awarded in such cases.[7]

849 (S.D. Ind. 1998) (enforcing employment contract between religious school and teacher); Emp't Div. v. Smith, 494 U.S. 872, 888 (1990) (holding that churches are not exempt from minimum wage laws); Prince v. Mass., 321 U.S. 1158 (1944) (holding that churches are not exempt from child labor laws); Minker v. Balt. Annual Conference of United Methodist Church, 894 F.2d 1354, 1360 (D.C. Cir. 1990) (permitting plaintiff to proceed on claim for breach of employment contract); Reardon v. Lemoyne, 454 A.2d 428 (N.H. 1982) (applying neutral principles test resolved the dispute by examining the employment contract just as the court would have in any other case).

4 McKelvey v. Pierce, 800 A.2d 840, 851 (N.J. 2002) (stating that if "the dispute can be resolved by application of purely neutral principles of law and without impermissible government intrusion (e.g., where the church offers no religious-based justification for its actions and points to no internal governance rights that would actually be affected), there is no First Amendment shield to litigation"); Minker v. Balt. Annual Conference of United Methodist Church, 894 F.2d 1354, 1358 (D.C. Cir. 1990) (explaining that the "neutral principles test ... permits a court to interpret provisions of religious documents involving property rights and other nondoctrinal matters as long as the analysis can be done in purely secular terms"). *But see* Heard v. Johnson, 810 A.2d 871, 882 (D.C. 2002) (dismissing breach of contract and defamation suit by pastor because it could not be resolved without intrusion on religious decisions); Kelsey v. Ray, 719 A.2d 1248, 1251 (D.C. 1998) (concluding that the claim could not be resolved without excessive intrusion); Baldwin v. First Methodist Episcopal Church of Opportunity, 140 P. 673 (Wash. 1914) (applying general contract principles regarding whether there was a contract between the church and the pastor regarding his salary).

5 Church of God of Prospect Plaza v. Fourth Church of Christ, Scientist, 431 N.Y.S.2d 834, 839 (1980) (holding that specific performance of the contract would "be highly detrimental to the purpose of the corporation and the interests of its members ... [s]pecific performance of this contract would leave the combined congregation of two churches without a house of worship"); First Baptist Church of Dearborn v. Solner, 67 N.W.2d 252, 253 (Mich. 1954) (holding that specific performance would not be appropriate to compel the defendants to sell to plaintiffs); Glad Tidings Church of Am. v. Hinkley, 226 P.2d 1016, 1022 (Ariz. 1951) (holding that specific performance would be inadequate); Rector of St. David's Church v. Wood, 34 P. 18, 20 (Or. 1893) (stating that "[c]ourts will not generally decree the specific performance of a contract to deliver personal property ... 'delivery of chattels which can be supplied by the vendor alone, are among those which will be specifically enforced'"); Croy v. Cobe Laboratories, Inc., 132 F. App'x. 229 (2005) (holding that specific performance is not an appropriate remedy for breach of an employment contract); Gargano v. Diocese of Rockville Centre, 888 F.Supp. 1274, 1287 (E.D. N.Y. 1995) (specific performance is not an available remedy to breaches of employment contracts).

6 Bourne v. Ctr. of Children, Inc., 838 A.2d 371, 378 (Md. Ct. Spec. App. 2003) (stating that "religious organizations must be allowed to select their own clergy, free from government interference"); Weishuhn v. Catholic Diocese of Lansing, No. 05-081808-CD, 2010 WL 290516 (Mich. Ct. App. Jan 26, 2010) (court holding that it could not decide the teacher's claim because the "[t]ermination of a ministerial employee by a religious institution is an absolutely protected action under the First Amendment, regardless of the reason for doing so"); Cooper v. Church of St. Benedict, 954 A.2d 1216, 1220 (Pa. 2008) ("For purposes of the ministerial exception, courts have applied a 'ministerial-function' test, pursuant to which the exception applies 'if primary duties include teaching, spreading the faith, church governance, supervision of a religious order, or supervision of participation in religious ritual and worship.") (internal citations omitted).

7 56 C.J.S. Measure of Damages § 123 (2007) (holding that "[t]he general rule is that the measure of damages for breach of an employment contract is the compensation which an employee who has been wrongfully discharged would have received had the contract been carried out according to its terms"); Landix v. Tulane Ave. Baptist Church, 155 So. 776 (La. Ct. App. 1934) ("[r]ecord held to show that under Baptist Church law, church conference specially called could dispense with services of paid officers and employees who were members of congregation, at any time even without cause, thus entitling dismissed

As Chapter 11 explains, however, courts will not decide ecclesiastical matters in order to interpret an employment contract.[8] For example, a court will not determine whether a minister has breached his or her moral duties as required by church teachings or whether the minister is religiously fit to serve in that capacity.[9] To the extent that courts may interpret portions of a contract without answering ecclesiastical questions, they generally do so.[10] For example, even if a court will not question whether there were valid religious

choirmaster to recover salary only up to time of dismissal, especially where dismissal was for misconduct, though he had been appointed for a full year"); Duhon v. Slickline, Inc., 449 So.2d 1147 (La. Ct. App. 1984) (stating that a party who establishes a breach of his or her employment contract is entitled to damages); Pierce v. Tenn. Coal, Iron & R.R. Co., 173 U.S. 1 (1899) (stating "that in an action for breach of contract the amount which would have been received, if the contract had been kept, is the measure of damages if the contract is broken").

8 *See* Chapter 11. *See also* Washington v. African Methodist Episcopal Church, Inc., No. 11 CV 6087, 2011 WL 4352404 (W.D.N.Y. Sept 16, 2011) (The court held that it lacked subject-matter jurisdiction because the pastor relied on the Book of Discipline in his allegations of his breach of employment contract claim.); Elvig v. Calvin Presbyterian Church, 397 F.3d 790, 792 (9th Cir. 2005) (stating that the First Amendment protects a church's right to hire, fire, and assign duties to its ministers because to allow courts to review those employment actions could interfere with rights guaranteed by the First Amendment).

9 McClure v. Salvation Army, 460 F.2d 553 (5th Cir. 1972) (stating that the relationship between a church and its ministers "must necessarily be recognized as of prime ecclesiastical concern. Just as the initial function of selecting a minister is a matter of church administration and government, so are the functions which accompany such a selection."); Bollard v. Cal. Province of the Soc'y of Jesus, 196 F.3d 198, 207 (2d Cir. 2008) (stating that churches should be free from state cause of action that would impinge on the church's right to "choose its ministers or to exercise its religious beliefs in the context of employing its ministers") Rweyemamu v. Cote, 520 F.3d 198, 208 (2d Cir. 2008) (Second circuit stated that "[t]he more 'pervasively religious' the relationship between an employee and his [or her] employer, the more salient the free exercise concern becomes."); Van Osdol v. Vogt, 908 P.2d 1122, 1126 n. 6 (Colo. 1996) (court noting that the plaintiff's claims "all relate directly to [the church's] choice of a minister. ... For a court to determine whether the defendants impermissibly caused [the] plaintiff damage would require the court to examine the reasoning behind [the church's] choice of a minister."); Minker v. Balt. Annual Conference of United Methodist Church, 894 F.2d 1354, 1359 (D.C. Cir. 1990) (The court refused to apply ministerial exception based on the minister's antidiscrimination claim derived from the Methodist Book of Discipline because it would "necessarily ... [involve] interpretation of the minister's occupational qualifications which requires an 'understanding of the genuine desire to embody and carry forth more effectively Christ's ministry.'"); Elvig v. Calvin Presbyterian Church, 375 F.3d 951, 961–2 (9th Cir. 2004) (holding that "the [c]hurch cannot be required to articulate a justification for its ministerial decisions"); Petruska v. Gannon Univ., 462 F.3d 294, 307–9 (3d Cir. 2006) (holding that "the First Amendment protects [the university's] right to restructure regardless of its reason for doing so" because the "choice of restructure constituted a decision about who would perform spiritual functions and about how those functions would be divided").

10 Dobrota v. Free Serbian Orthodox Church St. Nicholas, 952 P.2d 1190, 1194–5 (Ariz. Ct. App. 1998) (holding that a trial court is allowed to decide issues relating to unpaid salary, benefits and missing property); Leavy v. Congregation Beth Shalom, 490 F.Supp.2d 1011, 1027 (N.D. Iowa 2007) (holding that it could decide the insurance coverage and annual compensation adjustment claims because they could be made "by factual determinations that do not involve the court in internal, ecclesiastical matters"); Favalora Sidaway, 995 So.2d 1133, 1135 (Fla. Dist. Ct. App. 2008) (*per curiam*) (stating that "courts are not forbidden from examining a religious organization's internal laws or structure, especially where the inquiry is relevant to a third party's purely secular tort or contract claims"); Rweyemamu v. Cote, 520 F.3d 198, 207 (2d Cir. 2008) (stating that "although its name [ministerial exception] might imply an absolute barrier to suit; for example, a case may proceed if it involves a limited inquiry that 'combined with the ability of the district court to control discovery, can prevent a wide-ranging intrusion into sensitive religious matters'") (internal citations omitted); Reardon v. Lemoyne, 454 A.2d 428 (N.H. 1982) (stating that "in religious controversies involving property or contractual rights outside doctrinal realm, court may accept jurisdiction and render decision without violating First Amendment")

grounds for termination, it may enforce the terms of a severance provision or notice provision.[11] These issues are discussed further in Chapter 11.

This chapter will focus on several issues that arise in contract cases involving religious entities or individuals. These issues are cases that involve contracts touching on ecclesiastical questions,[12] charitable donations or devises to religious entities under contract law,[13] the few remaining "blue laws" effecting contract creation,[14] contractual provisions requiring the exhaustion of internal procedures of religious organizations,[15] religious discrimination in contracts,[16] and religious defenses in garden-variety contract cases (*hint:* they rarely ever work).[17]

## A. Contracts that Raise Ecclesiastical Questions

As you have seen elsewhere in this book, courts do not address ecclesiastical questions. This doctrine, called the "ecclesiastical abstention doctrine,"[18] can be heavily tested in

[11] United Methodist Church, Balt. Annual Conference v. White, 571 A.2d 790, 793 (D.C. 1990) (noting that "in extremely limited circumstances, courts have adjudicated conflicts between church and clergy when the issue has been whether church officials had the authority to effect a pastor's discharge, as distinct from whether the church's decision was correct"); Gipe v. Superior Court, 14 Cal. App. 3d 617, 629 (1981) (stating that "requiring a church to pay its discharged minister in accordance with its contract will have a significant chilling effect upon the church's exercise of its right to discharge its ministers on account of doctrinal or other ecclesiastical differences"); Jenkins v. Trinity Evangelical Lutheran Church, 356 Ill. App. 3d 504, 511 (2005) (holding that the church's right to discharge plaintiff was not intimately related to the promise of salary and benefits and could be enforced); McGarry v. St. Anthony of Padua Roman Catholic Church, 704 A.2d 1353 (N.J. Sup. Ct. 1998) (holding that the church "had an absolute right to terminate plaintiff's employment-at-will"); St. John's Greek Catholic Hungarian Russian Orthodox Church of Rahway v. Fedak, 233 A.2d 663 (N.J. Sup. Ct. 1967) (holding that although "the congregation was free to terminate the services of Father Krehel upon the giving of the required notice, we are in accord with his contention that the procedure followed in doing so fell short of that required for congregational action under the bylaws"); Ebenezer Baptist Church of Providence v. Thompson, 45 R.I. 263 (1923) (holding that the notice of termination was reasonable).

[12] *See infra* Section A.

[13] *See infra* Section A.

[14] *See infra* Section B.

[15] *See infra* Section C.

[16] *See infra* Section D.

[17] *See infra* Section E.

[18] The "ecclesiastical abstention doctrine" is derived from the Free Exercise and Establishment Clauses of the First Amendment. *See* J. Nowak & R. Rotunda, Constitutional Law 17.12, at 1413 (6th ed., 2000) ("Of course, the government cannot declare which party is correct in matters of religion, for that would violate the principles of both religion clauses. A judicial declaration of such matters would simultaneously establish one religious view as correct for the organization while inhibiting the free exercise of the opposing belief"); Presbyterian Church in the U.S. v. Mary Elizabeth Blue Hull Mem'l Presbyterian Church, 393 U.S. 440, 449 (1969). The Supreme Court has stated that religious organizations require "an independence from secular control or manipulation, in short, power to decide for themselves, free from state interference, matters of church governance as well as those of faith and doctrine." Kedroff v. St. Nicholas Cathedral, 344 U.S. 94, 116 (1952); *see also* Gonzalez v. Roman Catholic Archbishop of Manila, 280 U.S. 1, 7–8 (1929) (stating that "[i]n the absence of fraud, collusion, or arbitrariness, the decisions of the proper church tribunals on matters purely ecclesiastical, although affecting civil rights, are accepted in litigation before the secular courts as conclusive, because the parties in interest made them so by contract or otherwise"); Kedroff, 344 U.S. at 116–17 (holding that the ecclesiastical abstention doctrine "must now be said to have federal constitutional protection as part of the free exercise of religion against state interference"); Serbian Eastern Orthodox Diocese for the U.S.A. & Canada v. Milivojevich, 426 U.S. 696 (1976)

contract cases. Courts generally must interpret contracts to address legal issues regarding enforcement, creation, or dissolution of contracts.[19] Yet contracts sometimes have provisions that raise religious questions.[20] For example, if someone makes a contract with a church, but before performance a schism occurs within the church and neither entity will honor the contract, the contractor may need to determine which entity is the "church" for purposes of contract enforcement.[21] If the court is called on to answer this question, it would appear at first glance that the court would have to violate the ecclesiastical abstention doctrine.

Courts, however, are not completely powerless in these cases. It remains true, even in such contract cases, that courts cannot answer ecclesiastical questions,[22] but courts often look to the law developed in the area of church property disputes and schisms to address

(reaffirming *Watson* in that civil courts lacked "the competence of ecclesiastical tribunals in applying the law that governs ecclesiastical disputes").

[19] *See* Restatement (Second) of Contracts § 17 *Requirement of a Bargain* (stating that "the formation of a contract requires a bargain in which there is a manifestation of mutual assent to the exchange and a consideration"); Jones v. Wolf, 443 U.S. 606, 609 (1979) (applying principles of property law); Presbyterian Church, 393 U.S. 440, 450 (1969) (applying principles of property law); Minker v. Balt. Annual Conference of United Methodist Church, 894 F.2d 1354, 1360 (D.C. Cir. 1990) (applying principles of contract law); Reid v. Johnston, 85 S.E.2d 114 (N.C. 1955) (holding that courts have jurisdiction as to contract rights that involve or arise from a church controversy); Granite Rock Co. v. Int'l Broth. of Teamsters, 130 S.Ct. 2847, 2855–6 (2010) (stating "that where the dispute at issue concerns contract formation, the dispute is generally for courts to decide"); The Harriman, 76 U.S. 161, 173 (1869) (stating that "[i]t is the province of courts to enforce contracts – not to make or modify them. When there is neither fraud, accident, nor mistake, the exercise of dispensing power is not a judicial function"); Bronson v. Rodes, 74 U.S. 229, 245 (1868) (stating that "[i]t is the appropriate function of courts of justice to enforce contracts according to the lawful intent and understanding of the parties").

[20] Lewis v. Seventh Day Adventists Lake Region Conference, 978 F.2d 940, 942–3 (6th Cir. 1992) (holding that the court could not decide claims of breach of employment contract, promissory estoppel, intentional infliction of emotional distress, and a derivative spousal claim because resolution of those claims would violate the Free Exercise Clause); Minker v. Balt. Annual Conference of United Methodist Church, 894 F.2d 1354, 1358–60 (D.C. Cir. 1990) (holding that it could not decide claims involving age discrimination and breach of contract because those claims were based on the church's written constitution and thus would entail inquiry into ecclesiastical policy); Hutchinson v. Thomas, 789 F.2d 392, 395–6 (6th Cir. 1986) (dismissing defamation claim against church because resolution would require an inquiry into ecclesiastical decision); Natal v. Christian & Missionary Alliance, 1988 WL 159169 at *4, *8 (D.P.R. Dec. 15, 1988) (dismissing wrongful termination claim because termination decisions are exclusively within the churches control).

[21] The Supreme Court has stated that in "cases where there is a schism [in a congressional church] which leads to a separation into distinct and conflicting bodies, the rights of such bodies to the use of the property must be determined by the ordinary principles which govern voluntary associations. If the principle of government in such cases is that the majority rules, then the numerical majority of members must control the right to the use of the property. If there be within the congregation officers in whom are vested the powers of such control, then those who adhere to the acknowledged organism by which the body is governed are entitled to the use of the property." Watson v. Jones, 80 U.S. 679, 725 (1871). *See also* Wilson v. Presbyterian Church of John's Island, 19 S.C. Eq. 192 (1946) (determining which parties were actually still members of the church after a schism); Turbeville v. Morris, 26 S.E.2d 821 (S.C. 1943); Middleton v. Ellison, 78 S.E. 739 (S.C. 1913); Wallace v. Hughes, 131 Ky. 445 (1909); Black v. St. Bernadette Congregation of Appleton, 121 Wis.2d 560 (1984).

[22] Parizek v. Roncalli Catholic High School of Omaha, 655 N.W.2d 404 (Neb. Ct. App. 2002) (stating that "[a] church may enter into contracts, which contracts are enforceable in civil court; however, the courts may not inquire into contractual matters whose enforcement would require a searching and therefore impermissible inquiry into church doctrine"); Serbian Eastern Orthodox Diocese for the U.S. & Can. v. Milivojevich, 426 U.S. 696 (1976) (stating that civil courts are not competent to consider ecclesiastical decisions because the inquiry is guided by different analytical principles).

these situations.[23] Therefore, courts dealing with a hierarchical religious entity often look to any pronouncements by the highest authority within the church.[24] In cases involving

[23] Jones v. Crestview Southern Baptist Church, 192 P.3d 571, 573 (Colo. App. 2008) (stating that "[w]hile civil courts have jurisdiction to render decisions in religious controversies involving rights outside the doctrinal realm, such disputes must be resolved by application of secular or neutral principles of law, thereby avoiding any impermissible inquiry into ecclesiastical questions"); Jones v. Wolf, 443 U.S. 595, 604 (1979) (stating that "a State is constitutionally entitled to adopt neutral principles of law as a means of adjudicating a church property dispute"); Presbyterian Church v. Mary Elizabeth Blue Hull Mem'l Presbyterian Church, 393 U.S. 440, 449 (1969) (holding that "there are neutral principles of law, developed for use in all property disputes, which can be applied without 'establishing' churches to which property can be awarded"); Burgess v. Rock Creek Baptist Church, 734 F.Supp. 30, 32 (D. D.C. 1990) (discussing neutral principles doctrine as applied to church property disputes); Jenkins v. Trinity Evangelical Lutheran Church, 825 N.E.2d 1206 (Ill. App. Ct. 2005) (holding that there are "neutral principles applicable to property and contract disputes, as will permit civil court to resolve disputes arising in church setting, must be completely secular in operation, yet flexible enough to accommodate all forms of religious organization and polity, relying exclusively on objective, well-established concepts of property law familiar to lawyers and judges"); African Methodist Episcopal Zion Church v. Union Chapel A.M.E. Zion Church, 308 S.E.2d 73 (N.C. Ct. App. 1983) (stating that "[c]ourts have jurisdiction as to civil, contract and property rights which are involved in or arise from a church controversy"); Watson v. Jones, 80 U.S. 679, 725 (1871) (stating that when there is "a schism which leads to a separation into distinct and conflicting bodies, the rights of such bodies to the use of the property must be determined by the ordinary principles which govern voluntary associations. If the principle of government in such cases is that the majority rules, then the numerical majority of members must control the right to the use of the property"); Jones v. Wolf, 443 U.S. 595, 602 (1979) (applying the neutral principles approach to a church property dispute as long as it does not "involve consideration of doctrinal matters, whether the ritual and liturgy of worship or the tenants of faith").

[24] Episcopal Church Cases, 198 P.3d 66 (Cal. 2009) (holding that "secular courts called on to resolve church property disputes should proceed as follows: State courts must not decide questions of religious doctrine; those are for the church to resolve. Accordingly, if resolution of a property dispute involves a point of doctrine, the court must defer to the position of the highest ecclesiastical authority that has decided the point. But to the extent the court can resolve a property dispute without reference to church doctrine, it should apply neutral principles of law. The court should consider sources such as the deeds to the property in dispute, the local church's constitution, cannons, and rules, and relevant statutes, including statutes specifically concerning religious property."); Landix v. Tulane Ave. Baptist Church, 155 So. 776 (La. Ct. App. 1934) (finding that the "[r]ecord held to show that under Baptist church law, church conference specially called could dispense with services of paid officers and employees who were members of congregation, at any time even without cause, thus entitling dismissed choirmaster to recover salary only up to time of dismissal, especially where dismissal was for misconduct, though he had been appointed for a full year"); Watson v. Jones, 80 U.S. 679, 727 (1871) (stating that "whenever the questions of discipline, or of faith, or ecclesiastical rule, custom, or law have been decided by the highest of these church judicatories to which the matter has been carried, the legal tribunals must accept such decisions as final, and as biding on them, in their application to the case before them"); Gonzalez v. Roman Catholic Archbishop of Manila, 280 U.S. 1, 16 (1929) (holding that "[i]n the absence of fraud, collusion, or arbitrariness, the decisions of the proper church tribunals on matters purely ecclesiastical, although affecting civil rights, are accepted in litigation before the secular courts as conclusive, because the parties in interest made them so by contract or otherwise"); Kedroff v. St. Nicholas Cathedral of the Russian Orthodox Church in North America, 344 U.S 94 (1952) (holding that the state law violated the Free Exercise Clause by interfering with an internal church dispute and deciding who was the "true" church, further holding that civil courts must defer to the ecclesiastical authorities regardless of whether it is based on statute or common law); Jones v. Wolf, 443 U.S. 595, 604 (1979) (stating that the neutral principles method "requires a civil court to examine certain religious documents, such as a church constitution, for language of trust in favor of the general church"); Protestant Episcopal Church in the Diocese of N.J. v. Graves, 83 N.J. 572, 585 (1980) (holding "that when a hierarchical organization exists, civil courts must defer to the higher ecclesiastical authority in resolving a property dispute between a local parish and the general church"); Bruss v. Przybylo, 385 Ill. App. 3d 399, 424 (2008) (stating that "[i]n hierarchical churches the courts will usually defer to the chain of authority"); Bennison v. Sharp, 121 Mich. App. 705 (1982) (relying on the hierarchical theory in

congregational churches, courts look to the pronouncements of a majority of the congregation[25] unless congregational rules provide for other methods to determine the will of the congregation.[26] Moreover, in many cases, courts look to neutral principles of law,[27]

concluding that the right to use and control the property remained with the minority); Hope Presbyterian Church v. Presbyterian Church (U.S.A.), 242 Ore. App. 485 (2011) (relying on the hierarchical deference approach); Wheeler v. Roman Catholic Archdiocese of Bos., 389 N.E.2d 966, *cert denied*, 444 U.S. 899 (Mass. 1979) (stating that "[i]n a hierarchical church structure, a local church is but an integral and subordinate member of a larger, general church organization").

25 N. C. Christian Conference v. Allen, 72 S.E. 617 (N.C. App. 1911) (court looking to what the majority of the trustees had done); Presbyterian Congregation v. Johnson 1841 WL 4042 (Pa. 1841) (discussing the majority of the pew-holders and contributing members of the congregation); Watson v. Jones, 80 U.S. 679 (1871) (discussing that the court looks to what the majority of the congregation wants); Bouldin v. Alexander, 82 U.S. 131, 141 (1872) (stating that "[i]n a congregational church, the majority, if they adhere to the organization and to the doctrines, represents the church); Graham v. Lockhart, 256 S.E.2d 518, 519–20 (N.C. App. 1979) (holding that the court is "limited to determining that the majority voted to remove the defendant and the record shows that the majority of the congregation so voted"); Antioch Temple, Inc. v. Parekh, 383 Mass. 854, 860 (1981) (holding that "[a] congregational church, by contrast, 'is self-governing … strictly independent of other ecclesiastical associations, and so far as church government is concerned, owes no fealty or obligation to any higher authority'"); Reid v. Gholson, 327 S.E.2d 107 (Va. 1985) (distinguishing congregation churches from hierarchical ones by stating that "[t]hey are free to adopt constitutions, by-laws, and internal rules which will alter or regulate their proceedings, but even these must be enacted by majority vote. And in the absence of such voluntarily-adopted rules, each such congregation functions as a pure democracy. When the majority has spoken in a fairly-conducted congregational meeting held after proper notice to the membership, then the governing body of the church as expressed its will and, as in the case of an hierarchical church, its decision is constitutionally immune from judicial review.").

26 First Church of Brethren of Lewistown v. Snider, 79 A.2d 422 (Pa. 1951) (stating that "it is clear that the property vests in that faction, whether majority or minority, which continues to act in harmony with the laws, usages and customs accepted by the body before the dispute and dissension arose and that faction is the true congregation and corporation, if incorporated. An independent or congregational church is governed by the majority of its own membership so long as they act within the purposes of the organization, but, if connected with a given denomination, it is bound, not only by its rules and laws, but also by the laws and usages of the particular sector ecclesiastical organization with which it is affiliated."); Gibbs v. Gilead Ecclesiastical Soc'y, 38 Conn. 153 (1871) (stating that "the plaintiff's 'work in the gospel ministry' was to be in accordance with the congregational polity, and his pastoral relation subject to its usages and laws.… That polity is contained in the congregational theory of the nature of a Christian church; in the usages of the churches in respect to mutual communion and assistance which existed when the Platform was adopted, and which were not affected by its provisions; in all the work of the Synod of 1708 at Saybrook, including the 'Confession of Faith,' 'Heads of Agreement,' and 'Articles of Discipline'; in the self adopted constitutions, rules and by-laws of the consociations, and their interpretations and modifications of the Platform; and in the corresponding usages adopted by the consociations, associations, and churches, since associations and consociations were organized."); Solid Rock Baptist Church v. Carlton, 789 A.2d 149 (N.J. Sup. Ct. 2002) (stating that "[w]hile it is true that in a congregational church setting the majority may rule, it does not follow that if a congregational church is involved, the majority must rule").

27 Congregation Yetev Lev d'Satmar, Inc. v. Kahana, 9 N.Y.3d 282 (2007) (stating that "civil courts may decide church property disputes based on 'neutral principles' where they can, but must defer to ecclesiastical authorities when neutral principles will not resolve the case"); Presbyterian Church v. Mary Elizabeth Blue Hull Memorial Church, 393 U.S. 440, 443–4 (1969) ("Civil courts do not inhibit free exercise of religion merely by opening their doors to disputes involving church property. And there are neutral principles of law, developed for use in all property disputes."); Jones v. Wolf, 443 U.S. 595, 603 (1979) (holding that "the primary advantages of the neutral-principles approach are that it is completely secular in operation … relies exclusively on objective, well-established concepts of trust and property law familiar to lawyers and judges. It thereby promises to free civil courts completely from entanglement in questions of religious doctrine, polity, and practice."); Scotts African Union Methodist Protestant Church v. Conference of African Union First Colored Methodist Protestant Church, 98 F.3d 78 (3d Cir. 1996) (applying neutral principles of law approach); Carnes v. Smith, 222 S.E.2d 322 (Ga. 1976) (following neutral principles

including neutral principles of contract law,[28] which enable them to answer the underlying questions without having to make ecclesiastical decisions.[29] These neutral principles may include the religious entity's corporate charter,[30] governance documents,[31] neutral legal principles generally,[32] and, of course, the provisions of the contract itself.[33]

of law approach); Harris v. Apostolic Overcoming Holy Church of God, Inc., 457 So.2d 385, 387 (Ala. 1984) (applying neutral principles); Protestant Episcopal Church in the Diocese of L.A. v. Barker, 115 Cal. App. 3d 599 (1981) (applying neutral principles); Grutka v. Clifford, 445 N.E.2d 1015, 1019 (Ind. App. 1983) (applying neutral principles); Fluker Cmty. Church v. Hitchens, 419 So.2d 445, 447–8 (La. 1982) (applying neutral principles); Graffam v. Wray, 437 A.2d 627, 634 (Me. 1981) (applying neutral principles); Babcock Memorial Presbyterian Church v. Presbytery of Balt., 464 A.2d 1008, 1016 (Md. 1983) (applying neutral principles of law approach); Piletich v. Deretich, 328 N.W.2d 696, 701–2 (Minn. 1982) (applying neutral principles of law approach); Bishop & Diocese of Colo. v. Mote, 716 P.2d 85 (Colo. 1986) (applying neutral principles of law approach); Presbyterian Church v. Hull Church 393 U.S. 440, 449 (stating that "there are neutral principles of law, developed for use in all property disputes, which can be applied without 'establishing' churches to which property is awarded"); Md. & Va. Churches v. Sharpsburg Ch., 396 U.S. 367 (1970) (applying the neutral principles).

28 Berthiaume v. McCormack, 891 A.2d 539 (N.H. 2006) (relying on the plain language of the statute and deed); Odatalla v. Odatalla, 355 N.J. Super. 305 (2002) (applying principles of contract law to the case); Presbytery of Ohio Valley, Inc. v. OPC, Inc., 940 N.E.2d 1188 (Ind. Ct. App. 2010) (applying principles of contract law); In re Marriage of Obaidi, 154 Wash. App. 609 (2010) (applying principles of contract law); Hawkins v. Friendship Missionary Baptist Church, 69 S.W.3d 756 (Tex. Ct. App. 2002) (stating that courts can apply principles of contract law); Freedom Church v. Cent. Dist. Conf. of the Evangelical Free Church of Am., 2007 U.S. Dist. LEXIS 343 (Iowa App. Mar. 28, 2007) (applying neutral principles of contract law); Jae-Woo cha v. Korean Presbyterian Church, 55 Va. Cir. 480 (2000) (stating that courts can apply neutral principles of law approach).

29 McElroy v. Guilfoyle, 589 A.2d 1082 (N.J. Super. 1990) (stating that the "[t]emporal matters affecting civil, contract, or property rights of religious body and its members or clergy may be resolved in civil court, if dispute involves purely secular issues and can be resolved without entanglement with matters of church's faith, discipline or doctrine"); Md. & Va. Eldership of the Churches of God v. Church of God at Sharpsburg, Inc., 396 U.S. 367 (1970) (holding that "resolution of the dispute involved no inquiry into religious doctrine"); Serbian Eastern Orthodox Dioceses for the U.S. & Can. v. Milivojevich, 426 U.S. 696, 708 (1976) (holding that "where resolution of the disputes cannot be made without extensive inquiry … into religious law and polity," courts must accept the decision of the highest church body as binding).

30 Jones v. Wolf, 443 U.S. 595 (1979) (holding that when "adjudicating a church property dispute, a state is constitutionally entitled to adopt a 'neutral principles of law' analysis involving consideration of … local church's charter"); Maryland & Va. Churches v. Sharpsburg Church, 396 U.S. 367, 368 (1970) (applying "the terms of the local church charters").

31 Jones v. Wolf, 443 U.S. 595 (1979) (holding that when "adjudicating a church property dispute, a state is constitutionally entitled to adopt a 'neutral principles of law' analysis involving consideration of … state statutes governing the holding of church property … and the general church's constitution"); Md. & Va. Churches v. Sharpsburg Church, 396 U.S. 367, 368 (1970) (applying "the provisions in the constitution of the general church concerning the ownership and control of church property"); Babcock Memorial Presbyterian Church v. Presbytery of Balt. of the United Presbyterian Church in the U.S., 464 A.2d 1008 (Md. 1983) (court resolved church property dispute by relying on the hierarchical control over local church affairs in the UPCUSA Book of Order); Calvary Presbyterian Church of Balt. City v. Presbytery of Balt. of the United Presbyterian Church in the U.S., 386 A.2d 357 (Md. App. 1978) (same); Poesnecker v. Ricchio, 631 A.2d 1097 (Pa. Commw. 1993) (applying the rules of religious fraternal organization).

32 Elmora Hebrew Center, Inc. v. Fishman, 593 A.2d 725 (N.J. 1991) (stating that "[c]ourts have powers, and perhaps duty as well, to enforce secular contract rights, despite fact that contracting parties may base their rights on religious affiliations"); Jones v. Wolf, 443 U.S. 595 (1979) (applying general neutral principles of contract law); Md. & Va. Churches v. Sharpsburg Church, 396 U.S. 367, 368 (1970) (applying general neutral principles of contract law) (stating that it "requires a civil court to examine certain religious documents, such as a church constitution, for language of trust in favor of the general church").

33 Jones v. Wolf, 443 U.S. 595 (1979) (holding that when "adjudicating a church property dispute, a state is constitutionally entitled to adopt a 'neutral principles of law' analysis involving consideration of deed");

As a result, courts are sometimes able to address these disputes without violating the ecclesiastical abstention doctrine.[34] The key is that some means exist for the court to address the legal issues involved without making theological/religious determinations.[35] This remains true, even where the end result is that the court decides a case that could have involved an ecclesiastical question had the court not had secular means to decide the case.[36]

## B. Charitable Donations or Devises to Religious Entities under Contract Law

Situations involving the interpretation of contracts involving charitable devises and donations to religious entities are common. They run the gamut from garden-variety cases that

Md. & Va. Churches v. Sharpsburg Church, 396 U.S. 367, 368 (1970) (applying "the language of the deeds"); Presbytery of Donegal v. Calhoun, 99 Pa. Commw. 300 (1986) (stating that courts can look to the language of the contract); State Presbytery of the Cumberland Presbyterian Church v. Hudson, 344 Ark. 332 (2001) (applying the language of the deeds); First Presbyterian Church v. United Presbyterian Church, 62 N.Y.2d 110 (1984) (applying the language of the deeds); Ark. Annual Conf. of the AME Church, Inc. v. New Direction Praise & Worship Ctr., Inc., 375 Ark. 428 (2009) (applying the language of the deed); Bd. of Managers of the Diocesan Missionary v. Church of the Holy Comforter, 164 Misc. 2d 661 (Sup. Ct N.Y. Dutchess County 1993) (stating that courts should look to the language of the deed); Presbytery of Hudson Riv. of Presby. Church (U.S.A.) v. Trustees of First Presbyterian Church & Congregation of Ridgeberry, 72 A.D.3d 78 (N.Y. App. Div. 2010) (stating that courts should look to the language of the deed); Schmidt v. Catholic Diocese, 18 So.3d 814 (Miss. 2009) (stating that interpreting deeds is permissible in courts).

34 *See* cases cited *supra* note 22. *See also* Jones, 443 U.S. at 604 (stating that civil courts are not permitted to resolve ecclesiastical questions in church property dispute); Serbian Orthodox Diocese v. Milivojevich, 426 U.S. 696 (1976); Parizek v. Roncalli Catholic High School of Omaha, 11 Neb. App. 482, 486 (2002) ("A church may enter into contracts, which contracts are enforceable in civil court; however, the courts may not inquire into contractual matters whose enforcement would require a searching and therefore impermissible imquiry into church doctrine."). *But see* Carr v. Union Church of Hopewell, 186 Va. 411, 417 (1947) (permitting court jurisdiction where the issues of "[e]cclesiastical beliefs, matters of church doctrine and polity and the like were entirely absent").

35 *See* sources cited *supra* note 4. *See also* Southeastern Pennsylvania Synod of the Evangelical Lutheran Church in America v. Meena, 19 A.3d 1191, 1196 (Pa. Commw. Ct. 2011) {"The deference approach seeks to avoid the danger of government entanglement with religion because our courts have acknowledged that 'First Amendment values are plainly jeopardized when church property litigation is made to turn on the resolution by civil courts of controversies over religious doctrine and practice.'" [quoting Presbytery of Beaver-Butler v. Middlesex Presbyterian Church, 507 Pa. 255, 262 (1985)]}; Presbyerian Church in U.S. v. Mary Elizabeth Blue Hull Memorial Presbyterian Church, 393 US 440, 449 (1969) ("The Amendment therefore commands civil courts to decide church property disputes without resolving underlying controversies over religious doctrine. Hence, States, religious organizations, and individuals must structure relationships involving church property so as not to require the civil courts to resolve ecclesiastical questions."). For cases discussing the Ecclesiastical Abstention Doctrine, *see* sources cited *supra* note 18.

36 Despite the formerly harsh rule that a court may not decide a unless a "neutral principal of law" applies found in cases such as Watson v. Jones, 80 US 679 (1871), and Presbyterian Church v. Mary Elizabeth Blue Hull Memorial Church, 393 US 440 (1969), the current rule of law is being diluted, allowing secular courts to hear more cases. Calvary Christian Sch., Inc. v. Huffstuttler, 367 Ark. 117, 122–123 (2006). Some courts have permitted hearing only portions cases where there is a mix of ecclesiastical questions and secular questions, whereas others have refused to hear the case as a whole. *Compare* Drevlow v Lutheran Church, 991 F2d 468, (8th Cir. 1993) (dismissing claims that directly related to ecclesiastical questions while allowing remaining claims to proceed to trial) *with* Gaston v. Diocese of Allentown, 712 A2d 757 (Pa. 1998) (dismissing the plaintiff's complaint for lack of jurisdiction stating "the action was an attempt to involve civil courts in ecclesiastical rule," where a student was expelled from a catholic school). *See also,* cases cited *supra* note 4; cases cited *supra* note 22; cases cited *supra* note 23.

can be decided on the face of the contract or by contract interpretation of provisions unrelated to religious questions,[37] to cases that directly raise ecclesiastical questions.[38] Moreover, two lines of cases raise questions common in charitable contribution cases, namely, how to treat charitable devises in light of the doctrine of consideration,[39] or how to treat cases under the doctrine of detrimental reliance/promissory estoppel.[40] The first part of this chapter addressed the ecclesiastical issue. This section will focus on questions of enforcement of charitable donations and devises to religious entities, including questions regarding consideration and promissory estoppel.

### 1. *Contracts for Devises and Donations that Raise Ecclesiastical Questions*

As explained earlier, courts do not answer ecclesiastical questions, and this remains true in contract cases.[41] Cases involving donations or devises sometimes raise questions about whether a religious entity is entitled to enforce the contract for donation or devise if

[37] Salvation Army v. Strickland, 253 Ga. 758 (1985) (holding that the intangible personal properties held in trust by a chartable and religious organization was not exempt from taxation as property held in trust for exclusive benefit of religious or chartiable institution when the religious organization was required to pay income from the properties to donors or their designees during specified lifetimes); Vasselos v. Greek Orth. Community of St. Spyridon, 129 N.W.2d 243 (Wis. 1964)(reinstating the jury's verdict for nominal damages in favor of the plaintiff in a breach of contract claim where the plaintiff argued the monthly deposit to defendant the church was a conditional gift and defendant argued the deposit was either an unconditional gift or a conditional gift whose conditions had previously been waived. The contract was unrelated to religious questions because the money was on the condition that Greek would continue to be taught at the church (*id.*); Willard v. Trustees of Methodist Episcopal Church of Rockville Centre, 66 Ill. 55 (1872) (where a party made a subscription to a church before the church was officially incorporated, the party inured to the benefit of the corporation thereafter created); Washburn v. Acome, 131 NYS 963, 966 (N.Y. Sup. Ct. 1911)("It is a well-established principle ... that an unincorporated society cannot take by devise."). To explore the role of the Internal Revenue Service in charitable contribution cases, *see* Hernandez v. C.I.R., 490 US 680 (1989).

[38] Secular courts are not permitted to decide ecclesiastical questions under the ecclesiastical abstention doctrine and must instead adhere to neutral principals of law. *See generally* discussion in Section A. *See also* Gonzalex v. Roman Catholic Archbishop of Manila, 280 U.S. 1 (1929) (holding that the decision of church authorities as to qualification of applicant for chaplaincy are conclusive in secular courts); Jones, 443 U.S. at 604 (stating that "there may be cases where the ... constitution of a general church incorporates religious concepts. ... If in such a case the interpretation of the instruments of ownership would require the civil courts to resolve a religious controversy, then the court must defer to the resolution of the doctrinal issue by the authoritative ecclesiastical body.").

[39] *See* Congregation of Bnai Abraham v. Kanner, 200 Ill. App. 640, 641 (1915) ("A promise by the widow of a deceased member of a religious congregation to pay off an encumbrance on church property in consideration of funeral rites performed and to be performed upon the deceased, and empowering the trustees of the congregation to enforce the promise, held not to be a promise by anybody to anybody, except to the maker thereof, and not founded upon a valid consideration"); Mills v. Davison, 54 N.J. Eq. 659, 662 (1896) ("The deed is to the religious society and to their successors, with the words 'but not to their assigns' added. It was made for a nominal consideration, and was therefore a deed of gift."). For an early case of a contribution to a college, *see* Stewart v. Trustees of Hamilton College, 2 Denio 403 (S.C.N.Y. 1845) (holding that where an agreement is made for a donation of money to be made to a religious institution and there is nothing done on the part of the donee to receive and invest the money and apply the interest to the payment of salaries of its officers, there is not sufficient consideration to support the agreement).

[40] *See, e.g., In re* Munson's Estate, 54 Cal. App. 2d 590, 593 (1942) (holding that appellants could not defeat the testamentary intent of the deceased by arguing reliance on Section 41 of the California Probate Code, which limited charitable devises and legacies "to a share not in excess collectively of one-third of a decedents estate").

[41] *See* discussion in Section A. *Compare* sources cited *supra* note 18 *with* sources cited *supra* note 20.

the entity has changed its doctrines or affiliation since the contract was drafted.[42] The next subsection will address questions of enforceability generally, but this subsection will address cases where the contract is otherwise enforceable, but interpreting the contract potentially could involve a court in deciding whether new religious doctrines are in conflict with older ones, or a change in religious affiliation effects a change in religious doctrine adequate to frustrate the donor's intent.

As a general matter, courts apply neutral principles of law[43] and/or defer to the determination of the highest authority within a hierarchical church[44] or the majority within a congregational church[45] to address these issues. If, however, such principles do not enable the court to answer the legal question, the court is barred by the First Amendment from

[42] For an example of where the Court strongly suggested against allowing refunds of donations, *see* Molko v. Holy Spirit Ass'n for Unification of World Christianity, 224 Cal. Rptr. 817, 834 (Ct. App. 1986) *review granted and opinion superseded sub nom.* Holy Spirit Ass'n for Unification of World Christianity v. Superior Court of County of Alameda (Dole), 721 P.2d 40 (Cal. 1986), and *review granted and opinion superseded*, 721 P.2d 40 (Cal. 1986) and *aff'd in part, rev'd in part sub nom.* Molko v. Holy Spirit Assn., 46 Cal. 3d 1092, 762 P.2d 46 (1988) (stating that "it is not hard to imagine what would occur if each potential dissenter were told: contributing to a religious organization – your own or indeed that of a group you reject – will give you a judicial platform from which to air your religious differences with others and potentially win a favorable verdict; all you need do in order to overcome the normal bar to civil adjudication of ecclesiastical matters is sue for a refund! Not only would such an invitation declare open season on churches and their followers; it could at the same time make at least some religious groups resist the very attempt to solicit donations, while inducing others – those too desperate for resources to refrain from financial appeals – to rigidify their doctrines and freeze or at least conceal their own evolution for fear that doctrinal change, ordinarily immune from censorship, could trigger refund-seeking litigation. It is in part for reasons such as these that the [F]irst [A]mendment has been construed to mean that religious questions remain non-justiciable even when they do not reach civil courts independently but instead form preliminary or ancillary issues in an otherwise justiciable dispute.").

[43] *See* discussion *supra* Part I; cases cited *supra* note 22. *See also* Jones, 443 U.S. at 604 (holding that "a State is constitutionally entitled to adopt neutral principles of law as a means of adjudicating a church property dispute); Minker v. Baltimore Annual Conference of United Methodist Church, 894 F2d 1354, 1359 (D.C. Cir. 1990) ("It is true that not *all* provisions of a religious constitution are immune from civil court interpretation. ... the Court adopted the neutral principles test which permits a court to interpret provisions of religious documents involving property rights and other nondoctrinal [*sic*] matters as long as the analysis can be done in purely secular terms.").

[44] Jones, 443 U.S. at 602 (stating that "[a]s a corollary to this commandment, the Amendment requires that civil courts defer to the resolution of issues of religious doctrine or polity by the highest court of a hierarchical church organization"). *See also In re* Episcopal Church Cases, 45 Cal. 4th 467, 492 (2009) (stating that on issues of religious doctrine and internal church governance, the court much defers to the greater church's resolution); People *ex rel.* Muhammad v. Muhammad-Rahmah, 289 Ill. App. 3d 740, 744 (1997) (explaining that "[c]ourts must defer to the resolution reached by the church's highest ecclesiastical authority on questions of religious doctrine, faith or polity. ... However, where the court can resolve the dispute according to 'neutral principles of law,' without invading ecclesiastical doctrine, mandatory deference is not required."); Canovaro v. Brothers of Order of Hermits of St. Augustine, 326 Pa. 76, 87 (1937) (stating that "[t]he act of 1935 provides that whenever any property has heretofore been or shall hereafter be conveyed for the use of any church, congregation, or religious society or in trust for religious worship or sepulture, it shall be taken and held subject to the control and disposition of such officers or authorities of such church ... The act is comprehensive enough to include all property, real or personal, of churches, congregations, or religious societies acquired by gift, purchase, grant, or devise."); Elmora Hebrew Center, Inc. v. Fisherman, 125 N.J. 404, 414 (1991) (stating that where a church is governed by a hierarchical structure, the court is to defer to the decision reached by the highest church authority).

[45] Elmora Hebrew Center, Inc., 125 N.J. at 414 (stating that where the governing body of the church is a congregational structure, courts are to defer to the majority's resolutions); Watson v. Jones, 80 US 679, 725 (1871) (stating that civil courts are to enforce the property decisions made by a majority of members in a congregational church).

answering the question lest it violate the Establishment Clause by engaging in religious interpretation or the Free Exercise Clause by favoring one side in a dispute involving religious decisions.[46] As long as the court can decide the matter without deciding ecclesiastical questions, however, it will do so.[47] Commonly, courts will look to church bylaws,[48] incorporation documents,[49] general principles of contract law,[50] general principles of the law of evidence, other neutral principles of law,[51] determinations of the highest authority within a hierarchical church,[52] or determinations by the congregation's majority in congregational churches.[53]

46 Jones, 443 U.S. at 604 (1979) (stating that "there may be cases where the … constitution of a general church incorporates religious concepts. … If in such a case the interpretation of the instruments of ownership would require the civil courts to resolve a religious controversy, then the court must defer to the resolution of the doctrinal issue by the authoritative ecclesiastical body."). *See also* Elmora Hebrew Center, 125 N.J. at 413 (explaining that "courts can and do decide secular legal questions in cases involving some background issues of religious doctrine, so long as the courts do not intrude into the determination of the doctrinal issues").

47 *See* sources cited *supra* note 35; sources cited *supra* note 4. *See also* discussion in Section A.

48 *See* Korean United Presbyterian Church v. Presbytery of the Pacific, 230 Cal. App. 3d 480, 498 (1991) (explaining that "[t]he conclusion to be drawn from … [Jones v. Wolfe, 443 US 595 (1979)] is that a state court may resolve disputes over church property through use of neutral principles of law, focusing on sources such as … bylaws … if the civil court is required to resolve a religious controversy, it must then defer to the resolution of the doctrinal issue by the authoritative ecclesiastical body."); Rector, Wardens and Vestrymen of Christ Church in Savannah v. Bishop of Episcopal Diocese of Georgia, Inc., 305 Ga.App. 87, 88 (2010) (stating that "[n]eutral principles of law include state statutes, corporate charters, relevant deeds, and the organizational constitutions and bylaws of the denomination"); Viravonga v. Samakitham, 372 Ark. 562, 574 (2008) (using the church's bylaws to determine the affiliation of the temple); Central Coast Baptist Ass'n v. First Baptist Church of Las Lomas, 154 Cal. App. 4th 586, 842–3 (explaining that "[i]n cases where disputes over civil or property rights are involved in churches of congregational organization, a court may apply neutral principles of law to determine whether the bylaws and rules were being properly observed by those governing the church – for instance, whether meetings were conducted or elections were held in accordance with the applicable rules or pertinent principles of law"); El Bey v. Moorish Science Temple of America, Inc., 362 Md. 339, 351 (2001) (stating that the Maryland court has a legitimate interest resolving secular disputes of religious organizations by interpreting corporate charters or bylaws using neutral principles of law). For an example of the Court's respect of church bylaws, *see* Waverly Hall Baptist Church, Inc. v. Branham, 276 Ga. App. 818, 821 (2005) {explaining that "[i]t is plain that Georgia courts have jurisdiction over disputes involving a nonprofit corporation's board of directors as well as the disposition of church property by that board, as long as we respect the nonprofit corporation's right to determine its own membership roster and bylaws." [quoting Srisovana et al. v Cambodian Buddhist Society, Inc. et al., 269 Ga.App. 600, 602(1) (2004)]}.

49 *See* Korean United Presbyterian Church v. Presbytery of the Pacific, 230 Cal. App. 3d 480, 498 (1991) (stating that "[t]he conclusion to be drawn from … [Jones v. Wolfe, 443 U.S. 595 (1979)] is that a state court may resolve disputes over church property through use of neutral principles of law, focusing on sources such as … articles of incorporation … if the civil court is required to resolve a religious controversy, it must then defer to the resolution of the doctrinal issue by the authoritative ecclesiastical body"); Southern Ohio State Exec. Offices of Church of God v. Fairborn Church of God, 61 Ohio App. 3d 526, 538 (1989) (explaining that once a hierarchical relationship is found by the court, a civil court my look beyond deeds and articles of incorporation to church constitutions and similar documents to resolve a church's property dispute).

50 General Conference of Evangelical Methodist Church v. Faith Evangelical Methodist Church, 809 N.W.2d 117, 122 (Ct. App. Iowa 2011) (using general principles of contract law to determine that there was an offer and acceptance between parties and thus their agreement to be bound and formally affiliated); Jenkins v. Trinity Evangelical Lutheran Church, 356 Ill. App. 3d 504, 1213 (2005) (explaining that some claims against churches can be decided using contract law, such as wage and benefits disputes).

51 *See* sources cited *supra* note 43.

52 *See* sources cited *supra* note 44.

53 *See* sources cited *supra* note 45.

## 2. *Enforcement of Charitable Subscription Agreements Involving Religious Organizations*

Courts have long attempted to enforce charitable subscription agreements, including those involving religious entities, despite often obvious problems of consideration or proof of detrimental reliance.[54] A number of legal fictions[55] and factual distortions[56] have been used to achieve enforcement over the years. These will be discussed next.

Recently, however, the *Restatement (Second) of Contracts* acknowledged the enforceability of these agreements as a matter of contract law and public policy.[57] Therefore, jurisdictions that follow this provisions in the restatement need not rely on the grounds used by earlier courts because the restatement acknowledged the enforceability of charitable subscription contracts on their face based on the many years of decisions in a variety of jurisdictions attempting to find legal grounds within the doctrines of consideration or promissory estoppel to enforce such agreements. Of course, not all jurisdictions follow the restatement,[58] and even among those that do, not all have applied this particular section of the restatement.[59] Therefore, in a number of jurisdictions, courts still rely on a variety of other methods to enforce charitable subscriptions[60] or find them unenforceable for lack of consideration.[61]

54 *See* Underwood v. Waldron, 12 Mich. 73 (discussing what should be deemed as sufficient consideration for a charitable subscription for the use of a Michigan college); King v. Trustees of Boston Univ., 420 Mass. 52, 58–9 (1995) ("Before analyzing the first and second statements, we note the considerations governing our review. A primary concern in enforcing charitable subscriptions, as with enforcement of other gratuitous transfers such as gifts and trusts, is ascertaining the intention of the donor. … If donative intent is sufficiently clear, we shall give effect to that intent to the extent possible without abandoning basic contractual principles, such as specificity of the donor's promise, consideration, and reasonableness of the charity's reliance."); Jordan v. Mount Sinai Hospital of Greater Miami, Inc., 276 So.2d (Dist. Ct. App. Fla. 3d District 1973) (explaining that the general contract rule that a promise not supported by consideration is a *nudum pactum* and as such unenforceable, in its liberal sense, is applicable to charitable subscriptions).

55 Salsbury v. Northwestern Bell Telephone Co., 221 N.W.2d 609, 613 (S. Ct. Iowa 1974) (stating that "[w]e acknowledge as valid the criticism of cases which enforce charitable subscriptions only on a fictional finding of consideration. But we are reluctant to adopt promissory estoppel as the sole alternative basis for such enforcement."); Jordan v. Mount Sinai Hosp. of Greater Miami, Inc., 276 So.2d 102, 108 (Fla. Dist. Ct. App. 1973) *aff'd.* 290 So.2d 484 (Fla. 1974) (stating that "[c]ourts should act with restraint in respect to the public policy arguments endeavoring to sustain a mere charitable subscription. To ascribe consideration where there is none, or to adopt any other theory which affords charities a different legal rationale than other entities, is to approve fiction.").

56 For cases finding sufficient consideration present where, under the general law of contract, the case presents insufficient consideration, *see generally* Presbyterian Soc. of Knoxboro v. Beach, 74 N.Y. 72 (1878); Young Men's Christian Ass'n v. Estill, 140 Ga. 291 (1913); Martin v. Meles, 179 Mass. 114 (1901).

57 "A charitable subscription or a marriage settlement is binding under Subsection (1) without proof that the promise induced action or forbearance." RESTATEMENT (SECOND) OF CONTRACTS § 90(1) (1981).

58 *See, e.g.*, Williams v. Habul, 724 S.E.2d 104, 110 (Ct. App. N.C. 2012) (explaining that the restatement is persuasive but not binding authority in North Carolina); Canfield v. Security-First Nat. Bank, 13 Cal.2d 1, 30–1 (1939) [stating that the *Restatement (Second) of Contracts* is not binding authority in California].

59 *See, e.g.*, Olson v. Synergistic Technologies Business Systems, Inc., 628 N.W.2d 142, 151 (Sup. Ct. Minn. 2001) (only adopting the section and allowing relief to the extent that it would prevent injustice). However, other courts have adopted this section. *See, e.g.*, Murphy v. Burke, 454 Pa. 391, 399 n. 10 (1973); Hoffman v. Red Owl Stores, Inc., 26 Wis.2d 683, 696 (1965).

60 *See* sources cited *supra* note 55; sources cited *supra* note 56.

61 *E.g.*, Hamilton College v. Stewart, 1 N.Y. 581, 582 (1848) (holding that there is a lack of consideration and therefore an invalid charitable subscription where an endowment of a literary institution is meant to be the consideration for a fund designated for that object). *See also* sources cited *supra* note 54.

Consideration is a difficult issue for courts faced with whether or not to enforce charitable subscriptions. On the one hand, there is a long tradition of courts favoring enforcement of charitable subscriptions most likely because charities are seen as socially useful and public policy favors enforcement.[62] On the other hand, there is the obvious fact that promises made to charitable organizations to donate money or other valuable commodities are generally motivated by generosity, moral commitments, or perhaps even rewards in the afterlife.

Justice Cardozo, writing for the Supreme Court[63] and reflecting the opinions of numerous other courts, explained that in some cases the donor may be seeking recognition for himself or herself or whoever's name the donation is made in.[64] In these cases, if a building, fund, and so on is named after the donor or the donor's requested name or some other public acknowledgment is made, there may be consideration, even though the donor may have also been motivated by charitable concerns.[65] Moreover, although the naming of something on receipt or promise of a charitable subscription could be considered detrimental reliance by a charity,[66] it is possible that a court may find the naming to be a condition to a gratuitous promise, which would vitiate the

[62] *See, e.g.*, Salsbury v. Northwestern Bell Telephone Company, 221 N.W.2d 609, 611–12 (Iowa 1874) (stating that "[c]ases throughout the country clearly reflect a conflict between the desired goal of enforcing charitable subscriptions and the realities of contract law. The result has been strained reasoning which has been the subject of considerable criticism."); Allegheny College v. Nat'l Chautauqua County Bank of Jamestown, 246 N.Y. 369, 374 (1927) [stating that "[v]ery likely, conceptions of public policy have shaped, more or less subconsciously, the rulings thus made. Judges have been affected by the thought that 'defenses of that character' are 'breaches of faith towards the public, and especially towards those engaged in the same enterprise, and an unwarrantable disappointment of the reasonable expectations of those interested." (internal citations omitted)].

[63] Justice Cardozo was an associate judge of the New York Sate Court of Appeals from 1914–27, chief judge of the New York State Court of Appeals from 1928–32, and associae justice of the United State Supreme Court from 1932–1938. *Benjamin N. Cardozo, in* The Historcial Society of the Courts of the Sate of New York, *available at:* http://www.courts.state.ny.us/history/cardozo.htm (accessed Oct. 5, 2012). For Justice Cardozo's writing on this matter, *see* Allegheny College, 246 N.Y. at 376 (writing for the Court on dispute concerning the ability of a college to change the name of a scholarship whose funds were donated in a charitable subscription with the intention of having the name remain the same). Justice Cardozo wrote, "[t]he purpose of the founder would be unfairly thwarted or at least inadequately served if the college failed to communicate to the world, or in any event to applicants for the scholarship, the title of the memorial. By implication it undertook, when it accepted a portion of the 'gift,' that in its circulars of information and in other customary ways when making announcement of this scholarship, it would couple with the announcement the name of the donor" (*id.*).

[64] Allegheny College, 246 N.Y. at 377–8 (holding that sufficient consideration existed where the charitable subscription was given on the condition that the fund be made in the name of the donator and that there was an implied duty to continue using the name of the donator as a founder of the fund, thus creating a bilateral agreement).

[65] *See* Allegheny College, 246 N.Y. at 376 (finding sufficient consideration to support a charitable subscription where the plaintiff was to perpetuate the name of the founder of the memorial); Trustees of Baker University v. Clelland, 86 F.2d 14, 20 (8th Cir. 1936) (holding that sufficient consideration exists to support a charitable subscription where the recipient assumed the responsibility of seeing that the name of the donor was perpetuated throughout the college in association with the subscription).

[66] A charity that names a building, or some other tangible thing, after a donation is given or promised will often be unable to name the building, etc. … after someone else, therefore removing the naming rights from the charitable market so to speak. Moreover, the charity will likely have gone to some expense, such as adding new signage and publicity.

consideration argument.[67] Still, many courts that have addressed these situations have found detrimental reliance and consideration[68] or, in some cases, promissory estoppel.[69] Other bases for finding charitable subscription contracts enforceable are an implied promise by the charitable organization to continue its charitable or religious work,[70] an implied promise to use donations for the purpose designated by a charitable entity in a fund-raising campaign,[71] or finding consideration based on mutual promises by donors,[72]

67 *See, e.g.*, Loranger Const. Corp. v. E.F. Hauserman Co., 6 Mass. App. Ct. 152 (1978) (explaining that while application of promissory estoppel reduces formal protection against nonconsensual imposition of contract liability, the doctrine is limited by the requirement that the reliance must be reasonable; a promisor can prevent reasonable reliance by stating that the promise is only an invitation to negotiate or that it must be accepted within a reasonable time or by withdrawing his or her promise before detrimental reliance thereon by the promise).

68 Bethlehem Fabricators, Inc. v. British Overseas Airways Corp., 434 F.2d 840, 844 (U.S. Ct. App. 2d Cir. 1970) (stating that under New York law, enforcement of gratuitous promises inducing detrimental reliance is not limited to charitable subscription cases); Chapman v. Bomann, 381 A.2d 1123 (Me. 1978) (explaining that several Maine cases have held that reasonable and detrimental reliance on the promise of another person can act as a replacement for consideration, even in charitable subscription cases). *But see In re* Estate of Schmidt, 723 N.W.2d 454 (2006) (explaining that in Iowa there is no requirement to show detrimental reliance or consideration, and charitable subscriptions are binding without proof of either).

69 *See generally In re* Field's Estate, 11 Misc. 2d 427, 432–3 (1958) (explaining that where the Illinois statute of frauds was unavailable to defeat enforcement of alleged oral charitable subscriptions given to claimants by decedent during his lifetime as against his estate, in view of part performance by the decedent in his lifetime and reliance upon the oral promise by the donee, thereby invoking the doctrine of promissory estoppel precluding the decedent or his estate from raising any defense based on the statute of frauds); I. & I. Holding Corp. v. Gainsburg, 251 A.D. 550, 554 (N.Y. App. Div. 1937) (explaining that New York has adopted promissory estoppel as the equivalent of consideration in the realm of charitable subscriptions); Lake Bluff Orphanage v. Magill's Ex'rs, 305 Ky. 391, 394 (1947) (enforcing charitable subscriptions with the doctrine of promissory estoppel "where there is an agreement by individuals to subscribe funds for the accomplishment of an enterprise which would not otherwise be undertaken or continued" internal citations omitted).

70 *See In re* San Juan Dupont Plaza Hotel Fire Litigation, 687 F.Supp.2d 1, 3 (2010) (holding that the remaining unclaimed funds from a settlement that remained unclaimed for twenty years of the Animal Legal Defense Fund, a charitable organization, were to be used to continue its work. While the court did not specifically state that it reached its decision via an implied promise, it stated that it used the equitable *cy pres* doctrine to reach an equitable decision); Menorah Chapels At Millburn v. Needle, 386 N.J. Super. 100, 109 (App. Div. 2006) [holding that the contract for Jewish funeral services was not severable such that failure to provide ritual could be cured by price deduction. The Court further stated that neutral principals of law are secular legal rules that can be applied to religious parties or disputes and "[s]pecifically, courts should enforce express agreements or implied promises to comply with religious doctrine when they can determine compliance or non-compliance with such agreements by application of neutral principles of law" (internal quotations and citations omitted), *id.* at 109].

71 *See, e.g.*, *In re* De Brabant's Estate, 95 N.Y.S.2d 324 (Sur. 1949) (holding that where the decedent pledged $75,000 to claimant organization for purpose of building a student chapel and erection of the chapel was postponed, the fact that the chapel was not erected during her lifetime did not result in a failure of consideration for the pledge. The Court further stated that "[s]urely it was implied that the claimant was to conduct the fundraising campaign, of which the decedent's pledge formed a part, and that it would forbear from soliciting funds for the Chapel from other persons. Moreover, there was an implied promise by the claimant or its predecessor in interest to go forward with the project, of which the Chapel was an integral part." *Id.* at 335–6).

72 For an examination on the implications of multiple donors being treated with higher regard than single donors, *see* First Methodist Episcopal Church of Mt. Vernon v. Howard's Estate, 233 N.Y.S. 451, 455 (Sur. 1929) *aff'd sub nom.* First Methodist Episcopal Church of Mt. Vernon v. Estate of Howard, 250 N.Y.S. 906 (1931) (stating that "[w]hat applies to a single donor applies with double force to multiple donors to charitable funds).

and promissory estoppel based on the argument that the charity relied on the promised donation to its detriment.[73] The restatement's frank recognition that charitable subscriptions are enforceable as a matter of public policy regardless of whether they meet the strict requirements of the doctrine of consideration is refreshingly straightforward.

## C. Contracts and "Blue Laws"

Historically, a number of jurisdictions prohibited the execution of contracts on Sundays[74] and/or invalidated contracts to be performed on Sundays.[75] Courts found a variety of tools to validate such contracts, such as allowing contracts to be performed out of necessity[76] or for charitable purposes.[77] This exception included situations where performance would protect property from destruction[78] or where performance

[73] *See, e.g.*, Arrowsmith v. Mercantile-Safe Deposit & Trust Co., 313 Md. 334, 354, 545 A.2d 674, 684 (1988) (holding that the decedent's pledge to make a charitable contribution was unenforceable after the decedent's death due to lack of consideration for the contribution and because the charity had not relied on the pledge to its detriment).

[74] *See, e.g.*, Lovell v. Boston & M.R.Co., 75 NH 568, 78 A 621, 34 LRA NS 67 (holding that contracts executed in Vermont on Sundays were void); Gauthier v. Cole, (1883 C.C. Mich.) 17 F 716 (stating that Michigan statute prohibited contracts to do any type of work on Sunday); McAuliffe v. Vaughan, 135 Ga. 852 (1911) (stating that in Georgia, "[i]t has been held ... that where one, in pursuing his business or the work of his [or her] ordinary calling on the Sabbath, makes a contract, it is invalid, and cannot be enforced"); Thompson v. Weems, 111 F.2d 566, 568 (5th Cir. 1940) (holding that under Mississippi law, a life insurer could not make an insurance contract on Sunday and could not be required to execute or perform a previously made, valid contract on Sunday. *See also* Code Miss. 1930, § 1131).

[75] King v. Fleming, (1874) 72 Ill. 21, 22 Am. Rep. 131 (explaining that promissory notes were void when executed on a Sunday in Indiana); Williams v. State, 333 So.2d 613 (Ala. 1976) (finding that because contracts in Alabama are void on Sundays, and a check is a contract, that check is void if made and uttered on Sunday); Brouchu v. Haigh, 51 Mass. App. Dec. 174 (1973) (finding that, similar to *Williams v. State*, the delivery of a check on Sunday as part of payment of a contract made on the same day is void); Hammons v. State, 59 Ala. 164 (187) (stating that under Alabama Code of 1876 § 2138, contracts made on Sunday are prohibited unless the contract is "for the advancement of religion, or in the execution, or for the performance of some work of charity, or in case of necessity"); Thompson, 111 F.2d at 568 (holding that under Mississippi law, a life insurer could not make an insurance contract on Sunday and could not be required to execute or perform a previously made, valid contract on Sunday).

[76] *E.g.*, International Text Book Co. v. Ohl, 150 Mich. 131 (1907) (stating that "the Michigan Sunday law is not merely directed against the making of contracts, but prohibits the doing of all work, except works of necessity and charity"); McAuliffe v. Vaughan, 135 Ga. 852 (1911) (quoting Pen. Code 1910 §416 stating that "any person who shall pursue his business, or the work of his ordinary calling, on the Lord's Day, works of necessity or charity only excepted, shall be guilty of a misdemeanor"); White's Lumber & Supply Co. v. Collins, 191 So. 105, 106 (Miss. 1939) [Miss. Code § 1131 (1930)], prohibits work or employment on Sundays except in cases of necessity or charity, including the collection of a debt. Quoted in J. Sibley's dissent in Thompson, 111 F.2d at 568); Lovejoy v. Whipple, 18 Vt. 379, 383 (1846)(Vermont statute prohibits secular business or employment, except works of necessity or charity, including the execution of a note); De Forth v. Wisconsin & M.R. Co., 9 NW 17, 18 (Wis. 1881)(Wisconsin's Section 4695, Rev. St. 1878 prohibited any manner of business on Sundays except in the cases of necessity or charity, including the loaning of money and giving of a note.).

[77] *Id.*

[78] McGatrick v. Wason, 4 Ohio St. 566 (1855) (holding that a ship was justified in leaving port on a Sunday in violation of a state blue law in order to protect the ship from being damaged. The Court further stated,

involved caring for those in need.[79] Moreover, courts required that a defense based on "blue laws" be affirmatively pleaded,[80] and courts did not generally favor such defenses.[81] For example, as long as acceptance occurred on Monday, even if the other elements of the contract occurred on Sunday, courts often would allow the contract to stand.[82] Moreover, innocent purchasers were not subject to the defense.[83]

In recent years, many "blue laws" applicable to contracts have been repealed,[84] or they have gone generally unenforced.[85] Numerous challenges have been brought against these laws, and many have been repealed. Yet they remain in a few jurisdictions.[86] The Supreme Court upheld "blue laws" against challenge under the Establishment

"[I]t is no part of the design of the act to destroy, or impose onerous restrictions upon any lawful trade or business." *Id.* at 573. Along a similar vein, courts also recognized an economic necessity defense. *See id.* (stating that caring for property is a work of necessity).

79 *See* souces cited *supra* at note 76.

80 For example, for claims alleging discriminatory application of a "blue law," the burden of proof is often on the party asserting the discriminatory enforcement. *See, e.g.*, People v Acme Markets, Inc., 37 N.Y.2d 326, (1975). *See also* People v. Adler, 160 NYS 539, 541 (2d Dept. 1916) (holding that the defendant shoe maker was guilty of violating New York's blue laws by operating his factory on Sunday. Although the defendant was a Sabbatarian, exempting him from New York's no-labor-on-Sunday law, which he used as a defense, he was convicted because he could not prove to the Court that his labor "was done in such a manner as not to interrupt or disturb other persons in observing the first of the week as holy time." *Id.*).

81 *See generally* Chestnut v. Harbaugh, 78 Pa. 473 (1875) (holding that the Sunday Law of 1705 does not declare a Sunday contract void; however, the law will not lend its aid to enforce an executory contract so made).

82 *See, e.g.*, Harper v. State, 394 So.2d 311, 313 (Sup. Ct. Miss. 1981) (where a contract is negotiated and agreed on on a secular day, it will still be valid even if the contract is finalized and signed on a Sunday); Raynor v. Blatz Brewing Co., 76 N.W. 343, 344 (Sup. Ct. Wisc. 1898) (stating that there is a difference between contracts "made" on Sunday and contracts "executed" on Sunday. "A court held a contract made on Sunday was illegal, but they never held a contract executed on Sunday illegal." *Id.*).

83 Currie-McGraw Co. v. H. & J. Friedman, 135 Miss. 701, 100 So. 273, 274 (1924) (stating that "[t]his holder is an innocent purchaser… permit this defense would be to allow these defendants to take advantage of their own wrong, to profit by the fact that they had violated the Sunday law; while, on the other hand the plaintiff has violated no law and had no knowledge of its violation by the defendants. To permit this defense would be to allow the party who alone has been guilty of a breach of the law to set up his illegal act as a defense to a suit by an innocent party. This court will not entertain such a defense.").

84 *See* Me. Rev. Stat. tit. 16, § 353-A (stating that "[n]o deed, contract, receipt or other instrument in writing shall be voidable only because it was made, executed, dated or delivered on the Lord's Day"); Conn. Gen. Stat. Ann. § 53-302a (West) [held unconstitutional by Caldor's, Inc. v. Bedding Barn, Inc., 177 Conn. 304 (1979)]; 18 Pa. Cons. Stat. Ann. § 7363 (West) [held to be unconstitutional by the Pennsylvania Supreme Court in Kroger Co. v. O'Hara Tp., 392 A.2d 266 (1978)].

85 People v. Abrahams, 40 N.Y.2d 277, 279–80 (N.Y. 1976) (discussing the multitude of exceptions to "blue laws" in New York); People v. Acme Markets, Inc., 37 N.Y.2d 326, 331 (1975) (explaining that Sunday sales laws have fallen by the wayside so much as to be generally unenforced except when there is a specific complaint). *But see* State v. Cranston, 59 Idaho 561, 85 P.2d 682, 684 (1938) (stating that "[i]f the Sunday closing law is unwise, antiquated, unenforced or unenforceable (all non-judicial questions) the legislature is the place for those to go who are dissatisfied and there disclose their grievances").

86 *See, e.g.*, N.J. Stat. Ann. § 40A:64-1 (West) (prohibiting the sale of clothing, building and lumber supply materials, furniture, home or business or office furnishings, or household, business, or office appliances on Sunday except in cases of necessity and charity or in cases of isolated transactions); Okla. Stat. Ann. tit. 21, § 907 (West) (stating that "[t]he first day of the week being by very general consent set apart for rest and religious uses, the law forbids to be done on that day certain acts deemed useless and serious interruptions of the repose and religious liberty of the community. Any violation of this prohibition is Sabbath-breaking."

Clause[87] and the Free Exercise Clause,[88] but those cases did not involve the invalidation of contracts executed on Sunday or to be performed on Sunday.[89] It remains possible that the application of "blue laws" to invalidate an otherwise validly executed contract would violate the Establishment Clause of the Constitution or state constitutional equivalents.

## D. Exhaustion of Internal Organizational Remedies

Sometimes religious entities' bylaws or other stated tenets require the exhaustion of internal remedies or procedures before bringing a case to court.[90] In such cases, courts generally enforce these requirements as long as the court need not make ecclesiastical determinations.[91] In most of these cases, ecclesiastical determinations are unnecessary because the bylaws or other documents are reasonably clear about internal procedures and remedies.[92] In cases where religious tenets prevent civil suits generally for enforcement of contracts, the courts follow the processes explained earlier.[93] Therefore, sometimes they may find that a contract action cannot be pursued in civil court.[94] Yet other times they may find that neutral principles of contract law are available to decide the case and that there is no clear prohibition on the filing of such suits.[95] Of course, where the other party to a contract is not a member of the sect involved, this defense is generally unavailable to the religious entity, and the terms of the contract would determine what other remedies need to be exhausted before suit can be brought.

This would include unnecessary contracts.); Mass. Gen. Laws Ann. ch. 136, § 5 (West) (listing the penalty for conducting business, including those involving contracts, on Sunday).

87 McGowan v. State of Md., 366 U.S. 420, 445 (1961) (holding that even though sunday closing laws have their origins from religious roots, a state can still have secular goals in providing Sunday as a day of rest for its citizens. Furthermore, "it is common knowledge that the first day of the week has come to have special significance as a rest day in this country." *Id.* at 452); Braunfeld v. Brown, 366 U.S. 599, 609 (1961) (upholding Pennsylvania's sunday closing law).

88 *Id.*

89 McGowan v. State of Md., 366 U.S. 420, 445 (1961) (involving a statute that closed stores on Sundays); Braunfeld v. Brown, 366 U.S. 599, 609 (1961) (involving a statute that closed stores on Sundays).

90 *See* Sims v. Ransom, 67 N.Y.S.2d 416, 417–18 (Sup. Ct. 1946) (holding that plaintiffs case was over before it even started. The court said that "[t]he complaint is fatally defective in failing to allege that the plaintiffs have exhausted the remedies available to them under the constitution and by-laws of the church. It is a fundamental rule that 'even in cases otherwise warranting judicial interference,' the court will not, as a rule, take jurisdiction unless the complaining member has exhausted such remedies as may be provided by the laws of the association itself."); Florida High School Athletic Ass'n v. Melbourne Central Catholic High School, 867 So.2d 1281, 1288 (Fla. Dist. Ct. App. 2004) (explaining that private organizations have internal procedures that members are to exhaust before initiating an action in any outside court or tribunal).

91 *See* sources cited supra note 37; sources cited supra note 5. *See also* discussion in Section A.

92 *See generally*, cases cited *supra* note 48; cases cited *supra* note 49.

93 *See* discussion in Section A.

94 *See* Williams v. Arpie, 44 N.Y.2d 689, 691, 376 N.E.2d 909, 910 (1978) [citing Baxter v. McDonnell, 155 N.Y. 83, 97 (1898)] (stating that "[a]bsent any such express contract, disputes arising from the relationship between a member of a hierarchical religious organization and that organization are not subject to resolution in the civil courts); cases cited *supra* note 34. *See generally*, discussion in Section A.

95 *See* sources cited *supra* note 27.

## E. Discrimination in Contracting and/or in Contract Terms

Simply put, religious discrimination, including in contracting, is forbidden under federal and state laws (in many jurisdictions),[96] as well as the Constitution.[97] This does not mean that religious entities cannot favor coreligionists in some hiring decisions, but that is a topic covered in Chapter 11. The question here is whether religious entities can discriminate based on religion in other sorts of contracts. The short answer is no.[98] There are, however, exceptions. Where the contract is for secular objects, discrimination is not permitted. Where the contract is for religious objects, such as art, prayerbooks, and so on, religious entities may favor coreligionists in many jurisdictions. Some state antidiscrimination laws have specific exceptions for these circumstances, and in other cases, federal or state free exercise principles [or Religious Freedom Restoration Act (RFRA) laws] could require such exceptions. As a general matter, though, religious discrimination, like racial discrimination,[99] in contracting is illegal under federal and state law.[100]

[96] *See* 42 U.S.C.A. § 1981 (West) (stating that "[a]ll persons within the jurisdiction of the United States shall have the same right in every State and Territory to make and enforce contracts, to sue, be parties, give evidence, and to the full and equal benefit of all laws and proceedings for the security of persons and property as is enjoyed by white citizens"). *See also* Alaska Stat. § 18.80.200 (stating that "it is the policy of the state and the purpose of this chapter to eliminate and prevent discrimination in employment, in credit and financing practices, in places of public accommodation, in the sale, lease, or rental of real property because of… religion."); Alaska Stat. § 36.30.040 (requiring the commissioner to adopt regulations to eliminate and prevent discrimination in state contracting because of religion, among other characteristics); Tenn. Code Ann. § 7-4-206 (West) (stating that "[t]he metropolitan government shall monitor the expenditure of funds from the convention center fund to ensure that all contractors, vendors, suppliers and professional services providers receiving compensation from the fund do not discriminate in hiring, partnering, contracting or subcontracting on the basis of race, religion, ethnic background, or sex"); Ohio Rev. Code Ann. § 4112.02 (West) (stating that "[i]t shall be an unlawful discriminatory practice … [f]or any person to … refuse to sell, transfer, assign, rent, lease, sublease, or finance housing accommodations, refuse to negotiate for the sale or rental of housing accommodations, or otherwise deny or make unavailable housing accommodations because of race, color, religion, sex, military status, familial status, ancestry, disability, or national origin").

[97] *See, e.g.*, Ariz. Const. art. II, § 13 (stating that "[n]o law shall be enacted granting to any citizen, class of citizens, or corporation other than municipal, privileges or immunities which, upon the same terms, shall not equally belong to all citizens or corporations"); Ind. Const. art. I, § 2 (examining courts have interpreted this article to mean that Indiana courts have jurisdiction over contract disputes involving churches and may in certain circumstances review ecclesiastical decisions). *See* Baker v. AME Church Judicial Council, 320 F.Supp.2d 786 (N.D. Ind. 2004).

[98] *See generally* Ariz. Rev. Stat. Ann. § 41-3751 (stating that "[e]xcept as otherwise provided by law, a religious organization shall not discriminate against a person in regard to rendering assistance funded under any program described in this section on the basis of religion, a religious belief or refusal to participate in a religious practice, or on the basis of race, age, color, sex or national origin"). *See also* statutes cited *supra* note 96; sources cited *supra* note 97.

[99] The federal statute prohibiting racial discrimination in contracting states that "[a]ll persons within the jurisdiction of the United States shall have the same right in every State and Territory to make and enforce contracts, to sue, be parties, give evidence, and to the full and equal benefit of all laws and proceedings for the security of persons and property as is enjoyed by white citizens, and shall be subject to like punishment, pains, penalties, taxes, licenses, and exactions of every kind, and to no other." 42 U.S.C.A. § 1981 (West). For state statutes, *see, e.g.*, Minn. Stat. Ann. § 363A.17 (West) (stating that "to intentionally refuse to do business with, to refuse to contract with, or to discriminate in the basic terms, conditions, or performance of the contract because of a person's race, national origin, color, sex, sexual orientation, or disability, unless the alleged refusal or discrimination is because of a legitimate business purpose"); R.I. Gen. Laws Ann. § 42-112-1 (West) (stating that "[a] ll persons within the state, regardless of race, color, religion, sex, disability, age, or country of ancestral origin, have, except as is otherwise provided or permitted by law, the same rights to make and enforce contracts, to inherit, purchase, to lease, sell, hold, and convey real and personal property, to sue, be parties, give evidence, and to the full and equal benefit of all laws and proceedings for the security of persons and property, and are subject to like punishment, pains, penalties, taxes, licenses, and exactions of every kind, and to no other").

[100] *See* sources cited *supra* note 96.

Yet other issues arise. For example, may religious organizations discriminate based on sexual orientation in contracting in a jurisdiction that protects against such discrimination? If the state has an exception for religious entities,[101] or a RFRA law,[102] or if the state constitution has been interpreted to apply greater protections for exemptions to generally applicable laws than under the U.S. Constitution, the answer could possibly be yes.[103] Otherwise, the antidiscrimination law is generally applicable, and no exception need be made for a religious entity.

## F. Religious Defenses in Garden-Variety Contracts

This section addressed a number of situations in which religious entities may be treated differently from other entities in contracting (and a variety of situations where they are not). One final note is in order, however. Religious defenses rarely, if ever, work in garden-variety contract cases.[104] By this, we mean cases where the sole issue or issues are interpretation of secular provisions of a contract between a religious entity and another party where the focus of the contract is not directly a religious object. Therefore, in the vast majority of contract cases involving religious entities – like other entities – no special defense is available.[105] Religious entities regularly contract for secular objects such as office supplies, construction, climate control, parking, and so on. In most of these cases, the religious nature of one of the parties to the contract has no bearing on the case and provides no special defenses.[106]

101 The best example of this is employment contract cases. *See, e.g.*, Thorson v. Billy Graham Evangelistic Ass'n, 687 N.W.2d 652 (Minn. Ct. App. 2004) (holding that defendant nonprofit religious organization could discriminate against employee on the basis of her sexual orientation. The Court stated that "[b]ecause BGEA's business activities are exclusively related to its evangelical ministry, they are not secular business activities unrelated to the religious and educational purposes for which BGEA is organized. Accordingly, BGEA is exempt from the sexual-orientation provisions of the Minnesota Human Rights Act." *Id.* at 658).

102 The federal version of this type of statute requires that governments show compelling justification for substantially burdening an individual's right to religious exercise, even if the burden is the result of a generally applicable rule, unless the government can show that its regulation is the least restrictive means of furthering a compelling government interest. 42 U.S.C. §§ 2000bb *et seq.* (West). However, the U.S. Supreme Court held this statute to exceed Congress' power under Section 5 of the Fourteenth Amendment and to constitute congressional intrusion on state power. City of Boerne v. Flores, 521 US 507, 532–4 (1997). Despite the Supreme Court ruling, many states have enacted their own Religious Freedom Restoration Act laws. *See, e.g.*, Ill. Stat. Ch. 775 § 35/1 *et seq.*; N.M. Stat. Ann. § 28-22-1 *et seq.* (West); R.I. Gen. Laws Ann. § 42-80.1-1 *et seq.* (West).

103 *See* cases cited *supra* notes 102 & 103.

104 *See, e.g.*, Strickland, 253 Ga. at 758–9 (holding that the intangible personal properties held in trust by a chartable and religious organization were not exempt from taxation as property held in trust for exclusive benefit of religious or charitable institution when the religious organization was required to pay income from the properties to donors or their designees during specified lifetimes).

105 *See generally* Strickland, 253 Ga. at 758–9 (holding that a special defense was not available). For when the Court will hear cases involving religious entities due to not having to determine ecclesiastical questions, *see* cases cited *supra* note 49.

106 *See* Potts v. Longest & Tessier Co., 86 W. Va. 157 (1920) (deciding the contract dispute for the construction of a building between a religious society and construction company without mention of the religious nature of the one party).

# 10 Taxation

## A. Overview

Taxation is highly relevant in the law and religion context. Numerous issues have arisen regarding the relationship between religious entities or individuals and federal or state taxes. This chapter will explore these issues in detail. We note that perhaps the greatest tax expert in history, Boris Bittker, originated the idea for this book and wrote several chapters. Unfortunately, he did not have the opportunity to write the tax chapter before he passed away. Thus we humbly submit this chapter with the understanding that it will not likely meet the standards of perfection that Boris would have achieved. We hope that all readers will understand that any limitations or errors in this chapter are in no way attributable to Professor Bittker.

After this overview, the chapter begins with a brief examination of U.S. Supreme Court decisions relevant to religion and taxation. These decisions are revisited in greater detail in some of the subsequent sections. The purpose of the initial section is to set forth some of the basic ground rules established by the Supreme Court in tax cases under the Establishment and Free Exercise Clauses.

The next section of the Chapter addresses federal taxation, including § 501(c)(3) exemptions, church status, parsonage exemptions, and Social Security taxes. The final section addresses state and local taxation. The issues in this section include state and local income tax, property tax, and sales tax. Please note that this chapter does not address taxpayer standing issues because they are addressed at Chapter 4.E.1.

## B. The U.S. Supreme Court Landscape

A number of cases decided by the U.S. Supreme Court directly address the constitutional issues raised when tax exemptions are given to, or denied to, religious entities. This section will provide a brief overview of the most significant of these cases. The cases discussed in this section and other relevant Supreme Court decisions also will be discussed where relevant in subsequent sections of this chapter. These cases do not answer many of the diverse questions that arise in the tax context, but they do lay a foundation regarding what may or may not be constitutional.

In *Walz v. Tax Commisioners*,[1] the Supreme Court upheld a New York City property tax exemption for properties used for religious worship.[2] The exemption was challenged

[1] 397 U.S. 664 (1970).
[2] *Id.*

under the Establishment Clause.[3] It is essential to note that the property tax exemption in *Walz* also applied to nonreligious organizations, constituting "a broad class of property owned by nonprofit, quasi-public corporations which include hospitals, libraries, playgrounds, scientific, professional, historical, and patriotic groups."[4] Because the law did not benefit just religious entities and was designed to promote secular objectives, the Court held that the purpose of the exemptions did not advance or inhibit religion.[5] Moreover, the *Walz* Court held that the tax exemption was not a "subsidy" to religion, which would violate the Establishment Clause.[6] Later decisions by the Court, however, suggest that the distinction between exemption and subsidy discussed in *Walz* is no longer of constitutional importance.[7]

The *Walz* Court also addressed government entanglement with religion and held that the property tax exemption helped to avoid an entanglement with religion.[8] The Court noted that requiring secular tax authorities to collect taxes and assign value to houses of worship and all the fixtures within them (in order to calculate taxes) would involve a substantial entanglement between government and religion.[9] Moreover, it could foster another form of entanglement – that involving "political strife over aid to religion."[10] The *Walz* Court also mentioned the long history of similar tax exemptions back to the time of the framing of the Constitution.[11]

As will be seen later in this chapter, the most important lessons from *Walz* given subsequent cases are the relevance of not favoring religion or a specific religion[12] and the relevance of the long history of tax exemptions for religious entities.[13] It is essential that exemptions be given to an array of similarly situated entities and not simply to religious entities.[14] As will be seen, this is consistent with Internal Revenue Code (IRC) § 501 (c)(3)[15] but not with the treatment of "churches" under the tax code.[16]

In fact, in *Texas Monthly v. Bullock*,[17] a majority of the Court recognized that an exemption given only to publications promoting religion violates the Establishment Clause;[18] although that majority was splintered into a plurality and concurring opinion on other aspects of the holding.[19] The statute at issue in *Texas Monthly* exempted

3 *Id.*
4 *Id.* at 673.
5 *Id.* at 671–3.
6 *Id.* at 675–98.
7 *See, e.g.*, Texas Monthly, Inc. v. Bullock, 489 U.S. 1 (1989); Jimmy Swaggart Ministries v. Bd. of Equalization of Cal., 110 S.Ct. 688 (1990); Bd. of Educ. of Kiryas Joel Village Sch. Dist. v. Grumet, 512 U.S. 687 (1994); *cf.* Zelman v. Simmons-Harris, 536 U.S. 639 (2002).
8 Walz, 397 U.S. at 670, 674–9 (noting that the existence of the religious clauses is an involvement that seeks to mark boundaries to avoid excessive government entanglement with religion).
9 *Id.* at 674.
10 *Id.* at 694 (Harlan, J., concurring).
11 *Id.* at 676–80, 681–715 (discussing that tax exemptions for religious organizations are embedded in the long history of the United States).
12 *Id.* at 695.
13 *Id.*
14 *Id.* at 696–7.
15 IRC § 501(c)(3) (West 2010).
16 IRC § 501(h)(5) (West 2010).
17 Texas Monthly, Inc., 789 U.S. 1 (1989).
18 *Id.* at 4, 6–9.
19 *Id.* at 5, 789 U.S. at 25–30 (Blackmun, H., concurring).

religious publications from the Texas state sales tax.[20] It did not exempt nonreligious publications,[21] and despite the state's protestations to the contrary, it did not exempt even those publications addressing religious questions from a nonreligious perspective.[22] The relevant portion of the statute exempted "[p]eriodicals that are published or distributed by a religious faith and that consist wholly of writings promulgating the teaching of the faith and books that consist wholly of writings sacred to a religious faith."[23]

Both the plurality and the concurring opinion of Justices Blackmun and O'Connor, agreed that the tax exemption violated the Establishment Clause because it endorsed religion over nonreligion,[24] and there was no need to decide the case under the Free Press Clause given the Establishment Clause violation.[25] The main point of disagreement between the plurality and concurrence was over the relevance of the Free Exercise Clause.[26] Earlier cases suggested that the Free Exercise Clause may require that a state not tax religious literature distributed by religious entities.[27]

The plurality held that there was no evidence that the payment of a sales tax on printed material "would offend [believers'] religious beliefs or inhibit religious activity.[28] Moreover, the plurality noted that under *United States v. Lee*,[29] even if the payment of a sales tax burdened religion, the state might have an overriding interest in uniform application of the sales tax, which would be appropriately tailored to that concern.[30] Therefore, the plurality found that there was no possible violation of the Free Exercise Clause if the items were not exempt from the sales tax, and even if there were, the government interest could be adequate to support uniform application of the sales tax.[31]

The concurrence, however, did not see the need to address the Free Exercise Clause question because whether or not the government can tax religious publications by religious entities under the Free Exercise Clause, it cannot create an exemption *only* for those publications under the Establishment Clause.[32] Significantly, under the more recent decision in *Employment Div. v. Smith*,[33] the Free Exercise Clause concern would

20 Tex. Tax Code Ann. § 151.312 (West 1982) (Periodicals and writings, including those presented on audio tape, videotape, and computer disk, that are published and distributed by a religious, philanthropic, charitable, historical, scientific, or other similar organization that is not operated for profit but excluding an educational organization are exempted from the taxes imposed by this chapter.).

21 *Id.*

22 *Id.*

23 *Id.*

24 Texas Monthly, Inc., 789 U.S. at 25–30 (Blackmun, H., concurring).

25 *See id.* at 5–8 (plurality opinion); *id* at 25–7 (White, B., concurring) (stating that the statute should have been struck down under the Free Press Clause).

26 *Id.* at 5–26 (plurality opinion) (stating that taxing the publications may inhibit their ability to function to some extent, thereby going against the Free Exercise Clause); *id.* at 25–31 (concurring opinion) (stating that free speech is not inhibited enough to be an issue, so one must decide where the line between the Establishment Clause and the Free Exercise Clause lies).

27 *See* Murdock v. Com. of Pennsylvania, 319 U.S. 105 (1943) (holding that an ordinance requiring solicitors to purchase a license was an unconstitutional tax on the Jehovah's Witnesses right to freely exercise their religion); Walz v. Tax Commission, 397 U.S. 664 (1970) (holding that grants of tax exemption to religious organizations do not violate the Establishment Clause of the First Amendment).

28 Texas Monthly, Inc., 789 U.S. at 18.

29 *Id.* at 19–20 (plurality opinion) [citing United States v. Lee, 455 U.S. 252 (1982)].

30 *Id.*

31 *Id.* at 5–26.

32 *Id.* at 5–8.

33 485 U.S. 660 (1988).

seem a nonissue as long as the tax imposed is generally applicable.[34] Thus *Texas Monthly* is especially relevant under the Establishment Clause.

*United States v. Lee*,[35] which was cited by the *Texas Monthly* plurality,[36] however, is quite relevant to whether or not there is a right to be exempt from paying a tax under the Free Exercise Clause.[37] In *Lee*, an Amish employer did not pay the employee or employer portions of the Social Security tax for his Amish employees.[38] After the Internal Revenue Service (IRS) required him to pay, he paid a portion of what he was asked to pay and sued.[39] The Court held that burdens on religion may be justified if the burden is "essential to accomplish an overriding governmental interest."[40] In this case, that overriding interest was the uniform application of the Social Security tax.[41] In a portion of the opinion relevant to all taxes, the Court held

> The tax system could not function if denominations were allowed to challenge the tax system because tax payments were spent in a manner that violates their religious belief. Because the broad public interest in maintaining a sound tax system is of such a high order, religious belief in conflict with the payment of taxes affords no basis for resisting the tax [citations omitted].[42]

Other significant cases are consistent with *Lee*.[43] The one exception applies when a state charges a flat license tax on commercial sales.[44] Under that circumstance, the state cannot charge the tax on religious materials distributed for evangelical purposes.[45]

In another important case, *Bob Jones University v. United States*,[46] the Court held that the IRS need not give § 501(c)(3) status to religious schools that discriminate based on race.[47] The reason for this is that such entities violate public policy, and they

[34] *Id.* (it may be a concern, however, under Religious Freedom Restoration Acts).
[35] 455 U.S. 252 (1982).
[36] 789 U.S. at 19–20 (plurality opinion) [citing United States v. Lee, 455 U.S. 252 (1982)].
[37] 455 U.S. 252 (1982).
[38] *Id.* at 244.
[39] *Id.* at 254–5.
[40] *Id.* at 257.
[41] *Id.* at 258–9.
[42] *Id.* at 260.
[43] *See, e.g.*, Jimmy Swaggart Ministries v. Bd. of Equalization of Cal., 493 U.S. 378, 392 (1990) (concluding that a "generally applicable" sales tax on the sale of religious materials is not a "constitutionally significant burden" on religious practices or beliefs); Hernandez v. Comm'r, 490 U.S. 680, 684, 699 (1989) (holding that contributions made to churches in return for services are not tax deductible and finding that even if such a holding would burden religion, a burden would be justified because of the state's interest in maintaining a sound tax system); Tex. Monthly, Inc. v. Bullock, 489 U.S. 1, 5 (1989) [holding that exempting only religious periodicals from sales tax violates the Establishment Clause (U.S. Const. amend. I)]; Bob Jones Univ. v. United States, 461 U.S. 574, 595–6 (1983) (holding that racially discriminatory religious educational institutions may be denied tax-exempt status).
[44] Follett v. Town of McCormick, S.C., 321 U.S. 573, 576–7 (1944) (holding that a flat license tax on the sale of religious material by an evangelist is unconstitutional); Murdock v. Pennsylvania, 319 U.S. 105, 112–13 (1943) (holding that a flat license tax on the sale of religious material by an evangelist is unconstitutional and noting that "[a] state may not impose a charge for the enjoyment of a right granted by the federal constitution.").
[45] *See supra*, note 44.
[46] 461 U.S. 574 (1983).
[47] IRC § 501(c)(3) (2010) (exempting qualifying organizations from taxation); Bob Jones Univ, 461 U.S. at 595 ("It would be wholly incompatible with the concepts underlying tax exemption to grant the benefit of tax-exempt status to racially discriminatory educational entities.").

do not confer a public benefit consistent with the § 501(c)(3) notion of "charitable" institutions.[48] Thus the schools were not entitled to the charitable exemption under § 501(c)(3).[49]

Therefore, the government may have an adequate basis to impose taxes even where doing so burdens religion as long as the taxes are applicable regardless of religion.[50] Moreover, while the government certainly can exempt religious entities from taxes, it cannot exempt only religious entities from taxes.[51]

Finally, in *Hernandez v. Commissioner of the Internal Revenue Service*,[52] the Court held that payment for services rendered by a religious entity need not be treated as deductible by the IRS.[53] In *Hernandez*, members of the Church of Scientology were denied exemptions for payments made for auditing services.[54] These services were charged at a set fee, and free services were not available.[55] The Court held that such fee-for-service systems, even when central to a religious entity's theology, need not be treated as deductible charitable donations.[56]

With these general points in mind, let's turn our attention to the specific tax requirements that apply when religious entities are exempted from taxation. The analysis will first address federal law and then state law. Some of these issues also have been addressed by the Supreme Court, and those decisions will be integrated into the relevant sections of this chapter.

## C. Federal Taxation

A number of complex issues arise when the federal tax code is applied to religious entities. The most common issues that arise involve religious entities and § 501(c)(3) status.[57] Other issues involve church status under the tax code, which provides greater advantages than § 501(c)(3) status alone[58] but also raises potential Establishment Clause concerns.[59] A number of issues have arisen around the "federal parsonage exemption" as well,[60] and some courts and scholars have questioned its constitutionality.[61] Each of these issues involves numerous subquestions that will be addressed in the next three subsections. The fourth subsection addresses Social Security taxes.

48 IRC § 501(c)(3); Bob Jones Univ., 461 U.S. at 595 ("Racially discriminatory educational institutions cannot be viewed as conferring a public benefit within the 'charitable' concept.").
49 Bob Jones Univ., 461 U.S. at 605.
50 *See, e.g.*, Jimmy Swaggart Ministries v. Bd. of Equalization of Cal., 493 U.S. 378, 392 (1990); Hernandez v. Comm'r, 490 U.S. 680, 684, 699 (1989); Bob Jones Univ., 461 U.S. at 595–6; United States v. Lee, 455 U.S. 252, 258–60 (1982).
51 Tex. Monthly, Inc. v. Bullock, 489 U.S. 1, 5 (1989).
52 490 U.S. 680 (1989).
53 *Id.* at 684.
54 *Id.* at 686.
55 *Id.* at 691–2.
56 *Id.* at 692–4.
57 IRC § 501(c)(3) ["An organization described in subsection (c) … shall be exempt from taxation."].
58 IRC § 170(a)(1) (West 2013) ("There shall be allowed as a deduction any charitable contribution.").
59 IRC § 501(c)(3).
60 *Id.*
61 *Id.*

### 1. *Section 501(C)(3) Status*

Internal Revenue Code § 501(c)(3) enables certain organizations to be tax exempt.[62] Moreover, donations to these organizations are deductible for the donor.[63] Both of these are significant benefits to the qualifying organization, but to qualify for § 501(c)(3), organizations must meet a number of criteria.[64] A § 501(c)(3) organization has to be "organized and operated exclusively" for an exempt purpose.[65] Exempt purposes are "religious, charitable, scientific, testing for public safety, literary, or educational purposes, or to foster national or international amateur sports competition ... or the prevention of cruelty to children or animals."[66] This chapter is only concerned with religious entities and other charitable entities connected with religious entities.

Additionally, none of an exempt organizations' net earnings can inure to the "benefit of any private shareholder or individual."[67] This is commonly referred to as the "private inurement requirement,"[68] and it has led to a number of issues in the context of religious organizations.[69] Another important requirement for § 501(c)(3) status is that exempt

62 *Id.*

63 *See, e.g.*, Presbyterian & Reformed Pub. Co. v. Comm'r, 743 F.2d 148, 154 (3d Cir. 1984) (listing the "numerous cases denying tax-exempt status based upon private inurement").

64 *See, e.g.*, Church of Scientology of Ca. v. Comm'r, 823 F.2d 1310, 1318–19 (9th Cir. 1987) (finding that excessive royalty payments, exclusive control over church money, and receipt of high amounts of money are private inurement of the church leader); Church By Mail, Inc. v. Comm'r, 765 F.2d 1387, 1393 (9th Cir. 1985) (finding that excessive salaries paid to ministers is private inurement); Presbyterian & Reformed Pub. Co., 743 F.2d at 154 (finding that increased commercial activity is not private inurement when it does not "[inure] to the personal benefit of any individual"); Bubbling Well Church of Universal Love v. Comm'r, 670 F.2d 104, 106 (9th Cir. 1981) (finding that benefits to a pastor and his family with no proof of regular church activities is private inurement); Church of Transfiguring Spirit, Inc. v. Comm'r, 76 T.C. 1, 5 (1981) (denying tax-exempt status to a church wherein "virtually all" of its income was spent for the benefit of its leaders).

65 IRC § 501(c)(3).

66 *Id.*

67 *Id.*

68 IRC § 501(c)(3); Treas. Reg. § 1.501(c)(3)-1(b) (2008) [detailing the requirements for meeting the organizational component of § 501(c)(3) status]; *see, e.g.*, Hall v. Comm'r, 729 F.2d 632, 634 (9th Cir. 1984) {finding that an organization failed the organizational test for 501(c)(3) qualification because there was no evidence that its assets were dedicated "so that, upon dissolution, they would be distributed for an exempt purpose" [quoting Treas. Reg. 1.501(c)(3)-1(b)(4)]}; Bethel Conservative Mennonite Church v. Comm'r, 746 F.2d 388, 393 (7th Cir. 1984) {finding that a church's assets were "dedicated to an exempt purpose" thus meeting the organizational test for § 501(c)(3) status [quoting Treas. Reg. § 1.501(c)(3)-1(b)(4)]}; Church of the Chosen People v. United States, 548 F. Supp. 1247, 1253 (D. Minn. 1982) (finding that a plaintiff without a comprehensive doctrine and "external manifestations analogous to other religions" is not "exclusively or substantially organized for religious purposes").

69 IRC § 501(c)(3); Treas. Reg. § 1.501(c)(3)-1(c) (2008) [detailing the requirements for meeting the operational component of § 501(c)(3) status]; *see, e.g.*, IHC Health Plans, Inc. v. Comm'r, 325 F.3d 1188, 1200 (10th Cir. 2003) (denying tax exempt status to a religious organization whose primary activities were commercial); St. David's Health Care Sys. v. United States, 349 F.3d 232, 237–39 (5th Cir. 2003) [finding that the question of control in a partnership between a for-profit and a not-for-profit is determinative of whether the organization operates exclusively for an exempt purpose under § 501(c)(3)]; Living Faith, Inc. v. Comm'r, 950 F.2d 365, 367 (7th Cir. 1991) (finding that an organization that runs restaurants and health food stores operates with a "substantial commercial purpose" and thus does not operate exclusively for a tax-exempt purpose); Am. Ass'n of Christian Sch. Voluntary Employees Beneficiary Ass'n Welfare Plan Trust v. United States, 850 F.2d 1510 (11th Cir. 1988) [affirming that a trust established to provide insurance to Christian school employees did not meet the operational test to qualify as a § 501(c)(3) organization]; Church By Mail, Inc. v. Comm'r, 765 F.2d 1387, 1392 (9th Cir. 1985) (affirming the

organizations may not carry out political activity.[70] This means that exempt organizations should not financially support or devote a substantial part of their activities to "carrying on propaganda, or otherwise attempting, to influence legislation."[71] They may not "participate in, or intervene in (including the publishing or distributing of statements), any political campaign on behalf of (or in opposition to) any candidate for public office."[72]

Cases involving religious organizations have arisen under each requirement. Therefore, there are cases addressing (1) whether a religious organization is organized exclusively for an exempt purpose,[73] (2) whether a religious organization is operated exclusively for an exempt purpose,[74] (3) the meaning of and relationship between the terms "organized" and "operated,"[75] (4) the meaning of "exclusively,"[76] and, of course, what qualifies as an "exempt purpose" organization.[77] Moreover, there are numerous cases on both the private inurement prohibition[78] and the political activity prohibition.[79] Each of these will be addressed in turn.

denial of tax-exempt status to a church that was operated "for [a] substantial nonexempt purpose"); Bethel Conservative Mennonite Church, 746 F.2d at 392 (finding a church that offered a charitable "Medical Aid Plan" to its members to be "operated for an exempt purpose").

70 IRC § 501(c)(3); Treas. Reg. § 501(c)(3)-1; *see, e.g.*, Presbyterian and Reformed Pub. Co. v. Comm'r, 743 F.2d 148, 152–6 (3rd Cir. 1984) (addressing "at what point the successful operation of a tax-exempt organization … transformed that organization into a commercial enterprise" and making this determination by looking to "the purpose to which the … activity is directed"); Senior Citizens Stores, Inc. v. United States, 602 F.2d 711, 713 (5th Cir. 1979) ("The focus in deciding whether a corporation qualifies for tax exempt status is on the manner of operation of its business, not just whether it is organized under 'not-for-profit' corporate statutes.").

71 IRC § 501(c)(3); Treas. Reg. § 501(c)(3)-1 (detailing the requirements for organizations to be organized and operated "exclusively" for an exempt purpose); *see, e.g.*, Better Bus. Bureau of Washington, D.C., v. United States, 326 U.S. 279, 283 (1945) (establishing the meaning of "exclusively" by deciding "that the presence of a single [nonexempt] purpose, if substantial in nature, will destroy the exemption regardless of the number or importance of truly … [exempt] purposes."); Living Faith, Inc., 950 F.2d at 367; Church in Boston v. Comm'r, 71 T.C. 102, 107 (1978) [discussing the § 501(c)(3) requirement of exclusivity: "The term exclusively, however, has been construed not to mean 'solely' or 'absolutely without exception.' An organization which engages in nonexempt activities can obtain and maintain exempt status so long as such activities are only incidental and less than substantial."].

72 IRC § 501(c)(3); Treas. Reg. § 501(c)(3)-1(d) (2008) [explaining "exempt purpose" for § 501(c)(3) qualification]; *see, e.g.*, Bob Jones Univ. v. United States, 461 U.S. 574, 598 (U.S.S.C. 1983) (holding that an organization whose practices "violate fundamental public policy" cannot be found to be operating for an exempt purpose); IHC Health Plans, Inc., 325 F.3d at 1200; St. David's Health Care Sys., 349 F.3d at 237–9; Bethel Conservative Mennonite Church, 746 F.2d at 392; Presbyterian & Reformed Pub. Co., 743 F.2d at 156.

73 IRC § 501(c)(3); *see supra*, note 64.

74 IRC § 501(c)(3); *see, e.g.*, Branch Ministries v. Rossotti, 211 F.3d 137, 141–2 (D.C. Cir. 2000) [holding that a church's placement of political ads in newspapers violates the ban on political activity in § 501(c)(3)]; Christian Echoes Nat. Ministry, Inc. v. United States, 470 F.2d 849, 854 (10th Cir. 1972) (holding that substantial political activity by a religious organization disqualifies it from tax exemption).

75 IRC § 501(c)(3); Treas. Reg. § 1.501(c)(3)–1(c); Treas. Reg. § 1.501(c)(3)–1(b).

76 IRC § 501(c)(3); Treas. Reg. § 1.501(c)(3)–1(c); Treas. Reg. § 1.501(c)(3)–1(b).

77 Treas. Reg. § 1.501(c)(3)–1 ["In order to be exempt as an organization described in section 501(c)(3), an organization must be both organized and operated exclusively for one or more of the purposes specified in such section. If an organization fails to meet either the organizational test or the operational test, it is not exempt."].

78 *See supra* note 68.

79 *See supra* note 69.

### a. "Organized and Operated Exclusively for an Exempt Purpose"[80]

As mentioned earlier, a § 501(c)(3) organization has to be "organized and operated exclusively" for an exempt purpose.[81] Every element of this requirement is significant.[82] Thus the IRS and courts reviewing cases under this rule examine the meaning of "organized,"[83] "operated,"[84] "exclusively,"[85] and "exempt purpose."[86] Every element must be met for an organization to qualify as a § 501(c)(3) organization.[87] Moreover, the inquiry into each element can be highly fact sensitive.[88]

Perhaps the most straightforward element is the last one, "exempt purpose."[89] In general, if an organization meets the other elements and it serves one of the purposes listed in § 501(c)(3), it serves an exempt purpose.[90] If it is not organized and operated exclusively for that purpose, however, it is not exempt under § 501(c)(3).[91]

To be "organized" for an exempt purpose, the organization must demonstrate through documentation,[92] such as articlcs of incorporation,[93] trust instruments,[94] charter,[95] or bylaws,[96] that it is organized to further charitable objectives meeting one or more of the exempt purposes specified in § 501(c)(3).[97] Moreover, pursuant to IRC

[80] *See supra* notes 73–7.

[81] IRC § 501(c)(3); *see supra* notes 73–4.

[82] *See, e.g.*, Church of Transfiguring Spirit, Inc. v. Comm'r of Internal Revenue, 76 T.C. 1, 4 (1981); Fides Publisher Ass'n v. United States, 263 F. Supp. 924, 933 (1967); Am. Ass'n of Christian Sch. Voluntary Employees Beneficiary Ass'n Welfare Plan Trust v. United States, 663 F. Supp. 275, 277 (M.D. Ala. 1987); People of God Cmty. v. Comm'r of Internal Revenue, 75 T.C. 127, 131 (1980).

[83] *See infra* notes 92–101.

[84] *See infra* notes 102–6.

[85] *See infra* notes 107–13.

[86] Universal Life Church, Inc. v. United States, 372 F. Supp. 770, 776 (E.D. Cal. 1974); S. Church of Universal Bhd. Assembled, Inc. v. Comm'r of Internal Revenue, 74 T.C. 1223, 1228 (1980); Presbyterian & Reformed Pub. Co., 743 F.2d at 157–9.

[87] *See supra* note 82.

[88] *See* Tennessee Baptist Children's Homes, Inc. v. United States, 604 F. Supp. 210, 212–13 (M.D. Tenn. 1984) *aff'd*, 790 F.2d 534 (6th Cir. 1986) ("it should be clear that this was a very close case. It turned on the facts peculiar to it.").

[89] IRC § 501(c)(3) (listing the exempt purposes as "religious, charitable, scientific, testing for public safety, literary, or educational purposes, or to foster national or international amateur sports competition (but only if no part of its activities involve the provision of athletic facilities or equipment), or for the prevention of cruelty to children or animals.").

[90] *Id.*

[91] *Id.*

[92] Brian Ruud Int'l v. United States, 733 F. Supp. 396, 398-99 (D.D.C. 1989); Basic Unit Ministry of Alma Karl Schurig v. United States, 511 F. Supp. 166, 168 (D.D.C. 1981); Elisian Guild, Inc. v. United States, 412 F.2d 121, 123-24 (1st Cir. 1969); Tennessee Baptist Children's Homes, Inc., 604 F. Supp. at 212-13 *aff'd*, 790 F.2d 534 (6th Cir. 1986).

[93] Elisian Guild, Inc., 412 F.2d at 123-24; Church of the Chosen People (N. Am.Panarchate) v. United States, 548 F. Supp. 1247, 1253 (D. Minn. 1982); Living Faith, Inc. v. C.I.R., 950 F.2d 365, 367 (7th Cir. 1991); Passaic United Hebrew Burial Ass'n v. United States, 216 F. Supp. 500, 502 (D.N.J. 1963).

[94] There are no published cases involving the use of trust instruments in this context, but trust instruments are the sort of document that could be useful if those instruments demonstrate that the organization is funded by a trust for charitable purposes and has followed the requirements set out in the trust.

[95] Presbyterian & Reformed Pub. Co., 743 F.2d at 150.

[96] Bylaws addressing an exempt purposes specified in § 501(c)(3) would be good supplemental evidence in this context, but of course, articles of incorporation or a charter are better evidence. *See supra* notes 93 & 95 and accompanying text.

[97] IRC § 501(c)(3) (listing the exempt purposes as "religious, charitable, scientific, testing for public safety, literary, or educational purposes, or to foster national or international amateur sports competition (but only

§ 509(a)(3),[98] if the organization operates under the rubric of a supporting organization (usually a larger entity), this documentation must show the relationship between the organization and its governing body,[99] which is relevant to whether it is organized to meet an exempt purpose or purposes.[100] This is known as the "organizational" test.[101]

To be "operated" for an exempt purpose an organization must show that it in fact substantially operates for the purpose(s) for which it was organized.[102] It must also show that it operates in the manner in which it was organized to operate.[103] This has ramifications for the private inurement issues discussed later in this section.[104] I addition, pursuant to IRC § 509(a)(3),[105] if the organization operates under the rubric of a supporting organization, it must show that the supporting organization is in fact operating the organization seeking exemption for one or more of the exempt purposes.[106]

To be organized and operated "exclusively" for an exempt purpose, an organization seeking § 501(c)(3) status must show that it operates exclusively to fulfill an exempt purpose.[107] This requires that its primary goal(s) is to carry out exempt activities.[108] As a practical matter, however, the term "exclusively" in this context is not as strict as the common understanding of the term would suggest.[109] Courts have interpreted this term loosely[110] and have allowed entities to maintain or gain § 501(c)(3) status even if they engage in some incidental activities that are not exempt,[111] but these nonexempt activities cannot be a substantial or a primary focus of an exempt entity.[112] If the nonexempt

if no part of its activities involve the provision of athletic facilities or equipment), or for the prevention of cruelty to children or animals.").

98 IRC § 509(a)(3).

99 S. Church of Universal Bhd. Assembled, Inc., 74 T.C. at 1226; Am. Ass'n of Christian Sch. Voluntary Employees Beneficiary Ass'n Welfare Plan Trust, 663 F. Supp. at 278–9; Presbyterian & Reformed Pub. Co., 743 F.2d at 150–1.

100 *See supra* note 99.

101 Elisian Guild, Inc., 412 F.2d at 123; Universal Life Church, Inc. v. United States, 372 F. Supp. 770, 775 (E.D. Cal. 1974); Church of Spiritual Tech. v. United States, 26 Cl. Ct. 713, 730 (1992) *aff'd*, 991 F.2d 812 (Fed. Cir. 1993).

102 Basic Unit Ministry of Alma Karl Schurig v. United States, 511 F. Supp. 166, 168 (D.D.C. 1981); Freedom Church of Revelation v. United States, 588 F. Supp. 693 (D.D.C. 1984); S. Church of Universal Bhd. Assembled, Inc. v. Comm'r of Internal Revenue, 74 T.C. 1223, 1227 (1980); Elisian Guild, Inc., 412 F.2d at 124-25; Church of the Chosen People, 548 F. Supp. at 1253; S. Church of Universal Bhd. Assembled, Inc., 74 T.C. at 1227.

103 *Id.* (all sources).

104 *See infra* notes 114–56

105 IRC § 501(c)(3).

106 S. Church of Universal Bhd. Assembled, Inc., 74 T.C. at 1227; Am. Ass'n of Christian Sch. Voluntary Employees Beneficiary Ass'n Welfare Plan Trust, 663 F. Supp. at 278–9; Presbyterian & Reformed Pub. Co., 743 F.2d at 158–9.

107 Fides Publisher Ass'n, 263 F. Supp. at 936; Presbyterian & Reformed Pub. Co., 743 F.2d at 157–9; Church of Ethereal Joy v. Comm'r of Internal Revenue, 83 T.C. 20, 21 (1984).

108 *Id.* (both sources).

109 United Missionary Aviation, Inc. v. C.I.R., T.C. Memo. 1990-566 (T.C. 1990) *aff'd sub nom.* United Missionary v. C.I.R., 985 F.2d 564 (8th Cir. 1991); Passaic United Hebrew Burial Ass'n, 216 F. Supp. at 505; Church of the Chosen People (N. Am. Panarchate), 548 F. Supp. at 1253; Church of Transfiguring Spirit, Inc., 76 T.C. 1, 4 (1981).

110 *Id.* (all sources).

111 Tennessee Baptist Children's Homes, 604 F. Supp. at 213 *aff'd*, 790 F.2d 534 (6th Cir. 1986); Passaic United Hebrew Burial Ass'n, 216 F. Supp. at 506–7 (D.N.J. 1963).

112 Fides Publisher Ass'n, 263 F. Supp. at 936; Parker v. Commisioner, 365 F.2d 792, 798–9 (1966); Am. Ass'n of Christian Sch. Voluntary Employees Beneficiary Ass'n Welfare Plan Trust, 663 F. Supp. 275,

activity crosses the line so as to become substantial or primary, the entity would lose exempt status.[113]

### b. No Private Inurement[114]

The requirement that none of an exempt organization's net earnings can inure to the "benefit of any private shareholder or individual"[115] has led to a significant amount of litigation.[116] Some cases are rather straightforward. For example, cases where those in charge of an organization[117] or members of their family[118] are paid far more than the fair market value of their services.[119] Other cases are significantly harder. For example, a case where a church that has a sincerely held belief and tradition of caring for its members' spiritual and basic social needs provides health insurance for members at no cost to them.[120] As will be seen, in the first line of cases the entity rarely is able to gain or maintain exempt status,[121] but in the second situation (it is a single case),[122] the entity was allowed to keep its exempt status under § 501(c)(3).[123] Many cases, however, fall

277–8 (M.D. Ala. 1987); Church By Mail, Inc. v. C.I.R., 765 F.2d 1387, 1392 (9th Cir. 1985); Living Faith, Inc., 950 F.2d at 372–6; Scripture Press Found. v. United States, 285 F.2d 800 (Ct. Cl. 1961); Inc. Trustees of Gospel Worker Soc. v. U.S., Dep't of Treasury, 510 F. Supp. 374, 378–80 (D.D.C.); Freedom Church of Revelation v. United States, 588 F. Supp. 693, 696 (D.D.C. 1984).

113 *Id.* (all sources).

114 IRC § 501(c)(3).

115 *Id.*

116 *See infra* notes 117–56.

117 Airlie Found., Inc. v. United States, 826 F. Supp. 537, 550 (D.D.C. 1993) *aff'd*, 55 F.3d 684 (D.C. Cir. 1995); Founding Church of Scientology v. United States, 412 F.2d 1197, 1202 (Ct. Cl. 1969); Church in Boston v. Comm'r of Internal Revenue, 71 T.C. 102, 106–7 (1978); Church of Scientology of Ca. v. Comm'r, 823 F.2d 1310, 1317–19 (9th Cir. 1987); United States v. Daly, 756 F.2d 1076, 1083 (5th Cir. 1985); Church of Transfiguring Spirit, Inc., 76 T.C. 1, 4 (1981).

118 Airlie Found., 826 F. Supp. at 550; Unitary Mission Church of Long Island v. Comm'r of Internal Revenue, 74 T.C. 507, 513–15 (1980) *aff'd*, 647 F.2d 163 (2d Cir. 1981); Founding Church of Scientology, 412 F.2d 1197, 1202 (Ct. Cl. 1969); Church of Scientology of Ca., 823 F.2d at 1317–19 (9th Cir. 1987); Church of Transfiguring Spirit, Inc., 76 T.C. 1, 5–6 (1981).

119 *See supra* notes 117–18.

120 Am. Ass'n of Christian Sch. Voluntary Employees Beneficiary Ass'n Welfare Plan Trust, 663 F. Supp. at 277–78.

121 Treas. Reg. § 1.501(c)(3)–1 ("An organization is not … operated exclusively for one or more of the purposes specified … unless it serves a public rather than a private interest."); *See, e.g.*, Bob Jones Univ. v. United States, 461 U.S. 574, 591 (1983) ("Charitable exemptions are justified on the basis that the exempt entity confers a public benefit."); Presbyterian & Reformed Pub. Co. v. Comm'r, 743 F.2d 148, 153 (3d Cir. 1984) ("The policy underpinnings of the non-inurement rule derive from the common law belief that charities should promote the public good rather than private benefit."); Founding Church of Scientology v. United States, 412 F.2d 1197, 1199 (Ct. Cl. 1969) ("The statutory language [makes it clear] … that Congress intended to extend the exemption only when the sole beneficiary of the institutional operations was the public at large.").

122 Treas. Reg. § 1.501(c)(3)–1(c)(2) ("An organization is not operated exclusively for one or more exempt purposes if its net earnings inure in whole or in part to the benefit of private shareholders or individuals."); *See, e.g.*, St. David's Health Care Sys. v. United States, 349 F.3d 232, 237 (5th Cir. 2003) ["Even if St. David's performs important charitable functions, St. David's cannot qualify for tax-exempt status under § 501(c)(3) if its activities via the partnership substantially further the private, profit-seeking interests of HCA."]; Freedom Church of Revelation v. United States, 588 F. Supp. 693, 697 (D.D.C. 1984) ("The fact that plaintiff has shown independently that it did engage in some charitable work … is not enough to entitle plaintiff to continued recognition as an exempt organization.").

123 *See, e.g.*, Fed'n Pharmacy Servs., Inc. v. Comm'r, 625 F.2d 804, 809 (8th Cir. 1980) (finding that offering discounts only to members and regardless of financial need is a private not public benefit); Canada

somewhere in between these two scenarios.[124] Private inurement, like every other element under § 501(c)(3), is a highly fact-sensitive issue.[125]

Allowing private inurement, especially in the most egregious cases, would be inconsistent with the notion that § 501(c)(3) entities serve the public good.[126] Even if an entity serves the public good in some ways, if it allows private inurement, it is questionable whether it is truly organized and run for exempt purposes.[127] If a benefit is limited only to members of an organization, private inurement is generally found because the class being served is not the "public."[128]

The amount of private inurement does not matter.[129] Any private inurement violates the requirement.[130] Some cases in which private inurement led to revocation or denial of § 501(c)(3) status involved significant amounts of money or other benefits flowing to individuals.[131]

v. Comm'r, 82 T.C. 973, 986–7 (1984) (finding that an organization whose function is to provide rent-free community housing and land to its members inures to the members' benefit); *cf.*, Treas. Reg. § 1.501(c)(3)–1(d)(1)(iii) (providing an example of private inurement wherein the organization researches genealogy for members of one specific family and thus serves a private rather than a public purpose).

124 Treas. Reg. § 1.501(c)(3)–1(c)(2); Church of Scientology of Ca. v. Comm'r, 823 F.2d 1310, 1316 (9th Cir. 1987) ("The organization loses tax exempt status if even a small percentage of income inures to a private individual."); Founding Church of Scientology, 412 F.2d at 1202 (Addressing private inurement, "Congress … specifically intended that the amount or extent of benefit should not be the determining factor."); Church of Transfiguring Spirit, Inc. v. Comm'r, 76 T.C. 1, 5 (1981) {Addressing private inurement, "the amount or extent of such inurement or benefit is not determinative" [citing Unitary Mission Church of Long Island v. Comm'r, 74 T.C. 507, 513 (1980), *aff'd without published opinion*, 647 F.2d 163 (2d Cir. 1981)]}.

125 *See* sources cited *id.*

126 *See, e.g.*, Church of Scientology of Ca., 823 F.2d at 1317–19 (private inurement of leaders included living expenses, thousands of dollars of "debt repayments," excessive royalty income, and control of millions of dollars of church assets); Church By Mail, Inc. v. Comm'r, 765 F.2d 1387, 1392–3 (9th Cir. 1985) (finding that over $160,000 paid to ministers is excessive in comparison to what the church could reasonably pay for the same services); Tony & Susan Alamo Found. v. Comm'r, 63 T.C.M. (CCH) 2422, at *14 (T.C. 1992), *aff'd without published opinion*, 92 F.3d 1190 (8th Cir. 1996) (Private inurement of leaders included "substantial amounts of jewelry, furs, clothing, automobiles, personal residences, antiques, and currency being used exclusively by … [organization's leaders].").

127 *See, e.g.*, Church of Transfiguring Spirit, Inc., 76 T.C. at 4–5 (finding private inurement in the form of a housing allowance of $1,189.82 because this was "virtually all" of the church's income); Spokane Motorcycle Club v. United States, 222 F. Supp. 151, 153–4 (E.D. Wash. 1963) (finding that provision of "refreshments, goods and services" to members, although the "amounts were not large," constitutes private inurement).

128 *Cf.* Treas. Reg. § 1.501(c)(3)–1 (providing an example of private inurement wherein only $2,500 out of an organization's "substantial assets and revenues" is used to pay for the chief financial officer's personal expenses); Rev. Rul. 67-251, 1967-2 C.B. 196, at *1 (1967) (IRS advising business leagues that, though a "small percentage of total expenditures," financial aid and welfare services provided to members constitutes private inurement).

129 *See supra* notes 112–14 and 126–8.

130 *See, e.g.*, Hall v. Comm'r, 729 F.2d 632, 634 (9th Cir. 1984) (affirming the denial of tax-exempt status to a religious organization that serves "almost exclusively to funnel a rental allowance to its officers"); Church of the Chosen People v. United States, 548 F. Supp. 1247, 1253 (D. Minn. 1982) (finding private inurement of church leaders when their "entire rent" was paid for by the church); Unitary Mission Church of Long Island v. Comm'r, 74 T.C. 507, 514 (1980) *aff'd without published opinion*, 647 F.2d 163 (2d Cir. 1981) (finding parsonage allowances of unexplained amounts to be excessive); Church of Living Tree v. Comm'r, 71 T.C.M. (CCH) 3210, at *3 (T.C.1996) (finding that provision of rent-free housing to the organization leader – who deeded the property to the church – is private inurement).

131 *See, e.g.*, Page v. Comm'r, 58 F.3d 1342, 1348–9 (8th Cir. 1995) (finding private inurement when a church leader's "food, utilities, airplane maintenance, [and] provision of transportation" are paid for by the church account to which he is the primary contributor); Basic Unit Ministry of Alma Karl Schurig

Yet, in other cases, relatively small sums were involved,[132] especially when compared with the exempt entity's total budget.[133]

In addition to the above-mentioned cases where compensation exceeding the fair market value of services provided was paid to interested individuals,[134] cases in which private inurement has been found involve the provision of housing,[135] personal expenses,[136] food,[137] cars,[138] subsidized gifts,[139] vacations,[140] tuition payments,[141] interest-free loans or

v. Comm'r, 670 F.2d 1210, 1212 (D.C. Cir. 1982) (finding private inurement when 70 percent of the organization's expenses was used to pay the living expenses of members); S. Church of Universal Bhd. Assembled, Inc. v. Comm'r, 74 T.C. 1223, 1224–5 (1980) (finding that payment of minister's "utilities, fuel, maintenance, and repair expenses of the parsonage … food, postage, stationery, pots and pans, dishes, glassware, sheets, blankets, towels, and curtains," with church funds almost entirely contributed by the minister is private inurement); Church of Modern Enlightenment v. Comm'r, 55 T.C.M. (CCH) 1304 (T.C. 1988) *aff'd without published opinion*, 875 F.2d 307 (2d Cir. 1989) (finding that payment of church leader's "food, clothing, shelter and other necessities of life" when he is the sole contributor to the church and only employed part time with the church is private inurement), New Life Tabernacle v. Comm'r, 44 T.C.M. (CCH) 309 (T.C. 1982) (finding that payment of church member living expenses without quantification of the services performed in return is private inurement).

132 *See, e.g.*, Page, 58 F.3d at 1348–9; S. Church of Universal Bhd. Assembled, Inc., 74 T.C. at 1224–5; New Life Tabernacle, 44 T.C.M. (CCH) 309 (finding that "petitioner's activities of providing its members with food, clothing, shelter, automobiles, and personal allowances … constitute inurement").

133 *See, e.g.*, Page, 58 F.3d at 1348–9; Founding Church of Scientology v. United States, 412 F.2d 1197, 1201 (Ct. Cl. 1969) (finding provision of a vehicle to a church leader to be evidence of private inurement); New Life Tabernacle, 44 T.C.M. (CCH) 309.

134 *See, e.g.*, United States v. Daly, 756 F.2d 1076, 1083 (5th Cir. 1985) (finding evidence of private inurement in use of church funds to purchase "furs, cars, planes, boats, gold coins, and real estate"); Tony & Susan Alamo Found. v. Comm'r, 63 T.C.M. (CCH) 2422, at *14 (T.C. 1992), *aff'd without published opinion*, 92 F.3d 1190 (8th Cir. 1996) (Private inurement of leaders included "substantial amounts of jewelry, furs, clothing, automobiles, personal residences, antiques, and currency.").

135 *See, e.g.*, Bubbling Well Church of Universal Love v. Comm'r, 670 F.2d 104, 105 (9th Cir. 1981) (finding that church-paid travel to Europe with no facts detailing the trip purpose is evidence of private inurement); Basic Bible Church v. Comm'r, 74 T.C. 846, 857–8 (1980), *aff'd* Kile v. Comm'r, 739 F.2d 265 (7th Cir. 1984) (finding private inurement when "$4,000 was paid for travel with there being no evidence … how it furthered church purposes"); Unitary Mission Church, 74 T.C. at 515 (finding that payment for six trips without record of the trips' activities is evidence of private inurement).

136 *See, e.g.*, United States v. Jiggetts, 850 F.2d 690, at *4 (4th Cir. R. 32.1 1988) (unpublished) (finding that congregational funds used to pay for the pastor's daughter's college tuition, among other personal expenses, inured to the benefit of the church leader).

137 *See, e.g.*, Founding Church of Scientology, 412 F.2d at 1202 (finding that serving as a source of credit for church leaders is evidence of private inurement); Unitary Mission Church, 74 T.C. at 514 (finding that loans provided without evidence of fixed criteria or interest charged are private inurement); W. Catholic Church v. Comm'r, 73 T.C. 196, 211–14 (1979), *aff'd without published opinion*, 631 F.2d 736 (7th Cir. 1980) (finding that grants given without objective criteria for receipt are not exempt activity and that the church in this case functioned as an "incorporated pocketbook" for its leader).

138 *Cf.* Treas. Reg. § 1.501(c)(3)–1(f)(2)(iv) (providing an example of private inurement wherein the organization purchases assets from its trustees at more than fair market value); Hancock Acad. of Savannah, Inc. v. Comm'r, 69 T.C. 488, 494 (1977) (finding that a nonprofit school's purchase of goodwill at a cost exceeding its fair market value benefited individuals).

139 *See, e.g.*, Tony & Susan Alamo Found., 63 T.C.M. (CCH) at *14 (finding that purchase of expensive clothes, including furs, for organization leaders is evidence of private inurement); New Life Tabernacle v. Comm'r, 44 T.C.M. (CCH) 309 (T.C. 1982) (finding that payment for church member clothing, along with other living expenses, is evidence of private inurement).

140 *See, e.g.*, Church of Scientology of Ca. v. Comm'r, 823 F.2d 1310, 1315–19 (9th Cir. 1987) (finding evidence of private inurement in "debt repayments" wherein the church leader received a portion of the church's gross income as compensation for his efforts to found the religion).

141 *See* Daly, 756 F.2d 1076, 1083 (5th Cir. 1985) (finding evidence of private inurement in use of church funds to purchase "furs, cars, planes, boats, gold coins, and real estate").

grants,[142] asset purchases,[143] and a number of other benefits such as country club membership. Moreover, comingling of organizational funds and personal funds has been found to support a finding of private inurement.

There are cases, however, where courts or the IRS have found some private inurement to be acceptable because the private inurement is incidental to the organization effectuating an exempt purpose.[144] Thus, limiting burial at a religious cemetery only to coreligionists,[145] the provision of medical benefits to church members pursuant to church doctrine requiring taking care of members' basic needs,[146] and engaging in genealogic research for a specific religious group[147] have not been deemed private inurement even though only members benefit.[148] This is so because in each of these cases the courts and/or the IRS found that the private inurement was incidental to the exempt charitable/religious purpose of the entity.[149] Thus, even though only coreligionists of the exempt organization benefited, the reason for that limitation was consistent with the exempt purpose of those organizations.[150]

As one might expect given the private inurement requirement, an organization exempt under § 501(c)(3) must maintain adequate financial records to demonstrate that it meets all § 501(c)(3) requirements.[151] Moreover, a § 501(c)(3) organization must file appropriate forms, including Form 990, every year. "Churches," as defined by the IRS, however, are exempt from the annual reporting requirement.[152]

Because "churches" – as defined by the IRS – need not submit the same documentation as other § 501(c)(3) entities,[153] a number of interesting problems have arisen. These problems will be discussed in greater detail in the subsequent subsection devoted to "church" status. For now, it is adequate to note that some entities have sought "church"

142 *See, e.g.*, Founding Church of Scientology, 412 F.2d at 1202 (finding that serving as a source of credit for church leaders is evidence of private inurement); Tony & Susan Alamo Found. v. Comm'r, 63 T.C.M. (CCH) 2422, at *14 (T.C. 1992), *aff'd without published opinion*, 92 F.3d 1190 (8th Cir. 1996) (Private inurement of leaders included "substantial amounts of jewelry, furs, clothing, automobiles, personal residences, antiques, and currency being used exclusively by ... [organization's leaders]."); Canada v. Comm'r, 82 T.C. 973, 986–7 (1984) (finding that an organization whose function is to provide rent-free community housing and land to its members inures to the members' benefit).

143 *See, e.g.*, *American Woodworking Machinery & Equipment Show, Inc. v. United States*, 249 F.Supp. 392 (M.D.N.C.) (noting that an otherwise tax-exempt organization may engage in profit-making activities or supply minor services to individuals without losing its exemption where such profit-making activities or services are *incidental* to its primary exempt activities or services).

144 *Overview of Inurement/Private Benefit Issues in IRC 501(c)(3)*, 1990 EO CPE (1990); *available at*: http://www.irs.gov/pub/irs-tege/eotopicc90.pdf (accessed April 13, 2015).

145 Rev. Rul. 79–359, 1979–2 C.B. 226.

146 IRC § 501(c)(3) (noting that adequate financial records must be maintained under the aforementioned statutory provision).

147 *Id* [requiring any organization, except for churches, that has been granted tax-exempt status pursuant to § 501(c)(3) is required to file a Form 990 for each year its contributions received exceed $25,000].

148 *Id.*

149 *Id* (outlining that churches are seeking to apply for exempt status must apply for exemption on IRS Form 1023).

150 *See, e.g.*, Church or Scientology v. Comm'r, 83 T.C. 381 (1984) [finding that although the church filed Form 990, it did not qualify for exemption from taxation under IRC § 501(c)(3) because it operated for a substantial commercial purpose and its earnings benefited the founder, his family, and a private non-charitable corporation controlled by key church officials).

151 *Annual Exempt Organization Return: Who Must File*, IRS, *available at*: http://www.irs.gov/Charities-&-Non-Profits/Annual-Exempt-Organization-Return: Who-Must-File.

152 Treas. Reg. §1.6033-1(g).

153 *Id.*

status precisely to avoid financial accountability[154] because "churches" need not file the same documents that other § 501(c)(3) organizations are required to file every year.[155] Of course, most entities seeking "church" status are not involved in fostering private inurement, but some less scrupulous entities have sought "church" status to avoid divulging information that would show private inurement has occurred.[156] These schemes have been successful on occasion but have rarely succeeded over time.

### c. Political Involvement

One of the most controversial requirements for religious organizations under § 501(c)(3) is the requirement that § 501(c)(3) organizations refrain from political activity and lobbying.[157] There are three main areas of concern regarding this issue. Each will be addressed in a separate subsection.

First, the specific § 501(c)(3) (and related regulatory) requirements regarding lobbying and political activity. These indicate what is allowed, what is not allowed, and what remains unclear. They also indicate what the IRS may do if a religious § 501(c)(3) entity has been found in violation of the nonpoliticking requirement.[158]

The second issue is the relevance of § 501(c)(4) to the questions involved here.[159] Section 501(c)(4) provides a mechanism by which a religious entity can engage in political activity and/or lobbying under certain carefully drawn circumstances without losing tax-exempt status.[160] Yet using § 501(c)(4) status has serious implications because, while the entity itself remains tax exempt, donations to a § 501(c)(4) entity are not tax exempt.[161]

154 *See* Wendy Gerzog Shaller, *Churches and Their Enviable Tax Status*, 51 U. Pitt. L. Rev. 345, 351, 358 (1990) (arguing that some entities "misuse the 'church' form as a means of tax avoidance.").

155 Treas. Reg. § 1.6033-1(g).

156 *See* cases cited *supra* note 154.

157 IRC § 501(c)(3) (granting tax-exempt status to qualifying charitable organizations if "no substantial part of the activities of which is carrying on propaganda, or otherwise attempting, to influence legislation … and which does not participate in, or intervene in (including the publishing or distributing of statements), any political campaign on behalf of (or in opposition to) any candidate for public office"); Treas. Reg. § 1.501(c)(3)–1(c)(3) (clarifying what activities constitute "attempting to influence legislation" and defining terms relevant to the prohibition against participating in a political campaigns).

158 IRC § 501(c)(3); IRC § 7611 (1998) [detailing the process, requirements, and limitations for an IRS church tax inquiry and possible revocation of § 501(c)(3) status if the IRS "reasonably believes" the church is not exempt per the § 501(c)(3) requirements]; IRC § 4955 (1996) [detailing the tax penalties for political expenditures by a § 501(c)(3) organization]; IRC § 7409 (1987) [allowing action by the United States to enjoin § 501(c)(3) organizations who have engaged in prohibited political activity from making additional political expenditures and "for such other relief as may be appropriate to ensure that the assets of such organization are preserved for charitable or other purposes specified in § 501(c)(3)."]; Treas. Reg. § 301.7409–1 (1995) [detailing IRS process for addressing "flagrant political expenditures" by § 501(c)(3) organizations, including potential injunction against additional political spending (IRC § 7409)]; Treas. Reg. § 1.501(h)–3(a) ["Under section 501(h) … an organization that has elected the expenditure test and that normally makes expenditures in excess of the corresponding ceiling amount will cease to be exempt from tax under § 501(a) as an organization described in § 501(c)(3)"].

159 IRC § 501(c)(4) (2010).

160 IRC § 501(c)(4); Treas. Reg. § 1.501(c)(4)–1 ["A civic league or organization may be exempt as an organization described in § 501(c)(4) if – (i) It is not organized or operated for profit; and (ii) It is operated exclusively for the promotion of social welfare. … The promotion of social welfare does not include direct or indirect participation or intervention in political campaigns on behalf of or in opposition to any candidate for public office."].

161 IRC § 170 (c)(2)(D) (2013) [defining tax exempt charitable contributions as those to a qualifying organization "which is not disqualified for tax exemption under § 501(c)(3) by reason of … [political activity]."];

The third issue is whether the "no political involvement" requirement is constitutional when a religious organization cannot separate its religious and political doctrines.[162] The Supreme Court has held that requiring § 501(c)(3) religious entities to refrain from politics and lobbying is constitutional because of the § 501(c)(4) alternative,[163] but the Court has never addressed a situation where a religious entity's core religious values include issues such as pacifism or protecting the environment, and clergy give sermons around election time in which these issues are addressed and one candidate clearly is on the opposite side. This chapter will not focus much on this issue because the Supreme Court has settled the more common questions, and no court has directly confronted this issue. Discussion of this issue will be limited to the interaction between the IRS and All Saints Episcopal Church of Pasadena, California, where the issue was addressed – in part but without clear resolution – by the IRS.[164]

i. *§ 501(c)(3) and Political Activity: Statutory Provisions, Regulations, and Cases.* Section 501(c)(3) organizations receive significant financial benefits both because such organizations themselves are tax exempt[165] and because donations to these organizations are deductible for those making the donations.[166] Suggested reasons for these benefits are that § 501(c)(3) charitable organizations are nonprofit and provide substantial benefits to society.[167] The private inurement requirement discussed earlier helps to ensure that a § 501(c)(3) organization is nonprofit and serves a public purpose.[168] Refraining from political activity also may be consistent with serving society generally,[169] but

*See* Regan v. Taxation with Representation of Washington, 461 U.S. 540, 543 (1983) ["Taxpayers who contribute to § 501(c)(3) organizations are permitted by § 170(c)(2) to deduct the amount of their contributions on their federal income tax returns, while contributions to § 501(c)(4) organizations are not deductible.").

162 *See, e.g.*, Patricia Ward Biederman and Jason Felch, *Antiwar Sermon Brings IRS Warning*, L.A. Times, Nov. 7, 2005, *available at:* http://articles.latimes.com/2005/nov/07/local/me-allsaints7 (describing the IRS investigation of the All Saints Episcopal Church in Pasadena, California, for potential violation of the political activity prohibition, putting its tax-exempt status at risk, after a guest preacher gave a sermon in which he was critical of then-president and presidential candidate George Bush's war policies); Rebecca Trounson, *IRS Ends Church Probe but Stirs New Questions*, L.A. Times, Sept. 24, 2007, *available at:* http://articles.latimes.com/2007/sep/24/local/me-allsaints24 (explaining the close of the IRS investigation of All Saints Episcopal Church after two years, in which the IRS maintained the illegality of the sermon in question but did not pursue the investigation nor offer guidance on the political activity prohibition).

163 *See, e.g.*, Regan v. Taxation With Representation of Washington, 461 U.S. 540, 552 (1983) (Blackmun, J., concurring) ["The constitutional defect that would inhere in § 501(c)(3) alone is avoided by § 501(c)(4). … TWR may use its present § 501(c)(3) organization for its nonlobbying activities and may create a § 501(c)(4) affiliate to pursue its charitable goals through lobbying.").

164 *See supra* note 162.

165 IRC § 501(a) ["An organization described in subsection (c) … shall be exempt from taxation under this subtitle unless such exemption is denied under § 502 or § 503.").

166 IRC § 170(a)(1) (2013) ("There shall be allowed as a deduction any 'charitable contribution.'").

167 *See, e.g.*, Bob Jones Univ. v. United States, 461 U.S. 574, 591 (1983) ("Charitable exemptions are justified on the basis that the exempt entity confers a public benefit.").

168 IRC § 501(c)(3) (2010).

169 *See, e.g.*, Christian Echoes Nat. Ministry, Inc. v. United States, 470 F.2d 849, 853–4 (10th Cir. 1972) [explaining that organizations are granted tax exemption "because of the benefit the public obtains from their activities" and that "the limitations in § 501(c)(3) stem from the congressional policy that the United States Treasury should be neutral in *political affairs and that substantial activities directed to*

perhaps more important, because these organizations are tax exempt and donations to them are tax deductible, the government has an interest in not subsidizing political activities through tax benefits given to charitable entities.[170] Regardless of the reasons for the requirement that § 501(c)(3) organizations refrain from political activity, the basic requirements have commanded a lot of attention in the regulations,[171] cases,[172] and commentary.[173]

There are two requirements that preclude a § 501(c)(3) organization from engaging in politics.[174] First, a § 501(c)(3) organization may not engage in lobbying or attempting to influence legislation.[175] Second, a § 501(c)(3) organization may not participate or intervene in any political campaign.[176] The latter requirement includes advocating for any

*attempts to influence legislation or affect a political campaign should not be subsidized*"); Slee v. Comm'r, 42 F.2d 184, 185 (2d Cir. 1930) (providing an early rationale for political activity limitations by finding that an organization advocating for changes to the law "cannot be said to be 'exclusively' charitable, educational or scientific.").

170 *See, e.g.*, Regan v. Taxation With Representation of Washington, 461 U.S. 540, 550 (1983) ("Congress ... has the authority to determine whether the advantage the public would receive from additional lobbying by charities is worth the money the public would pay to subsidize that lobbying and other disadvantages that might accompany that lobbying. ... It is not irrational for Congress to decide that tax exempt charities ... should not further benefit at the expense of taxpayers at large by obtaining a further subsidy for lobbying.").

171 *See, e.g.*, Treas. Reg. § 1.501(c)(3)–1(c)(3); Treas. Reg. § 301.7409–1; Treas. Reg. § 1.501(c)(4)–1.

172 *See, e.g.*, Branch Ministries v. Rossotti, 211 F.3d 137, 141–2 (D.C. Cir. 2000) [holding that a church's placement of political ads in newspapers violates the ban on political activity in § 501(c)(3)]; Christian Echoes Nat. Ministry, Inc. v. United States, 470 F.2d 849, 854 (10th Cir. 1972) (holding that substantial political activity by a religious organization disqualifies it from tax exemption).

173 *See, e.g.*, Roger Colinvaux, *The Political Speech of Charities in the Face of Citizens United: A Defense of Prohibition*, 62 Case W. Res. L. Rev. 685, 685 (2012) {analyzing the prohibition of political activities by § 501(c)(3) organizations in the wake of the *Citizen's United* decision [citing Citizens United v. Fed. Election Comm'n, 558 U.S. 310 (2010)]}; Johnny Rex Buckles, *Does the Constitutional Norm of Separation of Church and State Justify the Denial of Tax Exemption to Churches That Engage in Partisan Political Speech?* 84 Ind. L.J. 447, 447 (2009) (arguing that separation of church and state does not justify the prohibition of political activity by churches); Siri Mielke Buller, *Lobbying and Political Restrictions on § 501(c)(3) Organizations: A Guide for Compliance in the Wake of Increased IRS Examination*, 52 S.D. L. Rev. 136, 136 (2007) [offering guidance for 501(c)(3) organizations regarding compliance with the rules surrounding political activity]; Jerome Park Prather, *Tax Exemption of American Churches and Other Nonprofits: One Election Cycle after Branch Ministries v. Rossotti*, 94 Ky. L.J. 139, 139 (2006) (exploring the relationship between churches and politics and the IRS limitations on political activity); Todd Brower, *Whose Voice Shall Be Heard? Lobbying Limitations on Section 501(c)(3) Charitable Organizations Held Constitutional in Regan v. Taxation with Representation*, 28 St. Louis U. L.J. 1017 (1984) [examining the § 501(c)(3) lobbying limitations and the unequal application of the limitations to organizations].

174 IRC § 501(c)(3).

175 IRC § 501(c)(3); Treas. Reg. § 1.501(c)(3)–1(c)(3)(ii) ["An organization will be regarded as attempting to influence legislation if the organization: (a) Contacts, or urges the public to contact, members of a legislative body for the purpose of proposing, supporting, or opposing legislation; or (b) Advocates the adoption or rejection of legislation."].

176 IRC § 501(c)(3); Treas. Reg. § 1.501(c)(3)–1(c)(3)(iii) ("An organization is an action organization if it participates or intervenes, directly or indirectly, in any political campaign on behalf of or in opposition to any candidate for public office. ... Activities which constitute participation or intervention in a political campaign on behalf of or in opposition to a candidate include, but are not limited to, the publication or distribution of written or printed statements or the making of oral statements on behalf of or in opposition to such a candidate."].

candidate in a federal, state, or local election,[177] and both requirements apply to federal, state, and local activity.[178]

LOBBYING AND RELATED ACTIVITIES. Section 501(c)(3) addresses lobbying and related activities by requiring that: "no substantial part of the activities" of an exempt organization may involve "carrying on propaganda, or otherwise attempting, to influence legislation [except as otherwise provided in subsection (h)]."[179] The Supreme Court upheld this requirement against a free speech and equal protection challenge in *Regan v. Taxation with Representation*.[180] The Court upheld it in part because § 501(c)(4) provided an alternative means for political lobbying prohibited under § 501(c)(3).[181] This will be discussed further later in this section.

Currently, most §501(c)(3) entities can elect to use §501(h) or be subject to the "substantial part" test discussed further later.[182] Section 501(h) does not apply to churches as defined later in this chapter, but it can apply to other religious § 501(c)(3) entities.[183] Section 501(h) allows organizations that choose to invoke it to spend no more than 20 percent of their budgets on lobbying.[184] Any expenditures in excess of this amount are subject to an excise tax, and if lobbying expenditures are regularly more than 150 percent of the 20 percent lobbying limit, the organization will lose its § 501(c)(3) status.[185]

177 Treas. Reg § 1.501(c)(3)–1(c)(3)(iii) ("The term candidate for public office means an individual who offers himself, or is proposed by others, as a contestant for an elective public office, whether such office be national, State, or local.").

178 Treas. Reg. § 1.501(c)(3)–1(c)(3)(ii) ("The term legislation … includes action by the Congress, by any State legislature, by any local council or similar governing body, or by the public in a referendum, initiative, constitutional amendment, or similar procedure."); Treas. Reg. § 1.501(c)(3)–1(c)(3)(iii).

179 IRC § 501(c)(3).

180 461 U.S. 540, 551 (1983).

181 *Id.* at 552 (Blackmun, J., concurring) ["The constitutional defect that would inhere in § 501(c)(3) alone is avoided by § 501(c)(4), … TWR may use its present § 501(c)(3) organization for its nonlobbying activities and may create a § 501(c)(4) affiliate to pursue its charitable goals through lobbying."].

182 IRC § 501(c)(3) (granting tax-exempt status to qualifying charitable organizations if "no substantial part of the activities of which is carrying on propaganda, or otherwise attempting, to influence legislation."); IRC § 501(h)(1) ("Exemption from taxation … shall be denied because a substantial part of the activities of such organization consists of carrying on propaganda, or otherwise attempting, to influence legislation, but only if such organization normally–(A) makes lobbying expenditures in excess of the lobbying ceiling amount for such organization for each taxable year, or (B) makes grass roots expenditures in excess of the grass roots ceiling amount for such organization for each taxable year.").

183 IRC §501(h)(5) {listing organizations that do not qualify for the 501(h) exception, organizations "(A) described in §170(b)(1)(A)(i) (relating to churches), (B) an integrated auxiliary of a church or of a convention or association of churches, or (C) a member of an affiliated group of organizations [within the meaning of §4911(f)(2)] if one or more members of such group is described in subparagraph (A) or (B)."}.

184 IRC § 4911(c)(2) ("If the exempt purpose expenditures are not over $500,000, the lobbying nontaxable amount is 20 percent of the exempt purpose expenditures.").

185 IRC § 4911(a)(1) ("There is hereby imposed on the excess lobbying expenditures of any organization to which this section applies a tax equal to 25 percent of the amount of the excess lobbying expenditures for the taxable year."); Treas. Reg. § 1.501(h)–3(a) ["Under § 501(h) … an organization that has elected the expenditure test and that normally makes expenditures in excess of the corresponding ceiling amount will cease to be exempt from tax under § 501(a) as an organization described in § 501(c)(3)"].

Churches and § 501(c)(3) entities that do not elect to invoke § 501(h) are subject to the "substantial part" test, which is derived from the language "*no substantial part* of the activities of which is carrying on propaganda, or otherwise attempting, to influence legislation [emphasis added]."[186] Courts and the IRS generally have interpreted the "substantial part" language in broad terms.[187] It certainly lacks the mathematical precision of § 501(h),[188] but this occasionally may be beneficial to a § 501(c)(3) organization.[189]

Unlike § 501(h), the "substantial part" test has no mathematical formula.[190] Thus it is subject to interpretation by the IRS and the courts.[191] A few courts have used a percentage test,[192] but that approach has been rejected by the IRS and most other courts.[193] Most courts to address the issue since around 2002 (and some before then) tended to take an approach similar to that set forth in IRS Publication 1828,[194] specifically the section addressing the meaning of "substantial part"[195]: the determination of substantial part should be "on the basis of all the pertinent facts and circumstances in each case."[196] Therefore, determining whether a § 501(c)(3) entity has violated the "substantial part" test requires a fact-sensitive case-by-case analysis.[197]

The "substantial part" approach does not prevent churches or other § 501(c)(3) organizations that do not invoke § 501(h) from ever addressing issues important to them, even politically charged issues.[198] It does, however, mean that they may not do so in a

186 IRC § 501(c)(3).

187 *See, e.g.*, Christian Echoes, 470 F.2d at 855 (Regarding political activities, "Congress intended that the limitations be given a broad or liberal interpretation."); Haswell v. U. S., 500 F.2d 1133, 1142 (Ct. Cl. 1974) (The limitation on substantial lobbying activity "should be liberally construed.").

188 *See* IRC § 501(h).

189 *Cf.* Treas. Reg. § 1.501(c)(3)–1(c)(2) ("An organization will not fail to meet the operational test merely because it advocates, as an insubstantial part of its activities, the adoption or rejection of legislation.").

190 *See, e.g.*, Christian Echoes, 470 F.2d at 855 ("The political activities of an organization must be balanced in the context of the objectives and circumstances of the organization to determine whether a substantial part of its activities was to influence or attempt to influence legislation.").

191 *See, e.g.*, *id.*; Haswell, 500 F.2d at 1142 ("A percentage test to determine whether the activities are substantial is not appropriate. Such a test obscures the complexity of balancing the organization's activities in relation to its objectives and circumstances in the context of the totality of the organization."); League of Women Voters of U.S. v. United States, 180 F. Supp. 379, 383 (Ct. Cl. 1960) (finding that an organization fails the substantial part test when "the influencing of legislation is the League's main purpose and reason for being").

192 *See, e.g.*, Seasongood v. Comm'r, 227 F.2d 907, 912 (6th Cir. 1955) [holding that spending "less than 5 percent of the time and effort" on alleged political activities was not "substantial" within the meaning of 501(c)(3)].

193 *See, e.g.*, Christian Echoes, 470 F.2d at 855 ("A percentage test to determine whether the activities were substantial obscures the complexity of balancing the organization's activities in relation to its objectives and circumstances."); Haswell, 500 F.2d at 1142; Krohn v. United States, 246 F. Supp. 341, 347–8 (D. Colo. 1965) (The apparent certainty of a percent test obscures the basic difficulties of balancing activities in the context of organizational objectives and circumstances.").

194 *Tax Guide for Churches and Religious Organizations: Benefits and Responsibilities under the Federal Tax Law* (Sept. 2003), *available at:* http://www.irs.gov/pub/irs-pdf/p1828.pdf.

195 *Id.* at 6.

196 *Id.*

197 *Id.* ["The IRS considers a variety of factors, including the time devoted (by both compensated and volunteer workers) and the expenditures devoted by the organization to the activity, when determining whether the lobbying activity is substantial."].

198 *Id.* at 5–6 ["An IRC § 501(c)(3) organization may engage in some lobbying, but too much lobbying activity risks loss of tax-exempt status. … Churches and religious organizations may, however, involve themselves in issues of public policy without the activity being considered as lobbying. For example, churches may conduct educational meetings, prepare and distribute educational materials, or otherwise consider public policy issues in an educational manner without jeopardizing their tax-exempt status."].

manner that attempts to influence legislation[199] or, as will be explained later, that participates or intervenes in a political campaign.[200] At least one court, however, has found attempts to mold public opinion on issues subject to legislation to violate the "substantial part" test.[201] The organization involved in that case, however, also had been involved in trying to effect legislation,[202] and the court's reasoning in that case conflicts with a number of other opinions.[203]

Thus a religious organization that is exempt under § 501(c)(3),[204] but which does not use § 501(h),[205] that opposes or supports a woman's right to choose an abortion may address the issue of abortion from a religious perspective,[206] but may not lobby for legislation that supports its position and may not support a political candidate who agrees with its position.[207] As will be seen, however, it can become a § 501(c)(4) organization and engage in lobbying to the extent permitted under that section,[208] or it can give up its tax-exempt status generally and engage in politics to the same degree as any other entity.[209]

PARTICIPATING IN OR EFFECTING POLITICAL CAMPAIGNS. Section 501(c)(3) addresses activities involving political campaigns in the following language: "[a § 501(c)(3) organization may] not participate in, or intervene in (including the publishing or distributing of statements), any political campaign on behalf of (or in opposition to) any candidate for public office."[210] The Treasury regulations enforcing this provision make it clear that public office applies to any federal, state, or local office.[211]

199 IRC § 501(c)(3); *see, e.g.*, Christian Echoes Nat. Ministry, Inc. v. United States, 470 F.2d 849, 855 (10th Cir. 1972) (affirming the revocation of tax exempt status for an organization with substantial political activity including promoting government policy change and legislation).

200 IRC § 501(c)(3); *see, e.g.*, Branch Ministries v. Rossotti, 211 F.3d 137, 139 (D.C. Cir. 2000) (affirming the revocation of tax exempt status for a church which "[f]our days before the 1992 presidential election ... placed full-page advertisements in two newspapers in which it urged Christians not to vote for then-presidential candidate Bill Clinton because of his positions on certain moral issues").

201 Christian Echoes, 470 F.2d at 855 (affirming the revocation of tax-exempt status for an organization with substantial political activity, including the "[attempt] to mold public opinion in civil rights legislation, Medicare, the Postage Revision Act of 1967, the Honest Election Law of 1967, the Nuclear Test Ban Treaty, the Panama Canal Treaty, firearms control legislation, and the Outer Space Treaty.").

202 *Id.* ("An essential part of the program of Christian Echoes was to promote desirable governmental policies consistent with its objectives through legislation.").

203 *See, e.g.*, Dulles v. Johnson, 273 F.2d 362, 367 (2d Cir. 1959) (finding that an organization that made recommendations to government officials regarding proposed legislation satisfied the requirement that influencing legislation was not a substantial part of its activities and reasoning that the organization's political activities were only a small part of its total activities and were aimed at improving the law rather than a "selfish purpose"); Seasongood v. C.I.R., 227 F.2d 907, 912 (6th Cir. 1955) (reasoning that, in addition to being only 5 percent of the organization's activities, efforts to influence legislation were considered to be with a "good faith purpose" and not "untoward" and hence were not violations of the "substantial part" rule).

204 IRC § 501(c)(3).

205 IRC § 501(h).

206 *See supra* notes 198–203 and accompanying text.

207 *See, e.g.*, Branch Ministries v. Rossotti, 211 F.3d 137, 139, 140 (D.C. Cir. 2000) (affirming the IRS's decision to revoke tax exempt status to a church based on its decision to purchase an advertisement against presidential candidate Bill Clinton in 1992 criticizing him, in part, for his support of abortion).

208 IRC § 501(c)(4); *see infra* 254–89 and accompanying text.

209 *See* Christian Echoes, 470 F.2d at 857 ("The taxpayer may engage in [political lobbying] without restraint, subject, however, to withhold of the [tax] exemption.").

210 IRC § 501(c)(3).

211 26 C.F.R. § 1.501(c)(3)–1(c)(3)(iii).

Moreover, a candidate is anyone running for office,[212] whether in a primary or a general election[213] and whether self-declared or nominated by a political party or others.[214] The regulations also make clear that participation in, or intervention in, a campaign through "publishing or distributing statements" includes both written and oral statements.[215]

Thus, giving a sermon that advocates for a particular candidate or against a particular candidate,[216] doing the same regarding a political party,[217] inviting a specific candidate for election-related reasons,[218] disseminating literature advocating for or against candidates,[219] approving or disapproving of candidates in writing or verbally,[220] and rating candidates – even in a nonpartisan manner[221] – all violate the campaign requirement.[222] It is important to note in regard to personal activities of organization leadership that a distinction is drawn between the personal activities of a § 501(c)(3) organization's leaders and any activity that may be seen as coming from the organization itself.[223] A sermon advocating for or against a candidate, distribution of political literature, and any other activity carrying the imprimatur of the § 501(c)(3) entity violates the rule.[224] Conversely, a clergy member or board member quietly volunteering to help a campaign as an individual, while not holding himself or herself out as being affiliated with the § 501(c)(3) entity, would not violate the rule barring other circumstances implicating the rule.[225]

212 *Id.*

213 *Id.*

214 *Id.*

215 *Id.*

216 Donald B. Tobin, *Political Campaigning by Churches and Charities: Hazardous for 501(c)(3)s, Dangerous for Democracy*, 95 GEO. L.J. 1313, 1351 (2007) ("[T]he individual cannot intervene in an election by using sermons, letters in the organization's publications, or organizational resources to promote or oppose a candidate.").

217 H. Chandler Combest, *Symbolism As Savior: A Look at the Irs Ban on Political Activity by Tax-Exempt Religious Organizations*, 61 ALA. L. REV. 1121, 1131 (2010) ("The IRS has held that a church may not make statements that directly support or oppose a candidate for public office, a slate of candidates, or a political party in a sermon, church bulletin, on a church website or in an editorial in a church publication.") (internal quotation omitted).

218 Rev. Rul. 2007-41, 2007-1 C.B. 1421 ("[A] forum for candidates could be operated in a manner that would show a bias or preference for or against a particular candidate"); *see also supra* notes 230–6.

219 Tobin, *supra* note 216.

220 *Id.*

221 *See* Ass'n of Bar of City of New York v. C.I.R., 858 F.2d 876, 880 (2d Cir. 1988) ("[The plaintiffs] argue, and we assume this to be so, that it evaluates judicial candidates on a nonpartisan basis. However, [§ 501(c)(3)] and pertinent regulations thereunder are not limited in their application to the partisan campaigns of candidates representing recognized political parties.").

222 IRC § 501(c)(3); *See supra* notes 216–21.

223 Tobin, *supra* note 216 ("Individual members of the organization, including its leaders, may speak out in their individual capacities. These activities, however, must be conducted in their personal capacities; the members cannot use their organization as a means of "amplifying" their speech. They may speak out against a particular issue or politician and may actively support a candidate for public office.").

224 Tobin, *supra* note 216 ("[T]he individual cannot intervene in an election by using sermons, letters in the organization's publications, or organizational resources to promote or oppose a candidate.").

225 Tobin, *supra* note 216 ("Individual members of the organization, including its leaders, may speak out in their individual capacities. These activities, however, must be conducted in their personal capacities; the members cannot use their organization as a means of 'amplifying' their speech. They may speak out against a particular issue or politician and may actively support a candidate for public office.").

One of the toughest issues that arises is determining whether a given example of issue advocacy does or does not involve lobbying or effecting campaigns.[226] The IRS has noted that in the context of political campaigns, as in lobbying, participation "depends upon all of the facts and circumstances of each case."[227] IRS Ruling 2007-41[228] can be helpful in illustrating some of the circumstances that do and do not violate the campaign provision, including issue advocacy.[229]

Another tough issue is candidate appearances at the §501(c)(3) organization or organization-sponsored events. This is also addressed in IRS Ruling 2007-41.[230] Inviting a political candidate to speak is not a per se violation of the campaign rule,[231] but it carries significant risk if the IRS finds it to be partisan or otherwise taking any position on an election.[232] The IRS will look at several factors in analyzing whether a candidate appearance violates the campaign rule. There are three main factors listed that the IRS will consider, but the ruling makes clear that the list is not exhaustive.[233] First, did the organization give equal opportunities for opposing candidates for the same position to participate at the appearance?[234] Second, did the organization indicate that it opposed or supported the candidate who appeared there?[235] Third, was political fund-raising conducted at the event where the candidate appeared?[236]

A related issue arises if the organization invites a candidate to speak but not in his or her capacity as a candidate. The key question here is whether the candidate is "publically recognized" by the organization as a candidate in relation to the appearance (including before and after the appearance).[237] If a candidate, for example, is an author and is invited to speak about a book he or she wrote and no mention is made of his or her candidacy, there would not likely be a problem under § 501(c)(3).[238] In contrast, if the person was invited as an author and as a candidate for an office, a violation is far more likely to be found.[239] This is reflected in the factors addressed in two IRS rulings, Ruling 20017-41[240] and Ruling 2007-25.[241] Factors to be considered include the reasons the individual was selected to speak,[242] the capacity in which the individual is speaking,[243] whether the election or candidacy is mentioned by the § 501(c)(3) organization or agents of the

226 Rev. Rul. 2007-41, 2007-1 C.B. 1421.

227 *Id.*

228 *Id.*

229 *Id.*

230 *Id.*

231 *Id.* (citing Rev. Rul. 74-574, 1974-2 C.B. 160) ("Providing a forum for candidates is not, in and of itself, prohibited political activity.").

232 *Id.* ("However, a forum for candidates could be operated in a manner that would show a bias or preference for or against a particular candidate.").

233 *Id.*

234 *Id.* ("Whether the organization provides an equal opportunity to participating to political candidate seeking the same office").

235 *Id.* ("Whether the organization indicates any support for or opposition to the candidate").

236 *Id.* ("Whether any political fundraising occurs.").

237 *Id.*

238 *Id.*

239 *Id.*

240 *Id.*

241 Rev. Rul, 2007-25.

242 Rev. Rul. 2007-41, 2007-1 C.B. 1421 ("Whether the individual is chosen to speak solely for reasons other than candidacy for public office").

243 *Id.* ("Whether the individual speaks only in a non-candidate capacity").

organization,[244] whether the event is nonpartisan,[245] and whether any campaign activity occurs at the event.[246] It is certainly advisable that there be a good non-campaign-related reason for having the candidate speak in his or her individual capacity[247] and that the campaign, candidacy, and related issues not be mentioned.[248]

Significantly, there are some election-related activities that do not violate § 501(c)(3).[249] For example, educating people on their right to vote,[250] "get out the vote" efforts,[251] and voter registration initiatives[252] are allowed as long as they are not done in a manner that advocates for or against a specific candidate, issue, or party.[253]

ii. *The § 501(c)(4) Option.* In *Regan v. Taxation with Representation*,[254] the Supreme Court upheld the lobbying restrictions under § 501(c)(3) in part because § 501(c)(4) provides a valid alternative for entities that promote social welfare and want to engage in some forms of political activity while maintaining tax-exempt status.[255] Section 501(c)(4)(A) adds to the list of exempt organizations

> (A) Civic leagues or organizations not organized for profit but operated exclusively for the promotion of social welfare, or local associations of employees, the membership of which is limited to the employees of a designated person or persons in a particular municipality, and the net earnings of which are devoted exclusively to charitable, educational, or recreational purposes.[256]

Section 501(c)(4)(B) makes the private inurement requirement applicable to all § 501(c)(4) organizations.[257] Yet § 501(c)(4) says nothing about political activity.[258] This, along with the Supreme Court's reliance on § 501(c)(4) as an alternative avenue for some political activity by exempt organizations,[259] has opened up the possibility of § 501(c)(3)

244 *Id.* ("Whether either the individual or any representative of the organization makes any mention of his or her candidacy or the election").

245 *Id.* ("Whether the organization maintains a nonpartisan atmosphere").

246 *Id.* ("Whether any campaign activity occurs in connection with the candidate's attendance.").

247 *See supra* notes 242–3, and accompanying text.

248 *See supra* notes 244–6, and accompanying text.

249 Rev. Rul. 78-248, 1978-1 C.B. 154 ("Certain 'voter education' activities conducted in a nonpartisan manner by an organization recognized as exempt under section 501(c)(3) of the Code will not constitute prohibited political activity disqualifying the organization from exemption.").

250 *Id.* ("'[V]oter education' activity . . . is not prohibited political activity within the meaning of section 501(c)(3) of the Code.").

251 Rev. Rul. 2007-41, 2007-1 C.B. 1421 ("[S]ection 501(c)(3) organizations may encourage people to participate in the electoral process through voter registration and get-out-the-vote drives, conducted in a non-partisan manner.").

252 *Id.*

253 *Id.* ("[V]oter education or registration activities conducted in a biased manner that favors (or opposes) one or more candidates is prohibited.").

254 Regan v. Taxation With Representation, 461 U.S. 540 (1983).

255 *Id.*

256 26 IRC § 501(c)(4)(A) (West 2010).

257 26 IRC § 501(c)(4)(B) (West 2010).

258 26 IRC § 501(c)(4) (West 2010).

259 *See, e.g.*, Regan v. Taxation With Representation of Wash., 461 U.S. 540, 543 (1983) ["§ 501(c)(4) organizations, but not § 501(c)(3) organizations, are permitted to engage in substantial lobbying to advance their exempt purposes."].

entities reorganizing as § 501(c)(4) entities[260] or even creating parallel § 501(c)(4) agencies as long as there is no inappropriate connection to the § 501(c)(3) entity, as discussed later.[261]

There are some significant differences between § 501(c)(3) and § 501(c)(4) entities.[262] First, § 501(c)(4) entities are themselves exempt from taxation, but donations to such entities are not deductible for donors.[263] Second, §501(c)(4) entities, for purposes relevant to the current discussion of religious entities, must be "operated exclusively for the promotion of social welfare."[264]

Treasury Regulation 1.502(c)(4)-1[265] sheds some light on this question because it is designed to help define "operated exclusively for the promotion of social welfare."[266] It reads in relevant part

> (2) Promotion of Social Welfare
>
> (i) In general. An organization is operated exclusively for the promotion of social welfare if it is primarily engaged in promoting in some way the common good and general welfare of the people of the community. An organization embraced within this section is one which is operated primarily for the purpose of bringing about civic betterments and social improvements. A social welfare organization will qualify for exemption as a charitable organization if it falls within the definition of charitable set forth in paragraph (d)(2) of § 1.501(c)(3)-1 and is not an action organization as set forth in paragraph (c)(3) of § 1.501(c)(3)-1.
>
> (ii) Political or social activities. The promotion of social welfare does not include direct or indirect participation or intervention in political campaigns on behalf of or in opposition to any candidate for public office. ... A social welfare organization that is not, at any time after October 4, 1976, exempt from taxation as an organization described in § 501(c)(3) may qualify under § 501(c)(4) even though it is an action organization described in § 1.501(c)(3)-1(c)(3)(ii) or (iv), if it otherwise qualifies under this section.[267]

Considering this regulation as a whole, part (i) could apply to many religious organizations,[268] and part (ii) simply means that such political activities do not in and of

260 *Id. at* 544 (noting that "[*Taxation with Representation of Washington*] ... can obtain tax deductible contributions for its non-lobbying activity by returning to the dual structure it used in the past, with a § 501(c)(3) organization for non-lobbying activities and a § 501(c)(4) organization for lobbying."].

261 *Id. at* 553 [noting that given the relationship between § 501(c)(3) and § 501(c)(4), the Court found that Congress' purpose in imposing lobbying restriction was to insure that no tax-deductable contributions are used to pay for substantial lobbying).

262 *Cf.* § 501(c)(4)(A) (West 2010) [articulating silence as to whether a tax-exempt organization under 501(c)(4) may engage in political activity but articulating that it must operate exclusively for the promotion of social welfare], *with* 26 IRC § 501(c)(3) (West 2010) (articulating that the organization must be organized for the purpose of "public good," and no part of its net earnings shall be used for private inurement, nor shall it engage in carrying on of propaganda or participate in influencing legislation politics or intervene in any political campaign on behalf of, or in opposition to, any candidate).

263 Taxation with Representation of Wash., 461 U.S. 540 at 543 (1983)[articulating that taxpayers contributions to IRC § 501(c)(4) organizations are not deductible, but acknowledging that taxpayers contributions to IRC § 501(c)(3) organizations are deductible].

264 Taxation with Representation of Wash., 461 U.S. 540 at 554 n. 4 (1983) [quoting IRC § 501(c)(4)].

265 Treas. Reg. § 1.501(c)(4)–1 (1990).

266 *Id.*

267 *Id.*

268 *Id.*

themselves count as part of the social welfare qualification.[269] Unlike § 501(c)(3) organizations, however, those activities are not precluded for § 501(c)(4) entities if the organization otherwise meets the social welfare requirement.[270] In fact, the IRS recognized this in Ruling 81-95.[271] Moreover, the term "exclusively for the promotion of social welfare" has been interpreted broadly by the IRS[272] and the courts.[273]

Therefore, many religious entities can meet the social welfare requirement.[274] First, many religious entities offer services to the community, such as food banks, shelters, and so on that would easily qualify as promoting social welfare.[275] Second, it could be argued that religious entities serve the social welfare of the community simply by functioning as religious entities.[276] Of course, some religious entities have already been recognized as qualifying.[277] Finally, a wide range of entities have been recognized as operating "exclusively for the promotion of social welfare," and by analogy, many religious organizations could qualify.[278]

Two distinct possibilities arise for religious organizations that seek to maintain tax-exempt status under § 501(c)(4) while being able to engage in some forms of political activity. First, a § 501(c)(3) organization could convert to a § 501(c)(4) organization.[279]

269 *Id.*

270 *Cf.* Treas. Reg. § 1.501(c)(4)–1 (1990) *with* Treas. Reg. § 1.504–1 (1990).

271 Rev. Rul. 81–95, 1981-C.B. 332.

272 *See, e.g.*, Quality Auditing Co., Inc. v. Comm'r of Internal Revenue, 114 T.C. 498, 504 (2000) ["In application of the organizational and operational tests, *exclusively* does not mean solely or absolutely without exception." (emphasis added)]; Nationalist Movement v. Commissioner, 102 T.C. 558, 576, 1994 WL 118959 (1994); Church in Boston v. Commissioner, 71 T.C. 102, 107, 1978 WL 3388 (1978).

273 *See, e.g.*, People's Educational Camp Soc. Inc. v. Comm'r of Internal Revenue, 331 F.2d 923, 930 (2d Cir. 1964) ("[C]ultural activities … such as lectures, concerts, plays, and art exhibits which were regularly held during the resort's summer season … did not involve the promotion of social welfare … considered in their relation to the total operation of [the commercial resort]."); Veterans Foundation v. United States, 281 F.2d 912 (10 Cir. 1960); Hanover Imp. Soc., Inc. v. Gagne, 92 F.2d 888, 891 (1 Cir. 1937) ("[E]mphasis on the broader term 'social welfare' is in line with the current regulations covering the subsection, which do not appear to give the word 'civic' any real independent limiting effect but which only deal with organizations 'operated primarily for the purpose of bringing about civic betterment and social improvements."); Amalgamated Housing Corp. v. Commissioner, 37 B.T.A. 817, 825, *aff'd per curiam*, 108 F.2d 1010 (2 Cir. 1940); *but cf.* Consumer-Farmer Milk Coop. v. Commissioner, 186 F.2d 68, 70 (2 Cir. 1950); United States v. Pickwick Elec. Membership Corp., 158 F.2d 272, 276 (6 Cir. 1946).

274 *See* Comm'r of Internal Revenue, 331 F.2d 923, 930 (2d Cir. 1964) ("This court has characterized the promotion of social welfare as involving the serving of 'purposes beneficial to the community as a whole,' or the promotion of the 'welfare of mankind' in the manner generally of the charitable, educational and religious organizations exempted by like provisions of the Code.")

275 *See, e.g.*, Walz, 397 U.S. 664, 708 (1970) (noting that churches perform some a variety of social welfare programs).

276 *See, e.g.*, Mutual Aid Ass'n of the Church of the Brethren v. United States, 759 F.2d 792, 796 (10th Cir. 1985) (holding that an unincorporated insurance association formed and promoted by church members to sell insurance protection to its members is not entitled to tax-exempt status as an organization primarily engaged in promotion of social welfare).

277 *Id.*

278 *See, e.g.*, Monterey Public Parking Corp. v. United States, 481 F.2d 175, 176 (9th Cir. 1973) (holding that corporation qualified for exemption from federal taxes as charitable corporation and social welfare organization where it was formed to construct and operate public off-street parking facility in central business district of city); Eden Hall Farm v. United States, 389 F.Supp. 858, 867 (W.D. Pa. 1975) (A nonprofit institution, which served Pittsburgh and surrounding community by providing a "country holiday" to thousands of working women qualified as tax-exempt social welfare organization.).

279 *Cf.* IRC § 501 (c)(4)(A) (West 2010) [articulating silence as to whether a tax-exempt organization under § 501(c)(4) may engage in political activity but articulating that it must operate exclusively for the

This approach raises fewer questions because as long as the organization qualifies as a § 501(c)(4) organization, it can engage in some political activity.[280] Donors would no longer be able to deduct their donations to the organizations, but the organization itself would be exempt.[281]

The second approach would be to set up parallel organizations, one maintaining § 501(c)(3) status, thus allowing donors to deduct their donations,[282] and the other operating under § 501(c)(4).[283] The § 501(c)(4) organization would be able to engage in political activity but would have to be a separate entity from the § 501(c)(3) organization.[284] This is exactly the sort of structure the Supreme Court suggested would be acceptable in *Regan v. Taxation with Representation*.[285] The Court also explained, however, that under such a structure, the § 501(c)(3) organization could "not subsidize the § 501(c)(4) organization."[286] In addition to not subsidizing each other, the § 501(c)(3) and § 501(c)(4) organizations could not function as one entity.[287] They would need to be legally and factually separate entities.[288] The *Regan* case did not involve a religious entity, but lower courts have recognized the applicability of its reasoning to religious entities.[289]

### 2. *Church Status*

Church's are treated differently from other organizations, including other religious organizations, under § 501(c)(3).[290] The term "church status" is awkward because it applies not just to churches but also to synagogues, temples, mosques, and so on.[291] The most significant benefits of "church status" are that churches are not required to receive a

promotion of social welfare], *with* 26 IRC § 501(c)(3) (West 2010) (articulating that the organization must be organized for the purpose of "public good," and no part of its net earnings shall be used for private inurement, nor shall it engage in carrying on of propaganda or participate in influencing legislation politics or intervene in any political campaign on behalf of, or in opposition to, any candidate).

280 IRC § 501(c)(4).

281 Taxation with Representation of Wash., 461 U.S. 540 at 543 (1983)[articulating that taxpayer contributions to IRC § 501(c)(4) organizations are not deductable but acknowledging that taxpayer contributions to IRC § 501(c)(3) organizations are deductable).

282 *Id.* at 552 [noting that Taxation with Representation of Washington may use its § 501(c)(3) organization for its nonpolitical activities and may create a § 501(c)(4) affiliate to pursue its charitable goals through political activism].

283 *Id.*

284 *Id.*

285 *Id.*

286 *Id.* at 541.

287 *Id.* at 552 ["A § 501(c)(3) organization's right to speak is not infringed, because it is free to make known its views on legislation through its § 501(c)(4) affiliate without losing tax benefits for its nonlobbying activities."].

288 *Id.*

289 *See, e.g.*, Church of Scientology of Cal. v. Comm'r of Internal Revenue, 83 T.C. 381, 452 (1984) (noting that "[t]he First Amendment does not shield a church from the constraints of the criminal law … and the Government … could insist its largesse not subsidize criminal activity").

290 26 IRC § 501(c)(3) (West 2010).

291 *See, e.g.*, National Ass'n of American Churches v. Comm'r of Internal Revenue, 82 T.C. 18, 34 (1984) [holding that a federation of churches is a religious organization within the meaning of § 501(c)(3)]; Rev. Rul. 80–114, 1980–1 CB 115 (providing in part that a nonprofit organization that provides care, comfort, and maintenance to persons seeking healing consistent with the teachings of the Christian Science Church through a medical care facility is exempt).

ruling from the IRS to have § 501(c)(3) status[292]; churches need not file annual informational returns or Form 990 to maintain § 501(c)(3) status,[293] reports that other § 501(c)(3) entities are required to file; and there are significant restrictions on the IRS's ability to investigate churches and specific procedures the IRS must follow if it does investigate a church.[294] Of course, if the IRS chooses to investigate and finds that an entity claiming church status does not meet the requirements to hold that status, the IRS may revoke church status.[295] If an entity loses church status, it still may remain a § 501(c)(3) entity as long as it meets all the requirements to qualify and maintain such status, including the filing of annual reports.[296]

This section will focus on the two major questions that arise in regard to church status. First, what are the requirements to maintain church status? This question may seem odd because churches simply can declare themselves so and do not need IRS approval to be considered a church for § 501(c)(3) purposes,[297] but of course, the IRS may challenge that status, and then the question becomes highly relevant.[298] This question also raises significant constitutional concerns. Second, what procedures are churches entitled to if the IRS chooses to challenge church status.

#### a. Maintaining Church Status

Church status is mentioned in 26 U.S.C. § 170(b)(1)(A)(I), which is part of a broader provision addressing deductions for individual contributions to charitable entities.[299] Yet the term "church" is not defined in that section. Religious entities need not apply for church status, but when that status is questioned by the IRS, two approaches generally have been used to analyze whether an entity should be able to maintain church status.[300] The first is a set of fourteen criteria set forth by the IRS.[301] The second is referred to as the "associational test."[302] The two approaches overlap in significant ways.[303]

The fourteen criteria are

> (1) a distinct legal existence; (2) a recognized creed and form of worship; (3) a definite and distinct ecclesiastical government; (4) a formal code of doctrine and discipline; (5) a distinct

[292] *Elimination of the Advance Ruling Process for New Organizations*, IRS; *available at:* http://www.irs.gov/Charities-&-Non-Profits/Charitable-Organizations/Elimination-of-the-Advance-Ruling-Process (accessed Jan. 24, 2014).

[293] Treas. Reg. § 1.6033–1(g).

[294] IRC § 7611.

[295] *Id.*

[296] *Id.*

[297] *Elimination of the Advance Ruling Process for New Organizations*, IRS; *available at:* http://www.irs.gov/Charities-&-Non-Profits/Charitable-Organizations/Elimination-of-the-Advance-Ruling-Process (accessed Jan. 24, 2014).

[298] IRC § 7611.

[299] *See* IRC § 170(b)(1)(A)(i).

[300] *Id.*

[301] *See* Spiritual Outreach Society v. Comm'r of Internal Revenue, 58 T.C.M. (CCH) 284 (1990); *See also* Jeramie Fortenberry, *What is a Church? Tests for Church Status under Tax Laws: The Intersection of the First Amendment and the Internal Revenue Code Raises Challenges*, Nonprofit Law Report; *available at:* http://www.nonprofitlawreport.com/what_is_a_church/ (accessed Oct. 10, 2014) (articulating the fourteen criteria considered).

[302] *See id.*

[303] *Id.*

religious history; (6) a membership not associated with any other church or denomination; (7) an organization of ordained ministers; (8) ordained ministers selected after completing prescribed studies; (9) a literature of its own; (10) established places of worship; (11) regular congregations; (12) regular religious services; (13) Sunday schools for religious instruction of the young; and (14) schools for the preparation of its ministers.[304]

The associational test requires that a church be a group of believers who regularly meet for "communal worship."[305] Thus courts using the associational approach look at whether individuals associate with each other for worship.[306] Many courts refer to both the fourteen criteria and the associational test,[307] but in recent years, the associational test has become more dominant in judicial opinions.[308] Of course, the IRS still considers both the fourteen criteria and the associational aspects of an entity.[309] As several courts have pointed out, it is fair to say that the two approaches often would lead to the same results because the most salient of the fourteen criteria relate to the associational nature of a church.[310]

It is hard to ignore the fact that both these approaches point toward what many would consider "traditional" churches and congregations.[311] In fact, courts have held that churches that use broadcast media,[312] mailings,[313] the Internet,[314] and other nontraditional means of assembly[315] are not entitled to "church status" under the IRC.[316] Courts also have required that churches "regularly" meet for worship, so occasionally meeting for worship has been held not to qualify,[317] especially when a number of the other indicia mentioned in the fourteen criteria are missing.[318] Such organizations are, of course, still entitled to § 501(c)(3) status if they meet the requirements.[319]

Thus most traditional congregations will be able to obtain "church status" regardless of faith or denomination. Less traditional congregations that maintain more traditional structures and that assemble together for worship will be able to maintain "church

304 Foundation of Human Understanding v. U.S., 614 F.3d 1383, 1387 n. 2 (Fed. Cir. 2010).

305 *Id.* at 1387; *see* Fortenberry, *supra* note 14, at 1 (stating that believers must meet regularly for communal worship).

306 *See* Foundation of Human Understanding, *supra* note 17, at 1389 ("The evidence of attendance at Foundation meetings or services is thus insufficient to satisfy the associational test because it does not establish the frequency or nature of the meetings, the consistency of the congregation, or the extent to which those meetings enabled members to associate with each other in worship.").

307 *Id.* at 1387, 1389.

308 *Id.* at 1389 ("We agree that the associational test is an appropriate test for determining church status under § 170, although we recognize that the associational test and the '14 criteria test' substantially overlap; as courts have pointed out, among the most important of the 14 criteria are the requirements of 'regular congregations' and 'regular religious services.'").

309 *Id.*

310 *Id.*

311 *See* Fortenberry, *supra* note 14, at 1.

312 *See* Foundation of Human Understanding, 614 F.3d at 1389.

313 *See generally id.*

314 *Id.* at 1391.

315 *Id.*

316 *Id.*

317 *Id.* at 1390 ("[T]he attendance of groups of people at occasional seminars in cities scattered across the country does not constitute a regular assembly of a cohesive group of people for worship.").

318 *Id.* at 1387 ("[T]he court looked to the 14 criteria for guidance and found that the Foundation satisfied some, but not all, of those criteria.").

319 *See* Bubbling Well Church of Universal Love, Inc., *supra* note 8, at 531.

status."[320] Yet congregations that do not regularly come together for worship under the associational test or that do not maintain the traditional indicia of a "church" will not likely be able to maintain "church status."[321]

Given the benefits bestowed by "church status," one would think that the act of defining what is and is not a church by the IRS and courts would violate the Establishment Clause and/or Free Exercise Clause. Yet courts have repeatedly held that because church status simply allows entities not to file annual forms and dispenses with the need for formal recognition as a § 501(c)(3) entity, it helps to prevent government involvement with religious entities.[322] Moreover, courts have held that because religious entities that are not "churches" still can maintain § 501(c)(3) status, the exception to the filing requirements for "churches" is not the sort of benefit that gives rise to violations under the Free Exercise or Establishment Clauses.[323] Thus both Establishment Clause and Free Exercise Clause challenges to "church status" under the IRC generally have failed.[324]

As a number of commentators and judges have pointed out, however, this is quite disturbing because it puts courts and the IRS in the business of deciding what a "church" is, even if only for limited purposes.[325] This is especially problematic when one considers that only "churches" are excluded from the filing requirements.[326] All other § 501(c)(3) entities, whether religious or not, must file the paperwork.[327] Thus the argument favoring exemptions for religious entities under § 501(c)(3) in the face of Establishment Clause concerns – that religious entities are only one of many types of nonprofit entities that serve a variety of communities – does not apply to the "church status" benefits.[328]

At some point there may be a successful challenge to "church status" based on the Establishment Clause, but that day does not seem near. Moreover, at some point a religious entity denied "church status" might bring a successful Free Exercise Clause claim because the "church status" determination is not generally applicable (it only applies to religion)[329] or successfully make a similar argument under the Religious Freedom Restoration Act (RFRA),[330] but even if this were to happen, it might lead to a granting of an exemption for that, and perhaps similarly situated entities, but the "church status" category would remain, even if a bit more inclusive.

### b. Procedures Available if the IRS Challenges an Entity's Church Status

As explained earlier, churches need not apply to the IRS for an advance decision that they meet the requirements for § 501(c)(3)[331] and need not file informational returns or

320 *See generally* Foundation of Human Understanding.
321 *See* Foundation of Human Understanding, *supra* note 31, at 1387.
322 Internal Revenue Service, *supra* note 3, at 3.
323 *See* Church of Scientology of Cal., *supra* note 10, at 383–4, 444, 448, 455–64 (articulating the courts holding and dispelling petitioner's claim of violations under the Free Exercise and Establishment Clauses).
324 *Id.*
325 *See* Fortenberry, *supra* note 14, at 1.
326 *See* IRS, *supra* note 3, at 3.
327 *See* IRC § 501(c)(3).
328 *See* Church of Scientology of Cal., *supra* note 10, at 383–4, 444, 448, 455–64.
329 *Id.*
330 42 U.S.C. § 2000bb (West 1993).
331 *Elimination of the Advance Ruling Process for New Organizations*, IRS; *available at:* http://www.irs.gov/Charities-&-Non-Profits/Charitable-Organizations/Elimination-of-the-Advance-Ruling-Process (accessed Jan. 24, 2014).

Form 990 with the IRS.[332] Yet one of the greatest protections enjoyed by those religious entities holding church status is the vast array of procedural protections they enjoy under the Church Audit Procedures Act (CAPA).[333] CAPA places significant restrictions on the ability of the IRS to initiate and conduct an investigation of whether a church is exempt under § 501(c)(3) based on its church status or whether the church has unreported taxable income or is engaged in activities that may be deemed taxable.[334] The following is an overview of CAPA procedures, but anyone involved in a challenge to church status should review every provision of CAPA in detail.[335]

First, an investigation cannot begin without a "reasonable belief" by a "high-level" Department of Treasury official.[336] If this requirement is met, the IRS must send a church written notice of the concerns giving rise to the investigation.[337] The church must be afforded a reasonable amount of time to reply with a written explanation, and the notice should specify a time within which the written explanation should be returned.[338] If the IRS still has concerns after the written explanation is received, or if no written explanation is received, the IRS can issue a second notice requiring review of the church's financial records.[339] The second notice should be issued within ninety days of receipt of the written explanation or the expiration of the time specified in the initial notice.[340]

Before the financial records are reviewed, the church has a right to request a conference with the IRS to discuss any IRS concerns.[341] The IRS has two years from the issuance of the second notice to complete the investigation.[342] The two-year period can be suspended if either the church or the IRS files judicial proceedings, the church fails to comply with reasonable request for financial information, or by mutual agreement between the IRS and the church.[343] If the investigation does not lead to revocation or other negative findings as defined in § 7611,[344] the IRS may not initiate a new investigation for five years, unless approved in writing by the Secretary of the Treasury or if the new investigation does not involve "the same or similar issues" as the first investigation.[345]

Thus most churches are never investigated by the IRS regarding their "church status," and when a church is investigated by the IRS, there is usually some evidence that the church is not exempt under § 501(c)(3) because it failed to meet one of the requirements of that section, the church does not meet the requirements for "church status," or the church has some taxable income regardless of whether it is otherwise exempt.[346]

332 Treas. Reg. § 1.6033–1(g).
333 26 U.S.C. § 7611.
334 *Id.*
335 *Id.*
336 *Id.*
337 *Id.*
338 *Id.*
339 *Id.*
340 *Id.*
341 *Id.*
342 *Id.*
343 *Id.*
344 *Id.*
345 *Id.*
346 *See* Mathew Encino, *Holy Profits: How Federal Law Allows for the Abuse of the Church Tax-Exempt Status*, 14 Hous. Bus. & Tax L.J. 78 (2014) (discussing how CAPA procedures make it difficult for the IRS to investigate and enforce violations of church tax-exempt status); *cf.* Foundation of Human Understanding v. United States, 614 F.3d 1383, 1389–90 (Fed Cir. 2010); Lutheran Soc'y Serv. of Minnesota v. United

If a church is investigated and the IRS decides to revoke church, or tax-exempt, status, the burden of proof to establish that the revocation of "church status" was in error falls on the church during any subsequent court proceedings.[347] In most cases where the IRS only questions "church status," even if a church loses that status, it will still be exempt under § 501(c)(3).[348]

### c. Parsonage Exemption

The "parsonage exemption" is a provision – or really two provisions – under the IRC that exempt property for ministers of the gospel from gross income for purposes of calculating income tax.[349] These provisions are found in IRC § 107.[350] The first provision exempts the value of a home provided by the church to ministers.[351] The second exempts "rental allowance(s)" paid to ministers for the purpose of renting or buying a home.[352] The second provision exempts from income "the rental allowance paid" to a minister "to the extent such allowance does not exceed the fair rental value of the home, including furnishings and appurtenances such as a garage, plus the cost of utilities."[353]

The term "minister of the gospel" is obviously underinclusive because use of the terms "minister" and "gospel" are from Protestant conceptions of clergy (i.e., the term "gospel" and use of the term "minister" rather than "priest," "rabbi," "imam," etc.). The term has been interpreted by courts and in Treasury regulations, however, to apply to all clergy who are serving in a ministerial role.[354] An IRS ruling states that functions performed by a "minister of the gospel" are "the performance of sacerdotal functions, the conduct of religious worship, the administration and maintenance of religious organizations and their integral agencies, and the performance of teaching and administrative duties at theological seminaries."[355] The IRS and the courts have excluded even ordained clergy who do not meet these requirements.[356]

Regulations enacted by the Department of Treasury explain what the term "home" means.[357] The regulations state that the home includes not only the "dwelling place" but also all furnishings within the home and attachments such as garages.[358] This is applied to both provisions in IRC § 107 but also reflects the language from subsection 2, which

States, 758 F.2d 1283, 1287 (8th Cir. 1985); American Guidance Found., Inc. v. United States, 490 F.Supp. 304 (D.D.C. 1980).

347 Foundation of Human Understanding, 614 F.3d at 1389–90; Foundation of Human Understanding v. United States, 88 Fed Cl. 203, 212 (2009) [citing Christian Echoes Nat'l Ministry, Inc. v. United States, 470 F.2d 849, 854 (10th Cir. 1972)].

348 *See, e.g.*, Foundation of Human Understanding, 614 F.3d at 1387 n. 1; Foundation of Human Understanding, 88 Fed Cl. at 208 n. 2; Spiritual Outreach Soc'y v. Comm'r, 927 F.2d 335, 337 n. 2 (8th Cir. 1990); Church of Visible Intelligence that Governs the Universe v. United States, 4 Cl Ct. 55, 65 (1983).

349 Justin Butterfield, Hiram Sasser & Reed Smith, *The Parsonage Exemption Deserves Broad Protection*, 16 TEX. REV. L. & POL. 251, 252 (2012).

350 IRC § 107.

351 *Id.* § 107(1).

352 *Id.* § 107(2).

353 *Id.*

354 Silverman v. Comm'r, 57 T.C. 727, 731 (1972); Salkov v. Comm'r, 46 T.C. 190, 194–5, 198 (1966).

355 Treas. Reg. § 1.107–1(a).

356 Tovas v. Comm'r, 67 T.C. 897, 906 (1977); Colbert v. Comm'r, 61 T.C. 449, 453, 456–7 (1974).

357 Treas. Reg. § 1.107-1(b).

358 *Id.*

applies the housing allowance to "the fair rental value of the home, including furnishings and appurtenances such as a garage, plus the cost of utilities."[359] Moreover, the cost of utilities may be covered.[360]

The regulations make clear, however, that any housing or housing allowance provided by the religious entity to a minister must be compensation for his or her services and not simply an extra perk.[361] This can be done by the religious entity in a number of ways that formally declare that the housing or housing allowance is compensation for service being rendered by the minister.[362] This should be done before payment of any housing allowance.[363] The most obvious way to do this is in the minister's employment contract,[364] but it also may be done through other official documents, such as minutes or resolutions by the religious entity.[365]

Given that the parsonage exemption allows "ministers of the gospel" to deduct the cost of housing from gross income, it would be fair to assume they should not be able to also deduct mortgage interest and property taxes paid for with these tax-free funds. However, under the tax code, they may do so.[366] Thus "ministers of the gospel" are entitled to the parsonage exemption and still may deduct mortgage interest and property taxes from their federal income tax.[367] The latter deductions are the same for all federal taxpayers, and there is no provision in the code for excluding those entitled to a parsonage exemption from those receiving these deductions.[368]

A case that arose in the 11th Circuit addressed whether more than one home can be covered under the parsonage exemption.[369] The 11th Circuit held that only one home can be exempted.[370] This makes sense given the language of IRC §107 as well as the purpose of that section.[371] Thus second homes, vacation homes, and similar properties are not likely covered under the parsonage exemption[372] and are definitely not covered by the parsonage exemption in the 11th Circuit.[373]

The parsonage exemption and especially the regulations used to interpret and enforce it[374] raise serious constitutional questions under the Establishment Clause.[375]

359 IRC § 107(2).
360 Rev. Rul. 59–350.
361 Treas. Reg. § 1.107–1(a).
362 *Id.* § 1.107–1(b).
363 *Id.*
364 *Id.*
365 *Id.*
366 IRC § 163(h)(3); § 164 (a)(1–2).
367 *Id.*
368 *Id.*
369 Comm'r v. Driscoll, 669 F.3d 1309, 1311 (11th Cir. 2012).
370 *Id.* at 1312–13.
371 *Id.* at 1311–12.
372 *Id.*
373 *Id.*
374 *See* Treas. Reg. § 1.61–2; § 1.107–1; § 1.1402(a)–11; § 601.201.
375 *See* Warren v. Comm'r, 332 F.3d 1012 (9th Cir. 2002); Freedom from Religion Found., Inc. v. Lew, 983 F. Supp. 2d 1051, (W.D. Wis., 2013); Freedom from Religion Found., Inc. v. Geithner, 644 F.3d 836 (9th Cir. 2011); Erwin Chemerinsky, *The Parsonage Exemption Violates the Establishment Clause and Should Be Declared Unconstitutional*, 24 Whitter L. Rev. 707 (2003); Butterfield, *supra* note 62; Dean T. Barnham, *The Parsonage Exclusion under the Endorsement Test: Last Gasp or Second Wind?* 13 Va. Tax. Rev. 397 (1993).

There is no clear answer from the Supreme Court or federal appellate courts to these questions yet,[376] but in a carefully reasoned decision in the U.S. District Court for the Western District of Wisconsin, the court held that the parsonage exemption violates the Establishment Clause.[377] For those interested in these issues, it is worth looking at this decision and at law review articles that address the constitutionality of the parsonage exemption.[378]

### d. A Note on Social Security Tax and Religion

Early on, Congress exempted self-employed individuals from paying Social Security taxes based on a sincere religious objection to doing so.[379] For example, many Amish believe that the community has a religious duty to support community members in need and that paying Social Security taxes conflict with this obligation.[380] Yet, in *United States v. Lee*,[381] the Court upheld the government's claim that this exemption does not apply to an Amish business that has employees.

Shortly after the *Lee* decision, Congress passed the Exemption Act of 1988,[382] which exempted religious employers who are members of certain recognized sects from paying Social Security taxes for their employees if they and their employees meet the requirements of the Exemption Act.[383] In order to be exempted, the employer must file an application for exemption, and that application must be approved.[384] Thus, regardless of RFRA and the current state of Free Exercise Clause jurisprudence, religious individuals and employers can be exempted from Social Security taxes if they meet the requirements of the Exemption Act of 1988.[385]

RFRA may be relevant in other tax cases. Recently, in *Burwell v. Hobby Lobby*,[386] a majority of the Court provided an exemption under RFRA to the Health and Human Services (HHS) mandate under the Affordable Care Act to a for-profit private employer.[387] The Court distinguished *Lee* because the Social Security tax was a "national system of taxation," and therefore, there was a compelling interest and narrow tailoring to deny an exemption.[388] The majority, however, ignored some of the key language in *Lee* and arguably mischaracterized the holding in Lee as narrower than it was.[389] The end result of this may be that exemptions to tax programs that are not part of what the Court calls a "national system of taxation" are available under RFRA.

376 The Ninth Circuit heard a case in 2011 that involved a constitutional challenge to the parsonage exemption. Freedom from Religion Found., 644 F.3d at 840. However, the court remanded the case to the district court without ruling on the constitutional issue. *Id.* at 839–40, 844.

377 Freedom from Religion Found., Inc. v. Lew, 983 F. Supp. 2d 1051, 1054 (W.D. Wis., 2013) (holding the parsonage exemption unconstitutional under the Establishment Clause).

378 *See supra* note 375.

379 IRC § 1402(g).

380 United States v. Lee, 455 U.S. 252, 257 (1982).

381 455 U.S. at 259–61.

382 26 U.S.C. § 3127.

383 *Id.*

384 *Id.*

385 *Id.*

386 U.S., 134 S. Ct. 2751 (2014).

387 *Id.* at 2759–60.

388 *Id.* at 2783–4.

389 *Id.* at 2803–4 (Ginsburg, J., dissenting).

## D. State Taxation

Many issues involving state taxation and religion have been addresses by the Supreme Court. Except in those rare instances in which a state tax exemption was found to be unconstitutional under the U.S. Constitution,[390] most state tax exemptions for religious entities or properties are constitutional as long as they meet a few requirements set forth by the Supreme Court.[391] Of course, state tax exemptions for religious entities still may violate state constitutions.[392]

### 1. *Generally Applicable State Tax Exemptions or Burdens*

As with the federal tax code, state tax exemptions that inure to the benefit of religious entities are constitutional as long as they are part of a broader system of exemptions. In *Mueller v. Allen*,[393] the Supreme Court upheld a state tax exemption for tuition, textbooks, and certain other expenses paid by families with students in school.[394] The exemption provided significant benefits for parents whose children attended private religious schools, which were the bulk of the private schools in the state.[395] Yet the Court held that because the exemption was not limited to religious schools and in fact benefited all families who had educational expenses for children in public or private primary and secondary schools – whether secular or religious – the exemption was constitutional.[396] *Mueller* remains good law and, if anything, has become a stronger precedent in light of subsequent cases.[397]

Relatedly, if a state tax is generally applied to all entities selling items for profit, there is no duty to provide a religious exemption to the state tax under the U.S. Constitution.[398] In *Jimmy Swaggert Ministries v. Board of Equalization of California*,[399] the Court held that California's 6 percent sales tax on tangible personal property could be applied to sales by Jimmy Swaggert Ministries.[400] The Court held that the collection of the state sales and use tax on sales of religious materials did not impose a substantial burden on Jimmy Swaggert Ministries' religious freedom under the federal Free Exercise Clause.[401] The Court distinguished *Murdock v. Pennsylvania*[402] and *Follett v. McCormick*,[403] which held that a flat tax could not be applied to the distribution of religious materials intending to evangelize.[404] According to the Court, the reason the taxes were unconstitutional

390 Texas Monthly, Inc. v. Bullock, 489 U.S. 1 (1989).
391 Mueller v. Allen, 463 U.S. 388 (1983).
392 *See, e.g.*, Metro. Gov't of Nashville & Davidson Cnty. v. Tennessee State Bd. of Equalization, 817 S.W.2d 953 (Tenn. 1991); *In re* Appeal of Springmoor, Inc., 498 S.E.2d 177 (N.C. 1998); Chittenden Town Sch. Dist. v. Dep't of Educ., 738 A.2d 539, 541 (Vt. 1999).
393 465 U.S. 388 (1983).
394 *Id.* at 390.
395 *Id.* at 401, 411.
396 *Id.* at 397–9.
397 *See* Zelman v. Simmons-Harris, 536 U.S. 639 (2002).
398 Jimmy Swaggert Ministries v. Bd. of Equalization of California, 493 U.S. 378 (1990); *cf.* Employment Division v. Smith, 494 U.S. 872 (1990).
399 493 U.S. 378.
400 *Id.* at 381, 397.
401 *Id.* at 391–2.
402 319 U.S. 105 (1943).
403 321 U.S. 573 (1944).
404 Murdock, 319 U.S. at 106–7, 113–14; Follett, 321 U.S. at 576, 578 (1944).

in those cases was that the flat taxes amounted to a prior restraint on religious speech,[405] which makes the tax in those cases different from a general sales tax.[406] The key is that the California sales tax was neutral and applied to all entities selling items whether for-profit, charitable, religious, or even governmental.[407] Therefore, it was not a prior restrain on speech, so the only harm is the small reduction in profit from the tax.[408] *Hernandez v. Commissioner of Internal Revenue*[409] had already made clear that the reduction in funds that could be used for religious activities caused by imposition of a sales tax is not a substantial burden on the free exercise of religion.[410]

The *Jimmy Swaggert Ministries* Court also held that the tax did not violate the Establishment Clause through entanglement between government and religion.[411] It is important to note, however, that the Court stated that it is possible "a more onerous tax rate, even if generally applicable,"[412] could create free exercise issues, and the subsequent decision in *Employment Division v. Smith*[413] would not likely require exemptions in cases of generally applicable state taxes, but a state constitution or RFRA might.

Therefore, a state tax exemption that includes religious entities and is part of a broader system of exemptions is constitutional.[414] This is true regardless of whether state income tax,[415] sales tax,[416] or other taxes are involved.[417] The subject of property taxes will be addressed separately, and there may be even broader protection for tax exemptions that benefit religious entities in the property tax context. Yet this does not mean that a state must exempt religious entities from a generally applicable sales, use, property, or other tax.

### 2. *State Tax Exemptions that Are Not Part of a Broader Exemption System*

If a tax exemption is granted only to religious entities or sales and not to similarly situated entities or sales, the Establishment Clause is violated.[418] In *Texas Monthly v. Bullock*,[419] the Supreme Court held that a Texas sales tax exemption that applied only to religious texts sold by a religious faith that promote the doctrines of that faith or the faith's sacred texts violated the Establishment Clause.[420] The Court held that such a tax lacks a secular purpose and unconstitutionally favors religion over nonreligion.[421]

405 Jimmy Swaggert Ministries, 493 U.S. at 386.
406 *Id.* at 389.
407 *Id.* at 389–90.
408 *Id.* at 390–1.
409 490 U.S. 680.
410 Jimmy Swaggert Ministries, 492 U.S. at 390–1 (citing Hernandez, 490 U.S. at 699).
411 *Id.* at 397.
412 *Id.* at 391.
413 494 U.S. 872.
414 *See supra* notes 406–26 and accompanying text.
415 Mueller, 465 U.S. at 397–9.
416 Jimmy Swaggert ministries, 493 U.S. at 389–90.
417 *See id.* at 392 (holding that the generally applicable use tax, like the generally applicable sales tax, did not violate the Establishment Clause); *cf.* Minneapolis Star & Tribune Co. v. Minnesota Comm'r of Revenue, 460 U.S. 575, 581 (1983) (finding that a use tax applied only to paper and ink used in publications violated the First Amendment because it was not generally applicable).
418 Texas Monthly, 489 U.S. at 1.
419 *Id.*
420 *Id.* at 5.
421 *Id.* at 14–16.

The Court was clear that if the tax were applicable to a wide enough array of publications, it could be constitutional, even if it incidentally benefited religion to include religious publications in that array.[422] This is, of course, consistent with the cases in Section D.1. Texas asserted the arguments that the exemption was necessary to protect the free exercise of religion and prevent entanglement between government and religion.[423] The Court rejected both arguments.[424] The Court held, and that holding was reaffirmed the next term in the *Jimmy Swaggert Ministries* decision discussed earlier, that there is no free exercise right to a tax exemption under a generally applicable tax.[425] The Court also held that the exemption created greater entanglement with religion than would applying the tax because the state would need to determine what counted as "religiously significant" for purposes of applying the exemption.[426] If a state chooses to exempt religious entities or content from sales, use, or most other taxes, it must do so as part of a broader exemption system.[427] The one exception that may be constitutional is exemptions for religious entities' under a state property tax, but this exception is quite narrow. It will be discussed in the next subsection.

### 3. *Religious Property Tax and Parsonage Exemptions*

Many jurisdictions have tax exemptions for property owned by religious entities that is used for religious purposes.[428] The substance, breadth, structure, and enforcement of these exemptions vary quite a bit from jurisdiction to jurisdiction,[429] but there are some general rules on constitutionality that apply to all these exemptions.

As noted in the discussion of the *Walz* case earlier,[430] these exemptions are constitutional as long as they are part of a wider array of property tax exemptions for similarly situated entities.[431] In *Walz*, the Court noted that property exemptions also were available to "a broad class of property owned by nonprofit, quasi-public corporations which include hospitals, libraries, playgrounds, scientific, professional, historical, and patriotic groups."[432] The Court also held that such exemptions are supported by the long history of property tax exemptions for property owned by religious entities and used for religious purposes.[433] Obviously, then, most state and local property tax exemptions for property owned by religious entities and used for religious purposes are constitutional because most such exemptions are part of a broader class of exemptions. Relatedly, and also based on the *Texas Monthly* case discussed earlier,[434] property tax exemptions that apply only to religious entities are constitutionally suspect. Of course, many religious entities also engage in charitable activity under the relevant state provisions and thus may be eligible for charitable exemptions for property that is

422 *Id.* at 10–12.
423 *Id.* at 17.
424 *Id.* at 18.
425 *Id.* at 19–20; *see supra* notes 399–417 and accompanying text.
426 Texas Monthly, 489 U.S. at 20.
427 *Id.* at 14–16.
428 *See infra* notes 437–91 and accompanying text.
429 *Id.*
430 *See supra* notes 1–11 and accompanying text.
431 Walz v. Tax Comm'n of New York, 397 U.S. 664 (1970).
432 *Id.* at 673.
433 *Id.* at 676–8.
434 *See supra* notes 419–27 and accompanying text.

not subject to a religious exemption,[435] although where and how these lines are drawn vary from state to state.[436]

Yet one type of property tax exemption that applies only to religious entities exists in many states: the parsonage exemption.[437] As with the federal parsonage exemption, there is a chance that these exemptions are unconstitutional despite their long historical pedigree because they only apply to parsonages, but for now these remain in many jurisdictions. Here we are referring to specific exemptions for parsonages. It is also possible that a parsonage that is part of church property may be exempt under a more general exemption.[438] These specific parsonage exemptions may one day be found unconstitutional despite their long historical pedigree because they obviously favor religion over nonreligion and they are not generally part of a broader exemption scheme.[439] Yet, for now, we will address the various models for these exemptions.

As of 2012, several states have a specific parsonage exemption provision in state statutes and references in the state constitution. These states are Arkansas,[440] Georgia,[441] Illinois,[442] Indiana,[443] Michigan,[444] Montana,[445] Nevada,[446] New York,[447] North Carolina,[448] North Dakota,[449] South Carolina,[450] Texas,[451] Virginia,[452] West Virginia,[453] and Wyoming.[454] A number of states also have a parsonage exemption under state statute but no specific state constitutional provision. These states are Connecticut,[455] Hawaii,[456] Maine,[457] Maryland,[458]

435 *See, e.g.*, Archdiocese of Portland v. Dep't of Revenue, 5 Or. Tax 111, 111 (1972), *aff'd*, 266 Or. 419, 513 P.2d 1137 (1973); *but see* Hubbard Press v. Tracy, 67 Ohio St. 3d 564, 1993 Ohio 3, 621 N.E.2d 396.

436 *See supra* notes 431–3 and accompanying text.

437 *See infra* notes 438–91 and accompanying text

438 *See infra* notes 466–89 and accompanying text.

439 *See* Warren v. Comm'r, 332 F.3d 1012 (9th Cir. 2002); Freedom from Religion Found., Inc. v. Lew, 983 F. Supp. 2d 1051 (W.D. Wis., 2013); Freedom from Religion Found., Inc. v. Geithner, 644 F.3d 836 (9th Cir. 2011); Erwin Chemerinsky, *The Parsonage Exemption Violates the Establishment Clause and Should be Declared Unconstitutional*, 24 Whitter L. Rev. 707 (2003); Butterfield, *supra* note 62; Dean T. Barnham, *The Parsonage Exclusion under the Endorsement Test: Last Gasp or Second Wind?* 13 Va. Tax. Rev. 397 (1993).

440 Ark. Code Ann. § 26-3-303 (West); Ark. Const. art. XVI, § 5(b).

441 Ga. Code Ann. § 48-5-41(a)(2.1–3); Ga. Const. art. VII, § 2, ¶ IV.

442 35 Ill. Comp. Stat. Ann. 200/15–40 (West); 200/15–65; Ill. Const. art. IX, § 6.

443 Ind. Code Ann. § 6-1.1-10-16(a) (West); § 6-1.1-10-21; § 14-33-7-4 (a)(1–2); Ind. Const. art. X, § 1(c)(1).

444 Mich. Comp. Laws Ann. § 205.54a (West); § 211.7(o)(1); § 211.7(s); Mich. Const. art. IX, § 4.

445 Mont. Code Ann. § 15-6-201(1)(b); Mont. Const. art. VIII, § 5(1)(b).

446 Nev. Rev. Stat. Ann. § 361.125(1) (West); § 361.140(1)(a); § 361.157(2)(i); Nev. Const. art. X, § 1(8).

447 N.Y. Real Prop. Tax Law § 420-a(1)(a) (McKinney); § 430; § 436(1); § 462; N.Y. Const. art. XVI, § 1.

448 N.C. Gen. Stat. Ann. § 105–278.3(a) (West); § 105–278.5(a)(1); N.C. Const. art. V, § 2(3).

449 N.D. Cent. Code Ann. § 57-02-08(7) (West); N.D. Const. art. X, § 5.

450 S.C. Code Ann. § 12-37-220(A)(3); S.C. Const. art. X, § 3(c).

451 Tex. Tax Code Ann. § 11.18(d) (West); § 11.20; Tex. Const. art. VIII, § 2(a).

452 Va. Code Ann. § 58.1–3606(A)(2) (West); § 58.1–3609; § 58.1–3617; § 58.1–3651; Va. Const. art. X, § 6(a)(6).

453 W. Va. Code Ann. § 11-3-9(a)(5–7) (West); W. Va. Const. art. X, § 1.

454 Wyo. Stat. Ann. § 39-11-105(a)(vii) (West); Wyo. Const. art. XV, § 12.

455 Conn. Gen. Stat. Ann. § 12–66 (West); § 12–81(12–15).

456 Haw. Rev. Stat. § 46–74.2 (West); § 246–32(b)(3).

457 Me. Rev. Stat. tit. 36, § 508(1); § 652(A).

458 Md. Code Ann., Tax-Prop. § 7–201 (West); § 7–204.

Massachusetts,[459] New Hampshire,[460] Rhode Island,[461] Vermont,[462] Washington[463] and Wisconsin.[464] Most of these states also have a general religious property tax exemption.[465]

Some states have a statute for religious exemptions but broader references in the state constitution that could support a parsonage exemption. These states are Arizona,[466] California,[467] and Colorado.[468] Some states have no specific parsonage exemption despite having a general religious exemption for property taxes. These states are Alabama,[469] Alaska,[470] Delaware,[471] Idaho,[472] Iowa,[473] Kansas,[474] Kentucky,[475] Louisiana,[476] Minnesota,[477] Florida,[478] Mississippi,[479] Missouri,[480] Nebraska,[481] New Jersey,[482] New Mexico,[483] Ohio,[484] Oklahoma,[485] Oregon,[486] Pennsylvania,[487] South Dakota,[488] and Utah.[489] Tennessee had a parsonage exemption by statute,[490] but it was struck down as a violation of the state constitution.[491]

459 Mass. Gen. Laws Ann. ch. 59, § 5 (West).
460 N.H. Rev. Stat. Ann. § 72:23(III).
461 R.I. Gen. Laws Ann. § 44-3-3 (West).
462 Vt. Stat. Ann. tit. 32, § 3832(2) (West).
463 Wash. Rev. Code Ann. § 84.36.020(2) (West).
464 Wis. Stat. Ann. § 70.11(4) (West).
465 *See, e.g.*, Conn. Gen. Stat. Ann. § 12–81(12–14) (West); Haw. Rev. Stat. § 246–32(b)(3); Md. Code Ann., Tax-Prop. § 7–204; N.H. Rev. Stat. Ann. § 72:23(III).
466 Ariz. Rev. Stat. Ann. § 42–11109(A); § 42–11129; § 42–11132(B); Ariz. Const. art. IX, § 2(2).
467 Cal. Rev. & Tax. Code § 206.2 (West); § 207; § 214(a); Cal. Const. art. XIII, § 3(f).
468 Colo. Rev. Stat. Ann. § 39-3-106(1) (West); § 39-3-116(1); Colo. Const. art X, § 5.1
469 Ala. Code § 10A-20-4.01(7); § 40-9-1; Ala. Const. art. IV, § 91; Ala. Const. art. XI, § 217(k).
470 Alaska Stat. Ann. § 29.45.030(a)(3) (West); Alaska Const. art. IX, § 4.
471 Del. Code Ann. tit. 9, § 8105 (West); Del. Const. art. VIII, § 1.
472 Idaho Code Ann. § 63-602B(1) (West); Idaho Const. art. VII, § 5.
473 Iowa Code Ann. § 427.1(8) (West).
474 Kan. Stat. Ann. § 79–201 (West); Kan. Const. art. XI, § 1(a)(4).
475 Ky. Rev. Stat. Ann. § 139.495 (West); § 367.650 (West); Ky. Const. § 170.
476 La. Rev. Stat. Ann. § 33:2828(A–B); La. Const. art. VII, § 21(B)(1)(a).
477 Minn. Stat. Ann. § 272.02(subd. 6) (West); § 273.19(subd. 1); Minn. Const. art. X, § 1.
478 Fla. Stat. Ann. § 196.012(1) (West); Fla. Const. art. VII, § 3(a).
479 Miss. Code. Ann. § 27-31-1(d) (West); § 79-11-501(a)(i)(A); Miss. Const. art. IV, § 112.
480 Mo. Ann. Stat. § 137.100(5) (West); Mo. Const. art. X, § 6(1).
481 Neb. Rev. Stat. § 77–202(1)(d); Neb. Const. art. VIII, § 2.
482 N.J. Stat. Ann. § 54:4-3.6 (West); § 54:4-3.6c; N.J. Const. art. VIII, § 1, ¶2.
483 N.M. Stat. Ann. § 7-36-7 (West); N.M. Const. art. VIII, § 3.
484 Ohio Rev. Code Ann. § 5709.06 (West); § 5709.07(A)(2–3); § 5709.12(E); Ohio Const. art. XII, § 2.
485 Okla. Stat. Ann. tit. 68, § 2887(7) (West); Okla. Const. art. X, § 6.
486 Or. Rev. Stat. Ann. § 307.130(2) (West); § 307.140(1).
487 53 Pa. Stat. Ann. § 7108 (West); 72 Pa. Stat. Ann. § 5020–204 (West); § 5453.202(a)(1); Pa. Const. art. VIII, § 2(a)(i).
488 S.D. Codified Laws § 10-4-15; S.D. Const. art. XI, § 6.
489 Utah Code Ann. § 59-2-1101(3)(d)(West); § 59-4-101(3)(c); Utah Const. art. XIII, § 3(1)(f).
490 Metro. Gov't of Nashville, 817 S.W.2d at 953.
491 *Id.*

# 11 Employment

Jennifer Ann Drobac and Jill L. Wesley*

At the beginning of a new millennium, employment discrimination on the basis of religious affiliation remains a problem in the United States. Even though Europeans settled here to escape religious persecution, the Equal Employment Opportunity Commission (EEOC) reported that it had received 3,811 allegations of employment discrimination on the basis of religion in 2012. This figure accounted for 3.8 percent of the agency's total caseload for the fiscal year. Although this number is small in comparison with other categories, such as discrimination based on sex (30,356 allegations) or race (33,512 allegations), the allegations of religious discrimination in employment have doubled since 1997, the first year for which statistics are available on the agency's website.[1] Of special concern is the increase in allegations of discrimination made by Muslims since the terrorist attacks of September 11, 2001.[2]

Although a complete review of law regarding religion and U.S. employment would take multiple volumes, this chapter summarizes the history of and recent trends in two aspects of the law in this area. The first section of this chapter surveys laws and case precedent that protect working religious adherents who claim discrimination, harassment, or a failure to accommodate. Adherents now bring most of their claims under Title VII of the Civil Rights Act of 1964[3] or equivalent state fair employment practice statutes.[4] However, isolated legislation, some arguably politically as well as

* Jennifer Ann Drobac, Professor of Law, Indiana University Robert H. McKinney School of Law, and Jill L. Wesley, Indiana University Robert H. McKinney School of Law. A draft of this chapter has been accepted to appear as *Religion and Employment Anti-Discrimination Law: Past, Present, and Post Hosanna-Tabor*, 69 NYU Ann. Surv. Am. L. 761 (2015). Special thanks to Professor R. George Wright for his comments and to our research assistants, Stacy McGuyre and Clifford Robinson. We also thank Oliver J. Richards and Sharon Steinerman at NYU Ann. Surv. Am. L. 

1 U.S. Equal Employment Opportunity Commission, *Charge Statistics FY1997 Through FY2012, available at:* http://eeoc.gov/eeoc/statistics/enforcement/charges.cfm (accessed April 28, 2013).

2 In the time period between the end of 2001 and 2011, charges filed by Muslims have risen from 15.8 percent to 21.8 percent of the total of religious discrimination in employment charges filed. U.S. Equal Employment Opportunity Commission, *Religion-Based Charges Files from 10/01/2000 through 3/31/2011 Showing Percentage Filed on the Basis of Religion-Muslim, available at:* http://www.eeoc.gov/eeoc/events/9-11-11_religion_charges.cfm (accessed April 28, 2013).

3 42 U.S.C.A. § 2000e-2 (West 2013). Civil Rights Act of 1964, Pub. L. No. 88-352, § 703, 78 Stat. 241, 255–7.

4 *See, e.g.*, Friedman v. S. Cal. Permanente Med. Group, 102 Cal. App. 4th 39, 125 Cal. Rptr. 2d 663 (2002) (holding that plaintiff's veganism was not a religious creed as defined by California's Fair Employment and Housing Act).

religiously motivated, offers additional protections. Recently passed "refusal clauses," also known as "conscience clauses," relate to the sale of contraceptives or the provision of pregnancy-termination services. They highlight the importance of targeted and specific statutes.[5] *Burwell v. Hobby Lobby Stores, Inc.*[6] addresses whether for-profit, private employers enjoy the same protections afforded by the Religious Freedom Restoration Act of 1993 (RFRA)[7] that religions may claim against governmental interference.

The second section of this chapter covers the protections for religious institutions that also operate as employers. The Supreme Court's 2012 decision in *Hosanna-Tabor Evangelical Lutheran Church and School v. E.E.O.C.*[8] indicates that the legal debate concerning the separation of church and state remains lively – at least where religious employers operate. The future direction of Court interpretation of that precedent remains obscure. Some analysts suggest that the Court limited *Hosanna-Tabor*'s reach, whereas others contend that its influence may be quite extensive. This chapter concludes with several observations about the evolution of religion and employment law.

## A. Causes of Action Available to Employees

Since its passage in 1964, Title VII of the Civil Rights Act has served as the primary legal vehicle for employment discrimination or harassment claims by religious adherents. However, a review of early religious discrimination claims brought under the First Amendment enhances an understanding of modern Title VII jurisprudence in at least three ways.

First, many of the early religious freedom cases highlight the tension between a court's mandate to remedy instances of religious discrimination and the historic separation of church and state. The First Amendment admonishes that "Congress shall make no law respecting an establishment of religion, or prohibiting the free exercise thereof."[9] Courts acknowledge that they walk the line between a violation of the Establishment Clause and validation of the Free Exercise Clause. Endorsement of religion becomes a particular concern when two religious adherents have opposing interests.[10] Neutrality, as well as the protection of religious freedom, surfaces as a primary goal of reviewing courts.

5 National Conference of State Legislatures, *Pharmacist Conscience Clauses: Laws and Information* (May 2012), *available at:* http://www.ncsl.org/issues-research/health/pharmacist-conscience-clauses-laws-and-information.aspx.

6 __U.S.__, 134 S. Ct. 2751 (2014).

7 42 U.S.C. §§ 2000bb *et seq.*

8 132 S. Ct. 694, 697 (2012).

9 U.S. Const. amend. I. The First Amendment is applicable to the states through the Fourteenth Amendment. *See, e.g.*, NAACP v. Alabama, 357 U.S. 449, 460–1 (1958) (freedom of association); Cantwell v. Connecticut, 310 U.S. 296, 303 (1940) (applying Free Exercise and Establishment Clauses to states).

10 *See, e.g.*, New York City Transit Auth. v. State, Executive Dept., Div. of Human Rights, 211 A.D.2d 220, 224, 627 N.Y.S.2d 360 (1995) *aff'd as modified*, 89 N.Y.2d 79, 674 N.E.2d 305 (1996). This court explained

> Simply put, to find the proper balance between the Free Exercise Clause and the Establishment Clause may not always be easy. Nevertheless, it is important to recognize that true religious liberty is damaged, not only where a penalty is attached to religious observance, but also where the State acts to promote the welfare of one religious group ahead of another. The Constitution firmly condemns both courses with the same neutral hand.

*Id. at* 224 (citation omitted).

Second, the early cases reveal how courts strained to verify an adherent's religious beliefs in evaluating free exercise claims. In general, courts examined what constitutes a religion and, more specifically, what constitutes a religious belief. Additionaly, courts explored how firmly established an adherent's belief had to be before it triggered First Amendment free exercise protection. Courts continue to struggle with these questions. They do so within the Title VII framework, guided by more recently passed religious protections and in reliance on early court precedent.

Third, the early employment religious discrimination cases reveal possible biases on the part of legislatures and courts against minority religious adherents, such as Jehovah's Witnesses and Muslims. The Supreme Court acknowledged the problem of disfavored religious identity in *Church of the Lukumi Babalu Aye, Inc. v. City of Hialeah* [11] when it dealt with a facially neutral law. The Court explained that "[f]acial neutrality is not determinative.... Official action that targets religious conduct for distinctive treatment cannot be shielded by mere compliance with the requirement of facial neutrality. The Free Exercise Clause protects against governmental hostility which is masked as well as overt."[12] The challenge for jurists is to identify masked hostility.

### 1. *First Amendment Employment Discrimination Claims*

Application of the First Amendment's Free Exercise and Establishment Clauses to employment law gained strength during the industrialization of the U.S. economy. As factory jobs lured more workers from the agricultural fields, conflicts concerning the accommodation of religious freedoms arose between workers and their employers. Court resolution of these disputes necessitated judicial recognition of the limitations on government involvement in religion set by the First Amendment. Without targeted legislation, however, minority groups, including religious adherents, continued to suffer discrimination in both the public and private sectors.

Beginning in the early nineteenth century,[13] individuals began to challenge state "blue laws"[14] that regulate some forms of commercial conduct on particular days,

[11] 508 U.S. 520, 534 (1993) (finding that a ban on killing animals violated the free exercise rights of Santería adherents who practice animal sacrifice as a form of religious devotion).

[12] *Id.* at 534. Even though the *Lukumi Babalu Aye* Court found the challenged ordinances facially neutral, it noted that the laws specifically targeted Santería sacrifice. *See id.* at 535–40.

[13] Commonwealth v. Wolf, 1817 WL 1768 (Pa. 1817) (imposing a penalty on Jewish plaintiff for breaking Sunday Sabbath).

[14] *Compare* Samuel Peters, A General History of Connecticut: From its First Settlement Under George Fenwick, to Its Latest Period of Amity with Great Britain Prior to the Revolution; Including a Description of the Country, and Many Curious and Interesting Anecdotes; with an Appendix, Pointing out the Causes of the Rebellion in America; Together with the Particular Part Taken by the People of Connecticut in Its Promotion (1829), *available at*: http://archive.org/details/generalhistoryof00peter (referencing "blue laws" as religious laws written in a blue bound book), *and* W.L. Kingsley, *Lying as a Fine Art: And the Claims of Rev. Samuel Peters as an Artist*, XVI Scribner's Monthly 275, 279–80 (1878), *available at*: http://www.unz.org/Pub/Century-1878jun-00275?View=PDFPages (disputing the existence of Connecticut's blue book of religious laws and referring to Peters as "lying.") *with* W.F. Poole, *A Popular Cyclopaedia of United States History* 2, The Dial; A Monthly Index of Current Literature, 209, 209–10 (1882), *available at*: http://babel.hathitrust.org/cgi/pt?view=image;size=100;id=mdp.39015030985850;page=root;seq=221;num=209) (providing an alternative origin of the term "blue laws." "The word 'blue,' or 'blew' – meaning fixed, faithful, constant – is as old as Chaucer's time; and when fixed principles went out of fashion in England on the

usually Sundays.[15] Most U.S. "blue laws" protect the Christian Sunday Sabbath or Christian holidays such as Christmas. For example, Indiana still bans vehicle[16] and off-premises alcohol sales on Sundays.[17] Arguably, these laws run afoul of the Establishment Clause by promoting Christianity. However, nonreligious justifications, such as the welfare and morality of the community, enable the surviving laws to withstand judicial scrutiny.[18]

Many of the early challenge suits involved employment-related "blue laws," usually laws that reserved Sunday as a day of rest and mandated Sunday business closures. Often those who challenged "blue law" restrictions did so because they observed a Sabbath other than Sunday and did not want to lose two days of income.[19] Some Sunday work prohibition laws remained in force through the middle of the twentieth century.[20] Only gradually did more leniency for Saturday sabbatarians and others develop.[21]

Avoiding religionist justifications for "blue laws," the Supreme Court echoed reasoning almost a century old in *Braunfeld v. Brown* (1961)[22]:

> [W]e cannot find a State without power to provide a weekly respite from all labor and, at the same time, to set one day of the week apart from the others as a day of rest, repose, recreation and tranquility – a day when the hectic tempo of everyday existence ceases and a more pleasant atmosphere is created, a day which all members of the family and community have the opportunity to spend and enjoy together.[23]

restoration of Charles II, whatever was fixed, serious and rigid in morals and religion was termed 'blue,' or 'true blue,' and was applied as a term of reproach to Puritans and Presbyterians.... The Connecticut code of 1650 was milder than that of Massachusetts, Virginia, or England; and yet to New Yorkers, who had no religion at all, it seemed strict, and hence 'blue.'").

15 Andrew J. King, *Sunday Law in the Nineteenth Century*, 64 Alb. L. Rev. 675, 676 (2000). King's article provides a full historical accounting of the challenges presented by the "blue laws."

16 Ind. Code Ann. § 24-4-6-1 (West 2013).

17 Ind. Code Ann. § 7.1-3-1-14 (West 2013).

18 Com. v. Has, 122 Mass. 40, 42 (1877). In *Com. v. Has*, the court explained, "the legislative authority to provide for its observance [the work cessation/Sabbath] is derived from [the state's] general authority to regulate the business of the community and to provide for its moral and physical welfare." *Id.* However, in other cases, judicial *dicta* revealed additional motivations. One court protected the Christian Sabbath for observation, explaining "that this is a Christian nation." State v. Barnes, 22 N.D. 18, 132 N.W. 215, 216 (1911). The *Barnes* court also suggested that Sunday is the one day of rest typically observed by "civilized peoples." *Id. at* 216; *see also id.* at 216–17 (documenting support for the designation of Sunday as a day of rest in history, dating back to A.D. 321).

19 *See, e.g.*, Scoles v. State, 47 Ark. 476, 1 S.W. 769 (1886) (finding Seventh-Day Adventist guilty of working on Sunday); Com. v. Starr, 144 Mass. 359, 11 N.E. 533 (1887) (affirming lower court decision that the statute prohibited the Jewish shopkeeper from remaining open on Sunday to serve other Jews.); State v. Blair, 130 Kan. 863, 288 P. 729 (1930) (considering a defendant who claimed no particular religion but resisted the imposition of a religious day of rest).

20 Town of W. Orange v. Carr's Dept. Store, 53 N.J. Super. 237, 147 A.2d 97 (County Ct. 1958) (finding that the store owner violated local ordinance when employees were in the store checking inventory on Sunday). In *Town of W. Orange*, the court allowed labor on the restricted day if work "performed is in his dwelling house, work shop or on his premises, and has not disturbed other persons in the observance of the first day of the week as the Sabbath." *Id.* at 245.

21 *See, e.g.*, Wallace v. Jaffree, 472 U.S. 38, 52–3 (1985) (explaining that "the Court has unambiguously concluded that the individual freedom of conscience protected by the First Amendment embraces the right to select any religious faith or none at all.")

22 366 U.S. 599 (1961).

23 *Id.* at 607.

The Supreme Court found it within the state's general police powers to designate one day of the week as a day of rest "when the atmosphere is one of calm and relaxation rather than one of commercialism."[24] The Court, like other courts that had examined the issue before, failed to consider that the designated day was sacred to some but not all citizens.

Though many of the old work-related "blue laws" have been repealed, most states still have remnant "blue laws."[25] The evolution of and remaining "blue laws" offer an important lens through which to view current legal practices that govern the expression and control of religion in the workplace. Veiled religious endorsements and possible biases warrant careful reading of judicial opinions and analysis of legislation. For example, one might argue that prohibitions on sex work (a.k.a. prostitution), while ostensibly passed for public health and morality reasons, reflect religious precepts against nonmarital recreational sex.[26] As this chapter moves through the workplace religious rights of both employees and employers, it draws attention to alleged mixed-motive legislation and possible subtle religious endorsements or prejudices.

#### a. Possible Court Bias against Minority Religious Adherents and the Tension with the Establishment Clause Implicated in Free Exercise Claims

Any government display of bias against or preference for a religion implicates First Amendment rights. This section highlights the difficult balance courts must strike between the protection of religious freedoms, guaranteed by the Free Exercise Clause, and the maintenance of religious neutrality, mandated by the Establishment Clause. One early employment case that raises questions about the application of laws of ostensibly neutral religious import is *Prince v. Massachusetts* (1944).[27] In *Prince*, the Court upheld Massachusetts's child labor laws against a Jehovah's Witness who allowed her ordained nine-year-old niece to distribute religious literature. The Court reasoned that the state has an interest in protecting children from exploitive labor. In doing so, the Court justified the infringement of free exercise and other constitutional rights by asserting public welfare, morality, and the protection of children.[28] Unlike the old "blue laws," prohibitions against the exploitation of children carry no obvious religious endorsement. However, the court decision may be tied to a masked hostility toward Jehovah's Witnesses and other minority religious adherents, as illustrated in other court

[24] *Id.* at 602.

[25] *See Blue Law, available at:* http://en.wikipedia.org/wiki/Blue_law#Examples_of_blue_laws_in_the_United_States_today_by_state; *see also Blue Laws in the United States, available at:* http://en.wikipedia.org/wiki/Blue_laws_in_the_United_States.

[26] *See* Kate DeCou, *U.S. Social Policy on Prostitution: Whose Welfare Is Served?* 24 New Eng. J. on Crim. & Civ. Confinement 427, 430–2 (1998); *see also* People v. Freaney, 108 A.D.2d 228, 230, 488 N.Y.S.2d 759, 761 (1985).

The *Freaney* court explained

> Interestingly, prostitution itself was not a common-law crime, unless the manner in which it was engaged constituted a public nuisance (2 Wharton's Criminal Law § 271 [14th ed.]). It became a crime by statute and, despite the suggestion that prostitution should be decriminalized and treated as a licensed, regulated activity, virtually all jurisdictions continue to punish prostitution for utilitarian reasons as well as religious and moral ones (ALI Model Penal Code § 251.2, cmt. at 456).

*Id.*

[27] 321 U.S. 158 (1944).

[28] *Id.* at 166–7.

cases, including, for example, child custody cases.[29] The reliance on neutral criteria allays some, but often not all, concerns.

If judicial or government officials display hostility to minority religious adherents, such as Jehovah's Witnesses, the animus carries other constitutional ramifications. When government officials prefer one religion over another or religion over no religious affiliation, the government's religious endorsement necessarily implicates Establishment Clause concerns. In *Everson v. Board of Education*,[30] the Court evaluated the First Amendment's Establishment Clause and held that "[n]either a State nor the Federal Government can set up a church. Neither can pass laws which aid one religion, aid all religions, or prefer one religion over another."[31] The Court perfected a test to determine whether governmental action violates the Establishment Clause in *Lemon v. Kurtzman*.[32] The three-part *Lemon* test requires that governmental action must (1) "have a secular legislative purpose," (2) have a "principal or primary effect … that neither advances nor inhibits religion," and (3) avoid "an excessive … entanglement with religion."[33] However, Supreme Court justices, constitutional law scholars, and others have criticized the *Lemon* test in the decades since its formulation.[34] In *Van Orden v. Perry*,[35] the Court acknowledged that "[m]any of our recent cases simply have not applied the test. Others have applied it only after concluding that the challenged practice was invalid under a different Establishment Clause test."[36]

In 1984, Justice O'Connor offered the "endorsement test" as an improvement on and replacement for the *Lemon* test. Over the years, the endorsement test has received the

[29] *Compare* Jennifer Ann Drobac, *For the Sake of the Children: Court Consideration of Religion in Child Custody Cases*, 50 Stan. L. Rev. 1609 (1998), *with* Prince, 321 U.S. at 170. The *Prince* Court held that "[p]arents may be free to become martyrs themselves. But it does not follow they are free, in identical circumstances, to make martyrs of their children before they have reached the age of full and legal discretion when they can make that choice for themselves." Prince, 321 U.S. at 170. Arguably, this dictum suggested that a child's martyrdom exacerbated the dangers to the *Prince* child and disparaged Mrs. Prince for her religiously associated behavior.

[30] 330 U.S. 1 (1947) (sustaining state reimbursement for cost of transporting children to parochial schools as an extension of the logic by which state-paid police protect schoolchildren regardless of whether they attend parochial schools).

[31] *Id.* at 15.

[32] 403 U.S. 602, 606–7 (1971) (invalidating a 15 percent salary supplement to private-school teachers of secular subjects).

[33] *Id.* at 612–13 [quoting Walz v. Tax Comm'n, 397 U.S. 664, 674 (1970)].

[34] *See, e.g.*, Wallace v. Jaffree, 472 U.S. 38, 63 (1985) (Powell, J., concurring) (referring to criticism by Justices O'Connor and Rehnquist); Kent Greenawalt, *Quo Vadis: The Status and Prospects of "Tests" Under the Religion Clauses*, 1995 Sup. Ct. Rev. 323, 359–79 (1995) (reviewing the fractured application of *Lemon* in subsequent cases). Donald Beschle comments, "Separationists find the [*Lemon*] test too loose in its acceptance of plausible secular state purposes and too pliable in its quest for a primary secular effect. Accomodationists point to the 'Catch-22' nature of the entanglement clause as an obstacle to conscientious legislative attempts to satisfy the 'effects' test." Donald. L. Beschle, *God Bless the Child?: The Use of Religion as a Factor in Child Custody and Adoption Proceedings*, 58 Fordham L. Rev. 383, 394 (1989).

[35] Van Orden v. Perry, 545 U.S. 677 (2005) (holding that Texas State Capitol Ten Commandment display carried an historical meaning and did not violate the Establishment Clause).

[36] *Id.* at 686 [citing Zelman v. Simmons-Harris, 536 U.S. 639 (2002), and Good News Club v. Milford Central School, 533 U.S. 98 (2001)].

most sustained interest.[37] In *Lynch v. Donnelly*,[38] Justice O'Connor suggested that the Establishment Clause prohibits two types of government action. In her concurring opinion, she explained:

> One is excessive entanglements with religious institutions, which may interfere with the independence of the institutions, give the institutions access to government or governmental powers not fully shared by nonadherents of the religion, and foster the creation of political constituencies defined along religious lines. The second and more direct infringement is government endorsement or disapproval of religion. Endorsement sends a message to nonadherents that they are outsiders, not full members of the political community, and an accompanying message to adherents that they are insiders, favored members of the political community. Disapproval sends the opposite message.[39]

The first prohibition closely resembles the third prong of the test, warning against "excessive entanglement." However, the second admonition – that government action must neither endorse nor disapprove of religion – is significantly different from the first two prongs of *Lemon*.

The *Lemon* "purpose" and "effects" prongs focus on the stated purpose and actual effects of governmental action or legislation. In her explanation of the endorsement test, Justice O'Connor advised that "[t]he proper inquiry under the purpose prong of *Lemon*, I submit, is whether the government intends to convey a message of endorsement or disapproval of religion."[40] In applying the endorsement test, a court asks what the government intends by its action, which is not necessarily the same as the stated purpose. Justice O'Connor also counseled

> [T]he effect prong of the test is properly interpreted not to require invalidation of a government practice merely because it in fact causes, even as a primary effect, advancement or inhibition of religion.... What is crucial is that a government practice not have the effect of communicating a message of government endorsement or disapproval of religion.[41]

This explanation emphasizes that the unconstitutionality of a message lies in its perception as government endorsement and not in whether the government has, in reality, advanced or inhibited religion. This test, which ferrets out the appearance of inappropriate endorsement, sweeps much more broadly than one that requires actual advancement or inhibition of religion.

37 *See, e.g.*, County of Allegheny v. ACLU, 492 U.S. 573, 595 (1989) (adopting Justice O'Connor's endorsement test for the first time). Professor Greenawalt explained, however, "A majority of Justices do agree that 'endorsement' is the crucial inquiry for certain kinds of cases, but no majority agrees on the proper formulation of that test for at least some of these cases." Greenawalt, *supra* note 34, at 361.

38 465 U.S. 668, 684–5 (1984) (finding that a city did not violate the Establishment Clause by displaying a nativity scene).

39 *Id.*

40 *Id.* at 691.

41 *Id.* at 691–2. Justice O'Connor added, "Every government practice must be judged in its unique circumstances to determine whether it constitutes an endorsement or disapproval of religion." *Id.* at 694.

In *Wallace v. Jaffree*,[42] Justice O'Connor further clarified the endorsement test. She said in her concurrence, "The relevant issue is whether an objective observer, acquainted with the text, legislative history, and implementation of the statute, would perceive it as a state endorsement."[43] Justice O'Connor's intelligent "objective observer" is not an average person on the street but one who, for example, is familiar with the legislative history of a statute.

Justice O'Connor gave more guidance concerning the objective observer in *Corporation of the Presiding Bishop of the Church of Jesus Christ of Latter-Day Saints v. Amos*.[44] She noted that something more than historical facts determine whether the objective observer perceives a message of endorsement: "Although evidentiary submissions may help answer it, the question is, like the question whether racial or sex-based classifications communicate an invidious message, in large part a legal question to be answered on the basis of judicial interpretation of social facts."[45] This elaboration leaves the qualifications of the objective observer frustratingly vague and confusing.

O'Connor's objective observer is the "reasonable person" in tort law who understands complex statutes and their legislative histories. This observer can both personify community ideals and engage in sophisticated judicial interpretation of the social elements that he or she personifies. What remains unclear, in part, is whether (and how) the objective observer represents all communities and how Justice O'Connor harmonizes the reasonable person's conclusions with those of the judicial historian and interpreter.

Courts continue to struggle with Establishment Clause jurisprudence that still makes reference to both the *Lemon* and endorsement tests.[46] In 2011, Justice Thomas noted the lack of guidance as he dissented from the denial of *certiorari* in a case involving government display of highway crosses for slain police officers. He lamented, "Our jurisprudence provides no principled basis by which a lower court could discern whether *Lemon*/endorsement, or some other test, should apply in Establishment Clause cases."[47] This overview of Establishment Clause jurisprudence (if it can be called that) helps one to understand the tension between Free Exercise Clause and Establishment Clause claims in the evolution of employment law cases. The tightrope that courts walk over the abyss of religious discrimination demonstrates that a misstep may result in the violation of constitutional protections.

[42] 472 U.S. 38 (1985).

[43] *Id.* at 76 (O'Connor, J., concurring); *see also* Corporation of the Presiding Bishop of the Church of Jesus Christ of Latter-Day Saints v. Amos, 483 U.S. 327, 348 (1987) (O'Connor, J., concurring) (citing *Wallace* and discussing the objective observer's perception of government action); Thornton v. Caldor, 472 U.S. 703, 711 (1985) (O'Connor, J., concurring) (referencing the objective observer's understanding of a state endorsing one particular day as the Sabbath).

[44] 483 U.S. 327 (1987).

[45] *Id.* at 348 (O'Connor, J., concurring) (quoting Lynch, 465 U.S. at 693–4). In *Capitol Square Review & Advisory Bd. v. Pinette* [515 U.S. 753 (1995)], Justice O'Connor wrote, "In this respect, the applicable observer is similar to the 'reasonable person' in tort law, who 'is not to be identified with any ordinary individual, who might occasionally do unreasonable things' but is 'rather a personification of a community ideal of reasonable behavior, determined by the [collective] social judgment." ' *Id.* at 779–80 (O'Connor, J., concurring) [quoting W. Keeton, D. Dobbs, R. Keeton & D. Owen, Prosser and Keeton on Law of Torts 175 (5th ed., 1984)].

[46] *See, e.g.*, Salazar v. Buono, 559 U.S. 700, 707–9 (2010) (remanding the case involving the display of a Latin cross on national land and the transfer of that land).

[47] Utah Highway Patrol Ass'n v. Am. Atheists, Inc., __ U.S. __, 132 S. Ct. 12, 14 (2011).

### b. Free Exercise and Establishment Clause Issues in Unemployment Benefits Cases

A large category of religious discrimination employment cases involves a state's denial of unemployment benefits. Claimant workers quit or were fired from their jobs because of a religious conflict. In *Sherbert v. Verner*,[48] a Seventh-Day Adventist sought unemployment benefits after she was terminated for refusing to work on her Saturday Sabbath. The U.S. Supreme Court reversed the South Carolina Supreme Court's denial of benefits. The Court held that "[t]he [South Carolina] ruling forces her to choose between following the precepts of her religion and forfeiting benefits, on the one hand, and abandoning one of the precepts of her religion in order to accept work, on the other hand."[49] In deciding the case, the *Sherbert* Court established a "balancing test" that "asks whether the law at issue substantially burdens a religious practice and, if so, whether the burden is justified by a compelling government interest."[50] This test tracks the "strict scrutiny" analysis used in *Wisconsin v. Yoder*, another case that considered the Free Exercise Clause.[51]

Justice Harlan's dissent in *Sherbert* deserves note for a number of reasons. First, he emphasized that the South Carolina law was one that the South Carolina Supreme Court had "uniformly applied ... in conformity with its clearly expressed purpose."[52] Second, Harlan expressed his concern that allowing an exception for Sherbert based on her religion amounted to a violation of the Establishment Clause. Harlan alluded to the tension between the Free Exercise and Establishment Clauses. He reasoned that South Carolina "must single out for financial assistance those whose behavior is religiously motivated, even though it denies such assistance to others whose identical behavior (in this case, an inability to work on Saturdays) is not religiously motivated."[53]

Finally, Justice Harlan referenced *Braunfeld v. Brown*.[54] Recall that *Braunfeld* was a "blue law" case that had upheld the right of a state to prohibit work and provide for a day of rest on Sunday, even if it imposed a cost on an individual citizen.[55] Harlan explained

> The secular purpose of the statute before us today is even clearer than that involved in *Braunfeld*. And just as in *Braunfeld* – where exceptions to the Sunday closing laws for Sabbatarians would have been inconsistent with the purpose to achieve a uniform day of rest and would have required case-by-case inquiry into religious beliefs – so here, an exception to the rules of eligibility based on religious convictions would necessitate judicial examination of those convictions and would be at odds with the limited purpose of the statute to smooth out the economy during periods of industrial instability.[56]

[48] 374 U.S. 398 (1963).
[49] *Id.* at 404.
[50] City of Boerne v. Flores, 521 U.S. 507 (1997) (confirming the *Sherbert* balancing test).
[51] *Wisconsin v. Yoder* involved a challenge by Amish parents of the Wisconsin compulsory education law. The Court held that the First and Fourteenth Amendments prevented the state from compelling Amish children to remain in school past the eighth grade until they are sixteen [406 U.S. 205 (1972)]. The Religious Freedom Restoration Act (RFRA) traces the compelling interest test traced back to *Wisconsin v. Yoder* {42 U.S.C.A. § 2000bb (West 2013) [stating that the purpose of the legislations is "to restore the compelling interest test as set forth in *Sherbert v. Verner*, 374 U.S. 398 (1963) and *Wisconsin v. Yoder*, 406 U.S. 205 (1972)"]}.
[52] Sherbert, 374 at 419 (Harlan, J., dissenting).
[53] *Id.* at 422. *But see* Von Stauffenberg v. Dist. Unemployment Comp. Bd., 459 F.2d 1128 (D.C. Cir. 1972) (holding that the exemption of religious organizations from unemployment compensation tax payment does not violate the Establishment Clause of the First Amendment).
[54] 366 U.S. 599 (1961).
[55] Sherbert, 374 at 421.
[56] *Id.* (Harlan, J., dissenting) (citations omitted, emphasis added).

Harlan regarded the *Sherbert* decision as a violation of the principle that the Court should avoid involvement with remedying a situation based on an individual's religious beliefs and should instead allow the statutes to fulfill their secular duty without judicial interference.

Thus the *Sherbert* Court supported a religious exception to a rule of otherwise neutral application. Subsequent unemployment decisions confirmed the *Sherbert* majority view that favored accommodation of religious practices and found no constitutional conflict.[57] However, Harlan's position foreshadowed the majority decision in *Employment Division, Department of Human Resources of Oregon v. Smith*,[58] which held that a neutral law of general applicability did not violate the Free Exercise Clause.[59]

In another major decision concerning unemployment benefits, *Thomas v. Review Board of the Indiana Employment Security Division*,[60] the Supreme Court again applied the *Sherbert* test. *Thomas* validated the free exercise rights of a Jehovah's Witness who had quit his job after a transfer to a position that required that he build military equipment in violation of his religion's tenets. The worker filed suit after a denial of unemployment benefits and later appealed from an Indiana Supreme Court decision that upheld the state's legitimate interests. In overturning the Indiana Supreme Court, the U.S. Supreme Court reaffirmed that "[a] person may not be compelled to choose between the exercise of a First Amendment right and participation in an otherwise available public program."[61]

The *Thomas* Court specifically disapproved of the Indiana Supreme Court's willingness to explore what actions Thomas should have taken on the basis of his religious beliefs. The Court reasoned that "[c]ourts should not undertake to dissect religious beliefs because the believer admits that he is 'struggling' with his position or because his beliefs are not articulated with the clarity and precision that a more sophisticated person might employ."[62] In this passage, one sees how the *Thomas* Court disapproved of unreasonable court examination or verification of the adherent's religious beliefs. The Court added that "it is not within the judicial function and judicial competence to inquire whether the petitioner or his fellow worker more correctly perceived the commands of their common faith. Courts are not arbiters of scriptural interpretation."[63] Thus, in both in both *Sherbert* and *Thomas*, the Supreme Court resolved the tension between the Free Exercise and Establishment Clauses in favor of the religious adherents. The Court applied a "balancing test" that permitted exceptions to laws of neutral applicability for the individual religious needs of citizens.[64]

57 *See generally* Abner S. Greene, *The Apparent Consistency of Religion Clauses Doctrine*, 21 WASH. U. J.L. & POL'Y 225, 260–1 (2006) [calling for "a more robust commitment to judicially created exemptions under the Free Exercise Clause (in tandem with legislatively crafted accommodations) to offset the ways in which religious citizens are asked to abstain from a full and express use of government to advance their theological ends"].

58 494 U.S. 872 (1990).

59 *Id.* at 872 (1990).

60 450 U.S. 707 (1981).

61 *Id.* at 708; *see also* Hobbie v. Unemployment Appeals Comm'n of Florida, 480 U.S. 136, 146 (1987) (citing *Sherbert* and *Thomas* in concluding "that Florida's refusal to award unemployment compensation benefits to appellant violated the Free Exercise Clause of the First Amendment").

62 *Id.* at 715.

63 *Id.* at 716.

64 *But see id.* at 720. Justice Rehnquist's *Thomas* dissent revisited Justice Harlan's emphasis on *Braunfeld*:

> [I]n this case, it cannot be said that the State discriminated against Thomas on the basis of his religious beliefs or that he was denied benefits *because* he was a Jehovah's Witness. Where, as here, a State has enacted a general statute, the purpose and effect of which is to advance the State's secular

The Supreme Court extended the *Sherbert* and *Thomas* holdings in *Frazee v. Illinois Department of Employment Security*.[65] Frazee opposed working on Sunday because of his personal religious beliefs and was denied unemployment benefits. Unlike Sherbert and Thomas, however, Frazee was not a member of an established religious sect or church, nor did he claim that his refusal to work on Sundays resulted from a "tenet, belief or teaching of an established religious body."[66] The Court held that Illinois had violated the Free Exercise Clause in denying Frazee unemployment benefits.[67] In reconciling its decision with *Sherbert* and *Thomas*, the Court explained, "Never did we suggest [in *Sherbert* and *Thomas*] that unless a claimant belongs to a sect that forbids what his [or her] job requires, his belief, however sincere, must be deemed a purely personal preference rather than a religious belief."[68] Thus the Court affirmed that First Amendment Free Exercise protection mandated neither affiliation with a particular religious sect nor verification of religious zeal and sincerity. Once again, the Court held for the religious adherent.

The most recent employment benefits case, *Employment Division, Department of Human Resources of Oregon v. Smith*,[69] involved two workers who were "fired from their jobs with a private drug rehabilitation organization because they ingested peyote for sacramental purposes at a ceremony of the Native American Church," of which they were members.[70] Smith and Black were held ineligible for employment benefits because they had been fired for misconduct.[71] The Oregon Court of Appeals overturned the decision of the Employment Board on the basis that the activities of Smith and Black were religious and, therefore, were protected by the Free Exercise Clause of the First Amendment.[72] The Supreme Court of Oregon upheld the decision of the Court of Appeals, using the reasoning of *Sherbert* and *Thomas*.[73]

In reversing the decision of Oregon's Supreme Court, the U.S. Supreme Court opined, "We have never held that an individual's religious beliefs excuse him [or her] from compliance with an otherwise valid law prohibiting conduct that the State is free to regulate. On the contrary, the record of more than a century of our free exercise jurisprudence

> goals, the Free Exercise Clause does not in my view require the State to conform that statute to the dictates of religious conscience of any group. As Justice Harlan recognized in his dissent in *Sherbert v. Verner, supra*: "Those situations in which the Constitution may require special treatment on account of religion are ... few and far between." Like him I believe that although a State could choose to grant exemptions to religious persons from state unemployment regulations, a State is not constitutionally compelled to do so.

*Id.* at 722–3 (Rehnquist, J. dissenting) [quoting Sherbert, 374 U.S. at 423 (other citations and footnotes omitted)]. Rehnquist stressed the neutrality of the state to justify his preferred outcome. Again, this theme surfaced later in *Smith*.

65 489 U.S. 829 (1989).

66 *Id.* at 831.

67 *Id.* at 829.

68 *Id.* at 832–3.

69 494 U.S. 872 (1990).

70 Smith, 494 U.S. at 874.

71 *Id.*

72 *Id.*

73 Smith v. Employment Div., Dept. of Human Res., 301 Or. 209, 216-17, 721 P.2d 445, 449 (1986) *vacated sub nom.* Employment Div., Dept. of Human Res. of State of Or. v. Smith, 485 U.S. 660 (1988) *and adhered to sub nom.* Smith v. Employment Div., 307 Or. 68, 763 P.2d 146 (1988) *rev'd sub nom.* Employment Div., Dept. of Human Res. of Oregon v. Smith, 494 U.S. 872.

contradicts that proposition."[74] The Court continued, "[T]he right of free exercise does not relieve an individual of the obligation to comply with a 'valid and neutral law of general applicability on the ground that the law proscribes (or prescribes) conduct that his [or her] religion prescribes (or proscribes).' "[75] Without overruling *Sherbert*, the Supreme Court followed the reasoning in the *Sherbert* and *Thomas* dissents. It left the legal community to reconcile the decisions in this line of cases.

The primary distinguishing factor between *Smith* and other similar religious freedom cases is that the Supreme Court declined to designate Smith's and Black's ingestion of peyote as religiously motivated. Rather, the Court emphasized that they had violated a criminal drug use statute.[76] This reasoning echoes that in *Prince v. Massachusetts*, in which the Court upheld the facially neutral child labor laws against the free exercise claims of a Jehovah's Witness. One wonders, based on the Court's treatment of Jehovah's Witnesses and the conjectures of bias following *Prince*, whether the Court would have come to the same conclusion in *Smith* if the rehab center had terminated Smith and Black for ingesting Christian sacramental wine. Arguably not, because the ingestion of sacramental wine does not otherwise constitute a crime involving a controlled substance. *Smith* and *Prince* also raise the notion that, in addition to facial neutrality, strong public policy, such as the war on drugs or protection of children from exploitative labor, trumps free exercise rights. If this is the case, however, the Court might simply have cited the compelling governmental interest and validated the challenged *Smith* statute using narrow grounds.

*Smith* marks the Court's retreat from the underlying reasoning in the *Sherbert*, *Thomas*, and *Frazee* holdings that free exercise protection mandated neither affiliation with a particular religious sect nor verification of religious sincerity. However, the *Smith* Court justified its rejection of the strict scrutiny standard in evaluating alleged free exercise violations by reasoning, "The government's ability to enforce generally applicable prohibitions of socially harmful conduct, like its ability to carry out other aspects of public policy, 'cannot depend on measuring the effects of a governmental action on a religious objector's spiritual development.' "[77]

The *Smith* Court explained that it invoked the compelling interest (strict scrutiny) test to evaluate free exercise claims only when the government had created a mechanism for individualized exemptions to generally applicable laws.[78] In *Sherbert*, the unemployment compensation administrative system allowed the state to analyze individual free exercise claims for exemption.[79] *Smith* noted that such cases "stand for the proposition that where the State has in place a system of individual exemptions, it may not refuse to extend that system to cases of 'religious hardship' without compelling reason."[80] In *Smith*, no mechanism existed for the evaluation of free exercise claims against the otherwise valid and neutral Oregon criminal drug laws, and the Court refused to extend the heightened scrutiny standard to that type of case.

74 Smith, 494 U.S. at 878–9.
75 *Id.* at 879.
76 *Id.* at 875–6.
77 *Id.* at 885 [quoting Lyng v. Northwest Indian Cemetery Protective Ass'n, 485 U.S. 439, 451 (1988)].
78 Smith, 494 U.S. at 884.
79 Sherbert, 374 U.S. at 405–6.
80 Smith, 494 U.S. at 884 [quoting Bowen v. Roy, 476 U.S. 693, 708 (1986)].

In response to *Smith*, Congress enacted the Religious Freedom Restoration Act of 1993 (RFRA).[81] Congress addressed its disapproval of *Smith*, stating "in *Employment Division v. Smith*, 494 U.S. 872 (1990) the Supreme Court virtually eliminated the requirement that the government justify burdens on religious exercise imposed by laws neutral toward religion."[82] Congress then codified the *Sherbert* compelling interest test, explaining, "Government may substantially burden a person's exercise of religion only if it demonstrates that application of the burden to the person – (1) is in furtherance of a compelling governmental interest; and (2) is the least restrictive means of furthering that compelling governmental interest."[83] In essence, Congress codified the strict scrutiny standard for Free Exercise Clause case evaluations.

The constitutionality of the RFRA came before the Supreme Court in *City of Boerne v. Flores*.[84] The original issue in the case concerned a dispute between the Catholic archbishop of San Antonio and the City of Boerne regarding whether the archbishop could invoke the RFRA to overcome the denial of a construction permit.[85] In coming to its conclusion that the RFRA was unconstitutional as applied to the states, the Court stated that "[b]road as the power of Congress is under the Enforcement Clause of the Fourteenth Amendment, RFRA contradicts vital principles necessary to maintain separation of powers and the federal balance."[86] *Boerne* references *Smith* and how it led Congress to pass the RFRA. The *Boerne* majority noted that the Court had declined to apply the *Sherbert* test in *Smith*.[87] Three Justices – O'Conner, Souter,[88] and Breyer[89] – registered their disagreement with the majority decision in *Boerne*. Justice O'Conner authored the lead dissent, arguing that the Court should take the opportunity presented by *Boerne* to revisit their *Smith* holding.[90] Her dissent advocated for a return to the *Sherbert* compelling interest test.[91]

More recently, in *Gonzales v. O Centro Espirita Beneficente Uniao Do Vegetal* [UDV] (2006),[92] the Court returned to the *Sherbert* test codified in RFRA. Specifically,

81 For a more complete discussion of RFRA and similar state statutes, *see* Christopher C. Lund, *Religious Liberty After Gonzales: A Look at State RFRAs*, 55 S.D. L. Rev. 466 (2010).

82 42 U.S.C.A. § 2000bb (West 2013).

83 42 U.S.C.A. § 2000bb-1 (West 2013).

84 521 U.S. 507 (1997).

85 *Id.* at 512.

86 *Id.* at 536.

87 *Id.* at 512–13.

88 *Id.* at 565.

89 *Id.* at 566.

90 *Id.* at 546. Justice O'Connor argued:

> [The Free Exercise Clause] is best understood as an affirmative guarantee of the right to participate in religious practices and conduct without impermissible governmental interference, even when such conduct conflicts with a neutral, generally applicable law. Before *Smith*, our free exercise cases were generally in keeping with this idea: where a law substantially burdened religiously motivated conduct – regardless whether it was specifically targeted at religion or applied generally – we required government to justify that law with a compelling state interest and to use means narrowly tailored to achieve that interest.

*Id.* (O'Connor, J. dissenting).

91 In response to *Boerne*, Congress enacted the Religious Land Use and Institutionalized Persons Act of 2000 (RLUIPA), pursuant to its Spending Clause and Commerce Clause authority. RLUIPA is limited in scope, targeting two areas of state and local action. As its title indicates, RLUIPA applies to land-use regulation and restrictions on the free exercise of religion by institutionalized persons. Sossamon v. Texas, 131 S. Ct. 1651, 1656, (2011).

92 546 U.S. 418 (2006).

the Court rejected that U.S. Customs inspectors had a compelling interest in banning the UDV's sacramental use of hoasca, a brewed tea that contains DMT, a hallucinogen regulated under Schedule I of the Controlled Substances Act.[93] The Court explained why the *Smith* peyote case no longer controlled the outcome in *Gonzales*: "[W]e [the Justices] rejected the interpretation of the Free Exercise Clause announced in *Sherbert v. Verner*, and, in accord with earlier cases, see *Smith*, held that the Constitution does not require judges to engage in a case-by-case assessment of the religious burdens imposed by facially constitutional laws."[94] However, RFRA reintroduced the requirement of a strict scrutiny analysis.[95] Addressing changes wrought by RFRA since *Smith*, the *Gonzales* Court explained, "RFRA requires the Government to demonstrate that the compelling interest test is satisfied through application of the challenged law 'to the person' – the particular claimant whose sincere exercise of religion is being substantially burdened. RFRA expressly adopted the compelling interest test 'as set forth in *Sherbert v. Verner.*' "[96] Conducting the strict scrutiny analysis mandated by RFRA, the Court then upheld the preliminary injunction sought by UDV against U.S. Custom Officials.

This discussion of employment benefits cases and Supreme Court First Amendment jurisprudence indicates that free exercise claims for employment discrimination remain viable under RFRA against federal government interference. Whether the Court will continue to analyze state action using a low-level *Smith* scrutiny or a strict scrutiny test, consistent with RFRA and *Gonzales*, remains unclear.

### c. Free Exercise and Establishment Clause Issues in Future Cases

Another question raised post-*Smith* and RFRA is whether for-profit corporations can, on behalf of their owners or shareholders, allege free exercise violations against the federal government. The Court recently addressed this issue only with respect to RFRA in *Burwell v. Hobby Lobby Stores, Inc.*[97] Hobby Lobby was attempting to use RFRA to avoid providing its employees with health care coverage for certain contraceptives. The Greens, owners of Hobby Lobby Stores "believe that life begins at conception and that it would violate their religion to facilitate access to contraceptive drugs or devices that operate after that point."[98] The corporation's owners alleged that provision of such coverage, mandated by the 2010 Patient Protection and Affordable Care Act (ACA),[99] violated their free exercise rights under RFRA.[100] The plain language of RFRA specifies that it applies to persons. RFRA reads: "Government shall not substantially burden a *person's* exercise of religion even if the burden results from a rule of general applicability."[101] RFRA does not specifically define "person." Therefore, the Court relied on the Dictionary Act. "Under the Dictionary Act, 'the wor[d] "person" ... include[s] corporations, companies,

93 21 U.S.C. § 801 *et seq.* (2000 ed. and Supp. I); *see* §§ 823 & 960(a)(1).
94 *Id.* at 424 (citations omitted).
95 Id.
96 *Id.* at 430–1 (citations omitted)
97 __ U.S. __, 134 S. Ct. 2751 (2014).
98 *Id.* at 2766.
99 42 U.S.C. § 18001 *et seq.* (2010).
100 Hobby Lobby, 134 S. Ct. at 2765–6.
101 42 U.S.C.A. § 2000bb-1(a) (West 2013) (italics added).

associations, firms, partnerships, societies, and joint stock companies, as well as individuals.' "[102] Thus the Court held that a "person" covered by RFRA includes a for-profit corporation such as Hobby Lobby.[103]

Arguably, *Hobby Lobby* has limited relevance to the subject of employment discrimination on the basis of religion. It is not technically an employment discrimination case in that the corporate employer was not employed by the federal government. Hobby Lobby employees were not suing their corporate employer for religious accommodation nor asserting their free exercise rights. The Court noted the limits of its *Hobby Lobby* decision:

> The principal dissent raises the possibility that discrimination in hiring, for example on the basis of race, might be cloaked as religious practice to escape legal sanction. Our decision today provides no such shield. The Government has a compelling interest in providing an equal opportunity to participate in the workforce without regard to race, and prohibitions on racial discrimination are precisely tailored to achieve that critical goal.[104]

Because the RFRA applies to for-profit corporations, however, one can expect to see further suits testing the range of RFRA protections.

Included the in ripple effect of *Hobby Lobby* is the risk of Establishment Clause claims brought by nonreligious employees. Hobby Lobby employees might argue, for example, that the ACA is a law of neutral application and that RFRA, as interpreted by the Hobby Lobby Court, endorses religious values over the rights to health care by the nonreligious employees and women, thereby discriminating against nonadherents and women. Until its parameters are clearer, *Hobby Lobby* is really beyond the scope of this chapter. However, the authors highlight *Hobby Lobby* as another case that may influence the future of employment-related First Amendment claims.

## 2. *Title VII of the Civil Rights Act of 1964*

In the nineteenth and early twentieth centuries, when workers faced no state action or government interference with their free exercise rights, they often had no recourse. The Constitution simply did not apply in disputes between private parties. In the mid-twentieth century, however, the Civil Rights Movement forced a national discussion concerning the Constitution's failure to secure basic civil rights, regardless of race. Congressional debate over appropriately responsive legislation widened the circle of citizens covered by the proposed laws. Legislative proposals included protections not only for racial minorities but also for women, religious adherents, and other minority groups. Congress passed the Civil Rights Act of 1964,[105] including Title VII's protection from religious discrimination in employment, which supplemented the protections originally provided by the First Amendment and by more general employment laws.

102 Hobby Lobby, 134 S. Ct. at 2768 (quoting 1 U.S.C. § 1).
103 *Id.* at 2767–75.
104 *Id.* at 2783 (citations omitted).
105 42 U.S.C.A. § 2000e-2 (West 2013). Civil Rights Act of 1964, Pub. L. No. 88-352, § 703, 78 Stat. 241, 255–7.

Today, Title VII of the Civil Rights Act of 1964 provides a primary legal cause of action for religious discrimination in employment. Title VII offers employees two main avenues for redress of grievances: a request for accommodation and a claim for discrimination on the basis of religion.[106] As will become apparent in the review of court application of Title VII's protections, several themes prevalent in First Amendment cases resurface. First, Title VII cases highlight the tension between a court's mandate to remedy instances of religious discrimination and the historical separation of church and state.[107] Second, Title VII cases also reveal how courts strain to verify an adherent's religious beliefs in evaluating claims. In general, courts broadly define "religion" and what constitutes a "religious belief."[108] Courts explore with great care how firmly established an adherent's belief must be before it triggers Title VII protection.

a. Failure to Accommodate: Section (j)

In an accommodation action, an employee typically alleges that an employer failed to allow the worker's religious practices, required by a religion or sect. For example, the employer might have denied the employee time off to observe his or her religion's Sabbath. Failure to accommodate religious practices accounts for a large percentage of religious discrimination in employment claims filed by workers.[109]

The original version of the 1964 Civil Rights Act narrowly defined "religion," and early court decisions did not equate a lack of accommodation with discrimination.[110] Senator Jennings Randolph, a practicing Seventh-Day Adventist and a Saturday sabbatarian,[111] believed that those early decisions would severely disadvantage worshippers like himself.[112] He succeeded in lobbying Congress to include an expanded definition when it amended the act in 1972.[113] Section (j) of the Civil Rights Act now specifies

[106] 29 C.F.R. § 1605.2 (West 2013) and 42 U.S.C.A. § 2000e-2(a) (West 2013).

[107] *See, e.g.*, E.E.O.C. v. Townley Eng'g & Mfg. Co., 859 F.2d 610, 613 (9th Cir. 1988) (finding no Title VII exemption for a religious, for-profit corporation and that it had discriminated against an atheist employee by requiring him to attend weekly devotional services on company time). In *Townley*, the court mentioned:

> We note that under the facts of this case, no construction of section 702 would avoid significant First Amendment questions. If we held that Townley was a 'religious corporation' under the meaning of section 702, and therefore exempt from Title VII's prohibition against religious discrimination, then we might be faced with a question the Supreme Court left open in *Corporation of the Presiding Bishop v. Amos*, 483 U.S. 327, 107 S.Ct. 2862, 97 L.Ed.2d 273 (1987): whether exemption of a religious corporation's for-profit activities violates the Establishment Clause."

*Id.* at 613 n. 2. The issue that *Townley* decided against the employer that claimed Title VII exemption is similar to the one that the Supreme Court will decide in *Hobby Lobby* regarding the for-profit corporation's appeal under RFRA.

[108] *See infra* at 30.

[109] *See* EEOC, *Statistics, Bases by Issue FY2010–FY2013*, *available at:* http://www.eeoc.gov/eeoc/statistics/enforcement/bases_by_issue.cfm.

[110] Dewey v. Reynolds Metals Co., 429 F.2d 324 (6th Cir. 1970), *aff'd by equally divided Court*, 402 U.S. 689 (1971); Riley v. Bendix Corp., 330 F.Supp. 583 (M.D. Fla.1971), *rev'd* 464 F.2d 1113 (5th Cir. 1972).

[111] *Randolph, Jennings* (1902–1998), in Biographical Directory of the United States Congress, *available at:* http://bioguide.congress.gov/scripts/biodisplay.pl?index=R000046 (accessed April 28, 2013).

[112] *See* Justice Marshall's dissent in *Trans World Airlines, Inc. v. Hardison* [432 U.S. 63, 88–9 (1977) (Marshall, J. dissenting)] for an overview of the possible effect of the decisions in *Dewey* and *Riley*.

[113] Hardison, 432 U.S. at 74–6.

that "[t]he term 'religion' includes all aspects of religious observance and practice, as well as belief, unless an employer demonstrates that he [or she] is unable to reasonably accommodate to an employee's or prospective employee's religious observance or practice without undue hardship on the conduct of the employer's business."[114]

To establish a failure to accommodate, the plaintiff must establish that "(1) he or she has a bona fide religious belief that conflicts with an employment requirement; (2) he or she informed the employer of this belief; [and] (3) he or she was disciplined for failure to comply with the conflicting employment requirement."[115] If the plaintiff succeeds in establishing a prima facie case, the burden then shifts to the employer to demonstrate that it could not reasonably accommodate the plaintiff's religious needs without undue hardship.[116] According to the United State Court of Appeals for the 4th Circuit in *E.E.O.C. v. Firestone Fibers & Textiles Co.*[117]:

> This is a two-prong inquiry. To satisfy its burden, the employer must demonstrate (1) that it provided the plaintiff with a reasonable accommodation for his or her religious observances, [and] (2) that such accommodation was not provided because it would have caused an undue hardship – that is, it would have "result[ed] in 'more than a cost' to the employer."[118]

In the years since Title VII's passage and amendment, litigants have challenged each prong of the prima facie case and employer burden, often in an attempt to define their seemingly amorphous terms.

### b. Religious Belief

With respect to the employee's religious belief, employers have questioned the religion itself, the sincerity of the employee's belief, and the necessity of the practices for which the employee sought accommodation. Courts examine consistency in the employee's religious practices but allow plaintiffs some latitude for occasional deviations from established practices or for individual interpretation of tenets. The early free exercise cases brought under the First Amendment arguably influence court treatment of employee religious beliefs and practices under Title VII. For example, in *Boomsma v. Greyhound Food Management, Inc.*,[119] the court expressed its concern "that plaintiff had substituted for a fellow employee for Sunday work on one occasion, and ... had performed Sunday duty for the Air Force National Guard."[120] The plaintiff failed to explain how his religious belief against working on Sundays permitted either of these activities. Relying on Second Circuit guidance, however, the court concluded that "the burden on the plaintiff to establish a bona fide religious belief 'is not a heavy one.'"[121]

114 42 U.S.C.A. § 2000e(j) (West 2013).

115 Philbrook v. Ansonia Bd. of Educ., 757 F.2d 476, 481 (2d Cir. 1985) *aff'd and remanded*, 479 U.S. 60 (1986).

116 Chalmers v. Tulon Co. of Richmond, 101 F.3d 1012 (4th Cir. 1996); *see also* 42 U.S.C.A. § 2000e (j).

117 515 F.3d 307 (4th Cir. 2008).

118 Firestone Fibers, 515 F.3d at 312 [quoting Ansonia Bd. of Educ. v. Philbrook, 479 U.S. 60, 67 (quoting Hardison, 432 U.S. at 84)].

119 639 F. Supp. 1448 (W.D. Mich. 1986).

120 *Id.* at 1453.

121 *Id.* (quoting Ansonia, 757 F.2d at 482).

The EEOC's formal definition of "religion" incorporates the evaluative principles that the Supreme Court espoused in *United States v. Seeger*[122] and *Welsh v. United States*.[123] The EEOC explained that "the Commission will define religious practices to include moral or ethical beliefs as to what is right and wrong which are sincerely held with the strength of traditional religious views."[124] Additionally, the employee's belief system need not be formally recognized or incorporated into an established religion.[125] The Supreme Court also later held in *Thomas v. Review Board of the Indiana Employment Security Division*,[126] that "religious beliefs need not be acceptable, logical, consistent, or comprehensible to others in order to merit First Amendment protection."[127]

Although the EEOC and the courts are reluctant to delve into whether a religious practice stems from a legitimate religion that qualifies for protection under Title VII,[128] occasionally courts find such an evaluation unavoidable. Courts typically examine an employee's religious beliefs if they appear to constitute a philosophical attitude rather than an established religion or if a particular belief system differs dramatically from what one would consider a valid expression of faith. For example, the California Court of Appeal held that an employee's veganism reflected his personal life philosophy rather than an organized religion.[129] Therefore, Title VII's accommodation mandate did not apply.[130] However, in contrast, the U.S. District Court for the Eastern District of Wisconsin held that the white supremacist belief system of "Creativity"[131] did qualify as a religion in the employee's life and that the employee was entitled to protection under Title VII.[132]

In *Malnak v. Yogi*, the Third Circuit explored generally whether a religion is eligible for protection under Title VII.[133] Referencing U.S. religious pluralism, a *Malnak*

[122] 380 U.S. 163, 183–5 (1965) (explaining that the "task is to decide whether the beliefs professed by a registrant are sincerely held and whether they are, in his own scheme of things, religious").

[123] 398 U.S. 333, 339–40 (1970)(holding that "the central consideration in determining whether the registrant's beliefs are religious is whether these beliefs play the role of a religion and function as a religion in the registrant's life.")

[124] 29 C.F.R. § 1605.1 (West 2013).

[125] The code states: "The fact that no religious group espouses such beliefs or the fact that the religious group to which the individual professes to belong may not accept such belief will not determine whether the belief is a religious belief of the employee or prospective employee." *Id.*

[126] 450 U.S. 707 (1981).

[127] *Id.* at 714.

[128] Redmond v. GAF Corp., 574 F.2d 897 (7th Cir. 1978) (explaining the interpretation of religion under the 1972 amendment to Title VII). The *Redmond* court held

> The Supreme Court has never had the occasion to interpret this phrase of the 1972 amendment, but the two circuits which have considered it, the Fifth and Sixth Circuits, both have concluded that it is not to be given a narrow or limited interpretation. We conclude that conduct which is "religiously motivated," i.e., "all forms and aspects of religion, however eccentric," is protected.

*Id.* at 900–1.

[129] Friedman v. S. Cal. Permanente Med. Group, 125 Cal. Rptr. 2d 663, 667 (Ct. App. 2002).

[130] *Id.* at 685.

[131] *See* Lawrence D. Rosenthal, *Title VII's Unintended Beneficiaries: How Some White Supremacist Groups Will Be Able to Use Title VII to Gain Protection from Discrimination in the Workplace*, 84 *Temp. L. Rev.* 443 (2012), for a discussion of how white supremacist groups have sought and obtained Title VII protection.

[132] Peterson v. Wilmur Communications, Inc., 205 F. Supp. 2d 1014 (E.D. Wis. 2002).

[133] 592 F.2d 197 (3d Cir. 1979).

concurrence reasoned, "Under the modern view, 'religion' is not confined to the relationship of man with his Creator, either as a matter of law or as a matter of theology."[134] A number of federal circuit courts have relied on Judge Adams's concurring analysis in *Malnak*.[135]

Judge Adams formulated a three-part test to be used in evaluating whether a set of beliefs earns protection as a religion under Title VII. The first part identifies "the content of the supposed religion, not to determine its truth or falsity, or whether it is schismatic or orthodox, but to determine whether the subject matter it comprehends is consistent with the assertion that it is, or is not, a religion."[136] The second step involves a determination of whether the belief system presented is comprehensive in its approach to answering life's "'ultimate' questions."[137] Third, a court must consider how well the "formal, external, or surface signs"[138] of the religion in question compare with those of other accepted religions. For example, these signs might include "formal services, ceremonial functions, the existence of clergy, structure and organization, efforts at propagation, observation of holidays and other similar manifestations associated with the traditional religions."[139] However, Judge Adams also highlighted that "a religion may exist without any of these signs."[140]

Although courts remain reluctant to question a given religious tradition, they more readily examine a self-professed adherent's sincerity and whether the accommodation request is based on religious motivations.[141] The inquiry includes whether professed religious dedication masks secular motives[142] If the employee strays at all from the

[134] *Id.* at 207. The Judge Adams further explained:

> It seems unavoidable, from *Seeger*, *Welsh*, and *Torcaso*, that the Theistic formulation presumed to be applicable in the late nineteenth century cases is no longer sustainable.... Even theologians of traditionally recognized faiths have moved away from a strictly Theistic approach in explaining their own religions. Such movement, when coupled with the growth in the United States, of many Eastern and non-traditional belief systems, suggests that the older, limited definition would deny "religious" identification to faiths now adhered to by millions of Americans.

*Id.* (footnote omitted).

[135] *See* Friedman v. S. Cal. Permanente Med. Group, 125 Cal. Rptr.2d 663, 678–9 (2002) [citing and stating in brackets: DeHart v. Horn, 227 F.3d 47, 52 n. 3 (3d Cir. 2000); Love v. Reed, 216 F.3d 682, 687 (8th Cir. 2000) ("adopting analysis based on Third Circuit ruling premised entirely on Judge Adams's concurring opinion in *Malnak*"); U.S. v. Meyers, 95 F.3d 1475, 1483 (10th Cir. 1996) ("analyzing religion issue using in part a Third Circuit ruling premised upon Judge Adams's Malnak concurring opinion"); Alvarado v. City of San Jose, 94 F.3d 1223, 1227 (9th Cir. 1996); Dettmer v. Landon, 799 F.2d 929, 931 (4th Cir. 1986); Grove v. Mead School Distr. No., 344 753 F.2d 1528, 1534 (9th Cir. 1985); Wiggins v. Sargent, 753 F.2d 663, 666 (8th Cir. 1985) ("adopting Third Circuit test"); Africa v. Com. of Pa., 662 F.2d 1025, 1033–4 (3d Cir. 1981)].

[136] Malnak, 592 F.2d at 208.

[137] *Id.* at 208–9.

[138] *Id.* at 209.

[139] *Id.*

[140] *Id.*

[141] *See* E.E.O.C. v. Abercrombie & Fitch Stores, Inc., 798 F. Supp. 2d 1272, 1284 (N.D. Okla. 2011) *rev'd on other grounds*, E.E.O.C. v. Abercrombie & Fitch Stores, Inc., 731 F.3d 1106 (10th Cir. 2013). Note that the Tenth Circuit reversed because "Ms. Elauf never informed Abercrombie prior to its hiring decision that her practice of wearing a hijab was based on her religious beliefs and ... that she would need an accommodation for the practice, because of a conflict between it and Abercrombie's clothing policy." Abercrombie, 731 F.3d at 1116. This holding helps to explain the notice obligation discussed below. *See infra* at 35.

[142] Int'l Soc. For Krishna Consciousness, Inc. v. Barber, 650 F.2d 430, 432 (2d Cir. 1981) ("Our openness is legitimately restricted only when underlying motives of deception and fraud hide behind a facade of

accepted tenets of his or her religious belief, an employer litigates the sincerity of the employee's belief to defeat the associated claim for workplace accommodation.[143] For example, clothing retailer Abercrombie & Fitch asserted doubts as to an employee's religious sincerity in two cases on point. In the first, an employee who had converted to the Apostolic faith after she was hired by Abercrombie requested to be able to wear modest clothing that did not conform to the retailer's "look" policy.[144] In denying the plaintiff's motion for summary judgment, the court noted Abercrombie's evidence that the employee had arrived to depositions wearing clothing almost identical to garments that the retailer required that she wear in the store.[145] In the second Abercrombie case, a female Muslim applicant who requested to wear her headscarf while working was refused employment because Abercrombie claimed the headscarf was contrary to its "look" policy.[146] In presenting its side of the case, the retailer challenged the sincerity of the teenager's beliefs on the basis that "she did not know the street address of her mosque, does not regularly attend Friday services, and does not pray five times a day or every day."[147] In issuing a summary-judgment decision in favor of the plaintiff, the court stated

> [Our] focus must be on the sincerity of Elauf's belief that she must wear a head scarf – not whether she observed all tenets of the Muslim faith – because it was her belief about head scarves that required accommodation. And the *purpose* of the inquiry, according to *Philbrook, supra,* is whether this belief is held as a matter of conscience or instead, animated by motives of deception and fraud.[148]

Thus, though employers suggest that any infraction constitutes evidence of insincerity, the courts require more for dismissal. Courts allow plaintiffs to grow in their religious practices and to vary the strength of their commitment over time.[149] Judges also acknowledge that plaintiffs are human and may not always meet the requirements of their faiths.[150] Finally, as evidenced earlier, adherents need not be experts in their faiths nor follow every rule to establish a prima facie case.

conscience and religious belief"); E.E.O.C. v. Chemsico, Inc., 216 F. Supp. 2d 940, 948 (E.D. Mo. 2002) (noting union concern that allowing the accommodation would result in an increase in accommodation requests and that the representative already receives "three to four fake notes on any given Saturday").

143 E.E.O.C. v. Alamo Rent-A-Car LLC, 432 F. Supp. 2d 1006, 1011 (D. Ariz. 2006) (rejecting employer's contention that employee's willingness to remove headscarf during prior Ramadan compromised the sincerity of her belief and holding that the analysis must focus on the facts at issue and employee's sincerity at that point in time); E.E.O.C. v. Red Robin Gourmet Burgers, Inc., C04-1291JLR, 2005 WL 2090677 (W.D. Wash. Aug. 29, 2005) (finding that employee covered religious tattoos on occasion but could articulate the difference between purposeful and incidental coverage).

144 E.E.O.C. v. Abercrombie & Fitch Stores, Inc., 4:08CV1470 JCH, 2009 WL 3517578 (E.D. Mo. Oct. 26, 2009).

145 *Id.* at 3.

146 Abercrombie, 798 F. Supp. 2d at 1275.

147 *Id.* at 1284.

148 *Id.* at 1285.

149 E.E.O.C. v. Ilona of Hungary, Inc., 108 F.3d 1569, 1575–6 (7th Cir. 1997) (responding to employer, who questioned sincerity of employee's Judaism because she did not observe every Jewish holiday, that such observance was not essential and strength of faith could vary over time).

150 E.E.O.C. v. Chemsico, Inc., 216 F. Supp. 2d 940, 950 (E.D. Mo. 2002) (finding that sincere religious belief of plaintiff, who was member of Church of God which did not allow sex before marriage and who had delivered a child out of wedlock, did not require that adherent never fell below religious standards).

Employers also contest whether the practice or observance for which the employee seeks accommodation is religious in nature and covered by section (j). For example, a court held for an employer that setting up for a church play constituted a voluntary social obligation that merited no religious accommodation.[151] In another example, an employee failed to demonstrate that religion, rather than a personal aversion, motivated the refusal to wear a gingerbread necklace during the holiday season.[152] Court analysis of practice remains tricky because, as noted earlier, an employee's religious beliefs need not derive from a recognized or organized religious tradition. However, the employee still must demonstrate that the alleged protected activity is grounded in a faith for which the employee can establish a record of observation.[153]

### c. Notified Employer of Belief

Courts have consistently held that an applicant or employee must notify the employer of his or her religious beliefs so that the employer is afforded an opportunity to accommodate related practices. This notification must be specific enough that the employer has a general understanding of what the employee's religious beliefs are and what accommodation of those beliefs might entail. The Seventh Circuit clarified that "[a]n employee has a duty to give fair notice of religious practices that might interfere with his [or her] employment. On the other hand, an employer cannot 'shield itself from liability by … intentionally remaining in the dark.'"[154]

No court expects an employer to be an expert in all religions,[155] nor to monitor continually its workforce for religious needs.[156] In *Reed v. Great Lakes Companies, Inc.*,

151 Wessling v. Kroger Co., 554 F. Supp. 548, 552 (E.D. Mich. 1982).

152 Kreilkamp v. Roundy's, Inc., 428 F. Supp. 2d 903, 908 (W.D. Wis. 2006).

153 *See, e.g.*, Abercrombie, 731 F.3d at 1119. The *Abercrombie* court explained

> First, an applicant or employee may engage in practices that are associated with a particular religion, but do so for cultural or other reasons that are not grounded in that religion. If so, an employer's discrimination against that individual for engaging in that practice … would not contravene Title VII's religion-discrimination provisions.

*Id.*

154 Xodus v. Wackenhut Corp., 619 F.3d 683, 686 (7th Cir. 2010) [citations omitted and quoting EEOC v. Sears, Roebuck & Co., 417 F.3d 789, 804 (7th Cir.2005)].

155 *Wilkerson v. New Media Tech. Charter Sch., Inc.* provides an example of a court's unwillingness to require that employers be familiar with every employees' nuanced faith traditions and accommodate the related practices. Wilkerson v. New Media Tech. Charter Sch. Inc., 522 F.3d 315, 319–20 (3d Cir. 2008) ("[W]e do not impute to the employer the duty to possess knowledge of particularized beliefs of religious sects."). In that case, the Third Circuit affirmed a ruling that an employer's general knowledge of an employee's Christian beliefs was not sufficient to put the employer on notice that the employee would need an accommodation at a ceremony where alcoholic drinks were served. Wilkerson, 522 F.3d at 319. In another example, the Seventh Circuit Court of Appeals held that an employer was not required to equate an applicant's use of the word "belief" with a particular religious tradition and that the applicant should have been more explicit regarding his need for accommodation. Xodus, 619 F.3d at 683. When Xodus applied for a position with Wackenhut Corp, the hiring manager told Xodus that he would need to cut his dreadlocks to comply with the organization's grooming policy. *Id.* at 685. In affirming the lower court, the appellate court explained, "Xodus claims that his use of the word 'belief' and the dreadlocks themselves sufficed to notify McCuller of the religious nature of his hairstyle. But unlike race or sex, a person's religion is not always readily apparent." *Id.* at 686.

156 Redmond, 574 F.2d at 902 ("We agree with defendant that accommodation is not so onerous as to charge an employer with the responsibility for continually searching for each potential religious conflict of every

the court explained that "[e]ven if he wears a religious symbol, such as a cross or a yarmulke, this may not pinpoint his particular beliefs and observances; and anyway employers are not charged with detailed knowledge of the beliefs and observances associated with particular sects."[157] Thus courts have held that the appearance of an employee does not create a duty for an employer to understand how that employee may need to be accommodated.

Debates arise about whether an employee need directly and explicity notify an employer of a need for religious accommodation to establish a prima facie case of a failure to accommodate.[158] For example, in the *Abercrombie* headscarf case, the district court held that the manager's past experience in hiring and the fact that the Muslim applicant wore a headscarf to her interview allowed for sufficient notice that the applicant would require an accommodation.[159] The court also noted that the hiring manager had contacted a district manager to discuss the possible need for an accommodation.[160] The Tenth Circuit reversed and remanded this case on the ground that "Ms. Elauf never informed Abercrombie *before* its hiring decision that her practice of wearing a hijab was based upon her religious beliefs and that she needed an accommodation for that practice."[161] Therefore, the court found that Abercrombie did not have notice of the need for accommodation.

Case law also emphasizes that employees should seek accommodation at the management level with the human resources unit rather than through a local manager.[162] Otherwise, employees who experience a change in management may need to renotify their employers of the need for accommodation.[163]

employee. The employee has the duty to inform his [or her] employer of his [or her] religious needs so that the employer has notice of the conflict.").

157 Reed v. Great Lakes Companies, Inc., 330 F.3d 931, 936 (7th Cir. 2003).

158 In *Hellinger v. Eckerd Corp.*, the court held that an applicant's reference to a need for accommodation served as sufficient notification [67 F. Supp. 2d 1359, 1363–4 (S.D. Fla. 1999)]. In *Hellinger*, the pharmacist candidate failed to inform the employer during the interview and on his application form that his Orthodox Jewish faith precluded him from selling condoms and that, as a result, he would need an accommodation (Hellinger, 67 F. Supp. 2d at 1361). The employer learned of the need when the hiring manager consulted one of Hellinger's references and decided against hiring the pharmacist based on the reference (*id.* at 1363). In denying the employer's motion for summary judgment, the court explained that the employer was not relieved of the obligation to accommodate because the employer received notice, even if not from the plaintiff (*id.* at 1363–4). The court stated

> It would be hyper-technical, based on the facts of this case, to require notice of the Plaintiff's religious beliefs to come only from the Plaintiff. The notice requirement is meant in part to allow the company an opportunity to attempt to reasonably accommodate the Plaintiff's beliefs. The Defendant was not deprived of the opportunity to attempt to accommodate the Plaintiff's beliefs merely because the notice did not come from the Plaintiff.

*Id.* The district court also cautioned that its ruling "does not place the burden of inquiry on the employer." *Id.* at 1364.

159 Abercrombie, 798 F. Supp. 2d at 1286.

160 *Id.*

161 Abercrombie, 731 F.3d at 1122 (italics added).

162 *See also* Johnson v. AutoZone, Inc., 768 F. Supp. 2d 1124, 1129 (N.D. Ala. 2011).

163 In *Miller v. Safeway, Inc.*, a native Alaskan wore his hair long because of his spiritual beliefs [102 P.3d 282, 285 (Alaska 2004)]. Although long hair violated the store's grooming policy for males, Miller received an accommodation from the local store manager who had hired him (*id.*). When Safeway purchased the chain for which Miller worked, his local accommodation continued only for another eighteen months (*id.* at 286). When Safeway slated Miller for a transfer to a different store, it informed him that he would

Finally, an employee must notify his or her employer in advance of the need for a religious accommodation. In *Johnson v. Angelica Uniform Group, Inc.*, an employee missed twelve days of work to observe the Holy Days established by the Worldwide Church of God and was subsequently fired.[164] The court upheld the district court's ruling that the employee had failed to establish a prima facie case because she had not informed the employer in advance of her need for accommodation.[165]

### d. Disciplined for Failure to Comply

In an adverse employment action, courts look for negative consequences similar to those that occur in other types of discrimination cases.[166] For example, a plaintiff might provide the court with evidence that he or she was "discharged or disciplined as a result of his [or her] failure to comply with an employer demand which conflicted with his [or her] religious beliefs."[167] However, a demotion that does not result in a salary reduction may legitimately accommodate the employee's religious practice.[168] Courts also have found an employee's requested transfer that resulted in a religious conflict as excusing the employer's need to accommodate.[169] Additionally, a "failure to promote with continued accommodation" was not sufficiently adverse to constitute a Title VII violation.[170]

After the employee successfully makes the prima facie case, the burden shifts to the employer. Circuit courts require employers to show (1) proof that the employer attempted a reasonable accommodation or (2) a demonstration that accommodation constituted an undue hardship.[171] They split on how to assign these burdens, however. The First, Third, and Fourth Circuits treat reasonable accommodation and undue hardship as two distinct defenses to a charge of religious discrimination.[172]

need to cut his hair or face termination (*id.*). In this case, if Miller had sought the accommodation at the organizational level, a record of his need for accommodation would have better protected him during the transition in the store ownership. The court granted Safeway summary judgment because of Miller's failure to give notice of a need for religious accommodation during the ownership transition (*id.* at 292–3).

164 762 F.2d 671, 672 (8th Cir. 1985).

165 Johnson, 762 F.2d at 673.

166 Lake v. B.F. Goodrich Co., 837 F.2d 449, 450 (11th Cir. 1988) (finding that employee was fired for failure to report to work for a weekend shift).

167 Wilshin v. Allstate Ins. Co., 212 F. Supp. 2d 1360, 1373 (M.D. Ga. 2002).

168 Mathewson v. Florida Game & Fresh Water Fish Comm'n, 693 F. Supp. 1044, 1050 (M.D. Fla. 1988) *aff'd sub nom.* Mathewson v. Florida Game & Freshwater Fish Comm'n, 871 F.2d 123 (11th Cir. 1989) (finding an accommodation for an employee offered a demotion without a salary reduction to enable him to avoid working on Saturdays).

169 Irvin v. Aubrey, 92 S.W.3d 87, 90 (Ky. Ct. App. 2001).

170 Johnson v. AutoZone, Inc., 768 F. Supp. 2d 1124, 1139–40 (N.D. Ala. 2011).

171 *See infra* notes 172–78 and accompanying text.

172 *See, e.g.*, E.E.O.C. v. Union Independiente de la Autoridad de Acueductos y Alcantarillados de Puerto Rico, 279 F.3d 49, 55 (1st Cir. 2002) (holding that after the plaintiff has established his prima facie case, "the burden shifts to the union to show that it made a reasonable accommodation of the religious practice or show that any accommodation would result in undue hardship"); United States v. Bd. of Educ. for Sch. Dist. of Philadelphia, 911 F.2d 882, 887 (3d Cir. 1990) (finding that there are two defenses, accommodation and undue hardship); Firestone Fibers, 515 F.3d at 312 [explaining that the employer's burden "is a two-prong inquiry," and employer "must demonstrate *either* (1) that it provided the plaintiff with a reasonable accommodation for his or her religious observances *or* (2) that such accommodation was not provided because it would have caused an undue hardship"].

In contrast, the other circuits view the employer's burden as a two-step process. The process begins with presentation of evidence of an attempt to accommodate. Then, if necessary, the employer continues with evidence of an undue burden.[173] The Ninth Circuit follows this process but adds a condition that the employer negotiate with the employee.[174] The Ninth Circuit also permits a demonstration of good-faith efforts as part of a showing of reasonable accommodation.[175]

e. Employee Responsibility for Accommodation

Some courts place the burden on the employee to suggest a reasonable accommodation to the employer. For example, in *Yott v. North American Rockwell Corp.*,[176] the Ninth Circuit stated, "The plaintiff has the burden of proving that he has offered to the employer an accommodation which is acceptable to him."[177] The Seventh Circuit specifically rejected this approach in *Redmond v. GAF Corp.*, reasoning that "While we feel plaintiff should be free, even encouraged, to suggest to his employer possible ways of accommodating his religious needs, we see nothing in the statute to support the position that this is part of plaintiff's burden of proof."[178]

173 Knight v. Connecticut Dept. of Pub. Health, 275 F.3d 156, 167 (2d Cir. 2001) (explaining that after an employee establishes his prima facie case, "the burden then shifts to the employer to show it could not accommodate the employees' religious beliefs without undue hardship"); Weber v. Roadway Exp., Inc., 199 F.3d 270, 273 (5th Cir. 2000) (stating that the burden shifts to the employer to demonstrate that it was unable to accommodate the employee's beliefs without undue hardship); Virts v. Consol. Freightways Corp. of Delaware, 285 F.3d 508, 516 (6th Cir. 2002) ("Once the plaintiff has established a prima facie case, the burden shifts to the defendant employer to show that it could not reasonably accommodate the employee without undue hardship."); Baz v. Walters, 782 F.2d 701, 705–6 (7th Cir. 1986) (holding that the employer's burden is "to demonstrate that he cannot accommodate the plaintiff's religious practice without undue hardship to his business"); Harrell v. Donahue, 638 F.3d 975, 979 (8th Cir. 2011) ("Title VII requires an employer to reasonably accommodate the religious beliefs of its employees unless the employer can demonstrate that doing so would impose an undue hardship."); Toledo v. Nobel-Sysco, Inc., 892 F.2d 1481, 1486 (10th Cir. 1989) ["Once a plaintiff has made out a prima facie case, 'the burden shifts to the employer to show that it was unable reasonably to accommodate the plaintiff's religious needs without undue hardship.'"(citations omitted)]; Morrissette-Brown v. Mobile Infirmary Med. Ctr., 506 F.3d 1317, 1321 (11th Cir. 2007) [stating that "the burden shifts to the defendant to 'demonstrate that he is unable to reasonably accommodate to an employee's or prospective employee's religious observance or practice without undue hardship on the conduct of the employer's business.'" (citations omitted)].

174 Opuku-Boateng v. State of Cal., 95 F.3d 1461, 1467 (9th Cir. 1996) {stating that after the employee establishes a prima facie case, "the burden shifts to the employer to show that it 'negotiate[d] with the employee in an effort reasonably to accommodate the employee's religious beliefs'" [quoting EEOC v. Hacienda Hotel, 881 F.2d 1504, 1513 (9th Cir.1989)]}. The court also held that if the negotiations fail to eliminate the religious conflict, "the employer must either accept the employee's proposal or demonstrate that it would cause undue hardship were it to do so." *Id.*

175 Anderson v. Gen. Dynamics Convair Aerospace Div., 589 F.2d 397, 401 (9th Cir. 1978) (concluding that the burden was on the employer and union "to prove that they made good faith efforts to accommodate Anderson's religious beliefs and, if those efforts were unsuccessful, to demonstrate that they were unable reasonably to accommodate his beliefs without undue hardship").

176 428 F. Supp. 763, 769 (C.D. Cal. 1977) *aff'd*, 602 F.2d 904 (9th Cir. 1979).

177 Yott v. N. Am. Rockwell Corp., 428 F. Supp. 763, 769 (C.D. Cal. 1977) *aff'd*, 602 F.2d 904 (9th Cir. 1979).

178 Redmond, 574 F.2d at 901.

### f. Vague Terms: Reasonable Accommodation and Undue Hardship

The employer's burden to accommodate, through an employee's proposal or otherwise, attracts additional litigation because of vague terms in the statute. When Congress amended Title VII of the Civil Rights Act in 1972, it mandated an employer "to reasonably accommodate" the "religious observance or practice" of employees or prospective employees as long as that effort to accommodate does not create an "undue hardship on the conduct of the employer's business."[179] The amended definitions section, however, failed to specify what Congress meant by "reasonably accommodate" and "undue hardship."[180] Courts in each circuit have interpreted and explored the terms.[181] One judge suggested that whether an accommodation is reasonable is "difficult to boil down to a set formula. Instead, the determination of reasonableness is quintessentially a fact-bound inquiry that depends on the unique circumstances of each case."[182]

179 42 U.S.C.A. § 2000e(j) (West 2012).

180 Am. Postal Workers Union, San Francisco Local v. Postmaster Gen., 781 F.2d 772, 775 (9th Cir. 1986) ("The 'reach' of the obligation has simply never been spelled out by Congress or the EEOC."); Beadle v. Hillsborough County Sheriff's Dept., 29 F.3d 589, 592 (11th Cir. 1994) ("The phrases 'reasonably accommodate' and 'undue hardship' are not defined within the language of Title VII.").

181 *See, e.g.*, Smith v. Pyro Min. Co., 827 F.2d 1081, 1085 (6th Cir. 1987) ("The reasonableness ... must be determined on a case-by-case basis; what may be a reasonable accommodation for one employee may not be reasonable for another"); Maroko v. Werner Enterprises, Inc., 778 F. Supp. 2d 993, 1003 (D. Minn. 2011) (noting that the "Eighth Circuit has counseled that the reasonableness of a proposed accommodation often 'is a question for the jury because it turns on fact-intensive issues such as work demands [and] the strength and nature of the employee's religious conviction'"); Williams v. S. Union Gas Co., 529 F.2d 483, 489 (10th Cir. 1976) ("The phrases 'reasonably accommodate' and 'undue hardship' are relative terms and cannot be given any hard and fast meaning."); Beadle, 29 F.3d at 592 (finding that definitions of reasonable accommodation and undue hardship are "unclear under the statute and must be determined on a case-by-case basis."). In *Hardison*, the Court determined

> Cases decided by the Courts of Appeals since the enactment of the 1972 amendments to Title VII similarly provide us with little guidance as to the scope of the employer's obligation. In circumstances where an employer has declined to take steps that would burden some employees in order to permit another employee or prospective employee to observe his Sabbath, the Fifth, Sixth, and Tenth Circuits have found no violation for failure to accommodate.

Hardison, 432 U.S. at 75 n. 10; *see also*, Williams v. Southern Union Gas Co., 529 F.2d 483 (10th Cir. 1976) (finding no issue of law and no violation because employer did not normally require plaintiff to work on his Sabbath); Reid v. Memphis Publishing Co., 521 F.2d 512 (6th Cir. 1975) (finding no evidence that accommodation would not have been an undue hardship for the employer); Johnson v. United States Postal Service, 497 F.2d 128 (5th Cir. 1974) (ruling that further accommodation in a small post office would have posed an undue hardship for the Postal Service); *but see* Draper v. United States Pipe & Foundry Co., 527 F.2d 515 (6th Cir. 1975) (finding no undue hardship where an accommodation would cause other workers to become disgruntled); Cummins v. Parker Seal Co., 516 F.2d 544 (6th Cir. 1975) (holding that mild, infrequent complaints by co-workers would not have amounted to an undue hardship in accommodation), *aff'd by equally divided Court*, 429 U.S. 65 (1976), *vacated*, Parker Seal Co. v. Cummins, 433 U.S. 903 (1977); Riley v. Bendix Corp., 464 F.2d 1113 (5th Cir. 1972) (finding no evidence of undue hardship). One might explain these apparent intracircuit conflicts by the differing facts of each case, but neither the Fifth nor the Sixth Circuit has suggested a theory of decision to justify the differing results that they have reached.

182 Haliye v. Celestica Corp., 717 F. Supp. 2d 873, 881 (D. Minn. 2010). A number of cases focus on whether shift swapping between employees constitutes a reasonable accommodation. Courts have expressed concern that if they force a shift swap in the spirit of accommodation for one employee, they could inadvertently create an accommodation issue for the employer and another employee. *See, e.g.*, Lee v. ABF Freight Sys., Inc., 22 F.3d 1019, 1023 (10th Cir. 1994) (finding that an employer need not deny the shift

The Supreme Court first weighed in on the issue of what might constitute a reasonable accommodation in *Ansonia Board of Education v. Philbrook*.[183] *Ansonia* concerned a high school teacher who had decided to join the Worldwide Church of God,[184] which required that he miss six days of school in observance of Holy Days.[185] The collective-bargaining agreement (CBA) that governed the school's leave policy allowed for only three days of leave for religious observances.[186] Philbrook and the school board favored different accommodations. Philbrook requested that the school board permit him to use personal business leave for religious observance or that he pay a substitute and receive his full pay for the days off.[187] However, the board wanted Philbrook to take unpaid leave when he exhausted his religious leave allowance.[188]

The Supreme Court held that Title VII required only that the employer provide the employee with an accommodation, not that it be without cost to the employee[189] or that it be the accommodation that the employee preferred.[190] The Court explained, "Neither the terms nor the legislative history of § 701(j) supports the Court of Appeals' conclusion that an employer's accommodation obligation includes a duty to accept the employee's proposal unless that accommodation causes undue hardship on the conduct of the

or job preferences of some employees to accommodate the religious needs of others.) Additionally, some caution against requiring one employee to rely on the "goodwill" of other employees in order to satisfy a religious need. *See, e.g.*, N. Shore Univ. Hosp. v. State Human Rights Appeal Bd., 82 A.D.2d 799, 800, 439 N.Y.S.2d 408 (1981) [holding that an employer has an affirmative duty to assist the employee because the employee "'should not [be] forced to rely upon the good will of [his or] her coworkers or [his or] her powers of persuasion, else be relegated to choosing between [his or] her religious beliefs and [his or] her employment'" (citation omitted)].

If the employer does offer shift swapping as a potential solution, the employer must actively assist the employee in finding someone with whom to swap. E.E.O.C. v. Aldi, Inc., CIV.A. 06-01210, 2008 WL 859249 (W.D. Pa. Mar. 28, 2008) (finding that where courts had accepted shift swapping as an appropriate accommodation, employers had taken additional action beyond the existing scheduling procedure); Kenner v. Domtar Indus., Inc., 04-CV-4021, 2006 WL 522468 (W.D. Ark. Mar. 3, 2006) (stating that the "employer could not rely on existence of a shift-swap policy when employer took no effort in response to employee's notification of the conflict"); Miller v. Drennon, 966 F.2d 1443 (4th Cir. 1992) (unpublished) (holding that the shift swapping accommodation was as reasonable as those upheld in other circuits); Brener v. Diagnostic Ctr. Hosp., 671 F.2d 141 (5th Cir. 1982) (ruling that hospital's policy of allowing pharmacists to trade shifts was a reasonable accommodation).

The Ninth, Tenth, and Eleventh Circuits have found shift swapping to be a reasonable accommodation. *See, e.g.*, Hudson v. W. Airlines, Inc., 851 F.2d 261 (9th Cir. 1988) (holding that "collective-bargaining agreement provided employee with reasonable accommodations to eliminate her religious conflicts ... [by allowing] employee to trade shifts with coworkers"); United States v. City of Albuquerque, 545 F.2d 110, 113 (10th Cir. 1976) (affirming the district court's holding that trading shifts was a reasonable accommodation); Beadle, 29 F.3d 589 (holding that a neutral rotating shift system and shift swaps within the system represent reasonable accommodations).

183 479 U.S. 60 (1986).

184 *Id.* at 62.

185 *Id.*

186 *Id.* at 63–4.

187 *Id.* at 64–5.

188 *Id.* at 70.

189 *Id.* (holding that it was reasonable for employee to take a day of unpaid leave).

190 At least one court determined that an employer could encounter more difficulty crafting an accommodation if the employee's belief system dictated that a religious violation resulted when anyone worked on the holy day. *See, e.g.*, U.S. E.E.O.C. v. J.P. Stevens & Co., Inc., 740 F. Supp. 1135, 1138 (M.D.N.C. 1990) (explaining that accommodation failed because employees refused to request that someone else commit what they considered to be a sin).

employer's business."[191] The Court cautioned that "[t]he extent of undue hardship on the employer's business is at issue only where the employer claims that it is unable to offer any reasonable accommodation without such hardship."[192] Although an employer might require the employee to take a day of unpaid leave for a religious observance, commented the Court, an employer has not offered a "reasonable accommodation when paid leave is provided for all purposes religious ones."[193]

*Ansonia* prompted two partial dissents. Justice Marshall wrote that a denial of pay constituted an adverse action rather than an accommodation.[194] For Marshall, further attempts at accommodation were required because the board's solution forced Philbrook "to choose between following his religious precepts with a partial forfeiture of salary and violating these precepts for work with full pay."[195] In stark contrast, Justice Stevens reasoned that no accommodation was necessary because Philbrook suffered an adverse consequence only because he took a day off of work, not because the school interfered with his religious practice.[196]

*Ansonia* provides some guidance to courts, employers, and employees regarding what constitutes a reasonable accommodation. However, accommodation cases tend to be relatively fact specific. Therefore, one should exercise caution in generalizing beyond the facts of a specific case. An Eighth Circuit district court used *Ansonia* as a signal that "it is not unreasonable to ask an employee to take unpaid leave while attempting to place him in another position."[197] However, the court noted that a mere possibility that an acceptable position might open up would not suffice as an accommodation.[198] Similarly, in *American Postal Workers Union, San Francisco Local v. Postmaster General*,[199] the Ninth Circuit held that an acceptable accommodation is one that "reasonably preserves the affected employee's employment status."[200] Additionally, the employer must update and adjust accommodations as work conditions change. For example, the Sixth Circuit held in *E.E.O.C. v. Arlington Transit Mix, Inc.*,[201] that an employer could not rely on a prior

191 Ansonia, 479 U.S. at 61 [Finding that an employer meets its legal obligation under § 701(j) when it offers a reasonable accommodation. Section 701(j) does not require that the employer prove that each of the employee's alternative accommodations would result in undue hardship.).

192 *Id.*

193 *Id.* at 71.

194 *Id.* at 74 (Marshall, J. dissenting) ("A forced reduction in compensation based on an employee's religious beliefs can be as much a violation of Title VII as a refusal to hire or grant a promotion.").

195 *Id.*

196 *Id.* at 81 (Stevens, J. dissenting). Justice Stevens wrote

> Every employee who takes a day off from work for an unauthorized purpose suffers the same inconvenience as Philbrook; each loses a day of pay and must make up the work associated with that day. The obligation to perform the work carries over, not because the employee has exercised his religion in the one case or satisfied a secular business need in another, but for the generic and shared reason that the employee was not paid for a day on which he was hired to do work. Since no statutory conflict between Philbrook's religion and his work duties occurred, the duty to accommodate his religious practices never arose.

*Id.* This reasoning appears consistent with Harlan's approach in *Braunfield* and Rehnquist's in *Thomas*.

197 Maroko, 778 F. Supp. 2d at 1002.

198 *Id.* at 1003 (disapproving that the plaintiff's employment would have been terminated if a position did not become available during the time of the leave).

199 781 F.2d 772 (9th Cir. 1986).

200 *Id.* at 776–7.

201 957 F.2d 219 (6th Cir. 1991).

accommodation to satisfy the employer's obligations under Title VII after the employee's schedule changed.[202]

### g. Vague Terms and Union Member Employees

Litigation over the meaning of "reasonable accommodation" and "undue hardship" has forced employers to navigate between employee accommodation and the obligations to honor CBAs and to deal fairly with unions, as mandated by the National Labor Relations Act.[203] The Supreme Court established priorities between competing interests and clarified the meaning of terms in *Trans World Airlines, Inc. v. Hardison*.[204]

Hardison, who joined the Worldwide Church of God after he began at TWA,[205] worked in a division that operated twenty-four hours a day, seven days a week.[206] Hardison informed his supervisor of his need to observe the church's Sabbath, from sundown on Friday to sundown on Saturday. His supervisor attempted to accommodate him and was initially successful in doing so.[207] However, when Hardison transferred to a different area, he lacked sufficient seniority for TWA to schedule him around his Sabbath on a regular basis.[208]

The *Hardison* decision serves a two-fold purpose. First, the Court reviewed the Sixth Circuit's position in *Dewey v. Reynolds Metals Co.* regarding the importance of CBAs.

202 E.E.O.C. v. Arlington Transit Mix, Inc., 957 F.2d 219, 222 (6th Cir. 1991) (finding that once the new schedule was implemented, the company should have made a reasonable attempt to accommodate employee's sincere religious needs).

203 29 U.S.C.A. § 151 *et seq.*

204 432 U.S. 63, 79 (1977); *but see* Dewey v. Reynolds Metals Co., 429 F.2d 324 (6th Cir. 1970) *aff'd*, 402 U.S. 689 (1971). In, *Dewey*, a Title VII case filed prior to the 1972 Section (j) amendments, an equally divided Supreme Court affirmed the Sixth Circuit's holding that an employer need not disrupt the schedules of other employees to accommodate the plaintiff's religious practices (*id.*). The Sixth Circuit held that "[t]he reason for Dewey's discharge was not discrimination on account of his religion; it was because he violated the provisions of the collective-bargaining agreement entered into by his union with his employer, which provisions were applicable equally to all employees" (*id.* at 330–1). The court expressed concern that its allowing Dewey to change his schedule for a religious reason "could create chaotic personnel problems and lead to grievances and additional arbitrations" (*id.*). The court continued, "The fundamental error of Dewey and the *amici curiae* is that they equate religious discrimination with failure to accommodate. We submit [that] these two concepts are entirely different. The employer ought not to be forced to accommodate each of the varying religious beliefs and practices of his employees" (*id.* at 335).

Other cases that comment on *Dewey* call its currency into question. For example, in *Michigan Dept. of Civil Rights ex rel. Parks v. Gen. Motors Corp., Fisher Body Div.* [412 Mich. 610, 635, 317 N.W.2d 16, 24 (1982)], the court found that

> *Dewey*, it must be observed, was decided before the 1972 amendment to Title VII defined "religion" to include religious observances and practices and imposed a reasonable accommodation duty on the employer. *Dewey* also preceded the United States Supreme Court decision in *Griggs v. Duke Power Co.*, which spoke of Title VII as proscribing "not only overt discrimination, but also practices that are fair in form, but discriminatory in operation." Further, the affirmance by an equally divided Supreme Court entitles *Dewey* to no precedential weight and its several alternative rationales, according to the Supreme Court, make its impact "inconclusive."

*Id.* (citation omitted).

205 Hardison, 432 U.S. at 67.

206 *Id.* at 66–7.

207 *Id.* at 67–8.

208 *Id.* at 68.

The Court stated, "Collective bargaining, aimed at effecting workable and enforceable agreements between management and labor, lies at the core of our national labor policy, and seniority provisions are universally included in these contracts."[209] This *Hardison* quotation confirms the primacy of CBAs and union seniority.

Second, the Court established the "*de minimis* standard" as a way for employers to judge whether the cost of a particular accommodation constituted an undue hardship. The Court explained:

To require TWA to bear more than a de minimis cost in order to give Hardison Saturdays off is an undue hardship.[15] Like abandonment of the seniority system, *to require TWA to bear additional costs when no such costs are incurred to give other employees the days off that they want would involve unequal treatment of employees on the basis of their religion*.[210] Here the Court sought to put all employees on equal footing regardless of their religious practices. Additionally, the Court's interest in preserving the integrity of the CBA and protecting union employers from additional grievances justified the *de minimis* standard to resolve the differences between the competing needs of employees, employers, and the union. This standard appears to present quite a hurdle, therefore, to employees.

Application of the *Hardison de minimis* analysis involves consideration of a variety of factors. Such factors may include (1) whether the employees are union members with an applicable CBA, (2) whether the accommodation would force the employer to assume additional payroll costs, (3) whether the accommodation would affect the employer's marketing brand or employee appearance, and (4) whether the accommodation might affect employee safety.[211]

209 *Id*. at 79. The Court continued, "Without a clear and express indication from Congress, we cannot agree with Hardison and the EEOC that an agreed-upon seniority system must give way when necessary to accommodate religious observances." *Id*.

210 *Id*. at 84 (emphasis added). The Court continued:

> By suggesting that TWA should incur certain costs in order to give Hardison Saturdays off the Court of Appeals would in effect require TWA to finance an additional Saturday off and then to choose the employee who will enjoy it on the basis of his religious beliefs. While incurring extra costs to secure a replacement for Hardison might remove the necessity of compelling another employee to work involuntarily in Hardison's place, it would not change the fact that the privilege of having Saturdays off would be allocated according to religious beliefs.

*Id*. at 84–5.

Justice Marshall dissented. He expressed concern especially for the potential erosion of tolerance for minority faiths. He wrote, "Particularly troublesome has been the plight of adherents to minority faiths who do not observe the holy days on which most businesses are closed – Sundays, Christmas, and Easter – but who need time off for their own days of religious observance" [*id*. at 85 (Marshall, J. dissenting)]. Marshall also spoke to the more general social effect:

> Today's decision deals a fatal blow to all efforts under Title VII to accommodate work requirements to religious practices.... An employer, the Court concludes, need not grant even the most minor special privilege to religious observers to enable them to follow their faith. As a question of social policy, this result is deeply troubling, for a society that truly values religious pluralism cannot compel adherents of minority religions to make the cruel choice of surrendering their religion or their job. And as a matter of law today's result is intolerable, for the Court adopts the very position that Congress expressly rejected in 1972, as if we were free to disregard congressional choices that a majority of this Court thinks unwise.

*Id*. at 86–7.

211 *See infra* notes 212–28 and accompanying text.

State and federal courts consistently find that employers need not disturb a negotiated CBA to accommodate an employee's religious practices.[212] In fact, courts often point to a neutral seniority system as itself an accommodation of employee needs.[213] This reasoning has its limitations, however. When one enterprising employer tried to use the seniority system at one of its unionized work locations to deny time off to an employee at a nonunionized site, the court declined to find evidence of an accommodation.[214]

Some judges express skepticism over a union seniority system as an accommodation because Title VII's employer obligations do not apply to unions.[215] Union representatives are free to insist on implementation of the CBA without fear of statutory repercussions. The Concurrence points out in *New York City Transit Authority v. State, Executive Department, Division of Human Rights* that the union did so insist, even though accommodation would have been fairly easy because of the sheer number of employees.[216]

212 Stolley v. Lockheed Martin Aeronautics Co., 228 F. App'x 379, 382 (5th Cir. 2007) (unpublished) (holding that the employer was not required to disrupt seniority system when the union was unwilling to waive provision in the CBA.); Haliye, 717 F. Supp. 2d at 879 ("This is not to say that there are no bright-line rules for determining whether a given accommodation is reasonable. For example, an employer is not required to deprive other employees of their contractual rights in order to accommodate an employee's religious needs."); *see also* In re New York City Transit Auth. v. State, Executive Dept., Div. of Human Rights, 211 A.D.2d 220, 223, 627 N.Y.S.2d 360, 362 (1995) *aff'd as modified*, 89 N.Y.2d 79, 674 N.E.2d 305 (1996) ("The courts are not free to downgrade the importance of union seniority rights."); Boomsma, 639 F. Supp. at 1454 (noting the neutrality of a scheduling system "particularly where such system is mandated by a collective bargaining agreement and operates through a seniority system"); Wren v. T.I.M.E.-D.C., Inc., 595 F.2d 441, 445 (8th Cir. 1979) (deciding that the employer was not required to depart from a seniority system to accommodate a religious need); Lee, 22 F.3d at 1023 (holding that "Title VII [does not] require an employer to violate a valid labor agreement to accommodate an employee").

213 *See, e.g.*, Firestone Fibers, 515 F.3d at 315. Relying on *Hardison*, the Fourth Circuit court reasoned

> Firestone's use of a seniority-based bidding system for working shifts "itself represent[s] a significant accommodation to the needs, both religious and secular, of all of [its] employees." This is because a "seniority system represents a neutral way of minimizing the number of occasions when an employee must work on a day that he would prefer to have off." When Jozwiakowski first reviewed Wise's request, he examined whether Wise could change shifts or positions. Unfortunately for Wise, Jozwiakowski could not grant such a move because Wise's preferred shift (7:00 a.m. to 3:00 p.m.) was occupied by employees with more seniority. As the district court noted, however, "[t]he fact that Wise does not currently benefit from the seniority system does not negate the reasonableness of the accommodation."

*Id.* (citation omitted).

214 New York & Massachusetts Motor Serv., Inc. v. Massachusetts Comm'n Against Discrimination, 401 Mass. 566, 574, 517 N.E.2d 1270, 1275 (1988).

215 *See, e.g.*, New York City Transit Auth. v. State, Executive Dept., Div. of Human Rights, 211 A.D.2d 220, 226, 627 N.Y.S.2d 360 (1995). In *New York City Transit Auth.*, a concurring opinion emphasized:

> My objection to the more or less automatic exemption of union seniority systems from civil rights statutes is that current State and Federal standards impose no obligation on the employer *and union* to accommodate an employee's religious beliefs, even where, as here, the employer is a quasi-public agency that derives a substantial portion of its operating revenue from public funding.... By requiring no effort at accommodation on the part of the employee union, the law invites intolerable discriminatory consequences through rigid adherence to contractual provisions.

*Id.* (citation omitted).

216 *Id.* Concerning the organization that employed over 33,000 workers, the concurrence expressed skepticism that "the accommodation of the occasional Sabbath observer would require another employee to forego the comfort of home and the company of offspring." *Id.* at 225. The Concurrence added, "It is clear from the record that the Transport Workers Union insisted on rigid adherence to the terms of its collective bargaining agreement and ultimately frustrated any attempt by the employer to permit its employee to take Saturdays off." *Id.* at 225–6.

The law incentivizes union and employer enforcement of the seniority structure guaranteed by a CBA much more than it than does a religious accommodation for a single employee.[217]

Courts routinely find that employer-borne accommodation costs, whether they result from an increase in salary or a decrease in production due to a missing worker, are not *de minimis*.[218] For example, in *United States v. City of Albuquerque*, the Tenth Circuit held that "Title VII does not require an employer … to bear the financial burden of an employee's religious convictions."[219] However, the EEOC reminds employers that they are always free to take on the additional costs to accommodate the needs of an employee.[220]

### h. Employee Appearance and Employer Brand

Courts also face conflicts over how an employee expresses religious beliefs through his or her appearance.[221] In one often-cited case, *Cloutier v. Costco Wholesale Corp.*,[222] an employee named Cloutier who had joined the Church of Body Modification pierced various parts of her body, including her face.[223] Local managers objected to the piercings as a violation of Costco's dress code and asked her to remove or cover them.

217 *Id.* at 222. (noting that the employer "declined" to contest issue with union).

218 Favero v. Huntsville Indep. Sch. Dist., 939 F. Supp. 1281, 1291 (S.D. Tex. 1996) *aff'd*, 110 F.3d 793 (5th Cir. 1997) (holding that "courts have repeatedly held that paying additional wages to accomplish an accommodation is an undue burden."); Mann v. Frank, 7 F.3d 1365, 1370 (8th Cir. 1993) ["'Any cost in efficiency or wage expenditure that is more than de minimis constitutes undue hardship.'" (quoting Hardison, 432 U.S. at 84)]; Red Robin Gourmet Burgers, C04-1291JLR, 2005 WL 2090677 (finding an undue hardship in "additional costs arising from lost efficiency or higher wages"); Lee, 22 F.3d 1 at 1023 ("The cost of hiring an additional worker or the loss of production that results from not replacing a worker who is unavailable due to a religious conflict can amount to undue hardship."); Hellinger, 67 F. Supp. 2d at 1364–5 (holding that precedent supported employer's argument that hiring additional pharmacy staff would be more than a *de minimis* cost).

219 423 F. Supp. 591 601 (D.N.M. 1975) *aff'd*, 545 F.2d 110 (10th Cir. 1976).

220 U.S. Equal Employment Opportunity Commission, *EEOC Best Practices for Eradicating Religious Discrimination in the Workplace, available at:* http://www.eeoc.gov/policy/docs/best_practices_religion.html (accessed April 28, 2013) (stating that "employers may of course choose voluntarily to incur whatever additional operational or financial costs they deem appropriate to accommodate an employee's religious need for scheduling flexibility").

221 Cloutier v. Costco Wholesale Corp., 390 F.3d 126, 136 (1st Cir. 2004). Courts considering Title VII religious discrimination claims also have upheld dress code policies that, like Costco's, are designed to appeal to customer preference or to promote a professional public image. *E.g.*, Hussein v. The Waldorf-Astoria, 134 F. Supp. 2d 591, 599 (S.D.N.Y.2001) ("Some courts have found that clean-shavenness is a bona fide occupational qualification in certain businesses and, in those situations, as long as the employer's grooming requirement is not directed at religion, enforcing the policy is not an unlawful discriminatory practice."), *aff'd*, 31 Fed. App'x 740 (2d Cir. 2002) (unpublished). The majority of religious discrimination cases in this arena appear to involve policies regulating facial hair. *E.g.*, EEOC v. Sambo's of Georgia, Inc., 530 F. Supp. 86 (N.D.Ga.1981) (holding that exempting a Sikh job applicant whose religious practice required that he wear a beard from a restaurant's no-facial-hair policy would constitute undue hardship); *cf.* Woods v. Safeway Stores, Inc., 420 F. Supp. 35, 43 (E.D. Va. 1976) (upholding an employer's no-beard policy against a claim of racial discrimination, finding that it served a legitimate business interest in maintaining an image of cleanliness to attract and retain customers), *aff'd*, 579 F.2d 43 (4th Cir. 1978).

222 390 F.3d 126 (1st Cir. 2004).

223 *Id.* at 128.

Cloutier objected.[224] Holding in favor of Costco, the First Circuit validated the retailer's right to cultivate a "neat, clean and professional image."[225] Similarly, in *E.E.O.C. v. Sambo's of Georgia, Inc.*, a Georgia district court upheld an employer's enforcement of grooming standards, commenting in dicta that even if those standards are "nothing more than an appeal to customer preference ... it is not the law that customer preference is an insufficient justification as a matter of law."[226]

### i. Safety

Employers also tend to prevail when religious dress or appearance preferences conflict with safety requirements.[227] For example, the Fifth Circuit held that a female applicant's request to wear skirts while working as a stocker at Sears would have constituted a safety hazard and de facto an undue hardship for the retailer.[228]

### j. Co-Worker Needs/Complaints

In defending an accommodation action, an employer may point to the need to maintain harmony in the workplace, especially when an accommodation would require a co-worker to take a less desirable schedule or to complete a larger share of the workload. However, courts typically require that co-worker complaints amount to more than a general inconvenience or constitute more than mere grumbling.[229]

224 *Id.*

225 *Id.* at 136.

226 530 F. Supp. 86, 91 (N.D. Ga. 1981).

227 McCarter v. Harris County, Tex., CIV.A. H-04-4159, 2006 WL 1281087 (S.D. Tex. May 5, 2006) (finding that the accommodation of allowing an employee to wear a skirt or dress when such attire increased job performance safety risks imposed an undue hardship on the employer); E.E.O.C. v. Kelly Services, Inc., 598 F.3d 1022, 1032 (8th Cir. 2010) (holding that a printer's refusal to hire a Muslim wearing a hijab constituted a legitimate safety concern and was not a pretext for discrimination); Bhatia v. Chevron U.S.A., Inc., 734 F.2d 1382 (9th Cir. 1984) (upholding the suspension of a Sikh employee who refused to shave after a new policy required employees to be clean-shaven so that respirator masks fit properly).

228 Johnson v. Sears Roebuck & Co., 66 F. App'x 523 (5th Cir. 2003).

229 *See, e.g.*, Brener, 671 F.2d at 147 (describing complaints of other employees as "mere grumbling underestimates the actual imposition on other employees in depriving them of their shift preference at least partly because they do not adhere to the same religion as Brener"); Burns v. S. Pac. Transp. Co., 589 F.2d 403, 407 (9th Cir. 1978) (holding that undue hardship requires more than grumbling or unhappiness; it requires an "imposition on co-workers or disruption of the work routine"). In *Cummins v. Parker Seal Co.* [516 F.2d 544 (6th Cir. 1975), *aff'd*, 429 U.S. 65 (1976), *judgment vacated on reh'g*, 433 U.S. 903 (1977), *and vacated*, 433 U.S. 903 (1977)], the court explained

> The objections and complaints of fellow employees, in and of themselves, do not constitute undue hardship in the conduct of an employer's business. If employees are disgruntled because an employer accommodates its work rules to the religious needs of one employee, under EEOC Regulation 1605 and 2000e(j) such grumbling must yield to the single employee's right to practice his [or her] religion. Moreover, the fact that Saturday Sabbath observance by one employee forces other employees to substitute during weekend hours does not demonstrate an undue hardship on the employer's business. It is conceivable that employee morale problems could become so acute that they would constitute an undue hardship. The EEOC, in interpreting Regulation 1605, has noted the possibility of undue hardship when the employer can make a persuasive showing that employee discontent will produce "chaotic personnel problems."

### k. No Hypotheticals

When holding that a particular circumstance constitutes an undue hardship, courts often require actual evidence of the hardship rather than speculation about negative consequences.[230] However, in an unpublished opinion from the Sixth Circuit, the court stated that the employer need not prove unequivocally that the accommodation will result in an undue hardship. The court reasoned that "[s]urely Congress did not intend that an employer must actually undertake an accommodation that will inevitably cause undue hardship."[231] Affirming the district court's summary judgment for the employer, the appellate court indicated that the office was too small for the employer to allow all the plaintiff's requested leave when she had already exhausted more than her accumulated time. The employer need not implement a particular accommodation in order to judge its effectiveness or cost.[232]

In *Cloutier*, the employee claimed that her appearance had not prompted any complaints of which she was aware.[233] The First Circuit acknowledged sister courts' similar hesitancy to rule on hypothetical hardships.[234] However, it still affirmed summary judgment for the employer. The court reasoned that the employee's desired accommodation "would be an undue hardship because it would adversely affect the employer's public image. Costco has made a determination that facial piercings, aside from earrings, detract from the 'neat, clean and professional image' that it aims to cultivate. Such a business determination is within its discretion."[235]

Cummins v. Parker Seal Co., 516 F.2d at 550 [citing EEOC Decision No. 72-0606 (Dec. 22, 1971), CCH EEOC DEC. P 6310, at 4555 (1972); EEOC Decision No. 71-463 (Nov. 13, 1970), CCH EEOC DEC. P 6206, at 4350 (1972)].

230 *See, e.g.*, E.E.O.C. v. Aldi, Inc., CIV.A. 06-01210, 2008 WL 859249 (W.D. Pa. Mar. 28, 2008) (chastising the employer for presenting only hypothetical generalizations of potential costs to support its claim of undue hardship); Smith, 827 F.2d at 1086 (finding that "[a]n employer must ... present evidence of undue hardship; it cannot rely merely on speculation"); Anderson, 589 F.2d at 402 (concluding that "[u]ndue hardship cannot be proved by assumptions nor by opinions based on hypothetical facts"); Alamo Rent-A-Car, 432 F. Supp. 2d at 1015 ("Alamo fails to support its assertion of undue burden with anything other than speculation, which is not a basis to establish a genuine material fact."); Abercrombie, 798 F. Supp. 2d at 1287 (ruling that the employer should have attempted "to collect or analyze data to corroborate his opinion" using the data from similar accommodations that had been granted). In *Draper v. U.S. Pipe & Foundry Co.*, the court stated

> [W]e are somewhat skeptical of hypothetical hardships that an employer thinks might be caused by an accommodation that never has been put into practice. The employer is on stronger ground when he has attempted various methods of accommodation and can point to hardships that actually resulted.

Draper, 527 F.2d at 520.

231 DePriest v. Dep't of Human Services of State of Tenn., 830 F.2d 193, 4 (6th Cir. 1987) (unpublished).

232 *Id.* at 1, 4; *but see* Red Robin Gourmet Burgers, C04-1291JLR, 2005 WL 2090677. The *Red Robin* court took issue with the employer's argument that it had presented "concrete evidence" in the form of a company profile and customer study. The court held that "Red Robin fails to present any evidence that visible tattoos are inconsistent with these goals (to present a family-oriented and kid-friendly image) generally, or that its customers specifically share this perception" (*id.* at 5). Instead, the court stated, the employer must present "evidence of 'actual imposition on co-workers or disruption of the work routine' to demonstrate undue hardship" [*id.* (citation omitted)].

233 Cloutier, 390 F.3d at 135.

234 *Id.*

235 *Id.* at 136.

### l. Special Case of Muslim Employees

As noted earlier, EEOC charges by Muslims of workplace religious discrimination or failure to accommodate have increased by 143 percent since 2001. They accounted for 21.8 percent in 2011.[236] Accommodation requests by Muslims typically focus on appearance, such as clearance to wear a beard or a headscarf.[237] Anecdotal evidence in several case histories indicates that Muslims tend to be unsuccessful in pursuing religious accommodation requests.[238] This phenomenon deserves further research.

In *E.E.O.C. v. GEO Group, Inc.*, a private prison denied three Muslim employees a variation from the uniform policy to allow them to wear headscarves.[239] Ruling for the employer prison, the Third Circuit cited safety concerns presented by the headscarves: the inability to identity the wearer adequately and the possibility that prisoners would use the headscarves to choke the female employees during a riot. The court wrote that "prison is not a summer camp"[240] and that the employer was entitled to take measures designed to prevent these dangers.[241]

In his dissent, Judge Tashima focused on safety risks that might constitute more than a *de minimis* cost for the employer. In doing so, he chastised the majority for applying the wrong legal standard. He argued that the employer, GEO Group, should have demonstrated that the headscarves presented a real, not just hypothetical, safety issue.[242] He suggested that "[a]n employer cannot evade liability for religious discrimination by merely asserting that it has a legitimate business interest, no matter how important, for refusing to accommodate an employee's religious practice."[243] *GEO Group* highlights a tension involving safety concerns. Court decisions that require actual evidence of undue hardship allow for potential safety risks. Those that grant the employers latitude to enforce dress codes and safety protocols allow for possible employer abuse of the discretionary latitude.

### m. Religious Discrimination

In addition to the mandate of religious accommodation, Title VII proscribes religious discrimination evident in adverse employment action or in a hostile work environment.[244]

[236] EEOC, *Religion-Based Charges, available at*: http://www.eeoc.gov/eeoc/events/9-11-11_religion_charges.cfm.

[237] E. Greyhound Lines Div. of Greyhound Lines, Inc. v. New York State Div. of Human Rights on Complaint of Ibraham, 311 N.Y.S.2d 465, *aff'd sub nom.*, E. Greyhound Lines Div. of Greyhound Lines, Inc. v. New York State Div. of Human Rights, 265 N.E.2d 745 (1970) (noting that the plaintiff wanted an accommodation to wear a beard); Webb v. City of Philadelphia, 562 F.3d 256, 260 (3rd Cir. 2009) (describing how a female Muslim police officer requested the right to wear a hijab or headscarf).

[238] E. Greyhound Lines, *supra*, 311 N.Y.S.2d at 465 (ruling that the complaint should have been dismissed and leaving decisions concerning dress code policy to the employer); Webb, *supra*, 562 F.3d at 260–1 (finding that a uniform dress code was important in establishing trust with the community as well as authority). *See* Sadia Aslam, *Hijab in the Workplace: Why Title VII Does Not Adequately Protect Employees from Discrimination on the Basis of Religious Dress and Appearance*, 80 UMKC L. Rev. 221 (2011), for a thorough discussion of related issues.

[239] E.E.O.C. v. GEO Group, Inc., 616 F.3d 265, 269 (3rd Cir. 2010).

[240] *Id.* at 275.

[241] *Id.* at 274 ("Even assuming khimars present only a small threat of the asserted dangers, they do present a threat which is something that GEO is entitled to attempt to prevent.").

[242] *Id.* at 284.

[243] *Id.* at 285.

[244] 42 U.S.C.A. § 2000e-2 (West 2013).

The elements of a prima facie case of religious discrimination track those for other areas of discrimination law, such as racial or sexual harassment.[245]

To establish a prima facie case of religious discrimination based on an adverse employment action under Title VII, the claimant must demonstrate (1) that he or she was a member of a protected class because of his or her religion, (2) that he or she experienced an adverse employment action, (3) that he or she was qualified for the job or performing to legitimate expectations, and (4) that he or she was replaced by a person outside the protected class or that he or she was treated differently than similarly situated employees.[246] To meet the requirements of the second prong, the employee must experience a "materially adverse employment action," which courts define as "a significant change in employment status, such as hiring, firing, failing to promote, reassignment with significantly different responsibilities, or a decision causing a significant change in benefits."[247]

To prove a discriminatorily hostile or abusive work environment, the plaintiff must show that "the harassment was (1) unwelcome, (2) because of religion, (3) sufficiently severe or pervasive to alter the conditions of employment and create an abusive atmosphere, and (4) imputable to the employer."[248] Typically, the plaintiff must prove that discriminatory statements made in the workplace were more than stray remarks and that the remarks played a part in whatever action was taken against the employee.[249]

245 *Compare* Jennifer Ann Drobac, Sexual Harassment Law: History, Cases, and Theory 71 (2005) (new edition anticipated 2015) *with* E.E.O.C. v. Sunbelt Rentals, Inc., 521 F.3d 306, 313–14 (4th Cir. 2008).

246 *See, e.g.*, Tepper v. Potter, 505 F.3d 508, 515 (6th Cir. 2007); Fischer v. Forestwood Co., Inc., 525 F.3d 972, 985 (10th Cir. 2008); Vetter v. Farmland Indus., Inc., 884 F. Supp. 1287, 1302 (N.D. Iowa 1995) (listing element that plaintiff "was performing his or her job at a level that met the employer's legitimate expectations").

247 Tepper, 505 F.3d at 515 (citations omitted).

248 Sunbelt Rentals, 521 F.3d at 313.

249 *Id.* at 316. (describing how the plaintiff was subjected to derogatory terms, such as "Taliban" and "towel head" on a regular basis, which was enough to establish an initial claim); Powell v. Bob Downes Chrysler-Plymouth, Inc., 865 F. Supp. 1340, 1349 (E.D. Mo. 1994) (noting that remarks made by defendant's wife could not be attributed to defendant and that plaintiff could not prove that defendant considered religion when the adverse decision was made); Kloss v. Ball State Univ., 2007 WL 4150208, 10 (S.D. Ind. Nov. 19, 2007) (holding that jokes and comments amounted to "several isolated statements over period of five years" and "do not rise above the level of teasing"); Johnson v. AutoZone, Inc., 768 F. Supp. 2d 1124, 1153 (N.D. Ala. 2011) ("Plaintiff's allegations are simply not enough, and courts in this circuit have consistently dismissed religious hostile work environment claims for similar infirmities of proof."); *see, e.g.*, Wheeles v. Nelson's Elec. Motor Services, 559 F. Supp. 2d 1260, 1272 (M.D. Ala. 2008) (dismissing religious harassment claim where plaintiff failed to satisfy "severe or pervasive" requirement and complained-of conduct was nothing more than "slightly insulting"); Mackmuhammad v. Cagle's, Inc., 379 Fed. App'x 801, 805–6 (11th Cir. 2010) (holding that Muslim employee was not subjected to religious harassment when manager referred to him as "Bin Laden" or "Muhammad-man" over company radio and intercom and when supervisors asked him about his religion and made comments about his religious dietary restrictions because such comments were at most insensitive and rude and did not rise to the level of severe and pervasive harassment); Richardson v. Dougherty County, Georgia, 185 Fed. App'x 785, 790–1 (11th Cir. 2006) (rejecting Title VII hostile work environment claim where supervisor referred to plaintiff more than fifty times as "preacher man" and made comments about his religion and request for accommodation, where such conduct was not objectively severe or pervasive); Jones v. United Space Alliance, L.L.C., 170 Fed. App'x 52, 55–6 (11th Cir. 2006) (dismissing hostile environment claim because complained-of conduct was not objectively severe or pervasive, where manager made derogatory remarks based on plaintiff's religion, co-worker removed flyer advertising plaintiff's church events, manager told him to remove lanyard with name "Jesus" on it, manager told him not to leave his bible on his desk, and he was asked to turn down religious music played at work).

Two cases in particular highlight the procedural and substantive application of antidiscrimination law. In *Jenkins v. New York City Transit Authority*, the defendant challenged the Title VII claim, arguing an absence of actionable religious disparate impact.[250] The Southern District Court of New York rejected this defense, noting that courts often dismiss disparate impact religious claims for "lack of evidence, rather than failure to state a claim."[251] In *Gadling-Cole v. West Chester University*, the plaintiff believed that homosexuality was a sin and claimed to have faced workplace harassment because of this belief.[252] A Pennsylvania district court found credence with plaintiff's religious discrimination claims and that sufficient facts supported the pleadings.[253] The court distinguished *Gadling-Cole* from cases involving sexual orientation harassment, not currently entitled to protection under Title VII.[254]

This distinction between religious discrimination and sexual orientation discrimination is important because Congress may soon extend Title VII to provide protection against discrimination based on sexual orientation.[255] At some point, a court might have to resolve two opposing claims of harassment or discrimination arising out of a single set of facts. One employee might claim that he or she has been the victim of harassment because of religious beliefs, whereas another might allege harassment because of sexual orientation. How a court will resolve such competing claims is difficult to predict, but the court will want to avoid an Establishment Clause violation by preferring one religious adherent over another or over a nonbeliever.

### 3. *"Refusal" or "Conscience" Laws*

Since the Supreme Court's *Roe v. Wade* [256] decision, many states have enacted "refusal laws" that allow health care providers to refuse to participate in pregnancy-termination or sterilization procedures that violate or are inconsistent with their religious beliefs.[257]

250 646 F. Supp. 2d 464, 471 (S.D.N.Y. 2009).

251 *Id.* [citing Barrow v. Greenville Indep. Sch. Dist., 480 F.3d 377, 382–3 (5th Cir. 2007); Soria v. Ozinga Bros., Inc., 704 F.2d 990, 994–7 (7th Cir. 1983); and Tucker v. Reno, 205 F. Supp. 2d 1169, 1174–5 (D. Or. 2002)]. The *Jenkins* court explained

> [T]his court granted an employer's motion to dismiss a disparate impact claim based on religious discrimination, but did so because the plaintiff had failed to meet the elements required to state a disparate impact claim. *See also* Collette v. St. Luke's Roosevelt Hosp., 132 F. Supp. 2d 256, 276–8 (S.D.N.Y.2001). These cases leave open the possibility that a disparate impact claim based on religious discrimination can be stated if it is properly pleaded. The defendants' argument that a disparate impact claim based on religious discrimination does not exist is therefore without merit.

*Id.*

252 2012 WL 1075809 (E.D. Pa. Mar. 30, 2012).

253 *Id.*

254 *Id.*

255 The Employment Non-Discrimination Act (ENDA) would prohibit employment discrimination on the basis of sexual orientation under federal law. *See* Employment Non-Discrimination Act of 2011, S. 811, 112th Cong. (2011). As with Title VII, ENDA would exempt private employers with fewer than fifteen employees, religious institutions, and private membership clubs. *See id.* at §§ 3a(4), 6, 11. This exemption for religious employers includes any "religious corporation, association, educational institution, or society." Title VII of Civil Rights Act of 1964, 42 U.S.C.A. § 2000e-1 (2006), as amended by Civil Rights Act of 1991, 42 U.S.C.A. § 1981a.

256 410 U.S. 113 (1973).

257 *See* Rachel Benson Gold, *Conscience Makes a Comeback in the Age of Managed Care*, The Guttmacher Report on Public Policy 1 (1998), *available at:* http://www.guttmacher.org/pubs/tgr/01/1/gr010101.html

Immediately following *Roe* in 1973, Congress passed the Public Health Service Act (PHSA),[258] also known as the "Church Amendment."[259] The PHSA safeguards federally funded health care providers from a requirement that they participate in abortion procedures when personnel raise moral or religious objections. The act further proscribes hospitals from mandating the performance of pregnancy termination as a condition of employment.[260] Laws that followed added to protections for religious adherents and their employer organizations.[261] Originally, these laws focused on abortion, but more recently, they have been expanded to protect pharmacists who refuse to dispense emergency contraception and to fill contraception prescriptions.[262]

Laws that protect religious adherents who refuse to provide medical and pharmaceutical services clearly disadvantage women and families who seek access to such services. Government involvement on either side arguably raises First Amendment Establishment Clause and Free Exercise Clause issues, in addition to Fourteenth Amendment equal protection and substantive due process concerns that are beyond the scope of this review. The 2010 passage of the Patient Protection and Affordable Care Act (ACA, colloquially known as "Obamacare")[263] only heightens the tension of this debate. In that legislation, Congress mandated that employers with fifty or more employees provide a minimal level of health care coverage for women.[264] Health Resources and Services Administration guidelines provided that plans must include coverage for all Food and Drug Administration–approved contraceptive methods, sterilization procedures, and

(accessed April 14, 2013); *see also* Erin Whitcomb, *A Most Fundamental Freedom of Choice: An International Review of Conscientious Objection to Elective Abortion*, 24 St. John's J. Legal Comment. 771 (2010).

258 42 U.S.C.A. § 300a-7 (1973).

259 Frank Church was the bill's sponsor, and the amendment carries his name. Maureen Kramlich, *Urban Law Journal Special Series: The Current State of Abortion Law and Reproductive Rights: The Abortion Debate Thirty Years Later: From Choice to Coercion*, 31 Fordham Urb. L.J. 783, 789 (2004); *see also* Whitcomb, *supra* note 257.

260 42 U.S.C.A. § 300a-7 (1973), at (c)(1)(A) (barring hospital discrimination "in the employment, promotion or termination of employment of any physician or health care personnel" who performed or assisted or refused to perform or assist in the lawful sterilization or abortion procedures for moral or religious reasons.); *see also* Whitcomb, *supra* note 257.

261 *E.g.*, Consolidated Appropriations Act of 2005, Pub. L. No. 108-447, §508(d)(1), 118 Stat. 2809, 3163 (2004). The Hyde-Weldon Conscience Protection Amendment, passed in 2005, closes loopholes associated with the PHSA.

262 *See, e.g.*, Ark. Code Ann. § 20-16-304(4) (West 2012) (permitting physician and pharmacist refusal to dispense contraceptives); Idaho Code Ann. § 18-611(2) (West 2013) ("No health care professional shall be required to provide any health care service that violates his or her conscience.").

263 Patient Protection and Affordable Care Act, Pub. L. No. 111-148, 124 Stat. 119 (2010).

264 26 U.S.C.A. § 4980H (c)(2)(A) (Supp. 2011) and 42 U.S.C.A. § 300gg-13(a) (Supp. 2011). The statute provides

> [a] group health plan and a health insurance issuer offering group or individual health insurance coverage shall, at a minimum provide coverage for and shall not impose any cost sharing requirements for – (1) evidence-based items or services that have in effect a rating of "A" or "B" in the current recommendations of the United States Preventive Services Task Force … (4) with respect to women, such additional preventive care and screenings not described in paragraph (1) as provided for in comprehensive guidelines supported by the Health Resources and Services Administration for purposes of this paragraph.

42 U.S.C.A. § 300gg-13(a) (Supp. 2011); *see also* Rose Shingledecker, *Note, No Good Deed: The Impropriety of the Religious Accommodation of Contraceptive Coverage Requirements in the Patient Protection and Affordable Care Act* 47 Ind. L. Rev. 301 (2014).

associated counseling.[265] A narrow exception for religious exemption resulted in more litigation and leads us to the next section concerning not only not-for-profit religious employers[266] but also for-profit, private corporate employers.

## B. Exceptions to Antidiscrimination Legislation Available to Not-for-Profit Religious Employers and For-Profit Private Corporate Employers

The Free Exercise and Establishment Clauses of the First Amendment limit court oversight of employees of religious institutions. Under the First Amendment, religious employers may build a workforce of coreligionists, as well as discharge ministerial employees, a term that is broadly defined, for any reason the religious employer chooses. Additionally, Title VII and Sections 702 and 703 in particular provide exceptions from its antidiscrimination policies for religious organizations.[267]

To explain these constitutional limits and religious employer exemptions, the second section of this chapter analyzes three aspects of government oversight of religious nonprofit employers. The first subsection examines whether an organization qualifies as a religious employer. The second subsection reviews the First Amendment's Freedom of Association Clause and a religious employer's right to hire coreligionists. The third subsection considers the ministerial exception and briefly reviews the Supreme Court's

265 U.S. Department of Health & Human Services, *Affordable Care Act Rules on Expanding Access to Preventive Services for Women* (Aug. 1, 2011), *available at:* http://www.healthcare.gov/news/factsheets/2011/08/womensprevention08012011a.html.

266 *See, e.g.*, Complaint & Demand for Jury Trial, Univ. of Notre Dame v. Sebelius, No. 3:12CV253, 2012 WL 1859163 (N.D. Ind. May 21, 2012). Jones Day represents the plaintiffs in twelve lawsuits filed by Catholic entities on May 21, 2012. The complaints reiterate common complaints and arguments. Shingledecker, *supra* note 264 (citing http://www.becketfund.org/hhsinformationcentral/).

267 42 U.S.C.A. § 2000e-1 (Section 702) (West 2013) specifies

> (a) Inapplicability of subchapter to certain aliens and employees of religious entities. This subchapter shall not apply to … a religious corporation, association, educational institution, or society with respect to the employment of individuals of a particular religion to perform work connected with the carrying on by such corporation, association, educational institution, or society of its activities.

*Id.*

42 U.S.C.A. § 2000e-2 (Section 703) (West 2013) adds

> (e) Businesses or enterprises with personnel qualified on basis of religion, sex, or national origin; educational institutions with personnel of particular religion. Notwithstanding any other provision of this subchapter, (1) it shall not be an unlawful employment practice for an employer to hire and employ employees, for an employment agency to classify, or refer for employment any individual, for a labor organization to classify its membership or to classify or refer for employment any individual, or for an employer, labor organization, or joint labor-management committee controlling apprenticeship or other training or retraining programs to admit or employ any individual in any such program, on the basis of his religion, sex, or national origin in those certain instances where religion, sex, or national origin is a bona fide occupational qualification reasonably necessary to the normal operation of that particular business or enterprise, and (2) it shall not be an unlawful employment practice for a school, college, university, or other educational institution or institution of learning to hire and employ employees of a particular religion if such school, college, university, or other educational institution or institution of learning is, in whole or in substantial part, owned, supported, controlled, or managed by a particular religion or by a particular religious corporation, association, or society, or if the curriculum of such school, college, university, or other educational institution or institution of learning is directed toward the propagation of a particular religion.

*Id.*

confirmation of that exception in *Hosanna-Tabor Evangelical Lutheran Church & School v. E.E.O.C.*[268]

### 1. *Is the Organization a Religious Employer?*

In order to limit government intrusion into its internal human resources processes, an organization must first prove its religious character. A number of court cases have explored whether an organization was essentially a religious institution and the associated burden of proof. These cases have not produced a comprehensive national standard. Moreover, *Hosanna-Tabor Evangelical Lutheran Church & School v. E.E.O.C.*,[269] discussed later, offers little clear guidance on the point.

In a recent case concerning employer qualification for religious exemption from Title VII, *Spencer v. World Vision, Inc.*,[270] the Ninth Circuit identified three different tests, none of which received a majority endorsement.[271] World Vision is a self-described Christian humanitarian organization that addresses the root causes of poverty and injustice. When World Vision hired Sylvia Spencer and two other "employees," it required that they submit personal statements about their "relationship with Jesus Christ," as well as comply with the organization's "Statement of Faith, Core Values, and Mission Statement."[272] When "World Vision discovered that the Employees denied the deity of Jesus Christ and disavowed the doctrine of the Trinity," it terminated them.[273] All three filed suit in the U.S District Court for the Western District of Washington, alleging that World Vision had violated Title VII. The district court granted summary judgment to World Vision, reasoning that World Vision was a religious employer under the framework set forth in *LeBoon v. Lancaster Jewish Community Center Ass'n*, discussed later.[274] The employees appealed, and the Ninth Circuit Court reviewed the case *de novo* to determine whether World Vision qualified for an exemption from Title VII because it (World Vision) is a religious organization.[275]

Judge O'Scannlain's *Spencer* concurrence suggested inquiry as to whether the institution "(1) is organized for a self-identified religious purpose (as evidenced by Articles of Incorporation or similar foundational documents), (2) is engaged in activity consistent with, and in furtherance of, those religious purposes, and (3) holds itself out to the public as religious."[276]

Judge Kleinfeld, who also concurred in *Spencer*, offered a reformulation of O'Scannlain's test that he (Kleinfeld) thought was too inclusive. He first advised asking whether an entity is organized for a religious purpose. Additionally, Kleinfeld proposed

268 132 S. Ct. 694 (2012). For a more in-depth analysis of *Hosanna-Tabor*, *see Leading Cases*, 126 Harv. L. Rev. 179 (2012).
269 132 S. Ct. 694 (2012).
270 633 F.3d 723 (9th Cir. 2011) *cert. denied*, 132 S. Ct. 96 (2011).
271 For further discussion of the *Spencer* decision, as well as the qualifications to be considered a religious employer, *see* Brandon S. Boulter, *Goldilocks and the Three-Judge Panel: Spencer v. World Vision, Inc. and the Religious Organization Exemption of Title VII*, 2011 B.Y.U. L. Rev. 33 (2011).
272 Spencer, 633 F.3d at 725.
273 *Id.*
274 *Id.* at 725–6 [discussing LeBoon v. Lancaster Jewish Community Center Ass'n, 503 F.3d 217 (3d Cir. 2007)].
275 Spencer, 633 F.3d at 726.
276 *Id.* at 734 (O'Scannlain, J. concurring).

asking whether the entity "is engaged primarily in carrying out that religious purpose, holds itself out to the public as an entity for carrying out that religious purpose, and does not engage primarily or substantially in the exchange of goods or services for money beyond nominal amounts."[277] Not only did Judge Kleinfeld add the fourth requirement, he also modified the first so as not to mandate incorporation or other formal organizational form.

Judge Berzon, who dissented, relied on two earlier Ninth Circuit decisions, *E.E.O.C. v. Townley Engineering & Manufacturing Co.*[278] and *E.E.O.C. v. Kamehameha Schools/Bishop Estate*.[279]. These decisions provided the basis for informal EEOC discussion of the "definition of an employer that qualifies as a religious organization."[280] Moreover, their facts help to demonstrate how far jurisprudence has evolved in the twenty-five years preceding the Court's *Hobby Lobby* decision.

Townley Manufacturing Company was a closely held corporation founded by Jake and Helen Townley, who were born-again Christians.[281] Helen Townley "made a covenant with God that their business 'would be a Christian, faith-operated business.'"[282] Therefore, the Townleys mandated employee attendance at weekly devotional services at their Florida plant.[283] In 1979, the company hired Louis Pelvas, an atheist, to work at its Arizona plant that had no devotional services until April 1984. Pelvas asked to be excused from the services in June 1984, but his supervisor denied this request. In October 1984, Pelvas filed a religious discrimination charge with the EEOC, and it brought suit.[284] Ultimately, the Ninth Circuit affirmed the district court's decision that found a violation of Title VII.[285] The Ninth Circuit held that Townley's requirement that an objecting employee attend the devotional services "cannot be reconciled with Title VII's prohibition against religious discrimination" and "that Congress did not intend section 702's exemption for religious corporations to shield corporations such at Townley."[286] However, the court did recognize that the Townleys, as individuals, have "rights under the Free Exercise Clause that Title VII cannot infringe."[287]

In holding that Townley Manufacturing Company was not entitled to an exception, as a religious organization, from the worker protections of Title VII, the court referenced the related legislative history. The court concluded that "[a]ll [in Congress] assumed that only those institutions with extremely close ties to organized religions would be covered. Churches, and entities similar to churches, were the paradigm."[288] The court noted that Townley Manufacturing Company was a secular organization that produced

277 *Id.* at 748 (Kleinfeld, J., concurring).
278 859 F.2d 610, 618 (9th Cir.1988).
279 EEOC v. Kamehameha Schools/Bishop Estate, 990 F.2d 458, 460 (9th Cir.1993).
280 Letter from Reed L. Russell, EEOC Legal Counsel to Kevin Cummings, Branch Chief, Business and Trade Services Department of Homeland Security (Dec. 28, 2007), *available at:* http://www.eeoc.gov/eeoc/foia/letters/2007/religious_organization_exception_dec_28_2007.html
281 Townley, 859 F.2d at 611–12.
282 *Id.* at 612.
283 *Id.*
284 *Id.*
285 *Id.* at 613.
286 *Id.*
287 *Id.*
288 *Id.* at 618.

mining equipment.[289] The court explained "that the beliefs of the owners and operators of a corporation are simply not enough in themselves to make the corporation 'religious' within the meaning of section 702."[290] In section D, this survey compares the *Townley* facts with the Supreme Court's recent *Hobby Lobby* decision. Important to this comparison is the Ninth Circuit's emphasis that Townley Manufacturing Company's articles of incorporation did not mention any religious purpose.[291]

In *Kamehameha*, Bernice Pauahi Bishop, a member of the Hawaiian royal family, used a charitable trust to found the Kamehameha Schools. The founding documents directed that all teachers be Protestants.[292] Carole Edgerton, who was not Protestant, applied for a position as a substitute French teacher and was told of the religious requirement. She subsequently filed a religious discrimination charge with the EEOC.[293] The schools sought an exemption to requirements of Title VII as a religious educational institution.[294] A district court held in favor of the schools and granted the exemption.[295] On appeal, the Ninth Circuit Court overturned the decision. In considering the exemption, it weighed several factors, including purpose and ownership, which described the schools.[296] It concluded that "the Schools are essentially a secular institution operating within a historical tradition that includes Protestantism, and the Schools' purpose and character is [*sic*] primarily secular, not primarily religious."[297]

Relying on *Townley* and *Kamehameha*, Judge Berzon, who dissented in *Spencer*, argued for a two-part analysis to determine whether the employer was a religious entity and entitled to the exemption. Quoting *Townley*, he reasoned, "First, '[a]ll significant religious and secular characteristics must be weighed to determine whether the corporation's purpose and character are primarily religious.'"[298] Quoting *Kamehameha*, he noted, "Second, '[w]e construe the statutory exemption [ ] narrowly,' with the understanding that 'only those institutions with extremely close ties to organized religion [are] covered.'"[299] Thus the *per curiam Spencer* opinion arguably undermined *Townley* and *Kamehameha* without clearly establishing a new test.

*LeBoon v. Lancaster Jewish Community Center Ass'n*,[300] a case noted in *Spencer* also was mentioned in the EEOC informal definition of a religious organization.[301] The

289 *Id.* at 619.
290 *Id.*
291 *Id.*
292 Kamehameha, 990 F.2d at 459.
293 *Id.*
294 *Id.*
295 *Id.*
296 *Id.* at 461. The Ninth Circuit weighed the following factors in determining whether the schools were entitled to the exemption for a religious institution: (1) ownership and affiliation: schools were not controlled by or affiliated with any particular sect; (2) purpose: schools instructed students in developing their own moral code rather than following those of a particular religion; (3) faculty: only 3 out of 250 teachers had religious duties, and none were required to maintain active membership in a church; (4) student body: fewer than one-third of on-campus students were Protestant; (5) student activities: student activities were varied and not of an overtly religious character but did include prayers at times; (6) curriculum: core courses were taught from a secular doctrine, and the schools did not instruct students in a Protestant doctrine. *Id.* at 461–4.
297 *Id.*at 463–4.
298 Spencer, 633 F.3d at 750 (Berzon, J., dissenting) (citations omitted).
299 *Id.*
300 503 F.3d 217 (3rd Cir. 2007)
301 Russell Letter, *supra note* 280.

Lancaster Jewish Community Center Association (LJCC) was a nonprofit organization charged with the mission to "enhance and promote Jewish life, identity, and continuity."[302] To fulfill its mission, the LJCC undertook a variety of activities, including the operation of a summer camp and preschool, the publication of a newspaper, and the promotion of events to celebrate Jewish holidays. The main sources of its income included the Lancaster Jewish Federation, the United Way, membership dues (membership was open to adherents of other religions), program fees, rents, and donations.[303] Linda LeBoon, an evangelical Christian, worked for nearly four years as a bookkeeper for the LJCC until she was terminated in 2002.[304] Two other employees had been terminated shortly before LeBoon for what she believed to be discriminatory reasons.[305] At the time LeBoon was terminated, the organization was in financial distress, and the interim executive director believed that another employee could assume LeBoon's duties.[306]

After her termination, LeBoon "filed suit in federal court alleging religious discrimination, retaliation, and wrongful discharge in violation of Pennsylvania's public policy."[307] LeBoon believed that she was fired either because she is a Christian or in retaliation for complaining about the firings of other employees.[308] A magistrate judge granted LJCC's motion for summary judgment, finding that LJCC was a religious employer and exempt from Title VII's prohibition against religious discrimination in employment.[309] LeBoon filed a motion for reconsideration based a "manifest error of fact regarding the percentage of the LJCC's funding that came from the Lancaster Jewish Federation Campaign."[310] The LJCC conceded the error, and the original order was vacated. On rehearing, the magistrate judge again held that the LJCC was a "religious organization exempted from the religious discrimination provisions of Title VII."[311]

Ultimately, the Third Circuit relied on nine factors in determining whether an organization was sufficiently religious to qualify for exemption:

> (1) whether the entity operates for a profit, (2) whether it produces a secular product, (3) whether the entity's articles of incorporation or other pertinent documents state a religious purpose, (4) whether it is owned, affiliated with or financially supported by a formally religious entity such as a church or synagogue, (5) whether a formally religious entity participates in the management, for instance, by having representatives on the board of trustees, (6) whether the entity holds itself out to the public as secular or sectarian, (7) whether the entity regularly includes prayer or other forms of worship in its activities, (8) whether it includes religious instruction in its curriculum, to the extent it is an educational institution, and (9) whether its membership is made up by coreligionists.[312]

302 Leboon, 503 F.3d at 221 (quotation marks in the original).
303 *Id.*
304 *Id.*
305 *Id.* at 221–2.
306 *Id.* at 222.
307 *Id.*
308 *Id.*
309 *Id.*
310 *Id.*
311 *Id.*
312 LeBoon, 503 F.3d at 226. In crafting the test, the court referenced Killinger v. Samford University, 113 F.3d 196 (11th Cir. 1997), Kamehameha Schools/Bishop Estate, 990 F.2d 458, Townley, 859 F.2d 610, and EEOC v. Mississippi College, 626 F.2d 477 (5th Cir. 1980).

The Third Circuit affirmed the lower court decisions and held that LJCC was a religious organization entitled to the exemption.[313]

Two Fourth Circuit decisions, *Fike v. United Methodist Children's Home of Virginia, Inc.*,[314] and *Silo v. CHW Medical Foundation*,[315] arrived at seemingly contradictory determinations regarding the extent to which an entity must reflect the principles of its founding organization in order to be considered a religious organization. In *Fike*, the court held that the United Methodist Children's Home, operating as a Christian home for orphans, demonstrated too little religious affiliation in its day-to-day activities for the court to consider it a religious employer exempt from Title VII.[316] However, in *Silo*, a Catholic hospital's operation was consistent with the church's founding mission of "healing and providing services to the sick and poor in the Catholic moral tradition."[317] The court exempted the hospital employer, even though the hospital "does not have a chaplaincy or chapel, does not sponsor or conduct religious services, prayer groups or Bible studies on its premises and does not publicly place or display Bibles, crucifixes or any other religious symbols."[318]

Although *Burwell v. Hobby Lobby Stores, Inc.*,[319] dealt with whether a private, for-profit *corporation* qualified as a *person* for the application of RFRA, it seemingly raises the question of whether such a corporation might also qualify as a religious employer. *Hobby Lobby* arguably strengthens the autonomy of religious, for-profit, corporate employers in relation to their employees against governmental interference. Therefore, one might wonder if cases such as *Townley* shed light on *Hobby Lobby*'s broader implications. Are "secular" employers that incorporate religion into the activities of the workplace more likely to qualify for the exemption post *Hobby Lobby*?

*Hobby Lobby* does not mention *Townley*, *Kamehameha*, or *LeBoon*. Because Hobby Lobby's owners asserted *their own* RFRA rights via the corporate entity against the government and the PPACA, the Court did not address whether Hobby Lobby Stores was a religious employer. Therefore, *Hobby Lobby* should have little influence on the application of Title VII to private, for-profit corporations. However, wonders never cease.

This collection of cases concerning qualification for exemption on the basis of religious character highlights the fractured and varied approaches to claims by religious adherents. Litigants anticipating such an issue in the future need to pay close attention to the continuing evolution of the law on this matter in their respective jurisdictions.

## 2. *The Right to Hire Coreligionists/Freedom of Association*

Once the organization establishes itself as a religious one, it may use shared religious values as the basis for hiring decisions.[320] In *Corp. of Presiding Bishop of Church of Jesus*

313 *Id.* at 226–31.
314 547 F. Supp. 286, 290 (E.D. Va. 1982), *aff'd*, 709 F.2d 284 (4th Cir. 1983).
315 27 Cal. 4th 1097, 45 P.3d 1162 (2002).
316 Fike, 547 F. Supp. at 290.
317 Silo, 27 Cal. 4th at 1101.
318 *Id.*
319 134 S. Ct. 2751.
320 *See supra* note 267 and especially 42 U.S.C.A. §2000e-2(2); *see also* Boy Scouts of Am. v. Dale, 530 U.S. 640 (2000). Although not a case that focused on paid employment, *Dale* held that religious organizations are free to affiliate with only those persons who share similar philosophical viewpoints. The Court

*Christ of Latter-Day Saints v. Amos*, Mayson worked as a building engineer at the Deseret Gymnasium for sixteen years. The gymnasium was a "nonprofit facility, open to the public," and operated by the Church of Jesus Christ of Latter-Day Saints.[321] The church fired Mayson because he "failed to qualify for a temple recommend, that is, a certificate that he is a member of the Church and eligible to attend its temples."[322] Mayson and a group of similarly situated employees filed suit, alleging violation of Title VII and other protections.

The Supreme Court held that a religious employer may select only those applicants who share its religious philosophy, even for nonreligious purposes, to advance its overall religious mission.[323] The Court also evaluated whether its ruling regarding the Title VII claim might work to promote the establishment of religion, in violation of the First Amendment. Using the *Lemon* test,[324] the Court concluded that "[a] law is not unconstitutional simply because it *allows* churches to advance religion, which is their very purpose. For a law to have forbidden 'effects,' *Government itself* must have advanced religion through its own activities and influence."[325] Arguably, *Amos* gives employers qualifying under the religious exception of Title VII great latitude in their personnel decisions.

In *Little v. Wuerl*, the Third Circuit published a direct endorsement of a religious institution's right to hire only coreligionists.[326] The *Wuerl* court upheld the dismissal of a Protestant teacher after she remarried, an act that allegedly violated Catholic doctrine.[327] The court explained that the Title VII exemption applied "whether or not every individual plays a direct role in the organization's 'religious activities.'"[328] The court "conclude[d] that the permission to employ persons 'of a particular religion' includes permission to employ only persons whose beliefs and conduct are consistent with the employer's religious precepts."[329] The court held that "it does not violate Title VII's prohibition of religious discrimination for a parochial school to discharge a Catholic or a non-Catholic teacher who has publicly engaged in conduct regarded by the school as inconsistent with its religious principles."[330]

### 3. *The Ministerial Exception*

In 1972, before Section 702 of Title VII, 42 U.S.C. §2000e-1 created an exemption for employees of religious entities, the Fifth Circuit considered Title VII's application to these workers. With *McClure v. Salvation* Army, the court established a ministerial

rejected government mandate that groups accept undesired members. The Court held, "The forced inclusion of an unwanted person in a group infringes the group's freedom of expressive association if the presence of that person affects in a significant way the group's ability to advocate public or private viewpoints." *Id.* at 648.

321 483 U.S. at 330.

322 *Id.*

323 483 U.S. 327 (1987) (holding that religious exemption to Title VII's prohibition against religious discrimination in employment for secular nonprofit activities of a religious organization did not violate Establishment Clause).

324 *See supra* notes 33 & 34 and accompanying text.

325 *Id.* at 328.

326 929 F.2d 944 (3rd Cir. 1991).

327 *Id.* at 946.

328 *Id.* at 951.

329 *Id.*

330 *Id.*

exception.[331] The court clarified that religious institutions had a right to govern themselves through their chosen ministers. Mrs. Billie McClure qualified as such a minister. McClure had entered the Salvation Army's training program in 1965 and had served the Salvation Army in a number of roles, including her final role as a secretary in the public relations department.[332] She had considered her role with the Salvation Army to be religious in nature, even when she was not performing religious duties.[333] After the Salvation Army terminated her employment, McClure filed discrimination charges with the EEOC alleging that she had "received less salary and fewer benefits than that accorded similarly situated male officers, [and] also that she had been discharged because of her complaints to her superiors and the Equal Employment Opportunity Commission [EEOC] with regard to these practices."[334]

In deciding *McClure*, the Fifth Circuit stressed the primacy of the relationship between ministers and churches. It explained that ministers are the "lifeblood" and "chief instrument" of the church.[335] The court's decision also referenced past Supreme Court decisions that recognized a "wall of separation" between church and state[336] and that churches had the "power to decide for themselves, free from state interference, matters of church government as well as those of faith and doctrine."[337]

In addressing the facts before it, the *McClure* court explained that application of Title VII would (without an implied free exercise exception) "cause the State to intrude upon matters of church administration and government which have so many times before been proclaimed to be matters of a singular ecclesiastical concern."[338] The court concluded that "Congress did not intend, through the nonspecific wording of the applicable provisions of Title VII, to regulate the employment relationship between church and minister" and, therefore, that it lacked jurisdiction to decide McClure's claim.[339] The 1972 *McClure* reasoning foreshadowed that of the Supreme Court nearly forty years later.

Since the Fifth Circuit's *McClure* decision, each of the federal circuits has similarly found a ministerial exception.[340] However, the Supreme Court did not confirm any such exception until 2011, when it decided *Hosanna-Tabor Evangelical Lutheran Church & School v. E.E.O.C.*,[341] which involved a retaliation suit by a "called" teacher,

331 460 F.2d 553 (5th Cir. 1972).

332 McClure v. Salvation Army, 323 F. Supp. 1100, 1103 (N.D. Ga. 1971), *aff'd*, 460 F.2d 553 (5th Cir. 1972).

333 *Id.* at 1104.

334 McClure, 460 F.2d at 555.

335 *Id.* at 558–9.

336 *Id.* at 558.

337 *Id.* at 560.

338 *Id.*

339 *Id.* at 560–1.

340 Natal v. Christian & Missionary Alliance, 878 F.2d 1575 (1st Cir. 1989); DeMarco v. Holy Cross High Sch., 4 F.3d 166 (2d Cir. 1993); Little v. Wuerl, 929 F.2d 944 (3rd Cir. 1991); Rayburn v. Gen. Conference of Seventh-Day Adventists, 772 F.2d 1164 (4th Cir. 1985); Hollins v. Methodist Healthcare, Inc., 474 F.3d 223 (6th Cir. 2007) *abrogated by* Hosanna-Tabor Evangelical Lutheran Church & Sch. v. E.E.O.C., 132 S. Ct. 694, (2012); Alicea-Hernandez v. Catholic Bishop of Chicago, 320 F.3d 698 (7th Cir. 2003); Scharon v. St. Luke's Episcopal Presbyterian Hospitals, 929 F.2d 360 (8th Cir. 1991); Bollard v. California Province of the Soc'y of Jesus, 196 F.3d 940 (9th Cir. 1999); Skrzypczak v. Roman Catholic Diocese of Tulsa, 611 F.3d 1238, (10th Cir. 2010), *cert. denied*, 132 S. Ct. 1088, 181 L. Ed. 2d 976 (U.S. 2012); Gellington v. Christian Methodist Episcopal Church, Inc., 203 F.3d 1299, 1302 (11th Cir. 2000).

341 132 S. Ct. 694 (2012). For a more in-depth analysis of *Hosanna-Tabor, see Leading Cases*, 126 Harv. L. Rev. 179 (2012).

Cheryl Perich, against a Lutheran school. Hosanna-Tabor hired Perich as a lay teacher in 1999.[342] After Perich completed the necessary training, Hosanna-Tabor asked Perich to become a "called" teacher or a commissioned minister, and she accepted.[343] During her employment with the school, Perich taught both secular and religious topics.[344]

Following a narcolepsy diagnosis, Perich took a disability leave.[345] She received medical clearance to return to work on February 22 and went to the school, fully aware that it had already hired a lay teacher to replace her.[346] The church congregation had already voted to release Perich from her calling. It offered to pay a portion of her health insurance premiums if she agreed to resign,[347] which she refused to do. The school's principal asked her to leave, but Perich refused until she was given written documentation that she had reported to work.[348] The school later terminated Perich for "insubordination and disruptive behavior" as well as for damaging her relationship with the school by threatening to take legal action.[349]

In *Hosanna-Tabor,* the Court held that the ministerial exception prevented court intervention in a ministerial employment decision. The Court so ruled even though the termination and related discrimination claim were ostensibly unrelated to matters of church religious doctrine.[350] Having confirmed the viability of a ministerial exception, the *Hosanna-Tabor* Court determined that a "called" teacher, such as Perich, was a minister for Hosanna-Tabor. The Court explained, "Perich [had] accepted the call and received a 'diploma of vocation' designating her a commissioned minister."[351] The EEOC and Perich claimed that "Hosanna-Tabor's asserted religious reason for firing Perich – that she violated the Synod's commitment to internal dispute resolution – was pretextual."[352] The Court responded that the "purpose of the exception is not to safeguard a church's decision to fire a minister only when it is made for a religious reason. The exception instead ensures that the authority to select and control who will minister to the faithful … is the church's alone."[353]

In reaching its conclusion, the *Hosanna-Tabor* Court had to distinguish *Smith,* the 1990 peyote–unemployment benefits case.[354] Recall that in *Smith,* the Court had held that "the right of free exercise does not relieve an individual of the obligation to comply with a 'valid and neutral law of general applicability on the ground that the law proscribes (or prescribes) conduct that his [or her] religion prescribes (or

342 *Hosanna-Tabor,* 132 S. Ct. at 700.
343 *Id.*
344 *Id.*
345 *Id.*
346 *Id.*
347 *Id.*
348 *Id.*
349 *Id.* (quotes in the original). Perich had threatened to sue under the Americans with Disabilities Act (ADA), 42 U.S.C. § 12101 *et seq.* (1990).
350 *Id.* at 710.
351 *Id.* at 700. Other factors influenced the Court's determination that Perich functioned as a minister. For example, she satisfied specific academic requirements, including eight theology courses, in order to "pass an oral examination by a faculty committee" (*id.* at 699). Perich "also taught a religion class four days a week, led the students in prayer and devotional exercises each day, and attended a weekly school wide chapel service. Perich led the chapel service herself about twice a year" (*id.* at 700).
352 *Id.* at 709.
353 *Id.*
354 *See supra* notes 74 & 75 and accompanying text.

proscribes).' "[355] Arguably, the ADA is a law of neutral application. Therefore, the right of free exercise would not relieve Hosanna-Tabor of the obligation to comply with its dictates, including its nonretaliation provisions. The *Hosanna-Tabor* Court found *Smith* inapposite. Writing for a unanimous Court, Justice Roberts explained

> It is true that the ADA's prohibition on retaliation, like Oregon's prohibition on peyote use, is a valid and neutral law of general applicability. But a church's selection of its ministers is unlike an *individual's* ingestion of peyote. *Smith* involved government regulation of only *outward physical acts*. The present case, in contrast, concerns government interference with an *internal church decision that affects the faith and mission of the church itself*. The contention that *Smith* forecloses recognition of a ministerial exception rooted in the Religion Clauses has no merit.[356]

The Court provided no guidance on how to distinguish "outward physical acts" from the act of employment termination that it considered "an internal church decision." One might speculate that the difference is one of practical significance for the independence of viable institutional churches. More particularly, institutional churches vary dramatically as to whom they recognize as a "minister." Some churches favor hierarchy and formal role differentiation, whereas others may count all their adult members as "ministers."

Commentators take a variety of perspectives on *Hosanna-Tabor*'s treatment of *Smith*. Professor McConnell suggests that *Hosanna-Tabor* marks "a shift in Religion Clauses jurisprudence from a focus on individual believers to a focus on the autonomy of organized religious institutions."[357] Another review of the decision notes "an untenable distinction between the facts of *Hosanna-Tabor* and *Smith* – a distinction that may have the unfortunate side effect of implying a new and ambiguous exception to *Smith*'s free exercise holding.[358] A third view, taken by Professor Laycock, emphasizes *Smith*'s refusal to "lend its [the Court's] power to one or the other side in controversies over religious authority or dogma."[359] He explains that the Court's cursory handling of *Smith* is consistent with *Smith*'s holding that it offered no precedential value in cases regarding religious authority.[360]

355 *Id.* at 879.

356 Hosanna-Tabor, 132 S. Ct. at 707 (emphasis added).

357 Michael W. McConnell, *Reflections on Hosanna-Tabor*, 35 Harv. J.L. & Pub. Pol'y 821, 835–6 (2012). Professor McConnell added

> [With *Hosanna-Tabor*] the Free Exercise Clause provides far greater protection to the "faith and mission" of religious institutions than to individual acts of religious exercise.... Perhaps it is a coincidence, but this shift in emphasis corresponds very roughly to the old divide between individualistic Protestantism and institutional Catholicism and might be the first evident fruit of the new Catholic majority on the Court.

*Id.* at 836. Other observers might not attribute the shift in emphasis to the new Catholic majority. However, Justice Brennan, a Catholic, displayed great interest in protecting individual religious conscience. *See generally* Kim Isaac Eisler, A Justice for All: William J. Brennan, Jr., and the Decisions That Transformed America (1993).

358 *Leading Cases*, 126 Harv. L. Rev. 176, 182 (2012).

359 Smith, 494 U.S. at 877 [citing Presbyterian Church in U.S. v. Mary Elizabeth Blue Hull Memorial Presbyterian Church, 393 U.S. 440, 445–52 (1969); Kedroff v. St. Nicholas Cathedral, 344 U.S. 94, 95–119 (1952); Serbian Eastern Orthodox Diocese v. Milivojevich, 426 U.S. 696, 708–25 (1976)]; *see also* Douglas Laycock, *Hosanna-Tabor and the Ministerial Exception*, 35 Harv. J.L. & Public Pol'y 839, 854 (2012) (discussing the application of *Smith*).

360 Laycock, *Hosanna-Tabor*, *supra* note 359 at 854–5.

In another review,[361] Elliot Williams contrasted the Court's holding in *Christian Legal Society v. Martinez*.[362] The *Martinez* Court had held that the First Amendment did not shield a religious student organization from compliance with a law school's nondiscrimination policy. Therefore, the Christian Legal Society had to extend voting rights and positions of authority to all comers or lose monetary and advertising benefits made available to student organizations.[363] Williams concluded that *Hosanna-Tabor* "significantly alters contemporary Free Exercise doctrine."[364] He proposed that "*Hosanna-Tabor* limited *Smith* and revitalized a category of behavior protected under the Free Exercise Clause of the First Amendment – 'decision[s] that affect the faith and mission of the church itself.'"[365] No doubt, the lower courts also will interpret *Hosanna-Tabor*'s import and meaning using a variety of perspectives regarding the relevance of *Smith*.

Concerning which employees qualify for the ministerial exception, Chief Justice Roberts noted that the *Hosanna-Tabor* opinion was limited to its facts.[366] The Court explained, "We are reluctant, however, to adopt a rigid formula for deciding when an employee qualifies as a minister. It is enough for us to conclude ... that the exception covers Perich, given all the circumstances of her employment."[367] The Court then reviewed those circumstances, including her training, titles, promotion within the church, perceptions concerning her status (both hers and the church's), and her religiously focused duties.[368] The Court considered both formal and functional factors.

In concluding that the ministerial exception, an affirmative defense,[369] barred Perich's retaliation action, the Court further limited its holding. The Court stated, "We express no view on whether the exception bars other types of suits, including actions by employees alleging breach of contract or tortious conduct by their religious employers. There will be time enough to address the applicability of the exception to other circumstances if and when they arise."[370]

### a. Qualifying Ministers

The *Hosanna-Tabor* concurrences emphasized that the Court did not adopt a bright-line rule for when the ministerial exception applies, nor did it provide a guiding definition of "minister." Justice Thomas wrote, "Judicial attempts to fashion a civil definition of 'minister' through a bright-line test or multi-factor analysis risk disadvantaging those religious

361 Elliott Williams, *Resurrecting Free Exercise in Hosanna-Tabor Lutheran Church & School v. EEOC, 132 S. CT. 694 (2012)*, 36 Harv. J.L. & Public Pol'y 391, 402 (2013)

362 130 S. Ct. 2971 (2010) (finding no constitutional violation when the law school mandated that that the school's officially recognized, religious affiliated student group follow the school's "all-comers" nondiscrimination policy).

363 Williams, 36 Harv. J.L. & Public Pol'y at 401.

364 *Id.* at 402.

365 *Id.* at 402 (quoting Hosanna-Tabor, 132 S. Ct. at 707).

366 *Id.* at 710 (2012). The unanimous Court held that "[t]he case before us is an employment discrimination suit brought on behalf of a minister, challenging her church's decision to fire her. Today we hold only that the ministerial exception bars such a suit." *Id.*

367 *Id.* at 707.

368 *Id.* at 707–8.

369 *Id.* at 709 n. 4.

370 *Id.* at 710.

groups whose beliefs, practices, and membership are outside of the 'mainstream' or unpalatable to some."[371]

Justice Alito, joined by Justice Kagan, cautioned against using formal title and ordination status as triggers for the exception's application.[372] He emphasized a functional approach, suggesting that "[t]hese [qualifying employees] include those who serve in positions of leadership, those who perform important functions in worship services, and in the performance of religious ceremonies and rituals, and those who are entrusted with teaching and conveying the tenets of the faith to the next generation."[373] He distinguished "a purely secular teacher [who] would not qualify for the 'ministerial' exception."[374] He explained, "[T]he constitutional protection of religious teachers is not somehow diminished when they take on secular functions in addition to their religious ones."[375] He concluded that Perich's qualification as a minister "rests not on respondent's ordination status or her formal title, but rather on her functional status as the type of employee that a church must be free to appoint or dismiss in order to exercise the religious liberty that the First Amendment guarantees."[376]

Because the *Hosanna-Tabor* majority offered no definition for "minister," lower courts will continue to operate as they have done historically on this matter. Numerous state and federal circuit courts agree that a religious organization need not have designated the employee as a "minister."[377] The employee need only be distinctively involved in the religious mission of the organization. Thus the lower courts have historically taken a more functional approach, similar to the one described by Justice Alito. These lower courts have found that positions ranging from choir director[378] to press secretary[379] qualify under the ministerial exception.

A few circuit courts have established tests to help determine if an employee qualifies under the ministerial exception.[380] In the Fifth Circuit, where the exception originated

371 *Id.* at 711 (Thomas, J., concurring). Justice Thomas reasoned that because "Hosanna-Tabor sincerely considered Perich [to be] a minister," her suit was "properly barred by the ministerial exception." *Id.*

372 *Id.* at 714 (Alito, J., concurring).

373 *Id.* at 712.

374 *Id.* at 715.

375 *Id.*

376 *Id.* at 716.

377 *See, e.g.*, Coulee Catholic Schools v. Labor and Industry Review Commission, 768 N.W.2d 868, 892 (Wis. 2009) (holding that the role of teacher was closely linked to an religious organization's mission and qualified for a religious exception to the state's employment discrimination statutes).

378 Starkman v. Evans, 198 F.3d 173, 176 (5th Cir. 1999) (holding that religious music plays a highly important role in the spiritual mission of the church and that job specifications required the choir director to be educated in religion and serve as a spiritual leader).

379 Alicea-Hernandez v. Catholic Bishop of Chicago, 320 F.3d 698, 704 (7th Cir. 2003) (finding that plaintiff served as a liaison between the church and the community to which it directed its message and for which she served an integral role in shaping).

380 Alcazar v. Corp. of the Catholic Archbishop of Seattle, 627 F.3d 1288, 1291 (9th Cir. 2010) (discussing tests adopted by other circuits and stating that it had declined to adopt one). The circuit courts have not adopted a uniform general test for making that determination. Some courts use the "primary duties" test, which asks whether the employee's primary duties are religious in nature. Skrzypczak v. Roman Catholic Diocese of Tulsa, 611 F.3d 1238, 1243–4 (10th Cir. 2010); E.E.O.C. v. Catholic University of America, 83 F.3d 455, 463 (D.C. Cir. 1996); Rayburn, 772 F.2d at 1168–9. Others appear to use a version of the "primary duties" test, though without expressly adopting it. Petruska v. Gannon Univ., 462 F.3d 294, 304 n. 6, 307 n. 10 (3rd Cir. 2006); Scharon v. St. Luke's Episcopal Presbyterian Hosps., 929 F.2d 360, 362–3 (8th Cir. 1991). At least one court has opted for a multifactor test. Starkman, 198 F.3d at 175–7; *see also* Tomic v. Catholic Diocese of Peoria, 442 F.3d 1036, 1039–41 (7th Cir. 2006) (discussing several factors).

before statutory codification,[381] the court recommends three factors. The first consideration focuses on whether an employer made employment decisions related to the position at issue using primarily religious criteria.[382] The second factor involves whether "the plaintiff was qualified and authorized to perform the ceremonies of the Church."[383] Third, the court considers whether the plaintiff "'engaged in activities traditionally considered ecclesiastical or religious' … including whether the plaintiff 'attends to the religious needs of the faithful.'"[384]

Other courts use different criteria. The Fourth Circuit adopted a "primary duties test,"[385] which centers on whether the primary duties of the aggrieved employee advanced the mission of the religious institution.[386] Building on the primary duties test, a Wisconsin state court developed a test based on mission functionality. This test analyzes "how important or closely linked the employee's work is to the fundamental mission of that organization."[387]

### b. Limits on the Ministerial Exception

While numerous religious organizations have used the ministerial exception to defend themselves against discrimination suits brought by current and former employees, the defense is not absolute.[388] In *E.E.O.C. v. Roman Catholic Diocese of Raleigh, N.C.*, the court concluded, "The ministerial exception does not insulate wholesale the religious employer from the operation of federal anti-discrimination statutes."[389] In *Petruska v. Gannon University*, the court "agree[d] with the implied findings of sister circuits that Congress would prefer a tailored exception to Title VII [rather] than a complete invalidation of the statute."[390]

381 *But see* Hosanna-Tabor, 132 S. Ct. at 714 (Alito, J., concurring)("The Fourth Circuit was the first to use the term 'ministerial exception.'")
382 Starkman, 198 F.3d at 176.
383 *Id.*
384 *Id.* [citing E.E.O.C. v. Sw. Baptist Theological Seminary, 651 F.2d 277, 286 (5th Cir. 1981) and E.E.O.C v. Mississippi College, 626 F.2d 477, 485 (5th Cir. 1980)].
385 Rayburn, 772 F.2d at 1169 [citing Bruce N. Bagni, *Discrimination in the Name of the Lord: A Critical Evaluation of Discrimination by Religious Organizations*, 79 Columbia L. Rev. 1514, 1545 (1979)]. The *Rayburn* court held that "[a]s a general rule, if the employee's primary duties consist of teaching, spreading the faith, church governance, supervision of a religious order, or supervision or participation in religious ritual and worship, he or she should be considered 'clergy.'" *Id.*
386 *Id.*
387 Coulee Catholic Sch., 768 N.W.2d at 882–3.
388 DeMarco v. Holy Cross High Sch., 4 F.3d 166 (2d Cir. 1993) (resolving a defense against an ADEA claim); Starkman, 198 F.3d 173 (5th Cir. 1999) (deciding a case involving an ADA claim); Combs v. Cent. Texas Annual Conference of United Methodist Church, 173 F.3d 343, 345 (5th Cir. 1999) (ruling in a Title VII action); Ogugua v. Archdiocese of Omaha, 8:07CV471, 2008 WL 4717121 (D. Neb. Oct. 22, 2008). The *Ogugua* court held that "[t]his Court recognizes that religious employers, such as the Archdiocese and SVdP, are free to discriminate on the basis of race, color, religion, sex, national origin, age, physical disability, and any other basis, with respect to the terms and conditions of employment of spiritual employees performing spiritual duties. A court cannot interfere in such decisions without becoming entangled in matters of religion in violation of the First Amendment's Establishment Clause." Ogugua, 2008 WL at 5 (footnotes omitted).
389 213 F.3d 795, 801 (4th Cir. 2000).
390 462 F.3d 294, 305 n. 8 (3d Cir. 2006).

### c. Sexual Harassment, Tort, and Breach of Contract Claims against Religious Employers

Investigations of sexual harassment claims made against ministers remain the one Title VII issue from which lower courts routinely decline to shield churches. In *Bollard v. California Province of the Society of Jesus*, the Ninth Circuit held that a novice priest could pursue a sexual harassment charge against the church.[391] The *Bollard* court reasoned that free exercise rationales offered no support for an exception to Title VII. The court stated, "The Jesuits do not offer a religious justification for the harassment Bollard alleges; indeed, they condemn it as inconsistent with their values and beliefs."[392] Given that determination, the court foresaw no danger that a sexual harassment action would permit the secular court to interfere in judgments on questions of religious faith or doctrine. Additionally, the court concluded, "The Jesuits' disavowal of the harassment also reassures us that application of Title VII in this context will have no significant impact on their religious beliefs or doctrines."[393] Instead of applying the ministerial exception, however, the court applied the *Sherbert* balancing test to evaluate whether Title VII's application would constitute an impermissible violation of the Free Exercise Clause.[394]

In a more recent sexual harassment case, *Elvig v. Calvin Presbyterian Church*, the Ninth Circuit allowed a plaintiff to proceed with her claims. The court reasoned that because Elvig had "stated narrower and thus viable sexual harassment and retaliation claims that do not implicate protected employment decisions," she could proceed with her claims without implicating the ministerial exception.[395]

This limitation on the exception is not exclusive to the Ninth Circuit. Another 2004 case, *Dolquist v. Heartland Presbytery*, relied on *Bollard* and the Ninth Circuit's reasoning to find that "the First Amendment does not preclude plaintiff from stating a claim for sexual harassment."[396] In *Dolquist*, the Kansas Federal District Court confirmed that "two state courts [New Jersey and Minnesota] have held that the First Amendment does not preclude ministers from suing for sexual harassment."[397]

Various circuits also have held churches accountable for breach of contract claims arising between the church and its ministerial staff. In *Rayburn v. General Conference of Seventh-Day Adventists*,[398] the Fourth Circuit reminded the parties that "churches are not – and should not be – above the law. Like any other person or organization, they may be held liable for their torts and upon their valid contracts."[399] The court added, "Their employment decisions may be subject to Title VII scrutiny, where the decision does not involve the church's spiritual functions."[400] Similarly, the D.C. Circuit in *Minker v. Baltimore Annual Conference of United Methodist Church* held that the plaintiff could

391 196 F.3d 940, 950 (9th Cir. 1999).
392 *Id.* at 947.
393 *Id.*
394 *Id.* at 948.
395 375 F.3d 951, 953 (9th Cir. 2004).
396 342 F. Supp. 2d 996, 1007 (D. Kan. 2004).
397 *Id.* at 1006 [citing McKelvey v. Pierce, 800 A.2d 840 (2002) and Black v. Snyder, 471 N.W.2d 715 (Minn. Ct. App. 1991)].
398 772 F.2d 1164 (4th Cir. 1985).
399 *Id.* at 1171.
400 *Id.*

proceed with a claim of breach of contract based on oral promises related to his employment opportunities within the church.[401]

The *Hosanna-Tabor* Court's disinclination to address application of the ministerial exception in circumstances such as these only invites future appeals for the Court to resolve these issues.[402] The *Hosanna-Tabor* Court admonished that the purpose of the ministerial exception is not only to protect terminations justified exclusively for religious reasons. Therefore, one can imagine a breach of contract case that could implicate a "minister."[403] One may wonder whether even Title VII sexual harassment claims will survive in future cases against religious institutions.

#### d. The Future of the Ministerial Exception

Supreme Court ratification of the ministerial exception leaves many open questions. Included among those questions are how the courts will further apply the ministerial exception to Title VII and other antidiscrimination claims and which religious employees will be covered by the exception. Current interpretations of the exception provide qualifying religious organizations with a wide berth in making employment decisions. Any constriction of the latitude may come more likely from congressional amendments of Title VII or other similar legislation than from courts.

## C. Conclusions

Fewer Americans proclaim themselves affiliated with a particular religious organization than they did historically.[404] According to a 2012 Pew poll, "One-fifth of the U.S. public – and a third of adults under 30 – are religiously unaffiliated today, the highest percentages ever in Pew Research Center polling."[405] A 2012 Gallup poll confirmed, "In particular, the percentage of Americans who do not have a specific religious identity has increased, while the percentage who identify as Protestant or some other non-Catholic Christian religion has decreased."[406] However, the Gallup poll also noted that "[s]ixty-nine percent of American adults are very or moderately religious, based on self-reports of the importance of religion in their daily lives and attendance at religious services."[407] Thus legal protection for religious workers, whether specifically affiliated or not, continues to serve a valuable function.

401 894 F.2d 1354, 1359 (D.C. Cir. 1990).

402 *See supra* note 370 and accompanying text.

403 *See supra* note 371 and accompanying text.

404 Pew Research Center, Forum on Religion & Public Life, *"Nones" on the Rise: One in Five Adults Have No Religious Affiliation* (Oct. 9, 2012), *available at:* http://www.pewforum.org/Unaffiliated/nones-on-the-rise.aspx.

405 *"Nones" on the Rise*, *supra* note 404, at 9. To gain more information about religious affiliations in the United States, *see* the recently launched DAAR, Digital Atlas of American Religion. Indiana University-Purdue University Indianapolis, *available at:* http://religionatlas.org. A chart on this site indicates that at least 46 percent of Americans affiliate with some type of religion. http://religionatlas.org/?page_id=44.

406 Frank Newport, Gallup Politics, *Seven in 10 Americans Are Very or Moderately Religious but Protestant Population Is Shrinking as "Unbranded" Religion Grows* (Dec. 4, 2012), *available at:* http://www.gallup.com/poll/159050/seven-americans-moderately-religious.aspx (accessed May 3, 2013).

407 *Id.* For a more general and fascinating discussion of modern trends, *see* Robert D. Putnam & David E. Campbell, American Grace: How Religion Divides and Unites Us (2012).

Protections for religious adherents and employers appear to remain strong in the United States. For example, Stanford Law School just launched its Religious Liberty Clinic.[408] The *Hosanna-Tabor* case reconfirms the Court's commitment to the free exercise of religion, including that of religious organizations. *Hobby Lobby* heralds the advent of religious protections from governmental interference for private, for-profit corporations as *persons* under the RFRA. However, the *Hosanna-Tabor* and *Hobby Lobby* cases also may suggest more jurisprudential respect for corporate organizational mission and independence than it does for religious free exercise.[409] How the balance of rights among individual religious adherents, religious corporations, and the government and between religious institutions and employees will evolve in the future remains unclear. Recent cases suggest, however, that courts remain committed to the separation of church and state in the context of employment.

408 Leslie A. Gordon, *Does a Prisoner Have a Right to a Mohel? Stanford's new clinic take on religious liberties cases*, ABA J. 12 (May 2013).

409 *Compare* Citizens United v. Federal Election Commission, 558 U.S. 310 (2010) (finding that corporate political spending is a form of speech protected under the First Amendment) *with* Hosanna Tabor, 132 S. Ct. 694 (2012) [finding that how religious groups select (or dismiss) their own members is protected by the Free Exercise Clause of the First Amendment]. One analyst recently noted

> In the eight years since Chief Justice Roberts joined the court, it has allowed corporations to spend freely in elections in the Citizens United case, has shielded them from class actions and human rights suits, and has made arbitration the favored way to resolve many disputes. Business groups say the Roberts court's decisions have helped combat frivolous lawsuits, while plaintiffs' lawyers say the rulings have destroyed legitimate claims for harm from faulty products, discriminatory practices and fraud.

Adam Liptak, *Corporations Find a Friend in the Supreme Court*, N.Y. Times (May 4, 2013), *available at:* http://www.nytimes.com/2013/05/05/business/pro-business-decisions-are-defining-this-supreme-court.html?ref=todayspaper. For a print version of this article, *see* Adam Liptak, *Friend of the Corporation*, N.Y.Times, May 5, 2013, BU1.

# 12 Land Use

Angela C. Carmella*

This chapter addresses the variety of laws that affect real property used by religious organizations (and to a lesser degree individuals) for religious purposes. It starts with the most obvious form of land use control: zoning. After a brief description of earlier jurisprudential trends, attention turns to federal law: the Religious Land Use and Institutionalized Persons Act of 2000 (RLUIPA), which governs the regulatory relationship between local governments and religious organizations. The chapter then moves from a consideration of zoning and RLUIPA to a host of other topics relevant to individuals and groups as they use their property for religious purposes: the law of nuisance and private restrictive covenants; laws relating to charity, sanctuary, and surveillance; laws against desecration of religious sites and disruption of religious services; historic preservation; and eminent domain. Note the special regard often given the house of worship as courts, legislatures, and agencies attempt to protect this preeminent locus of religious activity and symbol of religious pluralism while at the same time balancing other significant social, aesthetic, and economic considerations.

## A. Zoning Religious Land Use: Twentieth-Century State and Federal Developments

### 1. *Land Use Controls on Religious Properties*

Religious exercise, even when focused on matters transcendent, occurs here and now in a physical space. Thus it is not surprising that religious groups worship and conduct nearly all their ancillary activities – education, pastoral work, service to society – on real property and usually on real property that they own; alternatively, they rent space or meet in private homes.[1] Access to land and buildings is quite

* Professor of Law, Seton Hall University School of Law.

1 Of course, there are itinerant preachers and proselytizers, such as the Jehovah's Witnesses, who fought for the right to use public spaces (e.g., sidewalks, parks) for religious outreach. But even Jehovah's Witnesses worship in their own Kingdom Halls. In the 1994 Survey of Religious Organizations at the National Level, conducted for the DePaul University Center for Church/State Studies by the Northwestern University Survey Laboratory, 96 percent of religious groups surveyed reported that they hold religious services at least once a week; of those respondents, 89 percent own their houses of worship and 11 percent lease space for worship. *See* Angela C. Carmella, *Land Use Regulation of Churches*, *in* Religious Organizations in the United States 565, 566–7 (James A. Serritella ed., 2006). Note that in addition to church rentals of private property, church rental of public property that is made generally available to the community is common. *See, e.g.*, Vineyard Christian Fellowship v. City of Evanston, 250 F. Supp. 2d 961, 970 (N.D. Ill.

clearly a precondition to religious assembly and religious exercise.[2] As one federal judge commented,

> [p]laces of worship have in almost all religions been as integral to their religion as have Sunday School, preaching, hymn singing, prayer, and other forms of worship which we have traditionally recognized as the "exercise" of religion. Churches are the situs for the most sacred, traditional exercise of religion: baptisms, confirmations, marriages, funerals, sacramental services, ordinations, and rites of passage of all kinds.
>
> [T]he place of worship is central to the first amendment concept of free exercise as essentially the only place of religious "assembly" and the central place for the expression of religious "speech." Thus, when government agencies seek to encumber the use of buildings for religious worship, they are, in fact, impinging on speech, assembly, and religious exercise through the use of zoning ordinances.[3]

Land use regulations – zoning and planning in particular – focus on the kinds of negative impacts generated by various kinds of land use on surrounding properties, which often undermine municipal goals, and seek to control these "secondary effects" by categorizing and regulating uses and dimensions. These secondary effects include traffic, noise, congestion, and other environmental externalities; infrastructure burdens on sewers and roads and the increased need for safety services such as fire and police; changes to neighborhood character; threats to aesthetic and economic values; reductions in the tax base; and thwarting economic revitalization or the creation of districts of a particular character.

Zoning ordinances create three main use categories: in any given zone, there will be uses that are permitted "as of right" and uses that are forbidden; there also may be uses that are "conditional" – that is, they may be approved but with conditions attached to a "special" or "conditional use" permit intended to mitigate negative secondary impacts. Additionally, even a forbidden use might be permitted by a "variance process" on the finding of a particular hardship. There also may be a variety of special zones that provide additional flexibility, such as planned unit developments (PUDs) and cluster zones; rezoning also may be an option. And, of course, dimensional controls are a critical adjunct to use controls: they govern the height, bulk, density, and location of buildings; lot size and shape; aesthetics (in gross terms); and the relationship between the building and the lot. These controls also set out rules that indicate the kinds of dimensions that are as of right, permitted with conditions, or forbidden. Nonconforming uses and dimensions that predate zoning changes are "grandfathered" and continue (even after transfer) until abandoned or terminated by some event or occurrence.

As is the case for all real property, property used for religious purposes is subject to use and dimensional controls. Houses of worship are often categorized with other assembly

2003). This practice has been upheld in the face of Establishment Clause challenges. *See, e.g.*, Resnick v. E. Brunswick Twp. Bd. of Educ., 389 A.2d 944 (N.J. 1978); *but see* Bronx Household of Faith v. Bd. of Educ. of N.Y. City, 750 F.3d 184 (2d Cir. 2014) (upholding prohibition on church worship services in public school buildings), *cert. denied*, 135 S. Ct. 1730 (2015).

2 "Inherent in any religion is a community of worship, rather than just the faith or conduct of a lone worshiper. Physical access to a community of worship is crucial to a religious observer's ability to practice both faith and religious conduct within the community. A governmental regulation that precludes such access to the worshiping community presents a substantial burden to the religious exercise." Castle Hills First Baptist Church v. City of Castle Hills, No. SA-01-CA-1149-RF, 2004 WL 546792 (W.D. Tex. Mar. 17, 2004).

3 Messiah Baptist Church v. Cnty. of Jefferson, 859 F.2d 820, 828–9 (10th Cir. 1988) (McKay, J., dissenting).

uses, such as theaters, meeting halls, educational buildings, and other noncommercial uses. Religious schools, fellowship halls, and social services will be zoned depending on whether they are accessory to a house of worship or are the exclusive or primary use of a parcel. (The phenomenon of "megachurches," which combine the sanctuary with multiple and often nontraditional accessory uses, has proven a particular challenge for zoning officials.) Houses of worship and other adjunct uses may be excluded from residential neighborhoods; in fact, they may be excluded from many different zones: commercial, office/professional, industrial, agricultural, entertainment, and special zones for economic or downtown redevelopment. When religious groups seek to build a new structure in a particular zone or seek to change an existing building or its use, they often have to seek some form of permission from zoning authorities. Permission may be denied or restricted in some way. Preventing or restricting the location, expansion, or operation of religious uses by way of land use regulation has been a source of litigation for many decades.

## 2. *Losing the Connection between Religious Exercise and Land Use*

For most of the twentieth century, litigation involving religious land uses was brought at the state level.[4] Religious groups often sued for access to exclusively residential zones. In the decisions that resulted, most state courts recognized the connection between religious exercise and land use, prohibiting blanket exclusions of houses of worship from residential zones. Sometimes the prohibition was explicitly grounded on a church's freedom of worship and assembly,[5] but more often it was framed in terms of substantive due process.[6] Indeed, it was not unusual to find a presumption that houses of worship promoted the general welfare and morals of the community, which either conclusively outweighed negative secondary effects or could be rebutted in certain circumstances.[7] When neighbors complained of traffic, parking, noise, or decreased property values that would result from building a house of worship in the area, courts often refused to support zoning exclusions because "[r]eligious structures enjoy a constitutionally protected status which severely curtails the permissible extent of governmental regulation in the name of the police powers."[8] A minority of state courts began to reject any specific constitutional status for these buildings or their presumptively beneficial nature[9] and to give land use priority to ensure peaceful residential neighborhoods, undisturbed by the

4 *See generally* Mark W. Cordes, *Where to Pray? Religious Zoning and the First Amendment*, 35 U. KAN. L. REV. 697 (1987) (collecting cases); Laurie Reynolds, *Zoning and the Church: The Police Power versus the First Amendment*, 64 B.U. L. REV. 767 (1985) (collecting cases).

5 Bd. of Zoning Appeals of Meridian Hills v. Schulte, 172 N.E.2d 39, 44 (Ind. 1961).

6 "The primary rationale for invalidating such exclusions has not stemmed from concern with freedom of religion, but rather from a due process analysis which concludes that such exclusions are arbitrary and capricious and fail to promote the public health, safety, morals or welfare. In so holding, courts have reasoned that churches, by their very nature, are 'clearly in furtherance of the public morals and general welfare,' often emphasizing the moral guidance they provide to communities. Despite this frequent emphasis on substantive due process analysis, a close reading of these decisions suggests that religious freedom has also been involved in the courts' reasoning and has occasionally been articulated as a primary reason for invalidating locational restrictions." Cordes, *supra* note 4, at 706–7 (citations omitted).

7 *See generally* Cornell Univ. v. Bagnardi, 503 N.E. 2d 509 (N.Y. 1980).

8 Westchester Reform Temple v. Brown, 239 N.E.2d 891, 896 (N.Y. 1968).

9 *See, e.g.*, Congregation Kol Ami v. Abington Twp., 309 F.3d 120, 139 (3d Cir. 2002) (citing cases on both sides of the presumption issue and rejecting it).

noise and traffic caused by religious assembly uses.[10] Nevertheless, despite state-to-state variations in case law, most jurisdictions recognized the relationship between protecting houses of worship from zoning exclusions and facilitating religious exercise.

In the 1980s, when religious claimants started to bring zoning challenges in federal court, this basic connection between land use and religious exercise got severed. Borrowing directly from the minority courts' reasoning in religious zoning cases, federal courts employed rational basis review despite the prevailing strict scrutiny standard of *Sherbert v. Verner*.[11] The Eleventh Circuit denied the free exercise claim of a rabbi who was ordered by the town to cease using his home as a synagogue because he could go elsewhere – to a zone that allowed house of worship use.[12] The Sixth Circuit rejected the claim of a Jehovah's Witness congregation that had been denied a permit to build a Kingdom Hall in a residential zone.[13] Viewing the location of a church as a secular matter, the court found that constructing the church building "has no religious or ritualistic significance for the Jehovah's Witnesses … its freedom to worship is [only] tangentially related to worshipping in its own structure."[14] The Tenth Circuit likewise rejected the free exercise claim of a church excluded from an agricultural zone. The court found "no evidence that building a church, or building a church on a particular site, is intimately related to the religious tenets of the church."[15] Like the rabbi, these churches could simply relocate to other zones where religious assembly was permitted. Indeed, the Sixth Circuit thought the Jehovah's Witnesses had plenty of alternative locations, even when 90 percent of the municipality excluded houses of worship. A dissenting Tenth Circuit judge commented that "[t]o claim that this case is only concerned with the construction of a building is to miss the point."[16]

Many federal courts went out of their way to reject the connection between land use regulation and religious exercise, and even courts that entertained the notion of a connection considered it to be highly attenuated. Land use decisions that affected the location, construction, or expansion of religious property were viewed as causing only minor economic or aesthetic burdens as long as there was a theoretical alternative location within the municipality.[17] This approach, among other trends, resulted in near-total deference to land use regulation in the federal courts in the years leading up to *Employment Division v. Smith*,[18] as well as after.[19] Consistent with *Smith*'s antidiscrimination principle, only cases of overt, egregious hostility toward a particular congregation triggered

[10] Without a doubt, municipalities have legitimate interests in controlling secondary effects of assembly uses, such as traffic and noise. As religious land uses became more intense and their impacts more severe, the substantive due process argument became increasingly difficult to defend.

[11] 374 U.S. 398 (1963).

[12] Grosz v. City of Miami Beach, 721 F.2d 729 (11th Cir. 1983).

[13] Lakewood, Ohio Congregation of Jehovah's Witnesses v. City of Lakewood, 699 F.2d 303 (6th Cir. 1983).

[14] *Id.* at 306–7.

[15] Messiah Baptist Church v. Cnty. of Jefferson, 859 F.2d 820, 824–5 (10th Cir. 1988).

[16] *Id.* at 830 (McKay, J., dissenting).

[17] Christian Gospel Church, Inc. v. City & Cnty. of S.F., 896 F.2d 1221, 1224 (9th Cir. 1990); Messiah Baptist Church v. Cnty. of Jefferson, 859 F.2d 820, 824–5 (10th Cir. 1988); Grosz v. City of Miami Beach, 721 F.2d 729, 739–40 (11th Cir. 1983); Lakewood, Ohio Congregation of Jehovah's Witnesses, Inc. v. City of Lakewood, 699 F.2d 303, 304 (6th Cir. 1983).

[18] 494 U.S. 872 (1990).

[19] *See, e.g.*, Messiah Baptist Church v. Cnty. of Jefferson, 859 F.2d 820 (10th Cir. 1988); Christian Gospel Church, Inc. v. City & Cnty. of S.F., 896 F.2d 1221 (9th Cir. 1990); Grosz v. City of Miami Beach, 721 F.2d 729 (11th Cir. 1983); Cornerstone Bible Church v. City of Hastings, 948 F.2d 464 (8th Cir. 1991);

Free Exercise Clause protection. We see the antidiscrimination principle at work in a 1988 decision of the Fifth Circuit.[20] In that case, the court held that the Free Exercise Clause protected a Muslim organization that had been repeatedly denied permission to locate its mosque in a particular zone while many Christian church buildings had been permitted to locate there.

Thus the federal case law of the 1980s and 1990s reflected the widespread notion that land use regulation is a familiar, flexible, and necessary tool of local governments and deserves deference in the absence of discrimination.[21] Indeed, even the Supreme Court seemed to think that this deference was appropriate, based on several indicators. First, shortly after *Smith*, the Court's procedural actions in several historic preservation decisions suggested this position: it denied *certiorari* in a Second Circuit decision that had applied *Smith* to uphold the government's actions and remanded for reconsideration in light of *Smith* a state court decision that had applied strict scrutiny to strike the government's actions.[22] Second, the first post-*Smith* case to reach the Supreme Court, *Church of the Lukumi Babalu Aye v. City of Hialeah*, was a land use case of overt antidiscrimination, which gave the Court the opportunity to demarcate emphatically the line between neutral and hostile government actions.[23] Finally, this sense that nondiscriminatory land use regulation deserved deference was solidified in the Court's 1997 decision in *City of Boerne v. Flores*, where Justice Kennedy noted, "It is a reality of the modern regulatory state that numerous state laws, such as the zoning regulations at issue here, impose a substantial burden on a large class of individuals. When the exercise of religion has been burdened in an incidental way by a law of general application, it does not follow that the persons affected have been burdened any more than their fellow citizens, let alone burdened because of their religious beliefs."[24]

Rector of St. Bartholomew's Church v. City of N.Y. & Landmarks Preservation Comm'n, 914 F.2d 348 (2d Cir. 1990); Salvation Army v. Dep't of Cmty. Affairs, 919 F.2d 183 (3d Cir. 1990). Other federal courts took a similar approach in cases of accessory uses. *See, e.g.*, Christ College, Inc. v. Bd. of Supervisors, 944 F.2d 901 (4th Cir. 1991 unpublished) (school); First Assembly of God v. Collier Cnty., 27 F.3d 526 (11th Cir. 1994) (homeless shelter).

20 Islamic Ctr. of Miss., Inc. v. City of Starkville, 840 F.2d 293, 302–3 (5th Cir. 1988) (substantial burden found when permit denial was based on clear anti-Muslim discrimination); *see also* Marks v. City of Chesapeake, 883 F.2d 308, 309–10 (4th Cir. 1989) (city arbitrarily and capriciously denied permit when it placated religious objections of neighbors to a fortune teller/palmistry business).

21 Zoning, historic preservation, and eminent domain need only satisfy rational basis review in most contexts. Village of Euclid v. Ambler Realty, 272 U.S. 365, 388 (1926) ("If the validity of the legislative classification for zoning purposes be fairly debatable, the legislative judgment must be allowed to control."); Penn Central Transp. Co. v. City of N.Y., 438 U.S. 104 (1978) (historic preservation); Kelo v. City of New London, 545 U.S. 469 (2005) (eminent domain). Courts occasionally depart from rational basis to give heightened scrutiny under the Free Speech Clause to zoning controls aimed at adult establishments.

22 *See* Rector of St. Bartholomew's Church v. City of N.Y. & Landmarks Preservation Comm'n, 914 F.2d 348 (2d Cir. 1990), *cert. denied* 499 U.S. 905 (1991); First Covenant Church v. City of Seattle, 787 P.2d 1352 (Wash. 1990) (First Covenant I), *vacated and remanded*, 499 U.S. 901 (1991), *on remand*, 840 P.2d 174 (Wash. 1992) (First Covenant II).

23 508 U.S. 520 (1993). The city passed four land use ordinances all aimed at ensuring that the church – and only this church – could not establish a place of worship in the city because of its practice of ritual animal sacrifice. The laws contained so many exemptions for all sorts of animal killings that the only conduct to come within the scope of the law was this church's ritual sacrifice. The law was neither neutral nor generally applicable, so *Smith* did not apply, and the city could not meet the compelling interest requirement.

24 521 U.S. 507, 535 (1997) (holding RFRA unconstitutional as applied to state laws because it exceeds Congress's authority under Section 5 of the Fourteenth Amendment).

### 3. *Attempts to Restore the Connection between Religious Exercise and Land Use*

In the post-*Smith* world, courts had three avenues for employing a strict scrutiny standard of review in land use cases. First, several state courts interpreted their own state constitutions to require strict scrutiny in free exercise challenges to land use controls.[25] Second, a few courts focused on the fact that most land use decisions result from governmental "individualized assessments," where discretionary (and potentially discriminatory) evaluations are made, which *Smith* itself considered apt for strict scrutiny.[26] Discrimination did not need to be proven; as long as the government made assessments based on "criteria [that] invite consideration of the particular circumstances,"[27] strict scrutiny would apply. As the U.S. Supreme Court noted of its precedent, "Where the State has in place a system of individual exemptions, it may not refuse to extend that system to cases of 'religious hardship' without compelling reason."[28] Indeed, most land use controls are implemented through specialized and conditional permits, variances, rezoning, and the like, all of which require the discretionary evaluation of proposed developments.

The third avenue to strict scrutiny was the Religious Freedom Restoration Act (RFRA). Passed in 1993 in direct response to *Smith*, it explicitly required a strict scrutiny standard of review for substantial burdens on religious exercise, even those resulting from neutral general laws. "Substantial burden" was not defined in the statute, but several land use decisions under RFRA were quite generous in their understanding of what kinds of laws burdened religious exercise in violation of the statute.[29] In several decisions in which

25 Soc'y of Jesus v. Boston Landmarks Comm'n, 564 N.E.2d 571 (Mass. 1990); First Covenant II, *supra* note 22 (one ground among others). For an interesting discussion of separate state and federal interpretations, *see* City Chapel Evangelical Free, Inc. v. City of S. Bend *ex rel.* Dep't of Redevelopment, 744 N.E.2d 443 (Ind. 2001). On the interpretation of state constitutions to provide strict scrutiny review in all sorts of religious exercise cases, *see generally* William W. Bassett et al., Religious Organizations and the Law § 2.63 (West 2012).

26 First Covenant II, *supra* note 22 (historic preservation is a system of individualized exemptions); Alpine Christian Fellowship v. Cnty. Comm'rs, 870 F. Supp. 991 (D. Colo. 1994) (city denied permit, reviewed under strict scrutiny); Keeler v. Mayor & City Council of Cumberland, 940 F. Supp. 879 (D. Md. 1996) (historic preservation is a system of individualized exemptions); Korean Buddhist Dae Won Sa Temple of Haw. v. Sullivan, 953 P.2d 1315, 1344 n. 31 (Haw. 1998) (city's variance law creates a system of individualized exemptions). Some courts even continue to apply this today. *See, e.g.*, Hale O Kaula Church v. Maui Planning Comm'n, 229 F. Supp. 2d 1056 (D. Haw. 2002) (city denial of special permit is subject to strict scrutiny under Free Exercise Clause because it is a system of individualized exemptions). Another possible argument, that land use regulation involves regulating both religion and speech, as a "hybrid" under *Smith*, was used successfully in only one decision. *See* First Covenant II, *supra* note 22.

27 Employment Div., Dep't of Human Res. of Or. v. Smith, 494 U.S. 872, 884 (1990).

28 *Id.*

29 *See, e.g.*, W. Presbyterian Church v. Bd. of Zoning Appeals of Dist. of Columbia, 862 F. Supp. 538 (D.D.C. 1994) (Once a church is permitted to locate its worship in a neighborhood, it has the right to accessory uses such as ministering to poor as long as the program is not a nuisance; "acts of charity as an essential part of religious worship" are viewed as equivalent to prayer); Stuart Circle Parish v. Bd. of Zoning Appeals of the City of Richmond, 946 F. Supp. 1225, 1236 (E.D. Va. 1996) (zoning limits feeding and housing programs for homeless to thirty individuals for seven days in a seven-month period; plaintiff churches made "strong showing that feeding the poor constitutes a central tenet of religion," and court issued TRO, no irreparable injury to city and no compelling government interest because substantial disruption not shown); Jesus Ctr. v. Farmington Hills Zoning Bd. of Appeals, 544 N.W.2d 698, 704–5 (Mich. Ct. App. 1996) (nontraditional services for the poor found to be so integral to worship that once the house of worship is established, accessory uses must be allowed; substantial burden resulted from the municipality's attempt "to limit a church to activities and programs that are commonly practiced by other churches rather than allowing it to follow its faith even in unique and novel ways.").

municipalities denied churches permits to provide services for the homeless, courts found substantial burdens on religious exercise that were not justified by compelling governmental interests. Of course, not all courts took this approach because deference to land use regulation continued to be strong.[30] Case law under RFRA ended abruptly in 1997 when the statute was held unconstitutional as applied to states in *Boerne*.[31] State RFRAs passed since then codify a strict scrutiny review of substantial burdens on religious exercise.[32] When interpreting their state RFRAs in the land use context, state courts first have to decide whether they even apply to land use controls.[33] Though state RFRA claims often can be found in state decisions, these claims are easily ignored in federal court decisions.[34]

None of the rationales for moving to strict scrutiny gained sufficient traction to challenge the widespread deference to land use decisions. Thus, after *Boerne*, religious liberty proponents returned to Congress.[35] It remained clear to religious organizations and others that a statute was needed to reassert the fundamental connection between religious exercise and land use. The primary consideration was the potential for intolerance, hostility and discrimination in land use decisions, especially toward minority faiths.

[30] In the Eleventh Circuit, where Grosz continued to provide the interpretation for land use cases, we see *Smith*'s deferential approach and an alternative location analysis. Daytona Rescue Mission, Inc. v. City of Daytona Beach, 885 F. Supp. 1554 (M.D. Fla. 1995) (Denial of permission to serve homeless was not a substantial burden because there were alternative locations in which this land use was permitted; further, even if there had been a substantial burden, it was justified by a compelling interest in regulating shelters and food banks.); *see also* First Assembly of God v. Collier Cnty., 20 F.3d 419 (11th Cir. 1994) (denial of permit to operate homeless shelter raised no constitutional issue because zoning and building codes were neutral and generally applicable and not targeted at church; church could operate shelter in zone that permits them), *modified by* 27 F.3d 526 (11th Cir. 1994) (adding a footnote on RFRA's applicability but irrelevance because it was not raised by parties).

[31] City of Boerne v. Flores, 521 U.S. 507 (1997).

[32] As of 2010, there were sixteen state RFRAs. *See* Christopher Lund, *Religious Liberty after Gonzales: A Look at State RFRAs*, 55 S.D. L. Rev. 466 (2010) (collecting statutes at note 6); *see also* Douglas Laycock, *State RFRAs and Land Use Regulation*, 32 U.C. Davis L. Rev. 755 (1999).

[33] *Compare* Barr v. City of Sinton, 295 S.W.3d 287 (Tex. 2009) (state RFRA applies to zoning ordinance that banned pastor from using two homes to house and provide religious instruction to former prisoners; ordinance substantially and unjustifiably burdens his religious exercise), *with* Cambodian Buddhist Soc'y v. Planning & Zoning Comm'n, 941 A.2d 868 (Conn. 2008) (religious land use is not religious exercise under state RFRA).

[34] Professor Lund offers an important observation regarding why state RFRA claims do not get proper attention in federal court: "The first obstacle lies in the doctrine of supplemental jurisdiction. Under this doctrine, federal courts have the power to decide state-law claims connected to federal claims. So in a case with a Free Exercise (or RLUIPA) claim, a federal court has supplemental jurisdiction to hear a state RFRA claim as well. But the key is this. Federal courts will often not assert supplemental jurisdiction over state claims once all the federal claims have been resolved. So a federal court that rejects a plaintiff's federal Free Exercise claim (or RLUIPA claim) will usually then dismiss the plaintiff's suit entirely and never even get to any state RFRA claim that the plaintiff has also brought. This has happened quite frequently. And another point comes in here too. A federal court will also dismiss a state RFRA claim when the plaintiff is successful on his [or her] federal claims, on the theory that resolving the state RFRA claim is now an unnecessary waste of time. When you take those two points together, you see that federal courts have the power to decline to hear state RFRA cases altogether." Lund, *supra* note 32, at 483 (citations omitted).

[35] After RFRA failed on the grounds that it was not authorized under Section 5 of the Fourteenth Amendment, Congress turned its attention to a new possibility, the Religious Liberty Protection Act (RLPA), which relied on the Spending and Commerce Clause powers for authority. Religious Liberty Protection Act of 1999, H.R. 1691, 106th Cong. (1999). This legislation was never enacted, but related legislation was, in 2000. *See generally infra* Section B.

Local zoning officials could claim that a proposal would generate negative secondary effects as a pretext for discrimination – precisely the type of concern that relates to the government's ability to make "individualized assessments."

In addition to these kinds of concerns regarding discrimination, another kind of discrimination had taken root: a general municipal bias against religious uses. Although the biggest issue for religious groups at mid-twentieth century had been exclusion from residential neighborhoods, by the end of the century it became clear that churches were seeking access – and meeting municipal resistance – to many different types of zones. Based on the assumption that houses of worship (and other religious uses) are incompatible with many other types of uses, municipalities have denied access to just about every type of zone in addition to residential: in commercial, office/professional, industrial, agricultural, entertainment, mixed use, and redevelopment zones. But not all religious uses cause negative impacts, and if they do, their impacts can be mitigated by imposing conditions on approvals. Furthermore, governments sometimes allow intense nonreligious uses in a given zone while excluding similarly intense religious uses – without demonstrating how the same negative impacts are tolerable in one case but not the other. The implication of these trends was clear: religious groups could see diminishing opportunities for access to private property.

## B. The Religious Land Use and Institutionalized Persons Act of 2000 (RLUIPA)

### 1. *RLUIPA Introduction*

Three years after RFRA was held unconstitutional as applied to state laws, Congress enacted legislation to address two specific areas of government interference with free exercise: land use regulation and prison administration. In the land use context, it had become clear by the late 1990s that minority faiths were involved in a disproportionately large number of lawsuits, trying to vindicate rights involving the location of houses of worship and accessory uses.[36] During nine hearings held over a three-year period,[37] Congress considered extensive evidence of religious discrimination in the land use regulatory context. "Churches in general, and new, small, or unfamiliar churches in particular, are frequently discriminated against on the face of zoning codes and also in the highly individualized and discretionary processes of land use regulation. Zoning codes frequently exclude churches in places where they permit theaters, meeting halls, and other places where large groups of people assemble for secular purposes. Or the codes permit churches only with individualized permission from the zoning board, and zoning

[36] "While minority religions represent considerably less than 9 percent of the population, they are involved in over 49 percent of the cases involving the right to locate a church at a particular site, and in over 33 percent of the cases seeking approval of accessory uses of an existing church site (e.g., for sheltering or feeding the homeless). The disproportionate burden carried by minority religions becomes even more distressing if one takes into account cases involving non-denominational groups, or groups that cannot be classified on the basis of information in case reports. If these unclassified cases are counted, over 68 percent of reported location cases, and over 50 percent of accessory use cases, involve … [small] minority religions." Brief of the Church of Jesus Christ of Latter-Day Saints as Amicus Curiae in Support of Respondents, City of Boerne v. Flores, 521 U.S. 507 (1997) (No. 95-2074).

[37] Three before the Senate Committee on the Judiciary and six before the House Subcommittee on the Constitution.

boards use that authority in discriminatory ways."[38] The cosponsors of RLUIPA noted that these findings thwarted basic rights of religious organizations. "The right to assemble for worship is at the very core of the free exercise of religion. Churches and synagogues cannot function without a physical space adequate to their needs and consistent with their theological requirements. The right to build, buy, or rent such a space is an indispensable adjunct to the core First Amendment right to assemble for religious purposes."[39]

Cognizant of this critical link between real property and religious exercise, Congress enacted the Religious Land Use and Institutionalized Persons Act (RLUIPA) in 2000.[40] It contains four provisions that address the kinds of problems religious groups experience when dealing with zoning and landmarking authorities. The statute prohibits (1) substantial burdens on religious exercise that are not the least restrictive means of advancing a compelling governmental interest,[41] (2) treating religious assembly and institutional uses on less than equal terms with nonreligious assembly and institutional uses, (3) discrimination, and (4) exclusion and unreasonable limitation of religious land uses.[42] The

38 146 Cong. Rec. S7774-01 (Jul. 27, 2000) (joint statement of Sen. Hatch and Sen. Kennedy).

39 *Id.*

40 The body of scholarship commenting on this statute is extensive. For a sample of the positions and arguments, *see, e.g.*, Douglas Laycock & Luke W. Goodrich, *RLUIPA: Necessary, Modest, and Under-Enforced*, 39 Fordham Urb. L.J. 1021, 1025 (2012); Ira C. Lupu & Robert W. Tuttle, *The Forms and Limits of Religious Accommodation: The Case of RLUIPA*, 32 Cardozo L. Rev. 1907 (2011); Bram Alden, *Reconsidering RLUIPA: Do Religious Land Use Protections Really Benefit Religious Land Users*, 57 UCLA. L. Rev. 1779 (2010); Patricia Salkin & Amy Lavine, *The Genesis of RLUIPA and Federalism: Evaluating the Creation of a Federal Statutory Right and Its Impact on Local Government*, 40 Urb. L. Rev. 195 (2008).

41 Protection of Land Use as Religious Exercise:

> (a) Substantial burdens
> (1) General rule
> No government shall impose or implement a land use regulation in a manner that imposes a substantial burden on the religious exercise of a person, including a religious assembly or institution, unless the government demonstrates that imposition of the burden on that person, assembly, or institution –
> (A) is in furtherance of a compelling governmental interest; and
> (B) is the least restrictive means of furthering that compelling governmental interest.
> (2) Scope of application
> This subsection applies in any case in which –
> (A) the substantial burden is imposed in a program or activity that receives Federal financial assistance, even if the burden results from a rule of general applicability;
> (B) the substantial burden affects, or removal of that substantial burden would affect, commerce with foreign nations, among the several States, or with Indian tribes, even if the burden results from a rule of general applicability; or
> (C) the substantial burden is imposed in the implementation of a land use regulation or system of land use regulations, under which a government makes, or has in place formal or informal procedures or practices that permit the government to make, individualized assessments of the proposed uses for the property involved.

42 U.S.C. § 2000cc.

42 Protection of Land Use as Religious Exercise:

> (b) Discrimination and exclusion
> (1) Equal terms
> No government shall impose or implement a land use regulation in a manner that treats a religious assembly or institution on less than equal terms with a nonreligious assembly or institution.
> (2) Nondiscrimination
> No government shall impose or implement a land use regulation that discriminates against any assembly or institution on the basis of religion or religious denomination.

substantial burden provision mirrors the existing strict scrutiny permitted under *Smith* in cases of "individualized assessments" and is somewhat controversial.[43] The remaining three provisions on discrimination, exclusion, and limitation reflect fairly settled constitutional principles.[44] Given the legislative goal of protecting religious groups – particularly religious minorities – from hostile land use control, it should come as no surprise that "Jews, Muslims, Buddhists, and Hindus constitute only about 3 percent of the United States population. But in the first ten years under RLUIPA, they represented 34 percent of DOJ's [Department of Justice's] caseload. Cases involving racial-minority Christian congregations represented another 30 percent. Thus, 64 percent of all DOJ investigations involved racial or religious minorities."[45]

The statute directly reestablishes the link between real property and religious exercise by defining religious land use as religious exercise:

> The term "religious exercise" includes any exercise of religion, whether or not compelled by, or central to, a system of religious belief. ... *The use, building, or conversion of real property for the purpose of religious exercise shall be considered to be religious exercise* of the person or entity that uses or intends to use the property for that purpose.[46]

This definition explicitly rejects the narrow interpretation of the federal cases from the 1980s and 1990s.[47] Indeed, courts adjudicating RLUIPA claims have noted the dramatic departure from prior federal precedent.[48] This new definition "undermines the relevance of holdings"

> (3) Exclusions and limits
> No government shall impose or implement a land use regulation that –
> (A) totally excludes religious assemblies from a jurisdiction; or
> (B) unreasonably limits religious assemblies, institutions, or structures within a jurisdiction.

42 U.S.C. § 2000cc.

43 *See infra* Section B.2.

44 *See infra* Sections B.8 and B.9.

45 Laycock & Goodrich, *supra* note 40, at 1029. Note that the United States Department of Justice (DOJ) actively enforces RLUIPA. But settlements of RLUIPA litigation might not always satisfy the antidiscrimination goals of the legislation. *See, e.g.*, Moxley v. Town of Walkersville, 601 F. Supp. 2d 648 (D. Md. 2009) (municipality pays in excess of its yearly budget to buy land from Muslim group to prevent mosque construction), *discussed in* Laycock & Goodrich, *supra* note 40, at 1030–1.

46 42 U.S.C. § 2000cc-5(7)(A)(B) (emphasis supplied). The DOJ website reiterates that "religious groups simply cannot exercise their faiths without facilities adequate for their needs," *available at:* http://www.usdoj.gov/crt/housing/index.html.

47 Congress may prohibit more than what is prohibited by the Free Exercise Clause as long as the "prophylactic legislation is congruent and proportional to the injury to be prevented or remedied." City of Boerne v. Flores, 521 U.S. 507, 518 (1997).

48 *See, e.g.*, Grace United Methodist Church v. City of Cheyenne, 451 F.3d 643, 663 (10th Cir. 2006) ("[T]he statute substantially modified and relaxed the definition of 'religious exercise.'"); Civil Liberties for Urban Believers v. City of Chicago, 342 F.3d 752, 761 (7th Cir. 2003) ("This definition reveals Congress' intent to expand the concept of religious exercise contemplated both in" RFRA and the First Amendment. By expanding the definition to include land use and by eliminating the centrality test, "Congress necessarily contemplated that a broader range of governmental conduct could be prohibited as imposing a 'substantial burden' on religious exercise than the range of conduct that could be prohibited under free exercise jurisprudence."); Lighthouse Inst. for Evangelism v. City of Long Branch, 510 F.3d 253, 273–4 (3d Cir. 2007) ("[U]nlike RLUIPA, which explicitly defines as religious exercise: 'The use, building, or conversion of real property for the purpose of religious exercise,' the Free Exercise Clause does not define land use as religious exercise."); Midrash Sephardi v. Town of Surfside, 366 F.3d 1214, 1225–6 (11th Cir. 2004) (prior case law stood for the proposition that "zoning decisions do not generally impose a substantial burden on religious exercise" and that they suggest the need for the property use to be compelled by or central to the religion – which RLUIPA clearly rejects).

denying the religious significance of houses of worship, for "under the RLUIPA, the development of these properties would have been deemed 'religious exercise.'"[49] Indeed, even beyond this clear definition, courts are directed to give broad protection under the statute's rules of construction.[50]

Of course, the breadth of protection offered by RLUIPA is not the same thing as immunity from land use regulation, nor does it excuse churches from having to make application for special permits, variances, conditional use permits, rezoning, and the like. Particularly in connection with accessory uses, courts are aware that despite this expanded definition of "religious exercise," churches still must prove that use of the real property is religious in nature.[51]

Now that a large body of case law has been generated, we can see the major interpretive issues. Two of the four provisions have generated the most litigation: interpreting the breadth and applicability of the substantial burden provision and interpreting the proper scope and application of the equal terms provision. A detailed discussion of those sections follows. Keep in mind that critics continue to call the statute unnecessary intervention in local land use decisions, and supporters continue to assert that RLUIPA was necessary to reverse the overly deferential federal jurisprudence, especially with respect to covert forms of religious discrimination made possible by discretionary land use processes, and to ensure fair access to private property.[52]

## 2. *Substantial Burden: The Connection to an Individualized Assessment*[53]

RLUIPA provides a long list of defined terms, but "substantial burden" is not among them. Now that most federal circuits have had a chance to interpret the "substantial

[49] Congregation Kol Ami v. Abington Twp., No. Civ. A. 01-1919, 2004 WL 1837037, at *8 (E.D. Pa. Aug. 17, 2004), *amended on denial of reconsideration by* No. Civ. A. 01-1919, 2004 WL 2137819 (E.D. Pa. Sep. 21, 2004). *See also* Westchester Day Sch. v. Village of Mamaroneck, 504 F.3d 338, 347 (2d Cir. 2007) ("To remove any remaining doubt how broadly Congress aimed to define religious exercise, RLUIPA goes on to state that the Act's aim of protecting religious exercise is to be construed broadly and 'to the maximum extent permitted by the terms of this chapter and the Constitution.'").

[50] Rules of Construction:

> (g) Broad construction
> This chapter shall be construed in favor of a broad protection of religious exercise, to the maximum extent permitted by the terms of this chapter and the Constitution.
> (h) No preemption or repeal
> Nothing in this chapter shall be construed to preempt State law, or repeal Federal law, that is equally as protective of religious exercise as, or more protective of religious exercise than, this chapter.

42 U.S.C. § 2000cc-3.

[51] Of course, there are also the standard procedural requirements that must be met, such as statutes of limitation and jurisdictional matters. *See, e.g.*, Congregation Adas Yereim v. City of N.Y., 673 F. Supp. 2d 94 (E.D.N.Y. 2009); United States v. Maui Cnty., 298 F. Supp. 2d 1010 (D. Haw. 2003).

[52] *Compare* Marci A. Hamilton, *The Constitutional Limitations on Congress's Power Over Local Land Use: Why the Religious Land Use and Institutionalized Persons Act is Unconstitutional*, 2 ALB. GOV'T L. REV. 366, 412 (2009) (RLUIPA "has created havoc in local land use governance related to religious entities, altered politics at the local level, and cost taxpayers millions.") *with* Laycock & Goodrich, *supra* note 40, at 1025 ("[T]welve years of precedent show that RLUIPA was and is needed. Churches continue to face hostility and discrimination in the zoning context, and RLUIPA rightly assists courts in bringing the First Amendment to bear.").

[53] Judicial Relief:

burden" provision, we see that several definitions have emerged. Some circuits have only defined it with respect to the prison context, but others have specifically applied a definition in the land use context. Courts have noted that RLUIPA's strict scrutiny provision at Section 2000cc(a)(1) "codifies *Sherbert*,"[54] and in this connection they look to *Sherbert* and its progeny for interpretive guidance.

According to *Smith*, *Sherbert*'s focus is on the government's potential for antireligious discrimination based on the discretionary nature of an individualized evaluation, given the fact that *Sherbert* involved an unemployment compensation claim in a process that gave government administrators discretion to grant or deny benefits. Justice Scalia noted that *Sherbert*'s strict scrutiny "was developed in a context that lent itself to individualized governmental assessment of the reasons for the relevant conduct. … [O]ur decisions in the unemployment cases stand for the proposition that where the State has in place a system of individual exemptions, it may not refuse to extend that system to cases of 'religious hardship' without compelling reason."[55] Thus strict scrutiny remains the rule when the government makes individualized assessments.

RLUIPA's substantial burden provision, with its related strict scrutiny review, is closely linked to an understanding of land use control as a system of individualized assessments because the statute is "targeted solely to low visibility decisions with the obvious – and, for Congress, unacceptable – concomitant risk of idiosyncratic application."[56] Indeed, the main way to support a claim under the substantial burden provision is for the religious claimant to show that the government decision was a product of individualized assessment.[57]

Zoning and landmarking decisions are often found to constitute an individualized assessment under RLUIPA. Many courts find an individualized assessment when government may take into account particular details of the proposed use in deciding whether to permit

> (b) Burden of persuasion
> If a plaintiff produces prima facie evidence to support a claim alleging a violation of the Free Exercise Clause or a violation of section 2000cc of this title, the government shall bear the burden of persuasion on any element of the claim, except that the plaintiff shall bear the burden of persuasion on whether the law (including a regulation) or government practice that is challenged by the claim substantially burdens the plaintiff's exercise of religion.

42 U.S.C. § 2000cc-2.

54 Sts. Constantine & Helen Greek Orthodox Church v. City of New Berlin, 396 F.3d 895, 897 (7th Cir. 2005) [referring to Sherbert v. Verner, 374 U.S. 398 (1963)].

55 Employment Div., Dep't of Human Res. of Or. v. Smith, 494 U.S. 872, 884 (1990).

56 Freedom Baptist Church v. Twp. of Middletown, 204 F. Supp. 2d 857, 873–4 (E.D. Pa. 2002); *see also id.* at 868 ("[Z]oning ordinances must by their nature impose individual assessment regimes … [that] necessarily involve case-by-case evaluations of the propriety of the proposed activity against extant land use regulations."). But not all courts agree that zoning decisions involve individualized assessment. *See, e.g.*, Grace United Methodist Church v. City of Cheyenne, 451 F.3d 643, 651–3 (10th Cir. 2006); Lighthouse Inst. for Evangelism, Inc. v. City of Long Branch, 510 F.3d 253, 276 (3d Cir. 2007); Cambodian Buddhist Soc'y of Conn., Inc. v. Planning & Zoning of Comm. of the Town of Newtown, 941 A.2d 868, 892 (Conn. 2008); Greater Bible Way Temple of Jackson v. City of Jackson, 733 N.W.2d 734, 744 (Mich. 2007).

57 42 U.S.C. § 2000cc(a)(2)(C). An alternative way to support a substantial burden claim is to demonstrate under 42 U.S.C. § 2000cc(a)(2)(B) that the burden (or its removal), even if resulting from a generally applicable law, affects interstate commerce. *See, e.g.*, Westchester Day Sch. v. Village of Mamaroneck, 504 F.3d 338, 354 (2d Cir. 2007). The Spending Powers basis, set forth in 42 U.S.C. § 2000cc(a)(2)(A), is used primarily in the prison context.

or deny that proposed use, as occurs whenever there is a decision on an application for a special permit, variance, or rezoning.[58] As one court wrote, "No one contests that zoning ordinances must by their nature impose individual assessment regimes. That is to say, land use regulations through zoning codes necessarily involve case-by-case evaluations of the propriety of proposed activity against extant land use regulations. They are, therefore, of necessity different from laws of general applicability which do not admit to exceptions on Free Exercise grounds."[59]

But some courts add a discrimination requirement to the individualized assessment analysis. For these courts, the absence of religious bigotry compels a finding that the government's decision was not the product of an individualized assessment.[60] It is important to note, however, that despite the focus on the potential for discrimination, neither *Sherbert* nor *Smith* (in preserving rather than overruling *Sherbert*) requires a showing of discrimination in order to trigger strict scrutiny or to establish a substantial burden to religious exercise; nor does RLUIPA set forth such a requirement.

Given the central concern with the discretionary element within land use regulation, it is not surprising that when a religious claimant prevails on its RLUIPA burden claim, the facts usually indicate municipal behavior that is unfair, arbitrary, capricious, deceptive, and/or hostile. Even if the behavior does not rise to the level of discrimination under the separate discrimination provision of the statute or under the Equal Protection Clause, it is clear that courts are more likely to find a substantial burden because local governments have misused their power to thwart the basic rights of religious organizations.[61]

### 3. *Substantial Burden: Court Definitions*

Federal courts of appeal have taken widely varying approaches to defining "substantial burden" under RLUIPA. The Seventh Circuit made it hard to establish such a burden when it stated in *City League of Urban Believers (CLUB) v. City of Chicago* that "a land-use regulation that imposes a substantial burden on religious exercise is one that *necessarily bears direct, primary, and fundamental responsibility for rendering religious exercise* – including the use of real property for the purpose thereof within the regulated jurisdiction generally – *effectively impracticable*."[62] The Ninth Circuit, in *Guru Nanak Sikh Society of Yuba County v. Sutter County*, chose a far less rigid formulation when it offered a plain-language interpretation of substantial burden. "[F]or a land use regulation to impose a 'substantial

58 *See, e.g.*, Chabad Lubavitch of Litchfield Cnty., Inc. v. Borough of Litchfield, 768 F.3d 183 (2d Cir. 2014), *cert. denied*, 135 S. Ct. 1853 (2015); Guru Nanak Sikh Soc'y of Yuba City v. Cnty. of Sutter, 456 F.3d 978 (9th Cir. 2006); Midrash Sephardi v. Town of Surfside, 366 F.3d 1214 (11th Cir. 2004); Grace Church of N. Cnty. v. City of San Diego, 555 F. Supp. 2d 1126 (S.D. Cal. 2008); Vietnamese Buddhism Study Temple in Am. v. City of Garden Grove, 460 F. Supp. 2d 1165 (C.D. Cal. 2006); Living Water Church of God v. Twp. of Meridian, 258 Fed. Appx. 729 (6th Cir. 2007); Lighthouse Cmty. Church of God v. City of Southfield, Civ. Case No. 05-40220, 2007 WL 30280, at *7 (E.D. Mich. Jan. 3, 2007); Episcopal Student Found. v. City of Ann Arbor, 341 F. Supp. 2d 691 (E.D. Mich. 2004).

59 Freedom Baptist Church of Delaware Cnty. v. Twp. of Middletown, 204 F. Supp. 2d 857, 868 (E.D. Pa. 2002).

60 *See, e.g.*, Cambodian Buddhist Soc'y of Conn., Inc. v. Planning & Zoning of Comm. of the Town of Newtown, 941 A.2d 868 (Conn. 2008).

61 *See infra* Section B.6 for a discussion of representative decisions.

62 342 F.3d 752, 761 (7th Cir. 2003) (emphasis supplied). This difficult standard has not been consistently applied. *See, e.g.*, Sts. Constantine & Helen Greek Orthodox Church v. City of New Berlin, 396 F.3d 895 (7th Cir. 2005).

burden,' it must be 'oppressive' to a 'significantly great' extent. That is, a 'substantial burden' on 'religious exercise' must impose a significantly great restriction or onus upon such exercise."[63]

Other circuits have taken a middle way, interpreting "substantial burden" to involve pressure that directly coerces a religious group to alter its conduct or violate its beliefs.[64] These courts echo *Thomas v. Review Board of the Indiana Empl. Sec. Div.*,[65] one of *Sherbert*'s progeny, which found a substantial burden where the state "put[s] pressure on an adherent to modify his [or her] behavior and to violate his [or her] beliefs." One sees the influence of *Thomas* in *Midrash Sephardi, Inc. v. Town of Surfside*, where the Eleventh Circuit wrote that "a 'substantial burden' must place more than an inconvenience on religious exercise; a 'substantial burden' is akin to significant pressure which directly coerces the religious adherent to conform his or her behavior accordingly."[66] The Second Circuit agreed. In *Westchester Day Sch. v. Vill. of Mamaroneck*, the court required "government action that directly coerces the religious institution to change its behavior" in order to find a substantial burden.[67] Similarly, the Fourth Circuit noted in *Bethel World Outreach Ministries v. Montgomery County Council* that a religious claimant can demonstrate a substantial burden "by establishing that a government regulation puts substantial pressure on it to modify its behavior."[68]

The First Circuit in *Roman Catholic Bishop of Springfield v. City of Springfield* surveyed the various approaches taken by the other circuits and decided not to adopt an abstract test but rather to "identify some relevant factors and use a functional approach to the facts of a particular case."[69] Those factors include whether the regulation is arbitrary, capricious, or unlawful or targets religious practices or groups in a hostile way and whether the process, though facially neutral, will necessarily produce a negative result for the religious applicant.[70] Though the court did not choose a particular test, it clearly rejected any notion that the burden must be "disabling" or that it must involve coercion to change or abandon religious beliefs. It recognized that most courts have not been wooden in applying particular definitions, given that many factors enter into the analysis of what constitutes a substantial burden.

63 Guru Nanak Sikh Soc'y of Yuba City v. Cnty. of Sutter, 456 F.3d 978, 989 (9th Cir. 2006) [quoting San Jose Christian Coll. v. City of Morgan Hill, 360 F.3d 1024, 1034 (9th Cir. 2004)].

64 "The requirement that a religious plaintiff show pressure to violate its beliefs might be appropriate in the prison context, but not in the land use context where government "lacks comparable control. … [R]equiring a religious organization to prove that a land use regulation pressured it to violate its beliefs would be tantamount to eliminating RLUIPA's substantial burden protection in the land use context. It seems very unlikely that Congress intended this." Bethel World Outreach Ministries v. Montgomery Cnty. Council, 706 F.3d 548, 555 (4th Cir. 2013). *But see* Living Water Church of God v. Charter Twp. of Meridian, 258 Fed. App'x 729, 737 (6th Cir. 2007) (asking whether "government action place[s] substantial pressure on a religious institution to violate its religious beliefs or effectively bar a religious institution from using its property in the exercise of its religion?"). Courts have defined substantial burden in the RLUIPA prison provisions. *See e.g.*, Spratt v. R.I. Dep't of Corr., 482 F.3d 33, 38 (1st Cir. 2007); Lovelace v. Lee, 472 F.3d 174, 187 (4th Cir. 2006); Adkins v. Kaspar, 393 F.3d 559, 569 (5th Cir. 2004).

65 450 U.S. 707, 718 (1981).

66 366 F.3d 1214, 1227 (11th Cir. 2004).

67 504 F.3d 338, 349 (2d Cir. 2007); *see also* Chabad, 768 F.3d at 195–96.

68 706 F.3d 548, 556 (4th Cir. 2013).

69 724 F.3d 78, 95 (1st Cir. 2013).

70 *See infra* Section B.6.

### 4. *Substantial Burden: When Difficult to Establish*

Most RLUIPA challenges are brought after the local land use authority has denied permission to demolish and/or build or to expand existing facilities. Those denials can result from the application of a wide variety of provisions addressing parking, setbacks, lot area, and intensity and compatibility of uses. The religious claimants have to establish that the denial constitutes a substantial burden on religious exercise. Sometimes the proposal is not denied but is granted with conditions to mitigate negative impacts – and again, the religious group must establish that those conditions are burdensome. Substantiality "is a relative term" that "depends on its magnitude in relation to the [church's] needs and resources."[71] Thus a permit denial or conditions on a permit may be considered a substantial burden for one church but not for another. Although generalizations are difficult to make, some overarching principles can be set forth.

It is well settled that the requirement that the religious property owner obtain necessary permits or variances – together with the delay, cost, and uncertainty associated with the administrative process – is not, by itself, a burden.[72] Religious groups, like any property owner, are on actual or constructive notice of the land use regulations that affect their development goals, must seek approvals through an administrative process, and must bear the risk that they may not win the approval for the exact proposal made. Indeed, where there is no reasonable expectation of obtaining permission, courts usually do not find a burden.[73] Similarly, if it is clear after the denial of a proposal that an amended proposal (i.e., one that addresses the municipality's concerns) is likely to be approved, courts usually do not find a burden. In *Corp. of Presiding Bishop v. City of West Linn*,[74] the city denied a permit to build a house of worship in a residential zone because the project would generate numerous negative impacts. The church was encouraged to submit a new application because there were options it had not explored. The court noted that "[n]othing in the record indicates that the city would not approve a revised application that met its concerns."[75] The expense and delay that would be involved in the new application process were necessary to making an acceptable development plan.[76] Courts have, however, determined that in certain circumstances, reworking and resubmitting an application, along with the associated delays and costs, can indeed be unreasonable and create a substantial burden.[77]

[71] World Outreach Conference Ctr. v. City of Chicago, 591 F.3d 531, 539 (7th Cir. 2009).

[72] *See, e.g.*, Civil Liberties for Urban Believers v. City of Chicago, 342 F.3d 752 (7th Cir. 2003); Konikov v. Orange Cnty., Fla., 410 F.3d 1317 (11th Cir. 2005).

[73] *See, e.g.*, Vision Church v. Vill. of Long Grove, 468 F.3d 975 (7th Cir. 2007).

[74] 111 P.3d 1123 (Or. 2005).

[75] *Id.* at 1130.

[76] *Id. Accord,* House of Fire Christian Church v. Zoning Bd. of Adjustment of City of Clifton, 879 A.2d 1212, 1225 (N.J. App. Div. 2005). It also appears that expense and delay involved in the permitting process are not given much weight in the substantial burden determination when the church ultimately receives approvals. *See, e.g.*, Civil Liberties for Urban Believers v. City of Chicago, 342 F.3d 752, 761 (7th Cir. 2003) (where the plaintiff churches ultimately found properties on which to locate, zoning ordinances did "not render impracticable the use of real property in … [the jurisdiction] for religious exercise, much less discourage churches from locating or attempting to locate [there].").

[77] *See generally infra* Section B.6, particularly the discussion of Sts. Constantine & Helen Greek Orthodox Church v. City of New Berlin, 396 F.3d 895, 900–1 (7th Cir. 2005).

It is also well settled that mere inconvenience or financial hardship resulting from the denial of permission does not, by itself, constitute a substantial burden.[78] Thus no substantial burden exists when Orthodox Jews, who do not ride in cars to synagogue on the Sabbath, have to "walk a few extra blocks"[79] or when a cell phone tower on nearby property interferes with the view from the sanctuary[80]; both are considered to be inconveniences. But financial impacts might be a relevant factor in the finding of burden.[81]

When churches seek to expand facilities at their current location, interpretations of substantial burden are hard to predict because the decisions are so dependent on facts.[82] But it is true that courts are more likely to find no burden when existing facilities are adequate. One example is in the historic preservation context. The Episcopal Student Foundation sought to demolish its landmarked building to build a facility that would allow for expanded ministries and worship space. The court upheld the denial of permission, noting the many activities presently conducted in the building, and reminded the organization that if it wanted to expand these ministries and worship in a larger space, it could use its own building (terminating the commercial leases that currently limited its use of half the building) or rent space in a nearby church for worship.[83] Another court upheld the denial of a conditional use permit to operate in a new location because the existing house of worship was sufficient for the group's purposes, despite some physical limitations.[84] Yet another court upheld the denial of a permit to modernize a parochial school. Although a reasonable jury could have found the school's facilities to be "cramped and inadequate," the court found that "in light of the successful operation of the school for many years at or near its current location and its projected enrollment, a reasonable jury could find that the city's actions did not 'impose a significantly great restriction or onus upon the school's religious exercise.'"[85]

It may be difficult to establish a substantial burden if land use authorities grant some type of permission, even if it does not allow the exact development that was proposed. Religious groups sometimes sue governments when they obtain approval for something less than proposed, especially if they sought permission to build a facility of a certain size based on predictions of future membership and ministry. But future plans count for little when "[r]easonable size restrictions … do not affect the [current] ability of members … to worship together."[86] This is particularly true for megachurches that seek to build facilities far

[78] *See, e.g.*, Church of Scientology of Ga. v. City of Sandy Springs, Ga., 843 F. Supp. 2d 1328 (N.D. Ga. 2012).

[79] Midrash Sephardi, Inc. v. Town of Surfside, 366 F.3d 1214, 1228 (11th Cir. 2004).

[80] Omnipoint Communications, Inc. v. City of White Plains, 202 F.R.D. 402 (S.D.N.Y. 2001).

[81] *See, e.g.*, Karla L. Chaffee & Dwight H. Merriam, *Six Fact Patterns of Substantial Burden in RLUIPA: Lessons for Potential Litigants*, 2 ALB. GOV'T L. REV. 437, 455–7 (2009); Reaching Hearts Int'l., Inc. v. Prince George's Cnty., 368 Fed. Appx. 370 (4th Cir. 2010).

[82] Chaffee & Merriam, *supra* note 81, at 452–3.

[83] Episcopal Student Found. v. City of Ann Arbor, 341 F. Supp. 2d 691 (E.D. Mich. 2004); *accord*, Vineyard Christian Fellowship of Evanston v. City of Evanston, 250 F. Supp. 2d 961 (N.D. Ill. 2003) (group was able to use property for many religious uses except worship; expense of renting elsewhere for worship was not a substantial burden).

[84] Williams Island Synagogue, Inc. v. City of Aventura, 144 Fed. Appx. 857 (11th Cir. 2005).

[85] Academy of Our Lady of Peace v. City of San Diego, No. 09CV962-WQH-AJB, 2010 WL 1329014 (S.D. Cal. Apr. 1, 2010) (employing Ninth Circuit's substantial burden test), *writ of mandate claim denied*, 835 F. Supp. 2d 895 (S.D. Cal. 2011).

[86] Chaffee & Merriam, *supra* note 81, at 478.

larger and more multidimensional than most houses of worship. In *Vision Church v. Village of Long Grove*, the Seventh Circuit could not "fathom a situation in which limiting the church to a three-building, 55,000 square-foot facility would impose an unreasonable and substantial burden on religious exercise" for a congregation of 120 when that size would accommodate up to 1,000 members.[87] However, at least one court was quite solicitous of a megachurch's need to establish itself in a new location capable of accommodating a large congregation and varied ministry.[88]

It also may be difficult to establish a substantial burden if land use authorities grant conditional approvals. Numerous conditions limiting future development, use of outdoor areas, and the number of religious services have been found not to substantially burden a church.[89] Of course, one can imagine conditions placed on a permit that are so onerous as to constitute a substantial burden,[90] but more typically, the imposition of conditions on development is viewed as a reasonable mechanism for mitigating negative impacts of a project and a less restrictive alternative than denial of a permit. Indeed, the fact that the board refused to consider conditional approval of the project in *Westchester Day School* (issuing instead a flat denial) was critical to the court's finding of both a substantial burden and the board's failure to select a less restrictive alternative (even if its concerns had been compelling).[91] In a similar vein, the Fourth Circuit remanded a case to the district court on the substantial burden determination where the county had failed to consider any less restrictive alternatives to complete prohibition of church construction in an agricultural preserve.[92] Thus it is important to be aware of outright denials of permission to locate, build, or expand religious facilities because those might constitute substantial burdens.

### 5. *Substantial Burden: When Difficult to Establish – Alternative Location Analysis*

As with the federal case law from the pre-*Smith* era, the existence of alternative locations proves to be a critical factor in the finding of burden in RLUIPA cases.[93] In most cases,

[87] 468 F.3d 975, 1000 (7th Cir. 2006); *see also* Living Water Church of God v. Charter Twp. of Meridian, 258 Fed. Appx. 729 (6th Cir. 2007) (no substantial burden where proposal for 34,000 square foot religious school was permitted at only 14,000 square feet). *But see* Church of Scientology of Ga. v. City of Sandy Springs, Ga., 843 F. Supp. 2d 1328 (N.D. Ga. 2013) (denying summary judgment where church proposed to convert 32,000 square foot office building into 44,000 square foot church and city approved at 32,000 square feet).

[88] Cottonwood Christian Ctr. v. Cypress Redevelopment Agency, 218 F. Supp. 2d 1203 (C.D. Cal. 2002).

[89] Vision Church v. Village of Long Grove, 468 F.3d 975 (7th Cir. 2006).

[90] *See, e.g.*, Roman Catholic Diocese of Rockville Centre v. Incorporated Vill. of Old Westbury, No. 09 CV 5195 (DRH) (ETB), 2012 WL 1392365, at *8 (E.D.N.Y. Apr. 23, 2012). Additionally, conditions imposed on religious property development due to hostility toward the religious organization will fail. *See infra* Section B.6.

[91] 504 F.3d at 352–3.

[92] Bethel World Outreach Ministries v. Montgomery Cnty. Council, 706 F.3d 548, 559 (4th Cir. 2013). *See also* Congregation Rabbinical College of Tartikov, Inc. v. Village of Pomona, 915 F. Supp. 2d 574, 632 (S.D.N.Y. 2013) (Rabbinical college sufficiently alleged a substantial burden because a flat ban on worship facilities under a zoning/wetland ordinance meant that its facility could not be constructed.).

[93] Note a related discussion in Hollywood Cmty. Synagogue v. City of Hollywood, Fla., 436 F. Supp. 2d 1325 (S.D. Fla. 2006) (zoning ordinance was found to give "unbridled discretion" to zoning officials in violation of constitution, which suggests that an alternative location analysis is inconsistent with free speech jurisprudence, at least in a discretionary context that can result in an unconstitutional prior restraint on a place of worship); *and see id.* at 1336 ("[O]ne is not to have the exercise of his [or her] liberty of expression in

religious claimants will find it more difficult to prove a substantial burden if they are unable to demonstrate the lack of suitable alternative properties.[94] Conversely, the lack of reasonable alternatives can work in a religious group's favor, as it did in *Westchester Day School*. In that case, a religious school sought permission to expand at its current location; the Second Circuit held the denial baseless. The court asked whether the plaintiff had quick, reliable, and financially feasible alternatives; it did not. A "theoretical" alternative location made no sense for a long-term user such as *Westchester Day School*, which had been a good neighbor and only sought expansion of facilities on an already large piece of property where abutters were other large institutional users. The Ninth Circuit in *Guru Nanak* also found a substantial burden where there was no real possibility of obtaining permission to build at an alternative site.[95] Indeed, this emphasis on alternative locations has been rejected altogether by some courts,[96] and the very idea of searching for and paying for other property has been considered a violation of the unreasonable limitations provision of RLUIPA.[97]

### 6. *Substantial Burden: Unfairness or Discrimination in the Land Use Process*

In light of the difficulties religious groups may face in prevailing on RLUIPA claims, the advice of pragmatic practitioners to religious claimants is this: "1. Understand that RLUIPA's substantial burden provision does not alter a religious institution's obligation to comply with existing zoning regulations. 2. Rely on the law at the time of application and realize the law may change. 3. Assess current, not future needs. 4. Consider all reasonable alternatives."[98]

But sometimes religious groups suffer unfairness and injustice in the land use regulatory process. As noted earlier in the discussion of the individualized assessment, the

appropriate places abridged on the plea that it may be exercised in some other place." [quoting Schneider v. State of N.J., 308 U.S. 147, 163 (1939)].

94 *See, e.g.*, World Outreach Conference Ctr. v. City of Chicago, 591 F.3d 531 (7th Cir. 2009) (denial of demolition permit for landmarked building, where it wanted to build its family life center, was only "modest burden" on church because it could build on large empty lot it already owned); Petra Presbyterian Church v. Village of Northbrook, 489 F.3d 846 (7th Cir. 2007) (churches banned from industrial zone; church can go elsewhere); San Jose Christian Coll. v. City of Morgan Hill, 360 F.3d 1024, 1034–5 (9th Cir. 2004) (Denial of application for rezoning: "[W]hile the PUD ordinance may have rendered the College unable to provide education and/or worship at the … [site], there is no evidence in the record demonstrating that College was precluded from using other sites within the City."); Midrash Sephardi, Inc. v. Town of Surfside, 366 F.3d 1214, 1228 (11th Cir. 2004) (alternative locations a few blocks away); Wesleyan Methodist Church of Canisteo v. Village of Canisteo, 792 F. Supp. 2d 667 (W.D.N.Y. 2011) (denying church construction in industrial zone where zone was neutral/general and several alternative locations were available including building on existing site).

95 *See infra* notes 113–16 and accompanying text. *See also* Int'l Church of the Foursquare Gospel v. City of San Leandro, 673 F.3d 1059 (9th Cir. 2011), *cert. denied*, 132 S. Ct. 251 (2011) (evidence that no suitable alternative locations existed was relevant to determination of substantial burden).

96 Lighthouse Cmty. Church of God v. City of Southfield, Civ. Case No. 05-40220, 2007 WL 30280, at *9 (E.D. Mich. Jan. 3, 2007) ("[I]t is undisputed that Plaintiff cannot currently use its building for worship purposes. Worship services are fundamental to the practice and exercise of one's beliefs. Selling its current building and searching for another is not a mere inconvenience to Plaintiff. Instead, the Court finds the burden on Plaintiff is substantial.").

97 *See, e.g.*, Chabad of Nova, Inc. v. City of Cooper City, 575 F. Supp. 2d 1280, 1290 (S.D. Fla. 2008) (noting the "limited availability of property for the location of religious assemblies [and that] religious assemblies were subject to inflated costs in order to locate in the City"). *See infra* Section B.9.

98 Chaffee & Merriam, *supra* note 81, at 479–82.

possibility of governmental abuse through the discretionary application of land use controls to religious organizations is at the heart of RLUIPA's strict scrutiny provision. And regardless of the particular definition of "substantial burden," one element is common to most of the successful religious claims: bad behavior by land use authorities, described variously as conduct toward religious applicants in the land use process that is arbitrary, capricious, unlawful, unfair, in bad faith, deceptive, and/or hostile. "Under the substantial burden framework, a court may block application of a land use regulation … where the context raises an 'inference' of hostility to a religious organization, even when the evidence does not necessarily show explicit discrimination 'on the basis of religion' contemplated by" the discrimination and exclusion provisions.[99]

Recall that delay, cost, and uncertainty of the administrative process usually do not constitute a substantial burden. If local officials have treated the religious group unfairly or with hostility, however, courts look at the facts in an entirely different light. In *Reaching Hearts Int'l, Inc. v. Prince George's County*, for instance, the church spent hundreds of thousands of dollars for a seventeen-acre parcel in reliance on the county's actions, only to find that the zoning code had been amended in the interim and that the church's permission to build was limited to only 0.7 acre of that parcel – clearly not enough land for the house of worship, school, and parking. The court found that the resulting delay, uncertainty, and expense constituted a substantial burden on the church's religious exercise.[100]

In *Sts. Constantine & Helen Greek Orthodox Church, Inc. v. City of New Berlin*, the church applied for "institutional" use in a residential zone, but zoning officials were worried that if the church failed to raise money for its proposed house of worship, it would stay in its current location and sell the forty-acre parcel for some nonchurch institutional use.[101] Judge Posner noted that these fears were unfounded because the church had taken all necessary legal steps to reassure officials that it would not do so. In considering the absurdity of making the church "restart the permit process to satisfy the Planning Commission about a contingency for which the Church ha[d] already provided complete satisfaction,"[102] he concluded that "the repeated legal errors by the City's officials cast doubt on their good faith."[103]

> The burden here was substantial. The Church could have searched around for other parcels of land (though a lot more effort would have been involved in such a search than, as the City would have it, calling up some real estate agents), or it could have continued filing applications with the City, but in either case there would have been delay, uncertainty, and expense. That the burden would not be insuperable would not make it insubstantial.[104]

Judge Posner again showed his disdain for municipal hostility toward religious groups in *World Outreach Conference Ctr. v. City of Chicago*.[105] In that case, a church bought a

99 Sts. Constantine & Helen Greek Orthodox Church v. City of New Berlin, 396 F.3d 895, 900 (7th Cir. 2005).
100 584 F. Supp. 2d 766 (D. Md. 2008), *aff'd*, 368 Fed. Appx. 370 (4th Cir. 2010).
101 396 F.3d 895 (7th Cir. 2005).
102 *Id.* at 900.
103 *Id.* at 899.
104 *Id.* at 900–1.
105 591 F.3d 531, 539 (7th Cir. 2009).

YMCA building to operate a community center with recreational and residential facilities for the poor. The city insisted that the church could not continue the single residential occupancy use without a special permit and brought suit against the church in state court to press its argument. The suit, clearly meritless, was dropped six months later. Judge Posner called it malicious prosecution – "harassment by frivolous legal claims" – by city officials, which created a substantial burden under RLUIPA on this small church serving the poor, with "no possible justification for it."[106]

In *Grace Church of North County v. City of San Diego*,[107] a church with property in an industrial park received a conditional use permit for half the duration requested and with no reasonable expectation of an extension. The district court wrote

> At various levels of Defendants' mandatory CUP [conditional use permit] process, Grace Church experienced outright hostility to its application, decision-making that is seemingly arbitrary or pretextual, and ignorance regarding the requirements of controlling federal law regarding the application of land use laws to religious institutions. ... In addition to the burden presented by this process, the Court concludes that Grace Church faces substantial uncertainty regarding whether any future attempts to extend the current CUP would be successful.[108]

The municipality's reason for the permit limitation – that it had to preserve industrial lands – lacked merit because the industrial zone expressly permitted church and other nonindustrial uses.

Then there are cases in which the local officials deny the application, refusing to impose mitigating measures or to consider mitigating measures offered by the religious groups. In *Westchester Day School v. Village of Mamaroneck*,[109] where a Jewish school was denied permission to expand at its current location in a neighborhood of large institutional uses, the Second Circuit found that the zoning board's reasons for denying the expansion – traffic and parking impacts – were unsupported by the board's own experts and completely unrelated to preventing adverse impacts on the public; indeed, the zoning board had simply acted in the interest of a small group of neighborhood opponents and had refused to consider approving the project with mitigating conditions.[110] The court found that the outright denial caused a substantial burden because the school had no "ready alternatives."[111] The court wrote that "when an institution has *a ready alternative* – be it an entirely different plan to meet the same needs or the opportunity to try again in line with a zoning board's recommendations – its religious exercise has not been burdened. When the school has no ready alternatives, or where the alternatives require

106 *Id.* at 537–8. On remand, although the district court disagreed that the suit represented malicious prosecution, it did agree that the meritless lawsuit constituted a substantial burden on the church's religious exercise and awarded the church expenses and fees associated with defending it. World Outreach Conference Ctr. v. City of Chicago, No. 06-2891, 2013 WL 2477193 *10–*11 (N.D. Ill. June 10, 2013).

107 555 F. Supp. 2d 1126 (S.D. Cal. 2008).

108 *Id.* at 1136.

109 504 F.3d 338 (2d Cir. 2007).

110 The court found that the justifications "do not bear the necessary substantial relation to public health, safety, or welfare and [that] the zoning board's findings are not supported by substantial evidence." *Id.* at 351.

111 *Id.* at 352.

substantial delay, uncertainty and expense, a complete denial of the school's application might be indicative of a substantial burden."[112]

In an even more egregious case, *Guru Nanak Sikh Society v. County of Sutter*,[113] a Sikh community sought a conditional use permit to construct a temple in a residential zone. Despite the group's acceptance of numerous mitigation measures and the recommendation of the appropriate county authority, the planning commission denied the application because neighbors complained of possible noise and traffic. The Sikhs then obtained a larger parcel in an agricultural zone and sought a conditional use permit to build a smaller temple on it, in an effort to avoid impacts on neighbors altogether. (The land surrounding the new location was used primarily as orchards.) The planning commission approved, but then neighboring owners complained of possible traffic and lower property values.[114] The county board of supervisors reversed the planning commission on grounds that the temple would cause leapfrog development – even though many developments had already received approvals in this zone.[115] The Ninth Circuit found a substantial burden "based on two considerations: (1) that the County's broad reasons given for its tandem denials could easily apply to all future applications by Guru Nanak; and (2) that Guru Nanak readily agreed to every mitigation measure suggested by the Planning Division, but the County, without explanation, found such cooperation insufficient."[116] Moreover, the Ninth Circuit found no realistic possibility of an alternative location.

The refusal to consider mitigating conditions also was at issue in *Irshad Learning Center v. County of Dupage*,[117] in which a Muslim organization applied for a conditional use permit in a residential zone to locate a mosque and school in a building that had been used as a private school. The application was denied outright. Numerous procedural problems at the public hearings and the county's refusal to consider conditional approval were found to impose a substantial burden on the organization's religious exercise and to violate the organization's substantive due process rights. The court wrote, "Where the arbitrary, capricious, or unlawful nature of a defendant's actions suggests that a religious institution received less than even-handed treatment, the application of RLUIPA's substantial burden provision usefully 'backstops the explicit prohibition of religious discrimination in the later section of the Act.'"[118]

Although eminent domain and environmental statutes are not considered "land use regulations" subject to RLUIPA, in several cases where these were closely tied to the implementation of zoning decisions – and where there was egregious conduct by

112 *Id.* at 349.

113 465 F.3d 978 (9th Cir. 2006).

114 *Id.* at 983. The commission could approve the proposal only after finding that "the establishment, maintenance, or operation of the use or building applied for will or will not, under the circumstances of the particular case, be detrimental to the health, safety and general welfare of persons residing or working in the neighborhood of such proposed use, or be detrimental or injurious to property and improvement in the neighborhood or to the general welfare of the County." *Id.* at 986.

115 *Id.* at 987.

116 *Id.* at 981 (County's actions "greatly lessened the prospect of the Sikhs being able to construct a temple in the future, and ... the county inconsistently applied its development concerns" and "did not assert, much less prove, compelling interests for its action").

117 937 F. Supp. 2d 910 (N.D. Ill. 2013).

118 *Id.* at 942 [quoting Sts. Constantine & Helen Greek Orthodox Church, Inc. v. City of New Berlin, 396 F.3d 895, 900 (7th Cir. 2005)].

the local officials – a substantial burden was found. In *Cottonwood Christian Center v. Cypress Redevelopment Agency*, a megachurch that was outgrowing its current facility spent five years identifying and assembling an eighteen-acre parcel to use as a 300,000 square foot worship center (with a 4,700-seat sanctuary).[119] The church was told that its proposed use was a permitted use and that it needed to apply for a conditional use permit; initially, its application did not get reviewed because of unwarranted delays and then because of a moratorium on all permits. By the time city planners began their application review, the city had begun to consider various redevelopment plans for the site and shortly thereafter tried to take the Cottonwood property by eminent domain to use as a site for a Costco. A substantial burden was found: the church had "a religious need to have a large and multifaceted church,"[120] and its current location was inadequate. But most significantly, the court found "strong evidence the [city's] actions [were] not neutral but instead specifically aimed at discriminating against Cottonwood's religious uses."[121] The city had claimed that it had an interest in using the site to generate revenue and that it needed to eliminate blight. The court found the revenue-generating interest suspect and the concern with blight disingenuous. Urgent action to find a use for the site and to eliminate the decade-old blight had come only in response to the church's permit application. Indeed, if the city wanted to eliminate blight, the court said, it need only let the church build its center. Thus the city failed to justify the taking as the least restrictive alternative for advancing a compelling interest.

In *Fortress Bible Church v. Feiner*, the municipality used not eminent domain but environmental review as a way to make a zoning decision.[122] The church's facility was inadequate, so it bought a new parcel for its house of worship and school. The church submitted an environmental impact statement, but the town refused to go forward with the review; it also repeatedly rejected the church's efforts to address the town's concerns. The town said it was willing to consider a modified plan, but the court found this to be disingenuous. The finding of substantial burden

> is bolstered by the arbitrary, capricious and discriminatory nature of the Town's actions, taken in bad faith. The Town attempted to extort from the Church a payment in lieu of taxes, it ignored and then replaced its Planning Commissioner when he advocated on the Church's behalf, and Town staff intentionally destroyed relevant evidence. Further, the district court's finding regarding the Town's open hostility to the Church *qua* church was not clear error; the record reflects comments from members of the Board indicating that they were opposed to the project because it was "another church." The Town's desire to prevent the Church from building on its property relegated it to facilities that were wholly inadequate to accommodate its religious practice. We affirm the district court's finding that the Town violated the Church's rights under RLUIPA.[123]

These examples show that municipalities sometimes use their discretionary powers (including their assessment of negative secondary effects) as ways to exclude or restrict not just religious uses but particular religious groups – especially minority religious groups. In the examples provided, Jews, Muslims, Sikhs, and nonmainstream Christians suffered

[119] 218 F. Supp. 2d 1203 (C.D. Cal. 2002).
[120] *Id.* at 1227.
[121] *Id.* at 1224.
[122] 694 F.3d 208 (2d Cir. 2012).
[123] *Id.* at 219–20.

government hostility and indignities and were treated in arbitrary, capricious, malicious, and/or discriminatory ways. And in most of these cases, zoning authorities showed a complete lack of regard for the fundamental rights of religious groups by assuming that they possessed unlimited resources and unlimited options to build or expand in other locations. It is easier for a religious group to establish a substantial burden in these types of cases. Thus, in an attempt to prevent government misbehavior, knowledgeable practitioners advise local land use authorities to do the following: "1. Ensure zoning regulations provide equal treatment. 2. Provide for suitable alternative locations for religious use. 3. Produce an adequate and accurate record for decision. 4. Provide realistic suggestions that align governmental and [religious] institutional objectives. 5. Be willing to accept a conforming application."[124]

### 7. *Substantial Burden: Compelling Interest and Least Restrictive Alternative*

Most of the jurisprudential "action" in RLUIPA cases occurs at the first stage: finding a burden. In cases where no substantial burden is found, that is the end of the inquiry. In cases where a substantial burden is established, the court must then determine whether the government has established that no less restrictive alternative exists to advance a compelling interest. Land use regulations have long been held not to constitute compelling governmental interests, and this is no different in most RLUIPA cases.[125] Some courts do find land use regulation to promote a compelling interest.[126]

Sometimes courts will find, or theoretically posit, a compelling interest to discuss the municipality's failure to establish that its action is the least restrictive alternative.[127] This approach was taken in *Westchester Day School*, in which the court noted that the "mere invocation of the general characteristics of" the state's interest is not sufficient; the government must review the "harms posed by the particular use at issue."[128] And the less restrictive alternative available to the municipality was to grant conditional approval even had there been a compelling governmental interest. Even if traffic control had been shown to be a compelling governmental interest, mitigation measures (such as conditions for retiming traffic lights, rerouting traffic, limiting enrollment, requiring busing) would have been less restrictive alternatives to denying a permit.

124 Chaffee & Merriam, *supra* note 81, at 473–8.

125 *See, e.g.*, Covenant Christian Ministries, Inc. v. City of Marietta, 654 F.3d 1231, 1246 (11th Cir. 2011); Reaching Hearts Int'l, Inc. v. Prince George's Cnty., 368 Fed. Appx. 370 (4th Cir. 2010); Grace Church of N. Cnty. v. City of San Diego, 555 F. Supp. 2d 1126 (S.D. Cal. 2008); Mintz v. Roman Catholic Bishop of Springfield, 424 F. Supp. 2d 309 (D. Mass. 2006).

126 *See, e.g.*, Lighthouse Inst. for Evangelism, Inc. v. City of Long Branch, 510 F.3d 253 (3d Cir. 2007) (creating arts/commercial downtown center).

127 *See, e.g.*, Lighthouse Cmty. Church of God v. City of Southfield, Civ. Case No. 05-40220, 2007 WL 30280 (E.D. Mich. Jan. 3, 2007); Mintz v. Roman Catholic Bishop of Springfield, 424 F. Supp. 2d 309 (D. Mass. 2006); Cottonwood Christian Ctr. v. Cypress Redevelopment Agency, 218 F. Supp. 2d 1203 (C.D. Cal. 2002).

128 Westchester Day Sch. v. Vill. of Mamaroneck, 504 F.3d 338, 353 (2d Cir. 2007) [referring to the formulation in Gonzales v. O Centro Espirita Beneficente Uniao Do Vegetal, 546 U.S. 418 (2006)].

## 8. *Equal Terms: Court Definitions*

The equal terms provision states: "No government shall impose or implement a land use regulation in a manner that treats a religious assembly or institution on less than equal terms with a nonreligious assembly or institution."[129] Assembly and institutional uses are intense and typically affect traffic, parking, infrastructure, and the like. Thus RLUIPA's equal terms provision attempts to create some baseline equivalence between religious and nonreligious "assemblies and institutions" on the assumption that their uses will produce comparable negative impacts.[130] One might wonder why such language would be needed. After all, most of the predominant zoning issues of the twentieth century involved excluding houses of worship and accessory uses from residential zones. In that situation, there was no concern about differential treatment because all assembly and institutional uses were excluded. More recently, however, several trends have developed: religious land use has become more intense, varied, and multifaceted than ever before. Churches have attempted to locate religious uses not only in residential zones but in industrial, commercial, mixed-use, and agricultural areas as well, and local governments have been treating religious uses differently from other nonreligious uses for all sorts of purposes in all kinds of zones. In fact, municipalities often consider religious uses inappropriate for redevelopment zones where high economic and entertainment activity is clustered.[131]

The courts have taken a variety of approaches to the proper scope of comparison.[132] In the Eleventh Circuit, if the zoning ordinance is facially discriminatory, any nonreligious assembly or institution can be used as a comparator. This inquiry, by itself, would make it quite easy to find a violation of the equal terms provision, but the court added a requirement that the facially discriminatory ordinance pass strict scrutiny. In *Midrash Sephardi v. City of Surfside*, the city's zoning code excluded houses of worship while

129 42 U.S.C. § 2000cc(b)(1). This provision is applicable only to a "religious assembly or institution." A private, for-profit property owner was not an assembly or institution capable of bringing equal terms claim when denied permission to build a private chapel on its property. Anselmo v. Cnty. of Shasta, 873 F. Supp. 2d 1247 (E.D. Cal. 2012).

130 The equal terms provision does not prevent exclusive use zones. *See, e.g.*, Petra Presbyterian Church v. Village of Northbrook, 489 F.3d 846 (7th Cir. 2007) (industrial area that excludes all assembly uses, secular and religious, did not violate equal terms). *But see* Covenant Christian Ministries, Inc. v. City of Marietta, 654 F.3d 1231 (11th Cir. 2011) (exclusive residential zone is allowed, but where permitted uses in residential zone [recreation centers, parks, playgrounds] had same potential for negative impacts [i.e., disruption and traffic] as religious assembly uses, court found exclusion of religious uses facially invalid.).

131 *See, e.g.*, Opulent Life Church v. City of Holly Springs, 697 F.3d 279 (5th Cir. 2012); Centro Familiar Cristiano Buenas Nuevas v. City of Yuma, 651 F.3d 1163 (9th Cir. 2011); River of Life Kingdom Ministries v. Vill. of Hazel Crest, Ill., 611 F.3d 367 (7th Cir. 2010); Digrugilliers v. Consol. City of Indianapolis, 506 F.3d 612 (7th Cir. 2007); Lighthouse Inst. for Evangelism, Inc. v. City of Long Branch, 510 F.3d 253 (3d Cir. 2007); Midrash Sephardi, Inc. v. Town of Surfside, 366 F.3d 1214 (11th Cir. 2004).

132 Of course, the plaintiffs bear the burden of identifying the relevant differential treatment under any of these approaches. Where a religious group failed to demonstrate that secular properties in the historic district (even if proper comparators) were treated differently, it failed to establish that it had been "treated on less than equal terms." Chabad Lubavitch of Litchfield v. Borough of Litchfield, 853 F. Supp. 2d 214 (D. Conn. 2012). The major question common to all the circuits' approaches involves identifying a proper comparator. When this comparator is not offered, there can be no equal terms violation. *See, e.g.*, Church of Scientology of Ga., Inc. v. City of Sandy Springs, Ga., 843 F. Supp. 2d 1328 (N.D. Ga. 2012); Grace Church of Roaring Fork Valley v. Bd. of Cnty. Comm'rs of Pitkin Cnty., 742 F. Supp. 2d 1156 (D. Colo. 2010).

allowing private clubs and lodges in business districts because "churches and synagogues … contribute little synergy to retail shopping areas and disrupt the continuity of retail environments."[133] Looking at the words of the equal terms provision, the Eleventh Circuit found "that churches and synagogues, as well as private clubs and lodges, fall within the natural perimeter of 'assembly or institution'" and concluded that there was unequal treatment.[134] When the court subjected the religious exclusion to strict scrutiny review, the ordinance failed. The court noted that "Surfside's stated goal of retail synergy is pursued only against religious assemblies, but not other non-commercial assemblies, thus devaluing the religious reasons for assembling. … Because private clubs do not serve Surfside's economic and commercial goals but are nevertheless permitted in the business district indicates that the law pursues Surfside's interest only against conduct motivated by religious belief."[135]

For zoning ordinances that are facially neutral, the Eleventh Circuit takes a different approach. Plaintiffs challenge these on the grounds that they either single out religion by way of a "religious gerrymander"[136] or have been applied in a discriminatory way.[137] In the first case, the plaintiff must demonstrate that "the challenged zoning regulation separates permissible from impermissible assemblies or institutions in a way that burdens 'almost only' religious uses."[138] In the second case, the plaintiff must demonstrate that "a *similarly situated* nonreligious comparator received differential treatment under the challenged regulation. If a plaintiff offers no similarly situated comparator, then there can be no cognizable evidence of less than equal treatment, and the plaintiff has failed to meet its initial burden of proof."[139]

133 366 F.3d 1214, 1222 (11th Cir. 2004). *See also* Chabad of Nova, Inc. v. City of Cooper City, 575 F. Supp. 2d 1280 (S.D. Fla. 2008) (churches prohibited in business districts but many nonreligious assembly uses permitted, such as day care, movie theaters, arts schools, and meeting places).

134 366 F.3d at 1231.

135 *Id.* at 1234–5. *Accord*, New Life Ministries v. Charter Twp. of Mt. Morris, No. 05-74339, 2006 WL 2583254 (E.D. Mich. Sep. 7, 2006) (equal terms violation where nonreligious assembly uses were allowed in commercial district but not houses of worship and where no compelling interest justified the differential treatment). For a different approach, *see* Vineyard Christian Fellowship v. City of Evanston, 250 F. Supp. 2d 961, 978–9 (N.D. Ill. 2003) (on facts similar to Midrash, court finds equal protection violation).

136 *See, e.g.*, Primera Iglesia Bautista Hispana, Inc. v. Broward Cnty., 450 F.3d 1295, 1308 (11th Cir. 2006) (zoning required nonagricultural and nonresidential uses to be 1,000 feet from existing agricultural and residential uses; plaintiff failed to present evidence of gerrymander that burdened only religious uses). *See also* Congregation Rabbinical College of Tartikov, Inc. v. Village of Pomona, 915 F. Supp. 2d 574 (S.D.N.Y. 2013) (religious school sufficiently states equal terms claim, arguing that town's facially neutral zoning and wetlands ordinances were adopted in order to block construction of school on this site).

137 *See, e.g.*, Primera Iglesia, 450 F.3d at 1308 (Church failed to show evidence that a similarly situated nonreligious comparator was treated differently; school was not a similarly situated comparator because the school had received rezoning, whereas the church had been denied a variance.); Konikov v. Orange Cnty., Fla., 410 F.3d 1317 (11th Cir. 2005) (equal terms violation where two to three religious meetings a week were illegal, whereas two to three social or family meetings were legal); *see also* Rocky Mountain Christian Church v. Bd. of Cnty. Comm'rs of Boulder, Colo., 613 F.3d 1229 (10th Cir. 2010) (County treated church less favorably than school, its proper comparator, and improperly treated church's permit application as new application.).

138 Primera Iglesia, 450 F.3d at 1311.

139 *Id.* (emphasis in original).

The Third, Seventh, and Ninth Circuits do not craft their tests in relation to the facially discriminatory or facially neutral form of the zoning ordinance. To establish a violation of the equal terms provision, they require that the plaintiff show that a religious institution is treated less well than a similarly situated nonreligious comparator. The Seventh and Ninth Circuits mandate a comparator similarly situated with respect to "accepted zoning criteria."[140] The Third Circuit mandates evidence of a comparator "similarly situated as to *the regulatory purpose*."[141] In other words, if the municipality restricts only religious uses because of negative impacts unique to them, then it is justified in barring those religious uses while allowing other secular assembly uses. In *Lighthouse Institute for Evangelism v. City of Long Branch*, a New Jersey shore community adopted a redevelopment plan that sought to create a vibrant entertainment area. Because New Jersey has a law that prohibits liquor within 200 feet of a church, the city plan allowed theaters, cinemas, performance art venues, restaurants, bars and clubs, culinary schools, and dance studios but not houses of worship. The Third Circuit agreed with the city that "churches are not similarly situated to [these]" because of the state statute. "[I]t is clear that Long Branch could not create a downtown area where restaurants, clubs, bars, retail and entertainment facilities synergize if Long Branch could not issue liquor licenses throughout that area."[142]

140 The Seventh Circuit in River of Life Kingdom Ministries v. Vill. of Hazel Crest, 611 F.3d 367, 371–3 (7th Cir. 2010) (*en banc*), criticizes the tests of the Eleventh and Third Circuits. *Compare* Vision Church v. Village of Long Grove, 468 F.3d 975, 1002–3 (7th Cir. 2006) (not adopting a separate test but applying Eleventh Circuit analysis). The Ninth Circuit position is set out in Centro Familiar Cristiano Buenas Nuevas v. City of Yuma, 651 F.3d 1163, 1172–3 (9th Cir. 2011), which involved facially unequal treatment of religious and educational uses (requiring conditional use permits) when compared with other comparable uses permitted as of right. The religious uses were treated differently without justification based on "accepted zoning criteria," which include considerations of negative secondary effects. "The city violates the equal terms provision only when a church is treated on a less than equal basis with a secular comparator, similarly situated with respect to an accepted zoning criteria. The burden is not on the church to show a similarly situated secular assembly, but on the city to show that the treatment received by the church should not be deemed unequal, where it appears to be unequal on the face of the ordinance." *Id.* at 1173. *See also* Vietnamese Buddhism Study Temple v. City of Garden Grove, 460 F. Supp. 2d 1165 (C.D. Cal. 2006) (facially unequal treatment of religious and nonreligious assemblies violated equal terms provision).

141 Lighthouse Inst. for Evangelism v. City of Long Branch, 510 F.3d 253, 266 (3d Cir. 2007) (emphasis in original). This formulation is criticized in River of Life Kingdom Ministries v. Vill. of Hazel Crest, 611 F.3d 367, 371–3 (7th Cir. 2010) (*en banc*): "The problems that we have identified with the Third Circuit's test can be solved by a shift of focus from regulatory *purpose* to accepted zoning *criteria*. The shift is not merely semantic. 'Purpose' is subjective and manipulable, so asking about 'regulatory purpose' might result in giving local officials a free hand in answering the question 'equal with respect to what?' 'Regulatory criteria' are objective – and it is federal judges who will apply the criteria to resolve the issue. … [I]f religious and secular land uses that are treated the same … from the standpoint of an accepted zoning criterion, such as 'commercial district,' or 'residential district,' or 'industrial district,' that is enough to rebut an equal-terms claim." (emphasis in original).

142 Lighthouse Inst., 510 F.3d at 272. (Note also that the church could locate in the remaining 90 percent of the city.) While this redevelopment plan was held not to violate the equal terms provision, an earlier city ordinance in effect prior to the redevelopment plan was found to violate it. *Id.* The Seventh Circuit has addressed similar cases involving such liquor restrictions. *See, e.g.*, River of Life Kingdom Ministries v. Village of Hazel Crest, Ill., 611 F.3d 367 (7th Cir. 2010). In that case, churches were excluded from a plan to revitalize a commercial center. The court found no violation of equal terms because nonreligious assembly uses that do not generate tax revenues or energize the retail sector also were excluded: community centers, meeting halls, and libraries. In contrast to the Third Circuit's decision in *Lighthouse Institute*, however, state law cannot serve as a defense to a violation of federal law; the "Government cannot, by granting churches special privileges … furnish the reason for excluding churches from otherwise

The Fifth Circuit has crafted a test that is slightly different from those noted earlier. Rejecting the approach of the Eleventh Circuit and adopting something of a hybrid of the Third, Seventh, and Ninth Circuit approaches, the court wrote that '"less than equal terms' must be measured by the ordinance itself and the criteria by which it treats institutions differently." The court "must determine: (1) the regulatory purpose or zoning criterion behind the regulation at issue, as stated explicitly in the text of the ordinance or regulation; and (2) whether the religious assembly or institution is treated as well as every other nonreligious assembly or institution that is 'similarly situated' with respect to the stated purpose or criterion."[143] In *Elijah Group, Inc. v. City of Leon Valley*, the city had excluded churches from the B-2 business zone but had allowed secular nonretail institutions in the zone (as conditional uses).[144] Because of this, the church plaintiff was able to use its B-2 property for day care but not for religious services. The court found a violation of the equal terms provision "because ... [the ordinance] prohibits the Church from even applying for a SUP [special use permit] when, e.g., a nonreligious private club may apply for a SUP despite the obvious conclusion that the Church and a private club must be treated the same, i.e., on 'equal terms' by the ordinance, given the similar non–B-2 nature of each."[145]

The Second Circuit uses yet another test mandating a comparator similarly situated for all "functional intents and purposes" of the ordinance. In *Third Church of Christ, Scientist, of New York City v. City of New York*,[146] a church was prohibited from operating catering services when a hotel in the same zone was not. Both catering operations had violated their occupancy certificates, but the hotel only received violation notices. The court found the hotel to be a valid comparator to the church because "the Church's and the hotel's catering activities ... [are] *similarly situated with regard to their legality* under [the city's] law."[147] After determining the legality of both the church and hotel catering

suitable districts." *Id.* at 384 [quoting Digrugilliers v. City of Indianapolis, 506 F.3d 612, 614–15 (7th Cir. 2007)]. The Ninth Circuit also has addressed these types of cases. *See* Centro Familiar Cristiano Buenas Nuevas v. City of Yuma, 651 F.3d 1163 (9th Cir. 2011). In an all-too-familiar fact pattern, the city was trying to revitalize its Main Street and wanted to avoid the law that restricted liquor within 300 feet of houses of worship and schools. Although many uses were permitted as of right, all religious and educational uses required a conditional use permit – even those uses that did not trigger the 300-foot restriction. Therefore, the existence of this restriction did not justify the unequal treatment of religious groups, especially since the Arizona legislature had amended the law to allow for waiver by churches. When the plaintiff church was denied a conditional use permit, the court held that it made out prima facie case of unequal treatment under the equal terms provision. For more on liquor restrictions in the vicinity of houses of worship, *see infra* Section E.3.

143 Opulent Life Church v. City of Holly Springs, 697 F.3d 279, 292–3 (5th Cir. 2012). The court made clear that the circuit had not adopted the approach of any other circuit but had established its own approach the year before in *Elijah Group, Inc. v. City of Leon Valley* [643 F.3d 419, 424 (5th Cir. 2011)]. In *Opulent Life*, houses of worship were excluded from the Business Courthouse Square District (which allowed retail and office uses), but other noncommercial uses such as libraries, museums, and art galleries were allowed. The court found a clear violation. The burden is on the municipality to explain "the regulatory purpose and show that it treated religious facilities on equivalent terms as nonreligious institutions that are similarly situated." 697 F.3d at 293.

144 643 F.3d 419 (5th Cir. 2011). "In assessing the City's ordinance under the [Equal Terms] Clause, we conclude that the Clause does require the Church to show more than simply that its religious use is forbidden and some other nonreligious use is permitted. The 'less than equal terms' must be measured by the ordinance itself and the criteria by which it treats institutions differently." *Id.* at 424.

145 *Id.* at 424.

146 626 F.3d 667 (2d Cir. 2010).

147 *Id.* at 670 (emphasis added).

activities under the zoning ordinance, the court asked whether the city treated the similarly "legal" religious and nonreligious institutions on equal terms. The church and the hotel were found to be "similarly situated for all functional intents and purposes relevant here."[148] The court found a violation of the equal terms provision and upheld a permanent injunction against revoking the church's accessory use permit.

The First Circuit rejected an equal terms claim in *Roman Catholic Bishop of Springfield v. City of Springfield*, where the city had created a single-parcel historic district in order to prevent a recently closed church building from being sold and demolished.[149] Whereas the court noted that "circuits disagree as to the applicable comparator" in equal terms cases, it had no occasion to articulate its own test because the religious plaintiff in the case failed to establish any comparator whatsoever. The church had "compared itself to every secular institution in the ... [city], none of which are included in the single-parcel historic district." This argument failed.

### 9. *Discrimination: Exclusion and Limitation*

RLUIPA also incorporates the bedrock principle that the government may not discriminate on the basis of religion. If discrimination is the primary motivating factor for a government land use decision, RLUIPA is available to protect the injured religious group.[150] Municipal officials sometimes justify their decisions with alleged negative impacts (e.g., parking, traffic, congestion, noise, loss of tax revenue, incompatibility with goals of zone) when, in reality, these impacts are only a pretext for discrimination against a particular church. RLUIPA's nondiscrimination provision addresses this problem by forbidding any government to "impose or implement a land use regulation that discriminates against any assembly or institution on the basis of religion or religious denomination."[151] As in the *Starkville* decision in the federal jurisprudence of the 1980s, in which intentional discrimination toward a Muslim community was found to violate the constitution,[152] plaintiffs that demonstrate clear antireligious animus by governmental bodies likely will state a claim under this RLUIPA provision.

Although discrimination claims under RLUIPA often fail,[153] there are examples of unlawful government conduct. A good illustration is found in *Hollywood Community Synagogue, Inc. v. City of Hollywood*.[154] In that case, a Jewish congregation seeking permission to worship in a residential zone was met with harassment and selective

148 *Id.* at 668.

149 724 F.3d 78 (1st Cir. 2013).

150 There also may be constitutional claims under the Free Exercise Clause and Equal Protection Clause.

151 42 U.S.C. § 2000cc(b)(2).

152 *See supra* note 20 and accompanying text.

153 *See, e.g.*, World Outreach Conference Ctr. v. City of Chicago, 591 F.3d 531 (7th Cir. 2009); Church of Scientology of Ga. v. City of Sandy Springs, Ga., 843 F. Supp. 2d 1328 (N.D. Ga. 2012); Grace Church of Roaring Fork Valley v. Bd. of Cnty. Comm'rs of Pitkin Cnty., 742 F. Supp. 2d 1156 (D. Colo. 2010); Adhi Parasakthi Charitable, Med., Educ. & Cultural Soc'y of N. Am. v. Twp. of W. Pikeland, 721 F. Supp. 2d 361, 385–6 (E.D. Pa. 2010); Hale O Kaula Church v. Maui Planning Comm'n, 229 F. Supp. 2d 1056 (D. Haw. 2002). *See also* Irshad Learning Ctr. v. Cnty. of Dupage, 937 F. Supp. 2d 910, 937 (N.D. Ill. 2013) (being treated differently from other religious institutions is not sufficient proof of discrimination; plaintiff must offer "similarly situated comparators" that are "*prima facie* identical or directly comparable to plaintiff in all relevant respects").

154 430 F. Supp. 2d 1296, 1320–1 (S.D. Fla. 2006).

enforcement of code provisions, constant monitoring and investigation by local officials, and repeated issuance of violation notices. And like the zoning authority in *Starkville*, the Hollywood zoning board gave permission to numerous other houses of worship but uniquely denied permission to this synagogue. Furthermore, the zoning ordinance gave the board very broad discretion to deny the permit, which was found to have been denied on the basis of religious affiliation. Indeed, the district court found the criteria set out in the ordinance to be so "broad and imprecise" as to "empower ... [zoning authorities] to covertly discriminate against places of worship under the guise of 'compatibility' or other intangible considerations."[155] The city's criteria for making land use decisions, together with the application of those criteria, disregarded and devalued the need for a careful assessment of actual land use impacts.

RLUIPA's exclusion and limitation provision prohibits government from "impos[ing] or implement[ing] a land use regulation that – (A) totally excludes religious assemblies from a jurisdiction; or (B) unreasonably limits religious assemblies, institutions, or structures within a jurisdiction."[156] Courts sometimes find that this provision has been violated when an unusually and unnecessarily restrictive picture of religious land use emerges.[157] But a court might set a very high bar and not entertain the argument unless the ban on religious uses is total.[158]

### 10. *Nonworship Accessory Facilities: When Is a Use Not "Religious Exercise"?*

RLUIPA defines "religious exercise" to include "the use, building or conversion of real property for the purpose of religious exercise," and courts are often called on to determine the precise scope of this definition. As noted in Section B.1, the statute expressly provides a broad definition and a broad construction of the concept of religious exercise.[159] Obviously, traditional houses of worship and religious schools fall within this definition of religious exercise. What about other ancillary and auxiliary – "accessory" – uses?

Though the legislative history notes that there must be an outside limit to the class of accessory uses that comes within RLUIPA's scope,[160] many ancillary uses have been

155 Hollywood Cmty. Synagogue, Inc. v. City of Hollywood, 436 F. Supp. 2d 1325, 1337 (S.D. Fla. 2006).

156 42 U.S.C. § 2000cc(b)(3).

157 *See, e.g.*, Rocky Mountain Christian Church, 613 F.3d 1229, 1238–9 (10th Cir. 2010) (jury could conclude that land use regulations severely limited opportunities to worship); Congregation Rabbinical College of Tartikov v. Village of Pomona, 915 F. Supp. 2d 574 (S.D.N.Y. 2013) (ordinance preventing rabbinical college stated a claim under this provision); Chabad of Nova, Inc. v. City of Cooper City, 575 F. Supp. 2d 1280, 1290 (S.D. Fla. 2008) (unreasonable limitation on religious groups in search of alternative sites because they are "required to aggregate anywhere from 2 to 7 times the number of properties as the average land user and required to obtain more frontage than any other non-residential uses in the same district").

158 Vision Church v. Village of Long Grove, 468 F.3d 975, 990 (7th Cir. 2006) (requiring church to apply for special use permit did not amount to total ban, so it did not violate Exclusion Clause).

159 Religious exercise "includes any exercise of religion, whether or not compelled by, or central to, a system of religious belief." 42 U.S.C. § 2000cc-5(7)(A). "This chapter shall be construed in favor of a broad protection of religious exercise, to the maximum extent permitted by the terms of this chapter and the Constitution." 42 U.S.C. § 2000cc-3(g).

160 "The definition of 'religious exercise' under this Act includes the 'use, building, or conversion' of real property for religious exercise. However, not every activity carried out by a religious entity or individual constitutes religious exercise. In many cases, real property is used by religious institutions for purposes that are comparable to those carried out by other institutions. While recognizing that these activities or facilities may be owned, sponsored or operated by a religious institution, or may permit a religious

found to fall within the statutory definition of religious exercise. It is not surprising that many uses that are related to the nurture of the religious community are included. A parish center qualifies,[161] as does a proposed rebuilding that would accommodate an expanded campus ministry (with study groups and spiritual community in addition to worship).[162] A guesthouse for Jewish visitors to a hospital is religious exercise because visiting the sick is part of religious observance.[163] Even the deconsecration of a house of worship that will no longer be used for religious purposes is considered to be religious exercise under RLUIPA.[164] A rabbinical college and its accessory uses also qualify,[165] but in the case of religiously affiliated schools that teach a full curriculum, the religious plaintiff may have to show that a religious curriculum exists along with secular courses. One such plaintiff was required to demonstrate that a substantial number of classrooms and areas within the proposed expanded facility would be used exclusively or predominantly for religious uses in the Jewish curriculum before the court accepted its claim of "religious exercise" under the statute.[166]

Unsurprisingly, buildings used "for secular activities or to generate revenue to finance religious activities are not automatically protected."[167] An apartment complex, provided as housing to the poor, was not viewed as religious exercise under the statute.[168] A fortune teller/spiritual counselor who charges fees for services[169] and a for-profit day care for disabled children operating in church building[170] were not engaged in "religious exercise" within the meaning of RLUIPA. Indeed, if a religious group uses property for a commercial venture, its claim to religious exercise may fail the threshold requirement of sincerity. In *Grace United Methodist Church v. City of Cheyenne*, the church challenged the denial of a variance to put a commercial day-care center in a residential neighborhood.[171] The jury found that the church had failed to prove that it was engaged in sincere religious exercise, so it never reached the substantial burden inquiry. And in a unique case, the sole owner of a secular corporation involved in ranching operations sought the

institution to obtain addition funds to further its religious activities, this alone does not automatically bring these activities or facilities within the bill's definition of 'religious exercise.' For example, a burden on a commercial building, which is connected to religious exercise primarily by the fact that the proceeds from the building's operation would be used to support religious exercise, is not a substantial burden on religious exercise." 146 Cong. Rec. S7776 (July 27, 2000) (joint statement of Senators Hatch and Kennedy).

161 Mintz v. Roman Catholic Bishop of Springfield, 424 F. Supp. 2d 309 (D. Mass 2006).

162 Episcopal Student Found. v. City of Ann Arbor, 341 F. Supp. 2d 691, 700–1 (E.D. Mich. 2004).

163 Bikur Cholim, Inc. v. Village of Suffern, 664 F. Supp. 2d 267 (S.D.N.Y. 2009).

164 Roman Catholic Bishop of Springfield v. City of Springfield, 724 F.3d 78 (1st Cir. 2013).

165 Congregation Rabbinical College of Tartikov, Inc. v. Village of Pomona, 915 F. Supp. 2d 574 (S.D.N.Y. 2013).

166 Westchester Day Sch. v. Village of Mamaroneck, 504 F.3d 338, 348 (2d Cir. 2007) [court ensured that "each room the school planned to build would be used at least in part for religious education and practice. … In light of these findings, amply supported in the record, the expansion project is a 'building [and] conversion of real property for the purpose of religious exercise' and thus is religious exercise under § 2000cc-5(7)(B)"].

167 Mintz v. Roman Catholic Bishop, 424 F. Supp. 2d 309, 318 (D. Mass. 2006).

168 Greater Bible Way Temple v. City of Jackson, 733 N.W.2d 734 (Mich. 2007).

169 Moore-King v. Cnty. of Chesterfield, 708 F.3d 560, 570–1 (4th Cir. 2013).

170 Calvary Christian Ctr. v. City of Fredericksburg, 832 F. Supp. 2d 635 (E.D. Va. 2011) (distinguished from *Westchester Day School* on the grounds that the curriculum in this case was not religious).

171 451 F.3d 643 (10th Cir. 2006) (the fact that the jury had been instructed that religious exercise had to be fundamental under RLUIPA was wrong was harmless error; substantial burden not even relevant).

right to build a chapel on the corporation's grounds. When he challenged the denial of zoning permission to do so, the court allowed the plaintiff to proceed on a substantial burden claim but noted the "novelty of a non-religious property owner asserting rights under RLUIPA" because there are no RLUIPA cases "protecting the religious exercise rights of a non-religious organization."[172] It remains to be seen whether courts will find free exercise rights for secular entities under the statute.[173]

### 11. *Laws Other than Zoning and Landmarking: When Is It "Land-Use Regulation"?*

Some courts adjudicating RLUIPA claims have been called on to determine the breadth or narrowness of the term "land use regulation." The statute defines this term to include zoning and landmarking (i.e., historic preservation), and most cases fall easily within these categories.[174] But questions have arisen as to RLUIPA's applicability to laws outside of zoning and preservation. RLUIPA has been found to apply to sign regulations[175] but not to a mandatory sewer tap-in ordinance[176] or to annexation undertaken pursuant to a state annexation statute.[177] Governmental takings by eminent domain are generally not considered to be subject to RLUIPA,[178] but when eminent domain is used to effect a zoning plan, RLUIPA has been found to apply.[179] Similarly, environmental law normally would not count as land use regulation, but when it is used by a municipality as a vehicle

172 Anselmo v. Cnty. of Shasta, 873 F. Supp. 2d 1247 (2012). *But see* Reverge Anselmo v. Cnty. of Shasta, No. CIV. 2:12-00361 WBS EFB, 2013 WL 1934175 (E.D. Cal. May 9, 2013) (RLUIPA claim held not ripe for review).

173 For analysis of this issue outside the RLUIPA context, *see* Burwell v. Hobby Lobby Stores, Inc., 134 S. Ct. 2751, 2768–75 (2014) (RFRA applies to religious exercise of for-profit corporation).

174 Definitions:

> (5) Land use regulation
> The term "land use regulation" means a zoning or landmarking law, or the application of such a law, that limits or restricts a claimant's use or development of land (including a structure affixed to land), if the claimant has an ownership, leasehold, easement, servitude, or other property interest in the regulated land or a contract or option to acquire such an interest.

42 U.S.C. § 2000cc-5.

175 Trinity Assembly of God of Baltimore City, Inc. v. People's Counsel for Baltimore Cnty., 962 A.2d 404 (Md. 2008). *But see* E. End Eruv Ass'n, Inc. v. Village of Westhampton Beach, 828 F. Supp. 2d 526 (E.D.N.Y. 2011) (group obtained license from utility companies to affix strips to utility poles to define eruv, an area for walking on Sabbath; license not a property interest under RLUIPA, so no claim for burden when sign ordinance prevented eruv construction).

176 Second Baptist Church of Leechburg v. Gilpin Twp., 118 Fed. Appx. 615 (3d Cir. 2004).

177 Vision Church v. Village of Long Grove, 468 F.3d 975 (7th Cir. 2007).

178 *See infra* Section G.2.

179 *See, e.g.*, Cottonwood Christian Ctr. v. Cypress Redevelopment Agency, 218 F. Supp. 2d 1203 (C.D. Cal. 2002). The court held that RLUIPA applied because the authority to take, in order to eliminate blight, "as set forth in the Resolution of Necessity, is based on a zoning system developed by … [the city]. It would unquestionably limit or restrict Cottonwood's use or development of land." *Id.* at 1222 n. 9 (internal quotations removed). But the court noted that even if it was only considering the taking, it "would fall under RLUIPA's land use regulation." *Id. Cf.* Albanian Associated Fund v. Twp. of Wayne, Civ. Action No. 06-CV-3217 (PGS), 2007 WL 2904194, at *8 (D.N.J. Oct. 1, 2007), where the court did not reach the question of whether RLUIPA applies to eminent domain because "the RLUIPA challenge does not go to the actual taking, but rather the implementation of the open space plan which is land use regulation. The taking is merely the method of implementation."

for making zoning decisions, RLUIPA has been found to apply.[180] RLUIPA has been held not to apply to federal government decisions regarding the management of its own land.[181]

Does RLUIPA apply to building codes and other safety codes?[182] As a general rule, churches are required to comply with building and safety codes.[183] RLUIPA has been held not to apply to enforcement of the Americans with Disabilities Act.[184] Religious buildings, however, are exempt from the Americans with Disabilities Act, which does not apply its public accommodation provisions to "religious organizations or entities controlled by religious organizations, including places of worship."[185] Note that state and local laws might require religious buildings to provide wheelchair accessibility and other disability accommodations, however.[186]

### 12. *When Municipalities Remedy Their Violations*

RLUIPA provides that

> [a] government may avoid the preemptive force of any provision of this chapter by changing the policy or practice that results in a substantial burden on religious exercise, by retaining the policy or practice and exempting the substantially burdened religious exercise, by providing exemptions from the policy or practice for applications that substantially burden religious exercise, or by any other means that eliminates the substantial burden.[187]

Municipalities thus are free to correct defects in their ordinances and thereby preclude claims under the statute.[188]

### 13. *RLUIPA's Remedies*

RLUIPA provides for appropriate relief against governments and against any person acting under color of state law.[189] In addition to injunctive and declaratory

180 Fortress Bible Church v. Feiner, 694 F.3d 208 (2d Cir. 2012).

181 Navajo Nation v. U.S. Forest Serv., 535 F.3d 1058 (9th Cir. 2008) (RLUIPA not applicable to federal government's own land management decisions). RLUIPA also appears not to apply to other governmentally owned property. *See, e.g.*, Prater v. City of Burnside, 289 F.3d 417 (6th Cir. 2002) (city-owned roadway).

182 For an argument that RLUIPA should apply, *see* Shelly Ross Saxer, *Assessing RLUIPA's Application to Building Codes and Aesthetic Land Use Regulation*, 2 ALB. GOV'T L. REV. 623 (2009).

183 If the building and zoning codes are related for enforcement purposes, RLUIPA may apply. *See, e.g.*, Anselmo v. Cnty. of Shasta, 873 F. Supp. 2d 1247 (E.D. Cal. 2012) (where grant of building permit is contingent on no violation of other portions of county code). *See also* City of Sumner v. First Baptist Church, 639 P.2d 1358 (Wash. 1982) (encouraging flexibility when applying building code to religious school).

184 Anselmo, 873 F. Supp. 2d at 1256–7.

185 42 U.S.C. § 12187.

186 The ADA does not limit more expansive disability protections found in other federal statutes or state law. *See* 42 U.S.C. § 12201(b); *see also* Stevens v. Optimum-Health Inst.-San Diego, 810 F. Supp. 2d 1074 (S.D. Cal. 2011) (state disability law is not preempted by the ADA's religious exemption).

187 42 U.S.C. § 2000cc-3(e) (entitled "Governmental discretion in alleviating burdens on religious exercise").

188 *See, e.g.*, Civil Liberties for Urban Believers v. City of Chicago, 342 F.3d 752 (7th Cir. 2003) (city amended zoning ordinance to remedy discrimination by restricting clubs, lodges, and theaters in ways similar to churches).

189 42 U.S.C. § 2000cc-5(4) (defining government); *see also* 42 U.S.C. § 2000cc-2 ["Judicial Relief: a) Cause of action. A person may assert a violation of this chapter as a claim or defense in a judicial proceeding and obtain appropriate relief against a government. Standing to assert a claim or defense under this section shall be governed by the general rules of standing under Article III of the Constitution."].

relief,[190] it appears that money damages generally may be available. Whereas sovereign immunity prevents monetary awards in the prison context,[191] it does not preclude damage awards against municipalities.[192]

### 14. *Religious Use of One's Home: Applicability of RLUIPA, Fair Housing Act*

In our constitutional system, we provide special regard for freedoms in the home – rights of speech, association, privacy, and religious exercise.[193] Thus, when homeowners or tenants use their residences for religious purposes, we are immediately confronted with the conflict between their freedoms and the obligations owed to neighbors. For occasional uses that are clearly accessory to residential use, there should be no question that there is freedom to use property for religious purposes. From the perspective of zoning codes, small religious gatherings for spiritual, educational, or social purposes in private homes should be treated no differently than small gatherings of people in private homes for any licit purpose. They generate the same kinds of secondary impacts, regardless of the reason for meeting – impacts such as noise or traffic and parking problems, which we typically tolerate as part of residential life even if it temporarily inconveniences neighbors. Indeed, if both religious and secular gatherings generate similar impacts, but religious gatherings are treated differently and less favorably under a zoning code, this might violate RLUIPA's equal terms and/or discrimination provisions and perhaps even its substantial burden provision. Of course, at the other end of the spectrum, if a private home is used exclusively or primarily as a house of worship, zoning officials generally (and appropriately) treat it as a house of worship under the zoning code rather than as accessory to residential use.[194]

190 Note that the United States can enforce RLUIPA:

> Authority of United States to enforce this chapter
> The United States may bring an action for injunctive or declaratory relief to enforce compliance with this chapter. Nothing in this subsection shall be construed to deny, impair, or otherwise affect any right or authority of the Attorney General, the United States, or any agency, officer, or employee of the United States, acting under any law other than this subsection, to institute or intervene in any proceeding. 42 U.S.C. § 2000cc-2(f).

191 Sossamon v. Texas, 131 S. Ct. 1651 (2011) (Eleventh Amendment sovereign immunity bars monetary damages.).

192 *See, e.g.*, Centro Familiar Cristiano Buenas Nuevas v. City of Yuma, 651 F.3d 1163 (9th Cir. 2011); Reaching Hearts Int'l, Inc. v. Prince George's Cnty., 584 F. Supp. 2d 766 (D. Md. 2008) (awarding over $3.7 million in damages as well as injunctive relief), *aff'd*, 368 Fed. Appx. 370 (4th Cir. 2010); Lighthouse Inst. for Evangelism, Inc. v. City of Long Branch, 510 F.3d 253, 273 (3d Cir. 2007), *on remand*, No. CIV 00-3366 (WHW), 2010 WL 1491079 (D.N.J. Apr. 13, 2010); Chase v. City of Portsmouth, 428 F. Supp. 2d 487, 490 (E.D. Va. 2006).

193 *See, e.g.*, State v. Cameron, 498 A.2d 1217 (N.J. 1985). The New Jersey Supreme Court reviewed the question of "whether a municipal zoning ordinance that excludes 'churches and similar places of worship' from a residential use district can be applied to prohibit a minister from temporarily using his home to hold a one-hour religious service each week for his congregation. The minister claims that the ordinance does not, with sufficient clarity, forbid this religious activity, and, as applied against him, it is unconstitutionally vague. We agree." *Id.* at 1218. The court concluded that "the ordinance impinges directly on constitutionally protected interests. The threat or actuality of enforcement could undermine the rights to free exercise of religion, free speech, free assembly, and privacy. For these reasons, constitutional due process calls for the utmost clarity concerning the scope of the ordinance's intended prohibitions." *Id.* at 1221.

194 *See, e.g.*, Hollywood Cmty. Synagogue, Inc. v. City of Hollywood, 436 F. Supp. 2d 1325 (S.D. Fla. 2006) (Denial of special exception to locate a synagogue in a residential zone was unconstitutional;

Most of the cases, however, involve more of a hybrid situation, in which one's home serves as both residence and place of worship; in such cases, consideration will be given to the frequency of assembly uses and the impacts on the neighborhood. For some state (and most federal) courts that adopted a deferential position toward municipal zoning in the 1980s and 1990s, exclusions of worship uses from residential neighborhoods did not raise any constitutional issue as long as alternative locations existed. RLUIPA has called this approach into question.

Several important home worship cases involve home synagogues, which are common in Orthodox Jewish communities.[195] *Grosz v. City of Miami*[196] provides a good example of the deferential federal jurisprudence of the decade leading up to *Smith*. Rabbi Grosz operated a small home synagogue (called a "shul") in an accessory building (a detached garage) next to his home. Most of the congregants were family, friends, and neighbors, but occasionally members of the public (and visitors to South Florida) would come to his shul. Though he held services twice a day, most of them were small and caused no disruption to the neighborhood. The concerns focused on larger, less frequent gatherings. The Eleventh Circuit determined that Rabbi Grosz could move his shul to one of the many zones in which religious uses were allowed; excluding worship from the residential zone, where all similar uses were prohibited, did not violate the rabbi's free exercise rights.

In cases of overt discrimination, which are not governed by *Smith*'s deferential approach, the Free Exercise Clause and the Fair Housing Act (FHA) offer protection. When zoning codes disguise animus toward religious groups by restricting their home worship (either by the way codes are written or are enforced), a discrimination claim is actionable. In *LeBlanc-Sternberg v. Fletcher*,[197] the Second Circuit upheld a jury determination that the village had discriminated against Orthodox and Hasidic Jews in violation of the FHA when it passed a zoning ordinance intended to keep them from settling there.

After RLUIPA gave textual support for an approach that was more protective of religious land uses, different considerations came to be emphasized in home worship cases. Take, for instance, the home synagogue at issue in *Konikov v. Orange County*, a case in which Rabbi Konikov prevailed on an as-applied equal terms claim.[198] As head of a Chabad organization in the greater Orlando area, he held two to three religious meetings each week in his home. The enforcement division watched his home for sixty-eight days and determined that he was operating a synagogue without a special exception; as fines accrued, the municipality even placed a lien on the rabbi's property. It was clear, though, by the government's own admission, that if people gathered at a home two to three

criteria for issuing permit were broad and imprecise, allowing covert discrimination; no other place of worship had ever been denied permission to operate in residential zone.); Hollywood Cmty. Synagogue, Inc. v. City of Hollywood, 430 F. Supp. 2d 1296 (S.D. Fla. 2006) (RLUIPA substantial burden claim is dismissed, but equal terms claim survives.); Hollywood Cmty. Synagogue, Inc. v. City of Hollywood, 254 Fed. Appx. 769 (11th Cir. 2007) (affirming denial of motion to intervene by neighbors).

195 Congregants walk to synagogue, so multiple home synagogues exist to provide religious services within walking distance for everyone.

196 721 F.2d 729 (11th Cir. 1983), *superseded by statute as stated in* Midrash Sephardi, Inc. v. Town of Surfside, 366 F.3d 1214 (11th Cir. 2004).

197 67 F.3d 412 (2d Cir. 1995).

198 410 F.3d 1317 (11th Cir. 2005). The rabbi did not prevail on the substantial burden or facial equal terms claims.

times each week for family celebrations or to watch sports on television, these meetings would not violate the zoning code "so long as religion is not discussed." The court found this treatment of a religious assembly to be on less than equal terms compared with a non-religious assembly, in violation of RLUIPA.

Though ultimately vacated on procedural grounds, the decision of the district court in *Murphy v. New Milford Zoning Comm'n*[199] concluded that the statute protected homeowners who hosted a weekly prayer meeting of over twenty-five people, sometimes with up to twenty cars parked in the driveway and backyard, as well as on the cul-de-sac on which the owners lived. As in *Konikov*, zoning officials had decided that these meetings were not a customary accessory use in this residential zone. After a cease and desist order was issued, the homeowners argued successfully in the district court that the order substantially and unjustifiably burdened their free exercise and won a preliminary injunction.

RLUIPA plaintiffs are usually religious organizations but sometimes are individuals – especially in these home worship cases. An unusual situation was presented in *Anselmo v. County of Shasta*,[200] where a rancher who was the sole owner of a limited partnership, Seven Hills, was denied permission to build a private chapel on property owned by Seven Hills. Although the federal district court determined that the RLUIPA claim was not ripe for review,[201] an earlier decision by the same court on a motion to dismiss highlighted the secular, for-profit nature of the owner. The court wrote, "Although corporations and limited partnerships have broad rights, the court has been unable to find a single RLUIPA case protecting the religious exercise rights of a non-religious organization such as Seven Hills. Based on the lack of clear case law establishing that RLUIPA entitles property owners to exemption from zoning laws when those zoning laws prevent them from building a place of worship on their own property and the novelty of a non-religious property owner asserting rights under RLUIPA, the court concludes that plaintiffs' RLUIPA rights were not so clearly established that a reasonable officer would know that his conduct violated a clearly established right."[202]

## 15. *Establishment Clause Challenges to RLUIPA and Similar Laws*

For purposes of the First Amendment's Establishment Clause, the distinction between permissible and forbidden accommodations can be difficult to discern. Nevertheless, courts generally have been deferential to local governments in crafting religious exemptions or religion-protective treatment in zoning ordinances. The First Circuit upheld a Massachusetts state law that prohibits local zoning laws that exclude religious and educational uses, among others.[203] In what is known as the "Dover Amendment," the state law provides the following:

> No zoning ordinance or by-law shall regulate or restrict the interior area of a single family residential building *nor shall any such ordinance or by-law prohibit, regulate or*

[199] 289 F. Supp. 2d 87, 105 (D. Conn. 2003) (The town had failed to show that the order was the least restrictive means of furthering a compelling governmental interest.), *vacated* 402 F.3d 342 (2d Cir. 2005) (The claim was not ripe for review; plaintiffs should have appealed the order to zoning board and sought a variance instead of bringing suit.).

[200] Anselmo v. Cnty. of Shasta, 873 F. Supp. 2d 1247 (E.D. Cal. 2012).

[201] Reverge Anselmo v. Cnty. of Shasta, No. CIV. 2:12-00361 WBS EFB, 2013 WL 1934175 (E.D. Cal. May 9, 2013).

[202] Anselmo, 873 F. Supp. 2d at 1264; *see also supra* note 173.

[203] Boyajian v. Gatzunis, 212 F.3d 1 (1st Cir. 2000) (other uses included agricultural, child care, and solar energy).

> *restrict the use of land or structures for religious purposes* or for educational purposes *on land owned or leased* by the commonwealth or any of its agencies, subdivisions or bodies politic or *by a religious sect or denomination*, or by a nonprofit educational corporation; *provided, however, that such land or structures may be subject to reasonable regulations* concerning the bulk and height of structures and determining yard sizes, lot area, setbacks, open space, parking and building coverage requirements.[204]

The court emphasized that religious uses were part of a larger category of protected uses, that they were still subject to reasonable regulations, and that their inclusion was based on "Massachusetts' effort to eliminate local zoning discrimination ... [which] is fully in line with the Court's approval of government actions aimed at lifting burdens from the exercise of religion."[205] The Seventh Circuit found an exemption from permitting requirements for religious day care and preschools to be permissible under the Establishment Clause because it eliminated obstacles to free exercise, furthered church autonomy on issues of mission, involved no subsidy of religious activity by nonbeneficiaries, and promoted the separation of church and state.[206]

Many courts have found the land use portion of RLUIPA constitutional under the Establishment Clause.[207] The Supreme Court determined that the prison provision of RLUIPA did not violate the Establishment Clause but did not opine as to the land use provision in its decision.[208] Despite continued scholarly attention to the issue,[209] the Establishment Clause question has subsided in RLUIPA litigation, and its constitutionality has been assumed.

## C. Private Land Use Controls: Nuisance Lawsuits and Restrictive Covenants

In the prezoning era of the late nineteenth century, nuisance law and restrictive covenants served as the primary mechanisms of land use control. The increasing complexities of modern society created a need for coordinated, centralized planning, and zoning was born in the early 1900s. Despite the widespread acceptance of zoning over this last century, nuisance lawsuits and restrictive covenants continue to be highly relevant mechanisms of land use control. They are private methods of controlling religious land uses and also can be used by religious groups to control uses around them.[210]

204 Mass. Gen. Laws Ann. ch. 40A, § 3 (emphasis added).

205 Boyajian, 212 F.3d at 8.

206 Cohen v. City of Des Plaines, 8 F.3d 484 (7th Cir. 1993). *See also* Ehlers-Renzi v. Connelly Sch. of the Holy Child, 224 F.3d 283 (4th Cir. 2000) (No Establishment Clause violation occurs when parochial schools are exempt from the special permit requirement.); Concerned Citizens of Carderock v. Hubbard, 84 F. Supp. 2d 668 (D. Md. 2000) (No Establishment Clause violation occurs when places of worship are defined as permitted uses in single-family residential zones.). For a challenge of a permit grant, *see* Mintz v. Roman Catholic Bishop of Springfield, 424 F. Supp. 2d 309 (D. Mass. 2006) (No Establishment Clause violation occurs when zoning board grants permit to church for parish center in order to comply with RLUIPA; conditions on permit addressed neighbors' concerns.).

207 *See, e.g.*, Westchester Day Sch. v. Village of Mamaroneck, 504 F.3d 338, 355–6 (2d Cir. 2007); Midrash Sephardi, Inc. v. Town of Surfside, 366 F.3d 1214, 1240–2 (11th Cir. 2004).

208 Cutter v. Wilkinson, 544 U.S. 709 (2005).

209 *See, e.g.*, Hamilton, *supra* note 52.

210 With respect to nuisance, *see, e.g.*, St. John's Church in the Wilderness v. Scott, 296 P.3d 273 (Colo. Ct. App. 2012), *cert. denied*, No. 12SC658, 2013 WL 119791 (Colo. Jan. 7, 2013), *cert. denied*, 133 S. Ct. 2798 (2013) (affirming finding of private nuisance and grant of injunction against protesters who

## 1. *Nuisance*

No property owner has the right to commit nuisances, and religious owners are no exception.[211] When churches and religious individuals engage in activity on their property that substantially interferes with the use and enjoyment of neighboring property, nuisances are found. In fact, it appears that a religious "defense" to nuisance is typically not available to excuse the actions.[212] Cases involving individuals tend to focus on property uses such as displays of Christmas lights that cause traffic jams and excessive light.[213] Cases involving churches usually focus on accessory uses such as operating a soup kitchen or homeless shelter, which under certain circumstances can be incompatible with surrounding uses.[214] Indeed, nuisance law actually might define the outer limit of protections for religious uses. Courts sometimes will order a municipality to allow a use, such as a feeding program, to operate on the express condition that the program not create a nuisance.[215]

## 2. *Covenants that Exclude Houses of Worship*

The creation of an area devoted to an exclusive use can be accomplished by zoning code or by private restrictive covenant. Throughout the twentieth century, when many state courts began to give constitutional protection to religious land uses, churches were often allowed to locate in residential neighborhoods that had been zoned to be exclusively residential.[216] Based on the argument that judicial enforcement of covenants involves state action, churches also challenged the existence of private residential-only covenants.[217] After all, these covenants excluded houses of worship from residential areas just as effectively as residential-only zones under municipal ordinances.

These constitutional challenges to private restrictive covenants were unsuccessful in nearly all cases. Only one state appeals court accepted the state action argument.[218] Private restrictions were repeatedly held to put any new owners, including churches, on constructive or actual notice of the restriction regardless of any impact on religious

disturbed worship services). With respect to covenants, *see, e.g.*, Southeastern Jurisdictional Admin. Council, Inc. v. Emerson, 683 S.E.2d 366 (N.C. 2009) (unique religious character of Methodist retreat and residential community preserved by covenants).

211 "Freedom of religion does not provide anyone with the right to conduct a true nuisance." Wilkinson v. LaFranz, 574 So. 2d 403, 407 (La. Ct. App. 1991) (church soup kitchen).

212 *See generally* Alan Stephens, *Free Exercise of Religion Clause as Defense to Tort Liability*, 93 A.L.R. FED. 754 (orig. publ. 1989, updated) (collecting cases).

213 Osborne v. Power, 908 S.W.2d 340 (Ark. 1995).

214 *See generally* Shelly Ross Saxer, *When Religion Becomes a Nuisance: Balancing Land Use and Religious Freedom When Activities of Religious Institutions Bring Outsiders into the Neighborhood*, 84 KY. L.J. 507, 545–2 and n. 293 (1995–1996) (collecting cases and advocating for the use of nuisance against churches when their accessory uses involving service to the poor cause negative impacts on residential neighborhoods).

215 W. Presbyterian Church v. Bd. of Zoning Adjustment of Dist. of Columbia, 862 F. Supp. 538 (D.D.C. 1994) (city cannot stop church's feeding program, but court would enjoin if program became a nuisance).

216 *See supra* Section A.2.

217 This argument was made after the Supreme Court's decision in *Shelley v. Kraemer* [334 U.S. 1 (1948) (holding that judicial enforcement of a racially restrictive covenant constituted state action in violation of the Fourteenth Amendment)].

218 W. Hill Baptist Church v. Abbate, 261 N.E.2d 196 (Ohio Ct. C.P., Summit Cnty. 1969).

exercise.[219] Thus private covenants that exclude religious uses (or defeasible estates with the same effect) are generally enforceable. Of course, any covenant expressing religious discrimination would be unenforceable.[220]

RLUIPA's applicability to covenants that exclude religious uses is largely an open question. In *Adhi Parasakthi Charitable, Medical, Educational, and Cultural Society of North America v. Twp. of West Pikeland*,[221] the federal district court rejected the plaintiff religious organization's argument that enforcement of a restrictive covenant constitutes a substantial burden on religion under RLUIPA. The Hindu organization was unable to build a temple on its property, but the court found that the property was already restricted at the time of purchase. Thus, when the zoning board recognized the covenant and denied the permit, it caused no cognizable burden under RLUIPA. Dicta suggesting the possible applicability of RLUIPA can be found in at least one federal circuit court decision.[222]

### 3. *Covenants that Exclude Religious Objects and Uses in Common-Interest Communities*

A special category of covenants that restrict religious uses consists of covenants that restrict individuals from religious uses or decorations on their residential property within a common-interest community (CIC). CICs, which are governed by condominium associations and homeowner associations, are controlled extensively by covenants, conditions, and restrictions (CC&Rs) that are set out in a declaration and attached to all deeds

219 *See, e.g.*, Grace United Methodist Church v. City of Cheyenne, 451 F.3d 643 (10th Cir. 2006) (homeowner association had standing to intervene in church's RLUIPA suit challenging denial of variance to operate day-care center in residential zone in order to enforce restrictive covenant); Adhi Parasakthi Charitable, Med., Educ. & Cultural Soc'y of N. Am. v. Twp. of W. Pikeland, 721 F. Supp. 2d 361 (E.D. Pa. 2010) (court rejects plaintiff religious group's argument that enforcement of restrictive covenant constitutes substantial burden on religion under RLUIPA; government is simply enforcing restrictive covenant regardless of plaintiff's beliefs); Bd. of Zoning Appeals of Meridian Hills v. Schulte, 127 N.E.2d 39, 44 (Ind. 1961); Christ Methodist Church v. Macklanburg, 177 P.2d 1008 (Okla. 1947) (citing numerous cases holding that churches are bound by title restrictions); Voice of Cornerstone Church Corp. v. Pizza Prop. Partners, 160 S.W.3d 657 (Tex. Ct. App. 2005) (church is bound by restrictive covenant limiting uses to commercial/industrial); Church of Christ v. Metropolitan Bd. of Zoning Appeals, 371 N.E.2d 1331 (Ind. Ct. App. 1978); McDonald v. Chaffin, 529 S.W.2d 54 (Tenn. Ct. App. 1975) (house used as a church violated residential-only restriction); Ginsburg v. Yeshiva of Far Rockaway, 358 N.Y.S.2d 477, 482 (2d Dept. 1974) (residential use covenants are enforceable against religious institutions); Ireland v. Bible Baptist Church, 480 S.W.2d 467 (Tex. Ct. App. 1972) (injunction to compel removal of church structures that violate single-family residential covenants); Poughkeepsie N.Y. Congregation of Jehovah's Witnesses, N. Unit v. Booth, 323 N.Y.S.2d 181 (Supr. Ct. 1971) (covenants for residential and farm use exclude church); *and see generally* Robert G. Ritz, *Note: Restrictive Covenants and Religious Uses: The Constitutional Interplay*, 29 Syracuse L. Rev. 993 (1978) (collecting cases); Peter L. Maroulis, *Note, Restrictive Covenants as a Device to Control Religious Uses*, 12 Syracuse L. Rev. 347 (1961) (collecting cases).

220 *See* Restatement (Third) of Property: Servitudes § 3.1 (2000) (covenants that unreasonably burden a fundamental constitutional right violate public policy).

221 721 F. Supp. 2d 361 (E.D. Pa. 2010).

222 Konikov v. Orange Cnty., Fla., 410 F.3d 1317, 1324 n.3 (11th Cir. 2005) {Regarding residential-only restrictive covenant that expressly prohibited application for special permit, the court wrote, "Such a prohibition might constitute a constitutional violation and substantial burden in violation of RLUIPA [citing Shelley v. Kramer, 334 U.S. 1 (1948)]. We need not address this hypothetical issue, however, because Konikov never raised it."}.

of individually owned residences. In a condominium, the owner owns only the interior of his or her unit; the land as well as other areas of the buildings, such as hallways, balconies, and patios, are considered common areas, although an owner has exclusive rights to those elements (such as a balcony or patio) that are physically adjacent to the unit. In subdivisions managed by homeowners associations, an owner typically owns his or her home and the lot on which it sits. The CC&Rs can be quite detailed, frequently including controls on landscaping, paint color, location and type of parked vehicles, and pet restrictions.

Courts routinely accept the argument that an extensive web of restrictions is necessary to keep social and aesthetic order and to maintain property values in the CIC. Because a purchaser of a residence in a CIC becomes a member of the owners' association and accepts the servitude regime and governance structure, courts find that residents are on constructive, if not actual, notice of restrictions and therefore impliedly consent to them on purchase.

Sometimes the CC&Rs' restrictions include (or are interpreted to include) prohibitions against religious symbols on door frames or against religious objects in front of homes or on balconies, patios, or exterior walls of condominiums. They also may include bans on religious symbols and religious services in meeting rooms and other common areas intended for gatherings of residents. These restrictions might be generally applicable and religion neutral ("no placement of items anywhere in hallway") or targeted only at religious conduct ("no religious services in the common room"). Although there are many examples of these types of restrictions in the news, most have not been litigated.[223]

Because the restrictions affect residences, the FHA[224] and its ban on religious discrimination have been invoked to challenge restrictions on religious objects and uses. Many conflicts involve mezuzahs[225] on exterior door frames and succahs[226] on balconies or patios. In *Bloch v. Frischholz*, the condominium association repeatedly removed a mezuzah that a Jewish couple placed on the door post because it violated the rule against affixing or placing anything anywhere in the hallway.[227] The Seventh Circuit found that the couple could proceed on a claim of intentional discrimination under the FHA: issues for trial existed because the rule as reinterpreted was a marked departure from prior practice and because of allegations of anti-Semitic conduct on the part of the CIC leadership. In addition to the placement of religious objects, some CICs ban religious use of common areas. Several courts have upheld these bans,[228]

223 *See* Angela C. Carmella, *Religion-Free Environments in Common Interest Communities*, 38 PEPPERDINE L. REV. 57 (2010) (collecting news articles and cases).

224 42 U.S.C. § 3601–19 (2006) (prohibiting discrimination on the basis of race, color, religion, sex, national origin, disability, or familial status in the sale or rental of housing and in the terms and conditions of the sale or rental of housing).

225 A mezuzah is a small marker, about three to six inches long, that contains a small piece of rolled up parchment of biblical verse.

226 A succah is a small shelter or booth with sides but no roof used for celebrating the nine-day Festival of Tabernacles, or Succoth.

227 587 F.3d 771 (7th Cir. 2009) (reversing district court's grant of summary judgment to condominium association). In Gassman v. Frischholz, No. 5 C 5377, 2011 WL 2550797 (N.D. Ill. June 27, 2011), the court held that Bloch may pursue discrimination claims under a proof of discriminatory intent or a modified disparate impact theory.

228 Savanna Club Worship Serv., Inc. v. Savanna Club Homeowners' Ass'n., 456 F. Supp. 2d 1223 (S.D. Fla. 2005) (exclusion of all worship services from common space was not discriminatory under FHA because all faiths were treated the same); Neuman v. Grandview at Emerald Hills, Inc. 861 So. 2d 494 (Fla. Dist.

although federal policy states that religious uses should have access on the same terms as other uses.[229]

These types of conflicts have resulted in legislative resolutions in Illinois and Florida and pending legislation in Texas and New York.[230] It is also common for federal (and state) housing discrimination officials to get involved in addressing complaints.

### 4. *Covenants that Create Single-Religion Communities*

An exception to the religious discrimination provision of the FHA applies to housing that is controlled by religious groups, such as convents and monasteries. Churches therefore can transfer and restrict property in favor of their own members without concern of FHA enforcement. But the church's control over the property has to be definitive. In a case of a Catholics-only CIC, the exception did not apply (and a FHA violation was found) because the organization was not under the auspices or control of a church.[231]

### 5. *Covenants that Preserve Religious Use and Design*

Religious uses can be specified and preserved in an instrument of transfer, by covenant, or by defeasible fee. The religious building appearance and design also can be preserved by covenant. When we think of historic preservation, we usually think about the public designation of architectural treasures.[232] But any owner of historically or culturally significant property can decide to preserve it through private covenant (or facade easement), with a nonprofit organization holding the benefit of the covenant (or easement). Churches may take advantage of this option, which is typically available by statute.

## D. Heightened Government Interest in Specific Religious Land Uses

### 1. *Property Dedicated to Serving the Poor*

There is a "centuries old church tradition of sanctuary for those in need of shelter and aid"[233] that the law has recognized in many ways. Indeed, the assumption that houses of

Ct. App. 2003) (rule banning religious use of common areas did not unreasonably restrict condominium owners; case did not involve FHA).

229 Carmella, *supra* note 223, at n. 9.

230 *See generally id; see also* Amanda Hopkins, *What's Wrong with My Nativity Scene? Religiously Discriminating Restrictive Covenants in New York*, 13 RUTGERS J.L. & RELIGION 415 (2012) (urging passage of New York's Religious Symbols Bill).

231 United States v. Columbus Country Club, 915 F.2d 877 (3d Cir. 1990) {Prohibition on sales of summer bungalows to non-Catholics violates FHA, even though non-Catholics reside in community as tenants and guests; club does not get the benefit of the religious exemption from FHA, which requires that the organization be nonprofit and "operated, supervised, or controlled by or in conjunction with" a religious organization [citing 42 U.S.C. § 3607(a)]}. Other cases suggest that as long as there is no discrimination, covenants may be enforceable to retain religious character. *See, e.g.*, Southeastern Jurisdictional Admin. Council, Inc. v. Emerson, 683 S.E.2d 366 (N.C. 2009) (In Methodist retreat center and private residential community of 700 homes, where unique religious character was preserved by covenants, covenant requiring service fee payable to Methodist body was held enforceable.).

232 *See infra* Section F.

233 St. John's Evangelical Lutheran Church v. City of Hoboken, 479 A.2d 935, 938 (N.J. Super. Ct. Law Div. 1983). *See generally* Shelly Ross Saxer, *Faith in Action: Religious Accessory Uses and Land Use Regulation*, 2008 UTAH L. REV. 593.

worship would be put to additional, accessory uses – charitable and educational – has been built into zoning ordinances for over a century.[234]

Though churches have always engaged in charitable works, the rise in poverty and homelessness has meant that those works sometimes take on unique and novel forms of land use, which easily get on the government's regulatory radar. The services they provide to the poor often create conflict with neighbors (particularly in residential zones) and with cities trying to control the ways in which social services are delivered. Local governments can be quite aggressive in stopping unpermitted shelters[235] and will often fight churches that attempt to operate homeless missions in novel ways. In the early 1990s, Mother Teresa's Missionaries of Charity sought to renovate an empty building for the homeless in New York City for $500,000 but refused to install (for $100,000) a mandatory elevator the group said it would not use. The city would not waive this requirement, so the sisters abandoned the project.[236] There has been much criticism of the bureaucratization that creates obstacles to religious missions for the homeless – especially to churches with novel approaches to their missions – but sometimes the courts rescue churches from it.[237]

In New York City in the late 1990s and into the new century, the Fifth Avenue Presbyterian Church permitted the homeless who refuse indoor shelters to sleep on the steps of its house of worship because it considered this space a sanctuary for the homeless.[238] The church designated the landings at the tops of staircases (within arched entryways) for homeless persons to use between 9 p.m. and 7 a.m. The city notified the church that it would not permit this use of the church's property because the church had no license and because the use constituted a public nuisance. The church responded that "its outdoor sanctuary forms an integral part of its religious mission and that the police's removal of the homeless interferes with the Church's ministry and homeless outreach program."[239] The Second Circuit agreed with the church, and the city was first preliminarily and then permanently enjoined from interfering with the church's provision of shelter.[240] The court held, under the Free Exercise Clause of the First Amendment,

234 *See supra* Section B.10.

235 Westgate Tabernacle, Inc. v. Palm Beach Cnty., 14 So. 3d 1027, 1032 (Fla. Dist. Ct. App. 2009) (church operating shelter without permit challenged permit requirement as unnecessary and also challenged process as substantial burden, both unsuccessfully); *accord*, Family Life Church v. City of Elgin, 561 F. Supp. 2d 978, 981 (N.D. Ill. 2008). The requirement that a church apply for permits is not, in and of itself, a substantial burden under RLUIPA. *See supra* Section B.4.

236 Marshall J. Breger, *Regulatory Flexibility and the Administrative State*, 32 Tulsa L.J. 325, 353, n. 79 (1996).

237 *See, e.g.*, St. John's Evangelical Church v. City of Hoboken, 479 A.2d 935, 939 (N.J. Super. Ct. Law Div. 1983) (Homeless shelters should be subject to reasonable health and safety standards but exempt from those imposed on hotels.).

238 Fifth Ave. Presbyterian Church v. City of N.Y., 293 F.3d 570, 572 (2d Cir. 2002).

239 *Id.* at 574.

240 *Id.* at 576 (preliminary injunction); Fifth Ave. Presbyterian Church v. City of N.Y., No. 01 CIV. 11493 (LMM), 2004 WL 2471406 (S.D.N.Y. Oct. 29, 2004) (Permanent injunction: "It is ORDERED that the defendants are permanently enjoined from entering onto the property of the plaintiff Fifth Avenue Presbyterian Church described below for the purposes of dispersing or arresting any person who shall be sleeping or otherwise lawfully on that property, provided that nothing in this order shall limit the authority of the New York City Police Department to arrest any person for other conduct that is unlawful, or from removing from Church property anyone who is present there without the consent of the Church, or from removing homeless persons from Church property during a winter alert officially declared by the

that the city did not establish that dispersing the homeless would be the least restrictive means of advancing a compelling interest that would justify the substantial burden on protected religious exercise. It also rejected the city's public nuisance claim.[241]

In addition to church-run operations, a unique phenomenon has emerged: groups of homeless persons asking churches for permission to use their property temporarily to set up a "tent city," with the churches providing not only the space but also meals and restrooms. Cities may require permits for these kinds of temporary encampments.[242] Or they might be banned, as was the case in Woodinville, Washington, where a church was prevented entirely from hosting a tent city. In that case, though, the state's high court, sitting *en banc*, protected the church's right to do so under a robust reading of its own constitution.[243] In fact, after the case, the Washington legislature enacted a law allowing churches to host tent cities under government regulations that further health and safety but do not substantially burden churches.[244]

Judicial protection of a novel religious mission is evident in *Chosen 300 Ministries, Inc. v. City of Philadelphia*.[245] (While this case did not involve the use of real property held by religious organizations, it is worth noting in connection with other court decisions involving care of homeless populations.) Philadelphia banned outdoor feeding programs in an attempt to move all the homeless feeding programs indoors. But numerous religious ministries provided meals to the homeless outside, at locations where the homeless

New York City Department of Health. For the purposes of this order, the portion of the Church's property at issue constitutes the three staircases that extend from the Church building towards Fifth Avenue, and the two staircases that extend from the Church building toward 55th Street."), *aff'd but criticized*, 177 Fed. App'x 198 (2d Cir. 2006) (criticizing district court's assumption that sidewalk near church was public place and outside scope of injunction).

241 *Id.* at *4–*9 (relying on *Lukumi*, court noted how the city's actions were substantially underinclusive).

242 *See generally* Kelli Stout, *Comment: Tent Cities and RLUIPA: How a New Religious-Land-Use Issue Aggravates RLUIPA*, 41 Seton Hall L. Rev. 465 (2011).

243 *See* City of Woodinville v. Northshore United Church of Christ, 211 P.3d 406, 413 (Wash. 2009), *discussed in* Stout, *supra* note 242, at 488–90.

244 Wash. Rev. Code Ann. § 35.21.915 (West) provides

(1) A religious organization may host temporary encampments for the homeless on property owned or controlled by the religious organization whether within buildings located on the property or elsewhere on the property outside of buildings.

(2) A city or town may not enact an ordinance or regulation or take any other action that:

(a) Imposes conditions other than those necessary to protect public health and safety and that do not substantially burden the decisions or actions of a religious organization regarding the location of housing or shelter for homeless persons on property owned by the religious organization;

(b) Requires a religious organization to obtain insurance pertaining to the liability of a municipality with respect to homeless persons housed on property owned by a religious organization or otherwise requires the religious organization to indemnify the municipality against such liability; or

(c) Imposes permit fees in excess of the actual costs associated with the review and approval of the required permit applications.

(3) For the purposes of this section, "religious organization" means the federally protected practice of a recognized religious assembly, school, or institution that owns or controls real property.

(4) An appointed or elected public official, public employee, or public agency as defined in RCW 4.24.470 is immune from civil liability for (a) damages arising from the permitting decisions for a temporary encampment for the homeless as provided in this section and (b) any conduct or unlawful activity that may occur as a result of the temporary encampment for the homeless as provided in this section.

245 No. CIV.A. 12-3159, 2012 WL 3235317 (E.D. Pa. Aug. 9, 2012). *But see* First Vagabonds Church of God v. City of Orlando, 638 F.3d 756 (11th Cir. 2011) (If feeding homeless is expressive conduct, city can place reasonable restrictions on it consistent with Free Speech Clause.).

congregated. And just as the service-resistant homeless in *Fifth Avenue Presbyterian* who would not sleep in an indoor shelter needed outdoor shelter, the many service-resistant homeless who would not eat at an indoor facility needed outdoor feeding programs. The religious plaintiffs won a preliminary injunction against the city's ban on the grounds of likelihood of success on a claim under the Pennsylvania Religious Freedom Restoration Act (RFRA).[246] The ban substantially burdened the plaintiffs' religious mission and would not advance in the least restrictive manner the city's interest in ending homelessness and providing services to the homeless.

Governments have long relied on nonstate actors such as churches to deliver all kinds of social services. Whereas officials are properly concerned with health and safety matters, there remains a strong sense that regulation should have sufficient flexibility to accommodate innovative approaches and that local government should not encumber service providers with unnecessary burdens or delays. Judge Posner of the Seventh Circuit voiced this sentiment when he criticized Chicago's denial of permits to a religious organization for a single-residence occupancy building even after the Federal Emergency Management Agency (FEMA), with the support of state officials, had specifically requested that this organization house victims of Hurricane Katrina in the facility.[247]

### 2. *Property Providing Sanctuary to Immigrants*

Some churches have sheltered refugees or illegal immigrants in their houses of worship during several "sanctuary movements" since the 1980s, but there is no legal right to use a house of worship as a refuge from law enforcement.[248] This application of the notion of "sanctuary" is not protected religious exercise under the Free Exercise Clause or under federal statutes such as RFRA or RLUIPA and provides no immunity from arrest. Offering refuge in this way is an act of civil disobedience, attempting to draw attention to the plight of those being sheltered as well to protect them physically from government authorities. Immigration authorities do tend, however, to respect the sanctuary of persons inside a church, and it has long been unofficial policy not to conduct arrests in such circumstances.[249] Indeed, in a 2008 memorandum, U.S. Immigration and Customs

246 The act defines a "substantial burden" to be "an agency action which does any of the following: (1) Significantly constrains or inhibits conduct or expression mandated by a person's sincerely held religious beliefs. (2) Significantly curtails a person's ability to express adherence to the person's religious faith. (3) Denies a person a reasonable opportunity to engage in activities which are fundamental to the person's religion. (4) Compels conduct or expression which violates a specific tenet of a person's religious faith." 71 Pa. Stat. Ann. § 2403. Here plaintiffs argued that the ban constitutes a substantial burden under subsections (1), (2), or (3). Chosen 300 Ministries, Inc. v. City of Philadelphia, Civ. A. 12-3159, 2012 WL 3235317 (E.D. Pa. Aug. 9, 2012).

247 World Outreach Conference Ctr. v. City of Chicago, 591 F.3d 531 (7th Cir. 2009).

248 *See generally* Kara L. Wild, *The New Sanctuary Movement: When Moral Mission Means Breaking the Law, and the Consequences for Churches and Illegal Immigrants*, 50 Santa Clara L. Rev. 981 (2010); Kristina M. Campbell, *Humanitarian Aid is Never a Crime? The Politics of Immigration Enforcement and the Provision of Sanctuary*, 63 Syracuse L. Rev. 71 (2012); Cathleen Kaveny, *More than a Refuge: Why Immigration Officials Should Steer Clear of Churches*, 138 Commonweal, Nov. 4, 2011, WLNR 27356027 ("[H]ouses of worship have long been considered places of sanctuary, although the law has not always recognized that claim.").

249 "Since the 1970s, the unwritten rule has been 'no churches, no playgrounds, no schools,'" Sophia Tareen, *Officials Hesitant to Arrest Immigrants Who Seek Church Sanctuary*, USA Today, July 16, 2008, *available at:* http://usatoday30.usatoday.com/news/religion/2008-07-16-immigration-churches_N.htm.

Enforcement announced its policy not to target churches, schools, and other "sensitive locations" for immigration enforcement absent extenuating circumstances such as threatened violence or terrorism.[250] In some cases, federal authorities might even work with clergy to find short-term solutions for those being sheltered while more permanent solutions are sought.[251] This reluctance to enter houses of worship recognizes that these buildings are the location of protected First Amendment activity. But, of course, the story has had its complexities.

Beginning in the 1980s, hundreds of churches helped refugees fleeing from civil wars in El Salvador and Guatemala who were not eligible for political asylum in the United States.[252] By 1982, the Central American Sanctuary Movement had been established. Whereas some clergy and lay members were involved in secret efforts to smuggle refugees across the border, most movement members were involved in the very public provision of basic needs for the refugees.

Although federal authorities did not attempt to arrest refugees being sheltered in churches, they did move against the leadership of the Sanctuary Movement. Immigration and Naturalization Service (INS) agents infiltrated churches and gained the trust of unsuspecting church members in order to tape conversations and gain information. These investigative efforts led to criminal indictments and convictions of some clergy and lay leaders, which were later upheld in the face of constitutional challenges.[253] (Some of those convicted had only provided shelter to refugees.[254]) Their defenses under the Free Exercise Clause failed: the government's "overriding interest in policing its borders" outweighed any possible religious interest, and an exemption could not be limited, given the fact that Catholics, Methodists, Presbyterians, and Unitarians were involved in the movement.[255]

Churches also lost independent constitutional challenges to the secret tapings of their religious services.[256] They had argued that covert, warrantless surveillance of church services violated the Free Exercise Clause, pointing to a decrease in religious participation and suspension of some religious activities and growing distrust and fear among church members. But these investigations were found to be the least restrictive means of protecting the compelling interest in national borders because they were conducted in good faith and occurred within the scope of the church's invitation.

250 Kaveny, *supra* note 248.

251 U.S. Immigration and Customs Enforcement provided orders of supervision rather than deportation to Indonesian immigrants who had spent several years at a New Jersey church. Sue Epstein, *Indonesian Immigrants in Highland Park Freed from Church Sanctuary*, Feb. 26, 2013, *available at:* http://blog.nj.com/middlesex_impact/print.html?entry=/2013/02/indonesian_immigrants_in_highl.html.

252 While numbers vary, PBS News Hour reported that 500 congregations sheltered 1,000 refugees. *See Transcript, Churches Providing Sanctuary for Illegal Immigrants*, PBS NEWSHOUR, June 18, 2007, *available at:* http://www.pbs.org/newhour/bb/social_issues/jan-june07/sanctuary_06-18.html.

253 United States v. Aguilar, 883 F.2d 662 (9th Cir. 1989) (Meetings on church property were open to the public and news media, so no expectation of privacy or confidentiality arose; agents were "invited informers."); United States v. Merkt, 794 F.2d 950 (5th Cir. 1986); United States v. Elder, 601 F. Supp. 1574 (S.D. Tex. 1985) (Free Exercise Clause not a bar to prosecution of Roman Catholic charged with transporting undocumented aliens from El Salvador).

254 Wild, *supra* note 248, at 1004–5.

255 United States v. Aguilar, 883 F.2d at 696. *See also* Am. Baptist Churches in U.S.A. v. Meese, 712 F. Supp. 756 (N.D. Cal. 1989) (churches lack standing to challenge prosecutions).

256 *See, e.g.*, Presbyterian Church (U.S.A.) v. United States, 752 F. Supp. 1505, 1516 (D. Ariz. 1990), *on remand from* 870 F.2d 518 (9th Cir. 1989); United States v. Aguilar, 883 F.2d 662, 705 (9th Cir. 1989).

In the mid-2000s, when Congress was beginning to consider some particularly harsh immigration laws – including the criminalization of charity toward those in need without regard to their immigration status – the New Sanctuary Movement was born.[257] Mexican immigrant Elvira Arellano became the symbol of the movement: she took sanctuary in a Chicago church in 2006, where she remained for a year to avoid deportation and separation from her child.[258] She was arrested only after leaving the church and the city. Inspired by the church activism of the 1980s, this new movement focused on sheltering illegal immigrants already in the United States (with strong work histories and children born in the United States) in order to draw attention to the plight of thousands facing deportation and family breakup. Despite raids at factories, farms, and shopping areas, federal immigration authorities stayed out of churches.[259] This movement to shelter families is only one of many efforts to provide humanitarian aid, especially after states began to enact their own immigration laws.[260] But the house of worship remains a significant symbol and reality of sanctuary as immigration reform takes center stage.[261]

### 3. *Property Suspected of Being Used for Criminal or Terrorist Activity*

As is clear from the immigration context, government intelligence gathering occurs within houses of worship. In the post-9/11 world, surveillance of mosques in search of terrorists has been a widespread and controversial practice. Until then, law enforcement operated under some limitations, including a rule of "no surveillance or infiltration of religious organizations without any proof of criminal activity."[262] With a loosening of guidelines, however, by 2003, an inventory of mosques had been created, and the infiltration of mosques for intelligence gathering since then has increased.[263] This is not only

257 H.R. 4437, introduced in 2005, would have made it a felony to provide aid to those in the country illegally. The bill never became law.

258 *Transcript, Churches Providing Sanctuary for Illegal Immigrants*, PBS NEWSHOUR, June 18, 2007, *available at:* http://www.pbs.org/newhour/bb/social_issues/jan-june07/sanctuary_06-18.html. *See also* David van Biema, *A Church Haven for Illegal Aliens*, TIME, July 19, 2007, *available at:* http://www.time.com/time/magazine/article/0,9171,16455169,00.html; Jill Serjeant, *Immigrants Take Sanctuary in U.S. Churches*, REUTERS, May 9, 2007, *available at:* http://mobile.reuters.com/article/idUSN0924974520070510?irpc=932.

259 Tareen, *supra* note 249.

260 *See generally* Campbell, *supra* note 248.

261 *See* "Georgia Coalition organizes 'Day without Immigrants,'" EFE World News Service, June 30, 2011 (describing Georgia Sanctuary Zone movement, developing a network of businesses and churches to provide sanctuary sites to immigrants); Brady McCombs, *Church's Move to Offer Sanctuary Harkens to Controversy Years Ago*, ARIZ. DAILY STAR, Oct. 19, 2011, *available at:* 2011 WLNR 21630101 (describing a Catholic Church protecting a family from deportation).

262 Tom Lininger, *Sects, Lies, and Videotape: The Surveillance and Infiltration of Religious Groups*, 89 IOWA L. REV. 1201, 1228 (2004) (describing the long history of such government scrutiny, from black churches during the civil rights movement, through the sanctuary movement of the 1980s and Branch Davidians in the 1990s, up through today's Muslim communities).

263 *See generally* David A. Harris, *Law Enforcement and Intelligence Gathering in Muslim and Immigrant Communities after 9/11*, 34 N.Y.U. REV. L. & SOC. CHANGE 123 (2010); Jodie A. Kirshner, *U.S. and U.K. Approaches to the War on Terror: The Surveillance of Religious Worship*, 14 U. MIAMI INT'L & COMP. L. REV. 217 (2006) (discussing FBI intelligence gathering operations at mosques); Jon Sherman, *A Person Otherwise Innocent": Policing Entrapment in Preventative Undercover Counterterrorism Investigations*, 11 U. PA. J. CONST. L. 1475 (2009) (surveillance noted in larger context of terrorism cases). *See infra* Section E.4.

an issue of federal law; state and local law enforcement agencies are involved in these practices as well. After news broke in 2012 that the New York City Police Department (NYPD) had maintained a surveillance program in New Jersey targeting Muslims at various locations, including mosques, Muslim advocacy groups sued.[264] In 2013, it was reported that the NYPD had categorized a dozen New York City mosques as terrorist organizations.[265]

## E. Laws Protecting Religious Sites and Buildings

Religious groups owning real property can, like all owners, bring actions under trespass and nuisance law if others interfere with their rights to possession or with their use and enjoyment of property. In addition, numerous protections for houses of worship and other religious property can be found at the local, state, and federal levels.

### 1. *Protecting Natural Features that Have Religious Significance*

The Free Exercise Clause and the federal American Indian Religious Freedom Act provide little protection to Native American sacred sites.[266] But some scholars regard more recent trends in agency decision making to provide substantive protection. One such scholar noted that

> [c]urrently, federal land management agencies are responsible for the majority of decisions regarding Indian sacred sites located on federal land. Given that, in the past, land management agencies were often responsible for the decisions to destroy sacred sites, it is little wonder that most tribes and sacred sites supporters are dubious that these agencies will provide any real protection. But such mistrust may no longer be justified. Land management agencies are increasingly working to protect sacred sites, and in many instances such agencies are able to provide a form of protection that most of society would find preferable to the protections available through the courts or Congress.[267]

Some of this progress results in the protection of Native American sacred sites from being used in ways they consider to be desecration. Using a web of federal and state laws and

264 Hannan Adely & Nick Cunin, *Muslim Group to Sue NYPD Today over Spying*, N.J. RECORD, June 6, 2012, *available at*: 2012 WLNR 11853906. *See also* Asian Am. Legal Defense & Educ. Fund v. NYPD, 964 N.Y.S.2d 888 (N.Y. Sup. Ct. 2013) (plaintiffs sought records under state freedom of information law regarding policy guidelines for surveillance of Muslims, but court holds that these documents are exempt from disclosure law).

265 Adam Goldman & Matt Apuzzo, *NYPD Designates Mosques as Terrorism Organizations*, AP, Aug. 28, 2013, *available at*: http://bigstory.ap.org/article/nypd-designates-mosques-terrorism-organizations. *See also Editorial, Spying on Muslims*, N.Y. TIMES, Sep. 8, 2013 (criticizing NYPD's "indefensible program").

266 Lyng v. Northwest Indian Cemetery Protective Ass'n, 485 U.S. 439 (1988) (Destruction of Native American sites on federal land that is caused by government activity but does not involve coercive government action creates no cognizable free exercise claim.); American Indian Religious Freedom Act of 1978, 42 U.S.C. § 1996 (a policy statement regarding Native Americans' rights to religious freedom that creates no cause of action for enforcement).

267 Marcia Yablon, *Property Rights and Sacred Sites: Federal Regulatory Responses to American Indian Religious Claims on Public Land*, 113 YALE L.J. 1623, 1626 (2004). *See also* Michelle Kay Albert, *Obligations and Opportunities to Protect Native American Sacred Sites Located on Public Lands*, 40 COLUM. HUM. RTS. L. REV. 479 (2009).

related agency policies, Native Americans have won some protection for the integrity of natural features that have religious, cultural, and historical significance. The National Register of Historic Places and the environmental impact statement requirements under the National Environmental Policy Act, as well as analogous state laws, are among the vehicles enabling agencies to protect Native American sites. We see such examples as these: Arizona policy prohibits the use of materials from sacred sites such as Woodruff Butte in state construction projects[268]; the U.S. Forest Service bans rock climbing (which usually involves the installation of fixed anchors) at Cave Rock, a rock formation on the eastern shore of Lake Tahoe[269]; and the National Park Service asks visitors not to approach or walk under Rainbow Bridge in southern Utah, the world's largest natural bridge, in order to respect the spiritual significance of the area to Native Americans.[270] Courts have upheld these types of protections against Establishment Clause challenges because the locations are important not only as sacred sites to Native Americans but also as cultural resources to the entire nation.

### 2. *Prohibiting Desecration and Destruction of Religious Buildings*

Legislatures have enacted laws that specifically prohibit desecration or vandalism of houses of worship and other religious properties such as cemeteries and schools; protection is also often given to religious symbols as venerated objects.[271] Many states traditionally considered desecration of places of worship to be a misdemeanor or felony and have increased penalties in recognition of the rise in hate crimes aimed at persons and groups based on race, religion, and other characteristics. These crimes of religious vandalism, which include every kind of damage from defacement to destruction, involve actions intended to intimidate and oppress religious communities. Desecration laws have even been enacted at the federal level for specific contexts. Laws that criminalize desecration are generally considered to comport with the Establishment Clause because they so clearly protect the free exercise of religion and "are an appropriate response to the increased incidence and gravity of crimes committed in or against religious property"[272] and the concomitant chilling effects on religious assembly.

268 Cholla Ready Mix, Inc. v. Civish, 382 F.3d 969 (9th Cir. 2004) (secular purpose of preserving sites of religious, cultural and historic significance; no endorsement of Native American religions).

269 Access Fund v. U.S. Dep't of Agriculture, 499 F.3d 1036 (9th Cir. 2007) (secular purpose of preserving sites of religious, cultural, and historic significance; no endorsement of Native American religions).

270 Natural Arch & Bridge Soc'y v. Alston, 209 F. Supp. 2d 1207 (D. Utah 2002), *judgment aff'd*, 98 Fed. Appx. 711 (10th Cir. 2004) (Restriction was voluntary, not coercive; recognition of historic, cultural significance of religion does not violate Establishment Clause.). *See also* Bear Lodge Multiple Use Ass'n v. Babbitt, 175 F.3d 814 (10th Cir. 1999) (Climbers were asked to voluntarily refrain from climbing during Native American religious ceremonies; plaintiffs have no standing to bring Establishment Clause challenge.).

271 Antidesecration statutes often protect nonreligious as well as religious properties. *See generally* Zachary J. Wolfe, *Statutes Prohibiting Religiously Hostile Acts: Institutional Vandalism and Related State Statutes* §§ 14.1, 14.3, 14.4, *in* HATE CRIMES LAW (West) (database updated 2013) (collecting statutes). Some state laws have modeled their laws after Section 250.9 of the Model Penal Code.

272 Wolfe, *supra* note 271, at § 14.10. *See generally Note, Protecting Religious Exercise: The First Amendment and Legislative Responses to Religious Vandalism*, 97 HARV. L. REV. 547 (1983) (arguing against an Establishment Clause concern because these laws protect the free exercise of religion, as vandalism against the house of worship has economic, symbolic, and psychological impacts, in addition to chilling

During the 1980s, anti-Semitic bias incidents – including vandalism against synagogues – were on the rise, which prompted the amendment of criminal laws (through enhanced criminal penalties) to take into account the harsh reality that where people gather to worship can be a target for hate.[273] New York's aggravated harassment statutes were enacted in part to addresses damage to houses of worship.[274] Massachusetts enacted criminal legislation to supplement its existing law and to address desecration of houses of worship.[275] Indeed, the criminal laws of most states have some kind of explicit protection for religious property.[276]

Religious vandalism is addressed in two federal statutes as well.[277] In the 1990s, following a spate of arsons that destroyed more than sixty-six black churches in an eighteen-month period throughout the nation,[278] Congress passed the Church Arson Prevention Act of 1996.[279] The act provides enhanced criminal penalties for anyone who "intentionally defaces, damages, or destroys any religious real property, because of the religious character of that property, or attempts to do so" if "the offense is in

effects on religious assembly). For a collection of desecration cases, *see Validity and Construction of Statute or Ordinance Prohibiting Desecration of Church*, 90 A.L.R.3d 1128 (orig. publ. 1979, updated).

273 Some hate crimes laws ran afoul of the Free Speech Clause after *R.A.V. v. City of St. Paul* [505 U.S. 377 (1992) (facial invalidity of content-based hate speech ordinance)] and had to be amended. *See, e.g.*, State v. Vawter, 642 A.2d 349, 360 (N.J. 1994).

274 N.Y. Penal Law § 240.31(1) (McKinney) provides in part as follows: "A person is guilty of aggravated harassment in the first degree when with the intent to harass, annoy, threaten or alarm another person, because of the race, color, religion, or national origin of such person he [or she]: 1. Damages premises primarily used for religious purposes, or acquired … and maintained for the purposes of religious instruction, and the damage to the premises exceeds fifty dollars." For the origins and context of this new legislation, *see generally* Abraham Abramovsky, *Bias Crime: A Call for Alternative Responses*, 19 Fordham Urb. L.J. 875 (1992).

275 Mass. Gen. L. ch. 266, § 127A provides criminal penalties for "[a]ny person who willfully, intentionally and without right, or wantonly and without cause, destroys, defaces, mars, or injures a church, synagogue or other building, structure or place used for the purpose of burial or memorializing the dead, or a school, educational facility or community center" (as well as adjacent grounds and personal property within these buildings). For the origins and context of this legislation, *see generally* Virginia Nia Lee & Joseph M. Fernandez, *Legislative Responses to Hate-Motivated Violence: The Massachusetts Experience and Beyond*, 25 Harv. C.R.-C.L. L. Rev. 287 (1990).

276 *See* Ala. Code § 13A-11-12 (1975) (class A misdemeanor) (desecration of "venerated objects" – public monuments or places of worship or burial, or state or the American flag); Conn. Gen. Stat. § 46a–58 (prohibiting desecration of property, including houses of worship, by acts that mar, deface, damage "as a demonstration of irreverence or contempt"); N.J. Stat. Ann. § 2C:33–9 ("A person commits a disorderly persons offense if he [or she] purposely desecrates any public monument, insignia, symbol, or structure, or place of worship or burial. 'Desecrate' means defacing, damaging or polluting."); N.M. Stat. Ann. § 30-15-4 ("[d]esecration of a church consists of willfully, maliciously, and intentionally defacing a church or any portion thereof"). For additional examples of vandalism and desecration statutes, *see* Cal. Penal Code §§ 594.3 & 11411; Ga. Code Ann. § 16-7-26; Ky. Rev. Stat. Ann. § 525.110; Md. Code Ann., Criminal Law § 10-302; N.C. Gen. Stat. § 14-144; Okla. Stat. tit. 21, § 1765; R.I. Gen. Laws § 11-44-31; Wis. Stat. § 943.012. *See also supra* note 271 for collection of statutes.

277 18 U.S.C. §§ 247–8. *See also* Wolfe, *supra* note 271, §§ 14.1–14.11.

278 Civil Rights Monitor, *available at:* http://www.civilrights.org/monitor/vol8_no5_6/art4.html.

279 Pub. L. No. 104–155, 110 Stat. 1392. Congress found that "[t]he incidence of arson or other destruction or vandalism of places of religious worship, and the incidence of violent interference with an individual's lawful exercise or attempted exercise of the right of religious freedom at a place of religious worship pose a serious national problem" and that "[t]he incidence of arson of places of religious worship has recently increased, especially in the context of places of religious worship that serve predominantly African-American congregations."

or affects interstate or foreign commerce."[280] It also provides for enhanced criminal penalties (without the need to show an interstate commerce nexus) whenever anyone "intentionally defaces, damages, or destroys any religious real property because of the race, color, or ethnic characteristics of any individual associated with that religious property, or attempts to do so."[281] "Religious real property" is defined to include "any church, synagogue, mosque, religious cemetery, or other religious real property, including fixtures or religious objects contained within a place of religious worship."[282] No federal prosecution can be brought under this provision unless the attorney general certifies that it would be "in the public interest and necessary to secure substantial justice."[283] The law has been found constitutional under the Establishment Clause.[284]

Another federal statute passed in the mid-1990s that responded to specific events of the time was the Freedom of Access to Clinic Entrances Act (FACE).[285] A little-known provision of the statute, best known for its prohibition of the obstruction, interference with, or intimidation of women seeking to enter abortion clinics, protects religious worshippers at a place of worship as well as religious property.[286] In addition to authorizing legal action against those who injure, intimidate, or interfere with religious exercise at a place of worship, FACE also provides civil remedies and criminal penalties for anyone who "intentionally damages or destroys the property of a place of religious worship."[287]

Alteration or demolition of religious buildings, when done by their owners to accommodate changes in worship or congregational needs or to make the property more marketable, is controversial when those buildings have been declared architectural, cultural, or historic landmarks.[288] In those cases, the drastic changes to religious sites by the religious groups themselves is claimed as an aspect of the free exercise of religion and may fall within the scope of RLUIPA.[289]

### 3. *Controlling Uses in the Vicinity of a House of Worship*

Thus far this chapter has focused on the activities of religious groups, especially those conducted on their property. State or local zoning laws also often protect houses of worship, along with schools and residences, from the negative secondary effects of incompatible

280 18 U.S.C. § 247(a)(1) and (b). The church met the interstate commerce nexus in *United States v. Gillespie* [452 F.3d 1183 (10th Cir. 2006)] but did not in *United States v. Davies* [394 F.3d 182 (3d Cir. 2005)]. *See also* United States v. Ballinger, 395 F.3d 1218 (11th Cir. 2005) (constitutional under Commerce Clause).

281 18 U.S.C. § 247(c). Punishments are set forth in subsection (d).

282 *Id.* § 247(f).

283 *Id.* § 247(e).

284 United States v. Corum, 362 F.3d 489 (8th Cir. 2004).

285 18 U.S.C. § 248.

286 *Id.* § 248(a)(2)–(3).

287 *Id.* § 248(a)(3).

288 *See infra* § F.

289 *See, e.g.*, Roman Catholic Bishop of Springfield v. City of Springfield, 724 F.3d 78 (1st Cir. 2013). In this case, the bishop decided to close a house of worship and "deconsecrate" it in order to sell it for non-religious uses. The court described the process of deconsecration: it involves removing religious symbols from the building's exterior; if removal is not possible, then the symbols may be covered permanently. "Symbols that cannot be removed may also be destroyed – along with the building itself, if necessary – if [the bishop] … determines that destruction is necessary to avoid desecration." *Id.* at 85.

uses in the vicinity, such as bars and adult businesses.[290] Ordinances may prohibit these uses from locating within a certain number of feet of religious, educational, and residential properties. The Supreme Court, in *Larkin v. Grendel's Den*, noted that this method of protecting religious land use would be constitutional. In that case, the Court struck down a Massachusetts statute that gave churches and schools the unilateral power to prevent the issuance of liquor licenses to any businesses located within 500 feet.[291] The case was brought by a restaurant in Cambridge that had been denied a liquor license automatically on the objection of a nearby church. The Court held that giving this veto power to a church was an unconstitutional delegation of governmental power in violation of the Establishment Clause. Chief Justice Burger noted that the valid secular objective of protecting churches and schools from the "hurly-burly" typically associated with alcohol "can be readily accomplished by other means … [such as] through an absolute legislative ban on liquor outlets within reasonable prescribed distances from churches, schools, hospitals, and like institutions."[292]

This concern for "the right of the church to be free from offensive land uses in its vicinity"[293] represents a more traditional view of houses of worship in bucolic residential neighborhoods or in town centers with other large institutional uses such as courthouses and municipal buildings. Now that religious groups locate their places of worship in every zone imaginable – commercial, industrial, agricultural – some of these laws that offer zoning "protections" actually create new problems. Churches that want to locate in downtown areas where revitalization is occurring run into zoning prohibitions on the ground that houses of worship thwart economic redevelopment goals because their presence precludes the establishment of restaurants, bars, and other entertainment venues in the vicinity.[294]

### 4. *Protecting Access to Houses of Worship and Prohibiting Disruption of Religious Services*

Numerous state laws also provide protections for undisturbed worship.[295] These laws have their roots in the nineteenth century and, like the state laws involving vandalism, have

290 *See also* Md. Reclamation Associates, Inc. v. Harford Cnty., 994 A.2d 842 (Md. Ct. App. 2010) (no variance for landfill from 1,000-foot buffer zone protecting residences and institutional uses where landfill would be detrimental to adjacent church and graveyard significant in African-American history). Such protections are not always local. *See, e.g.*, Nat'l Min. Ass'n v. Kempthorne, 512 F.3d 702, 705 (D.C. Cir. 2008) {upholding federal rule against mining in "areas within three hundred feet of any occupied dwelling, public building, school, church, community, or institutional building, or within one hundred feet of a cemetery" [citing 30 U.S.C. § 1272(e)]}.

291 459 U.S. 116 (1982).

292 *Id.* at 124. "Plainly schools and churches have a valid interest in being insulated from certain kinds of commercial establishments, including those dispensing liquor. Zoning laws have long been employed to this end, and there can be little doubt about the power of a state to regulate the environment in the vicinity of schools, churches, hospitals, and the like by exercise of reasonable zoning laws." *Id.* at 121; *and see id.* at 124 nn. 7–8 (collecting state laws). *See also* VFW John O'Connor Post No. 4833 v. Santa Rosa Cnty., Fla., 506 F. Supp. 2d 1079 (N.D. Fla. 2007) (ordinance banning liquor within 2,500 feet of schools and churches was constitutional under Establishment Clause).

293 Digrugilliers v. Consolidated City of Indianapolis, 506 F.3d 612, 616 (7th Cir. 2007).

294 *See supra* Section B.8. Note that one solution is to allow religious groups to waive their rights under such state and local laws.

295 *See generally* Wolfe, *supra* note 271, § 14.7. *See, e.g.*, Cal. Penal Code § 302; Md. Code Ann., Criminal Law § 10-303; Mich. Comp. Laws §§ 750.169 & 752.525; Miss. Code Ann. § 97-35-17; N.Y. Penal Law

been modernized to reflect concern about hate crimes.[296] Some focus specifically on the ability of worshippers to gather peacefully. For instance, California law provides that

> [e]very person who intentionally disturbs or disquiets any assemblage of people met for religious worship at a tax-exempt place of worship, by profane discourse, rude or indecent behavior, or by any unnecessary noise, either within the place where the meeting is held, or so near it as to disturb the order and solemnity of the meeting, is guilty of a misdemeanor punishable by a fine not exceeding one thousand dollars ($1,000), or by imprisonment in a county jail for a period not exceeding one year, or by both that fine and imprisonment.[297]

Other laws, such as those like Maryland's, provide more generally for unhindered access to a place of worship: "A person may not, by force or threat of force, obstruct or attempt to obstruct another in the free exercise of that person's religious beliefs."[298] States also may have related laws, such as prohibitions on concealed handguns in a place of worship.[299] In addition to protecting rights of assembly and free exercise, these laws also express protection in terms of privacy.[300]

Several disruption cases occurred in the late 1960s, reflecting the racial turbulence of the time. These cases implicated federal civil right laws prohibiting a conspiracy to deprive members of a church of the right to freedom of worship.[301] In *Central Presbyterian Church v. Black Liberation Front*, not only federal law but also Missouri's state disruption law were found applicable to a volatile situation in which about twenty members of the Black Liberation Front entered a white church, making various demands and threatening to burn the church down.[302] Shortly thereafter, they burned the court's temporary restraining order in front of television cameras. The defendants were found to have violated federal civil rights law and the state disruption law. The

§§ 240.21 & 240.71; N.C. Gen. Stat. §§ 14-288.4 & 14-199; Okla. Stat. tit. 21 § 915; S.C. Code Ann. § 16-17-520; Tenn. Code Ann. § 39-17-306; Va. Code Ann. § 18.2-415; W. Va. Code § 943.012. General laws against public disturbance or breach of peace, as well as specific hate crimes laws, may overlap or provide coverage in states that do not have a specific prohibition. In New Jersey, for instance, the law protects against disruption of any meeting, procession, or gathering. *See* N.J. Stat. Ann. § 2C:33–8; *compare* Ark. Code Ann. § 5-71-207 (disrupting any lawful assembly or meeting is disorderly conduct).

296 *See generally Conduct Amounting to Offense of Disturbing Public or Religious Meeting*, 12 A.L.R. 650 (orig. publ. 1921, updated) (collecting cases); *see also* Carter v. Peters, 26 F.3d 697 (7th Cir. 1994) (Statute that increased penalties for crimes committed in houses of worship did not violate Establishment Clause.); Burke v. State, 943 N.E.2d 870 (Ind. Ct. App. 2011) (Burglary enhancement law did not violate Establishment Clause.).

297 Cal. Penal Code § 302.

298 Md. Code Ann., Criminal Law § 10-303.

299 *See, e.g.*, Ark. Code Ann. § 5-73-306(16)(A)(B) (Church may decide who may carry weapon on its property.).

300 "The government has a legitimate interest in protecting the privacy of places of worship." St. John's Church in the Wilderness v. Scott, 194 P.3d 475, 484 (Colo. Ct. App. 2008); *see also* St. David's Episcopal Church v. Westboro Baptist Church, Inc., 921 P.2d 821 (1996).

301 The Civil Rights Act of 1866, 42 U.S.C. § 1985(3), prohibits a conspiracy to deprive persons of any right of a citizen. The Civil Rights Act of 1870, 18 U.S.C. § 241, imposes criminal penalties "[i]f two or more persons conspire to injure, oppress, threaten, or intimidate any citizen in the free exercise or enjoyment of any right secured to him by the Constitution or laws of United States." *See* Central Presbyterian Church v. Black Liberation Front, 303 F. Supp. 894 (E.D. Mo. 1969); Action v. Gannon, 450 F.2d 1227 (8th Cir. 1971).

302 303 F. Supp. 894 (E.D. Mo. 1969) (applying Mo. Rev. Stat. § 562.250).

court said that the state law's purpose is to ensure religious freedom – "the right to peaceful religious services." The court issued a preliminary injunction because the defendants' "frequent attempts to intimidate the churches and their members … give every indication that unless restrained, they will continue to harass, disturb and oppress the plaintiffs."[303]

Some disruption statutes create a zone around the house of worship in which a person can be prosecuted for disturbing worship in a more peripheral way – such as shouting from across the street. These types of laws are vulnerable to challenge under the Free Speech Clause jurisprudence that has developed regarding protesters at abortion clinics and funerals.[304] In 2012, Missouri enacted the House of Worship Protection Act. The law criminalizes the act of disrupting a house of worship if a person

> 1) Intentionally and unreasonably disturbs, interrupts, or disquiets any house of worship by using profane discourse, rude or indecent behavior, or making noise either within the house of worship *or so near it as to disturb the order and solemnity of the worship services*; or 2) Intentionally injures, intimidates, or interferes with or attempts to injure, intimidate, or interfere with any person lawfully exercising the right of religious freedom in or outside of a house of worship or seeking access to a house of worship, whether by force, threat, or physical obstruction.[305]

Survivors Network of Those Abused by Priests (SNAP), a group that pickets and distributes leaflets outside of churches where alleged pedophile clergy have served, brought a facial challenge under the Free Speech Clause. Because the provision set out in italics can affect traditional public forums (such as public streets and sidewalks), which enjoy special First Amendment protection, the Eighth Circuit noted that "the government's ability to regulate speech in such places 'is very limited.'"[306] Reversing the district court's determination that the law involved content neutral regulation of time, place and manner of speech, the appellate court found that the statute was a content-based ban on only some kinds of speech because it "targeted … the expressive content of the protest message."[307] In holding that the law failed strict scrutiny, the Eighth Circuit noted that this statute was not necessary to promote the state's interest in protecting religious exercise: state law already prohibits anyone from obstructing the entrance to a house of worship.[308]

303 *Id.* at 901.

304 Madsen v. Women's Health Ctr., 512 U.S. 753 (1994) (State court injunction creating thirty-six-foot buffer zone around abortion clinic and restricting noise did not violate Free Speech Clause.); Hill v. Colorado, 530 U.S. 703 (2000) (Statute prohibiting knowing approach within eight feet of another at medical facility did not violate Free Speech Clause.); Snyder v. Phelps, 562 U.S. 443 (2010) (Funeral protesters' speech was protected under Free Speech Clause from state tort liability.).

305 Mo. Rev. Stat. § 574.035 (emphasis added). "House of worship" means "any church, synagogue, mosque, other building or structure, or public or private place used for religious worship, religious instruction, or other religious purpose." Mo. Rev. Stat. § 574.035(2).

306 Survivors Network of Those Abused by Priests v. Joyce, 779 F.3d 785, 789 (8th Cir. 2015) (internal citation omitted).

307 *Id.* at 792. The court distinguished Phelps-Roper v. City of Manchester, 697 F.3d 678 (8th Cir. 2012) (*en banc*) (upholding funeral protest ordinance barring protests within 300 feet of any funeral or burial site or within one hour before and after a funeral service).

308 Survivors Network, 779 F.3d at 794.

Several federal statutes mentioned in Section E.2 in connection with laws against religious vandalism – the Church Arson Prevention Act and the Freedom of Access to Clinic Entrances Act (FACE) – also seek to ensure unencumbered access to religious property for church members. The Church Arson Prevention Act provides that anyone who "intentionally obstructs, by force or threat of force, any person in the enjoyment of that person's free exercise of religious beliefs, or attempts to do so" is subject to the act as long as an interstate commerce nexus can be established.[309] Similarly, FACE provides that anyone who "by force or threat of force or by physical obstruction, intentionally injures, intimidates or interferes with or attempts to injure, intimidate or interfere with any person lawfully exercising or seeking to exercise the First Amendment right of religious freedom at a place of worship" is subject to the act.[310]

Antidisruption injunctions in individual cases can act like these statutes. In a recent Colorado case, a state court issued an injunction for a private nuisance against antiabortion demonstrators who, away from church property, carried signs showing aborted fetuses and made loud noise that disturbed an outdoor Palm Sunday service.[311] The injunction prevents the demonstrators from showing "gruesome images"[312] and from "shouting or yelling at or using any noise amplification device in a manner reasonably calculated to: (1) disturb parishioners' ability to worship; (2) interfere with the plaintiff church's ability to use its property for worship services and/or worship-related events ... and (4) deter parishioners from participating in worship services and/or worship-related events on plaintiff church's property."[313] In 2013, the Colorado Supreme Court denied review and let the injunction stand, and the U.S. Supreme Court denied *certiorari*.[314] The defendants' primary argument was that the "gruesome images" portion of the injunction violated the Free Speech Clause, but they also argued that the restrictions on noise were unjustified content-based restrictions.

### 5. *Protecting Religious Expression from Competing Expression*

In the case of *First Unitarian Church of Salt Lake City v. Salt Lake City Corporation*, the Tenth Circuit required a public easement for pedestrian access over property owned

309 18 U.S.C. § 247(a)(2).

310 *Id.* § 248(a)(2). *See also* 18 U.S.C. §§ 248(e)(2), (3), (4) (defining "interfere with," "intimidate," and "physical obstruction").

311 St. John's Church in the Wilderness v. Scott, 296 P.3d 273 (Colo. Ct. App. 2012), *cert. denied*, No. 12SC658, 2013 WL 119791 (Colo. Supr. Ct. 2013), *cert. denied*, 133 S. Ct. 2798 (2013).

312 Even though this part of the injunction was content based, the Colorado Court of Appeals found it to be narrowly tailored to promote the compelling interest in protecting children from exposure to gruesome images. *Id.* at 283–4.

313 St. John's in the Wilderness v. Scott, 194 P.3d 475, 486 (Colo. Ct. App. 2008). Note that the Colorado Court of Appeals found this part of the injunction constitutional because it was content neutral. *See id.* at 483–4.

314 St. John's Church in the Wilderness v. Scott, 296 P.3d 273 (Colo. Ct. App. 2012), *cert. denied*, No. 12SC658, 2013 WL 119791 (Colo. Supr. Ct. 2013), *cert. denied*, 133 S. Ct. 2798 (2013).

by a church to be treated as a public forum.[315] Salt Lake City sold a portion of a downtown public street to the Church of Latter-Day Saints (LDS Church) and retained an easement for pedestrian access and passage by the public. The transaction came as part of a redevelopment of the downtown that closed a part of Main Street and created a public plaza; the LDS Church improved the plaza area, making it fit "seamlessly into the Church's downtown campus."[316] The LDS Church owned the entire two-block area and, after the sale, the plaza area as well, which it used for religious exhibits, leafletting, and special events. The plaza also served as the entrance to Temple Square (the location of the Mormon Tabernacle and Salt Lake Temple). The easement document (retaining the easement in favor of the city) clearly stated that no public forum was intended and that the LDS Church had full control over the activities on the plaza (including the right to deny access to disorderly persons). The LDS Church, in short, could fill the space with its own expression.[317]

Several organizations, including a church, challenged these restrictions as a violation of the public forum doctrine of the Free Speech Clause. The appeals court found that the plaza, which had been a public sidewalk before the sale (and where the government had permitted public expression) and which now functioned like a public sidewalk retained its character as public property. Specifically, it found that the easement is a traditional public forum, despite the sale and the express intent of church and city to the contrary in the language creating the easement.[318] The court held that the city did not have the authority to prohibit all expressive activities on a public easement it reserved across otherwise private property. "If it wants an easement, the City must permit speech on the easement. Otherwise, it must relinquish the easement so the parcel becomes entirely private."[319]

The City and LDS Church had argued that restricting expression was a legitimate attempt to "protect the Church and the sanctity of its property from public speech."[320] The court responded by saying that the city is free to impose time, place, and manner restrictions in order to take the church's interests into account and "may seek to accommodate competing uses of the easement,"[321] but it rejected the church's argument that "permitting public speech on the easement would infringe on the Church's right of free expression."[322] "[T]he Church has no First Amendment right to be protected from public speech. The speech of others does not, as a matter of law, infringe on an individual's own free speech rights."[323]

315 308 F.3d 1114 (10th Cir. 2002).

316 *Id.* at 1119.

317 *Id.*

318 "The City's declaration is at odds with the objective characteristics of the property and the City's express purpose of providing a pedestrian throughway." *Id.* at 1131.

319 *Id.* at 1132. This is actually what happened later, when the city sold the easement to the LDS Church. That sale was challenged as a violation of the Establishment Clause but upheld in *Utah Gospel Mission v. Salt Lake City Corp.* [425 F.3d 1249 (10th Cir. 2005) (no public speech rights on private property)].

320 First Unitarian Church, 308 F.3d at 1132.

321 *Id.* at 1133. It is the city's role, not the church's, to regulate speech in the easement.

322 *Id.*

323 *Id.*

## F. Historic Preservation: Landmarking Religious Buildings

### 1. *Introduction*

Preservation laws, when applied to houses of worship and other religious properties, seem to be a logical extension of religious vandalism and disruption laws.[324] Those laws reflect our high regard for houses of worship and other religious properties as sensitive locations for protected First Amendment activity and symbols of diversity and religious freedom. Laws concerning preservation reflect an additional consideration: our regard for many of these buildings as places of great aesthetic, cultural, and historic value. Not only do we protect religious buildings from criminal acts by third parties, but we also protect many of them from changes desired by their owners that would harm their aesthetic, historic, or cultural significance. Indeed, while preservation ordinances typically do not require owner consent, houses of worship and other religious properties are sometimes designated landmarks at the request of the religious owners themselves, communities that are proud of the many significant roles their buildings have played.[325]

But once the coercive force of law shifts from preventing third-party harm to a house of worship to preventing its owner from making changes to it, arguments that free exercise is being unlawfully burdened begin to emerge. Owning a building subject to the jurisdiction of a landmarks commission means that virtually any change to the building must be approved by the commission after a public process involving scrutiny of the proposal. Although houses of worship are places of great beauty, they are not museums; they are actively used for sacral, charitable, educational, social, and other accessory purposes, and change is a natural part of their life. Religious groups might seek to expand buildings in order to accommodate changes in worship, mission, or membership; they might want to add or substitute new religious uses on the property; they might want to make architectural changes in order to accommodate changes in liturgy or theological developments; they might simply want a different building when the existing structure is a hindrance to their mission; or they might not want to divert funds from religious mission to repair and replace costly original materials, which is an added expense for many religious organizations on limited budgets. (Indeed, this diversion might force the church to change its priorities or to close or limit programs.) Thus, while some churches have actively and proudly sought landmark designation, others have fought it because of the restrictions and maintenance requirements it entails.

Free exercise challenges often fail for a variety of reasons. Sometimes they fail because there are alternatives that the church has not considered that would preserve the building (or at least those elements of greatest architectural significance) while also accommodating some or all of the church's needs. Sometimes free exercise claims fail because they ignore the very purpose of preservation: making it (nearly) impossible to demolish historic treasures in favor of lucrative real estate development. Arguments

324 Native Americans have used state and federal preservation law, such as the National Register for Historic Places, as a way of protecting from desecration and destruction features found in nature that have religious, cultural, and historic significance. *See supra* notes 268–70 and accompanying text.

325 Landmarking is not only about status for the owners, however. Because they are connected with property of high regard, ministries might be improved and more widely supported, and for religious buildings within historic districts, religious owners get the broader benefits of strong land use control over changes in the district.

that the free exercise of religion is being unlawfully burdened are harder to make when the church wants to transfer the property to a developer without landmark restrictions. Even though the money a church receives from a sale will fund religious activities, there is a clear difference between demolishing a church in order to make way for a nonreligious development and demolishing a church so that a new house of worship can be built in its place.[326]

There are about two thousand preservation ordinances throughout the nation.[327] Preservation promotes aesthetics, economic revitalization, and neighborhood stability. In contrast to zoning powers, through which municipalities focus on incompatibility and intensity of uses through use and dimensional controls, preservation powers allow municipalities to focus on the *design* of buildings with historic, cultural, and/or aesthetic importance.[328] Preservation also works in conjunction with other land use controls to define and promote the character of particular neighborhoods and districts. Indeed, municipal officials commonly use a coordinated mix of zoning, eminent domain, and preservation to promote the redevelopment of downtowns, waterfront areas, or other special zones according to a comprehensive plan. While preservation is typically managed at the local level, there are state and federal laws and registers, such as the National Register of Historic Places, that may provide separate statutory provisions and benefits and may support local preservation efforts.[329]

Most local preservation ordinances provide general criteria of age and aesthetic quality, which means that all buildings meeting these criteria are potential landmarks. Individual buildings and entire districts that meet the criteria can be designated for preservation by affirmative government action following a public process under a municipal landmarks commission. Once the building is designated as a landmark,

326 Economic burdens, which include not being able to sell property, are not cognizable as free exercise burdens in most cases, except in Washington. *See infra* Section F.4. On occasion, owners of historic churches have agreed to let wireless telecommunications equipment be placed inside church steeples. Preservation ordinances have not prevented them because the equipment is not visible to the public. *See, e.g.*, Brehmer v. Planning Bd. of Town of Wellfleet, 238 F.3d 117 (1st Cir. 2001); Cellco Partnership v. Town of Colonie, No. 1:10-CV-581 (GLS/ATB), 2011 WL 5975028 (N.D.N.Y. Nov. 28, 2011).

327 For a collection of cases and scholarship on historical landmark designations, *see* William W. Bassett et. al., Religious Organizations and the Law § 15.16 (West 2012). *See also* Ira C. Lupu & Robert Tuttle, *Historic Preservation Grants to Houses of Worship: A Case Study in the Survival of Separationism*, 43 B.C. L. Rev. 1139 (2002). Note that private preservation of historic landmarks (by restrictive covenant or facade easement held by a private nonprofit organization) might be available under state law as an alternative or adjunct to public preservation. *See supra* Section C.5.

328 Municipalities also promote neighborhood character through architectural design controls that govern new construction (with a process that might be administered by an architectural design review board), which, of course, can affect construction of new religious buildings. *See, e.g.*, Cambodian Buddhist Soc'y v. Planning & Zoning Comm'n, 941 A.2d 868, 897 (Conn. 2008) (fact that "the design of the proposed temple ... was not in harmony with the design of other buildings in the vicinity" was not a valid reason for denying a permit for construction of Buddhist temple with explicitly Asian design). Zoning controls also can have aesthetic impacts. *See e.g.*, Korean Buddhist Dae Won Sa Temple v. Sullivan, 953 P.2d 1315 (Haw. 1998) (Buddhist community argued that the height restriction on temple roof interfered with the balance and harmony of the buildings in its temple compound; court found only burdens of expense and inconvenience because the community could have chosen an alternative location.).

329 The National Historic Preservation Act, which created the National Register of Historic Places, requires federal agencies to consider the effects (when funding or licensing) of any "undertaking on any district, site, building, structure, or object that is included in or eligible for inclusion in the National Register." 16 U.S.C. § 470f.

there is a process to seek permission to make changes to the building. The owner seeks either a "certificate of appropriateness" or a "hardship exemption." Denial in either case means that the building cannot be changed as proposed. When religious properties re involved, church owners might claim that the free exercise of religion is unjustifiably burdened either under the Free Exercise Clause or, more recently, under RLUIPA. Ultimately, one must ask to what degree churches should be accountable to the public for maintaining a historic landmark: should they be treated like any owner of historically significant property? Or should their right to the "free exercise of religion" include the right to make changes to their buildings? Or should their free exercise be protected only to the extent that they continue to use the property directly and explicitly for religious use?

Most preservation ordinances do not exempt religious properties, but some courts have carved out exemptions in particular cases.[330] Washington and Massachusetts have been amenable to exemptions for exteriors and interiors, respectively.[331] California has enacted a broad statutory exemption for religious buildings that meet certain eligibility requirements, which its high court has upheld against an Establishment Clause challenge.[332] But the paucity of judicial and legislative exemptions does not tell the story of the political struggles on the ground between churches and preservationists that can result in accommodation of religious claims. Take, for instance, the situation of the Christian Scientist Church in Washington, D.C., which, in 2007, sought permission to demolish and replace its house of worship. The existing building, an example of aesthetically hideous Brutalist architecture, had become completely incompatible with the church's needs. This "set off a series of lawsuits, landmarking hearings and legal challenges involving the District government, the D.C. Preservation League, the Committee of 100, the church and its development partners. A settlement was finally reached in November 2010. But not until October 2012 did the Historic Preservation Review Board approve the concept design."[333] Thus, after six years, the proposed mixed-use development – office building, house of worship, retail, and parking – is close to final approval.[334] Examples abound, less conflict-ridden, of government agencies and nonprofit preservation organizations working with religious groups to devise solutions that both accommodate religious exercise and save architectural treasures if at all possible.[335]

### 2. *Preservation during the* Sherbert *and* Smith *Eras*

A few early challenges to preservation came during the *Sherbert* era when religious exercise was protected by a strict scrutiny standard of judicial review under the Free Exercise Clause. The claims involved the economic hardships of landmarked churches in

330 *See infra* Section F.4.

331 *See infra* notes 365–75 and accompanying text.

332 *See infra* notes 362–4 and accompanying text.

333 Michael Neibauer, *JBG, ICG Propose Redevelopment of Brutalist Downtown D.C. Church*, 2013 WLNR 4785248.

334 *Id.*

335 *See generally* Susan Corts Hill, *Is an Exemption from Historic Preservation Designation for Religious Institutions Needed in the District of Columbia?* (2008), *available at:* http://scholarship.law.georgetown.edu/hpps_papers/27.

Manhattan, where high costs of repair and maintenance, together with lost development opportunities, could be financially devastating. In fact, free exercise arguments were made alongside arguments that the landmark designation effected a taking of private property without just compensation. When the Society for Ethical Culture challenged the designation of its meeting house, which prevented it from developing the property for nonreligious uses, the New York Court of Appeals held that the Free Exercise Clause "does not entitle ... [the Society] to immunity from reasonable governmental regulations when it acts in purely secular matters."[336] In another case of unexploited land values, the Church of St. Paul and St. Andrew challenged a landmark designation that effectively scuttled its plans to renovate its church and build a commercial high rise on part of the property to provide for the church's financial survival. The New York Court of Appeals, while focused on the issue of ripeness, noted that a free exercise claim would exist only where designation directly prohibits or interferes with religious uses, which was not the case here.[337] As with religious challenges to zoning laws during the era of strict scrutiny, churches usually lost their free exercise claims against preservation laws.[338]

After *Smith* was decided, the constitutional framework became one of explicit deference to facially neutral laws of general applicability. In *Rector, Warden & Members of the Vestry of St. Bartholomew's Church v. City of New York*,[339] the Second Circuit embraced the *Smith* standard. The church in that case sought to demolish its seven-story community house, which was adjacent to its house of worship, and replace it with a fifty-nine-story office tower to fund religious activities. Although the Court noted that the designation and denial of a demolition permit "drastically restricted the Church's ability to raise revenues and to carry out its various charitable and ministerial programs," this did not result in an unconstitutional burden: the court found the landmarks law to be generally applicable and facially neutral.[340] Without evidence of a discriminatory motive or interference with its current level of operations, the First Amendment was not implicated.[341] Further, because the church could continue its present mission in the current facilities, the court found that no regulatory taking had occurred.[342]

Throughout the 1990s, courts used the *Smith* standard to rebuff church challenges to historic preservation. Designation alone was found not to implicate the Free Exercise

336 Soc'y for Ethical Culture v. Spatt, 415 N.E.2d 922, 926 (N.Y. 1980). The designation was not a taking because it did not "physically or financially prevent, or seriously interfere with the carrying out of the charitable purpose" of the society. Further, there was no interference in continuing religious activities. *Id.* at 925.

337 Church of St. Paul & St. Andrew v. Barwick, 496 N.E.2d 183 (N.Y. 1986).

338 *See supra* Section A.2.

339 914 F.2d 348 (2d Cir. 1990).

340 *Id.* at 355.

341 Indeed, the U.S. Supreme Court denied *certiorari* in this case [499 U.S. 905 (1991)] and at the same time remanded for reconsideration in light of *Smith* a decision of the Washington Supreme Court that had found a landmark designation of a church to constitute a violation of the Free Exercise Clause. *See* First Covenant Church v. City of Seattle, 787 P.2d 1352 (Wash. 1990) (*First Covenant I*), *vacated and remanded*, 499 U.S. 901 (1991), *on remand*, 840 P.2d 174 (Wash. 1992) (*First Covenant II*), discussed *infra* at Section F.4.

342 The economic burden argument is often coupled with a regulatory taking argument. These have been largely unsuccessful. Some courts have found regulatory takings. *See, e.g.*, Galich v. Catholic Bishop, 394 N.E.2d 572 (Ill. App. Ct. 1979); *see also* Lutheran Church in Am. v. City of N.Y., 316 N.E.2d 305 (N.Y. 1974) [but holding is in doubt after Penn Central Transp. Co. v. City of N.Y., 438 U.S. 104 (1978)].

Clause.[343] Moreover, denials of demolition permits[344] and of permission to disregard historic building materials[345] also did not implicate the clause because the preservation laws were considered neutral laws of general applicability. It is worth noting that the Supreme Court's 1997 decision in *City of Boerne v. Flores*,[346] which held RFRA unconstitutional as applied to the states, was a case about historic preservation. There the Court also focused on the neutral and general nature of the law. The case involved a Catholic Church in a historic district that was denied a permit to enlarge its building. Because of increasing membership, the church had outgrown its worship space, and the owners sought to demolish the house of worship (except the facade) and expand its facilities.

The archbishop sued the city under RFRA, alleging that the permit denial had substantially burdened the church without compelling justification. The city successfully defended with the argument that RFRA was unconstitutional. The Court assumed that historic preservation laws should be treated as generally applicable and facially neutral law under *Smith*'s rational basis standard of review rather than as an individualized assessment that would be subject to a strict scrutiny standard. Justice Kennedy wrote, "It is a reality of the modern regulatory state that numerous state laws, such as the zoning regulations at issue here, impose a substantial burden on a large class of individuals. When the exercise of religion has been burdened in an incidental way by a law of general application, it does not follow that the persons affected have been burdened any more than their fellow citizens, let alone burdened because of their religious beliefs."[347]

But some courts have rejected the assumption made by the Supreme Court in *Boerne* and by the Second Circuit in *St. Bartholomew's* that historic preservation involves neutral laws of general applicability, noting that the typical preservation ordinance contains a process by which exemptions could be granted based on individualized assessments of facts, which, under *Smith*, calls for strict scrutiny review. Under this paradigm, denials of permits to change or demolish could be found to constitute unjustified burdens on religious exercise. A federal district court took this position in *Keeler v. Mayor and City Council of Cumberland*, in which the bishop sought to demolish a church and monastery within a historic district to replace them with smaller liturgically appropriate buildings.[348] The line of Washington cases described in Section F.4 took this approach.

343 Metropolitan Baptist Church v. D.C. Dep't of Consumer-Regulatory Affairs-Historic Preservation Bd., 718 A.2d 119 (D.C. 1998) (designation alone not a burden; free exercise claim not ripe).

344 City of Ypsilanti v. First Presbyterian Church, No. 191379, 1998 WL 1993029 (Mich. Ct. App. Feb. 3, 1998) (not a violation of Free Exercise Clause under *Smith* to deny demolition permit and require church to maintain historic log cabin on its site because historic district ordinance was facially neutral and generally applicable).

345 First Church of Christ, Scientist v. Ridgefield Hist. Dist. Comm'n, 738 A.2d 224, 231 (Conn. Super. Ct. 1998) (where permission was denied to place vinyl siding on exterior of historic church; First Amendment [under *Smith*] "cannot be extended ... to avoid otherwise reasonable and neutral legal obligations imposed by government"), *aff'd*, 737 A.2d 989 (Conn. App. Ct. 1999) (*per curiam*).

346 521 U.S. 507 (1997) (holding RFRA unconstitutional as applied to the states because it exceeds Congress' authority under Section 5 of the Fourteenth Amendment).

347 *Id*. at 535.

348 Keeler v. Mayor & City Council of Cumberland, 940 F. Supp. 879 (D. Md. 1996) (denial of permit infringed free exercise; state may not refuse to extend individualized assessment system to cases of religious hardship without compelling justification); *see also* Mount St. Scholastica v. City of Atchison, 482 F. Supp. 2d 1281 (D. Kan. 2007) (Historic preservation is individualized assessment, so strict scrutiny applies; denial of permit to demolish administration building was substantial burden, and historic preservation is not a compelling governmental interest.).

The landmarks laws at issue there "invite individualized assessments of the subject property and the owner's use of such property" and are therefore not generally applicable.[349]

### 3. *Preservation under RLUIPA*

The advent of RLUIPA has not imposed a uniform analysis on church preservation challenges.[350] It also has not ended the use of the deferential *Smith* standard because some courts may continue to consider historic preservation laws to be facially neutral and generally applicable despite the fact that denials of permits to demolish or reconstruct buildings are made after an individualized assessment pursuant to exemption provisions of an ordinance.[351] And even where strict scrutiny is held to apply, churches are often unable to establish a substantial burden on religious exercise.[352]

But much like judicial concern over zoning decisions that reflect antireligious bias,[353] courts will look disapprovingly at historic preservation decisions that misuse discretion and target religious institutions in hostile ways. In *Roman Catholic Bishop of Springfield v. City of Springfield*, the city created a single-parcel historic district containing only a house of worship that had been closed a few weeks earlier.[354] Parishioners and other residents lobbied for designation to prevent the building from being sold and demolished. The First Circuit noted "some troubling circumstances surrounding the City's enactment of the Ordinance."[355] The court set its concern aside, however, because the bishop still had the opportunity to submit proposals to city landmark officials and obtain a hardship exemption. Thus the court held that the ordinance itself – which was only the designation of the building – did not violate the substantial burden provision.

RLUIPA challenges to preservation do not always involve restrictions on development of religious property that is landmarked; sometimes they involve the exclusion of religious

349 First Covenant Church v. City of Seattle, 840 P.2d 174, 181 (Wash. 1992).

350 *See generally supra* Section B. RLUIPA defines land use regulation as "zoning and landmarking" laws. Landmarking includes historic preservation. It also includes open-space preservation. *See* Albanian Associated Fund v. Twp. of Wayne, Civ. Action No. 06-CV-3217 (PGS), 2007 WL 2904194, at *8 (D.N.J. Oct. 1, 2007).

351 *See, e.g.*, City of Boerne v. Flores, 521 U.S. 507, 535 (1997) (dicta). *But see* Chabad Lubavitch of Litchfield Cnty., Inc. v. Borough of Litchfield, 853 F.Supp.2d 214, 224–5 (D. Conn. 2012) 768 F.3d 183, 193 (2d Cir. 2014) (preservation "undeniably demands an individualized assessment of applications to alter historic properties"), *cert. denied*, 135 S. Ct. 1853 (2015); Roman Catholic Bishop of Springfield v. City of Springfield, 724 F.3d 73 (1st Cir. 2013) (historic designation is the result of discretionary process and is not generally applicable).

352 *See, e.g.*, Roman Catholic Bishop of Springfield v. City of Springfield, 724 F.3d 73 (1st Cir. 2013) (no substantial burden from historic designation alone); World Outreach Conference Ctr. v. City of Chicago, 591 F.3d 539 (7th Cir. 2009) (no substantial burden from increased cost of maintaining landmark; court found that church could sell the landmark and use proceeds to finance new construction on another lot church already owned); Episcopal Student Found. v. City of Ann Arbor, 341 F. Supp. 2d 691, 704 (E.D. Mich. 2004) (no substantial burden where church denied permits for demolition and construction of new building for expanded ministries because church would have enough room if it stopped leasing out space to tenants); Trinity Assembly of God of Baltimore City, Inc. v. People's Counsel for Baltimore Cnty., 941 A.2d 560 (2008), *judgment aff'd*, 962 A.2d 404 (Md. 2008) (no substantial burden from denial of permission for larger sign, based on historic considerations).

353 *See supra* Section B.6.

354 724 F.3d 78 (1st Cir. 2013); *see also* Chabad, *supra* note 351.

355 *Id.* at 98.

uses from historic districts. A church successfully challenged such an exclusion under the equal terms provision of RLUIPA.[356] The religious organization had been denied a conditional use permit to operate a new church in the city's historic area because a church use was deemed inconsistent with the development of that district into a "tourism, entertainment and retail corridor." Churches were singled out as incompatible uses, whereas other assembly uses were not. Because churches had to obtain a permit while similarly situated secular membership assemblies did not, RLUIPA was violated.

### 4. *Legislative and Judge-Made Exceptions for Religious Properties*

In a few states, church plaintiffs have won exemptions from historic preservation in court; others have benefited from exemptions in state or local law. These exemptions do not prevent a church from obtaining landmark designation if that is desired.

Although most local ordinances cover churches, a few exempt them. Chicago and Pittsburgh are examples of cities that require owner involvement in the preservation decision.[357] In Chicago, the church must consent in order for a house of worship to be designated.[358] In Pittsburgh, the church itself has to nominate the religious building for designation.[359] New York City exempts the interiors of houses of worship.[360]

Exemptions have been upheld against Establishment Clause challenges.[361] California's statutory exemption applies broadly to all noncommercial property owned by religious institutions.[362] Religious owners are eligible for an exemption if they can prove a "substantial hardship," which can be demonstrated when preservation is likely to deprive the owner of economic return on its property, the reasonable use of its property, or the appropriate use of its property in the furtherance of its mission.[363] The Supreme Court of

[356] Centro Familiar Cristiano Buenas Nuevas v. City of Yuma, 651 F.3d 1163 (9th Cir. 2011). *But cf.* Chabad Lubavitch of Litchfield Cnty., Inc. v. Borough of Litchfield, 853 F. Supp. 2d 214 (D. Conn. 2012) (Requirement that anyone, secular or religious, proposing to build in historic district obtain certificate of appropriateness is not a substantial burden under RLUIPA; moreover, there was no showing that secular properties, even if appropriate comparators, were treated differently from plaintiff's property.).

[357] *See* Susan Corts Hill, *Is an Exemption from Historic Preservation Designation for Religious Institutions Needed in the District of Columbia?* (2008), *available at:* http://scholarship.law.georgetown.edu/hpps_papers/27.

[358] Chicago, Ill. Code ch. 2-120, § 660. *See* Alger v. City of Chicago, 753 F. Supp. 228 (N.D. Ill. 1990) (no standing to challenge exemption where demolition was too speculative).

[359] Pittsburgh, Pa. Code, tit. 11, ch. 1101.02–1101.03 (house of worship, rectory, convent).

[360] New York, N.Y. Admin. Code § 25-303 (2). *See also* Crimi v. Rutgers Presbyterian Church in City of N.Y., 89 N.Y.S. 2d 813 (Sup. Ct. N.Y. 1949) (Fresco painter could not sue church that destroyed a fresco it had commissioned on church wall.).

[361] Exemptions, of course, can be challenged on other grounds. *See, e.g.*, Springfield Preservation Trust v. Springfield Library & Museums Ass'n, 852 N.E.2d 83 (Mass. 2006) (preservation exemption unauthorized, but narrow exemption allowed for properties owned by Roman Catholic diocese and by museum and library association as of date of law's adoption).

[362] *See, e.g.*, California-Nevada Annual Conference of United Methodist Church v. City & Cnty. of S.F., 94 Cal. Rptr. 3d 64 (Cal. Ct. App. 2009) (Church property was noncommercial property and therefore exempt from preservation by state statute even though church intended to sell for demolition and development as a condominium site.). *But see* Or Khaim Hashalom v. City of Santa Monica, 118 Cal. Rptr. 3d 390 (Cal. Ct. App. 2010) (exemption held not to apply to an apartment complex because it was found to be a commercial enterprise).

[363] Cal. Govt. Code § 25373(c)(d).

California has upheld this exemption against an Establishment Clause challenge on the grounds that it had the secular purpose of avoiding free exercise violations.[364]

Several states have mandated religious exemptions from historic preservation. In a series of decisions in the 1990s, the Washington courts found substantial and unjustified burdens on free exercise. Beginning with *First Covenant Church v. City of Seattle*,[365] the Washington Supreme Court found that even after *Smith* changed the standard of review in free exercise cases, historic preservation laws would be subject to strict scrutiny under the state constitution as well as under two of *Smith*'s exceptions: as an individualized assessment and as implicating a "hybrid" of two constitutional protections for religion and speech.[366] The court determined that the hybrid approach applied because the designation of a house of worship involved the government in compelling a particular architectural statement, which implicated the Free Speech Clause in addition to the Free Exercise Clause.[367] The designation caused financial burdens by "grossly diminish[ing] the value of the Church's principal asset."[368] It also caused administrative burdens with its "liturgy exemption," which allowed the church to make architectural changes necessitated by changes in the liturgy, but only after the church met with government authorities to prove its case. When applying strict scrutiny, the court held that preservation was not a sufficiently compelling state interest to justify these burdens. Thus, whereas other courts have found designation alone not to burden a church's religious exercise,[369] *First Covenant* held that designation alone can indeed constitute a substantial burden.

In 1996, the Washington Supreme Court extended *First Covenant* in *First United Methodist Church v. Hearing Examiner for the Seattle Landmarks Preservation Board*, holding that even the *proposed* designation of a house of worship (in the form of a nomination that itself carries restrictions) "severely burdens" the church because it could interfere with a sale to a nonreligious owner, the proceeds of which would go to the

364 E. Bay Asian v. State of California, 13 P.3d 1122 (Cal. 2000) (exemption not an establishment under either state or federal constitution).

365 840 P.2d 174 (Wash. 1992) (First Covenant II).

366 In an earlier decision in the same case [*see* 787 P.2d 1352 (Wash. 1990) (First Covenant I)], the Washington Supreme Court held, under *Sherbert*, that the ordinance was an unconstitutional burden on the church's free exercise. The state's interest in historic preservation was not sufficiently compelling to justify the burden. Then *Smith* was decided. The city petitioned for *certiorari*, which was granted. The U.S. Supreme Court vacated the judgment and remanded for further consideration in light of *Smith* [499 U.S. 901 (1991)]. On remand, the Washington Supreme Court reinstated its original holding [840 P.2d 174 (Wash. 1992)]. *Smith* did not apply because the ordinance was not a neutral of general applicability; the ordinance applied only to the church. With *Smith* inapplicable, the court ruled that the ordinance violated the federal and state constitutions because the interest in historic preservation was not sufficiently compelling to justify the burden.

367 The "hybrid" argument was an independent ground for taking a case out of *Smith*'s rational basis review and requiring strict scrutiny review. In *First Covenant II*, the church made a speech-religion hybrid claim because it argued that the church's architecture was a form of religious expression. *But see* Adhi Parasakthi Charitable, Medical, Educational, & Cultural Soc'y of N. Am. v. Twp. of W. Pikeland, 721 F. Supp. 2d 361, 374 (E.D. Pa. 2010) ("The building of a place of worship will not be considered expressive conduct protected by the Free Speech Clause.").

368 840 P.2d at 184.

369 *See, e.g.*, Roman Catholic Bishop of Springfield v. City of Springfield, 724 F.3d 78 (1st Cir. 2013) (under RLUIPA); Metropolitan Baptist Church v. D.C. Dep't of Consumer-Regulatory Affairs-Historic Preservation Bd., 718 A.2d 119 (D.C. 1998) (under Free Exercise Clause).

church's religious mission.[370] The city conceded that it had no compelling governmental interest. A year later, the Washington Supreme Court protected a church's decision to demolish a school and replace it with a pastoral center.[371] The court found that the demolition permit ordinance – which involved a lengthy period of delay – would cause an administrative burden and violate the church's right to free exercise under the state constitution. More recently, a state appellate court held that a city could not require a church to consider alternatives to demolition of a sanctuary under environmental laws.[372] Because the church "cannot be required to maintain the sanctuary for purposes of landmark preservation, it also cannot be required to consider alternatives that, if imposed, would violate [the church's] constitutional rights."[373] The upshot of these cases, taken together, is that financial and administrative burdens, if demonstrated in a given case, are indeed considered burdens on religious exercise that can lead to an exemption.

Massachusetts' high court also has carved out an exemption from historic preservation laws. In 1990, the Supreme Judicial Court avoided *Smith* altogether by holding under its state constitution that the landmark preservation of the interior of a house of worship was unconstitutional. Finding that "the configuration of the church interior is so freighted with religious meaning that it must be considered part and parcel of the … worship,"[374] the court wrote

> The government interest in historic preservation, though worthy, is not sufficiently compelling to justify restraints on the free exercise of religion, a right of primary importance. In short, under our hierarchy of constitutional values we must accept the possible loss of historically significant elements of the interior of this church as the price of safeguarding the right of religious freedom. We conclude, in sum, that the landmark designation of the church interior unconstitutionally restrains religious worship. We further conclude that the conduct the commission attempted to regulate, renovation of the church interior, neither disturbs the public peace nor obstructs the religious worship of nonmembers of the church.[375]

370 916 P.2d 374 (Wash. 1996). Here the economic argument was persuasive. If a church "decides to sell its property in order to respond to the needs of its congregation, it has a right to do so without landmark restrictions creating administrative or financial burdens. The free exercise clause prevents government from engaging in landmark preservation when it has a coercive effect on religion. This protection does not cease if United Methodist sells its property. … [The landmark law] severely burdens free exercise of religion because it impedes United Methodist from selling its property and using the proceeds to advance its religious mission." *Id.* at 381.

371 Munns v. Martin, 930 P.2d 318 (Wash. 1997).

372 Friends of First United Methodist Church v. City of Seattle, 130 Wash. App. 1031 (Wash. Ct. App. 2005).

373 *Id.*

374 Soc'y of Jesus of New England v. Boston Landmarks Comm'n, 564 N.E.2d 571, 573 (1990). ("We conclude, therefore, that art. 2 protects the right freely to design interior spaces for religious worship, thus barring the government from regulating changes in such places, provided that no public safety question is presented.").

375 *Id.* at 574. Article 2 of the state constitution provides in relevant part: "[N]o subject shall be hurt, molested, or restrained, in his person, liberty, or estate, for worshipping GOD in the manner and season most agreeable to the dictates of his own conscience; or for his religious profession or sentiments; *provided he doth not disturb the public peace, or obstruct others in their religious worship.*" MASS. CONST. art. II (emphasis added).

### 5. *Public Grants to Assist Owners of Religious Landmarks and Establishment Clause Issues*

Numerous programs of public (and private) funding exist to mitigate the economic burdens on property owners of designated properties. The federal government used to follow a strict separationist policy of "no direct public monies" to churches for bricks and mortar on the theory that it violated of the Establishment Clause. But some exceptions emerged in the mid-1990s. For example, the Church Arson Prevention Act of 1996 (discussed in Section E.2) provides low-income reconstruction loans to nonprofits, including houses of worship, covered by the act; this has been found not to constitute an establishment violation.[376] Significant changes in Establishment Clause jurisprudence make it likely that churches that are designated will be able to seek public monetary assistance as long as funds are offered as part of a general program making benefits widely available to owners of historic properties.[377] In fact, several courts have upheld urban improvement programs that provide grants to churches on neutral eligibility criteria and for a secular purpose.[378] Indeed, under the Save the Treasures program of the National Park Service and National Trust for Historic Preservation – traditionally a thoroughly separationist program – grants have been made to Old North Church in Boston and Touro Synagogue on the grounds that the federal government has an "interest in preserving all sites of historic significance to the nation, without regard to their religious or secular character."[379]

## G. Religious Land Use and Eminent Domain

### 1. *Eminent-Domain Takings of Religious Buildings*

As is clear from Sections E.2 and F, the sovereign protects religious buildings from criminal vandalism and, through historic designation, often prevents religious groups from altering and razing their own buildings. Ironically, sometimes the sovereign itself seeks to demolish religious buildings for a public purpose through its power of eminent domain.

[376] *See* United States v. Corum, 362 F.3d 489 (8th Cir. 2004) (*see supra* note 278 and accompanying text).

[377] *See* Ira C. Lupu & Robert Tuttle, *Historic Preservation Grants to Houses of Worship : A Case Study in the Survival of Separationism*, 43 B.C. L. Rev. 1139 (2002). Lupu and Tuttle argue that if states can regulate religious properties with preservation, then it can subsidize those properties. (The implication of this argument is that religious properties that are exempt should not be eligible for funding.) They also argue that house of worship interiors should be exempt from preservation and therefore not eligible for public assistance.

[378] *See, e.g.*, Am. Atheists, Inc. v. City of Detroit Downtown Development Auth., 567 F.3d 278 (6th Cir. 2009) (Under facade improvement grant program, ninety-one projects received funds, nine of which were church sponsored; no Establishment Clause violation because monies were distributed on neutral criteria to recipients that were eligible as part of large class of property owners, and "Detroit sought to fix up its downtown, not establish a religion."). *See also* Saint Louis Univ. v. Masonic Temple Ass'n of St. Louis, 220 S.W.3d 721 (Mo. 2007) (Jesuit university received tax abatement for its arena development in blighted area pursuant to generally available program; no Establishment Clause violation because the construction had a secular purpose and program did not advance religion).

[379] Danielle Assad, *Direct Government Grants to Churches for Façade Improvements: The Fall of the Wall of Separation?* 86 U. Det. Mercy L. Rev. 509, 530–1 (2009).

States might have special rules or exemptions for certain takings involving religious property.[380] Typically, however, religious property is fully subject to the government's power to take. Government or its designated authority might take religious property along with many other parcels as part of a large urban revitalization project or might take only the individual religious building. At a minimum, the taking must satisfy the Fifth Amendment's Public Use and Just Compensation Clauses, which require that the property be paid for[381] and put to a broadly articulated public purpose.[382] Many states add constitutional or statutory restrictions or requirements, such as necessity or a finding of blight, to this federal minimum.[383]

Several interesting cases were decided during the *Sherbert* era, when eminent-domain takings of religious property were subjected to strict scrutiny judicial review. In the 1970s, the City of Denver's major urban renewal plan included the taking and demolition of a church building that had special historic and religious significance to the worshippers. The church fought the taking, but the Colorado Supreme Court found that despite the clear burden on religious exercise, the city had demonstrated a compelling interest in its comprehensive downtown revitalization plan. All the buildings, including the house of worship, had to be razed; no "reasonable alternative means of accomplish[ing]" the revitalization existed.[384] The Second Circuit also noted the applicability of strict scrutiny to the City of Yonkers' taking of two acres of grounds at a Catholic seminary to build housing. The court said that "it is well settled that a limitation by the government on the free exercise of religion is permitted only when the state can demonstrate that a compelling interest justifies the restriction and that no alternative means of accomplishing the state's compelling interest are available."[385] The court, quite solicitous of the seminary's need for tranquil space, remanded to consider the question of whether the taking of the seminary property was necessary to vindicate a compelling state interest.[386]

380 *See, e.g.*, City of Jordan v. Church of St. John the Baptist of Jordan, 764 N.W.2d 71 (Minn. Ct. App. 2009) (State statute required city to obtain consent of church governing body to obtain easement for signal light by eminent domain through church's property.); State of Ill. Med. Ctr. Comm'n v. United Church of the Med. Ctr., 491 N.E.2d 1327 (Ill. App. Ct. 1986) (exemption from eminent domain of property used exclusively for religious purposes not applicable in case where property was used for both religious and secular purposes). *See also* 24 Pa. Cons. Stat. § 7–721 (Pennsylvania statute prohibiting takings of church property for use as public school) ("[N]o board of school directors shall take by condemnation any burial ground, or any land belonging to any incorporated institution of learning, incorporated hospital association, or unincorporated church, incorporated or unincorporated religious association, which land is actually used or held for the purpose for which such burial ground, institution of learning, hospital association, church, or religious association was established."); *and see generally* Philip E. Hassman, *Eminent Domain Right to Condemn Property Owned or Used by Private Educational, Charitable, or Religious Organizations*, 80 A.L.R.3D 833 (orig. publ. 1977).

381 Although "just compensation" usually means market value, the measure of compensation might be different for religious, charitable, educational, and nonprofit uses under state law (e.g., replacement cost of buildings).

382 Kelo v. City of New London, 545 U.S. 469 (2005) (Taking for the purpose of economic development fulfills "public use" requirement.).

383 *See, e.g.*, Cnty. of Wayne v. Hathcock, 684 N.W.2d 765 (Mich. 2004) (necessity); Gallenthin Realty Development, Inc. v. Borough of Paulsboro, 924 A.2d 447 (N.J. 2007) (blight).

384 Pillar of Fire v. Denver Urban Renewal Auth., 509 P.2d 1250 (Colo. 1973) {Even condemnation of a church parking lot received strict scrutiny. In *Order of Friars Minor v. Denver Urban Renewal Auth.* [527 P.2d 804, 805 (Colo. 1974)], the court noted that condemnation is constitutional only when "there is a substantial public interest … which cannot be accomplished 'through any other reasonable means.'"}.

385 Yonkers Racing Corp. v. City of Yonkers, 858 F.2d 855, 872 (2d Cir. 1988).

386 *Id.*

After *Smith*, however, it may be difficult to make such claims under the Free Exercise Clause unless the taking targets a religious group in a *Lukumi*-like bid to drive the group out of town. Takings of large land areas for major projects easily would be seen as facially neutral with respect to religion and generally applicable to all properties identified for condemnation and thus subject to rational basis review. Even a taking of a single religious building might not be viewed as an individualized assessment if it is done pursuant to a general, religion-neutral statute and process.[387]

Strict scrutiny might be available by state constitutional interpretation or state statute. States are free to interpret their state free exercise provisions in a way that provides greater protection than the federal interpretation. *In City Chapel Evangelical Free, Inc. v. City of South Bend ex rel. Dep't of Redevelopment*, the church argued that the eminent domain of its chapel building was a material burden on its right to worship under the state constitution.[388] The Indiana Supreme Court remanded the case for a hearing on the issue; the federal claim, which it denied, did not control the state interpretation.

State RFRAs also provide for strict scrutiny.[389] The Florida RFRA was used in *Christian Romany Church Ministries, Inc. v. Broward County*, which involved a church challenging the condemnation of its house of worship and forced relocation. Though the court applied the state RFRA, it held that the taking did not cause a substantial burden on religious exercise and that the relocation was only an inconvenience.[390]

## 2. *Eminent Domain, RFRA, and RLUIPA*

Federal statutes might apply to provide a higher standard of review. RFRA would apply to federal takings, although there is no case law on point.[391] RLUIPA on its face applies only to land use regulation, defined as "zoning and landmarking," and there is no mention of eminent domain in the legislative history.[392] Courts have split on RLUIPA's applicability

387 Other arguments, such as a hybrid claim, also might fail. *See, e.g.*, City Chapel Evangelical Free, Inc. v. City of S. Bend *ex rel.* Dep't of Redevelopment, 744 N.E.2d 443 (Ind. 2001) (church not entitled to hearing on claim that taking of religious building had to be justified by compelling interest on a hybrid claim of free exercise and association rights under First Amendment).

388 *Id.*

389 *See supra* Section A.3.

390 980 So. 2d 1164 (Fla. Dist. Ct. App. 2008). "The church's insistence that a specific church building for holding worship services is fundamental to religious exercise under the statute is unpersuasive. Our supreme court expressly rejected any definition of substantial burden other than that compelling conduct or that forbidding conduct. By no stretch does an otherwise valid condemnation fall within these limits. There is nothing about this location that is unique or integral to the conduct of the religion." *Id.* at 1168.

391 In a church's RFRA challenge to a taking for purposes of O'Hare Airport expansion (which would force the relocation of a cemetery), the court held that "any burden on the exercise of religion caused by the City's airport expansion plan is not fairly attributable to the FAA." Without federal action, RFRA did not apply. Vill. of Bensenville v. Fed. Aviation Admin., 457 F.3d 52, 57 (D.C. Cir. 2006). *See infra* note 398 and accompanying text for the same church's RLUIPA challenge to the city's taking.

392 For a general discussion, *see* Kenneth G. Leonczyk, Jr., *RLUIPA and Eminent Domain: How a Plain Reading of a Flawed Statute Creates an Absurd Result*, 13 Tex. Rev. L. & Pol. 311 (2009). For a provocative article arguing against applying RLUIPA to eminent domain, *see* Christopher Serkin & Nelson Tebbe, *Condemning Religion: RLUIPA and the Politics of Eminent Domain*, 85 Notre Dame L. Rev. 1 (2009) (inviting municipalities to use or threaten to use eminent domain against religious groups that rely on RLUIPA to resist zoning decisions; governmental abuses will be restrained because municipalities have to pay religious groups for their property).

to takings.[393] There was even a failed attempt to amend the statute to include eminent domain in order to eliminate any uncertainty.[394]

In *Cottonwood Christian Center v. Cypress Redevelopment Agency*, the federal district court applied RLUIPA to a taking on the grounds that the eminent-domain action was closely tied to the implementation of municipal zoning decisions.[395] Closely related to the city's refusal to grant the church a conditional use permit was the city's decision to take the church's property for use as a Costco retail center. The church won a preliminary injunction against the taking. The court found "strong evidence the ... [city's] actions are not neutral but instead specifically aimed at discriminating against Cottonwood's religious uses."[396] The city had claimed that it had an interest in using the site to generate revenue and that it needed to eliminate blight, but the court found neither to be compelling. Indeed, the city had never been concerned with this site before the church purchased it. Moreover, it was clear that the best way to eliminate blight would be to permit the church development to go forward. The city failed to justify the taking, which substantially burdened the church's religious exercise, as the least restrictive alternative for advancing a compelling interest.

Other courts, finding RLUIPA inapplicable to eminent domain, have distinguished *Cottonwood* or found its reasoning unpersuasive. In *City and County of Honolulu v. Sherman*,[397] the government condemned fifty residential condominiums owned by First United Methodist Church under an ordinance authorizing takings for leasehold-to-fee simple conversions. The church argued that condemnation deprived it of the ability to use the property for religious purposes after the leases terminate. But the Hawaii Supreme Court found that eminent domain is not "land use regulation" under RLUIPA and, in contrast to *Cottonwood*, that not all eminent domain is grounded in a zoning system. The Seventh Circuit took a similar approach in *St. John's United Church of Christ v. City of Chicago*[398] when it held that RLUIPA did not apply to land acquisition for airport modernization that required the relocation of a church cemetery.[399]

As we know well from experience with the Free Exercise Clause and RLUIPA, the existence of strict scrutiny judicial review does not necessarily guarantee a close, hard look at government conduct. In most *Sherbert*-era decisions, and now in many RLUIPA zoning decisions, the existence of alternative locations – zones within a municipality that would accommodate religious uses – negates a substantial burden.[400] Thus, the

393 In *Albanian Associated Fund v. Twp. of Wayne*, Civ. Action No. 06-CV-3217 (PGS), 2007 WL 2904194 (D.N.J. Oct. 1, 2007)], the municipality sought to take the entire eleven-acre parcel owned by religious organization for purpose of keeping open space, even though eight to nine of those acres would have remained open after the proposed mosque was built. The court did not reach the question of whether RLUIPA applies to eminent domain because "the RLUIPA challenge does not go to the actual taking, but rather the implementation of the open space plan which is land use regulation. The taking is merely the method of implementation." *Id.* at *8.

394 *See* Matthew Baker, *RLUIPA and Eminent Domain: Probing the Boundaries of Religious Land Use Protection*, 2008 B.Y.U. L. Rev. 1213, 1238.

395 218 F. Supp. 2d 1203 (C.D. Cal. 2002).

396 *Id.* at 1224.

397 129 P.3d 542 (Haw. 2006).

398 502 F.3d 616 (7th Cir. 2007) (condemnation of religious cemetery for airport expansion).

399 *See also* Faith Temple Church v. Town of Brighton, 405 F.Supp.2d 250 (W.D.N.Y. 2005) (RLUIPA not applicable to zoning, Cottonwood unpersuasive); Congregation Adas Yereim v. City of N.Y., 673 F. Supp. 2d 94, 105–6 (E.D.N.Y. 2009) (RLUIPA not applicable to eminent domain).

400 *See supra* Sections A.2 and B.5.

reasoning goes, the church may be denied zoning approvals and unable to develop at this site, but it can find property elsewhere and build in that new location. If we extend this concept of alternative sites to eminent domain, we see that it would be quite difficult to establish a free exercise burden: the government is not simply telling a church to go find new property somewhere else; it is actually providing the religious condemnee with money to purchase or rent an alternative site.[401]

### 3. *Religious Beneficiaries of Eminent Domain*

Note too that a religious group might be the beneficiary of eminent domain rather than the condemnee. In the case of *In re Redevelopment Authority of City of Philadelphia*,[402] the city took a private home in a blighted area and transferred it to a religious entity for the purpose of building a religious school. On an Establishment Clause challenge, the Pennsylvania Supreme Court held that this conveyance of eminent-domain property to a religious entity, as part of a redevelopment plan, met the requirements of the *Lemon* test: the transaction had a secular purpose and primary secular effect – the elimination of blight – and involved no excessive entanglement of state in religious affairs.[403]

401 For a provocative argument that a forced move to a new location can mean the death of the church, *see generally* Leonczyck, *supra* note 392.

402 938 A.2d 341 (Pa. 2007).

403 Lemon v. Kurtzman, 403 U.S. 602 (1971).

# 13 Torts

Religious institutions and entities can be involved in tort cases just like other institutions and entities. Given constitutional considerations, however, there are some unique questions that arise when tort claims are brought against, or by, religious institutions or entities. These issues will be explored in this chapter in the context of the various tort causes of action that arise in religion contexts.

The sorts of tort claims that can arise when religious institutions and entities are involved include both intentional and negligence-based torts. These issues can arise from garden-variety tort claims such as a slip and fall on church property[1] or from more serious issues such as sexual abuse by clergy.[2] Some of the more common causes of action that arise, especially in clergy abuse cases, include negligent supervision,[3] negligent

1 *See, e.g.*, Mouhot v. Twelfth St. Baptist Church, 949 So.2d 668 (La. Ct. App. 2007) (finding a church negligent because it knowingly failed to remove a potentially hazardous floor mat that caused a seventy-one-year-old woman to fall); Stitt v. Holland Abundant Life Fellowship, 614 N.W.2d 88 (Mich. 2000) (denying visitor's cause of action against a church for the injuries sustained after she tripped and fell in the church's parking lot because the visitor entered the church's property for a noncommercial purpose); Graf v. St. Luke's Evangelical Church, 625 N.E.2d 851 (Ill. App. Ct. 1993) (recognizing a cause of action against a church that allowed or created an unnatural accumulation of snow and ice on its steps causing a guest to fall); Broad St. Christian Church v. Carrington, 234 So.2d 732 (Fla. Dist. Ct. App. 1970) (recognizing that a church may be liable to a grandmother who fell while attending her grandson's ordination, if it was determined that she was an invitee).

2 *See, e.g.*, Doe v. Norwich Roman Catholic Diocesan Corp., 309 F. Supp. 2d 247 (D. Conn. 2004) (determining a church could be liable for the sexual misconduct of its priest during counseling sessions because the priest sought to bring the victim closer to the church and thereby increase financial donations; thus the court determined that the actions were not clearly outside the scope of employment); Robertson v. Church of God, Int'l, 978 S.W.2d 120 (Tex. App. 1997) (finding church not liable for its minister's sexual assault of a massage therapist when therapy was unrelated to minister's work for the church); Konkle v. Henson, 672 N.E.2d 450 (Ind. Ct. App. 1996) (determining that a church may be liable for sexual misconduct of its minister under the doctrine of *respondeat superior* liability); Jeffrey E. v. Central Baptist Church, 243 Cal. Rptr. 128 (Cal. Ct. App. 1988) (recognizing that a church may be liable under the theory of *respondeat superior* for the sexual misconduct of its Sunday school teacher as long as the connection between the teacher's duties and misconduct is not too attenuated).

3 *See, e.g.*, R.A. v. First Church of Christ, 748 A.2d 692 (Pa. Super. Ct. 2000) (recognizing that a church, like a secular employer, can be held liable for negligent supervision of its employees); Mark K. v. Roman Catholic Archbishop of L.A., 79 Cal. Rptr. 2d 73, 78 (Cal. Ct. App. 1998) (finding that a church breached its duty to supervise a priest who had a "known propensity for engaging in sexual conduct with boys" by allowing him access to the children under certain circumstances); Rosado v. Bridgeport Roman Catholic Diocesan Corp., 716 A.2d 967 (Conn. Super. Ct. 1998) (recognizing that a church may be held liable for negligent supervision of its priest who sexually assaulted minors if the church knew or should have known

hiring and retention,[4] intentional infliction of emotional distress,[5] negligent infliction of emotional distress,[6] tortious breach of fiduciary duty,[7] assault and battery (by the clergy member or other abuser),[8] loss of consortium,[9] and false imprisonment.[10] As will be seen, these claims meet with varying levels of success.

of its priest's misconduct and failed to act); Bender v. First Church of the Nazarene, 571 N.E.2d 475 (Ohio Ct. App. 1989) (recognizing that a church does have a duty to supervise its agents but finding that there was no evidence the church either anticipated, or should have anticipated, that a volunteer would rape a six-year-old boy).

4 *See, e.g.*, Sanders v. Casa View Baptist Church, 898 F. Supp. 1169 (N.D. Tex. 1995) (finding that a church, which lacked knowledge of its minister's alleged tortious conduct, did not act negligently by hiring the priest because the church conducted a reasonable review of his competence and qualifications); Vione v. Tewell, 820 N.Y.S.2d 682, 687 (2006) (finding a valid negligent retention claim against a church because plaintiff's allegations made it clear that the church knew, or should have known, of its minister's "propensity to engage in harmful conduct, but decided to look the other way"); Byrd v. Faber, 565 N.E.2d 584 (Ohio 1991) (recognizing claims against religious institutions for negligent hiring but holding that such claims must be plead with greater specificity because of the inherent First Amendment issues); Smith v. Privette, 495 S.E.2d 395 (N.C. Ct. App. 1998) (recognizing a viable negligent retention claim against a church arising out of the alleged sexual misconduct of its minister).

5 *See, e.g.*, Sanders, 898 F. Supp. at 1178 (recognizing that a church can be vicariously liable for its minister's intentional torts if the minister's actions were known by the church, ratified by the church, or determined to be within the scope of minister's employment); Guinn v. Church of Christ of Collinsville, 775 P.2d 766 (Okla. 1989) (finding that the elders' disciplinary actions against a former parishioner, who had disassociated herself from the church, were proper grounds for her intentional infliction of emotional distress claim); Conley v. Roman Catholic Archbishop of S.F., 102 Cal. Rptr. 2d 679 (Cal. Ct. App. 2000) (finding that a priest, who reported acts of child abuse by a second priest, had a viable intentional infliction of emotional distress claim against the church when it sanctioned him for reporting the abuse).

6 *See, e.g.*, Roman Catholic Diocese of Jackson v. Morrison, 905 So. 2d 1213 (Miss. 2005) (finding that a mother's negligent infliction of emotional distress claim against the Roman Catholic Diocese arising out of alleged sexual abuse of her children by a former priest was not jurisdictionally barred); Doe v. Hartford Roman Catholic Diocesan Corp., 716 A.2d 960 (Conn. Super. Ct. 1998) (finding that the First Amendment does not bar a negligent infliction of emotional distress claim against a diocese); Davis v. Black, 591 N.E.2d 11 (Ohio Ct. App. 1991) (finding that the parish secretary had a viable negligent infliction of emotional distress claim arising out of the church's reaction to her allegations of sexual harassment by the pastor).

7 *See, e.g.*, Doe v. Evans, 814 So. 2d 370 (Fla. 2002) (finding that a church that engaged in marital counseling through its clergy had a fiduciary duty to its counselees); Moses v. Diocese of Colo., 863 P.2d 310 (Colo. 1993) (finding that a diocese, through its agents, assumed and breached a fiduciary duty to a parishioner when its bishop assumed control of the parishioner and used the sexually abused parishioner's trust to her detriment); C.J.C. v. Corporation of Catholic Bishop of Yakima, 985 P.2d 262 (Wash. 1999) (finding that a church had a duty to affirmatively act to prevent foreseeable harm to the children of its congregation).

8 *See, e.g.*, Tichenor v. Roman Catholic Church of the Archdiocese of New Orleans, 32 F.3d 953 (5th Cir. 1994) (categorizing a priest's illicit sexual conduct toward minors as assault and battery but finding that the one-year statutory limitation was applicable to such claims); Doe v. Hartz, 52 F. Supp. 2d 1027 (N.D. Iowa 1999) (recognizing a parishioner's claim of sexual abuse as a claim for assault and battery on which relief can be granted); Jones v. Trane, 591 N.Y.S.2d 927 (N.Y. App. Div. 1992) (recognizing a battery claim against a priest for his alleged sexual conduct toward an infant).

9 *See, e.g.*, Morrison, 905 So. 2d at 1243 (finding that a mother's loss of consortium claim arising out of alleged sexual molestation of her children by a former priest of the diocese was not jurisdictionally barred); Roe v. Archdiocese of St. Paul & Minneapolis, 518 N.W.2d 629 (Minn. Ct. App. 1994) (finding that a husband's loss of consortium claim against the church was derivative of his wife's claim of sexual assault by a priest, which was barred by the statute of limitations); Podolinski v. Episcopal Diocese of Pittsburgh, 23 Pa. D. & C.4th 385 (Pa. Com. Pl. 1995) (recognizing a spouse's loss of consortium claim against a religious organization).

10 *See, e.g.*, Hendricks v. Bauer, 709 S.W.2d 774 (Tex. App. 1986) (finding that a church is not liable for the tortious actions of its pastor, which included falsely imprisoning a repairman in a closet, when those actions were not within the scope of his employment nor in furtherance of church's business); Wood

Additionally, claims have been brought by or against religious entities for defamation,[11] trespass,[12] nuisance,[13] invasion of privacy,[14] conversion,[15] negligence,[16] and even products liability.[17] Again, these claims have varying amounts of success depending on

v. Berean Baptist Church, 1997 WL 33343376 (Mich. Ct. App. 1997) (finding a student's false imprisonment claim against a church arising out of an event where she was detained in a curtained area while attending vacation Bible school did not require reference to religious beliefs); Alpharetta First United Methodist Church v. Stewart, 472 S.E.2d 532 (Ga. Ct. App. 1996) (finding that counselee's tort claims against the church, which included false imprisonment, were barred by the statute of limitations).

11 *See, e.g.*, Conley v. Roman Catholic Archbishop of S.F., 102 Cal. Rptr. 2d 679, 683 (Cal. Ct. App. 2000) (finding that a priest who reported child abuse by a second priest had a viable defamation claim against the church that characterized his report in a publication as a "witch hunt"); Church of God, Inc., v. Shaw, 391 S.E.2d 666, 667 (Ga. Ct. App. 1990) (holding that a corporation church could only be liable for its agent's allegedly slanderous statement if it "expressly ordered and directed" the agent to say the exact statement); Mallette v. Church of God Int'l, 789 So. 2d 120 (Miss. Ct. App. 2001) (recognizing that a reverend could bring a defamation claim against a church if statements lacked ecclesiastical justification).

12 *See, e.g.*, Church of Christ in Hollywood v. Superior Court, 121 Cal. Rptr. 2d 810 (Cal. Ct. App. 2002) (finding that a church is allowed to exclude unwelcome trespassers from its premises); Capitol View Cmty. Church v. Achor Ctr., Inc., 571 S.E.2d 181 (Ga. Ct. App. 2002) (holding for the owner of a homeless shelter who sought to permanently enjoin members of an adjacent church from trespassing on owner's property); Horvitz v. St. John The Baptist Church Corp., 1998 Mass. App. Div. 143 (Mass Dist. Ct. 1998) (affirming the trial court's decision that a church was liable for trespass when its landscaping company entered onto the plaintiff's land).

13 *See, e.g.*, Baltimore & P. R. Co. v. Fifth Baptist Church of Wash., 137 U.S. 568 (1891) (finding that a church could maintain an nuisance action against a railroad company); St. David's Episcopal Church v. Westboro Baptist Church, Inc., 921 P.2d 821 (Kan. Ct. App. 1996) (discussing a church's nuisance and temporary injunction claims against another church arising from picketing incidents); Bible Baptist Church v. City of Cleburne, 848 S.W.2d 826 (Tex. App. 1993) (recognizing that a church's nuisance claim against a municipality may fit within the exception to governmental immunity if the sewage backup was determined to be a nonnegligent nuisance).

14 *See, e.g.*, Smith v. Calvary Christian Church, 614 N.W.2d 590 (Mich. 2000) (finding that a former church member who consented to the church's practices may not bring an invasion of privacy claim against the church for its disciplinary actions); Guinn v. Church of Christ of Collinsville, 775 P.2d 766 (Okla. 1989) (recognizing that a former parishioner's invasion of privacy claim against the church elders for their communication of the parishioner's religious disobedience to several congregations after the parishioner had disassociated herself from the church); Gunn v. Mariners Church, Inc., 84 Cal. Rptr. 3d 1, 10 (Cal. Ct. App. 2008) (finding that the "ministerial exception" precluded a former worship leader's invasion of privacy claim against his church arising from statements made in connection with the leader's termination of employment).

15 *See, e.g.*, Second Int'l Baha'i Council v. Chase, 106 P.3d 1168 (Mont. 2005) (finding that a court may resolve church property disputes, such as conversion, when it applies secular principles of law); Highway Church of Christ, Inc. v. Barber, 325 S.E.2d 305 (N.C. Ct. App. 1985) (upholding the trial court's dismissal of a church's claim for conversion against another church arising from a bond sales agreement); Horvitz, 1998 Mass. App. Div. at 143 (affirming a church's liability for conversion when its landscaping company removed a concrete slab wall from the adjacent lot); Church of Scientology of Cal. v. Armstrong, 283 Cal. Rptr. 917 (Cal. Ct. App. 1991) (finding that a church employee's conversion of church documents was justified by a reasonable belief that the church would cause him harm).

16 *See, e.g.*, Roman Catholic Diocese of Jackson v. Morrison, 905 So. 2d 1213 (Miss. 2005) (holding that the First Amendment did not bar negligence claims against a church arising from a former priest's sexual abuse of children); Doe v. Catholic Diocese of Cleveland, 813 N.E.2d 977 (Ohio Ct. App. 2004) (recognizing a negligence claim against a church that failed to protect a child molested by its priest but finding the claim barred by the statute of limitations); Bull St. Church of Christ v. Jenson, 504 S.E.2d 1, 6 (Ga. Ct. App. 1998) (finding a church negligent when it allowed a child molestation victim to "roam free in the church" when there were foreseeable dangers in doing so).

17 *See, e.g.*, Roman Catholic Diocese of Jackson v. Morrison, 905 So. 2d 1213 (Miss. 2005) (holding that the First Amendment did not bar negligence claims against a church arising from a former priest's sexual abuse of children); Doe v. Catholic Diocese of Cleveland, 813 N.E.2d 977 (Ohio Ct. App. 2004)

the facts of the cases and the jurisdictions in which they are filed. As you will see, one tort that is virtually never successful – at least not when characterized as such – is clergy malpractice.[18]

Various factors can affect outcomes in these cases. Obviously, the variety of tort law concepts among jurisdictions is a major factor.[19] Additionally, if a court must delve into ecclesiastical matters, the First Amendment generally will prevent it from doing so.[20] Relatedly, the availability of neutral principles of law to resolve the claim may be relevant.[21] Whether or not the victim is a member of the religious entity is also a key factor because it can have significant impact on whether constitutional norms are involved and to what degree.

This chapter will first address questions relating to the First Amendment. This will be followed by a discussion of each of the tort causes of action and relevant defenses. This

(recognizing a negligence claim against a church that failed to protect a child molested by its priest but finding the claim barred by the statute of limitations); Bull St. Church of Christ v. Jenson, 504 S.E.2d 1, 6 (Ga. Ct. App. 1998) (finding a church negligent when it allowed a child molestation victim to "roam free in the church" when there were foreseeable dangers in doing so).

18 *See, e.g.*, Nally v. Grace Community Church, 763 P.2d 948, 961 (Cal. 1988) (failing to extend the duty to prevent suicide to nontherapist counselor "who offer[ed] counseling to potentially suicidal person on secular or spiritual matters"); Hester v. Barnett, 723 S.W.2d 544, 554 (Mo. Ct. App. 1987) (finding no ministerial malpractice claim when a minister purposely disclosed confidential communications received as a spiritual advisor because the tradition that a minister does not divulge confidential communications describes "a moral, not a legal duty"); Borchers v. Hrychuk, 727 A.2d 388 (Md. Ct. Spec. App. 1999) (failing to recognize a clergy malpractice claim due to both the impracticability of defining a standard of care that would generalize across religions and the potential to burden free exercise of religion); Nardella v. Dattilo, 36 Pa. D. & C.4th 364 (Pa. Com. Pl. 1997) (failing to recognize clergy malpractice as a viable cause of action); Teadt v. Lutheran Church Mo. Synod, 603 N.W.2d 816 (Mich. Ct. App. 1999) (holding that a claim for a minister's breach of fiduciary duty during marital counseling sessions is equivalent to a clergy malpractice claim and is unrecognizable); R.A. v. First Church of Christ, 748 A.2d 692 (Pa. Super. Ct. 2000) (confirming that ministerial malpractice is not a recognized cause of action).

19 *Compare* Martinelli v. Bridgeport Roman Catholic Diocesan Corp., 196 F.3d 409 (2nd Cir. 1999) (finding a diocese that supervises its clergy members who engage in martial counseling creates a fiduciary duty between itself and counselees), *and* Doe v. Evans, 814 So. 2d 370 (Fla. 2002) (holding that a religious organization that holds itself out as a provider of marital counseling owes a fiduciary duty to its counselees), *with* S.H.C. v. Lu, 54 P.3d 174, 181 (Wash. Ct. App 2002) (holding that there was no "special relationship" between an adult victim of sexual abuse by a religious leader and the leader's religious organization to establish a fiduciary duty), *and* Brown v. Pearson, 483 S.E.2d 477 (S.C. Ct. App. 1997) (finding that a church owed no fiduciary duty to parishioner).

20 Watson v. Jones, 80 U.S. 679 (1871); Jones v. Wolf, 443 U.S. 595 (1979); *see, e.g.*, Gibson v. Brewer, 952 S.W.2d 239 (Mo. 1997) (holding that claims pertaining to a church's negligence in supervising, hiring, or retaining its clergy were barred by the First Amendment); Guinn v. Church of Christ of Collinsville, 775 P.2d 766 (Okla. 1989) (finding the trial court's refusal to award defendants summary judgment on the plaintiff's prewithdrawal tort claims against the church's elders constituted a governmental burden on the defendant's right to free exercise of religion); Swanson v. Roman Catholic Bishop of Portland, 692 A.2d 441 (Me. 1997) (finding that a negligent supervision claim against a church for its priest's alleged sexual misconduct during counseling was barred by the First Amendment).

21 Jones, 443 U.S. at 602; *see, e.g.*, Holmes v. Lorch, 329 F.Supp.2d 516 (S.D.N.Y. 2004) (applying neutral principles of agency law to determine whether to impute a church league basketball coach's misconduct to the church); Fortin v. Roman Catholic Bishop of Portland, 871 A.2d 1208, 1225 (Me. 2005) (finding that "courts do no inhibit the free exercise of religion by applying neutral principles of law to a civil dispute involving members of the clergy"); Jeffrey Scott E. v. Central Baptist Church, 243 Cal. Rptr. 128 (Cal. Ct. App. 1988) (applying neutral principles of agency law to find that a Sunday school teacher's acts of molestation could not be imputed to the church by the *respondeat superior* doctrine); J.M. v. Minnesota Dist. Council of the Assemblies of God, 658 N.W.2d 589 (Minn. Ct. App. 2003) (finding that the Establishment Clause is not implicated when neutral principles of law are applied, without particular regard to religious doctrine, to determine a church's duty to examine a pastor's employment history).

discussion will also address the role of the First Amendment in analyzing each cause of action. Many cases involve abuse by clergy, and the major question presented is whether, and under what causes of action, a religious entity may be liable for such conduct. The answer to this question is helpful when dealing with tort claims against religious entities under other torts as well.

## A. Tort Claims and the Religion Clauses

The religion clauses of the First Amendment to the United States Constitution,[22] as well as state constitutional provisions,[23] often raise questions when religious institutions are sued in tort.[24] As with cases involving church schisms and property disputes, the key question that arises is whether courts would need to determine ecclesiastical issues in order to decide the case.[25] Not surprisingly, the analysis from *Watson v. Jones*,[26] *Jones v. Wolf*,[27] and related cases[28] is often applied to determine these issues.

[22] U.S.C.A. Const. Amend. I ("Congress shall make no law respecting an establishment of religion, or prohibiting the free exercise thereof.").

[23] *See, e.g.*, Ala Const. Art. I, § 3 (holding that no religion shall be established by law nor given preference there under); West's Ann. Cal. Const. Art. I, § 4 (guaranteeing free exercise and enjoyment of religion and that the legislature shall make no law respecting the establishment thereof); F.S.A. Const. Art. I, § 3 (stating that there shall be no law respecting the establishment of religion or prohibiting the free exercise of religion); M.G.L.A. Const. Pt. 1, Art. 2 (preserving the right to freedom of religion); West's R.C.W.A. Const. Art. I, § 11 (guaranteeing absolute freedom of conscious in all religious matters).

[24] *See supra* note 19 and accompanying text. *See, e.g.*, Ehrens v. The Lutheran Church-Missouri Synod, 269 F.Supp.2d. 328 (S.D.N.Y. 2003) (holding that it would create excessive entanglement for court to decide whether church negligently retained cleric after allegations of sexual abuse because court would be functioning as ecclesiastical court); Richelle v. Roman Catholic Archbishop, 130 Cal. Rpt.2d 601 (Cal. Ct. App. 2003) (holding that the First Amendment does not prevent "imposition of a fiduciary duty on a pastor whose sexual misconduct breaches a confidential relation with a parishioner"); Malicki v. Doe, 814 So.2d 347 (Fla. 2002) (finding that the Free Exercise Clause does not bar negligent hiring and supervision claims against church in clergy sexual abuse case); Olson v. First Church of Nazarene, 661 N.W.2d 254 (Minn. 2003) (finding that the court need only apply neutral principles of law to discover whether an employment relationship existed between church and cleric accused of sexual penetration of a parishioner); Roman Catholic Diocese of Jackson v. Morrison, 905 So.2d 1213 (Miss. 2006) (holding that in clergy sexual abuse cases, examining the church's duty to protect against sexual molestation of children will not excessively entangle courts in religious matters); Smith v. Privette, 495 S.E.2d 395 (N.C. App. 1998) (finding that negligent retention and supervision claim against church in a sexual abuse case is not barred by the First Amendment); Vione v Tewell, 820 N.Y.S.2d 682 (N.Y. 2006) (holding that claims against a pastor and church for breach of fiduciary duty, negligent hiring and retention, and intentional infliction of emotional distress can be decided in "accordance with neutral principles of law without resort to religious tenets").

[25] Watson, 80 U.S. 679 (1871) (discussing whether a church structure is hierarchical or congregational and deferring to the decisions of the highest church tribunal on matters of doctrine). *Cf.* Ehrens v. Lutheran Church-Missouri Synod, 269 F.Supp.2d 328 (S.D.N.Y. 2003) (looking at *Watson* analysis on structure of the church); Schmidt v. Bishop, 779 F.Supp. 321 (S.D.N.Y. 1991) (holding that it would be "inappropriate and unconstitutional for this Court to determine after the fact that the ecclesiastical authorities negligently supervised or retained the defendant bishop"); Roman Catholic Diocese of Jackson v. Morrison, 905 So.2d 1213 (Miss. 2005) (discussing *Watson* "Doctrine of Church Autonomy"); Smith v. Privette, 495 S.E.2d 395 (N.C. Ct. App. 1998) (finding that doctrine of church autonomy does not bar plaintiff's claim of negligent retention and supervision against defendant church); Celnik v. Congregation B'nai Israel, 131 P.3d 102 (N.M. 2006) (applying *Watson* doctrine of church autonomy to preclude deciding whether rabbi was wrongfully discharged from employment).

[26] 80 U.S. 679 (1871).

[27] 443 U.S. 595 (1979).

[28] *See, e.g.*, Serbian Eastern Orthodox Diocese for the United States of America and Canada v. Milivojevich, 426 U.S. 696 (1976); Presbyterian Church in U.S. v. Mary Elizabeth Blue Hull Memorial Presbyterian

Therefore, courts often try to determine if the religious entity involved is hierarchical or congregational[29] and/or whether the case can be decided based on neutral principles of law.[30] Some courts rely on one or the other approach,[31] whereas others merge the two approaches,[32] as have many courts in church schism and property dispute cases. The *Watson* and *Wolf* analyses have been held to implicate both Free Exercise Clause and Establishment Clause concerns.[33] Free exercise is relevant because courts could infringe free exercise rights of religious institutions and individuals by determining ecclesiastical questions.[34] By deciding these questions courts may also create unconstitutional entanglement between government and religion,[35] thus violating the

Church, 393 U.S. 440 (1969); Kedroff v. St. Nicholas Cathedral of Russian Orthodox Church in North America, 344 U.S. 94 (1952).

29 *See supra* note 26.

30 *See supra* note 27.

31 *See, e.g.*, Schmidt v. Bishop, 779 F.Supp. 321 (S.D.N.Y. 1991) (holding that it would be "inappropriate and unconstitutional for this Court to determine after the fact that the ecclesiastical authorities negligently supervised or retainted the defendant bishop"); Smith v. Privette, 495 S.E.2d 395 (N.C. Ct. App. 1998) (finding that the doctrine of church autonomy does not bar plaintiff's claim of negligent retention and supervision against defendant church); Celnik v. Congregation B'nai Israel, 131 P.3d 102 (N.M. 2006) (applying *Watson* doctrine of church autonomy to preclude deciding whether rabbi was wrongfully discharged from employment).

32 *See, e.g.*, Smith v. Raleigh Dist. of the N. Carolina Conference of the United Methodist Church, 63 F.Supp.2d 694 (E.D.N.C. 1999) (holding that neutral principles of law apply to church lay employees, but *Watson* analysis applies to ministerial employees); Martinelli v. Bridgeport Roman Catholic Diocesan Corp., 10 F.Supp.2d 139 (D. Conn. 1998) (using hybrid of *Watson* and *Wolf* analysis); Sanders v. Casa View Baptist Church, 898 F.Supp. 1169 (N.D. Tex. 1995) (using both principles of church autonomy and neutral principles of law to bar a claim of wrongful discharge against church); Houston v. Mike High Adventist Academy, 846 F.Supp. 1449 (D. Colo. 1994) (finding that the allegations in the case could not be decided under either *Watson* or *Jones*); Moses v. Diocese of Colorado, 863 P.2d 310 (Colo. 1993) (discussing church autonomy and neutral principles of law); Malecki v. Doe, 814 So.2d 347 (Fla. 2002) (discussing both principles of church autonomy and neutral principles of law analyses); Roman Catholic Diocese of Jackson v. Morrison, 905 So.2d 1213 (Miss. 2005) (holding that *Watson* analysis still has valid judicial application but looking to traditional First Amendment analysis by applying Establishment Clause or Free Exercise Clause); C.J.C. v. Corp of the Catholic Biship of Yakima, 985 P.2d 262 (Wash. 1999) (stating that both church autonomy and neutral principles of law precluded plaintiff's allegations involving spiritual standards).

33 *See, e.g.*, Serbian Eastern Orthodox Diocese v. Milivojevich, 426 U.S. 696 (1976) (finding that *Watson* applied to free exercise concerns); Ehrens v. The Lutheran Church-Missouri Synod, 269 F.Supp.2d 328 (S.D.N.Y. 2003) (citing *Watson* on the Establishment Clause); Smith v. Raleigh Dist. of North Carolina Conference of United Methodist Church, 63 F.Supp.2d 694 (E.D.N.C. 1999) (citing *Watson* for both Free Exercise and Establishment Clause issues); Martinelli v. Bridgeport Roman Catholic Diocesan Corp., 10 F.Supp.2d 139 (D. Conn. 1998) (using both *Watson* and *Wolf* in Free Exercise Clause analysis); Moses v. Diocese of Colorado, 863 P.2d 310 (Colo. 1993) (citing both *Watson* and *Wolf* in analysis of Free Exercise Clause and Establishment Clause); C.J.C. v. Corp of the Catholic Bishop of Yakima, 985 P.2d 262 (Wash. 1999) (finding that *Watson* and *Wolf* barred claims under the First Amendment).

34 *See, e.g.*, Serbian Eastern Orthodox Diocese v. Milivojevich, 426 U.S. 696 (1976) (holding that in matters involving "discipline, faith, internal organization, or ecclesiastical rule, custom or law," courts would infringe on free exercise rights); DeCorso v. Watchtower Bible and Tract Society of New York, Inc., 829 A.2d 38 (Conn. App. 2003) (finding that plaintiff's negligent infliction of emotional distress claim was barred because court would have to delve into ecclesiastical matters); Guinn v. Church of Christ of Collinsville, 775 P.2d 766 (Okla. 1989) (finding that it would violate the Free Exercise Clause to rule on church disciplinary actions); Tidman v. Salvation Army, 1998 WL 391765 (Tenn. Ct. App.) (stating that cases involing the religious order and its clergy are outside the purview of the courts); *In re* Pleasant Glade Assembly of God, 991 S.W.2d 85 (Tex. Ct. App. 1998) (holding that all of plaintiff's claims were barred because court would have to delve into church doctrine to decide).

35 *See, e.g.*, Sanders v. Casa View Baptist Church, 898 F.Supp. 1169 (N.D. Tex. 1995) (finding that deciding minister's cross-claims for breach of contract and wrongful discharge would create excessive

Establishment Clause.[36] Although this analysis originated in church property dispute cases, it applies in tort cases as well.[37]

When a court determines that deciding a cause of action would raise ecclesiastical questions, the cause of action is ordinarily dismissed.[38] Other claims may remain, however, and courts generally have addressed various causes of action and the questions they raise using a case-by-case, issue-by-issue, analysis.[39] Some claims, such as clergy malpractice,[40] are universally found to raise issues that cannot be answered without violating the Constitution,[41] whereas other claims rarely raise constitutional concerns,[42] and still

entanglement); DeCorso v. Watchtower Bible and Tract Society of New York, Inc., 829 A.2d 38 (Conn. App. Ct. 2003) (holding that it would create unconstitutional entanglement to consider plaintiff's claim against religious corporation and elders); Burgess v. Rock Creek Baptist Church, 734 F.Supp. 30 (D.C. 1990) (stating that termination of plaintiff's church membership was a matter of "ecclesiastical cognizance" and would involve excessive entanglement in religion); Tidman v. Salvation Army, 1998 WL 391765 (Tenn. Ct. App. 1998) (finding that some causes of action would create excessive entanglement with religion).

36 *See, e.g.*, DeCorso v. Watchtower Bible and Tract Society of New York, Inc., 829 A.2d 38 (Conn. App. Ct. 2003) (holding that it would violate the Establishment Clause to consider plaintiff's claim against religious corporation and elders); Gaston v. Diocese of Allentown, 712 A.2d 757 (Pa. Super. Ct. 1998) (barring claims against parochial elementary school as a violation of both the Establishment Clause and the Free Exercise Clause); Franco v. The Church of Jesus Christ of Latter-Day saints, 21 P.3d 198 (Utah 2001) (holding that the Establishment Clause barred court from deciding claims for gross negligence, negligent infliction of emotional distress, and breach of fiduciary duty against church and pastor).

37 *See supra* notes 25–37.

38 *See, e.g.*, John Doe v. Capuchin Franciscan Friars, 520 F.Supp.2d 1124 (E.D. Mo. 2007) (analyzing individual claims and finding that claims for negligence did not violate either Establishment or Free Exercise Clauses); Conley v. Roman Catholic Archbishop of San Francisco, 102 Cal. Rptr. 679 (Cal. Ct. App. 2000) (holding that child abuse reporting statute did not create excessive entanglement with religion nor violate the free exercise clause of the First Amendment); Moses v. Diocese of Colorado, 863 P.2d 310 (Colo. 1993) (stating that recovery was not barred by first amendment but evidence only supported claims for negligent hiring and supervision and not for vicarious liability); Smith v. Tilton, 3 S.W.3d 77 (Tex. Ct. App. 1999) (barring some claims because they would create excessive entanglement but upheld cause of action for fraud, negligent misrepresentation, and breach of fiduciary duty).

39 *Id.*

40 *See supra* note 17. *See also* Sands v. Living Word Fellowship, 34 P.3d 955 (Alaska 2001) (finding that plaintiff's claims for negligent and intentional infliction of emotional distress were barred by religion clauses); Amato v. Greenquist, 679 N.E.2d 446 (Ill. App. Ct. 1997) (holding that all claims against the church could not be answered without violating First Amendment religion clauses); Gaston v. Diocese of Allentown, 712 A.2d 757 (Pa. Super. Ct. 1998) (barring claims against parochial elementary school as violation of both the Establishment Clause and the Free Exercise Clause); Franco v. The Church of Jesus Christ of Latter-Day saints, 21 P.3d 198 (Utah 2001) (holding that claims could not be adjudicated without violating the religion clauses).

41 *See, e.g.*, Ehrens. v. The Lutheran Church-Missouri Synod, 26 F.Supp.2d 328 (S.D.N.Y. 2003) (holding that the first amendment prevented the court from determining whether authorities negligently supervised pastor); Isely v. Capuchin Province, 880 F.Supp. 1138 (E.D. Mich. 1995) (finding that the Establishment Clause barred negligent hiring claim); Sanders v. Casa View Baptist Church, 898 F.Supp. 1169 (N.D. Tex. 1995) (holding that the First Amendment barred minister's claims for breach of contract and wrongful discharge against the church); Swanson v. Roman Catholic Bishop of Portland, 692 A.2d 441 (Me. 1997) (holding that the First Amendment barred plaintiff's claim of negligent supervision against the Catholic Church).

42 *See, e.g.*, JC2, ME, FH, PM, BO, BS and TS v. Grammond, 232 F.Supp.2d 1166 (D. Ore. 2002) (finding that the court is "not prevented from addressing church-related disputes, provided [that] the court refrains from considering doctrinal matters and resolves the dispute solely on neutral principles"); Konkle v. Henson, 672 N.E.2d 450 (Ind. Ct. App. 1996) (stating that the First Amendment did not bar secular tort claims); C.J.C. v. Corporation of the Catholic Bishop of Yakima, 985 P.2d 262 (Wash. 1999) (holding

others vary by jurisdiction, with some jurisdictions finding religion clause violations[43] and others finding no such violations.[44]

These causes of action and the analyses applied to them by various jurisdictions will be addressed in the following sections. For now, it is best to lay down the basics. That is, what sorts of claims are most likely to raise ecclesiastical questions, and what sorts of claims are least likely to do so? The easiest situation in this context is where a court would need to determine whether a church's behavior is consistent with its religious tenets in a context in which the answer is not otherwise obvious.[45] Courts will find that such issues cannot be decided by the civil judiciary.[46] In claims based on general negligence, such as a slip and fall,[47] traffic accidents,[48] or failure to supervise in a day-care setting,[49] especially when the

that "so long as liability is predicated on secular conduct and does not involve the interpretation of church doctrine or religious beliefs, it does not offend constitutional principles").

43 *See, e.g.*, Drevlow v. Lutheran Church, Mo. Synod, 991 F.2d 468 (8th Cir. 1993) (refusing to deter mine whether the Synod's employment decision was supported by its bylaws); JC2 v. Grammond, 232 F. Supp. 2d 1166, 1170 (D. Or. 2002) (finding that a court may not pass judgment on the "appropriateness, correctness or validity" of religious cannons to determine whether the church is vicariously liable for its minister's sexual misconduct); S.H.C. v. Lu, 54 P.3d 174 (Wash. Ct. App. 2002) (refusing to examine the reasonableness of certain religious beliefs that forbid temple members from questioning their Grandmaster's surreptitious behavior with young girls); Guinn v. Church of Christ of Collinsville, 775 P.2d 766 (Okla. 1989) (finding elders' disciplinary actions against a wayward parishioner who had not yet withdrawn from the church were not subject to judicial review).

44 *See, e.g.*, Doe v. Norwich Roman Catholic Diocesan Corporation, 268 F.Supp.2d 139 (D. Conn. 2003) (finding that negligent hiring and supervision claims would not cause excessive entanglement with religion and a violation of the First Amendment); Bear Valley Church of Christ v. DeBose, 928 P.2d 1315 (Colo. 1996) (stating that the First Amendment did not bar claim of negligent hiring in clergy sexual abuse case); Winkler v. Rocky Mountain Conference, 923 P.2d 152 (Colo. Ct. App. 1995) (holding that it does not violate the Establishment Clause to hold viable claims for breach of fiduciary duty, negligent hiring or supervision, and vicarious liability where supported by competent evidence); Olson v. Church of Nazarene, 661 N.W.2d 254 (Minn. Ct. App. 2003) (holding that the Establishment Clause did not preclude court from inquiry in connection with vicarious liability, negligent supervision, negligent retention claims).

45 *See, e.g.*, Drevlow, 991 F.2d at 471 (finding that a minister's claim that a Synod violated its bylaws by removing an eligible minister's name "from its list of eligible ministers falls squarely into the category of claims that are not justiciable by secular courts"); Ehrens v. Lutheran Church-Missouri Synod, 269 F. Supp. 2d 328 (S.D.N.Y. 2003) (finding that a court's attempt to define the duty of care a church must adhere to in determining a priest's continuing eligibility as a clergy member would be forbidden by the First Amendment); Gibson v. Brewer, 952 S.W.2d 239 (Mo. 1997) (finding that claims that a diocese negligently ordained a member of its clergy would require interpretation of religious policies and are forbidden by the First Amendment).

46 *Id.*

47 *See, e.g.*, Mouhot v. Twelfth St. Baptist Church, 949 So. 2d 668 (La. Ct. App. 2007) (finding a church negligent when it knowingly failed to remove a floor mat that caused a seventy-one-year-old women to fall and break her hip); Byrd v. Church of Christ Uniting, 597 N.Y.S.2d 211 (N.Y. App. Div. 1993) (recognizing that a church could be liable for an icy condition in its parking lot that caused an individual to fall if it knowingly failed to alleviate the treacherous condition within a reasonable time period); Graf v. St. Luke's Evangelical Lutheran Church, 625 N.E.2d 851 (Ill. App. Ct. 1993) (recognizing a negligence action against a church that allowed or created an unnatural accumulation of snow and ice on its steps causing a guest to fall).

48 *See, e.g.*, Ambrosio v. Price, 495 F. Supp. 381, 384 (D. Neb. 1979) (recognizing that a church may be liable for its priest's negligent operation of a motor vehicle while fulfilling his "priestly" responsibilities); Malloy v. Fong, 232 P.2d 241(Cal. 1951) (finding a religious organization liable for its employee's negligent operation of a motor vehicle); Garber v. Scott, 525 S.W.2d 114 (Mo. Ct. App. 1975) (authorizing a verdict against a church for its pastor's negligent operation of a motor vehicle while engaged in activities closely related to his employment with the church).

49 *See, e.g.*, Todd v. First Baptist Church of West Point, 993 So. 2d 827 (Miss. 2008) (*en banc*) (recognizing a parent's negligence claim against a church arising from an injury her daughter sustained while attending

claimant is a nonmember of the faith,[50] ecclesiastical questions are rarely, if ever, involved. Many cases, however, fall in between.

If a court must delve into the relationship between a religious entity and its clergy, First Amendment concerns may arise.[51] This often comes up in claims based on negligent hiring, retention, and supervision of clergy who have sexually abused members of the faith.[52] Many courts have found no First Amendment violation in situations where the religious entity had knowledge of the abuser's propensities and failed to act.[53] These

the church's day care); Douglas v. John Hus Moravian Church of Brooklyn, Inc., 778 N.Y.S.2d 77 (N.Y. App. Div. 2004) (discussing a child's negligent supervision claim against a church for the injuries he sustained while playing a game of tag at the church's day-care program); Ward v. Mount Calvary Lutheran Church, 873 P.2d 688 (Ariz. Ct. App. 1994) (discussing parents' negligence claim against church for the injuries their daughter sustained while attending day care; the court did not mention the First Amendment); Cutler v. St. John's United Methodist Church, 489 So. 2d 123 (Fla. Dist. Ct. App. 1986) (finding that a church may be liable when it fails to supervise children who attend church-sponsored events).

50 *See, e.g.*, Guinn, 775 P.2d at 778 (discussing the ramifications of a church's disciplinary actions against a former parishioner who had withdrawn her membership from the church); Robertson v. Church of God, Int'l, 978 S.W.2d 120 (Tex. App. 1997) (finding that a church was not a proximate cause of the damage caused by its minister's sexual misconduct with a massage therapist who had never attended any church service); R.A. *ex rel.* N.A. v. First Church of Christ, 748 A.2d 692 (Pa. Super. Ct. 2000) (discussing a negligent supervision claim against a church for its minister's sexual misconduct with a neighborhood girl who was not a member of the church). *See also* Stitt v. Holland Abundant Life Fellowship, 614 N.W.2d 88 (Mich. 2000) (discussing a church guest's negligence claim without implicating the First Amendment); Guinn, 775 P.2d at 779 (holding that a church's disciplinary actions taken against a former parishioner who had unequivocally withdrawn from the church were not protected by the First Amendment); Robertson, 978 S.W.2d at 124–25 (discussing a negligent hiring claim against a church that did not implicate the First Amendment).

51 *See, e.g.*, Farley v. Wisconsin Evangelical Lutheran Synod, 821 F. Supp. 1286 (D. Minn. 1993) (refusing to delve into the reasons a religious organization terminated its minister; such an inquiry implicates First Amendment concerns); Bowie v. Murphy, 624 S.E.2d 74, 78 (Va. 2006) ("[C]ourts lack subject matter jurisdiction to resolve issues of church governance and disputes over religious doctrines."); Roman Catholic Bishop of S.D. v. Superior Court, 50 Cal. Rptr. 2d 399, 406 (Cal. Ct. App. 1996) (holding that a court cannot require a church to supervise its clergy merely because they take a vow of celibacy).

52 *See, e.g.*, Gibson v. Brewer, 952 S.W.2d 239 (Mo. 1997) (discussing the First Amendment issues inherent within negligent hiring claims against a religious organization arising from a clergy member's sexual misconduct); J.M. v. Minnesota Dist. Council of the Assemblies of God, 658 N.W.2d 589 (Minn. Ct. App. 2003) (finding that a court's determination of how a church should use employment history in the context of a hiring decision would constitute an entanglement between church and state); Smith v. Privette, 495 S.E.2d 395, 398 (N.C. Ct. App. 1998) (acknowledging that a church's decision to "hire or discharge a minister is inextricable from religious doctrine and protected by the First Amendment"; the church is not afforded the same protection from judicial inquiry to the extent that it had knowledge of its priest's propensity to engage in sexual misconduct).

53 *See, e.g.*, Vione v. Tewell, 820 N.Y.S.2d 682 (2006) (finding a viable negligent retention claim against a church that knew its minister engaged in sexual relations with a parishioner's wife and the church actively discouraged the parishioner from initiating an investigation of the minister's conduct); Roman Catholic Diocese of Jackson v. Morrison, 905 So. 2d 1213 (Miss. 2005) (recognizing a mother's negligent supervision claim against a church that knew her children were in danger of being sexually molested but failed to take necessary steps to protect the children); Privette, 495 S.E.2d at 398 (finding that judicial inquiry about a church's knowledge of its minister's propensities to engage in sexual misconduct are not prohibited by the First Amendment); Mark K. v. Roman Catholic Archbishop of L.A., 79 Cal. Rptr. 2d 73 (Cal. Ct. App. 1998) (finding that a church breached its duty to supervise its priest, who had a known propensity to engage in deviant sexual conduct, by allowing him access to children in situations that posed a risk for sexual abuse).

claims, usually based in negligent supervision, raise fewer First Amendment concerns because they can be decided based on neutral principles of law.[54] Of course, other courts disagree.[55] This will be explored further in the section dealing with negligent supervision. Claims based in negligent hiring and retention, however, are frequently found to violate the First Amendment because the question of hiring and keeping clergy often involves significant theological concerns, such as whether the individual was called to the clergy or has the requisite religious training to carry out his or her religious duties.[56] Some courts disagree on this issue as well.[57] The majority view is that decisions to hire and retain clergy are inherently ecclesiastical questions,[58] whereas decisions and behavior related to supervising clergy who pose risks known to the religious entity need not

[54] *See, e.g.*, Malicki v. Doe, 814 So. 2d 347, 361 (Fla. 2002) (stating that, in the context of a negligent hiring and supervision claim, a court shall give no greater deference to the "tortious conduct committed on third parties by religious organizations" than it gives to nonreligious organizations that engage in analogous conduct); Moses v. Diocese of Colo., 863 P.2d 310 (Colo. 1993) (applying neutral principles of agency law to determine that a diocese should have taken steps to ensure that its priest was not in a position to abuse his power while conducting counseling); J.M., 658 N.W.2d at 594 (finding that a religious entity's standard of care derived from neutral principles of tort law does not contravene the First Amendment).

[55] *See, e.g.*, Schmidt v. Bishop, 779 F. Supp. 321, 332 (S.D.N.Y. 1991) (finding that a pastor "is not analogous to a common law employee" in the context of a negligent supervision claim against a religious organization); Ayon v. Gourley, 47 F. Supp. 2d 1246, 1250 (D. Colo. 1998) (finding that a negligent retention claim against the Roman Catholic Archdiocese was barred by the First Amendment because the employer-employee relationship between the church and its clergy was based on a "unique relationship conceived by church doctrine"); Swanson v. Roman Catholic Bishop of Portland, 692 A.2d 441 (Me. 1997) (finding an imposition of a principle-agent relationship between a church and its clergy, in the context of a negligent supervision claim, would require impermissible infringement on an ecclesiastical relationship).

[56] *See, e.g.*, Ayon, 47 F. Supp. 2d at 1250 ("The choice of individuals to serve as ministers is one of the most fundamental rights belonging to a religious institution."); Sanders v. Casa View Baptist Church, 898 F. Supp. 1169, 1179 (N.D. Tex. 1995) (granting church's summary judgment motion for a negligent hiring claim because the church conducted a reasonable review of its minister's "competence and qualifications"); Pritzlaff v. Archdiocese of Milwaukee, 672 N.W.2d 780, 790 (Wis. 1995) (finding that the First Amendment forbids a court from delineating what characteristics would ensure that someone was "competent to serve as a Catholic priest"); J.M., 658 N.W.2d at 594 (finding that a court's review of how a church uses a pastor's employment history in the context of an employment decision would constitute an excessive entanglement between church and state).

[57] *See, e.g.*, Doe v. Norwich Roman Catholic Diocesan Corp., 268 F. Supp. 2d 139 (D. Conn. 2003) (recognizing that most negligent hiring claims against a religious organization can be resolved without a court impermissibly interpreting religious doctrines or practices); Doe v. Evans, 814 So. 2d 370 (Fla. 2002) (finding that the First Amendment did not bar parishioner's negligent hiring claim against the church arising from its pastor's sexual misconduct during marriage counseling); Bear Valley Church of Christ v. Debose 928 P.2d 1315 (Colo. 1996) (distinguishing between illegal hiring or terminations suits, which are barred by the First Amendment, and negligent hiring claims against a church, which are not barred by the First Amendment; whereas the former inherently involves interpretation of church's internal practices, the latter merely requires a court to examine the dangers known to the church when it decides to hire a particular clergy member).

[58] *See, e.g.*, Sanders, 898 F.Supp. at 1182 (finding that a priest's wrongful discharge claim against a church was an ecclesiastical question due its administrative nature); Cha v. Korean Presbyterian Church of Washington, 553 S.E.2d 511, 515 (Va. 2001) ("[E]cclesiastical decisions regarding the appointment and removal of pastors are generally beyond the jurisdiction of secular courts."); Gibson, 952 S.W.2d at 246–7 (holding that negligent hiring claims against a religious organization are ecclesiastical questions); Privette, 495 S.E.2d at 398 (acknowledging that a religious organization's decision to hire or retain its clergy is "inextricable from religious doctrine").

raise such questions.[59] Of course, even here the analysis can be significantly affected by the facts and the jurisdiction where the case arose.[60]

As noted earlier, what may be called "garden variety" torts pose little potential for First Amendment concerns. A court can determine whether a person driving a vehicle owned by a religious entity was negligent without delving into ecclesiastical matters.[61] Similarly, if a congregant slips and falls in a church where a dangerous condition existed, a court generally need not determine ecclesiastical questions to determine liability.[62] Even here, though, exceptions exist. If a congregant is doing work on a church building as part of his or her religious convictions or duties and is hurt while doing so, it is possible that religious questions could arise in addition to the general tort questions that come up in such cases.[63] Ecclesiastical questions also may arise in determining whether a specific

[59] *See, e.g.*, Evans, 814 So.2d at 373 (holding that a parishioner's negligent supervision claim against a church can be based on neutral principles; accordingly, it does not raise ecclesiastical concerns); J.M., 658 N.W.2d at 598 (finding that a negligent supervision claim does not violate the First Amendment when it turns on the church's knowledge of its minister's propensity to engage in sexual misconduct with counselees); Doe v. Hartford Roman Catholic Diocesan Corp., 716 A.2d 960 (Conn. Super. Ct. 1998) (finding that a parishioner's negligent supervision claim against a diocese arising from the alleged sexual misconduct of its priest would not prejudice ecclesiastical tenets).

[60] *See, e.g.*, JC2 v. Grammond, 232 F. Supp. 2d 1166 (D. Or. 2002) (recognizing that a church's liability arising from its priest's sexual abuse of altar boys hinges on whether the minister's sexual misconduct was in furtherance of his ministerial duties); DeBose, 928 P.2d at 1323–4 (limiting the factual inquiry into a church's negligent supervision of a minister who sexually assaulted a child during counseling sessions to ensure that the court did not impermissibly pass judgment on religious doctrines); J.M., 658 N.W.2d at 594 (announcing that negligent hiring claims should be determined based on the "totality of the circumstances surrounding the hiring"); Roman Catholic Bishop v. Superior Court, 50 Cal. Rptr. 2d 399 (Cal. Ct. App. 1996) (finding that the record did not support the contention that a church should have known that its minister would sexually abuse a child); *compare* Isely v. Capuchin Province, 880 F. Supp. 1138 (E.D. Mich. 1995) (recognizing that a negligent supervision claim against a church could be decided without determining questions of an ecclesiastical nature), *and* Malicki v. Doe, 814 So. 2d 347 (Fla. 2002) (finding that the First Amendment does not bar negligent supervision claims against religious organizations), *with* Gibson, 952 S.W.2d at 247–8 (holding that a civil court's enforcement of a negligent supervision claim against a church would not accord the autonomy guaranteed by its First Amendment rights) *and* Swanson v. Roman Catholic Bishop of Portland, 692 A.2d 441, 445 (Me. 1997) (holding that "[p]astoral supervision is an ecclesiastical prerogative").

[61] *See* Abrosio v. Price, 495 F.Supp. 381 (D. Neb. 1979) (granting summary judgment for the plaintiff in a car accident case against defendant clergy but not against his employer).

[62] *See* Trinity Episcopal Church of Vero Beach v. Hoglund, 222 So.2d 781 (Ill. App. Ct. 1969) (finding defendant church liable for fall due to ice and snow accumulation on church steps); Fintak v. Catholic Bishop of Chicago, 366 N.E.2d 480 (Ill. App. Ct. 1977) (holding defendant church liable for plaintiff's slip and fall injury); Morgan v. Hartford Accident and Indemnity Company, 402 So.2d 640 (La. 1981) (finding defendant church liable for damages and for negligence for failure to warn about eight-inch step into gown room); Mouhot v. Twelfth Street Baptist Church, 949 So.2d 668 (La. Ct. App. 2007) (holding church liable for parishioner's injury as a result of a defective door mat); Strong v. Southside Baptist Church, 823 So.2d 608 (Miss. Ct. App. 2002) (finding church not liable for slip and fall injury of wedding guest because guest was sole proximate cause of injury); Stevens v. Bow Mills Methodist Church, 283 A.2d 488 (N.H. 1971) (holding defendant church liable for plaintiff's injuries due to a fall on the church premises); Fain v. O'Connell, 909 Sw.2d 790 (Tenn. 1995) (holding that summary judgment improperly granted for defendant bishop in case where plaintiff was injured during a fall on church property).

[63] *See* Fernquist v. San Francisco Presbytery, 313 P.2d 192 (Cal. Dist. Ct. App. 1957) (holding that court had to determine relationship between church and construction worker before it could determine liability); Catanzaro v. Central Congregational Co., Inc., 705 A.2d 533 (R.I. 1998) (holding church liable for injury to construction worker who was renovating church for failure to upkeep church property); Crocker v. Barr, 409 Se.2d 368 (S.C. 1991) (holding that a church could be held liable where volunteer congregant was injured while performing work on church property).

individual is an invitee, licensee, or trespasser on church property,[64] although in most circumstances neutral principles of law are available to make such a determination.[65]

The situations just discussed provide examples of claims that are either highly likely or highly unlikely to raise ecclesiastical concerns. Many claims fall somewhere in the middle. We will explore each tort in turn to address the sorts of issues that arise in the context of religious institutions and entities.

## B. Intentional Torts

A number of intentional torts have been raised in cases involving religious entities and institutions. These include assault,[66] battery,[67] conversion,[68] false

[64] *See* Fernquist v. San Francisco Presbytery, 313 P.2d 192 (Cal. Dist. Ct. App. 1957) (holding that for purposes of liability, plaintiff construction worker was a licensee and not merely an invitee or part of a joint venture); Schmanski v. Church of St. Casmir of Wells, 67 N.W.2d 644 (Minn. 1954) (holding that plaintiff was an invitee of church and not a parishioner); Byrd v. Arrowood, 455 Se.2d 672 (N.C. Ct. App. 1995) (holding that plaintiff's status as a member of the church or not would be proof required to succeed in slip and fall case); Springer v. Federated Church of Reno, 283 P.2d 1071 (Nev. 1955) (holding that a member of the church was the beneficiary of the church and as such could not recover in action against church).

[65] *See supra* note 68. *See also* Trinity Episcopal Church of Vero Beach, 222 So.2d 781 (Fla. Dist. Ct. App. 1969) (holding that a church member attending a meeting was an invitee); Strong v. Southside Baptist Church, 823 So.2d 608 (Miss. Ct. App. 2002) (holding that a wedding guest was an invitee); Fain v. O'Connell, 909 So.2d 790 (Tenn. 1995) (finding that no joint venture existed between church and members, thereby precluding suit against church association).

[66] *See* Vincent v. Raglin, 318 N.W.2d 629 (Mich. Ct. App. 1982) (holding that plaintiff pastor presented sufficient evidence for claim of assault and battery against owners and employees of a security guard service hired for his removal); McIntosh v. Johnson, 649 So.2d 190 (Miss. 1995) (holding that no action for assault was warranted by church against defendant); McGlynn v. St. Andrew the Apostle Church, 304 A.2d 372 (N.Y. 2003) (holding a church not responsible for injuries sustained by assault from intoxicated guest at party where church had rented premises out); City of Gaffney v. Putnam, 15 S.E.2d 130 (S.C. 1941) (finding that religious words spoken by a minister will not justify an assault or battery unless accompanied by an actual offer of physical violence); Kerley v. Germscheid, 106 N.W. 136 (S.D. 1906) (holding that sufficient contradictory evidence was presented in an assault and battery case between priest and stone mason for a jury to decide the matter); Pleasant Glade Assembly of God v. Schubert, 174 S.W.3d 388 (Tex. App. 2005) (finding that the First Amendment did not preclude plaintiff's claims for assault, battery, and false imprisonment against church, pastors, and several church members).

[67] *See* City of Gaffney v. Putnam, 15 S.E.2d 130 (S.C. 1941) (finding that religious words spoken by minister will not justify an assault or battery unless accompanied by actual offer of physical violence); Kerley v. Germscheid, 106 N.W. 136 (S.D. 1906) (holding that sufficient contradictory evidence was presented in assault and battery case between priest and stone mason for a jury to decide the matter); Pleasant Glade Assembly of God v. Schubert, 174 S.W.3d 388 (Tex. App. 2005) (finding that the First Amendment did not preclude plaintiff's claims for assault, battery, and false imprisonment against church, pastors, and several church members).

[68] *See* Maktab Tarighe Oveyssi Shah Maghsoudi, Inc. v. Kianfar, 179 F.3d 1244 (9th Cir. 1999) (finding that the court could decide conversion claim by one religious order against another by using neutral secular principles of law); First Methodist Church of Union Springs v. Scott, 226 So.2d 632 (Ala. 1969) (holding that the First Amendment denied the validity to state act that would have prevented dissenting members of a church from converting the property to unintended or different use due to change in social policies of the parent church); Second International Baha'i Council v. Chase, 106 P.3d 1168 (Mont. 2005) (holding that state interest in deciding property disputes did not bar its deciding religious corporation's conversion claims against corporate president as long as the dispute could be decided using neutral principles of law); Carjow, LLC v. Simmons, 563 S.E.2d 359 (S.C. Ct. App. 2002) (holding that

imprisonment,[69] trespass to land,[70] intentional infliction of emotional distress,[71] and libel.[72] Libel will be addressed in Section F of this chapter on defamation. The other causes of action will be addressed here. Of course, a key question in the intentional tort context is under what circumstances a religious entity or institution might be liable for torts committed by its employees and/or clergy.[73] Some intentional torts, such as assault or battery, are less likely to lead to direct institutional liability because they are generally

purchaser of a church could bring a claim for conversion of church pews that were removed by the former pastor); Libhart v. Copeland, 949 S.W.2d 783 (Tex. App. 1997) (finding for former church members in conversion and fraud claims against former pastor in connection with disposition of church's assets after its dissolution).

69 *See* Turner v. Church of Jesus Christ of Latter Day Saints, 18 S.W.3d 877 (Tex. App. 2000) (holding that the First Amendment did not bar former missionary's false imprisonment claims against church); Pleasant Glade Assembly of God v. Schubert, 174 S.W.3d 388 (Tex. App. 2005) (finding that the First Amendment did not preclude plaintiff's claims for assault, battery, and false imprisonment against church, pastors, and several church members).

70 *See* Dixon v. Edwards, 290 F.3d 699 (4th Cir. 2002) (deciding to grant declaratory and injunctive relief for bishop against a priest and vestry for control over parish property); Crist v. Village of Larchmont, 797 F.Supp. 309 (S.D.N.Y. 1992) (holding that abortion protester's arrest for trespass on church property did not violate protester's constitutional rights); Church of Christ in Hollywood v. Superior Court of Los Angeles, 121 Cal.Rptr.2d 810 (Cal. Ct. App. 2002) (finding church's claim for trespass against an expelled member could warrant granting of restraining order); Capitol View Community Church, 571 S.E.2d 181 (Ga. Ct. App. 2003) (holding that *res judicata* prevented church from appealing permanent injunction against its trespass by property owner); Mason v. Our Lady Star of the Sea Catholic Church, 154 S.W.3d 816 (Tex. App. 2005) (upholding dismissal of trespass claim by property owner against church that owned adjacent land alleging that improvements to the church land caused her property to flood).

71 *See* Doe v. Liberatore, 478 F.Supp.2d 742 (M.D. Pa. 2007) (dismissing plaintiff's intentional infliction of emotional distress claim because of lack of evidence that behavior was outrageous); Borchers v. Hrychuk, 727 A.2d 388 (Md. 1998) (alleging intentional infliction of emotional distress for sexual relationship that evolved out of church member and pastor marital counseling); John Doe CS v. Capuchin Franciscan Friars, 520 F.Supp.2d 1124 (E.D. Mo. 2007) (upholding plaintiff's claim for intentional infliction of emotional distress); Bouchard v. New York Archdiocese, 2006 WL 1375232 (S.D.N.Y. 2006) (upholding plaintiff's intentional infliction of emotional distress claim against church alleging scheme of concealment of priest's alleged sexual abuse); Faieta v. World Harvest Church, 891 N.E.2d 370 (Ohio 2008) (finding that evidence supported verdict against church provider for intentional infliction of emotional distress); Guinn v. Church of Christ of Collinsville, 775 P.2d 766 (Okla. 1989) (holding that former member's intentional infliction of emotional distress claims against church not barred by First Amendment).

72 *See* Church of Scientology Int'l v. Behar, 238 F.3d 168 (2nd Cir. 2001) (dismissing church's libel claim against publisher for magazine article); Drevlow v. Lutheran Church, Missouri Synod, 991 F.2d 468 (8th Cir. 1993) (holding that the First Amendment did not bar minister's libel claim against church); Bolduc v. Bailey, 586 F.Supp. 896 (D. Colo. 1984) (upholding priest and religious society's claim of defamation); Farley v. Wisconsin Evangelical Lutheran Synod, 821 F.Supp. 1286 (D. Minn. 1993) (holding that the First Amendment barred resolution of defamation claim made by minster against church organization); Church of Scientology of California v. Siegelman, 475 F.Supp. 950 (S.D.N.Y. 1979) (holding that statements made by defendant authors were replete with opinions and conclusions and thus could not be the basis for a defamation claim); Bowie v. Murphy, 624 S.E.2d 74 (Va. 2006) (holding that the First Amendment did not bar deacon's defamation claim against church).

73 *See* Bouchard v. New York Archdiocese, 2006 WL 1375232 (S.D.N.Y. 2006) (holding that church defendants could not be held vicariously liable for sexual misconduct of priest); Doe v. Liberatore, 478 F.Supp.2d 742 (M.D. Pa. 2007) (finding that a church could not be held liable for outrageous sexual abuse perpetrated by priest).

engaged in by an individual,[74] although the conduct giving rise to those torts may be actionable under claims such as negligent supervision[75] or (in a minority of jurisdictions) *respondeat superior* liability,[76] each of which will be discussed in later sections.

## 1. *Assault and Battery*

The torts of assault and battery are ancient torts.[77] Though the specifics of these torts can vary a bit between jurisdictions,[78] the general elements are usually the same.[79] One commits the tort of battery when one intentionally causes harmful or offensive contact with another person or persons, or a logical extension of that person or persons, without

[74] *See supra* notes 70–71.

[75] *Id. See also* Doe v. Holy See, 434 F.Supp.2d 925 (D. Or. 2006) (holding that the Holy See could be held liable for negligent supervision for priest's sexual abuse of minors); Beach v. Jean, 746 A.2d 228 (Conn. Super. Ct. 1999) (holding church and diocese not liable for negligent supervision of priest in sexual abuse action); Swanson v. Roman Catholic Bishop of Portland, 692 A.2d 441 (Me. 1997) (finding that the First Amendment barred negligent supervision claim against church for priest sexual assault); Hutchison v. Luddy, 896 A.2d 1260 (Pa. 2006) (affirming award of punitive damages against diocesan defendants on theory of negligent supervision in priest sexual abuse case).

[76] *See* Doe v. Holy See, 434 F.Supp.2d 925 (D. Or. 2006) (dismissing plaintiff's *respondeat superior* claim because he did not sufficiently plead evidence that sexual abuse was based on conduct resulting from commercial activities of the church); Iglesia Cristiana La Casa Del Senor, Inc. v. L.M., 783 So.2d 353 (Fla. Ct. App. 2001) (finding that a church is not liable under *respondeat superior* for pastor's sexual assault of minor because act was independent of employment); Doe v. South Central Spanish District of the Church of God, 2002 WL 31296620 (Tex. App.) (holding that sexual assault was outside the scope of employment so no employer liability); C.J.C. v. Corporation of the Catholic Bishop of Yakima, 985 P.2d 262 (Wash. 1999) (holding that diocese could not be held liable on *respondeat superior* for priest's sexual abuse of children).

[77] *See* N.H. v. Presbyterian Church, 998 P.2d 592 (Okla. 1999) (holding that national organization is not responsible under *respondeat superior* for priest's sexual misconduct); Doe v. Liberatore, 478 F.Supp.2d 742 (M.D. Pa. 2007) (finding that the First Amendment did not bar claims of sexual abuse against priest); Church of Jesus Christ of Latter-Day Saints v. Superior Court, 764 P.2d 759 (Az. App. 1988) (action brought by mother of sexually abused child against clergy and church); Roman Catholic Bishop of San Diego v. Superior Court of San Diego County, 50 Cal.Rptr.2d 399 (Cal. Ct. App. 1996) (ordering summary judgment be granted for defendants in negligent hiring and supervision action brought by minor arising from alleged priest's sexual abuse); Moses v. Diocese of Colorado, 863 P.2d 310 (Colo. 1993) (holding that the First Amendment did not bar sexual abuse claim against clergy and church); C.J.C. v. Corporation of the Catholic Bishop of Yakima, 985 P.2d 262 (Wash. 1999) (finding that priest's conduct constituted childhood sexual abuse).

[78] *See* Ehrens v. Lutheran Church, 385 F.3d 232 (2nd Cir. 2004) (holding that church is not liable for pastor's alleged sexual assault on minor church member when incidents occurred outside church property); Iglesia Cristiana La Case Del Senor, Inc. v. L.M., 783 So.2d 353 (Fla. Ct. App. 2001) (holding that church is not liable for pastor's sexual assault of a minor on theory of negligent supervision); Wende C. v. United Methodist Church, 827 N.E.2d 265 (N.Y. 2005) (finding no cause of action for sexual assault when evidence of consensual sexual relationship existed between pastor and church member); R.A. v. First Church of Christ, 748 A.2d 692 (Pa. Super. Ct. 2000) (holding that church could not be liable for minister's sexual assault of a minor who was not member of church and assault did not take place at or near church premises or church-sponsored activities).

[79] *See supra* notes 81 & 82. *See also* Winkler v. Rocky Mountain Conference of the United Methodist Church, 923 P.2d 152 (Colo. Ct. App. 1996) (holding that both pastor and conference breached fiduciary duty to plaintiff in suit alleging unwanted physical contact).

privilege or consent.[80] One commits the tort of assault when one places another person or persons in reasonable apprehension of an imminent battery.[81]

The torts of assault and battery arise in a surprising number of cases involving religious entities. The most common sort of case where these torts arise is clergy abuse.[82] Obviously, cases involving sexual assault,[83] other sorts of physical assault,[84] and other forms of sexual misconduct,[85] abusive behavior,[86] or threats[87] may lead to one or both of

[80] *See* John Doe CS v. Capuchin Franciscan Friars, 520 F.Supp.2d 1124 (E.D. Mo 2007) (holding that religious order could not be held liable for sexual misconduct under agency theory); Richelle L. v. Roman Catholic Archbishop, 130 Cal.Rptr.2d 601 (Cal. Ct. App. 2003) (finding that plaintiff's claims arising from sexual misconduct with reverend could not be adjudicated without violation of the First Amendment); Gibson v. Brewer, 952 S.W.2d 239 (Mo. 1997) (finding diocese not liable for priest's sexual misconduct); N.H. v. Presbyterian Church, 998 P.2d 592 (Okla. 1999) (holding that national organization not responsible under *respondeat superior* for priest's sexual misconduct).

[81] *See* JC2, ME, FH, PM, BO, BS and TS v. Grammond, 232 F.Supp.2d 1166 (D. Or. 2002) (holding that the First Amendment did not bar claims against church and priest for sexual abuse that occurred while they were alter boys); Bear Valley Church of Christ v. DeBose, 928 P.2d 1315 (Colo. 1996) (finding that the First Amendment is not a defense to plaintiff's claims alleging minister's inappropriate touching of a minor); Konkle v. Henson, 672 N.E.2d 450 (Ind. Ct. App. 1996) (dismissing action for *respondeat superior* against church for sexual molestation by minister because he was not acting in scope of employment); Fortin v. Roman Catholic Bishop of Portland, 871 A.2d 1208 (Me. 2005) (holding that victim of sexual abuse alleged sufficient facts to establish fiduciary relationship with diocese so as to give rise to a duty to protect).

[82] *See, e.g.*, JC2 v. Grammond, 232 F. Supp. 2d 1166 (D. Or. 2001) (remanding a parishioner's sexual battery claim against a church to state court); Bonner v. Roman Catholic Diocese of Boise, 913 P.2d 567 (Idaho 1996) (stating that acts of sexual abuse, including those perpetrated by clergy members, are at the very least acts of battery that will subject perpetrators to suit); Doe v. First United Methodist Church, 629 N.E.2d 402 (Ohio 1994) (discussing a congregant's claims, which included sexual battery, against First United Church arising from roughly three-hundred separate instances of sexual abuse by the church's choir director).

[83] *See, e.g.*, Doe v. Norwich Roman Catholic Diocesan Corp., 309 F. Supp. 2d 247 (D. Conn. 2004) (finding that a parishioner had viable claims against the diocese arising from instances of sexual abuse by a former priest); Doe v. Hartz, 52 F. Supp. 2d 1027 (N.D. Iowa 1999) (finding a parishioner's claims of sexual abuse by a cleric were tantamount to simple assault and battery claim); Pachulski v. Roman Catholic Diocese of Grand Rapids, 1999 WL 33441139 (Mich. App. 1999) (discussing a seventeen-year-old parishioner's assault and battery claims against the diocese, church, and a priest who allegedly gave the parishioner a full-body massage); Konkle v. Henson, 672 N.E.2d 450 (Ind. Ct. App. 1996) (finding that a religious institution was not liable for its minister's offensive touching of a young congregant).

[84] *See, e.g.*, Hartz, 52 F. Supp. 2d at 1067 (finding a viable assault claim against a cleric arising from a mere handshake); Pleasant Glade Assembly of God v. Schubert, 264 S.W.3d 1 (Tex. 2008) (discussing the tort claims against a religious group arising from instances where church members forcibly restrained another congregant), *cert. denied*, 129 S.Ct. 1003 (2009); Frame v. Comeaux, 735 So. 2d 753 (La. Ct. App. 1999) (dismissing an assault and battery charge against the diocese arising from its teacher's disciplinary actions against a student).

[85] *See, e.g.*, Bouchard v. New York Archdiocese, 2006 WL 1375232 (S.D.N.Y. 2006) (discussing parishioner's assault and battery claims against a priest and a religious institution arising from the priest's acts of sexual abuse that claimed to have healing power); Olson v. First Church of the Nazarene, 661 N.W.2d 254 (Minn. Ct. App. 2003) (discussing a parishioner's claim that a church was vicariously liable for its priest's sexual penetration); Moseley v. Second New St. Paul Baptist Church, 534 A.2d 346 (D.C. 1987) (discussing a church employer's amenability to tort liability arising from an incident where the church's janitor sexually assaulted two young boys).

[86] *See, e.g.*, Weiss v. Patrick, 453 F. Supp. 717 (D.R.I. 1978) (discussing several church members' abuse of another member who was believed to worship Satan); Schubert, 264 S.W.3d at 12–13 (dismissing claims of assault and battery against a church arising from an incident where church members forcibly placed their hands on a collapsed congregant and began to pray); Jones v. Trane, 591 N.Y.S.2d 927 (Sup. Ct. 1992) (suggesting that a priest's abusive behavior, which placed a minor parishioner in immediate apprehension of sexual contact, amounts to claim for assault, not malpractice).

[87] *See, e.g.*, Zawadzka v. Catholic Bishop of Chi., 785 N.E.2d 71 (Ill. App. Ct. 2003) (dismissing, on procedural grounds, a parishioner's battery claims arising from an incident where she was raped and impregnated

these torts. Other situations where the torts may arise is when violence erupts between church members and/or clergy or church employees[88] or where clergy or congregants target outsiders for physical violence or threats.[89] Of course, most of the time, the party liable is the clergy member or other employee of the religious entity and not the entity itself.[90] This is so because, as a general matter, vicarious liability in assault or battery cases is not recognized.[91]

by a priest who threatened to have her deported if she revealed that he was the father of her child); Wood *ex rel.* Wood v. Berean Baptist Church, 1997 WL 33343376 (Mich. Ct. App. 1997) (finding a viable assault and battery claim against a church arising from employee's confinement and verbal intimidation of a Sunday school student); Alpharetta First United Methodist Church v. Stewart, 472 S.E.2d 532, 533 (Ga. Ct. App. 1996) {discussing congregant's assault and battery claims against a religious institution arising from a minister's "manipulation of the [congregant's] 'transference' phenomenon" [citing Jacobsen v. Boyle, 397 S.E.2d 1 (Ga. Ct. App. 1990)]}.

88 *See, e.g.*, Moseley, 534 A.2d at 349 (dismissing a father's attempt to hold a church vicariously liable for injuries sustained by his two sons who were sexually assaulted by a church janitor because the janitor was not acting within the scope of his employment when he perpetrated the sexual assault); Vincent v. Raglin, 318 N.W.2d 629 (Mich. Ct. App. 1982) (mandating that a pastor who was forcibly ejected from church services be entitled to submit his assault and battery claims to a jury); Hook v. Snell, 304 P.2d 516 (Kan. Ct. App. 1956) (discussing a church member's assault and battery charge against an in-law arising from an incident that occurred after a church service); Whitney v. Hitchcock, 4 Denio 461 (N.Y. Sup. Ct. 1847) (discussing a father's assault and battery claim against a fellow church member who assaulted his daughter at an evening prayer meeting).

89 *See, e.g.*, Robertson v. Church of God, Int'l, 978 S.W.2d 120 (Tex. App. 1997) (discussing a massage therapist's claims against a church for its priest's sexual assault); Robinson v. Dunn, 683 So. 2d 894 (La. Ct. App. 1997) (dismissing a former pastor's assault and battery charge against the church deacons who forcibly removed him from a church meeting because the pastor's employment contract had expired and he had no right to attend the meeting); R.A. *ex rel.* N.A. v. First Church of Christ, 748 A.2d 692 (Pa. Super. Ct. 2000) (discussing an attempt to hold a religious institution liable for its priest's sexual assaults on a minor who was not a member of the church).

90 *See, e.g.*, Doe v. Holy See, 557 F.3d 1066, 1080 (9th Cir. 2009) (holding that an international religious organization is not subject to jurisdiction for the allegedly tortious actions of the "Archdiocese, the Chicago Bishop, and the Order"), *petition for cert. filed*, Jun 25, 2009 (No. 09-1); Holmes v. Lorch, 329 F. Supp. 2d 516 (S.D.N.Y. 2004) (remanding an assault and battery charge against a church-league basketball coach who molested one of his players while dismissing the same claim against the church); Soto v. Catholic Diocese of El Paso, 156 S.W.3d 881 (Tex. App. 2005) (dismissing a parishioner's tort claims against the religious institution arising from its former priest's sexual misbehavior because the parishioner failed to show tortious behavior on the part of the institution); Iglesia Cristiana La Casa Del Senor, Inc. v. L.M., 783 So. 2d 353 (Fla. Dist. Ct. App. 2001) (holding that a church is not vicariously liable for its pastor's sexual misconduct with a young congregant).

91 *See, e.g.*, Doe CS v. Capuchin Franciscan Friars, 520 F. Supp. 2d 1124, 1131 (E.D. Mo. 2007) {"The sexual misconduct of a priest against a student is not intended to further the employer's business, but rather results from 'purely private and personal desires.'" [quoting P.S. v. Psychiatric Coverage, Ltd., 887 S.W.2d 622, 624 (Mo. Ct. App. 1994)]}; C.J.C. v. Corporation of the Catholic Bishop of Yakima, 985 P.2d 262 (Wash. 1999) (stating that the imposition of vicarious liability on a religious institution for a priest's sexual misconduct would contravene Washington case law and public policy); Rita M. v. Roman Catholic Archbishop of L.A., 232 Cal. Rptr. 685 (Cal. Ct. App. 1986) (holding that priest's sexual misconduct cannot be the basis for a successful vicarious liability claim against a religious institution because such conduct is wholly outside the scope a priest's employment); Doe v. Hartford Roman Catholic Diocesan Corp., 716 A.2d 960 (Conn. Super. Ct. 1998) (holding that a church cannot be vicariously liable for its clergy's sexual abuse of minors).

Liability for the harm caused by these torts still may be imposed on a religious entity under claims for negligent supervision[92] or other causes of action,[93] but rarely is a religious institution liable for the torts of assault or battery,[94] although even here there are exceptions, usually when the religious entity itself promotes the assault or battery.[95] Courts, however, have little trouble imposing liability on clergy or other individuals within a religious entity for assault and/or battery.[96] These claims against the individual tortfeasors do not generally involve the courts in ecclesiastical matters,[97] and are more

[92] *See, e.g.*, Ehrens v. Lutheran Church, 385 F.3d 232 (2nd Cir. 2004) (affirming the summary disposition of a parishioner's negligent supervision claim against the Synod because the parishioner failed to identify evidence to support her contention that the Synod knew of its priest's sexual proclivities); Bear Valley Church of Christ v. DeBose, 928 P.2d 1315 (Colo. 1996) (finding that a church is amenable to suit for its negligent supervision of a priest who engaged in inappropriate massaging of youth he counseled); Olson v. First Church of the Nazarene, 661 N.W.2d 254, 264–5 (Minn. Ct. App. 2003) (stating that a negligent supervision claim against a religious institution "derives from the doctrine of *respondeat superior*" and turns on the "reasonableness" of the institution's supervision of its clergy); Smith v. Privette, 495 S.E.2d 395 (N.C. Ct. App. 1998) (finding that allegations of a cleric's sexual assaults and batteries on fellow church employees amounted to a viable negligent supervision claim against the religious organization that hired the cleric); Rosado v. Bridgeport Roman Catholic Diocesan Corp., 716 A.2d 967 (Conn. Super. Ct. 1998) (stating that a religious institution may be held liable for injuries caused by its pedophile clergy if the church knowingly failed or negligently supervised them).

[93] *See, e.g.*, Martinelli v. Bridgeport Roman Catholic Diocesan Corp., 196 F.3d 409 (2nd Cir. 1999) (discussing a former parishioner's breach of fiduciary duty claim against the diocese arising from a priest's sexual abuse); Tri v. J.T.T., 162 S.W.3d 552 (Tex. 2004) (discussing a conspiracy charge against a Buddhist organization arising from the rape of two female visitors by a monk); Napieralski v. Unity Church of Greater Portland, 802 A.2d 391 (Me. 2002) (dismissing an insurance agent's claims of negligence, negligent infliction of emotional distress, and negligent supervision against the church that employed the cleric who sexually assaulted the insurance agent outside the church premises); Byrd v. Faber, 565 N.E.2d 584 (Ohio 1991) (discussing a parishioner's claims against a church for fraud and negligent hiring of a priest who sexually assaulted the parishioner during counseling); Hartford Roman Catholic Diocesan Corp., 716 A.2d at 964 (finding a viable negligent infliction of emotional distress claim against a religious institution arising from its priest's sexual assault of a parishioner).

[94] *See, e.g.*, *Byrd*, 565 N.E.2d at 588 (dismissing claim that a church was vicariously liable for its priest's nonconsensual sexual assault of a parishioner); Frame v. Comeaux, 735 So. 2d 753 (La. Ct. App. 1999) (finding that a religious institution was not liable for its employee's disciplinary actions against a student); Jeffrey E. v. Central Baptist Church, 243 Cal. Rptr. 128 (Cal. Ct. App. 1988) (holding that a church was not liable for its Sunday-school teacher's sexual assault of a student); Moseley v. Second New St. Paul Baptist Church, 534 A.2d 346, 349 (D.C. 1987) (finding that a church is not liable for a sexual assault perpetrated by its janitor because the janitor was acting wholly outside the parameters of his employment duties at the church).

[95] *See, e.g.*, Capuchin Franciscan Friars, 520 F. Supp. 2d at 1132 (recognizing that a religious institution may be amenable to tort liability for its clergy's sexual assaults and batteries if the institution subsequently ratifies such behavior); Sanders v. Casa View Baptist Church, 898 F. Supp. 1169 (N.D. Tex. 1995) (recognizing that a church is amenable to liability for its clergy's intentional torts if it ratifies the tortious behavior); A.L.M. v. Diocese of Allentown, 68 Pa. D. & C.4th 111 (Pa. Com. Pl. 2004) (tolling the statute of limitations on parishioner's claims, which arose from a cleric's sexual abuse, based on the diocese's alleged active concealment of the clergy abuse).

[96] *See, e.g.*, Holmes v. Lorch, 329 F. Supp. 2d 516 (S.D.N.Y. 2004) (remanding an assault and battery charge against a church-league basketball coach who allegedly molested one of his players and made subsequent attempts to keep the child from reporting the abuse); Doe v. Hartz, 52 F. Supp. 2d 1027 (N.D. Iowa 1999) (finding that a parishioner had sufficiently alleged a factual basis that would allow her to recover against a priest for his sexual battery and assault); Bonner v. Roman Catholic Diocese of Boise, 913 P.2d 567 (Idaho 1996) (stating that acts of sexual abuse, including those perpetrated by clergy members, are at the very least acts of battery that will subject perpetrators to suit).

[97] *See, e.g.*, Hartz, 52 F. Supp. 2d at 1051 (finding that a priest may be amenable to liability for assault and battery; the court did not have any ecclesiastical concerns); Bowie v. Murphy, 624

consistent with the general principle that vicarious liability is unavailable for assault or battery.[98]

Courts have held explicitly that sexual and/or physical abuse is not part of the duties of clergy members or church employees, and therefore, finding these individuals liable for their conduct would not raise religious questions.[99] To the extent that physical assault or threats are argued to be part of a religious tradition, courts tend to find that the state's interest in protecting individuals from assault and battery outweighs any free exercise right asserted.[100] This is especially true because if one voluntarily submits to the conduct alleged to constitute the tort – a scenario that may raise ecclesiastical questions – one will not likely be able to prove that the conduct was harmful or offensive,[101] and the defense of consent will also potentially be available.[102]

S.E.2d 74 (Va. 2006) (discussing a deacon's assault charge against a church member without delving into ecclesiastical matters); Rosado v. Bridgeport Roman Catholic Diocesan Corp., 716 A.2d 967 (Conn. Super. Ct. 1998) (finding that tort liability can be imposed on a sexually abusive cleric when the cleric was ostensibly motivated by nonreligious desires).

98 *See, e.g.*, Bouchard v. New York Archdiocese, 2006 WL 1375232, at *4 (S.D.N.Y. 2006) ("Church may not be held vicariously liable for the sexual misconduct of an employee-priest … as such misconduct is clearly outside the scope of employment as a priest, and is unrelated to the furtherance of the Church Defendants' business."); Gibson v. Brewer, 952 S.W.2d 239 (Mo. 1997) (holding that a religious institution cannot be held liable for the intentional sexual misconduct of its clergy); Alpharetta First United Methodist Church v. Stewart, 472 S.E.2d 532 (Ga. Ct. App. 1996) (recognizing that pursuant to Georgia law, a church-employer may not be vicariously liable for torts arising from its minister's sexual misconduct, misconduct that is "purely personal in nature [and] unrelated to the [minister]'s duties"); R.A. *ex rel.* N.A. v. First Church of Christ, 748 A.2d 692, 699 (Pa. Super. Ct. 2000) (holding that a claim of vicarious liability against a religious institution is meritless when it is based on sexual misconduct by the institution's clergy).

99 *See, e.g.*, Sanders v. Casa View Baptist Church, 898 F. Supp. 1169 (N.D. Tex. 1995) (recognizing that a cleric's sexual misconduct is beyond the scope of his employment duties); Gibson, 952 S.W.2d at 246 (finding that a cleric's sexual misconduct cannot be the basis of institutional liability because such conduct is outside the "scope of employment of a priest and [is] in fact forbidden"); Konkle v. Henson, 672 N.E.2d 450 (Ind. Ct. App. 1996) (holding that a minister's sexual assault of a congregant was not authorized by the church or within the scope of his pastoral duties).

100 *See, e.g.*, Doe v. Norwich Roman Catholic Diocesan Corp., 309 F. Supp. 2d 247, 252 (D. Conn. 2004) (finding that a parishioner had a viable *respondeat superior* claim against a church arising from a priest's sexual abuse. Evidence showed that the priest's sexual misconduct was an attempt to bring the parishioner "closer to the Church and her religious faith, thereby increasing financial donations to the Church and volunteer time spent by plaintiff and her family in furtherance of the Church's business."); Malicki v. Doe, 814 So. 2d 347 (Fla. 2002) (stating the general proposition that government's interest in protecting its respective citizens often warrants adjudicating tort claims arising from clergy sexual misconduct); Rosado, 716 A.2d at 973 (stating that a mere assertion that tortious behavior was founded on religious beliefs cannot excuse a cleric from otherwise valid laws prohibiting such tortious behavior).

101 *See, e.g.*, Wende C. v. United Methodist Church, 827 N.E.2d 265 (N.Y. 2005) (finding that an adult church member had consented to the sexual relationship she had with a minister; thus a cause of action for battery could not be maintained); Olson v. First Church of the Nazarene, 661 N.W.2d 254 (Minn. Ct. App. 2003) (discussing a parishioner's assertion that the context of her spiritual counseling with a sexually abusive priest adversely affected her capacity to consent to sexual penetration); Jacqueline R. v. Household of Faith Family Church, Inc., 118 Cal. Rptr. 2d 264 (Cal. Ct. App. 2002) (finding that the claimant could not establish that she found the objectively consensual sexual contact with a pastor harmful or offensive).

102 *See, e.g.*, Wende C., 827 N.E.2d at 267 (sustaining a pastor's consent defense with regard to a battery claim brought by a congregant who had been sexually involved with the pastor for over a year); Olson, 661 N.W.2d at 262 (recognizing that consent is always a plausible defense to battery charges arising from a sexual relationship between a cleric and a parishioner); Jacqueline R., 118 Cal. Rptr. 2d at 270–1 (affirming the trial court's finding that the sexual relationship between a pastor and a congregant was consensual and thus could not be the basis for a claim of assault and battery).

## 2. *Conversion*

The tort of conversion generally includes the following elements: (1) one must intentionally[103] (2) appropriate the property (usually chattel property) of another[104] (3) for his or her own use or enjoyment[105] or (4) destroy the property, alter its nature, or wrongfully assume title of the property.[106] As with most torts, the details can vary between jurisdictions and contexts,[107] but for present purposes, this definition is adequate.

The tort of conversion has not arisen in many cases involving religious entities. The few cases where it has arisen have generally involved the conversion of church property by church members, clergy, or former clergy.[108] Usually the church is the entity alleging conversion.[109] In a small number of cases, a party that has a financial, real estate, and/or chattel interest in the property is the plaintiff, and the religious entity, its members, or

103 *See, e.g.*, St. Paul Church, Inc. v. Board of Trustees of the Alaska Missionary Conference of the United Methodist Church, Inc., 145 P.3d 541 (Alaska 2006) (stating that to establish a claim of conversion, plaintiff must prove that defendants intentionally interfered with the plaintiff's possessory interest in the property); General Convention of the New Jerusalem in the United States of America, Inc. v. MacKenzie, 874 N.E.2d 1084 (Mass. 2007) (stating that if the General Convention was the rightful owner of the church's assets, petitioner's conversion claim would not have been dismissed where the individual defendants knew they had no right to the disputed property but exercised acts of ownership and control over them anyway).

104 *See* St. Paul Church, Inc. v. Board of Trustees of the Alaska Missionary Conference of the United Methodist Church, Inc., 145 P.3d 541 (Alaska 2006) (stating that for a claim of conversion, plaintiff must prove that defendants' acts caused plaintiff's loss of property); Church of God of the Union Assembly, Inc. v. Carmical, 104 S.E.2d 912 (Ga. 1958) (finding a conversion where defendant church took plaintiff's tent); Carlson et. al. v. Fox, 31 S.E.2d 507 (Ga. 1944) (finding a conversion where seizure of church funds occurred by unauthorized parties); Johnson v. Oliver, 250 S.W.3d 182 (Tex. Ct. App. 2008) (finding a conversion where one church took a bus that belonged to another church).

105 *See* Church of God of the Union Assembly, Inc. v. Carmical, 104 S.E.2d 912 (Ga. 1958) (upholding conviction for conversion where defendant church took plaintiff's tent and used it in its own business); Johnson v. Oliver, 250 S.W.3d 182 (Tex. Ct. App. 2008) (finding a conversion where church founder took and used a bus that belonged to another church).

106 *See* St. Paul Church, Inc. v. Board of Trustees of the Alaska Missionary Conference of the United Methodist Church, Inc., 145 P.3d 541 (Alaska 2006) (upholding judgment for plaintiffs in conversion action where defendants withheld property and broke locks); Horvitz v. St. John the Baptist Church, 1998 WL 465836 (Mass. App. Ct.) (upholding nominal damages awarded to plaintiffs on their claim for conversion where church removed a concrete slab wall owned by plaintiffs when church was expanding its cemetery).

107 *See, e.g.*, Church of Scientology of California v. Armstrong, 23 Cal.Rptr. 917 (Cal. Ct. App. 1991) (finding conversion a defense where plaintiff believed his life or well-being to be in danger and the only way to defend himself was the taking of the documents in question); Carlson et. al. v. Fox, 31 S.E.2d 507 (Ga. 1944) (finding a conversion even where church funds were not being dissipated or used for improper purposes).

108 *See* Guardian Angel Polish National Catholic Church of Los Angeles, Inc. v. Grotnik, 13 Cal.Rptr.3d 552 (Cal. Ct. App. 2004) (finding that when local parish severed its ties with national church and brought action over rights to the property, the trial court erred in finding in favor of parish. Court of Appeals ordered the trial court to try the national church's conversion claim against parish.); Carlson v. Fox, 31 S.E.2d 507 (Ga. 1944) (upholding trial court ruling of conversion against board of directors illegally appointed by pastor for taking charge of church funds and usurping church deacons); Gaydos v. Imhoff, 245 S.W.3d 303 (Mo. Ct. App. 2008) (affirming judgment in favor of church for conversion claim against former president of board of directors for church's cemetery); Libhart v. Copeland, 949 S.W.2d 783 (Tex. Ct. App. 1997) (affirming decision for former church members against former pastor in action for conversion of church property).

109 *See* Maktab Tarighe Oveyssi Shah Maghsoudi, Inc. v. Kianfar, 179 F.3d 1244 (9th Cir. 1999) (finding that conversion claim made by a religious order against former members could be decided based on neutral

clergy are the defendants.[110] Courts most often recognize such claims against individuals,[111] such as a clergy member,[112] given the intentional nature of the tort.[113]

### 3. *False Imprisonment*

The tort of false imprisonment requires that the defendant, through threats or actions, causes the victim to be confined (or completely confined in many jurisdictions) for an unreasonable period of time within boundaries created by the defendant that allow no reasonable means of escape of which the victim is aware.[114] Fear of physical harm

principles of law and should not have been dismissed); Iglesia Evangelica Latina, Inc. v. Southern Pacific Latin American District of the Assemblies of God, 93 Cal.Rptr.3d 75 (Cal. Ct. App. 2009) (remanding for trial local church's conversion claim against district council after claim had been dismissed by superior court); Second International Baha'I Council v. Chase, 106 P.3d 1168 (Mont. 2005) (holding that religious organization's conversion action against religious leader for alleged conversion of corporate funds could be decided if corporation's board could be decided with neutral principles); Gaydos v. Imhoff, 245 S.W.3d 303 (Mo. Ct. App. 2008) (affirming judgment for a church in a conversion claim against president of board of directors for cemetery); Highway Church of Christ, Inc. v. Barber, 325 S.E.2d 305 (N.C. Ct. App. 1985) (recognizing church's claim for conversion against bishop of another church but dismissing the claim for lack of evidence); Cardwell v. Brown, 384 N.Y.S.2d 876 (N.Y. 1976) (affirming damages for church in conversion action against new board of directors of church for the usurpation of the management and control of the church); Johnson v. Oliver, 250 S.W.3d 182 (Tex. Ct. App. 2008) (affirming judgment for church and it's presiding officer in claim for conversion against another church and its founder).

110 *See* Church of God of the Union Assembly, Inc. v. Carmical, 104 S.E.2d 912 (Ga. 1958) (affirming jury decision for plaintiff in action by plaintiff against defendant church for conversion of plaintiff's tent); Dixon v. Hill, 620 S.E.2d 715 (N.C. Ct. App. 2005) (affirming decision against church in conversion claim brought by home residents for conversion of their property and money); Buyofski v. St. Stephens Roman Catholic Church, 2006 WL 2069149 (N.J. Super. Ct. App. Div.) (finding that statute of limitations did not bar plaintiff's conversion claim against defendant church and pastor); Carjow, LLC v. Simmons, 563 S.E.2d 359 (S.C. Ct. App. 2002) (upholding judgment for purchaser of church in conversion action against former pastor to recover possession of church pews and ceiling fans and lights).

111 *See* Highway Church of Christ, Inc. v. Barber, 325 S.E.2d 305 (N.C. Ct. App. 1985) (recognizing church's claim for conversion against bishop of another church but dismissing the claim for lack of evidence); Buyofski v. St. Stephens Roman Catholic Church, 2006 WL 2069149 (N.J. Super. Ct. App. Div.) (finding that statute of limitations did not bar conversion claim against pastor for conversion of stepmother's estate); Carjow, LLC v. Simmons, 563 S.E.2d 359 (S.C. Ct. App. 2002) (upholding judgment for purchaser of church in conversion claim against former pastor); Libhart v. Copeland, 949 S.W.2d 783 (Tex. Ct. App. 1997) (affirming decision for former church members against former pastor in action for conversion of church property).

112 *See* Highway Church of Christ, Inc. v. Barber, 325 S.E.2d 305 (N.C. Ct. App. 1985) (recognizing church's claim for conversion against bishop of another church but dismissing the claim for lack of evidence); Buyofski v. St. Stephens Roman Catholic Church, 2006 WL 2069149 (N.J. Super. Ct. App. Div.) (finding that statue of limitations did not bar plaintiff's conversion claim against pastor); Carjow, LLC v. Simmons, 563 S.E.2d 359 (S.C. Ct. App. 2002) (finding for purchaser of church property in conversion action against former pastor); Libhart v. Copeland, 949 S.W.2d 783 (Tex. Ct. App. 1997) (affirming decision for former church members against former pastor in action for conversion of church property).

113 *See* Buyofski v. St. Stephens Roman Catholic Church, 2006 WL 2069149 (N.J. Super. Ct. App. Div.) (finding that statute of limitations did not bar plaintiff's conversion claim against pastor for fiduciary duty conversion where it was alleged that defendant pastor intentionally converted decedent's assets).

114 *See* Blair v. Wills, 420 F.3d 823 (8th Cir. 2005) (stating that to proceed on a false imprisonment claim, plaintiff would have to show that he was confined without his consent and without legal justification); Snyder v. Evangelical Orthodox Church, 264 Cal.Rptr. 640 (Cal. Ct. App. 1989) {"[T]he tort of false imprisonment is the 'nonconsensual, intentional confinement of a person, without lawful privilege, for

generally supports a victim's claim that he or she had no reasonable means of escape of which he or she was aware.[115] Generally recognized defenses include consent or legal justification.[116]

Not surprisingly, there are few cases involving religious institutions/entities and false imprisonment. Even less surprising is that the few cases there are generally involve either the holding of a member of a faith (usually a "cult"), or former member, in order to keep that individual from leaving[117]; religious practices that involve physically restraining or holding a congregant against his or her will[118]; or similar scenarios designed to keep an individual from violating the faith's tenets. Even so, there are very few cases. Additionally, there are cases based on "deprogramming" people who became members of a "cult,"[119] but these cases, which generally do not involve religious entities in the deprogramming, are beyond the scope of this book.

As should be obvious, courts are reticent to reach issues that require determination of the validity of a religious practice,[120] especially where the individual alleging the claim of false imprisonment did not object at the time.[121] Therefore, if the facts giving rise to the claim of false imprisonment involve ritual practices and there is not ample evidence that the victim opposed the practice or opposed the practice in the specific instance on which

an appreciable length of time, however short.'" [citing Molko v. Holy Spirit Assn., 762 P.2d 46 (Cal. 1988)]}; Turner v. Church of Jesus Christ of Latter-Day Saints, 18 S.W.3d 877, 900 (Tex. Ct. App. 2000) [stating that in action for false imprisonment against church where plaintiff was admitted to behavioral science unit of hospital after missionary work, plaintiff would have to show that (1) church willfully directed, requested, or participated in plaintiff's detention (2) without his consent and (3) without the authority of law)].

115 *See* Peterson v. Sorlien, 299 N.W.2d 123, 128 (Minn. 1980) ("[I]f one is aware of a reasonable means of escape that does not present a danger of bodily or material harm, a restriction is not total and complete and does not constitute unlawful imprisonment."); Grace v. Dempsey, 43 N.W. 1127 (Wis. 1889) (affirming judgment for plaintiff in an action for false imprisonment where Catholic priest instructed parishioners to bring plaintiff to his house and plaintiff went for fear of physical harm if he refused).

116 *See* Blair v. Wills, 420 F.3d 823 (8th Cir. 2005) (parents' consent for minor child being held at church-run school was defense to minor's false imprisonment claim where parents were informed as to school's policies); Snyder v. Evangelical Orthodox Church, 264 Cal.Rptr. 640 (Cal. Ct. App. 1989) (holding that summary judgment was properly granted for defendant where evidence showed that plaintiff consented to remain in isolation for a week); Peterson v. Sorlien, 299 N.W.2d 123 (Minn. 1980) (stating that consent is a defense to an allegation of false imprisonment and that consent could be seen through one's behavior).

117 *See, e.g.*, Molko v. Holy Spirit Assn., 762 P.2d 46 (Cal. 1988) ("[A] person is falsely imprisoned 'if he [or she] is wrongfully deprived of his [or her] freedom to leave a particular place by the conduct of another'") [citing Schangafelt v. Seaboard Finance Co., 239 P.2d 42 (Cal. Ct. App. 1951)]; Whittaker v. Sandford, 85 A. 399 (Me. 1912) (finding false imprisonment where leader of religious sect prevented the wife of a member from leaving his boat so that the husband could persuade her to remain a member).

118 *See* Pleasant Glade Assembly of God v. Schubert, 264 S.W.3d 1 (Tex. 2008) (involving church members who physically restrained plaintiff during an episode at church youth group).

119 *See* Peterson v. Sorlien, 299 N.W.2d 123 (Minn. 1980) (plaintiff daughter brought false imprisonment charges against parents for attempting to deprogram her and have her leave the religious cult she belonged to).

120 *See* Pleasant Glade Assembly of God v. Schubert, 264 S.W.3d 1 (Tex. 2008) (holding that because the "laying of hands" was a part of the church's belief system, even if a particular member found the practice emotionally disturbing, it did not make the matter a secular one).

121 *See* Snyder v. Evangelical Orthodox Church, 264 Cal.Rptr. 640 (Cal. Ct. App. 1989) (finding that plaintiff's week in isolation was consensual, thus barring a false imprisonment claim against church).

he or she brings suit, courts generally find a First Amendment bar to such claims.[122] Where there is no religious justification, the fact that the defendant is a religious entity, without more, is not an adequate defense.[123]

### 4. *Intentional Infliction of Emotional Distress*

The tort of intentional infliction of emotional distress is hard to prove given its stringent requirements. Yet there have been a number of successful claims for intentional infliction of emotional distress involving clergy and/or religious entities.[124] There is some variation among jurisdictions regarding the elements of the tort and the stringency with which those elements are evaluated,[125] but the general elements of the tort are as follows: the defendant must act intentionally or recklessly,[126] the conduct must be extreme

122 *See* Molko v. Holy Spirit Assn., 762 P.2d 46 (Cal. 1988) (holding that threats of divine retribution are protected religious speech and cannot be the basis of a tort claim); Snyder v. Evangelical Orthodox Church, 264 Cal.Rptr. 640 (Cal. Ct. App. 1989) (finding that plaintiff's claim that he only consented to a week in isolation because of a threat that his sins would not be absolved was barred by the First Amendment as protected religious speech); Pleasant Glade Assembly of God v. Schubert, 264 S.W.3d 1 (Tex. 2008) (holding that the First Amendment prohibits courts from determining issues of religious doctrine and barring plaintiff's false imprisonment claim because it would make the court determine the validity of a religious practice); Turner v. Church of Jesus Christ of Latter-Day Saints, 18 S.W.3d 877, 897 (Tex. Ct. App. 2000) (holding that where plaintiff was held in behavioral science unit of hospital after being admitted by church and plaintiff brought false imprisonment claim against church, the claim was not barred by the First Amendment "because it does not involve the internal policies of the Church or matters of faith or ecclesiastical doctrine, and it does not actively involve the government in the Church's religious activities or excessively entangle the government with religion").

123 *See* Higgins v. Maher, 258 Cal.Rptr. 757, 761 (Cal. Ct. App. 1989) ("Regardless of the church's motives or objectives, or the circumstances giving rise, we would probably agree that torts such as battery, false imprisonment or conversion cannot be perpetrated upon its members with civil impunity.").

124 *See, e.g.*, Guinn v. Church of Christ of Collinsville, 775 P.2d 766 (Okla. 1989) (holding elders' of a church liable for intentional infliction of emotional distress for their continued disciplinary actions against a former congregant); Gibson v. Brewer, 952 S.W.2d 239 (Mo. 1997) (recognizing that a religious institution is amenable to liability for the severe emotional distress it intentionally inflicts); Amato v. Greenquist, 679 N.E.2d 446 (Ill. App. Ct. 1997) (recognizing a husband's intentional infliction of emotional distress claim against a pastor who abused his power as the couple's marriage counselor); Faieta v. World Harvest Church, 891 N.E.2d 370 (Ohio Com. Pl. 2008) (holding that the record supported an intentional infliction of emotional distress claim against a religious organization arising from physical abuse of a child by its employee), *aff'd*, 2008 WL 5423454 (Ohio Ct. App. 2008).

125 *Compare* Doe v. Liberatore, 478 F. Supp. 2d 742, 765 (M.D. Pa. 2007) ("[T]o prevail on an intentional infliction of emotional distress cause of action, a … [parishioner] must provide competent medical evidence to prove the existence of emotional distress); *with* Collins v. African Methodist Episcopal Zion Church, 2006 WL 1579718 (Del. Super. Ct. 2006) (citing Delaware precedent that holds a claim for intentional infliction of emotional distress "may be made even in the absence of accompanying bodily harm" [citing Cummings v. Pinder, 574 A.2d 843, 845 (Del. 1990)].

126 *See, e.g.*, Liberatore, 478 F. Supp. 2d at 765 (requiring intentional or reckless behavior on behalf of the diocese); Doe v. Hartz, 52 F. Supp. 2d 1027 (N.D. Iowa 1999) (requiring that a pastor intentionally or recklessly cause emotional distress); Vione v. Tewell, 820 N.Y.S.2d 682, 687 (Sup. Ct. 2006) (requiring an "intent to cause severe emotional distress"); Gibson, 952 S.W.2d at 249 (requiring the parents of a sexually abused boy to prove that the diocese either intentionally or recklessly caused severe emotional distress in order for the diocese to be susceptible to liability).

and outrageous,[127] and the defendant's conduct must cause emotional distress[128] and that distress must be severe.[129]

As noted earlier, intentional infliction of emotional distress claims have been raised against religious entities in a number of cases.[130] Such claims also have been brought against individual clergy members.[131] One of the most common factual scenarios for

[127] *See, e.g.*, Liberatore, 478 F. Supp. 2d at 765 (requiring alleged conduct to be extreme and outrageous in order to surmount a summary judgment motion on an intentional infliction of emotional distress claim); Hartz, 52 F. Supp. 2d at 1068 (finding that a pastor's unwelcomed touching and kissing of a parishioner is not the kind of behavior that meets the stringent requirements of outrageous conduct required to support a successful intentional infliction of emotional distress claim); Vione, 820 N.Y.S.2d at 687 (requiring that an intentional infliction of emotional distress alleges outrageous "conduct that exceeds the bounds of decency tolerable in civilized society"); Gibson, 952 S.W.2d at 249 (requiring conduct that is so outrageous in nature that it exceeds any bound of decency); Guinn, 775 P.2d at 783 {recognizing that the tort of intentional infliction of emotional distress requires a court to consider "the 'extreme' and 'outrageous' nature of the parties' conduct" [citing Eddy v. Brown, 715 P.2d 74, 77–8 (Okla. 1986)]}; Nally v. Grace Cmty. Church, 763 P.2d 948 (Cal. 1988) {requiring conduct that exceeds what is "usually tolerated in a civilized community" [quoting Davidson v. City of Westminster, 649 P.2d 894 (Cal. 1982)]}; Borchers v. Hrychuk, 727 A.2d 388 (Md. Ct. Spec. App. 1999) (discussing the extreme and outrageous conduct requirement for a successful intentional infliction of emotional distress claim arising from the sexual misconduct of a pastor during marriage counseling); Checkley v. Boyd, 107 P.3d 651, 660 (Or. Ct. App. 2005) {requiring that an intentional infliction of emotional distress claimant allege conduct that is "extraordinarily beyond the bounds of socially tolerable behavior" [citing McGanty v. Staudenraus, 901 P.2d 841 (Or. 1995)]}; DeCorso v. Watchtower Bible & Tract Soc'y of N.Y., Inc., 829 A.2d 38 (Conn. App. Ct. 2003) (discussing the spectrum of behavior that can and cannot satisfy the extreme and outrageous conduct requirement of an intentional infliction of emotional distress claim against a religious organization); Amato, 679 N.E.2d at 455 {finding a successfully pled intentional infliction of emotional distress claim against a pastor for his tortious abuse of power as a marriage counselor; conduct constituted extreme and outrageous behavior [citing Kolegas v. Heftel Broad. Corp., 607 N.E.2d 201, 212 (Ill. 1992)]}; Frith v. Shupp, 2002 WL 1981382 (Tex. App. 2002) (finding that a pastor's mere encouragement of a parishioner to dismiss her pending lawsuit against the church was not the type of outrageous conduct required to sustain an intentional infliction of emotional distress claim).

[128] *See, e.g.*, Liberatore, 478 F. Supp. 2d at 765 (requiring the diocese's behavior to cause emotional distress to surmount a summary judgment motion on an intentional infliction of emotional distress claim); Checkley, 107 P.3d at 660 (requiring proof that a religious congregation intended to cause the "plaintiff severe emotional distress or knew with substantial certainty that their conduct would cause such distress"); DeCorso, 829 A.2d at 42–3 (calling for causation to be averred by a claimant of intentional infliction of emotional distress).

[129] *See, e.g.*, Liberatore, 478 F. Supp. 2d at 765 (requiring that the diocese's intentionally outrageous behavior cause the parishioner to suffer severe emotional distress); Vione, 820 N.Y.S.2d at 687 (requiring severe emotional distress to be alleged for any intentional infliction of emotional distress claim); Gibson, 952 S.W.2d at 249 (requiring a parishioner to suffer severe emotional distress before the court will permit recovery from an religious institution pursuant to an intentional infliction of emotional distress claim); Nally, 763 P.2d at 961 (requiring claimant of an intentional infliction of emotional distress to allege that he or she suffered severe emotional distress).

[130] *See, e.g.*, Roman Catholic Diocese of Jackson v. Morrison, 905 So. 2d 1213 (Miss. 2005) (holding that a mother and her three children were not jurisdictionally barred from bringing their intentional infliction of emotional distress claims against the Roman Catholic Diocese arising from its priest's sexual abuse of children); Conley v. Roman Catholic Archbishop of S.F., 102 Cal. Rptr. 2d 679 (Cal. Ct. App. 2000) (discussing a former priest's intentional infliction of emotional distress claim against a religious institution for its retaliatory actions); Faieta v. World Harvest Church, 891 N.E.2d 370 (Ohio Com. Pl. 2008) (discussing a claim for intentional infliction of emotional distress against a church arising from its teacher's physical abuse of a child), *aff'd*, 2008 WL 5423454 (Ohio Ct. App. 2008).

[131] *See, e.g.*, Walker v. Dickerman, 993 F. Supp. 101 (D. Conn. 1997) (holding minister liable for an intentional infliction of emotional distress arising from his sexual abuse of a parishioner as a minor); Sanders

such claims is sexual abuse by clergy or other employees of a religious entity.[132] Such conduct by itself generally will not make the religious entity liable for intentional infliction of emotional distress.[133] Rather, cases where religious entities have been held liable for intentional infliction of emotional distress have involved attempts by religious entities to cover up the conduct,[134] the movement of known clergy sexual offenders from one church to another where the offender may have contact with those in the offender's target group(s),[135] threats by religious entities toward victims or their families to keep quiet about the conduct,[136] or gross intentional disregard for the safety

v. Casa View Baptist Church, 898 F. Supp. 1169 (N.D. Tex. 1995) (holding that church employees had a viable intentional infliction of emotional distress claim against a minister for his sexual misconduct with coworkers); Swanson v. Roman Catholic Bishop of Portland, 692 A.2d 441 (Me. 1997) (recognizing an intentional infliction of emotional distress claim against a priest for his acts of sexual misconduct during marriage counseling and his subsequent attempts to bestow false confidences on the counselee's husband); Vione, 820 N.Y.S.2d at 688 (dismissing a parishioner's intentional infliction of emotional distress claim against his former minister who engaged the parishioner's wife in a sexual relationship while acting as couple's marriage counselor); Amato, 679 N.E.2d at 455 (recognizing an intentional infliction of emotional distress claim against a pastor for his sexual misconduct).

132 *See, e.g.*, Sanders, 898 F. Supp. at 1178, 1181 (holding that the sexual misconduct of a church's clergy, without more, cannot suffice to sustain an intentional infliction of emotional distress claim against the church); Destefano v. Grabrian, 763 P.2d 275 (Colo. 1988) (discussing claims of intentional infliction of emotional distress against a religious institution and its members arising from clergy sexual misconduct); Borchers, 727 A.2d at 392 (affirming the dismissal of a congregant's intentional infliction of emotional distress claim against a church arising from its pastor's alleged sexual misconduct during marriage counseling).

133 *See, e.g.*, Liberatore, 478 F. Supp. 2d at 758 (holding that acts of sexual abuse by clergy are inherently outrageous and thus are outside the scope of employment. Accordingly, the priest's employer, a religious institution, will not be held vicariously liable for such conduct.); Gibson, 952 S.W.2d at 249 (dismissing an intentional infliction of emotional distress claim against the diocese arising from a clergy member's sexual misconduct with a minor child); Vione, 820 N.Y.S.2d at 687 (finding a minister's sexual misconduct with the congregants who attended his marriage counseling session insufficient to sustain an intentional infliction of emotional distress claim against the religious institution).

134 *See, e.g.*, Bouchard v. New York Archdiocese, 2006 WL 1375232 (S.D.N.Y. 2006) (refusing to dismiss a congregant's intentional infliction of emotional distress claim against the church arising from the church's alleged active concealment of its clergy's sexual misconduct); Gallas v. Greek Orthodox Archdiocese, 587 N.Y.S.2d 82, 86 (Sup. Ct. 1991) (finding that a religious organization's attempted "cover-up" of its clergy's sexual misconduct was sufficient to subject the organization to liability; the claim, however, was dismissed on statutory grounds.); Faieta, 891 N.E.2d at 404 (discussing a religious organization's attempts to cover up incidents of child abuse within its day-care system by "espousing and circulating a manufactured claim of rashes among [day-care] ... students to end any further inquiries into the incident").

135 *See, e.g.*, Bonson v. Diocese of Altoona-Johnstown, 67 Pa. D. & C.4th 419, 438–9 (Pa. Com. Pl. 2004) (finding a viable intentional infliction of emotional distress claim against diocesan defendants that knowingly concealed information concerning its priests' "predatory sexual impulses toward children and adolescents" while permitting, and in fact encouraging, children to be in "close proximity to the [dangerous] priests"); Burns v. First Congregational Church of Vernon, 2000 WL 1337671, at *5 (Conn. Super. Ct. 2000) (finding a viable intentional infliction of emotional distress claim when church knowingly failed to monitor a sexually deviant priest while permitting him access to locations "where he presented a danger-without-warning to prey" on children); Gagne v. O'Donoghue, 1996 WL 1185145 (Mass. Super. 1996) (implying that a diocese may be amenable to liability for the sexual misconduct of its clergy if it failed to act on information tending to show that it had knowledge of past instances of sexual misconduct by its perpetrating clergy).

136 *See, e.g.*, McKelvey v. Pierce, 800 A.2d 840 (N.J. 2002) (finding a seminary student's claim of harassment and sexual abuse by his mentors was a sufficient basis for his intentional infliction of emotional distress

of victims in light of knowledge held by the religious entity.[137] Even under these circumstances, some courts will not recognize claims against the religious entity itself because the sexual conduct was engaged in by the clergy member[138] and/or because decisions regarding clergy placement and discipline are internal church matters protected by the First Amendment.[139]

It is essential to reinforce that even though churches have been found liable for intentional infliction of emotional distress, intentional infliction of emotional distress is an intentional tort, and therefore they have been found directly liable rather than vicariously liable.[140] Religious entities are liable because of their own conduct that

claim against the diocese); Vione, 820 N.Y.S.2d at 687 (dismissing a parishioner's intentional infliction of emotional distress claim against a religious institution that discouraged the parishioner from filing a grievance against a priest who was engaged in an adulterous affair with the parishioner's wife); Faieta, 891 N.E.2d at 404 (discussing the threats a religious organization made toward the family of a physically abused minor).

137 *See, e.g.*, Doe v. Hartz, 52 F. Supp. 2d 1027, 1077 (N.D. Iowa 1999) (finding that a church may be vicariously liable for its priest's acts of sexual abuse if the church had knowledge of the priest's past misconduct, making the presently alleged sexual misconduct "a realistic threat"); Roman Catholic Diocese of Jackson v. Morrison, 905 So. 2d 1213, 1222 (Miss. 2005) (stating that a religious institution is amenable to liability if it knowingly failed to take "reasonable steps to protect" children susceptible to molestation); Osborne v. Payne, 31 S.W.3d 911 (Ky. 2000) (requiring that a diocese have knowledge of its perpetrating priest's history of sexually deviancy before the court would sustain an intentional infliction of emotional distress claim against the diocese).

138 *See, e.g.*, Bryan R. v. Watchtower Bible & Tract Soc'y of N.Y., Inc., 738 A.2d 839, 848 (Me. 1999) (dismissing an intentional infliction of emotional distress claim against the church arising from instances of sexual abuse by its clergy); Gibson, 952 S.W.2d at 249 (dismissing parents' intentional infliction of emotional distress claim against diocese arising from its priest's sexual assault of the plaintiffs' son); Vione, 820 N.Y.S.2d at 687–8 (dismissing an intentional infliction of emotional distress claim against the religious institution arising from the sexual misconduct of its clergy).

139 *See, e.g.*, Ayon v. Gourley, 47 F. Supp. 2d 1246 (D. Colo. 1998) (holding that the subject matter of certain claims against an archdiocese for outrageous conduct would require the court to delve into constitutionally protected church policies and doctrines); Bryan R., 738 A.2d at 848 (holding that intrachurch discipline for clergy sexual misconduct is an ecclesiastical issue and that subjecting a church to tort liability for such matters "would insert the State into matters … wholly forbidden by the Free Exercise Clause of the First Amendment"); Olson v. First Church of Nazarene, 661 N.W.2d 254 (Minn. Ct. App. 2003) (finding that information pertinent to a church's termination of its minister is inherently ecclesiastical and may not be the basis for an intentional infliction of emotional distress claim).

140 *See, e.g.*, Schovanec v. Archdiocese of Oklahoma City, 188 P.3d 158 (Okla. 2008) (finding that the archdiocese was not vicariously liable for the sexual misconduct of its priest); Morrison, 905 So. 2d at 1241 ("Churches and religious institutions are not traditional employers such that vicarious liability, through the doctrine of *respondeat superior*, exists as a matter of law, in all cases."); Gray v. Ward, 950 S.W.2d 232, 234 (Mo. 1997) ("Intentional sexual activity and intentional infliction of emotional distress do not fall within the scope of employment of a priest, and [thus] the Diocese cannot be held [vicariously] liable."); Destefano v. Grabrian, 763 P.2d 275, 287 (Colo. 1988) ("A priest's violation of his vow of celibacy is contrary to the instructions and doctrines of the Catholic church. When a priest has sexual intercourse with a parishioner it is [neither] part of the priest's duties nor customary within the business of the church. Such conduct is contrary to the principles of Catholicism"; accordingly, the religious institution, without more, cannot be held vicariously liable for such conduct.); Amato v. Greenquist, 679 N.E.2d 446 (Ill. App. Ct. 1997) (finding that a religious institution cannot be held vicariously liable for its pastor's self-serving actions that consequently inflicted emotional distress).

enabled,[141] covered up,[142] ratified,[143] or furthered the conduct of the individual clergy member[144] or because of the entity's own actions toward the victim.[145] It is the religious entity's outrageous conduct that gives rise to successful claims against the entity in jurisdictions that allow intentional infliction of emotional distress claims against religious entities.[146]

141 *See, e.g.*, O'Bryan v. Holy See, 556 F.3d 361 (6th Cir. 2009) (finding a viable intentional infliction of emotional distress claim against the Holy See arising from its employees' surreptitious supervision of known sexually deviant clergy, supervisory conduct that was pursuant to the Holy See's policy and in violation of international law), *petition for cert. filed*, 77 U.S.L.W. 3645 (U.S. May 7, 2009) (No. 08-1384); John Doe CS v. Capuchin Franciscan Friars, 520 F. Supp. 2d 1124 (E.D. Mo. 2007) (finding a viable intentional infliction of emotional distress claim against a religious organization that knowingly failed to alleviate the risk posed by its sexually deviant clergy); Bonson v. Diocese of Altoona-Johnstown, 67 Pa. D. & C.4th 419 (Pa. Com. Pl. 2004) (finding a diocese amenable to liability for intentional infliction of emotional distress arising from its encouragement of parents to allow their children within a close proximity of dangerous priests).

142 *See, e.g.*, Bouchard v. New York Archdiocese, 2006 WL 1375232 (S.D.N.Y. 2006) (refusing to dismiss a congregant's intentional infliction of emotional distress claim against the church to the extent that she alleged it knowingly concealed its clergy members' sexual misconduct); Doe v. Corporation of President of Church of Jesus Christ of Latter-Day Saints, 167 P.3d 1193 (Wash. Ct. App. 2007) (discussing a religious institution's liablility when its clergy actively discouraged a sexual abuse victim from reporting the sexual abuse of her father, who was also a member of the institution's clergy); Faieta v. World Harvest Church, 891 N.E.2d 370 (Ohio Com. Pl. 2008) (finding that a church was liable for intentional infliction of emotional distress arising from its attempts to cover up incidents of child abuse), *aff'd*, 2008 WL 5423454 (Ohio Ct. App. 2008).

143 *See, e.g.*, Capuchin Franciscan Friars, 520 F. Supp. 2d at 1127 (finding that a religious organization ratified its clergy's sexual misconduct when it knowingly failed to report such misconduct to the proper authorities); Sanders v. Casa View Baptist Church, 898 F. Supp. 1169 (N.D. Tex. 1995) (recognizing that a religious institution is amenable to suit for intentional infliction of emotional distress if it ratifies the tortious behavior of its clergy); Checkley v. Boyd, 107 P.3d 651 (Or. Ct. App. 2005) (requiring that a congregation ratify or consent to its clergy's tortious behavior before it can be held vicariously liable for the resulting emotional distress).

144 *See, e.g.*, Doe 1 *ex rel.* Doe 1 v. Roman Catholic Diocese of Nashville, 154 S.W.3d 22 (Tenn. 2005) (stating that a diocese's knowing failure to implement sufficient restrictions on a sexually deviant priest, which consequently allowed him access to children, is a factual question that merits reversing the trial court's summary disposition of an intentional infliction of emotional distress claim against the diocese); McKelvey v. Pierce, 800 A.2d 840 (N.J. 2002) (finding that a seminary student successfully pled a cause of action for intentional infliction of emotional distress against the diocese. The student alleged that the diocese provided an atmosphere that fostered and encouraged homosexual misconduct by its clergy.); Bonson, 67 Pa. D. & C.4th at 438 (finding a viable intentional infliction of emotional distress claim against the diocese that knowingly facilitated its sexually deviant clergy's access to vulnerable children).

145 *See, e.g.*, Guinn v. Church of Christ of Collinsville, 775 P.2d 766 (Okla. 1989) (holding church elders liable for their continued verbal attacks on a former parishioner); Bryan R. v. Watchtower Bible & Tract Soc'y of N.Y., Inc., 738 A.2d 839, 848 (Me. 1999) (implying that only a religious institution's extreme and outrageous conduct may be the basis for a viable intentional infliction of emotional distress claim against that institution); Meroni v. Holy Spirit Ass'n for the Unification of World Christianity, 506 N.Y.S.2d 174, 176 (N.Y. App. Div. 1986) ("[A] church may be held liable for intentional tortious conduct on behalf of its officers or members, even if that conduct is carried out as part of the church's religious practices."); Erickson v. Christenson, 781 P.2d 383, 387 (Or. Ct. App. 1989) (discussing a religious institution's conduct when it repeatedly required a sexually abused parishioner to confront her abuser before the institution would remove him from office).

146 *See, e.g.*, Capuchin Franciscan Friars, 520 F. Supp. 2d at 1127 (recognizing an intentional infliction of emotional distress claim against a religious order that knowingly permitted a sexually deviant

There are circumstances other than clergy abuse that have given rise to successful intentional infliction of emotional distress claims against religious entities,[147] but like the clergy abuse cases, it is the conduct of the entity that gives rise to institutional liability.[148] These cases include situations where former congregants are targeted by a religious entity for retaliatory or other outrageous speech or conduct that causes the required harm.[149] Additionally, there have been a few cases involving action toward current congregants,[150] clergy,[151] or other employees.[152] Otherwise, liability for

clergy member access to students); Franco v. Church of Jesus Christ of Latter-day Saints, 21 P.3d 198 (Utah 2001) (discussing the spectrum of behavior that may or may not constitute a successful claim for intentional infliction of emotional distress against a religious organization); Tucker v. Roman Catholic of Lafayette-In-Ind., 837 N.E.2d 596 (Ind. Ct. App. 2006) (dismissing a parishioner's intentional infliction of emotional distress claim against the church arising from instances of sexual abuse by parishioner's religious teacher; none of the evidence suggested the diocese intentionally caused parishioner harm.).

147 *See, e.g.*, Guinn, 775 P.2d at 782 (discussing institutional liability for intentional infliction of emotional distress arising from a church's denunciation of former congregant); Conley v. Roman Catholic Archbishop of S.F., 102 Cal. Rptr. 2d 679 (Cal. Ct. App. 2000) (discussing a priest's intentional infliction of emotional distress claim arising from the sanctions levied by his employer).

148 *See, e.g.*, Tucker, 837 N.E.2d at 603 (requiring the diocese to have intentionally caused emotional distress before it can be held liable for the sexual misconduct of its employees); Conley, 102 Cal. Rptr. 2d at 683 (finding that a religious organization is amenable to liability for intentional infliction of emotional distress based on its retaliation against clergy who reported child abuse within the church); Petrell v. Rakoczy, 2005 WL 1683600 (Mass. Super. 2005) (finding a parishioner's distress from her consensual sexual relationship with a priest was insufficient to sustain an intentional infliction of emotional distress claim against diocesan defendants).

149 *See, e.g.*, Poindexter v. Armstrong, 934 F. Supp. 1052 (W.D. Ark. 1994) (suggesting that a religious organization would be amenable to liability for intentional infliction of emotional distress if it attempted to forcefully subject former congregants to its religious teachings); Guinn, 775 P.2d at 783 (discussing institutional liability for intentional infliction of emotional distress arising from the church's denunciation of former congregant); Smith v. Tilton, 3 S.W.3d 77 (Tex. App. 1999) (finding that a religious institution's tortious statements to the widow of a former congregant could subject the organization to liability for intentional infliction of emotion distress if the statements were not based on religious beliefs. The court, however, dismissed the claim on procedural grounds).

150 *See, e.g.*, Gulbraa v. Corporation of the President of the Church of Jesus Christ of Latter-Day Saints, 159 P.3d 392 (Utah Ct. App. 2007) (holding that a church is amenable to liability for intentional infliction of emotional distress if it concealed the location of a congregant's abducted children); Doe v. Corporation of President of Church of Jesus Christ of Latter-Day Saints, 167 P.3d 1193 (Wash. Ct. App. 2007) (discussing an intentional infliction of emotional distress claim against a church arising from its clergy's attempts to discourage a parishioner from reporting her stepfather's sexual abuse); Wood *ex rel.* Wood v. Berean Baptist Church, 1997 WL 33343376 (Mich. Ct. App. 1997) (finding a viable intentional infliction of emotional distress claim against a church arising from an incident in which its employees confined a vacation Bible school student to a curtained area where they verbally intimidated the student).

151 *See, e.g.*, Ogle v. Hocker, 2008 WL 2224863 (6th Cir. 2008) (discussing a bishop's intentional infliction of emotional distress claim against another bishop for the latter's dissemination of false rumors regarding the former's sexual preferences); Conley, 102 Cal. Rptr. 2d at 683 (recognizing a pastor's intentional infliction of emotional distress claim against diocese based on its retaliation against the pastor for his attempts to report child abuse pursuant to California's Child Abuse and Neglect Reporting Act); Callahan v. First Congregational Church of Haverhill, 2001 WL 1839719 (Mass. Super. 2001) (finding a viable intentional infliction of emotional distress claim against church arising from its attempts to destroy an interim pastor's reputation while simultaneously eliminating his future employment opportunities).

152 *See, e.g.*, Madsen v. Erwin, 481 N.E.2d 1160 (Mass. 1985) (dismissing a former employee's intentional infliction of emotional distress claim against the church that terminated her employment based solely

intentional infliction of emotional distress only falls on the individual(s) who commit the outrageous conduct.[153]

### 5. *Trespass to Land*

In most jurisdictions, the tort of trespass requires that a defendant intentionally and physically invade another's real property without authorization.[154] The relevant intent for the tort of trespass to land is simply the intent to enter the property.[155] Therefore, even if an individual mistakenly believes that he or she has a right to enter the property, the requirements of the tort may be met.[156]

on her homosexual preferences); Davis v. Black, 591 N.E.2d 11 (Ohio Ct. App. 1991) (finding that a secretary had a viable claim against the church that terminated her employment after she filed a sexual harassment complaint against the church's rector); Craddock v. Church Cmty. Supported Living Ass'n, 2000 WL 33159150 (Conn. Super. 2000) (finding that the disparity of treatment between certain employees by the religious institution was a basis for an intentional infliction of emotional distress claim).

153 *See, e.g.*, Walker v. Dickerman, 993 F. Supp. 101 (D. Conn. 1997) (finding a minister liable for intentional infliction of emotional distress arising from minister's sexual abuse of a minor); Amato v. Greenquist, 679 N.E.2d 446 (Ill. App. Ct. 1997) (holding a pastor, not the religious institution, liable for intentional infliction of emotional distress); Erickson v. Christenson, 781 P.2d 383 (Or. Ct. App. 1989) (stating that the nature of a priest's relationship with his sexual abuse victims was essential for the court's determination of liability for intentional infliction of emotional distress); Collins v. African Methodist Episcopal Zion Church, 2006 WL 1579718 (Del. Super. Ct. 2006) (finding a viable intentional infliction of emotional distress claim against a pastor who repeatedly made sexually harassing and intimidating statements to a congregant).

154 *See, e.g.*, Church of Christ in Hollywood v. Superior Court of L.A., 121 Cal. Rptr. 2d 810, 815 (Cal. Ct. App. 2002) ("The essence of the cause of action for trespass is an 'unauthorized entry' onto the land of another."); Burt v. Beautiful Savior Lutheran Church of Broomfield, 809 P.2d 1064, 1067 (Colo. App. 1990) ("[T]respass is the physical intrusion upon property of another without the permission of the person lawfully entitled to the possession of the real estate."); Capitol View Cmty. Church v. Achor Ctr., Inc., 571 S.E.2d 181, 181–84 (Ga. Ct. App. 2002) (finding that "[t]he trial court did not err in granting summary judgment and entering [a] permanent injunction" when a reverend and his congregation repeatedly entered on the property of a homeless shelter, formerly a church, after such entering was forbade numerous times); Keck v. Woodring, 208 P.2d 1133, 1135 (Okla. 1948) (holding that a plaintiff, seeking damages for injuries suffered while on defendant's property, was a trespasser because plaintiff entered on defendant's land without express or implied invitation).

155 *See, e.g.*, Connecticut v. Steinmann, 569 A.2d 557, 559 (Conn. App. Ct. 1990) (holding that trespass "requires knowledge on the part of the accused that he is entering without license or privilege"); St. Paul Church, Inc. v. Bd. of Trs. of the Alaska Missionary Conference of the United Methodist Church, Inc., 145 P.3d 541, 558 (Alaska 2006) ("An intentional entry onto the land of another constitutes intentional trespass even if the trespasser believes that he or she has the right to be on the land."); Cockrell v. Pleasant Valley Baptist Church, 762 S.W.2d 879, 881 (Mo. Ct. App. 1989) (finding that the defendant church was liable for trespass when it "mistakenly but intentionally entered her property").

156 *See, e.g.*, Cockrell, 762 S.W.2d at 881 ("A party may be liable in trespass if he [or she] intends to do the act which results in the damage, although in so doing he [or she] did not intend to commit an act of trespass. The party may not even know that his [or her] act will constitute a trespass, and may act in good faith and through honest mistake."); Burt, 809 P.2d at 1067 ("[L]iability for trespass requires only an intent to do the act that itself constitutes, or inevitably causes, the intrusion."); Church of Christ, 121 Cal. Rptr. 2d at 815 (holding that it is the intentional invasion of another's property, not the underlying motivation, that constitutes a trespass).

The property of religious entities can be subject to actionable trespass, just as other private property can.[157] Thus religious entities can bring claims for trespass.[158] Moreover, categories such as invitee and licensee can be applied in the context of religious entities by jurisdictions that use such categories.[159] A key point, of course, is that the religious entity may have religious grounds for considering someone an invitee or licensee, and courts generally will defer to such determinations so as not to violate the Free Exercise Clause or the Establishment Clause.[160] Indeed, this is the unique question that arises in trespass involving religious entities. Who is entitled to be on the property, and what role does religious doctrine play in that determination?[161]

157 *See, e.g.*, Church of Christ, 121 Cal. Rptr. 2d at 812 ("We conclude that the church, like any nonsectarian property owner, may decide whom to allow on its premises."); St. Paul Church, Inc., 145 P.3d at 553 (adopting a "neutral-principles approach when resolving property disputes between religious organizations"); Decker v. Tschetter Hutterian Brethren, Inc., 594 N.W.2d 357, 364 (S.D. 1999) (holding that "[s]ecular courts will adjudicate disputes under the 'neutral principles of law' doctrine," meaning disputes should be determined under common property-law principles).

158 *See* Church of Christ of Long Beach v. Harper, 256 P. 476, 478 (Cal. Dist. Ct. App. 1927) ("The jurisdiction of a civil court to adjudge any ecclesiastical matter must result as a mere incident to the determination of some property right."); Church of Christ, 121 Cal. Rptr. 2d at 812 ("We conclude that the church, like any nonsectarian property owner, may decide whom to allow on its premises.").

159 *See, e.g.*, Keck, 208 P.2d at 1135 (stating that the plaintiff may not recover for damages sustained on trespassed property "even though he may have been an invitee or at the least licensee to other parts of the premises"); Frye v. Trs. of the Rumbletown Free Methodist Church, 657 N.E.2d 745, 747 (Ind. Ct. App. 1995) (characterizing the sole issue presented on appeal as to whether the individual "was an invitee, a licensee, or a trespasser when he entered the premises of the church parsonage"); Hambright v. First Baptist Church-Eastwood, 638 So. 2d 865, 867 (Ala. 1994) (refusing to depart from current standard of "classifying visitors as invitees, licensees, or trespassers for determining what duty the landowner may owe in a particular circumstance" when a member injured herself while attending church).

160 *See, e.g.*, Stitt v. Holland Abundant Life Fellowship, 614 N.W.2d 88, 96 (Mich. 2000) (holding that an individual attending church for religious services is a licensee and not an invitee because religious services do not contain a commercial purpose); Hambright, 638 So.2d at 868 (holding the plaintiff to be a licensee, rather than an invitee, under the definition that a licensee is one who enters another's property with consent but no business purpose); Frye, 657 N.E.2d at 750 (finding the plaintiff to be a licensee "with a privilege implied by custom" to enter church property).

161 *See* Presbyterian Church in U.S. v. Mary Elizabeth Blue Hull Mem'l Presbyterian Church 393 U.S. 440 (1969). The Court stated

> [T]he First Amendment severely circumscribes the role that civil courts may play in resolving church property disputes. It is obvious, however, that not every civil court decision as to property claimed by a religious organization jeopardizes values protected by the First Amendment. Civil courts do not inhibit free exercise of religion merely by opening their doors to disputes involving church property. And there are neutral principles of law, developed for use in all property disputes, which can be applied without 'establishing' churches to which property is awarded. But First Amendment values are plainly jeopardized when church property litigation is made to turn on the resolution by civil courts of controversies over religious doctrine and practice. If civil courts undertake to resolve such controversies in order to adjudicate the property dispute, the hazards are ever present of inhibiting the free development of religious doctrine and of implicating secular interests in matters of purely ecclesiastical concern. Because of these hazards, the First Amendment enjoins the employment of organs of government for essentially religious purposes. … [T]he Amendment therefore commands civil courts to decide church property disputes without resolving underlying controversies over religious doctrine.

*Id.* at 449. *See also* Hambright, 638 So.2d at 868 ("We have held that a person attending a church service is a licensee on the church premises."); De Mello v. St. Thomas the Apostle Church Corp. of Warren, 165 A.2d 500, 504 (R.I. 1960) (finding plaintiff to be an invitee on entering church premises for the purpose of voluntarily helping with a supper designed to raise funds for church); Coolbaugh v. St. Peter's

An area where these issues have been particularly dicey is where a church schism has taken place, and two or more different factions dispute the right to occupy the property.[162] In these cases, trespass claims may be brought against members of the competing faction who seek to enter or use the property.[163] Claims also have been brought by and against clergy members who have the support of one faction.[164]

These claims generally are handled under the principles governing church property disputes and schisms discussed in Chapter 8.[165] Thus the key question is whether the court must determine ecclesiastical questions to decide the matter.[166] If so, courts generally will not hear the claim.[167] If not, courts generally will decide the claim based on

Roman Catholic Church, 115 A.2d 662, 664 (Conn. 1955) (holding plaintiff not to be an invitee because entrance on church property to light a candle for daughter who was having a baby amounted to benefit for plaintiff and not church).

162 *See, e.g.*, Mary Elizabeth Blue Hull Mem'l Presbyterian Church, 393 U.S. at 449 (holding that "the [First] Amendment therefore commands civil courts to decide church property disputes without resolving underlying controversies over religious doctrine" during property dispute between two local churches that broke away from its larger, general church); Capitol View Cmty. Church, 571 S.E.2d at 181–4 (finding an expelled reverend and his congregation to be trespassers on the premises of former church that subsequently was sold to a homeless shelter); Jones v. Wolf, 443 U.S. 595, 597 (1979) (stating that in a case where a local congregation voted to disassociate from the national church, "[t]he question for decision is whether civil courts, consistent with the First and Fourteenth Amendments to the Constitution, may resolve the dispute on the basis of 'neutral principles of law,' or whether they must defer to the resolution of an authoritative tribunal of the hierarchical church"); Bishop & Diocese of Colo. v. Mote, 716 P.2d 85, 96 (Colo. 1986) (discussing the benefits and detriments of both the "neutral principles" and "polity" approaches to resolving property disputes among churches and ultimately adopting the "neutral principles" approach because of its unlikelihood for violating the First Amendment).

163 *See, e.g.*, Mary Elizabeth Blue Hull Mem'l Presbyterian Church, 393 U.S. at 441–4 (discussing national church's claim of trespass and property ownership against two local churches that disassociated from the national church); Wolf, 443 U.S. at 597 (discussing the resolution of nearly two-thirds of a church's members, including the pastor, to disassociate from its national, hierarchical church); Bennett v. Morgan, 66 S.W. 287, 288 (Ky. 1902) (discussing the dispute between a dissenting minority of church members with the doctrinal beliefs of the majority, including the majority's breaking into the church with an axe and subsequently changing the locks to prevent the minority's trespass on church premises).

164 *See, e.g.*, Bennett, 66 S.W. at 288 (case in which a majority factor, led by the pastor, sought to prevent a minority dissenting factor from trespassing on church property); Tucker v. Denson, 80 So. 373, 374 (Ala. 1918) (case in which a minority faction led by church trustees sought injunction based on claims of trespass by majority faction); Presbytery of Hudson River of Presbyterian Church v. Trustees of First Presbyterian Church & Congregation of Ridgeberry, 896 N.Y.S.2d 417, 419 (N.Y. App. Div. 2010) (case in which the majority loyal members of a church sought a declaratory judgment of a dissenting faction led by trustees).

165 *See supra* Chapter 8.

166 *ee* Mary Elizabeth Blue Hull Mem'l Presbyterian Church, 393 U.S. at 449 ("If civil courts undertake to resolve … controversies [over religious doctrine and practice] in order to adjudicate the property dispute, the hazards are ever present of inhibiting the free development of religious doctrine and of implicating secular interests in matters of purely ecclesiastical concern. … [T]he Amendment therefore commands civil courts to decide church property disputes without resolving underlying controversies over religious doctrine."); Presbytery of Riverside v. Cmty. Church of Palm Springs 152 Cal. Rptr. 854, 856, 860 (Cal. Ct. App. 2007) (upholding the rule of *Blue Hull Mem'l Presbyterian Church* in a case where the national church sought property possessed by disassociated local church); Avondale Church of Christ v. Merrill Lynch, No. E2007-02335-COA-R3-CV, 2008 WL 4853085, at *4–5 (Tenn. Ct. App. Nov. 10, 2008) (stating that courts must begin with the premise courts do not hold jurisdiction over disputes of a purely ecclesiastical nature, but "courts have exercised subject matter jurisdiction over intrachurch disputes involving civil or other property rights, as long as the resolution does not require excessive entanglement in matters of religion or church doctrine").

167 *See, e.g.*, St. John Chrysostom Greek Catholic Church v. Elko, 259 A.2d 419, 425 (Pa. 1969) (upholding the lower court's decision and jurisdiction over a church dispute because the result was "attained by

neutral principles of law[168] and/or through deference to the church hierarchy or congregational majority depending on the nature of the entity.[169] These are the mechanisms the U.S. Supreme Court has held to allow courts to address questions that might otherwise raise ecclesiastical concerns without determining ecclesiastical claims. The Court has held numerous times that civil courts may not determine ecclesiastical claims but may use the preceding mechanisms to determine the outcome in cases where these mechanisms can be used without deciding ecclesiastical questions.

Claims also have been brought by private parties against religious individuals and entities for trespass.[170] Religious entities and individuals enjoy no special right to trespass on private property[171] other than the rights that may be enjoyed by similar nonprofit organizations in some jurisdictions.[172] Where ecclesiastical questions are not raised at all, that

considering purely factual matters which relate to the kind of church [one] is … [and did not have] to consider the significance and relevance of church doctrine"); Harris v. Matthews, 643 S.E.2d 566, 570–1 (N.C. 2007) (denying jurisdiction to hear church dispute while holding that "[w]hen a congregational church's internal property dispute cannot be resolved using neutral principles of law, the courts must intrude no further and must instead defer to the decisions" of church members themselves or other local body designed specifically to determine ecclesiastical disputes); Masjid Al-Ihsaan, Inc. v. Ouda, 553 S.E.2d 331, 332–3 (Ga. Ct. App. 2001) (affirming dismissal of trespass claim because "[t]hat determination would be based on the mosque's internal procedures, which are beyond judicial review"); Gillespie v. Elkins S. Baptist Church, 350 S.E.2d 715, 718 (W. Va. 1986) ("Civil courts have generally held that they lack jurisdiction to hear and determine any controversy relating to purely ecclesiastical or spiritual practices."); Park Slope Jewish Ctr. V. Congregation B'nai Jacob, 686 N.E.2d 1330, 1332 (N.Y. 1997) (reversing lower court's dismissal of property dispute based on lack of jurisdiction and finding that property dispute could be resolved using the "neutral principles" approach).

168 *See, e.g.*, Mary Elizabeth Blue Hull Mem'l Presbyterian Church, 393 U.S. at 449 (establishing the "neutral principles" approach); Park Slope Jewish Ctr., 686 N.E.2d at 1332 (finding that property dispute could be resolved using the "neutral principles" approach); St. Paul Church, Inc., 145 P.3d at 553 (adopting a "neutral-principles approach when resolving property disputes between religious organizations"); Decker, 594 N.W.2d at 364 (holding that "[s]ecular courts will adjudicate disputes under the 'neutral principles of law' doctrine," meaning that disputes should be determined under common property-law principles); Mote, 716 P.2d at 96 (adopting the "neutral principles" approach because of its unlikelihood for violating the First Amendment).

169 *See, e.g.*, Wolf, 443 U.S. at 607 (applying a rule of majority representation in determining a property dispute among competing members of a church, believing it "would be consistent with both the neutral-principles analysis and the First Amendment"); Watson v. Jones, 80 U.S. 679, 725, 727 (1871) (stating that when a church is congregational in nature, "the rights of … [the competing groups] to the use of the property must be determined by the ordinary principles which govern voluntary associations"; however, when a church is hierarchical in nature, the court must defer to the decision of the highest tribunal of that organization); Mote, 716 P.2d at 96 (discussing the benefits and detriments of both the "neutral principles" and "polity" approaches to resolving property disputes among churches and ultimately adopting the "neutral principles" approach because of its unlikelihood for violating the First Amendment).

170 *See, e.g.*, Fairlawn Cemetery Ass'n v. First Presbyterian Church, 496 P.2d 1185, 1186–87 (Okla. 1972) (Cemetery operator sued church during construction for piling dirt against cemetery wall, which Court found to constitute a continuing trespass.); Gill v. First Christian Church, 117 S.E.2d 164, 165–6 (Ga. 1960) (Plaintiff sued church when debris and other runoff during construction entered on plaintiff's land.).

171 *See, e.g.*, Steinmann, 569 A.2d at 560 ("There is, however, no constitutional right to … 'freedom of worship' on private property where there is no license or privilege to be there.").

172 *See, e.g.*, Watchtower Bible & Tract Soc'y v. Vill. Of Stratton, 536 U.S. 150, 167–8 (2002) (holding that local law requiring solicitors to obtain a license from mayor to be a violation of the First Amendment's protection of freedom of speech as applied to Jehovah's Witnesses); Schneider v. New Jersey, 308 U.S. 147, 164 (1939) ("To require a censorship through license which makes impossible the free and unhampered distribution of pamphlets strikes at the very heart of the constitutional guarantees."). *But*

is, in garden-variety trespass cases,[173] religious property enjoys the same right to be free from trespass as other private property.[174]

## C. Negligence

Religious entities, like other entities, can and have been sued for negligence.[175] For a long time, religious entities were not subject to liability for negligence based on the doctrine of church immunity.[176] Today that doctrine no longer exists in most jurisdictions.[177] The doctrine of charitable immunity may apply to religious entities that otherwise meet the necessary requirements to fall under the doctrine,[178] but that doctrine in its current

*see* Ass'n of Cmty. Orgs. for Reform Now v. Town of East Greenwich, 453 F. Supp.2d. 394, 416 (D. R.I. 2006) (upholding a law requiring solicitors to obtain a license and abide by a curfew because the "ordinance leaves open alternative channels of communication through which … [the solicitor] can effectively communicate its message and/or solicit funds").

173 *See, e.g.*, Church of Christ, 121 Cal. Rptr. 2d at 819 (finding that the church's claim of trespass does not raise questions of religious doctrine); Fulbright v. Higginbotham, 34 S.W. 875, 877 (Mo. 1896) (finding that the claim of trespass does not require ecclesiastical questions to be answered but only who held whole title to the property in dispute).

174 *See, e.g.*, Church of Christ, 121 Cal. Rptr. 2d at 812 (Cal. Ct. App. 2002) ("We conclude that the church, like any nonsectarian property owner, may decide whom to allow on its premises.").

175 *See* Dove v. Hartz, 970 F.Supp. 1375 (N.D.Iowa 1997) (holding that negligent supervision claim brought against church in clergy sexual abuse case not barred by the First Amendment); Smith v. O'Connell, 986 F.Supp. 73 (D.R.I. 1997) (holding that the First Amendment did not bar minor's claim of sexual molestation against priest and church for negligent supervision); Bivin v. Wright 656 N.E.2d 1121, 1124–5 (Ill. 1995) (upholding husband and wife's negligent supervision claim against church for minister who engaged in sexual relationship with wife during marital counseling); Kenneth R. v. Roman Catholic Diocese of Brooklyn, 229 N.Y.S.2d 791 (N.Y. 1997) (finding that plaintiff stated a claim for negligent supervision and retention against the church in a case where plaintiff alleged that the church should have known of bishop's propensity to sexually abuse children); Catanzaro v. Central Congregational Co., Inc., 705 A.2d 533 (R.I. 1998) (holding church liable for injury to construction worker who was renovating church for failure to upkeep church property); Macedonia Baptist Church v. Gibson, 833 S.W.2d 557 (Tex. Ct. App. 1992) (upholding jury award for plaintiff injured by defective lightening rod on defendant's church building).

176 *See, e.g.*, Cook v. John N. Norton Memorial Infirmary, 202 S.W. 874 (Ky. Ct. App. 1918) (holding that the doctrine of charitable immunity precludes a charitable institution from being liable for tortious injury); Rhoda v. Aroostook General Hospital, 220 A.2d 530 (Me. 1967) (upholding doctrine of charitable immunity).

177 *See* Moses v. Dioceses of Colorado, 863 P.2d 310 (Colo. 1993) (holding that religious organizations do not have absolute immunity from tort liability); Smith v. Privette, 495 S.E.2d 395, 397 (N.C. App. 1998) (finding that the First Amendment does not grant religious organizations absolute immunity from tort liability) Kenneth R. v. Roman Catholic Diocese of Brooklyn, 229 A.D.2d 159, 165 (N.Y. 1997) (same); Strock v. Pressnell, 527 N.E.2d 1235, 1237 (Ohio 1988) {finding that the doctrine of charitable immunity has been abolished in Ohio [citing Albritton v. Neighborhood Centers Assn., 466 N.E.2d 867 (Ohio 1984)]}; Widell v. Holy Trinity Catholic Church, 121 N.W.2d 249 (Wis. 1963) (holding the old rule of church immunity no longer valid).

178 *See* Hemenway v. Presbyterian Hospital Association of Colorado, 419 P.2d 312 (Colo. 1966) (holding that the doctrine of charitable immunity precluded action against church due to hospital's negligence where plaintiff signed agreement to drop case unless court decided to overturn doctrine so that plaintiff might recover damages); Selwitz v. Temple Beth Sholom, Inc., 1940 WL 771 (Conn. Super. Ct.) (holding that the doctrine of charitable immunity still may apply to churches but not for acts of negligence); Pitcher v. Roman Catholic Bishop of Portland, 974 A.2d 286 (Me. 2009) (holding that bishop was entitled to assert charitable immunity as defense to negligent supervision claim); J. v. Victory Tabernacle Baptist Church, 372 S.E.2d 391 (Va. 1988) (holding that the charitable immunity of religious institutions holds except to the independent tort of negligent hiring).

form in most jurisdictions does not preclude liability for negligence claims.[179] Of course, the First Amendment may provide a defense in some contexts.[180]

This section is separated into four subsections. The first will address what may be termed "garden-variety negligence claims." These are negligence claims brought by or against religious entities and/or individuals in which the religious nature of the party makes no difference in the analysis of the claim and does not raise Free Exercise Clause or Establishment Clause questions.[181] The most obvious examples are cases involving automobiles.[182] The second and third subsections focus on claims where the religious nature of a party makes a difference or provides a potential defense to the claim. The most obvious examples are cases involving negligent hiring or supervision of clergy members or other employees.[183] The final subsection addresses vicarious liability.

179 *See* Mallow v. Fong, 232 P.2d 241 (Cal. 1951) (holding that the doctrine of charitable immunity does not apply to negligence claims); Sugrue v. St. Francis Xavier Church Corp., 1939 WL 905 (Conn. C.P.) (holding that the doctrine of charitable immunity does not preclude an action against the church for negligence or nuisance); Selwitz v. Temple Beth Sholom, Inc., 1940 WL 771 (Conn. Super. Ct.) (holding that the doctrine of charitable immunity did not apply where plaintiff was injured after paying consideration to attend a book club held on defendant's premises); Wilson v. Evangelical Lutheran Church of Reformation of Milwaukee, 230 N.W. 708 (Wis. 1930) (holding that the doctrine of charitable immunity will not preclude plaintiff from bringing negligence action against church for injuries sustained after falling down an unlit hallway in the church building).

180 *See, e.g.*, Ehrens v. The Lutheran Church-Missouri Synod, 26 F.Supp.2d 328 (S.D.N.Y. 2003) (holding that the First Amendment prevented court from determining whether authorities negligently supervised pastor); Isley v. Capuchin Province, 880 F.Supp. 1138 (E.D. Mich. 1995) (finding that the Establishment Clause barred negligent hiring claim); Swanson v. Roman Catholic Bishop of Portland, 692 A.2d 441 (Me. 1997) (holding that the First Amendment barred plaintiff's claim of negligent supervision against the Catholic Church).

181 *See* Dove v. Hartz, 970 F.Supp. 1375 (N.D.Iowa 1997) (holding that a negligent supervision claim brought against church in clergy sexual abuse case was not barred by the First Amendment); Smith v. O'Connell, 986 F.Supp. 73 (D.R.I. 1997) (holding that the First Amendment does not bar minor's claim of sexual molestation against priest and church for negligent supervision); Moses v. Diocese of Colorado 863 P.2d 310 (Colo. 1993) (holding that the First Amendment does not bar parishioner's claims against diocese and bishop for negligent hiring and supervision); Bivin v. Wright 656 N.E.2d 1121, 1124–25 (Ill. 1995) (finding that a negligent supervision claim brought by husband and wife against church is not barred by the First Amendment); Kenneth R. v. Roman Catholic Diocese of Brooklyn, 229 N.Y.S.2d 791 (N.Y. 1997) (finding that plaintiff's claim for negligent supervision and retention is not barred by the First Amendment); Catanzaro v. Central Congregational Co., Inc., 705 A.2d 533 (R.I. 1998) (holding a church liable for injury to a construction worker who was renovating church for failure to upkeep church property); Pleasant Glade Assembly of God v. Schubert, 174 S.W.3d 388 (Tex. Ct. App. 2005) (finding that the First Amendment does not preclude plaintiff's claims for assault, battery, and false imprisonment against church, pastors, and several church members) Carjow, LLC v. Simmons, 563 S.E.2d 359 (S.C. Ct. App. 2002) (holding that the purchaser of church property could bring claim for conversion of church pews that were removed by former pastor); Bowie v. Murphy, 624 S.E.2d 74 (Va. 2006) (holding that the First Amendment does not bar deacon's defamation claim against church).

182 *See, e.g.*, Essick v. Barksdale, 882 F.Supp. 365 (D.De. 1995) (holding defendant church's insurance carrier liable for injuries caused to plaintiff when church's employee caused car accident); Abrosio v. Prince, 495 F.Supp. 381 (D. Neb. 1979) (granting summary judgment for plaintiff in car accident case against defendant clergy but not against his employer); Malloy v. Fong, 232 P.2d 241 (Cal. 1951) (holding that charitable immunity does not preclude negligence suit against pastor and agent of church).

183 *See* Dove v. Hartz, 970 F.Supp. 1375 (N.D.Iowa 1997) (holding that negligent supervision claim brought against church in clergy sexual abuse case is not barred by the First Amendment); Smith v. O'Connell, 986 F.Supp. 73 (D.R.I. 1997) (holding that the First Amendment does not bar minor's claim of sexual molestation against priest and church for negligent supervision); Iglesia Cristiana La Casa Del Senor, Inc. v. L.M., 783 So.2d 353 (Fla. Dist. Ct. App. 2001) (finding that church is not liable on theory of

### 1. *Garden-Variety Negligence Claims*

Religious entities and individuals, like others, are subject to liability[184] and may sue for damages due to negligence.[185] Under tort law there are numerous negligence concepts, such as negligence per se,[186] *res ipsa loquitur*,[187] contributory negligence,[188] comparative

vicarious liability or negligent supervision for sexual assault by pastor); Bull Street Church of Christ v. Jensen, 504 S.E.2d 1 (Ga. Ct. App. 1998) (holding for plaintiff in negligent supervision claim against church); J.M. v. Minnesota District Council of the Assemblies of God, 658 N.W.2d 589 (Minn. Ct. App. 2003) (holding that adjudication of negligent hiring claim would involve excessive entanglement between church and state); Kenneth R. v. Roman Catholic Diocese of Brooklyn, 229 N.Y.S.2d 791 (N.Y. 1997) (finding that plaintiff's claim for negligent supervision and retention is not barred by the First Amendment); S.H.C. v. Lu, 54 P.3d 174 (Wash. Ct. App. 2002) (holding that adjudicating member of religious order's negligent supervision claim against religious organization would create excessive entanglement with religious doctrine).

184 *See* Abrosio v. Prince, 495 F.Supp. 381 (D. Neb. 1979) (granting summary judgment for plaintiff in car accident case against defendant clergy but not against his employer); Moses v. Diocese of Colorado, 863 P.2d 310 (Colo. 1993) (upholding jury's finding against defendant bishop for injuries sustained as a result of his sexual relationship with parishioner); Hutchison v. Luddy, 896 A.2d 1260 (Pa. Super. Ct. 2006) (upholding award for damages against both bishop and diocese where jury found liability in priest sexual abuse action); Catanzaro v. Central Congregational Co., Inc., 705 A.2d 533 (R.I. 1998) (holding church liable for injury to construction worker who was renovating church for failure to upkeep church property); Macedonia Baptist Church v. Gibson, 833 S.W.2d 557 (Tex. Ct. App. 1992) (upholding jury verdict for church member injured by faulty lightening rod installed by defendant church).

185 *See, e.g.*, Bismarck Baptist Church v. Wiedemann Industries, Inc., 201 N.W.2d 434 (N.D. 1972) (holding that church failed to establish cause of fire in negligence action against defendant manufacturer); Lutheran Church of the Good Shepherd of Baton Rouge v. Canfield, 233 So.2d 331 (La. Ct. App. 1970) (holding that plaintiff church failed to discharge its burden of proof in action against manufacturer for damages caused by faulty heating unit); First Baptist Church of Jefferson City v. Bybee Church Organs, 789 S.W.2d 829 (Mo. Ct. App. 1990) (finding that church's complaint against defendant manufacturer of organ system stated a cause of action for negligence); Reformed Church of the Ascension v. Theodore Hooven & Sons, Inc., 764 A.2d 1106 (Pa. Super. Ct. 2000) (holding that defendant painters owed a duty of reasonable care to plaintiff church while removing old paint and may be found liable for negligence); *cf.* Hiles v. Episcopal Diocese of Massachusetts, 773 N.E.2d 929 (Mass. 2002) (holding that although some claims can be adjudicated without violating the First Amendment, negligence action by priest against the diocese could not be decided without examining church doctrine).

186 *See* Houston v. Mile High Adventist Academy, 846 F.Supp. 1449 (D. Colo. 1994) (holding that plaintiff's negligence per se claim against the parochial school did not raise claim under state employment discrimination statute or under statute prohibiting discrimination on the basis of sex in any education program).

187 *See* Lutheran Church of the Good Shepherd of Baton Rouge v. Canfield, 233 So.2d 331 (La. Ct. App. 1970) (holding that doctrine of *res ipsa locquitur* was not available to plaintiff church that failed to show freedom from fault on all parties except manufacturer of defective heating units that allegedly caused fire); Bismark Baptist Church v. Wiedemann Industries, Inc., 201 N.W.2d 434 (N.D. 1972) (holding that in negligence action by church against manufacturer of baptistery, doctrine of *res ipsa locquitur* does not apply because the defendants were not in exclusive control of the instrumentality at the time of the accident).

188 *See* Winkler v. Rocky Mountain Conference of the United Methodist Church, 923 P.2d 152 (Colo. Ct. App. 1996) (holding that in female parishioner's suit against church and pastor alleging extreme and outrageous conduct, no jury instruction on contributory negligence was appropriate for intentional tort but was sufficient on negligent hiring claim); Bennet v. Gitzen, 484 P.2d 811 (Colo. Ct. App. 1971) (finding that in negligence case where child was injured on church property, a child under the age of seven cannot be considered to have contributed to his injuries for lack of capacity); Stapleman v. St. Joseph the Worker, 205 N.W.2d 677 (Minn. 1973) (reversing decision for plaintiff where alleged defendant's negligence in placing coat rack caused plaintiff's subsequent fall and injuries because plaintiff's contributory negligence was proximate cause of injuries).

negligence,[189] assumption of the risk,[190] intervening superseding causation,[191] gross negligence,[192] vicarious liability,[193] indemnification,[194] joint and several liability,[195] and so on. Religious entities are subject to these concepts, where applicable, like any other party.[196] The next subsection will address situations where there are differences in regard to religious entities or special exceptions. This subsection focuses on, as the title suggests, garden-variety claims. Thus, because religious entities and individuals are subject to the same concepts as others, the focus is on the sorts of claims that arise most frequently for religious entities.

[189] *See* Clark v. Lumbermans Mutual Insurance Co., 465 So.2d 552 (Fla. Ct. App. 1985) (holding that plaintiff's negligence claim against church where plaintiff was injured during church-sponsored canoe trip was barred because plaintiff was sole proximate cause of own injury); Shorter v. Drury, 695 P.2d 116 (Wash. 1985) (finding that plaintiff's signing of waiver refusing blood transfusion on religious grounds was an express assumption of the risk and survived enactment of the comparative negligence statute).

[190] *See* Bennet v. Gitzen, 484 P.2d 811 (Colo. Ct. App. 1971) (finding that in negligence claim where minor plaintiff was injured on church property, jury should not be instructed on assumption of the risk if child is under seven years of age); Shorter v. Drury, 695 P.2d 116 (Wash. 1985) (finding in medical malpractice suit where husband and wife refused blood transfusion and wife died that submitting issue of assumption of the risk to the jury did not violate the Free Exercise Clause of the First Amendment).

[191] *See* Andrade v. Unites States, 116 F.Supp.2d 778 (W.D. Tex. 2000) (Members of a religious group brought action against the United States and others following a fire that destroyed religious compound at the end of a fifty-one-day siege. The court held that even if the United States was negligent, the intervening criminal acts of certain members of the religious group in starting the fire were a superseding cause of injuries.); Bull Street Church of Christ v. Jensen, 504 S.E.2d 1 (Ga. App. 1998) (finding that church maintained liability for negligence by intervening criminal acts of priests because church had actual and constructive knowledge of priests' propensity for sexual abuse).

[192] *See* Craig v. State of Maryland, 155 A.2d 684 (Md. 1959) (holding that defendant parents whose child died when they failed to supply it with medical care was not gross negligence on their part); Franco v. Church of Jesus Christ of Latter-Day Saints, 21 P.3d 198 (Utah 2001) (holding that court could not adjudicate gross negligence action against church because it would create excessive entanglement with church doctrine).

[193] *See* Doe v. Liberatore, 478 F.Supp.2d 742 (M.D. Pa. 2007) (finding that church could not be held liable for outrageous sexual abuse perpetrated by priest); Bouchard v. New York Archdiocese, 2006 WL 1375232 (S.D.N.Y. 2006) (holding that church defendants could not be held vicariously liable for sexual misconduct of priest); M.K. v. Archdiocese of Portland in Oregon, 228 F.Supp. 1168 (D. Or. 2002) (finding that the First Amendment does not bar plaintiff's claim for *respondeat superior* against defendant church in sexual abuse case); Mt. Zion State Bank & Trust v. Central Illinois Annual Conference of the United Methodist Church, 556 N.E.2d 1270 (Ill. App. Ct. 1990) (holding that church could not be held vicariously liable for pastor's conduct where charged conduct was outside scope of pastor's employment); Odenthal v. Minnesota Conference of Seventh-Day Adventists, 657 N.W.2d 569 (Minn. Ct. App. 2003) (holding that the First Amendment does not bar court from hearing church member's vicarious liability claim against church for actions of minister); C.J.C. v. Corporation of the Catholic Bishop of Yakima, 985 P.2d 262 (Wash. 1999) (holding that diocese could not be held liable for priest's sexual abuse of children).

[194] *See, e.g.*, Pacific Insurance Co. v. Catholic Bishop of Spokane, 450 F.Supp.2d 1186 (E.D. Wash. 2006) (refusing to grant summary judgment on insurance company's indemnification claim against church for priests' alleged sexual abuse of parishioners); Fiske v. Church of St. Mary of the Angels, 804 F.Supp. 496 (W.D.N.Y. 1992) (granting summary judgment for the church on the issue of indemnification against general contractor whose employee was injured after falling from the church's steeple); Roman Catholic Diocese of Joliet, Inc. v. Interstate Fire Ins. Co., 685 N.E.2d 932 (Ill. App. 1997) (dismissing grant of summary judgment for church in action for indemnification from insurance company arising out of priest's sexual abuse of minor).

[195] *See* Pleasant Glade Assembly of God v. Schubert, 264 S.W.3d 1 (Tex. 2008) (reversing lower court's ruling against church as debtor with joint and several liability for acts of pastor and youth minister because plaintiff's claim was nonsecular); Doe v. Corporation of Church of Jesus Christ of Later-Day Saints, 167 P.3d 1193 (Wash. Ct. App. 2007) (holding that church could not be held jointly and severally liable for damages caused by codefendant stepfather for intentional acts of sexual abuse toward his stepdaughters where the church was aware of said acts and did not report them).

[196] *See, e.g.*, *supra* notes 184–95.

Negligence claims generally involve four elements: (1) duty,[197] (2) breach,[198] (3) causation,[199] and (4) damages.[200] As will be seen in the next subsection, the first two elements can raise important questions when the duty or breach relate to ecclesiastical matters.[201] In many cases, however, ecclesiastical matters are not involved.[202]

197 *See* Nally v. Grace Community Church of the Valley, 763 P.2d 948 (Cal. 1988) (finding that church owed no duty to prevent suicide of victim because victim participated in church's biblical counseling program); Bull Street Church of Christ v. Jensen, 504 S.E.2d 1 (Ga. Ct. App. 1998) (finding that church had a duty to use reasonable care to protect children from foreseeable risk of harm); Fortin v. Roman Catholic Bishop of Portland, 871 A.2d 1208 (Me. 2005) (holding that victim of sexual abuse alleged sufficient facts to establish fiduciary relationship with diocese so as to give rise to a duty to protect); Meyer v. Lindala, 657 N.W.2d 635 (Minn. Ct. App. 2004) (holding that religious congregation and its governing body owed no affirmative duty to protect victims of sexual abuse from other member); Todd v. First Baptist Church of West Point, 93 So.2d 827 (Miss. 2008) {stating that the elements of a prima facie case of negligence are duty, breach, causation, and damages [citing Grisham v. John Q. Long V.F.W. Post, No. 4057, Inc., 519 So.2d 413, 416 (Miss. 1998)]}; S.H.C. v. Lu, 54 P.3d 174 (Wash. Ct. App. 2002) (holding that no duty existed between the plaintiff member and the temple).

198 *See* Winkler v. Rocky Mountain Conference of the United Methodist Church, 923 P.2d 152 (Colo. Ct. App. 1996) (holding that both pastor and conference breached fiduciary duty to plaintiff in suit alleging unwanted physical contact); Bull Street Church of Christ v. Jensen, 504 S.E.2d 1 (Ga. App. 1998) (holding that church breached duty of care owed to victim by allowing her to wander unsupervised through church premises); Todd v. First Baptist Church of West Point, 93 So.2d 827 (Miss. 2008) {stating that the elements of a prima facie case of negligence are duty, breach, causation, and damages [citing Grisham v. John Q. Long V.F.W. Post, No. 4057, Inc., 519 So.2d 413, 416 (Miss. 1998)]}.

199 *See* Bull Street Church of Christ v. Jensen, 504 S.E.2d 1 (Ga. Ct. App. 1998) (holding that church's breach of duty and the reasonable foreseeability of harm were valid bases for jury to find church liable for victim's injuries); Todd v. First Baptist Church of West Point, 93 So.2d 827 (Miss. 2008) {stating that the elements of a prima facie case of negligence are duty, breach, causation, and damages [citing Grisham v. John Q. Long V.F.W. Post, No. 4057, Inc., 519 So.2d 413, 416 (Miss. 1998)]}; Robertson v. Church of God, International, 978 S.W.2d 120 (Tex. Ct. App. 1997) (holding that because contact between the plaintiff and defendant minister was personal in nature, the church's negligent supervision and retention of defendant was not a proximate cause of plaintiff's injuries).

200 *See* Bull Street Church of Christ v. Jensen, 504 S.E.2d 1 (Ga. Ct. App. 1998) (affirming jury award of damages to victim of sexual abuse in action against church for negligent supervision); Mrozka v. Archdiocese of St. Paul and Minneapolis, 482 N.W.2d 806 (Minn. Ct. App. 1992) (upholding jury award for compensatory and punitive damages where church admitted negligence in clergy sexual abuse case); Todd v. First Baptist Church of West Point, 93 So.2d 827 (Miss. 2008) {stating that the elements of a prima facie case of negligence are duty, breach, causation, and damages [citing Grisham v. John Q. Long V.F.W. Post, No. 4057, Inc., 519 So.2d 413, 416 (Miss. 1998)]}; Faieta v. World Harvest Church, 891 N.E.2d 370 (Ohio Ct. App. 2008) (upholding jury award of compensatory and punitive damages against church for negligent supervision where child was physically abused by teacher at church day care).

201 *See, e.g.*, Dausch v. Ryske, 52 F.3d 1425 (7th Cir. 1994) (holding that the First Amendment bars adjudicating breach of fiduciary duty claim against pastor and church); Ehrens v. Lutheran Church-Missouri Synod, 269 F.Supp.2d 328 (S.D.N.Y. 2003) (finding that the First Amendment bars sexual assault claims against church because defining a clergy's duty of care would foster excessive entanglement with religion); Isley v. Capuchin Province, 880 F.Supp. 1138 (E.D. Mich. 1995) (holding that in sexual abuse case against priest and church, the First Amendment bars questions of negligent hiring and retention because they would require interpretation of church doctrine); Richelle L. v. Roman Catholic Archbishop, 130 Cal. Rptr.2d 601, 616 (Cal. Ct. App. 2003) (holding that "a pastor may be subject to tort liability for sexually inappropriate and injurious conduct that breaches a fiduciary duty arising out of a confidential relation with a parishioner" but finding in the present case that the alleged injurious conduct was dictated by a sincerely held religious belief and so could not be decided on secular terms); Gray v. Ward, 950 S.W.2d 232 (Mo. 1997) (holding that the First Amendment bars claims against the diocese for negligent hiring and retention of clergy and negligent supervision of clergy and other independent acts of negligence); Franco v. Church of Jesus Christ of Latter-Day Saints, 21 P.3d 198 (Utah 2001) (holding that plaintiff's claims for gross negligence, negligent infliction of emotional distress, and breach of fiduciary duty are barred by the First Amendment because they would foster excessive government entanglement with church doctrine).

202 *See, e.g.*, Doe v. Norwich Roman Catholic Diocesan Corp., 268 F.Supp.2d 139 (D. Conn. 2003) (finding that inquiries into negligent supervision and employment can be conducted without entanglement

Religious entities have been sued over car accidents,[203] slip-and-fall accidents,[204] negligent maintenance of premises leading to harm,[205] and a variety of other personal-injury scenarios.[206] In contexts involving premises, questions can arise regarding whether someone is an invitee, licensee, or trespasser in jurisdictions where these categories matter.[207] Usually these questions can be answered without raising ecclesiastical matters, for

in religious matters); Bear Valley Church of Christ v. DeBose, 928 P.2d 1315 (Colo. 1996) (finding that negligent supervision and retention claims can be decided by a court without delving into ecclesiastical matters); Odenthal v. Minnesota Conference of Seventh-Day Adventists, 657 N.W.2d 569 (Minn. Ct. App. 2003) (finding that church member's negligent supervision and vicarious liability claims are not barred by the Free Exercise Clause); Mrozka v. Archdiocese of St. Paul and Minneapolis, 482 N.W.2d 806 (Minn. Ct. App. 1992) (holding that the Free Exercise Clause does not bar court from assessing punitive damages in clergy sexual abuse case against church), Roman Catholic Diocese of Jackson v. Morrison, 905 So.2d 1213 (Miss. 2005) (finding that the Establishment Clause and First Amendment do not bar the state jurisdiction to adjudicate breach of fiduciary duty and negligent hiring, supervision, and retention claims against defendant church); F.G. v. MacDonell, 696 A.2d 697 (N.J. 1997) (holding that the First Amendment does not bar a claim for breach of fiduciary duty against clergy in sexual abuse case); C.J.C. v. Corp. of the Catholic Bishop of Yakima, 985 P.2d 262 (Wash. 1999) (holding that the First Amendment does not bar claims against priest and church because the liability was based on secular conduct).

203 *See supra* note 182.

204 *See* Broad St. Christian Church v. Carrington, 234 So.2d 732 (Fla. Ct. App. 1970) (recognizing that a church may be liable to a grandmother who fell while attending her grandson's ordination); Fintak v. Catholic Bishop of Chicago, 366 N.E.2d 480 (Ill. App. Ct. 1977) (holding defendant church liable for plaintiff's slip and fall injury); Trinity Episcopal Church of Vero Beach v. Hoglund, 222 So.2d 781 (Ill. App. Ct. 1969) (finding defendant church liable for a fall due to ice and snow accumulation on church steps); Morgan v. Hartford Accident and Indemnity Company, 402 So.2d 640 (La. 1981) (finding defendant church liable for damages and for negligence for failure to warn about eight-inch step into gown room); Stitt v. Holland Abundant Life Fellowship, 614 N.W.2d 88 (Mich. 2000) (denying visitor's cause of action against church for the injuries sustained after she tripped and fell in church parking lot because visitor entered property for noncommercial purpose); Stevens v. Bow Mills Methodist Church, 283 A.2d 488 (N.H. 1971) (holding defendant church liable for plaintiff's injuries due to a fall on the church premises).

205 *See* Coolbaugh v. St. Peter's Roman Catholic Church of Bridgeport, 115 A.2d 662 (Conn. 1955) (finding that church had not been negligent in selection of sexton who placed wire on lawn that caused plaintiff's fall and so church not liable); Jensen v. Grace Lutheran Church of Clearwater, Inc., 163 So.2d 782 (Fla. Ct. App. 1964) (dismissing plaintiff's negligence claims against defendant church where duty of church was to refrain from wanton and willful negligence in maintenance of church entrance); Graf v. St. Luke's Evangelical Church, 625 N.E.2d 851 (Ill. Ct. App. 1993) (recognizing a negligence claim against a church that allowed or created an unnatural accumulation of snow and ice on it steps causing a guest to fall).

206 *See* Fernquist v. San Francisco Presbytery, 313 P.2d 192 (Cal. Dist. Ct. App. 1957) (holding that court had to determine relationship between church and construction worker before it could determine liability); Piney Grove Baptist Church v. Goss, 565 S.E.2d 569 (Ga. Ct. App. 2002) (denying church's motion for summary judgment on negligent hiring claim and premises liability where church member was injured while volunteering at construction of church fellowship hall); Clontz v. St. Mark's Evangelical Lutheran Church, 578 S.E.2d 654 (N.C. Ct. App. 2003) (upholding plaintiff's stated negligent supervision claim against church for injuries sustained while assisting with hayride at holiday festival); Catanzaro v. Central Congregational Co., Inc., 705 A.2d 533 (R.I. 1998) (holding church liable for injury to construction worker who was renovating church for failure to upkeep church property); Crocker v. Barr, 409 Se.2d 368 (S.C. 1991) (holding that church could be held liable where volunteer congregant was injured while performing work on church property).

207 *See* Fernquist v. San Francisco Presbytery, 313 P.2d 192 (Cal. Dist. Ct. App. 1957) (holding that for purposes of liability, plaintiff construction worker was a licensee and not merely an invitee or part of a joint venture); Broad St. Christian Church v. Carrington, 234 So.2d 732 (Fla. Ct. App. 1970) (recognizing that church may be liable for slip and fall if victim was an invitee); Schmanski v. Church of St. Casmir

example, where a worker or parishioner slips and falls.[208] Sometimes these categories do raise ecclesiastical questions,[209] usually when there are questions regarding whether a particular congregant or clergy member had a reason to be on the premises.[210] The latter

of Wells, 67 N.W.2d 644 (Minn. 1954) (holding that plaintiff was an invitee of church and not a parishioner); Byrd v. Arrowood, 455 Se.2d 672 (N.C. Ct. App. 1995) (holding that plaintiff's status as a member of the church or not would be proof required to succeed in slip and fall case); Springer v. Federated Church of Reno, 283 P.2d 1071 (Nev. 1955) (holding that a member of the church was the beneficiary of the church and as such could not recover in action against church); S.H.C. v. Lu, 54 P.3d 174 (Wash. Ct. App. 2002) (finding that inquiring into whether a religious member was a business invitee of the Temple and therefore temple owed her a duty to protect from reasonably foreseeable harmful conduct would involve excessive entanglement with religious doctrine).

208 *See, e.g.*, Broad St. Christian Church v. Carrington, 234 So.2d 732 (Fla. Ct. App. 1970) (recognizing that a church may be liable to a grandmother who fell while attending her grandson's ordination); Trinity Episcopal Church of Vero Beach v. Hoglund, 222 So.2d 781 (Ill. App. Ct. 1969) (finding defendant church liable for fall due to ice and snow accumulation on church steps); Clontz v. St. Mark's Evangelical Lutheran Church, 578 S.E.2d 654 (N.C. Ct. App. 2003) (upholding plaintiff's stated negligent supervision claim against church for injuries sustained while assisting with hayride at holiday festival); Catanzaro v. Central Congregational Co., Inc., 705 A.2d 533 (R.I. 1998) (holding church liable for injury to construction worker who was renovating church for failure to upkeep church property).

209 *See, e.g.*, Duncan v. Peterson, 835 N.E.2d 411, 422 (Ill. App. 2005) (pastor's claim for false light invasion of privacy claims could not be litigated as to whether church's revocation of his pastoral position was proper under church doctrine, but invasion of privacy tort claims could be litigated because deciding "whether defendants published a letter placing [plaintiff] in a false light … does not require extensive inquiry into religious law and polity"); Bass v. Aetna Ins. Co., 370 So.2d 511 (La. 1979) (running compelled by prayer during a church revival service was not a defense to negligence when parishioner ran into another church member who was bowed in prayer); McGowan v. Victory and Power Ministries, 757 So.2d 912 (La. App. 2000) (Church volunteers acted reasonably and were not liable for failing to prevent parishioner who fell when "'the Spirit of the Holy Ghost began to cause [plaintiff] to dance and shout in the Spirit of Praise.'"); Alexander v. Culp, 705 N.E.2d 378 (Ohio Ct. App. 1997) (declining to allow clergy malpractice claim against priest for negligent marriage counseling when such an inquiry could violate the First Amendment and cause of action could go forward independently on ordinary negligence); Harmotta v. Bender, 601 A.2d 837 (Pa. Super. Ct. 1992) (Trial court did not act in error when it refused to exclude Roman Catholic potential jurors from jury pool when those jurors were not also members of the defendant parish.); Shropshire v. Pure Holiness Church of God, 1991 WL 121460 (Tenn. Ct. App. 1991) (A member of an incorporated religious organization cannot bring action for damages against the organization because it is a joint enterprise and must instead bring against individual members.); *In re* Pleasant Glade Assembly of God, 991 S.W.2d 85, 89 (Tex. App. 1998) (claims for negligence, gross negligence, and professional negligence barred when the claims attacked the propriety of a church's actions in casting out demons because it would involve "an impermissible inquiry into whether they deviated from the standard of care of an ordinary" practitioner); Bhatia v. Mehak, Inc., 551 S.E.2d 358 (Va. 2001) (Caterers hired by Hindu organization were not entitled to charitable immunity when one of their employees spilled scalding tea on children during a religious ceremony.); Wojtanowski v. Franciscan Fathers Minor Conventuals of St. Josaphat's Church, 148 N.W.2d 54 (Wis. 1967) (question of fact existed whether candle-lighting ceremony was religious activity that would have fallen under charitable immunity).

210 *See, e.g.*, Coolbaugh v. St. Peter's Roman Catholic Church of Bridgeport, 115 A.2d 662 (Conn. 1955) (church entitled to charitable immunity when parishioner slipped and fell while on church premises to light candle; not an invitee but religious beneficiary); Robinson v. Dunn, 683 So. 2d 894 (La. Ct. App. 1997) (dismissing claim brought by former pastor plaintiff against church when he was physically removed from the pulpit in a reasonable manner); Stitt v. Holland Abundant Life Fellowship, 614 N.W.2d 88 (Mich. 2000) (holding that plaintiff church visitor on church property for purposes of attending Bible study was licensee and not invitee and thus entitled to a lower duty of care); Weigel v. Reintjes, 154 S.W.2d 412 (Mo. Ct. App. 1941) (Churchgoers and persons accepting the invitation to use the church are entitled to invitee status.); Ryan v. Holy Trinity Evangelical Lutheran Church, 815 A.2d 419 (N.J. 2003) (Charitable immunity act bars plaintiff in expectant mother support group injured by falling door from bringing action against church.); Bianchi v. South Park Presbyterian Church, 8

scenarios will be discussed in subsection 3.[211] The former are addressed by general tort principles in the relevant jurisdiction.[212]

A.2d 567 (N.J. 1939) (Social center was part of church's social education and action, which is in itself a primary function of religion, and thus plaintiff who slipped and fell at the social center was barred from bringing a negligence claim against the church for injuries resulting from the slip and fall.); Thomas v. Second Baptist Church of Long Branch, 766 A.2d 816 (N.J. Super. Ct. App. Div. 2001) (Congregant was a beneficiary when entering church regardless of actual intended purpose for entrance and was barred from litigating claim under charitable immunity.); Burgie v. Muench, 29 N.E.2d 439 (Ohio Ct. App. 1940) (Former church member in church for ladies' auxiliary club was there to partake as "beneficiary," and thus action was banned by charitable immunity doctrine.); Crocker v. Barr, 409 S.E.2d 368 (S.C. 1991) (Unincorporated church could be held liable for injuries of member sustained while member was performing voluntary construction in the church's attic.); Fain v. O'Connell, 909 S.W.2d 790 (Tenn. 1995) (Catholic school teacher plaintiff was not found to be in joint enterprise with another catholic church where she fell and was injured and thus was not barred from bringing negligence action against the church.); Shorter v. Drury, 695 P.2d 116 (Wash. 1985) (Submission of comparative negligence issue to jury stemming from deceased patient's refusal of blood transfusion during surgery was held not to be a violation of the First Amendment Free Exercise Clause when the refusal was based on religious beliefs.).

211 *See infra*, Section C.2.

212 *See, e.g.*, Albers v. Church of the Nazarene, 698 F.2d 852 (7th Cir. 1983) (Court applies Illinois law and upholds judgment for defendant day-care center operated on church premises, holding that a pile of sticks did not create a reasonable danger to children invitees on premises.); Ward v. Mount Calvary Lutheran Church, 873 P.2d 688 (Ariz. Ct. App. 1994) (*Res ipsa loquitur* is not applicable to a four-year-old child who broke leg at church day care.); Blackburn v. Broad Street Baptist Church, 702 A.2d 1331 (N.J. Sup. Ct. App. Div. 1997) (Rescue doctrine is inapplicable to trespasser on church property.); Fernquist v. San Francisco Prebystery, 313 P.2d 192 (Cal. 1957) (holding that church owed volunteer carpenter working on church dormitory an invitee duty of care for injury suffered during carpentry work); Bennett v. Gitzen, P.2d 811 (Colo. App. 1971) (holding church liable for injuries suffered by boy who rode bicycle down steep concrete ramp on church property when the ramp was an attractive nuisance and the church made no attempt to exclude children from that section of the property); Graf v. St. Luke's Evangelical Lutheran Church, 625 N.E.2d 851 (Ill. App. Ct. 1994) (holding that sufficient evidence existed that a jury could have found that the church had knowledge of an accumulation of snow and was negligent in failing to remove such); Todd v. First Baptist Church of West Point, 993 So.2d 827 (Miss. 2008) (holding that a genuine issue of material fact existed as to whether worker at church's day care met appropriate standard of care required for child care when a two-year-old was injured at church preschool); Manukas v. American Insurance Co., 237 A.2d 898 (N.J. Super. Ct. App. Div. 1968) (holding that a claim against church's insurance company is barred without first demonstrating church's negligence); Cuesta v. Immaculate Conception Roman Catholic Church, 562 N.Y.S.2d 537 (N.Y. App. Div. 1990) (holding that the church is not liable when volunteer umpire assumed risk of injury involved with softball); Boccaccino v. Our Lady of Pity Roman Catholic Church, 238 N.Y.S.2d 911 (N.Y. App. Div. 1963) (holding that the church is not liable for parishioner who slipped and fell when church had no notice to remedy wet conditions); Saul v. Roman Catholic Church of Santa Fe, 402 P.2d 48 (N.M. 1965) (holding that the church is liable under attractive nuisance doctrine when a child was hurt jumping a bike on mounds of dirt); Haessly v. Schrembs, 1928 WL 2610 (Ohio Ct. App. 1928) (holding that contributory negligence claim is barred for parishioner who was struck by a swinging door); First v. Zem Zem Temple, 686 A.2d 18 (Pa. Super. Ct. 1996) (holding that a genuine issue of fact existed as to whether church's dance floor at a wedding was defective and the proximate cause of plaintiff wedding guest's injuries); Catanzaro v. Central Congregational Church, 705 A.2d 533 (R.I. 1998) (holding that employee of construction company who was hurt while repairing gate had dropped the gate during construction and was 50 percent comparatively negligent); Thomas v. St. Mary's Roman Catholic Church, 283 N.W.2d 254 (S.D. 1979) (holding that church violated duty of reasonable care by having breakable glass near basketball court when high school player was injured during game); Macedonia Baptist Church, 833 S.W.2d 557 (Tex. App. 1992) (affirming jury verdict finding that the church negligently installed lightning protection equipment and thus the striking of a parishioner by lightning was not an "Act of God"); Rosendahl v. Lesourd Methodist Church, 412 P.2d 109 (Wash. 1966) (holding that a church member who fell from ladder that was furnished by church when it collapsed was contributorily

In all these garden-variety cases, once one learns that general tort concepts apply, one might find it more useful to look at a book on torts than at a book on law and religion. The key is knowing when general principles do not apply, and that is the subject of the next two subsections. Thus, in terms of tort liability, a car accident is a car accident whether a religious entity is involved or not, unless somehow an ecclesiastical question is raised.[213]

## 2. *Negligent Hiring, Supervision, Retention, and Other Negligence Issues*

Claims for negligent hiring, supervision, and retention raise a number of issues. These claims arise in a variety of circumstances. The most common is abuse of congregants or their family members by clergy.[214] Other claims can involve failure to adequately supervise employees under circumstances where injury is reasonably foreseeable.[215]

negligent due to patched and old nature of ladder); Parchem v. St. Cecilia's Congregation, 137 N.W.2d 90 (Wis. 1965) (action affirmed against church for woman who fell while walking down church steps due to improper installation of handrails).

213 *See* Malloy v. Fong, 232 P.2d 241 (Cal. 1951) (holding church liable for damages resulting from car accident when pastor was driving children from biblical study class to recreational area and was acting as agent of church); Gillet v. Watchtower Bible & Tract Society, 913 So.2d 618, 620 (Fla. Dist. Ct. App. 2005) (holding that plaintiff struck by fellow church member's car could not bring suit against defendant church because handing out pamphlets was on behalf of "Jehovah God" and did not make defendant an agent of the church for vicarious liability); Brillhart v. Scheier, 758 P.2d 219 (Kan. 1988) (Negligence of Catholic parish pastor could not be imputed to his diocese when the car accident arose while pastor had discretion and control over his activity regardless of whether the activity may have benefited the diocese.); Ambrosio v. Price, 495 F.Supp. 381, 384 (D. Nebraska 1979) (holding that passenger in automobile accident with priest who was driving an automobile owned by his church employer could not recover from the church when the priest's trip was a personal one and not in furtherance of "a priestly" responsibility); Williams v. Bright, 658 N.Y.S.2d 910, 913 (N.Y. App. Div. 1997) (remanded for new hearing on damages for injuries suffered in car accident when jury was instructed on "reasonable believer" standard for mitigating damages when plaintiff refused certain medical procedures due to beliefs as Jehovah's Witness); Anderson v. Burnett County, 558 N.W.2d 636 (Wis. Ct. App. 1996) (Car accident trial plaintiff was granted a new trial following verdict that found neither party negligent when jury was impeached due to negative comments about plaintiff's religious status as a Jehovah's Witness.).

214 *See, e.g.*, Napieralski v. Unity Church, 802 A.2d 391 (Me. 2002) (Church attendee who sold life insurance brought claim stemming from alleged sexual assault by reverend who allegedly assaulted her at home owned by church.); Ehrens v. Lutheran Church-Missouri Synod, 269 F.Supp.2d 328 (S.D.N.Y. 2003) (Plaintiff alleged that when he was a minor, the pastor developed a sexual relationship with him and committed sexual assault.); R.A. v. First Church of Christ, 748 A.2d 692 (Pa. Super. Ct. 2000) (holding church not vicariously liable for minister's alleged misconduct of sexually abusing minor); C.J.C. v. Catholic Bishop of Yakima, 985 P.2d 262 (Wash. 1999) (consolidated cases against priests and Catholic Church for various claims that priests molested altar boys and children of congregants over a wide-ranging period of time); S.H.C. v. Lu, 54 P.3d 174 (Wash. Ct. App. 2002) (actionable claims against Buddhist grandmaster on negligent and intentional infliction of emotional distress who told congregant that the only way to save her life was to take part in a religious ritual involving sexual intercourse); Funkhouser v. Wilson, 950 P.2d 501 (Wash. Ct. App. 1998) (Adult children who were allegedly sexually molested by Bible school teacher brought action against church and church members who allegedly knew of abuse.).

215 *See, e.g.*, Nutt v. Norwich Roman Catholic Diocese, 921 F.Supp 66, 74 (D. Conn. 1995) (holding that there was a material issue of fact as to whether Catholic priest's sexual abuse of altar boys was reasonably foreseeable when defendants were alleged to have notice of the priest's past treatment for sexual abuse of minors); Nally v. Grace Community Church of the Valley, 763 P.2d 948 (Cal. 1988) (claim for clergyman malpractice dismissed against church when pastoral counseling failed to prevent young man's suicide when suicide was a foreseeable risk); Coolbaugh v. St. Peter's Roman Catholic Church, 115 A.2d 662 (Conn. 1955) (Church was not liable for negligent hiring of sexton who placed wire on church lawn

The latter claims raise fewer issues than do claims related to abuse or other similar behavior.[216]

For example, failure to adequately supervise staff at a camp or religious school program generally could be addressed under normal negligence principles without raising serious ecclesiastical questions.[217] The same would be true for hiring a staff member to supervise an activity such as swimming where that staff member is unqualified

and thus could not be liable for plaintiff's tripping injury.); Bull Street Church of Christ v. Jensen, 504 S.E.2d 1 (Ga. Ct. App. 1998) (Church had a duty to protect victim child from reasonably foreseeable molestation by another child church known to have deviant sexual tendencies.); Doe v. Braco, 2002 WL 1923870 (Mass. Super. 2002) (finding that a jury question existed as to whether subsequent abuse of children was reasonably foreseeable when deacon knew of pastor's past sexual molestation of children at church functions); Schmanski v. Church of St. Casimir of Wells, 67 N.W.2d 644 (Minn. 1954) (holding that mere presence of janitor in an unlighted boiler room who startled woman hired to clean church was not a reasonably foreseeable cause of injury); C.J.C. v. Catholic Bishop of Yakima, 985 P.2d 262 (Wash. 1999) (Court held that the church had a duty to protect children from harm it reasonably knew or should have known could result from placing children under the care of its employees with propensities for sexual abuse.). *But see* Bender v. First Church of the Nazarene, 571 N.E.2d 475 (Ohio Ct. App. 1989) (holding that criminal sexual assault of a six-year-old by a fourteen-year-old volunteer at religious school was not reasonably foreseeable).

216 *See, infra*, notes 233–240, 248–257, and accompanying text.

217 *See* Jeffrey Scott E. v. Central Baptist Church, 243 Cal. Rptr. 128 (Cal. Ct. App. 1988) (affirming summary judgment for church Sunday school teacher's molestation that occurred outside scheduled class time at home visits and holding that such activities unrelated to the church were not reasonably foreseeable); Beach v. Jean, 746 A.2d 228 (Conn. Super. Ct. 1999) (negligent hiring and supervision claim against church dismissed because church had no actual notice or knowledge of any sexual propensities or past wrongdoings of minister); Clark v. Lumberman's Mutual Insurance Company, 465 So.2d 552 (Fla. Dis. Ct. App. 1985) (Twenty-one-year old plaintiff who dove head first into shallow water during Church canoe trip could not recover damages from church for failure to supervise.); Isely v. Capuchin Province, 880 F. Supp 1138 (E.D. Mich. 1995) (Duty to warn negligence could arise out of teacher-pupil relationship where the school's supervisory officials had knowledge of the activities of the teacher who was the subject of the complaints of priest sexual abuse at religious school.); Clontz v. St. Mark's Evangelical Lutheran Church, 578 S.E.2d 654, 659 (N.C. Ct. App. 2003) (Court held that plaintiff had alleged sufficient negligence claim for church's negligent supervision of children on a hayride at religious festival.); Popkin v. Jewish YMCA of Rochester, 122 N.Y.S.2d 559 (N.Y. App. Div. 1953) (Religious organization was not liable for injuries suffered by six year old girl at camp when sole proximate cause of injury was being struck by a noncamper on a bicycle despite fact that injury occurred during moment of alleged brief inattentiveness by the camp counselor.); Christofides v. Hellenic Eastern Orthodox Christian Church, 227 N.Y.S.2d 946 (N.Y. Mun. Ct. 1962) (Church was liable for injuries suffered by child in classroom who was stabbed by a classmate when the school teacher was absent from classroom and children were unsupervised for twenty-five minutes); Doe v. First United Methodist Church, 629 N.E.2d 402 (Ohio 1994) (Plaintiff would have had actionable claim against church for sexual assaults by teacher and choir director under theory of assault and battery had the claims not been barred by the applicable statute of limitations.); Mills v. Deehr, 2004 WL 1047720 (Ohio Ct. App. 2004) (dismissing claim for negligent supervision of nonclergy church basketball coach who sexually assaulted parishioner under analysis of *respondeat superior* that sexual assault was outside the scope of employment); Faieta v. World Harvest Church, 147 Ohio Misc.2d 51 (2008) (Verdict against church upheld, finding that church was liable for negligent supervision when it had knowledge of day-care provider's incompetence and abuse when the teacher could provide no reasonable explanation for children's injuries while in his sole care.); Hornback v. Archdiocese of Milwaukee, 752 N.W.2d 862, 872 (Wis. 2008) (Court dismissed a negligence claim against Catholic Church, finding that the standard of reasonable and ordinary care did not require church to "notify all subsequent employers within dioceses and parochial school systems across the country" of mere knowledge of religious school teacher's past sexual abuse or potential propensity for abuse.).

or retaining a staff member who has lost state-required certification in the relevant activity.[218] Conversely, claims for negligent hiring or retention of clergy or other church employees with a religious role, such as religious school teachers, can raise significant ecclesiastical concerns.[219] The same could be said for claims of negligent supervision of such individuals,[220] but for a number of reasons discussed later, some courts recognize negligent supervision claims while rejecting negligent hiring and retention claims.[221]

218 *See* Bourn v. Herring, 166 S.E.2d 89 (Ga. 1969) (holding that the church was not liable for failing to exercise ordinary care in supervising deceased boy who drowned at a church picnic when the boy was of ordinary capacity and responsible for his own safety, absent willful misconduct by the church); Piney Grove Baptist Church v. Goss, 565 S.E.2d 569 (Ga. Ct. App. 2002) (fact issue existed whether church was negligent for hiring contractor for construction project when the church apparently did not inquire into any of the contractor's qualifications for such work and contractor did not possess any certification for construction work); McGuire v. Baptist Encampment, 199 So. 192 (La. Ct. App. 1941) (holding that reverend who was head of Baptist camp was not negligent for failing to provide supervision of campers when boy drowned after taking boat out without permission and against camp rules); Brown v. Church of the Holy Name of Jesus, 252 A.2d 176 (R.I. 1969) (Rhode Island court, applying Massachusetts law, holds that the Massachusetts charitable immunity doctrine is inapplicable to wrongful death suit where boy drowned at church outing and no certified lifeguards were on duty.); Weston v. New Bethel Missionary Baptist Church, 598 P.2d 411 (Wash. Ct. App. 1979) (Church was barred from seeking indemnification from contractors for damages caused by collapse of a rockery when the church hired replacement contractors who did not follow the original engineering design for the rockery.).

219 *See* Ayon v. Gourley, 47 F. Supp. 2d 1246 (D. Colo. 1998) (holding that a negligent hiring claim asserted against archdiocese by plaintiff claiming sexual abuse would require impermissible inquiry into religious standards for selection of priests and thus is barred by First Amendment); Nally v. Grace Community Church of the Valley, 763 P.2d 948 (Cal. 1988) (Court rejected imposing same standard of care as licensed mental health care professionals on pastoral counselors.); Roman Catholic Bishop of San Diego v. Superior Court of San Diego County, 50 Cal. Rptr.2d 399 (Cal. Ct. App. 1996) (Court dismissed negligent supervision claim against Catholic Church when priest allegedly sexually abused a fifteen-year-old girl; court declined to impose greater duty to supervise priests based on church's religious tenets.); Moses v. Diocese of Colorado, 863 P.2d 310 (Colo. 1993) (recognizing that negligent hiring and supervision claims can be heard when pertaining only to secular conduct and that "courts must not become embroiled in disputes involving a religious organization if the court would be required to interpret or weigh church doctrine"); Gibson v. Brewer, 952 S.W.2d 239 (Mo. 1997) (Judicial inquiry into claims against diocese of negligent hiring, ordination, retention, and supervision of priest accused of sexually abusing a parishioner would violate the First Amendment.).

220 *See* Houston v. Mile High Adventist Academy, 846 F. Supp 1449, 1455 (D. Colo. 1994) (holding that negligent supervision claims against religious school when teachers impermissibly taught using sexually explicit material are barred by the First Amendment to the extent that the material was inconsistent with the religious tenets of the Seventh-Day Adventist Church); Richelle L. v. Roman Catholic Archbishop, 130 Cal. Rptr. 2d 601, 619 n.15 (Cal. Ct. App. 2003) (Court did not reach negligent supervision claim but noted in a footnote that if plaintiff had been able to sustain a claim against the reverend for sexual abuse, the question before the court would have hinged on whether the alleged sexual misconduct violated a vow of celibacy compelled by Catholic Church.); Gibson, 952 S.W.2d at 247 (holding that First Amendment barred negligent hiring, retention, and supervision claims against church for failing to supervise priest who sexually abused a boy because such an inquiry would require endorsing a church model of "hiring, ordination and retention of clergy"); Westbrook v. Penley, 231 S.W.3d 389 (Tex. 2007) (Professional counseling negligence claim could not be separated from religious pastoral malpractice claim, and thus claim is barred by First Amendment.).

221 *See, e.g.*, Tichenor v. Roman Catholic Church, 32 F.3d 953 (5th Cir. 1994) (holding that Mississippi does not recognize a cause of action for negligent hiring, even when a simple background check would have revealed former priest's background of sexual misconduct); Houston, 846 F. Supp at 1455 (Negligent supervision claims were properly alleged when the claims only addressed negligent supervision of religious teachers based on educational standards and not religious tenets.); Mt. Zion State Bank & Trust v. Central Illinois Annual Conference of the United Methodist Church, 556 N.E.2d 1270 (Ill. App. Ct. 1990) (rejecting negligent hiring verdict when it was not clear that the church's negligence in hiring pastor with history of child molestation was a proximate cause of his subsequent sexual assaults of minor children); Isley

Of course, some courts recognize the latter claims,[222] and others do not recognize negligent supervision claims.[223]

v. Capuchin Province, 880 F.Supp 1138, 1150 (E.D. Mich.) (Student brought claim against priests who molested him and their supervisors; rejection of negligent hiring claim because "questions of hiring and retention of clergy necessarily will require interpretation of church canons, and internal church policies and practices" in violation of the First Amendment.); J.M. v. Minnesota District Council of Assemblies of God, 658 N.W.2d 589 (Minn. Ct. App. 2003) (Court barred hiring and retention claims of pastor who began sexual relationship with congregant on basis that they implicated core, fundamental church tenets related to hiring practices.); Odenthal v. Minnesota Conference of Seventh-Day Adventists, 657 N.W.2d 569 (Minn. Ct. App. 2003) (recognizing negligent supervision claims related to secular counseling); Gray v. Ward, 950 S.W.2d 232 (Mo. 1997) (dismissing negligent hiring and retention claims against church for allowing priest to begin sexual relationship with victim when he was a child for negligent hiring and retention but allowing action for intentional failure to supervise when church allegedly knew of abuse and took no action); Smith v. Privette, 495 S.E.2d 395 (N.C. Ct. App. 1998) (holding that claim of negligent supervision was a common-law tort claim similar to premises liability that did not impermissibly inquire into religious hiring qualifications but rejecting possible negligent hiring claims as inextricable from religious tenets due to religious hiring qualifications that would necessarily be involved in such an inquiry); Byrd v. Faber, 565 N.E.2d 584 (Ohio 1991) (rejecting negligent hiring claim when claim was not pled with specific operative facts demonstrating knowledge of past criminal sexual history; doing so without specific facts would involve potential inquiry into religious practices); C.J.C. v. Catholic Bishop of Yakima, 985 P.2d 262 (Wash. 1999) (recognizing that churches are subject to the same duty of reasonable care in supervising employees as similar entities who oversee safety of children, such as schools).

222 *See, e.g.*, Doe v. Norwich Roman Catholic Diocesan Corp., 268 F.Supp.2d 139 (D. Conn. 2003) (finding that negligent hiring and supervisions claim could be brought under Connecticut law when priest allegedly sexually abused girl when she was fifteen to sixteen years old); Nutt, 921 F. Supp at 74 (Negligent supervision claim stemming from Catholic priest's alleged abuse of altar boys would not involve excessive entanglement because it would involve a secular analysis "of the defendants' possible role in allowing one of its employees to engage in conduct which they, as employers, as well as society in general, expressly prohibit."); Bear Valley Church of Christ v. DeBose, 928 P.2d 1315, 1323 (Colo. 1996) (upholding negligent hiring claim, distinguishing it from "illegal hiring or discharge of a minister," and explaining that the claim involves reasonable foreseeability of harm toward third parties, in case where minister engaged in inappropriate touching during child's counseling sessions); Winkler v. Rocky Mountain Conference, 923 P.2d 152 (Colo. App. 1995) (holding that the First Amendment does not bar claims of negligent hiring or supervision when pastor's inappropriate sexual behavior toward parishioner was not based on any religious tenet or belief); Malicki v. Doe, 814 So.2d 347, 361 (Fla. 2002) (recognizing that negligent hiring, retention, and supervision claims against church for actions by priest for claims of abuse when plaintiffs were church employees could be heard by the court under neutral application of tort law based on preventing reasonably foreseeable harm); Konkle v. Henson, 672 N.E.2d (Ind. Ct. App. 1996) (Negligent hiring and retention claim of minister who the church knew had a sexual relationship with a congregant when she was aged seven to twenty did not require any inquiry into religious doctrine or practice, and claim would not violate the First Amendment.); J.M. v. Minnesota District Council of Assemblies of G-d, 658 N.W.2d 589 (Minn. Ct. App. 2003) (holding that while negligent hiring claim would involve impermissible inquiry into religious tenets, negligent retention claim of pastor related to propensity to sexually violate parishioners could be evaluated under secular standards); Mrozka v. Archdiocese of St. Paul and Minneapolis, 482 N.W.2d 806 (Minn. Ct. App. 1992) (upholding trial award for damages resulting from retention of archbishop known to have abused multiple children during past tenures under negligence claim, allowing punitive damages); Roman Catholic Diocese v. Morrison, 905 So.2d 1213, 1224 (Miss. 2005) (holding that negligent hiring and retention claims related to hiring a priest who sexually molested children are common-law causes of action that have only a secular purpose, no primary effect of enhancing or inhibiting religion, and thus do not involve excessive entanglement with religion); Vione v. Tewell, 820 N.Y.S.2d 682 (N.Y. Sup. Ct. 2006) (holding that negligent hiring and retention claims against church and minister who began a sexual affair during marriage counseling could be evaluated under neutral principles due to large body of civil law on those claims); Hutchinson v. Luddy, 896 A.2d 1260 (Pa. Super. Ct. 2006) (upholding punitive damages against church for negligent retention claim when church knew or should have known about priest's sexual molestation of minor male and past inappropriate sexual tendencies).

223 *See, e.g.*, Ehrens, 269 F. Supp. 2d at 333 (holding that negligent supervision and retention claim against church for retaining pastor who allegedly sexually abused plaintiff when he was a minor is barred by the

The key is that claims based on negligent employment of clergy and other employees with religious roles can raise important ecclesiastical concerns.[224] These concerns include the right of religious entities to determine qualifications for a position based on religious principles and/or traditions,[225] the role of religious requirements in disciplining employees,[226]

First Amendment and would necessarily involve impermissible analysis for the standards and rules "as to the duty of care by which a denomination keeps its 'roster' of those priests ... authorized to accept canonical employment"); Isely, 880 F. Supp 1138 (federal court sitting in diversity not convinced that Wisconsin would, at the time, adopt yet unrecognized independent cause of action for negligent supervision); Napieralski, 802 A.2d 391 (Me. 2002) (Negligent supervision claim against minister who sexually assaulted woman in his own home during private personal visit unrelated to Church business or function despite the fact that the church owned the home dismissed due to Maine not recognizing negligent supervision cause of action.); Swanson v. Roman Catholic Bishop of Portland, 692 A.2d 441, 444 (Me. 1997) (holding that "[p]astoral supervision is an ecclesiastical prerogative" and that it would be improper to impose secular supervision standards on a church); Teadt v. Lutheran Church, 603 N.W.2d 816 (Mich. Ct. App 1999) (holding that negligent supervision claim was not independently actionable without first establishing wrongdoing by the church employee; without an actionable claim that the minister had violated some duty in beginning the sexual relationship, the parishioner could not establish that the church had been negligent in supervising him); Sanders v. Casa View Baptist Church, 898 F. Supp 1169 (N.D. Tex. 1995) (holding that church employees who brought claim for professional malpractice against minister who began sexual relationships during marriage counseling could not bring action against church for negligent supervision when marriage counseling was not one of the minister's duties); Feanco v. Church of Jesus Christ of Latter-Day Saints, 21 P.3d 198 (Utah 2001) (holding that claim against church for negligence stemming from counseling and referral to unlicensed counselor would be a clergy malpractice claim barred by the First Amendment); Shull v. Caroline Furnace Lutheran Camp and Retreat Center, 2004 WL 1320895 (Va. Cir. Ct. 2004) (Church camp not be held liable for negligence stemming from child who drowned at camp due to charitable immunity.); S.H.C., 54 P.3d 174 (holding that negligent supervision claim against Buddhist temple would necessarily involve questions of how obedient the temple should have been to the defendant Grandmaster and thus involve impermissible religious entanglement).

224 *See, e.g.*, Doe, 268 F. Supp. 2d 139 (holding that claim of negligent hiring and supervision would only be allowed to go forward if strictly limited to secular matters and did not raise issues related to inquiry of religious policies or practices); Ehrens, 269 F.Supp.2d at 333 (holding that negligent supervision and retention claim against church for retaining pastor who allegedly sexually abused plaintiff when he was a minor was barred by the First Amendment and would necessarily involve impermissible analysis for the standards and rules "as to the duty of care by which a denomination keeps its 'roster' of those priests ... authorized to accept canonical employment"); Fortin v. Roman Catholic Bishop of Portland, 871 A.2d 1208 (Me. 2005) (upholding claim for negligent supervision of priest who sexually abused victim when he was a child and noting that the Free Exercise Clause would only be violated if resolution of the claim interfered with a religious doctrine or practice); Isely, 880 F. Supp 1138 (E.D. Mich. 1995) (Negligent hiring claim would involve judicial inquiry into church canons and internal church policies and practices and thus would constitute excessive entanglement.); Byrd v. Faber, 565 N.E.2d 584 (Ohio 1991) (Negligent hiring claim was required to be pled with particularity due to potential entanglement stemming from inquiry into religious tenets as well as employment practices and policies.); Hutchinson, 896 A.2d 1260 (Court held that church was liable for negligent supervision stemming from Catholic priest's sexual molestation of young boy; court considered testimony that the bishop who oversaw the priest knew that Canon Law required him to investigate sexual molestation claims.).

225 *See* Ehrens, 269 F.Supp.2d at 333 (S.D.N.Y. 2003) (holding that negligent supervision claim would involve setting constitutionally impermissible duty of care standards for the hiring of clergy); J.M. v. Minnesota District Council of Assemblies of God, 658 N.W.2d 589 (Minn. Ct. App. 2003) (Court refused to recognize negligent hiring claim when doing so would involve impermissible inquiry into qualifications to serve as pastor as dictated by church doctrine.); Smith v. Privette, 495 S.E.2d 395 (N.C. Ct. App. 1998) (rejecting negligent hiring claim because it would involve impermissible inquiry into the religious tenets involved with hiring a minister).

226 *See* Sanders, 898 F. Supp 1169 (Plaintiffs who had sexual relationship with minister during unsanctioned marriage counseling brought claim that their firing for violation of the church's moral standards was a mere pretext for sex discrimination; court dismissed claim, upholding termination.); Winkler, 923 P.2d at

the role of forgiveness and belief in rehabilitation rather than dismissal in some religious traditions,[227] the role that church hierarchy plays in determining the need for and structure of supervisory relationships,[228] internal codes of discipline,[229] and the lack of a church

157 (Court rejected church's claim that handling of complaints against pastor who had inappropriate sexual contact with parishioners fell under church's internal Book of Discipline and thus was barred under the First Amendment.); Southeastern Conference Association of Seventh-Day Adventists v. Dennis, 862 So.2d 842, 844 (Fla. Dist. Ct. App. 2003) (Trial court did not have jurisdiction to adjudicate claim of minister for violation of internal church disciplinary procedures because such matters would inquiry into "matters of discipline, faith, internal organization, or ecclesiastical rule, custom, or law."); Roman Catholic Diocese v. Morrison, 905 So.2d 1213 (Miss. 2005) (holding that enforcing the duty to protect children against sexual molestation would not require impermissible inquiry into how a bishop supervises or disciplines his priests); Nardella v. Dattilo, 36 Pa. D. & C.4th 364 (1997) (dismissing claim for clergy malpractice, noting that the standards for how a priest's conduct and resulting disciplinary manners were to be left to the church, but upholding negligent supervision claim when church elders knew of sexually abusive behavior of counselee).

227 *See* Doe, 2002 WL 1923870 (Deacon of the Council of Elders encouraged parents to forgive new pastor when pastor allegedly fondled two boys in a pool at Church picnic.); Fortin, 871 A.2d 1225 (dismissing argument that Free Exercise Clause would be violated with resolution of negligent supervision claim because the claim would not involve analysis of any theological doctrines concerning "sin, penance, forgiveness [or] redemption"); Odenthal, 657 N.W.2d 569 (Negligent counseling claim was evaluated under neutral state counseling standards, not church's internal handbook, which had religious standards of forgiveness after repentance.); Gibson, 952 S.W.2d at 243 (Court refused to allow negligent supervision and rentention claim, citing First Amendment entanglement; parents reported alleged sexual fondling by priest of their son at sleepover in church rectory, and diocese officials said that it was "an innocent pat on the butt" and that the parents should "forgive and forget."); Feanco v. Church of Jesus Christ of Latter-Day Saints, 21 P.3d 198 (Utah 2001) (Girl who was molested by another fourteen-year-old LDS church member brought negligence claim, stating that the LDS negligently mishandled its pastoral counseling relationship by advising her to "forgive, forget, and seek Atonement.").

228 *See* Ayon, 47 F. Supp. 2d at 1246 (holding that a negligent supervision claim would involve impermissible examination into adequacy of supervisory procedures established by archidocese); Doe v. Evans, 814 So.2d 370, 374 (Fla. 2002) (holding that when a church allows its clergy to take on a fiduciary duty through marriage counseling, the church's relationship with the counselee also takes on a fiduciary nature and corresponding duty); Fortin, 871 A.2d at 1225 (holding that claim of negligent supervision of priest who molested plaintiff did not plead any facts that would lead to an inquiry into the relationship or communications between the church, bishop, and priest); Roman Catholic Diocese v. Morrison, 905 So.2d 1213 (Miss. 2005) (dismissing church's claim that negligent supervision claim would involve impermissible evaluation of the supervisory relationship between a bishop and his priests).

229 *See* Ayon, 47 F. Supp. 2d at 1250 (holding that negligent supervision claims that analyze "practices of disciplinary actions, reprimand write-ups and grievance procedures" in a church setting are barred by the First Amendment); Sanders, 898 F. Supp 1169 (First Amendment bars inquiry into whether minister's termination for having extramarital affairs with other church employees because such inquiry would involve analysis of ecclesiastical policies and standards.); Winkler, 923 P.2d 152, 157 (Court rejected church's claim that handling of complaints against pastor who had inappropriate sexual contact with parishioners fell under church's internal Book of Discipline and thus is barred under the First Amendment.); Konkle, 672 N.E.2d (Ind. Ct. App. 1996) (International church organization could not be liable for behavior that was not reported to the local church's internal judicial procedures, and only the local church could be liable for reasonably foreseeable harm resulting from minister's molestation.); Hiles v. Episcopal Diocese of Massachusetts, 773 N.E.2d 929, 937 (Mass. 2002) (Priest was barred from bringing slander claim against bishop because claim would require the Court "to determine whether the Church's disciplinary procedures were properly invoked" and thus impermissibly inquire into an ecclesiastical issues.); Doe, 2002 WL 1923870 (Deacon had a duty to report sexual abuse by pastor despite the fact that he learned of the abuse through voluntary counseling sessions and internal discipline was not his duty as voluntary member of Council of Elders.); Mzroka v. Archdiocese of St. Paul and Minneapolis, 482 N.W.2d 806, 811 (Minn. Ct. App. 1992) (Punitive damages did not raise excessive entanglement issues when "the reasonableness of its actions relating to a priest's placement

hierarchy to supervise clergy in some congregational settings.[230] Courts are often concerned about getting involved in such situations because of the likelihood of having to address ecclesiastical questions.[231] Some courts point out that these sorts of claims can be characterized as claims for clergy malpractice, which, as noted earlier, courts do not recognize.[232]

Yet, in many cases, courts are willing to address issues because negligence can be determined without any need to address ecclesiastical concerns.[233] For example, consider

or discipline was examined."); Hutchinson, 896 A.2d 1260 (Church and bishop held negligent in disciplining Catholic priest by reassigning him and giving him private warnings instead of warning potential third-party victims.).

230 *See* Doe v. Cunningham, 30 F.3d 879 (7th Cir. 1994) (holding that supervising organization was not liable for negligent supervision of pastor once it assigned pastor to an archbishop and local parish because supervising pastor at supervising organization had no power to make any personnel decisions regarding the tortfeasor pastor.); N.H. v. Presbyterian Church, 998 P.2d 592 (Okla. 1999) (National organization was unaware of the minister's acts and propensity to abuse children, and complaints were only made at several local ministries and thus could not be held liable for negligent hiring, retention, or supervision); Eckler v. General Council of the Assemblies of God, 784 S.W.2d 935 (Tex. App. 1990) (Court affirmed summary judgment on negligent supervision claim against national church for sexual misconduct of religious school teacher at local church when the local churches were independent, self-governing, and had their own bylaws.); *But see* Beach v. Jean, 746 A.2d 228 (Conn. Super. Ct. 1999) (Diocesan officials who oversaw local church regularly visited local church and inquired about priest's job performance and possible moral flaws.).

231 Doe v. Norwich Roman Catholic Diocesan Corp., 268 F. Supp.2d 139, 144 (D. Conn. 2003) ("[W]here resolution of disputes cannot be made without extensive inquiry … into religious law and polity … courts [should] not disturb the decisions of the highest ecclesiastical tribunal within a hierarchical church."); Isley v. Chapuchin Province, 880 F. Supp 1138, 1150 (E.D. Mich. 1995) (holding negligence claims that require a court to interpret Canon Law or internal church policies and practices violate the First Amendment "because such judicial inquires would constitute excessive entanglement with religion."); Bear Valley Church of Christ v. DeBose, 928 P.2d 1315, 1321 (Colo. 1996) (stating that if the priest's acts were motivated by sincere religious beliefs or consistent with religious practices, then the court would have to resolve a difficult First Amendment issue); Konkle v. Henson, 672 N.E.2d 450, 455 (Ind. App. 1996) (holding that "[t]he First Amendment … prohibits the court from determining underlying questions of religious doctrine and practice.").

232 Schmidt v. Bishop, 779 F. Supp. 321, 327 (S.D.N.Y. 1991) (holding that it would be impracticable to allow a claim for clergy malpractice because such a determination would "be intertwined with the religious philosophy of … ecclesiastical teachings of the religious entity."); Nally v. Grace Comm. Church of the Valley, 47 Cal.3d 278, 283, 290 (Cal. 1988) (dismissing the plaintiff's claim for clergy malpractice for failure to prevent their son's suicide because it did not state cause of action); Bear Valley Church of Christ, 928 P.2d at 1327 (holding that in Colorado a claim for clergy malpractice is not actionable); Franco v. The Church of Jesus Christ of Latter-Day Saints, 21 P.3d 198, 203 (Utah 2001) (finding courts throughout the United States to uniformly reject the claim of clergy malpractice because these claims would "entangle the courts in the examination of religious doctrine, practice, or church polity … [which] is prohibited by the Establishment Clause."); Byrd v. Faber, 566 N.E.2d 584, 587 (Ohio 1991) (Discussing "[t]he [A]ppellees' claim for clergy malpractice does not address any aspect of the clergy-communicant relationship not already actionable" and allowing recovery for type of claim would "grant a redundant remedy."); Richelle L. v. Roman Catholic Archbishop, 106 Cal.App.4th 257, 269 (Cal. Ct. App. 2003) (stating that although malpractice claims may be made against "physicians, psychotherapists, and attorneys," a claim for clergy malpractice does *not* exist in the law).

233 Norwich Roman Catholic, 268 F. Supp.2d at 146 (holding that claims for negligent supervision and employment can generally be reviewed without any entanglement in the church's doctrines or practices.); Bear Valley Church of Christ, 928 P.2d at 1324 (finding that the court may review a third party's claim alleging negligence of a religious institution's actions concerning its employees "without implicating or running afoul of the First Amendment"); Konkle, 672 N.E.2d at 456 (stating that review of a pastor's actions that were not religiously motivated only requires the court to apply "secular standards

a case where a clergy member in a hierarchical church is involved in sexually abusing children.[234] The relevant church hierarchy is aware of the behavior, and rather than removing the clergy member from contact with children, the church transfers him or her to another church where he or she abuses other children.[235] The church hierarchy never warns anyone at the new church of the past conduct.[236] When the victims of abuse at the new church sue, the church hierarchy claims that they could not terminate the clergy member because of faith in rehabilitation and forgiveness.[237] A court could not address the credibility or value of the church's retention defense,[238] but courts have held that under these circumstances, the church was negligent in supervising the clergy member even if the retention defense is accepted because it should not have allowed the

to secular conduct which is permissible under First Amendment standards"); Franco, 21 P.3d at 203 ("[T]he entanglement doctrine does not bar tort claims against clergy for misconduct not within the purview of the First Amendment, because the claims are unrelated to the religious efforts of a cleric."); Conley v. Roman Catholic Archbishop of San Francisco 85 Cal.App.4th 1126, 1130 (Cal. Ct. App. 2000) (discussing that a church's hierarchy is as open to tort liability as other social entities as long as the court does not review theological reasons for church's actions).

234 Nutt v. Norwich Roman Catholic Diocese, 921 F. Supp. 66, 70–1 (D. Conn. 1995) (priest accused of showing young boys X-rated films, taking them on overnight trips, and sexually molesting them in hotel rooms on numerous occasions); Bear Valley Church of Christ, 928 P.2d at1328 (The "minister admit[ed] to employing nudity and partial nudity in [his] counseling" sessions.); Bull Street Church of Christ v. Jensen, 504 S.E.2d 1, 6 (Ga. App. 1998) [A minister lured a four-year-old girl into a church classroom and "touched her privates and kissed her on the mouth." (internal quotations omitted)]; Mrozka v. Archdiocese of St. Paul and Minneapolis, 482 N.W. 2d 806, 809–10 (Minn. App. 1992) (A priest continuously sexually abused young boys in his congregation even after years of treatment and transfers to new parishes.).

235 Mrozka, 482 N.W.2d at 809 (stating that after learning of numerous incidents of sexual abuse, superiors transferred the clergy member to another church where he continued to sexually abuse young boys while much of this activity was ignored by his superiors); Hutchison ex rel. Hutchison v. Luddy, 896 A.2d 1260, 1270–1 (Pa. Super. Ct. 2006) (noting that the church bishop transferred a priest after receiving parents' complaint concerning the priest's inappropriate sexual behavior with their children); Diocese of Winona v. Interstate Fire & Cas. Co., 89 F.3d 1386, 1394 (Minn. 1996) [noting that after abusing young boys in numerous parishes, "the Diocese transferred … [the priest] to the Archdiocese in light of the needs of youthful parishioners to be free from Adamson's sexuality problem." (internal quotations omitted)].

236 Mrozka, 482 N.W.2d at 809 (after transferring the priest to the archdiocese, the bishop did not disclose to the archbishop the priest's history of sexually abusing young boys, and the sexual abuse continued.); Hutchison *ex rel.* Hutchison, 896 A.2d at 1261 (It was the "practice of [the] bishop and diocese, in handling complaints of priest pedophilia … [to] transfer priests who admitted molesting children without warning anyone at new parish.").

237 Roman Catholic Diocese of Jackson v. Morrison, 905 So.2d 1213, 1238 (Miss. 2005) (stating that the bishop must necessarily look to the teachings and demands of the Scriptures and Canon Law when disciplining a priest, believing that genuine conversion can occur; therefore, the priest can use his prior failing to teach others in his ministry); Fortin v. The Roman Catholic Bishop of Portland, 871 A.2d 1208, 1226 (Me. 2005) (The church argued that a judicial review of the negligence "claim will result in the court assessing, and approving or disapproving, fundamental theological doctrines concerning sin, penance, forgiveness and redemption" used in the church's retention and supervision of its priests); Odenthal v. Minnesota Conference of Seventh-Day Adventists, 657 N.W.2d 569, 575 (Minn. App. 2003) (The church "contends that scripture governs discipline within the church, and that if a minister trespasses but repents, scripture requires forgiveness.").

238 Roman Catholic Diocese of Jackson, 905 So. 2d at 1241 (The court refused to consider the "policies or practices … adopted by the Diocese" in determining whether a common-law duty was imposed.); Fortin, 871 A.2d at 1227 (When there is nothing on the record to show that resolution of a negligence claim will result in substantial burden on religious beliefs, then the court does not need to address the theological beliefs of the church.).

clergy member to have further contact with children under the circumstances,[239] and/or it should have warned the members or board of the new church.[240]

This raises the key issue in negligent supervision, hiring, and retention claims. It is key that these are not claims for vicarious liability.[241] The religious entity is liable for its own conduct or failure to act.[242] Vicarious liability for a clergy member's conduct could raise a number of religious issues.[243] Even without these additional ecclesiastical issues, it would be hard to prevail on such a claim because employers are rarely vicariously liable for intentional torts committed by employees,[244] and it would be nearly impossible to demonstrate that sexual abuse is within the scope of a clergy member's employment.[245]

239 Jones by Jones v. Trane, 591 N.Y.S.2d 927, 932 (N.Y. Sup. Ct. 1992) (stating that if the priest's "employers placed or continued him in a setting in which [the child] abuse occurred, the fact that the placement occurred in the course of internal administration of the religious units does not preclude holding the institutions accountable to the victim of their neglect in administration.").

240 Funkhouser v. Wilson, 950 P.2d 501, 510 (Wash. App. 1998) (Rational trier of fact could establish a breach of reasonable care when a church leader failed to warn the pastor or the board of another church leader's sexual abuse of two young girls.); Hutchison *ex rel.* Hutchison, 896 A.2d at 1276 (holding that the church was liable for resulting harm from failure to warn a new parish of the transferring priest's past of sexually abusing children); Roman Catholic Diocese of Jackson, 905 So. 2d at 1241–2 (holding that "[c]hurches and religious institutions are not traditional employers such that vicarious liability, through the doctrine of *respondeat superior*, exists as a matter of law, in all cases."); Mount Zion State Bank & Trust v. Cent. Ill. Annual Conference of United Methodist Church, 556 N.E.2d 1270, 1276 (Ill. App. Ct. 1990) (holding that a claim for vicarious liability could not be sustained against a church because of a pastor's acts of molestation).

241 Funkhouser, 950 P.2d at 663 (holding that church breached a reasonable duty of care when it failed to "take any action that would have prevented … [the church leader] from continuing" contact with children of the congregation); Konkle, 672 N.E.2d at 460 (stating that to prevail on claim of negligence against the church, the plaintiff must show that the church knew or had reason to know of harmful conduct by pastor and "failed to take appropriate action"); C.J.C. v. Corp. of Catholic Bishop of Yakima, 985 P.2d 262, 275–76 (Wash. 1999) (holding that the Church negligently caused harm when it failed to affirmatively act to prevent a harm from occurring by "placing its agent into" situations where it knew, or should have know, risk of harm would occur).; Winkler v. Rocky Mountain Conference of United Methodist Church, 923 P.2d 152, 159 (Colo. App. 1995) (holding that the conference became liable for their employee's actions when they knew or should have known that those actions would continue to subject third parties to harm).

242 Norwich Roman Catholic Diocesan, 268 F. Supp. 2d at 142, 146 (holding that a claim of *respondeat superior* could not be resolved without inquiry into religious practice and doctrinal matters); Roman Catholic Diocese of Jackson, 905 So.2d at 1241–2 (stating that claims of vicarious liability concern relationships that "are *by definition* of a religious nature, determined primarily by the religious beliefs and ecclesiastical doctrine of the particular religious group").

243 Norwich Roman Catholic Diocesan, 268 F. Supp. 2d at 142, 146 (holding that a claim of *respondeat superior* could not be resolved without inquiry into religious practice and doctrinal matters); Roman Catholic Diocese of Jackson, 905 So.2d at 1241–2 (stating that claims of vicarious liability concern relationships that "are by definition of a religious nature, determined primarily by the religious beliefs and ecclesiastical doctrine of the particular religious group").

244 Fearing v. Bucher, 977 P.2d 1163, 1166 n. 4 (Or. 1999) (stating that "an employee's intentional tort rarely, if ever, will have been authorized expressly by the employer").

245 Nutt, 921 F. Supp. at 70 (noting that acts of sexual molestation of minors by a priest were not "in furtherance of his employer's business and therefore within the scope of his employment"); Norwich Roman Catholic Diocesan, 268 F. Supp. 2d at 142 (finding that a claim of *respondeat superior* is inapplicable to hold a church liable for sexual abuse by priests "because such acts by the priests are not in furtherance of the church's business"); Byrd, 565 N.E.2d at 588 (stating that the doctrine of *respondeat superior* is inapplicable because the Seventh-Day Adventist organization does not hire or train its pastors to "rape, seduce, or otherwise physically assault members of his congregation"); Jeffrey E. v. Cent. Baptist Church, 197 Cal. App. 3d 718 (Cal. Ct. App. 1988) (holding that the claim for vicarious liability failed because

Thus it is important to remain focused on the fact that claims for negligent supervision, hiring, and retention are based on the religious entity's conduct vis-à-vis the offending clergy member and victims.[246]

This explains why claims for negligent hiring and retention are often frowned upon,[247] but claims for negligent supervision are more successful.[248] The former claims may put civil courts into the religiously charged issues that religious entities engage in when making decisions about clergy hiring and retention.[249] Negligent supervision claims are often focused on the religious entity's failure to adequately supervise those who it hires or retains when that entity has reason to believe congregants or others are being harmed by those individuals.[250] Knowledge of the harmful conduct or its likelihood can be

sexual molestation is not related to teaching Sunday school, nor is it required of a Sunday school teacher in scope of employment).

246 Funkhouser, 950 P.2d at 663 (holding that the church has a duty to "keep an eye on" the priest alleged of sexual molestation and to protect children in the congregation from this known harm); Bull Street Church of Christ, 504 S.E.2d at 6 (finding that a claim of negligence could be sustained because of the church's failure to supervise a priest known to engage in sexual acts with parish children and to protect those children from the known harmful conduct); Bear Valley Church of Christ, 928 P.2d at 1328 (finding that a claim of negligent hiring, retention, and supervision is proper when plaintiff alleges that the church failed to properly investigate allegations of sexual molestation and failed to properly supervise the minister after receiving notice of injurious acts); Hutchison *ex rel.* Hutchison, 896 A.2d at 1261 (finding the church liable for damages incurred by parishioners after receiving notice of a priest's acts of sexual molestation against young children and routinely ignoring the complaints by continuing to place the priest in situations with access to young children).

247 Ayon v. Gourley, 47 F.Supp.2d 1246, 1250 (D. Colo. 1998) (finding that any inquiry into the hiring practices of the church would violate the Free Exercise and Establishment Clauses by examining church policy and doctrine); Isely, 880 F. Supp. at 1150–1 (holding that a claim for negligent hiring should be dismissed because it would require the court to interpret Canon Law and delve into church policies and practices that would cause excessive entanglement in violation of the First Amendment); Byrd, 565 N.E.2d at 589 (noting in analyzing a claim for negligent "hiring [that] it is necessary to examine … employment policies and practices … [that are] infused with the religious tenets of the particular sect involved," which may cause "serious entanglement problems"); Gibson v. Brewer, 952 S.W.2d 239, 246–7 (Mo. 1997) (holding that the trial court did not err in "dismissing the claims of negligent hiring/ordination/retention … [because] judicial inquiry into hiring, ordaining, and retaining clergy would result in an endorsement of religion, by approving one model for church hiring, ordination, and retention of clergy.").

248 Isely, 880 F. Supp at 1151 (noting that unlike hiring matters, claims of negligent supervision can be handled without delving into church law and policy); Norwich Roman Catholic Diocesan, 268 F. Supp. 2d at 146 (noting that claims of negligent supervision "can generally be conducted without any entanglement in the religious doctrines and practices of the church").

249 Isley, 880 F. Supp at 1151 (dismissing a claim for negligent hiring because any inquiry into the church's decision of who is permitted to become or remain a priest would cause excessive entanglement in religion); Gray v. Ward, 950 S.W.2d 232 (Mo. 1997) (finding that claims against diocese for negligent hiring and retention are barred by the First Amendment); Byrd, 565 N.E.2d at 589 (discussing claims of negligent hiring by a religious organization necessarily require examination of their policies and practices, which may lead to serious entanglement problems under the First Amendment); Gibson, 952 S.W. 2d at 246–7 (Mo. 1997) (finding that questions of negligent hiring and retention "necessarily involve interpretation of religious doctrine, policy, and administration," which may cause excessive entanglement in violation of the First Amendment); Ayon, 47 F.Supp.2d at 1250 (finding that "consideration of the hiring policies of the Archdiocese Defendants would inevitably require examination of church policy and doctrine … [which] would violate both the Free Exercise and Establishment Clauses"); Schmidt, 779 F. Supp. 232 (holding that "any inquiry into the policies and practices of the Church … in hiring … their clergy raises … First Amendment problems of entanglement").

250 Vione v. Tewell, 820 N.Y.S. 2d 682, 687 (N.Y. Sup. 2006) (finding that a claim for negligent supervision was valid when the church failed to take action after learning of their employee's inappropriate behavior

central to these cases.[251] In some cases, courts require actual knowledge of past abusive conduct by the relevant clergy member or employee[252] or at the very least knowledge of current inappropriate behavior.[253] Other courts have applied constructive knowledge in circumstances where it would be unreasonable for the entity not to have known of the risk or harm.[254]

Where religious entities knowingly place an employee who has engaged in sexual or other physical abuse in a situation where that employee will have contact with those similarly situated to his or her past victims, courts are even more likely to find liability when the abuse happens again.[255] Under these circumstances, the court may find or presume a failure to adequately supervise because the clergy member or employee was able to abuse again.[256] A few courts do not recognize such claims even under these circumstances because of fear of having to determine ecclesiastical questions.[257]

Another common basis for such claims arises when a religious entity threatens the victim or his or her family with retaliation if claims are made public or tries to minimize the harm through counseling or other mechanisms.[258] Here it is the entity's conduct that directly gives rise to liability rather than failure to supervise an employee or

with a parishioner); Trane, 591 N.Y.S. 2d at 932 (holding that a claim for negligent supervision was valid when the church knew of their employee's past sexual misconduct and continued to place him in situations where the previous acts occurred); Diocese of Winona, 89 F.3d at 1394–6 (determining that the archdiocese negligently supervised a priest who was known to have molested young boys by placing him in a new parish where he continued to molest young boys).

251 Doe v. Evans, 814 So. 2d 370, 372 (Fla. 2002) (determining that the plaintiff's claim for negligent hiring and supervision was valid "based upon [the Diocese] knowledge of [the reverend's] prior sexual misconduct in similar circumstances"); Trane, 591 N.Y.S. 2d at 932 (stating that for the plaintiffs to have a valid claim, they must show that the church had "knowledge that the priest was likely to commit sexual abuse on youths with whom he was put in contact," and the "employers placed or continued him in a setting in which such abuse occurred"); Diocese of Winona, 89 F.3d at 1396 (finding the archdiocese liable for the harmful actions of their employee because they knowingly and repeatedly placed him in situations where he could continue to abuse); Mark K. v. Roman Catholic Archbishop of Los Angeles, 67 Cal. App. 4th 603, 612 (Cal. App. 2 Dist. 1998) (finding that a duty was breached when the church knowingly placed a priest with a history of sexual misconduct with boys "in [a] situation where there was potential for sexual abuse").

252 Kennedy v. Roman Catholic Diocese of Burlington, 921 F. Supp. 231, 234 (D. Vt. 1996) (stating that the plaintiff could not sustain a claim for negligence against the church because she failed to proffer evidence, circumstantial or otherwise, that the priest had the propensity to engage in sexual activity with parishioners and that the diocese was given knowledge of that fact); Williams v. United Pentecostal Church Intern., 115 S.W. 3d 612, 615–16 (Tex. App. [dash was typo so I deleted] Beaumont 2003) (holding that the church owed no duty of care when, even though the church was aware of general dangers of sexual abuse, there was no actual knowledge of prior sexual molestation by this particular church leader).

253 *Id.*

254 Trane, 591 N.Y.S. 2d at 932.

255 Roman Catholic Diocese of Jackson v. Morrison, 905 So.2d 1213 (Miss. 2005); *See also* cases cited *supra* note 251.

256 Vione v. Tewell, 820 N.Y.S. 2d 682, 687 (N.Y. Sup. 2006) (finding that a claim for negligent supervision was valid when the church failed to take action after learning of their employee's inappropriate behavior with a parishioner); Trane, 591 N.Y.S. 2d at 932 (holding that a claim for negligent supervision was valid when the church knew of their employee's past sexual misconduct and continued to place him in situations where the previous acts occurred); Diocese of Winona 89 F.3d at 1394–6 (determining that the archdiocese negligently supervised a priest who was known to have molested young boys by placing him in a new parish where he continued to molest young boys).

257 Ayon v. Gourley, 47 F.Supp.2d 1246, 1250 (D.Colo.1998), *aff'd*, 185 F.3d 873 (10th Cir. 1999); Ehrens v. Lutheran Church–Missouri Synod, 269 F.Supp.2d 328 (S.D.N.Y.2003).

258 A number of these cases are cited, *supra*, section B.4.

clergy member. Therefore, these claims can fall under the general negligence claims discussed earlier.

Moreover, there are a number of state statutes that specifically hold entities liable when they fail to adequately supervise an employee and/or negligently hire or retain an employee resulting in abuse. Some of these statutes have provisions that specifically apply to religious organizations. Still others extend the statute of limitations for such claims where the religious entity's own conduct inhibited or prevented timelier claims.

### 3. *Other Negligence Claims Likely to Raise Ecclesiastical Concerns*

Claims for negligent counseling or negligent ministering are rarely successful because these claims are either directly based in clergy malpractice or closely resemble clergy malpractice. As noted earlier, claims for clergy malpractice are virtually never successful.[259] There are, however, a few cases where claims for negligent counseling by a religious entity have been recognized.[260] These cases usually involve situations where the counselor held himself or herself out as engaging in secular counseling,[261] or where the counselor's secular credentials were touted,[262] or where such credentials were touted but did not exist.[263] In a few cases, claims were successful where the religious counselor knew or should have known that the patient needed secular help and discouraged such help[264] or failed to suggest such help.[265] More often than not, however, claims for failure to refer to secular counselors are unsuccessful because those claims raise ecclesiastical questions.[266]

### 4. *Vicarious Liability*

As noted earlier, vicarious liability may be available against religious entities in garden-variety tort claims. Therefore, concepts such as *respondeat superior* may apply in such cases. In cases where clergy or other church employees abuse congregants or others, sexually or otherwise, the clergy member or employee is almost always found to be

259 *See* cases cites, *supra* at note 232.

260 *See infra* notes 261–6.

261 Odenthal v. Minn. Conference of Seventh-Day Adventists, 649 N.W.2d 426 (Minn. 2002); Doe v. Evans, 814 So. 2d 370, 375 (Fla. 2002).

262 Dausch v. Rykse, 52 F.3d 1425, 1428, 1435 (7th Cir. 1994) (holding that pastor who held himself out to be a trained psychological counselor and undertook such counseling could be found liable for negligent counseling).

263 Sanders v. Casa View Baptist Church, 134 F.3d 331, 334, 338 (5th Cir. 1998) (holding that a minister who knew that his duties did not involve counseling but represented that he was qualified to provide marriage counseling could be sued for negligent counseling).

264 Moses v. Diocese of Colo., 863 P.2d 310, 318, 321 (Colo. 1993) (*en banc*) (holding that bishop and diocese who told a woman involved in a sexual relationship with a priest who was giving her counseling not to tell anyone about what happened was subject to suit for negligent counseling).

265 Lundman v. McKown, 530 N.W.2d 807, 821–3, 828–9 (Minn. Ct. App. 1995) (holding that a Christian science nurse and caregiver had a duty of care to sick child which they breached when they did not request secular medical help when it became necessary).

266 Germain v. Pullman Baptist Church, 980 P.2d 809 (Wash. Ct. App. 1999); Rose v. Washington Conference of Seventh-Day Adventists, 127 Wash. App. 1046 (2005) (unpublished); Amato v. Greenquist, 679 N.E.2d 446 (Ill. App. Ct. 1997); Nally v. Grace Cmty. Church, 763 P.2d 948 (Cal. 1988); Roppolo v. Moore, 93-2361 (La. App. 4 Cir. 1994); 644 So. 2d 206 *writ denied*, 94-3032 (La. 1995), 650 So. 2d 253.

acting outside the scope of employment,[267] although a few courts have held otherwise.[268] As explained earlier, the best way to find a religious entity liable for harm resulting from physical, mental, or sexual abuse is through a claim for negligent supervision or through another claim that focuses on the entity's conduct.

Moreover, vicarious liability does not generally apply to intentional torts, and most of the conduct in abuse cases falls within intentional torts. Again, there are exceptions to this general rule. The exceptions usually arise where a religious entity has been found to ratify the intentional conduct (and, of course, the entity can be liable for its own intentional conduct).[269] Claims for negligent supervision and direct negligence against the entity provide the better mechanism for victims in these cases, but as explained earlier, some courts have found even these claims to raise ecclesiastical concerns.

## D. Nuisance

Nuisance claims are based on tortious interference with the use or enjoyment of property, but unlike trespass, nuisance claims do not involve physical entry on the affected land by the alleged tortfeasor (or an item propelled onto the property by the tortfeasor).[270]

267 Nutt, 921 F. Supp. at 70 (noting that acts of sexual molestation of minors by priest were not "in furtherance of his employer's business and therefore within the scope of his employment"); Norwich Roman Catholic Diocesan, 268 F. Supp. 2d at 142 (finding that a claim of *respondeat superior* is inapplicable to hold a church liable for sexual abuse by priests "because such acts by the priests are not in furtherance of the church's business"); Byrd, 565 N.E.2d at 588 (stating the doctrine of *respondeat superior* to be inapplicable because the Seventh-Day Adventist organization does not hire or train its pastors to "rape, seduce, or otherwise physically assault members of his congregation"); Jeffrey E. v. Cent. Baptist Church, 197 Cal. App. 3d 718 (Cal. Ct. App. 1988) (holding that the claim for vicarious liability failed because sexual molestation is not related to teaching Sunday school, nor is it required of a Sunday school teacher in scope of employment).

268 *Cf.* S.H.C. v. Lu, 54 P.3d 174 (Wash. Ct. App. 2002) (actionable claims against Buddhist grandmaster on negligent and intentional infliction of emotional distress who told congregant that the only way to save her life was to take part in a religious ritual involving sexual intercourse).

269 *See, e.g.*, Gallas v. Greek Orthodox Archdiocese, 587 N.Y.S.2d 82, 86 (Sup. Ct. 1991) (finding that a religious organization's attempted "cover-up" of its clergy's sexual misconduct was sufficient to subject the organization to liability; the claim, however, was dismissed on statutory grounds); Faieta v. World Harvest Church, 891 N.E.2d 370 (Ohio Com. Pl. 2008) (holding that the record supported an intentional infliction of emotional distress claim against a religious organization arising from physical abuse of a child by its employee), *aff'd*, 2008 WL 5423454 (Ohio Ct. App. 2008); Bonson v. Diocese of Altoona-Johnstown, 67 Pa. D. & C.4th 419, 438–9 (Pa. Com. Pl. 2004) (finding a viable intentional infliction of emotional distress claim against diocesan defendants that knowingly concealed information concerning its priests' "predatory sexual impulses toward children and adolescents" while permitting, and in fact encouraging, children to be in "close proximity to the [dangerous] priests"); Bouchard v. New York Archdiocese, 2006 WL 1375232 (S.D.N.Y. 2006) (refusing to dismiss a congregant's intentional infliction of emotional distress claim against the church arising from the church's alleged active concealment of its clergy's sexual misconduct); Burns v. First Congregational Church of Vernon, 2000 WL 1337671, at *5 (Conn. Super. Ct. 2000) (finding a viable intentional infliction of emotional distress claim when church knowingly failed to monitor a sexually deviant priest while permitting him access to locations "where he presented a danger-without-warning to prey" on children); Gagne v. O'Donoghue, 1996 WL 1185145 (Mass. Super. 1996) (implying that a diocese may be amenable to liability for the sexual misconduct of its clergy if it failed to act on information tending to show that it had knowledge of past instances of sexual misconduct by its perpetrating clergy).

270 *See, e.g.*, Fifth Ave. Presbyterian Church v. City of New York, 293 F.3d 570, 576 (2d Cir. 2002) (finding that city failed to establish a public nuisance claim based on church's operation of a homeless shelter); Duncan v. United States, 48 F.2d 128, 133 (9th Cir. 1931) (recognizing that the use of profane language

There are generally two types of nuisance: (1) private nuisance and (2) public nuisance.[271] Religious entities have been involved in both sorts of situations,[272] albeit somewhat rarely compared with some of the other torts addressed in this chapter.

The elements of a private nuisance are based on interference with the use and enjoyment of land.[273] The defendant must not have physically entered the land because if the land was entered, the resulting tort would be a trespass not a nuisance.[274] Moreover, the defendant must act with the intent of interfering with the plaintiff's use and enjoyment of the land.[275] It is essential to clarify, however, that this element often can be met simply by showing that the defendant created or continued the condition that interferes with the plaintiff's use and enjoyment of the land knowing that the plaintiff's interests are being harmed or are substantially certain to be harmed if the condition is created or continued.[276] The interference with the use or enjoyment of the land actually must occur, but

has constituted a public nuisance); St. David's Episcopal Church v. Westboro Baptist Church, 921 P.2d 821, 828 (Kan. Ct. App. 1996) (finding th defendant liable for private nuisance because of picketing near church); Langan v. Bellinger, 203 A.D.2d 857, 858 (N.Y. 1994) (assessing a private nuisance claim based on noise).

271 *See, e.g.*, St. David's Episcopal Church, 921 P.2d at 827–8 (discussing the elements of private nuisance); Langan, 203 A.D.2d at 857–8 (discussing the requirements for a private nuisance claim); Louderback v. Orkin Exterminating Co., 26 F.Supp 2d 1298, 1309–10 (D. Kan. 1998) (discussing a public nuisance claim as opposed to a private nuisance claim).

272 *See, e.g.*, Fifth Ave. Presbyterian Church, 293 F.3d at 576 (discussing city's claim that church's homeless shelter constituted a public nuisance); St. David's Episcopal Church, 921 P.2d at 827–8 (discussing a private nuisance claim of one church against another); Langan, 203 A.D.2d at 857–8 (discussing a private nuisance claim against a church for music); Louderback, 26 F.Supp 2d at 1309–10 (discussing a public nuisance claim by a church against a pesticide company).

273 *See, e.g.*, Maranatha Temple, Inc. v. Enter. Prods. Co., 893 S.W.2d 92, 99 (Tex. App. 1995) (describing different categories of interference with use and enjoyment of property); St. David's Episcopal Church, 921 P.2d at 827–8 (finding interference with use and enjoyment of the property a necessary element); Langan, 203 A.D.2d at 857–8 (finding that an element of private nuisance is an interference with another's use of property); Louderback, 26 F.Supp 2d at 1309–10 (describing nuisance as generally requiring interference with another's rights); People *ex rel.* Birkett v City of Chicago, 758 N.E.2d 25, 27 (Ill. App. Ct. 2001) (plaintiff claiming noise from jet aircraft interfering with use of school buildings).

274 *See, e.g.*, Dalley v. Dykema Gossett, 788 N.W.2d 679, 691 (Mich. Ct. App. 2010) (finding that a trespass is the unlawful invasion of another's private property); First Baptist Church of Lombard v. Toll Highway Auth., 703 N.E.2d 978, 983–4 (Ill. App. Ct. 1998) (analyzing action that resulted in flooding as a trespass and the continuing condition of the highway as a nuisance); St. David's Episcopal Church, 921 P.2d at 825 (discussing the temporary restraining order that created a buffer zone between the picketing, which was a nuisance, and the plaintiff's property); Langan, 203 A.D.2d at 857–8 (describing the interference as noise that originated from the plaintiff's property).

275 *See, e.g.*, St. David's Episcopal Church, 921 P.2d at 827–8 (requiring that defendant act with an intent to interfere with the use or enjoyment of the land); Langan, 203 A.D.2d at 857–8 (discussing that liability required the interference to be intentional and unreasonable); Maranatha Temple, Inc., 893 S.W.2d at 99 (describing different categories of interference with use and enjoyment of property); Adkins v Thomas Solvent Co., 487 N.W.2d 715, 720–21 (Mich. 1992) (describing the general test for private nuisance, including the element of intent).

276 *See, e.g.*, St. David's Episcopal Church, 921 P.2d at 827–8 (finding that the intent element does not require a malicious intent but can be satisfied by full knowledge of the harm); Barnes v. St. Stephen's Missionary Baptist Church, 580 S.E.2d 587, 591 (Ga. Ct. App. 2003) (requiring that the church must have created or continued the act that caused the harm in order to be liable); Chambers v. Summerville United Methodist Church, 675 So.2d 1315, 1316 (Ala. Civ. App. 1996) (finding that the intent element is satisfied by creating or continuing an act that has the foreseeable consequence of proximately causing the interference).

the extent of the interference need not have been intended or anticipated.[277] Moreover, interference with the use and enjoyment of the land must be substantial or cause a substantial injury.[278] Finally, the interference must be unreasonable.[279]

The elements of a public nuisance require an unreasonable interference with a right common to the general public.[280] This interference with a public right must be unreasonable[281]; examples of unreasonable interference often involve substantial interference with public health and safety or with public comfort or convenience.[282] An interference also may be deemed unreasonable because the conduct involved is prohibited by state or local laws or administrative rules.[283] Finally, it is relevant whether the conduct

277 *See, e.g.*, Langan, 203 A.D.2d at 857–8 (describing the test for private nuisance, which includes actual interference but does not require the defendant to have intended the extent of the interference); St. David's Episcopal Church, 921 P.2d at 827–8 (finding that a necessary element is an actual interference with the use or enjoyment of the land); Chambers, 675 So.2d at 1316 (requiring actual interference but only requiring that the result was foreseeable, not anticipated); Maranatha Temple, Inc., 893 S.W.2d at 98–100 (discussing nuisance as requiring actual interference with use or enjoyment of land); Adkins, 487 N.W.2d at 720–1 (discussing the general test as requiring actual interference, although the extent need not be intended or anticipacted).

278 *See, e.g.*, Maranatha Temple, Inc., 893 S.W.2d at 98–9 (describing nuisance as requiring substantial interference); St. David's Episcopal Church, 921 P.2d at 827–8 (finding it necessary that the interference with the use or enjoyment of the land be substantial); Langan, 203 A.D.2d at 857–8 (requiring substantial interference); Adkins, 487 N.W.2d at 720–1 (discussing the general test as requiring substantial interference).

279 *See, e.g.*, *St. David's Episcopal Church*, 921 P.2d at 827–8 (finding it necessary that the interference be unreasonable); Langan, 203 A.D.2d at 857–8 (finding unreasonableness to be a prerequisite); Maranatha Temple, Inc., 893 S.W.2d 92, 98–9 (Tex. App. 1995) (describing nuisance as an unreasonable interference); Adkins, 487 N.W.2d at 720–1 (discussing the general test as requiring an unreasonable interference).

280 *See, e.g.*, Grace United Methodist Church v. City of Cheyenne, 451 F.3d 643, 671 (10th cir. 2006) (holding that the church's proposed day-care center would have been unlawful under the city's zoning ordinance); Fifth Ave. Presbyterian Church v. City of New York, 293 F.3d 570, 573–6 (2d Cir. 2002) (finding that the city failed to establish a public nuisance claim based on church's operation of a homeless shelter and alleged noncompliance with minimum standards of habitability); Tate v Akers, 565 F.2d 1166, 1170 (1977) (holding that the Seventh-Day Adventist Church door-to-door ministry did not constitute a nuisance as proscribed by ordinance); Louderback v. Orkin Exterminating Co., 26 F.Supp 2d 1298, 1309 (D. Kan. 1998) (describing a public nuisance as an "infringement of the rights of the state or community at large, as opposed to the rights of an individual").

281 *See, e.g.*, Maranatha Temple, Inc., 893 S.W.2d at 98–9 (describing nuisance as an substantial interference that is unreasonable); Louderback, 26 F.Supp 2d at 1309 (describing a public nuisance as an unreasonable interference with a public right); Capitol Properties Group, LCC v. 1247 Ctr. Street, LCC, 770 N.W.2d 105, 111 (Mich. Ct. App. 2009) (describing a public nuisance as involving and unreasonable interference with public rights); Askwith v. City of Sault Ste. Marie, 477 N.W.2d 448, 451 (Mich. Ct. App. 1991) (requiring a public nuisance to be an unreasonable interference with a public right).

282 *See, e.g.*, Askwith, 477 N.W.2d at 451 (providing that a public nuisance includes a significant interference with public safety); Capitol Properties Group, LCC, 770 N.W.2d at 111 (defining an element of public nuisance as a significant inference with the public's health, safety, comfort, or convenience); Louderback, 26 F.Supp 2d at 1309 (holding that the injection of pesticide into heating and air-conditioning duct work of the church did not constitute a public nuisance because, among other reasons, there was no evidence presented that the acts created a danger to public safety); Yarrick v. Village of Kent City, 473 N.W.2d 774, 776 (Mich. Ct. App. 1991) (finding that a man-made hole in a public park could constitute a public nuisance).

283 *See, e.g.*, Tate, 565 F.2d at 1169 (finding that the city's ordinance proscribed acts of uninvited solicitors, peddlers, and hawkers and that the city treated those actions as nuisances); Grace United Methodist Church, 451 F.3d at 674 (holding that the church's proposed day-care center would have been unlawful

is of a continuing nature or has caused long-lasting effects when the defendant knew or should have known that the condition created will have a substantial effect on public rights.[284] Needless to say, but we are saying it anyway, this is a rather malleable definition, and public nuisance law can vary greatly depending on the jurisdiction, the defendant party(s), and the circumstances.[285]

In virtually all nuisance cases involving religious entities, the religious entities, whether plaintiffs or defendants, are treated like all other plaintiff's and defendants. Therefore, most nuisance cases involving religious entities are legally indistinguishable from other nuisance cases.[286] There are, however, a few cases where the religious nature of the entity is relevant to the legal analysis.[287]

For example, there are several cases where churches provided food and/or shelter to the homeless as part of the church's religious mission or ministry.[288] Local citizens

under the city's zoning ordinance); Civil Liberties for Urban Believers v. City of Chicago, 342 F.3d 752, 766 (7th cir. 2003) (finding that the zoning ordinance that required churches to obtain a special use approval before operating in business or commercial districts is constitutional).

284 *See, e.g.*, Baltimore & P.R. Co. v. First Baptist Church of Washington, 137 U.S 568, 576 11 S.Ct. 185, 188 (1891) (finding that a fresh action will lie for every continuance of a nuisance); Capitol Properties Group, LCC, 770 N.W.2d at 111 (describing an element of public nuisance as unreasonable interference that the actor knew or should have known would produce long-lasting, significant effects on a public right); Barnes v. St. Stephen's Missionary Baptist Church, 580 S.E.2d 587, 591 (Ga. Ct. App. 2003) (requiring that a nuisance be of a repetitious or continuing nature and not just a single, isolated incident).

285 *See, e.g.*, Western Presbyterian Church v. Board of Zoning Adjustment, 862 F.Supp. 538, 546–7 (D.D.C. 1994) (finding that a church's program to feed the homeless on its property did not constitute a public nuisance and that application of the zoning ordinance would substantially burden free exercise of religion); Louderback v. Orkin Exterminating Co., 26 F.Supp.2d 1298, 1309–10 (D. Kan. 1998) (holding that interference with a large number of people's permissive use of a church did not constitute an infringement on a public right); Adkins v Thomas Solvent Co., 487 N.W.2d 715, 720–1 (Mich. 1992) (describing that while there is a general definition for nuisance in Michigan, whether a nuisance exists will be more dependent on the particular facts and circumstances of the case).

286 *See, e.g.*, Barnes, 580 S.E.2d at 591 (analyzing public nuisance claim against defendant church with general public nuisance principles); St. David's Episcopal Church v. Westboro Baptist Church, 921 P.2d 821, 827–8 (Kan. Ct. App. 1996) (analyzing private nuisance claim against defendant church with the general test); Langan v. Bellinger, 203 A.D.2d 857, 857–8 (N.Y. 1994) (using general test to assess private nuisance claim); Louderback, 26 F.Supp 2d at 1309–10 (requiring plaintiff church to prove all the elements of its public nuisance claim); Maranatha Temple, Inc. v. Enter. Prods. Co., 893 S.W.2d 92, 98–9 (Tex. App. 1995) (affirming summary judgment against plaintiff church because fear of lawful operation of industry did not constitute a nuisance).

287 *See, e.g.*, Tate v Akers, 565 F.2d 1166, 1170 (1977) (finding that defendant's door-to-door sale of church literature was primarily to spread the word of the gospel and was not proscribed solicitation); Western Presbyterian Church, 862 F.Supp. at 544 (finding that a church's program to feed the homeless was religious conduct and protected by the First Amendment); Jesus Center v. Farmington Hills Zoning Board of Appeals, 544 N.W.2d 698, 704 (Mich. Ct. App. 1996) (holding that requiring the church to relocate its homeless shelter apart from the place of worship constituted a substantial burden on the free exercise of religion); Fifth Ave. Presbyterian Church v. City of New York, 293 F.3d 570, 575 (2d Cir. 2002) (finding that the church had demonstrated a likelihood of success in proving that its provision of an outdoor sleeping area for the homeless was for the purpose of effectuating its deeply held religious belief).

288 *See, e.g.*, Western Presbyterian Church, 862 F.Supp. at 544 (finding that church's program to feed the homeless was motivated by a sincere religious belief); Jesus Center, 544 N.W.2d at 703–4 (finding that the shelter provided by the church for the homeless was part of its religious mission); Fifth Ave. Presbyterian Church, 293 F.3d at 575 (finding that the church had demonstrated a likelihood of success in establishing that its provision of an outdoor sleeping area for the homeless was part of its religious ministry).

complained about the supposed risks associated with such an operation.[289] Sometimes these complaints were based on concerns about increased crime or loitering,[290] and sometimes the concerns were tied to fears that the operation would have a negative impact on property values.[291] These cases often address the question of whether the sheltering and feeding of those in need is part of the religious entity's religious mission.[292] For the reasons mentioned in other chapters, courts will not generally question a religious entity's assertion that such care is part of its religious function.[293] Some courts, however, do explain why such care is part of the church's religious mission.[294] These courts usually do so by accepting and recounting the religious entity's religious rationale.[295]

289 *See, e.g.*, Western Presbyterian Church, 862 F.Supp. at 546 (finding that neighborhood organizations complained about the risk of increase in crime and the depreciation of property values associated with the influx of the homeless); Jesus Center, 544 N.W.2d at 700 (Residents complained that they feared for their safety and an increase in crime.); Fifth Ave. Presbyterian Church, 293 F.3d at 576 (City argued that the outdoor shelter area was unsafe for the homeless.).

290 *See, e.g.*, Western Presbyterian Church, 862 F.Supp. at 546 (finding that neighborhood organizations complained about the increase in crime caused by the homeless); Jesus Center, 544 N.W.2d at 700 (Residents complained that the homeless were loitering and trespassing.).

291 *See, e.g.*, Western Presbyterian Church, 862 F.Supp. at 546 (finding that neighborhood organizations complained that the increase in the homeless population would result in a decline in property values). *Cf.* BAM Historic Dist. Ass'n v. Koch, 723 F.2d 233, 237 (2nd cir. 1983) (Plaintiffs claimed that the operation of a homeless shelter in their neighborhood will cause a decline in property values.); Spring-Gar Cmty. Civic Ass'n v. Homes for the Homeless, Inc., 149 A.D.2d 581, 581 (N.Y. App. Div. 1989) (Neighborhood organization alleged that increased use of a building as a homeless shelter would decrease surrounding property values.).

292 *See, e.g.*, Western Presbyterian Church, 862 F.Supp. at 544 (finding that the church's program to feed the homeless was motivated by a sincere religious belief); Jesus Center, 544 N.W.2d at 703–4 (discussing whether the church's shelter program was in furtherance of its religious mission); Fifth Ave. Presbyterian Church, 293 F.3d at 574–5 (discussing whether the church's outdoor sheltering program is part of the church's religious ministry).

293 *See, e.g.*, Jesus Center, 544 N.W.2d at 703 (finding that the determination of whether certain activities are in furtherance of an organization's religious mission is a way in which religious entities define themselves; "[i]t is not the job of the courts to second guess 'what activities are sufficiently religious' to qualify for 'free exercise' protection."); Fifth Ave. Presbyterian Church, 293 F.3d at 574 (discussing that courts are not free to inquire into the centrality of a professed belief to the adherent's religion because to do so would be contrary to the meaning of free exercise).

294 *See, e.g.*, Western Presbyterian Church, 862 F.Supp. at 544 (discussing that the concept of charity is central to all major religions); Jesus Center, 544 N.W.2d at 703–4 (discussing that the act of caring for the poor has been part of the Christian tradition since its early times during the Roman Empire); Fifth Ave. Presbyterian Church, 293 F.3d at 574–5 (discussing an affidavit in which the church's homeless liaison discusses the scripture of the Bible and that there is no higher act of worship for a Christian than to give the love of God to the needy).

295 *See, e.g.*, Western Presbyterian Church, 862 F.Supp. at 544 (discussing the church's bylaws and passages from the Bible and accepting that they are sincere religious beliefs); Jesus Center, 544 N.W.2d at 703–4 (accepting the church's position that its shelter program is an expression of its faith); Fifth Ave. Presbyterian Church, 293 F.3d at 574–5 (accepting and recounting an affidavit professing the church's religious rationale).

Because zoning laws are also often involved in these cases,[296] and because nuisance law is generally applicable for Free Exercise Clause purposes,[297] courts have held that there is no duty to exempt a religious entity from general nuisance law or to require zoning variances that would otherwise not be required. This is so because of the doctrine set forth in *Employment Division v. Smith*,[298] which held that there is no duty under the Free Exercise Clause for government entities to provide exemption to generally applicable laws.[299] Still, the religious entity prevails in most of these cases either because the activity is not deemed to be a nuisance or because even if it could give rise to a nuisance, there was no evidence that a nuisance actually had occurred. In a few situations, the religious entity itself agreed to limit the times that the complained of services were provided so as to minimize the likelihood of the activity becoming or remaining a nuisance.

Another class of nuisance cases involving religious entities involves church bells or music that is argued to be loud enough to interfere with the use and enjoyment of land by neighbours.[300] These cases are few in number. In these cases, the religious character of the noise is often treated under general nuisance law, and normal questions about the volume and disturbance caused by the noise are the primary focus.[301] If the volume and/or time did interfere with use and enjoyment of others' land, it could constitute a nuisance[302] regardless of the fact that the cause was a religious entity.[303]

An interesting case involving religious protests by the infamous Westboro Baptist Church raised questions about whether religious protests can constitute a private nuisance despite First Amendment speech and religion concerns.[304] Westboro Church engaged in loud, offensive, and sometimes threatening protests near the plaintiff's property.[305] The plaintiff was an Episcopal Church.[306] The trial court issued a

[296] *See, e.g.*, Grace United Methodist Church v. City of Cheyenne, 451 F.3d 643, 647–9 (10th cir. 2006) (discussing the church's request for a zoning variance so that it could operate a day-care facility); Western Presbyterian Church, 862 F.Supp. at 542 (discussing the conflict between the free exercise of religion and the state's legitimate power to regulate the use of real property); Jesus Center v. Farmington Hills Zoning Board of Appeals, 544 N.W.2d 698, 699–700 (Mich. Ct. App. 1996) (discussing the factual background of the church's effort to obtain zoning approval for homeless shelter operation); Civil Liberties for Urban Believers v. City of Chicago, 342 F.3d 752, 755–9 (7th cir. 2003) (discussing Chicago's zoning classifications and the churches' requests for special use permits to operate churches in business and commercial districts).

[297] *See, e.g.*, Western Presbyterian Church, 862 F.Supp. at 545 (discussing RFRA and the heightened scrutiny above what is constitutionally prescribed for generally applicable laws); Jesus Center, 544 N.W.2d at 702–3 (discussing the applicability of the Free Exercise Clause as RFRA to the zoning ordinance); Grace United Methodist Church, 451 F.3d at 649–55 (discussing the free exercise of religion and that the zoning law was neutral and generally applicable); Civil Liberties for Urban Believers, 342 F.3d at 762–4 (analyzing Chicago's zoning laws as neutral and generally applicable); Tate v Akers, 565 F.2d 1166, 1170 (1977) (holding the city's nuisance law inapplicable to plaintiffs and avoiding the constitutional question).

[298] Employment Div. v. Smith, 494 U.S. 872 (1990) (There is generally no constitutional right to exemptions from laws of general applicability under the Free Exercise Clause.).

[299] *Id.*

[300] Langan v. Bellinger, 203 A.D.2d 857 (N.Y. App. Div. 1994).

[301] *Id.*

[302] *Id.*

[303] *Id.*

[304] St. David's Episcopal Church v. Westboro Baptist Church, 921 P.2d 821 (Kan. Ct. App. 1996).

[305] *Id.* at 828–9.

[306] *Id.* at 824.

temporary restraining order based on a claim of private nuisance, and the temporary restraining order ripened into a preliminary injunction.[307] Westboro appealed on First Amendment grounds based primarily on freedom of speech because the injunction limited the time and proximity to the church of the protests.[308] The trial court and court of appeals held that the private nuisance claim against Westboro was likely to succeed on the merits, although the appellate court noted that its holding was based on the incomplete state of the record at the time of the appeal, which was in large part due to Westboro's trial tactics.[309]

There are few public nuisance cases involving religious entities.[310] One of the above-mentioned cases involved attempts by New York City to arrest or disperse homeless individuals who were invited by a church to stay on church property. The City claimed a public nuisance,[311] but the church prevailed against the public nuisance claim under the First Amendment.[312] As with private nuisance claims, religious entities generally are treated similarly to nonreligious entities in public nuisance cases.

## E. Ultrahazardous Activities

As a general matter, religious entities are involved in cases implicating ultrahazardous activities on the same terms as most entities.[313] There are, however, very few cases. Churches have sued extermination companies and other entities who allegedly engaged in ultrahazardous activities claiming strict liability for damages.[314] Religious entities have not generally prevailed on such claims,[315] but this is true for such claims brought by any party regardless of whether it is a religious entity.

There is, however, one issue involving ultrahazardous activities unique to religious entities, namely, cases involving religious snake handling. Most of the extant cases were decided under public nuisance law, criminal law, or family law, but the question of ultrahazardous risks was addressed.[316] Very few of the snake-handling cases involve an in

307 *Id.* at 826–7.

308 *See generally id.*

309 *Id.* at 826–9.

310 Examples of these cases can be found, however. *See* Fifth Avenue Presbyterian Church v. City of New York, 293 F.3d 570 (2nd Cir. 2002); Louderback v. Orkin Exterminating Company, 26 F.Supp.2d 1298 (D. Kan. 1998); Swann v. Pack, 527 S.W.2d 99 (Tenn. 1975).

311 Fifth Avenue Presbyterian Church, *supra* note 310.

312 *Id.*

313 Bowyer & Johnson Construction Company v. White, 255 F.3d 482 (5th Cir. 1958)(applying general law in Mississippi regarding fire set by subcontractor working on church property; under general law, it was not clear that the fire was inherently dangerous for tort purposes, and regardless, contractor could not be liable for possibility that subcontractor might use fire for work it performs); Louderback v. Orkin Exterminating Company, 26 F.Supp.2d 1298 (D.Kansas 1998)(general rules for abnormally dangerous activities and public nuisance applied in case where church sued pesticide company for contamination).

314 *Id.*

315 *Id.*

316 *See, e.g.*, Swann v. Pack, 527 S.W.2d 99 (Tenn. 1975) (Snake handling is a common-law public nuisance because of the extreme danger it poses to the handlers and others.); Harden v. State, 216 S.W.2d 708 (Tenn. 1949) (criminal case addressing abnormal danger created by snake handling); State v. Massey, 51 S.E.2d 179 (N.C. 1949) (same); Lawson v. Commonwealth, 164 S.W.2d 972 (Ken. 1942) (same); Hill v. State, 88 So.2d 880 (Ala. Ct. App. 1956) (same); *cf.* Harris v. Harris, 343 So.2d 762 (Miss. 1977) (State supreme court overturned decision of chancery court to award custody to father in divorce decree because mother attended church that allowed snake handling. State Supreme Court noted the extreme

depth discussion of the law generally applicable to ultrahazardous activities,[317] but the courts seem to always assume – for good reason – that the handling of poisonous snakes by those not trained as herpetologists is a hazardous activity.[318] The question that generally arises is whether such conduct is privileged based on the Free Exercise Clause and/or state constitutional provisions[319] or whether the low rate of bites in such churches somehow takes the cases out of the ultrahazardous activity analysis. The latter argument has never been successful. Moreover, most of these cases involve state statutes banning snake handling by those not professionally trained to do so.[320] Some involve handling of any dangerous animal unless the handler is professionally trained to do so.[321]

These cases sometimes involve claims based on public nuisance because of the risks to public health and safety.[322] Also, many of the cases involve criminal prosecutions under state statutes, and thus, reasoning to a tort claim must be by analogy.[323] Still, the potential for an ultrahazardous activity claim by a bystander who is bitten is apparent given the reasoning in these cases.

The crux of these cases is the argument by the church or individual members named as defendants that snake handling in the church context is protected by the Free Exercise Clause to the U.S. Constitution or similar state constitutional provisions.[324] These claims have been uniformly unsuccessful.[325] This is so even when the compelling interest test has been applied.[326] One possible exception would be where a state specifically targeted religious snake handling and not other forms.[327] One case that today appears to have been wrongly decided against a church – if the prohibition against intentional discrimination were applied – involved a state law applied directly to religious snake handling that did not even require that the snakes be poisonous.[328] Of course, except in cases of intentional discrimination,[329] the compelling interest test generally only applies today where there are state religious freedom restoration acts (RFRAs) in place or where a "hybrid right" is interfered with.[330]

Today the cases would appear even easier because the laws in most of these states would be viewed as generally applicable.[331] The only possible way to prevail in such

danger that could exist in such an environment but also noted that there was no evidence that mother planned to handle snakes or expose child to area of church where snakes are handled.).

317 *Id.* (all cases).

318 *Id.*

319 Harris v. Harris, 343 So.2d 762 (Miss. 1977); State v. Massey, 51 S,E,2d 179; Harden v. State, 216 S.W.2d 708 (Tenn. 1949); Lawson v. Commonwealth, 164 S.W.2d 972 (Ken. 1942).

320 Swann v. Pack, 527 S.W.2d 99 (Tenn. 1975) (state statute); Harden v. State, 216 S.W.2d 708 (Tenn. 1949) (same); Lawson v. Commonwealth, 164 S.W.2d 972 (Ken. 1942) (same); Hill v. State, 88 So.2d 880 (Ala. Ct. App. 1956) (same); State v. Massey, 51 S.E.2d 179 (N.C. 1949) (city ordinance).

321 Swann, note 320, *supra* at 112.

322 *See generally id.*

323 Harden, *supra* note 320; State v. Massey, *supra* note 320; Lawson, *supra* note 320; Hill, *supra* note 320.

324 *See* cases cited at note 316, *supra*.

325 *Id.*

326 *See* Swann, *supra* note 320 at 11–14.

327 *See* Church of the Lukumi Babalu Aye v. City of Hialeah, 508 U.S. 520 (1993).

328 *See* Lawson, *supra* note 320.

329 *See* Church of the Lukumi Babalu Aye, supra note 327.

330 Employment Div. v. Smith, 494 U.S. 872 (1990) (addressing concept of "hybrid rights").

331 *Id.* (There is generally no constitutional right to exemptions from laws of general applicability under the Free Exercise Clause.).

a case would be if the state statute involved was aimed specifically at the religious practice,[332] and even then, government might be found to have a compelling interest, although narrow tailoring might remain an issue.

## F. Defamation

Defamation is a complex issue no matter what the factual scenario,[333] but this is even more true when religious entities are involved.[334] The law generally applicable to defamation claims applies in the context of religious entities.[335] Thus questions arise in defamation cases involving religious entities or individuals such as whether clergy members are public figures,[336] whether a given statement is true or false,[337] what community is the relevant community for determining the effect of the defamatory statement (i.e., if it is published within the congregation only, what effect does that have?),[338] and whether the statement was published.[339]

Still, numerous issues unique to cases involving religious entities arise. First, the courts often treat cases involving defamation claims brought by clergy differently from those brought by congregants.[340] Courts also often treat claims brought by those not affiliated with the religious entity involved differently from either situation mentioned earlier.[341] Moreover, in some cases it is the religious entity itself that brings a defamation claim.[342]

In all these cases, some common questions arise. When does the ecclesiastical abstention doctrine apply to defamation claims involving religious entities?[343] Are there neutral

332 *See* Church of the Lukumi Babalu Aye, *supra* note 327 (Law was unconstitutional because it was designed to discriminate against religious group.).

333 New York Times Co. v. Sullivan, 376 U.S. 254 (1964) (requiring public officls to prove "actual malice" to recover on a defamation claim); Gertz v. Robert Welch, Inc., 418 U.S. 323 (1974) (private individuals can recover actual damages without showing actual malice but may not recover punitive damages without such a showing); Harte-Hanks Commc'ns, Inc., v. Connaughton, 491 U.S. 657 (1989) (clarifying the "actual malice" standard); Milkovich v. Lorain Journal Co., 497 U.S. 1 (1990) (First Amendment does not require a separate "opinion privilege" limiting defamation law).

334 *See infra* notes 335–49, and accompanying text.

335 *See e.g.*, Miles v. Perry, 529 A.2d 199 (Conn. App. Ct. 1987); Steed v. St. Paul's United Methodist Church, 31,521 (La. App. 2 Cir. 1999), 728 So. 2d 931,*writ denied*, 99-0877 (La. 1999), 740 So. 2d 1290 (1990).

336 Readers Digest Assoc. Inc., v. Superior Court, 690 P.2d 610 (Cal. 1984); Davis v. Keystone Printing Serv., Inc., 507 N.E.2d 1358 (Ill. App. Ct. 1987); Miles, 529 A.2d 199; Contemporary Mission, Inc. v. New York Times Co., 842 F.2d 612 (2d Cir. 1988).

337 Abdelhak v. Jewish Press Inc., 985 A.2d 197 (N.J. Super. Ct. App. Div. 2009); Hartwig v. Albertus Magnus Coll., 93 F. Supp. 2d 200 (D. Conn. 2000).

338 Busby v. First Christian Church, 95 So. 869 (La. 1923); Mosley v. Evans, 630 N.E.2d 75 (Oh. Ct. App. 1993) (information published only to church members is entitled to qualified immunity so long as speaker did not act with actual malice).

339 Monahan v. Sims, 294 S.E.2d 548 (Ga. Ct. App. 1982); Busby, 95 So. 869; Church of Scientology of Cal, Inc. v. Green, 354 F. Supp. 800 (S.D.N.Y. 1973).

340 *Cf. infra* notes 346–59 and accompanying text, *with infra* notes 360–6 and accompanying text.

341 *Cf. infra* notes 346–66 and accompanying text, *with infra* notes 363–6 and accompanying text.

342 Reader's Digest Assn. v. Superior Court, 690 P.2d 610 (Cal. 1984); Church of Scientology of Minn. v. Minn. State Med. Ass'n Found., 264 N.W.2d 152 (Minn. 1978); Missouri Church of Scientology v. Adams, 543 S.W.2d 776 (Mo. 1976).

343 *See infra* notes 346–7, 354–9, & 363 and accompanying text.

principles of law that mitigate this doctrine in some cases, and if so, what are they?[344] As will be seen, the answer to the first two questions is "sometimes."[345]

The easiest defamation cases to address are those brought by clergy against the religious entity for statements made by church officials concerning a clergy member's religious qualifications or rejection of, or violation of, church doctrines. In these cases, the ecclesiastical abstention doctrine applies.[346] Courts will not get involved in assessing such claims because the underlying allegedly defamatory statements are between a religious entity and clergy member and, even once published, involve religious doctrine.[347] This combination of the religious entity–clergy relationship and the statements' involving religious doctrine makes these cases relatively easy to decide.[348]

What happens, however, when the clergy member alleges that a religious entity and/or its officials committed defamation based on things other than religious qualifications or theological questions? In most such cases the clergy member will lose because the religious entity/clergy relationship is infused with ecclesiastical concerns and the religious entity will be given broad leeway as to what falls under the label of ecclesiastical questions.[349] There are a few cases, however, where the publication by a religious entity or its officials has been either so far outside the realm of ecclesiastical question,[350] or the publication is so obviously false that a court need not address any ecclesiastical question to address its truthfulness.[351] In these cases neutral principles can be applied.[352] Moreover, the plaintiff has generally been allowed to proceed in the face of a motion to dismiss, and in many of these cases the plaintiff has won.[353]

The former cases generally involve allegations of criminal conduct[354] or the sorts of conduct that would support a claim for libel per se.[355] It is key that in the latter cases, even when they do not involve allegations of such conduct, a plaintiff will not succeed just because a nonbeliever would consider the allegedly defamatory statements to be obviously false.[356] For example, a minister would not succeed on a claim that he or she

344 *See infra* notes 350–2, 354–5, & 362–3 and accompanying text.

345 *See infra* notes 346–66 and accompanying text.

346 Horne v. Andrews, 589 S.E.2d 719 (Ga. Ct. App. 2003); McManus v. Taylor, 521 So. 2d 449 (La. Ct. App. 1988); Bourne v. Ctr. on Children, Inc., 838 A.2d 371 (Md. Ct. Spec. App. 2003); Sieger v. Union of Orthodox Rabbis of U.S. & Canada, Inc., 767 N.Y.S.2d 78 (N.Y. App. Div. 2003); Tran v. Fiorenza, 934 S.W.2d 740 (Tex. App. 1996); Goodman v. Temple Shir Ami, Inc., 712 So. 2d 775 (Fla. Dist. Ct. App. 1998).

347 *Id.* (all sources).

348 *Id.* (all sources).

349 Hiles v. Episcopal Diocese of Mass., 773 N.E.2d 929 (Mass. 2002); Callahan v. First Congregational Church Of Haverhill, 808 N.E.2d 301 (Mass. 2004) Downs v. Roman Catholic Archbishop of Balt., 683 A.2d 808 (Md. Ct. Spec. App. 1996); Cha v. Korean Presbyterian Church of Wash., 553 S.E.2d 511 (Va. 2001); Black v. Snyder, 471 N.W.2d 715 (Minn. Ct. App. 1991).

350 Gorman v. Swaggart, 524 So. 2d 915 (La. Ct. App. 1988); Callahan, 808 N.E.2d 301; Mallette v. Church of God Int'l, 789 So. 2d 120 (Miss. Ct. App. 2001); Ausley v. Shaw, 193 S.W.3d 892 (Tenn. Ct. App. 2005).

351 Duncan v. Peterson, 835 N.E.2d 411 (Ill. App. Ct. 2005).

352 *See supra* notes 350–1.

353 *Id.*

354 Hayden v. Schulte, 97-0422 (La. App. 4 Cir. 1997), 701 So. 2d 1354, *writ denied sub nom.* Patrick v. Schulte, 97-2941 (La. 1998), 709 So. 2d 737; Conley, 102 Cal. Rptr. 2d 679.

355 LeGrande v. Emmanuel, 889 So. 2d 991 (Fla. Dist. Ct. App. 2004); Stewart v. Ging, 327 P.2d 333 (N.M. 1958).

356 LeGrande, 889 So. 2d 991; *Conley*, 102 Cal. Rptr. 2d 679.

has been possessed by demons or some other supernatural force or evil inclinations.[357] The key here is that successful claims must be based on a publication about temporal conduct.[358] The publication should be false and cannot involve supernatural or metaphysical assertions.[359]

Another major issue that arises in defamation cases involving religious entities is the role the ecclesiastical abstention doctrine plays in cases brought by congregants against the religious entity. As with the clergy cases, civil courts generally avoid addressing ecclesiastical questions in these cases.[360] Thus, if a congregant or former congregant alleges defamation against the religious entity and/or its clergy and/or leadership, a court will not address issues pertaining to purely religious allegations made against the congregant.[361] Courts will, however, often use neutral principles of law where available in these cases.[362] For example, if the underlying factual allegation on which a religious claim is based is obviously false, or a reasonable person should have known that it was false, a court can address this without addressing the religious implications had the plaintiff actually engaged in the alleged conduct.[363] Thus, for example, if a congregant or former congregant is accused of being a thief or an adulterer, a court may hear the case as long as the focus is the truthfulness of the factual allegation involved rather than the religious implications.[364] Thus, if the allegation is that the congregant was a thief or adulterer in his or her heart rather than in the temporal world, a court will not hear the case because of the ecclesiastical abstention doctrine.[365] Obviously, in most jurisdictions, if the defamatory statement is not related to religious questions at all, the ecclesiastical abstention doctrine will not bar an action for defamation.[366]

357 *Cf.* First United Church, Inc. v. Udofia, 479 S.E.2d 146, 149 (Ga. Ct. App. 1996) (finding that parishioners of a church could not bring a defamation claim against a church for calling them witches and accusing them of practicing witchcraft.).

358 LeGrande, 889 So. 2d 991; Conley, 102 Cal. Rptr. 2d 679.

359 *But see* Ausley v. Shaw, 193 S.W.3d 892 (Tenn. Ct. App. 2005).

360 Pappas v. Passias, 707 N.Y.S.2d 178 (N.Y. App. Div. 2000); Brady v. Pace, 108 S.W.3d 54 (Mo. Ct. App. 2003); Glass v. First United Pentecostal Church of DeRidder, 95-1442 (La. App. 3 Cir. 6/12/96), 676 So. 2d 724; Kond v. Mudryk, 769 So. 2d 1073 (Fla. Dist. Ct. App. 2000); House of God Which is the Church of the Living God, the Pillar & Ground of the Truth Without Controversy, Inc. v. White, 792 So. 2d 491 (Fla. Dist. Ct. App. 2001).

361 *Id.* (all sources).

362 Berger v. Temple Beth-El of Great Neck, 756 N.Y.S.2d 94 (N.Y. App. Div. 2003); Kliebenstein v. Iowa Conference of United Methodist Church, 663 N.W.2d 404 (Iowa 2003); Lipscombe v. Crudup, 888 A.2d 1171 (D.C. 2005); Hester v. Barnett, 723 S.W.2d 544 (Mo. Ct. App. 1987).

363 Lipscombe, 888 A.2d 1171; Muresan v. Phila. Romanian Pentecostal Church, 962 P.2d 711 (Or. Ct. App. 1998).

364 Udofia, 479 S.E.2d 146; Hester, 723 S.W.2d 544.

365 A decision from the Court of Appeals of Georgia illustrates well the how courts treat these two different types of alleged defamations committed by a church. In *First United Church, Inc. v. Udofia*, the court held that the trial court had subject matter jurisdiction to hear a defamation claim which alleged that the church falsely accused the plaintiffs of committing crimes because analyzing these claims "would not require an impermissible inquiry in church doctrine." 479 S.E.2d at 149. On the other hand, the court held that the trial court did not have subject matter jurisdiction to consider allegations that the plaintiffs were witches and practiced witchcraft, because those allegations "related to religious faith, belief, and practice." *Id.*

366 Muresan, 962 P.2d 711; Cooper v. Grace Baptist Church of Columbus, Ohio, Inc., 612 N.E.2d 357 (Ohio Ct. App. 1992).

# 14 Criminal Law and Process

## A. Introduction

"[T]he power to create and enforce a criminal code" is, in the U.S. Supreme Court's words, "[f]oremost among the prerogatives of sovereignty."[1] It enables a sovereign to proscribe or prescribe conduct in furtherance of community health, safety, welfare, or morals and then to prosecute violations of those mandates using the full complement of the state's coercive powers.[2] To be sure, although governmental pervasiveness in the last century has perhaps blurred the line between regulation and criminalization, the latter nevertheless remains, conceptually at least, the paradigmatic expression of state authority.

As a practical matter, it is often the nature, extent, and basis of the punishment that distinguish criminal offenses from civil wrongs. Both transgressions, for example, can lead to minor or temporary incursions on liberty and, especially in the civil realm, to the confiscation of one's property.[3] But criminal offenses also can lead to greater stigma, to significant secondary consequences (e.g., disenfranchisement), to more severe restrictions on one's basic liberties (e.g., incarceration), and even to the termination of one's life (e.g., capital punishment), which substantially explains the heightened evidentiary burden on the prosecution.[4] Moreover, although both criminal punishment and civil liability are

1 Heath v. Alabama, 474 U.S. 82, 93 (1985); *see also* McCulloch v. Maryland, 17 U.S. (4 Wheat.) 316, 418 (1819) ("[T]he power of punishment appertains to sovereignty, and may be exercised, whenever the sovereign has a right to act, as incidental to his constitutional powers."); California v. Mesa, 813 F.2d 960, 966 (9th Cir. 1987) ("[A] polity's ability to protect its citizens from violence and other breaches of the peace through enforcement of criminal laws is the centermost pillar of sovereignty."), *aff'd*, 489 U.S. 121 (1989); Jeremy Rabkin, *Is EU Policy Eroding the Sovereignty of Non-Member States?* 1 U. CHI. J. INT'L L. 273, 277 (2000) ("One of the central elements of sovereignty is that each sovereign state is responsible for defining and enforcing its own criminal law within its own territory.").

2 *See* Motlow v. State, 145 S.W. 177, 183 (Tenn. 1912) ("The whole body of the criminal law is but a branch of [the police] power. Under this, not only may men, and even women, be restrained of their liberty, because the safety of the public requires their incarceration, but for the same reason their lives may be declared forfeit and taken from them."); State v. Ivey, 474 S.E.2d 501, 505 (W. Va. 1996) ("[T]he legislature, in the proper exercise of its police power, has the authority, within constitutional limits, to create and define crimes.").

3 The preferred remedy of the civil law is monetary compensation, categorized as one or more forms of damages, although equitable or injunctive relief is not uncommon. *See* DAN B. DOBBS, PAUL T. HAYDEN & ELLEN M. BUBLICK, 3 THE LAW OF TORTS §§ 479–83 (2d ed., 2011).

4 *See* Duro v. Reina, 495 U.S. 676, 688 (1990) ("The exercise of criminal jurisdiction subjects a person not only to the adjudicatory power of the tribunal, but also to the prosecuting power of the … [government], and involves a far more direct intrusion on personal liberties."); Adam H. Kurland, *First Principles of*

traditionally thought to have compensatory and deterrent functions, the former, unlike the latter, is often said to have incapacitative, rehabilitative, and retributive functions as well.[5]

It is precisely the significance of the criminal legal system, as the fullest and most drastic expression of legitimate state authority, that often makes the relationship between this system and the religious realm historically rich, contemporarily important, and frequently controversial. This relationship can be approached and examined in a variety of ways. Broadly viewed, one might examine the historical or empirical correlations between religion and a sovereign's criminal jurisprudence[6] or between religion and the prevention or occurrence of crime.[7] One might also examine the potential complementarity between religion and the criminal law in the regulation of harmful conduct,[8] or one might critique the criminal law from a particular religious perspective.[9]

*American Federalism and the Nature of Federal Criminal Jurisdiction*, 45 EMORY L.J. 1, 66 (1996) (noting "the unique and profound consequences of the criminal sanction – loss of liberty, if not life").

5 *See* WAYNE R. LAFAVE, 1 SUBSTANTIVE CRIMINAL LAW § 1.5 (2d ed., 2003) (discussing the theories of prevention, restraint, rehabilitation, deterrence, education, and retribution and noting potential conflicts among them); CHARLES E. TORCIA, 1 WHARTON'S CRIMINAL LAW § 1 (15th ed. rev'd, Sep. 2013) (hereinafter 1 WHARTON). For a discussion of differences between the law's treatment of conduct deemed criminal and its treatment of conduct deemed civilly wrong, *see* 1 WHARTON, *supra*, § 7 ("A crime is a public wrong since it implies injury to the state; a tort is a private wrong since it involves injury to an individual. In the case of a crime, the outraged state launches a criminal prosecution against the offender with a view toward punishing him [or her]; in the case of a tort, the injured individual brings a civil action against the wrongdoer to soothe his [or her] hurt. As a result of the criminal prosecution, the offender may be imprisoned; as a result of the civil action, the injured individual may recover money damages. The purpose of the criminal prosecution ultimately is to prevent crime and thereby to protect society; the purpose of the civil action is to compensate the injured individual and thereby to make him [or her] whole. In a criminal proceeding, the defendant's guilt must be established beyond a reasonable doubt; in a civil action, the defendant's liability may be established merely by a preponderance of the evidence.").

6 *See, e.g.*, J.M.B. CRAWFORD & JOHN F. QUINN, THE CHRISTIAN FOUNDATIONS OF CRIMINAL RESPONSIBILITY: A PHILOSOPHICAL STUDY OF LEGAL REASONING (1991); Joachim J. Savelsberg, *Religion, Historical Contingencies, and Institutional Conditions of Criminal Punishment: The German Case and Beyond*, 29 L. & SOC. INQUIRY 373 (2004).

7 *See generally* John Simpson & David Brownfield, *Religion and Crime*, in 3 ENCYCLOPEDIA OF CRIME & JUSTICE 1327–33 (Joshua Dressler ed., 2d ed., 2002) (reviewing the literature). Regarding the role, for example, of religion and faith-based organizations in the reduction of crime rates, *see* Byron R. Johnson, *Reviewing and Clarifying the Role of Religion in Reducing Crime and Delinquency*, FED. PROB., Dec. 2001, at 49 (broadly reviewing the literature). For various statistical analyses, *see* Paul Heaton, *Does Religion Really Reduce Crime?* 49 J.L. & ECON. 147 (Apr. 2006). For a review of religious sources of crime, *see* KAREL KURST-SWANGER, WORSHIP AND SIN: AN EXPLORATION OF RELIGION-RELATED CRIME IN THE UNITED STATES (2008).

8 *See, e.g.*, 1 LAFAVE, *supra* note 5, § 1.5 ("The criminal law is not, of course, the only weapon which society uses to prevent conduct which harms or threatens to harm these important interests of the public. Education, at home and at school, as to the types of conduct that society thinks good and bad, is an important weapon; religion, with its emphasis on distinguishing between good and evil conduct, is another.").

9 *See, e.g.*, CRIME, PUNISHMENT, AND DETERRENCE: AN AMERICAN-JEWISH EXPLORATION (David M. Gordis ed., 1991); U.S. CONFERENCE OF CATHOLIC BISHOPS, RESPONSIBILITY, REHABILITATION, AND RESTORATION: A CATHOLIC PERSPECTIVE ON CRIME AND CRIMINAL JUSTICE (2000), *available at*: http://www.usccb.org/sdwp/criminal.htm; Steven Davidoff, *A Comparative Study of the Jewish and the United States Constitutional Law of Capital Punishment*, 3 ILSA J. INT'L & COMP. L. 93 (1996). In the United States, after all, the criminal law is only partly informed by, and thus only partly congruent with, religious norms. *See* 1 LAFAVE, *supra* note 5, § 2.1 ("We have seen that some activities of a sexual nature were considered offenses against religion not punishable as common law crimes; for instance, private acts of fornication or adultery, and seduction. In general these activities are held not to constitute common law crimes in America.").

In this chapter, this relationship for the most part is presented topically. The overarching issue of the criminal law's application to religiously inspired conduct will first be examined both in general and with a specific focus on categories of crimes, from serious bodily harm to relatively minor offenses, as well as offenses against public morality or oneself. In addition, this chapter will address criminal liability resulting from the use of spiritual treatment, particularly for children in lieu of conventional medical care, as well as the criminal liability of clergy and religious institutions. The chapter then will focus on crimes against religious orthodoxy, such as blasphemy, fortune-telling, and witchcraft, as well as offenses against religious property, practices, or persons, such as church arson and hate crimes. Finally, the chapter will cover the constitutionally informed relationship between religion and the criminal process, from the selection and decision making of jurors, to various evidentiary issues such as the compulsion of testimony and the admissibility of a witness's or defendant's religion, to the use of religious authority by parties and judges.

## B. Application of Criminal Law to Religiously Based Conduct

### 1. *In General*

Among the best-known cases involving religion and the criminal law are those in which a person's religiously inspired conduct directly contravenes a criminal injunction, thereby raising the question of whether the person should, in light of the religious inspiration and the importance of conscience, be partially or even completely relieved of criminal liability.[10] Complicating this question is a tendency on the part of both prosecutors and defendants, when religiously inspired conduct has led to a serious crime, to approach the conflict with particularly unyielding dispositions. What is at stake from the government's perspective, after all, is nothing less than the legitimacy and reach of its sovereign jurisdiction,[11] as well as the equal enforcement of its laws,[12] whereas from the religious

[10] Also among the best-known cases, interestingly, are those at the other end of the spectrum, where civil and religious authority act *in concert* to proscribe conduct. *See, e.g.*, Scopes v. State, 289 S.W. 363 (Tenn. 1927); 1–3 The Salem Witchcraft Papers: Verbatim Transcriptions of the Court Records (Paul Boyer & Stephen Nissenbaum, eds., 1977) (revised by Benjamin C. Ray & Tara S. Wood, eds., 2011), *available at:* http://salem.lib.virginia.edu/texts/tei/swp.

[11] *See* Marci Hamilton, God vs. the Gavel: Religion and the Rule of Law (2005). Thus one finds categorical judicial declarations such as "[t]he law of the land is superior to any professed doctrines or beliefs, whether religious, secular, or pagan." Long v. State, 137 N.E. 49, 50 (Ind. 1922); *see also* Reynolds v. United States, 98 U.S. (8 Otto) 145, 166–7 (1879) ("Can a man excuse his practices to the contrary because of his religious belief? To permit this would be to make the professed doctrines of religious belief superior to the law of the land, and in effect to permit every citizen to become a law unto himself. Government could exist only in name under such circumstances.").

[12] *See, e.g.*, United States v. Brown, Nos. 89-5404 to -5407, 908 F.2d 968, 1990 WL 101946, at *7 (4th Cir. Jun. 21, 1990) (*per curiam*) (unpublished) (upholding a jury instruction providing in relevant part that "if one commits a crime under the belief, however sincere, that [his or] her conduct was religiously or morally required … that is no defense to the commission of a crime if the elements of the crime have been proved … beyond a reasonable doubt"), *cert. denied*, 498 U.S. 1029 (1991); United States v. Romano, 849 F.2d 812, 814 n. 3 (3d Cir. 1988) (affirming an evidentiary order excluding arguments based on, among other things, "divine law or other religious teachings"); United States v. Seward, 687 F.2d 1270, 1273 (10th Cir. 1982) (affirming the exclusion of "evidence of religious belief offered as a defense to this criminal charge"), *cert. denied sub nom.* Ahrendt v. United States, 459 U.S. 1147 (1983); Rice v. Commonwealth, 49 S.E.2d 342, 347 (Va. 1948) ("The constitutional protection of religious freedom … does not provide

claimant's vantage point, it is often the integrity of his or her relationship with God.[13] To be excused from the criminal law because one's conduct is religiously rather than nonreligiously inspired or, conversely, to be criminally prosecuted for following one's religious beliefs – either outcome can be understood as extremely problematic depending on one's point of view.[14]

Under the First Amendment, as presently interpreted, the general rule is that a religious basis for one's conduct neither diminishes nor enhances one's criminal liability.[15] That is, religion normally provides no defense to a criminal prosecution. In the words of then Circuit Judge John Paul Stevens, before his elevation to the Supreme Court,

> [i]f a religious, moral, or political purpose may exculpate illegal behavior, one might commit bigamy to avoid eternal damnation; steal from the rich to give alms to the poor; burn and destroy, not merely public records or perhaps buildings but even public servants as well, to implement a Utopian design.
>
> One who elects to serve mankind by taking the law into his own hands thereby demonstrates his conviction that his own ability to determine policy is superior to democratic decision making.[16]

In doctrinal terms, as long as a criminal law is neutral toward religion and generally applicable to materially similar conduct, the courts ordinarily will presume that it is constitutional and apply what is known as the "rationality" or "rational basis test."[17] In turn, the criminal defendant (or declaratory judgment plaintiff) must demonstrate – and it is a heavy evidentiary burden to satisfy – that the law or prosecution does not reasonably or rationally advance a legitimate government interest, such as the protection of health or safety.[18] Only if the particular criminal statute or prosecution targets religion or treats religion in a demonstrably selective manner,[19] or perhaps if another constitutional liberty is concurrently implicated, would the statute or prosecution be subjected to more rigorous scrutiny, thus increasing one's chances of diminished liability.

immunity from compliance with reasonable civil requirements imposed by the State. The individual cannot be permitted, on religious grounds, to be the judge of his [or her] duty to obey the regulatory laws enacted by the State in the interests of the public welfare ... Nor does the fact that defendants harbored no intent to commit a crime constitute a defense.").

13 *Cf.* Church of the Lukumi Babalu Aye, Inc. v. City of Hialeah, 508 U.S. 520, 577 (1993) (Souter, J., concurring in part and concurring in the judgment) ("The extent to which the Free Exercise Clause requires government to refrain from impeding religious exercise defines nothing less than the respective relationships in our constitutional democracy of the individual to government and to God.").

14 *See* J. Nelson Thomas, *Note, Prosecuting Religious Parents for Homicide: Compounding a Tragedy?* 1 VA. J. SOC. POL'Y & L. 409 (1994) (thus proposing a case-by-case rather than categorical approach based on a standard of responsible care).

15 *See* Employment Div. v. Smith, 494 U.S. 872 (1990).

16 United States v. Cullen, 454 F.2d 386, 392 (7th Cir. 1971) (footnote omitted).

17 Regarding the rational basis test, *see* Chapter 5.E.2.

18 Persons who intend to engage in conduct that is made illegal by a criminal law but who believe that the law is unconstitutional or otherwise invalid may have standing to sue the government (usually naming the person in charge of enforcing the law, such as the attorney general) seeking a declaratory judgment regarding the law's validity.

19 At least for purposes of equal protection, "in order to make out a claim of selective prosecution, the defendant must show: 1) that others similarly situated have not been prosecuted, and 2) that the Government's prosecution of him [or her] is selective, invidious, in bad faith or based on impermissible considerations such as race, religion, or his [or her] exercise of constitutional rights." United States v. Hayes, 589 F.2d 811, 819 (5th Cir. 1979), *cert. denied*, 444 U.S. 847 (1979).

This, in fact, is the general analytical standard for virtually all civil and criminal contexts in which free exercise disputes arise.[20] The Supreme Court adopted a similar standard at least as early as 1879,[21] and notwithstanding certain exceptions that developed in the 1960s and 1970s,[22] it was reestablished by the Court in 1990[23] and restated by that tribunal as recently as 2014.[24] As expressed by the late Judge Magruder, a much-respected member of the federal appellate bench, "[t]he civil authority can never concede the extreme claim that police regulations of general application not directed against any sect or creed – however widely the regulation may be accepted as being reasonable and proper – are constitutionally inapplicable to persons who sincerely believe the observance of them to be 'an insult to Almighty God.'"[25] In short, "[t]he guaranty of freedom of religion in the Bill of Rights is not a guaranty of immunity for violation of law,"[26] nor can it "be used as a means to escape civic duties."[27]

Only if this normal rule is deemed inappropriate, such as when a law or prosecution is somehow skewed against religion or when another more protective statute or constitutional provision applies,[28] does a substantial legal dispute arise between the dictates of the government and the position of the religious claimant. In such instances, the government action may be subjected to some level of heightened judicial review. Ordinarily, this is described as "strict scrutiny," under which the government action loses

20 *See* Chapter 5.A, C, & E. A potential exception, rooted as well in the Establishment Clause, is the so-called church autonomy doctrine, which categorically immunizes certain types of religious organizational decision making from legal scrutiny. *See* Hosanna-Tabor Evangelical Lutheran Church & Sch. v. EEOC, 132 S. Ct. 694 (2012) (selection of clergy, so-called ministerial exception); Serbian E. Orthodox Diocese for U.S. & Can. v. Milivojevich, 426 U.S. 696 (1976) (hierarchical church decision making). As discussed *infra* at section B.5, however, it is not clear that the church autonomy doctrine in any way precludes criminal, as opposed to civil, liability.

21 *See* Reynolds v. United States, 98 U.S. (8 Otto) 145, 162–7 (1879) (rejecting the notion that "religious belief can be accepted as a justification of an overt act made criminal by the law of the land"); Warner v. City of Boca Raton, 887 So. 2d 1023, 1027 (Fla. 2004) (explaining that prior to the 1960s, the Supreme Court's cases appeared to hold "that if a neutral law of general applicability was rationally related to a matter of governmental interest, it would not violate the Free Exercise Clause").

22 *See, e.g.*, Wisconsin v. Yoder, 406 U.S. 205 (1972) (criminal case); Sherbert v. Verner, 374 U.S. 398 (1963) (civil case). For many years following *Sherbert* and *Yoder*, it was thought that these cases stated the general rule rather than the exception. Such thinking was put to rest, however, in *Smith*.

23 *See* Employment Div. v. Smith, 494 U.S. 872 (1990).

24 *See* Burwell v. Hobby Lobby Stores, Inc., 134 S. Ct. 2751, 2760–1 (2014); *see also* Hosanna-Tabor, 132 S. Ct. at 706–7. The Court also restated the test, in a more impactful way, in City of Boerne v. Flores, 521 U.S. 507 (1997) [invalidating the state-applicable portion of the Religious Freedom Restoration Act (RFRA) as exceeding Congress's enforcement power under Section 5 of the Fourteenth Amendment because the RFRA required state and local governments to provide religious exemptions not required by the Free Exercise Clause as construed in *Smith*]; *see also* Darab v. United States, 623 A.2d 127, 133 (D.C. 1993) (noting that "the [*Smith*] Court rejected the argument that the religious motivation underlying the defendants' conduct placed them beyond the reach of a criminal law that was not specifically aimed at religion and was admittedly constitutional as applied to others").

25 City of Manchester v. Leiby, 117 F.2d 661, 666 (1st Cir. 1941), *cert. denied*, 313 U.S. 562 (1941).

26 Richter v. United States, 181 F.2d 591, 594 (9th Cir. 1950), *cert. denied*, 340 U.S. 892 (1950).

27 Darab, 623 A.2d at 133; *accord* People v. Ashley, 172 N.Y.S. 282, 285 (N.Y. App. Div. 1918) (noting that the "attempt to excuse violations of lawful salutary police regulations, enacted for the protection of the community, by appeals to constitutional rights and religious beliefs, does not find favor with the courts").

28 *See, e.g.*, Gonzales v. O Centro Espirita Beneficente Uniao do Vegetal, 546 U.S. 418 (2006) (holding that the application of a federal criminal controlled substances law against a particular religious denomination violated the Religious Freedom Restoration Act as amended).

its presumption of constitutionality – in fact, the law is essentially presumed unconstitutional – and the government must demonstrate that its action is a necessary or narrowly tailored means of achieving a compelling interest.[29] Even under this heightened scrutiny, however, criminal laws and their enforcement typically stand a good chance of being upheld because they many times serve compelling interests such as public safety, and their prohibitory nature is often considered necessary to achieve these interests. As is the case with law more broadly, however, this is a generalization to which there can be exceptions. Accordingly, the following sections address how these rules and levels of review play out in various subject-matter and factual contexts.

## 2. *Crimes against Persons or Property*

When one is charged with a felony or other major crime that causes tangible harm to an identifiable victim or victim's property, the Free Exercise Clause, even in its most protective form, provides little, if any, relief.[30] Examples of such crimes, many of which were traditionally classified as *mala in se*, would be "homicide … injuries to persons … (assaults, batteries, and … rape), and … crimes involving the wrongful misuse or taking or destruction of property (larceny, robbery, obtaining by false pretense, forgery, uttering, arson, etc.)."[31] At least three doctrinal reasons, as well as one theoretical premise, support or explain the relative impotence of the Free Exercise Clause when lodged against prosecutions for these types of major crimes.

First, most criminal laws will be categorized by courts as neutral and generally applicable, and to the extent that general applicability might be seen as a matter of degree, it is likely only to increase with the seriousness of the harm that any given criminal law prohibits.[32] Being neutral and generally applicable, under the current doctrinal regime, their constitutional validity thus will be assessed and most likely confirmed using the highly deferential rational basis test.[33] Second, as noted in the preceding subsection,

29 Regarding strict scrutiny, *see* Chapter 5.E.1.

30 *See* Am. Life League v. Reno, 47 F.3d 642, 656 (4th Cir. 1995) ("[W]e do not think the Free Exercise Clause shields conduct violating a criminal law that protects people and property from physical harm."), *cert. denied*, 516 U.S. 809 (1995); United States v. Meyers, 906 F. Supp. 1494, 1496 (D. Wyo. 1995) (describing as an "easy case" the question of whether "laws against murder may prohibit religiously motivated killing" or "laws against assault may prohibit religiously impelled physical attacks"), *aff'd*, 95 F.3d 1475 (10th Cir. 1996), *cert. denied*, 522 U.S. 1006 (1997); Gibson v. Brewer, 952 S.W.2d 239, 248 (Mo. 1997) (*en banc*) ("Religious conduct intended or certain to cause harm need not be tolerated under the First Amendment.").

31 Gerhardt v. State, 475 So. 2d 281, 283 n.6 (Fla. Dist. Ct. App. 1985). Another listing of "major crimes," the one used for federal criminal jurisdiction in relation to Indian country, can be found in 18 U.S.C. § 1153: "murder, manslaughter, kidnapping, maiming, a felony [involving sexual abuse], incest … felony assault … an assault against an individual who has not attained the age of 16 years, felony child abuse or neglect, arson, burglary, robbery, and … [certain felonies involving theft]."

32 *See, e.g.*, Ballard v. Walker, 772 F. Supp. 1335, 1341 (E.D.N.Y. 1991) (explaining that "[e]ven if petitioner's religious beliefs were bona fide, [he] still does not present an adequate defense for the crimes for which he was convicted" in light of *Employment Division v. Smith* [494 U.S. 872 (1990)] because the crimes with which he was charged "were not enacted to restrict religious beliefs").

33 The potential availability of statutory or common-law defenses such as necessity (*see* 1 WHARTON, *supra* note 5, § 90) is unlikely to render any given criminal law nongenerally applicable, at least as long as the reasons underlying the defenses are not inconsistent with the objectives of the criminal law. *See* Blackhawk v. Pennsylvania, 381 F.3d 202, 209 (3d Cir. 2004) ("A law fails the general applicability requirement if it burdens a category of religiously motivated conduct but exempts or does not reach a

even if strict scrutiny is invoked, the government normally would be able to defend its criminal laws as being necessary to achieve compelling interests, and this is especially true for those covering major crimes. Third, regardless of the level of scrutiny employed, free exercise claimants normally must demonstrate that the government has placed a substantial burden on their religious practice. In turn, to the extent that most religious traditions in the United States do not entail, much less command, the commission of harmful felonious conduct, claimants committing such conduct may have difficulty demonstrating that the criminal law or prosecution itself substantially burdens their religion. Finally, and more theoretically, a social contractual understanding of the Constitution suggests, if not requires, that citizens – the parties to the contract – agree not to cause meaningful harm to one another, which more generally corresponds to the complementary notions of natural rights, natural law, and the inherent limits of liberty.[34] To be sure, a number of state religious freedom provisions expressly circumscribe their protective scope by various police-power interests, such as "peace and safety," of the state.[35]

Accordingly, free exercise has not served as a successful defense to charges of, among other things, involuntary manslaughter,[36] unlawful entry,[37] rape,[38] assault,[39] domestic

substantial category of conduct that is not religiously motivated and that undermines the purposes of the law to at least the same degree as the covered conduct that is religiously motivated."); Mitchell Cnty. v. Zimmerman, 810 N.W.2d 1, 13 (Iowa 2012) ("Although there may be many secular exemptions to a statute, if none of them undermines the statutory purpose, then even their cumulative weight does not establish underinclusiveness.").

34 *Cf.* United States v. Bird, 124 F.3d 667, 690 (5th Cir. 1997) (observing that "[t]he regulation of violent actions by one person against another through criminal laws is the most elemental component of general police power"), *cert. denied*, 523 U.S. 1006 (1998).

35 *See, e.g.*, Ariz. Const. art. II, § 12; Cal. Const. art. I, § 4; Colo. Const. art. II, § 4; Conn. Const. art. I, § 3; Fla. Const. art. I, § 3; Ga. Const. art. I, § 1, ¶ IV; Idaho Const. art. I, § 4; Ill. Const. art. I, § 3; Me. Const. art. I, § 3; Md. Const. Decl. of Rts. art. 36; Mass. Const. pt. I, art. II; Minn. Const. art. I, § 16; Miss. Const. art. III, § 18; Mo. Const. art. I, § 5; Nev. Const. art. I, § 4; N.H. Const. pt. I, art. 5; N.Y. Const. art. I, § 3; N.D. Const. art. I, § 3; S.D. Const. art. VI, § 3; Wash. Const. art. I, § 11; Wyo. Const. art. I, § 18.

36 *See, e.g.*, Walker v. Superior Ct., 763 P.2d 852, 869–71 (Cal. 1988) (*en banc*) (allowing involuntary manslaughter prosecution to proceed for death of child, notwithstanding religious basis for parental decision to forego conventional medical care and using strict scrutiny), *cert. denied*, 491 U.S. 905 (1989); Commonwealth v. Twitchell, 617 N.E.2d 609 (Mass. 1993) (upholding involuntary manslaughter conviction where parents, for religious reasons, did not seek medical treatment for their child); State v. Beagley, 305 P.3d 147 (Or. Ct. App. 2013) (same, negligent homicide); Commonwealth v. Nixon, 761 A.2d 1151 (Pa. 2000) (same, involuntary manslaughter), *cert. denied*, 532 U.S. 1008 (2001); Commonwealth v. Barnhart, 497 A.2d 616 (Pa. Super. Ct. 1985) (same), *appeal denied*, 538 A.2d 874 (Pa. 1988), *cert. denied*, 488 U.S. 817 (1988); *see also* Bergmann v. State, 486 N.E.2d 653, 660–1 (Ind. Ct. App. 1985) (similar facts, affirming conviction for reckless homicide, notwithstanding religious beliefs); State v. Norman, 808 P.2d 1159, 1162–3 (Wash. Ct. App. 1991) (similar facts, affirming conviction of father for first-degree manslaughter, notwithstanding religious beliefs), *review denied*, 818 P.2d 1099 (Wash. 1991).

37 *See, e.g.*, Darab, 623 A.2d at 132–4 (rejecting free exercise challenge to unlawful entry prosecution).

38 *See, e.g.*, Alan Abrahamson, *Man Who Claimed Right to Sex with Wife Is Sentenced*, L.A. Times, Jan. 31, 1996, at 1 (describing conviction of a "man who said that his Catholic faith gave him the religious and constitutional right to have sex with his wife").

39 *See, e.g.*, State v. Baxter, 141 P.3d 92, 99–100 (Wash. Ct. App. 2006) (upholding conviction for second-degree assault of a child where a father attempted to circumcise his eight-year-old son at home). "[W]hile [the father] had the right to control his son's care and upbringing, that right did not extend to the type of harm he inflicted on his son, and his religious motive was not a valid defense to the corresponding criminal liability." *Id.*

violence,[40] child endangerment,[41] trespass,[42] violating child labor laws,[43] committing various forms of fraud,[44] burying a body without a permit,[45] issuing harassing or intimidating communications,[46] and threatening public officials.[47] Free exercise has provided an equally ineffective defense to prosecutions for serious crimes against the government or the public as a whole, such as seditious conspiracy,[48] evading one's tax obligations,[49] counterfeiting,[50] simulating legal process,[51] destroying government property,[52] refusing to register under the Selective Service Act,[53] or violating the nation's immigration laws.[54]

40 *See, e.g.*, Currie v. Michigan, No. 10-13133, 2010 WL 3324869, at *1 (E.D. Mich. Aug. 20, 2010) (unpublished); *cf. also* S.D. v. M.J.R., 2 A.3d 412, 422–6 (N.J. Super. Ct. App Div. 2010) (holding that defendant's religious beliefs did not provide a defense against a domestic violence complaint filed by his spouse).

41 *See, e.g.*, People v. Rippberger, 283 Cal. Rptr. 111, 123 (Cal. Ct. App. 1991); Commonwealth v. Foster, 764 A.2d 1076 (Pa. Super. Ct. 2000) (upholding convictions of parents for endangering the welfare of a child and criminal conspiracy arising from their use of prayer in lieu of conventional treatment for their child's cancer), *appeal denied*, 782 A.2d 542 (Pa. 2001).

42 *See, e.g.*, United States v. Acevedo-Delgado, 167 F. Supp. 2d 477, 481–2 (D.P.R. 2001) (finding a violation of neither the Free Exercise Clause nor RFRA); Commonwealth v. Cartwright, 856 N.E.2d 177, 179–80 (Mass. 2006); Dayton v. Drake, 590 N.E.2d 319, 322–3 (Ohio Ct. App. 1990), *dismissed*, 568 N.E.2d 689 (Ohio 1991); State v. Horn, 377 N.W.2d 176, 179 (Wis. Ct. App. 1985), *aff'd*, 407 N.W.2d 854 (Wis. 1987). Likewise, free exercise does not override a property owner's right to exclude, enforceable by an injunction against trespass, a violation of which can then be a criminal offense. *See, e.g.*, Planned Parenthood of Mid-Iowa v. Maki, 478 N.W.2d 637, 640 (Iowa 1991).

43 *See, e.g.*, Prince v. Massachusetts, 321 U.S. 158, 166 (1944).

44 *See, e.g.*, United States v. Carruthers, 152 F.2d 512, 517–18 (7th Cir. 1945) (upholding conviction for mail fraud despite allegedly religious content of defendant's conduct), *cert. denied*, 327 U.S. 787 (1946); Ballard, 772 F. Supp. at 1340–1 (refusing, on *habeas*, to vacate defendant's conviction for grand larceny or fortune-telling where his "promises to cure the complainants' spiritual problems were deliberate lies made with fraudulent intent"); Stephen Senn, *The Prosecution of Religious Fraud*, 17 FLA. ST. U. L. REV. 325 (1990).

45 *See, e.g.*, State v. Chambers, 477 A.2d 110, 112 (Vt. 1984), *appeal dismissed and cert. denied*, 469 U.S. 875 (1984).

46 *See, e.g.*, Baker v. State, 494 P.2d 68, 71 (Ariz. Ct. App. 1972) (phone calls); People v. Peterson, 715 N.E.2d 1221, 1229 (Ill. Ct. App. 1999) (letters), *appeal denied*, 723 N.E.2d 1167 (Ill. 1999), *cert. denied*, 529 U.S. 1077 (2000).

47 *See, e.g.*, United States v. Callahan, 702 F.2d 964, 966 (11th Cir. 1983) (*per curiam*) (upholding prosecution for making threats against the president-elect, even though accompanied by religious statements), *cert. denied*, 464 U.S. 840 (1983).

48 *See, e.g.*, United States v. Rahman, 189 F.3d 88, 116–17 (2d Cir. 1999), *cert. denied*, 528 U.S. 982 (1999), *and cert. denied*, 528 U.S. 1094 (2000).

49 *See, e.g.*, United States v. Sun Myung Moon, 718 F.2d 1210, 1226–8 (2d Cir. 1983), *cert. denied*, 466 U.S. 971 (1984).

50 *See, e.g.*, United States v. Grismore, 564 F.2d 929, 932–3 (10th Cir. 1977), *cert. denied*, 435 U.S. 954 (1978).

51 *See, e.g.*, Runningwolf v. State, 317 S.W.3d 829, 840–1 (Tex. Ct. App. 2010), *aff'd*, 360 S.W.3d 490 (Tex. Ct. Crim. App. 2012).

52 *See, e.g.*, United States v. Allen, 760 F.2d 447, 452–3 (2d Cir. 1985).

53 *See, e.g.*, United States v. Aguilar, 883 F.2d 662, 694–7 (9th Cir. 1989), *cert. denied*, 498 U.S. 1046 (1991); United States v. Schmucker, 815 F.2d 413, 417–18 (6th Cir. 1987); United States v. Bertram, 477 F.2d 1329, 1330 (10th Cir. 1973).

54 *See, e.g.*, United States v. Merkt, 794 F.2d 950, 954–7 (5th Cir. 1986), *cert. denied*, 480 U.S. 946 (1987); United States v. Elder, 601 F. Supp. 1574, 1576–80 (S.D. Tex. 1985). For a detailed examination of the "sanctuary movement," typically associated with defendants in religion-based immigration law violations, *see* Barbara Bezdek, *Religious Outlaws: Narratives of Legality and the Politics of Citizen Interpretation*, 62 TENN. L. REV. 899 (1995).

Indeed, to the extent that there are mitigating aspects of religion or religious belief in relation to serious felony charges, they are not, generally speaking, a function of religious freedom per se. One possible mitigating effect, for example, arises from the government's inability under the First Amendment, largely, if not entirely, the Establishment Clause, to assess the objective truth or falsity of religious beliefs[55] insofar as doing so would open the door to religious persecution and entangle the government in religious doctrine.[56] In turn, the government might be impeded from prosecuting a defendant for fraud, for instance, where allegedly fraudulent statements consist partly or wholly of religious assertions. As Professor William Marshall observes,

> [i]n prosecuting a faith healer for religious fraud ... the government may not ask the jury to evaluate whether the defendant intended to defraud on the basis of the veracity of the defendant's purportedly fraudulent assertions. No similar disability is imposed upon the government ... in prosecuting fraud based upon a defendant's nonreligious statements that, for example, the elixir she is selling can cure the victim's ills. That is, in cases not implicating religious belief, the government may prove intent to defraud by showing that a defendant's statement "if you buy this elixir, it will cure you" is not a credible assertion. The government cannot, however, prove fraud in its case against the faith healer by showing that the defendant's religiously based assertion "if you give me money, God will cure you" is similarly noncredible.[57]

A defendant's religious beliefs also may, in exceptional cases, adversely affect the government's ability to establish one or more of the elements of a charged crime, all of which it must prove beyond a reasonable doubt.[58] Specifically, there is a limited body of case law holding that a religious belief may – if sincerely maintained and sufficiently strong to override what most observers would consider objective reality – negate a mental element (*mens rea*) requiring actual appreciation or apprehension of the nature or ordinary consequences of one's conduct.[59] In *People v. Strong*,[60] for example, the defendant's religious faith led him to believe that "he could stop a follower's heartbeat and breathing and plunge knives into his chest without any injury to the person."[61] When he performed the ceremony on a new recruit, however, the ritual not only injured the recruit, it killed him. The defendant then was charged with second-degree manslaughter, which under

[55] *See* United States v. Ballard, 322 U.S. 78, 86–8 (1944). For different readings of *Ballard*, *see* Ronald J. Krotoszynski, Jr., *The Apostle, Mr. Justice Jackson, and the "Pathological Perspective" of the Free Exercise Clause*, 65 Wash. & Lee L. Rev. 1071 (2008); William P. Marshall, *Smith, Ballard, and the Religious Inquiry Exception to the Criminal Law*, 44 Tex. Tech L. Rev. 239 (2011).

[56] *See* Chapter 4.C.1.c and Chapter 5.D

[57] Marshall, *supra* note 55, at 241–2 (footnotes omitted). For further analysis, *see* Barry Nobel, *Religious Healing in the Courts: The Liberties and Liabilities of Patients, Parents, and Healers*, 16 Puget Sound L. Rev. 599, 668–81 (1993); Senn, *supra* note 44.

[58] Regarding this evidentiary standard, and more generally the prosecution's burden of proof, *see* Jefferson L. Ingram, Criminal Evidence §§ 3.5–3.6 (10th ed., 2009).

[59] *Cf.* Wayne R. LaFave, 2 Substantive Criminal Law § 15.4, at n. 28 (2d ed., 2003 rev'd Oct. 2013) ("[I]t is no interference with one's freedom of religion to convict of manslaughter one who, for religious reasons, fails to call a doctor when to fail to do so constitutes criminal negligence. Yet an honest religious belief that prayer is a better cure than medicine, that Providence can heal better than doctors, might serve to negate the awareness of risk which is required for manslaughter in those states which use a subjective test of criminal negligence.").

[60] 338 N.E.2d 602 (N.Y. 1975).

[61] *Id.* at 604.

state law required that he perceived the risk of death but consciously disregarded it. At trial, the defendant argued unsuccessfully that the jury also should have been able to consider a lesser charge of negligent homicide, which required only that he negligently or unreasonably failed to perceive the risk. On appeal, the state high court held that it was error to exclude the lesser, alternative charge in light of testimony that neither the defendant nor the victim perceived the risk and that the defendant had at least once performed the ritual without causing injury.[62]

Likewise, in *United States v. Lynch*,[63] a federal district court held that two defendants who violated its injunction against further protesting at a particular abortion clinic were not guilty of criminal contempt because, according to the court's findings, "neither [defendant] acted with the willfulness which criminal contempt requires."[64] Specifically, the court found "as a matter of fact that [the defendants'] sincere, genuine, objectively based and, indeed, conscience-driven religious belief, preclude[d] a finding of willfulness," which it defined as "deliberate conduct done with a bad purpose either to disobey or to disregard the law."[65]

Key to this small line of decisions, apparently, is whether the defendant is charged with a general-intent crime as opposed to a specific-intent crime. In an unpublished California case, for example, the Court of Appeal was quite explicit in distinguishing between these two categories of crime when upholding denial of the defendant's request to instruct the jury regarding his religious beliefs as a potential defense, albeit to a charge of involuntary intoxication rather than a more serious crime.[66] The appellant, for his part, "maintain[ed] that his beliefs ... showed [that] he was unable to form criminal intent, and that he was divinely inspired to medicate himself."[67] According to the Court, however, the defendant "was convicted of a general intent crime. Therefore, there was no requirement to disprove an intent element. [His] ... religious beliefs were of no relevance to the issues, and the trial court properly excluded testimony on this subject."[68]

At least two serious concerns accompany the attempt to negate intent, specific or otherwise, by means of one's religious beliefs. First, the small number of cases in which such a defense has prevailed, or has even been permitted, suggests that it is viewed quite negatively by judges, perhaps even bordering on frivolous in most instances. Second, the use

62 *See id.* at 604. For further discussion of *Strong* and the constitutional and other issues that it raises, *see* John S. Hilbert, *Comment, God in a Cage: Religion, Intent, and Criminal Law*, 36 BUFF. L. REV. 701 (1987).

63 952 F. Supp. 167 (S.D.N.Y. 1997), *appeal dismissed*, 162 F.3d 732 (2d Cir. 1998), *reh'g and reh'g en banc denied*, 181 F.3d 330 (2d Cir. 1999).

64 *Id.* at 170. For critical commentary on *Lynch*, *see* John C. Klotz, *Abortion Decision Undercuts Rule of Law*, NAT'L L.J., Feb. 24, 1997, at A23; Michael W. McConnell, *Breaking the Law, Bending the Law*, FIRST THINGS, June-July 1997, at 13; Tara Adams Ragone, *Note, In Contempt of Contempt? Religious Motivation as a Reason to Mitigate Contempt Sanctions*, 1999 ANN. SURV. AM. L. 195.

65 Lynch, 952 F. Supp. at 170 [citing BLACK'S LAW DICTIONARY (5th ed. 1979)]. *Compare* United States v. Baldwin, 770 F.2d 1550, 1557–8 (11th Cir. 1985) (refusing, in the context of criminal contempt, to find a person's conduct not "willful" merely because it was premised on religious beliefs, and defining willful as deliberate or intentional rather than inadvertent or negligent), *cert. denied*, 475 U.S. 1120 (1986). For appellate criticism of the *Lynch* court's finding, *see* United States v. Lynch, 181 F.3d 330, 331–2 (2d Cir. 1999) (Sack, J., concurring in the denial of rehearing *en banc*); *id.* at 335–7 (Cabranes, J., dissenting from the denial of rehearing *en banc*); United States v. Lynch, 162 F.3d 732, 746 (2d Cir. 1998) (Feinberg, J., dissenting).

66 *See* People v. Bellow, No. B149524, 2002 WL 374146, at *3 (Cal. Ct. App. Mar. 8, 2003) (unpublished).

67 *Id.*

68 *Id.*

of such a defense yields a rather unseemly implication, namely, that devout religiosity ought to have, in effect, the same legal status as mental deficiency[69] or juvenile naiveté.[70] To be sure, some jurisdictions even recognize a so-called deific decree basis for legal insanity,[71] pursuant to which "one who believes that he [or she] is acting under the direct command of God is no less insane because he [or she] nevertheless knows murder is prohibited by the laws of man. Indeed, it may actually emphasize his [or her] insanity."[72]

Thus far the analysis has centered largely on major crimes, particularly those involving harm to persons or property. More difficult questions can arise where the conduct at issue is by statute declared criminal but does not cause the sort of serious damage to life, health, or property that essentially places the statute beyond meaningful constitutional challenge. Crimes of this sort can include certain offenses against the public as a whole or against public morality (addressed in the next subsection), conduct causing tangible but comparatively minor harm, and a variety of *mala prohibita* or quasi-regulatory infractions.[73] In such circumstances, one's free exercise defense may have a greater (though perhaps still modest) likelihood of success, especially if heightened scrutiny is employed. In large part, this increased likelihood can be attributed to two causes. First, the government's interest is in fact less likely to be compelling or the prosecution of the conduct might not be necessary to achieve its interest, especially when, as may often be the case, the low-level criminal law already contains nonreligious exemptions. Second, permitting or exempting the conduct is less likely to be problematic from the standpoint

[69] *See* Grant H. Morris & Ansar Haroun, *"God Told Me To Kill": Religion or Delusion?* 38 SAN DIEGO L. REV. 973 (2001); Andrew J. Demko, *Note, Abraham's Deific Defense: Problems with Insanity, Faith, and Knowing Right from Wrong*, 80 NOTRE DAME L. REV. 1961 (2005); *cf.* John H. Garvey, *Free Exercise and the Values of Religious Liberty*, 18 CONN. L. REV. 779, 794–6 (1986) (comparing religion and insanity).

[70] *Cf. In re* William G., 963 P.2d 287 (Ariz. Ct. App. 1997) (acquitting a teenager of criminal damage because of his lack of awareness that riding shopping carts posed a substantial risk of damage to automobiles, which in fact he damaged).

[71] The original deific decree, of course, is God's directive to Abraham to "[t]ake your son, your only son Isaac, whom you love, and … offer him there as a burnt offering … Abraham built an altar there and laid the wood in order. He bound his son Isaac, and laid him on the altar, on top of the wood. Then Abraham reached out his hand and took the knife to kill his son." *Genesis* 22:2, 9–10 (NEW REVISED STANDARD VERSION).

[72] State v. Cameron, 674 P.2d 650, 654 (Wash. 1983) (*en banc*) [citing State v. Crenshaw, 659 P.2d 488 (Wash. 1983); People v. Schmidt, 110 N.E. 945 (N.Y. 1915)]; *see also* People v. Serravo, 823 P.2d 128, 139–40 (Colo. 1992) (*en banc*); State v. Worlock, 569 A.2d 1314, 1322 (N.J. 1990). For commentary, *see* Grant H. Morris & Ansar Haroun, *"God Told Me To Kill": Religion or Delusion?*, 38 SAN DIEGO L. REV. 973 (2001); Andrew J. Demko, *Note, Abraham's Deific Defense: Problems with Insanity, Faith, and Knowing Right from Wrong*, 80 NOTRE DAME L. REV. 1961 (2005); Christopher Hawthorne, *Note, "Deific Decree": The Short, Happy Life of a Pseudo-Doctrine*, 33 LOY. L.A. L. REV. 1755 (2000). At least one court has called into question the constitutionality of the "deific decree" doctrine. *See* Wilson v. Gaetz, 608 F.3d 347, 354 (7th Cir. 2010) ("[T]o distinguish between 'deific' and all other delusions and confine the insanity defense to the former would present serious questions under the First Amendment's establishment clause.").

[73] *See* Thomson v. State, 44 S.W.2d 171, 178 (Tex. Ct. App. 2001) {"Criminal offenses are characterized as either *malum in se*, meaning 'inherently evil' or *malum prohibitum*, meaning 'prohibited evil.' These distinctions are deeply rooted in American and English jurisprudence. *Malum in se* offenses traditionally include acts that are inherently immoral, such as murder, arson, or rape. A *malum prohibitum* offense is defined as: '[a]n act that is a crime merely because it is prohibited by statute, although the act itself is not necessarily immoral.' Examples of *mala prohibita* offenses include speeding, illegal dumping of trash, and possession of a firearm while under a domestic restraining order." (citations omitted) [quoting BLACK'S LAW DICTIONARY 971 (7th ed., 1999)]}.

of judicial intuition, particularly if a judge does not believe that the general goals of the criminal law, such as deterrence or rehabilitation, will be furthered by a conviction.[74]

Thus, for example, under heightened scrutiny, the government has not always succeeded in its efforts to enforce against religious objectors its criminal laws concerning wildlife protection,[75] preservation of roads,[76] or the use of government-specified vehicle signage.[77] Likewise, there is a long line of cases invalidating restrictions on religious expression, particularly the distribution of religious literature, although the role of the Free Speech Clause, either independently or in conjunction with religious freedom, often has been central to such cases.[78] Where, by comparison, heightened scrutiny is not employed or another protection such as free speech is not involved, challenges even to these low-level offenses (e.g., driving without a license) are highly unlikely to succeed, assuming that the law is not entirely irrational or arbitrary in its design or operation.[79]

### 3. *Crimes against Public Morality or Oneself*

Certain species of conduct made criminal by a number of jurisdictions are distinct either for causing harm primarily against norms of public morality (e.g., public nudity or bigamy) or for causing harm primarily against oneself (e.g., suicide or personal drug use). Often lacking in such crimes is direct physical injury to the person or property of anyone

74 *See, e.g.*, People v. Singh, 516 N.Y.S.2d 412, 415–16 (N.Y. City Ct. Queens Cnty. 1987) (in the prosecution of a Sikh for carrying an exposed knife as required by his religious beliefs, reluctantly holding that the Free Exercise Clause was not violated but then nevertheless dismissing the prosecution "as a matter of judicial discretion" because "[t]here exist compelling factors and circumstances that clearly demonstrate that conviction or prosecution of the said defendant upon the said accusatory instrument could constitute or result in injustice and would serve no useful purpose").

75 *See, e.g.*, Horen v. Commonwealth, 479 S.E.2d 553, 557, 559–60 (Va. Ct. App. 1997) (reversing misdemeanor convictions for possessing the feathers of protected birds, noting that there were several nonreligious exceptions in the statute and finding neither a compelling interest nor the least restrictive means); *see also* United States v. Hardman, 297 F.3d 1116 (10th Cir. 2002) (*en banc*). For further discussion of such cases, *see* Tina S. Boradiansky, *Comment, Conflicting Values: The Religious Killing of Federally Protected Wildlife*, 30 Nat. Resources J. 709 (1990).

76 *See, e.g.*, Mitchell Cnty. v. Zimmerman, 810 N.W.2d 1, 15–18 (Iowa 2012) (reversing citations for violation of a road surface protection ordinance, which provided for criminal and civil penalties, observing that there were several nonreligious exceptions in the ordinance and holding that the ordinance was not narrowly tailored to achieve the interest in road preservation).

77 *See, e.g.*, State v. Miller, 549 N.W.2d 235, 241–2 (Wis. 1996) (as applied to Amish, state's requirement of slow-moving vehicle sign was not the least restrictive means to ensure roadway safety, using strict scrutiny under the Wisconsin Constitution); State v. Hershberger, 462 N.W.2d 393, 397–9 (Minn. 1990) (same under the Minnesota Constitution).

78 *See, e.g.*, Watchtower Bible & Tract Soc'y of N.Y., Inc. v. Vill. of Stratton, 536 U.S. 150, 165–9 (2002) (invalidating an ordinance requiring those who distribute door-to-door literature first to obtain a permit); Marsh v. Alabama, 326 U.S. 501, 509 (1946) (holding that a privately operated municipality could not prosecute an individual for distributing religious literature); Murdock v. Pennsylvania, 319 U.S. 105, 108 (1943) (reversing convictions for unauthorized dissemination of religious literature, noting that "[t]he hand distribution of religious tracts is an age-old form of missionary evangelism – as old as the history of printing presses"); Cantwell v. Connecticut, 310 U.S. 296, 311 (1940) (similar).

79 *See, e.g.*, Tenison v. State, 38 P.3d 535, 539–40 (Alaska 2001) (not applying heightened scrutiny and upholding conviction for driving with an expired license, notwithstanding defendant's religion-based refusal to provide her Social Security Number in order to renew her license); Cosby v. State, 738 N.E.2d 709, 711–12 (Ind. Ct. App. 2000) (not applying heightened scrutiny and upholding misdemeanor conviction for driving, to church, without a valid license).

other than the individual or individuals engaging in the conduct. Accordingly, these are often called "victimless crimes,"[80] although this characterization may be both controversial and in some instances inapt. This subsection examines several activities that can stem from religious beliefs and generally can be classified as crimes against public morality or oneself: bigamy or polygamy, conduct involving alcohol or controlled substances, snake handling, suicide, and self-mutilation.

It should be noted at the outset that this subsection examines only notable or representative categories of conduct fitting within the broad domain of crimes against public morality or oneself and that others certainly do exist. For example, *Wisconsin v. Yoder*,[81] one of the best-known Free Exercise Clause cases, involved a state's criminal prosecution of Old Order Amish parents for noncompliance with a compulsory school attendance law – conduct that can be characterized as contravening the public good but not causing obvious injury to persons or property. Perhaps due in part to the comparatively innocuous nature of the defendants' conduct – they refused to send their children to school beyond the eighth grade, whereas state law required schooling until age sixteen – the convictions were ultimately reversed in that case.[82] Applying strict scrutiny, the Supreme Court found that the government had not demonstrated that mandating an additional year or two of formal schooling was, in the case of the defendants' children, actually necessary to achieve the state's concededly significant interest in creating an educated citizenry.[83] To a large extent, *Yoder* stands apart, both in substance and in result, from most conflicts involving religious defenses to criminal prosecutions, and the Court itself went out of its way to emphasize that no "harm to the physical or mental health of the child or to the public safety, peace, order, or welfare has been demonstrated or may be properly inferred."[84] To be sure, even other free exercise interpositions against compulsory school attendance laws have been largely unsuccessful when the parents seek to avoid *all* formal or state-certified schooling or when their religious beliefs are not as all-encompassing as those of the Amish in *Yoder*.[85]

Returning, then, to the representative survey of crimes against public morality or oneself, the first form of conduct to be examined is bigamy or polygamy, the

[80] *See* Deborah Zalesne, *Sexual Harassment Law in the United States and South Africa: Facilitating the Transition from Legal Standards to Social Norms*, 25 HARV. WOMEN'S L.J. 143, 189 (2002). One standard reference defines "victimless crime" as "[a] crime that is considered to have no direct victim, usu[ally] because only consenting adults are involved. Examples are possession of illicit drugs and deviant sexual intercourse between consenting adults." BLACK'S LAW DICTIONARY 429 (9th ed., 2009).

[81] 406 U.S. 205 (1972).

[82] Attesting to the comparatively noninjurious nature of the parents' conduct, the criminal punishment consisted of a five-dollar fine. *See id.* at 208.

[83] *See id.* at 221–9.

[84] *Id.* at 230.

[85] *See, e.g.*, Jernigan v. State, 412 So. 2d 1242, 1245–6 (Ala. Ct. Crim. App. 1982); Burrow v. State, 669 S.W.2d 441, 443–4 (Ark. 1984); State v. Patzer, 382 N.W.2d 631, 635–9 (N.D. 1986); State v. Schmidt, 505 N.E.2d 627, 629–30 (Ohio 1987), *cert. denied*, 484 U.S. 942 (1987); Howell v. State, 723 S.W.2d 755, 757–8 (Tex. Ct. App. 1986); State v. DeLaBruere, 577 A.2d 254, 263–72 (Vt. 1990). *Compare* State *ex rel.* Nagle v. Olin, 415 N.E.2d 279, 353–5 (Ohio 1980) (*per curiam*) (finding a free exercise violation where a child was attending an unchartered religious school and the state had gone "further than necessary to assure the state's legitimate interests in the education of children in private elementary schools"). *But see* People v. DeJonge, 501 N.W.2d 127, 139–44 (Mich. 1993) (finding a free exercise violation where state required use of certified teachers for home-schooled children because the state failed to show that its certification requirement was essential to its objective of ensuring adequate education).

criminalization of which appears largely to be a matter of moral offense.[86] Also known as "plural marriage," this practice is condoned or required by certain religions, today most notably in the United States by the Fundamentalist Church of Jesus Christ of Latter-Day Saints (FLDS).[87] The practice is effectively prohibited, however, by all fifty states[88] and is expressly prohibited by the state constitutions of Arizona, Idaho, New Mexico, Oklahoma, and Utah.[89] The most famous criminal prosecutions for bigamy occurred in the nineteenth century, when it was still undertaken by members of the Church of Jesus Christ of Latter-Day Saints, or Mormon Church, which is not affiliated with the FLDS.[90] From the 1860s to the 1880s, in response to Mormon practices, Congress passed a series of statutes prohibiting or otherwise penalizing bigamy or polygamy in federal territories,[91] leading to a variety of criminal prosecutions and civil disabilities.[92] In the late 1870s, the Supreme Court upheld the federal conviction of bigamist George Reynolds, finding it irrelevant that the alleged basis of Reynolds' conduct was his religious beliefs and declaring that "[l]aws are made for the government of

86 *See* Katharine B. Silbaugh, *Sex Offenses: Consensual*, *in* 4 Encyclopedia of Crime & Justice 1465, 1470 (Joshua Dressler ed., 2d ed., 2002) ("Bigamy is part of the criminal law of the United States apparently because it is an offense to Judeo-Christian faiths … The harm … is presumably moral offense to nonparties.").

87 *See Fundamentalist Church of Jesus Christ of Latter-Day Saints Fast Facts*, CNN, Apr. 22, 2014, *available at*: http://www.cnn.com/2013/10/31/us/fundamentalist-church-of-jesus-christ-of-latter-day-saints-fast-facts/. Some Native American traditions also can provide for plural marriage. *See* Mark Strasser, *Marriage, Free Exercise, and the Constitution*, 26 Law & Ineq. 59, 100–1 (2008). In addition, "it is suspected that there are a significant number of immigrant families engaging in polygamy in the United States." Jaime M. Gher, *Polygamy and Same-Sex Marriage: Allies or Adversaries within the Same-Sex Marriage Movement*, 14 Wm. & Mary J. Women & L. 559, 577 (2008).

88 *See* Gher, *supra* note 87, at 578; Strasser, *supra* note 87, at 101 & n. 310.

89 *See* Gher, *supra* note 87, at 578.

90 With an understanding of God developed from the traditions of *Old Testament* Israelite theocracy, Joseph Smith saw plural marriage (practiced by such influential men in church history as Abraham and Solomon) as essential to the religion, and in 1852, church leaders officially announced their commitment to the practice. In 1890, however, the church formally outlawed the practice. *See* Cleveland v. United States, 329 U.S. 14, 16 n. 1 (1946); Richard Lyman Bushman, Mormonism: A Very Short Introduction 89 (2008).

91 *See* Morrill Anti-Bigamy Act, 12 Stat. 501 (1862) (codified at Rev. Stat. § 5352) (prohibiting bigamy and imposing financial restrictions on church and nonprofit ownership); Poland Act, 18 Stat. 253 (1874) (redefining and transferring the jurisdiction of judicial and prosecutorial officers in the Utah territory and altering jury rules in ways that effectively kept polygamists off juries and facilitated their prosecution); Edmunds Act (or Edmunds Anti-Polygamy Act), 22 Stat. 30 (1882) (amending the Morrill Act by making polygamy a felony and prohibiting "bigamous" or "unlawful cohabitation," thereby facilitating prosecution without proof of actual multiple marriage); Edmunds-Tucker Act, 24 Stat. 635 (1887) (dissolving the Mormon church and an associated company; requiring an antipolygamy oath for prospective voters, jurors, and public officials; annulling territorial laws allowing illegitimate children to inherit; requiring civil marriage licenses and abrogating the common-law spousal privilege for polygamists, thereby facilitating polygamy prosecutions; and making additional changes to government structure and education) (repealed 1978). With regard to these laws, *see* Mary K. Campbell, *Mr. Peay's Horses: The Federal Response to Mormon Polygamy, 1854–1887*, 13 Yale J.L. & Feminism 29, 38–51 (2001) [discussing the Morrill Act, ch. 125, § 1, 12 Stat. 501 (1862) (codified at Rev. Stat. § 5352); the Poland Act, ch. 469, Part X, 13 Stat. 253 (1874); the Edmunds Act, ch. 47, Part X, 22 Stat. 30 (1882) (codified at 48 U.S.C. § 1461) (repealed 1983); and the Edmunds-Tucker Act, ch. 397, 24 Stat. 635 (1887) (codified at 28 U.S.C. § 633, 660) (repealed 1978)].

92 *See generally* Sarah Barringer Gordon, The Mormon Question: Polygamy and Constitutional Conflict in Nineteenth Century America (2002).

actions, and while they cannot interfere with mere religious belief and opinions, they may with practices."[93]

Since *Reynolds*, a number of courts have likewise rejected free exercise claims against criminal charges of bigamy or polygamy[94] or against adverse civil consequences resulting from one's engaging in this conduct.[95] Recent challenges, particularly to Utah's prohibition,[96] have not fared better,[97] even when concurrently asserting a due process–based sexual privacy argument based on expansive rulings by the Supreme Court.[98] A 2013 federal district court ruling did strike down the portion of Utah's law prohibiting "cohabit[ation] with another person," but the court distinguished that prohibition from, and indeed upheld, the ban on polygamy.[99] It remains to be seen whether additional changes in the legal treatment of same-sex conduct, and particularly same-sex marriage,[100] will have any secondary effect on the legal status of polygamy prohibitions.[101]

[93] Reynolds v. United States, 98 U.S. (8 Otto) 145, 166 (1879) (addressing challenge to Morrill Anti-Bigamy Act); *see also* Cleveland v. United States, 329 U.S. 14, 20 (1946) (upholding the inclusion of polygamy-related conduct within the federal prohibition on transporting in interstate commerce "any woman or girl for the purpose of prostitution or debauchery, or for any other immoral purpose"); Davis v. Beason, 133 U.S. 333 (1890) (addressing challenge to an Idaho territorial law similar to the Edmunds-Tucker Act), *overruled in part by* Romer v. Evans, 517 U.S. 620, 634 (1996); Miles v. United States, 103 U.S. (13 Otto) 304, 310–11 (1881).

[94] *See, e.g.*, State v. Fischer, 199 P.3d 663, 667–9 (Ariz. Ct. App. 2008); Long v. State, 137 N.E. 49 (Ind. 1922); State v. Green, 99 P.3d 820, 825–30 (Utah 2004) (upholding antibigamy statute against free exercise challenge); State v. Barlow, 153 P.2d 647 (Utah 1944) (unlawful cohabitation), *appeal dismissed*, 324 U.S. 829 (1945); State v. Gonzalez, No. 22829-1-III, 2005 WL 843751, at *3 (Wash. Ct. App. Apr. 12, 2005) (unpublished).

[95] *See, e.g.*, Potter v. Murray City, 760 F.2d 1065, 1066–70 (10th Cir. 1985) (rejecting the free exercise claim of a police officer discharged for bigamy, citing *Reynolds* and applying a strict scrutiny analysis), *cert. denied*, 474 U.S. 849 (1985).

[96] *See* UTAH CONST. art. III, § 1 ("Perfect toleration of religious sentiment is guaranteed. No inhabitant of this State shall ever be molested in person or property on account of his or her mode of religious worship; but polygamous or plural marriages are forever prohibited."); Utah Code Ann. § 76-7-101 (criminalizing bigamy as a third-degree felony).

[97] *See* Brown v. Buhman, 947 F. Supp. 2d 1170, 1194–7, 1203–4 (D. Utah 2013) (upholding as constitutional Utah's statutory prohibition); State v. Holm, 137 P.3d 726, 742 (Utah 2006) (same); *cf.* Bronson v. Swensen, 394 F. Supp. 2d 1329 (D. Utah 2005) (same), *vacated on jurisdictional grounds*, 500 F.3d 1099 (10th Cir. 2007). For analysis of claims made in *Bronson*, *see* Jacob Richards, *Comment, Autonomy, Imperfect Consent, and Polygamist Sex Rights Claims*, 98 CAL. L. REV. 197 (2010).

[98] In *Lawrence v. Texas* [539 U.S. 558 (2003)], the Supreme Court struck down a Texas statute criminalizing homosexual sodomy. The defendant in *Holm* unsuccessfully argued, citing *Lawrence*, that sexual conduct was a constitutionally protected act. *See* Holm, 137 P.3d at 742. For a discussion of the possible impact of certain constitutional developments on bigamy or polygamy's legal status, *see* Richard A. Vazquez, *Note, The Practice of Polygamy: Legitimate Free Exercise of Religion or Legitimate Public Menace? Revisiting Reynolds in Light of Modern Constitutional Jurisprudence*, 5 N.Y.U. J. LEGIS. & PUB. POL'Y 225 (2001).

[99] *See* Brown, 947 F. Supp. 2d at 1217–26 (invalidating the prohibition under the Free Exercise and Due Process Clauses).

[100] *See, e.g.*, United States v. Windsor, 133 S. Ct. 2675 (2013) (invalidating a general federal definition of marriage that excluded same-sex relationships). *Windsor* has led to a torrent of lower federal court invalidations of state prohibitions on same-sex marriage, largely on the theory that they violate the guarantee of equal protection. *See* http://www.freedomtomarry.org/states/.

[101] For differing views on this prospect, *see* Hema Chatlani, *In Defense of Marriage: Why Same-Sex Marriage Will Not Lead Us Down a Slippery Slope Toward the Legalization of Polygamy*, 6 APPALACHIAN J.L. 101 (2006); Gher, *supra* note 87; Charles P. Kindregan, Jr., *Religion, Polygamy, and Non-Traditional Families: Disparate Views on the Evolution of Marriage in History and the Debate over Same-Sex Unions*, 41 SUFFOLK U. L. REV. 19 (2007); Maura I. Strassberg, *Distinctions of Form or Substance: Monogamy,*

Another realm of conduct sometimes motivated by religion and primarily resulting in possible harm only to public morality or oneself (absent additional conduct, such as driving) is the consumption of alcohol such as wine, which can be a ritual or sacrament of a number of religions, most prominently Christianity and Judaism. In various jurisdictions and at different times in U.S. history, the production, transportation, sale, possession, and consumption of alcohol have been subject to regulation or criminalization. Most famously, Americans in 1919 ratified the Eighteenth Amendment, which prohibited "the manufacture, sale, or transportation of intoxicating liquors within, the importation thereof into, or the exportation thereof from the United States."[102] Congress, in turn, implemented the amendment principally by the National Prohibition Act, or Volstead Act. The statute itself had specific exemptions for religious as well as scientific and technological uses of alcohol, thus avoiding a conflict under the First Amendment regarding, especially, the manufacture, possession, and consumption of sacramental wine.[103] In 1933, the Twenty-First Amendment repealed the Eighteenth Amendment[104] and placed the authority to restrict the "transportation or importation into any State … for delivery or use therein of intoxicating liquors" into the hands of states,[105] which then generally regulated or prohibited alcohol but likewise provided exceptions (e.g., lowering the minimum consumption age or authorizing purchase from a nonstate seller) to accommodate, among other uses, religious practices.[106] Although no state today completely forbids the sale of alcohol, several counties and municipalities are "dry" in this sense, and some of these go so far as to prohibit consumption as well as sale, thus raising a free exercise issue to the extent that such prohibitions interfere with religious practices.[107] Given the

*Polygamy and Same-Sex Marriage*, 75 N.C. L. Rev. 1501 (1997); Ruth K. Khalsa, *Note, Polygamy as a Red Herring in the Same-Sex Marriage Debate*, 54 Duke L.J. 1665 (2005).

102 U.S. Const. amend. XVIII, § 1.

103 *See* Employment Div. v. Smith, 494 U.S. 872, 913 n. 6 (1990) (Blackmun, J., dissenting) [noting that "[d]uring Prohibition, the Federal Government exempted [the sacramental] use of wine from its general ban on possession and use of alcohol" (citing National Prohibition Act, Title II, § 3, 41 Stat. 308)]. *But cf.* Shapiro v. Lyle, 30 F.2d 971, 973 (W.D. Wash. 1929) (holding that the National Prohibition Act's quantity limit on sacramental wine did not violate the Free Exercise Clause), *appeal dismissed*, 36 F.2d 1021 (9th Cir. 1930).

104 *See* U.S. Const. amend. XXI, § 1.

105 *Id.* § 2.

106 *See, e.g.*, Ala. Code § 28-3-15(b); Ariz. Rev. Stat. § 4-244; Colo. Rev. Stat. § 18-13-122; Fla. Stat. § 564.03(5); Ga. Code § 3-3-23; Ill. Comp. Stat. ch. 235 § 5/6–20; Mich. Const. art. IV, § 40, *as interpreted in* Felix v. Milliken, 463 F. Supp. 1360, 1384–5 (E.D. Mich. 1978); Ohio Rev. Code § 4301.69(E)(1); 47 Pa. Stat. § 4–491(2); S.C. Code § 61-6-4070; Tenn. Code § 1-3-113(b)(2); Wash. Rev. Code § 66.44.270; Wis. Stat. § 125.07(1)(a)(3).

107 An alternative scenario, albeit one potentially involving a different analysis, is a policy of a prison (in an otherwise nondry jurisdiction) that imposes limitations on alcohol. *See, e.g.*, Gutierrez v. Corr. Corp. of Am., No. CV 10-0117-PHX-RCB, 2010 WL 4736618, at *3 (D. Ariz. Nov. 16, 2010) (unpublished) (rejecting free exercise challenge to such a policy, finding no substantial burden on the inmate's religious practice). A more litigated but not thoroughly resolved issue arises when a criminal defendant, as part of initial sentencing or as a condition of probation or parole, is prohibited from consuming alcohol but claims that such consumption is part of his or her religious practice. *See, e.g.*, Stergios v. United States, No. 2:12-CV-00237-GZS, 2013 WL 3045089, at *14 (D. Me. Jun. 17, 2013) (unpublished) (noting but deferring the issue). Conversely, at least one case has involved a claim that the involuntary provision of alcohol, by means of an injected tuberculosis test, would violate an inmate's religious tenet against alcohol consumption. *See* Canada v. Ray, Civ. Action No. 7:08-CV-00219, 2011 WL 565611, at *2 (W.D. Va. Feb. 9, 2011) (unpublished), *aff'd*, No. 11-6239, 437 Fed. App'x 263 (4th Cir. Jul. 6, 2011) (unpublished).

long-standing ritualistic or sacramental use of wine by recognizable religions, it has been argued that, notwithstanding *Smith* and even in the absence of a more protective religious freedom law, courts still would likely rule in favor of traditional religious practices should a conflict in a thoroughly dry jurisdiction arise.[108]

A much larger body of case law concerns the religious use of controlled substances, such as marijuana and certain hallucinogenic plant–derived chemicals, that in various respects are criminalized under federal and state law.[109] Arguably, the internal coherence or consistency of drug restrictions – regulating some, criminalizing others, and doing so to varying extents depending on the drug and the activity – is not always apparent,[110] but in general, it may be said that the First Amendment Free Exercise Clause has ordinarily not blocked their application to religiously based conduct. Numerous religious challenges to marijuana restrictions, for example, have been upheld under that clause,[111]

108 *See* Kenneth Marin, *Employment Division v. Smith: The Supreme Court Alters the State of Free Exercise Doctrine*, 40 Am. U. L. Rev. 1431, 1474 (1991). *But see* Erwin Chemerinsky, Constitutional Law, Principles and Policies § 12.3.2.3, at 1259 (3d ed., 2006) ("[P]rior to *Smith*, if a county had a law prohibiting all consumption of alcoholic beverages, there is no doubt that a free exercise exemption could have been obtained by a priest who wanted to use wine in communion or a Jewish family that wanted to use wine at a Sabbath or seder dinner. Yet, after *Smith*, it is clear that the priest or the Jewish family would lose in their free exercise claim. The prohibition of the consumption of alcohol is a neutral law of general applicability; it applies to all in the county and was not motivated by a desire to interfere with religion.").

109 In addition to drugs, federal law governs devices. In a series of cases involving a device called an "E-meter," the Church of Scientology argued that the government could not evaluate the religious effectiveness of the product, or the truth of the claims about its effectiveness, because doing so would violate the Free Exercise Clause. *See, e.g.*, Church of Scientology of Cal. v. Richardson, 437 F.2d 214 (9th Cir. 1971); Founding Church of Scientology of Wash., D.C. v. United States, 409 F.2d 1146 (D.C. Cir. 1969), *cert. denied*, 396 U.S. 963 (1969). In response, the government maintained that it was not assessing the validity of the claims of the device's efficacy but merely that the device was not labeled in compliance with the Food, Drug, and Cosmetic Act. Ultimately, a compromise was reached: only ordained ministers and members of the church could use the devices, and only for religious matters, and each device must contain a warning about the nonscientific nature of the instrument. *See, e.g.*, United States v. Article or Device "Hubbard Electrometer," 333 F. Supp. 357 (D.D.C. 1971).

110 Alcohol, for example, can be a potent intoxicant that, if misused, may cause a variety of bodily and social harms, including death. Yet so prevalent and accepted are the manufacture, sale, and use of alcohol that it is generally, by itself, not a target of the criminal law. For the most part, it is only when these activities result in other measurable harms, such as public intoxication or driving while under the influence of alcohol, that the criminal justice system comes into play.

111 *See, e.g.*, United States v. Greene, 892 F.2d 453, 456–7 (6th Cir. 1989), *cert. denied*, 495 U.S. 935 (1990); Olsen v. DEA, 878 F.2d 1458, 1461–3 (D.C. Cir. 1989), *cert. denied*, 495 U.S. 906 (1990); Olsen v. Iowa, 808 F.2d 652, 652 (8th Cir. 1986); United States v. Rush, 738 F.2d 497, 511–13 (1st Cir. 1984), *cert. denied*, 471 U.S. 1120 (1985); United States v. Middleton, 690 F.2d 820, 824–6 (11th Cir. 1982), *cert. denied*, 460 U.S. 1051 (1983); United States v. Spears, 443 F.2d 895, 895–6 (5th Cir. 1971) (*per curiam*), *cert. denied*, 404 U.S. 1020 (1972); Leary v. United States, 383 F.2d 851, 859–60 (5th Cir. 1967), *rev'd on other grounds*, 395 U.S. 6 (1969); Multi Denominational Ministry of Cannabis & Rastafari, Inc. v. Gonzales, 474 F. Supp. 2d 1133, 1143–4 (N.D. Cal. 2007), *aff'd*, No. 08-16083, 365 Fed. App'x 817 (9th Cir. Feb. 16, 2010) (unpublished); Rheuark v. State, 601 So. 2d 135, 139–40 (Ala. Ct. Crim. App. 1992); Whyte v. United States, 471 A.2d 1018, 1020–1 (D.C. 1984); State v. Adler, 118 P.3d 652, 659–61 (Haw. 2005) (finding marijuana prohibition legal under Hawaii Constitution); State v. Fluewelling, 249 P.3d 375, 377–8 (Idaho 2011); Rupert v. Portland, 605 A.2d 63, 68 (Me. 1992); Commonwealth v. Nissenbaum, 536 N.E.2d 592, 595–6 (Mass. 1989); State v. Olsen, 315 N.W.2d 1, 7–9 (Iowa 1982); Burton v. State, 194 S.W.3d 686, 688 (Tex. Ct. App. 2006); Trujillo v. State, 2 P.3d 567, 577 (Wyo. 2000); *cf. also* State v. Pedersen 679 N.W.2d 368, 376 (Minn. Ct. App. 2004) (holding that the defendant's medicinal marijuana use did not stem from sincerely held religious beliefs); People v. Trippet, 66 Cal. Rptr. 2d 559, 565–6 (Cal. Ct. App. 1997) (same); State v. Brashear, 593 P.2d 63, 68–71 (N.M. Ct. App. 1979) (similarly finding that the defendant's marijuana use was not based on sincere

even though marijuana can play an important role in Rastafarian and other beliefs systems.[112] More successful have been religious freedom claims by members of the Native American Church regarding their traditional use of hallucinogen-containing peyote[113] – initially by judicial rulings[114] and then by administrative and statutory exemptions[115] – although the unique and sometimes tortured history of Native American relations in the United States may have provided an influential backdrop to this line of cases.[116] Indeed, efforts of individuals or groups to analogize their religious drug use to that of the Native American use of peyote have, at least under the Free Exercise Clause, been largely unsuccessful.[117]

Although the government under the First Amendment ordinarily can apply its criminal drug laws against religious conduct, there can be exceptions, as the peyote cases illustrate. This is especially true if some kind of heightened scrutiny is triggered under the Free Exercise Clause, just as heightened scrutiny available under other religious freedom laws has occasionally thwarted criminal prosecutions. The most notable contemporary example of the latter phenomenon is the 2006 decision in *Gonzales v. O Centro Espirita Beneficente Uniao do Vegetal*,[118] in which the U.S. Supreme Court, applying strict scrutiny pursuant to the Religious Freedom Restoration Act (RFRA),[119]

religious beliefs, though stating, in dictum, that even had there been a burden on free exercise, the government would have prevailed).

112 *See* Guam v. Guerrero, 290 F.3d 1210, 1212 n. 2 (9th Cir. 2002) (noting the role of marijuana in the Rastafarian religion), *cert. denied*, 519 U.S. 907 (1996); Religion and American Law: An Encyclopedia 210 (Paul Finkelman ed., 2000) (observing that "Rastafarians and the Ethiopian Zion Coptic Church use marijuana extensively").

113 *See* Omer C. Stewart, Peyote Religion: A History (1987). "The plant *Lophophora williamsii*, a small, spineless cactus found in the Rio Grande Valley of Texas and northern Mexico, produces peyote, which grows in small buttons on the top of the cactus. Peyote's principal constituent is mescaline. When taken internally by chewing the buttons or drinking a derivative tea, peyote produces several types of hallucinations, depending primarily on the user. In most subjects, it causes extraordinary vision marked by bright and kaleidoscopic colors, geometric patterns, or scenes involving humans or animals. In others, it engenders hallucinatory symptoms similar to those produced in cases of schizophrenia, dementia praecox, or paranoia. Beyond its hallucinatory effect, peyote renders for most users a heightened sense of comprehension; it fosters a feeling of friendliness toward other persons." People v. Woody, 394 P.2d 813, 816–17 (Cal. 1964).

114 *See, e.g.*, State v. Whittingham, 504 P.2d 950. 951–5 (Ariz. Ct. App. 1973); People v. Woody, 394 P.2d 813, 815–22 (Cal. 1964); Whitehorn v. State, 561 P.2d 539, 544–5 (Okla. Ct. Crim. App. 1977).

115 *See* 21 C.F.R. § 1307.31 [current administrative exemption, formerly at 21 C.F.R. § 320.3(c)(3)]. In 1994, Congress codified and expanded the peyote exemption. *See* American Indian Religious Freedom Act Amendments of 1994, Pub. L. No. 103–344, § 2, 108 Stat. 3125 (Oct. 6, 1994) (codified at 42 U.S.C. § 1996a).

116 Not all such cases, moreover, have yielded successful free exercise claims. *See, e.g.*, State v. Soto, 537 P.2d 142, 144 (Or. Ct. App. 1975) (upholding conviction of Native American for possession of mescaline, the hallucinogen found in peyote, despite a claim of religious use).

117 *See, e.g.*, Olsen, 878 F.2d at 1463–5; United States v. Rush, 738 F.2d 497, 512–13 (1st Cir. 1984), *cert. denied*, 470 U.S. 1004 (1985); Whyte, 471 A.2d at 1021; Fluewelling, 249 P.3d at 378–79; People v. Crawford, 328 N.Y.S.2d 747, 749–55 (N.Y. Dist. Ct. Suffolk Cnty. 1972), *aff'd*, 340 N.Y.S.2d 848 (N.Y. Supr. Ct. 1973); Lewellyn v. State, 592 P.2d 538, 542–3 (Okla. Ct. Crim. App. 1979).

118 546 U.S. 418 (2006).

119 Pub. L. No. 103-141, 107 Stat. 1488 (Nov. 16, 1993) (codified as amended at 42 U.S.C. §§ 2000bb to 2000bb-4). RFRA originally prohibited the federal *and state* governments from "substantially burden[ing] a person's exercise of religion" unless it was the least restrictive means of achieving a compelling interest. Intended to displace Employment Div. v. Smith, 494 U.S. 872 (1990), the statute was declared unconstitutional as applied to states. *See* City of Boerne v. Flores, 521 U.S. 507 (1997). Three years later, Congress enacted the Religious Land Use and Institutionalized Persons Act (RLUIPA), Pub.

held that the federal government failed to show that it had a compelling interest in applying the Controlled Substances Act specifically against a religious group's use of a certain hallucinogen classified as a Schedule I substance by that statute. "Under the more focused inquiry required by RFRA and the compelling interest test," the Court said, "the Government's mere invocation of the general characteristics of Schedule I substances, as set forth in the Controlled Substances Act, cannot carry the day."[120] Specifically, the statute itself authorizes the federal government to make exceptions if consistent with public health and safety, and for several decades, it had exempted the religious use of peyote (also a Schedule I hallucinogen) by members of the Native American Church[121]; thus it was required but failed to explain why it could not also craft an exception in this case. In short, if a heightened standard of constitutional review such as strict scrutiny is employed, and if it is employed rigorously, then the likelihood of defeating a drug prosecution or conviction on religious grounds, particularly for simple possession or use, can increase significantly.[122]

Yet another strand of criminal law prohibiting conduct that is primarily injurious only to public morals or participating individuals concerns the handling of venomous snakes. Certain Pentecostal faith traditions, located largely in the Appalachian region of the United States, advocate the handling of such snakes to demonstrate the strength of their beliefs and the presence of the Holy Spirit, following the purported words of Jesus that "'these signs will accompany those who believe: by using my name they will cast out demons; they will speak in new tongues; they will pick up snakes in their hands, and if they drink any deadly thing, it will not hurt them; they will lay their hands on the sick, and they will recover.'"[123] The leading case involving the restriction of snake handling by religious practitioners is the Tennessee Supreme Court's 1975 decision in *State ex rel.*

L. No. 106-274, 114 Stat. 803-07 (Sept. 22, 2000) (codified at 42 U.S.C. §§ 2000cc to 2000cc-5), which applies to state and local governments but is limited to government decisions concerning land use and institutionalized persons. RFRA, as amended, apparently remains valid as applied to the federal government – hence its use in the *O Centro* case.

120 O Centro, 546 U.S. at 432.

121 *See id.* at 432–3 [referencing 21 U.S.C. § 822(d) and 21 C.F.R. § 1307.31, respectively].

122 *Cf.* Multi Denominational Ministry, 474 F. Supp. 2d at 1146–7 (implying that the RFRA might protect Rastafarian religious use of marijuana but rejecting a RFRA claim for an injunction against enforcement of federal law against a variety of marijuana-related activities beyond its sacramental use); State v. Pedersen 679 N.W.2d 368, 376–7 (Minn. Ct. App. 2004) (holding that the defendant's medicinal marijuana use did not stem from sincerely held religious beliefs, but "tak[ing] th[e] opportunity to note ... that the state's sole reliance on the legislature's enactment of statutes prohibiting the possession of marijuana to defeat a claim under [the Minnesota Constitution's religious freedom guarantee, which calls for strict scrutiny] is plainly inadequate"). *But see* State v. Hardesty, 214 P.3d 1004, 1008–10 (Ariz. 2009) (*en banc*) (upholding marijuana possession conviction under the strict scrutiny entailed by Arizona's Free Exercise of Religion Act, Ariz. Rev. Stat. § 41-1493.01, finding no less restrictive alternatives to achieve the state's compelling interest).

123 *Mark* 16:17–18 (NRSV). *See generally* Fred W. Brown & Jeanne McDonald, The Serpent Handlers: Three Families and Their Faith (2000); Thomas Burton, Serpent-Handling Believers (1993); Dennis Covington, Salvation on Sand Mountain: Snake Handling and Redemption in Southern Appalachia (1995); Ralph Hood & W. Paul Williamson, Them That Believe: The Power and Meaning of the Christian Serpent-Handling Tradition (2008); David L. Kimbrough, Taking Up Serpents: Snake Handlers of Eastern Kentucky (1995); *Contemporary Serpent Handling Sects of Appalachia*, Va. Commw. Univ. World Religions & Spirituality Project, *available at:* http://www.has.vcu.edu/wrs/profiles/SerpentHandlers.htm.

*Swann v. Pack.*[124] At the request of a district attorney (seeking to abate a public nuisance), a Tennessee circuit court permanently enjoined a minister (Liston Pack) as well as a church elder from "handling, displaying or exhibiting dangerous and poisonous snakes" anywhere in the county,[125] finding that such conduct violated a state law disallowing "any person, or persons, to display, exhibit, handle or use any poisonous or dangerous snake or reptile in such a manner as to endanger the life or health of any person."[126] The Court of Appeals modified the injunction, limiting it to the handling of snakes in the presence of consenting adults, but the Tennessee Supreme Court held that the modification was unwarranted and directed the trial judge to "enter an injunction perpetually enjoining and restraining all parties respondent from handling, displaying or exhibiting dangerous and poisonous snakes or from consuming strychnine or any other poisonous substances, within the confines of the State of Tennessee."[127] Employing a type of heightened scrutiny under both the U.S. and Tennessee Constitutions, the Court – independent of the criminal statute, but shedding light on its validity – found not only that the defendants were creating a public nuisance by handling the snakes in front of congregants but, further, that "the state has a right to protect a person from himself [or herself] and to demand that he [or she] protect his [or her] own life" and that the defendants' religious conduct was effectively outweighed by the state's "compelling interest in protecting the life and promoting the health of its citizens."[128]

As the *Pack* case indicates, a state may be able to prohibit, by tort if not criminal law, conduct that is injurious only to oneself, even if undertaken out of religious convictions. This may extend, of course, to attempted suicide and, more likely, to efforts that assist another in such an attempt.[129] As the D.C. Circuit noted several decades ago, relying in part on the *Reynolds* bigamy case, "[i]f self-homicide is a crime, there is no exception to

[124] 527 S.W.2d 99 (Tenn. 1975), *cert. denied*, 424 U.S. 954 (1976); *see also* Hill v. State, 88 So. 2d 880, 883–5 (Ala. Ct. App. 1956), *cert. denied*, 88 So. 2d 887 (Ala. 1956); Lawson v. Commonwealth, 164 S.W.2d 972, 973–6 (Ky. Ct. App. 1942); State v. Massey, 51 S.E.2d 179, 180 (N.C. 1949), *appeal dismissed*, 336 U.S. 942 (1949); Harden v. State, 216 S.W.2d 708, 710–11 (Tenn. 1948).

[125] *See* Pack, 527 S.W.2d at 102.

[126] *Id.* at 103 n. 1 (quoting Tenn. Code § 39–2208). The current version of the statute, codified in 1989, makes it a Class C misdemeanor "for a person to display, exhibit, handle, or use a poisonous or dangerous snake or reptile in a manner that endangers the life or health of any person." Tenn. Code § 39-17-101(a). Kentucky, too, has a snake-handling statute, but its specific criminalization of just religious activity differs from Tennessee's and arguably renders it constitutionally problematic. *See* Ky. Rev. Stat. § 437.060 ["Any person who displays, handles or uses any kind of reptile in connection with any religious service or gathering shall be fined not less than fifty dollars ($50) nor more than one hundred dollars ($100)."].

[127] Pack, 527 S.W.2d at 114.

[128] *Id.* at 113.

[129] Needless to say, there is no means or reason to try to punish a person who has successfully committed suicide, but the illegality of such an act can adversely affect the legal interests of others. At English common law, the result of a person's suicide was the forfeiture of all the decedent's "good and chattels to the king." 4 William Blackstone, *Commentaries* at *190. In the United States, a person's suicide can preclude his or her beneficiaries from receiving life insurance proceeds. *See, e.g.*, Estate of Tedrow v. Std. Life Ins. Co. of Ind., 558 N.W.2d 195, 197–8 (Iowa 1997); Estate of Galloway v. Guaranty Income Life Ins. Co., 725 P.2d 827, 828 (N.M. 1986). This result may obtain even if a policy does not specifically list suicide as a cause for denying benefits. *See, e.g.*, Supr. Commandery v. Ainsworth, 71 Ala. 436, 446–77 (1882). Some states bar the denial of life insurance benefits if the decedent was not sane at the time of suicide (*see, e.g.*, Mo. Rev. Stat. § 376.620), whereas others bar the denial of such benefits regardless of the decedent's mental state. *See, e.g.*, Colo. Rev. Stat. § 10-7-109; N.D. Cent. Code § 26.1-33-37; Va. Code § 38.2-3106 (if policy is held for two years).

the law's command for those who believe the crime to be divinely ordained."[130] Although "a majority of states no longer criminalize suicide,"[131] some states have retained their common-law prohibitions against it,[132] and most states criminalize suicide assistance.[133] Few, if any, cases directly address religiously motivated suicide, but there is at least one decision indicating that the Free Exercise Clause, invoked by a would-be decedent, will not shield those who assist in a suicide from criminal prosecution.[134] According to the court in that case, the would-be decedent's "claim is less compelling than that presented in [*Employment Division v. Smith*] because he does not just seek a limited exemption from the assisted suicide statute for himself so that he may freely practice his religion without fear of criminal prosecution. He also seeks exemptions for third parties – his wife and his physician – based on his personal religious beliefs, which may or may not be shared by the others."[135] Finding that the state's law criminalizing assisted suicide "is a valid, religiously-neutral, and generally-applicable criminal statute that prohibits conduct a state is free to regulate," the court then explained "that there was no evidence [that the would-be decedent] could have proffered regarding the importance of assisted suicide to his belief system which would exempt him, or his designated third persons, on First Amendment grounds from the provisions of the statute."[136]

Similarly, the Free Exercise Clause likely does not prevent the government, through criminal law or alternative means, from prohibiting other acts of serious self-harm – more than tattooing or short-term fasting, for instance – notwithstanding their possible religious bases or dimensions.[137] This is hardly an abstract issue because "[m]any religions, including sects of Hindu, Muslim, and Christianity, practice self-harm as a form of worship."[138] In a somewhat extreme case arising in Connecticut, for example, an individual was involuntarily committed to a mental health facility to prevent him from acting

130 Application of President & Dirs. of Georgetown College, Inc., 331 F.2d 1000, 1009 (D.C. Cir. 1964), *cert. denied*, 377 U.S. 978 (1964). The *Reynolds* Court itself had asked, rhetorically, "Suppose [that] one believed that human sacrifices were a necessary part of religious worship, would it be seriously contended that the civil government under which he lived could not interfere to prevent a sacrifice? Or if a wife religiously believed it was her duty to burn herself upon the funeral pile of her dead husband, would it be beyond the power of the civil government to prevent her carrying her belief into practice?" Reynolds, 98 U.S. (8 Otto) at 166.

131 Browne C. Lewis, *A Graceful Exit: Redefining Terminal to Expand the Availability of Physician-Facilitated Suicide*, 91 Or. L. Rev. 457, 464 (2012).

132 *See* Wackwitz v. Roy, 418 S.E.2d 861, 864 (Va. 1992) [noting that this is the case in Virginia as well as Alabama, Massachusetts, New Jersey, North Carolina, and South Carolina and citing S. Life & Health Ins. Co. v. Wynn, 194 So. 421 (Ala. Ct. App. 1940); Commonwealth v. Mink, 123 Mass. 422 (1877); State v. Carney, 55 A. 44 (N.J. 1903); State v. Willis, 121 S.E.2d 854 (N.C. 1961); State v. Levelle, 13 S.E. 319 (S.C. 1891), *overruled on other grounds by* State v. Torrence, 406 S.E.2d 315 (S.C. 1991)].

133 *See* Justine R. Young, *Dead Wrong: The Problems with Assisted Suicide Statutes and Prosecutions*, 6 Stan. L. & Pol'y Rev. 123, 123 (1994).

134 *See* Sanderson v. People, 12 P.3d 851, 853–4 (Colo. Ct. App. 2000); *see also* Calon v. Apfel, No. 98-3190, 185 F.3d 873, 1999 WL 415340, at *2 (10th Cir. 1999) (unpublished) (summarily rejecting a free exercise challenge to state law prohibitions on assisted suicide).

135 Sanderson, 12 P.3d at 854.

136 *Id.*

137 The Federal Bureau of Prisons, for example, explicitly prohibits religiously based self-mutilation, among other things. *See* John W. Popeo, *Note, Combating Radical Islam in Prison within the Legal Dictates of the Free Exercise Clause*, 32 New Eng. J. on Crim. & Civ. Confinement 135, 148 (2006).

138 Natalie Rezek, *Is Self-Harm by Cutting a Constitutionally Protected Right?*, 12 Quinnipiac Health L.J. 303, 323 (2009).

on what he described as the word of God, which by his own account had already prompted him to remove both an eye and a hand.[139] Upholding his commitment, the state supreme court found no violation of the Free Exercise Clause, notwithstanding the religious nature of the individual's purported motivations for his conduct[140] because it agreed with the trial court that his acts of self-harm were not, in fact, "the manifestations of a religious belief but indications of a mental illness."[141] Arguably, "[t]he opinion is confused, since it treats his claim as one arising under the first amendment, yet relegates him to continued detention as mentally ill"[142]; nevertheless, it illustrates the principle that the Free Exercise Clause does not necessarily pose an obstacle to a government's efforts to prevent serious self-harm.

### 4. *Crimes Resulting from Spiritual Healing*

As a matter of common and perhaps constitutional law, competent adults generally have the right to refuse medical treatment,[143] and some courts have specifically recognized a right to refuse such treatment for religious reasons even if the person dies as a consequence.[144] By contrast, when making medical decisions for one's children or other dependents, one's own right to refuse medical treatment (whatever the reason) has little, if any, bearing. The analysis potentially can become complicated, however, when the decision maker forgoes conventional medical treatment for his or her dependent on the basis of a good-faith belief that spiritual healing is the appropriate course of action.[145] That is, the decision maker does not forgo all treatment but provides spiritual care in lieu of conventional medical care and does so based on sincerely held religious beliefs.[146]

139 *See* Mayock v. Martin, 245 A.2d 574, 575 (Conn. 1968), *cert. denied*, 393 U.S. 1111 (1969).

140 *See id.* at 578.

141 *Id.* at 577.

142 J. Morris Clark, *Guidelines for the Free Exercise Clause*, 83 Harv. L. Rev. 327, 364 n. 145 (1969).

143 *See* Cruzan v. Dir., Mo. Dep't of Health, 497 U.S. 261, 269–77 (1990) (reviewing state common and statutory law). The Court then noted that "[t]he principle that a competent person has a constitutionally protected liberty interest in refusing unwanted medical treatment may be inferred from our prior decisions." *Id.* at 278.

144 *See, e.g.*, *In re* Osborne, 294 A.2d 372, 375 (D.C. 1972); Pub. Health Trust of Dade Cnty. v. Wons, 541 So.2d 96 (Fla. 1989); *In re* Estate of Brooks, 205 N.E.2d 435, 442 (Ill. 1965); *In re* Brown, 478 So.2d 1033, 1039 (Miss. 1985); *In re* Milton, 505 N.E.2d 255, 260 (Ohio 1987), *cert. denied*, 484 U.S. 820 (1987). A religious basis for the competent adult's decision is presumably not necessary. *See, e.g.*, McKay v. Bergstedt, 801 P.2d 617 (Nev. 1990).

145 *Compare, e.g.*, People v. Pierson, 68 N.E. 243, 246–7 (N.Y. 1903) (holding that religious freedom, per the state's constitution, did not provide a defense to a charge of failing to provide medical care to one's child), *with* State v. Lockhart, 664 P.2d 1059 (Okla. Crim. Ct. App. 1983) (affirming an instruction to a jury that parental good faith reliance on spiritual means could serve as a defense of justification against a misdemeanor charge of failing to provide medical care to one's child).

146 Perhaps not surprisingly, there is a great deal of secondary literature on spiritual healing, particularly in relation to children. *See, e.g.*, Peggy DesAutels, Margaret P. Battin & Larry May, Praying for a Cure: When Medical and Religious Practices Conflict (1999); Shawn Francis Peters, When Prayer Fails: Faith Healing, Children, and the Law (2008); Jennifer E. Chen, *Family Conflicts: The Role of Religion in Refusing Medical Treatment for Minors*, 58 Hastings L.J. 643 (2007); Jennifer M. Collins, *Crime and Parenthood: The Uneasy Case for Prosecuting Negligent Parents*, 100 Nw. U. L. Rev. 807 (2006); Jared A. Goldstein, *Is There a "Religious Question" Doctrine? Judicial Authority to Examine Religious Practices and Beliefs*, 54 Cath. U. L. Rev. 497 (2005); Richard A. Hughes, *The Death of Children by Faith-Based Medical Neglect*, 20 J.L. & Religion 247 (2004); Adam Lamparello, *Taking God Out of the Hospital: Requiring Parents to Seek Medical Care for Their Children Regardless of Religious Belief*, 6 Tex. F. on C.L. & C.R. 47 (2001); Elizabeth A. Lingle, *Treating Children by*

Broadly defined, "spiritual" or "faith healing" refers to efforts aimed at curing or ameliorating physical or psychological ailments through religious belief, prayer, or ritual.[147] The methods and conceptualization of spiritual healing vary widely among religious traditions. In several, spiritual healing is undertaken in conjunction with conventional medical treatment, whereas in others, such as Christian Science and certain Native American religions, it may be undertaken in place of conventional treatment, even for serious medical conditions.[148] These variations often reflect differences concerning how the processes and consequences of spiritual healing are conceptualized. To some, spiritual healing methods are believed to invite divine intervention or to harness supernatural entities or energies, which, in turn, may effect a cure or amelioration of the patient's ailment. To others, spiritual healing serves largely as an expression of devotion and obedience to divine will, the fruits of which may not be realized in the material, temporal realm. To others still, especially those who reject divine intervention, there may simply be an expectation that the use of prayer will yield primarily psychic benefits to the patient and the participating religious community. Religions also differ with regard to who may practice spiritual healing. Although most do not restrict laity from engaging in general practices such as prayer, more specific healing practices or rituals in some traditions may be confined either to clerics – for example, a priest or shaman – or to church-authorized practitioners.[149]

*Faith: Colliding Constitutional Issues*, 17 J. Legal Med. 301 (1996); Nobel, *supra* note 57; Emily Catalano, *Comment, Healing or Homicide? When Parents Refuse Medical Treatment for Their Children on Religious Grounds*, 18 Buff. Women's L.J. 157 (2010); Ivy B. Dodes, *Note, "Suffer the Little Children ...": Toward a Judicial Recognition of a Duty of Reasonable Care Owed Children by Religious Faith Healers*, 16 Hofstra L. Rev. 165 (1987); Kei Robert Hiraswa, *Note, Are Parents Acting in the Best Interests of Their Children when They Make Medical Decisions Based on Their Religious Beliefs?*, 44 Fam. Ct. Rev. 316 (2006); Laura M. Plastine, *Comment, "In God We Trust: When Parents Refuse Medical Treatment for Their Children Based on Their Sincere Religious Beliefs*, 3 Seton Hall Const. L.J. 123 (1993); J. Nelson Thomas, *Note, Prosecuting Religious Parents for Homicide: Compounding a Tragedy?*, 1 Va. J. Soc. Pol'y & L. 409 (1994).

147 *See* Sana Loue, *Parentally Mandated Religious Healing for Children: A Therapeutic Justice Approach*, 27 J.L. & Religion 397, 397–9 (2012) [explaining that approaches to spiritual healing "encompass a wide range of practices, ranging from prayer, meditation, and the laying on of hands, to exorcism, speaking in tongues, Spiritism, shamanic intervention, and various rituals of Santeria" (footnotes omitted)].

148 With regard to Christian Science, *see* Christian Science: A Sourcebook of Contemporary Materials (1991); Church of Christ, Scientist, *available at*: http://christianscience.com; James T. Richardson & John Dewitt, *Christian Science Spiritual Healing, the Law, and Public Opinion*, 34 J. Church & St. 749 (1992). According to one author, communities that "espouse one or more forms of religious healing while discouraging reliance on conventional medical treatments ... include the Christian Science Church, the Church of the First Born, End Time Ministries, Faith Tabernacle, Followers of Christ Church, Bible Believers' Fellowship, Christ Assembly, Christ Miracle Healing Center, Church of God Chapel, Church of God of the Union Assembly, Holiness Church, Jesus Through Jon and Judy, 'No Name' Fellowship, Northeast Kingdom Community Church, and The Source." Loue, *supra* note 147, at 399.

149 *Cf., e.g.*, 1983 Code of Canon Law c.1003, § 1 (limiting to priests the administration of the sacrament of anointing of the sick), *available at*: http://www.vatican.va/archive/ENG1104/__P3L.HTM. The nature of the patient's participation in the spiritual healing process also can vary among and within religious faiths. For example, it may be practiced without the physical presence or even the awareness of the patient, a technique that in certain circles is called "remote, absent, or distant healing." Prayers of healing said by congregations or distant acquaintances also might be considered efforts at remote healing, although they are often viewed as being intercessory, as opposed to unmediated, in nature. Alternatively, spiritual healing practices may involve the patient directly, such as by touching (or the laying on of hands), by praying or reciting scripture or stories with the patient, by the patient's repentance or atonement, by the use of

The medical community largely understands that one's spiritual health may affect and be affected by one's physical and mental health, and modern research has generally confirmed the potential therapeutic efficacy of prayer and faith.[150] Neither the mainstream medical community nor the criminal law, however, is oblivious to the physical dangers that may attend the rejection of conventional medical care, and in certain instances – especially decision making on behalf of others such as children – the legal system can and will intervene to prevent or punish such dangers. Indeed, where a child's welfare is involved, implicated is not simply the state's police power but also its *parens patriae* authority, which specifically enables it to protect minors in place of, and sometimes against the wishes of, their parents. As expressed by one state appellate court,

> [t]he parents' right to control their children's upbringing is cardinal. But the State, as *parens patriae*, may limit this right in the general interest of the youth's well-being. The State may interfere with the parents' rights to raise their children only where it "seeks to prevent harm or a risk of harm to the child." When parents defy the State's actions in protecting children, criminal liability may attach, even when the parents are acting in the interest of the child's religious upbringing.[151]

In the first instance, this authority can be used to impose a duty on parents to provide medical care to their children, one that may conflict with an exclusive regimen of spiritual treatment.[152] If this duty is violated, the government then may be able to assume temporary custody of a child for the administration of medical care, notwithstanding parental religious beliefs.[153] And if, because the state did or could not act in time, harm to the child actually results, then the parents can be criminally charged.[154] Importantly,

objects such as beads or crystals, by the administration of oils or water, by fasting or dietary restrictions, and, in some Christian traditions, by receipt of communion bread or wine.

150 Regarding the potential efficacy of religious or spiritual practices, *see* HAROLD G. KOENIG ET AL., HANDBOOK OF RELIGION AND HEALTH (2000); JEFF LEVIN, GOD, FAITH, AND HEALTH: EXPLORING THE SPIRITUALITY-HEALTH CONNECTION (2002).

151 State v. Baxter, 141 P.3d 92, 99 (Wash. Ct. App. 2006) [quoting *In re* Custody of Smith, 969 P.2d 21, 29 (Wash. 1998), *aff'd sub nom.* Troxel v. Granville, 530 U.S. 57 (2000)]. *Baxter* did not involve spiritual healing as such but rather a father's attempted home circumcision of his eight-year-old son.

152 *See In re* D.L.E., 645 P.2d 271, 275–6 (Colo. 1982) ["[T]he family itself is not beyond regulation in the public interest as against a claim of religious liberty, and neither the rights of religion nor rights of parenthood are beyond limitation. Acting to guard the general interest in the youth's well-being, the authority of the state, as *parens patriae*, is not nullified merely because a parent grounds his [or her] claim to control the child's course of conduct on religion or conscience. The right to practice religion freely does not include the right or liberty to expose the community or the child to ill health or death." (citations omitted)].

153 *See In re* E.G., 549 N.E.2d 322, 325 (Ill. 1989) ("An infant child ... can be compelled to accept life-saving medical treatment over the objections of [his or] her parents."); Morrison v. State, 252 S.W.2d 97, 100–2 (Mo. Ct. App. 1952); *In re* Guardianship of L.S. & H.S., 87 P.3d 521, 527 (Nev. 2004); State v. Perricone, 181 A.2d 751, 759 (N.J. 1962) ("[C]ourts have held that the refusal of parents, on religious grounds, to submit their infant child to a blood transfusion necessary to save its life or mental health amounted to statutory neglect, and therefore it was proper to appoint a guardian and to award custody to him [or her] for the limited purpose of authorizing transfusions."), *cert. denied*, 371 U.S. 890 (1962).

154 *See, e.g.*, Bergmann v. State, 486 N.E.2d 653, 660–1 (Ind. Ct. App. 1985) (affirming reckless homicide conviction, notwithstanding parental religious beliefs); Commonwealth v. Twitchell, 617 N.E.2d 609 (Mass. 1993) (same, involuntary manslaughter); State v. Beagley, 305 P.3d 147 (Or. Ct. App. 2013) (same, negligent homicide); State v. Hays, 964 P.2d 1042, 1046–7 (Or. Ct. App. 1998) (same), *review denied*, 977 P.2d 1170 (Or. 1998), *cert. denied*, 527 U.S. 1006 (1999); Commonwealth v. Nixon, 761 A.2d 1151 (Pa. 2000) (same, involuntary manslaughter), *cert. denied*, 532 U.S. 1008 (2001); Commonwealth

a number of state laws explicitly allow spiritual healing in place of conventional medical treatment, especially by parents in relation to their children, without fear of legal consequence such as a finding of child neglect or abuse.[155] But these exemptions are often limited to cases of nonserious harm.[156] By legal presumption, moreover, their relevance is confined to the specific statute in which they are found and, therefore, may not shield a parent from liability under another criminal or civil law.[157]

Courts recognize that liability under such circumstances can impose a substantial burden on the parents' religious beliefs and practices such that the Free Exercise Clause is clearly implicated.[158] But that clause (like other religious freedom laws) entails a weighing or balancing of competing interests, and even prior to *Employment Division v. Smith*, this process overwhelmingly indicated that parents may not subject their unemancipated, nonmature children to spiritual treatment, particularly when conventional care is eschewed, if doing so would pose a demonstrable danger to life or health.[159] This is true even under the highest standard of strict scrutiny because, according to the judicial consensus, the government has a compelling interest in children's welfare, and ordinarily the only means to achieve that interest is by imposing forced medical care[160] or

v. Barnhart, 497 A.2d 616 (Pa. Super. Ct. 1985) (same), *appeal denied*, 538 A.2d 874 (Pa. 1988), *cert. denied*, 488 U.S. 817 (1988); State v. Norman, 808 P.2d 1159, 1162–3 (Wash. Ct. App. 1991) (same, first-degree manslaughter), *review denied*, 818 P.2d 1099 (Wash. 1991).

155 For current compilations, *see* Children's Healthcare Is a Legal Duty, Inc., *Religious Defenses in State Penal Codes* (Jul. 15, 2014), *available at:* http://childrenshealthcare.org/wp-content/uploads/2014/07/State-exemptions-criminal2.pdf; Children's Healthcare Is a Legal Duty, Inc., *Religious Exemptions to Medical Treatment of Children in State Civil Codes* (Jul. 15, 2014), *available at:* http://childrenshealthcare.org/wp-content/uploads/2014/07/State-exemptions-civil3.pdf. *See also* Hermanson v. State, 604 So. 2d 775, 776 n. 1 (Fla. 1992); Paula A. Monopoli, *Allocating the Costs of Parental Free Exercise: Striking a New Balance Between Sincere Religious Belief and a Child's Right to Medical Treatment*, 18 PEPP. L. REV. 319, 320 nn.4 & 5 (1991). For critical analysis of such exemptions, *see* Ashley Dose, *Government Endorsement of Living on a Prayer*, 30 J. LEGAL MED. 515 (2009); Rebecca Williams, *Note, Faith Healing Exceptions versus Parens Patriae: Something's Gotta Give*, 10 FIRST AMEND. L. REV. 692 (2012).

156 If such limitations are not sufficiently clear, however, a statute or statutory scheme may be deemed unconstitutionally vague. *See, e.g.*, Hermanson v. State, 604 So.2d 775, 781–3 (Fla. 1992); State v. McKown, 475 N.W.2d 63, 67–9 (Minn. 1991), *cert. denied*, 502 U.S. 1036 (1992).

157 *See, e.g.*, Commonwealth v. Foster, 764 A.2d 1076 (Pa. Super. Ct. 2000) (holding that an exemption under a child abuse statute did not preclude a conviction for involuntary manslaughter), *appeal denied*, 782 A.2d 542 (Pa. 2001); Commonwealth v. Nixon, 718 A.2d 311, 313–15 (Pa. Super. Ct. 1998) (same), *aff'd*, 761 A.2d 1151 (Pa. 2000), *cert. denied*, 532 U.S. 1008 (2001); State v. Neumann, 832 N.W.2d 560, 577 (Wis. 2013) [explaining that "the text of the treatment-through prayer-provision, Wis. Stat. § 948.03(6) [exempting such treatment from a charge of child abuse], does not and cannot lead parents to expect that they are immune from criminal prosecution for second-degree reckless homicide"], *cert. denied*, 134 S. Ct. 544 (2013).

158 *See* Commonwealth v. Barnhart, 497 A.2d 616, 624 (Pa. Super. Ct. 1985) (recognizing that the involuntary manslaughter conviction of parents who failed for religious reasons to provide medical treatment "directly penalizes … [the parents] in the practice of their religion"), *appeal denied*, 538 A.2d 874 (Pa. 1988), *cert. denied*, 488 U.S. 817 (1988).

159 *See* Schmidt v. Mut. Hosp. Servs., Inc., 832 N.E.2d 977, 982 (Ind. Ct. App. 2005) ["[A]lthough an adult generally cannot be forced to undergo medical treatment against his [or her] religious principles, a parent's decision to refuse lifesaving medical treatment for a minor child must yield to the State's interest in protecting the health and welfare of the child." (footnote omitted)]; CHARLES E. TORCIA, 2 WHARTON'S CRIMINAL LAW § 175 (15th ed. rev'd, Sept. 2013) ("Ordinarily, if a defendant is under a legal duty to provide medical care, his [or her] religious belief is no defense to an unlawful homicide prosecution." (citing cases)].

160 *See* Roman Catholic Archdiocese of L.A. v. Superior Ct. of L.A. Cnty., 32 Cal. Rptr. 3d 209, 214 (Cal. Ct. App. 2005) ("While it is true the right to religious freedom holds a special place in our history and

by "[i]mposing criminal sanctions on a person who is responsible for [his or her] child's death" in order to "establish that parents must comply with the law and … [to] discourag[e] other parents from failing to provide medical care for children with life-threatening conditions."[161] As the Supreme Court has famously stated, "[p]arents may be free to become martyrs themselves. But it does not follow that they are free, in identical circumstances, to make martyrs of their children."[162] Thus parental decisions that would effectively make martyrs of their children may be judicially overridden,[163] and absent a statutory exemption, parents and possibly practitioners relying exclusively on spiritual healing may be held civilly and criminally responsible for the harm that accrues from forgoing conventional medical treatment.[164] Correspondingly, the government likely can restrict spiritual healing when it might independently cause additional harm, or at least additional serious harm, and can impose civil or criminal liability should such harm result.[165] Only where the available or proposed conventional medical treatment is itself comparably dangerous or uncertain does it appear that courts might be willing to defer to parental decision making,[166] essentially because the use of conventional care is no longer demonstrably necessary to preserve the child's health. As noted earlier, all of this is quite different from the situation of competent adults, who may choose for themselves to forego conventional medical treatment and pursue spiritual healing, even if it exacerbates their condition or precipitates their demise.[167]

culture, there also must be an accommodation by religious believers and institutions to the rules of civil society, particularly when the state's compelling interest in protecting children is in question."), *cert. denied*, 547 U.S. 1071 (2006).

161 Hays, 964 P.2d at 1047. "The state's interest does not end when a child dies; the state has an interest in protecting those children who are still alive. Imposing criminal sanctions on a person who is responsible for one child's death will further that interest by establishing that parents must comply with the law and by discouraging other parents from failing to provide medical care for children with life-threatening conditions … Once the child has died, a prosecution is the only way to vindicate the state's interest as to that child and to encourage compliance with the law as to other children." *Id.*

162 Prince v. Massachusetts, 321 U.S. 158, 170 (1944).

163 *See, e.g., In re* Guardianship of L.S., 87 P.3d 521, 522 (Nev. 2004) (*per curiam*) ("conclud[ing] that when the parents refused to consent to medically necessary care for … [their child] based on their religious convictions, the district court did not abuse its discretion in appointing … [a hospital] as a temporary guardian to make decisions to provide medically necessary, life-saving treatment for … [the child]"); *In re* Hamilton, 657 S.W.2d 425 (Tenn. Ct. App. 1983) (*per curiam*) (similar).

164 *See, e.g.,* Walker v. Superior Ct., 763 P.2d 852 (Cal. 1988), *cert. denied*, 491 U.S. 905 (1989); Commonwealth v. Twitchell, 617 N.E.2d 609 (Mass. 1993); Lundman v. McKown, 530 N.W.2d 807 (Minn. Ct. App. 1995), *cert. denied*, 516 U.S. 1092 (1996), *and cert. denied*, 516 U.S. 1099 (1996); Commonwealth v. Foster, 764 A.2d 1076 (Pa. Super. Ct. 2000) (upholding convictions of parents, members of the Faith Tabernacle Church, for endangering the welfare of a child and criminal conspiracy arising from their use of prayer in lieu of conventional treatment for their child's cancer), *appeal denied*, 782 A.2d 542 (Pa. 2001); Commonwealth v. Nixon, 718 A.2d 311 (Pa. Super. Ct. 1998) (upholding convictions of parents, members of the Faith Tabernacle Church, for involuntary manslaughter and endangering the welfare of a child arising from their use of prayer in lieu of conventional medical treatment for their child's diabetic ketoacidosis), *aff'd*, 761 A.2d 1151 (Pa. 2000), *cert. denied*, 532 U.S. 1008 (2001).

165 In the civil context, for example, additional resulting harm may proportionately diminish a patient's monetary compensation from an alleged tortfeasor. *See* Munn v. Algee, 924 F.2d 568, 573–4 (5th Cir. 1991), *cert. denied*, 502 U.S. 900 (1991). As one court has stated, "[t]he freedom to act upon one's religious convictions does not encompass the privilege of imposing tort liability on another for injuries resulting, not from another's tortious conduct, but rather from the voluntary practice of one's religious convictions." Corlett v. Caserta, 562 N.E.2d 257, 262 (Ill. Ct. App. 1990).

166 *See, e.g.,* Newmark v. Williams, 588 A.2d 1108, 1117–21 (Del. 1991).

167 Mature minors may or may not possess a right to refuse medical treatment. *Compare, e.g., In re* E.G., 549 N.E.2d 322, 328 (Ill. 1989) (finding that "a mature minor may exercise a common law right to consent to

### 5. *Crimes by Religious Leaders or Institutions*

From the High Middle Ages through the early nineteenth century, English law recognized in various forms the so-called benefit of clergy, which divested civil courts of jurisdiction over all but the most serious capital offenses committed by clergy (and eventually others feigning clerical status), thus effectively sparing them, at least for first offenses, from sentences of death.[168] Although adopted by a number of the American colonies, especially in the Anglican-oriented South,[169] in the new nation the privilege was rejected at the outset by the federal courts[170] and, by the mid-nineteenth century, by all state courts.[171]

In the contemporary United States, accordingly, clergy and churches generally may be prosecuted for their criminal offenses to the same extent that the government prosecutes ordinary individuals and entities for conduct that violates the criminal law.[172] That is, just as the religious basis of one's conduct by itself does not ordinarily yield a defense, neither does one's institutionalized religious status somehow shield one from criminal liability.[173] As summarized by a state appeals court, "[b]ecause churches, their congregations, and hierarchy exist and function within the civil community, they are … amenable to rules governing … criminal conduct."[174] In short, as long as a criminal statute is

or refuse medical care"), *with* O.G. v. Baum, 790 S.W.2d 839, 842 (Tex. Ct. App. 1990) (refusing to follow *In re E.G.*, finding that "the law is not settled … concerning whether a 16-year-old has constitutional and common-law rights to refuse a blood transfusion").

168 *See* John H. Langbein, *Shaping the Eighteenth-Century Criminal Trial: A View from the Ryder Sources*, 50 U. Chi. L. Rev. 1, 37–41 (1983); Note, *Felony Murder as a First Degree Offense: An Anachronism Revisited*, 66 Yale L.J. 427, 428–30 (1957). "In its inception '[t]he privilege known to later generations as benefit of clergy was a concession made by royal law to the Church in the aftermath of the Becket controversy.' The ecclesiastical representative who attended medieval trials controlled the privilege. If he endorsed an accused's claim to be a cleric, the royal court released the accused to the ecclesiastical court." Langbein, *supra*, at 37 (footnote omitted) [quoting John H. Baker, *Introduction to* 2 The Reports of Sir John Spelman 327 (John H. Baker ed., 1978)].

169 *See, e.g.*, Jeffrey K. Sawyer, *"Benefit of Clergy" in Maryland and Virginia*, 34 Am. J. Legal Hist. 49, 54–64 (1990).

170 *See* Act of Apr. 30, 1790, ch. 9, § 31, 1 Stat. 112, 119 (providing that "the benefit of clergy shall not be used or allowed, upon conviction of any crime, for which, by any statute of the United States, the punishment is or shall be declared to be death").

171 *See* Susan F. Mandiberg, *Why Sentencing by a Judge Satisfies the Right to Jury Trial: A Comparative Law Look at Blakely and Booker*, 40 McGeorge L. Rev. 107, 119–20 (2009).

172 *See, e.g.*, United States v. Beasley, 72 F.3d 1518 (11th Cir. 1996) (affirming RICO convictions of several leaders and members of a religious group), *cert. denied sub nom.* James v. United States, 518 U.S. 1027 (1996), *and cert. denied sub nom.* Ben Yahweh v. United States, 519 U.S. 866 (1996); United States v. Sun Myung Moon, 718 F.2d 1210 (2d Cir. 1983) (affirming conviction of religious leader for various federal tax violations), *cert. denied*, 466 U.S. 971 (1984); United States v. Lewis, 644 F. Supp. 1391 (W.D. Mich. 1986) (finding members of a religious communal sect guilty of subjecting children to involuntary servitude in violation of federal law), *aff'd*, 840 F.2d 1276 (6th Cir. 1988), *cert. denied*, 488 U.S. 894 (1988); People v. Hodges, 13 Cal. Rptr. 2d 412, 418–20 (Cal. Super. Ct. App. Dep't 1992) (affirming convictions of clergy for failure to comply with child abuse reporting statute); Guinan v. State, 65 So. 3d 589, 593–4 (Fla. Dist. Ct. App. 2011) (affirming conviction of priest for grand theft); State v. Bussman, No. A08-0858, 2009 WL 2015416 (Minn. Ct. App. Jul. 14, 2009) (unpublished) (affirming conviction of priest for sexual assault); William W. Bassett, W. Cole Durham, Jr. & Robert T. Smith, 3 Religious Organizations and the Law § 11:75 (rev'd Dec. 2013) (stating and elaborating on the general rule).

173 *See* Lewis, 644 F. Supp. at 1395 (stating "the obvious fact that religious leaders are no more immune from criminal prosecution than other citizens").

174 Williams v. Gleason, 26 S.W.3d 54, 59 (Tex. Ct. App. 2000), *cert. denied*, 533 U.S. 902 (2001).

neutral and generally applicable, as well as neutrally and generally applied, the religious status of the defendant normally has no obvious bearing on the constitutionality of its prosecutorial application.

This is a general rule, however, and religious status may, in particular circumstances, functionally or even formally influence a criminal legal analysis. As a practical matter, for example, legal actions involving clergy or religious institutions may be more likely than actions against laypersons to implicate religious or theological doctrines, the presence of which can then preclude prosecution or litigation because of the Establishment Clause's prohibition on excessive entanglement.[175] Additionally, and also as a practical matter, to the extent that a criminal defendant wishes to assert a free exercise defense, clergymember status may render some elements, such as sincerity or substantial burden, easier to establish to the court's satisfaction, depending, of course, on the nature of the free exercise claim asserted. Finally, it appears that some prosecutors have traditionally been disinclined to pursue charges (or at least the same charges) against clergy, especially those of mainstream or powerful churches,[176] although the sexual abuse revelations of recent years have likely eroded this customary prosecutorial reluctance.[177]

In some instances, the impact of religious clerical or institutional status may be adverse from the defendant's point of view, such as when such defendants may face heightened criminal liability because of their special relationship with congregants. Minnesota law, for example, enhances the penal classifications for certain sexual offenses when "the actor is or purports to be a member of the clergy" and the offending conduct "occurred during the course of a meeting in which the complainant sought or received religious or spiritual advice, aid, or comfort from the actor in private" or "during a period of time in which the complainant was meeting on an ongoing basis with the actor to seek or receive religious or spiritual advice, aid, or comfort in private."[178] Under the Establishment Clause, this enhanced classification scheme has been upheld against facial challenges because the statutes provide comparable enhancements when the crimes are committed by certain other nonreligious actors,[179] though its application in one case was invalidated

175 *See, e.g.*, State v. Burckhard, 592 N.W.2d 523, 526 (N.D. 1999) (affirming dismissal of a criminal charge against a priest for alleged theft of parish funds, where the court determined, based on a bishop's letter, that assessing the priest's authority in relation to the funds would have required an ecclesiastical determination of Canon Law and would have caused excessive entanglement in violation of the state and federal constitutions); Bradley J. B. Toben & Kris Helge, *Sexual Misconduct with Congregants or Parishioners: Crafting a Model Statute*, 1 Brit. J. Am. Legal Stud. 189, 204–5 (2012) [noting that "when the counseling of a congregant or parishioner is mixed in character (both secular and religious), but the inducement to sex arises solely from spiritual, religious or theological advice or guidance, the entanglement doctrine may be invoked as a constitutional impediment to prosecution"]. With regard to doctrinal entanglement in general, *see* Chapter 4.C.1.c.

176 *See* Timothy D. Lytton, *Clergy Sexual Abuse Litigation: The Policymaking Role of Tort Law*, 39 Conn. L. Rev. 809, 867–8 (2007) (noting this reluctance).

177 For analysis of prosecuting church leaders for clergy sexual abuse, *see* Michael F. Aylward, *Constitution, Crime, Clergy: First Amendment Implications of Sexual Abuse Claims*, 70 Def. Couns. J. 196 (2003); John S. Baker, Jr., *Prosecuting Dioceses and Bishops*, 44 B.C. L. Rev. 1061 (2003).

178 Minn. Stat. Ann. §§ 609.344, subd. 1(l) (sexual penetration), 609.345, subd. 1(l) (sexual contact).

179 *See* State v. Wenthe, 839 N.W.2d 83, 88–92 (Minn. 2013) [so holding with regard to Minn. Stat. § 609.344 subd. 1(l)(i)]; State v. Bussman, 741 N.W.2d 79, 89–92 (Minn. 2007) [affirming, by an equally divided court, that holding of the intermediate appellate court with regard to Minn. Stat. § 609.344 subd. 1(l)(ii)]; Doe v. F.P., 667 N.W.2d 493, 499-500 (Minn. Ct. App. 2003) [so holding with regard to both statutes, Minn. Stat. §§ 609.344 subd. 1(l), 609.345 subd. 1(l)].

when the trial court "allowed the religious doctrine of [a church] to become entangled with the criteria set out in the … statute for determining the criminality of [the defendant's] conduct."[180]

Lastly, there is, derived from one or both First Amendment religion clauses, a doctrinal amalgam that is often cast in terms of church autonomy,[181] and one might reasonably surmise that such a church autonomy doctrine would have something to say about the imposition of criminal liability. To date, however, this has not been the case. Insofar as the doctrine is concerned largely with internal church decision making, it may not immunize religious leaders or institutions from criminal liability for the external manifestations of their conduct. To be sure, several courts have suggested that no such immunity exists,[182] and the Second Circuit (in a case involving the criminal prosecution of a religious leader) has expressed this view in fairly blunt terms:

> To foreclose a court from analyzing a church's activities as needed to determine whether those activities violated a statute, on the ground that the First Amendment forbids such inquiry, would mean that there are no restraints or limitations on church activities … The "free exercise" of religion is not so unfettered. The First Amendment does not insulate a church or its members from judicial inquiry when a charge is made that their activities violate a penal statute.[183]

Courts have certainly held, in all events, that notions of church autonomy do not shield religious entities from evidentiary directives, such as subpoenas *duces tecum* (seeking, for example, financial or personnel records), issued in the course of a criminal investigation or prosecution.[184]

180 Bussman, 741 N.W.2d at 94. The defendant was subsequently convicted again, and that conviction was affirmed on appeal. *See* State v. Bussman, No. A08-0858, 2009 WL 2015416 (Minn. Ct. App. Jul. 14, 2009) (unpublished).

181 *See* Chapter 5.H (examining the ministerial exception) and Chapter 8 (examining the church property and schism cases).

182 *See, e.g.*, Minker v. Baltimore Annual Conf. of United Methodist Church, 894 F.2d 1354, 1357 (D.C. Cir. 1990) (rejecting the notion that, under the ministerial exception, "courts would be prevented from enforcing homicide statutes against churches that selected their pastors by making them play russian roulette"); Brazauskas v. Fort Wayne-S. Bend Diocese, Inc., 796 N.E. 286, 294 n. 6 (Ind. 2003) (hypothesizing that "a defendant charged with conspiracy to commit murder via terroristic attacks could not insulate himself [or herself} from liability merely by claiming that the agreement element of the crime occurred within a protected discussion of church doctrine or policy"), *cert. denied*, 541 U.S. 902 (2004).

183 United States v. Sun Myung Moon, 718 F.2d 1210, 1227 (2d Cir. 1983), *cert. denied*, 466 U.S. 971 (1984).

184 *See, e.g.*, Roman Catholic Archdiocese of L.A. v. Superior Court of L.A. Cnty., 32 Cal. Rptr. 2d 209 (Cal. Ct. App. 2005), *cert. denied*, 547 U.S. 1071 (2006); People v. Campobello, 810 N.E.2d 307, 315–17 (Ill. Ct. App. 2004) (upholding subpoena; citing cases); Soc'y of Jesus of New Eng. v. Commonwealth, 808 N.E.2d 272, 277–9 (Mass. 2004) (holding that the church autonomy doctrine of the Free Exercise Clause does not prohibit the issuance of *subpoena duces tecum* against a religious organization and a clergy member, as part of a prosecution of the clergy member, for personnel documents concerning the clergy member); *cf. also* Roman Catholic Archdiocese of Jackson v. Morrison, 905 So. 2d 1213, 1247 (Miss. 2005) (refusing, in a civil context, to recognize "a privilege under the First Amendment to refuse to produce religious-oriented documents"); *see generally* Marc L. Terry, *Disclosure of Church Archives in Cases of Criminal Misconduct by Clergymen*, 1 SUFFOLK J. TRIAL & APP. ADVOC. 95 (1995).

## C. Criminalization of Conduct Specifically Related to Religion

### 1. *Crimes against Religious Orthodoxy: Blasphemy, Soothsaying, and Sorcery*

This subsection addresses various forms of conduct that, at least historically, have been criminalized insofar as they contravene the religious orthodoxy of the citizenry, not merely in the general sense of being immoral or sinful but also in the specific sense of engaging in practices that are essentially heterodox in relation to the ambient religious beliefs of the community. These include blasphemy as well as spiritualistic activities such as fortune-telling, astrology or astromancy, crystallomancy, palm reading, necromancy, witchcraft, sorcery, and the like.[185] As the following paragraphs will illustrate, many of these traditional offenses have been removed from state criminal codes, and those provisions that remain are seldom, if ever, enforced and are likely to be found unconstitutional under the Establishment Clause, Free Exercise Clause, or Free Speech Clause.

The first of these, blasphemy, which is functionally a subset of sacrilegious expression, can be defined as "maliciously reviling God or religion" or "speaking evil of the Deity with an impious purpose to derogate from the divine Majesty."[186] Blackstone, for instance, defined blasphemy in English common law as "denying [God's] being or providence" or making "contumelious reproaches of our Saviour Christ" or "profane scoffing at the holy scripture, or exposing it to contempt and ridicule."[187] Like defamation, blasphemy could be either written or spoken, and to be criminal, it must have been either uttered in the presence of others or published in some manner.[188] At common law, as suggested by Blackstone's definition, the justification for punishing blasphemy was based on the theory that Christianity was part of the law of the land and that the state had a prerogative to defend and preserve the law, including the Christian faith.[189] A secondary motivation was that permitting blasphemy would undermine the sanctity of official oaths, rendering them ineffective.[190]

In colonial America, blasphemy cases occurred but never with great frequency. "Even in the seventeenth century, when the rate of North American blasphemy prosecutions was at its highest, such prosecutions were unusual. At the peak, there were eleven cases in

185 The offenses are found among those addressed in chapter 4 ("Of Offences against God and Religion") of the fourth book of William Blackstone's Commentaries on the Laws of England, *available at:* http://oll.libertyfund.org/titles/blackstone-commentaries-on-the-laws-of-england-in-four-books-vol-2. Blackstone covers, more thoroughly, (1) apostasy, (2) heresy, (3) offenses against the established church, (4) blasphemy, (5) swearing or cursing, (6) witchcraft, conjuration, enchantment, or sorcery, (7) religious impostors, (8) simony, "or the corrupt presentation of any one to an ecclesiastical benefice for gift or reward," (9) profaning the Sabbath, (10) drunkenness, and (11) open and notorious lewdness.

186 Charles E. Torcia, 4 Wharton's Criminal Law § 513 (15th ed. rev'd, Sep. 2013) (hereinafter 4 Wharton). For more in-depth discussions of the history and justification for blasphemy laws, *see* Blasphemy in Britain and America 1800–1930 (David Nash ed., 2010) (four volumes); Leonard Levy, Blasphemy: Verbal Offense against the Sacred, from Moses to Salman Rushdie (1993); David Nash, Blasphemy in the Christian World: A History (2007); *Note, Blasphemy,* 70 Colum. L. Rev. 694 (1970).

187 4 Blackstone, *Commentaries*, at *59.

188 *See* 4 Wharton, *supra* note 186, § 513.

189 *See id.*

190 *See, e.g.*, State v. Mockus, 113 A. 39, 42–3 (Me. 1921), *disavowed in part by* State v. John W., 418 A.2d 1097, 1102 n. 3 (Me. 1980).

the 1660s, six in the 1670s, and six more in the 1680s, nearly all in New England."[191] In the eighteenth century, there were only ten such prosecutions, and "[b]y the nineteenth century, prosecutions for blasphemy were extraordinarily rare"[192] partly because of state constitutional protections and partly because of a changing dynamic between state and English common law.[193] At the same time, the largely religious or theological rationales for blasphemy prohibitions were gradually replaced in American jurisprudence by the notion that such prohibitions were necessary to prevent breaches of the peace.[194] Some modern state codes continue to make blasphemy a crime,[195] but these statutes are rarely, if ever, enforced, and when challenged, they have failed under the Establishment Clause, the Free Speech Clause, or both.[196] In short, American law generally has rejected blasphemy laws as unconstitutional, though similar laws are in effect in other countries, often pertaining to Islam rather than Christianity.[197]

191 Christopher Thomas Anglim, Religion and the Law: A Dictionary 55 (1999).

192 *Id.*

193 *See id.* at 55–6; Sarah Barringer Gordon, *Blasphemy and the Law of Religious Liberty in Nineteenth-Century America*, 52 Am. Q. 682 (2000).

194 *See, e.g.*, Oney v. Okla. City, 120 F.2d 861, 865 (10th Cir. 1941) (facially upholding a municipal ordinance prohibiting, among other things, "the uttering, publication, circulation, or distribution of any words or language casting contumelious reproach or profane ridicule on God, Jesus Christ, the Holy Ghost, the Holy Scripture, or the Christian or any other religion, calculated to cause a breach of the peace" because "it is plainly directed against actions calculated to cause a breach of the peace and disturb public order" and "[i]ts object is to prevent the inciting of violence"); Lynch v. Muskogee, 47 F. Supp. 589, 592 (D. Okla. 1942) (similar, following Oney); State v. Chandler, 2 Del. (2 Harr.) 553, 557, 568–9 (Del. Ct. Gen. Sess. 1837); Commonwealth *ex rel.* Brown v. Rundle, 227 A.2d 895, 896–7 & n. 4 (Pa. 1967) (facially though cursorily upholding a state blasphemy prohibition), *cert. denied*, 387 U.S. 937 (1967).

195 *See, e.g.*, Mass. Gen. Laws ch. 272, § 36 ("Whoever wilfully blasphemes the holy name of God by denying, cursing or contumeliously reproaching God, his creation, government or final judging of the world, or by cursing or contumeliously reproaching Jesus Christ or the Holy Ghost, or by cursing or contumeliously reproaching or exposing to contempt and ridicule, the holy word of God contained in the holy scriptures shall be punished by imprisonment in jail for not more than one year or by a fine of not more than three hundred dollars, and may also be bound to good behavior."); Mich. Comp. Laws § 750.102 ("Any person who shall wilfully blaspheme the holy name of God, by cursing or contumeliously reproaching God, shall be guilty of a misdemeanor."); 21 Okla. St. § 901 (2007) ("Blasphemy consists in wantonly uttering or publishing words, casting contumelious reproach or profane ridicule upon God, Jesus Christ, the Holy Ghost, the Holy Scriptures or the Christian or any other religion."); *id.* § 902 ("If it appears beyond reasonable doubt that the words complained of were used in the course of serious discussion, and with intent to make known or recommend opinions entertained by the accused, such words are not blasphemy."); *id.* § 903 ("Blasphemy is a misdemeanor."); *see also* S.C. Code § 16-17-520 ("Any person who shall … (c) … use blasphemous … language at or near the place of … [any meeting, society, assembly or congregation convened for the purpose of religious worship] shall be guilty of a misdemeanor.").

196 *See* Kalman v. Cortes, 723 F. Supp. 2d 766, 784–807 (E.D. Pa. 2010) (invalidating Pennsylvania's blasphemy statute under the Establishment and Free Speech Clauses); State v. West, 263 A.2d 602, 603–5 (Mt. Ct. Spec. App. 1970) (invalidating Maryland's blasphemy statute because it lacked a secular purpose and was nonneutral in relation to religion); *cf. also* Joseph Burstyn, Inc. v. Wilson, 343 U.S. 495, 505–6 (1952) (invalidating state prohibition on sacrilegious speech as applied to a film); Leonard v. Robinson, 477 F.3d 347, 359–60 (6th Cir. 2007) (questioning the constitutional application of Michigan's blasphemy statute); Original Fayette Cnty. Civic & Welfare League, Inc. v. Ellington, 309 F. Supp. 89, 92 (W.D. Tenn. 1970) (invalidating under the Free Speech and Due Process Clauses a state law prohibiting "rude, boisterous, offensive, obscene or blasphemous language in any public place").

197 *See* U.S. Commission on International Religious Freedom, Annual Report 173–4 (2014) (listing forty-three known persons currently imprisoned for blasphemy in Egypt, Pakistan, and Saudi Arabia).

Blasphemy is perhaps the most obvious but by no means the only offense against religious orthodoxy within American criminal law. Various jurisdictions, for example, also have placed either criminal or regulatory restrictions on occult-like soothsaying activities such as fortune telling, astrology, tarot card reading, and palmistry, at least when they are offered to the public on a commercial basis.[198] In the main, these laws have reflected two chief rationales. The first is the government's desire to prevent fraud[199] – especially against "the gullible, superstitious, and unwary"[200] – the assumption being that activities such as fortune-telling and palmistry are little more than "hocus pocus."[201] Accordingly, some laws prohibit such activities only when undertaken with deceit.[202] Second, these restrictions also

198 *See, e.g.*, N.Y. Penal Law § 165.35 ("A person is guilty of fortune-telling [a clsss B misdemeanor] when, for a fee or compensation which he [or she] directly or indirectly solicits or receives, he [or she] claims or pretends to tell fortunes, or holds himself [or herself] out as being able, by claimed or pretended use of occult powers, to answer questions or give advice on personal matters or to exorcise, influence or affect evil spirits or curses; except that this section does not apply to a person who engages in the aforedescribed conduct as part of a show or exhibition solely for the purpose of entertainment or amusement."); 21 Okla. St. § 931 ("It shall be unlawful [as a misdemeanor] for any person or persons, pretending or professing to tell fortunes by the use of any subtle craft, means or device whatsoever, either by palmistry, clairvoyancy or otherwise, plying his or her trade, art or profession within the State of Oklahoma, to make any charge therefor either directly or indirectly or to receive any gift, donation or subscription by any means whatsoever for the same."); 18 Pa. Consol. Stat. § 7104(a) ("A person is guilty of a misdemeanor of the third degree if he [or she] pretends for gain or lucre, to tell fortunes or predict future events, by cards, tokens, the inspection of the head or hands of any person, or by the age of anyone, or by consulting the movements of the heavenly bodies, or in any other manner, or for gain or lucre, pretends to effect any purpose by spells, charms, necromancy, or incantation, or advises the taking or administering of what are commonly called love powders or potions, or prepares the same to be taken or administered, or publishes by card, circular, sign, newspaper or other means that he [or she] can predict future events, or for gain or lucre, pretends to enable anyone to get or to recover stolen property, or to tell where lost property is, or to stop bad luck, or to give good luck, or to put bad luck on a person or animal, or to stop or injure the business or health of a person or shorten his life, or to give success in business, enterprise, speculation, and games of chance, or to win the affection of a person, or to make one person marry another, or to induce a person to make or alter a will, or to tell where money or other property is hidden, or to tell where to dig for treasure, or to make a person to dispose of property in favor of another."); S.C. Code § 16-17-690 ("It shall be unlawful to engage in the business, trade or profession of fortunetelling, palmistry, phrenology, clairvoyance or the prediction of future events by cards or other means or to offer to tell fortunes or predict future events by palmistry, astrology, clairvoyance, cards or other means as an inducement to promote some other business, trade or profession. Any person violating the provisions of this section shall be guilty of a misdemeanor and upon conviction shall be subject to a fine of not less than twenty-five dollars nor more than one hundred dollars or imprisonment for not less than fifteen nor more than thirty days."). In addition, some states specifically authorize their political subdivisions to regulate, tax, or prohibit such activities. *See, e.g.*, Cal. Gov't Code § 50027; Ga. Code § 36-1-15; S.D. Codified Laws § 9-34-16.

199 *See, e.g.*, Ballard v. Walker, 772 F. Supp. 1335, 1341 (E.D.N.Y. 1991); White v. Adams, 343 S.W.2d 793, 794 (Ark. 1961); *In re* Bartha, 134 Cal. Rptr. 39, 43 (Cal. Ct. App. 1976); State v. Kenilworth, 54 A. 244, 245 (N.J. 1903); People v. Ashley, 172 N.Y.S. 282, 284 (N.Y. Supr. Ct. App. Div. 1918); Davis v. State, 160 N.E. 473, 475 (Ohio 1928), *error dismissed*, 277 U.S. 571 (1928).

200 Bartha, 134 Cal. Rptr. at 43; *see also* White, 343 S.W.2d at 794 (remarking that "fortune telling may be a fraudulent means of preying upon the ignorant, the superstitious, and the gullible"); People v. Rosenberg, 159 N.Y.S.2d 912, 915 (N.Y. City Magis. Ct. Borough of Brooklyn 1957).

201 Bridewell v. City of Bessemer, 46 So. 2d 568, 571 (Ala. Ct. App. 1950).

202 *See, e.g.*, Cal. Penal Code § 332(a) ("Every person who by ... pretensions to fortune telling, trick, or other means whatever, by use of cards or other implements or instruments ... fraudulently obtains from another person money or property of any description, shall be punished as in the case of larceny of property of like value for the first offense."); Mass. Gen. Laws ch. 266, § 75 ("Whoever, by a game, device, sleight of hand, pretended fortune telling or by any trick or other means by the use of cards or other implements or instruments, fraudulently obtains from another person property of any description shall be punished as in the case of larceny of property of like value.").

have reflected, at least in some of their original forms, not merely a scientifically but also a religiously informed "disbelief in [the] human power to prophesy human events"[203] that is ultimately rooted or embodied in scriptural admonitions.[204]

Generally speaking, courts have upheld restrictions or bans on fortune-telling and similar practices, particularly if done for money, when challenged as violating the constitutional guarantees of due process,[205] equal protection,[206] privileges and immunities,[207] freedom of religion,[208] and the bar on impairing contractual obligations.[209] For many years, such laws also survived challenges based on the freedom of speech,[210] but more recent decades have witnessed their increasing invalidation on this ground,[211] with courts often deeming the speech to be fully protected and the laws to be content based and unable to satisfy the attendant level of judicial scrutiny.[212] At the same time, courts have become less persuaded by the proposition that fortune-telling and similar expression are intrinsically fraudulent (or that the government should even be making such a judgment) and thus have been less receptive to fraud prevention as a reason to restrict such expression, at least absent a requirement and proof of actual fraud.[213]

203 People v. Malcolm, 154 N.Y.S. 919, 921 (N.Y. Ct. Gen. Sess. 1915); *see also* Mitchell v. City of Birmingham, 133 So. 13, 14 (Ala. 1931); White, 343 S.W.2d at 794.

204 *See* Mitchell, 133 So. at 14; Ashley, 172 N.Y.S. at 283–4.

205 *See, e.g.*, Gladstone v. Galton, 145 F.2d 742, 745 (9th Cir. 1944); White, 343 S.W.2d at 793–4; Bartha, 134 Cal. Rptr. at 43; Williams v. Jenkins, 83 S.E.2d 614, 616 (Ga. 1954); Davis, 160 N.E. at 474–5. *But cf.* Marks v. City of Chesapeake, Va., 883 F.2d 308, 311–13 (4th Cir. 1989) (holding that denial of conditional use permit to person seeking to use property for a palmistry and fortune-telling business, where denial reflected some citizens' irrational fears that such activities are "heretical," worked an unconstitutional deprivation of property without due process); Johnson v. Alexander, 219 So. 2d 66 (Fla. Dist. Ct. App. 1969) (similar).

206 *See, e.g.*, Gladstone, 145 F.2d at 745; White, 343 S.W.2d at 793–4.

207 *See, e.g.*, Davis, 160 N.E. at 474–5.

208 *See, e.g.*, Allinger v. Los Angeles, 77 Cal. Rptr. 256, 260–1 (Cal. Ct. App. 1969); Bartha, 134 Cal. Rptr. at 42–3; St. Louis v. Hellscher, 242 S.W. 652, 653 (Mo. 1922); Dill v. Hamilton, 291 N.W. 62, 64–5 (Neb. 1939); People v. Ballard, 533 N.Y.S.2d 558, 559 (N.Y. App. Div. 1988), *appeal denied*, 539 N.E.2d 593 (N.Y. 1989); Ashley, 172 N.Y.S. at 285–6; People v. Brossard, 33 N.Y.S.2d 369, 372 (N.Y. Cnty. Ct. Erie Cnty. 1942); Haas v. State, 28 Ohio C.D. 1, 3–5 (Ohio Ct. App. 1917); McMasters v. State, 207 P. 566, 568–69 (Okla. Ct. Crim. App. 1922); State v. Neitzel, 125 P. 939, 940 (Wash. 1912). Even before the modern era, some religious freedom challenges to such laws succeeded. *See, e.g.*, State v. De Laney, 122 A. 890, 891 (N.J. 1923); Commonwealth v. Blair, 92 Pa. Super. 169, 171–2 (Pa. Super. Ct. 1927).

209 *See* Gladstone, 145 F.2d at 745.

210 *See, e.g.*, Bartha, 134 Cal. Rptr. at 43; Williams, 83 S.E.2d at 616; Davis, 160 N.E. at 475.

211 *See, e.g.*, Argello v. City of Lincoln, 143 F.3d 1152, 1152–3 (8th Cir. 1998); Adams v. City of Alexandria, 875 F. Supp. 2d 685, 689–91 (W.D. La. 2012); Trimble v. City of New Iberia, 73 F.Supp. 2d 659, 666–7 (W.D. La. 1999); Angeline v. Mahoning Cnty. Agric. Soc., 993 F. Supp. 627. 631–5 (N.D. Ohio 1998); Rushman v. City of Milwaukee, 959 F.Supp. 1040, 1043–5 (E.D. Wis. 1997); Spiritual Psychic Sci. Church v. City of Asuza, 703 P.2d 1119, 1122–30 (Cal. 1985), *overruled in part by* Kasky v. Nike, Inc., 45 P.3d 243 (Cal. 2002), *cert. dismissed*, 539 U.S. 654 (2003); Nefedro v. Montgomery Cnty., 996 A.2d 850, 861–4 (Md. 2010); Marks v. Roseburg, 670 P.2d 201, 203–4 (Or. Ct. App. 1983), *review denied*, 678 P.2d 738 (Or. 1983).

212 *See, e.g.*, Argello, 143 F.3d at 1152–3; Adams, 875 F. Supp. at 689–91.

213 *See, e.g.*, Argello, 143 F.3d at 1153 ("[T]he ordinance [cannot] be upheld as a prohibition against fraud. It does not require that fortunetellers *know* that they are conveying false information, or that they have no power of seeing into the future. For all we know, certain persons genuinely believe that they have such powers. In this belief they may be mistaken, but that is not a decision that government is free to make under our Constitution."); Adams, 878 F. Supp. 2d at 690–1; Trimble, 73 F. Supp. 2d at 667; City of Chicago v. Westergren, 173 Ill. App. 562, 564 (Ill. Ct. App. 1912) ("However unreasonable such ideas and beliefs may appear to many, it is certain, and so indicated in this record, that a large number

A final realm of conduct historically subject to prohibition, at least partly for reasons of religious orthodoxy, is the practice of sorcery, witchcraft, wizardry, or other forms of conjuring or magical arts. Under the laws of early modern England, sorcery or witchcraft was a serious offense. In the sixteenth and seventeenth centuries, according to Blackstone, "all persons invoking any evil spirit, or consulting, covenanting with, entertaining, employing, feeding, or rewarding, any evil spirit; or taking up dead bodies from their graves to be used in any witchcraft, sorcery, charm, or enchantment; or killing or otherwise hurting any person by such infernal arts, should be guilty of felony without benefit of clergy, and suffer death."[214] Indeed, the "law punishes with death not only the sorcerers themselves, but also those who consult them."[215] By the middle of the eighteenth century, however, when Blackstone was writing his *Commentaries*, England had substantially diminished its criminalization and punishment of sorcery largely because of the abuse of witchcraft accusations by persons simply seeking retribution against neighbors,[216] though it still retained misdemeanor punishments – "a year's imprisonment, and standing four times in the pillory" – for those "pretending to use witchcraft, tell fortunes, or discover stolen goods, by skill in the occult sciences."[217]

The English colonists in the New World brought with them the religious and legal injunctions against witchcraft and other occultist practices.[218] The most famous American witchcraft trials, of course, are those centered in the Massachusetts colonial town of Salem.[219] In early 1692, the daughter and niece of Salem minister Samuel Parris began

of people have faith and confidence in spirit mediumship; and we are of the opinion that the belief therein and honest practice thereof without fraudulent means, tricks or devices cannot be held criminal."); Nefredo, 996 A.2d at 863. For further discussion of free speech issues, *see* Nicole Brown Jones, *Comment, Did Fortune Tellers See This Coming? Spiritual Counseling, Professional Speech, and the First Amendment*, 83 Miss. L.J. 639 (2014).

214 4 Blackstone, *Commentaries*, at *61 [citing 33 Hen. VIII, ch. 8 (1541), 1 Jac. I, ch. 12 (1604)]. "And if any person should attempt by sorcery to discover hidden treasure, or to restore stolen goods, or to provoke unlawful love, or to hurt any man or beast, though the same were not effected, he or she should suffer imprisonment and pillory for the first offence, and death for the second." *Id. See* Brian P. Levack, *Possession, Witchcraft, and the Law in Jacobean England*, 52 Wash. & Lee L. Rev. 1613 (1995). Regarding the evidentiary aspects, *see* Orna Alyagon Darr, *Experiments in the Courtroom: Dynamics and Spectacles of Proof in Early Modern English Witch Trials*, 39 Law & Soc. Inquiry 152. Regarding the potential scriptural bases for prohibiting if not punishing witchcraft or occultism, using the Christian Bible, *see Exodus* 22:18; *Deuteronomy* 18:10–12; *Acts* 8; *Galations* 5:20; *cf. Revelation* 21:8.

215 4 Blackstone, *Commentaries* *60.

216 *See id.* *61–*62 [citing 9 Geo. II, ch. 5 (1735)]. "These acts continued in force till lately, to the terror of all antient females in the kingdom: and many poor wretches were sacrificed thereby to the prejudice of their neighbours and their own illusions; not a few having, by some means or other, confessed the fact at the gallows." *Id.* *61.

217 *Id.*

218 *See, e.g.*, James v. Commonwealth, 12 Serg. & Rawle 220, 227–8 (Pa. 1825) (noting the Pennsylvania colony's adoption and enforcement of an early seventeenth-century English statute on witchcraft). The first colonial execution for witchcraft was the 1647 hanging of Alse Young of Windsor, Connecticut. *See Witches and Witchcraft—The First Person Executed in the Colonies, available at:* http://www.jud.ct.gov/lawlib/history/witches.htm.

219 *See* John Butler, Grant Wacker & Randall Balmer, Religion in American Life: A Short History 60–1 (2d ed., 2011); Mary Beth Norton, In the Devil's Snare: The Salem Witchcraft Crisis of 1692 (2002). For primary sources, *see Salem Witch Trials—Documentary Archive and Transcription Project, available at:* http://salem.lib.virginia.edu/home.html. For a recent overview of some of the theories regarding the Salem witchcraft hysteria, *see* Anthony Brandt, *An Unholy Mess*, Am. Hist., Dec. 2014, at 34.

having convulsive fits, which the family attributed to the witchcraft of several town residents. As the number of supposedly afflicted girls increased, so did the quantity and range of allegations, eventually leading over the course of the year to numerous witchcraft trials and convictions, often based on so-called spectral evidence, that is, claims by the accusers "that they were … tormented by witches in spectral forms that only they could see."[220] "When the dust finally settled in 1693, over 160 persons had been accused, 19 convicted witches had been executed by hanging, another 5 had died in prison, and 1 had been tortured to death."[221] Largely as a consequence of these trials and executions, colonial America, similar to Great Britain, thereafter experienced a decline in witchcraft prosecutions.[222] Today, much like the historic offenses of blasphemy and fortune-telling, prohibitions or restrictions relating to witchcraft and its variants not only are uncommon but when enforced or challenged presumably would run afoul of the First Amendment religion and speech guarantees. To be sure, the rise of Wicca as a recognized religion for constitutional and statutory purposes has essentially transformed a realm of conduct that had previously been punishable by death into one that is today manifestly protected by law.[223]

### 2. *Crimes against Religious Property, Practices, or Persons*

Addressed in this subsection are crimes consisting of conduct directed specifically at buildings and property, activities, or persons as a result of their religious character. It thus includes, for example, arson and other damage to structures and properties based on their religious affiliation or on the religious identity of their owners or occupants; interference with worship or other exercises of religion; and so-called religious hate crimes, that is, otherwise standard criminal offenses that are committed against persons based on their perceived religious beliefs or identity.

The federal government and most states have laws that criminalize damage to places of worship or other properties because of their religious affiliation or significance or that enhance punishment where a property is targeted because of the religion of its owners or users.[224] Such laws, which also may protect other structures or property used by the

220 Michael D. Bailey, Historical Dictionary of Witchcraft 124 (2003). "Such evidence might be supplied by another accused witch, who would testify to having seen someone in attendance at a witches' sabbath (many authorities maintained that witches traveled to sabbaths only in spirit), or by victims who would testify to having seen the form of a witch tormenting them. Many authorities argued that, although these specters might not be the witch herself, God would never allow the devil or a demon to impersonate an innocent person while working evil." *Id.* at 123–4.

221 John Corrigan, *Cosmology*, *in* Religion in American History 29, 46 (Amanda Porterfield & John Corrigan, eds., 2010).

222 For its part, "[i]n 1714, the Massachusetts assembly reversed the convictions of those accused and executed at Salem and called upon the colony to repent for its delusions." Butler et al., *supra* note 219, at 62.

223 *See, e.g.*, O'Bryan v. Bureau of Prisons, 349 F.3d 399, 400–1 (7th Cir. 2003) (effectively recognizing Wicca as a religion under RFRA); Brown v. Woodland Joint Unified Sch. Dist., 27 F.3d 1373, 1378 (9th Cir. 1994) (assuming that it is a religion under the Establishment Clause); Dettmer v. Landon, 799 F.2d 929, 932 (4th Cir. 1986) (deeming it a religion under the Free Exercise Clause), *cert. denied*, 483 U.S. 1007 (1987); Rouser v. White, 630 F. Supp.2d 1165, 1181 (E.D. Cal. 2009) (effectively recognizing it as a religion under RLUIPA); Van Koten v. Family Health Mgmt., Inc., 955 F. Supp. 898, 902 (N.D. Ill. 1997) (deeming it, at least for pleading purposes, a religion under Title VII of the Civil Rights Act of 1964), *aff'd*, 134 F.3d 375 (7th Cir. 1998) (*per curiam*) (unpublished).

224 *See, e.g.*, Pub. L. No. 100-346, § 1, 102 Stat. 644 (Jun. 24, 1988) (codified as amended at 18 U.S.C. § 247); Ala. Code § 13A-11-12; Ariz. Rev. Stat. § 13-1604(A)(1); Ark. Code §§ 5-38-301(a)(2)(D), 5-71-215(a)

public, generally can be justified as preserving and furthering both individual and institutional free exercise. As one commentator observed,

> [s]wastika-daubings, arsons, firebombings, and other acts of vandalism against religious institutions interfere in varied and far-reaching ways with the unfettered exercise of religion. Such acts often destroy property endowed with spiritual and historic value and may also be a source of unrest and psychological scars for the adherents of affected religious groups. Repairing the damage caused by vandalism drains the assets of religious institutions; these costs, together with the fears of congregants, may force curtailment of religious activities. Acts of vandalism and violence that mar communal religious experiences thus may well reduce the number of people who choose to observe their religion openly.[225]

To be sure, these laws have occasionally been challenged under the Establishment Clause – the idea being that they advance or endorse religion or favor religion over nonreligion – but courts have uniformly upheld them,[226] as have courts likewise upheld laws enhancing punishment for the commission of other crimes in or near places of worship.[227] The federal statute, in particular, has been upheld as well against a challenge that it exceeds the power of Congress under the Commerce Clause.[228]

(3); Cal. Penal Code §§ 423.2(f), 594.3, 11413; Colo. Rev. Stat. § 18-9-113; Conn. Gen. Stat. § 46a-58; 11 Del. Code § 1331; Fla. Stat. § 806.13; Ga. Code § 16-7-26; Haw. Rev. Stat. § 711-1107; Idaho Stat. § 18-7902(b); Ill. Comp. Stat. ch. 720 §§ 5/5-5-3.2(a)(11), 5/21–1.2(a)(1); Ind. Code § 35-43-1–2(b)(1); Kan. Stat. § 21-4111(a)(2)(D); Ky. Stat. §§ 525.110(1)(a), 525.113; La. Rev. Stat. § 14:225(A)(1); 17-A Me. Rev. Stat. § 507; Md. Crim. Law §§ 10-302, 10-305; Mass. Gen. Laws ch. 266 §§ 98, 127A; Mich. Comp. Laws § 750.147b; Minn. Stat. §§ 609.595, 609.5631; Miss. Code § 97-17-39; Mo. Stat. § 574.085.1(1); Mont. Code § 45-5-221(1)(c); Neb. Rev. Stat. § 28-111; Nev. Rev. Stat. § 206.125.1(a); N.J. Stat. §§ 2C:33-9-11; N.M. Stat. § 30-15-4; N.Y. Penal Law § 240.31; N.C. Gen. Stat. §§ 14-49(b1), 62.2, 144; Ohio Rev. Code § 2927.11(A)(1), (6); 21 Okla. Stat. § 1765; Or. Rev. Stat. § 166.075; 18 Pa. Consol. Stat. §§ 3307, 5509; R.I. Gen. Laws § 11-44-31; S.C. Code § 16-11-535; Tenn. Code §§ 39-14-301(b)(2), 39-17-311(a)(1); Tex. Penal Code §§ 28.03(f), 28.08(d); Va. Code §§ 18.2.127, 18.2.138; Wash. Rev. Code §§ 9.61.160, 9A.36.080(1)(b); Wis. Stat. § 943.012(1).

225 *Note, Protecting Religious Exercise: The First Amendment and Legislative Responses to Religious Vandalism*, 97 Harv. L. Rev. 547, 554–5 (1983) (footnote omitted).

226 *See* United States v. Corum, 362 F.3d 489, 496–7 (8th Cir. 2004) [upholding 18 U.S.C. § 247(a)(2) and (b)], *cert. denied*, 543 U.S. 1056 (2005); United States v. Scott, No. 98-40974, 202 F.3d 265, 1999 WL 1131952, at *1–*3 (5th Cir. Nov. 16, 1999) (*per curiam*) (unpublished) [upholding 18 U.S.C. § 247(a)(1)]; Todd v. State, 643 So. 2d 625, 628–30 (Fla. Dist. Ct. App. 1994) [upholding Fla. Stat. § 806.13(2)], *review denied*, 651 So. 2d 1197 (Fla. 1995), *cert. denied*, 515 U.S. 1143 (1995); People v. Carter, 592 N.E.2d 491, 495–8 (Ill. Ct. App. 1992) (upholding predecessor Illinois statute), *appeal denied*, 602 N.E.2d 461 (Ill. 1992); State v. Vogenthaler, 548 P.2d 112, 113–14 (N.M. Ct. App. 1976) (upholding predecessor New Mexico statute).

227 *See, e.g.*, Carter v. Peters, 26 F.3d 697, 698–9 (7th Cir. 1994) (upholding a state sentencing law that treated, as an aggravating factor, the occurrence of a crime in or on the grounds of a place of worship immediately before, during, or immediately after worship services), *cert. denied*, 513 U.S. 1003 (1994); Rice v. State, 754 So. 2d 881, 883–4 (Fla. Dist. Ct. App. 2000) (upholding a statutory sentence enhancement for drug offenses within 1000 feet of a place of worship), *review denied*, 779 So. 2d 272 (Fla. 2000); People v. Falbe, 727 N.E.2d 200, 206–9 (Ill. 2000) (same); Burke v. State, 943 N.E.2d 870, 874–6 (Ind. Ct. App. 2011), *transfer denied*, 950 N.E.2d 1207 (Ind. 2011); Dimaio v. State, 951 So. 2d 581, 587–8 (Miss. Ct. App. 2006) (upholding a statutory sentence enhancement for burglary or petit larceny committed in a place of worship); Maxwell v. State, 141 P.3d 564, 567–9 (Okla. Ct. Crim. App. 2006) (upholding a state law criminalizing houses of prostitution within 1000 feet of a church).

228 *See* United States v. Ballinger, 395 F.3d 1218, 1225–43 (11th Cir. 2005) (*en banc*), *cert. denied*, 546 U.S. 829 (2005). For additional analysis of the statute's application, given its commerce-based

Federal and state statutes also protect various types of religious practices. Federal law, for example, makes it a crime to "intentionally obstruct, by force or threat of force, any person in the enjoyment of that person's free exercise of religious beliefs, or attempt to do so,"[229] as well as to conspire "to injure, oppress, threaten, or intimidate any person ... in the free exercise or enjoyment" of religious freedom as guaranteed by federal constitutional and statutory law.[230] In addition, many states have laws that criminalize disturbing or interfering with religious worship or assembly.[231] Similar to federal law, some states also criminalize interference with religious practice more generally,[232] and a few specifically prohibit compulsion of religious profession or practice.[233] Importantly, these various statutes, which essentially embrace the common law's restriction on disturbing religious services,[234] are aimed at conduct by *all* citizens or groups, not just by government actors, the latter of which are constrained by other criminal laws[235] and, more broadly, by state and federal constitutional guarantees and by religious freedom statutes such as the Religious Freedom Restoration Act (RFRA) and its state counterparts. Like the religious property statutes, state laws protecting religious practices generally

jurisdictional element and relationship to 18 U.S.C. § 844(i), *see* United States v. Lamont, 330 F.3d 1249, 1251–9 (9th Cir. 2003); United States v. Odom, 252 F.3d 1289, 1293–7 (11th Cir. 2001), *cert. denied*, 535 U.S. 1058 (2002). Regarding the construction of "free exercise of religious beliefs" in section (a)(2), which prohibits "intentionally obstruct[ing], by force or threat of force, any person in the enjoyment of that person's free exercise of religious beliefs," *see* United States v. Barlow, 41 F.3d 935, 941–4 (5th Cir. 1994), *cert. denied*, 514 U.S. 1030 (1995), *and cert. denied sub nom.* Lebaron v. United States, 514 U.S. 1097 (1995).

229 18 U.S.C. § 247(a)(2).

230 *Id.* § 241. *See, e.g.*, United States v. Allen, 341 F.3d 870 (9th Cir. 2003) (affirming convictions under Section 241 for interfering with federal statutory right to use places of public accommodation free of racial and religious discrimination), *cert. denied*, 541 U.S. 975 (2004). *See also* 18 U.S.C. § 245(b)(2).

231 *See, e.g.*, Cal. Penal Code §§ 302(a), 423.2(b), (d); Mich. Comp. Laws § 752.525; Minn. Stat. § 609.28; Mo. Stat. § 574.035; Nev. Rev. Stat. § 201.270; N.M. Stat. § 30-13-1(A); N.Y. Penal Law §§ 240.21, 240.70(c), (d), 240.71; N.C. Gen. Stat. § 14-288.4(a)(7); 21 Okla. Stat. § 915; S.C. Code § 16-17-520; Va. Code § 18.2–415(B); *cf. also* Mich. Comp. Laws § 91.1(1)(i) (authorizing certain municipalities to prevent disturbances of religious meetings).

232 *See, e.g.*, Cal. Penal Code § 11412 ("Any person who, with intent to cause, attempts to cause or causes another to refrain from exercising his or her religion or from engaging in a religious service by means of a threat, directly communicated to such person, to inflict an unlawful injury upon any person or property, and it reasonably appears to the recipient of the threat that such threat could be carried out is guilty of a felony."); 21 Okla. Stat. § 914 ("Every person who willfully prevents, by threats or violence, another person from performing any lawful act enjoined upon or recommended to such person by the religion which he [or she] professes, is guilty of a misdemeanor."); S.D. Codified Laws § 22-19B-4 ("Any person who, by threats or violence, intentionally prevents another person from performing any lawful act enjoined upon or recommended by the religion which such person professes is guilty of a Class 1 misdemeanor.").

233 *See, e.g.*, 21 Okla. Stat. § 913 ("Any willful attempt, by means of threats or violence to compel any person to adopt, practice or profess any particular form of religious belief, is a misdemeanor."); S.D. Codified Laws § 22-19B-5 ("Any person who intentionally attempts, by threats or violence, to compel another person to adopt, practice, or profess any particular form of religious belief is guilty of a Class 1 misdemeanor.").

234 *See* 4 WHARTON, *supra* note 186, § 506; *see, e.g.*, State v. Wright, 41 Ark. 410, 412 (Ark. 1883); State v. Jasper, 15 N.C. (4 Dev.) 323, 325–7 (N.C. 1833); State v. Watkins, 130 S.W. 839, 839–40 (Tenn. 1910).

235 *See, e.g.*, 18 U.S.C. § 242; Catlette v. United States, 132 F.2d 902, 907 (4th Cir. 1943) (affirming convictions of law enforcement officers for violating this section, then codified at 18 U.S.C. § 52, for the officers' mistreatment of "victims solely by reason of their membership in the religious sect known as Jehovah's Witnesses, and their practices founded on their beliefs").

have survived challenges under the First Amendment religion clauses[236] and the Free Speech Clause.[237]

Lastly, the criminal law can extend to conduct against persons based on their perceived or actual religious affiliation. Although criminal prohibitions on religious discrimination as such have existed for many decades,[238] these newer laws against "hate crimes," as they are often designated, reflect a more recent cultural shift in the meaning of equal citizenship and a concerted effort to penalize bigotry as an especially pernicious dimension of criminal conduct.[239] According to the Federal Bureau of Investigation, in 2012 there were 1,166 criminal offenses motivated by religious bias, as reported by law enforcement agencies.[240] Of these, nearly 60 percent were anti-Jewish, 12.8 percent were anti-Islamic, 6.8 percent were anti-Catholic, 2.9 percent were anti-Protestant, and 16 percent involved multiple or unspecified religions.[241]

Although the Supreme Court has indicated that the Free Speech Clause prohibits the criminalization of expression or expressive conduct because of the particular message that it conveys in relation to victims, such as hatred of a victim's religion,[242] the Court has countenanced the enhancement of a defendant's sentence where some aspect of a defendant's criminal conduct, such as the selection of his or her victim, was motivated by prejudice against a victim's religion, race, or other characteristic.[243] Today, forty-five

236 *See, e.g.*, Hill v. State, 381 So. 2d 206, 210–12 (Ala. Ct. Crim. App. 1979) (upholding under the religion clauses a former Alabama statute making it a crime to "wilfully interrupt or disturb any assemblage of people met for religious worship, by noise, profane discourse, rude or indecent behavior or any other act, at or near the place of worship"), *writ denied*, 381 So. 2d 213 (Ala. 1980); Riley v. Dist. of Columbia, 283 A.2d 819, 824–5 (D.C. 1971) (upholding under the religion clauses a since-repealed DC statute making it a crime "to molest or disturb any congregation engaged in any religious exercise or proceedings in any church or place of worship"), *cert. denied*, 405 U.S. 1066 (1972); People v. McDaniel, 661 N.Y.S.2d 904, 906 (N.Y. Supr. Ct. App. Term 1997) (upholding N.Y. Penal Law § 240.21 under the Establishment Clause), *appeal denied*, 685 N.E.2d 219 (N.Y. 1997).

237 *See, e.g.*, Survivors Network of Those Abused by Priests, Inc. v. Joyce, 941 F. Supp. 2d 1078, 1088–90 (E.D. Mo. 2013) (upholding Mo. Stat. § 574.035 under the Free Speech Clause); Riley, 283 A.2d at 824.

238 *See, e.g.*, 18 U.S.C. § 245(b)(2) (originally enacted in 1968, criminalizing religious discrimination in various federally-protected activities); 42 U.S.C. § 3631 (also enacted in 1968, making it a crime "by force or threat of force [to] willfully injure, intimidate or interfere with, or attempt to injure, intimidate or interfere with" any person "because of his [or her] … religion" in relation to a housing transaction); *cf. also* 42 U.S.C. § 1985(3).

239 *See* James F. Short, Jr., *Criminology: Modern Controversies, in* 1 Encyclopedia of Crime & Justice 464, 466–7 (Joshua Dressler ed., 2d ed., 2002) (noting that "crimes motivated by 'hate' or 'bias' became a part of the legal and social lexicon of the United States only in the 1980s" and that "[b]y bringing hate or bias motivation under the criminal law, the United States, in effect, embarked on a social and legal experiment to sanction and control behavior that has long been a part of the history of the country").

240 *See* FBI, *2012 Hate Crime Statistics: Incidents and Offenses, available at:* http://www.fbi.gov/about-us/cjis/ucr/hate-crime/2012/topic-pages/incidents-and-offenses/incidentsandoffenses_final.

241 *See id.* For criticism of the report based on alleged underreporting, *see* Anti-Defamation League, *2012 Hate Crime Statistics Report "Seriously Flawed,"* Nov. 25, 2013, *available at:* http://www.adl.org/press-center/press-releases/hate-crimes/adl-2012-hate-crime-statistics-report-flawed.html.

242 *See* R.A.V. v. City of St. Paul, Minn., 505 U.S. 377, 391–6 (1992) (invalidating a municipal ordinance making it a crime to "place on public or private property a symbol, object, appellation, characterization or graffiti, including, but not limited to, a burning cross or Nazi swastika, which one knows or has reasonable grounds to know arouses anger, alarm or resentment in others on the basis of race, color, creed, religion or gender").

243 *See* Wisconsin v. Mitchell, 508 U.S. 476, 484–90 (1993). "[W]hereas the ordinance struck down in R.A.V. was explicitly directed at expression (*i.e.*, 'speech' or 'messages') … the statute in … [*Mitchell*] is aimed at conduct unprotected by the First Amendment." *Id.* at 487.

states have criminal laws providing for the punishment, or enhanced punishment, of such conduct.[244] Some states also have laws that specifically penalize various forms of religious intimidation,[245] including particular acts such as cross burning or the defacement of the victim's property by means of a religiously intimidating symbol.[246]

In 2009, the federal government enacted its own hate crime statute,[247] which among other things makes it a crime to "willfully cause bodily injury to any person or, through the use of fire, a firearm, a dangerous weapon, or an explosive or incendiary device, attempt to cause bodily injury to any person, because of the actual or perceived … religion … of any person."[248] The federal statute can be invoked only if the U.S. attorney general certifies that a state lacks jurisdiction or has requested the federal government to assume jurisdiction, that a state has prosecuted but the resulting "verdict or sentence … left demonstratively unvindicated the Federal interest in eradicating bias-motivated violence," or that a federal prosecution "is in the public interest and necessary to secure substantial justice."[249] To date, the federal hate crimes law has been upheld against a variety of constitutional challenges, though not specifically in prosecutions involving religion.[250] The most notable religion-related case under the statute thus far, involving Amish-on-Amish forcible beard cutting,[251] yielded a very narrow reading of the statute's causation element, which textually requires that the injury or attempted injury be "because of the actual or perceived … religion" of the victim. In particular, the Sixth Circuit ruled that the victim's actual or perceived religion must be a but-for cause of the offending conduct and that if the perpetrator would have engaged in the conduct apart from the victim's actual or perceived religion – even if the specific form that the injury took was religiously significant, as with the beard cutting – then the statute is not violated.[252]

244 *See* Jessica Malloy-Thorpe & David Hemken, *Hate Crime Regulation and Challenges*, 13 Geo. J. Gender & L. 289, 296 (2012). Of the available approaches, "[s]entencing enhancement … is the most common form of hate crime sanction." 1 Encyclopedia of Crime & Justice, *supra* note 239, at 467.

245 *See, e.g.*, Colo. Rev. Stat. § 18-9-121(2); Conn. Gen. Stat. §§ 53a-181j(a), 181k(a)–181l(a); Idaho Code § 18-7902; Mass. Gen. Laws ch. 265 § 39(a); N.J. Stat. 2C:16-1(a); 21 Okla. Stat. § 850; Or. Rev. Stat. §§ 165.165(1), 166.155(1)(c).

246 *See, e.g.*, Cal. Penal Code § 11411(c) (2007) (making it a crime to "burn or desecrate a cross or other religious symbol, knowing it to be a religious symbol, on the private property of another without authorization for the purpose of terrorizing the owner or occupant of that private property or in reckless disregard of the risk of terrorizing the owner or occupant of that private property" or to "burn, desecrate, or destroy a cross or other religious symbol, knowing it to be a religious symbol, on the property of a primary school, junior high school, or high school for the purpose of terrorizing any person who attends or works at the school or who is otherwise associated with the school"); S.D. Codified Laws §§ 22-19B-1(2), 22-19B-2 (criminalizing intimidation or harassment on the basis of religion, including by "defac[ing]" property, and then defining "deface" to include "cross-burnings or the placing of any word or symbol commonly associated with racial, religious, or ethnic terrorism on the property of another person without that person's permission").

247 Matthew Shepard and James Boyd, Jr. Hate Crimes Protection Act, Pub. L. No. 111-84, Div. E, §§ 4701–4713, 123 Stat. 2835 (Oct. 28, 2009) (codified in relevant part at 18 U.S.C. § 249).

248 18 U.S.C. §§ 249(a)(1), (a)(2)(A).

249 *Id.* § 249(b)(1)(A)–(D).

250 *See, e.g.*, United States v. Hatch, 722 F.3d 1193, 1208–9 (10th Cir. 2013) (equal protection), *cert. denied*, 134 S. Ct. 1538 (2014); United States v. Jenkins, 909 F. Supp. 2d 758, 775–8 (E.D. Ky. 2012) (equal protection, due process, free speech).

251 Regarding the facts and cultural underpinnings of the case, *see* Donald B. Kraybill, Renegade Amish: Beard Cutting, Hate Crimes, and the Trial of the Bergholz Barbers (2014).

252 *See* United States v. Miller, 767 F.3d 585 (6th Cir. 2014).

## D. Criminal Processes and Procedures

### 1. *Religious Garb in the Courtroom*

Criminal trials periodically involve parties, witnesses, attorneys, or spectators who seek to follow or express their religious beliefs through the wearing of particular clothing or jewelry.[253] Judicial rules or courthouse policies, however, may effectively prohibit or restrict the wearing of certain items such as head coverings, thereby creating a conflict and, in turn, a potential claim under one or more provisions of the U.S. Constitution, particularly the First Amendment religion and speech clauses, in federal court, under the RFRA, or in state court, under one or more state constitutional or statutory guarantees.

Requirements or restrictions regarding apparel or jewelry may vary by the personnel involved in the trial process – lawyers may be subject to certain rules, witnesses to others[254] – and may be imposed in furtherance of multiple objectives, including minimizing security risks,[255] maintaining courtroom decorum,[256] preserving the right to confront witnesses[257] or the ability of the court or jurors to assess witness credibility,[258] or preventing jurors from being unduly influenced by the messages associated with certain

253 *See* State v. Fergerstrom, 101 P.3d 652, 665–70 (Haw. Ct. App. 2004) (reviewing several cases), *aff'd*, 101 P.3d 225 (Haw. 2004); Samuel J. Levine, *Religious Symbols and Religious Garb in the Courtroom: Personal Values and Public Judgments*, 66 FORDHAM L. REV. 1505 (1998).

254 *See, e.g.*, Kan. 6th Jud. Dist. Ct. R. 1.8 ("When appearing in court, all attorneys shall be suitably attired, and to the extent possible shall advise their clients to be similarly attired in apparel other than shirts without collars, shorts, sandals, overalls, torn or tattered jeans."); *id.* R. 1.10 ("In keeping with the dignity and serious nature of court proceedings, proper attire is required in the courtrooms. No participant in a case may appear in t-shirts, tank-tops, tube-tops, cut-offs, shorts, excessive or distractive facial jewelry or other inappropriate clothing."); Mo. 15th Jud. Circ. Ct. R. 9.4(c) ("Attorneys appearing before the court and their clients shall be dressed in appropriate attire consistent with professional standards and the dignity of the court. Inappropriate attire may result in a party or an attorney not being permitted to proceed before the court until corrections in conduct and/or appearance by the party or the attorney is corrected to the reasonable satisfaction of the court before which an appearance is being made. The same rule applies to witnesses."); Nev. 3d Jud. Dist. R. 10 (setting forth different requirements for attorneys and for litigants, witnesses, and jurors); W. Va. Trial Ct. R. 4.07 ("Counsel shall at all court appearances present themselves attired in a manner befitting their profession and indicative of their respect for the court, and shall admonish their clients and witnesses concerning inappropriate courtroom attire.").

255 *See, e.g.*, Spanks-El v. Finley, No. 85C9259, 1987 WL 10307 (N.D. Ill. Apr. 30, 1987) (unpublished) (addressing a courthouse rule requiring removal of head coverings, for a security search, prior to entry), *aff'd*, No. 87-1857, 845 F.2d 1023 (7th Cir. Apr. 12, 1988) (unpublished).

256 *See, e.g.*, Mich. 6th Jud. Circ. Ct. R. 8.115(B) ("Court proceedings shall be conducted in a manner that protects the dignity and seriousness of the proceedings. Conduct by any person that may interfere with the decorum of the court is prohibited and may result in removal of that person from the court."); Or. Uniform Trial Ct. R. 3.010(1) ("All persons attending the court must be dressed so as not to detract from the dignity of court. Members of the public not dressed in accordance with this rule may be removed from the courtroom."), *discussed in* State v. Allen, 832 P.2d 1248 (Or. Ct. App. 1992); *see also* *Fergerstrom*, 101 P.3d at 670 (explaining that a court could permissibly prohibit "a mode of dress that is obscene, disruptive, distractive, or depreciative of the solemnity of the judicial process, or that will create an atmosphere of unfairness").

257 *See* Steven R. Houchin, Comment, *Confronting the Shadow: Is Forcing a Muslim Witness to Unveil in a Criminal Trial a Constitutional Right, or an Unreasonable Intrusion?*, 36 PEPP. L. REV. 823, 854–8 (2009).

258 *See, e.g.*, Mich. R. Evid. 611(b) ["The court shall exercise reasonable control over the appearance of parties and witnesses so as to (1) ensure that the demeanor of such persons may be observed and assessed by the fact-finder and (2) ensure the accurate identification of such persons."].

clothing or symbols.[259] Some of these rules prospectively make accommodations for particular types of religious garb, such as head coverings,[260] but many times they state general, exceptionless directives, leaving it to the trial judge, as a matter of traditional discretion and in accordance with constitutional or other guarantees, to decide whether or not an accommodation for a particular individual should be provided.[261]

Based on the case law and the existing doctrine of religious liberty, it appears that a request by a person seeking to wear religious apparel or jewelry in a courtroom generally has a substantial likelihood of prevailing when the request is framed in terms of free exercise.[262] In part, this likelihood reflects the probable availability of triggering heightened scrutiny of

259 *See, e.g.*, United States v. Yahweh, 779 F. Supp. 1342, 1343 (S.D. Fla. 1992) (discussing concern about "the possible intimidating effect upon a jury in a four months long trial, or longer, with charges in the indictment of such violent crimes and conduct when the spectator area would apparently be saturated with a sea of spectators garbed in a white 'uniform' of sorts"); Sonoma Cnty. (Cal.) Super. Ct. Local R. 25.1 ("The court may prohibit, in a courtroom, the wearing or displaying of clothing, tattoos, or other items that reasonably could be considered to intimidate witnesses or others present or to undermine the integrity of the judicial process.").

260 *See, e.g.*, Ill. 8th Jud. Circ. Ct. R. 1.11(c)(6) ("No caps or hats may be worn by males or females while court is in session except for religious or medical purposes.").

261 By tradition, and today typically codified by rule, "a judge has the inherent authority, right and duty to maintain dignity, decorum and order in the courtroom and to reasonably control the manner of dress, manners and conduct in the courtroom for the good of the administration of justice." State *ex rel.* Burrell-El v. Autrey, 752 S.W.2d 895, 900 (Mo. Ct. App. 1988). Being matters of judicial discretion, trial court decisions regarding attire in the courtroom are, in turn, deferentially reviewed for abuse of discretion, though that standard may give way to *de novo* review if the appellate court detects an underlying error of law, including an error in interpreting and applying the Free Exercise Clause or other religious freedom guarantee.

262 *See, e.g.*, Tyson v. Damore, No. Civ. A. 03-5297, 2004 WL 1837033, at *9–*11 (E.D. Pa. Aug. 13, 2004) (unpublished) (holding that a courthouse deputy violated the free exercise of a witness in a criminal trial by arresting him for disorderly conduct after he refused to remove his religious cap); Yahweh, 779 F. Supp. at 1344–5 (allowing defendants to wear their religious garb – "white-robed uniforms with white turbans" – though not allowing courtroom spectators to do so); Joseph v. State, 642 So. 2d 613, 615 (Fla. Dist. Ct. App. 1994) (quashing a trial court order insofar as it "prohibited petitioner from wearing at trial any clothing depicting or making reference either by word, picture or symbol to his religious beliefs, ideals, affiliations or followings"), *cause dismissed*, 5 So. 3d 669 (Fla. 2009); McMillan v. State, 265 A.2d 453, 457 (Md. 1970) (reversing contempt conviction of criminal defendant who refused to remove religious head cover at his arraignment); State v. Tate, 682 N.W.2d 169, 179 (Minn. Ct. App. 2004) (determining that the trial court "arguably infringed on [a criminal defendant's] constitutional right to the free exercise of religion by ordering him to wear his cross inside his sweater"); Burrell-El, 752 S.W.2d at 901–2 (vacating finding of criminal contempt against a criminal defendant who, for religious reasons, refused to remove his fez); Ryslik v. Krass, 652 A.2d 767, 769, 772 (N.J. Super. Ct. App. Div. 1995) (upholding right of clergy defendant in a civil trial to testify in clerical garb); Close-It Enterprises, Inc. v. Weinberger, 407 N.Y.S.2d 587, 588 (N.Y. App. Div. 1978) (holding that civil defendant, who refused to remove his yarmulke, was wrongfully excluded from the courtroom); People v. Drucker, 418 N.Y.S.2d 744, 746–7 (N.Y. City Crim. Ct. Queens Cnty. 1979) (upholding the free exercise right of a clergy witness in a criminal trial to wear his clerical attire); *In re* Palmer, 386 A.2d 1112, 1116 (R.I. 1978) (holding that petitioner in a civil action was entitled to wear a prayer cap); State v. Hodges, 695 S.W.2d 171 (Tenn. 1985) (holding that trial court should have made further inquiry into a criminal defendant's admittedly bizarre but allegedly religiously based request to appear in court in a concoction of fur, paint, and various articles such as eye goggles and a stuffed snake); *see also* Atkin v. Parana, No. Civ-86-1075E, 1987 WL 16459 (W.D.N.Y. Sep. 1, 1987) (unpublished); Fergerstrom, 101 P.3d at 670–1 (assuming that a trial court's decision to allow a witness to wear religious clothing in addition to, but not – as requested – instead of, traditional Western clothing may have been invalid and erroneous); Green v. State, 209 S.W.3d 831, 833–4 (Tex. Ct. App. 2006) (holding the that trial court properly overruled the defendant's objection to the prosecutor's wearing of a small cross around her neck during trial because

the challenged restriction, assuming that the person making the request is sincere and the restriction actually burden's a religious practice. To be sure, even under the Free Exercise Clause as construed in *Employment Division v. Smith*, heightened scrutiny of the court or administrative decision should obtain insofar as the denial of the request ultimately results from an individualized government assessment rather than the systematic application of a neutral and generally applicable law.[263] Alternatively, to the extent that religious clothing and jewelry implicate not only free exercise but free speech as well, requests to wear such items arguably pose hybrid claims under *Smith*, thus potentially also triggering heightened scrutiny on that basis.[264]

Should heightened scrutiny be employed, the court would have to assess the strength of one or more countervailing interests depending on the scenario. These can include the earlier-noted rationales for courtroom attire rules – that is, maintaining security, preserving decorum, securing the ability to confront and assess witnesses, and preventing unwanted influence of the jury – as well as any other interests of the government or constitutional rights of the defendant, such as a fair and impartial trial characterized by due process. The court then would have to assess whether restricting the religious clothing or jewelry is truly necessary to achieve the applicable interests. In general, it appears that these interests seldom do require total restrictions on religious garb. As summarized by one federal district court, "[a]lthough the cases discussing this issue are few in number, the holdings are consistent ... that once a court's reasonable needs for security and decorum are met, an individual who holds sincere religious beliefs cannot be precluded from wearing a head covering with religious significance in a courtroom."[265] In addition, should the court or a party be concerned that allowing the religious attire might unduly influence the jury, the court can attempt to mitigate that concern by allowing extensive *voir dire* and, later, by using corrective jury instructions,[266] thereby employing "a less intrusive alternative than restricting [the claimant's] manner of dress and impinging on his [or her] possible constitutional right to free exercise of religion."[267]

A more complex and even smaller set of cases addresses the scenario of a cleric who, while serving as criminal defense counsel, requests that he or she be able to wear his or her clerical garb in the courtroom. Such cases are more complex precisely because of the special role and duties of attorneys, and, in turn, their greater regulability, within

the prosecutor's conduct did not violate the Establishment Clause), *petition stricken by* No. PD-1969-06, 2007 WL 1217924 (Tex. Ct. Crim. App. Apr. 25, 2007) (*per curiam*) (unpublished).

263 Regarding this potential exception under *Smith*, *see* Chapter 5.F.3.

264 Regarding this potential exception under *Smith*, *see* Chapter 5.F.4.

265 Tyson, 2004 WL 1837033, at *9.

266 *See, e.g.*, Joseph, 642 So. 2d at 615 ("If the trial court feels the need to instruct the jurors or venire persons to disregard such religious dress in performing their duties and to explain petitioner's [First Amendment] right, such instruction would be consistent with the First Amendment and the trial court's control of its courtroom."); Fergerstrom, 101 P.3d at 670 ("[A]ny positive or negative potential bias that might be caused by any other attire worn by the party or the witness can and should be addressed during the jury selection process, the trial, and in the instructions to the jury."); Ryslik, 652 A.2d at 772 ("Any potential bias that could be caused by defendant's religious garb can be and here actually was addressed during the jury selection process and generally should be reiterated during the jury charge."); Drucker, 418 N.Y.S.2d at 746 ("The potential prejudice to a defendant [of a complaining witness appearing in clerical garb] may be circumvented by a carefully practiced voir dire coupled with strong limiting instructions to the jury concerning their evaluation of a witness' credibility.").

267 Ryslik, 652 A.2d at 772.

the criminal trial process.[268] The leading case of this genre is *La Rocca v. Lane*,[269] which involved a Roman Catholic priest who desired to wear his clerical shirt and collar while representing a criminal defendant in a jury trial. The trial judge had prohibited him from doing so, agreeing with the prosecutor's objection that the clerical attire "might influence even one juror, and perhaps prejudice a juror for or against the defendant."[270] The priest-attorney, however, "argued that a directed removal of his clerical garb by the court would violate his client's right to be represented by counsel of her own choice, and would also violate his right to free exercise of religion."[271] The New York Court of Appeals, that state's highest court, ultimately sided with the trial judge. On the one hand, it noted that "a juror might view differently statements made by a member of the clergy than those made by others, and might ascribe a greater measure of veracity and personal commitment to the rightness of his client's cause."[272] On the other hand, it surmised that "religious prejudices … often insidious and usually denied, might spill over from a lawyer-cleric of whatever faith to the client," that the client (despite her choice of attorney) might be deprived of a fair trial as a result, and that ultimately it is "the court which must insure a fair trial."[273] In the end, the court determined that the "risk that a fair trial could not be had outweighed" the attorney's right to wear his clerical garb, at least in a trial before a jury.[274]

268 *See* Friedman v. Dist. Ct., 611 P.2d 77, 78 (Alaska 1980) ("Attorneys occupy a different position in relation to the courts than do ordinary citizens. Attorneys are officers of the court. The privilege of practicing law is subject to certain conditions, among which is that an attorney must observe reasonable rules of courtroom behavior and decorum. Courts have long controlled the manner in which attorneys may appear before them."); La Rocca v. Lane, 366 N.Y.S.2d 456, 460 (N.Y. App. Div. 1975) (noting that "the relationship between the court and an attorney is more intimate and more subject to regulation than is the status of a spectator, witness, or party, although certainly there is residual power in the court even to regulate that status"), *aff'd*, 338 N.E.2d 606 (N.Y. 1975), *cert. denied*, 424 U.S. 968 (1976).

269 338 N.E.2d 606 (N.Y. 1975).

270 *Id.* at 609.

271 *Id.* He "also stated that he had been 'designated' by his bishop to appear in court as a Catholic priest wearing his clerical garb." *Id.* The court later observed that "[w]hile this designation or direction is uncontroverted, the record does not establish in any degree why this designation or direction was made, or whether it was absolute or conditional. Nor does petitioner now make much of the point, assuming that he still relies on it, which one should assume. But assuming that that is so may not change the result in the case, once it is determined reasonably that the paramount judicial duty to assure a fair trial is involved." *Id.* at 613.

272 *Id.* at 613.

273 *Id.*

274 The other case in this genre, arising in the same court system, is Gold v. McShane, 426 N.Y.S.2d 504 (N.Y. App. Div. 1980), which followed *La Rocca* and blocked enforcement of an order by the trial judge in People v. Rodriguez, 424 N.Y.S.2d 600 (N.Y. Supr. Ct. Kings Cnty. 1979), that, despite the *La Rocca* decision, had attempted to permit Father La Rocca in a different case to wear his clerical attire. The Second Circuit, when presented with La Rocca's claim in a separate civil rights action, held that collateral estoppel barred further litigation of the matter. *See* La Rocca v. Gold, 662 F.2d 144, 148–9 (2d Cir. 1981). In completely unrelated litigation, the Second Circuit the next year distinguished the situation in *La Rocca* – "a lawyer who happens also to be a priest" – from the situation of "a priest who happens also to be a pro se plaintiff in a civil action" and saw "no reason why [the latter's] assumption of the further role of advocate in his own behalf should be conditioned on his doffing his everyday clerical garb." O'Reilly v. N.Y. Times Co., 692 F.2d 863, 869 n. 8 (2d Cir. 1982). *See also* Susannah A. Nesmith, *Accused Satanist Gets His Day in Court*, MIAMI HERALD, Aug. 13, 2007, *available at:* http://www.miamiherald.com/news/breaking_dade/story/201519.html (reporting that a satanist accused of murder was allowed to

## 2. *Religion and Jurors*

### a. Selection and Removal

One area of potential confusion or uncertainty today is the role that a prospective juror's religious beliefs can lawfully play in the jury selection process. Broadly speaking, challenges to (or strikes of) prospective jurors or venirepersons can be *for cause*, where the challenger must explain why the juror cannot fairly and impartially apply the law, or *peremptory*, where the challenger ordinarily need not articulate such a basis, the idea being "that a party has a degree of latitude to eliminate from the jury persons whom he or she may perceive as likely to be unsympathetic without having to show grounds for disqualification for bias."[275] The following paragraphs will examine the potential relevance or role of a juror's religion within each type of challenge.

With regard to challenges for cause, the prosecutor or defense counsel ordinarily has an unlimited number of strikes but must provide a sound basis for each requested elimination of a prospective juror.[276] Whether or not the religion of prospective jurors can be elicited on *voir dire* is normally within the trial court's discretion,[277] and courts may differ on whether they consider it to be a legitimate matter of inquiry in the first instance.[278] Generally speaking, if a prospective juror indicates that his or her religious beliefs would interfere with rendering a fair and impartial verdict based on the governing law, then that person can justifiably be eliminated for cause, whether at the request of a party or by the court's own authority.[279] Accordingly, a for-cause strike of a Jehovah's Witness minister

represent himself wearing "an all-black outfit, a cap he says is related to his religion and special Satanic jewelry").

275 Arthur T. von Mehren & Peter L. Murray, Law in the United States 211 (2d ed., 2007).

276 *See* Gray v. Mississippi, 481 U.S. 648, 652 n. 3 (1987) ["A motion to excuse a venire member for cause of course must be supported by specified causes or reasons that demonstrate that, as a matter of law, the venire member is not qualified to serve. There is no limitation on the number of venire members who may be challenged for cause." (citation omitted)].

277 *See* People v. Velarde, 616 P.2d 104, 105 (Colo. 1980) ["[I]t has consistently been held that it is within the discretion of the trial judge whether to make inquiry of the jurors on voir dire as to their religious affiliations." [citing Gold v. United States, 378 F.2d 588 (9th Cir. 1967); Pope v. United States, 372 F.2d 710 (8th Cir. 1967), *vacated on other grounds*, 392 U.S. 651 (1968); Yarborough v. United States, 230 F.2d 56 (4th Cir. 1956), *cert. denied*, 351 U.S. 969 (1956)]].

278 *See, e.g.*, Brandborg v. Lucas, 891 F. Supp. 352, 358 (E.D. Tex. 1995) {"Religion has often been a question of prospective jurors. However, when religion is unrelated to the issue at trial it is not a proper subject for inquiry." [citing United States v. Barnes, 604 F.2d 121 (2d Cir. 1979), *cert. denied*, 446 U.S. 907 (1980); United States v. Daily, 139 F.2d 7 (7th Cir. 1943)]}; Riley v. State, 496 A.2d 997, 1006 (Del. 1985) ["As a general rule, a person otherwise competent to serve on a jury is not disqualified from sitting merely because of religious beliefs or associations. However, religious affiliations of prospective jurors may be a proper subject of voir dire examination if: (1) religious beliefs are involved in an issue in the case; (2) a religious organization is a party to the litigation; or (3) 'special circumstances' raise the possibility of religious prejudice." (citation omitted)], *cert. denied*, 478 U.S. 1022 (1986); State v. Betts, 646 S.W.2d 94, 98–99 (Mo. 1983) (*en banc*) (noting the trial court's discretion over *voir dire* and then explaining that "religious affiliations do not constitute qualification or disqualification for jury service" but that a juror's opinions "about the merits of the law" can be material "when they are so unyielding as to preclude a juror from following the court's instructions"), *overruled on other grounds by* Joy v. Morrison, 254 S.W.3d 885 (Mo. 2008) (*en banc*).

279 *See* United States v. Burrous, 147 F.3d 111, 117 (2d Cir. 1998) ["The district court may remove, for just cause, a juror who indicates during deliberation that he [or she] is unable to render a verdict because of a personal religious objection, unless it appears that the purported objection might mask a disagreement

was upheld where a court determined that "[a] general tenet of Jehovah's Witnesses is that they cannot sit in judgment of another person" and the juror acknowledged this tenet, even explaining that there could be "some counseling which might enable him to serve as a juror but the counseling might take four days."[280] Given those circumstances, it was found that the trial court could have reasonably concluded that, absent the counseling, which presumably posed logistical concerns, the juror's "religious beliefs … would have prevented or substantially impaired the performance of his duties as a juror."[281] By contrast, sufficient cause will rarely exist if the challenge rests on speculation about the juror's views or beliefs (and, in turn, the juror's ability to apply the law) based solely on the juror's religious affiliation or identity, especially if the juror does not explicitly purport to adhere strictly to the relevant teachings or tenets of his or her denomination. One rare and perhaps dated instance in which such for-cause strikes were sanctioned involved a defendant charged with criminal libel that included blatantly anti-Semitic messages, where the defense counsel sought to strike potential jury members who were Jewish on the theory that their affiliation alone would likely prevent impartiality in their deliberations.[282]

The religion of prospective jurors likely will come under particular scrutiny and may elicit for-cause challenges in the prosecution of crimes in which the death sentence may be sought.[283] Ordinarily, a religious opposition to capital punishment that would prevent or substantially impair a prospective juror's performance is a valid basis for eliminating that person through a for-cause challenge,[284] and such an elimination will violate neither the jury trial rights of the defendant[285] nor the religious rights of the prospective juror.[286] However, prospective jurors who merely express concerns or general objections

among jurors regarding the merits of the case." (citations omitted)], *cert. denied*, 525 U.S. 939 (1998); *accord* United States v. Decoud, 456 F.3d 996, 1018 (9th Cir. 2006), *cert. denied*, 551 U.S. 1116 (2007); United States v. Geffrard, 87 F.3d 448, 451–2 (11th Cir. 1996), *cert. denied*, 519 U.S. 985 (1996).

280 State v. Tucker, 512 S.E.2d 99, 103–4 (S.C. 1999), *cert. denied*, 527 U.S. 1042 (1999).

281 *Id.* at 104; *see also* Miles v. United States, 103 U.S. (13 Otto) 304, 310 (1881) (in a bigamy prosecution, upholding the exclusion of prospective jurors who embraced Mormon teaching on polygamy because "a jury composed of men entertaining such a belief could not have been free from bias or prejudice on the trial for bigamy, of a person who entertained the same belief, and whose offence consisted in the act of living in polygamy"); Casey v. Roman Catholic Archbishop of Baltimore, 143 A.2d 627, 632 (Md. 1958) ("[I]f the religious affiliation of a juror might reasonably prevent him [or her] from arriving at a fair and impartial verdict in a particular case because of the nature of the case, the parties are entitled to ferret out, or preferably have the court discover for them, the existence of bias or prejudice resulting from such affiliation.").

282 *See* Potter v. State, 216 S.W. 886, 888 (Tex. Ct. Crim. App. 1919) ("In our opinion such jurors were disqualified, and the questions should have been permitted, and challenge for cause should have have [*sic*] been sustained, if made."). *Compare* Coleman v. United States, 379 A.2d 951, 953–4 (D.C. 1977) (upholding trial court's refusal to grant defendant's request to remove all Catholic jurors where defendants were charged with, among other things, armed robbery of two Catholic priests inside a Catholic church).

283 *See* People v. Williams, 148 P.3d 47, 62 (Cal. 2006) ["Although exclusion of a prospective juror on grounds of religious affiliation is improper, it is not necessarily true that inquiry into such affiliation is forbidden during voir dire. Membership in a particular religious denomination or sect indicated on a jury questionnaire may alert the trial court and counsel to a potential bias in favor of or against the death penalty that requires further exploration at voir dire." (citation omitted)], *cert. denied*, 552 U.S. 874 (2007).

284 For an early rendition of this general rule, *see* Commonwealth v. Lesher, 17 Serg. & Rawle 155, 157–60 (Pa. 1828).

285 *See* Lockhart v. McCree, 476 U.S. 162 (1986).

286 *See, e.g.*, State v. Clark, 990 P.2d 793, 802–3 (N.M. 1999) (so holding with regard to juror religious freedom under the New Mexico Constitution); State v. Warren, 499 S.E.2d 431, 441–2 (N.C. 1998) (same under the U.S. and North Carolina Constitutions), *cert. denied*, 525 U.S. 915 (1998); Wolf v. Sundquist,

with regard to imposing the death penalty but who do not evidence a complete inability or unwillingness to do so generally cannot be struck or removed for cause because this could narrow the jury pool only to those without any qualms about capital punishment, therefore depriving a defendant of the constitutional right to a fair and impartial jury.[287] The key question, once again, "is whether the juror's views would 'prevent or substantially impair the performance of his [or her] duties as a juror in accordance with his [or her] instructions and his [or her] oath'" such that "the trial judge is left with the definite impression that a prospective juror would be unable to faithfully and impartially apply the law."[288]

In addition to challenges for cause, parties may exercise a limited number of peremptory challenges, which by their nature require no articulation of cause.[289] The role of religion in the peremptory challenge context is somewhat more complicated than in the for-cause context principally for two reasons. First, the very idea of the peremptory challenge is that an attorney should be permitted to strike a prospective juror based on the attorney's experience and intuition through a process that is inherently speculative, not always amenable to easy articulation, and potentially undermined by external constraints.[290] In the words of the Utah Supreme Court,

955 S.W.2d 626, 629–33 (Tenn. Ct. App. 1997) (same under the Tennessee Constitution). For criticism of this assessment of juror religious liberty, *see* Brian Galle, Note, *Free Exercise Rights of Capital Jurors*, 101 Colum. L. Rev. 569 (2001).

287 *See* Buchanan v. Kentucky, 483 U.S. 402, 416 (1987) ("[N]ot all who oppose the death penalty are excludable for cause. Those who indicate that they can set aside temporarily their personal beliefs in deference to the rule of law may serve as jurors."); Witherspoon, 391 U.S. at 522 (holding that "a sentence of death cannot be carried out if the jury that imposed or recommended it was chosen by excluding veniremen for cause simply because they voiced general objections to the death penalty or expressed conscientious or religious scruples against its infliction"); State v. Anderson, 4 P.3d 369, 373–4 (Ariz. 2000) (*en banc*); James J. Gobert, Ellen Kreitzberg & Charles H. Rose III, Jury Selection. The Law, Art and Science of Selecting a Jury § 7:52 (3d ed., updated Dec. 2013) ("A juror may not be excused simply based on his or her personal views or beliefs including when a juror has a conscientious or religious objection to capital punishment. A juror may only be excused for cause if he or she is unable to set aside any personal beliefs or would be unable to follow the law.").

288 Wainwright v. Witt, 469 U.S. 412, 424, 426 (1985) [quoting Adams v. Texas, 448 U.S. 38, 45 (1980)]. *See, e.g.*, Ortiz v. Quarterman, 504 F.3d 492, 502 (5th Cir. 2007) (upholding on *habeas* review a for-cause strike where the juror was asked whether "she could 'ever, sitting as a juror, no matter – no matter what the evidence showed, vote to inflict the death penalty,' and she replied 'No, sir.'"), *cert. denied*, 553 U.S. 1035 (2008).

289 *See* Gray, 481 U.S. at 652 n. 3 [noting that "[s]tates traditionally have limited the number of peremptory challenges allotted to litigants because peremptory challenges ordinarily can be exercised without articulating reasons, subject to constitutional limitations" (citation omitted)]; United States v. Elliott, 89 F.3d 1360, 1365 (8th Cir. 1996) (noting that "peremptory strikes, for which no reasons need be given (absent a *Batson* challenge), are different from challenges for cause, which by definition require a showing of cause"), *cert. denied*, 519 U.S. 1118 (1997); State v. Reiners, 644 N.W.2d 118, 123 (Minn. Ct. App. 2002) (noting that, in contrast to challenges for cause, a "party making a peremptory challenge is not required to show that the challenged juror could not be impartial"), *aff'd*, 664 N.W.2d 826 (Minn. 2003). In federal criminal trials, the number of available peremptory challenges varies by the type of crime and the party. In misdemeanor trials, both the government and the defense have three; in noncapital felony trials, the government has six, whereas the defense has ten; and in trials where the government seeks the death penalty, both sides have twenty. *See* Fed. R. Crim. P. 24(b).

290 *See* Swain v. Alabama, 380 U.S. 202, 220 (1965) ["The essential nature of the peremptory challenge is that it is one exercised without a reason stated, without inquiry and without being subject to the court's control. While challenges for cause permit rejection of jurors on a narrowly specified, provable and legally cognizable basis of partiality, the peremptory permits rejection for a real or imagined partiality

> [p]eremptory challenges are designed to allow an attorney an opportunity to remove a juror, not because he or she is prejudiced as to the particular facts of the case, but for more general biases that affect how a juror may perceive and evaluate witnesses, parties, and evidence. Juror attitudes revealed during voir dire may indicate dimly perceived, yet deeply rooted, psychological biases or prejudices that may not rise to the level of a for-cause challenge but nevertheless support a peremptory challenge.[291]

In turn, a trial court's discretion "should be liberally exercised in favor of allowing counsel to elicit information from prospective jurors."[292] To be sure, an important component of a trial's fairness is "the right of counsel to ask *voir dire* questions designed to discover attitudes and biases, both conscious and subconscious, even though they 'would not have supported a challenge for cause.' All that is necessary for a *voir dire* question to be appropriate is that it allow 'defense counsel to exercise his [or her] peremptory challenges more intelligently.'"[293]

Second, however, some courts have concluded that religion-based peremptory challenges may violate the guarantee of equal protection, extrapolating from the U.S. Supreme Court's rulings in *Batson v. Kentucky*[294] and *J.E.B. v. Alabama ex rel. T.B.*[295] These decisions hold that peremptory challenges cannot be premised solely on a prospective juror's race or gender, respectively, and that when a peremptory challenge is plausibly alleged to rest on race or gender, the striking party must then provide a race-neutral or gender-neutral rationale for the challenge.[296] The Court has not decided, however, whether the reasoning of *Batson* and *J.E.B.* should extend to peremptory challenges based on a juror's religion and, in particular, the juror's mere denominational

that is less easily designated or demonstrable." (citations omitted)], *overruled on other grounds by* Batson v. Kentucky, 476 U.S. 79 (1986); Hayes v. State, 94 So. 3d 452, 460 (Fla. 2012) (noting that peremptory challenges "have traditionally been exercised according to a party's unfettered discretion"); State v. Dow, 375 S.W.3d 845, 850 (Mo. Ct. App. 2012) {"A venireperson's 'hesitation and body language during questioning' are legitimate bases for using a peremptory strike. One of the differences between a peremptory strike and a challenge for cause is that, in choosing to exercise a peremptory strike, an attorney or party 'is allowed a subjective evaluation of the honesty and accuracy of the statement of the venireperson.'" (citation omitted) [respectively quoting State v. Morrow, 968 S.W.2d 100, 114 (Mo. 1998) (*en banc*), *cert. denied*, 525 U.S. 896 (1998), and State v. Rollins, 321 S.W.3d 353, 368 (Mo. Ct. App. 2010), *cert. denied*, 131 S. Ct. 2115 (2011)]}; State v. Eason, 445 S.E.2d 917, 921 (N.C. 1994) [noting that "the exercise of peremptory challenges is frequently more art than science and is based on legitimate hunches and past experience" (internal quotation marks omitted)], *cert. denied*, 513 U.S. 1096 (1995).

291 State v. Worthen, 765 P.2d 839, 845 (Utah 1988).

292 *Id.*

293 *Id.* (citation omitted) [quoting State v. Ball, 685 P.2d 1055, 1060 (Utah 1984)]; *see also* United States v. Ible, 630 F.2d 389, 394–5 (5th Cir. 1980) (viewing "with grave concern" the trial court's "denial of [the defendant's] proposed voir dire question concerning the jurors' moral or religious beliefs about alcohol" where the defendant's alleged intemperance was at issue).

294 476 U.S. 79 (1986).

295 511 U.S. 127 (1994).

296 *See* Purkett v. Elem, 514 U.S. 765, 767–8 (1995) (*per curiam*) {"Under our *Batson* jurisprudence, once the opponent of a peremptory challenge has made out a prima facie case of racial discrimination (step one), the burden of production shifts to the proponent of the strike to come forward with a race-neutral explanation (step two). If a race-neutral explanation is tendered, the trial court must then decide (step three) whether the opponent of the strike has proved purposeful racial discrimination. The second step of this process does not demand an explanation that is persuasive, or even plausible. 'At this [second] step of the inquiry, the issue is the facial validity of the prosecutor's explanation. Unless a discriminatory intent is inherent in the prosecutor's explanation, the reason offered will be deemed race neutral.'" (citations omitted) [quoting Hernandez v. New York, 500 U.S. 352, 360 (1991) (plurality opinion)]}.

affiliation, thus spawning division among lower federal and state courts[297] as well as a great deal of commentary.[298]

There are, arguably, good reasons for the division among courts. On the one hand, religion or religious affiliation is, like race, a suspect classification under the Equal Protection Clause,[299] and there do persist in the country various degrees of uninformed or irrational prejudice and stereotyping of certain religious groups.[300] As the Connecticut Supreme Court has remarked,

> [a]lthough one's religious *beliefs* may render a prospective juror unsuitable for service in a particular case, one's religious *affiliation*, like one's race or gender, bears no relation to that person's ability to serve as a juror ... Moreover, to allow the exclusion of an otherwise qualified venireperson simply on account of that person's religious affiliation would amount to permitting jury selection procedures that promote 'state-sponsored group stereotypes rooted in, and reflective of, historical prejudice.' "[301]

On the other hand, unlike the historical circumstances surrounding race and its influence on the legal process, "there is no indication that irrational religious bias so pervades the peremptory challenge as to undermine the integrity of the jury system."[302] Moreover, while "[a]ttributing to women or African Americans as a group any specific

297 *Compare, e.g.*, United States v. Brown, 352 F.3d 654, 667–9 (2d Cir. 2003) (extending *Batson* to religious affiliation); State v. Purcell, 18 P.3d 113, 120 (Ariz. Ct. App. 2001) (same); People v. Martin, 75 Cal. Rptr. 2d 147, 151 (Cal. Ct. App. 1998) (same), *and* State v. Hodge, 726 A.2d 531, 550–3 (Conn. 1999) (same), *cert. denied*, 528 U.S. 969 (1999), *and* Highler v. State, 854 N.E.2d 823, 829 (Ind. 2006) (same), *with* United States v. Williams, 44 M.J. 482, 485 (C.A.A.F. 1996) (declining to extend *Batson* to religious affiliation), *and* State v. Davis, 504 N.W.2d 767 (Minn. 1993) (same), *and* Devoe v. State, 354 S.W.3d 457, 472 (Tex. Ct. Crim. App. 2011) [same, reaffirming the holding of Casarez v. State, 913 S.W.2d 468, 494–6 (Tex. Ct. Crim. App. 1994) (*en banc*)]. *Cf. also* Gold v. United States, 378 F.2d 588, 594 (9th Cir. 1967) (pre-*Batson*, upholding a trial court's refusal to inquire into the religious background of the jurors upon *voir dire* examination based on the trial court's determination that such inquiry would have been improper); Turner v. Roman Catholic Diocese of Burlington, Vt., 987 A.2d 960, 987 (Vt. 2009) (implying that removing a juror based solely on religious affiliation might be unconstitutional under a *Batson*-type analysis).

298 *See, e.g.*, Robert W. Gurry, *The Jury Is Out: The Urgent Need for a New Approach in Deciding When Religion-Based Peremptory Strikes Violate the First and Fourteenth Amendments*, 18 Regent U. L. Rev. 91 (2005); Daniel M. Hinkle, *Peremptory Challenges Based on Religious Affiliation: Are They Constitutional?* 9 Buff. Crim. L. Rev. 139 (2005); John H. Mansfield, *Peremptory Challenges to Jurors Based upon or Affecting Religion*, 34 Seton Hall L. Rev. 435 (2004); Benjamin Hoorn Barton, *Note, Religion-Based Peremptory Challenges after Batson v. Kentucky and J.E.B. v. Alabama: An Equal Protection and First Amendment Analysis*, 94 Mich. L. Rev. 191 (1995); Amy B. Gendleman, *Comment, The Equal Protection Clause, the Free Exercise Clause and Religion-Based Peremptory Challenges*, 63 U. Chi. L. Rev. 1639 (1996).

299 *See* Chapter 6.B.3.

300 *See, e.g.*, Gallup Center for Muslim Studies, *In U.S., Religious Prejudice Stronger Against Muslims*, Jan. 21, 2010, *available at:* http://www.gallup.com/poll/125312/religious-prejudice-stronger-against-muslims.aspx.

301 Hodge, 726 A.2d at 553 (quoting J.E.B., 511 U.S. at 128).

302 Davis, 504 N.W.2d at 771 (also observing that "religious bigotry in the use of the peremptory challenge is not as prevalent, or flagrant, or historically ingrained in the jury selection process as is race"). Complicating the matter further is that the U.S. Supreme Court's denial of *certiorari* in *Davis* was accompanied by a dissenting opinion from Justice Thomas, joined by Justice Scalia, which claimed that the Minnesota Supreme Court's reasoning in *Davis* was inconsistent with the U.S. Supreme Court's subsequently issued decision in *J.E.B. See* Davis v. Minnesota, 511 U.S. 1115 (1994) (Thomas, J., dissenting from denial of *certiorari*).

moral, political, or social belief is overly broad because membership in the group does not depend upon subscription to the belief," such attribution in the case of religion is not necessarily "overly broad, and therefore not invidious, when the belief is an article of faith" of the religion to which the prospective juror acknowledges adherence.[303]

Many courts, whether or not they have formally extended *Batson* to religion, essentially recognize in the peremptory challenge context a distinction (noted earlier by the Connecticut Supreme Court) between a prospective juror's religious *affiliation* as such and the particular religious *beliefs or conduct* of a prospective juror that could more plausibly indicate how that person may perform as a juror.[304] According to the Seventh Circuit, while noting but not deciding the potential applicability of the *Batson* approach, "[i]t would be improper and perhaps unconstitutional to strike a juror on the basis of his [or her] being a Catholic, a Jew, [or] a Muslim" but it "would be proper to strike him [or her] on the basis of a belief that would prevent him [or her] from basing his [or her] decision on the evidence and instructions, even if the belief had a religious backing; suppose for example that his [or her] religion taught that crimes should be left entirely to the justice of God."[305] Thus, in one case, the North Carolina Supreme Court upheld the peremptory strike of a Jehovah's Witness, noting that she "was not stricken solely because she was a Jehovah's Witness"; rather "the prospective juror, because of her strong personal and religious convictions, expressed reservations about the death penalty and was stricken because of these reservations."[306]

As a practical matter, issues involving the religion of jurors do not end with the selection process. Once a trial has commenced, and even well into the deliberative process, jurors may make statements or otherwise indicate that they are ultimately incapable of fairly and impartially judging the facts or abiding by the applicable legal rules. When this apparent incapability is religiously based (as when it is not), the judge must decide whether the juror can and should be excused or removed. Ordinarily, the standard for removal is "just cause" or "good cause,"[307] and the basic rule, as recited by the Second Circuit, is that

[303] Casarez, 913 S.W.2d at 496. "Because all members of the group share the same faith by definition, it is not unjust to attribute beliefs characteristic of the faith to all of them." *Id.*

[304] *See, e.g.*, United States v. DeJesus, 347 F.3d 500, 510 (3d Cir. 2003) ("not reach[ing] the issue of whether a peremptory strike based solely on religious affiliation would be unconstitutional" though distinguishing between beliefs or activity and affiliation, the former of which may constitutionally be used as a basis for challenging a juror), *cert. denied*, 541 U.S. 1086 (2004); United States v. Stafford, 136 F.3d 1109, 1114 (7th Cir. 1998) ("It is necessary to distinguish among religious affiliation, a religion's general tenets, and a specific religious belief."), *modified*, 136 F.3d 1115 (7th Cir. 1998), *cert. denied*, 525 U.S. 849 (1998); State v. Fuller, 862 A.2d 1130, 1140 (N.J. 2004) ("We discern … an emerging consensus to extend the equal protection analysis of *Batson* and *J.E.B.* to peremptory challenges based solely on religious affiliation and to find those challenges unconstitutional. Challenges based on religious beliefs or religious activities, however, are generally permitted.").

[305] Stafford, 136 F.3d at 1114. The Court continued: "In between and most difficult to evaluate from the standpoint of *Batson* is a religious outlook that might make the prospective juror unusually reluctant, or unusually eager, to convict a criminal defendant." *Id.*

[306] Eason, 445 S.E.2d at 921. "The prosecutor did not learn that [the prospective juror] was a Jehovah's Witness, and move to excuse her, without further inquiry to discover how her religious beliefs might affect her ability to follow the law." *Id.* at 922.

[307] *See, e.g.*, Fed. R. Crim. P. 23(b)(2)–(3) (authorizing the court, either on its own or at the parties' request, to proceed in the absence of a juror excused for "good cause").

> [t]he [trial] court may remove, for just cause, a juror who indicates during deliberation that he [or she] is unable to render a verdict because of a personal religious objection, unless it appears that the purported objection might mask a disagreement among jurors regarding the merits of the case. Where the dismissal does not unduly taint the proceedings, the remaining eleven jurors may proceed to render verdict. These decisions are entrusted to the discretion of the trial court, and will only be reversed in cases where that discretion is abused.[308]

As this passage indicates, when a juror is removed, if the governing law permits (and typically subject to the trial judge's discretion), the deliberations may proceed even in the absence of that juror as long as the defendant consents or the court determines that the removal would not violate the defendant's constitutional jury rights.[309]

#### b. Objections to Service

Jury duty occasionally can give rise to conflicts triggering the Free Exercise Clause or analogous religious freedom guarantees. For some prospective jurors, the very task of rendering a verdict in any case may pose an issue of conscience. This can be a problem for groups such as conservative Anabaptists[310] and, as noted previously, Jehovah's Witnesses, whose religious tenets may preclude sitting in judgment of another person and, more generally, may bar jury service insofar as it "contribut[es] to the mechanisms of a worldly government"[311] and impermissibly "endorse[s] legitimate government authority."[312] For others, the task of serving as a juror may be problematic only in particular instances, such as capital cases, whereas for still others whose religious beliefs do not prohibit jury service as such, it may turn out that a specific practice of their religion, such as observing a holy day or attending services, happens to conflict with the trial schedule or with particular court rules.

To the extent that the conflict takes the form of a free exercise claim, and assuming that the religious claimant is sincere and that some kind of heightened scrutiny is triggered, then the court will need to assess the importance and necessity of having the particular claimant serve as a juror notwithstanding the claimant's religious objection.[313] In

308 Burrous, 147 F.3d at 117 (citations omitted); *see also* Geffrard, 87 F.3d at 451–2.

309 For ordinary federal criminal trials, courts have upheld the trial judge's authority to proceed with an eleven-member jury. *See, e.g.*, United States v. Ahmad, 974 F.2d 1163, 1164 (9th Cir. 1992); United States v. Smith, 789 F.2d 196, 204–5 (3d Cir. 1986), *cert. denied*, 479 U.S. 1017 (1986).

310 *See* Michael Hattfield, *The Anabaptist Conscience and Religious Exemption to Jury Service*, 65 N.Y.U. Ann. Surv. Am. L. 269 (2009).

311 State v. Everly, 146 S.E.2d 705, 706–7 (W. Va. 1966).

312 Encyclopedia of Religion in America 1108 (Charles H. Lippy & Peter W. Williams, eds., 2010) (noting Jehovah's Witnesses' "persistent refusal to partake in political activities such as voting in elections or joining pressure groups" and their "object[ion] to both jury and military service on the grounds that both practices endorse legitimate governmental authority"). In particular, Jehovah's Witnesses "regard world powers and political parties as the unwitting allies of Satan." Britannica Encyclopedia of World Religions 563 (Wendy Doniger ed., 2006). A converse situation arose in United States v. Lewis, 638 F. Supp. 573 (W.D. Mich. 1986), where the criminal defendants argued that "their religious beliefs forb[ade] them from submitting to the judgment of lay jurors" such that "the government's refusal to consent to their waiver of trial by jury ... infringe[d] their free exercise of religion as guaranteed under the First Amendment." *Id.* at 575. Ultimately, the district court ruled in the defendants' favor. *See id.* at 577–81.

313 Generally speaking, heightened scrutiny will require that the claimant show that jury service imposes a substantial burden on his or her sincere religious practice and, further, that either (1) the jury

cases of complete objection to jury duty, typically involving Jehovah's Witnesses, a number of mid-twentieth-century decisions ruled favorably for the prospective juror, finding that the excusal of the objector would undermine neither the empanelment process nor the government's authority more generally.[314] As a practical matter, this result accords with the reality that such a juror could and presumably would be lawfully challenged and removed for cause should his or her threshold objection not result in excusal before the *voir dire* stage.

Regarding religious conflicts with the trial schedule – such as, for example, when it encompasses the Jewish holidays of Rosh Hashanah and Yom Kippur – trial courts typically have discretion to excuse from service prospective jurors who would encounter these conflicts,[315] much as judges have discretion to excuse jurors for serious secular conflicts involving medical issues or family obligations.[316] Such excusals, moreover, do not by themselves ordinarily violate a defendant's constitutional jury rights, such as the right to a jury representing a fair cross section of the community.[317] Likewise, where

selection-excusal process amounts to a scheme of "individualized governmental assessment" under Employment Div. v. Smith, 494 U.S. 872, 884 (1990) or is not generally applicable because prospective jurors are excused for nonreligious reasons such as medical, employment, or family conflicts [*see* Church of the Lukumi Babalu Aye, Inc. v. City of Hialeah, 508 U.S. 520, 542–6 (1993)] or (2) another religious freedom law that is more protective than the Free Exercise Clause, such as a state statute or constitutional provision or (in federal court) RFRA, applies. Regarding the sources and components of heightened scrutiny, *see* Chapter 5.A, E, & F.

314 *See, e.g.*, United States v. Hillyard, 52 F. Supp. 612, 615 (E.D. Wash. 1943) (dismissing an action for contempt against a Jehovah's Witness who refused to serve as a juror, finding that the refusal did "not amount to a breaking out 'into overt acts against peace and good order'" and did not diminished "the prestige of th[e] court"); *In re* Jenison, 125 N.W.2d 588, 589 (Minn. 1963) (*per curiam*) (holding that "until and unless further experience indicates that the indiscriminate invoking of the First Amendment poses a serious threat to the effective functioning of our jury system, any person whose religious convictions prohibit compulsory jury duty shall henceforth be exempt"); Everly, 146 S.E.2d at 708 (reversing a contempt conviction of a Jehovah's Witness who refused to serve as a juror and finding that his refusal would not "affect the peace and safety of the state and [that] there [was] no showing that an adequate number of competent jurors could not be obtained otherwise in order for the state's interest to be protected").

315 *See, e.g.*, Grech v. Wainwright, 492 F.2d 747, 749–50 (5th Cir. 1974) (holding that excusing Jewish potential jurors was proper when the beginning of the trial coincided with Yom Kippur); Grech v. State, 243 So. 2d 216, 217–18 (Fla. Dist. Ct. App. 1971) (same), *cert. denied*, 247 So. 2d 439 (Fla. 1971); People v. Robinson, 881 N.Y.S.2d 77, 77 (N.Y. App. Div. 2009) (holding that the trial court "properly exercised its discretion when it excused all prospective jurors who would have been unavailable due to a two-day religious observance that immediately preceded a weekend"), *leave to appeal denied*, 920 N.E.2d 101 (N.Y. 2009).

316 Likewise, courts have discretion to alter the trial schedule to accommodate the religious practices of parties, and often do so, though free exercise claims by defendants arguing that the trial court should have done so in a particular instance have met with mixed results. *Compare, e.g.*, People v. Gilliam, 626 N.Y.S.2d 245, 245–6 (N.Y. App. Div. 1995) (ruling for defendant who requested an adjournment of *voir dire*), *with* Hoyt v. Lewin, 444 F. Supp. 2d 258, 273–4 (S.D.N.Y. 2006) (ruling against defendant), *and* State v. Pride, 1 S.W.3d 494, 505–7 (Mo. Ct. App. 1999) (same), *cert. denied*, 529 U.S. 1004 (2000), *and* People v. Morgan, 697 N.Y.S.2d 259, 260 (N.Y. App. Div. 1999) (same), *leave to appeal denied*, 728 N.E.2d 988 (N.Y. 2000).

317 *See, e.g.*, Scott v. Dugger, 891 F.2d 800, 804 (11th Cir. 1989), *cert. denied*, 498 U.S. 881 (1990); Grech, 492 F.2d at 749–50; United States v. Myrick, No. 97CR197, 1998 WL 832647, at *8 (N.D. Ill. Nov. 17, 1998) (unpublished); Turrentine v. State, 965 P.2d 955, 966–7 (Okla. Ct. Crim. App. 1998); *cf. also* People v. Marrero, 487 N.Y.S.2d 853, 855 (N.Y. Supr. Ct. App. Div. 1985) ["The mere fact that a voir dire of a jury is conducted on a Jewish holiday does not constitute an infringement of the right to a jury composed of a fair cross-section of the community." (citations omitted)].

a juror has been seated and observes the trial but is then excused due to a religious conflict – perhaps the trial runs longer than anticipated, thus overlapping with a religious holiday – the trial judge by rule or practice then may have the authority to suspend the deliberations until the juror returns or, if that is deemed problematic, simply to proceed in the juror's absence.[318]

### c. Deliberations and Decision Making

The confidentiality of juror deliberations is fundamental to the American criminal justice system, as illustrated by Federal Rule of Evidence 606's general prohibition (during an assessment of the verdict's validity) against juror testimony regarding "any statement made or incident that occurred during the jury's deliberations; the effect of anything on that juror's or another juror's vote; or any juror's mental processes concerning the verdict or indictment."[319] Even that evidentiary rule, however, has exceptions for juror testimony about whether "extraneous prejudicial information was improperly brought to the jury's attention" or "an outside influence was improperly brought to bear on any juror."[320] These exceptions effectively preserve a defendant's right, grounded in due process and the Sixth Amendment, to a jury verdict that is reached fairly and impartially based solely on the facts adduced during the trial and the applicable law as determined by the presiding judge.[321]

One potential source of extraneous information or outside influence, and thus one potential threat to a defendant's constitutional rights, is religion, such as a juror's possession of a Bible in the jury room or a juror's reference to scripture or the activity of juror prayer during deliberations.[322] In general, however, the juror conduct will lead to a mistrial or a new trial only if it is found to be prejudicial – "the federal standard [is] that extraneous evidence is presumptively prejudicial"[323] – and if the state cannot show that "the jurors' consideration of the extrinsic evidence was harmless to the defendant"[324] in

318 *See, e.g.*, United States v. Stratton, 779 F.2d 820, 832 (2d Cir. 1985) [upholding trial court's excusal under Fed. R. Civ. P. 23(b) of a juror who asked to observe a four and a half day religious holiday because "the trial judge was entitled to conclude that an adjournment of 4½ days would be less desirable than an eleven-juror verdict"), *cert. denied*, 476 U.S. 1162 (1985), *and cert. denied sub nom.* Parness v. United States, 477 U.S. 906 (1986).

319 Fed. R. Evid. 606(b)(1). Rule 606(b)(1) codifies "the common-law rule [that] generally 'prohibited the admission of juror testimony to impeach a jury verdict.'" Robinson v. Polk, 438 F.3d 350, 359 (4th Cir. 2006) [quoting Tanner v. United States, 483 U.S. 107, 117 (1987)], *cert. denied*, 549 U.S. 1003 (2006).

320 *See* Fed. R. Evid. 606(b)(2)(A)–(B). A third exception allows a juror to testify about whether "a mistake was made in entering the verdict on the verdict form." *Id.* 606(b)(2)(C).

321 *See* Robinson, 438 F.3d at 360; *see also* Robinson v. Polk, 444 F.3d 225, 226 (4th Cir. 2006) (Wilkinson, J., concurring in the denial of rehearing *en banc*) {"The Sixth Amendment jury-trial right 'guarantees to the criminally accused a fair trial by a panel of impartial, indifferent jurors.' At its core, the right contemplates that jurors will render their decision based on the law and the facts presented." (citation omitted) [quoting Irvin v. Dowd, 366 U.S. 717, 722 (1961)]}, *cert. denied*, 549 U.S. 1003 (2006).

322 *See, e.g.*, Dean Sanderford, *The Sixth Amendment, Rule 606(B), and the Intrusion into Jury Deliberations of Religious Principles of Decision*, 74 Tenn. L. Rev. 167 (2007); Gregory M. Ashley, *Note, Theology in the Jury Room: Religious Discussion as "Extraneous Material" in the Course of Capital Punishment Deliberations*, 55 Vand. L. Rev. 127 (2002).

323 McNair v. Campbell, 416 F.3d 1291, 1303 (11th Cir. 2005) [citing Turner v. Louisiana, 379 U.S. 466, 473 (1965); Remmer v. United States, 347 U.S. 227, 229 (1954)], *cert. denied*, 547 U.S. 1073 (2006).

324 *Id.* at 1307.

light of the totality of the circumstances, including "the nature of the extrinsic evidence, how the evidence reached the jury, and the strength of the [government's] case."[325] It should be noted that this calculus may vary from jurisdiction to jurisdiction and also that a quite different and more governmentally deferential approach is normally applied when a verdict is being challenged not directly but collaterally, as through a petition for writ of *habeas corpus*.

Despite the seemingly restrictive and demanding language of these standards, juror conduct involving religion, including the reading of scripture in the jury room, is often deemed to be not improper or, even if improper, to constitute harmless error. In one case from Utah, for example, a jury member told her fellow jurors during deliberations that after praying for a sign, she had received a revelation: if the defense counsel failed to look her in the eye during closing argument, then she should vote to convict.[326] The defense counsel, it turns out, did not during oral argument look her in the eye. The jury subsequently returned a verdict of guilty.[327] Rejecting the defendant's attempt to impeach the jury's verdict as having been prejudiced by the juror's revelation, the Utah Supreme Court determined that

> [p]rayer is almost certainly a part of the personal decision-making process of many people, a process that is employed when serving on a jury. There is no necessary inconsistency between proper performance as a juror and reliance on prayer or supposed responses to prayer. So long as a juror is capable of fairly weighing the evidence and applying the law to the facts, one may not challenge that juror's decision on grounds that he or she may have reached it by aid of prayer or supposed responses to prayer.[328]

In turn, the Court held that "prayer and supposed responses to prayer are not included within the meaning of the words 'outside influence'" under the state-law counterpart to Rule 606(b).[329] The Utah Supreme Court's view appears to represent the majority position.[330] Accordingly, the general rule employed by most courts is that absent any showing of prejudice resulting from juror prayer, there is no actionable legal violation (in the sense of warranting a mistrial or, on appeal, reversal), whether in terms of evidentiary rules, due process, or other constitutional guarantees.[331]

Many courts likewise have refused to nullify a jury verdict based solely on the presence or use of a Bible during jury deliberations,[332] although these determinations appear to

[325] *Id.* at 1308. In addition, the reviewing court should consider "the heavy burden on the State." *Id.* at 1307–8.

[326] *See* State v. DeMille, 756 P.2d 81, 83 (Utah 1988) [applying Utah R. Evid. 606(b), which largely tracks the federal rule].

[327] *See id.*

[328] *Id.* at 84.

[329] *Id.*

[330] *See, e.g.*, McNair v. State, 706 So. 2d 828, 838 (Ala. Ct. Crim. App. 1997), *cert. denied*, 523 U.S. 1064 (1998).

[331] *See, e.g.*, State v. Copeland, 530 So. 2d 526, 544 (La. 1988), *cert. denied*, 489 U.S. 1091 (1989); New Jersey v. Scherzer, 694 A.2d 196, 259 (N.J. Super. Ct. 1997); State v. Williams, 832 N.E.2d 783, 790 (Ohio Ct. App. 2005), *appeal not allowed*, 839 N.E.2d 403 (Ohio 2005).

[332] *See, e.g.*, McNair, 706 So. 2d at 838; Jones v. Francis, 312 S.E.2d 300, 303 (Ga. 1984), *cert. denied*, 469 U.S. 873 (1984); State v. Langley, 711 So. 2d 651 (La. 1998) (addressed in unpublished appendix). *But see* People v. Harlan, 109 P.3d 616, 631–2 (Colo. 2005) (holding to the contrary in a death penalty case and finding that the jury's reference to the Bible during deliberations amounted to the improper use of extraneous information, being neither in evidence nor part of the judge's instructions, and that

be highly factual and potentially dependent on how the Bible was used by jurors, including which verses, if any, were read.[333] The Ninth Circuit, for its part, has held that the use of certain biblical passages in capital jury deliberations need not be deemed an exposure to prejudicial extraneous material where the passages, such as an eye for an eye, are generally known within common parlance.[334] Employing a different line of reasoning, the Fourth Circuit has explained that unlike other potential extrinsic influences on jurors, "the reading of Bible passages invites the listener to examine his or her own conscience from within. In this way, the Bible is not an 'external' influence. In addition, reading the Bible is analogous to the situation where a juror quotes the Bible from memory, which assuredly would not be considered an improper influence."[335] Still other courts have ruled that whereas the Bible may be considered a potentially influential extraneous text, its use generally will be deemed harmless error absent proof of actual effect on the outcome of the jury's deliberations.[336] At the very least, there does not appear to be any "*per se* rule that juror discussion of the Bible in the jury room during deliberations creates an incurable taint that forecloses any possibility of curative instruction and requires a mistrial."[337] Likewise, discussion by jurors of biblical doctrines, without a Bible physically being in the jury room, also has been an insufficient basis to undermine the jury's verdict.[338]

Although most courts, when determining whether or not religious input has prejudicially influenced a jury verdict, employ the common-law test for prejudice, some commentators have argued that this test should be replaced or augmented by Establishment Clause analysis because, as the cases appear to illustrate, criminal defendants are seldom successful when challenging alleged religious influences in juror deliberations.[339]

the scriptural verses were unduly prejudicial insofar as they could have influenced the choice between imposing death or a life sentence), *cert. denied*, 546 U.S. 928 (2005).

333 The Old Testament of the Christian Bible has a considerable amount of text with the seeming potential to influence a jury's decision making, particularly in the sentencing phase of a capital trial. *See, e.g.*, *Genesis* 9:6 ("Whoever sheds the blood of a human, by a human shall that person's blood be shed.") (NRSV); *Exodus* 21:23–5 ("If any harm follows, then you shall give life for life, eye for eye, tooth for tooth, hand for hand, foot for foot, burn for burn, wound for wound, stripe for stripe.") (NRSV).

334 *See* Fields v. Brown, 503 F.3d 755, 780 (9th Cir. 2007), *cert. denied*, 552 U.S. 1314 (2008); *accord* Sechrest v. Baker, 816 F. Supp. 2d 1017, 1055 (D. Nev. 2011) (finding no misconduct by prosecutor's statements – "thank the Good Lord"; "by God"; and "out of the mouths of babes" – insofar as the statements "are figures of speech" that, although they "derive from religious sources, and while they include mention of God and the Bible, they actually carried little religious meaning" and by using them the prosecutor "did not convey any religious doctrine to the jury" and "did not summon religious authority as support for his position").

335 Robinson, 438 F.3d at 363–4; *see also* Burch v. Corcoran, 273 F.3d 577, 590–1 (4th Cir. 2001), *cert. denied*, 535 U.S. 1104 (2002); Jeremy B. Sporn, *Legal Injection? The Constitutionality of the Bible in Capital Sentencing Deliberations*, 83 Tul. L. Rev. 813, 821–8 (2009) (discussing the circuit court rulings).

336 *See* Oliver v. Quarterman, 541 F.3d 329, 331 (5th Cir. 2008), *cert. denied*, 556 U.S. 1181 (2009); People v. Danks, 82 P.3d 1249, 1268–9 (Cal. 2004) (holding that consulting with a pastor and bringing in passages to distribute to the jury in capital proceedings was juror misconduct but that they did not rise to the level of prejudice to warrant a mistrial), *cert. denied*, 543 U.S. 961 (2004); Keen v. State, No. W2004-02159-CCA-R3PD, 2006 WL 1540258, at *32 (Tenn. Ct. App. Jun. 5, 2006) (unpublished), *cert. denied*, 550 U.S. 938 (2007); Lenz v. Warden of Sussex I State Prison, 593 S.E.2d 292, 298-31 (Va. 2004), *cert. denied*, 542 U.S. 953 (2004).

337 United States v. Lara-Ramirez, 519 F.3d 76, 89 (1st Cir. 2008).

338 *See, e.g.*, Young v. State, 12 P.3d 20, 48–9 (Okla. Ct. Crim. App. 2000), *cert. denied*, 532 U.S. 1055 (2001).

339 *See Recent Cases – Capital Sentencing – Juror Prejudice*, 119 Harv. L. Rev. 646, 651–3 (2005).

Professors Gary Simson and Stephen Garvey, for instance, propose that the role of religious materials in sentencing determinations should be governed by the Establishment Clause insofar as a jury's decision is backed by the power of the state. In particular, they argue that the role of religion in jury decision making may be analyzed under either the purpose prong of *Lemon*, which requires that government actions have a legitimate secular purpose and not exhibit a predominant religious purpose, or the endorsement test, which prohibits the government from endorsing or disfavoring religion from the objective vantage point of a reasonable observer.[340]

### 3. *Religion and Evidence*

#### a. The Clergy-Penitent or Religious Communications Privilege

The objective of a legal trial, including a criminal trial, is to reach a judgment in conformity with the facts and the governing law. Much of the time, the law provides for a vigorous pursuit of factual truth; thus evidence may be subpoenaed, testimony compelled, and noncompliance with a court's evidentiary ruling punished by a finding and order of contempt. But the law embodies other values – some mandated by the Constitution, others positively declared by statute, and still others inherited and maintained by the common law – and these values at times may compete with truth maximization. One means by which these competing values are manifested is a "privilege," that is, an "evidentiary rule that gives a witness the option to not disclose the fact asked for, even though it might be relevant."[341]

The focus here is on the privilege for certain confidential religious communications, traditionally known as the "priest-penitent" or "clergy-penitent privilege." The Supreme Court, for example, has several times acknowledged the existence of the privilege as a matter of common law.[342] State court recognition of the privilege appears to have originated in New York in 1813, when a court of that state refused to compel a Catholic priest to testify regarding the identity of a thief who had confessed to the priest and asked him to return stolen goods to their rightful owner.[343] Four years later, a different New York court distinguished the 1813 decision and held that a defendant's communication to a Protestant minister was not privileged,[344] relying on the "distinction between auricular confessions made to a priest in the course of discipline, according to the canons of the

340 *See* Gary J. Simson & Stephen P. Garvey, *Knockin' on Heaven's Door: Rethinking the Role of Religion in Death Penalty Cases*, 86 Cornell L. Rev. 1090, 1120–30 (2001). These purpose and endorsement inquiries are addressed in Chapter 4.C.1.

341 Black's Law Dictionary 1317 (9th ed., 2009).

342 *See* Edward J. Imwinkelried, The New Wigmore: Evidentiary Privileges § 6.2.3 (2d ed. 2010, updated 2014) [noting Totten v. United States, 92 U.S. 105 (1875), United States v. Nixon, 418 U.S. 683 (1974), and Trammel v. United States, 445 U.S. 40 (1980), as instances where the Court recognized the existence of the priest-penitent privilege as a matter of common law]; Michael J. Mazza, *Comment, Should Clergy Hold the Priest-Penitent Privilege?* 82 Marq. L. Rev. 171, 178–80 (1998) (same).

343 *See* Mazza, *supra* note 342, at 181 [referring to the case of People v. Phillips (N.Y. Ct. Gen. Sess. Jun. 14, 1813), which was not officially reported but was reprinted both in William Sampson, The Catholic Question in America 95–114 (1813) and in *Privileged Communications to Clergymen*, 1 Cath. Law. 199, 200–9 (1955)].

344 *Id.* [discussing People v. Smith, 2 City Hall Recorder (Rogers) 77 (N.Y. Ct. of Oyer & Terminer 1817), also reprinted in *Privileged Communications to Clergymen*, *supra* note 343, at 209–13].

church, and those made to a minister of the gospel in confidence, merely as a friend or adviser."[345]

Just over a decade later, New York enacted a statute recognizing the clergy-penitent privilege,[346] and today a privilege for religious communications is codified in all states as well as the District of Columbia.[347] In federal courts, the privilege continues to be recognized as a matter of common law and, unlike the states, is not specifically embodied in a statute or evidentiary rule.[348] Though it can "differ significantly from state to state, there are generally four elements that must be satisfied to establish the privilege. There must be (1) a communication, (2) made in confidence, (3) to a cleric, (4) who was acting in his or her professional capacity."[349] As with other privileges, the religious communications privilege often may serve the instrumental purpose of encouraging candor in protected relationships by a promise of confidentiality.[350] Ultimately, however, it may be difficult to defend on that basis alone,[351] and in fact, the privilege applies even where

345 *Privileged Communications to Clergymen*, *supra* note 343, at 211.

346 *See* N.Y. Rev. Stat. 1828, pt. 3, ch. 7, tit. 3, § 72, reprinted in *Privileged Communications to Clergymen*, *supra* note 343, at 213. The privilege in New York survives in codified form for civil actions (*see* N.Y. Civ. Prac. L. & Rules § 4505), though it appears to apply to criminal actions as well. *See* People v. Harris, 934 N.Y.S.2d 639, 645–6 (N.Y. Supr. Ct. Kings Cnty. 2011).

347 *See* David Blaikie & Diana Ginn, The Legal Guide for Religious Institutions 166 (2010); Imwinkelried, *supra* note 342, § 6.2.3. "The common law recognized no privilege for confidential communications or confessions to a religious advisor, and without state statutes providing for the privilege, it would not exist. At present, all 50 states have enacted privilege statutes that cover confidential communications between religious leaders and followers and have attempted to be inclusive in order to cover genuine religions and faiths." Ingram, *supra* note 58, § 10.6.A, at 368 (footnotes omitted).

348 In 1972, the Supreme Court proposed the codification of several individual privileges (communications to clergy among them, designated as Federal Rule of Evidence 506) [*see* Rules of Evidence for United States Courts and Magistrates, 56 F.R.D. 183, 247–9 (1972)], but Congress ultimately declined to enact specific privileges and instead codified a general provision, Federal Rule of Evidence 501, while still allowing federal courts to recognize specific privileges via federal common law on a privilege-by-privilege, case-by-case basis. *See* S. Rep. No. 93-1277, at 11 (1974); H.R. Rep. No. 93-650, at 8 (1973). Cognizant of Congress' intention to codify only a general privileges section to the Federal Rules of Evidence, the Court effectively reaffirmed a religious communications privilege in United States v. Nixon, 418 U.S. 683, 709 (1974) ("[G]enerally, an attorney or a priest may not be required to disclose what has been revealed in professional confidence."). The original (1975) version of Rule 501 provided in relevant part: "Except as otherwise required by the Constitution of the United States or provide by act of Congress or in rules prescribed by the Supreme Court pursuant to statutory authority, the privilege of a witness, person, government, state, or political subdivision thereof shall be governed by the principles of the common law as they may be interpreted by the courts of the United States in the light of reason and experience." Pub. L. No. 93-595, § 1, 88 Stat. 1926 (Jan. 2, 1975). As amended in 2011, Rule 501 is cosmetically different but materially similar, providing in relevant part that "[t]he common law – as interpreted by United States courts in the light of reason and experience – governs a claim of privilege unless … [the U.S. Constitution, a federal statute, or rules prescribed by the Supreme Court] provides otherwise." Fed. R. Evid. 501. Congress did subsequently codify the attorney-client privilege at Fed. R. Evid. 502.

349 Blaikie & Ginn, *supra* note 347, at 167.

350 *See, e.g.*, Trammel v. United States, 445 U.S. 40, 51 (1980) ("The priest-penitent privilege recognizes the human need to disclose to a spiritual counselor, in total and absolute confidence, what are believed to be flawed acts or thoughts and to receive priestly consolation and guidance in return.").

351 *See* Imwinkelried, *supra* note 342, § 6.2.3(a) (noting that "[i]f the penitent is a sincere fideist, he or she would probably make the confession even absent the assurance of confidentiality furnished by an evidentiary privilege").

the penitent's act of confession essentially fulfills a religious obligation under the tenets of his or her faith.[352]

The first common element, that of a communication, is relatively straightforward and normally extends not only to conventional verbal expressions but also to observations.[353] The element of confidentiality, by comparison, is somewhat more complicated. The communication must be accompanied by a reasonable expectation of confidentiality such that statements made in a public setting or in the presence of third parties who are not necessary for the communication generally will not qualify for the privilege.[354] However, the privilege will not be forfeited by the presence of a third party if that party "is essential to and in furtherance of a communication to a member of the clergy"[355] or if, despite the third party's presence, the penitent "believe[s] the communication [will] remain private and such belief is reasonable."[356] Furthermore, "most jurisdictions hold that the privilege is waived if the holder of the privilege voluntarily discloses privileged material to non-ordained unnecessary third parties."[357]

Regarding the requirement that the communication's recipient be a member of the clergy, this is usually a matter of statutory definition or construction, subject at some level to First Amendment considerations.[358] Most statutes are comparatively broad or

352 *See* Ingram, *supra* note 58, § 10.6.B, at 370 ("The privilege generally applies to a voluntary confession, as well as to one made under a mandate of the church.").

353 *See id.* ("The privilege generally applies … to observations as well as to communications.").

354 *See* United States v. Webb, 615 F.2d 828, 828 (9th Cir. 1980) (*per curiam*) (holding that a confession to a prison chaplain with a security officer present was not protected); People v. Trammel, 345 P.3d 945, 948 (Colo. Ct. App. 2014), *cert. denied*, No. 14SC335, 2015 WL 1205596 (Colo. Mar. 16, 2015) (citing cases); State v. Hedger, 768 P.2d 1331, 1334 (Idaho 1989) (holding that a statement made when approaching a pastor after a Sunday service that was within earshot of another church member was not privileged because there was no reasonable expectation of confidentiality); State v. Willis, 75 A.3d 1068, 1072 (N.H. 2013) (holding that the privilege did not apply when defendant made statement to pastor in presence of defendant's wife and pastor's wife, the latter of "whom the trial court found to be an 'extraneous' third party' "); State v. West, 345 S.E.2d 186, 189 (N.C. 1986) (similar).

355 *In re* Grand Jury Investigation, 918 F.2d 374, 386 (3d Cir. 1990); *accord* United States v. Shelton, 64 M.J. 32, 45 (C.A.A.F. 2006) [applying Mil. R. Evid. 503(b)(2)]; State v. Martin, 975 P.2d 1020, 1029 (Wash. 1999) (*en banc*).

356 State v. Archibeque, 221 P.3d 1045, 1050 (Ariz. Ct. App. 2009); *see also* State v. Ellis, 756 So. 2d 418, 420–1 (La. Ct. App. 1999) (finding that the privilege attached to meeting involving penitent, pastor, penitent's wife, and victim of penitent's conduct as well as victim's wife, where both penitent and pastor viewed the meeting as confidential), *writ denied*, 831 So. 2d 268 (La. 2002). In cases finding "a waiver when a third party was present during the confession" typically "the third party was someone other than the communicant's spouse and usually not a person the communicant could appropriately rely upon to keep statements confidential." Archibeque, 221 P.3d at 1051 n. 2 [citing Perry v. State, 655 S.W.2d 380 (Ark. 1983); People v. Diercks, 411 N.E.2d 97 (Ill. Ct. App. 1980); State v. Gooding, 989 P.2d 304 (Mont. 1999); People v. Brown, 368 N.Y.S.2d 645 (N.Y. Supr. Ct. N.Y. Cnty. 1974); State v. West, 345 S.E.2d 186 (N.C. 1986)].

357 Ingram, *supra* note 58, § 10.6.D, at 372.

358 *See* Mazza, *supra* note 42, at 183–4. A privilege for religious communications must necessarily conform to the First Amendment. On the one hand, its recognition may be seen as consistent with the Free Exercise Clause interests of both the penitent and the cleric, particularly if the latter is bound by religious tenet or church law not to disclose such communications. *See* Ronald J. Columbo, *Forgive Us Our Sins: The Inadequacies of the Clergy-Penitent Privilege*, 73 N.Y.U. L. Rev. 225, 235 (1998); Mary Harter Mitchell, *Must Clergy Tell? Child Abuse Reporting Requirements versus the Clergy Privilege and Free Exercise of Religion*, 71 Minn. L. Rev. 723, 776–7, 799–806 (1987). On the other hand, the privilege's recognition could create Establishment Clause problems (and potentially other constitutional problems) to the extent that it too indiscriminately favors religious over nonreligious communications or is not applied evenhandedly among religions. *See* Waters v. O'Connor, 103 P.3d 292, 296–7 (Ariz.

even vague, thus allowing the inclusion of clergy from many different faiths, but all statutes typically require that the cleric be connected to an otherwise legally recognized or organized religion.[359] Courts have expressed differing views on whether the clergy member must in fact by ordained by the religious organization.[360] Finally, the privilege will only attach to communications when the recipient is consulted and acting in the professional capacity or character of a cleric.[361] In particular, the intended or actual nature of the communication must involve some kind of spiritual or distinctly pastoral activity, such as confession, absolution, counseling, or guidance.[362] Accordingly, "[t]he mere fact that a communication was made to a clergyman or documentation was transmitted to a clergyman is insufficient in itself to invoke the privilege"; rather, the communication must have been "made in the context of a confession or spiritual matter."[363]

Absent the privilege, in fact, witnesses ordinarily can be compelled to testify, even without immunity and even if so doing would violate religious law.[364] However, should the privilege be found applicable, and assuming that it has not been waived, "then either the cleric and/or the person who confided in the cleric cannot be forced to disclose the communication."[365] As for who actually holds and can waive the privilege, there is variation among the states, much of it determined by statutory differences. "The majority of the jurisdictions consider the clergy-penitent privilege to be for the benefit of the penitent. Therefore, the penitent may claim the privilege or waive the privilege as he or she sees fit."[366] In turn, "[t]he general rule is that if the penitent waives the privilege, the clergy member may be required to testify about the communication."[367] In some states,

Ct. App. 2004) (explaining that the term "clergyman" in the state privilege statute cannot be "limited to members of religious organizations having an ordained clergy" because "[s]uch a restrictive definition would raise serious concerns under the Establishment Clause"); Columbo, *supra*, at 236; Mitchell, *supra*, at 777–85.

359 *See* Mazza, *supra* note 342, at 183–4.

360 *Compare, e.g.*, Waters, 103 P.3d at 297 (rejecting an ordination requirement but holding that a church music director did not qualify under the state privilege statute), *and In re* Murtha, 279 A.2d 889 (N.J. App. Div. 1971) (holding a nun in contempt of court for refusing to testify based on the court's finding that the nun did not perform functions comparable to those of a priest for the purpose of invoking the statutory privilege), *certification denied*, 281 A.2d 278 (1971), *with* Eckmann v. Bd. of Educ. of Hawthorn Sch. Dist. No. 17, 106 F.R.D. 70, 72–3 (E.D. Mo. 1985) (extending the privilege to a nun because she was acting in the capacity of a spiritual adviser).

361 *See* Ingram, *supra* note 58, § 10.6.C, at 370–1 ("In order for a communication to be privileged under most statutes, it must have been made to a clergy member in his or her professional capacity or character."). "When the communication is not made within the requisite nature of the confidential disclosure of a penitent seeking religious advice or consolation from a clergy member, a court should not recognize the privilege." *Id.* § 10.6.C, at 371.

362 *See* United States v. Gordon, 655 F.2d 478, 486 (2d Cir. 1981); R. Michael Cassidy, *Sharing Sacred Secrets: Is It (Past) Time for a Dangerous Person Exception to the Clergy-Penitent Privilege?*, 44 Wm. & Mary L. Rev. 1627, 1648 (2003).

363 Hutchinson v. Luddy, 606 A.2d 905, 909 (Pa. Super. Ct. 1992) [citing United States v. Gordon, 655 F.2d 478 (2d Cir. 1981); United States v. Wells, 446 F.2d 2 (2d Cir. 1971); Keenan v. Gigante, 390 N.E.2d 1151 (N.Y. 1979)], *appeal discontinued*, 611 A.2d 712 (Pa. 1992).

364 *See, e.g.*, United States v. Huss, 482 F.2d 38, 51 (2d Cir. 1973) (with immunity); Matter of Fuhrer, 419 N.Y.S.2d 426, 431–32 (N.Y. Supr. Ct. Richmond Cnty. 1979) (without immunity); State v. Bing, 253 S.E.2d 101, 102 (S.C. 1979) (without immunity).

365 Blaikie & Ginn, *supra* note 347, at 166.

366 Ingram, *supra* note 58, § 10.6.D, at 372. *See also* Mazza, *supra* note 342, at 187 (noting several states where this is clearly the case).

367 Ingram, *supra* note 58, § 10.6.D, at 372.

however, "the clergy member is deemed to be a holder of the privilege on the theory that the state should neither force a member of the clergy to violate, nor punish him or her for refusing to violate, church doctrine where the church teaching requires clergy to maintain secrecy as to confidential statements made in the course of religious counseling."[368]

b. Credibility and Religion

Historically, "[f]ears that nonbelievers would have no incentive to be truthful led to the … practice in many American jurisdictions of preventing persons who had no religious belief from serving as witnesses."[369] The modern view, by contrast, is that "one's religious belief or lack thereof should not be a basis upon which a court or jury should evaluate testimonial capacity or credibility."[370] Accordingly, the contemporary evidence rules of the federal and state courts uniformly prohibit the use of a witness's possession or lack of religious beliefs to demonstrate that the witness, on that basis alone, is or is not credible or competent,[371] a prohibition that in many states is also embodied in their own constitutions.[372] Illustrative of these proscriptions is Rule 610 of the *Federal Rules of*

368 *Id. See also* Mazza, *supra* note 342, at 187 (noting such jurisdictions).

369 INGRAM, *supra* note 58, § 8.15, at 264.

370 *Id.* § 8.15, at 264, 265. This prohibition includes "using religion as a tool to bolster a witness's credibility." *Id.* § 8.15, at 264. "Religious belief was a prerequisite to ancient common law capacity to take an oath and thus to competency of the witness. At common law religious belief evolved from a question of competency to one of credibility and thereafter came to be a matter of privilege in the witness. The latter, fully applied, would exclude appropriate inquiry relative to interest, bias, and the like." Annotation to Wis. Stat. § 906.10. Not addressed here is the oath or affirmation requirement imposed on witnesses and deponents and the extent to which it has raised and may continue to raise constitutional issues. For representative cases, *see* Doe v. Phillips, 81 F.3d 1204, 1210 (2d Cir. 1996), *cert. denied*, 520 U.S. 1115 (1997); United States v. Ward, 989 F.2d 1015, 1018–20 (9th Cir. 1992); Gordon v. Idaho, 778 F.2d 1397, 1401 (9th Cir. 1985); State v. Bowlin, 850 S.W.2d 116, 117–18 (Mo. Ct. App. 1993); Scott v. State, 80 S.W.3d 184, 191–3 (Tex. Ct. App. 2002). For academic commentary, *see* Frederick B. Jonassen, *"So Help Me?": Religious Expression and Artifacts in the Oath of Office and the Courtroom Oath*, 12 CARDOZO PUB. L., POL'Y & ETHICS J. 303 (2014); Eugene L. Milhizer, *So Help Me Allah: An Historical and Prudential Analysis of Oaths as Applied to the Current Controversy of the Bible and Quran in Oath Practices in America*, 70 OHIO ST. L.J. 1 (2009).

371 *See, e.g.*, Fed. R. Evid. 610; Ala. R. Evid. 610; Ark. Code § 16-41-101, R. 610; Cal. Evid. Code § 789; Colo. Rev. Stat. § 13-90-110; Fla. Stat. § 90.611; Ga. Code § 24-9-3; Hawaii Rev. Stat. § 626-1, R. 610; Idaho Stat. § 9-201; Ind. Code § 34-45-2-12; Ind. R. Evid. 610; Iowa Code R. 5.610; Kan. Stat. § 60-430; La. Code Evid. art. 610; Md. Rules R. 5-610; Mich. Comp. Laws § 600.1436; Mich. R. Evid. 610; Mont. R. Evid. 610; Neb. Rev. Stat. § 27-610; Nev. Rev. Stat. 50.105; N.H. R. Evid. 610; N.J. R. Evid. 610; N.M. R. Ann. 11-610; N.C. Gen. Stat. § 8C-1, R. 610; 12 Okla. Stat. § 2610; Or. Rev. Stat. § 40.365, R. 610; 42 Pa. Consol. Stat. § 5902; Pa. R. Evid. 610; S.C. R. Evid. 610; S.D. Codified Laws § 19-14-17, Rule 610; Tex. R. Evid. 610; Utah Code § 78-24-1; Utah R. Evid. 610; Vt. Stat. § 1606; Wash. R. Evid. 610; W. Va. R. Evid. 610; Wis. Stat. Ann. 906.10; *cf. also* Guam Code § 610; Mil. R. Evid. 610; P.R. Laws tit. 32, app. IV, R. 48; V.I. Code tit. V, § 858.

372 *See, e.g.*, ARIZ. CONST. art. II, § 12 ("[N]or shall any person be incompetent as a witness or juror in consequence of his [or her] opinion on matters of religion, nor be questioned touching his [or her] religious belief in any court of justice to affect the weight of his [or her] testimony."); ARK CONST. art. II, § 26 ("[N]or shall any person be rendered incompetent to be a witness on account of his [or her] religious belief."); CAL. CONST. art. 1, § 4 ("A person is not incompetent to be a witness or juror because of his or her opinions on religious beliefs."); IND. CONST. art. 1, § 7 ("No person shall be rendered incompetent as a witness, in consequence of his [or her] opinions on matters of religion."); IOWA CONST. art. I, § 4 ("[N]o person shall be deprived of any of his [or her] rights, privileges, or capacities, or disqualified from the performance of any of his [or her] public or private duties, or rendered incompetent to give evidence in any court of law or equity, in consequence of his [or her] opinions on the subject of religion.");

*Evidence*, which categorically declares that "[e]vidence of a witness's religious beliefs or opinions is not admissible to attack or support the witness's credibility."[373] This and similar rules typically do not, however, erect a complete bar on evidence relating to religion. To the contrary, evidence of a witness's religious affiliation, beliefs, or practices theoretically may be introduced for any purpose other than undermining or supporting the witness's credibility, such as showing that "an aspect of religion might have an effect on bias or motive for impeachment purposes."[374] More generally, courts have held that "[a] person's beliefs, superstitions, or affiliation with a religious group is properly admissible where probative of an issue in a criminal prosecution."[375]

The use of religion in relation to witnesses not only must comply with the applicable evidentiary rules limiting such use to an allowable purpose such as showing bias but also must comply with evidentiary rules prohibiting unduly prejudicial evidence[376] and,

MICH. CONST. art. I, § 18 ("No person shall be rendered incompetent to be a witness on account of his [or her] opinions on matters of religious belief."); NEB. CONST. art. I, § 4 ("[N]or shall any person be incompetent to be a witness on account of his [or her] religious beliefs."); NEV. CONST. art. I, § 4 ("[N]o person shall be rendered incompetent to be a witness on account of his [or her] opinions on matters of his [or her] religious belief."); N.Y. CONST. art. I, § 3 ("[N]o person shall be rendered incompetent to be a witness on account of his or her opinions on matters of religious belief."); N.D. CONST. art. I, § 3 ("[N]o person shall be rendered incompetent to be a witness or juror on account of his [or her] opinion on matters of religious belief."); OHIO CONST. art. I, § 7 ("[N]or shall any person be incompetent to be a witness on account of his [or her] religious belief."); OR. CONST. art. I, § 6 ("No person shall be rendered incompetent as a witness, or juror in consequence of his [or her] opinions on matters of religeon [*sic*]; nor be questioned in any Court of Justice touching his [or her] religeous [*sic*] belief to affect the weight of his [or her] testimony."); TEX. CONST. art. I, § 5 ("No person shall be disqualified to give evidence in any of the Courts of this State on account of his [or her] religious opinions, or for the want of any religious belief."); UTAH CONST. art. I, § 4 ("[N]or shall any person be incompetent as a witness or juror on account of religious belief or the absence thereof."); WASH. CONST. art. I, § 11 ("[N]or shall any person be incompetent as a witness or juror, in consequence of his opinion on matters of religion, nor be questioned in any court of justice touching his [or her] religious belief to affect the weight of his [or her] testimony."); WYO. CONST. art. I, § 18 ("[N]o person shall be rendered incompetent ... to serve as a witness or juror, because of his [or her] opinion on any matter of religious belief whatever.").

373 Fed. R. Evid. 610.

374 INGRAM, *supra* note 58, § 8.15 at 264 [citing Slagle v. Bagley, 457 F.3d 501, 517 (6th Cir. 2006), *cert. denied*, 551 U.S. 1134 (2007)].

375 United States v. Beasley, 72 F.3d 1518, 1527 (11th Cir. 1996), *cert. denied sub nom.* James v. United States, 518 U.S. 1027 (1996), *and cert. denied sub nom.* Ben Yahweh v. United States, 519 U.S. 866 (1996); *accord* United States v. Shalom, No. 95-1768, 113 F.3d 1236, 1997 WL 225514, at *4 (6th Cir. May 1, 1997) (*per curiam*) (unpublished) (agreeing with *Beasley*), *cert. denied*, 522 U.S. 890 (1997); State v. Sanchez, 127 P.3d 212, 218 (Idaho Ct. App. 2005) ("[A] witness's beliefs or affiliation with a religious group is properly admissible where probative of an issue in a criminal prosecution."); State v. Leitner, 34 P.3d 42, 55 (Kan. 2001) (explaining that "the introduction of evidence of a person's membership or participation in a religious group or association" requires that "such evidence should be related to the commission of the crime charged or should be used to show a person's possible bias or motive").

376 *See, e.g.*, Fed. R. Evid. 403 (authorizing the trial court's exclusion of otherwise "relevant evidence if its probative value is substantially outweighed by a danger of one or more of the following: unfair prejudice, confusing the issues, misleading the jury, undue delay, wasting time, or needlessly presenting cumulative evidence"); Beasley, 72 F.3d at 1527 (upholding admission of defendant's religious beliefs and practices and finding that the trial court did not improperly apply Fed. R. Evid. 403); United States v. Sun Myung Moon, 718 F.2d 1210, 1233 (2d Cir. 1983) (same), *cert. denied*, 466 U.S. 971 (1984); State v. Kimbrell, 360 S.E.2d 691, 694 (N.C. 1987) (holding that admission of the defendant's satanic and occultist activities, introduced by the prosecutor over the defendant's objection, constituted reversible error where "[t]he outcome of the trial depended on the jury's perception of the relative veracity of the witnesses" and the "questions about devil worship, satanic bibles, graveyard seances, and the like" had "little or no probative value").

ultimately, with constitutional guarantees such as equal protection, due process, and the First Amendment religion clauses.[377] The concern about undue prejudice arises precisely because one of the primary reasons for barring religion as a means of attacking or bolstering credibility is "to guard against the prejudice which may result from disclosure of a witness's faith."[378]

#### c. The Defendant's Religious Affiliation, Beliefs, Statements, or Practices

In addition to the codified limits on enhancing or undermining witness credibility solely on the basis of religion, there also exist limits specifically on the extent to which a defendant's religion – his or her affiliation, beliefs, statements, or practices – may be introduced at trial or used in sentencing.[379] Should the defendant choose to testify, of course, then the aforementioned limitations relating to credibility will apply. Correspondingly, a defendant's religious beliefs or affiliation can be admitted and employed in order to show bias[380] or to demonstrate some other relevant aspect of the prosecution,[381] subject to potential constitutional constraints and, of course, to the applicable rules generally governing the admission of evidence.[382] For example, in a state prosecution of a cleric for sexually assaulting a minor within his congregation, evidence of "the tenets of defendant's church, including defendant's religious authority and the congregation's concern with the appropriate behavior of teenage churchgoers, provided an important context

[377] *See, e.g.*, Beasley, 72 F.3d at 1527–8 (holding that admission of the defendant's religious practices, "where relevant to a trial issue," did not violate the First Amendment); Hampton v. Richard, No. Civ. 5:12-14401, 2014 WL 1260162, at *14 (E.D. Mich. Mar. 26, 2014) (unpublished) (same); State v. Dreiling, 54 P.3d 475, 499 (Kan. 2002) (same), *cert. denied*, 538 U.S. 944 (2003).

[378] United States v. Sampol, 636 F.2d 621, 666 (D.C. Cir 1980) (explaining that this is the purpose of Fed. R. Evid. 610).

[379] Some state laws, in addition to prohibiting religion as a basis for establishing or undermining witness credibility, delineate with some specificity the evidentiary nature, limits, and uses of a party's religious beliefs. *See, e.g.*, Kan. Stat. § 60-430 ("Every person has a privilege to refuse to disclose his or her theological opinion or religious belief unless his or her adherence or nonadherence to such an opinion or belief is material to an issue in the action other than that of his or her credibility as a witness.").

[380] *See, e.g.*, United States v. Abel, 469 U.S. 45, 52 (1984) (holding that "[a] witness' and a party's common membership in an organization, even without proof that the witness or party has personally adopted its tenets, is certainly probative of bias").

[381] *See* Beasley, 72 F.3d at 1527 ["A person's beliefs, superstitions, or affiliation with a religious group is properly admissible where probative of an issue in a criminal prosecution." (citing Sun Myung Moon, 718 F.2d at 1233)]; *accord* Shalom, 1997 WL 225514, at *4; United States v. Hakim, No. 02-CR-131, 2002 WL 31151174, at *4–*5 (E.D. Pa. Sep. 24, 2002) (unpublished); Sanchez, 127 P.3d at 218; State v. Dreiling, 54 P.3d 475, 499 (Kan. 2002) (allowing the government to introduce evidence of a defendant's religion when his or her "religious practices involve beliefs and statements … tend to establish a motive for the defendant to commit the crime"), *cert. denied*, 538 U.S. 944 (2003).

[382] *See, e.g.*, Fed. R. Evid. 403 (authorizing federal courts to "exclude relevant evidence if its probative value is substantially outweighed by a danger of … unfair prejudice, confusing the issues, [or] misleading the jury"); United States v. Haldar, 751 F.3d 450, 457 (7th Cir. 2014) (finding that the prosecutor's opening statement, which referred to the defendant's position within a religious organization, did not impermissibly comment on the defendant's religion and did not violate Fed. R. Evid. 403 as being unfairly prejudicial); Beasley, 72 F.3d at 1527 (finding no violation of the First Amendment or Fed. R. Evid. 403 or 610 by the introduction of defendants' religious beliefs and practices where their religion's "teachings were used to justify, rationalize, and promote crime" and where a defendant "himself sought to interject religion into his cross-examination by responding to numerous questions with a religious/Biblical response").

for the [alleged] incidents" and thus was deemed admissible without violating the First Amendment or the state's evidentiary rule regarding religion and witness credibility.[383] Similarly, "[t]he government may present evidence of the defendant's religious beliefs if they are relevant to show the defendant's motive or any mental state that is an element of the offense" and also may "offer evidence of religious beliefs if relevant to an affirmative defense raised by the accused."[384]

It is not just the prosecutor, however, who may try to sway the jury with some aspect of the defendant's religiosity. Defendants themselves, without testifying, also may try to do so by, for example, prominently displaying a Bible at the defense table or wearing religious items such as a cross. They may even contend, in some cases plausibly, that they have a right to do so under the First Amendment.[385] However, a number of courts have held that a trial judge, exercising discretionary authority over courtroom and trial management, may restrict or even forbid the display of a Bible at counsel's table without violating religious freedom if the restriction is intended to maintain the fairness of the trial.[386] In one high-profile case, moreover, the defendant attempted not to sway but to eliminate the jury, requesting a bench trial out of fear that his nonmainstream beliefs – the defendant was Sun Myung Moon, founder of the Unification Church – would adversely influence the jury's decision making. The government refused to consent to a bench trial, however, and the Second Circuit ultimately ruled that the trial judge's denial of his request was permissible under the First and Sixth Amendments.[387]

383 *See* People v. Bautista, 77 Cal. Rptr. 3d 824, 842–3 (Cal. Ct. App. 2008).

384 *See* Roger Park & Tom Lininger, The New Wigmore: Impeachment and Rehabilitation § 7.6 (2d ed. 2010, updated 2014).

385 *See, e.g.*, Caldwell v. State, 243 So. 2d 422, 424 (Fla. Dist. Ct. App. 1971), *appeal dismissed*, 247 So. 2d 326 (Fla. 1971); State v. Albertson, No. A04-2277, 2006 WL 466454, at *1–*2 (Minn. Ct. App. Feb. 28, 2006) (unpublished); People v. Williams, 864 N.Y.S.2d 405, 206 (N.Y. App. Div. 2008), *leave to appeal denied*, 901 N.E.2d 771 (N.Y. 2008); Alexander v. State, 282 S.W.3d 143, 147–8 (Tex. 2009), *cert. denied*, 559 U.S. 1010 (2010); *see also* State v. Tate, 682 N.W.2d 169, 174-5 (Minn. Ct. App. 2004) (holding that while asking a defendant to tuck a large cross worn around his neck under his shirt without inquiring into the sincerity of his religious beliefs was in error but not a prejudicial one nor in violation of any fundamental right to a fair jury trial or in violation of the Free Exercise Clause).

386 *See, e.g.*, Albertson, 2006 WL 466454, at *2 ("[T]he district court is charged with restricting disruptive conduct at trial, including the regulation of religious displays. A compelling interest of conducting a trial in a secular, impartial, orderly manner justified the district court's order. Because the district court inquired into the purpose of the Bible, had a compelling interest in conducting an orderly, impartial trial, and allowed appellant to hold the Bible in his lap, the district court did not err in ordering appellant to conceal his Bible."); Williams, 864 N.Y.S.2d at 406 ["The court did not violate defendant's right to free exercise of his religion when it prohibited him from displaying his Bible in the presence of the jury, an act that would have posed the risk of evoking sympathy. The compelling interest of guaranteeing a fair trial to both sides justified the court's incidental restriction on defendant's religious practices." (citations omitted)]; Alexander, 282 S.W.3d at 147–8 (finding that "simply displaying a Bible on the counsel table does not constitute the 'exercise' of religion" where there was "no showing that [the defendant's] religious practices or beliefs required him to prominently display his Bible during trial" or that "he had it for reference or even for comfort"; accordingly, the trial court's direction "to keep the Bible in a place less visible than on top of counsel table" was proper when "issued for the purpose of conducting an orderly trial, so that the jury would be uninfluenced by factors external to the evidence adduced").

387 *See* United States v. Sun Myung Moon, 718 F.2d 1210 (2d Cir. 1983). For critical analysis, in light of the *Moon* case, of the government's refusal to consent to bench trials and religious prejudice, *see* Charles J. Ogletree, *Reverend Moon and the Black Hebrews: Constitutional Protection of a Defendant's Religion in Criminal Cases*, 22 Harv. C.R.-C.L. L. Rev. 191 (1987) (proposing a *Batson*-like justification requirement for such refusals).

A defendant's religiosity may be a matter of contested admissibility not only during the guilt phase of a trial but also, if guilt is found, during sentencing. At present, jurisdictions differ tremendously regarding the extent to which, and manner in which, a defendant's religious background or profile can be used as either a mitigating or an aggravating sentencing factor. For example, "[a]lthough many courts have traditionally allowed information about a defendant's religion to be presented to the sentencing judge, several courts have recently stated that a defendant's religious belief, or lack thereof, is an inappropriate aggravating sentencing factor."[388] This emerging categorical position is seemingly consistent both with the long-standing free exercise principle that religious beliefs as such are absolutely protected[389] and, at least in some instances, with the Supreme Court's holding in *Dawson v. Delaware*[390] that the First Amendment freedom of association "prevents … [the government] from employing evidence of a defendant's abstract beliefs at a sentencing hearing when those beliefs have no bearing on the issue being tried."[391] Such a position is arguably less tenable, however, when the defendant's religious beliefs are in fact related to the underlying crime itself or otherwise have a logical bearing on the objectives of sentencing, such as the feasibility of rehabilitation, the likelihood of deterrence, or conversely, the need for incapacitation. In this regard, even the *Dawson* Court qualified its holding by emphasizing that "the Constitution does not erect a *per se* barrier to the admission of evidence concerning one's beliefs and associations at sentencing simply because those beliefs and associations are protected by the First Amendment."[392]

Thus "the government may show that the defendant is part of a sect that advocates violence, because his future violent propensities are relevant in a sentencing hearing"[393] and it "may also introduce evidence of religious rituals that occurred contemporaneously with the crime, because sentencing requires consideration of offense conduct."[394] In one case, the Seventh Circuit held that was the government could introduce a defendant's anti-Semitic statements where the defendant had been convicted of destroying property

388 Carissa Byrne Hessick & F. Andrew Hessick, *Recognizing Constitutional Rights at Sentencing*, 99 Cal. L. Rev. 47, 55 (2011) (footnote omitted). *See, e.g.*, State v. Ninham, 797 N.W.2d 451, 477 (Wis. 2011) (explaining that a trial court "may not base its sentencing decision upon the defendant's or the victim's religion"), *cert. denied*, 133 S. Ct. 59 (2012).

389 *See, e.g.*, Employment Div. v. Smith, 494 U.S. 872, 877 (1990). "The Free Exercise Clause categorically prohibits government from regulating, prohibiting, or rewarding religious beliefs as such" [McDaniel v. Paty, 435 U.S. 618, 626 (1978) (plurality opinion)], and "neither a State nor the Federal Government can constitutionally force a person 'to profess a belief or disbelief in any religion.'" Torcaso v. Watkins, 367 U.S. 488, 495 (1961) [quoting Everson v. Bd. of Educ., 330 U.S. 1, 15 (1947)].

390 503 U.S. 159 (1992).

391 *Id.* at 168. It also may be consistent with the sentencing guidelines, if any, applicable to a given jurisdiction. *See, e.g.*, U.S. Sentencing Guidelines § 5H.1.10 (2013) (providing as a policy statement that a defendant's creed and religion, among other enumerated factors, "are not relevant in the determination of a sentence").

392 Dawson, 503 U.S. at 165.

393 Park & Lininger, *supra* note 384, § 7.8 [citing Miller-El v. Johnson, 261 F.3d 445, 455 (5th Cir. 2001), *rev'd on other grounds*, 537 U.S. 322 (2003); Davis v. State, 329 S.W.3d 798, 805–6 (Tex. Ct. Crim. App. 2010), *cert. denied*, 132 S. Ct. 128 (2011)]. *See also* State v. Brumwell, 249 P.3d 965, 971–3, 975 (Or. 2011) (*en banc*) (holding that inquiry into the defendant's satanic beliefs during sentencing was permissible because such beliefs were relevant to motive for prior crimes and, in turn, relevant to likelihood of future criminal conduct, and further that such inquiry did not violate the First Amendment), *cert. denied*, 132 S. Ct. 1028 (2012).

394 Park & Lininger, *supra* note 384, § 7.8 [citing People v. Shatner, 673 N.E.2d 258, 268–9 (Ill. 1996), *cert. denied*, 520 U.S. 1231 (1997)].

at a Jewish community center precisely because the statements thus were "indicative of motive and future dangerousness."[395] As the court explained, "[l]ack of remorse and poor rehabilitative potential are traditionally very important considerations for any sentencing judge," and by considering the defendant's anti-Semitic remarks, "the sentencing court was not punishing [him] for his abstract beliefs but rather for his concrete application of those misguided beliefs in criminal activity."[396] Even under the D.C. Circuit's demanding standard of *United States v. Lemon*,[397] a sentencing determination may take into account religious affiliation if there is "sufficiently reliable evidence that the defendant was a member of or closely affiliated with [a particular religious organization], that the [religious organization] had certain illegal aims, and that the defendant intended to further those illegal aims."[398]

### 4. *The Use of Religious Arguments or Authority by Parties and Judges*

The permissibility of invoking religious authority in the guilt or sentencing phases of a criminal trial, particularly in a way that could influence those processes, presents a complicated interaction of criminal procedural rights, the constitutional rights of free exercise and free speech, among others, and the duties and ethics of attorneys, judges, or both. Regarding the use of religious authority by parties, the available precedents suggest that a case-by-case, heavily circumstantial analysis is and perhaps ought to be the preferred approach depending on the nature of the authority invoked as well as the manner, stage, and type of case in which it is employed. With regard to the judicial use of religious authority, the available precedents, though somewhat fewer in number, suggest that these variables are similarly considered but, at the same time, that judges generally have less latitude than do the parties, perhaps because of the need to maintain impartiality (including its appearance) as well as the more direct governance of the Establishment Clause in relation to judicial action. This constrained latitude is especially characteristic of the judge's function in sentencing, despite the traditional discretion accorded to judges when engaged in that task.

Prosecutors and defense attorneys may have good practical reason to rely on religious sources when arguing to the jury, given the potential resonance, if not authoritative

395 Kapadia v. Tally, 229 F.3d 641, 648 (7th Cir. 2000).

396 *Id. See also* State v. Ross, 696 P.2d 706, 710 (Ariz. Ct. App. 1984) (finding no error where the sentencing judge noted a religious reference in a letter by the defendant to the victim, not as "a common on ... [the defendant's religion]" but as evidence of the defendant's effort "to play upon the victim's religious beliefs to gain sympathy"). Correspondingly, a victim's religious faith may be introduced within the context of a victim impact statement if it is relevant to the impact of the crime. *See, e.g.*, United States v. Bernard, 299 F.3d 467, 479 (5th Cir. 2002) [allowing evidence that the victims were youth ministers "[b]ecause religion played a vital role in ... [the victims'] lives," and "it would be impossible to describe their uniqueness as individual human beings without reference to their faith." (internal quotations omitted)], *cert. denied*, 539 U.S. 928 (2003).

397 723 F.2d 922 (D.C. Cir. 1983). For a discussion of *Lemon*, *see* Ogletree, *supra* note 387.

398 Lemon, 723 F.2d at 941; *see also id.* at 939–40 ("[T]he first amendment proscribes punishment of an individual for membership in a protected [religious] organization unless the organization has illegal aims and the individual intends to further those aims."); *accord* United States v. Stewart, 686 F.3d 156, 169 (2d Cir. 2012) ("It is impermissible to sentence a defendant more harshly based on associations that do not relate to specific criminal wrongdoing, for example, or for beliefs that some might find morally reprehensible."), *cert. denied*, 134 S. Ct. 54 (2013).

nature, that such sources may have, consciously or unconsciously, in many a juror's mind. It is this potential for extralegal influence, however, that engenders unease among trial and appellate courts precisely because "[t]he jury's decision is to be based upon the evidence presented at trial and the legal instructions given by the court."[399] As has been noted,

> [w]hether offered by the government or by defense counsel, appeals to the jury based on religious values are inescapably powerful. The familiar narratives about Cain and Abel, taking an eye for an eye, casting the first stone, and turning the other cheek are emotionally compelling even to the nonreligious person. Jurors who accept a prosecutor's argument that a higher authority requires (or alternatively does not allow) the death penalty would not then rely solely on evidence and law in reaching a decision. Nor would jurors properly evaluate aggravating and mitigating factors or give the defendant the individualized assessment required by the Eighth Amendment. An argument by either side that relieves jurors of their responsibility by making them ministers of a divine command also violates the right to a decision guided by law and evidence.[400]

In turn, many courts discourage the use by attorneys of scriptural invocations when arguing to juries[401] insofar as "references to the Bible might improperly inflame the passions and prejudices of the jury, thereby denying the defendant due process."[402] Nor is a denial of due process as such the only possible constitutional problem; also potentially implicated may be the Eighth Amendment,[403] as indicated by the preceding quotation, and perhaps even the Establishment Clause.[404]

399 Sandoval v. Calderon, 241 F.3d 765, 776 (9th Cir. 2000), *cert. denied*, 534 U.S. 847 (2001), *and cert. denied*, 534 U.S. 943 (2001).

400 Geraldine Szott Moohr & Roger Sherman, *Book Review*, 24 J.L. & RELIGION 749, 750 (2009) [reviewing MONICA K. MILLER, RELIGION IN CRIMINAL JUSTICE (2006)]; *see also* Sandoval, 241 F.3d at 776 ["[A]ny suggestion that the jury may base its decision on a 'higher law' than that of the court in which it sits is forbidden. The obvious danger of such a suggestion is that the jury will give less weight to, or perhaps even disregard, the legal instructions given it by the trial judge in favor of the asserted higher law." (citations omitted)].

401 *See* Lis Wiehl, *Judges and Lawyers Are Not Singing from the Same Hymnal When It Comes to Allowing the Bible in the Courtroom*, 24 AM. J. TRIAL ADVOC. 273, 273–4 (2000) [citing Carruthers v. State, 528 S.E.2d 217, 221 (Ga. 2000), *overruled on other grounds by* Vergara v. State, 657 S.E.2d 863 (Ga. 2008); People v. Rohn, 296 N.W.2d 315, 317–18 (Mich. Ct. App. 1980), *overruled on other grounds by* People v. Perry, 594 N.W.2d 477 (Mich. 1999); Commonwealth v. Brown, 711 A.2d 444, 456 (Pa. 1998); Commonwealth v. Chambers, 599 A.2d 630, 644 (Pa. 1991)].

402 *Id.* [citing Cunningham v. Zant, 928 F.2d 1006, 1020 (11th Cir. 1991); People v. Wrest, 839 P.2d 1020, 1028 (Cal. 1992); Rohn, 296 N.W.2d at 318]. For additional commentary, much of it focused on religious arguments in capital trials, *see* John H. Blume & Sheri Lynn Johnson, *Don't Take His Eye, Don't Take His Tooth, and Don't Cast the First Stone: Limiting Religious Arguments in Capital Cases*, 9 WM. & MARY BILL RTS. J. 61 (2000); H. Lyssette Chavez & Monica K. Miller, *Religious References in Death Sentence Phases of Trials: Two Psychological Theories That Suggest Judicial Rulings and Assumptions May Affect Jurors*, 13 LEWIS & CLARK L. REV. 1037 (2009); David L. Paavola, *I Know Exactly What You Mean: Recognizing the Danger of Coded Appeals to Religious Prejudice in Capital Cases*, 62 S.C. L. REV. 639 (2011); Elizabeth A. Brooks, *Note, Thou Shalt Not Quote the Bible: Determining the Propriety of Attorney Use of Religious Philosophy and Themes in Oral Arguments*, 33 GA. L. REV. 1113 (1999); Brian C. Duffy, *Note, Barring Foul Blows: An Argument for a Per Se Reversible-Error Rule for Prosecutors' Use of Religious Arguments in the Sentencing Phase of Capital Cases*, 50 VAND. L. REV. 1335 (1997).

403 *See, e.g.*, Sandoval, 241 F.3d at 776 ("In a capital case … the prosecution's invocation of higher law or extra-judicial authority violates the Eighth Amendment principle that the death penalty may be constitutionally imposed only when the jury makes findings under a sentencing scheme that carefully focuses the jury on the specific factors it is to consider in reaching a verdict."); *see also* Farina v. Sec'y, Fla. Dep't of Corr., No. 12-13260, 536 Fed. App'x 966, 983–4 (11th Cir. Sep. 30, 2013) (*per curiam*) (unpublished).

404 *Cf., e.g.*, People v. Williams, 233 P.3d 1000, 1046 (Cal. 2010) (assuming, without deciding, that the prosecutor's religious references during closing argument may have violated the Establishment Clause),

The general norm against invoking religious references, though broadly applicable to both prosecutors and defense counsel, appears to apply with particular force to the former,[405] and "courts overwhelmingly have taken a disapproving approach to the prosecutorial use of religious imagery and references during trials,"[406] especially during the sentencing or penalty phase of capital trials.[407] Such references often, though not always, have been found to constitute prosecutorial misconduct; less often, however, have they been deemed sufficiently prejudicial and unredressed (or irremediable) to warrant a declaration of mistrial at the trial level, a finding of reversible error on appeal, or the invalidation of a conviction on collateral review.[408] When the prosecutor's statements are extensive

*cert. denied*, 131 S. Ct. 1602 (2011); State v. Johnson, 944 A.2d 416, 427–8 (Conn. Ct. App. 2008) (noting this argument by the defendant but deeming it unpreserved), *certification denied*, 953 A.2d 650 (Conn. 2008); Dilworth v. State, No. 13-07-00520-CR, 2008 WL 5732155, at *3 (Tex. Ct. App. Dec. 4, 2008) (unpublished) (same); *see also* Jackson v. Epps, No. 4:03CV461-P, 2010 WL 3853158, at *26–*29 (N.D. Miss. Sep. 28, 2010) (unpublished) (rejecting such a claim under the cause-and-prejudice standard of habeas review), *aff'd*, No. 10-70029, 447 Fed. App'x 535 (5th Cir. Oct. 13, 2011) (unpublished), *cert. denied*, 132 S. Ct. 2379 (2012).

405 This is perhaps not surprising given the prominence of the prosecutor and the potential imbalance of power and authority within the courtroom. *See* Bennett L. Gershman, Prosecutorial Misconduct § 4:1 (2d ed. rev. 2014–2015) ("The prosecutor is the most dominant figure in the American criminal justice system. The prosecutor decides whether or not to bring criminal charges; who to charge; what charges to bring; whether a defendant will stand trial, plead guilty, or enter a correctional program in lieu of criminal charges; and whether to confer immunity from prosecution. The prosecutor, in short, holds the power to invoke or deny punishment.").

406 State v. Ceballos, 832 A.2d 14, 32 (Conn. 2003). "In contrast to the majority approach, other jurisdictions permit, but do not encourage, the use of religious references as an oratorical device. Such references, however, are generally prohibited when offered in direct support of the imposition of capital punishment upon a defendant." *Id.* at 33–4 (citations omitted). For a fuller typology, *see* Monica K. Miller & Brian H. Bornstein, *Religious Appeals in Closing Arguments: Impermissible Input or Benign Banter?*, 29 Law & Psychol. Rev. 29, 31 (2005) ["Courts have reacted to the use of religious appeals in a variety of different ways. Approaches have varied by jurisdiction, but some include: prohibiting all appeals, generally accepting all appeals, and issuing limitations on certain types of appeals. Some courts have rationalized that the potential effects of a religious appeal have been counterbalanced by the judge's instructions or by further instructions from the attorney. Other courts have deemed religious appeals to be harmless in light of the totality of the evidence against the defendant. Finally, some jurisdictions have adopted the rule of 'fair response,' which allows religious appeals if the opposing attorney also used appeals." (footnotes omitted)].

407 *See* Ceballos, 832 A.2d at 32 n. 32 (noting that "the majority of the case law on this issue has developed within the context of prosecutorial religious references made during the sentencing phases of death penalty trials" though further noting that "[t]hese holdings … certainly are not inapplicable in a trial for the purpose of determining the defendant's guilt, especially when the state's case is not particularly strong"). Regarding the restriction of religious references by defense counsel as well, *see* Edmonds v. Commonwealth, Nos. 2007-SC-000350-MR, 2007-SC-000359-MR, 2009 WL 4263142, at *10 (Ky. Nov. 25, 2009) (*per curiam*) (unpublished) (upholding a trial court's refusal to permit the defendant "to compare himself to Jesus being put to death on the cross"); Commonwealth v. Daniels, 644 A.2d 1175, 1182–3 (Pa. 1994) (disallowing defense counsel from arguing against the death penalty on scriptural or other religious grounds); State v. Patterson, 482 S.E.2d 760, 766 (S.C. 1997), *cert. denied*, 522 U.S. 853 (1997); State v. Reid, 164 S.W.3d 286, 347 (Tenn. 2005) (affirming a trial court's finding that a prosecutor's scriptural "reference was of a religious nature and constituted error, but … was harmless" insofar as the "reference did not affect the verdict to the prejudice" of the defendant); *see also* Nixon v. State, 533 So. 2d 1078, 1100–1 (Miss. 1987) (holding that the prosecutor's invocation of religion was not reversible error in part, apparently, because of defense counsel's own use of religion), *cert. denied*, 490 U.S. 1102 (1989), *and overruled on other grounds by* Wharton v. State, 734 So. 2d 985 (Miss. 1998).

408 *See* Ceballos, 832 A.2d at 32 ("In a majority of … jurisdictions [that disapprove of prosecutorial religious references], the courts have concluded that … [such] references … [are] always improper. These courts, however, do not concomitantly conclude that all improper religious remarks constitute harmful or reversible error. Rather, the majority approach follows the initial determination of impropriety with

and egregiously inflammatory – for example, arguing to jurors "that by sentencing ... [the defendant] to death, the jury would be 'doing what God says'" and "that imposing the death penalty and destroying ... [the defendant's] mortal body might be the only way to save ... [his or her] eternal soul"[409] – the determinations of misconduct and prejudice are simple,[410] but many times the prosecutor's reference may be more isolated or indirect, or defense counsel may fail to object to the reference or otherwise preserve the issue for appeal and may even legitimize the prosecutor's conduct by independently invoking scripture or making religious references on behalf of the defendant. Ultimately, the permissibility and legal effect of parties' scriptural or other religious invocations appear to entail a jurisdiction-dependent and, for most courts, largely contextual analysis.

A modest number of cases and several academic works also address the extent to which judges, in their decision making or opinion writing, may themselves rely on or advert to religious values, premises, or sources of authority such as religious texts.[411] Relatedly, some rulings address the extent to which a judge may effectively imbue a trial with religious expression or practices, such as by displaying the Ten Commandments behind the bench,[412]

a subsequent analysis as to whether the defendant was prejudiced by the inappropriate remarks."). *See, e.g.*, Bains v. Cambra, 204 F.3d 964, 974–5, 977–8 (9th Cir. 2000) (on collateral review, finding that a prosecutor's religion-related closing arguments involved constitutional error with potentially prejudicial effect, but ultimately concluding that the error was harmless), *cert. denied*, 531 U.S. 1037 (2000).

409 Sandoval, 241 F.3d at 776.

410 *See id.* (concluding with little difficulty that the prosecutor's argument "was both improper and highly prejudicial").

411 Scholarly works include Mark B. Greenlee, *Faith on the Bench: The Role of Religious Belief in the Criminal Sentencing Decisions of Judges*, 26 U. Dayton L. Rev. 1 (2000); Wendell L. Griffen, *The Case for Religious Values in Judicial Decision-Making*, 81 Marq. L. Rev. 513 (1998); Scott C. Idleman, *The Limits of Religious Values in Judicial Decisionmaking*, 81 Marq. L. Rev. 537 (1998); Jack B. Weinstein, *Does Religion Have a Role in Criminal Sentencing?*, 23 Touro L. Rev. 539 (2007); Sanja Zgonjanin, *Quoting the Bible: The Use of Religious References in Judicial Decision-Making*, 9 N.Y. City L. Rev. 31 (2005). More generally, *see* Daniel G. Ashburn, *Appealing to a Higher Authority? Jewish Law in American Judicial Opinions*, 71 U. Det. Mercy L. Rev. 295 (1994); Stephen L. Carter, *The Religiously Devout Judge*, 64 Notre Dame L. Rev. 932 (1989); Teresa S. Collett, *"The King's Good Servant, but God's First": The Role of Religion in Judicial Decisionmaking*, 41 S. Tex. L. Rev. 1277 (2000); J. Michael Medina, *The Bible Annotated: Use of the Bible in Reported American Decisions*, 12 N. Ill. L. Rev. 187 (1991); Mark C. Modak-Truran, *Reenchanting the Law: The Religious Dimension of Judicial Decision Making*, 53 Cath. U. L. Rev. 709 (2004). Mark Greenlee has developed a taxonomy of views regarding the role of religion in judicial decision making, using four models: separatist, publicist, privatist, and wholist. *See* Greenlee, *supra*, at 13–23. "The separatist model maintains that religious convictions should not be relied upon during either deliberation or justification. In other words, religious convictions and legal analysis belong to separate realms and should not be mixed." *Id.* at 13. The publicist model disallows the use of religious convictions during deliberation but relies on religious conviction to justify the judicial decision (*see id.* at 16), whereas "[t]he privatist model flips the realm of permissible reliance from justification to deliberation. It allows for reliance upon religious convictions during deliberations about, but not during justifications of, judicial decisions." *Id.* at 16–17. Finally, the wholist model provides "that religious convictions must or may be relied upon in deliberation and justification." *Id.* at 18.

412 *See, e.g.*, ACLU of Ohio Found., Inc. v. DeWeese, 633 F.3d 424, 432–5 (6th Cir. 2011) (holding that a trial judge violated the Establishment Clause by hanging the a Ten Commandments poster in his courtroom), *cert. denied*, 132 S. Ct. 368 (2011); ACLU of Ohio Found., Inc. v. Ashbrook, 375 F.3d 484, 491–5 (6th Cir. 2004) (same), *cert. denied*, 545 U.S. 1152 (2005). For commentary on the case of Alabama Judge (later Chief Justice) Roy Moore, who eventually came to be known as the "Ten Commandments Judge," *see* S. Joshua Briskman, *Comment, Prayer and the Ten Commandments in the Courtroom: Were the Actions of Circuit Judge Roy Moore Constitutional?*, 25 Am. J. Trial Advoc. 343 (2001); Dustin Zander, *Note, Thou Shalt Not Post the Ten Commandments on the Courtroom Wall: Judge Roy Moore and the Constitution*, 9 Kan. J.L. & Pub. Pol'y 371 (1999).

by using prayers at the opening of court sessions,[413] or by separately leading jurors in prayer.[414] For the most part, the focus here is on the actual employment of religious authority in the process of judicial decision making, particularly in the context of criminal sentencing.

Judges traditionally have significant discretion in their criminal sentencing determinations.[415] Such determinations, however, must abide by any applicable sentencing guidelines and, of course, by constitutional constraints such as equal protection and due process.[416] As the Fourth Circuit has explained,

> a sentencing court can consider the impact a defendant's crimes have had on a community and can vindicate that community's interests in justice. To a considerable extent a sentencing judge is the embodiment of public condemnation and social outrage. As the community's spokesperson, a judge can lecture a defendant as a lesson to that defendant and as a deterrent to others.
>
> Sentencing discretion, however, must be exercised within the boundaries of due process ... Courts have held that sentences imposed on the basis of impermissible considerations ... violate due process ... [S]imilar principles apply when a judge impermissibly takes his [or her] own religious characteristics into account in sentencing.
>
> Our Constitution, of course, does not require a person to surrender his or her religious beliefs upon the assumption of judicial office. Courts, however, cannot sanction sentencing procedures that create the perception of the bench as a pulpit from which judges announce their personal sense of religiosity and simultaneously punish defendants for offending it. Whether or not the trial judge has a religion is irrelevant for purposes of sentencing.[417]

According to several courts, the Fourth's Circuit's "due process logic ... extend[s] only to those circumstances where impermissible personal views expressed at sentencing were the basis of the sentence."[418] That is, although a judge's particular invocation of scripture

413 *See, e.g.*, N.C. Civil Liberties Union Legal Found. v. Constangy, 947 F.2d 1145, 1149–53 (4th Cir. 1991) (holding that the practice, by a judge primarily handling criminal misdemeanors, violated the Establishment Clause), *cert. denied*, 505 U.S. 1219 (1992); Martinez v. State, 984 P.2d 813, 827–9 (Okla. Ct. Crim. App. 1999) (finding that a judge's prayer did not create a basis for a new trial but "warn[ing] trial judges against the practice of offering prayer before criminal trials due to the strong potential for error in the trial proceedings"); *see also* United States v. Walker, 696 F.2d 277, 281–2 (4th Cir. 1982) (criticizing as "needlessly risky" but finding nonprejudicial a judge's practice of having a minister deliver a prayer before opening each trial), *cert. denied sub nom.* Bashlor v. United States, 464 U.S. 891 (1983).

414 *See, e.g.*, State v. Bjorklund, 604 N.W.2d 169, 225 (Neb. 2000) (determining that the practice amounted to harmless error, where the judge "made no comment on the evidence, the law, or the defendant, and ... the jurors did not interpret his words as such"), *cert. denied*, 531 U.S. 843 (2000), *and abrogated on other grounds by* State v. Mata, 745 N.W.2d 229, 278 (Neb. 2008).

415 *See* Hessick & Hessick, *supra* note 388, at 51–3. In turn, "[t]he traditional principle guiding appellate courts faced with challenges to sentences ... is to defer to the discretion of a trial court. As a general rule, 'a federal appellate tribunal will not review a judgment of sentence that is within the statutory maximum unless there be a showing of illegality or abuse of discretion.'" United States v. Bazzano, 570 F.2d 1120, 1130–1 (3d Cir. 1977) (footnote omitted) [quoting United States v. Fessler, 453 F.2d 953, 954 (3d Cir. 1972)], *cert. denied*, 436 U.S. 917 (1978).

416 *See* United States v. De La Cruz, 870 F.2d 1192, 1196 (7th Cir. 1989) ["A trial judge has wide discretion in sentencing which will not be disturbed ... absent a gross abuse of discretion ... This axiom of appellate review applies with great force where ... the sentence imposed is within the statutory limits. However, the trial judge's discretion is, of course, circumscribed by the constitutional rights of the defendant." (citations omitted)]; Hessick & Hessick, *supra* note 388, at 53–5.

417 United States v. Bakker, 925 F.2d 728, 740 (4th Cir. 1991) (footnote and citations omitted).

418 United States v. Traxler, 477 F.3d 1243, 1249 (10th Cir. 2007) [citing Arnett v. Jackson, 393 F.3d 681, 687–8 (6th Cir. 2005), *cert. denied*, 546 U.S. 886 (2005); United States v. Salama, 974 F.2d 520, 522–3

or other religious authority or principles may be imprudent and even amount to legal error, it will not give rise to reversible or other fatal error, whether on due process or other grounds, unless it is shown to have biased or otherwise influenced the nature or duration of the sentence ultimately imposed on the defendant.[419] Moreover, as the Ohio Supreme Court has noted, "a *per se* rule prohibiting all references to religious texts by a sentencing judge would amount to th[e] ... imposition of a particular and restrictive model of judicial decisionmaking" that "would prohibit references to religious convictions in the oral or written justifications of judicial decisions, even though such considerations may unavoidably surface during the judge's private deliberations."[420]

(4th Cir. 1992), *cert. denied*, 507 U.S. 943 (1993); United States v. Roth, 934 F.2d 248, 253 (10th Cir. 1991)], *cert. denied*, 552 U.S. 909 (2007).

419 *See, e.g.*, United States v. Cronin, No. 10-4871, 429 Fed. App'x 241, 243 (4th Cir. May 18, 2011) (*per curiam*) (unpublished) {determining that "[t]he district court's invocation of God's blessings on the victims present at sentencing d[id] not indicate that religion was 'an inappropriate driving force or improper consideration' in the sentence imposed" [quoting United States v. Hoffman, 626 F.3d 993, 999 (8th Cir. 2010), *cert. denied*, 131 S. Ct. 3004 (2011)]}; *Hoffman*, 626 F.3d at 998–9 (holding that sentencing judge's reference to eternal punishment was not an abuse of discretion where it did not affect the sentence imposed); Torres v. State, 124 So. 3d 439 (Fla. Dist. Ct. App. 2013) (vacating a defendant's sentence and remanding for resentencing by a different judge after concluding that "the trial judge's comments [during the sentencing hearing] ... [could] reasonably be construed to suggest that the trial judge based [the defendant's] sentence, at least in part, on religion" and therefore denied the defendant due process); State v. Pattno, 579 N.W.2d 503, 534–6, 543 (Neb. 1998) (holding that trial judge's reading of scripture condemning homosexuality indicated actual bias against defendant convicted of sexual assault and ultimately vacating the sentence and remanding to a different judge for resentencing), *cert. denied*, 525 U.S. 1068 (1999); People v. Carter, 424 N.Y.S.2d 15, 15–16 (N.Y. App. Div. 1980) (determining that "[t]he trial court's use at sentencing of an aphorism ascribed to a religious work in describing the allegedly predatory characteristics evinced by th[e] defendant was not an establishment of religion by the State in violation of the Federal or State Constitutions" and did "not taint ... [the sentence] with the court's personal religious beliefs"), *cert. denied*, 449 U.S. 861 (1980); State v. Earls, 758 S.E.2d 654, 659–60 (N.C. Ct. App. 2014) (finding that sentencing judge's scriptural references were unwarranted but did not amount to legal error); State v. Betters, 835 N.W.2d 249, 255 (Wis. Ct. App. 2013) (finding that trial court's multiple religious references during sentencing were not shown to have actually affected the sentencing decision in light of traditional sentencing criteria).

420 State v. Arnett, 724 N.E.2d 793, 800 (Ohio 2000).

# 15 Family Law

Cynthia Lee Starnes*

This chapter examines key issues at the intersection of religion and family law. The chapter begins with a brief look at the states' accommodation of religious choice in laws governing entry into marriage. Next, the chapter explores the rich topic of religion and custody of children, examining (1) the role of religion as a positive or negative factor in the choice of a primary custodian, (2) restrictions on a parent's behavior or time with the child for reasons related to religion, and (3) enforcement of parental agreements concerning the child's religious upbringing. The chapter then turns to adoption, examining religious matching laws and judicial inquiries into the religion of prospective adoptive parents. Finally, the chapter explores religious choices about divorce, in particular, the question of whether a civil court will enforce a religiously grounded marriage contract.

## A. Entering Marriage: Solemnization

In the United States, marriage has always been the subject of civil authority. The state, rather than the church or the individual, controls access to and exit from the relationship. Marriage may begin with a private agreement, but this agreement gives way to a series of nonnegotiable terms imposed by the state.[1] Simply put, marriage is a status arising from a contract.[2] In an increasing number of instances, however, the state defers to private choices about marriage. A simple and long-standing example of this deference lies in state laws that give parties freedom to solemnize their marriage through a religious ceremony.

Every state permits religious solemnization of marriage.[3] State statutes vary, however, in their willingness to defer to private choices about religious solemnization. Some

* Professor of Law and the John F. Schaefer Chair of Matrimonial Law, Michigan State University College of Law. For their excellent and tireless research assistance, I thank Amanda Jones, Stephanie May, Mitch Olsen, and Sarah Primrose. For her excellent and speedy citation check, I thank Allison Eicher. Finally, I add my hearty thanks to the amazing reference librarians at MSU College of Law, especially on this project to Barbara Bean.

1 As the U.S. Supreme Court stated long ago, "Other contracts may be modified, restricted, or enlarged, or entirely released upon the consent of the parties. Not so with marriage. The relation once formed, the law steps in and holds the parties to various obligations and liabilities." Maynard v. Hill, 125 U.S. 190, 211–12 (1888).

2 *See, e.g.*, Unif. Marriage & Divorce Act § 201 (1973) (hereinafter UMDA) ("Marriage is a personal relationship between a man and a woman arising out of a civil contract to which the consent of the parties is essential.")

3 *See, e.g.*, Md. Code, Ann. Fam. Law § 2-401 (LexisNexis 2006); Mich. Comp. Laws Ann. § 551.101 (2007); N.Y. Dom. Rel Law § 13 (McKinney 2012); Wis. Stat. Ann. § 765.05 (West 2009).

statutes are quite broad, permitting solemnization, for example, "in accordance with any mode of solemnization recognized by any religious denomination."[4] Other statutes are more particularized, identifying specific religious faiths and religious officials who may solemnize a marriage.[5] Some states permit solemnization in religious organizations that have no ministers or priests.[6] Some statutes specify that the religious officiant must perform the ceremony in accord with religious rules or customs.[7]

4 Colo. Rev. Stat. § 14-2-109(1) (2006). *See also* Del. Code Ann. tit. 13, § 106 (West Supp. 2010) (authorizing solemnization by "a clergyperson or minister of any religion."); D.C. Code § 46-406 (LexisNexis Mar. 2012 Supp.) (providing that "every minister of any religious society … may be authorized by any judge … to celebrate marriages"); Idaho Code Ann. § 32-303 (2012) (permitting solemnization by a "priest or minister of the gospel of any denomination."); Mont. Code Ann. § 40-1-301 (2012) (providing that a marriage may be solemnized "in accordance with any mode of solemnization recognized by any religious denomination."); N.J. Stat. Ann. § 37:1–13 (West 2011 Supp.) (permitting solemnization by "every minister of every religion"); Ohio Rev. Code Ann. § 3101.08 (LexisNexis 2008) (permitting solemnization by "[a]n ordained or licensed minister of any religious society or congregation within this state who is licensed to solemnize marriages"); Or. Rev. Stat. Ann. § 106.120 (West 2012) (allowing solemnization by "a clergyperson of any religious congregation"); S.D. Codified Laws § 25-1-30 (2003) (permitting solemnization by "any person authorized by a church to solemnize marriages."); *and* Wash. Rev. Code Ann. § 26.04.050 (West 2012 Supp.) (providing that "any regularly licensed or ordained minister or any priest of any church or religious denomination" can solemnize a marriage).

5 *See, e.g.*, Ala. Code § 30-1-7 (2012) ("Marriages may be solemnized by any licensed minister of the gospel in regular communion with the Christian Church. … The people called Mennonites, Quakers or any other Christian society … may solemnize according to their forms."); La. Rev. Stat. Ann. § 9:202 (West 2008) ("A marriage ceremony may be performed by a priest, minister, rabbi, clerk of the Religious Society of Friends."); Me. Rev. Stat. Ann. tit. 19-A, § 655 (2012) ("[a] person licensed to preach by an association of ministers, religious seminary or ecclesiastical body"); Mass. Gen. Laws Ann. ch. 207, §§ 38, 39 (West 2007) (Solemnization may be performed by "an ordained deacon in the United Methodist Church or in the Roman Catholic Church … rabbi of the Jewish faith … authorized representative of a Spiritual Assembly of the Baha'is … priest or minister of the Buddhist religion; minister in fellowship with the Unitarian Universalist Association … a leader of an ethical Cultural Society … or under the oversight of a Friends or Quaker Monthly meeting."); Okla. Stat. Ann. tit. 43, § 7 (West 2001) (Solemnization may be performed by a preacher, minister, priest, rabbi, or ecclesiastical dignitary.); S.C. Code Ann. § 20-1-20 (2012) ("Only ministers of the Gospel, Jewish rabbis, officers authorized to administer oaths in this State, and the chief or spiritual leader of a Native American Indian entity recognized by the South Carolina Commission for Minority Affairs … are authorized to administer a marriage ceremony in this State"); Tex. Fam. Code Ann. § 2.202 (2012) (Solemnization may be performed by "a licensed or ordained Christian minister or priest, a Jewish rabbi, a person who is an officer of a religious organization and who is authorized by the organization to conduct a marriage ceremony.").

6 *See, e.g.*, Ky. Rev. Stat. Ann. § 402.050 (LexisNexis 1999) (authorizing solemnization by "a religious society that has no officiating minister or priest"); Me. Rev. Stat. Ann. 19-A § 658 (2012) (authorizing "a marriage solemnized among Quakers or Friends in the form practiced in their meeting, or solemnized among members of the Baha'i faith"); Okla. Stat. tit. 43 § 7 (West 2001) (providing that "[m]arriages between persons belonging to the society called Friends, or Quakers, the spiritual assembly of the Baha'is or the Church of Jesus Christ of Latter-Day Saints, which have no ordained minister, may be solemnized by the persons and in the manner prescribed by and practiced in any such society, church, or assembly").

7 *See, e.g.*, Ala. Code § 30-1-7(b) (2012) (permitting solemnization "by the pastor of any religious society according to the rules ordained or custom established by such society"); N.D. Cent. Code § 14-03-09 (2004) (permitting solemnization by "any person authorized by the rituals and practices of any religious persuasion"); 23 Pa. Cons. Stat. Ann. § 1503(b) (West 2010) (permitting solemnization "according to the rules and customs of the society"); Tenn. Code Ann. § 36-3-301(a)(2) (2012) (providing that "any such minister, preacher, pastor, priest, rabbi or other spiritual leader must be ordained or otherwise designated in conformity with the customs of a church, temple or other religious group or organization; and such customs must provide for such ordination or designation by a considered, deliberate, and responsible act"); *and* W. Va. Code Ann. § 48-2-403 (LexisNexis 2004) (requiring that "religious representative authorized to celebrate the rites of marriage shall perform the ceremony of marriage according to the rites and

Few cases have arisen under these solemnization statutes. One question that has been litigated concerns religious organizations in which every member is, or can be, a minister. A few courts have held that where a statute requires proof of ordination, members of the Universal Life Church, who may become ministers simply by asking to be ordained, are not eligible to solemnize marriages.[8] By contrast, another court held that a member of the Jehovah's Witnesses could solemnize a marriage because all members of that faith are ministers.[9]

We turn now to the important and complex topic of religion issues affecting custody of children.

## B. Custody of Children

Custody disputes present some of the most difficult cases in family law.[10] A judge's task is to see beyond acrimony and passion to determine the parenting arrangement that will serve the child's best interest. Yet, even as judges strive to assess the child's interests, they must take care not to tread on the parents' constitutionally protected authority to direct the child's upbringing, a right augmented in religion cases by the Free Exercise and Establishment Clauses of the First Amendment.[11] Not surprisingly, custody decision making has been described as a task worthy of the wisdom of Solomon.[12]

The best interest of the child has long been the standard for custody decision making in the United States. State law, either by statute or by judicial decision, guides judges by identifying multiple factors relevant to the child's best interest. But these factors typically

ceremonies of his or her religious denomination, church, synagogue, spiritual assembly or religious organization and the laws of the State of West Virginia").

8 *See, e.g.*, State v. Lynch, 272 S.E.2d 349 (N.C. 1980); Cramer v. Commonwealth, 202 S.E.2d 911 (Va. 1974), *cert denied*, 419 U.S. 875 (1974); Ravenal v. Ravenal, 338 N.Y.S.2d 324 (N.Y. Spec. Term 1972); Paramore v. Brown, 448 P.2d 699 (Nev. 1968).

9 *See, e.g.*, State *ex rel.* Hayes v. O'Brien, 114 N.E. 2d 729 (Ohio 1953).

10 As one court observed, litigation involving the religious upbringing of children is "likely to evoke strong and passionate reactions by the protagonists, to cause the general public to take sides, and to incite acrimonious debate among religious groups." Zummo v. Zummo, 574 A.2d 1130, 1132 (Pa. Super. Ct. 1990) [quoting Leo Pfeffer, *Religion in the Upbringing of Children*, 35 B.U. L. Rev. 333 (1955)].

11 The seminal Supreme Court cases on parental rights are Meyer v. Nebraska, 262 U.S. 390, 399 (1923) (stating that the liberty guarantee includes the right "to marry, establish a home and bring up children") and Pierce v. Soc'y of Sisters, 268 U.S. 510, 535 (1925) (stating that "[t]he child is not the mere creature of the state; those who nurture him and direct his destiny have the right, coupled with the high duty, to recognize and prepare him for additional obligations"). In the 1970s, the Court again recognized the importance of parental rights. *See* Stanley v. Illinois, 405 U.S. 645, 651 (1972) (observing that the "rights to conceive and to raise one's children have been deemed 'essential'); *and* Wisconsin v. Yoder, 406 U.S. 205, 232 (1972) (recognizing that the "primary role of the parents in the upbringing of their children is now established beyond dispute as an enduring American tradition"). *See also* Troxel v. Granville, 530 U.S. 57, 72–3 (2000) (stating that a state may not "infringe on the fundamental right of parents to make child rearing decisions simply because a state judge believes a 'better' decision could be made"); and Emp't Div. v. Smith, 494 U.S. 872, 881–2 (1990) (recognizing that the combination of parental and religious rights creates a "hybrid" right that requires rigorous review of neutral, generally applicable laws that infringe this right).

12 *See, e.g.*, Zummo, 574 A.2d at 1132 ("Under the best of circumstances … [custody decision making] is a task requiring Solomonic judgment."). The story of King Solomon's task of identifying which of two women was a child's true mother is described in the Judeo-Christian Bible at I Kings 3:23–7. As the court in *Zummo* pointed out, custody courts face the "more agonizing choice between two claimants whose assertions of parentage are both unquestionably true." *Id.* at 1135.

are not weighted and not exclusive, ultimately leaving the custody decision to the broad discretion of an individual trial judge who is considered best positioned to weigh the facts of a particular case.[13]

Traditional best-interest decision making assumes that judges must choose one parent to serve as the child's custodian. The last three decades have seen a dramatic challenge to this assumption as courts increasingly embrace the notion that the child's interest is best served by the continuing involvement of both parents. Custody orders thus often provide for some form of shared parenting.[14] Parents may share *physical* custody, *legal* custody (the right to make important decisions for the child), or both.[15] Consistent with the movement away

13 The Michigan best-interest statute, for example, lists twelve factors relevant to custody; the last is "[a]ny other factor considered by the court to be relevant." Mich. Comp. Laws § 722.23 (2007) provides

> Sec. 3. As used in this act, "best interests of the child" means the sum total of the following factors to be considered, evaluated, and determined by the court:
>
> (a) The love, affection, and other emotional ties existing between the parties involved and the child.
> (b) The capacity and disposition of the parties involved to give the child love, affection, and guidance and to continue the education and raising of the child in his or her religion or creed, if any.
> (c) The capacity and disposition of the parties involved to provide the child with food, clothing, medical care or other remedial care recognized and permitted under the laws of this state in place of medical care, and other material needs.
> (d) The length of time the child has lived in a stable, satisfactory environment, and the desirability of maintaining continuity.
> (e) The permanence, as a family unit, of the existing or proposed custodial home or homes.
> (f) The moral fitness of the parties involved.
> (g) The mental and physical health of the parties involved.
> (h) The home, school, and community record of the child.
> (i) The reasonable preference of the child, if the court considers the child to be of sufficient age to express preference.
> (j) The willingness and ability of each of the parties to facilitate and encourage a close and continuing parent-child relationship between the child and the other parent or the child and the parents.
> (k) Domestic violence, regardless of whether the violence was directed against or witnessed by the child.
> (l) Any other factor considered by the court to be relevant to a particular child custody dispute.

14 The "joint custody" movement swept through states in the 1980s and 1990s. By 1999, thirty-four states had enacted joint custody statutes of some type. Doris Jonas Freed & Timothy B. Walker, *Family Law in the 50 States*, 22 Fam. L. Q. 367, 467 (1989).

15 The Massachusetts custody statute provides a helpful description of the distinction between sole and shared custody and between physical and legal custody:

> "Sole legal custody," one parent shall have the right and responsibility to make major decisions regarding the child's welfare including matters of education, medical care and emotional, moral and religious development.
>
> "Shared legal custody," continued mutual responsibility and involvement by both parents in major decisions regarding the child's welfare including matters of education, medical care and emotional, moral and religious development.
>
> "Sole physical custody," a child shall reside with and be under the supervision of one parent, subject to reasonable visitation by the other parent, unless the court determines that such visitation would not be in the best interest of the child.
>
> "Shared physical custody," a child shall have periods of residing with and being under the supervision of each parent; provided, however, that physical custody shall be shared by the parents in such a way as to assure a child frequent and continued contact with both parents.

Mass. Gen. Laws Ann. ch. 208 § 31 (West 2007). For a comparable definition of "legal custody," *see* Iowa Code § 598.1(3), (5) (West 2005) (describing legal custody as "decision making affecting the child's legal status, medical care, education, extracurricular activities, and religious instruction"). Unfortunately, not

from binary custody models, this section generally uses the terms "primary custodian" or "primary caretaker" to describe the parent with majority responsibility for the child's physical care and "secondary custodian" or "secondary caretaker" to describe the parent with minority responsibility.[16]

### 1. *General Disinclination to Consider Religion in Custody Decision Making*

In 1817, poet Percy Bysshe Shelley lost custody of his children partly because he was an avowed atheist.[17] Much has changed since Shelley's day. Constitutional protections generally prevent contemporary courts from basing custody decisions on a dislike of atheists,[18] on a per se evaluation of the merits of the parents' religious faiths,[19] or on a weighing of the parents' respective religiosity.[20] The U.S. Supreme Court has long recognized that parents' fundamental right to direct the upbringing of their children[21] includes a right to direct the child's religious training,[22] a right that does not disappear at

all courts specify whether "shared custody" refers to legal or physical custody, which causes considerable confusion in the cases and commentary.

16 This usage follows the American Law Institute's lead in urging abandonment of traditional terminology, such as "custodian" and "noncustodian," which suggests a winner-take-all custody model. *See* American Law Institute, Principles of the Law of Family Dissolution: Analysis and Recommendations § 2.05 (2002) (hereinafter ALI Principles). The ALI would generally replace the best-interest custody model with an "approximation" model, under which each parent's custodial responsibility after divorce would quantitatively approximate that parent's share of child care prior to divorce. *See* ALI Principles § 2.08(1). The institute also recommends a rebuttable presumption in favor of joint legal custody. *Id.* at § 2.09.

17 Shelley v. Westbrooke, 37 Eng. Rep. 850, 851 (Ch. 1817). *Shelley* was one of the first English cases to depart from the rule of absolute paternal rights to children. In Shelley's case, the children's mother had died, and the court decided that the maternal grandparents were better candidates for custody than their atheist father.

18 *See, e.g.*, Montgomery Cnty. Dept. of Soc. Serv. v. Sanders, 381 A.2d 1154, 1161 n. 10 (Md. Ct. Spec. App. 1978) ("pronouncement that atheists or persons with 'irreligious principles' are unfit parents is without the ambit of the First Amendment"); and Zummo, 574 A.2d at 1151 ["[T]he First Amendment … precludes a preference for some religion over none, regardless of the *secular* benefits presumed to be at stake." (emphasis in original)].

19 As one court warned, the attitude of a court hearing a custody dispute should be one of "strict impartiality between religions." Osteraas v. Osteraas, 859 P.2d 948, 951 (Idaho 1993). *See also* Zucco v. Garrett, 501 N.E.2d 875, 880 (Ill. App. Ct. 1986) (stating that "religion, in and of itself, must play no role in judicial determinations as to child custody"); *and* Wojnarowicz v. Wojnarowicz, 137 A.2d 618, 621 (N.J. Super. Ct. Ch. Div. 1958) (stating that "intervention in matters of religion is a perilous adventure upon which the judiciary should be loath to embark").

20 *See, e.g.*, Osteraas, 859 P.2d at 954 (Trial court erred in comparing parents' respective religious devoutness but permissibly examined the ethical traits parents would teach children.); *and* Zummo, 574 A.2d at 1152 ("a preference in custody disputes in favor of an active participant in organized religion would violate the Establishment Clause"). For cases in which courts have declined to count a parent's lack of religiosity as a negative factor, *see* Placencia v. Placencia, 3 S.W.3d 497, 502 (Tenn. Ct. App. 1999) (finding no evidence that the father's failure to provide the child with a religious education negatively impacted the child); *In re* Marriage of Oswald, 847 P.2d 251, 253 (Colo. App. 1993) (noting a lack of evidence that mother's failure to consistently take children to church threatened their mental or physical health); *and* Burrows v. Brady, 605 A.2d 1312, 1317 (R.I. 1992) (stating that "a trial justice is not empowered to give preference to a particular religion merely because of its formalized or informalized nature … [or]to favor a consistent approach and disfavor an inconsistent approach to religion").

21 *See supra* note 12.

22 *See* Wisconsin v. Yoder, 406 U.S. at 232 (recognizing "the fundamental interest of parents, as contrasted with that of the State, to guide the religious future and education of their children"); and Prince v. Massachusetts, 321 U.S. 158, 165–6 (1944) (recognizing the "rights of children to exercise their religion, and of parents to give them religious training and to encourage them in the practice of religious belief").

divorce.[23] The right to autonomy in raising one's child, together with the Free Exercise and Establishment Clauses, thus limits the power of the state, acting through a custody court, to fashion orders based on religion. Accordingly, courts have generally declined to base custody on religious factors.

*Osteraas v. Osteraas*[24] provides a good example of this disinclination. In *Osteraas*, the trial judge removed primary custody from the mother partly because she was "completely inactive in any religion."[25] The Idaho Supreme Court reversed, warning that disfavor of nonreligious parents violates the Free Exercise Clause by signaling such parents that they must choose between their beliefs and custody of their children.[26] Preference for a religious parent over a nonreligious one, reasoned the court, also violates the Establishment Clause by appearing to advance a religion.[27] A preference for parents who participate in organized religion, explained another court, "places the authority, influence, support and power of the government on the side of organized religion, a non-secular result that the establishment clause is designed to prevent."[28]

Yet the disinclination to inquire into religion is not absolute. As the U.S. Supreme Court has recognized, "neither rights of religion nor rights of parenthood are beyond limitation."[29] In the custody context, the challenge is thus to identify permissible limitations on parents' constitutional rights. This task requires two steps: (1) identifying cases in which religion is permissibly considered and (2) assessing whether a judicial order based on religious factors is carefully crafted to protect the child's best interest without unnecessarily infringing the parents' constitutional rights.[30] This double challenge may arise in three contexts: (1) choosing a primary custodian based on a parent's religious belief and practice (or lack thereof), (2) limiting a parent's behavior or time with the child for reasons related to religion, and (3) enforcing a parental agreement relating to the child's religious upbringing against the wishes of one parent. We turn first to the role of religion in the judicial choice of a primary custodian.

*See also* Emp't Div. v. Smith, 494 U.S. at 881 n. 1 [noting that "[t]he Court's holding in *Pierce* stands as a charter of the rights of parents to direct the religious upbringing of their children" (quoting Wisconsin v. Yoder at 233)].

23 *See* Zummo, 574 A.2d at 1139 (reasoning that divorce does not extinguish or diminish constitutionally protected parental authority over children because such a view would be inconsistent with recognition of such parental authority even where parents were never married). Because parental rights do not depend on marriage, some of the custody cases in this chapter involve disputes between parents who were never married.

24 Osteraas v. Osteraas, 859 P.2d 948 (Idaho 1993).

25 *Id.* at 951.

26 *Id.* at 952.

27 *Id.* at 953. A preference for churchgoers also raises equal protection concerns because studies show that more women attend church than men. *See* Zummo, 574 A.2d at 1152 n. 38.

28 Zucco, 501 N.E.2d at 881.

29 Prince, 321 U.S. at 166 (affirming conviction of child's custodian for violating statute forbidding children from selling magazines in street or public places).

30 *See In re* Marriage of McSoud, 131 P.3d 1208, 1216 (Colo. App. 2006) (infringement of parental rights "permissible only if it is necessary to promote a compelling state interest and does so in the least restrictive manner possible"); Zummo, 574 A.2d at 1140 (any infringement of parental rights "would have to be the least intrusive measures adequate to protect the ... [child's] interests"); *and* Khalsa v. Khalsa, 751 P.2d 715, 721 (N.M. Ct. App. 1988) (any restrictions on a parent's visitation rights must be "narrowly tailored so as to minimize interference with the parents' religious freedom").

## 2. *Religion as a Factor in the Choice of a Primary Custodian*

Notwithstanding the general reluctance of most courts to consider religion in custody cases, a parent's religious beliefs and practices (or lack thereof) have sometimes counted as a factor in the court's choice of a primary custodian. This factor may carry either positive or negative weight. We begin by considering the positive role religion has sometimes played in a parent's battle for primary custody.

### a. Religion as a Positive Factor in the Choice of a Primary Custodian

Parents who participate in organized religion have sometimes received favorable treatment in custody courts. This preference may be traced to a perception that a religious parent is well suited to ensure the child's moral and spiritual well-being or, less often, to a sometimes candidly stated preference for churchgoers.

i. *The Child's Moral and Spiritual Well-Being.* Courts sometimes consider the child's "moral" or "spiritual" well-being in determining the custodial arrangement that will serve his or her best interests.[31] Indeed, some state statutes specifically authorize courts to consider these factors.[32] In a related factor, some statutes authorize courts to consider a parent's

[31] In Gancas v. Schultz, 683 A.2d 1207 (Pa. Super. Ct. 1996), for example, the court reversed a lower court's ruling partly because it failed to consider factors that affect the child's moral and spiritual well-being. "Religion," said the court, "while not determinative, 'is an important matter and should be given some consideration in child custody matters."' *Id.* at 1213 [quoting Boylan v. Boylan, 577 A.2d 218, 219 (Pa. Super. Ct. 1990), *overruled on other grounds by* G.B. v. M.M.B., 670 A.2d 714 (Pa. Super. Ct. 1996)]. *See also* Schaefer v. Cusack, 722 A.2d 73, 76 (Md. Ct. Spec. App. 1998) {"a court may properly consider … [the] spiritual and moral well-being of the child" [quoting Hild v. Hild, 157 A.2d 442, 446 (Md. 1960)]}; Burnham v. Burnham, 304 N.W.2d 58, 61 (Neb. 1981) (A court must consider "not only the spiritual and temporal welfare but also the minor's further training, education, morals, and the ability of the proposed guardian to best take care of the child."); Dean v. Dean, 232 S.E.2d 470, 471–2 (N.C. Ct. App. 1977) {"[J]udge's concern is to place the child in an environment which will best promote the full development of his physical, mental, moral and spiritual faculties." [quoting Blackley v. Blackley, 204 S.E.2d 678, 681 (N.C. 1974)]}; Com *ex rel.* Pruss v. Pruss, 344 A.2d 509, 510 (Pa. Super. Ct. 1975) ("[t]he best interests of … [a child] are not limited to physical well-being, but include moral, intellectual, and spiritual welfare"); and Burrows, 605 A.2d at 1315 ("All other considerations are subordinate to the child's intellectual, moral, physical, and spiritual well-being.").

[32] *See, e.g.*, Alaska Stat. § 25.24.150(c)(1) (West 2010) [requiring court to consider "the physical, emotional, mental, *religious* and social needs of the child" (emphasis added)]; Haw. Rev. Stat. § 571-46(5) (West 2011) [authorizing court to hear testimony to determine "what is for the best physical, mental, moral, and *spiritual* well-being of the child" (emphasis added)]; La. Civ. Code Ann. art. 134(2) (1994) (listing as a relevant factor "[t]he capacity and disposition of each party to give the child … spiritual guidance"); Mass. Gen. Laws Ann. ch. 208 § 31 (West 2007) [stating that "[w]hen considering the happiness and welfare of the child, the court shall consider whether or not the child's present or past living conditions adversely affect his physical, mental, *moral* or emotional health" (emphasis added)]; and S.C. Code Ann. § 20-3-160 (1976) (court may "make such orders touching … what … security shall be given for … the best spiritual as well as other interests of the children"). The Alaska statute has been narrowly construed. *See* Bonjour v. Bonjour, 592 P.2d 1233, 1239–40 (Alaska 1979) (limiting statute "to cases where particular religious practices or beliefs pose a substantial threat of or would result in actual physical, emotion [*sic*] or mental injury to the child or will otherwise have a harmful effect on the child" or where the child has "actual religious needs"). While a statutory reference to moral or spiritual factors directs a court's attention to these issues, the absence of such a statutory reference will typically not preclude a court from considering them since most statutory lists of relevant factors are nonexclusive.

"moral fitness," apparently as evidence of that parent's capacity to ensure the child's moral well-being.[33]

The distinction between morality and spirituality is sometimes blurred in custody cases. As one court opined, "[r]eligion and morality are so closely interwoven in the lives of most people that it is difficult to say whether good moral character could be molded in a child without some religious training."[34] In judging the "moral environment" in which children are raised, one court noted approvingly that the father "conscientiously adheres to religious teachings," whereas the mother, who had an "adulterous affair," had "unquestionably been less than moral."[35] Other courts have questioned the legitimacy of using religious activity as a proxy for moral fitness. Examination of parents' ethical traits, warned one court, must "not serve as a pretext, inadvertent or otherwise, for delving into an inquisition of either parent's religion or degree of devotion."[36]

Apart from the question of a child's general moral and spiritual well-being, courts sometimes conclude that a child has specific "religious" or "spiritual" needs.[37] Such a child may have a religious identity so that his or her well-being depends on an opportunity to continue prior religious training.[38] This consideration may translate into a

[33] *See, e.g.*, La. Civ. Code Ann. art. 134(6) (1994) (listing as a relevant factor the "moral fitness of each party, insofar as it affects the welfare of the child"); Mich. Comp. Laws § 722.23(f) (2005) (authorizing courts to consider "[t]he moral fitness of the parties" in determining the child's best interests); N.D. Cent. Code § 14-09-06.2(1)(f) (2009) (including in list of best-interest factors "the moral fitness of the parents, as that fitness impacts the child"); and Utah Code Ann. § 30-3-10(1)(a)(i) (2006) (including in list of relevant factors the "demonstrated moral standards of each of the parties"). *See also* Alaska Stat. § 25.24.150(c)(1),(2) (2010) (requiring court to consider "the capacity and desire of each parent" to meet the child's religious needs).

[34] Robert O. v. Judy E, 395 N.Y.S.2d 351, 352 (N.Y. Fam. Ct. 1977).

[35] McNamara v. McNamara, 181 N.W.2d 206, 209 (Iowa 1970). *See also* Lipsey v. Lipsey, 450 So.2d 1095, 1097 (Ala. Civ. App. 1984) (stating that the father "was the parent most concerned with the children's care and religious nurture" and that he "takes [the children] to church and attempts to instill in them proper moral values"); Fitzgerald v. Fitzgerald, 464 A.2d 110, 112 (D.C. 1983) (noting that a parent's "regularly attend[ing] church, an institution which assists in moral training, and tak[ing] his child along" "properly can enter a custody determination"); Davidson v. Coit, 899 So.2d 904, 911 (Miss. Ct. App. 2005) (concluding that because the father "regularly takes the children to church ... there was evidence to support the chancellor's decision to weigh the moral fitness factor in his favor"); Blevins v. Bardwell, 784 So.2d 166, 175 (Miss. 2001) (reasoning that consideration of parent's ability to provide a "future religious example" could "theoretically" fall within the category of "moral fitness"); Latimer v. Farmer, 602 S.E.2d 32, 36 (S.C. 2004) (stating that the "[f]ather has taken the responsibility for the moral upbringing of Child by taking her to church and reading her Bible stories"); *and* Kisling v. Allison, 541 S.E.2d 273, 276 (S.C. Ct. App. 2001) (stating that "[a] child's regular attendance in a house of worship arguably suggests the child live[d] in a home where moral development is fostered").

[36] Osteraas, 859 P.2d at 954 n. 6. The court in *Osteraas* shunned the word "moral" in favor of "ethical" because the former has "religious connotations." *See also* Zucco, 501 N.E.2d at 880 ("A party's 'religiousness,' standing alone, is an uncertain guide to his fitness as a parent.").

[37] The Alaska custody statute expressly authorizes courts to consider the child's religious needs in determining her best interest. *See* Alaska Stat. § 25.24.150(c)(1) (West 2010). *See also* S.C. Code Ann. § 20-3-160 (1976) (best-interest factors include which parent can best satisfy the "spiritual interests" of the child).

[38] For an example of statutory recognition of the child's interest in continuing prior religious training, *see* Mich. Comp. Laws § 722.23(b) (2005) (listing as one factor in determining the child's best interest "[t]he capacity and disposition of the parties involved to give the child love, affection, and guidance and to continue the education and raising of the child in his or her religion or creed, if any"). For a broad interpretation of this language, *see In re* Barlow, 273 N.W. 2d 35, 44 (Mich. 1978) (stating that even for children without prior religious training, "consideration of religious factors serves to promote values highly prized in our society").

preference for the parent who is better positioned to continue that training – often the parent who practices the religion in which the child was raised.

In *MacLagan v. Klein*,[39] for example, the father was Jewish, the mother was Christian, and the six-year-old child had been raised in the Jewish faith. The trial court granted the father sole decision-making authority over the child's religious training, and the mother appealed, arguing that the judge improperly preferred the father's religion. The appellate court affirmed, holding that the trial judge properly considered that the parties had agreed to rear the child in the Jewish faith,[40] that the child "had a positive sense of identity as a Jew," and that the child had experienced "stress and anxiety as a result of her exposure to two competing religions."[41]

Courts have sometimes been hesitant to conclude that a child has developed a religious identity. In *Bonjour v. Bonjour*,[42] for example, the trial judge awarded primary custody of the five-year-old child to the father partly on the ground that the father could best meet the child's religious needs.[43] The father was involved in "an organized religious community" and had been "principally involved in … [the child's] religious education," whereas the mother was a "non-churchgoing Christian" who "evidenced a passive interest" in the child's religious development.[44] On appeal, the court remanded, cautioning that a child's "religious needs" may be considered only if they are "actual" rather than "presumed."[45] The court observed that the trial judge had not found that the child had religious needs and that, as a threshold matter, a religious identity requires that a child be mature enough to choose among religions or to choose to avoid religion.[46] The trial judge,

39 MacLagan v. Klein, 473 S.E. 2d 778 (N.C. Ct. App. 1996), *overruled on other grounds* by Pulliam v. Smith, 501 S.E.2d 898 (S.C. 1998).

40 For a discussion of the effect of parental agreements on a child's religious upbringing, *see* Section B.4 of this chapter.

41 MacLagan, 473 S.E.2d at 785–7. For a discussion of restrictions on parental activity on the ground that exposure to inconsistent religions is harmful to the child, *see* Section B.3.b of this chapter. In another case involving a child with prior religious training, the court in *In re* Davis, 30 S.W.3d 609 (Tex. App. 2000), affirmed an order granting a father's petition to modify his visitation to allow him to take his daughters, who were fifteen and six, to catechism classes and to allow the older daughter to attend confirmation classes. During the marriage, the parents had raised their children in the Catholic Church, but after the divorce, the mother stopped attending church. In the court's view, the older child, who was sixteen, had "reached an age of importance in the exercise of religious beliefs." *Id.* at 615. *See also* McCain v. McCain, 580 N.W.2d 485 (Mich. Ct. App. 1998) (holding that trial judge reasonably considered father more prepared to continue children's religious training because the mother had left the family church), *and* Gancas, 683 A.2d at 1213 (remanding case in which judge awarded primary custody to father without considering the child's spiritual welfare, namely, that the mother was taking the child to church, whereas the father, "an admitted agnostic, does not attend church.")

42 Bonjour v. Bonjour, 592 P.2d 1233 (Alaska 1979).

43 *Id.* at 1239.

44 *Id.* at 1236 n. 4 & 1237 n. 5.

45 *Id.* at 1244. The *Bonjour* court gave two examples of a child whose mature preference might appropriately affect the custody decision: a fifteen-year old child who (1) is a "devout adherent to a particular religion" or (2) has "a profound aversion to formal religious training of any sort." *Id.* at 1239–40.

46 As the court noted, the question of maturity will vary from case to case. The court cited with approval *Wojnarowicz* (137 A.2d 618), in which the court held that children aged three, five, and seven were not mature enough to form an "intelligent opinion" about religion. Bonjour, 592 P.2d at 1240 n.14. In *Zummo* (574 A.2d at 1149), the court observed that although a uniform age of maturity is not set, "children twelve or older are generally considered mature enough to assert a religious identify, while children eight and under are not." The *Zummo* court rejected the lower court's statement that the children, aged three, four,

concluded the court, moved "too far down the path of religious philosophy," entangling itself in an inappropriate judicial inquiry.[47]

In an exception to its general position that custody should be decided without regard to religion,[48] the American Law Institute would allow consideration of religious activity to the "minimum degree necessary" to protect "the child's ability to practice a religion that has been a significant part of the child's life."[49] The exception is limited to "children who have experienced an upbringing for a substantial period in a particular religious tradition and have developed their own identity in, or allegiance to, that religion."[50]

Beyond the cases in which a child has developed a religious identity lies a collection of more troubling cases in which courts have expressly preferred a churchgoing parent to a nonreligious or less-religious parent.

ii. *Preferences for Churchgoing Parents.* In a surprising number of cases, given constitutional constraints on religious preferences, custody courts have commented favorably on a parent's church attendance.[51] Churchgoing (or nonchurchgoing), however,

and eight, had a religious identity, noting among other things, the mother's statement that the childrens' Jewish education had just begun. *Id.* at 1149.

47 Bonjour, 592 P.2d at 1243. *See also* Zummo, 574 A.2d at 1149 ["In order to avoid arrogating to itself unconstitutional authority to declare orthodoxy in determining religious identity, courts only recognize a *legally* cognizable religious identity when such an identity is asserted by the child itself, and then only if the child has reached sufficient maturity and intellectual development to understand the significance of such an assertion." (emphasis in original)].

48 ALI Principles *supra* note 17, § 2.12 cmt. d.

49 *Id.* § 2.12(1)(c). The ALI reasons that "at some point in the development of a religious identity, a child may acquire his or her own interest in religious freedom that warrants consideration along with the parents' interests." *Id.* § 2.12 cmt. d. A second exception involves cases in which a parent's religious activity threatens harm to the child. For a discussion of the "harm standard" for parents' religious activity as a negative factor, *see* Section B.2.b of this chapter.

50 ALI Principles, *supra* note 17, § 2.12 cmt. d.

51 *See, e.g.*, Strickland v. Strickland, 235 So.2d 833, 835 (Ala. 1970) (noting that the father regularly took his children to church); Lipsey, 450 So.2d at 1097 (noting that the father takes the children to church and "attempts to instill in them proper moral values"); Moore v. Smith, 499 S.W.2d 634, 637 (Ark. 1973) (noting testimony that the "[father] was a member of his church, attended with reasonable regularity, and … [took] his son with him"); Todd v. Casciano, 569 S.E.2d 566, 570 (Ga. Ct. App. 2002) (noting that the father "attended church regularly"); Carey v. Carey, 211 N.W.2d 342, 345 (Iowa 1973) (noting the father's "conscientious efforts to further [the children's] church attendance and religious education"); Lewis v. Lewis, 537 P.2d 204, 208 (Kan. 1975) (noting that the father is a member of the Methodist Church and that he takes the children to church with him); Welch v. Welch, 307 So.2d 737, 739 (La. Ct. App. 1975) (noting that the father and children "attend church together every Sunday"); Weigand v. Houghton, 730 So.2d 581, 587 (Miss. 1999) (noting that the "mother has seen that [the child] is taken to church and undergone religious training" and that the chancellor "weighed this factor heavily in her favor"); Wilson v. Wilson, 590 P.2d 1136, 1139 (Mont. 1979) (noting the father's "regular church attendance and his willingness to assist the children in their moral and spiritual development"); *In re* King, 181 S.E.2d 221, 221 (N.C. Ct. App. 1971) (noting that the mother "participates in local church and college activities"); Latimer, 602 S.E.2d at 36 (noting that the "[f]ather has taken the responsibility for the moral upbringing of Child by taking her to church and reading her Bible stories"); Johnson v. Johnson, 536 S.W.2d 620, 621 (Tex. Civ. App. 1976) (noting that the father "wants the children to attend church"). *See also* Peacock v. Peacock, 903 So. 2d 506, 513–14 (La. Ct. App. 2005) (concluding that both parents provide the child "with spiritual guidance, sending her to church and going with her"). For a case in which a court noted the "irregularity" of the father's church attendance and questioned the sincerity of his "religious commitment," *see* Shainwald v. Shainwald, 395 S.E.2d 441, 446 (S.C. Ct. App. 1990) (upholding award of custody to the father nonetheless).

rarely plays a *determinative* role; rather, it is weighed along with other best-interest factors.[52]

When a court prefers a churchgoing parent, it implicitly disfavors a less religious or nonchurchgoing parent who is competing for primary custody.[53] Indeed, courts have sometimes noted disapprovingly that a parent who does not attend church is not likely to take the child to church.[54] In these and other cases, courts have contrasted the behavior of a nonchurchgoing parent with what is thought to be the more commendable behavior of the other parent who takes the child to church.[55] Given the First Amendment concerns raised in preferring

52 As some courts have stated, churchgoing may be considered as long as it is not the sole or dispositive factor in the custody decision. *See, e.g.*, Turner v. Turner, 824 So.2d 652, 655–6 (Miss. Ct. App. 2002) (stating that religion cannot be the sole basis for a custody decision but concluding that the father's churchgoing was not "unduly emphasized"); and Gancas, 683 A.2d at 1213 [stating that "[r]eligion while not determinative, 'is an important matter and should be given some consideration in child custody matters'" (quoting Boylan, 577 A.2d at 219)]; *and* Pountain v. Pountain, 503 S.E.2d 757, 761 (S.C. Ct. App. 1998) (stating that "[a]lthough the religious beliefs of parents are not dispositive in a child custody dispute, they are a factor relevant to determining the best interest of a child"). For cases in which a court favorably weighed a parent's churchgoing but ultimately awarded primary custody to the other parent, *see* Cousins v. Smith, 491 S.W.2d 587, 590 (Ark. 1973) (noting that "[p]erhaps the matter of greatest concern is the contrast in church attendance habits in these homes," with only the mother taking the children to church regularly, but upholding order granting father custody based on other factors); *and* Deason v. Deason, 759 So.2d 219, 221 (La. Ct. App. 2000) (noting that "[t]he father only casually attends churches of his religious denomination, while the mother is a member and regularly attends one specific church of her religious denomination," but affirming order granting father primary custody based on other factors).

53 *See* Zucco, 501 N.E.2d at 881 (noting that "giving preference to parents who are active adherents of organized religion … punish[es] parents who do not believe in God or going to church by making it less likely that they will gain custody of their children"). For a discussion of courts' general disinclination to weigh parents' respective religiosity, *see* Section B.1 of this chapter.

54 Plum v. Plum, 478 S.W.2d 882, 883 (Ark. 1972) (noting that the "[father] did not attend church and would not require his children to attend"); Gallo v. Gallo, 440 A.2d 782, 786 n. 4 (Conn. 1981) (noting that the father "had made no effort to have … [the child] receive any religious education, although the boy has demonstrated to his mother through his inquiries an interest in his Creator and the church Sunday School"); Brown v. Brown, 877 So.2d 1228, 1232 (La. Ct. App. 2004) (noting that the mother never said she was "interested in these children making and attending church services"); Dean, 232 S.E.2d at 471 (noting trial court finding that the mother's "failure to take … [the child] to church and Sunday School was jeopardizing his spiritual values"); Pountain, 503 S.E.2d at 759 (noting that the mother professes to be a Christian, whereas the father is an agnostic); *and In re* Davis, 30 S.W.3d at 614 (noting that "after the divorce [the] mother stopped attending church").

55 Firestone v. Parker, 451 So.2d 329, 330 (Ala. Civ. App. 1984) (noting that "the father takes the child to church, but there is no indication that the mother does so"); Sanders v. Sanders, 435 So.2d 123, 124 (Ala. Civ. App. 1983) (noting that the mother "took … [the children] to church regularly, and the father did not take them to church"); Woodard v. Woodard, 244 So.2d 595, 597 (Ala. Civ. App. 1971) (noting that "during the time that … [the mother] had custody of the child, she had never taken him to Sunday School, whereas he was taken to Sunday School nearly every Sunday by his father and stepmother"); Crowson v. Crowson, 742 So.2d 107, 111 (La. Ct. App. 1999) (noting that the father "attends church with … [the child] and helps him say his prayers at night," whereas the mother "no longer attends services"); Tweedel v. Tweedel, 484 So.2d 260, 262 (La. Ct. App. 1986) (noting that "[t]he child attends church regularly with the mother and receives religious instruction, [whereas] [t]he father testified that he has not brought the child to church because the child did not want to go and that he would not force the child to go to church"); Quinn v. Quinn, 412 So.2d 649, 655 (La. Ct. App. 1982) (noting that "[w]ith the father the child would be in a religious, churchgoing environment [whereas mother] did not attend church with the father and child while they lived together"); Storlien v. Storlien, 386 N.W.2d 812, 813 (Minn. Ct. App. 1986) (noting that the mother "is a religious person who attends church on a regular basis [and] would probably provide more constant attention to the children's religious education and training than would … [the father who] was not a member of any organized religion and did not attend church services"); Blevins, 784

a religious parent over a less religious or nonreligious one, it is not surprising that courts have attempted to justify a preference for churchgoers in secular terms. Some courts have stated that churchgoing evidences a parent's "moral fitness"[56] and past efforts to further the child's moral development.[57] A few courts have elaborated on this justification. As one judge opined about parents who were both nonchurchgoers,

> I was a little bit distraught in finding that there was no particular affiliation with a church. Probably 95 percent of the criminals that I see before me come from homes where there's no … established religious affiliation.[58]

As another court reasoned,

> [c]hurches are traditionally places of calm and concern. At virtually no expense to parents, churches offer children the opportunity for interaction with groups of other children as well as adults, in an environment conducive to character-building.[59]

The general reluctance of courts to base custody on an evaluation of the merits of a parent's religious activity (or lack thereof) ensures that the preference for churchgoers is a minority

So. 2d at 175 (noting that although the father "does at times pray with … [the child] and has attended a non-denominational 'house of prayer,' [the mother] seems much more committed and consistent in her Catholic upbringing"); *In re* Guardianship of J.N.T., 910 So. 2d 631, 634 (Miss. Ct. App. 2005) (noting that, in a contest between nonparents, one party "does not attend church and it seems she does not really care for the institution of marriage," whereas the other party attends church with his wife); Turner, 824 So.2d at 655 (noting that the father "has consistently taken the child to church," whereas "[t]here has been little religious training shown by the mother"); Pacheco v. Pacheco, 770 So.2d 1007, 1010–11 (Miss. Ct. App. 2000) (noting that the father "took his daughter to church with him," whereas "there was no evidence as to religious activity taking place with … [the mother] and her daughter since the separation"); Graci v. Graci, 590 N.Y.S.2d 377, 379 (N.Y. App. Div. 1992) (noting that mother "takes the children to church; [the father] does not"); Gancas, 683 A.2d at 1213 (noting the mother's testimony that "she takes … [the child] to church whenever … [the child] is with her [whereas the] [f]ather, an admitted agnostic, does not attend church"); Sutherland v. Sutherland, 831 S.W.2d 283, 286–7 (Tenn. Ct. App. 1991) (noting that "[t]he mother is very involved with church and teaches in the Sabbath school. She takes … [the child] with her to church when she has him for visitation. On the other hand, the father is not very involved in church activities.").

56 *See, e.g.*, Blevins, 784 So.2d at 175 (stating that trial court's consideration of "future religious example," which included evidence that father "did not remember the last time he was inside a church," was permissible evidence of "moral fitness of the parents" or "other factors relevant to the parent-child relationship"); Davidson, 899 So.2d at 911 (noting that because the father "regularly takes the children to church," there was "evidence to support the chancellor's decision to weigh the moral fitness factor in his favor"); Mixon v. Sharp, 853 So.2d 834, 840 (Miss. Ct. App. 2003) (noting as a factor in favor of father's "moral fitness" that he "is a Sunday school teacher at his church, and until recently, was a church officer"). *See also* Carey, 211 N.W.2d at 345 (stating that a parent's "conscientious efforts to further [the children's] church attendance and religious education" was permissible to show parent's "affection and concern, and dedication to the children's best interest." For a discussion of "moral fitness" as a best-interest factor, *see* Section B.2.a.i of this chapter.

57 *See, e.g.*, Fitzgerald, 464 A.2d at 111 (noting that the father, but not the mother, had "seen fit to expose the child to … institutional training … [and that] the church is an excellent institution which can help to train in morals"); *and* Kisling, 541 S.E.2d at 276 (noting that "[a] child's regular attendance in a house of worship arguably suggests [that] the child lives in a home where moral development is fostered").

58 Carson v. Carson, 401 N.W.2d 632, 635–6 (Mich. Ct. App. 1986) (concluding that because neither party was religious, the parents were "equal" in this regard).

59 McLemore v. McLemore, 762 So.2d 316, 320 (Miss. 2000) (holding that order requiring parents to ensure that the children attend church did not violate First Amendment but nevertheless modifying order to state that parents should be "vitally interested" in child's regular spiritual training).

position. A trial court's preference for churchgoing, however, may be held harmless if other factors support the custody decision.[60]

Though the religious faith of some parents has improved their case for primary custody, the religious faith of other parents has undercut that case. We turn now to the recurring scenario in which courts count a parent's religion as a negative factor in the custody contest.

### b. Religion as a Negative Factor in the Choice of a Primary Custodian

As we have seen, the parental right to direct the child's religious upbringing, together with the Free Exercise and Establishment Clauses of the Constitution, generally insulates parents' religious beliefs and practices from judicial scrutiny in a custody contest.[61] But when a parent's religious practices threaten to harm the child, that activity may count as a negative factor in the custody decision. Authority to consider harm is sometimes traced to *Wisconsin v. Yoder*.[62] Recognizing "the rights of parents to direct the religious upbringing of their children," the Supreme Court in *Yoder* held that Amish parents could not be penalized for failing to comply with state compulsory school attendance laws.[63] The Court cautioned, however, that "the power of the parent, even when linked to a free exercise claim, may be subject to limitation ... if it appears that parental decisions will jeopardize the health or safety of the child, or have a potential for significant social burdens."[64] A parent's religious practices thus may count as a negative, sometimes dispositive factor in the custody contest if those practices threaten the child's physical or mental well-being. Courts employ a variety of tests to determine whether parental religious practices meet this threshold. Most courts take one of three approaches.[65]

[60] *See, e.g.*, Osteraas, 859 P.2d at 954 (stating that consideration of a parent's religion may be harmless error where there is other evidence sufficient to support a custody order and remanding for determination of whether there was such evidence); and Zucco, 501 N.E.2d at 879 (stating that there is no reversible error where evidence of a parent's religious affiliation is admitted only to gather "insight into the entire family picture" but concluding that trial judge improperly cited religion as one of two factors that tipped the scale in favor of father).

[61] *See* Section B.1 of this chapter.

[62] Wisconsin v. Yoder, 406 U.S. 205 (1972). *See, e.g.*, *In re* Marriage of Hadeen, 619 P.2d 374, 380 (Wash. Ct. App. 1980) ["Cases involving religion as an aspect of a custody dispute generally comport with the language of *Wisconsin v. Yoder* ... regarding a showing that the parental decisions will jeopardize the child's health or safety." (citation omitted)]; *In re* Marriage of Weiss, 49 Cal. Rptr. 2d 339, 342 (Cal. Dist. Ct. App. 1996) ["The United States Supreme Court specifically has held parental authority in matters of religious upbringing may be encroached upon only upon a showing of a 'substantial threat' of harm to the 'physical or mental health of the child or to the public safety, peace, order, or welfare.'" (quoting Wisconsin v. Yoder)]; *and* Zummo, 547 A.2d at 1140 ["If the other parent objects [to one parent's religious indoctrination of the child] and seeks restrictions, the objecting parent must establish a substantial risk of harm in the absence of restriction proposed." (citing Wisconsin v. Yoder)]. *See also* Pater v. Pater, 588 N.E.2d 794, 798–9 (Ohio 1992) ["[A] parent's actions are not insulated from the domestic relations court's inquiry just because they are based on religious beliefs, especially actions that will harm the child's mental or physical health." (citing Prince, 321 U.S. 158)].

[63] Wisconsin v. Yoder, 406 U.S. at 233.

[64] *Id.* at 233–4. *See also* Prince, 321 U.S. at 166 (stating that "neither rights of religion nor rights of parenthood are beyond limitation" and affirming conviction of child's custodian for violating statute forbidding children from selling magazines in street or public places).

[65] Not every court that gives a parent's religious practices negative effect identifies the standard of "harm" required for such consideration. *See, e.g.*, Roberts v. Roberts, 586 S.E.2d 290, 295 (Va. Ct. App. 2003) (affirming order denying father in-person visitation on evidence of his "bitter denunciation of mother to the children, his eschatological threats concerning mother and, on occasion, the children, and his

Under the first approach, courts set a low threshold for harm, applying what is essentially the "best-interest test." These courts consider a parent's religious beliefs and practices if they appear adverse to the child's best interest.[66] As one court explained, a court may consider "evidence of the religious views or practices of a party seeking custody … to the extent that such views or practices are demonstrated to bear upon the physical or emotional welfare of the child."[67]

The oft-cited case of *Burnham v. Burnham*[68] provides a good example of this first approach. In *Burnham*, the court reversed an order granting custody to the mother, concluding that her religious beliefs "if continued … will have a deleterious effect not only on the relationship between the father and his daughter but upon the well-being of the child herself."[69] In particular, the court noted (1) the mother's belief that her marriage and the child were both illegitimate, (2) the mother's willingness to cut the child out of her life if she disobeyed church rules, and (3) the racist views held by the mother and, apparently, her church.[70]

In a second approach, many courts allow consideration of parents' religious beliefs and practices only to the extent they pose a "reasonable" or "substantial" likelihood of harm.[71] *Harris v. Harris*[72] provides a good example of this approach. In *Harris*, the

active undermining the ability of mother and the children to maintain a proper and wholesome relationship" without identifying a general test for determining when a parent's religious practices should be considered).

66 *See, e.g.*, Hoedebeck v. Hoedebeck, 948 P.2d 1240, 1242 (Okla. Civ. App. 1997) (stating that "the court may not decide that one religion is better or worse than another, but it does have the duty to determine the best interests of the children"); *and* Birch v. Birch, 463 N.E.2d 1254, 1257 (Ohio 1984) (reasoning that the "obligation of the court to consider the best interests of the children serves to protect them from emotionally unstable and fanatically misguided custodial parents, whether the parents' behavior is religiously motivated or otherwise, while simultaneously safeguarding the parents' fundamental constitutional freedom to raise their children as they deem proper").

67 Bienenfeld v. Bennett-White, 605 A.2d 172, 182 (Md. Ct. Spec. App. 1992).

68 304 N.W.2d 58 (Neb. 1981).

69 *Id.* at 62.

70 *Id.* at 60–1. The court quoted a letter in which the mother wrote: "I have discovered that there exists in this world, a master plot on the part of the Jews and Communists, to gain control of the world." *Id.* at 60. *See also* Bienenfeld, 605 A.2d at 182 (stating that mother's religious views were relevant to the children's emotional well-being to the extent that her "fidelity" to those views threatened the children's relationship with their father); Hoedebeck, 948 P.2d at 1242 (concluding that modification order granting the father sole custody was in the children's best interest after the mother's religious conversion prompted her to deny unsupervised visitation to the grandparents, to use the children as messengers to communicate with the father, and to pressure the children to hide things from the father, resulting in the children becoming "detached [and] weepy"); Birch, 463 N.E.2d at 1255–6 (affirming order denying custody to both parents and finding that the mother's adoption of "ultra-conservative" religion led her to insist that "the children be clothed so that little of their body shows, even in the hottest days of summer," to leave the children unsupervised because "God would look after them," and to make the children "rise before dawn on Sundays to attend multiple church services"); *and* Holder v. Holder, 872 N.E.2d 1239, 1243 (Ohio Ct. App. 2007) (noting that while custody was not at issue, the mother's "unrelenting refusal to place … [the child's] needs above her own religious convictions clearly justified the trial court's grant of sole custody of … [the child] to … [the father]"). For a case in which a court rejected a trial court's conclusion that a father's new "life in the Lord" did not negatively affect the children's best interest, *see* Stolarick v. Novak, 584 A.2d 1034, 1036 (Pa. Super. Ct. 1991).

71 *See, e.g.*, *In re* Marriage of Short, 698 P.2d 1310, 1313 (Colo. 1985) ("[E]vidence of a party's religious beliefs or practices is relevant and admissible in a custody proceeding if … such beliefs or practices are reasonably likely to cause present or future harm to the physical or mental development of the child."); *and In re* Marriage of Hadeen, 619 P.2d 374, 382 (Wash. Ct. App. 1980) (religious beliefs and practices considered only to the extent that they pose a "reasonable and substantial likelihood of immediate or future impairment" of the child's mental or physical well-being).

72 343 So.2d 762 (Miss. 1977).

trial court granted the father's modification petition, awarding him primary custody and restricting the mother's visitation to periods in the father's home.[73] The mother attended "religious services where reptiles were handled in close proximity to said child, where there was some shouting, [and] speaking in the unknown tongue."[74] "This situation," said the trial judge, "could do nothing but disturb and scare a small child."[75] The court concluded that although the mother was a "fit and proper person in every respect," her involvement in a "religious sect" was "detrimental to the growth, welfare and intellectual development of a five-year-old child."[76] On appeal, the court reversed, finding "no proof that this child was subjected to any danger of being bitten by a poisonous snake."[77] The mother's parental right, said the court, does not include the right to expose the child to physical danger, but in this case there was no evidence that the mother had done so or was likely to do so. Snakes, noted the court, have never been handled by any of the regular members of the mother's church.[78] Moreover, the mother had never handled a snake herself and stated that she would not do so.[79] The court concluded that the trial judge had no authority to dictate the mother's religion absent evidence that her religious practices exposed the child to "physical danger or to what society in general deems immoral practices."[80]

In a variation on the second approach, some courts require that the risk of harm to the child appear imminent.[81] In *Osier v. Osier*,[82] for example, a court awarded custody to the father, finding dispositive the refusal of the mother, a Jehovah's Witness, to consent

73 *Id.* at 762.
74 *Id.* at 763.
75 As the court explained, "church members believe that a person anointed by God to handle a snake can do so without harm. But so far it appears that none of the members of the … [mother's church] has ever felt so anointed." *Id.* at 764.
76 *Id.* at 763.
77 The child had only once attended a service in which snakes were handled, and that was in the company of the father, the mother having decided to keep the child away because she suspected snakes would be involved in the service. *Id.*
78 *Id.*
79 *Id.* at 764.
80 *Id.* In a case taking a similar approach, the court in *In re Marriage of Hadeen* (619 P.2d at 379–80) awarded custody of four of the couple's five children to the father after concluding that the mother "is in complete submission to … [her church] to the exclusion of other *reasonable* relationships." *Id.* at 382 (emphasis added). The mother's church taught that "spirit filled people" could lie and curse to "natural people" and endorsed a "strict code of discipline" that included isolation, fasting, and physical punishment "as a means of gaining parental control of children." *Id.* at 375–6. This code of discipline prompted the mother on one occasion to spank her daughter for two hours with a Ping-Pong paddle while the other children held her down. *Id.* at 375. Notwithstanding this evidence, an appellate court remanded for a new trial. The trial judge, said the court, opined, but did not find, that the mother's "submission" to her church "posed a substantial threat of endangering the children's mental or physical welfare." *Id.* at 382–3. For a case in which a court rejected the mother's claim that the practices of the father's church, "including the performance of exorcisms and the belief that a wife should be subservient to her husband" were harmful to the child, *see In re* Marriage of Wang, 896 P.2d 450, 450 (Mont. 1995) (affirming order awarding primary custody to father despite court's failure to make specific findings relating to effect of father's religious beliefs on child's best interest). *See also* Alaniz v. Alaniz, 867 S.W.2d 54, 57 (Tex. Ct. App. 1993) [jury (charged with custody decisions in Texas) could consider mother's religious "beliefs, teachings, or practices … [if they] were either illegal, immoral, or harmful rather than just unusual or abnormal"].
81 *See, e.g.*, Peterson v. Peterson, 474 N.W.2d 862, 869 (Neb. 1991) (parent's religious practices should not be considered unless they pose an "immediate and substantial threat" to child); *and* Garrett v. Garrett, 527 N.W.2d 213, 221 (Neb. Ct. App. 1995) (same).
82 410 A.2d 1027 (Me. 1980).

to any necessary blood transfusion for the child.[83] The mother's religious beliefs, concluded the trial judge, "endanger … [the child's] physical well-being."[84] On appeal, the court remanded, stressing that a court may not take a parent's religious practices into account "unless such practices pose an immediate and substantial threat to the temporal well-being of the child."[85] Noting that the child was an active eight-year-old boy of normal health, the court explained that it did "not know what specific evidence, if any, was available concerning … [the child's] proneness to accidents or to illnesses requiring blood transfusions."[86] "Furthermore," said the court, "facts such as the statistical frequency of blood transfusions for normal children aged eight and older and the degree of risk involved in taking or refusing blood or chemical substitutes, are not the proper subjects of judicial notice."[87]

Consistent with this emphasis on "imminent harm," the American Law Institute has taken the position that in working out a custodial arrangement, a parent's religious practices may be considered "to the minimum degree necessary to protect the child from severe and almost certain harm."[88]

In a third approach to the harm requirement, some courts maintain that a parent's religious practices should not affect the custody decision unless those practices have actually harmed the child. The major case in this category is *Quiner vs. Quiner*.[89] The mother in *Quiner* was a member of a church that taught "separation," a concept that requires members to shun relationships and activities with nonmembers, who are believed to be "spiritually unclean."[90] Separation supports a rigid code of conduct, under which school children are counseled "to eat their own box lunch alone and secluded from their schoolmates" and are discouraged (or forbidden) from participating in extracurricular activities or playing with other children outside school.[91] All forms of entertainment are discouraged or forbidden, including "card playing, dominoes, checkers and chess,"

83 *Id.* at 1028–9.

84 *Id.* at 1029.

85 *Id.* at 1030 n. 5 (emphasis in original). The court reasoned that "'[the] right to practice religion freely does not include liberty to expose … the child … to ill health or death.'" Osier at 1030 (quoting Prince, 321 U.S. at 166–7). In a second prong to its test, the court stated that if a court finds that a parent's religious practice poses an "immediate and substantial threat to the child's well-being," the court should protect the child's best interest by crafting an order that "makes the least possible intrusion upon the constitutionally protected interests of the parent." Osier, 410 A.2d at 1031. The court cited with approval *Levitsky v. Levitsky* [190 A.2d 621 (Md. 1963)], in which the court, after finding that the mother's religious practices were a "serious threat" to the child's life, nevertheless granted her custody but entered an order eliminating the need for her consent to any blood transfusions. Osier, 410 A.2d at 1031.

86 Osier at 1031 n. 7.

87 *Id. See also* Garrett, 527 N.W.2d 213 (mother's religious practices, including discouraging the children from celebrating birthdays and holidays, or saying the pledge of allegiance at school, and her unwillingness to allow them blood transfusions not sufficient to establish imminent harm to children); *and* Peterson, 474 N.W.2d at 869–70 ("[M]other's excessive use of corporal punishment poses an immediate and substantial threat to the temporal well-being of her children," which supported a change of custody even if mother's First Amendment rights were implicated.).

88 ALI Principles, *supra* note 17, at § 2.12(1)(c). This position is stated as an exception to the ALI's general rule that the religious activities of a parent should ordinarily not be considered. *See id.* § 2.12 cmt. d. A second exception would allow consideration of religion "to protect the child's ability to practice a religion that has been a significant part of the child's life." *Id.* For a discussion of the effect of a child's prior religious practice on custody, *see* Section B.2.a.i of this chapter.

89 59 Cal. Rptr. 503 (Cal. Ct. App. 1967)

90 Quiner *supra* at 508.

91 *Id.*

radio, television, theater, and music.[92] Children may not have toys.[93] Based on the mother's "zealous belief and espousal of the principle of separation," the trial judge concluded that the best interests of the child were served by awarding custody to the father.[94]

On appeal, the court reversed. While agreeing with the trial judge that custody in the mother "may possibly breed definite antipathy to [the] father," the court reasoned that the mother's enforcement of the principle of separation might actually do just the opposite, inspiring the child to reject the life his mother advocated and to become more attached to his father.[95] In a much-referenced passage, the court warned

> Precisely because a court cannot *know* one way or another, with any degree of certainty, the proper or sure road to personal security and happiness or to religious salvation, which latter to untold millions is their primary and ultimate best interest, evaluation of religious teaching and training and its projected as distinguished from immediate effect (psychologists and psychiatrists to the contrary notwithstanding) upon the physical, mental and emotional well-being of a child, must be forcibly kept from judicial determinations. Numerous profound thinkers have fixed convictions that *all* religion is bad, particularly so in the rearing of children. If a court has the right to weigh the religious beliefs or lack of them of one parent against those of the other, for the purpose of making the precise conclusion as to which one is for the best interests of a child, we open a Pandora's box which can never be closed.[96]

Accordingly, the court concluded

> [C]ourts have no power to tell parents who teach nothing secularly immoral, unlawful or against public policy, how to shape the minds of their children, particularly on the subject of accepted religious belief. Evidence must be produced which will sustain a finding that there is actual impairment of physical, emotional and mental well-being contrary to the best interests of the child.[97]

Other courts have agreed that consideration of a parent's religious practices should depend on a showing of actual harm to the child.[98]

The choice of the child's primary custodian does not always signal an end to custody disputes. In a recurring scenario, one parent seeks the court's aid in attempting to control

92 *Id.*

93 *Id.*

94 *Id.* at 510. On appeal, the court found it "obvious" that "the mother was deprived of custody because of her espousal of the principle of separation and for no other reason." *Id.* at 517.

95 *Id.* at 513.

96 *Id.* at 516–17 (emphasis in original).

97 *Id.* at 516.

98 *See, e.g.*, Leppert v. Leppert, 519 N.W.2d 287, 290 (N. D. 1994) (concluding that mother's vilification of father to children and evidence that two children, who had been home schooled by the mother, lagged behind their peers demonstrated that the mother's religious beliefs "constituted extreme danger to children" requiring reversal of trial court's award of custody of three of five children to mother); Pater, 588 N.E.2d at 797 (concluding that mother's refusal to allow child to celebrate holidays, participate in extracurricular activities, or salute the flag "do[es] not appear to directly endanger the child's physical or mental health" and so does not support denial of custody to mother); Jakab v. Jakab, 664 A.2d 261, 265–6 (Vt. 1995) {affirming lower court's denial of custody to father because even if father's religious faith "required him to hit his children with a paddle, a fireplace poker or a strap … religious practices may be considered in custody and visitation decisions if they 'have a direct and immediate negative impact on the physical and mental health of the child'" [quoting Varnum v. Varnum, 586 A.2d 1107, 1111 (Vt. 1990)]}; *and* Varnum, 586 A.2d at 1109 (stating that mother's physical discipline of children, which included spanking with a spoon, a ladle, and a paddle and "striking them about the face and body using both her hands

the other parent's behavior with the child. Often the targeted behavior relates to the child's religious upbringing.

### 3. *Parental Restrictions Related to Religion*

In a recurring scenario, one parent attempts to control the other parent's activity with the child for reasons related to religion. A primary custodian, for example, may seek an order (1) requiring the other parent to facilitate the child's attendance at religious services during visitation or (2) prohibiting the other parent from exposing the child to a religion that differs from the one chosen by the primary custodian.

#### a. Parental Compulsion: Requiring One Parent to Facilitate the Other Parent's Plan for the Child's Religious Upbringing

Courts have sometimes granted one parent's request that the other parent facilitate a plan for the child's religious training. These orders often require a secondary custodian to transport the child to religious services or classes.[99] In *Johns v. Johns*,[100] for example, a judge ordered the father "to see that the children attend Sunday School and Church" in furtherance of the primary-caretaker mother's "consistent course of religious instruction."[101] An appellate court affirmed the order, noting that "[m]oral instruction is, like every other aspect of education, the result of accumulated and consistent effort over time."[102] Similarly, in *Overman v. Overman*,[103] a court ordered the father to transport his son to catechism class during his Saturday morning visitation,[104] and in *Zummo v. Zummo*,[105] the father was ordered to present his children at synagogue for Sunday school during visitation.[106]

In *Chasan v. Mintz*,[107] both parents supported the child's training in the Jewish faith, but the father objected to an order requiring him to transfer the child to the mother's home for attendance at religious services during his Sunday visitation. The New Hampshire Supreme Court found no abuse of discretion in the order, notwithstanding the father's plea that his relocation increased the travel time necessary for him to comply.[108]

As justification for these orders, courts sometimes cite the primary custodian's right to direct the child's religious training. This right is often recognized by statute.[109] As one

and other implements" amounted to child abuse and supported award of custody to father even though mother's discipline was "apparently" religiously inspired).

99 In a less common scenario involving parents of different faiths, one court directed "that each party will impress upon the children the need for religious tolerance and not permit any third party to attempt to teach them otherwise." Frank v. Frank, 833 A.2d 194, 199 (Pa. Super. Ct. 2003). This order was affirmed on appeal, although the vagueness of the order would surely make policing difficult.

100 918 S.W.2d 728 (Ark. Ct. App. 1996)

101 *Id.* at 730.

102 *Id.*

103 497 N.E.2d 618 (Ind. Ct. App. 1986).

104 *Id.* at 619.

105 574 A.2d 1130.

106 *Id.* at 1132.

107 409 A.2d 787 (N.H. 1979).

108 *Id.* at 788.

109 *See, e.g.*, Ariz. Rev. Stat. Ann. § 25–410(A) (2001) (stating that except as otherwise agreed, or in cases of harm to the child, "the custodian may determine the child's upbringing, including the child's …

court observed, "[t]he law is clear that the primary caretaker has the right to determine the religious upbringing of the children in his or her charge," and courts will not interfere with that determination.[110] Accordingly, the court in *Pardue v. Pardue*[111] upheld an order conditioning the father's visitation rights on his compliance with the mother's plan for the child's religious instruction. As primary caretaker, explained the court, the mother "has the right to demand that her children have their religious education and training fostered in the church of her choice according to the schedule of her choice."[112]

Some courts have suggested that the primary caretaker's right to raise and educate children in a chosen religion is exclusive.[113] Other courts have disagreed, reasoning, for example, that "during visitation periods," a secondary caretaker "retain[s] unlimited prerogative to direct the children's religious upbringing."[114] Some courts have recognized a secondary custodian's parental rights during periods with the child but have nonetheless upheld restrictions on such parents. In these cases, courts may view the restriction as simply an "accommodation"[115] to the primary custodian and a mere "inconvenience" to the secondary parent,[116] justified by the best interest of the child.

religious training"); Colo. Rev. Stat. Ann. § 14-10-130(A) (West 1999) (stating that except as otherwise agreed, or in cases of harm to the child, "the person or persons with responsibility for decision-making may determine the child's upbringing, including his or her … religious training"); 750 Ill. Comp. Stat. Ann. 5/608 (2009); Ind. Code Ann. § 31-17-2-17 (West 1997) (stating that except as otherwise agreed, or in cases of harm to the child, "the custodian may determine the child's upbringing, including the child's … religious training"); Ky. Rev. Stat. Ann. § 403.330 (West 1998) (same); Mo. Rev. Stat. § 452.405 (West 1998) (same); Mont. Code Ann. § 40-4-218 (1997) (same); Wash. Rev. Code Ann. §26.10.170 (2005) (same).

110 Feldman v. Feldman, 874 A.2d 606, 611 (N.J. Super. Ct. 2005). In *Feldman*, the court affirmed an order prohibiting the secondary caretaker from enrolling the children "in training and education classes … over the primary caretaker's objections" but did not bar the secondary caretaker from "having the children exposed to religious services or holidays." *Id.* at 608.

111 285 So.2d 552 (La. Ct. App. 1973).

112 *Id.* at 555. *See also* Chapman v. Chapman, 352 N.W.2d 437, 441 (Minn.Ct. App. 1984) (reinstating order requiring father to take child to Mass during visitation and stating that courts must defer to custodial parent's decision on religion unless it endangers the child).

113 *See, e.g.*, Overman, 497 N.E.2d at 619 (stating that Indiana statute gives custodial parent the right to determine the child's religious training and that the "non-custodial parent must not impose his or her religious views on the child"); and Lange v. Lange, 502 N.W.2d 143, 146 (Wis. Ct. App. 1993) (stating that Wisconsin law gives the custodial parent "the sole right to choose the religion of the children"). *See also* Andros v. Andros, 396 N.W.2d 917, 923–4 (Minn. Ct. App. 1986) (stating that the trial court's order properly gave the legal and physical custodian "exclusive control of the children's religious training").

114 Bienenfeld, 605 A.2d at 183 (affirming the order that "specifically tailored the … [secondary custodian's] visitation rights to coincide with particular religious holidays, so that her children would be able to fulfill the religious obligations imposed by her faith"). *See also* Zummo, 574 A.2d at 1140 (stating that "each parent has parental authority during lawful periods of custody or visitation" and that a parent may "pursue whatever course of religious indoctrination … that parent sees fit … during periods of lawful custody or visitation"); *and In re* Marriage of McSoud, 131 P.3d at 1215 (stating that the parent without decision-making authority "retains a constitutional right to educate the child to that parent's religion").

115 *See, e.g., In re* Marriage of Tisckos, 514 N.E.2d 523, 528–9 (Ill. App. Ct. 1987) (describing visitation order requiring the father to deliver the child to the mother's residence on Sunday mornings for church services as "in the nature of an accommodation to be made on behalf of the child by the noncustodial parent"); *and* Zummo, 574 A.2d at 1157 (finding a "material and controlling distinction" between orders that prohibit a parent from taking the child to religious services and orders that require a parent to transport the child to religious services and describing the latter as a constitutional accommodation of the other parent's rights).

116 *See, e.g.*, Johns, 918 S.W.2d at 731 (stating that inconvenience to the father does not justify setting aside an order requiring him to take the children to Sunday school and church if order is consistent with

Secondary custodians have charged that orders compelling them to facilitate the other parent's plan for the child's religious upbringing violate the Free Exercise and Establishment Clauses of the Constitution or state constitutions. Some courts have rejected these charges, reasoning that a transportation order does not require the parent to himself or herself attend religious sessions.[117] Other courts have been less tolerant of transportation orders, reasoning that such orders present parents with a forced choice: either attend the service or relinquish part of the time available to spend with the child. In *Carrico v. Blevins*,[118] for example, the court rejected a transportation order that effectively required the mother either "to attend church with her son or suffer the penalty of losing a portion of her visitation time."[119] Similarly, in *Brown v. Szakal*,[120] the court held that a secondary-caretaker father could not be required constitutionally to observe the Jewish Sabbath and dietary laws of the mother's religion during visitation with the child.[121]

Even when a transportation order does not compel the secondary custodian to attend religious services, the order may be constitutionally infirm if it compels the parent to violate his or her own religion, such as, for example, where that religion prohibits transportation of one's child to a different religion.[122] Finally, the transportation order should be the least restrictive means to accommodate the primary custodian's religious choice for the child. If a less intrusive approach, such as rescheduling parenting time, will accomplish the same end, the transportation order may be constitutionally infirm.[123]

An order requiring a secondary custodian to see that children attend the primary custodian's chosen religious services also may raise questions about *the child's* free exercise rights. In *Watts v. Watts*,[124] for example, a judge conditioned the mother's weekend visitation on her taking the children to Sunday school and church. The father, who was the primary caretaker, made the familiar argument that the mother's constitutional rights

children's best interest); *and* Overman, 497 N.E.2d at 619 (transporting son to catechism, which lasts 1.5 hours, is not an "unreasonable interference with father's visitation rights").

117 *See, e.g.*, Johns, 918 S.W.2d at 731 (order requiring father to see that the children attend religious services placed no limitation on father's religious freedom because it did not require him to attend religious services); *In re* Marriage of McSoud, 131 P.3d at 1219 (noting, for purposes of remand, that the order would improperly infringe on the mother's right to religious freedom if court interpreted it to require the mother to accompany the child to religious services during parenting time); *and* McLemore, 762 So. 2d at 318–20 [holding that the order requiring parents to "assume responsibility for the attendance of the children in church each Sunday" did not require the parents to attend church but modifying the order to state that parents should be "vitally interested" in children's regular spiritual training (emphasis omitted)].

118 402 S.E.2d 235 (Va. Ct. App. 1991).

119 *Id.* at 237. The court added that the order violated the state constitution, which prohibits a state from requiring a citizen to attend any "religious worship." *Id.* at 237–8.

120 514 A.2d 81 (N.J. Super. Ct. Ch. Div. 1986).

121 *Id.* at 83.

122 *See, e.g.*, *In re* Marriage of McSoud, 131 P.3d at 1219–20 (noting that in challenging transportation order, the mother presented no evidence that her religion prohibited her from transporting the children to religious services different from her own).

123 *See, e.g.*, *id.* at 1220 (noting that the court issuing the transportation order did not indicate that it had considered less restrictive means, including "rescheduling the activities to occur during father's parenting time, requiring that father provide the necessary transportation during mother's parenting time, or affording mother additional parenting time to compensate for any significant interruption to her parenting time").

124 563 S.W.2d 314 (Tex. Civ. App. 1978).

were not violated because she was not required to attend church herself.[125] The court concluded, however, that even if the order did not violate the mother's rights, it violated the rights of the children under the Texas Constitution.[126] The children, observed the court, might not want religious training.[127]

### b. Parental Prohibition: Requiring a Parent to Refrain from Exposing the Child to Religious Beliefs and Practices

In a scenario that has troubled many courts, one parent seeks an order prohibiting or limiting the other parent from exposing the child to certain religious beliefs or practices. Most often the primary custodian seeks to limit the child's exposure to a religion that differs from the one he or she has chosen for the child. Concern over the secondary custodian's constitutional right to parent, together with First Amendment protections, has led most courts to decline to impose such restrictions in the absence of evidence that they are necessary to protect the child from harm.

In the oft-cited case of *Munoz v. Munoz*,[128] the court endorsed the general view that courts should not restrict a parent's right to expose the child to religious beliefs or practices unless there is a "clear and affirmative showing" of harm to the child.[129] The "obvious reason" for this rule, said the court, is that "constitutionally, American courts are forbidden from interfering with religious freedoms or to take steps preferring one religion over another."[130] In *Munoz*, the court reversed an order prohibiting the father from taking the children to Catholic services or classes during visitation.[131] The mother, who was Mormon, had sought the order. Rejecting the notion that "duality of religious beliefs, per se, creates a conflict upon young minds," the court found insufficient the mother's mere speculation that such dual exposure was confusing to the child.[132]

Most courts have followed the general rule set out in *Munoz* that a restriction on a parent's religions activity with the child must be supported by a showing of actual or potential harm to the child.[133] Many courts also have agreed with *Munoz* that speculation

125 *Id.* at 317.

126 *Id.* The court quoted Article I, § 6 of the Texas Constitution:

> No man shall be compelled to attend, erect or support any place of worship, or to maintain any ministry against his consent. No human authority ought, in any case whatever, to control or interfere with the rights of conscience in matters of religion, and no preference shall ever be given by law to any religious society or mode of worship.

Tx. Const., Art. I, § 6.

127 Watts, 563 S.W.2d at 317.

128 489 P.2d 1133 (Wash. 1971) (*en banc*).

129 *Id.* at 1135.

130 *Id.*

131 *Id.* at 1134.

132 *Id.* at 1136.

133 *See, e.g., In re* Marriage of McSoud, 131 P.3d at 1220 (reversing an order that allowed the mother to take the child to church "only so long as she supports [the child's] participation and attendance at church with father" because there was no evidence that the child suffered "substantial physical or emotional harm from attending either parent's church"); Mesa v. Mesa, 652 So.2d 456, 457 (Fl. Dist. Ct. App. 1995) (vacating, because of an absence of proof of harm to the child, an order that the "children shall not attend the mother's religious services, nor shall she in any way endeavor to educate her children into her religious practice or that of the church to which she attends directly or indirectly"); Khalsa v. Khalsa,

about the general propensity of dual religious exposure to cause harm is not enough.[134] Nor is a parent's general testimony that the child is stressed or confused sufficient.[135] As one court explained, restrictions on a secondary custodian's religious activity with the child must be supported by a "*factual* showing, not mere conclusions and speculation."[136] Indeed, some courts have suggested that exposure to conflicting religions actually may be healthy for children.[137] A few courts have taken a contrary view, opining that exposure to different religions is generally confusing to children.[138]

751 P.2d 715, 720 (N.M. Ct. App. 1988) (stating that "[i]n justifying a prohibition of religious restrictions on visitation rights, physical or emotional harm to the child cannot be assumed, but must be demonstrated in detail"); Pater, 588 N.E.2d at 801 (reversing an order prohibiting the mother from teaching or exposing the child to her Jehovah's Witness beliefs because of the absence of proof that such exposure harmed the child); *and In re* Marriage of Jensen-Branch, 899 P.2d 803, 809 (Wash. Ct. App. 1995) [stating that even when parents do not share decision-making authority, each remains "free to teach the children about religion *independently*" unless such teaching would cause actual or potential harm to the child (emphasis in original)].

134 *See, e.g., In re* Marriage of McSoud, 131 P.3d at 1216–17 (Harm to the child from exposure to conflicting religions should not be assumed.); Felton v. Felton, 418 N.E.2d 606, 607 (Mass. 1981) ("[H]arm to the child from conflicting religious instructions or practices, which would justify such a limitation, should not be simply assumed or surmised; it must be demonstrated in detail."); Hanson v. Hanson, 404 N.W.2d 460, 464 (N. D. 1987) ("To justify the placement of religious restrictions on visitation rights, the physical or emotional harm to the child resulting from the conflicting religious instructions or practices cannot be simply assumed or surmised, but must be demonstrated in detail."); *and* Zummo, 574 A.2d at 1155 ["[C]ourts have rejected speculation by parents and by experts as to potential future emotional harm to a *particular* child based upon the assumption that such exposure is *generally* harmful." (emphasis in original)].

135 *See* Felton, 418 N.E.2d at 610.

136 Robertson v. Robertson, 575 P.2d 1092, 1093 (Wash. Ct. App. 1978) (concluding that mother's affidavit that teachings of the Jehovah's Witnesses "confuses and alarms [the] children" was insufficient). *See also* Kendall v. Kendall, 687 N.E.2d 1228, 1232 (Mass. 1997) ("'[W]holly uncorroborated testimony' of a parent [is] insufficient to demonstrate harm."); Hanson, 404 N.W.2d at 465 n. 2 ("[G]eneral testimony of a parent, as in this case, that the children are "confused" or "upset" by the duality of their parents' religious beliefs does not suffice."); Khalsa, 751 P.2d at 720 ("[A] custodial parent's general testimony that the child is upset or confused because of the non-custodial parent's religious practice is insufficient to demonstrate harm."); *and* Munoz, 489 P.2d at 1135 ("[S]peculation on the part of the parents that it was 'confusing' to the 6-year-old son" is insufficient.).

137 As one court explained,

> [t]here may also be a value in letting the child see, even at an early age, the religious models between which it is likely to be led to choose in later life. And it is suggested, sometimes, that a diversity of religious experience is itself a sound stimulant for a child.

Felton, 418 N.E.2d at 607. *See also In re* Marriage of McSoud, 131 P.3d at 1217 (agreeing with courts stating that "merely exposing a child to a second religion need not be harmful, and indeed may be healthy for the child."); Zummo, 574 A.2d. at 1155 n. 45 (citing courts stating that bireligious exposure would be beneficial); Frank, 833 A.2d at 199 (observing that while exposure to parents' conflicting religious beliefs may cause stress, "[s]tress … is not always harmful nor is it always to be avoided and protected against"); and Fatemi v. Fatemi, 489 A.2d 798, 801 (Pa. Super. Ct. 1985) (speaking to a visitation restriction not based on religion but observing that the "process of children's maturation requires that they view and evaluate their parents in the bright light of reality").

138 In *Morris v. Morris* [412 A.2d 139 (Pa. Super. Ct. 1979)], for example, a court prohibited the father, a Jehovah's Witness, from taking his daughter on door-to-door religious solicitations during visitation. The mother, who had primary custody, was raising the child in the Catholic Church. "[I]t is beyond dispute," said the court, "that a young child reared into two inconsistent religious traditions will quite probably experience some deleterious physical or mental effects." *Id.* at 142. The court further noted the testimony of a clinical psychologist who, after interviewing the child for thirty minutes, stated that "considerable

One court described the types of evidence that might establish harm sufficient to support a restriction on a secondary custodian's religious activity with the child. Such evidence includes testimony that the child's "general demeanor, attitude, school work, appetite, health or outlook has been affected ... [by the] conflict," corroborated by "church, school, medical or psychiatric authorities, [or] associates, in or out of school."[139] Even when such evidence suggests that the child is experiencing distress, it may be difficult to establish that this condition is a product of exposure to the parents' conflicting religions rather than to some other cause, such as the divorce itself.[140]

*Funk v. Ossman*[141] provides a helpful example of harm caused by a child's exposure to different religious faiths. In *Funk*, a trial judge enjoined the father from taking his eight-year-old son to "formal Jewish religious training or indoctrination" during visitation.[142] The mother, who was a lay minister in the Lutheran church, did not object to the child going to synagogue but protested that the father was training the child in Judaism. An appellate court affirmed the injunction, concluding that the child's exposure to multiple religions was indeed harming the child. The court noted the testimony of a child psychologist that the child was experiencing anxiety, manifested in encopresis (soiling his pants), which ceased when he stopped attending Jewish Sunday school.[143]

Similarly, in *Kendall v. Kendall*,[144] the court upheld a restriction on the secondary custodian based on evidence of demonstrated harm to the child. The parents in *Kendall* had agreed when they married that they would raise their children in the Jewish faith. At the time of their divorce, the mother had become an Orthodox Jew and the father a

inconsistency" in the parents' beliefs "would cause [the] child to disregard the teaching of either parent" and that taking the child on door-to-door solicitations would "probably, although not necessarily, result in some psychological impairment." *Id.* at 146. Reasoning that it is not possible to predict harm with absolute certainty and that waiting until the child is actually harmed is inadvisable, an appellate court affirmed the restriction. *Id.* at 146–7. *See also* LeDoux v. LeDoux, 452 N.W.2d 1, 6 (Neb. 1990) (Grant, J., concurring) ("I do not see how one parent with one set of religious beliefs and one parent with a different, conflicting set of religious beliefs can raise their minor children with full training and instruction in each parent's beliefs without reducing their minor children to a totally confused, psychologically disastrous state.").

139 Felton, 418 N.E.2d at 611 [quoting Pope v. Pope, 267 S.W.2d 340, 343 (Mo. Ct. App. 1954) (reversing restriction on visitation)].

140 *See, e.g., In re* Marriage of Mentry, 190 Cal. Rptr. 843, 847 (Cal. Ct. App. 1983) ("There was evidence that the boy had social adjustment problems in school for which he had received psychological counseling, but no evidence relating these problems, or periodic stomach aches which both children assertedly suffered, to conflict over religion."); Compton v. Gilmore, 560 P.2d 861, 863 (Idaho 1977) (Trial court did not find that child's "'strange,' 'unusual' and 'aggressive behavior after visits with her father ... was in any way caused by the religious differences of the parents."); Kirchner v. Caughey, 606 A.2d 257, 262 (Md. 1992) ("A factual finding of a causal relationship between the religious practices and the actual or probable harm to a child is required – mere conclusions and speculations will not suffice."); *and* Pater, 58 N.E.2d at 801 ("Because a divorce is a stressful event for a child, a court must carefully separate the distress caused by that event from any distress allegedly caused by religious conflict."))..

141 724 P.2d 1247, 1251 (Ariz Ct. App. 1986).

142 *Id.* at 1249.

143 The court opined that the child "feels that he is a mediator and must please both parents, including pleasing them over the religious issue." *Id.* at 1251. *See also* LeDoux, 452 N.W.2d at 5 (identifying an "immediate and substantial threat to [the son's] well-being" in the form of stress stemming partly from his "involuntary exposure to disparate religions" and manifested in wetting and "the equivalent of a nightmare").

144 687 N.E.2d at 1230.

"fundamentalist Christian."[145] The mother sought an order limiting the children's exposure to the father's religion, which allegedly taught that those who do not accept his faith "are 'damned to go to hell' where there will be 'weeping and gnashing of teeth.' "[146] Concluding that the children's exposure to two religions was "substantially damaging" them, the trial court ordered both parents to refrain from indoctrinating the children in a manner that "substantially promotes their ... alienation from either parent or their rejection of either parent."[147] The order imposed multiple restrictions on the father:

> The ... [father] shall not take the children to his church ... nor engage them in prayer or bible study if it promotes rejection rather than acceptance, of their mother or their own Jewish self-identity. The ... [father] shall not share his religious beliefs with the children if those beliefs cause the children significant emotional distress or worry about their mother or about themselves. Thus, for example, ... [the father] may have pictures of Jesus Christ hanging on the walls of his residence, and that will not serve as any basis for restricting his visitation with his children. But ... [the father] may not take the children to religious services where they receive the message that adults or children who do not accept Jesus Christ as their lord and savior are destined to burn in hell. By way of further example, ... [the father] may not shave off [the oldest child's] payes.[148]

In affirming the order, the Massachusetts Supreme Court reasoned that the evidence "paints a strong picture of the reasonably projected course if the children continue to be caught in the cross-fire of their parents' religious difference: ... [the father's] religion may alienate the children from their custodial parent (she is bad, she will burn in hell), and may diminish their own sense of self-worth and self-identity (Jews are bad, Jews will burn in hell). At minimum they will be called upon to 'choose' between their parents, in itself a detrimental result."[149] While recognizing that the existence of substantial harm was a "close question," the court concluded that "[t]he case law does not require the court to wait for a formal psychiatric breakdown."[150]

Courts have sometimes struck down restrictions that are not carefully crafted. Limitations on a parent's religious conduct with the child must be narrowly tailored to protect the child while minimizing interference with a parent's religious freedom.[151] In

[145] *Id.*
[146] *Id.*
[147] *Id.* at 1231.
[148] *Id.*
[149] *Id.* at 1235.
[150] *Id.*
[151] Khalsa, 751 P.2d at 721. In *Khalsa*, the court identified three factors relevant to the legitimacy of a restriction on a parent's religious activity with a child:

1. Whether there exists detailed factual evidence demonstrating that the conflicting beliefs or practices of the parents pose substantial physical or emotional harm to the child;
2. Whether restricting the religious interaction between the parent and child will necessarily alleviate this harm; and
3. Whether such restrictions are narrowly tailored so as to minimize interference with the parents' religious freedom.

*Id.* Applying this test, the court in *Khalsa* found no evidence that the children were harmed by exposure to the father's Sikh religion during visitation and so held erroneous a lower court order enjoining the father from encouraging the children to participate in Sikh religious activities during visitation. *Id. See also* LeDoux, 452 N.W.2d at 5 (stating that the restriction must ensure the child's best interest with "the least possible intrusion upon the constitutionally protected interests of the parent").

*Kirchner v. Caughey*,[152] for example, the court vacated an order prohibiting the father from having the child "participate in any church or church-related activity" because the order was overly broad, reaching "activities such as church picnics, bicycle rodeos, and the like that the record does not show would be harmful to the child."[153] Similarly, an order stating that the mother "shall not teach or expose the child to the Jehovah's Witnesses' beliefs in any form" was deemed overbroad because it "could be construed as forbidding any discussion of the Bible."[154]

A few courts have taken the position that the child's exposure to multiple religions may be restricted even without a showing that such exposure is harming the child. These courts have sometimes suggested that the primary custodian's right to direct the child's religious training precludes the other parent from engaging the child in different religious training.[155] In *Lange v. Lange*,[156] for example, the mother obtained an order prohibiting the father from "imposing his religious views on the children" contrary to the Lutheran doctrine she had chosen as the primary caretaker. The father had evidently convinced the children that because the mother was Lutheran, she was going to hell, effectively causing the children to reject the mother's choice of religion.[157] In upholding the order, the appellate court noted that Wisconsin law gives the custodial parent "the sole right to choose the religion of the children."[158] This right, reasoned the court, "is meaningless without protection from subversion" and so justifies a court in fashioning "reasonable restrictions" to protect the custodian's choice.[159]

The child's preference sometimes plays a role in parental disputes over the child's religious practices. In *In re Marriage of Boldt*,[160] for example, the custodial father planned to have his twelve-year-old son circumcised as part of the child's conversion to the Jewish

[152] 606 A.2d 257 (Md. 1992).

[153] *Id.* at 262.

[154] Pater, 58 N.E.2d at 801.

[155] For a discussion of the primary custodian's right to direct the child's religious upbringing, *see* Section B.3.a of this chapter.

[156] 502 N.W.2d 143 (Wis. Ct. App. 1993)

[157] *Id.* at 147. For a case in which a court refused to restrain a secondary custodian from taking children to services in a conflicting religion on the ground that she was *not* attempting to subvert the primary custodian's choice of religion, *see* Wood v. DeHahn, 571 N.W.2d 186, 189 (Wis. Ct. App. 1997) (contrasting intent of secondary custodian in *Lange*).

[158] Lange at 146.

[159] Lange at 146. A dissenting judge argued that the restriction could pass constitutional scrutiny only on a showing that the father's actions had a "grave, damaging effect on the parties' children." *Id.* at 154 (Dykman, J. dissenting). *See also* A.G.R. *ex rel.* Conflenti v. Huff, 815 N.E.2d 120, 124–6 (Ind. Ct. App. 2004) (finding reasonable an order prohibiting the father from allowing the child to participate in holiday-related activities, which contravened faith in which custodial mother was raising child); *In re* Paternity of K.R.H., 784 N.E.2d 985, 992–93 (Ind. Ct. App. 2003) (affirming an order restricting the secondary custodian from taking the child to church unless the church was Roman Catholic on the ground that the custodial parent has the right to control the child's religious training); *and* Andros, 396 N.W.2d at 923–4 (upholding a visitation order structured to prevent a secondary parent from taking his children to church on the ground that Minnesota law gives "the custodial parent … control of the children's religious upbringing."). In *In re Marriage of Murga* [163 Cal. Rptr. 79, 82 (Cal. Ct. App. 1980)], the court took a different view, stating that "while the custodial parent undoubtedly has the right to make ultimate decisions concerning the child's religious upbringing, a court will not enjoin the noncustodial parent from discussing religion with the child or involving the child in his or her religious activities in the absence of a showing that the child will be thereby harmed."

[160] 176 P.3d 388 (Or. 2008).

faith.[161] The mother, a member of the Russian Orthodox Church, opposed the circumcision and sought a modification of custody or, in the alternative, an order enjoining the father from proceeding with the circumcision.[162] The trial court granted the injunction, but the Oregon Supreme Court reversed and remanded the case to determine the child's preference.[163] While noting that the decision to circumcise a male child generally falls to the custodial parent, the court expressed concern over the mother's allegation that the child objected to the circumcision.[164] Forcing a twelve-year-old child to undergo a circumcision against his will, reasoned the court, "*could* seriously affect the relationship between ... [the child] and father, and could have a pronounced effect on father's capability to properly care for ... [the child]."[165]

In an interesting twist on the usual scenario in which one parent seeks to restrict the other parent's religious activity with the child, one court *sua sponte* ordered both parents to "shelter" the child from their "non-mainstream religious beliefs and rituals."[166] The parents were practicing Wiccans, and neither had moved for such a restriction. On appeal by both parents, an appellate court struck the restriction. The court acknowledged that the parental right to direct the child's religious upbringing may be limited if unrestricted religious practices "would endanger the child's physical health or significantly impair the child's emotional development."[167] In this case, however, neither party alleged and the trial judge did not find that the parents' religious practices were endangering the child. Consequently, the trial judge lacked authority to limit the parents' right to direct the child's religious training.[168]

Some parents have attempted to avoid or resolve disputes about the child's religious upbringing by entering a private agreement. When one parent subsequently changes his or her mind and objects to enforcement of the agreement, a court must decide whether the parents' agreement is binding. We turn now to this question.

### 4. *Parental Agreements Concerning the Child's Religious Upbringing*

Parental agreements about the child's religious training add another layer of complexity to custody decision making.[169] These agreements may take the form of (1) a premarital

161 *Id.* at 389.
162 *Id.* at 389–90.
163 *Id.*
164 *Id.* at 394.
165 *Id.* (emphasis in original) For a case finding deference to a child's preference inappropriate, *see* Hicks v. Hicks, 868 A.2d 1245 (Pa. Super. Ct. 2005). The mother in *Hicks* wanted to baptize the child over the father's objection. The trial judge ruled that the issue be deferred until the child, then a third-grader, reached age thirteen and could herself decide whether she wanted to be baptized. *Id.* at 1247. On the mother's appeal, the court reversed, finding no evidence that the baptism would threaten harm to the child and concluding that giving the child the power to decide the issue usurped the custodial mother's right to determine the child's religious upbringing. *Id.* at 1252–3.
166 Jones v. Jones, 832 N.E.2d 1057, 1059 (Ind. Ct. App. 2005). In the court's words, "Wicca [is] a form of paganism." *Id.* at 1058.
167 *Id.* at 1060.
168 *Id.* at 1061.
169 When parents agree to raise a child in a particular faith and follow through on that agreement during marriage, the result may be that the child, if mature enough, has developed a religious identity. *See, e.g.*, MacLagan, 473 S.E. 2d at 784 (where parents raised the child in the Jewish faith pursuant to agreement,

agreement (also known as an "antenuptial" or "prenuptial agreement") entered prior to marriage, (2) a marital agreement entered during an ongoing marriage, or (3) a separation or settlement agreement entered when divorce is on the horizon. Many courts have struggled with requests by one parent to enforce an agreement regarding the child's religious upbringing over the objection of the other parent. On either constitutional or contract grounds, most courts have declined to enforce these agreements.

Constitutional concerns begin with the Establishment Clause. Courts have sometimes warned that enforcement of parental agreements about religion would draw judges into inappropriate religious inquiries. The leading case of *Zummo v. Zummo*[170] provides a good example of this danger. In *Zummo*, the parties entered an oral premarital agreement that provided that "any children will be raised in the Jewish faith."[171] The mother thought the agreement required "exclusive Jewish religious indoctrination," whereas the father thought it required a formal Jewish education but permitted exposure to Catholic Mass.[172] The trial judge took the mother's view, prohibiting the father from taking the children to religious services "contrary to the Jewish faith."[173] On appeal, the court noted the many questions posed by the order enforcing the agreement:

> What constitutes a "religious service?" Which are "contrary" to the Jewish faith? What for the matter is the "Jewish" faith? Orthodox, Conservative, Reform, Reconstructionist, Messianic, Humanistic, Secular and other Jewish sects might differ widely on this point.[174]

Not surprisingly, the court vacated the prohibition, noting that "[b]oth the subject matter and the ambiguities of the order make excessive entanglement in religious matters inevitable."[175]

and the child "had a positive sense of identity as a Jew"). For a discussion of the child's past religious training as a factor in the choice of a primary custodian, *see* Section B.2.a.i of this chapter.

170 574 A.2d 1130, 1132 (Pa. Super. Ct. 1990).

171 *See id.* at 1141.

172 *Id.* at 1145.

173 *Id.* at 1142. The order further specified that it should not be construed to prevent the father from taking the children to "weddings, funerals, or family gatherings" or including the children in "events involving family traditions at Christmas and Easter." *Id.*

174 *Id.* at 1146. An agreement that the child shall be reared in the Roman Catholic Religion raises many similar questions. As one court asked:

> What constitutes "rearing" a child in the religion or cultus of this church, or of any church? Must ... [the child] be taken to church once a week, or once in two weeks, on Sunday? If mid-week services are held, must ... [the child] be taken to them? Is it required that ... [the child] attend catechism class? Must ... [the child] attend a parochial school if the particular denomination in question maintains such schools? What fast days must be observed, what Lenten observances followed? Would it be sufficient if the child be required to conform to a part of these things, and, if so, which part? Or are all of them required? The difficulty would be the same, no matter what church might be named in such a decree as the one now before us.

Lynch v. Uhlenhopp, 78 N.W.2d 491, 497 (Iowa 1956) (holding that mother could not be held in contempt for violating an agreement, entered by stipulation at divorce, that the child "be reared in the Roman Catholic Religion" because of its vagueness and uncertainty). *Id.* at 493.

175 Zummo, 574 A.2d at 1146. The court upheld another portion of the order requiring the father to present the children at synagogue for Sunday school during his visitation. *Id.* at 1132. For a discussion of orders compelling a secondary custodian to transport children to religious services consistent with the primary custodian's plan for the children's religious upbringing, *see* Section B.3.a of this chapter.

Courts also have noted free exercise issues associated with enforcement of parental agreements to raise the child in an identified faith. The primary concern is that holding an objecting parent to such an agreement encroaches on the freedom to change one's mind about religion and to expose one's child to changed beliefs.[176] This potential is especially acute in cases of premarital agreements entered many years earlier. As one court explained,

> [t]he freedom to choose any religion necessarily comprehends the freedom to change religions. Great changes in religious beliefs by individuals are a feature of Western history; e.g., Saul of Tarsus on the road to Damascus; Constantine and the cross in the sky; Martin Luther and the cathedral door at Worms, to cite a few. We would reduce the right to the free exercise of religion by half if we did not recognize the right to change one's religious mind. ... [M]oreover ... parental aspirations of women and men often evolve after the birth of a child.[177]

As the court in *Zummo* stated,

> [r]eligious freedom was recognized by our founding fathers to be *inalienable*. It remains so today. Thus, while we agree that a parent's religious freedom may yield to other compelling interests, we conclude that it may not be bargained away.[178]

Contract law sometimes presents another hurdle to enforcement of parental agreements about religion. An agreement that is ambiguous or vague enough to raise Establishment Clause concerns may be too indefinite to be enforceable under contract law.[179] A parental agreement also may be the product of duress or undue influence.[180] An alleged oral or implied-in-fact agreement may be difficult to prove.[181] In the case of a premarital agreement,

176 *See* Zummo at 1146 (stating that enforcement of agreements concerning a child's religious upbringing "plainly encroaches upon the fundamental right of individuals to question, to doubt, and to change their religious convictions, and to expose their children to their changed beliefs").

177 Abbo v. Briskin, 660 So.2d 1157, 1159 (Fla. Dist. Ct. App. 1995).

178 Zummo, 574 A.2d at 1148 (emphasis in original). Other courts have stated that parental agreements are not determinative, citing general constitutional concerns. *See, e.g., In re* Marriage of Weiss, 49 Cal. Rptr. 2d 339 (premarital agreement to raise children in the Jewish faith not enforceable on First Amendment grounds); Kirchner, 606 A.2d 257 [Parents' oral agreement (at time of child's birth) to raise her as a Catholic is not sufficient basis for restricting father's exposure of child to different religion, citing constitutional concerns.); *and* Hornung v. Hornung, 485 N.W.2d 335, 338 (Neb. Ct. App. 1992) (Parents' agreement during marriage to raise children as Catholics does not justify order requiring father to take children to Catholic Mass during visitation, noting "the court's constitutionally required religious neutrality.").

179 *See* Lynch, 78 N.W.2d at 496–7 (parents' stipulation that child "be reared in the Roman Catholic Religion" is too vague and uncertain to be enforced against mother in a contempt action); *and* Zummo, 574 A.2d at 1145 (Vagueness of order prohibiting father from taking children to "religious services contrary to the Jewish" faith makes it unenforceable on both contract and constitutional grounds.).

180 *See, e.g.*, Schwarzman v. Schwarzman, 388 N.Y.S.2d 993, 996 (Sup. Ct. 1976) (Mother's oral agreement "when she was in great anxiety, in the early stages of pregnancy and unmarried" to raise child as a Jew is not enforceable partly because mother never really adopted Judaism.).

181 *See, e.g., In re* Marriage of Bennett, 587 N.E. 2d 577 (Ill. App. Ct. 1992) (Father failed to prove elements of an implied-in-fact contract to raise the children in the Jewish faith, citing the contract requirements of offer, acceptance, and consideration.); *and* Diemer v. Diemer, 168 N.E.2d 654 (N.Y. 1960) (finding insufficient evidence to support father's allegation that parties entered oral premarital agreement to raise the child in the Protestant faith). A writing requirement is generally required for an enforceable premarital agreement. *See, e.g.*, Unif. Premarital Agmt Act § 2 (1983).

there is often a question about whether the parents intended the agreement to be enforced at divorce or rather to apply only during marriage.[182]

In a few cases, courts have refused to enforce parental agreements on the ground that the terms of such agreements conflict with state custody law. A parental agreement, say some courts, cannot override a judge's role in determining the child's best interest.[183] Other courts have refused to enforce agreements about the child's religious training to the extent that their terms conflict with statutory provisions for shared parental responsibility[184] or with the primary custodian's right to direct the child's religious upbringing.[185]

Despite the constitutional and contract concerns surrounding parental agreements about the child's religious training, courts have sometimes enforced them. Enforcement becomes more likely when the agreement is part of a settlement (rather than a premarital) agreement, when its terms are clearly and narrowly drawn, and when New York law applies.

In *Gruber v. Gruber*,[186] for example, the parents' separation agreement provided that "the children shall attend a yeshivah or school providing Jewish religious training until the completion of the 12th grade."[187] The agreement further provided that all "important decisions" about the children would be "the subject of joint consultation."[188] Notwithstanding the agreement, the father, who had primary custody at the time, removed the two children from a yeshivah and enrolled them in public schools without the mother's knowledge or consent.[189] The mother sought to force the father to reenroll the children in an Orthodox Jewish school, but the trial judge more generally directed the father to enroll the children in "a Jewish religious school that is supplemental to their public education" until their Bar Mitzvah.[190]

On appeal, the court reversed, stating that the language of the parents' agreement was "crystal clear" and that it required the children's enrollment in a full-time yeshivah or Jewish day school rather than a supplemental Hebrew school providing limited religious training.[191] Moreover, said the court, the explicit language of the agreement called

182 *See, e.g.*, Stevenot v. Stevenot, 520 N.Y.S.2d 197 (N.Y. App. Div. 1987) (concluding that oral agreement to raise children in the Congregational Church was not enforceable because parties were not contemplating divorce when they entered the agreement).

183 *See, e.g.*, Stanton v. Stanton, 100 S.E.2d 289 (Ga. 1957) (Parents' premarital agreement to raise children in the husband's religion could not override the discretion of the court to determine the child's best interest.); *and* Hehman v. Hehman, 178 N.Y.S.2d 328 (N.Y. Spec. Term 1958) (Prenuptial agreement designating the child's religious affiliation as Lutheran is not binding where best interest of thirteen-year-old child require court to consider the child's preference.).

184 *See, e.g.*, Sotnick v. Sotnick, 650 So.2d 157 (Fla. Dist. Ct. App. 1995) (agreement to raise child in the Jewish faith not enforceable because right to direct child's religious upbringing is controlled by state statute, which recognizes shared parental responsibility).

185 *See, e.g.*, *In re* Marriage of Wolfert, 598 P.2d 524 (Colo. App. 1979) (Premarital agreement to rear children in the Catholic faith does not trump statutory right of custodial parent to determine the child's religious upbringing.); *and In re* Marriage of Nuechterlein, 587 N.E.2d 21 (Ill. App. Ct. 1992) (Premarital agreement to raise children as Lutherans will not control because state law gives custodial parent the right to determine the child's religious upbringing). For a discussion of the primary custodian's right to direct the child's religious upbringing, *see* Section B.3.a of this chapter.

186 451 N.Y.S.2d 117 (N.Y. App. Div. 1982).

187 *Id.* at 118.

188 *Id.*

189 *Id.*

190 *Id.* at 118–19.

191 *Id.* at 122.

for religious training until the children complete the twelfth grade, not just until their Bar Mitzvah. New York law, said the court, recognizes the right of separating parents to contract about their children's religious training as long as their agreement is in the best interest of the children.[192] Such an agreement will be enforced unless the party in breach proves that compliance with the agreement would be detrimental to the child's best interest.[193] Because there was no evidence in this case that their enrollment in a yeshivah was harming the children, the court ordered the father to enroll the children in a full-time yeshivah or Jewish day school through their completion of the twelfth grade.[194]

In a recent case arising outside New York, the parents agreed at the time of their divorce that they would raise their children in the Protestant faith.[195] The divorce decree implementing this agreement provided

> Based upon the express agreement of the parties that the minor children be raised in the Protestant faith, the Court orders that each party hereto is enjoined from promoting another religious belief system/faith to the minor children unless both parties should consent.[196]

An Arkansas court held the father in contempt for violating the agreement "by promoting another religious belief system/faith" to his sons without the mother's consent.[197] On appeal, the court affirmed, rejecting the father's argument that the contempt order violated his First Amendment rights.[198] The order, said the court, "merely effectuated the parties' agreement."[199]

While a handful of courts have enforced parental agreements about the child's religious training, the majority rule outside New York is that these agreements are generally

192 *Id.* at 120. In another New York case, *Perlstein v. Perlstein* [429 N.Y.S.2d 896 (N.Y. App. Div. 1980)], the parents' separation agreement provided that the child would be raised and educated as an Orthodox Jew and that if the mother violated these provisions, custody would revert to the father. Without the father's knowledge or consent, the mother enrolled the child in a public school, and the father sought a change of custody under the terms of the agreement. A trial court dismissed the father's petition, but an appellate court remanded for a new trial, noting that the right of parents to contract about their children's religious lifestyle is well established in New York. As the parent resisting enforcement of the agreement, the mother bore the burden of showing that compliance with the agreement would be detrimental to the child. The court added that given the mother's "exclusive custody" of the child for the past five years, it might be "too late to enforce religious orthodoxy on the child." *Id.* at 901–02. *See also* Smith v. Smith, 17 Fam. L. Rep. 1024 (N.Y. Fam. Ct., Monroe Cty., 1990) (enforcing agreement requiring mother to raise child as Catholic even after changing her religion). *But see* Glauber v. Glauber, 600 N.Y.S.2d 740 (N.Y. App. Div. 1993) (agreements to arbitrate custody of children are not enforceable).

193 Gruber, 451 N.Y.S.2d at 120.

194 *Id.* at 122. *See also* Spring v. Glawon, 454 N.Y.S.2d 140, 141 (N.Y. App. Div. 1982) (affirming order requiring mother to remove child from religious school because of parents' agreement that "child shall have no religious upbringing without the express written permission of both parties").

195 Rownak v. Rownak, 288 S.W. 3d 672 (Ark. Ct. App. 2008).

196 *Id.* at 673.

197 *Id.*

198 *Id.* at 674.

199 *Id.* at 675. *See also* Gottlieb v. Gottlieb, 175 N.E.2d 619, 627 (Ill. App. Ct. 1961) (stating that agreements about the child's religious upbringing that are incorporated into a decree should not be "lightly cast aside"); Wagshal v. Wagshal, 238 A.2d 903 (Md. 1968) (holding that the chancellor erred in striking from the decree a requirement, based on the parents' agreement, that the child would be raised in the Jewish faith); *and* Bienenfeld, 605 A.2d 172 (changing custody from mother to father partly because mother violated agreement that children would be exposed to both the Orthodox Jewish and Episcopal faiths), *cert. denied*, 612 A.2d 256 (Md. 1992).

not enforceable over the objection of one parent. We now turn to issues involving religion and adoption.

## C. Religion and Adoption

Religion issues in adoption cases fall into two general categories. The first set of cases involves "religious matching" – a process that pairs the child with adoptive parents of an identified religious faith. In the second set of cases, a court considers the religion (or nonreligion) of prospective adoptive parents as one factor in determining whether placement will serve the child's best interest.

Most religious-matching cases begin with a birth parent's express preference for adoptive parents of a particular religion, usually the religion of the birth parent.[200] Deference to a birth parent's religious preference is sometimes authorized by state statute.[201] A Delaware statute, for example, provides that "[i]f either natural parent ... specifies the religion in which he or she desires the child to be raised, the Department or licensed agency shall make placement in accordance with such statement."[202] A New York matching statute goes further, imputing a religious preference to a birth parent who has not expressed one. Under New York law, a presumption arises "that the birth parent wishes the child to be reared in the religion of the birth parent."[203] The rationale for matching statutes is sometimes identified as a deference to the birth parent's right to control the child's religious

[200] The New York matching statute recognizes that a birth parent may choose a religion that is not her own. *See* N.Y. Soc. Serv. Law § 373(7) (2009) ("Religious wishes of a parent shall include wishes that the child be placed in the same religion as the birth parent or in a different religion from the birth parent or with indifference to religion or with religion a subordinate consideration.").

[201] *See, e.g.*, Ark. Code Ann. § 9-9-102(b) (2011) ("If the genetic parent or parents of the child express a preference for placing the child in a foster home or an adoptive home of the same or a similar religious background to that of the genetic parent or parents, the court shall place the child with a family that meets the genetic parent's religious preference, or if a family is not available, to a family of a different religious background that is knowledgeable and appreciative of the child's religious background."); Mass. Gen. Laws Ann. ch. 210 § 5B (2007) ("If ... the parent or parents of said child requested a religious designation for the child, the court may grant a petition for adoption of the child only to a person or persons of the religious designation so requested, unless a placement for adoptive custody based on such request would not have been in the best interests of the child. If a request for religious designation is not given effect, such reasons in support of such determination shall be made a part of the records of the proceedings."); Mont. Code Ann. § 42-4-201 (1997) (Best interest factors include the religion of a prospective adoptive parent "as it relates to the express preference of a birth parent or a child to be placed with an adoptive parent of a particular religious faith or denomination."); N.Y. Soc. Serv. Law § 373(7) (2009) (Statutory provisions on matching according to child's religious preference "shall, so far as consistent with the best interests of the child, and where practicable, be applied so as to give effect to the religious wishes of the birth mother, and of the birth father whose consent would be required for the child's adoption."); R.I. Gen. Laws § 15-7-13 (1975) ["[A] child shall be placed in an adoptive home of any religious faith or persuasion that may be designated by the natural parent(s) so far as practicable." (emphasis added)]; *and* Wis. Stat. Ann. § 48.82(3) (2011) ("When practicable and if requested by the birth parent, the adoptive parents shall be of the same religious faith as the birth parents of the person to be adopted."). *See also* 23 Pa. Cons. Stat. Ann. § 2725 (1992) ["The intermediary *may* honor the preference of the natural parents as to the religious faith in which the adoptive parents intend to rear the adopted child." (emphasis added)].

[202] Del. Code tit. 13,§ 911(a) (2009).

[203] N.Y. Soc. Serv. Law § 373(7) (2009).

upbringing[204] or, more pragmatically, as a means to increase the willingness of a religious parent to place the child for adoption.

Matching also may be based on the religious preference or religious background of the child.[205] A much-discussed provision of the New York Constitution, for example, provides that the child "shall be ... placed, when practicable ... in the custody of a person, of the same religious persuasion as the child."[206] When a mature child expresses a religious preference, a court may conclude that placement with adoptive parents who practice that religion is important to the child's well-being.[207] Some courts have taken a broader view, reasoning that adoptive parents need not practice the same religion as the child as long as they are willing to accommodate the child's religious preference.[208] Of course, gauging whether a child is mature enough to have a religious preference can be a difficult judicial task and raises many of the same questions previously discussed in the context of choosing a primary custodian.[209]

Courts have sometimes determined a child's religious identity based on the child's subjection to a religious ritual. In a case involving a neglected four-year-old boy, for example, a court determined that the boy was Jewish based on his ritual circumcision as an infant, notwithstanding the father's subsequent decision to have the child baptized in the Roman Catholic Church.[210]

204 *See, e.g.*, Scott v. Family Ministries, 135 Cal. Rptr. 430, 437 (1976) (deferring to birth parent's preference is consistent with the "common law right of a natural parent to control the religious upbringing of his child"). *But see In re* Efrain C., 314 N.Y.S.2d 255, 265 (N.Y. Fam. Ct. 1970) (reasoning that the parental right to determine the child's religious upbringing "is attenuated by the fact that he is surrendering his responsibility for his child."). For a discussion of the parental right to direct the child's religious upbringing in the context of custody disputes, *see* Section B.3.a of this chapter.

205 *See, e.g.*, 750 Ill. Stat. Ann. 50 § 15 (1985) ("The court in entering a judgment of adoption shall, whenever possible, give custody through adoption to a petitioner or petitioners of the same religious belief as that of the child."); La. Child. Code Ann. art. 683(D) (2004) ("In committing a child to the custody of an individual or a private agency or institution, the court shall, whenever practicable, select a person, agency, or institution of the same religious affiliation as the child or his parents."); Mont. Code Ann. § 42-4-201 (1997) [Best interest factors include the religion of a prospective adoptive parent "as it relates to the express *preference of* a birth parent or *a child* to be placed with an adoptive parent of a particular religious faith or denomination." (emphasis added)]; *and* N.Y. Soc. Serv. Law § 373(3) (2009) ("In appointing guardians of children, and in granting orders of adoption of children, the court shall, when practicable, appoint as such guardians, and give custody through adoption, only to a person or persons of the same religious faith as that of the child.").

206 N.Y. Const. art. VI, § 32. This section provides in full,

> [w]hen any court having jurisdiction over a child shall commit it or remand it to an institution or agency or place it in the custody of any person by parole, placing out, adoption or guardianship, the child shall be committed or remanded or placed, when practicable, in an institution or agency governed by persons, or in the custody of a person, of the same religious persuasion as the child.

207 For a discussion of the child's religious identity in the choice of a primary custodian, *see* Section B.2.a.i of this chapter.

208 *See, e.g.*, Matter of Baby Girl Z, 454 N.Y.S.2d 941, 943 (A.D.2d 1989), *appeal denied*, 555 N.Y.S.2d 691 (Key issue in determining whether birth mother's religious preference would be honored was not the religious background of the adoptive father but rather the religion in which the child would be raised.).

209 For a discussion of the child's religious identity as a factor in the choice of a primary custodian, *see* Section B.2.a.i of this chapter.

210 *In re* Glavas, 121 N.Y.S.2d 12, 18–19 (1953) (reasoning that a change young child's religion requires the consent of both parents). *See also In re* Santos, 105 N.Y.S. 2d 716, 717–18 (1951) (vacating an order committing seven- and eight-year-old sisters to Jewish agency for adoption because as infants both children

Matching statutes have survived constitutional challenge when interpreted to make matching a relevant but not exclusive or dispositive factor in determining whether an adoptive placement is in the child's best interest.[211] Religious matching thus should not be the sole reason for granting or denying an adoption petition.[212] State statutes often limit the role of matching to cases in which it is "practicable," consistent with the child's best interest, or will not result in hardship to the child.[213] Religious matching has been found impracticable where the child is difficult to place because of a physical disability,[214] where other circumstances make placement difficult and matching would

had been baptized Roman Catholic). Under an earlier version of the Massachusetts matching statute, the mother's religion was imputed to the child when the child's religion was in dispute. *See* Petitions of Goldman, 121 N.E.2d 843, 846 (Mass. 1954) (stating that "a child too young to understand any religion, even imperfectly, nevertheless may have a religion," which is the religion of the parents or the mother).

211 As the Massachusetts Supreme Court explained long ago in rejecting a constitutional challenge to its matching statute: "All religions are treated alike. There is no subordination of one sect to another. No burden is placed upon anyone for maintenance of any religion. No exercise of religion is required, prevented or hampered." Petitions of Goldman, 121 N.E.2d 843, 846 (Mass. 1954), *cert denied*, 348 U.S. 942 (1955). It is not clear that this reasoning would suffice under contemporary constitutional jurisprudence. For a case rejecting constitutional challenges to New York's matching law, *see* Dickens v. Ernesto, 281 N.E.2d 153, 154–7 (N.Y. Ct. App.), *appeal dismissed*, 407 U.S. 917 (1972) (rejecting Establishment Clause challenge on ground that matching laws prioritize the child's best interest and religion is not an exclusive or controlling factor). For a constitutional challenge to New York's matching statute as applied to foster care placements, *see* Wilder v. Bernstein, 848 F.2d 1338, 1346–9 (2d Cir. 1988) (holding that religious matching is permitted but not required by the First Amendment and that the state should make "reasonable efforts" to accommodate the religious preference of legal parents and foster children).

212 *See, e.g.*, Cooper v. Hinrichs, 140 N.E.2d 293, 276 (Ill. 1957) (noting that the best interests of the child is the "polestar" in adoption cases and that "the religious factor … does not … bar adoption irrespective of all other factors"); Petitions of Goldman, 121 N.E.2d 843, 846 (Mass. 1954), *cert denied*, 348 U.S. 942 (1955) (concluding that matching statute "merely ascribes somewhat more weight than was before ascribed to the religion of the natural parents"); Petition of Gally, 107 N.E.2d 21, 25 (Mass. 1952) (finding no legislative intent that "identity of religion should be the sole or necessarily the principal consideration"); Dickens v. Ernesto, 281 N.E.2d 153, 155 (1972), *appeal dismissed*, 407 U.S. 917 (1972) (stating that "[i]t is thus apparent, first, that religion is but one of many factors in the placement of a child for adoption and, second, that placement in conformity with 'the religious wishes of the parents of the child,' though desirable, is not mandatory."); *In re* Adoption of E, 279 A.2d 785, 793–6 (N.J. 1971) (holding that denial of adoption on sole ground of religious matching violates the First Amendment); *and* Orzechowski v. Perales, 582 N.Y.S.2d 341, 347–8 (N.Y. Sup.Ct. 1992) (stating that religion may not be "the sole or determinative factor" in adoption placements).

213 *See, e.g.*, Del. Code tit. 13,§ 911(c) (2009) (giving court discretion to waive requirement that natural parent's preference be honored to avoid "a hardship for the child to be adopted in obtaining a suitable and prompt placement"); La. Child. Code Ann. art. 683(D) (2004) (requiring court "whenever practicable" to select a person of the same religion as the child or his parents); Mass. Gen. Laws Ann. ch. 210 § 5B (2007) (Court must place child according to parent's preference "unless a placement for adoptive custody based on such request would not have been in the best interests of the child."); N.Y. Soc. Serv. Law § 373(3) (2009) (requiring court "when practicable" to place child with adoptive parents of the same religion as the child); R.I. Gen. Laws § 15-7-13 (1975) (requiring the court to place child in a home of the same faith as the natural parent "so far as practicable") *and* Wis. Stat. Ann. § 48.82(3) (2011) (requiring the court to honor birth parents' religious preference "[w]hen practicable"). For an example of stronger statutory language, *see* 750 Ill. Stat. Ann. 50 § 15 (1985) (requiring the court "whenever possible" to give custody through adoption to parents of the same religion as the child). Early on, the Illinois Supreme Court interpreted this language to mean that a court should not "bar adoption irrespective of all other factors merely because the adopting parents are of a different religious persuasion than the child." *See* Cooper, 140 N.E.2d, at 276.

214 *See, e.g.*, Frantum v. Dep't of Pub Welfare, 133 A.2d 408, 411–12 (Md. 1957) (affirming denial of adoption of physically disabled child by older Lutheran parents where mother preferred Catholic parents but allowing subsequent petition if more suitable parents are not found within six months); *and* Petition of

lead to rejection of otherwise well-suited parents,[215] or where matching would delay the child's placement.[216] Deference to a birth parent's preference has been held unnecessary where parental rights were terminated rather than surrendered voluntarily.[217] The many constraints on matching avoid the harsh results sometimes seen when matching plays a dispositive role.[218]

Apart from the matching cases, religion generally plays only a minimal role in adoption decisions. *Scott v. Family Ministries*[219] provides a good example. In *Scott*, representatives of World Vision, an evangelical Christian relief organization, brought orphans to the United States from Cambodia, delivered the children to a licensed California adoption agency, and instructed the agency to place the children in Christian homes. Dr. Scott, an Episcopalian, sought to adopt a child for whom he had provided medical care, but the agency turned him down because he and his wife were not members of an evangelical Protestant church. On appeal, the court observed that the agency, operating under state license, was subject to constitutional restrictions on state action. The agency, concluded the court, could not constitutionally use religion as a factor in selecting adoptive parents unless the birth parents expressed a preference that the child be raised in a particular religion.[220]

The court's duty to ensure that an adoptive placement is in the child's best interest has led some courts to inquire into the religion (or nonreligion) of prospective adoptive parents.[221] This inquiry is sometimes cast as an effort to assess the moral fitness of prospective parents and their ability to ensure the child's moral and spiritual well-being. A Montana statute, for example, recognizes that the religion of prospective adoptive parents is relevant "as it relates to the ability to provide the child with an opportunity for religious or spiritual and ethical development."[222] An inquiry into religiosity, however, raises many of the same Free Exercise and Establishment Clause concerns previously discussed in the context of parents competing for primary custody of children.[223] Courts

Gally, 107 N.E.2d at 24 & 25 [religious matching not practicable where prospective adoptive parents took sick infant (now two years old) into their home and nursed her to health].

215 *See, e.g., In re* Adoption of Michael D., 322 N.Y.S.2d 532, 533–34 (N.Y. Sup. Ct. 1971) (concluding that best interests of child were served by allowing Mormon parents, with whom child had lived for over three years, to adopt her even though child was baptized a Roman Catholic).

216 *See, e.g.,* Efrain C., 314 N.Y.S.2d at 263 (stating that "[i]n view of the emphasis placed by child care experts on a wholesome and stable environment in early infancy – each day in the early years bringing either development or retardation – a delay of more than a month or two in a child's adoptive placement in order to secure religious conformity must be deemed detrimental"). *See also* Frantum, 133 A.2d at 412 (setting six-month limit on search for younger, religiously matched parents).

217 *See* In Adoption of Brooke, 679 N.E.2d 569, 681 (Mass. App. Ct. 1997).

218 *See, e.g.,* Petitions of Goldman, 121 N.E.2d at 845 (affirming denial of petition by Jewish couple with whom children had lived for three years because birth mother was Catholic, and Catholic families were available and willing to adopt).

219 Scott v. Family Ministries, 135 Cal. Rptr. 430 (1976).

220 *Id.* at 437–40.

221 *See, e.g., In re* Bourque, 245 So.2d 525, 530 (La. Ct. App. 1971) (noting that prospective adoptive parents rarely attended church while children were in their custody and concluding that their failure to provide the children with "adequate religious training" was an important factor that may be considered on application for final adoption).

222 Mont. Stat. § 42-4-201(c) (2009). Some statutes require state agencies to include information about the religion of a prospective adoptive parent in the adoption report, evidently to be used in the court's determination of whether a placement is in the child's best interest. *See, e.g.,* Ariz. Rev. Stat. Ann. § 8-105(F)(4) (2009) (report to the court shall include the "religious background of the applicant").

223 *See* Section B of this chapter.

thus have cautioned that religion should play only a limited, nondispositive role in determining the child's best interest.[224] A lack of religiosity thus should not be the sole ground for disqualifying otherwise qualified prospective adoptive parents.[225]

## D. Religion and Divorce

As we have seen, state laws accommodate religious choices about marriage by authorizing religious solemnization. We turn now to the question of whether the state also will accommodate religious choices about divorce. The issue most frequently arises when one spouse asks a civil divorce court to enforce a religiously grounded marriage contract.

Marriage contracts typically are entered as part of a Jewish or Islamic wedding ceremony. The Jewish marriage contract, the *ketubah*, traditionally includes a provision that the couple will comply with Jewish law, that the husband will support the wife, and, in some instances, that the husband will pay the wife a specific sum of money in the event of divorce. The Islamic marriage contract, the *mahr* (or *sadaq*) agreement, typically requires the husband to pay the wife a specified sum (the *mahr*), a portion of which is due at the time of marriage and another portion at the wife's election, usually at divorce or the husband's death. Efforts to enforce a *ketubah* or a *mahr* agreement have met with varied success. We first explore terms requiring the husband to make a financial payment to the wife at divorce.

### 1. *Agreements Requiring Financial Payments at Divorce*

In a number of cases, one spouse has asked a civil divorce court to enforce the financial terms of a religious contract, usually a *mahr* agreement. The success of this effort first depends on whether the agreement satisfies the general requirements for enforcement of a contract. To the extent that the agreement meets these "neutral principles of law," it may be enforced, even it was entered as part of a religious marriage ceremony.[226] Application of general contract law to *mahr* agreements, however, has raised numerous questions.

As a threshold matter, a religiously grounded marriage contract may be unenforceable in a civil court if the parties viewed the agreement as a religious or cultural ritual without legal effect.[227] Nor will a marriage contract be enforced if the bride signed under duress.

224 *See, e.g.*, Dickens, 281 N.E.2d at 155 ("Religion has always been a relevant and important, though not controlling, consideration in this State in the placement of children for adoption."); *and* Commonwealth v. White, 169 A.2d 69, 73 (Pa. 1961) ("Proper religious training of a child is most important and a factor which must be given the most serious consideration. ... However, such factor, while of great weight, is not controlling.").

225 *See In re* Adoption of "E," 279 A.2d 785, 792–3 (N.J. 1971) (noting that while religiosity may evidence moral fitness to adopt, "we do not believe that any reasonable man no matter how devout in his own beliefs, would contend that morality lies in the exclusive province of one or of all religions or of religiosity in general").

226 *See* Odatalla v. Odatalla, 810 A.2d 93, 96–7 (N.J. Super. 2002) ("*Mahr* agreement is not void simply because it was entered into during an Islamic ceremony," but enforcement depends on satisfaction of neutral principles of law.); *and* Aziz v. Aziz, 488 N.Y.S.2d 123, 124 (Sup. Ct. Queens Co. 1985) ("[S]ecular terms [of *mahr* agreement] are enforceable as a contractual obligation, notwithstanding that it was entered into as part of a religious ceremony.").

227 As one husband described a *ketubah*, it is "poetry or art rather than a contract." *In re* Marriage of Goldman, 554 N.E.2d 1016, 1020 (Ill. App. Ct. 1990). The *mahr* is sometimes a nominal sum, suggesting

The *mahr* agreement typically is negotiated by the groom and the bride's father or other male relative, giving the bride little opportunity to bargain over its terms.[228] This circumstance alone, however, has been held insufficient to establish duress.[229]

Additionally, the terms of a *mahr* agreement may be too uncertain or indefinite to support an enforcement order. If, for example, the agreement provides that it will be governed by "Islamic law," a court may be hard-pressed to determine whether this choice invokes "the Shafi'i, Hanafi, Maliki, [or] Hanban" interpretation of Islam.[230] As one court concluded, "[a]n agreement whose only substantive term in any language is that the marriage has been made in accordance with 'Islamic law' is hopelessly uncertain as to its terms and conditions."[231]

Even if the intended school of Islamic law can be ascertained, asking a civil court to apply that law may require an inquiry into religious doctrine. The *mahr* agreement is typically quite short[232] and may fail to answer questions important to its application. Must the husband pay the *mahr* if the wife is the one who files for divorce?[233] Does the *mahr*, however small, supplant state divorce law, precluding the wife from receiving alimony

a symbolic rather than legal meaning. *See, e.g., In re* Marriage of Shaban, 105 Cal. Rptr. 2d 863, 865–6 (Ct. App. 2001) (*Mahr* agreement provided for an immediate payment of the equivalent of roughly $1 at marriage and $30 at divorce.).

228 *See id.* at 865 (noting that the *mahr* agreement was signed by the groom and the bride's father, who acted as the bride's representative) *and* Akileh v. Elchahal, 666 So.2d 246, 248 (Ct. App. Fla. 1996) (noting that the bride's father negotiated the *mahr* agreement without her participation). Even if she is given an opportunity to negotiate a *mahr*, the bride may be disparately positioned to do so, having little experience in dealing with men outside her family. In *Akileh*, for example, the court noted that the bride "had never socialized with a man outside the presence of her family." Akileh at 247.

229 In *Chaudry v. Chaudry* [388 A.2d 1000 (N.J. Super. 1978)], for example, an appellate court rejected a trial court's holding that a *mahr* agreement was unenforceable because the bride had no choice but to enter it. At divorce, the agreement, which was signed in Pakistan, limited the wife's financial rights against her physician husband to $1,500. Although the appellate court held the agreement enforceable, it quoted at length the trial court's observations regarding the Pakistani bride's position:

> While the State does recognize [premarital] agreements, it is essentially because there is a freedom of choice between the parties, and if they with full knowledge of their rights and with proper guidance and counseling come to a certain determination to waive or give up rights this certainly may be enforced in the proper case in this State; but, where as here there was no choice given to the … [wife] under the law of Pakistan and the Islamic law, which I do not criticize. … she had no choice. She had to waive, give up or not claim support or alimony in the event of a divorce, and it cannot be said that with that choice she chose to do it, because there was no choice involved. To that extent it is so clearly contrary to the public policy of this State that I decline to enforce it.

*Id.* at 1003.

230 Shaban, 105 Cal. Rptr. 2d at 869 n. 4 (noting that "Islamic law" may refer to any one of these four schools of interpretation).

231 *Id.* at 865–7. Actually, the *mahr* agreement in *Shaban* identified "a dowry of 500 Egyptian pounds and 25 piasters due from the husband to wife's 'proxy,' i.e., her father," and stated that twenty-five piasters had already been paid, with the balance due at divorce or the husband's death.

232 The *mahr* agreement in *Shaban*, for example, was a "one-page piece of paper written in Arabic.") *Id.* at 865.

233 *See, e.g., In re* Marriage of Dajani, 251 Cal. Rptr. 871, 871–2 (Ct. App. 1985) (noting conflicting expert testimony before trial court regarding whether under Islamic law wife forfeits deferred *mahr* by filing for divorce, but ultimately holding *mahr* agreement unenforceable because it violated public policy by encouraging divorce); *and* Akileh, 666 So.2d at 247–8 (noting testimony of wife's Islamic expert that wife did not forfeit right to *sadaq* by filing for divorce and conflicting testimony of husband that an Islamic court disqualified his sister for a *sadaq* because she wanted the divorce).

and a statutorily authorized share of community or marital property?[234] To the extent that the answers to such questions depend on an interpretation of Islamic law, enforcement of the agreement may require the court to become an arbiter, inappropriately entangling the court in Islamic religious doctrine.

If a *ketubah* or *mahr* agreement is classified as a premarital agreement,[235] public-policy concerns pose more enforcement hurdles.[236] Most important, under the traditional rule, a premarital agreement is not enforceable if its terms encourage divorce.[237] To the extent that a marriage contract aims to protect the wife by creating a financial disincentive for the husband to seek a divorce,[238] it may conversely create a financial incentive for the wife to do so herself. In *In re Marriage of Noghrey*,[239] for example, the court refused to enforce a *ketubah* that provided that on divorce the wife would receive a house and $500,000 or one-half of the husband's assets, whichever is greater. The agreement, said the court, was unenforceable because it encouraged the wife "to seek a dissolution, and with all deliberate speed, lest the husband suffer an untimely demise, nullifying the contract, and the wife's right to the money and property."[240]

Notwithstanding these challenges, courts have sometimes enforced the financial terms of religious contracts. In *Odatalla v. Odatalla*,[241] for example, a New Jersey court enforced a *mahr* agreement requiring the husband to pay the wife $10,000 at divorce.[242] The agreement, stated the court, "is nothing more and nothing less than a simple contract between two consenting adults … and does not contravene any statute or interests of society."[243] Similarly, in *Akileh v. Elchahal*,[244] a Florida court enforced a *mahr*

234 *See* Chaudry, 388 A.2d at 1006 (interpreting *mahr* to supplant any financial rights wife would otherwise have under state divorce law).

235 Because *ketubah* and *mahr* agreements are typically entered into at the time of marriage, a number of courts have described them as premarital agreements. *See, e.g.*, Dajani, 251 Cal. Rptr. at 872; Akileh, 666 So.2d at 247; *and* Chaudry, 388 A.2d at 1002. *But see* Shaban, 105 Cal. Rptr. 2d at 867 (noting trial court's conclusion that *mahr* agreement was not a premarital agreement but simply a marriage certificate identifying the parties and witnesses); *and* Ahmed v. Ahmed, 261 S.W.3d 190 (Tex. App. 2008) (concluding that *mahr* agreement was not a premarital agreement because it was entered six months after civil marriage ceremony).

236 The Uniform Premarital Agreement (UPAA), for example, provides that a premarital agreement is not enforceable if it is not voluntarily entered or if it was unconscionable at execution and a disclosure requirement is not met. Unif. Premarital Agmt Act § 6(a). *See, e.g.*, Atassi v. Atassi, 451 S.E.2d 371 (N.C. Ct. App. 1995) (concluding that Syrian marriage contract did not satisfy requirements of the UPAA).

237 *See* Dajani, 251 Cal. Rptr. at 872 ["Prenuptial agreements which 'facilitate divorce or separation by providing for a settlement only in the event of such an occurrence are void as against public policy.'" (citations omitted)].

238 *See* Shaban, 105 Cal. Rptr. 2d at 869 n. 6 (observing that in Jewish and Islamic law, a dowry compensates the wife for the husband's right to divorce at will and that if the deferred dower is high enough, it deters the husband from exercising that right).

239 215 Cal. Rptr. 153, 155 (6th Dist. 1985).

240 Noghrey at 156–7. *See also* Dajani, 251 Cal. Rptr. at 871 n. 3, 872–3 (concluding that *mahr* agreement requiring husband to pay roughly $1,700 at divorce encouraged "profiteering by divorce" and was thus unenforceable) (quoting Noghrey, 215 Cal. Rptr. at 153). For a view that *Dajani* was wrongly decided because "[a] dowry worth only $1,700, payable upon dissolution, is insufficient to seriously jeopardize a viable marriage," *see In re* Marriage of Bellio, 129 Cal. Rptr. 2d 556, 559 (Cal. Ct. App. 2003).

241 810 A.2d 93 (N.J. Super. Ct. 2002)

242 *Id.* at 98.

243 *Id. See also* Chaudry, 388 A.2d 1000 (enforcing, over wife's objection, *mahr* agreement that limited the wife's financial rights at divorce to $1,500).

244 666 So.2d 246.

agreement requiring the husband to pay the wife $50,000 at divorce,[245] and in *Aziz v. Aziz*,[246] a New York court enforced a *mahr* agreement requiring the husband to pay the wife $5,000 at divorce.[247]

## 2. *Agreements to Obtain a Religious Divorce*

More controversial than the financial payment cases are cases involving agreements to obtain a religious divorce. In a recurring scenario, a couple marries in the Jewish faith, and at the time of their civil divorce, the wife seeks to compel her husband to provide a *get*. The *get* is a bill of religious divorce, which frees the wife to remarry in the Jewish faith.[248] Without a *get*, the wife is an *agunah* (a "tied" woman).[249] If an *agunah* attempts to remarry, she is cast as an adulteress, and if she has subsequent children, they are deemed illegitimate and unable to marry other Jews.[250]

Not surprisingly, given the significant consequences associated with failure to obtain a *get*, wives have sometimes asked civil courts to compel reluctant husbands to obtain or initiate procedures to obtain a *get*.[251] The wife's request typically takes the form of an action to compel the husband to specifically perform his promise to provide a *get*.[252] Establishing the husband's promise is a crucial first step, for without a contractual foundation, the court may conclude that it lacks authority to grant the wife's request.[253] Some courts have determined that the *ketubah* contains an implied term requiring the husband to provide a *get* in the event of a civil divorce. In *Minkin v. Minkin*,[254] for example, the parties' *ketubah* included the traditional language that the parties will "conform to the provisions of the laws of Moses and Israel."[255] These laws, observed the court, require a husband to provide a *get* to a wife who has committed adultery.[256] Because the husband had alleged the wife's adultery, the court concluded that the *ketubah* required him to provide her with a *get*.[257]

245 *Id.* at 247.
246 Aziz, 488 N.Y.S.2d 123.
247 *Id.* at 124.
248 Aflalo v. Aflalo, 685 A.2d 523, 524 n. 1 (Super Ct. N.J. 1996).
249 *Id.* at 527.
250 *Id.*
251 *See, e.g.*, Koeppel v. Koeppel, 138 N.Y.S.2d 366, 370 (N.Y. Sup. Ct. 1954) (Wife sought specific performance of husband's promise, in pre-annulment agreement, to "appear before a Rabbi or Rabbinate ... and execute any and all papers and documents required by and necessary to effectuate a dissolution of their marriage in accordance with the ecclesiastical laws of the Faith and Church of said parties.").
252 Specific performance, rather than damages, is the remedy sought because a monetary award would not give the wife the benefit of her bargain. *See id.* at 371 (observing that wife had no adequate remedy at law against husband who refused to obtain a religious divorce as promised).
253 *See* Victor v. Victor, 866 P.2d 899, 901 (Ct. App. Ariz. 1994) (finding nothing in Arizona statutes that gives court authority to order a husband to grant a religious divorce and noting that "a religious divorce is not germane to the civil dissolution"); *and* Turner v. Turner, 192 So.2d 787, 788–9 (Ct. App. Fla. 1967) (stating that Florida divorce statute does not authorize court to require party to secure a religious divorce).
254 Minkin v. Minkin, 434 A.2d 665 (N.J. Super. Ct. Ch. Div. 1981).
255 *Id.* at 665–6.
256 *Id.*
257 *Id.* at 666. *See also* Goldman, 554 N.E.2d at 1020, 1022 (interpreting the words "[b]e thou my wife according to the law of Moses and Israel" to mean that status of marriage would be governed by Othodox Jewish law, which requires the husband to provide a *get* on divorce); *and* Burns v. Burns, 538 A.2d 438,

More often a husband's promise to provide a *get* is expressly stated in a separation agreement or other agreement entered when marital troubles have arisen. In *Scholl v. Scholl*,[258] for example, the parties' "Stipulation of Settlement" included a provision that the "[h]usband shall forthwith cooperate with Wife in allowing her to obtain a Jewish Divorce known as a *GET*."[259] Wives have sometimes charged that they paid too high a price for such promises, acceding to a husband's demands for financial or custodial concessions in return for his promise to provide a *get*. In a few cases, courts have held such agreements unenforceable on this ground, concluding that the wife's consent was obtained under duress.[260]

If the court determines that the husband made and broke an enforceable promise to provide a *get*, the court must then tackle the troubling question of whether specific enforcement of that promise would violate the First Amendment. Judicial answers to this question have been inconsistent. New York courts have held that a court can specifically enforce a promise to obtain a religious divorce without violating the First Amendment.[261] Courts in Illinois

440–1 (N.J. Super. Ct. Ch. Div. 1987) (noting that the *ketubah* required parties to conform to law of Moses and Israel and listing five circumstances in which this law requires a husband to secure a *get*). *But see* Victor, 866 P.2d at 902 (Language in *ketubah* that parties will comply with the "laws of Moses and Israel" is too vague to support terms requiring husband to obtain a *get*.); *and* Mayer-Kolker v. Kolker, 819 A.2d 17, 20–1 (N.J. Super. Ct. 2003) (concluding that reference to "law of Moses and Israel" was too imprecise to enforce).

258 621 A.2d 808 (Del. Fam. Ct. 1992).

259 *Id.* at 809. *See also* Kaplinsky v. Kaplinsky, 603 N.Y.S.2d 574, 575 (Sup. Ct. 1993) (Stipulation of settlement provided that husband would "remove any and all barriers to the wife's remarriage."); Waxstein v. Waxstein, 395 N.Y.S.2d 877, 880 (Sup. Ct. 1976) (Separation agreement provided that "parties shall obtain a *GET* from a duly constituted Rabbinical court."), *aff'd*, 394 N.Y.S.2d 153 (App. Div. 1977); *and* Rubin v. Rubin, 348 N.Y.S.2d 61, 63 (Fam. Ct. 1973) (separation agreement provided that parties would cooperate in obtaining a Jewish divorce).

260 *See, e.g.*, Segal v. Segal, 650 A.2d 996, 997–8 (N.J. App.Div. 1996) (concluding that husband's refusal to consent to a *get* unless wife acceded to all his demands constituted "extreme pressure" requiring invalidation of deed); Burns, 538 A.2d at 439–40 (describing husband's offer to secure a *get* if wife invested $25,000 in trust for daughter as "akin to extortion"); *and In re* Golding v. Golding, 581 N.Y.S.2d 4, 6 (N.Y. App. Div. 1992) (holding that the wife "did not freely and voluntarily enter into the [settlement] agreement, but was compelled to do so by her husband's invocation of his power to refuse to give her a Jewish divorce"). *See also* Perl v. Perl, 512 N.Y.S.2d 372, 375 (N.Y. App. Div. 1987) (noting the "unequal allocation of power between spouses to terminate a religious marriage and "the very real possibility" that the wife's consent to settlement agreement was coerced). For a case in which the court rejected the wife's claim of duress, *see* Rubin, 348 N.Y.S.2d at 67–8 (noting that wife's "vigor" in negotiations and the number of negotiated amendments to the settlement agreement undercut her claim of undue influence). *See also* Greenberg v. Greenberg, 656 N.Y.S.2d 369, 369–70 (App. Div. 1997) (rejecting wife's argument that she executed general release prior to arbitration under threat that she would otherwise be subject to writ issued against one who disobeys rabbinical decrees).

261 *See, e.g.*, Kaplinsky, 603 N.Y.S.2d at 575 (affirming order holding husband in contempt for failing to provide *get* as required by parties' stipulation of settlement); Waxstein, 395 N.Y.S.2d 877, 881 (requiring husband to obtain or initiate proceedings to obtain a *get*); *and* Koeppel, 138 N.Y.S.2d at 369–71 (stating that husband's failure to comply with promise in preannulment agreement to cooperate in obtaining a religious divorce left wife with no adequate remedy at law and denying husband's motion for summary judgment). In an interesting twist on the usual scenario, the *wife* in *Rubin v. Rubin* refused to cooperate in obtaining a *get* despite a provision in the parties' agreement that made her cooperation a condition precedent to the husband's duty to pay a lump sum of money (348 N.Y.S.2d at 68). When the wife sued the husband to collect the amount due, the court ordered the husband to "consult a Rabbi of his choice for the purpose of having notice sent to … [the wife] either to appear or to accept a *get*" and held that if a *get* is obtained within two weeks, husband shall pay wife the $3,740 due under the agreement, but that if a *get* is not so obtained, wife's petition shall be dismissed. *Id.*

and Delaware have agreed,[262] an Arizona court has disagreed,[263] and the New Jersey courts are split.[264]

In the leading case of *Minkin*,[265] a New Jersey court rejected the husband's claim that an order requiring him to provide a *get* would violate the First Amendment.[266] Such an order, reasoned the court, would merely require the husband to do what he promised to do in the *ketubah*.[267] "Acquisition of a *get*," said the court, "is not a religious act, but a severance of a contractual relationship between two parties."[268] Citing a rabbi's testimony, the court explained that "the *get* does not involve a religious ceremony or require a rabbi's presence, and although the husband is required to take the initiative, he does not have to be a believer, state any doctrine or creed, or even acknowledge his Jewishness." The court added that the state permits clergy to perform marriages in religious ceremonies and that this practice "has never been considered to be an excessive entanglement with religion."[269] The *get* procedure, concluded the court, "cannot be construed as any more religious than the marriage ceremony itself."[270] Other courts have taken positions similar to that of *Minkin*, reasoning that specific performance orders merely require a husband to do what he promised to do,[271] that such orders

262 *See* Scholl, 621 A.2d 808, 813 (Fam. Ct. Del. 1992) (directing husband to obtain an Orthodox *get* within 60 days); *and In re* Marriage of Goldman, 554 N.E.2d 1016, 1021 (Ill. App. Ct. 1990) (affirming order requiring husband to give wife an Orthodox *get*).

263 *See* Victor, 866 P.2d 899, 901 (stating that the First Amendment prohibits a court from requiring a religious act and that the *ketubah* was not an enforceable agreement). *See also* Turner v. Turner, 192 So. 2d 787, at 788–9 (Fla. 1996) (holding that the lower court had no authority to order husband to cooperate with wife in obtaining a Jewish divorce but not mentioning whether husband had at any time promised to obtain a *get*). In an older case, a Pennsylvania court held that it had no authority to order a husband to appear before a "Hebrew clergyman and there make oral or written declaration that he agrees to free … [the wife] from the bonds of matrimony," notwithstanding the wife's claim that the husband made an oral premarital promise that he would adhere to all Hebrew practices and submit all disputes to a rabbi. Price v. Price, 16 Pa. D. & C. 290, 290–1 (Ct. Common Pleas 1932).

264 *Compare* Minkin, 434 A.2d 665 (holding that the court may order the husband to obtain a *get* without violating the First Amendment) *and* Burns, 538 A.2d 438 (ordering husband to initiate proceedings for a *get* or alternatively to authorize preparation of a *get* on his behalf) *with* Aflalo, 685 A.2d 523 (declining to require husband to provide a *get*).

265 434 A.2d 665.

266 *Id.* at 668.

267 *Id.* at 666.

268 *Id.* at 667. The court added that "entry of an order compelling the … [husband] to secure a *get* would have the clear secular purpose of completing a dissolution of the marriage." *Id.* at 668.

269 *Id.* at 668.

270 *Id.*

271 *See* Scholl, 621 A.2d at 812 (stating that an order requiring husband to obtain a *get* "would not be constitutionally infirm … but would be proper to compel Husband to do what he already promised"); Goldman, 554 N.E.2d at 1024 (stating that order required husband "to do nothing more than what he promised to do when he signed the *ketubah*" and finding his free exercvise claim was without merit); *and* Koeppel, 138 N.Y.S.2d at 373 (stating that specific performance would "merely require the … [husband] to do what he voluntarily agreed to do" and rejecting the husband's contention that specific performance would violate his First Amendment rights). *See also* Avitzur v. Avitzur, 446 N.E.2d 136, 138 (Ct. App. NY 1983) (noting that wife did not seek to compel the husband to obtain a *get* but "merely seeks to enforce an agreement made by … [husband] to appear before and accept the decision of a designated tribunal").

are based on "neutral principles" of law,[272] and that they do not require a husband to engage in a religious act.[273]

These propositions, however, have not gone uncontested. In *Aflalo v. Aflalo*,[274] another New Jersey court refused to follow the *Minkin* lead, concluding that an order compelling a husband to cooperate in obtaining a Jewish divorce would violate his First Amendment rights.[275] The *Aflalo* court found "unconvincing" the *Minkin* court's statement that obtaining a *get* is not a religious act, noting that the court reached this conclusion only after choosing among the testimony of several rabbis.[276] This process required the court to decide religious doctrine, inappropriately entangling the court in religious affairs and casting the court in the role of "arbiter of what is 'religious.'"[277] Moreover, warned the *Aflalo* court, an order compelling a husband to provide a *get* provokes "the unsettling vision of future enforcement proceedings," including fines and imprisonment.[278] "The specter of [a husband] being imprisoned or surrendering his religious freedoms because of action by a civil court is the very image which gave rise to the First Amendment."[279] As a practical matter, added the court, "*Minkin* fails to recognize that coercing the husband to provide the 'get' would not have the effect sought" because under Jewish law a *get* must be given voluntarily.[280]

An alternative to an action to enforce a promise to obtain a religious divorce lies in New York's controversial "*Get* Statute." This statute authorizes a court to condition the

[272] *See, e.g.*, Goldman, 554 N.E.2d at 1023 (stating that court may apply "objective, well-established principles of secular law, or 'neutral principles of law,'"and concluding that the order requiring husband to obtain a *get* "avoids an excessive entanglement with religion"). *See also* Avitzur, 446 N.E.2d at 138 (reasoning that an agreement to bring marital disputes to a religious tribunal is entitled "to no less dignity than any other civil contract").

[273] *See* Scholl, 621 A.2d at 812 (stating that order requiring husband to obtain a *get* would not require him "to participate in a religious ceremony or perform acts contrary to his religious belief"); *and* Goldman, 554 N.E.2d at 1024 (noting that "[e]xpert testimony established that the *get* procedure was secular in nature and did not require ... [the husband] to engage in any act of worship or to express any religious belief").

[274] 685 A.2d 523 (N.J. Super. 1996).

[275] *Id.* at 525.

[276] *Id.* at 528.

[277] *Id.*

[278] *Id.* at 530. The court cited two New York cases: Megibow v. Megibow, 612 N.Y.S.2d 758, 760 (N.Y. Sup. Ct. 1994) (directing the husband to cooperate with wife in obtaining a *get* and stating that the process shall be initiated within twenty days and completed within ninety days and that husband's failure to cooperate "may result in punishment for contempt"), and Kaplinsky, 603 N.Y.S.2d at 575 (holding that the court properly held husband in contempt for failing to deliver a *get* and stating that court may enforce contempt order through imprisonment and withholding economic benefits from husband). *But see* Scholl, 621 A.2d at 811 (stating that a court may not enforce an order of specific performance against husband by incarcerating him); *and* Waxstein, 395 N.Y.S.2d 877 at 881 (same).

[279] Aflalo, 685 A.2d at 530.

[280] *Id.* at 529–30. As the court observed, the terms of a *get* provide that "the husband does 'willingly consent, being under no restraint, to release, to set free, and put aside thee, my wife.'" *Id.* at 529. *See also* Margulies vs. Margulies, 344 N.Y.S.2d 482, 484 (N.Y. App. Div. 1973) (noting that court had been told "that since a Jewish divorce can only be granted upon the representation that it is sought by the husband of his own free will, any such divorce, if obtained under compulsion by the court, would in any event be a nullity" and vacating order committing husband to jail for fifteen days with an "opportunity to purge himself" of contempt if he participated in a religious divorce).

grant of a civil divorce on a showing that the party seeking the divorce has "taken all steps solely within his ... power to remove all barriers to the ... [other party's] remarriage."[281] The statute thus empowers a court to delay or deny a civil divorce to a husband who seeks a divorce but refuses to provide his wife with a *get*. In an additional provision added in 1992, the *Get* Statute provides that "the court shall, where appropriate, consider the effect of a barrier to remarriage" on the factors relevant to disposition of property and maintenance (alimony) awards, effectively authorizing a court to impose financial penalties on a husband who fails to provide his wife with a religious divorce.[282] This new section covers cases in which the wife, rather than the husband, seeks the divorce. The Get Statute gives New York courts a powerful, noncontractual, if controversial, tool for nudging a reluctant spouse to obtain a religious divorce.

### 3. *Agreements to Submit to the Jurisdiction of a Religious Tribunal*

In a premarital or subsequent contract, parties may agree to appear before a religious tribunal for counseling or arbitration. If one spouse subsequently refuses to so appear, the other spouse may seek an order of specific performance from a civil court. In *Avitzur v. Avtzur*,[283] for example, the parties' *ketubah* included an agreement "to recognize the Beth Din ... as having authority to counsel us in the light of Jewish tradition ... and to summon either party at the request of the other, in order to enable the party so requesting to live in accordance with the standards of the Jewish law of marriage throughout his or her lifetime."[284] The husband later obtained a civil divorce but refused to appear before the Beth Din as promised, which prevented the wife from obtaining a religious divorce.[285] The wife thus sought an order compelling the husband's appearance before the Beth Din.[286] The court granted the order, reasoning that the wife was merely asking the court to enforce a contractual obligation "closely analogous to an antenuptial agreement to arbitrate a dispute"[287] The *ketubah*, said the court, "should ordinarily be entitled to no less dignity than any other civil contract to submit a dispute to a nonjudicial forum."[288]

In a more common scenario, parties abide by their promise to submit marital disputes to the jurisdiction of a religious tribunal, an arbitration order is issued, and one spouse seeks judicial confirmation of the order over the objection of the other spouse. In such cases, a court will verify that the agreement to arbitrate was not the product of duress or

281 N.Y. Dom. Rel. Law. § 253(3) (McKinney 1999). This subsection provides in full

> No final judgment of annulment or divorce shall thereafter be entered unless the plaintiff shall have filed and served a sworn statement: (i) that, to the best of his or her knowledge, he or she has, prior to the entry of such final judgment, taken all steps solely within his or her power to remove all barriers to the defendant's remarriage following the annulment or divorce; or (ii) that the defendant has waived in writing the requirements of this subdivision.

282 N.Y. Dom. Rel. Law. § 236 5B(5)(h) (property), (6)(d) (maintenance) (McKinney 1999).
283 446 N.E.2d 136.
284 *Id.* at 137.
285 *Id.*
286 *Id.*
287 *Id.* at 138.
288 *Id.* The court added that like other forum selection clauses, the selection must not violate state law or public policy. *Id.*

other unconscionability.[289] Additionally, the court may inquire into the arbitration process to verify compliance with procedural safeguards or at least to ensure a modicum of "basic fairness."[290] Finally, terms dealing with children may be given special scrutiny to ensure that they serve the child's best interest.[291]

289 *In re* Marriage of Popack, 998 P.2d 464, 468 (Colo Ct. App. 2000). For cases in which a wife charged that her consent to a settlement agreement was coerced by her husband's threat to withhold a *get*, *see supra* note 261. For a case in which a court rejected a wife's claim that she executed a general release prior to arbitration under threat that she would otherwise be subject to a writ issued against one who disobeys rabbinical decrees, *see* Greenberg, 656 N.Y.S.2d at 369–70.

290 *See* Kovacs v. Kovacs, 633 A.2d 425, 433 (Md. Ct. Spec. App. 1993) (recognizing that parties may waive application of procedures required by state arbitration act but stating that a court must ensure arbitration procedures meet standards of "basic fairness"), *and* Stein v. Stein, 707 N.Y.S.2d 754, 758–9 (Sup. Ct 1999) (declining to confirm a decision of the Beth Din that failed to comply with a statutory waiting period but recognizing that parties can waive procedural safeguards in writing).

291 In *Kovacs* (633 A.2d 425), for example, a civil court was asked to enforce a Beth Din arbitration award. The court confirmed the alimony and property portions of the award but held that provisions affecting children must be the subject of independent judgment by the reviewing civil court. *Id.* at 432. *See also* Popack, 998 P.2d at 469 (concluding that while child custody, visitation, and child support are arbitrable, the court retains jurisdiction, on the request of either party, to decide *de novo* all issues relating to children), *and* Stein v. Stein, 707 N.Y.S.2d 754, 758 (Sup. Ct. 1999) (declining to confirm provisions of Beth Din decision addressing child custody and visitation).

# 16 Public Education

## A. Historical Context: Education in the Colonies

Colonial Massachusetts gave public education a firm legal foundation in 1642 by ordering parents to ensure that their children were taught "to read and understand the principles of religion and the capital laws of the country."[1] As schooling became institutionalized throughout the colonies, teachers were widely required to be persons of "piety and good character," a provision that was tantamount to a religious test for appointment.[2] Formal education was vastly augmented by the vocational training, including reading and arithmetic ("cyphering"), provided by master craftsmen to their apprentices.

As the avalanche of church-state litigation in the twentieth and twenty-first centuries amply illustrates, education in both public and parochial schools has struggled to come to terms with the remnants of its early religious roots. A leading observer of the status of religion in American education has offered this summary:

> God's place within the public schools of the United States has been debatable, and subject to controversy, for as long as there have been public schools. In colonial America, religion played a central role in the schools of every colony, but the understanding of religion differed substantially from colony to colony. With the coming of nationhood and the separation of church and state on the federal level, the public school was pressed into service as a new kind of national church, commissioned to create and carry the common culture and morality of the nation. Since citizens differed dramatically in their definitions of this culture and morality, and especially since newly arrived Catholics, newly freed African Americans, and newly conquered Native Americans all had still other ideas, the content of the nation's common creed – and especially the appropriateness of its more overtly religious dimensions – was a subject of fierce debate and continuing change throughout the nineteenth century.
>
> By the end of that century, due as much to exhaustion as any thoughtful will, schools had dropped the more obviously religious – and generally Protestant Christian – trappings of the school faith, replacing them with a generic commitment to democracy reinforced by a set of patriotic symbols, including flags and flag salutes and the

1 Samuel Eliot Morison, The Intellectual Life of Colonial New England 66 (NYU Press 1956).

2 *See* Lawrence A. Cremin, American Education, The Colonial Experience, 1607-1783 at 87 (Harper & Row 1970). For descriptions of the earliest colonial schools, *see* Robert Francis S. Saybolt, The Public Schools of Colonial Boston, 1632–1775 (Harvard Univ. Press 1935) and, by the same author, Source Studies in American Colonial Education, The Private School (Univ. of Ill. Press 1925); Morison *supra* note 1, "The Public Grammar Schools," ch. IV.

omnipresent pictures of George Washington and Abraham Lincoln. Some religious symbols – bible reading and prayer in a minority of states, Christmas carols and pious references in most communities – continued well into the twentieth century.[3]

## B. Historical Context: Religion and Education in the Early Nineteenth Century

### 1. *Introduction*

It may be hyperbole to describe public education in colonial days and the early nineteenth century as the child of religion and the churches; but the two institutions were intermingled in a way that refuted any claim of a wall between church and state within the states and that today would impel charges that the Establishment Clause and perhaps the Free Exercise Clause were being violated. There were numerous instances of discrimination against religious minorities, especially Catholics, who opposed the overt or latent Protestant practices.[4] No such attacks manifested in the early days, however, for two good legal reasons, which were supported, indeed overwhelmed, by a basic fact of cultural life. As to the legal reasons: first, almost all of the colonial and early nineteenth-century schools were launched and supported by towns and other local agencies, with occasional support from the states. These political bodies were not limited by the Establishment Clause of the First Amendment; it was not incorporated into the Fourteenth Amendment (and hence applied to the states) by the Supreme Court for almost a century.[5] In the interim, the states could have established official religions, if they chose, free from any federal constitutional barriers. Second, although the Establishment Clause limited action by Congress, federally supported schools were few and far between, and those that existed were supported by Congress under constitutional provisions that, arguably, were not subject to the Establishment Clause, such as federal jurisdiction over the nation's territories and possessions, military bases, Native American reservations, and other enclaves that were not incorporated into the Union.

### 2. *Religion and Public Education: The Influence of Horace Mann*

In the first half of the nineteenth century, Horace Mann (1796–1859), rivaled only by John Dewey (1859–1952) as America's leading philosopher and theorist of public education, devoted his keen intellect and formidable energy to the task of formulating and promoting a universal program of free tax-supported public education.[6] During a twelve-year tenure as Secretary of the Massachusetts Board of Education (a misleading appellation because his agency supervised no schools and had only advisory authority), he issued a series of annual reports from 1837 to 1848 dealing with every aspect of the nascent institution – a public commitment to universal free education, the training of

3 James W. Fraser, Between Church and State, Religion and Public Education in a Multicultural America 3 (St. Martin's Press 1999); *see also* Frank Lambert, The Founding Fathers and the Place of Religion in America (Princeton Univ. Press 2003).

4 Frank S. Ravitch, School Prayer and Discrimination: The Civil Rights of Religious Minorities and Dissenters 3–18 (Northeastern Univ. Press 1999).

5 *See* Everson v. Board of Education, 330 U.S. 1 (1947) (incorporating the Establishment Clause).

6 *See* Jonathan Messerli, Horace Mann, Biography (Knopf 1972).

teachers, modes of instruction, school buildings, supervisors, finance, curriculum, public libraries, discipline, and so forth – that had an immense influence, though his writings are known today mainly by educational bureaucrats.[7]

Mann, a moralist at heart, believed in "the absolute right of every human being that comes into the world to an education," an axion creating "the correlative duty of every government to see that the means of education are provided for all.[8] To Mann, education is "the balance wheel of the nation's social machinery,"[9] and he was particularly concerned with "the moral foundations of a common educational program in a religiously diverse society.[10] This is not the place for a full account, or even a summary, of Mann's program to discharge the government's duty, but his views about the role of religion in his program deserve attention, particularly because they are reflected in the history of the American public school system and have turned out in our day to be the root of much constitutional litigation.

The obvious mode of avoiding bitter and endless religious dissension in the school system that might have appealed to Mann if he had not been a creature of the nineteenth century – a purely secular institution, leaving religious instruction to the family and the churches – was dismissed by him without discussion: "I do not suppose that a man can be found in Massachusetts who would declare such a [secular] system to be his first choice."[11] Mann instead concluded that "certain common principles could be culled from the several sectarian creeds and made the core of a body of religious doctrine on which all could agree." For Mann, these were the great principles of "natural religion" – the truths that had been given in the Bible and demonstrated in the course of history.[12] Mann expanded on this common body of thought (modeled *pro tanto* on the Massachusetts schools of his day) when he rebuffed the hostile allegation that he proposed to expel religion from his ideal educational system, making it "un-Christian":

> If the Bible, then, is the exponent of Christianity; if the Bible contains the communications, precepts, and doctrines, which make up the religious system called and known as Christianity; if the Bible makes known those truths, which, according to the faith of Christians, are able to make men wise unto salvation; and if this Bible is in the schools, how can it be said that Christianity is excluded from the schools; or how can it be said that the school system, which adopts and uses the Bible, is an anti-Christian, or an un-Christian system?[13]

An acute scholar has tersely observed that the close resemblance of this religious message to Mann's "own optimistic, humanistic Unitarianism did not seem to trouble him."[14]

7 Mann's Annual Reports are reprinted in HORACE MANN, ANNUAL REPORTS ON EDUCATION (Lee and Shepard 1872).

8 HORACE MANN, TENTH ANNUAL REPORT (Horace Man League 1952); THE REPUBLIC AND THE SCHOOL, HORACE MANN ON THE EDUCATION OF FREE MEN 63 (Lawrence A. Cremin ed., Columbia Univ. Press 1957).

9 CREMIN, *supra* note 2 at 87.

10 *Id.* at 12.

11 *Id.* at 107–8.

12 *Id.* at 13. *See Creating an American Common School and a Common Faith: Horace Mann and the Protestant Public Schools, 1789–1860, in* FRASER, *supra* note 3, at 23–44; *see also* PAUL C. GUTJAHR, AN AMERICAN BIBLE, A HISTORY OF THE GOOD BOOK IN THE UNITED STATES, 1777–1880 (Stanford Univ. Press 2002), ch. 4.

13 *Id.* at 105–6.

14 *Id.* at 13.

The nonsectarian liberal Protestantism that came to saturate Mann's ideal school system, however, was anathema to many of the Roman Catholics whose children attended the Massachusetts common schools of the day.[15] Mann did not greet their complaints in the spirit of compromise; to the contrary, for him and his Protestant compatriots, the complainants were more in need of conversion than serious consideration. Lyman Beecher, for example, smugly announced: "Let the Catholics mingle with us as Americans and come with their children under the full action of our common schools and republican institutions, and the various powers of assimilation and we are prepared cheerfully to abide the consequences."[16] In a sense, Mann found himself in a vicious circle of his own making: because the nonsectarian Protestantism of his schools offended the Catholics, one of their responses was the creation of their own parochial schools, and this development was, in Mann's view, a threat to his goal in a single system of universal public education.[17]

In memory of his massive achievements in building America's system of free public education, Horace Mann's name adorns the facades of many public school buildings. The record of history would be augmented if a few courthouses bore his name to memorialize the litigation generated by his confidence that the liberal Protestant ethic would be happily accepted by all his fellow citizens. Despite his great achievements, he was a creature of the early nineteenth century, and his choice to favor a pan-Protestant approach over a sectarian Protestant approach was actually forward thinking for that era, but in New England as in other parts of the nation, that was *no solace* to Catholics and others who did not subscribe to the Protestant ethos or did not believe that it should be inculcated through the public schools.[18]

## C. The Constitutional Structure of Free Public Education

The nation's public school system is built on three basic legal principles, which are embodied in the constitutional and statutory laws of every state. First, all children between specified ages (typically five to sixteen) must attend school; second, parents may elect to send their children to parochial or other nonpublic schools or to educate them at home if the alternative program satisfies the state's educational requirements; and third, children and their parents are subject to truancy laws if they do not comply with the mandatory school attendance law. The second and third of these basic principles are, of course, secondary to the first; were it not for the mandatory educational requirement, there would be no need for the option to attend a nonpublic school or for penalties for violating the first principle.

Although these three principles are observed by every state in the union (and by the federal government in the District of Columbia),[19] there is no Supreme Court decision that squarely upholds the constitutionality of the mandatory school attendance

[15] Robert H. Lord, John E. Sexton & Edward T. Harrington, History of the Archdiocese of Boston, 2 In the Various Stages of Its Development, 1604–1943 at 585–602 (Sheed & Ward, 1944).

[16] Fraser, *supra* note 3, at 34.

[17] Cremin, *supra* note 2, at 23 (religious schools as "direct threats" to the common school).

[18] Ravitch, *supra* note 4, at 3–18.

[19] *See, generally*, D. Edmund Reutter, Jr., The Law of Public Education (3d ed, Foundation Press 1985).

principle.[20] In a nation of litigators, this is surprising because the state commandeers the better part of the child's life for more than a decade. In dictum and comment, however, the Supreme Court has crushed in advance any attempt to delegitimate the mandatory school attendance laws. Thus, in *Brown v. Board of Education* (1954), a case of such importance that no remark could have slipped into the opinion inadvertently, the justices unanimously subscribed to these views:

> Today education is perhaps the most important function of state and local governments. Compulsory school attendance laws and the great expenditures for education both demonstrate our recognition of the importance of education to our democratic society."[21]

Similarly, in *Wisconsin v. Yoder* (1972), exempting Old Order Amish school children from Wisconsin's compulsory school attendance law on completing the eighth grade, Chief Justice Burger, speaking for the Court, unmistakably presupposed that the law was constitutional, except when applied to unusual situations, observing:

> We should ... note that compulsory education and child labor laws find their historical origin in common humanitarian instincts, and that the age limits of both laws have been coordinated to achieve their related objectives.... The two kinds of statutes – compulsory school attendance and child labor laws – tend to keep children of certain ages off the labor market and in school; this regimen in turn provides opportunity to prepare for a livelihood of a higher order than that which children could pursue without education and protects their health in adolescence.[22]

Two earlier Supreme Court decisions, often cited as ruling that state compulsory school attendance laws are constitutional, do not quite qualify, but they also presuppose that the compulsion is constitutional. The first is *Meyer v. Nebraska* (1923), which invalidated a state prohibition on using German to teach in any public, denominational, or private school unless the student had completed the eighth grade on the ground that the "statute as applied is arbitrary and without reasonable relation to any end within the competency of the state."[23] The plaintiff relied on the Due Process Clause of the Fourteenth Amendment but did not question "the power of the state to compel attendance at some school and to make reasonable regulations for all schools."[24] The Court very likely accepted this concession but did not explicitly rule that it was a valid statement of the law.

The second decision that is often cited as legitimating the universal compulsory school attendance laws also falls frustratingly short of a crisp ruling, namely, *Pierce v. Society of Sisters* (1925).[25] In this case, the court unanimously invalidated an Oregon statute

20 *See, generally*, Philip B. Kurland, *The Supreme Court, Compulsory Education, and the First Amendment's Religion Clauses*, 75 W. Va. L. Rev. 213 (1973).

21 Brown v. Board of Education, 347 U.S. 483, 493 (1954).

22 Wisconsin v. Yoder, 406 U.S. 205, 228 (1972); Shawn Francis Peters, The Yoder Case: Religious Freedom, Education, and Parental Rights (Univ. of Press of Kansas 2003).

23 Meyer v. Nebraska, 262 U.S. 390, 403 (1923) (divided court) (law applied to teacher in Lutheran school); *see also* Farrington v. Tokushiga, 273 U.S. 284 (1927) (*Meyer* principle applied to regulation of schools in territory of Hawaii under Due Process Clause of Fifth Amendment).

24 *Meyer*, 262 U.S. at 402. For the "substantive due process" doctrine, *see, generally*, Laurence H. Tribe, American Constitutional Law 1332–81 (3d ed., 2000).

25 Pierce v. Society of Sisters, 268 U.S. 510 (1925). The Oregon statute exempted a few categories of parents (e.g., those residing at a considerable distance from any public school).

requiring every parent, guardian, or other person having control or charge or custody of a child between eight and sixteen years to send him or her "to a public school." This public school monopoly law was narrowly enacted by an electoral initiative led by an ignoble crew of nativists, Ku Klux Klanners, Scottish Rite Masons, and anti-Catholics, who pushed for similar measures in a dozen states in the early 1920s.[26] In a terse opinion, the Court announced:

> Under the doctrine of *Meyer v. Nebraska*, we think it entirely plain that the [Oregon] Act ... unreasonably interferes with the liberty of parents and guardians to direct the upbringing and education of children under their control. The fundamental theory of liberty upon which all governments in this Union repose excludes any general power of the state to standardize its children by forcing them to accept instruction from public teachers only. The child is not the mere creature of the state; those who nurture him and direct his destiny have the right, coupled with the high duty, to recognize and prepare him for additional obligations.[27]

This case bans a state requirement that every child attend a *public* school, but it did not disrupt enforcement of the normal school attendance laws, which require *school* attendance, not *public school* attendance. Although *Pierce* makes no mention of religion – perhaps because the Supreme Court had not yet applied the Establishment Clause of the First Amendment to the states – it is often construed to mean that parochial schools satisfy state school attendance laws.

## D. *Everson v. Board of Education* and the Incorporation of the Establishment Clause

Although the Supreme Court has never come clearly to grips with the constitutionality of the universal state compulsory school attendance laws, in 1947 the justices seized hold of a minor element of the nation's educational system – a municipality's reimbursement of the bus fares paid by parents to send their children to local parochial schools and upheld the constitutionality of this practice.[28] In order to do so, the Court first had to determine whether the Establishment Clause, which had not yet been incorporated through the Fourteenth Amendment, should be incorporated and thus made applicable to the states (and local governments). The Court held that the Establishment Clause is indeed incorporated through the Fourteenth Amendment.[29]

The majority opinion and Justice Rutledge's dissenting opinion are largely devoted to a reconstruction of the history leading to the enactment of the religion clauses of the First Amendment. Both emphasize the church-state views of Madison and Jefferson, virtually ignoring the opinions of their Virginia and constitutional compatriots. In later church-state cases, the justices often emulated the opinions of Justices Black and Rutledge in *Everson* by interpreting the Establishment Clause as though the writings

[26] *See* David B. Tyack, *The Perils of Pluralism: The Background of the Pierce Law*, 74 Am. Hist. Rev. 74 (1968); Freedom and Education: Pierce v. Society of Sisters Reconsidered (Donald P. Kommers & Miachel J. Wahoske eds., Center for Civil Rights, Notre Dame Law School 1978).

[27] Pierce, 268 U.S.at 534–5.

[28] Everson v. Board of Education, 330 U.S. 1, 18 (1946) (divided court).

[29] *Id.* at 15–16.

of Madison and Jefferson were the only source of enlightenment.[30] Other opinions, which reject a separationist approach, stress only the counterhistory.[31]

Justice Black's somewhat one-sided excursion into history led him, in the end, to issue this resounding, much-quoted manifesto in *Everson*:

> The "establishment of religion" clause of the First Amendment means at least this: neither a state nor the Federal Government can set up a church. Neither can pass laws which aid one religion, aid all religions, or prefer one religion over another. Neither can force nor influence a person to go to or to remain away from church against his will or force him to profess a belief or disbelief in any religion. No person can be punished for entertaining or professing religious beliefs or disbeliefs, for church attendance or non-attendance. No tax in any amount, large or small, can be levied to support any religious activities or institutions, whatever they may be called, or whatever form they may adopt to teach or practice religion. Neither a state nor the Federal Government can, openly or secretly, participate in the affairs of any religious organizations or groups and vice versa.[32]

When quoting these stirring words, however, the commentators rarely point out that they prepare the reader for the exact opposite, namely, a ruling that the challenged reimbursement of the children's bus fares was – despite this rhetoric – constitutional.[33] Justice Jackson, dissenting in *Everson* for himself and Justice Frankfurter, spells out this anticlimactic result, first with a literary irony and then with a metaphor:

> [T]he undertones of the [Black] opinion, advocating complete and uncompromising separation of Church from State, seem utterly discordant with its conclusion yielding support to their commingling in educational matters. The case which irresistibly comes to mind as the most fitting precedent is that of Julia who, according to Byron's reports, "whispering 'I will ne'er consent,' – consented." …
>
> I cannot read the history of the struggle to separate political from ecclesiastical affairs … without a conviction that the Court today is unconsciously giving the clock's hands a backward turn.[34]

## E. Public School Cooperation with Religious Instruction: "Shared," "Released," and "Dismissed" Time

### 1. *Introduction*

In the period beginning shortly before we entered World War I and continuing until the 1950s, many Protestants, lay and clergy, became dissatisfied with church-sponsored Sunday school as the principal mode of providing their children with religious instruction

[30] Engel v. Vitale, 370 U.S. 421 (1962); Abington Township v. Schempp, 374 U.S. 203 (1963).

[31] Marsh v. Chambers, 463 U.S. 783 (1983); Lynch v. Donnelly, 465 U.S. 668 (1984); Wallace v. Jaffree, 472 U.S. 38, 40 n. 1 (1985); Wallace v. Jaffree, 472 U.S. 38, 91–113 (Rehnquist, J., dissenting).

[32] Everson, 330 U.S. at 15–16. The American Civil Liberties Union (ACLU) filed an *amicus curiae* brief arguing that the *Everson* ordinance was unconstitutional. Noting that the District of Columbia required its local street car and bus lines to grant a reduced fare to all school children (cited by the appellees to support their claim that the *Everson* ordinance was constitutional), the ACLU assented that the DC law was "merely a matter of rate-fixing," not involving the expenditure of any public funds. Brief of ACLU as *Amicus Curiae* at 27 n. 2, Everson v. Bd. of Education, 330 U.S. 1 (1947) (No. 52), 1946 WL 50128.

[33] Everson, 330 U.S. at 18.

[34] *Id.* at 19 & 28 (Jackson, J., dissenting).

partly for a reason later voiced by Justice Frankfurter: "By appearing to make religion a one-day-a-week matter, the Sunday school, which acquired national acceptance, tended to relegate the child's religious education, and thereby his [or her] religion, to a minor role not unlike the enforced piano lesson."[35] The Protestant leaders sought a remedy with the "released-time experiment," which drew on the public schools to provide religious education on weekdays for children whose parents wished to enroll them in one of three variations of "released time":[36]

1. A plan under which religious teachers provided instruction in the public school building to the electing children, while the nonelection pupils were kept together in study halls, the library, or the gym ("shared time"). Thus all children spent the same hours in school, and all received the same instruction in their secular, nonreligious subjects.
2. A plan, which did not use the public school building, under which the electing students were released to go for religious instruction in their church's building, whereas the nonelecting children remained in the public school for a period of study or other nonessential instruction ("released time").
3. A plan under which the public school would open later or close earlier on one or more days, leaving the nonelecting students free to use the time as they chose, whereas the electing students would receive religious instruction in their denomination's church or center ("dismissed time").

The terminology was not hard and fast; the first two plans often and all three sometimes bear the generic label "released time."

### 2. *"Shared" or "Released" Time*

In *McCollum v. Board of Education* (1948), the Supreme Court held that a "shared time" plan adopted by the Board of Education of Champaign, Illinois, to provide religious instruction in the local public school system violated the Establishment Clause.[37] The Court described the plan as follows:

> In 1940 interested members of the Jewish, Roman Catholic, and a few of the Protestant faiths formed a voluntary association called the Champaign Council on Religious Education. They obtained permission from the Board of Education to offer classes in religious instruction to public school pupils in grades four to nine inclusive. Classes were made up of pupils whose parents signed printed cards requesting that their children be permitted to attend; they were held weekly, thirty minutes for the lower grades, forty-five minutes for the higher. The council employed the religious teachers at no expense to the school authorities, but the instructors were subject to the approval and supervision of the superintendent of schools. The classes were taught in three separate

[35] McCollum v. Board of Education, 333 U.S. 203, 221–2 (1948) (opinion of Frankfurter, J.).

[36] For a detailed account of these plans and variations on them, *see The Released-Time Experiment*, *in* Leo Pfeffer, Church, State, and Freedom 311–73 (Beacon Press 1953). The pre-1950 material in Pfeffer's work draws on Anson Phelps Stokes, Church and State in the United States (Harper & Bros. 1950) and on its one-volume revision and summary, Anson Phelps Stokes & Leo Pfeffer, Church and State in the United States (Harper & Row 1964).

[37] McCollum, 333 U.S. at 465–6. *See*, *generally*, Anson Phelps Stokes, II Church and State in the United States 515 (Harper & Bros. 1950).

> religious groups by Protestant teachers, Catholic priests, and a Jewish rabbi, although for the past several years there have apparently been no classes instructed in the Jewish religion. Classes were conducted in the regular classrooms of the school building. Students who did not choose to take the religious instruction were not released from public school duties; they were required to leave their classrooms and go to some other place in the school building for pursuit of their secular studies. On the other hand, students who were released from secular study for the religious instruction were required to be present at the religious classes. Reports of their presence or absence were to be made to their secular teachers.[38]

After characterizing the plan as a "utilization of the tax-established and tax-supported public school system to aid religious groups to spread their faith,"[39] the Court noted that counsel for the school board recognized that the program was barred by the Establishment Clause "if we adhere to the views expressed by both the majority and the minority Justices in the *Everson* case."[40] The school board, therefore, asked the Court to reconsider and repudiate its "dicta" in *Everson* and rule instead that "historically the First Amendment was intended to forbid only government preference of one religion over another, not an impartial governmental assistance of all religions."[41] Having rejected this theory in deciding *Everson* less than a year earlier, the Court not surprisingly refused to reconsider that ruling. Writing for the Court, however, Justice Black, possibly with an eye focused on the potential for an inflamed public reaction to its decision, rejected in advance any accusation that it "manifest[s] a governmental hostility to religion or religious teachings."[42]

Justice Black's opinion for the Court in *McCollum* was powerfully buttressed by an extended concurring opinion by Justice Frankfurter, with whom Justices Jackson, Rutledge, and Burton joined – the four who had dissented in the *Everson* case. In his opinion, Justice Frankfurter reviewed the history of public school education in the United States, noting the early prohibition in Massachusetts, New York, and other states of "sectarian doctrine," with the result that "long before the Fourteenth Amendment subjected the States to new limitations [e.g., the Establishment Clause of the First Amendment], the prohibition of furtherance by the State of religious instruction became the guiding principle, in law and feeling, of the American people"; thus the separation of church and state in the field of education "was not imposed upon unwilling States by force of superior [federal] law."[43] Frankfurter then cited samples of the "prolific literature" on the "released time" movement, noting that it took many forms and that the Court was passing only on the plan before it because other plans might differ in aspects "that may well

[38] McCollum, 333 U.S. at 207–10.

[39] *Id.* at 210.

[40] *Id.* at 211. *See* Everson v. Board of Education, 330 U.S. 1 (1947). *Everson* held, by a divided Court, that the use of public funds to reimburse the parents of children attending parochial schools for bus transportation to and from school, but both the majority and dissenting justices agreed that "[n]either a state nor the Federal Government can … pass laws which aid one religion, aid all religions, or prefer one religion over another… [n]o tax in any amount, large or small, can be levied to support any religious activities or institutions, whatever they may be called, or whatever form they may adopt to teach or practice religion." McCollum, 333 U.S. 210.

[41] *Id.* at 211.

[42] *Id.*

[43] *McCollum*, 333 U.S. at 215 (opinion of Frankfurter, J.).

be constitutionally different."[44] He also called attention to the French system – known in the United States as "dismissed time" – under which the school day is shortened once a week "to allow all children to go where they please, leaving those who so desire to go to a religious school."[45]

### 3. *New York's Variation on "Released" Time*

In *Zorach v. Clauson* (1952), the Court confronted, only a few years after *McCullom* was decided, a New York program for religious instruction that resembled the French plan except that the students who did not leave school to attend religious classes were kept in their regular public school building.[46] The New York plan was described and contrasted with the *McCollum* plan by the Court:

> New York City has a program which permits its public schools to release students during the school day so that they may leave the school buildings and school grounds and go to religious centers for religious instruction or devotional exercises. A student is released on written request of his parents. Those not released stay in the classrooms. The churches make weekly reports to the schools, sending a list of children who have been released from public school but who have not reported for religious instruction.
>
> This "released time" program involves neither religious instruction in public school classrooms nor the expenditure of public funds. All costs, including the application blanks, are paid by the religious organizations. The case is therefore unlike *McCollum v. Board of Education* ... which involved a "released time" program from Illinois. In that case the classrooms were turned over to religious instructors. We accordingly held that the program violated the First Amendment which (by reason of the Fourteenth Amendment) prohibits the states from establishing religion or prohibiting its free exercise.[47]

The constitutionality of the New York plan was challenged by taxpayers and residents with children in its public schools, who alleged that in essence it was not different from the plan rejected in the *McCollum* case:

> Their argument, stated elaborately in various ways, reduces itself to this: the weight and influence of the school is put behind a program for religious instruction; public school teachers police it, keeping tab on students who are released; the classroom activities come to a halt while the students who are released for religious instruction are on leave; the school is a crutch on which the churches are leaning for support in their religious training; without the cooperation of the schools this "released time" program, like the one in the *McCollum* case, would be futile and ineffective.[48]

Justice Douglas, speaking for the Court, rejected the "suggestion" that the New York plan "involves the use of coercion to get public school students into religious classrooms" because there was no evidence in the record supporting this contention, and the New York Court of Appeals, which had upheld the plan's constitutionality, ruled that a

44 *Id.* at 231.
45 *Id.* at 230.
46 Zorach v. Clausen, 343 U.S. 306 (1952).
47 *Id.* at 308–9.
48 *Id.* at 309–10.

trial on this issue was barred because the plaintiffs had failed to raise "the issue of maladminstration" in the manner required by the state's rules of procedure.[49]

In the absence of coercion, the Court could discern no constitutional taint in the plan. In so ruling, the Court agreed with the proposition that the separation of church and state "must be complete and unequivocal," but it also asserted that

> [t]he First Amendment, however, does not say that in every and all respects there shall be a separation of Church and State. Rather, it studiously defines the manner, the specific ways, in which there shall be no concert or union or dependency one on the other. That is the common sense of the matter. Otherwise the state and religion would be aliens to each other – hostile, suspicious, and even unfriendly. Churches could not be required to pay even property taxes. Municipalities would not be permitted to render police or fire protection to religious groups. Policemen who helped parishioners into their places of worship would violate the Constitution. Prayers in our legislative halls; the appeals to the Almighty in the messages of the Chief Executive; the proclamations making Thanksgiving Day a holiday; "so help me God" in our courtroom oaths – these and all other references to the Almighty that run through our laws, our public rituals, our ceremonies would be floating the First Amendment. A fastidious atheist or agnostic could even object to the supplication with which the Court opens each session: "God save the United States and this Honorable Court."[50]

Turning from these potential ramifications of the plaintiffs' argument to its impact on the public school system if adopted, the Court asserted that if accepted, it would make it unconstitutional to release individual students or groups of students from public schools to attend religious services:

> A Catholic student applies to his [or her] teacher for permission to leave the school during hours on a Holy Day of Obligation to attend a mass. A Jewish student asks his [or her] teacher for permission to be excused for Yom Kippur. A Protestant wants the afternoon off for a family baptismal ceremony. In each case the teacher requires parental consent in writing. In each case the teacher, in order to make sure the student is not a truant, goes further and requires a report from the priest, the rabbi, or the minister. The teacher in other words cooperates in a religious program to the extent of making it possible for [his or] her students to participate in it. Whether [he or] she does it occasionally for a few students, regularly for one, or pursuant to a systematized program designed to further the religious needs of all the students does not alter the character of the act.[51]

In drawing these slippery slope analogies, the Court failed to mention that the released time plan did not excuse students from school attendance so that they could discharge a religious obligation, whereas the allegedly analogous releases from public schools on religious holidays may have been required by the Free Exercise Clause.

[49] Zorach, 343 U.S. at 311 & n. 7. For the exclusion from the case of proffered evidence of coercion, *see* Leo Pfeffer, God, Caesar, and the Constitution 190–91 (Beacon Press 1975); *see also id.* at 192, commenting on Justice Douglas' record in church-state separation cases and observing "it seems almost as though he had decided to devote the rest of his life to making atonement for his aberration in *Zorach v. Clauson.*"

[50] Zorach, 343 U.S. at 312–13.

[51] Zorach, 343 U.S. at 313.

Justice Douglas concluded the opinion with a peroration that is often quoted in other cases and in public debate:

> We are a religious people whose institutions presuppose a Supreme Being. We guarantee the freedom to worship as one chooses ... When the state encourages religious instruction or cooperates with religious authorities by adjusting the schedule of public events to sectarian needs, it follows the best of our traditions. For it then respects the religious nature of our people and accommodates the public service to their spiritual needs. To hold that it may not would be to find in the Constitution a requirement that the government show a callous indifference to religious groups. That would be preferring those who believe in no religion over those who do believe....
>
> We follow the *McCollum* case. But we cannot expand it to cover the present released time program unless separation of Church and State means that public institutions can make no adjustments of their schedules to accommodate the religious needs of the people. We cannot read into the Bill of Rights such a philosophy of hostility to religion.[52]

Justice Black dissented, arguing that the case was controlled by *McCollum* because, in his view, use of the public school buildings for religious instruction in the *McCollum* plan was only one of its deficiencies, not a *sine qua non* for the decision. For Justice Black, coercion was inherent in the plan under review in *Zorach*:

> Here the sole question is whether New York can use its compulsory education laws to help religious sects get attendants presumably too unenthusiastic to go unless moved to do so by the pressure of this state machinery. That this is the plan, purpose, design and consequence of the New York program cannot be denied. The state thus makes religious sects beneficiaries of its power to compel children to attend secular schools. Any use of such coercive power by the state to help or hinder some religious sects or to prefer all religious sects over nonbelievers or vice versa is just what I think the First Amendment forbids....
>
> State help to religion injects political and party prejudices into a holy field. It too often substitutes force for prayer, hate for love, and persecution for persuasion. Government should not be allowed, under cover of the soft euphemism of "co-operation," to steal into the sacred area of religious choice.[53]

Justices Frankfurter and Jackson also dissented, arguing that the *Zorach* plan called on the coercive power of the state to recruit students for religious instruction. Jackson concluded his brief dissent with this harsh judgment:

> The wall which the Court [in *McCollum*] was professing to erect between Church and State has become even more warped and twisted than I expected. Today's judgment will be more interesting to students of psychology and of the judicial processes than to students of constitutional law.[54]

[52] Zorach, 343 U.S. at 313–15. The much-quoted, and sometimes deplored, first sentence of this extract was diluted, if not muddied, by Justice Douglas, dissenting in *McGowan v. Maryland* [366 U.S. 420, 563 (1961)]; the Puritan influence "helped shape our constitutional law and our common law" by giving priority to individual conscience and individual judgment.

[53] Zorach, 343 U.S. at 343 U.S. at 318–20 (Black, J., dissenting).

[54] *Id.* at 325 (Jackson, J., dissenting).

As of 2014, released-time programs that follow the approach taken in *Zorach* are constitutional and have been upheld by the lower courts.[55]

## F. Prayers, Bible Reading, and Similar Religious Practices in Public Schools

### 1. *Early Cases*

Prior to incorporation of the Establishment Clause, cases were brought in state courts to challenge school prayer under state constitutions and statutes. Some of these cases found these practices to be unconstitutional.[56] Yet others found them to be consistent with the state constitution and laws.[57]

### 2. *School Prayer after Incorporation:* Engel *and* Abington

In *Engel v. Vitale* (1962), the Supreme Court struck down a New York requirement that public school students recite the following prayer in the presence of a teacher at the beginning of every school day:

> Almighty God, we acknowledge our dependence upon Thee, and we beg Thy blessings upon us, our parents, our teachers and our Country.[58]

Although the suit attacking this requirement was brought by the parents of children who claimed that the "Regents' Prayer" (so-called because it was drafted by the New York Board of Regents) "was contrary to [their and their children's] beliefs, religions, or religious practices," the Court did not rely on the Free Exercise Clause of the First Amendment presumably because objecting children were excused from participation, and the New York courts had ruled that the school authorities must allow exemptions for objecting students.[59]

The Supreme Court rested, instead, on the First Amendment's prohibition of laws "respecting an establishment of religion," saying that this prohibition must at least mean that it is no part of the business of government to compose official prayers for recitation by any group of the American people.[60] In support of this rationale, the Court

[55] Moss v. Spartanburg Cnty. Sch. Dist. Seven, 683 F.3d 599 (4th Cir. 2012) *cert. denied*, 133 S. Ct. 623, 184 L.Ed. 2d 396 (2012); Pierce *ex rel.* Pierce v. Sullivan W. Cent. Sch. Dist., 379 F.3d 56 (2d Cir. 2004); Lanner v. Wimmer, 662 F.2d 1349, 1351 (10th Cir. 1981).

[56] *See e.g.*, State *ex rel.* Weiss v. Dist. Bd. of Sch. Dist. No. 8 of City of Edgerton, 44 N.W. 967, 971 (Wis. 1890); Herold v. Parish Bd. of Sch. Dirs., 68 So. 116 (La. 1915); Tudor v. Bd. of Ed. of Borough of Rutherford, 100 A.2d 857 (N.J. 1953); Brown v. Orange Cnty. Bd. of Pub. Instruction, 128 So.2d 181 (Fla. Dist. Ct. App. 1960) *aff'd*, 155 So.2d 371 (Fla. 1963).

[57] Billard v. Bd. of Educ., 76 P.422, 423 (Kan. 1904); Spiller v. Inhabitants of Woburn, 94 Mass. 127 (1866).

[58] Engel v. Vitale, 370 U.S. 421, 422 (1962); *see, generally*, Arthur E. Sutherland, Jr., *Establishment According to Engel*, 76 HARV. L. REV. 25 (1962); Ernest J. Brown, *Quis Custodiet Ipsos Custodes? – The School Prayer Cases*, 1963 SUP. CT. REV. 1 (1963). For the political aftermath of the school prayer cases, *see* William M. Beaney & Edward N. Beiser, *Prayer and Politics: The Impact of Engel and Schempp on the Political Process*, 13 J. PUB. L. 475 (1963). Reflecting its political context – New York state's *Engel* prayer has been dubbed "a Three-Faiths public religion." RICHARD E. MORGAN, THE SUPREME COURT AND RELIGION 133 (Free Press, 1972).

[59] Engel, 370 U.S. at 423. For the effect of *Engel v. Vitale* on the showing that must be made to establish a plaintiff's standing to sue, *see* Sutherland, *supra* note 59, at 27.

[60] Engel, 370 U.S. at 425.

reviewed the political disputes in England over the contents of the *Book of Common Prayer*, which it described as one of the reasons causing "many of our early colonists to leave England and seek religious freedom in America."[61] Although they then used their newfound authority to establish their own religions in their new residences, this "unfortunate" turnabout led, in its turn, to "a widespread awareness among many Americans of the dangers of a union of Church and State" when the Constitution was adopted:

> They knew the anguish, hardship and bitter strife that could come when zealous religious groups struggled with one another to obtain the Government's stamp of approval from each King, Queen, or Protector that came to temporary power. The Constitution was intended to avert a part of this danger by leaving the government of this country in the hands of the people rather than in the hands of any monarch. But this safeguard was not enough. Our Founders were no more willing to let the content of their prayers and their privilege of praying whenever they pleased be influenced by the ballot box than they were to let these vital matters of personal conscience depend upon the succession of monarchs. The First Amendment was added to the Constitution to stand as a guarantee that neither the power nor the prestige of the Federal government would be used to control, support or influence the kinds of prayer the American people can say – that the people's religions must not be subjected to the pressures of government for change each time a new political administration is elected to office.[62]

The Court went on to reject New York's claim that the "Regents' Prayer" was rendered acceptable because it was "nondenominational"[63] and was not imposed on pupils over their own or their parents' objections:

> Neither [of these facts] can serve to free it from the limitations of the Establishment Clause, as it might from the Free Exercise Clause, of the First Amendment, both of which are operative against the States by virtue of the Fourteenth Amendment.... The Establishment Clause, unlike the Free Exercise Clause, does not depend upon any showing of direct governmental compulsion and is violated by the enactment of laws which establish an official religion whether those laws operate directly to coerce non-observing individuals or not.... When the power, prestige and financial support of government is placed behind a particular religious belief, the indirect coercive pressure upon religious minorities to conform to the prevailing officially approved religion is plain. But the purposes underlying the Establishment Clause go much further than that. Its first and most immediate purpose rested on the belief that a union of government and religion tends to destroy government and to degrade religion.[64]

In harmony with this "separation" theme – and perhaps hoping to strike a preemptive blow against an anticipated torrent of public criticism – the Court denied that its

61 *Id.*

62 *Id.* at 427, 429–30.

63 Commenting on this feature of the prayer, Professor Paul Freund tartly observed that "[t]he Regents' prayer in New York was an effort to enlarge pan-Protestantism and pan-Christianity to pan-religion through a kind of to-whom-it-may-concern prayer." FREUND, RELIGION AND THE PUBLIC SCHOOLS, THE LEGAL ISSUE 13 (Harvard Univ. Press, 1985).

64 Engel, 370 U.S. at 430–1. Justice Douglas argued that New York's prayer and practice were too far removed from "the strictly historic meaning" of an establishment of religion, but he concurred in the Court's decision because "New York oversteps the bounds [of the First Amendment] when it finances a religious exercise." *Id.* at 439 (Douglas, J., concurring).

interpretation of the Establishment Clause indicated "hostility toward religion or toward prayer," asserting

> Nothing ... could be more wrong.... It is neither sacrilegious nor antireligious to say that each separate government in this country should stay out of the business of writing or sanctioning official prayers and leave that purely religious function to the people themselves and to those the people choose to look to for religious guidance.[65]

In a footnote to this remark, the Court offered a dictum that, as time would show, would not mollify its critics but that may have annoyed its hard-core protagonists:

> There is, of course, nothing in the decision reached here that is inconsistent with the fact that school children and others are officially encouraged to express love for our country by reciting historical documents such as the Declaration of Independence which contain references to the Deity or by singing officially espoused anthems which include the composer's professions of faith in a Supreme Being, or with the fact that there are many manifestations in our public life of belief in God. Such patriotic or ceremonial occasions bear no true resemblance to the unquestioned religious exercise that the State of New York has sponsored in this instance.[66]

Justice Stewart dissented, asserting that "what is relevant to the issue here is not the history of an established church in sixteenth century England or in eighteenth century America, but the history of the religious traditions of our people, reflected in countless practices of the institutions and officials of our government."[67] Stewart fleshed out this claim by listing a host of invocations of the Deity, commencing with the Supreme Court crier's call, "God save the United States and this Honorable Court,"[68] and then closed his dissent with a sardonic question: "[I]s the Court suggesting that the Constitution permits judges and congressmen and Presidents to join in prayer, but prohibits school children from doing so?"[69]

The repeated references in *Engel v. Vitale* to the constitutional impropriety of a prayer drafted by government officials led some to predict that the ruling of unconstitutionality in *Engel v. Vitale* could be confined to an officially drafted prayer. This speculative bubble was quickly deflated, however, when the Supreme Court ruled in *School District of Abington v. Schempp* (1963) that two more school prayer practices were unconstitutional: (1) a Pennsylvania statutory requirement that at least ten verses from the Bible be read, without comment, in every public school at the opening of each school day, with exemptions at the written request of the pupil's parent or guardian,[70] and (2) a Baltimore rule similarly requiring the reading, without comment, of a chapter in the Bible and/or the "Lord's Prayer," also subject to an exemption if a child's parent so requested.[71] After reviewing its earlier establishment and free exercise cases, the court observed in *Schempp*:

> The wholesome "neutrality" of which this Court's cases speak thus stems from a recognition of the teachings of history that powerful sects or groups might bring about a

65 *Id.* at 434 & 435.
66 *Id.* at 435 n. 21.
67 *Id.* at 446 (Stewart, J., dissenting).
68 *Id.*
69 *Id.* at 450 n. 9.
70 Abington v. Schempp, 374 U.S. 203, 206 (1963).
71 *Id.* at 211.

> fusion of governmental and religious functions or a concert or dependency of one upon the other to the end that official support of the State or Federal Government would be placed behind the tenets of one or of all orthodoxies. This the Establishment Clause prohibits. And a further reason for neutrality is found in the Free Exercise Clause, which recognizes the value of religious training, teaching and observance and, more particularly, the right of every person to freely choose his own course with reference thereto, free of any compulsion from the state. This the Free Exercise Clause guarantees. Thus, as we have seen, the two clauses may overlap.[72]

The Court then announced

> The test [of constitutionality under the Establishment Clause] may be stated as follows: what are the purpose and the primary effect of the enactment? If either is the advancement or inhibition of religion then the enactment exceeds the scope of legislative power as circumscribed by the Constitution. That is to say that to withstand the strictures of the Establishment Clause there must be a secular legislative purpose and a primary effect that neither advances nor inhibits religion.[73]

The Court ruled that both of the Bible-reading programs under review failed to pass the applicable test:

> Applying the Establishment Clause principles to the cases at bar we find that the States are requiring the selection and reading at the opening of the school day of verses from the Holy Bible and the recitation of the Lord's Prayer by the students in unison. These exercises are prescribed as part of the curricular activities of students who are required by law to attend school. They are held in the school buildings under the supervision and with the participation of teachers employed in those schools.... The trial court in ... [the Pennsylvania case] has found that such an opening exercise is a religious ceremony and was intended by the State to be so. We agree with the trial court's finding as to the religious character of the exercises. Given that finding, the exercises and the law requiring them are in violation of the Establishment Clause.[74]

The Court's disposition in the *Baltimore* case took a few more sentences, but the Court reached the same result:

> There is no ... specific finding as to the religious character of the exercises in ... [the Baltimore case] and the State contends ... that the program is an effort to extend its benefits to all public school children without regard to their religious belief. Included within its secular purposes, it says, are the promotion of moral values, the contradiction to the materialistic tends of our times, the perpetuation of our institutions and the teaching of literature.... But even if its purpose is not strictly religious, it is sought to be accomplished through readings, without comment, from the Bible. Surely the place of the Bible as an instrument of religion cannot be grainsaid, and the State's recognition of the pervading religious character of the ceremony is evident from the rule's specific permission of the alternative use of the Catholic Douay version as well as the ... [provision] permitting nonattendance at the exercises. None of these factors is consistent with the contention that the Bible is here used either as an instrument for nonreligious moral inspiration or as a reference for the teaching of secular subjects.[75]

72 *Id.* at 222
73 *Id.*
74 *Id.* at 223.
75 *Id.* at 223–4. The nonattendance option was not part of the program as originally adopted but was added after a lower federal court struck down the original plan. *Id.* at 207 n. 1.

Finally, the Court rejected a defense, proffered to support the constitutionality of the Bible reading, that had gained some public support, namely, that the Establishment and Free Exercise Clauses *required* religious exercises in the public schools, lest a "religion of secularism" come to prevail:

> It is insisted that unless these religious exercises are permitted a "religion of secularism" is established in the schools. We agree of course that the State may not establish a "religion of secularism" in the sense of affirmatively opposing or showing hostility to religion, thus "preferring those who believe in no religion over those who do believe." ... In addition, it might well be said that one's education is not complete without a study of comparative religion or the history of religion and its relationship to the advancement of civilization. It certainly may be said that the Bible is worthy of study for its literary and historic qualities. Nothing we have said here indicates that such study of the Bible or of religion, when presented objectively as part of a secular program of education, may not be effected consistently with the First Amendment. But the exercises here do not fall into these categories. They are religious exercises, required by the States in violation of the command of the First Amendment that the Government maintain strict neutrality, neither aiding nor opposing religion.[76]

Justice Douglas concurred in the decision, as he had in *Engel v. Vitale*, arguing that the vice of the Bible-reading requirement was that "through the mechanism of the State, all of the people are being required to finance a religious exercise that only some of the people want and that violates the sensibilities of others."[77] Justice Brennan also concurred, with an unusually copious opinion, asserting that the historical record relating to the intent of the Founding Fathers "is at best ambiguous," that "statements can readily be found to support either side" of the issue before the Court, and that "our religious composition makes us a vastly more diverse people than were our forefathers."[78] Justice Brennan also observed that "daily religious exercises in the schools served broader goals than compelling formal worship or God of fostering church attendance," but he concluded that even when "devoid of sectarian bias," school prayers were "nonetheless religious."[79]

### 3. Lee v. Weisman *and the "Coercion Test"*

The *Engel* and *Schempp* cases struck down state-imposed prayer and Bible reading at the beginning of each day in the state's public schools, but both cases hinted that the Establishment Clause did not necessarily ban all public ceremonies with a religious aura. The Court did not decide another school prayer case for almost thirty years. During that time, the Court applied the "*Lemon* test" (the first two elements of which were set forth in *Abington Tp. v. Schempp*)[80] and the "endorsement test"[81] to a number of religious

76 *Id.* at 225–6.
77 *Id.* at 229 (Douglas, J., concurring).
78 *Id.* at 237, 240 (Brennan, J., dissenting).
79 *Id.* at 271.
80 The *Lemon* test requires that "[f]irst, the statute must have a secular legislative purpose; second, its principal or primary effect must be one that neither advances nor inhibits religion; finally, the statute must not foster 'an excessive government entanglement with religion.'" Lemon v. Kurtzman, 403 U.S. 602 (1971). For applications of the *Lemon* test, *see* Wallace, 472 U.S. 38; Edwards v. Aguillard, 482 U.S. 578, 587 (1987); Stone v. Graham, 449 U.S. 39 (1980); Allegheny v. ACLU, 492 U.S. 573 (1989).
81 Allegheny, 492 U.S. 573; Edwards, 482 U.S. 578.

practices carried out by government. It became clear that the public school context presents some unique issues and that the rules applied in that context may not be applicable in all other contexts. Thus, when addressing legislative prayer, the Court applied what might be called the "tradition test" because of the unique and long-standing tradition of legislative prayer.[82] In *Lee v. Weisman*, however, the Court extended its Establishment Clause jurisprudence to prohibit prayer at the graduation ceremonies of public schools.[83] The practice under review was described by the Court as follows:

> For many years it has been the policy of the Providence [Rhode Island] School Committee and the Superintendent of Schools to permit principals to invite members of the clergy to give invocations and benedictions at middle school and high school graduations.... It has been the custom of Providence school officials to provide invited clergy with a pamphlet entitled "Guidelines for Civic Occasions," prepared by the National Conference of Christians and Jews. The Guidelines recommend that public prayers at nonsectarian civic ceremonies be composed with "inclusiveness and sensitivity," but they acknowledge that "[p]rayer of any kind may be inappropriate on some civic occasions." ... The principal gave Rabbi Gutterman [the chosen clergyman for the ceremony under analysis by the Court] the pamphlet before the graduation and advised him the invocation and benediction should be nonsectarian.[84]

At the ceremony, the students stood for the Pledge of Allegiance and remained standing for Rabbi Gutterman's prayers.[85] The Court estimated that the invocation and benediction, including a "respectful moment of silence," took up only a minute or two.[86]

The Court ruled that Rhode Island's practice violated the Establishment Clause. In so holding, the Court first rejected the argument that graduation day prayers are an innocent outcropping of a pervasive "civic religion" that is consistent with the Establishment Clause. The Court then cited earlier cases expressing "heightened concerns with protecting freedom of conscience from subtle coercion in the elementary and secondary schools," noted that various studies in psychology supported "the common assumption that adolescents are often susceptive to pressure from their peers towards conformity,"[87] and concluded that the pressure on students to conform to the school-sponsored religious ceremony in light of this peer pressure could not be placed on students by the government at a graduation, an event of great "singular importance."[88]

There were two concurring opinions in *Lee v. Weisman*. Justice Blackmun, with whom Justices Stevens and O'Connor joined, stressed the consistency of the Court's decisions with its earlier Establishment Clause cases but explained that coercion is not necessary for a successful Establishment Clause claim.[89] Justice Blackmun found that the practices in *Lee* also would violate the *Lemon*/endorsement test.[90] Justice Souter, also joined by Justices Stevens and O'Connor, wrote separately to emphasize (1) that

[82] Marsh, 463 U.S. at 786–9; Lynch, 465 U.S. at 678–91 (applying a similar approach to a Christmas display, which included a crèche, in a public park).
[83] Lee v. Weisman, 505 U.S. 577 (1992).
[84] *Id.* at 581.
[85] *Id.* at 583.
[86] *Id.*
[87] *Id.* at 592–3.
[88] *Id.* at 598.
[89] *Id.* at 604–5 (Blackmun, J., concurring).
[90] *Id.* at 609.

the Establishment Clause is violated not only by state practices that aid one religion or prefer one over another but also by those that aid all religions[91] and (2) that the "coercion of religious conformity" is not a necessary element of an Establishment Clause violation.[92]

Justice Scalia dissented, joined by Chief Justice Rehnquist and Justices White and Thomas. He charged that the Court's holding "lays waste a tradition that is as old as public-school graduation ceremonies themselves, and that is a component of an even more long-standing American tradition of nonsectarian prayer to God at public celebrations generally," using as "the bulldozer of [the Court's] social engineering … a boundless, and doubtlessly manipulable, test of psychological coercion, which promises to do for the Establishment Clause what the *Durham* rule did for the insanity defense."[93] After ridiculing the coercion concept and suggesting that the Pledge of Allegiance "ought to be the next project for the Court's bulldozer," Justice Scalia argued that there was a "deeper flaw" in the Court's opinion, namely, its failure to recognize that "the hallmark of historical establishments of religion was coercion of religious orthodoxy and of financial support by force of law and threat of penalty."[94] Late in his dissent, Justice Scalia conceded that there were two "happy products" of the Court's decision in *Lee v. Weisman*: first, that by "essentially ignoring" the *Lemon* case, the Court had evidently buried it,[95] and second, that the *Lee v. Weisman* decision was "only a jurisprudential disaster and not a practical one" because it could easily be evaded by announcing at the beginning of graduation exercises that "while all are asked to rise for the invocation and benediction, none is compelled to join in them nor will be assumed, by rising, to have done so."[96] It is not clear whether this advisory opinion, a device for which the justices are not paid, was given tongue-in-cheek.

### 4. *"Voluntary, Student-Initiated" Prayer*

When the Court next decided a school prayer case it was unclear what test would be applied: the "*Lemon* test," the "endorsement test" as a gloss on *Lemon* or as a separate test, and/or the "coercion test" from *Lee*. In addition, after *Lee* was decided, schools sometimes allowed what became known as "voluntary, student-initiated" prayer. Voluntary, student-initiated prayer was often facilitated by school policies that allowed students to vote on whether to have a student deliver a prayer and often on which student or students would do so.[97] The idea was that if students voted on the prayer and the prayer giver, there would be no the state action, and the prayer could be treated as private speech.[98] The lower courts were split on the issue, with the majority of lower courts to consider the issue finding this sort of prayer unconstitutional.[99]

[91] *Id.* at 610 (Souter, J., concurring).
[92] *Id.* at 618.
[93] *Id.* at 632 (Scalia, J., dissenting).
[94] *Id.* at 639, 640.
[95] *Id.* at 644.
[96] *Id.* at 644–5.
[97] *See* Ravitch, *supra* note 4, at 44–73.
[98] *Id.* (explaining that this argument is problematic under both the Establishment and Free Speech Clauses).
[99] ACLU v. Black Horse Pike Reg'l Bd. of Educ., 84 F.3d 1471 (3d Cir. 1996); Jones v. Clear Creek Indep. Sch. Dist., 930 F.2d 416 (5th Cir. 1991); Ingebretsen v. Jackson Pub. Sch. Dist., 88 F.3d 274, 282 (5th Cir. 1996).

In *Santa Fe Independent School District v. Doe*,[100] the Court applied the *Lemon*, endorsement, and coercion tests, as well as free speech principles, finding "voluntary, student-initiated prayer" at public high school football games to be unconstitutional.[101] The school's program was set out in an intricately drafted document that bears every indication of the burning of midnight oil by a squad of lawyers; if any high school coach or principal was involved, it was surely as a bemused, if not bewildered, bystander. The program called for a secret student vote on whether there should be an invocation before home varsity football games, and if so, a student was to be elected to select and deliver the invocation.[102] If, however, there ensued a court order forbidding enforcement of this program, the following default policy would come into play:

> The [school] board has chosen to permit students to deliver a brief invocation and/or message to be delivered during the pre-game ceremonies of home varsity football games to solemnize the event, to promote good sportsmanship and student safety, and to establish the appropriate environment for the competition.
>
> Upon advice and direction of the high school principal, each spring, the high school student council shall conduct an election, by the high school student body, by secret ballot, to determine whether such a message or invocation will be a part of the pre-game ceremonies and if so, shall elect a student from a list of student volunteers, to deliver the statement or invocation. The student volunteer who is selected by his or her classmates may decide what statement or invocation to deliver, consistent with the goals and purposes of this policy. Any message and/or invocation delivered by a student must be nonsectarian and nonproselytizing.[103]

The first policy, which allowed sectarian invocations, was in fact enjoined by a court order, so the default position prescribed in the second policy took center stage.[104]

The Supreme Court, in a six-to-three decision, invalidated the program.[105] The Court held that the policy was coercive under *Lee* because it created pressure on nonconforming students to come late to the games, miss the games, aquiesce.[106] The Court explained that football games are an important part of the high school experience and that students could not be put to this choice.[107] This aspect of the opinion seems to overlook the language in *Lee* that graduation is an event of "singular" importance and therefore school-sponsored religious ceremonies could not be allowed at graduations.[108] The Court found, however, that the policy also imposed direct coercion on players, band members, and cheeleaders, who had to be there for the game and might fear retaliation if they did not participate.[109]

The Court also found that the policy endorsed religion.[110] Part of this finding was based on the long history of blatant Establishment Clause violations by the Santa Fe

100 530 U.S. 290 (2000).
101 *Id.*
102 *Id.* at 297.
103 *Id.* at 298 n. 6.
104 *Id.* at 299.
105 Doe, 530 U.S. at 292–3.
106 *Id.* at 311–13.
107 *Id.* at 312.
108 *See* Lee v. Weisman, 505 U.S. 577, 598 (1992).
109 Doe, 530 U.S. at 311.
110 *Id.* at 301–9.

School District, of which the football game prayer policies were only a small part.[111] The other practices were found unconstitutional by lower courts[112] and were not at issue before the Supreme Court, but their existence was relevant to how a reasonable observer would perceive the policy.[113] This was especially so given the context in which the prayer was given:

> Once the student speaker is selected and the message composed, the invocation is then delivered to a large audience assembled as part of a regularly scheduled, school-sponsored function conducted on school property. The message is broadcast over the school's public address system, which remains subject to the control of school officials. It is fair to assume that the pregame ceremony is clothed in the traditional indicia of school sporting events, which generally include not just the team, but also cheerleaders and band members dressed in uniforms sporting the school name and mascot. The school's name is likely written in large print across the field and on banners and flags. . . .
>
> In this context the members of the listening audience must perceive the pre-game message as a public expression of the views of the majority of the student body delivered with the approval of the school administration.[114]

The Court also found that for similar reasons the policy violated the purpose prong of the *Lemon* test, which the Court held applied to facial challenges under the Establishment Clause.[115]

Moreover, the Court addressed the school district's arguments that the policy promoted student free speech and therefore was not state-sponsored prayer but rather student-initiated prayer, and that the prayer was nonsectarian and nonproselytizing and therefore did not violate the Establishment Clause.[116] The Court held that the speech was not truly student initiated because the vote was created by school policy.[117] Moreover, the school had adequate control over the game, and therefore, any speech that occurred there could not be fairly considered private speech.[118] Even if it were considered private speech, the Court noted, the school would be favoring the speech of the majority, which it cannot do under the Establishment Clause when that speech is religious[119] or under the Free Speech Clause generally.[120]

The Court rejected the school district's argument that the nonsectarian, nonproselytizing requirement saved the policy.[121] The Court explained that *Engel*, *Abington*, and *Lee* all rejected this argument.[122]

Chief Justice Rehnquist filed a dissenting opinion for himself and Justices Scalia and Thomas.[123] Justice Rhenquist questioned the Court's ruling that the policy was invalid on its face because it would not necessarily lead to prayer, and he suggested that the

111 *Id.* at 309.
112 *Id.*
113 *Id.* at 308.
114 *Id.* at 307–8.
115 *Id.* at 314–17.
116 *Id.* at 302.
117 *Id.*
118 *Id.*
119 *Id.* at 304–5.
120 *Id.*
121 *Id.* at 305.
122 *Id.*
123 *Id.* at 318 (Rehnquist, J., dissenting).

policy could be challenged on an as-applied basis if it led to Establishment Clause violations.[124] He also argued that the majority decision "bristles with hostility to all things religious in public life"[125] and conflicted with precedent because in his view the policy could have had a secular purpose and the speech was private, not public speech.[126]

Since *Santa Fe*, a number of lower courts have addressed the issue of "voluntary, student-initiated prayer" at public school graduations.[127] These courts have generally found the practices to be unconstitutional if they are based on policies similar to the one in *Santa Fe*.[128] Graduation ceremonies are not generally considered public forums for speech, and therefore, any speech that occurs as the result of a school policy such as that in *Santa Fe* would not be truly private speech.[129] One exception is the puzzling decision by the Eleventh Circuit Court of Appeals in *Adler v. Duval County School Bd.*,[130] on remand from the Supreme Court after *Santa Fe*.[131] The decision is in conflict with most other cases decided since *Santa Fe*[132] and seemingly with the ruling in *Santa Fe* itself.[133]

Yet, even putting the Eleventh Circuit's odd decision aside, there are serious issues that still arise when a student is not elected in a context where prayer is likely to occur, but rather gives a prayer as a valedictorian or salutatorian or as an elected class speaker in a context where there was no reason to expect prayer to be the focus of the speech.[134] Questions also arise when schools review these sorts of speeches in advance and censor out prayer.[135] A number of courts have held that school districts may review student speeches ahead of time and may require that religious references, especially sectarian or proselytizing ones, be removed.[136] Central to these cases is the notion that graduation is not a public forum, and therefore, it is school controlled.[137] This means that the school district may act based on legitimate pedagogic concerns and is given great discretion in this regard.[138] If a district is concerned that it would violate the Establishment Clause to allow religious speech at a school-sponsored event, courts have generally allowed the district to preclude the religious speech.[139] A few courts have held, however, that schools may not censor valedictory and similar speeches for religious content.[140]

124 *Id.* at 318–19, 326

125 *Id.* at 318.

126 *Id.* at 321–2.

127 Workman v. Greenwood Cmty. Sch. Corp., 1:10-CV-0293-SEB-TAB, 2010 WL 1780043 (S.D. Ind. Apr. 30, 2010); Deveney v. Bd. of Educ. of Cnty. of Kanawha, 231 F. Supp. 2d 483 (S.D.W. Va. 2002); Appenheimer v. Sch. Bd. of Washington Cmty. High Sch. Dist. 308, 01-1226, 2001 WL 1885834 (C.D. Ill. May 24, 2001).

128 *See supra* note 129.

129 Deveney, 231 F. Supp. 2d at 487–8; Appenheimer, 2001 WL 1885834 at *7–*8.

130 250 F.3d 1330 (2001).

131 *Id.* at 1332.

132 *See supra* note 127 and accompanying text.

133 *See* Adler, 250 F.3d at 1342–7 (Kravitch, J., dissenting).

134 *See* Doe v. Madison Sch. Dist., 177 F.3d 789 (9th Cir. 1998, vacated on other grounds).

135 Lassonde v. Pleasonton Unified Sch. Dist., 320 F.3d 979 (9th Cir. 2003); A.M. *ex rel.* McKay v. Taconic Hills Cent. Sch. Dist., 510 F. App'x 3 (2d Cir. 2013) *cert. denied*, 134 S. Ct. 196, 187 L. Ed. 2d 44 (U.S. 2013); Cole v. Oroville Union High School Dist., 228 F.3d 1092 (9th Cir. 2000).

136 *Id.* (all sources)..

137 *Id.*

138 *Id.*

139 *Id.*

140 Griffith v. Butte Sch. Dist. No. 1, 244 P.3d 321, 333 (Mont. 2010).

What happens if a school does not review a student speech prior to graduation, and a religious speech or prayer is ultimately given? A major issue is whether the school had any reason to know that a prayer or religious speech would be given.[141] If there is a pattern of prayer in such speeches over the years or the school seems to favor or promote religious references, there may be an Establishment Clause violation.[142] If it is an unexpected occurrence, however, the school may not have violated the Establishment Clause.[143] Moreover, unless there is reason to believe that similar religious references or prayer will be repeated by future speakers, the district may have no duty to act.[144] At least one court has upheld school discipline against the speaker, however, when the speaker used a graduation speech to proselytize despite a school policy prohibiting proselytizing speech at graduation.[145]

### 5. *Other Public School Prayer and Religious Practices Issues*

A number of other issues have arisen in regard to religion at graduation ceremonies and in other contexts. The most common is singing sectarian music at graduation ceremonies. A number of courts have held that singing religious music at a public high school graduation ceremony is unconstitutional[146] or that a school can prohibit such music in order to be inclusive and/or avoid an Establishment Clause violation.[147]

Moreover, cases have arisen regarding religious speech by teachers or coaches.[148] It should be obvious that teachers cannot pray with or preach to their students, but more subtle situations arise. For example, a coach may be precluded from joining in "student-initiated prayer" by his or her team because to join in would be to endorse religion and may be coercive for those who do not participate.[149] Teachers may not pray with students at school,[150] but voluntary prayer groups in the faculty lounge or other areas that students do not have access to has been upheld as long as administrators are not involved and no one is forced to participate.[151]

141 *Cf.* Doe v. Madison Sch. Dist., 177 F.3d 789 (9th Cir. 1998, vacated on other grounds); Doe *ex rel.* Doe v. Sch. Dist. of City of Norfplk, 340 F.3d 605, 610–13 (8th Cir. 2003).

142 This would be consistent with the purpose and primary effect/endorsement analysis in a number of cases, most notably *Santa Fe v. Doe* [530 U.S. 290 (2000)].

143 Doe *ex rel.* Doe v. City of Norfolk, 340 F.3d at 613.

144 *Cf.* Doe v. Madison Sch. Dist., 177 F.3d 789 (9th Cir. 1998, vacated on other grounds)

145 Corder v. Lewis Palmer School Dist. No. 38, 566 F.3d 1219 (10th Cir. 2009).

146 Skarin v. Woodbine Cmty. Sch. Dist., 204 F. Supp. 2d 1195, 1198 (S.D. Iowa 2002); *cf.* S.D. v. St. Johns Cnty. Sch. Dist., 632 F. Supp. 2d 1085 (M.D. Fla. 2009) (Plaintiffs established a likelihood of success on the merits for an Establishment Clause violation when school allowed performance of a song about God at an elementary school assembly.).

147 Ashby v. Isle of Wright Cnty. Sch. bd., 354 F. Supp. 2d 616, 629–30 (E.D. Va. 2004); Nurre v. Whitehead, 580 F.3d 1087, 1099 (9th Cir. 2009); *cf.* Stratechuk v. Bd. of Educ., S. Orange-Maplewood Sch. Dist., 587 F.3d 597 (3d Cir. 2009) (prohibiting performances at school-sponsored elementary school events did not violate student's free exercise rights).

148 *See infra* notes 154–6.

149 Borden v. Sch. Dist. of Twp. Of East Brunswick, 523 F.3d 153, 176–9 (3rd Cir. 2008); Doe v. Duncanville Indep. Sch. Dist., 70 F.3d 402 (5th Cir. 1995).

150 Doe v. Wilson Cnty. Sch. Sys., 564 F. Supp. 2d 766, 801–3 (M.D. Tenn. 2008); Holloman *ex rel.* Holloman v. Harland, 370 F.3d 1252, 1285–9 (11th Cir. 2004).

151 Eder v. City of New York, 06 CIV. 13013, 2009 WL 362706 7–*10 (S.D.N.Y. Feb. 12, 2009); Wigg v. Sioux Falls Sch. Dist. 49-5, 382 F.3d 807 (8th Cir. 2004).

There also have been a number of cases regarding choral music by public school choirs and/or at public school events.[152] Most courts to addess these issues have held that religious components need not be stripped from music classes or choir repertoires in order to avoid violating the Establishment Clause.[153] A school, teacher, or music director may not, however, favor religious music over other music in a manner that coerces students to participate or endorses religion.[154] Moreover, students cannot be punished for refusing to participate in religious choral music that violates the tenets of their faith.[155] These issues come up quite often, and whether or not a particular situation violates the Constitution is a highly fact-sensitive inquiry.

## 6. *Moments of Silence in Public Schools for Meditation or Prayer*

In 1978, Alabama enacted a statute providing that at the beginning of the public school day, the teachers in charge of grades one through six "shall announce that a period of silence, not to exceed one minute in duration, shall be observed for meditation, and during any such period silence shall be maintained and no activities engaged in."[156] In 1981, a second statute was enacted providing that the teacher "may announce that a period of silence not to exceed one minute in duration shall be observed for meditation or voluntary prayer, and during any such period no other activities shall be engaged in."[157] In 1982, a third statute was enacted providing that "any teacher or professor in any public educational institution within the state of Alabama, recognizing that the Lord God is one, at the beginning of any homeroom or any class, may pray, may lead willing students in prayer, or may lead the willing students in the following [state-drafted] prayer to God."[158]

All three statutes were attacked in *Wallace v. Jaffree*[159] as unconstitutional by the parents of three pupils in the Alabama elementary school system. The federal district court held that there was "nothing wrong" with the 1978 law, which made no mention of prayer and presumably permitted the pupils to pray silently, to daydream, or even to think about their lessons as they wished.[160] The plaintiff did not appeal this determination.[161] The district court accepted the plaintiff's claim that the 1981 and 1982 laws were condemned by the Supreme Court's earlier holdings but then "embarked on a fresh examination of

152 S.D. v. St. Johns County School Dist., 632 F. Supp. 2d 1085 (M.D. Fl. 2009); Stratechuk v. Board of Educ., South Orange-Maplewood School Dist., 587 F.3d 597 (3rd Cir. 2009); Bauchman for Bauchman v. W. High Sch., 132 F.3d 542 (10th Cir. 1997); Doe v. Duncanville Indep. Sch. Dist., 70 F.3d 402 (5th Cir. 1995).

153 *See supra* note 157.

154 *See* Lisa Ness Seidman, *Religious Music in the Public Schools: Music to Establishment Clause Ears?* 65 Geo. Wash. L. Rev. 466, 492 (1997) ("[R]eligious music programs can potentially violate the constitutional prohibition against establishment. They may endorse religion, coerce student participation in religious activities, or have the purpose or primary effect of advancing religion.").

155 *See* S.D., 632 F. Supp. 2d 1085 (holding as unconstitutional the school's requirement that eight-year-olds sing a religious song or forgoe attendance at the end-of-the-year assembly)

156 Wallace v. Jaffree, 472 U.S. 38, 40 n. 1 (1985).

157 *Id.* at 40 n. 2.

158 *Id.* at 40 n. 3

159 Wallace, 472 U.S. 38.

160 *Id.* at 41 & n. 4.

161 *Id.* at 41.

the question [of] whether the First Amendment imposes any barrier to the establishment of an official religion by the State of Alabama."[162] On the basis of "newly discovered evidence" that the Supreme Court "erred" in holding that Alabama could not do so because the First Amendment did not apply to the states (a ridiculous holding by a district court that is bound by Supreme Court decisions), the district court refused to enjoin enforcement of the 1981 and 1982 statutes.[163] The Court of Appeals for the Eleventh Circuit reversed,[164] and the case then went to the Supreme Court, which summarily affirmed the appellate court's verdict of unconstitutionality for the 1982 statute and limited the appeal to the validity of the 1981 meditation-or-prayer law.[165]

The Supreme Court affirmed the Court of Appeals' conclusion that the 1981 statute was unconstitutional, even though it offered students an option between prayer and meditation during the moment of silence. The Court began its analysis by quoting its ruling in *Lemon v. Kurtzman* (1971) that Establishment Clause claims were subject to three "cumulative criteria":

> Every analysis in this area must begin with consideration of the cumulative criteria developed by the Court over many years. Three such tests may be gleaned from our cases. First, the statute must have a secular legislative purpose; second, its principal or primary effect must be one that neither advances nor inhibits religion.... [F]inally, the statute must not foster "an excessive government entanglement with religion."[166]

The Court then turned to the first criterion, under which a statute cannot stand if it "does not have a clearly secular purpose."[167] The Court found that the 1981 statute was devoid of any secular purpose because the remarkably candid legislator who sponsored it admitted that its function was "the return of voluntary prayer in our public schools" and that he had "no other purpose in mind."[168] Moreover, since Alabama's 1978 meditation statute already permitted students to engage in silent prayer if they so desired, the Court could identify no additional objective for the 1981 statute except "to convey a message of state endorsement and promotion of prayer."[169]

Significantly, moment-of-silence laws are usually constitutional as long as they are not based on a religious purpose.[170] This is especially so if prayer is not mentioned, or if prayer is mentioned, it is just one of several examples mentioned in the statute. A number of lower courts have addresses moment-of-silence laws that include prayer as an example of what might be done during the moment of silence or that have added prayer as an example.[171] Whether this is constitutional is affected by the purpose of

162 *Id.* at 45.

163 *Id.* at 48. For the district court's opinion – described as "remarkable" by the Supreme Court for its extreme interpretation and failure to follow binding precedent, *see* 554 F. Supp. 1004 (S.D. Ala. 1983).

164 705 F.2d 1526 (1983).

165 For these preliminary bouts in the battle, *see* Jaffree v. Mobile County, 459 U.S. 1314 (1983) (Justice Powell, as circuit justice; district court obligated to follow *Engel* and *Schempp* cases); Wallace v. Jaffree, 466 U.S. 924 (1984) (probable jurisdiction noted, limited to constitutionality of 1981 statute).

166 Wallace, 472 U.S. at 55–6 [quoting Lemon v. Kurtzman, 403 U.S. 602, 612–13 (1971)].

167 Wallace, 472 U.S. at 56.

168 *Id.* at 56–7 & n. 43.

169 *Id.* at 58–9.

170 *Id.* at 67 (O'Connor, J., concurring)

171 Sherman *ex rel.* Sherman v. Koch, 623 F.3d 501 (7th Cir. 2010); Brown v. Gilmore, 258 F.3d 265 (4th Cir. 2001).

including prayer as an example[172] and whether it is listed along with other, nonreligious examples.[173]

It is also essential that the moment-of-silence law be applied in a manner that does not favor religion, even if it is facially constitutional. There are examples of these laws being applied in a manner that is unconstitutional, even if the law is constitutional on its face.[174] For example, a moment-of-silence law in West Virginia was applied by a school district in a way that favored prayer and disfavored religious minorities.[175] This was found to be unconstitutional.[176]

## G. Creationism and Intelligent Design in Public Schools

In 1928, Arkansas enacted an "antievolution statute," which was an adaption of the Tennessee law that produced the famous *Scopes* trial in 1927.[177] The Arkansas law made it unlawful for a teacher in any state-supported school or university "to teach the theory or doctrine that mankind ascended or descended from a lower order of animal"[178] or to use a textbook that teaches this doctrine or theory. The penalty for violation was a fine in an amount not exceeding $500 and dismissal from the offender's position.[179]

In *Epperson v. Arkansas* (1968), the Supreme Court acknowledged that "public education in our Nation is committed to the control of state and local authorities" and that "[c]ourts do not and cannot intervene in the resolution of conflicts which arise in the daily operation of school systems and which do not directly and sharply implicate basic constitutional values," but it did not then bow out, instead ruling that the statute violated the Establishment Clause of the First Amendment.[180] The case began with a complaint by a high school teacher of biology, who alleged that the law subjected her to "a literal dilemma" because the text prescribed by the school administration, on the recommendation of its teachers of biology, contained a chapter setting forth the prohibited theory. After noting that "the statute might presently [be] more of a curiosity than a vital fact of life" in Arkansas and Mississippi (which had a similar law on its books),[181] the Supreme Court ruled that the teacher's appeal from the Arkansas Supreme Court's decision upholding the law "is properly [heard] here, and it is our duty to decide the issues presented."[182]

172 Sherman, 623 F.3d at 515–16; Brown, 258 F.3d at 275–7.
173 Sherman, 623 F.3d at 515–16; Brown, 258 F.3d at 275–7.
174 *See* Walter v. W. Virginia Bd. of Educ., 610 F. Supp. 1169 (S.D.W. Va. 1985).
175 *Id.* at 1170–4.
176 *Id.* at 1177.
177 *See, generally,* Edward J. Larson, *The Scopes Trial and the Evolving Concept of Freedom,* 85 VA. L. REV. 503 (1999).
178 The idea that *Homo sapiens* evolved from some less complex living organism is accepted as fact in the scientific community. However, the idea that *Homo sapiens* evolved *from a single genealogical tree* is a theory, not a fact. *See* W. Ford Dolittle, *Uprooting the Tree of Life,* SCI. AM., Feb. 2000, at 87.
179 Epperson v. Arkansas, 393 U.S. 97 (1968).
180 *Id.* at 104. The decision was unanimous, though Justices Black, Harlan, and Stewart concurred rather than joining in the Court's opinion, written by Justice Fortas. *Id.* at 109, 114, 115.
181 *Id.* at 102. The Tennessee statute was repealed in 1967. *Id.* at 102, n. 8.
182 *Id.* at 102.

After a brief, almost perfunctory review of its far from conclusive earlier church-state decisions, the Court struck down the Arkansas statute:

> While study of religions and of the bible from a literary and historic viewpoint, presented objectively as part of a secular program of education, need not collide with the First Amendment's prohibition, the State may not adopt programs or practices in its public schools or colleges which "aid or oppose" any religion.... In the present case, there can be no doubt that Arkansas has sought to prevent its teachers from discussing the theory of evolution because it is contrary to the belief of some that the Book of Genesis must be the exclusive source of doctrine as to the origin of man. No suggestion has been made that Arkansas' law may be justified by considerations of state policy other than the religious views of some of its citizens. It is clear that fundamentalist sectarian conviction was and is the law's reason for existence. Its antecedent, Tennessee's "monkey law" candidly stated its purpose: to make it unlawful "to teach any theory that denies the story of the Divine Creation of man as taught in the bible, and to teach instead that man has descended from a lower order of animals." Perhaps the sensational publicity attendant upon the *Scopes* trial induced Arkansas to adopt less explicit language. It eliminated Tennessee's reference to "the story of the Divine Creation of man" as taught in the Bible, but there is no doubt that the motivation for the law was the same: to suppress the teaching of a theory which, it was thought, "denied" the divine creation of man.
>
> Arkansas' law cannot be defended as an act of religious neutrality. Arkansas did not seek to excise from the curricula of its schools and universities all discussion of the origin of man. The law's effort was confined to an attempt to blot out a particular theory because of its supposed conflict with the Biblical account, literally read. Plainly, the law is contrary to the mandate of the First, and a violation of the Fourteenth, Amendment to the Constitution.[183]

Justice Black concurred in the Court's decision, notwithstanding his doubts (1) whether the case presented a justiciable controversy, (2) whether the Arkansas legislators were motivated not by religious beliefs but by prudence, impelling them to remove a controversial subject from the curriculum, (3) difficulty in determining whether the Court's decision infringes the religious freedom of those who consider evolution "an anti-religious doctrine," and (4) whether "a person hired to teach school children takes with him [or her] into the classroom a constitutional right to teach sociological, economic, political, or religious subjects that the school's managers do not want discussed."[184] Black, therefore, would have either struck down the Arkansas statute as too vague to enforce or would have remanded the case to the State Supreme Court (which had failed to decide whether the statute prohibited any explanation of evolution or only teaching that the theory was true) for clarification of its holding and opinion.[185] Justice Harlan concurred in ruling that the statute constituted a forbidden establishment of religion but objected to dicta in the opinion suggesting that it was unconstitutionally vague and interfered with free

[183] *Id.* at 106–9. In its final sentence, the Court cited the Fourteenth Amendment, which makes the First Amendment, including its religion clauses, applicable to the states. For discussion of this "incorporation" doctrine, *see supra* Subsection F.1..

[184] Epperson, 393 U.S. at 109–14 (Black, J., concurring). [unecessary to include this].

[185] Epperson, 393 U.S. at 114 (Black, J., concurring). For the Arkansas Supreme Court's two-sentence *per curiam* opinion, *see id.* at 101 n. 7. Commenting on the state court's dodging of this issue, the Court observed that it "perhaps reflect[s] the discomfort which the statute's quixotic prohibition necessarily engenders in the modern mind." *Id.* at 102.

speech,[186] and Justice Stewart concurred on the ground, bypassed by the Court, that the law was "so vague as to be invalid under the Fourteenth Amendment."[187]

Thirteen years passed before the Court again addressed the question of creationism in the public schools. In the interim, lower courts addressed the issue, most famously in *McLean v. Arkansas Bd. of Educ.*,[188] where a federal district court held unconstitutional a "Balanced Treatment Act" requiring that creation science be taught if evolution is taught.[189] A similar law in Louisiana made its way to the Supreme Court.

On July 20, 1981, Louisiana Governor David C. Treen signed the "Balanced Treatment for Creation-Science and Evolution in Public School Instruction Act" into law. The law was sponsored by State Senator Bill Keith, who introduced a related bill in June 1980.[190] The stated purpose of the law was to promote academic freedom,[191] but it did so by requiring that "creation science" must be taught whenever evolution is taught in Louisiana public schools.[192] There was no explicit prohibition on teaching creation science before the law was enacted,[193] and under the law, there was no requirement that either creation science or evolution be taught.[194] The only requirement was that teachers must teach creation science if they teach evolution.

The Louisiana law was a "balanced-treatment law." These laws were supported by the creation-science movement.[195] Creation scientists argued that these laws were designed to promote academic freedom and free speech.[196] The Louisiana law was challenged in federal court shortly after it was signed.[197] The resulting decision issued by the Supreme Court in 1987 is known as *Edwards v. Aguillard*.[198]

In *Edwards*, the Court held that the Louisiana law was unconstitutional because its purpose was to promote a religious concept, creation science, and not to promote academic freedom.[199] The *Edwards* Court focused exclusively on whether the Louisiana "Balanced Treatment Act" had a valid secular purpose.[200] After looking at the language of the Louisiana law,[201] the statements of Senator Keith who introduced it,[202] statements by other legislators and government officials,[203] and statements by those who testified before the legislature on the bill,[204] the Court held that the purpose of the law was to promote

186 *Id.* at 115–16 (Harlan, J., concurring). Justice Stewart's reliance on the Fourteenth Amendment was presumably intended to refer to its Due Process Clause.

187 *Id.* at 116 (Stewart, J., concurring).

188 529 F. Supp. 1255 (E.D. Ark. 1982).

189 *Id.* at 1272.

190 Edwards v. Aguillard, 482 U.S. 578, 587 (1987).

191 *Id.* at 586.

192 *Id.* at 581, 586.

193 *Id.* at 587.

194 *Id.* at 586–9.

195 *See, generally*, Robert Pennock, Tower of Babel: The Evidence Against the New Creationism (MIT Press 1999).

196 Edwards, 482 U.S. at 596.

197 *Id.* at 581–2.

198 482 U.S. 578 (1987).

199 *Id.* at 586–9, 591–3, 596–7.

200 *Id.*

201 *Id.* at 581, 586–9.

202 *Id.* at 587, 591–3.

203 *Id.* at 591.

204 *Id.* at 591 n. 13.

creationism and to favor the views of certain Christian denominations.[205] The Court did not accept the state's argument that the law was designed to promote academic freedom.[206] It found instead that the law could not serve the purpose of promoting academic freedom because the law limited rather than expanded such freedom.[207]

Weighing heavily against the claim of a valid secular purpose were the facts that the law's proponents spoke in explicitly religious terms and that creation science posits that human beings were placed on earth by a supernatural creator.[208] Moreover, the Court found that the law was designed to counter evolution with creationism "at every turn,"[209] which served the religious beliefs of certain religious groups.[210] To make matters worse for the state, the law provided support for additional creation-science teaching materials but not for the development of additional evolution materials,[211] and the law explicitly provided protection for teachers who taught creation science but not for those who taught evolution (even though if one was taught, the other must be taught under the law).[212]

Significantly, the *Edwards* decision, and the defeat of "balanced-treatment acts" in other courts,[213] became an impetus for what would eventually become the intelligent-design (ID) movement. In fact, it seems clear that ID was designed, in part, to avoid some of the problems that doomed creation science in the courtroom. So far, only one court has addressed ID in public school science classrooms in any detail, and it is to that case that we now turn.

In *Kitzmiller v. Dover Area School District*,[214] a federal district court held that the inclusion of a disclaimer favoring ID in classrooms, the purchase and placement of ID texts in the school library, and conduct by some school board members violated the Establishment Clause of the First Amendment.[215] The key issue in the case was whether ID is religion or science.[216] This issue was so important because if ID is a religiously grounded concept, including it in science classrooms, even through a mandatory disclaimer, would violate the Establishment Clause.[217] If ID were science, however, there might be an argument that it could be included in such classes despite its religious underpinnings. If ID is neither religion nor science, there is no constitutional issue because if it is not religious, the Establishment Clause could not be violated,[218] although teaching ID as science still would raise serious educational concerns that could

205 *Id.* at 592–4, 596–7.

206 *Id.* at 586–8.

207 *Cf. id.* at 587–9 ("[U]nder the Act's requirements, teachers who were once free to teach any and all facets of this subject are now unable to do so.").

208 *Id.* at 587–94.

209 *Id.* at 589.

210 *Id.* at 588–9, 592–3.

211 *Id.* at 588.

212 *Id.*

213 Edwards, 482 U.S. 578; Waters, 515 F.2d 485 (finding Tennessee's balanced-treatment law unconstitutional); McLean, 529 F. Supp. 1255 (same for Arkansas act).

214 400 F. Supp. 2d 707 (E.D. Pa. 2005).

215 *Id.*

216 *Id.*

217 *Id.* at 711–23, 735–46.

218 *Cf.* Kitzmiller, 400 F. Supp. 2d at 711–23 (pointing out constitutional issues arise because ID is a religious theory not just because it is bad science).

be addressed at the state level. Thus the best-case scenario for the school board would have been a finding that ID is not religious and is science. The best-case scenario for those opposing the school board's ID policy would be a finding that ID is not science and is religiously based.

The court heard testimony from leading philosophers of science,[219] biologists,[220] and ID proponents.[221] After hearing all this testimony and evaluating documentary evidence such as manuscripts of an ID textbook that was virtually identical to a creation-science text with "intelligent designer" substituted for God and "intelligent design" for "creation," the court held that ID is not science and that it is a religiously grounded theory.[222] The court's holding that ID is a religiously based theory and not a scientific theory was central to its reasoning under the Establishment Clause.[223] The Supreme Court had already held in *Edwards*[224] that religiously based theories of creation (in that case "creation science") could not be taught in public school science classes without running afoul of the Establishment Clause.[225]

Theologians and philosophers of science testified that ID is not a scientific theory and that it is a religious theory.[226] Moreover, the ID proponents' top witnesses had a hard time explaining how ID is science and not religiously grounded:

> Moreover, it is notable that both Professors Behe and Minnich [two leading defense experts] admitted [that] their personal view is that the designer is God and Professor Minnich testified that he understands many leading advocates of ID to believe the designer to be God. Although proponents of the ID [movement] occasionally suggest that the designer could be a space alien or a time-traveling cell biologist, no serious alternative to God as the designer has been proposed by members of the ID [movement], including Defendants' expert witnesses. In fact, an explicit concession that the intelligent designer works outside the laws of nature and science and a direct reference to religion is *Pandas*" [the leading ID textbook] rhetorical statement, "What kind of intelligent agent was it [the designer]" and answer: "On its own science cannot answer this question. It must leave it to religion and philosophy."[227]

Once the *Kitzmiller* court determined that ID is not science and that it is religion, the outcome that the school board policies violated the Establishment Clause was unavoidable.[228] Adding to the obvious outcome was the remarkable behavior by some school board members. Members had threatened teachers,[229] had burned an evolution mural found in a classroom,[230] had laundered the purchase of ID books for the school library through a local church,[231] had made brazenly sectarian statements in their official

219 *Id.* at 719, 721, 735–6.
220 *Id.* at 724–5, 727–9, 737–8, 740, 743–4.
221 *Id.* at 718–23, 735–45.
222 *Id.* at 735–46.
223 *Id.*
224 482 U.S. 578 (1987).
225 *Id.*
226 *Id.* at 718.
227 *Id.* at 718–19.
228 *Id.*
229 *Id.* at 749–50, 755, 762.
230 *Id.* at 753.
231 *Id.* at 753–6.

capacities,[232] had engaged in sectarian attacks on board members and members of the public who disagreed with them,[233] and had lied on the stand and in depositions.[234]

The court applied the endorsement and *Lemon* tests to the school board policy.[235] It held that the disclaimer and the other events surrounding the disclaimer (including the acquisition of ID textbooks for the school library) violated the endorsement test[236] and the purpose and effects prongs of the *Lemon* test.[237] Thus the school board policy violated the Establishment Clause.[238] Because the court found that ID is not science and that overwhelming evidence proved that it is religiously grounded, the court held that the ID policy violated both the purpose and effects elements of the endorsement test.[239]

The evidence demonstrated that the purpose of implementing the ID policy was to endorse the majority school board members' religious views[240] and that there is no secular purpose that would support teaching ID as science.[241] Therefore, the policy would make a reasonable observer familiar with the history of the policy feel that the board was creating political and religious insiders and outsiders based on religious views.[242] The board argued that the purpose of the policy was to promote critical-thinking skills and improve science education.[243] Certainly exposure to different ideas and values might support teaching ID in comparative religion or philosophy classes,[244] but because the court held that ID is not a scientific theory, there is no secular purpose for teaching it in science classes.[245]

The board fared no better when the court analyzed the effects of the policy under the endorsement test. The court held that because ID is religious and not science, the effect of the disclaimer and book purchases was to endorse religion.[246] Thus, when the policy was implemented, the disclaimer was read in classes, and ID books were added to the library in a well-advertised manner, a reasonable observer would believe that such actions had the effect of creating political and religious insiders and outsiders.[247] There was substantial evidence to back up the notion that indeed this is exactly what happened in Dover when the policy was being debated and after it was passed and implemented.[248] This same analysis essentially applied to the *Lemon* effects test as well.[249] The court used the same reasoning to hold that the primary effect of the Dover policy was to promote the religious theory of ID.[250]

232 *Id.* at 748–53.
233 *Id.*
234 *Id.* at 748, 752.
235 *Id.* at 712–14.
236 *Id.* at 714–35, 765.
237 *Id.* at 746–65.
238 *Id.* at 765–6.
239 *Id.* at 745–6, 765.
240 *Id.*
241 *Id.* at 735–43.
242 *Id.* at 745–6.
243 *Id.* at 762–3.
244 *Id.* at 765.
245 *Id.* at 735–46, 763–5.
246 *Id.* at 745–6, 763–4 (holding that school board policy and actions violated effects inquiry under endorsement and *Lemon* tests).
247 *Id.*
248 *Id.* at 748–62.
249 *Id.* at 763–5.
250 *Id.*

The court's discussion of the school board's purpose under the *Lemon* test went beyond the discussion of purpose under the endorsement test.[251] The court specifically addressed the behavior and statements of particular school board members to demonstrate that the board policy had no secular purpose and was designed primarily to promote the religious views of certain board members.[252] It is important to note, however, that even without such behavior, the fact that the court held that ID is not science and is religious was enough to violate the endorsement test and the effects test under *Lemon*.[253]

Of course, the decision of a federal district court does not have the precedential value of an appeals court decision. Yet the *Kitzmiller* court's careful analysis of the science versus religion issue likely will be followed by other courts because it is the first decision directly addressing the constitutionality of an ID policy in science classrooms and also because so many leading figures representing both sides of the issue testified at trial.[254] However, the school board's behavior in *Kitzmiller* was so brazen that courts confronted with similar policies from better-behaved school boards could use the Dover school board's conduct to distinguish *Kitzmiller*. Significantly, the Dover School Board's behavior was not the primary focus of the court's analysis on the science versus religion issue.[255] It is that issue that was key to the ultimate outcome in the case.[256] Therefore, even without the behavior of school board members, the case most likely would have come out the same way.[257]

## H. Religion Elsewhere in the School Curriculum

There is no question that schools need not exclude religious content from the curriculum.[258] As the Court in *Abington v. Schempp* noted, doing so would skew the ways in which history and other subjects are taught.[259] Therefore, the role of religion in history, art, and literature need not be ignored or excluded from public schools.[260] The key is that the material must be taught in an objective way that does not favor or promote any particular religious view as right or wrong, true or false.[261] This may be characterized as the rule of "teach it, don't preach it!"

Schools may teach comparative religion courses and may include the role of religion and religious texts in history, art, literature, and other places where it is relevant to the curriculum.[262] Several organizations have tried to promote "Bible history" and

251 *Id.* at 748–62.
252 *Id.*
253 *Id.* at 711–46.
254 *See, generally, id.*
255 *Id.* at 720–3, 735–45.
256 *See, generally, id.*
257 *Id.* at 746–63.
258 Abington, 374 U.S. at 225, 300; Lee, 505 U.S. at 597–8.
259 Abington, 374 U.S. at 225, 300; *see also* Engel, 370 U.S. at 434 ("The history of man is inseperable from the history of religion.").
260 *See supra* notes 265 & 266.
261 Abington, 374 U.S. at 225 ("Nothing we have said here indicates that such study of the Bible or of religion, when presented objectively as part of a secular program of education, may not be effected consistently with the First Amendment.")
262 *See supra* notes 265–8.

similar classes.[263] Many of these likely would be found unconstitutional because they teach the "Bible as history" rather than just the role of the Bible in history[264] or teach the Bible as the word of God in a literaure class rather than as a text to be studied like others.[265] These sorts of courses appear to be backdoor attempts to get religion, usually Christianity, into the curriculum and therefore would be unconstitutional.[266] However, courses that do not have such a purpose and are more balanced in their presentation of the material are likely to survive constitutional scrutiny.[267] To do so, however, the course must look at the material objectively without presuming its truth.[268]

## I. Religious Symbols and Displays in the Classroom or School Building

In *Stone v. Graham* (1980), the Supreme Court summarily reversed an equally divided Kentucky Supreme Court that had affirmed a trial court's decision upholding the constitutionality of a Kentucky law requiring a copy of the Ten Commandments, purchased with private contributions, to be posted in every public classroom of the state, accompanied by a notice ("in small print") that "[t]he secular purpose of the Ten Commandments is clearly seen in its adoption as the fundamental legal code of Western Civilization and the Common Law of the United States."[269] After quoting the three-prong *Lemon* test, the Supreme Court ruled that the Kentucky statute "had no secular legislative purpose, and is therefore unconstitutional."[270] Elaborating on this conclusion, the Court stated:

> The Ten Commandments are undeniably a sacred text in the Jewish and Christian faiths, and no legislative recitation of a supposed secular purpose can blind us to that fact. The Commandments do not confine themselves to arguably secular matters, such as honoring one's parents, killing or murder, adultery, stealing, false witness, and covetousness.... Rather, the first part of the Commandments concerns the religious duties of believers; worshiping the Lord God alone, avoiding idolatry, not using the Lord's name in vain, and observing the Sabbath Day.
>
> This is not a case in which the Ten Commandments are integrated into the school curriculum, where the Bible may constitutionally be used in an appropriate study of history, civilization, ethics, comparative religion, or the like.... Posting of religious texts on the wall serves no such educational function. If the posted copies of the Ten Commandments are to have any effect at all, it will be to induce the schoolchildren to read, meditate upon, perhaps to venerate and obey, the Commandments. However desirable this might be as a matter of private devotion, it is not a permissible state objective under the Establishment Clause.[271]

263 Gibson v. Lee Cnty. Sch. Bd., 1 F. Supp. 2d 1426, 1428 (M.D. Fla. 1998); Wiley v. Franklin, 468 F. Supp. 133, 139 (E.D. Tenn. 1979); Crockett v. Sorenson, 568 F. Supp. 1422, 1430 (W.D. Va. 1983).

264 Herdahl v. Pontotoc Cnty. Sch. Dist., 933 F. Supp. 582, 593 (N.D. Miss. 1996).

265 Doe v. Porter, 370 F.3d 558 (6th Cir. 2004); Hall v. Bd. of Sch. Comm'rs of Conecuh Cnty., 656 F.2d 999, 1001–3 (5th Cir. 1981).

266 *See supra* notes 270–2.

267 Daugherty v. Vanguard Charter Sch. Acad., 116 F. Supp. 2d 897, 912–16 (W.D. Mich. 2000).

268 Crockett, 568 F. Supp. at 1431 (W.D. Va. 1983) ("[A Bible course] should be taught in an objective manner with no attempt made to indoctrinate the children as to either the truth or falsity of the biblical materials.").

269 Stone v. Graham, 449 U.S. 39, 41 (1980).

270 Stone, 449 U.S. at 41.

271 Stone, 449 U.S. at 41–2.

The Court brushed aside the state's claim that the posters were paid for by private contributions because their posting in the classrooms provides "the official support" that triggers application of the Establishment Clause, as did the state treasurer's services as a collecting agent for the private contributions.[272]

Although the Court explicitly distinguished the situation before it from one in which the poster was used in a course in history or ethics, it is possible that a trial court might conclude, on a full record, that the pupils (or some of them) were coerced even in a profusely secular context not merely to memorize and understand the Ten Commandments but to treat them as rules of conduct. In our society, there is an inherent and ineradicable difference between a chart setting out the Ten Commandments and one illustrating the Seven Wonders of the Ancient World, the division of the Soviet Union after the cold war, or even the Code of Hammurabi. Still, the Court might conclude that any "coercive" effect of the Ten Commandments derives primarily from the pupil's home environment – the temperament inculcated by the family and brought by the pupil to school – rather than from classroom study or even that any coercive effect is simultaneously offset or dissipated by the aura of relativism that a course in comparative ethics or religion inevitably imparts (to the alarm of devout parents).

It is clear, then, that public schools cannot display religious symbols in classrooms or school buildings. This leaves (at least) two questions open. First, what constitutes a "religious symbol" in the school context? Second, what about student displays where students are allowed to pick topics to write about or otherwise address (art, etc.)?

The first question is addressed in Chapter 17 of this book, devoted to religious symbolism.[273] It is clear that schools may not post the Ten Commandments, nativity scenes, and similar displays, but what about general holiday displays involving Christmas trees and reindeer? Courts have generally allowed these,[274] especially where other seasonal holidays are included.[275] But teachers may not require students to create Christmas art or the like.[276]

The second question has been addressed in a number of cases,[277] including the Third Circuit's decision in the *Medford* case, where a school was found not to have violated

[272] *Id.* at 42.

[273] *See infra* Chapter 17.

[274] Skoros v. City of New York, 437 F.3d 1, 16–39 (2d Cir. 2006); Clever v. Cherry Hill Twp. Bd. of Educ., 838 F. Supp. 929, 931 (D.N.J. 1993)

[275] Clever, 838 F. Supp. at 940 ("To the extent [that] the record reflects the actual implementation of that policy, the calendars for November and December, which celebrate a wide variety of religious and secular holidays, confirm that its intent is being fairly implemented.").

[276] *Cf.* S.D., 632 F. Supp. 2d 1085 (holding as unconstitutional the school's requirement that an eight-year-old sing a song about God or forgoe attendance at the end-of-the-year assembly); *cf.* U.S. Dep't of Educ., *Religious Expression and Prayer in Class Assignments*, in GUIDANCE ON CONSTITUTIONALLY PROTECTED PRAYER IN PUBLIC ELEMENTARY AND SECONDARY SCHOOLS (Feb. 7, 2003), *available at:* http://www2.ed.gov/policy/gen/guid/religionandschools/prayer_guidance.html:

> Students may express their beliefs about religion in homework, artwork, and other written and oral assignments free from discrimination based on the religious content of their submissions. Such home and classroom work should be judged by ordinary academic standards of substance and relevance and against other legitimate pedagogical concerns identified by the school. Thus, if a teacher's assignment involves writing a poem, the work of a student who submits a poem in the form of a prayer (for example, a psalm) should be judged on the basis of academic standards (such as literary quality) and neither penalized nor rewarded on account of its religious content.

[277] Peck *ex rel.* Peck v. Baldwinsville Cent. Sch. Dist., 426 F.3d 617 (2d Cir. 2005); Curry v. Sch. Dist., 452 F. Supp. 2d 723 (E.D. Mich. 2006); *cf.* Demmon v. Loudoun County Pub. Schs, 342 F. Supp. 2d 474

the Constitution when a teacher refused to hang a student's work with the work of other students because he chose to focus on a religious theme in an open assignment.[278] The general rule, when the assignment is not publically displayed (and most likely in some jurisdictions even if it is publically displayed), however, is that if an assignment allows students to address a question from a variety of perspectives, religious perspectives may not be excluded or discriminated against.[279] For example, if a teacher assigns the class to write a report on the person who has influenced them the most, and students are able to decide who, a student may not be treated differently if he or she picks Jesus or another religious figure.[280]

## J. Equal Access to Public School Buildings: The "Limited Public Forum" Principle

### 1. *Introduction*

In *Widmar v. Vincent* (1981), the Supreme Court invalidated, on free speech grounds, a state university's regulation prohibiting student use of the university's facilities "for purposes of religious worship or religious teaching."[281] The context for this ruling was a record showing that the university had created a "public forum" by allowing a wide diversity of student groups to present their programs in its buildings; thus the no-religion restriction was an exception to a generally applicable university policy requiring justification:

> Through its policy of accommodating their meetings, the University has created a forum generally open for use by student groups. Having done so, the University has assumed an obligation to justify its discriminations and exclusions under applicable constitutional norms....
>
> In order to justify discriminatory exclusion from a public forum based on the religious content of a group's intended speech, the University must ... satisfy the standard of review appropriate to content-based exclusions. It must show that its regulation is necessary to serve a compelling state interest and that it is narrowly drawn to achieve that end....
>
> We are not oblivious to the range of an open forum's likely effects. It is possible – perhaps even foreseeable – that religious groups will benefit from access to University facilities. But this Court has explained that a religious organization's enjoyment of

(E.D. Va. 2004) (holding that school violated a family's free speech rights when it prohibited bricks with a Latin cross on a school fund-raising project when other secular symbols were allowed).

278 C.H. *ex rel.* Z.H. v. Oliva, 195 F.3d 167, 177 (3d Cir. 1999) (3d Cir. 2000).

279 U.S. Dep't of Educ., *Religious Expression and Prayer in Class Assignments*, in Guidance on Constitutionally Protected Prayer in Public Elementary and Secondary Schools (Feb. 7, 2003), *available at:* http://www2.ed.gov/policy/gen/guid/religionandschools/prayer_guidance.html:

> Students may express their beliefs about religion in homework, artwork, and other written and oral assignments free from discrimination based on the religious content of their submissions. Such home and classroom work should be judged by ordinary academic standards of substance and relevance and against other legitimate pedagogical concerns identified by the school. Thus, if a teacher's assignment involves writing a poem, the work of a student who submits a poem in the form of a prayer (for example, a psalm) should be judged on the basis of academic standards (such as literary quality) and neither penalized nor rewarded on account of its religious content.

280 *Cf. id.*

281 Widmar v. Vincent, 454 U.S. 263, 265 (1981).

merely "incidental" benefits does not violate the prohibition against the "primary advancement" of religion.[282]

*Widmar* involved the rights of university students, and it left open the possibility of a contrary result for meetings of students in elementary and secondary schools – indeed, hinting at a contrary result by noting that university students are "young adults" who "are less impressionable than younger students" and "should be able to appreciate that the University's policy is one of neutrality toward religion."[283] This issue was resolved, however, through the Court's response to a federal statute requiring equal access for religious non-curriculum-related student groups after school hours where the school opens itself to other non-curriculum-related student groups and by a decision directly addressing equal access in the elementary school context.

## 2. *The Equal Access Act*

The federal Equal Access Act, enacted in 1984, makes it unlawful for any public secondary school that receives federal financial assistance and that maintains "a limited open forum" to deny equal access to or discriminate against any students wishing "to conduct a meeting within that limited open forum on the basis of the religious, political, philosophical, or other content of the speech at such meetings."[284] Under the act, a "limited open forum" exists when a public secondary school allows "one or more non-curriculum-related student groups to meet on school premises during noninstructional time."[285] This legislation in effect extended the reasoning of the *Widmar* case to public secondary schools that receive federal funds.

In *Board of Education v. Mergens*, the Supreme Court encountered the 1984 federal law in the context of a suit brought by a group of students at a Nebraska high school against the local school board, complaining that they had been denied the right to form a Christian club with the same privileges as other student groups.[286] The proposed club's purpose was, among other things, to permit students to read and discuss the Bible and to pray together, but membership was to be voluntary and open to all students regardless of their religious affiliation. The students' application was denied on the ground that permitting a religious club at the school would violate the Establishment Clause.[287] The Supreme Court affirmed the Court of Appeals, which held that the Equal Access Act applied to the students' proposal and did not violate the Establishment Clause.[288]

More than half the prevailing opinion was devoted to questions of statutory construction, primarily the crucial phrase "non-curriculum-related student group," because the act applied only if the school permitted one or more groups of this type to meet on

282 *Id.* at 267, 269–70, 273–4. *See, generally, Equal Access: The Widmar and Bender Cases, in* RODNEY K. SMITH, PUBLIC PRAYER AND THE CONSTITUTION (Scholarly Resources 1987).

283 454 U.S. at 274 n. 14.

284 20 USC § 4071(a).

285 *Id.*

286 Board of Education v. Mergens, 496 U.S. 226, 232–3. The school in *Mergens* received federal funds, thus subjecting it to the terms of the Equal Access Act. *Id.* at 233. [this is addressed elsewhere so unecessary here.]

287 *Id.* at 232–3.

288 *Id.* at 234. For the Court of Appeals' opinion, *see* 867 F.2d 1076 (8th Cir. 1989).

the campus before or after classes.[289] The Court observed that this phrase was "unfortunately" not defined by the act and that the legislative history was "less than helpful"; both parties to the suit before it could cite language favoring its own interpretation.[290] In the end, the Court concluded that the statutory phrase means "any student group that does not *directly* relate to the body of courses offered by the school."[291] This interpretation is consistent, the Court pointed out, with the intent of Congress "to provide a low threshold for triggering the Act's requirements."[292] After inspecting ten of the school's approximately thirty student clubs (all dutifully listed in an appendix to the prevailing opinion), the Court identified three qualifying clubs (scuba diving, chess, and peer advocates) demonstrating that the school maintained a "limited open forum" within the meaning of the act, and the Court accordingly ruled that the denial of the complainants' right to form a Christian club violated the act.[293]

The Court then turned to the contention that the act, as thus applied, violated the Establishment Clause. Eight justices agreed in rejecting this claim, but they set out their views in three separate opinions. Justice O'Connor, with whom Chief Justice Rehnquist and Justices White and Blackmun joined, summarized and rejected the school board's arguments. The school board's principal contention was that the act has the primary effect of advancing religion.

> Specifically, petitioners urged that, because the student religious meetings are held under school aegis, and because the states' compulsory attendance laws bring the students together (and thereby provide a ready-made audience for student evangelists), an objective observer in the position of a secondary school student will perceive official school support for such religious meetings.[294]

In response to this argument, Justice O'Connor asserted that "secondary school students are mature enough and are likely to understand that a school does not endorse or support student speech that it merely permits on a nondiscriminatory basis."[295] She also noted that Congress had expressed the same conviction and commented that "we do not lightly second-guess such legislative judgment particularly where the judgments are based in part on empirical determinations."[296] Justice O'Connor also pointed out that the act expressly limited participation of school officials at meetings of student religious groups, thereby reducing the likelihood that students would treat the teachers as role models. She added:

> To be sure, the possibility of student peer pressure remains, but there is little if any risk of official state endorsement or coercion where no formal classroom activities are involved and no school officials actively participate. Moreover, petitioners' fear of a mistaken inference of endorsement is largely self-imposed, because the school itself has control over

289 Mergens, 496 U.S. at 235–6.
290 *Id.* at 237–8.
291 *Id.* at 239 (emphasis in original).
292 *Id.* at 240.
293 *Id.* at 245–7.
294 *Id.* at 249.
295 *Id.* at 250. This observation suggests that the same result might have been reached by extending the rationale of the *Widmar* case to high schools, thus making it unnecessary for the Court to deal with the Equal Access Act.
296 *Id.* at 251.

> any impressions it gives its students.... To the extent a school makes clear that the recognition of respondents' proposed club is not an endorsement of the views of the club's participants ... students will reasonably understand that the school's official recognition of the club evinces neutrality toward, rather than endorsement of, religious speech.[297]

Justice O'Connor also rejected the argument that a student religious club would imply official endorsement of or preference for religion or a particular religious belief because of the wide spectrum of officially recognized student clubs at the high school under examination, as well as the freedom of its students to organize additional clubs:

> Under the Act, a school with a limited open forum may not lawfully deny access to a Jewish students' club, a Young Democrats club, or a philosophy club devoted to the study of Nietzsche. To the extent that a religious club is merely one of many different student-initiated voluntary clubs, students should perceive no message of government endorsement of religion.[298]

Finally, Justice O'Connor rejected the school board's last argument, namely, that by complying with the act's requirements, the school would risk an excessive entanglement between government and religion because the club's faculty sponsor "would be charged with actively directing the activities of the group, guiding its leaders, and ensuring balance in the presentation of controversial ideas."[299] O'Connor's reply was to call attention to the act's statutory limits on the activities of school officials. Moreover, she asserted that a denial of equal access to the proposed religious club "might well create greater entanglement problems in the form of invasive monitoring to prevent religious speech at meetings at which such speech might occur."[300]

Concurring in the judgment, Justices Kennedy and Scalia joined in a separate opinion objecting to the plurality's use of the "endorsement" concept in passing on the act's constitutionality. To them, "the word endorsement has insufficient content to be dispositive," and they added that "it is inevitable that a public high school 'endorses' a religious club, in a common-sense use of the term, if the club happens to be one of many activities that the school permits students to choose in order to further the development of their intellect and character in an extracurricular setting."[301] They would have decided the case by applying two principles:

> The first is that the government cannot "give direct benefits to religion in such a degree that it in fact 'establishes a [state] religion or religious faith, or tends to do so.'" ... Any incidental benefits that accompany official recognition of a religious club under the criteria set forth in the ... [Act] do not lead to the establishment of religion under the standard.... The second principle ... is that the government cannot coerce any student to participate in a religious activity.... The Act is consistent with this standard as well.[302]

Justice Marshall, with whom Justice Brennan joined, wrote a separate concurrence, agreeing that the act as applied to the high school before the Court could withstand

297 *Id.* at 252. For this point, the opinion cites *Widmar v. Vincent*, discussed *infra* notes 281–3 and accompanying text.
298 *Id.*
299 *Id.*
300 *Id.* at 253.
301 *Id.* at 261 (Kennedy, J., concurring).
302 *Id.* at 260–1.

Establishment Clause scrutiny, but he was troubled by the fact that the school had no other political or ideological clubs. Because the proposed religious club would be the only group advocating a controversial viewpoint, he felt that the school must "fully dissociate itself from the Club's religious speech and avoid appearing to sponsor or endorse the Club's goals," particularly because the club "could provide a fertile ground for peer pressure," as recognized by the plurality, and because the school environment, as structured by the state, may facilitate the coercion of members of minority religions.[303]

Justice Stevens, the lone dissenter in *Mergens*, objected to the breadth of the "limited open forum" as created by the majority; he would have confined the term "non-curriculum-related" to a group whose purpose, in whole or in part, is to advocate "partisan theological, political, or ethical views."[304] Because the school before the Court had not recognized any such student clubs, it had not created a "limited open forum" and hence was not subject to the act's equal access rules.[305] Objecting to the Court's ruling, he observed:

> The Court's construction of this Act … leads to a sweeping intrusion by the federal government into the operation of our public schools, and does so despite the absence of any indication that Congress intended to divest local school districts of their power to shape the educational environment. If a high school administration continues to believe that it is sound policy to exclude controversial groups, such as political clubs, the Ku Klux Klan, and perhaps gay rights advocacy groups, from its facilities, it now must also close its doors to traditional extracurricular activities that are noncontroversial but not directly related to any course being offered at the school. Congress made frequent reference to the primacy of local control in public education, and the legislative history of the Act is thus inconsistent with the Court's rigid definition of "noncurriculum related groups." Indeed, the very fact that Congress omitted any definition in the statute itself is persuasive evidence of an intent to allow local officials broad discretion in deciding whether to create limited public fora.[306]

### 3. Good News Club

*Good News Club* is in many ways a straightforward speech case.[307] The school district allowed a variety of noncurricular student groups access to school facilities when school was not in session.[308] Both parties agreed that the district provided a "limited public forum" for a variety of groups at the school.[309] The religious club was denied access because the religious character of its meetings were the equivalent of religious instruction. The district argued that the denial of access under such circumstances was in compliance with New York law.[310] It was specifically the group's deeply religious mission, as

303 *Id.* at 268, 270 (Marshall, J., concurring).
304 *Id.* at 270–1, 276 (Stevens, J., dissenting).
305 *Id.* at 277–8.
306 *Id.* at 290–1.
307 533 U.S. 98, 106–12 (2001).
308 *Id.* at 102, 108.
309 *Id.* at 108 (The district, however, disputed the scope of the forum.). N.Y. Educ. Law § 414 (McKinney 2000) (stating purposes for which schools may be opened for public use).
310 *Id.*

well as its proselytizing nature, that gave the school district pause.[311] Thus, from a free speech perspective, the issue was one of viewpoint discrimination.[312] Therefore, the district could only exclude the group if excluding it was narrowly tailored to serve a compelling government interest.

The district argued that its compelling interest was compliance with the Establishment Clause because the group was intensely religious, believed in proselytizing, was run by outside adults, and most important, was geared for elementary school students who are young and impressionable.[313] The Court held that the nature of the speech was not determinative when the school created a limited public forum. Once a limited public forum is created, the speech is not likely to be viewed as government speech, and because parental consent was required, students would not perceive the group as school sponsored, and in fact, exclusion of the group might make students feel that the school is hostile toward religion.[314] The majority held that absent coercion of some sort, religious speech in a limited public forum will not give rise to an Establishment Clause violation.[315] The Court further held that if children are allowed to attend the challenged meeting in the public school building only with their parents' consent, the existence of improper "coercion" depends on whether the parents would feel coerced.[316]

Justice Breyer concurred but did not think that the record was adequate to determine whether children might perceive endorsement of religion,[317] and he made it clear that endorsement should be the central inquiry. Justices Souter and Stevens each filed dissenting opinions.[318] These opinions stressed the religious nature of the group and its focus on targeting elementary school children.[319] The dissents argued that elementary school children are too young to understand whether such a group is school sponsored or not and may feel pressure to participate from their peers.[320]

### 4. *Teacher Supervision of Non-Curriculum-Related Religious Groups*

The Equal Access Act requires that any school employee who attends the meetings of a religious group under the terms of the act must do so only in a custodial capacity.[321] This means that school employees cannot sponsor, substantively supervise, or endorse religious clubs that meet under the act.[322] This requirement also applies under the Establishment Clause. Even if a group can constitutionally meet in a limited public forum, if a school employee is viewed as favoring or endorsing the group, Establishment Clause concerns may arise. This is especially true if the employee is a teacher or principal. As a general matter, the best advice is that school employees do not get involved in any religious group meeting in a limited public forum opened by the school unless

311 Good News Club, 533 U.S. at 107–10.
312 *Id.* at 107–10.
313 *Id.* at 115.
314 *Id.* at 118.
315 *Id.* at 111–12.
316 *Id.* at 115.
317 *Id.* at 129–30 (Breyer, J., concurring).
318 *Id.* at 130 (Stevens, J., dissenting); *id.* at 134 (Souter, J., dissenting).
319 *See id.* at 130–46.
320 *Id.*
321 20 U.S.C. § 4071(c)(3).
322 20 U.S.C. § 4072(3).

in a custodial manner.[323] If the school requires that any such group be "supervised" by a teacher or administrator, an exception can be made for religious groups,[324] or any teacher or administrator who supervises a religious group may not promote the group or be involved in any of the group's religious content or activities.[325]

### 5. *Closing a Public or Limited Public Forum*

Schools need not create a limited public forum. There is no constitutional problem if a school chooses to limit access only to curriculum-related groups. Yet what if a school chooses to close a limited public forum in order to prevent a religious club from meeting? Or a school district predominated by a particular religious viewpoint chooses to close a limited public forum rather than let a lesbian, gay, bisexual, and transgender (LGBT) or atheist group meet? The answer depends on why and how the forum is closed and whether alternative vehicles for student expression are also shut down.

If a school closes a forum based on religious or antireligious objections to a particular group, the closing of the forum might violate the Establishment Clause and/or the Free Speech Clause (content or viewpoint discrimination).[326] If, however, the school has a legitimate pedagogic reason for doing so, courts often will defer to the school.[327] Of course, the forum must be truly closed. If the school allows the forum to remain open for favored groups, excluded groups would have a valid claim.[328] It is also important that students not be excluded from exercising their *Tinker* rights,[329] so even if a school closes a limited public forum, thus excluding non-curriculum-related groups, it may not prevent students from engaging in religious or other speech in a reasonable, time, place and manner.

### 6. *Other Contexts for Equal Access to Public School Buildings*

In addition to their primary use for education, public school buildings are often used after-hours as places of public assembly – for lectures, concerts, political meetings, voting, athletic contests, and other functions, sometimes specified by statutes or regulations and sometimes left to custom and tradition. There is a substantial body of law governing these after-hour uses of school buildings. These uses take on a constitutional dimension when the buildings, or parts thereof, become "limited public forums."[330] The term "limited" is used because of the restrictions required to protect the primary function of the buildings for education. The resulting free speech issues are beyond the

[323] *Cf.* 20 U.S.C. § 4071(c)(3).

[324] *Cf. id.*

[325] *Cf. id.*; Graham B. Forrester, *Note: A Practical Guide to the Establishment Clause for Teachers, Principals and Consumers*, 2001 NEXUS, 257, 26–68 (Spring 2001) ("[T]eachers, principals or other school officials may attend [religious group meetings] but not participate in the event.").

[326] DiLoreto v. Downey Unified Sch. Dist. Bd. of Educ., 196 F.3d 958 (9th Cir. 1999).

[327] McMillen v. Itawamba Cnty. Sch. Dist., 702 F. Supp. 2d 699 (N.D. Miss. 2010); J.S. *ex rel.* Smith v. Holly Area Sch., 749 F. Supp. 2d 614 (E.D. Mich. 2010).

[328] Demmon v. Loudoun Cnty. Pub. Sch., 342 F. Supp. 2d 474 (E.D. Va. 2004).

[329] *See* Tinker v. Des Moines Indep. Cmty. Sch. Dist., 393 U.S. 503 (1969).

[330] "Arfora," for those with a Latinate taste.

scope of this work,[331] except for the following case and its progeny, which focus directly on access to public school buildings.

In *Lamb's Chapel v. Center Moriches School District*, the Supreme Court rejected a school district's claim that it would violate the Establishment Clause if it allowed a church to use its facilities to exhibit a religious-oriented film series on family values and childrearing.[332] State law authorized the after-hours use of school facilities for a great variety of activities ranging from social, civic, and recreational meetings to voting,[333] but a state court had held that because the statutory list did not include religious meetings, they were not permissible, and the school district accordingly rejected the church's application.[334] The Supreme Court first ruled that New York law allowed the public to engage in such a wide array of communicative uses in the buildings that they had become "limited public forums" and that this status prohibited denying access to a speaker solely to suppress its point of view on an otherwise permissible subject.[335] The Court then rejected the school district's theory that allowing the religiously oriented film to be exhibited would violate the Establishment Clause, thus supplying the district with a compelling interest to deny access. This theory, the Court ruled, was inconsistent with the *Widmar* and *Lemon* cases.[336] Because the film would be shown in a limited public forum, it would not reasonably be viewed as government speech, and without evidence that it was favored by the school district, it could not violate the Establishment Clause.[337]

Justice Scalia concurred in the judgment but objected to the use of the *Lemon* test. He asserted that "[l]ike some ghoul in a late-night horror movie that repeatedly sits up in its grave and shuffles abroad, after being repeatedly killed and buried, *Lemon* stalks our Establishment Clause jurisprudence once again, frightening the little children and school attorneys of Center Moriches Union Free School District."[338] Justice Scalia then asserted that, "giving *Lamb's Chapel* nondiscriminatory access to school facilities cannot violate … [the Establishment Clause] because it does not signify state or local embrace of a particular religious sect."[339]

331 *See, generally*, Ronald D. Rotunda & John E. Nowak, Treatise on Constitutional Law §§ 20–45 (2d ed., West); Laurence Tribe, Constitutional law §§12–24 (2d ed.). For cases on this subject under state law, *see* C. T. Foster, *Use of Public School Premises for Religious Purposes During Nonschool Time*, 79 ALR 2d. 1148 (1961).

332 508 U.S. 384 (1993).

333 N.Y. Educ. Law § 414 (McKinney 2000).

334 Lambs Chapel, 508 U.S. at 387.

335 The Court noted that the breadth of the permissible uses came close to making the building in *Lamb's Chapel* a "traditional public forum" but did not pass on this possibility because it was unnecessary to decide the case. *Id.* at 391–2.

336 *Id.* at 395.

337 Lambs Chapel, 508 U.S. at 390–7.

338 *Id.* at 398 (Scalia, J., concurring). Justice Scalia accompanied his denunciation of *Lemon* with a compendium of earlier opinions rejecting its validity. *Id.* at 398–9.

339 *Id.* at 401 (Scalia, J., concurring). Justice Scalia accompanied his denunciation of *Lemon* with a compendium of earlier opinions rejecting its validity.

# 17 Religious Symbolism on Government Property

## A. Introduction

Courts have repeatedly grappled with the issues raised when government displays religious symbols or religious symbols are displayed by others on government property. Cases involve a variety of religious symbols, for example, Ten Commandments displays,[1] crèches (nativity scenes),[2] Latin crosses,[3]

1 *See* McCreary County v. ACLU of Kentucky, 545 U.S. 844, 125 S.Ct. 2722 (2005) (striking down courthouse displays including Ten Commandments where displays were created as a means to post the Ten Commandments in the courthouses); Van Orden v. Perry, 545 U.S. 677, 125 S.Ct. 2854 (2005) (plurality opinion) (upholding display of Ten Commandments monument donated by the Fraternal Order of Eagles in 1961 on the grounds between the Texas State Capitol and State Supreme Court building); Stone v. Graham, 449 U.S. 39 (1981) (*per curiam*) (striking down Kentucky statute that required the posting of the Ten Commandments in each public school classroom in the state); *see also* ACLU of Ohio v. DeWeese, 633 F.3d 424, 426 (6th Cir. 2011) (holding that a poster of the Ten Commandments hung by a judge in an Ohio courtroom violated the establishment clause); ACLU of Kentucky v. Grayson Cnty., Ky., 591 F.3d 837 (6th Cir. 2010) (upholding courthouse display of Ten Commandments that was part of a larger display of the "Foundations of American Law and Government"); Green v. Haskell Cnty. Bd. of Comm'rs, 568 F.3d 784 (10th Cir. 2009) (striking down display of Ten Commandments on the lawn of a county courthouse); Card v. City of Everett, 520 F.3d 1009 (9th Cir. 2008) (upholding a Ten Commandments monument on the lawn of Old Everett City Hall by comparing the monument to the one upheld in *Van Orden*); ACLU of Kentucky v. Mercer Cnty., Ky., 432 F.3d 624 (6th Cir. 2005) (upholding a display including the Ten Commandments in a courthouse that was materially indistinguishable from the final display in *McCreary County* because the display lacked a religious purpose); ACLU of Nebraska v. City of Plattsmouth, Neb., 419 F.3d 772 (8th Cir. 2005) (*en banc*) (upholding a monument of the Ten Commandments in a public park); King v. Richmond County, 331 F.3d 1271 (11th Cir. 2003) (upholding use of small seal that included a depiction of the Ten Commandments, but not the text, along with other images); Glassroth v. Moore, 335 F.3d 1282 (11th Cir. 2003) (striking down display of large granite Ten Commandments monument placed in the rotunda of Alabama state courthouse in the middle of the night by former chief justice of the Alabama Supreme Court); Freethought Soc'y of Greater Philadelphia v. Chester County, 334 F.3d 247 (3d Cir. 2003) (upholding display of small Ten Commandments plaque on old entrance to county courthouse, where plaque was placed on the building in 1920 and old entrance where plaque was located was no longer in use); Adland v. Russ, 307 F.3d 471 (6th Cir. 2002) (striking down display of monument donated by the Fraternal Order of Eagles in 1961 on grounds of the state capitol); Books v. City of Elkhart, 235 F.3d 292 (7th Cir. 2000) (same for monument donated in 1958 and located on grounds of city municipal building).

2 *See, e.g.*, Lynch v. Donnelly, 465 U.S. 668 (1984) (upholding display of crèche by City of Pawtucket as part of broader seasonal display); County of Allegheny v. ACLU of Greater Pittsburgh, 492 U.S. 573 (1989) (striking down display of crèche on grand staircase of courthouse where chèche was not part of broader display).

3 *See, e.g.*, Salazar v. Buono, 559 U.S. 700, 130 S. Ct. 1803 (2009) (upholding land transfer of small parcel of government land containing Latin cross used as war memorial to private citizen); Capitol Square Review

menorahs,[4] and Christmas trees.[5] The analysis in these cases has been the focus of a great deal of scholarly criticism.[6] Most of that criticism is beyond the scope of this chapter. The goal of this chapter is to equip you with knowledge of the leading cases addressing religious symbolism on government property and the legal approaches courts have used, and are currently using, in these cases.

## B. Religious Symbolism Cases

The U.S. Supreme Court has decided a number of cases involving the display of religious objects or symbols by government entities on public property. In *Lynch v. Donnelly*[7] and in *County of Allegheny v. ACLU*,[8] the Court addressed the display of nativity scenes – crèches – by government entities. *County of Allegheny* also involved the display of a large menorah next to an even larger Christmas tree accompanied by a sign saluting liberty.[9]

In *Stone v. Graham*,[10] the Court addressed a Kentucky statute that required a copy of the Ten Commandments to be placed on a wall in all public school classrooms in the state. More recently, in *McCreary County v. ACLU of Kentucky*,[11] the Court struck down courthouse displays in two Kentucky counties that included the Ten Commandments, and in *Van Orden v. Perry*,[12] the Court upheld the display of a Ten Commandments monument on the grounds of the Texas State Capitol. In *Pleasant Grove v. Summum*,[13] the Court upheld a town's refusal to erect a monument reflecting the Seven Aphorisms of the Summum religion even though the town had a Ten

Bd. v. Pinette, 515 U.S. 753 (1995) (upholding display of Latin cross by Ku Klux Klan on the grounds of state capitol because cross was displayed in public forum open to all kinds of speech); Separation of Church and State Committee v. City of Eugene Oregon, 93 F.3d 617 (9th Cir. 1996) (striking down fifty-one-foot-tall Latin cross that was erected in city park and that was designated as a war memorial after the court struck down its display in an earlier decision); Ellis v. City of La Mesa, 990 F.2d 1518 (9th Cir. 1993) (striking down the display of two large Latin crosses in separate public parks and the use of a Latin cross in the city's official insignia under the no preference clause of the California Constitution).

4 *See, e.g.*, Allegheny, 492 U.S. 573 (upholding display of a menorah along with a large Christmas tree and a sign saluting liberty at city-county building).

5 *Id.*

6 *See, e.g.*, Alan Brownstein, *A Decent Respect for Religious Liberty and Religious Equality: Justice O'Connor's Interpretation of the Religion Clauses of the First Amendment*, 32 McGeorge L. Rev. 837, 855–8 (2001) (criticizing the Court's minimization of the impact government display of religious objects can have on religious minorities); Laura Underkuffler-Freund, *The Separation of the Religious and the Secular: A Foundational Challenge to First Amendment Theory*, 36 Wm. & Mary L. Rev. 837, 871–2, 971–2 (1995) (criticizing the Court's desacrilization of religious symbols); Kenneth L. Karst, *The First Amendment, The Politics of Religion and the Symbols of Government*, 27 Harv. C.R.-C.L. L. Rev. 503 (1992) (criticizing the Court's minimization of the impact government display of religious objects can have on religious minorities); Frank S. Ravitch, *Religious Objects as Legal Subjects*, 40 Wake Forest L. Rev. 1011 (2005); Timothy Zick, *Cross Burning, Cockfighting, and Symbolic Meaning: Toward a First Amendment Ethnography*, 45 Wm. & Mary L. Rev. 2261 (2004) (criticizing the Court's desacrilization of religious symbols).

7 465 U.S. 668 (1984).

8 492 U.S. 573 (1989).

9 *Id.* at 587, 614.

10 449 U.S. 39 (1981) (*per curiam*).

11 545 U.S. 844 (2005).

12 545 U.S. 677 (2005) (plurality opinion).

13 555 U.S. 460 (2009).

Commandments monument on the same property.[14] The Court addressed the issue as a government speech issue[15] and did not address the possible – some would say probable – Establishment Clause violation in the case.

In *Salazar v. Buono*,[16] the Court upheld a land transfer that enabled a Latin cross which had served as a war memorial to remain on land that had been public prior to the land transfer.[17] Finally, in *Capitol Square Review* and *Advisory Board v. Pinette*,[18] the Court addressed the placement of a large cross on government property that was a public forum. In *Capitol Square*, the public forum issue was dispositive of the outcome.[19] Each of these cases will be discussed in this chapter. In addition, there are a number of lower court decisions addressing everything from large Latin crosses[20] to Ten Commandments monuments.[21] A number of these cases also will be discussed herein.

This section will set forth the ways in which courts have approached a variety of religious objects and symbols. The section will be organized around the objects themselves. Thus there will be separate subsections devoted to crèches, crosses, menorahs, Ten Commandments displays, Christmas trees, and other holiday displays. Naturally, some of these objects overlap in a given display, and this too will be discussed. A major focus, however, will be Ten Commandments displays because the recent Supreme Court cases involving these displays set forth the current legal standards applicable to many religious displays.

### 1. *Crèches*

In *Lynch v. Donnelly*,[22] the Court considered whether a crèche (a nativity scene) placed in a park in Pawtucket, Rhode Island, as part of a larger Christmas display that included such things as a Santa Claus house and plastic reindeer violated the Establishment Clause.[23] The city owned the display and clearly supported and sponsored its erection in the park.[24] Thus this was a case involving a government-supported display. The Court held that the display was constitutional, only paying lip service to the *Lemon* test, which

14 *Id.*
15 *Id.* at 470–1.
16 559 U.S. 700 (2010).
17 *Id.*
18 515 U.S. 753 (1995).
19 *Id.*
20 A surprising number of cases have involved government display of crosses. For example, Carpenter v. City & County of San Francisco, 93 F.3d 627 (9th Cir. 1996); Separation of Church and State Comm. v. City of Eugene, 93 F.3d 617 (9th Cir. 1996); Ellis v. City of La Mesa, 990 F.2d 1518 (9th Cir. 1993); Murray v. City of Austin, 947 F.2d 147 (5th Cir. 1991); Harris v. City of Zion, 927 F.2d 1401 (7th Cir. 1991); Mendelson v. City of St. Cloud, 719 F. Supp. 1065 (M.D. Fla. 1989); Jewish War Veterans of the United States v. United States, 695 F. Supp. 1 (D.D.C. 1987); ACLU v. City of St. Charles, 622 F.Supp. 1542 (N.D. Ill. 1985); Eugene Sand & Gravel, Inc. v. City of Eugene, 558 P.2d 338 (1976) (*en banc*); Lowe v. City of Eugene, 463 P.2d 360 (1969) (*en banc*); *see also* Paulsen v. City of San Diego, 294 F.3d 1124 (9th Cir. 2002) (involving sale of public land on which large Latin cross stood under circumstances that raised constitutional concerns under state establishment clause); Gonzales v. North Township, 4 F.3d 1412 (7th Cir. 1993) (involving crucifix).
21 *See supra* note 1.
22 465 U.S. 668 (1984).
23 *Id.*
24 *Id.* at 671–2.

was the then-prevailing test for Establishment Clause claims.[25] In reality, the Court used analysis similar to that which it had used in *Marsh v. Chambers*[26] to uphold the practice of legislative prayer. The Court noted the long history of various forms of government interaction with religion, such as legislative chaplains. The Court acknowledged the religious meaning of the crèche yet held that holiday displays such as the one in Pawtucket are part of a long tradition connected to the winter holiday season and that Christmas has a secular meaning in addition to its religious meaning.[27]

The Court focused heavily on the importance of the broader context of the display, which included "a Santa Claus house, reindeer pulling a sleigh, candy-striped poles, a Christmas tree, carolers, cutout figures" of a "clown, an elephant, and a teddy bear, hundreds of colored lights, [and] a large banner that [read] 'Seasons Greetings.'"[28] It also noted the display's connection to the secular/commercial aspects of the holiday. In this context, the display as a whole represented the secular aspects of Christmas.[29] Thus, while the crèche is a religious symbol,[30] it did not foster a government establishment of religion in the context of the broader display and the holiday season because that context demonstrated both a secular purpose and a primary effect that neither advanced nor inhibited religion.[31] The Court referred to the crèche as a "passive" object.[32] Though this is patently ridiculous from a theological and artistic perspective, the Court has continued to use the term "passive" to refer to religious symbols.[33] The Court also found no entanglement because of the low cost of the display and held that political divisiveness, which was an element of entanglement at that time, was insufficient by itself to support an Establishment Clause claim.[34] In short, the Court acknowledged the fact that a crèche is a religious symbol but essentially ignored or minimized any significant discussion of the challenged object itself.

In a concurring opinion, Justice O'Connor introduced the "endorsement test."[35] The endorsement test has become highly influential in cases involving government-supported or -endorsed religious symbols.[36] It is hard to know whether the current Court will continue to use the endorsement test given Justice O'Connor's retirement and Justice Alito taking her place, but for now, the endorsement test is important in many religious symbolism cases. Justice O'Connor wrote:

> The Establishment Clause prohibits government from making adherence to a religion relevant in any way to a person's standing in the political community. Government can

[25] *Id.* at 678–85, 687.
[26] 463 U.S. 783 (1983).
[27] Lynch, 465 U.S. at 674–8, 682, 686–7.
[28] *Id.* at 671.
[29] *Id.* at 679–83, 685–6.
[30] *d.* at 687; Steven D. Smith, *Separation and the "Secular": Reconstructing the Disestablishment Decision*, 67 Tex. L. Rev. 955, 1002–3 (1989) (Some critics of the decision misunderstand the majority's secularization position; that position did not result from a conclusion that the crèche lost its religious meaning because of its placement, but rather the majority employed a broad notion of the secular and found that the religious symbol served a secular purpose in the context involved.).
[31] Lynch, 465 U.S. at 679–85, 687.
[32] *Id.* at 685.
[33] Van Orden, 545 U.S. at 682, 686.
[34] Lynch at 683–5.
[35] *Id.* at 687 (O'Connor, J., concurring).
[36] For example, in the Court's first religious symbolism case after *Lynch*, the Court applied the endorsement test [County of Allegheny v. ACLU, 492 U.S. 573 (1989)], and the test has been applied in numerous religious symbolism cases by lower courts.

> run afoul of that prohibition in two principal ways. One is excessive entanglement with religious institutions, which may interfere with the independence of the institutions, give the institutions access to government or governmental powers not fully shared by nonadherents of the religion, and foster the creation of political constituencies defined along religious lines [citation omitted]. The second and more direct infringement is government endorsement or disapproval of religion. Endorsement sends a message to nonadherents that they are outsiders, not full members of the political community, and an accompanying message to adherents that they are insiders, favored members of the political community. Disapproval sends the opposite message.[37]

Later in her concurring opinion she characterized the inquiry into the display as follows:

> The central issue in this case is whether Pawtucket has endorsed Christianity by its display of the crèche. To answer that question, we must examine both what Pawtucket intended to communicate in displaying the crèche and what message the City's display actually conveyed. The purpose and effect prongs of the *Lemon* test represent these two aspects of the meaning of the City's action.[38]

Justice Brennan filed a dissenting opinion joined by Justices Blackman, Marshall, and Stevens,[39] and Justice Blackman filed a dissenting opinion joined by Justice Stevens.[40] The dissenting opinions pointed out that had the Court applied the *Lemon* test in the manner it had in other cases under the Establishment Clause, the government-sponsored crèche would not have survived scrutiny.[41] Justice Brennan's dissenting opinion also pointed out that placing a patently religious symbol representing an event central to Christian theology in the context of a broader display of items connected to the Christmas holiday is likely to favor the dominant Christian tradition and thus could not be saved by relying on the commercialized aspects of the holiday.[42] Such government action favoring one religion would violate the *Lemon* test.[43] Moreover, both dissents argued that by minimizing the religious import of the crèche in the context of the display, the Court both degraded the religious meaning of the symbol and the holiday and failed to address the exclusionary message the display sent to non-Christians.[44]

In *Allegheny*, the Court also addressed a crèche display.[45] As will be discussed later, that case also involved the display of a menorah and a Christmas tree.[46] The Court's analysis of the crèche used the endorsement approach set forth by Justice O'Connor in *Lynch*.[47] As in *Lynch*, the physical context of the crèche display was central to the Court's decision.[48] The crèche was owned by the Holy Name Society, a Roman Catholic organization, and was located on the grand staircase of the county courthouse. It was not surrounded by sundry plastic figures and other "secular" symbols of the "holiday season,"

37 Lynch, 465 U.S. at 687–8 (O'Connor, J., concurring).
38 *Id.* at 690 (O'Connor, J., concurring).
39 *Id.* at 694 (Brennan, J., dissenting).
40 *Id.* at 726 (Blackmun, J., dissenting).
41 *Id.* at 697–714 (Brennan, J., dissenting); *id.* at 626–7 (Blackmun, J., dissenting).
42 *Id.* at 697, 700–2 (Brennan, J., dissenting).
43 *Id.*
44 *Id.* at 708–9 (Brennan, J., dissenting); *id.* at 726–7 (Blackmun, J., dissenting).
45 County of Allegheny v. ACLU, 492 U.S. 573 (1989).
46 *Id.*
47 *Id.* at 592–4.
48 *Id.* at 598–600.

as had been the crèche in *Lynch*.[49] It was surrounded on three sides by a wooden fence, and red and white poinsettia plants were placed around the crèche.[50] There was a sign denoting that the crèche was donated by the Holy Name Society, and there were also two small evergreen trees decorated with a red bow, but these basically blended into the manger scene depicted in the crèche.[51]

Justice Blackmun, writing for the Court, held that the display of the crèche violated the Establishment Clause because unlike the crèche in *Lynch*, the crèche in the Allegheny County courthouse sent a message endorsing Christianity, and "nothing in the crèche's setting detract[ed] from that message."[52] Government may "acknowledge Christmas as a cultural phenomenon" but may not celebrate it as a "Christian holy day."[53] The crèche, which has an obvious religious message, is a celebration of the religious aspects of the holiday.[54] Interestingly, *Lynch* and *Allegheny* together stand for the proposition that the crèche can somehow become adequately secularized if it is part of a larger holiday display celebrating the "secular aspects" of Christmas.[55] The Court did not hold that the crèche loses its religious nature based on its context[56] but rather that in some contexts its religious message is appropriately secularized such that government may display it.[57]

Justice Kennedy, in an opinion joined by Chief Justice Rehnquist and Justices Scalia and White, strongly dissented from this portion of the Court's holding.[58] Justice Kennedy would have upheld the display of the crèche based on his reading of *Lynch* and *Marsh*.[59] Instead of applying the endorsement test, he would have applied a test based on religious coercion.[60] Significantly, he recognized the religious nature of the crèche.[61] There are also a number of decisions by lower courts involving crèches, and they are generally consistent with the Court's reasoning in *Lynch* and *Allegheny*.[62]

### 2. *Crosses*

Perhaps the most famous case involving the display of a cross on government property is *Capitol Square Review Board v. Pinette*,[63] which involved the display of a large cross on the grounds of the Ohio State Capitol. The cross was placed there by the Ku Klux Klan, a notorious hate group.[64] The Court held that the square was a public forum for speech

49 *Id.* at 580–1, 598–600.
50 *Id.* at 580.
51 *Id.*
52 *Id.* at 598–602.
53 *Id.* at 601.
54 *Id.* at 598–601.
55 *See, generally*, Allegheny, 492 U.S. 598; Lynch, 465 U.S. 668.
56 *See* Smith, *supra* note 30.
57 *Id.*
58 Allegheny, 492 U.S. at 655 (Kennedy, J., concurring in part and dissenting in part).
59 *Id.* at 662–3, 679.
60 *Id.* at 664–74, 677–9.
61 *Id.* at 662–4.
62 Lower court decisions that claim to be consistent with the Court's approach in *Lynch* and *Allegheny* include ACLU v. Schundler, 168 F.3d 92 (3rd Cir. 1999); Elewski v. City of Syracuse, 123 F.3d 51 (2d Cir. 1997); Am. Jewish Cong. v. City of Beverly Hills, 90 F.3d 379 (9th Cir. 1996); Smith v. County of Albemarle, 895 F.2d 953 (4th Cir. 1990); Jocham v. Tuscola County, 239 F. Supp. 2d 714 (E.D. Mich. 2003).
63 515 U.S. 753 (1995).
64 *Id.* at 758.

purposes.[65] Because the government wanted to exclude the cross from the square and the square was a public forum, the state needed to show a compelling governmental interest to support the exclusion of the religious message.[66] This is so because the state's actions in attempting to exclude the cross constituted content discrimination.[67] The state's reason for excluding the cross was compliance with the Establishment Clause.[68] The Court acknowledged that compliance with the Establishment Clause could constitute a compelling government interest,[69] but the state's action in this case was not mandated by the Establishment Clause because the Establishment Clause does not prohibit private religious expression in a public forum.[70] Thus the state could not exclude the cross without violating the Free Speech Clause.[71]

A plurality of the Court rejected what it referred to as the "transferred endorsement test" – essentially the endorsement test advocated by Justice O'Connor.[72] "Transferred endorsement" was the plurality's shorthand for the idea that the state could be liable for endorsement of religion if a reasonable observer would perceive the expression of private actors on public land as endorsed by the government.[73] The plurality rejected the idea that actions of private individuals could be endorsed by government in a public forum, even if an outsider might mistake the private action for state action.[74]

The Court's opinion involved little discussion of the nature of the religious object involved because it was resolved primarily under the Free Speech Clause. Yet the dissenting opinions evidenced a great concern about the religious nature of the cross and the message its placement on the capitol square would send.[75] Justice Stevens' dissenting opinion demonstrated concern about the perspective of religious outsiders.[76] For example, when a nonbeliever or religious minority passes the capitol square and sees a large cross, it is quite possible that the cross will be perceived as a symbol of majoritarian dominance even if the viewer realizes that the government did not erect it.[77] This is bolstered by the fact that the majority religion in the United States generally (including, of course, Ohio) is Christianity (although there are certainly a diversity of Christian sects and denominations).[78] Thus it is likely that to the extent that religious symbols are exhibited on the square and religious messages are shared, the vast majority of the messages

65 *Id.* at 758, 761.
66 *Id.* at 761.
67 *Id.*
68 *Id.*
69 *Id.* at 761–2.
70 *Id.* at 762–70.
71 *Id.* at 765–770.
72 *Id.* at 764 (plurality opinion).
73 *Id.* at 764–70 (plurality opinion).
74 *Id.*
75 *Id.* at 797 (Stevens, J., dissenting); *id.* at 817 (Ginsburg, J., dissenting).
76 *Id.* at 799–800.
77 *Cf. id.* at 798 (Stevens, J., concurring) (Some citizens might perceive the cross "as a message of exclusion – a statehouse sign calling powerfully to mind their outsider status"); *see also* STEPHEN M. FELDMAN, PLEASE DON'T WISH ME A MERRY CHRISTMAS: A CRITICAL HISTORY OF THE SEPARATION OF CHURCH AND STATE (1997) (discussing perceptions of Christian dominance in American history and the difference between insider and outsider views regarding religion in public life).
78 *See, e.g.*, Mark G. Valencia, *Comment, Take Care of Me When I Am Dead: An Examination of American Church-State Development and the Future of American Religious Liberty*, 49 SMU L. REV. 1579, 1634 (1996) ("The vast majority of American adults (86.5%) identify themselves as Christian").

will be Christian or at the very least reflective of mainstream Western religions.[79] Thus Justice Stevens suggested that the resulting message to nonbelievers and religious minorities may be, to use Justice O'Connor's language, that they are outsiders and not full members of the community.[80] For Justice Stevens, the fact that the square was a public forum did not change this fact.[81]

The key to understanding *Capitol Square* is to understand that even though it involved a cross on public property, it is primarily a free speech case because that property was a public forum. Therefore, when religious symbolism cases involve private speech in a public forum (which may include limited or designated public forums), the likelihood is that the display will be constitutional unless there is evidence of government favoritism. If there is evidence of government favoritism, the Establishment Clause arguments are much stronger both directly and as a defense to a free speech claim. Remember that despite the plurality opinion suggesting otherwise, a majority of the justices in *Capitol Square* would have allowed an Establishment Clause defense to the free speech claim under appropriate facts. The disagreement among the justices on that issue was whether the facts in *Capitol Square* were adequate to support an Establishment Clause claim.

In *Salazar v. Buono*,[82] the Court suggested that the transfer of government land to a private entity on which a Latin cross had been erected in 1934 to serve as a war memorial was constitutional.[83] The facts of the case are somewhat unusual, but a brief discussion of *Salazar* is helpful because the case provides guidance on the validity of land transfers to preserve religious displays. The district court held before the land transfer that the cross on government property was an unconstitutional endorsement of religion.[84] During the appeal, Congress passed an act that transferred the land on which the cross stood to a private entity.[85] Prior to that, Congress passed several laws that precluded the use of government funds to remove the cross.[86] The land transfer was the primary focus of the case when it reached the U.S. Supreme Court after the district court applied the same injunction it had applied to the original display to the transfer, suggesting that Congress had an unconstitutional motive for the land transfer.[87]

The Court noted that "[t]he landtransfer statute was a substantial change in circumstances bearing on the propriety of the requested relief."[88] It held that the district court should not have dismissed "Congress's motives as illicit."[89] The Court held that the lower court should have considered the reasons for the congressional action, including the fact that Congress was attempting to comply with the original court order without

79 This is reflected in *Lynch v. Donnelly* [465 U.S. 668 (1984)] and *County of Allegheny v. ACLU* [492 U.S. 573 (1989)], where a crèche (*Lynch*) and a Christmas tree and menorah (as well as a crèche) (*Allegheny*) were the displays at issue. It is also reflected in the types of objects that are generally involved in cases in the lower courts. *See, generally*, Part C (discussing a number of court decisions involving crèches, crosses, menorahs, Ten Commandments monuments, and objects such as Christmas trees and Santas).

80 Allegheny, 492 U.S. at 798–802, (Stevens, J., dissenting).

81 *Id.* at 807 (Stevens, J., dissenting).

82 559 U.S. 700 (2010).

83 *Id.*

84 *Id.* at 708.

85 *Id.* at 709–10.

86 *Id.* at 709.

87 *Id.* at 710–11.

88 *Id.* at 715.

89 *Id.*

dismantling a war memorial.[90] The Court also held that the initial placement of the cross on government property by a private entity was not state action attempting to favor a "particular creed."[91] The Court also noted that the cross stood for almost seventy years before the initial injunction was granted, and this was relevant to the meaning of the cross even today.[92] According to the Court,

> [t]he landtransfer statute embodies Congress's legislative judgment that this dispute is best resolved through a framework and policy of accommodation for a symbol that, while challenged under the Establishment Clause, has complex meaning beyond the expression of religious views. That judgment should not have been dismissed as an evasion, for the statute brought about a change of law and a congressional statement of policy applicable to the case.[93]

As a result, the Court remanded the case for further proceedings considering the Court's analysis.[94] The Court acknowledged that there may be constitutionally significant issues that arise from the land transfer[95] but that the lower courts should not simply assume that dismantling the display is the only way to address these issues.[96] Other options, such as signs noting the private sponsorship of the display or other alternatives, might resolve the issue.[97] The case is heavily focused on the specific facts underlying both the injunction and the way in which the land-transfer statute and procedural history of the case interacted.[98] The Court's reasoning suggests that land transfers may be one option for long-standing religious monuments that have allegedly taken on a nonreligious aspect and that presumably are not located near government buildings. Yet the facts and location of the monument are so unique that the case may have little application in other contexts, such as displays in front of government buildings, if there is not a public forum.[99]

*Capitol Square* and *Salazar* are the only Supreme Court cases involving the display of a cross on government property, and both were decided without addressing what would happen if a cross were displayed in a nonpublic forum on government land. There are, however, a number of cases in the lower courts that address the latter issue. For example, in *Separation of Church and State Committee v. City of Eugene*,[100] the United States Court of Appeals for the Ninth Circuit held that a fifty-one-foot-tall concrete Latin cross that had been erected in a public park and subsequently designated a war memorial violated the Establishment Clause.[101] The cross was illuminated on certain holidays.[102] In a *per curium* opinion, the court held that the display endorsed Christianity:

90 *Id.* at 716–17.
91 *Id.* at 715.
92 *Id.* at 716.
93 *Id.* at 717.
94 *Id.* at 722.
95 *Id.* at 721–2.
96 *Id.* at 722.
97 *Id.*
98 *See, generally*, Salazar, 559 U.S. 700.
99 *See* Amanda Reid, *Private Memorials on Public Space: Roadside Crosses at the Intersection of the Free Speech Clause and the Establishment Clause*, 92 Neb. L. Rev. 124, 171 (2013) ("The narrow grounds of the *Salazar* decision leave unresolved many of the questions that are raised by the presence of a memorial cross on public land.").
100 93 F.3d 617 (9th Cir. 1996).
101 *Id.* at 618–20.
102 *Id.* at 618.

> There is no question that the Latin cross is a symbol of Christianity, and that its placement on public land by the City of Eugene violates the Establishment Clause. Because the cross may reasonably be perceived as government endorsement of Christianity, the City of Eugene has impermissibly breached the First Amendment's "wall of separation" between church and state [footnote omitted].[103]

Thus the court acknowledged in unequivocal terms that the cross is a religious symbol.[104]

Judge O'Scannlain filed an opinion concurring in the result.[105] He would have engaged in a more fact-sensitive inquiry into the context of the display, but like the majority, he acknowledged the potential religious message of the cross in the context at issue.[106] Moreover, there have been a number of surprisingly similar cases decided under the federal Constitution and several state constitutions.[107] Most of these cases treat crosses as obvious religious symbols.[108]

### 3. *Menorahs*

As noted earlier, the *Allegheny* decision also addressed the placement of a menorah outside a city-county building.[109] The menorah was owned by Chabad-Lubavich, a Hasidic Jewish group,[110] and was placed near a large Christmas tree and a sign saluting liberty.[111] The Court acknowledged the religious nature and history of the menorah and the holiday of Chanukah,[112] which the menorah is related to.[113] Yet the Court held that the context of the menorah – situated near the Christmas tree and a sign saluting liberty – did not endorse Judaism or religion generally.[114] Rather, the Court held that the display sent a message

103 *Id.* at 620.

104 *Id.*

105 *Id.* at 620 (O'Scannlain, J., concurring in the result).

106 *Id.* at 624–6 (O'Scannlain, J., concurring in the result).

107 Trunk v. City of San Diego, 629 F.3d 1099 (9th Cir. 2011) (striking down a large cross on a veterans' memorial atop Mount Soledad); Carpenter v. City & County of San Francisco, 93 F.3d 627 (9th Cir. 1996); Separation of Church and State Comm. v. City of Eugene, 93 F.3d 617 (9th Cir. 1996); Ellis v. City of La Mesa, 990 F.2d 1518 (9th Cir. 1993) (striking down the display of two large Latin crosses in separate public parks and the use of a Latin cross in the city's official insignia under the no preference clause of the California Constitution); Murray v. City of Austin, 947 F.2d 147 (5th Cir. 1991); Harris v. City of Zion, 927 F.2d 1401 (7th Cir. 1991); Mendelson v. City of St. Cloud, 719 F. Supp. 1065 (M.D. Fla. 1989); Jewish War Veterans of the United States v. United States, 695 F. Supp. 1 (D.D.C. 1987); ACLU v. City of St. Charles, 622 F.Supp. 1542 (N.D. Ill. 1985); Eugene Sand & Gravel, Inc. v. City of Eugene, 558 P.2d 338 (Or. 1976) (*en banc*); Lowe v. City of Eugene, 463 P.2d 360 (Or. 1969) (*en banc*) (striking down a cross on city property in part based on the Oregon Constitution); *see also* Paulson v. City of San Diego, 294 F.3d 1124 (9th Cir. 2002) (*en banc*) (involving sale of public land on which large Latin cross stood under circumstances that raised constitutional concerns under state establishment clause); Gonzales v. North Township, 4 F.3d 1412 (7th Cir. 1993) (striking down a crucifixion as a memorial for service men in a public park); Meyer v. Oklahoma City, 496 P.2d 789 (Okla. 1972) (affirming a fifty-foot cross controlled by the city on fair grounds under the Oklahoma Constitution).

108 *See supra* note 107.

109 Allegheny, 492 U.S. 573.

110 *Id.* at 587. Although the menorah was owned by Chabad, it was "stored, erected, and removed each year by the city. *Id.*

111 *Id.* at 582.

112 *Id.* at 583–5.

113 *Id.* at 582–7.

114 *Id.* at 617–20.

recognizing religious pluralism and cultural diversity.[115] The Court viewed the display as representing the winter holiday season rather than a specific religion or holiday.[116] In her concurring opinion, Justice O'Connor stressed that the message sent by the display to a reasonable observer was a message of tolerance and good tidings for the holiday season.[117]

Justices Brennan and Stevens authored opinions dissenting from the Court's holding regarding the menorah.[118] Justice Brennan, joined by Justices Marshall and Stevens, agreed with the majority that Chanukah and the menorah are religious but disagreed that the context of the display could adequately secularize the menorah.[119] Justice Stevens, in an opinion joined by Justices Brennan and Marshall, argued that "the Establishment Clause should be construed to create a strong presumption against the display of religious symbols on public property."[120] Both Justice Brennan and Justice Stevens were concerned that the Court's decision would offend both believers and nonbelievers by minimizing the religious meaning of the object involved – in this case a menorah – and by minimizing the impact such displays have on religious outsiders and nonbelievers.[121] A number of lower courts have followed the *Allegheny* Court's analysis.

### 4. *Ten Commandments Displays*

In *Stone v. Graham*,[122] the Court held that a Kentucky law requiring the posting of the Ten Commandments in every public school classroom in the state violated the Establishment Clause. The law required the inclusion of a notation "concerning the purpose of the display" that focused on the "secular application of the Ten Commandments" in legal codes.[123] *Stone* is a short *per curium* opinion,[124] but it is notable for purposes of the discussion herein. Specifically, the Court stated, "[t]he Ten Commandments are undeniably a sacred text in the Jewish and Christian faith, and no legislative recitation of a supposed secular purpose can blind us to that fact."[125] As this passage suggests, the Court held that the law failed the secular purpose prong of the *Lemon* test because there was no valid secular purpose for mandating the posting of a sacred text on the walls of every public school classroom in the state.[126]

In 2005, the Supreme Court decided two cases that set the parameters for analysis of religious symbols in the twenty-first century and perhaps also clarified some of the conflict between the reasoning in the *Lynch* and *Allegheny* cases. The 2005 cases involved widely different facts, even though both involved Ten Commandments displays. The

115 *Id.* at 619–20.
116 *Id.* at 617–20.
117 *Id.* at 635–6 (O'Connor, J., concurring in part and concurring in the judgment).
118 *Id.* at 637 (Brennan, J., concurring in part and dissenting in part); *id.* at 646 (Stevens, J., concurring in part and dissenting in part).
119 *Id.* at 643–5 (Brennan, J., concurring in part and dissenting in part).
120 *Id.* at 650–1 (Stevens, J., concurring in part and dissenting in part).
121 *Id.* at 644–6 (Brennan, J., concurring in part and dissenting in part); *id.* at 650–2 (Stevens, J., concurring in part and dissenting in part).
122 449 U.S. 39 (1981) (*per curiam*).
123 *Id.* at 39 n. 1.
124 *Id.* at 39–43.
125 *Id.* at 41.
126 *Id.* at 40–3.

analysis from these cases, however, as was true of *Lynch* and *Allegheny*, applies beyond the specific objects involved in the cases.[127]

In *ACLU v. McCreary County*,[128] the Court held that Ten Commandments displays in two separate county courthouses were unconstitutional.[129] The Court relied on the secular purpose prong of the *Lemon* and endorsement tests.[130] The history of the displays in question played a significant role in the Court's analysis. Each of the displays originally consisted of a framed copy of the Ten Commandments taken from the King James version of the Bible.[131] The courthouse displays were readily visible to those using the courthouse.[132] In response to a lawsuit aimed at forcing the counties to remove the displays, the counties modified the displays to include a variety of other documents, including "an excerpt from the Declaration of Independence ... the Preamble to the Kentucky Constitution ... the national motto of "In God We Trust" ... [and] a page from the *Congressional Record*" declaring 1983 the year of the Bible.[133] Each of the documents mentioned God, and some documents were edited to include only the religious references contained in them.[134] The district court granted the plaintiffs' request for a preliminary injunction despite these modifications to the displays.

In response, the counties posted a third version of the displays that included fuller versions of some of the same documents contained in the second version but also included some additional documents that did not reference God.[135] The new displays also included a "prefatory document" that claimed that the displays contained "documents that played a significant role in the foundation of our system of law and government."[136] This document suggested that the Ten Commandments influenced the Declaration of Independence but made no attempt to connect the Ten Commandments to the other items in the display.[137]

The majority opinion was authored by Justice Souter.[138] The opinion focused heavily on the history of the display and the lack of a secular purpose evinced by that history.[139] The Court's analysis began with a quote from *Stone* recognizing that the Ten Commandments "are undeniably a sacred text in the Jewish and Christian faiths."[140] The Court's secular purpose analysis used the *Lemon* test but explained that the purpose analysis in that test is meant to ensure government neutrality between religions "and between

127. Staley v. Harris County, 461 F.3d 504 (5th Cir. 2009) (Bible display that was originally constitutional when dedicated in the 1950s as a part of a monument to a philanthropist who happened to be religious but fell into disrepair became unconstitutional when rebuilt by judge who ran on returning religion to the public square platform and focused the attention of the rededicated monument on the Bible itself rather than the philanthropist and engaged in sectarian dedication ceremony).

128. 545 U.S. 844, 125 S.Ct. 2722 (2005).

129. *Id.*

130. *Id.*

131. *Id.* at 2722–3.

132. *Id.*

133. *Id.* at 2729.

134. *Id.* at 2739.

135. *Id.* at 2730–1.

136. *Id.* at 2730–1, 2739–41.

137. *Id.* at 2739–41.

138. *Id.* at 2722.

139. *Id.*

140. *Id.* at 2732.

religion and nonreligion."[141] The Court then applied endorsement analysis, explaining that when government favors religion or a particular religion, it sends a message to "nonadherents 'that they are outsiders, not full members of the political community, and an accompanying message to adherents that they are insiders, favored members" of the political community.[142]

The majority openly addressed the argument put forth by the county that secular purpose analysis is impossible because it requires the courts to know the thoughts and minds of government actors. Justice Souter wrote for the majority:

> The eyes that look to purpose belong to an "objective observer," one who takes account of the traditional external signs that show up in the "text, legislative history, and implementation of the statute,“ or comparable official act.[143]

The Court explained that if an objective observer would perceive the predominant purpose behind a government action as religious, the government is "taking religious sides."[144] In determining what an objective observer would perceive, the history and context of the display – of which the observer is presumed to be aware – are quite important.[145]

The Court recognized that the *Stone* Court found the Ten Commandments to be an "instrument of religion" and that this was decisive under the facts in that case.[146] Still the Court held that there is no per se rule against displaying the Ten Commandments under all circumstances.[147] The majority acknowledged the theological significance of the commandments and the impact of their divine origin.[148] In so doing, the Court pointed out that the text of the commandments is a powerful indication of their religious nature and the likely religious purpose in displaying them.[149] The opinion explained that where the text of the Ten Commandments is absent, it is less likely that an observer would perceive the depiction of tablets as religious,[150] and conversely, when the text is present, "the insistence of the religious message is hard to avoid" absent a context that suggests "a message going beyond an excuse to promote [a] religious point of view."[151] As a result, when the government places the text of the Ten Commandments "alone in public view" – as the counties did in the first of the three displays – the religious purpose is obvious.[152] Moreover, surrounding the text with other historical documents, whose main connection is that they contain religious references, would only make a reasonable observer more likely to perceive a religious purpose.[153]

The counties' third display, which included a number of secular documents and the text of the Ten Commandments, was ostensibly intended to represent the foundations

141 *Id.* at 2733.
142 *Id.*
143 *Id.* at 2734.
144 *Id.* at 2732–4.
145 *Id.* at 2734–7.
146 *Id.* at 2737–8.
147 *Id.*
148 *Id.* at 2738–9.
149 *Id.*
150 *Id.*
151 *Id.*
152 *Id.* at 2739.
153 *Id.*

of American law.[154] The Court recognized that in a vacuum such a display might have a secular purpose,[155] but in light of the history of the courthouse displays and the odd choices of historical documents – that is, including the Magna Carta and Declaration of Independence but not the Constitution or the Fourteenth Amendment[156] – the displays could not survive secular purpose analysis.[157] The Court found especially odd attempts to link the Ten Commandments, with their divine origin, and the Declaration of Independence, which derives governmental power from the people.[158]

The Court held that neutrality, although an elusive and variable concept, is an important focus of the religion clauses because the Framers were concerned about the civic divisiveness that can be caused when the government takes sides in religious debates.[159] This militates against the constitutionality of government displays that evince a religious purpose.[160] The Court rejected the dissent's brand of strict originalism because there are historical arguments that support both sides.

Justice O'Connor, who joined the majority, filed a concurring opinion.[161] She argued that given the religious divisiveness in nations without some level of separation, and given the success of the American experiment with separation – both for religion and for society more generally – it makes little sense to reject core Establishment Clause principles and allow the government to favor one religion or set of religions over others or over nonreligion.[162] She cited to the American tradition of religious voluntarism and wrote that when government endorses one religious tradition or another, it can distort the marketplace of ideas and foster divisiveness.[163] Displays such as those in McCreary County violate the endorsement principle.[164]

Justice Scalia filed a strongly worded dissent that was joined by Justice Thomas and Chief Justice Rehnquist and in part by Justice Kennedy.[165] Justice Scalia relied on originalist arguments to assert that the government can endorse monotheistic religious traditions as long as it does not discriminate against other religious views or play favorites when it comes to funding or other aid.[166] Justice Scalia pointed to a number of statements and actions by various Framers endorsing monotheism, as well as to a number of historical practices that do the same.[167] As Justice Souter pointed out for the majority, Justice Scalia's history is quite selective, and it leaves out other historical information that may suggest support for a broader separation or that may suggest a favoring of Protestant religious views rather than monotheism generally.[168] Justice Scalia also criticized the

154 *Id.* at 2739–40.
155 *Id.* at 2741.
156 *Id.*
157 *Id.* at 2739–41.
158 *Id.* at 2740–1.
159 *Id.* at 2742–3.
160 *Id.* at 2743–5.
161 *Id.* at 2746 (O'Connor, J., concurring).
162 *Id.*
163 *Id.* at 2746–7.
164 *Id.* at 2747.
165 *Id.* at 2748 (Scalia, J., dissenting).
166 *Id.*
167 *Id.* at 2748–53.
168 Justice Souter, of course, while acknowledging these problems, goes on to rely on originalist arguments himself. *Id.* at 2743–5 (majority opinion).

majority for its focus on secular purpose, arguing that determining legislative purpose is not a fruitful task for the judiciary and that purpose analysis can cause a great deal of mischief.[169] Justice Scalia would require government coercion or government action that proselytizes or disparages a particular religion(s) to find a religious display unconstitutional.[170]

*Van Orden v. Perry*[171] was decided the same day as *McCreary County* but involved very different facts. *Van Orden* is a split decision. Justice Rehnquist wrote the opinion for a plurality of justices. Significantly, there are four justices in the plurality and four dissenting justices.[172] Thus Justice Breyer's opinion concurring in the judgment seems to be the key opinion. This is quite similar to the famous *Bakke* case,[173] where the Court was split four to four, and Justice Powell's concurring opinion became the key precedent.[174]

*Van Orden* involved the display of a Ten Commandments monument on the ground between the Texas State Capitol building and the State Supreme Court building.[175] The monument was one of a number of monuments scattered around the grounds of the capitol.[176] Its location did not call any special attention to it. The monument was donated in 1961 by the Fraternal Order of Eagles, and the Eagles paid the cost of erecting it.[177] There was little evidence of the legislative intent behind accepting the monument, and there was no evidence of the sort of religiously motivated purpose evident in *McCreary County*.[178]

The plurality opinion held that the Establishment Clause has a dual nature. It recognizes "the strong role played by religion and religious traditions throughout our nation's history" and at the same time recognizes that "governmental intervention in religious matters can itself endanger religious freedom."[179] The plurality applied analysis quite similar to that applied in *Lynch*; it did not apply either the *Lemon* test or the endorsement test.[180] Thus the plurality focused on the "unbroken history of official acknowledgments by all three branches of government of the role of religion in American life," as asserted in *Lynch*.[181] The opinion then recited several historical examples supporting this and cited cases such as *Marsh v. Chambers*[182] and *Lynch* in combination with dicta from other cases.[183] This is followed with discussion of the religious monuments and sculptures adorning federal buildings in the District of Columbia, including the Supreme Court. This is used as evidence that the Ten Commandments can have a secular meaning as well as a religious meaning, namely, the decalogue's historical role in American law and culture.[184] Significantly, this seems to conflict with the Court's earlier holding

169 *Id.* at 2757–63 (Scalia, J., dissenting).
170 *Id.* at 2761–2.
171 545 U.S. 677, 125 S.Ct. 2854 (2005) (plurality opinion).
172 *See, generally, id.*
173 Regents of Univ. of Cal. v. Bakke, 438 U.S. 265 (1978)
174 *Id.*
175 *Id.* at 2858 (plurality opinion).
176 *Id.*
177 *Id.*
178 *Id.* at 2858, 2864 n. 11.
179 *Id.* at 2859.
180 *Id.* at 2861–4.
181 *Id.* at 2861.
182 463 U.S. 783 (1983).
183 Van Orden, 125 S. Ct. at 2861–2 (plurality opinion).
184 *Id.* at 2862–3.

in *Stone*,[185] but the plurality distinguishes *Stone*, arguing that *Stone* involved the public schools, where heightened Establishment Clause analysis has generally been applied.[186]

The plurality repeated the somewhat ridiculous statement from *Lynch* that the religious object (in this case the Ten Commandments monument) is "passive."[187] Second, it explained that monuments such as the one in Texas can have "a dual significance, partaking of both religion and government."[188] As long as the monument "partakes" of an appropriate secular "significance," the religious "significance," while still there, is not determinative under the Establishment Clause.[189]

Justice Thomas wrote a concurring opinion repeating his call in earlier cases to reevaluate incorporation of the Establishment Clause[190] and arguing that to the extent that clause is incorporated, the touchstone of Establishment Clause analysis should be legal coercion.[191] Justice Thomas argued that the Court's endorsement approach "either gives insufficient weight to the views of nonadherents and adherents alike, or it provides no principled way to choose between those views."[192]

As mentioned earlier, Justice Breyer's concurring opinion is key to applying the *Van Orden* decision. Justice Breyer viewed *Van Orden* as a "borderline" case to which no legal test can be appropriately applied.[193] This leaves only the "exercise of legal judgment" for determining the outcome.[194] Justice Breyer stressed, however, that legal judgment is "not a personal judgment": "Rather … it must reflect and remain faithful to the underlying purposes of the clauses, and it must take account of context and consequences measured in light of those purposes."[195]

Like the plurality, Justice Breyer wrote that the purpose of the Establishment Clause is to maintain some level of separation between church and state while avoiding hostility to religion, although it seems clear that Justice Breyer weighed these factors differently than the plurality.[196] Justice Breyer asserted that avoiding religious divisiveness is a major goal of the Establishment Clause but that this can cut both ways.[197] Therefore, the type of religious purpose evidenced in *McCreary County* is unconstitutional, but so would be attempts by the "government to purge from the public sphere all that in any way partakes of the religious."[198]

Justice Breyer noted that long-standing religious displays do not generally raise the same Establishment Clause concerns as new attempts to display religious objects because the long-standing displays are less likely to be divisive, assuming that their context and purpose adequately secularize them.[199] This seems to be an attempt to protect against

185 Stone, 449 U.S. 39 (*per curiam*).
186 Van Orden, 125 S. Ct. at 2863–4 (plurality opinion).
187 *Id.* at 2861, 2864.
188 *Id.* at 2864.
189 *See, generally, id.*
190 *Id.* (Thomas, J., concurring).
191 *Id.* at 2865.
192 *Id.* at 2867.
193 *Id.* at 2869 (Breyer, J., concurring in the judgment).
194 *Id.*
195 *Id.*
196 *Id.* at 2868–9.
197 *Id.* at 2871.
198 *Id.* at 2868, 2871.
199 *Id.* at 2871.

Establishment Clause challenge most long-standing government displays that include religious themes – recognition of a form of symbolic ceremonial Deism, if you will. Justice Breyer rejected much of the plurality's reasoning and seems to carve out a narrow group of cases involving long-standing religious monuments or displays whose physical and historical context makes them appear less divisive than they might appear in other historical or physical settings.

Justice Stevens wrote a dissenting opinion that focused heavily on the religious nature of the Ten Commandments.[200] He pointed out the intense theological disputes that can arise in relation to the choice of text for the Ten Commandments, and he focused heavily on the concepts of neutrality and separation.[201] Justice Stevens expressed great concern about the potential divisiveness of a display with such obvious theological significance. In light of that theological significance, he distinguished displays of the Ten Commandments that focus on the Commandments' text from other displays with religious content the Court has upheld.[202] In his view, such displays inherently create religious insiders and outsiders and thus violate the neutrality and separation principles.[203]

Justice Souter wrote a dissenting opinion in which he argued that the context of the Texas display, especially the fact that the full text of the Ten Commandments appears on the monument, demonstrates a form of religious favoritism that violates the neutrality principle (and implicitly endorses religion).[204] He argued that unless context alters the message, government cannot display "an obviously religious text" consistently with the neutrality principle.[205] Justice Souter looked at the purposes of the Fraternal Order of Eagles in donating the monument and the state's purpose for placing the monument on the capitol grounds as well as the physical attributes of the monument – which included sizing and capitalizing words that reinforce the most religious aspects of the text – and concluded that the state was clearly sending a religious message by displaying the monument.[206] He rejected the state's arguments that the purpose was to recognize the Ten Commandments' role as one of the foundations of secular law in Texas and the nation as a whole.[207] He pointed out that the Ten Commandments are a divine injunction to follow the laws stated therein and that the monument was designed so as to accentuate the divine.[208] Justice Souter also argued that the physical setting on the twenty-two-acre capitol grounds along with sixteen other monuments does not alter the message sent by the Ten Commandments because there is no common theme among the monuments.[209] He chided the plurality for relying on generalities in earlier cases rather than on more relevant cases such as *Stone*,[210] and he argued that the plurality's attempt to limit *Stone* to the classroom setting was against the lessons of that case and other precedent.[211]

200 *Id.* at 2873 (Stevens, J., dissenting).
201 *Id.*
202 *Id.*
203 *Id.* at 2874–5.
204 *Id.* at 2892 (Souter, J., dissenting).
205 *Id.*
206 *Id.* at 2893.
207 *Id.* at 2895–6.
208 *Id.* at 2893.
209 *Id.* at 2895.
210 *Id.* at 2895–6.
211 *Id.* at 2896–7.

The law relating to public display of religious objects by government entities may at first glance seem unclear after *McCreary County* and *Van Orden*, but despite their differing reasoning and outcomes, some general parameters and rules emerge from the decisions. First, if a display does not have a secular purpose, it is unconstitutional because a majority of the Court in *McCreary County* held that the secular purpose prong of the *Lemon* test (as merged with a focus on endorsement) applies to these monuments. Second, a long-standing display that is contextualized by other displays and that was not subject to complaints for most of its history and for which there is a secular purpose (or where the purpose is unknown) is most likely constitutional as long as it does not favor one sect or religion.

Finally, if there is an adequate secular purpose, but the display would not survive under Justice Breyer's *Van Orden* approach, the answer is unclear, but it seems that the Court would apply the effects approach from *Lemon*, as augmented by endorsement analysis. Dicta in *McCreary County* seem to support this approach, and the *McCreary County* majority would apply the *Lemon*/endorsement approach except in the limited context of Justice Breyer's *Van Orden* concurrence (Justice Breyer was part of the *McCreary County* majority). Therefore, it appears that a majority of the Court would apply the *Lemon* and endorsement tests or something resembling these tests to the effects of government-supported Ten Commandments (and perhaps other) displays. Perhaps, then, it is not an exaggeration to say that context is everything when analyzing religious displays on government property.

Two decisions by the United States Court of Appeals for the Eleventh Circuit, each of which preceded *McCreary County* and *Van Orden*, demonstrate the important role context can play in cases involving government use or display of the Ten Commandments. In *King v. Richmond County*,[212] the Eleventh Circuit upheld the use of a small county seal with a picture of the Ten Commandments on it. The seal did not contain the text of the Ten Commandments,[213] and no one in the county knew why the Ten Commandments icon was included in the seal because the seal had been created in the late nineteenth century.[214] There was some speculation that it was meant to symbolize law because the seal was generally used to authenticate legal documents, and when it was developed, many citizens were illiterate.[215] The court applied the *Lemon* test as augmented by the endorsement test and thus inquired as to whether the primary purpose or effect of the seal was to endorse religion (entanglement was not an issue in the case).[216] The court discussed in detail the importance of context in religious symbolism cases and held that, in context, the seal neither had the purpose or effect of endorsing religion given its size, placement, use, the inclusion of secular symbols in the seal, and the fact that the seal did not include the text of the Ten Commandments.[217] The decision seems consistent with *McCreary County* and *Van Orden*, even though it predated those decisions.

212 331 F.3d 1271 (11th Cir. 2003).

213 *Id.* at 1274 (the seal depicted the Roman numerals I to X but not the text of the Ten Commandments).

214 *Id.* (The seal had been used "for more than 130 years," but no one knew the "purpose for the seal's design.").

215 *Id.* at 1277.

216 *Id.* at 1276–86.

217 *Id.* at 1277–86.

In *Glassroth v. Moore*,[218] the Eleventh Circuit held that the placement of a large granite Ten Commandments monument in the rotunda of the state courthouse by the chief justice of the Alabama Supreme Court violated the Establishment Clause. Chief Justice Moore installed the monument in the middle of the night with a film crew from Coral Ridge Ministries, an Evangelical Christian group, filming the installation.[219] The monument included the full text of the King James version of the Ten Commandments, and all other text was smaller and below the Ten Commandments, which were on the top of the monument in tablet form.[220]

Justice Moore never consulted the other justices before installing the monument,[221] and he refused to remove the monument when ordered to do so by a federal court.[222] Significantly, Justice Moore made several statements demonstrating his view that the monument was a religious object.[223] The case received a great deal of media attention, but as a matter of constitutional law, the case was easy to decide because Justice Moore's behavior erased any doubt that his purpose in erecting the monument was to promote religion, specifically Christianity.[224] Moreover, given the circumstances surrounding the monument's installation and its location and context in the courthouse (including frequent prayer vigils), the effect of the monument was to endorse religion and specifically Christianity.[225] Thus the court held that the monument violated the first two prongs of the *Lemon* test (the court also analyzed the effects prong through the lens of the endorsement test).[226] There is no question that this case is consistent with *McCreary County* and that *Van Orden* would not likely apply given Justice Moore's remarkably sectarian behavior.

A number of cases have been decided since *McCreary County* and *Van Orden*. These cases run the gamut in their facts and analysis. Some cases have found a religious display evinced a purpose to endorse religion and therefore held the display unconstitutional.[227] Some of these cases involved Ten Commandments displays,[228] but others involved other religious symbols.[229] Some cases have found the effects of a religious

218 335 F.3d 1282 (11th Cir. 2003).
219 *Id.* at 1286.
220 *Id.* at 1285–6.
221 *Id.* at 1285.
222 *Id.* at 1288.
223 *Id.* at 1286–7.
224 *Id.* at 1296–7.
225 *Id.* at 1297.
226 *Id.* at 1296–7.
227 Staley v. Harris County, 461 F.3d 504 (2006); DeWeese, 633 F.3d 424 (holding that the judge had a religious purpose for hanging a poster of the Ten Commandments in his courtroom).
228 DeWeese, 633 F.3d 424 (holding that the judge had a religious purpose for hanging a poster of the Ten Commandments in his courtroom); Green, 568 F.3d 784 (striking down display of Ten Commandments on the lawn of a county courthouse because it had the effect of promoting religion).
229 Staley, 461 F.3d 504 (Bible display that was originally constitutional when dedicated in the 1950s as a part of a monument to a philanthropist who happened to be religious but fell into disrepair became unconstitutional when rebuilt by judge who ran on returning religion to the public square platform and focused the attention of the rededicated monument on the bible itself rather than the philanthropist and engaged in sectarian dedication ceremony); Trunk, 629 F.3d 1099 (striking down the Mt. Soledad cross memorial because it had the effect of promoting religion); Am. Atheists, Inc. v. Duncan, 616 F.3d 1145, 1150 (10th Cir. 2010) (striking down roadside cross memorials because they had the effect of promoting religion).

display endorse religion.[230] Other cases have upheld religious displays on government property in circumstances similar to *Van Orden*, where the display was not a central focus on the government property and had been there for a long time without complaint.[231] Yet a few cases seem to apply a *Van Orden*–type analysis to situations where the religious display sits directly in front a government building and is not contextualized in such a way as to make it similar to the monument that Justice Breyer found presented a "borderline" case in *Van Orden*.[232] The latter cases are likely wrongly decided, but unless overturned, they remain good law in the jurisdictions that decided them.

Another case worth mentioning, although it is more worth mentioning as an exception rather than the rule, is *Pleasant Grove City v. Summum*.[233] The city had accepted the donation of eleven permanent monuments, including a Ten Commandments monument, and had controlled the land and monuments for many years.[234] A group of adherents to the Summum religion asked to display a monument reflecting the Seven Aphorisms of Summum.[235] The city declined, claiming that it accepted monuments that deal with city history or that are donated by groups with a long-standing connection with the community.[236] Summum sued, arguing that the city was engaged in viewpoint discrimination in violation of the Free Speech Clause.[237]

The Supreme Court held that the display was government speech and therefore there was no free speech issue.[238] The precedent dealing with private displays in public forums, such as *Capitol Square*, did not apply because this was government speech, and the land was not a public forum.[239] Significantly, the Court did not address the Establishment Clause issue that arises because the city allowed the Ten Commandments monument and seemed to favor more long-standing religions over others.[240] The case is primarily

230 *See, e.g.*, Green, 568 F.3d 784 (striking down display of Ten Commandments on the lawn of a county courthouse because it had the effect of promoting religion); Trunk, 629 F.3d 1099 (striking down the Mt. Soledad cross memorial because it had the effect of promoting religion); Duncan, 616 F.3d 1145 (striking down roadside cross memorials because they had the effect of promoting religion); Felix v. City of Bloomfield, 1:12-CV-00125-JAPRHS, 2014 WL 3865948 (D.N.M. Aug. 7, 2014) (striking down Ten Commandments statute on in front of the New Mexico City Municipal Building because it had the effect of promoting religion).

231 Card, 520 F.3d 1009 (9th Cir. 2008); Red River Freethinkers v. City of Fargo, 13-1934, 2014 WL 4178341 (8th Cir. Aug. 25, 2014); ACLU Nebraska Found. v. City of Plattsmouth, Neb., 419 F.3d 772, 774 (8th Cir. 2005); Freedom From Religion Found., Inc. v. Weber, 951 F. Supp. 2d 1123, 1125 (D. Mont. 2013); Twombly v. City of Fargo, 388 F. Supp. 2d 983, 984 (D.N.D. 2005); ACLU of Ohio v. Bd. of Comm'rs of Lucas Cnty., Ohio, 444 F. Supp. 2d 805, 807 (N.D. Ohio 2006); Russelburg v. Gibson Cnty., Ind., 3:03-CV-149-RLY-WGH, 2005 WL 2175527 (S.D. Ind. Sept. 7, 2005).

232 ACLU Nebraska Found. v. City of Plattsmouth, Neb., 419 F.3d 772, 780 (8th Cir. 2005) (Bye, J., dissenting) ("Texas's display of its Ten Commandments monument [in *Van Orden*], while much like Plattsmouth's monument, is surrounded by seventeen additional monuments and twenty-one historical markers. … Conversely, Plattsmouth's monument rests alone among the park's trees and recreational equipment.").

233 555 U.S. 460 (2009).

234 *Id.* at 464–5.

235 *Id.* at 465.

236 *Id.* at 465–6.

237 *Id.* at 466.

238 *Id.* at 470–2.

239 *Id.* at 467–70.

240 *See, generally*, Pleasant Grove, 55 U.S. 460 (Court addresses speech issues only and does not address Establishment Clause issues potentially raised by city's maintenance of the Ten Commandments monument and refusal of Summum's monument.).

useful in explaining that free speech doctrine does not apply to government speech in a nonpublic forum, but beyond that it says little about the constitutionality of Ten Commandments monuments generally.[241]

### 5. *Christmas Trees and Other Holiday Displays*

The constitutionality of the display of Christmas trees and other similar holiday displays by government was essentially resolved by the Court's reasoning in *Lynch* and *Allegheny*, where the Court presumed that such displays were constitutional.[242] The opinions of the Court in both cases scarcely questioned the constitutionality of Christmas trees and objects such as Santas, elves, and plastic reindeer.[243] Even Justice Brennan's opinion concurring in part and dissenting in part in *Allegheny*, which suggests that a Christmas tree can have significant religious meaning in some contexts, seems to assume that a Christmas tree by itself is not a religious object.[244] Lower courts have followed suit.[245]

## C. Conclusion

A few general conclusions emerge from the religious symbolism cases. First, if the display is private speech in a public forum (or limited public forum), it is likely constitutional unless government has somehow favored the religious speech.[246] Second, courts should seriously consider whether the purpose behind religious displays on public property that does not constitute a public forum are to endorse religion.[247] The same is likely true for the effects of such displays.[248] Third, however, when the religious display is a long-standing one that does not represent just one faith and the display has a secular purpose (or the purpose is not known) and the display is reflective of the religious traditions of the nation (or state), it is likely constitutional,[249] especially if it is contextualized by other objects and/or is not a central focus on government property.[250]

241 *Id.*
242 *See, generally*, Lynch, 465 U.S. 668; Allegheny, 492 U.S. 573.
243 *Id.*
244 Allegheny, 492 U.S. at 639 (Brennan, J., concurring in part and dissenting in part).
245 ACLU of New Jersey v. Schundler, 168 F.3d 92 (3d Cir. 1999); Sechler v. State Coll. Area Sch. Dist., 121 F. Supp. 2d 439, 444 (M.D. Pa. 2000); Grutzmacher v. Cnty. of Clark, 33 F. Supp. 2d 896 (D. Nev. 1999); Doe v. City of Warren, 889 F.2d 1087 (6th Cir. 1989) (unpublished); King v. Vill. of Waunakee, 517 N.W.2d 671 (Wis. 1994).
246 Capitol Square, 515 U.S. 753.
247 ACLU v. McCreary County, 545 U.S. 844, 125 S.Ct. 2722 (2005).
248 *See supra* note 230.
249 Van Orden, 545 U.S. 677 (2005).
250 *Id.* at 702 (Breyer, J., Concurring in the judgment).

# 18 Special Contexts: Prisons and the Military

This chapter addresses the application of the First Amendment religion clauses as well as other religion-related laws to the special contexts of prisons and the military. Much like public education, these contexts warrant separate treatment because of the pervasive governmental authority and control found within them and the attendant custodial or quasi-custodial nature of the relationship between the government and many of the persons subject to that authority and control. Additionally, each context is defined by levels of expertise and experience on the part of the officials charged with their operation and a corresponding level of judicial deference that is typically not present in other settings. Of course, most of the relevant laws – the Free Exercise Clause, the Establishment Clause, the Religious Freedom Restoration Act (RFRA), and, in the case of state prisons, the Religious Land Use and Institutionalized Persons Act (RLUIPA) – remain applicable, but the unique characteristics and interests found within each context tend to alter, at times significantly, the interpretation and implementation of the terms and doctrines of these laws.

## A. Prisons: In General

The interplay between religion and incarceration has a long and involved history. "Churches were among the first institutions to provide asylum for accused criminals. The establishment of prisons and penitentiaries followed religious tenets that encouraged offenders to do penance for their crimes and to reject a criminal lifestyle while being isolated from others."[1] The contemporary reality, perhaps related to this history, is that the context of incarceration seems to generate a disproportionate number of religious freedom claims, which, in turn, generate a large number of judicial decisions.

[1] Harry S. Dammer, *Religion in Prisons*, *in* 2 Encyclopedia of Prisons and Correctional Facilities 834, 834–5 (2005). As this text suggests, the historical interrelationship between religion and incarceration, though not more recounted here, is significant. *See* Andrew Skotnicki, Religion and the Development of the American Penal System (2000); Larry E. Sullivan, *History of Religion in Prison*, *in* 1 Encyclopedia of Prisons and Correctional Facilities 420–2 (2005). "The term 'penitentiary' – related to 'penance' – was first used in eighteenth-century Pennsylvania to describe institutions established for convicts to reflect and repent." *Developments in the Law – In the Belly of the Whale: Religious Practice in Prison*, 115 Harv. L. Rev. 1891, 1892 (2002) (citation omitted). However, "[b]y the following century this rehabilitative ideal had disintegrated, resulting in a cruel and often chaotic environment for offenders." *Id. See also* Todd R. Clear, George F. Cole & Michael D. Reisig, American Corrections 47–9 (9th ed., 2011).

The causes for this pattern, to the extent it is an accurate observation, are several and fairly evident. The mere fact of confinement, for example, increases the likelihood that religious practices will somehow be constrained. Although "[t]he right to exercise religious practices and beliefs does not terminate at the prison door … [t]he free exercise right … is necessarily limited by the fact of incarceration, and may be curtailed in order to achieve legitimate correctional goals or to maintain prison security."[2]

In addition, prison regulations are such that in the balance of liberty versus order, the latter will be favored to a degree that unincarcerated citizens presumably would be unwilling to tolerate. Although most prison administrators likely recognize that religion has significant therapeutic and rehabilitative potential,[3] they also understand that religious beliefs and practices can be a front for less benign or noble motives and that religious freedom claims can be one means of gaming or exploiting the system.[4] "Research has indicated that in addition to using religion for parole release, inmates may practice religion while in prison for a variety of other self-interested reasons. They may try to influence the chaplain or warden to improve their living conditions (e.g., special food, transfer to another prison wing or institution), to meet up with and exchange contraband from other inmates at religious functions, to meet volunteers, and to gain protection from other inmates."[5] Finally, and relatedly, prisoners may have ample time, sufficient resources, and few disincentives to assert a full range of alleged legal wrongs, restrictions on free exercise being merely one subgroup of such claims. This is not to suggest, of course, that prisoner claims are per se frivolous or insincere – some are, some are not – but is to recognize the reality of incarcerated life and culture, particularly for those serving repeat or extended sentences.[6]

Prisoner claims can be sorted into a number of broad subject-matter categories. Following an overview of the general applicable standards, the next section will walk

2 McElyea v. Babbitt, 833 F.2d 196, 197 (9th Cir. 1987) (*per curiam*).

3 *See* Clear et al., *supra* note 1, at 388 (noting potential benefits of religious prison programs, though also noting ambiguous social science findings); Dammer, *supra* note 1, at 838–9 (similar).

4 *See* Taylor G. Stout, *Note, The Costs of Religious Accommodation in Prisons*, 96 Va. L. Rev. 1201, 1209–11 (2010) (documenting this exploitation specifically by gangs). Regarding the culture and causes of inmate manipulation of correctional staff, which can include religious personnel, *see* Gary F. Cornelius, The Correctional Officer: A Practical Guide (2d ed., 2010), ch. 11, *excerpted in part at:* http://www.correctionsone.com/correctional-psychology/articles/3328579-Avoiding-inmate-manipulation/.

5 Dammer, *supra* note 1, at 838.

6 As one federal district judge observed, "The establishment of a new religion while in prison must be viewed with a certain suspicion. On the other hand, one cannot rule out the possibility that the belief in such a religion and the desire to pursue its teachings are sincerely held. Furthermore, while it would be easy to mock such beliefs coupled with mail order ordination certificates, it must be recognized that adherence to religious principles may have a beneficial impact on incarcerated individuals, and therefore, should be encouraged." Jacques v. Hilton, 569 F. Supp. 730, 731 (D.N.J. 1983), *aff'd*, 738 F.2d 422 (3d Cir. 1984); *see also* Yellowbear v. Lampert, 741 F.3d 48, 54 (10th Cir. 2014) (noting that there may be "those who, facing the difficult realities of prison life, are tempted to seek special dispensations through fraudulent assertions of faith"); *Comment, The Religious Rights of the Incarcerated*, 125 U. Pa. L. Rev. 812, 861 n. 306 (1977) ("A sincerity inquiry is especially important in prison free exercise cases because the bleakness of institutional life may create an incentive falsely to allege religious motivation for acts, such as growing a beard, that will be tolerated only if done in pursuit of a religious belief held in good faith.").

through several of these topical categories. Then there will be a brief treatment of claims by correctional staff, including clergy. Before undertaking these surveys of prisoner and staff claims, however, two caveats should be noted. The first is that many of the judicial decisions cited in the prison-related sections, unlike most cases cited in this book, are unreported or unpublished and, as a result, may not be available to those who lack access to subscription legal databases. This is not ideal, of course, especially because courts may consider such unreported decisions to be noncitable or nonbinding precedent.[7] It is, however, a unique and unavoidable consequence of the subject matter because prisoner cases are frequently not published in standard reporters and certainly less often than most other areas of law.[8]

The second caveat, which in time will be explained more fully, is that the recent case law involving religious freedom, including especially cases involving prisoners, is no longer dominated by claims under the First Amendment Free Exercise Clause as such but rather, or also, by claims under RLUIPA,[9] RFRA,[10] and a variety of state religious freedom laws or guarantees,[11] most of which emerged after the Supreme Court's restrictive interpretation of the Free Exercise Clause in *Employment Division v. Smith*.[12] Correspondingly, the cases decided under one of these religious freedom laws may be of only persuasive or nonbinding authority for cases arising under the others, making it critical to discern the precise legal framework under which one is proceeding and the relative authority of rulings derived from other laws.

Notwithstanding this second caveat, it should be pointed out that courts do tend to rely, sometimes heavily, on pre-*Smith* free exercise cases when addressing claims

7 *See, e.g.*, Fed. R. App. P. 32.1 (effectively allowing courts to restrict citation to unpublished or "non-precedential" opinions issued before January 1, 2007).

8 It has been observed, for example, that unpublished cases seem disproportionately to involve "immigration matters, criminal appeals, prisoners' rights (including *habeas*), and civil rights cases." David C. Vladeck & Mitu Gulati, *Judicial Triage: Reflections on the Debate over Unpublished Opinions*, 62 Wash. & Lee L. Rev. 1667, 1704 (2005) (reporting results from a limited, "unscientific" survey); *see also* David Greenwald & Frederick A.O. Schwarz, Jr., *The Censorial Judiciary*, 35 U.C. Davis L. Rev. 1133, 1158 (2002) (noting "specific classes of appeals that generate unpublished opinions with disproportionate frequency, such as appeals from denials of prisoner *pro se* petitions and from rulings in civil rights and social security cases").

9 Pub. L. No. 106–274, 114 Stat. 803 (Sept. 22, 2000) (codified at 42 U.S.C. §§ 2000cc to 2000cc-5).

10 Pub. L. No. 103–141, 107 Stat. 1488 (Nov. 16, 1993) (codified as amended at 42 U.S.C. §§ 2000bb to 2000bb-4).

11 *See* Chapter 5.A (listing state guarantees); Lee Boothby & Nicholas P. Miller, *Prisoner Claims for Religious Freedom and State RFRAs*, 32 U.C. Davis L. Rev. 573 (1999); Benjamin S. Fischer, *Note, Power to the Prisoner: The Importance of State Religious Freedom Acts in Preserving the Religious Liberties of Prisoners*, 10 J.L. & Pol'y 233 (2001). In addition to these general guarantees of religious freedom, many states have enacted statutes or promulgated regulations that specifically ensure inmate access to religious services, clergy, texts, or other items, thereby facilitating free exercise and forestalling its infringement by prison staff. *See, e.g.*, Ala. Code § 14-3-46 (ensuring provision of Bibles and other religious publications); Colo. Rev. Stat. § 17-42-101 (protecting inmates' freedom of worship); N.H. Rev. Stat. §§ 622:22, 622.23 (providing for religious instruction, ministration, and freedom of worship of inmates); Wis. Stat. §§ 301.33, 302.39 (providing for clergy-conducted services, religious ministration, and inmate access to the Bible).

12 494 U.S. 872 (1990).

under both RLUIPA[13] and RFRA.[14] This reliance stems from the explicit statement by Congress in RFRA that its purpose was to reinstate the free exercise standards that pertained prior to *Smith*[15] and then its decision to use in RLUIPA the same standards used in RFRA. In addition, and for these and other reasons, RFRA and RLUIPA rulings have been effectively treated by some courts as precedentially equivalent.[16] Despite their application to separate prison systems – RFRA to federal,[17] RLUIPA to state[18] – both laws function to such a similar, if not identical, extent that RFRA cases tend to serve as binding precedent in RLUIPA cases and vice versa.[19] This chapter, in all events, will

13 *See, e.g.*, Guru Nanak Sikh Soc'y of Yuba City v. Cnty. of Sutter, 456 F.3d 978, 988 (9th Cir. 2006) ("The Supreme Court's free exercise jurisprudence is instructive in defining a substantial burden under RLUIPA."); Lovelace v. Lee, 472 F.3d 174, 187 (4th Cir. 2006) (when defining "substantial burden under RLUIPA, "follow[ing] the Supreme Court's guidance in the Free Exercise Clause context"); Grace United Methodist Church v. City of Cheyenne, 451 F.3d 643, 661 (10th Cir. 2006) ["RLUIPA's legislative history reveals that 'substantial burden' is to be interpreted by reference to the Religious Freedom Restoration Act of 1993 (RFRA) and First Amendment jurisprudence." (citation omitted) (citing 146 CONG. REC. 7774-01, 7776)]; Civil Liberties for Urban Believers v. City of Chicago, 342 F.3d 752, 760 (7th Cir. 2003) (same), *cert. denied*, 541 U.S. 1096 (2004); Ragland v. Angelone, 420 F. Supp. 2d 507, 513 (W.D. Va. 2006) ("[I]n applying the RLUIPA standard, courts seek instruction from strict scrutiny precedents, addressing constitutional or RFRA claims."), *aff'd*, No. 06-6575, 193 Fed. App'x 218 (4th Cir. Aug. 2, 2006) (unpublished), *cert. denied*, 549 U.S. 1306 (2007); Westchester Day Sch. v. Village of Mamaroneck, 417 F. Supp. 2d 477, 546 (S.D.N.Y. 2006) {stating that "Congress 'intended that the term [substantial burden]' be interpreted by reference to Supreme Court jurisprudence" and that it "not ... be given any broader interpretation than the Supreme Court's articulation of the concept of substantial burden [on] religious exercise" [quoting Cambodian Buddhist Soc'y of Conn., Inc. v. Newtown Planning & Zoning Comm'n, No. CV 030350572S, 2005 WL 3370834, at *6 (Conn. Super. Ct. Nov. 18, 2005) (unpublished) (quoting 146 CONG. REC. at S7776)]}, *aff'd*, 504 F.3d 338 (2d Cir. 2007).

14 *See* Midrash Sephardi, Inc. v. Town of Surfside, 366 F.3d 1214, 1236 (11th Cir. 2004) (explaining that "RFRA sought to ... restore ... the pre-*Smith* standard"), *cert. denied*, 543 U.S. 1146 (2005); United States v. Hardman, 297 F.3d 1116, 1143 (10th Cir. 2002) (Hartz, J., concurring) (concluding that "pre-*Smith* Supreme Court opinions that purport to be consistent with *Sherbert* and *Yoder* are persuasive authority with respect to the interpretation of RFRA"); C.L.U.B. v. City of Chicago, 157 F. Supp. 2d 903, 917 (N.D. Ill. 2001) (explaining that RFRA "sought to rescind *Smith* and restore what proponents refer to as the pre-*Smith* standard"), *aff'd*, 342 F.3d 752 (7th Cir. 2003), *cert. denied*, 541 U.S. 1096 (2004).

15 Congress expressly stated that one of RFRA's two "purposes" was "to restore the compelling interest test as set forth in *Sherbert v. Verner* [374 U.S. 398 (1963)] and *Wisconsin v. Yoder* [406 U.S. 205 (1972)] and to guarantee its application in all cases where free exercise of religion is substantially burdened." 42 U.S.C. § 2000bb(b)(1); *see* Gonzales v. O Centro Espirita Beneficente Uniao do Vegetal, 546 U.S. 418, 431–2 (2006). Given that essentially the same test was then imposed by RLUIPA, it has not been difficult for at least some courts to conclude that "[b]oth RFRA *and RLUIPA* sought to rescind [*Smith*] and to restore the pre-*Smith* 'compelling interest/least restrictive means' standard when a plaintiff challenged the application of neutral, generally applicable laws to religious practices." Murphy v. Zoning Comm'n of Town of New Milford, 148 F. Supp. 2d 173, 183 n.6 (D. Conn. 2001) (emphasis added). This understanding of RLUIPA is arguably enhanced by its express mandate that it "shall be construed in favor of a broad protection of religious exercise, to the maximum extent permitted by the terms of this chapter and the Constitution." 42 U.S.C. § 2000cc-3(g).

16 One such other reason is that Congress, when it enacted RLUIPA, simultaneously amended RFRA, incorporating within RFRA a definition of "exercise of religion" set forth in RLUIPA. *See* 42 U.S.C. § 2000bb-2(4) [using the definition found at *id.* § 2000cc-5(7)(a)].

17 *Id.* § 2000bb-2(1)-(2) (limiting the application of RFRA to the federal government and to various federal territories and possessions).

18 42 U.S.C. § 2000cc-5(4)(A) (limiting the application of RLUIPA's main provisions, §§ 2000cc and 2000cc-1, to state and local governments).

19 *See, e.g.*, Fowler v. Crawford, 534 F.3d 931, 938 (8th Cir. 2008) (applying a RFRA case essentially as binding precedent in a RLUIPA case), *cert. denied*, 556 U.S. 1105 (2009).

attempt to identify non–First Amendment cases, when quoted or cited, with either of these acronyms.

## 1. *The Reasonableness Test*

As with most constitutional liberties, the exercise of religion is necessarily and legitimately limited by incarceration.[20] One's status as a convicted criminal, coupled with the unique nature of the prison environment, makes such limitations not only justified but also unremarkable.[21] Thus "[w]hat might be viewed as an unreasonable infringement of a fundamental constitutional right were it to occur outside prison may be valid in prison as long as the infringement is reasonably related to legitimate penological objectives, which include rehabilitation, deterrence, and security."[22] To be sure, at least one federal appellate court, before *Smith*, remarked that "[t]he 'free' exercise of religion … is rather a misnomer in the prison setting."[23] Nevertheless, the Supreme Court has admonished that "federal courts must take cognizance of the valid constitutional claims of prison inmates. Prison walls do not form a barrier separating prison inmates from the protections of the Constitution."[24] In turn, the Court has explained that "a prison inmate retains those First Amendment rights that are not inconsistent with his [or her] status as a prisoner or with the legitimate penological objectives of the corrections system."[25]

In terms of constitutional doctrine, these circumstances have yielded a "'reasonableness' test [that is] less restrictive than that ordinarily applied to cognizable infringements of fundamental constitutional rights."[26] This test, which derives from *Turner v. Safley*[27] and which the Court explicitly extended to free exercise claims in *O'Lone v. Estate of Shabazz*,[28] provides that "when a prison regulation impinges on inmates' constitutional rights, the regulation is valid if it is reasonably related to legitimate

[20] *See* Pell v. Procunier, 417 U.S. 817, 822 (1974); McElyea v. Babbitt, 833 F.2d 196, 197 (9th Cir. 1987) (*per curiam*) (noting that "[t]he free exercise right … is necessarily limited by the fact of incarceration"); Hartmann v. Cal. Dep't of Corr. & Rehab., 707 F.3d 1114, 1122 (9th Cir. 2013) (noting that a "prisoner's right to freely exercise his [or her] religion … is limited by institutional objectives and by the loss of freedom concomitant with incarceration"). This is the case with most, but not all, constitutional liberties. For instance, in *Johnson v. California* [543 U.S. 499 (2005)], the Court indicated that the equal protection standard for racial discrimination in the prison context was the same as that developed in the civilian context.

[21] *See* O'Lone v. Estate of Shabazz, 482 U.S. 342, 348 (1987) ("The limitations on the exercise of constitutional rights arise both from the fact of incarceration and from valid penological objectives – including deterrence of crime, rehabilitation of prisoners, and institutional security.); Rooks v. Zavares, No. Civ. A. 99-B-631, 2001 WL 34047959, at *6 (D. Colo. Jan. 25, 2001) (unpublished) {"The courts have recognized that, to accommodate prison institutional needs and objectives, it is necessary to place major restrictions on prisoners' First Amendment rights." [citing Jones v. N.C. Prisoners' Labor Union, Inc., 433 U.S. 119, 129–30 (1977)]}.

[22] Mosier v. Maynard, 937 F.3d 1521, 1525 (10th Cir. 1991).

[23] Johnson-Bey v. Lane, 863 F.2d 1308, 1310 (7th Cir. 1988).

[24] Turner v. Safley, 482 U.S. 78, 84 (1987) (citation omitted); *see also* Cruz v. Beto, 405 U.S. 319, 322 n. 2 (1972) ("[R]easonable opportunities must be afforded to all prisoners to exercise the religious freedom guaranteed by the First and Fourteenth Amendments without fear of penalty.").

[25] Pell, 417 U.S. at 822.

[26] O'Lone, 482 U.S. at 349. *Turner* and *O'Lone* provide the constitutional standard. RLUIPA – and, for federal defendants, RFRA – imposes the higher standard of strict scrutiny.

[27] 482 U.S. 78 (1987).

[28] *See* O'Lone, 482 U.S. at 350.

penological interests."[29] There are several features of the test – often called the "*Turner* standard" or "*Turner* test" – that warrant elaboration, especially given the Court's own accompanying commentary and over two decades of lower court rulings.

First, in free exercise cases, the application of *Turner* is often (but not always) prefaced by a threshold requirement that the claimant demonstrate a substantial burden on his or her religious practice,[30] similar, if not identical, to the requirement developed outside the prison context under the First Amendment[31] and expressly included in both RFRA[32] and RLUIPA.[33] Many claims, in fact, never proceed beyond this initial requirement.[34] Among other circumstances, courts have refused to find a substantial burden simply because a prison does not affirmatively supply particular religious materials to an inmate[35] or does not allow a prisoner to start a weekly study group.[36] In analyzing this

[29] Turner, 482 U.S. at 89. This standard supplanted a variety of other, divergent tests that had existed to that point. For an overview of the prior law, *see Comment, The Religious Rights of the Incarcerated*, 125 U. Pa. L. Rev. 812 (1977). *Turner* does not necessarily supply the standard for all constitutional claims by prisoners, but it does govern many claims arising under the First Amendment.

[30] *Compare* Levitan v. Ashcroft, 281 F.3d 1313, 1320 (D.C. Cir. 2002) (applying a substantial burden requirement at the outset of a *Turner-O'Lone* analysis), *and* Eastwood v. Kicklighter, No. 7:10CV00096, 2010 WL 2326540, at *3 (W.D. Va. Jun. 8, 2010) (unpublished) (applying a substantial burden requirement), *and* Ordneal v. Dretke, 435 F. Supp. 2d 608, 618 (S.D. Tex. 2006) {"To establish a free exercise clause violation, plaintiff must demonstrate both that defendants have (1) 'placed a substantial burden on the observation of a central religious belief or practice,' and (2) that the defendants' conduct is not 'reasonably related to legitimate penological interests.'" [quoting Hernandez v. Comm'r, 490 U.S. 680, 699 (1999), and O'Lone, 482 U.S. at 349, respectively]}, *and* Phipps v. Morgan, No. CV-04-5108-MWL, 2006 WL 543896, at *6 (E.D. Wash. Mar. 6, 2006) (unpublished) (applying a substantial burden requirement), *and* Wilson v. Moore, 270 F. Supp. 2d 1328, 1348–49 (N.D. Fla. 2003) (same), *with* Williams v. Morton, 343 F.3d 212, 217 (3d Cir. 2003) ["The Prison Officials argue that [under *Turner*] it is ... a prerequisite for the inmate to establish that the challenged prison policy 'substantially burdens' his or her religious beliefs. There is no support for that assertion." (citation omitted)], *with* Ford v. McGinnis, 352 F.3d 582, 592 (2d Cir. 2003) (noting the split between the D.C. and Third Circuits and, because no party challenged or briefed the issue, "assum[ing] that the substantial burden test applies").

[31] *See* Chapter 5.C.

[32] *See* 42 U.S.C. § 2000bb-1.

[33] *See id.* § 2000cc-1.

[34] *See, e.g.*, Goodrick v. Sonnen, No. 12-35076, 505 Fed. App'x 654, 655 (9th Cir. Jan. 17, 2013) (unpublished) (affirming dismissal of an inmate's free exercise and RLUIPA claims because he "failed adequately to allege how the challenged policy burdened the exercise of his religious beliefs"); Gladson v. Iowa Dep't of Corr., 551 F.3d 825, 834 (8th Cir. 2009) (similar); Baranowski v. Hart, 486 F.3d 112, 125 (5th Cir. 2007) (similar), *cert. denied*, 552 U.S. 1062 (2007); Sledge v. Cummings, 69 F.3d 548 (10th Cir. 1995) (unpublished) (similar, under RFRA), *cert. denied*, 517 U.S. 1145 (1996).

[35] *See, e.g.*, Eley v. Herman, No. 1:04-CV-416-TS, 2006 WL 1722364, at *6 (N.D. Ind. June 21, 2006) (unpublished) {"Since a Koran was essential to the Plaintiff's religious exercise, by not having it, he was suffering a detriment to his religious exercise. Moreover, had the jail provided him a Koran, it would have alleviated this void in his practice of faith. But that is not to say that, by not giving him a Koran, the jail imposed any burden upon him. If the Plaintiff suffered a hardship, it was not one created by the jail. No evidence exists that the policy not to give him a Koran prohibited him from getting a Koran on his own ... [N]either the Constitution nor RLUIPA place [*sic*] any duty on jails to provide inmates with religious materials." [citing Borzych v. Frank, 439 F.3d 388, 390 (7th Cir. 2006); Cutter v. Wilkinson, 544 U.S. 709, 720 n. 5 (2005)]}; *see also* Adkins v. Kaspar, 393 F.3d 559, 571 (5th Cir. 2004) ("The requirement of an outside volunteer – which is a uniform requirement for all religious assemblies at [the prison] with the exception of Muslims – does not place a substantial burden on [the claimant's] religious exercise ... All things considered, we are convinced that the acts of the defendants have not placed a substantial burden on [the claimant's] free exercise of his YEA religion, within the contemplation of the RLUIPA."), *cert. denied*, 545 U.S. 1104 (2005).

[36] *See, e.g.*, Kaufman v. McCaughtry, 419 F.3d 678, 683 (7th Cir. 2005) (explaining that, under the First Amendment, the prisoner failed to show a substantial burden on his religious practice because

threshold factor, some courts appear essentially to apply a sliding scale, where the less substantial the burden on the claimant's religious practice, the weaker or more minimal is the penological interest that prison officials will need to assert to overcome it.[37]

Independent of the burden requirement, the *Turner* Court articulated four factors, the so-called *Turner* factors, that determine the overall reasonableness and thus ultimate validity of a prison policy or regulation. First, "there must be a 'valid, rational connection' between the prison regulation and the legitimate governmental interest put forward to justify it."[38] As part of this validity and rationality, "the efforts of prison administrators, when assessed in their totality, must be evenhanded ... [and] cannot discriminate against a particular religion."[39] Second, there must be "alternative means of exercising the right that remain open to prison inmates."[40] Third, a prison's "accommodation of the asserted constitutional right" should not have "a significant 'ripple effect' on fellow inmates or on prison staff" in terms of negative "ramifications on the liberty of others or on the use of the prison's limited resources for preserving institutional order."[41] Fourth and finally, there should be no "obvious, easy alternatives" to the prison's existing approach. "This is not a 'least restrictive alternative' test: prison officials do not have to set up and then shoot down every conceivable alternative method of accommodating the claimant's constitutional complaint. But if an inmate claimant can point to an alternative that fully accommodates the prisoner's rights at de minimis cost to valid penological interests, a court may consider that as evidence that the regulation does not satisfy the reasonable relationship standard."[42]

Comparatively speaking, *Turner* "is not a demanding standard,"[43] and case law indicates that the government likely has the evidentiary burden only on the first factor[44] – a burden described by courts as "slight"[45] and "relatively limited"[46] – with the prisoner shouldering the evidentiary burden for the remainder of the test.[47] When assessing these four factors, moreover, courts begin with a number of conceptual premises that, in general, are also

there was no evidence that he could not effectively practice atheism without the benefit of a weekly study group).

37 Makin v. Colo. Dep't of Corr., 183 F.3d 1205, 1213 (10th Cir. 1999) (explaining that "[a] complete denial of the ability to observe a religious practice is not required to demonstrate an infringement, though the fact that a spiritual experience was only diminished rather than denied may factor into the strength of the penological interests necessary to justify the infringement").

38 Turner, 482 U.S. at 89 [quoting Block v. Rutherford, 468 U.S. 576, 586 (1984)]. "Moreover, the governmental objective must be a legitimate and neutral one." *Id.* at 90.

39 Al-Alamin v. Gramley, 926 F.2d 680, 686 (7th Cir. 1991) (explaining that "the treatment of all inmates must be qualitatively comparable").

40 Turner, 482 U.S. at 90.

41 *Id.*

42 *Id.* at 90–1 (citation omitted).

43 Reed v. Faulkner, 842 F.2d 960, 962 (7th Cir. 1988).

44 *See* Walker v. Sumner, 917 F.2d 382, 385–6 (9th Cir. 1990) ["[D]eference does not mean abdication. Prison officials must 'put forward' a legitimate governmental interest to justify their regulation, and must provide evidence that the interest proferred is the reason why the regulation was adopted or enforced." (citation omitted) (quoting Turner, 482 U.S. at 89)].

45 Sharp v. Johnson, 669 F.3d 144, 156 (3d Cir. 2012), *cert. denied*, 133 S. Ct. 41 (2012).

46 Salahuddin v. Goord, 467 F.3d 263, 275 (2d Cir. 2006).

47 *See* Sharp, 669 F.3d at 156 [interpreting Overton v. Bazzetta, 539 U.S. 126, 132 (2003)]; Jackson v. Pollard, No. 06-3000, 208 Fed. App'x 457, 460 (7th Cir. Nov. 2, 2006) (unpublished); Figel v. Overton, No. 04-1038, 121 Fed. App'x 642, 646 n. 2 (6th Cir. Feb. 4, 2005) (unpublished); Williams v. Morton, 343 F.3d 212, 217 (3d Cir. 2003) ("[T]he burden is not on the state to prove the validity of the challenged prison regulation but instead is on the inmate to disprove it.").

favorable to the government. From the outset, for example, the decisions, policies, and regulations of prison officials, like those of the military, ought to receive a level of deference greater than that of ordinary governmental officials.[48] Part of this deference reflects the unusual environment in which prison officials must operate and their special knowledge of that environment; part of it no doubt also reflects the judiciary's corresponding lack of expertise or experience with such an environment.[49] Thus, among other things, the "evaluation of penological objectives is committed to the considered judgment of prison administrators, 'who are actually charged with and trained in the running of the particular institution under examination.'"[50]

Furthermore, the pool of legitimate penological interests is broad. Obviously within that pool are concerns such as institutional security, the health and safety of inmates and staff, and the traditional interests of rehabilitation and deterrence.[51] In addition, a purely administrative concern such as "simplified food service, ... budget constraints,"[52] or "[p]romoting the efficient allocation of prison resources has been recognized as a legitimate governmental interest."[53] Even if this were not the case, moreover, "[c]orrectional administrators acknowledge that many economic or efficiency institutional concerns can be repackaged as security issues."[54] In a RLUIPA case, for example, one federal district court reasoned that "[f]iscal, staffing, and space considerations are a part of maintaining security and preserving order" and that "[m]aintaining security and preserving order are compelling government interests."[55]

Finally, many of the presumptions and reasonable inferences generally will favor the government rather than the challenger, depending, of course, on the stage of the litigation and the type of motion before the court. Prison policies, like all government actions, enjoy a presumption of constitutionality at the outset, and it is the challenger who carries

[48] *See* O'Lone v. Estate of Shabazz, 482 U.S. 342, 349 (1987); Jackson v. Bush, No. 3:06cv133/MCR/EMT, 2006 WL 2331026, at *6 (N.D. Fla. Aug. 9, 2006) (unpublished) {adopting Magistrate Judge's Report and Recommendation: "Prison administrators should be given great deference in adopting and executing policies and practices. Absent substantial evidence in the record indicating that officials exaggerated their response to considerations of order, discipline, and security, courts ordinarily should defer to their judgment" [citing Bell v. Wolfish, 441 U.S. 520, 547 (1979); McCorkle v. Johnson, 881 F.2d 993 (11th Cir. 1989)]}.

[49] *See* Turner, 482 U.S. at 84–85 ("Running a prison is an inordinately difficult undertaking that requires expertise, planning, and the commitment of resources, all of which are peculiarly within the province of the legislative and executive branches of government. Prison administration is, moreover, a task that has been committed to the responsibility of those branches, and separation of powers concerns counsel a policy of judicial restraint."); McManus v. Bass, No. Civ. A. 2:05CV117, 2006 WL 753017, at *9 (E.D. Va. Mar. 22, 2006) (unpublished) ("In rejecting a strict scrutiny standard, the Supreme Court determined that prison officials, rather than courts, should make difficult judgments necessary to maintain institutional order and discipline and that courts should defer to prison officials' reasonable exercise of discretion since courts do not have the expertise to administer state prisons.").

[50] O'Lone, 482 U.S. at 349 [quoting Bell v. Wolfish, 441 U.S. 520, 562 (1979)].

[51] *See* Pell v. Procunier, 417 U.S. 817, 822–3 (1974) (describing deterrence, rehabilitation, and institutional security as legitimate penological objectives).

[52] Williams v. Morton, 343 F.3d 212, 217 (3d Cir. 2003).

[53] Jewell v. Gonzales, 420 F. Supp. 2d 406, 427 (W.D. Pa. 2006) [citing Williams v. Morton, 343 F.3d 212 (3d Cir. 2003); Breakiron v. Neal, 166 F. Supp. 2d 1110 (N.D. Tex. 2001)]; *accord* Al-Alamin v. Gramley, 926 F.2d 680, 686 (7th Cir. 1991) (explaining that "economic concerns are legitimate penological demands").

[54] *Developments in the Law*, *supra* note 1, at 1894 n. 19.

[55] Orafan v. Goord, 411 F. Supp. 2d 153, 160 (N.D.N.Y. 2006) (RLUIPA case), *vacated on other grounds*, No. 06-2951-PR, 249 Fed. App'x 217 (2d Cir. Sep. 28, 2007) (unpublished).

the ultimate responsibility to show that a policy is invalid. The burden, in other words, "is not on the state to prove the validity of the challenged prison regulation but instead is on the inmate to disprove it."[56] However, even prison policies or actions that might ordinarily be constitutional under *Turner* can fail the reasonableness test if they appear to be applied in an unjustifiably excessive, redundant, or selective manner.[57]

## 2. *The Impact of* Smith *and then RFRA and RLUIPA*

*Turner* and *O'Lone* were both handed down in 1987. Just three years later, the Supreme Court decided *Employment Division v. Smith*,[58] which changed the general landscape for free exercise, limiting the opportunities for strict scrutiny and leaving most challenges to the low-level standard of rationality or rational basis review.[59] *Smith* did not explicitly overrule any cases, however, thus leaving intact the *Turner-O'Lone* standard for prisons, which, though also a low-level form of scrutiny, is nonetheless potentially different from mere rationality review. As the Seventh Circuit has observed, "*O'Lone* ... requires prison authorities to 'accommodate' an inmate's religious preferences if consistent with security and other legitimate penological concerns," but "[a]ccommodation is what *Smith* says the free exercise clause does not require; and it's hard to believe that prisoners have more rights than nonprisoners."[60] Accordingly, "[m]any courts have grappled with the question of how ... *Smith* interacts with ... *Turner* and *O'Lone*."[61] The D.C. Circuit has proposed three possibilities:

> One possibility is that *Smith* supplanted the *Turner* analysis, because *Smith* can be read to say that religious inmates should never be entitled to exemptions from generally applicable, religion-neutral prison regulations. Another possibility is that *Smith* simply has no application in the unique and highly regulated prison context, so *Turner* and *O'Lone* continue to govern. A third possibility is that both *Smith* and *O'Lone/Turner* are applicable, but at different stages of analysis. Under this view, *Smith* is relevant in determining the scope of a person's free exercise right in the first instance, while *Turner* and *O'Lone* are employed in determining how that right may be circumscribed in the specialized prison context. Thus, a prisoner asserting a right to smoke marijuana

56 Williams v. Morton, 343 F.3d 212, 217 (3d Cir. 2003) [citing Overton v. Bazzetta, 539 U.S. 126 (2003)].

57 *See, e.g.*, Boles v. Neet, 486 F.3d 1177, 1182–83 (10th Cir. 2007) (denying qualified immunity to a warden who applied a clothing policy to a religiously objecting inmate and who identified no legitimate penological objective served by the policy's application); Jean-Laurent v. Wilkerson, 438 F. Supp. 2d 318, 326 (S.D.N.Y. 2006) (explaining that strip searches of inmates are generally constitutional insofar as they advance the penologically legitimate interest in security but that a second search, seemingly advancing no legitimate interest, could violate both the Free Exercise Clause and RLUIPA), *aff'd*, No. 09-1929-PR, 461 Fed. App'x 18 (2d Cir. Feb. 8, 2012) (unpublished). As stated decades ago by the Third Circuit, "[T]he federal courts have been sensitive to certain particularized complaints, foremost among which have been allegations of religious discrimination. In such cases, the courts have not hesitated to intervene where prison officials have unreasonably attempted to curtail the practice of religion by prison inmates." Gittlemacker v. Prasse, 428 F.2d 1, 4 (3d Cir. 1970).

58 494 U.S. 872 (1990).

59 *See, generally*, Joseph Thomas Wilson, *Comment, The Big Man in the Big House: Prisoner Free Exercise in Light of Employment Division v. Smith*, 73 La. L. Rev. 219 (2012).

60 Grayson v. Schuler, 666 F.3d 450, 453 (7th Cir. 2012).

61 Levitan v. Ashcroft, 281 F.3d 1313, 1318 (D.C. Cir. 2002). *See, e.g.*, Grayson v. Schuler, 666 F.3d 450, 452–3 (7th Cir. 2012) (noting the uncertainty); Boles v. Neet, 486 F.3d 1177, 1181–2 (10th Cir. 2007) (same).

> for religious purposes in prison would never reach the *Turner* analysis, because he [or she] would lack a First Amendment right under *Smith* to smoke marijuana in the first instance, whether in prison or elsewhere.[62]

As this court further noted, "[m]ost Courts of Appeals have taken the second approach, simply continuing to apply *Turner* and *O'Lone* in analyzing prisoners' constitutional rights."[63] Nevertheless, it remains an "open question"[64] whether and to what extent one's constitutional free exercise right in prison differs, at least in theory, from its civilian counterpart. Irrespective of how this question is resolved, it is potentially overshadowed by the enactment of RFRA and RLUIPA, which impose a different and higher standard in federal and state prisoner challenges, respectively.

Of course, strict scrutiny in the prison context pursuant to these statutes, though higher than the constitutional standard, is not necessarily as rigorous as the traditional conception of strict scrutiny. With regard to RLUIPA's strict scrutiny standard, for example, the Supreme Court has clearly indicated that courts should exercise a more traditional level of deference toward the decisions of prison administrators:

> [The Court has] no cause to believe that RLUIPA would not be applied in an appropriately balanced way, with particular sensitivity to security concerns. While the Act adopts a "compelling governmental interest" standard, context matters in the application of that standard. Lawmakers supporting RLUIPA were mindful of the urgency of discipline, order, safety, and security in penal institutions. They anticipated that courts would apply the Act's standard with due deference to the experience and expertise of prison and jail administrators in establishing necessary regulations and procedures to maintain good order, security and discipline, consistent with consideration of costs and limited resources.[65]

Thus, while the government is still required to demonstrate that a challenged policy is the least restrictive means of achieving a compelling interest (assuming that the inmate has triggered that standard), courts are more likely, when compared with the nonprison setting, to credit the government's fact-based assessment of whether its interests actually can be served as well by alternative means. The same, presumably, is true with regard to RFRA, which can apply to the federal prison context.[66]

Finally, it should be noted that RLUIPA and RFRA claimants may, because of the nature and text of those statutes, face limitations not faced by claimants under the Free Exercise Clause. Under RLUIPA, for example, the Supreme Court has held that RLUIPA's spending-power-based provision does not waive state sovereign immunity such that monetary damages cannot be recovered by prisoners in suits against states or state agents named in their official capacities.[67] Likewise, some lower courts have held that

62 Levitan, 281 F.3d at 1318–19.

63 *Id.* at 1319 [citing Kikumura v. Hurley, 242 F.3d 950, 956–58 (10th Cir. 2001); Flagner v. Wilkinson, 241 F.3d 475, 481–7 (6th Cir. 2001); Green v. Polunsky, 229 F.3d 486, 489–91 (5th Cir. 2000); DeHart v. Horn, 227 F.3d 47, 51–60 (3d Cir. 2000) (*en banc*); Hakim v. Hicks, 223 F.3d 1244, 1247–9 & n. 3 (11th Cir. 2000); Ward v. Walsh, 1 F.3d 873, 876–7 (9th Cir. 1993); Salaam v. Lockhart, 905 F.2d 1168, 1171 n. 7 (8th Cir. 1990)].

64 Lewis v. Sternes, 712 F.3d 1083, 1085 (7th Cir. 2013).

65 Cutter v. Wilkinson, 544 U.S. 709, 722–3 (2005).

66 *See* Hoevenaar v. Lazaroff, 422 F.3d 366, 370–71 (6th Cir. 2005) (indicating that the same level of deference should obtain under RFRA), *cert. denied*, 549 U.S. 875 (2006).

67 *See* Sossamon v. Texas, 131 S. Ct. 1651, 1658–61 (2011).

RFRA does not waive the federal government's sovereign immunity and thus disallows monetary relief against the federal government or its agents in official-capacity suits.[68] At the same time, several lower courts also have held that RLUIPA does not permit suits against state prison officials in their individual capacities, thereby foreclosing a potential alternative avenue of monetary relief.[69]

### 3. *The Guarantee of Equal Protection*

Of particular concern to prison officials, administratively, can be the presence of inmate populations exhibiting numerous and wide-ranging religious beliefs and practices. With the growth of the nation's religious diversity, "a number of nontraditional faith groups ... have surfaced in correctional facilities. These include variations of the four traditional groups [Catholic, Protestant, Muslim, and Jewish], in addition to Hindus, Mormons, Native Americans, Buddhists, Rastafarians, Hispanic religions (Curanderismo, Santería, Espiritismo), Jehovah's Witnesses, and Christian Scientists. Two of the newest faith groups ... are Wicca and Satanism."[70] In general, as the religious diversity of a prison's population increases, so will the number and variety of accommodation requests, thereby giving rise to security, logistical, fiscal, and other issues. As the Seventh Circuit has remarked, the "issue of religious discrimination in prison poses one of the knottiest problems in First Amendment jurisprudence, since prison officials face significant challenges in maintaining security and safety, as well as substantial constraints on budget and staffing, and balancing these concerns with a wide range of religious practices can be daunting."[71] At the same time, it may be increasingly difficult for prison staff to assess whether or not a particular practice is religious and whether or not a claimant's beliefs are sincerely held.

Potentially complicating the task of prison officials in this regard is the constitutional mandate, apart from the First Amendment, of equal protection, which arises from the Fifth and Fourteenth Amendments.[72] In particular, when restricting or accommodating religious practices, the government must "'treat similarly situated people alike,' a protection that applies to prison inmates."[73] Courts have allayed some of the administrative concern over having to accommodate the entire spectrum of

[68] *See, e.g.*, Webman v. Fed. Bureau of Prisons, 441 F.3d 1022 (D.C. Cir. 2006); *see id.* at 1026 n. 2 (listing several federal district court cases so concluding).

[69] *See, e.g.*, Washington v. Gonyea, 731 F.3d 143, 145–6 (2d Cir. 2013) (holding that RLUIPA does not create a cause of action to sue prison officials in their individual capacity; citing other circuit courts so holding); Sharp v. Johnson, 669 F.3d 144, 154–5 (3d Cir. 2012) ("RLUIPA does not permit an action against [state prison officials] in their individual capacities. [The state] ... not [the officials] ... was the direct recipient of any federal funds. Thus, RLUIPA cannot impose direct liability on ... [the officials], who were not parties to the contract created between ... [the state] and the federal government."), *cert. denied*, 133 S. Ct. 41 (2012).

[70] Dammer, *supra* note 1, at 837–8.

[71] Easterling v. Pollard, No. 12-1532, 528 Fed. App'x 653, 657 (7th Cir. Jul. 22, 2013) (unpublished).

[72] This mandate is found in the text of the Fourteenth Amendment; *see* U.S. Const. amend. XIV, § 1, which binds state and local governments, and it has been read into the Due Process Clause of the Fifth Amendment, which binds the federal government. *See* Adarand Constructors, Inc. v. Pena, 515 U.S. 200, 215 (1995); Bolling v. Sharpe, 347 U.S. 497, 500 (1954).

[73] Murphy v. Mo. Dep't of Corr., 372 F.3d 979, 984 (8th Cir. 2004) (citation omitted) [quoting Rouse v. Benson, 193 F.3d 936, 942 (8th Cir. 1999)], *cert. denied*, 543 U.S. 991 (2004).

religious practices by refusing to adopt a standard of exact equality among religions regardless of cost.[74] "[N]ot 'every religious sect or group within a prison – however few in numbers – must have identical facilities or personnel.'"[75] Rather, "the treatment of all inmates must be qualitatively comparable."[76] Furthermore, the courts' refusal to require full accommodation of every inmate's individual religious practices has led to an emphasis not on "whether the inmates have been denied specific religious accommodations, but [on] whether, more broadly, the prison affords the inmates opportunities to exercise their faith."[77] Some courts have also held that an inmate's "situation must be considered in comparison with inmates confined in the [same] correctional system" and "that it is insufficient to merely argue that a prisoner is being treated differently by comparing his [or her] situation with prisoners located in another state."[78] In addition, regarding the issue of whether a prison policy's differential treatment of inmates or their practices is rationally or reasonably related to legitimate penological interests, courts will "giv[e] due deference to the expertise of prison officials."[79] Practically speaking, then, the assessment of a religion-related equal protection claim may be not much different from or more demanding than a free exercise claim (assuming no heightened scrutiny), and several courts have held that the *Turner* test governs both types of claims.[80]

In order even to arrive at that test, however, the inmate must make certain showings. If the inmate is alleging specifically that the prison's differential treatment is directly affecting his or her religious practices, then the prisoner must show "[1] that he [or she] is treated differently than a similarly situated class of inmates, [2] that the different treatment burdens [his or her free exercise of religion] … and [3] that the different treatment

[74] *See* Hartmann v. Cal. Dep't of Corr. & Rehab., 707 F.3d 1114, 1123 (9th Cir. 2013) ["The Equal Protection Clause requires the State to treat all similarly situated people equally. This does not mean, however, that all prisoners must receive identical treatment and resources." (citation omitted)]; Thompson v. Commonwealth of Ky., 712 F.2d 1078, 1081 (6th Cir. 1983) (rejecting the notion "that either the prisons or the courts must engage in … strict numerical analysis … or create a system of ratios or quotas in order to comply with the dictates of the Equal Protection Clause").

[75] Sossamon v. Lone Star State of Tex., 560 F.3d 316, 336 (5th Cir. 2009) [quoting Adkins v. Kaspar, 393 F.3d 559, 566 (5th Cir. 2004)], *aff'd*, 131 S. Ct. 1651 (2011).

[76] Al-Alamin v. Gramley, 926 F.2d 680, 686 (7th Cir. 1991).

[77] Freeman v. Tex. Dep't of Crim. Justice, 369 F.3d 854, 861 (5th Cir. 2004) (citations omitted).

[78] Smith v. Thompson, Civ. A. No. 3:09-48-DCR, 2010 WL 2923197, at *10 (E.D. Ky. Jul. 23, 2010) (unpublished) [citing Stewart v. McManus, 924 F.2d 138 (8th Cir. 1991); Daniels v. Thompson, Civ. A. No. 3:09-11-DCR, 2009 WL 960192 (E.D. Ky. Apr. 7, 2009) (unpublished); Tucker v. Angelone, 954 F. Supp. 134, 136 (E.D. Va. 1997)].

[79] Murphy, 372 F.3d at 985.

[80] *See* Sossamon, 560 F.3d at 336; DeHart v. Horn, 227 F.3d 47, 61 (3d Cir. 2000) (*en banc*) ("*Turner* is equally applicable [to an inmate's equal protection claim], and the appropriate analysis for this claim is the same as that for [his] Free Exercise claim."); McGlothlin v. Murray, 993 F. Supp. 389, 406–7 (W.D. Va. 1997), *aff'd*, Nos. 97-6449 & 97-6634, 151 F.3d 1029 (4th Cir. Jul. 1, 1998) (unpublished), *cert. denied*, 526 U.S. 1022 (1999); *cf.* Reed v. Faulkner, 842 F.2d 960, 962 (7th Cir. 1988) ["[*Turner*] is not a demanding standard, and it implies that if either … [the claimant] is not … sincere … or the regulation limiting the length of male inmates' hair strikes a reasonable balance between the interest in religious liberty and the needs of prison safety and security, he must lose on his free-exercise claim. And if the exception for American Indians is nonarbitrary he must lose on his equal protection claim as well … because the religious dimension of the discrimination is governed by the religion clauses of the First Amendment, leaving for the equal protection clause only a claim of arbitrariness unrelated to the character of the activity allegedly discriminated against." (citations omitted)].

bears no rational relation to any legitimate penal interest."[81] A failure to establish any of these three elements will doom the prisoner's claim. Alternatively, if the inmate is alleging simply that the prison is differentially treating different religions, then the prisoner must show that there is intentional or purposeful discrimination either between or among religions or on the basis of religious beliefs or affiliation. A more complete analysis of religion-related equal protection claims is found in Chapter 6.[82]

### 4. *Exhaustion, Consolidation, and Pleading Requirements*

The federal government and many states have statutory provisions restricting the ability of prisoners to bring suits challenging aspects of their incarceration, including alleged violations of religious free exercise.[83] In addition, there are several jurisdictional or common-law doctrines that preclude the institution of lawsuits where a claimant has not yet run the gauntlet of administrative processes, including, in the case of prisoners, those mandated by the correctional institution.[84] Lastly, prisoners must abide by established rules of pleading, though, as will be discussed, courts have some discretion to reform defects in pleading, particularly in a *pro se* civil rights lawsuit, which is a litigation genre characteristic of religious freedom claims brought by prisoners.

At the federal level, Congress has enacted the Prison Litigation Reform Act (PLRA),[85] which provides that "[n]o action shall be brought with respect to prison conditions under [42 U.S.C. §] 1983 ... or any other Federal law, by a prisoner confined in any jail, prison, or other correctional facility until such administrative remedies as are available are exhausted."[86] As summarized by one federal district court, the PLRA's "exhaustion requirement ... is mandatory and 'applies to all prisoners seeking redress for prison circumstances or occurrences.' [It] ... 'afford[s] corrections officials time and opportunity to address complaints internally before allowing the initiation of a federal case' and, where possible, to 'satisfy the inmate, thereby obviating the need for litigation.'"[87] Importantly, this exhaustion requirement applies to religious freedom claims whether they arise from federal constitutional or statutory law.[88] Thus it makes no difference whether the claimant is alleging a violation of the First Amendment, RFRA, or RLUIPA,[89] the last of which

81 *Id.*; *see also* Adkins v. Kaspar, 393 F.3d 559, 566 (5th Cir. 2004) {"To succeed on his Equal Protection claim, [the prisoner] ... 'must prove purposeful discrimination resulting in a discriminatory effect among persons similarly situated.'" [quoting Muhammad v. Lynaugh, 966 F.2d 901, 903 (5th Cir. 1992)]}.

82 For additional treatment of religious discrimination under the Equal Protection Clause, *see* John W. Palmer, Constitutional Rights of Prisoners § 7.3 (9th ed., 2010).

83 *See, e.g.*, 42 U.S.C. § 1997e(a); 10 Del. Code Ann. § 8804; La. Rev. Stat. § 15:1184; Mass. Gen. Laws Ann. 127 § 38F; Mich. Comp. Laws Ann. § 600.5503. Wis. Stat. Ann. § 893.735.

84 *See* Cutter v. Wilkinson, 544 U.S. 709, 723 n. 12 (2005).

85 Pub. L. No. 104–134, 110 Stat. 1321 (Apr. 26, 1996) (codified in scattered sections of 18, 28 & 42 U.S.C.).

86 42 U.S.C. § 1997e(a).

87 Sample v. Lappin, 424 F. Supp. 2d 187, 190–1 (D.D.C. 2006) (citation omitted) [quoting Porter v. Nussle, 534 U.S. 516, 520, 524–5 (2002)]. For a discussion of the exhaustion requirement, including its background and underlying principles, *see* Woodford v. Ngo, 548 U.S. 81, 84–93 (2006).

88 *See* Franklin v. Rees, No. Civ. A. 405CVP67M, 2005 WL 1653609 (W.D. Ky. July 1, 2005) (unpublished).

89 *See, e.g.*, Brunskill v. Boyd, No. 04-15152, 141 Fed. App'x. 771, 2005 WL 1208632, at *5 (11th Cir. May 10, 2005) (unpublished) (dismissing Equal Protection Clause claim of religious discrimination for failure to exhaust administrative remedies under the PLRA); Jackson v. Dist. of Columbia, 254 F.3d 262, 266–7 (D.C. Cir. 2001) (PLRA applies to RFRA claims); *see also* Woodford v. Ngo 548 U.S. 81 (2006) (holding that prisoners who have allowed their opportunity to file internal prison grievances to lapse and who no

specifically declares that "nothing in … [it] shall be construed to amend or repeal the Prison Litigation Reform Act."[90] In addition, "[a] litigant's failure to raise issues during an administrative appeal can constitute a failure to exhaust administrative remedies."[91] However, a prisoner who exhausts administrative processes for one religious freedom claim may not need to exhaust administrative processes for a subsequently added religious freedom claim that basically alleges a violation based on the same facts.[92]

Similar restrictions exist at the state level as well. Maryland, for example, prohibits a prisoner from "maintain[ing] a civil action until the prisoner has fully exhausted all administrative remedies for resolving the complaint or grievance."[93] In Texas, likewise, prisoners are required to "exhaust their administrative remedies … [to] further the legitimate, even compelling, state interest in protecting scarce judicial resources from the continued onslaught of prisoners who abuse the judicial system by filing frivolous civil lawsuits."[94] Furthermore, the federal courts require that prisoners in state facilities must first exhaust state prisons' grievance processes to satisfy the PLRA exhaustion requirement.[95]

While the rules concerning exhaustion are generally unfavorable for prison claimants, the same cannot be said of pleading requirements, which in most jurisdictions (including the federal courts) are designed to facilitate the full development and exposition of a plaintiff's claims.[96] This is particularly evident in the context of *pro se* litigation, which is often the nature of inmate suits. Although " '[d]istrict judges have no obligation to act as counsel or paralegal to *pro se* litigants,' "[97] nevertheless, they have broad discretion to construe *pro se* complaints liberally.[98] In general, "[c]ourts are reluctant to dismiss the claim of a prisoner proceeding *pro se* solely on procedural grounds, and usually allow

longer have any remedies available have not properly exhausted their administrative remedies and, thus, may not take their claims to federal court).

90 42 U.S.C. § 2000cc-2(e).

91 Kikumura v. Hurley, 242 F.3d 950, 956 (10th Cir. 2001).

92 *See* DeHart v. Horn, 390 F.3d 262, 275 (3d Cir. 2004) (holding that claimant "is not required to re-exhaust his RLUIPA claim" when added to replace the originally filed and basically identical RFRA claim). But the subsequent RLUIPA claim actually must be pled, and a court need not construe a previously pled RFRA claim as a RLUIPA claim. *See* Wyatt v. Terhune, 315 F.3d 1108, 1115–16 (9th Cir. 2003) ["Although we construe a *pro se* prisoner's pleadings liberally, we decline to construe [the prisoner's] RFRA claim as a RLUIPA claim or to consider the merits of [the prisoner's] RLUIPA claim for the first time on appeal." (citation omitted)], *cert. denied*, 540 U.S. 810 (2003).

93 Md. Code Ann., Cts. & Jud. Proc. § 5-1003(a)(1); *see* Evans v. Maryland, 396 Md. 256, 914 A.2d 25, 29 (Md. 2006) ["In 1997, the [Maryland] General Assembly enacted the Prisoner Litigation Act (PLA) in order to complement the Federal Prison Litigation Reform Act (42 U.S.C. § 1997e), enacted by Congress a year earlier."].

94 Sanders v. Palunsky, 36 S.W.3d 222, 226 (Tex. Ct. App. 2001).

95 *See* Webb v. Baker, No. 1:05-CV-1300, 2006 WL 1876964, at *1 (S.D. Ind. Jul. 5, 2006) (unpublished) {"The pleadings and the evidentiary record show that plaintiff Webb failed to properly utilize the administrative remedy process available to him at Wabash Valley with respect to the claim that his Quaran was confiscated and destroyed. No grievance filed by Webb alerted prison authorities to the presence of a claim of the exercise of religious freedom." [citing Woodford v. Ngo, 548 U.S. 81, 90–1 (2006); Riccardo v. Rausch, 375 F.3d 521, 524 (7th Cir. 2004), *cert. denied*, 544 U.S. 904 (2005)]}.

96 Regarding the history and interpretation of Fed. R. Civ. P. 8, which largely governs pleading in the federal district courts, *see* Christopher M. Fairman, *The Myth of Notice Pleading*, 45 ARIZ. L. REV. 987, 990–6 (2003).

97 Myles v. United States, 416 F.3d 551, 552 (7th Cir. 2005) [quoting Pliler v. Ford, 542 U.S. 225 (2004)].

98 *Id.* [citing Haines v. Kerner, 404 U.S. 519 (1972)].

prisoners to correct deficiencies by amendment."[99] A norm of liberal construction is considered important "particularly where civil rights claims are involved,"[100] and this includes claims for religious freedom.

Pursuant to the PLRA, however, even when the prisoner is proceeding *pro se*, courts will dismiss a complaint if it is "frivolous [or] malicious, … fails to state a claim upon which relief may be granted" or "seeks monetary relief from a defendant who is immune from such relief."[101] In addition, some courts effectively require that a prisoner's religious freedom claim be pled under both the First Amendment and RFRA or RLIUPA (assuming that the prisoner seeks the benefit of both) by treating claims pled under one of these as a cause of action separate from the other.[102] Thus a claim asserting only the Free Exercise Clause need not and may not be construed as also encompassing a RFRA or RLUIPA claim.[103] That being said, a court likely has the discretionary authority to take cognizance of such a claim and, within the bounds of due process, may do so based on equitable considerations.[104] As noted earlier, moreover, courts generally favor allowing prisoners and other *pro se* litigants to amend their original complaints, which could include adding an omitted a constitutional or statutory religious freedom claim as long as the applicable rules of civil procedure permit such amendment.[105]

Because a court's authority to construe a prisoner's religious freedom claim is discretionary, a claim that is not pled with sufficiency effectively may be waived, whether it

[99] *Procedural Means of Enforcement under 42 U.S.C. § 1983*, 42 Geo. L.J. Ann. Rev. Crim. Proc. 1095, 1113–15 (2013) (footnote omitted).

[100] Balistreri v. Pacifica Police Dep't, 901 F.2d 696, 699 (9th Cir. 1990).

[101] 28 U.S.C. § 1915A(b).

[102] *See* Marria v. Broaddus, 200 F. Supp. 2d 280 (S.D.N.Y. 2002) (analyzing plaintiff's religious freedom claims separately under both First Amendment principles and the provisions of RLUIPA); *see also* Murphy v. Mo. Dep't of Corr., 372 F.3d 979 (8th Cir. 2004) (addressing prisoner's constitutional Free Exercise Clause claim separately from his statutory claim under RLUIPA), *cert. denied*, 543 U.S. 991 (2004).

[103] *See, e.g.*, Jones v. Goord, 435 F. Supp. 2d 221, 260 (S.D.N.Y. 2006) ("RLUIPA is an independent cause of action, not a directive to courts instructing how [*sic*] evaluate claims brought under the First Amendment. Under RLUIPA, an inmate 'may assert a … claim … in a judicial proceeding and obtain appropriate relief against a government' [42 U.S.C. § 2000cc-2(a)]. Nothing in the text of the statute requires a federal court to apply RLUIPA in all cases where it could be applied. Rather, the statute says that the claim may be 'assert[ed],' implying that some affirmative action is required by the party relying on the statute.").

[104] *See, e.g.*, Dingle v. Zon, No. 02-0058, 189 Fed. App'x 8, 10 (2d Cir. 2006) (unpublished) ("Because the complaint could support a claim under RLUIPA – despite that the face of the complaint alleges only specific, constitutional violations – the district court has an obligation to consider the claim."); Moore v. Cross, No. 05-2875, 2007 WL 835417, at *12 (D. Minn. Mar. 15, 2007) (unpublished) (reading *pro se* prisoner plaintiff's RLUIPA claim as a RFRA claim because prisoner was in federal, not state, prison); Fayson v. Earle, No. Civ. 04-219-KAJ, 2006 WL 3220062, at *3 n. 5 (D. Del. Nov. 7, 2006) (unpublished) ("[The prisoner] does not specifically raise RLUIPA … [but] [b]ecause her [First] Amended Complaint is to be liberally construed, I will consider it as raising a RLUIPA claim."); Clark v. Briley, No. 03 C 3852, 2005 WL 2369330, at * 3 (N.D. Ill. Sept. 26, 2005) (unpublished) ("Although Clark did not raise the issue of RLUIPA in his complaint, we are mindful of the fact that he is a *pro se* litigant and interpret his complaint liberally to include such a claim.").

[105] *See, e.g.*, Nelson v. Miller, Civ. No. 03-254-JPG, 2006 WL 1891855, at *1 (S.D. Ill. July 10, 2005) (unpublished) (under Fed. R. Civ. P. 15, allowing addition of an Establishment Clause claim that was "premised upon allegations contained in the original complaint" but disallowing addition of a Free Exercise Clause claim involving "entirely new allegations which did not even arise until two years after the issues at the heart of the original complaint").

arises under the First Amendment,[106] RLUIPA,[107] or RFRA.[108] Furthermore, a prisoner's claim may be deemed abandoned or waived if not adequately argued at the trial level or sufficiently developed on appeal,[109] although, once again, it remains in a court's discretion nevertheless to consider a waived or abandoned claim.[110]

Lastly, it should be noted that a prisoner's claim concerning an alleged violation of his or her constitutional rights, including the free exercise of religion, requires that prison officials be more than negligent,[111] consistent with the more general liability rules for alleged constitutional violations under 42 U.S.C. § 1983.[112] This bar on negligence suits has been extended to suits under RLUIPA because allowing prisoners to proceed with negligence suits "under RLUIPA would undermine [the] deference [due to prison administrators] by exposing prison officials to an unduly high level of judicial scrutiny."[113] In short, prisoners' religious freedom claims, if premised on nothing more than governmental negligence, will rarely, if ever, succeed.[114]

### 5. *The Civil Rights of Institutionalized Persons Act*

Suits by prisoners are not the only means to vindicate alleged violations of their religious freedom. The Civil Rights of Institutionalized Persons Act (CRIPA),[115] for example,

106 *See, e.g.*, Jenner v. McDaniel, No. 03–1422, 123 Fed. App'x 900, 903 (10th Cir. 2005) (unpublished) (prisoner's failure to object before the district court concerning the magistrate judge's determination that the First Amendment's Establishment Clause was not implicated waived the claim).

107 *See, e.g.*, Jones v. Goord, 435 F. Supp. 2d 221, 262 (S.D.N.Y. 2006) {"A RLUIPA claim, like any other claim, can be waived if it is not brought in a timely fashion." [citing Fifth Ave. Presbyterian Church v. City of N.Y., 293 F.3d 570, 576 (2d Cir. 2002)]}.

108 *See, e.g., In re* Watson, 403 F.3d 1, 7 (1st Cir. 2005); Bethesda Lutheran Homes & Servs., Inc. v. Leean, 122 F.3d 443, 449 (7th Cir. 1997); United States v. Amer, 110 F.3d 873, 879 n. 1 (2d Cir. 1997); Cochran v. Morris, 73 F.3d 1310, 1317 n. 3 (4th Cir. 1996).

109 *See* Kerr v. Farrey, 95 F.3d 472, 481 (7th Cir. 1996) (holding that the appellant waived his free exercise and RFRA claims because he "failed to develop" his religious liberty argument on appeal); Long v. Bd. of Educ. of Jefferson Cnty., Ky., 121 F. Supp. 2d 621, 628 (W.D. Ky. 2000) (concluding that the plaintiff's free exercise claim "appear[s] to have been abandoned since [it was] omitted from Plaintiffs' Response to Defendant's Motion for Summary Judgment and w[as] not presented during a conference in chambers"), *aff'd*, No. 00-6710, 21 Fed. App'x 252 (6th Cir. 2001) (unpublished); Burton v. State, 194 S.W.3d 686 (Tex. Ct. App. 2006) (holding that a defendant waived an as-applied free exercise challenge by not asserting it before the trial court).

110 *See* Fisher v. Texas, 169 F.3d 295, 304–5 (5th Cir. 1999) (reasoning that it was within the court's discretion to consider an issue that was implicitly waived by the state before the district court).

111 *See* Gallagher v. Shelton, 587 F.3d 1063, 1070 (10th Cir. 2009) ("[A]n isolated act of negligence would not violate an inmate's First Amendment right to free exercise of religion."); Lovelace v. Lee, 472 F.3d 174, 201 (4th Cir. 2006) ("[N]egligent acts by officials causing unintended denials of religious rights do not violate the Free Exercise Clause. [An inmate] … must assert conscious or intentional interference with his [or her] free exercise rights to state a valid claim under [42 U.S.C.] § 1983."); Railford v. Wallens Ridge State Prison, No. CIVA 7:06CV00421, 2006 WL 2350162, at *1 (W.D. Va. Aug. 11, 2006) (unpublished); Shaheed v. Winston, 885 F. Supp. 861, 868 (E.D. Va. 1995).

112 *See* Wilson v. Cross, 845 F.2d 163, 165 (8th Cir. 1988) ("[T]he constitutional tortfeasor must have acted intentionally because negligence is not actionable under § 1983." [citing Daniels v. Williams, 474 U.S. 327, 328 (1986)].

113 Lovelace, 472 F.3d at 194.

114 In addition, the PLRA may limit the ability of prisoners to recover damages for free exercise violations. *See* Searles v. Van Bebber, 251 F.3d 869, 876 (10th Cir. 2001), *cert. denied*, 536 U.S. 904 (2002); Hughes v. Heimgartner, No. 12-3250-SAC, 2013 WL 760600, at *3 (D. Kan. Feb. 27, 2013) (unpublished).

115 Pub. L. No. 96–247, 94 Stat. 349, 349 (1980) (codified as amended at 42 U.S.C. §§ 1997a-1997j).

gives the U.S. Attorney General the ability to bring claims against states for perceived abuses of constitutional rights.[116] Under 42 U.S.C. § 1997a, the Attorney General may initiate an action against any state (or agent of a state) if there is a reasonable belief that the state's actions have caused institutionalized persons to "suffer grevious harm, and that such deprivation is pursuant to a pattern or practice of resistance to the full enjoyment of ... [constitutional rights]."[117] In these circumstances, the Attorney General is entitled to sue or to intervene on behalf of the United States in an existing suit for the minimum equitable relief necessary to stop the deprivation of rights.[118] Consistent with other laws governing civil rights litigation,[119] a prevailing party may receive attorney's fees at the discretion of the court.[120]

In the decades since its passage, CRIPA has been expressly tied by reference into much of the more recent legislation thus far discussed. For example, RLUIPA's directive that "[n]o government shall impose a substantial burden on the religious exercise of a person residing in or confined to an institution" is explicitly controlled by the definition of "institution" in Section 1997,[121] which includes facilities that house the "mentally ill, disabled, or retarded, or chronically ill or handicapped" and "juveniles" and also includes pretrial detention facilities and correctional facilities.[122] As such, the rules for claims by prisoners under RLUIPA should apply identically to claims under RLUIPA made by residents of state-run long-term care facilities, group homes, mental institutions, and rehabilitation centers.[123]

## B. Prisons: Claims by Inmates

When an inmate alleges that his or her right to the free exercise of religion has been violated by a prison regulation, the inmate, besides needing to prove that the regulation is not reasonably related to legitimate penological interests,[124] "must [first] establish that his or her beliefs are (1) sincere and (2) religious in nature."[125] The elements of sincerity and religiousness are principally covered in Chapters 5 and 7, but some illustrations and observations may be helpful at this juncture. With regard to the element of sincerity, for example, a suit in which an inmate claimed that he was deprived access to Tarot cards was dismissed on summary judgment because he "neither alleged nor submitted any proof that he sincerely holds to any religious belief that mandates the

116 *See* 42 U.S.C. § 1997a(a).

117 *Id.*; *see also* United States v. Erie Cnty., N.Y., 724 F. Supp. 2d 357 (W.D.N.Y. 2010) (holding that CRIPA is a valid exercise of congressional power and that the statute is constitutional in its application by the U.S. Department of Justice).

118 42 U.S.C. § 1997a(a); *see also id.* § 1997c.

119 *See, e.g., id.* § 1988.

120 *See id.* § 1997a(b); *see also id.* § 1997(d)(1)(A) (stating that the PLRA's general limitation on receiving attorney's fees does not apply where "the fee was directly and reasonably incurred in proving an actual violation of the plaintiff's rights").

121 *Id.* § 2000cc-1(a).

122 *Id.* § 1997.

123 *See, e.g.*, DeSimone v. Bartow, No. 09-2541, 355 Fed. App'x 44, 46 (7th Cir. Dec. 8, 2009) (unpublished) (addressing a RLUIPA claim by an individual civilly committed in a state mental health facility).

124 *See supra* Section A.1.

125 *Substantive Rights Retained by Prisoners*, 42 Geo. L.J. Ann Rev. Crim. Proc. 1045, 1058 (2013) (footnote omitted).

use of Tarot cards."[126] Deciding if an inmate's beliefs are sincerely held, however, does not require, and indeed may not allow, an inquiry into "whether, as an objective matter, the belief is 'accurate or logical.'"[127] Thus, in another case, a Jewish rabbi's view than an inmate who claimed to be Jewish was "not 'in fact Jewish' according to the 'practice of the Jewish religion'" was not determinative of whether the inmate's alleged Jewish beliefs were sincerely held.[128] In particular, determining whether the inmate's beliefs were sincerely held did not depend on "whether he ... [was] in fact a Jew under Judaic law."[129]

Sincerity alone is not enough, however, and a prisoner who sincerely holds beliefs that are not ultimately deemed religious will have no claim under the Free Exercise Clause.[130] "First Amendment protection only attaches to beliefs rooted in religion, as opposed to purely secular beliefs or personal preferences."[131] Ordinarily, the threshold for religiousness is not especially high,[132] and "'religious beliefs need not be acceptable, logical, consistent, or comprehensible to others in order to merit First Amendment protection.'"[133] Some courts, in order to structure their assessment of whether or not a belief system constitutes a religion, employ various objective criteria. For example, a court might ask whether a claimant's belief system "addresses fundamental and ultimate questions having to do with deep and imponderable matters," "is comprehensive in nature" and "consists of a belief-system as opposed to an isolated teaching," and exhibits "certain formal and external signs."[134] When invoking such criteria, however, a court generally should not use them as "a rigid 'test' for defining a religion."[135]

If an inmate succeeds in demonstrating that his or her beliefs are sincerely held and religious in nature, and also that a practice stemming from those beliefs has been sufficiently burdened by the government, then the next analytical step depends on the legal

126 Farid v. Smith, 850 F.2d 917, 926 (2d Cir. 1988). As this case suggests, the sincerely held belief must relate directly to the practice on which the requested accommodation is based. Too attenuated a relationship between one's asserted beliefs and one's desired practice may be treated as a lack of sincerity, as in *Farid*, or a failure to prove a cognizable burden on one's religion. *See* Spies v. Voinovich, 173 F.3d 398, 406–7 (6th Cir. 1999) (reasoning that a plaintiff whose religion mandated that he observe a vegetarian diet, which the prison provided him, did not have a constitutional right to a vegan diet, which his religion did not mandate but which, the court surmised, he preferred).

127 Jackson v. Mann, 196 F.3d 316, 320 (2d Cir. 1999); *see also* Ford v. McGinnis, 352 F.3d 582, 591 (2d Cir. 2003) (reasoning that "any perceived lack of objective validity to Ford's belief" did not matter in determining whether his belief was sincerely held).

128 Jackson, 196 F.3d at 320.

129 *Id.* at 321.

130 *See, e.g.*, Jolly v. Coughlin, 76 F.3d 468, 476 (2d Cir. 1996) (noting that, in addition to determining whether the inmate's belief is subjectively sincere, a court needs to determine whether "the belief is religious in nature"); Africa v. Commonwealth of Pa., 662 F.2d 1025, 1032–6 (3d Cir. 1981) (determining that the organization to which an inmate belonged, and on the basis of which he requested a special diet, was not a religion under the Free Exercise Clause), *cert. denied*, 456 U.S. 908 (1982); *see also Ford*, 352 F.3d at 590 (quoting *Jolly*).

131 Love v. Reed, 216 F.3d 682, 687 (8th Cir. 2000) [citing Thomas v. Review Bd. of the Ind. Employment Sec. Div., 450 U.S. 707, 713 (1981); Ochs v. Thalacker, 90 F.3d 293, 296 (8th Cir. 1996)].

132 *See* United States v. Meyers, 906 F. Supp. 1494, 1501 (D. Wyo. 1995) (RFRA case), *aff'd*, 95 F.3d 1475 (10th Cir. 1996), *cert. denied*, 522 U.S. 1006 (1997).

133 Thomas, 450 U.S. at 714.

134 Love, 216 F.3d at 687 {quoting *Africa v. Pennsylvania* [662 F.2d 1025, 1032 (3d Cir. 1981)] and explaining that the Third Circuit has used "three 'useful indicia'" in defining a religion).

135 *Id.* (quoting Africa, 662 F.2d at 1032 n. 13).

source of the prisoner's claim. If it is the Free Exercise Clause, then the analysis will be conducted under *Turner* and *O'Lone*, or perhaps *Smith*, or both standards.[136] If it is RFRA or RLUIPA, then the evidentiary burden will shift to the government, which must demonstrate that its regulation or policy, as applied to the prisoner, is the least restrictive means of achieving a compelling interest, though courts, as noted, will apply that otherwise rigorous test with appropriate deference to the decisions of prison administrators.[137] With these basic elements and analytical standards in mind, the focus over the following subsections is on particular categories of prisoner claims.

### 1. *Grooming*

Several religious belief systems mandate or prohibit particular hairstyles or other modes of grooming. Rastafarians, for instance, subscribe to the Nazirite Vow, derived from *Numbers* 6:1–21 of the *Old Testament*, which they believe prohibits the cutting of hair.[138] Also, many Muslims maintain long or facial hair, such as beards or mustaches, as part of their observance of Islam.[139] Likewise, certain Native American customs regarding long hair have strong religious dimensions.[140] For some Native Americans, "[h]air is only supposed to be cut as a sign of grieving for the recently dead, and shorn locks are often placed with the deceased so that they may be carried into the afterlife."[141]

As one might expect, however, correctional institutions often have rules regulating the length of prisoners' hair or restricting the presence of facial hair.[142] Typically, these rules are defended for reasons of safety and hygiene.[143] One oft-cited safety or security

136 *See supra* Section A.2.

137 *See id.*

138 *See* Reed v. Faulkner, 842 F.2d 960, 962 (7th Cir. 1988) [explaining that within Rastafarianism, "men should not shave, cut, or comb their hair (hence the 'dreadlocks,' which apparently are the natural result of letting one's hair grow wild)"]. For additional reading, *see* Reed v. Faulkner, 653 F. Supp. 965, 973–4 app. A (N.D. Ind. 1987); Derek O'Brien & Vaughan Carter, *Chant Down Babylon: Freedom of Religion and the Rastafarian Challenge to Majoritarianism*, 18 J.L. & Religion 219 (2002); Timothy B. Taylor, *Redemption Song: An Update on the Rastafarians and the Free Exercise Clause*, 9 Whittier L. Rev. 663 (1988); Melissa R. Johnson, *Positive Vibration: An Examination of Incarcerated Rastafarian Free Exercise Claims*, 34 New Eng. J. on Crim. & Civ. Confinement 391 (2008); Timothy B. Taylor, *Note, Soul Rebels: The Rastafarians and the Free Exercise Clause*, 72 Geo. L.J. 1605 (1984); *Rastafarianism, available at:* http://religiousmovements.lib.virginia.edu/nrms/rast.html.

139 *See* Gartrell v. Ashcroft, 191 F. Supp. 2d 23 (D.D.C. 2002).

140 *See* Mosier v. Maynard, 937 F.3d 1521, 1526 n. 3 (10th Cir. 1991) (noting cases where Native Americans have asserted religiously based hair-length claims).

141 Diaz v. Collins, 114 F.3d 69, 72 n. 18 (5th Cir. 1997); *see also* Pollock v. Marshall, 845 F.2d 656, 657 (6th Cir. 1988) ("The Lakota American Indians believe that hair is sacred and should not be cut.").

142 *See, e.g.*, 15 Cal. Code Reg. § 3062 ("Inmate Grooming Standards"); Ga. Dep't of Corr., Inmate Handbook § V(g) ("Violations Pertaining to Personal Appearance and Sanitation"); *id.* § VII(C) ("Personal Hygiene"); Nev. Dep't of Corr. Admin. Reg. 705 ("Inmate Grooming and Personal Hygiene"); Ohio Admin. Code § 5120-9-25 ("Appearance and grooming of male inmates"); *id.* § 5120-9-25.1 ("Appearance and grooming of female inmates"); Va. Dep't of Corr., Div. of Ops. Proc. 864.1 ("Offender Grooming and Hygiene"); *see, generally*, Dawinder S. Sidhu, *Religious Freedom and Inmate Grooming Standards*, 66 U. Miami L. Rev. 923 (2012).

143 *See, e.g.*, Warsoldier v. Woodford, 418 F.3d 989, 1002 (9th Cir. 2005) (RLUIPA case) (holding that the California Department of Corrections' hair length regulation was underlined by a "compelling interest in maintaining prison security, health and hygiene."); Robinson v. Foti, 527 F. Supp. 1111, 1114 (E.D. La. 1981) (Prison claimed hygiene and security as reasons behind regulation that inmate cut his dreadlocks.).

rationale, for example, is that such rules make it harder for an inmate, particularly an escapee, to alter his or her appearance in relation to his or her photos on file with the prison.[144] Another is that "long hair … facilitates the transfer of contraband and weapons."[145] As summarized by the Eleventh Circuit in a RLUIPA case, "[i]t is … beyond dispute that [a prison system] … has compelling interests in security, discipline, hygiene, and safety within its prisons and in the public's safety in the event of escapes and alteration of appearances."[146]

Some correctional systems or facilities create religious (as well as medical) exceptions to grooming regulations,[147] but others attempt to enforce their regulations categorically. In general, the courts have accepted prison officials' arguments that, under *Turner*, grooming regulations are rationally connected to legitimate penological interests in security such that the application of the regulations normally will not violate prisoners' free exercise rights.[148] Even under RFRA's or RLUIPA's standard of strict scrutiny, courts largely agree that prisons have multiple compelling governmental interests at stake, security foremost among them, although they sometimes differ on whether a prison has demonstrated that full enforcement of a strict grooming policy actually furthers or is the least restrictive means of furthering these interests.[149] The Ninth Circuit, for example, found that a prison had failed to make this showing because it could not "explain why prisons in other jurisdictions … are able to meet the same compelling interests of prison safety and security without requiring short hair or permitting a religious exemption."[150] By contrast, the Eleventh Circuit held that a prison system had demonstrated "that its exceptionless short-hair policy for male inmates is the least restrictive means of furthering the compelling governmental interests [in security, discipline, hygiene, and safety within its prisons and in the public's safety in the event of escapes and alteration of appearances]."[151] Among other things, the prison had "shown that [the inmates'] proposed alternative – allowing an exemption for Native American inmates,

144 *See* Harris v. Chapman, 97 F.3d 499, 503–4 (11th Cir. 1996); *see also* Brown v. Ridge, No. Civ. A. 04-0759-A, 2006 WL 1581167, at *13–*14 (W.D. La. Jan. 19, 2006) (Magis. Rpt. & Rec.) (unpublished) [citing Diaz v. Collins, 114 F.3d 69, 72–3 (5th Cir. 1997) (other citations omitted)].

145 Diaz, 114 F.3d at 73.

146 Knight v. Thompson, 723 F.3d 1275, 1283 (11th Cir. 2013) *judgment vacated for reconsideration*, 135 S. Ct. 1173 (2015).

147 *See* Warsoldier, 418 F.3d at 999 (noting that the Colorado Department of Corrections "expressly provides for a religious exemption to its grooming regulations").

148 *See* Kuperman v. Wrenn, 645 F.3d 69, 74–7 (1st Cir. 2011); Taylor v. Johnson, 257 F.3d 470, 472 (5th Cir. 2001) (*per curiam*) (finding that a prison grooming policy effectively forbidding a Muslim prisoner from wearing a beard was reasonably related to legitimate penological interests in safety); Fromer v. Scully, 874 F.2d 69, 74 (2d Cir. 1989); Pollock v. Marshall, 845 F.2d 656, 659–60 (6th Cir. 1988); *see also* Diaz, 114 F.3d at 73 (RFRA case) {"We agree with our colleagues in the Eighth and Eleventh Circuits that a prison regulation on hair length is related to security and, as such, involves a compelling state interest." [citing Harris v. Chapman 97 F.3d 499 (11th Cir. 1996); Hamilton v. Schriro, 74 F.3d 1545 (8th Cir. 1996)]}.

149 *See, e.g.*, Holt v. Hobbs, 135 S. Ct. 853 (2015) (RLUIPA); Kuperman, 645 F.3d at 79–80 (RLUIPA); Fegans v. Norris, 537 F.3d 897, 903–6 (8th Cir. 2008) (RLUIPA); May v. Baldwin, 109 F.3d 557, 564 (9th Cir. 1997) (RFRA), *cert. denied*, 522 U.S. 921 (1997).

150 *See* Warsoldier, 418 F.3d at 1001; *see also* Fluellen v. Goord, No. 06-CV-602E(Sr), 2007 WL 4560597, at *7 (W.D.N.Y. Mar. 12, 2007) (unpublished); Muhammad v. Crosby, No. 4:05cv193-WS, 2007 WL 604937, at *3–*4 (N.D. Fla. Feb. 22, 2007) (unpublished) (explaining that the Eleventh Circuit's decision finding prison's grooming policy valid under RFRA would not change under RLUIPA because "the standard of review is basically the same").

151 Knight, 723 F.3d at 1284 (RLUIPA case).

requiring exempted inmates to search their own hair, and using a computer program to manipulate inmate photographs – does not eliminate the [the prison's] security, discipline, hygiene, and safety concerns."[152] For instance, "inmates can manipulate searches of their own hair to conceal weapons and contraband, and using a computer program to alter photographs does nothing to address the impediments that long hair causes for the identification of inmates within the prisons. [Their] … proposed alternative also does nothing to assuage the [prison's] concerns about gang-formation and hair-pulling during fights, or the concealment of infections and infestations."[153]

## 2. *Jewelry, Headgear, or Garb*

Correctional institutions typically also have regulations that restrict, to varying degrees, the wearing of jewelry, headgear, or nonstandard clothing.[154] Just as some religions dictate hair length or facial hair, however, certain religions require or exhort adherents to don specific items of jewelry, headgear, or garb, often as a sign of devotion and humility before God or as a means of evangelizing or otherwise expressing one's faith. Prisoners, for example, have asserted claims that their religious beliefs and practices entail the wearing of, among other things, headbands,[155] headdresses,[156] beads,[157] crosses or crucifixes,[158] yarmulkes,[159] fezzes,[160] turbans,[161] kufis,[162] and crowns.[163]

Restrictions on nonstandard headgear or clothing, much like grooming requirements, are typically premised on safety- and security-related concerns that weapons, drugs, or other contraband may be more easily concealed and their detection hampered or that certain forms of religious garb actually may be symbols of gang affiliation.[164]

152 Knight, 723 F.3d at 1284–5.

153 *Id.* at 1285.

154 *See, e.g.*, Ga. Dep't of Corr., Inmate Handbook § V(g)(6) (making it a violation to "[w]ear on the person, body, or clothing of earrings, ornamental buckles, beads, pendants, medallions, or other items of decoration or jewelry" with the exception of "[w]atches, standard size individual finger rings, religious medals, or crosses").

155 *See, e.g.*, Standing Deer v. Carlson, 831 F.2d 1525 (9th Cir. 1987); Wilson v. Moore, 270 F. Supp. 2d 1328, 1353 (N.D. Fla. 2003).

156 *See, e.g.*, Blair-Bey v. Ludlow, No. 97-15941, 1999 WL 51493, 168 F.3d 497 (9th Cir. 1999) (unpublished).

157 *See, e.g.*, Alameen v. Coughlin, 892 F. Supp. 440 (E.D.N.Y. 1995); Campos v. Coughlin, 854 F. Supp. 194 (S.D.N.Y. 1994).

158 *See, e.g.*, Sasnett v. Litscher, 197 F.3d 290 (7th Cir. 1999), *abrogated by* Bridges v. Gilbert, 557 F.3d 541 (7th Cir. 2009); Vandyke v. S.W. Va. Reg'l Jail Auth., No. CIVA 7:06CV00267, 2006 WL 2475898 (W.D. Va. Aug. 25, 2006) (unpublished); Mark v. Nix, 983 F.2d 138 (8th Cir. 1993) (*per curiam*); Escobar v. Landwehr, 837 F. Supp. 284 (W.D. Wis. 1993).

159 *See, e.g.*, Young v. Lane, 922 F.2d 370 (7th Cir. 1991).

160 *See, e.g.*, Portley-El v. Zavaras, No. 99-1028, 1999 WL 542631, 188 F.3d 519 (10th Cir. 1999) (unpublished), *cert. denied*, 528 U.S. 1088 (2000); Jackson-Bey v. Hanslmaier, 115 F.3d 1091 (2d Cir. 1997).

161 *See, e.g.*, Jefferson v. Gonzales, No. 05-442, 2006 WL 1305224, at *3 (D.D.C. May 10, 2006), *aff'd*, No. 06-5219, 2006 WL 6467214 (D.C. Cir. Dec. 26, 2006) (unpublished).

162 *See, e.g.*, Shepard v. Peryam, 657 F. Supp. 2d 1331 (S.D. Fla. 2009).

163 *See, e.g.*, Benjamin v. Coughlin, 905 F.2d 571, 578–9 (2d Cir. 1990) (as part of Rastafarian practice); Panayoty v. Annucci, 898 F. Supp. 2d 469, 482–3 (N.D.N.Y. 2012) (Magis. J. Rpt. & Recomm.) (as part of the Nation of Gods and Earth religion), *adopted by* No. 9:11-CV-159, 2012 WL 4378127 (N.D.N.Y. Sep. 25, 2012) (unpublished).

164 *See, e.g.*, Young v. Lane, 922 F.2d 370, 375 (7th Cir. 1991) (noting that prison officials justified "their policy concerning uniform headgear … on the basis of security concerns" related to "conceal[ing]

Some courts have ruled in favor of inmates when the head covering or other clothing, if fit tightly to the head or body, does not in fact enhance concealment or inhibit detection of prohibited items, especially if the context in which the prisoner desires to wear the headgear or clothing is such that smuggling or concealment is not an issue.[165] Thus inmates might be able to wear certain tightly fitting headgear, such as Jewish yarmulkes or Native American headbands, and might be able to do so in their cells or during religious services,[166] or when being transported to the hospital,[167] but not in common areas or during meals.[168] As a general matter, however, courts frequently find that headgear and clothing restrictions are rationally connected to legitimate penological interests and thus valid under *Turner* and *O'Lone*.[169] In addition, prison officials are entitled, without violating the First Amendment, "to draw a distinction between, on the one hand, religious emblems that are common to the members of other umbrella religious groups, easy to recognize, and difficult to abuse as a gang symbol and, on the other hand, emblems that are unique to each prisoner and [pose] ... potential security risks."[170] Even under the heightened scrutiny of RLUIPA or RFRA, headgear and clothing restrictions have been upheld.[171] But a prison should not prevail under that standard when, as in the case of a Native American inmate who was prohibited from wearing a medicine bag under his clothing, the prison makes "no showing that ... [denying the request] is the least restrictive means of furthering its interest in enhanced prison security and ... [does] not show that medicine bags pose a genuine threat to prison security."[172]

contraband and ... gang identification"); Benjamin v. Coughlin, 905 F.2d 571, 578 (2d Cir. 1990) (noting that corrections regulations restricted "the wearing of crowns to designated areas" based on "legitimate security reasons" such as "[p]reventing the smuggling of contraband, such as weapons and drugs"), *cert. denied*, 498 U.S. 951 (1990); Rogers v. Scurr, 676 F.2d 1211, 1215 (8th Cir. 1982) (noting that "prison officials have explained the purpose of their policy of prohibiting the wearing of caps and robes outside prayer meetings; they urge that such attire makes it too easy to conceal contraband").

165 *See* Benjamin, 905 F.2d at 579 (noting relative security concerns among different types of religious headgear based on "the size of the headgear and the ease with which contraband can be secreted"); Jefferson, 2006 WL 1305224, at *3 (distinguishing between a turban, which may "enable an inmate to conceal weapons and drugs," and a kufi, "which is a thin, sometimes transparent, tight-fitting cap" in which it "is difficult for an inmate to conceal contraband").

166 *See, e.g.*, Young, 922 F.2d at 375.

167 *See, e.g.*, Boles v. Neet, 486 F.3d 1177, 1182–3 (10th Cir. 2007) (finding a violation where warden prohibited a Jewish inmate from wearing a yarmulke during transport between prison and hospital and warden did not connect the prohibition to a legitimate penological objective).

168 *See, e.g.*, Standing Deer, 831 F.2d at 1528–9.

169 *See, e.g.*, Davis v. Clinton, 74 Fed. App'x 452, 455 (6th Cir. 2003) (unpublished) (upholding prohibition on daily wearing of religious clothing); Muhammad v. Lynaugh, 966 F.2d 901, 902–3 (5th Cir. 1992) (upholding restriction on Muslim inmates' wearing of kufi caps, where weapons could be hidden under caps); Benjamin, 905 F.2d at 579 (upholding restriction on wearing of Rastafarian crowns to designated areas because of "the enhanced potential for concealing contraband and the obvious increase in guard/inmate contact that would result from searches of crowns"); Butler-Bey v. Frey, 811 F.2d 449, 451 (8th Cir. 1987) (upholding restriction on fezzes, which could be used to smuggle contraband); Rogers, 676 F.2d at 1215–16 (upholding ban on prayer caps and robes outside of prayer meetings in order to prevent concealment of contraband).

170 Kaufman v. Pugh, 733 F.3d 692, 699 (7th Cir. 2013) (specifically referring to the Establishment Clause's general prohibition on denomination discrimination).

171 *See, e.g.*, Jefferson, 2006 WL 1305224, at *3–*4.

172 Craddick v. Duckworth, 113 F.3d 83, 85 (7th Cir. 1997).

With regard to jewelry and jewelry-like items, prison officials typically cite two major concerns: *first*, that such items, if made of metal, glass, hard plastic, or certain minerals, can be fashioned into weapons and, *second*, that they may be used as a form of gang identification. The first concern ordinarily prevails in court, even under heightened scrutiny, especially when a prison is willing to allow inmates to possess other alternative religious items that cannot be converted into weapons or tools.[173] For example, in a RLUIPA suit brought by a Native American inmate, it was alleged that prison officials prohibited the inmate "from possessing headbands, ribbon shirts, jewelry, looms and shells for traditional ceremonial dances."[174] The court determined that, under the prison policies, inmates could not in fact "possess headbands, ribbon shirts, jewelry and looms" but that Native American inmates "may use an abalone shell during the sweat lodge ceremony." Upholding the restrictions, the court found that they served compelling interests in "security and safety" given the many potential uses of the items: "(1) beads used in headbands . . . [and] jewelry could be used to make a crude weapon; (2) beads and jewelry can be fashioned into a key capable of unlocking handcuffs; (3) metal jewelry, beads or spacers can be melted down to create unauthorized objects such as edged weapons, keys and badges; (4) ribbon shirts, jewelry, looms, shells and rattles create a security concern due to the possibility of items being hidden with the objects; and (5) headbands and ribbon shirts could be used to conceal an inmate's identity, which could facilitate escape."[175]

### 3. *Clergy, Services, or Facilities*

"Nearly all state and federal correctional institutions provide support for at least some of the four traditional faith groups – Catholic, Protestant, Muslim, and Jewish."[176] This institutional support can take a number of forms. For many religious traditions, one obvious means of support is the provision of clergy, from full- or part-time chaplains to outside volunteers.[177] To be sure, "[c]haplains have been part of the U.S. prison system since its beginnings. From the first penitentiary set up by Quakers in the Walnut Street Jail in Philadelphia, the clergy have been able to enter penal institutions to provide religious training, counseling, and support."[178] Consistent with this tradition, many states

173 *See, e.g.*, Piskanin v. Hammer, No. 07-2518, 269 Fed. App'x 159, 162 (3d Cir. Mar. 18, 2008) (unpublished) (upholding confiscation of an inmate's religious medal/necklace in order to prevent self-harm, where inmate was placed on suicide watch); Finley v. Bramlett, No. 88–2762, 847 F.2d 815, 1989 WL 41675, at *2 (9th Cir. 1989) (unpublished) (similar); Skenandore v. Endicott, No. 05-C-0234, 2006 WL 2587545, at *21 (E.D. Wis. Sep. 6, 2006) (unpublished); VanDyke v. S.W. Va. Reg'l Jail Auth., No. CIVA 7:06CV00267, 2006 WL 2475898, at *3 (W.D. Va. Aug. 25, 2006) (unpublished) (upholding the confiscation of an inmate's crucifix because the crucifix, though itself "not sharp or pointed . . . could be sharpened into a weapon posed a potential threat to security" and because a prison official "specifically advised [the inmate] that he could possess a crucifix made of cloth or thread").

174 Skenandore, 2006 WL 2587545, at *21.

175 *Id.*

176 Dammer, *supra* note 1, at 837–8.

177 "In the case when an individual or small group of inmates wish to practice a religion that is not familiar to a current chaplain, a contract chaplain, outside volunteer, or spiritual advisor who specializes in that faith perspective may be brought into the institution to minister to inmates. Chaplains, contract chaplains, volunteers, and spiritual advisors are also referred to as 'faith representatives.'" *Id.* at 837.

178 Melvina Sumter, *Chaplains*, *in* 1 Encyclopedia of Prisons and Correctional Facilities 112 (2005). For survey data on the roles and perspectives of prison chaplains, *see* The Pew Forum on

authorize chaplaincies or the involvement of outside clergy or religious advisors at their correctional facilities.[179]

In addition, prisons can support inmate religious freedom by making facilities available for services, instruction, or other religious programs and by providing a regular schedule of services or programs, and many state laws also specifically address these matters.[180] Accordingly, "[i]t is not uncommon for a large prison to have numerous religious services on a daily basis. In contrast, jails may limit religious practice to a single service for all denominations called a 'multifaith service.' Institutions, particularly those of high security, may also use 'cell-by-cell' ministry, whereby the chaplains from different denominations visit inmates individually as requested."[181]

As for what is guaranteed by the Free Exercise Clause in terms of access to clergy, services, and facilities within a correctional institution, prisoners must be provided reasonable and reasonably similar resources, subject to institutional interests, including fiscal and logistical considerations. As the Supreme Court has explained, not "every religious sect or group within a prison – however few in number – must have identical facilities or personnel. A special chapel or place of worship need not be provided for every faith regardless of size; nor must a chaplain, priest, or minister be provided without regard to the extent of the demand. But reasonable opportunities must be afforded to all prisoners to exercise the religious freedom guaranteed by the First and Fourteenth Amendments."[182] Thus the employment of chaplains for some religions does not mean that prison officials must "employ chaplains of each and every faith to which prisoners might happen to subscribe."[183] Indeed, "it is well-settled that the First Amendment does

Religion & Public Life, Religion in Prisons: A 50-State Survey of Prison Chaplains (Mar. 22, 2012), *available at*: http://www.pewforum.org/files/2012/03/Religion-in-Prisons.pdf.

179 *See, e.g.*, Ala. Code § 14-3-12; Ariz. Rev. Stat. § 31–206; Cal. Penal Code § 5009(b)–(c); Colo. Rev. Stat. § 17-42-101(4); 730 Ill. Comp. Stat. 5/3-7-2(g); Ky. Rev. Stat. 197.270; La. Rev. Stat. § 857; 34-A Me. Rev. Stat. § 3236; Mich. Comp. Laws § 800.291; Minn. Stat. §§ 241.05, 641.16; Miss. Code Ann. § 47-5-85; Mo. Stat. § 217.235; Nev. Dep't of Corr. Religious Practice Manual § 5(A); N.C. Gen. Stat. § 148-10.1; 57 Okla. Stat. § 5; Or. Rev. Stat. § 179.375; Wash. Rev. Code §§ 72.01.210, 72.01.220; Wis. Stat. § 301.33(1)–(2). Washington's state constitution specifically contemplates such chaplaincies. *See* Wash. Const. art. I, § 11 (providing that "this article shall not be so construed as to forbid the employment by the state of a chaplain for such of the state custodial, correctional, and mental institutions ... as in the discretion of the legislature may seem justified").

180 *See, e.g.*, Ariz. Rev. Stat. § 31-206(B) (providing that "chaplains shall hold services at the state prison at least twice each month"); *id.* § 41-2804.01 (providing for religious programs at juvenile correctional facilities); Colo. Rev. Stat. § 17-42-101(2) (providing for services and access to religious facilities); Miss. Code Ann. § 47-5-85 (requiring "an area at each facility of the correctional system for religious worship to be conducted by the [state correctional] chaplain's office"); Nev. Dep't of Corr. Admin. Reg. 810 ("Religious Faith Group Activities and Programs"); Nev. Dep't of Corr. Religious Practice Manual § 5(B) ("Chapel Schedule"); N.H. Rev. Stat. § 622:22 (requiring that correctional institutions "provide for suitable religious instruction and ministration to the inmates"). Massachusetts specifically guarantees inmates' religious exercise by its constitution. *See* Mass. Const. amend. art. 18, § 4 ("Nothing herein contained shall be construed to deprive any inmate of a publicly controlled reformatory, penal or charitable institution of the opportunity of religious exercises therein of his [or her] own faith; but no inmate of such institution shall be compelled to attend religious services or receive religious instruction against his [or her] will, or, if a minor, without the consent of his [or her] parent or guardian.").

181 Dammer, *supra* note 1, at 838.

182 Cruz v. Beto, 405 U.S. 319, 322 n. 2 (1972).

183 Johnson-Bey v. Lane, 863 F.2d 1308, 1312 (7th Cir. 1988); *see also id.* at 1310 (explaining that prison officials "need not employ chaplains representing every faith with at least one adherent among the prison population").

not require [the] prison administration to provide inmates with the chaplain of their choice."[184] As summarized by the Eighth Circuit, "[t]he Constitution does not ... require that a religious advisor be provided for every sect in a penitentiary. Nor is a prisoner entitled to insist on a religious advisor whose beliefs are completely congruent with his [or her] own. Only when a prisoner's sole opportunity for group worship arises under the guidance of someone whose beliefs are significantly different from his [or her] own is there a possibility that the prisoner's free exercise rights are substantially burdened in this manner."[185]

As for the availability of and access to religious services and programs, although there is some authority that prisons have no obligation in the first instance,[186] a total ban on religious services, absent some kind of high-security or quarantine situation to justify it, would hardly seem to be the provision of a reasonable opportunity for inmates to practice their religion.[187] Prison officials can, however, "restrict the time, place or manner" in which religious services take place as long as such restrictions satisfy the applicable standard.[188] In turn, inmates generally may not dictate to prison officials where religious services should be held,[189] "need not ... [be] allow[ed] ... to conduct their own religious services[190] or to conduct services without prison supervision,[191] and normally have no right to leave the institution to exercise their religion.[192] Some courts have even upheld

184 Hartmann v. Cal. Dep't of Corr. & Rehab., 707 F.3d 1114, 1122 (9th Cir. 2013); *see also* Al-Alamin v. Gramley, 926 F.2d 680, 687 (7th Cir. 1991) (holding that a prison need not pay for a full-time Muslim cleric as long as inmates otherwise had a reasonable opportunity to practice their religion); Ward v. Walsh, 1 F.3d 873, 880 (9th Cir. 1993) (holding that a prison did not need to provide an inmate with an Orthodox rabbi); Gittlemacker v. Prasse, 428 F.2d 1, 4 (3d Cir. 1970) ("The requirement that a state interpose no unreasonable barriers to the free exercise of an inmate's religion cannot be equated with the suggestion that the state has an affirmative duty to provide, furnish, or supply every inmate with a clergyman or religious services of his [or her] choice.").

185 Weir v. Nix, 114 F.3d 817, 820–1 (8th Cir. 1997) (citations omitted); *see also* Brown, 368 F. Supp. 2d at 1021–2.

186 *See* Larry v. Goetz, No. 06-C-197-C, 2006 WL 1495784, at *6 (W.D. Wis. May 18, 2006) (unpublished) (The Establishment Clause "does not obligate correctional institutions to offer religious services to inmates; it requires only that if services are provided, they are extended to all religious groups.").

187 *See, e.g.*, Alley v. Vasquez, No. 88-2886, 878 F.2d 385, 1989 WL 69929, at *2–*3 (9th Cir. Jun. 23, 1989) (unpublished) (upholding a lockdown, even though it interfered with religious services and ministration, due to heightened security concerns following the fatal stabbing of a correctional officer); Brown v. Johnson, 743 F.2d 408, 412 (6th Cir. 1984) (upholding a ban on one type of ministry because specifically of security and violence concerns), *cert. denied*, 469 U.S. 1215 (1985).

188 *See* O'Lone v. Estate of Shabazz, 482 U.S. 342, 358 (1987) (so stating with regard to the specialized standard of the Free Exercise Clause).

189 *See* Price v. Scott, No. 3:05-CV-401 AS, 2006 WL 2361817, at *3 (N.D. Ind. Aug. 14, 2006) (unpublished) ("Neither the First Amendment nor RLUIPA permits an inmate to dictate to prison officials the location of religious services.").

190 Johnson-Bey, 863 F.2d at 1310; *accord* Anderson v. Angelone, 123 F.3d 1197, 1198–9 (9th Cir. 1997) (holding that a state "prohibition on inmate-led religious services does not violate the First Amendment" and finding that "[r]equiring an outside minister to lead religious activity among inmates undoubtedly contributes to prison security" and "helps ensure that inmate activity is supervised by responsible individuals and lessens the possibility that inmate religious groups will subvert prison authority"); Cooper v. Tard, 855 F.2d 125, 129 (3d Cir. 1988) (holding that because religious gatherings tend to create alternative authorities within the prison population, they are properly considered a security risk and may be disallowed).

191 *See, e.g.*, Butler-Bey v. Frey, 811 F.2d 449, 452 (8th Cir. 1987).

192 *See, e.g.*, Green v. McKaskle, 788 F.2d 1116, 1126 (5th Cir. 1986); Beasley v. Konteh, 433 F. Supp. 2d 874 (N.D. Ohio 2006) (holding that neither the Free Exercise Clause nor RLUIPA "require[s] prison officials to transport [a prisoner] to an Orthodox Jewish Synagogue for conversion to Judaism").

rules permitting collective worship only to those religious groups with a certain minimum number of adherents in the prison.[193]

Prison officials' relative latitude in deciding the level of access that prisoners may have to religious clergy, services, and facilities does not, however, permit them to discriminate intentionally against minority faiths.[194] "[T]he efforts of prison administrators, when assessed in their totality, must be evenhanded" and "cannot discriminate against a particular religion."[195] To be evenhanded, their decisions must be based on considerations such as institutional security, actual demographic demands, and available resources. Even if this leads to a policy or arrangement that favors majority or traditional faiths, such a policy or arrangement will be upheld as long as it can be deemed neutral and as long as all prisoners otherwise have a reasonable opportunity to observe their religion.[196] The efforts of prison officials also must not be coercive, as discussed with regard to rehabilitative programs in Section 19.04(B). A prison may not "compel or even encourage inmates' attendance at religious services, and it most certainly cannot attempt to influence the religious messages which the chaplains convey to the prisoners."[197]

With regard specifically to facilities, Native American prisoners may present unique requests based on particular observances associated with their faith traditions, highlighting the extent to which those faiths differ both conceptually and in practice from Western religions. "Rather than going to church, the traditional Native might attend a sweat lodge; rather than accepting bread from the Holy Priest, they may smoke a ceremonial pipe to come into Communion with the Great Spirit; and rather than kneeling with their hands placed together in prayer, they may let sweetgrass be feathered over their entire being for spiritual cleansing and allow the smoke to carry their prayers into the heavens."[198]

Needless to say, sweat lodges have not be traditional fixtures at correctional institutions, and access to and use of smoking materials may pose safety, security, and logistical issues for prison administrators. Nevertheless, some state laws specifically and rather extensively provide for the accommodation of Native American religious practices in prison,[199] and

193 Spies v. Voinovich, 173 F.3d 398, 404–5 (6th Cir. 1999); Childs v. Duckworth 705 F.2d 915, 920 (7th Cir. 1983) ("Perhaps the most obvious of the First Amendment rights that are necessarily curtailed by confinement are those associational rights that the First Amendment protects outside of the prison walls.").

194 *See* Johnson-Bey, 863 F.2d at 1312.

195 Al-Alamin v. Gramley, 926 F.2d 680, 686 (7th Cir. 1991).

196 *See* Freeman v. Tex. Dep't of Crim. Justice, 369 F.3d 854, 859–62 (5th Cir. 2004) (upholding under *Turner* a state prison policy that "provides weekly religious services for what it considers to be the five 'major faith sub-groups' in its prisons: Roman Catholic; Christian/non-Roman Catholic; Jewish; Muslim; and Native American" and "also offers a variety of supplemental devotional opportunities" for denominations that do not easily fit into these categories; finding that the policy is neutral – that there was "no evidence that [the] policy is targeted toward the … [claimant's religion] or favors one religious group over another" – even though it plainly singled out "major" religions for structured accommodation); *see also* Boxer X v. Donald, No. 05–14904, 169 Fed. App'x 555, 560, 2006 WL 463243, at *4 (11th Cir. Feb. 28, 2006) (unpublished) (reasoning that it is sufficient if the prison "provides congregational services based on generic abstractions of actual denominational faiths" as long as the policy "does not affect, for example, the ability to consult outside ministers, read and maintain religious materials in the prison cell, or perform individual religious exercises").

197 Montano v. Hedgepeth, 120 F.3d 844, 850 n. 10 (8th Cir. 1997).

198 Harry Derbitsky, *Native American Spirituality*, *in* 1 ENCYCLOPEDIA OF PRISONS AND CORRECTIONAL FACILITIES 627 (2005).

199 *See, e.g.*, Ariz. Dep't of Corr. Order Manual § 904.03, ¶ 1.4 (Jan. 28, 2013); Colo. Rev. Stat. § 17-42-102; Nev. Dep't of Corr., Religious Practice Manual § 9 (Feb. 12, 2014); N.M. Stat. § 33-10-4; Utah Code Ann. § 64-13-40; *cf.* Ariz. Rev. Stat. § 31-206(c).

"approximately half the states in the United States allow Native sweat lodge ceremonies [in their prison systems]."[200] To date, the case law under the Free Exercise Clause and RLUIPA has varied regarding whether a prison must accommodate a Native American inmate's request to use a sweat lodge,[201] though it is fairly clear that such requests may be denied in maximum security settings.[202] It is also relatively clear that where a sweat lodge is in place, a prison need not hire an outside religious advisor to oversee ceremonies in the lodge,[203] and further, if the prison has established a reasonable schedule for using the sweat lodge, it need not grant requests to use the lodge outside of that schedule.[204]

### 4. *Reading Materials*

Many states authorize or require the provision of, or at least the availability of, religious books or instructional materials for prisoners at their correctional institutions.[205] Minnesota, for example, provides that "[e]very keeper of a jail shall provide for each prisoner able and willing to read it a copy of the Bible or the sacred book of another religion, at the expense of the county,"[206] whereas Alabama directs that the state "Board of Corrections must procure a sufficient number of Bibles and other religious and improving reading matter for the convicts, not to exceed in cost $500 in any one year, and it shall be the duty of the chaplain to distribute the same among the convicts."[207] Some statutes and regulations place rather clear limitations on the nature of the reading materials to be made available. Kentucky and Kansas, for example, provide that inmates who request religious publications or instructional materials may receive them but only if they impose no cost on the institution and pose no threat to institutional security.[208]

200 Derbitsky, *supra* note 198, at 628; *see* Farrow v. Stanley, No. Civ. 02-567-PB, 2005 WL 2671541, at *12 (D.N.H. Oct. 20, 2005) (noting that "[a] number of the nation's state and federal prisons provide Native American inmates with access to a sweat lodge" and citing examples).

201 *Compare* Fowler v. Crawford, 534 F.3d 931, 938–43 (8th Cir. 2008) (RLUIPA case) (no accommodation required where inmate requested construction of a sweat lodge and provision of fire, rocks, shovels, deer antlers, split wood, and other items, and prison officials expressed security concerns about the use of items as weapons and the inability of guards to view and supervise activities within the sweat lodge), *cert. denied*, 556 U.S. 1105 (2009), *and* Haight v. Thompson, No. 5:11-CV-00118, 2013 WL 1092969, at *8–*12 (W.D. Ky. Mar. 15, 2013) (unpublished) (denial of request violates neither the Free Exercise Clause nor RLUIPA), *and* Wilson v. Moore, 270 F. Supp. 2d 1328, 1353 (N.D. Fla. 2003) (denial of request does not violate the Free Exercise Clause), *and* Tart v. Young, 168 F. Supp. 2d 590, 593 (W.D. Va. 2001) (same), *with* Yellowbear v. Lampert, 741 F.3d 48 (10th Cir. 2014) (remanding under RLUIPA where prison failed to demonstrate that barring access to a sweat lodge was the least restrictive means to achieve a compelling interest), *and Farrow*, 2005 WL 2671541, at *7–*9 (finding that prison officials had not yet satisfied RLUIPA's standard in denying access to a sweat lodge).

202 *See, e.g.*, Hamilton v. Schriro, 74 F.3d 1545 (8th Cir. 1996) (Free Exercise Clause and RFRA), *cert. denied*, 519 U.S. 874 (1996); Allen v. Toombs, 827 F.2d 563 (9th Cir. 1987).

203 *See* Brown *ex rel.* Indigenous Inmates at N.D. State Prison v. Schuetzle, 368 F. Supp. 2d 1009, 1022 (D.N.D. 2005).

204 *See* Thomas v. Gunter, 103 F.3d 700, 703 (8th Cir. 1997); Skenandore v. Endicott, No. 05-C-0234, 2006 WL 2587545, at *15 (E.D. Wis. Sep. 6, 2006) (unpublished) (upholding under RLUIPA a prison's time limits on sweat lodge use).

205 *See, e.g.*, Ala. Code § 14-3-46; Kan. Stat. § 75–5223; Ky. Rev. Stat. §§ 197.275, 441.145; Mass. Gen. Laws ch. 127, § 93; Minn. Stat. § 641.16; 57 Okla. Stat. § 5; Tenn. Code § 41-21-211; Wis. Stat. § 301.33(3).

206 Minn. Stat. § 641.16.

207 Ala. Code § 14-3-46.

208 *See* Kan. Stat. § 75-5223; Ky. Rev. Stat. §§ 197.275, 441.145.

State laws also can provide for the availability of or access to religious materials other than publications, such as "objects of a religious nature" or "sacred objects."[209] These various laws exist because government officials recognize the importance of such publications and items to many religions and because prisoners frequently request access to religious books or other religious items to observe, facilitate, or augment the practice of their religion. Particularly for scriptural religions such as Christianity, Judaism, and Islam, the role of sacred texts obviously can be central to religious practice and formation. In some circumstances, a religion's central texts, which usually contain the religion's tenets, are held to be sacred, even to the point where desecration of the text is understood as an unforgivable offense.

In general, the Free Exercise Clause "does not impose an affirmative obligation on the government to provide an inmate with the accoutrements of his [or her] religion, especially where the inmate is able to purchase the items himself [or herself]."[210] Nor does RLUIPA or RFRA appear to change this principle. The Supreme Court, when upholding RLUIPA, did so partly because it expected that the statute's application, first by prison officials and then by courts, would take adequate account of the burdens on correctional institutions and other inmates, specifically adding that "RLUIPA does not require a State to pay for an inmate's devotional accessories."[211] But the Free Exercise Clause, per *Turner* and *O'Lone*, does obligate prisons otherwise to allow inmates a reasonable opportunity to observe their religions, including by means of religious texts and publications. Thus, for example, although prisons may enact neutral and reasonable restrictions on the number of books that inmates can have in their cells at any given time[212] and need not provide inmates access to the exact version or translation of a religious text,[213] they may not simply prohibit inmate access to all religious texts,[214] much less to all reading materials,[215] nor can they permit access only to texts concerning specific religions while denying access to texts concerning others.[216] Under the heightened scrutiny of RLUIPA and RFRA, moreover, even their neutral and reasonable restrictions may not stand. In

209 Colo. Rev. Stat. § 17-42-101(3) ("The department shall permit access to objects of a religious nature where possession of such objects would not unduly burden the reasonable security interests of the correctional facility. Prison officials shall accord appropriate respect for sacred objects. When the reasonable security interests of the correctional facility necessitate the inspection of any sacred object, such inspection shall be done visually.").

210 Larry v. Goetz, No. 06-C-197-C, 2006 WL 1495784, at *6 (W.D. Wis. May 18, 2006) (unpublished).

211 Cutter v. Wilkinson, 544 U.S. 709, 720 n. 8 (2005) [citing Charles v. Verhagen, 348 F.3d 601, 605 (7th Cir. 2003)].

212 *See* Roy v. Arizona, No. CV-03-2150-PHX-SRB, 2006 WL 120328, at *13 (D. Ariz. Jan. 13, 2006) (unpublished).

213 *See* Earl v. Gould, No. 1:03CV109-1-MU, 2006 WL 983887, at *2 (W.D.N.C. Apr. 11, 2006) (unpublished) ("Plaintiff has not established that [the defendant's] conduct substantially burdened his exercise of his religion ... Plaintiff was provided with a Quran ... [N]ot being provided with a specific translation of a religious text does not substantially burden Plaintiff when Plaintiff was provided several common versions of the religious text.").

214 *See* McElyea v. Babbitt, 833 F.3d 196, 199 (9th Cir. 1987) (noting that a prison "cannot erect a barrier to an inmate's access to religious reading material absent a security or penological interest").

215 *See* Parnell v. Waldrep, 511 F. Supp. 764, 767–8 (W.D.N.C. 1981) (finding unconstitutional a ban on "virtually all reading materials").

216 *See* Parnell, 764 F. Supp. at 768 (finding an Establishment Clause violation where a "jail, while prohibiting receipt of most other reading materials, established an exception for Bibles and 'little Christian tracts'").

one case, for instance, the Third Circuit invalidated a limit on ten books per cell, finding that the limit imposed a substantial burden on an inmate's religious practice and that the corrections officials were "unable to show that its ten-book policy is the least restrictive means to further its compelling governmental interest in the safety and health of prisoners and prison employees."[217]

In addition to regulating access to reading materials already in an institution, prison regulations often restrict the receipt of mailed materials advocating illegal activities or racial, religious, or national violence, typically in furtherance of institutional safety and security. Prison officials normally are free to enforce such restrictions,[218] but if the materials are not in fact likely to induce violence or undermine prison safety – if religious publications advocate, say, racial purity but not violence – then the officials will need to advance another legitimate or compelling interest to prohibit inmates from receiving such materials.[219] In an Eighth Circuit case, for example, prison officials imposed a ban on all literature and materials from the Church of Jesus Christ Christian, a religious organization with a substantial incarcerated following and well known for its white supremacist message.[220] The court ruled that the literature could not be summarily labeled "likely to be disruptive or produce violence" without an actual examination of each piece of mail such that the prison's categorical ban was unconstitutional.[221] Where a particularized review of religious materials reveals some parts to be inflammatory or likely to incite violence, however, prison officials then may block receipt of the entire publication or body of materials and need not engage in redaction, particularly when there is "evidence showing that the costs to implement such a procedure would be prohibitive."[222]

### 5. *Special Diets*

Another realm of potential conflict between inmate religious freedom and prison administration involves inmate requests for special diets in accordance with their religious tenets.[223] Because food and drink are necessities of life and otherwise not regularly available to inmates, just as prisons must provide these things in general, they must ordinarily

217 Washington v. Klem, 497 F.3d 272, 274 (3d Cir. 2007).

218 *See, e.g.*, Chriceol v. Phillips, 169 F.3d 313, 315–16 (5th Cir. 1999); Shabazz v. Parsons, 127 F.3d 1246, 1249 (10th Cir. 1997); Winburn v. Bologna, 979 F. Supp. 531, 534–5 (W.D. Mich. 1997) (upholding under both the Free Exercise Clause and RFRA a ban on receiving "material that promotes racial supremacy and violence" where there was "no easy alternative to barring such potential violence causing materials").

219 *See* Murphy v. Mo. Dep't of Corr., 814 F.2d 1252, 1257 (8th Cir. 1987) (holding that "[a] total ban on Aryan Nations materials is more restrictive of prisoner First Amendment rights than is necessary to maintain prison security" and that the restriction must be limited "to those materials that advocate violence or that are so racially inflammatory as to be reasonably likely to cause violence at the prison"); Rooks v. Zavares, No. Civ. A. 99-B-631, 2001 WL 34047959, at *12 (D. Colo. Jan. 25, 2001) (unpublished).

220 *See* Williams v. Brimeyer, 116 F.3d 351, 353 (8th Cir. 1997).

221 *See id.* at 352 n. 2, 353–4.

222 Shabazz v. Parsons, 127 F.3d 1246, 1249 (10th Cir. 1997).

223 For additional reading, *see* Shannon A. Burns, *Perfect Piety? Transgression and Redemption within the Legal Structures Affording Prisoners the Right to a Religious Diet*, 50 U. LOUISVILLE L. REV. 153 (2011); Jamie Aron Forman, *Note, Jewish Prisoners and Their First Amendment Right to a Kosher Meal: An Examination of the Relationship between Prison Dietary Policy and Correctional Goals*, 65 BROOKLYN L. REV. 477 (1999); Benjamin Pi-wei Liu, *Comment, A Prisoner's Right to Religious Diet beyond the Free Exercise Clause*, 51 UCLA L. REV. 1151 (2004).

attempt to honor requests for special diets based on religious needs unless their refusal satisfies the standard of *Turner* and *O'Lone*.[224] Accordingly, policies concerning the accommodation of religious diets for prisons can be found in both federal law[225] and the laws of several states.[226] Pursuant to the *Turner* and *O'Lone* standard, courts will assess "whether there is a rational connection between the prison's refusal to give [an inmate] his [or her] requested diet and a legitimate penological interest" and, if so, "whether the refusal is reasonable in light of the nature of the prison's penological interest, [the inmate's] interest in practicing his [or her] religion, the overall effect on the prison community of granting his [or her] request, and the availability of ways to accommodate [the inmate's] request at *de minimis* cost to valid penological interests."[227] Legitimate penological concerns in this context obviously can include safety and security but also may include an "interest in an efficient food system and in avoiding inmate jealousy"[228] as well as "the reduction of administrative and budgetary burdens."[229] Recognizing these many interests, the Fifth Circuit thus has stated that "prisons need not respond to particularized religious dietary requests.... [I]f one such dietary request is granted, similar demands will proliferate, with two possible results: either accommodation of such demands will place an undue burden on the prison system, or the prisons would become entangled with religion while drawing fine and searching distinctions among various free exercise claimants."[230] With regard to whether an inmate has alternative means of religious practice, when assessing the refusal of a requested diet, these alternatives need not be dietary in nature; rather, courts have simply looked at other ways that the inmate is able to practice or express his or her faith.[231] Notwithstanding this latitude under *Turner* and *O'Lone*, prison officials may not, in their provision or denial of religious dietary requests, any more than their

224 *See* Gallagher v. Shelton, 587 F.3d 1063, 1070 (10th Cir. 2009) ("[A]n inmate's right to free exercise of religion includes the right to a diet that conforms with their religious beliefs."); McElyea v. Babbitt, 833 F.3d 196, 198 (9th Cir. 1987) ("Inmates ... have the right to be provided with food sufficient to sustain them in good health that satisfies the dietary laws of their religion.").

225 *See* 28 C.F.R. §§ 547.20(b), 548.20. "The Bureau provides inmates requesting a religious diet reasonable and equitable opportunity to observe their religious dietary practice within the constraints of budget limitations and the security and orderly running of the institution and the Bureau through a religious diet menu. The inmate will provide a written statement articulating the religious motivation for participation in the religious diet program." *Id.* § 548.20(a).

226 *See, e.g.*, Alaska Dep't of Corr. Policies & Procedures 805.03 (Oct. 15, 1986); Ariz. Dep't of Corr. Order Manual § 904.03, ¶ 1.5 (Jan. 28, 2013); Cal. Dep't of Corr. & Rehab. Operations Manual ch. 5, art. 51, § 54080.14; Nev. Dep't of Corr. Admin. Reg. 814 (Jun. 17, 2012); N.Y. Comp. Codes R. & Regs. tit. 9, § 7024.6; S.D. Dep't of Corr. Pol'y 1.5.F.2 (Jan. 13, 2014); Va. Dep't of Corr. Food Service Manual ch. 4 (Jul. 1, 2012); Wyo. Dep't of Corr. Pol'y & Proc. 5.601 (Jun. 15, 2013).

227 DeHart v. Horn, 227 F.3d 47, 52 (3d Cir. 2000) (*en banc*).

228 *Id.* at 53; *see also* Ashelman v. Wawrzaszek, 111 F.3d 674, 677 (9th Cir. 1997) (noting that a "prison has a legitimate interest in running a simplified food service"); Kahey v. Jones, 836 F.2d 948, 950 (5th Cir. 1988) (commenting that a correctional institution "has a legitimate governmental interest in running a simplified prison food service rather than a full-scale restaurant").

229 Shakur v. Schriro, 514 F.3d 878, 886 (9th Cir. 2008).

230 Kahey, 836 F.2d at 950; *see also* Andreola v. Wisconsin, No. 05-1931, 171 Fed. App'x 514, 515–16 (7th Cir. 2006) (unpublished) ["[T]he First Amendment does not require prisons to accommodate every element of each inmate's faith; there are so many variations that the enterprise would be both costly and unavailing (for perfect implementation cannot be assured at any cost). It also would open the system to abuse, for prisoners might make 'religious' demands motivated more by matters of taste than matters of faith ... [I]t is enough to accommodate religious dietary needs shared by a significant number of prisoners; inmate-specific diets are not required."].

231 *See, e.g.*, Shakur, 514 F.3d at 886; DeHart, 227 F.3d at 54.

treatment of other religion-based requests, intentionally discriminate against certain religions, and their "treatment of all inmates must be qualitatively comparable."[232]

Although some inmates' prevail on their dietary claims under the Free Exercise Clause,[233] their probability of doing so should increase under RFRA or RLUIPA, particularly because budgetary interests (a principal basis for refusing dietary requests) are alone less likely to be considered compelling, and to the extent that a prison already may be providing some dietary accommodations, it may have more difficulty explaining why any additional request undermines a compelling interest or why denying that request is the least restrictive alternative available to the institution.[234] However, this certainly depends on the nature and context of the request. Where, for example, a Jewish inmate requests a kosher diet, but the Jewish inmate population is extremely small and the prison's "budget is not adequate to cover the increased expense of either providing a separate kosher kitchen or bringing in kosher food from the outside," its "ability to provide a nutritionally appropriate meal to other offenders would be jeopardized (because the payments for kosher meals would come out of the general food budget for all inmates)," and "such a policy would breed resentment among other inmates," a court likely will find, as did the Fifth Circuit in such a case, that the strict scrutiny standard of RLUIPA is satisfied.[235]

### 6. *Objections to Medical Procedures*

Some religions disallow or discourage various medical procedures that otherwise might be administered on a routine or emergency basis. Jehovah's Witnesses, for example, are well known for opposing blood transfusions in reliance on their interpretation of scripture,[236] whereas Christian Scientists strongly encourage but does not necessarily or always require spiritual healing over conventional medical treatment.[237] Inmates also have alleged that certain tests or inoculations that contain substances such as alcohol or pork derivatives and that procedures such as piercing the skin are forbidden by their religious beliefs.[238] Objections to medical testing or treatments, however, often conflict with the policies or initiatives or prisons, which have an obligation to provide basic medical care for their populations. Indeed, prison officials can be held liable if they evidence deliberate disregard for the medical needs of those in their custody,[239] including the

232 Al-Alamin v. Gramley, 926 F.2d 680, 686 (7th Cir. 1991) (stating these principles generally, without specific regard for the type of request).

233 *See, e.g.*, Williams v. Bitner, 455 F.3d 186, 191 & n. 5 (3d Cir. 2006); Beerheide v. Suthers, 286 F.3d 1179 (10th Cir. 2002); Makin v. Colo. Dep't of Corr., 183 F.3d 1205, 1211–14 (10th Cir. 1999).

234 *See, e.g.*, Jova v. Smith, 582 F.3d 410, 417 (2d Cir. 2009) (remanding under RLUIPA for least restrictive means analysis related to a dietary request), *cert. denied*, 559 U.S. 1077 (2010); Koger v. Bryan, 523 F.3d 789, 800–1 (7th Cir. 2008) (finding RLUIPA strict scrutiny test unsatisfied in both respects with regard to a dietary request).

235 *See* Baranowski v. Hart, 486 F.3d 112, 125–6 (5th Cir. 2007), *cert. denied*, 552 U.S. 1062 (2007).

236 *See Jehovah's Witness*, *in* BRITANNICA ENCYCLOPEDIA OF WORLD RELIGIONS 563 (Michael Frassetto ed., 2006).

237 *See Christian Science*, *in* BRITANNICA ENCYCLOPEDIA, *supra* note 236, at 235.

238 *See, e.g.*, Hughes v. Chesney, No. Civ. 3:CV-00-17, 2005 WL 2300353, at *3 (M.D. Pa. Sep. 21, 2005) (unpublished) (Inmate alleged that "a tuberculosis test … contained a pork derivative" and that "the consumption of pork in any way violates his religious beliefs."); Africa v. Horn, 998 F. Supp. 557, 559 (E.D. Pa. 1998) (Inmate alleged that religious beliefs prohibited piercing of the skin with a needle.).

239 *See* Estelle v. Gamble, 429 U.S. 97, 104–5 (1976) (concluding that the Eighth Amendment is violated when prisons show "deliberate indifference to [the] serious medical needs of prisoners").

failure to prevent exposure to communicable diseases such as tuberculosis, which can be especially problematic in the prison environment.[240]

In general, prisoners do not have a right under the Free Exercise Clause to reject medical treatment or testing that is mandated generally across the prison population and is rationally connected to maintaining the health or safety of that population.[241] Thus, for example, prisons ordinarily can require tuberculosis testing[242] or can at least require monitoring of those who object to testing[243] and also can normally compel treatment in the case of a positive test.[244] Likewise, prisoners who object on religious grounds to medical testing or treatment may be quarantined or, in some circumstances, even forcibly treated against their will.[245] The same result usually obtains even under the heightened scrutiny of RFRA or RLUIPA, given that health and safety interests can be compelling and that the control of communicable diseases can require universal testing and treatment.[246] DNA sampling of inmates, for criminal investigational purposes, generally also has been upheld against religious objections.[247]

### 7. *Additional Claims*

Beyond the categories discussed earlier, prisoners have raised a variety of additional religious freedom claims. Muslim prisoners, for example, have alleged that strip searches

240 *See* McCormick v. Stalder, 105 F.3d 1059, 1062 n. 2 (5th Cir. 1997) {"[P]rison officials face potential liability for failure to take adequate steps to control the spread of tuberculosis." [citing Plummer v. United States, 580 F.2d 72, 76–7 (3d Cir. 1978); DeGidio v. Pung, 920 F.2d 525, 528 (8th Cir. 1990)]}.

241 *See* Ballard v. Woodard, 641 F. Supp. 432, 436–7 (W.D.N.C. 1986).

242 *See, e.g.*, Soder v. Williamson, Civ. No. 4:07-CV-1851, 2008 WL 3200839, at *4 (M.D. Pa. Aug. 7, 2008) (unpublished), *aff'd*, No. 08-4400, 336 Fed. App'x 206 (3d Cir. Jun. 5, 2009) (unpublished); Hasenmeier-McCarthy v. Rose, 986 F. Supp. 464, 467–8 (S.D. Ohio 1998); *see also* Dunn v. White, 880 F.2d 1188, 1197–8 (10th Cir. 1989) (holding that a "plaintiff's vague allegation that he declined AIDS testing on generic 'religious grounds' does not implicate" a religious exemption from AIDS testing), *cert. denied*, 493 U.S. 1059 (1990); Ballard, 641 F. Supp. at 437.

243 *See* Jolly v. Coughlin, 76 F.3d 468, 477–80 (7th Cir. 1996) (holding that RFRA may demand monitoring as a less restrictive means to testing); Jihad v. Wright, 929 F. Supp. 325, 329–31 (N.D. Ind. 1996) (similar).

244 *See* McCormick v. Stalder, 105 F.3d 1059, 1061–2 (5th Cir. 1997) (holding that mandatory treatment did not violate the Eighth or Fourteenth Amendment, not specifically assessing a religious objection).

245 *See, e.g.*, *Dunn*, 880 F.2d at 1198 (holding that a threat of punishment for denying medical tests on religious grounds is not sufficient to give rise to a due process claim); Africa, 998 F. Supp. at 560 (holding that prison authorities "did not violate the constitution by effectively requiring plaintiff to take a [tuberculosis skin] test or remain in segregated housing for twelve months" and, in fact, "in doing so prison authorities respected plaintiff's wish, whether religiously based or otherwise, not to be tested"); Ballard, 641 F. Supp. at 438 (reasoning that because "the State's interest in preventing health problems in its prison system is so compelling that it overrides [a] prisoner's First Amendment religious rights" and finding "that the force was used in this case [in] the course of protecting a legitimate state interest").

246 *See, e.g.*, Johnson v. Sherman, No. CIV S-04-2255-LKK-EFB-P, 2007 WL 1029856, at *4 (E.D. Cal. Apr. 2, 2007) (Magis. J. Recomm. & Rpt.) (unpublished) (RLUIPA), *adopted by* 2007 WL 1894263 (E.D. Cal. Jul. 2, 2007) (unpublished); Karolis v. N.J. Dep't of Corr., 935 F. Supp. 523, 527–9 (D.N.J. 1996) (RFRA).

247 *See, e.g.*, Shaffer v. Saffle, 148 F.3d 1180, 1182 (10th Cir. 1998) (finding no free exercise violation where the inmate failed to "contend the [DNA sampling] statute … is not neutral or generally applicable" or to allege that "the statute was applied to him differently because of his religious beliefs"), *cert. denied*, 525 U.S. 1005 (1998).

transgress their belief that they should not be seen naked by strangers.[248] In general, however, reasonable strip searches will not violate inmate religious freedom insofar as they necessarily advance the legitimate and indeed compelling interests in safety and security. However, the use of *excessive* strip searches, not independently justifiable in furtherance of safety and security, has been held to violate a prisoner's religious freedom.[249] Another area of litigation involves the beliefs of some prisoners that they must adopt new names as part of their religious identity. The problem arises when such a prisoner wants the prison to use the new name but has not actually changed his or her *legal* name. This can cause confusion for prison administrations, which routinely maintain records based the legal names of inmates. Some courts have found that a prison's refusal to recognize a inmate's adopted religious name does not violate the inmate's religious freedom.[250] However, to the extent that such a right is recognized,[251] courts have held that it will not be violated where a prison institutes a dual-name policy, allowing for use of both names.[252] Should a prison have such a policy, moreover, an inmate must comply with it[253] and has no corresponding "constitutional right to have his [or her] pre-existing prison records altered to reflect his [or her] newly adopted name."[254]

Prisons sometimes also have regulations restricting the persons or organizations to which an inmate may direct checks written from the inmate's prison account, and a religious freedom claim may arise when such restrictions bar the inmate from sending a check specifically to a religious group. In general, courts, at least those using a *Turner-O'Lone* analysis, have upheld such restrictions, finding "that there is a rational, legitimate connection between the disbursement restrictions and the institutional goal of providing for the safety and security of the prison by controlling the flow of funds to help control illegal activities and the pressuring of inmates by inmates."[255] Without such restrictions, prison officials would have to assess in each instance "whether the person or organization to whom a 'donation' is requested is in fact a religious organization and not someone who, for the moment, is fronting as such, whether the inmate has any genuine connection of a religious nature with the requested recipient, and whether the 'donation' represents some response to undue pressure or threat to the inmate."[256] Because such issues "are not readily determinable," it would be "an unnecessarily heavy

[248] *See, e.g.*, Jean-Laurent v. Wilkinson, 438 F. Supp. 2d 318, 323–4 (S.D.N.Y. 2006), *aff'd*, No. 09-1929-PR, 461 Fed. App'x 18 (2d Cir. Feb. 8, 2012) (unpublished).

[249] *See id.*

[250] *See, e.g.*, Howard v. Wilson, No. 04-61018, 176 Fed. App'x 468, 469 (5th Cir. 2006) (unpublished); Mathews v. Morales, 23 F.3d 118 (5th Cir. 1994); Spies v. Voinovich, 173 F.3d 398, 406 (6th Cir. 1999).

[251] *See* Malik v. Brown, 71 F.3d 724, 727–9 (9th Cir. 1995).

[252] *See* United States v. Baker, 415 F.3d 1273 (11th Cir. 2005) (*per curiam*); *see also* Hakim v. Hicks, 223 F.3d 1244, 1249 (11th Cir. 2000) (finding that prison's regulation prohibiting use of a prisoner's religious name was unreasonable under the *Turner* standard).

[253] *See, e.g.*, Mutawakkil v. Huibregtse, 735 F.3d 524, 526–8 (7th Cir. 2013) (requirements of dual name policy did not violate RLUIPA); Fawaad v. Jones, 81 F.3d 1084, 1086–7 (11th Cir. 1996) (requirements of dual name policy did not violate RFRA); Azeez v. Fairman, 795 F.2d 1296, 1300–1 (7th Cir. 1986) (requirements of dual name did not violate the Free Exercise Clause).

[254] Baker, 415 F.3d at 1274 [citing Barrett v. Virginia, 689 F.2d 498, 503 (4th Cir. 1982); Imam Ali Abdullah Akbar v. Canney, 634 F.2d 339, 340 (6th Cir. 1980)].

[255] Blankenship v. Gunter, 707 F. Supp. 1137, 1139 (D. Neb. 1988), *aff'd*, 898 F.2d 625 (8th Cir. 1990); *see also* VanDyke v. S.W. Va. Reg'l Jail Auth., No. CIVA 7:06CV00267, 2006 WL 2475898, at *3 (W.D. Va. Aug. 25, 2006) (unpublished).

[256] Blankenship, 707 F. Supp. at 1139.

burden" on prison officials to compel them "to make an investigation of every request for transfer of funds."[257]

## C. Prisons: Claims by Correctional Employees and Clerics

Most religious freedom claims in the prison context are asserted by inmates, but occasionally such claims are asserted by correctional employees, including paid chaplains.[258] Correctional employees' religious freedom claims do not fall under RLUIPA because the employees are not institutionalized, but federal correctional employees may use RFRA and the Free Exercise Clause, and state correctional employees may use the Free Exercise Clause and their state's law of religious freedom. Although correctional employees' religious freedom rights are not constitutionally limited like those of inmates, their status as public employees may, when compared with civilians, lead to some diminishment of rights.[259] Moreover, the environment in which they are employed may lead to the validation of workplace restrictions or conditions that would not ordinarily be upheld outside the prison context.

Religious freedom claims initiated by correctional employees have typically involved challenges to dress codes[260] or grooming regulations, particularly restrictions on hair length.[261] Like traditional law enforcement agencies, most, if not all, prisons have uniform and grooming policies that may limit employee hair length, facial hair, and the like. However, these policies clash with some religions (e.g., the Rastafari movement and certain Native American belief systems) that require adherents to keep their hair long or braided.[262] To the extent that strict scrutiny governs the religious freedom analysis, then the prison must show that its policy is the least restrictive means of achieving a compelling government interest. Although such policies generally will be found to further compelling interests, such as fostering discipline and uniformity among employees,

257 *Id.*

258 Though apparently not often. *See* Francis v. Keane, 888 F. Supp. 568, 576 (S.D.N.Y. 1995) (noting that "there are almost no cases addressing free exercise claims by correctional officers").

259 *See* Finnie v. Lee Cnty., Miss., 907 F. Supp. 2d 750, 767 (N.D. Miss. 2012) {noting, in case involving a corrections officer, that "numerous courts have retreated from the typical strict scrutiny review to adopt some other less rigorous analytical framework in public employment free exercise cases" [citing Fraternal Order of Police Newark Lodge No. 12 v. City of Newark, 170 F.3d 359, 365–6 n. 7 (3d Cir. 1999); Baz v. Walters, 782 F.2d 701, 708 (7th Cir. 1986); Shatkin v. Univ. of Tex. at Arlington, No. 4:06-CV-882-Y, 2009 WL 614788, at *7 (N.D. Tex. 2009) (unpublished); Draper v. Logan Cnty. Pub. Library, 403 F. Supp. 2d 608 (W.D. Ky. 2005)]}.

260 *See, e.g.*, Finnie, 907 F. Supp. 2d at 762–9 (addressing free exercise challenge by female juvenile detention officer to regulation requiring that she wear pants, which she claimed violated her religious beliefs); Seabrook v. City of N.Y., No. 99-9169, 2000 WL 349276, 210 F.3d 355 (2d Cir. Apr. 4, 2000) (*per curiam*) (unpublished) (affirming denial of injunctive relief to female correctional officers who alleged that wearing pants, as required by prison regulation, violated their religious beliefs, under the U.S. and N.Y. Constitutions).

261 *See, e.g.*, Booth v. Maryland, 327 F.3d 377, 380–3 (4th Cir. 2003) (remanding Rastafarian jail guard's free exercise claim to determine whether the religiously neutral grooming policy had been unevenly implemented); Francis, 888 F. Supp. at 572–80 (addressing challenge by Rastafarian correctional officers to grooming regulation); Humphrey v. Lane, 728 N.E.2d 1039 (Ohio 2000) (addressing challenge by Native American correctional employee to hair length regulation), *cert. denied*, 531 U.S. 912 (2000); Rourke v. N.Y. Dep't of Corr. Servs., 615 N.Y.S.2d 470 (N.Y. App. Div. 1994) (same).

262 *See supra* notes 138–41 and accompanying text.

ensuring employee safety, and projecting a uniform professional image to inmates and the public,[263] full enforcement of the policies may not actually be necessary to achieve the prison's objectives. In turn, if an employee can wear his or her hair in a manner that deviates from the policy but does not undermine the prison's interests, then, under strict scrutiny, the prison policy should not be enforceable against the employee.[264]

Lastly, claims are occasionally brought by clergy or associated religious personnel often regarding access to correctional facilities and alleging discriminatory treatment among religions. To date, such claims, when pursued under the Free Exercise Clause, have not be successful. According to the courts, the clergy have no independent free exercise right to enter a correctional facility, or they lack standing to raise such a claim either on their own behalf or on behalf of inmates (so-called third party standing).[265]

## D. Prisons: Establishment Clause Claims

While prisoner claims make up a large part of civil litigation in the country, relatively few of these are brought under the Establishment Clause. According to a survey by the U.S. Commission on Civil Rights, Establishment Clause claims made up only about 2.2 percent of the religion-based claims filed by prisoners between 2001 and 2006.[266] Although violations of the Establishment Clause in prison are not especially common, when alleged, they are treated with relative gravity in light of the custodial nature of the state-prisoner relationship, the inherently restrictive nature of incarceration, and thus the heightened potential for coercion.[267] At the same time, the "[g]overnmental provision of various items to facilitate the exercise of religious freedoms" that "would undoubtedly give rise to cognizable claims under the Establishment Clause … in the free world" is often allowed and "in some instances mandated within the prison context."[268]

A general exposition of the Establishment Clause and its many principles, doctrines, and tests can be found in Chapter 4. Highlighted here will be three particular dimensions of the prison context in which Establishment Clause claims, to varying degrees

263 *Compare* Humphrey, 728 N.E.2d at 1046 (so holding using a comparable analysis under Ohio Const. art. I, § 7), *with* Rourke, 615 N.Y.S.2d at 472–3 (finding that the state failed to provide any legitimate interests in support of its policy strictly regulating employee hair length).

264 *See, e.g.*, Francis, 888 F. Supp. at 575 (holding, on summary judgment, that the correctional facility defendants had not demonstrated that a grooming policy as applied to two Rastafarian correctional officers was "the least restrictive means of advancing the state's asserted interests in safety, discipline and *esprit de corps*"); Humphrey, 728 N.E.2d at 1046 (finding, under the strict scrutiny test of Ohio Const. art. I, § 7, that allowing a correctional officer to wear his hair pinned under his uniform cap was a less restrictive means of achieving the government's interests).

265 *See, e.g.*, McCollum v. Cal. Dep't of Corr. & Rehab., 647 F.3d 870, 878–80 (9th Cir. 2011); O'Malley v. Brierley, 477 F.2d 785, 788–93 (3d Cir. 1973).

266 Gerald A. Reynolds et al., U.S. Commission on Civil Rights, Enforcing Religious Freedoms in Prison (2008).

267 Warner v. Orange Cnty. Dep't of Probation, 115 F.3d 1068, 1075–6 (2d Cir. 1997) (recognizing that due to the custodial nature and high stakes of correctional programs, these circumstances may be as or more coercive, natively, than situations involving children and establishment in schools).

268 Monmouth Cnty. Correctional Inst'l Inmates v. Lanzaro, 834 F.2d 326, 341 (3d Cir. 1987) (citations omitted), *cert. denied*, 486 U.S. 1006 (1988); *see also* Gittlemacker v. Prasse, 428 F.2d 1, 4 (3d Cir. 1970 (noting that "provid[ing] facilities for worship and the opportunity for … clergy to visit the institution … may be rationalized on the basis that since society has removed the prisoner from the community where he [or she] could freely exercise his [or her] religion, it has an obligation to furnish or supply him [or her] with the opportunity to practice his [or her] faith during confinement").

of success, have been asserted. These are, *first*, the validity of religious freedom accommodations not required by the Free Exercise Clause; *second*, the possibility of religious coercion, particularly in relation to mandated participation in rehabilitative programs; and *third*, the permissibility of having prison systems employ and direct chaplains.

### 1. *Religious Accommodations*

*Cutter v. Wilkinson*,[269] a U.S. Supreme Court decision, is perhaps the best-known Establishment Clause case involving the prison context, but the constitutional grievance in that case was raised not by inmates but by prison officials. In particular, they alleged that RLUIPA was facially unconstitutional insofar as it "improperly advances religion in violation of the First Amendment's Establishment Clause."[270] After all, if various religious accommodations are not required by the Free Exercise Clause, then a statute such as RLUIPA that mandates those accommodations but does not mandate comparable treatment of nonreligious requests could be seen as favoring or advancing religion and only religion. The Supreme Court, however, unanimously disagreed and upheld RLUIPA against their facial challenge. As it had in prior cases (though not with regard to a broad statute such as RLUIPA or RFRA), the Court "'recognized that the government may … accommodate religious practices … without violating the Establishment Clause'"[271] and "that 'there is room for play in the joints between' the Free Exercise and Establishment Clauses, allowing the government to accommodate religion beyond free exercise requirements, without offense to the Establishment Clause."[272] More specifically, the Court found "RLUIPA's institutionalized-persons provision compatible with the Establishment Clause because it alleviates exceptional government-created burdens on private religious exercise" – burdens on "persons who are unable freely to attend to their religious needs and are therefore dependent on the government's permission and accommodation for exercise of their religion"[273] – and because courts "[p]roperly applying RLUIPA … must take adequate account of the burdens a requested accommodation may impose on nonbeneficiaries,"[274] including an institution's need to maintain order and safety,"[275] and "must be satisfied that the Act's prescriptions are and will be administered neutrally among different faiths."[276] In short, and with these understandings, the prisoner accommodation scheme of RLUIPA "fits within the corridor between

269 544 U.S. 709 (2005).

270 *Id.* at 713.

271 *Id.* [quoting Hobbie v. Unemployment Appeals Comm'n of Fla., 480 U.S. 136, 144–5 (1987)].

272 *Id.* [quoting Locke v. Davey, 540 U.S. 712, 718 (2004)]; *see also id.* at 719 {"Our decisions recognize that 'there is room for play in the joints' between the Clauses, some space for legislative action neither compelled by the Free Exercise Clause nor prohibited by the Establishment Clause." (citation omitted) [quoting Walz v. Tax Comm'n of City of N.Y., 397 U.S. 664, 669 (1970)]}. *See, e.g.*, Goodvine v. Swiekatowski, 594 F. Supp. 2d 1049 (W.D. Wis. 2009) (noting that providing religious texts to prisoners to facilitate their free exercise falls in the permissible free space between the clauses, while providing only Bibles, and not Qur'ans or other religious texts, may exceed that free space and begin to impermissibly establish a religion).

273 Cutter, 544 U.S. at 721.

274 *Id.* at 720.

275 *Id.* at 722.

276 *Id.* at 720 (citation omitted).

the Religion Clauses: On its face, the Act qualifies as a permissible legislative accommodation of religion that is not barred by the Establishment Clause."[277]

Three aspects of *Cutter* merit emphasis. First, though it involved RLUIPA, its upholding of that statute strongly suggests that other across-the-board accommodation schemes, such as RFRA, the land use provisions of RLUIPA, and comparable state statutes or constitutional standards, also could survive a facial attack under the Establishment Clause.[278] This is important because federal prisoners must use RFRA, not RLUIPA, and because RLUIPA by its own terms might not apply to all prisoners in state or local custody, thus necessitating possible reliance on state religious freedom laws.[279] Second, RLUIPA was upheld in *Cutter* against a *facial* challenge, that is, a claim that the statute is unconstitutional as written, without regard to the facts of any particular accommodation situation. Accordingly, the Court did not foreclose Establishment Clause challenges to specific applications of RLUIPA,[280] and it went out of its way to emphasize certain considerations that, if absent, might have led to a different outcome, namely, that the statute's application will alleviate exceptional burdens, will take adequate account of the institution's and other prisoners' interests, and will be neutral among religions. On this point the Court could not have been clearer: "Should inmate requests for religious accommodations become excessive, impose unjustified burdens on other institutionalized persons, or jeopardize the effective functioning of an institution, the facility would be free to resist the imposition."[281] Third and lastly, it seems notable that the *Cutter* Court did not directly or systematically apply to RLUIPA the test of *Lemon v. Kurtzman*,[282] its long-standing but sometimes ignored three part analysis for assessing alleged Establishment Clause violations.[283] This doctrinal deviation could reflect the instability of the *Lemon* test, or it simply could reflect the Court's flexible approach to the Establishment Clause when assessing government efforts to accommodate religious practices.[284] In all events, it has led to some lower court uncertainty regarding the proper Establishment Clause analysis to be used specifically in the prison context and, further, how the *Turner* test might be

277 *Id.*

278 This has been the general judicial consensus regarding RFRA both prior to and after *Cutter*. *See, e.g.*, Hankins v. Lyght, 441 F.3d 96, 107–9 (2d Cir. 2006) (finding no Establishment Clause violation); Christians v. Crystal Evangelical Free Church, 141 F.3d 854, 861–3 (8th Cir. 1998) (same), *cert. denied*, 525 U.S. 811 (1998); EEOC v. Catholic Univ. of Am., 83 F.3d 455, 470 (D.C. Cir. 1996) (same).

279 RLUIPA's institutionalized persons provisions only apply to "a program or activity that receives Federal financial assistance" [42 U.S.C. § 2000cc-1(b)(1)] or where "the substantial burden [on an institutionalized person's free exercise] affects, or removal of that substantial burden would affect, commerce with foreign nations, among the several States, or with Indian tribes" [*id.* § 2000bb-1(b)(2)]. Although "[e]very State ... accepts federal funding for its prisons," *Cutter* (544 U.S. at 716 n. 4) it is unclear whether every local jail, for example, should or must be considered part of its state's prison program.

280 *See* Cutter, 544 U.S. at 725 ["In upholding RLUIPA's institutionalized-persons provision, we emphasize that ... [the prison officials] 'have raised a facial challenge to [the Act's] constitutionality, and have not contended that under the facts of any of [prisoners'] specific cases ... applying RLUIPA would produce unconstitutional results.'" (quoting district court opinion)].

281 *Id.* at 726.

282 403 U.S. 602 (1971). "First, the statute must have a secular legislative purpose; second, its principal or primary effect must be one that neither advances nor inhibits religion; finally, the statute must not foster 'an excessive government entanglement with religion.'" *Id.* at 612–13 (citation omitted) (quoting Walz, 397 U.S. at 674).

283 *See* Cutter, 544 U.S. at 717 & n. 6 (noting the lower court's use of the *Lemon* test and then simply remarking that it would "resolve this case on other grounds").

284 *See* Chapter 4.D.2 (addressing both possibilities, particularly the latter).

related to that analysis.[285] Other courts, however, have "consistently analyzed Establishment claims without mentioning the *Turner* standard, even when applying that standard to Free Exercise claims in the same case."[286]

## 2. *Coercion and Rehabilitation Programs*

Many mainstream religions see prison ministry as an important calling and respond by subsidizing programs that otherwise might be too expensive for the state itself to provide. At the same time, some of these privately subsidized religious programs may deliver services that are equally effective or perhaps more so than those delivered by nonreligious providers.[287] Several states, in turn, have been receptive to such programs.[288] What many religious organizations may seek in return for their lower-cost, higher-return alternative, however, is the opportunity to employ religiously based methods or even to evangelize to prisoners.[289]

This prospect creates a host of possible Establishment Clause issues – from endorsement to entanglement – but one of the most obvious is the potential for religious coercion. Prisoners, like civilians, may not be coerced into attending religious programs or receiving religious services either directly by imposing penalties for nonparticipation or indirectly by conditioning any nontrivial benefit or interest on their involvement with such programs or services.[290] In short, the "government may not coerce anyone to support or participate in religion or its exercise."[291]

285 *See, e.g.*, Salahuddin v. Perez, No. 99 Civ. 10431, 2006 WL 266574, at *9 (S.D.N.Y. Feb. 2, 2006) (unpublished).

286 Ams. United for Separation of Church & State v. Prison Fellowship Ministries, Inc. 509 F.3d 406, 426 (8th Cir. 2007).

287 *See, e.g.*, *id.* at 417 (describing how the religious program provider, InnerChange, was able to underbid the secular provider, Emerald Correctional Management, while still providing the added value of a licensed substance abuse program); Inouye v. Kemna, 504 F.3d 705, 714 n. 10 (9th Cir. 2007) {noting that there are "some data to suggest that the programs, as part of a larger treatment strategy, have helped many people maintain their sobriety, at least for a period of time" (citing Max Dehn, *How It Works: Sobriety Sentencing, The Constitution, and Alcoholics Anonymous*, 10 Mich. St. U.J. Med. & L. 255, 269–74 (2006)]}; Freedom from Religion Found., Inc. v. McCallum, 324 F.3d 880, 882 (7th Cir. 2003) ("The success of Alcoholics Anonymous is evidence that Christianity can be a valuable element in a program for treating addiction."). For critical discussion of the Eighth Circuit case, *Americans United, see* Winnifred Fallers Sullivan, Prison Religion: Faith-Based Reform and the Constitution (2009).

288 *See, e.g.*, Fla. Stat. § 944.803(1) (finding that "faith- and character-based programs offered in state and private correctional institutions and facilities have the potential to facilitate inmate institutional adjustment, help inmates assume personal responsibility, and reduce recidivism").

289 *Prison Fellowship Ministries*, 509 F.3d at 414 ("[T]he application of Biblical principles is not an agenda item – it is the agenda.").

290 *See* Jackson v. Nixon, 747 F.3d 537, 541–3 (8th Cir. 2014) (finding potential coercion where progress toward early parole appeared to be conditioned on participation in a rehabilitative program with religious components); Prison Fellowship Ministries, 509 F.3d at 421–3 (finding a religious prison rehabilitative program unconstitutional because amenities were made available to members that were not available to members of similar, secular programs); Kerr v. Farrey, 95 F.3d 472, 479–80 (7th Cir. 1996) (holding that requiring an inmate's attendance at Narcotics Anonymous meetings, where failure to attend would result in "significant penalties" such as "classification to a higher security risk category and adverse notations in his prison record that could affect his chances for parole," violated the Establishment Clause); Rachel F. Calabro, *Comment, Correction Through Coercion: Do State Mandated Alcohol and Drug Treatment Programs in Prisons Violate the Establishment Clause?* 47 DePaul L. Rev. 565 (1998); *see also* Warner v. Orange Cnty. Dep't of Probation, 115 F.3d 1068, 1075 (2d Cir. 1997) (holding that requiring a probationer to attend Alcoholics Anonymous meetings, which had a central religious component, violated the Establishment Clause).

291 Lee v. Weisman, 505 U.S. 557, 587 (1992) [quoting Lynch v. Donnelly, 465 U.S. 668, 678 (1984)].

Accordingly, "[s]everal courts have held that forcing inmates to participate in religion-based substance abuse programs, such as the twelve-step program used by Alcoholics Anonymous and Narcotics Anonymous, violates the Establishment Clause of the First Amendment."[292] In order for the coercion to be found unconstitutional under the Establishment Clause, however, the object of the coercion must be sufficiently religious in nature. For example, courts have found Alcoholics Anonymous' therapy method constitutionally problematic because it "involve[s] a substantial religious component" and "place[s] a heavy emphasis on spirituality and prayer, both in conception and in practice."[293] By contrast, therapeutic programming during which other participants discuss religion and the facilitators mention it only briefly for context does not sufficiently involve religion so as to make mandatory participation unconstitutionally coercive.[294]

Coercion also will not be found if a religiously based program is optional, either because participation in it is truly voluntary (i.e., nonparticipation will not adversely affect any interest of the prisoner)[295] or because a nonreligious alternative program is made available to prisoners.[296] In addition, there is obviously no coercion where a prisoner independently chooses to participate in such a program, fully understanding that it has religious dimensions. For example, in a funding-related challenge to a state corrections department's use of a religiously based halfway house for parolees who violated the terms of their release,[297] the court found that because prisoners were offered choices regarding whether to move into the halfway house (instead of accepting revocation of their parole) and into which house they could move (there being both religious and nonreligious options), a parolee's selection of the religious option should be viewed as a private voluntary choice, not attributable to government.[298] Of course, even if a religiously

[292] Catala v. Comm'r, No. Civ. 05-CV-106-JD, 2005 WL 3133036, at *1 (D.N.H. Nov. 22, 2005) (unpublished) [citing Warner, 115 F.3d at 1074, Kerr, 95 F.3d at 474; Bobko v. Lavan, No. Civ. 1:CV-04-0158, 2005 WL 1309072, at *3 (M.D. Pa. May 31, 2005) (unpublished), *aff'd*, No. 05-3184, 157 Fed. App'x 516 (3d Cir. 2005) (unpublished); Turner v. Hickman, 342 F. Supp. 2d 887, 895 (E.D. Cal. 2004)]; *see also* Nusbaum v. Terrangi, 210 F. Supp. 2d 784, 787–9 (E.D. Va. 2002); Ross v. Keelings, 2 F. Supp. 2d 810, 816–18 (E.D. Va. 1998); Griffin v. Coughlin, 673 N.E.2d 98, 108 (N.Y. 1996), *cert. denied*, 519 U.S. 1054 (1997).

[293] Warner, 115 F.3d at 1070; *see also* Inouye, 504 F.3d at 712–14 (holding that a parole officer's requirement that a parolee attend an Alcoholics Anonymous/Narcotics Anonymous program violated the Establishment Clause).

[294] *See* Gray v. Johnson, 436 F. Supp. 2d 795, 799–801 (W.D. Va. 2006).

[295] *See, e.g.*, Henderson v. Frank, No. 05-2684, 190 Fed. App'x 507, 509 (7th Cir. Aug. 3, 2006) (unpublished) (rejecting an inmate's challenge to a religiously based behavior modification program where the inmate "never provided any evidence that he was denied parole, advancement through the level system, or a transfer for refusing to complete a behavior modification program").

[296] *See, e.g.*, Bobko v. Levan, No. 05-3184, 157 Fed. App'x 516, 517 (3d Cir. 2005) (unpublished) (holding that required participation in a therapeutic program as a condition of parole was not religiously coercive where "defendants submitted evidence establishing that ... a secular approach to recovery ... [was also] available in the ... program"); Arnold v. Tenn. Bd. of Paroles, 956 S.W.2d 478, 484 (Tenn. 1997) (noting that "to require a prisoner to attend or participate in ... a treatment program would constitute a violation of the Establishment Clause" if the program is religious and "there are no alternative secular treatment programs offered"); Griffin, 673 N.E.2d at 108 (finding an Establishment Clause violation where participation in Alcoholics Anonymous was "mandated" and it was the "exclusive drug addiction and alcoholism rehabilitation program").

[297] McCallum, 324 F.3d at 881.

[298] *See id.* at 881–2 ["The choice must be private, to provide insulating material between government and religion. It *is* private; it is the offender's choice." (emphasis in original)].

based program is not coercive, that finding will not immunize it from other possible Establishment Clause concerns, such as endorsement or discrimination.[299]

### 3. *Chaplains*

Chaplains have been involved in the rehabilitative work of prisons and in caring for the spiritual needs of the incarcerated for as long as prisons have existed in this country. Indeed, "[e]arly prison chaplains in the United States held positions of relative importance, since they were part of a penal system created by religious groups."[300] As a result, they have come to be ... a fixture in the prison setting,[301] and "[m]ost of the direct influence of religion in corrections has been accomplished through the work of correctional chaplains."[302] Several state laws authorize chaplaincies or the involvement of clergy or religious advisors at their correctional facilities,[303] and the Federal Bureau of Prisons, as of 2007, employed 251 prison chaplains, with federal prisons typically having at least two full-time chaplains on staff.[304] The U.S. Commission on Civil Rights estimates that the number of active chaplains is actually many times that, given how many clergy choose to volunteer their time ministering in prison.[305]

Although the notion of chaplains serving as state employees or providers of government-funded religious services may seem to create obvious Establishment Clause issues, courts have repeatedly held that the employment and use of prison chaplains are, as a general matter, constitutional.[306] Just as prisons may and in some instances must

299 *See, e.g.*, Williams v. Lara, 52 S.W.3d 171, 191–2 (Tex. 2001) (holding that a county jail program, even if voluntary, violated the Establishment Clause because it "endorse[d] one religious view while excluding others, and thus convey[ed] the impermissible message of official preference for one specific religious view").

300 Dammer, *supra* note 1, at 837. "They were responsible for visiting inmates, providing services and sermons, and also served as teachers, librarians, and record keepers. Because of the limited budgets of correctional institutions, the early chaplains were often called upon to be the sole educator in many American prisons. The 'schooling' often consisted of the chaplain standing in a dark corridor with a lantern hanging from the cell bars, extolling the virtues of repentance." *Id.*

301 This reality may, by itself, justify the constitutionality of government-employed chaplains in the prison setting under the historical practice theory of *Marsh v. Chambers* [463 U.S. 783 (1983)] and, more recently, *Town of Greece, N.Y. v. Galloway* [134 S. Ct. 1811 (2014)].

302 Dammer, *supra* note 1, at 836.

303 *See, e.g.*, Ala. Code § 14-3-12; Ariz. Rev. Stat. § 31–206; Cal. Penal Code § 5009(b)–(c); Colo. Rev. Stat. § 17-42-101(4); Ky. Rev. Stat. 197.270; La. Rev. Stat. § 857; 34-A Me. Rev. Stat. § 3236; Mich. Comp. Laws § 800.291; Minn. Stat. §§ 241.05, 641.16; Miss. Code Ann. § 47-5-85; Mo. Stat. § 217.235; N.C. Gen. Stat. § 148-10.1; 57 Okla. Stat. § 5; Or. Rev. Stat. § 179.375; Wash. Rev. Code §§ 72.01.210, 72.01.220; Wis. Stat. § 301.33(1)–(2).

304 Gerald A. Reynolds et al., U.S. Comm'n on Civil Rights, Enforcing Religious Freedoms in Prison 16 (2008).

305 *See id.* at 16–17 (estimating that most federal prisons had between 27 and 150 volunteer chaplains, whereas some state facilities surveyed had several hundred during the twelve-month survey period).

306 *See, e.g.*, Hartmann v. Cal. Dep't of Corr. & Rehab., 707 F.3d 1114, 1126 (9th Cir. 2013) ("Prison employment of full-time chaplains to assist inmates in their religious exercise is a permissible accommodation within the established parameters of the First Amendment."); Montano v. Hedgepeth, 120 F.d 844, 850 n. 10 (8th Cir. 1997) (noting that "states might commit a technical violation of the Establishment Clause by ... hiring prison chaplains" but that "this is condoned as a permissible accommodation for persons whose free exercise rights would otherwise suffer"); Johnson-Bey v. Lane, 863 F.2d 1308, 1312 (7th Cir. 1988) ("[P]risoners ... have restricted or even no access to religious services unless government takes an active role in supplying those services ... The religious establishments that result are minor and seem

provide for inmates' secular needs by employing doctors, social workers, and educators, they also are permitted, if not required, to provide for inmates' spiritual needs by hiring clergy and arranging for religious advisors and volunteers.[307] As one district court has commented, "[i]n prisons, where the government has significant control over inmates' lives, 'a niche has necessarily been carved into the establishment clause to require the government to afford opportunities for worship.' Thus ... 'the establishment clause has been interpreted in the light of the affirmative demands of the free exercise clause.' "[308] In addition to their religious responsibilities, chaplains can play limited roles in prison administrative processes, such as serving as a witness at executions[309] and providing reports for parole consideration,[310] but they "cannot intervene excessively in the affairs of prison administration" insofar as "prison chaplains' exercise of substantial governmental authority may constitute excessive religious entanglement in the affairs of the state."[311] With regard to volunteer clergy, there is no rule against allowing religious personnel into cellblocks to minister to prisoners, but prison officials must not allow the coerced proselytization of those in their care.[312]

Courts also generally have upheld a variety of approaches to prison hiring of chaplains and the allocation of chaplain services. The Seventh Circuit, for example, has explained that "[p]risons are entitled to employ chaplains"[313] but "need not employ chaplains of each and every faith to which prisoners might happen to subscribe," especially given limited budgets and administrative capabilities, although it has also admonished that prison officials, in the provision of chaplaincy services, may not "discriminate against minority faiths except to the extent required by the exigencies of prison administration."[314] The Eleventh Circuit has even indicated that "the mere fact that a prison chaplain is of one

consistent with, and indeed required by, the overall purpose of the First Amendment's religion clauses, which is to promote religious liberty."); Theriault v. Silber, 547 F.2d 1279, 1280 (5th Cir. 1977) (*per curiam*) (summarily rejecting an Establishment Clause challenge to the "employment of chaplains in federal prisons"), *cert. denied*, 434 U.S. 871 (1977); Bates v. Or. Dep't of Corr., Civ. No. 93-674-FR, 1994 WL 123112, at *2 (D. Or. Aug. 11, 1994) (unpublished); Horn v. People of Cal., 321 F. Supp. 961, 965 (E.D. Cal. 1968), *aff'd*, 436 F.2d 1375 (9th Cir. 1970), *cert. denied*, 401 U.S. 976 (1971); Duffy v. State Personnel Bd., 232 Cal. Rptr. 622, 630–1 (Cal. Ct. App. 1991).

307 *See* Theriault v. Carlson, 339 F. Supp. 375, 380–1 (N.D. Ga. 1972), *rev'd on other grounds*, 495 F.2d 390 (5th Cir. 1974).

308 Muhammad v. City of N.Y. Dep't of Corr., 904 F. Supp. 161, 198 (S.D.N.Y. 1995) (citation omitted) [quoting United States v. Kahane, 396 F. Supp. 687, 698 (E.D.N.Y.), *ordered modified by* 527 F.2d 492 (2d Cir. 1975)], *appeal dismissed*, 126 F.3d 119 (2d Cir. 1997).

309 *See, e.g.*, Wyo. Stat. § 7-13-908(a)(iii)–(iv).

310 *See* Remmers v. Brewer, 494 F.2d 1277, 1278 (8th Cir. 1974) (*per curiam*), *cert. denied*, 419 U.S. 1012 (1974).

311 Theriault v. A Religious Office in the Structure of the Gov't Requiring a Religious Test as a Qualification, 895 F.2d 104, 107 (2d Cir. 1990).

312 *See* Campbell v. Cauthron, 623 F.2d 503, 509 (8th Cir. 1980) (holding that "jail officials must take steps ... to ensure that no inmate is subjected to forced religious indoctrination" by religious volunteers who had been authorized to enter the cell block).

313 Johnson-Bey v. Lane, 863 F.2d 1308, 1312 (7th Cir. 1988).

314 *Id.*; *see also* Hartmann, 707 F.3d at 1126 (discerning a possible Establishment Clause violation where a "prison administration has created staff chaplain positions for five conventional faiths, but fails to employ any neutral criteria in evaluating whether a growing membership in minority religions warrants a reallocation of resources used in accommodating inmates' religious exercise needs" and noting that "a prison administration accommodating inmates' rights under the First Amendment must do so without unduly preferring one religion over another").

particular faith does not constitute an Establishment Clause violation."[315] Rules requiring that religious services be led by an outside cleric or religious advisor rather than allowing inmate-led services have generally also met with court approval, as long as the prison officials make reasonable efforts to obtain the services of volunteer chaplains.[316]

## E. The Military: Introduction

The maxim that "there are no atheists in foxholes" is not entirely accurate,[317] but the fact remains that most members of the armed forces have specific, and at times heightened, spiritual needs. The federal government, based partly on its quasi-custodial relationship to service members, is necessarily tasked with addressing these spiritual demands, much as it supplies service members with sufficient food, housing, and medical care.[318] Correspondingly, the government is entitled to fund and control certain activities in the military setting that otherwise would be viewed as impermissibly establishing a state religion, such as hiring clergy, furnishing hymnals and other religious materials, and even constructing places of worship. As Justice Stewart once observed, "[s]pending federal funds to employ chaplains for the armed forces might be said to violate the Establishment Clause. Yet a lonely soldier stationed at some far-away outpost could surely complain that a government which did not provide him [or her] the opportunity for pastoral guidance was affirmatively prohibiting the free exercise of his [or her] religion."[319]

At the same time, the government potentially may restrict the religious freedom of service members in ways that would be entirely forbidden if imposed on the civilian populace. Like the prison context examined earlier in this chapter, the military context generates special government interests that can uniquely limit an individual's religious rights. National security, the operational readiness and effectiveness of the armed forces, and the requisite maintenance of a specialized military culture built on discipline, honor, loyalty, and obedience to lawful authority are interests of sufficient gravity – and

315 Ingram v. Ault, 50 F.3d 898, 900 (11th Cir. 1995) (*per curiam*) (internal quotations omitted) (not so holding itself, but approvingly quoting the district court's language); *see also* Card v. Dugger, 709 F. Supp. 1098, 1110 (M.D. Fla. 1988) (finding no Establishment Clause violation where forty-five of forty-seven full-time chaplains in state correctional system were Protestant Christian in the absence of evidence that hiring was religiously discriminatory and that inmates' spiritual needs were not being met), *aff'd*, 871 F.2d 1023 (11th Cir. 1989).

316 *See* Adkins v. Kaspar, 393 F.3d 559, 564–5 (5th Cir. 2004); Cooper v. Tard, 855 F.2d 125, 129–30 (3d Cir. 1988); Hadi v. Horn, 830 F.2d 779, 784–7 (7th Cir. 1987). Nor is a prison "required to excuse inmates to attend religious services outside of the prison." Johnson-Bey, 863 F.2d at 1310.

317 *See, e.g.*, Philip K. Paulson, *I Was an Atheist in a Foxhole*, THE HUMANIST, Sep.–Oct. 1989, *available at:* http://americanhumanist.org/humanism/I_Was_an_Atheist_in_a_Foxhole; *Atheists in Foxholes, in Cockpits, and on Ships*, *available at:* http://militaryatheists.org/atheists-in-foxholes/.

318 Members of the National Guard are ordinarily under state rather than federal authority (so-called Title 32 status), with the governor of their respective state serving as their commander in chief. However, they can be ordered into federal active duty (so-called Title 10 status), in which case the U.S. president serves as their commander in chief. *See* AIR FORCE OPERATIONS AND THE LAW: A GUIDE FOR AIR, SPACE, AND CYBER FORCES 221 (2d ed., 2009). This chapter will generally refer only to the federal government, and any analysis pursuant to the Free Exercise Clause should not differ if the service member is in the National Guard under state authority.

319 Sch. Dist. of Abington Twp., Pa. v. Schempp, 374 U.S. 203, 309 (Stewart, J., dissenting).

relative civilian unfamiliarity – that courts are unusually deferential to military regulations and judgments.[320] In the words of the Supreme Court,

> [w]hile the members of the military are not excluded from the protection granted by the First Amendment, the different character of the military community and of the military mission requires a different application of those protections. The fundamental necessity for obedience, and the consequent necessity for imposition of discipline, may render permissible within the military that which would be constitutionally impermissible outside it.[321]

These special circumstances by no means remove military governance from the purview of constitutional scrutiny by the courts, and judicial deference to military policies will necessarily diminish as the policies affect matters peripheral to the core mission and functions of the armed forces.[322] On the whole, however, the unique mission, expertise, and culture of the armed forces have led the judiciary to accord military officials a wide berth in their judgments on how best to govern those under their command, even when that governance impinges on otherwise cognizable constitutional interests. The next two sections examine how this dynamic plays out under the Free Exercise and Establishment Clauses, which are covered more generally in Chapters 5 and 4, respectively.

## F. The Military: Religious Freedom Claims

The Free Exercise Clause applies to the federal government in its relation to service members, but the scope of those service members' religious freedom is limited by several factors, chief among these being the aforementioned specialized culture of the military, the corresponding judicial deference to military judgments, and the fact that the relationship between the government and service members is, fundamentally, that of employer to employee. Accordingly, as one district court has remarked, "claims of religious infringement to military conduct occup[y] a judicial space of their own."[323] The process of asserting a free exercise claim also differs in the military relative to the civilian and non-public-employment spheres in that the Department of Defense as well as each branch of the armed services has in place directives, instructions, or regulations

320 *See* Lebron v. Rumsfeld, 670 F.3d 540, 559 (4th Cir. 2012) (noting "the reluctance by courts to intrude into matters of military governance"), *cert. denied*, 132 S. Ct. 2751 (2012); Hartmann v. Stone, 68 F.3d 973, 984–5 (6th Cir. 1995) ("The military exists to preserve the security of the United States, and in doing so it protects the freedoms of the citizenry ... This function has required courts to defer to [military] judgment on many aspects of internal operations ... [T]he military considers the maintenance of uniformity and the discipline it engenders to be a necessary ingredient of its preparedness, and the courts do not look any further."); Veitch v. Danzig, 135 F. Supp. 2d 32, 36 (D.D.C. 2001) (noting the "federal courts' historic reluctance 'to intrude upon the authority of the Executive in military and national security affairs'" [quoting Dep't of Navy v. Egan, 484 U.S. 518, 530 (1988)].

321 Parker v. Levy, 417 U.S. 733, 758 (1974).

322 *See, e.g.*, Hartmann, 68 F.3d at 985–6 (invalidating an Army policy under the Free Exercise Clause where the policy "control[led] the conduct of people not in the Armed Forces" – i.e., families of soldiers – and a "link to [the Army's] combat mission" was not "discernible"); Rigdon v. Perry, 962 F. Supp. 150, 162 (D.D.C. 1997) (invalidating a military policy under RFRA where the military officials, among other things, "failed to submit any evidence showing how [the claimants' religious expression] ... would in any way ... create a clear danger to the loyalty, discipline or morale of the troops").

323 Larson v. U.S. Navy, 486 F. Supp. 2d 11, 28 (D.D.C. 2007).

governing the religious freedom of service members, either as free-standing policies[324] or as exceptions to grooming, uniform, or other general standards.[325] In compliance with these rules, service members generally must pursue their claims, at least in the first instance, through separate administrative and judicial mechanisms within the military.[326]

Illustrative of these unique dynamics and processes is the case of *Goldman v. Weinberger*, decided by the U.S. Supreme Court in 1986.[327] Goldman, an Orthodox Jewish rabbi and Air Force captain, served as a clinical psychologist at a military-run mental health institution. After being disciplined for wearing his yarmulke in violation of an Air Force regulation governing headgear, Goldman challenged the regulation pursuant to the Free Exercise Clause.[328] Under the then-prevailing standard of that clause, at least the one applicable to civilian claims, Goldman's suit presumably would have triggered strict scrutiny, and the government would have had to demonstrate that prohibiting him from wearing the yarmulke was necessary to achieve a compelling interest.[329]

324 *See, e.g.*, Dep't of Defense Instruction 1300.17 (rev'd Jan. 22, 2014) ("Accommodation of Religious Practices within the Military Services"); Air Force Instruction 1-1, ¶¶ 2.11 (Aug. 7, 2012) ("Government Neutrality Regarding Religion" and "Free Exercise of Religion and Religious Accommodation"); Army Reg. 600-20, ¶ 5–6 (Sep. 20, 2012) ("Accommodating religious practices"); Sec'y of the Navy Instruction 1730.8B (Oct. 2, 2008) ("Accommodation of Religious Practices").

325 *See, e.g.*, Air Force Instruction 36-2903 (Jul. 18, 2011, rev'd Jun. 1, 2012) (setting forth grooming and uniform standards with specific provisions for religious accommodation); Navy Personnel Manual 1050-280, at ¶ 5(a)(3) (Aug. 22, 2002) (allowing "special liberty" or leave "for observance of major religious events, requiring the individual to be continuously absent from work or duty"); Navy Uniform Regulations (NAVPERS 15665I) 1101, at § 4 (containing exceptions to headgear rules for religious services). In addition, the Army occasionally grants limited religious exceptions to Army Regulation 670–1, which sets forth grooming and uniform standards. *See* Thomas R. Lamont, *The Thirteenth Charles L. Decker Lecture in Administrative and Civil Law*, 212 MIL. L. REV. 222, 228 (2012).

326 In addition to these intramilitary administrative processes, service member suits for damages may be uniquely blocked by the *Feres* doctrine, a judicially crafted exception to the federal government's waiver of immunity for alleged tortious conduct, including violations of constitutional rights, "where the injuries arise out of or are in the course of activity incident to service." Feres v. United States, 340 U.S. 135, 146 (1950) [construing the Federal Tort Claims Act, 28 U.S.C. § 1346(b)]; *see* Lombard v. United States, 690 F.2d 215, 228 (D.C. Cir. 1982) (applying *Feres* to constitutional claims), *cert. denied*, 462 U.S. 1118 (1983); Tobin v. Pryce, 983 F. Supp. 880, 887–8 (D. Neb. 1997) (holding that *Feres* barred a free exercise claim).

327 475 U.S. 503 (1986); *see also* Khalsa v. Weinberger, 779 F.2d 1393 (9th Cir. 1985) (a similar case involving the wearing of Sikh turbans, with identical results, wherein the court's analysis rests on a slippery-slope-type rationale); Veitch v. Danzig, 135 F. Supp. 2d 32 (D.D.C. 2001) (a widely publicized case in which the district court finds that a court-marshaled chaplain's religious issues are insubstantial, given the fact of his overarching duty as an officer). Interestingly, *Goldman* predates *Employment Division v. Smith* and, along with other cases from the 1980s, arguably presages *Smith*'s reasoning if not its doctrinal reconfiguration.

328 *See id.* at 505–6. The regulation provided that the only persons authorized to wear headgear indoors were armed military police performing their duties. An exception was made for Captain Goldman to wear his yarmulke indoors, on the condition that he wear it only indoors. After he rejected the condition and his attorney contacted the Air Force General Counsel, the exception was withdrawn, and disciplinary proceedings were initiated. He then brought suit. *See id.* at 505. These are the facts from the Court's opinion. For a more robust factual exposition, *see* Samuel J. Levine, *Untold Stories of Goldman v. Weinberger: Religious Freedom Confronts Military Uniformity*, 66 A.F. L. REV. 205 (2010).

329 The standard for assessing free exercise claims in the military was not entirely clear. *Compare* Sherwood v. Brown, 619 F.2d 47, 48 (9th Cir. 1980) (*per curiam*) (using strict scrutiny), *with* Bitterman v. Sec'y of Defense, 553 F. Supp. 719, 722–3 (D.D.C. 1982) (expressing uncertainty as to appropriate standard, ultimately using something like strict scrutiny). *See* Thomas R. Folk, *Military Appearance Requirements and the Free Exercise Clause*, 98 MIL. L. REV. 53 (1982) (noting the conflict among courts).

The Court made clear from the outset of the case, however, that strict scrutiny was not an appropriate standard in the military context, noting that it had "repeatedly held that 'the military is, by necessity, a specialized society separate from civilian society'" and "'must insist upon a respect for duty and a discipline without counterpart in civilian life,' in order to prepare for and perform its vital role."[330]

Instead, said the Court, judicial "review of military regulations challenged on First Amendment grounds is far more deferential than constitutional review of similar laws or regulations designed for civilian society."[331] In particular, "when evaluating whether military needs justify a particular restriction on religiously motivated conduct, courts must give great deference to the professional judgment of military authorities concerning the relative importance of a particular military interest."[332] As for evidence offered by Goldman that religious exceptions are desirable and will increase morale, the Court bluntly stated that "whether or not expert witnesses may feel that religious exceptions to ... [the regulation] are desirable is quite beside the point. The desirability of dress regulations in the military is decided by the appropriate military officials, and they are under no constitutional mandate to abandon their considered professional judgment."[333] Though acknowledging that the regulations may make "military life ... more objectionable for ... [Goldman] and probably others,"[334] the Court nevertheless concluded that the they "reasonably and evenhandedly regulate dress in the interest of the military's perceived need for uniformity" and ultimately ruled that the Goldman's free exercise of religion was not violated.[335]

Less than two years after *Goldman*, Congress responded by enacting a statute to govern the wearing of religious apparel while in uniform.[336] At first blush, the statute seems rather protective, guaranteeing that "a member of the armed forces may wear an item of religious apparel while wearing the uniform of the member's armed force."[337] However, additional provisions indicate that "the wearing of an item of religious apparel" may be prohibited if it is determined, pursuant to military regulations promulgated under the statute, either "that the wearing of the item would interfere with the performance of the member's military duties"[338] or "that the item of apparel is not neat and conservative."[339]

This particular statutory response aside, the more significant developments arising after *Goldman* have concerned the appropriate standard of scrutiny for military religious freedom claims. The first of these occurred in 1990, when the Supreme Court, in *Employment Division v. Smith*,[340] held that the strict scrutiny standard, which many believed to be the default standard (outside the military) for *prima facie* free exercise infringements, would henceforth be available only if the challenged law or policy is not

330 Goldman, 475 U.S. at 506–7 (citations omitted) [quoting Parker v. Levy, 417 U.S. 733, 743 (1974), and Schlesinger v. Councilman, 420 U.S. 738, 757 (1975), respectively].

331 *Id.* at 507.

332 *Id.*

333 *Id.* at 509.

334 *Id.*

335 *Id.* at 510.

336 Pub. L. No. 100–180, div. A, tit. V, § 508(a)(2), 101 Stat. 1086 (Dec. 4, 1987) (codified at 10 U.S.C. § 774).

337 10 U.S.C. § 774(a).

338 *Id.* § 774(b)(1).

339 *Id.* § 774(b)(2).

340 494 U.S. 872 (1990).

neutral or generally applicable and perhaps in limited other circumstances.[341] In the absence of strict scrutiny, courts presumably should apply the highly deferential rational basis test.[342] The second development occurred in 1993, when Congress responded to *Smith* by enacting the Religious Freedom Restoration Act (RFRA),[343] which statutorily reinstated strict scrutiny as the default standard whenever a claimant can demonstrate that a law or policy substantially burdens a religious practice, even if the law or policy is neutral and generally applicable. Though RFRA's application to state and local governments was ruled unconstitutional in 1997,[344] it remains, at least by its text and by acquiescence, applicable to actions of the federal government.[345]

These developments, in turn, generate two questions: *first*, whether the correct Free Exercise Clause standard for the military context is that of *Goldman* or that of *Smith* and, *second*, whether RFRA applies to the military (and, if so, whether it applies in the same way that it applies outside the military). As to the first question, *Smith* approvingly mentions *Goldman*[346] and certainly does not overrule it – *Smith*, in fact, overruled no cases – suggesting that *Goldman* provides the appropriate standard. To some extent, the answer to this question may be inconsequential given the apparent similarity between the two standards, but lower courts and litigants ought to know which case supplies the governing framework. As to the second question, one's answer is, by contrast, potentially quite significant because RFRA most assuredly imposes a different and higher standard than either *Goldman* or *Smith*.

To date, the cases indicate that RFRA does apply to the federal military context,[347] which is also the position taken in some service branch instructions.[348] This position is certainly consistent with the statute's language, which nowhere exempts the military, as well as its legislative history, which evinces an expectation by Congress that RFRA would be so applied but with appropriate deference to military decision making.[349] It is this apparent expectation, to be sure, that will determine whether courts will apply to

[341] *See* Chapter 5.F.

[342] *See* Chapter 5.E.3.

[343] Pub. L. No. 103–141, 107 Stat. 1488 (Nov. 16, 1993) (codified as amended at 42 U.S.C. §§ 2000bb to 2000bb-4).

[344] *See* City of Boerne v. Flores, 521 U.S. 507 (1997).

[345] *See* 42 U.S.C. § 2000bb-2(1); Gonzales v. O Centro Espirita Beneficente Uniao do Vegetal, 546 U.S. 418 (2006) (applying RFRA, where the federal government did not challenge its constitutionality). Several lower courts have explicitly upheld RFRA's application to the federal government. *See, e.g.*, Blackhawk v. Pennsylvania, 381 F.3d 202, 212 (3d Cir. 2004); O'Bryan v. Bureau of Prisons, 349 F.3d 399, 401 (7th Cir. 2003); Henderson v. Kennedy, 265 F.3d 1072, 1073 (D.C. Cir. 2001), *cert. denied*, 535 U.S. 986 (2002); Guam v. Guerrero, 290 F.3d 1210, 1219–21 (9th Cir. 2002); Kikumura v. Hurley, 242 F.3d 950, 958–9 (10th Cir. 2001); Christians v. Crystal Evangelical Free Church, 141 F.3d 854, 859–61 (8th Cir. 1998), *cert. denied*, 525 U.S. 811 (1998).

[346] *See* Smith, 494 U.S. at 884.

[347] *See, e.g.*, Lipton v. Peters, No. Civ. SA-99-0235-EP, 1999 WL 33289705, at *3 (W.D. Tex. Oct. 12, 1999) (unpublished), *aff'd*, No. 00-50200, 240 F.3d 1074 (5th Cir. Nov. 30, 2000) (unpublished); Rigdon v. Perry, 962 F. Supp. 150, 160–2 (D.D.C. 1997); United States v. Webster, 65 M.J. 936, 944–8 (Army Ct. Crim. App. 2008), *review denied*, 67 M.J. 9 (C.A.A.F. 2008).

[348] *See, e.g.*, Air Force Instruction 31-205 ¶ 6.5.4 (Apr. 7, 2004, rev'd Jul. 6, 2007) (recognizing its application to those in military correctional custody).

[349] *See* Jeffrey Lakin, *Note, Atheists in Foxholes: Examining the Current State of Religious Freedom in the United States Military*, 9 FIRST AMEND. L. REV. 713, 729–30 (2011) (summarizing the House and Senate reports).

military RFRA claims a robust, civilian-type version of strict scrutiny[350] or will instead adjust the scrutiny, or the impact of that scrutiny, in deference to military judgments, just as the Supreme Court has explained that courts applying another federal religious freedom statute in the prison context should do so in a way that accords significant deference to prison officials.[351] As the Court explained with regard to that statute, "[w]hile the Act adopts a 'compelling governmental interest' standard, '[c]ontext matters' in the application of that standard."[352] In light of RFRA's legislative history and the judiciary's traditional deference to military decisions, there is good reason to believe that a comparable perspective will attend the judicial application of RFRA's strict scrutiny standard in the military context.[353]

## G. The Military: Establishment Clause Claims

The Establishment Clause, which prohibits Congress from making any "law respecting an establishment of religion,"[354] applies without question to governmental actions in the military context. As with the Free Exercise Clause, however, the uniqueness of that context can affect the force or relevance of doctrines formulated in cases involving only civilians. On the one hand, the deference traditionally accorded by the judiciary to military decisions may lead to the tempering or even the nonapplication of certain Establishment Clause tests. For example, the Second Circuit's decision upholding the Army's chaplaincy program,[355] discussed in greater length in Section I, specifically found it inappropriate to apply the Supreme Court's principal Establishment Clause test partly because of the long-standing nature of the program but also partly because the program rested ultimately on the constitutional authority of Congress over military affairs. On the other hand, the custodial and hierarchical nature of the military context can lead to heightened judicial concern about certain Establishment Clause problems, such as religious coercion and discrimination, that ordinarily arise only with public school students and prison inmates.

Apart from the potential Establishment Clause issues relating to conscription and military chaplaincies, which are addressed respectively in the next two sections, there are few suits involving Establishment Clause challenges in the military context, although a common theme in a number of these is alleged coercion or compulsion of religious activity.[356]

350 *See, e.g.*, Gonzales v. O Centro Espirita Beneficente Uniao do Vegetal, 546 U.S. 418 (2006) (using full-blown strict scrutiny under RFRA and holding that the federal government failed to demonstrate a compelling interest in the application of the Controlled Substances Act to a particular religious practice).

351 *See* Cutter v. Wilkinson, 544 U.S. 709 (2005) (addressing Section 3 of the Religious Land Use and Institutionalized Persons Act, 42 U.S.C. § 2000cc-1).

352 *Id.* at 722–3 (citation omitted) [quoting Grutter v. Bollinger, 539 U.S. 306, 327 (2003)].

353 *Cf., e.g.*, Webster, 65 M.J. at 946, 947–8 (in a case involving RFRA and the Free Exercise Clause, explaining that "[t]he *Goldman* decision instructs courts to apply judicial deference when strictly scrutinizing the military's burden on the free exercise of religion" and then finding the strict scrutiny test satisfied).

354 U.S. Const. amend. I.

355 Katcoff v. Marsh, 755 F.2d 223 (2d Cir. 1985).

356 *See* Anderson v. Laird, 466 F.2d 283 (D.C. Cir. 1972) (invaliding a requirement that students at the federal military academies attend chapel services), *cert. denied*, 409 U.S. 1076 (1972); Spadone v. McHugh, Civ. Action No. 11-01601-BJR, 2014 WL 46456 (D.D.C. Jan. 7, 2014) (dismissing as moot a claim by a former West Point cadet alleging forced recital of the Cadet's Prayer as part of an investigative hearing at which he was accused of plagiarism); Weinstein v. U.S. Air Force, 468 F. Supp. 2d 1366 (D.N.M. 2006) (dismissing

The leading case of this genre is *Anderson v. Laird*,[357] a D.C. Circuit Court ruling that struck down regulations requiring cadets and midshipmen at the nation's military academies to attend religious services. The three-judge panel was divided two to one in the judgment, and the two in the majority each provided his own opinion, but these two judges both agreed that the requirements were invalid under the Establishment Clause because they compelled religious observance, penalizing those who failed to adhere to the requirements "by reprimands, demerits, punishment marching tours, confinement to quarters, and possible expulsion."[358] In the view of one of the two judges in the majority, "[t]he Establishment Clause assures that the exercise of religion will be truly free – will be voluntary, and not imposed" – and this "essential requirement of voluntarism is breached by the compulsory Academy regulations."[359]

## H. The Military: Conscription and Conscientious Objection

### 1. *Historical Development and Statutory Framework*

Prior to the Civil War, conscription was performed by the state governments, corresponding to the reality that the armed forces consisted primarily of state-level militia units.[360] In turn, "[t]he early problem of conscientious objectors was strictly one of local … or state concern."[361] The states often provided, in their constitutions or other laws, exemptions for adherents to pacifist faiths,[362] most notably the Society of Friends, or Quakers.[363] Congress for the first time authorized conscription in 1863,[364] and in an amendment the following year it exempted from combat duty persons who "are conscientiously opposed to the bearing of arms, and who are prohibited from doing so by the rules and articles of faith [of their] … religious denominations."[365] The Confederacy had already incorporated a similar exemption in its own draft law of 1862.[366]

for lack of standing a claim by recent Air Force Academy graduates alleging various forms of religious coercion, harassment, and proselytization); *cf.* Mellen v. Bunting, 327 F.3d 355 (4th Cir. 2003) (invalidating a requirement that students stand at attention during a supper prayer at a state-operated military academy), *cert. denied*, 541 U.S. 1019 (2004). Two exceptions are Winkler v. Gates, 481 F.3d 977 (7th Cir. 2007) (dismissing, for lack of standing, a federal taxpayer's claim alleging that a federal statute requiring the U.S. military to assist the Boy Scouts with its jamboree violated the Establishment Clause), and Jewish War Veterans of U.S. v. United States, 695 F. Supp. 3, 11–14 (D.D.C. 1988) (holding that a sixty-five-foot Latin cross, erected on a Marine Corps base in Hawaii as a memorial for missing soldiers, violated the Establishment Clause).

357 466 F.2d 283 (D.C. Cir. 1972).

358 *Id.* at 285 (opinion of Bazelon, C. J.).

359 *Id.* at 297 (opinion of Leventhal, J.).

360 Correspondingly, prior to American independence, conscription was effected at the colonial level. *See* William L. Shaw, *Selective Service: A Source of Military Manpower*, 13 MIL. L. REV. 35, 40–1 (1961).

361 Robert R. Russell, *Development of Conscientious Objector Recognition in the United States*, 20 GEO. WASH. L. REV. 409, 412 (1952).

362 *See* United States v. Seeger, 380 U.S. 163, 170 (1965).

363 Regarding the pre-Revolutionary era, *see* Michael W. McConnell, *The Origins and Historical Understanding of the Free Exercise of Religion*, 103 HARV. L. REV. 1409, 1468 (1990) (noting colonial exemptions).

364 Enrollment Act, ch. 75, 12 Stat. 731 (Mar. 3, 1863). *See* Shaw, *supra* note 360, at 42–4 (discussing various aspects of the 1863 law).

365 Act of Feb. 24, 1864, ch. 13, § 17, 13 Stat. 6, 9, *quoted in* Gillette v. United States, 401 U.S. 437, 443 n. 8 (1971). *See* Russell, *supra* note 361, at 418–19 (discussing the 1864 amendment).

366 *See* Russell, *supra* note 361, at 419–20 (discussing the 1862 act as well as other Confederate conscription efforts); Shaw, *supra* note 360, at 44–6 (same); *see also* William L. Shaw, *The Confederate Conscription*

The Selective Service Act of 1917,[367] also known as the "Conscription Act" or "Military Draft Act," likewise exempted any person "whose religious convictions are against war or participation therein in accordance with the creed or principles of [and who belong to] … any well-recognized religious sect or organization at present organized and existing and whose existing creed or principles forbid its members to participate in war in any form."[368] Thus, for example, the act exempted members of the Quaker and Anabaptist communities.[369] Challenges to the conscription scheme and its exemptions were summarily rejected by the Supreme Court, which explained that it would not even analyze "the proposition that an establishment of a religion or an interference with the free exercise thereof repugnant to the First Amendment resulted from the exemption clauses … because we think its unsoundness is too apparent to require us to do more."[370]

After World War I, the Court also indicated that the exemption of conscientious objectors was a matter of legislative grace, not constitutional right, though it acknowledged the long tradition of providing such exemptions. In *United States v. Macintosh*,[371] the Court declared that

> [t]he conscientious objector is relieved from the obligation to bear arms in obedience to no constitutional provision, express or implied; but because, and only because, it has accorded with the policy of Congress thus to relieve him.… The privilege of the native-born conscientious objector to avoid bearing arms comes, not from the Constitution, but from the acts of Congress. That body may grant or withhold the exemption as in its wisdom it sees fit; and, if it be withheld, the native-born conscientious objector cannot successfully assert the privilege. No other conclusion is compatible with the well-nigh limitless extent of the war powers … which include, by necessary implication, the power, in the last extremity, to compel the armed service of any citizen in the land, without regard to his objections or his views in respect of the justice or morality of the particular war or of war in general.[372]

The Selective Training and Service Act of 1940,[373] also known as the "Burke-Wadsworth Act," retained the conscientious objector exemption but removed the organizational affiliation requirement, instead requiring simply that a person "by reason of religious

*and Exemption Acts*, 6 Am. J. Legal Hist. 368 (1962). The original Confederate statute, Conscription Act (Confed. Cong., 1st Cong., 1st Sess., act 31) (Apr. 16, 1862), was amended on Apr. 21, 1862, to exempt, among other persons, "all persons who have been and now are members of the society of Friends and the association of Dunkards, Nazarenes and Mennonists, in regular membership in their respective denominations: Provided, Members of the society of Friends, Nazarenes, Mennonists and Dunkards shall furnish substitutes or pay a tax of five hundred dollars each into the public treasury."

367 Pub. L. No. 65–12, ch. 15, 40 Stat. 76 (May 18, 1917). *See* Shaw, *supra* note 360, at 47–50 (discussing various aspects of the 1917 law).

368 Pub. L. No. 65–12, ch. 15, § 4, 40 Stat. at 78 (codified at former 50 U.S.C. app. § 204); *see* Russell, *supra* note 361, at 420–2 (discussing conscientious objection under the 1917 law).

369 *See* John Whiteclay Chambers II, To Raise an Army: The Draft Comes to Modern America 216–17 (1987); William W. Hartzog, American Military Heritage 120 (2006).

370 Arver v. United States, 245 U.S. 366, 389–90 (1918).

371 283 U.S. 605 (1931), *overruled in part by* Girouard v. United States, 328 U.S. 61 (1946).

372 *Id.* at 623–4; *see also* United States v. Schwimmer, 279 U.S. 644, 650–3 (1929), *overruled in part by* Girouard v. United States, 328 U.S. 61 (1946); Shaw, *supra* note 360, at 50–1 (discussing the *Hamilton* case).

373 Pub. L. No. 76–783, 54 Stat. 885 (Sep. 16, 1940).

training and belief" be "conscientiously opposed to participation in war in any form."[374] If the person's opposition extended only to combat service, then he would be assigned a noncombatant role; if it extended to all military service, then he would "be assigned to work of national importance under civilian direction."[375] One consequence of eliminating the requirement of affiliation with a recognized pacifist denomination was that courts themselves had to determine what types of training and belief were sufficiently "religious" to qualify for the exemption. The Ninth Circuit, for example, held that the exemption was intended to encompass "an individual's belief in his responsibility to an authority higher and beyond any worldly one" but not "a conscientious social belief, or a sincere devotion to a high moralistic philosophy"[376] or a belief "based entirely upon philosophical, social or political policy."[377] "[N]o matter how pure and admirable ... [an applicant's] standard may be, and no matter how devotedly he adheres to it, [a] philosophy and morals and social policy without the concept of deity cannot be said to be religion in the sense of that term as it is used in the statute."[378] Likewise, the Second Circuit held that the exemption did not extend to a belief "based on philosophical and political considerations" such as a "conviction that war is a futile means of righting wrongs or of protecting the state, that it is not worth the sacrifice, that it is waged for base ends, or is otherwise indefensible."[379]

In 1948, Congress enacted a revised Selective Service Act,[380] also known as the "Elston Act" and, by later amendment, the "Universal Military Training and Service Act."[381] Like its predecessors, this statute contained a conscientious objector exemption for those who opposed all war on the basis of "religious training and belief," although it defined this phrase to mean "a relation to a Supreme Being involving duties superior to those arising from any human relation, but ... not includ[ing] essentially political, sociological, or philosophical views or a merely personal moral code."[382] The Supreme Court

374 *Id.* § 5(g), 54 Stat. at 889 [codified at former 50 U.S.C. app. § 305(g)], *quoted in* Girouard, 328 U.S. at 66. Congress in the 1940 statute, absent presidential authorization to the contrary, withheld from the courts the power to review the accuracy of exemption denials under the statute {*id.* § 10(a)(2), 54 Stat. at 893 [codified at former 50 U.S.C. app. § 310(a)(2)]}, but courts held that as long as the applicant submitted to induction, they could effectively review such denials collaterally by means of a writ of *habeas corpus*. *See, e.g.*, United States v. Kauten, 133 F.2d 703, 706–7 (2d Cir. 1943); United States v. Bowles, 131 F.2d 818 (3d Cir. 1942), *aff'd*, 319 U.S. 33 (1943). For general analysis, *see* Russell, *supra* note 361, at 422–7; Shaw, *supra* note 360, at 51–4.

375 Pub. L. No. 76–783, § 5(g), 54 Stat. at 889.

376 Berman v. United States, 156 F.2d 377, 380 (9th Cir. 1946), *cert. denied*, 329 U.S. 795 (1946).

377 *Id.* at 382.

378 *Id.* at 381.

379 Kauten, 133 F.2d at 707. "There is a distinction between a course of reasoning resulting in a conviction that a particular war is inexpedient or disastrous and a conscientious objection to participation in any war under any circumstances. The latter, and not the former, may be the basis of exemption under the Act. The former is usually a political objection, while the latter, we think, may justly be regarded as a response of the individual to an inward mentor, call it conscience or God, that is for many persons at the present time the equivalent of what has always been thought a religious impulse." *Id.* at 708.

380 Pub. L. No. 80–759, 62 Stat. 604 (Jun. 24, 1948) (codified as amended at 50 U.S.C. app. §§ 451–73).

381 Pub. L. No. 82–51, 65 Stat. 75 (Jun. 19, 1951). *See* Russell, *supra* note 361, at 427–9 (discussing the 1948 and 1951 statutes); Shaw, *supra* note 360, at 54–6 (same).

382 Pub. L. No. 80–759, § 6(j), 62 Stat. at 612–13 [codified at 50 U.S.C. app. § 456(j)]. *See* Shaw, *supra* note 360, at 60–3 (discussing the exemptions for religious ministers and conscientious objection under the statute).

confronted the revised exemption in *United States v. Seeger*,[383] which involved a draftee who refused to submit to induction based on conscientious beliefs that were arguably religious, though largely agnostic, and thus presumably outside of Congress's "Supreme Being" definition of religious belief. Ruling for Mr. Seeger, the Court construed the exemption to include "[a] sincere and meaningful belief which occupies in the life of its possessor a place parallel to that filled by the God of those admittedly qualifying for the exemption."[384] "Local boards and courts," the justices said, "are not free to reject beliefs because they consider them 'incomprehensible.' Their task is to decide whether the beliefs professed by a registrant are sincerely held and whether they are, in his own scheme of things, religious."[385]

Five years later, in *Welsh v. United States*,[386] the Court again addressed the conscientious objector exemption under the 1948 statute. This time, a plurality of justices held that the exemption also should have been extended to an individual who sought conscientious objector status based on his beliefs, which he described as concerning morality[387] and "certainly religious in the ethical sense of the word,"[388] even though he specifically crossed out "religious training and" on the conscientious objector form.[389] The determinative factors, these justices held, are that a registrant's "opposition to war stem from [his] moral, ethical, or religious beliefs about what is right and wrong and that these beliefs be held with the strength of traditional religious convictions."[390]

In 1967, Congress amended the Selective Service Act, and among other things deleted the "Supreme Being" language of the 1948 statute in accordance with *Seeger*.[391] The 1967 version is materially identical to the current version, which in relevant part provides that the statute shall not

> be construed to require any person to be subject to combatant training and service in the armed forces of the United States who, by reason of religious training and belief, is conscientiously opposed to participation in war in any form. As used in this subsection, the term "religious training and belief" does not include essentially political, sociological, or philosophical views, or a merely personal moral code.[392]

As this language indicates, one's animating beliefs cannot consist of "essentially political, sociological, or philosophical views, or a merely personal moral code," although the *Seeger* and *Welsh* decisions – especially Mr. Welsh's initial refusal to use the word

383 380 U.S. 163 (1965).
384 *Id.* at 176.
385 *Id.* at 184–5.
386 398 U.S. 333 (1970) (plurality opinion).
387 *See id.* at 343.
388 *Id.* at 341.
389 *See id.* at 337, 341. "In his original application in April 1964, Welsh stated that he did not believe in a Supreme Being, but in a letter to his local board in June 1965, he requested that his original answer be stricken and the question left open." *Id.* at 337 n. 3.
390 *Id.* at 340. "If an individual deeply and sincerely holds beliefs that are purely ethical or moral in source and content but that nevertheless impose upon him a duty of conscience to refrain from participating in any war at any time, those beliefs certainly occupy in the life of that individual 'a place parallel to that filled by … God' in traditionally religious persons. Because his beliefs function as a religion in his life, such an individual is as much entitled to a 'religious' conscientious objector exemption … as is someone who derives his conscientious opposition to war from traditional religious convictions." *Id.*
391 *See* Pub. L. No. 90–40, § 1(7), 81 Stat. 100, 104 (Jun. 30, 1967).
392 50 U.S.C. app. § 456(j).

"religious" and the *Welsh* Court's own statements that "moral" or "ethical" beliefs can qualify – arguably removed "personal moral code" or at least some personal moral codes from the realm of excluded beliefs.

The draft ended in 1973, eventually resulting in the all-volunteer military that the nation has today. Although the next subsection will address some basic First Amendment issues concerning conscription, mentioned here will be two issues that have arisen under the previously quoted exemption in the years following the draft's conclusion. The first concerns mandatory registration for the Selective Service System, which was reinstated in 1980 by presidential proclamation[393] and persists to the present day.[394] Some registrants naturally wish either to avoid registration completely on the basis of conscientious objection or to include within their registration an application for conscientious objector status. However, even though registration is considered a military rather than a civilian activity,[395] regulations provide that a registrant cannot seek conscientious objector status until he is actually inducted and undergoes the classification process. In turn, lower courts since 1980, as they did in earlier eras, have held that the registration requirement itself does not violate the Free Exercise Clause.[396]

The second issue concerns current service members who wish to change their status to that of conscientious objector, with the aim of either avoiding particular duties or deployments or, more often, being discharged from the military altogether.[397] Given that the Free Exercise Clause by itself does not appear to shield a conscientious objector from *mandatory* conscription, it naturally follows that "[d]ischarge of a voluntary enlistee for conscientious objection is a privilege granted by the executive branch, not a constitutional right."[398] In turn, and not surprisingly, the cases that have reached the courts – the military grants some requests, with no ensuing litigation[399] – have met with mixed results,[400] where the court, typically reviewing a petition for writ of *habeas corpus*,

393 Proclamation No. 4771 (Jul. 2, 1980) [promulgated at 3 C.F.R. 82 (1981)], *available at:* http://www.archives.gov/federal-register/codification/proclamations/04771.html, *and discussed in* Wayte v. United States, 470 U.S. 598, 600–1 (1985).

394 *See Selective Service System, Who Must Register, available at:* https://www.sss.gov/FSwho.htm.

395 The Court originally categorized it as civilian (*see* Hamilton, 293 U.S. at 259–60) but has since characterized it as the first step of military activity. *See* Rostker v. Goldberg, 453 U.S. 57, 75 (1981).

396 *See, e.g.*, United States v. Schmucker, 815 F.2d 413, 417–18 (6th Cir. 1987); United States v. Rutt, No. 86-1591, 818 F.2d 867, 1987 WL 37416, at *2 (6th Cir. 1987) (unpublished); Garman v. U.S. Postal Serv., 509 F. Supp. 507, 509 (N.D. Ind. 1981) [citing United States v. Baechler, 509 F.2d 13, 15 (4th Cir. 1974); United States v. Bertram, 477 F.2d 1329, 1330 (10th Cir. 1973); United States v. Bigman, 429 F.2d 13 (9th Cir. 1970); Richter v. United States, 181 F.2d 591, 593 (9th Cir. 1950); United States v. Crocker, 308 F. Supp. 998 (D. Minn. 1970), *aff'd*, 435 F.2d 601 (8th Cir. 1971)]. Nor does it violate a right to privacy or otherwise deprive registrants of their liberty without due process of law. *See* Detenber v. Turnage, 701 F.2d 233, 234–5 (1st Cir. 1983).

397 Department of Defense regulations governing conscientious objection were previously published at 35 C.F.R. pt. 75, but they have been unpublished for the last several years. Nevertheless, the current criteria and general procedures may be found in Department of Defense Instruction 1300.06 (May 5, 2007). In addition, individual branches have their own directives and accompanying processes. *See* Air Force Instruction 36-3204 (Jul. 15, 1994); Army Reg. 600-43 (Aug. 21, 2006); Marine Corps Order 1306.16E (Nov. 21, 1986).

398 Watson v. Green, 569 F.3d 115, 127 (2d Cir. 2009), *reh'g en banc denied*, 587 F.3d 156 (2d Cir. 2009).

399 *See A Closer Look: Conscientious Objection*, Aug. 24, 2007 (noting that 179 of 405 requests between 2002 and 2007 had been granted), *available at:* http://www.pbs.org/now/shows/334/conscientious-objection.html.

400 *See, e.g.*, Kanai v. McHugh, 638 F.3d 251, 267–8 (4th Cir. 2011) [finding basis in fact for denying conscientious objector (CO) discharge of U.S. Military Academy cadet], *cert. denied*, 132 S. Ct. 381

normally determines only whether there is a factual basis in the record for denying the change of status or the discharge as a conscientious objector.[401]

## 2. *First Amendment Issues*

As the preceding subsection illustrates with regard to the various draft statutes, constitutional questions necessarily attend military conscription, from the power of Congress to institute it in the first instance to the potential deprivations of liberty resulting from its implementation. In terms of the religion clauses, conscription gives rise to at least three basic questions: *first*, is a conscientious objector exemption of any kind *required* by the Free Exercise Clause; *second*, if not, is such an exemption *permissible* under the Establishment Clause; and *third*, whether such an exemption is required or permissible, are there limits that these clauses impose on the nature or scope of the exemption?

Regarding the first question, the Supreme Court has indicated that exempting conscientious objectors is not required by the Free Exercise Clause, and the current free exercise framework of *Employment Division v. Smith* presumably would not change that assessment.[402] *Seeger* and *Welsh*, after all, though informed by constitutional considerations, were ultimately constructions of the federal conscription statute. That is, even though that the Supreme Court may have interpreted the statutory exemption broadly to avoid possible issues under the religion clauses, it did not rule that such an exemption had to be included in the statute in the first place. To the contrary, the Court had given indications in cases prior to *Seeger* and *Welsh* that the Free Exercise Clause does not by

(2011); Watson, 569 F.3d at 130–4 (finding no basis in fact for denial of CO discharge); Hanna v. Sec'y of Army, 513 F.3d 4 (1st Cir. 2008) (affirming district court finding of no factual basis for denying CO discharge); Aguayo v. Harvey, 476 F.3d 971 (D.C. Cir. 2007) (finding sufficient factual basis for denying CO discharge), *cert. denied*, 552 U.S. 1256 (2008); Alhassan v. Hagee, 424 F.3d 518, 522–5 (7th Cir. 2005) (same); Roby v. U.S. Dep't of Navy, 76 F.3d 1052, 1058–9 (9th Cir. 1996) (same); Rogowskyj v. Conway, Civ. Action No. 06-1930-ESH, 2007 WL 779390, at *4–*5 (D.D.C. Mar. 13, 2007) (unpublished) (same); Daly v. Claytor, 472 F. Supp. 752 (D. Mass. 1979) (finding some deficiencies but not a total lack of basis for denying a discharge and thus remanding to the Navy for a new hearing).

401 *See* Alhassan v. Hagee, 424 F.3d 518, 522 (7th Cir. 2005) {"In order to prevail, the government has the burden of proving that there was a 'basis in fact' for its denial of [the service member's] application. Our review of a decision supported by a basis in fact standard of review is limited, and has been described by the ninth circuit as 'the narrowest review known to the law.' The reviewing court does not weigh the evidence for itself or ask whether there is substantial evidence to support the military officials' denial of the applicant's request for conscientious objector status." (citations omitted) [quoting Estep v. United States, 327 U.S. 114, 122 (1946), and Woods v. Sheehan, 987 F.2d 1454, 1456 (9th Cir. 1993), respectively)]}; Lipton v. Peters, No. 00-50200, 240 F.3d 1074 (5th Cir. Nov. 30, 2000) (unpublished) {"Our review of the Air Force's denial of a conscientious-objector discharge is extremely narrow. Such a denial must be sustained if this court can discern any basis in fact for it." (citation omitted) [citing Dewalt v. Commanding Officer, Ft. Benning, Ga, 476 F.2d 440, 442 (5th Cir. 1973); Silverthorne v. Laird, 460 F.2d 1175, 1179 (5th Cir. 1972)]}.

402 Nor does the Free Exercise Clause or RFRA provide relief to taxpayers who oppose military expenditures. *See* Adams v. Comm'r, 170 F.3d 173, 175–80 (3d Cir. 1999) (RFRA case), *cert. denied*, 528 U.S. 1117 (2000). The Third Circuit noted that the Supreme Court, before *Smith*, had twice rejected free exercise challenges to tax obligations – first in *United States v. Lee* [455 U.S. 252 (1982)] and then in *Hernandez v. Comm'r* [490 U.S. 680 (1989)] – and that "*Lee* and *Hernandez* are both part of a line of cases that have refused to recognize free exercise challenges to the payment of taxes or penalties imposed due to a refusal to pay taxes as a protest against the military activities of the United States." *Id.* at 178 (citing numerous circuit court decisions).

its own force compel an exemption,[403] and one year after *Welsh*, in *Gillette v. United States*,[404] the Court reaffirmed those earlier indications.[405] Even under strict scrutiny, whether triggered through the RFRA or through an exception to *Smith*'s main rule, the government almost certainly could require military service of some kind, though perhaps it could not demonstrate that classifying *all* conscriptees as potential combatants is truly necessary to achieve its compelling objectives.

Regarding the second question, it is clearly permissible to provide an exemption for conscientious objectors even if the Free Exercise Clause does not mandate one. This is implicit in the many conscientious objector cases that the Supreme Court has decided, and it accords with the Court's view toward permissible or discretionary free exercise accommodation. As the Court explained in 2005, its "decisions recognize that 'there is room for play in the joints' between the Clauses, some space for legislative action neither compelled by the Free Exercise Clause nor prohibited by the Establishment Clause."[406] Particularly where, as in the conscription situation, the government has by its own actions created a dilemma of conscience for persons of faith, it is entitled to lessen or eliminate that predicament by providing a partial or complete accommodation.[407]

Addressing the third question, then, the government is entitled to set up a permissible or discretionary accommodation – here a conscientious objection exemption to military conscription – as long as the accommodation does not transgress other constitutional limitations, chiefly the Establishment Clause. Thus a conscientious objector exemption may be problematic if, among other things, the burden on religious practice that it alleviates is not significant or not government imposed,[408] the exemption does not impose undue costs on third parties who do not benefit from the exemption,[409] or the exemption

403 *See, e.g.*, Hamilton v. Regents of Univ. of Cal., 293 U.S. 245, 264 (1934); Jacobson v. Massachusetts, 197 U.S. 11, 29 (1905).

404 401 U.S. 437 (1971).

405 *See id.* at 461 n. 23 (noting that the Court had "previously suggested that relief for conscientious objectors is not mandated by the Constitution" [citing Hamilton, 293 U.S. at 264; United States v. Macintosh, 283 U.S. 605, 623–4 (1931)].

406 Cutter v. Wilkinson, 544 U.S. 709, 719 (2005) [quoting Walz v. Tax Comm'n of City of N.Y., 397 U.S. 664, 669 (1970)].

407 *See id.* at 720; Corp. of Presiding Bishop of Church of Jesus Christ of Latter-Day Saints v. Amos, 483 U.S. 327, 336 (1987) ("[I]t is a permissible legislative purpose to alleviate significant governmental interference with the ability of religious organizations to define and carry out their religious missions.").

408 *See* Cutter, 544 U.S. at 720 (upholding a federal religious freedom statute in part because "it alleviates exceptional government-created burdens on private religious exercise"); Tex. Monthly, Inc. v. Bullock, 489 U.S. 1, 15, 18 n. 18 (1989) (plurality opinion) (explaining that a discretionary accommodation is problematic when it "cannot reasonably be seen as removing a significant state-imposed deterrent to the free exercise of religion" or is not "designed to alleviate government intrusions that might significantly deter adherents of a particular faith from conduct protected by the Free Exercise Clause"); Amos, 483 U.S. at 336 (upholding exemption to federal civil rights law because it "alleviate[s] significant governmental interference" with the conduct of religious organizations); Children's Healthcare Is a Legal Duty, Inc. v. Min De Parle, 212 F.3d 1084, 1094 (8th Cir. 2000) (explaining that "government-imposed burdens upon religion, although not severe enough to require accommodation under the Free Exercise Clause," must "be sufficiently onerous to permit Congress to alleviate them without transgressing the Establishment Clause"), *cert. denied*, 532 U.S. 957 (2001).

409 *See* Cutter, 544 U.S. at 720 (upholding a federal religious freedom statute in part because courts can "take adequate account of the burdens a requested accommodation may impose on nonbeneficiaries"); Tex. Monthly, 489 U.S. at 15, 18 n. 8 (finding it problematic that a discretionary accommodation "burdens nonbeneficiaries markedly" or would "impose substantial burdens on nonbeneficiaries while allowing others to act according to their religious beliefs"); Estate of Thornton v. Caldor, Inc., 472 U.S. 703, 709–10 & n. 9 (1985).

is preferential rather than neutral among religions.[410] Though the limitation on nonbeneficiary costs may seem problematic in relation to conscription – after all, another person must be conscripted to fill the combat or noncombat role not filled by the conscientious objector[411] – perhaps the relatively small number of qualifying objectors and the overall scale of federal military conscription make the third-party costs sufficiently diffuse as to render the exemption acceptable.

As for the last limitation, the Court itself held during the Vietnam War that the conscientious objector exemption "does not discriminate on the basis of religious affiliation or religious belief, apart of course from beliefs concerning war" but, rather, "says that anyone who is conscientiously opposed to all war shall be relieved of military service."[412] In that case, an applicant for the exemption was not "conscientiously opposed to participation in war in any form" as phrased in the statute; rather, he was opposed only to participating in an unjust war, which he considered the U.S. military operations in Southeast Asia to be.[413] In turn, he claimed that denying him conscientious objector status was tantamount to discrimination between religions or religious beliefs. The Court, however, upheld the exemption as written, finding that the exemption "does not single out any religious organization or religious creed for special treatment,"[414] that "the affirmative purposes underlying ... [the exemption] are neutral and secular," and "that valid neutral reasons exist for limiting the exemption to objectors to all war."[415]

## I. The Military: Chaplaincies

Since the earliest times in history, invoking the blessings of the divine upon dangerous undertakings, especially military ones, has been an important tradition in most cultures. From Homer's *Iliad* to Tolstoy's *War and Peace*, reverence, sacrifice, and petition to God (or the gods) have for many been as integral to military operations as the strategies of generals and the logistics of quartermasters. This was true for General Washington during the American Revolution, who viewed chaplains as "absolutely essential for ... assuring the army that God was on their side,"[416] and it was true in 1944 when General Eisenhower, in his message to the armed forces destined for Normandy, spoke of their

410 *See* Cutter, 544 U.S. at 720, 723–4; Bd. of Educ. v. Grumet, 512 U.S. 687, 706–7 (1994); Walz, 397 U.S. at 672–3.

411 The exemption can potentially excuse one from all military service but not from alternative public service. In particular, it provides that "[a]ny person claiming exemption from combatant training and service because of such conscientious objections whose claim is sustained by the local board shall, if he is inducted into the armed forces under this title, be assigned to noncombatant service as defined by the President, or shall, if he is found to be conscientiously opposed to participation in such noncombatant service, in lieu of such induction, be ordered by his local board ... to perform for a period [of twenty-four months] ... such civilian work contributing to the maintenance of the national health, safety, or interest as the Director [of the Selective Service System] may deem appropriate." 50 U.S.C. app. § 456(j).

412 Gillette, 401 U.S. at 450.

413 *See id.* at 439. By comparison, he "had stated his willingness to participate in a war of national defense or a war sponsored by the United Nations as a peace-keeping measure." *Id.*

414 *Id.* at 451.

415 *Id.* at 455.

416 Thomas A. Kidd, God of Liberty: A Religious History of the American Revolution 116 (2010).

"Great Crusade" and urged all involved to "beseech the blessing of Almighty God upon this great and noble undertaking."[417]

Soldiers, sailors, and colonists arriving in the New World were often accompanied by clergy.[418] The exploration and colonization of the Americas commenced during a period of intense religious ferment – Reformation and Counter-Reformation – in Europe, including Great Britain.[419] Religious and political aims often overlapped.[420] The English flag was the Cross of St. George, Spaniards used the Cross of Burgundy, and the French *Fleur de Lis* in the Middle Ages was "regarded … as an emblem of illumination and as an attribute of the Lord."[421] Spanish outposts bore religious names: San Francisco, Sacramento, San Antonio; Jesuit missions along the Great Lakes were vanguards of the French Empire; and the Church of England was the established church of the Virginia Colony.[422] For the sake of a successful voyage at sea, victory in battle, or blessings and bounty for a colony, a chaplain to lead prayers, to baptize and bury colonists, and to attest to the righteousness of one's mission would have been deemed essential.

Over time, the role of the expeditionary chaplain has shifted from being seen as one who imparts God's blessing on an endeavor to that of a specialist who serves the members of the armed forces.[423] The United States essentially led the way in this transformation of the military chaplaincy largely because of its own demographic and constitutional features. Historically, whereas Russian troops could be assumed to be Orthodox, British troops Anglican, and Austrian troops Catholic, the religious diversity of the United States and its lack of an established church demanded that it chart a different course.

### 1. *Historical Development*

#### a. The Revolutionary War

Despite a lack of religious uniformity in the American ranks, political and military authorities in the fledgling nation, much like their European contemporaries, made efforts to provide for the spiritual care of their armed forces.[424] The *Rules for the Regulation of the Navy of the United Colonies of North-America*, dating to 1775, illustrate the Continental Congress's commitment to the spiritual welfare of sailors and to maintaining piety among the naval forces.[425] Article 2 provided that "[t]he Commanders of the ships of the Thirteen United Colonies are to take care that divine service be performed twice a day on board, and sermon preached on Sundays, unless bad weather or other extraordinary accidents prevent it," and Article 3 "strictly enjoined" the captain to punish anyone who

417 Gen. Dwight D. Eisenhower, *Order of the Day* (1944), *available at:* http://www.ourdocuments.gov/doc.php?flash=true&doc=75&page=transcript.

418 *See* Jon Butler et al., Religion in American Life: A Short History 49 (2d ed., 2011).

419 *See id.* at 6.

420 *See id.*

421 J. E. Cirlot, A Dictionary of Symbols 109 (Jack Sage, trans., 2d ed., 1971) (citation omitted).

422 *See id.* at 80.

423 *See* Kidd, *supra* note 416, at 116–17.

424 Parker C. Thompson, From Its European Antecedents to 1791: The United States Army Chaplaincy at xvii (1978).

425 *See Rules for the Regulation of the Navy of the United Colonies of North-America* (Nov. 28, 1775), *available at:* http://www.history.navy.mil/faqs/faq59-5.htm.

"shall be heard to swear, curse, or blaspheme the name of God."[426] As with many early U.S. military codes, these naval regulations closely mirrored existing regulations of the British Royal Navy.[427] In 1776, the Second Continental Congress issued further instructions pertaining to naval chaplains, including their base pay and their shares of prize percentages when enemy ships were captured.[428] The first Continental Navy chaplain is believed to have been Reverend Benjamin Balch, a Congregationalist minister whose father served as a chaplain in the Royal Navy.[429] Balch was no doubt chosen in part because the Continental Navy drew heavily from New England's seafaring towns, where Congregationalists made up large portions of the population.[430]

The Continental Congress also was mindful of the need to provide religious support for ground troops. While ships at sea, owing to their isolation, would need a chaplain to provide religious services, it may have been theoretically possible to let interested soldiers avail themselves of local clergy and churches. The Congress, however, implicitly rejected this notion in 1775, authorizing the Continental Army to have its own chaplains at a pay rate of $20 per month.[431] The very diversity of the American religious landscape may have influenced Congress's decision. After all, New England Congregationalists could hardly be expected to substitute Anglican services for their own simply because the army had marched into Virginia. Additionally, the presence of chaplains in the army could, at least in theory, serve as a bulwark against drunkenness, gambling, and other vices among soldiers that could undermine military discipline.[432] In all, 218 chaplains served in the Continental Army, and 25 were killed.[433]

General Washington followed up Congress's 1775 authorization with an order on July 9, 1776, aimed at securing the appointment of qualified chaplains:

> The honorable Continental Congress having been pleased to allow a chaplain to each regiment, the colonels or commanding officers of each regiment are directed to procure chaplains accordingly, persons of good character and exemplary lives, and to see that all inferior officers and soldiers pay them suitable respect. The blessing and protection of Heaven are at all times necessary, but especially so in times of public distress and danger. The General hopes and trusts, that every officer and man will endeavor to live and act as becomes a Christian soldier, defending the dearest rights and liberties of his country.[434]

This particular order indicates that Washington was conscious not only of the religious needs of his troops and the critical role of chaplains in this regard but also of the

426 *Id.*

427 *See* 1 Clifford M. Drury, The History of the Chaplain Corps, United States Navy: 1778–1939, at 2 (1948).

428 *See id.* at 3.

429 *See id.* at 4.

430 *See* Charles H. Metzger, *Chaplains in the American Revolution*, 31 Cath. Hist. Rev. 31, 50–1 (1945).

431 Thompson, *supra* note 424, at 107. "Before the war, chaplains generally had served the colonial militias under a volunteer and rotation system." Derek H. Davis, Religion and the Continental Congress, 1774–1789: Contributions to Original Intent 80 (2000).

432 *Id.*

433 *Military Chaplains: A Historian's View from the American Revolution to Iraq*, Christian Sci. Monitor, Oct. 30, 2007, *available at:* http://www.csmonitor.com/2007/1030/p25s02-usmi.html/(page)/2 (interview with U.S. Chaplain Corps historian John Brinsfield).

434 Quoted in Davis, *supra* note 431, at 80.

relationship between religion and the behavior of those under his command, whom he hoped would "live and act as becomes a Christian soldier." In November 1775, in fact, he had issued a harsh rebuke to soldiers who were planning to celebrate Guy Fawkes Night, presumably by burning an effigy of the Pope.[435] Although his principal concern seemed to be the diplomatic repercussions of such a celebration for relations with Canada, with its large French Catholic population, Washington's remarks arguably reveal a deeper theme regarding the proper place of religion in the American military context. Unlike many European armies, repeatedly entangled as they had been in Protestant-Catholic conflicts over the previous centuries, the Continental Army was not conceived as fighting under the banner of a particular religion – be it Congregationalist, Presbyterian, or Anglican – nor, correspondingly, was it viewed as being entitled to special blessings on that account. Rather, Washington desired that the diverse religious sensibilities of Americans be respected, following a "policy of 'generous toleration'" and believing that the Army's cause was best furthered when men of different denominations could serve alongside each other without interdenominational enmity.[436]

### b. The Nineteenth Century

By the mid-nineteenth century, immigration was altering the demographics of the United States and, consequently, of the military. The period of the Mexican-American War (1846–1848) thus became pivotal in terms of the understanding of the role that religion played in a military context. Some viewed the war as a "crusade by Protestant America to subdue Catholic Mexico."[437] Indeed, the officer corps remained largely the purview of the Protestant elite, but the enlisted ranks now included a far larger percentage of Catholics than had been present during the Revolution.[438] Likely out of fear that war might be seen as a Protestant Crusade, and in a first for the U.S. military chaplaincies, President James Knox Polk personally ordered Catholic chaplains to be attached to the U.S. Army during the war while apparently making no order for Protestant chaplains.[439] Polk, a distant relative of the Scottish Reformer John Knox, was a strong advocate of religious tolerance, recalling that he was refused baptism because of a conflict between

[435] Washington's remarks were as follows: "As the Commander in Chief has been apprized of a design form'd for the observance of that ridiculous and childish custom of burning the Effigy of the pope – He cannot help expressing his surprise that there should be Officers and Soldiers in this army so void of common sense, as not to see the impropriety of such a step at this Juncture; at a Time when we are soliciting, and have really obtain'd, the friendship and alliance of the people of Canada, whom we ought to consider as Brethren embarked in the same Cause. The defence of the general Liberty of America: At such a juncture, and in such Circumstances, to be insulting their Religion, is so monstrous, as not to be suffered or excused; indeed instead of offering the most remote insult, it is our duty to address public thanks to these our Brethren, as to them we are so much indebted for every late happy Success over the common Enemy in Canada." Paul F. Boller, *George Washington and Religious Liberty*, 17 Wm. & Mary Q. 486, 492 (Oct. 1986).

[436] *Id.* at 495.

[437] Herman A. Norton, Struggling for Recognition: The United States Army Chaplaincy 1791–1865, at 65 (1977).

[438] *See* Ted C. Hinckley, *American Anti-Catholicism during the Mexican War*, 31 Pac. Hist. Rev. 121, 135–6 (1964).

[439] *See* Norton, *supra* note 437, at 66.

a Presbyterian pastor and his Deist father.[440] Polk had a mild interest in Methodism and was eventually baptized on his deathbed.[441]

The President began working with New York Bishop John Hughes to arrange for American Catholic priests to accompany the U.S. Army into Mexico. Hughes himself personally volunteered to travel to Mexico to assure Mexican clergy that the United States had no intention of persecuting Catholics.[442] The overture would go unrealized, however. As Polk and Hughes prepared the way for employing Catholic clergy as military chaplains, a backlash emerged. A Presbyterian minister, William McCalla, began publically decrying Polk's actions.[443] In his diary, Polk wrote that "unless I appointed the Rev. McCalla a chaplain, the petitioners intended to go before the public and attack the administration upon religious grounds because of the employment of these Catholic priests."[444]

Polk had originally envisioned priests working to ensure harmony between the U.S. forces and the Mexican populace, but his initiative was drastically scaled back to just two Jesuits, recommended by Bishop Hughes, joining the Chaplain Corps.[445] Although this did represent a significant move in terms of diversifying the chaplaincy, it also proved far from adequate. One of these first Catholic chaplains, Fr. Anthony Rey, former vice president of Georgetown College, met a grisly end. "Against the advice of the U.S. officers, he set out for Matamoras, preaching to a congregation of Americans and Mexicans at Ceralvo.... [H]is body was discovered, pierced with lances, a few days later."[446] This left Fr. John McElroy, the future founder of Boston College, as the lone Catholic military chaplain in a war involving multiple fronts, armies, and naval units and left Catholic military personnel woefully underserved.[447]

Just as the Mexican War had forced the military to come to grips with the increased presence of Catholics within the ranks, the newly founded Mormon faith also had to be considered. Tensions between Mormons and other Americans had been high and at times even violent. Despite this, with Polk's sanction, the government urged Mormons to form up combat units to serve in the Mexican War. Mormon leader Brigham Young wrote approvingly of the idea: "The President wants to do us good and secure our confidence.

440 *See* Earl Irvin West, *Religion in the Life of James K. Polk*, 26 Tenn. Hist. Q. 357, 359 (1967).

441 *See id.* at 371.

442 John Seigenthaler, James K. Polk: The 11th President 1845–1849, at 15 (2003).

443 *See* West, *supra* note 440, at 369–70.

444 Seigenthaler, *supra* note 442, at 16.

445 West, *supra* note 440, at 370.

446 Nicholas Weber, *Anthony Rey*, *in* 13 The Catholic Encyclopedia (1912), *available at*: http://www.newadvent.org/cathen/13017c.htm.

447 Scenes such as a shelled church, described by an Englishman serving in the U.S. Army, would no doubt have had a severe impact on Catholic soldiers: "Several shells had fallen through the dome, on the marble floor, the fragments of which had made sad mutilations of the pictures and effigies of the saints and virgins of the various shrines ... one of these shells had killed and wounded about twenty of the unfortunate inhabitants who had fled to its shelter as a sanctuary of safety during the bombardment." George Ballentine, The Mexican War, by an English Soldier 165 (1860). Some Catholic American soldiers deserted and formed the San Patricio Battalion of the Mexican Army. *See* Hinckley, *supra* note 438, at 135. "As the majority of these deserters were Irish, the cause commonly assigned by the officers for their desertion, was, that as they were Roman Catholics they imagined they were fighting against their religion in fighting the Mexicans." Ballentine, *supra* at 281. Most of the deserters met with a bad end: those who did not die on the battlefield were captured and executed, including thirty who were hung the moment that the American flag was raised over the Mexican fortress of Chapultepec.

The outfit of this five hundred men costs us nothing, and their pay will be sufficient to take their families over the mountains. There is war between Mexico and the United States, to whom California must fall a prey, and if we are the first settlers the old citizens cannot have a Hancock or Missouri pretext to mob the Saints. The thing is from above for our own good."[448] The resulting "Mormon Battalion," the only religiously based unit in the history of the U.S. Army, would make an arduous march from Council Bluffs to Sacramento, California, capturing the outpost at Tucson, Arizona, along the way.[449]

By the time of the Civil War, the military chaplaincy had essentially emerged in its modern form as a professional component of the military serving the specific religious needs of the troops. All told, the Union forces included 32 naval chaplains, 32 post chaplains, 178 hospital chaplains, and 2,138 regimental chaplains, providing services to over 2.2 million men.[450] One interesting aspect of the Civil War chaplaincy is the election of chaplains by the soldiers, particularly within the Confederate state militias.[451] Although the popular election of chaplains increased the diversity of the chaplain corps, more or less allowing it to meet the specific religious needs of the troops, soldiers who found themselves religious minorities within their regiments were still left without the sort of spiritual care they may have sought. On the other side of the battlefield, among the Union troops, the commanding officers chose the chaplains, subject to approval by the state's governor final appointment by the U.S. War Department.[452]

In terms of the religious makeup of the chaplains, Methodism's numbers reflect its phenomenal growth during the "Second Great Awakening." Over one-quarter of Union chaplains and over one-third of Confederate chaplains were Methodist. Although American Methodism at the time of the Civil War was deeply divided on several issues, especially slavery (indeed, the main northern and southern branches of Methodism did not reunite until 1939),[453] these numbers reflect an extremely vibrant, dynamic, and evangelical faith that had broad appeal in mid-nineteenth-century America. For the Union, Methodist chaplains outnumbered the chaplains of the faiths that had been dominant during the Revolution – Presbyterian (12 percent), Episcopalian (7 percent), and Congregationalist (6 percent) – combined.[454] Confederate chaplains, though paid less than their Union counterparts and not given a specific uniform,[455] exhibited a demographic profile similar to that of the Union, with Methodists, Presbyterians, Baptists, and Episcopalians being the most common – a reminder, perhaps, of how much the

448 Joseph D. Brown, The Mormon Trek West 50–2 (1980).

449 *See* David B. Gracy II & Helen J.H. Rugeley, *From the Mississippi to the Pacific: An Englishman in the Mormon Battalion*, 7(2) Arizona and the West 127, 151 (1965).

450 *See* Richard G. Williams, Jr., *A Great Deal of Good: The Word and Impact of Chaplains During the American Civil War* 3 (Oct. 2011), *available at:* http://www.essential.civilwar.vt.edu/assets/files/ECWC%20TOPIC%20Chaplains%20Essay.pdf.

451 *See* Bell I. Wiley, *"Holy Joes" of the Sixties: A Study of Civil War Chaplains*, 16(3) Huntington Libr. Q. 287 (1953).

452 *Id.* at 288.

453 For additional information, *see* Philip Stone, *How the Methodist Church Split in the 1840s*, From the Archives Blog (Wofford College) (Jan. 30, 2013), *available at:* http://blogs.wofford.edu/from_the_archives/2013/01/30/how-the-methodist-church-split-in-the-1840s/; Philip Stone, *Methodist Reunification*, From the Archives Blog (Wofford College) (Nov. 7, 2013), *available at:* http://blogs.wofford.edu/from_the_archives/2013/11/07/methodist-reunification/.

454 *See* Williams, *supra* note 450, at 3.

455 *See id.* at 2.

North and South actually had in common despite their entanglement in a bitter and bloody war.[456]

After significant congressional debate and controversy surrounding the salary and qualifications of U.S. army chaplains, an 1861 statute reflecting the prevalence of Christianity in the nation mandated that "there shall be allowed to each regiment one chaplain, who ... must be a regular ordained minister of a Christian denomination."[457] This mandate effectively ensured that the government would be dealing with organized denominations rather than self-proclaimed clergy and unaffiliated evangelists.[458] Methodism proved to be ecclesiastical enough to satisfy the statute but still informal and evangelistic enough to have broad appeal in the army.[459] Whereas Catholic, Lutheran, and Episcopal clergy would have spent several years in study preparing for ordination, it was observed with regard to the nineteenth century that Methodist ordination in the early and mid-nineteenth century was often based more on practical ability, though aspiring Methodist chaplains still had to undergo apprenticeships and doctrinal examinations.[460]

Not only did the 1861 act screen out independent and unaffiliated would-be chaplains, its language also excluded non-Christians. Rabbi Arnold Fischel, chaplain to the Board of Delegates of American Israelites, quickly set himself to the task of ending the exclusionary limitation of military chaplain positions to Christians. Writing of his efforts, he said:

> I undertook the twofold task of officiating as chaplain to the Jewish soldiers on the Potomac, and agitating the repeal of the Act of Congress by which Jewish Ministers are excluded from the office of Chaplain in the U.S. Army. Shortly after my arrival in Washington, I had an interview with the President, delivered to him the letter of the Board, and requested him to use his influence for the repeal of the law, which excluded from office a class of citizens who by the Constitution are entitled to complete political equality. The President did not hesitate to express his full concurrence in my views, and promised that he would take the matter into serious consideration.[461]

In July of 1862, Congress acted, and the wording "a Christian denomination" was altered to "some religious denomination."[462] Four rabbis eventually would enter the Union

456 *See id.*

457 Act of July 22, 1861, ch. 9, § 9, 12 Stat. 268, 270, *available at:* http://www.lawfareblog.com/wp-content/uploads/2013/10/Act-of-July-22-1861-12-Stat.-281.pdf.

458 *See* Norton, *supra* note 437, at 89.

459 *See id.* at 90.

460 *See* Nathan O. Hatch, The Democratization of American Christianity 140 (1989) ("The Methodist commitment to leave no circuit unattended forced their leadership to channel young converts into preaching assignments very quickly. Education for eager young Methodist recruits was a hands-on experience. They moved into exhorting and preaching while they served apprenticeships as class leaders, and they moved into circuits as understudies to more experienced preachers."); Rollin W. Quimby, *Congress and the Civl War Chaplaincy*, 10(3) Civil War Hist. 246, 255 (1964).

461 Rabbi Arnold Rischel, *Report to the Board of Delegates* (Apr. 3, 1862), *available at:* http://www.jewish-history.com/civilwar/af040362.html.

462 *See* Act of July 17, 1862, ch. 200, § 8, 12 Stat. 594, 595 (1862). The new language provided that "no person shall be appointed a chaplain in the United States army who is not a regularly ordained minister of some religious denomination, and who does not present testimonials of his present good standing as such minister, with a recommendation for his appointment as an army chaplain from some authorized ecclesiastical body, or not less than five accredited ministers belonging to said religious denomination." *Id.*

forces as chaplains, adding an entirely new level of diversity to what was already one of the most diverse chaplain corps in the world.[463]

By the end of the nineteenth century, many of the issues relating to military chaplains had seemingly been resolved. Their status as paid, full-time professionals was established, as was their primary role of ministering to the specific and diverse religious needs of the soldiers rather than acting as the military's liaisons to Heaven. Although the nation's demographics had posed challenges for the relationship between the military and various religious bodies, these had been overcome: President Polk saw the chaplaincy opened to non-Protestants, and President Lincoln saw it further extended to non-Christians. Moreover, whereas Polk had struggled to appoint two Catholic chaplains to serve, by the time of the Spanish-American War in 1898, non-Protestant chaplain officers were regularly accorded positions of equal trust and significant responsibility. Illustrative is Fr. William Reaney, who, while serving aboard Admiral Dewey's flagship *Olympia*, acted as an intermediary and set up negotiations between Dewey and the Spanish Archbishop of Manila.[464] Reaney's efforts are rather similar to what Polk and Bishop Hughes may have envisioned during the Mexican-American War.

### c. The Twentieth Century

The earliest years of the twentieth century witnessed a temporary return to the nation's traditional isolationism and, with it, a decline in military numbers, including its chaplaincies.[465] With America's 1917 entry into World War I and a remobilization of personnel, however, came a revival of the military chaplaincy corps, this time headed to the battlefields of Europe. With support from the American public and most American churches, the United States entered "the war to end all wars," as President Wilson famously called it, with a strong sense that the nation had a divine mandate to lead the Allied powers to victory and to usher in perpetual peace for humanity.[466] Just under 150 chaplains accompanied the American Expeditionary Forces' arrival in Europe in 1917,[467] and as the size and involvement of the American military grew, so did the need for the chaplains. Cognizant of this need and of the disparity between chaplain and troop numbers, Congress in May of 1918 authorized one chaplain for every 1,200 troops.[468] By the end of the conflict, 2,217 chaplains had been commissioned by the U.S. Army.[469]

463 *See* NORTON, *supra* note 437, at 91–2. At the same time that the government demonstrated its concern for the religiously diverse needs of its troops, some Union citizens viewed the war as akin to a religious crusade. An editor of the influential Republican abolitionist newspaper, the *New York Tribune*, spoke of the war as one of "Law, liberty and righteousness" and urged that the Union Army "must fight it as their Puritan forefathers, with Bible and Psalm book in hand." JOHN W. BRINSFIELD, FAITH IN THE FIGHT: CIVIL WAR CHAPLAINS 7 (2003).

464 *See History Revealed in Priest's Eulogy*, N.Y. TIMES, Nov. 21, 1915, at 19, *available at*: http://query.nytimes.com/mem/archive-free/pdf?res=F50F17FA3E5F17738DDDA80A94D9415B858DF1D3.

465 There were only 213,557 troops under the control of the War Department, compared with over 3.5 million by the 1918 Armistice. *See* EARL F. STOVER, UP FROM HANDYMAN: THE UNITED STATES ARMY CHAPLAINCY 1865–1920, at 186–7 (1977).

466 *See id.*

467 *See id.*

468 *See* Pub. L. No. 65–158, § 15, 40 Stat. 561 (May 25, 1918); STOVER, *supra* note 465, at 186–7.

469 *See* STOVER, *supra* note 465, at 188.

Reflecting the nation's demographics, the chaplaincy corps in World War I was heavily but not disproportionately Protestant, with roughly two Protestant chaplains for every Catholic chaplain.[470] For the first time since the Civil War, moreover, Jewish chaplains provided services for the troops.[471] Perhaps because of their heavy workload, the chaplain corps conducted large "interfaith masses" for all the troops, regardless of denomination.[472] These services often consisted of an Episcopal chaplain giving a sermon, a Lutheran chaplain reciting scripture, and a Catholic chaplain singing the Mass.[473] A common view among the chaplains was that their primary duty was to serve the Army as a whole and only secondarily to be representatives of their denominations.[474] To be sure, Christian ministers served Jewish troops, and rabbis served Christian troops.[475] Episcopal Bishop Charles Brent, a friend of General John J. Pershing and appointed the Senior General Chaplain by Pershing himself, was a strong proponent of church unity and ecumenicalism throughout his life and possibly influenced the corps' interdenominational approach.[476]

The primary duties of the chaplaincy corps were similar to those of chaplains in past wars, consisting of conducting services for the troops or being available for troops who sought out spiritual counsel – but when battle began, the chaplains' role became much more than preaching and prayer. Chaplains frequently assisted first aid units and attended to the physical and spiritual needs of the wounded who lay on the battlefield, and some even risked their own lives to rescue the injured from further harm in no-man's land.[477] Indeed, the chaplains served both God and their country: twenty-seven chaplains were decorated for their bravery or wounds in battle, and eleven chaplains were killed or died from battle wounds during the course of U.S involvement in the war.[478] After battle, chaplains attended to proper burials of the fallen troops, ensuring that the decedent's name, unit, and date of death were present on his gravestone and that the coordinates of the burial site were properly recorded for the sake of the deceased's loved ones.[479] Beyond their duties for the American soldiers, interestingly, some of the Christian chaplains conducted religious services for German and Austrian prisoners of war, and one chaplain, stationed in Siberia, even organized a choir and orchestra comprised of prisoners of war, demonstrating how unity in faith could transcend even the deep geopolitical divisions between the Allies and Central Powers.[480] Yet, despite these efforts and the fact that the war was seen by many as the "war to end all wars," as history showed, the United States would face familiar European foes again just a few decades later.

470 *See id.* at 208.

471 *See id.* at 189.

472 *See id.*

473 However, when an archbishop heard of a Catholic chaplain's participation in the interfaith ceremony, the chaplain was chastised for violating the canon law of the Catholic Church. *See id.*

474 *See id.*

475 *See id.*

476 *See id.* at 220; Frank E. Sugeno, *Charles Henry Brent, Apostle for Unity*, 79 Anglican & Episcopal Hist. 75 (2001).

477 *See* Stover, *supra* note 465, at 193.

478 *See id.* at 194.

479 *See id.* at 195.

480 *See id.* at 197.

The entry of the United States into World War II differed significantly from its entry into World War I. Despite presidential pledges to keep the nation out of each war – Wilson in the 1916 election, Roosevelt in 1940 – the government was already preparing for war and had in place substantial forces, even before the bombing of Pearl Harbor in December 1941.[481] This included chaplains, of which there were roughly 1,500 prior to America's official entry into the war.[482] By 1945, almost 9,000 chaplains were on duty for the Army, serving over 8 million troops.[483]

The Office of the Chief of Chaplains, which had been created in 1920, established denominational quotas, but achieving these proved to be a formidable task.[484] Whereas the quota set for Catholic priests (2,250) reached 88 percent fulfillment by the end of the war, the quota for so-called Negro churches was only 22 percent fulfilled.[485] By the date of the Japanese surrender, 5,620 Protestant chaplains, 2,278 Catholic chaplains, and 243 Jewish chaplains had served over the course of the war.[486] Christian Science, Quaker, Eastern Orthodox, and Mormon chaplains, while small in number, also served, but because adherents to those faiths were so widely dispersed across the fronts, the chaplains were generally assigned to headquarters for more efficient travel in the discharge of their ministerial duties.[487] With respect to Jewish rabbis, while also relatively small in number, their presence overseas was most readily felt on liberation of the Nazi concentration camps.[488] For many Holocaust survivors, the arrival of the Jewish chaplains on liberation was essential to restoring their spiritual and physical well-being.[489]

Many of the chaplains' religious or spiritual duties in World War II – preaching, counseling, tending to the sick and wounded, and ensuring proper burial – were similar to those of chaplains in past American conflicts. World War II chaplains, however, also went to great lengths to establish strong bonds with the troops they served. With the increased use of airplanes during the war, some chaplains, dubbed the "parachute padres," even attended "Jump School" (at that time, the U.S. Army Parachute School) so as to gain the full trust and acceptance of their troops, further demonstrating their primary function of serving not their denomination but the personnel and objectives of the U.S. Army.[490] This commitment to become an integral part of soldiers' lives also was shown by the chaplaincy's devotion to troops in battle. One famous example involved the four chaplains aboard the U.S. transport ship *Dorchester*, which was torpedoed by a German U-boat in February 1943. As the ship descended to the icy depths of the North Atlantic, the chaplains – a Reformed Jewish rabbi, a Catholic priest, and two Protestant ministers – prayed for the safety of the troops and even gave away their life jackets so

[481] *See* Robert L. Gushwa, The Best and Worst of Times: The United States Army Chaplaincy 1920–1945, at 97 (1977).
[482] *See id.* at 98.
[483] *See id.* at 99.
[484] *See id.* at 99–100
[485] *See id.* at 100.
[486] *See id.* at 99.
[487] *See id.* at 100.
[488] *See id.* at 183.
[489] *See id.* at 183–5.
[490] *See id.* at 112.

that others might survive.[491] In all, there were 478 casualties among chaplains in World War II.[492]

In the post–World War II era, and especially in the last generation, changing religious demographics have posed new challenges for the military[493] and, in turn, for military chaplaincy programs.[494] As the country and the military have increased both in their religious diversity and in their emphasis on recognizing this diversity, the need to accommodate soldiers of an ever-greater variety of religious backgrounds has become a matter of significance. At the same time, the relative decline of many mainline Protestant denominations and the rise of outspoken evangelical and secular segments of American society have had an impact on the relationship between religion and the military, including its chaplain corps.

### 2. *Constitutionality*

The leading case on the constitutionality of military chaplaincies is *Katcoff v. Marsh*,[495] a Second Circuit decision from 1985.[496] The initial lawsuit was filed by two Harvard law students challenging the U.S. Army's chaplaincy program and especially the government's funding of it. Specifically, it alleged that that the program lacked a secular purpose, had the primary effect of advancing religion, and fostered an excessive entanglement of religion, all in violation of the Establishment Clause standards articulated in *Lemon v. Kurtzman*.[497] The Second Circuit acknowledged the logical validity of these allegations in light of *Lemon* but deemed them not controlling under the circumstances.[498] Instead, the appeals court followed the Supreme Court's lead in *Marsh v. Chambers*,[499] which just two years prior had upheld state legislative prayer (delivered by a paid chaplain) largely because of an unbroken national tradition of federal legislative prayer. According to the Second Circuit, "neither the Establishment Clause nor statutes creating and maintaining the Army chaplaincy may be interpreted as if they existed in a sterile vacuum. They must be viewed in the light of the historical background of

491 *See id.* at 127–8; Dan Kurzman, No Greater Glory: The Four Immortal Chaplains and the Sinking of the Dorchester in World War II (2004); Francis Beauchesne Thornton, Sea of Glory: The Magnificent Story of the Four Chaplains (repr. 2012) (1953); *The Saga of the Four Chaplains*, Four Chaplains Memorial Foundation, *available at:* http://www.fourchaplains.org/story.html.

492 *See* Gushwa, *supra* note 481, at 141–2.

493 *See* Military Leadership Diversity Commission, *Religious Diversity in the U.S. Military* (Issue Paper No. 22) (Jun. 2010), *available at:* http://www.militaryatheists.org/resources/MLDC-RIPSdemographics.pdf. For a discussion of the Vietnam War, in particular, *see* Jacqueline E. Whitt, Bringing God to Men: American Military Chaplains and the Vietnam War (2014).

494 *See, e.g.*, Kim Philip Hansen, Military Chaplains and Religious Diversity (2012); Alan Cooperman, *For Gods and Country*, Wash. Post, Feb. 19, 2007 (discussing a Christian Army chaplain who, after converting to Wicca, applied unsuccessfully to serve as a Wiccan chaplain), *available at:* http://www.washingtonpost.com/wp-dyn/content/article/2007/02/18/AR2007021801396.html.

495 755 F.2d 223 (2d Cir. 1985).

496 For a thorough exposition of the First Amendment issues raised in *Katcoff* and by military chaplaincies more generally, *see* Ira C. Lupu & Robert W. Tuttle, *Instruments of Accommodation: The Military Chaplaincy and the Constitution*, 110 W. Va. L. Rev. 89 (2007).

497 403 U.S. 602, 612–13 (1971).

498 *See* Katcoff, 755 F.2d at 232.

499 463 U.S. 783 (1983).

their enactment to the extent that it sheds light on the purpose of the Framers of the Constitution."[500]

Three considerations, in particular, directed the constitutional analysis. The first was the fact that "[i]n providing our armed forces with a military chaplaincy Congress has perpetuated a facility that began during Revolutionary days before the adoption of our Constitution, and that has continued ever since then, with the size of the chaplaincy growing larger in proportion to the increase in the size of our Army."[501] Even more significant was that "[u]pon the adoption of the Constitution and before the December 1791 ratification of the First Amendment Congress authorized the appointment of a commissioned Army chaplain."[502] In short, just like federal legislative prayer, Congress's provision for military chaplaincies had an "'unambiguous and unbroken history of more than 200 years.'"[503]

The second key consideration was the object of the court's inquiry, namely, an exercise of the federal government's powers in relation to the military, coupled with traditional judicial deference to decisions concerning the military. "The present case," noted the court, "involves … other provisions of our Constitution, which must not only be respected but, to the extent possible, interpreted compatibly with the Establishment Clause."[504] Most notably, the case directly implicated "the War Power Clause of Art. I, § 8, which provides in pertinent part that Congress shall have the power to 'provide for the common Defence,' 'to raise and support Armies,' and to 'make Rules for the Government and Regulation of the land and naval Forces.'"[505] Acknowledging that "military conduct is not immune from judicial review when challenged as violative of the Bill of Rights,"[506] nevertheless, the court said, "caution dictates that when a matter provided for by Congress in the exercise of its war power and implemented by the Army appears reasonably relevant and necessary to furtherance of our national defense it should be treated as presumptively valid and any doubt as to its constitutionality should be resolved as a matter of judicial comity in favor of deference to the military's exercise of its discretion."[507]

The third and final consideration was that military chaplaincies, while possibly contradicting the spirit of the Establishment Clause, were congruent with the Free Exercise

500 Katcoff, 755 F.2d at 232.

501 *Id.* at 225.

502 *Id.*

503 *Id.* at 232 (quoting Marsh, 463 U.S. at 792). Regarding the historical pedigree of employing military chaplains, *see* David E. Fitzkee & Linell A. Letendre, *Religion in the Military: Navigating the Channel Between the Religion Clauses*, 59 AIR FORCE L. REV. 1, 44–5 (2007) ["The existence of military chaplains began prior to the adoption of the Constitution. The First Continental Congress authorized the numbers of military chaplains as well as their pay. Military chaplains' duties in the late 1700s included leading prayer services, visiting the troops, and counseling commanders. During the Revolutionary War, General Washington even issued a general order requiring all officers and soldiers to pray and fast on 17 May 1776. This evidence shows that chaplains led troops in prayer since the very beginning of our nation's history." (footnotes omitted)]; William A. Wildhack III, *Navy Chaplains at the Crossroads: Navigating the Intersection of Free Speech, Free Exercise, Establishment, and Equal Protection*, 51 NAVAL L. REV. 217, 225 (2005) (discussing Abraham Baldwin, who was a Revolutionary War–era Army chaplain and one of Georgia's signatories to the U.S. Constitution).

504 Katcoff, 755 F.2d at 233.

505 *Id.*

506 *Id.*

507 *Id.* at 234.

Clause. "It is readily apparent that this Clause, like the Establishment Clause, obligates Congress, upon creating an Army, to make religion available to soldiers who have been moved by the Army to areas of the world where religion of their own denominations is not available to them."[508] Indeed, noted the court, "[u]nless the Army provided a chaplaincy it would deprive the soldier of his right under the Establishment Clause not to have religion inhibited and of his right under the Free Exercise Clause to practice his freely chosen religion."[509]

Taking into account these considerations, the Second Circuit then explained that the appropriate Establishment Clause inquiry is not the three-part test of *Lemon* but instead "whether, after considering practical alternatives, the chaplaincy program is relevant to and reasonably necessary for the Army's conduct of our national defense."[510] In turn, the court found that some kind of chaplaincy program for the Army is "essential,"[511] that the plaintiffs' proposed alternative of a privately funded program "is so inherently impractical as to border on the frivolous"[512] and might not even be effective,[513] "that from time to time Congress [considered but] rejected proposals for abolition of the military chaplaincy in favor of dependence on civilian or other alternatives,"[514] that the "purpose and effect of the program is [*sic*] to make religion, religious education, counseling and religious facilities available to military personnel and their families under circumstances where the practice of religion would otherwise be denied as a practical matter to all or a substantial number,"[515] and that "the morale of our soldiers, their willingness to serve, and the efficiency of the Army as an instrument for our national defense rests [*sic*] in substantial part on the military chaplaincy, which is vital to our Army's functioning."[516] With a few potential qualifications, the court thus upheld the Army's chaplaincy program as consistent with the Establishment Clause.[517]

### 3. *Current and Emerging Issues*

The foundational First Amendment issues concerning the validity of military chaplaincies appear essentially to have been resolved by *Katcoff*, a decision that the Supreme Court has subsequently cited with approval.[518] However, additional issues under the religion clauses or RFRA continue to arise in relation to the chaplaincy programs of the armed services. In large measure, these issues often reflect broader changes and

508 *Id.*
509 *Id.*
510 *Id.* at 235.
511 *Id.*
512 *Id.* at 236.
513 *See id.* at 236–7.
514 *Id.* at 237.
515 *Id.*
516 *Id.*
517 For consideration on remand, the Second Circuit noted that "[i]n a few areas" – i.e., certain military personnel in large cities and retired military personnel and their families – "the reasonable necessity for certain activities of the military chaplaincy is not readily apparent." *Id.* at 237–8. These possible limitations are explored in Malcolm H. Wilkerson, *Picking Up Where Katcoff Left Off: Developing a Framework for a Constitutional Military Chaplaincy*, 66 Okla. L. Rev. 245 (2014).
518 *See* Cutter v. Wilkinson, 544 U.S. 709, 722 (2005); *see also* Lee v. Weisman, 505 U.S. 577, 626 (1992) (Souter, J., concurring).

attendant conflicts in American society, such as the increasing pluralism or diversification of the religious landscape or the growing tolerance or acceptance of same-sex orientation, conduct, or marriage.

Whereas *Katcoff* was brought by two civilians with no military connection, some of today's constitutional issues involving the chaplain corps are being raised by chaplains themselves. To some extent, this is not surprising. As federal employees and specifically as service members, many core aspects of their daily operations are governed by military policies, whether embedded in congressional statutes, regulations and instructions, or commanders' orders. These policies dictate chaplain qualifications, hiring, assignment, duties, promotion, and separation as well as the nature and allocation of the services they provide.[519] The military can even regulate, to a great degree, the apparel of clergy in furtherance of the same objectives of discipline and uniformity that undergird its regulation of nonclerical personnel.[520] Thus it is reasonable to expect occasional allegations that one or more these rules may not be religiously neutral, or not always be neutrally applied, or to encounter conflicts between these rules and the religious beliefs and practices of chaplains.

Extending over a decade, for example, has been litigation by current and former military chaplains alleging, among other things, that the U.S. Navy's system for promoting chaplains is religiously discriminatory in violation of both the Establishment Clause and the guarantee of equal protection.[521] They have claimed, specifically, that various practices employed in the promotion process favor Catholic and liturgical Protestant clergy while disadvantaging non-liturgical Christian clergy.[522] Although the D.C. Circuit, in at least its fourth decision in the litigation, ruled against the chaplains in late 2013, that ruling concerned only a motion for preliminary injunctive relief; thus the litigation will continue, perhaps for several more years.

Future issues may stem from conflicts between military directives and the religious expression or practices of chaplains, either as individuals or on behalf of their denominations. Consider in this regard the 2010 repeal of the "Don't Ask, Don't Tell" policy[523] or the 2013 invalidation of the federal definition of marriage as heterosexual only[524] and the possible impact of these developments on military chaplains whose religious traditions consider same-sex sexual relationships, including marriage, to be problematic. *Stars*

[519] *See, e.g.*, 10 U.S.C. § 3547 (setting forth basic duties for Army chaplains); *id.* § 6031 (same for Navy chaplains); *id.* § 8547 (same for Air Force chaplains); Army Field Manual 1-05 (Oct. 2012) ("Religious Support").

[520] *See, e.g.*, Army Pamphlet 670-1, ¶ 20-6 (Mar. 31, 2014) ("Chaplain's apparel"); *id.* ¶ 21-10(c)(10)–(12) (dictating insignia for chaplains, chaplain assistants, and chaplain candidates). Army Pamphlet 670-1 implements Army Regulation 670-1 (Mar. 31, 2014) ("Wear and Appearance of Army Uniforms and Insignia").

[521] *See In re* Navy Chaplaincy, 738 F.3d 425 (D.C. Cir. 2013), *cert. denied*, 135 S. Ct. 86 (2014).

[522] *See id.* at 427–8. Specifically, they seek "to enjoin three current Navy selection board policies – (1) staffing the seven-member selection boards with two chaplains, (2) enabling members to keep their votes secret via the 'sleeves,' and (3) allowing the Chief of Chaplains or his deputy to serve as the selection board president – that they claim result in disparate treatment of the non-liturgical candidates." *Id.* at 427.

[523] Don't Ask, Don't Tell Repeal Act of 2010, Pub. L. No. 111–321, 124 Stat. 3515 (Dec. 22, 2010) (repealing 10 U.S.C. § 654).

[524] *See* United States v. Windsor, 133 S. Ct. 2675 (2013) [invalidating, under the Fifth Amendment Due Process Clause, 1 U.S.C. § 7 as amended by Section 3 of the Defense of Marriage Act, Pub. L. No. 104–199, 110 Stat. 2419 (1996)].

*and Stripes* reported in the lead up to the repeal that conservative Christian chaplains and groups feared that the repeal would mean "that sermons against gay marriage or counseling advising against gay relationships could lead to demotions and dismissal for chaplains."[525] It further noted that based on these concerns, "some evangelical Christian groups ... [were] contemplating pulling their ministers out of the ranks,"[526] a prospect that could jeopardize the religious interests or needs of many service members. With regard to same-sex marriages, some military installations currently allow such ceremonies, though at present it appears that a chaplain is not required to perform a same-sex wedding if it contradicts the chaplain's denominational teachings.[527]

To the extent that the military eventually does promulgate regulations that, for example, prohibit clergy comments critical of same-sex conduct or relationships or mandate the performance of same-sex weddings, there will no doubt be strong resistance to such regulations by some chaplains. Although the doctrine of church autonomy might categorically shield their civilian counterparts if similar laws were to be enacted outside the military, it is not certain that this doctrine has application in the context of military chaplaincies. This leaves RFRA and its strict scrutiny framework, which would ask whether any particular military regulation – assuming that its application substantially burdens the chaplain's free exercise of religion – is the least restrictive means to achieve a compelling interest. If, in turn, the traditional judicial deference to military decisions informs this analysis, then one can expect mixed results depending on the relationship between the object of the regulation (e.g., the substance of a counseling session versus the performance of a wedding) and the military's objectives of discipline, morale, unit cohesion, and the like.[528]

525 Leo Shane III, *Conservatives Insist "Don't Ask, Don't Tell" Repeal Will Harm Chaplains*, Stars & Stripes, Apr. 30, 2010, *available at:* http://www.stripes.com/news/conservatives-insist-don-t-ask-don-t-tell-repeal-will-harm-chaplains-1.101690.

526 *Id.*

527 *See* Mitch Snow, *Chaplains Won't Perform Same-Sex Ceremonies at Utah AFB*, Stars & Stripes, Jan. 1, 2014, *available at:* http://www.stripes.com/news/us/chaplains-won-t-perform-same-sex-ceremonies-at-utah-afb-1.260110.

528 *See* Michael E. Schauss, *Putting Fire & Brimstone on Ice: The Restriction of Chaplain Speech during Religious Worship Services*, Army Lawyer, Feb. 2013, at 17, 26–7 (arguing that a commander's order to a chaplain prohibiting sermons that effectively disparage service members based on their sexual orientation could survive strict scrutiny in furtherance of goals such as discipline, unit cohesion and morale, and mission accomplishment).

# Appendix A: Federal Constitutional Provisions

**U.S. Const. art. I, § 7, cl. 2:** Every Bill which shall have passed the House of Representatives and the Senate, shall, before it become a Law, be presented to the President of the United States.... If any Bill shall not be returned by the President within ten Days (Sundays excepted) after it shall have been presented to him, the Same shall be a Law, in like Manner as if he had signed it, unless the Congress by their Adjournment prevent its Return, in which Case it shall not be a Law.

**U.S. Const. art. VI, cl. 3:** The Senators and Representatives before mentioned, and the Members of the several State Legislatures, and all executive and judicial Officers, both of the United States and of the several States, shall be bound by Oath or Affirmation, to support this Constitution; but no religious Test shall ever be required as a Qualification to any Office or public Trust under the United States.

**U.S. Const. art. VII:** The Ratification of the Conventions of nine States, shall be sufficient for the Establishment of this Constitution between the States so ratifying the same.

done in Convention by the Unanimous Consent of the States present the Seventeenth Day of September in the Year of our Lord one thousand seven hundred and Eighty seven and of the Independence of the United States of America the Twelfth.

**U.S. Const. amend. I:** Congress shall make no law respecting an establishment of religion, or prohibiting the free exercise thereof; or abridging the freedom of speech, or of the press, or the right of the people peaceably to assemble, and to petition the Government for a redress of grievances.

**U.S. Const. amend. V:** No person shall be held to answer for a capital, or otherwise infamous crime, unless on a presentment or indictment of a Grand Jury, except in cases arising in the land or naval forces, or in the Militia, when in actual service in time of War or public danger; nor shall any person be subject for the same offence to be twice put in jeopardy of life or limb; nor shall be compelled in any criminal case to be a witness against himself, nor be deprived of life, liberty, or property, without due process of law; nor shall private property be taken for public use, without just compensation.

**U.S. Const. amend. XIV**

**Section 1.** All persons born or naturalized in the United States, and subject to the jurisdiction thereof, are citizens of the United States and of the State wherein they reside. No State shall make or enforce any law which shall abridge the privileges or immunities of citizens of the United States; nor shall any State deprive any person of life, liberty, or property, without due process of law; nor deny to any person within its jurisdiction the equal protection of the laws.

**Section 5.** The Congress shall have power to enforce, by appropriate legislation, the provisions of this article.

# Appendix B: State Constitutional Provisions

## Alabama

**Ala. Const. preamble:** We, the people of the State of Alabama, in order to establish justice, insure domestic tranquility, and secure the blessings of liberty to ourselves and our posterity, invoking the favor and guidance of Almighty God, do ordain and establish the following Constitution and form of government for the State of Alabama:

**Ala. Const. art. I, § 3:** That no religion shall be established by law; that no preference shall be given by law to any religious sect, society, denomination, or mode of worship; that no one shall be compelled by law to attend any place of worship; nor to pay any tithes, taxes, or other rate for building or repairing any place of worship, or for maintaining any minister or ministry; that no religious test shall be required as a qualification to any office or public trust under this state; and that the civil rights, privileges, and capacities of any citizen shall not be in any manner affected by his religious principles.

**Ala. Const. art. I, § 3.01:**

**Section I.** The amendment shall be known as and may be cited as the Alabama Religious Freedom Amendment.

**Section II.** The Legislature makes the following findings concerning religious freedom:

(1) The framers of the United States Constitution, recognizing free exercise of religion as an unalienable right, secured its protection in the First Amendment to the Constitution, and the framers of the Constitution of Alabama of 1901, also recognizing this right, secured the protection of religious freedom in Article I, Section 3.
(2) Federal and state laws "neutral" toward religion may burden religious exercise as surely as laws intended to interfere with religious exercise.
(3) Governments should not burden religious exercise without compelling justification.
(4) In Employment Division v. Smith, 494 U.S. 872 (1990), the United States Supreme Court virtually eliminated the requirement that the government justify burdens on religious exercise imposed by laws neutral toward religion.
(5) The compelling interest test as set forth in prior court rulings is a workable test for striking sensible balances between religious liberty and competing governmental interests in areas ranging from public education (pedagogical interests and religious rights, including recognizing regulations necessary to alleviate interference with the educational process versus rights of religious freedom) to national

defense (conscription and conscientious objection, including the need to raise an army versus rights to object to individual participation), and other areas of important mutual concern.

(6) Congress passed the Religious Freedom Restoration Act, 42 U.S.C., § 2000bb, to establish the compelling interest test set forth in prior federal court rulings, but in City of Boerne v. Flores, 117 S.Ct. 2157 (1997), the United States Supreme Court held the act unconstitutional stating that the right to regulate was retained by the states.

**Section III.** The purpose of the Alabama Religious Freedom Amendment is to guarantee that the freedom of religion is not burdened by state and local law; and to provide a claim or defense to persons whose religious freedom is burdened by government.

**Section IV.** As used in this amendment, the following words shall have the following meanings:

(1) **Demonstrates.** Meets the burdens of going forward with the evidence and of persuasion.
(2) **Freedom of Religion.** The free exercise of religion under Article I, Section 3, of the Constitution of Alabama of 1901.
(3) **Government.** Any branch, department, agency, instrumentality, and official (or other person acting under the color of law) of the State of Alabama, any political subdivision of a state, municipality, or other local government.
(4) **Rule.** Any government statute, regulation, ordinance, administrative provision, ruling guideline, requirement, or any statement of law whatever.

**Section V.** (a) Government shall not burden a person's freedom of religion even if the burden results from a rule of general applicability, except as provided in subsection (b).

(b) Government may burden a person's freedom of religion only if it demonstrates that application of the burden to the person.

(1) Is in furtherance of a compelling governmental interest; and

(2) Is the least restrictive means of furthering that compelling governmental interest.

(c) A person whose religious freedom has been burdened in violation of this section may assert that violation as a claim or defense in a judicial, administrative, or other proceeding and obtain appropriate relief against a government.

**Section VI.** (a) This amendment applies to all government rules and implementations thereof, whether statutory or otherwise, and whether adopted before or after the effective date of this amendment.

(b) Nothing in this amendment shall be construed to authorize any government to burden any religious belief.

(c) Nothing in this amendment shall be construed to affect, interpret, or in any way address those portions of the First Amendment of the United States Constitution permitting the free exercise of religion or prohibiting laws respecting the establishment of religion, or those provisions of Article I, Section 3, of the Constitution of Alabama of 1901, regarding the establishment of religion.

**Section VII.** (a) This amendment shall be liberally construed to effectuate its remedial and deterrent purposes.

(b) If any provision of this amendment or its application to any particular person or circumstance is held invalid, that provision or its application is severable and does not affect the validity of other provisions or applications of this amendment.

### Alaska

**Alaska Const. preamble:** We the people of Alaska, grateful to God and to those who founded our nation and pioneered this great land, in order to secure and transmit to succeeding generations our heritage of political, civil, and religious liberty within the Union of States, do ordain and establish this constitution for the State of Alaska.

**Alaska Const. art. I, § 4:** No law shall be made respecting an establishment of religion, or prohibiting the free exercise thereof.

**Alaska Const. art. VII, § 1:** The legislature shall by general law establish and maintain a system of public schools open to all children of the State, and may provide for other public educational institutions. Schools and institutions so established shall be free from sectarian control. No money shall be paid from public funds for the direct benefit of any religious or other private educational institution.

### Arizona

**Ariz. Const. preamble:** We, the people of the state of Arizona, grateful to Almighty God for our liberties, do ordain this Constitution.

**Ariz. Const. art. II, § 12:** The liberty of conscience secured by the provisions of this constitution shall not be so construed as to excuse acts of licentiousness, or justify practices inconsistent with the peace and safety of the state. No public money or property shall be appropriated for or applied to any religious worship, exercise, or instruction, or to the support of any religious establishment. No religious qualification shall be required for any public office or employment, nor shall any person be incompetent as a witness or juror in consequence of his opinion on matters of religion, nor be questioned touching his religious belief in any court of justice to affect the weight of his testimony.

**Ariz. Const. art. XI, § 7:** No sectarian instruction shall be imparted in any school or State educational institution that may be established under this Constitution, and no religious or political test or qualification shall ever be required as a condition of admission into any public educational institution of the State, as teacher, student, or pupil; but the liberty of conscience hereby secured shall not be so construed as to justify practices or conduct inconsistent with the good order, peace, morality, or safety of the State, or with the rights of others.

**Ariz. Const. art. XX, ¶ 1:** Perfect toleration of religious sentiment shall be secured to every inhabitant of this State, and no inhabitant of this State shall ever be molested in person or property on account of his or her mode of religious worship, or lack of the same.

### Arkansas

**Art. Const. preamble:** We, the People of the State of Arkansas, grateful to Almighty God for the privilege of choosing our own form of government; for our civil and religious liberty; and desiring to perpetuate its blessings, and secure the same to ourselves and posterity; do ordain and establish this Constitution.

**Ark. Const. art. II, § 24:** All men have a natural and indefeasible right to worship Almighty God according to the dictates of their own consciences; no man can, of right, be compelled to attend, erect, or support any place of worship; or to maintain any ministry against his consent. No human authority can, in any case or manner whatsoever, control or interfere with the right of conscience; and no preference shall ever be given, by law, to any religious establishment, denomination or mode of worship, above any other.

**Ark. Const. art. II, § 25:** Religion, morality and knowledge being essential to good government, the General Assembly shall enact suitable laws to protect every religious denomination in the peaceable enjoyment of its own mode of public worship.

**Ark. Const. art. II, § 26:** No religious test shall ever be required of any person as a qualification to vote or hold office; nor shall any person be rendered incompetent to be a witness on account of his religious belief; but nothing herein shall be construed to dispense with oaths or affirmations.

**Art. Const. art. XIX, § 1:** No person who denies the being of a God shall hold any office in the civil departments of this State, nor be competent to testify as a witness in any Court.

## California

**Cal. Const. preamble:** We, the People of the State of California, grateful to Almighty God for our freedom, in order to secure and perpetuate its blessings, do establish this Constitution.

**Cal. Const. art. I, § 4:** Free exercise and enjoyment of religion without discrimination or preference are guaranteed. This liberty of conscience does not excuse acts that are licentious or inconsistent with the peace or safety of the State. The Legislature shall make no law respecting an establishment of religion.

A person is not incompetent to be a witness or juror because of his or her opinions on religious beliefs.

**Cal. Const. art. IX, § 8:** No public money shall ever be appropriated for the support of any sectarian or denominational school, or any school not under the exclusive control of the officers of the public schools; nor shall any sectarian or denominational doctrine be taught, or instruction thereon be permitted, directly or indirectly, in any of the common schools of this State.

**Cal. Const. art. IX, § 9(f):** ... The university shall be entirely independent of all political or sectarian influence and kept free therefrom in the appointment of its regents and in the administration of its affairs, and no person shall be debarred admission to any department of the university on account of race, religion, ethnic heritage, or sex.

**Cal. Const. art. XVI, § 5:** Neither the Legislature, nor any county, city and county, township, school district, or other municipal corporation, shall ever make an appropriation, or pay from any public fund whatever, or grant anything to or in aid of any religious sect, church, creed, or sectarian purpose, or help to support or sustain any school, college, university, hospital, or other institution controlled by any religious creed, church, or sectarian denomination whatever; nor shall any grant or donation of personal property or real estate ever be made by the state, or any city, city and county, town, or other municipal corporation for any religious creed, church, or sectarian purpose whatever; provided, that nothing in this section shall prevent the Legislature granting aid pursuant to Section 3 of Article XVI.

## Colorado

**Colo. Const. preamble:** We, the people of Colorado, with profound reverence for the Supreme Ruler of the Universe, in order to form a more independent and perfect government; establish justice; insure tranquility; provide for the common defense; promote the general welfare and secure the blessings of liberty to ourselves and our posterity, do ordain and establish this constitution for the "State of Colorado."

**Colo. Const. art. II, § 4:** The free exercise and enjoyment of religious profession and worship, without discrimination, shall forever hereafter be guaranteed; and no person shall be denied any civil or political right, privilege or capacity, on account of his opinions concerning religion; but the liberty of conscience hereby secured shall not be construed to dispense with oaths or affirmations, excuse acts of licentiousness or justify practices inconsistent with the good order, peace or safety of the state. No person shall be required to attend or support any ministry or place of worship, religious sect or denomination against his consent. Nor shall any preference be given by law to any religious denomination or mode of worship.

**Colo. Const. art. IX, § 8:** No religious test or qualification shall ever be required of any person as a condition of admission into any public educational institution of the state, either as a teacher or student; and no teacher or student of any such institution shall ever be required to attend or participate in any religious service whatsoever. No sectarian tenets or doctrines shall ever be taught in the public school, nor shall any distinction or classification of pupils be made on account of race or color, nor shall any pupil be assigned or transported to any public educational institution for the purpose of achieving racial balance.

## Connecticut

**Conn. Const. preamble:** The People of Connecticut acknowledging with gratitude, the good providence of God, in having permitted them to enjoy a free government; do, in order more effectually to define, secure, and perpetuate the liberties, rights and privileges which they have derived from their ancestors; hereby, after a careful consideration and revision, ordain and establish the following constitution and form of civil government.

**Conn. Const. art. I, § 3:** The exercise and enjoyment of religious profession and worship, without discrimination, shall forever be free to all persons in the state; provided, that the right hereby declared and established, shall not be so construed as to excuse acts of licentiousness, or to justify practices inconsistent with the peace and safety of the state.

**Conn. Const. art. I, § 20:** No person shall be denied the equal protection of the law nor be subjected to segregation or discrimination in the exercise or enjoyment of his or her civil or political rights because of religion, race, color, ancestry, national origin, sex or physical or mental disability.

**Conn. Const. art. VII:** It being the right of all men to worship the Supreme Being, the Great Creator and Preserver of the Universe, and to render that worship in a mode consistent with the dictates of their consciences, no person shall by law be compelled to join or support, nor be classed or associated with, any congregation, church or religious association. No preference shall be given by law to any religious society or denomination in the state. Each shall have and enjoy the same and equal powers, rights and privileges, and may support and maintain the ministers or teachers of its society or denomination, and may build and repair houses for public worship.

## Delaware

**Del. Const. preamble:** Through Divine goodness, all people have by nature the rights of worshiping and serving their Creator according to the dictates of their consciences, of enjoying and defending life and liberty, of acquiring and protecting reputation and property, and in general of obtaining objects suitable to their condition, without injury by one to another; and as these rights are essential to their welfare, for due exercise thereof, power is inherent in them; and therefore all just authority in the institutions of political society is derived from the people, and established with their consent, to advance their happiness; and they may for this end, as circumstances require, from time to time, alter their Constitution of government.

**Del. Const. art. I, § 1:** Although it is the duty of all men frequently to assemble together for the public worship of Almighty God; and piety and morality, on which the prosperity of communities depends, are hereby promoted; yet no man shall or ought to be compelled to attend any religious worship, to contribute to the erection or support of any place of worship, or to the maintenance of any ministry, against his own free will and consent; and no power shall or ought to be vested in or assumed by any magistrate that shall in any case interfere with, or in any manner control the rights of conscience, in the free exercise of religious worship, nor a preference given by law to any religious societies, denominations, or modes of worship.

**Del. Const. art. I, § 2:** No religious test shall be required as a qualification to any office, or public trust, under this State.

**Del. Const. art. X, § 3:** No portion of any fund now existing, or which may hereafter be appropriated, or raised by tax, for educational purposes, shall be appropriated to, or used by, or in aid of any sectarian, church or denominational school; provided, that all real or personal property used for school purposes, where the tuition is free, shall be exempt from taxation and assessment for public purposes.

## Florida

**Fla. Const. preamble:** We, the people of the State of Florida, being grateful to Almighty God for our constitutional liberty, in order to secure its benefits, perfect our government, insure domestic tranquility, maintain public order, and guarantee equal civil and political rights to all, do ordain and establish this constitution.

**Fla. Const. art. I, § 3:** There shall be no law respecting the establishment of religion or prohibiting or penalizing the free exercise thereof. Religious freedom shall not justify practices inconsistent with public morals, peace or safety. No revenue of the state or any political subdivision or agency thereof shall ever be taken from the public treasury directly or indirectly in aid of any church, sect, or religious denomination or in aid of any sectarian institution.

**Fla. Const. art. X, § 2(a):** The militia shall be composed of all ablebodied inhabitants of the state who are or have declared their intention to become citizens of the United States; and no person because of religious creed or opinion shall be exempted from military duty except upon conditions provided by law.

## Georgia

**Ga. Const. preamble:** To perpetuate the principles of free government, insure justice to all, preserve peace, promote the interest and happiness of the citizen and of the family, and transmit to posterity the enjoyment of liberty, we the people of Georgia, relying upon the protection and guidance of Almighty God, do ordain and establish this Constitution.

**Ga. Const. art. I, § 1, ¶ III:** Each person has the natural and inalienable right to worship God, each according to the dictates of that person's own conscience; and no human authority should, in any case, control or interfere with such right of conscience.

**Ga. Const. art. I, § 1, ¶ IV:** No inhabitant of this state shall be molested in person or property or be prohibited from holding any public office or trust on account of religious opinions; but the right of freedom of religion shall not be so construed as to excuse acts of licentiousness or justify practices inconsistent with the peace and safety of the state.

**Ga. Const. art. I, § 2, ¶ VII:** No money shall ever be taken from the public treasury, directly or indirectly, in aid of any church, sect, cult, or religious denomination or of any sectarian institution.

## Hawaii

**Haw. Const. preamble:** We, the people of Hawaii, grateful for Divine Guidance, and mindful of our Hawaiian heritage and uniqueness as an island State, dedicate our efforts to fulfill the philosophy decreed by the Hawaii State motto, "Ua mau ke ea o ka aina i ka pono."

**Haw. Const. art. I, § 4:** No law shall be enacted respecting an establishment of religion, or prohibiting the free exercise thereof, or abridging the freedom of speech or of the press or the right of the people peaceably to assemble and to petition the government for a redress of grievances.

**Haw. Const. art. I, § 5:** No person shall be deprived of life, liberty or property without due process of law, nor be denied the equal protection of the laws, nor be denied the enjoyment of the person's civil rights or be discriminated against in the exercise thereof because of race, religion, sex or ancestry.

**Haw. Const. art. I, § 9:** No citizen shall be denied enlistment in any military organization of this State nor be segregated therein because of race, religious principles or ancestry.

**Haw. Const. art. X, § 1:** The State shall provide for the establishment, support and control of a statewide system of public schools free from sectarian control, a state university, public libraries and such other educational institutions as may be deemed desirable, including physical facilities therefor. There shall be no discrimination in public educational institutions because of race, religion, sex or ancestry; nor shall public funds be appropriated for the support or benefit of any sectarian or nonsectarian private educational institution, except that proceeds of special purpose revenue bonds authorized or issued under section 12 of Article VII may be appropriated to finance or assist:

1. Not-for-profit corporations that provide early childhood education and care facilities serving the general public; and
2. Not-for-profit private nonsectarian and sectarian elementary schools, secondary schools, colleges and universities.

**Haw. Const. art. XII, § 7:** The State reaffirms and shall protect all rights, customarily and traditionally exercised for subsistence, cultural and religious purposes and possessed by ahupua'a tenants who are descendants of native Hawaiians who inhabited the Hawaiian Islands prior to 1778, subject to the right of the State to regulate such rights.

## Idaho

**Idaho Const. preamble:** We, the people of the state of Idaho, grateful to Almighty God for our freedom, to secure its blessings and promote our common welfare do establish this Constitution.

**Idaho Const. art. I, § 4:** The exercise and enjoyment of religious faith and worship shall forever be guaranteed; and no person shall be denied any civil or political right, privilege, or capacity on account of his religious opinions; but the liberty of conscience hereby secured shall not be construed to dispense with oaths or affirmations, or excuse acts of licentiousness or justify polygamous or other pernicious practices, inconsistent with morality or the peace or safety of the state; nor to permit any person, organization, or association to directly or indirectly aid or abet, counsel or advise any person to commit the crime of bigamy or polygamy, or any other crime. No person shall be required to attend or support any ministry or place of worship, religious sect or denomination, or pay tithes against his consent; nor shall any preference be given by law to any religious denomination or mode of worship. Bigamy and polygamy are forever prohibited in the state, and the legislature shall provide by law for the punishment of such crimes.

**Idaho Const. art. IX, § 5:** Neither the legislature nor any county, city, town, township, school district, or other public corporation, shall ever make any appropriation, or pay from any public fund or moneys whatever, anything in aid of any church or sectarian or religious society, or for any sectarian or religious purpose, or to help support or sustain any school, academy, seminary, college, university or other literary or scientific institution, controlled by any church, sectarian or religious denomination whatsoever; nor shall any grant or donation of land, money or other personal property ever be made by the state, or any such public corporation, to any church or for any sectarian or religious purpose; provided, however, that a health facilities authority, as specifically authorized and empowered by law, may finance or refinance any private, not for profit, health facilities owned or operated by any church or sectarian religious society, through loans, leases, or other transactions.

**Idaho Const. art. IX, § 6:** No religious test or qualification shall ever be required of any person as a condition of admission into any public educational institution of the state, either as teacher or student; and no teacher or student of any such institution shall ever be required to attend or participate in any religious service whatever. No sectarian or religious tenets or doctrines shall ever be taught in the public schools, nor shall any distinction or classification of pupils be made on account of race or color. No books, papers, tracts or documents of a political, sectarian or denominational character shall be used or introduced in any schools established under the provisions of this article, nor shall any teacher or any district receive any of the public school moneys in which the schools have not been taught in accordance with the provisions of this article.

**Idaho Const. art. XXI, § 19:** It is ordained by the state of Idaho that perfect toleration of religious sentiment shall be secured, and no inhabitant of said state shall ever be molested in person or property on account of his or her mode of religious worship.

## Illinois

**Ill. Const. preamble:** We, the People of the State of Illinois – grateful to Almighty God for the civil, political and religious liberty which He has permitted us to enjoy and seeking His blessing upon our endeavors – in order to provide for the health, safety and welfare of the people; maintain a representative and orderly government; eliminate poverty and inequality; assure legal, social and economic justice; provide opportunity for the fullest development of the individual; insure domestic tranquility; provide for the common defense; and secure the blessings of freedom and liberty to ourselves and our posterity–do ordain and establish this Constitution for the State of Illinois.

**Ill. Const. art. I, § 3:** The free exercise and enjoyment of religious profession and worship, without discrimination, shall forever be guaranteed, and no person shall be denied any civil or political right, privilege or capacity, on account of his religious opinions; but the liberty of conscience hereby secured shall not be construed to dispense with oaths or affirmations, excuse acts of licentiousness, or justify practices inconsistent with the peace or safety of the State. No person shall be required to attend or support any ministry or place of worship against his consent, nor shall any preference be given by law to any religious denomination or mode of worship.

**Ill. Const. art. I, § 17:** All persons shall have the right to be free from discrimination on the basis of race, color, creed, national ancestry and sex in the hiring and promotion practices of any employer or in the sale or rental of property.

These rights are enforceable without action by the General Assembly, but the General Assembly by law may establish reasonable exemptions relating to these rights and provide additional remedies for their violation.

**Ill. Const. art. I, § 20:** To promote individual dignity, communications that portray criminality, depravity or lack of virtue in, or that incite violence, hatred, abuse or hostility toward, a person or group of persons by reason of or by reference to religious, racial, ethnic, national or regional affiliation are condemned.

**Ill. Const. art. X, § 3:** Neither the General Assembly nor any county, city, town, township, school district, or other public corporation, shall ever make any appropriation or pay from any public fund whatever, anything in aid of any church or sectarian purpose, or to help support or sustain any school, academy, seminary, college, university, or other literary or scientific institution, controlled by any church or sectarian denomination whatever; nor shall any grant or donation of land, money, or other personal property ever be made by the State, or any such public corporation, to any church, or for any sectarian purpose.

## Indiana

**Ind. Const. preamble:** TO THE END, that justice be established, public order maintained, and liberty perpetuated; WE, the *People* of the *State* of *Indiana*, grateful to

ALMIGHTY GOD for the free exercise of the right to choose our own form of government, do ordain this *Constitution*.

**Ind. Const. art. I, § 2:** All people shall be secured in the natural right to worship ALMIGHTY GOD, according to the dictates of their own consciences.

**Ind. Const. art. I, § 3:** No law shall, in any case whatever, control the free exercise and enjoyment of religious opinions, or interfere with the rights of conscience.

**Ind. Const. art. I, § 4:** No preference shall be given, by law, to any creed, religious society, or mode of worship; and no person shall be compelled to attend, erect, or support, any place of worship, or to maintain any ministry, against his consent.

**Ind. Const. art. I, § 5:** No religious test shall be required, as a qualification for any office of trust or profit.

**Ind. Const. art. I, § 6:** No money shall be drawn from the treasury, for the benefit of any religious or theological institution.

**Ind. Const. art. I, § 7:** No person shall be rendered incompetent as a witness, in consequence of his opinions on matters of religion.

## Iowa

**Iowa Const. preamble:** WE THE PEOPLE OF THE STATE OF IOWA, grateful to the Supreme Being for the blessings hitherto enjoyed, and feeling our dependence on Him for a continuation of those blessings, do ordain and establish a free and independent government, by the name of the State of Iowa. . . .

**Iowa Const. art. I, § 3:** The general assembly shall make no law respecting an establishment of religion, or prohibiting the free exercise thereof; nor shall any person be compelled to attend any place of worship, pay tithes, taxes, or other rates for building or repairing places of worship, or the maintenance of any minister, or ministry.

**Iowa Const. art. I, § 4:** No religious test shall be required as a qualification for any office, or public trust, and no person shall be deprived of any of his rights, privileges, or capacities, or disqualified from the performance of any of his public or private duties, or rendered incompetent to give evidence in any court of law or equity, in consequence of his opinions on the subject of religion; and any party to any judicial proceeding shall have the right to use as a witness, or take the testimony of, any other person not disqualified on account of interest, who may be cognizant of any fact material to the case; and parties to suits may be witnesses, as provided by law.

## Kansas

**Kan. Const. preamble:** We, the people of Kansas, grateful to Almighty God for our civil and religious privileges, in order to insure the full enjoyment of our rights as American citizens, do ordain and establish this constitution of the state of Kansas. . . .

**Kan. Const. Bill of Rts. § 7:** The right to worship God according to the dictates of conscience shall never be infringed; nor shall any person be compelled to attend or support any form of worship; nor shall any control of or interference with the rights of conscience be permitted, nor any preference be given by law to any religious establishment or mode of worship. No religious test or property qualification shall be required for any office of public trust, nor for any vote at any elections, nor shall any person be incompetent to testify on account of religious belief.

**Kan. Const. art. VI, § 6(c):** No religious sect or sects shall control any part of the public educational funds.

**Kan. Const. art. I, § 8:** The militia shall be composed of all able-bodied male citizens between the ages of twenty-one and forty-five years, except such as are exempted by the laws of the United States or of this state; but all citizens of any religious denomination whatever who from scruples of conscience may be adverse to bearing arms shall be exempted therefrom, upon such conditions as may be prescribed by law.

## Kentucky

**Ky. Const. preamble:** We, the people of the Commonwealth of Kentucky, grateful to Almighty God for the civil, political and religious liberties we enjoy, and invoking the continuance of these blessings, do ordain and establish this Constitution.

**Ky. Const. Bill of Rts. § 1:** All men are, by nature, free and equal, and have certain inherent and inalienable rights, among which may be reckoned:

...

Second: The right of worshipping Almighty God according to the dictates of their consciences.

...

**Ky. Const. Bill of Rts. § 5:** No preference shall ever be given by law to any religious sect, society or denomination; nor to any particular creed, mode of worship or system of ecclesiastical polity; nor shall any person be compelled to attend any place of worship, to contribute to the erection or maintenance of any such place, or to the salary or support of any minister of religion; nor shall any man be compelled to send his child to any school to which he may be conscientiously opposed; and the civil rights, privileges or capacities of no person shall be taken away, or in anywise diminished or enlarged, on account of his belief or disbelief of any religious tenet, dogma or teaching. No human authority shall, in any case whatever, control or interfere with the rights of conscience.

**Ky. Const. § 189:** No portion of any fund or tax now existing, or that may hereafter be raised or levied for educational purposes, shall be appropriated to, or used by, or in aid of, any church, sectarian or denominational school.

**Ky. Const. § 232:** The manner of administering an oath or affirmation shall be such as is most consistent with the conscience of the deponent, and shall be esteemed by the General Assembly the most solemn appeal to God.

## Louisiana

**La. Const. preamble:** We, the people of Louisiana, grateful to Almighty God for the civil, political, economic, and religious liberties we enjoy, and desiring to protect individual rights to life, liberty, and property; afford opportunity for the fullest development of the individual; assure equality of rights; promote the health, safety, education, and welfare of the people; maintain a representative and orderly government; ensure domestic tranquility; provide for the common defense; and secure the blessings of freedom and justice to ourselves and our posterity, do ordain and establish this constitution.

**La. Const. art. I, § 3:** No person shall be denied the equal protection of the laws. No law shall discriminate against a person because of race or religious ideas, beliefs, or affiliations. No law shall arbitrarily, capriciously, or unreasonably discriminate against a person because of birth, age, sex, culture, physical condition, or political ideas or affiliations. Slavery and involuntary servitude are prohibited, except in the latter case as punishment for crime.

**La. Const. art. I, § 8:** No law shall be enacted respecting an establishment of religion or prohibiting the free exercise thereof.

**La. Const. art. I, § 12:** In access to public areas, accommodations, and facilities, every person shall be free from discrimination based on race, religion, or national ancestry and from arbitrary, capricious, or unreasonable discrimination based on age, sex, or physical condition.

**La. Const. art. X, § 8(B):** No classified employee shall be discriminated against because of his political or religious beliefs, sex, or race. A classified employee so discriminated against shall have the right of appeal to the appropriate commission pursuant to Section 12 of this Part. The burden of proof on appeal, as to the facts, shall be on the employee.

**La. Const. art. X, § 46(B):** No classified state police officer shall be discriminated against because of his political or religious beliefs, sex, or race. A classified state police officer so discriminated against shall have the right of appeal to the commission. The burden of proof on appeal, as to the facts, shall be on the state police officer.

## Maine

**Me. Const. preamble:** We the people of Maine, in order to establish justice, insure tranquility, provide for our mutual defense, promote our common welfare, and secure to ourselves and our posterity the blessings of liberty, acknowledging with grateful hearts the goodness of the Sovereign Ruler of the Universe in affording us an opportunity, so favorable to the design; and, imploring God's aid and direction in its accomplishment, do agree to form ourselves into a free and independent State, by the style and title of the State of Maine and do ordain and establish the following Constitution for the government of the same.

**Me. Const. art. I, § 3:** All individuals have a natural and unalienable right to worship Almighty God according to the dictates of their own consciences, and no person shall be hurt, molested or restrained in that person's liberty or estate for worshipping God in the manner and season most agreeable to the dictates of that person's own conscience, nor for that person's religious professions or sentiments, provided that that person does not disturb the public peace, nor obstruct others in their religious worship; – and all persons demeaning themselves peaceably, as good members of the State, shall be equally under the protection of the laws, and no subordination nor preference of any one sect or denomination to another shall ever be established by law, nor shall any religious test be required as a qualification for any office or trust, under this State; and all religious societies in this State, whether incorporate or unincorporate, shall at all times have the exclusive right of electing their public teachers, and contracting with them for their support and maintenance.

**Me. Const. art. VII, § 5:** Persons of the denominations of Quakers and Shakers, Justices of the Supreme Judicial Court, Ministers of the Gospel and persons exempted by the laws of the United States may be exempted from military duty, but no other able-bodied person of the age of 18 and under the age of 45 years, excepting officers of the militia who have been honorably discharged, shall be so exempted.

## Maryland

**Md. Const. preamble:** We, the People of the State of Maryland, grateful to Almighty God for our civil and religious liberty, and taking into our serious consideration the best means of establishing a good Constitution in this State for the sure foundation and more permanent security thereof....

**Md. Const. Decl. of Rts. art. 36:** That as it is the duty of every man to worship God in such manner as he thinks most acceptable to Him, all persons are equally entitled to protection in their religious liberty; wherefore, no person ought by any law to be molested in his person or estate, on account of his religious persuasion, or profession, or for his religious practice, unless, under the color of religion, he shall disturb the good order, peace or safety of the State, or shall infringe the laws of morality, or injure others in their natural, civil or religious rights; nor ought any person to be compelled to frequent, or maintain, or contribute, unless on contract, to maintain, any place of worship, or any ministry; nor shall any person, otherwise competent, be deemed incompetent as a witness, or juror, on account of his religious belief; provided, he believes in the existence of God, and that under His dispensation such person will be held morally accountable for his acts, and be rewarded or punished therefor either in this world or in the world to come.

Nothing shall prohibit or require the making reference to belief in, reliance upon, or invoking the aid of God or a Supreme Being in any governmental or public document, proceeding, activity, ceremony, school, institution, or place.

Nothing in this article shall constitute an establishment of religion.

**Md. Const. Decl. of Rts. art. 37:** That no religious test ought ever to be required as a qualification for any office of profit or trust in this State, other than a declaration of belief in the existence of God; nor shall the Legislature prescribe any other oath of office than the oath prescribed by this Constitution.

## Massachusetts

**Mass. Const. preamble:** ... We ... the people of Massachusetts, acknowledging, with grateful hearts, the goodness of the great Legislator of the universe, in affording us, in the course of His providence, an opportunity, deliberately and peaceably, without fraud, violence or surprise, of entering into an original, explicit, and solemn compact with each other; and of forming a new constitution of civil government, for ourselves and posterity; and devoutly imploring His direction in so interesting a design, do agree upon, ordain and establish the following Declaration of Rights, and Frame of Government, as the Constitution of the Commonwealth of Massachusetts.

**Mass. Const. pt. I, art. II:** It is the right as well as the duty of all men in society, publicly, and at stated seasons to worship the SUPREME BEING, the great Creator and Preserver of the universe. And no subject shall be hurt, molested, or restrained, in his person, liberty, or estate, for worshipping GOD in the manner and season most agreeable to the dictates of his own conscience; or for his religious profession or sentiments; provided he doth not disturb the public peace, or obstruct others in their religious worship.

**Mass. Const. pt. I, art. III:** As the public worship of GOD and instructions in piety, religion and morality, promote the happiness and prosperity of a people and the security of a republican government; – therefore, the several religious societies of this commonwealth, whether corporate or unincorporate, at any meeting legally warned and holden for that purpose, shall ever have the right to elect their pastors or religious teachers, to contract with them for their support, to raise money for erecting and repairing houses for public worship, for the maintenance of religious instruction, and for the payment of necessary expenses: and all persons belonging to any religious society shall be taken and held to be members, until they shall file with the clerk of such society, a written notice, declaring the dissolution of their membership, and thenceforth shall not be liable for any grant or contract which may be thereafter made, or entered into by such society: – and all religious sects and denominations, demeaning themselves peaceably, and as good citizens of the commonwealth, shall be equally under the protection of the law; and no subordination of any one sect or denomination to another shall ever be established by law.

**Mass. Const. pt. I, art. III:**

**Section 1.** No law shall be passed prohibiting the free exercise of religion.

**Section 2.** No grant, appropriation or use of public money or property or loan of credit shall be made or authorized by the commonwealth or any political subdivision thereof for the purpose of founding, maintaining or aiding any infirmary, hospital, institution, primary or secondary school, or charitable or religious undertaking which is not publicly owned and under the exclusive control, order and supervision of public officers or public agents authorized by the commonwealth or federal authority or both, except that appropriations may be made for the maintenance and support of the Soldiers' Home in Massachusetts and for free public libraries in any city or town, and to carry out legal obligations, if any, already entered into; and no such grant, appropriation or use of public money or property or loan of public credit shall be made or authorized for the purpose of founding, maintaining or aiding any church, religious denomination or society. Nothing herein contained shall be construed to prevent the commonwealth from making grants-in-aid to private higher educational institutions or to students or parents or guardians of students attending such institutions.

**Section 3.** Nothing herein contained shall be construed to prevent the commonwealth, or any political division thereof, from paying to privately controlled hospitals, infirmaries, or institutions for the deaf, dumb or blind not more than the ordinary and reasonable compensation for care or support actually rendered or furnished by such hospitals, infirmaries or institutions to such persons as may be in whole or in part unable to support or care for themselves.

**Section 4.** Nothing herein contained shall be construed to deprive any inmate of a publicly controlled reformatory, penal or charitable institution of the opportunity of religious exercises therein of his own faith; but no inmate of such institution shall be compelled to attend religious services or receive religious instruction against his will, or, if a minor, without the consent of his parent or guardian.

**Section 5.** This amendment shall not take effect until the October first next succeeding its ratification and adoption by the people.

**Mass. Const. amend. art. 48, pt. 2:**

**Section 2.** No measure that relates to religion, religious practices or religious institutions; or to the appointment, qualification, tenure, removal, recall or compensation of judges; or to the reversal of a judicial decision; or to the powers, creation or abolition of courts; or the operation of which is restricted to a particular town, city or other political division or to particular districts or localities of the commonwealth; or that makes a specific appropriation of money from the treasury of the commonwealth, shall be proposed by an initiative petition; but if a law approved by the people is not repealed, the general court shall raise by taxation or otherwise and shall appropriate such money as may be necessary to carry such law into effect.

## Michigan

**Mich. Const. ch. 1 preamble:** We, the people of the State of Michigan, grateful to Almighty God for the blessings of freedom, and earnestly desiring to secure these blessings undiminished to ourselves and our posterity, do ordain and establish this constitution.

**Mich. Const. art. I, § 2:** No person shall be denied the equal protection of the laws; nor shall any person be denied the enjoyment of his civil or political rights or be discriminated against in the exercise thereof because of religion, race, color or national origin. The legislature shall implement this section by appropriate legislation.

**Mich. Const. art. I, § 4:** Every person shall be at liberty to worship God according to the dictates of his own conscience. No person shall be compelled to attend, or, against his consent, to contribute to the erection or support of any place of religious worship, or to pay tithes, taxes or other rates for the support of any minister of the gospel or teacher of religion. No money shall be appropriated or drawn from the treasury for the benefit of any religious sect or society, theological or religious seminary; nor shall property belonging to the state be appropriated for any such purpose. The civil and political rights, privileges and capacities of no person shall be diminished or enlarged on account of his religious belief.

**Mich. Const. art. I, § 18:** No person shall be rendered incompetent to be a witness on account of his opinions on matters of religious belief.

**Mich. Const. art. VIII, § 1:** Religion, morality and knowledge being necessary to good government and the happiness of mankind, schools and the means of education shall forever be encouraged.

**Mich. Const. art. VIII, § 2:** The legislature shall maintain and support a system of free public elementary and secondary schools as defined by law. Every school district shall provide for the education of its pupils without discrimination as to religion, creed, race, color or national origin.

## Minnesota

**Minn. Const. preamble:** We, the people of the state of Minnesota, grateful to God for our civil and religious liberty, and desiring to perpetuate its blessings and secure the same to ourselves and our posterity, do ordain and establish this Constitution.

**Minn. Const. art. I, § 16:** The enumeration of rights in this constitution shall not deny or impair others retained by and inherent in the people. The right of every man to worship God according to the dictates of his own conscience shall never be infringed; nor shall any man be compelled to attend, erect or support any place of worship, or to maintain any religious or ecclesiastical ministry, against his consent; nor shall any control of or interference with the rights of conscience be permitted, or any preference be given by law to any religious establishment or mode of worship; but the liberty of conscience hereby secured shall not be so construed as to excuse acts of licentiousness or justify practices inconsistent with the peace or safety of the state, nor shall any money be drawn from the treasury for the benefit of any religious societies or religious or theological seminaries.

**Minn. Const. art. I, § 17:** No religious test or amount of property shall be required as a qualification for any office of public trust in the state. No religious test or amount of property shall be required as a qualification of any voter at any election in this state; nor shall any person be rendered incompetent to give evidence in any court of law or equity in consequence of his opinion upon the subject of religion.

**Minn. Const. art. XIII, § 2:** In no case shall any public money or property be appropriated or used for the support of schools wherein the distinctive doctrines, creeds or tenets of any particular Christian or other religious sect are promulgated or taught.

## Mississippi

**Miss. Const. preamble:** We, the people of Mississippi in convention assembled, grateful to Almighty God, and invoking his blessing on our work, do ordain and establish this constitution.

**Miss. Const. art. III, § 18:** No religious test as a qualification for office shall be required; and no preference shall be given by law to any religious sect or mode of worship; but the free enjoyment of all religious sentiments and the different modes of worship shall be held sacred. The rights hereby secured shall not be construed to justify acts of licentiousness injurious to morals or dangerous to the peace and safety of the state, or to exclude the Holy Bible from use in any public school of this state.

**Miss. Const. art. VIII, § 208:** No religious or other sect or sects shall ever control any part of the school or other educational funds of this state; nor shall any funds be appropriated toward the support of any sectarian school, or to any school that at the time of receiving such appropriation is not conducted as a free school.

**Miss. Const. art. XIV, § 265:** No person who denies the existence of a Supreme Being shall hold any office in this state.

## Missouri

**Mo. Const. preamble:** We, the people of Missouri, with profound reverence for the Supreme Ruler of the Universe, and grateful for His goodness, do establish this Constitution for the better government of the state.

**Mo. Const. art. I, § 5:** That all men have a natural and indefeasible right to worship Almighty God according to the dictates of their own consciences; that no human authority can control or interfere with the rights of conscience; that no person shall, on account of his religious persuasion or belief, be rendered ineligible to any public office or trust or profit in this state, be disqualified from testifying or serving as a juror, or be molested in his person or estate; but this section shall not be construed to excuse acts of licentiousness, nor to justify practices inconsistent with the good order, peace or safety of the state, or with the rights of others.

**Mo. Const. art. I, § 6:** That no person can be compelled to erect, support or attend any place or system of worship, or to maintain or support any priest, minister, preacher or teacher of any sect, church, creed or denomination of religion; but if any person shall voluntarily make a contract for any such object, he shall be held to the performance of the same.

**Mo. Const. art. I, § 7:** That no money shall ever be taken from the public treasury, directly or indirectly, in aid of any church, sect or denomination of religion, or in aid of any priest, preacher, minister or teacher thereof, as such; and that no preference shall be given to nor any discrimination made against any church, sect or creed of religion, or any form of religious faith or worship.

**Mo. Const. art. IX, § 8:** Neither the general assembly, nor any county, city, town, township, school district or other municipal corporation, shall ever make an appropriation or pay from any public fund whatever, anything in aid of any religious creed, church or sectarian purpose, or to help to support or sustain any private or public school, academy, seminary, college, university, or other institution of learning controlled by any religious creed, church or sectarian denomination whatever; nor shall any grant or donation of personal property or real estate ever be made by the state, or any county, city, town, or other municipal corporation, for any religious creed, church, or sectarian purpose whatever.

## Montana

**Mont. Const. preamble:** We the people of Montana grateful to God for the quiet beauty of our state, the grandeur of our mountains, the vastness of our rolling plains, and desiring to improve the quality of life, equality of opportunity and to secure the blessings of liberty for this and future generations do ordain and establish this constitution.

**Mont. Const. art. II, § 4:** The dignity of the human being is inviolable. No person shall be denied the equal protection of the laws. Neither the state nor any person, firm, corporation, or institution shall discriminate against any person in the exercise of his civil or political rights on account of race, color, sex, culture, social origin or condition, or political or religious ideas.

**Mont. Const. art. II, § 5:** The state shall make no law respecting an establishment of religion or prohibiting the free exercise thereof.

**Mont. Const. art. X, § 6:** (1) The legislature, counties, cities, towns, school districts, and public corporations shall not make any direct or indirect appropriation or payment from any public fund or monies, or any grant of lands or other property for any sectarian purpose or to aid any church, school, academy, seminary, college, university, or other literary or scientific institution, controlled in whole or in part by any church, sect, or denomination.

(2) This section shall not apply to funds from federal sources provided to the state for the express purpose of distribution to non-public education.

**Mont. Const. art. X, § 7:** No religious or partisan test or qualification shall be required of any teacher or student as a condition of admission into any public educational institution. Attendance shall not be required at any religious service. No sectarian tenets shall be advocated in any public educational institution of the state. No person shall be refused admission to any public educational institution on account of sex, race, creed, religion, political beliefs, or national origin.

## Nebraska

**Neb. Const. preamble:** We, the people, grateful to Almighty God for our freedom, do ordain and establish the following declaration of rights and frame of government, as the Constitution of the State of Nebraska.

**Neb. Const. art. I, § 4:** All persons have a natural and indefeasible right to worship Almighty God according to the dictates of their own consciences. No person shall be compelled to attend, erect or support any place of worship against his consent, and no preference shall be given by law to any religious society, nor shall any interference with the rights of conscience be permitted. No religious test shall be required as a qualification for office, nor shall any person be incompetent to be a witness on account of his religious beliefs; but nothing herein shall be construed to dispense with oaths and affirmations. Religion, morality, and knowledge, however, being essential to good government, it shall be the duty of the Legislature to pass suitable laws to protect every religious denomination in the peaceable enjoyment of its own mode of public worship, and to encourage schools and the means of instruction.

**Neb. Const. art. VII, § 11:** Notwithstanding any other provision in the Constitution, appropriation of public funds shall not be made to any school or institution of learning not owned or exclusively controlled by the state or a political subdivision thereof; PROVIDED, that the Legislature may provide that the state or any political subdivision thereof may contract with institutions not wholly owned or controlled by the state or any political subdivision to provide for educational or other services for the benefit of children under the age of twenty-one years who are handicapped, as that term is from time to time defined by the Legislature, if such services are nonsectarian in nature.

All public schools shall be free of sectarian instruction.

The state shall not accept money or property to be used for sectarian purposes; PROVIDED, that the Legislature may provide that the state may receive money from the federal government and distribute it in accordance with the terms of any such federal grants, but no public funds of the state, any political subdivision, or any public corporation may be added thereto.

A religious test or qualification shall not be required of any teacher or student for admission or continuance in any school or institution supported in whole or in part by public funds or taxation.

## Nevada

**Nev. Const. preamble:** We the people of the State of Nevada Grateful to Almighty God for our freedom in order to secure its blessings, insure domestic tranquility, and form a more perfect Government, do establish this Constitution.

**Nev. Const. art. I, § 4:** The free exercise and enjoyment of religious profession and worship without discrimination or preference shall forever be allowed in this State, and no person shall be rendered incompetent to be a witness on account of his opinions on matters of his religious belief, but the liberty of consciene [*sic*] hereby secured, shall not be so construed, as to excuse acts of licentiousness or justify practices inconsistent with the peace, or safety of this State.

**Nev. Const. art. XI, § 3:** The right of any citizen of the state to vote, hold office or sit upon juries, shall never be restricted, abridged or impaired on account of religion, race, language or color, or inability to speak, read or write the English or Spanish languages except as may be otherwise provided in this constitution.

**Nev. Const. art. XI, § 9:** No sectarian instruction shall be imparted or tolerated in any school or University that may be established under this Constitution.

**Nev. Const. art. XI, § 10:** No public funds of any kind or character whatever, State, County or Municipal, shall be used for sectarian purpose.

**Nev. Const. art. XII, § 9:** No religious test shall ever be required as a condition of admission into the public schools or any educational institution of this state, either as a teacher or student, and no teacher or student of such school or institution shall ever be required to attend or participate in any religious service whatsoever.

**Nev. Const. art. XXI, § 1:** Perfect toleration of religious sentiment shall be secured, and no inhabitant of this state shall ever be molested in person or property on account of his or her mode of religious worship. Polygamous or plural marriages and polygamous cohabitation are forever prohibited.

## New Hampshire

**N.H. Const. pt. I, art. 4:** Among the natural rights, some are, in their very nature unalienable, because no equivalent can be given or received for them. Of this kind are the Rights of Conscience.

**N.H. Const. pt. I, art. 5:** Every individual has a natural and unalienable right to worship God according to the dictates of his own conscience, and reason; and no subject shall be hurt, molested, or restrained, in his peers on, liberty, or estate, for worshipping God in the manner and season most agreeable to the dictates of his own conscience; or for his religious profession, sentiments, or persuasion; provided he doth not disturb the public peace or disturb others in their religious worship.

**N.H. Const. pt. I, art. 6:** As morality and piety, rightly grounded on high principles, will give the best and greatest security to government, and will lay, in the hearts of men, the strongest obligations to due subjection; and as the knowledge of these is most likely to be propagated through a society, therefore, the several parishes, bodies, corporate, or religious societies shall at all times have the right of electing their own teachers, and of contracting with them for their support or maintenance, or both. But no person shall ever be compelled to pay towards the support of the schools of any sect or denomination. And every person, denomination or sect shall be equally under the protection of the law; and no subordination of any one sect, denomination or persuasion to another shall ever be established.

**N.H. Const. pt. I, art. 13:** No person, who is conscientiously scrupulous about the lawfulness of bearing arms, shall be compelled thereto.

## New Jersey

**N.J. Const. preamble:** We, the people of the State of New Jersey, grateful to Almighty God for the civil and religious liberty which He hath so long permitted us to enjoy, and looking to Him for a blessing upon our endeavors to secure and transmit the same unimpaired to succeeding generations, do ordain and establish this Constitution.

**N.J. Const. art. I, ¶ 3:** No person shall be deprived of the inestimable privilege of worshipping Almighty God in a manner agreeable to the dictates of his own conscience; nor under any pretense whatever be compelled to attend any place of worship contrary to his faith and judgment; nor shall any person be obliged to pay tithes, taxes, or other rates for building or repairing any church or churches, place or places of worship, or for the maintenance of any minister or ministry, contrary to what he believes to be right or has deliberately and voluntarily engaged to perform.

**N.J. Const. art. I, ¶ 4:** There shall be no establishment of one religious sect in preference to another; no religious or racial test shall be required as a qualification for any office or public trust.

**N.J. Const. art. I, ¶ 5:** No person shall be denied the enjoyment of any civil or military right, nor be discriminated against in the exercise of any civil or military right, nor be segregated in the militia or in the public schools, because of religious principles, race, color, ancestry or national origin.

## New Mexico

**N.M. Const. preamble:** We, the people of New Mexico, grateful to Almighty God for the blessings of liberty, in order to secure the advantages of a state government, do ordain and establish this constitution.

**N.M. Const. art. II, § 11:** Every man shall be free to worship God according to the dictates of his own conscience, and no person shall ever be molested or denied any civil or political right or privilege on account of his religious opinion or mode of religious worship. No person shall be required to attend any place of worship or support any religious sect or denomination; nor shall any preference be given by law to any religious denomination or mode of worship.

## New York

**N.Y. Const. preamble:** WE, THE PEOPLE of the State of New York, grateful to Almighty God for our Freedom, in order to secure its blessings, DO ESTABLISH THIS CONSTITUTION.

**N.Y. Const. art. I, § 3:** The free exercise and enjoyment of religious profession and worship, without discrimination or preference, shall forever be allowed in this state to all humankind; and no person shall be rendered incompetent to be a witness on account of his or her opinions on matters of religious belief; but the liberty of conscience hereby secured shall not be so construed as to excuse acts of licentiousness, or justify practices inconsistent with the peace or safety of this state.

**N.Y. Const. art. I, § 11:** No person shall be denied the equal protection of the laws of this state or any subdivision thereof. No person shall, because of race, color, creed or religion, be subjected to any discrimination in his or her civil rights by any other person or by any firm, corporation, or institution, or by the state or any agency or subdivision of the state.

**N.Y. Const. art. VI, § 32:** When any court having jurisdiction over a child shall commit it or remand it to an institution or agency or place it in the custody of any person by parole, placing out, adoption or guardianship, the child shall be committed or remanded or placed, when practicable, in an institution or agency governed by persons, or in the custody of a person, of the same religious persuasion as the child.

**N.Y. Const. art. XI, § 3:** Neither the state nor any subdivision thereof, shall use its property or credit or any public money, or authorize or permit either to be used, directly or indirectly, in aid or maintenance, other than for examination or inspection, of any school or institution of learning wholly or in part under the control or direction of any religious denomination, or in which any denominational tenet or doctrine is taught, but the legislature may provide for the transportation of children to and from any school or institution of learning.

### North Carolina

**N.C. Const. preamble:** We, the people of the State of North Carolina, grateful to Almighty God, the Sovereign Ruler of Nations, for the preservation of the American Union and the existence of our civil, political and religious liberties, and acknowledging our dependence upon Him for the continuance of those blessings to us and our posterity, do, for the more certain security thereof and for the better government of this State, ordain and establish this Constitution.

**N.C. Const. art. I, § 13:** All persons have a natural and inalienable right to worship Almighty God according to the dictates of their own consciences, and no human authority shall, in any case whatever, control or interfere with the rights of conscience.

**N.C. Const. art. I, § 19:** No person shall be taken, imprisoned, or disseized of his freehold, liberties, or privileges, or outlawed, or exiled, or in any manner deprived of his life, liberty, or property, but by the law of the land. No person shall be denied the equal protection of the laws; nor shall any person be subjected to discrimination by the State because of race, color, religion, or national origin.

**N.C. Const. art. I, § 26:** No person shall be excluded from jury service on account of sex, race, color, religion, or national origin.

**N.C. Const. art. V, § 8:** Notwithstanding any other provisions of this Constitution, the General Assembly may enact general laws to authorize the State, counties, cities or towns, and other State and local governmental entities to issue revenue bonds to finance or refinance for any such governmental entity or any nonprofit private corporation, regardless of any church or religious relationship, the cost of acquiring, constructing, and financing health care facility projects to be operated to serve and benefit the public.... The power of eminent domain shall not be used pursuant hereto for nonprofit private corporations.

**N.C. Const. art. V, § 12:** Notwithstanding any other provisions of this Constitution, the General Assembly may enact general laws to authorize the State or any State entity to issue revenue bonds to finance and refinance the cost of acquiring, constructing, and financing higher education facilities to be operated to serve and benefit the public for any nonprofit private corporation, regardless of any church or religious relationship.... The power of eminent domain shall not be used pursuant hereto.

**N.C. Const. art. VI, § 8:** The following persons shall be disqualified for office: First, any person who shall deny the being of Almighty God....

**N.C. Const. art. IX, § 1:** Religion, morality, and knowledge being necessary to good government and the happiness of mankind, schools, libraries, and the means of education shall forever be encouraged.

**N.C. Const. art. XI, § 4:** Beneficent provision for the poor, the unfortunate, and the orphan is one of the first duties of a civilized and a Christian state. Therefore the General Assembly shall provide for and define the duties of a board of public welfare.

## North Dakota

**N.D. Const. preamble:** We, the people of North Dakota, grateful to Almighty God for the blessings of civil and religious liberty, do ordain and establish this constitution.

**N.D. Const. art. I, § 3:** The free exercise and enjoyment of religious profession and worship, without discrimination or preference shall be forever guaranteed in this state, and no person shall be rendered incompetent to be a witness or juror on account of his opinion on matters of religious belief; but the liberty of conscience hereby secured shall not be so construed as to excuse acts of licentiousness, or justify practices inconsistent with the peace or safety of this state.

**N.D. Const. art. VIII, § 1:** A high degree of intelligence, patriotism, integrity and morality on the part of every voter in a government by the people being necessary in order to insure the continuance of that government and the prosperity and happiness of the people, the legislative assembly shall make provision for the establishment and maintenance of a system of public schools which shall be open to all children of the state of North Dakota and free from sectarian control. This legislative requirement shall be irrevocable without the consent of the United States and the people of North Dakota.

**N.D. Const. art. VIII, § 5:** All colleges, universities, and other educational institutions, for the support of which lands have been granted to this state, or which are supported by a public tax, shall remain under the absolute and exclusive control of the state. No money raised for the support of the public schools of the state shall be appropriated to or used for the support of any sectarian school.

**N.D. Const. art. XI, § 16:** The reserve militia of this state consists of all able-bodied individuals eighteen years of age and older residing in the state, unless exempted by the laws of the United States or of this state. The active militia is the national guard of this state and consists of individuals who volunteer and are accepted unless exempted by the laws of the United States or of this state. An individual whose religious tenets or conscientious scruples forbid that individual to bear arms may not be compelled to do so in times of peace, but that individual shall pay an equivalent for a personal service.

**N.D. Const. art. XIII, § 1:** Perfect toleration of religious sentiment must be secured, and no inhabitant of this state may ever be molested in person or property on account of that person's mode of religious worship.

## Ohio

**Ohio Const. preamble:** We, the people of the State of Ohio, grateful to Almighty God for our freedom, to secure its blessings and promote our common welfare, do establish this Constitution.

**Ohio Const. art. I, § 7:** All men have a natural and indefeasible right to worship Almighty God according to the dictates of their own conscience. No person shall be compelled to attend, erect, or support any place of worship, or maintain any form of worship, against his consent; and no preference shall be given, by law, to any religious society; nor shall any interference with the rights of conscience be permitted. No religious test shall be required, as a qualification for office, nor shall any person be incompetent to be a witness on account of his religious belief; but nothing herein shall be construed to dispense with oaths and affirmations. Religion, morality, and knowledge, however, being essential to good government, it shall be the duty of the General Assembly to pass suitable laws, to protect every religious denomination in the peaceable enjoyment of its own mode of public worship, and to encourage schools and the means of instruction.

**Ohio Const. art. VI, § 1:** The principal of all funds, arising from the sale, or other disposition of lands, or other property, granted or entrusted to this State for educational and religious purposes, shall be used or disposed of in such manner as the General Assembly shall prescribe by law.

**Ohio Const. art. VI, § 2:** The general assembly shall make such provisions, by taxation, or otherwise, as, with the income arising from the school trust fund, will secure a thorough and efficient system of common schools throughout the State; but, no religious or other sect, or sects, shall ever have any exclusive right to, or control of, any part of the school funds of this state.

### Oklahoma

**Okla. Const. preamble:** Invoking the guidance of Almighty God, in order to secure and perpetuate the blessing of liberty; to secure just and rightful government; to promote our mutual welfare and happiness, we, the people of the State of Oklahoma, do ordain and establish this Constitution.

**Okla. Const. art. I, § 2:** Perfect toleration of religious sentiment shall be secured, and no inhabitant of the State shall ever be molested in person or property on account of his or her mode of religious worship; and no religious test shall be required for the exercise of civil or political rights. Polygamous or plural marriages are forever prohibited.

**Okla. Const. art. II, § 5:** No public money or property shall ever be appropriated, applied, donated, or used, directly or indirectly, for the use, benefit, or support of any sect, church, denomination, or system of religion, or for the use, benefit, or support of any priest, preacher, minister, or other religious teacher or dignitary, or sectarian institution as such.

### Oregon

**Or. Const. art. I, § 2:** All men shall be secure in the Natural right, to worship Almighty God according to the dictates of their own consciences.

**Or. Const. art. I, § 3:** No law shall in any case whatever control the free exercise, and enjoyment of religeous [*sic*] opinions, or interfere with the rights of conscience.

**Or. Const. art. I, § 4:** No religious test shall be required as a qualification for any office of trust or profit.

**Or. Const. art. I, § 5:** No money shall be drawn from the Treasury for the benefit of any religeous [*sic*], or theological institution, nor shall any money be appropriated for the payment of any religeous [*sic*] services in either house of the Legislative Assembly.

**Or. Const. art. I, § 6:** No person shall be rendered incompetent as a witness, or juror in consequence of his opinions on matters of religeon [*sic*]; nor be questioned in any Court of Justice touching his religeous [*sic*] belief to affect the weight of his testimony.

### Pennsylvania

**Pa. Const. preamble:** WE, the people of the Commonwealth of Pennsylvania, grateful to Almighty God for the blessings of civil and religious liberty, and humbly invoking His guidance, do ordain and establish this Constitution.

**Pa. Const. art. I, § 3:** All men have a natural and indefeasible right to worship Almighty God according to the dictates of their own consciences; no man can of right be compelled to attend, erect or support any place of worship, or to maintain any ministry against his consent; no human authority can, in any case whatever, control or interfere with the rights of conscience, and no preference shall ever be given by law to any religious establishments or modes of worship.

**Pa. Const. art. I, § 4:** No person who acknowledges the being of a God and a future state of rewards and punishments shall, on account of his religious sentiments, be disqualified to hold any office or place of trust or profit under this Commonwealth.

## Rhode Island

**R.I. Const. preamble:** We, the people of the State of Rhode Island and Providence Plantations, grateful to Almighty God for the civil and religious liberty which He hath so long permitted us to enjoy, and looking to Him for a blessing upon our endeavors to secure and to transmit the same, unimpaired, to succeeding generations, do ordain and establish this Constitution of government.

**R.I. Const. art. I, § 3:** Whereas Almighty God hath created the mind free; and all attempts to influence it by temporal punishments or burdens, or by civil incapacitations, tend to beget habits of hypocrisy and meanness; and whereas a principal object of our venerable ancestors, in their migration to this country and their settlement of this state, was, as they expressed it, to hold forth a lively experiment that a flourishing civil state may stand and be best maintained with full liberty in religious concernments; we, therefore, declare that no person shall be compelled to frequent or to support any religious worship, place, or ministry whatever, except in fulfillment of such person's voluntary contract; nor enforced, restrained, molested, or burdened in body or goods; nor disqualified from holding any office; nor otherwise suffer on account of such person's religious belief; and that every person shall be free to worship God according to the dictates of such person's conscience, and to profess and by argument to maintain such person's opinion in matters of religion; and that the same shall in no wise diminish, enlarge, or affect the civil capacity of any person.

## South Carolina

**S.C. Const. preamble:** We, the people of the State of South Carolina, in Convention assembled, grateful to God for our liberties, do ordain and establish this Constitution for the preservation and perpetuation of the same.

**S.C. Const. art. I, § 2:** The General Assembly shall make no law respecting an establishment of religion or prohibiting the free exercise thereof, or abridging the freedom of speech or of the press; or the right of the people peaceably to assemble and to petition the government or any department thereof for a redress of grievances.

**S.C. Const. art. VI, § 2:** No person shall be eligible to the office of Governor who denies the existence of the Supreme Being. . . .

**S.C. Const. art. VIII, § 1:** The militia of this State shall consist of all able-bodied male citizens of the State between the ages of eighteen and forty-five years, except such persons as are now or may be exempted by the laws of the United States or this State, or who from religious scruples may be adverse to bearing arms, and shall be organized, officered, armed, equipped and disciplined as the General Assembly may by law direct.

**S.C. Const. art. XI, § 4:** No money shall be paid from public funds nor shall the credit of the State or any of its political subdivisions be used for the direct benefit of any religious or other private educational institution.

**S.C. Const. art. XVII, § 4:** No person who denies the existence of the Supreme Being shall hold any office under this Constitution.

### South Dakota

**S.D. Const. preamble:** We, the people of South Dakota, grateful to Almighty God for our civil and religious liberties, in order to form a more perfect and independent government, establish justice, insure tranquillity [*sic*], provide for the common defense, promote the general welfare and preserve to ourselves and to our posterity the blessings of liberty, do ordain and establish this Constitution for the state of South Dakota.

**S.D. Const. art. VI, § 3:** The right to worship God according to the dictates of conscience shall never be infringed. No person shall be denied any civil or political right, privilege or position on account of his religious opinions; but the liberty of conscience hereby secured shall not be so construed as to excuse licentiousness, the invasion of the rights of others, or justify practices inconsistent with the peace or safety of the state.

No person shall be compelled to attend or support any ministry or place of worship against his consent nor shall any preference be given by law to any religious establishment or mode of worship. No money or property of the state shall be given or appropriated for the benefit of any sectarian or religious society or institution.

**S.D. Const. art. XXI, § 1:** The design of the great seal of South Dakota shall be as follows: … Properly divided between the upper and lower edges of the circle shall appear the legend, "Under God the People Rule" which shall be the motto of the state of South Dakota. …

### Tennessee

**Tenn. Const. art. I, § 3:** That all men have a natural and indefeasible right to worship Almighty God according to the dictates of their own conscience; that no man can of right be compelled to attend, erect, or support any place of worship, or to maintain any minister against his consent; that no human authority can, in any case whatever, control or interfere with the rights of conscience; and that no preference shall ever be given, by law, to any religious establishment or mode of worship.

**Tenn. Const. art. I, § 4:** That no political or religious test, other than an oath to support the Constitution of the United States and of this State, shall ever be required as a qualification to any office or public trust under this State.

**Tenn. Const. art. 9, § 1:** Whereas Ministers of the Gospel are by their profession, dedicated to God and the care of souls, and ought not to be diverted from the great duties of their functions; therefore, no Minister of the Gospel, or priest of any denomination whatever, shall be eligible to a seat in either House of the Legislature.

**Tenn. Const. art. 9, § 2:** No person who denies the being of God, or a future state of rewards and punishments, shall hold any office in the civil department of this State.

## Texas

**Tex. Const. preamble:** Humbly invoking the blessings of Almighty God, the people of the State of Texas, do ordain and establish this Constitution.

**Tex. Const. art. I, § 4:** No religious test shall ever be required as a qualification to any office, or public trust, in this State; nor shall any one be excluded from holding office on account of his religious sentiments, provided he acknowledge the existence of a Supreme Being.

**Tex. Const. art. I, § 5:** No person shall be disqualified to give evidence in any of the Courts of this State on account of his religious opinions, or for the want of any religious belief, but all oaths or affirmations shall be administered in the mode most binding upon the conscience, and shall be taken subject to the pains and penalties of perjury.

**Tex. Const. art. I, § 6:** All men have a natural and indefeasible right to worship Almighty God according to the dictates of their own consciences. No man shall be compelled to attend, erect or support any place of worship, or to maintain any ministry against his consent. No human authority ought, in any case whatever, to control or interfere with the rights of conscience in matters of religion, and no preference shall ever be given by law to any religious society or mode of worship. But it shall be the duty of the Legislature to pass such laws as may be necessary to protect equally every religious denomination in the peaceable enjoyment of its own mode of public worship.

**Tex. Const. art. I, § 7:** No money shall be appropriated, or drawn from the Treasury for the benefit of any sect, or religious society, theological or religious seminary; nor shall property belonging to the State be appropriated for any such purposes.

## Utah

**Utah Const. preamble:** Grateful to Almighty God for life and liberty, we, the people of Utah, in order to secure and perpetuate the principles of free government, do ordain and establish this CONSTITUTION.

**Utah Const. art. I, § 4:** The rights of conscience shall never be infringed. The State shall make no law respecting an establishment of religion or prohibiting the free exercise thereof; no religious test shall be required as a qualification for any office of public trust or for any vote at any election; nor shall any person be incompetent as a witness or juror on account of religious belief or the absence thereof. There shall be no union of Church and State, nor shall any church dominate the State or interfere with its functions. No public money or property shall be appropriated for or applied to any religious worship, exercise or instruction, or for the support of any ecclesiastical establishment.

## Vermont

**Vt. Const. ch. I, art. 3:** That all persons have a natural and unalienable right, to worship Almighty God, according to the dictates of their own consciences and understandings, as in their opinion shall be regulated by the word of God; and that no person ought to, or of right can be compelled to attend any religious worship, or erect or support any place of worship, or maintain any minister, contrary to the dictates of conscience, nor can any person be justly deprived or abridged of any civil right as a citizen, on account of religious sentiments, or peculia[r] mode of religious worship; and that no authority can, or ought to be vested in, or assumed by, any power whatever, that shall in any case interfere with, or in any manner control the rights of conscience, in the free exercise of religious worship. Nevertheless, every sect or denomination of christians ought to observe the sabbath or Lord's day, and keep up some sort of religious worship, which to them shall seem most agreeable to the revealed will of God.

## Virginia

**Va. Const. art. I, § 11:** That no person shall be deprived of his life, liberty, or property without due process of law; that the General Assembly shall not pass any law impairing the obligation of contracts, nor any law whereby private property shall be taken or damaged for public uses, without just compensation, the term "public uses" to be defined by the General Assembly; and that the right to be free from any governmental discrimination upon the basis of religious conviction, race, color, sex, or national origin shall not be abridged, except that the mere separation of the sexes shall not be considered discrimination....

**Va. Const. art. I, § 16:** That religion or the duty which we owe to our Creator, and the manner of discharging it, can be directed only by reason and conviction, not by force or violence; and, therefore, all men are equally entitled to the free exercise of religion, according to the dictates of conscience; and that it is the mutual duty of all to practice Christian forbearance, love, and charity towards each other. No man shall be compelled to frequent or support any religious worship, place, or ministry whatsoever, nor shall be enforced, restrained, molested, or burthened [*sic*] in his body or goods, nor shall otherwise suffer on account of his religious opinions or belief; but all men shall be free to profess and by argument to maintain their opinions in matters of religion, and the same shall in nowise diminish, enlarge, or affect their civil capacities. And the General Assembly shall not prescribe any religious test whatever, or confer any peculiar privileges or advantages on any sect or denomination, or pass any law requiring or authorizing any religious society, or the people of any district within this Commonwealth, to levy on themselves or others, any tax for the erection or repair of any house of public worship, or for the support of any church or ministry; but it shall be left free to every person to select his religious instructor, and to make for his support such private contract as he shall please.

**Va. Const. art. IV, § 16:** The General Assembly shall not make any appropriation of public funds, personal property, or real estate to any church or sectarian society, or any association or institution of any kind whatever which is entirely or partly, directly or indirectly, controlled by any church or sectarian society. Nor shall the General Assembly make any like appropriation to any charitable institution which is not owned or controlled by the Commonwealth; the General Assembly may, however, make appropriations to nonsectarian institutions for the reform of youthful criminals and may also authorize counties, cities, or towns to make such appropriations to any charitable institution or association.

**Va. Const. art. VIII, § 11:** The General Assembly may provide for loans to, and grants to or on behalf of, students attending nonprofit institutions of higher education in the Commonwealth whose primary purpose is to provide collegiate or graduate education and not to provide religious training or theological education. The General Assembly may also provide for a State agency or authority to assist in borrowing money for construction of educational facilities at such institutions, provided that the Commonwealth shall not be liable for any debt created by such borrowing. The General Assembly may also provide for the Commonwealth or any political subdivision thereof to contract with such institutions for the provision of educational or other related services.

**Va. Const. art. X, § 6:** (a) Except as otherwise provided in this Constitution, the following property and no other shall be exempt from taxation, State and local, including inheritance taxes:

...

(2) Real estate and personal property owned and exclusively occupied or used by churches or religious bodies for religious worship or for the residences of their ministers....

## Washington

**Wash. Const. preamble:** We, the people of the State of Washington, grateful to the Supreme Ruler of the Universe for our liberties, do ordain this constitution.

**Wash. Const. art. I, § 11:** Absolute freedom of conscience in all matters of religious sentiment, belief and worship, shall be guaranteed to every individual, and no one shall be molested or disturbed in person or property on account of religion; but the liberty of conscience hereby secured shall not be so construed as to excuse acts of licentiousness or justify practices inconsistent with the peace and safety of the state. No public money or property shall be appropriated for or applied to any religious worship, exercise or instruction, or the support of any religious establishment: PROVIDED, HOWEVER, That this article shall not be so construed as to forbid the employment by the state of a chaplain for such of the state custodial, correctional, and mental institutions, or by a county's or public hospital district's hospital, health care facility, or hospice, as in the discretion of the legislature may seem justified. No religious qualification shall be required for any public office or employment, nor shall any person be incompetent as a witness or juror, in consequence of his opinion on matters of religion, nor be questioned in any court of justice touching his religious belief to affect the weight of his testimony.

**Wash. Const. art. IX, § 4:** All schools maintained or supported wholly or in part by the public funds shall be forever free from sectarian control or influence.

**Wash. Const. art. XXVI:** The following ordinance shall be irrevocable without the consent of the United States and the people of this state:

First. That perfect toleration of religious sentiment shall be secured and that no inhabitant of this state shall ever be molested in person or property on account of his or her mode of religious worship....

## West Virginia

**W. Va. Const. preamble:** Since through Divine Providence we enjoy the blessings of civil, political and religious liberty, we, the people of West Virginia, in and through the provisions of this Constitution, reaffirm our faith in and constant reliance upon God and seek diligently to promote, preserve and perpetuate good government in the state of West Virginia for the common welfare, freedom and security of ourselves and our posterity.

**W. Va. Const. art. III, § 11:** Political tests, requiring persons, as a prerequisite to the enjoyment of their civil and political rights, to purge themselves by their own oaths, of past alleged offences, are repugnant to the principles of free government, and are cruel and oppressive. No religious or political test oath shall be required as a prerequisite or qualification to vote, serve as a juror, sue, plead, appeal, or pursue any profession or employment. Nor shall any person be deprived by law, of any right, or privilege, because of any act done prior to the passage of such law.

**W. Va. Const. art. III, § 15:** No man shall be compelled to frequent or support any religious worship, place or ministry whatsoever; nor shall any man be enforced, restrained, molested or burthened [*sic*], in his body or goods, or otherwise suffer, on account of his religious opinions or belief, but all men shall be free to profess and by argument, to maintain their opinions in matters of religion; and the same shall, in nowise, affect, diminish or enlarge their civil capacities; and the Legislature shall not prescribe any religious test whatever, or confer any peculiar privileges or advantages on any sect or denomination, or pass any law requiring or authorizing any religious society, or the people of any district within this state, to levy on themselves, or others, any tax for the erection or repair of any house for public worship, or for the support of any church or ministry, but it shall be left free for every person to select his religious instructor, and to make for his support, such private contracts as he shall please.

**W. Va. Const. art. VI, § 47:** No charter of incorporation shall be granted to any church or religious denomination. Provisions may be made by general laws for securing the title to church property, and for the sale and transfer thereof, so that it shall be held, used, or transferred for the purposes of such church, or religious denomination.

## Wisconsin

**Wis. Const. preamble:** We, the people of Wisconsin, grateful to Almighty God for our freedom, in order to secure its blessings, form a more perfect government, insure domestic tranquility and promote the general welfare, do establish this constitution.

**Wis. Const. art. I, § 18:** The right of every person to worship Almighty God according to the dictates of conscience shall never be infringed; nor shall any person be compelled to attend, erect or support any place of worship, or to maintain any ministry, without consent; nor shall any control of, or interference with, the rights of conscience be permitted, or any preference be given by law to any religious establishments or modes of worship; nor shall any money be drawn from the treasury for the benefit of religious societies, or religious or theological seminaries.

**Wis. Const. art. I, § 19:** No religious tests shall ever be required as a qualification for any office of public trust under the state, and no person shall be rendered incompetent to give evidence in any court of law or equity in consequence of his opinions on the subject of religion.

**Wis. Const. art. I, § 23:** Nothing in this constitution shall prohibit the legislature from providing for the safety and welfare of children by providing for the transportation of children to and from any parochial or private school or institution of learning.

**Wis. Const. art. I, § 24:** Nothing in this constitution, shall prohibit the legislature from authorizing, by law, the use of public school buildings by civic, religious or charitable organizations during nonschool hours upon payment by the organization to the school district of reasonable compensation for such use.

**Wis. Const. art. X, § 3:** The legislature shall provide by law for the establishment of district schools, which shall be as nearly uniform as practicable; and such schools shall be free and without charge for tuition to all children between the ages of 4 and 20 years; and no sectarian instruction shall be allowed therein; but the legislature by law may, for the purpose of religious instruction outside the district schools, authorize the release of students during regular school hours.

## Wyoming

**Wyo. Const. preamble:** We, the people of the State of Wyoming, grateful to God for our civil, political and religious liberties, and desiring to secure them to ourselves and perpetuate them to our posterity, do ordain and establish this Constitution.

**Wyo. Const. art. I, § 18:** The free exercise and enjoyment of religious profession and worship without discrimination or preference shall be forever guaranteed in this state, and no person shall be rendered incompetent to hold any office of trust or profit, or to serve as a witness or juror, because of his opinion on any matter of religious belief whatever; but the liberty of conscience hereby secured shall not be so construed as to excuse acts of licentiousness or justify practices inconsistent with the peace or safety of the state.

**Wyo. Const. art. I, § 19:** No money of the state shall ever be given or appropriated to any sectarian or religious society or institution.

**Wyo. Const. art. VII, § 8:** Provision shall be made by general law for the equitable allocation of such income among all school districts in the state. But no appropriation shall be made from said fund to any district for the year in which a school has not been maintained for at least three (3) months; nor shall any portion of any public school fund ever be used to support or assist any private school, or any school, academy, seminary, college or other institution of learning controlled by any church or sectarian organization or religious denomination whatsoever.

**Wyo. Const. art. VII, § 12:** No sectarian instruction, qualifications or tests shall be imparted, exacted, applied or in any manner tolerated in the schools of any grade or character controlled by the state, nor shall attendance be required at any religious service therein, nor shall any sectarian tenets or doctrines be taught or favored in any public school or institution that may be established under this constitution.

**Wyo. Const. art. X, § 12:** Railroad and telegraph lines heretofore constructed or that may hereafter be constructed in this state are hereby declared public highways and common carriers, and as such must be made by law to extend the same equality and impartiality to all who use them, excepting employees and their families and ministers of the gospel, whether individuals or corporations.

**Wyo. Const. art. XXI, § 25:** Perfect toleration of religious sentiment shall be secured, and no inhabitant of this state shall ever be molested in person or property on account of his or her mode of religious worship.

**Wyo. Const. art. XXI, § 28:** The legislature shall make laws for the establishment and maintenance of systems of public schools which shall be open to all the children of the state and free from sectarian control.

# Appendix C: Selected Federal Statutes

### *10 U.S.C. § 774. Religious apparel: wearing while in uniform*

(a) **General Rule.** – Except as provided under subsection (b), a member of the armed forces may wear an item of religious apparel while wearing the uniform of the member's armed force.
(b) **Exceptions.** – The Secretary concerned may prohibit the wearing of an item of religious apparel –
  (1) in circumstances with respect to which the Secretary determines that the wearing of the item would interfere with the performance of the member's military duties; or
  (2) if the Secretary determines, under regulations under subsection (c), that the item of apparel is not neat and conservative.
(c) **Regulations.** – The Secretary concerned shall prescribe regulations concerning the wearing of religious apparel by members of the armed forces under the Secretary's jurisdiction while the members are wearing the uniform. Such regulations shall be consistent with subsections (a) and (b).
(d) **Religious Apparel Defined.** – In this section, the term "religious apparel" means apparel the wearing of which is part of the observance of the religious faith practiced by the member.

### *11 U.S.C. § 548 [Religious Liberty and Charitable Donation Protection Act of 1998, Pub. L. No. 105–183, 112 Stat. 517 (June 19, 1998) (codified at 11 U.S.C. §§ 544, 546, 548, 707, 1325)]*

**Section 548. Fraudulent transfers and obligations:**

(a)(1) The trustee may avoid any transfer of an interest of the debtor in property, or any obligation incurred by the debtor, that was made or incurred on or within one year before the date of the filing of the petition, if the debtor voluntarily or involuntarily–
  (A) made such transfer or incurred such obligation with actual intent to hinder, delay, or defraud any entity to which the debtor was or became, on or after the date that such transfer was made or such obligation was incurred, indebted; or
  (B) (i) received less than a reasonably equivalent value in exchange for such transfer or obligation; and

(ii) (I) was insolvent on the date that such transfer was made or such obligation was incurred, or became insolvent as a result of such transfer or obligation;

(II) was engaged in business or a transaction, or was about to engage in business or a transaction, for which any property remaining with the debtor was an unreasonably small capital; or

(III) intended to incur, or believed that the debtor would incur, debts that would be beyond the debtor's ability to pay as such debts matured.

(2) A transfer of a charitable contribution to a qualified religious or charitable entity or organization shall not be considered to be a transfer covered under paragraph (1)(B) in any case in which.–

(A) the amount of that contribution does not exceed 15 percent of the gross annual income of the debtor for the year in which the transfer of the contribution is made; or

(B) the contribution made by a debtor exceeded the percentage amount of gross annual income specified in subparagraph (A), if the transfer was consistent with the practices of the debtor in making charitable contributions.

(b) The trustee of a partnership debtor may avoid any transfer of an interest of the debtor in property, or any obligation incurred by the debtor, that was made or incurred on or within one year before the date of the filing of the petition, to a general partner in the debtor, if the debtor was insolvent on the date such transfer was made or such obligation was incurred, or became insolvent as a result of such transfer or obligation.

(c) Except to the extent that a transfer or obligation voidable under this section is voidable under section 544, 545, or 547 of this title, a transferee or obligee of such a transfer or obligation that takes for value and in good faith has a lien on or may retain any interest transferred or may enforce any obligation incurred, as the case may be, to the extent that such transferee or obligee gave value to the debtor in exchange for such transfer or obligation.

(d) (1) For the purposes of this section, a transfer is made when such transfer is so perfected that a bona fide purchaser from the debtor against whom applicable law permits such transfer to be perfected cannot acquire an interest in the property transferred that is superior to the interest in such property of the transferee, but if such transfer is not so perfected before the commencement of the case, such transfer is made immediately before the date of the filing of the petition.

(2) In this section –

(A) "value" means property, or satisfaction or securing of a present or antecedent debt of the debtor, but does not include an unperformed promise to furnish support to the debtor or to a relative of the debtor;

(B) a commodity broker, forward contract merchant, stockbroker, financial institution, or securities clearing agency that receives a margin payment, as defined in section 101, 741, or 761 of this title, or settlement payment, as defined in section 101 or 741 of this title, takes for value to the extent of such payment;

(C) a repo participant that receives a margin payment, as defined in section 741 or 761 of this title, or settlement payment, as defined in section 741 of this title, in connection with a repurchase agreement, takes for value to the extent of such payment; and

(D) a swap participant that receives a transfer in connection with a swap agreement takes for value to the extent of such transfer.

(3) In this section, the term "charitable contribution" means a charitable contribution, as that term is defined in section 170(c) of the Internal Revenue Code of 1986, if that contribution–

(A) is made by a natural person; and

(B) consists of.–

(i) a financial instrument (as that term is defined in section 731(c)(2)(C) of the Internal Revenue Code of 1986); or

(ii) cash.

(4) In this section, the term "qualified religious or charitable entity or organization" means–

(A) an entity described in section 170(c)(1) of the Internal Revenue Code of 1986; or

(B) an entity or organization described in section 170(c)(2) of the Internal Revenue Code of 1986.

### *18 U.S.C. § 247. Damage to religious property; obstruction of persons in the free exercise of religious beliefs*

(a) Whoever, in any of the circumstances referred to in subsection (b) of this section –

(1) intentionally defaces, damages, or destroys any religious real property, because of the religious character of that property, or attempts to do so; or

(2) intentionally obstructs, by force or threat of force, any person in the enjoyment of that person's free exercise of religious beliefs, or attempts to do so;

shall be punished as provided in subsection (d).

(b) The circumstances referred to in subsection (a) are that the offense is in or affects interstate or foreign commerce.

(c) Whoever intentionally defaces, damages, or destroys any religious real property because of the race, color, or ethnic characteristics of any individual associated with that religious property, or attempts to do so, shall be punished as provided in subsection (d).

(d) The punishment for a violation of subsection (a) of this section shall be –

(1) if death results from acts committed in violation of this section or if such acts include kidnapping or an attempt to kidnap, aggravated sexual abuse or an attempt to commit aggravated sexual abuse, or an attempt to kill, a fine in accordance with this title and imprisonment for any term of years or for life, or both, or may be sentenced to death;

(2) if bodily injury results to any person, including any public safety officer performing duties as a direct or proximate result of conduct prohibited by this section, and the violation is by means of fire or an explosive, a fine under this title or imprisonment for not more that 40 years, or both;

(3) if bodily injury to any person, including any public safety officer performing duties as a direct or proximate result of conduct prohibited by this section, results from the acts committed in violation of this section or if such acts

include the use, attempted use, or threatened use of a dangerous weapon, explosives, or fire, a fine in accordance with this title and imprisonment for not more than 20 years, or both; and

(4) in any other case, a fine in accordance with this title and imprisonment for not more than one year, or both.

(e) No prosecution of any offense described in this section shall be undertaken by the United States except upon the certification in writing of the Attorney General or his designee that in his judgment a prosecution by the United States is in the public interest and necessary to secure substantial justice.

(f) As used in this section, the term "religious real property" means any church, synagogue, mosque, religious cemetery, or other religious real property, including fixtures or religious objects contained within a place of religious worship.

(g) No person shall be prosecuted, tried, or punished for any noncapital offense under this section unless the indictment is found or the information is instituted not later than 7 years after the date on which the offense was committed.

*18 U.S.C. § 249 [Matthew Shepard and James Boyd, Jr. Hate Crimes Protection Act, Pub. L. No. 111–84, Div. E, § 4707, 123 Stat. 2835, 2838–41 (Oct. 28, 2009)]*

(a) In General. –

(1) Offenses involving actual or perceived race, color, religion, or national origin. – Whoever, whether or not acting under color of law, willfully causes bodily injury to any person or, through the use of fire, a firearm, a dangerous weapon, or an explosive or incendiary device, attempts to cause bodily injury to any person, because of the actual or perceived race, color, religion, or national origin of any person –

(A) shall be imprisoned not more than 10 years, fined in accordance with this title, or both; and

(B) shall be imprisoned for any term of years or for life, fined in accordance with this title, or both, if –

(i) death results from the offense; or

(ii) the offense includes kidnapping or an attempt to kidnap, aggravated sexual abuse or an attempt to commit aggravated sexual abuse, or an attempt to kill.

(2) Offenses involving actual or perceived religion, national origin, gender, sexual orientation, gender identity, or disability. –

(A) In general. – Whoever, whether or not acting under color of law, in any circumstance described in subparagraph (B) or paragraph (3), willfully causes bodily injury to any person or, through the use of fire, a firearm, a dangerous weapon, or an explosive or incendiary device, attempts to cause bodily injury to any person, because of the actual or perceived religion, national origin, gender, sexual orientation, gender identity, or disability of any person –

(i) shall be imprisoned not more than 10 years, fined in accordance with this title, or both; and

(ii) shall be imprisoned for any term of years or for life, fined in accordance with this title, or both, if –

(I) death results from the offense; or
(II) the offense includes kidnapping or an attempt to kidnap, aggravated sexual abuse or an attempt to commit aggravated sexual abuse, or an attempt to kill.

(B) Circumstances described. – For purposes of subparagraph (A), the circumstances described in this subparagraph are that –
(i) the conduct described in subparagraph (A) occurs during the course of, or as the result of, the travel of the defendant or the victim –
(I) across a State line or national border; or
(II) using a channel, facility, or instrumentality of interstate or foreign commerce;
(ii) the defendant uses a channel, facility, or instrumentality of interstate or foreign commerce in connection with the conduct described in subparagraph (A);
(iii) in connection with the conduct described in subparagraph (A), the defendant employs a firearm, dangerous weapon, explosive or incendiary device, or other weapon that has traveled in interstate or foreign commerce; or
(iv) the conduct described in subparagraph (A) –
(I) interferes with commercial or other economic activity in which the victim is engaged at the time of the conduct; or
(II) otherwise affects interstate or foreign commerce.

(3) Offenses occurring in the special maritime or territorial jurisdiction of the united states. – Whoever, within the special maritime or territorial jurisdiction of the United States, engages in conduct described in paragraph (1) or in paragraph (2)(A) (without regard to whether that conduct occurred in a circumstance described in paragraph (2)(B)) shall be subject to the same penalties as prescribed in those paragraphs.

(4) Guidelines. – All prosecutions conducted by the United States under this section shall be undertaken pursuant to guidelines issued by the Attorney General, or the designee of the Attorney General, to be included in the United States Attorneys' Manual that shall establish neutral and objective criteria for determining whether a crime was committed because of the actual or perceived status of any person.

(b) Certification Requirement. –
(1) In general. – No prosecution of any offense described in this subsection may be undertaken by the United States, except under the certification in writing of the Attorney General, or a designee, that –
(A) the State does not have jurisdiction;
(B) the State has requested that the Federal Government assume jurisdiction;
(C) the verdict or sentence obtained pursuant to State charges left demonstratively unvindicated the Federal interest in eradicating bias-motivated violence; or
(D) a prosecution by the United States is in the public interest and necessary to secure substantial justice.

(2) Rule of construction. – Nothing in this subsection shall be construed to limit the authority of Federal officers, or a Federal grand jury, to investigate possible violations of this section.

*20 U.S.C. §§ 4071–4074 [**Equal Access Act, Pub. L. No.** 98–377, §§ 802–805, 98 **Stat.** 1302 (**Aug.** 11, 1984)].*

**Section 4071. Denial of equal access prohibited:**

(a) Restriction of limited open forum on basis of religious, political, philosophical, or other speech content prohibited

It shall be unlawful for any public secondary school which receives Federal financial assistance and which has a limited open forum to deny equal access or a fair opportunity to, or discriminate against, any students who wish to conduct a meeting within that limited open forum on the basis of the religious, political, philosophical, or other content of the speech at such meetings.

(b) "Limited open forum" defined

A public secondary school has a limited open forum whenever such school grants an offering to or opportunity for one or more noncurriculum related student groups to meet on school premises during noninstructional time.

(c) Fair opportunity criteria

Schools shall be deemed to offer a fair opportunity to students who wish to conduct a meeting within its limited open forum if such school uniformly provides that –

(1) the meeting is voluntary and student-initiated;
(2) there is no sponsorship of the meeting by the school, the government, or its agents or employees;
(3) employees or agents of the school or government are present at religious meetings only in a nonparticipatory capacity;
(4) the meeting does not materially and substantially interfere with the orderly conduct of educational activities within the school; and
(5) nonschool persons may not direct, conduct, control, or regularly attend activities of student groups.

(d) Construction of subchapter with respect to certain rights

Nothing in this subchapter shall be construed to authorize the United States or any State or political subdivision thereof –

(1) to influence the form or content of any prayer or other religious activity;
(2) to require any person to participate in prayer or other religious activity;
(3) to expend public funds beyond the incidental cost of providing the space for student-initiated meetings;
(4) to compel any school agent or employee to attend a school meeting if the content of the speech at the meeting is contrary to the beliefs of the agent or employee;
(5) to sanction meetings that are otherwise unlawful;

(6) to limit the rights of groups of students which are not of a specified numerical size; or
(7) to abridge the constitutional rights of any person.

(e) Federal financial assistance to schools unaffected

Notwithstanding the availability of any other remedy under the Constitution or the laws of the United States, nothing in this subchapter shall be construed to authorize the United States to deny or withhold Federal financial assistance to any school.

(f) Authority of schools with respect to order, discipline, well-being, and attendance concerns

Nothing in this subchapter shall be construed to limit the authority of the school, its agents or employees, to maintain order and discipline on school premises, to protect the well-being of students and faculty, and to assure that attendance of students at meetings is voluntary.

**Section 4072. Definitions:**
As used in this subchapter –

(1) The term "secondary school" means a public school which provides secondary education as determined by State law.
(2) The term "sponsorship" includes the act of promoting, leading, or participating in a meeting. The assignment of a teacher, administrator, or other school employee to a meeting for custodial purposes does not constitute sponsorship of the meeting.
(3) The term "meeting" includes those activities of student groups which are permitted under a school's limited open forum and are not directly related to the school curriculum.
(4) The term "noninstructional time" means time set aside by the school before actual classroom instruction begins or after actual classroom instruction ends.

**Section 4073. Severability:**
If any provision of this subchapter or the application thereof to any person or circumstances is judicially determined to be invalid, the provisions of the remainder of the subchapter and the application to other persons or circumstances shall not be affected thereby.

**Section 4074. Construction:**
The provisions of this subchapter shall supersede all other provisions of Federal law that are inconsistent with the provisions of this subchapter.

### 26 U.S.C. § 170. *Charitable, etc., contributions and gifts*

(a) Allowance of deduction. –
  (1) General rule. – There shall be allowed as a deduction any charitable contribution (as defined in subsection (c)) payment of which is made within the taxable year. A charitable contribution shall be allowable as a deduction only if verified under regulations prescribed by the Secretary.

  . . .

(b) Percentage limitations. –

(1) Individuals. – In the case of an individual, the deduction provided in subsection (a) shall be limited as provided in the succeeding subparagraphs.

(A) General rule. – Any charitable contribution to –

(i) a church or a convention or association of churches,

(ii) an educational organization which normally maintains a regular faculty and curriculum and normally has a regularly enrolled body of pupils or students in attendance at the place where its educational activities are regularly carried on,

(iii) an organization the principal purpose or functions of which are the providing of medical or hospital care or medical education or medical research, if the organization is a hospital, or if the organization is a medical research organization directly engaged in the continuous active conduct of medical research in conjunction with a hospital, and during the calendar year in which the contribution is made such organization is committed to spend such contributions for such research before January 1 of the fifth calendar year which begins after the date such contribution is made,

(iv) an organization which normally receives a substantial part of its support (exclusive of income received in the exercise or performance by such organization of its charitable, educational, or other purpose or function constituting the basis for its exemption under section 501(a)) from the United States or any State or political subdivision thereof or from direct or indirect contributions from the general public, and which is organized and operated exclusively to receive, hold, invest, and administer property and to make expenditures to or for the benefit of a college or university which is an organization referred to in clause (ii) of this subparagraph and which is an agency or instrumentality of a State or political subdivision thereof, or which is owned or operated by a State or political subdivision thereof or by an agency or instrumentality of one or more States or political subdivisions,

(v) a governmental unit referred to in subsection (c)(1),

(vi) an organization referred to in subsection (c)(2) which normally receives a substantial part of its support (exclusive of income received in the exercise or performance by such organization of its charitable, educational, or other purpose or function constituting the basis for its exemption under section 501(a)) from a governmental unit referred to in subsection (c)(1) or from direct or indirect contributions from the general public,

(vii) a private foundation described in subparagraph (F), or

(viii) an organization described in section 509(a)(2) or (3),

shall be allowed to the extent that the aggregate of such contributions does not exceed 50 percent of the taxpayer's contribution base for the taxable year.

. . .

(c) Charitable contribution defined. – For purposes of this section, the term "charitable contribution" means a contribution or gift to or for the use of –

. . .

(2) A corporation, trust, or community chest, fund, or foundation –
   (A) created or organized in the United States or in any possession thereof, or under the law of the United States, any State, the District of Columbia, or any possession of the United States;
   (B) organized and operated exclusively for religious, charitable, scientific, literary, or educational purposes, or to foster national or international amateur sports competition (but only if no part of its activities involve the provision of athletic facilities or equipment), or for the prevention of cruelty to children or animals;
   (C) no part of the net earnings of which inures to the benefit of any private shareholder or individual; and
   (D) which is not disqualified for tax exemption under section 501(c)(3) by reason of attempting to influence legislation, and which does not participate in, or intervene in (including the publishing or distributing of statements), any political campaign on behalf of (or in opposition to) any candidate for public office.

A contribution or gift by a corporation to a trust, chest, fund, or foundation shall be deductible by reason of this paragraph only if it is to be used within the United States or any of its possessions exclusively for purposes specified in subparagraph (B). Rules similar to the rules of section 501(j) shall apply for purposes of this paragraph.

### 26 U.S.C. § 501. *Exemption from tax on corporations, certain trusts, etc.*

(a) Exemption from taxation. – An organization described in subsection (c) or (d) or section 401(a) shall be exempt from taxation under this subtitle unless such exemption is denied under section 502 or 503.

. . .

(c) List of exempt organizations. – The following organizations are referred to in subsection (a):

. . .

   (3) Corporations, and any community chest, fund, or foundation, organized and operated exclusively for religious, charitable, scientific, testing for public safety, literary, or educational purposes, or to foster national or international amateur sports competition (but only if no part of its activities involve the provision of athletic facilities or equipment), or for the prevention of cruelty to children or animals, no part of the net earnings of which inures to the benefit of any private shareholder or individual, no substantial part of the activities of which is carrying on propaganda, or otherwise attempting, to influence legislation (except as otherwise provided in subsection (h)), and which does not participate in, or intervene in (including the publishing or distributing of statements), any political campaign on behalf of (or in opposition to) any candidate for public office.

   . . .

(d) Religious and apostolic organizations. – The following organizations are referred to in subsection (a): Religious or apostolic associations or corporations, if such associations or corporations have a common treasury or community treasury, even if such associations or corporations engage in business for the common benefit of the members, but only if the members thereof include (at the time of filing their returns) in their gross income their entire pro rata shares, whether distributed or not, of the taxable income of the association or corporation for such year. Any amount so included in the gross income of a member shall be treated as a dividend received.

...

(h) Expenditures by public charities to influence legislation. –

(1) General rule. – In the case of an organization to which this subsection applies, exemption from taxation under subsection (a) shall be denied because a substantial part of the activities of such organization consists of carrying on propaganda, or otherwise attempting, to influence legislation, but only if such organization normally –

(A) makes lobbying expenditures in excess of the lobbying ceiling amount for such organization for each taxable year, or

(B) makes grass roots expenditures in excess of the grass roots ceiling amount for such organization for each taxable year.

(2) Definitions. – For purposes of this subsection –

(A) Lobbying expenditures. – The term "lobbying expenditures" means expenditures for the purpose of influencing legislation (as defined in section 4911(d)).

(B) Lobbying ceiling amount. – The lobbying ceiling amount for any organization for any taxable year is 150 percent of the lobbying nontaxable amount for such organization for such taxable year, determined under section 4911.

(C) Grass roots expenditures. – The term "grass roots expenditures" means expenditures for the purpose of influencing legislation (as defined in section 4911(d) without regard to paragraph (1)(B) thereof).

(D) Grass roots ceiling amount. – The grass roots ceiling amount for any organization for any taxable year is 150 percent of the grass roots nontaxable amount for such organization for such taxable year, determined under section 4911.

(3) Organizations to which this subsection applies. – This subsection shall apply to any organization which has elected (in such manner and at such time as the Secretary may prescribe) to have the provisions of this subsection apply to such organization and which, for the taxable year which includes the date the election is made, is described in subsection (c)(3) and –

(A) is described in paragraph (4), and

(B) is not a disqualified organization under paragraph (5).

(4) Organizations permitted to elect to have this subsection apply. – An organization is described in this paragraph if it is described in –

(A) section 170(b)(1)(A)(ii) (relating to educational institutions),

(B) section 170(b)(1)(A)(iii) (relating to hospitals and medical research organizations),

(C) section 170(b)(1)(A)(iv) (relating to organizations supporting government schools),

(D) section 170(b)(1)(A)(vi) (relating to organizations publicly supported by charitable contributions),
(E) section 509(a)(2) (relating to organizations publicly supported by admissions, sales, etc.), or
(F) section 509(a)(3) (relating to organizations supporting certain types of public charities) except that for purposes of this subparagraph, section 509(a)(3) shall be applied without regard to the last sentence of section 509(a).

(5) Disqualified organizations. – For purposes of paragraph (3) an organization is a disqualified organization if it is –
(A) described in section 170(b)(1)(A)(i) (relating to churches),
(B) an integrated auxiliary of a church or of a convention or association of churches, or
(C) a member of an affiliated group of organizations (within the meaning of section 4911(f) (2)) if one or more members of such group is described in subparagraph (A) or (B).

(6) Years for which election is effective. – An election by an organization under this subsection shall be effective for all taxable years of such organization which –
(A) end after the date the election is made, and
(B) begin before the date the election is revoked by such organization (under regulations prescribed by the Secretary).

(7) No effect on certain organizations. – With respect to any organization for a taxable year for which –
(A) such organization is a disqualified organization (within the meaning of paragraph (5)), or
(B) an election under this subsection is not in effect for such organization, nothing in this subsection or in section 4911 shall be construed to affect the interpretation of the phrase, "no substantial part of the activities of which is carrying on propaganda, or otherwise attempting, to influence legislation," under subsection (c)(3).

. . .

(i) Prohibition of discrimination by certain social clubs. – Notwithstanding subsection (a), an organization which is described in subsection (c)(7) shall not be exempt from taxation under subsection (a) for any taxable year if, at any time during such taxable year, the charter, bylaws, or other governing instrument, of such organization or any written policy statement of such organization contains a provision which provides for discrimination against any person on the basis of race, color, or religion. The preceding sentence to the extent it relates to discrimination on the basis of religion shall not apply to –

(1) an auxiliary of a fraternal beneficiary society if such society –
(A) is described in subsection (c)(8) and exempt from tax under subsection (a), and
(B) limits its membership to the members of a particular religion, or

(2) a club which in good faith limits its membership to the members of a particular religion in order to further the teachings or principles of that religion, and not to exclude individuals of a particular race or color.

### *26 U.S.C. § 1402. Definitions*

(g) Members of certain religious faiths. –

(1) Exemption. – Any individual may file an application (in such form and manner, and with such official, as may be prescribed by regulations under this chapter) for an exemption from the tax imposed by this chapter [Tax on Self-Employment Income] if he is a member of a recognized religious sect or division thereof and is an adherent of established tenets or teachings of such sect or division by reason of which he is conscientiously opposed to acceptance of the benefits of any private or public insurance which makes payments in the event of death, disability, old-age, or retirement or makes payments toward the cost of, or provides services for, medical care (including the benefits of any insurance system established by the Social Security Act). Such exemption may be granted only if the application contains or is accompanied by –

(A) such evidence of such individual's membership in, and adherence to the tenets or teachings of, the sect or division thereof as the Secretary may require for purposes of determining such individual's compliance with the preceding sentence, and

(B) his waiver of all benefits and other payments under titles II and XVIII of the Social Security Act on the basis of his wages and self-employment income as well as all such benefits and other payments to him on the basis of the wages and self-employment income of any other person,

and only if the Commissioner of Social Security finds that –

(C) such sect or division thereof has the established tenets or teachings referred to in the preceding sentence,

(D) it is the practice, and has been for a period of time which he deems to be substantial, for members of such sect or division thereof to make provision for their dependent members which in his judgment is reasonable in view of their general level of living, and

(E) such sect or division thereof has been in existence at all times since December 31, 1950.

An exemption may not be granted to any individual if any benefit or other payment referred to in subparagraph (B) became payable (or, but for section 203 or 222(b) of the Social Security Act, would have become payable) at or before the time of the filing of such waiver.

(2) Period for which exemption effective. – An exemption granted to any individual pursuant to this subsection shall apply with respect to all taxable years beginning after December 31, 1950, except that such exemption shall not apply for any taxable year –

(A) beginning (i) before the taxable year in which such individual first met the requirements of the first sentence of paragraph (1), or (ii) before the time as of which the Commissioner of Social Security finds that the sect or division thereof of which such individual is a member met the requirements of subparagraphs (C) and (D), or

(B) ending (i) after the time such individual ceases to meet the requirements of the first sentence of paragraph (1), or (ii) after the time as of which the Commissioner of Social Security finds that the sect or division thereof of which he is a member ceases to meet the requirements of subparagraph (C) or (D).

(3) Subsection to apply to certain church employees. – This subsection shall apply with respect to services which are described in subparagraph (B) of section 3121(b)(8) (and are not described in subparagraph (A) of such section).

### 42 U.S.C. § 1983. *Civil action for deprivation of rights*

Every person who, under color of any statute, ordinance, regulation, custom, or usage, of any State or Territory or the District of Columbia, subjects, or causes to be subjected, any citizen of the United States or other person within the jurisdiction thereof to the deprivation of any rights, privileges, or immunities secured by the Constitution and laws, shall be liable to the party injured in an action at law, suit in equity, or other proper proceeding for redress, except that in any action brought against a judicial officer for an act or omission taken in such officer's judicial capacity, injunctive relief shall not be granted unless a declaratory decree was violated or declaratory relief was unavailable. For the purposes of this section, any Act of Congress applicable exclusively to the District of Columbia shall be considered to be a statute of the District of Columbia.

### 42 U.S.C. § 1996 [*American Indian Religious Freedom Act of 1978, Pub. L. No. 95–341, § 1, 92 Stat. 469 (Aug. 11, 1978)*]

On and after August 11, 1978, it shall be the policy of the United States to protect and preserve for American Indians their inherent right of freedom to believe, express, and exercise the traditional religions of the American Indian, Eskimo, Aleut, and Native Hawaiians, including but not limited to access to sites, use and possession of sacred objects, and the freedom to worship through ceremonials and traditional rites.

### 42 U.S.C. § 1996a [*American Indian Religious Freedom Act Amendments of 1994, Pub. L. No. 103–344, § 2, 108 Stat. 3125 (Oct. 6, 1994)*]

(a) Congressional findings and declarations

The Congress finds and declares that –

(1) for many Indian people, the traditional ceremonial use of the peyote cactus as a religious sacrament has for centuries been integral to a way of life, and significant in perpetuating Indian tribes and cultures;

(2) since 1965, this ceremonial use of peyote by Indians has been protected by Federal regulation;

(3) while at least 28 States have enacted laws which are similar to, or are in conformance with, the Federal regulation which protects the ceremonial use of peyote by Indian religious practitioners, 22 States have not done so, and this lack of uniformity has created hardship for Indian people who participate in such religious ceremonies;

(4) the Supreme Court of the United States, in the case of Employment Division v. Smith, 494 U.S. 872 (1990), held that the First Amendment does not protect Indian practitioners who use peyote in Indian religious ceremonies, and also raised uncertainty whether this religious practice would be protected under the compelling State interest standard; and

(5) the lack of adequate and clear legal protection for the religious use of peyote by Indians may serve to stigmatize and marginalize Indian tribes and cultures, and increase the risk that they will be exposed to discriminatory treatment.

(b) Use, possession, or transportation of peyote

(1) Notwithstanding any other provision of law, the use, possession, or transportation of peyote by an Indian for bona fide traditional ceremonial purposes in connection with the practice of a traditional Indian religion is lawful, and shall not be prohibited by the United States or any State. No Indian shall be penalized or discriminated against on the basis of such use, possession or transportation, including, but not limited to, denial of otherwise applicable benefits under public assistance programs.

(2) This section does not prohibit such reasonable regulation and registration by the Drug Enforcement Administration of those persons who cultivate, harvest, or distribute peyote as may be consistent with the purposes of this section and section 1996 of this title.

(3) This section does not prohibit application of the provisions of section 481.111(a) of Vernon's Texas Health and Safety Code Annotated, in effect on October 6, 1994, insofar as those provisions pertain to the cultivation, harvest, and distribution of peyote.

(4) Nothing in this section shall prohibit any Federal department or agency, in carrying out its statutory responsibilities and functions, from promulgating regulations establishing reasonable limitations on the use or ingestion of peyote prior to or during the performance of duties by sworn law enforcement officers or personnel directly involved in public transportation or any other safety-sensitive positions where the performance of such duties may be adversely affected by such use or ingestion. Such regulations shall be adopted only after consultation with representatives of traditional Indian religions for which the sacramental use of peyote is integral to their practice. Any regulation promulgated pursuant to this section shall be subject to the balancing test set forth in section 3 of the Religious Freedom Restoration Act (Public Law 103–141; 42 U.S.C. 2000bb-1).

(5) This section shall not be construed as requiring prison authorities to permit, nor shall it be construed to prohibit prison authorities from permitting, access to peyote by Indians while incarcerated within Federal or State prison facilities.

(6) Subject to the provisions of the Religious Freedom Restoration Act (Public Law 103–141; 42 U.S.C. 2000bb-1) [42 U.S.C.A. § 2000bb et seq.], this section shall not be construed to prohibit States from enacting or enforcing reasonable traffic safety laws or regulations.

(7) Subject to the provisions of the Religious Freedom Restoration Act (Public Law 103–141; 42 U.S.C. 2000bb-1), this section does not prohibit the Secretary of Defense from promulgating regulations establishing reasonable limitations on

the use, possession, transportation, or distribution of peyote to promote military readiness, safety, or compliance with international law or laws of other countries. Such regulations shall be adopted only after consultation with representatives of traditional Indian religions for which the sacramental use of peyote is integral to their practice.

(c) Definitions

For purposes of this section –

(1) the term "Indian" means a member of an Indian tribe;
(2) the term "Indian tribe" means any tribe, band, nation, pueblo, or other organized group or community of Indians, including any Alaska Native village (as defined in, or established pursuant to, the Alaska Native Claims Settlement Act (43 U.S.C. 1601 et seq.)), which is recognized as eligible for the special programs and services provided by the United States to Indians because of their status as Indians;
(3) the term "Indian religion" means any religion–
    (A) which is practiced by Indians, and
    (B) the origin and interpretation of which is from within a traditional Indian culture or community; and
(4) the term "State" means any State of the United States, and any political subdivision thereof.

(d) Protection of rights of Indians and Indian tribes

Nothing in this section shall be construed as abrogating, diminishing, or otherwise affecting –

(1) the inherent rights of any Indian tribe;
(2) the rights, express or implicit, of any Indian tribe which exist under treaties, Executive orders, and laws of the United States;
(3) the inherent right of Indians to practice their religions; and
(4) the right of Indians to practice their religions under any Federal or State law.

***42 U.S.C. §§ 2000bb to 2000bb-4 [Religious Freedom Restoration Act of 1993, Pub. L. No. 103–141, 107 Stat. 1488 (as amended)].***

**Section 2000bb. Congressional findings and declaration of purposes:**

(a) Findings

The Congress finds that –

(1) the framers of the Constitution, recognizing free exercise of religion as an unalienable right, secured its protection in the First Amendment to the Constitution;
(2) laws "neutral" toward religion may burden religious exercise as surely as laws intended to interfere with religious exercise;
(3) governments should not substantially burden religious exercise without compelling justification;

(4) in Employment Division v. Smith, 494 U.S. 872 (1990) the Supreme Court virtually eliminated the requirement that the government justify burdens on religious exercise imposed by laws neutral toward religion; and
(5) the compelling interest test as set forth in prior Federal court rulings is a workable test for striking sensible balances between religious liberty and competing prior governmental interests.

(b) Purposes

The purposes of this chapter are –

(1) to restore the compelling interest test as set forth in Sherbert v. Verner, 374 U.S. 398 (1963) and Wisconsin v. Yoder, 406 U.S. 205 (1972) and to guarantee its application in all cases where free exercise of religion is substantially burdened; and
(2) to provide a claim or defense to persons whose religious exercise is substantially burdened by government.

**Section 2000bb-1. Free exercise of religion protected:**

(a) In general

Government shall not substantially burden a person's exercise of religion even if the burden results from a rule of general applicability, except as provided in subsection (b) of this section.

(b) Exception

Government may substantially burden a person's exercise of religion only if it demonstrates that application of the burden to the person –

(1) is in furtherance of a compelling governmental interest; and
(2) is the least restrictive means of furthering that compelling governmental interest.

(c) Judicial relief

A person whose religious exercise has been burdened in violation of this section may assert that violation as a claim or defense in a judicial proceeding and obtain appropriate relief against a government. Standing to assert a claim or defense under this section shall be governed by the general rules of standing under article III of the Constitution.

**Section 2000bb-2. Definitions:**

As used in this chapter –

(1) the term "government" includes a branch, department, agency, instrumentality, and official (or other person acting under color of law) of the United States, or of a covered entity;
(2) the term "covered entity" means the District of Columbia, the Commonwealth of Puerto Rico, and each territory and possession of the United States;
(3) the term "demonstrates" means meets the burdens of going forward with the evidence and of persuasion; and
(4) the term "exercise of religion" means religious exercise, as defined in section 2000cc-5 of this title.

**Section 2000bb-3. Applicability:**

(a) In general

This chapter applies to all Federal law, and the implementation of that law, whether statutory or otherwise, and whether adopted before or after November 16, 1993.

(b) Rule of construction

Federal statutory law adopted after November 16, 1993 is subject to this chapter unless such law explicitly excludes such application by reference to this chapter.

(c) Religious belief unaffected

Nothing in this chapter shall be construed to authorize any government to burden any religious belief.

**Section 2000bb-4. Establishment clause unaffected:**

Nothing in this chapter shall be construed to affect, interpret, or in any way address that portion of the First Amendment prohibiting laws respecting the establishment of religion (referred to in this section as the "Establishment Clause"). Granting government funding, benefits, or exemptions, to the extent permissible under the Establishment Clause, shall not constitute a violation of this chapter. As used in this section, the term "granting," used with respect to government funding, benefits, or exemptions, does not include the denial of government funding, benefits, or exemptions.

*42 U.S.C. §§ 2000cc to 2000cc-5 [Religious Land Use and Institutionalized Persons Act of 2000, Pub. L. No. 106–274, 114 Stat. 803–07 (Sept. 22, 2000)].*

**Section 2000cc. Protection of land use as religious exercise:**

(a) Substantial burdens
  (1) General rule

No government shall impose or implement a land use regulation in a manner that imposes a substantial burden on the religious exercise of a person, including a religious assembly or institution, unless the government demonstrates that imposition of the burden on that person, assembly, or institution –

(A) is in furtherance of a compelling governmental interest; and
(B) is the least restrictive means of furthering that compelling governmental interest.

(2) Scope of application

This subsection applies in any case in which –

(A) the substantial burden is imposed in a program or activity that receives Federal financial assistance, even if the burden results from a rule of general applicability;
(B) the substantial burden affects, or removal of that substantial burden would affect, commerce with foreign nations, among the several States,

or with Indian tribes, even if the burden results from a rule of general applicability; or

(C) the substantial burden is imposed in the implementation of a land use regulation or system of land use regulations, under which a government makes, or has in place formal or informal procedures or practices that permit the government to make, individualized assessments of the proposed uses for the property involved.

(b) Discrimination and exclusion

(1) Equal terms

No government shall impose or implement a land use regulation in a manner that treats a religious assembly or institution on less than equal terms with a nonreligious assembly or institution.

(2) Nondiscrimination

No government shall impose or implement a land use regulation that discriminates against any assembly or institution on the basis of religion or religious denomination.

(3) Exclusions and limits

No government shall impose or implement a land use regulation that –

(A) totally excludes religious assemblies from a jurisdiction; or

(B) unreasonably limits religious assemblies, institutions, or structures within a jurisdiction.

**Section 2000cc-1. Protection of religious exercise of institutionalized persons:**

(a) General rule

No government shall impose a substantial burden on the religious exercise of a person residing in or confined to an institution, as defined in section 1997 of this title, even if the burden results from a rule of general applicability, unless the government demonstrates that imposition of the burden on that person –

(1) is in furtherance of a compelling governmental interest; and

(2) is the least restrictive means of furthering that compelling governmental interest.

(b) Scope of application

This section applies in any case in which –

(1) the substantial burden is imposed in a program or activity that receives Federal financial assistance; or

(2) the substantial burden affects, or removal of that substantial burden would affect, commerce with foreign nations, among the several States, or with Indian tribes.

**Section 2000cc-2. Judicial relief:**

(a) Cause of action

A person may assert a violation of this chapter as a claim or defense in a judicial proceeding and obtain appropriate relief against a government. Standing to assert a claim or defense under this section shall be governed by the general rules of standing under Article III of the Constitution.

(b) Burden of persuasion

If a plaintiff produces prima facie evidence to support a claim alleging a violation of the Free Exercise Clause or a violation of section 2000cc of this title, the government shall bear the burden of persuasion on any element of the claim, except that the plaintiff shall bear the burden of persuasion on whether the law (including a regulation) or government practice that is challenged by the claim substantially burdens the plaintiff's exercise of religion.

(c) Full faith and credit

Adjudication of a claim of a violation of section 2000cc of this title in a non-Federal forum shall not be entitled to full faith and credit in a Federal court unless the claimant had a full and fair adjudication of that claim in the non-Federal forum.

(d) Omitted

(e) Prisoners

Nothing in this chapter shall be construed to amend or repeal the Prison Litigation Reform Act of 1995 (including provisions of law amended by that Act).

(f) Authority of United States to enforce this chapter

The United States may bring an action for injunctive or declaratory relief to enforce compliance with this chapter. Nothing in this subsection shall be construed to deny, impair, or otherwise affect any right or authority of the Attorney General, the United States, or any agency, officer, or employee of the United States, acting under any law other than this subsection, to institute or intervene in any proceeding.

(g) Limitation

If the only jurisdictional basis for applying a provision of this chapter is a claim that a substantial burden by a government on religious exercise affects, or that removal of that substantial burden would affect, commerce with foreign nations, among the several States, or with Indian tribes, the provision shall not apply if the government demonstrates that all substantial burdens on, or the removal of all substantial burdens from, similar religious exercise throughout the Nation would not lead in the aggregate to a substantial effect on commerce with foreign nations, among the several States, or with Indian tribes.

**Section 2000cc-3. Rules of construction:**

(a) Religious belief unaffected

Nothing in this chapter shall be construed to authorize any government to burden any religious belief.

(b) Religious exercise not regulated

Nothing in this chapter shall create any basis for restricting or burdening religious exercise or for claims against a religious organization including any religiously affiliated school or university, not acting under color of law.

(c) Claims to funding unaffected

Nothing in this chapter shall create or preclude a right of any religious organization to receive funding or other assistance from a government, or of any person to receive government funding for a religious activity, but this chapter may require a government to incur expenses in its own operations to avoid imposing a substantial burden on religious exercise.

(d) Other authority to impose conditions on funding unaffected

Nothing in this chapter shall –

(1) authorize a government to regulate or affect, directly or indirectly, the activities or policies of a person other than a government as a condition of receiving funding or other assistance; or
(2) restrict any authority that may exist under other law to so regulate or affect, except as provided in this chapter.

(e) Governmental discretion in alleviating burdens on religious exercise

A government may avoid the preemptive force of any provision of this chapter by changing the policy or practice that results in a substantial burden on religious exercise, by retaining the policy or practice and exempting the substantially burdened religious exercise, by providing exemptions from the policy or practice for applications that substantially burden religious exercise, or by any other means that eliminates the substantial burden.

(f) Effect on other law

With respect to a claim brought under this chapter, proof that a substantial burden on a person's religious exercise affects, or removal of that burden would affect, commerce with foreign nations, among the several States, or with Indian tribes, shall not establish any inference or presumption that Congress intends that any religious exercise is, or is not, subject to any law other than this chapter.

(g) Broad construction

This chapter shall be construed in favor of a broad protection of religious exercise, to the maximum extent permitted by the terms of this chapter and the Constitution.

(h) No preemption or repeal

Nothing in this chapter shall be construed to preempt State law, or repeal Federal law, that is equally as protective of religious exercise as, or more protective of religious exercise than, this chapter.

(i) Severability

If any provision of this chapter or of an amendment made by this chapter, or any application of such provision to any person or circumstance, is held to be unconstitutional, the remainder of this chapter, the amendments made by this chapter, and the application of the provision to any other person or circumstance shall not be affected.

**Section 2000cc-4. Establishment Clause unaffected:**

Nothing in this chapter shall be construed to affect, interpret, or in any way address that portion of the First Amendment to the Constitution prohibiting laws respecting an establishment of religion (referred to in this section as the "Establishment Clause"). Granting government funding, benefits, or exemptions, to the extent permissible under the Establishment Clause, shall not constitute a violation of this chapter. In this section, the term "granting," used with respect to government funding, benefits, or exemptions, does not include the denial of government funding, benefits, or exemptions.

**Section 2000cc-5. Definitions;**

In this chapter:

(1) Claimant

The term "claimant" means a person raising a claim or defense under this chapter.

(2) Demonstrates

The term "demonstrates" means meets the burdens of going forward with the evidence and of persuasion.

(3) Free Exercise Clause

The term "Free Exercise Clause" means that portion of the First Amendment to the Constitution that proscribes laws prohibiting the free exercise of religion.

(4) Government

The term "government" –

(A) means –
(i) a State, county, municipality, or other governmental entity created under the authority of a State;
(ii) any branch, department, agency, instrumentality, or official of an entity listed in clause (i); and
(iii) any other person acting under color of State law; and
(B) for the purposes of sections 2000cc-2(b) and 2000cc-3 of this title, includes the United States, a branch, department, agency, instrumentality, or official of the United States, and any other person acting under color of Federal law.

(5) Land use regulation

The term "land use regulation" means a zoning or landmarking law, or the application of such a law, that limits or restricts a claimant's use or development of land (including a structure affixed to land), if the claimant has an ownership, leasehold, easement, servitude, or other property interest in the regulated land or a contract or option to acquire such an interest.

(6) Program or activity

The term "program or activity" means all of the operations of any entity as described in paragraph (1) or (2) of section 2000d-4a of this title.

(7) Religious exercise

(A) In general

The term "religious exercise" includes any exercise of religion, whether or not compelled by, or central to, a system of religious belief.

(B) Rule

The use, building, or conversion of real property for the purpose of religious exercise shall be considered to be religious exercise of the person or entity that uses or intends to use the property for that purpose.

### *42 U.S.C. §§ 2000e to 2000e-17 (selected provisions) [Civil Rights Act of 1964, Pub. L. No. 88–352, Title VII, § 703, 78 Stat. 255 (July 2, 1964) (as amended)]*

**Section 2000e(j):**

The term "religion" includes all aspects of religious observance and practice, as well as belief, unless an employer demonstrates that he is unable to reasonably accommodate to an employee's or prospective employee's religious observance or practice without undue hardship on the conduct of the employer's business.

**Section 2000e-1(a). Applicability to foreign and religious employment:**

This subchapter shall not apply to an employer with respect to the employment of aliens outside any State, or to a religious corporation, association, educational institution, or society with respect to the employment of individuals of a particular religion to perform work connected with the carrying on by such corporation, association, educational institution, or society of its activities.

. . .

**Section 2000e-2. Unlawful employment practices:**

(a) Employer practices

It shall be an unlawful employment practice for an employer –

(1) to fail or refuse to hire or to discharge any individual, or otherwise to discriminate against any individual with respect to his compensation, terms, conditions, or privileges of employment, because of such individual's race, color, religion, sex, or national origin; or

(2) to limit, segregate, or classify his employees or applicants for employment in any way which would deprive or tend to deprive any individual of employment opportunities or otherwise adversely affect his status as an employee, because of such individual's race, color, religion, sex, or national origin.

. . .

(e) Businesses or enterprises with personnel qualified on basis of religion, sex, or national origin; educational institutions with personnel of particular religion

Notwithstanding any other provision of this subchapter, (1) it shall not be an unlawful employment practice for an employer to hire and employ employees, for an employment agency to classify, or refer for employment any individual, for a labor organization to classify its membership or to classify or refer for employment any individual, or for an employer, labor organization, or joint labor-management committee controlling apprenticeship or other training or retraining programs to admit or employ any individual in any such program, on the basis of his religion, sex, or national origin in those certain instances where religion, sex, or national origin is a bona fide occupational qualification reasonably necessary to the normal operation of that particular business or enterprise, and (2) it shall not be an unlawful employment practice for a school, college, university, or other educational institution or institution of learning to hire and employ employees of a particular religion if such school, college, university, or other educational institution or institution of learning is, in whole or in substantial part, owned, supported, controlled, or managed by a particular religion or by a particular religious corporation, association, or society, or if the curriculum of such school, college, university, or other educational institution or institution of learning is directed toward the propagation of a particular religion.

...

**Section 2000e–16. Employment by Federal Government:**

(a) Discriminatory practices prohibited; employees or applicants for employment subject to coverage

All personnel actions affecting employees or applicants for employment (except with regard to aliens employed outside the limits of the United States) in military departments as defined in section 102 of title 5, in executive agencies as defined in section 105 of title 5 (including employees and applicants for employment who are paid from nonappropriated funds), in the United States Postal Service and the Postal Regulatory Commission, in those units of the Government of the District of Columbia having positions in the competitive service, and in those units of the judicial branch of the Federal Government having positions in the competitive service, in the Smithsonian Institution, and in the Government Printing Office, the Government Accountability Office, and the Library of Congress shall be made free from any discrimination based on race, color, religion, sex, or national origin.

...

**Section 2000e–16b. Discriminatory practices prohibited:**

(a) Practices

All personnel actions affecting the Presidential appointees described in section 1219 of title 2 or the State employees described in section 2000e–16c of this title shall be made free from any discrimination based on –

(1) race, color, religion, sex, or national origin, within the meaning of section 2000e–16 of this title;

...

**Section 2000e–16c. Coverage of previously exempt State employees:**

(a) Application

The rights, protections, and remedies provided pursuant to section 2000e–16b of this title shall apply with respect to employment of any individual chosen or appointed, by a person elected to public office in any State or political subdivision of any State by the qualified voters thereof –

(1) to be a member of the elected official's personal staff;
(2) to serve the elected official on the policymaking level; or
(3) to serve the elected official as an immediate advisor with respect to the exercise of the constitutional or legal powers of the office.

...

*42 U.S.C. § 3604 [Fair Housing Act, Pub. L. No. 90–284, tit. VIII, 82 Stat. 81 (Apr. 11, 1968) (codified as amended at §§ 3601–3631)]*

**Section 3604. Discrimination in the sale or rental of housing and other prohibited practices:**

As made applicable by section 3603 of this title and except as exempted by sections 3603(b) and 3607 of this title, it shall be unlawful –

(a) To refuse to sell or rent after the making of a bona fide offer, or to refuse to negotiate for the sale or rental of, or otherwise make unavailable or deny, a dwelling to any person because of race, color, religion, sex, familial status, or national origin.
(b) To discriminate against any person in the terms, conditions, or privileges of sale or rental of a dwelling, or in the provision of services or facilities in connection therewith, because of race, color, religion, sex, familial status, or national origin.
(c) To make, print, or publish, or cause to be made, printed, or published any notice, statement, or advertisement, with respect to the sale or rental of a dwelling that indicates any preference, limitation, or discrimination based on race, color, religion, sex, handicap, familial status, or national origin, or an intention to make any such preference, limitation, or discrimination.
(d) To represent to any person because of race, color, religion, sex, handicap, familial status, or national origin that any dwelling is not available for inspection, sale, or rental when such dwelling is in fact so available.
(e) For profit, to induce or attempt to induce any person to sell or rent any dwelling by representations regarding the entry or prospective entry into the neighborhood of a person or persons of a particular race, color, religion, sex, handicap, familial status, or national origin.

. . .

*42 U.S.C. §§ 12112–12113 [Americans with Disabilities Act, Pub. L. No. 101–336, Tit. I, § 103, 104 Stat. 33342 (July 26, 1990) (codified as amended at 42 U.S.C. §§ 12101–12213)]*

**Section 12112. Discrimination:**

(a) General rule

No covered entity shall discriminate against a qualified individual on the basis of disability in regard to job application procedures, the hiring, advancement, or discharge of employees, employee compensation, job training, and other terms, conditions, and privileges of employment.

(b) Construction

As used in subsection (a) of this section, the term "discriminate against a qualified individual on the basis of disability" includes –

(1) limiting, segregating, or classifying a job applicant or employee in a way that adversely affects the opportunities or status of such applicant or employee because of the disability of such applicant or employee;
(2) participating in a contractual or other arrangement or relationship that has the effect of subjecting a covered entity's qualified applicant or employee with a

disability to the discrimination prohibited by this subchapter (such relationship includes a relationship with an employment or referral agency, labor union, an organization providing fringe benefits to an employee of the covered entity, or an organization providing training and apprenticeship programs);

(3) utilizing standards, criteria, or methods of administration –
 (A) that have the effect of discrimination on the basis of disability; or
 (B) that perpetuate the discrimination of others who are subject to common administrative control;

(4) excluding or otherwise denying equal jobs or benefits to a qualified individual because of the known disability of an individual with whom the qualified individual is known to have a relationship or association;

(5) (A) not making reasonable accommodations to the known physical or mental limitations of an otherwise qualified individual with a disability who is an applicant or employee, unless such covered entity can demonstrate that the accommodation would impose an undue hardship on the operation of the business of such covered entity; or
 (B) denying employment opportunities to a job applicant or employee who is an otherwise qualified individual with a disability, if such denial is based on the need of such covered entity to make reasonable accommodation to the physical or mental impairments of the employee or applicant;

(6) using qualification standards, employment tests or other selection criteria that screen out or tend to screen out an individual with a disability or a class of individuals with disabilities unless the standard, test or other selection criteria, as used by the covered entity, is shown to be job-related for the position in question and is consistent with business necessity; and

(7) failing to select and administer tests concerning employment in the most effective manner to ensure that, when such test is administered to a job applicant or employee who has a disability that impairs sensory, manual, or speaking skills, such test results accurately reflect the skills, aptitude, or whatever other factor of such applicant or employee that such test purports to measure, rather than reflecting the impaired sensory, manual, or speaking skills of such employee or applicant (except where such skills are the factors that the test purports to measure).

**Section 12113. Defenses:**

(a) In general

It may be a defense to a charge of discrimination under this chapter that an alleged application of qualification standards, tests, or selection criteria that screen out or tend to screen out or otherwise deny a job or benefit to an individual with a disability has been shown to be job-related and consistent with business necessity, and such performance cannot be accomplished by reasonable accommodation, as required under this subchapter.

(b) Qualification standards

The term "qualification standards" may include a requirement that an individual shall not pose a direct threat to the health or safety of other individuals in the workplace.

...

(d) Religious entities
(1) In general

This subchapter shall not prohibit a religious corporation, association, educational institution, or society from giving preference in employment to individuals of a particular religion to perform work connected with the carrying on by such corporation, association, educational institution, or society of its activities.

(2) Religious tenets requirement

Under this subchapter, a religious organization may require that all applicants and employees conform to the religious tenets of such organization.

...

### *50 U.S.C. app. § 456(g), (j) [Military Selective Service Act, ch. 625, Title I, § 6, 62 Stat. 609 (June 24, 1948) (as amended)]*

(g) (1) Regular or duly ordained ministers of religion, as defined in this title [sections 451 to 471a of this Appendix], shall be exempt from training and service, but not from registration, under this title [said sections].

(2) Students preparing for the ministry under the direction of recognized churches or religious organizations, who are satisfactorily pursuing full-time courses of instruction in recognized theological or divinity schools, or who are satisfactorily pursuing full-time courses of instruction leading to their entrance into recognized theological or divinity schools in which they have been preenrolled, shall be deferred from training and service, but not from registration, under this title [sections 451 to 471a of this Appendix]. Persons who are or may be deferred under the provisions of this subsection shall remain liable for training and service in the Armed Forces under the provisions of section 4(a) of this Act [section 454(a) of this Appendix] until the thirty-fifth anniversary of the date of their birth. The foregoing sentence shall not be construed to prevent the exemption or continued deferment of such persons if otherwise exempted or deferrable under any other provision of this Act.

...

(j) Nothing contained in this title [sections 451 to 471a of this Appendix] shall be construed to require any person to be subject to combatant training and service in the armed forces of the United States who, by reason of religious training and belief, is conscientiously opposed to participation in war in any form. As used in this subsection, the term "religious training and belief" does not include essentially political, sociological, or philosophical views, or a merely personal moral code. Any person claiming exemption from combatant training and service because of such conscientious objections whose claim is sustained by the local board shall, if he is inducted into the armed forces under this title [said sections], be assigned to noncombatant service as defined by the President, or shall, if he is found to be conscientiously opposed to participation in such noncombatant service, in lieu of such induction, be ordered by his local board, subject to such regulations as the President may prescribe, to perform for a period equal to the period prescribed in section 4(b) [section 454(b) of this Appendix] such civilian work contributing to the maintenance of the national health, safety, or interest as the Director may deem appropriate and any such person who knowingly fails or neglects to obey any such order from his local board shall be deemed, for the purposes of section 12 of this title [section 462 of this Appendix], to have knowingly failed or neglected to perform a duty required of him under this title [said sections]. The Director shall be responsible for finding civilian work for persons exempted from training and service under this subsection and for the placement of such persons in appropriate civilian work contributing to the maintenance of the national health, safety, or interest.

# Index